The Handybook for Genealogists

United States of America

Eleventh Edition

Published by Everton Publishers
Logan, Utah

President and Publisher: Walter Fuller
Editorial Development: My Ancestors Found
Design and Production: WestWords, Inc.
Printer: Banta Publications Group

ISBN: 1-890895-05-9—Book without CD
       1-890895-06-7—Book with CD

Printed in Harrisonburg, VA.

Table of Contents

Preface

We have made every effort to insure that the data contained in this book is the most current information possible. We realize, however, that much of the Handybook information is time sensitive and therefore ask for the help of our readers in keeping each edition up to date. If you have additions or updates, please send them to the following:

Everton Publishers
PO Box 368
Logan, Utah 84323-0368

The 11th Edition of the Handybook has been another monumental effort and we wish to acknowledge some of those who have been responsible for its success: Jennifer H. Johnson, Bridget Cook, Sarah Bird, Brenda Bird, Jane K. Anderson, and Kimberly A. Savage of My Ancestors; and Jared Sterzer and the staff of WestWords, Inc. We would also like to thank Adrian Ettlinger and Arthur Lassagne for help in updating county creation dates in this edition.

We offer this book to our readers in hopes that it may help you make cherished connections with your family—both past and present.

Holly

Holly T. Hansen
Editor

Introduction

Since 1947, the *Handybook for Genealogists* has been a "must have" tool for researchers. It contains a vast amount of information on U.S. counties, which is critical to family history research because the greatest amount of vital records are kept on a county level.

With the *Handybook,* you can quickly identify which records are held by each county and the type of information contained within each record type. You also have at your fingertips addresses, phone numbers, email addresses, and website URLs that make it easy to contact county record keepers.

In addition to county information, the *Handybook* includes the following for each state in the U.S.:

- A brief history of each state
- Information on vital records held at the state level
- A list of societies and repositories within each state
- An extensive bibliography of publications

Always consult the general information on a state before proceeding to the state and county listings that follow. Records are kept by individual jurisdictions. Each country keeps records on its citizens, and a state government holds different record types than the local county government. Using each jurisdiction will help you find your ancestors more effectively. Using the sources listed in the *Handybook* can save you hours of research.

Among the valuable resources held by national governments are census, military service and pensions records, land holdings, treaties, great historical libraries and other valuable collections that tell the story of individuals and the world in which they lived. Records held by the state include land, tax, birth, marriage and death records. Some records, such as immigration, emigration and naturalization records, can be located at all levels of jurisdiction—national, state and county. The *Handybook* gives contact information for offices that maintain records which allow you to quickly locate and request copies of valuable documents. Where known, internet addresses have also been included.

Using the County Information

After reading the general information for a state, you will find an alphabetic list for each state's counties, including counties that no longer exist. You can trace a county by its parent county or the territory from which it was created. There is an index to help you locate each county on the state county map. County creation dates are included to help you build a timeline for your research and locate the correct county records to search. These listings contain valuable data useful in helping you trace your ancestry and add life to your family tree.

Below is an example of a county entry and a key to reading the information.

County	Map	Date	Parent County or Territory From Which Organized
Website	Index	Created	Address/Details
Iron*	**N2**	**31 Jan 1850**	**Original county**
			Iron County; 68 S 100 E; PO Box 429; Parowan, UT 84761; Ph. 435.477.8341.
			Details: (Formerly Little Salt Lake Co. Name changed to Iron 3 Dec 1850) (County Clerk has marriage records from 1887; County Recorder has land records from 1852; Clerk District Court has divorce, probate & court records.)

County. This is the current name of the county (or Louisiana parish or Alaska borough). If the name has changed, the former name appears in alphabetical order with a reference to the current name. A county that has been discontinued is also noted.

*Asterisk. An asterisk (*) following a county's name indicates its inclusion in the Historical Records Survey.

Website. The URL of the official county website or USGENWEB address.

Map Index. The coordinates used to locate this county on the state maps at the back of the Handybook.

Date Created. The date the county, parish, or borough was created or incorporated.

Parent County or Territory From Which Organized. The name of the county or counties from which this county was formed. Some counties were formed at the same time the state or territory was organized (original counties), while others were organized from previous entities such as a state or territory (in the eastern United States), or a Mexican municipality (in the American southwest).

Information on parent counties can help you know which government office has custody of records for a specific time period. Even if a family did not physically change residence, the location of records on that family could have moved as jurisdictional boundaries changed.

For example, a family living in what was to become Ford County, Illinois between 1788 and 1865, may have records in the custody of nine different offices. Working backwards, Ford County was organized in 1859 from land previously belonging to Clark County. Clark County was formed in 1819 from land previously belonging to Crawford County, which was formed in 1816 from a part of Edwards County. Edwards County was organized in 1814 from parts of both Madison and Gallatin counties. Madison had been split off of St. Clair County in 1812, while Gallatin was organized from a part of Randolph County in 1812. In turn, St. Clair County was formed from the old Northwest Territory in 1790, while Randolph County was organized from the Northwest Territory in 1795. To get all of the records on your family, you would consult the archives of all nine of these government units.

Address. The contact information including the address and phone number of the main offices of this county or parish.

Details. Information about the history of the county and the records held at the county level.

Explanation of the Historical Records Survey

When the Great Depression hit the United States in 1929, the American economy hit rock bottom. In 1933, President Franklin D. Roosevelt introduced "The New Deal," a series of programs designed to pick America up and get the economy moving again.

The Works Progress Administration (WPA) was one of these programs. The WPA employed out-of-work Americans who were certified by local agencies as meeting certain qualifications.

The WPA was born in 1935. In 1939, the WPA was renamed the Works Projects Administration. Over the years, the WPA would employ nearly 8.5 million Americans. Interestingly, half of those workers were employed in New York City. The WPA existed for only eight years, but provided a valuable resource for genealogists. Originally organized in 1935 as part of the Federal Writers Project, the Historical Records Survey (HRS) documented resources for research into American history. In 1939 it became a unit of the Research and Records Program.

The WPA was organized into regional, state, and local divisions. Much of the work performed by the HRS was done for the National Archives and Records Administration (NARA), as well as state archives and state historical societies.

The HRS was responsible for creating the soundex indexes of the Federal Census. The HRS also compiled indexes of vital statistics, cemetery interments, school records, military records, maps, newspapers, etc. The list went on. Surveys of public record archives were conducted and inventories created in most states between the years 1936 and 1943. While few of these inventories give full transcripts, they do name the records that were available in the respective archives at the time of the survey. These inventories often give the condition of the various records, where they were stored and the dates of commencement and conclusion of the records. Microfilms of these indexes were later made by other organizations.

After the WPA was dissolved, the records, now in the hands of state archives and historical societies, were microfilmed, indexed and made available for use. However, many other records were placed into boxes and stored away. Also, a few have been destroyed, and in some cases, destroyed deliberately.

A checklist of publications was originally published by the WPA as W.P.A. Technical Series, Research and Records Bibliography Number 7. It has been reprinted by the Genealogical Publishing Company in Baltimore, Maryland as the *Check List of Historical Records Survey Publications, Bibliography of Research Projects Reports,* by Sargent B. Child and Dorothy B. Holmes. You may obtain a microform copy through the Family History Library in Salt Lake City, Utah. The microfilm numbers are 874,113 item 2; a second filming numbered 9244683 item 4; and microfiche number 6016392.

United States of America

Capital: Washington, District of Columbia

History records the mainland of the North American Continent was first sighted by the Spanish explorer and treasure hunter Don Juan Ponce de Leon on Easter, March 27, 1513. He claimed the land for Spain and called it *La Florida,* interpreted as "Land of Flowers." Between 1513 and 1563 the government of Spain launched six expeditions to settle La Florida; all failed. Jean Ribaut, a French explorer, and his party built Fort Caroline in 1562 and by 1564 they had succeeded in establishing a colony on the St. Johns River. This settlement was destroyed when the Spaniard Don Pedro Menendez de Aviles, his soldiers, and settlers founded St. Augustine in 1565. St. Augustine is generally regarded as the first permanent European settlement in what is now the United States.

In 1607, Captain John Smith, accompanied by 105 settlers, established the English colony of Jamestown, in what is now Virginia. This started a land rush that would last for centuries. Plymouth Colony was established in 1620, Peter Minuit purchased Manhattan Island in 1626, the establishment of Maryland as a Roman Catholic colony occurred in 1634, and numerous other settlements followed.

Exploration, religion, and the desire for land appear to be the driving factor in these first waves of migration to the New World. The French settled in the area of the Great Lakes, in what is now upstate New York and the province of Quebec, and along the coast of the Gulf of Mexico, in what was to become Mississippi and Louisiana. The Dutch established towns in New York, New Jersey, and Pennsylvania. Germans and other German-speaking groups fleeing religious persecution established colonies in New York, Pennsylvania, and the Carolinas. The British settled up and down the Atlantic and Gulf coasts.

The land was occupied by great numbers of Native American peoples long before the arrival of explorers and those seeking new land and religious freedom. Many of the natives aided the newcomers, some listened to and accepted Christianity, and many were driven from their homes suffering death from warfare, slavery, and European diseases. The

clash of cultures existing during the formative years of America has caused long lasting effects.

The white population grew from about 4,600 in 1630 to over 100,000 in 1670 to over a quarter of a million by 1700. When space became limited on the coasts, people of all origins moved inland. Even though each settler viewed it as a land of opportunity, various visions of opportunity and loyalty to different political and religious systems caused friction. Eventually, major confrontations broke out between the English colonists and the French, resulting in King George's War in 1744 and the French Indian War (the Seven Years War) in 1754. The resulting treaty, in 1763, expanded British influence in areas of Canada and the lower American Colonies.

However, as Britain's American Colony continued to grow to over two million by 1770, its citizens became increasingly uncomfortable with the absentee rule of the British Crown. A series of unpopular taxes enacted between 1764 and 1774 led to the seating of the first Continental Congress in 1774, and eventually to a Declaration of Independence by thirteen colonies in 1776, formally creating a new nation. By the time the Revolutionary War came to an end in 1781, almost 250,000 men had served the American cause, with about 34,000 casualties on the American side.

Although the colonies of the new nation had a working agreement in the Articles of Confederation, a more formal, binding document was needed to ensure that the various states would not disintegrate. At a convention in Philadelphia in 1787, a constitution was written and proposed to the individual states. That constitution was ratified and put into effect in 1789.

One of the provisions of the new constitution required a census of the population every ten years, beginning in 1790. That first census included only the names of the heads of households, and showed a population of 3,929,214. By the next federal census in 1800, the population count had risen to 5,308,483.

In 1803 the geographic size of the United States was doubled by the purchase from France of an area stretching from the Gulf Coast to what is now Montana. Total cost for the new real estate was $15 million. In 1819, Spain ceded the Florida peninsula and Gulf coastal territory west to Louisiana to the United States.

Even while the country was acquiring land to the south and west, its citizens were still fending off the British. The War of 1812 lasted until 1815, with 285,000 Americans fighting to maintain their freedom from Britain, at a cost of 7,000 casualties.

Although bonds had been raised to purchase lands from the French, the United States still had difficulty raising funds for the veterans of its wars. Instead, huge tracts of western lands were opened for exclusive use as "bounties" for those who had served in U.S. military actions. The prospect of free, open land in the west lured many veterans and their families into the new states and territories of Ohio, Indiana, Illinois, Michigan, Alabama, Mississippi, Arkansas, and Missouri.

But again, conflicts between settlers arose due to their divergent cultural backgrounds. Slavery in various states and territories was a source of conflict, and on several occasions it threatened to split the nation. Henry Clay's Missouri Compromise of 1820 set boundaries for freedom and slavery, but was only a temporary measure. In 1835 Texas declared its independence from Mexico and joined the United States in 1845. Following the war with Mexico from 1846 to 1848, Mexico ceded vast portions of the American West to the United States, including California, Arizona, New Mexico, Nevada, Utah, and part of Colorado.

The opening of these new lands with their apparent unlimited possibilities exacerbated the debate on the slavery issue, and where slavery should be allowed. In 1850 Henry Clay proposed another compromise but this new compromise could not solve the problem. By the end of the 1850s several southern states had become disenchanted with the process, and openly talked of secession from the rest of the nation.

Between 1861 and 1865, the Civil War (also known as the War Between the States) racked the nation. Over two million men served in the Union forces, and over a million served in the forces of the Confederacy. By the end of the war, casualties among Union forces were about 360,222, with more than 258,000 suffered by the Confederacy. Some estimates place total casualties closer to 700,000 for both sides combined.

Although it would take decades for the wounds of that war to heal, westward expansion in the United States continued. To encourage settlement in new lands, the Homestead Act was passed in 1862, granting free land to those who would settle it. In 1867 Alaska was purchased from Russia for $7.2 million. The first transcontinental railroad was completed in 1869, allowing easier, quicker access to frontier territories.

The effect of these developments on the population of the country was dramatic. During the decade of the Civil War, the population grew by only seven million, from thirty-one million to thirty-eight million. But the population rose to over fifty million by 1880, to almost sixty-three mil-

lion by 1890, and to over seventy-six million by the turn of the century.

Between 1820 and 1920, over thirty million immigrants arrived on America's shores. The major ports for the immigrants were New York, Boston, Baltimore, Philadelphia, New Orleans, and San Francisco. But numerous other ports on the Atlantic, Pacific, and Gulf coasts also welcomed immigrants, and large numbers entered overland, crossing the Canadian and Mexican borders.

Eventually, the numbers of immigrants, and their cultural diversity, created a backlash that caused the welcome mat to be removed. In 1921 Congress established a quota system limiting the amount of immigrants that would be accepted. This system did not undergo major modification until 1965, vastly reducing the number of immigrants during that forty-five year span. Even so, the population of the United States grew from 106 million in 1920 to almost 180 million by 1960.

In the meantime, the United States was involved in three military actions. Its participation in the First World War lasted from 1917 to 1918, involved about five million American servicemen, and resulted in 320,000 casualties. The Second World War involved sixteen million Americans from 1941 to 1945, with a million casualties. The United States sent six million men to serve in the Korean War (1950–1953), with 160,000 casualties.

In 1959 Alaska was admitted to the Union as the forty-ninth state, with Hawaii following as the fiftieth state later the same year.

American military involvement in Vietnam between 1963 and 1973 involved nine million servicemen, and resulted in 200,000 casualties.

In January and February of 1991, America and a coalition of 32 nations (including Britain, Egypt, France, and Saudi Arabia) became involved in a war with Iraq over that country's seizure of land in Kuwait. This was called the Persian Gulf War, which included Operation Desert Storm.

In 1995 and 1996 the United States acted with other NATO peacekeepers to prevent further bloodshed and a civil war in what was formerly the Eastern Block country of Yugoslavia.

On September 11, 2001, a terrorist attack on the World Trade Center in New York City and the Pentagon in Washington, D.C. killed nearly 3000 people. Shortly after, the U.S. government announced a War on Terrorism that has had a profound effect, both nationally and internationally.

The U.S. invasion of Afghanistan (code named Operation Enduring Freedom) began in October of 2001, in the wake of Sept. 11, 2001, in opposition to the Taliban government and operations of Al Qaeda. Post-invasion occupation has continued since 2002.

2003 brought an invasion of Iraq (the Second Persian Gulf War, or Iraq War) by the United States and Britain with support from a coalition of 48 other governments. On May 1, 2003, President George W. Bush declared the end of major combat operations. This was also followed by post-war occupation and combat that is still underway.

Federal Resources

The federal government of the United States does not have responsibility for the maintenance of vital records (births, marriages, divorces and deaths). But there are several important record types in federal repositories that are valuable to family historians. Many of these are in the custody of the United States National Archives in Washington, D.C. and in its several regional facilities throughout the nation. A list of these archives is included in the United States section of this book.

There are many federal records that genealogists find useful in their pursuit of ancestry. Following are summaries of some useful types of federal records:

Population Census Schedules: By constitutional mandate, a census of the population of the United States is conducted every ten years. These decennial censuses began in 1790 and have continued since. From 1790 through 1840 the federal censuses contained only the names of the heads of households, with a numeric breakdown of the members of the household by gender, age and race. Beginning in 1850 the federal population schedules have shown every resident of the country with his or her name, age, gender, occupation, and state or country of birth. Industry and Manufacturing schedules exist for 1850, 1860 and 1870. Mortality schedules exist for 1850, 1860, 1870 and 1880. Slave schedules are available for 1850 and 1860. Social statistics schedules are available for 1850, 1860 and 1870. More recent censuses may also show such data as literacy, parents' birthplaces, marital status, the number of years married, whether naturalized, the year of immigration to the United States, and more.

In 2002 federal population schedules were made available for 1790 through 1930. The 1890 federal census is available, but the original schedules were largely destroyed, with only scattered pages surviving for a small number of localities and showing just a few thousand residents.

These schedules have been microfilmed by the National Archives and are widely available through the LDS Family History Library in Salt Lake City and more than 4,000 Family History Centers located throughout the world. There are additional sources, such as state libraries and archives, local libraries, and commercial interests. Most are now commercially available via the Internet and on CD-ROM, specifically designed for genealogical research.

These population schedules are generally arranged geographically, with each enumerator following a route designed to cover all of the residences in his or her assigned area. These enumeration districts were logically assigned, following streets, towns, townships, and county boundaries.

There are statewide indexes for a large portion of the available federal censuses, although many of these contain only the names of the heads of the households rather than all of the names that appear on the original schedules. Digital indexes continue to be created for use in helping the genealogist to access census records quickly and efficiently.

Mortality schedules are also available from most of the same sources as the federal censuses, and all of them have been every-name indexed. Like the population schedules, the federal mortality schedules are organized geographically. Generally they show the name of each person who died twelve months prior to the census, his or her age, gender, race, marital status, occupation, month and cause of death.

Immigration Records: Immigration records, commonly called "ship passenger arrival records," may provide evidence of a person's arrival in the United States as well as foreign birthplace. The National Archives and Records Administration (NARA) has immigration records for various ports for the years 1800 to 1959. Prior to January 1, 1820, the United States Federal Government did not require captains or masters of vessels to present passenger lists to U.S. officials. We are seeing immigration records come online via the Internet at an ever increasing rate.

These lists are arranged by port, then by date, and finally by ship. Each generally shows the name of the ship, the port from which it sailed, when it arrived in the United States, and its captain. Individual data, recorded for every passenger on the ship, includes the passenger's name, age, gender, occupation, former residence, and destination. Even the names of those who were born on board or who died during the voyage should be recorded.

There are indexes to most of these arrival lists, the exception being the lists for the port of New York for 1847 through 1896. These passenger arrival lists and their indexes are available on microfilm from the National Archives, the Family History Library and its Family History Centers, some state and local libraries, and a number of commercial entities. With the advent of the Internet we are beginning to see new indexes become available that we have not had access to in the past.

To locate other passenger lists from 1538 to 1959, consult the books dealing with immigration and ship passenger lists listed in the bibliography section of this chapter.

Military Records: The United States National Archives is the official repository for records of military personnel who have been discharged from the U.S. Air Force, Army, Marine Corps, and Navy. Those records available for public examination at the National Archives are a valuable source of information about an individual's military service, family and medical history. Because of their research value, NARA has microfilmed many of these records, primarily those created before 1900. For more information you may want to use the following website: www.archives.gov/veterans/military-service-records/get-service-records.html. Some of these records are also available at the LDS Family History Library and its affiliated Family History Centers.

Following is a list of useful military records for genealogical research:

- **Enlistment records,** give the recruit's name, age, gender, residence, and unit. Some may include the names of parents, spouse or children.

- **Service records,** detail the participation in periodic musters, battles, and other actions, as well as wounds, hospitalizations, reassignments, etc.
- **Pension applications,** include details of service, documentation of relationships, and in some cases include depositions made by individuals who served in the same unit giving additional details of their military service.

Societies and Repositories

Afro-American Historical and Genealogical Society, Inc., National; PO Box 73067; Washington, D.C. 20056-3067; www.aahgs.org

American College of Heraldry; www.americancollegeofheraldry.org

American Family Records Association; PO Box 15505; Kansas City, MO 64106

American Historical Society of Germans from Russia; 631 D. Street; Lincoln, NE 68502-1199; (402) 474-3363; www.ahsgr.org

American Indian Institute; The University of Oklahoma; 555 Constitution St.; Suite 237; Norman, OK 73037-7820; (405) 325-4127; tel.occe.ou.edu/aii/contact_us.htm

American-Canadian Genealogical Society; PO Box 668; Manchester, NH 03105; www.acgs.org

American-French Genealogical Society; PO Box 830; Woonsocket, RI 02895-0870; (401) 765-6141; www.afgs.org

American-Portuguese Genealogical Society, Inc.; PO Box 644; Tanton, MA 02780

American-Schleswig-Holstein Heritage Society; PO Box 313; Davenport, IA 52805-0313; www.ashhs.org

Association of Professional Genealogists, PO Box 350998; Westminster, CO 80035-0998; (303) 422-9371; www.apgen.org

Civil War Descendants Society; PO Box 233; Athens, AL 35611

Colonial Dames of America in the State of New York; National Society of Library; 215 East 71st St.; New York, NY 10021

Daughters of the Union Veterans of the Civil War 1861–1865; 503 S. Walnut; Springfield, IL 62704

Family History Library of The Church of Jesus Christ of Latter-day Saints, 35 North West Temple; Salt Lake City, UT 84150-3400; (801) 240-2331; www.familysearch.org

Federation of Genealogical Societies; PO Box 200940; Austin, TX 78720-0940; (888) fgs-1500; www.fgs.org

First World War, Order of the; PO Box 7062–GH; Gainesville, FL 32605-7062

Flemish Americans, Genealogical Society of; 18740 Thirteen Mile Road; Roseville, MI 48066

Genealogical Center Library; PO Box 71343; Marietta, GA 30007-1343

German American Heritage Center; 712 West 2nd Street; Davenport, IA 52802-1410; (563) 322-8844; www.gahc.org

Heritage Quest Lending Library; PO Box 329; Bountiful, UT 84011-0329; (800) 760-2455; www.heritagequest.com

Hispanic Historical and Ancestral Research, Society of; SHHAR, PO Box 490; Midway City, CA 92655-0490; www.SHHAR.org

Immigrant Genealogical Society; PO Box 7369; Burbank, CA 91510-7369; (661) 259-6648; feefhs.org/igs/frg-igs.html

Institute of Genealogy and History for Latin America; 2191 S. 2200 E.; Mt. Springs, UT 84757; (435) 867-8422

International Society for British Genealogy and Family History; PO Box 3115; Salt Lake City, UT 84110-3115

Jewish Genealogical Societies, Association of; 1485 Teaneck Road; Teaneck, NJ 07666; www.iajgs.org

Library of Congress; Local History & Genealogy Division; 101 Independence Ave. SE, Thomas Jefferson Building, LJ G42; Washington, D.C. 20540-4660; www.loc.gov/rr/genealogy/

Loyalist Descendants (American Revolution), Society of; PO Box 848, Desk 120; Rockingham, NC 28379

Mayflower Descendants, General Society of; Box 3297; Plymouth, MA 02361-3297; (508) 746-3188; www.mayflower.org

Mexican War Veterans, Descendants of; 1114 Pacific Drive; Richardson, TX 75081; www.dmwv.org

National Genealogical Society Library; 4527 17th St.; North Arlington, VA 22207-2399; (703) 525-0050; www.ngsgenealogy.org

National Huguenot Society; 9033 Lyndale Ave. S. Suite 108; Bloomington, MN 55420-3535; (952) 885-9776; www.huguenot.netnation.com

National Society Daughters of the American Revolution Library; 1776 D Street, N.W.; Washington, D.C. 20006-5303; www.dar.org

National Society Sons of the American Revolution Library; 1000 South Fourth St.; Louisville, KY 40203; (502) 589-1776; www.sar.org

New England Historic Genealogical Society; 101 Newbury St.; Boston, MA 02116; (617) 536-5740; www.newenglandancestors.org

Norwegian-American Genealogical Association; N-AGA c/o Minnesota Genealogical Society, 5768 Olson Memorial Hwy; Golden Valley, MN 55422-5014; (763) 595-9347; www.norwegianamerican.org

Norwegian-American Museum, Vesterheim; 523 W. Water Street, PO Box 379; Decorah, IA 52101-0379; (319) 382-9681; www.vesterheim.org

Orphan Train Heritage Society of America; (OTHSA) 614 East Emma Ave., #115; Springdale, AR 72764-4634; (501) 756-2780

Palatine Library, Palatines to America, Capital Univ.; Box 101; Columbus, OH 43209-2394; (614) 236-8281; www.genealogy.org/~palam/

Railroad Retirement Board, United States of America; 844 Rush St.; Chicago, IL 60611-2092; (800) 808-0772; www.rrb.gov

Second World War, Order of the; PO Box 357062-HSC; Gainesville, FL 32635-7062; (352) 377-4164

Southern Society of Genealogists, Inc.; Box 295; Centre, AL 35960; (205) 475-5261

Stagecoach Library for Genealogical Research; 1840 South Wolcott Ct.; Denver, CO 80219; (Rental library); (303) 922-8856

Swenson Swedish Immigration Research Center; Augustana College, 639 38th Street; Rock Island, IL 61201-2296; (309) 794-7204; www.augustana.edu/swenson/

Virginia Society of the Sons of the American Revolution; 3600 West Broad, Suite 446; Richmond, VA 23230-4918

White House Historical Association; PO Box 27624; Washington, D.C. 20038-7624; (202) 737-8292; www.whitehousehistory.org

National Archives and Records Administration Centers

The National Archives and Records Administration; 8601 Adelphi Road; College Park, MD 20740-6001; (866) 272-6272; fax: (301) 837-0483

NARA's Pacific Alaska Region (Anchorage); 654 West Third Avenue; Anchorage, AK 99501-2145

NARA's Southeast Region (Atlanta); 1557 St. Joseph Avenue; East Point, GA 30344-2593

NARA's Northeast Region (Boston); Frederick C. Murphy Federal Center; 380 Trapelo Road; Waltham, MA 02452-6399

NARA's Great Lakes Region (Chicago); 7358 South Pulaski Road; Chicago, IL 60629-5898

NARA's Great Lakes Region (Dayton); 3150 Springboro Road; Dayton, OH 45439-1883

NARA's Rocky Mountain Region (Denver); Bldg. 48, Denver Federal Center; West 6th Avenue and Kipling Street; Denver, CO 80225-0307

NARA's Southwest Region (Fort Worth); 501 West Felix Street, Building 1; Fort Worth, TX 76115-3405

NARA's Central Plains Region (Kansas City); 2312 East Bannister Road; Kansas City, MO 64131

NARA's Pacific Region (Laguna Niguel, CA); 24000 Avila Road, 1st Floor, East Entrance; Laguna Niguel, CA 92677-3497

NARA's Central Plains Region (Lee's Summit, MO); 200 Space Center Drive; Lee's Summit, MO 64064-1182

NARA's Northeast Region (New York City); 201 Varick Street; New York, NY 10014-4811

NARA's Mid Atlantic Region (Center City Philadelphia); 900 Market Street; Philadelphia, PA 19107-4292

NARA's Mid Atlantic Region (Northeast Philadelphia); 14700 Townsend Road; Philadelphia, PA 19154-1096

NARA's Northeast Region (Pittsfield, MA); 10 Conte Drive; Pittsfield, MA 01201-8230

NARA's Pacific Region (San Francisco); 1000 Commodore Drive; San Bruno, CA 94066-2350

NARA's Pacific Alaska Region (Seattle); 6125 Sand Point Way NE; Seattle, WA 98115-7999

National Personnel Records Center; Civilian Personnel Records; 111 Winnebago Street; St. Louis, MO 63118-4126

National Personnel Records Center; Military Personnel Records; 9700 Page Avenue; St. Louis, MO 63132-5100

Office of Record Services - Washington, D.C. (NW); National Archives at College Park; 8601 Adelphi Road, Room 3400; College Park, MD 20740-6001

Washington National Records Center (WNRC); 4205 Suitland Road; Suitland, MD 20746-8001

Bibliography

Archives and Libraries

American Library Directory: A Classified List of Libraries in the United States and Canada. With Personal and Statistical Data. New York: R. R. Bowker, annual.

Bentley, Elizabeth Petty, and Debra Ann Carl, comps. *Directory of Family Associations.* 3rd ed. Turlock, California: Marietta Pub. Co., 1996. 4th ed. Baltimore: Genealogical Publishing Co., Inc., 2001.

Cavanaugh, Karen B. *A Genealogist's Guide to the Ft. Wayne, Indiana, Public Library*; Owensboro, Kentucky: McDowell Publications, 1980.

Daughters of the American Revolution Library. Library Catalog. 3 vols. Washington, D.C.: Daughters of the American Revolution, 1982–1992.

Directory of Archives and Manuscript Repositories in the United States. 2nd ed. Phoenix Press, 1988.

Downs, Robert B. *American Library Resources: A Bibliographical Guide.* Boston: Gregg Press, 1972.

Encyclopedia of Associations. 3 vols. 32nd ed. Detroit: Gale Research Co., 1987–.

Filby, P. William. *Directory of American Libraries With Genealogy or Local History Collections.* Wilmington, Delaware: Scholarly Resources, 1988.

Guide to Genealogical Research in the National Archives. Washington, D.C.: National Archives Trust Fund Board, 1985.

Hereditary Register of the United States of America. Annual. Yoncalla, Oregon: Hereditary Register Publications, 1972–.

Makower, Joel and Linda Zaleskie. *The American History Sourcebook.* New York: Prentice-Hall, 1998.

Meyer, Mary K., ed. *Directory of Genealogical Societies in the U.S.A. and Canada.* 11th ed. Mt. Airy, Maryland: Mary K. Meyer, 1996.

Neagles, James C. *The Library of Congress: A Guide to Genealogical and Historical Research.* Salt Lake City: Ancestry Publishing, 1990.

Parch, Grace D., ed. *Directory of Newspaper Libraries in the United States and Canada.* New York: Project of the Newspaper Division, Special Libraries Assoc., 1976, 10th Edition

Parker, J. Carlyle. *Going to Salt Lake City to do Family History Research.* 3rd ed. Turlock, California: Marietta Publishing Company, 1996.

Roberts, Jayare, and Dorothy Hebertson, comps. *Register of U.S. Lineage Societies.* Salt Lake City: Family History Library, 1990.

Schaefer, Christina K. *The Center: Guide to Genealogical Research in the National Capitol Area.* Baltimore: Genealogical Publishing, 1996.

Sinko, Peggy Tuck. *Guide to Local and Family History at the Newberry Library.* Salt Lake City: Ancestry, 1987.

Szucs, Loretto Dennis, and Sandra Hargraves Luebking. *The Archives: A Guide to the National Archives Field Branches.* Salt Lake City: Ancestry, 1988.

Warren, Paula Stuart and James W. *Your Guide to the Family History Library: How to Access the World's Largest Genealogy Resource.* Cincinnati, Ohio: Betterway Books, 2001.

Wheeler, Mary Bray, ed. *Directory of Historical Organizations in the United States and Canada.* 14th ed. Nashville, Tennessee: American Association for State and Local History, 1990.

Zakailik, Joanne A., ed. *Directory of Special Libraries and Information Centers.* 17th ed. Detroit: Gale Research Co., 1994.

Bible Records

Bible Records, ca. 1141–1982. National Genealogical Society (Arlington, Virginia). (Salt Lake City: Filmed by the Genealogical Society of Utah, 1995). Bible records were collected from members of the National Genealogical Society.

Edmondson, Chan. *Revolutionary War Period Bible, Family, and Marriage Records Gleaned from Pension Applications,* 10 vol. Dallas, Tex.: C. Edmondson, 1990.

Kirkham, E. Kay. *An Index to Some of the Bibles and Family Records of the United States: 35,500 References as Taken From NSDAR Files and Elsewhere....* Logan, Utah: Everton Publishers, 1979.

Kirkham, E. Kay. *An Index to Some of the Bibles and Family Records of the United States: 45,500 References as Taken From the Microfilm at the Genealogical Society of Utah.* Logan, Utah: Everton Publishers, 1984.

Lester, Memory Aldridge. *Old Southern Bible Records: Transcriptions of Births, Marriages and Deaths from Family Bibles, Chiefly of the 18th and 19th Centuries.* Baltimore: Clearfield Co., 1990.

Biography

American Biographical Index. 6 vols. London: Bowker-Saur, 1993.

Biographical Books, 1816–1949 and 1950–1980. New York: Bowker, 1983, 1980.

Black Biography, 1190–1950: A Cumulative Index. 3 vols. Alexandria, VA: Chadwyck-Healey, 1991.

Cimbala, Diane J., Jennifer Cargill, and Brian Alley. *Biographical Sources: A Guide to Dictionaries and Reference Works.* Phoenix L Oryx Press, 1986.

Dictionary of American Biography. New York: Charles Scribner's Sons, 1928–1988.

Herbert, Mirana C., and Barbara McNeil. *Biographical and Genealogy Master Index,* 2nd ed, vols., Detroit: Gale Research, 1980–.

Herbert, Miranda C., and Barbara McNeil. *Historical and Biographical Dictionaries, Master Index: a Consolidated Index to Biographical Information Concerning Historical Personages in over 35 of the Principal Retrospective Biographical Dictionaries.* Detroit: Gale Research Co., 1980.

Index to Biographies in Local Histories in the Library of Congress. Baltimore: Magna Carta Book, 1979.

Library of Congress Index to Biographies in State and Local Histories. Baltimore: Magna Carta Book Co., 1979.

Rider, Fremont, ed. *The American Genealogical-Biographical Index to American, Biographical and Local History Materials.* (AGBI). Series 2. Middletown, Connecticut: Godfrey Memorial Library, 1952–.

Slocum, Robert B., ed. *Biographical Dictionaries and Related Works,* 2 vols. 2nd ed. Detroit: Gale Research, 1986.

Cemeteries

American Blue Book of Funeral Directors. New York: Kates-Boyston Publications, 1932–.

American Blue Book of Funeral Directors. New York: The American Funeral Director, biennial.

Annese, Domenico. "*Construction: Cemetery Design Standards.*" *Landscape Architecture* (January 1983): 85987.

Brown, John Gary. *Soul in the Stone: Cemetery Art from America's Heartland*. Lawrence, Kansas: University Press of Kansas, 1994.

Burek, Deborah, ed. *Cemeteries of the United States*. Detroit: Gale Research Co., 1994.

Cemeteries of the U.S.: A Guide to Contact Information for U.S. Cemeteries and Their Records. 1st ed. Detroit: Gale Research, 1994.

Kot, Elizabeth Gorrell and James D. Kot. *United States Cemetery Address Book, 1994–1995*. Vallejo, California Indices Publishing, 1994.

Meyer, Richard E. ed. *Cemeteries and Gravemarkers: Voices of American Culture*. Ann Arbor: UMI Research Press, 1989.

National Directory of Morticians. Youngstown, Ohio: National Directory of Morticians, 1959–.

National Yellow Book of Funeral Directors. Youngstown, Ohio: Nomis Publications, c1989–.

Nishiura, Elizabeth. *American Battle Monuments: A Guide to Battlefields and Cemeteries of the United States Armed Forces*. Detroit: Omnigraphics, 1989.

Stemmons, Jack and Diane. *Cemetery Record Compendium*. Logan, Utah: Everton Publishers, 1979.

Wallis, Charles L. *American Epitaphs: Grave and Humorous*. New York: Dover Publications, 1975.

Census Records

A Census of Pensioners for Revolutionary or Military Services, 1840. Published With] *A General Index to a Census of Pensioners*. Two Volumes in One. (1841, 1965), repr. 1996. Clearfield Company.

Buckway, G. Eileen. *U.S. 1910 Federal Census: Unindexed States: A Guide to Finding Census Enumeration Districts for Unindexed Cities, Towns and Villages*. Salt Lake City: Family History Library, 1992.

Census Enumeration Districts 1830–1890 and 1910–1950. National Archives Microfilm Publication T-1224, 146 rolls.

Davidson, Katherine H., and Charlotte Am. Ashby, comps. *Preliminary Inventory of the Records of the Bureau of the Census*. Preliminary Inventory No. 161. Washington, D.C.: National Archives and Records Service, 1964.

Dollarhide, William. *The Census Book: A Genealogist's Guide to Federal Census Facts, Schedules and Indexes*. Bountiful, Utah: Heritage Quest, 1999.

Dubester, Henry J. *State Censuses: An Annotated Bibliography of Censuses of Population Taken After the Year 1790 by the States mid Territories of the United States*. Reprint. Knightstown, Indiana: Bookmark, 1975.

Hamilton, Ann B. *Researcher's Guide to United States Census Availability, 1790–1920*. Bowie, Maryland: Heritage Books, 1987.

Indexes to Manufacturers' Census of 1920: An Edited Printing of the Original Indexes and Information. Reprint. Knightstown, Indiana: Bookmark, n.d.

Jackson, Ronald V, Jr. *Early American Series*. Salt Lake City: Accelerated Indexing Systems, 1981–84.

Kemp, Thomas Jay. *The American Census Handbook*. Wilmington, Delaware: Scholarly Resources, Inc., 2001.

Konrad, J. *Directory of Census Information Sources*. Summit Publications, 1984.

Lainhart, Ann S. *State Census Records*. Baltimore: Genealogical Publishing, 1992.

National Archives and Records Administration. *Federal Population and Mortality Schedules, 1790–1910, in the National Archives and the States*. Washington, D.C.: National Archives, 1986. 2 microfiche.

National Archives and Records Administration. *Cartographic Records of the Bureau of the Census*. Preliminary Inventory No. 103. Washington, D.C.: National Archives, 1958.

National Archives Trust Fund Board. *Federal Population Census, 1790–1890: A Catalog of Microfilm Copies of the Schedules*. Rev. Washington, D.C.: National Archives Trust Fund Board, 2001.

National Archives Trust Fund Board. *Federal Population Census, 1900: A Catalog of Microfilm Copies of the Schedules*. Rev. Washington, D.C.: National Archives Trust Fund Board, 2000.

National Archives Trust Fund Board. *Federal Population Census, 1910: A Catalog of Microfilm Copies of the Schedules*. Rev. Washington, D.C.: National Archives Trust Fund Board, 2000.

National Archives Trust Fund Board. *Federal Population Census, 1920: A Catalog of Microfilm Copies of the Schedules*. Rev. Washington, D.C.: National Archives Trust Fund Board, 1992.

Parker, J. Carlyle. *City, County, Town and Township Index to the 1850 Federal Census Schedules*. Detroit: Gale Research Co., 1979.

Stephenson, Charles, "The Methodology of Historical Census Record Lineage: A User's Guide to the Soundex," *Journal of Family History* 5 (1) (Spring 1980): 112–15. Reprinted in Prolguc 12 (2) (Fall 1980): 151–53.

Steuart, Bradley W. *The Soundex Reference Guide: Soundex Codes to Over 125,000 Surnames*. Bountiful, Utah: Precision Indexing, 1990.

Street Indexes to the 29 Largest Cities in the 1910 Census. National Archives Microfiche Publication M-1283.

Thorndale, William and William Dollarhide. *Map Guide to the U.S. Federal Census, 1790–1920*. Baltimore: Genealogical Publishing Co, 1987.

Thorndale, William. "Census Indexes and Spelling Variants." *APG (Association of Professional Genealogists) Newsletter 4* (5) (May 1982): 6–9. Reprinted in *The Source: A Guidebook of American Genealogy*, edited by Arlene Eakle and Johni Cerny. Salt Lake City: Ancestry, 1984, pp. 17–20.

U.S. Bureau of the Census. *200 Years of U.S. Census Taking: Population and Housing Questions, 1790–1990*. Washington, D.C.: Government Printing Office, 1989.

U.S. Congress. Senate. *The History and Growth of the United States Census. Prepared by the Senate Committee on the Census* by Carroll D. Wright. S. Doc. 194, 56 Cong, I sess. Serial 385b. Reprint. 1967.

U.S. Library of Congress. Census Library Project. *State Censuses: An Annotated Bibliography of Censuses of Population Taken After the Year 1790 by States and Territories of the United States of the United States.* Prepared by Henry J. Dubester. Washington, D.C.: Government Printing Office, 1948.

United States. Bureau of the Census. *Cross Index to Selected City Streets and Enumeration Districts.* Washington, D.C.: National Archives, 1984.

United States. Bureau of the Census. 11th Census, 1890. *Schedules Enumerating Union Veterans and Widows of Union Veterans of the Civil War.* Washington, D.C.: National Archives, 1948.

Wright, Carroll D. *The History and Growth of the United States Census.* Reprint. New York: Johnson, 1966.

Church Records

Ahlstrom, Sydney E. *A Religious History of the American People.* New Haven, Connecticut: Yale University Press, 1972.

Allison, William H. *Inventory of Unpublished Material for American Religious History in Protestant Church Archives and Their Repositories.* Washington, D.C.: Carnegie Institute, 1910.

Check List of Historical Records Survey Publications. WPA, 1943. Reprint. Baltimore: Genealogical Publishing Co., *1969.*

Church and Synagogue Libraries. Metuchen, New Jersey: The Scarecrow Press, 1980.

Ganstadt, Edwin Scott. *Historical Atlas of Religions in America.* New York: Harper & Row, 1962.

Hefner, Loretta L. *The WPA Historical Records Survey: A Guide to the Unpublished Inventories, Indexes and Transcripts.* Chicago: Society of American Archivists, 1980.

Hill, Thomas. *Monthly Meetings in North America: An Index.* 2nd ed. Cincinnati: n.p, 1993.

Hinshaw, William Wade. *Encyclopedia of American Quaker Genealogy.* 6 vols. Ann Arbor, Michigan: Edwards Brothers, 1936–1950. Reprint. Baltimore: Genealogical Publishing Co, 1973, 1994.

Hostetter, C. Nelson. *Anabaptist-Mennonites Nationwide USA.* Morgantown, Pennsylvania: Masthof Press, 1997.

Jacquet, Constant H. *Yearbook of American and Canadian Churches.* Nashville: Abingdon Press, annual.

Kirkham, E. Kay. *A Survey of American Church Records.* Logan, Utah: Everton Publishers, 1978.

Mead, Frank S. *Handbook of American Denominations.* 8th ed. Nashville: Aningdon Press, 1985.

Melton, John Gordon, ed. *National Directory of Churches, Synagogues and Other Houses of Worship.* 4 vols. Detroit: Gale Research, 1994.

Melton, John Gordon. *The Encyclopedia of American Religions.* Detroit: Gale Research, 1989.

Pettee, Julia. *List of Churches: Official Forms of the Names for Denominational Bodies with Brief Descriptive and Historical Notes.* Chicago: American Library Association, 1948.

Rodda, Dorothy. *Directory of Church Libraries.* Philadelphia: Drexel Press, 1967.

Suelflow, August R. *A Preliminary Guide to Church Records Repositories.* St. Louis: Church Archives Committee, Society of American Archivists, 1969.

Sweet, William Warren. *Religion on the American Frontier, 1183–1840: A Collection of Source Materials.* New York: Cooper Square Publishers, 1940, 1964.

The Official Catholic Directory. Chicago: Hoffman Bros., 1886–1997.

Court Records

Askin, Jayne. *Search: A Handbook for Adoptees and Birth-parents.* 2nd ed. Phoenix, Arizona: Oryx Press, 1992.

Bentley, Elizabeth Petty. *County Courthouse Book.* Genealogical Publishing, 1995.

Black, Henry Campbell. *Black's Law Dictionary: Definitions of the Terms and Phrases of American and English Jurisprudence, Ancient and Modern.* St. Paul: West Publishing, 1991.

Blume, William and Elizabeth Gaspar Brown. *Digests and Lists Pertaining to the Development of Law and Legal Institutions in the Territories of the United States: 1787–1954.* 6 vols. Ann Arbor: University Microfilm, 1965–79.

BRB Publication Research and Editorial Staff. *The Sourcebook of Federal Courts, U.S. District and Bankruptcy: The Definitive Guide to Searching for Case Information at the Local Level Within the Federal Court System.* Tempe, Arizona: BRB Publications, 1993.

Burton, William C. *Burton's Legal Thesaurus.* 3rd ed. Columbus, Ohio: McGraw Hill Professional Publishing, 2001.

Eichholz, Alice, ed. *Ancestry's Red Book: American State, County & Town Sources.* Salt Lake City, Utah: Ancestry, 1992.

Evans, Barbara Jean. *The New A to Zax: A Comprehensive Genealogical Dictionary for Genealogists and Historians.* 2nd ed. Champaign, Illinois: B. J. Evans, 1990.

Hasse, Adelaide R. *Materials for a Bibliography of the Public Archives of the Thirteen Original States Covering Colonial Period and State Period to 1789.* 1908. Reprint. New York: Argonaut Press, 1966.

Jeffrey, William, Jr. "Early New England Court Records: A Bibliography of Published Material." *Boston Public Library Quarterly* 1954, as reprinted in *American Journal of Legal History* (1957): 119–47.

Klunder, Virgil L. *Lifeline: The Action Guide to Adoption Search.* Cape Coral, Florida: Caradium Publishing, 1991.

Low, Erick Baker. *A Bibliography on the History of the Organizational and Jurisdiction of State Courts.* Williamsburg: National Center for State Courts, 1980.

McReynolds, Michael. *List of Pre-1840 Federal District Court Records Located in Federal Record Centers.* Washington, D.C.: Government Printing Office, 1972. Special List, 31.

National Association of State Libraries. *A Checklist of Legislative Journals of the States of the USA.* New York: Oxford Press, 1938.

National Association of State Libraries. *Preliminary Checklists of Session Laws, to 1922.* New York: Oxford Press, 1934.

Ray, Susanne Smith, et al., comp. *A Preliminary Guide to the Pre-1904 County Records in the National Archives Branch.* Richmond: Virginia State Library and Archives, 1987.

Salmon, Marylynn. *Women and the Law of Property in Early America.* Chapel Hill: University of North Carolina Press, 1986.

Sourcebook of Federal Courts: U.S. District and Bankruptcy. Public Record Research Library. Tempe, Arizona: BRB Publications, 1993.

Szucs, Loretto Dennis and Sandra Hargraves Luebking. *The Archives: A Guide to the National Archives Field Branches.* Salt Lake City: Ancestry, 1988. (Extensive bibliography for Court Records, pp. 232–38).

The Handybook for Genealogists, 11th ed. Logan, Utah: Everton Publishers Inc., 2002.

Tompkins, Dorothy Campbell. *Court Organizations and Administration: A Bibliography.* Berkeley: University of California Press, 1973.

Washington Division of Archives and Records Management. *Frontier Justice: Abstracts and Indexes to the Records of the Territorial District Courts, 1853–1889.* Olympia, Washington: Secretary of State, 1987.

Dictionaries

Dictionary Catalog of the Local History and Genealogy Division. Boston: G. K. Hall, 1974.

Dictionary of American Biography. New York: Charles Scribner's Sons, 1928–1988.

Dictionary of Indian Tribes of the Americas. Newport Beach, California: American Indian Publishers, 1993.

Oxford English Dictionary. Oxford, England: Clarendon Press, 1931–1986.

Directories

American Library Directory. New York: R.R. Bowker Co., annual.

Ayer Directory of Publications. Bala Cynwyd, Pennsylvania: Ayer Press, annual.

Bentley, Elizabeth Petty and Debra Ann Carl, comps. *Directory of Family Associations.* 4th ed. Baltimore: Genealogical Publishing Co., Inc., 2001.

Bentley, Elizabeth Petty. *The Genealogist's Address Book.* 4th ed. Baltimore: Genealogical Publishing Co., Inc., 1998.

Burton, Robert E. "City Directories in the United States, 1784–1820: A Bibliography with Historical Notes." M.S. Thesis, University of Michigan, 1956.

Catalog of City, County, and State Directories Published in North America. New York North American Directory Publishers, 1967.

City Directories of the United States Pre 1860 Through 1901: Guide to the Microfilm Collection. Woodbridge, Connecticut: Research Publications, 1983.

Klein, Bernard. *Guide to American Directories.* 5th ed. Englewood Cliffs, New Jersey: Prentice-Hall, 1962.

National Historical Publications and Records Commission. *Directory of Archives and Manuscript Depositories in the United States.* Washington, D.C.: National Archives and Records Service, 1978.

National Historical Publications and Records Commission. *Directory of Archives and Manuscript Repositories in the United States.* 2nd ed. Phoenix: Oryx Press, 1988.

Parch, Grace D., ed. *Directory of Newspaper Libraries in the United States and Canada.* New York: Project of the Newspaper Division, Special Libraries Assoc., 1976.

Smith, Betty P. *Directory of Historical Societies and Agencies in the United States and Canada.* 14th ed. Nashville: American Association for State and Local History, 1990.

Spear, Dorothea N. *Bibliography of American Directories Through 1860.* Worcester, Massachusetts: American Antiquarian Society, 1961.

Street Directory of the Principal Cities of the United States... to April 1908. 5th ed. 1908. Detroit: Gale Research Co., 1973.

Emigration, Immigration, Migration and Naturalization

Allen, James Paul and Eugene James Turner. *We the People: An Atlas of America's Diversity*. New York: McMillian, 1988.

Anuta, Michael J. *Ships of Our Ancestors*. 2nd ed. Baltimore: Genealogical Publishing Co., 1993.

Appel, John J. *Immigrant Historical Societies in the USA*. New York: Amo Press, 1980.

Appel, John J. *The New Immigration*. New York: Pitman Publishers, 1971.

Auerbach, Frank L. *Immigration Laws of the United States*. Indianapolis: Bobbs-Merrill, 1961.

Bodnar, John. *The Transplanted: A History of Immigrants in Urban America*. Bloomington: Indiana University Press, 1987.

Bolino, August C. *The Ellis Island Source Book*. Washington, D.C.: Kensington Historical Press, 1985.

Boyer, Carl. *Ship Passenger Lists, National and New England (1600–1825)*. Newhall, California: C. Boyer, 1977. Covers Lancour entries 1–71.

Boyer, Carl. *Ship Passenger Lists, New York and New Jersey (1600–1825)*. Newhall, California: C. Boyer, 1978. Covers Lancour entries 72–115.

Boyer, Carl. *Ship Passenger Lists, the South (1538–1825)*. Newhall, California: C. Boyer, 1979. Covers Lancour entries 198E–243.

Boyer, Carol. *Ship Passenger Lists, Pennsylvania and Delaware (1641–1825)*. Newhall, California: C. Boyer, 1980. Covers Lancour entries 116–197.

Buenker, John D., Nicholas C. Burckel, and Rudolph J. Vecoli. *Immigration and Ethnicity: A Guide to Information Sources*. Detroit: Gale Research Co., 1977.

Carmack, Sharon DeBartolo. *A Genealogist's Guide to Discovering Your Emigrant & Ethnic Ancestors*. Cincinnati: Betterway Books, 2000.

Coldham, Peter Wilson. *Bonded Passengers to America*. Vol. I–IX. Baltimore: Genealogical Publishing Co., 1993.

Coldham, Peter Wilson. *Emigrants in Chains*. Baltimore: Genealogical Publishing Co., 1992.

Coldham, Peter Wilson. *Supplement to the Complete Book of Immigrants in Bondage, 1614–1775*. Baltimore: Genealogical Publishing Co., 1992.

Coldham, Peter Wilson. *The Complete Book of Emigrants in Bondage, 1614–1755*. Baltimore: Genealogical Publishing Co., 1988.

Coldham, Peter Wilson. *The Complete Book of Immigrants, 1607–1660*. Baltimore: Genealogical Publishing Co., 1987.

Coldham, Peter Wilson. *The Complete Book of Immigrants, 1661–1699*. Baltimore: Genealogical Publishing Co., 1990.

Coldham, Peter Wilson. *The Complete Book of Immigrants, 1700–1750*. Baltimore: Genealogical Publishing Co., 1992.

Coldham, Peter Wilson. *The Complete Book of Immigrants, 1751–1776*. Baltimore: Genealogical Publishing Co., 1993.

Colletta, John P. *They Came in Ships*. 2nd ed. Salt Lake City, Utah: Ancestry, Inc., 1993.

Cordasco, Francescoa, ed. *A Bibliography of American Immigration History*. Fairfield, New Jersey: Augustus M. Kelly Publishers, 1978.

Cordasco, Francescoa, ed. *The Immigrant Woman in North America*. Metuchen, New Jersey: Scarecrow Press, 1985.

Cordasco, Francescoa, ed. *The New American Immigration: Evolving Patterns of Legal and Illegal Emigration: A Bibliography of Selected References*. New York: Garland, 1987.

Douglas, Lee V. *A Select Bibliography of Works: Norwegian-American Immigration and Local History. Research Guide No. 6*. Washington, D.C.: Library of Congress, Local History & Genealogy Reading Room, n.d..

Douglass, Lee V. *Danish Immigration to America: An Annotated Bibliography of Resources at the Library of Congress. Research Guide No. 28*. Washington, D.C.: Library of Congress, Local History & Genealogy Reading Room, n.d..

Filby, P. William, ed. *Passenger and Immigration Lists Bibliography, 1538–1900*. 2nd ed. Detroit, Michigan: Gale Research Co., 1988.

Filby, P. William, et al. *Passenger and Immigration Lists Index*, 15 vols. Detroit, Gale Research Co., 1981–.

Glazier, Ira A., ed. *The Famine Immigrants: Lists of Irish Immigrants Arriving at the Pan of New York, 1846–1851*. 8 vols. Baltimore: Genealogical Publishing Co., 1983–1986.

Guillet, Edwin C. *The Great Migration: The Atlantic Crossing by Sailing Ship Since 1770*. Rev. Ed. Toronto: University Press, 1963.

Handlin, Oscar, ed. *Immigration as a Factor in American History*. Englewood Cliffs, New Jersey: Prentice-Hall, Inc., 1959.

Handlin, Oscar, ed. *The Uprooted: The Epic Story of the Great Migrations that Made the American People*. Reprinted, 2nd ed. Enlarged, Boston: Little Brown & Co., 1973.

History of the Immigration and Naturalization Service. Washington, D.C.: Government Printing Office, 1988.

Hoglund, A. William. *Immigrants and Their Children in the United States: A Bibliography of Doctoral Dissertations, 1885–1982*. New York: Garland, 1986.

Hotten, John Camden. *The Original Lists Of Persons Of Quality Who Went From Great Britain to the American Plantations, 1600–1700. Localities Where They Formerly Lived in the Mother Country, the Names of the*

Ships in which They Embarked and Other Interesting Particulars. (1874), repr. 2003. Clearfield Company.

Kennedy, John F. *A Nation of Immigrants.* New York: Harper and Row, 1964.

Konvitz, Milton R. *Civil Rights in Immigration.* Ithaca, New York: Cornell University Press, 1953.

Kraut, Alan M. *The Huddled Masses: The Immigrant in American Society.* Arlington Heights, Illinois: Harlan Davidson, 1982.

Lancour, Harold, comp. *A Bibliography of Ship Passenger Lists, 1518–1825; Being a Guide to Published Lists of Early Immigrants to North America.* 3rd ed. New York: New York Public Library, 1978.

Lind, Marilyn. *Immigration, Migration and Settlement in the United States: A Genealogical Guidebook.* Cloquet, Minnesota: The Linden Press, 1985.

Miller, Olga K. *Migration, Emigration, Immigration.* Logan, Utah: Everton Publishers, 1981.

Moody, Suzanna and Joel Wurt, eds. *The Immigration History Research Center: A Guide to Collections.* New York: Greenwood Press, 1991.

Morrison, Joan and Charlotte Fox Zabusky. *American Mosaic: The Immigrant Experience in the Words of Those Who Lived It.* 2nd ed. Pittsburgh: University of Pittsburgh Press, 1993.

Morton, Allen. *Directory of European Steamship Arrivals: for the Years 1890 to 1930 at the Port of New York and for the Years 1904 to 1926 at the Ports of New York, Philadelphia, Boston and Baltimore.* 1931. Reprint, Genealogical Publishing, 1980, 1987.

Neagles, James C., and Lila Lee Neagles. *Locating Your Immigrant Ancestor.* Logan, Utah: Everton Publishers, 1975.

Tepper, Michael. *American Passenger Arrival Records: A Guide to the Records of Immigrants Arriving at American Ports by Sail and Stream.* 2nd ed. Baltimore: Genealogical Publishing Co., 1993.

Tepper, Michael. *Emigrants to Pennsylvania, 1641–1819: A Consolidation of Ship Passenger Lists from the Pennsylvania Magazine of History and Biography.* Baltimore: Genealogical Publishing Co., 1978.

Tepper, Michael. *Immigrants to the Middle Colonies: A Consolidation of Ship Passenger Lists and Associated Data from the New York Genealogical and Biographical Record.* Baltimore: Genealogical Publishing Co., 1978.

Tepper, Michael. *New World Immigrants: A Consolidation of Ship Passenger Lists and Associated Data from Periodical Literature.* 2 vols. Baltimore: Genealogical Publishing Co., 1988.

Tepper, Michael. *Passengers to America: A Consolidation of Ship Passenger Lists from the New England Historical and Genealogical Register.* Baltimore: Genealogical Publishing Co., 1977.

The Church of Jesus Christ of Latter-day Saints. *Research Outline: Tracing Immigrant Origins.* Salt Lake City: Family History Library, 1992.

The Great Migration Begins: Immigrants to New England 1620–1633. CD-ROM ed. Salt Lake City: Ancestry, 2000.

Wood, Virginia Steele. *Immigrant Arrivals: A Guide to Published Sources.* Rev. ed. Washington, D.C: Library of Congress, Local History & Genealogy Reading Room, n.d.

Gazetteers

Abate, Frank R., ed. *American Places Dictionary: A Guide to 45,000 Populated Places, Natural Features, and Other Places in the United States.* 4 vols. Detroit: Omnigraphics, 1994.

Abate, Frank R., ed. *Omni Gazetteer of the United States of America: Providing Name, Location, and Identification for Nearly 1,500,000 Populated Places, Structures, Facilities, Locales, Historic Places, and Geographic Features in the Fifty States...* 11 vols. Detroit: Omnigraphics, 1994.

Bahn, Gilbert S. *American Place Names of Long Ago. A Republication of the Index of Cram's Unrivaled Atlas of the World as based on the Census on 1890.* Baltimore: Genealogical Publishing Co., 1998.

Fanning's Illustrated Gazetteer of the United States. New York: Ensign, Bridgman, and Fanning, 1855.

Gannett, Henry. *The Origin of Certain Place Names in the United States.* 2nd ed. Baltimore: Clearfield Co., 1996.

Kane, Joseph Nathan. *The American Counties: A Record of the Origin of the 3,012 Counties, Dates of Creation and Organization, Area, 1960 Population, Historical Data, etc. of the 50 States.* New York: Scarecrow Press, 1962.

Seltzer, Leon E. *The Columbia-Lippincott Gazetteer of the World.* Morningside Heights, New York: Columbia University Press, 1952.

Genealogy

A Complement to Genealogies in the Library of Congress: A Bibliography. Reprint. Baltimore: Genealogical Publishing Co., Inc., 2001.

Clark, Patricia L., and Dorothy Huntsman, eds. *American Genealogical Biographical Key Title Index.* Salt Lake City: Genealogical Society of Utah, 1990.

Dictionary Catalog of the Local History and Genealogy Division. Boston: G. K. Hall, 1974.

Genealogical Index of the Newberry Library. 4 vols. Boston: G. K. Hall, 1960.

Genealogies Cataloged in the Library of Congress Since 1986. Washington, D.C.: Cataloging Distribution Service, Library of Congress, 1992.

Greenlaw, William Prescott. *The Greenlaw Index of the New England Historic Genealogical Society.* Boston: G. K. Hall, 1979.

Index to American Genealogies: And to Genealogical Material contained in all works as Town Histories, County Histories, Local Histories, Historical Society Publications, Biographies, Historical Periodicals, and Kindred Works. Baltimore: Genealogical Publishing, 1984.

Index to Personal Names in the National Union Catalog of Manuscript Collections, 1959–1984. 2 vols. Alexandria, Virginia: Chadwyck-Healey, 1988.

Index to Some of the Family Records of the Southern States: 35,000 Microfilm References from the N.S.D.A.R. Files and Elsewhere. Logan, Utah: Everton Publishers, 1979.

Kaminkow, Marion J., ed. *A Complement to Genealogies in the Library of Congress*. Baltimore: Magna Carta Book Co., 1981.

Kaminkow, Marion J., ed. *United States Local Histories in the Library of Congress, A Bibliography*. Baltimore: Magna Carta Book Co., 1972.

Kaminkow, Marion J., *Genealogies in the Library of Congress: A Bibliography*. 2 vols. 2 supplements, 1972–76, 1976–86. Baltimore: Magna Carta Book, 1972. Reprint. Baltimore: Genealogical Publishing Co., 2001.

Koons, Bee Barton. *Teaching Genealogy to Young People*. 2004. Heritage Books.

National Union Catalog of Manuscript Collections (NUCMC). Annual. Washington, D.C.: Library of Congress, 1959–.

New York Public Library. *Dictionary Catalog of the Local History and Genealogy Division*. 18 vols. Boston: G.K. Hall, 1974.

Rider, Fremont, ed. *The American Genealogical-Biographical Index to American, Biographical and Local History Materials*. Middletown, Connecticut: Godfrey Memorial Library, 1999, 2000.

Schreiner-Yantis, Netti. *Genealogical and Local History Books in Print*. Springfield, Virginia: Genealogical Books in Print, 1976–.

Virkus, Frederick A., ed. *Abridged Compendium of American Genealogy: First Families of the United States*. 7 vols. 1925–1942. Reprint, Baltimore: Genealogical Publishing, 1987.

Handbooks and Guidebooks

American Society of Genealogists. *Genealogical Research: Methods and Sources*. 2 vols. Rev. ed. Washington, D.C.: American Society of Genealogists, 1980, 1983.

Greenwood, Val D. *The Researcher's Guide to American Genealogy*, 3rd edition. Baltimore: Genealogical Publishing Co., Inc., 2000.

Guide to Genealogical Research in the National Archives. Washington, D.C.: National Archives Trust Fund Board, 1985.

Hall, H. Byron, ed. *Lest We Forget: A Guide to Genealogical Research in the Nation's Capital*.

Annandale, Virginia: Annandale and Oakton Stakes of the Church of Jesus Christ of Latter-day Saints, 1989, c1965.

Hefner, Loretta L. *The W.P.A. Historical Records Survey: A Guide to Unpublished Inventories, Indexes and Transcripts*. Chicago: Society of American Archivists, 1980.

Kemp, Thomas Jay. *International Vital Records Handbook*. Baltimore: Genealogical Publishing Co., Inc., 2001.

Kemp, Thomas Jay. *The American Census Handbook*. Wilmington, Delaware: Scholarly Resources, Inc., 2001.

Kirkham, E. Kay. *A Handy Guide to Record Searching in the Larger Cities of the United States, Including a Guide to Their Vital Records and Some Maps with Street Indexes with Other Information of Genealogical Value*. Logan, Utah: Everton Publishers, 1974.

Kirkham, E. Kay. *A Survey of American Church Records*. Logan, Utah: Everton Publishers, 1978.

Kirkham, E. Kay. *The Handwriting of American Records for a Period of 300 Years*. Logan, Utah: Everton Publishers, 1973.

Lackey, Richard S. *Cite Your Sources: A Manual for Documenting Family Histories and Genealogical Records*. Reprint. Jackson, Mississippi: University Press of Mississippi, 1986.

Makower, Joel and Linda Zaleskie. *The American History Sourcebook*. New York: Prentice-Hall, 1998.

Mead, Frank S. *Handbook of Denominations*. New York: Arlington Press, 1965.

Meyerink, Kory L., ed. *Printed Sources: A Guide to Published Genealogical Records*. Salt Lake City: Ancestry Publishing, 1998.

Mills, Elizabeth Shown, ed. *Professional Genealogy: A Manual for Researchers, Writers, Editors, Lecturers and Librarians*. Baltimore: Genealogical Publishing Co., 2001.

Mills, Elizabeth Shown. *Evidence!: Citation & Analysis for the Family Historian*. Baltimore: Genealogical Publishing Co., 2000.

Neagles, James C. *The Library of Congress: A Guide to Genealogical and Historical Research*. Salt Lake City: Ancestry, 1990.

Pfeiffer, Laura Szucs. *Hidden Sources: Family History in Unlikely Places*. Salt Lake City: Ancestry Publishing, 2000.

Rubincam, Milton. *Pitfalls in Genealogical Research*. Salt Lake City: Ancestry Pubs., 1987.

Schreiner-Yantis, Netti. *Genealogical and Local History Books in Print*. Springfield, Virginia: Genealogical Books in Print, 1981.

Sherrill, Paul Drake and Beth Sherrill. *Missing Pieces—How to Find Birth Parents and Adopted Children. A Search and Reunion Guidebook*. 2004. Heritage Books.

Smolenyak, Megan and Ann Turner. *Trace Your Roots with DNA Using Genetic Tests to Explore Your Family Tree.* 2005.

Stevenson, Noel C. *Evidence: A Guide to the Standard of Proof Relating to Pedigree, Ancestry, Heirship, and Family History.* Rev. ed. Lagunna Hills, California: Aegean Park Press, 1989.

Stryker-Rodda, Harriet. *Understanding Colonial Handwriting.* Baltimore: Genealogical Publishing. 1986.

Szucs, Loretto Dennis and Sandra Hargreaves Luebking, eds. *The Source: A Guidebook for American Genealogy.* Rev. ed. Salt Lake City: Ancestry Incorporated, 1997.

Wright, Norman E. *Preserving Your American Heritage: A Guide to Family and Local History.* Provo, Utah: Brigham Young University Press, 1981.

Historical Geography

Adams, James Truslow. *Atlas of American History.* New York: Charles Scribner's Sons, 1943.

Atlas of American History. New York: Charles Scribner's Sons, 1984.

Grim, Ronald E. *Historical Geography of the United States: A Guide to Information Sources.* Detroit: Gale Research, 1982.

Holt, Alfred. *American Place Names.* New York: Thomas Y. Crowell, 1938.

Kane, Joseph Nathan. *The American Counties: Origins of Names, Dates of Creation and Organization, Area, Population, Historical Data, and Published Sources.* 4th ed. Metuchen, New Jersey: Scarecrow Press, 1983.

Kirkham, E. Kay. *A Genealogical and Historical Atlas of the United States of America.* Logan, Utah: Everton Publishers, 1976.

Sealock, Richard B., ed., et al. *Bibliography of Place-Name Literature, United States and Canada.* 3rd ed. Chicago: American Library Assoc., 1982.

The Handybook for Genealogists. Logan, Utah: Everton Publishers Inc., 2002.

History

Atlas of American History. New York: Charles Scribner's Sons, 1984.

Buenker, John D., Gerald Michael Greenfield, and William J. Murin. *Urban History: A Guide to Information Sources.* Detroit: Gale Research Co., 1981.

Dictionary Catalog of the Local History and Genealogy Division. Boston: G. K. Hall, 1974.

Dictionary of American History, Revised ed., 8 vol. New York: Charles Scribner's Sons, 1976.

Douglas, Lee V. *A Select Bibliography of Harks: Norwegian-American Immigration and Local History. Research Guide No. 6.* Washington, D.C.: Library of Congress, Local History & Genealogy Reading Room, n.d.

Filby, P. William. *A Bibliography of American County Histories.* Baltimore: Genealogical Publishing Co., 1985. 10th Edition.

Handlin, Oscar, ed. *Immigration as a Factor in American History.* Englewood Cliffs, New Jersey: Prentice-Hall, Inc., 1959.

Handlin, Oscar, ed. *The Uprooted: The Epic Story of the Great Migrations that Made the American People.* Reprinted, 2nd ed. Enlarged, Boston: Little Brown & Co., 1973.

Holden, Robert John and Donna Jean Holden. *The Hunting Pioneers 1720–1840, Ultimate Backwoodsmen on the Early American Frontier.* 2000. Heritage Books.

Kaminkow, Marion J., ed. *United States Local Histories in the Library of Congress, A Bibliography.* 5 vols. Baltimore: Magna Carta Book Co., 1975–1976.

Schlesinger, Jr., Arthur M. *The Almanac of American History.* Greenwich, Connecticut: Bison Books, 1983.

Schreiner-Yantis, Netti. *Genealogical and Local History Books in Print.* Springfield, Virginia: Genealogical Books in Print, 1981.

United States Local Histories in the Library of Congress, A Bibliography. Baltimore: Magna Carta Book Co., 1975.

Webster's Guide to American History: A Chronological, Geographical, and Biographical Survey and Compendium. Springfield, Massachusetts: G&C Merriam, 1971.

Land and Property

Billington, Ray Allen and Martin Ridge. *Western Expansion, A History of the American Frontier.* 5th ed. New York: Macmillan Publishing Co., 1982.

Bureau of Land Management. *Manual of Instruction for the Survey of the Public Lands of the United States.* Technical Bulletin 6. Washington, D.C.: Department of the Interior, 1973.

Bureau of Land Management. *Public Land Bibliography.* Washington, D.C.: Bureau of Land Management, 1962.

Department of the Interior. *Catalog of the United States Geological Survey Library.* 24 vols. plus a supplement of 11 vols. and a second of 4. Boston: G.K. Hall, 1964, 1972–1974.

Digested Summary and Alphabetical List of Private Claims Which Have Been Presented to the House Representatives.... Baltimore: Genealogical Publishing Co., 1970.

Donaldson, Thomas. *The Public Domain: Its History with Statistics.* House Misc. Doc. 45 pt. 4, 47th Cong., 2nd Sess. 1884. Reprint. New York: Johnson Reprint, 1970.

Hibbard, Benjamin Horace. *A History of the Public Domain Policies.* New York: Peter, Smith, 1939.

Higham, John. *Strangers in the Land Patterns of American Nativism, 1860–1925.* Rutgers, New Jersey: Rutgers

University Press, 1955. Reprint, New York: Atheneum, 1963–1981.

Hone, Wade. *Land and Property Research in the United States*. Salt Lake City: Ancestry, 1997.

Kirkham, E. Kay. *The Land Records of America and Their Genealogical Value*. Salt Lake City: Deseret Book, 1964.

Lee, Lawrence B. "American Public Land History: A Review Essay" *Agricultural History* 55 (1981): 284–99.

McMullin, Phillip W., ed. *Grassroots of America*. Reprint. Greenville, South Carolina: Southern Historical Press, 1993.

National Archives. *Guide to Genealogical Research in the National Archives*. Washington, D.C.: National Archives and Records Service, 2000.

Robbins, Roy Marvin. *Our Landed Heritage: The Public Domain, 1776–1970*. 2nd ed. Lincoln: University of Nebraska Press, 1976.

Rohrbough, Malcolm J. *The Land Office Business: The Settlement and Administration of American Public Lands, 1789–1837*. Belmont, California: Wadsworth Publishing Co., 1990.

Salmon, Marylynn. *Women and the Law of Property in Early America*. Chapel Hill: University of North Carolina Press, 1986.

Smith, Clifford Neal. *Federal Land Series: A Calendar of Archival Materials on the Land Patents Issued by the United States Government, with Subject, Tract and Name Indexes*. 4 vols. Reprint. Baltimore: Clearfield Co., 1999.

Stevenson, Richard W. *Land Ownership Maps*. Washington, D.C.: Library of Congress, 1967.

Treat, Payson Jackson. *The National Land System, 1185–1820*. New York: E.B. Treat, 1910.

United States Congress. *American State Papers, Class VIII,: Public Lands and The American State Papers, Class IX,: Claims*. 9 vols. Washington, D.C.: Gale and Seaton, 1832–61. Reprint, Greenville, South Carolina: Southern Historical Press, 1994.

United States Congress. House. *Digested Summary and Alphabetical List of Private Claims Which Have Been Presented to the House of Representatives*. Washington, D.C.: Library of Congress, [19–].

Yoshpe, Harry P., and Phillip P. Brower. *Preliminary Inventory of the Land-Entry Papers of the General Land Office*. Preliminary Inventory 22 Washington, D.C.: National Archives, 1949. Reprint. San Jose, California: Rose Family Association, 1996.

Maps and Atlases

Androit, Jay. *Township Atlas of the United States*. McClean, Virginia: Documents Index, 1991.

Atlas of American History, 2nd ed., revised. New York: Charles Scribner's Sons, 1984.

Cobb, David A., comp. *Guide to U.S. Map Resources*. Chicago: American Library Association, 1986.

Geography and Map Section of the Library of Congress. "Fire Insurance Maps in the Library of Congress." Washington, D.C.: 1981.

Kirkham, E. Kay. *A Genealogical and Historical Atlas of the United States of America*. Logan, Utah: Everton Publishers, 1976.

Library of Congress. Geography and Map Division. *Land Ownership Maps*. Washington, D.C.: Library of Congress, 1983.

Library of Congress. Geography and Map Division. *Land Ownership Maps: A Checklist of Nineteenth Century United States County Maps in the Library of Congress*. Washington, D.C.: Library of Congress, 1967.

Library of Congress. *Panoramic Maps of Cities in the United States and Canada: A Checklist of Maps of the Collections of the Library of Congress, Geography and Map Division*. 2nd ed. Washington, D.C.: Library of Congress, 1984.

Long, John H., ed. *Historical Atlas and Chronology of County Boundaries, 1788–1980*. 5 vols. Boston: G. K. Hall, 1984.

Long, John H., ed., [State] *Atlas of Historical County Boundaries*. New York: Charles Scribner's sons, 1996–.

Madower, Joel, ed. *The Map Catalog*. New York: Vintage Books, 1986.

Meinig, D. W. *The Shaping of America: A Geographical Perspective on 500 Years of History*. 2 vols. New Haven, Connecticut: Yale University Press, 1986.

Moffat, Riley Moore. *Map Index to Topographic Quadrangles of the United States, 1882–1940*. Occasional paper: Western Association of Map Libraries, no. 10 Santa Cruz, California: Western Association of Map Libraries, 1986.

Rand-McNally Commercial Atlas and Marketing Guide. New York: Rand-McNally & Co., annual.

Shelley, Michael H. *Ward Maps of United States Cities: A Selective Checklist of Pre-1900 Maps in the Library of Congress*. Washington, D.C.: N.p., 1975.

The American Heritage Pictorial Atlas of United States History. New York: American Heritage Publishing, 1966.

Thorndale, William and William Dollarhide. *Map Guide to the U.S. Federal Census, 1790–1920*. Baltimore: Genealogical Publishing Co., 1987.

Thrower, Norman J.W. "The County Atlases of the United States." Surveying and Mapping 21 (1961): 365–73.

United States. *Geological Survey. Topographic Maps of the United States*. Scale varies. Suitland, Maryland: National Archives and Records Service, 1976–.

Walsh, Jim. *Maps Contained in the Publications of the American Bibliography, 1639–1819: An Index and Checklist*. Metuchen, New Jersey: Scarecrow Press, 1988.

Ward Maps of United States Cities. Washington, D.C.: Library of Congress, [1975?].

Military Records

D.A.R. *Patriot Index*. Washington, D.C.: National Society, Daughters of the American Revolution, 1979.

Davis, Lenwood G. *Blacks in the American Armed Forces, 1776–1983*: A Bibliography. Westport, Connecticut: Greenwood Press, 1985.

Deputy, Marilyn, and Pat Barben. *Register of Federal United States Military Records, A Guide to Manuscript Sources at the Genealogical Library Salt Lake City and the National Archives in Washington, D.C.* 3 vols. Bowie, Maryland: Heritage Books, 1986.

Family History Library. *U.S. Military Records: Research Outline*. Salt Lake City: The Church of Jesus Christ of Latter-day Saints, 1998.

Giller, Sadye, William H. Dumont and Louise M. Dumont. *Index of Revolutionary War Pension Applications*. Washington, D.C.: National Genealogical Society, 1966.

Groene, Bertram H. *Tracing Your Civil War Ancestor*. Revised. Winston-Salem, North Carolina: John F. Blair, 1995.

Heitman, Francis B. *Historical Register and Dictionary of the United States Army, from Its Organization September 29, 1789 to March 2, 1903.* 2 vols. 1965. Reprint. Baltimore: Genealogical Publishing Co., 1994.

Horowita, Lois. *A Bibliography of Military Name Lists From Pre-1615 to 1900: A Guide to Genealogical Sources*. Metuchen, New Jersey: The Scarecrow Press, 1990.

Hughes, Mark, comp. *The Unpublished Roll of Honor*. Baltimore: Genealogical Publishing Co., Inc. 1996.

Index of Rolls of Honor in the Lineage Books. Washington, D.C.: DAR, 1939–.

Index to Revolutionary War Pension Applications in the National Archives. National Genealogical Society Special Publication No. 40. Washington, D.C.: NGS, 1976.

Johnson, Richard S. *How to Locate Anyone Who Is or Has Been in the Military*. 7th ed. Spartanburg, South Carolina: MIE Publishing, 1996.

Kinnell, Susan K. *Military History of the United States; an Annotated Bibliography*. Santa Barbara, California: ABC-CLIO, 1986.

Kirkham, E. Kay. *Some of the Military Records of America (Before 1900): Their Use and Values in Genealogical and Historical Research*. Salt Lake City: Deseret Book Co., 1964.

Lane, Jack C. *Americans Military Past: A Guide to Information Sources*. Detroit: Gale Research, 1980.

Military Service Records: A Select Catalog of National Archives Microfilm Publications. Washington, D.C.: National Archives Trust, 1985.

Mulligan, Timothy P. comp. *Guide to Records Relating to U.S. Military Participation in World War II*. Washington, D.C.: National Archives and Records Administration, 1996.

Neagles, James C., and Lila L. Neagles. *Locating Your Revolutionary War Ancestors: A Guide to the Military Records*. Logan, Utah: Everton Publishers, 1983.

Neagles, James C. *U.S. Military Records: A Guide to Federal and State Sources, Colonial America to the Present*. Salt Lake City: Ancestry, 1994.

Patriot Index Centennial Edition. Washington, D.C.: National Society DAR, 1994.

Poulos, Paula Nassen, ed. *A Woman's War Too: U.S. Women in the Military in World War II*. Washington, D.C.: National Archives and Records Administration, 1996.

Powell, William H. *List of Officers of the Army of the United States From 1779 to 1900 Embracing a Register of All Appointments by the President of the United States in the Volunteer Service During the Civil War and of Volunteer Officers of the United States June I, 1900.* Detroit: Gale Research Co. 1967.

Purdy, Virginia C., and Robert Gruber, comps. *American Women and the U.S. Armed Forces: A Guide to the Records of Military Agencies in the National Archives Relating to American Women*. Washington, D.C.: National Archives and Records Administration, 1992.

Reamy, Martha and William Reamy, comps. *Index to the Roll of Honor*. Baltimore: Genealogical Publishing Co., 1995.

Ryan, Gary D., and Timothy K. Nenninge, eds. *Soldiers and Civilians: The U.S. Army and the American People*. Washington, D.C.: National Archives and Records Administration, 1987.

Tozeski, Stanley R. *Preliminary Inventory of the Records of the U.S. Military Academy*. Washington, D.C.: National Archives and Records Service, 1976.

U.S. Quartermaster's Department. Roll of Honor. 27 Vols. Reprint. Baltimore: Genealogical Publishing Co., Inc., 1994.

U.S. Veterans Administration. *Abstracts of Service Records of Naval Officers ("Records of Officers") 1798–1893*. M330, 19 rolls. Washington, D.C.: National Archives Microfilm Publications.

U.S. Veterans Administration. *Registers of Enlistments in the United States Army, 1789–1914*. M233, 80 rolls. Washington, D.C.: National Archives Publications, 1963.

White, Virgil D. *Genealogical Abstracts of Revolutionary War Pension Files*. 3 vol. Waynesboro, Tennessee: National Historical Publishing Co., 1990–1992.

White, Virgil D. *Index to War of 1812 Pension Files*. 2 vol. Waynesboro, Tennessee: National Historical Pub. Co., 1992.

White, Virgil D. *Index of U.S. Marshals, 1789–1960*. Waynesboro, Tennessee: National Historical Pub. Co., 1988.

White, Virgil D. *Index to Mexican War Pension Files.* Waynesboro, Tennessee: National Historical Pub. Co., 1989.

White, Virgil D. *Index to Old Wars Pension Files, 1815–1926.* Waynesboro, Tennessee: National Historical Publishing, 1993.

White, Virgil D. *Index to Pension Applications for Indian Wars Service Between 1817 and 1898.* Waynesboro, Tennessee: National Historical Pub. Co., 1997.

White, Virgil D. *Index to U.S. Military Pension Applications of Remarried Widows for Service Between 1812 and 1911.* Waynesboro, Tennessee: National Historical Publishing Co., 1999.

White, Virgil D. *Index to Volunteer Soldiers in Indian Wars and Disturbances, 1815–1858.* Waynesboro, Tennessee: National Historical Publishing Co., 1994.

White, Virgil D. *Index to Volunteer Soldiers, 1784–1811.* Waynesboro, Tennessee: National Historical Pub. Co., 1987.

White, Virgil D. *Index to Medal of Honor Recipients, 1863–1978.* Waynesboro, Tennessee: National Historical Pub. Co., 1999.

Minorities

Archeacon, Thomas J. *Becoming American: An Ethnic History.* New York: The Free Press, 1983.

Bodnar, John. *The Transplanted: A History of Immigrants in Urban America.* Bloomington, Indiana: Indiana University Press, 1985.

Carmack, Sharon DeBartolo. *A Genealogist's Guide to Discovering Your Emigrant & Ethnic Ancestors.* Cincinnati: Betterway Books, 2000.

Colletta, John Philip. *Finding Italian Roots. The Complete Guide for Americans.* 2nd Edition. 2003.

Ethnographic Bibliography of North America. 4th ed. 5 vols. Behavior Science Bibliographies. New Haven, Connecticut: Human Relations Area Files, 1975; supplement (3 vols.), 1990.

Lieberson, Stanley. *Ethnic Patterns in American Cities.* New York: Free Press, 1963.

Mindel, Charles H., and Robert W. Habenstein. *Ethnic Families in America: Patterns and Variations.* New York: Elsevier Science Publishing Co., 1981.

Murdock, George P., and Timothy J. O'Leary, eds. *Ethnographic Bibliography of North America, 1975 and Supplement to the 1975 Edition.* 1990.

Nemecek. Paul M. *Historical and Cultural Essays on Czechs in America.* 2004.

Smith, Jessie C. *Ethnic Genealogy: A Resource Guide.* Westport, Connecticut: Greenwood Press, 1983.

Sowell, Thomas. *Ethnic America: A History.* New York: Basic Books, 1981.

Szucs, Loretto Dennis and Sandra Hargraves Luebking. *The Source: A Guidebook of American Genealogy.*

Revised ed. Salt Lake City, Utah: Ancestry Incorporated, 1997. Extensive bibliography on United States ethnic sources in Chapter 13, *"Immigration: Finding Immigrant Origins."*

Thernatrom, Stephen, ed. *Harvard Encyclopedia of American Ethnic Groups.* Cambridge, Massachusetts: Harvard University Press, 1980.

Tracing Immigrant Origins: Research Outline. Salt Lake City: Family History Library, 1992.

Wasserman, Paul and Alice E. Kennington. *Ethnic Information Sources of the United States: A Guide to Organizations, Agencies, Foundations, Institutions, Media, Commercial and Trade Bodies, Government Programs, Research Institutes, Libraries and Museums, Religious Organizations, Banking Firms, Festivals and Fairs, Travel and Tourist Offices, Airlines and Ship Lines, Bookdealers and Publishers' Representatives, and Books, Pamphlets, and Audiovisual on Specific Ethnic Groups.* 2nd ed. 2 vols. Detroit: Gale Research Co., 1983.

Wertsmann, Vladimir F. *Romanians in the United States & Canada. A Guide to Ancestry and Heritage Research.* North Salt Lake, Utah: Heritage Quest, 2002.

Wynar, Lubomyr R., and Anna T. Wynar. *The Encyclopedic Directory of Ethnic Newspapers and Periodicals in the United States.* 2nd ed. Littleton, Colorado: Libraries Unlimited, 1976.

Wynar, Lubomyr R. *Encyclopedia Directory of Ethnic Organizations in the United States.* Littleton, Colorado: Libraries Unlimited, 1976.

African-Americans

African American Genealogical Sourcebook. New York: Gale Research, 1995.

Black Studies: A Select Catalog of National Archives Microfilm Publications. Washington, D.C.: National Archives, 1984.

Burkett, Randall K., Nancy Hall Burkett, and Henry Louis Gates, Jr., eds. *Black Biographical Dictionaries 1790–1950.* Alexandria, Virginia: Chadwyck-Healy, Inc., [198–].

Burroughs, Tony. *Black Roots: A Beginner's Guide to Tracing the African American Family Tree.* New York: Fireside Div. Of Simon & Schuster, 2001.

Campbell, Georgetta Merritt. *Extant Collections of Early Black Newspapers: A Research Guide to the Black Press, 1880–1915, With an Index to the Boston Guardian, 1902–1904.*

Fears, Mary Louvenis Jackson. *Slave Ancestral Research: It's Something Else.* Bowie, Maryland: Heritage Books, 1995.

Frazier, Thomas R. *Afro-American History: Primary Sources.* Chicago: The Dorsey Press, 1988.

Gutman, Herbert George. *The Black Family in Slavery and Freedom, 1750–1925.* New York: Vintage Books, 1976.

Ham, Debra Newman, and Beverly Brannan, eds. *The African-American Mosaic: A Library of Congress*

Resource Guide for the Study of Black History and Culture. Washington, D.C.: Library of Congress, 1993.

Henritze, Barbara K. *Bibliographic Checklist of African American Newspapers.* Baltimore, Maryland: Genealogical Publishing Co., 1995.

Kelbaugh, Ross J. *Introduction to African American Photographs, 1840–1950.* 2005.

Newspapers and Periodicals by and About Black People. North Carolina Central University. School of Library Science. African-American Materials Project. Boston: G.K. Hall, 1978.

Records of Ante-Bellum Southern Plantations from the Revolution through the Civil War. Frederic, Maryland: University Publications of America, 1985–.

Rose, James and Alice Eichholz. *Black Genesis.* Detroit: Gale Research, 1978.

Schubert, Frank N. *On the Trail of the Buffalo Soldier: Biographies of African Americans in the U.S. Army, 1866–1917.* Wilmington, Delaware: Scholarly Resources, 1995.

Streets, David H. *Slave Genealogy: A Research Guide with Case Studies.* Bowie, Maryland: Heritage, 1986.

Thackery, David T. *A Bibliography of African American Family History at the Newberry Library.* Chicago: The Newberry Library, 1993.

Thackery, David T., and Dee Woodtor. *Case Studies in Afro-American Genealogy.* Chicago: The Newberry Library, 1989. Troy, New York: Whitston Publishing Co., 1981.

Wadelington, Charles Weldon. *Tips on Collecting and Preserving Black Family History: A Guide for the Beginner.* Raleigh, North Carolina: North Carolina Afro-American Genealogical Society, 1986.

Woodtor, Dee Farmer. *Finding a Place Called Home: A Guide to African-American Genealogy and Historical Identity.* New York: Random House, 1999.

Young, Tommie Morton. *Afro-American Genealogy Sourcebook.* New York: Garland Publishing, Inc., 1987.

Hispanic

Byers, Paula K, ed. *Hispanic American Genealogy Sourcebook.* New York: Gale Research, 1995.

Camarillo, Albert. *Latinos in the United States: A Historical Bibliography.* Santa Barbara, California: ABC-Clio, 1986.

Codinach, Guadalupe Jimenez. *The Hispanic World, 1492–1898: A Guide to Photo Reproduced Manuscripts from Spain in the Collections of the United States, Guam and Puerto Rico—El mundo hispanico 1492–1898: guia de copias fotograficas de manuscritos espanoles existentes en los Estados Unidos de America, Guam y Puerto Rico.* Washington, D.C.: Library of Congress, 1994.

Fernandez-Shaw, Carlos. *The Hispanic Presence in the United States from 1492 to Today.* New York: Facts on File, 1987.

Flores, Norma and Patsy Ludwig. *A Beginner's Guide to Hispanic Genealogy.* San Mateo, California: Western Book/Journal Press, 1993.

Hispanic American Genealogical Sourcebook. New York: Gale Research, 1995.

Platt, Lyman D. *Census Records for Latin America and Hispanic United States.* Baltimore: Genealogical Publishing Co., 1998.

Platt, Lyman D. *Spanish Surname Histories.* Orem, Utah: Automated Archives, 1984.

Ryskamp, George and Peggy Ryskamp. *A Student's Guide to Mexican American Genealogy.* Phoenix, Arizona: Onyx Press, 1996.

Ryskamp, George R. *Finding Your Hispanic Roots.* Baltimore, Maryland: Genealogical Publishing Co., Inc., 1997.

Ryskamp, George R. *Tracing Your Hispanic Heritage.* Riverside, California: Hispanic Family History Research, 1984.

Jewish Americans

Blau, Joseph Leon. *The Jews of the United States, 1790–1840: A Documentary History.* New York: Columbia University Press, 1963.

Daniels, Judith M. *The Concise Dictionary of American Jewish Biography.* 2 vols. Brooklyn: Carlson Publishing, 1994.

Dimont, Max. *The Jews in America: The Roots, History, and Destiny of American Jews.* New York: Simon and Schuster, 1978.

Diner, Hasia R. *A Time for Gathering: The Second Migration, 1820–1880.* Baltimore: Johns Hopkins University Press, 1992.

Faber, Eli, and Henry L. Feingold, eds. *A Time for Planting: The First Migration, 1654–1820.* Baltimore: Johns Hopkins University Press, 1992.

Goodstein, Nancy. *Jewish Records in the Family History Library Catalog.* 9 vols. Salt Lake City: Family History Department, Church of Jesus Christ of Latter-day Saints, 2000.

Gorr, Samuel. *Jewish Personal Names: Their Origin, Derivation and Diminutive Forms.* Teaneck, New Jersey: Avotaynu, 1992.

Guggenheimer, Heinrich W. *Jewish Family Names and Their Origins: An Etymological Dictionary.* Hoboken, New Jersey: Ktav, 1992.

Harvey, John Frederick. *Church and Synagogue Libraries.* Metuchen, New Jersey: The Scarecrow Press, 1980.

Kohn, Gary J. *The Jewish Experience: A Guide to Manuscript Sources in the Library of Congress.* Cincinnati: American Jewish Archives, 1986.

Kurzweil, Arthur. *The Encyclopedia of Jewish Genealogy.* 3 vols. Northvale, New Jersey: Jason Aronson, 1991.

Marcus, Jacob Rader. *United States Jews, 1776–1989.* 4 vols. Detroit: Wayne State University Press, 1989.

Marx, Alexander. *Studies in Jewish History and Booklore.* New York: Jewish Theological Seminary of America, 1944.

Mason, Philip P. *Directory of Jewish Archival Institutions.* Detroit: Published for the National Foundation for Jewish Culture by Wayne State University Press, 1975.

Rischin, Moses. *Jews of the American West.* Detroit: Wayne State University, 1991.

Rudd, Hynda L. *Mountain West Pioneer Jewry: An Historical and Genealogical Source Book (from origins to 1885).* Los Angeles: Will Kramer, 1980.

Sachar, Howard M. *A History of the Jews in America.* New York: Alfred A. Knopf, 1994, c1992.

Scharfman, I. Harold. *Jews on the Frontier-. An Account of Jewish Pioneers and Settlers on the American Frontier.* Malibu, California: Joseph Simon/Pangloss Press, 1990, 1977.

Schleifer, Jay. *A Student's Guide to Jewish American Genealogy.* Phoenix, Arizona: Oryx Press, 1996.

Segall, Aryeh. *Guide to Jewish Archives.* Jerusalem, New York: World Council on Jewish Archives, 1981.

Sorin, Gerald. *A Time for Building: The Third Migration, 1880–1920.* Baltimore: Johns Hopkins University, 1992.

Stern, Malcolm H. *First American Jewish Families: 600 genealogies, 1654–1988.* 3rd ed. Baltimore: Ottenheimer, 1991.

Zubatsky, David S., and Irwin M. Berebt. *Jewish Genealogy: A Sourcebook of Family Histories and Genealogies.* Reprint. Teaneck, New Jersey: Avotaynu, Inc., 1996.

Names

Bardsley, Charles W. *Curiosities of Puritan Nomenclature.* 1880. Reprint. Baltimore: Clearfield Co., 1996.

Baring-Gould, Sabine. *Family Names and Their Story.* Baltimore: Genealogical Publishing Co., 1968.

Bowman, William Dodgson. *The Story of Surnames.* 1932. Reprint. Detroit: Gale Research, 1968.

Hook, J. N. *Family Names: How Our Surnames Came to America.* New York: Macmillan Pub., 1982.

Latham, Edward. *A Dictionary of Names, Nicknames and Surnames of Persons, Places and Things.* Detroit: Gale Research, 1966.

Loughead, Flora Haines Apponyi. *Dictionary of Given Names with Origins and Meanings.* 2nd ed. Glendale, California: Arthur H.Clark, 1974, 1933.

Moody, Sophy. *What is Your Name? A Popular Account of the Meanings and Derivations of Christian Names.* 1863. Reprint. Detroit: Gale Research, 1976.

Payton, Geoffrey. *Webster's Dictionary of Proper Names.* Springfield, Massachusetts: G. & C. Merriam, 1970.

Room, Adrian. *Brewer's Dictionary of Names.* Oxford: Cassell, 1992.

Rose, Christine. *Nicknames Past and Present.* 3rd ed. rev. and enl. San Jose, California: Rose Family Association, 1998.

Smith, Elsdon C. *American Surnames.* Baltimore: Genealogical Publishing Co., 1986.

Smith, Elsdon C. *New Dictionary of American Family Names.* New York: Harper & Row, 1973.

Smith, Elsdon C. *Personal Names: A Bibliography.* New York: New York Public Library, 1952.

Smith, Elsdon C. *The Story of Our Names.* New York: Harper, 1950.

Stein, Lou. *Clues to Family Names.* 2nd ed. rev. Bowie, Maryland: Heritage Books, 1988.

Surnames in the United States Census of 1790: An Analysis of National Origins of the Population. Baltimore: Genealogical Pub. Co., 1969.

Vallentine, John F. *Locality Finding Aids for United States Surnames.* Logan, Utah: Everton Publishers, 1977.

Native Races

American Indians: A Select Catalog of National Archives Microfilm Publications. Washington, D.C.: National Archives and Records Administrations, 1994.

Barr, Charles B. *Guide to Sources of Indian Genealogy.* Independence, MO: C.B. Barr, 1989.

Bataille, Gretchen M., ed. *Native American Women: A Bibliographical Dictionary.* Garland Publishing, New York, 1993.

Bowen, Jeff. Transc. *Eastern Cherokee by Blood, 1906–1910. Volume I—Applications 1–3000 from the U.S. Court of Claims, 1906–1910. Cherokee-Related Records of Special Commissioner Guion Miller.* Baltimore: Genealogical Publishing Co., Inc., 2005.

Bowen, Jeff. *Indian Wills, 1911–1921. Records of the Bureau of Indian Affairs. Book One.* Baltimore: Genealogical Publishing Co., Inc., 2005.

Byers, Paula K., ed. *Native American Genealogical Sourcebook.* Detroit: Gale Research Inc, 1995.

Carter, Kent. *The Dawes Commission and the Allotment of the Five Civilized Tribes, 1893–1914.* Provo, Utah: Ancestry, 1999.

Champagne, Duane, ed. *The Native North American Almanac.* Detroit, Michigan: Gale Research, 1994.

Cohen, Felix. *Handbook of Federal Indian Law. Reprint of the 1942 edition.* Albuquerque: University of New Mexico Press.

D'Arcey McNickle Center for History of the American Indian. Pasadena, California: Salem Press, 1991.

Danby, James P., ed. *Native American Periodicals and Newspapers, 1828–1982; Bibliography, Publishing Record, and Holdings.* Westport, Connecticut: Greenwood Press, 1984.

Davis, Mary B., ed. *Native America in the Twentieth Century: An Encyclopedia.* New York: Garland Publishing, 1994.

Dewitt, Donald L. *American Indian Resource Materials in the Western History Collection,* University of Oklahoma. Norman: University of Oklahoma Press, 1990.

Dictionary of Indian Tribes of the Americas. 4 vols. Newport Beach, California: American Indian Publishers, 1993.

Driver, Harold E. *Indians of North America.* Chicago: University of Chicago Press, 1961.

Duffy, Laurie Beth. *Who's Looking for Whom in Native American Ancestry.* 2 vols. Bowie, Maryland: Heritage Books, Inc., 1997, 1999.

Furtaw, Julia C., ed. *Native Americans Information Directory.* Detroit, Michigan: Gale Research, 1993.

Gannett, Henry A. *A Gazetteer of Indian Territory.* Washington, D.C.: Government Printing Office, 1905.

Gideon, D.C. *Indian Territory—Descriptive, Biographical and Genealogical, Including the Landed Estates, County Seats, With General History of the Territory.* Chicago: The Lewis Publishing Co, 1901.

Hill, Edward E. *Guide to Records in the National Archives of the United States Relating to American Indians.* Washington, D.C.: U.S. Government Printing Office, 1981.

Hill, Edward E. *The Office of Indian Affairs, 1824–1880: Historical Sketches.* New York: Clearwater Publishing Co., 1974.

Hirschfelder, Arlene and Martha Kreipe de Montano. *The Native American Almanac: A Portrait of Native America Today.* New York: Prentice-Hall, 1993.

Hirschfelder, Arlene and Paulette Miolin. *The Encyclopedia of Native American Religions: An Introduction.* Facts on File, 1992.

Hoxie, Frederick E., and Harvey Markowitz. *Native Americans: An Annotated Bibliography.* Pasadena, California: Salem Press, 1991.

Indian Reservations: A State and Federal Handbook. Confederation of American Indians. Jefferson, North Carolina: McFarland, 1986.

Kirkham, E. Kay. *Our Native Americans: Their Records of Genealogical Value: Volume I Federal Government Records, Oklahoma Historical Society Records, Genealogical Society of Utah Listings.* Logan, Utah: Everton Publishers, 1980.

Kirkham, E. Kay. *Our Native Americans: Their Records of Genealogical Value.* Volume 2. Logan, Utah: Everton Publishers, 1984.

Leirch, Barbara. *A Concise Dictionary of Indian Tribes in North America.* Algonac, Michigan: Reference Publications, 1979.

Lipps, Oscar Hiram. *Laws and Regulations Relating to Indians and Their Lands.* Lewiston, Idaho: Lewiston Printing and Binding Co, 1913.

McClure, Tony Mack, Ph.D. *Cherokee Proud: A Guide for Tracing and Honoring Your Cherokee Ancestors.* Chunannee Books.

McDowell, Janet A. *The Dispossession of the American Indian, 1887–1834.* Bloomington: Indiana University Press, 1991.

Native American Periodicals and Newspapers, 1828–1982: A Bibliography, Publishing Records and Holdings. Westport, Connecticut: Greenwood Press, 1984.

Native American Women: Telling their Lives. Lincoln: University of Nebraska Press, 1984.

Mills Lennon, Rachal. *Tracing Ancestors among the Five Civilized Tribes. Southeastern Indians Prior to Removal.* Baltimore, Maryland: Genealogical Publishing Co., Inc., 2002.

Pangburn, Richard. *Indian Blood II: Further Adventures in Finding Your Native American Ancestor.* Louisville, Kentucky: Butler Books, 1996.

Pangburn, Richard. *Indian Blood: Finding Your Native American Ancestor.* Louisville, Kentucky: Butler Books, 1993.

Russell, George L. *American Indian Digest.* Phoenix, Arizona: Thunderbird Enterprises, 1994.

Sturdevant, William C., ed. *Handbook of North American Indians.* Washington, D.C.: Smithsonian Institution Press, 1978–.

Swanton, John R. *The Indian Tribes of North America.* Smithsonian Institution Press, Washington, D.C., 1979.

U.S. Department of the Interior Library. *Bibliographic and Historical Index of American Indians and Persons Involved in Indian Affairs.* 8 vols. Boston: G.K. Hall, 1966.

Waldman, Carl. *Atlas of the North American Indian.* Reprint. New York: Facts on File Publications, 1985.

Waldman, Carl. *Encyclopedia of Native American Tribes.* New York: Facts on File Publications, 1988.

Waldman, Carl. *Who Was Who in Native American History.* New York: Facts on File Publications, 1990.

Witcher, Burt Bryan. *A Bibliography of Sources for Native American Family History.* Fort Wayne, Indiana: Allen County Public Library, 1988.

Naturalization and Citizenship

Directory of Courts Having Jurisdiction in Naturalization Proceedings. United States Department of Justice, Immigration and Naturalization Service. Washington, D.C.: Microfilmed by the Library of Congress Photoduplication Service, 1992.

Kettner, James H. *The Development of American Citizenship, 1608–1870.* Chapel Hill, North Carolina: Published for the Institute of Early American History and Culture by the University of North Carolina Press, 1978.

Neagles, James C. *Locating Your Immigrant Ancestor: A Guide to Naturalization Records*. Logan, Utah: Everton Publishers, 1986.

Newman, John J. *American Naturalization Records, 1790–1990: What They Are and How to Use Them*. Bountiful, Utah: Heritage Quest, 1998.

Schaeter, Christina K. *Guide to Naturalization Records of the United States*. Baltimore: Genealogical Publishing Co., 1997.

Smith, Darrell Hevenor. *The Bureau of Naturalization: Its History, Activities and Organization*. New York: AMS Press, 1974.

Szucs, Loretto Dennis. *They Became Americans: Finding Naturalization Records and Ethnic Origins*. Salt Lake City: Ancestry Inc., 1998.

Udell, Oilman G. *Naturalization Laws*. Washington D.C.: Government Print Office, 1968.

Newspapers

Allbaugh, Gaylord P. *History and Annotated Bibliography of American Religious Periodicals and Newspapers Established From 1730 Through 1830*. 2 vols. Worcester, Massachusetts: American Antiquarian Society, 1994.

American Newspaper Directory, (annual). 1869–1908. New York: George P. Rowell and Co.

Brigham, Clarence Saunders. *History and Bibliography of American Newspapers, 1690–1820*. 2 vols. Worcester, Massachusetts: American Antiquarian Society, 1975.

Center for Research Libraries. *The Center for Research Libraries Catalogue: Newspapers*. 2nd ed. Chicago: The Center, 1978.

Gale Directory of Publications: An Annual Guide to Newspapers, Magazines, Journals, and Related Publications; Formerly Ayer Directory of Publications; Published Annually since 1869. Detroit, Michigan: Gale Research, 1987–.

Gregory, Winifred. *American Newspapers, 1821–1936: A Union List of Files Available in the United States and Canada*. New York: H.W. Wilson Co., 1937, reprint 1967.

Guide to Microforms in Print, (annual). 1961– Munich: K.G. Saur. Annual Catalog of microform titles, including newspapers.

Heuvel, Jon Vanden. *Untapped Sources: America's Newspaper Archives and Histories*. New York: Gannett Foundation Media Center, 1991.

Lathem, Edward Connery. *Chronological Tables of American Newspapers, 1690–1820; Being a Tabular Guide to Holdings of Newspapers Published in America Through the Year 1820*. Worcester, Massachusetts: American Antiquarian Society, 1972.

Library of Congress Catalog Management and Publication Division. *Newspapers in Microform, United States*

1848–1912. Washington, D.C.: Catalog Publication Division Progressing Department, 1984.

Milner, Anita. *Newspaper Genealogical Column Directory*. Bowie, Maryland: Heritage Books, 1992.

Milner, Anita. *Newspaper Indexes: A Location and Subject Guide for Researchers*. Metuchen, New Jersey: Scarecrow Press, 1979.

Newspapers in Microform: United States, 1948–1983. 2 vols. Washington, D.C.: Library of Congress, 1984.

Parch, Grace D., ed. *Directory of Newspaper Libraries in the United States and Canada*. New York: Project of the Newspaper Division, Special Libraries Assoc., 1976.

Rowell, George Presbury. *Rowell's American Newspaper Directory: Containing a Description of all the Newspapers and Periodicals Published in the United States and Territories, Dominion of Canada and Newfoundland, and of the Towns and Cities in Which They are Published, Together With a Statement or Estimate of the Average Number of Copies.... 40 vols*. New York: Geo. P. Rowell & Co., 1869–1908.

Serials and Newspapers in Microform (annual). Ann Arbor, Michigan: University Microfilms International. Annual catalog of microfilmed newspapers for sale.

Swigart, Paul E. *Chronological Index of Newspapers for the Period 1801–1952 in the Collections of the Library of Congress*. 3 vols. plus supplement. (Washington, D.C.: Microfilmed by Library of Congress Photoduplication Service, 199–?).

Union List of Serials in Libraries of the United States and Canada. 3rd ed. 5 vols. New York: H.W. Wilson, 1965.

United States Newspaper Program National Union List. 4th ed. Dublin, Ohio: Online Computer Library Center, 1993. Microfiche.

Wynar, Luhomyr Roman. *Encyclopedic Directory of Ethnic Newspapers and Periodicals in the United States*. Littleton, Colorado: Libraries Unlimited, 1976.

Obituaries

Jarboe, Betty M. *Obituaries: A Guide to Sources*. Boston: G. K. Hall, 1989.

Levy, Felice D. *Obituaries on File*. 2 vols. New York: Facts on File, 1979. (These books are a compilation of the obituaries that have appeared in Facts on File from the beginning of the journal in the late 1940's through 1978).

The New York Times Obituaries Index. New York: The Times, 1970.

Online Sources

Crowe, Elizabeth Powell. *Genealogy Online*, 6th Edition. New York: Osborne/McGraw-Hill, 2002.

Howells, Cyndi. *Cyndi's List: A Comprehensive List of 70,000 Genealogy Sites on the Internet*. Baltimore: Genealogical Publishing Co., Inc., 2001.

Schafer, Christina K. *Instant Information on the Internet: A Genealogist's No-Frills Guide to the 50 States and the District of Columbia*. Revised. Baltimore: Genealogical Publishing Company, 2000.

Periodicals–Genealogy

Everton's Genealogical Helper. 1947–. Published by Everton Publishers, Inc., Logan, Utah.

Genealogical Computing. 1981–. Published by Ancestry.com, Salt Lake City, Utah.

Genealogical Journal. 1972–. Published by the Utah Genealogical Association, Salt Lake City, Utah.

Heritage Quest: The International Genealogy Forum. 1985–. Published by Heritage Quest, Bountiful, Utah.

National Genealogical Society Quarterly. 1912–. Published by the National Genealogical Society, Arlington, Virginia.

New England Historical and Genealogical Register.1847–. Published by the New England Historic and Genealogical Society, Boston, Massachusetts.

The American Genealogist. 1922–. Published by Dr. David Greene. Domorest, Georgia.

Sources and Indexes

Biography of Genealogical and Local History Periodicals With Union List of Major U.S. Collections. Fort Wayne, Indiana: Allen Count Public Library Foundation, 1990.

Boyer, Carl III. *Donald Jacobus' Index to Genealogical Periodicals*. Newhall, California: Boyer Publications, 1983.

Carson, Dina C. *Directory of Genealogical and Historical Publications in the U.S. and Canada*. Niwot, Colorado: Iron Gate Publishing, 1992.

Genealogical Guide Master Index of Genealogy in the Daughters of the American Revolution Magazine Volumes 1–84 (1892–1950) with Supplement Volumes 85–89 (1950–1966) Combined Edition. Compiled by Elizabeth Benton Chapter, NSDAR, Kansas City, Missouri, 1951. Reprint. Baltimore: Genealogical Publishing Co., 1994.

Jacobus, Donald Lines. *Index to Genealogical Periodicals*. Baltimore: Genealogical Publishing Co., 1978.

Periodical Source Index (PERSI). Ft. Wayne, Indiana: Allen County Public Library Foundation, 1987–.

Quigley, Maud. *Index to Family Names in Genealogical Periodicals*. Grand Rapids, Michigan: Western Michigan Genealogical Society, 1981.

Sperry, Kip. *Index to Genealogical Periodical Literature, 1960–1977*. Detroit: Gale Research Co., 1979.

Towle, Laird C., and Catherine M. Mayhew. *Genealogical Periodical Annual Index*. Bowie, Maryland: Heritage Books, annual.

Postal and Shipping Guides

Bowen, Eli. *The United States Post-Office Guide*. New York: Arno Press, 1976.

Bullinger's Postal and Shipping Guide for the United States and Canada, annual. Westwood, New Jersey: Bullinger's Guides, 1871–.

Conkling, Roscoe Platt. *The Butterfield Overland Mail, 1857–1869: Its Organization and Operation Over the Southern Route to 1861, Subsequently Over the Central Route to 1866, and Under Wells, Fargo and Company in 1869*. 3 vols. Glendale, California: Arthur H. Clark Co., 1947.

Hafen, LeRoy R. *The Overland Mail*. Lawrence, Massachusetts: Quarterman Pub., 1976.

Record of Appointment of Postmasters, October 1789–1832. Washington, D.C.: The National Archives, 1980.

Simmons, Don. *Post Offices in the United States*. Melber, Kentucky: Simmons Historical Publications, 1991.

United States Directory of Post Offices. Washington, D.C.: U.S. Postal Department, Annual.

United States Official Postal Guide. Washington D.C.: U.S. Government Printing Office, 1879–.

Webster's Atlas and Zip Code Directory. Springfield, Massachusetts: G. & C. Merriam, 1981. (Includes maps).

Probate Records

Carter, Fran. *Searching American Probate Records*. Bountiful, Utah: American Genealogical Lending Library, 1993.

Coldham, Peter Wilson. *American Wills & Administrations in the Prerogative Court of Canterbury, 1610–1857*. Baltimore, Maryland: Genealogical Publishing Co., 1989.

Coldham, Peter Wilson. *American Wills Proved in London, 1611–1775*. Baltimore, Maryland: Genealogical Publishing, 1992.

Dobson, David. *Scottish-American Wills, 1650–1900*. Baltimore: Genealogical Publishing, 1991.

Vital Records

Kemp, Thomas Jay. *International Vital Records Handbook*. 4th ed. Baltimore: Genealogical Publishing Co., Inc., 2000.

Stemmons, Jack and Diane Stemmons. *The Vital Records Compendium: Comprising a Directory of Vital Records and Where They May be Located*. Logan, Utah: Everton Publishers, 1979.

Notes

Alabama

Capital: Montgomery

Territory: 1817

State: 1819 (22nd)

We dare defend our rights

The Spanish explorers Panfilo de Narvaez and Cabeza de Vaca were among the first non-Indians to pass through this area in 1528. The first settlers were Spanish and French, perhaps arriving as early as 1699. The first community founded was Mobile in 1702, which was settled by the French. France governed the area from 1710 to 1763, when England gained control. Settlers during this period came from South Carolina and Georgia, as well as England, France, and Spain.

To avoid participation in the Revolutionary War, many British sympathizers left Georgia in 1775 to settle in the Alabama area. Planters from Georgia, Virginia, and the Carolinas followed in 1783. That same year, Britain ceded the Mobile area to Spain, leaving the remainder of present-day Alabama to Georgia. In 1795 the Alabama region became part of the Territory of Mississippi.

In the early 1800's, emigrants from the Carolinas and Virginia came to the central and western parts of Alabama, especially in areas along the Tombigbee and Black Warrior Rivers. The Scotch-Irish from Tennessee settled the Tennessee Valley district in northern Alabama in 1809. During the War of 1812, American forces captured Mobile from the Spanish and defeated the Creek Indians. This led to the removal of the Creeks and other Indian tribes and opened the area to settlement. An influx of settlers, many of whom brought slaves with them, resulted in the formation of the Alabama Territory in 1817. Seven counties were formed at that time and St. Stephens became the capital. In November of 1818, the city of Cahaba became the capital, replacing the site of Huntsville. Tuscaloosa became the capital in 1826, followed in 1846 by Montgomery, the present capital.

Representatives of Alabama's 22 counties gathered in Huntsville for a convention in 1819. On 14 December, 1819, Alabama became the 22nd state.

Alabama seceded from the Union in 1861. About 2,500 men from Alabama served in the Union forces and an estimated 100,000 men served in the Confederate forces. Alabama was readmitted to the Union in 1868.

Look for vital records in the following locations:

- **Birth and death records:** State Department of Health Bureau of Vital Statistics. Records are incomplete prior to 1908.
- **Marriage records:** State Department of Health Bureau of Vital Statistics post 1936. Check individual county and city courthouses for prior marriages generally dating back to the formation of each county.
- **Divorce records:** Supreme Court of the Territory and General Assembly. Most divorce proceedings were filed with local Chancery courts. In 1917, the Chancery courts were merged with the Circuit Court for each county.
- **Naturalizations:** Scattered throughout court minute books, especially county circuit records.
- **Census records:** Alabama Department of Archives and History. Early census records for French settlements near Mobile are available. Incomplete territorial and state census records exist for 1816, 1818, 1820, 1831, 1850, 1855, 1860 and 1880. State census records are available. A special census of Confederate Veterans was taken in 1907, which has been abstracted, indexed, and published.

Alabama Vital Records Department of Public Health
PO Box 5625
Montgomery, Alabama 36103-5625
(334) 206-5418
http://ph.state.al.us/chs/VitalRecords/Death/DEATH.html

Alabama Department of Archives and History
624 Washington Avenue
Montgomery, Alabama 36103-0100
(334) 242-4435
www.archives.state.al.us/

Alabama

Societies and Repositories

Alabama Department of Archives & History; 624
Washington Avenue; Montgomery, AL 36130-0100;
(334) 242-4435; dpendlet@archives.state.al.us;
www.archives.state.al.us/index.html.

Alabama Division, United Daughters of the Confederacy;
16149 Highway 10, East; Pine Apple, AL 36768;
www.members.home.net/aladivudc.

Alabama Historical Association (AHA); c/o ADAH 624
Washington Ave.; Montgomery, AL 36130.

Alabama Public Library Service; 6030 Monticello Drive;
Montgomery, AL 36130; www.apls.state.al.us.

Autauga Genealogical Society; PO Box 680668; Prattville,
AL 36068-0668; jkbrown2@knology.net;
www.rootsweb.com/~alags.

Baldwin County Genealogical Society; PO Box 108;
Foley, AL 36536.

Barbour County Genealogy & Local Historical Society; c/o
Eufaula Carnegie Library 217 No. Eufaula Ave.;
Eufaula, AL 36027.

Birmingham African-American Genealogy Study Group;
Birmingham, AL; (205) 925-7979; annistine@cs.com.

Birmingham Genealogical Society, Inc.; PO Box 2432;
Birmingham, AL 35201; MaryAliceT@aol.com;
www.birminghamgenealogy.org.

Black Warrior River Chapter, SAR; 3032 Firethorne Dr.;
Tuscaloosa, AL 35405; (205) 553-1695;
tlneathery@prodigy.net;
http://members.aol.com/blkwriver.

Bullock County Historical Society; PO Box 663;
Union Springs, AL 36089.

Butler County Historical Society/Library; 309 Ft. Dale St.;
Greenville, AL 36037.

Central Alabama Genealogical Society; PO Box 125;
Selma, AL 36701.

Chattahoocee Valley Historical Society; 3419 20th Ave.;
Cobb Memorial Archives; Valley, AL 36854.

Choctaw County Genealogical Society; 620 County Rd. 4;
Butler, AL 36904; randallm@tds.net;
www.rootsweb.com/~alccgs.

Civil War Descendants Society; PO Box 233; Athens, AL
35611.

Coosa County Historical Society; PO Box 5; Rockford, AL
35136.

Cullman Chapter, SAR; 1468 County Road 1559; Cullman,
AL 35058; (256) 796-6859; phenry@corrcomm.net.

Dale County Genealogical and Historical Society; 320
James Street; Ozark, AL 36360; (334) 774-0888;
http://web.snowhill.com/~marian/a.society.genealogical.
historical.html.

DeKalb County Genealogical Society; PO Box 681087;
Fort Payne, AL 35968-1612; w4ctk@farmerstel.com;
www.dekalbsociety.freeservers.com.

Etowah Chapter, SAR; 1001 Padenreich Ave.; Gadsden, AL
35903; (256) 546-8067.

Genealogical Society of East Alabama, Inc.; PO Box 2992;
Opelika, AL 36803.

Genealogy Society of Washington County; PO Box 399;
Chatom, AL 36518; http://members.aol.com/
JORDANJM2/WCGS.html.

General Richard Montgomery Chapter, SAR; 3813 Marie
Cook Drive; Montgomery, AL 36109; (334) 272-2174.

Hueytown Historical Society; 3264 Fieldale Drive;
Hueytown, AL 35023; (205) 497-0689;
repcurry@aol.com; www.hueytown.org/historical.

Jackson County Historical Association, Inc.; PO Box 1494;
Scottsboro, AL 35768.

John Henry Lentz Chapter, SAR; AL; (256) 420-3985;
repcurry@aol.com.

Lamar County Genealogical Society; PO Box 357; Vernon,
AL 35592;
www.fayette.net/carruth/genealogysociety.htm.

Leeds Historical Society; 2623 Madison Avenue Apt. 1282;
Moody, AL 35004; stagecoach@leedsalabama.com;
http://leedsalabama.com/historical_society.htm.

Limestone County Historical Society; PO Box 82; Athens,
AL 35611.

Lowndes County Historical & Genealogical Society;
HCR 2, Box 350; Minter, AL 36761.

Marion County Genealogical Society; PO Box 360;
Winfield, AL 35594.

Mobile Genealogical Society, Inc.; PO Box 6224; Mobile,
AL 36606; www.siteone.com/clubs/mgs.

Montgomery County Historical Society; 512 South Court
Street; PO Box 1829; Montgomery, AL, 36102;
mchs@mont.mindspring.com;
www.mindspring.com/~mchs/.

Montgomery Genealogical Society, Inc.; PO Box 230194;
Montgomery, AL 36123-0194;
www.rootsweb.com/~almgs.

Natchez Trace Genealogical Society; PO Box 420;
Florence, AL 35631.

North Central Alabama Genealogical Society; PO Box 13;
Cullman, AL 35056-0013; lthurman@hiwaay.net;
http://home.hiwaay.net/~lthurman/society.htm.

Pea River Historical and Genealogical Society;
109 Main Street; Enterprise, AL 36330;
www.angelfire.com/al2/peariverhistgensoc/index.html.

Piedmont Historical and Genealogical Society; PO Box 47;
Spring Garden, AL 36275.

Pike County Historical & Genealogical Society;
Route 2, Box 272; Goshen, AL 36035;
www.rootsweb.com/~alpike/hsp.htm.

Richard Henry Lee Chapter, SAR; 869 Cary Drive;
Auburn, AL 36830; (334) 887-9661;
jrretired@prodigy.net.

Shelby County Historical Society, Inc.;
1854 Old Courthouse; PO Box 457; Columbiana, AL
35051-0457; Seales_Family@msn.com;
www.rootsweb.com/~alshelby/schs.html.

Society of the Desc. of Washington's Army at Valley Forge,
Alabama Brigade; 7905 Ensley Dr., SW; Huntsville, AL
35802-2959.

Sons of the American Revolution, Alabama Society; 507
Bonnet Hill Circle; Mobile, AL 36609.

Southeast Alabama Genealogical Society (SEAGS);
PO Box 246; Dothan, AL 36302.

St. Clair Historical Society; PO Box 125; Odenville, AL
35120.

Tennessee Valley Chapter, SAR; 5460 Chickasaw Drive;
Guntersville, AL 35976-2802; (256) 582-0313;
raybetwhitt@AOL.com.

Tennessee Valley Genealogical Society; PO Box 1568;
Huntsville, AL 35807; cshazel@mindspring.com;
http://hiwaay.net/~white/TVGS/sitemap.html.

Tennessee Valley Historical Society; PO Box 149;
Sheffield, AL 35660-0149;
http://home.hiwaay.net/~krjohn.

Tuscaloosa Genealogical Society, Morning Group;
2020 Third Court E; Tuscaloosa, AL 35401.

Walker County Genealogical Society; PO Box 3408;
Jasper, AL 35502.

Washington County Historical Society; PO Box 456;
Chatom, AL 36518.

Wilcox Historical Society; PO Box 464; Camden, AL
36726; www.wilcoxwebworks.com/history.

Winston County Genealogical Society; PO Box 112;
Double Springs, AL 35553;
winstoncounty@hotmail.com;
http://wcgs.ala.nu/wcgs.htm.

Wiregrass Chapter, SAR; 200 E. Silver Oak Dr.; Enterprise,
AL 36330; (334) 347-0661; johnrx@snowhill.com.

Bibliography and Record Sources

General

Abernathy, Thomas Perkins. *The Formative Period in
Alabama, 1815–1828.* Tuscaloosa, Alabama: University
of Alabama Press, 1990.

Alabama Genealogical Records; Alabama Genealogical
Records Commission, DAR, 1964–1965. Reprint.
Microfilm. Salt Lake City: Genealogical Society of
Utah, 1970.

Alabama Research Outline. Series US-States, No. 1. Salt
Lake City: Family History Library, 1988.

Austin, Jeannette H. *Alabama Bible Records.* Riverdale,
Georgia: Jeanette Austin, 1987.

Barefield, Marilyn Davis. *Researching in Alabama: A
Genealogical Guide.* Easley, South Carolina: Southern
Historical Press, 1987.

Brewer, W. *Alabama: Her History, Resources, War Record,
and Public Men from 1540 to 1872.* (1872) Reprint
1995. Baltimore: Clearfield Co., 2001.

Daughters of the American Revolution (Alabama). *Some
Early Alabama Churches, Established Before 1870.* Salt
Lake City: Filmed by the Genealogical Society of Utah,
1978.

DuBose, Joel C. *Notable Men of Alabama; Personal &
Genealogical.* 1904. Reprint on Microfiche.
Spartanburg, South Carolina: The Reprint Co., 1976.

Elliott, Wendy L. *Research in Alabama.* Bountiful, Utah:
American Genealogical Lending Library, 1987.

Foscue, Virginia O. *Place Names in Alabama.* Tuscaloosa,
Alabama: University of Alabama Press, 1989.

Gandrud, Pauline M., and Kathleen P. Jones. *Alabama
Records.* 244 vols. Easley, South Carolina: Southern
Historical Press, 1981.

Newspapers on Microfilm, Samford University Library.
Birmingham: Samford University Library, 1970.

Oliver, Lloyd F. *Index to Colonel James Edmonds
Saunders' Early Settlers of Alabama.* Tomball, Texas:
Genealogical Publications, 1978.

Owen, Thomas McAdory *History of Alabama and
Dictionary of Alabama Biography.* 4 vols. Chicago: The
S. J. Clarke Publishing Co., 1921.

Rogers, William Warren, Robert David Ward, Leah Rawls
Atkins, and Wayne Flynt. *Alabama: The History of a
Deep South State.* Tuscaloosa, Alabama: University of
Alabama Press, 1994.

Southerland, Henry Deleon Jr. and Jerry Elijah Brown. *The
Federal Road Through Georgia, the Creek Nation, and
Alabama, 1806–1836.* 1989. Tuscaloosa, Alabama:
University of Alabama Press, 1990.

Strickland, Jean and Patricia N. Edwards. *Residents of the
Mississippi Territory.* 5 vols. Moss Point, Mississippi: J.
Stickland, 1995.

Stubbs, Elizabeth Saundars Blair. *Early Settlers of
Alabama; With "Notes and Genealogies."* Reprint.
Baltimore: Clearfield Co., 1991.

Atlases, Maps and Gazetteers

Berney, Saffold. *Hand-book of Alabama.* Birmingham:
Roberts and Son, 1892.

Dodd, Donald B., and Borden D. Dent. *Historical Atlas of
Alabama.* University, Alabama: University of Alabama
Press, 1974.

Harris, W. Stuart. *Dead Towns of Alabama.* University,
Alabama: University of Alabama Press, 1977.

Long, John H., ed. *Atlas of Historical County Boundaries
Alabama.* New York: Simon & Schuster, 1996.

Mason, Sara Elizabeth. *A List of Nineteenth Century Maps
of the State Of Alabama.* Birmingham, Alabama:
Birmingham Public Library, 1973.

Thorndale, William and William Dollarhide. *Map Guides to the U.S. Federal Census, 1790–1920; Alabama, 1800–1920.* Baltimore: Genealogical Publishing Co., 1987.

Yesterday's Faces of Alabama; A Collection of Maps, 1822–1909. Montgomery, Alabama: Society of Pioneers of Montgomery, 1978.

Censuses

Available Census Records and Census Substitutes

Federal Census 1830, 1840, 1850, 1860, 1870, 1880, 1900, 1910, 1920, 1930

State/Territorial Census 1816, 1818, 1820, 1831, 1850, 1855, 1866, 1880

Early Alabama Settlers 1816

Confederate Veterans 1907, 1921, 1927

Federal Mortality Schedules 1850, 1860, 1870, 1880

Alabama 1907 Census of Confederate Soldiers. Cullman, Alabama; Gregath Publishing Co., 1982–1983.

Dollarhide, William. *The Census Book; A Genealogist's Guide to Federal Census Facts, Schedules and Indexes.* Bountiful, Utah: Heritage Quest, 1999.

Kemp, Thomas Jay. *The American Census Handbook.* Wilmington, Delaware: Scholarly Resources, Inc., 2001.

Lainhart, Ann S. *State Census Records.* Baltimore: Genealogical Publishing Co., Inc., 1992.

McMillan, James B., and William A. Read. *Indian Place Names in Alabama.* Revised ed. Tuscaloosa, Alabama: University of Alabama Press, 1984.

Owen, Marie Bankhead. *Alabama Census Returns, 1820, and an Abstract of Federal Census of Alabama, 1830.* Reprinted from the Alabama Historical Quarterly (1944) Vol. 6, No. 3. Baltimore: Genealogical Pub. Co., 1996.

Szucs, Loretto Dennis and Matthew Wright. *Finding Answers in U.S. Census Records.* Ancestry Publishing, 2001.

Court Records, Probate and Wills

Alabama Society, Daughters of the American Revolution. *Index to Alabama Wills 1808–1870.* Reprint. Baltimore: Genealogical Publishing Co., 1977.

Immigration

Connick, Lucille Mallon. *Lists of Ships' Passengers, Mobile, Alabama.* 2 vols. Mobile, Alabama; Lucille Connick, 1988–1989.

Mitchell, Mrs. Lois Dumas. *Mobile Ship News.* (Manuscript) Mobile, Alabama, 1964.

United States. Bureau of Customs. *A Supplemental Index to Passenger Lists of Vessels Arriving At Atlantic & Gulf Coast Ports (Excluding New York) 1820–1874.* Washington, D.C.; Filmed by the National Archives Record Services, 1960.

United States. Bureau of Customs. *Copies of Lists of Passengers Arriving At Miscellaneous Ports on the Atlantic and Gulf Coasts and At Ports on the Great Lakes, 1820–1873.* Washington, D.C.; The National Archives, 1964.

United States. Circuit Court (Alabama; Northern District). *Declarations of Intention, Huntsville, 1875–1894.* Microfilm of originals in the National Archives Center in East Point, Georgia. Salt Lake City: Filmed by the Genealogical Society of Utah, 1989. Microfilm, 1 roll.

United States. Immigration and Naturalization Service. *Index to Passenger Lists of Vessels Arriving At Miscellaneous Ports in Alabama, Florida, Georgia, and South Carolina, 1890–1924.* Washington, D.C.; Microphotographed by Immigration and Naturalization Service, 1957.

Land

Ainsworth, Fern. *Private Land Claims; Alabama, Arkansas, Florida.* Natchitoches, Louisiana: Fern Ainsworth, 1978.

Barefield, Marilyn Davis Hahn. *Old Cahaba Land Office Records and Military Warrants, 1817–1853.* Birmingham, Alabama: Southern University Press, 1986.

Cowart, Margaret Matthews. *Old Land Records of [county], Alabama.* Huntsville, Alabama; Margaret Matthews Cowart, 1980–1986.

*De Ville, Winston. *English Land Grants in West Florida; A Register for the States of Alabama, Mississippi, and Parts of Florida and Louisiana, 1766–1776.* Ville Platte, Louisiana: Winston De Ville, 1986.

Douthat, James L. Robert. *Armstrong's Survey Book of Cherokee Lands; Lands Granted from the Treaty of 27 February 1819.* Signal Mountain, Tennessee: Institute of Historic Research, 1993.

Old Huntsville Land Office Records and Military Warrants, 1810–1854. Easley, South Carolina: Southern Historical Press, 1985.

Old Sparta and Elba Land Office Records and Military Warrants, 1822–1860. Easley, South Carolina; Southern Historical Press, 1983.

Old St. Stephen's Land Office Records and American State Papers, Public Lands. Easley, South Carolina; Southern Historical Press, 1983.

Old Tuscaloosa Land Office Records and Military Warrants, 1821–1855. Easley, South Carolina; Southern Historical Press, 1984.

United States. Bureau of Land Management *Card Files.* Washington, D.C.; Bureau of Land Management, 19–. Microfilm, 160 rolls.

United States. Department of the Interior. Bureau of Land Management. *Alabama Pre-1908 Patents; Homesteads, Cash Entry, Creek Indian Treaty and Choctaw Indian Scrip.* Springfield, Virginia; BLM Eastern States, 1996. CD-ROM.

Military

Alabama, Department of Archives and History. *Alabama State Troops (militia), 1873–1898.* Microfilm of originals in the Alabama Department of Archives and History in Montgomery, Alabama. Salt Lake City: Filmed by the Genealogical Society of Utah, 1986. Microfilm, 5 Rolls.

Alabama, Department of Archives and History. *Revolutionary Soldiers in Alabama, Being a List of Names Compiled from Authentic Sources, of Soldiers of the American Revolution, Who Resided in the State of Alabama.* Montgomery, Alabama: Brown Printing Co., 1967.

Barefield, Marilyn Davis Hahn. *Old Cahaba Land Office Records and Military Warrants, 1817–1853.* Birmingham, Alabama: Southern University Press, 1986.

Black, Clifford. *An Index to Alabama Society Sons of the American Revolution, Members and their Ancestors, 1903–1996.* Signal Mountain, Tennessee: Mountain Press, 1996.

Douthat, James. L. *Volunteer Soldiers In the Cherokee War—1836–1839.* Signal Mountain, Tennessee: Mountain Press, 1995.

Fritot, Jesse R. *Pension Records of Soldiers of the Revolution Who Removed to Florida, with Record of Service.* [S.I.]: AR National Society, Jacksonville Chapter, 1946.

Old Huntsville Land Office Records and Military Warrants, 1810–1854. Easley, South Carolina: Southern Historical Press, 1985.

Old Sparta and Elba Land Office Records and Military Warrants, 1822–1860. Easley, South Carolina: Southern Historical Press, 1983.

Old Tuscaloosa Land Office Records and Military Warrants, 1821–1855. Easley, South Carolina: Southern Historical Press, 1984.

*Owen, Thomas M. *Revolutionary Soldiers in Alabama.* Alabama State Archives Bulletin 5, 1911. Reprint. Baltimore: Clearfield, Colorado, 1991.

Penny, Morris M., and J. Gary Laine. *Law's Alabama Brigade in the War between the Union and the Confederacy.* Shippensburg, Pennsylvania: White Mane Pub., 1996.

Potter, Johnny L. T. N. *First Tennessee & Alabama Independent Vidette Cavalry, 1863–1864, roster; companies A, B, C, D, E, F, G, H.* Chattanooga, Tennessee: Mountain Press, 1995.

Sifakis, Stewart. *Compendium of the Confederate Armies; Alabama.* Galveston, Texas: Frontier Press, 1992.

United States. Record and Pension Office. *Compiled Service Records of Volunteer Union Soldiers who Served in Organizations from the State of Alabama.* Washington, D.C.: The National Archives, 1959. Microfilm, 10 rolls.

United States. Selective Service System. *Alabama, World Ward I Selective Service System Draft Registration Cards, 1917–1918.* Washington, D.C.: The National Archives, 1987–1988.

Vital and Cemetery

Alabama Cemetery Records. Typescript. Salt Lake City: Genealogical Society of Utah, 1942–45.

Alabama, Department of Health (Montgomery, Alabama*).* *Marriage Certificates, 1936–1992; Index, 1936–1959.* Salt Lake City: Filmed by the Genealogical Society of Utah, 1993. Microfilm, multiple rolls.

Bible and Cemetery Records. Birmingham, Alabama: Birmingham Genealogical Society, 1963.

Dodd, Jordan R., and Norman L. Moyes. *Alabama Marriages, Early to 1825.* Bountiful, Utah: Precision Indexing, 1991.

England, Flora Dainwood. *Alabama Notes.* 4 vols. Reprint. Baltimore: Genealogical Publishing Co., 1977.

Foley, Helen S. *Marriage and Death Notices from Alabama Newspapers and Family Records, 1819–1890.* Easley, South Carolina: Southern Historical Press, 1981.

Gandrud, Pauline Jones. *Marriage, Death and Legal Notices from Early Alabama Newspapers, 1818–1880.* (1981) Reprint. Greenville, South Carolina: Southern Historical Press, 1994.

Marriage, Death, and Legal Notices From Early Alabama Newspapers, 1819–1893. Easley, South Carolina: Southern Historical Press, 1981.

County Website	Map Index	Date Created	Parent County or Territory From Which Organized Address/Details
Autauga www.rootsweb.com/~alautaug/	J7	21 Nov 1818	**Montgomery** Autauga County; 134 North Court St Ste 106; Prattville, AL 36067; Ph. (334) 361-3725 **Details:** (Judge of Probate has Probate, land & military Records; Clerk Circuit Court has Divorce & court Records; Records Office has marriage Records from early 1800's; Health Department has birth & death Records)
Baine		7 Dec 1866	**Blount, Calhoun, Cherokee, DeKalb, Marshall, St. Clair** Baine County; AL **Details:** (Abolished 3 Dec 1867. Established as Etowah County 1 Dec 1868) County Terminated 1867
Baker		30 Dec 1868	**Autauga, Bibb, Perry, Shelby** Baker County; AL **Details:** (see Chilton) Name changed to Chilton 17 Dec 1874
Baldwin www.co.baldwin.al.us/	P3, P4	21 Dec 1809	**Washington, part of Florida** Baldwin County; 1 Court Sq; PO Box 239; Bay Mintte, AL 36507; Ph. (334) 937-9561 **Details:** (Probate Court has marriage Records from 1810, Probate Records from 1809 & land Records from 1808; Clerk Circuit Court has Divorce & court Records)
Barbour www.rootsweb.com/~albarbou/barbour.html	L10	18 Dec 1832	**Creek Cession, part of Pike** Barbour County; 1800 Fifth Ave N; PO Box 398; Clayton, AL 36016-0398; Ph. (334) 775-8371 **Details:** (Judge of Probate has Marriage, Probate & land Records from 1800's; Clerk Circuit Court has Divorce Records from 1860 & Court Records from 1912)
Benton		18 Dec 1832	**Creek Cession of 1832** Benton County; AL **Details:** (see Calhoun) Name changed to Calhoun 29 Jan 1858 County Terminated in 1858
Bibb www.dbtech.net/bibbco/	H6	7 Feb 1818	**Monroe, Montgomery** Bibb County; 157 SW Davidson Dr; Centreville, AL 35042; Ph. (205) 926-4747 **Details:** (Formerly Cahawba County. Name changed to Bibb 2 Dec 1820) (County Clerk has Marriage, Probate & land Records from 1818; Clerk Circuit Court has Divorce & Court Records)
Blount www.rootsweb.com/~alblount/	E7	6 Feb 1818	**Cherokee Cession, Montgomery** Blount County; 220 2nd Ave E Rm 106; PO Box 45; Oneonta, AL 35121; Ph. (256) 625-4160 **Details:** (County Archivist has Probate Records from 1824, Marriage, land & Burial Records from 1820; Clerk Circuit Court has Divorce & Court Records)
Bullock www.intersurf.com/~johnjanr/bullock.html	K9	5 Dec 1866	**Barbour, Macon, Montgomery, Pike** Bullock County; PO Box 71; Union Springs, AL 36089; Ph. (334) 738-2250 **Details:** (Probate Judge has Probate & Military Records; County Commissioner has Divorce & land Records; Clerk Circuit Court has Court Records)

County Website	Map Index	Date Created	Parent County or Territory From Which Organized Address/Details
Butler www.rootsweb.com/~albutler/	M7	**13 Dec 1819**	**Conecuh, Montgomery** Butler County; 700 Court Sq; PO Box 756; Greenville, AL 36037-0756; Ph. (334) 382-3512 **Details:** (Courthouse Burned April 1853) (Probate Judge has Birth & death Records 1894–1919, Marriage, Probate & land Records from 1853)
Cahawba		**7 Feb 1818**	**Monroe, Montgomery** Cahawba County; AL **Details:** (see Bibb) Name changed to Bibb 4 Dec 1820
Calhoun www.rootsweb.com/~alcalhou/	F9	**18 Dec 1832**	**Creek Cession of 1832** Calhoun County; 1702 Noble St Ste 103; PO Box 610; Anniston, AL 36201; Ph. (256) 236-8231 **Details:** (Formerly Benton County. Name changed to Calhoun 29 Jan 1858) (Probate Judge has Marriage Records 1834–1979 & land Records 1865–1979; Register in Chancery has Divorce Records; Clerk Circuit Court has Court Records)
Chambers www.rootsweb.com/~alchambe/	I10	**18 Dec 1832**	**Creek Cession of 1832** Chambers County; 18 Alabama Ave; Lafayette, AL 36862; Ph. (334) 864-7181 **Details:** (Probate Office has Marriage Records from 1833, Probate & land Records from 1843; Clerk Circuit Court has Divorce & Court Records)
Cherokee www.rootsweb.com/~alcherok/	E10	**9 Jan 1836**	**Cherokee Cession 1835** Cherokee County; 102 W Main St; Centre, AL 35960; Ph. (256) 927-3363 **Details:** (Records Burned in 1882) (Probate Judge has Marriage, Probate, land & Military discharge Records from 1882; Clerk Circuit Court has Divorce & Court Records)
Chilton www.chilton.al.us/	I7	**30 Dec 1868**	**Autauga, Bibb, Perry, Shelby** Chilton County; PO Box 557; Clanton, AL 35045; Ph. (205) 755-1555 **Details:** (Formerly Baker County. Name changed to Chilton 17 Dec 1874) (Clerk Circuit Court has Probate & Divorce Records, Court Records from 1868; Probate Judge has Marriage & land Records)
Choctaw www.rootsweb.com/~alchoCourta/index.htm	K3	**29 Dec 1847**	**Sumter, Washington** Choctaw County; 117 S Mulberry Ave; Butler, AL 36904; Ph. (205) 459-2155 **Details:** (County Clerk has Marriage, Probate & land Records from 1873; Clerk Circuit Court has Court & Divorce Records)
Clarke www.rootsweb.com/~alclarke/clarke.html	M4	**10 Dec 1812**	**Washington** Clarke County; 117 Court St; PO Box 548; Grove Hill, AL 36451; Ph. (334) 275-3251 **Details:** (Probate Judge has Marriage & Probate Records from 1814 & land Records from 1820; Clerk Circuit Court has Divorce & Court Records; Health Clinic has Birth & Death Records)
Clay www.geocities.com/sg_russell/clal.htm	G9	**7 Dec 1866**	**Randolph, Talladega** Clay County; PO Box 187; Ashland, AL 36251; Ph. (256) 354-7888 **Details:** (Probate Court has land Records from 1861, Probate Records from 1865 & Marriage Records from 1872; County Court has Death Records 1920–1940 & Voting Registration 1906–1936)

County Website	Map Index	Date Created	Parent County or Territory From Which Organized Address/Details
Cleburne www.rootsweb.com/~alcleBurial/	F10	6 Dec 1866	**Calhoun, Randolph, Talladega** Cleburne County; 120 Vickery St; Heflin, AL 36264; Ph. (256) 463-5655 **Details:** (Probate Judge has Birth & Death Records 1911–1921, Marriage & Probate Records from 1867 & land Records from 1884)
Coffee www.rootsweb.com/~alcoffee/	N9	29 Dec 1841	**Dale** Coffee County; 230 Court St; PO Box 402; Elba, AL 36323; Ph. (334) 897-2211 **Details:** (Probate Judge has Marriage Records from 1877 & land Records from early 1800's; Clerk Circuit Court has Divorce & Court Records)
Colbert www.colbertcounty.org/	C4	6 Feb 1867	**Franklin** Colbert County; 201 N Main St; Tuscumbia, AL 35674-2060; Ph. (256) 386-8500 **Details:** (Abolished same year created, re-established 1869) (Probate Judge has Marriage, Probate & land Records; Clerk Circuit Court has Divorce Records; County Health Department has Birth, Death & Burial Records)
Conecuh www.rootsweb.com/~alconecu/	N6	13 Feb 1818	**Monroe** Conecuh County; PO Box 347; Evergreen, AL 36401-0347; Ph. (334) 578-2095 **Details:** (Probate Judge has Marriage, Probate & land Records)
Coosa www.rootsweb.com/~alcoosa/coosa.html	H8	18 Dec 1832	**Creek Cession of 1832** Coosa County; PO Box 10; Rockford, AL 35136; Ph. (256) 377-2420 **Details:** (Probate Records Office has a few Birth & Death Records 1920–1945, Marriage, Divorce, Probate, land & Military Records from 1834; Circuit Court Office has Court Records from 1834)
Cotaco		6 Feb 1818	**Cherokee Turkeytown Cession** Cotaco County; AL **Details:** (see Morgan) Name changed to Morgan 14 June 1821; County Terminated in 1821
Covington www.rootsweb.com/~alcoving/	O8	7 Dec 1821	**Henry** Covington County; 260 Hillcrest Drive; PO Box 188; Andalusia, AL 36420; Ph. (334) 428-2610 **Details:** (Records Burned 1895) (Probate Judge has Marriage, Probate & land Records; Clerk Circuit Court has Court & Divorce Records)
Crenshaw www.rootsweb.com/~alcrensh/	M8	24 Nov 1866	**Butler, Coffee, Covington, Lowndes, Pike** Crenshaw County; PO Box 227; Luvern, AL 36049-0227; Ph. (334) 335-6568 **Details:** (Probate Judge has Marriage, Probate & land Records from 1866; Clerk Circuit Court has Divorce & Court Records)
Cullman www.co.cullman.al.us/	E6	24 Jan 1877	**Blount, Morgan, Winston** Cullman County; 500 2nd Ave SW; Cullman, AL 35055-4155; Ph. (256) 739-3530 **Details:** (Probate Judge has Marriage, Divorce, Probate, Court & land Records from 1877, old newspapers)

County Website	Map Index	Date Created	Parent County or Territory From Which Organized Address/Details
Dale	N10	22 Dec 1825	**Covington, Henry, Pike** Dale County; 202 Hwy 123 S Ste. C; Ozark, AL 36360; Ph. (334) 774-6025 **Details:** (Probate Judge has Marriage & Probate Records from 1884 & land Records; Clerk Circuit Court has Court & Divorce Records from 1885; County Health Department has Birth Records)
Dallas www.prairiebluff.com/algenweb/dallas/	K6	9 Feb 1818	**Montgomery, Creek Cession of 1814** Dallas County; PO Box 987; Selma, AL 36702-0997; Ph. (334) 874-2560 **Details:** (Probate Judge has Marriage Records from 1818, Divorce Records from 1917, Probate Records from 1821 and land Records from 1820)
Decatur		1821	**Jackson** Decatur County **Details:** County Terminated 1824
De Kalb www.tourdekalb.com/	D9	9 Jan 1836	**Cherokee Cession of 1835** De Kalb County; 111 Grand Ave SW; Fort Payne, AL 35967-1863; Ph. (256) 845-8500 **Details:** (Probate Judge has Marriage, Divorce, Probate & land Records; County Health Department has Birth, Death & Burial Records; Clerk Circuit Court has Court Records)
Elmore www.rootsweb.com/~alelmore/	J8	15 Feb 1866	**Autauga, Coosa, Montgomery, Tallapoosa** Elmore County; 100 Commerce St Rm 207; PO Box 338; Wetumpka, AL 36092-0338; Ph. (334) 567-1159 **Details:** (Probate Judge has Marriage & land Records from 1867, Birth & Death Records 1909–1913, Probate Records from 1866 & Military Discharge Records from 1919)
Escambia www.rootsweb.com/~alescamb/	O6	10 Dec 1868	**Baldwin, Conecuh** Escambia County; PO Box 848; Brewton, AL 36427-0848; Ph. (334) 867-0208 **Details:** (County Clerk has Marriage Records from 1897, Probate & land Records from 1869)
Etowah www.etowahcounty.org/	E9	7 Dec 1868	**Blount, Calhoun, Cherokee, DeKalb, Marshall. St. Clair** Etowah County; 800 Forrest Ave; Gadsden, AL 35901-3641; Ph. (256) 549-5300 **Details:** (Formerly Baine County, abolished 3 Dec 1867. Re-established as Etowah County 1 Dec 1868) (Probate Judge has Marriage, Divorce, Probate & land Records from 1867)
Fayette www.rootsweb.com/~alfayett/	F4	20 Dec 1824	**Marion, Pickens, Tuscaloosa** Fayette County; 103 1st Ave NW; PO Box 819; Fayette, AL 35555-0819; Ph. (205) 932-4510 **Details:** (Probate Judge has Birth Records 1884–1941, Death Records 1899–1941, Marriage Records from 1866, Probate Records from 1844, land Records from 1848 & Military Discharge Records from 1919)
Franklin www.franklinalabama.com/	D4	6 Feb 1818	**Cherokee & Chickasaw Cession of 1816** Franklin County; 410 N Jackson St; PO Box 1028; Russellville, AL 35653; Ph. (256) 332-8850 **Details:** (Records Burned 1890) (Probate Judge has Marriage, Probate & land Records from 1890; Clerk Circuit Court has Court Records from 1923 & Divorce Records)

County Website	Map Index	Date Created	Parent County or Territory From Which Organized Address/Details
Geneva www.alaweb.com/~gcounty/	O9	26 Dec 1868	**Dale, Henry, Coffee** Geneva County; PO Box 430; Geneva, AL 36340-0430; Ph. (334) 684-5610 **Details:** (Probate Judge has Marriage Records from 1898, Birth Records 1909–1918, Death Records 1909–1941, Probate Records from 1883, land Records from 1898 & Military Discharge Records from 1930)
Greene http.home.earthlink.net/~rodbush/GreeneHP.htm	I3	13 Dec 1819	**Marengo, Tuscaloosa** Greene County; PO Box 656; Eutaw, AL 35462-0656; Ph. (205) 372-3349 **Details:** (Probate Judge has Marriage Records from 1823, Probate Records from 1821, land Records from 1820 & Military Discharge Records)
Hale www.halecoal.org/	I4	30 Jan 1867	**Greene, Marengo, Perry, Tuscaloosa** Hale County; 1001 Main St; PO Box 396; Greensboro, AL 36744-1510; Ph. (334) 624-4257 **Details:** (Probate Judge has Marriage, Divorce, Probate, Court & land Records from 1868)
Hancock		12 Feb 1850	**Walker** Hancock County; AL **Details:** (see Winston) Name changed to Winston 22 Jan 1858
Henry www.rootsweb.com/~alhenry/	M11	13 Dec 1819	**Conecuh** Henry County; 101 Court Sq Ste A; Abbeville, AL 36310-2135; Ph. (334) 585-3257 **Details:** (Probate Judge has Marriage Records from 1821, land Records from 1824, Birth Records 1895–1922, Death Records 1895–1906 & Probate Records from 1839)
Houston www.houstoncounty.org/	O11	9 Feb 1903	**Dale, Geneva, Henry** Houston County; PO Box 6406; Dothan, AL 36302-6406; Ph. (334) 677-4741 **Details:** (Health Department has Birth, Death & Burial Records; Probate Office has Marriage, Probate & land Records from 1903; Clerk Circuit Court has Court Records from 1903; Register in Chancery has Divorce Records from 1903)
Jackson http.fly.hiwaay.net/~prm/jcalgenweb.html	B9	13 Dec 1819	**Cherokee Cession of 1816** Jackson County; 102 E Laurel St, Ste 47; PO Box 397; Scottsboro, AL 35768-0397; Ph. (256) 574-9280 **Details:** (Probate Judge has Marriage Records from 1851, Probate Records from 1850, land Records from 1835 & 1900 Civil War Vets list; Clerk Circuit Court has Court Records from 1920 & Divorce Records from 1895; County Health Department has Birth & Death Records; Public Library has cemetery Records)
Jefferson www.jeffcointouch.com/ieindex.asp	F6	13 Dec 1819	**Blount** Jefferson County; 716 Richard Arrington, Jr Blvd N; Birmingham, AL 35203; Ph. (205) 325-5300 **Details:** (Probate Judge has Marriage Records from 1818, Probate Records from 1870 & land Records from 1820)
Jones		4 Feb 1867	**Marion, Fayette** Jones County; AL **Details:** (see Lamar) Abolished 13 Nov 1867. Re-established as Sanford County 8 Oct 1868. Name changed to Lamar 8 Feb 1877

County	Map	Date	Parent County or Territory From Which Organized
Website	Index	Created	Address/Details

Lamar   F3   1877   **Marion, Fayette**
www.lamar.net/

Lamar County; PO Box 338; Vernon, AL 35592; Ph. (205) 695-7333
Details: (Formerly Jones County. Abolished 13 Nov 1867 and re-established as Sanford County 8 Oct 1868. Name changed to Lamar 8 Feb 1877) (Probate Office has Marriage Records 1867–1997, Probate and land Records; Circuit Clerk Office has Divorce and Court Records)

Lauderdale   B4   6 Feb 1818   **Cherokee, Chickasaw & ChoCourtaw Cession in 1816**
www.rootsweb.com/~allAuditorer/index.htm

Lauderdale County; PO Box 1059; Florence, AL 35631-1059; Ph. (256) 760-5750
Details: (Probate Judge has Marriage & Probate Records)

Lawrence   C5   6 Feb 1818   **Cherokee, Chickasaw & ChoCourtaw Cession in 1816**
www.rootsweb.com/~allawren/

Lawrence County; 750 Main St; Moulton, AL 35650-1553; Ph. (256) 974-0663
Details: (Probate Judge has Marriage, Divorce, Probate & land Records from 1810; Clerk Circuit Court has Court Records)

Lee   J10   5 Dec 1866   **Chambers, Macon, Russell, Tallapoosa**
www.rootsweb.com/~allee/

Lee County; 215 S 9th St; PO Box 666; Opelika, AL 36801-4919; Ph. (334) 745-9767
Details: (Probate Judge has Marriage & land Records from 1867, Military Discharge Records from 1919 & Probate Records from 1861)

Limestone   B6   6 Feb 1818   **Cherokee & Chickasaw Cession in 1816**
www.co.limestone.al.us/

Limestone County; 102 W Washington St; Athens, AL 35611-2597; Ph. (256) 233-6400
Details: (County Archive has Birth & Death Records 1881–1913, Marriage Records 1832–1900, Divorce Records 1896–1947, Probate, land & Court Records 1818–1900, tax Records 1861–1900, newspapers 1868–1985; Probate Judge has Marriage, Probate & land Records after 1900; Clerk Circuit Court has Court Records after 1900 & Divorce Records after 1947)

Lowndes   K7   20 Jan 1830   **Butler, Dallas, Montgomery**
www.rootsweb.com/~allownde/

Lowndes County; PO Box 65; Hayneville, AL 36040-0065; Ph. (334) 548-2331
Details: (Judge of Probate has Marriage & land Records from 1830, Birth & Death Records from 1879, Probate Records from 1870 & Military Discharge Records from 1919)

Macon   K10   18 Dec 1832   **Creek Cession of 1832**
www.intersurf.com/~johnjanr/macon.html

Macon County; 101 E Northside St; Tuskegee, AL 36083-1757; Ph. (334) 727-5120
Details: (Probate Judge has Marriage, Probate & land Records from 1835; Clerk Circuit Court has Court Records from 1868)

Madison   B7   13 Dec 1808   **Cherokee & Chickasaw Cession 1806–1807**
www.co.madison.al.us/

Madison County; 100 North Side Sq; Huntsville, AL 35801-4820; Ph. (256) 532-3327
Details: (Probate Judge has Marriage, Probate & land Records from 1809; Clerk Circuit Court has Divorce & Court Records; County Health Department has Death & Burial Records)

County	Map	Date	Parent County or Territory From Which Organized
Website	Index	Created	Address/Details

Marengo K4   **6 Feb 1818**   **ChoCourtaw Cession of 1816**
www.rootsweb.com/~almareng/
Marengo County; 101 E Coats Ave; PO Box 480715; Linden, AL 36748-1546; Ph. (334) 295-2200
Details: (Probate Judge has Marriage, Probate & land Records; Register in Chancery has Divorce Records; Clerk Circuit Court has Court Records)

Marion E4   **13 Feb 1818**   **Tuscaloosa**
www.rootsweb.com/~almarion/marion1.htm
Marion County; PO Box 460; Hamilton, AL 35570-1595; Ph. (205) 921-3172
Details: (Records Burned 1883) (Probate Judge has Birth & Death Records 1909–1919, Marriage Records from 1887, Probate Records from 1885, land Records from 1887 & Military Discharge Records from 1920)

Marshall D8   **9 Jan 1836**   **Blount, Cherokee Cession 1835, Jackson**
www.marshallco.org/www/
Marshall County; 424 Blount Ave; Guntersville, AL 35976-0000; Ph. (256) 571-7701
Details: (Probate Judge has Marriage, Probate & land Records from 1836 & Birth & Death Records from 1920)

Mobile P3   **1 Aug 1812**   **West Florida**
www.mobilecounty.org/
Mobile County; 109 Government St; Mobile, AL 36602-3108; Ph. (334) 690-8700
Details: (Probate Judge has Marriage Records from 1813, Probate Records from 1812 & land Records from 1813)

Monroe M5   **29 Jun 1815**   **Creek Cession 1814, Washington**
www.rootsweb.com/~almonroe/
Monroe County; County Courthouse; PO Box 8; Monroeville, AL 36461; Ph. (334) 743-4107
Details: (Courthouse fire destroyed all Records prior to 1833) (Probate Judge has Marriage, Probate & land Records from 1832; 1816 Census of Monroe County Public by Monroe Journal, Monroeville, AL)

Montgomery K8   **6 Dec 1816**   **Monroe**
www.mc-ala.org/
Montgomery County; PO Box 1667; Montgomery, AL 36102; Ph. (334) 832-1210
Details: (Probate Judge has Marriage Records from 1928, Probate Records from 1817 & land Records from 1819; AL Department of Archives & History has Marriage Records 1817–1928; Clerk of Board of Revenue has Divorce Records from 1852 & Court Records from 1917)

Morgan C6   **1821**   **Cherokee Turkeytown Cession**
www.co.morgan.al.us/
Morgan County; 302 Lee St NE; Decatur, AL 35601-1999; Ph. (256) 351-4737
Details: (Formerly Cotaco County. Name changed to Morgan 14 June 1821) (Probate Judge has Marriage & Probate Records from 1818)

Perry J5   **13 Dec 1819**   **Montgomery, Creek Cession of 1814**
www.rootsweb.com/~alperry/index.htm
Perry County; PO Box 478; Marion, AL 36756; Ph. (334) 683-2200
Details: (County Clerk has Marriage, Probate & land Records)

County	Map	Date	Parent County or Territory From Which Organized
Website	Index	Created	Address/Details

Pickens G3 **19 Dec 1820** **Tuscaloosa**
www.rootsweb.com/~alpicken/pcpage.htm
Pickens County; PO Box 460; Carrollton, AL 35447;
Ph. (205) 367-2020
Details: (Probate Judge has Marriage, Probate & land Records from 1876; Clerk Circuit Court has Divorce & Court Records)

Pike L9 **17 Dec 1821** **Henry, Montgomery**
www.intersurf.com/~johnjanr/pike.html
Pike County; 120 W Church St; PO Box 1147; Troy, AL 36081;
Ph. (334) 566-6374
Details: (Probate Judge has Marriage, Probate & land Records from 1830, Birth Records 1881–1904, Death Records 1881–1891 & 1902–1905)

Randolph G10 **18 Dec 1832** **Creek Cession 1832**
www.rootsweb.com/~alrandol/
Randolph County; PO Box 249; Wedowee, AL 36278;
Ph. (256) 357-4933
Details: (Courthouse Burned 1897, Records destroyed) (Health Department in Roanoke has Birth & Death Records, Probate Judge has Marriage Records from 1897, Probate Records from 1897, Military pensions 1904–1909, Newspapers, Probate Records, & Guardianship Records. Circuit Clerk has Court, Divorce, and Immigration Records. Tax Commisioner has Land & Property Maps & Tax Records. Registrar of Deeds has Land Records from 1897)

Russell K11 **18 Dec 1832** **Creek Cession 1832**
www.rootsweb.com/~alrussel/
Russell County; PO Box 969; Phenix, AL 36868; Ph. (334) 298-6426
Details: (County Health Department has Birth & Death Records; Clerk Circuit Court has Divorce & Court Records; Judge of Probate has Marriage, Probate & land Records from 1833)

Sanford **8 Oct 1868** **Jones**
Sanford County; AL
Details: (see Lamar) Formed from abolished Jones County. Name changed to Lamar 8 Feb 1877

Shelby G7 **7 Feb 1818** **Montgomery**
www.shelbycountyalabama.com/index.shtm
Shelby County; Main St; PO Box 467; Columbiana, AL 35051;
Ph. (205) 669-3740
Details: (Probate Judge has Marriage, Probate & land Records from 1824)

St. Clair F8 **20 Nov 1818** **Shelby**
www.rootsweb.com/~alstclai/
St. Clair County; PO Box 397; Ashville, AL 35953-0397;
Ph. (256) 594-2100
Details: (Probate Judge has Marriage, Probate & land Records from 1800; Clerk Circuit Court has Divorce & Court Records)

Sumter J3 **18 Dec 1832** **ChoCourtaw Cession of 1830**
www.rootsweb.com/~alsumter/index.htm
Sumter County; Franklin St; PO Box 70; Livingston, AL 35470;
Ph. (205) 652-2731
Details: (Probate Judge has a few Birth Records 1888–1918, Marriage & Probate Records from 1833, land Records & historical voters maps)

County	Map	Date	Parent County or Territory From Which Organized
Website	Index	Created	Address/Details

Talladega   G8   **18 Dec 1832**

www.rootsweb.com/~altallad/

Creek Cession of 1832

Talladega County; PO Box 755; Talladega, AL 35160;
Ph. (256) 362-4175

Details: (Chancery Court has Divorce Records 1888–1892; Department of Health has Birth & Death Records from 1897; Probate Court has Marriage Records from 1834, Land & Probate Records from 1833, & Military Records from 1930; Clerk of Circuit Court has Court Records from 1833)

Tallapoosa   I9   **18 Dec 1832**

Creek Cession of 1832

Tallapoosa County; 125 N Broadnax St, Rm 131; Dadeville, AL 36853; Ph. (256) 825.-4268

Details: (Probate Judge has a few Birth & Death Records 1881–1991, Marriage & Probate Records from 1835; Clerk Circuit Court has Divorce & Court Records; 90 acres were swapped between Tallapoosa & Coosa Counties in 1963)

Tuscaloosa   G5   **6 Feb 1818**

www.tuscco.com/

Cherokee & ChoCourtaw Cession 1816

Tuscaloosa County; 714 Greensboro Ave; Tuscaloosa, AL 35401-1895; Ph. (205) 349-3870

Details: (Probate Judge has Marriage & Probate Records from 1823)

Walker   F5   **26 Dec 1823**

www.walkercounty.com/

Marion, Tuscaloosa

Walker County; PO Box 1447; Jasper, AL 35502; Ph. (205) 384-3404

Details: (Records Burned 1877) (Probate Judge has Marriage & Probate Records)

Washington   N3   **4 June 1800**

http.members.aol.com/JORDANJM2/
washingtn.html

Mississippi Terr.

Washington County; PO Box 146; Chatom, AL, 36518-0146; Ph. (334) 847-2208

Details: (Probate Judge has Marriage Records from 1826, land Records from 1799, Military Discharge Records from 1919, Birth & Death Records from 1920 & Probate Records from 1825)

Wilcox   L5   **13 Dec 1819**

www.prairiebluff.com/algenweb/wilcox/

Monroe, Dallas

Wilcox County; 12 Water St; PO Box 488; Camden, AL 36726-0656; Ph. (334) 682-9112

Details: (Probate Judge has Marriage, Probate & land Records from 1819)

Winston   D5   **22 Jan 1858**

www.rootsweb.com/~alwinsto/

Walker

Winston County; PO Box 147; Double Springs, AL 35553; Ph. (205) 489-5026

Details: (Formerly Hancock County. Name changed to Winston 22 Jan 1858) (Probate Judge has Marriage, Probate & land Records from 1891; Clerk Circuit Court has Divorce & Court Records)

Alaska

Capital: Juneau

Territory: 1912

State: 1959 (49th)

North to the future

Russians established Alaska's first permanent, non-native settlement at Kodiak Island in 1784. Soon thereafter, British and American traders began to enter the area. Sitka was permanently settled by the Russians in 1804 and served as the center of government until 1906. The southern and eastern boundaries of Alaska were established by treaties with the United States and Britain between 1824 and 1828. Another boundary adjustment was made in 1903 between Alaska and British Columbia.

Alaska remained under Russian control until Russia was defeated in the Crimean War. Following this defeat, Russia sold Alaska to the United States on March 30, 1867. From 1867 to 1884, Alaska was administered first by the War Department, then by the Treasury Department, and then by the Navy Department. American settlement was sparse until the discovery of gold near Juneau in 1880. The first Organic Act, passed by Congress in 1884, provided a governor and federal courts to Alaska, with Sitka as the government's headquarters. State statute provided that persons in use of or occupying land at the beginning of civil government, May 17, 1884, would not be disturbed. The first General Land Office opened in Sitka in 1885, followed by offices in Juneau in 1902 and Nome in 1907. The Klondike strike in 1896 resulted in an influx of settlers. Further discoveries of gold at Nome in 1898 and placer fields at Fairbanks in 1902 continued the rush of settlers.

Alaska was a district until the Act of 1912 named it a U.S. Territory and Juneau was named the capital. It became a state in 1959. There are 16 Boroughs and 11 geographical census areas.

Look for vital records in the following locations:

- **Birth, death, marriage and divorce records:** The Bureau of Vital Statistics, Department of Health and Social Services in Juneau has birth, delayed birth, marriage, divorce (since 1950), and death records. State registration began in 1913 and was generally complied with by 1945.

- **Naturalizations:** Residents of Alaska in 1867 became citizens of the United States. Naturalization records for later settlers are filed in the judicial districts. Records for some districts are at the Alaska State Archives. Old territorial records of Fairbanks, Juneau, and Nome have been transferred to the Superior Court. Naturalization records after September 1906 are at the National Archives in Seattle, Washington.

- **Land records:** The jurisdiction of Alaska's land records is either federal or state. Organized boroughs also maintain land records, but receive their information from the state. Judicial Districts were created between 1897 and 1901, covering these areas:
  - First Judicial District. Provided a courthouse in Juneau and covered Southeastern Alexander Archipelago and the cities of Ketchikan, Wrangell, Sitka, and Juneau.
  - Second Judicial District. Provided a courthouse in Nome and covered the northern area including Nome and Barrow.
  - Third Judicial District. Provided a courthouse in Anchorage and covered the southern area including Anchorage, Kodiak and the Aleutian Islands.
  - Fourth Judicial District. Provided a courthouse in Fairbanks and covered the central area including Fairbanks, Bethel and Toksook Bay.

  Alaska remained a district until the Act of 1912 made Alaska a United States Territory and established the capital at Juneau. Statehood was granted in 1959. Currently, Alaska has 16 Boroughs and 11 geographical Census Areas.

- **Court records:** When researching Alaska's early court records there are three important time periods to remember:
  - 1884–1912—Alaska was a civil and judicial district; Sitka was the seat of government. Three divisions were created at Eagle City, Juneau and St. Michael.

Alaska

- 1912–1959—The Federal territorial court system was implemented.
- 1959–Present—The State court system was implemented.

All records for 1884–1959 are located at the Alaska State Archives or the National Archives Pacific Region (Alaska). Some records are in manuscript collections. Generally, records from 1959 to the present are in the office of the Clerk of Court in each judicial district. Older records are periodically transferred to the Alaska State Archives.

Department of Health and Social Services Bureau of Vital Statistics
5441 Commercial Boulevard
Juneau, AK 99801
(907) 465-3391; Fax (907) 465-3618
www.hss.state.ak.us/dph/bvs/

Alaska State Archives
141 Willoughby Avenue
Juneau, AK 99801
(907) 465-2270; Fax (907) 465-2465
www.archives.state.ak

National Archives—Alaska Region
Federal Office Building
654 West Third Ave., Room 012
Anchorage, AK 99501-2145
(907) 271-2441; Fax (907) 271-2442

Societies and Repositories

Alaska Society, SAR; 3310 Checkmate Drive; Anchorage, AK 99508-4924; (907) 333-4693; hrookus@alaska.com.

Alaska State Archives; 141 Willoughby Avenue; Juneau, AK 99801-1720; (907) 465-2270; archives@eed.state.ak.us; www.archives.state.ak.us.

Alaska State Library; PO Box 110571; Juneau, AK 99811; (907) 465-2920; asl@eed.state.ak.us; www.library.state.ak.us.

Anchorage Genealogical Society; PO Box 242294; Anchorage, AK 99524-2294.

Eagle Historical Society; PO Box 23; Eagle City, AK 99738; ehsmus@aptalaska.net; www.eagleak.org.

Fairbanks Genealogical Society; Fairbanks, AK; www.ptialaska.net/~fgs.

Gastineau Genealogical Society; 3270 Nowell Ave.; Juneau, AK 99801.

NARA, Pacific Alaska Region (Anchorage); 654 West Third Avenue; Anchorage, AK 99501-2145; (907) 262-7820; alaska.archives@nara.gov; www.archives.gov/facilities/pacific_alaska_region.html.

Palmer Historical Society, PO Box 1925; Palmer, AK 99645.

SAR, Alaska Society; 1925 N. Salem Dr.; Anchorage, AK 99504.

Wrangell Genealogical Society; PO Box 928EP; Wrangell, AK 99929.

Bibliography and Record Sources

General

Alaska Oral History Index. Fairbanks: University of Alaska Fairbanks, 1984.

The Alaska-Yukon Gold Book: A Roster of the Progressive Men and Women Who Were the Argonauts of the Klondike Gold Stampede. Seattle: Sourdough Stampede Association, 1930.

Bancroft, Hubert Howe. *History of Alaska, 1730–1885*. San Francisco: A.L. Bancroft, 1886.

Bradbury, Connie Malcolm and David Albert Hales. *Alaska Sources a Guide to Historical Records and Information Resources*. North Salt Lake: Heritage Quest, 2001.

Brooks, Maria. *Alaska Women's Oral History Collection: Catalogue with Subject Index*. Anchorage: Anchorage Community College, 1983.

De Armond, Robert N. *The Founding of Juneau*. Juneau, Alaska: Gastineau Channel Centennial Association, 1967.

Falk, Marvin W. *Alaskan Maps: A Cartobibliography of Alaska to 1900*. New York: Garland Pub., 1983.

Family History Library. *Alaska: Research Outline*. Salt Lake City: Corp. of the President of The Church of Jesus Christ of Latter-day Saints, 1988.

Ferrell, Ed. *Biographies of Alaska-Yukon pioneers*. 3 vols. 1850–1950. Bowie, Maryland: Heritage Books, c1994–1997.

Galbraith, William R. *The Alaska Newspaper Tree*. Fairbanks: Elmer Rasmuson Library, 1975.

Hone, Wade E. *Land and Property Research in the United States*. Salt Lake City: Ancestry Incorporated, 1997.

Hulley, Clarence Charles. *Alaska, 1741–1953/9*. Portland, Oregon: Binfords & Mort, 1953.

Hunt, William R. *Alaska, a Bicentennial History*. New York: W. W. Norton and Co., 1976.

Jackson, Ronald Vern and Gary Ronald Teeples. *Alaskan Records, 1870–1907/9*. North Salt Lake, Utah: Accelerated Indexing Systems International, c1976.

Lada-Mocarski, Valerian. *Bibliography of Books on Alaska Published Before 1868*. New Haven, Connecticut: Yale University Press, 1969.

MacLean, Edna A. *Genealogical Record of Barrow Eskimo Families*. Barrow, Alaska: Naval Research Laboratory, 1971.

Naske, Claus-M., and Slotnick, Herman E. *Alaska: A Picture of the 49th State*. Norman, Oklahoma: University of Oklahoma Press, 1987.

Parham, R. Bruce. *How to Find Your Gold Rush Relative: Sources on the Klondike and Alaska Gold Rushes (1896-1914)*. Anchorage, Alaska: National Archives and Records Administration, Pacific Alaska Region, 1997.

Pierce, Richard A. *Russian America: A Biographical Dictionary*. Kingston, Ontario, Canada: Limestone Press, 1990.

Ricks, Melvin Byron. *Melvin Ricks' Alaska Bibliography: An Introductory Guide to Alaskan Historical Literature*. Portland, Oregon: Binford & Mort, 1977.

Shalkop, Antoinette. *The Alaskan Russian Church Archives: Records of the Russian Orthodox Greek Catholic Church of North America—Diocese of Alaska*. Washington: Manuscript Division, Library of Congress, 1984.

Sherwood, Morgan B. *Alaska and its History*. Seattle, Washington: University of Washington Press, 1967.

Ulibarri, George S. *Documenting Alaskan History: Guide to Federal Archives Relating to Alaska*. Fairbanks, Alaska: University of Alaska Press, 1982.

University of Washington (Seattle) Library. *The Dictionary Catalog of the Pacific Northwest Collection of the University of Washington (Seattle) Libraries*. 6 vols. Boston: G.K. Hall and Co., 1972.

Wharton, David. *The Alaska Gold Rush*. Bloomington, Indiana: Indiana University Press, 1972.

Woerner, R. K. *The Alaska Handbook*. Jefferson, North Carolina: McFarland & Co., 1986.

Atlases, Maps and Gazetteers

Alaska Atlas and Gazetteer. 4th ed. Freeport, Maine: DeLorme Mapping Co., 1995.

Baker, Marcus. *Geographic Dictionary of Alaska*. Washington, D.C.: Library of Congress Photoduplication Service, 1963. Microfilm.

Geographic Dictionary of Alaska. Washington, D.C.: Government Printing Office, 1902.

Orth, Donald J. *Dictionary of Alaska Place Names*. Washington, D.C.: Government Printing Office, 1902.

Phillips, James W. *Alaska-Yukon Place Names*. Seattle: University of Washington Press, 1973.

Schorr, Alan Edward. *Alaska Place Names*. Juneau, Alaska: Denali Press, 1991.

Census

Dollarhide, William. *The Census Book: A Genealogist's Guide to Federal Census Facts, Schedules and Indexes*. Bountiful, Utah: Heritage Quest, 1999.

Kemp, Thomas Jay. *The American Census Handbook*. Wilmington, Delaware: Scholarly Resources, Inc., 2001.

Lainhart, Ann S. *State Census Records*. Baltimore: Genealogical Publishing Co., Inc., 1992.

Szucs, Loretto Dennis and Matthew Wright. *Finding Answers in U.S. Census Records*. Ancestry Publishing, 2001.

Thorndale, William. *Map Guide to the U.S. Federal Census, 1790–1920*. Baltimore: Genealogical Publishing Co., 1987.

Court Records, Probate, and Wills

District and Territorial Court System: Record Group Inventory. Juneau, Alaska: State Archives, 1987.

Emigration, Immigration, Migration and Naturalization

Parham, R. Bruce. *Indexes to Naturalization Records of the U.S. District Court for the District, Territory & State of Alaska (Third division), 1903–1991*. Seattle: National Archives and Records Administration, Pacific Alaska Region, 1997. 22 Microfilm.

Rasmussen, Janet E. *New Land, New Lives: Scandinavian Immigrants to the Pacific Northwest*. Seattle: University of Washington Press, c1993.

United States. Immigration and Naturalization Service. *Alphabetical Index of Alien Arrivals at Eagle, Hyder, Ketchikan, Nome, and Skagway, Alaska, June 1906–August 1946: M2016*. College Park, Maryland: National Archives and Records Administration, 1997. Microfilm.

Land and Property

Alaska Department of Natural Resources. *Alaska Mining Claims Cross-Reference Index*. Juneau, Alaska: Alaska Department of Natural Resources, 2002. Online database www.dnr.state.ak.us.

Fisher, Raymond Henry. *Records of the Russian-American Company, 1802, 1817–1867*. Washington, D.C.: National Archives, National Archives and Records Service, General Services Administration, 1971.

Russian-American Company Records, 1802–1867. 92 vols. Washington, D.C.: National Archives, 1942.

U.S. Congress. House. *Message from the President of the United States in Relation to the Transfer of Territory from Russia to the United States, January 28, 1868*. 40th Cong., 2d sess. H. Exec. Doc. 125. Washington, D.C.: G.P.O., 1868–1912.

Military

Grant, Bruce. *American Forts Yesterday and Today*. New York: E. P. Dutton & Co., 1965.

United States. Selective Service System. *Alaska, World War I Selective Service System Draft Registration Cards, 1917–1918. National Archives Microfilm Publications, M1509*. Washington, D.C.: National Archives, 1987–1988. 4 Microfilm.

Vital and Cemetery Records

Dorosh, Elizabeth and John. *Index to Baptisms, Marriages, and Deaths in the Archives of the Russian Orthodox*

Greek Catholic Church in Alaska, 1900–1936. Washington, D.C.: Library of Congress, 1964.

Index to Baptisms, Marriages and Deaths in the Archives of the Russian Orthodox Greek Catholic Church in Alaska, 1816–1866. Washington, D.C.: Library of Congress, 1973.

Index to Baptisms, Marriages and Deaths in the Archives of the Russian Orthodox Greek Catholic Church in Alaska 1867–1889. Washington, D.C.: Library of Congress, 1986.

County Website	Map Index	Date Created	Parent County or Territory From Which Organized Address/Details
Aleutians East Borough www.aleutianseast.org/	K9	1987	Aleutians East Borough County; PO Box 349; Sand Point, AK 99501-0349; Ph. (907) 383-5334
Aleutians West Census Area	N11		Aleutians West Census Area County; AK
Anchorage Borough www.ci.anchorage.ak.us./	G7		Anchorage Borough County; PO Box 196650; Anchorage, AK 99519-6650; Ph. (907) 343-4311
Bethel Census Area future website at http://usgenweb.com/	J7		Bethel Census Area County; PO Box 388; Bethel, AK 99559; Ph. (907) 543-2047
Bristol Bay Borough www.theborough.com/	I8	Oct 1962	Bristol Bay Borough County; PO Box 189; Naknek, AK 99633-0189; Ph. (907) 246-4224 **Details:** (Borough Cemetery has Burial & Cemetery Records from 1991, *Marked Business & Commerce, Census, Land & Property, Land & Property -- Maps, and Tax, but did not tell what office or court holds these records*
Denali Borough G6 www.mtaonline.net/~dbgovt/borough.html			Denali Borough County; AK
Dillingham Census Area future website at http://usgenweb.com/	I8		Dillingham Census Area County; PO Box 889; Dillingham, AK 99576; Ph. (907) 842-5211
Fairbanks North Star Borough www.co.fairbanks.ak.us/	F5	1 Jan 1964	Fairbanks North Star Borough County; 809 Pioneer Rd; PO Box 71267; Fairbanks, AK 99707; Ph. (907) 459-1000
Haines Borough B8 www.haines.ak.us/		29 Aug 1968	Haines Borough County; PO Box 1209; Haines, AK 99827-1209; Ph. (907) 766-711

County	Map	Date	Parent County or Territory From Which Organized
Website	Index	Created	Address/Details

Juneau, City and
Bourough B8 30 Sept 1963
www.juneau.org/
city_clerk@ci.juneau.ak.us

Juneau, City and Bourough County; 155 S Seward St; Juneau, AK 99801; Ph. (907) 586-5278
Details: (City Clerk has Cemetery, Land, and Tax Records from 1900)

Kenai Peninsula
Borough G7 12 Dec 1963
www.borough.kenai.ak.us/

Kenai Peninsula Borough County; 144 N Binkley; Soldotna, AK 99669; Ph. (907) 262-4441

Ketchikan Gateway
Borough A10
www.borough.ketchikan.ak.us/

Ketchikan Gateway Borough County; 344 Front St; Ketchikan, AK 99901-6431; Ph. (907) 228-6625

Kodiak Island
Borough H9 24 Sept 1963
www.kib.co.kodiak.ak.us/

Kodiak Island Borough County; 710 Mill Bay Rd; Kodiak, AK 99615; Ph. (907) 486-9300

Lake and Peninsula
Borough I8 Apr 1989
www.bristolbay.com/~lpboro/

Lake and Peninsula Borough County; PO Box 495; King Salmon, AK 99613-0495; Ph. (907) 246-3421

Matanuska-Susitna
Borough G6 1964
http://borough.co.mat-su.ak.us/

Matanuska-Susitna Borough County; 350 E Dahlia Ave; PO Box 1608; Palmer, AK 99645-1608; Ph. (907) 745-4801

Nome Census
Area K5
future website at http://usgenweb.com/

Nome Census Area County; 61 Hunter Way; Nome, AK 99762; Ph. (907) 443-6663

North Slope
Borough H3 1 Jul 1972
www.co.north-slope.ak.us/

North Slope Borough County; PO Box 69; Barrow, AK 99723-0069; Ph. (907) 852-2611

Northwest Arctic
Borough J4 2 Jun 1986
future website at http://usgenweb.com/

Northwest Arctic Borough County; PO Box 1110; Kotzebue, AK 99752-1110; Ph. (907) 442-2500

Prince of Wales-Outer
Ketchika B10

Prince of Wales-Outer Ketchika County; AK

Sitka Borough B9 2 Dec 1971
www.cityofsitka.com/

Sitka Borough County; 100 Lincoln St; Sitka, AK 99835-7563; Ph. (907) 747-1812

Skagway-Hoonah-Angoon
Census A C8

Skagway-Hoonah-Angoon Census A County; AK

Alaska

County Website	Map Index	Date Created	Parent County or Territory From Which Organized Address/Details
Southeast Fairbanks Census Area	**E5**		Southeast Fairbanks Census Are County; AK
Valdez Cordova Census Area	**E7**		Valdez Cordova Census Area County; AK
Wade Hampton Census Area	**K6**		Wade Hampton Census Area County; AK
Wrangell-PetersBurg Census Area	**B9**		Wrangell-PetersBurg Census Area County; AK
Yakutat Borough future website at http://usgenweb.com/	**D8**	**7 Sept 1971**	Yakutat Borough County; PO Box 160; Yukutat, AK 99689; Ph. (907) 784-3323
Yukon-Koyukuk Census Area	**G4**		Yukon-Koyukuk Census Area County; AK

Arizona

Capital: Phoenix

Territory: 1863

State: 1912 (48th)

God enriches

The first explorers came to Arizona in search of gold and treasures, attracted by tales of the fabulous "Seven Cities of Cibola." European explorers came into the region as early as 1539. About 150 years later, Catholic missionaries came to proselytize the Indians. The first permanent, non-Indian settlement began in 1776 at the present site of Tucson. Arizona was under the control of Mexico in the section known as New Mexico in 1821. Early settlers generally came into the Gila Valley from the Sonora and Sinaloa states of Mexico.

Following the Mexican War, the portion of Arizona north of the Gila River became part of the United States. The lower portion of Arizona was purchased from Mexico in 1854 under terms of the Gadsden Purchase. Arizona was part of the territory of New Mexico, which was organized in 1850. Following this organization, members of the Church of Jesus Christ of Latter-day Saints began moving from Utah to settle in Arizona. In 1863, Arizona Territory was formed. Prescott was the territorial capital. During the Civil War, the New Mexico territory had about 200 soldiers fighting for the Confederacy and more than 6,000 for the Union.

From 1852 to 1863, the New Mexico district, probate, and supreme courts had jurisdiction for the Arizona area.

In 1870, Arizona had less than 10,000 residents. The population increased twenty-fold over the following 40 years. In the next half century, the population more than tripled. Phoenix became the capital in 1889. The foreign-born population of Arizona in descending order came from Mexico, Canada, England, Wales, Germany, Russia, Italy, Poland, Austria, Sweden, Greece, Ireland, Scotland, Yugoslavia, and Czechoslovakia.

Look for vital statistics in the following locations:

- **Birth and death records:** Vital Records Section, Department of Health Service after 18 March, 1909; check with county seats from 1887 to 18 March, 1909.
- **Marriage records:** Clerk of the Superior Court of each county. From 1891 to 1912, clerks of probate courts issued marriage licenses.

- **Divorce records:** Clerk of the Superior Court of the county in which the license was issued. The earliest divorce records were granted by the territorial legislature and are published in the Territorial Statutes. Until 1912, the district court of each county kept these records. District courts had countywide jurisdiction over records of chancery, criminal cases, and divorces from 1864 to 1912. After 1912, superior courts had jurisdiction for most areas.
- **Naturalizations:** Filed in the district court of the county where the examination was conducted. From 1906 until 1912, the clerk of the U.S. district courts in Tucson, Tombstone, Phoenix, Prescott, and Solomonville recorded naturalizations. After 1912 (1919 for Maricopa County), naturalization records were filed in the superior courts.
- **Land records:** Office of the recorder of the county where the land is located.
- **Census records:** Incomplete territorial census records for the years 1864, 1866, 1867, 1869, 1871, 1872, and 1873 are available at the Department of Libraries, Archives and Public Records. Arizona was included in the New Mexico federal census for 1860.

Office of Vital Records Arizona Department of Health Service
150 North 18th Avenue
Phoenix, Arizona 85007
(602) 542-1000; (602) 542-0883 fax
www.azdhs.gov/vitalrcd/death_index.htm

Department of Libraries, Archives, and Public Records
Old Capitol Building
1700 West Washington, 3rd Floor
Phoenix, Arizona 85007
www.dlapr.lib.az.us/archives/

Societies and Repositories

Arizona Genealogical Advisory Board; PO Box 5641; Mesa, AZ 85211-5641; www.azgab.org.

Arizona Historical Society; Tucson, AZ; ahsref@vms.arizona.edu; http://w3.arizona.edu/~azhist.

Arizona Pioneer's Historical Society; 949 East Second St.; Tucson, AZ 85719.

Arizona State Genealogical Society; PO Box 42075; Tucson, AZ 85733-2075; (520) 275-2747; www.rootsweb.com/~asgs.

Arizona State Library, Archives and Public Records; State Capitol, Suite 342; 1700 W. Washington; Phoenix, AZ 85007; (602) 542-4159; archive@lib.az.us; http://lib.az.us/archives/index.html.

Arizona Sun Chapter, AHSGR; 1857 Leisure World; Mesa, AZ 85206; (480) 654-3767; babithr@amug.org; www.ahsgr.org/azsun.html.

Black Family Historical Society of Arizona; PO Box 1515; Gilbert, AZ 85299-1515.

Casa Grande Valley Historical Society; 110 W. Florence Blvd.; Casa Grande, AZ 85222-4033; (520) 836-2223; info@cgvhs.org; www.cgvhs.org.

Central Arizona Division, Arizona Historical Society; 1300 N. College Ave.; Tempe, AZ 85281.

Cherokee Family Ties; 516N. 38th St.; Mesa, AZ 85208.

Cochise Chapter, Arizona SAR; AZ; ringgold1@mindspring.com.

Cochise Genealogical Society; 1001 D. Avenue; Douglas, AZ 85607-2251.

Coconino County Genealogical Society; 649 E. Edison; Williams, AZ 86046.

Czech and Slovak Genealogical Society of Arizona; 4921 E. Exeter Blvd.; Phoenix, AZ 85018-2942; djanca@worldnet.att.net; www.rootsweb.com/~azcsgsa.

Daughters of The American Revolution, Arizona State; 17239 N. 59th Pl.; Scottsdale, AZ 85254.

Family History Society of Arizona, The; PO Box 63094; Phoenix, AZ 85082-3094; www.fhsa.org.

Genealogical Society of Pinal County, Arizona, Inc.; 1107 E. 10th St.; Casa Grande, AZ 85222.

Genealogical Society of Yuma, Arizona; PO Box 2905; Yuma, AZ 85366-2905; (928) 344-2280; patburtch@aol.com; www.gsya.org.

Genealogical Workshop of Mesa; PO Box 6052; Mesa, AZ 85216; windy@worldnet.att.net; http://members.home.net/gwom.

Green Valley Chapter, Arizona SAR; AZ; CKPLATTII@juno.com.

Green Valley Genealogical Society; PO Box 1009; Green Valley, AZ 85622-1009; www.rootsweb.com/~azgvgs.

Jerome Historical Society; PO Box 156; Jerome, AZ 86331; Director@jeromehistoricalsociety.org; www.jeromehistoricalsociety.org/index.html.

Jewish Historical Society of Southern Arizona, Committee on Genealogical; 4181 E. Pontatoc Canyon Dr.; Tucson, AZ 85718.

Lake Havasu Genealogical Society; PO Box 953; Lake Havasu City, AZ 86405-0953; (928) 855-5113; chascoulbourn@citlink.net; www.rootsweb.com/~azlhgs.

Mohave County Genealogical Society; 400 West Beale Street; Kingman, AZ 86401.

Navajo County Genealogical Society; PO Box 1403; Winslow, AZ 86047.

Northern Arizona Chapter, Arizona SAR; AZ; aurand@sedona.net.

Northern Arizona Genealogical Society; PO Box 695; Prescott, AZ 86302; www.rootsweb.com/~aznags.

Northern Gila County Genealogical Society; PO Box 952; Payson, AZ 85547; (928) 474-2139; ngcgs@npgcable.com; http://users.rootsweb.com/~azngcgs/index.html.

Oracle Historical Society; PO Box 10; Oracle, AZ 85623; www.ferberts.com/ohs.

Palo Verde Chapter, Arizona SAR; dhheler@worldnet.att.net.

Phoenix Chapter, Arizona SAR; AZ; NEWTSPHX@aol.com.

Phoenix Genealogical Society; PO Box 39703; Phoenix, AZ 85069-8703.

Prescott Chapter, Arizona, SAR; AZ; jhanny@cableone.net.

Prescott Historical Society; 415 West Gurley St.; Prescott, AZ 86301.

Rio Colorado Division, Arizona Historical Society; 240 S. Madison; Yuma, AZ 85364.

Saguaro Chapter, Arizona SAR; AZ; Kardonb@aol.com.

Sedona Genealogy Club; PO Box 4258; Sedona, AZ 86340; http://fp.sedona.net/genealogy/index.htm.

Sierra Vista Genealogical Society; Sierra Vista, AZ ; www.rootsweb.com/~azsvgs.

Skyline Chapter, Arizona SAR; AZ; Rcrawford@aol.com.

Sun Cities Genealogical Society; 12600 113th Ave., Suite C-6; PO Box 1448; Youngtown, AZ 85363.

Tempe Historical Society; 809 E. Southern Avenue; Tempe, AZ 85282; www.tempe.gov/museum/ahistsoc.htm.

Tri-State Genealogical Society; PO Box 6045; Mohave Valley, AZ 86440.

Tucson Chapter, Arizona SAR; AZ; dickzoo@worldnet.att.net.

West Valley Genealogical Society; 12222 N. 111th Ave; Youngtown, AZ 85363-1225; www.rootsweb.com/~azwvgs/WVHome.htm.

Bibliography and Record Sources

General

A Historical and Biographical Record of the Territory of Arizona. Chicago: McFarland & Poole, 1896.

Arizona Historical Society. *Official Directory of Arizona Historical Museums and Related Support Organizations.* Tucson, Arizona: Arizona Historical Society, 1997.

Arizona History Today. Tucson, Arizona: Arizona Historical Society, 1997–. Serial.

Arizona Research Outline. Series U.S.-States, No. 3. Salt Lake City: Family History Library, 1988.

Beers, Henry Putney. *Spanish and Mexican Records of the American Southwest: A Bibliographical Guide to Archive and Manuscript Sources.* Tucson: University of Arizona Press, 1979.

Directory of Churches and Religious Organizations in Arizona. Phoenix: Division of Professional and Service Projects, WPA, 1940.

Farish, Thomas Edwin. *History of Arizona.* 8 vols., San Francisco: Filmer Bros. Electrotype Co. Reprint of Phoenix: N.P., 1915–18.

Hayden, Carl. *Carl Hayden Biographical Files, ca. 1825–1927.* (Tempe, Arizona: Arizona State University).

Lutrell, Estelle. *Newspapers and Periodicals of Arizona, 1859–1911.* Tucson: University of Arizona, 1950.

Portrait and Biographical Record of Arizona. Chicago: Chapman Publishing Co., 1901.

Powell, Donald M. *Arizona Gathering II, 1950–1969: An Annotated Bibliography.* Tucson: University of Arizona Press, 1973.

Powell, Donald M. *Arizona Gathering II: An Annotated Bibliography, 1950–1969.* Tucson: University of Arizona Press, 1973.

*Spiros, Joyce V. Hawley. *Genealogical Guide to Arizona and Nevada.* Gallup, New Mexico: Verlene Publishing, 1983.

Surname Index for the Arizona Sentinel, 1872–1905. Yuma, Arizona: Genealogical Society of Yuma, Arizona, 1997.

Wiggins, Marvin E. *Mormons and Their Neighbors: An Index of Over 75,000 Biographical Sketches from 1820 to the Present.* 2 vols. (Provo, Utah: Brigham Young University, 1984).

Wyllys, Rufus Kay. *Arizona: The History of a Frontier State.* Phoenix: Hobson and Herr, 1950.

Atlases, Maps and Gazetteers

Barnes, Will C. *Arizona Place Names.* Revised. Tucson: University of Arizona Press, 1982.

Dreyfuss, John J. *History of Arizona's Counties and Courthouses.* Tucson: National Society of the Colonial Dames of America in the State of Arizona, 1972.

Granger, Byrd H. *Arizona's Names: X Marks the Place.* Tucson, Arizona: Falconer Pub. Co., 1983.

Herman, James E., and Barbara H. Sherman. *Ghost Towns of Arizona.* Norman, Oklahoma: University of Oklahoma Press, 1969.

Theobold, John and Lillian Theobold. *Arizona Territory: Post Offices and Postmasters.* Phoenix: Arizona Historical Foundation, 1961.

Thorndale, William and William Dollarhide. *Map Guides to the U.S. Federal Censuses, 1790–1920: Arizona, 1860–1920.* Baltimore: Genealogical Publishing, 1987.

Walker, Henry P. and Don Bufkin. *Historical Atlas of Arizona.* Norman, Oklahoma: University of Oklahoma Press, 1979.

Censuses

Available Census Records and Census Substitutes

Federal Census 1860, 1870, 1880, 1900, 1910, 1920, 1930

Federal Mortality Schedules 1870, 1880

State/Territorial Census 1850, 1860, 1864, 1866, 1867, 1869

Dollarhide, William. *The Census Book: A Genealogist's Guide to Federal Census Facts, Schedules and Indexes.* Bountiful, Utah: Heritage Quest, 1999.

Kemp, Thomas Jay. *The American Census Handbook.* Wilmington, Deleware: Scholarly Resources, Inc., 2001.

Lainhart, Ann S. *State Census Records.* Baltimore: Genealogical Publishing Co., Inc., 1992.

Szucs, Loretto Dennis and Matthew Wright. *Finding Answers in U.S. Census Records.* Ancestry Publishing, 2001.

United States. Bureau of the Census. *Cross Index to Selected City Streets and Enumeration Districts, 1910 Census.* Washington, D.C.: National Archives, 1984.

Court Records, Probate, and Wills

A Guide to Arizona Courts. Phoenix, Arizona: Arizona Supreme Court Office of The Courts, 1997.

James, Jessamine Bland. *Will Books 1 & 2, Years 1866–1900, Pima County, Territory of Arizona.* Typescript. Salt Lake City: Filmed by the Genealogical Society of Utah, 1970.

Immigration

Arizona. Superior Court (Cochise County). *Citizenship Petitions Denied and Granted, 1929–1955.* Microfilm of original records at the Cochise County Courthouse in Bisbee, Arizona. Salt Lake City: Filmed by the Genealogical Society of Utah, 1997. Microfilm.

United States. District Court (Arizona Territory: 2nd Judicial District). *Naturalizations, 1882–1912; Index, 1864–1911.* Microfilm of records located at the National Archives, Pacific Southwest Region, Laguna Niguel, California. Salt Lake City: Filmed by the Genealogical Society of Utah, 1989. Microfilm, multiple rolls.

Land

Miscellaneous Archives Relating to New Mexico Land Grants, 1695–1842. Albuquerque: University of New Mexico Library, 1955–1957. Text in Spanish.

New Mexico (Territory). Secretary's Office. *Records of Land Titles, 1847–1852.* Albuquerque, New Mexico: University of New Mexico Library, 1955–1957.

New Mexico (Territory). Surveyor-General's Office. *Record of Private Land Claims Adjudicated By the U.S. Surveyor General, 1855–1890.* Salt Lake City: Filmed by the Genealogical Society of Utah, 1955–1957. Microfilm, multiple rolls.

Twitchell, Ralph E. *The Twitchell Archives, 1685–1898.* Albuquerque, New Mexico: Filmed by the University of New Mexico Library, 1955–1957. Microfilm, 6 rolls.

United States. Land Office (Prescott, Arizona). *Land Entry Decisions by the Commission of General Land Office, Prescott, Arizona: Homestead Claims and Applications, Mineral Entries, Railroad Land Claims, etc.* Microfilm of records located at the National Archives, Pacific Southwest Region, Laguna Niguel, California. Salt Lake City: Filmed by the Genealogical Society of Utah, 1989. Microfilm, 13 rolls.

United States. Land Office (Prescott, Arizona). *Land Records, 1847–1907.* Microfilm of records located at the National Archives Pacific Southwest Region, Laguna Niguel, California. Salt Lake City: Filmed by the Genealogical Society of Utah, 1989. Microfilm, 3 rolls.

United States. Surveyor General (Arizona). *Records of Mineral Surveys, Homestead Surveys, and Private Land Claims.* Microfilm of records located at the National Archives, Pacific Southwest Region, Laguna Niguel, California. Salt Lake City: Filmed by the Genealogical Society of Utah, 1989. Microfilm, 2 rolls.

Van Ness, John R., and Christine Van Ness. *Spanish and Mexican Land Grants in New Mexico and Colorado.* Manhattan, Kansas: Ag Press, 1981.

Vigil, Donaciano. *Vigil's Index, 1681–1846.* Albuquerque: University of New Mexico Library, 1955–1957. Text in Spanish.

Military

Alexander, David V. *Arizona Frontier Military Place Names: 1846–1912.* Las Cruces, New Mexico: Yucca Tree Press, 1998.

Altshuler, Constance Wynn. *Chains of Command: Arizona and the Army, 1856–1875.* Tucson, Arizona: Arizona Historical Society, 1981.

Arizona Pioneers' Historical Society (Tucson, Arizona). *The Army in the West, A Guide to Microfilmed Records in the Library of the Arizona Pioneers' Historical Society.* Tucson, Arizona: W.C. Cox Co., 1974.

Brandes, Ray. *Frontier Military Posts of Arizona* (Globe, Arizona: Dale S. King, 1960; Gabbert, Howard Markland.)

Hortsch, Frances A. *Arizona's Memorial to Vietnam Veterans.* Phoenix, Arizona: Phoenix Genealogical Society, 1987.

The Rough Riders: A Brief Study and Indexed Roster of the 1st Regiment, U.S. Volunteer Cavalry, 1898. Tucson, Arizona: Arizona State Genealogical Society, 1992.

United States. Adjutant General's Office. *Index to Compiled Service Records of Confederate.* Washington, D.C.: The National Archives, 1962.

United States. Adjutant General's Office. *Index to Compiled Service Records of Volunteer Union Soldiers who served in Organizations from the Territory of Arizona, 1861–1865.* Washington, D.C.: National Archives. Central Plains Region, 1964.

United States. Selective Service System. *Arizona, World War I Selective Service System Draft Registration Cards, 1917–1918.* Washington, D.C.: National Archives, 1987–1988.

Ynfante, Charles. *Arizona During the Second World War, 1941–1945, a Survey of Selected Topics.* Dissertation. (Ph.D.) Flagstaff, Arizona: Northern Arizona University, 1997.

Vital and Cemetery

Arizona Cemetery Records. Salt Lake City: Genealogical Society of Utah, 1959.

Arizona Death Records: An Index Compiled from Mortuary, Cemetery, Church Records. Tucson: Arizona State Genealogical Society, n.d.

Arizona Statewide Archival and Records Project, Work Projects Administration. *Guide to Public Vital Statistics Records in Arizona.* Phoenix, Arizona.: [s.n.], 1941.

ARIZONA, CA, ID, NV, 1850–1951. [S.l.]: Brøderbund, 1996. CD-ROM

Arizona. Department of Health Services. *Arizona Birth Certificates, 1855–1924.* Microfilm of original records at the Arizona Department of Library, Archives and Public Records Management Division in Phoenix, Arizona. Salt Lake City: Filmed by the Genealogical Society of Utah, 1998–1999. Microfilm, 51 rolls.

Arizona. Department of Health Services. *Birth and Death Records for Various Arizona Counties, 1887–1912.* Salt Lake City: Filmed by the Genealogical Society of Utah, 1998.

Arizona. Department of Health Services. *Death Certificates (Arizona), ca. 1870–1949.* Microfilm of original records at the Arizona Department of Library, Archives and Public Records, Records Management Division in Phoenix, Arizona. Salt Lake City: Filmed by the Genealogical Society of Utah, 1998–1999. Microfilm, 93 rolls.

*Whiteside, Dora M. *Northern Arizona Territorial Death and Burial Records 1870–1910.* Prescott, Arizona: D. Whiteside, 1988.

County Website	Map Index	Date Created	Parent County or Territory From Which Organized Address/Details
Apache www.co.apache.az.us/	E11	**14 Feb 1879**	**Yavapai** Apache County; 70 West 3rd S; PO Box 428; St. Johns, AZ 85936-0428; Ph. (520) 337-4364 **Details:** (Clerk Superior Court has Marriage, Divorce, Probate & Court Records from 1879; County Recorder has land Records from 1879)
Castle Dome		**1860**	**Original county** Castle Dome County; AZ **Details:** (see Yuma) Name changed to Yuma 21 Dec 1864; County Terminated 1864
Cochise www.co.cochise.az.us/	O10	**1 Feb 1881**	**Pima** Cochise County; PO Box CK; Bisbee, AZ 85603-0000; Ph. (520) 432-8604 **Details:** (Clerk Superior Court has Marriage, Divorce, Probate & Court Records; County Recorder has land Records)
Coconino http://co.coconino.az.us/	F6	**19 Feb 1891**	**Yavapai** Coconino County; Flagstaff Justice Court; 100 E Birch Ave; Flagstaff, AZ 86001-4696; Ph. (520) 774-5011 **Details:** (Clerk Superior Court has Marriage, Divorce, Court & Probate Records from 1891; County Recorder has land Records
Ewell		**1860**	**Original county** Ewell County; AZ **Details:** (see Pima) Name changed to Pima 15 Dec 1864; County Terminated 1863
Gila www.rootsweb.com/~azgila/index.htm	J8	**8 Feb 1881**	**Maricopa, Pinal** Gila County; 1400 E Ash St; Globe, AZ 85501-1414; Ph. (520) 425-3231 **Details:** (County Clerk has Marriage Records from 1881, Divorce, Probate & Court Records from 1914; County Recorder has Land Records
Graham www.graham.az.gov/	L10	**10 Mar 1881**	**Apache, Pima** Graham County; 800 Main St; Safford, AZ 85546-2829; Ph. (520) 428-3250 **Details:** (Clerk Superior Court has Marriage, Probate, Divorce & Court Records from 1881 & Naturalization Records 1903–1973; County Recorder has Land Records)
Greenlee www.rootsweb.com/~azgreenl/index.html	K11	**10 Mar 1909**	**Graham** Greenlee County; PO Box 908; Clifton, AZ 85533; Ph. (520) 865-2072 **Details:** (Clerk Superior Court has Marriage, Divorce, Probate & Court Records from 1911; County Recorder has land Records)
La Paz www.co.la-paz.az.us/	J3	**2 Nov 1983**	**Yuma** La Paz County; 1108 Joshua Ave; Parker, AZ 85344-6477; Ph. (520) 669-6115 **Details:** (Clerk Superior Court has Marriage, Divorce, Probate & Court Records; County Recorder has land Records)
Maricopa www.maricopa.gov/	K5	**14 Feb 1871**	**Yavapai, Yuma, Pima** Maricopa County; 301 W Jefferson; Phoenix, AZ 85003-2225; Ph. (602) 506-3572 **Details:** (Clerk Superior Court has Marriage Records from 1877, Divorce Records from 1930, Probate & Court Records from 1871; County Recorder has land Records)

County Website	Map Index	Date Created	Parent County or Territory From Which Organized Address/Details
Mesilla		1860	**Original County** Mesilla County; **Details:** County Terminated in 1863
Mohave www.co.mohave.az.us/	E3	21 Dec 1864	**Original county** Mohave County; 401 E Spring St; PO Box 7000; Kingman, AZ 86401; Ph. (928) 753-0713 **Details:** (Clerk Superior Court has Marriage Records from 1888, Divorce, Probate & Court Records from 1850; County Recorder has land Records)
Navajo www.co.navajo.az.us/	E9	21 Mar 1895	**Apache** Navajo County; PO Box 668; Holbrook, AZ 86025-0668; Ph. (520) 524-4000 **Details:** (Clerk Superior Court has Marriage, Divorce, Probate & Court Records; County Recorder has land Records)
Pah-Ute		1865	**Mohave** Pah-Ute County; **Details:** County Terminated in 1871
Pima www.co.pima.az.us/	N7	15 Dec 1864	**Original county** Pima County; 130 W Congress St; Tucson, AZ 85701-1333; Ph. (520) 740-8661 **Details:** (Formerly Ewell County Name changed to Pima) (Clerk Superior Court has Marriage, Divorce, Probate & Court Records from 1863)
Pinal www.co.pinal.az.us/	L7	1 Feb 1875	**Pima, Yavapai** Pinal County; 100 N Florence; Florence, AZ 85232; Ph. (520) 868-6000 **Details:** (Clerk Superior Court has Marriage, Probate & Court Records from 1875 & Divorce Records from 1883; County Recorder has land Records)
Santa Cruz www.santacruzcountyaz.org/	O8	15 Mar 1899	**Pima, Cochise** Santa Cruz County; 2150 North Congress Dr, Suite 215; PO Box 1265; Nogales, AZ 85628-1265; Ph. (520) 375-7700 **Details:** (Clerk Superior Court has Marriage, Divorce, Probate & Court Records from 1899, Military Records 1907–1922, Naturaliza- tion Records 1888–1985 & Adoption Records from 1940)
Yavapai www.co.yavapai.az.us/	H5	21 Dec 1864	**Original county** Yavapai County; 1015 Fair St; Prescott, AZ 86301; Ph. (520) 639-8110 **Details:** (Clerk Superior Court has Marriage, Divorce, Probate & Court Records; County Recorder has land Records)
Yuma www.co.yuma.az.us/	L3	21 Dec 1864	**Original county** Yuma County; 168 S 2nd Ave; Yuma, AZ 85364; Ph. (520) 329-2170 **Details:** (Formerly Castle Dome County. Name changed to Yuma) (Clerk Superior Court has Marriage, Divorce, Probate & Court Records from 1863)

Arkansas

Capital: Little Rock

Territory: 1819

State: 1836 (25th)

The people rule

In 1541, Hernando de Soto became the first European to explore the Arkansas area. Louis Joliet and Jacques Marquette also explored the region in 1673 followed by Rene Robert Cavelier, sieur de la Salle, in 1682. La Salle claimed all the Mississippi Valley for France and named it Louisiana. This claim resulted in increased French activity in the area and the establishment of the Arkansas Post in 1686. Major Indian tribes of the area were the Quapaw, also known as the Akansa or Arkansas, the Osage, and the Caddo.

In 1762, France ceded Louisiana to Spain. The Spanish opened the area to settlement by Americans in 1783, but less than 1,000 came prior to the turn of the century. In 1801, Spain returned the area to France. The United States purchased Louisiana in 1803.

Following the Louisiana Purchase, Arkansas was opened to settlement with land at very low prices. As a result, thousands of settlers from the mideast and southeast areas of the United States came to Arkansas. Many of the early settlers were English, Irish, or Scottish and came from Kentucky or Tennessee. The formation of the Missouri Territory in 1812 included Arkansas. Arkansas County was formed the following year. Additional settlers came to claim bounty land for service in the War of 1812 and to grow cotton. Many of these settlers came from Virginia and the Carolinas through Tennessee, Mississippi, or Missouri.

Arkansas Territory was formed in 1819, when Missouri applied for statehood. The territory included present-day Oklahoma until June 15, 1836, when Arkansas became a state. Arkansas seceded from the Union in 1861. About 8,000 soldiers from Arkansas fought for the Union and an estimated 50,000 for the Confederacy.

Arkansas was readmitted to the Union in 1868. After the Civil War, large groups of southern European immigrants came to the rich lands between the Arkansas and the White Rivers. Many Poles came directly to Pulaski County and many Italians moved to the northwest section of the state to raise fruit. The building of railroads in the late 19th century caused the population to nearly triple from 1870 to 1900.

Look for vital records in the following locations:

- **Birth and death records:** The Division of Vital Records, Arkansas Department of Health from 1914.
- **Marriage records:** The Division of Vital Records, Arkansas Department of Health from 1917. County Clerks also keep marriage records.
- **Divorce records:** The Division of Vital Records, Arkansas Department of Health from 1921. Chancery courts have countywide jurisdiction over equity, divorce, probate, and adoption proceedings.
- **Land records:** The Arkansas State Land Office has original land plats of the U.S. Government surveys of Arkansas and original entries by township and range.
- **Naturalizations:** Generally filed in the circuit court in each county, although some were filed with the U.S. District Courts at Fort Smith, Little Rock, and Fort Worth, Texas.
- **Census records:** A territorial census for 1830 is available and has been indexed. The Arkansas History Commission has sheriffs' censuses for several counties in 1829 and for Arkansas County in 1823.

The Arkansas History Commission
One Capitol Mall
Little Rock, AR 72201
(501) 682-6900
www.ark-ives.com/

Arkansas Department of Health Division of Vital Records
4815 West Markham Street, Slot 44
Little Rock, AR 72205-386
(501) 661-2174
www.healthyarkansas.com/certificates/certificates.html

The Arkansas State Land Office
109 State Capitol
Little Rock, AR 72201
(501) 324-9222

Societies and Repositories

Ancestors Unknown; 404 Angus; Conway, AR 72032.

Arkansas Genealogical Society; PO Box 17653; Little Rock, AR 72222; askags@agsgenealogy.org; www.rootsweb.com/~args.

Arkansas Historical Association; Historical Dept., Ozark Hall 12 University of Arkansas; Fayetteville, AR 72701.

Arkansas History Commission and State Archives; One Capitol Mall; Little Rock, AR 72201; www.ark-ives.com.

Arkansas State Library; One Capitol Mall; Little Rock, AR 72201; (501) 682-2053; www.asl.lib.ar.us.

Ashley County Genealogical Society; PO Drawer R; Crossett, AR 71635; (870) 364-2885.

Batesville Genealogical Society; PO Box 3883; Batesville, AR 72503-3883.

Baxter County, Arkansas Historical and Genealogical Society; PO Box 1611; Mountain Home, AR 72654-1611; kjhamer@centurytel.net; www.geocities.com/Athens/2101/bchgs.html.

Benton County Historical Society; PO Box 1034; Bentonville, AR 72712; BCHSARk@Juno.com; www.uark.edu/depts/globmark/bchsar.

Bradley County Genealogical Society; PO Box 837; Warren, AR 71671-0837; www.rootsweb.com/~arbradle/bradcogensoc.shtml.

Carroll County Historical Society; PO Box 249; Berryville, AR 72616-0249; www.rootsweb.com/~arcchs.

Clark County Genealogical and Historical Association; PO Box 516; Arkadelphia, AR 71923.

Clay County Genealogical Club; c/o Piggott Public Library; 361 West Main; Piggott, AR 72454.

Cleburne County Historical Society; PO Box 794; Heber Springs, AR 72543.

Craighead County Historical Society; PO Box 1011; Jonesboro, AR 72403-1011.

Crawford County Genealogical Society; PO Box 276; Alma, AR 72921.

Crawford County Historical Society; 929 E. Main St.; Van Buren, AR 72956.

Crowley's Ridge Genealogical Society; Box 2091; State University, AR 72467.

Department of Arkansas Heritage; 1500 Tower Building 323 Center Street; Little Rock, AR 72201; info@arkansasheritage.com; www.arkansasheritage.com.

Enoch Ashley Chapter, NSDAR; 2613 Dauphine Dr.; Rogers, AR 72756.

Frontier Researchers, Genealogical Society; PO Box 2123; Fort Smith, AR 72902.

Garland County Historical Society; 222 McMahan Dr.; Hot Springs, AR 71913-6243; (501) 623-6766; bjmclane@direclynx.net.

General Lafayette Chapter, SAR; Fayetteville, AR ; (501) 442-6098; dennisboyer@netzero.net; www.geocities.com/Heartland/Ridge/4629.

Grand Prairie Genealogical Society; c/o Stuttgart Public Library; 2002 So Buerkle St.; Stuttgart, AR 72160; www.rootsweb.com/~ararkans/grandpra.htm.

Greene County Historical and Genealogical Society; c/o Greene County Library; 120 N 12th St; Paragould, AR 72450.

Hempstead County Genealogical Society; PO Box 1158; Hope, AR 71902-1158.

Heritage Club, The; 218 Howard; Nashville, AR 71852.

Historical and Genealogical Society of Marion County Arkansas; PO Box 761; Yellville, AR 72687.

Hot Springs County Arkansas Historical & Genealogical Society; PO Box 674; Malvern, AR 72104.

Independence County Historical Society; Box 1412; Batesville, AR 72501.

Izard County Arkansas Historical Society; PO Box 306; Pineville, AR 72566.

Johnson County Historical Society; PO Box 505; Clarksville, AR 72830.

Logan County Historical Society; PO Box 40; Magazine, AR 72943-0040.

Madison County Genealogical and Historical Society; PO Box 427; Huntsville, AR 72740.

Melting Pot Genealogical Society; PO Box 936; Hot Springs, AR 71902.

Montgomery County Historical Society; PO Box 520; Mount Ida, AR 71957.

Nevada County Depot Museum Association; 403 W. First St. South; Prescott, AR 71857.

Newton County Historical Society; PO Box 360; Jasper, AR 72641; www.mcrush.com/history.

Northwest Arkansas Genealogical Society; PO Box 796; Rogers, AR 72757-0796.

Ouachita County Historical Society; 926 Washington Northwest; Camden, AR 71701.

Ouachita-Calhoun Genealogical Society; PO Box 2092; Camden, AR 71701; www.rootsweb.com/~arcalhou/societie.htm#societies.

Pike County Archives & History Society; PO Box 238; Murfreesboro, AR 71958; (870) 285-3187; www.rootsweb.com/~arpcahs.

Pope County Historical Association; 1120 N. Detroit; Russellville, AR 72801.

Randolph County Historical & Genealogical Society; 111 West Everett St.; Pocahontas, AR 72455;

(870) 892-5617; darhist@tcac.net; www.geocities.com/Heartland/Orchard/8659.

Saline County Historical Commission; c/o Gunn Museum of Saline County; 218 S. Market St.; Benton, AR 72015.

Saline County History & Heritage Society; PO Box 1712; Benton, AR 72018-1712; www.rootsweb.com/~arsaline/schhs.html.

Scott County Historical & Genealogical Society; PO Box 1560; Waldron, AR 72958.

Sevier County Genealogical Society, Inc.; 717 N. Maple; DeQueen, AR 71832.

Southeast Arkansas Genealogical Society; c/o Drew County Historical Museum; 404 S. Main; Monticello, AR 71655; genealogy71655@yahoo.com.

Southwest Arkansas Genealogical Society; 1022 Lawton Circle; Magnolia, AR 71753.

Stone County Historical Society; PO Box 210; Mountain View, AR 72560; http://rootsweb.com/~arscgs.

Union County Genealogical Society; c/o Barton Library; East 5th and No. Jefferson St; El Dorado, AR 71730.

Van Buren County Historical Society; PO Box 1023; Clinton, AR 72031-1023; museum@artelco.com; http://gozarks.com.

Washington County Arkansas Genealogical Society; PO Box 41; Fayetteville, AR 72702-0041; wcags@hotmail.com; www.rootsweb.com/~arwcags.

Yell County Historical and Genealogical Society; Box 622; Dardanelle, AR 72834; www.rootsweb.com/~aryell/yhs.htm.

Bibliography and Record Sources

General

Allsop, Fred W. *History of the Arkansas Press for a Hundred Years and More.* (1922) Reprint. Greenville, South Carolina: Southern Historical Press, Inc., 1978.

Arkansas Genealogical Collection. Daughters of the American Revolution (Arkansas). Salt Lake City: Filmed by the Genealogical Society of Utah, 1970–71.

Clark, Georgia H. and R. Bruce Parham, comps. *Arkansas County and Local Histories: A Bibliography.* Fayetteville, Arkansas: [s.n.], 1976.

Family History Library. *Research Outline: Arkansas.* Salt Lake City, Utah: Family History Library, Salt Lake City Distribution Center, 1988.

Finley, Randy. *From Slavery to Uncertain Freedom: The Freedmen's Bureau in Arkansas, 1865–1869.* Galveston, Texas: Frontier Press, 1996.

Goodspeed Publishing Company. *Biographical & Historical Memoirs of Arkansas: General History of Arkansas.* (1884) Reprint. Greenville, South Carolina: Southern Historical Press, Inc., 1984.

Goodspeed Publishing Company. *History of Central Arkansas.* (1889) Reprint. Greenville, South Carolina: Southern Historical Press, Inc., 1984.

Goodspeed Publishing Company. *History of Eastern Arkansas.* (1890) Reprint. Greenville, South Carolina: Southern Historical Press, Inc., 1984.

Goodspeed Publishing Company. *History of Northeast Arkansas.* (1884) Reprint. Greenville, South Carolina: Southern Historical Press, Inc., 1984.

Goodspeed Publishing Company. *History of Northwestern Arkansas.* (1889) Reprint. Greenville, South Carolina: Southern Historical Press, Inc., 1984.

Goodspeed Publishing Company. *History of South Arkansas.* (1884) Reprint. Greenville, South Carolina: Southern Historical Press, Inc., 1984.

Goodspeed Publishing Company. *History of Western Arkansas.* (1891) Reprint. Greenville, South Carolina: Southern Historical Press, Inc., 1984.

Goodspeed Publishing Company. *A Reminiscent History of the Ozark Region of Arkansas and Missouri.* (1894) Reprint. Greenville, South Carolina: Southern Historical Press, Inc., 1988.

Hallum, John. *Biographical and Pictorial History of Arkansas.* (1887) Reprint. Greenville, South Carolina: Southern Historical Press, Inc., 1978.

Historical Records Survey, Division of Community Service Programs, Work Projects Administration. *Union List of Arkansas Newspapers, 1819–1942: a Partial Inventory of Arkansas Newspaper Files Available in Offices of Publishers, Libraries, and Private Collections in Arkansas.* Little Rock, Arkansas: Historical Records Survey, 1942.

Payne, Dorothy. *Arkansas Pensioners 1818–1900.* Easley, South Carolina: Southern Historical Press, 1985.

Pope, William F. *Early Days in Arkansas: Being for the Most Part the Personal Recollections of an Old Settler.* (1895) Reprint. Greenville, South Carolina: Southern Historical Press, Inc., 1978.

Reeves, Lucy Marion. *Arkansas Families: Glimpses of Yesterday Columns from the Arkansas Gazette.* Conway, Arkansas: Arkansas Research, 1996.

Riggins, J. H. *Lest We Forget, or Character Gems Gleaned from South Arkansas.* (1910) Reprint. Greenville, South Carolina: Southern Historical Press, Inc., 1978.

Roberts, Lewis E. *The By-Name Index to the Centennial History of Arkansas.* 3 vols. Conway, Arkansas: Arkansas Research, 1994.

Ragsdale, William Oates. *They Sought a Land, A Settlement in Arkansas River Valley, 1840–1870.* Fayetteville, Arkansas: University of Arkansas Press, 1997.

Shinn, Josiah H. *Pioneers and Makers of Arkansas.* (1908) Reprint. Baltimore, Maryland: Clearfield Company, 1991.

Thomas, David Yancey. *Arkansas and Its People, a History, 1541–1930*. New York: American Historical Society, 1930.

Wagoner, Claudia. *Arkansas Researchers' Handbook*. Fayetteville, Arkansas: Research Plus, 1986.

Atlases, Maps and Gazetteers

Allen, Desmond Walls. *Arkansas Township Digest: Minor Civil Divisions, 1820–1990*. Conway, Arkansas: Arkansas Research, 1994.

Arkansas Atlas and Gazetteer. Freeport, Maine: DeLorme Mapping Co., 1997.

Baker, Russell Pierce. *Arkansas Township Atlas: a History of the Minor Civil Divisions in Each Arkansas County*. Hot Springs, Arkansas: Arkansas Genealogical Society, 1984, 1985.

Smith, Richard M. *The Atlas of Arkansas: Official Atlas of the State of Arkansas*. Fayetteville: University of Arkansas Press, 1989.

Thorndale, William and William Dollarhide. *Map Guides to the U.S. Federal Censuses, 1790–1920: Arkansas, 1810–1920*. Bountiful, Utah, American Genealogical Lending Library, 1987.

Works Projects Administration. Historical Records Survey. *List of Post Offices in Arkansas as Shown in Early Newspaper Files, 1817–1874*. Little Rock: Arkansas History Commission, n.d.

Censuses

Available Census Records and Census Substitutes

Federal Census 1830, 1840, 1850, 1860, 1870, 1880, 1900, 1910, 1920, 1930

Federal Mortality Schedules 1850, 1860, 1870, 1880

Confederate Veterans 1911

Jackson, Ronald Vern and Gary Ronald Teeples, eds. *Arkansas Sheriff's Censuses, 1823 & 1829*. Bountiful, Utah: Accelerated Indexing Systems, 1978, c1976 (Salt Lake City: Ambassador Press, 1978).

McLane, Bobbie Jones and Desmond Walls Allen. *1850 Census of Central Arkansas: Hot Spring, Jefferson, Montgomery, Perry, Prairie, Pulaski, Saline, Scott, and Yell Counties*. Conway, Arkansas: Arkansas Research, 1995.

McLane, Bobbie Jones and Desmond Walls Allen. *1850 Census of Eastern Arkansas: Arkansas, Chicot, Crittenden, Desha, Greene, Mississippi, Monroe, Phillips, Poinsett, and St. Francis Counties*. Conway, Arkansas: Arkansas Research, 1995.

McLane, Bobbie Jones, and Desmond Walls Allen. *1850 Census of North Central Arkansas: Conway, Fulton, Independence, Izard, Jackson, Lawrence, Marion, Randolph, Searcy, Van Buren, and White Counties*. Conway, Arkansas: Arkansas Research, 1995.

McLane, Bobbie Jones and Desmond Walls Allen. *1850 Census of Northwest Arkansas: Benton, Carroll, Crawford, Franklin, Johnson, Madison, Newton, Pope, and Washington Counties*. Conway, Arkansas: Arkansas Research, 1995.

McLane, Bobbie Jones and Desmond Walls Allen. *1850 Census of Southern Arkansas: Ashley, Bradley, Clark, Dallas, Drew, Hempstead, Lafayette, Ouachita, Pike, Polk, Sevier, and Union Counties*. Conway, Arkansas: Arkansas Research, 1995.

McLane, Bobbie Jones and Desmond Walls Allen. *Arkansas 1850 Census Every Name Index*. Conway, Arkansas: Arkansas Research, 1995.

Morgan, James Logan. *1820 Census of the Territory of Arkansas (Reconstructed)* (1984) Reprint. Conway, Arkansas: Arkansas Research, 1992.

Thorndale, William and William Dollarhide. *Map Guides to the U.S. Federal Censuses, 1790–1920: Arkansas, 1810–1920*. Bountiful, Utah: American Genealogical Lending Library, 1987.

Court Records, Probates, and Wills

Ruple, Jack Damon. *Genealogist's Guide to Arkansas Courthouse Research*. Arkansas: s.n., 1989.

Stevenson, Mrs. James Harold and Mrs. Edward Lynn Westbrooke, eds. *Index to Wills and Administrations of Arkansas from the Earliest to 1900*. Jonesboro, Arkansas: Vowels Print. Co., 1986.

Szucs, Loretto Dennis and Matthew Wright. *Finding Answers in U.S. Census Records*. Ancestry Publishing, 2001.

Taunton, Joan Thurman. *Abstracts of Arkansas Reports, January 1837 through January 1861*. Hot Springs, Arkansas: Arkansas Genealogical Society, 1988.

Immigration

Baker, Jack D. *Cherokee Emigration Rolls, 1817–1835*. Oklahoma City, Oklahoma: Baker Pub. Co., 1977.

Index to Naturalization Records in Arkansas, 1809–1906. Little Rock, Arkansas: Immigration and Naturalization Records Indexing Project Service Division. United States Work Projects Administration, 1942.

United States. Work Projects Administration (Arkansas). *Immigration and Naturalization Records Indexing Project. Index to naturalization records in Arkansas, 1809–1906*. Washington, D.C.: Library of Congress, Photoduplication Service, [19--].

Land

Allen, Desmond Walls and Bobbie Jones McLane. *Arkansas Land Patents: Eastern Arkansas Counties (Clay, Craighead, Crittenden, Cross, Greene, Lee, Mississippi, Monroe, Phillips, Poinsett, and St. Francis Counties, granted through 30 June 1908)*. 1991. Indexed. Conway, Arkansas: Arkansas Research.

Arkansas. Commissioner of State Lands. *Spanish Land Claims; Tract Books, ca. 1803–1900*. Salt Lake City:

Filmed by the Genealogical Society of Utah, 1981. Microfilm, 37 rolls.

Arkansas. Surveyor General. *Land Records*. Original records in the State Land Office, Little Rock, Arkansas. Salt Lake City: Filmed by the Genealogical Society of Utah, 1981. Microfilm, 3 rolls.

Christensen, Katheren. *Arkansas Military Bounty Grants (War of 1812)*. Hot Springs, Arkansas: Arkansas Ancestors, 1971.

First Settlers of the Missouri Territory. 2 vols. Nacogdoches, Texas: Ericson Books, 1983.

Ingmire, Frances T. *Citizens of Missouri*. 3 vols. St. Louis: F. T. Ingmire, 1984.

United States. Bureau of Land Management. *Card Files*. Washington, D.C.: Bureau of Land Management, 19--.

United States. Department of the Interior. Bureau of Land Management. *Arkansas General Land Office Records (pre-1908)*. Springfield, Virginia: BLM Eastern States, 1993.

Military

Allen, Desmond Walls. *Arkansas Union Soldiers Pension Application Index*. Conway, Arkansas: Arkansas Research, 1987.

Allen, Desmond Walls. *Arkansas' Damned Yankees: Index to Union Soldiers in Arkansas Regiments*. Conway, Arkansas: Arkansas Research, 1987.

Allen, Desmond Walls. *Arkansas' Mexican War Soldiers*. Conway, Arkansas: Arkansas Research, 1988.

Allen, Desmond Walls. *Arkansas' Spanish American War Soldiers*. Conway, Arkansas: Arkansas Research, 1988.

Allen, Desmond Walls. *First Arkansas Confederate Mounted Rifles*. Conway, Arkansas: Arkansas Research, 1988.

Allen, Desmond Walls. *Forty-fifth Arkansas Confederate Cavalry*. Conway, Arkansas: Arkansas Research, 1988.

Allen, Desmond Walls. *The Fourteenth Arkansas Confederate Infantry*. Conway, Arkansas: Arkansas Research, 1988.

Allen, Desmond Walls. *Index to Arkansas Confederate Pension Applications*. Conway, Arkansas: Arkansas Research, 1991.

Allen, Desmond Walls. *Index to Arkansas Confederate Soldiers*. 3 vols. Conway, Arkansas: Arkansas Research, 1990.

Allen, Desmond Walls. *The Seventh Arkansas Confederate Infantry*. Conway, Arkansas: Arkansas Research, 1988.

Allen, Desmond Walls. *The Thirty-eighth Arkansas Confederate Infantry*. Conway, Arkansas: Arkansas Research, 1988.

Allen, Desmond Walls. *The Twenty-seventh Arkansas Confederate Infantry*. Conway, Arkansas: Arkansas Research, 1987.

Christ, *Rugged and Sublime: The Civil War in Arkansas*. Galveston, Texas: Frontier Press, 1994.

Christensen, Katheren, comp. *Arkansas Military Bounty Grants (War of 1812)*. Hot Springs, Arkansas: Arkansas Ancestors, 1971.

Dougan. *Confederate Arkansas: The People and Policies of a Frontier State in Wartime*. Reprint. Galveston, Texas: Frontier Press, 1994.

Ingmire, Frances. *Arkansas Confederate Veterans and Widows Home Records*. Signal Mountain, Tennessee: Mountain Press, n.d.

Ingmire, Frances T., comp. *Arkansas Confederate Veterans and Widows Pension Applications*. Athens, Georgia: Iberian Publishing Company, 1985.

McLane, Bobbie J. and Capitola Glazner, eds. *Arkansas 1911 Census of Confederate Veterans*. S.l.: s.n., 1977–1981.

Payne, Dorothy. *Arkansas Pensioners, 1818–1900: Records of Some Arkansas Residents Who Applied to the Federal Government for Benefits Arising from Services in Federal Military Organizations* (Revolutionary War. War of 1812. Indian and Mexican Wars). Greenville, South Carolina: Southern Historical Press, Inc., 1985.

Sifakis, Stewart. *Compendium of the Confederate Armies: Florida and Arkansas*. Galveston, Texas: Frontier Press, 1992.

Turnbo, Silas Claborn. *History of the Twenty-seventh Arkansas Confederate Infantry*. Conway, Arkansas: Arkansas Research, n.d.

United States. Selective Service System. *Arkansas, World War I Selective Service System Draft Registration Cards, 1917–1918*. Washington, D.C.: The National Archives, 1987–1988.

Vital and Cemetery

Allen, Desmond Walls. *Arkansas Death Record Index, 1914–1923*. Conway, Arkansas: Arkansas Research, 1996.

Allen, Desmond Walls. *Arkansas Death Record Index, 1924–1933*. Conway, Arkansas: Arkansas Research, 1997.

Allen, Desmond Walls. *Arkansas Death Record Index, 1934–1940*. Conway, Arkansas: Arkansas Research, 1996.

Allen, Desmond Walls. *Central Arkansas Death Record Index, 1914–1923: Garland, Grant, Hot Spring, Lonoke, Perry, Prairie, Pulaski, and Saline Counties*. Conway, Arkansas: Arkansas Research, 1996.

Allen, Desmond Walls. *Central Arkansas Death Record Index, 1934–1940: Garland, Grant, Hot Spring, Lonoke, Perry, Prairie, Pulaski, and Saline Counties*. Conway, Arkansas: Arkansas Research, 1996.

Allen, Desmond Walls. *Eastern Arkansas Death Record Index, 1914–1923: Clay, Craighead, Crittenden, Cross, Greene, Lee, Mississippi, Monroe, Phillips, Poinsett,* and St. Francis Counties. Conway, Arkansas: Arkansas Research, 1996.

Allen, Desmond Walls. *Eastern Arkansas Death Record Index, 1934–1940: Clay, Craighead, Crittenden, Cross, Greene, Lee, Mississippi, Monroe, Phillips, Poinsett, and St. Francis Counties.* Conway, Arkansas: Arkansas Research, 1996.

Allen, Desmond Walls. *North Central Arkansas Death Record Index, 1914–1923: Baxter, Cleburne, Conway, Faulkner, Fulton, Independence, Izard, Jackson, Lawrence, Randolph, Sharp, Stone, Van Buren, White, and Woodruff Counties.* Conway, Arkansas: Arkansas Research, 1996.

Allen, Desmond Walls. *Southeastern Arkansas Death Record Index. 1914–1923: Arkansas, Ashley, Bradley, Chicot, Cleveland, Desha, Drew, Jefferson, and Lincoln Counties.* Conway, Arkansas: Arkansas Research, 1996.

Allen, Desmond Walls. *Southeastern Arkansas Death Record Index. 1934–1940: Arkansas, Ashley, Bradley, Chicot, Cleveland, Desha, Drew, Jefferson, and Lincoln Counties.* Conway, Arkansas: Arkansas Research, 1996.

Allen, Desmond Walls. *Southwestern Arkansas Death Record Index, 1914–1923: Calhoun, Clark, Columbia, Dallas, Hempstead, Howard, Lafayette, Little River, Miller, Nevada, Ouachita, Pike, Sevier, and Union Counties.* Conway, Arkansas: Arkansas Research, 1996.

Allen, Desmond Walls. *Southwestern Arkansas Death Record Index, 1934–1940: Calhoun, Clark, Columbia, Dallas, Hempstead, Howard, Lafayette, Little River, Miller, Nevada, Ouachita, Pike, Sevier, and Union Counties.* Conway, Arkansas: Arkansas Research, 1996.

Allen, Desmond Walls. *Western Arkansas Death Record Index, 1914–1923: Crawford, Franklin, Johnson, Logan, Montgomery, Polk, Pope, Scott, Sebastian, and Yell Counties.* Conway, Arkansas: Arkansas Research, 1996.

Allen, Desmond Walls. *Western Arkansas Death Record Index, 1934–1940: Crawford, Franklin, Johnson, Logan, Montgomery, Polk, Pope, Scott, Sebastian, and Yell Counties.* Conway, Arkansas: Arkansas Research, 1996.

Arkansas, 1850–1900. S.l.: Brøderbund, 1999. CD-ROM.

Arkansas Biographical Card File Index, 1819–1950. Microreproduction of originals housed at the Arkansas History Commission, Little Rock. Salt Lake City: Filmed by the Genealogical Society of Utah, 1994. Microfilm, 53 rolls.

Arkansas Death Indexes, 1914–1923, 1934–1946, 1948, 1914–1948. Hot Springs, Arkansas: Arkansas Genealogical Society, 1999. 214 Microfiche.

Arkansas Historical Survey Project, Division of Community Service Programs, Work Projects Administration. *Guide to Vital Statistic Records in Arkansas: Volume II, Church Archives.* Little Rock, Arkansas: Historical Records Survey.

Chism, Stephen J. *The Arkansas Gazette Obituaries Index, 1819–1879.* Greenville, South Carolina: Southern Historical Press, Inc., 1990.

Morgan, James Logan. *Arkansas Marriage Notices, 1819–1845.* (1984) Reprint. Conway, Arkansas: Arkansas Research, 1992.

Morgan, James Logan. *Arkansas Marriage Records, 1808–1835.* (1981) Reprint. Conway, Arkansas: Arkansas Research, 1994.

Morgan, James Logan. *Arkansas Newspaper Abstracts, 1819–1845.* (1981) Reprint. Conway, Arkansas: Arkansas Research, 1992.

Morgan, James Logan. *Arkansas Newspaper Index, 1819–1845: Index to Obituaries, Biographical Notes and Probate and Chancery Notices from Arkansas Newspapers, 1819–1845.* Newport, Arkansas.: Morgan Books, ©1981.

Prudence Hall Chapter, DAR. *Index to Sources for Arkansas Cemetery Inscriptions.* North Little Rock, Arkansas.: D. A. R., 1976.

County Website	Map Index	Date Created	Parent County or Territory From Which Organized Address/Details
Arkansas www.rootsweb.com/~ararkans/	K8	**31 Dec 1813**	**Original county** Arkansas County; 101 Court Sq; DeWitt, AR 72042; Ph. (870) 946-4349 **Details:** (County Clerk has Probate Records from 1809 & Marriage Records from 1838; Clerk Circuit Court has land Records, Divorce & Court Records from 1803 & Military Discharge Records from 1917)
Ashley www.rootsweb.com/~arashley/arashley_Index1.html	O7	**30 Nov 1848**	**Chicot, Union, Drew** Ashley County; 215 E Jefferson St; Hamburg, AR 71646; Ph. (870) 853-2020 **Details:** (County Clerk has Marriage Records from 1848, Probate & land Records; Clerk Circuit Court has Divorce Records)

County	Map	Date	Parent County or Territory From Which Organized
Website	Index	Created	Address/Details

Baxter   E6   24 Mar 1873   **Fulton, Izard, Marion, Searcy**
www.baxtercountyonline.com/baxgen/
Baxter County; Courthouse Sq; 1 E 7th St; Mountain Home, AR 72653; Ph. (870) 425-3475
Details: (County Clerk has Marriage, Death, Probate, Divorce, Land, and Court Records)

Benton   E2   30 Sep 1836   **Washington**
www.co.benton.ar.us/
Benton County; 215 E Central; Bentonville, AR 72712;
Ph. (479) 271-1031
Details: (County Clerk has Marriage Records from 1861 & Probate Records from 1859; Clerk Circuit Court has Divorce, Court & land Records)

Boone   E4   9 Apr 1869   **Carrol, Madison**
www.rootsweb.com/~arboone/boone.html
Boone County; 100 N Main St; Harrison, AR 72602;
Ph. (870) 741-8428
Details: (County Clerk has Marriage & Probate Records from 1869; Clerk Circuit Court has Divorce, Court & land Records)

Bradley   N6   18 Dec 1840   **Union**
www.rootsweb.com/~arbradle/
Bradley County; 101 E Cedar St; Warren, AR 71671-0000;
Ph. (870) 226-3464
Details: (County Clerk has Marriage Records from 1846 & Probate Records from 1850; Clerk Circuit Court has Divorce, Court & land Records)

Calhoun   N6   6 Dec 1850   **Dallas, Ouachita**
www.rootsweb.com/~arcalhou/
Calhoun County; Main St; Hampton, AR 71744; Ph. (870) 798-2517
Details: (County Clerk has Marriage & land Records from 1851, Divorce, Probate & Court Records from 1880)

Carroll   F3   1 Nov 1833   **Izard**
www.rootsweb.com/~arcarrol/Carroll.html
Carroll County; 210 W Church St; Berryville, AR 726164233;
Ph. (870) 423-2022
Details: (County Clerk has Marriage & Probate Records from 1870; Clerk Circuit Court has land, Court & Divorce Records from 1870)

Chicot   O8   1820   **Arkansas**
www.seark.net/~sabra/chicotco.html
Chicot County; 108 Main St; Lake Village, AR 716530000;
Ph. (870) 265-8000
Details: (County Clerk has Marriage & Probate Records from 1839; Clerk Circuit Court has Court Records from 1824, land & Divorce Records)

Clark   L4   15 Dec 1818   **Arkansas**
www.pastracks.com/states/arkansas/clark/
Clark County; Courthouse Sq; 401 Clay St; Arkadelphia, AR 71923;
Ph. (870) 246-4491
Details: (County Clerk has Marriage Records from 1821 & Probate Records from 1800; Clerk Circuit Court has Divorce, Court & land Records)

Clay   E10   6 Dec 1875   **Randolph, Greene**
www.rootsweb.com/~arclay/
Clay County; PO Box 306; Piggott, AR 72454; Ph. (870) 598-2813
Details: (Formerly Clayton County Name changed to Clay 6 Dec 1875; Records Burned in 1893) (Clerk Circuit Court has land, Divorce & Court Records from 1893; County Clerk has Marriage & Probate Records from 1893)

County Website	Map Index	Date Created	Parent County or Territory From Which Organized Address/Details
Clayton		24 Mar 1873	**Randolph, Greene** Clayton County; AR; **Details:** (see Clay) Name changed to Clay 6 Dec 1875
Cleburne www.rootsweb.com/~arclebur/	H7	20 Feb 1883	**White, Van Buren, Independence** Cleburne County; 301 W Main St; Heber Springs, AR 72543; Ph. (501) 362-4620 **Details:** (County Clerk has Marriage, Probate, Divorce, Court & land Records from 1883)
Cleveland www.rootsweb.com/~arclevel/index.html	M6	17 Apr 1873	**Dallas, Bradley, Jefferson, Lincoln** Cleveland County; Main & Magnolia Sts; PO Box 348; Rison, AR 71665; Ph. (870) 325-6521 **Details:** (Formerly Dorsey County Name changed to Cleveland 5 Mar 1885) (County Clerk has Marriage Records from 1880, Divorce, Probate & Court Records)
Columbia www.rootsweb.com/~arcolumb/	O4	17 Dec 1852	**Lafayette, Hempstead, Ouachita** Columbia County; 1 Court Sq, #1; Magnolia, AR 71753; Ph. (870) 235-3774 **Details:** (County Clerk has Marriage & land Records from 1853, Divorce & Court Records from 1860 & Probate Records; County Library has Cemetery Records)
Conway www.rootsweb.com/~arconway/	H5	20 Oct 1825	**Pulaski** Conway County; 117 S Moose St; Morrilton, AR 72110; Ph. (501) 354-9621 **Details:** (County Clerk has Marriage Records from 1858 & Probate Records; Clerk Circuit Court has Divorce, Court & land Records)
Craighead www.craigheadcounty.org/	G10	19 Feb 1859	**Mississippi, Greene, Poinsett** Craighead County; 511 S Main St; Jonesboro, AR 72401; Ph. (870) 933-4520 **Details:** (County Clerk has Marriage & Probate Records from 1878 & tax Records; Clerk Circuit Court has Court & Divorce Records from 1878 & land Records from 1900)
Crawford www.rootsweb.com/~arcrawfo/	H1	18 Oct 1820	**Pulaski** Crawford County; 300 Main St; Van Buren, AR 72956; Ph. (501) 474-1312 **Details:** (County Clerk has Marriage & Probate Records from 1877; Clerk Circuit Court has Court & land Records from 1877 & Divorce Records)
Crittenden www.rootsweb.com/~arcritte/	I11	22 Oct 1825	**Phillips** Crittenden County; 100 Court St; Marion, AR 72364; Ph. (870) 739-4434 **Details:** (County Clerk has Marriage & Probate Records; Clerk Circuit Court has Divorce, Military & Court Records; County Assessor has land Records)
Cross www.rootsweb.com/~arcross/	I10	15 Nov 1862	**Crittenden, Poinsett, St. Francis** Cross County; 705 Union Ave E #8; Wynne, AR 72396; Ph. (870) 238-5735 **Details:** (County Clerk has Marriage & Probate Records from 1863, tax & County Court Records from 1865; Clerk Circuit Court has Court & land Records from 1865; Chancery Circuit Clerk has Divorce Records from 1866; County Historical Society has newspapers from 1935, Cemetery Records & Family History)

County	Map	Date	Parent County or Territory From Which Organized
Website	Index	Created	Address/Details

Dallas   M5   **1 Jan 1845**
www.rootsweb.com/~ardallas/dallas1.htm

Clark, Bradley
Dallas County; 206 W 3rd St; Fordyce, AR 71742; Ph. (870) 352-7179
Details: (County Clerk has Marriage Records from 1855, land Records from 1845, Probate, Divorce & Court Records)

Desha   M8   **12 Dec 1838**
http://home.earthlink.net/~reitzamm/index.html

Arkansas, Chicot
Desha County; Robert Moore Ave; PO Box 188; Arkansas City, AR 71630; Ph. (870) 877-2323
Details: (County Clerk has Marriage Records from 1865 & Probate Records; Clerk Circuit Court has Divorce, Court & land Records)

Dorsey   **17 Apr 1873**
www.rootsweb.com/~ardorsey/

Dallas, Bradley, Jefferson, Lincoln
Dorsey County; AR
Details: (see Cleveland) Name changed to Cleveland 5 Mar 1885

Drew   N7   **26 Nov 1846**
http://members.tripod.com/~BackwardsBRanch/gwdc.html

Arkansas, Bradley
Drew County; 210 S Main St; Monticello, AR 71655; Ph. (870) 460-6260
Details: (County Clerk has Marriage & Probate Records; Clerk Circuit Court has Divorce, Military & Court Records; County Assessor has land Records)

Faulkner   I6   **12 Apr 1873**
http://members.tripod.com/~BackwardsBRanch/gwfc.html

Pulaski, Conway
Faulkner County; 801 Locust St; Conway, AR 72032; Ph. (501) 450-4910
Details: (County Clerk has Marriage, Probate & Court Records from 1873)

Franklin   H3   **19 Dec 1837**
www.rootsweb.com/~arfrankl/

Crawford
Franklin County; 211 W Commercial St; Ozark, AR 72949-0000; Ph. (501) 667-3607
Details: (County Clerk has Marriage Records from 1850, Probate Records from 1838 & land Records from 1899)

Fulton   E7   **21 Dec 1842**
www.rootsweb.com/~arfulton/

Izard
Fulton County; PO Box 278; Salem, AR 72576-0278; Ph. (870) 895-3310
Details: (County Clerk has Marriage Records from 1887, Divorce, land, Probate & Court Records from 1891)

Garland   K4   **5 Apr 1873**
www.garlandcounty.org/

Saline
Garland County; 501 Ouachita Ave; Hot Springs, AR 71901; Ph. (501) 622-3610
Details: (County Clerk has Marriage & Probate Records; Clerk Circuit Court has Divorce, Court & land Records)

Grant   L6   **4 Feb 1869**

Jefferson, Hot Springs, Saline
Grant County; 101 W Center St Room 106; Sheridan, AR 72150; Ph. (870) 942-2631
Details: (County & Circuit Clerk has Divorce, Guardianship, Land, Marriage, Probate, Tax, Court, & Other Historical Records from 1877)

Greene   F10   **5 Nov 1833**
www.rootsweb.com/~argreene/greene1.html

Lawrence
Greene County; PO Box 62; Paragould, AR 72451-0364; Ph. (870) 239-6311
Details: (County Clerk has Marriage, Probate, Court & land Records from 1876; Clerk Circuit Court has Divorce Records)

County Website	Map Index	Date Created	Parent County or Territory From Which Organized Address/Details
Hempstead www.rootsweb.com/~arhempst/	M3	15 Dec 1818	**Arkansas** Hempstead County; PO Box 1420; Hope, AR 71801-1420; Ph. (870) 777-2241 **Details:** (County Clerk has Marriage & Probate Records from 1823 & land Records from 1900)
Hot Spring www.rootsweb.com/~arhotspr/	L5	2 Nov 1829	**Clark** Hot Spring County; 210 Locust St; Malvern, AR 72104; Ph. (501) 332-2291 **Details:** (County Clerk has Marriage Records from 1825 & Probate Records from 1834; Clerk Circuit Court has Court & Divorce Records)
Howard www.genealogyshoppe.com/arhoward/	L2	17 Apr 1873	**Pike, Hempstead, Polk, Sevier** Howard County; 421 N Main St; Nashville, AR 71852; Ph. (870) 845-7502 **Details:** (County Clerk has Marriage & Probate Records from 1873 & some Cemetery Records; Clerk Circuit Court has Divorce, Court & Land Records from 1873)
Independence http://fly.hiwaay.net/~dmglenn/independ.htm	G8	23 Oct 1820	**Lawrence, Arkansas** Independence County; 192 E Main St; Batesville, AR 72501; Ph. (870) 793-8828 **Details:** (County Clerk has Marriage Records from 1826 & Probate Records from 1839; Clerk Circuit Court has Divorce, Court & land Records; County Library has Burial Records)
Izard www.pastracks.com/states/arkansas/izard/	F7	27 Oct 1825	**Independence** Izard County; PO Box 327; Melbourne, AR 72556; Ph. (870) 368-4328 **Details:** (Line between Izard & Sharp Counties changed 9 Mar 1877) (County Clerk has Marriage, Divorce, Probate, Court & land Records from 1889)
Jackson www.rootsweb.com/~arjackso/	G9	5 Nov 1829	**Independence** Jackson County; 208 Main St; Newport, AR 72112; Ph. (870) 523-7420 **Details:** (County Clerk has Marriage Records from 1843 & Probate Records from 1845; Clerk Circuit Court has Divorce & Court Records from 1845 & land Records)
Jefferson www.rootsweb.com/~arjeffer/index.html	K7	2 Nov 1829	**Arkansas, Pulaski** Jefferson County; 101 W Barraque St; Pine Bluff, AR 71601; Ph. (870) 541-5360 **Details:** (County Clerk has Marriage Records from 1830 & Probate Records from 1845; Clerk Circuit Court has Divorce, Court & land Records)
Johnson www.oklahoma.net/~pvtspark/johnson.html	H3	16 Nov 1833	**Pope** Johnson County; 215 W Main St; PO Box 57; Clarksville, AR 72830; Ph. (501) 754-3967 **Details:** (County Clerk has Marriage Records from 1855 & Probate Records from 1844; Clerk Circuit Court has Divorce, Court & land Records; Extension Office has Burial Records)

County Website	Map Index	Date Created	Parent County or Territory From Which Organized Address/Details
Lafayette www.rootsweb.com/~arlafaye/	O3	**15 Oct 1827**	**Hempstead** Lafayette County; 2 Courthouse Sq; Lewisville, AR 71845; Ph. (870) 921-4633 **Details:** (County Clerk has Marriage Records from 1848 & Probate Records from 1828; County Court Records from 1838; Tax Records from 1862; Clerk Circuit Court has Divorce Records from 1840; Civil Records from 1970; Land Records from 1827; Circuit Records from 1828)
Lawrence http://members.tripod.com/~BackwardsBRanch/lc.html	F9	**15 Jan 1815**	**New Madrid, Mo** Lawrence County; PO Box 553, 315 W Main; Walnut Ridge, AR 72476; Ph. (870) 886-1111 **Details:** (County Clerk has Marriage & Probate Records)
Lee www.rootsweb.com/~arlee2/lee.htm	J10	**17 Apr 1873**	**Phillips, Monroe, Crittenden, St. Francis** Lee County; 15 E Chestnut St; Marianna, AR 72360; Ph. (870) 295-7715 **Details:** (County Clerk has Marriage, Probate & tax Records from 1873; Clerk Circuit Court has Divorce, Military & Court Records from 1873)
Lincoln www.rootsweb.com/~arlee2/lee.htm	M7	**28 Mar 1871**	**Arkansas, Bradley, Desha, Drew, Jefferson** Lincoln County; 300 S Drew St; Star City, AR 71667; Ph. (870) 628-5114 **Details:** (County Clerk has Marriage, Probate & land Records from 1871 & tax Records)
Little River www.rootsweb.com/~arlittle/	M2	**5 Mar 1867**	**Hempstead** Little River County; 351 N 2nd St; Ashdown, AR 71822; Ph. (870) 898-7208 **Details:** (County Clerk has Marriage & Probate Records from 1880; Clerk Circuit Court has Divorce & land Records)
Logan www.rootsweb.com/~arlogan/index.htm	I3	**14 Dec 1875**	**Pope, Franklin, Johnson, Scott, Yell** Logan County; Courthouse Sq; Paris, AR 72855; Ph. (501) 963-2618 **Details:** (Formerly Sarber Coutny Name changed to Logan 14 Dec 1875) (County Clerk has Marriage & Probate Records; Clerk Circuit Court has Divorce, Court & land Records)
Lonoke www.rootsweb.com/~arlonoke/	J7	**16 Apr 1873**	**Pulaski, Prairie** Lonoke County; 3rd & N Center St; PO Box 431; Lonoke, AR 72086-0431; Ph. (501) 676-2368 **Details:** (County Clerk has Marriage & Probate Records) (Some Records of Lonoke County are in Des Arc, Prairie County, AR)
Lovely		**1826**	**Northwest Arkansas & Northeast Oklahoma** Lovely County; AR **Details:** (Lost to Oklahoma & Terminated 1827)
Madison http://members.aol.com/ptice/argenweb-mc.htm	F3	**30 Sep 1836**	**Washington** Madison County; 1 Main St; PO Box 37; Huntsville, AR 72740-0037; Ph. (501) 738-6721 **Details:** (County Clerk has Marriage & Probate Records from 1901)

County	Map	Date	Parent County or Territory From Which Organized
Website	Index	Created	Address/Details

Marion   F5   **29 Sept 1836**   **Izard**
www.rootsweb.com/~armarion/

Marion County; 300 E Old Main; PO Box 385; Yellville, AR 72687; Ph. (870) 449-6226

Details: (Formerly Searcy County. Name changed to Marion 29 Sept 1836) (County Clerk has Marriage, Divorce, Probate, Court, & Land Records from 1888; Courthouse Burned Aug 12 1887: No Records before this date, Except for some documents that were recorded)

Miller   N2   **Dec 1874**   **Lafayette**
www.rootsweb.com/~armiller/

Miller County; 400 Laurel St; Texarkana, AR 71854; Ph. (870) 744-1501

Details: (County Clerk has Marriage, Probate & land Records from 1875; Clerk Circuit Court has Divorce & Court Records)

Miller, old   **1 Apr 1820**   **Hempstead**

Miller, old County; AR ;

Details: (Abolished 1836. Re-establisted Dec 1874 from Lafayette County)

Mississippi   G11   **1 Nov 1833**   **Crittenden**
http://mcagov.missconet.com/

Mississippi County; 200 W Walnut; Blytheville, AR 72315; Ph. (870) 763-3212

Details: (County Clerk has Marriage Records from 1850 & Probate Records from 1865; Clerk Circuit Court has Divorce & Court Records from 1866 & land Records from 1865)

Monroe   J9   **2 Nov 1829**   **Phillips, Arkansas**
www.rootsweb.com/~armonro2/

Monroe County; 123 Madison St; Clarendon, AR 72029-2794; Ph. (870) 747-3921

Details: (County Clerk has Marriage Records from 1850 & Probate Records from 1839; Clerk Circuit Court has Divorce Records from 1839, Court Records from 1830 & land Records from 1829)

Montgomery   K3   **9 Dec 1842**   **Hot Springs**
www.rootsweb.com/~armontgo/

Montgomery County; 105 Hwy 270 E; PO Box 369; Mount Ida, AR 71957; Ph. (870) 867-3521

Details: (County Clerk has Birth, Burial, Cemetery, Business, Census, & Death Records & Newspapers)

Nevada   M4   **20 Mar 1871**   **Hempstead, Columbia, Ouachita**
www.rootsweb.com/~arnevada/

Nevada County; 215 E 2nd St S; Prescott, AR 71857; Ph. (870) 887-3115

Details: (County Clerk has Marriage & Probate Records from 1871 & Cemetery Records; Clerk Circuit Court has Divorce, Court & land Records from 1871)

Newton   G4   **14 Dec 1842**   **Carroll**
www.rootsweb.com/~arnewton/

Newton County; Court St; Jasper, AR 82641-0435; Ph. (870) 446-5125

Details: (County Clerk has Land & Marriage Records from 1866 & Court & Probate Records from 1880; Department of Health has Birth & Death Records from 1914)

Ouachita   M5   **29 Nov 1842**   **Union**
www.rootsweb.com/~arouachi/index.html

Ouachita County; 145 Jackson St; Camden, AR 71701; Ph. (870) 837-2220

Details: (County Clerk has Marriage & Probate Records from 1875; Clerk Circuit Court has Divorce, Court & land Records)

County Website	Map Index	Date Created	Parent County or Territory From Which Organized Address/Details
Perry www.rootsweb.com/~arperry/	J5	**18 Dec 1840**	**Conway** Perry County; PO Box 358; Perryville, AR 72126-0358; Ph. (501) 889-5126 **Details:** (County Clerk has Marriage, Divorce, Probate, Court & land Records from 1882)
Phillips www.rootsweb.com/~arphill2/phillips.htm	K9	**1 May 1820**	**Arkansas, Hempstead** Phillips County; 600 Cherry St; Helena, AR 72342; Ph. (870) 338-5505 **Details:** (County Clerk has Marriage Records from 1831 & Probate Records from 1850; Clerk Circuit Court has Divorce, Court & land Records from 1820)
Pike www.rootsweb.com/~arpike/	L3	**1 Nov 1833**	**Clark, Hempstead** Pike County; PO Box 219; Murfreesboro, AR 71958; Ph. (870) 285-2231 or (870) 285-2743 **Details:** (County Clerk has Marriage Records, Register of Wills; Probate Court has Probate Records from 1895; Clerk Circuit Court has Divorce, Court, Land & MilitaryDischarge Records from 1895
Poinsett www.rootsweb.com/~arpoinse/	H10	**28 Feb 1838**	**Greene, St. Francis** Poinsett County; 401 Market St; HarrisBurg, AR 72432; Ph. (870) 578-4410 **Details:** (County Clerk has Marriage Records from 1873 & Probate Records; Clerk Circuit Court has Divorce, Court & land Records)
Polk www.rootsweb.com/~arpolk/	K2	**30 Nov 1844**	**Sevier** Polk County; 507 Church Ave; Mena, AR 71953; Ph. (501) 394-8123 **Details:** (County Clerk has Marriage Records from 1885, Probate Records from 1900 & Cemetery Records; Clerk Circuit Court has Divorce, land and Court Records from 1885 & Military Records)
Pope www.rootsweb.com/~arpope2/	H4	**2 Nov 1829**	**Crawford** Pope County; 100 W Main St; Russellville, AR 72801; Ph. (501) 968-6064 **Details:** (County Clerk has Marriage & Probate Records from 1831, County Court Records from 1857, voter & Death Records from 1965; Clerk Circuit Court has Divorce, land, Military & Court Records)
Prairie www.rootsweb.com/~arprairi/	J8	**25 Nov 1846**	**Pulaski, Monroe** Prairie County; PO Box 278; Des Arc, AR 72040-0278; Ph. (870) 256-3741 **Details:** (Part of the county was taken from Monroe in 1869. Check Monroe County for Records prior to this date) (County Clerk in DeValls Bluff, AR has Marriage, Divorce, Probate, Court & land Records from 1885, Naturalization Records 1907–1912 & Military Discharge Records from 1917)
Pulaski www.co.pulaski.ar.us/index.htm	J6	**15 Dec 1818**	**Arkansas** Pulaski County; 401 W Markham St; Little Rock, AR 72201; Ph. (501) 340-8500 **Details:** (County Clerk has Marriage Records from 1838, Probate Records from 1820, voter Registration Records from 1952, real estate tax Records from 1828, Personal Probate tax Records from 1869 & poll tax from 1892; Clerk Circuit Court has Court, land & Naturalization Records; Clerk Chancery Court has Divorce Records; History Commission has Probate Court Records before 1920.

County Website	Map Index	Date Created	Parent County or Territory From Which Organized Address/Details
Randolph www.randolphchamber.com/	E9	1835	**Lawrence** Randolph County; 107 W Broadway; Pocahontas, AR 72455; Ph. (870) 892-5822 **Details:** (County Clerk has Marriage & Probate Records from 1837; Circuit Clerk has Divorce, land, Military & Court Records from 1836)
Saline www.salinecounty.org/	J5	2 Nov 1835	**Pulaski, Hempstead** Saline County; 215 North Main Ste 9; Benton, AR 72015; Ph. (501) 303-5630 **Details:** (County Clerk has Marriage & Probate Records from 1836 & land Records from 1871)
Sarber		22 Mar 1871	**Pope, Franklin, Johnson, Scott, Yell** Sarber County; AR **Details:** (see Logan) Name changed to Logan 14 Dec 1875
Scott www.rootsweb.com/~arscott/scott.htm	J2	5 Nov 1833	**Pulaski, Crawford, Pope** Scott County; 100 W 1 St Ste 1; Waldron, AR 72958; Ph. (501) 637-2155 **Details:** (County & Circuit Clerk has Marriage, Divorce, Probate, land & Court Records from 1882)
Searcy www.pastracks.com/states/arkansas/searcy/	G5	13 Dec 1838	**Marion** Searcy County; Courthouse Sq; PO Box 297; Marshall, AR 72650-0297; Ph. (870) 448-3554 **Details:** (County Clerk has Marriage, Divorce, Probate & Court Records from 1881 & land Records from 1866)
Sebastian www.rootsweb.com/~arsebast/sebast.htm	I1	6 Jan 1851	**Scott, Polk, Crawford, Van Buren** Sebastian County; 35 S 6th; Fort Smith, AR 72901; Ph. (501) 782-5065 **Details:** (County Clerk has Marriage Records from 1865 & Probate Records from 1866; Clerk Circuit Court has Divorce, Court & land Records)
Sevier www.genealogyshoppe.com/arsevier/	L2	17 Oct 1828	**Hempstead, Miller** Sevier County; 115 N 3rd; De Queen, AR 71832; Ph. (870) 642-2425 **Details:** (County Clerk has Marriage & Probate Records from 1829; Clerk Circuit Court has Divorce, Court & land Records)
Sharp www.sharpcounty.org/	F8	18 Jul 1868	**Lawrence** Sharp County; PO Box 307; Ash Flat, AR 72513; Ph. (870) 994-7338 **Details:** (Line between Sharp & Izard changed 1877) (County Clerk has Marriage, Probate, Divorce, Court & land Records from 1880)
St. Francis Check for future website at http://usgenweb.com/	I10	13 Oct 1827	**Phillips** St. Francis County; 313 S Izard St; Forrest City, AR 72335-3856; Ph. (870) 261-1725 **Details:** (County Clerk has Marriage Records from 1875, Probate Records from 1910 & tax Records; Clerk Circuit Court has Divorce, Court & land Records)
Stone www.pastracks.com/states/arkansas/stone/	G6	21 Apr 1873	**Izard, Independence, Searcy, Van Buren** Stone County; HC 71 Box 1; PO Box 1427; Mountain View, AR 72560-0427; Ph. (870) 269-5550 **Details:** (County Clerk has Marriage & Divorce Records from 1873; Clerk Circuit Court has Probate, land, Military & Court Records from 1873)

County	Map	Date	Parent County or Territory From Which Organized
Website	Index	Created	Address/Details

Union   O5   **2 Nov 1829**   **Hempstead, Clark**
www.rootsweb.com/~arunion/
Union County; 101 N Washington; El Dorado, AR 71730;
Ph. (870) 864-1910
Details: (County Clerk has Marriage & Probate Records from 1846; Clerk Circuit Court has Divorce, Court & land Records)

Van Buren   H6   **11 Nov 1833**   **Independence, Conway, Izard**
www.rootsweb.com/~arvanBurial/
Van Buren County; Main & Griggs; Clinton, AR 72031;
Ph. (501) 745-4140
Details: (County Clerk has Marriage, Court & land Records from 1859, Divorce Records from 1874 & Probate Records from 1860)

Washington   G2   **17 Oct 1828**   **Crawford**
www.co.washington.ar.us/Archives
Washington County Archives; 4 South College, Suite 202;
Fayetteville, AR 72701; Ph. (479) 444-1543
Details: (Department of Health has Birth & Death records from 1914, City Library has Burial & Cemetery Records, Census, and Newspapers, County Archive has Business & Commerce Records from 1886, Court Records from 1829, Divorce Records from 1839, Guardianship Records from 1837, Land Records from 1830, Marriage Records from 1845; Military Records from 1829, Naturalization Records from 1829, Probate Records from 1837, and Tax Records from 1868

White   I7   **23 Oct 1835**   **Pulaski, Jackson, Independence**
www.cswnet.com/~wccomp/
White County; 300 N Spruce St; Searcy, AR 72143; Ph. (501) 279-6200
Details: (County Clerk has Marriage, Divorce, Probate, Court, land, tax & Miscellaneous Records)

Woodruff   I9   **26 Nov 1862**   **Jackson, St. Francis**
www.rootsweb.com/~arwoodru/
Woodruff County; 500 N 3rd St; Augusta, AR 72006-0356;
Ph. (870) 347-5206
Details: (County Clerk has Marriage & Probate Records from 1865; Clerk Circuit Court has Divorce, Court & land Records)

Yell   J4   **5 Dec 1840**   **Pope, Scott**
www.rootsweb.com/~aryell/
Yell County; 5th & Main; PO Box 219; Danville, AR 72833;
Ph. (479) 495-4850
Details: (County Clerk has Court, Divorce, Guardianship, Land, Marriage, Military, Probate, & Tax Records)

Notes

California

I have found it

Capital: Sacramento
State: 1850 (31st)

Juan Cabrillo discovered California in 1542. The English, due to Sir Francis Drake's visit in 1579, also laid claim to the land. However, the Spanish were the first to establish settlements. San Diego was settled in 1769 and Monterey in 1770. Junipero Serra set up a chain of Franciscan missions throughout the state, which served as religious and economic centers. The Russians built Fort Ross in 1812 to serve as a trading post. In 1841 Fort Ross was abandoned. After Mexican independence in 1821, California became mainly a collection of large ranches. In 1839, a Swiss, John Augustus Sutter, established the "Kingdom of New Helvetia" in the Sacramento River Valley. Two years later Americans began traveling overland to California in significant numbers. Early in the Mexican War, American forces occupied California. John C. Fremont, the American soldier and explorer, headed a short-lived Republic of California in 1846. In 1848, California was ceded to the United States. Just nine days earlier, gold was discovered at Sutter's Mill. This discovery led to the California Gold Rush of 1849, which brought more than 100,000 people to California from all over the United States, Asia, Australia, and Europe.

This mass migration enabled California to attain the required number of inhabitants to be admitted to the Union in 1850. During the Civil War, 15,700 soldiers from California fought for the Union. Many Chinese immigrants who came for the gold rush helped build the transcontinental railroad, which was completed in 1869. A railroad rate war in 1884 and a real estate boom in 1885 led to another wave of immigration. Foreign-born Californians, in descending order, came from Mexico, Canada, Italy, England, Wales, Russia, Germany, Sweden, Ireland, Scotland, Poland, Austria, France, Denmark, Norway, Switzerland, Portugal, Greece, Yugoslavia, Hungary, Netherlands, Spain, Finland, Czechoslovakia, Romania, Lithuania, and Belgium.

Look for vital records in the following locations:

- **Birth and death records:** Office of Vital Records since 1905. Prior to 1 July, 1905, records are available from the county recorders and the health departments of many larger cities.
- **Marriage records:** Office of Vital Records since 1905. Prior to 1 July, 1905, records are available from the county recorders and the health departments of many larger cities.
- **Divorce records:** County clerks have divorce, probate, civil court and other records.
- **Naturalizations:** County offices of the Superior Courts and U.S. Circuit Courts in Los Angeles and San Francisco.
- **Land records:** Real estate deeds are filed in the County Recorder's office. Pre-statehood lists, termed padrons, of Spanish, Mexican, and Indian residents have been published.
- **Census records:** California State Archives has some census records for major California cities from 1897 to 1938.

California Department of Health Services Office of Vital Records — M.S. 5103
PO Box 997410
Sacramento, CA 95899-7410
(916) 445-4171
www.dhs.ca.gov/hisp/chs/ovr/OrderCert.htm

California State Archives
Room 130, 1020 "O" Street
Sacramento, CA 95814
(916) 653-7715
www.ss.ca.gov/archives/archives.htm

Societies and Repositories

African American Genealogical Society of Northern California; PO Box 27485; Oakland, CA 94602-0985; president@aagsnc.org; www.aagsnc.org.

African-American Genealogical Society, California; PO Box 8442; Los Angeles, CA 90008-0442.

Afro-American Genealogical Society, California; Afro-American Museum; 600 State Dr., Exposition Par; Los Angeles, CA 90037.

Alhambra Historical Society; 1550 W. Alhambra Rd.; PO Box 6687; Alhambra, CA 91802.

Altadena Heritage; PO Box 218; Altadena, CA 91003.

Altadena Historical Society; PO Box 144; Altadena, CA 91003.

Amador County Genealogical Society; 10193 Buena Vista Dr.; Jackson, CA 95642.

Angel Island Association; PO Box 866; Tiburon, CA 94920; Val.Sherer@angelisland.org; www.angelisland.org.

Antelope Valley Chapter, DAR, CA; avdar@yahoo.com; www.geocities.com/Heartland/Prairie/1776.

Antelope Valley Genealogical Society; PO Box 1049; Lancaster, CA 93534-1049; www.qnet.com/~toiyabe/avgs.

Anza Valley Historical Society; PO Box 391134; Anza, AZ 92539-1134.

Augustan Society; PO Box 75; Daggett, CA 92327-0075; (760) 254-9223; robertcleve@yahoo.com; www.augustansociety.org.

Azusa Historical Society; City Hall Complex; 213 E. Footlhill Blvd.; Azusa, CA 91702.

Balkan and Eastern European American Genealogical and Historical Society; 4843 Mission St.; San Francisco, CA 94112.

Berkeley Historical Society; PO Box 1190; Berkeley, CA 94701-1190; berkhist@juno.com; www.ci.berkeley.ca.us/histsoc.

British Family Historical Society of Los Angeles; 22941 Felbar Ave.; Torrance, CA 90505.

British Isles Genealogical Research Association; PO Box 19775; San Diego, CA 92159-0775.

Burbank Historical Society; 1015 W. Olive Ave.; Burbank, CA 91506.

Butte Chapter, CASSAR; CA; Boydstun@mindspring.com.

Calabasas Historical Society; PO Box 8067; Calabasas, CA 91371.

Calaveras Genealogical Society; PO Box 184; Angels Camp, CA 95222-0184.

California Genealogical Society; 1611 Telegraph Ave, Suite 200; Oakland, CA 94612-2152; library@calgensoc.org; www.calgensoc.com.

California History and Genealogy Room; Fresno Co. Public Library; 2420 Mariposa St; Fresno, CA 93721; (559) 488-6270; www.fresnolibrary.org/calif/index.html.

California Mission Studies Association; PO Box 3357; Bakersfield, CA 93385-3357; www.ca-missions.org/contact.html.

California State Archives; 1020 "O" Street; Sacramento, CA 95814; (916) 653-2246; ArchivesWeb@ss.ca.gov; www.ss.ca.gov/archives/archives.htm.

California State Genealogical Alliance; PO Box 311; Danville, CA 94526-0311; sheilabe@syv.com; www.csga.com.

California State Library; Library and Courts Building; 914 Capitol Mall; Sacramento, CA 95814; (916) 654-0261; cslsirc@library.ca.gov; www.asl.lib.ar.us.

Carlsbad Historical Society; PO Box 252; Carlsbad, CA 92018-0252; www.carlsbad.ca.us/chs.html.

Central California Chapter, AHSGR; 3233 N. West Avenue; Fresno, CA 93705-3402; ahsgrfr@mindspring.com; www.ahsgr.org/cacentra.html.

Central Coast Chapter, CASSAR; CA; GEWilley@onemain.com.

Clan Diggers Genealogical Society, Inc. of the Kern River Valley; PO Box 531; Lake Isabella, CA 93240.

Clayton Historical Society; PO Box 94; Clayton, CA 94517-0094; http://94517.com/chs.

Coachella Valley Chapter, CASSAR; CA; remlap2@aol.com.

Computer Genealogy Society of San Diego (CGSSD); PO Box 370357; San Diego, CA 92137-0357; cgssd-board@ucsd.edu; www.cgssd.org.

Computer Rooters; 9491 Lake Natoma Dr.; Orangevale, CA 95662-5050.

Conejo Valley Genealogical Society, Inc.; PO Box 1228; Thousand Oaks, CA 91358-0228; cvgsweb@prodigy.net; www.rootsweb.com/~cacvgs.

Contra Costa County Genealogical Society; PO Box 910; Concord, CA 94522; www.geocities.com/Heartland/Plains/4335/cccgs/cccgs.html.

Contra Costa County Historical Society; 610 Main Street; Martinez, CA 94553; cchistry@ix.netcom.com; www.ccnet.com/~xptom/ccchs.

Covina Valley Historical Society; 125 E. College St.; Covina, CA 91723.

Covina, Calif. Chapter, DAR; 2441 SN. Cameron Ave.; Covina, CA 91724.

Cupertino Historical Society; Cupertino, CA; www.cupertino.org/update/civic/chs.htm.

Dalton Genealogical Society; 880 Ames Court; Palo Alto, CA 94303.

Delta Chapter, CASSAR; CA; rsarhill@modesto.net.

Delta Genealogical Interest Group; PO Box 157; Knightsen, CA 94548.

Downey Historical Society; PO Box 554; Downey, CA 90241-0554.

Duarte Historical Society; PO Box 263; Duarte, CA 91009.

Eagle Rock Valley Historical Society; 2035 Colorado Blvd.; Eagle Rock, CA 90041.

East Bay Genealogical Society; PO Box 20417; Oakland, CA 94620-0417; www.katpher.com/EBGS/EBGS.html.

East Kern Genealogical Society; PO Box 961; North Edwards, CA 93523-0961.

Echo Park Historical Society; 1471 Fairbanks Pl.; Los Angeles, CA 90026; EPHIST@aol.com.

Encino Historical Society; 16756 Moorpark St.; Encino, CA 91436.

Escondido Genealogical Society; PO Box 2190; Escondido, CA 92033-2190.

Eureka California Senior Center; 1910 California St.; Eureka, CA 95501.

Forestville Historical Society; PO Box 195; Forestville, CA 95436; www.sonic.net/forestville.

Fresno County Genealogical Society; PO Box 1429; Fresno, CA 93716-1429.

Fresno Historical Society; 7160 West Kearney Boulevard; Fresno, CA 93706; FrHistSoc@aol.com; www.valleyhistory.org.

Genealogical and Historical Council of the Sacramento Valley; PO Box 214749; Sacramento, CA 95821-0749; (916) 682-3381; ijones@ns.net; http://feefhs.org/ghcsv/frgghcsv.html.

Genealogical Association of Sacramento; PO Box 292145; Sacramento, CA 95829-2145.

Genealogical Club of Sun City; PO Box 175; Sun City, CA 92586-0175.

Genealogical Society of Coachella Valley; PO Box 124; Indio, CA 92202.

Genealogical Society of Hispanic America of Southern California; PO Box 2472; Santa Fe Springs, CA 90670.

Genealogical Society of Madera; PO Box 495; Madera, CA 93639.

Genealogical Society of Morongo Basin; PO Box 234; Yucca Valley, CA 92286; www.yuccavalley.com/genealogy.

Genealogical Society of North Orange County, (GSNOCC); PO Box 706; Yorba Linda, CA 92885-0706.

Genealogical Society of Riverside; PO Box 2557; Riverside, CA 92516; gaubuchon@aol.com; www.geocities.com/Heartland/Woods/6250.

Genealogical Society of Santa Cruz County; PO Box 72; Santa Cruz, CA 95063.

Genealogical Society of Siskiyou County; PO Box 225; Yreka, CA 96097.

Genealogical Society of Stanislaus County; PO Box A; Modesto, CA 95352-3660; http://compuology.com/cagenweb/gssc.html.

Genealogy Society of Vallejo-Benicia; 734 Marin Street; Vallejo, CA 94590; www.rootsweb.com/~cagsv

General George Washington Chapter, CASSAR; CA; TippitoeSH@aol.com.

General Patton Chapter, CASSAR; CA; H2Ham@aol.com; http://members.aol.com/sarpatton/homepage.htm.

German Immigrant Genealogical Society; PO Box 7369; 1310 B West Magnolia Blvd; Burbank, CA 91510-7369; (818) 353-2341; http://feefhs.org/igs/frg-igs.html.

German Research Association; PO Box 11293; San Diego, CA 92111.

Glendale Historical Society; PO Box 4173; Glendale, CA 91202.

Glendora Genealogical Group; PO Box 1141; Glendora, CA 91740-1141; lorman@adelphia.net; www.geocities.com/ccstone_us/GlenGenGrp.htm.

Glendora Historical Society; 314 N. Glendora Ave.; PO Box 532; Glendora, CA 91740.

Gold Country Chapter, CASSAR; CA; ELY@foothill.net; www.jps.net/perky.

Golden Gate Chapter, AHSGR; 2725 Belmont Canyon Road; Belmont, CA 94002-1204; (650) 591-5143; Bobloiss@aol.com.

Harbor Chapter, CASSAR; CA; pinsational@earthlink.net; http://home.earthlink.net/~rodbush/sar.htm.

Hayward Area Genealogical Society; PO Box 754; Hayward, CA 94543.

Hemet-San Jacinto Genealogical Society; PO Box 2516; Hemet, CA 92343.

Hi-Desert Genealogical Society; PO Box 1271; Victorville, CA 92393; http://vvo.com/comm/hdgs.htm.

Historical Society of Centinela Valley; 7634 Midfield Ave.; Los Angeles, CA 90045.

Historical Society of Long Beach; PO Box 1869; Long Beach, CA 90801-1869; (562) 495-1210; hslb@historicalsocietylb.org; www.historicalsocietylb.

Historical Society of Monterey Park; 781 S. Orange Ave.; PO Box 172; Monterey Park, CA 91754.

Historical Society of Southern California; 200 E. Ave. 43; Los Angeles, CA 90031; HSSC@socalhistory.org; www.socalhistory.org.

Historical Society of the Upper Mojave Desert; PO Box 2001; Ridgecrest, CA 93556-2001; (760) 375-7385; ldpracc@ridgecrest.ca.us; www.ridgecrest.ca.us/~matmus/Hist.html.

Historical Society of West Covina; PO Box 4597; West Covina, CA 91793.

Huguenot Society of California; CA; mwatson@genealogyoncd.com.

Humboldt County Genealogical Society; 2336 G Street; Eureka, CA 95501.

Hungarian-American Friendship Society; c/o Doug Holmes; 1035 Starbrook Drive; Galt, CA 95632; HAFS@dholmes.com; www.dholmes.com/hafs.html.

Indian Wells Valley Genealogical Society; 131 Los Flores; Ridgecrest, CA 93555.

Jewish Genealogical Society of Los Angeles; PO Box 55443; Sherman Oaks, CA 91413-0443; (818) 712-9031; sonia@jgsla.org; www.jewishgen.org/jgsla.

Jewish Genealogical Society of Orange County; 2370–1D Via Mariposa West; Laguna Hills, CA 92653.

Jewish Genealogical Society of Sacramento; 5631 Kiva Dr.; Sacramento, CA 95841.

Jewish Genealogical Society of San Diego; 255 South Rios Ave.; Solana Beach, CA 92075.

JPL Genealogy Club; CA; (818) 354-7758; Jay.Holladay@jpl.nasa.gov; www.jplerc.org/genealog.

Kern Chapter CASSAR; CA; TWSpears62@cs.com.

Kern County Genealogical Society; PO Box 2214; Bakersfield, CA 93303.

La Puente Valley Historical Society; PO Box 522; La Puente, CA 91744.

La Rochelle Chapter, Huguenot Society of California; CA; kaylaw@earthlink.net; www.huguenot.netnation.com/states/california/index.html.

Lake County Genealogical Society; PO Box 1323; Lakeport, CA 95453.

Lake Elsinore Genealogical Society; Box 807; Lake Elsinore, CA 92531-0807.

Leisure World Genealogical Workshop; c/o Leisure World Library; 2300 Beverly Manor Rd.; Seal Beach, CA 90740.

Little Landers Historical Society; 10110 Commerce Ave.; Tujunga, CA 91043; (818) 352-3420; BoltonHallNews@msn.com; http://digitallibrary.csun.edu/heritage_network/llhs.html.

Livermore-Amador Genealogical Society; PO Box 901; Livermore, CA 94550; www.l-ags.org/index.html.

Lodi, California Chapter, AHSGR; 3525 Veneman Ave. No.; Modesto, CA 95356-2435; (209) 524-6330; blauweg@aol.com.

Lomita Historical Society; 24016 Benhill Ave.; PO Box 549; Lomita, CA 90717.

Los Angeles City Historical Society; PO Box 41046; Los Angeles, CA 90041.

Los Angeles Westside Genealogical Society; PO Box 10447; Marina Del Rey, CA 90295-6447; www.genealogy-la.com/lawgs.shtml.

Los Banos Genealogical Society, Inc.; PO Box 2525; Los Banos, CA 93635.

Marin County Genealogical Society; PO Box 1511; Novato, CA 94949-1511; president@maringensoc.org; www.maringensoc.org.

Martinez Historical Society; PO Box 14; Martinez, CA 94553; www.martinezhistory.org/index2.html.

Mendocino Coast Genealogical Society; PO Box 762; Fort Bragg, CA 95437.

Mendocino County Historical Society, Inc.; Held-Poage Research Library; 603 W. Perkins St.; Ukiah, CA 95482-4726; (707) 462-6969.

Merced County Genealogical Society; PO Box 3061; Merced, CA 95340; Ntin768062@aol.com; www.rootsweb.com/~camcgs/home.htm.

Monterey Bay Chapter, CASSAR; CA; jsl@redshift.com; www.mccnet.com/sar.html.

Monterey County Genealogical Society; PO Box 8144; Salinas, CA 93912-9144

Monterey County Historical Society; PO Box 3576; Salinas, CA 93912; mchs@dedot.com; http://users.dedot.com/mchs.

Moraga Historical Society; PO Box 103; Moraga, CA 94556; mhistory@silcon.com.

Mt. Diablo Chapter, AHSGR; 11 Wandel Drive; Moraga, CA 94556-1829; siebert@are.berkeley.edu.

Mt. Diablo Genealogical Society; PO Box 4654; Walnut Creek, CA 94596.

Napa Valley Genealogical and Biographical Society; 1701 Menlo Ave.; Napa, CA 94558; (707) 252-2252; nvgbs@napanet.net; www.napanet.net/~nvgbs.

NARA, Pacific Region (Laguna Nigel); 24000 Avila Road, Laguna Nigel, CA 92677-3497

NARA, Pacific Region (San Francisco); 1000 Commodore Drive; San Bruno, CA 94066-2350; (650) 876-9009; daniel.nealand@nara.gov; www.archives.gov/facilities/ca/san_francisco.html.

Native Daughters of the Golden West; 555 Baker St.; San Francisco, CA 94117-1405.

Native Sons of the Golden West; 414 Mason St.; San Francisco, CA 94102.

Nevada County Genealogical Society; PO Box 176; Cedar Ridge, CA 95924; jpvaughn@jps.net; www.rootsweb.com/~cancgs.

North Coast Chapter, CASSAR; CA; bjhoyle@humboldt1.com.

North Lake Tahoe Historical Society; PO Box 6141; Tahoe City, CA 96145; (530) 583-1762; nlths@tahoecountry.com; www.tahoecountry.com/nlths/index.html.

North San Diego County Genealogical Society, Inc.; PO Box 581; Carlsbad, CA 92008.

Orange County Chapter, CASSAR; CA; kekoalou@aol.com; http://members.xoom.com/nationalink.

Orange County Genealogical Society; PO Box 1587; Orange, CA 92856-1587; kinkatcher@aol.com; http://occgs.com.

Pacific Palisades Historical Society; PO Box 1299; Los Angeles, CA 90272.

Pajaro Valley Genealogical Society; 53 North Dr.; Freedom, CA 95019.

Palm Springs Genealogical Society; PO Box 2093; Palm Springs, CA 92263-2093.

Paradise Genealogical Society, Inc.; 5587 Scottwood Rd; PO Box 460; Paradise, CA 95967-0460

Pasadena Genealogical Society; PO Box 94774; Pasadena, CA 91109-4774.

Pasadena Heritage; 80 West Dayton; Pasadena, CA 91105.

Pasadena Historical Society; 470 W. Walnut St.; Pasadena, CA 91103.

Patterson Genies; 13218 Sycamore; Patterson, CA 95363.

Pico Rivera History and Heritage Society; PO Box 313; Pico Rivera, CA 90666.

Placer County Genealogical Society; PO Box 7385; Auburn, CA 95604-7385; toff@pacbell.net; www.webcom.com/gunruh/pcgs.html.

Plumas County Historical Society; 500 Jackson St.; Quincy, CA 95971-9412.

Polish Genealogical Society of California; PO Box 307; Buena Park, CA 90621-0307; Information@pgsca.org; http://feefhs.org/pol/pgsca/frgpgsca.html.

Pomona Valley Genealogical Society; PO Box 296; Pomona, CA 91766.

Questing Heirs Genealogical Society; PO Box 15102; Long Beach, CA 90815-0102; (562) 437-4337; Realmac@aol.com; www.cagenweb.com/questing.

Redding Chapter, CASSAR; CA; poomback@c-zone.net.

Redlands Area Genealogy Society; PO Box 1024; Redlands, CA 92373; dlhunter@earthlink.net; www.rahs.org/genealogy.

Redondo Beach Historical Society; PO Box 978; Redondo Beach, CA 90277; RBHistSoc@aol.com; http://members.aol.com/RBHistSoc.

Redwood Empire Chapter, CASSAR; CA; JohnMacNab@aol.com.

Redwood Genealogical Society; Box 645; Fortuna, CA 95540

Renegade Root Diggers; 9171 Fargo Ave.; Hanford, CA 93230.

Root Cellar Sacramento Genealogical Society; PO Box 254; Citrus Heights, CA 95811-0265; (916) 481-4930; schang007@comcast.net.

Root Diggers, Lucerne Valley Genealogical Association; c/o Lucerne Valley Library; PO Box 408; Lucerne Valley, CA 92356.

Roseville Genealogical Society; PO Box 459; Roseville, CA 95678; llarson@foothill.net; www.rootsweb.com/~carvgs/rgs.htm.

Sacramento Chapter, CASSAR; CA; TChilton@telis.org; www.bigfoot.com/~sarsac/.

Sacramento German Genealogical Society; PO Box 660061; Sacramento, CA 95866.

Sacramento Valley Chapter, AHSGR; 624 Shangri Lane; Sacramento, CA 95825-5505; (916) 925-5054; rmbmlb@attbi.com; http://ahsgr_sac.tripod.com.

Samuel Ramsey Chapter, California State Society DAR; CA; http://members.home.net/swelch/cssdar/chapters/samuel_ramsey.

San Bernardino Valley Genealogical Society; PO Box 2220; San Bernardino, CA 92405.

San Clemente Historical Society; PO Box 283; San Clemente, CA 92674-0283; www.ocnow.com/community/groups/sanclemente/index.html.

San Diego Chapter CASSAR; CA; SARTravis@aol.com.

San Diego Genealogical Society; 1050 Pioneer Way, Suite E; El Cajon, CA 92020-1943; sdgs2000@yahoo.com; www.rootsweb.com/~casdgs.

San Diego Historical Society; PO Box 81825; San Diego, CA 92138; www.sandiegohistory.org/histsoc.html.

San Diego, California Chapter. The National Society Daughters of the War of 1812; San Diego, CA ; Pjcposey@aol.com; www.rootsweb.com/~nysdcdw.

San Fernando Valley Genealogical Society; PO Box 3486; Winnetka, CA 91396-3486; eburrelle@netzero.net; www.rootsweb.com/~casfvgs.

San Fernando Valley Historical Society; PO Box 7039; Mission Hills, CA 92346-7039.

San Francisco Bay Area Jewish Genealogical Society; PO Box 471616; San Francisco, CA 94147; jfrankel@lmi.net; www.jewishgen.org/sfbajgs.

San Francisco Chapter, CASSAR; CA; PracPower@aol.com.

San Gorgonio Pass Genealogical Society; 1050 Brinton Ave.; Banning, CA 92220.

San Joaquin Genealogical Society; PO Box 4817; Stockton, CA 95204-0817; www.rootsweb.com/~sjgs.

San Luis Obispo County Genealogical Society, Inc.; PO Box 4; Atascadero, CA 93423-0004.

San Marino Historical Society; PO Box 80222; San Marino, CA 91118-8222.

San Mateo County Genealogical Society; PO Box 5083; San Mateo, CA 94402-0083; hchrisman@aol.com; www.smcgs.org.

San Ramon Valley Genealogical Society; PO Box 305; Diablo, CA 94528.

Santa Barbara County Genealogical Society; 316 Castillo St, Santa Barbara; PO Box 1303; Goleta, CA

93116-1303; (805) 884-9909; sbcgs@msn.com; www.cagenweb.com/santabarbara/sbcgs.

Santa Clara County Historical and Genealogical Society; 2635 Homestead Rd.; Santa Clara, CA 95051; (408) 615-2900; SCCHGS@hotmail.com; www.rootsweb.com/~cascchgs.

Santa Clarita Valley Historical Society; 24107 San Fernando Rd.; Newhall, CA 91321.

Santa Maria Valley Genealogical Society; PO Box 1215; Santa Maria, CA 93456.

Santa Monica Historical Society; 1345 3rd Street Promenade; PO Box 3059; Santa Monica, CA 90408-3059.

Scott Valley Genealogical Group; Etna, CA; www.sisqtel.net/~nwhipple/svgg.html.

Sequoia Genealogical Society; 113 North F Street; Tulare, CA 93274; (559) 685-2342.

Shasta Genealogical Society; PO Box 994652; Redding, CA 96099-4652; sgs106@hotmail.com; www.rootsweb.com/~cascogs.

Silicon Valley Chapter, CASSAR; CA; circle@inow.com; www.geocities.com/svsar.

Sloughhouse Area Genealogical Society; Sloughhouse, CA; www.rootsweb.com/~casags.

Society of Hispanic Historical and Ancestral Research; PO Box 490; Midway City, CA 92655-0490; mimilozano@aol.com; http://members.aol.com/shhar.

Society of Mayflower Descendants in the State of California; 405 Fourteenth St., Terrace Level; Oakland, CA 94612.

Solano County Genealogical Society, Inc.; PO Box 2494; Fairfield, CA 94533.

Sonoma County Genealogical Society; PO Box 2273; Santa Rosa, CA 95405-0273; audreyrae@earthlink.net; www.scgs.org.

Sons of Liberty Chapter, CASSAR; CA; glenn_gujda@paramount.com; www.geocities.com/sons_of_liberty_sar/.

South Bay Cities Genealogical Society; PO Box 11069; Torrance, CA 90510-1069; sbcgs@hotmail.com; www.rootsweb.com/~casbcgs.

South Coast Chapter, CASSAR; CA; CMPorter@hotmail.com; www.southcoastSAR.org.

South Orange County Genealogical Society; PO Box 4513; Mission Viejo, CA 92690-4513; www.rootsweb.com/~casoccgs.

Southern California Chapter, AHSGR; 16371 Silver Lane; Huntington Beach, CA 92647; (714) 847-6481; ahhart@aol.com; www.ehrman.net/ahsgr/casocal.html.

Southern California Chapter, OGS; 14837 Los Robles Avenue; Hacienda Heights, CA 91745-2615; (626) 333-1194; bjcbogie@aol.com.

Southern California Genealogical Society; 417 Irving Dr.; Burbank, CA 91504-2408; scgs@earthlink.net; www.scgsgenealogy.com.

Southern California Jewish Historical Society; 6505 Wilshire Blvd.; Los Angeles, CA 90048.

Spanishtown Historical Society; Box 62; Half Moon Bay, CA 94019.

St. Ives Historical Society; 21661 Lyn St.; California City, CA 93505; dflood@ccis.com; www.saintives.com.

Sutter-Yuba Genealogical Society; PO Box 523; Marysville, CA 95901-1523; RTonjes775@aol.com; http://rootsweb.com/~casygs.

Taft Genealogical Society; PO Box 1411; Taft, CA 93268.

Tehama Genealogical and Historical Society; PO Box 415; Red Bluff, CA 96080.

Temple City Historical Society; PO Box 1379; Temple City, CA 91780; www.ci.temple-city.ca.us/comunorg/histsoc.htm.

The California Mennonite Historical Society; 4824 E. Butler; Fresno, CA 93727-5097; peter_klassen@csufresno.edu; www.fresno.edu/affiliation/cmhs.

The Davis Genealogical Club and Library; c/o The Davis Senior Center; 646 A Street; Davis, CA 95616-3602; mholt@jps.net; http://feefhs.org/ghcsv/dgc/frg-dgcl.html.

The Historical Society of Pomona Valley; 1460 East Holt Blvd. Suite 78; Pomona, CA 91767; ogallivan@earthlink.net; www.osb.net/pomona.

Topanga Historical Society; PO Box 1214; Topanga, CA 90290; www.topangaonline.com/hsociety.html.

Tracy Area Genealogical Society; Tracy Historical Museum; 1141 Adam Street; Tracy, CA 95376; (209) 832-1106; TAGSCA@sbcglobal.net; http://rootsweb.com/~catags/frmain.htm.

TRW Genealogical Society; One Space Park S-1435; Redondo Beach, CA 90279.

Tule Tree Tracers; 41 W. Thurman Ave.; Porterville, CA 93257.

Tuolumme County Genealogical Society; 158 W Bradford Ave; PO Box 3956; Sanora, CA 95370

Vandenberg Genealogical Society; PO Box 81; Lompoc, CA 93438-0081.

Venice Historical Society; PO Box 12844; Venice, CA 90295; (310) 967-5170; info@veniceofamerica.org; www.veniceofamerica.org.

Ventura County Genealogical Society; PO Box 24608; Ventura, CA 93002; www.rootsweb.com/~cavcgs.

Whittier Area Genealogical Society; PO Box 4367; Whittier, CA 90607-4367.

Whittier Historical Society; 6755 Newlin Ave; Whittier, CA 90601; www.whittierbiz.com/info/museum.htm#Whittier%20Historical%20Society.

Workman and Temple Family Homestead Museum; 15415 East Don Julian Road; City of Industry, CA 91745-1029; info@homesteadmuseum.org; www.homesteadmuseum.org.

Yolo County Archives; 226 Buckeye St.; Woodland, CA 95695.

Yolo County Historical Society; PO Box 1447; Woodland, CA 95776; www.yolo.net/ychs.

Yorba Linda Heritage Museum and Historical Society; PO Box 396; Yorba Linda, CA 92885-0396.

Yucaipa Valley Genealogical Society; PO Box 32; Yucaipa, CA 92399.

Bibliography and Record Sources

General

Bancroft, Hubert H. *California Pioneer Register and Index, 1542–1848, Including Inhabitants...1769–1800 and a List of Pioneers (1884–1901)*. Reprint. Baltimore, Maryland: Clearfield Co., 1990.

Bolton, Herbert E. *The Spanish Borderlands: A Chronicle of Old Florida and the Southwest*. (1921), reprint. Galveston Texas: Frontier Press, 1996.

California Genealogical Society. *Genealogy Success Stories: Personal Problem-solving Accounts That Encourage, Enlighten and Inspire You*. San Francisco, California: California Genealogical Society, 1995.

California Local History: A Bibliography and Union List of Library Holdings. 2nd ed. Stanford, California: Stanford University Press, 1970. Supplement (covering 1961 to 1970), 1976.

California Research Outline. Series U.S.-States, No. 5. Salt Lake City: Family History Library, 1988.

Faulkinbury, Jim W. *The Foreign-Born Voters of California in 1872*. Sacramento, California: Jim W. Faulkinbury, 1994.

Hunt, Rockwell Dennis, ed. *California and Californians*. Chicago: Lewis Publishing Co., 1932.

Nicklas, Laurie. *The California Locator. A Directory of Public Records for Locating People Dead or Alive in California*. Modesto, California: Laurie Nicklas, 1996.

Parker, J. Carlyle. *An Index to the Biographies in 19th Century California County Histories*. (1979). Reprint. Turlock, California: Marietta Pub. Co., 1994.

Phelps, Alonzo. *Contemporary Biography of California's Representative Men...*2 vols. San Francisco: A.L. Bancroft and Co., 1881.

Pompey, Sherman L. *Genealogical Records of California*. Fresno, California: Sherman L. Pompey, 1968.

Smith, Clifford N. *Gold! German Transcontinental Travelers to California, 1849–1851*. McNeal, Arizona: Westland Publications, 1988.

Solano County Genealogical Society, Inc. *Index to the DAR "Records of the Families of the California Pioneers," Volumes 1–27*. Fairfield, California: Solano Co. Gen Soc., 1988.

Southern California Genealogical Society. *Sources of Genealogical Help in California Libraries*. Rev. ed. 1996. Burbank, California: The Society.

Southern California Genealogical Society. *American Indian Related Books in the SCGS Library*. Burbank, California: The Society.

Southern California Genealogical Society. *UCLA Library: Sources of. Genealogical Help*. Burbank, California: The Society.

Atlases, Maps and Gazetteers

Beck, Warren A., and Ynez D. Haase. *Historical Atlas of California*. Norman: University of Oklahoma Press, 1974.

California City and Unincorporated Place Names. Sacramento: California Division of Highways, 1971.

Coy, Owen C. *California County Boundaries: A Study of the Division of the States into Counties and the Subsequent Changes in their Boundaries, with Maps*. Berkeley: California Historical Survey Commission, 1923. Reprint. Rev. ed. Fresno, California: Valley Publishers, 1973.

Durrennberger, Robert W. *Patterns on the Land: Geographical, Historical, and Political Maps of California*. Palo Alto, California: National Press Books, 1965.

Gudde, Erwin G. *California Place Names: The Origin and Etymology of Current Geographical Names*. 3rd ed. Rev. and Enl. Berkeley: University of California Press, 1969.

Hanna, Phil L., comp. *The Dictionary of California Land Names*. Los Angeles: Automobile Club of Southern California, 1946.

Patera, Edward L. *History of California Post Offices, 1849–1990 / H. E. Salley: Includes Branches and Stations, Rural Free Delivery Routes, Navy Numbered Branches, Highway and Railway Post Offices*. 2nd ed. Lake Grove, Oregon: The Depot, 1991.

Preston, Ralph N. *Early California: Early Forts, Old Mines, Old Town Sites*. Northern ed. Corvallis, Oregon: Western Guide Publishers, 1974. Reprinted as *Early California Atlas: Northern Edition*. 2nd ed. Portland, Oregon: Binford & Mort Publishers, 1983.

Salley, Harold E. *History of California Post Offices, 1849–1976: Includes Branches and Stations, Navy Numbered Branches, Highway and Railroad Posts*. La Mesa, California: Postal History Association, 1977.

Sanchez, Nellie Van de Grift. *Spanish and Indian Place Names of California—Their Meaning and Their Romance*. San Francisco: A.M. Robertson, 1930.

Southern and Central California Atlas and Gazetteer. 3rd ed. Freeport, Maine: DeLorme Mapping Co., 1994.

United States. Geological Survey. *California, Index to Topographic and Other Map Coverage*. Reston, Virginia: United States Geological Survey. National Mapping Program, 1983.

Censuses

Available Census Records and Census Substitutes

Federal Census 1850 (except Contra Costa, San Francisco and Santa Clara Counties), 1860, 1870, 1880, 1900, 1910, 1920, 1930

Federal Mortality Schedules 1850, 1860, 1870, 1880

State Federal Census 1852

Patron Census 1790

California State Genealogical Alliance. *The California 1890 Great Register of Voters Index*. 3 vols. North Salt Lake, Utah: Heritage Quest, 2001.

Dollarhide, William. *The Census Book: A Genealogist's Guide to Federal Census Facts, Schedules and Indexes*. Bountiful, Utah: Heritage Quest, 1999.

Kemp, Thomas Jay. *The American Census Handbook*. Wilmington, Delaware: Scholarly Resources, Inc., 2001.

Lainhart, Ann S. *State Census Records*. Baltimore: Genealogical Publishing Co. Inc., 1992.

Szucs, Loretto Dennis and Matthew Wright. *Finding Answers in U.S. Census Records*. Ancestry Publishing, 2001.

Thorndale, William. *Map Guide to the U.S. Federal Census, 1790–1920*. Baltimore: Genealogical Publishing Co., 1987.

United States. Bureau of Internal Revenue. *Internal Revenue Assessment Lists for California, 1862–1866*. Washington, D.C.: The National Archives, 1988. 33 microfilm.

Court Records, Probate, and Wills

California. State Archives (Sacramento). *Index to Records of Appellate Court Cases, 1900–1930*. Microfilm of original records at the State Archives, Sacramento, Calif. Salt Lake City: Filmed by the Genealogical Society of Utah, 1975. 2 microfilm.

California. State Archives (Sacramento). *Index to Records of Supreme Court Cases, 1850–1930*. Microfilm of original records at the State Archives, Sacramento, California. Salt Lake City: Filmed by the Genealogical Society of Utah, 1975. 2 microfilm.

California. State Archives (Sacramento). *Index to Transcripts of Court Cases in State Archives, Attorney General, State of California*. Microfilm of original records at the State Archives, Sacramento, California. Salt Lake City: Filmed by the Genealogical Society of Utah, 1975.

Dilts, Bryan Lee, comp. *1860 California Census Index: Head of Households and Other Surnames in Household Index*. 2nd ed. Bountiful, Utah: AGLL, 1984.

Nicklas, Laurie. *California County Courthouse Records: A Directory of Vital Records found in Each County Office in California*. Modesto, California: L. Nicklas, 1998.

Immigration

California State Library (Sacramento). *Pioneer Index File (California), 1906–1935*. Microfilm of card file located at the California State Library, Sacramento. Salt Lake City: Filmed by the Genealogical Society of Utah, 1991. 10 microfilm.

California. Circuit Court (Northern District). *Selected Indexes to Naturalization Records of the U.S. Circuit & District courts, Northern, & Southern districts of California*. Washington, D.C.: National Archives. Central Plains Region, 1984. 3 microfilm.

California. Superior Court. *Naturalization Records, 1887–1940*. Salt Lake City: Filmed by the Genealogical Society of Utah, 1987–1988. 246 microfilm.

Carr, Peter E. *San Francisco Passenger Departure Lists–Vols. I–IV*. San Luis Obispo, California: TCI Genealogical Resources, 1991–1993.

Lewis, Oscar. *Sea Routes to the Gold Fields, the Migration by Water to California in 1849–1852*. New York: Alfred A. Knopf, 1949.

United States. Bureau of Customs. *Alphabetical Index of Ships' Arrival at the Port of San Francisco, California, from ca. 1840 to 1 December 1954*. Washington, D.C.: National Archives. Central Plains Region, 1987.

United States. District Court (California: Northern District). *Declarations of Intention, 1846–1903*. Microfilm of original records at the Federal Records Center, San Bruno, California. Salt Lake City: Filmed by the Genealogical Society of Utah, 1975. 4 microfilm.

United States. District Court (California: Northern District). *Index to Naturalization in the U.S. District Court for the Northern District of California, 1860–1989*. Microfilm of records located at the National Archives, Pacific Sierra Region, San Bruno, California. Salt Lake City: Filmed by the Genealogical Society of Utah, 1992–1993. 165 microfilm.

United States. District Court (California: Southern District). *Declarations of Intention, 1927–1948*. Microreproduction of the original records at the Federal Archives and Records Center, Laguna Niguel, California. Salt Lake City: Filmed by the Genealogical Society of Utah, 1978. 44 microfilm.

United States. District Court (California: Southern District: Central Division). *General Card Index to Naturalized Citizens, 1915–1978*. Microfilm of original index cards located in the National Archives, Los Angeles Branch, Laguna Niguel, California. Salt Lake City: Filmed by the Genealogical Society of Utah, 1989. 114 microfilm.

United States. District Court (California: Southern District: Central Division). *Index Cards to Overseas Military Petitions of U.S. District Court for the Southern District of California, Central Division, Laguna Niguel.* Microfilm of original index cards located in the National Archives, Los Angeles Branch, Laguna Niguel, California. Salt Lake City: Filmed by the Genealogical Society of Utah, 1989. 2 microfilm.

United States. *Immigration and Naturalization Service. Crew Lists of Vessels Arriving at San Francisco, California, 1905–1921.* Washington, D.C.: The National Archives, 1988. 35 microfilm.

United States. *Immigration and Naturalization Service. Manifests of Alien Arrivals at San Ysidro (Tia Juana) California, April 21, 1908–December 1952.* College Park, Maryland: National Archives and Records Administration, 1999. 20 microfilm.

United States. Immigration and Naturalization Service. *Passenger Lists of Vessels Arriving at San Pedro/Wilmington/Los Angeles, California, June 29, 1907–June 30, 1948:* Record Group 85, M1764. Washington, D.C.: National Archives and Records Administration, 1998. 18 microfilm.

United States. *Immigration and Naturalization Service. Registers of Chinese Laborers Arriving at San Francisco, 1882–1888.* Washington, D.C.: The National Archives, 1988. 12 microfilm.

Land

Avina, Rose Hollenbaugh. *Spanish and Mexican Land Grants in California.* New York: Arno Press, 1976.

Bowman, J. N. *Index to the Spanish-Mexican Private Land Grant Records and Cases of California.* Bancroft Library, University of California, 1970.

California. Surveyor-general's Office. *Spanish Archives, 1833–1845.* Microfilm of original records at the State Archives, Sacramento, California. Salt Lake City: Filmed by the Genealogical Society of Utah, 1975. 14 microfilm.

Cowan, Robert Granniss. *Ranchos of California: A List of Spanish Concessions, 1775–1822, and Mexican Grants, 1822–1846.* Fresno, California: Academy Library Guild, 1956.

Deeter, Judy A. *Veterans Who Applied for Land in Southern California 1851–1911.* The author, Mission Viejo, California, 1993.

Lingenfelter Collection (California). *Northern California Bounty Land Grantees under Acts of 1847–1855.* Microfilm of originals in the Meriam Library, Special Collections, California State University, Chico, California. Salt Lake City: Filmed by the Genealogical Society of Utah, 1990.

Shumway, Burgess McK. *California Ranchos: Patented Private Land Grants Listed by County.* Edited by Michael and Mary Burgess. Athens, Georgia: Iberian Publishing Co., 1941.

United States. District Court (California: Northern District). *Private Land-Grant Case Files in the Circuit Court of*

the Northern District of California, 1852–1910. Microfilm of original records located in the Bancroft Library, Berkeley, California. Washington, D.C.: The National Archives, 1988. 28 microfilm.

United States. Land Office (Los Angeles, California). *Land Records, 1851–1936.* Microfilm of records located at the National Archives, Pacific Southwest Region Office, Laguna Niguel, California. Salt Lake City: Filmed by the Genealogical Society of Utah, 1989. 61 microfilm.

Military

Breithaupt, Richard Hoag, Jr. *Sons of the Revolution in the State of California, Centennial Register, 1893–1993.* Universal City, California: Walika, 1994.

California. Adjunct General's Office. *Records of California Men in the War of the Rebellion, 1861 to 1867.* Sacramento, California: State Office, 1890.

California. Adjutant General's Office. *California Military Records in the State Archives, 1858–1923.* Microfilm of original records at the State Archives, Sacramento, California. Salt Lake City: Filmed by the Genealogical Society of Utah, 1975. 35 microfilm.

California. State Council of Defense. *Records of Californians Who Served in World War I.* Microfilm of original records at the California State Library. Salt Lake City: Filmed by the Genealogical Society of Utah, 1975. 17 microfilm.

Carr, Elmer J. *Honorable Remembrance: The San Diego Master List of the Mormon Battalion.* S.l.: s.n., 1978.

Harlow, Neal. *California Conquered: War and Peace on the Pacific, 1846–1850.* Berkeley, California: University of California Press, 1982.

MacFarland, Olive K. H. *War Service Records, 1914–1919, California Chapters, Daughters of the American Revolution.* Salt Lake City: Filmed by the Genealogical Society of Utah, 1995. 14 microfiches.

Orton, Richard H. *Records of California Men in the War of the Rebellion, 1861 to 1867.* Tucson, Arizona: Filmed by W.C. Cox, 1974.

Pompey, Sherman L. *A List of Mexican War Veterans Buried in California.* Fresno, California: Sherman L. Pompey, 1968.

Sánchez, Joseph P. *Spanish Bluecoats, The Catalonian Volunteers in Northwestern New Spain, 1767–1810.* Albuquerque, New Mexico: University of New Mexico Press, 1990.

Thompson, J. S. *Records of the Mormon Battalion.* Microfilm of original published: Reno, Nevada: J.S. Thompson, 1995. Salt Lake City: Filmed by the Genealogical Society of Utah, 1995.

United States. Adjutant General's Office. *Index to Compiled Service Records of Volunteer Soldiers Who Served During Indian Wars and Disturbances, 1815–1858.* Washington, D.C.: The National Archives, 1966. 42 microfilm.

United States. Army. Military Department. *Records of the 10th Military Department, 1846–1851.* Washington, D.C.: The National Archives, 1955. 7 microfilm.

United States. District Court California: Southern District: Central Division. *Index Cards to Overseas Military Petitions of U.S. District Court for the Southern District of California, Central Division, Laguna Niguel.* Microfilm of original index cards located in the National Archives, Los Angeles Branch, Laguna Niguel, California. Salt Lake City: Filmed by the Genealogical Society of Utah, 1989. 2 microfilm.

United States. Selective Service System. *California, World War I Selective Service System Draft Registration Cards, 1917–1918.* Washington, D. C.: The National Archives, 1987–1988. 158 microfilm.

Vital and Cemetery

Bruner, Helen Maria. *California's Old Burying Grounds: Prepared for the National Society of Colonial Dames Resident in the State of California.* Tucson, Arizona: W.C. Cox Co., 1974.

California Death Records. The California Department of Health Services Office of Health Information and Research vital Statistics Section. http://vitals.rootsweb.com/ca/death/search.cgi, 1998–2001.

California State Library (Sacramento). *List of Deaths Copied from Records in the California State Library.* Sacramento: California State Library, n.d.

California State Library (Sacramento). *Mortuary Records 1849–1900 (Northern California).* Microfilm of card file located in Special Collections, California State Library, Sacramento. Salt Lake City: Filmed by the Genealogical Society of Utah, 1991. 13 microfilm.

California State Library (Sacramento). *Vital Statistics Index, California State Library, Sacramento, California: ca. 1800's–1920.* Microfilm of card file located in Special Collections, California State Library, Sacramento, California. Salt Lake City: Filmed by the Genealogical Society of Utah, 1991. 10 microfilm.

California State Register. *California Vital Records Indexes.* Sacramento, California: Office of the State Registrar, 1983. Microfiche.

California. Department of Public Health. *California Death Index, 1940–1990.* Sacramento, California: Office of State Registrar, 1991. 524 microfiche.

California. State Registrar. *California Marriage Records Indexes, 1960–1985.* Sacramento, California: Office of the State Registrar, 1983. 664 microfiches.

California. State Registrar. *Index to Deaths, 1905–1988.* Microfilm of records located at the Office of the State Registrar, Sacramento, and at the Butte County Courthouse, Oroville. Salt Lake City: Filmed by the Genealogical Society of Utah, 1990. 7 microfilm.

Cemetery Records of California. 11 vols. Typescript. Salt Lake City: Genealogical Society of Utah, 1954–63.

Culbertson, Judi. *Permanent Californians: An Illustrated Guide to the Cemeteries of California.* Chelsea, Vermont: Chelsea Green Pub. Co., 1989.

Daughters of the American Revolution (California). *Vital Records from Cemeteries in California, to 1962.* Salt Lake City: Filmed by the Genealogical Society of Utah, 1968. 4 microfilm.

Graves and Sites on the Oregon and California Trails: A Chapter in OCTA's Efforts to Preserve the Trails. Independence, Missouri: Oregon-California Trails Association, 1991.

Historical Records Survey (California*). Guide to Public Vital Statistics Records in California.* San Francisco: Northern California Historical Records Survey, 1941.

Kit, Elizabeth Gorrell and Shirley Pugh Thompson. *California Cemetery Inscription Sources: Print and Microform.* Vallejo, California: Indices Publishing, 1994.

Morebeck, Nancy Justus. *Northern California Marriage Index 1850–1860.* Vacaville, California: Nancy Justus Morebeck, 1993.

Nicklas, Laurie. *California County Courthouse Records: A Directory of Vital Records Found in Each County Office in California.* Modesto, California: L. Nicklas, 1998.

Oregon-California Trails Association (Independence, Missouri). *Graves and Sites on the Oregon and California Trails: A Chapter in OCTA's Efforts to Preserve the Trails.* Independence, Missouri: Oregon-California Trails Association, 1991.

Paradise Genealogical Society. *Genealogical Library Collection Shelf List, Paradise Genealogical Society.* Paradise, California: Paradise Gen. Soc., 1995.

Parker, J. Carlyle. *A Personal Name Index to Orton's "Records of California Men in the War of the Rebellion, 1861 to 1867.* (1978). Reprint. Turlock, California: Marietta Pub. Co., 1994.

Parker, Jimmy B. *Vital Records (Births and Deaths) of Indians of Round Valley Agency 1890–1899, 1906–1915, 1924.* Salt Lake City: Genealogical Society, 1972.

County Website	Map Index	Date Created	Parent County or Territory From Which Organized Address/Details
Alameda www.co.alameda.ca.us/	H4	25 Mar 1853	**Contra Costa, Santa Clara** Alameda County; 1106 Madison St; Rm 101; Oakland, CA 94607; Ph. (510) 272-6362 **Details:** (County Clerk has Marriage Records from 1854, Probate, Divorce, Court & land Records from 1853, Birth Records 1919–1988 [some from 1873] & Death Records 1905–1988 [some from 1876])
Alpine www.alpinecountyca.com	G6	16 Mar 1864	**El Dorado, Amador, Calaveras, Mono, Tuolumne** Alpine County; 99 Water St; PO Box 158; Markleeville, CA 96120; Ph. (530) 694-2281 **Details:** (County Clerk has Marriage & Naturalization Records; County Recorder has Birth, Death, Marriage, Maps, Land, & Tax Records; Court Clerk has Divorce, Probate, & Court Records; Archives has Historical Records, Census, & Newspapers)
Amador www.co.amador.ca.us/	G5	11 May 1854	**Calaveras, El Dorado** Amador County; 500 Argonaut Ln; Jackson, CA 95642; Ph. (209) 223-6468 **Details:** (Clerk Superior Court has Divorce, Probate & Court Records; County Archives has Naturalization Records; County Clerk has Birth & Death Records from 1872)
Branciforte		18 Feb 1850	**Original county** Branciforte County; CA **Details:** (see Santa Cruz) Name changed to Santa Cruz 5 Apr 1850
Butte www.buttecounty.net/	F4	18 Feb 1850	**Original county** Butte County; 25 County Center Dr; Oroville, CA 95965; Ph. (530) 538-7691 **Details:** (County Recorder has Marriage Records from 1851, Birth & Death Records from 1859 & land Records; County Clerk has Divorce, Probate & Court Records from 1850; Meriam Library, CA State University, Chico, has Divorce, Probate & Court Records 1850–1879 & Naturalization Records 1850–1960)
Calaveras www.co.calaveras.ca.us/	H5	18 Feb 1850	**Original county** Calaveras County; 891 Mountain Ranch Rd; San Andreas, CA 95249; Ph. (209) 754-6376 **Details:** (County Recorder has Birth Records from 1860, Marriage, Death & Divorce Records from 1882, Probate & Court Records from 1866, land Records from 1852 & mining claims from 1850)
Colusa www.cagenweb.com/colusa/	F3	18 Feb 1850	**Original county** Colusa County; 546 Jay St; Colusa, CA 95932-2443; Ph. (530) 458-0500 **Details:** (Spelling changed 1854 to Colusa from Colusi; Colusa County was created in 1850 but attached to Butte County for administration until it was organized in Jan 1851; From 1850 to 1854 county was spelled Colusi) (County Clerk has Birth Records from 1873, Marriage Records from 1853, Death Records from 1889, Probate, Court, land & assessment rolls from 1851, Great Registers from 1866 & Military rolls
Contra Costa www.co.contra-costa.ca.us/	H3	18 Feb 1850	**Original county** Contra Costa County; 730 Las Juntas St; PO Box 350; Martinez, CA 94553; Ph. (925) 646-2360 **Details:** (County Recorder has Birth & Death Records; County Clerk has Marriage, Divorce, Probate & Court Records)

County Website	Map Index	Date Created	Parent County or Territory From Which Organized Address/Details
Coso		1864	**Inyo** Coso County; CA **Details:** Former name for Inyo County 1864–1866
Del Norte www.co.del-norte.ca.us/	B1	2 Mar 1857	**Klamath** Del Norte County; 981 H St; Crescent City, CA 95531; Ph. (707) 464-7204 **Details:** (County Clerk has Divorce, Probate & Court Records from 1848; County Recorder has Birth, Marriage, & Death Records from 1873, land Records from 1853, leases & agreements 1857–1954)
El Dorado www.co.el-dorado.ca.us/	G5	18 Feb 1850	**Original county** El Dorado County; 360 Fair Ln; Placerville, CA 95667; Ph. (530) 621-5490 **Details:** (County Clerk has Divorce, Probate & Court Records; County Recorder has Birth, Marriage, Death, Burial, land & Military Records)
Fresno www.fresno.ca.gov/portal/Default.asp	J6	19 Apr 1856	**Merced, Mariposa, Tulare** Fresno County; 2221 Kern St; Fresno, CA 93721; Ph. (559) 488-3003 **Details:** (County Clerk has Birth, Marriage, & Death Records from 1855)
Glenn www.countyofglenn.net	E3	11 Mar 1891	**Colusa** Glenn County; 526 W Sycamore St; PO Box 391; Willows, CA 95988; Ph. (530) 934-6400 **Details:** (County Clerk has Birth, Death, Deeds, Marriage, Passport, & Other Historical Records)
Humboldt www.co.humboldt.ca.us/	D1	12 May 1853	**Trinity, Klamath** Humboldt County; 825 5th St; Eureka, CA 95501; Ph. (707) 476-2384 **Details:** (County Clerk has Divorce, Probate & Court Records from 1853; County Recorder has Birth, Marriage, Death, Burial & land Records)
Imperial www.co.imperial.ca.us/	O11	6 Aug 07	**San Diego** Imperial County; 940 W Main St; El Centro, CA 92243; Ph. (760) 482-4220 **Details:** (County Clerk has Marriage, Divorce, Probate & Court Records from 1907; County Recorder has Birth, Marriage, & Death Records from 1907)
Inyo www.countyofinyo.org/	J8	22 Mar 1866	**Tulare, Mono** Inyo County; 168 N Edwards St; PO Box F; Independence, CA 93526; Ph. (760) 878-0218 **Details:** (Formerly Coso County, 1864–1866) (County Clerk has Birth & Death Records from 1904, Marriage & land Records from 1866 & mining Records from 1872)
Kern www.co.kern.ca.us/	L7	2 Apr 1866	**Tulare, Los Angeles** Kern County; 1655 Chester Ave; Bakersfield, CA 93301; Ph. (661) 868-6400 **Details:** (County Clerk-Recorder has Birth, Marriage, Death & land Records from 1850, Divorce, Probate, Court & Register Voting Records from 1866; An exchange of territory with San Bernardino County took place in 1963)

County Website	Map Index	Date Created	Parent County or Territory From Which Organized Address/Details
Kings www.countyofkings.com/	K6	**22 Mar 1893**	**Tulare** Kings County; 1400 W Lacey Blvd; Hanford, CA 93230; Ph. (559) 582-3211 **Details:** (County Clerk has Birth, Marriage, Death, Divorce, Probate, Court, land & Naturalization Records from 1893)
Klamath		**25 Apr 1851**	**Original county** Klamath County; CA **Details:** (Dissolved 28 Mar 1874)
Lake www.co.lake.ca.us/cntyhome.html	F3	**20 May 1861**	**Napa** Lake County; 255 N Forbes St; Lakeport, CA 95453; Ph. (707) 263-2368 **Details:** (County Recorder holds Birth, Death, Land, Property, Marriage, & Military Records; Assessor has Land Records; Cemetery District has Burial & Cemetery Records; County Clerk has Ficticious Business Name Statements; Superior Court has Court, Divorce, Probate, Guardianship, & Newspaper Records; Tax Collector has Tax Records; Museum has other Historical Records)
Lassen www.cagenweb.com/tp/lassen/	D5	**1 Apr 1864**	**Plumas, Shasta** Lassen County; 220 S Lassen St, Ste 5; Susanville, CA 96130; Ph. (530) 251-8234 **Details:** (County Clerk has Divorce, Probate, Court & Naturalization Records from 1864; County Recorder has Marriage Records from 1864, land Records from 1857, Birth & Death Records from 1907, some prior to 1907 but incomplete before 1929)
Los Angeles www.co.la.ca.us/	M8	**18 Feb 1850**	**Original county** Los Angeles County; 12400 E Imperial Hwy; PO Box 1024; Norwalk, CA 90650; Ph. (562) 462-2137 **Details:** (County Clerk has Divorce Records from 1880, Probate & Court Records from 1850; County Recorder has Birth, Marriage, Death & land Records)
Madera www.madera-county.com/	I6	**11 Mar 1893**	**Fresno** Madera County; 209 W Yosemite Ave; Madera, CA 93637; Ph. (559) 675-7700 **Details:** (County Clerk has Birth, Marriage, Death, Divorce, Probate, Court & land Records from 1893 & some voting Records)
Marin www.marin.org/	H2	**18 Feb 1850**	**Original county** Marin County; 3501 Civic Center Dr; San Rafael, CA 94903; Ph. (415) 499-6094 **Details:** (County Recorder has Birth & Death Records from 1863, Marriage Records from 1856, land Records from 1852; County Clerk has Divorce & Court Records from 1900 & Probate Records from 1880)
Mariposa www.mariposacounty.org/	I6	**18 Feb 1850**	**Original county** Mariposa County; 5100 Bullion St; PO Box 35; Mariposa, CA 95338; Ph. (209) 966-5719 **Details:** (County Clerk has Divorce, Probate & Court Records; County Recorder has Birth, Marriage, Death, & Burial Records)

County	Map	Date	Parent County or Territory From Which Organized
Website	Index	Created	Address/Details

Mendocino   F2   18 Feb 1850   **Original county**
www.co.mendocino.ca.us/

Mendocino County; 501 Low Gap Rd Rm 1090; Ukiah, CA 95482; Ph. (707) 463-4221
Details: (Superior Court has Divorce & Court Records from 1858 & Probate Records from 1872; County Recorder has Birth, Marriage, Death, & land Records) (Some old Records in Sonoma County)

Merced   I5   19 Apr 1855   **Mariposa**
www.co.merced.ca.us/

Merced County; 2222 M St; Merced, CA 95340; Ph. (209) 385-7627
Details: (County Clerk has Divorce, Probate & Court Records from 1855; County Recorder has Birth, Marriage, Death, & Burial Records)

Modoc   C5   17 Feb 1874   **Siskiyou**
www.rh2o.com/modoc/

Modoc County; 204 Court St; PO Box 131; Alturas, CA 96101-0131; Ph. (530) 233-6205
Details: (County Clerk has Divorce, Probate, Court & voter Registration Records from 1874; County Recorder has Birth, Marriage, & Death Records)

Mono   H7   24 Apr 1861   **Calaveras, Fresno**
www.monocounty.org/

Mono County; Bryant Annex 2; PO Box 537; Bridgeport, CA 93517; Ph. (760) 932-5241
Details: (County Clerk has Birth & Marriage Records from 1861, Death, Burial, Divorce, Probate, Court & land Records from 1900)

Monterey   K4   18 Feb 1850   **Original county**
www.co.monterey.ca.us/

Monterey County; 240 Church St; PO Box 29, 240 Church St; Salinas, CA 93902; Ph. (831) 755-5041
Details: (County Recorder has Birth & Death Records & Marriage Records from 1893; Clerk Superior Court has Probate & land Records; County Court has Divorce & Court Records)

Napa   G3   18 Feb 1850   **Original county**
www.co.napa.ca.us/internet/

Napa County; 900 Coombs; PO Box 298; Napa, CA 94559-0298; Ph. (707) 253-4246
Details: (County Clerk-Recorder has Birth & Death Records from 1873, Marriage & land Records from 1850; Court Executive Officer has Divorce, Probate & Court Records from 1850)

Nevada   F5   25 Apr 1851   **Yuba**
www.mynevadacounty.com/

Nevada County; 950 Maidu Ave; Nevada City, CA 95959; Ph. (530) 265-1221
Details: (County Clerk has Birth, & Death Records from 1873, Marriage & land Records from 1856, Divorce, Probate & Court Records from 1880)

Orange   N8   11 Mar 1889   **Los Angeles**
www.oc.ca.gov/

Orange County; 12 Civic Center Pl; Santa Ana, CA 92701; Ph. (714) 834-2500
Details: (County Recorder has Birth, Marriage, Death & land Records; County Clerk has Divorce, Probate & Court Records from 1964)

Placer   F5   25 Apr 1851   **Yuba, Sutter**
www.placer.ca.gov/

Placer County; 2954 Richardson Dr; Auburn, CA 95603; Ph. (530) 886-5600
Details: (County Clerk-Recorder has Birth, Marriage, & Death Records from 1873 & land Records from 1850; County Clerk has Probate Records from 1851 & Court Records from 1880)

County Website	Map Index	Date Created	Parent County or Territory From Which Organized Address/Details
Plumas www.countyofplumas.com/	E5	**18 Mar 1854**	**Butte** Plumas County; 520 Main St; Quincy, CA 95971; Ph. (530) 283-6218 **Details:** (County Clerk has Divorce Records from 1860; County Recorder has Birth, Marriage, Death, Probate, Court & land Records from 1860; County Museum Archive has biographies and photographs)
Riverside www.co.riverside.ca.us/	N10	**11 Mar 1893**	**San Diego, San Bernardino** Riverside County; 4080 Lemon St 1st Fl; PO Box 12004; Riverside, CA 92502; Ph. (909) 486-7000 **Details:** (County Clerk-Recorder has Birth, Marriage, Death & land Records from 1893; Superior Court has Divorce, Probate & Court Records from 1893)
Sacramento www.co.sacramento.ca.us/	G4	**18 Feb 1850**	**Original county** Sacramento County; 600 8th St; PO Box 839; Sacramento, CA 95812-0893; Ph. (916) 874-6334 **Details:** (County Clerk has Divorce, Probate & Court Records from 1880; County Recorder has Birth, Marriage, Death & land Records)
San Benito www.san-benito.ca.us/	J4	**12 Feb 1874**	**Monterey** San Benito County; 440 5th St 2nd Fl; Hollister, CA 95023; Ph. (831) 636-4029 **Details:** (County Clerk has Birth, Marriage, Death, Burial, land & Naturalization Records from 1894; Superior Court has Divorce, Probate & Court Records)
San Bernardino www.co.san-bernardino.ca.us/	L10	**26 Apr 1853**	**Los Angeles, San Diego** San Bernardino County; 22 W Hospitality Ln; San Bernardino, CA 92415; Ph. (909) 387-8306 **Details:** (County Clerk has Marriage Licenses from 1887, Divorce & Probate Records from 1856, Court Records from 1853 & land Records from 1854; County Recorder has Birth & Death Records from 1853 & Marriage Records from 1857)
San Diego www.co.san-diego.ca.us/	O9	**18 Feb 1850**	**Original county** San Diego County; 1600 Pacific Hwy; San Diego, CA 92101; Ph. (619) 238-8158 **Details:** (County Clerk-Recorder has Birth Records from 1857, Marriage Records from 1856, Death Records from 1873 & land Records from 1850's; Superior Court has Probate, Court & Divorce Records)
San Francisco www.ci.sf.ca.us/	H3	**18 Feb 1850**	**Original county** San Francisco County; 1 Dr Carlton B Goodlett Pl; San Francisco, CA 94102; Ph. (415) 554-4950 **Details:** (Superior Court Clerk has Divorce, Probate & Court Records; County Recorder has Marriage Records; Department of Public Health has Birth Records)
San Joaquin www.co.san-joaquin.ca.us/	H4	**18 Feb 1850**	**Original county** San Joaquin County; 24 S Hunter St #304; PO Box 1968; Stockton, CA 95201; Ph. (209) 468-8075 **Details:** (County Clerk has Divorce, Probate & Court Records from 1851; County Recorder has Birth, Marriage, Death & land Records)

California

County Website	Map Index	Date Created	Parent County or Territory From Which Organized Address/Details
San Luis Obispo L5 www.sloclerkrecorder.org		**18 Feb 1850**	**Original county** San Luis Obispo County; 1055 Monterey St Rm D120 Government Center; San Luis Obispo, CA 93408; Ph. (805) 781-5080 **Details:** (County Clerk-Recorder has Birth Records from 1873, Death, Land, & Marriage Records from 1850, Census, Divorce, Guardianship, Immigration, Naturalization, Newspapers, Probate, & Tax Records)
San Mateo I3 www.co.sanmateo.ca.us/		**19 Apr 1856**	**San Francisco** San Mateo County; 400 County Center; Redwood City, CA 94063; Ph. (650) 363-4712 **Details:** (County Clerk-Recorder has Birth, Marriage, & Death Records from 1866, Divorce, Court & land Records from 1880 & Probate Records from 1856)
Santa Barbara M6 www.countyofsb.org/index.asp		**18 Feb 1850**	**Original county** Santa Barbara County; 105 E Anapamu Rm #204; Santa Barbara, CA 93101; Ph. (805) 568-2550 **Details:** (Superior Court has Divorce, Probate, Court & Naturalization Records; County Clerk-Recorder has Birth, Marriage, Death & land Records from 1850)
Santa Clara I4 www.co.santa-clara.ca.us/		**18 Feb 1850**	**Original county** Santa Clara County; 70 W Hedding St 1st Fl; San Jose, CA 95110-1768; Ph. (408) 299-2481 **Details:** (County Recorder has Birth & Death Records from 1873, Marriage Records from 1850, land Records from 1846 & Military Records from 1920; County Clerk has Divorce, Probate & Naturalization Records)
Santa Cruz I3 www.co.santa-cruz.ca.us/		**18 Feb 1850**	**Original county** Santa Cruz County; 701 Ocean St; Santa Cruz, CA 95060; Ph. (831) 454-2800 **Details:** (Formerly Branciforte County. Name changed to Santa Cruz 5 Apr 1850) (County Recorder has Marriage & land Records from 1850, Birth & Death Records from 1905 & Military Records from 1930; Clerk Superior Court has Divorce, Probate & Court Records)
Shasta D3 www.co.shasta.ca.us/		**18 Feb 1850**	**Original county** Shasta County; 1643 Market St; PO Box 990880; Redding, CA 96099; Ph. (530) 225-5730 **Details:** (County Clerk has Divorce, Probate & Court Records from 1880; County Recorder has Birth, Marriage, & Death Records)
Sierra E5 www.sierracounty.ws/index.shtml		**16 Apr 1852**	**Yuba** Sierra County; 100 Courthouse Sq Ste 11; PO Box D; Downieville, CA 95936; Ph. (530) 289-3295 **Details:** (County Recorder has Birth Records from 1857, Marriage & land Records from 1852 & Death Records from 1862; Superior Court has Divorce, Probate, Court & Naturalization Records from 1852)

County Website	Map Index	Date Created	Parent County or Territory From Which Organized Address/Details
Siskiyou www.co.siskiyou.ca.us/	**C3**	**22 Mar 1852**	**Shasta, Klamath** Siskiyou County; 311 Fourth St; PO Box 338; Yreka, CA 96097; Ph. (530) 842-8065 **Details:** (County Recorder has Birth, Marriage, Death & Burial Records; Court Services has Divorce, Probate & Court Records from 1853; County Clerk has Election Records, Board of Supervisor's minutes from 1860)
Solano www.co.solano.ca.us/	**G3**	**18 Feb 1850**	**Original county** Solano County; 701 Texas St; Fairfield, CA 94533; Ph. (707) 421-6265 **Details:** (County Recorder has Birth, Marriage, Death & land Records; County Clerk has Divorce, Probate & Court Records from 1850)
Sonoma www.sonoma-county.org/	**G2**	**18 Feb 1850**	**Original county** Sonoma County; 2300 County Center Dr; LaPlaza Building B177; Santa Rosa, CA 95403; Ph. (707) 565-3800 **Details:** (County Recorder has Birth, Marriage, Death, Burial & land Records; County Clerk has Divorce, Probate & Court Records from 1850)
Stanislaus www.co.stanislaus.ca.us/	**H4**	**1 Apr 1854**	**Tuolumne** Stanislaus County; 1021 I St; Modesto, CA 95354; Ph. (209) 525-5250 **Details:** (County Clerk-Recorder has Marriage Records from 1870, Birth & Death Records from 1900; Clerk Superior Court has Divorce, Probate & Court Records from 1854; County Recorder has land Records from 1854)
Sutter www.co.sutter.ca.us/	**F4**	**18 Feb 1850**	**Original county** Sutter County; 433 2nd St; Yuba City, CA 95992; Ph. (530) 822-7120 **Details:** (County Clerk-Recorder has Birth & Death Records from 1873, Marriage, land & Military Records from 1850; Civil Division of Courts has Divorce, Probate & Court Records)
Tehama www.co.tehama.ca.us	**E3**	**9 Apr 1856**	**Colusa, Butte, Shasta** Tehama County; 633 Washington St Room 11; PO Box 250; Red Bluff, CA 96080; Ph. (530) 527-3350 mageorge@co.tehama.ca.us **Details:** (Court Records are available at Superior Court)
Trinity www.trinitycounty.org/	**E2**	**18 Feb 1850**	**Original county** Trinity County; 101 Court St; PO Box 1258; Weaverville, CA 96093; Ph. (530) 623-1215 **Details:** (County Recorder has Birth & Death Record indexes 1873–1905, Birth & Death Records from 1905, Marriage Record indexes 1857–1905, Marriage Records from 1905 & Naturalization Records 1850–1940; Court Services has Divorce & Court Records from 1881, Probate Records from 1887 & land Records)
Tulare www.co.tulare.ca.us/	**K7**	**20 Apr 1852**	**Mariposa** Tulare County; 221 S Mooney Blvd; Visalia, CA 93291; Ph. (559) 733-6418 **Details:** (County Clerk-Recorder has Birth & Marriage Records from 1852, Death Records from 1873 & Military Records from 1919; Clerk Superior Court has Divorce, Probate, Court & Naturalization Records; County Assessor has land Records)

California

County	Map	Date	Parent County or Territory From Which Organized
Website	Index	Created	Address/Details

Tuolumne   H6   **18 Feb 1850**   **Original county**
www.tuolumnecounty.com/

Tuolumne County; 2 S Green St; Sonora, CA 95370-4679;
Ph. (209) 533-5570
Details: (County Clerk-Recorder has Birth Records from 1858, Marriage Records from 1850, Death Records from 1859, Burial Records from 1916, Divorce, Probate, Court & land Records from 1850 & old newspapers 1862–1948)

Ventura   M7   **22 Mar 1872**   **Santa Barbara**
www.countyofventura.org/dept.asp

Ventura County; 800 S Victoria Ave; Ventura, CA 93009;
Ph. (805) 654-2267
Details: (County Clerk-Recorder has Birth, Marriage, Death Records from 1873 & land Records from 1850; Clerk Superior Court has Divorce, Probate & Court Records from 1873; Some land went to Kern & Los Angeles Counties in boundary change)

Yolo   G3   **18 Feb 1850**   **Original county**
www.co.yolo.ca.us/

Yolo County; 625 Court St; PO Box 1130; Woodland, CA 95695;
Ph. (530) 666-8130
Details: (County Clerk has Birth, Marriage, Death & land Records, Divorce, Probate & Court Records from 1850)

Yuba   F4   **18 Feb 1850**   **Original county**
www.co.yuba.ca.us/

Yuba County; 935 14th St; Marysville, CA 95901; Ph. (530) 741-6547
Details: (County Clerk has Marriage Records from 1865, Divorce, Probate & Court Records from 1850 & voting Records from 1866)

Colorado

Capital: Denver

Territory: 1861

State: 1876 (38th)

Nothing without providence

Early Spanish explorers traveling through the Colorado area heard exciting tales of gold and silver from the Indians. Many treasure seekers searched throughout the Southwest and Rocky Mountain areas for these elusive fortunes. Spain and France alternated control until 1803 when all areas, except those south and west of the Arkansas River, were sold to the United States.

In 1806, Zebulon Pike was sent to explore the area. Others, such as Stephen Long in 1819 and John Fremont in 1842, also came. The remainder of present-day Colorado became part of the United States in 1848. Fur traders prospered in the area, but not until 1851 was the first town, San Luis, established. In 1854, Colorado was divided among the territories of Kansas, Nebraska, Utah, and New Mexico.

Settlement remained sparse until gold was discovered in 1858, when the Pikes Peak gold rush lured 50,000 people to Colorado. Denver, Golden, Boulder, and Pueblo were established as supply bases. The miners organized Arapaho County of the Kansas Territory in 1858. The following year the residents created the Territory of Jefferson, but Congress failed to recognize it.

The Territory of Colorado was finally organized in 1861, although some of its counties date their creation from 1859. The 1860 census for Colorado (then part of Kansas) shows 33,000 men and 1,500 women. During the Civil War, less than 5,000 men fought for the Union.

The completion of the transcontinental railroad in 1869 linked Colorado to both coasts and provided impetus for increased migration. Colorado gained statehood in 1876. The western part of the state was officially opened to settlement in 1881. Ute Indians were moved to reservations in Utah. At the time of the last major gold strike at Cripple Creek in 1890, the state boasted a population of 400,000.

Look for vital records in the following locations:

- **Birth and death records:** Vital Records Office, Colorado Department of Health holds state records from 1907. Search county and town clerk records between January 1876 and 1907.
- **Marriage records**: Kept by the county clerks from the organization of the county.
- **Divorce records**: Kept by the county clerks from the organization of the county. Probate records and wills are also in the offices of the county clerks, except for Denver, where there is a separate probate court.
- **Land records**: The first general land office in Colorado was established in 1863. Most land office records are at the National Archives, Denver Branch. County recorders kept private land records. Spanish land grants prior to 1862 were processed in the New Mexico Office. The U.S. Surveyor processed claims from 1855 to 1890.
- **Census records:** An 1860 Territorial Census was taken in the four territories of which Colorado was a part. The Utah part was not yet settled. The Nebraska part is listed under "unorganized territory." The Kansas part is listed in the Arapahoe County schedules, and the New Mexico part is listed in the Taos and Mora county schedules.

Vital Records Office Colorado Department of Health
4300 Cherry Creek Drive South
HSVRD-VR-A1
Denver, CO 80246-1530
(303) 692-2200
www.cdphe.state.co.us/hs/birth.html

Colorado State Archives
1313 Sherman, Room 1B20
Denver, CO 80203
(303) 866-2358; Fax: (303) 866-2257
www.colorado.gov/dpa/doit/archives/

Colorado

National Archives, Denver Branch
Denver Federal Center Building 48
West 6th Avenue and Kipling
Denver, Colorado 80225-0307
(303) 236-0817; Fax (303) 236-9354

Societies and Repositories

Archuleta County Genealogical Society; PO Box 1611;
Pagosa Springs, CO 81147;
www.rootsweb.com/~cosjhs/acgs.htm.

Aspen Historical Society; 620 West Bleeker Street; Aspen,
CO 81611.

Association of Professional Genealogists; PO Box 350998;
Westminster, CO 80035-0998; (303) 422-9371;
admin@apgen.org; www.apgen.org.

Aurora Genealogical Society of Colorado; PO Box 31732;
Aurora, CO 80041-0732.

Black Genealogical Search Group; PO Box 40674; Denver,
CO 80204-0674.

Black Genealogy Search Group/Blair-Caldwell African
American Research Library; 2401 Welton Street;
PO Box 40701; Denver, CO 80204-0701.

Boulder Genealogical Society; PO Box 3246; Boulder, CO
80307-3246; www.rootsweb.com/~bgs.

Boulder, Colorado Genealogical Group; 856 Applewood
Dr.; Lafayette, CO 80026.

Broomfield Genealogy Society; Broomfield, CO;
(303) 469-0724; rojam@prodigy.net;
www.rootsweb.com/~cobgs.

CGS/Computer Interest Group; 6437 W. Arbor Dr.;
Littleton, CO 80123-3927.

Colorado Association of Professional Genealogists;
PO Box 350877; West Minster, CO 80035-0877.

Colorado Chapter, Ohio Genealogical Society; Box 1106;
Longmont, CO 80502-1106.

Colorado Council of Genealogical Societies;
PO Box 40270; Denver, CO 80204-0270;
www.rootsweb.com/~coccgs.

Colorado Genealogical Society; PO Box 9218; Denver, CO
80209-0218.

Colorado High Plains Chapter, American Historical Society
of Germans from Russia; 530 Fairhurst; Sterling, CO
80751.

Colorado Springs Chapter, American Historical Society of
Germans from Russia; 70 Watch Hill Dr. Apt. A;
Colorado Springs, CO 80906-7935.

Colorado State Archives; 1313 Sherman Street—
Room 1B-20; Denver, CO 80203; (303) 866-2358;
archives@state.co.us;
www.colorado.gov/dpa/doit/archives/.

Colorado State Library; 201 East Colfax Avenue,
Room 309; Denver, CO 80203; (303) 866-6900;
www.cde.state.co.us/index_library.htm.

Columbine Genealogical and Historical Society, Inc.;
PO Box 2074; Littleton, CO 80161-2074;
(303) 841-3712; delliott@chisp.net;
www.rootsweb.com/~cocghs/index.htm.

Czech and Slovak Search Group; 209 S. Ogden; Denver,
CO 80209-2321.

Denver Metro Chapter, AHSGR; 13245 Grove Way;
Broomfield, CO 80020; rsandm@aol.com;
www.ahsgr.org/codenver.htm.

Eagle County Historical Society; PO Box 192; Eagle, CO
81631.

Foothills Genealogical Society of Colorado, Inc.;
PO Box 150382; Lakewood, CO 80215-0382;
Erskine@Ecentral.com; www.rootsweb.com/~cofgs.

Fore-Kin Trails Genealogical Society; 2392 E. Miami Rd.;
Montrose, CO 81401-6007.

Four Corners Genealogical Society; PO Box 2636;
Durango, CO 81302.

Fremont County Genealogical Society; Local History
Center CCPL; 516 Macon Ave.; Canon City, CO 81212.

Frontier Historical Society; 1001 Colorado Ave.;
Glenwood Springs, CO 81601.

Genealogical Research Society of Durango; 2720 Delwood;
Durango, CO 80301.

Genealogical Society of Hispanic America; PO Box 606;
Denver, CO 80209-0606.

Historical and Genealogical Researchers; PO Box 123;
Trinidad, CO 80456;
www.usgennet.org/usa/co/town/trinidad.

International Society for British Genealogy and Family
History; PO Box 350459; Westminster, CO 80035-0459;
www.isbgfh.org.

Jewish Genealogical Society of Colorado;
1982 S. Oneida St.; Denver, CO 80224.

Lafayette-Louisville Genealogical Society;
1022 S. Pegasus Pl.; Lafayette, CO 80026;
www.rootsweb.com/~collgs/index.html.

Larimer County Genealogical Society; PO Box 9502;
Fort Collins, CO 80505-9502; (970) 214-1618;
TyCCurtis@aol.com; http://jymis.com/~lcgs/index.htm.

Logan County Genealogical Society; PO Box 294; Sterling,
CO 80751.

Longmont Genealogical Society; PO Box 6081; Longmont,
CO 80501-2077; l-j-smith@prodigy.net;
www.rootsweb.com/~colgs/index.htm.

Longs Peak Chapter, COSSAR; CO;
JWSummers@aol.com.

Melon Valley Chapter, American Historical Society of
Germans from Russia; 708 So. 13th Street; Rocky Ford,
CO 81067-2132; (719) 254-3819.

Mesa County Genealogical Society; PO Box 1506;
Grand Junction, CO 81502-1506; www.gj.net/mcgs.

Mountain Genealogists Society; 25 Conifer Dr.; Evergreen,
CO 80439.

NARA, Rocky Mountain Region (Denver); Building 48-Denver Federal Center. West 6th Ave, Denver, CO 80225

Northern Colorado Chapter, American Historical Society of Germans from Russia; 1104 West Magnolia; Fort Collins, CO 80521; (970) 484-9771; ronfarm15@aol.com; www.ahsgr.org/conorthe.html.

Old Colorado City Historical Society; One South 24th Street; Colorado Springs, CO; history@oldcolo.com; http://history.oldcolo.com.

Palatines to America, Colorado Chapter; 7079 S. Marshall St.; Littleton, CO 80123-4607.

Pikes Peak Genealogical Society; PO Box 1262; Colorado Springs, CO 80901.

Prowers County Genealogical Society; PO Box 928; Lamar, CO 81052-0928.

Rio Blanco County Historical Society; 565 Park Street; PO Box 413; Meeker, CO 81641; (970) 878-9982; www.rootsweb.com/~coriobla/wrm.htm.

Rocky Mountain Jewish Historical Society; Center for Judaic Studies; 2000 East Asbury; Denver, CO 80208; nreichma@du.edu; www.du.edu/~ctrjuds/cjsrmjhs.html.

San Juan Historical Society; PO Box 1711; Pagosa Springs, CO 81147; www.rootsweb.com/~cosjhs/museum.htm

Sedgwick County Genealogy Society; PO Box 86; Julesburg, CO 80737; www.rootsweb.com/~cosedgwi/society.htm.

Sheridan Historical Society; 4101 S. Federal Blvd.; Sheridan, CO 80110-5399; www.rootsweb.com/~coshs.

Southeastern Colorado Genealogical Society, Inc.; PO Box 4207; Pueblo, CO 81003-0207.

Sons of the American Revolution, Colorado Society; 255 Moline St.; Aurora, CO 80010.

Summit Historical Society; 309 N. Main; PO Box 745; Breckenridge, CO 80424; rporter@amigo.net; http://summithistorical.org.

Ute Pass Historical Society; PO Box 6875; Woodland Park, CO 80866; Info@UtePassHistoricalSociety.org; www.utepasshistoricalsociety.org.

Weld County Genealogical Society; PO Box 278; Greeley, CO 80631; putnam@frii.com; www.rootsweb.com/~cowcgs.

White River Trace Genealogical Society; 425 12th St.; Meeker, CO 81641.

WISE Search Group; 1840 S. Wolcott Court; Denver, CO 80219-4309.

Yuma Area Genealogical Society; PO Box 24; Yuma, CO 80759.

Bibliography and Record Sources

General

Bauer, William, James L. Ozment, and John H. Willard. *Colorado Postal History: The Post Offices*. Crete, Nebraska: JB Publishing Co, 1971.

Bromwell, Henriette Elizabeth. *Colorado Portrait and Biography Index*. 4 vols. Denver, Colorado.: Western History Dept., Denver Public Library: Dakota Microfilm Service, 1979, [1982?].

Burdick, Liz and Kay Merrill. *Colorado Collections*. Microfilm. Salt Lake City: Genealogical Society of Utah, 1983.

Clint, Florence R. *Colorado Area Key, A Comprehensive Study of Genealogical Record Sources of Colorado, Including Maps and a Brief General History*. Fountain Valley, California: Eden Press, 1968.

Colorado Genealogical Society, Inc. *Surname Index to the Colorado Genealogist, Vols. 1–10* (1939–1949), Parts I and II. 1969. Microfiche.

Colorado Families: A Territorial Heritage. Denver: Colorado Genealogical Society, 1981.

Colorado Research Outline. Series US-State, no. 6. Salt Lake City: Family History Library. 1988.

Genealogical Index to the Records of the Society of Colorado Pioneers. Denver: Colorado Genealogical Society, Inc., 1990.

Oehlerts Donald E., *Guide to Colorado Newspapers, 1859–1963*. Denver: Bibliographical Center for Research, 1964.

Pioneers of the Territory of Southern Colorado. 4 vols. Monte Vista, Colorado: C.B.I. Offset Printers, 1980.

Portrait and Biographical Record of the State of Colorado: Containing Portraits and Biographies of Many Well Known Citizens of the Past and Present. 2 vol. Chicago: Chapman Pub. Co., 1899.

Subject Index to the Colorado Genealogist, Vols. 1–42 (1939-1981), Parts I and II. Denver: Colorado Genealogical Society, Inc. 1982. Microfiche.

Surname Index to the Colorado Genealogist, Vols. 11–20 (1950-1959), Parts I and II. Denver: Colorado Genealogical Society, Inc. 1974. Microfiche.

Surname Index to the Colorado Genealogist, Vols. 21–41 (1960-1980), Parts I and II. Denver: Colorado Genealogical Society, Inc. 1984. Microfiche.

Wynar, Bohdan S., and Roberta J. Depp, eds. *Colorado Bibliography*. Littleton, Colorado: Libraries Unlimited, 1980.

Atlases, Maps and Gazetteers

Bauer, William H., James L. Ozment, and John H. Willard. *Colorado Postal History: The Post Offices*. Crete, Nebraska: J-B Publishing Co., 1971.

Crofutt, George A. *A Crofutt's Grip Sack Guide to Colorado: A Complete Encyclopedia of the State, Resources and Condensed Authentic Descriptions of Every City, Town, Village, Station, Post Office and Important Mining Camp in the State*. 1885. 2nd ed. Boulder, Colorado: Johnson Books, 1981.

Dallas, Sandra. *Colorado Ghost Towns and Mining Camps*. Norman, Oklahoma: University of Oklahoma Press, 1985.

Dawson, J. Frank. *Place Names in Colorado.* Denver: J.F. Dawson Publishing Colorado, 1954.

Eichler, George R. *Colorado Place Names: Communities, Counties, Peaks, Passes ...* Boulder, Colorado: Johnson Pub., 1980.

Gannett, Henry. *A Gazetteer of Colorado.* Washington, D.C.: Government Printing Office, 1906.

Thorndale, William and William Dollarhide. *Map Guides to the U.S. Federal Censuses, 1790–1920: Colorado, 1860–1920.* Baltimore: Genealogical Publishing Co., 1987.

Censuses

Available Census Records and Census Substitutes

Federal Census 1860 (with Kansas), 1870, 1880, 1900, 1910, 1920

Federal Mortality Schedules 1870, 1880

State/Territorial Census 1885

Dollarhide, William. *The Census Book: A Genealogist's Guide to Federal Census Facts, Schedules and Indexes.* Bountiful, Utah: Heritage Quest, 1999.

Kemp, Thomas Jay. *The American Census Handbook.* Wilmington, Delaware: Scholarly Resources, Inc., 2001.

Lainhart, Ann S. *State Census Records.* Baltimore: Genealogical Publishing Co., 1992.

Szucs, Loretto Dennis and Matthew Wright. *Finding Answers in U.S. Census Records.* Ancestry Publishing, 2001.

Thorndale, William and William Dollarhide. *Map Guides to the U.S. Federal Censuses, 1790–1920: Colorado, 1860–1920.* Baltimore: Genealogical Publishing Co., 1987.

Court Records, Probate, and Wills

MacDougall, Ella Ruland. *Abstracts of Early Probate Records.* n.p., n.d.

United States. Works Progress Administration (Colorado*). Inventory of Federal Archives in the States, Series 02, Federal Courts, no. 6, Colorado.* Denver, Colorado: Colorado Historical Records Survey, 1939.

Immigration

Crayne-Trudell, Patricia. *Naturalization Records: Index to U.S. District Court—Denver, Colorado.* Lakewood, Colorado: Foothills Genealogical Society of Colorado, 1997.

Hafen, LeRoy R. ed. *Colorado and Its People: A Narrative and Topical History of the Centennial State. Vol. 2.* New York: Lewis Historical Publishing Co., 1948.

United States. District Court (Colorado). *Declarations of Intention, 1877–1952; Naturalization Dockets, 1906–1916; Petitions, 1906–1950; Miscellaneous Records, 1883–1922.* Washington, D.C.: National Archives. Central Plains Region, 1988. Microfilm, 79 rolls.

Land

Arapahoe County (Colorado). Recorder of Deeds. *Deed Records, 1860–1934.* Microfilm of original records at the Colorado State Archives in Denver, Colorado. Salt Lake City: Filmed by the Genealogical Society of Utah, 1992–1993. Microfilm, multiple rolls.

Beers, Henry Putney. *Spanish and Mexican Records of the American Southwest: A Bibliographic Guide to Archive and Manuscript Sources.* Tucson: University of Arizona Press, 1979. New Mexico (Territory).

Miscellaneous Archives Relating to New Mexico Land Grants, 1695–1842. Albuquerque, New Mexico: University of New Mexico Library, 1955–1957. Microfilm, 2 rolls.

New Mexico (Territory). Surveyor-General's Office. *Record of Private Land Claims Adjudicated by the U.S. Surveyor General, 1855–1890.* Albuquerque, New Mexico University of New Mexico Library, 1955–1957. Microfilm, 25 rolls.

New Mexico (Territory). Surveyor-General's Office. *Record of Private Land Claims Adjudicated By the U.S. Surveyor General, 1855–1890.* Albuquerque, New Mexico: University of New Mexico Library, 1955–1957.

Van Ness, John R., and Christine Van Ness. *Spanish and Mexican Land Grants in New Mexico and Colorado.* Manhattan, Kansas: AG Press, 1981.

Vigil, Donaciano. *Vigil's index, 1681–1846.* Albuquerque, New Mexico: University of New Mexico Library, 1955–1957.

Westphall, Victor. *Mercedes Reales: Hispanic Land Grants of the Upper Rio Grande Region.* Albuquerque, New Mexico: University of New Mexico Press, c1983.

Military

Colorado. National Guard. Military Affairs. *Civil War Index Cards, 1861–1865.* Microfilm of original records at the Colorado State Archives in Denver, Colorado. Salt Lake City: Filmed by the Genealogical Society of Utah, 1992. Microfilm, 4 rolls.

Harper, Frank. *Just Outside of Manila: Letters from Members of the First Colorado Regiment in the Spanish-American and Philippine-American Wars.* Denver, Colorado: Colorado Historical Society, 1992.

Hollister, Ovando James. *Colorado Volunteers in New Mexico, 1862.* Chicago: R. R. Donnelley, 1962.

Pompey, Sherman L. *Confederate Soldiers Buried in Colorado.* Independence, California: Historical and Genealogical Publishing Co., 1965. Each soldier is listed alphabetically under the state from which he served.

United States. Adjutant General's Office. *Index to Compiled Service Records of Volunteer Union Soldiers Who Served in Organizations from the Territory of Colorado.* Washington, D.C.: National Archives. Central Plains Region, 1964. Microfilm, 3 rolls.

United States. Selective Service System. *Colorado, World War I Selective Service System Draft Registration Cards, 1917–1918.* Washington, D.C.: The National Archives, 1987–1988. Microfilm, 41 rolls.

Williams, Ellen. *Three Years and a Half in the Army, or, History of the Second Colorados.* Washington, D.C.: Filmed by Library of Congress Photoduplication Service, 1976.

Vital and Cemetery

Colorado. Department of Health. *Statewide Marriage Index, 1900–1939, 1975–1992.* Denver: Colorado State Archives, 1975–1992. Microfilm, 106 rolls.

Colorado Genealogical Society. *Colorado Marriages 1858–1939* (CD-ROM).

Guide to Vital Statistics Records in Colorado, Vol. 2. Church Archives. Denver: Colorado Historical Records Survey W.P.A., 1942.

Historical Records Survey (Colorado). *Guide to Vital Statistics Records in Colorado.* 2 vols. Denver: The Survey, 1942.

Marriages of Arapahoe County, Colorado, 1859–1901: Including Territory That Became Adams, Denver, and Other Counties. Denver: Colorado Genealogical Society, 1986.

McQueary, Lela O. *Colorado Cemetery Inscriptions.* Englewood, Colorado: K. R. Merrill, 1987.

Merrill, Kay R. *Colorado Cemetery Directory*, Denver Colorado Council of Genealogical Societies, 1985.

Territorial Vital Records: Births, Divorces, Guardianship, Marriages, Naturalization, Wills; 1800s thru 1906 Utah Territory, AZ, CO, ID, NV, WY, Indian Terr.; LDS Branches, Wards; Deseret News Vital Recs.; J.P. Marriages; Meth. Marriages. St. George, Utah: Genealogical CD Publishing, 1994. 1 CD-ROM Disc.

Wommack, Linda. *From the Grave: A Roadside Guide to Colorado's Pioneer Cemeteries.* Caldwell, Idaho: Caxton Press, 1998.

County Website	Map Index	Date Created	Parent County or Territory From Which Organized Address/Details
Adams www.co.adams.co.us/	**G4**	**15 Apr 1901**	**Arapahoe** Adams County; 450 S 4th Ave; Brighton, CO 80601-3196; Ph. (303) 654-6020 **Details:** (County Clerk has Marriage & land Records from 1902, some Burial Records, some land Records from Arapahoe County prior to 1901, school census 1902–1964 & Military Discharge Records; 17th Judicial District Court Clerk has Divorce Records; Probate Court has Probate Records; Hall of Justice has Court Records)
Alamosa www.alamosacounty.org	**J10**	**8 Mar 1913**	**Costilla, Conejos** 402 Edison Ave.; PO Box 659; PO Box 630; Alamosa, CO 81101; Ph. (719) 589-3626/6681 ccockrum@alamosacounty.org hollylowder@alamosacounty.org **Details:** (County Clerk has Birth Records from 1900, Death Records from 1902, Land Records from 1890, Marriage & Military Records from 1913, Burial & Cemetery; Clerk of District Court has Court, Divorce, Guardianship, & Probate Records; Tax Rolls from 1913)
Arapahoe www.co.arapahoe.co.us/	**G5**	**1 Nov 1861**	**Original county, Kansas Territory** Arapahoe County; 5334 S Prince St; Littleton, CO 80166-0001; Ph. (303) 795-4200 **Details:** (First formed in 1855 as Territorial County. See Kansas 1860 for Census Records) (County Clerk has Marriage & land Records from 1902 & Burial Records to 1941; County Court has Divorce, Probate & Court Records)

County Website	Map Index	Date Created	Parent County or Territory From Which Organized Address/Details
Archuleta	M11	14 Apr 1885	**Conejos** Archuleta County; PO Box 2589; Pagosa Springs, CO 81147; Ph. (970) 264-5633 **Details:** (San Juan Basin Health Department has Birth & Death Records; Town has Burial Records; Clerk has Death Records, Land & Marriage Records from 1885; District Court has Divorce & Probate Records; Ruby Sisson Library has Newspapers; Assessor has Tax Records)
Baca www.rootsweb.com/~cobaca/	C11	16 Apr 1889	**Las Animas** Baca County; 741 Main St; Springfield, CO 81073-1548; Ph. (719) 523-4372 **Details:** (County Clerk has Marriage & land Records from 1889; Clerk District Court has Divorce, Probate & Court Records from 1910)
Bent www.rootsweb.com/~cobent/	D9	11 Feb 1870	**Greenwood, Pueblo** Bent County; PO Box 350; Las Animas, CO 81054-0350; Ph. (719) 456-1353 **Details:** (County Clerk-Recorder has Marriage & land Records from 1888 & Military Discharge Records; Nursing Service has Birth & Death Records; Combine Court has Divorce, Probate & Court Records)
Boulder www.co.boulder.co.us/	I4	1 Nov 1861	**Original county** Boulder County; 2020 13th St; PO Box 471; Boulder, CO 80302; Ph. (303) 441-7770 **Details:** (County Clerk-Recorder has Marriage Records from 1863, land Records from 1864 & Military Discharge Records from 1917; County Health Department has Birth & Death Records from 1872; County Court has Probate, Divorce & Court Records)
Broomfield www.ci.broomfield.co.us/	I4	15 Nov 2001	**Adams, Boulder, Jefferson, Weld** Broomfield County; One DesCombes Dr; Broomfield, CO 80020; Ph. (303) 438-6390 **Details:** (Colorado's newest county)
Carbonate		1 Nov 1861	**Original county** Carbonate County; CO **Details:** (see Lake County) Name changed to Lake 10 Feb 1879
Chaffee www.chaffeecounty.org	K7	1879	**Original county** Chaffee County; 132 Crestone Ave; PO Box 699; Salida, CO 81201-1566; Ph. (719) 539-2814 **Details:** (Formerly Lake County. Name changed to Chaffee 10 Feb 1879) (Judicial Building has Court Records; Other Offices have archives)
Cheyenne www.rootsweb.com/~cocheyen/index.htm	D7	25 Mar 1889	**Bent, Elbert** Cheyenne County; 615 N 5 W; PO Box 567; Cheyenne Wells, CO 80810; Ph. (719) 767-5685 **Details:** (Registrar has Birth, Death, & Burial Records; County Clerk has Marriage Records from 1889 & land Records from 1888; District Court has Divorce & Probate Records; County Judge has Court Records)

County	Map	Date	Parent County or Territory From Which Organized
Website	Index	Created	Address/Details

Clear Creek J5 **1 Nov 1861** **Original county**
www.co.clear-creek.co.us/
Clear Creek County; 405 Argentine St; Georgetown, CO 80444-2000;
Ph. (303) 679-2339
Details: (County Clerk has Marriage & land Records from 1862)

Conejos K11 **1 Nov 1861** **Original county**
www.rootsweb.com/~coconejo/
Conejos County; 6683 County Rd 13; PO Box 157; Conejos, CO
81129-0157; Ph. (719) 376-5422
Details: (Formerly Guadalupe County. Name changed to Conejos
7 Nov 1869) (Clerk of Courts has Probate Records; County Clerk has
Birth, Marriage, & Death Records; County Assessor has land Records)

Costilla I11 **1 Nov 1861** **Original county**
www.rootsweb.com/~cocostil/index.htm
Costilla County; 354 Main St; PO Box 100; San Luis, CO
81152-0100; Ph. (719) 672-3372
Details: (County Clerk has Marriage & land Records from 1853;
Clerk District Court has Divorce, Probate & Court Records)

Crowley F8 **29 May 1911** **Bent, Otero**
www.rootsweb.com/~cocrowle/
Crowley County; 110 E 6th St; Ordway, CO 81063-0000;
Ph. (719) 267-4643
Details: (County Clerk has Marriage & land Records)

Custer I9 **9 Mar 1877** **Fremont**
www.geocities.com/Heartland/Meadows/3456/
custer1.html
Custer County; 205 S 6th St; PO Box 150; Westcliffe, CO 81252;
Ph. (719) 783-0441
Details: (County Clerk has Marriage & Burial Records)

Delta N7 **11 Feb 1883** **Gunnison**
www.rootsweb.com/~codelta/
Delta County; 501 Palmer St; Delta, CO 81416-1753;
Ph. (970) 874-2150
Details: (County Clerk has Birth Records from 1920, Marriage,
Death & land Records from 1883 & School Census 1891–1964; Clerk
District Court has Divorce, Probate & Court Records)

Denver H5 **18 Mar 1901** **Arapahoe**
www.denvergov.org/
Denver County; 1437 Bannock St Ste 200; Denver, CO 80202;
Ph. (303) 640-3012
Details: (Has annexed territory from Arapahoe, Adams & Jefferson
Counties on several occasions) (County Clerk has Marriage Records
from 1902 & land Records from 1859; Clerk District Court has
Divorce Records from 1967, Probate & Court Records from 1858)

Dolores P10 **19 Feb 1881** **Ouray**
www.rootsweb.com/~codolore/index.html
Dolores County; 409 N Main St; PO Box 194; Dove Creek, CO
81324; Ph. (970) 677-2381
Details: (County Clerk has Birth & Death Records from 1894,
Marriage & land Records from 1881; County Court has Probate &
Court Records)

Douglas H6 **1 Nov 1861** **Original county**
www.douglas.co.us/
Douglas County; 301 Wilcox St; Castle Rock, CO 80104-2454;
Ph. (303) 660-7446;
Details: (County Clerk has Marriage Records from 1867 & land
Records from 1864)

County Website	Map Index	Date Created	Parent County or Territory From Which Organized Address/Details
Eagle www.eagle-county.com/	L5	11 Feb 1883	**Summit** Eagle County; 500 Broadway; Eagle, CO 81631-0850; Ph. (970) 328-8710 **Details:** (County Clerk has Birth & Marriage Records from 1883, Death & land Records; Clerk District Court has Divorce, Probate & Court Records)
El Paso www.elpasoco.com	G7	1 Nov 1861	**Original county, Kansas Territory** El Paso County; 200 S Cascade Ave; PO Box 2007; Colorado Springs, CO 80903; Ph. (719) 520-6216 **Details:** (Established 1859 as Kansas Territory) (Health Department has Birth Records from 1890 & Death Records from 1893; County Clerk has Marriage & Land Records from 1861 & Military Discharge Records from 1919; Clerk District Court has Divorce & Probate Records; County Court has Court Records)
Elbert www.rootsweb.com/~coelbert/	G6	2 Feb 1874	**Douglas, Greenwood** Elbert County; 215 Comanche St; Kiowa, CO 80117-0037; Ph. (303) 621-3129 **Details:** (County Clerk has Marriage Records from 1893 & land Records from 1874; Clerk of Combined Courts has Divorce, Probate & Court Records)
Fremont www.fremontco.com/	I8	1 Nov 1861	**Original county, Kansas Territory** Fremont County; 615 Macon Rm 100; Canon City, CO 81212; Ph. (719) 276-7330 **Details:** (Established as Kansas Territory in 1859) (County Clerk has Marriage & land Records; Clerk District Court has Divorce, Probate & Court Records)
Garfield www.garfield-county.com/	P5	10 Feb 1883	**Summit** Garfield County; 109 8th St Ste 200; Glenwood Springs, CO 81601; Ph. (970) 945-5004 **Details:** (County Clerk has Birth, Marriage, Death & land Records from 1883 & Military Records from 1910; District Court has Divorce, Probate & Court Records)
Gilpin http://stanwyck.com/CCGilpin/	I4	1 Nov 1861	**Original county** Gilpin County; 203 Eureka St; PO Box 366; Central City, CO 80427-0366; Ph. (303) 582-5321 **Details:** (County Clerk has Marriage Records from 1881 & land Records from 1861; Clerk District Court has Divorce & Probate Records)
Grand www.co.grand.co.us/	K4	2 Feb 1874	**Summit** Grand County; 308 Byers Ave; PO Box 264; Hot Sulphur Springs, CO 80451; Ph. (970) 725-3347 **Details:** (Local Registrar has Birth, Death & Burial Records; County & District Court has Divorce, Probate & Court Records; County Assessor has land Records; County Clerk has Marriage Records from 1874)
Greenwood		1870	**El Paso, Pueblo** Greenwood County; CO **Details:** County Terminated 1874. Bent and Elbert Counties formed from Greenwood

County Website	Map Index	Date Created	Parent County or Territory From Which Organized Address/Details
Guadalupe		1 Nov 1861	**Original county** Guadalupe County; CO **Details:** (see Conejos) Name changed to Conejos 7 Nov 1869
Gunnison www.co.gunnison.co.us/	M7	9 Mar 1877	**Lake** Gunnison County; 200 E Virginia Ave; Gunnison, CO 81230-2297; Ph. (970) 641-1516 **Details:** (County Clerk has Marriage Records from 1874 & land Records from 1879; Clerk County Court has Divorce & Probate Records from 1877 & Court Records from 1900; Gunnison Department of Social Services has Birth, Death, & Burial Records from 1910)
Hinsdale www.rootsweb.com/~cohinsda/	M9	10 Feb 1874	**Conejos** Hinsdale County; 317 N Henson St; Lake City, CO 81235-0277; Ph. (970) 944-2228 **Details:** (County Clerk has Marriage & land Records from 1875; County Court has Divorce, Probate & Court Records)
Huerfano www.rootsweb.com/~cohuerfa/	I10	1 Nov 1861	**Original county** Huerfano County; 401 Main St #204; Walsenburg, CO 81089-2034; Ph. (719) 738-2380 **Details:** (County Clerk has Marriage & land Records; Clerk District Court has Divorce, Probate & Court Records)
Jackson www.rootsweb.com/~cojackso/index.htm	K3	5 May 1909	**Grand, Larimer** Jackson County; PO Box 337; Walden, CO 80480; Ph. (970) 723-4334 **Details:** (County Clerk has Marriage & land Records from 1909; County Registrar has Birth & Death Records; Clerk District Court has Divorce, Probate & Court Records; County Cemetery Officer has Cemetery Records from 1909)
Jefferson http://206.247.49.21/ext/index.htm	I5	1 Nov 1861	**Original county** Jefferson County; 100 Jefferson City Pkwy #2530; Golden, CO 80419-2530; Ph. (303) 271-8168 **Details:** (County Clerk has Marriage Records from 1868 & land Records from 1860; County Health Department has Birth, Death, & Burial Records; Clerk District Court has Divorce Records; County Court has Probate & Court Records)
Kiowa www.kiowacountycolo.com/	D8	11 Apr 1889	**Cheyenne, Bent** Kiowa County; 1305 Goff; Eads, CO 81036-0000; Ph. (719) 943-8521 **Details:** (County Clerk has Marriage & land Records from 1889; Clerk District Court has Divorce, Probate & Court Records)
Kit Carson www.rootsweb.com/~cokitcar/index.htm	D6	11 Apr 1889	**Elbert** Kit Carson County; 251 16th St; Burlington, CO 80807-0249; Ph. (719) 346-8638 **Details:** (County Clerk has Marriage & land Records from 1889 & Burial Records from 1902; Clerk District Court has Birth, Death, Divorce, Probate & Court Records)
La Plata http://co.laplata.co.us/	N11	10 Feb 1874	**Conejos, Lake** La Plata County; 1060 E 2nd Ave; Durango, CO 81301-5157; Ph. (970) 382-6200 **Details:** (County Clerk has Marriage Records from 1878 & Land Records from 1876; Clerk District Court has Divorce & Probate Records; County Court has Court Records; San Juan Basin Health Department has Birth & Burial Records)

County Website	Map Index	Date Created	Parent County or Territory From Which Organized Address/Details
Lake www.usgw.org/co/lake/lake.html	K6	1 Nov 1861	**Original county** Lake County; 505 Harrison Ave; Leadville, CO 80461-0917; Ph. (719) 486-1410 **Details:** (Formerly Carbonate County. Name changed to Lake 1 Nov 1861) (County Clerk has Marriage Records from 1869, land Records from 1861 & some Burial Records 1885–1903; Clerk District Court has Divorce, Probate & Court Records)
Larimer www.co.larimer.co.us/	J2	1 Nov 1861	**Original county** Larimer County; 200 W Oak St; PO Box 1190; Fort Collins, CO 80522-1190; Ph. (970) 498-7860 **Details:** (County Clerk has Marriage & land Records from 1862; County Health Department has Birth & Death Records)
Las Animas www.usroots.com/~colorado/index.htm	G10	9 Feb 1866	**Huerfano** Las Animas County; 200 E 1st St; Trinidad, CO 81082; Ph. (719) 846-3314 **Details:** (County Clerk has Marriage Records from 1887, land Records from 1883 & Military Discharge Records from 1918; County Health Department has Birth & Death Records; Clerk District Court has Divorce, Probate & Court Records)
Lincoln www.rootsweb.com/~colincol/	E7	11 Apr 1889	**Elbert** Lincoln County; 103 3rd Ave; PO Box 39; Hugo, CO 80821; Ph. (719) 743-2444 **Details:** (County Clerk has Marriage & land Records from 1889; Clerk District Court has Divorce, Probate & Court Records)
Logan http://raq3-1.kci.net/	E2	25 Feb 1887	**Weld** Logan County; 315 Main St; Sterling, CO 80751-4349; Ph. (970) 522-1544 **Details:** (County Clerk-Recorder has Marriage Records from 1887 & Military Records from 1914; County Health Department has Birth & Death Records; County Assessor has land Records from 1875; District Court has Probate, Naturalization & Divorce Records; County Court has Court Records)
Mesa www.co.mesa.co.us/	O6	14 Feb 1883	**Gunnison** Mesa County; 2424 Hwy 6 & 50; PO Box 20,000-5010; Grand Junction, CO 81502; Ph. (970) 244-1607 **Details:** (County Clerk has Marriage & land Records from 1883; County Health Department has Birth, Death, & Burial Records; District Court has Divorce, Probate & Court Records; County Archives has some Burial Records; 1885 census taken)
Mineral www.creede.com/	M10	27 Mar 1893	**Hinsdale** Mineral County; 1201 N Main St; PO Box 70; Creede, CO 81130; Ph. (719) 658-2440 **Details:** (County Clerk has Marriage Records from 1893 & Military Records from 1945; District Court has Divorce, Probate, Court & Naturalization Records; County Assessor has land Records)
Moffat www.co.moffat.co.us/	O3	27 Feb 1911	**Routt** Moffat County; 221 W Victory Way; Craig, CO 81625; Ph. (970) 824-9109 **Details:** (County Clerk has Marriage, land & Military Records from 1911; Public Health Department has Birth & Death Records; County Court has Divorce, Probate & Court Records)

County Website	Map Index	Date Created	Parent County or Territory From Which Organized Address/Details
Montezuma www.swcolo.org/	**P11**	**16 Apr 1889**	**La Plata** Montezuma County; 109 W Main St Ste 302; Cortez, CO 81321; Ph. (970) 565-3728 **Details:** (Clerk District Court has Divorce, Probate & Court Records; County Clerk has Birth, Marriage, Death & land Records)
Montrose www.rootsweb.com/~comontro/	**P8**	**11 Feb 1883**	**Gunnison** Montrose County; 320 S 1st St; Montrose, CO 81401; Ph. (970) 249-3362 **Details:** (County Clerk has Birth & Death Records from 1907, Marriage Records from 1883 & land Records from 1882)
Morgan www.rootsweb.com/~comorgan/	**F3**	**19 Feb 1889**	**Weld** Morgan County; PO Box 596; Fort Morgan, CO 80701-2307; Ph. (970) 867-5616 **Details:** (County Clerk has Marriage & land Records from 1889; County Health Department has Birth & Death Records from 1910; Clerk District Court has Divorce & Probate Records from 1889; County Court has Court Records from 1889)
Otero www.rootsweb.com/~cootero/	**F9**	**25 Mar 1889**	**Bent** Otero County; 13 W 3rd St; La Junta, CO 81050-0000; Ph. (719) 384-8701 **Details:** (County Clerk has Marriage Records from 1892 & land Records from 1889; Clerk County Court has Divorce & Probate Records; Clerk District Court has Court Records)
Ouray www.co.ouray.co.us/	**N9**	**18 Jan 1877**	**Hinsdale, San Juan** Ouray County; 541 4th St; Ouray, CO 81427; Ph. (970) 325-4961 **Details:** (Formerly Uncompahgre County. Name changed to Ouray 2 Mar 1883) (County Clerk has Marriage & land Records from 1881; County Treasury has Birth Records from 1877 & Death Records from 1894; Court Clerk has Divorce, Probate & Court Records)
Park http://co.park.co.us/	**J6**	**1 Nov 1861**	**Original county** Park County; 501 Main St; Fairplay, CO 80440; Ph. (719) 836-2771 **Details:** (County Clerk has Marriage Records from 1893 & land Records; Clerk District Court has Divorce, Probate & Court Records)
Phillips www.rootsweb.com/~cophilli/	**C2**	**27 Mar 1889**	**Logan** Phillips County; 221 S Interocean Ave; Holyoke, CO 80734-1534; Ph. (970) 854-3131 **Details:** (County Clerk has Marriage & land Records from 1889; District Court has Probate Records; County Court has Divorce & Court Records; Local Registrars have Birth, Death, & Burial Records)
Pitkin www.pitkingov.com/	**M6**	**23 Feb 1881**	**Gunnison** Pitkin County; 530 E Main St #101; Aspen, CO 81611-1993; Ph. (970) 920-5180 **Details:** (County Clerk-Recorder has Birth, Marriage, & Death Records from 1890 & land Records from 1883; Clerk of Courts has Probate Records)
Platte		**1872**	**Weld** Platte County **Details:** County Terminated in 1874

County Website	Map Index	Date Created	Parent County or Territory From Which Organized Address/Details
Prowers www.rootsweb.com/~coProbatewer/	C9	**11 Apr 1889**	**Bent** Prowers County; 300 S Main St; Lamar, CO 81052-2857; Ph. (719) 336-4337 **Details:** (County Clerk has Marriage, Land & some Death Records from 1889; District Court has Divorce & Court Records; County Court has Probate Records)
Pueblo www.co.pueblo.co.us/	G9	**1 Nov 1861**	**Original county** Pueblo County; 215 W 10th St; Pueblo, CO 81003; Ph. (719) 583-6624 **Details:** (County Clerk has Marriage Records from 1867, Military Records from 1944 & land Records; City County Health Department has Birth & Death Records; District Court has Divorce, Probate, Court & Naturalization Records)
Rio Blanco www.rootsweb.com/~coriobla/	P4	**25 Mar 1889**	**Summit** Rio Blanco County; PO Box I; Meeker, CO 81641-1067; Ph. (970) 878-5068 **Details:** (County Clerk-Recorder has Birth & Death Records from 1898, Marriage & land Records from 1897; Clerk District Court has Divorce, Probate & Court Records)
Rio Grande www.rootsweb.com/~coriogra/	K10	**10 Feb 1874**	**Conejos, Costilla** Rio Grande County; 925 6th St; PO Box 160; Del Norte, CO 81132-0160; Ph. (719) 657-2744 **Details:** (County Clerk-Recorder has Marriage Records from 1876 & land Records from 1874; Clerk County Court has Divorce, Probate & Court Records)
Routt www.co.routt.co.us/	M3	**29 Jan 1877**	**Grand** Routt County; 522 Lincoln Ave; PO Box 773598; Steamboat Springs, CO 80487; Ph. (970) 879-1710 **Details:** (County Clerk has Marriage Records from 1893 & land Records from 1885; County Health Department has Birth & Death Records; Clerk District Court has Divorce, Probate & Court Records)
Saguache http://slv.org/saguachecounty	K9	**29 Dec 1866**	**Costilla** Saguache County; 501 4th St; PO Box 655; Saguache, CO 81149; Ph. (719) 655-2512 **Details:** (County Clerk has Marriage & Land Records from 1874; Public Registrar has Birth Records)
San Juan www.rootsweb.com/~cosanjua/	N10	**31 Jan 1876**	**La Plata** San Juan County; PO Box 466; Silverton, CO 81433-0466; Ph. (970) 387-5671 **Details:** (County Treasury has Birth Records from 1880 & Death Records from 1901; County Clerk has Marriage Records from 1880, Military Records from 1941 & land Records; Clerk District Court has Divorce, Probate & Court Records)
San Miguel www.sanmiguelcounty.org	P9	**1883**	**Ouray** San Miguel County; 333 W. Colorado Ave; PO Box 548; Telluride, CO 81435; Ph. (970) 728-3954 **Details:** (Formerly Ouray County. Name changed to San Miguel 2 Mar 1883) (County Clerk/Recorder has Marriage Records from the early 1800s; Clerk/Combined Courts has Divorce, Probate, & Court Records from 1883; County Recorder has Land Records from 1890; County Treasurer has Birth Records from 1897 & Death Records from 1906)

County	Map	Date	Parent County or Territory From Which Organized
Website	Index	Created	Address/Details

Sedgwick   C2   **9 Apr 1889**   **Logan**
www.rootsweb.com/~cosedgwi/index.htm
Sedgwick County; 315 Cedar St Suite 220; Julesburg, CO 80737-0003; Ph. (970) 474-3346
Details: (County Clerk has Marriage & land Records from 1889; Clerk District Court has Divorce, Probate & Court Records)

South Arapahoe   **1902**   **South Arapahoe**
Details: Name changed to Arapahoe in 1903

Summit   K5   **1 Nov 1861**   **Original county**
www.co.summit.co.us/
Summit County; 208 E Lincoln St; PO Box 68; Breckenridge, CO 80424-0068; Ph. (970) 453-2561
Details: (County Clerk has Marriage & land Records)

Teller   I7   **23 Mar 1899**   **El Paso**
www.co.teller.co.us/
Teller County; 101 W Bennett Ave; Cripple Creek, CO 80813-0959; Ph. (719) 689-2951
Details: (County Clerk has Marriage & land Records from 1899; Clerk District Court has Divorce, Probate & Court Records)

Uncompahgre   **18 Jan 1877**   **Hinsdale, San Juan**
Uncompahgre County, CO;
Details: (see Ouray) Name changed to Ouray 2 Mar 1883

Washington   E4   **9 Feb 1887**   **Weld, Arapahoe**
Washington County; 150 Ash Ave; PO Box L; Akron, CO 80720; Ph. (970) 345-6565
Details: (Clerk & Recorders Office has Birth, Death, Land, Marriage, Military, School Census, & Other Historical Records from 1887; County Assessor has Land & Tax Records; Court Clerk has Court, Divorce, Guardianship, Immigration, Naturalization, & Probate Records)

Weld   G2   **1 Nov 1861**   **Original county**
www.co.weld.co.us/
Weld County; 1402 17th St; Greeley, CO 80631-1123; Ph. (970) 353-3840
Details: (County Clerk has Marriage & land Records; Clerk District Court has Divorce, Probate & Court Records)

Yuma   C4   **15 Mar 1889**   **Washington, Arapahoe**
www.rootsweb.com/~coyuma/yuma.htm
Yuma County; 310 Ash St; PO Box 467; Wray, CO 80758-0426; Ph. (970) 332-5809
Details: (County Clerk has Marriage Records from 1889 & land Records from 1897)

Notes

The Handybook for Genealogists

Connecticut

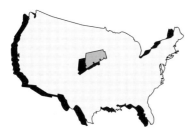

Capital: Hartford

Ninth Colony

State: 1788 (5th)

*He who transplanted,
still sustains*

The Dutch seafarer, Adriaen Block, was the first European in Connecticut when he sailed up the Connecticut River in 1614. In 1633, Dutch settlers from New Amsterdam built a fort and trading post at present-day Hartford. Glowing reports from John Oldham and others, combined with disgust for the intolerance of the Massachusetts Bay Colony, led to a migration from Massachusetts to Connecticut starting about 1634. Most of the settlers of Newtown (Cambridge), Watertown, and Dorchester moved to the central part of Connecticut, establishing the towns of Wethersfield, Windsor, and Suckiang (Hartford). These towns joined together in 1639 to form the Connecticut Colony, a relatively democratic colony. Meanwhile, in 1638, a party of Puritans founded New Haven, which with Milford, Stamford, and Guilford, formed the New Haven Colony.

The New Haven Colony was theocratic and used the Old Testament as the legal code. The decade of the 1640's saw a heavy influx of settlers from England. In 1662, John Winthrop, governor of the Connecticut Colony, was granted a charter that defined the boundaries as extending from Massachusetts to Long Island Sound and from Narragansett Bay to the Pacific Ocean. The New Haven Colony finally agreed to be absorbed into the Connecticut Colony in 1665. The next forty years were marked by migration westward, sometimes entire towns moved to a new setting.

By 1740, Connecticut was settled and organized into incorporated towns. Towns have remained the basic governing unit and it is at that level where many of the records are found. Connecticut had many boundary disputes with other colonies, especially Rhode Island, Massachusetts, and New York. In 1754, Connecticut settlers colonized the Wyoming Valley in Pennsylvania. Connecticut exchanged its rights to the territory west of its present boundary for the Western Reserve in Ohio and in 1799 gave up its claims to the Wyoming Valley in Pennsylvania. In 1800, the Western Reserve was incorporated in the Northwest Territory as Trumbull County, and Connecticut's present boundaries were set.

Connecticut played an important part in the Revolutionary War, as more than 40,000 of its men served. In 1777,

Danbury was burned, and in 1779, New Haven, Fairfield, and Norwalk were pillaged. Benedict Arnold largely destroyed New London and Groton in 1781. The 1790 Census shows a population of 223,236, most of whom came from England. Others came from Scotland, Ireland, France, and Holland.

Connecticut had more home industries than any other colony. Household gadgets invented and manufactured in the homes were carried all over the United States by "Yankee peddlers." The building of factories in the United States and the potato crop failures in Ireland brought 70,000 Irish, as well as settlers from Germany, Canada, Scandinavia, Italy, Poland, Lithuania, Czechoslovakia, and Hungary. During the Civil War, Connecticut supplied about 55,000 troops to the Union Army.

Look for vital records in the following locations:

- **Birth and death records:** Connecticut State Department of Public Health, Vital Records Section. Check with town clerk records prior to 1 July, 1897. Only the person, his parents, an attorney, or a member of a genealogical society in Connecticut may search birth records.
- **Marriage records:** Connecticut State Department of Public Health, Vital Records Section. Check with town clerk records prior to 1 July, 1897.
- **Divorce records:** Clerk of the Superior Court. Wills, inventories, and administrations of estates are in the probate districts. The boundaries of these districts often differ from town and county boundaries. There are 118 probate districts for the 169 towns. Many probate records are now in the Connecticut State Library.
- **Naturalizations:** U.S. Circuit Court in Hartford or in the county Superior Courts.

Almost every city in the state has printed histories that contain much genealogical information, especially about early inhabitants. Many family histories exist in manuscript form only, but many of these have been indexed to facilitate research. Although libraries will not do research, they provide names of researchers or give information about indexes, if the request is accompanied by a self-addressed stamped envelope.

Connecticut State Department of Public Health Vital Records Section
410 Capital Avenue
PO Box 340308
MS#11VRS
Hartford, CT 06134-0308
(860) 509-7897; Fax (860) 509-7964
www.dph.state.ct.us/OPPE/hpvital.htm

Connecticut State Library
231 Capitol Avenue
Hartford, CT 06106
(860) 757-6500
www.cslib.org/

Societies and Repositories

Amity and Woodbridge Historical Society; c/o Thomas Darling House; 1907 Litchfield Tpke.; Woodbridge, CT 06525; awhs@homestead.com; www.woodbridgehistory.org.

Aspinock Historical Society of Putnam; 208 School Road; Putnam, CT 06260.

Barkhamsted Historical Society; PO Box 94; Pleasant Valley, CT 06063; bhs@barkhamstedhistory.org; www.barkhamstedhistory.org.

Branford Historical Society-Harrison House; PO Box 504; Branford, CT 06405.

Brookfield, Connecticut Historical Society; PO Box 5231; Brookfield, CT 06804; www.danbury.org/org/brookhc.

Brooklyn Historical Society; PO Box 90; Brooklyn, CT 06234-0090.

Burlington Historical Society; PO Box 1215; Burlington, CT 06013.

Canterbury Historical Society; PO Box 2; Canterbury, CT 06331.

Canton Historical Society; 11 Front St.; Collinsville, CT 06022-1112.

Chaplin Historical Society; Chaplin Street; Chaplin, CT 06235.

Cheshire Historical Society; 43 Church Drive; PO Box 231; Cheshire, CT 06410; edwinkania@cox.net; http://users.rcn.com/andersonel/chs.htm.

Chester Historical Society, The; 9 West Main Street; PO Box 204; Chester, CT 06412; info@chesterhistoricalsociety.org; www.chesterhistoricalsociety.org/contact_us.htm.

Clinton Historical Society; CT; http://clintonct.com/hists.htm.

Colebrook Historical Society; PO Box 85; Colebrook, CT 06021.

Columbia Historical Society; 21 Edgarton Road; Columbia, CT 06237.

Connecticut Ancestry Society; The Ferguson Library; One Public Library Plaza; Stamford, CT 06904-1000.

Connecticut Ancient Order of Hibernians; CT; Fkearneyjr@aol.com; www.ctaoh.com.

Connecticut Historical Commission; 59 South Prospect Street; Hartford, CT 06106.

Connecticut Historical Society; One Elizabeth Street; Hartford, CT 06105; judith_e_johnson@chs.org; www.chs.org.

Connecticut Professional Genealogists Council; PO Box 4273; Hartford, CT 06147-4273.

Connecticut Society of Genealogists, Inc.; PO Box 435; Glastonbury, CT 06033-0435; www.csginc.org.

Connecticut State Library & Archives; Connecticut State Library; 231 Capitol Avenue; Hartford, CT 06106; (860) 757-6595; MJones@cslib.org; www.cslib.org/archives.htm.

Connecticut Valley Tobacco Historical Society, Inc.; PO Box 241; Windsor, CT 06095; www.tobaccohistsoc.org/connecti.htm.

Cornwall Historical Society; 7 Pine St., Box 115; Cornwall, CT 06753.

Coventry Historical Society; PO Box 534; Coventry, CT 06238; coventrycthistory@yahoo.com; http://geocities.com/coventrycthistory.

Cromwell Historical Society; 395 Main Street; Cromwell, CT 06416.

Danbury Historical Society; 43 Main St; Danbury, CT 06810; dmhs@danburyhistorical.org; www.danburyhistorical.org.

Darien Historical Society; 45 Old Kings Highway North; Darien, CT 06820; www.darien.lib.ct.us/townhall/about%5Fdarien/tour/historical_society.htm.

Deep River Historical Society; 245 Main Street; Deep River, CT 06417.

Derby Historical Society; 37 Elm Street; Ansonia, CT 06401; Derbyhistoricalsoc@juno.com; http://derbyhistorical.org.

Descendants of the Founders of Ancient Windsor; PO Box 39; Windsor, CT 06095-0039.

East Granby Historical Society; Box 188; East Granby, CT 06026; www.eastgranby.com/HistoricalSociety.

East Haddam Historical Society Museum; 264 Town Street; PO Box 27; East Haddam, CT 06423-0027.

East Haven Historical Society; 200 Tyler St.; PO Box 120052; East Haven, CT 06512.

East Windsor Historical Society; PO Box 363; East Windsor Hill, CT 06028; http://eastwindsorhistory.home.att.net.

Easton Historical Society; PO Box 121; Easton, CT 06612; www.tomorrowseaston.com/guestwebpages/ historicalsociety/historicalsociety.htm.

Ellington Historical Society; PO Box 73; Ellington, CT 06029.

Enfield Historical Society; 1294 Enfield Street; PO Box 586; Enfield, CT 06083; mkm-of-enfct@att.net; http://home.att.net/~mkm-of-enfct.

Essex Historical Society; PO Box 123; Essex, CT 06426; (978) 767-7888; www.essexhistory.org/default.htm.

Fairfield Historical Society; 636 Old Post Rd.; Fairfield, CT 06430; info@fairfieldhs.org; www.fairfieldhs.org.

Falls Village—Canaan Historical Society; Falls Village Depot; Railroad Street, PO Box 206; Falls Village, CT 06031.

Farmington Historical Society; PO Box 1645; Farmington, CT 06034.

Finnish American Heritage Society of Connecticut; PO Box 252; Canterbury, CT 06331; info@fahs-ct.org; www.fahs-ct.org/.

Franklin Historical Society; PO Box 73; Franklin, CT 06254.

French-Canadian Genealogical Society of Connecticut, Inc.; PO Box 928; Tolland, CT 06084-0928; ivarobin@ix.netcom.com; www.fcgsc.org.

Gaylordsville Historical Society; PO Box 25; Gaylordsville, CT 06755; kosier@gaylordsville.org; www.gaylordsville.org.

Godfrey Memorial Library; 134 Newfield Street; Middletown, CT 06457-2534; (860) 346-4375; www.godfrey.org.

Goshen Historical Society; 21 Old Middle Road; PO Box 457; Goshen, CT 06756-0457; www.goshenhistoricalsociety.org.

Guilford Historical Society; 171 Boston Street; PO Box 363; Guilford, CT 06437; info@GuilfordKeepingSociety.com; www.guilfordhistoricalsociety.com.

Haddam Historical Society; PO Box 97; Haddam, CT 06438; Thankfularnold@juno.com.

Hamden Historical Society; PO Box 5512; Hamden, CT 06518.

Hampton Historical Society; PO Box 12; Hampton, CT 06247.

Hartland Historical Society; PO Box 221; East Hartland, CT 06027; mnurge@earthlink.net; http://vvv.munic.state.ct.us/hartland/historical.htm.

Harwinton Historical Society; PO Box 84; Harwinton, CT 06791.

Hebron Historical Society; PO Box 43; Hebron, CT 06248; APiggott@aol.com; www.hebron.f2s.com.

Historical Society of East Hartford; PO Box 380166; East Hartford, CT 06108-0166; (860) 568-7305; hseh@lycos.com; www.hseh.org.

Historical Society of Town of Greenwich; Bush-Holley House; 39 Strickland Rd; Cos Cob, CT 06878; www.hstg.org.

Jewish Genealogical Society of Connecticut; 394 Sport Hill Rd.; Easton, CT 06612.

Killingly Historical Society; 196 Main St.; Danielson, CT 06239; www.qvctc.commnet.edu/brian/KHS/kilz1.html.

Lebanon Historical Society; 856 Trumbull Highway; PO Box 151; Lebanon, CT 06249; lebanon.hist.soc@snet.net; www.lebanonct.org/historic_sites.html.

Litchfield Historical Society; East and South Streets; Litchfield, CT 06759; www.litchfieldct.com/twn/lhistsoc.html.

Lyme Historical Society, Inc.; Florence Griswold Museum, 96 Lyme St.; Old Lyme, CT 06371.

Madison Historical Society; Allis-Bushnell House; 853 Boston Post Road; Madison, CT 06443.

Manchester Historical Society; 106 Hartford Road; Manchester, CT 06040; www.manchesterhistory.org.

Middlebury Historical Society; PO Box 104; Middlebury, CT 06762; www.middlebury-ct.org/historical.shtml.

Middlefield Historical Society; 405 Main Street; Middlefield, CT 06455.

Middlesex County Historical Society; 151 Main St.; Middletown, CT 06457; middlesexhistory@wesleyan.edu.

Middlesex Genealogical Society; PO Box 1111; Darien, CT 06820-1111; mgs2@optonline.net; www.darien.org/mgs.

Milford Historical Society; 34 High Street; Milford, CT; mhsoc@usa.net; www.geocities.com/SiliconValley/ Park/3831.

Monroe Historical Society; Box 212; Monroe, CT 06468; www.monroehistoricsociety.org.

Montville Historical Society; PO Box 1786; Montville, CT 06353.

Morris Historical Society; PO Box 234; Morris, CT 06763.

Mystic River Historical Society; PO Box 245; Mystic, CT 06355-0245.

Mystic Seaport; PO Box 6000; Mystic, CT 06355-0990; www.mysticseaport.org.

New Canaan Historical Society; 13 Oenoke Ridge; New Canaan, CT 06840; newcanaan.historical@snet.net; www.nchistory.org.

New Fairfield Historical Society; PO Box 8156; New Fairfield, CT 06812-8156.

New Hartford Historical Society; PO Box 41; New Hartford, CT 06057; nhhs@juno.com; www.town.new-hartford.ct.us/nhhs/index.html.

New Haven Colony Historical Society; 114 Whitney Ave.; New Haven, CT 06510.

New London County Historical Society; 11 Blinman Street; New London, CT 06320; (860) 443-1209; nlchsinc@aol.com; www.newlondonhistory.org.

New Milford Historical Society; PO Box 566; 6 Aspetuck Ave.; New Milford, CT 06776; www.nmhistorical.org.

Newtown Historical Society; 6 Bari Drive; Newtown, CT 06470.

Noank Historical Society; 17 Sylvan St. Box 454; Noank, CT 06340.

Norfolk Historical Society; 13 Village Green; PO Box 288; Norfolk, CT 06058; norfolkhistorical@snet.net.

North Haven Historical Society; 27 Broadway; North Haven, CT 06473; www.geocities.com/northhavenhistoricalsociety/home.htm.

North Stonington Historical Society; 1 Wyassup Rd.; PO Box 134; North Stonington, CT 06359; www.nostoningtonhistsoc.homestead.com.

Norwalk Historical Society; PO Box 335; 2 East Wall Street; Norwalk, CT 06852; MillHillPark@post.com; www.geocities.com/Heartland/Trail/8030.

Old Saybrook Historical Society; PO Box 4; Old Saybrook, CT 06475; www.oldsaybrook.com/History/society.htm.

Orange Historical Society; PO Box 784; Orange, CT 06477; questions@orangehistory.org; www.orangehistory.org.

Polish Genealogical Society of Connecticut and the Northeast, Inc.; 8 Lyle Rd.; New Britain, CT 06053; pgsne2@aol.com; www.pgsctne.org.

Portland Historical Society; Box 98; Portland, CT 06480; mcdougall@eisner.decus.org; www.geocities.com/portlandhistsoc.

Preston Historical Society; Town Hall, 389 Route 2; Preston, CT 06365; LindaCh5@aol.com.

Rocky Hill Historical Society; PO Box 185; Rocky Hill, CT 06067; info@rockyhillhistory.org; www.rockyhillhistory.org.

Salmon Brook Historical Society; 208 Salmon Brook Street; Granby, CT 06035; (860) 653-9713; www.salmonbrookhistorical.org.

Saybrook Colony Founders Association; PO Box 1635; Old Saybrook, CT 06475-1000; www.rootsweb.com/~ctscfa.

Sharon Historical Society; 18 Main Street; PO Box 511; Sharon, CT 06069; (860) 364-5688; director@sharonhist.org; www.sharonhist.org.

Shelton Historical Society; PO Box 2155; 70 Ripton Road; Shelton, CT 06484; shltn.hst.soc@snet.net.

Sherman Historical Society; Sherman, CT 06784; info@shermanhistorical.org; www.shermanhistorical.org/page1.html.

Simsbury Genealogical and Historical Research Library; 749 Hopmeadow Street; Simsbury, CT 06070; genehist@micro-net.com.

Simsbury Historical Society; 800 Hopmeadow Street; PO Box 2; Simsbury, CT 06070; www.ohwy.com/ct/s/simhisso.htm.

Society of Mayflower Descendants in Connecticut; 36 Arundel Ave.; Hartford, CT 06107.

South Windsor Historical Society; PO Box 216; 11 Beldon Road; South Windsor, CT 06074; http://southwindsorhistory.home.att.net.

Southington Genealogical Society; Southington Historical Center; 239 Main St; Southington, CT 06489.

Southington Historical Society; Southington, CT 06489; http://southington.com/History.

Stamford Historical Society; 1508 High Ridge Road; Stamford, CT 06903; shsadmin@flvax.ferg.lib.ct.us; www.stamfordhistory.org.

Stonington Historical Society; 40 Palmer Street; Stonington, CT 06378; www.stoningtonhistory.org.

Stratford Historical Society; 967 Academy Hill; PO Box 382; Stratford, CT 06497; judsonhousestfd@aol.com; www.stratfordhistoricalsociety.com.

The Avon Historical Society, Inc.; PO Box 448; Avon, CT 06001; www.avonct.com/historicalsociety/home.htm.

The Connecticut Trust for Historic Preservation; 940 Whitney Avenue; Hamden, CT 06517-4002; contact@cttrust.org; www.cttrust.org.

The Jewish Historical Society of Greater New Haven; PO Box 3251; New Haven, CT 06515-0351.

The Jewish Historical Society of Greater Stamford; PO Box 16918; Stamford, CT 06905-8901; www.stamfordhistory.org/jhsgs.htm.

The Mansfield Historical Society; PO Box 145; Storrs, CT 06268; info@mansfield-history.org; www.mansfield-history.org.

The Naugatuck Historical Society; PO Box 317; Naugatuck, CT 06770; (203) 723-8282; tjablonowski@prodigy.net; http://naugatuckhistory.com.

The Old Woodbury Historical Society Inc; Box 705; Woodbury, CT 06798.

The Ridgefield Historical Society; 400 Main Street; Ridgefield, CT 06877; info@ridgefieldhistoricalsociety.org; www.ridgefieldhistoricalsociety.org.

The Society of Middletown First Settlers Descendants; Middletown, CT; bobbijo@innercite.com; www.rootsweb.com/~ctsmfsd/Index.html.

The Somers Historical Society, Inc.; PO Box 652; Somers, CT 06071; mcml98@aol.com; www.somershistoricalsociety.org.

Thompson Historical Society; PO Box 47; Thompson, CT 06277; thompsonhistorical@snet.net; www.thompsonhistorical.org.

Trumbull Historical Society; 1856 Huntington Turnpike (Rte. 108); PO Box 312; Trumbull, CT 06611-0312; http://trumbull.ct.us/history.

Vernon Historical Society; PO Box 2055; Vernon, CT 06066; VernonHistSoc@juno.com.

Wallingford Historical Society; PO Box 73; Wallingford, CT 06492-0073.

West Hartford Historical Society and Noah Webster House Museum; 227 South Main Street; West Hartford, CT 06107; www.ctstateu.edu/noahweb.

West Haven Historical Society; 219 Court Street; West Haven, CT 06516.

Westbrook Historical Society; 1196 Boston Post Road; Westbrook, CT 06498.

Weston Historical Society; PO Box 1092; Weston, CT 06883; whs@wvfd.com; www.wvfd.com/whs.htm.

Westport Historical Society; 25 Avery Place; Westport, CT 06880; wheeler@whsoc.com; www.westporthistory.org.

Wethersfield Historical Society; 150 Main St.; Wethersfield, CT 06109; weth.hist.society@snet.net; www.wethhist.org.

Willington Historical Society; 48 Red Oak Hill; Willington, CT 06279.

Wilton Historical Society; Wilton Heritage Museum; 249 Danbury Rd.; Wilton, CT 06897.

Winchester Historical Society; 225 Prospect St.; Winsted, CT 06098.

Windham Historical Society; PO Box 105; Windham, CT 06226; www.windhamhistory.org.

Windsor Historical Society; 96 Palisado Ave.; Windsor, CT 06095; www.townofwindsorct.com/Historic%20Homes.htm.

Wintonbury Historical Society; PO Box 7454; Bloomfield, CT 06002-7454.

Wolcott Historical Society; PO Box 6410; Wolcott, CT 06716; wallou@arrl.net; www.wolcotthistory.org.

Woodstock Historical Society; PO Box 65; Woodstock, CT 06281; www.uvm.edu/~histpres/vtiana/woodstockhs.html.

Bibliography and Record Sources

General

Bailey, Frederic W. *Early Connecticut Marriages as Found on Ancient Church Records Prior to 1800.* 7 vols. New Haven: Bureau of American Ancestry for Family Research, 1896–1906.

Beardsley, E. Edwards. *The History of the Episcopal Church in Connecticut.* 2 vols. New York: Hurd and Houghton, 1865.

Bickford, Christopher P., and J. Bard McNulty. *John Warner Barber's Views of Connecticut Towns, 1834–36.* Hartford, Connecticut: Connecticut Historical Society, 1990.

Bingham, Harold J. *History of Connecticut.* 4 vols. New York: Lewis Historical Publishing Company, 1962.

Bolles, J. R. and Anna B. Williams. *The Rogerenes: Some Hitherto Unpublished Annals Belonging to the Colonial History of Connecticut.* With Appendix of Rogerene writings. (1904), Reprint, Salem, Massachusetts: Higginson Books, 1990.

Booth, Maud. *Universalist Church in Connecticut: Papers, 1791–1951.* Microreproduction of original records at the Connecticut State Library. Salt Lake City: Filmed by the Genealogical Society of Utah, 1976.

Brown, Barbara W. *Black Roots in Southeastern Connecticut, 1650–1900.* Detroit: Gale Research Company, 1980.

Burpee, Charles W. *Burpee's The Story of Connecticut.* 4 vols. New York: American Historical Co., 1939.

Connecticut Research Outline. Series US-States, no. 7, Salt Lake City: Family History Library, 1988.

Connecticut State Library (Hartford, Connecticut). *Connecticut Archives, Indians, 1647–1789.* 2 vols. Microfilm of original published: Hartford, Connecticut: [s.n.], 1922.

Connecticut State Library, *Guide to Archives in the Connecticut State Library.* 3rd ed. Hartford, Connecticut: Connecticut State Library, 1981.

Connecticut, 1600s–1800s. [S.l.]: Brøderbund, 2000. CD-ROM.

Crandall, Ralph J. ed. *Genealogical Research in New England.* Baltimore: Genealogical Publishing Co., 1984.

Cutter, William Richard, et al. *Genealogical and Family History of the State of Connecticut. A Record of the Achievements of Her People in the Making of a Commonwealth and the Building of a Nation.* In four volumes. Partially indexed. (1911) reprint, Baltimore: Clearfield Co., 1995.

Dayton, Cornelia Hughes. *Women Before the Bar: Gender, Law & Society in Connecticut: 1639–1789.* Galveston, Texas: Frontier Press, 1995.

Duffy, Ward E. *Who's Who in Connecticut.* New York City: Lewis Historical Publishing Company, 1933.

Genealogical and Biographical Records of American Citizens: Connecticut. 26 vols. Hartford, Connecticut: 1929–1949.

Giles, Barbara S. *Connecticut Genealogical Resources: Including Selected Bibliographies.* Seattle, Washington: Fiske Genealogical Foundation, 1991.

Greenlaw, William Prescott. *The Greenlaw Index of the New England Historic Genealogical Society.* 2 vols. Boston: G. K. Hall, 1979.

Guide to Vital Statistics in the Church Records of Connecticut. New Haven, Connecticut: Connecticut Historical Records Survey, 1942.

Hale, Charles R. *Hale Collection.* Microfilm of typescript at the Connecticut State Library. Salt Lake City: Filmed by the Genealogical Society of Utah, 1949–1950.

Hall, Lu Verne V. *New England Family Historie: State of Connecticut.* Bowie, Maryland: Heritage Books, 1999.

Hart, Samuel, et al. *Encyclopedia of Connecticut Biography, Genealogical-Memorial: Representative*

Citizens. 11 vols. Boston: American Historical Society, 1917–23.

Hart, Samuel. *Representative Citizens of Connecticut, Biographical, Memorial.* New York: American Historical Society, 1916.

Hinman, Royal R. *A Catalogue of the Names of the First Puritans Settlers of the Colony of Connecticut; with the Time of Their Arrival in the Colony and Their Standing in Society...* (1846) Reprint, Baltimore: Clearfield Co., 1996.

Historical Records Survey (Connecticut), *Inventory of the Church Archives of Connecticut, Presbyterians.* Salt Lake City: Filmed by the Genealogical Society of Utah, 1972.

Historical Records Survey (Connecticut). *Guide to Vital Statistics in the Church Records of Connecticut.* New Haven, Connecticut: The Survey, 1942.

Historical Records Survey (Connecticut). *Inventory of the Church Archives of Connecticut, Lutheran.* New Haven, Connecticut: The Survey, 1941.

Historical Records Survey (Connecticut). *Inventory of the Church Archives of Connecticut, Protestant Episcopal.* New Haven, Connecticut: The Survey, 1940.

Ireland, Norma Olin and Winifred Irving. *Cutter Index: A Consolidated Index of Cutter's Nine Genealogy Series.* Fallbrook, California: Ireland Indexing Service, 197?

Jacobus, Donald Lines. *Families of Ancient New Haven.* With an Index Vol. by Helen L. Scranton. 9 vols. in 3. Reprint, Baltimore: Genealogical Publishing, 1997.

Jacobus, Donald Lines. *Lists of Officials...of Connecticut Colony...1936 through...1677 and of New Haven Colony...[with] Soldiers in the Pequot War...*Reprint, Baltimore: Clearfield Co., 1996.

Jarvis, Lucy Cushing. *Sketches of Church life in Colonial Connecticut: Being the Story of the Transplanting of the Church of England into Forty-Two Parishes of Connecticut, with the Assistance of the Society for the Propagation of the Gospel.* New Haven: Tuttle, Morehouse & Taylor, 1902.

Kemp, Thomas J. *Connecticut Researcher's Handbook.* Detroit: Gale Research, 1981.

Lindberg, Marcia Wiswall, ed. *Genealogist's Handbook for New England Research.* 2nd ed. Boston: New England Historic Genealogical Society, 1993.

List of Church Records in the Connecticut State Library. Hartford: Connecticut State Library, 1976.

Mather, Frederick Gregory. *The Refugees of 1776 from Long Island to Connecticut.* Baltimore: Genealogical Publishing Co., 1972.

Morrison, Betty Jean. *Connecting to Connecticut.* Glastonbury: Connecticut Society of Genealogists, 1995.

New England Historic Genealogical Society. *English Origins of New England Families: from the New England Historical and Genealogical Register. First*

Series. 3 vols. Baltimore: Genealogical Publishing Co., 1985.

Osborn, Norris Galpin, ed. *Men of Mark in Connecticut.* 5 vols. Hartford: Connecticut: W.R. Goodspeed, 1906–1910.

Parks, Roger, ed. *Connecticut: A Bibliography of Its History.* Hanover, New Hampshire: University of New England, 1986.

Perry, Charles Edward. *Founders and Leaders of Connecticut, 1633–1783.* Boston, Massachusetts: D. C. Heath, ©1934.

Report of the Temporary Examiner of Public Records. Hartford, Connecticut: Case, Lockwood and Brainard, 1904.

Rider, Fremont, ed. *American Genealogical- Biographical Index. Vols. 1–186.* Middletown, Connecticut: The Godfrey Memorial Library, 1952.

Savage, James. *A Genealogical Dictionary of the First Settlers of New England ...4 vols. 1860–1862.* Reprint, Baltimore: Genealogical Publishing Company, 1965.

Spalding, John A. *Illustrated Popular Biography of Connecticut.* 2 vols. Hartford, Conn.: Press of the Case, Lockwood & Brainard Company, 1891.

Sperry, Kip. *Connecticut Sources for Family Historians and Genealogists.* Logan, Utah: Everton Publishers.

Stone, Earle L. Historical Records Survey (Connecticut). *Inventory of the Church Archives of Connecticut, Presbyterians.* Salt Lake City: Filmed by the Genealogical Society of Utah, 1972.

The First Laws of the State of Connecticut. (1784), Reprint, Wilmington, Delaware: Scholarly Resources, 1982.

The Public Records of the Colony of Connecticut (1636–1776). 15 vols. Hartford: Case, Lockwood & Brainard Co., 1850–1890.

The Public Records of the State of Connecticut 1776–1792. 7 vols. Hartford: Lockwood & Brainard, 1894–1948.

Trumbull, Benjamin. *A Complete History of Connecticut, Civil and Ecclesiastical: From the Emigration of its First Planters, from England, in the Year 1630, to the Year 1764; and to the Close of the Indian Wars; with an Appendix Containing the Original Patent of New England.* 2 vols. New London, Connecticut: H. D. Utley, 1898.

Ullman, Helen S. *Nutmegger Index: An Index to Non-Alphabetical Articles and a Subject Index to the Connecticut Nutmegger Volume 1–28, 1968–1996.* Rockport, Maine: Picton Press and Connecticut State Society of Genealogists, 1996.

Atlases, Maps and Gazetteers

Denis, Michael J. *Connecticut Towns and Counties: What was What, Where and When.* Oakland, Maine: Danbury House Books, 1985.

Gannett, Henry. *A Geographic Dictionary of Connecticut and Rhode Island*. Baltimore: Genealogical Publishing Company, 1978.

Hughes, Arthur H. *Connecticut Place Names*. Hartford: Connecticut Historical Society, 1976.

Lunt, Dudley. *The Bounds of Delaware*. Wilmington, Louisiana: Historical Society of Delaware, 1952.

Patera, Alan H. *The Post Offices of Connecticut*. Burtonville, Maryland: The Depot, 1977.

Pease, John C. *A Gazetteer of the States of Connecticut and Rhode Island: Written with Care and Impartiality from Original and Authentic Materials, Consisting of Two Parts ... with an Accurate and Improved Map of Each State*. New Haven, Connecticut: Yale University Microfilming Unit, 1989.

Sellers, Helen Earle. *Connecticut Town Origins: Their Names Boundaries, Early Histories and First Families*. Chester, Connecticut: Pequot Press, 1973.

Town and City Atlas of the State of Connecticut. Boston: D.H. Hurd and Co., 1893.

Censuses

Available Census Records and Census Substitutes
Federal Census 1790, 1800, 1810, 1820, 1830, 1840, 1850, 1860, 1870, 1880, 1900, 1010, 1920, 1930

State/Territorial Census 1670

Federal Mortality Schedules 1850, 1860, 1870, 1880

Connecticut 1670 Census. Oxford, Massachusetts: Holbrook Research Institute, 1977.

Connecticut State Library (Hartford, Connecticut). *Index of Connecticut Census Records from 1790–1850*. Microfilm of original records at the Connecticut State Library in Hartford, Connecticut. Salt Lake City: Filmed by the Genealogical Society of Utah, 1950. 95 microfilm.

Dollarhide, William. *The Census Book: A Genealogist's Guide to Federal Census Facts, Schedules and Indexes*. Bountiful, Utah: Heritage Quest, 1999.

Gannett, Henry. *A Geographic Dictionary of Connecticut and Rhode Island*. Washington, D.C.: Government Printing Office, 1894. Reprint. Baltimore: Genealogical Publishing Co., 1978

Hughes, Arthur H., and Allen S. Morse. *Connecticut Place Names*. Hartford: Connecticut Historical Society, 1976.

Kemp, Thomas Jay. *The American Census Handbook*. Wilmington, Delaware: Scholarly Resources, Inc., 2001.

Szucs, Loretto Dennis and Matthew Wright. *Finding Answers in U.S. Census Records*. Ancestry Publishing, 2001.

Thorndale, William. *Map Guide to the U.S. Federal Census, 1790–1920*. Baltimore: Genealogical Publishing Co., 1987.

Court Records, Probate and Wills

Connecticut State Library (Hartford, Connecticut). *Guide to Archives in the Connecticut State Library*. 3rd Ed. Hartford, Connecticut: Connecticut State Library, 1981.

Connecticut State Library (Hartford, Connecticut). *Probate Estate Files, 1881–1915*. Microfilm of original records in the Connecticut State Library, Hartford. Salt Lake City: Filmed by the Genealogical Society of Utah, 1990–1994. 576 microfilm.

Connecticut State Library (Hartford, Connecticut). *Probate Files Collection*. Microfilm of original records in the Connecticut State Library. Salt Lake City: Filmed by the Genealogical Society of Utah, 1977–1979. 1622 microfilm.

Connecticut. Inheritance Tax Division. *Estate Record Card Index, 1915–1926*. Microfilm of original records in the Connecticut State Archives, Hartford. Salt Lake City: Filmed by the Genealogical Society of Utah, 1989. 19 microfilm.

Connecticut. Particular Court. *Records of the Particular Court of Connecticut, 1639–1663*. Bowie, Maryland: Heritage Books, 1987.

Ditz, Toby L. *Property and Kinship: Inheritance in Early Connecticut, 1750–1820*. Princeton, New Jersey: Princeton University Press, 1986.

General Index to Probate Records: All Districts in Connecticut 1641–1948. Microfilm of originals in Hartford, Connecticut. Salt Lake City: Filmed by the Genealogical Society of Utah, 1957–1958. 67 microfilm.

Manwaring, Charles William, comp. *A Digest of the Early Connecticut Probate Records*. Hartford, Connecticut: R.S. Peck & Co., 1904–1906. Hartford District 1635 to 1750 in three volumes. Reprint. Baltimore: Genealogical Publishing Co., 1995.

Manwaring, Charles William. *A Digest of the Early Connecticut Probate Records*. 3 vols. Reprint. Baltimore: Genealogical Publishing Co., 1995.

The Public Records of the Colony of Connecticut (1636–1776). 15 vols. (Hartford, Connecticut: Case, Lockwood & Brainard Co., 1850–1890.

Immigration

Filby, P. William. *Passenger and Immigration Lists Index*, 15 vols. Detroit: Gale Research, 1981.

United States. Bureau of Customs. *A Supplemental Index to Passenger Lists of Vessels Arriving At Atlantic & Gulf Coast Ports (Excluding New York) 1820–1874*. Washington, D.C.: Filmed by the National Archives Record Services, 1960. Microfilm.

United States. Bureau of Customs. *Copies of Lists of Passengers Arriving At Miscellaneous Ports on the Atlantic and Gulf Coasts and At Ports on the Great Lakes, 1820–1873*. Washington, D.C.: The National Archives, 1964. Microfilm.

United States. Immigration and Naturalization Service. *St. Albans District Manifest Records of Aliens Arriving from Foreign Contiguous Territory: Arrivals At*

Canadian Border Ports from January 1895 to June 30, 1954: Indexes (Soundex), 1895–1924. Washington, D.C.: National Archives Records Service, 1986.

Land

Burr, Jean Chandler, comp. and ed. *Lyme Records 1667–1730: A Literal Transcription of the Minutes of the Town Meetings with Marginal Notations, to which hath been Appended Land Grants and Ear Marks.* Stonington, Connecticut: Pequot Press, 1968.

Colonial Land Records of Connecticut, 1640–1846. 5 vols. Microfilm of originals at the Connecticut State Library in Hartford, Connecticut. Salt Lake City: Filmed by the Genealogical Society of Utah, 1954. 3 microfilm.

Ditz, Toby L. *Property and Kinship: Inheritance in Early Connecticut, 1750–1820.* Princeton, New Jersey: Princeton University Press, 1986.

Hartford (Connecticut). *Town Clerk. Land Records, 1639–1901; General Index, 1639–1865.* Microfilm of originals in the Town Hall, Hartford, Connecticut. Salt Lake City: Filmed by the Genealogical Society of Utah, 1947–1949, 1983, 1986. Microfilm.

Judd, Sylvester. *Land Lotteries and Divorces of Connecticut 1755–1789 with Index.* Microfilm of originals at the Connecticut State Library in Hartford, Connecticut. Salt Lake City: Filmed by the Genealogical Society of Utah, 1954. 2 microfilm.

Susquehanna Company. *Susquehanna Settlers [and] Western Lands.* Microfilm of original records filmed at the Connecticut State Library in Hartford, Connecticut. Salt Lake City: Filmed by the Genealogical Society of Utah, 1954. 2 microfilm.

Winthrop, Robert Charles. *Robert C. Winthrop Collection: Connecticut Manuscripts 1631–1794.* Microfilm of originals at the Connecticut State Library in Hartford, Connecticut. Salt Lake City: Filmed by the Genealogical Society of Utah, 1954.

Military

Bates, Alfred C. ed. *Rolls of the Connecticut Men in the French and Indian War, 1755–1762.* 2 vols. (1903, 1905), reprint 1997. Baltimore: Clearfield Co., 1997.

Buckingham, Thomas. *Roll and Journal of Connecticut Service in Queen Anne's War 1710–1711.* New Haven, Connecticut: Acorn Club of Connecticut, 1916.

Cemetery Inscriptions, Records of Veterans, and Other Miscellaneous Records from the Connecticut State Library. Microfilm. Salt Lake City: Genealogical Society of Utah, 1979.

Collections of the Connecticut Historical Society, vols. 9 and 10. Hartford: Connecticut Historical Society, 1905.

Connecticut Adjunct General, *Record of Service of Connecticut Men in the War of the Revolution, War of 1812, Mexican War.* Hartford, Connecticut: Case, Lockwood & Brainard, 1889.

Connecticut Adjunct General. *Catalogue of Connecticut Volunteer Organizations.* Hartford, Connecticut: adjunct general, 1869.

Connecticut Adjunct General. *Record of Service of Connecticut Men, III, Mexican War.* Hartford, Connecticut: Case, Lockwood and Brainard, 1889.

Connecticut Adjutant General, *Records of Service of Connecticut Men in the I. War of the Revolution, II. War of 1812, III. Mexican War.* Hartford: Case, Lockwood and Brainard Co., 1889.

Connecticut Historical Society. *Rolls and Lists of Connecticut Men in the Revolution, 1775–1783.* Collections of the Connecticut Historical Society, vols. 8, 12. Hartford, Connecticut: 1901–09. Reprint. Baltimore: Heritage Books, 1996.

Connecticut Historical Society. *Rolls of Connecticut Men in the French and Indian War, 1755–1762.* 2 vols. Hartford, Connecticut, 1903–1905.

Connecticut Society Daughter of the American Revolution. *Connecticut Revolutionary Pensioners.* (1919) Reprint. Baltimore: Clearfield Co., 1997.

Connecticut State Library. *Connecticut Archives: Revolutionary War (Selected Papers), Series 1-3, 1763–1820.* Microfilm of originals at the Connecticut State Library in Hartford, Connecticut. Salt Lake City: Filmed by the Genealogical Society of Utah, 1954.

Connecticut. Governor. *Military Census Questionnaires, 1917–1918.* Microfilm of original records in the Connecticut State Archives, Hartford. Salt Lake City: Genealogical Society of Utah, 1988–1989. 454 microfilm.

Croffut, W. A. *The Military and Civil History of Connecticut during the War of 1861–65: Comprising a Detailed Account of the Various Regiments and Batteries, Through March, Encampment, Bivouac and Battle: Also Instances of Distinguished Personal Gallantry, and Biographical Sketches of Many Heroic Soldiers: Together with a Record of the Patriotic Action of Citizens at Home, and of the Liberal Support Furnished by the State in its Executive and Legislative Departments.* New York: Ledyard Bill, 1868.

Judd, Sylvester. *Connecticut Archives: War of 1812 (selected papers, 1812–1819.)* Salt Lake City: Filmed by the Genealogical Society of Utah, 1954. 2 microfilm.

Judd, Sylvester. *Connecticut Archives: Selected Papers of Colonial Wars.* Microfilm of originals at the Connecticut State Library in Hartford, Connecticut. Salt Lake City: Filmed by the Genealogical Society of Utah, 1954. 7 microfilm.

Record of Service of Connecticut Men in the Army and Navy of the United States During the War of the Rebellion. Hartford: Case, Lockwood & Brainard Co., 1889.

Rolls of Connecticut Men in the French and Indian War: 1755–1762. 2 vols. Hartford, Connecticut: Connecticut Historical Society, 1903–1905.

Roster of Soldiers, Sailors and Marines of the War of 1812, the Mexican War, and the War of the Rebellion. Lincoln, Nebraska: Nebraska State Genealogical Society, 1988.

Shepard, James. *Connecticut Soldiers in the Pequot War of 1637.* Meriden, Connecticut: Journal Publishing Co., 1913.

Society of the Colonial Wars. *Register of Pedigrees and Services of Ancestors.* Hartford, Connecticut: The society, 1941

The Public Records of the Colony of Connecticut (1636–1775), 15 vols. Hartford, Connecticut: 1850–1890.

U.S. Bureau of Pensions. *Pension Records of the Revolutionary Soldiers from Connecticut.* Washington, D.C.: Government Printing Office, 1919.

United States. Selective Service System. *Connecticut World War I Selective Service System Draft Registration Cards, 1917–1918.* National Archives Microfilm Publications, M1509. Washington, D.C.: National Archives, 1987–1988.

United States. Veterans Administration. *Revolutionary War Pension and Bounty-land-warrant Application Files.* Microfilm of original records in the National Archives, Washington, D.C. Washington, D.C.: The National Archives, 1969.

White, David O. *Connecticut's Black Soldiers, 1775–1783.* Chester, Connecticut: Pequot Press, 1973.

Vital and Cemetery

Arnold, James N. *Index to James N. Arnold Tombstone Records' Collection.* Microfilm of index cards at Knight Memorial Library, Providence, Rhode Island. Salt Lake City: Filmed by the Genealogical Society of Utah, 1992. 12 microfilm.

Bailey, Frederick. *Early Connecticut Marriages, as Found on Ancient Church Records Prior to 1800.* 1896–1906. Reprinted with integrated errata. 7 books in 1 vol. Baltimore: Genealogical Publishing Co., 1982.

Barbour, Lucius, comp. *Barbour Collection: Connecticut Vital Records Prior to 1850.* Microfilm of original records at the State Library Hartford, Connecticut. Salt Lake City: Filmed by the Genealogical Society of Utah, 1949.

Bible Records from Connecticut, Index Cards. Salt Lake City: Genealogical Society of Utah, 1949. Microfilm.

Bowman Collection: *Connecticut Vital Records in Massachusetts (1790's to Late 1800's).* Microfilm of card file in the Connecticut State Library, Hartford, Connecticut. Salt Lake City: Filmed by the Genealogical Society of Utah, 1949. Microfilm.

Connecticut State Library (Hartford, Connecticut). *Vital Records, A–Y: An Index to the Connecticut Historical Society Bulletin, Vols. 1–8.* Microfilm of original at the State Library in Hartford, Connecticut. Salt Lake City: Filmed by the Genealogical Society of Utah, 1949. Microfilm.

Daughters of the American Revolution (Connecticut). *Genealogical Collection.* Salt Lake City: Filmed by the Genealogical Society of Utah, 1970–1971.

Hale, Charles R. *Hale Collection.* Microfilm of typescript at the Connecticut State Library. Salt Lake City: Genealogical Society of Utah, 1949–1950. Microfilm.

Hearn, Daniel. *Connecticut Gravestones, Early to 1800.* Microfilm. Salt Lake City: Genealogical Society of Utah, 1989.

Ledogar, Edwin Richard. *Vital Statistics of Eastern Connecticut, Western Rhode Island, South Central Massachusetts.* 2 vols. Reprint. Arvada, Colorado: Ancestors Publishers, 1995.

Slater, James A. *The Colonial Burying Grounds of Eastern Connecticut and the Men Who Made Them.* Hamden, Connecticut: Published for the Academy by Archon Books, 1987.

Torrey, Clarence Almon. *New England Marriages Prior to 1700.* Andover, Massachusetts: Northeast Document Conservation Center, 1983.

County Website	Map Index	Date Created	Parent County or Territory From Which Organized Address/Details
Fairfield www.rootsweb.com/~Courtfairfi/	O9	10 May 1666	**Original county** Fairfield County; 1061 Main St; Bridgeport, Court 6604; Ph. (203) 579-6527 **Details:** (Town Clerks have Birth, Marriage, Death & land Records from 1700; Probate Judge has Probate Records) Towns Organized Before 1800: Brookfield 1788, Danbury 1685, Fairfield 1639, Greenwich 1640, Huntington (Shelton) 1789, New Fairfield 1740, Newtown 1711, Norwalk 1651, Redding 1767, Ridgefield 1708, Stanford 1641, Trumball 1798, Weston 1787.
Hartford www.rootsweb.com/~Courthartfo/	J4	10 May 1666	**Original county** Hartford County; 95 Washington St; Hartford, Court 6103; Ph. (203) 566-3170 **Details:** (Town & City Clerks have Birth, Marriage, Death, Burial & land Records; Probate Judge has Probate Records) Towns Organized Before 1800: Berlin 1785, Bristol 1785, Canton 1740, East Hartford 1783, East Windsor 1768, Enfield 1683, Farmington 1645, Glastonbury 1693, Granby 1786, Hartford 163, Granby 1786, Hartford 1635, Hartland, 1761, Sinsbury 1670, Southington 1779, Suffield 1674, Wethersfield 1634, Windsor 1633.
Litchfield www.geocities.com/TheTropics/1926/litchfield.html	M4	14 Oct 1751	**Hartford, Fairfield** Litchfield County; PO Box 247; Litchfield, Court 6759; Ph. (203) 567-0885 **Details:** (Clerk Superior Court has Divorce & Court Records from 1800's; Town Clerks have Birth, Marriage, Death & land Records; Probate Judge has Probate Records) Towns Organized Before 1800: Barkhamstead 1799, Bethlehem 1787, Canaan 1739, Colebrook 1799, Cornwall 1740, Goshen 1739, Harwinton 1737, Kent 1739, Litchfield 1719, New Hartford 1738, New Milford 1712, Norfolk 1758, Plymouth 1795, Roxbury 1796, Salisbury 1741, Sharon 1739, Torrington 1740, Washington 1779, Warren 1768, Watertown 1780, Winchester 1771, Woodbury 1673.
Middlesex www.rootsweb.com/~Courtmiddle/midlsxco.htm	H7	2 May 1785	**Hartford, New London, New Haven** Middlesex County; 265 DeKoven Dr; Middletown, Court 6457; Ph. (860) 344-2966 **Details:** (Town Clerks have Birth, Marriage, Death & land Records; Clerk Superior Court has Divorce & Court Records from 1800; Probate Judge has Probate Records) Towns Organized Before 1800: Chatham 1767, Durham 1704, East Haddam 1734, Haddam 1668, Killingsworth 1667, Middletown 1651, Saybrook 1635
New Haven www.geocities.com/TheTropics/1926/newhaven.html	K8	10 May 1666	**Original county** New Haven County; 235 Church St; New Haven, Court 6510; Ph. (203) 787-7908 **Details:** (Town Clerks have Birth, Marriage, Death & land Records; County Clerk has Divorce & Court Records; Probate Court has Probate Records) Towns Organized Before 1800: Branford 1639, Cheshire 1780, East Haven 1785, Guilford 1639, Hamden 1786, Meriden 1796, Millford 1639, New Haven 1638, North Haven 1786, Oxford 1798, Seymour 1672, Southbury 1787, South Derby 1675, Wallingford 1670, Waterbury 1686, Wolcott 796, Woodbridge 1784.

County	Map	Date	Parent County or Territory From Which Organized
Website	Index	Created	Address/Details

New London   D7   **10 May 1666**   **Original county**
www.rootsweb.com/~Courtnewlon/index.htm

New London County; 181 State St; New London, Court 6320;
Ph. (860) 447-5204
Details: (Clerk Superior Court has Divorce Records; Town Clerks have Birth, Marriage, Death & land Records from 1659 & Burial Records from 1893; Probate Judge has Probate Records)
   Towns Organized Before 1800: Bozrah 1786, Colchester 1698, Franklin 1786, Groton 1705, Lebanon 1700, Lisbon 1786, Lyme 1665, Montville 1786, New London 164, Norwich 1659, Preston 1687, Stonington 1649, Voluntown 1721.

Tolland   G4   **13 Oct 1785**   **Windham**
http://users.rcn.com/lmerrell/tolland.html

Tolland County; 69 Brooklyn St; Rockville, Court 06066-3643;
Ph. (860) 875-6294
Details: (Town Clerks have Birth, Marriage, Death & land Records; Probate Judge has Probate Records; Clerk Superior Court has Court Records)
   Towns Organized Before 1800: Bolton 1730, Coventry 1712, Ellington 1786, Hebron 1708, Mansfield 1702, Somers 1734, Stafford 1719, Tolland 1715, Union 1734, Vernon 1716, Wilington 172.

Windham   D4   **12 May 1726**   **Hartford, New London**
http://users.rcn.com/lmerrell/windham.html

Windham County; 155 Church St; Putnam, Court 6260;
Ph. (860) 928-2779
Details: (Town Clerks have Birth, Marriage, Death & land Records from 1692 & Burial Records from 1900; Probate Judge has Probate Records; Clerk Superior Court has Divorce Records)
   Towns Organized Before 1800: Ashford 1714, Brooklyn 1786, Canterbury 1703, Hampton 1786, Killingly 1708, Plainfield 1699, Pomfret 1713, Sterling 1794, Thompson 1785, Windham 1692, Woodstock (New Roxbury) 1686.

Notes

Delaware

Capital: Dover

First State

State: 1787 (1st)

Liberty and independence

Henry Hudson discovered Delaware in 1609 while in the service of the Dutch East India Company as he searched for the fabled Northwest Passage through North America to the Pacific Ocean. A year later, English explorer Samuel Argall sailed into the Delaware Bay and named the area for Virginia's governor, Lord De La Warr. Based on information provided by Hudson and other Dutch navigators, the Dutch West India Company was formed in 1621. In 1629, this company adopted a charter to grant land in the New World. They bought land adjoining the Delaware River and in 1631 David Pietersen de Vries established a camp on Lewes Beach, which failed. In 1638, the New Sweden Company outfitted an expedition to establish the first permanent settlement in Delaware at Wilmington. It was called Fort Christina.

The Dutch seized Fort Christina in 1655, making it part of New Netherland. The following year, the first Finnish colonists came to Delaware. In 1664, the English conquered New Netherland. Many English settlers came shortly afterward, mainly from Virginia, Maryland, New Jersey, New York, and Europe, and mingled with the Dutch and Swedes. In 1682, Delaware was granted to William Penn, but the people in Delaware objected so strongly that they were granted their own assembly in 1703. Meanwhile, Maryland claimed the southern and western parts of Delaware from 1684 to 1763, when Mason and Dixon established the western boundary of Delaware as well as the boundary between Pennsylvania and Maryland.

Delaware was a colony of great religious diversity. The Swedes brought their religion, as did the Dutch. Irish settlers brought the Presbyterian faith after 1698. Roman Catholics, as early as 1730, settled in the northern part of Delaware. French Catholics came from the West Indies in 1790.

Many of the settlers of the northern part of Delaware moved on to Pennsylvania, Maryland, and New Jersey. Delaware was on the front line of the Revolutionary War for nearly a year. This necessitated changing the capital from New Castle to Dover. Delaware became the first state to ratify the Constitution on 7 December, 1787. Although Delaware was a slave state during the Civil War, it overwhelmingly supported the Union. Over 16,000 men served the Union, while only several hundred served the Confederacy.

Due to slow transportation in its early days, Delaware's counties were divided into districts, called hundreds. These correspond to townships. Emigrants came primarily from Italy, Poland, Russia, Ireland, Germany, and England.

Look for vital records in the following locations:

- **Birth and death records:** Statewide registration of births began in 1861, stopped in 1863, and resumed in 1881. The Delaware Office of Vital Statistics in Dover, Delaware has birth and death records from 1861. Since all records are filed by year, it is necessary to have the year before a search can be initiated.

- **Marriage records:** State registrations of marriages began in 1847 and are also available from the Bureau of Vital Statistics. Counties began keeping marriage records as early as 1832.

- **Land records:** County recorders have deeds, mortgages, and leases from the late 1600's to the present.

- **Wills and probate records:** The Registrar of Wills has kept probate records from 1682 to the present. Some probate records are at the Bureau of Archives and Records Management, Hall of Records. The Bureau also has documents from the Swedish colonial period, the Dutch settlement, the Duke of York regime, and the Penn proprietorship. Most of its records date from statehood, including probate records; state, county, and municipal records; business records; and many others. Some early colonial records are in the archives of the states of New York and Pennsylvania.

Office of Vital Statistics Division of Public Health
Box 637
Dover, Delaware 19903
(302) 739-4700; Fax (888) 459-2943
www.dhss.delaware.gov/dhss/dph/ss/vitalstats.html

Delaware

Delaware Public Archives
121 Duke of York Street
Dover, Delaware 19902
(302) 744-5000
www.state.de.us/sos/dpa/

Societies and Repositories

Caesar Rodney Chapter, DESSAR; Delaware;
JackCLewis@aol.com.

Delaware County Historical Society; DE;
http://users.mwci.net/~delhi/hist_soc.htm.

Delaware Digital Library; DE; www.lib.de.us.

Delaware Genealogical Society; 505 Market Street Mall;
Wilmington, DE 19801; DEPatriot@aol.com;
http://delgensoc.org.

Delaware Public Archives; 121 Duke of York Street; Dover,
DE 19901; (302) 744-5000; archives@state.de.us;
www.state.de.us/sos/dpa.

Division of Historical and Cultural Affairs; Dept. of State;
Hall of Records; 21 The Green; Dover, DE 19901.
(302) 736-7400

Fort Delaware Society; PO Box 553; Delaware City, DE
19706; FtDSociety@del.net; www.del.net/org/fort.

General John Dagworthy Chapter, DESSAR;
alex.mcclure@dol.net.

Historical Society of Delaware; 505 Market Street;
Wilmington, DE 19801; hsd@hsd.org; www.hsd.org.

Jewish Federation of Delaware; 100 W. 10th Street, Suite
301; Wilmington, DE 19801-1628.

Jewish Historical Society of Delaware; 505 Market Street
Mall; Wilmington, DE 19801; jhsdel@hotmail.com;
http://hsd.org/jhsd.htm.

Major Peter Jaquett Chapter, DESSAR;
rdowning@udel.edu.

Major Robert Kirkwood Chapter, DESSAR;
DEPatriot@aol.com; www.sar.org/dessar/kirkwood.htm.

Bibliography and Record Sources

General

Arellano, Fay Louise Smith. *Delaware Trails: Some Tribal
Records 1842–1907.* Reprint. Baltimore: Clearfield Co.,
1997.

Bendler, Bruce A. *Colonial Delaware Assemblymen,
1682–1775.* Westminster, Maryland: Family Line
Publications, 1989.

Bendler, Bruce. *Colonial Delaware Records 1681–1713.*
Westminster, Maryland: Family Line Publications, 1992.

*Biographical and Genealogical History of the State of
Delaware: Containing Biographical and Genealogical
Sketches of Prominent and Representative Citizens, and
Many of the Early Settlers.* Tucson, Arizona: Filmed by
W. C. Cox, 1974.

Burr, Horace. *The Records of Holy Trinity (Old Swedes)
Church, Wilmington, Delaware, for 1697–1773.*
Wilmington, Delaware: Historical Society of Delaware,
1890.

Clark, Allen B. *This Is Good Country: A History of the
Amish of Delaware, 1915–1988.* Gordonville,
Pennsylvania: Gordonville Print Shop, 1989.

Clark, Patricia L., and Dorothy Huntsman, eds. *American
Genealogical Biographical Key Title Index.* Salt Lake
City: Genealogical Society of Utah. 1990.

Clark, Raymond B. *Delaware Church Records: A
Collection of Baptisms, Marriages, Deaths and Other
Records and Tombstone Inscriptions, From 1686–1880;
Five Important Religious Groups: Baptist, Episcopal,
Methodist, Presbyterian and Quaker with Historical
Sketches of the Churches or Groups . . . .* St. Michaels,
Maryland: R. B. Clark, 1986.

Coghlan, Gladys M. *Index to History of Delaware,
1609–1888.* Wilmington, Delaware: Historical Society
of Delaware, 1976.

Daughters of the American Revolution (DAR), Delaware.
Old Bible Records. 13 vols. Newark, Delaware: n.p.,
1944–1973.

Delaware Genealogical Research Guide. Delaware
Genealogical Society, 1989.

Delaware Public Archives Commission. *Delaware
Archives.* 3 vols. Wilmington, Delaware: James and
Walls, Printers, 1875.

*Directory of Churches and Religious Organizations in
Delaware.* Dover, Delaware: Historical Records Survey,
1942.

Doherty, Thomas P., ed. *Delaware Genealogical Research
Guide.* Delaware Genealogical Society, 1997.

Eckert, Jack. *Guide to the Records of Philadelphia Yearly
Meeting.* Philadelphia, Pennsylvania: Haverford
College, Records Committee of Philadelphia Yearly
Meeting, Swarthmore College, 1989.

Ferris, Benjamin. *A History of the Original Settlements on
the Delaware. . .& A History of Wilmington.*
Wilmington, Delaware: Wilson & Heald, 1846.

Frech, Mary L. *Chronology and Documentary Handbook of
the State of Delaware.* Dobbs Ferry, New York: Oceana
Publications, 1973.

Giles, Barbara S. comp. *Selected Delaware Bibliography
and Resources.* Seattle: B. S. Giles, 1990.

Hart, Matilda Spicer. *The Delaware Historical and
Genealogical Recall.* 1936. Reprint, Wilmington
Delaware: Delaware Genealogical Society, 1984.

Hartford Times Scrapbooks Index. Microreproduction of
original ms. and typescript at the Public Library, Grand
Rapids, Michigan. Salt Lake City: Filmed by the
Genealogical Society of Utah, 1974. 8 microfilm.

Historical Records Survey (Delaware). *Inventory of the
County Archives of Delaware. No. 1. New Castle*

County. Dover, Delaware: The Public Archives Commission, 1941.

Historical Research Committee. Delaware Society of the Colonial Dames of America. *A Calendar of Wills, New Castle County, 1682–1800.* New York: 1911. Reprint. Baltimore: Genealogical Publishing Co., 1969.

Holley, Barbara Ann, ed. *Directory of Libraries and Information Sources in the Philadelphia Area (Eastern Pennsylvania, Southern New Jersey, and Delaware).* Philadelphia: Special Libraries Association, Philadelphia Chapter, 1977.

Hugh M. Morris Library, Reference Dept. *Bibliography of Delaware, 1960–1974.* Newark: University of Delaware, 1976.

Johnson, Amandus. *The Swedish Settlements on the Delaware, 1638–1664.* 2 vols. 1911. Reprint, Baltimore: Genealogical Publishing Co., 1969.

Mattern, Joanne and Harold B. Hancock, comps. *A Preliminary Inventory of the Older Records in the Delaware Archives.* Dover, Delaware: Delaware Public Archives, 1978.

Mattsson, Algot. *New Sweden the Dream of an Empire.* Goteborg: Tre Bocker, 1987.

Nelson, Ralph D. *Delaware 1782 Tax Assessment and Census.* Wilmington, Delaware: Delaware Genealogical Society, 1994.

Public Archives Commission. *Delaware Archives.* 5 vols. Wilmington, Delaware: The Commission, 1911–.

Redden, Robert, ed. *Delaware Genealogical Society Surname Index.* Wilmington, Delaware: Delaware Genealogical Society, 1995.

Reed, Henry Clay and Marion Bjhomason Reed, comps. *A Bibliography of Delaware through 1960.* Newark: University of Delaware Press for the Institute of Delaware History and Culture, 1966.

Reed, Henry Clay and Marion Bjhomason Reed, comps. *Delaware, A History of the First State.* 3 vols. New York: Lewis Historical Publishing Company, 1947.

Rider, Fremont, ed. *American Genealogical- Biographical Index.* Vols. 1–186+. Middletown, Connecticut: Godfrey Memorial Library, 1952–.

Riggs, John Beverley. *A Guide to Manuscripts in the Eleutherian Mills Historical Library. . .* Greenville, Delaware: Eleutherian Mills Historical Library, 1970.

Rising, Johan Claesson. *The Rise and Fall of New Sweden: Governor Johan Rising's Journal 1654–1655.* Stockholm: Almqvist & Wiksell International, 1988. Uddevalla: Bohus Laningens boktr.

Scharf, John Thomas. *History of Delaware, 1609–1888.* 2 vols. Tucson, Arizona: W. C. Cox, 1974.

Scott, Kenneth and Janet Clarke. *Abstracts from the Pennsylvania Gazette, 1748–1755.* Baltimore: Genealogical Publishing, 1977.

Special Libraries Association. Philadelphia Chapter. *Directory of Libraries and Information Sources in the Philadelphia Area (Eastern Pennsylvania, Southern New Jersey and Delaware).* Philadelphia: [s.n.], 1977.

Todd, Robert W. *Methodism of the Peninsula, or, Sketches of Notable Characters and Events in the History of Methodism in the Maryland and Delaware Peninsula.* Philadelphia: Methodist Episcopal Book Rooms, 1886.

Turner, Joseph Brown. *Genealogical Collection of Delaware Families.* Salt Lake City: Genealogical Society of Utah, 1948.

United States. Bureau of Internal Revenue. *Internal Revenue Assessment Lists for Delaware, 1862–1866.* Washington, D.C.: National Archives, 1988.

Virdin, Donald Odell. *Delaware Family Histories and Genealogies.* St. Michaels, Maryland: Raymond B. Clark, 1984.

Weis, Fredrick Lewis. *The Colonial Clergy of Maryland, Delaware, and Georgia.* Baltimore: Genealogical Publishing, 1978.

Williams, E. Melvin. *History of Delaware, Past and Present.* 4 vols. New York: Lewis Historical Pub., 1929.

Wright, F. Edward. *Colonial Families of Delaware,* Vol. 6. Colonial Roots.

Wright, F. Edward. *Colonial Families of Delaware.* Westminster, Maryland: Willow Bend and Family Line Publications, 1998, 1999, 2000.

Atlases, Maps and Gazetteers

Beers, Daniel G. *Atlas of the State of Delaware. . .* Philadelphia: Pomeroy and Beers, 1868.

Bounds, Harvey C. *A Postal History of Delaware.* Newark, Delaware: Press of Kells, 1938.

Heck, L. W. *Delaware Place Names.* Washington, D.C.: U.S. Government Printing Office, 1966.

Gannett, Henry. *A Gazetteer of Maryland and Delaware.* Baltimore: Genealogical Publishing Co., 1976.

Long, John H., ed. *Delaware, Maryland, District of Columbia Atlas of Historical County Boundaries.* New York: Charles Scribner's Sons, Simon & Schuster Macmillan, 1996.

Maryland-Delaware Atlas & Gazetteer. Freeport, Maine: DeLorme Mapping, 1993.

Scott, Joseph. *A Geographical Description of the States of Maryland and Delaware: Also of the Counties, Towns, Rivers, Bays and Islands with a List of the Hundreds in Each County.* Kimber, Conrad, 1807.

Smith, Chester M. *The Postal History of Maryland, the Delmarva Peninsula and the District of Columbia: The Post Offices and First Postmasters from 1775 to 1984.* Burtonsville, Maryland: The Depot, 1984.

United States. Geological Survey. *Delaware Geographic Names: Alphabetical Finding List.* Reston, Virginia: U.S.G.S. Topographic Division, [1981].

U.S. Geological Survey. *National Gazetteer of the United States: Delaware 1983.* Washington, D.C.: Government Printing Office, 1984.

Delaware

Censuses

Available Census Records and Census Substitutes

Federal Census 1800, 1810, 1820, 1830, 1840, 1850, 1860, 1870, 1880, 1900, 1910, 1920, 1930

Federal Mortality Schedules 1870, 1880

Reconstructed State Census 1782

Residents 1693

Militia Rolls 1803–1807

Tax Lists 1681–1713

Quit Rents 1702–1713

Rent Rolls 1681–1688

Adams Apple Press. *The First Tax List for the Province of Pennsylvania and the Three Lower Counties, 1693.* Bedminster, Pennsylvania: The Press, 1994.

Craig, Peter Stebbins. *The 1693 Census of the Swedes on the Delaware.* Winter Park, Florida: SAG Publications, 1993.

DeValinger, Leon, Jr. *Reconstructed Census of Delaware.* Arlington, Virginia: National Genealogical Society, n.d.

Dollarhide, William. *The Census Book: A Genealogist's Guide to Federal Census Facts, Schedules and Indexes.* Bountiful, Utah: Heritage Quest, 1999.

Hancock, Harold B. *The Reconstructed Delaware Census of 1782.* Wilmington, Delaware: Delaware Genealogical Society, 1973.

Jackson, Ronald Vern and Gary Ronald Teeples. *Early Delaware Census Records, 1665–1697.* Bountiful, Utah: Accelerated Indexing Systems, 1977.

Lainhart, Ann S. *State Census Records.* Baltimore: Genealogical Publishing Co., Inc., 1992.

Kemp, Thomas Jay. *The American Census Handbook. Wilmington, Delaware: Scholarly Resources, Inc., 2001.*

Szucs, Loretto Dennis and Matthew Wright. *Finding Answers in U.S. Census Records.* Ancestry Publishing, 2001

Thorndale, William. *Map Guide to the U.S. Federal Census, 1790–1920.* Baltimore: Genealogical Publishing Co., 1987.

Court Records, Probate and Wills

Many records for the Courts of Delaware are found in the collections of the Delaware Public Archives, Dover, Delaware. The collection includes: dockets, calendars, petitions, sessions, orphan court minutes, appearance dockets, case files, court records, chancery records, miscellaneous records, etc. The collection inventory is online at www.state.de.us/sos/dpa/collections/guideintro.htm

DeValinger, Leon, Jr. *Calendar of Kent County, Delaware, Probate Records, 1680–1850.* Dover, Delaware: Public Archives Commission, 1944.

DeValinger, Leon, Jr., *Calendar of Sussex County, Delaware, Probate Records, 1680–1850.* Dover, Delaware: Public Archives Commission, 1964.

Documents Relating to the Colonial History of the State of New York. Albany, New York: The Argus Co., 1877.

Gehring, Charles T. *Delaware Papers.* 2 vols. Baltimore, Maryland: Genealogical Publishing Co., 1977–1981.

Smith, Carl T. *Philadelphia Administrations, 1683–1744 [abstracts].* Microfilm of original 2 vol. work at the Historical Society of Pennsylvania. Salt Lake City: Filmed by the Genealogical Society of Utah, 1964.

The First Laws of the State of Delaware 4 vols. (1797) Reprint. Wilmington, Delaware: Scholarly Resources.

Virdin, Donald O. *Colonial Delaware Wills and Estates to 1880; An Index.* Bowie, Maryland: Heritage Books, 1994.

Emigration, Immigration, Migration and Naturalization

Boyer, Carl. *Ship Passenger Lists: Pennsylvania and Delaware (1641–1825).* Newhall, California: The Compiler, 1980.

Coldham, Peter Wilson. *The Complete Book of Emigrants, 1607–1776 and Emigrants in Bondage, 1614–1775.* Novato, California: Brøderbund Software, 1996.

Delaware. Superior Court. *Naturalization Papers, Transcripts and Originals, A–Z.* Microfilm of the original records from the Hall of Records in Dover, Delaware. Salt Lake City: Genealogical Society of Utah, 1949.

Filby, P. William. *Philadelphia Naturalization Records.* Detroit: Gale Research, 1982.

United States. Bureau of Customs. *Copies of Lists of Passengers Arriving at Miscellaneous Ports on the Atlantic and Gulf Coasts.* National Archives Microfilm Publication.

United States. Bureau of Customs. *A Supplemental Index to Passenger Lists of Vessels Arriving At Atlantic & Gulf Coast Ports (Excluding New York) 1820–1874.* Washington, D.C.: Filmed by the National Archives Record Services, 1960.

United States. District Court (Delaware). *Naturalization Records, 1795–1932.* Microfilm of original records at the National Archives Branch, Philadelphia Branch. Salt Lake City: Genealogical Society of Utah, 1990. Microfilm, 27 rolls.

Land and Property

Bendler, Bruce A. *Colonial Delaware Records 1681–1713.* Westminster, Maryland: Family Line Publications, 1990.

Delaware Fugitive Records: An Inventory of the Official Land Grant Records Relating to the Present State of Delaware. Dover: Department of State, Division of Historical and Cultural Affairs, 1980.

Hone, Wade E. *Land and Property Research in the United States.* Salt Lake City: Ancestry Incorporated, 1997.

Kent County (Delaware). Recorder of Deeds. *Deed Record of Kent County, Delaware, 1680–1850; General Index,*

1680–1873. Salt Lake City: Filmed by the Genealogical Society of Utah, 1948.

Myers, Albert Cook, ed. *Walter Wharton's Land Survey Register, 1675–1679*. Wilmington, Delaware: The Historical Society of Delaware, 1955.

New Castle County (Delaware). Recorder of Deeds. *Deed Books of New Castle Co., Delaware, 1673–1850; General Index, 1640–1873*. Salt Lake City: Filmed by the Genealogical Society of Utah, 1949.

Original Land Titles in Delaware, Commonly Known as the Duke of York Record: Being an Authorized Transcript from the Official Archives of the State of Delaware, and Comprising the Letters Patent, Permits, Commissions, Surveys, Plats and Confirmations by the Duke of York and Other High Officials, from 1646 to 1679, with Revised Index. Wilmington, Delaware: Sunday Star Print, [1899]. Reprint. Baltimore: Clearfield Co., 1997.

Pennsylvania. Land Office. *Applications for Warrants, 1734–1865*. Salt Lake City: Genealogical Society of Utah, 1975.

Pennsylvania. Surveyor General's Office. *Applications for Warrants, 1755–1886*. Salt Lake City: Genealogical Society of Utah, 1976.

Pennsylvania. Surveyor General's Office. *Proprietary Papers, 1682–1850*. Salt Lake City: Genealogical Society of Utah, 1976.

Sussex County (Delaware). County Recorder. *Deed Records of Sussex Co., Delaware, 1693–1850*. Salt Lake City: Filmed by the Genealogical Society of Utah, 1948.

Weinberg, Allen and Thomas E. Slattery. *Warrants and Surveys of the Province of Pennsylvania Including the Three Lower Counties 1759*. 1965 Reprint. Knightstown, Indiana: Bookmark, 1975.

Military

Conner, William H., and Leon DeValinger, Jr. *Delaware's Role in World War II*. 2 vols. Dover, Delaware: Public Archives Commission, 1955.

Delaware. Public Archives Commission. *Delaware Archives*. 5 vols. Wilmington, Delaware: [s.n.], 1911–.

Peden, Henry C. Jr., *Colonial Delaware Soldiers and Sailors, 1638–1776*. Westminster, Maryland: Family Line Publications, 1995.

Peden, Henry C. Jr. *Delaware Militia in the War of 1812*. 2003. Colonial Roots.

Peden, Henry C. Jr., *Revolutionary Patriots of Delaware, 1775–1783*. Westminster, Maryland: Family Line Publications, 1996.

Roster of Soldiers, Sailors and Marines of the War of 1812, the Mexican War, and the War of the Rebellion... 4 vols. Lincoln, Nebraska: Nebraska State Genealogical Society, 1988.

United States. Adjutant General's Office. *General Index to Compiled Military Service Records of Revolutionary War Soldiers*. Washington, D.C.: National Archives, 1942.

United States. Adjutant General's Office. *Index to Compiled Service Records of Volunteer Union Soldiers Who Served in Organizations from the State of Delaware*. Washington, D.C.: The National Archives, 1964.

United States. Selective Service System. *Delaware World War I Selective Service System Draft Registration Cards, 1917–1918*. National Archives Microfilm Publications. Washington, D.C.: National Archives, 1987–1988.

White, Virgil D. *Index to Revolutionary War Service Records*. 4 vols. Waynesboro, Tennessee: National Historical Publishing, 1995.

Whitely, William G. *The Revolutionary Soldiers of Delaware*, Wilmington, Delaware: James and Walls, Printers, 1875.

Vital and Cemetery Records

Cope, Gilbert. *A List of Marriage License Bonds... in New Castle County, Delaware, 1744–1836*. Salt Lake City: Genealogical Society of Utah, 1965.

Delaware Bureau of Vital Statistics. *Birth Records, 1861–1913*. Microfilm of original records at the Hall of Records in Dover, Delaware. Salt Lake City: Filmed by the Genealogical Society of Utah, 1949. 37 microfilm.

Delaware Bureau of Vital Statistics. *Birth Records, Prior 1913 (1861-1912) – 1923*. Microfilm of original records at the Hall of Records in Dover, Delaware. [S.l.]: International Microfilmers, 1972. 39 microfilm.

Delaware Bureau of Vital Statistics. *Death Records, 1855–1910*. Microfilm of original records at the Hall of Records in Dover, Delaware. Salt Lake City: Filmed by the Genealogical Society of Utah, 1949. 50 microfilm.

Delaware Bureau of Vital Statistics. *Death Records, 1910–1955*. Microfilm of original records at the Hall of Records in Dover, Delaware ([S.l.]: International Microfilmers, 1973.) 75 microfilm.

Delaware Bureau of Vital Statistics. *Index Cards of Delaware Marriages, Baptisms, Births and Deaths, Ca. 1680–1934*. Microfilm of original index (typescript) at the Delaware State Archive Hall of Records in Dover. Salt Lake City: Filmed by the Genealogical Society of Utah, 1949. 18 microfilm.

Delaware Bureau of Vital Statistics. *Index Cards to Delaware Marriages, Baptisms, Births, and Deaths, 1680–1913*. Microfilm of original index (typescript) at the Delaware State Archive Hall of Records in Dover. Salt Lake City: Genealogical Society of Utah, 1949. Microfilm, 18 reels.

Delaware Bureau of Vital Statistics. *Marriage records, pre-1913 (1865-Jan 1913) – 1954*. Microfilm of original records at the Hall of Records in Dover, Delaware. Dover, Delaware: Filmed by the Bureau of Archives & Records Microfilm Service, 1993–1994. 133 microfilm.

Clark, Raymond B., ed. *Delaware Tombstone Inscriptions*. St. Michaels, Maryland: R. B. Clark, 1989.

Delaware

Dill, Raymond Walter. *Souls in Heaven, Names in Stone, Kent County, Delaware Cemetery Records.* Baltimore: Gateway Press, 1989.

Hudson, Millard F. *Cemetery Records of Sussex County, Delaware.* Salt Lake City: Genealogical Society of Utah, 1948.

Richards, Mary Fallon. *Deaths from the Delaware Gazette, 1854–1859, 1861–1864.* Wilmington, Delaware: Delaware Genealogical Society, 1995.

Richards, Mary Fallon. *Marriages from the Delaware Gazette, 1854–1859, 1861–1864.* Wilmington, Delaware: Delaware Genealogical Society, 1996.

Tatnall, Walter G. *Tombstone Records, New Castle County, Kent County, and Sussex County, Delaware.* Salt Lake City: Genealogical Society of Utah, 1949.

County	Map	Date	Parent County or Territory From Which Organized
Website	Index	Created	Address/Details

Deale | | 1680 | **Hoarekill**
Deale County; DE
Details: County Terminated in 1682

Hoarekill | | 8 Aug 1673 | **Original county**
Hoarekill County; DE
Details: Alternate Spelling "Whorekill"(see Deale) Name changed to Deale 30 Jun 1680. Name changed to Sussex 4 Dec 1682.

Kent   J5 | | 1642 | **St. Jones**
www.rootsweb.com/~dekent/ | | | Kent County; 414 Federal St; Dover, DE 19901; Ph. (302) 744-2347
Details: (Formerly St. Jones County. Name changed to Kent by 31 Dec 1683) (Clerk of Peace has Marriage Records; Clerk Superior Court has Divorce & Court Records; Recorder of Deeds has land Records from 1680; Register of Wills has Probate Records)

New Amstel | | 8 Aug 1673 | **Original county**
New Amistel County; DE
Details: (see New Castle) Name changed to New Castle by 31 Dec 1674

New Castle   E4 | | 8 Aug 1673 | **New Amistel**
www.co.new-castle.de.us/ | | | New Castle County; 800 N French St; Wilmington, DE 19801; Ph. (302) 571-7545
Details: (Formerly New Amistel County. Name changed to New Castle by 31 Dec 1674) (Clerk of Peace has Marriage Records from 1911; Prothonotary has Divorce & Court Records; Register of Wills has Probate Records; Recorder Deeds has land Records)

St. Jones | | 1680 | **Upland**
St. Jones County; DE
Details: County Terminated in 1682 (see Kent) Name changed to St. Jones 30 Jun 1680. Name changed to Kent by 31 Dec 1683

Sussex   O6 | | 1682 | **Deale**
www.sussexcounty.net/ | | | Sussex County; 2 The Cir; PO Box 589; Georgetown, DE 19947; Ph. (302) 855-7785
Details: (Formerly Deale County. Name changed to Sussex 4 Dec 1682) (Recorder of Deeds has land Records from 1693; Register of Wills has Probate Records)

Upland | | 8 Aug 1673 | **Original county**
Upland County; DE
Details: County Terminated in 1681 (see St. Jones & Kent) Name changed to St. Jones 30 Jun 1680. Name changed to Kent by 31 Dec 1683

Notes

District of Columbia

Territory of Washington, D.C.

Organized: 1790

Seat of Government: 1800

Justice for all

In 1783, the Continental Congress voted to establish a federal city. The site was selected by George Washington in 1790 as a political compromise between the northern and southern states. The capital of the United States covers about 70 square miles on the northeast side of the Potomac River, about 38 miles southwest of Baltimore. Maryland ceded parts of Montgomery, including Georgetown, and Prince George's County to the United States for its capital in the late 1780's. Virginia also ceded part of Fairfax County, including Alexandria. These counties continued to govern the area until about 1801. Virginia kept permanent custody of the records from Alexandria.

Congress convened for the first time in Washington in 1800 and Thomas Jefferson's inaugural in March 1801 was its first inauguration. Growth was very slow, increasing from 8,000 in 1800 to only 75,000 in 1860. In 1801, the counties of Washington and Alexandria were established in the District. The city of Washington was incorporated in 1802. The British captured Washington during the War of 1812 and burned most of the public buildings and records. During the Civil War, Washington was again threatened, but survived unscathed. Slavery was abolished in the District of Columbia in 1862.

The land ceded by Virginia for the District was returned to Virginia in 1846. The city's status was changed to that of a federal territory in 1871. Georgetown became part of the city of Washington, D.C., in 1895. Since then, the city of Washington, D.C., has had the same boundaries as the District of Columbia.

- **Birth and death records:** Registration of birth and death records began in 1874, with general compliance by 1915 for births and 1880 for deaths, although some earlier death records exist. The Department of Human Services, Vital Records Section in Washington, D.C., is the custodian for these records.

- **Marriage records:** The Superior Court of the District of Columbia, Marriage License Bureau in Washington, D.C., keeps marriage records. Registration began in 1811.

- **Divorce records:** Divorce proceedings prior to September 1956 are available from the Clerk of the U.S. District in Washington, D.C. Divorce docket, 1803–1848, is in the General Branch, Civil Archives Division, National Archives and Record Administration in Maryland. The administration receives mail at the Washington, D.C. address noted below.

- **Court records:** The National Archives also has records for the U.S. Circuit Court for the District of Columbia and Washington County Court records. Other records include building permits for the District for 1877–1949, Internal Revenue assessment lists for 1862–1866, and other tax books for Georgetown and the city and county of Washington.

- **Wills:** Clerk of the Probate Court, U.S. Courthouse has original wills from 1801 to the present. The courts in Virginia and Maryland kept probate records prior to 1801.

- **Land records:** Recorder of Deeds in Washington, D.C., holds all real estate records. Prior to 1895, deeds and wills for Georgetown were registered in Montgomery County, Maryland. Some of the records for Georgetown for 1800–1879 are available from the National Archives, microfilm M605.

- **More records:** The National Society, Daughters of the American Revolution in Washington, D.C., maintains a library of more than 40,000 volumes consisting of manuscripts and genealogical records, tombstone inscriptions, etc. The Genealogical Department of the Library of Congress in Washington, D.C., and the National Archives are two of the richest sources of genealogical material for Washington, D.C., and the entire United States.

Department of Health Vital Records Division

825 North Capitol Street NE
Washington, D.C. 20002
(202) 442-5999
www.dchealth.dc.gov/services/vital_records/index.shtm

District of Columbia Office of Public Records

John A. Wilson Building
1350 Pennsylvania Avenue, NW
Washington, D.C. 20004
(202) 727-1000
http://os.dc.gov/os/cwp/
view.asp?a=1207&Q=522721&osNav=/31376/

General Branch, Civil Archives Division, National Archives and Record Administration

Washington, D.C. 20409

Recorder of Deeds

515 D Street, N.W.
Washington, D.C. 20001
(202) 727-5374

Clerk of the U.S. District

333 Constitution Avenue, N.W.
Washington, D.C. 20001
(202) 273-0042

Register of Wills and Clerk of the Probate Court

U.S. Courthouse
500 Indiana Avenue, N.W.
Washington, D.C. 20001

National Society, Daughters of the American Revolution

1776 D Street, N.W.
Washington, D.C. 20006
(202) 628-1776

Societies and Repositories

Afro-American Historical and Genealogical Society, Inc.; PO Box 73067; Washington, D.C. 20056-3067; (301) 292-2751; Info@aahgs.org; www.aahgs.org.

Department of Veterans Affairs/National Cemetery Administration (40); 810 Vermont Ave. NW; Washington, D.C. 20420; (202) 273-5221; www.cem.va.gov.

District of Columbia Office of Public Records; John A. Wilson Building; 1350 Pennsylvania Avenue; Washington, D.C. 20004; (202) 727-1000; http://os.dc.gov/info/pubrec/pubrec.shtm.

District of Columbia Society, SAR; 725 15th Street, N.W. Ste 607, Washington D.C., 20005; dcssar@aol.com; www.sar.org/dcssar.

Jewish Special Interest Group; 3701 Connecticut Ave., NW #228; Washington, D.C. 20008.

National Society Daughters of American Colonists; 2205 Massachusetts Ave. N.W.; Washington, D.C. 20008.

Nation's Capitol Area Chapter, AHSGR; 2328—19th Street, NW; Washington, D.C. 20009; (202) 232-8827; ritabill@erols.com; www.ahsgr.org/dcapitol.html.

The National Society Children of the American Revolution; 1776 D Street NW Room 224; Washington, D.C. 20006-5392.

U.S. National Archives & Records Administration (NARA); National Archives Building; 700 Pennsylvania Ave.; Washington, D.C. 20408; www.nara.gov.

White House Historical Association; 740 Jackson Place, N.W.; Washington, D.C. 20506.

Bibliography and Record Sources

General

Allen, Ethan. *Washington; or, the Revolution: A Drama Founded Upon the Historic Events of the War for American Independence.* Washington, D.C.: National Cash Register, 1975. 5 microfiches.

American Biographical Directories, District of Columbia. . . 1908–0908. Washington, D.C.: Potomac Press, 1908.

A Biographical Congressional Directory, 1774 to 1900: The Continental Congress: September 5, 1774, to October 21, 1788, Inclusive [and] the United States Congress: the First Congress to the Fifty-seventh Congress, March 4, 1789, to March 4, 1903, Inclusive Washington, D.C.: Government Printing Office, 1903.

American Biographical Directories, District of Columbia, 1908–1909. Washington, D.C.: Potomac Press, 1908.

Angevine, Erma Miller. *Research in the District of Columbia.* Arlington, Virginia: National Genealogical Society, 1992.

Benton, Mildred, ed. *Library and Reference Facilities in the Area of the District of Columbia.* 12th ed. American Society for Information Science, 1986.

Cook, Eleanor Mildred Vaughan. *Guide to the Records of your District of Columbia Ancestors.* Silver Spring, Maryland: Family Line, 1987.

Daily National Intelligencer (Washington, D.C.).—No. 1 (Oct. 31, 1800).Washington, D.C.: Library of Congress, 1959.

A Directory of Churches and Religious Organizations in the District of Columbia, 1939. Washington, D.C.: District of Columbia Historical Records Survey, 1939.

Georgetown, Maryland (Montgomery County). *Property Tax Records: 1800–1820, 1862–1879.* Washington, D.C.: Filmed by the National Archives, 1965.

Georgetown, Maryland (Montgomery County). *Records, 1791–1878.* Washington, D.C.: The National Archives, 1965.

Green, Constance McLaughlin. *Washington: A History of the Capital, 1800–1950.* Princeton: Princeton University Press, 1964.

Hall, H. Byron. *Lest We Forget: A Guide to Genealogical Research in the Nation's Capital.* Annandale, Virginia: Annandale Stake, Church of Jesus Christ of Latter-day Saints, 1986.

Howe, Henry. *Historical Collections of Virginia: Containing a Collection of the Most Interesting Facts, Tradition, Biographical Sketches, Anecdotes, etc. Relating to its History and Antiquities, Together with Geographical and Statistical Description, to Which is Appended an Historical and Descriptive Sketch of the District of Columbia.* Charleston, South Carolina: Babcock, 1845.

Inventory of Church Archives in the District of Columbia: the Protestant Episcopal Church, Diocese of Washington. 2 vols. Washington, D.C.: Historical Records Survey, 1940.

Kranz, Sharlene. *Capital Collections: Resources for Jewish Genealogical Research in the Washington D.C. Area.* Bethesada, Maryland: Jewish Genealogical Society of Greater Washington, 1995.

Lewis, David L. *District of Columbia: A Bicentennial History.* New York: Norton, 1976.

Mackall, S. Somervell. *Early Days of Washington.* Washington: Neale Co., 1899.

National Archives and Records Administration. *Guide to Washington National Records Center Services.* Washington: National Archives and Records Administration.

Official Register of the United States: Containing a List of Officers and Employees in the Civil, Military, and Naval Service. Washington, D.C.: U.S. Gov't Printing Office, 1863–.

Pippenger, Wesley E. *District of Columbia Ancestors: A Guide to Records of the District of Columbia.* Westminster, Maryland: Family Line, 1997.

Pippenger, Wesley E. *The 1853 Washington and Georgetown Directory.* Revised 2004. Colonial Roots.

Porter, John Addison. *The City of Washington, Its Origin and Administration.* Baltimore: John Hopkins University, 1885.

Proctor, John Clagett. *Washington, Past and Present.* 4 vols. New York: Lewis Historical Publishing Co., 1930.

Provine, Dorothy S. *District of Columbia Free Negro Registers, 1821–1861.* 2 vols. Bowie, Maryland: Heritage Books, 1996.

Provine, Dorothy S. *District of Columbia Indentures of Apprenticeship, 1801–1893.* Lovettsville, Virginia: Willow Bend and Family Line Publications, 1998.

Provine, Dorothy S. *Preliminary Inventory of the Records of the Government of the District of Columbia. Record Group 351.* Washington, D.C.: National Archives and Records Service, 1976.

Schaefer, Christina K. *The Center: A Guide to Genealogical Research in the National Capitol Area.* Baltimore: Genealogical Publishing, 1996.

Smith, Chester M. *The Postal History of Maryland, the Delmarva Peninsula and the District of Columbia: The Post Offices and First Postmasters from 1775 to 1984.* Burtonsville, Maryland: The Depot, 1984.

Tindall, William. *Standard History of the City of Washington: From a Study of the Original Sources.* Knoxville, Tennessee: H.W. Crew, 1914.

Truett, Randall Bond. *Washington, D.C.: A Guide to the Nation's Capital.* New York: Hastings House, 1968.

United States. National Archives and Records Service. *Guide to Genealogical Research in the National Archives.* Washington, D.C.: National Archives and Records Service, 1985.

United States. Congress. *Federal Assessment, 1790–1805, Maryland, District of Columbia.* [Baltimore]: Maryland, Hall of Records Commission, 1965.

United States. Congress. *Official Congressional Directory. 1865–.*Washington, D.C.: U.S. Government Printing Office.

United States. National Archives and Records Service. *Preliminary Inventory of the Records of the Government of the District of Columbia, Record Group 351.* Washington, D.C.: National Archives and Records Service, 1976.

U.S. Department of State. *Register of Officers and Agents, Civil, Military, and Naval, in the Service of the United States.* Washington, D.C.: Government Printing Office, 1816–. Annual.

Webb, William B. *Centennial History of the City of Washington, D.C.* Dayton, Ohio: United Brethren Publishing House, 1892.

Williamson, Stanley. *Who's Who in the Nation's Capital.* Washington, D.C.: Ransdell, Inc., Biennial.

Atlases, Maps and Gazetteers

Long, John H. *Delaware, Maryland, District of Columbia Atlas of Historical County Boundaries.* New York: Charles Scribner's Sons, Simon & Schuster Macmillan, 1996.

Martin, Joseph. *A New and Comprehensive Gazetteer of Virginia, and the District of Columbia: Containing a Copious Collection of Geographical, Statistical, Political, Commercial, Religious, Moral and Miscellaneous Information, Collected and Compiled from the Most Respectable, and Chiefly from Original Sources.* Charlottesville, Virginia: J. Martin, 1835 (Moseley & Tompkins, printers.)

National Geographic Society (United States). Cartographic Division. *Round About the Nation's Capital with Descriptive Notes.* Washington, D.C.: The Society, 1956.

Truett, Randall Bond. *Washington, D.C.: A Guide to the Nation's Capital.* Original edition 1942. New York: Hastings House, 1968.

United States. Office of Geographic Research. Branch of Geographic Names. *District of Columbia Geographic Names.* Reston, Virginia: United States. Branch of Geographic Names, 1981. 2 microfiche.

Census

Available Census Records and Census Substitutes

Federal Census 1790 (with Maryland), 1800, 1810, 1820 (includes Alexandria County, Virginia), 1830 (includes Alexandria County, Virginia), 1840 (includes Alexandria County, Virginia), 1850, 1860, 1870, 1880, 1890, 1900, 1910, 1920, 1930

Federal Mortality Schedules 1850, 1860, 1870, 1880

Union Veterans and Widows 1890

State/Territorial Census 1867

Brown, Mary Ross. *An Illustrated Genealogy of the Counties of Maryland and the District of Columbia as a Guide to Locating Records: Including Detailed Maps Showing the Wards of the City of Baltimore in the Federal Censuses of 1850, 1860, 1870 & 1880.* S.l.: s.n., 1967.

Dollarhide, William. *The Census Book: A Genealogist's Guide to Federal Census Facts, Schedules and Indexes.* Bountiful, Utah: Heritage Quest,1999.

Kemp, Thomas Jay. *The American Census Handbook.* Wilmington, Delaware: Scholarly Resources, Inc., 2001.

Szucs, Loretto Dennis and Matthew Wright. *Finding Answers in U.S. Census Records.* Ancestry Publishing, 2001

Thorndale, William. *Map Guide to the U.S. Federal Census, 1790–1920.* Baltimore: Genealogical Publishing Co., 1987.

Court Records, Probate and Wills

Abstracts of Wills in the District of Columbia, 1776–1815: Compiled from Records in the Office of the Register of Wills. 2 vols. Washington: [s.n.], 1945–1946.

Bell, Mrs. Alexander H. *Abstracts of Wills in the District of Columbia, 1776–1815,* 2 vols. Washington, D.C.: Bell, 1946.

District of Columbia. Orphans Court. *Indentures of Apprenticeship Recorded in the Orphans Court,*

Washington County, District of Columbia, 1802–1811. Washington, D.C.: National Archives & Records Admin., 2000.

District of Columbia. *Register of Wills. Probate Records— 1801–1930, 1801–1930.* Microfilm of originals at the Office of Public Records, Washington, D.C. Salt Lake City: Filmed by the Genealogical Society of Utah, 1996–1997. 133 microfilm.

Hynson, Jerry M. *District of Columbia D.C. Department of Corrections Runaway Slave Book, 1848–1863: U.S. District Court for the District of Columbia Fugitive Slave Cases, 1862–1863.* Westminster, Maryland: Willow Bend Books, 1999.

Langille, Letitia A. *Wills, Book IV, Dated 1799 to 1837: As Recorded in the Office of Register of Wills, Municipal Court, Washington, D.C.* Microfilm of typescript ([50], 104 leaves) at the National Library of the D.A.R., Washington, D.C. Salt Lake City: Filmed by the Genealogical Society of Utah, 1972.

Pippenger, Wesley E. *District of Columbia Probate Records: Will books 1 through 6, 1801–1852 and Estate Files, 1801–1852.* Westminster, Maryland: Family Line, 1996.

Provine Dorothy S. *Index to District of Columbia Wills [1801–1920].* Baltimore: Genealogical Pub. Co., 1992.

United States. Circuit Court (District of Columbia*). Habeas Corpus Case Records: 1820–1863.* Washington, D.C.: National Archives. Central Plains Region, 1963. 2 microfilm.

United States. Circuit Court (District of Columbia). *Minutes of the U.S. Circuit Court for the District of Columbia, 1801–1863.* Washington, D.C.: National Archives. Central Plains Region, 1975. 6 microfilm.

United States. District Court (District of Columbia). *Records of the United States District Court for the District of Columbia Relating to Slaves, 1851–1863.* Washington, D.C.: Filmed by the National Archives, 1963. 2 microfilm.

Virginia. County Court (Alexandria County). *Will books, 1800–1878; Index to Wills, 1800–1951.* Microfilm of original records at the Alexandria City Courthouse in Alexandria, Virginia and the Arlington County Courthouse in Arlington, Virginia. Salt Lake City:The Genealogical Society of Utah, 1951. 6 microfilm.

Emigration, Immigration, Migration and Naturalization

"Early Circuit Court Naturalizations." *National Genealogical Society Quarterly.* Arlington, Virginia: National Genealogical Society Quarterly, vols. 41–45.

United States. Bureau of Customs. *Copies of Lists of Passengers Arriving At Miscellaneous Ports on the Atlantic and Gulf Coasts and At Ports on the Great Lakes, 1820–1873.* Washington, D.C.: The National Archives, 1964.

United States. District Court (District of Columbia). *Records of the United States District Court for the District of Columbia Relating to Slaves, 1851–1863*. Washington, D.C.: Filmed by the National Archives, 1963.

Land

District of Columbia. Recorder of deeds. *Land Records, 1792–1886; General Index to Deeds, 1792–1919*. Salt Lake City: Filmed by the Genealogical Society of Utah, 1972.

Gahn, Bessie Wilmarth. *Original Patentees of Land at Washington Prior to 1700*. 1936, Reprint. Baltimore: Genealogical Publishing Co., 1969.

Georgetown, Maryland (Montgomery County). *Property Tax Records: 1800–1820, 1862–1879*. Washington, D.C.: Filmed by the National Archives, 1965. 9 microfilm.

Georgetown, Maryland (Montgomery County). *Real Estate Belonging to the District of Columbia: 1860–1869*. Washington, D.C.: Filmed by the National Archives, 1965.

Montgomery County (Virginia). County Clerk. *General Index to Deeds, 1773–1933; Deeds, 1773–1868; Wills, 1773–1797*. Microfilm of original records in the District of Columbia Courthouse (Washington, D.C.). Salt Lake City: Filmed by the Genealogical Society of Utah, 1953. 694 microfilm.

Pippenger, Wesley E. *District of Columbia Original Land Owners, 1791–1800*. Westminster, Maryland: W.E. Pippenger, 1999.

Prince George County (Virginia). *Clerk of County Court. Deed Books, 1842–1858*. Salt Lake City: Filmed by the Genealogical Society of Utah, 1948.

Virginia. Corporation Court (Alexandria (Independent City)). *Virginia. Corporation Court (Alexandria (Independent City)). Deed Books, 1783–1865; Index, 1793–1870*. Salt Lake City: Filmed by the Genealogical Society of Utah, 1951.

Military

Pierce, Alycon Trubey. *Selected Final Pension Payment Vouchers, 1818–1864, District of Columbia*. Leesburg, Virginia: Willow Bend and Family Line Publications, 1998.

Sluby, Paul E., comp. *Civil War Cemeteries of the District of Columbia Metropolitan Area*. Washington, D.C.: Columbian Harmony Society, 1982.

United States. Adjutant General's Office. *Index to Compiled Service Records of Volunteer Union Soldiers Who Served in Organizations from the District of Columbia*. Washington, D.C.: The National Archives, 1964.

United States. Selective Service System. *District of Columbia, World War I Selective Service System Draft Registration Cards, 1917–1918*. National Archives Microfilm Publications, M1509. Washington, D.C.: National Archives, 1987–1988.

United States, Quartermaster's Department. *Roll of Honor, Vol. 1, Names of Soldiers Who Died in Defense of the American Union: Interred in the National Cemeteries at Washington, D.C. from August 3, 1861–June 30, 1865*. Washington, D.C.: Government Print Office, 1869.

Virginia. Office of the Comptroller. *Confederate Pension Applications, Virginia, acts of 1888, 1900, 1902; index, 1888–1934*. Microreproduction of original records at the Virginia State Library and Archives in Richmond, Virginia. Salt Lake City: Filmed by the Genealogical Society of Utah, 1988. 219 microfilm.

Wells, Charles J. *Maryland and District of Columbia Volunteers in the Mexican War*. Westminster, Maryland: Family Line Pub., 1991.

Vital and Cemetery Records

Congressional Cemetery Association (Washington, D.C.). *Cemetery Records, 1820–1988*. Microfilm of original records at the Washington Congressional Cemetery Association. Salt Lake City: Filmed by the Genealogical Society of Utah. 13 microfilm.

District of Columbia. Clerk of the Superior Court. *Marriage Records, 1811–1854, 1870–1921; Index, 1811–1986*. Microfilm of originals at the D.C. Records Office. Salt Lake City: Filmed by the Genealogical Society of Utah, 1997. 98 microfilm.

District of Columbia. Clerk of the Superior Court. *Marriage Records, 1907–1950*. Microfilm of originals at the D.C. Records Center. Salt Lake City: Filmed by the Genealogical Society of Utah, 1997. 38 microfilm.

District of Columbia. Health Department. *Birth Records, 1874–1897*. Microfilm of originals at the Health Department, Washington, D.C. Salt Lake City: Filmed by the Genealogical Society of Utah, 1995. 31 microfilm.

District of Columbia. Health Department. *Death Records, 1855–1949*. Microfilm at the Health Department in Washington, D.C. Salt Lake City: Filmed by the Genealogical Society of Utah, 1995. 180 microfilm.

District of Columbia. Health Department. *Foreign Death Certificates, 1888–1933*. Microfilm of originals and the District Records Center. Salt Lake City: Filmed by the Genealogical Society of Utah, 1997. 14 microfilm.

District of Columbia. Health Department. *Record of Disinterment, 1912–1940*. Microfilm of originals at the D.C. Records Center. Salt Lake City: Filmed by the Genealogical Society of Utah, 1997. 3 microfilm

Leach, Frank William, comp. *Extracts of Some of the Marriages and Deaths Printed in the National Intelligencer, Washington, D.C. Between the Years 1806–1858*. Salt Lake City: Filmed by the Genealogical Society of Utah, 1965.

Martin, George. *Marriage and Death Notices from the National Intelligencer (Washington, D.C.) 1800–1850*.

Washington, D.C.: National Genealogical Society Bookstore, 1976. 3 microfilm.

Pippenger, Wesley E. *District of Columbia Marriage Licenses: Registers*. Westminster, Maryland: Family Line, 1994–.

Register of Burials in District of Columbia Cemeteries, 1847–1938. Microreproduction of original records (6 v.) at the D.A.R. Library, Washington, D.C. Salt Lake City: Filmed by the Genealogical Society of Utah, 1971.

Ridgely, Helen West. *Historic Graves of Maryland and the District of Columbia: With the Inscriptions Appearing on the Tombstones in Most of the Counties of the State and in Washington and Georgetown*. Baltimore: Genealogical Publishing Co., 1967.

Sluby, Paul Edward, Sr. *Blacks in the Marriage Records of the District of Columbia, Dec. 23, 1811–June 16, 1870*. 2 vols. Washington, D.C.: Columbian Harmony Society, c1988.

Sluby, Paul E., Sr. *Civil War Cemeteries of the District of Columbia Metropolitan Area*. Washington, D.C.: Columbian Harmony Society, 1982.

Sluby, Paul E., Sr. *Selected Small Cemeteries of Washington, D.C.* Washington, D.C.: Columbian Harmony Society, 1987.

United States 1691–1850 Marriage Index. Bountiful, Utah: Heritage Quest, 1998.

Walker, Homer A. *Historical Court Records of Washington, District of Columbia*. Washington: s.n., 19–?.

Washington Hebrew Congregation (Washington, D.C.). *Interment List, 1856–1911*. Microreproduction of original records at the American Jewish Archives, Cincinnati, Ohio. Salt Lake City: Filmed by the Genealogical Society of Utah, 1977.

Wright, F. Edward. *Marriage Licenses of Washington, D.C., 1811–1830*. Silver Spring, Maryland: Family Line Pub., 1988.

County Website	Map Index	Date Created	Parent County or Territory From Which Organized Address/Details
District of Columbia www.dchomepage.net/dchomepage/main.htm		1790	**Montgomery VA, Prince Georges VA** District of Columbia County; 500 Indiana Ave NW; Washington, D.C. 20001-2131; Ph. (202) 879-1010

Florida

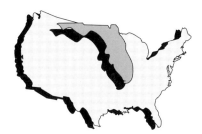

Capital: Tallahassee

Territory: 1822

State: 1845 (27th)

In God we trust

Long before its discovery by Europeans, Florida was populated by native Indian groups. Its original inhabitants included the Timucua, Apalachee, and Calusa peoples. The Seminole tribe migrated from Georgia and eventually became the dominant tribe.

Juan Ponce de Leon, the Spanish explorer who was searching for gold and the legendary fountain of youth, named and claimed the area in 1513 for Spain. Early settlement attempts failed, but in 1564 France established Fort Caroline and Spain founded St. Augustine a year later. Spain destroyed Fort Caroline, which made St. Augustine the first permanent non-native North American settlement.

Meanwhile, the British, Scotch, and Irish were settling the colonies and slowly encroaching on Florida territory. In 1762, during the Seven Years' War, the British captured Havana and Cuba. By the Treaty of Paris in 1763, Spain agreed to trade Florida for Havana.

By proclamation in 1763, the King of England established East and West Florida, divided by the Chattahoochee and Apalachicola Rivers. The largest settlement during the next twenty years was at New Smyrna in 1767. Up to 1,500 colonists from Italy, Greece, and the island of Minorca settled here. In 1783, Great Britain returned Florida to Spain in exchange for some islands in the West Indies.

In 1810 and 1812, the United States annexed portions of West Florida to Louisiana and the Mississippi Territory. Unable to govern the area, Spain ceded the remainder of West Florida and all of East Florida to the United States in 1819. Only about 5,000 non-native settlers lived in Florida at the time. In 1822, Florida was organized into a territory and in 1824 Tallahassee was laid out as the capital. Early settlers were predominantly Irish, but also included the Greeks from Southern Greece and the Dodecanese Islands, who worked as sponge divers and were affiliated with the Orthodox Greek Catholic Church. Former Virginians and Carolinians settled the middle section of Florida in the 1820's.

The Seminole Wars (1835–1842), brought about by poor treatment of the Indians, resulted in removal of the Indians to present-day Oklahoma. Growth really began in the 1840's as the population grew 56 percent. Most of the growth in East Florida during this time came from Georgia, Alabama, North Carolina and South Carolina. Florida became a state on March 3, 1845.

By 1860, the population had grown to 78,000. Half of the people were native-born while 22 percent came from Georgia, 11 percent from South Carolina and 5 percent from North Carolina. Florida seceded from the Union in 1861. Over 1,000 men fought for the Union and an estimated 20,000 fought for the Confederacy. Florida was readmitted into the Union in 1868. A post-Civil War boom lasted to the turn of the century due to the building of railroads and resorts. Another boom occurred from 1921 to 1925, resulting in the formation of Florida's last 13 counties.

Look for vital records in the following locations:

- **Birth and death records:** Statewide registration of births and deaths began in 1899, with general compliance by 1920. The Office of Vital Statistics in Jacksonville holds incomplete records of deaths from 1877 to 1917 and complete records since then. Some birth and death records are in city or county health departments. Jacksonville has birth and death records from 1893 to 1913, Pensacola from 1897 to 1916, and St. Petersburg prior to 1917.

- **Marriage and divorce records, wills:** The Office of Vital Statistics in Jacksonville has records of marriages from June 1927 to date as well as divorce records. Marriage records prior to June 1927 are in the office of the County Judge, generally in the county of the bride's residence. County judges also have the records of wills. Divorce records prior to 1927 are filed in the Circuit Court Clerk's office where the divorce was granted.

- **Census records:** Colonial, territorial, and state census records exist for 1783, 1786, 1790, 1793, 1814, 1825, 1837, 1845, 1855, 1865, 1868, 1875, 1885, 1895, and 1935. These are kept at the Florida State Archives, Florida Division of Archives, History, and Records Management in Tallahassee.

Department of Health Office of Vital Statistics
PO Box 210
1217 Pearl Street
Jacksonville, Florida 32231-0042
(904) 359-6900, ext 9000
www.doh.state.fl.us/planning_eval/vital_statistics/deaths.htm

Florida Bureau of Archives and Records Management
500 S. Bronough Street
Tallahassee, Florida 32399
(850) 245-6700
http://dlis.dos.state.fl.us/barm/

Societies and Repositories

Afro-American Historical and Genealogical Society, Central Florida Chapter; PO Box 1347; Orlando, FL 32802-1347; KOM222@yahoo.com; www.rootsweb.com/~flcfaahg/member.html.

Alachua County Genealogical Society; PO Box 12078; Gainesville, FL 32604; www.afn.org/~acgs.

Amelia Island Genealogical Society; PO Box 6005; Fernandina Beach, FL 32035-6005; (904) 261-2139; www.net-magic.net/biz-directory/genelogy.htm.

Apalachicola Historical Society, Inc; PO Box 75; Apalachicola, FL 32329; http://mailer.fsu.edu/~rthompso/fchs_adr.html.

Baker County Historical Society; PO Box 856; Macclenny, FL 32063; http://rootsweb.com/~flbaker/books.html.

Bay County Genealogical Society; PO Box 662; Panama City, FL 32402-0662; www.rootsweb.com/~flbay/genealogical.htm.

Big Lake Family History Society; PO Box 592; Okeechobee, FL 34973-0592.

Bonita Springs Genealogy Club; PO Box 366471; Bonita Springs, FL 34136.

Bowling Green Historical Council; PO Box 478; Bowling Green, FL 33834.

Boynton Beach Historical Society; Boynton Beach, FL; www.gopbi.com/community/groups/BBHS/index.html.

Brevard Chapter, SAR; 467 Bridgetown Ct.; Satellite Beach, FL 32937-3813; (321) 773-8369.

Broward County Historical Commission; 151 S.W. 2nd Street; Fort Lauderdale, FL 33301; www.co.broward.fl.us/history.htm.

Cape Canaveral Chapter (TROACC); PO Box 254186; PAFB, FL 32925-4186; (321) 768-2194; jcmurf@cfl.rr.com; www.brevardelderlaw.com/ troaccfam.htm.

Central Florida Chapter, SAR; PO Box 1015; Longwood, FL 32750-1015; (407) 767-5101; rrgaines@bellsouth.net.

Central Florida Genealogical Society, Inc.; PO Box 536309; Orlando, FL 32853-6309; cfgs@geocities.com; www.geocities.com/Heartland/Ranch/4580.

Charlotte Chapter, SAR; 4220 Pinecress Drive; Punta Gorda, FL 33982-1829; (941) 639-7264.

Charlotte County Genealogical Society; PO Box 494707; Port Charlotte, FL 33949-4707.

Citrus County Genealogical Society; PO Box 2211; Inverness, FL 34451-2211.

Citrus Springs Genealogical Society; 1826 W. Country Club Blvd; Citrus Springs, FL 34434.

Clay County Genealogical Society; PO Box 1071; Green Cove Springs, FL 32043.

Clearwater Chapter, SAR; 16135 4th St.E.; Redington Beach, FL 33708; (727) 319-6385; nelson91292@aol.com.

Daytona-Ormond Chapter, SAR; 20 Lazy Eight Drive; Daytona Beach, FL 32124-6776; (386) 788-0074; wmrace@mindspring.com.

Deland Chapter, SAR; PO Box 466; Deland, FL 32721; (904) 738-7462.

Descendants of the Knights of the Bath; PO Box 7062 GH; Gainesville, FL 32605-7062; partin@gnv.fdt.net.

DeSoto County Historical Society; PO Box 1824; Arcadia, FL 34265.

Dixie County Historical Society; PO Box 928; Cross City, FL 32628.

East Hillsborough Historical Society; Quintilla Geer Bruton Archives Center; 605 N. Colli; Plant City, FL 33566.

Emerald Coast Chapter, SAR; 31 Emory Street; Mary Esther, FL 32569-2009; (850) 243-2879; matheson31@home.com.

Englewood Genealogical Society; PO Box 795; Englewood, FL 34295.

Flagler Chapter, SAR; 82 Flamingo Drive; Palm Coast, FL 32137; (904) 445-7797.

Florida Department of State, Division of Library & Information Services; Bureau of Archives & Records Management; 500 S. Br; Tallahassee, FL 32399-0250; (850) 245-6700; BARM@mail.dos.state.fl.us; http://dlis.dos.state.fl.us/barm/fsa.html.

Florida Genealogical Society, Inc.; PO Box 18624; Tampa, FL 33679-8624.

Florida Historical Society; 1320 Highland Avenue; Melbourne, FL 32935; Flahistoricalsoc@aol.com; www.florida-historical-soc.org.

Florida State Genealogical Society; PO Box 10249; Tallahassee, FL 32302.

Fort Lauderdale Chapter, SAR; 1693 NW 97th Terrace; Coral Springs, FL 33071-5908; (954) 341-9285; VA60inf@aol.com.

Ft. Lauderdale Historical Society; 219 SW 2 Avenue; Ft. Lauderdale, FL 33301.

Gainesville Chapter, SAR; Registrar/Genealogist; PO Box 7062; Gainesville, FL 32605-7062.

Genealogical Group of Seminole County; PO Box 180993; Casselberry, FL 32178-0993.

Genealogical Society of Broward County, Florida; PO Box 485; Ft. Lauderdale, FL 33302; (954) 565-6193; sandyslm@bellsouth.net; www.rootsweb.com/~flgsbc/index.html.

Genealogical Society of Collier County; PO Box 7933; Naples, FL 33941-7933; www.naples.net/presents/gscc.

Genealogical Society of Flagler County; PO Box 35-4671; Palm Coast, FL 32135-4671; GSFCFL@cs.com; www.geocities.com/GSFCFL.

Genealogical Society of Greater Miami; PO Box 162905; Miami, FL 33116-2905; vdbjfb@bellsouth.net; www.rootsweb.com/~flgsgm.

Genealogical Society of Hernando County; PO Box 1793; Brooksville, FL 34605-1793; www.hcpl.lib.fl.us/genealogy.

Genealogical Society of North Brevard County; PO Box 997; Titusville, FL 32781-0897; www.nbbd.com/npr/gsnb/index.html.

Genealogical Society of Okaloosa County (Florida); PO Box 1175; Fort Walton Beach, FL 32549; (850) 243-4589; margmarieh@cox.net; www.rootsweb.com/~flokaloo/gsocinfo.htm.

Genealogical Society of Okeechobee; PO Box 371; Okeechobee, FL 34973-0371; rmorley@strato.net; www.rootsweb.com/~flgso.

Genealogical Society of Santa Rosa County; Milton Library; 805 Alabama St; Milton, FL 32570; pwariner@bellsouth.net; www.geocities.com/Heartland/Hills/3238/aboutus.htm.

Genealogical Society of Sarasota, Inc.; PO Box 1917; Sarasota, FL 34230-1917; www.rootsweb.com/~flgss.

Genealogical Society of South Brevard County; PO Box 786; Melbourne, FL 32902-0786; www.rootsweb.com/~flgssb.

Genealogical Society of Southeast Volusia County; PO Box 995; Edgewater, FL 32132.

Genealogy Club of Osceola County; PO Box 701295; St. Cloud, FL 34770-1295; AnnBergelt@aol.com; www.rootsweb.com/~flosceol/genclub.htm.

Geneva Historical and Genealogical Society; PO Box 145; Geneva, FL 32732; genevaHGS@aol.com; www.usgennet.org/usa/fl/county/seminole/Geneva/society.htm.

Gulf County Genealogical Society; PO Box 541; Port Saint Joe, FL 32457; www.geocities.com/Heartland/Meadows/5551/gcgsfl.html.

Halifax Genealogical Society; 30 Beach St.; Ormond Beach, FL 32174; www.halifaxhistorical.org.

Hamilton County Historical Society; FL ; www.rootsweb.com/~flhchms/index.htm.

Highlands County Genealogical Society; 116 East Main Street; Avon Park, FL 33825; msue617@yahoo.com; www.heartlineweb.org/hcgs.

Historic Ocala/Marion County Genealogical Society; PO Box 1206; Ocala, FL 34478-1206.

Imperial Polk Genealogical Society; PO Box 10; Kathleen, FL 33849; tracer@floridadetective.net; www.ipgs.org.

Indian River Genealogical Society, Inc.; PO Box 1850; Vero Beach, FL 32961-1850; Pat2u2@aol.com; www.rootsweb.com/~flindigs.

International Genealogical Fellowship of Rotarians, I. F. R. Genealogical; 5721 Antietam Dr.; Sarasota, FL 34231.

Jacksonville Chapter, SAR; 4484 Charter Point Blvd.; Jacksonville, FL 32277-1002; (904) 744-7312; twhetst@junix.ju.edu.

Jacksonville Genealogical Society, Inc.; PO Box 60756; Jacksonville, FL 32236-0756; MCHAUNCEY@msn.com; http://users.leading.net/~jgs.

Jewish Genealogical Society of Broward County; PO Box 17251; Ft. Lauderdale, FL 33318-7251.

Jewish Genealogical Society of Greater Miami; 8340 SW 151 St.; Miami, FL 33158.

Jewish Genealogical Society of Greater Orlando; PO Box 941332; Maitland, FL 32794; http://members.aol.com/JGSGO.

Jewish Genealogical Society of Palm Beach County, Inc.; PO Box 7796; Delray Beach, FL 33482-7796; www.jewishgen.org/jgspbci.

Jewish Genealogical Society of Southwest Florida; Sarasota, FL; (941) 921-1433; klapshein@aol.com.

Jewish Special Interest Group; 1601 Cougar Ct.; Winter Spring, FL 32708-3855.

Keystone Genealogical Society; PO Box 50; Monticello, FL 32344.

Kinseekers Genealogical Society of Lake County; PO Box 492711; Leesburg, FL 34749-2711.

Kinseekers of Lake County, Florida; 35305 Johns Lane; Eustis, FL ; (352) 589-5517; Busybee517@wmconnect.com.

Lake City Chapter, SAR; Rt. 15, Box 1230; Lake City, FL 32024; (904) 752-021; ljohns@isgroup.net.

Lakeland Chapter, SAR; 4203 Lake Marianna Drive, W.; Winter Haven, FL 33881-9034; (863) 956-4934; jspann@pclc.lib.fl.us.

Lake-Sumter Chapter, SAR; 5640 Twin Palms Rd.; Fruitland Park, FL 34731-6047; (352) 326-3333; moodyr@juno.com.

Lee County Genealogical Society; PO Box 150153; Cape Coral, FL 33915-0153.

Lehigh Acres Genealogical Society; PO Box 965; Lehigh Acres, FL 33970-0965.

Lemon Bay Historical and Genealogical Society; PO Box 1245; Englewood, FL 34295-1245.

Levy County Genealogy Society; c/o Levy County Journal; PO Box 159; Bronson, FL 32631.

Madison County, Florida Genealogical Society; PO Box 136; Madison, FL 32341-0136; mgreeson@digitalexp .com; www.rootsweb.com/ ~flmadcgs.

Major John Devane Chapter, SAR; 3710 East Midway Road; Plant City, FL 33565-2228; (813) 752-0875.

Manasota Genealogical Society; 1405 4th Ave. W.; Bradenton, FL 34205-7507; www.rootsweb.com/~flmgs.

Marco Island Historical Society; PO Box 2282; Marco Island, FL 34146; www.marco-island-florida.com/ history/home2.htm.

Marion Genealogical Society; PO Box 1206, Ocala, FL 34478-1206; (352) 291-2559; http://mariongenealogy.tripod.com.

Martin County Genealogical Society, Inc.; PO Box 275; Stuart, FL 34995; (561) 286-8458; dotw@gate.net; www.rootsweb.com/~flmcgs.

Miami Chapter, SAR; 9720 SW 142 Drive; Miami, FL 33176; (305) 233-0678; wtuttle118@aol.com.

Micanopy Historical Society; Micanopy, FL; micanopy@afn.org; www.afn.org/~micanopy.

Ocala Chapter, SAR; 8201 SW 108 Place Road; Ocala, FL 34481; (352) 861-1570; Sttorry@aol.com.

Order of the Second World War; PO Box 7062-GH; Gainesville, FL 32605-7062.

Osceola County Department, Genealogical Research; 326 Eastern Ave.; St. Cloud, FL 32769.

Osceola County Historical Society; 750 North Bass Road; Kissimmee, FL 34746-6307; www.flamuseums.org/fam/ flamuseums/pages/241.htm.

Palm Beach Chapter, SAR; 200 Andrews Avenue 3H; Delray Beach, FL 33483; (561) 272-1051; gerrym@gdw.net.

Palm Beach County Genealogical Society; PO Box 1746; West Palm Beach, FL 33402-1746; pbgenlib@juno.com; www.rootsweb.com/~flpalmbe.

Panama City Chapter, SAR; 6 Forest Grove Place; Ft. Walton Beach, FL 32548-6354; (850) 862-5078; emeraldcst@aol.com.

Pasco County Genealogical Society, Inc.; PO Box 2072; Dade City, FL 33525-2072; jpparr340@aol.com; www.rootsweb.com/~flpcgs.

Pastfinders of South Lake County; 620 Montrose; Clermont, FL 34711.

Pensacola Chapter, SAR; 10 Seminole Trail; Pensacola, FL 32506-3552; (850) 455-1732; jedlake1@earthlink.net.

Pinellas Genealogical Society; PO Box 1614; Largo, FL 33779-1614; www.rootsweb.com/~flpgs.

Polk County Historical Association; PO Box 2749; Bartow, FL 33980-2749.

Putnam County Genealogical Society; PO Box 2354; Palatka, FL 32178-2354; bmorris@gbso.net; www.afn.org/~pcgs.

Putnam County Historical Society; 100 Madison Street; Palatka, FL; www.rootsweb.com/~flpchs.

Ridge Genealogical Society; 1104 Voncile St.; Lake Wales, FL 33853.

Roots and Branches Genealogical Society; PO Box 612; DeLand, FL 32721-0612.

Saramana Chapter, SAR; 1444 Pine Bay; Sarasota, FL 34231-3535; (941) 924-1444; palmil@kudos.net.

Sebring Historical Society; PO Box 3313; Sebring, FL 33871-3313; www.heartlineweb.org/shs.

Seminole County Historical Society, Inc.; PO Box 409; Sanford, FL 32771-0409; http://members.tripod.com/ ~UNX3/seminolecounty.html.

Slovenian Genealogical Society; 7605 Harvey Street; Pensacola, FL 32506-5022; Rleskov@aol.com; www.sloveniangenealogy.org/chapters/Florida.htm.

Sons of the American Revolution; PO Box 7062; Gainesville, FL 32605-7062.

Southern Genealogist's Exchange Society, Inc., The; 6215 Sauterne Drive; PO Box 2801; Jacksonville, FL 32203-2801; (904) 778-1000; sgesjax@juno.com; http://sgesjax.tripod.com.

St. Augustine Chapter, SAR; 116 Knotty Pine Trail; Ponte Vedra Beach, FL 32082; (904) 280-3013; congem@bellsouth.net.

St. Augustine Genealogical Society; St. Johns County Public Library; 1960 N. Ponce de L; St. Augustine, FL 32084; www.geocities.com/glwilson_us/Stauggen.html.

St. Lucie Historical Society, Inc.; PO Box 578; Fort Pierce, FL 34954-0578; SLCHistoricalSoc@aol.com; www.rootsweb.com/~flslchs.

St. Lucie River Chapter, SAR; 3506 NW Oak Glen Drive; Jensen Beach, FL 34957-3414; (561) 692-4379; wthatcher@adelphia.net.

St. Petersburg Chapter, SAR; 4915 Bay Street NE, #325; St. Petersburg, FL 33703-4068; (727) 527-0019; MDMiller60@aol.com.

Suncoast Genealogical Society, Inc.; PO Box 1294; Palm Harbor, FL 34682-1294.

Suwannee Valley Genealogical Society; PO Box 967; Live Oak, FL 32064-0967; www.rootsweb.com/~flsvgs/svgs.htm.

Tallahassee Chapter, SAR; 6719 Alan A Dale Trail; Tallahassee, FL 32308-1655; (850) 893-7999; MurrayKing@aol.com.

Tallahassee Genealogical Society; PO Box 4371; Tallahassee, FL 32315; www.rootsweb.com/~fltgs.

Tampa Chapter, SAR; 19126 Amelia Circle; Lutz, FL 33549; (813) 949-4746; Cimmax@msn.com.

Taylor County Historical Society; 118 East Main St.; Perry, FL 32347.

The Brevard Genealogical Society, Inc.; PO Box 1123; Cocoa, FL 32923-1123; (321) 635-8758; jcrubins@bellsouth.net; www.rootsweb.com/~flbgs.

The Halifax Historical Society; 252 South Beach Street; Daytona Beach, FL 32114; mail@halifaxhistorical.org; www.halifaxhistorical.org.

The St. Augustine Historical Society; 271 Charlotte Street; St. Augustine, FL 32084; sahs@aug.com; www.oldcity.com/oldhouse/historical.html.

Treasure Coast Chapter, SAR; 13934 Cedro Court; Ft. Pierce, FL 34951; (561) 460-7859.

Treasure Coast Genealogical Society; PO Box 12582; Fort Pierce, FL 34979-2582; TreasureCoastGS@aol.com; www.rootsweb.com/~fltcgs.

Villages Genealogical Society; The Villages, FL 32159; www.angelfire.com/fl3/genie3/new_index.html.

Volusia Genealogical and Historical Society, Inc.; PO Box 2039; Daytona Beach, FL 32015.

Wakulla County Historical Society; PO Box 151; Crawfordville, FL 32326-0151.

West Florida Genealogical Society; PO Box 947; Pensacola, FL 32594-0947; ebowalsh@bellsouth.net; www.rootsweb.com/~flescamb/wfgs2.htm.

West Pasco Genealogical Society; 5636 Club House Dr.; New Port Richey, FL 34653-4405; http://homepages .rootsweb.com/~wpcgs/wpsgmember.htm.

West Volusia Historical Society, Inc.; 137 West Michigan Avenue; DeLand, FL 32720; www.volusia.com/ delandhouse/index.htm.

Bibliography and Record Sources

General

Bentley, George R. *The Episcopal Diocese of Florida, 1892–1975.* Gainesville, Florida: University of Florida Press, 1989.

Biographical Card Index [Florida]. St. Augustine, Florida: 1974. Microfilm, 18 rolls.

Bodziony, Gill Todd. *Genealogy and Local History: A Bibliography.* Rev. ed. Tallahassee: State Library of Florida, 1978.

Bolton, Herbert E. *The Spanish Borderlands: A Chronicle of Old Florida and the Southwest.* (1921) Reprint. Galveston, Texas: Frontier Press, 1996.

Bouknecht, Carol Cox. *Florida Prison Records, 1875 through 1899.* Tallahassee, Florida: Carol Cox Bouknecht, 1993.

Byrd, Beverly. *Genealogy and Local History: A Bibliography, 5th Supplement.* Tallahassee, Florida: Department of State. Division of Library Services, 1983.

Catalog of the Florida State Archives. Tallahassee, Florida: Department of State, 1975.

Catholic Church. Cathedral (St. Augustine, Florida). *Church Records, 1594–1924.* Salt Lake City: Genealogical Society of Utah, 1977.

Chapin, George M. *Florida, 1513–1913.* 2 vols. Chicago: S. J. Clarke Publishing Co., 1914.

Covington, James Warren. *The Story of Southwestern Florida.* 2 vols. New York: Lewis Historical Pub. Co., 1957.

Curley, Michael Joseph. *Church and State in the Spanish Floridas, 1783–1822.* New York: AMS Press, 1974.

Cutler, Harry Gardner. *History of Florida, Past and Present; Historical and Biographical.* 3 vols. Chicago and New York: Lewis Publishing Co., 1923.

Dagen, Paul L. *Seedtime and Harvest: 1942–1987 History of Alabama Northwest Florida District Mennonite Churches.* S.l.: s.n., 198–?.

Dovell, Junius E. *Florida: Historic- Dramatic- Contemporary,* 4 vols. New York: Lewis Historical Publishing Co., 1952.

Florida Research Outline. Series U.S.-States, no. 10. Salt Lake City: Family History Library, 1988.

Florida State Archives. Public Records Unit. *Microfilmed Records of Florida Counties.* Tallahassee, Florida: Florida State Archives, 1975–1977.

Gannon, Michael V. *The Cross in the Sand; The Early Catholic Church in Florida, 1513–1870.* Gainesville, Florida: University of Florida Press, 1965.

George, Paul S. *A Guide to the History of Florida.* New York: Greenwood Press, 1989.

Guide to Depositories of Manuscript Collections in the United States: Florida. Jacksonville, Florida: Florida Historical Records Survey Project, 1940.

Hann, John H. *A History of the Timucua Indians and Missions.* Gainesville, Florida: University Press of Florida, 1996.

Harris, Michael H., comp. *Florida History: A Bibliography.* Metuchen, New Jersey: Scarecrow Press, 1972.

Herbsman, Yael. *Index to Florida Jewish History in the American Israelite, 1854–1900.* Gainesville, Florida: University of Florida George A. Smathers Libraries, 1992.

Historical Records Survey (Florida). *A Preliminary List of Religious Bodies in Florida.* Jacksonville: Historical Records Survey, 1939.

Historical Records Survey (Florida). *Guide to Public Vital Statistics Records in Florida.* Jacksonville, Florida: Florida Historical Records Survey, 1941.

Index to the Archives of Spanish West Florida, 1782–1810, with an introduction by Stanley Clisby Arthur. New Orleans: Polyanthos Press, 1975.

Inventory of the Church Archives of Florida: Baptist Bodies. Jacksonville: Historical Records Survey, 1939–1940.

Kersey, Harry. *The Seminole and Miccosukee Tribes: A Critical Bibliography.* Bloomington, Indiana: Indiana University Press, 1987.

Kleback, Lisa Pazics. *Florida State Genealogical Society, Inc., Surname Directory.* The society: 1995.

Lantz, Raymond C. *Seminole Indians of Florida 1850–1874.* 2 vols. Baltimore: Heritage Books, Inc., 1994.

Lantz, Raymond C. *Seminole Indians of Florida 1875–1879.* Baltimore: Heritage Books Inc., 1995.

McAvoy, Thomas T. *Guide to the Microfilm Edition of the Records of the Diocese of Louisiana and the Floridas, 1576–1803.* Notre Dame, Indiana: University of Notre Dame Archives, 1976.

McGriff, Delbra D. *The Black Experience: A Guide to Afro-American Resources in the Florida State Archives.* Tallahassee: Florida Department of State Division of Library and Information Services, 1991.

Milanich, Jerald T. *Florida's Indians from Ancient Times to the Present.* Gainesville, Florida: University Press of Florida, 1998.

Moore-Wilson, Minnie. *The Seminoles of Florida.* 2003.

Nulty. *Confederate Florida: The Road to Olustee.* Galveston, Texas: Frontier Press, 1992.

Oesterreicher, Michel. *Pioneer Family: Life on Florida's Twentieth-Century Frontier.* Galveston, Texas: Frontier Press, 1996.

Peeler, Banks J. *A Story of the Southern Synod of the Evangelical and Reformed Church, 1740–1968.* Salisbury, North Carolina: Southern Synod of the Evangelical and Reformed Church, 1968.

Robie, Diane C. *Searching in Florida, A Reference Guide to Public and Private Records.*

Secretary of the Treasury. 1830 Private Land Claims in East Florida. Report No. 25 to the 21st Congress of the United States. Signal Mountain, Tennessee: Mountain Press, 1992.

Smith, George G. *The History of Methodism in Georgia and Florida: From 1785 to 1865.* Macon, Georgia: Jno. W. Burke and Co., 1877.

Southern Genealogist's Exchange Society. *Pioneers of Florida's First Coast.* Cullman, Alabama: Gregath, 1991.

St. Augustine Historical Society (Florida). *Biographical and Genealogical File.* Salt Lake City: Filmed by the Genealogical Society of Utah, 1974. Microfilm, 9 rolls.

St. Augustine Historical Society (Florida). *Biographical Card Index.* Salt Lake City: Filmed by the Genealogical Society of Utah, 1974. Microfilm, 18 rolls.

Taylor, Anne Wood and Mary Lee Barnes Harrell. *Florida Connections Through Bible Records, Volume I.* Tampa, Florida: Florida State Genealogical Society, 1993.

Taylor, Anne Wood. *Florida Pioneers and Their Descendants,* Vol I. Florida State Gen. Soc., 1992.

Thomas, David Hurst. *Missions of Spanish Florida.* New York: Garland, 1991.

Thrift, Charles Tinsley Jr. *The Trail of the Florida Circuit Rider: An Introduction to the Rise of Methodism in Middle and East* Florida. Lakeland, Florida: The Florida Southern College Press, 1944.

United States. Department of State. *Territorial Papers of Florida, 1777–1824.* Washington, D.C.: National Archives and Records Administration, 1946. 11 microfilm.

Wolfe, William A., and Janet Bingham Wolfe. *Names and Abstracts from the Acts of the Legislative Council of the Territory of Florida.* Tampa, Florida: Florida State Genealogical Society, 1991.

Atlases, Maps and Gazetteers

Bradbury, Alford G. *A Chronology of Florida Post Offices.* Sewall's Point, Florida: Florida Classics Library, 1993.

Cline, Howard F. *Provisional Historical Gazeteer [sic] with Locational Notes on Florida Colonial Communities.* New York: Garland Pub., 1974.

Fernald, Edward A. Tallahassee, Florida: Florida State University Foundation, 1981 Rose Printing.

Florida Atlas and Gazetteer. Freeport, Maine: DeLorme Mapping, c1987.

Florida Gazetteer and Business Directory. Jacksonville, Florida: R. L. Polk & Co., 1908.

Long, John H., ed. *Atlas of Historical County Boundaries: Florida.* New York: Simon & Schuster, 1996.

Morris, Allen Covington. *Florida Place Names.* Coral Gables, Florida: University of Miami Press, 1974.

Puetz, C. J., comp. *Florida County Maps.* Lyndon Station, Wisconsin: Thomas Publishing Co., 1988.

Censuses

Available Census Records and Census Substitutes

Federal Census 1830, 1840, 1850, 1860, 1870, 1880, 1900, 1910, 1920, 1930

State/Territorial Census 1783, 1786, 1790, 1793, 1814, 1825, 1837, 1845, 1855, 1865, 1868, 1875, 1885, 1895, 1935

Federal Mortality Schedules 1850, 1860, 1880

Dollarhide, William. *The Census Book: A Genealogist's Guide to Federal Census Facts, Schedules and Indexes.* Bountiful, Utah: Heritage Quest, 1999.

Florida. Department of Education. *Census of School Age Youth (6–21 years of age), 1896–1924.* Microfilm of records located at state archives, Tallahassee, Florida. Salt Lake City: Filmed by the Genealogical Society of Utah, 1990. 2 microfilm.

Florida. Division of Elections. *Florida Territorial and State Election Records, 1826–1865.* Microfilm of records located at state archives, Tallahassee, Florida. Salt Lake City: Filmed by the Genealogical Society of Utah, 1990. 9 microfilm.

Florida. Secretary of State. *Voter Registration Rolls, 1867–1905.* Microfilm of records at Bureau of Archives and Records Management, Tallahassee, Florida. Salt Lake City: Filmed by the Genealogical Society of Utah, 1990. 2 microfilm.

Florida. Tax Commission. *Tax Rolls of Florida Counties, Some are Incomplete, 1839–1891.* Salt Lake City: Filmed by the Genealogical Society of Utah, 1956. 66 microfilm.

Kemp, Thomas Jay. *The American Census Handbook.* Wilmington, Delaware: Scholarly Resources, Inc., 2001.

Lainhart, Ann S. *State Census Records.* Baltimore: Genealogical Publishing Co., Inc., 1992.

Michaels, Brian E. *Voters in the First Statewide Election, May 26, 1845.* Tampa, Florida: Florida Genealogical Society, 1987.

Mills, Donna Rachael. *Florida's First Families: Translated Abstracts of Pre-1821 Spanish Censuses.* Tuscaloosa, Florida: Mills Historical Press, 1992.

Szucs, Loretto Dennis and Matthew Wright. *Finding Answers in U.S. Census Records.* Ancestry Publishing, 2001

Tallahassee Genealogical Society, Inc. *Florida Voter Registration Lists 1867–68.* Tallahassee Genealogical Society, 1992.

Thorndale, William. *Map Guide to the U.S. Federal Census, 1790–1920.* Baltimore: Genealogical Publishing Co., 1987.

Court Records, Probate and Wills

County clerk is the custodian of the court, probate and will records. Refer to each county for those records.

Historical Records Survey (Florida). *Inventory of Federal Archives in the States, Series 02, Federal Courts; no. 09, Florida.* Jacksonville, Florida: Historical Records Survey, 1940.

United States. District Court (Florida: Southern District). *Admiralty Final Records of the U.S. District Court for the Southern District of Florida.* Microfilm of original records in the Regional Archives Branch of the Federal Archives and Records center, Atlanta, Georgia. (Washington, D.C.: National Archives and Records Service, 1984.) 13 microfilm.

Emigration, Immigration, Migration and Naturalization

García, María Cristina. *Havana, USA; Cuban Exiles and Cuban Americans in South Florida, 1959–1994.* Berkeley, California: University of California Press, 1996.

United States. Bureau of Customs. *A Supplemental Index to Passenger Lists of Vessels Arriving At Atlantic & Gulf Coast Ports (Excluding New York) 1820–1874.* Washington, D.C.: Filmed by the National Archives Record Services, 1960.

United States. Bureau of Customs. *Copies of Lists of Passengers Arriving At Miscellaneous Ports on the Atlantic and Gulf Coasts and At Ports on the Great Lakes, 1820–1873.* Washington, D.C.: The National Archives, 1964.

United States. District Court (Alabama: Southern District). *Declarations of Intentions, Naturalizations, and Petitions, 1855–1960.* Microfilm of originals at the National Archives in East Point, Georgia. Salt Lake City: Filmed by the Genealogical Society of Utah, 1987–1989. 9 microfilm.

United States. Immigration and Naturalization Service. *Index to Passenger Lists of Vessels Arriving At Miscellaneous Ports in Alabama, Florida, Georgia, and South Carolina, 1890–1924.* Washington, D.C.: Microphotographed by Immigration and Naturalization Service, 1957.

United States. Immigration and Naturalization Service. *Passenger Lists of Vessels Arriving At Key West, 1898–1920.* Washington, D.C.: Immigration and Naturalization Service, 1946.

Land and Property

Ainsworth, Fern. *Private Land Claims: Alabama, Arkansas, Florida.* Natchitoches, Louisiana: the author, 1978.

Davidson, Alvie L. *Florida Land: Records of the Tallahassee and Newnansville General Land Office, 1825–1892.* Bowie, Maryland: Heritage Books, 1989.

DeVille, Winston. *English Land Grants in West Florida: A Register for the States of Alabama, Mississippi, and Parts of Florida and Louisiana, 1766–1776.* Ville Platte, Louisiana: the author, 1986.

East Florida. Governor. *Spanish Land Grant Archives, 1764–1844.* Salt Lake City: Filmed by the Genealogical Society of Utah, 1977.

Florida. Division of State Lands. *Homestead Application Files, 1881–1905.* Microfilm of records at Florida State Archives, Tallahassee, Florida. Salt Lake City: Filmed by the Genealogical Society of Utah, 1990. 6 microfilm.

Florida. Division of State Lands. *Homestead Swampland Claim Files, 1846–1918; Index, 1846–1853.* Microfilm of records located at state archives, Tallahassee, Florida. Salt Lake City: Filmed by the Genealogical Society of Utah, 1990. 3 microfilm.

Historical Records Survey, Division of Professional and Service Projects. Works Progress Administration. *Spanish Land Grants in Florida: Briefed Translations from the Archives of the Board of Commissioners for Ascertaining Claims and Titles to Land in the Territory of Florida.* 5 vols. Tallahassee, Florida: State Library Board, 1940–41.

Hone, Wade E. *Land and Property Research in the United States.* Salt Lake City: Ancestry Incorporated, 1997.

McMullin, Phillip W. *Grassroots of America.* Salt Lake City: Gendex Corp., 1972.

Snider, Billie Ford. *Spanish Plat Book of Land Records of the District of Pensacola, Province of West Florida,*

British and Spanish Land Grants, 1763–1821. Pensacola, Florida: Antique Compiling, 1994.

Spanish Florida Land Records, 1764–1849. Microfilm of records at Florida State Archives, Tallahassee, Florida, [n.d.].

Spanish Land Grants in Florida: Briefed Translations from the Archives of the Board of Commissioner. 5 vols. Tallahassee: Historical Records Survey, 1940–1941.

United States. Commissioners for ascertaining claims to lands and titles in East Florida. *Land Claims, 1824–1828.* Salt Lake City: Filmed by the Genealogical Society of Utah, 1977.

Military

Chatelain, Verne Elmo. *The Defenses of Spanish Florida, 1565 to 1763.* Baltimore, Maryland: Baltimore Press, 1941.

Davis, T. Frederick. *"Florida's Part in the War with Mexico."* Florida Historical Quarterly 20 (January 1941): 235–239.

Florida State Militia, State Troops and National Guard, 1870–1918. Microfilm of records located at state archives, Tallahassee, Florida. Salt Lake City: Filmed by the Genealogical Society of Utah, 1990. 7 microfilm.

Florida. Comptroller's Office. *Pension Claims of Confederate Veterans and Their Widows Beginning 1885–1955.* Salt Lake City: Filmed by the Genealogical Society of Utah, 1955.

Hartman, David W., and David Coles. *Biographical Rosters of Florida's Confederate & Union Soldiers 1861–1865.* 6 vols. Wilmington, North Carolina: Broadfoot Publishing, 1995.

National Archives and Records Services. *Compiled Service Records, Volunteer Soldiers, Florida Indian Wars, 1835–1858* Washington, D.C.: Filmed by the National Archives, 1979.

Robertson, Fred L. *Soldiers of Florida in the Seminole Indian–Civil and Spanish-American Wars.* Bethesda, Maryland: University Publications of America, 1990.

Sifakis. *Compendium of the Confederate Armies: Florida and Arkansas.* Galveston, Texas: Frontier Press, 1992.

Soldiers of Florida in the Seminole Indian Civil and Spanish-American Wars. Live Oak, Florida: Democrat Book and Job Print, 1909.

United States. Adjutant General's Office. *Compiled Service Records of Confederate Soldiers Who Served in Organizations from the State of Florida, 1861–1865.* Washington, D.C.: National Archives, 1955, 1959.

United States. Adjutant General's Office. *Index to Compiled Service Records of Volunteer Soldiers Who Served During Indian Wars and Disturbances, 1815–1858.* Washington, D.C.: The National Archives, 1966.

United States. Adjutant General's Office. *Index to Compiled Service Records of Volunteer Union Soldiers Who Served in Organizations from the State of Florida.* Washington, D.C.: The National Archives, 1958.

United States. Adjutant General's Office. *World War I Navy Card Roster, 1917–1920 (Florida).* Microfilm of records located at state archives, Tallahassee, Florida. Salt Lake City: Filmed by the Genealogical Society of Utah, 1990. 4 microfilm.

United States. Record and Pension Office. *Compiled Service Records of Volunteer Union Soldiers Who Served in Organizations from the State of Florida.* Washington, D.C.: The National Archives, 1962.

United States. Selective Service System. *Florida, World War I Selective Service System Draft Registration Cards, 1917–1918. National Archives Microfilm Publications, M1509.* Washington, D.C.: National Archives, 1987–1988.

United States. Veterans Administration. *Pension Index File, Alphabetical; have the Veterans Administrative Contact and Administrative Services, Administrative Operations Services, 1861–1934.* Washington, D.C.: Veterans Administration, Publications Service, 1953.

United States. Veterans Administration. *Pension Index Files, Indian Wars, 1892–1926.* Washington, D.C.: Veterans' Administration, 1959.

United States. War Department. *World War II Honor List of Dead and Missing, State of Florida.* Salt Lake City: Filmed by the Genealogical Society of Utah, 1976.

White, Virgil D. *Register of Florida CSA Pension Applications.* Waynesboro, Tennessee: National Historical Pub. Co., 1989.

Vital and Cemetery Records

A. P. Boza Funeral Home (Tampa, Florida). *Funeral Home Records, 1929–1965.* Salt Lake City: Filmed by the Genealogical Society of Utah, 1975.

Cemetery Records of Florida and Georgia (Compiled by Members of the Florida Stake). Salt Lake City: Genealogical Society of Utah, 1960. Microfilm, 16 rolls.

Florida Combined Death Index, 1877–1969. Microfilm of records at Florida Dept. of Health and Rehabilitative Services, Jacksonville, Florida. Salt Lake City: Filmed by the Genealogical Society of Utah, 1992. 305 microfiche.

Florida Combined Marriage Index, 1927–1969. Microfilm of records at Florida Dept. of Health and Rehabilitative Services, Jacksonville, Florida. Salt Lake City: Filmed by the Genealogical Society of Utah, 1991. 471 microfiche.

Florida. State Board of Health. Bureau of Vital Statistics. *Florida Combined Divorce and Annulment Index, 1927–1969.* Microfilm of original records at Florida Dept. of Health and Rehabilitative Services, Jacksonville, Florida. Salt Lake City: Filmed by the Genealogical Society of Utah, 1991. 143 microfiche.

Florida. State Board of Health. Bureau of Vital Statistics. *Report of Divorce Granted and Report of Marriage Annulled, 1927–1950.* Jacksonville, Florida: Filmed by the Florida Vital Statistics Office. 141 microfilm.

Hayes, E. H. *Cemetery Records of Florida.* 9 vols. Typescript. Salt Lake City: Genealogical Society of Utah, 1946.

Historical Records Survey (Florida). *Guide to Public Vital Statistics Records in Florida.* Jacksonville, Florida: Florida Historical Records Survey, 1941.

Historical Records Survey (Florida). *Guide to the Supplementary Vital Statistics from Church Records in Florida.* 3 vols. Jacksonville: Historical Records Survey, 1942.

Jacksonville Branch Genealogical Library (Florida). *Vital Records Card File for Northern Florida and Southern Georgia, 1895–1945.* Microfilm of records in the Jacksonville Branch Genealogical Library, Jacksonville, Florida. Salt Lake City: Genealogical Society of Utah, 1977. 17 microfilm.

Veterans Graves Registration Project. *Register of Deceased Veterans, Florida.* Salt Lake City: Genealogical Society of Utah, 1953.

County	Map	Date	Parent County or Territory From Which Organized
Website	Index	Created	Address/Details

Alachua E9 **29 Dec 1824** **Duval, St. Johns**
www.co.alachua.fl.us/index_layers.html
Alachua County; 201 E University Ave; PO Box 600; Gainesville, FL 32601; Ph. (352) 374-3636
Details: (County Clerk has incomplete Marriage Records from 1837, Probate Records from 1840, land Records from 1848 & Court Records)

Baker D9 **8 Feb 1861** **New River**
www.nefcom.net/users/bcbcc/
Baker County; 339 E MacClenny Ave; MacClenny, FL 32063-2100; Ph. (904) 259-3121
Details: (County Judge has Marriage & Probate Records; Clerk Circuit Court has Divorce & Court Records from 1880)

Bay D4 **24 April 1913** **Calhoun**
www.bocc.co.bay.fl.us/
Bay County; 300 E 4th St; PO Box 2269; Panama City, FL 32402; Ph. (850) 763-9061
Details: (Health Department has Birth & Death Records; Clerk Circuit Court has Marriage, Probate, Divorce, Court & land Records from 1913)

Benton **24 Feb 1843** **Alachua**
Benton County; FL
Details: County Terminated 1850 (see Hernando) Formerly Hernando County. Name changed to Benton 6 Mar 1844. Name changed back to Hernando 24 Dec 1850.

Bradford D9 **21 Dec 1858** **Columbia**
www.rootsweb.com/~flbradfo/
Bradford County; PO Box B; Starke, FL 32091-1286; Ph. (904) 964-6280
Details: (Formerly New River County. Name changed to Bradford 6 Dec 1861) (County Clerk has Marriage Records from 1875, Probate & Court Records from 1892 & land Records from 1876)

Brevard H11 **1855** **Mosquito**
http://manatee.brev.lib.fl.us/
Brevard County; 400 S St; Titusville, FL 32780; Ph. (321) 633-1924
Details: (Formerly St. Lucie County. Name changed to Brevard 6 Jan 1855) (Clerk Circuit Court has Marriage Records from 1868, land Records from 1871, Divorce & Court Records from 1879, Probate Records from 1917 & Military Discharge Records from 1919; County Health Department has Death Records from 1985 & Birth Records; some Records prior to 1885 destroyed

Broward K11 **30 April 1915** **Dade, Palm Beach**
www.co.broward.fl.us/
Broward County; 201 SE 6th St; Fort Lauderdale, FL 33301; Ph. (954) 765-4578
Details: (Clerk Circuit Court has Marriage, Probate, Divorce, Court & land Records from 1915)

Calhoun C4 **26 Jan 1838** **Franklin**
www.rootsweb.com/~flcalhou/index.htm
Calhoun County; 20859 Central Ave E, Room 130; Blountstown, FL 32424; Ph. (850) 674-4545
Details: (County Judge has Marriage Records from 1880 & Probate Records from 1900; County Clerk has Divorce, Court Records from 1900 & Land Records from 1880)

County Website	Map Index	Date Created	Parent County or Territory From Which Organized Address/Details
Charlotte www.co.charlotte.fl.us/	**J9**	**23 April 1921**	**DeSoto** Charlotte County; 350 E Marion Ave; PO Box 511687; Punta Gorda, FL 33950; Ph. (941) 637-2199 **Details:** (Clerk Circuit Court has Marriage, Divorce, Probate, Court & land Records from 1921)
Citrus www.bocc.citrus.fl.us/	**F9**	**2 June 1887**	**Hernando** Citrus County; 111 W Main St; Inverness, FL 34450; Ph. (352) 637-9470 **Details:** (Office of History. Resources has Marriage Records 1887–1945, Cemetery, Probate, land & Court Records from 1887 & Military Discharge Records 1919–1969; County Health Department has Birth & Death Records)
Clay www.claycountygov.com/	**D10**	**31 Dec 1858**	**Duval** Clay County; PO Box 698; Green Cove Springs, FL 32043-0698; Ph. (904) 284-6317 **Details:** (Clerk Circuit Court has Marriage, Probate, Court & land Records from 1872 & Divorce Records from 1859; County Health Department has Birth & Death Records from 1973)
Collier www.co.collier.fl.us/	**K10**	**8 May 1923**	**Lee** Collier County; 3301 Tamiami Trail E; Naples, FL 33962-4902; Ph. (941) 732-2646 **Details:** (County Judge has Marriage & Probate Records; Clerk Circuit Court has Divorce, Court & land Records from 1923)
Columbia www.columbiacountyfla.com/	**D8**	**4 Feb 1832**	**Alachua** Columbia County; 145 N Hernando St; PO Box 2069; Lake City, FL 32055; Ph. (386) 758-1041 **Details:** (Clerk Circuit Court has Birth Records from 1943, Marriage & land Records from 1875, Divorce & Court Records from 1892 & Probate Records from 1895; County Public Health Unit has Birth, Death & Burial Records)
Dade		**4 Feb 1836**	**Monroe** Dade County; FL **Details:** (Name changed to Miami-Dade 1997)
De Soto http://co.desoto.fl.us/	**I10**	**19 May 1887**	**Manatee** De Soto County; 115 Oak St; Arcadia, FL 33821; Ph. (863) 993-4876 **Details:** (County Judge has Probate Records from 1887; Clerk Circuit Court has Divorce, Court & land Records from 1887)
Dixie www.dixie-county.com/	**E7**	**25 April 1921**	**Lafayette** Dixie County; PO Box 1206; Cross City, FL 32628; Ph. (352) 498-1200 **Details:** (Clerk Circuit Court has Marriage Records from 1973, Divorce, Probate, Court & land Records)
Duval www.coj.net/	**D10**	**12 Aug 1822**	**St. Johns** Duval County; 330 E Bay St; Jacksonville, FL 32202; Ph. (904) 630-2028 **Details:** (Clerk Circuit Court has Divorce, Court & land Records from 1921; County Judge has Marriage & Probate Records)

County Website	Map Index	Date Created	Parent County or Territory From Which Organized Address/Details
Escambia www.co.escambia.fl.us/	C1	**21 Jul 1821**	**One of two original Counties** Escambia County; 223 S Palafox Pl.; Pensacola, FL 32501; Ph. (850) 595-4310 **Details:** (Clerk County Court has Marriage, Probate & Court Records from 1821; County Health Department has Birth & Death Records; Comptroller has land Records from 1821)
Flagler http://flaglercounty.org/county1.htm	E10	**28 April 1917**	**St. Johns** Flagler County; 200 E Moody Blvd.; Bunnell, FL 32110; Ph. (386) 437-7414 **Details:** (Clerk Circuit Court has Marriage, Divorce, Probate, Court & land Records from 1917)
Franklin www.franklincountyflorida.com/	F5	**8 Feb 1832**	**Jackson** Franklin County; 33 Market St; Apalachicola, FL 32320; Ph. (850) 653-8861 **Details:** (County Judge has Marriage & Probate Records; Clerk Circuit Court has Divorce, Court & land Records)
Gadsden www.rootsweb.com/~flgadsde/	C5	**24 Jun 1823**	**Jackson** Gadsden County; 10 E Jefferson St; PO Box 1799; Quincy, FL 32351; Ph. (850) 875-8622 **Details:** (County Judge has Marriage & Probate Records; Clerk Circuit Court has Divorce, Court & land Records)
Gilchrist www.co.gilchrist.fl.us/	E8	**4 Dec 1925**	**Alachua** Gilchrist County; 112 S Main St; Trenton, FL 32693; Ph. (352) 463-3170 **Details:** (Clerk Circuit Court has Marriage, Divorce, Probate & Court Records from 1926)
Glades www.geocities.com/Heartland/Prairie/6173/ glades.html	J10	**23 April 1921**	**DeSoto** Glades County; PO Box 10; Moore Haven, FL 33471; Ph. (863) 946-0361 **Details:** (Clerk of Courts has Marriage, Divorce, land, Probate & Court Records from 1921 & Burial Records from 1925; County Health Department has Birth & Death Records from 1921)
Gulf www.gulfcountybusiness.com/	D4	**6 June 1925**	**Calhoun** Gulf County; 1000 Cecil G. Costin Sr. Blvd; Port St. Joe, FL 32456; Ph. (850) 229-6112 **Details:** (Clerk Circuit Court has Marriage, Probate, Divorce, Court, land & Military Discharge Records from 1925)
Hamilton www.rootsweb.com/~flhamilt/hamilton.html	C8	**26 Dec 1827**	**Jefferson** Hamilton County; 207 NE 1st St; Jasper, FL 32052; Ph. (904) 792-1288 **Details:** (County Judge has Marriage & Probate Records; Clerk Circuit Court has Divorce & Court Records from 1881 & land Records from 1837)

County	Map	Date	Parent County or Territory From Which Organized
Website	Index	Created	Address/Details

Hardee   I9   **23 April 1921**   **DeSoto**
www.hardeecounty.net/start.html

Hardee County; 412 W Orange St; Wauchula, FL 33873;
Ph. (863) 773-4174
Details: (Clerk Circuit Court has Marriage, Death, Divorce, Probate, Court & land Records from 1921)

Hendry   K10   **11 May 1923**   **Lee**
www.hendryfla.net/

Hendry County; 25 E Hickpochee Ave; PO Box 1760; LaBelle, FL 33975; Ph. (863) 675-5217
Details: (Clerk Circuit Court has Marriage, Divorce, land, Probate & Court Records from 1923 & Burial Records from 1953; County Health Department has Birth & Death Records)

Hernando   G9   **24 Feb 1843**   **Alachua**
www.co.hernando.fl.us/

Hernando County; 20 N Main St; Brooksville, FL 34601;
Ph. (352) 754-4201
Details: (Name changed to Benton 6 March 1844. Name changed back to Hernando 24 Dec 1850) (Clerk County Court has Marriage Records; Clerk Circuit Court has Divorce, Probate, Court & land Records from 1877)

Highlands   I10   **23 April 1921**   **DeSoto**
www.heartlineweb.org/highlandsbcc/

Highlands County; 590 S Commerce Ave; Sebring, FL 33870;
Ph. (863) 402-6565
Details: (Clerk Circuit Court has Marriage, Divorce, Probate, Court & land Records from 1921)

Hillsborough   H9   **25 Jan 1834**   **Alachua**
www.hillsboroughcounty.org/

Hillsborough County; 419 N Pierce St; Tampa, FL 33602;
Ph. (813) 276-8100
Details: (County Judge has Marriage & Probate Records; Clerk Circuit Court has Divorce & land Records)

Holmes   C4   **8 Jan 1848**   **Jackson**
www.rootsweb.com/~flholmes/holmes.htm

Holmes County; 201 N Oklahoma St; Bonifay, FL 32425;
Ph. (850) 547-1100
Details: (Clerk Circuit Court has Marriage, Probate, Divorce, Court & land Records)

Indian River   H11   **30 May 1925**   **St. Lucie**
www.myfloridacounty.com/mfCourtemplate/
view.jsp?countyid=INDIANRIVER

Indian River County; 1840 25th St; Vero Beach, FL 32960;
Ph. (561) 567-8000
Details: (Clerk Circuit Court has Marriage, Divorce, Probate, Court & land Records from 1925; County Health Department has Birth & Death Records)

Jackson   C4   **12 Aug 1822**   **Escambia**
members.aol.com/BettyMaeS/index.html

Jackson County; 2864 Madison St; PO Box 510; Marianna, FL 32447; Ph. (850) 482-9552
Details: (Clerk Circuit Court has Marriage Records from 1845, land Records from 1824, Divorce, Probate, Military & Court Records from 1900)

County Website	Map Index	Date Created	Parent County or Territory From Which Organized Address/Details
Jefferson www.co.jefferson.fl.us	C6	6 Jan 1827	**Leon** Jefferson County; Courthouse Rm #10; PO Box 547; Monticello, FL 32344; Ph. (850) 342-0218 clerkcdb@hotmail.com **Details:** (Clerk Circuit Court has Marriage Records from 1840, Divorce Records from 1900, Probate & Court Records from 1850 & land Records from 1827)
Lafayette www.rootsweb.com/~fllafaye/lafayette.html	D7	23 Dec 1856	**Madison** Lafayette County; Main St; PO Box 88; Mayo, FL 32066; Ph. (904) 294-1600 **Details:** (County Judge has Marriage & Probate Records; Clerk Circuit Court has Divorce Records from 1902, Court Records from 1907 & land Records from 1893)
Lake www.lakegovernment.com/	G10	27 May 1887	**Orange** Lake County; 315 W Main St; PO 7800; Tavares, FL 32778; Ph. (352) 742-4100 **Details:** (Clerk Circuit Court has Marriage, Divorce, Court & land Records from 1887, Probate Records from 1893 & adoption Records; County Health Department has Death Records)
Lee www.lee-county.com/	J10	13 May 1887	**Monroe** Lee County; 2115 2nd St; Fort Myers, FL 33901; Ph. (239) 335-2283 **Details:** (Clerk Circuit Court has Marriage, Divorce, Probate, Court & land Records)
Leon www.co.leon.fl.us/leon.htm	C6	29 Dec 1824	**Gadsden** Leon County; 301 S Monroe St; PO Box 726; Tallahassee, FL 32302; Ph. (850) 577-4000 **Details:** (Clerk Circuit Court has Marriage, Divorce, Probate, Court & land Records from 1825 & Military Discharge Records from 1914; County Health Department has Birth, Death & Burial Records)
Levy www.rootsweb.com/~fllevy/	F8	10 Mar 1845	**Alachua** Levy County; 355 Court St; Bronson, FL 32621; Ph. (352) 486-5229 **Details:** (Clerk Circuit Court has Marriage, Divorce, Probate, Court & land Records from 1850)
Liberty www.geocities.com/PicketFence/Street/2205/	D5	15 Dec 1855	**Gadsden** Liberty County; Hwy 20; PO Box 399; Bristol, FL 32321; Ph. (850) 643-2237 **Details:** (County Judge has Marriage & Probate Records; Clerk Circuit Court has Divorce, Court & land Records)
Madison www.maDischargeonfl.org/	C7	26 Dec 1827	**Jefferson** Madison County; PO Box 237; Madison, FL 32341; Ph. (850) 973-1500 **Details:** (Clerk Circuit Court has Marriage, Probate & Court Records from 1838, land Records from 1831 & Divorce Records)
Manatee www.co.manatee.fl.us/	I9	9 Jan 1855	**Hillsborough** Manatee County; 1115 Manatee Ave W; PO Box 25400; Bradenton, FL 34206; Ph. (941) 749-1800 **Details:** (Clerk Circuit Court has Marriage, Divorce, Probate, Court & land Records from 1857)

County	Map	Date	Parent County or Territory From Which Organized
Website	Index	Created	Address/Details

Marion   F9   **14 Mar 1844**   **Alachua**
www.rootsweb.com/~flmarion/index.html

Marion County; 110 NW 1st Ave; PO Box 1030; Ocala, FL 34478;
Ph. (352) 620-3904

Details: (Recording Office has land, Divorce, Probate & Court Records; Clerk of Courts has Marriage Records; County Health Department has Birth & Death Records)

Martin   J12   **30 May 1925**   **Palm Beach**
www.martin.fl.us/

Martin County; 2401 SE Monterey Rd; Stuart, FL 34995;
Ph. (561) 288-5576

Details: (Clerk Circuit Court has Marriage, Divorce, Probate, Court & land Records from 1925; County Health Department has Birth, Death & Burial Records)

Miami-Dade   L11   **13 Nov 1997**   **Monroe, Dade**
http://miamidade.gov/

Miami-Dade County; 111 NW First St., Ste 220; Miami, FL 33128;
Ph. (305) 375-5124

Details: (Organized from Dade County 1997) (County Judge has Marriage & Probate Records; Clerk Circuit Court has divorce & land Records from 1890)

Monroe   L10   **3 July 1823**   **St. Johns**
www.co.monroe.fl.us/

Monroe County; 500 Whitehead St; Key West, FL 33040;
Ph. (305) 292-3540

Details: (Clerk Circuit Court has Marriage, Divorce, Probate, Court & land Records from 1853)

Mosquito   **29 Dec 1824**   **St Johns**

Mosquito County; FL

Details: County Terminated 1845 (see Orange) Name changed to Orange 30 Jan 1845

Nassau   C10   **29 Dec 1824**   **Duval**
www.nassauclerk.com

Nassau County; PO Box 456; Fernandina Beach, FL 32034;
Ph. (904) 548-4600

Details: (Clerk Circuit Court has Marriage, Divorce, Probate, Court & land Records from 1800s)

New River   **21 Dec 1858**   **Columbia**

New River County; FL

Details: (see Bradford) Name changed to Bradford 6 Dec 1861

Okaloosa   C2   **3 Jun 1915**   **Santa Rosa**
www.co.okaloosa.fl.us/

Okaloosa County; 101 E James Lee Boulevard; Crestview, FL 32536;
Ph. (850) 689-5800

Details: (County Judge has Marriage & Probate Records; Clerk Circuit Court has Divorce, Court & land Records from 1915)

Okeechobee   I11   **8 May 1917**   **Brevard**
www.rootsweb.com/~flokeech/index.html

Okeechobee County; 304 NW 2nd St; Okeechobee, FL 34972;
Ph. (863) 763-6441

Details: (Clerk Circuit Court has Marriage, Divorce, Probate & Court Records from 1917 & land Records from 1880's; County Health Department has Birth & Death Records)

County Website	Map Index	Date Created	Parent County or Territory From Which Organized Address/Details
Orange www.orangecountyfl.net/Default.asp	**G10**	**1845**	**St. Johns** Orange County; 425 N Orange Ave; Orlando, FL 32801-3547; Ph. (407) 863-6321 **Details:** (Formerly Mosquito County 1824–1845. Name changed to Orange 30 Jan 1845) (Clerk Circuit Court has Marriage Records from 1890, Court & Probate Records from 1869)
Osceola www.osceola.org/	**H10**	**12 May 1887**	**Brevard** Osceola County; 2 Courthouse Sq Ste 2000; Kissimmee, FL 34741-5188; Ph. (407) 343-3500 **Details:** (Clerk Circuit Court has Marriage, Divorce, Probate, Court & land Records from 1887)
Palm Beach www.co.palm-beach.fl.us/	**J12**	**30 Apr 1909**	**Dade** Palm Beach County; 301 N Olive Ave; West Palm Beach, FL 33401-4705; Ph. (561) 355-2754 **Details:** (County Judge has Marriage & Probate Records; Clerk Circuit Court has Divorce, Court & land Records)
Pasco www.pascocounty.com/	**G9**	**2 Jun 1887**	**Hernando** Pasco County; 38053 Live Oak Ave; New Port Richey, FL 33523; Ph. (352) 521-4545 **Details:** (Clerk Circuit Court has Divorce, Court & land Records from 1887, Marriage & Probate Records)
Pinellas www.co.pinellas.fl.us/bcc/	**H8**	**23 May 1911**	**Hillsborough** Pinellas County; 315 Court St; Clearwater, FL 33756; Ph. (727) 464-3000 **Details:** (Clerk Circuit Court has Marriage, Divorce, Probate, Court & land Records from 1912)
Polk www.polk-county.net/	**H10**	**8 Feb 1861**	**Brevard** Polk County; 255 N Broadway Ave; Bartow, FL 33830-3912; Ph. (863) 534-4540 **Details:** (Boundaries changed 1871) (Clerk Circuit Court has Marriage, Divorce, Probate, Court & land Records from 1861)
Putnam www.co.putnam.fl.us/	**E10**	**13 Jan 1849**	**Alachua** Putnam County; 410 St Johns Ave; PO Box 758; Palatka, FL 32178; Ph. (386) 329-0361 **Details:** (Clerk Circuit Court has Marriage, Divorce, Probate, Court & land Records from 1849, Naturalization Records 1849–1914, Miscellaneous Records from 1800, Cemetery Records survey)
Santa Rosa www.co.santa-rosa.fl.us/	**C2**	**18 Feb 1842**	**Escambia** Santa Rosa County; 6865 Caroline St; Milton, FL 32570; Ph. (850) 623-0135 **Details:** (Courthouse Burned in 1869) (County Archives has Marriage, Divorce, Probate & Court Records from 1869; Deed Room, Main Courthouse has land Records from 1869)
Sarasota www.co.sarasota.fl.us/	**I8**	**14 May 1921**	**Manatee** Sarasota County; 2000 Main St; Sarasota, FL 34237; Ph. (941) 362-4066 **Details:** (Clerk Circuit Court has Marriage, Probate, Court & land Records from 1921 & Divorce Records from 1945; County Health Department has Birth & Death Records)

County Website	Map Index	Date Created	Parent County or Territory From Which Organized Address/Details
Seminole www.co.seminole.fl.us/	**G11**	**25 Apr 1913**	**Orange** Seminole County; 301 N Park Ave; Sanford, FL 32771; Ph. (407) 665-4330 **Details:** (County Judge has Marriage & Probate Records; Clerk Circuit Court has Divorce, Court & land Records from 1915)
St. Johns www.co.st-johns.fl.us	**D10**	**21 Jul 1821**	**One of two original counties** St. Johns County; 4010 Lewis Speedway Blvd; Saint Augustine, FL 32084; Ph. (904) 819-3600 reccoc2@co.st-johns.fl.us **Details:** (Clerk of Court has Marriage & Land Records from 1821, Divorce, Guardianship, Probate, & Court Records from 1970, Tax Records from 1950; Vital Statistics has Birth Records)
St. Lucie www.stlucieco.gov/	**I12**	**1844**	**Brevard** St. Lucie County; 2300 Virginia Ave; Fort Pierce, FL 34982; Ph. (561) 462-1400 **Details:** (Clerk Circuit Court has Marriage, Probate, Divorce, Court & land Records from 1905; County Health Department has Death & Burial Records)
Sumter http://bocc.co.sumter.fl.us/	**G9**	**8 Jan 1853**	**Marion** Sumter County; 209 N Florida St; Bushnell, FL 33513-9402; Ph. (352) 793-0200 **Details:** (Clerk Circuit Court has Marriage & land Records from 1853, Probate Records from 1856, Divorce Records from 1900, Court Records from 1913 & delayed Birth Records 1943–1972)
Suwannee www.rootsweb.com/~flsuwann/suwannee.htm	**D8**	**21 Dec 1858**	**Columbia** Suwannee County; 224 Pine Ave; Live Oak, FL 32060; Ph. (940) 364-3450 **Details:** (Clerk Circuit Court has Marriage, Divorce, land, Probate, Military Discharge & Court Records from 1859; County Health Department has Death Records)
Taylor http://perry.gulfnet.com/new_perry/taylor.htm	**D7**	**23 Dec 1856**	**Madison** Taylor County; PO Box 620; Perry, FL 32348; Ph. (850) 838-3500 **Details:** (Clerk Circuit Court has Marriage Records from 1908, Divorce Records from 1898, land Records from 1857, Probate Records from 1941, Court Records from 1946 & Military Discharge Records from 1914)
Union www.rootsweb.com/~flunion/index.htm	**D9**	**20 May 1921**	**Bradford** Union County; 15 NE First St; Lake Butler, FL 32054-1600; Ph. (904) 496-4241 **Details:** (Clerk Circuit Court has Divorce & Court Records)
Volusia www.volusia.org/	**F11**	**29 Dec 1854**	**Orange** Volusia County; 123 W Indiana; De Land, FL 32720; Ph. (904) 736-5920 **Details:** (Clerk Circuit Court has Marriage, Divorce, Court, Probate & land Records)
Wakulla http://mailer.fsu.edu/~rthompso/wakulla.html	**D6**	**11 Mar 1843**	**Leon** Wakulla County; Hwy 319; Crawfordville, FL 32327-0337; Ph. (850) 926-0905 **Details:** (Courthouse Burned in 1896) (Clerk Circuit Court has Marriage, Divorce, Probate, Court & land Records from 1896; County Health Department has some Birth Records)

County	Map	Date	Parent County or Territory From Which Organized
Website	Index	Created	Address/Details

Walton   **C3**   **29 Dec 1824**   **Escambia**
www.rootsweb.com/~flwalton/walton.htm

Walton County; 571 East Nelson Ave; PO Box 1260; De Funiak Springs, FL 32433-0000; Ph. (850) 892-8118
Details: (Clerk Circuit Court has Marriage Records from 1885, Probate Records from 1882, Divorce, Court & land Records, newspaper Records from 1905; County Health Department has Birth & Death Records)

Washington   **C4**   **9 Dec 1825**   **Jackson**
www.rootsweb.com/~flwashin/

Washington County; 711 3rd St; Chipley, FL 32428;
Ph. (850) 638-6200
Details: (Clerk Circuit Court has Marriage, Divorce, Probate, land & Court Records from 1890)

Georgia

Capital: Atlanta

State: 1788 (4th)

Wisdom, justice, and moderation

Creek and Cherokee Indians populated Georgia when it was discovered by Spanish explorer Hernando de Soto in 1540. Until 1732, the Spanish and English had sporadic disputes over the future state of Georgia. In 1732, King George II granted the land between the Savannah and Altamaha Rivers to prominent Englishmen. One of these Englishmen was James Oglethorpe, who came to Georgia to help achieve the goals of the new colony. Residents set out to provide a buffer between the Carolinas and Florida and establish a refuge for those who would otherwise be sent to debtors' prison. In 1733, Oglethorpe and 35 families settled Savannah. The next year Augusta was established and a group of Protestant refugees from Salzburg settled Ebenezer, in present-day Effingham County. Other settlers arrived from Switzerland, Germany, Italy, the Scottish Highlands, and Moravia in the next five years. In 1740, Georgia was divided into two counties. Savannah County was north of the Altamaha and Frederica County was south of the Altamaha. Many of the Moravians, who had come from North Carolina, moved from Georgia to Bethlehem and Nazareth, Pennsylvania, when their efforts to convert the Indians failed.

In 1752, Georgia's charter was surrendered and Georgia became a crown colony, claiming all the land between North Carolina and Florida, and the Atlantic Ocean to the Mississippi. From 1758 to 1777, Georgia was divided into the following 12 parishes: St. James, St. Matthew, St. John, St. Paul, St. George, St. Andrew, St. Philip, St. David, St. Patrick, St. Thomas, St. Mary, and Christ Church. These parishes were formed into seven large counties in 1777. Georgia gained statehood in 1788. In a dispute over states' rights in the 1790s, Georgia refused to carry out a Supreme Court decision against it, which led to the passage of the 11th amendment in 1798. That same year, the Territory of Mississippi, which later became the states of Alabama and Mississippi, was created from the western half of Georgia. Georgia's present boundaries were set in 1802.

Many families were drawn to Georgia in the early 1800s by land lotteries. Families who had lived in the territory for at least one year were allowed to draw for land areas as large as 400 acres. These lotteries were held in 1805, 1807, 1820, 1821, 1827, and 1832. Lists of lottery participants are held in the office of the Secretary of State. Some of these lists have been microfilmed and are available through the Family History Library in Salt Lake City, Utah.

Georgia seceded from the Union in 1861. More than 100,000 men fought for the Confederacy. More than 12,000 Union soldiers died as prisoners in Anderson, Georgia and are buried in a national cemetery in Sumter County. A published cemetery list by the Quartermaster General's Office entitled "Roll of Honor, Volume 3" is available.

Look for vital records in the following locations:

- **Birth and death records:** Vital Records Service, State Department of Human Resources in Atlanta, Georgia has birth and death records from 1919 to the present. Certified copies of birth records are issued at county and state offices to the person, a parent, or a legal representative. The index is closed to the public. Many earlier birth records are available from county offices at Atlanta, Savannah, and Macon. Death certificates are also issued at county and state offices. Indexes are closed to the public. Marriage records available from County Clerks or the County Clerk of the Ordinary Court.

- **Marriage records:** Clerk of the Court of Ordinary.

- **Divorce and civil court records:** The Superior Court Clerk keeps divorce and civil court records.

- **Naturalization records:** Shown in the minutes of the Superior, District, or City Court where the hearing was held. Also on microfilm at the Georgia Department of Archives and History in Atlanta, Georgia.

- **Land records:** Land deeds are recorded in the office of the Court of Ordinary as well as on microfilm and printed abstract form. The same court also holds records of homesteads, land warrants, licenses, indentures and pauper registers.

- **Wills:** The Clerk of the Court of Ordinary has wills from 1777 to 1798 and after 1852.
- **Voter registration records:** Clerk of the Court of Ordinary.
- **Census records:** State censuses taken for various years from 1786 to 1890 have survived for some counties and are located at the Georgia Department of Archives and History. Indexes to many state censuses have been published. Some county census records are also available for the years 1827 to 1890.
- **Military records:** A published roster of Georgia Confederate infantry soldiers compiled by Lillian Henderson and entitled *Roster of the Confederate Soldiers of Georgia, 1861–1865,* is available in six volumes through the Family History Library in Salt Lake City and its Family History Centers. The original Georgia pension records for Confederate veterans and index are at the Georgia Department of Archives and History in Atlanta, Georgia.

Georgia Department of Human Resources Vital Records
2600 Skyland Drive, NE
Atlanta, Georgia 30319-3640
(404) 679-4701
www.georgia.gov

The Georgia Archives
5800 Jonesboro Road
Morrow, Georgia 30260
(678) 364-3700
www.sos.state.ga.us/archives/

National Archives Atlanta Branch
1557 St. Joseph Avenue
East Point, Georgia 30334-2593
(404) 763-7477; Fax (404) 763-7033

Societies and Repositories

Abraham Baldwin Chapter, GASSAR; 314 W. Residence Ave.; Albany, GA 31701-2319; (229) 439-9489; wdm3bellsouth.net.

Alma-Bacon County Historical Society; 406 Mercer St.; Alma, GA 31510.

Alpharetta Historical Society, Inc.; PO Box 1386; 1835 Old Milton Pkwy.; Alpharetta, GA 30009-1386; mdwdw@aol.com.

Altamaha Chapter, SAR; 1381 Odum Hwy; Jesup, GA 31545-6947; (912) 427-3123; vdukes@accessatc.com.

American Cherokee Confederacy, Inc.; 619 Pine Cove Rd.; Albany, GA 31705-6906.

Andrew College Archives; Pitts Library; 413 College St.; Cuthbert, GA 31740.

Appling County Heritage Center, Inc.; PO Box 87; Baxley, GA 31513.

Ashantilly Center; PO Box 1449; Darien, GA 31305; coordinator@ashantilly.org.

Athens Chapter, GASSAR; 1541 Arrowhead Rd.; Greensboro, GA 30642-2001; (706) 453-7193; jhubert@pgtv.net.

Athens Historical Society; PO Box 7745; Athens, GA 30604-7745.

Atlanta Chapter, GASSAR; 1475 Mt. Paran Rd., N.W.; Atlanta, GA 30327-3749; (404) 233-1330; long.e.c.qk@worldnet.att.net.

Atlanta History Center; 130 West Paces Ferry Rd.; Atlanta, GA 30305; www.atlantahistorycenter.com.

Augusta Genealogical Society; PO Box 3743; Augusta, GA 30914-3743; www.augustagensociety.org.

Augusta Museum of History; 560 Reynolds St.; Augusta, GA 30901; mh@csra.net; www.augustamuseum.org.

Augusta-Richmond County Historical Society; 2500 Walton Way; Augusta, GA 30904-2200; vgreene@aug.edu.

Banks County Historical Society; PO Box 473; Homer, GA 30547-0473; tomjones@alltel.net; www.rootsweb.com/~gabchs/html.

Barnesville-Lamar County Historical Society; PO Box 805; Barnesville, GA 30204.

Bartow County Genealogical Society; PO Box 993; Cartersville, GA 30120-0993; www.geocities.com/Heartland/Park/9465/bartowcoga.html.

Blue Ridge Mountain Chapter, GASSAR; 1781 Possum Trot Place; Blairsville, GA 30512-6010; (706) 745-9513; bruskie@whitelion.net.

Bonaventure Historical Society; PO Box 5954; Savannah, GA 31414-5954.

Brantley County Historical and Preservation Society; PO Box 1096; Nahunta, GA 31553; (912) 462-5961; hueyham@hotmail.com.

Bulloch County Historical Society; PO Box 42; Statesboro, GA 30458.

Burke County Genealogical Society; 183 Knight Rd.; Waynesboro, GA 30830; jknight@burke.net; http://members.aol.com/J2525/gen.htm.

Button Gwinnett Chapter, GASSAR; 2674 Conifer Green Way; Dacula, GA 30019-3126; (770) 338-0495; jafdacula@aol.com.

Byron Area Historical Society; PO Box 755; Byron, GA 31008.

Candler County Historical Society; PO Box 325; Metter, GA 30439.

Captain John Collins Chapter, GASSAR; 4531 Paper Mill Rd.; Marietta, GA 30067; (770) 955-1303; guzy@mindspring.com.

Carroll County Genealogical Society; PO Box 576; Carrollton, GA 10117; mfword@aol.com; http://ccgs.westgeorgia.org.

Carroll County Historical Society; PO Box 1308; Carrollton, GA 30117; chestnut185@aol.com.

Casimir Pulaski Chapter, GASSAR; 842 Old Center Point Rd.; Carrollton, GA 30117-6728; (770) 834-7594; mdrey@bellsouth.net.

Catoosa County Historical Society; PO Box 113; Ringgold, GA 30736; joywm@aol.com.

Central Georgia Genealogical Society; PO Box 2024; Warner Robins, GA 31093; www.cggs.org.

Chattooga County Historical Society; PO Box 626; Summerville, GA 30747.

Cherokee County, Georgia Historical Society; PO Box 1287; Canton, GA 30114; bagwellandspears@mindspring.com; www.rockbarn.org/index.htm.

Clan Buchanan Society in America; c/o Odom Library; PO Box 1110; Moultrie, GA 31776.

Clark-Oconee Genealogical Society of Athens, Georgia; PO Box 6403; Athens, GA 30604.

Clay County Library; PO Box 275; Fort Gaines, GA 31751-0275; turnj@mail.clay.public.lib.ga.us.

Coastal Georgia Historical Society; PO Box 21136; St. Simons Is., GA 31522; ssilight@darien.net; www.saintsimonslighthouse.org.

Cobb County Genealogical Society, Inc.; PO Box 1413; Marietta, GA 30061-1413; CCGS@mindspring.com; www.rootsweb.com/~gaccgs.

Cobb Landmarks and Historical Society, Inc.; 145 Denmead St.; Marietta, GA 30060.

Coweta County Genealogical Society, Inc.; PO Box 1014; Newnan, GA 30264.

Coweta Falls Chapter, GASSAR; 4143 Spirea Dr.; Columbus, GA 31907-2643; (706) 561-5347; billyhilton81@yahoo.com.

Crawford County Historical Society; PO Box 394; Roberta, GA 31078.

Dade County Historical Society; PO Box 512; Trenton, GA 30752-0512; sueforrester@hotmail.com.

Dalton Chapter, GASSAR; 620 Emmons Dr.; Dalton, GA 30720-3915; (706) 278-7616; g.wright@alltel.net.

Decatur County Genealogical Society; PO Box 7492; Bainbridge, GA 31718; branchroot@aol.com.

Decatur County Historical Society; PO Box 682; Bainbridge, GA 31718.

DeKalb Historical Society; Old Courthouse on the Square; 101 E. Court Square; Decatur, GA 30030; dhs@dekalbhistory.org; www.dekalbhistory.org.

Delta Genealogical Society; c/o Rossville Public Library; 504 McFarland Ave.; Rossville, GA 30741-1255; rwilliv@mindspring.com; www.rootsweb.com/~gadgs.

Dodge Historical Society, Inc; 407 Eastman Way; Eastman, GA 31023; opound@peachnet.campuscwix.net.

Douglas County Genealogical Society; PO Box 5667; Douglasville, GA 30154; jirene@mediaone.net; www.douglascountygenealogicalsociety.org.

Early County Historical Society; PO Box 564; Blakely, GA 31723; kolomoki@alltel.net.

East Georgia Genealogical Society; PO Box 117; Winder, GA 30680; gaeggs@email.com; www.rootsweb.com/~gaeggs.

Eatonton-Putnam County Historical Society; 104 Church St.; Eatonton, GA 31024.

Edward Telfair Chapter, GASSAR; 1 Washington Ave.; Savannah, GA 31405-3104; (912) 238-1201; juliandk@aol.com.

Elbert County Historical Society; PO Box 1033; Elberton, GA 30635; (706) 283-1185.

Emanuel County Historic Preservation Society; PO Box 353; Swainsboro, GA 30401; derden@ega.peachnet.edu.

Etowah Valley Historical Society; PO Box 1886; Cartersville, GA 30120; evhs@evhsonline.org; www.evhsonline.org.

Evans County Historical Society, Inc.; PO Box 6; Claxton, GA 30417.

Fairfax Resolves Chapter, SAR; 12147 Holly Knoll Circle; Great Falls, GA 22066; (703) 430-6745; wginn@worldnet.att.net.

Fannin County Ancestral Hunters; GA; http://homepages.rootsweb.com/~fcgs.

Fayette County Historical Society; PO Box 421; Fayetteville, GA 30214; http://historyfayettecoga.org.

Flowery Branch Chapter of the Hall County Historical Society; PO Box 1994; Flowery Branch, GA 30542; boatfarm@aol.com.

Franklin County Historical Society; PO Box 541; Carnesville, GA 30521; epatterson@hartcom.net.

Genealogical Center Library; PO Box 71343; Marietta, GA 300007-1343; gencenlib@aol.com; http://homepages.rootsweb.com~gencenlb/index.html.

Genealogical Society of Muscogee County, Original; W.C. Bradley Memorial Library; 120 Bradley Dr.; Columbus, GA 31906.

George Walton Chapter, GASSAR; 3166 Floyd St.; Covington, GA 30014-2421; (770) 787-3495; bdobbs@georgia.org.

Georgia Genealogical Society; PO Box 54575; Atlanta, GA 30308-0575; don@martechpc.net; www.gagensociety.org.

Georgia Historical Society; 501 Whitaker Street; Savannah, GA 31401; www.georgiahistory.com.

Georgia Public Library Service; 1800 Century Pl Ne Ste 150; Atlanta, GA 30345-4300; www.georgialibraries.org/public.

Georgia State Archives; 5800 Jonesboro Road; Morrow, GA 30260; (678) 364-3700; reference@sos.state.ga.us; www.georgiaarchives.org.

Gordon County Historical Society; PO Box 342; Calhoun, GA 30701.

Grady County Historical Society; PO Box 586; Cairo, GA 31728; rcline@mail.grady.public.lib.ga.us.

Greene County Historical Society; PO Box 238; Greensboro, GA 30642.

Griffin-Spalding Historical Society; PO Box 196; Griffin, GA 30224; gshistso@bellsouth.net.

Guale Historical Society; PO Box 398; St. Mary, GA 31558.

Gwinnett Historical Society, Inc.; PO Box 261; Lawrenceville, GA 30246; ghs@gwinnetths.org; www.gwinnetths.org.

Hall County Historical Society; PO Box 2999; Gainesville, GA 30501; HCHS@hallcountyhistoricalsociety.org; www.hallcountyhistoricalsociety.org.

Hart County Historical Society; PO Box 96; Hartwell, GA 30643; sbohill@aol.com.

Historical Society of Forsyth County, Inc; PO Box 1334; Cumming, GA 30028; www.angelfire.com/ga3/hsofci.

Historical Society of the Georgia National Guard, Inc.; 201 Spring Hill Terrace; Roswell, GA 30075; www.hsgng.org.

Huxford Genealogical Society; PO Box 595; Homerville, GA 31634; www.huxford.com.

Jefferson County Historical Society, Inc.; PO Box 491; Louisville, GA 30434.

Jewish Genealogical Society of Georgia; 245 Dalrymple Rd.; Atlanta, GA 30328; www.jewishgen.org/ajgs/jgsg.

John Milledge Chapter, GASSAR; PO Box 824; Milledgeville, GA 31061-0824; (478) 452-3710.

Johnson County Historical Society; PO Box 87; Wrightsville, GA 31096; deshistpub@hotmail.com.

Joseph Habersham Chapter, GASSAR; 452 River Forest Run; Cleveland, GA 30528-2578; (706) 865-3345; kopugh@hemc.net.

Kennesaw Historical Society, Inc.; c/o Kennesaw Civil War Museum; 2829 Cherokee St.; Kennesaw, GA 30144; robertcjones@mindspring.com; www.mindspring.com/~robertcjones/khs/khs.htm.

Kennesaw Mountain Historical Association; 900 Kennesaw Mountain Dr.; Kennesaw, GA 30152.

LaGrange Chapter, GASSAR; 503 Merrill Lane; LaGrange, GA 30241-1488; (706) 882-2372; hannerspm@aol.com.

Lake Park Area Historical Society; PO Box 803; Lake Park, GA 31636-0803; cslocumb@datasys.net; www.datasys.net/lakepark.

Laurens County Historical Society, Inc.; PO Box 1461; Dublin, GA 31040; history@nlamerica.com; http://organizations.nlamerica.com/historical.

Lee County Historical Society; PO Box 393; Leesburg, GA 31763.

Liberty County Historical Society; PO Box 982; Hinesville, GA 31310.

Lincoln County Historical Society; PO Box 869; Lincolnton, GA 30817.

Lower Altamaha Historical Society; PO Box 1405; Darien, GA 31305; meyer43@darientel.net.

Lowndes County Historical Society & Museum; PO Box 434; 305 W. Central Avenue; Valdosta, GA 31603; lownhist@surfsouth.com.

Lyman Hall Chapter, GASSAR; 110 Saddlehorn Court; Woodstock, GA 30188-2055; (678) 493-2400; aagroup@worldnet.att.net.

Macon County Historical Society; PO Box 571; Montezuma, GA 31063; randafear@corinthian.net.

Marble Valley Historical Society; PO Box 815; Jasper, GA 30143; mvhs@marblevalley.org; http://marblevalley.org.

Marshes of Glynn Chapter, GASSAR; 105 Jackson Court St.; Simons Is., GA 31522-9771; (912) 634-6269; rreeves437@aol.com.

McIntosh Chapter, GASSAR; 5 1st Ave.; East Newnan, GA 30265-1743; (770) 253-7852; corley@mail3.newnanutilities.org.

Meriwether Historical Society; PO Box 741; Greenville, GA 30222.

Middle Georgia Chapter, GASSAR; PO Box 4261 St.; Simons Is., GA 31522-4261; (912) 375-9373.

Middle Georgia Historical Society, Inc.; PO Box 13358; Macon, GA 31208-3358.

Mill Creek Chapter, GASSAR; 308 Savannah Ave.; Statesboro, GA 30458-5259.

Morgan County Historical Society; 277 S. Main St.; Madison, GA 30650.

Muscogee Genealogical Society; PO Box 761; Columbus, GA 31902; ldowd@mindspring.com; www.muscogeegenealogy.com.

NARA, Southeast Region (Atlanta); 1557 St. Joseph Avenue; East Point, GA 30344-2593; (404) 763-7383; susanne.dewberry@nara.gov; www.archives.gov/facilities/ga/atlanta.html.

Newnan-Coweta Historical Society; PO Box 1001; Newnan, GA 30264; www.newnan.com/nchs/index.html.

Newton County Historical Society; PO Box 2415; Covington, GA 30015-2415.

Northeast Georgia Historical and Genealogical Society; PO Box 907085; Gainesville, GA 30501.

Northwest Georgia Historical and Genealogical Society; PO Box 5063; Rome, GA 30162-5063; www.rootsweb.com/~ganwhags.

Noxubee County Historical Society; 411 South Jefferson Street; PO Box 392; Macon, GA 39341.

Ocmulgee Chapter, GASSAR; 902 Westwood Dr.; Warner Robins, GA 31088-5869; (478) 953-3838; tjbllngr@home.net.

Old Clinton Historical Society; 154 Randolph St.; Gray, GA 31032.

Orphans Cemetery Assciation, Inc.; PO Box 4411; Eastman, GA 31023.

Paulding County Historical Society; PO Box 333; Dallas, GA 30132.

Peach County Historical Society; c/o Ann Brown; 201 Miller Street; Fort Valley, GA 31030; www.rootsweb.com/~gapchs.

Piedmont Chapter, GASSAR; 120 Cannonade Dr.; Alpharetta, GA 30004-4096; (770) 475-1463; get20@juno.com.

Pierce County Historical and Genealogical Society; PO Box 443; Blackshear, GA 31516; http://piercecounty.www.50megs.com.

Polk County Historical Society; PO Box 203; Cedartown, GA 30125; polkhist@mindspring.com.

Prater's Mill Foundation; PO Drawer H; Varnell, GA 30756; pratersmill@dalton.net; www.pratersmill.org.

Rabun County Historical Society, Inc.; PO Box 921; Clayton, GA 30525; www.rootsweb.com/~garchs.

Richmond Hill Historical Society, Inc.; PO Box 381; Richmond Hill, GA 31324; www.richmondhillga.com.

Rockdale County Genealogical Society; c/o Nancy Guinn Library; 864 Green St; Conyers, GA 30012; heloisesmith@msu.com.

Rockdale County Historical Society; PO Box 351; Conyers, GA 30012; www.geocities.com/Yosemite/Trails/3379/rchs.htm.

Rome Area Heritage Foundation, Inc.; PO Box 6181; Rome, GA 30161; leigh_callan@mail.fc.peachnet.edu.

Rome Chapter, GASSAR; 76 Acorn Road, SE; Rome, GA 30161-7707; (706) 235-5713.

Roopville Historical Society & Archive; PO Box 285; Roopville, GA 30170.

Roswell Historical Society; PO Box 1636; Roswell, GA 30077; www.accessatlanta.com/community/groups/roswellhistory.

Samuel Butts Chapter, GASSAR; 1648 Old Conyers Rd.; Stockbridge, GA 30281-2748; (770) 474-8088; canewcomer@earthlink.net.

Samuel Elbert Chapter, GASSAR; 2072 Pulliam Mill Rd.; Dewey Rose, GA 30634-2704; (706) 283-0629; gunnells@elberton.net.

Savannah Area Genealogical Society; PO Box 15385; Savannah, GA 31416.

Savannah River Valley Genealogical Society; PO Box 895; Hartwell, GA 30643; www.srvgs.org.

Smyrna Historical & Genealogical Society; 2861 Atlanta Street; Smyrna, GA 30082; www.rootsweb.com/~gashgs.

South Georgia Genealogical Society; PO Box 3307; Thomasville, GA 31799-3307.

Southwest Georgia Genealogical Society; PO Box 4672; Albany, GA 31706; swggs@swggs.org; www.swggs.org.

Sparta-Hancock County Historical Society; 353 E. Broad St.; Sparta, GA 31087.

Stephens County Historical Society; PO Box 125; Toccoa, GA 30577.

Taliaferro County Historical Society; PO Box 32; Crawfordville, GA 30631.

Tattnall County Historical Society; PO Box 2012; Reidsville, GA 30453.

Taylor County Historical-Genealogical Society; PO Box 1925; Butler, GA 31006.

Terrell County Historic Preservation Society; PO Box 63; Dawson, GA 31742; eduskin@surfsouth.

The Genealogical Society of Henry & Clayton Counties, Inc.; PO Box 1296, 71 Macon St.; McDonough, GA 30253; gensociety@juno.com; www.rootsweb.com/~gagshcc.

The Historical Society of Colquitt County, Inc.; PO Box 1961; Moultrie, GA 31776-1961.

The Historical Society of Douglas County, Inc.; PO Box 2018; Douglasville, GA 30133; (770) 942-0395.

The Historical Society of Walton County, Inc.; PO Box 1733; Monroe, GA 30655.

Thomas County Historical Society; PO Box 1922; Thomasville, GA 31799; history@rose.net; www.rose.net/~history/index.htm.

Thomaston-Upson Archives; PO Box 1137; Thomaston, GA 30286-0015; tuarch@alltel.net; http://alltel.net/~tuarch.

Thomasville Genealogical, History & Fine Arts Library; PO Box 1597; Thomasville, GA 31799.

Thronateeska Heritage Center; 100 Roosevelt Ave.; Albany, GA 31701; www.heritagecenter.org.

Toombs County Historical Society; PO Box 2825; Vidalia, GA 30474.

Treutlen County Historical Society, Inc.; 206 Second St., S.; Soperton, GA 30457.

Troup County Historical Society; 136 Main Street; PO Box 1051; LaGrange, GA 30241; info@trouparchives.org; www.trouparchives.org.

Tybee Island Historical Society; PO Box 366; Tybee Island, GA 31328.

Union County Historical Society; PO Box 35; Blairsville, GA 30514-0035; afarabee@alltel.net; www.ngeorgia.com/uchs.html.

Upson Historical Society; PO Box 363; Thomaston, GA 30296; www.rootsweb.com/~gauhs.

Valdosta Chapter, GASSAR; 2520 Jerry Jones Dr.; Valdosta, GA 31602-1645; (229) 242-5087; bcarswell@datasys.net.

Vienna Historic Preservation Society; 1321 E. Union St.; Vienna, GA 31092; www.historicvienna.org.

Walker County Historical Society; PO Box 707; Lafayette, GA 30728.

Washington County Historical Society; PO Box 6088; Sandersville, GA 31082.

Wayne County Historical Society; 125 N. East Broad St.; Jesup, GA 31546.

West Georgia Genealogical Society; c/o Troup County Archives; PO Box 1051; LaGrange, GA 30241.

White County Historical Society; PO Box 1139; Cleveland, GA 30528.

Whitfield-Murray Historical Society; Crown Garden and Archives; 715 Chattanooga Ave.; Dalton, GA 30720.

Wilkinson County Historical Society; PO Box 159; Gordon, GA 31031.

William Few Chapter, GASSAR; 4850 Wrightsboro Road GA; Grovetown, GA 30813; (706) 860-2205; user864418@aol.com.

William Miller Chapter, GASSAR; 1200 Pruitt Dr.; Waycross, GA 31501-6065; (912) 283-4071.

Wiregrass Genealogical Society; 45 25th Street; Eastman, GA 31023; (478) 272-5424; remullis@nlamerica.com; www.rootsweb.com/~gawgs.

Wiregrass Genealogical Society; Rte 2, Box 468; Cochran, GA 31014; www.rootsweb.com/~gawgs.

Worth County Historical Society; 1610 West St.; Sylvester, GA 31791-7531; nelldt@planttel.net.

Bibliography and Record Sources

General

Adams, Marilyn. *Georgia Local and Family History Sources in Print.* Clarkston, Georgia: Heritage Research, 1982.

Alexander, Adele Logan. *Ambiguous Lives: Free Women of Color in Rural Georgia, 1789–1879.* Fayetteville, Arkansas: University of Arkansas Press, 1991.

An Index to Georgia Tax Digests. 5 vols. Spartanburg, South Carolina: The Reprint Co., 1986.

Austin, Jeanette H. *Georgia Bible Records.* Baltimore: Genealogical Publishing Co., 1985.

Austin, Jeanette Holland. *Georgia Institute Records.* Baltimore: Genealogical Publishing Co., 1986.

Austin, Jeanette Holland. *The Georgians: Genealogies of Pioneer Families.* (1984), Reprint, Baltimore: Genealogical Publishing, 1986.

Biographical Souvenir of the States of Georgia and Florida. Chicago: F. A. Battey and Co., 1889.

Blair, Ruth. *Some Early Tax Digests of Georgia.* (1926) Reprint, Greenville, South Carolina: Southern Historical Press, 1971.

Bragg. Joe Brown's Army: *The Georgia State Line, 1862–1865.* 1987. Galveston, Texas: Frontier Press, 1987.

Brandenburg, John David and Rita Binkley Worthy. *Index to Georgia's 1867–1868 Returns of Qualified Voters and Registration Oath Books (White).* 1995. Atlanta, Georgia: the authors, 1995.

Bryan, Mary G. *Passports Issued by Governors of Georgia, 1785–1809.* Arlington, Virginia: National Genealogical Society, n.d.

Bryan, Mary G., and William H. Dumont. *Passports Issued by Governors of Georgia, 1810 to 1829. . .* Arlington, Virginia; National Genealogical Society, n.d.

Campbell, Jesse H. *Georgia Baptists: Historical and Biographical* (1847) Reprint, Greenville, South Carolina: Southern Historical Press, 1993.

Candler, Allen D., et al. *The Colonial Records of the State of Georgia, 1732–1784.* 32 vols. Atlanta, Georgia: State Printers, 1904–1989.

Coleman, Kenneth. *Dictionary of Georgia Biography.* Athens: University of Georgia Press, 1983.

Coulter, E. Merton and Albert B. Saye. *A List of the Early Settlers of Georgia.* (1949, 1967) 2nd ed. Baltimore: Clearfield Co., 1996.

Davis, *The Fledgling Province: Social and Cultural Life in Colonial Georgia, 1733–1776.* Galveston, Texas: Frontier Press, 1976.

Davis, Robert Scott, Jr. *A Researcher's Library of Georgia History, Genealogy, and Records Sources, Vol. I.* Greenville, South Carolina: Southern Historical Press, 1987.

Davis, Robert Scott, Jr. *A Researcher's Library of Georgia History, Genealogy, and Records Sources, Vol. II.* Greenville, South Carolina: Southern Historical Press, 1991.

Davis, Robert Scott, Jr. *Research in Georgia: With a Special Emphasis Upon the Georgia Department of Archives and History.* (1981) Greenville, South Carolina: Southern Historical Press, 1991.

Davis, Robert Scott, Jr. *The Georgia Black Book, Volume I: Morbid, Macabre, and Disgusting Records of Genealogical Value.* (1982) Reprint, Greenville, South Carolina: Southern Historical Press, 1992.

Davis, Robert Scott, Jr. *Research in Georgia.* Easley, South Carolina: Southern Historical Press, 1981.

Davis, Robert Scott. *A Guide to Native American (Indian) Research Sources at the Georgia Department of Archives and History.* Jasper, Georgia: R. S. Davis, 1985.

Davis, Robert Scott. *Georgians Past: Special Files of Georgia Settlers and Citizens, Subjects and Counties, 1733–1970s.* Milledgeville, Georgia: Boyd Pub., 1997.

Dorsey, James E. *Georgia Genealogy and Local History: A Bibliography.* Spartanburg, South Carolina: Reprint Co., 1983.

Dumont, William H. *Colonial Georgia Genealogical Data 1748–1783.* Arlington, Virginia: National Genealogical Society, n.d.

Early Georgia settlers, 1700s–1800s. [S.l.]: Brøderbund, 2000. CD-ROM.

Fries, Adelaide L. *The Moravians in Georgia, 1735–1740.* (1905) Reprint. Baltimore, Maryland: Clearfield Co., 1993.

Genealogical Material from Legal Notices in Early Georgia Newspapers. Greenville, South Carolina: Southern Historical Press, 1989.

Gentry, Lelia Thornton. *Historical Collections of the Georgia Chapters Daughters of the American Revolution. Vol. 4: Old Bible Records and Land Lotteries.* (1932) Reprint. 1995. Baltimore, Maryland: Clearfield Co., 1995.

Georgia Biographical Dictionary: People of All Times and Places Who Have Been Important to the History and Life of the State. New York: Somerset Pub., 1994.

Georgia Department of Archives and History. *A Preliminary Guide to Eighteenth-Century Records Held by the Georgia Department of Archives and History.* Atlanta: The Department, 1976.

Georgia Newspapers on Microfilm at the UGA Libraries: A Listing of Georgia Newspaper Holdings on Microfilm in the University of Georgia Libraries. (N.p.: 1978.)

Georgia Pioneers. 23 vols. Albany, Georgia: Georgia Pioneers Genealogical Society, 1964–1987.

Georgia Research Outline. Series US-States., no. 11. Salt Lake City: Family History Library, 1988.

Georgia. State Tax Commissioner. *Index to Tax Digests, 1787–1899.* (Salt Lake City: Filmed by the Genealogical Society of Utah, 1947).

Gilmer, Gov. George R. *Gilmer's Georgians (Sketches of Early Settlers of Upper Georgia, the Cherokees and the Author).* (1855, 1926) Reprint. Athens, Georgia: Iberian Publishing,

Grice, Warren. *Georgia Through Two Centuries.* 3 vols. New York: Lewis Historical Pub. Co., 1966.

Harwell, Richard Barksdale, comp. *Confederate Imprints at the Georgia Historical Society.* Savannah, Georgia: Georgia Historical Society, 1975.

Hawes, Lilla M., and Karen E. Osvald, comps. *Checklist of Eighteenth Century Manuscripts in the Georgia Historical Society.* Savannah, Georgia: Georgia Historical Society, 1976.

Hawes, Lilla Mills and Albert S. Britt, Jr., eds. *The Search for Georgia's Colonial Records.* Savannah, Georgia: Georgia, 1976.

Higgins, Margaret Elliott, ed. *Georgia Genealogical Gems.* Arlington, Virginia; National Genealogical Society.

Historical Collections of Georgia Chapters Daughters of the American Revolution, Vol. 1: Seventeen Georgia Counties. (1926, 1931). Reprint. Baltimore: Clearfield Co., 1995.

History of the Baptist Denomination in Georgia. Atlanta: J. P. Harrison & Co., 1881.

Hollingsworth, Leon S. *Leon S. Hollingsworth Genealogical Card File.* Atlanta, Georgia: R. J. Taylor, Jr. Foundation, 1980.

Howell, Clark. *History of Georgia.* 4 vols. Chicago: S. J. Clarke Pub. Co., 1926.

Huxford, Folks. *Pioneers of Wiregrass Georgia.* 9 vols. Homerville, Georgia: F. Huxford, 1951–1993.

Inventory of the Church Archives of Georgia: Atlanta Association of Baptist Churches. Atlanta: Georgia Historical Records Survey, 1941.

Jones, George F. *The Germans of Colonial Georgia, 1733–1783.* Rev. ed., Baltimore: Clearfield Company, 1996.

Knight, Lucian Lamar. *A Standard History of Georgia and Georgians.* 6 vols. Chicago: Lewis Publishing Co., 1917.

Lawrence, Harold. *Methodist Preachers in Georgia 1783–1900.* Tignall, Georgia: Boyd Pub., 1984.

Lucas, Silas Emmett, Jr. *Some Georgia County Records.* 7 vols. Reprint. Greenville, South Carolina: Southern Historical Press, 1991–1994.

Memoirs of Georgia: Containing Historical Accounts of the State's Civil, Military, Industrial and Professional Interests, and Personal Sketches of Many of Its People. 2 vols. Atlanta: Southern Historical Association, 1895.

Miller, Zell. *Great Georgians.* Franklin Springs, Georgia: Advocate Press, 1983.

Northen, William J. *Men of mark in Georgia: A Complete and Elaborate History of the State from Its Settlement To The Present Time, Chiefly Told in Biographies and Autobiographies of The Most Eminent Men of Each Period of Georgia's Progress and Development.* 7 vols. 1907–1912. Reprint, Spartanburg, South Carolina: The Reprint Co., 1974.

Robertson, David H. *Georgia Genealogical Research: A Practical Guide.* Stone Mountain, Georgia: David H. Robertson, 1989.

Rowland, Arthur Ray and James E. Dorsey. *A Bibliography of the Writings on Georgia History 1890–1970.* Rev. ed. Spartanburg, South Carolina: The Reprint Company Publishers, 1978.

Schweitzer, George K. *Georgia Genealogical Research.* Knoxville, Tennessee: George K. Schweitzer, 1987.

Simpson, John Eddins. *Georgia History: A Bibliography.* Mutuchen, New Jersey: Scarecrow Press, 1976.

Smith, George Gillman. *The Story of Georgia and the Georgia People, 1732 to 1860.* 2nd ed. (ca.1901) Reprint. Baltimore: Clearfield Co., 1968.

Southerland, Henry Deleon, Jr. and Jerry Elijah Brown. *The Federal Road Through Georgia, the Creek Nation, and Alabama, 1806–1836.* Galveston, Texas: Frontier Press, 1989.

Strobe, P. A. *Saltzbergers and Their Descendants, Being the History of a Colony of German, Lutheran, Protestants Who Emigrated to Georgia in 1734.* (1855) Reprint. Greenville, South Carolina: Southern Historical Press, 1980.

Subject and Surname Index to Newspapers (Daily Georgian, Etc.). Atlanta, Georgia: Department of Archives and History. Salt Lake City: Filmed by the Genealogical Society of Utah, 1960.

Warnock, Robert Holcomb. *Georgia Sources for Family History.* Atlanta, Georgia: Georgia Genealogical Society, 1995.

Warren, Mary Bondurant and Eve B. Weeks. *Whites Among the Cherokees.* Athens, Georgia: Iberian Publishing Co., n.d.

Warren, Mary Bondurant and Jack Moreland Jones. *Georgia Governor and Council Journal, 1761–1767.* Athens, Georgia: Iberian Publishing Co., 1992.

White, George. *Historical Collections of Georgia. Containing the Most Interesting Facts, Traditions, Biographical Sketches, Etc., Relating to Its History and Antiquities, from Its First Settlement to the Present Time.* 3rd ed. Reprint. Baltimore: Clearfield Co., 1996.

Williams. *The Georgia Gold Rush; Twenty-Niners, Cherokees, and Gold Fever.* Galveston, Texas: Frontier Press, 1993.

Wood, Virginia Steele and Ralph Van Wood, eds. *The Reuben King Journal, 1800–1806.* 1971. Savannah, Georgia: The Georgia Historical Society, 1971.

WPA Georgia: *The WPA Guide to Its Town and Countryside.* Galveston, Texas: Frontier Press, n.d.

Wylly, Charles Spalding. *The Seed That Was Sown in The Colony of Georgia: The Harvest and the Aftermath, 1740–1870.* New York and Washington: Neale Publishing, 1910.

Atlases, Maps and Gazetteers

Blake, Janice Gayle. *Pre-Nineteenth Century Maps in the Collection of the Georgia Surveyor General Department.* Atlanta: Surveyor General Department, 1976.

Bonner, James C. *Atlas for Georgia History.* Milledgeville, Georgia: Georgia College Duplicating Department, 1969.

Bryant, Pat. *Georgia Counties: Their Changing Boundaries,* 2d ed. Atlanta: State Printing Office, 1983.

Candler, Allen D. Georgia: *Comprising Sketches of Counties, Towns, Events, Institutions, and Persons, Arranged in Cyclopedic Form.* 4 vols. Atlanta: State Historical Assoc., 1906.

Georgia. Surveyor General. *Surveyor-General's Maps and Maps of Counties of Georgia, Arranged in Alphabetical Order.* Atlanta: Georgia Department of State, Microfilm division.

Goff, John H. *Placenames* of Georgia. Athens, Georgia: University of Georgia Press, 1975.

Hall. *Original County Map of Georgia: Showing Present and Original Counties and Land Districts.* Atlanta: Hall Brothers, 1895.

Hemperley, Marion R. *Cities, Towns, and Communities of Georgia Between 1847–1962: 8,500 Places and the County in Which Located.* Easley, South Carolina: Southern Historical Press, 1980.

Hemperley, Marion R. *Georgia Early Roads and Trails Circa 1730–1850.* Atlanta: Georgia Surveyor General Department, 1979.

Hemperley, Marion R. *Map of Colonial Georgia, 1773–1777.* Atlanta: Georgia Surveyor General Department, 1979.

Hodler, Thomas W., and Howard A. Schretter. *The Atlas of Georgia.* Athens, Georgia: Institute of Community and Area Development, 1986.

Johnsen, Margaret A. *Nineteenth Century Maps in the Collection of the Georgia Surveyor General Department.* Atlanta: Surveyor General Department, 1981.

Krakow, Kenneth K. *Georgia Place-Names.* Macon, Georgia: Winship Press, 1975.

Long, John H. *Atlas of Historical County Boundaries: Georgia.* New York: Simon & Schuster, 2001.

Sherwood, Adiel. *A Gazetteer of the State of Georgia Containing a Particular Description of the State, Its Resources, counties, Towns, Villages and Whatever is Usual in Statistical Works.* 4th ed. Rev. and corrected. Atlanta: Cherokee Printing Co., 1970.

Censuses

Available Census Records and Census Substitutes

Federal Census 1820 (except Franklin, Rabun and Twiggs Counties), 1830, 1840, 1850, 1860, 1870, 1880, 1900, 1910, 1920, 1930

Federal Mortality Schedules 1850, 1860, 1870, 1880

Early Settlers 1733–1742

Land Allotments 1741–1754

Land Lottery 1805, 1807, 1820, 1821, 1827, 1832

Reconstructed Census 1790

Cornell, Nancy J. *1864 Census for Reorganizing the Georgia Militia.* Baltimore: Genealogical Publishing Co., 2000.

De Lamar, Marie and Elisabeth Rothstein. *The Reconstructed 1790 Census of Georgia.* (1976), Reprint, Baltimore: Genealogical Publishing, 1989.

Dollarhide, William. *The Census Book: A Genealogist's Guide to Federal Census Facts, Schedules and Indexes.* Bountiful, Utah: Heritage Quest, 1999.

Kemp, Thomas Jay. *The American Census Handbook.* Wilmington, Delaware: Scholarly Resources, Inc., 2001.

Lainhart, Ann S. *State Census Records.* Baltimore: Genealogical Publishing Co., Inc., 1992.

Substitutes for Georgia's Lost 1790 Census. Albany, Georgia: Delwyn Assoc., 1975.

Szucs, Loretto Dennis and Matthew Wright. *Finding Answers in U.S. Census Records.* Ancestry Publishing, 2001.

Taylor, R. J., Jr. *An Index to Georgia Tax Digests.* 5 vols. Spartanburg, South Carolina: The Reprint Co., 1986, 1986.

Thorndale, William. *Map Guide to the U.S. Federal Census, 1790–1920.* Baltimore: Genealogical Publishing Co., 1987.

Court Records, Probate and Wills

Abstracts of Colonial Wills of the State of Georgia, 1733–1777. Spartanburg, South Carolina: The Reprint Co., 1981.

Austin, Jeanette Holland. *Index to Georgia Wills.* (1976) Reprint. Greenville, South Carolina: Southern Historical Press, 1985.

Austin, Jeanette Holland. *Georgia Intestate Records.* (1986) Reprint. Baltimore: Genealogical Publishing, 1995.

Brooke, Ted O. *In the Name of God, Amen: Georgia Wills, 1733–1860: An Index.* Atlanta: Pilgrim Press, 1976.

Candler, Allen D. *Statutes Enacted by the Royal Legislature of Georgia From Its First Session in 1754 to 1768.* Atlanta: The Legislature, 1910.

Early Colonial Records of Georgia: Including Wills, Letters of Administration, Inventories of Estates, Letters of Guardianship, Probate and Administration Letters, Minutes, Appraisements, etc., 1754–1778. Microreproduction of original ms. at the State Archives, Atlanta, Georgia. Salt Lake City: Filmed by the Genealogical Society of Utah, 1957. 7 microfilm.

Early Georgia Wills. Salt Lake City: American Heritage Research, 1976.

Geiger, Linda A. Woodward. *Index to Georgia's Federal Naturalization Records to 1950 (excluding military petitions).* Atlanta, Georgia: Georgia Genealogical Society, 1996.

Index to Probate Records of Colonial Georgia, 1733–1778. Atlanta: R. J. Taylor, Jr., Foundation, 1983.

Lane, Jane Warren Hollingsworth. *Court Records, Georgia Counties.* Salt Lake City: Filmed by the Genealogical Society of Utah, 1940, 1971.

Thaxton, Donna B. *Georgia Indian Depredation Claims.* Americus, Georgia: Thaxton Company, 1988.

Emigration, Immigration, Migration and Naturalization

Bryan, Mary. *Passports Issued by Georgia Governors, 1785–1809, and 1810–1820.* 2 vols. Washington, D.C.: National Genealogical Society, 1959, 1964.

Hemperley, Marion. "Federal Naturalization Oaths: Savannah, Georgia, 1790–1860." *Georgia Historical Quarterly,* 51, no. 4 (1967): 454–87.

Immigrants from Great Britain to the Georgia Colony. Morrow, Georgia: Genealogical Enterprises, 1970.

Miller, Stephen Franks. *The Bench and Bar of Georgia: Memoirs and Sketches With An Appendix, Containing a Court Roll From 1790 to 1857, etc.* 2 cols. Philadelphia: J. B. Lippincott, 1858.

United States. Circuit Court (Georgia). *Minutes, 1790–1842 ; Index to Plaintiffs and Defendants, 1790–1860.* Microreproduction of original records which are part of the Records of District Courts of the United States, Record Group 21, and are housed in the Federal Archives and Records Center, Atlanta, Georgia. Washington, D.C.: National Archives and Record Service. 3 microfilm.

United States. District Court (Alabama: Southern District). *Declarations of Intentions, Naturalizations, and Petitions, 1855–1960.* Microfilm of originals at the National Archives in East Point, Georgia. Salt Lake City: Filmed by the Genealogical Society of Utah, 1987–1989. 9 microfilm.

United States. District Court (Georgia: Northern District: Atlanta). Naturalization Certificate Stubs, 1907–1926. Microfilm of original housed at the National Archives in East Point, Georgia. Salt Lake City: Filmed by the Genealogical Society of Utah, 1989.

United States. District Court (Georgia: Savannah District). *Index to Aliens Admitted to Citizenship, 1906–1989.* Microreproduction of original records filmed at the U.S. Courthouse, Savannah, Georgia. Salt Lake City: Filmed by the Genealogical Society of Utah, 1989. 2 microfilm.

United States. District Court (Georgia: Southern District). *General Index Books, 1789–1928 ; Minute Books and Bench Dockets, 1789–1870.* Microreproduction of original records which are part of the Records of District Courts of the United States, Record Group 21, and are housed in the Atlanta Regional Branch of the National Archives, East Point, Georgia. Washington, D.C.: National Archives and Record Service, 1981. 3 microfilm.

United States. District Court (Georgia: Southern District). *Naturalization Records, 1790–1940.* Microreproduction of original records filmed at the United States Courthouse, Savannah, Georgia. Salt Lake City: Filmed by the Genealogical Society of Utah, 1990. 7 microfilm.

United States. Immigration and Naturalization Service. *Index to Passenger Lists of Vessels Arriving At Miscellaneous Ports in Alabama, Florida, Georgia, and South Carolina, 1890–1924.* Washington, D.C.: Microphotographed by Immigration and Naturalization Service, 1957.

United States. Immigration and Naturalization Service. *Savannah Passenger Lists* [United States]: Microphotographed by Immigration and Naturalization Service, 1946.

Land and Property

Bryant, Pat. *Entry of Claims for Georgia Landholders, 1733–1755.* Atlanta: State Printing Office, 1975.

Cadle, Farris W. *Georgia Land Surveying History and Law.* Athens, Georgia: University of Georgia Press, 1991.

Davis, Robert S., Jr., and Silas E. Lucas, comps. *The Georgia Land Lottery Papers, 1805–1914: Genealogical Data from the Loose Papers Filed in the Georgia Surveyor General Office Concerning the Lots Won in the State Land Lotteries and the People Who Won Them.* Easley, South Carolina: Southern Historical Press, 1979.

Davis, Robert Scott, Jr., *The 1833 Land Lottery of Georgia and Other Missing Names of Winners in the Georgia Land Lotteries.* Greenville, South Carolina: Southern Historical Press, 1991.

Georgia (Colony). Governor. *Colonial Records of Georgia, 1750–1829.* Microreproduction of original ms. at the State Archives, Atlanta, Georgia. Salt Lake City: Filmed by the Genealogical Society of Utah, 1957. 25 microfilm.

Georgia, Department of Archives and History. *Revolutionary Soldiers Receipts for Georgia Bounty Grants.* Atlanta, Georgia: Foote and Davies Co., 1928.

Georgia, Secretary of State. *Authentic List of All Land Lottery Grants Made to Veterans of the Revolutionary War by the State of Georgia, Taken from Official State Records in the Surveyor-General Department, Housed in the Georgia Department of Archives and History, Atlanta, GA, 1955.* 2nd ed. Atlanta, Georgia: Secretary of State, 1966.

Georgia. Department of State. *Land Office Records, Index.* Atlanta: Georgia Department of State, Microfilm Division, 19–.

Georgia. Surveyor General *Land Lottery Records, 1841–1870; Surveyor's Filed Notes, 1806–1860.* Atlanta: Georgia Dept. of Archives and History, 1967.

Georgia. Surveyor General. *Headrights and Land Grants of Georgia, 1756–1939.* Atlanta: Georgia Department of State, Microfilm Division, 1953–1954.

Georgia. Surveyor General. *Land Lottery Surveys.* Atlanta: Georgia Dept. Archives and History, 1967.

Georgia. Surveyor General. *Reverted Lottery Land Records, 1815–1872; Register of Grants, 1834–1847.* Atlanta: State Dept. of Archives and History, 1967.

Georgia. Surveyor General. *Surveyor-General's Records, Headright Surveys.* Atlanta: Georgia Department of State, Microfilm Division, 19–.

Hemperley, Marion R. *The Georgia Surveyor General Department: A History and Inventory of Georgia's Land Office.* Atlanta: State Printing Office, 1982.

Hone, Wade E. *Land and Property Research in the United States.* Salt Lake City: Ancestry Incorporated, 1997.

Houston, Martha Lou. *Reprint of Official Register of Land Lottery of Georgia 1827.* (1928) Reprint. Baltimore: Clearfield Co., 1992.

Index to the Headright and Bounty Grants of Georgia 1756–1909. Vidalia, Georgia: Georgia Genealogical Reprints, 1970.

Lucas, Silas Emmett, Jr. *Index to the Headright and Bounty Grants in Georgia from 1756–1909.* Revised Edition. Greenville, South Carolina: Southern Historical Press, 1992.

Lucas, Silas Emmett, Jr. *The 1827 Land Lottery of Georgia.* (1975) Reprint. Greenville, South Carolina: Southern Historical Press, 1986.

Lucas, Silas Emmett, Jr. *The 1832 Gold Lottery of Georgia.* (1976) Reprint. Greenville, South Carolina: Southern Historical Press, 1987.

Lucas, Silas Emmett, Jr. *The 1832 Gold Lottery of Georgia: Containing a List of the Fortunate Drawers in Said Lottery.* Easley, South Carolina: Southern Historical Press, 1976.

Lucas, Silas Emmett, Jr. *The Fourth or 1821 Land Lotteries of Georgia.* (1973), Reprint. Greenville, South Carolina: Southern Historical Press, 1986.

Lucas, Silas Emmett, Jr. *The Second or 1807 Land Lottery of Georgia.* (1968) Reprint, Greenville, South Carolina: Southern Historical Press, 1987.

Lucas, Silas Emmett, Jr. *The Third or 1820 Land Lotteries of Georgia.* (1983) Reprint. Greenville, South Carolina: Southern Historical Press, 1986.

Lucas, Silas Emmett, Jr. and Robert Scott Davis, Jr. eds. *The Georgia Land Lottery Papers, 1805–1914.* (1979) Reprint. Greenville, South Carolina: Southern Historical Press, 1987.

Mathews, Nathan and Kaydee Mathews. *Abstracts of Georgia Land Plat Books A & B.* Fayetteville, Georgia: Nathan and Kaydee Mathews, 1995.

Richardson, Marian M., and Jessie J. Mize. *1832 Cherokee Land Lottery, Index to Revolutionary Soldiers, Their Widows and Orphans Who Were Fortunate Drawers.* Danielsville, Georgia: Heritage Press, 1969.

Sears, Joan N. *The First One Hundred Years of Town Planning in Georgia.* Atlanta: Cherokee Pub. Co., 1979.

Smith, James F. *The 1832 Cherokee Land Lottery of Georgia.* (1838) Reprint. Greenville, South Carolina: Southern Historical Press, 1991.

Southern California Genealogical Society. *Land! Georgia Land Lotteries: Oregon Donation Land: Oregon Donation Land: Oklahoma Land Rushes.* Burbank, California: Southern California Genealogical Society, n.d.

Warren, Mary Bondurant. *1832 Cherokee Gold Lottery.* Athens, Georgia: Iberian Publishing Co., n.d.

Wood, Ralph V., and Virginia S. Wood. *The 1805 Land Lottery of Georgia.* Cambridge, Massachusetts: Greenwood Press, 1964.

Military

Arnold, H. Ross and Hank Burnham, comps. *Georgia Revolutionary War Soldiers' Graves.* 2 vols. Athens, Georgia: Iberian Publishing Co., 1993.

Boss, Bert E. *The Georgia State Memorial Book* (N.p.: 1921.

Brightwell, Juanita S. *Index to the Confederate Records of Georgia.* Spartanburg, South Carolina: Reprint Co., 1982.

Candler, Allen D. *The Confederate Records of the State of Georgia.* Atlanta, Georgia: C.P. Byrd, state printer, 1909–1911.

Candler, Allen D. *The Revolutionary Records of the State of Georgia.* 3 vols. Atlanta, Georgia.: The Franklin-Turner Co., 1908.

Clark, Murtie June. *Colonial Soldiers of the South, 1732–1774*. Baltimore: Genealogical Publishing Co., 1983.

Davis, Robert Scott, Jr. *Georgia Citizens and Soldiers of the American Revolution*. (1979). Greenville, South Carolina: Southern Historical Press, 1983.

Georgia Adjutant Generals Office. *Military Records, 1782–1899*. 6 vols. [N.p.]. Salt Lake City: Filmed by the Genealogical Society of Utah, 1957.

Georgia Executive Department. *Military Commissions in the State Militia, 1798–1860*. Microfilm of originals in the state archives at Atlanta, Georgia. Salt Lake City: Filmed by the Genealogical Society of Utah, 1957. 18 microfilm.

Georgia, 1851–1900. [S.l.]: Brøderbund, 1998. CD-ROM.

Georgia, State Division of Confederate Pensions and Records. *Roster of the Confederate Soldiers of Georgia 1861–1865*. Reprint, Hapeville, Georgia: Logina & Porter, 1959–1964.

Georgia. Department of Archives and History. *Confederate Pension Rolls*. Atlanta: Filmed by the State of Georgia Department of Archives and History, 1963. Microfilm, 634 rolls.

Georgia. Department of Health and Vital Statistics (Atlanta, Georgia). *Death index, 1919–1993*. Salt Lake City: Filmed by the Genealogical Society of Utah, 1995. 381 microfiche.

Georgia. Department of Health and Vital Statistics (Atlanta, Georgia). *Divorce Register Index, 1965–1992*. Salt Lake City: Filmed by the Genealogical Society of Utah, 1995. 149 microfiche.

Georgia. Department of Health and Vital Statistics (Atlanta, Georgia). *Marriage Register Index, 1964–1992*. Salt Lake City: Filmed by the Genealogical Society of Utah, 1995. 341 microfiche.

Georgia. Secretary of State. *Georgia Military Records, 1779–1842*. Microfilm of originals in the state archives at Atlanta, Georgia. Salt Lake City: Filmed by the Genealogical Society of Utah, 1947. 3 microfilm.

Hemperley, Marion R. *Military Certificates of Georgia, 1776–1800*. Atlanta: State Printing Office, 1983.

Hendersen, Lillian, comp. *Roster of the Confederate Soldiers of Georgia, 1861–1865*, 6 vols. Hapeville, Georgia: Longino & Porter, Inc., 1960–1964.

Houston, Martha Lou. *Six Hundred Revolutionary Soldiers and Widows of Revolutionary Soldiers Living in Georgia, 1827–1828*. Athens, Georgia: Heritage Press, 1965.

Index to the Headright Bounty Grants, 1756–1909. Rev. ed. Greenville, South Carolina: Southern Historical Press, 1992.

Jackson, Ronald Vern. *Georgia 1860 Mortality*. North Salt Lake, Utah: Accelerated Indexing Systems International, 1986.

Jackson, Ronald Vern. *Mortality Schedule Georgia 1850*. Bountiful, Utah: Accelerated Indexing Systems, 1979.

Johnson, James M. *Militiamen, Rangers, and Redcoats: The Military in Georgia, 1754–1776*. Macon, Georgia: Mercer University Press, 1992.

Johnson. *Militiamen, Rangers, and Redcoats; The Military in Georgia, 1754–1776*. Galveston, Texas: Frontier Press, 1992.

Knight, Lucian L. *Georgia's Roster of the Revolution. Containing a List of the State Defenders: Officers and Men; Partisans and Regulars; Whether Enlisted from Georgia or Settled in Georgia After the Close of Hostilities*. (1920) Reprint. Baltimore: Clearfield Co, 1996.

Kratovil, Judy Swaim. *Index to War of 1812 Service Records for Volunteer Soldiers from Georgia*. Atlanta, Georgia: J. S. Kratovil, 1986, 1986.

McCall, Mrs. Howard H. *Roster of Revolutionary Soldiers in Georgia*. 3 vols. Reprint. Baltimore: Clearfield Co., 1996.

Miles, Jim. *Georgia Civil War Sites: A Comprehensive Guide to 300 Civil War Battlefields, Forts, Museums, and Cemeteries in Georgia*. Warner Robins, Georgia: J & R Graphics, c1987.

Revolutionary Soldier's Receipts for Georgia Bounty Grants. Atlanta: Foote and Davies Co., 1928.

Sifakis. *Compendium of Confederate Armies: South Carolina and Georgia*. Galveston, Texas: Frontier Press, 1995.

Thaxton, Carlton J. *A Roster of Spanish-American War Soldiers for Georgia*. Americus, Georgia: Carlton Thaxton, 1984.

United States. Selective Service System. *Georgia, World War I Selective Service System Draft Registration Cards, 1917–1918*. National Archives Microfilm Publications, M1509. Washington, D.C.: National Archives, 1987–1988.

United States. War Department. Office of Adjutant General. *Georgia World War I Statement of Service Summary Card Files, ca. 1920–1929*. Microreproduction of originals housed in the Department of Archives and History in Atlanta, Georgia. Salt Lake City: Filmed by the Genealogical Society of Utah, 2001. 7 microfilm.

Volunteer Soldiers in the Cherokee War—1836–1839. Signal Mountain, Tennessee: Mountain Press, n.d.

Vital and Cemetery Records

Austin, Jeanette Holland. *30,638 Burials in Georgia*. Baltimore: Genealogical Publishing, 1995.

Brooke, Ted O. *Georgia Cemetery Directory and Bibliography of Georgia Cemetery Reference Sources*. Marietta, Georgia: T.O. Brooke, 1985.

Cemetery Records of Georgia, 16 vols. Salt Lake City: Genealogical Society of Utah, 1946–1952.

Georgia Department of Archives and History, Atlanta, Georgia. *Marriages, 1805–1866; Marriage Index, 1805–1866*. Microfilm of originals at the state archives in Atlanta, Georgia. Salt Lake City: Filmed by the Genealogical Society of Utah, 1957. 3 microfilm.

Georgia Society of the Colonial Dames of America. *Some Early Epitaphs in Georgia. Foreword and sketches by Mrs. Peter W. Meldrim.* Durham, North Carolina: Sceman Printery, 1924.

Guide to Public Vital Statistics Records in Georgia. Atlanta: Historical Records Survey, 1941.

Ingmire, Frances T. *Colonial Georgia Marriage Records from 1760–1810.* St. Louis: Frances T. Ingmire, 1895.

Jacksonville Branch Genealogical Library (Florida). *Vital Records Card File for North Florida and South Georgia, 1895–1945.* Microfilm of records in the Jacksonville Branch Genealogical Library, Jacksonville, Florida. Salt Lake City: Filmed by the Genealogical Society of Utah, 1977, 1980. 17 microfilm.

Lane, Mrs. Julian C., comp. *Marriage Records of Effingham County, Georgia, 1780–1875.* Statesboro, Georgia: Mrs. Julian C. Lane, 1940.

Liahona Research. *Georgia Marriages, 1801–1825: A Research Tool.* Bountiful, Utah: Precision Indexing, 1992.

Liahona Research. *Georgia Marriages, Early to 1800: A Research Tool.* Bountiful, Utah: Precision Indexing, 1990.

Maddox, Joseph T. *37,000 Early Georgia Marriages.* Irwinton, Georgia: Joseph T. Maddox, 1976.

Maddox, Joseph T. *Early Georgia Marriage Round-up.* Irwinton, Georgia: Joseph T. Maddox, 1975.

Maddox, Joseph T. *Early Georgia Marriages.* Irwinton, Georgia: Joseph T. Maddox, 1980.

Maddox, Joseph T., and Mary Carter. *40,000 Early Georgia Marriages.* Irwinton, Georgia: Joseph T. Maddox, 1977.

Marriages and Obituaries from Early Georgia Newspapers. Greenville, South Carolina: Southern Historical Press, 1989.

Overby, Mary McKeown. *Obituaries Published by "The Christian Index," 1822–1899.* Macon, Georgia: Georgia Baptist Historical Society, 1975, 1982.

Rocker, Willard. *Marriages and Obituaries from the Macon Messenger, 1818–1865.* Greenville, South Carolina: Southern Historical Press, 1988.

Shaw, Aurora. *1850 Georgia Mortality Schedule or Census.* Reprint. Greenville, South Carolina: Southern Historical Press, 1982.

United States Quartermaster's Department. *Roll of Honor: Names of Soldiers Who Died in Defense of the American Union, Interred in. . .* 27 vols. Government Printing Office, 1865–1871. Salt Lake City: Filmed by the Genealogical Society of Utah, 1981. 3 microfilm.

United States. Works Progress Administration (Georgia). *General Index to Savannah Newspapers, Savannah, Georgia, 1763–1845.* (Salt Lake City: Filmed by the Genealogical Society of Utah, 1959, 1989).

Warren, Mary B. *Marriages and Deaths 1763–1820. Abstracted from Extant Georgia Newspapers.* 2 vols. Danielsville, Georgia: Heritage Papers, 1968.

Warren, Mary B., ed. *Georgia Marriages 1811 Through 1820 Prepared from Extant Legal Records and Published Sources.* Danielsville, Georgia: Heritage Papers, 1988.

Warren, Mary Bondurant and Sarah Fleming White. *[Georgia] Marriages and Deaths, 1820 to 1830, Abstracted from Extant Newspapers.* (1972). Reprint. Athens, Georgia: Iberian Publishing Co., 1893.

County Website	Map Index	Date Created	Parent County or Territory From Which Organized Address/Details
Appling http://plant.sgc.peachnet.edu/~jbellis/genweb/ appling/appling.html	**M9**	**15 Dec 1818**	**Creek Indian Lands** Appling County; 83 S Oak St; Baxley, GA 31513-2097; Ph. (912) 367-8100 **Details:** (Records begin 1879, some 1859; Probate Court has Birth, Marriage, Death & Burial Records: Clerk Superior Court has Divorce, Probate & Court Records)
Atkinson www.geocities.com/Heartland/Lane/3390/	**O7**	**15 Aug 1917**	**Coffee, Clinch** Atkinson County; PO Box 518; Pearson, GA 31642-0518; Ph. (912) 422-3391 **Details:** (Clerk Superior Court has Divorce, Probate & Court Records from 1919; Probate Court has Birth & Death Records from 1929, Marriage & Land Records from 1919)
Bacon www.rootsweb.com/~gabacon/bchom.htm	**N8**	**27 Jul 1914**	**Appling, Pearce, Ware** Bacon County; 301 N Pierce St; PO Box 356; Alma, GA 31510-1957; Ph. (912) 632-4915 **Details:** (Clerk Superior Court has Divorce, Court & Land Records from 1915; Probate Court has Birth, Marriage, Death & Probate Records from 1915)
Baker www.rootsweb.com/~gabaker/	**O3**	**12 Dec 1825**	**Early** Baker County; 1 Baker Pl; PO Box 607; Newton, GA 31770-0000; Ph. (912) 734-3007 **Details:** (Probate Court has Birth & Death Records from 1930, Marriage & Probate Records from 1875; Clerk Superior Court has Land, Divorce & Court Records)
Baldwin www.genealogy-quest.com/Georgia/Baldwin/	**I7**	**11 May 1803**	**Creek Indian Lands** Baldwin County; 121 N Wilkinson; Milledgeville, GA 31061-3346; Ph. (912) 445-4791 **Details:** (Probate Court has Birth, Marriage, Death, Burial & Probate Records; County Clerk has Divorce, Court & Land Records from 1861)
Banks www.rootsweb.com/~gabanks/	**E6**	**11 Dec 1858**	**Franklin, Habersham** Banks County; PO Box 130; Homer, GA 30547-0130; Ph. (706) 677-2320 **Details:** (Probate Court has Birth, Marriage & Probate Records; Clerk Superior Court has Court & Land Records)
Barrow www.rootsweb.com/~gabarrow/	**F5**	**7 Jul 1914**	**Jackson, Walton, Gwinnett** Barrow County; 233 E Broad St; Winder, GA 30680-1973; Ph. (770) 307-3005 **Details:** (Probate Court has Birth, Marriage, Death, Burial & Probate Records; Clerk Superior Court has Divorce, Court & Land Records from 1915)
Bartow www.geocities.com/Heartland/Park/9465/ bartowcoga.html	**F3**	**3 Dec 1832**	**Cherokee** Bartow County; 135 W Cherokee Ave; PO Box 543; Cartersville, GA 30120-0543; Ph. (770) 387-5030 **Details:** (Formerly Cass County 1832–1861. Name changed to Bartow 6 Dec 1861) (Probate Court has Birth, Marriage & Probate Records; Clerk Superior Court has Divorce Records from 1862, Court Records from 1869, Land Records from 1837 & Military Discharge Records)

County Website	Map Index	Date Created	Parent County or Territory From Which Organized Address/Details
Ben Hill www.benhillco.com/	**M7**	**31 Jul 1906**	**Irwin, Wilcox** Ben Hill County; 401 E Central Ave; Fitzgerald, GA 31750; Ph. (229) 426-5135 **Details:** (County Clerk has Divorce, Court & Land Records from 1907; Probate Judge has Birth, Marriage, Death, Burial & Probate Records)
Berrien www.rootsweb.com/~gaberrie/	**O7**	**25 Feb 1856**	**Lowndes, Coffee, Irwin** Berrien County; 105 E Washington Ave; PO Box 446; Nashville, GA 31639; Ph. (912) 686-5421 **Details:** (Clerk Superior Court has Divorce & Court Records from 1856 & Land Records; Probate Court has Birth & Death Records from 1919, Marriage & Probate Records from 1856)
Bibb www.rootsweb.com/~gabibb/bibb.htm	**J5**	**9 Dec 1822**	**Jones, Monroe, Twiggs, Houston** Bibb County; 601 Mulberry St; Macon, GA 31201-2672; Ph. (912) 749-6527 **Details:** (County Health Department has Birth, Death & Burial Records; Probate Court has Marriage & Probate Records; County Clerk has Divorce, Court & Land Records from 1823)
Bleckley www.rootsweb.com/~gableckl/	**K6**	**30 Jul 1912**	**Pulaski** Bleckley County; 306 2nd St SE; Cochran, GA 31014-1633; Ph. (912) 934-3200 **Details:** (Clerk Superior Court has Divorce, Probate, Court & Land Records)
Brantley www.rootsweb.com/~gabrantl/	**O9**	**14 Aug 1920**	**Charlton, Pierce, Wayne** Brantley County; PO Box 398; Nahunta, GA 31553-0398; Ph. (912) 462-5256 **Details:** (Clerk Superior Court has Birth, Divorce, Probate & Court Records from 1921)
Brooks http://personal.mia.bellsouth.net/mia/Marriage/i/ miamibig/brooks/	**P6**	**11 Dec 1858**	**Lowndes, Thomas** Brooks County; Hwy 76 & Hwy 33; PO Box 272; Quitman, GA 31643-0000; Ph. (912) 263-5561 **Details:** (Clerk of Courts has Land Records from 1800's, Divorce & Court Records; Probate Court has Marriage & Probate Records; County Health Department has Birth & Death Records)
Bryan www.rootsweb.com/~gabryan/	**L11**	**19 Dec 1793**	**Chatham** Bryan County; PO Box 430; Pembroke, GA 31321-0000; Ph. (912) 653-3839 **Details:** (Probate Judge has Marriage, Probate, Birth & some Death Records; County Clerk has Divorce Records from 1920, Court & Land Records from 1793)
Bulloch www.rootsweb.com/~gabulloc/	**K10**	**8 Feb 1796**	**Bryan, Screven** Bulloch County; 1 Courthouse Sq; PO Box 347; Statesboro, GA 30459; Ph. (912) 764-6245 **Details:** (Probate Court has Birth, Marriage & Probate Records; Clerk Superior Court has Divorce & Court Records from 1891 & Land Records from 1876)

County Website	Map Index	Date Created	Parent County or Territory From Which Organized Address/Details
Burke http://members.aol.com/J2525/index.html	**I10**	**5 Feb 1777**	**Original county org. from St. George Parish** Burke County; 111 E 6th St; PO Box 89; Waynesboro, GA 30830-0000; Ph. (706) 554-2324 **Details:** (Courthouse burned in Jan 1856. All Records prior to that date destroyed) (Probate Court has Birth & Death Records from 1927, Marriage & Probate Records from 1856)
Butts www.lofthouse.com/USA/ga/butts/	**I5**	**24 Dec 1825**	**Henry, Monroe** Butts County; 25 Third St; PO Box 320; Jackson, GA 30233-0320; Ph. (770) 775-8200 **Details:** (Probate Court has Birth, Marriage, Death & Probate Records; Clerk Superior Court has Divorce, Court & Land Records from 1825)
Calhoun http://members.tripod.com/~rakmun/	**N3**	**20 Feb 1854**	**Baker, Early** Calhoun County; 111 School St; PO Box 111; Morgan, GA 31766; Ph. (912) 849-4835 **Details:** (Clerk Superior Court has Divorce, Land, Military & Court Records from 1854; Probate Court has Birth, Marriage, Death, Burial & Probate Records)
Camden www.rootsweb.com/~gacamden/	**P10**	**5 Feb 1777**	**Original county org. from St. Thomas & St. Mary Parishes** Camden County; 4th St & Courthouse Sq; PO Box 99; Woodbine, GA 31569-0000; Ph. (912) 576-5601 **Details:** (Fire 1870, few Records lost) (Clerk Superior Court has Divorce, Court & Land Records; Probate Court has Birth, Marriage, Death & Probate Records)
Campbell www.rootsweb.com/~gacampbe/		**20 Dec 1828**	**Carroll, Coweta, De Kalb, Fayette** Campbell County; GA **Details:** (see Fulton) Annexed by Fulton County 1 Jan 1932
Candler www.rootsweb.com/~gacandle/	**K9**	**1914**	**Bulloch, Emanuel, Tattnall** Candler County; 705 N Lewis St; Metter, GA 30439-0000; Ph. (912) 685-2835 **Details:** (County Clerk has Birth, Marriage & Death Records from 1915, Divorce, Court & Land Records from 1914)
Carroll http://carrollcoga.com/	**H2**	**11 Dec 1826**	**Creek Indian Lands** Carroll County; 423 College St; PO Box 338; Carrollton, GA 30117; Ph. (770) 830-5801 **Details:** (Clerk Superior Court has Divorce Records from 1900, Land & Court Records from 1828; Probate Court has Marriage & Probate Records from 1827; County Health Department has Birth & Death Records)
Cass www.geocities.com/Heartland/Park/9465/bartowcoga.html		**3 Dec 1832**	**Cherokee** Cass County, GA **Details:** (see Bartow) Name changed to Bartow 1862
Catoosa www.catoosa.com/	**D2**	**5 Dec 1853**	**Walker, Whitfield** Catoosa County; 7694 Nashville St; Ringgold, GA 30736-1799; Ph. (706) 965-2500 **Details:** (Clerk Superior Court has Court & Divorce Records from 1853 & Land Records; Probate Court has Marriage & Probate Records from 1853)

County	Map	Date	Parent County or Territory From Which Organized
Website	Index	Created	Address/Details

Charlton   P9   **18 Feb 1854**   **Camden**
www.rootsweb.com/~gacharlt/
Charlton County; 100 Third St; Folkston, GA 31537-0000;
Ph. (912) 496-2549
Details: (Courthouse burned in 1877) (Probate Judge has Birth, Marriage, Death, Burial & Probate Records; Clerk Superior Court has Divorce, Court & Land Records from 1877)

Chatham   L12   **5 Feb 1777**   **Original county org. from St. Phillip & Christ Church Parishes**
www.co.chatham.ga.us/
Chatham County; 133 Montgomery St; Savannah, GA 31401-3230;
Ph. (912) 652-7127
Details: (Probate Court has Birth, Marriage, Death & Probate Records; Clerk Superior Court has Divorce & Court Records from 1783, Land Records from 1785 & Naturalization Records from 1801)

Chattahoochee   K3   **13 Feb 1854**   **Muscogee, Marion**
www2.netdoor.com/~cch/CHA/
Chattahoochee County; PO Box 299; Cusseta, GA 31805-0000;
Ph. (706) 989-3602
Details: (Probate Court has Marriage & Probate Records from 1854, Birth & Death Records from 1919; Clerk Superior Court has Divorce, Court & Land Records from 1854)

Chattooga   E1   **28 Dec 1838**   **Floyd, Walker**
www.rootsweb.com/~gachatto/
Chattooga County; PO Box 211; Summerville, GA 30747-0211;
Ph. (706) 857-0700
Details: (Clerk Courts has Divorce Records from early 1900's & Court Records; Ordinance Office has Birth, Marriage, Death, Burial & Probate Records)

Cherokee   F3   **26 Dec 1831**   **Cherokee Lands**
www.rootsweb.com/~gacherok/
Cherokee County; 90 N St; Canton, GA 30114-2794;
Ph. (770) 479-1953
Details: (Clerk Superior Court has Divorce, Court & Land Records from 1833; Probate Court has Birth, Marriage, Death, Burial & Probate Records)

Christ Church   **1758**   **Creek Cession of 1733**
Christ Church County, GA
Details: County Terminated 1777 (see Chatham) Organized as an early parish & became part of Chatham County 5 Feb 1777

Clarke   G6   **5 Dec 1801**   **Jackson**
www.athensclarkeco.com/
Clarke County; 325 E Washington St Rm 200; PO Box 1868; Athens, GA 30601; Ph. (706) 613-3031
Details: (Clerk Superior Court has Divorce, Land & Court Records from 1801 & Military Records from 1922; County Health Department has Birth & Death Records from 1919; Probate Court has Marriage & Probate Records from 1801)

Clay   N2   **16 Feb 1854**   **Early, Randolph**
www.fortgaines.com/
Clay County; 210 S Washington; PO Box 550; Fort Gaines, GA 39851-0550; Ph. (229) 768-2631
Details: (Clerk Superior Court has Divorce & Land Records, Probate Court has Marriage & Probate Records)

Clayton   H4   **30 Nov 1858**   **Fayette, Henry**
www.co.clayton.ga.us/
Clayton County; 9151 Tara Blvd Ste. 1CL01; Jonesboro, GA 30236-4912; Ph. (770) 477-3401
Details: (Clerk's Office has Court, Divorce, Land, Military, & Other Records)

County Website	Map Index	Date Created	Parent County or Territory From Which Organized Address/Details
Clinch www.rootsweb.com/~gaclinch/	**P8**	**14 Feb 1850**	**Ware, Lowndes** Clinch County; 100 Court Sq; Homerville, GA 31634-1400; Ph. (912) 487-2667 **Details:** (All Records burned in 1856 & 1867) (Probate Court has Birth & Death Records from 1919, Marriage & Probate Records from 1867; Clerk Superior Court has Divorce & Court Records from 1867, Land Records from 1868, voters list from 1890 & old County newspapers from 1895)
Cobb http://co.cobb.ga.us/	**G3**	**3 Dec 1832**	**Cherokee** Cobb County; 100 Cherokee St. Marietta, GA 30060; Ph. (760) 528-3300 **Details:** (Fire in 1864; Records lost) (Department of Health has Birth & Death Records from 1919; Probate Court has Marriage & Probate Records from 1865; Clerk of Superior Court has Land & Court Records from 1865 & Divorce Records)
Coffee www.geocities.com/Heartland/Prairie/5941/	**N7**	**9 Feb 1854**	**Clinch, Irwin, Ware, Telfair** Coffee County; 101 So Peterson Ave; Douglas, GA 31533; Ph. (912) 384-4799 **Details:** (Clerk Superior Court has Divorce, Court & Land Records from 1854 & some Military Discharge Records from 1919; Probate Court has Marriage & Probate Records; County Health Department has Birth & Death Records)
Colquitt www.rootsweb.com/~gacolqu2/	**O5**	**25 Feb 1856**	**Lowndes, Thomas** Colquitt County; 1220 S Main St; PO Box 517; Moultrie, GA 31768; Ph. (912) 891-7400 **Details:** (Fire in 1881; Records lost) (Probate Court has Birth, Marriage, Death & Probate Records; Clerk Superior Court has Divorce, Court & Land Records)
Columbia www.co.columbia.ga.us/	**H9**	**10 Dec 1790**	**Richmond** Columbia County; PO Box 498; Evans, GA 30809; Ph. (760) 868-3300 **Details:** (Clerk of Courts has Land Records from 1700's, Court Records from 1900's & Divorce Records from 1945; Probate Court has Birth, Marriage, Death & Probate Records)
Cook www.rootsweb.com/~gacook/	**O6**	**3 Dec 1832**	**Berrien** Cook County; 212 N Hutchinson Ave; Adel, GA 31620; Ph. (912) 896-2266 **Details:** (Clerk Superior Court has Divorce, Land & Court Records from 1919; Probate Court has Birth, Marriage, Death & Probate Records from 1918)
Coweta www.coweta.ga.us/	**H3**	**11 Dec 1826**	**Creek Indian Lands** Coweta County; 200 Court Sq; Newnan, GA 30263; Ph. (770) 254-2690 **Details:** (Probate Court has Birth & Death Records from 1919, Marriage & Probate Records from 1828; Clerk Superior Court has Divorce, Court & Land Records from 1828)
Crawford www.rootsweb.com/~gacrawfo/gacrawford.htm	**J5**	**9 Dec 1822**	**Houston** Crawford County; PO Box 1059; Roberta, GA 31078; Ph. (912) 836-3782 **Details:** (Clerk Superior Court has Divorce & Court Records from 1850 & Land Records)

County Website	Map Index	Date Created	Parent County or Territory From Which Organized Address/Details
Crisp www.rootsweb.com/~gacrisp/	M5	17 Aug 1905	**Dooly** Crisp County; 210 7th St S; Cordele, GA 31015; Ph. (912) 276-2672 **Details:** (Clerk Superior Court has Divorce, Court & Land Records from 1905; Probate Court has Marriage & Probate Records; County Health Department has Birth & Death Records)
Dade www.rootsweb.com/~gadade/index.htm	D1	25 Dec 1837	**Walker** Dade County; PO Box 613; Trenton, GA 30752-0000; Ph. (706) 657-4625 **Details:** (County Clerk has Divorce, Court & Land Records)
Dawson www.dawsonco.org/	E4	3 Dec 1857	**Lumpkin, Gilmer** Dawson County; PO Box 192; Dawsonville, GA 30534-0192; Ph. (706) 265-3164 **Details:** (Clerk Superior Court has Divorce, Court & Land Records from 1857; Probate Court has Birth, Marriage, Death, Burial & Probate Records from 1858)
De Kalb www.rootsweb.com/~gadekalb/	G4	9 Dec 1822	**Fayette, Gwinett, Henry** De Kalb County; Courthouse; Decatur, GA 30030; Ph. (404) 371-2781 **Details:** (Courthouse burned 1842 & 1916) (Clerk of Superior Court has Divorce, Court, & Land Records from 1842; Probate Court has Marriage & Probate Records from 1842)
Decatur www.rootsweb.com/~gadecatu/	P3	8 Dec 1823	**Early** Decatur County; 1400 E Shotwell St; PO Box 735; Bainbridge, GA 31717-0735; Ph. (229) 248-3030 **Details:** (Probate Court has Marriage Records from 1823 & Probate Records; Clerk Superior Court has Divorce, Court & Land Records from 1823)
Dodge http://plant.sgc.peachnet.edu/~jbellis/genweb/dodge/dodge.html	L7	26 Oct 1870	**Montgomery, Pulaski, Telfair** Dodge County; 407 Anson Ave; PO Box 818; Eastman, GA 31023-0818; Ph. (478) 374-4361 **Details:** (Probate Court has Birth, Marriage, Death & Probate Records; Clerk Superior Court has Divorce, Court & Land Records)
Dooly www.rootsweb.com/~gadooly/	L5	15 May 1821	**Creek Indian Lands** Dooly County; PO Box 348; Vienna, GA 31092-0322; Ph. (912) 268-4228 **Details:** (Fire destroyed early Records) (Clerk Superior Court has Divorce & Court Records from 1846 & Land Records from 1850; Probate Court has Birth, Marriage, Death, Burial & Probate Records)
Dougherty www.albany.ga.us/doughertyco.htm	N4	15 Dec 1853	**Baker** Dougherty County; 222 Pine Ave; Albany, GA 31703-5301; Ph. (912) 431-2198 **Details:** (Clerk Superior Court has Divorce & Court Records from 1856 & Land Records from 1854; Probate Court has Birth, Marriage, Death & Probate Records)
Douglas www.County.douglas.ga.us/	G3	17 Oct 1870	**Carroll, Campbell** Douglas County; 8700 Hospital Dr; Douglasville, GA 30134-4501; Ph. (770) 920-7252 **Details:** (Probate Court has Birth, Marriage, Death & Probate Records; Clerk Superior Court has Divorce, Court & Land Records from 1870)

County Website	Map Index	Date Created	Parent County or Territory From Which Organized Address/Details
Early www.rootsweb.com/~gaearly/	N2	15 Dec 1818	**Creek Indian Lands** Early County; PO Box 849; Blakely, GA 31723; Ph. (229) 723-3033 **Details:** (Many Records lost, first Marriage Book, 1854) (Clerk of Court has Cemetery, Divorce, Land, Military & Court Records)
Echols www.rootsweb.com/~gaechols/index.html	P7	13 Dec 1858	**Clinch, Lowndes** Echols County; PO Box 190; Statenville, GA 31648-0190; Ph. (229) 559-5642 **Details:** (Most Records burned 1897) (Clerk Superior Court has Divorce, Court & Land Records)
Effingham www.effga.com/	K11	5 Feb 1777	**Original county org. from St. Mathews & St. Phillips Parishes** Effingham County; 901 N Pine St; Springfield, GA 31329-0000; Ph. (912) 754-2101 **Details:** (Some Records lost in Civil War & fire 1890) (Probate Court has Birth & Death Records from 1927, Marriage & Probate Records from 1790; Clerk Superior Court has Divorce & Court Records from 1777)
Elbert www.arches.uga.edu/~laaron/	F8	10 Dec 1790	**Wilkes** Elbert County; 10 W Church St; Elberton, GA 30635-1498; Ph. (706) 283-2005 **Details:** (Clerk Superior Court has Divorce, Court, Land & Cemetery Records from 1790 & Military Records from 1922; Probate Court has Birth, Marriage, Death, Burial & Probate Records)
Emanuel www.rootsweb.com/~gaemanue/	K9	10 Dec 1812	**Montgomery, Bulloch** Emanuel County; 201 N Main St; PO Box 787; Swainsboro, GA 30401-2042; Ph. (912) 237-8911 **Details:** (Probate Court has Birth, Marriage, Death & Probate Records; Clerk Superior Court has Divorce, Court & Land Records from 1812)
Evans www.rootsweb.com/~gaevans/	L10	11 Aug 1914	**Bulloch, Tattnall** Evans County; 3 Freeman St; Claxton, GA 30417-0000; Ph. (912) 739-3868 **Details:** (Probate Court has Birth, Marriage, Death, Burial & Probate Records; Clerk Superior Court has Divorce, Court & Land Records from 1915)
Fannin www.fannincounty.org/	D4	21 Jan 1854	**Gilmer, Union** Fannin County; 420 W Main St; PO Box 1300; Blue Ridge, GA 30513; Ph. (706) 632-2039 **Details:** (Department of Health has Birth & Death Records from 1919; Probate Court has Marriage & Probate Records from 1854; Clerk of Superior Court has Divorce, Court, & Land Records from 1854)
Fayette www.FayetteChamber.org	H4	15 May 1821	**Creek Indian Lands** Fayette County; 200 Courthouse Sq; PO Box 130; Fayetteville, GA 30214; Ph. (770) 461-9983 **Details:** (Probate Court has Birth, Marriage, Death & Probate Records; Clerk Superior Court has Divorce, Court & Land Records)
Floyd www.floydcountyga.org/	F2	3 Dec 1832	**Cherokee** Floyd County; 3 Government Plaza; Rome, GA 30161; Ph. (706) 291-5190 **Details:** (Probate Court has Marriage & Probate Records; Clerk Superior Court has Divorce, Court & Land Records from 1883)

County Website	Map Index	Date Created	Parent County or Territory From Which Organized Address/Details
Forsyth www.County.forsyth.ga.us/	**F4**	**3 Dec 1832**	**Cherokee** Forsyth County; 100 W Courthouse Sq; Cumming, GA 30040-0128; Ph. (770) 781-2120 **Details:** (Clerk of Courts has Land Records from 1830's, Divorce & Court Records; Probate Court has Birth, Marriage, Death & Probate Records)
Franklin www.rootsweb.com/~gafrankl/	**E7**	**25 Feb 1784**	**Cherokee Indian Lands** Franklin County; Courthouse Sq; PO Box 159; Carnesville, GA 30521-0000; Ph. (706) 384-2483 **Details:** (Clerk Superior Court has Divorce & Court Records from 1900 & Land Records from 1860; some Records prior to 1850 in GA Archives)
Fulton www.County.fulton.ga.us/	**G3**	**20 Dec 1853**	**DeKalb, Campbell, Milton** Fulton County; 136 Pryor St SW; Atlanta, GA 30303-3405; Ph. (404) 730-5300 **Details:** (Probate Court has Marriage & Probate Records; Clerk Superior Court has Divorce, Court & Land Records from 1854)
Gilmer www.rootsweb.com/~gagilmer/	**D4**	**3 Dec 1832**	**Cherokee** Gilmer County; 1 Westside Sq; Elllijay, GA 30540; Ph. (706) 635-4361 **Details:** (Probate Court has Birth & Death Records from 1927, Marriage Records from 1835 & Probate Records; Clerk Superior Court has Divorce Records from 1909, Land Records from 1833, Military Records from 1902 & Court Records from 1900)
Glascock www.rootsweb.com/~gaglasco/	**I8**	**19 Dec 1857**	**Warren** Glascock County; 62 E Main St; Gibson, GA 30810-0231; Ph. (706) 598-2084 **Details:** (Probate Court has Birth, Marriage, Death & Probate Records; Clerk Superior Court has Divorce, Court & Land Records)
Glynn www.glynncounty.org/	**O11**	**5 Feb 1777**	**Original county org. from St. David & St. Patrick Parishes** Glynn County; 701 H St; Brunswick, GA 31520-6750; Ph. (912) 554-7272 **Details:** (Probate Court has Marriage Records from 1845 & Probate Records from 1792; Clerk Superior Court has Divorce & Court Records from 1792 & Land Records 1824–1829 burned, all Records to 1818 damaged)
Gordon www.gordoncounty.org/	**E3**	**13 Feb 1850**	**Cass, Floyd** Gordon County; 101 Boston Rd; Calhoun, GA 30701-2244; Ph. (706) 629-3795 **Details:** (Records destroyed 1864) (Clerk Superior Court has Divorce & Court Records from 1864 & Land Records; Probate Court has Birth, Marriage, Death, Burial & Probate Records)
Grady www.rootsweb.com/~gagrady/	**P4**	**17 Aug 1905**	**Decatur, Thomas** Grady County; 250 N Broad St; Cairo, GA 31728-4101; Ph. (912) 377-2912 **Details:** (Clerk Superior Court has Divorce, Court & Land Records from 1906)

County Website	Map Index	Date Created	Parent County or Territory From Which Organized Address/Details
Greene www.greenecountyga.gov	H7	3 Feb 1786	**Washington** Greene County; 113 N Main, Ste 113; Greensboro, GA 30642; Ph. (706) 453-3346 **Details:** (Probate Court has Marriage Records from 1786, Birth Records from 1880, Death Records from 1919, Wills from 1787, Census, Newspapers; Clerk of Superior Court has Land & Property Records; Tax Commissioner has Tax Records)
Gwinnett www.County.gwinnett.ga.us/cgi-bin/bvgwin/egov/page.jsp	G5	15 Dec 1818	**Cherokee & Creek Indian Lands** Gwinnett County; 75 Langley Dr; PO Box 880; Lawrenceville, GA 30046; Ph. (770) 822-8100 **Details:** (Courthouse burned 1871; few Records saved) (Clerk Superior Court has Divorce, Court & Land Records)
Habersham www.co.habersham.ga.us/	E6	15 Dec 1818	**Cherokee Indian Lands** Habersham County; 555 Monroe St #35; Clarkesville, GA 30523-0227; Ph. (706) 754-2923 **Details:** (Clerk of Court has Birth Records from 1920, Cemetery Records from 1927, Divorce, Land, & Court Records from 1819, Military Records from 1900, & Probate Records; Chamber of Commerce has Business & Commerce Records; Probate Court has Death, Guardianship, Marriage Records, & Newspapers; State has Immigration & Naturalization Records; Tax Commissioner has Tax Records)
Hall www.hallcounty.org/	E5	15 Dec 1818	**Cherokee Indian Lands** Hall County; 116 Spring St; Gainesville, GA 30501; Ph. (770) 531-7025 **Details:** (Tornado destroyed courthouse in 1936; most Records lost, except deeds) (Clerk of Superior Court has Divorce Records from 1900, Court & Land Records from 1819; Probate Court has Marriage & Probate Records)
Hancock www.rootsweb.com/~gahancoc/index.html	I7	17 Dec 1793	**Greene, Washington** Hancock County; Courthouse Sq; Sparta, GA 31087-0000; Ph. (706) 444-6644 **Details:** (Probate Court has Birth & Death Records from 1927, Marriage Records from 1805 & Probate Records; Clerk Superior Court has Divorce & Court Records from 1919 & Land Records from 1794)
Haralson www.rootsweb.com/~gaharals/	G1	26 Jan 1856	**Carroll, Polk** Haralson County; PO Box 489; Buchanan, GA 30113-0488; Ph. (770) 646-2002 **Details:** (Probate Court has Birth, Marriage, Death, Burial & Probate Records; Clerk Superior Court has Divorce, Court & Land Records)
Harris www.rootsweb.com/~gaharris/index.html	J2	14 Dec 1827	**Muscogee, Troup** Harris County; PO Box 528; Hamilton, GA 31811-0528; Ph. (706) 628-4944 **Details:** (Probate Court has Marriage & Probate Records; Clerk Superior Court has Land Records from 1827, Divorce & Court Records from 1927; County Health Department has Birth & Death Records)

County Website	Map Index	Date Created	Parent County or Territory From Which Organized Address/Details
Hart www.geocities.com/RainForest/9478/hartcoga.html	E7	**7 Dec 1853**	**Elbert, Franklin** Hart County; PO Box 279; Hartwell, GA 30643-0279; Ph. (706) 376-2024 **Details:** (Probate Court has Birth, Marriage, Death, Burial & Probate Records; Clerk Superior Court has Divorce, Court & Land Records from 1856)
Heard	I2	**22 Dec 1830**	**Carroll, Coweta, Troup** Heard County; 161 Shady St.; PO Box 990; Franklin, GA 30217; Ph. (706) 675-6507 **Details:** (Fire in 1894) (Probate Court has Birth & Death Records from 1927, Newspapers from 1894, Marriage & Probate Records; County Museum/Library has Burial, Cemetery, Census, & Other Historical Records; Chamber of Commerce has Business & Commerce Records; Superior Court has Court, Divorce, Guardianship, Immigration, Land, Military, & Naturalization Records; County Assessor has Land & Tax Records)
Henry www.County.henry.ga.us/	H4	**15 May 1821**	**Creek Indian Lands** Henry County; 345 Phillips Dr; McDonough, GA 30253-3425; Ph. (770) 954-2400 **Details:** (Clerk Superior Court has Divorce, Court & Land Records from 1821)
Houston www.rootsweb.com/~gahousto/	K5	**15 May 1821**	**Creek Indian Lands** Houston County; 200 Carl Vinson Pkwy; Warner Robins, GA 31088-5808; Ph. (478) 542-2105 **Details:** (Probate Court has Birth & Death Records from 1927, Marriage Records from 1833 & Probate Records from 1827; Clerk Superior Court has Divorce, Court & Land Records from 1822)
Irwin www.geocities.com/gholback_1999/gairwin.html	N6	**15 Dec 1818**	**Creek Indian Lands** Irwin County; 207 S Irwin Ave; PO Box 186; Ocilla, GA 31774-1098; Ph. (229) 468-5356 **Details:** (Clerk Superior Court has Divorce, Land & Court Records from 1821 & Military Records from 1900; Probate Court has Birth, Marriage, Death & Burial Records from 1920 & Probate Records from 1850)
Jackson www.rootsweb.com/~gajackso/	F6	**11 Feb 1796**	**Franklin** Jackson County; 67 Athens St; PO Box 68; Jefferson, GA 30549-0068; Ph. (706) 367-6360 **Details:** (Clerk Superior Court has Land & Probate Records from 1796, Marriage Records from 1803, Birth Records from 1919, Death Records from 1927 & tax Records from 1800)
Jasper www.rootsweb.com/~gajasper/	H6	**1812**	**Baldwin** Jasper County; Courthouse on the Sq; Monticello, GA 31064; Ph. (706) 468-4901 **Details:** (Formerly Randolph County 1807–1811. Name changed to Jasper 10 Dec 1812) (Clerk Superior Court has Land Records from 1808, Divorce, Military & Court Records from 1900)
Jeff Davis http://plant.sgc.peachnet.edu/~jbellis/genweb/jeffdavis/jd.html	M8	**18 Aug 1905**	**Appling, Coffee** Jeff Davis County; Jeff Davis St; PO Box 602; Hazlehurst, GA 31539-0000; Ph. (912) 375-6611 **Details:** (Clerk Superior Court has Divorce, Court & Land Records from 1905)

County Website	Map Index	Date Created	Parent County or Territory From Which Organized Address/Details
Jefferson http://members.aol.com/J2525/jeff.htm	I8	**20 Feb 1796**	**Burke, Warren** Jefferson County; 202 E Broad St; PO Box 658; Louisville, GA 30434-1622; Ph. (478) 625-7922 **Details:** (Records not complete; Clerk of Courts has Land & Court Records from 1865, Divorce Records from 1900's & Marriage Records; Probate Court has Probate Records; County Health Department has Birth & Death Records)
Jenkins www.rootsweb.com/~gajenkin/	J10	**17 Aug 1905**	**Bullock, Burke, Emanuel, Screven** Jenkins County; Harvey St; PO Box 797; Millen, GA 30442-0797; Ph. (478) 982-4683 **Details:** (Probate Court has Marriage & Probate Records; Clerk Superior Court has Divorce, Court & Land Records from 1905)
Johnson www.rootsweb.com/~gajohnso/	J8	**11 Dec 1858**	**Emanuel, Laurens, Washington** Johnson County; PO Box 269; Wrightsville, GA 31096-0269; Ph. (912) 864-3388 **Details:** (Clerk Superior Court has Divorce, Court & Land Records from 1858)
Jones www.rootsweb.com/~gajones/	I6	**10 Dec 1807**	**Baldwin** Jones County; PO Box 1359; Gray, GA 31032-1359; Ph. (478) 986-6671 **Details:** (Probate Court has Birth & Death Records from 1924, Marriage & Probate Records from 1811; Clerk Superior Court has Land & Court Records)
Kinchafoonee		**16 Dec 1853**	**Stewart** Kinchafoonee County, GA **Details:** (see Webster) Name changed to Webster 21 Feb 1856
Lamar www.rootsweb.com/~galamar/	I4	**17 Aug 1920**	**Monroe, Pike** Lamar County; 326 Thomaston St; Barnesville, GA 30204-1616; Ph. (770) 358-5145 **Details:** (Clerk Superior Court has Divorce, Court & Land Records from 1921)
Lanier www.flash.net/~miamibig/lanier/	P7	**7 Aug 1920**	**Berrien, Lowndes, Clinch** Lanier County; 100 W Main St; Lakeland, GA 31635; Ph. (912) 482-2088 **Details:** (Clerk Superior Court has Divorce & Court Records from 1921 & Land Records; Probate Court has Birth, Marriage, Death & Probate Records from 1921)
Laurens www.rootsweb.com/~galauren/	K7	**10 Dec 1807**	**Wilkinson** Laurens County; 101 N Jefferson St; Dublin, GA 31021-6198; Ph. (478) 272-3210 **Details:** (Probate Court has Marriage & Probate Records; Clerk Superior Court has Divorce, Court & Land Records from 1807; County Health Department has Birth & Death Records)
Lee www.lee.ga.us/	M4	**11 Dec 1826**	**Creek Indian Lands** Lee County; PO Box 889; Leesburg, GA 31763-0056; Ph. (912) 759-6000 **Details:** (Courthouse fire 1858; all Records lost) (Clerk Superior Court has Marriage, Divorce & Court Records)

County Website	Map Index	Date Created	Parent County or Territory From Which Organized Address/Details
Liberty www.petersnn.org/libertyco/	**M11**	**5 Feb 1777**	**Original county org. from St. Andrew, St. James & St. Johns Parishes** Liberty County; Courthouse Sq; PO Box 829; Hinesville, GA 31313-3240; Ph. (912) 876-2164 **Details:** (Probate Judge has Marriage & Probate Records from late 1700's, Birth Records from 1919 & Death Records from 1927; Clerk of Courts has Divorce, Court & Land Records from 1756; some early Records lost)
Lincoln www.rootsweb.com/~galincol/index.html	**G8**	**20 Feb 1796**	**Wilkes** Lincoln County; 210 Humphrey St; PO Box 340; Lincolnton, GA 30817-0000; Ph. (706) 359-4444 **Details:** (Probate Court has Birth Records from 1920, Marriage Records from 1810, Death Records from 1930 & Probate Records from 1796; Clerk Superior Court has Divorce & Court Records from 1796 & Land Records from 1790)
Long www.rootsweb.com/~galong/index.html	**M10**	**14 Aug 1920**	**Liberty** Long County; McDonald St; Ludowici, GA 31316-0000; Ph. (912) 545-2123 **Details:** (Probate Court has Birth, Marriage, Death, Burial & Probate Records; Clerk Superior Court has Divorce, Court, Land & adoption Records from 1920)
Lowndes www.lowndescounty.com/	**P7**	**23 Dec 1825**	**Irwin** Lowndes County; 325 W Savannah Ave; PO Box 1349; Valdosta, GA 31601; Ph. (229) 333-5127 **Details:** (Probate Court has Marriage & Probate Records; Clerk Superior Court has Divorce, Court & Land Records from 1858)
Lumpkin www.rootsweb.com/~galumpki/	**E5**	**3 Dec 1832**	**Cherokee, Habersham, Hall** Lumpkin County; 99 Courthouse Hill Ste A; Dahlonega, GA 30533-1167; Ph. (706) 864-3742 **Details:** (Probate Court has Birth, Marriage, Death, Burial & Probate Records; Clerk Superior Court has Divorce, Court & Land Records from 1833)
Macon www.rootsweb.com/~gamacon/index.html	**K4**	**14 Dec 1837**	**Houston, Marion** Macon County; Sumter St; PO Box 297; Oglethorpe, GA 31068-0000; Ph. (912) 472-7021 **Details:** (Courthouse burned 1857; all Records lost) (Clerk Superior Court has Divorce, Court & Land Records; Probate Court has Marriage & Probate Records from 1857, Birth & Death Records from 1927)
Madison www.madisonco.us	**F7**	**5 Dec 1811**	**Clarke, Elbert, Franklin, Jackson, Oglethorpe** Madison County; 91 Albany Ave; Danielsville, GA 30633-0147; Ph. (706) 795-6365 **Details:** (Probate Court has Birth, Marriage, Death, Burial & Probate Records; Clerk Superior Court has Divorce, Court & Land Records from 1812)
Marion www.rootsweb.com/~gamarion/	**K3**	**14 Dec 1827**	**Lee, Muscogee** Marion County; Courthouse Sq; Buena Vista, GA 31803-0000; Ph. (912) 649-2603 **Details:** (Courthouse fire 1845; all Records lost) (Clerk Superior Court has Divorce, Court & Land Records)

County Website	Map Index	Date Created	Parent County or Territory From Which Organized Address/Details
McDuffie www.County.mcduffie.ga.us/	H8	18 Oct 1870	**Columbia, Warren** McDuffie County; 337 Main St; PO Box 158; Thomson, GA 30824-0028; Ph. (706) 595-2134 **Details:** (Probate Court has Birth, Marriage, Death & Probate Records from 1872; Clerk Superior Court has Divorce Records from 1872, Court Records & Land Records from 1870)
McIntosh www.gabooks.com/genmain.htm	N11	19 Dec 1793	**Liberty** McIntosh County; PO Box 584; Darien, GA 31305-0584; Ph. (912) 437-6671 **Details:** (Many Records lost during Civil War; Courthouse fire 1931) (Clerk Superior Court has Divorce, Court, Probate & Land Records)
Meriwether http://personal.atl.bellsouth.net/atl/Marriage/s/msaffold/meriweth.htm	I3	14 Dec 1827	**Troup** Meriwether County; PO Box 428; Greenville, GA 30222-0428; Ph. (706) 672-1314 **Details:** (Probate Court has Birth Records from 1927, Marriage Records from 1828, Death Records from 1929 & Probate Records from 1838; Clerk Superior Court has Divorce, Court & Land Records from 1827 & Military Discharge Records)
Miller www.rootsweb.com/~gamiller/	O3	26 Feb 1856	**Baker, Early** Miller County; 155 S 1st St Ste 2; Colquitt, GA 31737-1284; Ph. (912) 758-4104 **Details:** (Courthouse fire 1873; all Records lost) (Probate Court has Birth Records from 1919, Marriage Records from 1904, Death Records from 1950 & Probate Records from 1900; Clerk Superior Court has Land, Divorce & Court Records)
Milton www.mindspring.com/~ednab/		18 Dec 1857	**Cherokee, Cobb, Forsyth** Milton County; GA **Details:** (see Fulton) Annexed by Fulton County 1 Jan 1932
Mitchell www.rootsweb.com/~gamitche/index.html	O4	21 Dec 1857	**Baker** Mitchell County; PO Box 187; Camilla, GA 31730-0000; Ph. (912) 336-2000 **Details:** (Courthouse fire 1869; Superior Court Records and some other Records were saved) (Clerk Superior Court has Divorce Records from 1857 & Court Records from 1847)
Monroe www.rootsweb.com/~gamonroe/index.html	I5	15 May 1821	**Creek Indian Lands** Monroe County; PO Box 189; Forsyth, GA 31029-0189; Ph. (912) 994-7000 **Details:** (Probate Court has Marriage & Probate Records from 1824, Birth Records from 1927 & Death Records from 1940; Clerk Superior Court has Court & Land Records from 1821 & Divorce Records)
Montgomery http://plant.sgc.peachnet.edu/~jbellis/genweb/montgomery/montgomery.html	L8	19 Dec 1793	**Washington** Montgomery County; Railroad Ave; PO Box 295; Mount Vernon, GA 30445-0000; Ph. (912) 583-2363 **Details:** (Probate Court has Birth & Death Records from 1918, Marriage Records from 1807 & Probate Records from 1793; Clerk Superior Court has Divorce & Court Records from 1800 & Land Records from 1793; most original Records prior to 1890 are in State Archives)

County Website	Map Index	Date Created	Parent County or Territory From Which Organized Address/Details
Morgan www.morgan.public.lib.ga.us/county/	H6	10 Dec 1807	**Baldwin** Morgan County; PO Box 168; Madison, GA 30650-0168; Ph. (706) 342-0725 **Details:** (County Health Department has Birth Records; Probate Court has Marriage, Death, Burial & Probate Records; Clerk Superior Court has Divorce, Court & Land Records from 1807)
Murray www.rootsweb.com/~gamurray/index.htm	D3	3 Dec 1832	**Cherokee** Murray County; 101 N 3rd Ave; Chatsworth, GA 30705-0000; Ph. (706) 695-2932 **Details:** (Probate Court has Birth & Death Records from 1924, Marriage Records from 1842 & Probate Records from 1890; Clerk Superior Court has Court Records from 1834)
Muscogee www.rootsweb.com/~gamuscog/muscogee.htm	K3	11 Dec 1826	**Creek Indian Lands** Muscogee County; 100 10th St; PO Box 1340; Columbus, GA 31902; Ph. (706) 653-4013 **Details:** (Clerk Superior Court has Divorce, Court & Land Records from 1838)
Newton www.County.newton.ga.us/	H5	24 Dec 1821	**Henry, Jasper, Walton** Newton County; 1113 Usher St; Covington, GA 30014; Ph. (770) 784-2000 **Details:** (Clerk Superior Court has Divorce, Court & Land Records from 1822 & Military Records from 1917)
Oconee www.oconeecounty.com/	G6	25 Feb 1875	**Clarke** Oconee County; 23 N Main St; PO Box 1099; Watkinsville, GA 30677-2438; Ph. (706) 769-3940 **Details:** (Probate Court has Birth, Marriage, Death & Probate Records; Clerk Superior Court has Divorce, Court & Land Records from 1875)
Oglethorpe www.rootsweb.com/~gaogleth/	G7	19 Dec 1793	**Wilkes** Oglethorpe County; PO Box 261; Lexington, GA 30648-0261; Ph. (706) 743-5270 **Details:** (Courthouse fire 1941) (Probate Court has Birth, Marriage, Death & Probate Records; Clerk Superior Court has Divorce, Court & Land Records from 1794)
Paulding www.paulding.gov/	G2	3 Dec 1832	**Cherokee** Paulding County; 11 Courthouse Sq; Dallas, GA 30132-1401; Ph. (770) 445-7527 **Details:** (Clerk Superior Court has Divorce & Court Records from 1876 & Land Records from 1848)
Peach www.rootsweb.com/~gapeach/	K5	18 Jul 1924	**Houston, Macon** Peach County; 205 W Church St; PO Box 468; Fort Valley, GA 31030-4155; Ph. (912) 825-2535 **Details:** (Probate Court has Birth, Marriage, Death & Probate Records from 1925; Clerk Superior Court has Divorce, Court & Land Records from 1925)
Pickens www.rootsweb.com/~gapicken/	E3	5 Dec 1853	**Cherokee, Gilmer** Pickens County; 52 N Main St; Jasper, GA 30143-0000; Ph. (706) 692-2014 **Details:** (Probate Court has Birth, Marriage, Death, Burial & Probate Records; Clerk Superior Court has Divorce, Court & Land Records from 1854)

County	Map	Date	Parent County or Territory From Which Organized
Website	Index	Created	Address/Details

Pierce N9 **18 Dec 1857** — **Appling, Ware**
http://personal.jax.bellsouth.net/jax/r/s/rskhdr/
Pierce/pierce.htm

Pierce County; PO Box 679; Blackshear, GA 31516-0679;
Ph. (912) 449-2022
Details: (Courthouse fire 1874) (Probate Court has Birth Records from 1926, Marriage Records from 1875, Death Records from 1924 & Probate Records; Clerk Superior Court has Divorce & Court Records from 1875 & Land Records)

Pike I4 **9 Dec 1822** — **Monroe**
www.rootsweb.com/~gapike/index.htm

Pike County; PO Box 377; Zebulon, GA 30295-0377;
Ph. (706) 567-3406
Details: (Clerk Superior Court has Court & Land Records from 1823)

Polk F2 **20 Dec 1851** — **Paulding, Floyd**
www.rootsweb.com/~gapolk/

Polk County; PO Box 268; Cedartown, GA 30125-0268;
Ph. (770) 749-2100
Details: (Probate Court has Birth, Marriage, Death & Probate Records; Clerk Superior Court has Divorce, Court & Land Records from 1852)

Pulaski L6 **13 Dec 1808** — **Laurens**
www.rootsweb.com/~gapulask/index.htm

Pulaski County; PO Box 29; Hawkinsville, GA 31036-0029;
Ph. (478) 783-4154
Details: (Probate Court has Birth, Death, Guardianship, Marriage, and Probate Records; Superior Court has Court, Divorce, Land, Military, and Newspaper Records; City Hall has Cemetery, Business & Commerce Records)

Putnam H6 **10 Dec 1807** — **Baldwin**
www.rootsweb.com/~gaputnam/index.html

Putnam County; 100 S Jefferson Ave; Eatonton, GA 31024;
Ph. (706) 485-4501
Details: (Clerk Superior Court has Divorce & Court Records from 1807; Probate Court has Birth Records from 1866, Marriage & Probate Records from 1808, Death Records from 1919 & tax digest 1812–1848)

Quitman M2 **10 Dec 1858** — **Randolph, Stewart**
http://home.earthlink.net/~bwjohnson/
quit_mn.htm

Quitman County; PO Box 114; Georgetown, GA 31754-0114;
Ph. (912) 334-2578
Details: (Courthouse burned) (Clerk Superior Court has Birth Records from 1927, Marriage Records from 1919, Death Records, Divorce & Court Records from 1923 & Land Records from 1879)

Rabun D6 **21 Dec 1819** — **Cherokee Indian Lands**
www.usgennet.org/usa/region/southeast/garabun/

Rabun County; 25 Courthouse Sq #7; Clayton, GA 30525-0925;
Ph. (706) 782-3615
Details: (Probate Court has Marriage & Probate Records; Clerk Superior Court has Divorce, Court & Land Records)

Randolph M3 **20 Dec 1828** — **Lee**
http://home.earthlink.net/~bwjohnson/
rand_mn.htm

Randolph County; 208 Court St; Cuthbert, GA 31740-0000;
Ph. (229) 732-6440
Details: (Probate Court has Marriage & Probate Records from 1835; Clerk Superior Court has Divorce, Court & Land Records from 1835)

Randolph, old **10 Dec 1807** — **Baldwin**

Randolph, old County; GA
Details: (see Jasper) Name changed to Jasper 10 Dec 1812

County	Map	Date	Parent County or Territory From Which Organized
Website	Index	Created	Address/Details

Richmond   H9   5 Feb 1777
http://augusta.County.richmond.ga.us/

Original county org. from St. Paul Parish
Richmond County; 530 Green St; Augusta, GA 30911-0001;
Ph. (760) 821-2460
Details: (Clerk Superior Court has Land Records from 1778 &
Court Records; Probate Court has Marriage & Probate Records)

Rockdale   H5   18 Oct 1870
www.rockdalecounty.org/dale.cfm?pid=1

Henry, Newton
Rockdale County; 922 Court St NE; Conyers, GA 30207-4540;
Ph. (770) 929-4021
Details: (Probate Court has Marriage & Probate Records from 1870
& Death Records from 1930; Clerk Superior Court has Land, Divorce
& Court Records)

Schley   L4   22 Dec 1857
www.rootsweb.com/~gaschley/schley.htm

Marion, Sumter
Schley County; PO Box 352; Ellaville, GA 31806-0000;
Ph. (912) 937-2609
Details: (Probate Court has Birth, Death & Burial Records from
1927, Marriage Records from 1858 & Probate Records; Clerk Superior Court has Divorce, Court & Land Records from 1857)

Screven   J11   14 Dec 1793
www.rootsweb.com/~gascreve/

Burke, Effingham
Screven County; 216 Mims Rd; Sylvania, GA 30467-0159;
Ph. (912) 564-2622
Details: (Probate Court has Birth & Death Records from 1927, Marriage & Probate Records from 1817; Clerk Superior Court has Divorce
& Court Records from 1816 & Land Records from 1790)

Seminole   P3   8 Jul 1920
www.rootsweb.com/~gasemino/index.html

Decatur, Early
Seminole County; 200 S Knox Ave; Donalsonville, GA 31745;
Ph. (912) 524-2525
Details: (Probate Court has Birth, Marriage, Death & Probate
Records; Clerk Superior Court has Divorce, Court & Land Records
from 1921)

Spalding   I4   20 Dec 1851
www.rootsweb.com/~gaspaldi/

Fayette, Henry, Pike
Spalding County; 132 W Solomon St; Griffin, GA 30223-3312;
Ph. (770) 467.4745
Details: (Clerk Superior Court has Divorce, Court & Land Records
from 1852)

St. Andrew   1758

Creek Cession of 1733
St. Andrew County; GA
Details: (see Liberty) Organized as an early parish & became part of
Liberty County 5 Feb 1777

St. David   1765

Creek Cession of 1763
St. David County; GA
Details: (see Glynn) Organized as an early parish & became part of
Glynn County 5 Feb 1777

St. George   1758

Creek Cession of 1733
St. George County; GA
Details: (see Burke) Organized as an early parish & became Burke
County 5 Feb 1777

St. James   1758

Creek Cession of 1733
St. James County; GA
Details: (see Liberty) Organized as an early parish & became part of
Liberty County 5 Feb 1777

County Website	Map Index	Date Created	Parent County or Territory From Which Organized Address/Details
St. John		1758	**Creek Cession of 1733** St. John County; GA **Details:** (see Liberty) Organized as an early parish & became part of Liberty County 5 Feb 1777
St. Mary		1765	**Creek Cession of 1763** St. Mary County; GA **Details:** (see Camden) Organized as an early parish & became part of Camden County 5 Feb 1777
St. Matthew		1758	**Creek Cession of 1733** St. Matthew County; GA **Details:** (see Effingham) Organized as an early parish & became part of Effingham County 5 Feb 1777
St. Patrick		1765	**Creek Cession of 1763** St. Patrick County; GA **Details:** (see Glynn) Organized as an early parish & became part of Glynn County 5 Feb 1777
St. Paul		1758	**Creek Cession of 1733** St. Paul County; GA **Details:** (see Richmond) Organized as an early parish & became Richmond County 5 Feb 1777
St. Philip		1758	**Creek Cession of 1733** St. Philip County; GA **Details:** (see Chatham & Effingham) Organized as an early parish & became part of Chatham & Effingham Counties 5 Feb 1777
St. Thomas		1765	**Creek Cession of 1763** St. Thomas County; GA **Details:** (see Camden) Organized as an early parish & became part of Camden County 5 Feb 1777
Stephens www.rootsweb.com/~gastephe/	E6	18 Aug 1905	**Franklin, Habersham** Stephens County; 150 W Doyle St; PO Box 386; Toccoa, GA 30577-0000; Ph. (706) 886-9496 **Details:** (County Health Department has Birth & Death Records; Probate Court has Marriage & Probate Records; Clerk Superior Court has Divorce, Court & Land Records from 1906)
Stewart http://home.earthlink.net/~bwjohnson/ stew_mn.htm	L3	23 Dec 1830	**Randolph** Stewart County; PO Box 157; Lumpkin, GA 31815-0157; Ph. (912) 838-6220 **Details:** (Probate Court has Birth, Death & Burial Records from 1927, Marriage Records from 1828 & Probate Records; Clerk Superior Court has Divorce, Court & Land Records from 1830)
Sumter www.sumter-ga.com/	L4	26 Dec 1831	**Lee** Sumter County; PO Box 295; Americus, GA 31709-0295; Ph. (912) 924-3090 **Details:** (County Health Department has Birth, Death & Burial Records; Probate Court has Marriage & Probate Records; Clerk Superior Court has Divorce, Court & Land Records from 1831)

County Website	Map Index	Date Created	Parent County or Territory From Which Organized Address/Details
Talbot www.rootsweb.com/~gatalbot/	**J3**	**14 Dec 1827**	**Muscogee** Talbot County; Courthouse Sq; PO Box 155; Talbotton, GA 31827-0000; Ph. (706) 665-3220 **Details:** (Probate Court has Birth, Marriage, Death & Probate Records; Clerk Superior Court has Divorce, Court & Land Records)
Taliaferro http://web.infoave.net/~taliaferro/	**H7**	**24 Dec 1825**	**Green, Hancock, Oglethorpe, Warren, Wilkes** Taliaferro County; 113 Monument St SE; PO Box 114; Crawfordville, GA 30631-0000; Ph. (706) 456-2123 **Details:** (Probate Court has Birth Records from 1927, Death Records from 1920, Marriage & Probate Records from 1826, Land grants from 1750 & church Records from 1802; Clerk Superior Court has Divorce & Court Records from 1826)
Tattnall www.tattnall.com/	**M9**	**5 Dec 1801**	**Montgomery** Tattnall County; Main & Brazell Sts; Reidsville, GA 30453-0000; Ph. (912) 557-6761 **Details:** (Probate Court has Birth, Marriage, Death & Probate Records; Clerk Superior Court has Divorce Records from 1880, Court & Land Records)
Taylor www.rootsweb.com/~gataylor/gataylor.htm	**K4**	**15 Jan 1852**	**Macon, Marion, Talbot** Taylor County; 1 Courthouse Sq; PO Box 536; Butler, GA 31006; Ph. (478) 862-5594 **Details:** (Probate Court has Marriage & Probate Records from 1852; Clerk Superior Court has Divorce & Land Records from 1852, Military Discharge Records from 1922 & Court Records)
Telfair http://plant.sgc.peachnet.edu/~jbellis/genweb/telfair/telfair.html	**M7**	**10 Dec 1807**	**Wilkinson** Telfair County; 713 Telfair Ave; McRae, GA 31055-0000; Ph. (229) 868-6525 **Details:** (Probate Judge has Marriage & Probate Records; Clerk Superior Court has Divorce, Court & Land Records; County Health Department has Birth & Death Records)
Terrell http://home.earthlink.net/~bwjohnson/terr_mn.htm	**M4**	**16 Feb 1856**	**Lee, Randolph** Terrell County; 513 S Main St; Dawson, GA 31742; Ph. (229) 995-2631 **Details:** (Clerk of Superior Court has Divorce, Court, & Land Records from 1856; Probate Court has Marriage & Probate Records from 1856)
Thomas www.thomascountyboc.org/	**P5**	**23 Dec 1825**	**Decatur, Irwin** Thomas County; 225 N Broad St; Thomasville, GA 31792; Ph. (229) 225-4108 **Details:** (County Health Department has Birth & Death Records; Probate Court has Marriage & Probate Records; Clerk Superior Court has Divorce & Court Records from 1919 & Land Records from 1826)
Tift www.tiftcounty.org/	**N6**	**17 Aug 1905**	**Berrien, Irwin, Worth** Tift County; 225 N Tift Ave; Tifton, GA 31794-4463; Ph. (229) 386-7810 **Details:** (Probate Court has Marriage & Probate Records; Clerk Superior Court has Divorce, Court & Land Records from 1905)

County	Map	Date	Parent County or Territory From Which Organized
Website	Index	Created	Address/Details

Toombs   **L9**   **18 Aug 1905**   **Emanuel, Tattnall, Montgomery**
http://plant.sgc.peachnet.edu/~jbellis/genweb/
toombs/toombs.html

Toombs County; 100 Courthouse Sq; Lyons, GA 30436-0000;
Ph. (912) 526-3501

Details: (Probate Court has Birth, Marriage, Death, Burial & Probate Records from 1905; Clerk Superior Court has Divorce, Court & Land Records from 1905)

Towns   **D5**   **6 Mar 1856**   **Rabun, Union**
www.rootsweb.com/~gatowns/

Towns County; 48 River St Ste E; Hiawassee, GA 30546-0178;
Ph. (706) 896-2130

Details: (Probate Court has Birth & Death Records from 1927, Marriage Records from 1885 & Probate Records; Clerk Superior Court has Divorce, Land & Military Records from 1865)

Treutlen   **K8**   **21 Aug 1917**   **Emanuel, Montgomery**
www.rootsweb.com/~gatreutl/

Treutlen County; 200 Georgia Ave; Soperton, GA 30457-0000;
Ph. (912) 529-4215

Details: (Probate Court has Birth, Marriage, Death & Probate Records from 1919; Clerk Superior Court has Divorce, Court & Land Records from 1919)

Troup   **I2**   **11 Dec 1826**   **Creek Indian Lands**
www.troupcountyga.org/

Troup County; 136 Main Street; PO Box 1051; LaGrange, GA 30241;
Ph. (404) 884-1828

Details: (Probate Court has Marriage & Estate Records; Clerk of Court's Office has Deeds; Health Department has Birth & Death Records; County Archives has Court, Land, Military, Tax, Voter, School, Census, & Miscellaneous Records)

Turner   **M6**   **18 Aug 1905**   **Dooly, Irwin, Wilcox, Worth**
www.rootsweb.com/~gaturner/

Turner County; 219 E College Ave; Ashburn, GA 31714-1275;
Ph. (229) 567-2011

Details: (Clerk Superior Court has Divorce & Court Records from 1906 & Land Records; Probate Court has Birth, Marriage, Death, Burial & Probate Records)

Twiggs   **K6**   **14 Dec 1809**   **Wilkinson**
www.rootsweb.com/~gatwiggs/index.htm

Twiggs County; PO Box 202; Jeffersonville, GA 31044;
Ph. (478) 945-3350

Details: (Clerk Superior Court has Land, Court & Divorce Records; Probate Court has Birth, Marriage, Death & Probate Records)

Union   **D5**   **3 Dec 1832**   **Cherokee**
www.ancestraldesigns.com/union/

Union County; 114 Courthouse St; Blairsville, GA 30512;
Ph. (706) 745-2611

Details: (Probate Court has Birth, Marriage, Death & Probate Records; Clerk Superior Court has Divorce, Court & Land Records)

Upson   **J4**   **15 Dec 1824**   **Crawford, Pike**
www.rootsweb.com/~gaupson/gaupson.htm

Upson County; PO Box 889; Thomaston, GA 30286-0889;
Ph. (706) 647-7012

Details: (Probate Court has Marriage Records from 1825 & Probate Records from 1920; Clerk Superior Court has Divorce, Court & Land Records from 1825 & newspaper files from 1870)

County Website	Map Index	Date Created	Parent County or Territory From Which Organized Address/Details
Walker www.County.walker.ga.us/	**D1**	18 Dec 1833	**Murray** Walker County; 103 S Duke St; Lafayette, GA 30728-0445; Ph. (706) 638-1742 **Details:** (Courthouse fire 1883) (Clerk Superior Court has Divorce, Court & Land Records from 1883; Probate Judge has Marriage & Probate Records; County Health Department has Birth & Death Records)
Walton www.waltoncountyga.org/	**G5**	15 Dec 1818	**Creek Indian Lands** Walton County; PO Box 585; Monroe, GA 30655-0585; Ph. (770) 267-1301 **Details:** (Probate Court has Marriage & Probate Records from 1819; Clerk Superior Court has Land Records from 1819 & Divorce Records from 1900; Magistrate Court has Court Records from 1900; County Health Department has Birth & Death Records from 1919)
Ware www.rootsweb.com/~gaware/	**O8**	15 Dec 1824	**Appling** Ware County; 800 Church St; Waycross, GA 31501-3501; Ph. (912) 287-4340 **Details:** (Records burned 1854) (Probate Court has Marriage & Probate Records from 1874; Clerk of Courts has Land & Court Records)
Warren www.rootsweb.com/~gawarren/	**H8**	19 Dec 1793	**Columbia, Richmond, Wilkes, Hancock** Warren County; 100 Warren St; Warrenton, GA 30828-0000; Ph. (706) 465-2262 **Details:** (Probate Court has Birth, Marriage, Death & Probate Records; Clerk Superior Court has Divorce, Court & Land Records)
Washington www.rootsweb.com/~gawashin/ washingtoncounty001.htm	**J8**	25 Feb 1784	**Creek Indian Lands** Washington County; PO Box 271; Sandersville, GA 31082-0271; Ph. (912) 552-2325 **Details:** (Probate Court has Birth, Marriage & Probate Records; Clerk Superior Court has Divorce, Court & Land Records from 1865)
Wayne www.County.wayne.ga.us/	**N10**	11 May 1803	**Creek Indian Lands** Wayne County; 242 E Walnut St; PO Box 918; Jesup, GA 31598; Ph. (912) 427-5930 **Details:** (Probate Court has Birth, Marriage, Death & Probate Records; Clerk Superior Court has Divorce, Court & Land Records)
Webster www.rootsweb.com/~gawebste/	**L3**	16 Dec 1853	**Stewart** Webster County; Washington St & Hwy 280 ; PO Box 29; Preston, GA 31824-0000; Ph. (229) 828-3525 **Details:** (Formerly Kinchafoonee County 1853–1856. Name changed to Webster 21 Feb 1856) (Probate Court has Birth, Marriage, Death, Burial & Probate Records; Clerk Superior Court has Divorce, Court & Land Records)
Wheeler www.rootsweb.com/~gawebste/	**L8**	14 Aug 1912	**Montgomery** Wheeler County; 209 W Forest Ave; Alamo, GA 30411-0000; Ph. (912) 568-7137 **Details:** (County Health Department has Birth & Death Records from 1927; Probate Court has Marriage & Probate Records from 1913; Clerk Superior Court has Divorce, Court & Land Records from 1913)

County Website	Map Index	Date Created	Parent County or Territory From Which Organized Address/Details
White www.rootsweb.com/~gawhite/	D5	22 Dec 1857	**Habersham** White County; 59 S Main St #BIRTH; Cleveland, GA 30528-0185; Ph. (706) 865-2613 **Details:** (Probate Court has Birth, Marriage, Death & Probate Records; Clerk Superior Court has Divorce, Court & Land Records from 1858 & Military Discharge Records)
Whitfield www.geocities.com/Heartland/Plains/3242/whtfld.htm	D2	30 Dec 1851	**Murray** Whitfield County; 300 W Crawford St; PO Box 248; Dalton, GA 30722-0248; Ph. (706) 275-7451 **Details:** (Probate Court has Birth & Death Records from 1927, Marriage & Probate Records from 1852; Clerk Superior Court has Divorce, Court & Land Records from 1852)
Wilcox www.rootsweb.com/~gawilcox/	L6	22 Dec 1857	**Dooly, Irwin, Pulaski** Wilcox County; 103 N Broad St; Abbeville, GA 31001; Ph. (912) 467-2737 **Details:** (Probate Court has Birth & Death Records from 1927, Marriage Records from 1886 & Probate Records; Clerk Superior Court has Land Records from 1870, Divorce & Court Records from 1900 & Military Records from 1917)
Wilkes www.rootsweb.com/~gawilkes/	G8	5 Feb 1777	**Original county-Creek & Cherokee Indian Lands** Wilkes County; 23 E Court St Rm 205; Washington, GA 30673-1570; Ph. (706) 678-2423 **Details:** (Probate Court has Birth, Marriage, Death & Probate Records from 1792; Clerk Superior Court has Divorce & Court Records from 1778, Land Records from 1777 & Military Discharge Records)
Wilkinson www.accucomm.net/~wilcoboc/	J7	11 May 1803	**Original county-Creek Indian Lands** Wilkinson County; PO Box 250; Irwinton, GA 31042; Ph. (478) 946-2221 **Details:** (Courthouse burned in 1852 & 1924; Land Records were not burned in 1924) (Clerk Superior Court has some Divorce Records & Land Records from 1852)
Worth www.rootsweb.com/~gaworth/	N5	20 Dec 1853	**Dooly, Irwin** Worth County; 201 N Main St; Sylvester, GA 31791-2178; Ph. (229) 776-8205 **Details:** (Probate Court has Birth Records from 1897, Marriage Records from 1854, Death Records from 1919 & Probate Records from 1880; Cle3rk Superior Court has Divorce, Court & Land Records)

Notes

Hawaii

Capital: Honolulu
Territory: 1900
State: 1959 (50th)

*The life of the land is
perpetuated in righteousness*

The original Hawaiians, who probably settled the islands between 300 and 600 A.D., were of Polynesian origin. Captain James Cook discovered the Hawaiian Islands in 1778 and named them the Sandwich Islands. The 390-mile chain of islands includes the following eight main islands: Hawaii, Kahoolawe, Maui, Lanai, Molokai, Oahu, Kauai, and Nihau. Between 1782 and 1810, King Kamehameha united the islands under his rule. American whalers began stopping at the islands and missionaries arrived in 1820, bringing with them Western culture.

The Kamehameha dynasty continued, and in 1851 Kamehameha III placed the islands under protection of the United States. Sugar production began in 1835 and it soon became the dominant industry. A coup, incited by U.S. sugar interests, resulted in the monarchy's overthrow in 1893 and the establishment of the Republic of Hawaii on July 4, 1894. The republic continued until 1898 when the islands were ceded to the United States. Two years later, Hawaii became a U.S. territory.

When the Europeans arrived, some 300,000 native Hawaiians lived on the islands. Protestant missionaries from New England began arriving in Hawaii in 1820. Settlers and laborers started coming about a decade later, mostly from the Orient. By 1853, disease brought by visiting traders had slashed the population to about 75,000. The islands continued to witness an influx of foreigners well past the turn of the century with surges in the sandalwood, whaling, and sugar industries, plus the advent of a new cash crop—pineapple. On August 21, 1959, Hawaii became America's 50th state.

Look for vital records in the following locations:

- **Birth, death, marriage and divorce records:** Statewide registration of births began in 1842, but few records exist until 1896. General compliance was not reached until 1929. Copies of birth, death, marriage, and divorce records are available through Vital Statistics, State Department of Health in Honolulu.
- **Court records:** Circuit courts have probate records from the 1840s. Microfilms of probates from 1845 to 1900 are at the Hawaii State Archives, Iolani Palace Grounds in Honolulu.
- **Census records:** Colonial census records exist for some parts of Hawaii for 1866, 1878, 1890, and 1896. The last three are at the Hawaii State Archives. Also at the Archives are two "census files," 1840 to 1866 and 1847 to 1896, which contain miscellaneous records such as school census records, population lists, and vital record summaries.

State of Hawaii Department of Health
PO Box 3378
Honolulu, Hawaii 96801
(808) 586-4533
www.hawaii.gov/health/vital-records

Hawaii State Archives Historical Records Branch
Kekauluohi Building, Iolani Palace Grounds
Honolulu, Hawaii 96813
(808) 586-0329; Fax (808) 586-0330
www.state.hi.us/dags/archives/welcome.html

Societies and Repositories

Bishop Museum & Bishop Museum Library; PO Box 19000-A; Honolulu, HI 96817-0916; www.bishopmuseum.org.

Daughters of the American Revolution, Aloha Chapter; 1914 Makiki Heights Dr.; Honolulu, HI 96922.

Hawaii Chinese History Center; 111 North King Street, Room 410; Honolulu, HI 96817.

Hawaii County Genealogical Society; PO Box 931; Keaau, HI 96749.

Hawaii Mission Children's Society Library; 553 South King Street; Honolulu, HI 96813.

Hawaii State Archives; Kekauluohi Building; Iolani Palace Grounds; Honolulu, HI 96813; (808) 586-0329; archives@hawaii.gov; www.hawaii.gov/dags/archives.

Hawaii State Public Library System; HI; www.librarieshawaii.org.

Hawaiian Historical Society; 560 Kawaiahao St.; Honolulu, HI 96813; www.hawaiianhistory.org.

Kona Historical Society; PO Box 398; Captain Cook, HI 96704; khs@konahistorical.org; www.konahistorical.org.

Lyman House Memorial Museum; 276 Haili Street; Hilo, HI 96720.

Maui Genealogical Society; 38A Alania Place; Kihei, HI 96753; www.maui.net/~mauifun/mgs.htm.

Maui Historical Society; 2375 - A Main Street; Wailuku, HI 96793; aileyh@aloha.net; www.mauimuseum.org.

Portuguese Genealogical Society of Hawaii; 810 N. Vineyard Blvd. Room 11; Honolulu, HI 96817; www.lusaweb.com/genealogy/html/phgs.cfm.

Sandwich Islands Genealogical Society; PO Box 235039; Honolulu, HI 96823-3500; www.hpcug.org/ancestors/sigs.html.

SAR, Hawaii Society; 1564 Piikea St.; Honolulu, HI 96819.

United Puerto Rican Association of Hawaii, Inc.; 1249 N. School St.; Honolulu, HI 96817.

Bibliography and Record Sources

General

Alcantara, Ruben R. *The Filipinos in Hawaii: An Annotated Bibliography*. Honolulu, Hawaii: Social Science Research Institute, University of Hawaii, 1972.

Britsch, R. Lanier. *Moramona: the Mormons in Hawaii*. Laie, Hawaii: Institute for Polynesian Studies, 1989.

Chinese in Hawaii. Records from various sources: Hawaiian Archives—Extracts from "The Friend"—Cemetery inscriptions—Church records. Salt Lake City: Filmed by the Genealogical Society of Utah, 1982.

Cole, William A., and Elwin W. Jensen. *The Cole-Jensen Collection: Oral Genealogies and Genealogical Information Collected from the Polynesian Peoples and from the Pacific Islands*. Salt Lake City: Filmed by the Genealogical Society of Utah, 1984.

Conrad, Agnes C. *"Family History Sources in Hawaii," Hawaii Library Association Journal, 33 June 1974, p. 3–10*. Honolulu: Hawaii Library Association.

Conrad, Agnes C. *Genealogical Sources in Hawaii*. Honolulu, Hawaii: Hawaii Library Association, 1987.

Day, Arthur Grove. *History Makers of Hawaii: A Biographical Dictionary*. Honolulu, Hawaii: Mutual Publishing of Honolulu, 1984.

de Freitas, Joaquim Francisco. *Portuguese-Hawaiian Memories*. Honolulu, Hawaii: J. F. Freitas, 1930.

Gardner, Arthur L. *The Koreans in Hawaii: An Annotated Bibliography*. Honolulu, Hawaii: University of Hawaii, Social Science Research Institute, 1970.

Hawaii Research Outline. Series U.S. States, no. 12. Salt Lake City: Family History Library, 1988.

Hawaiian Journal of History. Honolulu: Hawaiian Historical Society, 1967—(Hong Kong: Libra Press).

Hawaiian Mission Children's Society (Honolulu, Hawaii). *Portraits of American Protestant Missionaries to Hawaii*. Washington: Microfilmed [by] the Library of Congress Photoduplication Service, 1992.

Hilleary, Perry Edward. *Men and Women of Hawaii: 1954, A Biographical Encyclopedia of Persons of Notable Achievement and Historical Account of the Peoples Who Have Distinguished Themselves Through Personal Success and Through Public Service*. Honolulu, Hawaii: Business Consultants, 1954.

Hunter, Louise H. *Buddhism in Hawaii*. Honolulu, Hawaii: University of Hawaii Press, 1971.

Judd, Bernice. *Voyages to Hawaii before 1860: A Record, Based on Historical Narratives in the Libraries of the Hawaiian Mission Children's Society and the Hawaiian Historical Society, Extended to March 1860*. Reprint. Honolulu: University Press of Hawaii, 1974.

Judd, Henry Pratt. *Men and Women of Hawaii: 1954*. Honolulu: Business Consultants, 1954.

Kaina, Maria. *Target Your Hawaiian Genealogy and Others As Well: A Family Guide Provided by the Hawaii State Public Library System*. Honolulu: Hawaii State Public Library System, 1991.

Kuykendall, Ralph S. *The Hawaiian Kingdom*. 3 vols. Honolulu: University of Hawaii Press, 1966–1968.

Langdon, Robert. *Where the Whalers Went: An Index to the Pacific Ports and Islands Visited by American whalers (and some other ships) in the 19th Century*. Canberra: Pacific Manuscripts Bureau, 1984.

Lind, Andrew W. *Hawaii's People*. Honolulu, Hawaii: University Press of Hawaii, 1974.

Lueras, Leonard. *Kanyaku imin: A Hundred Years of Japanese Life in Hawaii*. Honolulu, Hawaii: International Savings and Loan Association, 1985.

Luster, Arlene D. C. *A Directory of Libraries and Information Sources in Hawaii and the Pacific Islands*. Rev. ed. Honolulu: Hawaii Library Association, 1972.

Mardfin, Jean K. *Hawaiian Genealogy Project; Directory of Secondary Sources*. Honolulu, Hawaii: Office of Hawaiian Affairs, 1995.

Matsuda, Mitsugu. *The Japanese in Hawaii, 1868–1967: A Bibliography of the First Hundred Years*. Honolulu, Hawaii: University of Hawaii, 1968.

McGuire, Mrs. Elwood J. *Descendants of New England Protestant Missionaries to the Sandwich Islands (Hawaiian Islands), 1820–1900: An Alphabetically Arranged Copy of Births, Marriages, and Deaths from the Records of the Hawaiian Mission Children's Society Library, Honolulu, Hawaii*. Honolulu, Hawaii: Privately Printed, Hawaii State Regent, NSDAR, 1984.

McKinzie, Edith Kawelohea. *Hawaiian Genealogies: Extracted from Hawaiian Language Newspapers*. 2 vols. Honolulu: Brigham Young University–Hawaii, 1983–1986.

Mellen, Kathleen Dickenson. *An Island Kingdom Passes: Hawaii Becomes American*. New York: Hastings House, 1958.

Mookini, Esther T. *The Hawaiian Newspapers*. Honolulu: Topgallant Publishing Co., 1974.

Mulholland, John F. *Hawaii's Religions*. Rutland, Vermont: Charles E. Tuttle Co., 1970.

Nordyke. Eleanor C. *The Peopling of Hawaii*. Honolulu: University Press of Hawaii, 1989.

Nupepa Kuokoa (Honolulu, Hawaii). Honolulu: Univ. of Hawaii Library, Archives of Hawaii.

Ohai, Jean B. *Chinese Genealogy and Family Book Guide: Hawaiian and Chinese Sources*. Honolulu, Hawaii: Hawaii Chinese History Center, 1975.

Oliver, Douglas L. *The Pacific Islands*. Honolulu, Hawaii: University Press of Hawaii, 1961.

Oukah, Oukah. *Hawaiian Royal and Noble Genealogies*. 2nd ed. Dallas: Triskelion Press, 1998.

Peterson, Barbara Bennett. *Notable Women of Hawaii*. Honolulu, Hawaii: University of Hawaii Press, 1984.

Siddall, John William. *Men of Hawaii: Being a Biographical Reference Library, Complete and Authentic, of the Men of Note and Substantial Achievement in the Hawaiian Islands*. 5 vols. Honolulu, Hawaii: Honolulu Star-Bulletin, 1917–1930, 1936.

Taylor, Albert Pierce. *Under Hawaiian Skies: A Narrative of the Romance, Adventure and History of the Hawaiian Islands, A Complete Historical Account. . .* Honolulu, Hawaii: Advertiser Pub. Co., Ltd., 1926.

Young, Nancy Foon. *The Chinese in Hawaii: An Annotated Bibliography*. Honolulu, Hawaii: Social Science Research Institute, University of Hawaii, n.d.

Atlases, Maps and Gazetteers

Alexander, W. D., comp. *Hawaiian Geographic Names*. Washington, D.C.: United States Coast and Geodetic Survey, 1902.

Armstrong, R. Warwick. *Atlas of Hawaii*. 2nd ed. Honolulu, Hawaii: University of Hawaii Press, 1983.

Coulter, John W., comp. *A Gazetteer of the Territory of Hawaii*. Research Publications, no. 11. Honolulu: University of Hawaii, 1935. Reprint. Ann Harbor, Michigan: University Microfilm.

Fitzpatrick, Gary L., comp. *Hawaii: A List of Early Maps in the Library of Congress and a Summary of Services of Current Maps and Cartographic Information*. Washington, D.C.: Library of Congress, 1980.

Lindsey, Jessie H. *District and County Guide of the Territory of Hawaii*. N.p., 1947.

Pukui, Mary Kawena. *Place Names of Hawaii*. Honolulu: University Press of Hawaii, 1974.

United States. Board on Geographic Names. *Hawaiian Islands: Official Standard Names*. Washington, D.C.: Government Printing Office, 1956.

Censuses

Available Census Records and Census Substitutes

Federal Census 1900 (incomplete), 1910, 1920

Island Census 1890

State/Colonial Census 1866, 1896, 1840–1866, 1847–1896

Dollarhide, William. *The Census Book: A Genealogist's Guide to Federal Census Facts, Schedules and Indexes*. Bountiful, Utah: Heritage Quest, 1999.

Kemp, Thomas Jay. *The American Census Handbook*. Wilmington, Delaware: Scholarly Resources, Inc., 2001.

Lainhart, Ann S. *State Census Records*. Baltimore: Genealogical Publishing Co., Inc., 1992.

Szucs, Loretto Dennis and Matthew Wright. *Finding Answers in U.S. Census Records*. Ancestry Publishing, 2001.

Thorndale, William. *Map Guide to the U.S. Federal Census, 1790–1920*. Baltimore: Genealogical Publishing Co., 1987.

Court Records, Probate and Wills

Hawaii. Circuit Courts. *Probate Records, 1848–1916*. Microfilms of original records in the Archives of Hawaiian Islands. Salt Lake City: Filmed by the Genealogical Society of Utah, 1976. 3 microfilm.

Hawaiian Islands. Circuit Court. *Probate Records, 1845–1900*. Salt Lake City: Filmed by the Genealogical Society of Utah, 1977.

Emigration, Immigration, Migration and Naturalization

Hawaii. Department of the Interior. *Letters of Denization, 1846–1898*. Salt Lake City: Filmed by the Genealogical Society of Utah, 1977.

Hawaii. Department of the Interior. *List of British Subjects Who Have Received Special Rights of Citizenship [ca. 1892–1898].* Salt Lake City: Filmed by the Genealogical Society of Utah, 1977.

Hawaii. Supreme Court. *Naturalization Records, 1874–1904.* Salt Lake City: Filmed by the Genealogical Society of Utah, 1977.

Index to Naturalization Records, 1840–1892. Microfilm of original records at the State Archives of Hawaii (Iolani Palace Grounds) in Honolulu. Salt Lake City: Filmed by the Genealogical Society of Utah, 1999.

Judd, Bernice. *Voyages to Hawaii Before 1860: A Record, Based on Historical Narratives in the libraries of the Hawaiian Mission Children's Society and the Hawaiian Historical Society, Extended to March 1860.* Honolulu, Hawaii: University Press of Hawaii, 1974.

Portugal. Consulado Geral (Honolulu). *Ship Passenger Lists, 1878–1913.* Salt Lake City: Filmed by the Genealogical Society of Utah, 1977. (online database—ftp://ftp .rootsweb.com/pub/usgenweb/hi/shiplists/portug.txt)

United States. District Court (Hawaii). *Index to Naturalizations [petitions] in the U.S. District Court for the District of Hawaii, 1900–1975.* Washington, D.C.: National Archives and Records Administration, 1996. 23 microfilm.

Land and Property

British Commission Land Claims, 1843. Honolulu: Pau Hana Press. 1995.

Chinden, Jon J. *The Great Mahele: Hawaii's Land Division of 1848.* Honolulu: University Press of Hawaii, ca. 1958.

Chinen, Jon J. *Original Land Titles in Hawaii.* N.p., 1961.

Hawaii, Registrar of Bureau of Conveyances. *Deeds and Other Records, 1844–1900.* Honolulu: Department of Land and Natural Resources, ca. 1970. 108 microfilm.

Hawaii. Department of Land and Natural Resources. *Award Books, 1836–1855.* Salt Lake City: Filmed by the Genealogical Society of Utah, 1964. 12 microfilm.

Hawaii. Department of Land and Natural Resources. *Foreign Testimony, 1846–1862.* Salt Lake City: Filmed by the Genealogical Society of Utah, 1964. 4 microfilm.

Hawaii. Department of Land and Natural Resources. *Native Registers, 1846–1848.* Salt Lake City: Filmed by the Genealogical Society of Utah, 1964. 4 microfilm.

Hawaii. Department of Land and Natural Resources. *Native Testimony, 1844–1854.* Salt Lake City: Filmed by the Genealogical Society of Utah, 1864. 4 microfilm.

Hawaii. Department of Land and Natural Resources. *Patents Upon Confirmation of Land Commission, 1847–1961.* Salt Lake City: Filmed by the Genealogical Society of Utah, 1964. 19 microfilm.

Hone, Wade E. *Land and Property Research in the United States.* Salt Lake City: Ancestry Incorporated, 1997.

Office of the Commissioner of Public Lands of the Territory of Hawaii. *Indices of Awards Made by the Board of Commissioners to Quiet Land Titles in the Hawaiian Islands.* Honolulu: Hawaii Territorial Office, 1929.

Parker, Linda S. *Native American Estate: The Struggle Over Indian and Hawaiian Lands.* Honolulu, Hawaii: University of Hawaii Press, 1989.

Military

Duus, Masayo Umezawa. *Unlikely Liberators: The Men of the 100th and the 442nd.* Honolulu, Hawaii: University of Hawaii Press, 1987.

Leslie's Official History of the Spanish-American War: A Pictorial and Descriptive Record of the Cuban Rebellion, The Causes That Involved the United States, And A Complete Narrative of Our Conflict with Spain on Land and Sea, Supplemented with Fullest Information Respecting Cuba, Puerto Rico, the Philippines and Hawaii. . . . Washington: Leslie's Weekly, 1899.

United States Department of the Interior. National Park Service, USS Arizona Memorial. *A Comprehensive List of the Names of All Civilians and Military Personnel Killed in the Attack on Pearl Harbor, Dec 7, 1941, Honolulu, Hawaii.* (online database—ftp://ftp.rootsweb .com/pub/usgenweb/hi/military/pearl.txt)

United States. Selective Service System. *Hawaii, World War I Selective Service System Draft Registration Cards, 1917–1918.* National Archives Microfilm Publications, M1509. Washington, D.C.: National Archives, 1987–1988.

Vital and Cemetery Records

Arnold, Barry. *Hawaii Birth Register.* North Sydney, New South Wales: CD-ROM Services, 1995. CD-ROM.

Hawaii (Kingdom). Board of Health. *Reports of Burials, Kingdom of Hawaii, 1861–1892.* Microfilm of originals at the State Dept. of Health, Honolulu. Salt Lake City: Filmed by the Genealogical Society of Utah, 1978.

Hawaii (Territory). Board of Health. *Birth Records, 1896–1903.* Microfilm of originals in the State Department of Health, Honolulu. Salt Lake City: Filmed by the Genealogical Society of Utah, 1978. 17 microfilm.

Hawaii (Territory). Board of Health. *Death Records, 1904–1909.* Microfilm of original records at the State Department of Health in Honolulu, Hawaii. Salt Lake City: Filmed by the Genealogical Society of Utah, 1994.

Hawaii (Territory). Board of Health. *Death Records, 1909–1925; Index 1909–1949.* Microfilm of original records at the Department of Health, Honolulu. Salt Lake City: Filmed by the Genealogical Society of Utah, 1991. 74 microfilm.

Hawaii (Territory). Board of Health. *Death Registers, 1896–1903.* Microfilm of originals in the State Department of Health, Honolulu. Salt Lake City: Filmed by the Genealogical Society of Utah, 1978. 17 microfilm.

Hawaii (Territory). Board of Health. *Delayed Birth Records, 1904–1925.* Microfilm of original records at the State Department of Health, Honolulu. Salt Lake City: Filmed by the Genealogical Society of Utah, 1993–1994. 132 microfilm.

Hawaii (Territory). Board of Health. *Marriage Records, 1904–1909.* Microfilm of original records at the State Department of Health in Honolulu, Hawaii. Salt Lake City: Filmed by the Genealogical Society of Utah, 1994.

Hawaii (Territory). Board of Health. *Marriage Records, 1909–1925; Indexes 1909–1949.* Microfilm of original records at the State Department of Health, Honolulu. Salt Lake City: Filmed by the Genealogical Society of Utah, 1991. 61 microfilm.

Hawaii Cemetery Records. 2 vols. Typescript. Salt Lake City: Mrs. Jessie H. Lindsay and the Genealogical Society of Utah, 1942–1954.

Hawaii. Circuit Courts. *Divorce Records, 1849–1915.* Microfilm of originals made at Archives of Hawaii in Honolulu. Salt Lake City: Filmed by the Genealogical Society of Utah, 1977. 34 microfilm.

Hawaii. Circuit Courts. *Divorce Records, 1849–1915.* Microfilm of original records in the Archives of Hawaii in Honolulu. Salt Lake City: Filmed by the Genealogical Society of Utah, 1977. 141 microfilm.

Hawaii. Department of Health. *Restricted. Divorce Records Index, 1951–1990.* Microfilm of original records at the State Department of Health in Honolulu. Salt Lake City: Filmed by the Genealogical Society of Utah, 1996. 3 microfilm.

Index to Archives of Hawaii Collection of Marriage Records, 1826–1910. Honolulu, Hawaii: Bishop Museum. Salt Lake City: Filmed by the Genealogical Society of Utah, 1979.

Index to Births, Marriages, and Deaths in Hawaii Newspapers Prior to 1950. Microfilm. 6 reels. Salt Lake City: Filmed by the Genealogical Society of Utah, 1977.

Zabriskie, George Olin. *Tombstone Inscriptions from the Royal Mausoleum.* The author, 1969.

County Website	Map Index	Date Created	Parent County or Territory From Which Organized Address/Details
Hawaii www.hawaii-county.com/	C10	1905	**Hilo** Hawaii County; 25 Aupuni St; Hilo, HI 96720; Ph. (808) 961-8255 **Details:** (State Health Department has Marriage, Death, Birth, wills, Probate and land Records)
Honolulu www.co.honolulu.hi.us/	K3	1905	**Honolulu** Honolulu County; 530 S King St; Honolulu, HI 96813; Ph. (808) 523-4352 **Details:** (Named Oahu 1905–1909) (State Health Department has Marriage, Death, Birth, wills, Probate and land Records)
Kalawao Future website at www.rootsweb.com/~higenweb/hawaii.htm#COUNTIES	H5	1905	**Maui** Kalawao County; Isle of Molokai; Kalaupapa, HI; Ph. (808) 553-5800 **Details:** (State Health Department has Marriage, Death, Birth, wills, Probate and land Records)
Kauai www.kauaigov.org/	O1	1905	**Lihue** Kauai County; 4963 Rice St; Lihue, HI 96766; Ph.(808) 241-6371 **Details:** (State Health Department has Marriage, Death, Birth, wills, Probate and land Records)
Maui www.co.maui.hi.us/	E6	1905	**Wailuku** Maui County; 200 S High St; Wailuku, HI 96793; Ph. (808) 270-7748 **Details:** (State Health Department has Marriage, Death, Birth, wills, Probate and land Records)
Oahu		1905	Oahu County **Details:** Name changed to Honolulu 1909

Notes

Idaho

Capital: Boise
Territory: 1863
State: 1890 (43rd)

Let it be perpetual

daho was first populated by Shoshone, Northern Paiute, Bannock, and Nez Perce tribes, with the first inhabitants dating back some 10,000 years. The first white explorers in the area were Meriwether Lewis and William Clark, who arrived in 1805. David Thompson, a British fur trader, established the first trading post in 1809; other traders followed and built Fort Hall along the Snake River in 1834. Other outposts built near modern-day Pocatello served as important stopping points along the Oregon Trail. Idaho became part of the Oregon Territory in 1848, and a decade later it was made part of the Washington Territory.

The area's population began growing steadily in the 1860s, with the southern part of the state being settled first. Mormon immigrants from Northern Europe founded Idaho's first permanent settlement at Franklin, in Cache Valley, in 1860. A series of gold rushes in the river valleys of northern Idaho between 1860 and 1863 led to a mining boom. On 3 March, 1863, the Idaho Territory was formed from the Washington and Dakota Territories. The Idaho Territory included all of Montana and nearly all of Wyoming in addition to Idaho. With the organization of the Montana Territory in 1864 and the Wyoming Territory in 1868, Idaho took on its present shape. Indian conflicts hampered settlement until the 1880's, when the Native Americans moved to reservations. Another mining boom and the coming of railroads brought more settlers in the 1880's. In about 1910, large irrigation systems and districts were constructed around the Snake River. This opened up new areas for farming and brought many western and mid-western farmers to the area.

Look for vital records in the following locations:

- **Birth and death records:** The first birth records came from midwives in the 1870's. Midwives sent their reports to county clerks. Counties were required to keep birth and death records between January 1907 and July 1911. Since then statewide birth and death records have been kept at the Idaho Center for Vital Statistics in Boise.
- **Marriage and divorce records:** Idaho Center for Vital Statistics has marriage and divorce records from 1947. County recorders have records of marriages. No licenses were required before 11 March 1895.
- **Wills and probate records:** County clerks' offices.
- **Land records:** County recorder.
- **Census records:** Idaho settlers were included in the Oregon Territorial census of 1850, Washington Territory in 1860, and Idaho Territory in 1870 and 1880. The 1860 Census of Idaho County is included in the Spokane County, Washington enumeration. Parts of southern Idaho were included in the 1860 and 1870 census records of Cache County, Utah. Statewide indexes and mortality schedules are available for the census of 1870 and 1880.

Bureau of Health Policy and Vital Statistics
PO Box 83720
Boise, Idaho 83720-0036
(208) 334-5988
www.healthandwelfare.idaho.gov

Idaho State Historical Society Library and Archives
Historical Library
450 N. Fourth St.
Boise, Idaho 83702
(208) 334-3357
www.idahohistory.net/library_archives.html

Societies and Repositories

Adams County Historical Society; PO Box 352; New Meadows, ID 93654.

Bonner County Genealogical Society; PO Box 27; Dover, ID 83827-0027; www.rootsweb.com/~idbcgs

Bonneville County Historical Society; Bonnneville Museum; 200 N. Eastern Ave; Idaho Falls, ID 83402-4029.

Boundary County Historical Society; PO Box 808; Bonners Ferry, ID 83805.

Caldwell, Idaho Genealogical Group; c/o Carol Murphy; 3504 S. Illinois; Caldwell, ID 83605.

Canyon County Historical Society; PO Box 595; Nampa, ID 83651

Caribou County Historical Society; PO Box 775; Soda Springs, ID 93276.

Clearwater County Historical Society; PO Box 1454; Orofino, ID 83544.

Eagle Rock Railroad Historical Society, Inc.; PO Box 2685; Idaho Falls, ID 83404; (208) 522-4242; copies@srv.net; www.ida.net/org/errhsi.

Elmore County Historical Foundation; PO Box 204; Mountain Home, ID 93647.

Family Scanner Chapter, IGS; PO Box 581; Caldwell, ID 83605.

Gooding County Historical Society; PO Box 580; Gooding, ID 83330.

Idaho County Chapter, IGS; Grangeville Centennial Library; 215 W. North; Grangeville, ID 83530.

Idaho Genealogical Society, Inc.; PO Box 1854; Boise, ID 83701-1854; (208) 345-8838; www.lili.org/idahogenealogy.

Idaho State Historical Society Library & Archives; Merle Wells Archives Building; 2205 Old Penitentia; Boise, ID 83712; (208) 334-2620; sguerber@ishs.state.id.us; www.idahohistory.net/library_archives.html.

Idaho State Library; 325 West State Street; Boise, ID 83702; (208) 334-2150; lili@isl.state.id.us; www.lili.org.

Ilo-Vollmer Historical Society; PO Box 61; Craigmont, ID 83523.

Kamiah Genealogical Society; Box 322; Kamiah, ID 83536.

Kootenai County Genealogical Society; Hayden Lake Library; 8385 North Government Way; Hayden, ID 83835; www.usgennet.org/usa/id/county/kootenai/kcgs.

Latah County Historical Society; 110 Adams St.; Moscow, ID 83843.

Lewis County Historical Society; Rt. 2, Box 10; Kamiah, ID 83536.

Luna House Historical Society; 0310 Third St.; Lewiston, ID 83501.

Minidoka County Historical Society; PO Box 21; Rupert, ID 93350.

Nez Perce Historical Society; PO Box 86; Nez Perce, ID 83543.

Old Fort Boise Historical Society; PO Box 942; Parma, ID 93660.

Payette County Historical Society; PO Box 476; Payette, ID 83661.

Pocatello Branch Genealogical Society; PO Box 4272; Pocatello, ID 83201.

Shoshone County Genealogical Society; PO Box 783; Kellogg, ID 83837.

South Bannock County Historical Society & Museum; PO Box 387, 110 E. Main St.; Lava Hot Springs, ID 83246.

South Custer County Historical Society; PO Box 355; Mackay, ID 83251.

Treasure Valley Chapter, IGS; 325 W. State Street; Boise, ID 83702.

Twin Rivers Genealogical Society; PO Box 386; Lewiston, ID 83501.

Upper Snake River Valley Historical Society; PO Box 244; Rexburg, ID 83440.

Bibliography and Record Sources

General

An Illustrated History of North Idaho: Embracing Nez Perce, Idaho, Latah, Kootenai and Shoshone Counties, State of Idaho. Spokane, Washington: Western Publishing Company, 1903.

An Illustrated History of the State of Idaho: Containing A History of the State of Idaho from the Earliest Period of its Discovery to the Present Time, Together with Glimpses of its Auspicious Futures; Illustrations. . .and Biographical Mention of Many Pioneers and Prominent Citizens of Today. 4 vols. in 2. Chicago: Lewis Publishing Co., 1899.

Arnold, Royal Ross. *Indian Wars of Idaho.* Caldwell, Idaho, The Caxton Printers, Ltd., 1932.

Arrington, Leonard J. *History of Idaho.* 2 vols. Moscow, Idaho: University of Idaho Press; Idaho State Historical Society, 1994.

Attebery, Louie W. *Idaho Folk Life: Homesteads to Headstones.* Salt Lake City: University of Utah Press, 1985.

Battien, Pauline. *The Gold Seekers: . . .A 200 Year History of Mining in Washington, Idaho, Montana & lower British Columbia.* Colville, Washington: Statesman-Examiner 1989.

Beal, Merrill D. *A History of Southeastern Idaho: An Intimate Narrative of Peaceful Conquest by Empire Builders. . . .* Caldwell, Idaho: Caxon Printers, Ltd., 1942.

Beal, Merrill D. and Merle W. Wells. *History of Idaho.* 3 vols. New York: Lewis Historical Publishing Co., 1959.

Bieter, Pat. *The Basques in Idaho.* Boise: Idaho State Historical Society.

Sketches of the Inter-Mountain States: Together with Biographies of Many Prominent and Progressive Citizens Who Have Helped in the Development and History-Making of this Marvelous Region, 1847, 1909, Utah, Idaho, Nevada. Salt Lake City: Salt Lake Tribune, 1909.

Smith, Lorayne Orton. Zest for Living: Southern Idaho Senior Profiles. Dallas, Texas: Taylor Publishing, 1991.

Southern California Genealogical Society. Sources of Genealogical Help in Idaho. Burbank, California: Southern California Genealogical Society, n.d.

Swetnam, Susan Hendricks. Lives of the Saints in Southeast Idaho: An Introduction to Mormon Pioneer Life Story Writing. Moscow, Idaho: University of Idaho Press and Idaho State Historical Society, 1991.

The Mining Industry in Idaho: A Short Bibliography of Sources on Mines and Mining in the Idaho State Historical Society Library and Archives. Boise: The Historical Society, 1992.

Thousands of Idaho Surnames: Abstracted From Rejected Federal Land Applications. 5 vols. Portland, Oregon: Genealogical Forum of Portland, Oregon, 1980–1987.

University of Idaho. Idaho State Documents Catalog Contains 22,632 Catalog Cards on 38 microfiche Cards and Provides Bibliographic Information on Idaho State Documents from the Territorial Period to 1980. Boise, Idaho, Mountain States Microfilm, n.d.

Walker, Deward Edgar. Indians of Idaho. Moscow: University Press of Idaho, 1978.

Wiggins, Marvin E. Mormons and Their Neighbors: An Index of Over 75,000 Biographical Sketches from 1820 to the Present. 2 vols. Provo, Utah: Harold B. Lee Library, Brigham Young University, 1984.

Writers' Program (Idaho). The Idaho Encyclopedia. Tucson, Arizona: W. C. Cox Co., 1974.

Atlases, Maps and Gazetteers

An Atlas of Idaho Territory, 1863–1890. Boise, Idaho: Idaho Historical Society, 1978.

Boone, Lalia Phipps. Idaho Place Names: A Geographical Dictionary. Moscow, Idaho: University of Idaho Press, 1988.

Gazetteer of Cities, Villages, Unincorporated Communities, and Landmark Sites in the State of Idaho. 3rd ed. Idaho Department of Highways, 1966.

Kramer, Fritz L. "Idaho Town Names." State Historical Department Biennial Report 23 (1951–1952): 14–114.

Patera, Alan H., and John S. Gallagher. A Checklist of Idaho Post Offices. Burtonsville, Maryland: The Depot, ©1984 (Lake Oswego, Oregon: Raven Press).

Preston, Ralph N. Maps of Early Idaho. Corvallis, Oregon: Western Guide Publishers, 1972.

Randall, Art. A Short History and Postal Records of Idaho Towns: Ada County Through Washington County. S.l.: A. Randall, 1994.

Route of the Oregon Trail in Idaho: From Thomas Fork Valley at the Wyoming State Line Westward to Fort Boise at the Oregon State Line. Boise, Idaho: Idaho Dept. of Highways, 1963.

Schell, Frank R. Ghost Towns and Live Ones: A Chronology of the Post Office Dept. in Idaho, 1861–1973. Twin Falls, Idaho, 1973.

Wells, Merle William. An Atlas of Idaho Territory, 1863–1890. Boise, Idaho: Idaho Historical Society, 1978.

Censuses

Available Census Records and Census Substitutes

Federal Census 1870, 1880, 1900, 1910, 1920, 1930

Federal Mortality Schedules 1870, 1880

Dollarhide, William. The Census Book: A Genealogist's Guide to Federal Census Facts, Schedules and Indexes. Bountiful, Utah: Heritage Quest, 1999.

Kemp, Thomas Jay. The American Census Handbook. Wilmington, Delaware: Scholarly Resources, Inc., 2001.

Lainhart, Ann S. State Census Records. Baltimore: Genealogical Publishing Co., Inc., 1992.

Pompey, Sherman Lee. 1863 Census of Some Prominent Men in the Idaho Territory. Salt Lake City: Filmed by the Genealogical Society of Utah, 1970.

Szucs, Loretto Dennis and Matthew Wright. Finding Answers in U.S. Census Records. Ancestry Publishing, 2001.

Thorndale, William. Map Guide to the U.S. Federal Census, 1790–1920. Baltimore: Genealogical Publishing Co., 1987.

Upper Snake River Valley Family History Center. 1910 Idaho Census Index. 1993. Bountiful, Utah. AGLL.

Williams, Gene F., comp. Idaho Territorial Voters Poll Lists, 1863. Boise, Idaho: Williams Printing, 1996.

Court Records, Probate and Wills

Bianchi, Carl F. Justice for The Times: A Centennial History of the Idaho State Courts. Boise, Idaho: Idaho Law Foundation, Inc., 1990.

Idaho State Supreme Court Justices, 1890–1970, and Idaho District Judges, 1890–1989. Boise: Idaho Historical Society, 1971–1989.

Minutes of the Idaho Territorial Supreme Court, 1866–1891. Boise, Filmed by the Idaho Historical Society, 1961.

U. S. District Court, Idaho Territory, 1866–1890. Moscow, Idaho: University of Idaho Law Library. n.d. 11 microfilm.

Emigration, Immigration, Migration and Naturalization

Route of the Oregon Trail in Idaho: From Thomas Fork Valley at the Wyoming State Line Westward to Fort Boise at the Oregon State Line. Boise, Idaho: Idaho Dept. of Highways, 1963.

Brooks, Juanita. *History of the Jews in Utah and Idaho.* Salt Lake City: Western Epics, 1973.

Buckendorf, Madeline and Elizabeth P. Jacox. *Directory of Oral History Resources in Idaho.* S.l.: Idaho State History Society, 1982.

Catholic Church. Church of the Blessed Sacrament (Montpelier, Idaho). *Church Records, 1897–1985.* Salt Lake City: Filmed by the Genealogical Society of Utah, 1986–1987. 2 microfilm.

Church of Jesus Christ of Latter-day Saints. Cassia Stake (Idaho). *The First one hundred years: Cassia-Oakley Idaho Stake, 1887–1987.* S.n.: Church of Jesus Christ of Latter-day Saints. Cassia Stake (Idaho), n.d.

Daughters of the American Revolution. Alice Whitman Chapter (Lewiston, Idaho). *Idaho Genealogical Records.* Microfilm of original records in the D.A.R. Library in Washington, D.C. Salt Lake City: Filmed by the Genealogical Society of Utah, 1970.

Defenbach, Byron. *Idaho, The Place and Its People: A History of the Gem State from Prehistoric to Present Day.* 3 vols. Chicago: American Historical Society, Inc., 1933.

Directory of Churches and Religious Organizations of Idaho. Boise, Idaho: Historical Records Survey, 1940.

Drexler, Joan, comp. *Blackrobes Journey, 1840–1990: To the Loving Memory of the Devoted Pioneer Catholic Clergy and to the Priests, Sisters and Laity of the Current Church Community.* S.l.: s.n., 1990.

Etulain, Richard W. *Idaho History: A Bibliography.* Rev. ed. Pocatello: Idaho State University Press, 1979.

Forbush, Harold Sanford. *Education in the Upper Snake River Valley: The Public Schools, 1880–1950.* Rexburg, Idaho: H.S. Forbush, 1992 (Ricks College Press).

French, Hiram Taylor. *History of Idaho: A Narrative Account of its Historical Progress, Its People and Its Principal Interests.* 3 vols. Chicago: Lewis Pub., 1914.

Gobble, John R. *Lineages of the Members (Past and Present), Idaho Society, Sons of the American Revolution, 1909 through 1961. . . .* Idaho Falls, Idaho: J. R. Gobble, 1962.

Hailey, John. *The History of Idaho.* Boise, Idaho: Syms-York Co., 1910.

Hawley, James H. *History of Idaho: The Gem of the Mountains.* 4 vols. Chicago: S. J. Clarke Publishing Co., 1920.

Hill, Lila. *Early Methodism in Idaho: Extracts from News Articles and Historical Notes; Oregon-Idaho Conference of the United Methodist Church.* Salem, Oregon: United Methodist Church. Oregon-Idaho Conference. Commission on Archives and History, 1996.

Howell, Erle. *Methodism in the Northwest.* S.N.: n.p., n.d.

Hult, Ruby El. *Steamboats in the Timber.* 2d ed. Portland, Oregon: Binfords & Mort, 1968.

Idaho Ethnic Heritage. 3 vols. S.l.: Idaho Centennial Commission and Idaho State Historical Society, 1990.

Idaho Genealogical Society (Boise, Idaho). *Roma[...] Catholic Diocese of Boise, Catholic Chancery of Idaho, Master Index.* 25—vols. Boise, Idah[...] Genealogical Society.

Idaho Genealogical Society. *Footprints Through [...]* 3 vols. Boise, Idaho: Idaho Genealogical Soci[...] Boise, Idaho: Williams Printing.

Idaho Local History: A Bibliography with a Che[...] Library Holdings. Moscow, Idaho: University [...] Idaho, 1976.

Idaho Research Outline. Series U.S.-States, no. [...] Lake City: Family History Library, 1988.

Indian Peoples of Idaho. 2d ed. Boise, Idaho: B[...] University Press, 1979.

Jensen, Dwight William. *Discovering Idaho, A [...]* Caldwell, Idaho: Caxton Printers, 1977.

Kestler, William, John Meyers, and James L. H[...] *Scattered Graves.* S.l.: s.n., 1998.

Kirk, John Ohara. *Idaho 100: Stories from Idah[...] Citizens.* Helena, Montana: Falcon Press, 19[...]

L. D. S. Individual Histories (Idaho). 2 vols. S.l[...]

Lawless, Elaine J. *Guide to the Idaho Folklore [...]* Boise, Idaho: Idaho Folklife Center, Idaho St[...] Historical Society, 1983.

Miller, Donald C. *Ghost Towns of Idaho.* Bould[...] Pruett Pub. Co., 1976.

Nelson, Milo G., and Charles A. Webbert. *Idah[...] History: A Bibliography With a Checklist of [...] Holdings.* Moscow, Idaho: University Press [...] 1976.

Newspapers in the Idaho Historical Society Mi[...] Collection. Boise, Idaho: Idaho State Histori[...] 1999.

Osborn-Ryan, Sharon E. *Cumulative Baptism I[...] Catholic Church Records of the Pacific Nor[...]* Oregon Heritage Press, 1999.

Penson-Ward, Betty. *Idaho Women in History.* [...] Idaho: Northwest Printing, 1991–.

Powell, Barbara V. *Citizens of North Idaho.* M[...] Washington: B.V. Powell, 1986.

Quinn, Larry D. *A History of Magic Valley.* Tw[...] Idaho: Publishing West Associates, 1996.

Sappington, Roger Edwin. *The Brethren Along [...] River: A History of the Church of the Breth[...] and Western Montana.* Elgin, Illinois: Breth[...] 1966.

Schmick, Judy. *Idaho Surname Index.* Boise, I[...] Genealogical Society, 1989.

Schoenberg, Wilfred P. *A History of the Catho[...] the Pacific Northwest, 1743–1983.* Washing[...] Pastoral Press, 1987.

Simpson, Claude. *Panhandle Personalities, B[...] From The Idaho Panhandle.* Moscow, Idah[...] of Idaho Press, 1984.

United States. Bureau of Land Management. *Emigrant Trails of Southeastern Idaho*. Boise, Idaho: U.S. Dept. of the Interior, Bureau of Land Management, 1976.

United States. District Court (Idaho*). Naturalization Records, Central District, Moscow, Idaho, 1892–1935*. Microfilm of originals in the Federal courthouse in Boise, Idaho. Salt Lake City: Filmed by the Genealogical Society of Utah, 1987.

United States. District Court (Idaho). *Naturalization Records, Eastern District, Pocatello, Idaho, 1893–1945*. Microfilm of originals in the Federal courthouse in Boise, Idaho. Salt Lake City: Filmed by the Genealogical Society of Utah, 1987. 4 microfilm.

United States. District Court (Idaho). *Naturalization Records, Northern District, Coeur d'Alene, Idaho, 1909–1929*. Microfilm of originals in the Federal courthouse in Boise, Idaho. Salt Lake City: Filmed by the Genealogical Society of Utah, 1987. 3 microfilm.

United States. District Court (Idaho). *Naturalization Records, Southern District, Boise, Idaho, 1891–1934*. Microfilm of originals in the Federal courthouse in Boise, Idaho. Salt Lake City: Filmed by the Genealogical Society of Utah, 1987. 4 microfilm.

Land and Property

Avery, J. A. *Stockman's Guide [Southeastern Idaho]*. Idaho: Downey Idahoan, 1913.

Early homestead, timber culture act, reclamation land, and mining claim records for Idaho are found at the Bureau of Land Management and the Idaho Historical Society Archives in Boise, Idaho. Additionally, land and mining entries are found in the individual county records.

Genealogical Forum of Portland, Oregon. *Thousands of Idaho Surnames: Abstracted From Rejected Federal Land Applications*. 5 vols. Portland, Oregon: Genealogical Forum of Portland, Oregon, 1980–1987.

Hone, Wade E. *Land and Property Research in the United States*. Salt Lake City: Ancestry Incorporated, 1997.

Idaho Genealogical Society (Boise, Idaho). *Idaho State Brand Records and Indexes*. 4 vols. Boise, Idaho: The Society, 1988.

United States. Land Office (Idaho). *Land Records, 1868–1913*. Salt Lake City: Filmed by the Genealogical Society of Utah, 1989. 23 microfilm.

Military

Haulsee, W. M. et al. *Soldiers in the Great War*. 3 vols. (Washington, D.C.: Soldiers Record Publishing Assoc., 1920.)

Holloway, James Lafayette. *We Served in the Military, World War II*. Salt Lake City: Filmed by the Genealogical Society of Utah, 1998.

United States. Selective Service System. *Registration Cards of Men Born Between April 1877 and February 1897 (4th Draft Registration), Record Group 147*. Seattle, Washington: National Archives Record's Administration, Pacific Alaska Region, 1940–1947.

United States. Adjutant General's Office. *Index to Compiled Service Records of Volunteer Union Soldiers Who Served in Organizations From The Territory of Washington*. Washington, D.C.: The National Archives, 1964.

United States. Selective Service System. *Idaho, World War I Selective Service System Draft Registration Cards, 1917–1918*. National Archives Microfilm Publications, M1509. Washington, D.C.: National Archives, 1987–1988.

World War II Military Records of Pocatello and Surrounding Areas. Salt Lake City: Filmed by the Genealogical Society of Utah, 1990. 4 microfilm.

Vital and Cemetery Records

AZ, CA, ID, NV, 1850–1951. S.l.: Brøderbund, c1996. CD-ROM.

Cemetery Records of Idaho. 12 vols. Originals located in the Idaho Historical Society Genealogical Collection, Boise, Idaho. Salt Lake City: Genealogical Society of Utah, 1952–1968.

Church of Jesus Christ of Latter-day Saints. Genealogical Society. *Cemetery Records of Idaho Index*. 2 vols. Salt Lake City: The Society, 1954–1955.

Guide to Public Vital Statistics Records In Idaho, State and County. Boise, Idaho: Historical Records Survey, 1942.

Idaho. Department of Health and Welfare. *Death Certificates, 1911–1937; Index, 1911–1932*. Microfilm of originals at the Department of Health and Welfare in Boise, Idaho. Salt Lake City: Filmed by the Genealogical Society of Utah, 1988. 63 microfilm.

Miscellaneous Marriage Records Index. Salt Lake City: Filmed by the Genealogical Society of Utah, 1972. 19 microfilm.

Western States Historical Marriage Index. Rev. Rexburg, Idaho: BYU Idaho, 2002. Online database http://abish .byui.edu/special Collections/fhc.gbsearch.htm.

Woolf, Kathleen. *Death and Burial Records Compiled from Headstones, Sexton Records, Burial Permits, Early Ward Records, and Some Immediate Family Sources*. Microfilm of records at Family History Center, Idaho Falls, Idaho. Salt Lake City: Filmed by the Genealogical Society of Utah, 1994. 58 microfilm.

County Website	Map Index	Date Created	Parent County or Territory From Which Organized Address/Details
Ada www.rootsweb.com/~idada/	**N3**	**22 Dec 1865**	**Boise** Ada County; 650 Main St. Boise, ID 83702-5986; Ph. (208) 383-4417 **Details:** (County Clerk has Marriage Records from 1890, Land Records from 1864, Divorce, Probate, & Court Records)
Adams www.County.adams.id.us/	**K2**	**3 Mar 1911**	**Washington** Adams County; 107 Michigan Ave; Council, ID 83612-0048; Ph. (208) 583-4561 **Details:** (County Clerk has Marriage, Divorce, Probate, Court & Land Records from 1900)
Alturas		**1864**	**Original county** Alturas County; ID **Details:** (see Blaine) Abolished 1895 to create Blaine & Lincoln Counties
Bannock www.County.bannock.id.us/	**P10**	**6 Mar 1893**	**Bear Lake** Bannock County; 624 E Center St; Pocatello, ID 83201-6274; Ph. (208) 236-7340 **Details:** (County Clerk has Birth & Death Records from 1902, Marriage Records from 1893, Divorce, Probate & Court Records)
Bear Lake www.oregontrailcenter.org/bearlakeco.html	**Q12**	**5 Jan 1875**	**Oneida** Bear Lake County; 7 E Center St; Paris, ID 83261-0000; Ph. (208) 945-2212 **Details:** (County Clerk has Birth Records 1907–1911, Death Records 1907–1915, Marriage & Land Records from 1875 & Divorce Records from 1884)
Benewah www.rootsweb.com/~idbenewa/ben_indx.htm	**F2**	**23 Jan 1915**	**Kootenai** Benewah County; 701 College Ave; Saint Maries, ID 83861-0000; Ph. (208) 245-2234 **Details:** (County Clerk has Marriage, Burial, Divorce, Probate, Court & Land Records from 1915)
Bingham www.County.bingham.id.us/	**O10**	**13 Jan 1885**	**Oneida** Bingham County; 501 N Maple St; Blackfoot, ID 83221-1700; Ph. (208) 785-8040 **Details:** (County Clerk has Marriage & Land Records from 1885, Divorce & Court Records from 1900, Probate Records from 1892, Naturalization Records, Community minutes from 1855 & school Census 1898–1933)
Blaine	**N7**	**5 Mar 1895**	**Alturas** Blaine County; 206 1st Ave S, Ste. 200; PO Box 400; Hailey, ID 83333; Ph. (208) 788-5500 **Details:** (State of Idaho Vital Statistics has Birth & Death Records; Court Clerk has Divorce & Probate Records; County Recorder has Land, Marriage, & Military Discharge Records; County Treasurer has Tax Records)
Boise www.County.boise.id.us/	**M3**	**1863**	**Original county** Boise County; 420 Main St; Box BC; Idaho City, ID 83631-0157; Ph. (208) 392-4431 **Details:** (County Clerk has Marriage Records from 1868, Divorce Records from 1904, Probate & Land Records from 1865 & Court Records from 1867; some Records are not complete due to fires)

County Website	Map Index	Date Created	Parent County or Territory From Which Organized Address/Details
Bonner www.County.bonner.id.us/	**C2**	**21 Feb 1907**	**Kootenai** Bonner County; 215 S 1st Ave; Sandpoint, ID 83864-1392; Ph. (208) 265-1432 **Details:** (County Clerk has Birth & Death Records 1907–1911, Marriage, Divorce & Court Records from 1907, Probate Records from 1890 & Land Records from 1889)
Bonneville www.County.bonneville.id.us/	**N11**	**7 Feb 1911**	**Bingham** Bonneville County; 605 N Capital Ave; Idaho Falls, ID 83402-3582; Ph. (208) 529-1350 **Details:** (County Clerk has Marriage, Divorce, Land, Probate & Court Records from 1911)
Boundary www.boundary-idaho.com/	**B2**	**23 Jan 1915**	**Bonner, Kootenai** Boundary County; PO Box 419; Bonners Ferry, ID 83805; Ph. (208) 267-2242 **Details:** (County Clerk has Marriage, Land, Probate & Court Records, some Birth, Death, Divorce & Military Records)
Butte www.rootsweb.com/~idbutte/	**M8**	**6 Feb 1917**	**Bingham** Butte County; 248 W Corand; PO Box 737; Arco, ID 83213-0737; Ph. (208) 527-3021 **Details:** (County Clerk has Marriage, Burial, Divorce, Probate & school Records from 1917, Court Records from 1895 & Land Records from 1890)
Camas www.rootsweb.com/~idcamas/	**N5**	**6 Feb 1917**	**Blaine** Camas County; 501 Soldier Rd; PO Box 430; Fairfield, ID 83327-0430; Ph. (208) 764-2242 **Details:** (County Clerk has Marriage, Divorce & Court Records from 1917 & incomplete Burial Records; Probate Court has Probate Records from 1890)
Canyon www.canyoncounty.org/	**N2**	**7 Mar 1891**	**Owyhee, Ada** Canyon County; 1115 Albany; Caldwell, ID 83605-3542; Ph. (208) 454-7504 **Details:** (County Clerk has some Birth & Death Records 1907–1911, Marriage Records from 1895 & Land Records from 1892; Discharge Court has Divorce Records from 1892; Magistrate Court has Probate & Court Records from 1892)
Caribou www.rootsweb.com/~idcaribo/	**P11**	**11 Feb 1919**	**Bannock** Caribou County; 159 S Main St; PO Box 775; Soda Springs, ID 83276-0775; Ph. (208) 547-4324 **Details:** (County Clerk has Marriage Records from 1919, Divorce, Probate, Court & Land Records)
Cassia www.cassiacounty.org/	**Q7**	**20 Feb 1879**	**Oneida** Cassia County; 1459 Overland Ave; Burley, ID 83318; Ph. (208) 878-5240 **Details:** (County Recorder has Birth & Death Records from 1907–1911; County Clerk has Marriage, Divorce, Probate, Land, Military & Court Records from 1879 & some Naturalization Records)
Clark http://rootsweb.com/~idclark/clark.htm	**L9**	**1911**	**Fremont** Clark County; 320 W Main St; PO Box 205; Dubois, ID 83423-0205; Ph. (208) 274-5304 **Details:** (County Clerk has Marriage, Divorce, Court & Land Records from 1919)

County Website	Map Index	Date Created	Parent County or Territory From Which Organized Address/Details
Clearwater www.clearwatercounty.org	**G3**	**27 Feb 1911**	**Nez Perce** Clearwater County; 150 Michigan Ave; PO Box 586; Orofino, ID 83544; Ph. (208) 476-5615 rchristensen@clearwatercounty.org **Details:** (All Records from 1911 - Court's Office has Court, Divorce, Guardianship, & Probate Records; Recorder's Office has Land, Marriage, & Military Records; Treasurer's Office has Tax Records)
Custer www.County.custer.id.us/	**L6**	**8 Jan 1881**	**Alturas, Lemhi** Custer County; 801 Main St; PO Box 385; Challis, ID 83226; Ph. (208) 879-2360 **Details:** (County Clerk has Marriage, Divorce, Court & Land Records from 1872; Probate Court has Probate Records)
Elmore www.rootsquest.com/~idaho/elmore/	**N4**	**7 Feb 1889**	**Alturas, Ada** Elmore County; 150 S 4th E St; Mountain Home, ID 83647-3028; Ph. (208) 287-2133 **Details:** (County Clerk has Birth & Death Records 1907–1911, Marriage, Divorce, Probate, Court & Land Records from 1889)
Franklin www.rootsweb.com/~idfrankl/	**Q11**	**30 Jan 1913**	**Oneida** Franklin County; 39 W Oneida St; Preston, ID 83263-1234; Ph. (208) 852-1090 **Details:** (County Clerk has Marriage Records from 1913, Court & Land Records)
Fremont www.County.fremont.id.us/	**L11**	**4 Mar 1893**	**Bingham, Lemhi** Fremont County; 151 W 1st N; St. Anthony, ID 83445; Ph. (208) 624-7332 **Details:** (County Clerk has Birth & Death Records 1907–1911, Marriage, Divorce, Probate, Land, Court & Naturalization Records from 1893 & Military Records from 1919)
Gem www.County.gem.id.us/	**M2**	**19 Mar 1915**	**Boise, Canyon** Gem County; 415 E Main St; Emmett, ID 83617; Ph. (208) 365-4561 **Details:** (County Clerk has Marriage, Divorce, Court, Land & Military Records from 1915; County Magistrate has Probate Records)
Gooding www.rootsweb.com/~idgoodin/	**O5**	**27 Mar 1905**	**Lincoln** Gooding County; 624 Main St; PO Box 417; Gooding, ID 83330-0417; Ph. (208) 934-4841 **Details:** (County Clerk has Marriage, Divorce, Probate, Court & Land Records from 1913)
Idaho www.rootsquest.com/~idaho/idaho/	**I4**	**4 Feb 1864**	**Original county** Idaho County; 320 W Main St Rm 5; Grangeville, ID 83530-1948; Ph. (208) 983-2751 **Details:** (County Recorder has Birth & Death Records 1907–1911 & Marriage Records from 1868; County Clerk has Land Records from 1862, Divorce & Court Records from 1888)
Jefferson www.County.jefferson.id.us/	**M10**	**18 Feb 1913**	**Fremont** Jefferson County; 134 N Clark St; Rigby, ID 83442; Ph. (208) 745-7756 **Details:** (County Clerk has Marriage, Divorce, Probate, Court & Land Records from 1914)
Jerome www.County.jerome.id.us/	**P6**	**8 Feb 1919**	**Gooding, Lincoln** Jerome County; 300 N Lincoln Ave; Jerome, ID 83338-2344; Ph. (208) 324-8811 **Details:** (County Clerk has Marriage, Divorce, Probate, Court & Land Records from 1919)

County Website	Map Index	Date Created	Parent County or Territory From Which Organized Address/Details
Kootenai www.co.kootenai.id.us	E2	**22 Dec 1864**	**Nez Perce** Kootenai County; 451 Government Way; PO Box 9000; Coeur d' Alene, ID 83816-9000; Ph. (208) 446-1480 kcro@kcgov.us **Details:** (Created in 1864, but not organized until 1881) (County Recorder has Birth & Death Records 1907–1912, Marriage, Divorce, Probate & Court Records from 1881)
Latah www.latah.id.us/	F2	**1888**	**Nez Perce** Latah County; 522 S Adams; PO Box 8068; Moscow, ID 83843; Ph. (208) 882-8580 **Details:** (Created & organized by U.S. congressional enactment, said to be the only County in the U.S. so created) (County Clerk-Recorder has Birth & Death Records 1907–1911, Marriage, Land & Military Discharge Records from 1888 & Naturalization Records 1845–1898; Discharge Court has Probate Records from 1896, Court Records from 1891 & Divorce Records from 1940)
Lemhi www.rootsweb.com/~idlemhi/	J6	**9 Jan 1869**	**Idaho** Lemhi County; 206 Courthouse Dr; Salmon, ID 83467; Ph. (208) 756-2815 **Details:** (County Clerk-Recorder has Birth & Death Records 1907–1911, Marriage, Probate, Land, Divorce, Military, Court & Naturalization Records from 1869)
Lewis www.rootsquest.com/~idaho/lewis/	H2	**3 Mar 1911**	**Nez Perce** Lewis County; 510 Oak St; Nezperce, ID 83543-0000; Ph. (208) 937-2661 **Details:** (County Clerk has Marriage, Divorce, Probate, Court & Land Records from 1911)
Lincoln www.rootsweb.com/~idlincol/	O6	**18 Mar 1895**	**Alturas** Lincoln County; 111 W B St; Shoshone, ID 83352-0000; Ph. (208) 886-7641 **Details:** (County Clerk has some Birth & Death Records 1895–1913, Marriage, Divorce, Probate, Court & Land Records from 1895 & some school Records)
Madison www.County.madison.id.us/	M11	**18 Feb 1913**	**Fremont** Madison County; 134 E Main; PO Box 389; Rexburg, ID 83440-0389; Ph. (208) 356-3662 **Details:** (County Clerk has Marriage, Divorce, Probate, Court & Land Records from 1914)
Minidoka www.minidoka.id.us/	P7	**28 Jan 1913**	**Lincoln** Minidoka County; 715 G St; Rupert, ID 83350-0000; Ph. (208) 436-9511 **Details:** (County Clerk has Marriage, Divorce, Probate, Court & Land Records from 1913)
Nez Perce www.County.nezperce.id.us/	H2	**4 Feb 1864**	**Original county** Nez Perce County; 1230 Main St; PO Box 896; Lewiston, ID 83501-0896; Ph. (208) 799-3090 **Details:** (County Clerk has Birth & Death Records 1900–1911, Marriage, Divorce, Probate, Court & Land Records from 1860)
Oneida www.rootsweb.com/~idoneida/	Q9	**22 Jan 1864**	**Original county** Oneida County; 10 Court St; Malad City, ID 83252; Ph. (208) 766-4116 **Details:** (County Clerk has Birth & Death Records 1907–1911, Marriage Records from 1866, Military Records from 1919, Naturalization Records from 1869, Divorce, Probate, Court & Land Records)

County Website	Map Index	Date Created	Parent County or Territory From Which Organized Address/Details
Owyhee http://owyheecounty.net/	**P3**	**31 Dec 1863**	**Original county** Owyhee County; Hwy 78; Murphy, ID 83650-0128; Ph. (208) 495-2421 **Details:** (County Clerk has Birth & Death Records 1907–1913, Marriage Records from 1895, Divorce & Court Records from 1864 & Naturalization Records 1893–1911)
Payette www.rootsquest.com/~idaho/payette/	**M2**	**28 Feb 1917**	**Canyon** Payette County; 1130 3rd Ave N; Payette, ID 83661; Ph. (208) 642-6000 **Details:** (County Clerk has Marriage, Divorce, Probate, Court & Land Records from 1917 & Military Discharge Records from 1919)
Power www.rootsweb.com/~idpower/index.html	**P9**	**30 Jan 1913**	**Bingham, Blaine, Oneida** Power County; 543 Bannock Ave; American Falls, ID 83211-1200; Ph. (208) 226-7611 **Details:** (County Clerk has Marriage Records from 1914 & Divorce Records from 1916; Probate Court has Probate Records; Magistrate Court has Court Records; Assessor's Office has Land Records)
Shoshone www.rootsweb.com/~idshosho/	**E3**	**4 Feb 1864**	**Original county** Shoshone County; 700 Bank St; Wallace, ID 83873-1049; Ph. (208) 752-3331 **Details:** (County Clerk has Birth & Death Records 1907–1911, Marriage Records from 1875, Divorce Records from 1887, Probate Records from 1885, Court Records from 1884 & Land Records from 1871)
Teton http://homepages.rootsweb.com/~bar19/teton.htm	**M12**	**26 Jan 1915**	**Madison, Fremont, Bingham** Teton County; 89 N Main St; PO Box 756; Driggs, ID 83422-0756; (Ph.) 208-354.2905 **Details:** (County Clerk has Marriage, Divorce, Probate, Court & Land Records from 1916)
Twin Falls www.rootsweb.com/~idtwinfa/	**Q5**	**21 Feb 1907**	**Cassia** Twin Falls County; 425 Shoshone St N; PO Box 126; Twin Falls, ID 83303-0126; Ph. (208) 736-4000 **Details:** (County Clerk-Recorder has Birth & Land Records from 1907 & Military Records from 1919; Court Services has Divorce, Probate & Court Records from 1907)
Valley www.infowest.com/personal/w/wcraig/ valleycounty/index.html	**K4**	**26 Feb 1917**	**Boise, Idaho** Valley County; 219 N Main St; PO Box 737; Cascade, ID 83611; Ph. (208) 382-4297 **Details:** (County Recorder has Marriage Records from 1929 & Land Records from 1904; County Clerk has Divorce Records from 1950, Probate Records from 1934, Military & Court Records from 1917)
Washington www.ruralnetwork.net/~wcassr/	**L2**	**20 Feb 1879**	**Boise** Washington County; 256 E Court St; Weiser, ID 83672-0670; Ph. (208) 549-2092 **Details:** (County Clerk has Birth & Death Records 1907–1911, Marriage, Divorce, Probate, Court & Land Records from 1879)

Illinois

Capital: Springfield
Territory: 1809
State: 1818 (21st)

State sovereignty, national union

When explorers arrived in the 17th century, the principal inhabitants of the region were the Illinois, a confederation of Algonquian-speaking tribes. In 1673, Jacques Marquette and Louis Joliet became the first known Europeans to explore Illinois. The French established permanent settlements in 1699 at Cahokia and 1703 at Kaskaskia. At the end of the French and Indian War (1754–1763), Illinois was ceded to Great Britain. Many French settlers fled to St. Louis, Natchez, and other towns at this time. Virginians began to move into the region about 1769. The area was attached to Quebec in 1774.

During the Revolutionary War, George Rogers Clark captured Kaskaskia and Cahokia, securing the lands north of the Ohio River for the United States. Virginia claimed all the land north of the Ohio River for itself, but ceded it to the United States in 1784. In 1787, Illinois became part of the Northwest Territory. Three years later, Illinois became part of the Indiana Territory. The Illinois Territory was formed in 1809, with the Wisconsin region being transferred to the Michigan Territory in 1818.

The first settlers came by way of the Ohio River from North Carolina, Tennessee, Virginia, Kentucky, Maryland, and Pennsylvania. They settled in the southern part of the state. At the time of statehood in 1818, most of the population still resided in the southern part of the state. In about 1825, settlers from the New England states and New York came on the Erie Canal, the Great Lakes, or the National Road to settle the northern portion of the state. Industrial growth in the 1830's and 1840's brought thousands of Irish, southern Europeans, and Germans to man the factories around Lake Michigan. The expulsion of Sauk and Fox warriors in 1832 ended the last Indian threats to settlement. Transportation improvements between 1838 and 1856 stimulated migration into the state. The National Road reached Vandalia in 1838; the Illinois-Michigan Canal opened in 1848; and the Illinois Central Railroad was completed in 1856. Members of the Church of Jesus Christ of Latter-day Saints, also known as Mormons, came to Illinois in 1839 and founded Nauvoo on the Mississippi River. At one time it was the state's most populous city. Illinois sent about 255,000 men to fight the Confederacy.

Look for vital records in the following locations:

- **Birth and death records:** Division of Vital Records, State Department of Public Health, Springfield, Illinois. Statewide registration of births and deaths began in 1916. Certified copies are issued only to legally authorized (related) persons. Uncertified copies are issued for genealogical purposes. Some county clerks have birth and death records from 1877 to 1916, with a few as early as 1838.

- **Marriage and divorce records:** County clerks. Marriage licenses were not required until 1877, but some counties have records as early as 1790. Divorces were granted by the legislature and the circuit courts in the early 1800's. The Superior Court of Cook County in Chicago has custody of divorces and the county court clerks have custody of the divorce records.

- **Court and real estate records:** Counties with a population of more than 70,000 had probate courts prior to 1960. Counties with fewer people handled probate matters in the county court. Since 1960, probate matters have been handled by the circuit court. The court recorder of deeds handles all matters pertaining to real estate.

- **Census records:** Territorial and state censuses were taken in 1810, 1818, 1820, 1825, 1835, 1840, 1845, 1855, and 1865. Some residents were also listed in the 1807 Indiana Territorial census.

- **Military records:** Department of Veterans Affairs, Springfield, Illinois. VA maintains files with names of about 600,000 veterans buried in Illinois. They are listed in alphabetical order. A cemetery listing, by county, notes veteran burials. An index file of peacetime soldiers and those with unknown service is also available. Soldiers' discharge records are available at county courthouses. The State Archivist, Archives Building in Springfield might also have useful records.

Division of Vital Records Illinois Department of Public Health
605 West Jefferson Street
Springfield, IL 62702-5097
(217) 782-6553; Fax (217) 785-3209
www.idph.state.il.us/vitalrecords/deathinfo.htm

Illinois State Archives
Norton Building
Capitol Complex
Springfield, IL 62756
(217) 782-4682; Fax (217) 524-3930
www.cyberdriveillinois.com/departments/archives/archives.html

National Archives Chicago Branch
7358 South Pulaski Road
Chicago, IL 60629-5898
(312) 353-0162

Societies and Repositories

Afro-American Historical and Genealogical Society, Little Egypt; 703 S. Wall St. #5; Carbondale, IL 62901.

Afro-American Historical and Genealogical Society; 12516 S. Lowe St.; Chicago, IL 60628.

Alliance Chapter, Illinois NSDAR; Urbana-Champaign, IL; www.rootsweb.com/~ilacdar.

American Bicentennial Chapter, ILSSAR; 657 Darien Court; Hoffman Estates, IL 60194-2573; (847) 884-7751.

Assenisipia Chapter, SAR; PO Box 663; Manteno, IL 60950-0663; strude@aol.com.

Bloomington-Normal Genealogical Society; PO Box 489; Normal, IL 61761-0488.

Bond County Genealogical Society; PO Box 172; Greenville, IL 62246.

Brookfield Historical Society; 8820–1/2 Brookfield Avenue; Brookfield, IL 60513-1670; BHSRequest@hotmail.com; www.gailla.com/bhs.

Bureau County Genealogical Society; 629 S. Main Street; Princeton, IL 61356-2012; www.rootsweb.com/~ilbcgs.

Carroll County Genealogical Society; PO Box 347; Savanna, IL 61074; www.internetni.com/~ahaliotis/index2.html.

Cass County Historical/Genealogical Society; PO Box 11; Virginia, IL 62691; www.rootsweb.com/~ilcchgs.

Champaign Genealogical Society; c/o Champaign County Historical Archives; 201 S. Ra; Urbana, IL 61801-3283; kjeanne@juno.com.

Chicago Genealogical Society; PO Box 1160; Chicago, IL 60690-1160; chgogs@chgogs.org; http:/chgogs.org.

Chicago Historical Society; North Ave. and Clark St.; Chicago, IL 60614.

Chillicothe Historical Society; PO Box 181; Chillicothe, IL 61523-0181; chhs@osclink.com; www.chillicothehistorical.org.

Christian County Genealogical Society; PO Box 28; Taylorville, IL 62568; jbiond@ctitech.com; www.homepage.macomb.com/~tkuntz/christianco.htm.

Clay County Genealogical Society; 114 So. Church St.; PO Box 94; Louisville, IL 62858; (618) 665-4544; ccgs@wabash.net; www.rootsweb.com/~ilclay.

Clinton County Historical Society; 1091 Franklin St.; Carlyle, IL 62231; (618) 594-2683; www.carlyle.il.us/mus.htm.

Colchester Area Historical Society; 3975 E. 650th St.; Colchester, IL 62326.

Coles County Illinois Genealogical Society; PO Box 592; Charleston, IL 61920; www.rootsweb.com/~ilcoles/ccgs.htm.

Cook Memorial Public Library District; 413 N Milwaukee Ave; Libertyville, IL 60048; www.cooklib.org.

Crawford County Historical Society and Museum; PO Box 554; Robinson, IL 62454-0554; (618) 592-3310; oldcrawf@frsb.net; www.rootsweb.com/~ilcchs.

Cumberland and Coles County of Illinois Genealogical Society; Rt. 1, Box 141; Toledo, IL 62468.

Decatur (Macon County) Genealogical Society; PO Box 1548; Decatur, IL 62525-1548; www.rootsweb.com/~ildcgs.

DeKalb County Archives at the Joiner History Room; Sycamore Public Library; 103 E State St; Sycamore, IL 60178; joinerhistoryroom@co.de-kalb.il.us.

Des Plaines Historical Society; 789 Pearson St.; Des Plaines, IL 60016.

DeWitt County Genealogical Society; Box 632; Clinton, IL 61727; carolegeo@bwsys.com.

Dundee Township Historical Society; 426 Highland Ave.; Dundee, IL 60118.

Dunton Genealogical Society; 500 North Dunton; Arlington Heights, IL 60004.

DuPage County Genealogical Society; PO Box 3; Wheaton, IL 60189-0003; SMontg7300@aol.com; www.dcgs.org.

Edgar County Genealogical Society; PO Box 304; Paris, IL 61944-0304.

Edgar County Historical Society; 408 North Main; Paris, IL 61944-1549.

Edgewater Historical Society; C/O Marie Morrissette; 5555 N. Sheridan Rd. #1203; Chicago, IL 60640; Info@EdgewaterHistory.org; http://edgewaterhistory.org.

Edwards County Historical Society; 212 W. Main Street; Albion, IL 62806; www.rootsweb.com/~iledward/ehistsoc.html.

Effingham County Genealogical Society; PO Box 1166; Effingham, IL 62401; www.rootsweb.com/~ileffing/lookups.htm.

Ela Historical Society; 95 E. Main Street; Lake Zurich, IL 60047; www.lzarea.org/ehs.

Elgin Area Historical Society; 360 Park Street; Elgin, IL 60120; www.elginhistory.org.

Elgin Genealogical Society; PO Box 1418; Elgin, IL 60121-1418; http://nsn.nslsilus.org/elghome/egs/index.html.

Evanston Historical Society; 225 Greenwood; Evanston, IL 60201; l-cabot@northwestern.edu; www.evanstonhistorical.org.

Fayette County Genealogical Society; Box 177; Vandalia, IL 62471.

Fellowship of Brethren Genealogists; 1451 Dundee Ave.; Elgin, IL 60120.

Forest Park Historical Society; c/o Forest Park Library; 7555 Jackson Ave.; Forest Park, IL 60130.

Fort LaMotte Genealogical and Historical Society; c/o LaMotte Twp. Library; Palestine, IL 62451.

Fox Lake Area Historical Society; PO Box 4; Fox Lake, IL 60020; rsutton@lnd.com; www.rootsweb.com/~ilflahs/histsoc.html.

Fox Valley Genealogical Society; PO Box 5435; Naperville, IL 60567-5435; http://members.aol.com/fvgs1/index.html.

Freeburg Historical and Genealogical Society; Box 69; Freeburg, IL 62243.

Fulton County Historical and Genealogical Society; PO Box 593; Canton, IL 61520.

Genealogical Forum of Elmhurst, Illinois; 120 E. Park; Elmhurst, IL 60126.

Genealogical Society of DeKalb County, Illinois; PO Box 295; Sycamore, IL 60178.

Genealogical Society of Southern Illinois; c/o John A. Logan College; Rt. 2 Box 145; Carterville, IL 62918-9599; www.jal.cc.il.us/Gssi.org.html.

Glen Ellyn Historical Society; PO Box 283; Glen Ellyn, IL 60138; historical@glen-ellyn.com; www.glen-ellyn.com/historical.

Golden Historical Society, Inc.; Box 148; Golden, IL 62339; (217) 696-2360; www.windmill.org.

Great River Genealogical Society; c/o Quincy Public Library; 526 Jersey St.; Quincy, IL 62301-3996; www.outfitters.com/~grgs.

Greater Harvard Area Historical Society; 301 Hart Blvd.; PO Box 505; Harvard, IL 60033.

Greene County Historical and Genealogical Society; PO Box 137; Carrollton, IL 62016; www.rootsweb.com/~ilgreene/gcgs.htm.

Henry County Genealogical Society; PO Box 346; Kewanee, IL 61443; www.rootsweb.com/~ilhcgs/ index.html.

Henry Historical and Genealogical Society; 610 North St.; Henry, IL 61537.

Historical Society of OPRF; PO Box 771; Oak Park, IL 60303-0771; lipo@enteract.com; www.oprf.com/oprfhist.

Huguenot Society of Illinois; IL; rmyers6195@aol.com; www.execpc.com/~sril/ilhs.html.

Illiana Genealogical and Historical Society; PO Box 207; Danville, IL 61932.

Illinois State Archives; Margaret Cross Norton Building; Capitol Complex; Springfield, IL 62756; (217) 782-4682; www.cyberdriveillinois.com/departments/archives/archives.html.

Illinois State Genealogical Society; PO Box 10195; Springfield, IL 62791-0195; mdpulliam@prodigy.net; www.tbox.com/isgs.

Illinois State Library; Gwendolyn Brooks Building; 300 S. 2nd Street; Springfield, IL 62701-1796; (217) 785-5600; www.sos.state.il.us/library/isl/isl.html.

Iroquois County Genealogical Society; Old Courthouse Museum; 103 W. Cherry St.; Watseka, IL 60970; iroqgene@techinter.com; www.rootsweb.com/~ilicgs.

Jackson County Historical Society; 1616 Edith Street; Murphysboro, IL 62966; http://home.globaleyes.net/loganmus/JCHSEgypt.htm.

Jacksonville Area Genealogical and Historical Society; 416 S. Main St.; Jacksonville, IL 62650-2904.

Jasper County Genealogical and Historical Society; 100 S. Van Buren; Newton, IL 62448.

Jefferson County Genealogical Society; PO Box 1131; Mt. Vernon, IL 62864; www.rootsweb.com/~iljeffer/gensociety.htm.

Jersey County Historical Society; 601 N. State St.; Jerseyville, IL 62052-1103; (618) 498-3514; www.rootsweb.com/~iljersey/JCHS.htm.

Jewish Genealogical Society of Illinois; PO Box 515; Northbrook, IL 60065-0515; (847) 509-0201; jrfraz@core.com; www.jewishgen.org/jgsi.

Johnson County Genealogical and Historical Society; PO Box 1207; Vienna, IL 62995; jcghs@onecliq.net; www.johnsoncountyil.net.

Kane County Genealogical Society; PO Box 504; Geneva, IL 60134; www.rootsweb.com/~ilkcgs.

Kankakee Valley Genealogical Society; PO Box 442; Bourbonnais, IL 60914; www.kvgs.org/index.html.

Kishwaukee Genealogists; PO Box 5503; Rockford, IL 61125-0503.

Knox County Genealogical Society; PO Box 13; Galesburg, IL 61402-0013; www.rootsweb.com/~ilknox/knindex.htm.

Knox County Historical Society; PO Box 1757; Galesburg, IL 61402-1757; jward@knox.edu; http://knoxchs.homestead.com.

LaHarpe Historical and Genealogical Society; Box 289; LaHarpe, IL 61450.

Lake County, Illinois Genealogical Society; PO Box 721; Libertyville, IL 60048-0721; www.rootsweb.com/~illcgs.

Lake Defiance! Chapter, ILSSAR; IL; LtZap@aol.com.

LaSalle County Genealogical Guild; 115 West Glover St.; Ottawa, IL 61350; www.rootsweb.com/~illcgg.

Lawrence County Genealogical Society; R #1, Box 44; Bridgeport, IL 62417.

Lee County Genealogical Society; PO Box 6; Dixon, IL 61021-0063; www.rootsweb.com/~illee.

Lemont Area Historical Society; PO Box 126; Lemont, IL 60439; Barbb1938@cs.com; www.township.com/lemont/historical.

Lexington Genealogical and Historical Society; 318 W. Main St.; Lexington, IL 61753.

Lithuanian American Genealogy Society; c/o Balzekas Museum of Lithuanian Culture; 6500 Pul; Chicago, IL 60629-5136; http://feefhs.org/baltic/lt/frg-lags.html.

Macoupin County Genealogical Society; PO Box 95; Staunton, IL 62088-0095; www.rootsweb.com/~ilmacoup/m_gensoc.htm.

Madison County Genealogical Society; PO Box 631; Edwardsville, IL 62025-0631; www.plantnet.com/mcgs/.

Marion County Genealogical and Historical Society; PO Box 342; Salem, IL 62881.

Marissa Historical and Genealogical Society; PO Box 27; Marissa, IL 62257.

Marshall County Historical Society; 566 N. High St.; Lacon, IL 61540.

Mascoutah Historical Society; 306 W. Main; Mascoutah, IL 62258; www.mascoutah.com/Historical/webpg.htm.

Mason County Genealogical & Historical Society; PO Box 446; Havana, IL 62644-0446; www.havana.lib.il.us/community/mcghs.html.

Massac County Genealogical Society; PO Box 1043; Metropolis, IL 62960; debala715@yahoo.com; www.rootsweb.com/~ilmcgs.

McDonough County Genealogical Society; PO Box 202; Macomb, IL 61455; www.macomb.com/mcgs.

McHenry County Historical Society; PO Box 434; Union, IL 60180; www.crystallakenet.org/mchs.

McHenry County Illinois Genealogical Society; PO Box 184; Crystal Lake, IL 60039-0184; mcigs@mcigs.org; www.mcigs.org.

McLean County Genealogical Society; PO Box 488; Normal, IL 61761.

Mennonite Historical and Genealogical Society, Illinois; PO Box 819; Metamora, IL 61548.

Mercer County Historical Society; Essley-Noble Museum; 1406 SE 2nd Ave.; Aledo, IL 61231; www.rootsweb.com/~ilmercer/mchs.htm.

Monroe County Genealogical Society; PO Box 381; Columbia, IL 62236; www.rootsweb.com/~ilmonroe/gs.htm.

Montgomery County Genealogical Society; PO Box 212; Litchfield, IL 62056.

Morgan Area Genealogical Association; 405 Jackson Parkway; Springfield, IL 62704-1923; saleguas@motion.net; www.rootsweb.com/~ilmaga/index.html.

Moultrie County Historical and Genealogical Society; PO Box 588; Sullivan, IL 61951-0588; (217) 728-2076; cardinal_61951@yahoo.com; www.354.com/bethany/genealogy.htm.

Mount Prospect Historical Society; 101 South Maple Street; Mount Prospect, IL 60056-3203; mphist@aol.com; www.mphist.org/mphshome.htm.

NARA, Great Lakes Region (Chicago); 7358 South Pulaski Road; Chicago, IL 60629-5898; (773) 581-7816; chicago.archives@nara.gov; www.archives.gov/facilities/il/chicago.html.

North Suburban Genealogical Society; Winnetka Public Library; 768 Oak St.; Winnetka, IL 60093.

Northern Illinois Chapter, AHSGR; 208 Cold Spring Ct.; Palatine, IL 60067; (847) 397-7604; Cgorr@aol.com; www.ahsgr.org/ilnorthe.html.

Northwest Suburban Council of Genealogists; PO Box AC; Mt. Prospect, IL 60056.

Odell Historical and Genealogical Society; PO Box 82; Odell, IL 60460.

Ogle County Historical Society; 6th and Franklin Streets; Oregon, IL 61061.

Ogle County Illinois Genealogical Society; PO Box 251; Oregon, IL 61061.

Palatines to America, Illinois Chapter; PO 9638; Peoria, IL 61612-9638.

Peoria County Genealogical Society; PO Box 1489; Peoria, IL 61655-1489; www.usgennet.org/usa/il/county/peoria/pcgs.html.

Piatt County Historical and Genealogical Society.; PO Box 111; Monticello, IL 61856.

Pike and Calhoun Counties Genealogical Society; Box 104; Pleasant Hill, IL 62366; www.intersurf.com/~johnjanr/hsp.htm.

Polish Genealogical Society of America; 984 N. Milwaukee Ave.; Chicago, IL 60622; PGSAmerica@aol.com; www.pgsa.org.

Putnam County Historical Society; PO Box 74; Hennepin, IL 61327; www.rootsweb.com/~ilputnam/pchs.htm.

Randolph County Genealogical Society; 600 State St., Room 306; Chester, IL 62233; www.rootsweb.com/~ilrcgs/index.htm.

Richland County Genealogical and Historical Society; Box 202; Olney, IL 62450.

Rock Island County Historical Society; 822 - 11th Avenue; Moline, IL 61265-1221; RICHS@netexpress.net; www.netexpress.net/~richs.

Rock Island County Illinois Genealogical Society; PO Box 3912; Rock Island, IL 61204-3912; (309) 787-1826; rujan2000&at;aol.com; www.rootsweb.com/~ilbgsrim/index.html.

Rogers Park / West Ridge Historical Society; 6424 N. Western; Chicago, IL 60645-5422; mjdoyle44@aol.com; www.wecaretoo.com/Organizations/IL/rpwrhs.html.

Saline County Genealogical Society; PO Box 4; Harrisburg, IL 62946.

Sangamon County Genealogical Society; PO Box 1829; Springfield, IL 62705-1829; dbutton2@aol.com; www.rootsweb.com/~ilsangam/scgs/scgs.htm.

SAR, Illinois Society; PO Box 2314; Naperville, IL 60567.

Schuyler Jail Museum Genealogical and Historical Society; 2005 Congress; Rushville, IL 62681.

Shelby County Historical and Genealogical Society; 151 South Washington; Shelbyville, IL 62565; shgensoc@bmmhnet.com; www.shelbycohistgen.org.

Sons of Union Veterans of the Civil War, Illinois Dept.; PO Box 2314; Naperville, IL 60567.

South Suburban Genealogical and Historical Society; 3000 W. 170th Place; Hazel Crest, IL 60429-1174; (708) 335-3340; SSGHS@usa.net; www.rootsweb.com/~ssghs.

St. Clair County, Illinois Genealogical Society; PO Box 431; Belleville, IL 62222-0431; www.compu-type.net/rengen/stclair/stchome.htm.

Stark County Genealogical Society; 207 West Main St.; PO Box 83; Toulon, IL 61483.

Stark County Historical Society; West Jefferson; Toulon, IL 61483.

Stephen Decatur Chapter, NSDAR; Decatur, IL; decaturdar@aol.com; www.rootsweb.com/~ilsdcdar.

Stephenson County Genealogical Society; PO Box 514; Freeport, IL 61032.

Stephenson County Historical Society; 110 Coates Place; Freeport, IL 61032.

Sterling-Rock Falls Historical Society; 1005 E. 3rd St.; PO Box 65; Sterling, IL 61081.

Swedish-American Historical Society, The; 3225 W. Foster Ave, Box 48; Chicago, IL 60625; (773) 583-5722; info@swedishamericanhist.org; www.swedishamericanhist.org.

Tazewell County Genealogical & Historical Society; PO Box 312; 719 N. 11th St.; Pekin, IL 61555-0312; tcghs@email.com; www.rootsweb.com/~iltcghs.

The Czech & Slovak American Genealogy Society of Illinois; PO Box 313; Sugar Grove, IL 60554; HOSNA@worldnet.att.net; www.csagsi.org.

Thornton Township Historical Society/Genealogical Society; 154 E. 154th St.; Harvey, IL 60426.

Tinley Moraine Genealogists; PO Box 521; Tinley Park, IL 60477.

Union County Genealogical/Historical Research Committee; 101 East Spring St.; Anna, IL 62906.

United States of America Railroad Retirement Board; 844 Rush St.; Chicago, IL 60611; www.rrb.gov.

Warren County Illinois Genealogical Society; PO Box 761; Monmouth, IL 61462.

White County Historical Society/Mary Smith Fay Genealogy Library; 203 North Church; PO Box 121; Carmi, IL 62821; (618) 382-8425; WCHSgenealogylib@surffirst.net; www.rootsweb.com/~ilwcohs.

Whiteside County Genealogists; Box 145; Sterling, IL 61081.

Will-Grundy Counties Genealogical Society; PO Box 24; Willmington, IL 60481.

Williamson County Historical Society; 105 South Van Buren St.; Marion, IL 62959; charla@thewchs.com; www.thewchs.com/index.htm.

Winnebago and Boone Counties Genealogical Society; PO Box 10166; Rockford, IL 61131-0166.

Winnetka Historical Society; PO Box 365; Winnetka, IL 60093; www.northstarnet.org/wnkhome/history/index.html.

Zion Genealogical Society; c/o the Zion Benton Public Library; 2400 Gabriel Av; Zion, IL 60099; ZionGenSoc@aol.com; http://nsn.nslsilus.org/wkkhome/zion/index.html.

Bibliography and Record Sources

General

American State Papers: Documents, Legislative and Executive of the Congress of the United States. Salt Lake City; La Crosse, Wisconsin: Brookhaven Press. Salt Lake City: Filmed by the Genealogical Society of Utah, 1959, 1975, 1977.

Bailey, Robert E. *A Summary Guide to Local Governmental Records in the Illinois Regional Archives.* Springfield, Illinois: Illinois State Archives, Office of the Secretary of State, 1992.

Bailey, Robert E. *Descriptive Inventory of the Archives of the State of Illinois.* 2nd ed. Springfield, Illinois: Office of the Secretary of State, Illinois State Archives, 1997.

Bateman, Newton and Paul Selby. *Historical Encyclopedia of Illinois.* 2 vols. Chicago, Illinois: Munsell, 1913

Beckstead, Gayle and Mary Lou Kozub. *Searching in Illinois: A Reference Guide to Public and Private Records.* Costa Mesa, California: ISC Publications, 1984.

Buck, Solon Justus. *Travel and Description, 1765–1865: Together With a List of County Histories, Atlases and Biographical Collections and a List of Territorial and State Laws.* Springfield, Illinois: Trustees of the Illinois State Historical Library, 1914.

Carrier, Lois A. *Illinois: Crossroads of a Continent.* 1993. Galveston, Texas: Frontier Press, 1993.

Church of Jesus Christ of Latter-day Saints. Historical Department. *Index to Journal History*. Salt Lake City: Filmed by the Historical Dept., 1973. 58 microfilm.

Clayton, John. *The Illinois Fact Book and Historical Almanac, 1673–1968*. Carbondale, Illinois: Southern Illinois University Press, 1970.

Coffey, Achilles. *A Brief History of the Regular Baptists, Principally of Southern Illinois*. Elizabethtown, Illinois: Nelson Pub., 1984.

Davidson, Alexander and Bernard Stuve. *A Complete History of Illinois from 1673 to 1884*. Springfield, Illinois: H. W. Roker, 1884.

Dunne, Edward Fitzsimons. *Illinois, The Heart of the Nation*. 5 vols. Chicago: Lewis Pub., 1933.

Eddy, Thomas Mears. *The Patriotism of Illinois: A Record of the Civil and Military History of the State in the War for the Union, With a History of the Campaigns in Which Illinois Soldiers Have Been Conspicuous, Sketches of Distinguished Officers, The Roll of the Illustrious Dead, Movements of the Sanitary and Christian Commissions*. 2 vols. Chicago: Clarke, 1865.

Encyclopedia of Biography of Illinois. 3 vols. Chicago: Century Publishing and Engraving Co., 1892–1902.

Ford, Governor Thomas. *A History of Illinois from Its Commencement as a State in 1818 to 1847*. (1854) Reprint. Galveston, Texas: Frontier Press, 1995.

Genealogical Index of the Newberry Library, Chicago. 4 vols. Boston: G. K. Hall, 1960.

Genealogical Sources in Chicago, Illinois 1835–1900. Chicago: Chicago Genealogical Society, 1982.

Gilman, Agness Geneva. *Who's Who in Illinois, Women, Makers of History*. Chicago: The Eclectic Publishers, 1927.

Gooldy, Pat and Ray Gooldy. *Manual for Illinois Genealogical Research*. Indianapolis, Indiana: Ye Olde Genealogie Shoppe, 1994.

Hastings, Robert J. ed. *We Were There: An Oral History of the Illinois Baptist State Association, 1907–1976*. Springfield, Illinois: The Association, ©1976.

Haynes, Nathaniel Smith. *History of the Disciples of Christ in Illinois, 1819–1914*. Cincinnati: Standard Pub. Co., 1915.

Heckman, John. *Brethren in Northern Illinois and Wisconsin*. Elgin, Illinois: Brethren Publishing House, 1941.

Historical Records Survey (Illinois). *Guide to Church Vital Statistics Records in Illinois*. Chicago: The Survey, 1942.

Historical Records Survey (Illinois). *Guide to Depositories of Manuscript Collections in Illinois (preliminary edition)*. Chicago: Illinois Historical Records Survey Project, 1940.

Hoffmann, John. *A Guide to the History of Illinois*. New York: Greenwood Press, 1991.

Howard, Richard P. *Illinois: A History of the Prairie State*. Grand Rapids, Michigan: William B. Eerdmans Publishing Co., 1972.

Illinois Biographical Dictionary: People of All Times and All Places Who Have Been Important to the History and Life of The State. Reprint. New York: Somerset, 1993.

Illinois Libraries: Newspapers in the Illinois State Historical Library. Springfield, Illinois: Illinois State Library, 1979–1991.

Illinois Quaker Meeting Records. Kokomo, Indiana: Shelby Pub. and Printing, 1996.

Illinois Research Outline. Series U.S.-States, no. 14. Salt Lake City: Family History Library, 1988.

Illinois State Genealogical Society. *Guide to Illinois Researchers & Local Societies*. Springfield, Illinois: Illinois State Genealogical Society, 1996.

Illinois State Genealogical Society. *Illinois Libraries with Genealogical Collections*. Reprint. Springfield, Illinois: Illinois State Genealogical Society, 1993.

Illinois State Genealogical Society. *Prairie Pioneers*. Springfield, Illinois: Illinois State Genealogical Society.

Irons, Victoria, and Patricia C. Brennan. *Descriptive Inventory of the Archives of the State of Illinois*. Springfield, Illinois: Illinois State Archives, 1978.

Kimball, Stanley B. *Sources of Mormon History in Illinois, 1839–1848: An Annotated Catalog of The Microfilm Collection at Southern Illinois University*. 2nd ed. Carbondale, Illinois: Central Publications, Southern Illinois University, 1966.

Lunde, Mrs. O. B. *Illinois State Genealogical Society Surname Index*. Decatur, Illinois: Illinois State Genealogical Society, 1981.

McCormick, Henry. *The Women of Illinois*. Illinois: Pantagraph Printing and Stationery, 1913.

Melton, J. Gordon. *Log Cabins to Steeples: The Complete Story of the United Methodist Way in Illinois Including All Constituent Elements of the United Methodist Church*. Illinois: Commissions on Archives and History; Northern, Central and Southern Illinois Conferences, 1974.

Men of Illinois. Chicago: Halliday Witherspoon, 1902.

Newspapers in the Illinois State Historical Library. Springfield, Illinois: Illinois State Historical Library, 1964–1970.

Norton, Augustus T. *History of the Presbyterian Church in the State of Illinois: vol. 1*. St. Louis: W.S. Bryan, 1879, 1879.

Notable Men of Illinois and Their State. Chicago: Chicago Daily Journal, 1912.

O'Hara, Margaret. *Finding Your Chicago Ancestor . . .* n.p.: M. O'Hara, 1981.

Pease, Theodore Calvin. *The County Archives in the State of Illinois*. Springfield, Illinois: Trustees of the Illinois State Historical Library, 1915.

Pease, Theodore Calvin. *The Frontier State (IL), 1818–1848*. Springfield, Illinois: Illinois Centennial Commission, 1918.

Pennewell, Almer M. *The Methodist Movement in Northern Illinois*. Sycamore, Illinois: The Sycamore Tribune, 1942.

Plains People; the Midwest (Indiana, Illinois, Iowa, Missouri): Research Sources and Bibliographies. Seattle, Washington: Fiske Genealogical Foundation, 1990.

Records Relating to the Mormons in Illinois, 1839–1848 (dated 1840–1852) and Memorials of Mormons to Congress, 1840–1844. Washington: National Archives. Central Plains Region, 1964.

Robson, Charles. *The Biographical Encyclopedia of Illinois of the Nineteenth Century*: Philadelphia: Galaxy Pub. Co., 1875.

Schweitzer, George K. *Illinois Genealogical Research*. Knoxville, Tennessee: George K. Schweitzer, 1996.

Scott, Franklin William. *Newspapers and Periodicals of Illinois, 1814–1879*. Springfield, Illinois: Trustees of the Illinois State Historical Library, 1910.

Smith, George Washington. *History of Illinois and Her People*. 6 vols. Chicago: American Historical Society, 1927.

Smith, Willard H. *Mennonites in Illinois*. Scottdale, Pennsylvania: Herald Press, 1983.

Szucs, Loretto D. *Chicago and Cook County: A Guide to Research*. Salt Lake City: Ancestry, 1996.

The United States Biographical Dictionary and Portrait Gallery of Eminent and Self-made Men: Illinois Volume. 2 vols. Chicago and New York: American Biographical Publishing Co., 1876.

Tregillis, Helen Cox. *The Indians of Illinois: A History and Genealogy*. Decorah, Iowa: Anundsen Publishing Co., 1983.

Turnbaugh, Roy C. *A Guide to County Records in the Illinois Regional Archives*. Springfield, Illinois: Illinois State Archives, 1983.

Volkel, Lowell M. *Illinois Libraries with Genealogical Collections*. Springfield, Illinois: Illinois State Genealogical Society, 1992.

Volkel, Lowell M., and Marjorie Smith. *How to Research a Family with Illinois Roots*. Indianapolis: Ye Olde Genealogie Shoppe, 1977.

White, Elizabeth Pearson. "Illinois Settlers and Their Origins." *National Genealogical Society Quarterly*, vol. 74, no. 1 (March 1986), pp. 7–17.

Wolf, Joseph C. *A Reference Guide for Genealogical and Historical Research in Illinois*. Detroit: Detroit Society for Genealogical Research, 1967.

Atlases, Maps and Gazetteers

Adams, James N., comp. *Illinois Place Names*. Springfield, Illinois: Illinois State Historical Society, 1989.

Beck, Lewis Caleb. *A Gazetteer of the States of Illinois and Missouri. . . 1823*. Reprint. New York: Arno Press, 1975.

Carpentier, Charles F. *Counties of Illinois: Their Origin and Evolution. . . .* Springfield: State Journal Co., 1919.

Illinois Atlas & Gazetteer. Freeport, Maine: DeLorme Mapping, 1991.

Kelly, Sheila. *County and Township Gazetteer; Notes on the Location of Illinois County Seats*. Springfield, Illinois: Illinois State Archives, 1988.

Maps of Illinois Counties in 1876: Together with the Plat of Chicago and Other Cities. 1876. Reprint. Knightstown, Indiana: Mayhill Pub, 1972.

Origin and Evolution of Illinois Counties. [S.l.]: State of Illinois, 1989.

Peck, J. M. *A Gazetteer of Illinois in Three Parts: Containing a General View of the State, A General View of Each County, and a Particular Description of Each Town, Settlement, Stream, Prairie, Bottom, Bluff, etc. Alphabetically Arranged*. 2nd ed. Entirely rev., corrected and enl. Philadelphia: Grigg & Elliott, 1837. Reprint with a new place-name and index. Bowie, Maryland: Heritage Books, 1993.

Powell, Paul. *Counties of Illinois: Their Origin and Evolution with Twenty-Three Maps Showing the Original and the Present Boundary Lines of Each County of the State*. Springfield, Illinois: Secretary of State, 1972.

Vogel, Virgil J. *Indian Place Names in Illinois*. Springfield, Illinois: Illinois State Historical Library, 1963.

Warner and Beers. *Maps of Illinois Counties in 1876, Together with the Plan of Chicago and Other Cities and a Sampling of Illustrations*. Chicago: Union Atlas Co., 1876. Reprinted as *Atlas of the State of Illinois to Which Are Added Various General Maps and Illustrations*. Knightstown, Indiana: Mayhill Publications, 1972.

Censuses

Available Census Records and Census Substitutes

Federal Census 1820, 1830, 1840, 1850, 1860, 1870, 1880, 1900, 1910, 1920, 1930

Federal Mortality Schedules 1850, 1860, 1870, 1880

State/Territorial Census 1810, 1818, 1820, 1825, 1835, 1845, 1855, 1865

Dollarhide, William. *The Census Book: A Genealogist's Guide to Federal Census Facts, Schedules and Indexes*. Bountiful, Utah: Heritage Quest, 1999.

Genealogical Research Series Pamphlet No. 5 State Census Records. Springfield, Illinois: Illinois State Archives [n.d,] online at www.sos.state.il.us/departments/archives/research_series/rseries5.html.

Kemp, Thomas Jay. *The American Census Handbook*. Wilmington, Delaware: Scholarly Resources, Inc., 2001.

Lainhart, Ann S. *State Census Records*. Baltimore: Genealogical Publishing Co., Inc., 1992.

Name Index to Early Illinois Records. Springfield, Illinois: Illinois State Archives, 1975. 248 microfilm.

Szucs, Loretto Dennis and Matthew Wright. *Finding Answers in U.S. Census Records*. Ancestry Publishing, 2001.

Illinois

Thorndale, William. *Map Guide to the U.S. Federal Census, 1790–1920.* Baltimore: Genealogical Publishing Co., 1987.

Court Records, Probate and Wills

Clayton, John. *The Illinois Fact Book and Historical Almanac, 1673–1968.* Carbondale, Illinois: Southern Illinois University Press, 1970.

Crossley, Frederic Bears. *Courts and Lawyers.* 3 vols. Chicago: American Historical Society, 1916.

Edgar, Jim. *Illinois Probate Act and Related Laws, Effective January 5, 1988.* Rev. St. Paul, Minnesota: West Publishing Co., 1988.

Genealogical Research Series Pamphlet No. 2 Probate Records. Springfield, Illinois: Illinois State Archives, n.d. online at www.sos.state.il.us/departments/archives/research_series/rseries2.html

Palmer, John. *The Bench and Bar of Illinois: Historical and Reminiscent.* 2 vols. Chicago: Lewis Pub., 1899.

Rubincam, Milton. *"Migrations to Illinois, 1673–1860."* In *Illinois State Genealogical Society Quarterly,* vol. 4, no. 3 (October 1972), pp. 127–34. Springfield, Illinois: The Society, 1969–.

Territory of Illinois. County Court. *Court Records, 1796–1818.* Springfield, Illinois: Office of the Secretary of State, Micrographics Division, Source Documents Unit, 1986

Emigration, Immigration, Migration and Naturalization

United States. Circuit Court (Illinois: Northern District). *Oaths of Allegiance, 1872–1906.* Microfilm of original records housed in the Chicago Branch of the National Archives, Chicago, Illinois. Salt Lake City: Filmed by the Genealogical Society of Utah, 1985.

United States. Circuit Court (Illinois: Northern District). *Petitions for Naturalization, 1906–1911.* Microfilm of original records housed in the Chicago Branch of the National Archives, Salt Lake City: Filmed by the Genealogical Society of Utah, 1985. 10 microfilm.

United States. Circuit Court (Illinois: Southern District). *Naturalization Records, 1856–1903.* Microfilm of original records housed in the Chicago Branch of the National Archives, Chicago, Illinois. Salt Lake City: Filmed by the Genealogical Society of Utah, 1986.

United States. District Court (Illinois: Eastern District). *Naturalization Records, 1906–1932.* Microfilm of original records housed in the Chicago Branch of the National Archives, Chicago, Illinois. Salt Lake City: Filmed by the Genealogical Society of Utah, 1986. 4 microfilm.

United States. District Court (Illinois: Northern District). *Declarations of Intentions, 1903–1931; Index, 1906–1930.* Microfilm of original records housed in the Chicago Branch of the National Archives, Chicago, Illinois. Salt Lake City: Filmed by the Genealogical Society of Utah, 1985. 45 microfilm.

United States. District Court (Illinois: Northern District). *Naturalization Petitions, 1872–1902.* Microfilm of original records housed in the Chicago Branch of the National Archives, Chicago, Illinois. Salt Lake City: Filmed by the Genealogical Society of Utah, 1985.

United States. District Court (Illinois: Northern District). *Oaths of Allegiance, 1872–1903.* Microfilm of original records housed in the Chicago Branch of the National Archives, Chicago, Illinois. Salt Lake City: Filmed by the Genealogical Society of Utah, 1985.

United States. District Court (Illinois: Northern District). *Soundex Index to Naturalization Petitions for U.S. District & Circuit Courts, Northern District of Illinois and Immigration and Naturalization Service District 9, 1840–1950.* Salt Lake City: Filmed by the Genealogical Society of Utah, 1988. 183 microfilm.

United States. District Court (Illinois: Northern District: Eastern Division). *Records of Naturalizations and Name Changes; First set, 1926–1980; Second Set, 1980–1988.* Microreproduction of original manuscripts at the United States District Court, Chicago, Illinois. Salt Lake City: Filmed by the Genealogical Society of Utah, 1991–1992. 149 microfilm.

United States. District Court (Illinois: Southern District: Peoria). *Declarations of Intention, 1907–1936; Petitions for Naturalization, 1908–1930; Index, 1905–1954.* Microfilm of original records housed in the Chicago Branch of the National Archives, Chicago, Illinois. Salt Lake City: Filmed by the Genealogical Society of Utah, 1986. 13 microfilm.

United States. District Court (Illinois: Southern District: Springfield). *Naturalization Records, 1906–1952.* Microfilm of original records housed in the Chicago Branch of the National Archives, Chicago, Illinois. Salt Lake City: Filmed by the Genealogical Society of Utah, 1986. 3 microfilm.

Land and Property

Carlson, Theodore Leonard. *The Illinois Military Tract: A Study of Land Occupation, Utilization and Tenure.* Urbana: University of Illinois Press, 1951.

Genealogical Research Series Pamphlet No. 1, Land Sale Records. Springfield, Illinois: Illinois State Archives, n.d. online at www.sos.state.il.us/departments/archives/research_series/rseries1.html

Hone, Wade E. *Land and Property Research in the United States.* Salt Lake City: Ancestry Incorporated, 1997.

Illinois State Genealogical Society. *Hames Collection: Pre-Statehood Land Records.* Springfield, Illinois: Illinois State Genealogical Society.

Illinois. Auditor's Office. *Early Illinois Land Records, 1829–1865.* Springfield, Illinois: Office of the Secretary of State, Micrographics Division, Documents Unit, 1960.

Murphy, Charla, Mary Jo Moore, and Jean Burke, comps. *Original Lands Grants, 1824–1870*. Marion, Illinois: Williamson County Historical Society, 1997.

Record of the Services of Illinois Soldiers. . . . Springfield, Illinois: H. W. Rokker, 1882.

United States. Bureau of Land Management. *Card Files*. Microfilm of original card files located at the Bureau of Land Management's Eastern States Office in Alexandria, Virginia. Washington, D.C.: Bureau of Land Management, [19–]. 160 microfilm.

United States. General Land Office. *Federal Land Records, Tract Books of Illinois, 1826–1873*. Springfield, Illinois: Filmed by Office of the Secretary of State, Record Management Division, 1966. 19 microfilm.

United States. General Land Office. *Public Domain Sales Land Tract Record Listing, 1814–1925 (Index)*. Springfield, Illinois: Illinois State Archives, 1984.

United States. Veterans Administration. *War of 1812, Military Bounty Land Warrants, 1815–1858*. Washington, D.C.: The National Archives, 1971.

Volkel, Lowell M. *War of 1812 Bounty Land Patents in Illinois*. Thompson, Illinois: Heritage House, 1977.

Walker, James D. *War of 1812 Bounty Lands in Illinois*. Thomson, Illinois: Heritage House, 1977.

Military

Barnet, James. *The Martyrs and Heroes of Illinois in the Great Rebellion: Biographical Sketches*. Reprint. Bethesda, Maryland.: University Publications of America, 1993.

Fighting Men of Illinois: An Illustrated Historical Biography. Reprint. Tucson, Arizona: W. C. Cox, 1974.

Genealogical Research Series Pamphlet No. 3, Military Records. Springfield, Illinois: Illinois State Archives, n.d. online at www.sos.state.il.us/departments/archives/research_series/rseries3.html.

Hicken. *Illinois in the Civil War*. Galveston, Texas: Frontier Press, 1991.

Illinois Adjutant General's Office. *Record of the Service of Illinois Soldiers in the Black Hawk War, 1831–1832, and the Mexican War, 1846–1848*. Springfield, Illinois: H. W. Q. Rokker, 1882.

Illinois Soldier's and Sailor's Home at Quincy. 2 vols. Thomson, Illinois: Heritage House, 1980.

Illinois State Genealogical Society. *Remembering Illinois Veterans*. Springfield, Illinois: Illinois State Genealogical Society, 1992.

Illinois. Adjutant General. *Report of the Adjutant General of the State of Illinois*. Springfield, Illinois: Rokker, 1886.

Illinois. Assessors. *Militia Rolls, 1862–1863*. Salt Lake City: Filmed by the Genealogical Society of Utah, 1977.

Northcott, Dennis and Thomas Brooks. *Grand Army of the Republic, Department of Illinois, Transcription of the Death Rolls, 1879–1947*. 2003.

Publishers Subscription Co., ed. *Fighting Men of Illinois: An Illustrated Historical Biography*. Tucson, Arizona: W. C. Cox, 1974.

Roster of Men from Illinois Who Served in the United States Navy During the War of the Rebellion, 1861–1866. Salt Lake City: Genealogical Society of Utah, 1974, 1975.

Smith, John H. *Illinois Regiment*. Indianapolis, Indiana: Ye Olde Genealogie Shoppe.

Soldiers' and Patriots' Biographical Album: Containing Biographies and Portraits of Soldiers and Loyal Citizens in the American Conflict, Together with the Great Commanders of the Union Army, Also a History of the Organizations Growing Out of the War: Union Veteran Publishing Co., 1892.

Soldiers Burial Places in State of Illinois for Wars, 1774–1898. Microfilm of original record in Springfield, Illinois at the Illinois Veterans Commission. Salt Lake City: Filmed by the Genealogical Society of Utah, 1975. 31 microfilm.

Soldiers of the American Revolution Buried in Illinois. Springfield, Illinois: Illinois State Genealogical Society, 1975.

United States. Selective Service System. *Illinois, World War I Selective Service System Draft Registration Cards, 1917–1918*. National Archives Microfilm Publications, M1509. Washington, D.C.: National Archives, 1987–1988.

Walker, Harriet J. *Revolutionary Soldiers Buried in Illinois*. (1918) Reprint. Baltimore: Clearfield Company, 1992.

Walker, Harriet J. *Soldiers of the American Revolution Buried in Illinois: From the Journal of the Illinois State Historical Society*. Baltimore: Genealogical Publishing Co., 1967. Clearfield Co.

White, Virgil D., trans. *Index to War of 1812 Pension Files*. 1st Ed. Waynesboro, Tennessee: National Historical Pub. Co., 1989.

Wilson, James Grant. *Biographical Sketches of Illinois Officers Engaged in the War Against the Rebellion of 1861*. Chicago: James Barnet, 1862.

Vital and Cemetery Records

Cemetery Records of Illinois. 13 vols. Typescript. Salt Lake City: Genealogical Society of Utah, 1960–1966.

Cole, Arthur Charles. *The Era of the Civil War: 1848–1870*. (1919) Reprint. Galveston, Texas: Frontier Press, 1987.

Department of Veterans Affairs. *Veterans National Cemetery Records, Illinois*. Salt Lake City: Filmed by the Genealogical Society of Utah, 1981.

Guide to Public Vital Statistics Records in Illinois. 1941. Reprint. Thompson, Illinois: Heritage House, 1976.

Illinois State Genealogical Society. Devanny, Mrs. John S., comp. *Soldiers of the American Revolution Buried in Illinois*. Springfield, Illinois: 1975.

Illinois State Genealogical Society. *Illinois Marriage Records Index: 1763–1916*. Springfield, Illinois: Filmed by the Archives and the Society, 1994. 94 microfiche.

Illinois Veterans Commission (Springfield, Illinois). *Soldier's Burial Places in the State of Illinois for Wars, 1774–1898*. Springfield: Illinois Veterans Commission, 1975. Microfilm, 31 rolls.

Illinois. Department of Public Health. State Registrar. *Illinois Births, Prior to Act, Excluding Chicago: 1842, 1849–1872*. Microreproduction of original manuscripts at the Public Board of Health, Springfield, Illinois. Salt Lake City: Filmed by the Genealogical Society of Utah, 1995. 6 microfilm.

Illinois. Public Board of Health. Archives. *Death Certificates for the State of Illinois, 1916–1945, Excluding Chicago with the Exception of Stillbirths: Index, 1916–1938*. Microreproduction of original at the Public Board of Health, Archives, Springfield, Illinois. Salt Lake City: Filmed by the Genealogical Society of Utah, 1988–1992. 666 microfilm.

Index of Illinois Marriages, Earliest to 1900. Springfield, Illinois: Illinois State Genealogy Society, 1997. CD-ROM.

Mortality Schedules of Illinois, 1850–1880. Microfilm copy of original records located at the National Archives, Washington D.C. Illinois: Records Management Division, Secretary of State's Office, 1967. 7 microfilm.

Newbill, Leona Hopper. *Cook County, Illinois Marriage License Records, 1870–1880*. Salt Lake City: Filmed by the Genealogical Society of Utah, 1970.

Newspaper Research Committee, comp. *Vital Records from Chicago Newspapers*. Chicago: Chicago Genealogy. Society, 1971–.

Sanders, Walters. *Marriages from Illinois Counties*. 6 vols. Litchfield, Illinois: Walter Sanders, 1976.

Soldiers Burial Places in State of Illinois for Wars, 1774–1898. Salt Lake City: Filmed by the Genealogical Society of Utah, 1975.

Vangeison, Aaron. *Guide to Public Vital Statistics Records in Illinois*. Thomson, Illinois: Heritage House, 1976.

Vital Records from Chicago Newspapers, Volume 1–7, 1833–1848. Chicago: Chicago Genealogical Society, Newspaper Research Committee, 1971.

Volkel, Lowell. *Illinois 1850 Mortality Schedule with Index*. 3 vols. Thomson, Illinois: Heritage House, 1977, 1972.

Volkel, Lowell. *Illinois 1870 Mortality Schedule with Index*. 5 vols. Indianapolis, Indiana: Heritage House, 1985–1987.

Walker, Mrs. Harriet J. *Revolutionary Soldiers Buried in Illinois*. Los Angeles: Standard Printing Co., 1917. Reprint. Baltimore: Genealogical Publishing Co., 1967. Clearfield Co. reprint 1999.

County Website	Map Index	Date Created	Parent County or Territory From Which Organized Address/Details
Adams www.co.adams.il.us/	I2	**13 Jan 1825**	**Pike** Adams County; 507 Vermont St; Quincy, IL 62301-2934; Ph. (217) 277-2150 **Details:** (County Clerk has Birth & Death Records from 1878 & Marriage Records from 1825; Clerk Circuit Court has Divorce, Probate & Court Records)
Alexander www.rootsweb.com/~ilalexan/alexander.htm	Q7	**4 Mar 1819**	**Johnson** Alexander County; 2000 Washington Ave; Cairo, IL 62914-1717; Ph. (618) 734-7000 **Details:** (County Clerk has Birth & Death Records from 1878, Marriage & Land Records from 1819; Clerk Circuit Court has Divorce, Probate & Court Records)
Bond www.rootsweb.com/~ilbond/	L7	**4 Jan 1817**	**Madison** Bond County; 203 W College; Greenville, IL 62246-0407; Ph. (618) 664-0449 **Details:** (County Clerk has Birth & Death Records from 1877, Marriage Records from 1817, Land Records from 1870 & Military Discharge Records; Clerk Circuit Court has Divorce, Probate & Court Records)

County	Map	Date	Parent County or Territory From Which Organized
Website	Index	Created	Address/Details

Boone   **B8**   **4 Mar 1837**   **Winnebago**
www.rootsweb.com/~ilboone/boone.htm

Boone County; 601 N Main St; Belvidere, IL 61008-2600;
Ph. (815) 544-3103
Details: (County Clerk has Birth, Marriage & Death Records from 1877 & Land Records from 1838; Clerk Circuit Court has Divorce, Probate & Court Records)

Brown   **I3**   **1 Feb 1839**   **Schuyler**
www.rootsweb.com/~ilbrown/brown.htm

Brown County; 1 Court St; Mount Sterling, IL 62353-1241;
Ph. (217) 773-3421
Details: (County Clerk has Birth Records from 1860, Marriage Records from 1841, Death Records from 1878, Land Records from 1817 & Military Discharge Records from 1918; Clerk Circuit Court has Divorce, Probate, Court & Naturalization Records)

Bureau   **D6**   **28 Feb 1837**   **Putnam**
www.rootsweb.com/~ilgenweb/lists/bureaulist.htm

Bureau County; 700 S Main St; Princeton, IL 61356;
Ph. (815) 875-2014
Details: (County Clerk has Birth & Death Records from 1878, Marriage & Land Records from 1837 & Military Records from 1865; Clerk Circuit Court has Divorce, Probate, Court & Naturalization Records)

Calhoun   **K3**   **10 Jan 1825**   **Pike**
www.rootsweb.com/~ilcalhou/

Calhoun County; 102 County Rd; Hardin, IL 62047-0000;
Ph. (618) 576-2351
Details: (County Clerk has Birth & Death Records from 1877, Marriage & Land Records from 1825)

Carroll   **B5**   **22 Feb 1839**   **Jo Daviess**
www.serve.com/bmosher/ilcr/carroll.htm

Carroll County; Rt 78 & Rapp Rd; Mount Carroll, IL 61053-0000;
Ph. (815) 244-0221
Details: (County Clerk has Birth & Death Records from 1877, Marriage Records from 1839 & Land Records)

Cass   **I4**   **3 Mar 1837**   **Morgan**
www.rootsweb.com/~ilcass/cass.htm

Cass County; 100 E Springfield St; Virginia, IL 62691-0000;
Ph. (217) 452-7217
Details: (County Clerk has Birth Records from 1860, Marriage Records from 1837, Death Records from 1878 & Land Records; Clerk Circuit Court has Divorce, Probate & Court Records)

Champaign   **H10**   **20 Feb 1833**   **Vermilion**
http://node-02.advancenet.net/~coclerk/

Champaign County; 1776 E Washington St; Urbana, IL 61802;
Ph. (217) 384-3720
Details: (County Clerk has Birth & Death Records from 1878 & Marriage Records from 1833; Clerk Circuit Court has Divorce, Probate & Court Records; Recorder of Deeds has Land & Military Records)

Christian   **J7**   **1 Feb 1840**   **Sangamon, Shelby**
www.rootsweb.com/~ilchrist/

Christian County; 101 S Main St; Taylorville, IL 62568-1599;
Ph. (217) 824-4969
Details: (Formerly Dane County. Name changed to Christian 1 Feb 1840) (County Clerk has Birth & Death Records from 1878, Marriage Records from 1840 & Land Records from 1856; Clerk Circuit Court has Divorce, Probate & Court Records from 1875)

County Website	Map Index	Date Created	Parent County or Territory From Which Organized Address/Details
Clark www.clarkcountyil.org/	**K11**	**22 Mar 1819**	**Crawford** Clark County; 501 Archer Ave; Marshall, IL 62441; Ph. (217) 826-8311 **Details:** (County Clerk has Birth & Death Records from 1877, Marriage Records from 1819 & Land Records from 1818; Clerk Circuit Court has Divorce, Probate & Court Records)
Clay www.rootsweb.com/~ilclay/	**M9**	**23 Dec 1824**	**Wayne, Lawrence, Fayette** Clay County; County Courthouse; PO Box 160; Louisville, IL 62858-0000; Ph. (618) 665-3626 **Details:** (County Clerk has Birth, Death & Burial Records from 1878, Marriage Records from 1824, Land Records from 1825 & Military Discharge Records; Clerk Circuit Court has Divorce, Probate & Court Records)
Clinton www.rootsweb.com/~ilclint2/	**M6**	**27 Dec 1824**	**Washington, Bond, Fayette, Crawford** Clinton County; 851 Franklin; PO Box 308; Carlyle, IL 62231-0000; Ph. (618) 594-2464 **Details:** (County Clerk has Birth & Death Records from 1877, Marriage Records from 1825 & Land Records from 1818; Clerk Circuit Court has Divorce, Probate & Court Records)
Coles www.rootsweb.com/~ilcoles/coles.htm	**J10**	**25 Dec 1830**	**Clark, Edgar** Coles County; 6th & Monroe St; PO Box 227; Charleston, IL 61920-0207; Ph. (217) 348-0501 **Details:** (County Clerk has Birth & Death Records from 1878, Marriage & Land Records from 1830)
Cook www.co.cook.il.us/	**C11**	**15 Jan 1831**	**Putnam** Cook County; PO Box 642570; Chicago, IL 60664; Ph. (312) 603-5656 **Details:** (County Vital Records has Birth, Marriage & Death Records from 1872)
Crawford www.rootsweb.com/~jadmire/ilcrawf/	**L11**	**31 Dec 1816**	**Edwards** Crawford County; One Courthouse Sq; Robinson, IL 62454-2146; Ph. (618) 546-1212 **Details:** (County Clerk has Birth & Death Records from 1877, Marriage Records from 1817, Land Records from 1816 & Burial Records from 1975; Clerk Circuit Court has Divorce, Probate & Court Records, physical certificates, old school Records & tax Records)
Cumberland www.rootsweb.com/~ilcumber/	**K10**	**2 Mar 1843**	**Coles** Cumberland County; 140 Courthouse Sq.; PO Box 146; Toledo, IL 62468; Ph. (217) 849-2631 **Details:** (Fire in 1885 destroyed all Records) (County Clerk has Marriage, Death, Birth, Burial, & Land Records from 1885; Circuit Clerk has Court, Divorce, & Probate Records from 1885)
Dane		**15 Feb 1839**	**Sangamon, Shelby** Dane County; IL **Details:** (see Christian) Name changed to Christian 1 Feb 1840

County Website	Map Index	Date Created	Parent County or Territory From Which Organized Address/Details
De Kalb www.dekalbcounty.org/	C8	4 Mar 1837	**Kane** De Kalb County; 110 E Sycamore St; Sycamore, IL 60178-1497; Ph. (815) 895-7149 **Details:** (County Clerk has incomplete Birth & Death Records 1878–1916, complete from 1916, Marriage & Land Records from 1837, Naturalization Records from 1850 & poll Records 1858–1872; Clerk Circuit Court has Divorce & Court Records from 1850 & Probate Records from 1859)
De Witt www.rootsweb.com/~ildewitt/	H8	1 Mar 1839	**Macon, McLean** De Witt County; 201 W Washington St; Clinton, IL 61727-1639; Ph. (217) 935-2119 **Details:** (County Clerk has Birth, Death & Burial Records from 1877, Marriage & Land Records from 1839; Clerk Circuit Court has Divorce, Probate & Court Records from 1839)
Douglas www.rootsweb.com/~ildougla/douglas.htm	J10	8 Feb 1859	**Coles** Douglas County; 401 S Center St; Tuscola, IL 61953-1603; Ph. (217) 253-2411 **Details:** (County Clerk has Birth, Marriage, Death & Land Records from 1859, some Burial Records & Military Discharge Records; Clerk Circuit Court has Divorce, Probate & Court Records)
Du Page www.dupageco.org/	C10	9 Feb 1839	**Cook** Du Page County; 421 N County Farm Rd; Wheaton, IL 60187-3978; Ph. (630) 682-7035 **Details:** (County Clerk has Birth & Death Records from 1879, Marriage Records from 1839, Probate & Court Records; County Recorder has Land Records)
Edgar www.rootsweb.com/~iledgar/edgar.htm	J11	3 Jan 1823	**Clark** Edgar County; 115 W Court St; Paris, IL 61944; Ph. (217) 466-7433 **Details:** (County Clerk has Birth & Death Records from 1877, Marriage Records from 1823, Probate & Land Records from 1827; Clerk Circuit Court has Divorce & Court Records)
Edwards www.rootsweb.com/~iledward/	N10	28 Nov 1814	**Madison, Gallatin** Edwards County; 50 E Main St; Albion, IL 62806-1262; Ph. (618) 445-2115 **Details:** (County Clerk has Birth & Death Records from 1877, Marriage & Land Records from 1815; Clerk Circuit Court has Divorce, Probate & Court Records)
Effingham www.co.effingham.il.us/	L9	15 Feb 1831	**Fayette, Crawford** Effingham County; 101 N 4th St; PO Box 628; Effingham, IL 62401; Ph. (217) 342-6535 **Details:** (County Clerk has Birth & Death Records from 1878 [incomplete prior to 1916], Marriage & Land Records from 1833 & Military Records from 1919; Clerk Circuit Court has Divorce, Probate & Court Records)
Fayette	L8	14 Feb 1821	**Bond, Wayne, Clark, Jefferson** Fayette County; 221 S 7th St; PO Box 401; Vandalia, IL 62471; Ph. (618) 283-5000 **Details:** (County Clerk-Recorder has Birth & Death Records from 1877, Marriage & Land Records from 1821 & Military Records from 1917; Clerk Circuit Court has Divorce, Probate & Court Records)

County	Map	Date	Parent County or Territory From Which Organized
Website	Index	Created	Address/Details

Ford   G10   **17 Feb 1859**   **Clark**

www.prairienet.org/fordiroq/ford.htm

Ford County; 200 W State St Rm 101; Paxton, IL 60957;
Ph. (217) 379-2721

Details: (County Clerk has Birth & Death Records from 1878, Marriage & Land Records from 1859; Clerk Circuit Court has Divorce, Probate & Court Records)

Franklin   O8   **2 Jan 1818**   **White, Gallatin**

www.rootsweb.com/~ilfrankl/index2.html

Franklin County; PO Box 607; Benton, IL 62812-2264;
Ph. (618) 438-3221

Details: (County Clerk has Birth & Death Records from 1877 & Marriage Records from 1836; Clerk Circuit Court has Probate & Court Records from 1843)

Fulton   G5   **28 Jan 1823**   **Pike**

www.outfitters.com/illinois/fulton/

Fulton County; 100 N Main St; Lewistown, IL 61542-1445;
Ph. (309) 547-3041

Details: (County Clerk has Birth & Death Records from 1878, Marriage Records from 1824 & Land Records from 1823; Clerk Circuit Court has Divorce, Probate & Court Records)

Gallatin   P10   **14 Sep 1812**   **Randolph**

www.rootsweb.com/~ilgalla2/

Gallatin County; W Lincoln Blvd; Shawneetown, IL 62984-0550;
Ph. (618) 269-3025

Details: (County Clerk has Birth & Death Records from 1878, Marriage Records from 1830 & Land Records from 1800; Clerk Circuit Court has Probate Records from 1860)

Greene   K4   **20 Jan 1821**   **Madison**

www.rootsweb.com/~ilgreene/green.htm

Greene County; 519 N Main St; Carrollton, IL 62016;
Ph. (217) 942-5443

Details: (County Clerk has Birth & Death Records from 1877, Marriage & Land Records from 1821 & Military Records from 1862; Clerk Circuit Court has Divorce, Probate, Court & Naturalization Records)

Grundy   E9   **17 Feb 1841**   **LaSalle**

www.rootsweb.com/~ilgrundy/

Grundy County; 111 E Washington St; Morris, IL 60450-2268;
Ph. (815) 941-3222

Details: (County Clerk has Birth Records from 1877, Death Records from 1878, Marriage & Land Records from 1841 & Burial Records from 1976; Clerk Circuit Court has Divorce, Probate & Court Records from 1841)

Hamilton   N9   **8 Feb 1821**   **White**

www.rootsweb.com/~ilhamilt/

Hamilton County; 100 S Jackson St.; McLeansboro, IL 62859-1489;
Ph. (618) 643-2721

Details: (County Clerk has Birth & Death Records from 1878, Marriage Records from 1821, Land Records from 1835 & Military Records from 1865)

Hancock   G2   **13 Jan 1825**   **Pike, Unorg. Terr.**

www.rootsweb.com/~ilhancoc/

Hancock County; Box 39; Carthage, IL 62321; Ph. (217) 357-3519

Details: (County Clerk has Birth & Death Records from 1914 & Marriage Records from 1829; County Recorder has Land & Military Records from 1829; Clerk Circuit Court has Divorce, Probate, Court & Naturalization Records)

County	Map	Date	Parent County or Territory From Which Organized
Website	Index	Created	Address/Details

Hardin   Q10   2 Mar 1839   **Pope**
www.rootsweb.com/~ilhardi2/
Hardin County; Main St; Elizabethtown, IL 62931;
Ph. (618) 287-2251
Details: (County Clerk has Birth, Marriage, Death & Land Records from 1884; Clerk Circuit Court has Divorce, Probate & Court Records from 1970)

Henderson   F3   20 Jan 1841   **Warren**
www.outfitters.com/illinois/henderson/
Henderson County; PO Box 308; Oquawka, IL 61469-0308;
Ph. (309) 867-2911
Details: (County Clerk has Birth, Marriage & Death Records from 1878 & Land Records from 1841; Clerk Circuit Court has Divorce, Probate & Court Records from 1841)

Henry   E5   13 Jan 1825   **Fulton**
www.henrycty.com/
Henry County; 307 W Center St; Cambridge, IL 61238;
Ph. (309) 937-3575
Details: (County Clerk has incomplete Birth & Death Records from 1877, Marriage Records from 1837 & Land Records from 1835; Clerk Circuit Court has Divorce, Probate & Court Records from 1880 & Naturalization Records 1870–1940)

Iroquois   G11   26 Feb 1833   **Vermilion**
www.prairienet.org/fordiroq/iroquois.htm
Iroquois County; 1001 E Grant St; Watseka, IL 60970-1810;
Ph. (815) 432-6960
Details: (County Clerk has Birth & Death Records from 1878, Marriage Records from 1868 & Land Records from 1835; Clerk Circuit Court has Divorce & Court Records from 1855 & Probate Records from 1865; Old Courthouse Museum may have some Records)

Jackson   P7   10 Jan 1816   **Randolph, Johnson**
www.co.jackson.il.us/
Jackson County; 1001 Walnut St; Murphysboro, IL 62966-2177;
Ph. (618) 687-7360
Details: (County Clerk has Birth, Death & Burial Records from 1872, Marriage Records from 1842 & Land Records; Clerk Circuit Court has Divorce, Probate & Court Records)

Jasper   L10   15 Feb 1831   **Clay, Crawford**
www.rootsweb.com/~iljasper/
Jasper County; 100 W Jourdan St; Newton, IL 62448-1973;
Ph. (618) 783-3124
Details: (County Clerk has Birth & Death Records from 1877, Marriage & Land Records from 1835; Clerk Circuit Court has Divorce, Probate & Court Records)

Jefferson   N8   26 Mar 1819   **Edwards, White**
www.rootsweb.com/~iljeffer/
Jefferson County; 100 S 10th St; Mount Vernon, IL 62864-4086;
Ph. (618) 244-8020
Details: (County Clerk has Birth Records from 1878, Death Records from 1877, Marriage & Land Records from 1819)

Jersey   L4   28 Feb 1839   **Greene**
www.rootsweb.com/~iljersey/
Jersey County; 102 W Pearl St; Jerseyville, IL 62052-1675;
Ph. (618) 498-5571
Details: (County Clerk has Birth & Death Records from 1878, Marriage & Land Records from 1839, Divorce Records from 1840, Probate Records from 1850 & Court Records from 1845)

County	Map	Date	Parent County or Territory From Which Organized
Website	Index	Created	Address/Details

Jo Daviess   **A5**   **17 Feb 1827**   **Henry, Mercer, Putnam**
www.rootsweb.com/~iljodavi/index.html
Jo Daviess County; 330 N Bench St; Galena, IL 61036-1828;
Ph. (815) 777-0161
Details: (County Clerk has Birth & Death Records from 1877 with a few earlier & Marriage Records from 1830; Clerk Circuit Court has Probate Records from 1830, Divorce & Court Records from 1850 & Land Records from 1828)

Johnson   **Q8**   **14 Sep 1812**   **Randolph**
www.rootsweb.com/~iljohnso/
Johnson County; 400 Court Sq; Vienna, IL 62995-0096;
Ph. (618) 658-3611
Details: (County Clerk has Birth & Death Records from 1878, Marriage Records from 1834 & Land Records from 1815; Clerk Circuit Court has Divorce, Probate & Court Records)

Kane   **C9**   **16 Jan 1836**   **LaSalle**
www.rootsweb.com/~ilkane/
Kane County; 719 S Batavia Ave; Geneva, IL 60134;
Ph. (630) 232-5951
Details: (County Clerk has Birth & Death Records from 1878 & Marriage Records from 1836; Clerk Circuit Court has Divorce & Court Records; Probate Court has Probate Records; Supervisor of Assessments has Land Records)

Kankakee   **E10**   **11 Feb 1853**   **Iroquois, Will**
www.kankakecountyclerk.com
Kankakee County; 189 E Court St; Kankakee, IL 60901;
Ph. (815) 937-2990 dhendrickson@k3county.net
Details: (County Clerk has Birth Records from 1878, Death Records from 1877 & Marriage Records from 1853; Clerk Circuit Court has Divorce, Probate, Court & Naturalization Records; County Recorder has Land & Military Records)

Kendall   **D9**   **19 Feb 1841**   **LaSalle, Kane**
www.rootsweb.com/~ilkendal/
Kendall County; 111 W Fox St; Yorkville, IL 60560;
Ph. (630) 553-4183
Details: (County Clerk has Birth & Death Records from 1877, Marriage & Land Records from 1841; Clerk Circuit Court has Divorce, Probate, Court & Naturalization Records)

Knox   **F5**   **1830**   **Fulton**
www.knoxclerk.org
Knox County; 200 S Cherry St; Galesburg, IL 61401;
Ph. (309) 345-3815 info@knoxclerk.org
Details: (County Clerk has Birth & Death Records from 1878 & Marriage Records from 1830)

La Salle   **D8**   **15 Jan 1831**   **Putnam, Vermilion**
www.outfitters.com/illinois/lasalle/
La Salle County; 707 E Etna Rd; Ottawa, IL 61350; Ph. (815) 434-8202
Details: (County Clerk has Birth & Death Records from 1877 & Marriage Records from 1832; Clerk Circuit Court has Divorce & Court Records; Probate Office has Probate Records; Recorder of Deeds has Land Records)

Lake   **A10**   **1 Mar 1839**   **McHenry**
www.lakecountyfl.com/
Lake County; 18 N County St; Waukegan, IL 60085-4339;
Ph. (847) 360-3610
Details: (County Clerk has Birth Records from 1871, Marriage Records from 1839 & Death Records from 1877; Clerk Circuit Court has Divorce, Probate & Court Records; Recorder of Deeds has Land Records)

County Website	Map Index	Date Created	Parent County or Territory From Which Organized Address/Details
Lawrence www.rootsweb.com/~illawren/index.htm	**M11**	**16 Jan 1821**	**Crawford, Edwards** Lawrence County; 1100 State St; Lawrenceville, IL 62439-0000; Ph. (618) 943-2346 **Details:** (County Clerk has Birth Records from 1877, Death Records from 1878, Marriage & Land Records from 1821 & Cemetery book; Clerk Circuit Court has Divorce, Probate & Court Records; City Clerks have Burial Records)
Lee www.outfitters.com/illinois/lee/	**C7**	**27 Feb 1839**	**Ogle** Lee County; 112 E 2nd St; Dixon, IL 61021; Ph. (815) 288-3309 **Details:** (County Clerk has Birth Records from 1858, Marriage Records from 1839, Death Records from 1877, Burial, Land & Military Records; Clerk Circuit Court has Divorce, Probate, Court & Naturalization Records)
Livingston www.crtelco.com/~annette1/	**F9**	**27 Feb 1837**	**LaSalle, McLean** Livingston County; 112 W Madison St; Pontiac, IL 61764; Ph. (815) 844-2006 **Details:** (County Clerk has Birth Records from 1878 with a few 1856–1877, Death & Burial Records from 1878, Marriage & Land Records from 1837 & Military Discharge Records from 1861; Clerk Circuit Court has Divorce, Probate & Court Records)
Logan	**H7**	**15 Feb 1839**	**Sangamon** Logan County; 601 Broadway St; Lincoln, IL 62656; Ph. (217) 732-4148 **Details:** (County Clerk has Birth & Death Records from 1878, Marriage Records from 1857, Land Records from 1839; Circuit Clerk has Divorce, Probate, & Court Records from 1857)
Macon www.rootsweb.com/~ilmacon/	**I8**	**19 Jan 1829**	**Shelby** Macon County; 141 S Main St; Decatur, IL 62523; Ph. (217) 424-1305 **Details:** (County Clerk has Birth Records from 1850, Marriage Records from 1829, Death Records from 1877 & Burial Records from 1964; Clerk Circuit Court has Divorce, Probate & Court Records)
Macoupin www.rootsweb.com/~ilmacoup/macoupin.htm	**K5**	**17 Jan 1829**	**Madison, Greene** Macoupin County; 233 E 1st S St; Carlinville, IL 62626-0000; Ph. (217) 854-3214 **Details:** (County Clerk has Birth & Death Records from 1877, Marriage & Land Records from 1829; Clerk Circuit Court has Divorce, Probate & Court Records)
Madison www.co.madison.il.us/	**M5**	**14 Sep 1812**	**St. Clair** Madison County; 155 N Main St; Edwardsville, IL 62025-1999; Ph. (618) 692-6290 **Details:** (County Clerk has Birth Records from 1860, Marriage Records from 1813 & Death Records from 1878; Clerk Circuit Court has Divorce, Probate & Court Records)
Marion www.rootsweb.com/~ilmarion/marionco.htm	**M8**	**24 Jan 1823**	**Fayette, Jefferson** Marion County; 100 E Main St; Salem, IL 62881-0000; Ph. (618) 548-3400 **Details:** (County Clerk has Birth Records from 1878, Marriage Records from 1821, Death Records from 1877 & Land Records from 1823; Clerk Circuit Court has Divorce & Court Records from 1858 & Probate Records from 1840)

County	Map	Date	Parent County or Territory From Which Organized
Website	Index	Created	Address/Details

Marshall   F7   **19 Jan 1839**   **Putnam**
www.rootsweb.com/~ilmarsha/index.htm

Marshall County; 122 N Prairie St; Lacon, IL 61540;
Ph. (309) 246-6325

Details: (County Clerk has Birth Records from 1878, Marriage & Land Records from 1839, Death Records from 1877, Cemetery Records from 1857 & Military Records from 1861; Clerk Circuit Court has Divorce, Probate & Court Records)

Mason   H5   **20 Jan 1841**   **Tazewell, Menard**
www.masoncountyil.org

Mason County; PO Box 77; Havana, IL 62644; Ph. (309) 543-6661

Details: (County Recorder as from 1841 Land & Property Records/Plats; Marriage from 1841; Birth & Death and some Cemetery Records from 1878; Military Records from 1860; Circuit Clerk has Court Records & Divorce, Immigration, Guardianship, and Naturalization/Citizenship; Probate/Wills; Missing Original Marriage Licenses for 1931 and 1932)

Massac   R8   **8 Feb 1843**   **Pope, Johnson**
www.rootsweb.com/~ilmassac/

Massac County; PO Box 429; Metropolis, IL 62960-0429;
Ph. (618) 524-5213

Details: (County Clerk has Birth Records from 1858, Marriage Records from 1843, Death Records from 1878, Land Records from 1855 & Military Records; Clerk Circuit Court has Divorce, Probate, Court & Naturalization Records)

McDonough   G3   **25 Jan 1826**   **Schuyler**
www.outfitters.com/illinois/mcdonough/

McDonough County; 1 Courthouse Sq; Macomb, IL 61455;
Ph. (309) 833-2474

Details: (County Clerk has Birth Records from 1858, Marriage Records from 1830, Death Records from 1877 & Land Records from 1812; City Clerk has Burial Records; Clerk Circuit Court has Divorce, Probate & Court Records)

McHenry   B9   **16 Jan 1836**   **Cook**
www.co.mchenry.il.us/

McHenry County; 2200 N Seminary Ave; Woodstock, IL 60098;
Ph. (815) 334-4242

Details: (County Clerk has Birth & Death Records from 1877 & Marriage Records from 1837; Recorder of Deeds has Land Records from 1841 & Military Records; Clerk Circuit Court has Divorce & Court Records from 1836 & Probate Records from 1840)

McLean   G8   **25 Dec 1830**   **Tazewell, Unorg. Terr**
www.mcleancountyil.gov/countyclerk

McLean County; 115 E Washington St, Rm 102; PO Box 2400;
Bloomington, IL 61702-2400; Ph. (309) 888-5190
countyclerk@mcleancountyil.gov

Details: (County Clerk has Birth & Death Records from 1860 & Marriage Records from 1831; Clerk Circuit Court has Divorce, Probate & Court Records; County Recorder has Land Records)

Menard   I6   **15 Feb 1839**   **Sangamon**
www.rootsweb.com/~ilmenard/index.html/

Menard County; 102 S 7th St; PO Box 456; Petersburg, IL 62675-0456; Ph. (217) 632-2415

Details: (County Clerk has Birth & Death Records from 1877, Marriage & Land Records from 1839; Clerk Circuit Court has Divorce, Probate & Court Records from 1839)

County Website	Map Index	Date Created	Parent County or Territory From Which Organized Address/Details
Mercer www.rootsweb.com/~ilmercer/	E3	13 Jan 1825	**Unorg. Terr., Pike** Mercer County; 100 SE 3rd St; PO Box 66; Aledo, IL 61231; Ph. (309) 582-7021 **Details:** (County Clerk has Birth Records from 1857, Marriage Records from 1835, Death Records from 1877 & Military Records from 1866; County Recorder has Land Records from 1833; Clerk Circuit Court has Divorce, Probate, Court & Naturalization Records from 1835)
Monroe www.rootsweb.com/~ilmonroe/	N5	6 Jan 1816	**Randolph, St. Clair** Monroe County; 100 S Main St; Waterloo, IL 62298; Ph. (618) 939-8681 **Details:** (County Clerk has Birth & Death Records from 1878, Marriage & Land Records from 1816; Clerk Circuit Court has Probate Records from 1845, Court Records from 1843, Naturalization & Divorce Records)
Montgomery www.rootsweb.com/~ilmontgo/	K6	12 Feb 1821	**Bond, Madison** Montgomery County; 1 Courthouse Sq; PO Box 595; Hillsboro, IL 62049; Ph. (217) 532-9530 **Details:** (County Clerk has Birth & Death Records from 1877, Marriage & Land Records from 1821; Clerk Circuit Court has Divorce, Probate & Court Records)
Morgan www.rootsweb.com/~ilmorgan/morgan.htm	J5	31 Jan 1823	**Sangamon** Morgan County; 300 W State St; Jacksonville, IL 62650; Ph. (217) 245-4619 **Details:** (County Clerk has Birth, Death & Burial Records from 1878, Marriage Records from 1827, Divorce Records from 1831, Probate Records from 1836 & Court Records from 1828)
Moultrie	J9	16 Feb 1843	**Shelby, Macon** Moultrie County; 10 S Main St; Sullivan, IL 61951-0000; Ph. (217) 728-4389 **Details:** (County Clerk has Birth Records from 1859, Marriage & Land Records from 1840, Death Records from 1877 & Burial Records from 1961; Clerk Circuit Court has Divorce, Probate & Court Records)
Ogle www.oglecounty.org/	B7	16 Jan 1836	**Jo Daviess** Ogle County; 4th & Washington St; Oregon, IL 61061; Ph. (815) 732-1110 **Details:** (County Clerk has Birth Records from 1860, Death Records from 1878, Marriage & Land Records from 1837; Clerk Circuit Court has Divorce, Probate & Court Records)
Peoria www.co.peoria.il.us/	F6	13 Jan 1825	**Fulton** Peoria County; 324 S Main St Rm 101; Peoria, IL 61604; Ph. (309) 672-6059 **Details:** (County Clerk has Birth & Death Records from 1877 & Marriage Records from 1825; Clerk Circuit Court has Divorce, Probate & Court Records; Recorder of Deeds has Land Records; Peoria twp Census taken 1888 & 1899)

County Website	Map Index	Date Created	Parent County or Territory From Which Organized Address/Details
Perry www.rootsweb.com/~ilperry/	P7	29 Jan 1827	**Randolph, Jackson** Perry County; RR 1; Pinckneyville, IL 62274-0000; Ph. (618) 357-5116 **Details:** (County Clerk has incomplete Birth Records 1879–1916, complete from 1916, incomplete Marriage Records from 1827 & Death Records from 1879; Clerk Circuit Court has Divorce, Probate & Court Records from 1827)
Piatt www.co.piatt.il.us/	I9	27 Jan 1841	**DeWitt, Macon** Piatt County; 101 W Washington St; Monticello, IL 61856; Ph. (217) 762-9487 **Details:** (County Clerk has Birth & Death Records from 1877, Marriage Records from 1841 & Land Records from 1852; Clerk Circuit Court has Divorce, Probate & Court Records from 1841)
Pike www.pikeil.org/	J3	31 Jan 1821	**Madison, Bond, Clark** Pike County; 100 E Washington St; Pittsfield, IL 62363-0000; Ph. (217) 285-6812 **Details:** (County Clerk has Birth & Death Records from 1877, Marriage Records from 1827 & Land Records from 1821; Clerk Circuit Court has Divorce, Probate & Court Records)
Pope www.rootsweb.com/~ilpope/	Q9	10 Jan 1816	**Gallatin, Johnson** Pope County; 400 Main St; PO Box 216; Golconda, IL 62938; Ph. (618) 683-4466 **Details:** (County Clerk has Birth Records from 1877, some from 1862, Death Records from 1878, Marriage & Land Records from 1816, Probate Records 1816–1950, Military Discharge Records from 1865, militia roll 1861–1862, 1845 & 1865 state Census; Clerk Circuit Court has Probate Records from 1950, Court Records from 1816, Divorce & Naturalization Records)
Pulaski www.rootsweb.com/~ilpulask/pulaski.htm	R7	3 Mar 1843	**Johnson** Pulaski County; 2nd & High St; Mound City, IL 62963-0218; Ph. (618) 748-9360 **Details:** (County Clerk has Birth Records from 1866, Marriage Records from 1861, Death Records from 1882, Burial Records from 1950 & tax Records from 1851; Clerk Circuit Court has Divorce, Probate & Court Records)
Putnam www.rootsweb.com/~ilputnam/index.htm	E7	13 Jan 1825	**Fulton** Putnam County; 120 N 4th St; Hennepin, IL 61327; Ph. (815) 925-7016 **Details:** (County Clerk has Birth & Death Records from 1878, Marriage, Probate & Court Records from 1831)
Randolph www.rootsweb.com/~ilrandol/	O6	5 Oct 1795	**NW Territory, St. Clair** Randolph County; 1 Taylor St; Chester, IL 62233; Ph. (618) 826-2510 **Details:** (County Clerk has Birth Records from 1857, Death Records from 1877, Marriage Records from 1804, Land Records from 1768 & Burial Records; Clerk Circuit Court has Probate & Court Records from 1809)
Richland www.rootsweb.com/~ilrichla/index.htm	M10	24 Feb 1841	**Clay, Lawrence** Richland County; 103 W Main St; Olney, IL 62450-0000; Ph. (618) 392-3111 **Details:** (County Clerk has Birth & Death Records from 1878 & Marriage Records from 1841; Clerk Circuit Court has Divorce, Probate & Court Records)

County	Map	Date	Parent County or Territory From Which Organized
Website	Index	Created	Address/Details

Rock Island   D3   **9 Feb 1831**   **Jo Daviess**
www.co.rock-island.il.us/
Rock Island County; 1504 3rd Ave; Rock Island, IL 61201-8646;
Ph. (309) 786-4451
Details: (County Clerk has Birth Records from 1877, Marriage Records from 1833 & Death Records from 1878; Clerk Circuit Court has Divorce, Probate, Court & Naturalization Records; Recorder of Deeds has Land Records)

Saline   P9   **25 Feb 1847**   **Gallatin**
www.rootsweb.com/~ilsaline/
Saline County; 10 W Poplar St; Harrisburg, IL 62946;
Ph. (618) 253-8197
Details: (County Clerk has Birth Records from 1877, Death Records from 1878, Marriage & Land Records from 1848; Clerk Circuit Court has Divorce, Probate & Court Records; City Clerk has Burial Records)

Sangamon   J6   **30 Jan 1821**   **NW Territory**
www.co.sangamon.il.us/
Sangamon County; 200 S 9th St; Springfield, IL 62701-1629;
Ph. (217) 753-6700
Details: (County Clerk has Birth & Death Records from 1877 & Marriage Records from 1821; Clerk Circuit Court has Divorce, Probate & Court Records; Supervisor of Assessments has Land Records; Recorder of Deeds has Military Records)

Schuyler   H3   **13 Jan 1825**   **Pike, Fulton**
www.rootsweb.com/~ilschuyl/
Schuyler County; RR 1; PO Box 43E; Rushville, IL 62681;
Ph. (217) 322-4734
Details: (County Clerk has Birth & Death Records from 1877, Marriage & Land Records from 1825 & Military Records; Clerk Circuit Court has Divorce, Probate, Court & Naturalization Records; Schuyler County Jail Museum has Cemetery, Census, school, tax & family Records)

Scott   J4   **16 Feb 1839**   **Morgan**
www.rootsweb.com/~ilscott/scott.htm
Scott County; 23 E Market St; Winchester, IL 62694;
Ph. (217) 742-3178
Details: (County Clerk has Birth Records from 1860, Death Records from 1877, Marriage & Land Records from 1839; Clerk Circuit Court has Divorce, Probate & Court Records)

Shelby   K8   **23 Jan 1827**   **Fayette**
www.rootsweb.com/~ilshelb2/shelby.htm
Shelby County; 301 E Main St; Shelbyville, IL 62565;
Ph. (217) 774-5220
Details: (County Clerk has Birth Records from 1848, Marriage Records from 1827, Death Records from 1878 & Land Records from 1833; Clerk Circuit Court has Probate Records)

St. Clair   N5   **27 Apr 1790**   **NW Territory**
www.stclaircountyclerk.com
St. Clair County; 10 Public Sq; Belleville, IL 62220;
Ph. (618) 277-6600
Details: (County Clerk has Birth Records from 1874, Death Records from 1878, Marriage Records from 1763)

Stark   E6   **2 Mar 1839**   **Knox, Putnam**
www.outfitters.com/illinois/stark/
Stark County; 130 W Main St; PO Box 97; Toulon, IL 61483-0000;
Ph. (309) 286-5911
Details: (County Clerk has Birth Records from 1855, Marriage Records from 1839 & Death Records from 1878; Clerk Circuit Court has Divorce, Probate & Court Records)

County	Map	Date	Parent County or Territory From Which Organized
Website	Index	Created	Address/Details

Stephenson A6 **4 Mar 1837** **Jo Daviess, Winnebago**
www.rootsweb.com/~ilstephe/
Stephenson County; 15 N Galena Ave; Freeport, IL 61032;
Ph. (815) 235-8289
Details: (County Clerk has Birth & Death Records from 1878, Marriage & Land Records from 1837, Probate & Court Records from 1894)

Tazewell G6 **31 Jan 1827** **Sangamon**
www.usgennet.org/usa/il/county/tazewell/index.html
Tazewell County; 11 S 4th St; Pekin, IL 61554-0000;
Ph. (309) 477-2264
Details: (County Clerk has Birth & Death Records from 1878 & Marriage Records from 1827; Clerk Circuit Court has Burial, Divorce, Probate & Court Records; Recorder of Deeds has Land Records)

Union Q7 **2 Jan 1818** **Johnson**
www.hostville.com/ilun/
Union County; 311 W Market St; Jonesboro, IL 62952-0000;
Ph. (618) 833-5711
Details: (County Clerk has Birth Records from 1862, Death Records from 1877, Marriage & Land Records from 1818)

Vermilion H11 **18 Jan 1826** **Unorg. Terr., Edgar**
www.co.vermilion.il.us/
Vermilion County; 6 N Vermilion St; Danville, IL 61832;
Ph. (217) 431-2615
Details: (County Clerk has Birth Records from 1858, Marriage Records from 1826 & Death Records from 1877; Clerk Circuit Court has Divorce, Probate, Court & Naturalization Records; Recorder of Deeds has Land & Military Records)

Wabash N11 **27 Dec 1824** **Edwards**
www.rootsweb.com/~ilwabash/
Wabash County; 401 N Market St; Mount Carmel, IL 62863;
Ph. (618) 262-4561
Details: (County Clerk has Birth & Death Records from 1877, Marriage & Land Records from 1857, Probate & Court Records 1857–1965, Cemetery & Naturalization Records; Clerk Circuit Court has Divorce Records)

Warren F4 **13 Jan 1825** **Pike**
www.outfitters.com/illinois/warren/
Warren County; 100 W Broadway; Monmouth, IL 61462;
Ph. (309) 734-8592
Details: (County Clerk has Birth & Death Records from 1877, Marriage & Land Records from 1833 & Military Records; Clerk Circuit Court has Divorce, Probate, Court & Naturalization Records from 1825)

Washington N7 **2 Jan 1818** **St. Clair**
http://mypage.direct.ca/Marriage/mid/northam.html
Washington County; 101 E St Louis St; Nashville, IL 62263-1599;
Ph. (618) 327-8314
Details: (County Clerk has Birth, Death & Burial Records from 1877, Marriage Records from 1832 & Land Records from 1818; Clerk Circuit Court has Divorce, Probate & Court Records)

Wayne N9 **26 Mar 1819** **Edwards**
www.rootsweb.com/~ilwayne/index.htm
Wayne County; 301 E Main St; Fairfield, IL 62837-2013;
Ph. (618) 842-5182
Details: (County Clerk has Birth, Marriage, Death & Burial Records from 1886 & Land Records; Clerk Circuit Court has Probate, Divorce & Court Records)

County Website	Map Index	Date Created	Parent County or Territory From Which Organized Address/Details
White www.rootsweb.com/~ilwhite2/	O10	**9 Dec 1815**	**Gallatin** White County; PO Box 187; Carmi, IL 62821; Ph. (618) 382-7211 **Details:** (County Clerk has Birth & Death Records from 1877, & Marriage Records from 1816; Circuite Court Clerk has Probate & Court Records from 1816; County Recorder has Land Records from 1816)
Whiteside www.whiteside.org/	C5	**16 Jan 1836**	**Jo Daviess, Henry** Whiteside County; 200 E Knox St; Morrison, IL 61270; Ph. (815) 772-5189 **Details:** (County Clerk has Birth & Death Records from 1878, Marriage Records from 1839, Military Records 1861–1865 & tax Records from 1840; Clerk Circuit Court has Divorce, Probate & Court Records; County Recorder has Land Records)
Will www.willcountyillinois.com/	D10	**12 Jan 1836**	**Cook, Iroquois, Unorg. Terr.** Will County; 302 N Chicago St; Joliet, IL 60432; Ph. (815) 740-4615 **Details:** (County Clerk has Birth & Death Records from 1877 & Marriage Records from 1836; Clerk Circuit Court has Divorce, Probate, Court & Naturalization Records; County Treas has Land Records; Recorder of Deeds has Military Records)
Williamson www.people.ku.edu/~place/williamson.html	P8	**28 Feb 1839**	**Franklin** Williamson County; 200 W Jefferson St; Marion, IL 62959; Ph. (618) 997-1301 **Details:** (County Clerk has Birth Records from 1876, Marriage Records from 1839, Death Records from 1877 & Land Records; City Clerk has Burial Records; Clerk Circuit Court has Divorce, Probate & Court Records)
Winnebago www.rootsweb.com/~ilwinneb/winncnty.htm	A7	**16 Jan 1836**	**Jo Daviess** Winnebago County; 400 W State St; Rockford, IL 61101; Ph. (815) 987-3050 **Details:** (County Clerk has Birth & Death Records from 1876 & Marriage Records from 1839; Clerk Circuit Court has Divorce, Probate & Court Records; County Recorder has Land Records)
Woodford www.rootsweb.com/~ilwoodfo/	F7	**27 Feb 1841**	**Tazewell, McLean** Woodford County; 115 N Main St; Eureka, IL 61530-1273; Ph. (309) 467-2822 **Details:** (County Clerk has Birth & Death Records from 1877 & Marriage Records from 1841; County Recorder has Land Records from 1841; Clerk Circuit Court has Divorce, Probate & Court Records)

Notes

Indiana

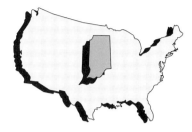

Capital: Indianapolis
Territory: 1800
State: 1816 (19th)

The crossroads of America

When French fur traders explored the Indiana region in the 17th century, the Miami, Potawatomi, and Delaware tribes were present. The French explorer, La Salle, first entered Indiana in 1679. Between 1700 and 1735, the French built Fort Miami near Fort Wayne. They also built Fort Ouiatenon, on the Wabash River, and Vincennes, on the lower Wabash, to protect their trading interests. Only Vincennes became a permanent settlement. In 1763, the area became British, but Indian uprisings made settlement difficult. During the Revolutionary War, George Rogers Clark captured Vincennes from the British and helped to end the Indian troubles. With the end of the war, Clarksville, opposite Louisville, Kentucky, was settled in 1784. Following establishment of the Northwest Territory, land was opened to Revolutionary War veterans and others.

Indiana Territory was organized in 1800. Michigan Territory was taken from it in 1805 and Illinois Territory in 1809. The last Indian resistance was finally overcome at the battle of Tippecanoe in 1811. Statehood was granted in 1816. The first counties to be settled were Knox, Harrison, Switzerland, and Clark. Most of the settlers in these counties came from Virginia, Kentucky, and the Carolinas. A group of Swiss immigrants settled in the southeast part of the state. Many Germans and Irish came to Indiana around 1830. New Englanders flocked to the state around 1850, settling in the northern counties. Quakers left Tennessee and the Carolinas to establish themselves in Wayne and Randolph counties away from slavery. Factory growth in the Calumet area attracted many central Europeans to the northwest part of Indiana. Indiana remained in the Union during the Civil War and furnished about 196,000 soldiers to the cause.

Look for vital records in the following locations:

- **Birth and death records:** Birth records from October 1907 are located at the Indiana State Department of Health, Division of Vital Statistics in Indianapolis. General compliance didn't occur until 1917. Death records date from 1900. Prior to 1900, birth and death records are located in the local health office of each county, generally beginning about 1882.

- **Marriage and divorce records:** County clerk's office prior to 1958 where the license was issued. Divorces were granted by the state legislature from 1817 to 1851. Since 1853, the court of common pleas in each county has divorce jurisdiction.

- **Court records:** Only Marion and St. Joseph Counties presently have probate courts. The other county records are kept by the clerk of the circuit court or the county clerk. Early probate records are in the court of common pleas, circuit courts, or probate courts (generally between 1829 and 1853).

- **Land records:** County recorder. The earliest land records, from 1789 to 1837, are published and indexed. Land records prior to 1807 were handled in Cincinnati, Ohio.

- **Census records:** State or territorial censuses were taken in some areas in 1807, 1810, and 1820. A few fragments of county and state census records exist for 1853, 1856, 1857, and 1877. These are available at the Indiana State Library in Indianapolis.

Vital Records Department State Department of Health
2 North Meridian Street
Indianapolis, IN 46204
(317) 233-1325
www.in.gov/isdh/bdcertifs/
birth_and_death_certificates.htm

Indiana Commission on Public Records
Records Center/State Archives
6400 East 30th Street, IN, Indiana 46219
(317) 591-5325
www.state.in.us/icpr/records_center/
www.state.in.us/icpr/archives/

Indiana State Library
140 North Senate Avenue
Indianapolis, IN 46204-2296
(317) 232-3689; (317) 232-3728 fax

Societies and Repositories

Adams County Historical Society; Box 262; Decatur, IN 46733.

Alexander Hamilton Chapter, SAR; 7135 Koldyke Dr; Fishers, IN 46038.

Alexandria Monroe Township Historical and Genealogical Society; RR 1 Box 402; Alexandria, IN 46001.

Alexis Coquillard Chapter, SAR; IN; glamb10100@aol.com.

Allen County Genealogical Society of Indiana; PO Box 12003; Ft. Wayne, IN 46862; www.ipfw.edu/ipfwhist/historgs/acgsi.htm.

Allen County Public Library, Historical Genealogy Department; 200 E. Berry; PO Box 2270; Fort Wayne, IN 46801-2270; (260) 421-1225; www.acpl.lib.in.us.

Bartholomew County Genealogical Society, Inc.; PO Box 2455; Columbus, IN 47202.

Bartholomew County Historical Society; 524 Third St.; Columbus, IN 47201.

Benton County Historical Society; 602 E. 7th St.; Fowler, IN 47944.

Blackford County Historical Society; PO Box 264; Hartford City, IN 47348; www.bchs-in.org.

Blair Society for Genealogical Research; 20 Parkwood Drive; Brownsburg, IN 46211-1922; (317) 852-5078; EPBlair@aol.com; http://blairsociety.org.

Boone County Historical Society; PO Box 141; Lebanon, IN 46052.

Brown County Genealogical Society; PO Box 1202; Nashville, IN 47448-1202; www.rootsweb.com/~inbcgs/title.htm.

Brown County Indiana Historical Society; 1934 SR 135 N; PO Box 668; Nashville, IN 47448; (812) 988-6089; BCArchive@hotmail.com.

Carroll County Historical Society; Ground Floor Court House; PO Box 277; Delphi, IN 46923; http://dcwi.com/~cchs/cchs.html.

Cass County Genealogical Society; PO Box 373; Logansport, IN 46947.

Clarence Cook Chapter, SAR; 809 N. East Street; Indianapolis, IN 46202-3424; (317) 917-0238; jackcooganmoore@aol.com; www.geocities.com/insSAR-south/clarcook.html.

Clark County Historical Society/Howard Steamboat Museum, Inc.; 1101 E. Market Street; PO Box 606; Jeffersonville, IN 47131-0606; (812) 283-3728; www.steamboatmuseum.org.

Clay County Genealogical Society, Inc.; PO Box 56; Center Point, IN 47840-0056; ccgslib@ticz.com; www.ccgsilib.org.

Clinton County Genealogical Society; c/o Frankfort Community Public Library; 209 W. Clin; Frankfort, IN 46041.

Clinton County Historical Society, Inc. and Historical Museum; 301 E. Clinton St.; Frankfort, IN 46041.

Continental Chapter, SAR; 1611 N. Tillotson Ave; Muncie, IN 47304-2500; m.jkreps1@juno.com; www.geocities.com/inssar-south/cont.html.

Crawford County, Indiana Historical & Genealogical Society; PO Box 139; Leavenworth, IN 47137.

Daniel Guthrie Chapter, SAR; 4630 Chatham Dr.; Bloomington, IN 47404-1319; legler2@bluemarble.net; www.geocities.com/inssar-south/daniguth.html.

DeKalb County Genealogical Society; c/o Eckhart Public Library; 603 S. Jackson St.; Auburn, IN 46706.

DeKalb County Historical Society; Box 686; Auburn, IN 46706.

Delaware County Historical Alliance; 120 E. Washington St.; Muncie, IN 47305-1734.

Dubois County Genealogical Society; PO Box 84; Ferdinand, IN 47532-0084.

Elkhart County Genealogical Society; PO Box 1031; Elkhart, IN 46515-1031; joybel@michiana.org; www.rootsweb.com/~inelkhar/ecgs.htm.

Elwood-Pipecreek Genealogical Society; c/o Elwood Public Library; 1600 Main St.; Elwood, IN 46036.

Fountain County Genealogical Society; 2855 S. Kingman Rd.; Kingman, IN 47952.

Fountain County Historical Society; PO Box 99; Kingman, IN 47952.

Fulton County Historical Society, Genealogical Section; 3063 S. 425 E.; Rochester, IN 46975; (574) 223-4436; fchs@rtcol.com; www.icss.net/~fchs.

Genealogical Society of Marion County; PO Box 2292; Indianapolis, IN 46206-2292; darrah@prodigy.net; www.rootsweb.com/~ingsmc/.

Genealogical Society of Whitley County; PO Box 224; Columbia City, IN 46725-0224; 260 - 691-2241; http://home.whitleynet.org/genealogy.

General Thomas Posey Chapter, SAR; 624 W 6th St; Mount Vernon, IN 47620; (812) 838-5960; wmagibbs@peoplepc.com; www.geocities.com/inssar-south/thospose.htm.

George Rogers Clark Chapter, SAR; 2816 Avondale Road; Vincennes, IN 47591; www.geocities.com/inssar-south/georclar.html.

Gibson Historical Society; PO Box 516; Princeton, IN 47670.

Greene County Genealogical Society; PO Box 164; Bloomfield, IN 47424.

Hamilton County Historical Society; PO Box 397; Noblesville, IN 46060.

Hancock County Historical Society, Inc.; PO Box 375; Greenfield, IN 46140-0375.

Harrison County Historical Society; 117 W. Beaver St.; Corydon, IN 47112.

Hendricks County Genealogical Society; 101 South Indiana St.; Danville, IN 46122.

Henry County Historical Society; 606 South 14th St.; New Castle, IN 47362.

Hoosier Pioneer Patriots Chapter, SAR; 733 Pennsylvania Ave; Sellersburg, IN 47172; (812) 246-2066; franklinsteph@hotmail.com; www.geocities.com/inssar-south/hoospion.html.

Howard County Genealogical Society; PO Box 2; Oakford, IN 46965; www.rootsweb.com/~inhoward/hcgs/index.html.

Howard County Historical Society; 1200 West Sycamore; Kokomo, IN 46901; www.howardcountymuseum.org.

Huntington County Genealogical Society; Huntington City Twp. Public Library; 200 W Market S; Huntington, IN 46750.

Indiana Genealogical Society; PO Box 10507; Fort Wayne, IN 46852-0507; blwarren49@aol.com; www.indgensoc.org

Indiana Historical Society; 315 W. Ohio Street; Indianapolis, IN 46202.

Indiana State Archives; 6440 E. 30th St.; Indianapolis, IN 46219; (317) 591-5325; arc@icpr.state.in.us; www.in.gov/icpr/archives.

Indiana State Library; 140 North Senate Avenue; Indianapolis, IN 46204-2296; www.statelib.lib.in.us.

Jackson County Genealogical Society; 415 1/2 S. Poplar St.; Brownstown, IN 47220.

Jasper County Historical Society; Augusta St.; Rensselaer, IN 47971.

Jay County Genealogy; 109 South Commerce Street; Portland, IN 47371; jaycogen@jayco.net; www.rootsweb.com/~injay.

Jay County Historical Society; PO Box 1292; Portland, IN 47371.

Jefferson County Historical Society; 615 West First Street; Madison, IN 47250; jchs@seidata.com; www.seidata.com/~jchs/jchs.htm.

Jennings County Genealogical Society; PO Box 863; North Vernon, IN 47265.

John Hay Chapter, SAR; 4913 W Luther Rd; Floyds Knobs, IN; (812) 923-8586; www.geocities.com/inssar-south/johnhay.html.

John Martin Chapter, SAR; 76 S. Thorpe Place; West Terre Haute, IN 47885; (812) 533-2319; KESLAW@aol.com; www.geocities.com/inssar-south/johnmart.html.

Johnson County Historical Society; 150 West Madison St.; Franklin, IN 46131.

Kosciusko County Historical Society; Genealogical Section; PO Box 1071; Warsaw, IN 46580.

La Porte County Genealogical Society; 904 Indiana Ave.; La Porte, IN 46350.

La Porte County Historical Society; LaPorte County Complex; 809 State Street; La Porte, IN 46350-3329; www.lapcohistsoc.org.

LaGrange County Historical Society, Inc.; R.R. 1; LaGrange, IN 46761.

Lexington Historical Society, Inc.; 5764 South State Rd. 203; Lexington, IN 47138.

Marion County Historical Society; 140 N. Senate; Indianapolis, IN 46204.

Marion-Adams Genealogical Society; 309 Main St.; Sheridan, IN 46069.

Martin County Historical Society, Inc.; PO Box R4; Shoals, IN 46504.

Mennonite Historical Library; 1700 S. Main Street; Goshen, IN 46526; (574) 535-7418; mhl@goshen.edu; www.goshen.edu/mhlwww.goshen.edu/mhl.

Merrillville-Ross Township Historical Society; 13 W. 73rd Avenue; Merrillville, IN 46410; www.rootsweb.com/~inlake/ross.htm.

Miami County Genealogical Society; PO Box 542; Peru, IN 46970; mus2@netusa1.net; www.rootsweb.com/~inmiami/gensoc.html.

Miami County Museum/Miami County Historical Society; 51 North Broadway; Peru, IN 46970; (765) 473-9183; archivist@miamicountymuseum.com; www.miamicountymuseum.com.

Monroe County Historical Society; 202 E. Sixth Street; Bloomington, IN 47408; (812) 332-2517; mchm@kiva.net; www.kiva.net/~mchm.

Morgan County History & Genealogical Association; PO Box 1012; Martinsville, IN 46151-0012; (765) 349-2985; www.rootsweb.com/~inmchaga/mchagai.html.

Noble County Genealogical Society; 813 E. Main St.; Albion, IN 46701.

Northern Indiana Historical Society; 112 So. Lafayette Blvd.; South Bend, IN 44601.

Northwest Indiana Genealogical Society; PO Box 595; Griffith, IN 46319; www.rootsweb.com/~inlake/nwigs.htm.

Northwest Territory Genealogical Society; Lewis Historical Society--LRC 22; Vincennes University; Vincennes, IN 47591; dbeeson@vunet.vinu.edu.

Ohio County Historical Society; PO Box 194; Rising Sun, IN 47040; www.risingsun.cc/comm/HistSociety.html.

Orange County Genealogical Society; PO Box 344; Paoli, IN 47454; www.usgennet.org/usa/in/county/orange/gensoc.htm.

Owen County Historical & Genealogical Society; PO Box 569; Spencer, IN 47460; lesndeb@ccrtc.com; www.owen.in.us/owenhist/owen.htm.

Palatines to America, Indiana Chapter; PO Box 40435; Indianapolis, IN 46240-0435.

Perry County Historical Society; c/o Mrs. James J. Groves; General Delivery; Rome, IN 47574.

Pike County Historical Society; PO Box 216; Petersburg, IN 47567.

Porter County Public Library Genealogical Group; 103 Jefferson St.; Valparaiso, IN 46393.

Posey County Historical Society; PO Box 171; Mt. Vernon, IN 47620.

Posey-Vanderburg Chapter, SAR; 612 Drexel Dr; St Phillips, IN; (812) 985-3421; www.geocities.com/inssar-south/posevand.html.

Randolph County Genealogical Society; R.R. 3 Box 61; Winchester, IN 47394.

Randolph County Historical Society; Rt. 3, Box 60A; Winchester, IN 47394.

Ripley County Historical Society, Inc.; 125 Washington Street; PO Box 525; Versailles, IN 47042; rchslib@seidata.com; www.seidata.com/~rchslib.

Scott County Genealogical Society; 5764 S. State Rd. 203; Lexington, IN 47139.

Seth Jewel Chapter, SAR; 1106 Greg St.; Auburn, IN 46706-1507; insSAR1@prodigy.net; www.geocities.com/inssar-south/sethjewe.html.

Simon Kenton Chapter, SAR; 470 E Amsler Rd; Rensselaer, IN 47978; (219) 886-5200; CraigJ@netnitco.net; www.geocities.com/inssar-south/simokent.html.

South Bend Area Genealogical Society; c/o Mishawaka Public Library; 209 Lincolnway Way E.; Mishawaka, IN 46544; www.rootsweb.com/~insbags/index.htm.

Southern Indiana Genealogical Society; PO Box 665; New Albany, IN 47151-0665; www.rootsweb.com/~insigs.

Spencer County Historical Society; 210 Walnut St.; Rockport, IN 47635.

Starke County Geneological Society; 152 W. Culver Road; Knox, IN 46534; tbrettin@skyenet.net; www.maplewoodfarm.com/ strkctygen.htm.

Steuben County Genealogical Society; Carnegie Library; 322 S. Wayne; Angola, IN 46703.

Sullivan County Historical Society; 10 S. Court St.; Sullivan, IN 47882-1510.

The Society of Indiana Pioneers; 450 West Ohio Street; Indianapolis, IN 46202; www.indianapioneers.com.

The Tippecanoe County Historical Association; 1001 South Street; Lafayette, IN 47901; mail@tcha.mus.in.us; www.tcha.mus.in.us.

Tippecanoe County Area Genealogical Society; 909 South St.; Lafayette, IN 47901.

Tri-County Genealogical Society; 23184 Pocket Rd. W.; Batesville, IN 47006.

Tri-State Genealogical Society; c/o Willard Library; 21 First Avenue; Evansville, IN 47710; vakarine@evansville.net; www.rootsweb.com/~intsgs.

Union County Historical Society; 6 E. Seminary St.; Liberty, IN 47353.

Vigo County Historical Society; 1411 So. 6th St.; Terre Haute, IN 47802; http://web.indstate.edu/community/vchs/home.html.

Wabash County Genealogical Society; PO Box 825; Wabash, IN 46992; llt@hoosierlink.net; www.rootsweb.com/~inwabash/wcgs.html.

Wabash County Historical Society; Wabash County Museum; 89 W. Hill St.; Wabash, IN 46992.

Warren County Historical Society; PO Box 176; Williamsport, IN 47993.

Washington County Historical Society; 307 E. Market St.; Salem, IN 47904.

Wayne County Genealogy Society; St. John's Lutheran Church; PO Box 2599; Richmond, IN 47375.

Wells County Historical Society; PO Box 143; Bluffton, IN 46714-0143; www.wchs-museum.org/wchsociety.htm.

White County Genealogical Society; 101 South Bluff St.; Monticello, IN 47960.

William Henry Harrison Chapter, SAR; 1733 Shenandoah Dr; Lafayette, IN 47905-4041; (765) 447-5973; parkave1@gte.net; www.geocities.com/inssar-south/willharr.html.

William Knight Chapter, SAR; 94 Pin Oak Road; Greencastle, IN 46135; (765) 653-6834.

William Van Gordon Chapter, SAR; 3047 Lake Side Dr; Highland, IN 46322; (219) 924-0416; www.geocities.com/inssar-south/willgord.html.

Bibliography and Record Sources

General

A Biographical History of Eminent and Self-made Men of the State of Indiana. 2 vols. Cincinnati: Western Biographical Publishing Co., 1880.

A Directory of Churches and Religious Organizations in Indiana. 3 vols. Indianapolis: Historical Records Survey, 1941.

Beatty, John D. *Research in Indiana.* Arlington, Virginia: National Genealogical Society, 1992.

Bender, Harold S. *The Mennonites of Indiana, 1835–1929.* Salt Lake City: Filmed by the Genealogical Society of Utah, 1990.

Blanchard, Charles. *History of the Catholic Church in Indiana.* 2 vols. Logansport, Indiana: A. W. Bowen & Co., 1898.

Buley, R. Carlyle. *The Old Northwest: Pioneer Period, 1815–1840.* Indianapolis: Indiana Historical Society, 1950

Caby, John Frank. *The Origin and Development of the Missionary Baptist Church in Indiana.* Franklin, Indiana: Franklin College, 1942.

Carty, Mickey Dimon. *Searching in Indiana: A Reference Guide to Public and Private Records.* Costa Mesa, California: ISC Pub., 1985.

Cavanaugh, Karen B. *A Genealogist's Guide to the Ft. Wayne, Indiana, Public Library.* Owensboro, Kentucky: McDowell Pub., 1980.

Clayton, Ellen Cox. *Memories of Yesterday in Indiana: A Brief History of the Early Days of the Church of Jesus Christ of Latter-Day Saints in Indiana.* S.l.: s.n., 196–.

Cumback, Will. *Men of Progress, Indiana: A Selected List of Biographical Sketches and Portraits of the Leaders in Business, Professional and Official Life, Together with Brief Notes on the History and Character of Indiana.* Indianapolis: The Indianapolis Sentinel, 1899.

Dillon, John B. *A History of Indiana.* Indianapolis: Bingham and Doughty, 1859.

Dorrel, Ruth and Thomas D. Hamm. *Abstracts of the Records of the Society of Friends in Indiana,* Vol. 1. Rev. ed. Indianapolis: Indiana Historical Society, 1996.

Dorrel, Ruth. *Indiana Source Book VI; Genealogical Material from the Hoosier Genealogist, 1982–1981.* Indianapolis: Indiana Historical Society, 1992.

Dorrel, Ruth. *Indiana Source Book VII; Genealogical Material from the Hoosier Genealogist, 1989–1990.* Indianapolis: Indiana Historical Society, 1994.

Dorrel, Ruth. *Pioneer Ancestors of Members of the Society of Indiana Pioneers.* Indianapolis: Indiana Historical Society, 1983.

Dunn, Jacob Piatt. *Indiana and Indianans.* 5 vols. Chicago and New York: The American Historical Society, 1919.

Dunn, Jacob Piatt. *Memorial and Genealogical Record of Representative Citizens of Indiana.* A. W. Bowen, 1914. Ed. de luxe [sic].

Esarey, Logan. *History of Indiana from Its Exploration to 1922.* 3 vols. Dayton, Ohio: Dayton Historical Society, 1923.

Esarey, Logan. *The Indiana Home.* (1953) Reprint. Galveston, Texas: Frontier Press, 1976.

Franklin, Charles. *Indiana Territorial Pioneer Records, 1801–1820.* S.l.: Heritage House, 1983–1985.

Fraustein, Rebah M. and Willard Heiss. *Indiana Source Book IV; Genealogical Material from the Hoosier Genealogist, 1979–1981.* Indianapolis: Indiana Historical Society, 1986.

Fraustein, Rebah M. *Indiana Source Book V; Genealogical Material from the Hoosier Genealogist, 1982–1984.* Indianapolis: Indiana Historical Society, 1990.

Gibbs. *Indiana's African American Heritage.* Galveston, Texas: Frontier Press, 1993.

Gooldy, Pat and Charles M. Franklin. *Indiana Wills Phase I (to 1850) and Phase II (1851–1898).* Indianapolis: Ye Olde Genealogie Shoppe.

Gooldy, Pat and Ray Gooldy. *Manual for Indiana Genealogical Research.* Indianapolis: Ye Olde Genealogie Shoppe, 1991.

Griffis, Joan A. Illiana. *Ancestors Volume 5, 1993, 1994, 1995, Genealogy Column in the Commercial News, Danville, Illinois.* Danville, Illinois: Joan A. Griffis, 1996.

Harter, Stuart. *Indiana Genealogy and Local History Sources Index.* Fort Wayne, Indiana: Stuart Harter, 1985.

Heiss, William. *Indiana Source Book I; Genealogical Material from the Hoosier Genealogist, 1961–1966.* Indianapolis: Indiana Historical Society, 1977.

Heiss, William. *Indiana Source Book II: Genealogical Material from the Hoosier Genealogist, 1967–1972.* Indianapolis: Indiana Historical Society, 1981.

Heiss, William. *Indiana Source Book III; Genealogical Material from the Hoosier Genealogist, 1973–1979.* Indianapolis: Indiana Historical Society, 1982.

Hine, Darlene Clark. *The Black Women in the Middle West Project: A Comprehensive Resource Guide, Illinois and Indiana; Historical Essays, Oral Histories, Biographical Profiles, and Document Collections.* Indianapolis, Indiana: Indiana Historical Bureau, 1986.

Hinshaw, Gregory P. *Indiana Friends Heritage 1821–1996, The 175th Anniversary History of Indiana Yearly Meeting of Friends (Quakers),* 1996.

Index to Encyclopedia of American Quaker Genealogy by William Wade Hinshaw. S.l.: Genealogical Pub. Co., 1999.

Indiana Biographical Index. West Bountiful, Utah: Genealogical Indexing Associates. 1983.

Indiana Research Outline. Series U.S.-States, no. 15. Salt Lake City: Family History Library, 1988.

Indiana Source Book: Genealogical Material from the Hoosier Genealogist, 1979–1981. Indianapolis: Indiana Historical Society, 1987.

Men of Indiana: In Nineteen Hundred and One. Indianapolis: Benesch, 1901.

Miller, Carolynne L. *Aids for Genealogical Searching in Indiana: A Bibliography.* Detroit: Detroit Society for Genealogical Research, 1970.

Miller, Carolynne L. *Indiana Sources for Genealogical Research in the Indiana State Library.* Indianapolis: Indiana Historical Society, 1984.

Miller, John W. *Indiana Newspaper Bibliography: Historical Accounts of all Indiana Newspapers Published from 1804 to l980 and Locational Information for all Available Copies, Both Original and Microfilm.* Indianapolis, Indiana: Indiana Historical Society, 1982.

Newhard, Malinda E. E. *A Guide to Genealogical Records in Indiana.* Harlan, Indiana: M. Newhard, 1979.

Parker, Jimmy B., and Lyman de Platt. *Indiana Biographical Index.* West Bountiful, Utah: Genealogical Indexing Associates, 1983.

Pumroy, Eric and Paul Brockman. *A Guide to Manuscript Collections of the Indiana Historical Society and Indiana State Library.* Indexed. Indianapolis: Indiana Historical Society, 1986.

Reed, George Irving. *Encyclopedia of Biography of Indiana*. Chicago: Century Publishing, 1895.

Rehmer, R. F. *Lutherans in Pioneer Indiana*. Lafayette, Indiana: Commercial Print., 1972.

Riker, Dorothy. *Genealogical Sources Reprinted from the Genealogical Section, Indiana Magazine of History*. Indianapolis: Indiana Historical Society, 1979.

Riker, Dorothy. *Indiana Source Books Index, Vols. 1–3*. Indianapolis: Indiana Historical Society, 1983.

Robbins, Coy D. *Indiana Negro Registers, 1852–1865*. Bowie, MD: Heritage Books, 1994.

Robinson, Mona. *Who's Your Hoosier Ancestor? Genealogy for Beginners*. Bloomington, Indiana: Indiana University Press, 1992.

Rudolf, L. C., and Judith E. Endelman. *Religion in Indiana, A Guide to Historical Resources*. Indiana University Press, 1986.

Rudolph. *Hoosier Faiths: A History of Indiana's Churches and Religious Groups*. Galveston, Texas: Frontier Press, 1995.

Scheiber, Harry N. *The Old Northwest: Studies in regional history, 1787–1910*. Lincoln, Nebraska: University of Nebraska Press, 1969.

Schweitzer, George K. *Indiana Genealogical Research*. Knoxville, Tennessee: George K. Schweitzer, 1996.

Smith, John L. *Indiana Methodism: A Series of Sketches and Incidents, Grave and Humorous Concerning Preachers and People of the West; with an Appendix Containing Personal Recollections, Public Addresses and other Miscellany*. Valparaiso, Indiana: J.L. Smith, 1892.

Southern California Genealogical Society. *Sources of Genealogical Help in Indiana*. Burbank, California: Southern California Genealogical Society.

Stott, W. T. *Baptist Church History, Indiana*. S.l.: s.n., 1908.

Taylor, Robert M., Jr., and Connie A. McBirney, eds. *Peopling Indiana: The Ethnic Experience*. Galveston, Texas: Frontier Press, 1996.

Thompson, Donald E. *Preliminary Checklist of Archives and Manuscripts in Indiana Repositories*. Indianapolis: Indiana Historical Society, 1980.

Thornbrough, Emma Lou. *The Negro in Indiana Before 1900: A Study of a Minority*. Bloomington, Indiana: Indiana University Press, 1993.

Wedel, Carolynne L. *Aids for Genealogical Searching in Indiana: A Bibliography*. Rev. ed. Detroit: Detroit Society for Genealogical Research, 1970.

Woollen, William Wesley and Jacob Platt Dunn. *Executive Journal of Indiana Territory*. (1900) Reprint. Indianapolis: Indiana Historical Society, 1985.

Woollen, William Wesley *Biographical and Historical Sketches of Early Indiana*. Indianapolis: Hammond, 1883.

Atlases, Maps and Gazetteers

Atlas of Indiana, 92 County maps. Includes detailed maps of individual counties, all the back roads, streams, lakes, towns, etc. Galveston, Texas. Frontier Press, n.d.

Baker, J. David. *The Postal History of Indiana*. 2 vols. Louisville, Kentucky: Leonard H. Hartman, 1976.

Baker, Ronald L., and Marvin Carmony. *Indiana Place Names*. Bloomington, Indiana: Indiana University Press, 1975.

Ball, T. H. *Northwestern Indiana, from 1800 to 1900: A View of Our Region Through the Nineteenth Century*. Chicago: Donohue & Hanneberry, 1900.

Chamberlain, E. *The Indiana Gazetteer, or, Topographical Dictionary of the State of Indiana*. Indianapolis: E. Chamberlain, 1849.

Franklin, Charles. *Genealogical Atlas of Indiana*. Indianapolis, Indiana: Heritage House, 1985.

Illustrated Historical Atlas of the State of Indiana. Chicago: Baskin, Forster, 1876.

Indiana Gazetteer, or Topographical Dictionary of the State of Indiana. 3rd ed. (1850) Reprint, Salem, Massachusetts: Higginson Book Co., 1993.

List of Indiana Post Offices. Microfilm of originals (3 x 5 cards) at the Indiana State Library in Indianapolis, Indiana. Salt Lake City: Filmed by the Genealogical Society of Utah, 1986.

Maps of Indiana Counties in 1876. (1968) Reprint. Indianapolis: Indiana Historical Society, 1979.

New Topographical Atlas and Gazetteer of Indiana. 1871. Reprint. Evansville, Indiana: Unigraphic, Inc., 1975.

Pence, George and Nellie C. Armstrong. *Indiana Boundaries: Territorial, State, and County*. (1933) Reprint. Indianapolis: Indiana Historical Society, 1967.

Scott, John. *The Indiana Gazetteer or Topographical Dictionary*. 1826. Reprint. Indianapolis: Indiana Historical Society, 1954.

Sinko, Peggy Tuck. *Indiana Atlas of Historical County Boundaries*. John H. Long, editor. Charles Scribners Sons, 1996.

Wilson, George R. *Early Indiana Trails and Surveys*. (1919) Reprint. Indianapolis: Indiana Historical Society, 1991.

Censuses

Available Census Records and Census Substitutes

Federal Census 1820, 1830, 1840, 1850, 1860, 1870, 1880, 1900, 1910, 1920

State/Territorial Census 1807, 1853, 1856, 1857, 1859, 1866, 1871, 1877

Federal Mortality Schedules 1850

Voters 1809

Revolutionary War Pensioners 1835

Dollarhide, William. *The Census Book: A Genealogist's Guide to Federal Census Facts, Schedules and Indexes.* Bountiful, Utah: Heritage Quest, 1999.

Franklin, Charles M. *Indiana Territorial Pioneer Records, 1801–1820.* S.l.: Heritage House, ©1983–1985.

Fraustein, Rebah M. *Census of Indiana Territory for 1807.* (1980) Reprint. Indianapolis: Indiana Historical Society, 1990.

Heiss, Willard. *1820 Federal Census for Indiana.* (1966) Reprint. Indianapolis: Indiana Historical Society, 1975.

Indiana. Adjutant General. *Enrollment of the Late Soldiers, Their Widows and Orphans of the Late Armies of the United States, Residing in the State of Indiana for the Year 1886–1894.* Microfilm of records located at the Indiana State Library, Indianapolis. Salt Lake City: Filmed by the Genealogical Society of Utah, 1988–1990. 89 microfilm.

Kemp, Thomas Jay. *The American Census Handbook.* Wilmington, Delaware: Scholarly Resources, Inc., 2001.

Lainhart, Ann S. *State Census Records.* Baltimore: Genealogical Publishing Co., Inc., 1992.

Szucs, Loretto Dennis and Matthew Wright. *Finding Answers in U.S. Census Records.* Ancestry Publishing, 2001.

Thorndale, William and William Dollarhide. *County Boundary Map Guides to the U.S. Federal Censuses, 1790–1920: Indiana, 1800–1920.* 1987. Bountiful, Utah. AGLL.

United States. Bureau of Internal Revenue. *Internal Revenue Assessment Lists for Indiana, 1862–1866.* Washington, D.C.: The National Archives, 1987. 42 microfilm.

Court Records, Probate and Wills

Franklin, Charles M. *Index to Indiana Wills: Phase 1, Through 1850 and Phase 2, 1850 Through 1880.* 2 Vols. Indianapolis: Heritage House, 1986–87.

Griffin, Warren B. *Preliminary Inventory: Records of the U.S. Courts for the District of Indiana.* Chicago: Federal Record Center, 1967.

Howe, Daniel Wait. *The Laws and Courts of Northwest and Indiana Territories.* Indiana Historical: Bowen-Merrill Co., 1886.

Moudy, Vera Mae. *Directory, Wills and Estates Information in Genealogy Dept., Indiana State Library.* Indianapolis, Indiana: Ye Olde Genealogie Shoppe, 1981.

Newman, John J. *Research in Indiana Courthouses: Judicial and Other Records.* (1981) Reprint Indianapolis: Indiana Historical Society, 1990.

Taylor, Charles W. *Biographical Sketches and Review of the Bench and Bar of Indiana: Containing Biographies and Sketches of Eminent Judges and Lawyers of Indiana, Together With a History of the Judiciary of the State and Review of the Bar from the Earliest Times to the Present with Anecdotes, Reminiscences, etc. . . . .* 2 vols. Indianapolis, Indiana: Bench and Bar Pub. Co., 1895.

The Laws of Indiana Territory, 1801–1809. Springfield, Illinois: Trustees of the Illinois State Historical Library, 1930.

United States. National Archives and Records Service. *Preliminary Inventory, Records of the United States Courts for the District of Indiana, (record group 21).* Chicago: Federal Records Center, 1967.

Emigration, Immigration, Migration and Naturalization

An Index to Indiana Naturalization Records Found in Various Order Books of the Ninety-two Local Courts Prior to 1907. Indianapolis: Indiana Historical Society, 1981.

Burns, Lee. *The National Road in Indiana.* Indianapolis: C. E. Pauley, 1920.

Enochs, Richard A. *From A to B: Migration Research: Birds of a Feather.* Fort Wayne, Indiana: Indiana Genealogical Society, 1994.

Indiana State Archives. (Indianapolis*). Indiana Naturalization Records prior to 1951.* Indianapolis, Indiana: Indiana State Archives, 2002. Online database—www.state.in.us/serv/icpr_naturalization.

United States. District Court (Illinois: Northern District). *Soundex Index to Naturalization Petitions for U.S. District & Circuit Courts, Northern District of Illinois and Immigration and Naturalization Service District 9, 1840–1950.* Salt Lake City: Filmed by the Genealogical Society of Utah, 1988. 183 microfilm.

Land and Property

Cowan, Janet C. *Jeffersonville Land Entries 1808–1818.* Indianapolis: the author, 1984.

Hone, Wade E. *Land and Property Research in the United States.* Salt Lake City: Ancestry Incorporated, 1997.

Indiana Historical Society (Indianapolis, Indiana). *This Land of Ours: The Acquisition and Disposition of the Public Domain; Papers Presented at an Indiana American Revolution Bicentennial Symposium, Purdue University, West Lafayette, Indiana, April 29 and 30, 1978.* Indianapolis, Indiana: The Society, 1978.

Indiana State Archives. (Indianapolis*). Land and Homestead Records.* Indianapolis, Indiana: Indiana State Archives, 2002. Online database—www.state.in.us/icpr/webfile/archives/homepage.html.

Lux, Leonard. *The Vincennes Donation Lands.* Indianapolis: Indiana Historical Society, 1949.

McMullin, Phillip W., ed. *Grassroots of America.* Salt Lake City: Gendex Corp., 1972.

Smith, Clifford N., ed. *French and British Land Grants in the Post Vincennes (Indiana) District, 1750–1784.*

Indiana

Selections from The American State Papers. McNeal, Arizona: Westland Publications, 1996.

This Land of Ours: The Acquisition and Disposition of the Public Domain. Indianapolis: Indiana Historical Society, 1978.

Waters, Margaret R. *Indiana Land Entries.* 2 Vols. Reprint. Knightstown, Indiana: Bookmark, 1977. Index of land entries for the Cincinnati Land District, 1801 to 1840, and Vincennes Land District, 1807 to 1877.

Military

Dorrel, Ruth. *Index to Admission Book, Indiana Soldiers and Sailors Home, 1868 through 1995.* Indianapolis, Indiana: Indiana Historical Society, 1997.

Franklin, Charles W. *Indiana, War of 1812 Soldiers: Militia.* Indianapolis: Ye Olde Genealogie Shoppe, 1984.

General Assembly of Indiana. *Record of Indiana Volunteers in the Spanish-American War 1898–1899.* Indianapolis: W. B. Burford, 1900.

Index to Indiana Enrollments of Soldiers, Their Widows and Orphans, 1886, 1890 and 1894. Microfilm of index cards located at the Indiana State Library, Indianapolis. Salt Lake City: Filmed by the Genealogical Society of Utah, 1988. 13 microfilm.

Index to Indiana Volunteers in the Mexican War. Microfilm of index cards located at the Indiana State Library, Indianapolis. Salt Lake City: Filmed by the Genealogical Society of Utah, 1988.

Indiana Adjutant General's Office. *Indiana in the War of the Rebellion.* 8 vols. Indianapolis: W.H.H. Terrell, 1869.

Indiana Historical Commission (Indianapolis). *Gold Star Honor Roll: A Record of Indiana Men and Women Who Died in the Service of the United States and the Allied Nations in the World War, 1914–1918.* Microfilm of original published: Indianapolis: Indiana Historical Commission, 1921. Salt Lake City: Filmed by the Genealogical Society of Utah, 1990.

Indiana Records of Soldier Births, Enlistments, Discharges, Some Deaths, etc., ca. 1869–1964. Microreproduction of index cards at the Northern Indiana Historical Society Museum, South Bend, Indiana. Salt Lake City: Filmed by the Genealogical Society of Utah, 1990.

Indiana State Archives. (*Indianapolis Civil War Resources.* Indianapolis, Indiana: Indiana State Archives, 2002. Online database—www.state.in.us/icpr/webfile/archives/homepage.html.

Indiana. Adjutant General. *Report.* Indianapolis: Adjutant General, 1865–1869.

Perry, Oran. *Indiana in the Mexican War.* Indianapolis: W.B. Burford, contractor for state printing, 1908.

Record of Indiana Volunteers in the Spanish-American War, 1898–1899. Indianapolis: W. B. Burford, 1900.

Terrell, W. H. H., comp. *Report of the Adjutant General of the State of Indiana.* 8 vols. Indianapolis: Indiana Adjutant General's Office, 1869.

Trapp, Glenda K. *Index to the Report of the Adjutant General of the State of Indiana.* Evansville, Indiana: the author, 1986.

United States. Adjutant General's Office. *Muster Pay and Receipt Rolls of Indiana Territory Volunteers or Military of the Period of the War of 1812.* 4 Vols. Washington, D.C.: Adjutant General. n.d.

United States. Adjutant General's Office. *Index to Compiled Service Records of Volunteer Union Soldiers Who Served in Organizations from the State of Indiana, 1861–1865.* Washington, D.C.: The National Archives, 1964.

United States. Selective Service System. *Indiana, World War I Selective Service System Draft Registration Cards, 1917–1918. National Archives Microfilm Publications, M1509.* Washington, D.C.: National Archives, 1987–1988.

United States. War Department. The Adjutant General's Office. *World War I Indiana Enrollment Cards, 1919.* Microfilm of originals in the Indiana State Archives in Indianapolis, Indiana. Salt Lake City: Filmed by the Genealogical Society of Utah, 1990. 35 microfilm.

Waters, Margaret R. *Revolutionary Soldiers, Buried in Indiana [Bound with:] Supplement.* 2 Vols. In 1 (1949, 1954). Reprint. Baltimore: Clearfield Company, 1992.

Wolfe, Barbara. *Index to Revolutionary Soldiers in Indiana.* Indianapolis: Ye Olde Genealogie Shoppe.

World War I Nurses Enrollment Cards, Indiana. Microfilm of card file located at the Indiana State Archives, Indianapolis. (Salt Lake City: Filmed by the Genealogical Society of Utah, 1991).

Vital and Cemetery Records

Cemetery Records of Indiana. 6 vols. Salt Lake City: Genealogical Society, 1954–64.

Cox, Carroll O. *Cemetery Records (Illinois and Indiana).* (Transcript). Salt Lake City: Genealogical Society of Utah, 1983. 2 microfiche.

Dodd, Jordan R., and Norman L. Moyes, comps. *Indiana Marriages, Early to 1825.* Bountiful, Utah: Precision Indexing, Inc., 1991.

Guide to Public Vital Statistics Records in Indiana. Indianapolis: Historical Records Survey, 1941.

Historical Records Survey (Indiana). *Miscellaneous Records of Indiana, 1827–1922.* S.l.: s.n., 1968. 10 microfilm.

Indiana State Library Genealogy Division. *Cemetery Database.* Indianapolis, Indiana: Indiana State Library Genealogy Division, 2002. Online Database—www.statelib.lib.in.us/www/indiana/genealogy/links.html#databases

Indiana, 1851–1900. S.l.: Brøderbund, 1998. CD ROM.

Indiana State Library. Genealogy Division. *Database to an Index of Indiana Marriages Through 1850.* Indianapolis, Indiana: Indiana State Library Genealogy Division, 2002. Online database—www.statelib.lib.in.us/www/indiana/genealogy/links.html#databases.

Indiana State Library, Genealogical Division. *Cemetery Locator File*. Microfilm of original records in the Indiana State Library, Indianapolis, Indiana. Salt Lake City: Filmed by the Genealogical Society of Utah, 1980. 4 microfilm.

Slater-Putt, Dawne Lisa. *Pre-1882 Indiana Births, From Secondary Sources*. Fort Wayne, Indiana: Heritage Pathways, Inc., 1999.

Vincent, Stephen A. *Southern Seed, Northern Soil: African-American Farm Communities in the Midwest*

1765–1900. Bloomington, Indiana: Indiana University Press, 1999.

Volkel, Lowell. *Indiana 1850 Mortality Schedule*. 3 vols. S.l.: L. M. Volkel, 1971.

Volkel, Lowell. *Illinois Mortality Schedule, 1860*. Indianapolis, Indiana: Heritage House, 1979.

Volkel, Lowell. *1870 Illinois Mortality Schedules*. Indianapolis, Indiana: Heritage House, 1985–1987.

County Website	Map Index	Date Created	Parent County or Territory From Which Organized Address/Details
Adams www.adams-county.com	F11	1824	Allen, Randolph Adams County; 112 S 2nd St; PO Box 189; Decatur, IN 46733; Ph. (260) 724-5309 Details: (County Health Department has Birth & Death Records; Clerk of the Circuit Court has Court, Divorce, Guardianship, Marriage, and Probate Records; County Recorder has Land & Property Records; County Treasurer has Tax Records)
Allen www.indico.net/counties/ALLEN/	D11	17 Dec 1823	Unorg. Terr., Randolph Allen County; 715 S Calhoun St Rm 200; Fort Wayne, IN 46802; Ph. (260) 449-7245 Details: (Department of Health has Birth & Death Records; Records Management Division has Burial, Cemetery, Marriage, & Naturalization Records; Central Services Division has Court, Guardianship, Divorce, & Probate Records; Recorder's Office has Land & Property Records; Veteran's Affairs Office has Military Records; Treasurer's Office has Tax Records)
Bartholomew www.rootsweb.com/~inbartho/barth.html	L8	8 Jan 1821	Unorg. Terr., Jackson Bartholomew County; 440 3rd St; PO Box 924; Columbus, IN 47202-0924; Ph. (812) 379-1600 Details: (County Clerk has Marriage, Divorce, Probate & Court Records from 1821, some Naturalization, Cemetery & Military Records; County Recorder has Land Records from 1821; Vit Stat has Birth & Death Records from 1882)
Benton www.bentoncounty.org/	F3	18 Feb 1840	Jasper Benton County; 706 E 5th St Ste #12; Fowler, IN 47944-1556; Ph. (765) 884-1728 Details: (Clerk Circuit Court has Marriage Records from 1841, Divorce & Court Records from 1800's, Probate Records from 1852 & Naturalization Records; County Recorder has Land & Military Records; County Health Department has Birth & Death Records from 1882)
Blackford www.rootsweb.com/~inblackf/index.htm	G10	15 Feb 1838	Jay Blackford County; 110 W Washington St; Hartford City, IN 47348; Ph. (765) 348-1620 Details: (County Clerk has Marriage, Divorce, Probate & Court Records from 1839; City & County Health Officers have Birth & Death Records; County Recorder has Land Records; County Coroner has Burial Records)

County Website	Map Index	Date Created	Parent County or Territory From Which Organized Address/Details
Boone www.bccn.boone.in.us/	H6	29 Jan 1830	**Hendricks, Marion** Boone County; 212 Courthouse Sq; Lebanon, IN 46052-2150; Ph. (765) 482-3510 **Details:** (County Clerk has Marriage Records from 1831, Divorce, Probate & Court Records from 1830; County Health Department has Birth & Death Records; County Recorder has Land Records)
Brown www.browncounty.org/	L7	4 Feb 1836	**Monroe, Bartholomew, Jackson** Brown County; Main St and Van Buren St; Nashville, IN 47448; Ph. (812) 988-5510 **Details:** (Some Records lost in 1873 fire) (County Health Department has Birth & Death Records from 1882; County Clerk has Marriage, Probate & Court Records from 1836, Divorce Records from 1850, Court ordered Birth Records from 1942; County Recorder has Land Records from 1874)
Carroll www.carlnet.org/	F6	1828	**Unorg. Terr.** Carroll County; 101 W Main St; Delphi, IN 46923; Ph. (765) 564-4485 **Details:** (County Clerk has Marriage, Divorce, Probate & Court Records from 1828; County Health Officer has Birth, Death & Burial Records from 1882; County Recorder has Land Records from 1828; Public Library in Delphi has newspapers from 1841; County Historical Society has Burial Records)
Cass www.rootsweb.com/~incass/county.html	E7	1829	**Carroll** Cass County; 103 Cass County Government Bldg; Logansport, IN 46947-3114; Ph. (219) 753-7740 **Details:** (County Health Department has Birth & Death Records; County Clerk has Marriage & Probate Records from 1892, Divorce & Court Records from 1894; County Auditor has Land Records)
Clark www.rootsweb.com/~inclark/	O9	3 Feb 1801	**Knox** Clark County; City Court Bldg 501 E Court Ave; Jeffersonville, IN 47130; Ph. (812) 285-6244 **Details:** (County Clerk has Marriage & Probate Records from 1850 & Court Records; County Recorder has Land Records; County Health Department has Birth & Death Records)
Clay www.claycountyin.org/	K4	12 Feb 1825	**Owen, Putnam, Vigo, Sullivan** Clay County; 609 E Nation Ave; Brazil, IN 47834-2797; Ph. (812) 448-9024 **Details:** (County Health Department has Birth & Death Records; County Clerk has Marriage, Divorce, Probate & Court Records from 1851; County Recorder has Land Records from 1825, some Naturalization & Burial Records)
Clinton www.rootsweb.com/~inclinto/	G6	29 Jan 1830	**Tippecanoe** Clinton County; 265 Courthouse Sq; Frankfort, IN 46041; Ph. (765) 659-6335 **Details:** (County Health Department has Birth & Death Records; County Clerk has Marriage & Probate Records from 1830, Divorce & Court Records from 1888; County Recorder has Land Records)
Crawford www.rootsweb.com/~incrawfo/	P6	29 Jan 1818	**Orange, Harrison, Perry** Crawford County; 316 S Court; English, IN 47118-0375; Ph. (812) 338-2565 **Details:** (County Clerk has Marriage Records from 1818, Divorce, Probate & Court Records from 1860; County Health Department has Birth & Death Records; County Recorder has Land Records)

County Website	Map Index	Date Created	Parent County or Territory From Which Organized Address/Details
Daviess www.indico.net/counties/DAVIESS/	N4	1817	**Knox** Daviess County; County Courthouse; PO Box 739; Washington, IN 47501; Ph. (812) 254-8664 **Details:** (County Clerk has Marriage, Divorce, Probate & Court Records from 1817)
De Kalb www.dekalbnet.org/	C11	7 Feb 1835	**Allen, La Grange** De Kalb County; 100 S Main St; PO Box 810; Auburn, IN 46706; Ph. (219) 925-2112 **Details:** (County Health Department has Birth & Death Records; County Clerk has Marriage & Court Records from 1837, Probate Records from 1855 & school Records 1903–1932; County Recorder has Land Records)
Dearborn www.dearborncounty.org/	L11	7 Mar 1803	**Clark** Dearborn County; 215-B W High St; Lawrenceburg, IN 47025; Ph. (812) 537-8867 **Details:** (Clerk Circuit Court has Marriage Records from 1826, Divorce, Probate & Court Records; County Health Officer has Birth & Death Records; County Recorder has Land Records)
Decatur www.indico.net/counties/DECATUR/	L9	1822	**Unorg. Terr.** Decatur County; 150 Courthouse Sq Ste 5; Greensburg, IN 47240; Ph. (812) 663-8223 **Details:** (County Clerk has Marriage Records from 1822, Divorce, Probate & Court Records; Board of Health has Birth & Death Records)
Delaware www.dcclerk.org/	H10	26 Jan 1827	**Randolph** Delaware County; 100 W Main St; Muncie, IN 47305; Ph. (765) 747-7726 **Details:** (County Clerk has Marriage, Divorce, Probate & Court Records from 1827)
Dubois www.rootsweb.com/~indubois/dubgen.htm	O5	1818	**Pike** Dubois County; 1 Courthouse Sq; Jasper, IN 47546; Ph. (812) 481-7035 **Details:** (Records Library has Marriage, Divorce, Probate, Land, Court & Naturalization Records from 1839 & Military Records from 1864; County Health Department has Birth & Death Records from 1882)
Elkhart www.elkhartcountyindiana.com	B8	29 Jan 1830	**Allen, Cass** Elkhart County; Courthouse Sq; Goshen, IN 46526-3297; Ph. (219) 535-6430 **Details:** (County Health Department has Birth & Death Records; County Clerk has Marriage, Divorce, Probate & Court Records from 1830; County Recorder has Land Records. Some Records are held at the Elkhart County Archives, 3022 W Wilden, Goshen, IN 46528— (574) 535-6668)
Fayette www.indico.net/counties/FAYETTE/	J10	1819	**Wayne, Franklin** Fayette County; 401 N Central Ave; PO Box 607; Connersville, IN 47331-0607; Ph. (765) 825-1813 **Details:** (Clerk Circuit Court has Marriage, Probate, Divorce & Court Records from 1819 & Naturalization Records from 1924)

Indiana

County Website	Map Index	Date Created	Parent County or Territory From Which Organized Address/Details
Floyd www.rootsweb.com/~infloyd/floydigw.html	P8	2 Jan 1819	**Harrison, Clarke** Floyd County; 311 W 1st St; New Albany, IN 47150-3501; Ph. (812) 948-5413 **Details:** (County Health Department has Birth & Death Records; County Clerk has Marriage Records from 1819, Divorce & Court Records from 1863 & Probate Records from 1819)
Fountain http://glenmar.com/~emoyhbo/	H3	1826	**Montgomery** Fountain County; 301 4th St; PO Box 183; Covington, IN 47932; Ph. (765) 793-2192 **Details:** (County Health Department has Birth & Death Records from 1885; County Clerk has Marriage Records from 1827, Divorce, Probate & Court Records from 1830; County Recorder has Land Records from 1828)
Franklin www.rootsweb.com/~infrankl/	K11	1811	**Clark, Dearborn, Jefferson** Franklin County; 634 Main St; Brookville, IN 47012-1405; Ph. (765) 647-3322 **Details:** (County Clerk has Marriage, Divorce, Probate & Court Records from 1811; County Recorder has Land Records from 1811; County Health Department has Birth & Death Records from 1882; Public Library has Cemetery Records from 1817 & Naturalization Records from 1820)
Fulton www.fultoncounty-in.org/	D7	7 Feb 1835	**Allen, Cass, St. Joseph** Fulton County; 815 Main St; Rochester, IN 46975; Ph. (219) 223-2911 **Details:** (County Clerk has Marriage, Divorce, Probate & Court Records from 1836; County Health Department has Birth & Death Records; County Recorder has Land Records)
Gibson www.usroots.com/~jmurphy/gibson/gibson.htm	P3	9 Mar 1813	**Knox** Gibson County; 101 N Main St; Princeton, IN 47670; Ph. (812) 386-8401 **Details:** (County Health Department has Birth & Death Records; County Clerk has Marriage Records from 1813, Divorce, Probate & Court Records from 1820)
Grant ww1.comteck.com/~tdtw98a/grant.htm	G9	10 Feb 1831	**Delaware, Madison, Cass** Grant County; County Courthouse; Marion, IN 46953; Ph. (765) 668-8121 **Details:** (County Health Department has Birth & Death Records; County Clerk has Marriage, Divorce, Probate & Court Records from 1831; County Auditor has Land Records)
Greene www.in-map.net/counties/GREENE/	M4	5 Jan 1821	**Daviess, Sullivan** Greene County; PO Box 229; Bloomfield, IN 47424; Ph. (812) 384-8532 **Details:** (County Clerk has Marriage, Divorce & Court Records from 1821, Probate Records from 1823 & Naturalization Records 1854–1906; County Recorder has Land Records from 1824, Military Records & some Cemetery Records; County Health Department has Birth Records from 1885 & Death Records from 1893)

County Website	Map Index	Date Created	Parent County or Territory From Which Organized Address/Details
Hamilton www.co.hamilton.in.us/	H8	8 Jan 1823	**Unorg. Terr., Marion** Hamilton County; Public Sq; Noblesville, IN 46060; Ph. (317) 776-9629 **Details:** (County Health Department has Birth & Death Records; County Clerk has Marriage, Divorce, Probate & Court Records from 1833; County Recorder has Land Records)
Hancock www.hccn.org/	I8	26 Jan 1827	**Madison** Hancock County; 9 E Main St; Greenfield, IN 46140; Ph. (317) 462-1109 **Details:** (County Clerk has Marriage, Divorce, Probate & Court Records from 1828; County Recorder has Land Records; County Health Department has Birth & Death Records from 1882)
Harrison www.jbntelco.com/~straub/	P7	11 Oct 1808	**Knox, Clark** Harrison County; 300 N Capitol Ave; Corydon, IN 47112-1139; Ph. (812) 738-4289 **Details:** (County Health Department has Birth & Death Records from 1882; County Clerk has Marriage, Probate & Court Records from 1809, Divorce Records from 1815 & Land Records from 1807)
Hendricks www.indico.net/counties/HENDRICKS/	J6	1824	**Unorg. Terr., Putnam** Hendricks County; 51 W Main St; PO Box 599; Danville, IN 46122; Ph. (317) 745-9231 **Details:** (County Health Department has Birth & Death Records from 1882; County Clerk has Marriage, Divorce, Probate & Court Records from 1823; County Auditor has Land Records)
Henry www.indico.net/counties/HENRY/	I10	1822	**Unorg. Terr.** Henry County; 101 S Main St; New Castle, IN 47362; Ph. (765) 529-6401 **Details:** (County Health Department has Birth & Death Records from 1882; County Clerk has Marriage, Divorce, Probate & Court Records from 1822; County Recorder has Land Records from 1823 & Cemetery deeds from 1925)
Howard www.co.howard.in.us/	G8	1846	**Carroll, Cass, Miami, Grant, Hamilton** Howard County; 104 N Buckeye St; PO Box 9004; Kokomo, IN 46904; Ph. (765) 456-2204 **Details:** (Formerly Richardville County. Name changed to Howard 28 Dec 1846) (County Clerk has Marriage, Divorce, Probate & Court Records from 1844; County Recorder has Land Records; County Health Department has Birth, Death & Burial Records)
Huntington www.huntington.in.us/	E9	2 Feb 1832	**Allen, Grant** Huntington County; 201 N Jefferson St. Rm 103; Huntington, IN 46750; Ph. (219) 358-4819 **Details:** (County Health Department has Birth & Death Records from 1882; County Clerk has Marriage Records from 1847, Court Records from 1840, Probate & Divorce Records from 1850; County Recorder has Land Records from 1834)
Jackson www.rootsweb.com/~injackso/	M7	1816	**Washington, Clark, Jefferson** Jackson County; 111 S Main St.; Brownstown, IN 47220; Ph. (812) 358-6116 **Details:** (County Health Department has Birth & Death Records; County Clerk has Marriage, Divorce, Probate & Court Records from 1816; County Auditor has Land Records)

County Website	Map Index	Date Created	Parent County or Territory From Which Organized Address/Details
Jasper www.lanewood.com/	D4	7 Feb 1835	**White, Warren** Jasper County; 115 W Washington; Rensselaer, IN 47978; Ph. (219) 866-4927 **Details:** (Courthouse burned in 1862; all Records destroyed) (County Health Department has Birth & Death Records; County Clerk has Marriage & Divorce Records from 1865, Probate & Court Records from 1864)
Jay www.rootsweb.com/~injay/	G11	7 Feb 1835	**Randolph, Delaware** Jay County; Main & Walnut; Portland, IN 47371; Ph. (219) 726-4951 **Details:** (County Health Department has Birth & Death Records from 1882; County Clerk has Marriage Records from 1843, Divorce Records from 1882, Probate Records from 1836 & Court Records from 1837; County Auditor has Land Records from 1836)
Jefferson www.indico.net/counties/JEFFERSON/	M10	1811	**Dearborn, Clark** Jefferson County; 300 E Main St #203; Madison, IN 47250; Ph. (812) 265-8921 **Details:** (County Health Department has Birth, Death & Burial Records; County Clerk has Marriage, Divorce, Probate & Court Records; County Recorder has Land Records)
Jennings www.rootsweb.com/~injennin/	M9	1817	**Jefferson, Jackson** Jennings County; 275 E Main St; N. Vernon, IN 47265; Ph. (812) 346-5907 **Details:** (County Clerk has Marriage & Probate Records; County Recorder has Land Records; County Health Department has Birth & Death Records)
Johnson	K7	1823	**Unorg. Terr.** Johnson County; County Courthouse 1st Floor; Franklin, IN 46131; Ph. (317) 736-3708 **Details:** (County Health Department has Birth, Death & Burial Records from 1882; County Clerk has Marriage, Divorce, Probate & Court Records from 1830; County Recorder has Land Records)
Knox www.accessknoxcounty.com/	N3	20 Jun 1790	**Northwest Territory** Knox County; 101 N 7th St; Vincennes, IN 47591; Ph. (812) 885-2521 **Details:** (County Clerk has Marriage Records from 1807, Divorce Records, Probate Records from 1806 & Court Records from 1790; County Recorder has Land Records; County Health Department has Birth & Death Records)
Kosciusko www.rootsweb.com/~inkosciu/	C8	7 Feb 1835	**Elkhart, Cass** Kosciusko County; 121 N Lake St; Warsaw, IN 46580; Ph. (219) 372-2331 **Details:** (County Health Department has Birth & Death Records from 1882; County Clerk has Marriage, Divorce, Probate & Court Records from 1836; County Recorder has Land Records; Twp Trustees have Burial Records)
La Grange www.lagrangecounty.org/	B10	2 Feb 1832	**Elkhart, Allen** La Grange County; 105 N Detroit St; La Grange, IN 46761-1853; Ph. (219) 463-6371 **Details:** (County Health Department has Birth & Death Records from 1882; County Clerk has Marriage, Divorce, Probate & Court Records from 1832; County Recorder has Land Records from 1832)

County Website	Map Index	Date Created	Parent County or Territory From Which Organized Address/Details
La Porte www.lc-link.org/	B5	9 Jan 1832	**St. Joseph** La Porte County; 813 Lincoln Way; La Porte, IN 46350; Ph. (219) 326-6808 **Details:** (County Clerk has Marriage Records from 1832, Divorce, Probate & Court Records from 1834; County Recorder has Land Records; County Health Department has Birth, Death & Burial Records)
Lake www.lakecountyin.com/	C3	28 Jan 1836	**Porter, Newton** Lake County; 2293 N Main St; Crown Point, IN 46307; Ph. (219) 755-3440 **Details:** (County Health Department has Birth & Death Records; Clerk Circuit Court has Marriage, Divorce, Probate & Court Records from 1837; County Recorder has Land Records)
Lawrence www.rootsweb.com/~inlawren/lawrengw.htm	M6	7 Jan 1818	**Orange** Lawrence County; County Courthouse; Bedford, IN 47421; Ph. (812) 275-7543 **Details:** (County Clerk has Marriage, Probate, Divorce & Court Records from 1818; County Health Department has Birth & Death Records; County Recorder has Land Records from 1818 & Military Records)
Madison www.rootsweb.com/~inmadiso/index.htm	H9	4 Jan 1823	**Unorg. Terr., Marion** Madison County; 16 E 9th; Anderson, IN 46016; Ph. (765) 641-9457 **Details:** (County Health Department has Birth Records from 1891 & Death Records from 1895; County Clerk has Marriage Records from 1884, Divorce, Probate & Court Records from 1880; County Auditor has Land Records from 1867; County Board of Health has school Records 1904–1932)
Marion www.indygov.org/	J7	1822	**Unorg. Terr.** Marion County; 200 E Washington; Indianapolis, IN 46204; Ph. (317) 327-4740 **Details:** (County Clerk has Marriage & Divorce Records; County Recorder has Birth, Death & Land Records; Probate Court has Probate Records)
Marshall www.co.marshall.in.us/	C7	7 Feb 1835	**St. Joseph, Elkhart** Marshall County; 211 W Madison St; Plymouth, IN 46563-1762; Ph. (219) 936-8922 **Details:** (County Health Department has Birth, Death & Burial Records from 1882; County Clerk has Marriage, Divorce, Probate & Court Records from 1836; County Recorder has Land Records)
Martin www.rootsweb.com/~inmartin/index.htm	N5	17 Jan 1820	**Daviess, Dubois** Martin County; Capitol St; PO Box 120; Shoals, IN 47581-0170; Ph. (812) 247-3651 **Details:** (County Health Department has Birth & Death Records; County Clerk has Marriage & Probate Records from 1820, Divorce & Court Records from 1842; County Recorder has Land Records)
Miami www.rootsweb.com/~inmiami/index.html	E8	2 Feb 1832	**Cass** Miami County; 21 Court St; PO Box 184; Peru, IN 46970; Ph. (756) 472-3901 **Details:** (County Health Department has Birth, Death & Burial Records; County Clerk has Marriage, Divorce, Probate & Court Records from 1843)

County Website	Map Index	Date Created	Parent County or Territory From Which Organized Address/Details
Monroe www.co.monroe.in.us/	L6	**14 Jan 1818**	**Orange** Monroe County; 301 N College Ave; PO Box 547; Bloomington, IN 47402; Ph. (812) 349-2613 mmccoy@co.monroe.in.us **Details:** (County Clerk has Divorce, Guardianship, Marriage, Naturalization, & Probate Records)
Montgomery www.wico.net/~zacho/montco/	H5	**1823**	**Parke, Putnam** Montgomery County; 100 E Main St; Crawfordsville, IN 47933-1715; Ph. (765) 364-6400 **Details:** (County Health Department has Birth & Death Records from 1882; County Clerk has Marriage, Divorce, Probate & Court Records from 1823 & some Naturalization Records; County Recorder has Land Records from 1823; Public Library has Cemetery Records from 1823)
Morgan http://scican2.scican.net/Home/scican_home.htm	K6	**1822**	**Unorg. Terr.** Morgan County; PO Box 1556; Martinsville, IN 46151; Ph. (765) 342-1025 **Details:** (County Clerk has Marriage, Probate & Court Records; County Recorder has Land Records; Board of Health has Birth & Death Records)
Newton www.rootsweb.com/~innewton/	D3	**7 Feb 1835**	**Unorg. Terr.** Newton County; Courthouse Sq; PO Box 49; Kentland, IN 47951; Ph. (219) 474-6081 **Details:** (Attached to St. Joseph, Warren & White Counties before re-creation & organization from Jasper County 8 Dec 1859) (County Clerk has Marriage, Divorce, Probate & Court Records from 1860; County Health Department has Birth & Death Records from 1882; County Recorder has Land Records from 1860)
Noble www.usgennet.org/usa/in/county/noble/	C10	**7 Feb 1835**	**Elkhart, LaGrange, Allen** Noble County; 101 N Orange St; Albion, IN 46701-1097; Ph. (219) 636-2736 **Details:** (County Health Department has Birth & Death Records; County Clerk has Marriage, Divorce, Probate & Court Records from 1859; County Auditor has Land Records; City Clerk has Burial Records)
Ohio www.rootsweb.com/~inohio/	M11	**4 Jan 1844**	**Dearborn** Ohio County; 413 Main St; Rising Sun, IN 47040; Ph. (812) 438-2610 **Details:** (County Clerk has Marriage, Divorce, Probate & Court Records from 1844)
Orange www.co.orange.in.us/	O6	**1816**	**Washington, Knox, Gibson** Orange County; Court St; Paoli, IN 47454; Ph. (812) 723-2649 **Details:** (County Health Department has Birth Records from 1882, Death & Burial Records; County Clerk has Marriage, Divorce, Probate & Court Records from 1816; County Recorder has Land Records from 1816)
Owen www.owencounty.org/index.html	K5	**1819**	**Daviess, Sullivan** Owen County; Main St; PO Box 146; Spencer, IN 47460; Ph. (812) 829-5015 **Details:** (County Health Department has Birth & Death Records from 1882; County Clerk has Marriage & Court Records from 1819, Divorce Records from 1832 & Probate Records from 1833; County Recorder has Land Records from 1819)

County Website	Map Index	Date Created	Parent County or Territory From Which Organized Address/Details
Parke www.rootsweb.com/~inparke/	J4	9 Jan 1821	**Unorg. Terr., Vigo** Parke County; 116 W High St #204; Rockville, IN 47872; Ph. (765) 569-5132 **Details:** (County Health Department has Birth Records from 1902 & Death Records from 1882; County Auditor has Marriage, Divorce, Probate & Court Records from 1833; County Recorder has Land Records from 1833)
Perry www.usroots.com/~jmurphy/perry/perry.htm	P6	7 Sept 1814	**Warrick, Gibson** Perry County; 2219 Payne St; Tell City, IN 47586; Ph. (812) 547-3741 **Details:** (County Clerk has Marriage, Divorce, Probate & Court Records from 1813; County Recorder has Land Records from 1813; County Health Department has Birth & Death Records from 1890)
Pike	O4	1817	**Gibson, Perry** Pike County; 801 Main St; Petersburg, IN 47567; Ph. (812) 354-6025 **Details:** (County Health Department has Birth & Death Records from 1887; Circuit Court Clerk has Marriage, Divorce, Civil, State, & Guardianship Records from 1817; County Recorder has Land Records)
Porter www.porterco.org/	B4	7 Feb 1835	**St. Joseph** Porter County; 16 E Lincolnway #209; Valparaiso, IN 46383; Ph. (219) 465-3450 **Details:** (Attached to St. Joseph County prior to organization 6 Feb 1836) (County Health Department has Birth & Death Records; County Clerk has Marriage, Divorce, Probate & Court Records from 1836; County Auditor has Land Records)
Posey www.rootsweb.com/~inposey/	P2	7 Sept 1814	**Warrick, Knox, Gibson** Posey County; PO Box 606; Mt. Vernon, IN 47620; Ph. (812) 838-1306 **Details:** (County Clerk has Marriage, Divorce, Probate & Court Records from 1815; County Health Department has Birth & Death Records from 1882; County Recorder has Land Records from 1815 & some Military Discharge Records)
Pulaski www.rootsweb.com/~inpulask/	D5	7 Feb 1835	**Cass, St. Joseph** Pulaski County; 112 E Main St; Winamac, IN 46996-1344; Ph. (219) 946-3313 **Details:** (County Clerk has Marriage, Divorce, Probate & Court Records from 1839; County Recorder has Birth & Death Records from 1882 & Land Records)
Putnam www.rootsweb.com/~inputnam/	J5	1822	**Unorg. Terr., Vigo, Owen** Putnam County; 1 Courthouse Sq St; PO Box 546; Greencastle, IN 46135-0546; Ph. (765) 653-2648 **Details:** (County Health Department has Birth & Death Records; County Clerk has Marriage Records from 1822, Divorce & Probate Records from 1825 & Court Records from 1828; County Recorder has Land Records)

County Website	Map Index	Date Created	Parent County or Territory From Which Organized Address/Details
Randolph www.rootsweb.com/~inrandol/	**H11**	**10 Jan 1818**	**Wayne** Randolph County; 100 S Main St; PO Box 230; Winchester, IN 47394; Ph. (765) 584-4214 **Details:** (County Health Department has Birth & Death Records; County Clerk has Marriage, Divorce, Guardianship, Immigration, Probate & Court Records; County Recorder has Land Records from 1818 & newspapers from 1876; Historical Society has Burial & Cemetery Records; County Library has Census; Treasurer's Office has Tax Records; State Archive has Naturalization Records)
Richardville		**15 Jan 1844**	**Carroll, Cass, Miami, Grant, Hamilton** Richardville County; IN **Details:** (see Howard) Name changed to Howard 28 Dec 1846
Ripley www.seidata.com/~ripleych/	**L10**	**27 Dec 1816**	**Dearborn, Jefferson** Ripley County; PO Box 177; Versailles, IN 47042; Ph. (812) 689-6115 **Details:** (County Health Department has Birth & Death Records; County Clerk has Marriage, Divorce, Probate & Court Records from 1818; County Recorder has Land Records)
Rush www.rootsweb.com/~inrush/	**J9**	**1822**	**Unorg. Terr.** Rush County; PO Box 429; Rushville, IN 46173-0429; Ph. (765) 932-2086 **Details:** (County Health Department has Birth, Death & Burial Records from 1882; County Clerk has Marriage, Divorce, Probate & Court Records from 1822; County Recorder has Land Records)
Scott www.scottcounty-in.gov	**N9**	**12 Jan 1820**	**Clark, Jefferson, Jennings** Scott County; 1 E McClain Ave, Ste G-30; Scottsburg, IN 47170; Ph. (812) 752-8450 pcarlisl@purdue.edu **Details:** (Some Original Records have been transferred to Scott County Genealogical Society. Clerk has marriage, Probate, Divorce, & Court Records; Recorders Office has Deeds, Military Records, mortgages, & Miscellaneous Recorded Items; Cicuit Court has Estate Information; Health Department has Birth & Death Records from 1882)
Shelby www.rootsweb.com/~inshelby/index.htm	**K8**	**1822**	**Unorg. Terr.** Shelby County; 407 S Harrison St; PO Box 198; Shelbyville, IN 46176-2161; Ph. (317) 392-6320 phyllismillerfleming@starband.net **Details:** (County Clerk has Court, Divorce, Guardianship, Marriage, Probate Records from 1822 and Naturalization Records from 1854; County Records has Land & Property Records from 1822; County Auditor has Tax & Commissioner's Records, as well as Children's Home Records; Marriage application books 1883–1906, lost books from Clerk's vault were stored in another county while courthouse basement was renovated. Now a few indices are missing—early common pleas, suits decided plaintiff 1896–1906, complete records probate book 1, maybe others.)
Spencer www.spencerco.org/	**Q4**	**10 Jan 1818**	**Warrick, Perry** Spencer County; 200 Main St; Rockport, IN 47635-1478; Ph. (812) 649-6027 **Details:** (County Health Department has Birth Records from 1882 & Death Records from 1830; Cemetery trustees have Burial Records; County Clerk has Marriage Records from 1818, Divorce & Court Records from 1883, Probate Records from 1848 & Naturalization Records 1852–1929; County Recorder has Land Records)

County Website	Map Index	Date Created	Parent County or Territory From Which Organized Address/Details
St. Joseph www.rootsweb.com/~instjose/	B7	29 Jan 1830	**Cass** St. Joseph County; 101 S Main St; South Bend, IN 46601; Ph. (219) 235-9635 **Details:** (County Health Department has Birth, Death & Burial Records; County Clerk has Marriage, Divorce, Probate & Court Records; County Assessor has Land Records)
Starke www.rootsweb.com/~instarke/	C6	7 Feb 1835	**St. Joseph** Starke County; PO Box 395; Knox, IN 46534; Ph. (219) 772-9128 **Details:** (County Clerk has Marriage, Divorce, Probate & Court Records from 1850; County Auditor has Land Records from 1850; County Health Department has Birth & Death Records)
Steuben www.indico.net/counties/STEUBEN/	B11	7 Feb 1835	**LaGrange** Steuben County; 55 Public Sq.; Angola, IN 46703; Ph. (219) 668-1000 **Details:** (County Health Department has Birth & Death Records; County Clerk has Marriage, Divorce, Probate & Court Records from 1837 & Land Records from mid-1800's)
Sullivan www.rootsweb.com/~insulliv/	L3	1817	**Knox** Sullivan County; 100 Courthouse Sq. #304; Sullivan, IN 47882; Ph. (812) 268-4657 **Details:** (County Clerk has Marriage, Divorce, Probate & Court Records from 1850)
Switzerland http://myindianahome.net/gen/switz/index.html	M11	7 Sep 1814	**Dearborn, Jefferson** Switzerland County; 212 W Main St; Vevay, IN 47043; Ph. (812) 427-3175 **Details:** (County Health Department has Birth, Death & Burial Records; County Clerk has Marriage, Divorce, Court & Probate Records from 1814; County Recorder has Land Records)
Tippecanoe www.county.tippecanoe.in.us/	G5	20 Jan 1826	**Unorg. Terr., Parke** Tippecanoe County; 301 Main St; Lafayette, IN 47901; Ph. (765) 423-9326 **Details:** (Clerk Circuit Court has Marriage Records from 1830, Death Records, Divorce Records from 1850, Probate & Court Records from 1832 & Naturalization Records)
Tipton www.rootsweb.com/~intipton/index.htm	G8	15 Jan 1844	**Hamilton, Cass, Miami** Tipton County; 101 E Jefferson; Tipton, IN 46072; Ph. (765) 675-2795 **Details:** (County Clerk has Marriage Records from 1844, Divorce, Probate & Court Records from 1850)
Union www.geocities.com/Heartland/Woods/9061/	J11	5 Jan 1821	**Wayne, Franklin, Fayette** Union County; 26 W Union St; Liberty, IN 47353; Ph. (765) 458-6121 **Details:** (Clerk Circuit Court has Marriage, Divorce, Probate & Court Records from 1821; County Health Department has Birth Records from 1882 & Death Records from 1907)
Vanderburgh www.vanderburghgov.org/	P3	7 Jan 1818	**Gibson, Posey, Warrick** Vanderburgh County; Circuit Center Cts Bldg Rm 216; PO Box 216; Evansville, IN 47732; Ph. (812) 435-5160 **Details:** (County Clerk has Marriage Records from 1916, Divorce Records from 1969, Probate Records from 1850 & Court Records from 1877; County Health Department has Birth & Death Records from 1882; County Recorder has Land Records from 1818 & Military Records from 1865; Willard Library has many of the older Records)

County Website	Map Index	Date Created	Parent County or Territory From Which Organized Address/Details
Vermillion www.rootsweb.com/~invermil/	I3	2 Jan 1824	**Parke** Vermillion County; Courthouse Sq; Newport, IN 47966-0008; Ph. (765) 492-3500 **Details:** (County Health Department has Birth & Death Records from 1882; County Clerk has Marriage, Divorce, Probate & Court Records from 1824; County Recorder has Land Records)
Vigo www.vigocountyin.com/	K3	21 Jan 1818	**Sullivan** Vigo County; 333 Wabash Ave; PO Box 8449; Terre Haute, IN 47808; Ph. (812) 462-3214 **Details:** (County Clerk has Marriage, Probate & Court Records from 1818 & Divorce Records from 1825)
Wabash www.rootsweb.com/~inwabash/	E8	2 Feb 1832	**Cass, Grant** Wabash County; 1 W Hill St; Wabash, IN 46992; Ph. (219) 563-0661 **Details:** (County Clerk has Marriage, Divorce, Probate & Court Records from 1835; County Health Department has Birth & Death Records; County Recorder & Museum has Burial Records)
Warren www.warrenco.net/	G3	19 Jan 1827	**Fountain** Warren County; 125 N Monroe St; Williamsport, IN 47993; Ph. (765) 762-3510 **Details:** (County Clerk has Marriage & Divorce Records from 1827, Probate Records from 1829 & Court Records from 1828; County Recorder has Land Records from 1827; County Health Department has Birth & Death Records from 1882)
Warrick www.indico.net/counties/WARRICK/	P3	9 Mar 1813	**Knox** Warrick County; 107 W Locust St; Boonville, IN 47601; Ph. (812) 897-6160 **Details:** (County Health Department has Birth, Death & Burial Records; County Clerk has Marriage Records from 1819, Divorce, Court & Probate Records from 1813; County Recorder has Land Records)
Washington 165.138.44.13/washington/	N7	1814	**Clark, Harrison, Jefferson** Washington County; 99 Public Sq; Salem, IN 47167; Ph. (812) 883-5748 **Details:** (County Health Department has Birth & Death Records from 1882; County Clerk has Marriage, Divorce, Probate & Court Records from 1814 & newspapers from 1891; County Recorder has Land Records; County Historical Society has many family Records)
Wayne www.co.wayne.in.us/	I11	1811	**Clark, Dearborn** Wayne County; 301 E Main; Richmond, IN 47374; Ph. (765) 973-9220 **Details:** (County Clerk has Marriage Records from 1810, Divorce & Court Records from 1873 & Probate Records from 1818; City-County Health Officer has Birth, Death & Burial Records)
Wells www.rootsweb.com/~inwells/	E10	7 Feb 1835	**Allen, Delaware, Randolph** Wells County; 102 W Market St; Bluffton, IN 46714; Ph. (219) 824-6479 **Details:** (County Health Department has Birth & Death Records; County Clerk has Marriage, Divorce & Court Records from 1837 & Probate Records from 1838; County Recorder has Land Records)

County Website	Map Index	Date Created	Parent County or Territory From Which Organized Address/Details
White www.rootsweb.com/~inwhite/	E5	**1 Feb 1834**	**Carroll** White County; 110 North Main St; PO Box 350; Monticello, IN 47960; Ph. (219) 583-7032 **Details:** (County Clerk has Marriage, Divorce, Probate & Court Records from 1834; County Recorder has Land Records; County Health Department has Birth, Death & Burial Records)
Whitley www.indico.net/counties/WHITLEY/	D9	**7 Feb 1835**	**Elkhart, Allen** Whitley County; 101 W Van Buren St; Columbia City, IN 46725; Ph. (219) 248-3102 **Details:** (County Clerk has Marriage Records from 1836, Divorce & Court Records from 1853 & Probate Records; County Health Department has Birth & Death Records from 1882; County Recorder has Land Records)

Notes

Iowa

Capital: Des Moines

Territory: 1838

State: 1846 (29th)

*Our liberties we prize and
our rights we will maintain*

When Marquette and Joliet discovered Iowa, Native American tribes (Sauk, Fox, Iowa, and Sioux) were well established there. The occasional fur trapper wandered through the country, too. However, it was Julien Dubuque who came in 1788 and began negotiating with Indians to develop the area's resources. Through the permission of the Fox Indians, Dubuque established a mining settlement near the present-day city that bears his name. With the Louisiana Purchase in 1803, the United States acquired the territory and built Fort Madison and Fort Armstrong. Dubuque was abandoned following its founder's death in 1810. Little further settlement occurred until the Fox and Sauk tribes were forced to cede more than 9,000 square miles of Iowa territory in 1833. With the opening of this land, settlers flocked to the area. The first settlers came from the eastern and southern states, the majority of whom originally came from the British Isles.

Iowa was part of the Territory of Indiana immediately after its purchase, then part of the Territory of Louisiana. From 1812 to 1821, Iowa was part of the Missouri Territory. When Missouri became a state in 1821, Iowa was left without government and remained so until 1834. In 1838, Iowa became a territory, following two years each as a part of the Michigan and Wisconsin Territories. In 1846, Iowa became a state with Iowa City as its capital. Des Moines became the capital in 1857.

Immediately prior to and after statehood, thousands of immigrants flocked to Iowa. The principal groups were:
- Scandinavians, to the central and western sections
- Hollanders, to the south central section
- Germans, along the Mississippi River
- Scottish and Welsh, to the mining towns of the southern counties
- Czechs to the east central section

Iowa sided with the Union in the Civil War, sending more than 76,000 men to serve in the Union army.

Look for vital records in the following locations:

- **Birth and death records:** Some counties began keeping birth and death records as early as 1870. It was not required until 1880 and general compliance did not occur until 1924. Delayed registration of births also took place by 1940. The clerk of the district court keeps these files. The Bureau of Vital Records, Iowa State Department of Public Health in Des Moines, has birth, marriage, and death records after July 1, 1880. Copies are available only to immediate family members, so relationship and reason for seeking information must be stated when writing. Statewide indexes by year are available. The birth index begins July 1, 1880. The death index begins January 1891. Parentage is not listed on any death record until July 1904.

- **Marriage and divorce records:** Marriage records from as early as 1850 can be obtained from county clerks. Many are transcribed and published. Early divorce records are located in the district courts. Transcribed copies were sent to the state beginning in 1906. The State Historical Society of Iowa in Des Moines has additional information.

- **Court records and wills:** Probate courts were created when Iowa became a territory. These were eventually discontinued and probate matters assigned to the district court. Copies of wills and probates can be obtained from district court clerks.

- **Census records:** Territorial censuses were taken in 1836, 1838, 1844, and 1846. However, copies exist for only a few counties. State censuses were taken in 1847, 1849, 1851, 1852, 1853, 1854, 1856, 1885, 1895, 1905, 1915, and 1925. A few town censuses were also taken in the 1880's and 1890's.

Iowa Department of Public Health
Bureau of Health Statistics
Lucas State Office Building
Des Moines, IA 50319-0075
(515) 281-4944
www.idph.state.ia.us/eh/health_statistics.asp

State Historical Society of Iowa
East 12th and Grand Avenue
Des Moines, IA 50319
www.iowahistory.org/

Societies and Repositories

Adair County Anquestors Genealogical Society; c/o Greenfield Public Library; PO Box 328; Greenfield, IA 50849-0328; www.rootsweb.com/~iaadair/society.htm.

Adams County Genealogical Society; PO Box 117; Prescott, IA 50859-0177.

Allamakee County Historical Society; PO Box 95; Waukon, IA 52172; www.rootsweb.com/~iaachs.

American/Schleswig-Holstein Heritage Society (ASHHS); 121 West Bryant Street; PO Box 506; Walcott, IA 52773-0506; (563) 284-4184; ASHHS@ASHHS.org; www.ashhs.org.

Ankeny Genealogical Chapter; 1110 N. W. 2nd St.; Ankeny, IA 50021-2320.

Appanoose County Iowa Genealogical Society; 1601 S 16th St; Centerville, IA 52544-3040; www.usgennet.org/usa/ia/county/appanoose/acgs.html.

Audubon County Genealogical Society; 505 Brayton St; Audubon, IA 50025-1301.

Benton County Genealogical Society; c/o Donnette Gossen; 1808 9th Ave.; Belle Plaine, IA 52208; www.rootsweb.com/~iabenton/bcgs.htm.

Benton County Historical Society; PO Box 22; Vinton, IA 52349; www.rootsweb.com/~iabenton/bchs/bchs.htm.

Boone County Genealogical Society; PO Box 453; Boone, IA 50036; www.rootsweb.com/~iabcgs/index.htm.

Boone County Historical Society; 602 Story Street; Boone, IA 50036; bchs@opencominc.com.

Botna Valley Genealogical Society, East Pottawattamie County; PO Box 633; Oakland, IA 51560-0633.

Bremer County Genealogical Society; Attn: Bill Bravener; 903 1st Street SE; Tripoli, IA 50676.

Buchanan County Genealogical Society; 103 4th Ave. SE, Box 4; Independence, IA 50644.

Buena Vista County Historical Society; Box 882; Storm Lake, IA 50598.

Buena Vista Genealogical Society; 221 W. Railroad St.; Storm Lake, IA 50599.

Butler County Genealogical Society; Clarksville Public Library; 103 W. Greene St.; Clarksville, IA 50619; ejohnson@forbin.com; www.pafways.org/genealogy/societies/butler.htm.

Calhoun County Genealogical Society; 426 5th St; Rockwell City, IA 50579-1415.

Carroll Conty, Iowa Genealogical Society; PO Box 21; Carroll, IA 51401-0021.

Cass County, Iowa Genealogical Society; 507 Poplar St; c/o Atlantic Public Library; Atlantic, IA 50022-1241.

Cedar County Genealogical Society; PO Box 52; Tipton, IA 52772-0052; www.rootsweb.com/~iacedar/ccgs.htm.

Cedar County Historical Society; 409 Sycamore St.; Tipton, IA 52772-1649.

Central Community Historical Society; R. R. 2, Box 98; DeWitt, IA 52742; www.rootsweb.com/~iaclinto/gensoc/cencomm.htm.

Central Iowa Genealogical Society; Box 945; Marshalltown, IA 50158-0945; www.marshallnet.com/~manor/genea/cigs.html.

Charter-Pierce Memorial Internet Genealogical Society; 3221 Villa Vista Drive; Des Moines, IA 50316-1338; (515) 266-5326; webbp@dwx.com; www.charter-pierce.org.

Cherokee County Historical Society; PO Box 247; Clegborn, IA 51014-0247.

Chickasaw County Genealogical Society; PO Box 434; New Hampton, IA 50659; www.rootsweb.com/~iachicka/CK_CCGS.htm.

Clarke County Genealogical Society; c/o Osceola Public Library; 300 S. Fillmore; Osceola, IA 50213-1414; www.rootsweb.com/~iaclarke/ccgs.html.

Clarke County Historical Society; Hwy. 69 South; Osceola, IA 50213; www.rootsweb.com/~iaclarke/hissoc.html.

Clayton County Genealogical Society; Box 846; Elkader, IA 52043-0846; www.rootsweb.com/~iaccgs.

Clinton County Genealogical Society; Box 2062; Clinton, IA 52732-2062.

Crawford County Genealogical Society; PO Box 26; Vail, IA 51465.

Dallas County Genealogical Society; Box 264; Dallas Center, IA 50063-0264.

Danish American Heritage Society; c/o James Iverson; 4105 Stone Brooke Road; Ames, IA 50010; iversenji@uswest.net; www.dana.edu/dahs.

Daughters of Union Veterans, Iowa Dept.; 105 S. 4th St.; Guthrie Center, IA 50115-1639.

Decorah Genealogical Association; c/o Decorah Public Library (East Entrance); 202 Win; Decorah, IA 52101-1812; ddiggers@hotmail.com; www.harveyshobbyhut.com/genealogy.

Delaware County Genealogical Society; 300 N. Franklin St.; Manchester, IA 52057-1520.

Des Moines County Genealogical Society; PO Box 493; Burlington, IA 52601-0493.

Dubuque County-Key City Genealogical Society; PO Box 13; Dubuque, IA 52004-0013; dckcgs@yahoo.com; www.rootsweb.com/~iadckcgs.

Dyersville Area Historical Society; 120 3rd SW; Dyersville, IA 52040.

Emmet County Genealogical Society; Estherville Public Library; 613 Central Ave.; Estherville, IA 51334-2294.

Fayette County Genealogical Society; 100 N Walnut; West Union, IA 52175-1347; www.rootsweb.com/~iafayett/iafirst6.htm.

Franklin County Genealogical Society; c/o Hampton Iowa Public Library; 4 Federal St.; South Hampton, IA 50441-1934.

Fremont County Historical Society; Box 671; Sidney, IA 51652-0337.

Gateway Genealogical Society; 618 14th Ave.; Camanche, IA 52730.

Greater Sioux County Genealogical Society; c/o Sioux Center Public Library; 327 First Ave. N.E; Sioux Center, IA 51250-1801; www.rootsweb.com/~iasioux/gscgs.htm.

Greene County, Iowa Genealogical Society; PO Box 133; Jefferson, IA 50129-0133; www.rootsweb.com/~iagreene.

Grundy County Genealogical Society; 708 West St.; Reinbeck, IA 50669-1365.

Guthrie County Genealogical Society; PO Box 96; Jamaica, IA 50128-0096.

Hamilton (Co) Heritage Hunters; 943 1st St; Webster City, IA 50595-2001.

Hancock County Genealogical Society; Box 81; Klemme, IA 50449-0081; (641) 587-2324; www.pafways.org/genealogy/societies/hancock.htm.

Hardin County, Iowa Genealogical Society; PO Box 401; Eldora, IA 50627-0401.

Harrison County, Iowa Genealogical Society; 2810 190th Trail; Woodbine, IA 51579; hcgs51579@prodigy.net; www.rootsweb.com/~iaharris/hcgs.htm.

Howard-Winneshiek Genealogical Society; 320 N. Elm St.; PO Box 362; Cresco, IA 52136; djsowers@powerbank.net; www.rootsweb.com/~iawinnes/wcgs.htm

Humboldt County Genealogical Society; 30 6th St. North; Humboldt, IA 50548; www.pafways.org/genealogy/societies/humboldt.htm.

Ida County Genealogical Society; 1111 S. Main St.; Ida Grove, IA 51445-1708.

Ida County Historical Society; 501 Zobel Lane; Ida Grove, IA 51445; www.rootsweb.com/~iaida/directory/idahis.htm.

Iowa City Genealogical Society; PO Box 822; Iowa City, IA 52244-0822; www.rootsweb.com/~iajohnso/icgensoc.htm.

Iowa County Historical Society; PO Box 288; Marengo, IA 52301.

Iowa Genealogical Society; 628 E. Grand Ave.; Des Moines, IA 50309-1924; igs@iowagenealogy.org; www.iowagenealogy.org.

Iowa Lakes Genealogical Society; 601 Monroe St.; Emmetsburg, IA 50536.

Jackson County Genealogical Chapter; Box 1065; Maquoketa, IA 52060-1065; www.rootsweb.com/~iajackso/JCGenie.html.

Jasper County Genealogical Society; PO Box 163; Newton, IA 50208.

Jefferson County Genealogical Society; 2791 240th St.; Fairfield, IA 52556-8518; www.rootsweb.com/~iajeffer/JCGS.htm.

Johnson County Historical Society; PO Box 5081; Coralville, IA 51141.

Jones County Genealogical Society; PO Box 174; Anomosa, IA 52205-0174; www.rootsweb.com/~iajones/research/research.htm#jcgs.

Keo-Mah Genealogical Society, Inc., Chapter of IGS; Keo-Mah Library; 103 N. 3rd St.; PO Box 616; Oskaloosa, IA 52577-0616; (641) 673-9373; www.geocities.com/Heartland/Acres/2263.

Lee County Genealogical Society; PO Box 303; Keokuk, IA 52632-0303; dasprung@interl.net; www.rootsweb.com/~ialeecgs.

Lime Creek / Winnebago County Genealogical Society; 135 N 11th Street; Forest City, IA 50436-1630; (641) 585-2584; www.pafways.org/genealogy/societies/winnebago.htm.

Linn County, Iowa Genealogical Society; 813 1st Ave. S.E.; PO Box 175; Cedar Rapids, IA 52406-0175.

Louisa County Genealogical Society; PO Box 202; Wapello, IA 52653; www.rootsweb.com/~ialcgs.

Lucas County Genealogical Society; c/o Chariton Public Library; 803 Braden Avenue; Chariton, IA 50049-1742; www.rootsweb.com/~ialucas/Lucasinfor.htm.

Madison County Genealogical Society; PO Box 26; Winterset, IA 50273-0026.

Marion County Genealogical Society; PO Box 395; Knoxville, IA 50138; www.rootsweb.com/~iamcgs/Index.html.

Mills County Genealogical Society; c/o Glenwood Public Library; 109 N. Vine St.; Glenwood, IA 51534-1516.

Monona County Genealogical Society; Box 16; Onawa, IA 51040-0016.

Monroe County Genealogical Society; c/o Albia Public Library; 203 Benton Ave. E.; Albia, IA 52531.

Montgomery County Genealogical Society; 320A Coolbaugh; Red Oak, IA 51566-2416.

Montgomery County Iowa Historical Society; 2700 N 4th Street; PO Box 634; Red Oak, IA 51566; (712) 623-3708; www.rootsweb.com/~iamontgo/montcent.htm.

Muscatine County Genealogical Society; 323 Main; Muscatine, IA 52761-2867.

Nishnabotna Genealogical Society; 1028 Road M 56; Harlan, IA 51537-6020; www.rootsweb.com/~iashelby/scgs.htm.

North Central Iowa Genealogical Society; PO Box 237; Mason City, IA 50402-0237; cbpcpapc@netins.net; www.pafways.org/genealogy/societies/northcentraliowa/index.htm.

Northeastern Iowa Genealogical Society; 503 South Street; Waterloo, IA 50701-1517; http://iowa-counties.com/blackhawk/gene.htm

Northwest Iowa Genealogical Society; 45 First St. SW.; Le Mars, IA 5103–3696; jwintger@lemarscomm.net.

Oelwein Area Genealogical Society; PO Box 389; Oelwein, IA 50662-0389; iaoags@hotmail.com; www.rootsweb.com/~iaoags.

Oelwein Area Historical Society; 900 2nd Avenue SE; Oelwein, IA ; iaoahs@hotmail.com; www.rootsweb.com/~iaoahs.

OHS Ostfriesian Heritage Society; 18419 205th St.; Grundy Center, IA 50638.

Old Fort Genealogical Society; PO Box 1; Fort Madison, IA 52627-0001; ofgensoc@interl.net; http://freepages.genealogy.rootsweb.com/~oldfort.

Page County Genealogical Society; Rural Route 2, Box 236; Shenandoah, IA 51610.

Palo Alto County Genealogical Society; c/o Emmetsburg Public Library; 707 N. Superior; Emmetsburg, IA 50536-2410.

Pocahontas County Genealogical Society; c/o Pocahontas Public Library; 14 Second Ave. N.W.; Pocahontas, IA 50574; (712) 335-7411; audrey@ncn.net; www.rootsweb.com/~iapocaho.

Pocahontas County/Laurens Genealogical Society; Laurens Public Library; 273 N. Third St.; Laurens, IA 50554; www.rootsweb.com/~iapcilgs.

Pottawattamie County Genealogical Society; PO Box 394; Council Bluffs, IA 51502-0394; www.rootsweb.com/~iapottaw/PCGS.htm.

Poweshiek County Historical & Genealogical Society; Box 280; Montezuma, IA 50171-0280; http://showcase.netins .net/web/powshk/index.htm.

Rashid Memorial Library; 3421 Avenue L; Fort Madison, IA 52627; (319) 372-2987.

Ringgold County Genealogical Society; c/o Betty Jo Ruby; 202 Adams St; Diagonal, IA 50845-1001.

Sac County Genealogical Society; PO Box 54; Sac City, IA 50583-0054; www.rootsweb.com/~iasac/gensociety/gensoc.htm.

SAR, Iowa Society; 403 S. Walnut; Mt. Pleasant, IA 52641.

Scott County Iowa Genealogical Society; PO Box 3132; Davenport, IA 52808-3132.

State Library of Iowa; 1112 East Grand Avenue; Des Moines, IA 50319; (515) 281-4105; www.silo.lib.ia.us.

Story County Chapter of the Iowa Genealogical Society; c/o Visitors Bureau' 1601 Golden Aspen Dr. Ste 110; Ames, IA 50010; www.rootsweb.com/~iastory/chapter.htm.

Tama County Tracers Genealogical Society; 200 North Broadway; Toledo, IA 52342-0084.

Taylor County Genealogical Society; Box 8; Gravity, IA 50848-0008.

Tree Stumpers; Rt. 1, Box 65; Meriden, IA 51037.

Union County Genealogical Society; c/o Gibson Memorial Library; 310 N. Maple; Creston, IA 50801.

Van Buren County Genealogical Society; PO Box 158; Keosauqua, IA 52565; www.rootsweb.com/~iavanbur/index.htm.

Wapello County Genealogical Society; PO Box 163; Ottumwa, IA 52501; www.rootsweb.com/~iawapegs.

Warren County Genealogical Society; 306 W. Salem; Indianola, IA 50125-2438.

Washington County Genealogical Society; PO Box 446; Washington, IA 52353.

Wayne County Genealogical Society; Le Compte Library; Corydon, IA 50060-1518.

Webster County Genealogical Society; PO Box 1594; Fort Dodge, IA 50501; www.rootsweb.com/~iawebste/webgenso.htm.

West Liberty Historical Society; 600 E. 4th St.; West Liberty, IA 52776.

Woodbury County Genealogical Society; PO Box 624; Sioux City, IA 51102-0624.

Wright County Genealogical Searchers; PO Box 225; Clarion, IA 50525-0225; gramstad@trvnet.net; www.pafways.org/genealogy/societies/wright.htm.

Bibliography and Record Sources

General

A Bibliography Of Iowa Newspapers, 1836–1976. Iowa: Iowa State Historical Dept., Division of the State Historical Society, 1979.

A Memorial and Biographical Record of Iowa. 2 vols. 1896. Reprint. Marceline, Missouri: Walsworth Publishing Co., 1978.

Andreas, A. T. *Andreas' Illustrated Historical Atlas Of The State Of Iowa, 1875*. Chicago: Lakeside Press, 1875.

Blanchard, Charles. *Religion in Iowa*. Salt Lake City: Filmed by the Genealogical Society of Utah, 1976.

Burgess, JoAnn and Rita Goranson. *Bible Records from Iowa Libraries and Museums*. 4 Vols. N.p., 1977.

Christensen, Thomas Peter. *A History of the Danes in Iowa*. New York: Arno Press, 1979.

Church of Jesus Christ of Latter-day Saints, The. Historical Department. *Journal History*. Salt Lake City: Filmed by the Historical Dept., 1968, 1973. 248 microfilm.

Citizens Historical Association (Indianapolis, Indiana). *Biographical Sketches of Iowans*. Salt Lake City: Filmed by the Genealogical Society of Utah, 1976. 3 microfilm.

Daughters of the American Revolution (Iowa). *Iowa Pioneer Families*. Salt Lake City: Filmed by the Genealogical Society of Utah, 1971. 1 microfilm.

Dawson, Patricia and David Hudson. *Iowa History and Culture: A Bibliography Of Materials Published Between 1952 And 1986*. Ames, Iowa: State Historical Society of Iowa, 1989.

Farmers of Iowa: A List of Farmers of Each County with Post Office n.p. 1892. Salt Lake City: Filmed by the Genealogical Society of Utah, 1978.

Fleming, James. *Goodenows Who Originated in Sudbury, Massachusetts 1638* A.D. Shepherdstown, West Virginia: Goodenow Family Association, 1994.

Fulton, A. R. *The Red Men of Iowa*. Des Moines, Iowa: Mills, 1882.

Gingerich, Melvin. *The Mennonites in Iowa: Marking The One-Hundredth Anniversary Of The Coming Of The Mennonites To Iowa*. Iowa City, Iowa: State Historical Society of Iowa, 1939.

Goedeke, Norma and Shirley Graham. *Swedish Settlements In Iowa And Western Illinois*. Galesburg, Illinois: Knox County Genealogical Society, 1992.

Gue, Benjamin F. *History of Iowa from the Earliest Times to the Beginning of the Twentieth Century*. 4 vols. New York: Century History Co., 1903.

Gue, Benjamin F. and Benjamin F. Shambaugh. *Biographies and Portraits of the Progressive Men of Iowa: Leaders in Business, Politics and the Professions; Together with an Original and Authentic History of the State*. 2 vols. Des Moines: Conaway and Shaw, 1899.

Gue, Benjamin F. *History of Iowa from the Earliest Times to the Beginning of the Twentieth Century*. 4 vols. New York: Century History Co., 1903.

Hamer, Maryanna. *History of the Church of the Brethren on the Northern Plains*. S.l.: s.n., 1977.

Harlan, Edgar Rubey. *A Narrative History of the People of Iowa: With Special Treatment of their Chief Enterprises in Education, Religion, Valor, Industry, Business, etc.* 5 vols. American Historical Society, 1931.

Harris, Katherine, comp. *Guide to Manuscripts*. Iowa City, Iowa: State Historical Society of Iowa, 1973.

Hinshaw, William Wade. *The William Wade Hinshaw Index to Iowa Quaker Meeting Records*. 11 vols. S.l.: s.n., 19–.

Historical Records Survey (Iowa). *Guide to Depositories of Manuscript Collections in the United States, Iowa*. Des Moines: Iowa Historical Records Survey, 1940.

History of Western Iowa: Its Settlement And Growth; A Comprehensive Compilation Of Progressive Events Concerning The Counties, Cities, Town And Villages. . .With An Authentic History Of The State Of Iowa. Iowa City, Iowa: Western Pub., 1882.

Iowa American Revolution Bicentennial Commission. *Century Farm Application*. Salt Lake City: Filmed by the Genealogical Society of Utah, 1978.

Iowa Biographical Dictionary: People of All Times and Places Who Have Been Important to The History and Life of The State. New York: Somerset, 1996.

Iowa Churches: a File at the Iowa Wesleyan College in Mt. Pleasant, Iowa. Salt Lake City: Filmed by the Genealogical Society of Utah, 1975.

Iowa Genealogical Society (Des Moines, Iowa*). Pioneer Certificates, 1800s–1991*. Microfilm of original records located at the Iowa Genealogical Society, Des Moines, Iowa. Salt Lake City: Filmed by the Genealogical Society of Utah, 1987. 14 microfilm.

Iowa Research Outline. Series U.S.-States, no. 16. Salt Lake City: Family History Library, 1988.

Iowa. State Department of History and Archives. *Biographical Data Collection*. Salt Lake City: Filmed by the Genealogical Society of Utah, 1978.

Iowa. State Department of History and Archives. *Biography Files*. Microfilm made from originals at the Iowa State Historical Department in Des Moines. Salt Lake City: Filmed by the Genealogical Society of Utah, 1978. 6 microfilm.

Iowa. State Department of History and Archives. *Family Record Collection*. Microfilm of manuscript at Iowa State Historical Department in Des Moines. Salt Lake City: Filmed by the Genealogical Society of Utah, 1978. 6 microfilm.

Iowa. State Department of History and Archives. *Fifty-Year Iowa Farm Families*. Microfilm made from originals at the Iowa State Historical Department in Des Moines. Salt Lake City: Filmed by the Genealogical Society of Utah, 1978. 2 microfilm.

Johnson, P. Adelstein. *The First Century of Congregationalism in Iowa, 1840–1940*. S.l.: Congregational Christian Conference of Iowa, 1945.

Jones, Louis Thomas. *The Quakers of Iowa*. Iowa City: State Historical Society, 1914.

MacBride, Thomas Huston. *In Cabins and Sod-Houses*. Iowa City: State Historical Society, 1928.

Mitchell, G. P. *A Century of Iowa Baptist History, 1834–1934.*: Pella, Iowa: Baptist Record, 1934.

Morford, Charles. *Biographical Index to the County Histories of Iowa*. Vol. 1. Baltimore: Gateway Press, 1979.

Ministerial Biographies: A File in the Iowa Wesleyan College in Mt. Pleasant, Iowa. Salt Lake City: Filmed by the Genealogical Society of Utah, 1975.

Palen, Margaret Krug. *German Settlers of Iowa: Their Descendants And European Ancestors*. Bowie, Maryland: Heritage Books, 1994.

Peterson, Becki. *Iowa County Records Manual*. Iowa City: State Historical Society of Iowa, 1987.

Petersen, William John. *Iowa History Reference Guide*. Iowa City: State Historical Society of Iowa, 1952.

Petersen, William John. *The Story Of Iowa: The Progress Of An American State*. 4 vols. New York: Lewis Historical Pub. Co., 1952.

Presbyterian Church in the U.S.A. Iowa Synod. *The Presbyterian Church in Iowa, 1837–1900; History*. Rapids, Iowa: Jones & Wells, 1907.

Rodabaugh, Willis P. *A History of the Church of the Brethren In Southern Iowa*. Elgin, Illinois: Brethren Pub. House, 1924.

Sofferan, Janice and Dorothy Warren, comps. *Northwest Iowa Pioneers*. S.l.: s.n., 1978?.

Sopp, Elsie L. *Personal Name Index to the 1856 City Directories of Iowa*. Detroit: Gale Research Co., 1980.

United States Biographical Dictionary and Portrait Gallery of Eminent and Self-Made Men. Chicago: American Biographical Pub. Co., 1878.

Tolzmann, Don Heinrich. *Upper Midwest German Biographical Index*. Bowie, Maryland: Heritage Books, 1993.

Tucker, Elva Louise. *The History of the Universalist Church in Iowa, 1843–1943*. Salt Lake City: Filmed by the Genealogical Society of Utah, 1976.

Vogel, George A. W. *Seventy-Five Years of God's Grace, a History of the Lutheran Church—Missouri Synod in Iowa, 1879–1954*. S.l.: Resolution of the Iowa District East and the Iowa District West, 1954.

Wortman, Verv V. *United Presbyterian Church of Iowa*. Salt Lake City: Filmed by the Genealogical Society of Utah, 1976.

Atlases, Maps and Gazetteers

Alphabetical Listing Of Iowa Post Offices, 1833–1970. S.l.: s.n.

Andreas, A. T. *Illustrated Historical Atlas of the State of Iowa, 1875*. Chicago: Lakeside Press, 1875.

Curtis, Peter H., comp. *Fire Insurance Maps of Iowa Cities and Towns: A List of Holdings*. Iowa City, Iowa: Iowa State Historical Department, 1983.

Dilts, Harold E. *From Ackley to Zwingle: The Origins Of Iowa Place Names*. 2nd ed. Ames, Iowa: Iowa State University Press, 1993.

Hair, James T. *Iowa State Gazetteer*. Chicago: Bailey & Hair, 1865.

Hills, Leon C. *History and Legends of Place Names in Iowa: The Meaning of Our Map*. 2nd ed. Omaha, Nebraska: Omaha School Supply Co., 1938.

Huebinger, M. *Atlas of the State of Iowa*. Davenport: Iowa Publishing Co., 1904.

Maps Taken from County Histories, Etc. and Filed Separately At the Iowa State Historical Society. Salt Lake City: Filmed by the Genealogical Society of Utah, 1976.

Mott, David C. *Abandoned Towns, Villages, and Post Offices of Iowa*. Council Bluffs: J. W. Hoffman and S. L. Purington Publishing, 1973.

Patera, Alan H. *Iowa Post Offices, 1833–1986*. Lake Oswego, Oregon: The Depot, 1986.

Polk, R. L. *Iowa State Gazetteer and Business Directory*. St. Paul: Polk; A.C. Danser, 1882–.

Ramsey, Guy Reed. *Postmarked Iowa: A List of Discontinued and Renamed Post Offices*. Crete, Nebraska: J-B Publishing Co., 1976.

Censuses

Available Census Records and Census Substitutes

Federal Census 1840, 1850, 1860, 1870, 1880, 1900, 1910, 1920

Federal Mortality Schedules 1850, 1860, 1870, 1880

State/Territorial Census 1836, 1838, 1840–1849, 1851, 1852, 1854, 1856, 1859, 1885, 1895, 1905, 1915, 1925

Sac and Fox Indian Census 1847

Dollarhide, William. *The Census Book: A Genealogist's Guide to Federal Census Facts, Schedules and Indexes*. Bountiful, Utah: Heritage Quest, 1999.

Kemp, Thomas Jay. *The American Census Handbook*. Wilmington, Delaware: Scholarly Resources, Inc., 2001.

Lainhart, Ann S. *State Census Records*. Baltimore: Genealogical Publishing Co., Inc., 1992.

Szucs, Loretto Dennis and Matthew Wright. *Finding Answers in U.S. Census Records*. Ancestry Publishing, 2001.

Thorndale, William. *Map Guide to the U.S. Federal Census, 1790–1920*. Baltimore: Genealogical Publishing Co., 1987.

United States. Bureau of Internal Revenue. *Internal Revenue Assessment Lists For Iowa, 1862–1866*. Washington, D.C.: The National Archives, 1988. 16 microfilm.

Court Records, Probate and Wills

Court records, wills and probate records are found in the individual county offices. Many have been transferred to the Iowa State Archives in Des Moines. See the county pages for further information.

Daughters of the American Revolution (Iowa). *Iowa Grave Records And Genealogical Data, 1800–1900*. Microfilm Made From Originals At The Iowa State Historical Department In Des Moines, Iowa. Salt Lake City: Filmed by the Genealogical Society of Utah, 1978. 4 microfilm.

Daughters of the American Revolution. Independence Pioneers Chapter (Missouri). *Wills, 1655–1871.* Independence, Missouri: The D.A.R. chapter, 1970–1971.

Emigration, Immigration, Migration and Naturalization

Palen, Margaret Krug. *German Settlers of Iowa: Their Descendants and European Ancestors.* Bowie, Maryland: Heritage Books, 1994.

Stellingwerff, J. *Amsterdamse Emigranten: Onbekende Brieven Uit De Prairie Van Iowa, 1846–1873.* Amsterdam: Buijten & Schipperheijn, 1975.

Land and Property

Hone, Wade E. *Land and Property Research in the United States.* Salt Lake City: Ancestry Incorporated, 1997.

Iowa American Revolution Bicentennial Commission. *Century Farm Applications.* Microfilm made from originals at the Iowa State Historical Department in Des Moines. Salt Lake City: Filmed by the Genealogical Society of Utah, 1978. 8 microfilm.

Iowa and the Civil War: A Reference Guide. Iowa City, Iowa: State Historical Society of Iowa.

Iowa. Land Department. *Abstract of Lands in Iowa Counties, Which Were Entered, or Sold At the Land Offices.* Microfilm of originals at the Iowa State Historical Department. Salt Lake City: Filmed by the Genealogical Society of Utah, 1978. 5 microfilm.

Iowa. Land Department. *Des Moines River Lands, 1847–1904.* Microfilm of typescript and original copy in the office of Secretary of State, Des Moines, Iowa. Salt Lake City: Filmed by the Genealogical Society of Utah, 1977. 6 microfilm.

Iowa. Land Department. *Miscellaneous Land Records, 1839–1930.* Microfilm of typescript and originals in office of Secretary of State, Des Moines, Iowa. Salt Lake City: Filmed by the Genealogical Society of Utah, 1977. 6 microfilm.

Iowa. Land Department. *School Land Grants, 1849–1917.* Microfilm of original copies at the office of Secretary of State, Des Moines, Iowa. Salt Lake City: Filmed by the Genealogical Society of Utah, 1977. 19 microfilm.

Iowa. Land Department. *Swamp Land Records, 1859–1921.* Microfilm of the typescript in the office of Secretary of State, Des Moines, Iowa. Salt Lake City: Filmed by the Genealogical Society of Utah, 1977. 3 microfilm.

Iowa. Land Department. *Tract Books of Iowa Land Districts, 1838–1910.* Microfilm of the original. Salt Lake City: Filmed by the Genealogical Society of Utah, 1977. 45 microfilm.

Lokken, Roscoe L. *Iowa: Public Land Disposal.* Iowa City: State Historical Society of Iowa, 1942.

Swierenga, Robert P. *Pioneers and Profits: Land Speculation on the Iowa Frontier.* Ames, Iowa: Iowa State University Press, 1968.

Military

Iowa. Adjutant General. *List of Ex-Soldiers, Sailors and Marines Living in Iowa.* Des Moines, Iowa: adjutant general. 1886.

Iowa. War records survey. *Graves Registration Division. Iowa Veterans Buried Out Of State: Graves Registration Service, A Division Of The Adjutant General's Department.* Microfilm of original records in the Iowa State Historical Department, Des Moines. Salt Lake City: Filmed by the Genealogical Society of Utah, 1978. 11 microfilm.

Roster and Record of Iowa Soldiers in the War of the Rebellion. Des Moines, Iowa: state printer, 1908–1911.

Roster Of Soldiers, Sailors And Marines Of The War Of 1812, The Mexican War, And The War Of The Rebellion. . . Lincoln, Nebraska: Nebraska State Genealogical Society, 1988.

Swisher, Jacob A. *The Iowa Department Of The Grand Army Of The Republic.* Iowa City, Iowa: State Historical Society of Iowa, 1936.

The Northern Border Brigade: A Story Of Military Beginnings. Salt Lake City: Filmed by the Genealogical Society of Utah, 1976.

United States. Record and Pension Office. *Compiled Service Records Of Volunteer Soldiers Who Served During The Mexican War In Mormon Organizations.* Washington, D.C.: National Archives. Central Plains Region, 1961. 3 microfilm.

United States. Selective Service System. *Iowa, World War I Selective Service System Draft Registration Cards, 1917–1918. National Archives Microfilm Publications, M1509.* Washington, D.C.: National Archives, 1987–1988.

Vital and Cemetery Records

Dolan, John P., and Lisa Lacher. *Guide To Public Records Of Iowa Counties.* Des Moines: Connie Wimer, 1986.

Fretwell, Sheila S. *Iowa Marriages Before Statehood, 1835–1846.* Waterloo, Iowa: Sheila S. Fretwell, 1985.

Guide to Public Vital Statistics in Iowa. Des Moines: Historical Records Survey, 1941.

Iowa Cemetery and Grave Records by the Grave Registration Project of the Works Progress Administration and the Daughters of the American Revolution. Microfilm made from originals at the Iowa State Historical Department in Des Moines. Salt Lake City: Genealogical Society of Utah, 1978. Microfilm, 21 rolls.

Iowa. State Department of History and Archives. *Iowa Cemeteries.* Microfilm made from originals at the Iowa State Historical Department in Des Moines. Salt Lake

City: Filmed by the Genealogical Society of Utah, 1978. 7 microfilm.

Iowa. State Department of History and Archives. *Iowa Cemetery and Grave Records By Grave Registration Project of the W.P.A. and D.A.R.* Microfilm made from originals at the Iowa State Historical Department in Des Moines. Salt Lake City: Filmed by the Genealogical Society of Utah, 1978. 21 microfilm.

Iowa. State Department of History and Archives. *Iowa Marriages, Ca. 1844–1900.* Microfilm made from originals at the Iowa State Historical Department in Des Moines. Salt Lake City: Filmed by the Genealogical Society of Utah, 1978.

Liahona Research. *Iowa Marriages, Early to 1850.* Bountiful, Utah: AGLL, 1990.

Work Projects Administration (Iowa War Records Survey). *Iowa Veterans Buried Out of State General's Department.* Microfilm of original records in the Iowa State Historical Department, Des Moines. Salt Lake City: Filmed by the Genealogical Society of Utah, 1978. 11 microfilm.

County Website	Map Index	Date Created	Parent County or Territory From Which Organized Address/Details
Adair www.rootsweb.com/~iaadair/	**L9**	**15 Jan 1851**	**Pottawattamie** Adair County; PO Box L; Greenfield, IA 50849-1290; Ph. (515) 743-2445 **Details:** (Attached to Pottawattamie & Cass Counties prior to organization 6 May 1854) (Clerk District Court has Birth & Death Records from 1880, Marriage Records from 1870, Divorce, Probate & Clerk Records from 1852)
Adams www.co.adams.ia.us/	**M9**	**15 Jan 1851**	**Pottawattamie** Adams County; 500 9th St; Corning, IA 50841; Ph. (515) 322-4711 **Details:** (Organized 7 Mar 1853) (Clerk District Court has Birth & Death Records from 1880, Marriage Records from 1853, Divorce Records from 1910, Probate & Clerk Records from 1860; County Recorder has Land Records)
Allamakee www.allamakeecounty.com/	**D3**	**20 Feb 1847**	**Unorg. Terr.** Allamakee County; 110 Allamakee St; PO Box 248; Waukon, IA 52172-1794; Ph. (563) 568-6351 **Details:** (Attached to Clayton County prior to organization 6 Mar 1849) (County Recorder has Birth & Death Records from 1880, Marriage Records from 1849 & Land Records from 1851; Clerk Courts has Divorce, Probate & Clerk Records from 1852 & Naturalization Records from 1849)
Appanoose www.rootsweb.com/~iaappano/app.htm	**H10**	**17 Feb 1843**	**Unorg. Terr.** Appanoose County; County Courthouse; Centerville, IA 52544; Ph. (515) 856-6101 **Details:** (Attached to Davis & Van Buren Counties prior to organization 3 Aug 1846) (Clerk District Court has Birth & Death Records from 1880, Marriage Records from 1846, Divorce, Probate & Clerk Records from 1847 & Naturalization Records 1868–1953; County Recorder has Land & Military Discharge Records from 1850)
Audubon www.auduboncounty.org/	**M8**	**15 Jan 1851**	**Pottawattamie** Audubon County; County Courthouse; Audubon, IA 50025; Ph. (712) 563-4275 **Details:** (Attached to Cass County prior to organization 9 Jul 1855) (Clerk District Court has Birth, Death & Burial Records from 1880, Marriage Records from 1856, Divorce Records from 1867, Clerk Records from 1861 & Probate Records from 1855; County Recorder has Land Records)

County	Map	Date	Parent County or Territory From Which Organized
Website	Index	Created	Address/Details

Bancroft | | 15 Jan 1851 | **Unorg. Terr.**
Bancroft County; IA
Details: (Merged into Kossuth 1855)

Benton | F6 | 21 Dec 1837 | **Dubuque**
Benton County; 111 E 4th St; PO Box 719; Vinton, IA 52349-1771;
Ph. (319) 472-2766
Details: (Attached to Jackson & Linn Counties prior to organization 1 Mar 1846) (County Clerk of Court has Burial, Cemetery, Court, Divorce, Guardianship, Immigration, Naturalization, & Probate Records; County Recorder has Birth, Death, Marriage, Military, & Tax Records; County Assessor has Land Records)

Black Hawk | G5 | 17 Feb 1843 | **Buchanan**
www.co.black-hawk.ia.us/
Black Hawk County; 316 E 5th St; Waterloo, IA 50703-4712;
Ph. (319) 833-3012
Details: (Attached to Buchanan, Benton & Delaware Counties prior to organization 17 Aug 1853) (Clerk District Court has Marriage Records from 1854, Divorce & Probate Records from 1880, Birth & Death Records from 1880)

Boone | K7 | 13 Jan 1846 | **Unorg. Terr.**
www.booneiowa.homestead.com/index.html
Boone County; County Courthouse; Boone, IA 50036;
Ph. (515) 432-6291
Details: (Attached to Polk & Linn Counties prior to organization 1 Oct 1849) (Clerk District Court has Birth & Death Records from 1880, Marriage & Probate Records from 1850, Divorce Records from 1900, Clerk Records from 1851, school Records 1889–1925 & Naturalization Records 1867–1916; County Recorder has Land Records)

Bremer | G4 | 15 Jan 1851 | **Unorg Terr.**
www.co.bremer.ia.us/
Bremer County; 415 E Bremer Ave; PO Box 328; Waverly, IA 50677-3536; Ph. (319) 352-5661
Details: (Attached to Buchanan County prior to organization 15 Aug 1853) (County Recorder has Birth, Marriage, Death & Land Records from 1800's; Clerk Courts has Divorce, Probate & Clerk Records)

Buchanan | E5 | 21 Dec 1837 | **Dubuque**
www.buchanancounty.com/
Buchanan County; 210 5th Ave NE; Independence, IA 50644-1959;
Ph. (319) 334-2196
Details: (Attached to Dubuque & Delaware Counties prior to organization 4 Oct 1847) (Clerk District Court has Birth & Death Records from 1880, Marriage Records from 1848, Divorce, Probate & Clerk Records from 1845)

Buena Vista | N4 | 15 Jan 1851 | **Unorg. Terr.**
www.co.buena-vista.ia.us/
Buena Vista County; 215 E 5th St; PO Box 1186; Storm Lake, IA 50588-1186; Ph. (712) 749-2546
Details: (Attached to Woodbury County prior to organization 20 Nov 1858) (Clerk District Court has Birth, Marriage, Death & Probate Records from 1880, Divorce & Clerk Records from 1877)

Buncombe | | 15 Jan 1851 | **Unorg. Terr.**
Buncombe County; IA
Details: (see Lyon) Name changed to Lyon 1861

County Website	Map Index	Date Created	Parent County or Territory From Which Organized Address/Details
Butler www.butlercoiowa.org/	**H4**	**15 Jan 1851**	**Unorg. Terr.** Butler County; PO Box 325; Allison, IA 50602; Ph. (319) 267-2487 **Details:** (Attached to Buchanan & Black Hawk Counties prior to organization 2 Oct 1854) (Clerk District Court has Birth & Death Records from 1880, Marriage Records from 1854, Probate Records from early 1800's, Divorce & Clerk Records from 1861)
Calhoun www.rootsweb.com/~iacalhou/	**M5**	**15 Jan 1851**	**Unorg. Terr.** Calhoun County; PO Box 273; Rockwell City, IA 50579-0273; Ph. (712) 297-8122 **Details:** (Formerly Fox County. Name changed to Calhoun 1852) (Clerk District Court has Birth, Death & Probate Records from 1880, Marriage Records from 1863, Burial Records from 1900, Divorce Records from 1906 & Clerk Records from 1872)
Carroll www.rootsweb.com/~iacarrol/Carroll.html	**M6**	**15 Jan 1851**	**Pottawattamie** Carroll County; PO Box 867; Carroll, IA 51401-0867; Ph. (712) 792-4327 **Details:** (Attached to Shelby & Guthrie Counties prior to organization 17 Aug 1855) (Clerk District Court has Birth & Death Records from 1880, Marriage Records from 1868, Divorce Records from 1923, Probate Records from 1858, Clerk Records from 1871, Naturalization Records from 1873, tax roll 1934 & state census; County Recorder has Land Records)
Cass www.nishna.net/tourism.html	**M8**	**15 Jan 1851**	**Pottawattamie** Cass County; 7th St Courthouse; Atlantic, IA 50022; Ph. (712) 243-2105 **Details:** (Organized 7 Mar 1853) (Clerk District Court has Birth & Death Records from 1880, Marriage Records from 1877, Divorce Records from 1906, Probate Records from 1870 & Clerk Records from 1865)
Cedar www.iowacity.com/cedarco/#cedar	**D7**	**21 Dec 1837**	**Dubuque** Cedar County; 400 Cedar St; Tipton, IA 52772-1752; Ph. (319) 886-2101 **Details:** (County Recorder has Birth, Death & Burial Records from 1880, Marriage & Land Records; Clerk District Court has Probate & Clerk Records from 1839 & Divorce Records from 1850)
Cerro Gordo future website at www.usgenweb.com/	**I3**	**15 Jan 1851**	**Unorg. Terr.** Cerro Gordo County; 220 N Washington Ave; Mason City, IA 50401-3254; Ph. (515) 421-3058 **Details:** (Attached to Floyd County prior to organization 29 Dec 1855) (County Recorder has Birth, Marriage, Death & Land Records from 1882; Clerk Courts has Divorce, Probate & Clerk Records)
Cherokee www.rootsweb.com/~iacherok/cherokee.htm	**O4**	**15 Jan 1851**	**Unorg. Terr.** Cherokee County; PO Box F; Cherokee, IA 51012; Ph. (712) 225-6735 **Details:** (Attached to Woodbury County prior to organization 2 Oct 1858) (Clerk District Court has Birth & Death Records from 1880, Marriage Records from 1872, Divorce, Probate, Clerk & some Cemetery Records)

County Website	Map Index	Date Created	Parent County or Territory From Which Organized Address/Details
Chickasaw www.chickasawcoia.org	**G3**	**15 Jan 1851**	**Unorg. Terr.** Chickasaw County; Prospect St; PO Box 311; New Hampton, IA 50659; Ph. (641) 394-2100/2068 **Details:** (Attached to Fayette County prior to organization 12 Sep 1853) (County Auditor has Birth, Burial, Cemetery, Census, Court, Death, Divorce, Land, Marriage, Probate, Tax, & Other Historical Records)
Clarke www.rootsweb.com/~iaclarke/	**K9**	**13 Jan 1846**	**Unorg. Terr.** Clarke County; 117 1/2 S Main St; Osceola, IA 50213-1299; Ph. (515) 342-2213 **Details:** (Attached to Lucas & Kishkekosh Counties prior to organization 21 Aug 1851) (Clerk District Court has Birth & Death Records from 1880, Marriage Records from 1850, Probate & Clerk Records from 1865 & Divorce Records from 1905; County Recorder has Land Records)
Clay www.co.clay.ia.us/	**N3**	**15 Jan 1851**	**Unorg. Terr.** Clay County; 215 W 4th St; Spencer, IA 51301-3822; Ph. (712) 262-4335 **Details:** (Attached to Woodbury County prior to organization 15 Oct 1858) (Clerk District Court has Probate Records from 1871, Divorce Records from 1906 & Clerk Records from 1869; County Auditor has Land Records)
Clayton www.rootsweb.com/~iaclayto/index.html	**D4**	**21 Dec 1837**	**Dubuque** Clayton County; 111 High St SE; Elkader, IA 52043; Ph. (319) 245-2204 **Details:** (Clerk District Court has Birth & Divorce Records from 1880, Marriage Records from 1848, Death Records 1880–1921 & from 1941, Probate & Clerk Records from 1840 & Naturalization Records from 1858; County Recorder has Land Records from 1839)
Clinton www.clintoncountyiowa.com/	**B7**	**21 Dec 1837**	**Dubuque** Clinton County; 1900 N 3rd St; PO Box 157; Clinton, IA 52732-0157; Ph. (319) 243-6210 **Details:** (Attached to Scott County prior to organization 5 Jan 1841) (Clerk District Court has Birth & Death Records 1880–1935 & from 1941, Marriage & Probate Records from 1840, Divorce & Clerk Records from mid-1800's; County Recorder has Land Records from 1840)
Cook		**1838**	**Des Moines** Cook County; IA **Details:** (Attached to Muscatine. Eliminated 18 Jan 1838 to Muscatine)
Crawford www.rootsweb.com/~iacrawfo/	**O6**	**1 Jan 1851**	**Pottawattamie, Unorg. Terr.** Crawford County; 1202 Broadway; PO Box 546; Denison, IA 51442; Ph. (712) 263-2242 **Details:** (Attached to Shelby County prior to organization 3 Sep 1855) (County Recorder has Birth & Death Records from 1880, Marriage Records from 1855, Land Records from 1859 & Military Records; Clerk Courts has Divorce Records from 1906, Probate Records from 1869, Clerk Records from 1866 and some Naturalization Records)

County	Map	Date	Parent County or Territory From Which Organized
Website	Index	Created	Address/Details

Crocker 1871 **Kossuth**

Crocker County; IA

Details: (Eliminated 11 Dec 1871 to Kossuth)

Dallas K7 **13 Jan 1846** **Unorg. Terr.**
www.co.dallas.ia.us/

Dallas County; 801 Court St; PO Box 38; Adel, IA 50003;
Ph. (515) 993-5804

Details: (Attached to Polk & Mahaska Counties prior to organization 1 Mar 1847) (Clerk District Court has Birth & Death Records from 1880, Marriage Records from 1850, Divorce Records from 1881, Probate Records from 1863 & Clerk Records from 1860; County Recorder has Land Records)

Davis G10 **17 Feb 1843** **Unorg. Terr.**
www.rootsweb.com/~iadavis/davis.htm

Davis County; 100 Courthouse Sq; Bloomfield, IA 52537-1600;
Ph. (515) 664-2011

Details: (Attached to Van Buren County prior to organization 1 Mar 1844) (Clerk District Court has Birth & Death Records from 1880, Marriage Records from 1844, Divorce, Probate & Clerk Records from 1844)

Decatur J10 **13 Jan 1846** **Unorg. Terr.**
www.rootsweb.com/~iadecatu/

Decatur County; 207 Main St; Leon, IA 50144-1647;
Ph. (515) 446-4331

Details: (Attached to Davis County prior to organization 6 May 1850; Courthouse burned in 1874) (County Clerk has Birth, Death, Divorce & Probate Records from 1880, Marriage & Land Records from 1874 & some Military Discharge & Cemetery Records)

Delaware D5 **21 Dec 1837** **Dubuque**
www.rootsweb.com/~iadelawa/

Delaware County; 301 E Main; PO Box 527; Manchester, IA 52057-0527; Ph. (319) 927-4942

Details: (Organized 19 Nov 1841) (Clerk District Court has Birth & Death Records from 1880, Marriage, Divorce & Clerk Records from 1851 & Probate Records from 1849; County Recorder has Land Records)

Des Moines D10 **1 Oct 1834** **Michigan Terr.**
www.rootsweb.com/~iadesmoi/

Des Moines County; 513 Main St; PO Box 158; Burlington, IA 52601; Ph. (319) 753-8262

Details: (Clerk District Court has Birth Records from 1880, Death Records 1880–1921 & from 1941, Marriage, Divorce, Probate & Clerk Records from 1835 & Naturalization Records from 1840)

Dickinson N2 **15 Jan 1851** **Unorg. Terr.**
www.co.dickinson.ia.us/

Dickinson County; 18th & Hill County Courthouse; Spirit Lake, IA 51360; Ph. (712) 336-1138

Details: (Attached to Woodbury County prior to organization 3 Aug 1857) (Clerk District Court has Birth, Marriage, Death, Burial, Divorce, Probate & Clerk Records from 1880; County Recorder has Land Records)

County Website	Map Index	Date Created	Parent County or Territory From Which Organized Address/Details
Dubuque www.rootsweb.com/~iadubuqu/	C5	1 Oct 1834	**Michigan Terr.** Dubuque County; 720 Central Ave; Dubuque, IA 52001; Ph. (319) 589-4418 **Details:** (Clerk District Court has Birth & Death Records from 1880, Marriage Records from 1840, Divorce Records from 1900, Probate Records from 1835 & Clerk Records from 1836; County Recorder has Land Records from 1836)
Emmet www.emmet.org/pmc/	M2	15 Jan 1851	**Unorg. Terr.** Emmet County; 609 1st Ave N; Estherville, IA 51334; Ph. (712) 362-3325 **Details:** (Attached to Boone & Webster Counties prior to organization 7 Feb 1859) (Clerk District Court has Birth Records from 1883, Marriage & Death Records from 1890, Divorce Records from 1915 & Probate Records from 1885)
Fayette www.rootsweb.com/~iafayett/	E4	21 Dec 1837	**Dubuque** Fayette County; 114 N Vine St; West Union, IA 52175; Ph. (319) 422-3234 **Details:** (Attached to Clayton County prior to organization 26 Aug 1850) (County Recorder has Birth & Death Records from 1880, Marriage Records from 1851 & Land Records from 1855; Clerk Courts has Divorce Records from 1897, Probate Records from 1869, Clerk Records from 1852 & Naturalization Records)
Floyd www.rootsweb.com/~iafloyd/	H3	15 Jan 1851	**Unorg. Terr.** Floyd County; 101 S Main St; Charles City, IA 50616; Ph. (515) 228-7111 **Details:** (Attached to Fayette & Chickasaw Counties prior to organization 4 Sep 1854) (County Recorder has Birth, Death, & Marriage Records from 1854—Missing 1921–1941; Land Records from 1854; Military Records from 1864; Naturalization Records from 1882)
Fox		1853	**Unorg. Terr.** Fox County; IA **Details:** (see Calhoun) Name changed to Calhoun 22 Jan 1853
Franklin www.pafways.org/iagenweb/franklin/	I4	15 Jan 1851	**Unorg. Terr.** Franklin County; 12 1st Ave NW; Hampton, IA 50441; Ph. (515) 456-5626 **Details:** (Attached to Chickasaw, Fayette & Hardin Counties prior to organization 3 Mar 1856) (Clerk Circuit Court has Birth & Death Records from 1880, Marriage Records from 1855, Probate Records from 1864, Divorce & Clerk Records from 1869; County Recorder has Land Records)
Fremont www.rootsweb.com/~iafremon/	O10	24 Feb 1847	**Unorg. Terr.** Fremont County; PO Box 549; Sidney, IA 51652-0549; Ph. (712) 374-2031 **Details:** (Attached to Appanoose County prior to organization 10 Sep 1849) (Clerk District Court has Birth & Death Records from 1880, except 1935–1941, limited Marriage Records from 1848, Divorce, Probate & Clerk Records; County Recorder has Land Records)

County Website	Map Index	Date Created	Parent County or Territory From Which Organized Address/Details
Greene www.co.greene.ia.us	L6	15 Jan 1851	**Unorg. Terr.** Greene County; 114 N Chestnut; County Courthouse; Jefferson, IA 50129-2114; Ph. (515) 386-5680 auditor@co.greene.ia.us **Details:** (Attached to Dallas County prior to organization 25 Aug 1853) (Recorder's Office has Birth & Land Records from 1880, Death Records from 1896, Marriage Records from 1850, Military Records from 1919, & Naturaliation Records; Clerk of Court has Court & Divorce Records from 1880, & Guardianship & Probate Records form 1850; Auditor's Office has Land Records from 1880, Census, Newspapers, & Tax Records; Townships/Cities have Burial Records; State has Birth Records 1921–1941)
Grundy www.grundycounty.org	H5	15 Jan 1851	**Unorg. Terr.** Grundy County; 706 G Ave; Grundy Center, IA 50638; Ph. (319) 824-3234 info@gccourthouse.org **Details:** (Attached to Buchanan & Black Hawk Counties prior to organization 25 Dec 1856) (County Recorder has Birth, Death, Immigration, Land, Marriage, Military, Naturalization, & Other Historical Records; Clerk District Court has Court, Divorce, Guardianship, & Probate Records; County Treasurer has Tax Records)
Guthrie www.rootsweb.com/~iaguthri/html/index.html	L8	15 Jan 1851	**Unorg. Terr.** Guthrie County; 200 N 5th St; Guthrie Center, IA 50115-1331; Ph. (515) 747-3415 **Details:** (Clerk District Court has Birth & Death Records from 1880, Marriage Records from 1852, Divorce Records from 1883, Probate Records from 1881 & Clerk Records from 1916)
Hamilton www.hamiltoncounty.org/	J5	8 Jan 1857	**Webster** Hamilton County; County Courthouse; Webster City, IA 50595-3158; Ph. (515) 832-4640 **Details:** (Clerk District Court has Birth, Marriage, Death, Divorce, Probate & Clerk Records from 1880)
Hancock www.pafways.org/iagenweb/hancock/	J3	15 Jan 1851	**Unorg. Terr.** Hancock County; 855 State St; Garner, IA 50438-1645; Ph. (515) 923-2532 **Details:** (Attached to Boone & Webster Counties prior to organization 25 Nov 1858) (Clerk District Court has Birth, Marriage, Death, Burial & Divorce Records from 1880, Probate & Clerk Records from 1856)
Hardin www.co.hardin.ia.us/	I5	15 Jan 1851	**Unorg. Terr.** Hardin County; 1215 Edgington Ave; Courthouse; Eldora, IA 50627; Ph. (641) 858-2320 **Details:** (Attached to Marshall County prior to organization 2 Mar 1853) (Clerk of District Court has Probate, Divorce, & Court Records; County Recorder has Birth, Marriage, & Death Records; County Auditor has Land Records)
Harrison www.rootsweb.com/~iaharris/	P7	15 Jan 1851	**Pottawattamie** Harrison County; 113 N 2nd Ave; Logan, IA 51546-1331; Ph. (712) 644-2665 **Details:** (Organized 7 Mar 1853) (Clerk District Court has Birth & Death Records from 1880, Marriage & Divorce Records from 1853, Probate Records from 1869, Clerk Records from 1850 & some Burial Records)

County	Map	Date	Parent County or Territory From Which Organized
Website	Index	Created	Address/Details

Henry   **E10**   **7 Dec 1836**   **Des Moines**
www.co.henry.ia.us.com

Henry County; 100 E Washington St; Mount Pleasant, IA 52641;
Ph. (319) 385-0756 supervisors@co.henry.ia.us
Details: (County Recorder has Birth, Burial, Cemetery, Death, Land, Marriage, & Military Records; County Auditor has Census & Land Records; County Clerk has Divorce, Guardianship & Probate Record; County Treasurer has Tax Records)

Howard   **G2**   **15 Jan 1851**   **Unorg. Terr.**
www.crescoia.com/howardcounty/index.html

Howard County; 218 N Elm St; Cresco, IA 52136-1522;
Ph. (319) 547-2661
Details: (Attached to Floyd County prior to organization 15 Sep 1855) (Clerk District Court has Birth, Marriage & Death Records from 1880, Divorce & Clerk Records from 1876 & Probate Records from 1877; County Recorder has Land Records from 1855)

Humboldt   **L4**   **31 Aug 1857**   **Webster, Kossuth**
www.pafways.org/iagenweb/humboldt/

Humboldt County; County Courthouse; Dakota City, IA 50529-9999;
Ph. (515) 332-1806
Details: (Clerk District Court has Birth Records from 1880, Marriage Records from 1858, Death Records from 1895, Divorce Records from 1890, Probate Records from 1873 & Clerk Records from 1892)

Humboldt, old   **15 Jan 1851**   **Unorg. Terr.**

Humboldt, old County; IA
Details: (Attached to Boone. Abolished 24 Jan 1855 & absorbed by Kossuth & Webster Counties)

Ida   **O5**   **15 Jan 1851**   **Unorg. Terr.**
www.rootsweb.com/~iaida/

Ida County; 401 Moorehead St; Ida Grove, IA 51445-1429;
Ph. (712) 364-2628
Details: (Attached to Woodbury County prior to organization 1 Jan 1859) (Clerk District Court has Birth, Marriage, Death, Divorce, Probate & Clerk Records from 1880; County Recorder has Land Records)

Iowa   **F7**   **17 Feb 1843**   **Keokuk**
www.rootsweb.com/~iaiowa/

Iowa County; Court Ave; PO Box 266; Marengo, IA 52301;
Ph. (319) 642-3914
Details: (Attached to Poweshiek & Johnson Counties prior to organizaton 1 Jul 1845) (County Recorder has Birth & Death Records from 1880, Marriage Records from 1851, Cemetery Records from 1867 & Land Records; Clerk District Court has Probate, Clerk & Divorce Records)

Jackson   **B6**   **21 Dec 1837**   **Dubuque**
www.rootsweb.com/~iajackso/

Jackson County; 201 W Platt St; Maquoketa, IA 52060-2243;
Ph. (319) 652-4946
Details: (Clerk District Court has Birth & Death Records from 1880, Marriage Records from 1850, Divorce Records from 1906, Probate Records from 1869 & Clerk Records from 1858)

County Website	Map Index	Date Created	Parent County or Territory From Which Organized Address/Details
Jasper http://iagenweb.org/jasper/	**I7**	**13 Jan 1846**	**Unorg. Terr.** Jasper County; 101 First St. N Room 104; Newton, IA 50208; Ph. (641) 792-3255 **Details:** (Attached to Mahaska County prior to organization 1 Mar 1846) (County Recorder has Birth & Death Records from 1880, Marriage Records from 1846, & Land & Military Records from 1855; Clerk of District Court has Probate Records from 1882 & Court Records from 1857)
Jefferson www.rootsweb.com/~iajeffer/index.htm	**F10**	**21 Jan 1839**	**Henry, Unorg. Terr.** Jefferson County; PO Box 984; Fairfield, IA 52556-0984; Ph. (515) 472-3454 **Details:** (Clerk District Court has Birth, Death, Divorce & Clerk Records from 1880, Marriage Records from 1839 & Probate Records from 1850; County Recorder has Land Records)
Johnson www.johnson-county.com/	**E8**	**21 Dec 1837**	**Dubuque, Cook, Muscatine** Johnson County; 913 S Dubuque St; Iowa City, IA 52240; Ph. (319) 356-6093 **Details:** (Attached to Cedar County prior to organization 4 Jul 1838) (County Recorder has Birth Records from 1882, Marriage Records from 1839, Death Records from 1880, Land & Military Records; Clerk Courts has Divorce, Probate & Clerk Records)
Jones www.co.jones.ia.us/	**D6**	**21 Dec 1837**	**Dubuque** Jones County; High St; Anamosa, IA 52205; Ph. (319) 462-4341 **Details:** (Attached to Jackson County prior to organization 1 Jun 1839) (Clerk District Court has Birth & Death Records from 1880, Marriage & Probate Records from 1840, Divorce Records from 1895 & Clerk Records; County Recorder has Land & Military Discharge Records from 1864)
Keokuk www.rootsweb.com/~iakeokuk/	**F8**	**21 Dec 1837**	**Dubuque** Keokuk County; Courthouse Sq; Sigourney, IA 52591-1499; Ph. (515) 622-2210 **Details:** (Attached to Johnson, Washington & Cedar Counties prior to organization 1 Mar 1844) (Clerk District Court has Birth & Death Records from 1880, Marriage, Divorce, Probate & Clerk Records from 1845; County Recorder has Land Records)
Kishkekosh		**17 Feb 1843**	**Unorg. Terr.** Kishkekosh County; IA **Details:** (see Monroe) Name changed to Monroe 1 Aug 1846
Kossuth www.pafways.org/iagenweb/kossuth/	**L3**	**15 Jan 1851**	**Unorg. Terr.** Kossuth County; 114 W State St; Algona, IA 50511-2613; Ph. (515) 295-3240 **Details:** (Attached to Boone & Webster Counties prior to organization 1 Mar 1856) (Clerk District Court has Birth Records 1880–1935 & from 1941, Death & Burial Records from 1880, Marriage Records from 1857, Probate Records from 1877, Divorce & Clerk Records)

County	Map	Date	Parent County or Territory From Which Organized
Website	Index	Created	Address/Details

Lee E11 **7 Dec 1836** **Des Moines**
www.leecounty.org
www.iowalandrecords.org

Lee County; 933 Ave H; Fort Madison, IA 52627; Ph. (319) 372-2592 also 25 N 7th St; Keokuk, IA 52632; Ph. (319) 524-1126
Details: (County Recorder, Keokuk, has Birth Records from 1880, Marriage & Probate Records from 1873, Death Records from 1867; County Clerk has Divorce Records from 1906 & Clerk Records from 1898; County Recorder, Ft. Madison, has Birth & Death Records 1880–1921 & from 1941 & Probate Records from 1838; County Recorder has Land Records)

Linn E6 **21 Dec 1837** **Dubuque**
www.co.linn.ia.us/

Linn County; 50 3rd Ave Bridge; Cedar Rapids, IA 52401-1704; Ph. (319) 398-3411
Details: (Attached to Jackson County prior to organization 1 Jun 1839) (Clerk District Court has Birth Records 1880–1934 & from 1941, Death Records 1880–1919 & from 1941, Marriage Records from 1840, Divorce, Probate & Clerk Records from 1860)

Louisa D9 **7 Dec 1836** **Des Moines**
www.rootsweb.com/~ialouisa/

Louisa County; 117 S Main St; Wapello, IA 52653-1547; Ph. (319) 523-4541
Details: (Clerk District Court has Birth & Death Records from 1880, Marriage Records from 1842, Divorce, Probate & Clerk Records)

Lucas I10 **13 Jan 1846** **Unorg. Terr.**
www.rootsweb.com/~ialucas/Main.htm

Lucas County; 916 Braden Ave; Chariton, IA 50049; Ph. (515) 774-4421
Details: (Attached to Monroe County prior to organization 4 Jul 1849) (Clerk District Court has Birth & Death Records from 1880, Marriage Records from 1849, Divorce & Clerk Records from 1900 & Probate Records from 1850)

Lyon Q2 **1861** **Unorg. Terr.**
www.rootsweb.com/~ialyon/

Lyon County; 206 S 2nd Ave; Rock Rapids, IA 51246-1597; Ph. (712) 472-2623
Details: (Formerly Buncombe County. Name changed to Lyon 11 Sep 1862. Attached to Woodbury County prior to organization 1 Jan 1872) (Clerk District Court has Birth, Marriage, Death, Divorce, Probate, Clerk & Land Records from 1880)

Madison K9 **13 Jan 1846** **Unorg. Terr.**
www.madisoncounty.com/

Madison County; PO Box 152; Winterset, IA 50273-0152; Ph. (515) 462-3771
Details: (Attached to Mahaska County prior to organization 19 Feb 1849) (Clerk District Court has Birth & Death Records from 1880, Marriage Records from 1855, Burial Records from 1849, Divorce & Clerk Records from 1861 & Probate Records from 1852; County Recorder has Land Records)

Mahaska H9 **17 Feb 1843** **Unorg. Terr.**
www.co.muscatine.ia.us/

Mahaska County; 106 S 1st St; PO Box 30; Oskaloosa, IA 52577-0030; Ph. (515) 673-8187
Details: (Attached to Washington County prior to organization 1 Mar 1844) (Clerk District Court has Birth & Death Records from 1880, Marriage, Divorce, Probate & Clerk Records from 1844)

County Website	Map Index	Date Created	Parent County or Territory From Which Organized Address/Details
Marion www.marioncountyiowa.com/	I9	**4 Aug 1845**	**Unorg. Terr.** Marion County; 214 E Main St; PO Box 497; Knoxville, IA 50138-0497; Ph. (515) 828-2211 **Details:** (Clerk District Court has Birth & Death Records from 1880, Marriage Records from 1846, Divorce & Probate Records from 1845)
Marshall www.co.marshall.ia.us/	H6	**13 Jan 1846**	**Unorg. Terr.** Marshall County; 17 E Main St; Marshalltown, IA 50158-4906; Ph. (515) 754-6373 **Details:** (Attached to Jasper & Linn Counties prior to organization 1 Oct 1849) (Clerk District Court has Birth & Death Records from 1880, Marriage, Probate, Clerk & Divorce Records from 1850)
Mills www.rootsweb.com/~iamills/	O10	**15 Jan 1851**	**Pottawattamie** Mills County; 518 Sharp St; Glenwood, IA 51534; Ph. (712) 527-4880 **Details:** (Clerk District Court has Divorce, Probate & Clerk Records from 1880; County Recorder has Birth, Marriage, Death & Land Records)
Mitchell www.rootsweb.com/~iamitche/	H2	**15 Jan 1851**	**Unorg. Terr.** Mitchell County; 508 State St; Osage, IA 50461; Ph. (515) 732 3726 **Details:** (Attached to Chickasaw & Fayette Counties prior to organization 2 Oct 1854) (County Recorder has Birth & Death Records from 1880, Marriage Records from 1871, Land Records from 1854 & Military Records from 1890; Clerk Courts has Divorce, Probate, Clerk & Naturalization Records from 1880)
Monona www.rootsweb.com/~iamonona/	P6	**15 Jan 1851**	**Pottawattamie** Monona County; 610 Iowa Ave; PO Box 53; Onawa, IA 51040-1699; Ph. (712) 423-2575 **Details:** (Attached to Harrison County prior to organization 3 Apr 1854) (Clerk District Court has Birth & Death Records from 1880, Marriage Records from 1857, Burial Records from 1950, Divorce & Clerk Records from 1856 & Probate Records from 1858)
Monroe www.iamonroe.org/	H9	**1 Aug 1846**	**Unorg. Terr.** Monroe County; 10 Benton Ave E; Albia, IA 52531; Ph. (515) 932-5212 **Details:** (Formerly Kishkekosh County. Name changed to Monroe 1 Aug 1846. Attached to Wapello & Jefferson Counties prior to organization 1 Jul 1845) (Clerk District Court has Birth & Death Records from 1880, Marriage, Divorce, Probate & Clerk Records from 1845; County Recorder has Land & Military Discharge Records)
Montgomery www.rootsweb.com/~iamontgo/	N10	**15 Jan 1851**	**Pottawattamie** Montgomery County; 105 Coolbaugh St; Red Oak, IA 51566; Ph. (712) 623-4986 **Details:** (Attached to Adams County prior to organization 5 Aug 1853) (Clerk District Court has Birth & Death Records from 1880, Marriage Records from 1856, Divorce & Clerk Records from 1873 & Probate Records from 1860; County Recorder has Land Records)

County Website	Map Index	Date Created	Parent County or Territory From Which Organized Address/Details
Muscatine www.co.muscatine.ia.us/	**D8**	**7 Dec 1836**	**Des Moines** Muscatine County; 401 E 3rd St; PO Box 327; Muscatine, IA 52761-4166; Ph. (319) 263-6511 **Details:** (County Recorder has Birth & Death Records 1880–1921 & from 1942, Marriage & Land Records from 1838 & Military Records; Clerk Courts has Divorce, Probate & Clerk Records)
O'Brien www.obriencounty.com/	**O3**	**15 Jan 1851**	**Unorg. Terr.** O'Brien County; 155 S Hayes Ave; Primghar, IA 51245; Ph. (712) 757-3255 **Details:** (Attached to Woodbury County prior to organization 7 Apr 1860) (County Recorder has Birth, Marriage & Death Records from 1880, Land Records from 1857 & Military Records from 1917; Clerk Courts has Divorce, Probate & Clerk Records from 1880)
Osceola www.osceolacountyia.com/	**O2**	**15 Jan 1851**	**Unorg. Terr.** Osceola County; 300 7th Ave; PO Box 156; Sibley, IA 51249; Ph. (712) 754-3595 **Details:** (Attached to Woodbury County prior to organization 1 Jan 1872) (Clerk of District Court has Birth, Death, Divorce, Probate, & Court Records from 1880 & Marriage Records from 1872)
Page www.rootsweb.com/~iapage/index.htm	**N10**	**24 Feb 1847**	**Unorg. Terr.** Page County; 112 E Main St; Clarinda, IA 51632-2197; Ph. (712) 542-3214 **Details:** (Attached to Appanoose County prior to organization 22 Mar 1852) (Clerk Courts has Divorce, Probate & Clerk Records; County Recorder has Birth, Marriage, Death & Land Records)
Palo Alto www.celticcousins.net/paloalto/index.htm	**M3**	**15 Jan 1851**	**Unorg. Terr.** Palo Alto County; 11th & Broadway; Emmetsburg, IA 50536; Ph. (712) 852-3603 **Details:** (Attached to Boone & Webster Counties prior to organization 29 Dec 1858) (Clerk District Court has Birth Records 1880–1904, Marriage Records from 1880, some Death Records from 1880, Divorce, Clerk & Probate Records)
Plymouth www.rootsweb.com/~iaplymou/	**Q4**	**15 Jan 1851**	**Unorg. Terr.** Plymouth County; 3rd Ave & 2nd St SE; Le Mars, IA 51031; Ph. (712) 546-6100 **Details:** (Attached to Woodbury County prior to organization 27 Oct 1858) (Clerk District Court has Birth, Death, Divorce & Probate Records from 1880, Marriage & Clerk Records from 1869; County Recorder has Land Records)
Pocahontas www.rootsweb.com/~iapocaho/	**M4**	**15 Jan 1851**	**Unorg. Terr.** Pocahontas County; Court Sq County Courthouse; Pocahontas, IA 50574; Ph. (712) 335-3361 **Details:** (Attached to Boone & Webster Counties prior to organization 11 May 1859) (County Recorder has Birth, Marriage & Death Records from 1880 & Land Records; Clerk District Court has Divorce & Clerk Records from 1860, Probate Records from 1872 & Naturalization Records)

County Website	Map Index	Date Created	Parent County or Territory From Which Organized Address/Details
Polk www.co.polk.ia.us/	J7	**13 Jan 1846**	**Unorg. Terr.** Polk County; 500 Mulberry St; Des Moines, IA 50309-4238; Ph. (515) 286-3845 **Details:** (County Recorder has Birth Records 1880–1921 & from 1942, Marriage Records from 1880, Death Records from 1941 & adoption Records to 1927; Clerk Courts has Probate Records from 1855, Clerk Records from 1850, Divorce Records from 1870 & Naturalization Records 1870–1928)
Pottawattamie www.pottcounty.com/	O9	**21 Sep 1848**	**Unorg. Terr.** Pottawattamie County; 227 S 6th St; Council Bluffs, IA 51501-4209; Ph. (712) 328-5604 **Details:** (Clerk Courts has Birth & Death Records 1880–1921 & from 1941, Marriage Records from 1840, Divorce Records from 1907 & Probate Records from 1898)
Poweshiek www.rootsweb.com/~iapowesh/	G8	**17 Feb 1843**	**Keokuk** Poweshiek County; 302 W Main St; Montezuma, IA 50171; Ph. (515) 623-5644 **Details:** (Attached to Mahaska & Iowa Counties prior to organization 3 Apr 1848) (Clerk District Court has Birth, Death, Divorce & Clerk Records from 1880, Marriage & Probate Records from 1860; County Recorder has Land Records)
Ringgold www.rootsweb.com/~iaringgo/	L10	**24 Feb 1847**	**Unorg. Terr.** Ringgold County; 109 W Madison St; Mount Ayr, IA 50854; Ph. (515) 464-3234 **Details:** (Attached to Taylor & Appanoose Counties prior to organization 31 Jan 1855) (Clerk District Court has Birth, Marriage, Death, Divorce, Probate & Clerk Records from 1880; County Recorder has Land Records)
Risley		**15 Jan 1851**	**Unorg. Terr.** Risley County; IA **Details:** (see Webster) Merged into Webster County 22 Jan 1853
Sac www.saccounty.org/	N5	**15 Jan 1851**	**Unorg. Terr.** Sac County; 100 NW State St; PO Box 386; Sac City, IA 50583-0368; Ph. (712) 662-7791 **Details:** (Attached to Woodbury & Greene Counties prior to organization 7 Apr 1856. Courthouse burned 1888, some charred Records recovered) (Clerk District Court has Birth, Marriage, Burial, Divorce, Probate & Clerk Records from 1888; County Recorder has Land Records from 1856)
Scott www.scottcountyiowa.com/	B8	**21 Dec 1837**	**Dubuque, Cook, Muscatine** Scott County; 416 W 4th St; Davenport, IA 52801-1187; Ph. (563) 326-8648 (Clerk of Courts) or (563) 326-8621 **Details:** (County Auditor has Property Transfer Books from 1865; County Recorder has Birth, Death, & Marriage Records; Bi-State Regional Commision has Census Records (Ph. (309) 793-6300); Clerk of Courts has Probate Records 1965–2005, Davenport Library has all other Probate Records)

County Website	Map Index	Date Created	Parent County or Territory From Which Organized Address/Details
Shelby www.iowacourtonline.org www.judicial.state.ia.us	N7	15 Jan 1851	**Pottawattamie** Shelby County; 612 Court; PO Box 431; Harlan, IA 51537; Ph. (712) 755-5543 **Details:** (Organized 7 Mar 1853) (Clerk Courts has Probate, Divorce & Clerk Records from 1869 & Naturalization Records from 1854; County Recorder has Birth & Death Records from 1880, Marriage Records from 1853, Land Records from 1854 & Military Records from 1919)
Sioux www.siouxcounty.org/	Q3	15 Jan 1851	**Unorg. Terr.** Sioux County; 210 Central Ave SE; Orange City, IA 51041-1751; Ph. (712) 737-2286 **Details:** (Attached to Woodbury County prior to organization 1 Jan 1860) (Clerk District Court has Birth & Death Records from 1880, Marriage, Probate & Clerk Records from 1870 & Divorce Records from 1908)
Slaughter		18 Jan 1838	**Henry, Louisa, Muscatine** Slaughter County; IA **Details:** (see Washington) Name changed to Washington 25 Jan 1839
Story www.storycounty.com/	J6	13 Jan 1846	**Unorg. Terr.** Story County; 900 6th St; Nevada, IA 50201-2004; Ph. (515) 382-6581 **Details:** (Attached to Boone, Polk & Linn Counties prior to organization 1 Jun 1853) (Clerk District Court has Birth & Death Records from 1880, Marriage, Divorce, Probate & Clerk Records from 1854)
Tama www.rootsweb.com/~iatama/	G6	17 Feb 1843	**Benton** Tama County; 100 W High St; PO Box 306; Toledo, IA 52342; Ph. (515) 484-3721 **Details:** (Attached to Benton & Linn Counties prior to organization 4 Jul 1853) (Clerk District Court has Birth & Death Records from 1880, Marriage Records from 1853, Divorce Records from 1908, Probate Records from 1895 & Clerk Records from 1859)
Taylor www.rootsweb.com/~iataylor/	M10	24 Feb 1847	**Unorg. Terr.** Taylor County; 405 Jefferson St; Bedford, IA 50833; Ph. (712) 523-2095 **Details:** (Attached to Appanoose County prior to organization 26 Feb 1851) (Clerk District Court has Birth, Death & Burial Records from 1880, Marriage Records from 1854, Divorce & Clerk Records from 1858 & Probate Records from 1863; County Recorder has Land Records)
Union http://lserver.aea14.k12.ia.us/SWP/jbriley/ucgen/ucgenhome.html	L10	15 Jan 1851	**Pottawattamie** Union County; 300 N Pine St; Creston, IA 50801-2430; Ph. (515) 782-7315 **Details:** (Organized 1 Mar 1853) (Clerk District Court has Birth, Death, Divorce, Probate & Clerk Records from 1880 & Marriage Records from 1856; County Assessor has Land Records)

County	Map	Date	Parent County or Territory From Which Organized
Website	Index	Created	Address/Details

Van Buren F10 **7 Dec 1836** **Des Moines**
www.villagesofvanburen.com

Van Buren County; 406 St Dodge St; PO Box 475; Keosauqua, IA 52565-0475; Ph. (319) 293-3129 jfinney@vbcoia.org
Details: (A fire in 1896 destroyed some Auditor Records but originating documents are still available at the Recorder's office. The fire destroyed mostly county school records. Many school records in 1970 were turned over to the local school districts.) (Clerk of District Court has Court Records from 1836, Divorce, Immigration, & Naturalization Records from 1890, Guardianship & Probate Records from 1837; Recorder has Birth & Death Records from 1890, Land & Marriage Records from 1837, & Military Records from 1860; Auditor has Land Records from 1860, & Tax Records from 1837)

Wahkaw **15 Jan 1851** **Unorg. Terr.**

Wahkaw County; IA
Details: (see Woodbury) Name changed to Woodbury 22 Jan 1853

Wapello G10 **17 Feb 1843** **Unorg. Terr.**
www.rootsweb.com/~iawapell/

Wapello County; 4th & Court Sq; Ottumwa, IA 52501-2599; Ph. (515) 683-0060
Details: (Attached to Jefferson County prior to organization 1 Mar 1844) (Clerk Courts has Divorce, Probate & Clerk Records from 1844; County Recorder has Birth, Marriage, Death & Land Records)

Warren J9 **13 Jan 1846** **Unorg. Terr.**
www.rootsweb.com/~iawarren/

Warren County; PO Box 379; Indianola, IA 50125-0379; Ph. (515) 961-1033
Details: (Attached to Mahaska County prior to organization 10 Feb 1849) (Clerk District Court has Birth, Death, Divorce, Probate & Clerk Records from 1880 & Marriage Records from 1850)

Washington E8 **25 Jan 1839** **Henry, Louisa, Muscatine**
http://co.washington.ia.us/

Washington County; PO Box 391; Washington, IA 52353-0391; Ph. (319) 653-7741
Details: (Formerly Slaughter County. Name changed to Washington 25 Jan 1839) (Clerk District Court has Birth & Death Records from 1880, Marriage Records from 1844, Divorce, Probate & Clerk Records from 1836 & some Naturalization Records; County Recorder has Land Records)

Wayne I10 **13 Jan 1846** **Unorg. Terr.**

Wayne County; PO Box 435; Corydon, IA 50060; Ph. (641) 872-1676
Details: (Attached to Davis County prior to organization 27 Jan 1851) (County Recorder has Birth & Death Records from 1880, Marriage Records from 1851, & Land & Town Property from 1852; Marriage Records were moved from Clerk of Court to Recorder's Office in 1995; Some Cemetery Index Books)

Webster L5 **22 Jan 1853** **Yell, Risley**
www.webstercountyia.org/

Webster County; 703 Central Ave; Fort Dodge, IA 50501; Ph. (515) 576-7115
Details: (Formerly Risley & Yell Counties. Name changed to Webster 22 Jan 1853) (Clerk District Court has Birth Records from 1876, Marriage Records from 1853, Death & Clerk Records from 1860, Divorce Records from 1870 & Probate Records from 1855; County Auditor has Land Records)

County Website	Map Index	Date Created	Parent County or Territory From Which Organized Address/Details
Winnebago www.rootsweb.com/~iawinneb/index.htm	**J2**	**15 Jan 1851**	**Unorg. Terr.** Winnebago County; 126 S Clark St; Forest City, IA 50436-1793; Ph. (515) 582-4520 **Details:** (Attached to Boone & Webster Counties prior to organization 1 Nov 1857) (Clerk Courts has Birth & Death Records from 1880, Marriage, Divorce, Probate & Clerk Records from 1865; County Registrar has Burial Records)
Winneshiek www.rootsweb.com/~iawinnes/index.htm	**E3**	**20 Feb 1847**	**Unorg. Terr.** Winneshiek County; 201 W Main St; Decorah, IA 52101-1775; Ph. (319) 382-2469 **Details:** (Attached to Clayton County prior to organization 1 Mar 1851) (Clerk District Court has Birth & Death Records from 1880, Marriage Records from 1851, Divorce & Clerk Records from 1855 & Probate Records from 1853)
Woodbury www.woodbury-ia.com/	**P5**	**22 Jan 1853**	**Unorg. Terr.** Woodbury County; 101 Court St; Sioux City, IA 51101-1909; Ph. (712) 279-6616 **Details:** (Formerly Wahkaw County. Name changed to Woodbury 22 Jan 1853. Organized 7 Mar 1853) (Clerk District Court has Birth & Death Records from 1880, Marriage Records from 1880 & some from 1854, Divorce Records from 1857, Probate Records from 1868, Clerk Records from 1850 & adoption Records from 1920)
Worth www.rootsweb.com/~iaworth/	**I2**	**15 Jan 1851**	**Unorg. Terr.** Worth County; 1000 Central Ave; Northwood, IA 50459-1523; Ph. (515) 324-2840 **Details:** (Attached to Fayette, Chickasaw, Floyd & Mitchell Counties prior to organization 13 Oct 1857) (Clerk District Court has incomplete Birth Records from 1880, Marriage Records from 1858, Death Records 1880–1919, Divorce Records from 1879, Probate & Clerk Records from 1857 & Naturalization Records; County Auditor has Land Records)
Wright www.wrightcounty.org/	**J4**	**15 Jan 1851**	**Unorg. Terr.** Wright County; PO Box 306; Clarion, IA 50525-0306; Ph. (515) 532-3113 **Details:** (Attached to Boone & Webster Counties prior to organization 1 Oct 1855) (Clerk District Court has Birth, Death & Probate Records from 1880, Marriage Records from 1860, Divorce & Clerk Records from 1873 & Naturalization Records 1857–1929; County Recorder has Land Records; City Clerks & libraries have Burial Records)
Yell		**15 Jan 1851**	**Unorg. Terr.** Yell County; IA **Details:** (see Webster) Merged Webster County 22 Jan 1853

Notes

Kansas

Capital: Topeka

Territory: 1854

State: 1861 (34th)

To the stars through adversity

Kansas was part of the Louisiana Purchase in 1803. Government expeditions to the area reported it to be a desert, starting the myth of the Great American Desert. Indians from the East were moved into the area to brave what was believed to be a harsh desert. The relationship was hostile between Native Americans (Kansa, Osage, Pawnee, and Wichita) and would-be settlers. The hostility increased when the Santa Fe Trail traversed the state beginning in 1821. To protect travelers, forts were established along the trail, beginning with Fort Leavenworth in 1827. Later, the Oregon Trail crossed northeastern Kansas.

Kansas remained unorganized territory until 1854 when the Kansas-Nebraska Act created the Kansas and Nebraska territories. Kansas had the same boundaries as today except that its western boundary was the "summit of the Rocky Mountains." The Kansas-Nebraska Act also stipulated that the people of a territory would decide by majority vote whether Kansas would be a free or a slave state. This act stimulated migration to Kansas as both pro and antislavery forces tried to gain the upper hand. The violence that marked the years from 1854 to statehood in 1861 led to the term "Bleeding Kansas." Kansas ultimately voted to be a free state. The population in 1861 was 10,000, consisting primarily of Southerners and New Englanders, along with others from Illinois, Indiana, Ohio, and Kentucky.

During the Civil War, Kansas had more than 20,000 Union soldiers. Its men suffered the highest mortality rate of any state in the Union. Many of the remaining Indian tribes in the state moved to Oklahoma by 1867. The few that refused to go fought against other settlers until 1878. A post-Civil War boom occurred due to the Homestead Act and railroad growth. Many Civil War veterans took up homesteads in the state and other settlers came from Germany, Russia, Sweden, England, and Mexico.

Look for vital records in the following locations:

- **Birth and death records:** Office of Vital Statistics, Kansas State Department of Health in Topeka has birth and death records since 1 July, 1911. A few counties began keeping birth and death records in 1885. These can be obtained from county clerks. Some cities also have birth and death records from 1910 to 1940.
- **Marriage and divorce records:** Office of Vital Statistics, Kansas State Department of Health, has marriage records from 1 May, 1913, and divorce records from 1 July, 1951. County clerks and probate court clerks also kept marriage records. Divorces prior to 1951 are on file with the district court.
- **Court records and wills:** After July 1951, probate judges began handling probate matters, wills, and in most counties civil court records.
- **Land records:** County recorders and county assessors keep real estate records.
- **Census records:** State and territorial censuses exist for 1855, 1865, 1875, 1885, 1895, 1905, 1915, and 1925. All censuses are available at the Kansas State Historical Society in Topeka. Some counties have voter censuses for 1856, 1857, and 1859.

Office of Vital Statistics Curtis State Office Building
1000 Southwest Jackson Street, Suite 120
Topeka, Kansas 66612-2221
(785) 296-1500; Fax: (785) 368-6368
www.kdhe.state.ks.us/vital/death.html

The National Archives Kansas City Branch
2306 East Bannister Road
Kansas City, Kansas 64131

Kansas State Historical Society
6425 SW 6th St
Topeka, Kansas 66615
(785) 272-8681
www.kshs.org/

Kansas

Societies and Repositories

Anderson County Genealogical Society; PO Box 194; Garnett, KS 66032; http://kanza.net/%7Eswguinn/ acgs.html.

Atchison County Kansas Genealogical Society; c/o Atchison Library; PO Box 303; Atchison, KS 66002; http://skyways.lib.ks.us/genweb/society/atchison/ackgs.htm.

Branches and Twigs Genealogical Society; 455 North Main; Kingman, KS 67068; ospec@terraworld.net; http://skyways.lib.ks.us/genweb/kingman/branches.html.

Chanute Genealogical Society; 800 W. 14th St.; Chanute, KS 66720-2699; www.rootsweb.com/~kscgs.

Chautauqua County Historical and Genealogical Society; PO Box 227; Sedan, KS 67361; millerv@onemain.com; http://freida-wells.tripod.com/ChautauquaCountyKansas.

Cherokee County Kansas Genealogical / Historical Society, Inc.; PO Box 33; Columbus, KS 66725-0033; cckghs@columbus-ks.com; http://skyways.lib.ks.us/kansas/genweb/cherokee/society/cckghs.html.

Cloud County Genealogical Society; PO Box 2027; Concordia, KS 66901; CloudGen@care2.com; www.dustdevil.com/towns/concordia/history/ccgs.

Cowley County Genealogical Society; 1518 E. 12th.; Winfield, KS 67156-3923; (620) 221-4591.

Crawford County Genealogical Society; c/o Pittsburg Public Library; 308 N. Walnut; Pittsburg, KS 66762.

Decatur County Genealogical Society; 307 N. Rodehaver; Oberlin, KS 67749.

Douglas County Historical Society; Watkins Community Museum of History; 1047 Massachus; Lawrence, KS 66044-2923.

Finney County Genealogical Society; PO Box 592; Garden City, KS 67846.

Flint Hills Genealogical Society; PO Box 555; Emporia, KS 66801-0555; lyoncoks@bigfoot.com; http://skyways.lib.ks.us/genweb/society/emporia/index.html.

Fort Hays, Kansas Genealogical Society; c/o Forsyth Library; FHS University; Hays, KS 67601.

Franklin County Genealogical Society; PO Box 353; Ottawa, KS 66067; www.ukans.edu/~hisite/franklin/fcgs.

Genealogical Society of Douglas County; PO Box 3664; Lawrence, KS 66046-0664; http://skyways.lib.ks.us/kansas/genweb/douglas/ dckgs.htm.

Golden Wheat Chapter, AHSGR; 2029 University; Wichita, KS 67213-3375; (316) 283-3129; edrif@msn.com; www.ahsgr.org/ksgolden.html.

Halstead Historical Society/Halstead Heritage Museum and Depot; 116 East First; PO Box 88; Halstead, KS 67056; (316) 835-2267; HistoricalSociety@HalsteadKansas.com; www.HistoricalSociety.HalsteadKansas.com.

Harper County Genealogical Society; Harper Public Library; 1002 Oak; Harper, KS 67058; (620) 962-5211; peterson@kanokla.net; http://skyways.lib.ks.us/kansas/genweb/society/harper.

Heart of American Chapter, AHSGR; 117 E. Minneapolis Street; Salina, KS 67401-6024; (913) 827-0782.

Hereditary Order of the Descendants of the Loyalists & Patriots of the American Revolution; 608 South Overlook Drive; Coffeyville, KS 67337-2531; (316) 251-2383.

Heritage Seekers of SW Kansas Chapter, AHSGR; 511 Baughman; Ulysses, KS 67880; (316) 356-2228.

Historical Society of the Downs Carnegie Library; South Morgan Ave.; Downs, KS 67437.

Hodgeman County Genealogical Society; PO Box 441; Jetmore, KS 67954.

Jefferson County Genealogical Society; PO Box 174; Oskaloosa, KS 66066-0174; jcgs1979@yahoo.com; http://skyways.lib.ks.us/kansas/genweb/jefferso/jfcogen.html.

Johnson County Genealogical Society; PO Box 12666; Shawnee Mission, KS 66292-2666; jpbill@swbell.com; http://history.cc.ukans.edu/heritage/society/jcgs/jcgs_main.html.

Kansas City Area Chapter, AHSGR; 4441 W 52nd Terrace; Roeland Park, KS 66205; (913) 362-7635.

Kansas Council of Genealogical Societies, Inc.; PO Box 3859; Topeka, KS 66604-6858.

Kansas Genealogical Society, Inc.; PO Box 103; Dodge City, KS 67846; www.dodgecity.net/kgs.

Kansas Society, DAR; 1000 W. 55th St. S.; Wichita, KS 67217.

Kansas State Historical Society; 6425 SW 6th Avenue; Topeka, KS 66615-1099; (785) 272-8681; www.kshs.org.

Kansas State Library; State Capitol Building; Topeka, KS 66612-1593; (785) 296-3296; eric@kslib.info; http://skyways.lib.ks.us/kansas/KSL.

Labette County Genealogical Society; c/o Mrs. Tina Rice; Box 544; Parsons, KS 67357; http://skyways.lib.ks.us/kansas/genweb/society/parsons.

Linn County Historical Society; Box 137; Pleasanton, KS 66075.

Lyon County Historical Society; 118 E. 6th Street; Emporia, KS 66801.

Marion County Genealogical Society; 401 S. Cedar; Marion, KS 66861-1331; http://skyways.lib.ks.us/genweb/society/marion.

Marshall County Historical Society; 1207 Broadway; Marysville, KS 66508.

Miami County Genealogical Society; PO Box 123; Paola, KS 66071.

Midwest Historical and Genealogical Society, Inc.; 1203 North Main; PO Box 1121; Wichita, KS 67201-1121; (316) 264-3611; http://skyways.lib.ks.us/kansas/genweb/mhgs.

Montgomery County Genealogical Society; PO Box 444; Coffeyville, KS 67337; www.rootsweb.com/%7Eksmontgo.

Nemaha County Genealogical Society; 113 N. 6th St.; Seneca, KS 66538.

North Central Kansas Genealogical Society; Box 251; Cawker City, KS 67430; http://skyways.lib.ks.us/kansas/towns/Cawker/library._html#soci.

Northeast Kansas Chapter, AHSGR; 4625 NW Geronimo Trail; Topeka, KS 66618; (785) 246-2821; f.a.jacobs@worldnet.att.net; www.ahsgr.org/ksnorthe.html.

Northwest Kansas Genealogical & Historical Society; 700W. 3rd; Oakley, KS 67748.

Norton County Genealogical Society; 101 E. Lincoln; Norton, KS 67654.

Old Fort Genealogical Society of Southeast Kansas; 502 S. National Ave.; Fort Scott, KS 66701; http://skyways.lib.ks.us/kansas/genweb/society/ftscott.

Osage County Historical Society & Research Center; 631 Topeka; PO Box 361; Lyndon, KS 66451; (785) 828-3477; research@kanza.net; www.osagechs.org.

Osborne County Genealogical and Historical Society Inc.; 929 North 2nd St.; Osborne, KS 67473-1629.

Phillips County Genealogical Society; PO Box 114; Phillipsburg, KS 67661; http://skyways.lib.ks.us/genweb/phillips/plgensoc.html.

Post Rock Chapter, AHSGR; 18350 Homer Rd; Russell, KS 67665; (785) 483-3976.

Rawlins County Genealogical Society; PO Box 405; Atwood, KS 67730; http://skyways.lib.ks.us/genweb/rawlins/rawgenesoc.html.

Reno County Genealogical Society; PO Box 5; Hutchinson, KS 67504-0005; http://renocountyks.homestead.com.

Republic County Genealogical Society; Rt. 1; Belleville, KS 66935.

Riley County Genealogical Society; 2005 Claflin Rd.; Manhattan, KS 66502-3415; www.rileycgs.com.

Sherman County Historical and Genealogical Society; PO Box 684; Goodland, KS 67735; http://skyways.lib.ks.us/genweb/sherman/shchs.html.

Smoky Valley Genealogical Society and Library, Inc.; 211 W. Iron, Suite 205; Salina, KS 67401-2613; http://skyways.lib.ks.us/kansas/genweb/ottawa/smoky.html.

Southeast Kansas Genealogical Society; PO Box 393; Iola, KS 66749-0671.

St. Marys Historical Society; 710 Alma St.; St. Marys, KS 66536.

Stafford County Historical and Genealogical Society; 201 S. Park; PO Box 249; Stafford, KS 67578-0249.

Stevens County Genealogical Society; HC 01, Box 12; Hugoton, KS 67951.

Sumner County Genealogical Society; Box 402; Wellington, KS 67152; www.rootsweb.com/%7Eksscgs.

Sunflower Chapter, AHSGR; 874 Samara; Munjor, KS 67601; (785) 625-6411; www.ahsgr.org/kssunflo.html.

Topeka Kansas Genealogical Society; PO Box 4048; Topeka, KS 66604-0048; TGS@networksplus.net; www.networksplus.net/donno.

Wichita County Genealogical Society; 201 N. 4th St.; PO Box 1561; Leoti, KS 67861; (620) 375-2316; genealogy@wichitacountymuseum.org; http://wichitacountymuseum.org/gensociety.htm.

Wichita Genealogical Society; Wichita Public Library; PO Box 3705; Wichita, KS 67201-3705; (316) 721-6794; http://skyways.lib.ks.us/orgs/wgs.

Wyandotte County Genealogical Society; PO Box 4228; Kansas City, KS 66104-0228.

Wyandotte County Historical Society & Museum; 631 N. 126th St.; Bonner Springs, KS 66012; www.kumc.edu/wcedc/museum/wcmuseum.html.

Bibliography and Record Sources

General

A Biographical History Of Central Kansas. 2 vols. New York: Lewis Pub. Co., 1902.

Adams, F. G. *Homestead Guide of Kansas and Nebraska.* Waterville, Kansas: 1873.

Anderson, Eileen. *Kansas Newspapers: A Directory of Newspaper Holdings in Kansas.* Topeka, Kansas: The Board, 1984.

Anderson, Lorene and Alan W. Farley. "Bibliography of Town and County Histories of Kansas." *Kansas Historical Quarterly* 21 (Autumn 1955): 513–51.

Anderson, Robert D., ed. "Searching in Kansas." *Journal of Genealogy.* vol. 2 (May 1977). Omaha, Nebraska: Anderson Publishing Co.

Andreas, A. T. *History of the State of Kansas: Containing a Full Account of Its Growth From an Uninhabited Territory to a Wealthy and Important State, of Its Early Settlement, a Supplementary History and Description of Its Counties, Cities, Towns and Villages, Their Advantages, Industries and Commerce, to Which are Added Biographical Sketches and Portraits of Prominent Men and Early Settlers.* 2 vols. Marceline, Missouri: Walsworth Pub. Co., 1976.

Baldwin, Sara Mullin. *Illustriana Kansas: Biographical Sketches of Kansas Men and Women of Achievement*

Who Have Been Awarded Life Membership in Kansas Illustriana Society. Hebron, Nebraska: Illustriana Inc., 1933.

Barry, Louise. *The Beginning of the West: Annals of the Kansas Gateway to the American West, 1540–1854*. Topeka: Kansas State Historical Society, 1972.

Berckefeldt, Denis. *Kansas County Records*. Kansas: A Pathfinders Publication.

Blackmar, Frank Wilson. *Kansas: A Cyclopedia of State History, Embracing Events, Institutions, Industries, Counties, Cities, Towns, Prominent Persons, Etc. . . With a Supplementary Volume Devoted to Selected Personal History And Reminiscence*. 3 vols. in 4. Chicago: Standard Pub. Co., 1912.

Bright, John D., ed. *Kansas: The First Century*. 4 vols. New York: Lewis Historical Publishing Co., 1956.

Burton, Arthur T. *Black, Buckskin and Blue: African American Scouts and Soldiers on the Western Frontier*. Austin, Texas: Eaton Press, 1999.

Connelley, William Elsey. *A Standard History of Kansas and Kansans*. 5 vols. Chicago: Lewis Pub. Co., 1918.

Correll, Charles M. *A Century of Congregationalism In Kansas, 1854–1954*. Topeka, Kansas: The Kansas Congregational and Christian Conference, ©1953 (Wichita, Kansas: McCormick-Armstrong Co.)

Craik, Elmer LeRoy. *A History of the Church of the Brethren in Kansas*. Mc Pherson, Kansas: E. Craik, 1972.

Curtis, Mary B. "Bibliography of Kansas: The Formative Years." *Magazine of Bibliographies* 1 (2) December 1972.

DeZurko, Edward R. *Early Kansas Churches*. Manhattan, Kansas: Kansas State College, 1949.

Dick, Everett. *The Sod House Frontier, 1854–1890: A Social History of the Northern Plains from the Creation of Kansas & Nebraska to the Admission of the Dakotas*. Lincoln, Nebraska: University of Nebraska, 1979, 1954.

Fitzgerald, Mary Paul. *Beacon on the Plains*. Leavenworth, Kansas: Saint Mary College, ©1939.

Gordon, Jacob U. *Narratives of African Americans in Kansas, 1870–1992: Beyond The Exodus Movement*. Lewiston, New York: E. Mellen Press, 1993.

Graves, William Whites. *The First Protestant Osage Missions, 1820–1837*. Oswego, Kansas: Carpenter Press, 1949.

Guide to Public Vital Statistics Records in Kansas. Topeka: Historical Records Survey, 1942.

Harper, Katherine C. *List of Books and Manuscripts in Kansas State DAR Library*. Mullinville, Kansas: Dodge City Chapter, DAR, 1972.

Haury, David A. *Guide to the Microfilm Collections of the Kansas State Historical Society*. Topeka, Kansas: Kansas State Historical Society, 1991.

Hinshaw, William Wade. *The William Wade Hinshaw Index to Kansas Quaker Meeting Records*. 4 vols. Kokomo, Indiana: Selby Pub. & Printing, 1991.

Historical and Descriptive Review of Kansas: With Special Reference to the Advantages of the Towns Named in the Index, Their Prosperous Institutions and Progressive Men. 3 vols. Topeka: Jno. Lethem, 1890–1891.

Hodge, Robert A. *Kansas Orphan Train Riders—These We Know*. Emporia, Kansas: R. A. Hodge, 1996.

Johnson, Samuel A. *The Battle Cry of Freedom: The New England Emigration Aid Company in the Kansas Crusade*. Westport, Connecticut: Greenwood Press, 1977.

Kansas Pioneers. Topeka, Kansas: Topeka Genealogical Society, 1976.

Kansas Research Outline. Series U.S.-States, no 17. Salt Lake City: Family History Library, 1988.

Kansas State Historical Society (Topeka, Kansas). *History of Kansas Newspapers: A History of the Newspapers and Magazines Published in Kansas from the Organization of Kansas Territory, 1854, to January 1, 1916 Together with Brief Statistical Information of the Counties, Cities and Towns of the State*. Topeka, Kansas: Kansas State Printing Plant, 1916.

Miner, H. Craig. *West of Wichita: Settling the High Plains of Kansas, 1865–1890*. Lawrence: University Press of Kansas, 1986.

Pioneer Women: Voices from the Kansas Frontier. New York: Simon and Schuster, 1981.

Portrait and Biographical Record of Southeastern Kansas: Containing Biographical Sketches of Prominent and Representative Citizens of the Counties, Together with Biographies and Portraits of All the Presidents of the United States and the Governors of the State of Kansas. Chicago: Biographical Pub. Co., 1894.

Roenigk, Adolph. *Pioneer History of Kansas*. Lincoln, Kansas: A. Roenigk. Denver: The Great Western Pub. Co., 1933.

Rooney, Doris Dockstader, et al. *Kansas Genealogical Society Six-Generation Ancestor Tables*. Dodge City, Kansas: Kansas Genealogical Society, 1976.

Scheck, Floyd. *Genealogy Records of Families of Germans from Russia*. Salt Lake City: Filmed by the Genealogical Society of Utah, 1992. 7 microfilm.

Shortridge, James R. *Peopling the Plains: Who Settled Where in Frontier Kansas*. Lawrence, Kansas: University Press of Kansas, 1995.

Smith, Patricia D. *Kansas Biographical Index: Statewide and Regional Histories*. Garden City, Kansas: Patricia D. Smith, 1994.

Sweet, William Henry. *A History of Methodism in Northwest Kansas*. Kansas: Kansas Wesleyan University, 1920.

Taylor, Blanche Mercer. *Plenteous Harvest: The Episcopal Church in Kansas, 1837–1972*. Kansas: The Diocese, ©1973 Topeka, Kansas: Printed by Josten's/American Yearbook Co.

The Forgotten Settlers of Kansas. Vols. 1–17. Topeka: Kansas Council of Genealogical Societies, 1983.

The United States Biographical Dictionary: Kansas. Chicago and Kansas City: S. Lewis & Co., 1879.

Tuttle, Charles Richard. *A New Centennial History of the State Of Kansas: Being a Full and Complete Civil, Political and Military History of the State, From Its Earliest Settlement to the Present Time*. Madison, Wisconsin: Inter-state Book Co., 1876.

United States. Department of State. *Territorial Papers of Kansas, 1854–1861*. Microfilm of originals in the National Archives in Washington, D.C., Washington, D.C.: The National Archives, 1953. 2 microfilm.

Unrau, William E. *The Kansas Indians, a History of the Wind People, 1673–1873*. Norman, Oklahoma: University of Oklahoma Press, 1971.

Atlases, Maps and Gazetteers

Baughman, Robert W. *Kansas in Maps*. Topeka: Kansas State Historical Society, 1961.

Baughman, Robert W. *Kansas Post Offices, May 29, 1828 to Aug. 3, 1961*. Topeka: Kansas Postal History Society, 1961.

Gannett, Henry A. *A Gazetteer of Kansas*. Washington, D.C.: U.S. Government Printing Office, 1898.

Gill, Helen G. *The Establishment of Counties in Kansas, 1855–1903*. Kansas Historical Society Collections 8. n.p., 1904.

Graden, Debra. *Kansas Towns & Cities as of 1912: Includes a List of Extinct Towns [and a] Bonus Index of Biographies from Volumes 1, 2, & 3 Extracted from "Kansas."* Leavenworth, Kansas: Grey Ink, c1997.

Kansas Atlas and Gazetteer. Freeport, Maine: DeLorme Mapping Co., 1997.

McCoy, Sondra Van Meter. *1001 Kansas Place Names*. Lawrence, Kansas: University Press of Kansas, 1989.

Official State Atlas of Kansas, Compiled from Government Surveys, County Records and Personal Investigations. L. H. Leverts and Co. (1887). Reprint by Kansas Council of Genealogical Societies, 1982.

Rydjord, John. *Kansas Place-Names*. Norman, Oklahoma: University of Oklahoma Press, 1972.

Socolofsky, Homer E., and Huber Self. *Historical Atlas of Kansas*. Norman, Oklahoma: University of Oklahoma Press, 1972.

Some Lost Towns of Kansas: And Extinct Geographical Locations. n.p.: Reprint of Kansas Historical Collections, vol. 12.

Censuses

Available Census Records and Census Substitutes

Federal Census 1860, 1870, 1880, 1900, 1910, 1920

Federal Mortality Schedules 1860, 1870, 1880

State/Territorial Census 1855, 1856, 1857, 1858, 1859, 1865, 1875, 1885, 1895, 1905, 1915, 1925

Dollarhide, William. *The Census Book: A Genealogist's Guide to Federal Census Facts, Schedules and Indexes*. Bountiful, Utah: Heritage Quest, 1999.

Kemp, Thomas Jay. *The American Census Handbook*. Wilmington, Delaware: Scholarly Resources, Inc., 2001.

Lainhart, Ann S. *State Census Records*. Baltimore: Genealogical Publishing Co., Inc., 1992.

Szucs, Loretto Dennis and Matthew Wright. *Finding Answers in U.S. Census Records*. Ancestry Publishing, 2001.

Thorndale, William. *Map Guide to the U.S. Federal Census, 1790–1920*. Baltimore: Genealogical Publishing Co., 1987.

United States. Bureau of Internal Revenue. *Internal Revenue Lists For Kansas, 1862–1866*. Microfilm of originals in the National Archives in Washington, D.C. Washington, D.C.: National Archives. Central Plains Region, 1985. 3 microfilm.

Court Records, Probate and Wills

Berckefeldt, Denis. *Kansas County Records*. Kansas: A Pathfinders Publication.

Court, probate and will records are found in the individual county court houses. Refer to the county information pages for further information.

United States. District Court (Kansas). *Slave Compensation Records, 1866–1867*. Microfilm of originals in the National Archives Branch in Kansas City, Missouri. Salt Lake City: Filmed by the Genealogical Society of Utah, 1991.

Emigration, Immigration, Migration and Naturalization

Carman, J. Neale. *Foreign-Language Units of Kansas*. Lawrence, Kansas: University of Kansas Press, 1962.

Robertson, Clara H. *Kansas Territorial Settlers of 1860 Who Were Born in Tennessee, Virginia, North Carolina and South Carolina*. Baltimore: Genealogical Publishing Co., 1976.

United States. District Court (Kansas). *Index to Naturalizations, 1856–1897; Declaration of Intention 1862–1897*. Microfilm of originals in the National Archives Branch in Kansas City, Missouri. Salt Lake City: Filmed by the Genealogical Society of Utah, 1990. 2 microfilm.

United States. District Court (Kansas: First Division). *Declarations Of Intention, 1908–1942; Naturalizations, 1865–1984*. Microfilm of originals in the National

Archives Branch in Kansas City, Missouri. Salt Lake City: Filmed by the Genealogical Society of Utah, 1990. 13 microfilm.

United States. District Court (Kansas: Second Division). *Declarations Of Intention, 1909–1947; Naturalizations, 1909–1979.* Microfilm of originals in the National Archives Branch in Kansas City, Missouri. Salt Lake City: Filmed by the Genealogical Society of Utah, 1990. 14 microfilm.

United States. District Court (Kansas: Third Division*). Declarations Of Intention, 1915–1964; Naturalizations, 1916–1966.* Microfilm of originals in the National Archives Branch in Kansas City, Missouri. Salt Lake City: Filmed by the Genealogical Society of Utah, 1990. 2 microfilm.

Land and Property

Adams, F. G. *Homestead Guide of Kansas and Nebraska.* Waterville, Kansas: 1873.

Homestead Guide of Kansas and Nebraska: Waterville, Kansas: F. G. Adams, 1873.

Hone, Wade E. *Land and Property Research in the United States.* Salt Lake City: Ancestry Incorporated, 1997.

United States. General Land Office. *Field Notes from Selected General Land Office Township Surveys.* Washington, D.C.: The National Archives, 1979. 281 microfilm.

Military

Decker, Eugene Donald. *A Selected, Annotated Bibliography of Sources in the Kansas State Historical Society Pertaining to Kansas in the Civil War.* Emporia, Kansas: State Teacher's College. 1961.

Kansas Adjutant General's Office. *Report of the Adjutant General, C. K. Holliday, December 31, 1864.* Leavenworth, Kansas: Adjutant General. 1865.

Kansas Adjutant General's Office. *Report of the Adjutant General, T. J. Anderson, of the State of Kansas in 1861–1865.* 2 Vols. Topeka, Kansas: Adjutant General, 1967–1870.

Kansas. Adjutant General's Office. *Kansas Troops in the Volunteer Service of the United States in the Spanish and Philippine Wars, Mustered in Under the First and Second Calls of the President of the United States: May 9, 1898–October 28, 1899.* Washington, D.C.: Filmed by the Library of Congress, Photoduplication Service, 1989.

Loosbrock, Richard J. *The History of the Kansas Department of the American Legion.* Topeka, Kansas: Kansas Dept. of the American Legion, 1968.

Ostertag, John A. *Fighting Twentieth, History and Official Souvenir: An Account of the Kansas Volunteers in the Spanish-American War, 1898–1899.* St. Joseph, Missouri: 1989.

Pompey, Sherman Lee. *An Honor Roll of Kansas Civil War Veterans.* Kingsburg, California: Pacific Specialists, 1972.

United States. Adjutant General's Office. *Index to Compiled Service Records of Volunteer Union Soldiers Who Served in Organizations from the State of Kansas.* Washington, D.C.: The National Archives, 1964.

United States. Bureau of Indian Affairs. Potawatomi Agency. *Records of Indians in World War I.* Kansas City, Missouri: Federal Archives and Records Center, 1977.

United States. Selective Service System. *Kansas, World War I Selective Service System Draft Registration Cards, 1917–1918. National Archives Microfilm Publications, M1509.* Washington, D.C.: National Archives, 1987–1988.

Vital and Cemetery Records

Cemetery Records in Southeastern Kansas and Southwestern Missouri. Microfilm. Salt Lake City: Genealogical Society of Utah, 1984.

Cemetery Records of Kansas (Compiled by Members of the Kansas Mission). 18 Vols. Typescript. Salt Lake City: Genealogical Society of Utah, 1956–.

Ford, Don L. *Abandoned and Semi-Active Cemeteries of Kansas. 3 Vols.* Decorah, Iowa: Anundsen Publishing, 1983–1985.

Historical Records Survey (Kansas). *Guide To Public Vital Statistics Records In Kansas.* Topeka, Kansas: The Survey, 1942.

Jackson, Ronald Vern. *Kansas 1860 Mortality Schedule.* Bountiful, Utah: Accelerated Indexing Systems, 1980.

Jackson, Ronald Vern. *Mortality Schedule, Kansas 1870.* Bountiful, Utah: Accelerated Indexing Systems, 1979.

Jackson, Ronald Vern. *Mortality Schedule, Kansas 1880.* Bountiful, Utah: Accelerated Indexing Systems, 1979.

Ostertag, John A. *Births, Marriages, Deaths and Other News Items and Events.* 11 vols. St. Joseph, Missouri: J. A. Ostertag, 1989–1999.

County Website	Map Index	Date Created	Parent County or Territory From Which Organized Address/Details
Allen www.allencounty.org/	C8	30 Aug 1855	**Original county** Allen County; 1 N Washington St; Iola, KS 66749-2841; Ph. (316) 365-7491 **Details:** (Clerk District Court has Marriage Records from 1856, Divorce, Probate & Court from 1860 & Naturalization Records 1871–1929; Register of Deeds has Land & Military Records from 1860)
Anderson http://skyways.lib.ks.us/genweb/anderson/index.html	C7	30 Aug 1855	**Original county** Anderson County; 100 E 4th Ave; Garnett, KS 66032; Ph. (785) 448-6886 **Details:** (Clerk District Court has Marriage, Divorce, Probate & Court Records from 1857; County Appraiser has Land Records from 1900)
Arapahoe		1855	**Original county** Arapahoe County; KS **Details:** (Disorganized) Became Colorado Terr. in 1861
Atchison http://skyways.lib.ks.us/genweb/atchison/index.html	C4	30 Aug 1855	**Original county** Atchison County; 423 N 5th St; Atchison, KS 66002; Ph. (913) 367-1653 at_county-clerk@wan.kdor.state.is.ut.gov **Details:** (County Clerk has Birth Records 1891–1906 & Death Records 1891–1911; Court Clerk has Divorce, Marriage, Probate, Court, & Naturalization Records; Registrar of Deeds has Land, Military Discharge, School, & Cemetery Records
Barber http://skyways.lib.ks.us/genweb/barber/index.html	J10	26 Feb 1867	**Marion** Barber County; 120 E Washington Ave; Medicine Lodge, KS 67104-1421; Ph. (316) 886-3961 **Details:** (Spelled Barbour until 1883) (Probate Court has Probate Records; Register of Deeds has Land Records; County Clerk has Birth, Marriage & Death Records)
Barton www.bartonks.com/	K7	26 Feb 1867	**Marion** Barton County; 1400 Main St; PO Box 1089; Great Bend, KS 67530-1089; Ph. (316) 793-1870 **Details:** (County Clerk has Birth & Death Records 1892–1911 & Cemetery Records; Register of Deeds has Land, school & Military Discharge Records; Clerk District Court has Marriage, Probate & Naturalization Records)
Billings		1873	**Original county** Billings County; KS **Details:** (see Norton) Temporary name for Norton, Name changed to Norton 26 Feb 1867. Name changed to Billings 6 Mar 1873. Name changed back to Norton 19 Feb 1874.
Bourbon www.bourboncountyks.org/	B8	30 Aug 1855	**Original county** Bourbon County; 210 S National Ave; Fort Scott, KS 66701-1328; Ph. (316) 223-3800 **Details:** (Clerk Court has Divorce Records from 1870; Probate Judge has Marriage & Probate Records from 1870 & Court Records from 1963)
Breckenridge		1855	**Original county** Breckenridge County; KS **Details:** (see Lyon) Name changed to Lyon 5 Feb 1862

County	Map	Date	Parent County or Territory From Which Organized
Website	Index	Created	Address/Details

Brown   D3   30 Aug 1855
http://skyways.lib.ks.us/genweb/butler/index.html

Original county
Brown County; 601 Oregon St; Hiawatha, KS 66434;
Ph. (785) 742-2581
Details: (County Name spelled Browne 1855–1857) (Clerk District Court has Divorce, Probate & Court Records from 1800's & Marriage Records; Register of Deeds has Land Records from 1857)

Buffalo   1873

Unorg. Terr.
Buffalo County; KS
Details: (see Gray, old) Became Gray County 1881, disappeared 1883 to Gray & Finney Counties

Butler   F8   30 Aug 1855
www.bucoks.com/

Original county
Butler County; 205 W Central Ave; El Dorado, KS 67042;
Ph. (316) 322-4232
Details: (County Clerk has Birth & Death Records 1887–1912 & Land Records from 1887; Clerk District Court has Marriage, Divorce, Probate & Court Records)

Calhoun   30 Aug 1855

Original county
Calhoun County; KS
Details: (see Jackson) Name changed to Jackson 11 Feb 1859

Chase   F7   11 Feb 1859
http://skyways.lib.ks.us/genweb/chase/index.html

Butler, Wise
Chase County; PO Box 529; Courthouse Sq; Cottonwood Falls, KS 66845; Ph. (Register of Deeds) (620) 273-6398 or (County Clerk) (620) 273-6423 or (Clerk of District Court) (620) 273-6319
Details: (Register of Deeds has Land Records from 1859, Death Records from 1859, Cemetery Records, & Marriage Records; County Clerk has Census; Clerk of District Court has Court, Probate, Marriage, & Divorce Records.

Chautauqua   E10   3 Mar 1875
http://skyways.lib.ks.us/genweb/chautauq/index.html

Howard
Chautauqua County; 215 N Chautauqua; Sedan, KS 67361;
Ph. (316) 725-3282
Details: (Register of Deeds has Death & Burial Records from 1871, Land Records from 1870 & Military Records from 1940; Probate Judge has Marriage & Probate Records; Clerk District Court has Divorce & Court Records)

Cherokee   B10   18 Feb 1860
http://skyways.lib.ks.us/genweb/cherokee/index.html

Unorg. Terr.
Cherokee County; 300 E Maple; Columbus, KS 66725;
Ph. (316) 429-2159
Details: (Formerly McGee County. Name changed to Cherokee 18 Feb 1860) (Register of Deeds has Land Records from 1866, Probate Court has Probate Records from 1870; County Clerk has Birth, Marriage & Death Records)

Cheyenne   Q3   6 Mar 1873
http://skyways.lib.ks.us/genweb/cheyenne/index.html

Unorg. Terr.
Cheyenne County; PO Box 985; St. Francis, KS 67756-0646;
Ph. (785) 332-2401
Details: (Clerk District Court has Marriage Records from 1886, Divorce, Court & Probate Records from 1892; Register of Deeds has Land Records from mid-1800's & Military Discharge Records from 1919)

County Website	Map Index	Date Created	Parent County or Territory From Which Organized Address/Details
Clark http://skyways.lib.ks.us/genweb/clark/index.html	**M10**	**1867**	**Ford** Clark County; 913 Highland St; Ashland, KS 67831; Ph. (316) 635-2753 **Details:** (County Clerk has Birth Records 1904–1910; City Clerk has Birth & Burial Records from 1910; Probate Judge has Marriage & Probate Records; Clerk District Court has Divorce & Court Records; Register of Deeds has Land Records)
Clay http://skyways.lib.ks.us/genweb/clay/index.html	**G5**	**20 Feb 1857**	**Original county** Clay County; 712 5th St; PO Box 98; Clay Center, KS 67432-0098; Ph. (785) 632-2552 **Details:** (County Clerk has Birth, Marriage & Death Records 1885–1911; Clerk District Court has Divorce, Probate & Court Records; Register of Deeds has Land Records)
Cloud www.CloudCountyKs.org	**H4**	**26 Feb 1867**	**Original county** Cloud County; 811 Washington St; PO Box 96; Concordia, KS 66901; Ph. (785) 243-8121 tferguso@dustdevil.com **Details:** (Formerly Shirley County. Name changed to Cloud 26 Feb 1867) (Register of Deeds has Birth Records from 1885–1910, Burial Records, Land, Milittary, & School Records; Historical Society has Business Records & Newspapers, Frank Carlson Library has Census Records; Probate Court has Court, Guardianship, Marriage, & Probate Records; Vital Statistics has Death Records; District Court has Divorce, Immigration, & Naturalization Records)
Coffey www.coffeycountyks.org/	**D7**	**30 Aug 1855**	**Original county** Coffey County; 6th & Neosho; Burlington, KS 66839; Ph. (316) 364-2191 **Details:** (Clerk District Court has Birth & Death Records 1892–1910, Marriage Records from 1855, Divorce, Probate & Court Records from 1857; Register of Deeds has Land Records from 1857; Historical Society & Public Library have Cemetery books)
Comanche http://skyways.lib.ks.us/genweb/comanche/index.html	**L10**	**26 Feb 1867**	**Marion** Comanche County; 201 S New York; PO Box 776; Coldwater, KS 67029; Ph. (316) 582-2361 comcorod@giantcomm.net **Details:** (County Clerk has Birth & Death Records 1891–1911; Magistrate Judge has Marriage Records from 1891, Probate & Court Records; Clerk District Court has Divorce Records; Register of Deeds has Land & School Records)
Cowley www.cowleycounty.org/	**F10**	**26 Feb 1867**	**Butler** Cowley County; 311 E 9th Ave; Winfield, KS 67156; Ph. (316) 221-4066 **Details:** (City Clerk has Birth Records; Probate Court has Marriage, Divorce & Probate Records from 1870 & Death Records; Clerk District Court has Court Records; Appraisers Office has Land Records)
Crawford www.crawfordcountykansas.org/	**B9**	**13 Feb 1867**	**Bourbon, Cherokee** Crawford County; PO Box 249; Girard, KS 66743-0249; Ph. (316) 724-6115 **Details:** (County Clerk has Birth & Death Records 1886–1911 & Burial Records 1860's–1976; Clerk District Court has Marriage, Divorce, Probate, Court & Naturalization Records; Register of Deeds has Land Records from 1869 & Military Records)

Kansas

County Website	Map Index	Date Created	Parent County or Territory From Which Organized Address/Details
Davis		30 Aug 1855	**Original county** Davis County; KS **Details:** (see Geary) Name changed to Geary 28 Feb 1889
Decatur http://skyways.lib.ks.us/genweb/decatur/ index.html	N3	6 Mar 1873	**Unorg. Terr.** Decatur County; 120 E Hall; PO Box 89; Oberlin, KS 67749; Ph. (785) 475-8107 **Details:** (Clerk District Court has Birth, Marriage & Death Records 1885–1913, Divorce & Court Records from 1881, Probate Records from 1891 & Naturalization Records from 1880; Register of Deeds has Land Records from 1878 & Military Discharge Records from 1862)
Dickinson www.dkcoks.com/	G6	20 Feb 1857	**Davis, Unorg. Terr.** Dickinson County; 109 E 1st St; Abilene, KS 67410-0248; Ph. (785) 263-3774 **Details:** (County Clerk has incomplete Birth Records from 1892, Marriage & Death Records from 1892)
Doniphan http://skyways.lib.ks.us/genweb/doniphan/ index.html	C3	30 Aug 1855	**Original county** Doniphan County; Main St; Troy, KS 66087; Ph. (785) 985-3513 **Details:** (Clerk District Court has Birth & Death Records 1898–1910, Marriage, Divorce, Probate & Court Records from 1856; Register of Deeds has Land Records from 1858; A yearly County Census is taken)
Dorn		30 Aug 1855	**Original county** Dorn County; KS **Details:** (see Neosho) Name changed to Neosho 3 Jun 1861
Douglas www.douglas-county.com/	C6	30 Aug 1855	**Original county** Douglas County; 111 E 11th; Lawrence, KS 66044; Ph. (785) 841-7700 **Details:** (Clerk District Court has Probate & Court Records from 1863 & Naturalization Records 1867–1953; Register of Deeds has Land Records; Spencer Research Library has Marriage Records 1863–1912)
Edwards http://skyways.lib.ks.us/genweb/edwards/ index.html	L8	7 Mar 1874	**Kiowa** Edwards County; 312 Massachusetts Ave; Kinsley, KS 67547-1099; Ph. (316) 659-3121 **Details:** (Probate Judge has Marriage, Divorce, Probate & Court Records from 1874; Register of Deeds has Land Records from 1874)
Elk http://skyways.lib.ks.us/genweb/elk/index.html	E9	3 Mar 1875	**Howard** Elk County; 127 N Pine St; Howard, KS 67349; Ph. (316) 374-2490 **Details:** (Courthouse burned in 1906) (Clerk District Court has Birth & Death Records 1885–1911, Marriage & Probate Records from 1875, Divorce & Court Records from 1906 & Land Records from 1871)
Ellis www.ellisco.net/	L6	26 Feb 1867	**Unorg. Terr.** Ellis County; 1204 Fort St; Hays, KS 67601; Ph. (785) 628-9410 **Details:** (County Clerk has Birth, Marriage & Death Records 1886–1911; Clerk District Court has Divorce, Probate, Court & Naturalization Records; Register of Deeds has Land, Military Discharge & school Records)

County Website	Map Index	Date Created	Parent County or Territory From Which Organized Address/Details
Ellsworth http://skyways.lib.ks.us/genweb/ellswort/index.html	**I6**	**26 Feb 1867**	**Marion, Unorg. Terr.** Ellsworth County; 210 N Kansas Ave; PO Box 396; Ellsworth, KS 67439; Ph. (785) 472-3022 **Details:** (Probate Judge has Marriage & Probate Records; City Clerk has Death & Burial Records; Clerk District Court has Divorce Records; County Court has Court Records; Register of Deeds has Land Records)
Finney www.finneycounty.org/	**O8**	**1883**	**Marion** Finney County; 3119 N 9th St; PO Box M; Garden City, KS 67846-0450; Ph. (316) 272-3051 **Details:** (Formerly Sequoyah County. Name changed to Finney 21 Feb 1883) (Probate Judge has Marriage & Probate Records from 1885; Clerk District Court has Divorce & Court Records from 1885)
Foote		**1881**	**Marion** Foote County; KS **Details:** (see Gray, old) Became Gray County 1881 & disappeared 1883
Ford www.fordcounty.net/	**M9**	**1867**	**Unorg. Terr., Marion** Ford County; 100 Gunsmoke; Dodge City, KS 67801; Ph. (316) 277-3184 **Details:** (City Clerk has Birth, Death & Burial Records; Probate Judge has Marriage, Probate & Court Records; Clerk District Court has Divorce Records; County Clerk has Land Records)
Franklin www.co.franklin.ks.us/	**C6**	**30 Aug 1855**	**Original county** Franklin County; 315 S Main; Ottawa, KS 66067; Ph. (785) 242-1471 **Details:** (Clerk District Court has Marriage, Divorce, Probate & Court Records; Register of Deeds has Land & Military Records)
Garfield		**5 Mar 1887**	**Finney, Hodgeman** Garfield County; KS **Details:** (see Finney) Annexed to Finney, 1893
Geary http://skyways.lib.ks.us/genweb/geary/index.html	**F5**	**28 Feb 1889**	**Original county** Geary County; 8th & Franklin; Junction City, KS 66441; Ph. (785) 238-3912 **Details:** (Formerly Davis County. Name changed to Geary 28 Feb 1889) (Probate Court has Marriage & Probate Records from 1860; Clerk District Court has Divorce Records from 1860; County Court has Court Records from 1937; Register of Deeds has Land Records from 1858)
Godfrey		**30 Aug 1855**	**Original county** Godfrey County; KS **Details:** (see Seward, old) Name changed to Seward 3 Jun 1861
Gove http://skyways.lib.ks.us/genweb/gove/index.html	**N6**	**1867**	**Unorg. Terr.** Gove County; 520 Washington St; PO Box 128; Gove, KS 67736-0128; Ph. (785) 938-2300 **Details:** (Register of Deeds has Land Records; Probate Court has Probate Records)

County Website	Map Index	Date Created	Parent County or Territory From Which Organized Address/Details
Graham http://skyways.lib.ks.us/genweb/graham/index.html	M5	26 Feb 1867	**Unorg. Terr.** Graham County; 410 N Pomeroy; Hill City, KS 67642-1645; Ph. (785) 674-5433 **Details:** (Probate Judge has Marriage & Probate Records; Clerk District Court has Divorce & Court Records; Register of Deeds has Land Records)
Grant www.grantcoks.org/	P9	6 Mar 1873	**Unorg. Terr.** Grant County; 108 S Glenn; Ulysses, KS 67880-2551; Ph. (620) 356-1335 clerk@pld.com **Details:** (Clerk of District Court has Divorce, Marriage, Probate, & Court Records; Register of Deeds has Land Records from 1873; County Clerk has Census Records 1915–1982; Cemetery Office has Cemetery Records for all Cemeteries; Grant County Library has Local Newspapers on Microfilm)
Gray http://skyways.lib.ks.us/genweb/gray/index.html	N9	5 Mar 1887	**Finney, Ford** Gray County; PO Box 487; Cimarron, KS 67835-0487; Ph. (316) 855-3618 **Details:** (Probate Judge has Marriage Records from 1887 & Probate Records from 1885; Clerk District Court has Divorce Records from 1887; Register of Deeds has Land Records from 1887; County Clerk has tax roll Census from 1889 & school Records)
Gray, old		1881	**Foote, Buffalo** Gray, old County; KS **Details:** (Disappeared in 1883; Reorg. 5 Mar 1887)
Greeley http://skyways.lib.ks.us/genweb/greeley/index.html	Q7	6 Mar 1873	**Unorg. Terr.** Greeley County; 208 Harper St; PO Box 277; Tribune, KS 67879-0277; Ph. (316) 376-4256 **Details:** (City Clerk has Birth Records; Probate Judge has Marriage & Probate Records; County Court has Court Records; Register of Deeds has Land Records)
Greenwood http://skyways.lib.ks.us/genweb/greenwoo/index.html	E8	30 Aug 1855	**Original county** Greenwood County; 311 N Main; PO Box 268; Eureka, KS 67045-1321; Ph. (316) 583-7421 **Details:** (County Clerk has Birth Records 1885–1947, Marriage Records 1885–1911 & Death Records 1885–1965; Clerk District Court has Divorce, Probate & Court Records; Register of Deeds has Land & Military Records)
Hageman		1867	**Marion** Hageman County **Details:** (See Hodgeman) Name changed to Hodgeman County in 1868
Hamilton http://skyways.lib.ks.us/genweb/hamilton/index.html	Q8	6 Mar 1873	**Unorg. Terr.** Hamilton County; 219 N Main St; Syracuse, KS 67878; Ph. (316) 384-5629 **Details:** (Probate Judge has Marriage & Probate Records from 1886; City Clerk has Death & Burial Records; Clerk District Court has Divorce Records; County Clerk has Land Records from 1884)

County Website	Map Index	Date Created	Parent County or Territory From Which Organized Address/Details
Harper www.harpercounty.org/	I10	26 Feb 1867	**Marion** Harper County; 200 N Jennings Ave; Anthony, KS 67003; Ph. (316) 842-5555 **Details:** (Probate Judge has Marriage & Probate Records; Clerk District Court has Divorce & Court Records; Register of Deeds has Land Records)
Harvey http://skyways.lib.ks.us/genweb/harvey/index.html	H8	29 Feb 1872	**McPherson, Sedgwick, Marion** Harvey County; PO Box 687; 800 N Main; Newton, KS 67114; Ph. (316) 284-6950 **Details:** (Birth Records do not exist; District Clerk has Marriage, Divorce, Probate, & Court Records from 1872; Register of deeds has Land & Naturalization Records from 1872, & Military Discharge Records; County Historical Museum & Archives has Cemetery Records, Newspapers, Other Historical Records (www.hchm.org))
Haskell www.haskellcounty.org/	O9	5 Mar 1887	**Finney** Haskell County; PO Box 518; Sublette, KS 67877-0518; Ph. (316) 675-2263 **Details:** (Department of Legal Statistics has Birth & Death Records; Probate Judge has Marriage & Probate Records; Clerk District Court has Divorce Records)
Hodgeman	M8	1868	**Marion** Hodgeman County; 500 Main St; PO Box 247; Jetmore, KS 67854-0247; Ph. (316) 357-6421 **Details:** (City Clerk has Birth, Death & Burial Records from 1911; Probate Judge has Marriage & Probate Records from 1887; Clerk District Court has Divorce & Court Records from 1887; Register of Deeds has Land Records from 1879)
Howard		1870	**Original county** Howard County; KS **Details:** (see Elk & Chautauqua) Org. as Godfrey County. Name changed to Seward, old, 3 Jun 1861. Name changed to Howard 26 Feb 1867. Howard divided to form Elk & Chautauqua Counties 11 Mar 1875. County was Terminated in 1875
Hunter		30 Aug 1855	**Original county** Hunter County; KS **Details:** (see Butler) Name changed to Butler 1864
Irving		2 Feb 1905	Irving County; KS **Details:** (County Terminated 1864)
Jackson http://skyways.lib.ks.us/genweb/jackson/index.html	D4	11 Feb 1859	**Original county** Jackson County; 400 New York Ave; Holton, KS 66436; Ph. (785) 364-2891 **Details:** (Formerly Calhoun County. Name changed to Jackson 11 Feb 1859) (County Clerk has Birth & Death Records 1903–1911; Probate Judge has Marriage Records from 1867, Probate Records from 1857 & Court Records from 1900; Clerk District Court has Divorce Records; Register of Deeds has Land Records from 1858)

County Website	Map Index	Date Created	Parent County or Territory From Which Organized Address/Details
Jefferson http://skyways.lib.ks.us/genweb/jefferso/index.html	C5	30 Aug 1855	**Original county** Jefferson County; 300 W Jefferson St; PO Box 321; Oskaloosa, KS 66066-0321; Ph. (785) 863-2272 **Details:** (Probate Judge has Marriage & Probate Records; Clerk District Court has Divorce Records; Register of Deeds has Land Records)
Jewell	I3	26 Feb 1867	**Unorg. Terr.** Jewell County; 307 N Commercial St.; Mankato, KS 66956; Ph. (785) 378-4070 **Details:** (Register of Deeds has Birth, Marriage, & Death Records 1886–1909 & Landownership Maps 1884, 1908, 1921, & 1930)
Johnson www.jocoks.com/	B6	30 Aug 1855	**Original county** Johnson County; 111 S Cherry; Olathe, KS 66061; Ph. (913) 764-8484 ext. 5335 **Details:** (Clerk District Court has Divorce & Court Records from 1861; Probate Court has Marriage & Probate Records)
Kansas		1873	**Unorg. Terr.** Kansas County; KS **Details:** (see Morton) Disappeared 1883. Reorganized 18 Feb 1886 as Morton County.
Kearny http://skyways.lib.ks.us/genweb/kearny/index.html	P8	6 Mar 1873	**Unorg. Terr.** Kearny County; 305 N Main St; Lakin, KS 67860; Ph. (316) 355-6422 **Details:** (County Clerk has Birth, Marriage & Death Records 1900–1910; Clerk District Court has Divorce & Court Records from 1894 & Probate Records from 1895; Register of Deeds has Land Records from 1894; County Clerk & County Historical Society have newspapers; County Appraiser has local Census from 1913)
Kingman http://skyways.lib.ks.us/genweb/kingman/index.html	I9	29 Feb 1872	**Reno** Kingman County; 130 N Spruce St; Kingman, KS 67068; Ph. (316) 532-2521 **Details:** (County Clerk has Death Records & local census; Clerk District Court has Marriage, Divorce, Probate & Court Records; County Appraiser has Land Records)
Kiowa http://skyways.lib.ks.us/genweb/kiowa/index.html	L9	10 Feb 1886	**Comanche, Edwards** Kiowa County; 211 E Florida; Greensburg, KS 67054; Ph. (316) 723-3366 **Details:** (Clerk District Court has Marriage, Probate & Naturalization Records; Register of Deeds has Land Records from 1886 & Military Discharge Records)
Kiowa, old		26 Feb 1867	**Marion** Kiowa, old County; KS **Details:** (Kiowa County absorbed by Edwards & Comanche Counties in 1875. Kiowa recreated 10 Feb 1886, being formed from parts of Edwards & Comanche)
Labette www.labettecounty.com/	C10	7 Feb 1867	**Neosho** Labette County; 501 Merchant St; PO Box 387; Oswego, KS 67356; Ph. (316) 795-2138 **Details:** (County Clerk has Birth Records 1885–1896 & Death Records 1885–1889; Probate Judge has Marriage & Probate Records from 1870; Clerk District Court has Divorce & Court Records from 1870; Register of Deeds has Land Records from 1875; A yearly County Census taken 1915–1979)

County Website	Map Index	Date Created	Parent County or Territory From Which Organized Address/Details
Lane http://trails.net/laneco/	**N7**	**6 Mar 1873**	**Unorg. Terr.** Lane County; 144 S Ln; PO Box 788; Dighton, KS 67839; Ph. (316) 397-5552 **Details:** (Magistrate Court has Marriage, Divorce, Probate & Court Records; Register of Deeds has Land Records; City of Dighton has Burial Records)
Leavenworth www.leavenworthcounty.org/	**C5**	**30 Aug 1855**	**Original county** Leavenworth County; 601 S Third St Ste 3051; Leavenworth, KS 66048-2781; Ph. (913) 684-0700 **Details:** (Probate Judge has Marriage & Probate Records from 1855; Register of Deeds has Land Records; Clerk District Court has Court & Naturalization Records from 1855)
Lincoln http://skyways.lib.ks.us/genweb/lincoln/index.html	**I5**	**26 Feb 1867**	**Unorg. Terr.** Lincoln County; 216 E Lincoln; Lincoln, KS 67455-2097; Ph. (785) 524-4757 **Details:** (County Clerk has some Cemetery, Land & Court Records & some local Census Records from 1913; Clerk District Court has Marriage, Divorce, Probate, Court & Naturalization Records from 1870; Register of Deeds has Land Records from 1870 & Military Discharge Records from 1880)
Linn http://skyways.lib.ks.us/genweb/linn/index.html	**B7**	**30 Aug 1855**	**Original county** Linn County; PO Box BIRTH; Mound City, KS 66056-0601; Ph. (913) 795-2668 **Details:** (Clerk District Court has Probate & Court Records from 1855; Register of Deeds has Land Records & Military Records from 1900; County Library/Museum has Birth, Marriage & Death Records from 1855, Divorce Records, Cemetery Records from 1910, Military Records 1861–1865 & newspapers from 1864)
Logan http://skyways.lib.ks.us/genweb/logan/index.html	**P6**	**24 Feb 1887**	**Wallace** Logan County; 710 W 2nd; Oakley, KS 67748; Ph. (785) 672-3654 **Details:** (Formerly St. John County. Name changed to Logan 24 Feb 1887) (City Clerk has Birth, Death & Burial Records; Probate Judge has Marriage & Probate Records; Clerk District Court has Divorce & Court Records; County Clerk has Land Records from 1885)
Lykins		**30 Aug 1855**	**Original county** Lykins County; KS **Details:** (see Miami) Name changed to Miami 3 June 1861
Lyon www.lyoncounty.org/	**E7**	**5 Feb 1862**	**Original county** Lyon County; 430 Commercial; Emporia, KS 66801-4000; Ph. (620) 342-4950 **Details:** (Formerly Breckenridge County. Name changed to Lyon 5 Feb 1862) (Clerk District Court has Marriage Records from 1861, Divorce Records from 1860, Probate Records from 1859 & Court Records from 1858; Register of Deeds has Land Records from 1856; City Clerk has Birth & Death Records)
Madison		**1855**	**Original county** Madison County; KS **Details:** Divided to Greenwood & Lyon Counties, 1862 County Terminated 1861

County Website	Map Index	Date Created	Parent County or Territory From Which Organized Address/Details
Marion http://skyways.lib.ks.us/genweb/marion/index.html	G7	1860	**Original county** Marion County; 204 S 4th St; PO Box 219; Marion, KS 66861; Ph. (316) 382-2185 **Details:** (County Clerk has Birth & Death Records 1885–1911; Clerk District Court has Marriage Records from 1800's, Divorce, Probate & Court Records; Register of Deeds has school Records 1873–1964 & Land Records)
Marshall http://skyways.lib.ks.us/genweb/marshall/index.html	F3	30 Aug 1855	**Original county** Marshall County; 1201 Broadway; Marysville, KS 66508-1844; Ph. (785) 562-5361 **Details:** (County Clerk has Birth Records 1885–1911 & Death Records 1889–1911; Clerk District Court has Marriage, Divorce, Probate & Court Records; Register of Deeds has Land Records)
McGee		30 Aug 1855	**Unorg. Terr.** McGee County; KS **Details:** (see Cherokee) Name changed to Cherokee 18 Feb 1860
McPherson www.mcphersoncountyks.us	H7	26 Feb 1867	**Marion** McPherson County; 117 N Maple St; PO Box 425; McPherson, KS 67460; Ph. (316) 241-3656 **Details:** (County Clerk has Birth Records 1874–1911, Marriage Records 1887–1911, Death Records 1886–1911 & local Census 1932; Clerk District Court has Divorce & Court Records from 1873, Probate Records from 1870 & Naturalization Records; Register of Deeds has Land Records)
Meade http://skyways.lib.ks.us/genweb/meade/index.html	N10	8 Jan 1873	**Unorg. Terr.** Meade County; 200 N Fowler St; PO Box 278; Meade, KS 67864; Ph. (316) 873-8700 **Details:** (Reorganized 7 Mar 1885) (Probate Judge has Birth, Marriage, Probate & Court Records; City Clerk has Burial Records; Clerk District Court has Divorce Records; Register of Deeds has Land Records)
Miami www.miamicountyks.org/	B6	3 June 1861	**Original County** Miami County; 201 S Pearl St Ste 102; Paola, KS 66071; Ph. (913) 294-3976 **Details:** (Formerly Lykins County. Name changed to Miami 3 June 1861) (Register of Deeds has Land Records from 1857; Probate Court has Probate & Marriage Records from 1857, Birth & Death Records; Clerk District Court has Court & Naturalization Records)
Mitchell http://skyways.lib.ks.us/genweb/mitchell/index.html	I4	26 Feb 1867	**Unorg. Terr.** Mitchell County; 111 S Hersey Ave; Beloit, KS 67420; Ph. (785) 738-3652 **Details:** (Probate Judge has Marriage & Probate Records; Clerk District Court has Divorce Records; Register of Deeds has Land Records)
Montgomery http://skyways.lib.ks.us/genweb/montgome/index.html	D10	26 Feb 1867	**Wilson** Montgomery County; 217 E Myrtle; PO Box 446; Independence, KS 67301; Ph. (316) 330-1200 **Details:** (County Clerk has Birth & Death Records 1886–1911; Probate Court has Marriage & Probate Records from 1870; Clerk District Court has Divorce & Court Records from 1870; Register of Deeds has Land Records from 1870)

County	Map	Date	Parent County or Territory From Which Organized
Website	Index	Created	Address/Details

Morris   **F6**   **11 Feb 1859**
http://skyways.lib.ks.us/genweb/morris/index.html

Original county
Morris County; 501 W Main St; Council Grove, KS 66846;
Ph. (316) 767-5518
Details: (Formerly Wise County. Name changed to Morris 11 Feb 1859) (Probate Judge has Marriage & Probate Records; City Clerk has Burial & Death Records; Clerk District Court has Divorce & Court Records; Register of Deeds has Land Records)

Morton   **Q10**   **18 Feb 1886**
http://skyways.lib.ks.us/genweb/morton/index.html

Kansas
Morton County; 1025 Morton St; PO Box 1116; Elkhart, KS 67950-1116; Ph. (316) 697-2157
Details: (Created as Kansas County 1873. Reorganized as Morton County 18 Feb 1886) (County Clerk has Marriage Records from 1887, Divorce & Court Records from 1900 & Land Records from 1887)

Nemaha   **E3**   **30 Aug 1855**
http://skyways.lib.ks.us/genweb/nemaha/index.html

Original county
Nemaha County; 607 Nemaha St; Seneca, KS 66538;
Ph. (785) 336-2146
Details: (County Clerk has Birth, Marriage & Death Records 1885–1911; Clerk District Court has Marriage, Probate & Court Records from 1857)

Neosho   **C9**   **3 Jun 1861**
http://skyways.lib.ks.us/genweb/neosho/index.html

Original county
Neosho County; 100 S Main St; PO Box 138; Erie, KS 66733;
Ph. (620) 244-3800
Details: (Formerly Dorn County. Name changed to Neosho 3 Jun 1861) (Probate Court has Probate Records from 1866 & Marriage Records from 1864; Clerk of District Court has Naturalization Records from 1868; Register of Deeds has Land Records from 1866)

Ness   **M7**   **26 Feb 1867**
http://skyways.lib.ks.us/genweb/ness/index.html

Unorg. Terr.
Ness County; 202 W Sycamore St; Ness City, KS 67560-1558;
Ph. (785) 798-2401
Details: (Probate Judge has Marriage & Probate Records; Clerk Courts has Divorce Records; City Clerk has Court Records; Register of Deeds has Land Records)

Norton   **M4**   **26 Feb 1867**
http://skyways.lib.ks.us/genweb/norton/index.htm

Unorg. Terr.
Norton County; 101 S Kansas Ave; Norton, KS 67654-0070;
Ph. (785) 877-5710
Details: (Name changed to Billings 6 Mar 1873. Name changed back to Norton 19 Feb 1874) (Clerk District Court has Marriage & Divorce Records; Probate Court has Probate & Court Records; Register of Deeds has Land Records from 1874 & some Cemetery Records; City Clerks have Birth & Death Records)

Oro   **7 Feb 1859**

Original county
Oro County; KS
Details: County Terminated 1861 (see Norton & Billings) Name changed to Norton 26 Feb 1867. Name changed to Billings 6 Mar 1873. Name changed back to Norton 19 Feb 1874.

County Website	Map Index	Date Created	Parent County or Territory From Which Organized
			Address/Details

Osage D6 **11 Feb 1859** **Original county**
www.osageco.org/
Osage County; 717 Topeka Ave; Lyndon, KS 66451-0226;
Ph. (785) 828-4812
Details: (Formerly Weller County. Name changed to Osage 11 Feb 1859) (County Clerk has Birth Records 1886–1921, Marriage Records 1885–1911 & Death Records 1885–1909; Clerk District Court has Divorce Records from 1863; County Court has Court Records from 1929; Register of Deeds has Land Records from 1858)

Osborne K5 **26 Feb 1867** **Unorg. Terr.**
http://skyways.lib.ks.us/genweb/osborne/index.html
Osborne County; 423 W Main St; Osborne, KS 67473;
Ph. (785) 346-5911
Details: (Probate Judge has Marriage, Probate & Court Records, Divorce Records from 1872; Register of Deeds has Land Records)

Otoe **16 Feb 1860** **Marion**
Otoe County; KS
Details: County Terminated 1864 (see Butler) Became part of Butler County, 1861

Ottawa H5 **27 Feb 1860** **Unorg. Terr.**
http://skyways.lib.ks.us/genweb/ottawa/index.html
Ottawa County; 307 N Concord; Minneapolis, KS 67467;
Ph. (785) 392-2279
Details: (County Clerk has Marriage, Divorce & Probate Records; City Officers have Birth Records from 1911 & Death Records; Register of Deeds has Land Records)

Pawnee L7 **26 Feb 1867** **Marion**
http://skyways.lib.ks.us/genweb/pawnee/index.html
Pawnee County; 715 Broadway; Larned, KS 67550;
Ph. (316) 285-3721
Details: (Clerk District Court has Marriage Records from 1873, Divorce, Probate, Court & Naturalization Records; Register of Deeds has Land Records; City Clerk has Birth & Death Records 1897–1911 & Burial Records from 1886; Census taken in 1886)

Peketon **1860** **Unorganized Territory**
Peketon, KS
Details: (Clerk District Court has Marriage Records from 1873, Divorce, Probate, Court & Naturalization Records; Register of Deeds has Land Records; City Clerk has Birth & Death Records 1897–1911 & Burial Records from 1886; Census taken in 1886)

Phillips L4 **26 Feb 1867** **Unorg. Terr.**
http://skyways.lib.ks.us/genweb/phillips/index.html
Phillips County; 301 State St; Phillipsburg, KS 67661;
Ph. (785) 543-5513
Details: (Probate Judge has Marriage & Probate Records; City Clerk has Death & Burial Records; Clerk District Court has Divorce & Court Records; County Clerk has Land Records)

Pottawatomie F4 **20 Feb 1857** **Riley, Calhoun**
www.pottcounty.org/
Pottawatomie County; 207 N First; Westmoreland, KS 66549-0187;
Ph. (785) 457-3314
Details: (County Clerk has Birth, Marriage & Death Records 1885–1910; Unified Court System has Divorce, Probate & Court Records; Register of Deeds has Land Records)

County Website	Map Index	Date Created	Parent County or Territory From Which Organized Address/Details
Pratt www.prattcounty.org/	**J9**	**26 Feb 1867**	**Marion** Pratt County; 300 S Ninnescah St; Pratt, KS 67124; Ph. (316) 672-7761 **Details:** (Clerk District Court has Marriage, Divorce, Probate & Court Records; Register of Deeds has Land & Military Records)
Rawlins http://skyways.lib.ks.us/genweb/rawlins/index.html	**P4**	**6 Mar 1873**	**Unorg. Terr.** Rawlins County; 607 Main St; Atwood, KS 67730-1896; Ph. (785) 626-3351 **Details:** (Register of Deeds has Land Records; Probate Court has Probate Records)
Reno www.rngov.reno.ks.us/	**I8**	**26 Feb 1867**	**Marion** Reno County; 206 W First; Hutchinson, KS 67501-5245; Ph. (620) 694-2934 **Details:** (County Clerk has Birth & Death Records 1890–1910 & Cemetery Records 1865–1978; Clerk District Court has Divorce Records; Probate Judge has Probate Records)
Republic http://skyways.lib.ks.us/genweb/republic/index.html	**H3**	**27 Feb 1860**	**Original county** Republic County; 1815 M St Rt 1; Belleville, KS 66935; Ph. (785) 527-5691 **Details:** (Register of Deeds has Land Records; Probate Court has Probate Records)
Rice http://skyways.lib.ks.us/genweb/rice/index.html	**I7**	**26 Feb 1867**	**Marion** Rice County; 101 W Commercial St; Lyons, KS 67554; Ph. (316) 257-2232 **Details:** (Clerk District Court has Marriage Records from 1872, Divorce, Probate & Court Records; Register of Deeds has Land Records from 1871; City Clerk has Birth Records 1895–1910 & Burial Records)
Richardson		**30 Aug 1855**	**Original county** Richardson County; KS **Details:** (see Wabaunsee) Name changed to Wabaunsee 11 Feb 1859
Riley www.rileycountyks.gov	**F5**	**30 Aug 1855**	**Original county** Riley County; 110 Courthouse Plaza; Manhattan, KS 66502-6018; Ph. (785) 565-6200 **Details:** (County Clerk has Birth & Death Records 1885–1886 & 1892–1909; City Clerk has Birth & Death Records from 1910; Probate Court has Probate Records; Register of Deeds has Land Records)
Rooks http://skyways.lib.ks.us/genweb/rooks/index.html	**L5**	**26 Feb 1867**	**Unorg. Terr.** Rooks County; 115 N Walnut St; Stockton, KS 67669-1663; Ph. (785) 425-6718 **Details:** (Clerk District Court has Birth & Death Records 1888–1905, Marriage & Divorce Records from 1888, Probate Records from 1881 & Court Records; Register of Deeds has Land Records)
Rush http://skyways.lib.ks.us/genweb/rush/index.html	**L7**	**26 Feb 1867**	**Unorg. Terr.** Rush County; 715 Elm St; La Crosse, KS 67548; Ph. (785) 222-2731 **Details:** (City Clerk has Birth, Death & Burial Records; Probate Judge has Marriage Records from 1876, Probate & Court Records; Clerk District Court has Divorce Records; Register of Deeds has Land Records)

County Website	Map Index	Date Created	Parent County or Territory From Which Organized Address/Details
Russell http://skyways.lib.ks.us/genweb/russell/index.html	**K6**	**26 Feb 1867**	**Unorg. Terr.** Russell County; 401 N Main St; PO Box 113; Russell, KS 67665; Ph. (785) 483-4641 **Details:** (County Clerk has Birth, Death, & Marriage Records 1885–1911; Russell Historical Society has Newspapers.) (Russell Historical Society 331 N Kansas. Russell, KS 67665. Ph. (785) 483-3637)
Saline www.co.saline.ks.us/	**H6**	**15 Feb 1860**	**Original county** Saline County; 300 W Ash; Salina, KS 67401; Ph. (785) 827-1961 **Details:** (Probate Judge has Marriage & Probate Records; Register of Deeds has Land Records)
Scott http://skyways.lib.ks.us/genweb/scott/index.html	**O7**	**6 Mar 1873**	**Unorg. Terr.** Scott County; 303 Court St; Scott City, KS 67871-1122; Ph. (316) 872-2420 **Details:** (City Clerk has Birth & Death Records; Probate Judge has Marriage & Probate Records; County Clerk has Burial Records; Clerk Courts has Divorce & Court Records)
Sedgwick www.sedgwick.ks.us/	**H8**	**26 Feb 1867**	**Butler, Marion** Sedgwick County; 525 N Main St; Wichita, KS 67203; Ph. (316) 383-7666 **Details:** (District Probate Court has Marriage & Probate Records from 1870; District Civic Court has Court Records; County Clerk has Land Records from 1887; Community Health Dept. (1900 E. 9th, Wichita, KS 67214) has Birth & Death Records)
Sequoyah		**1873**	**Marion** Sequoyah County; KS **Details:** (see Finney) Name changed to Finney 21 Feb 1883
Seward http://skyways.lib.ks.us/genweb/seward/index.html	**O10**	**1873**	**Unorg. Terr.** Seward County; 415 N Washington; Liberal, KS 67901; Ph. (316) 626-0211 **Details:** (City Clerk has Birth, Death & Burial Records; Probate Judge has Marriage & Probate Records; Clerk District Court has Divorce & Court Records; Register of Deeds has Land Records; County Clerk has newspapers from 1873)
Seward, old		**3 Jun 1861**	**Original county** Seward, old County; KS **Details:** (Formerly Godfrey County. Name changed to Seward 3 June 1861. Name changed to Howard 26 Feb 1867. Howard divided into Elk & Chautauqua Counties 11 Mar 1875)
Shawnee www.co.shawnee.ks.us/	**D5**	**30 Aug 1855**	**Original county** Shawnee County; 200 SE 7th St.; Topeka, KS 66603; Ph. (785) 233-8200 **Details:** (Clerk of District Court has Guardianship Records; Register of Deeds has Land & Military Records; Probate Court has Marriage Records from 1856 & Divorce Records from 1900; County Clerk has Birth & Death Records from 1894–1911)
Sheridan http://skyways.lib.ks.us/genweb/sheridan/index.html	**N4**	**6 Mar 1873**	**Unorg. Terr.** Sheridan County; PO Box 899; Hoxie, KS 67740-0899; Ph. (785) 675-3361 **Details:** (County Clerk has incomplete Birth & Death Records 1887–1910; Clerk District Court has Marriage, Divorce, Probate & Court Records; Register of Deeds has Land Records)

County Website	Map Index	Date Created	Parent County or Territory From Which Organized Address/Details
Sherman http://skyways.lib.ks.us/genweb/sherman/ index.html	Q4	6 Mar 1873	**Unorg. Terr.** Sherman County; 813 Broadway; Goodland, KS 67735-3056; Ph. (785) 899-4800 **Details:** (County Clerk has Newspapers from 1898, School & Census Records; City Clerk has Birth & Death Records, Land Records from 1887; Probate Judge has Marriage & Probate Records from 1886; Clerk District Court has Divorce & Court Records from 1887; Register of Deeds has Land Records from 1886)
Shirley		27 Feb 1860	**Original county** Shirley County; KS **Details:** (see Cloud) Name changed to Cloud 26 Feb 1867
Smith http://skyways.lib.ks.us/genweb/smith/index.html	K3	26 Feb 1867	**Unorg. Terr.** Smith County; 218 S Grant St; Smith Center, KS 66967; Ph. (785) 282-6533 **Details:** (Probate Judge has Marriage & Probate Records from 1875; Clerk District Court has Divorce & Court Records from 1875; County Clerk has Land Records from 1872)
St. John		4 Mar 1881	**Wallace** St. John County; KS **Details:** (see Logan) Name changed to Logan 24 Feb 1887
Stafford http://skyways.lib.ks.us/genweb/stafford/ index.html	J8	26 Feb 1867	**Marion** Stafford County; 209 N Broadway St; St. John, KS 67576; Ph. (316) 549-3509 **Details:** (Register of Deeds has Land Records; Probate Court has Probate Records)
Stanton http://skyways.lib.ks.us/genweb/stanton/index.html	Q9	6 Mar 1873	**Unorg. Terr.** Stanton County; 201 N Main; PO Box 190; Johnson, KS 67855; Ph. (620) 492-2140 **Details:** (Absorbed by Hamilton County 1883. Reorganized Feb 1887) (State Department of Human Resources has Birth & Death Records; Registrar of Deeds has Burial, Land, & Military Records; Chamber of Commerce has Business Records; County Clerk has Census; Clerk of District Court has Court, Divorce, Marriage, & Probate Records; County Treasury has Tax Records; Historical has other Historical Records)
Stevens http://skyways.lib.ks.us/genweb/stevens/index.html	P10	6 Mar 1873	**Indian Lands** Stevens County; 200 E 6th St; Hugoton, KS 67951-2652; Ph. (316) 544-2541 **Details:** (Probate Court has Probate Records; Register of Deeds has Land Records)
Sumner http://co.sumner.ks.us/	H10	26 Feb 1867	**Butler, Marion** Sumner County; 500 N Washington; Wellington, KS 67152; Ph. (316) 326-3395 **Details:** (Probate Judge has Marriage & Probate Records; Clerk District Court has Divorce Records; County Clerk has Land Records)

County Website	Map Index	Date Created	Parent County or Territory From Which Organized Address/Details
Thomas http://skyways.lib.ks.us/genweb/thomas/index.html	P5	6 Mar 1873	**Unorg. Terr.** Thomas County; 300 N Court Street; Colby, KS 67701; Ph. (785) 462-2561 **Details:** (County Clerk has Birth, Marriage & Death Records 1885–1910 & Burial Records from 1910; Clerk District Court has Marriage, Probate, Divorce, Court & Naturalization Records from 1885; Register of Deeds has Land Records from 1884 & Military Discharge Records)
Trego http://skyways.lib.ks.us/genweb/trego/index.html	M6	26 Feb 1867	**Unorg. Terr.** Trego County; 216 Main St; WaKeeney, KS 67672-2189; Ph. (785) 743-5773 **Details:** (Probate Judge has Marriage & Probate Records; Clerk District Court has Divorce & Court Records)
Wabaunsee http://skyways.lib.ks.us/genweb/wabaunse/index.html	E6	11 Feb 1859	**Original county** Wabaunsee County; 215 Kansas St; Alma, KS 66401; Ph. (785) 765-3414 **Details:** (Formerly Richardson County. Name changed to Wabaunsee 11 Feb 1859) (County Clerk has Birth, Marriage & Death Records 1892–1910; Clerk District Court has Divorce, Probate & Court Records)
Wallace http://skyways.lib.ks.us/genweb/wallace/index.html	Q6	2 Mar 1868	**Unorg. Terr.** Wallace County; 313 Main St; Sharon Springs, KS 67758; Ph. (785) 852-4282 **Details:** (County Clerk has Birth Records 1895–1911; Clerk of District Court has Death, Naturalization, Guardianship, Marriage Divorce, Probate, & Court Records; Register of Deeds has Land Records)
Washington http://skyways.lib.ks.us/genweb/washingt/index.html	G4	1859	**Unorg. Terr.** Washington County; 214 C St; Washington, KS 66968-1928; Ph. (785) 325-2974 **Details:** (County Clerk has Birth, Marriage & Death Records 1887–1911; Clerk District Court has Marriage Records from 1868, Divorce, Probate & Court Records from 1873 & Naturalization Records 1870–1938; Register of Deeds has Land Records)
Washington, old		1855	**Original county** Washington, old County; KS **Details:** (County disappeared in 1857 and reappeared as Peketon area or Marion County)
Weller		30 Aug 1855	**Original county** Weller County; KS **Details:** (see Osage) Name changed to Osage 11 Feb 1859
Wichita http://skyways.lib.ks.us/genweb/wichita/index.html	P7	6 Mar 1873	**Indian Lands** Wichita County; 206 S 4th St; PO Drawer 968; Leoti, KS 67861-0279; Ph. (316) 375-4454 **Details:** (Probate Judge has Marriage & Probate Records from 1887 & Court Records; City Clerk has Death & Burial Records from 1887; Clerk District Court has Divorce Records from 1887; Register of Deeds has Land Records from 1885)

County Website	Map Index	Date Created	Parent County or Territory From Which Organized Address/Details
Wilson http://skyways.lib.ks.us/genweb/wilson/index.html	**D9**	**30 Aug 1855**	**Original county** Wilson County; 615 Madison St; Fredonia, KS 66736; Ph. (316) 378-2186 **Details:** (Probate Judge has Marriage, Probate & Court Records; Clerk District Court has Divorce Records; Register of Deeds has Land Records)
Wise		**30 Aug 1855**	**Original county** Wise County; KS **Details:** (see Morris) Name changed to Morris 11 Feb 1859
Woodson www.woodsoncounty.net/	**D8**	**30 Aug 1855**	**Original county** Woodson County; 105 W Rutledge; Yates Center, KS 66783; Ph. (316) 625-3162 **Details:** (County Clerk has Birth Records 1885–1911, Marriage Records from 1860, Divorce & Probate Records from 1863, Court Records from 1934 & Land Records from 1861)
Wyandotte www.wycokck.org/	**B5**	**29 Jan 1859**	**Leavenworth, Johnson** Wyandotte County; 710 N 7th St; Kansas City, KS 66112; Ph. (913) 573-2800 **Details:** (City Clerk has Birth & Death Records; Probate Judge has Marriage & Probate Records; Clerk District Court has Divorce Records; Register of Deeds has Land Records)

Notes

Kentucky

Capital: Frankfort

State: 1792 (15th)

United we stand, divided we fall

Kentucky was primarily hunting grounds for the Shawnee, Wyandot, Delaware, and Cherokee tribes before the arrival of white settlers in the mid-1700s. Long before explorers helped open the way for settlers in Kentucky, the entire area was claimed by Virginia as part of Augusta County. Dr. Thomas Walker explored the eastern part of Kentucky around 1750, making Kentucky the first area west of the Allegheny Mountains to be settled by American pioneers.

The first permanent settlement was at Harrodsburg in 1774. The next year, Colonel Richard Henderson of North Carolina formed the Transylvania Company. He purchased almost half of Kentucky from Indian tribes. This purchase included all of the land between the Kentucky River in the central part of the state and the Cumberland River in the extreme western part. That same year, Boone established Boonesboro. In the late 1760s, Boone blazed the Wilderness Trail through the Appalachian Mountains' Cumberland Gap, enabling more westward migration. In 1776, the Kentucky area was taken away from Fincastle County, Virginia. It became Kentucky County, Virginia.

Conflicts with Indian tribes, provoked by the British, were continuous until Gen. George Rogers Clark captured British forts in Indiana and Illinois in 1778, during the Revolutionary War. Following the war, scores of new settlers poured into the area. In 1780, Kentucky County was divided into three counties; Fayette, Jefferson, and Lincoln; which were in turn divided into nine counties within a decade.

This early period of settlement was one of much bloodshed and danger as the Indians tried to protect their lands. Early settlers came mainly from Maryland, North Carolina, Pennsylvania, Tennessee, and Virginia. They were mainly of German, English, Irish, and Scottish descent.

Kentucky became a state in June 1792. After the Louisiana Purchase in 1803, migration and settlement in Kentucky increased. Immigrants from Russia, Italy, Poland, and Austria came to the area. The War of 1812 involved many Kentucky men. Although neutral in the Civil War, more than 75,000 Kentucky men fought for the Union and up to 60,000 fought for Confederate forces.

The extreme western tip of Kentucky is sometimes referred to as the Jackson Purchase Region since it was purchased in 1818 from the Chickasaw Indians during Andrew Jackson's presidency. It includes Calloway, Marshall, McCracken, Graves, Fulton, Hickman, Carlisle, and Ballard counties.

Look for vital records in the following locations:

- **Birth and death records:** Office of Vital Statistics, Department of Health Services in Frankfort, Kentucky beginning on 1 January, 1911. Prior to 1911 the following birth and death records are also located there:
  City of Louisville—birth records from 1898, death records from 1866
  City of Lexington—birth records from 1906, death records from 1898
  City of Covington—birth records from 1896, death records from 1880
  City of Newport—birth records from 1890, death records from 1880
  Records of births and deaths from some counties as early as 1851 are held by the Kentucky Historical Society in Frankfurt.

- **Marriage and divorce records:** Counties generally have marriage records from within a few years of their organization. Statewide collection of marriage and divorce records began on 1 June, 1958. Divorces prior to 1849 were granted by the state legislature. From 1849 to 1959, divorces were usually recorded by the circuit court and were often interfiled with other court matters.

- **Wills and court records:** County clerks keep wills and other probate records. Copies are also available at the Department of Libraries and Archives, Public Records Division in Frankfort and through the Kentucky Historical Society.

- **Naturalization records:** Filed in the district courts in Bowling Green, Catlettsburg, Covington, Frankfort, London, Louisville, Owensboro, and Paducah. The office of the Clerk of the Circuit Court also has these records.
- **Census records:** Many counties administered school censuses between 1870 and 1932 (mostly 1895 to 1910), which list all members of the family.

Office of Vital Statistics Department of Health Services
275 East Main Street
Frankfort, Kentucky 40621
(502) 564-4212
http://chfs.ky.gov/dph/vital

Department of Libraries and Archives
Public Records Division
300 Coffee Tree Road
PO Box 537
Frankfort, Kentucky 40601
(502) 564-8300
www.kdla.ky.gov/home.htm

Kentucky Historical Society
100 W. Broadway
Frankfort, Kentucky 40601
(502) 564-1792 or (877) 444-7867

Societies and Repositories

Adair County Genealogical Society; PO Box 613; Columbia, KY 42728; nowaydn@kih.net; www.rootsweb.com/~kyacgs.

Ancestral Trails Historical Society; PO Box 573; Vine Grove, KY 40175.

Ballard-Carlisle Historical-Genealogical Society; Box 279; Wickliffe, KY 42087; www.ballardconet.com/bchgs.

Bell County Historical Society; Box 1344; Middlesboro, KY 40965.

Big Sandy Chapter, SAR; PO BOX 182; Prestonburg, KY 41653.

Breathitt County Genealogical Society; c/o Breathitt County Public Library; 1024 College A; Jackson, KY 41339.

Breckinridge County Historical Society; PO Box 498; Hardinsburg, KY 40143; (502) 756-2867; breckcohistsoc@geocities.com; www.geocities.com/Heartland/Estates/6025.

Brown County Genealogical Society; c/o Kentucky History Center; 100 West Broadway; Frankfort, KY 40601.

Bullitt County Genealogical Society; PO Box 960; Shepherdsville, KY 40165.

Captain Charles Gatliff Chapter, SAR; 170 Florence Ave; Williamsburg, KY 40769.

Captain James Campen Chapter, SAR; 544 Shawnee Bay Road; Benton, KY 42025.

Captain John Scott Chapter, SAR; 2205 Stamping Ground Rd.; Georgetown, KY 40234.

Captian John Metcalfe Chapter, SAR; 934 Bell Dr.; Madisonville, KY 42431.

Charles Duncan Chapter, SAR; 8084 Scottsville Road; Alvaton, KY 42122.

Christian County Genealogical Society; 1101 Bethel St.; Hopkinsville, KY 42240.

Clay County Genealogical and Historical Society, Inc.; PO Box 394; Manchester, KY 40962-0394; http://members.tripod.com/~Sue_1/clay.html.

Corbin Genealogical Society; PO Box 353; Corbin, KY 40701.

Crittenden County Genealogical Society; 204 West Carlisle; So. Crittenden County Library; Marion, KY 42064.

Eastern Kentucky Genealogical Society; Box 1544; Ashland, KY 41101.

Fayette County, Kentucky Genealogical Society; PO Box 8113; Lexington, KY 40533-8113; hotrod863@aol.com; www.rootsweb.com/~kyfcgs.

Filson Club, The; 1310 So. Third St.; Louisville, KY 40208; www.filsonhistorical.org/

Floyd County Historical & Genealogical Society; Prestonburg, KY; jimdaniels@pcc.uky; www.geocities.com/Heartland/Ridge/2060/histsociety.html.

Fulton County Genealogical Society; PO. Box 1031; Fulton, KY 42041.

Garrard County Historical Society; 129 Redwood; Richmond, KY 40475.

Genealogical Society of Hancock County; Old Courthouse; Hawesville, KY 42348.

George Mason Chapter, SAR; 310 Market Street; Maysville, KY 41056.

Graves County Genealogical Society; PO Box 5002; Mayfield, KY 42066.

Grayson County Historical Society; PO Box 84; Leitchfield, KY 42754.

Green County Historical Society; PO Box 276; Greensburg, KY 42743.

Harlan Heritage Seekers; PO Box 853; Harlan, KY 40931.

Harrodsburg Historical Society, Genealogical Committee; Box 316; Harrodsburg, KY 40330.

Hart County Historical Society; PO Box 606; Munfordville, KY 42765.

Henderson County Historical and Genealogical Society; 132-B South Green Street; PO Box 303; Henderson, KY 42429-0303.

Hickman County Historical Society; Rt. 3, Box 255; Clinton, KY 42031.

Hopkins County Genealogical Society; PO Box 51; Madisonville, KY 42431; www.rootsweb.com/~kyhopkin/hcgs/index.html.

Jewish Genealogical Society of Louisville; Israel T. Namani Library; 3600 Dutchmans Ln.; Louisville, KY 40205.

John Marire Chapter, SAR; 112 Cox Mill Ct.; Hopkinsville, KY 42240.

John Weaver Chapter SAR; 1239 State St.; Bowling Green, KY 42101.

Johnson County Historical/Genealogical Society; 444 Main St.; PO Box 788; Paintsville, KY 41240.

Kentucky Department for Libraries and Archives; 300 Coffee Tree Road; PO Box 537; Frankfurt, KY 40602-0537; (502) 564-8300; www.kdla.net.

Kentucky Genealogical Society; PO Box 153; Frankfort, KY 40602-0153; kygs@aol.com; www.kygs.org.

Kentucky Historical Society; PO Box H; Frankfort, KY 40602-2108.

Kentucky Society of Pioneers; 1129 Pleasant Ridge Rd.; Utica, KY 42376.

Knott County Historical & Genealogical Society & Library; PO Box 1023; Hindman, KY 41822; www.geocities.com/Athens/Oracle/5468.

Knox County Historical Society, Inc.; PO Box 528; Barbourville, KY 40906.

LaFayette Chapter, SAR; 405 E. Main; Georgetown, KY 40324.

Laurel County Historical Society; PO Box 816; London, KY 40743; lchistsoc@kih.net; www.users.kih.net/%7Elchistsoc/histsoc/index.htm.

Letcher County Historical and Genealogical Society; PO Box 312; Whitesburg, KY 41858; creda@setel.com; www.home.mpinet.net/bcaudill/kygenweb/lchgs.htm.

Lewis County Historical Society; PO Box 212; Vanceburg, KY 41179.

Lieutenant Robert Moseley Chapter, SAR; 2786 Russell Road; Utica, KY 42376.

Logan County Genealogical Society, Inc.; PO Box 853; Russellville, KY 42276-0853.

Louisville Genealogical Society; PO Box 5164; Louisville, KY 40255-0164.

Louisville Thruston Chapter, SAR; PO Box 496; Pewee Valley, KY 40056.

Lyon County Historical Society; PO Box 994; Eddyville, KY 42038.

Magoffin County Historical Society; PO Box 222; Salyersville, KY 41465; magoffin@foothills.net; www.rootsweb.com/~kymhs.

Marshall County, Kentucky Genealogical Society; PO Box 373; Benton, KY 42025.

Mason County Genealogical Society; PO Box 266; Maysville, KY 41056.

McCracken County Genealogical Society; 4640 Buckner Lane; Paducah, KY 42001.

Metcalfe County Historical Society; Rt. 1, Box 371; Summer Shade, KY 42166.

Muhlenberg County Genealogical Society; Public Library; 117 S. Main St.; Greenville, KY 42345.

National Society Daughters of the Union 1861–1865, Inc.; PO Box 7041; Louisville, KY 40257-7041.

Nelson County Genealogical Roundtable; PO Box 409; Bardstown, KY 40004.

Pike County Society for Historical and Genealogical Research; PO Box 97; Pikeville, KY 41502; (606) 432-8698; cwmadd@eastky.net; www.rootsweb.com/~kypike/pikesociety.htm.

Pulaski County Historical Society; Public Library Bldg.; PO Box 36; Somerset, KY 42502.

Rockcastle County Historical Society; PO Box 930; Mt. Vernon, KY 40456.

Rowan County Historical Society; 236 Allen Ave.; Morehead, KY 40351.

Russell County Historical Society; PO Box 544; Jamestown, KY 42629.

Southern Kentucky Genealogical Society; 309 West Villa Drive; PO Box 1782; Bowling Green, KY 42102-1782; (270) 792-8367; dukebuggy@insightbb.com; http://members.aol.com/kygen/skgs.

Spencer County Historical and Genealogical Society; PO Box 266; Taylorsville, KY 40071.

The Campbell County Historical and Genealogical Society; 19 East Main Street; Alexandria, KY 41001; campbellcohistorynews@juno.com; www.rootsweb.com/~kycchgs.

Vanlear Historical Society; PO Box 12; Vanlear, KY 41265.

Webster County Historical & Genealogical Society; PO Box 215; Dixon, KY 42409-0215; lgc32738@apex.net; www.rootsweb.com/~kywebste/wch_gs.htm.

West-Central Kentucky Family Research Association; PO Box 1932; Owensboro, KY 42302-1932; wckfra@yahoo.com; www.rootsweb.com/~kywckfra/ www.rootsweb.com/~kywckfra.

Woodford County Historical Society Library & Museum; 121 Rose Hill; Versailles, KY 40383; woodford@qx.net; www.rootsweb.com/~kywchs.

Bibliography and Record Sources

General

Allen, William B. *A History of Kentucky.* 1872, Reprint. Ann Arbor, Michigan: University Microfilms, 1973.

Ardery, Julia Hoge Spencer. *Ardery Collection, ca. 1750–1970.* Salt Lake City: Filmed by the Genealogical Society of Utah, 1970.

Barton, E. E. *Barton Collection of Northern Kentucky Families.* Salt Lake City: Filmed by the Genealogical Society of Utah, 1963.

Coleman, John Winston. *A Bibliography of Kentucky History.* Lexington: University of Kentucky Press, 1949.

Cook, Michael Lewis. *Kentucky Index of Biographical Sketches in State, Regional, and County Histories.* Evansville, Indiana: Cook Publications, 1986.

Cox, Mrs. Edgar L., and Thomas W. Westerfield. *Kentucky Family Records.* 19 vols. Owensboro, Kentucky: West-Central Kentucky Family Research Association, 1970–1995.

Daughters of the American Revolution (Kentucky). *Genealogical Collection.* Salt Lake City: Filmed by the Genealogical Society of Utah, 1971.

Draper, Lyman Copeland. *Draper Manuscript Collection.* Chicago: Filmed by the University of Chicago Library, 1815–1891.

Dunnigan, Alice Allison. *The Fascinating Story of Black Kentuckians: Their Heritage and Traditions.* Washington, D.C.: Associated Pub., 1982.

Early Kentucky Settlers, 1700s–1800s. S.l.: Brøderbund, 2000. CD-ROM.

Early Kentucky Tax Records: From the Register of the Kentucky Historical Society. Baltimore: Genealogical Publishing Company, 1984.

Elliott, Sam Carpenter. *1792 to 1892 the Illustrated Centennial Record, of the State of Kentucky: Containing a Complete List of the Executive, Judicial and Legislative Departments of the State, and Kentuckians Who Have Occupied High Official Positions Under the United States and State Governments Since 1792.* Louisville, Kentucky: Geo. G. Fetter Print. Co., 1892.

Fowler, Ila Earle. *Kentucky Pioneers and Their Descendants.* Genealogical Pub. Co. (1967).

Genealogies of Kentucky Families: From the Filson Club History Quarterly. Baltimore: Genealogical Publishing Co., 1981.

Genealogies of Kentucky Families: From the Register of the Kentucky Historical Society. 2 vols. Baltimore: Genealogical Publishing Co., 1981.

Green, Thomas Marshall. *Historic Families of Kentucky.* Baltimore, Maryland: Clearfield Co., Inc., 2002.

Gresham, John M. *Biographical Cyclopedia of the Commonwealth of Kentucky.* Chicago: J. M. Gresham, 1896.

Hathaway, Beverly W. *Inventory of County Records of Kentucky.* Salt Lake City: Accelerated Indexing Systems, 1974.

Hathaway, Beverly W. *Kentucky Genealogical Research Sources.* West Jordan, Utah: Allstate Research Co., 1974.

Hogan, Roseann Reinemuth. *Kentucky Ancestry: A Guide to Genealogical and Historical Research.* Salt Lake City: Ancestry, 1992.

Inside Kentucky: Containing a Bibliography of Source Materials on Kentucky. Frankfort, Kentucky: 1974.

J. M. Armstrong Company. *The Biographical Encyclopedia of Kentucky, of the Dead and Living Men of the Nineteenth Century.* (1876) Reprint. Greenville, South Carolina: Southern Historical Press, 1980.

Johnson, W. D. *Biographical Sketches of Prominent Negro Men and Women of Kentucky: With Introductory Memoir of the Author, and Prefatory Remarks Showing the Difference Between American and British Slave Holders; Also Opinions of Leading Thinkers of the Race.* (Lexington, Kentucky: Filmed by the Margaret I. King Library, University of Kentucky, 1953).

Kentucky Historical Society (Frankfort, Kentucky). *Bibliography Of County Resources.* 3 vols. Frankfort, Kentucky: Kentucky Historical Society, 1990.

Kentucky Historical Society Index to Tax List[s]. Frankfort, Kentucky: The Society: 1973.

Kentucky Research Outline. Series U.S.-States, no. 18. Salt Lake City: Family History Library, 1988.

Kozee, William Carlos. *Early Families of Eastern and Southeastern Kentucky, and Their Descendants.* Strasburg, Virginia: Shenandoah Publishing House, 1961.

McDowell, Samuel R. *Who's Who in Kentucky Genealogy: a Biographical and Professional Profile of 595 Prominent Researchers in Kentucky Genealogy, With Over 6550 Surnames in Which They are Particularly Interested.* Utica, Kentucky: McDowell Publications, 1985.

Perrin, William Henry. *Kentucky; A History of the State: Embracing a Concise Account of the Origin and Development of the Virginia Colony; Its Expansion Westward, and the Settlement of the Frontier Beyond the Alleghenies; the Erection of Kentucky as an Independent State and Its Subsequent Development.* 7 vols. Easley, South Carolina: Southern Historical Press, 1979.

Polk, Johnson E. *A History of Kentucky and Kentuckians: The Leaders and Representative Men in Commerce, Industry and Modern Activities.* 3 vols. Chicago, New York: Lewis, 1912.

Schweitzer, George K. *Kentucky Genealogical Research.* Knoxville: George K. Schweitzer, 1983.

Shane Manuscript Collection. Salt Lake City: Filmed by the Genealogical Society of Utah, 1966–1967.

Smith, Zachary F. *The History of Kentucky: From Its Earliest Discovery and Settlement, to the Present Date. . .Its Military Events and Achievements, and Biographic Mention of Its Historic Characters.* Louisville, Kentucky: Courier Journal, 1886.

Southard, Mary Young. *Who's Who in Kentucky: A Biographical Assembly of Notable Kentuckians.* Louisville, Kentucky: Standard Print, 1936.

Spencer, John H. *A History of Kentucky Baptists: From 1769 to 1885, Including More Than 800 Biographical Sketches.* Cincinnati: J. R. Baumes, 1886.

Teague, Barbara. *Guide to Kentucky Archival And Manuscript Collections.* Frankfort, Kentucky: Kentucky Department for Libraries and Archives, Public Records Div., 1988–.

The Biographical Encyclopedia of Kentucky. 1 vol. in 2. Cincinnati: J. M. Armstrong, 1878.

Van Meter, Benjamin Franklin. *Genealogies and Sketches of Some Old Families Who Have Taken Prominent Part in the Development of Virginia and Kentucky Especially: And Later of Many Other States of This Union.* Louisville, Kentucky: J. P. Morton, 1901.

Walker, Emma Jane, et al. *Kentucky Bible Records.* 6 Vols. Lexington: Kentucky Society, Daughters of the American Revolution, 1962–1981.

Wallis, Frederick A. *A Sesqui-Centennial History of Kentucky: A Narrative Historical Edition, Preserving the Record of the Growth and Development of the Commonwealth, and Chronicling the Genealogical and Memorial Records of Its Prominent Families and Personages.* 4 vols. Hopkinsville, Kentucky: Historical Record Association, 1945.

Webb, Benjamin J. *The Centenary of Catholicity in Kentucky.* 1884. Reprint Utica, Kentucky: McDowell Publications.

Westerfield, Thomas W., and Samuel McDowell. *Kentucky Genealogy and Biography.* 9 vols. Owensboro, Kentucky: Genealogical Reference, 1969–.

Wilson, Samuel M. *Collection of Samuel M. Wilson of Lexington, Kentucky.* Salt Lake City: Filmed by the Genealogical Society of Utah, 1958.

Atlases, Maps and Gazetteers

Atlas of Kentucky. Galveston, Texas: Frontier Press.

Clark, Thomas D. *Historic Maps of Kentucky.* Lexington, Kentucky: University Press of Kentucky, 1979.

Field, Thomas P. *A Guide to Kentucky Place Names.* Lexington, Kentucky: University of Kentucky, 1961.

Kentucky Places and People. 1895–1896. Reprint of R. L. Polk and Company's "Kentucky State Gazetteer and Business Directory." Utica, Kentucky: McDowell Publications, 1984.

Kleber, John E. *The Kentucky Encyclopedia.* Lexington, Kentucky: University Press of Kentucky, 1992.

Long, John H. *Kentucky: Atlas of Historical County Boundaries.* New York: Charles Scribner's Sons, 1995.

Murphy, Thelma M. *Kentucky Post Offices, 1794–1819.* Indianapolis: s.n., 1975.

Patera, Alan H. *A Checklist of Kentucky Post Offices.* Lake Grove, Oregon: The Depot, 1989.

Rennick, Robert M. *Kentucky's Bluegrass: A Survey of the Post Offices.* Lake Grove, Oregon: Depot, 1993–.

Rennick, Robert M. *Kentucky Place Names.* Lexington: University Press of Kentucky, 1984.

Rone, Wendell Holmes. *An Historical Atlas of Kentucky and Her Counties: Davies County, 1850–1965.* Owensboro, Kentucky: Progress Printing Co., 1965.

United States. Office of Geographic Research. Branch of Geographic Names. *Kentucky Geographic Names.* Reston, Virginia.: United States. Branch of Geographic Names, 1981.

Census Records

Available Census Records and Census Substitutes

Federal Census, 1810, 1820, 1830, 1840, 1850, 1860, 1870, 1880, 1900, 1910, 1920, 1930

Federal Mortality Schedules 1850, 1860, 1870, 1880

Tax Lists 1790, 1795, 1800

Union Veterans and Widows 1890

Non-resident Tax Lists 1794–1805

School Census 1870–1932

Dollarhide, William. *The Census Book: A Genealogist's Guide to Federal Census Facts, Schedules and Indexes.* Bountiful, Utah: Heritage Quest, 1999.

Jacobs, Curtis. *The Jacobs Collection.* Microfilm of manuscripts housed at the Beauregard Parish Library, De Ridder, Louisiana. Salt Lake City: Filmed by the Genealogical Society of Utah, 1990. 20 microfilm.

Kemp, Thomas Jay. *The American Census Handbook.* Wilmington, Delaware: Scholarly Resources, Inc., 2001.

Kentucky Historical Society. Microfilm Department. *Kentucky Historical Society Index to Tax List.* Frankfort, Kentucky: The Society, 1973.

Lainhart, Ann S. *State Census Records.* Baltimore: Genealogical Publishing Co., Inc., 1992.

Schreiner-Yantis, Netti. *The 1787 Census of Virginia: An Accounting of the Name of Every White Male Tithable Over 21 Years, the Number of White Males Between 16 & 21 Years, the Number of Slaves Over 16 & Those Under 16 Years, Together With a Listing of Their Horses, Cattle & Carriages, and Also the Names of All Persons to Whom Ordinary Licenses and Physician's Licenses Were Issued.* 3 vols. Springfield, Virginia: Genealogical Books in Print, 1987.

Szucs, Loretto Dennis and Matthew Wright. *Finding Answers in U.S. Census Records.* Ancestry Publishing, 2001.

Thorndale, William and William Dollarhide. *Map Guide to the U.S. Federal Census, 1790–1920.* Baltimore: Genealogical Publishing Co., 1987.

Court Records, Probate and Wills

Cook, Michael L. *Virginia Supreme Court District of Kentucky: Order Books, 1783–1792.* Evansville, Indiana: Cook Publications, 1988.

Davis, Virginia. "McLean County Administrators Bonds—1867–1800." *Bluegrass Roots* 18 (1): 13–20 (Spring 1991).

Griffin, Warren B. *Preliminary Inventory Records of the United States Courts from the District of Kentucky, Record Group 21.* Chicago: Federal Records Center, 1968.

Ireland, Robert M. *The County Courts in Antebellum Kentucky.* Lexington: The University Press of Kentucky, 1972.

Jackson, Ronald Vern. *Index to Kentucky Wills to 1851, the Testators.* Bountiful, Utah: Accelerated Indexing Systems, 1977.

Jillson, Willard Rouse. *Old Kentucky Entries and Deeds: A Complete Index to All of the Earliest Land Entries. Military Warrants. Deeds and Wills of the Commonwealth of Kentucky.* Louisville: Standard Printing Co., (1926). Reprint. Baltimore: Genealogical Publishing Co., 1987.

King, Junie Estelle Stewart. *Abstract [sic] of Early Kentucky Wills and Inventories.* 1933. Reprint. Baltimore: Genealogical Publishing Co., 1969.

McAdams, Ednah Wilson. *Kentucky Pioneer and Court Records.* 1929. Reprint. Baltimore: Genealogical Publishing Company, 1981.

Warrants. *Deeds and Wills of the Commonwealth of Kentucky.* Louisville: Standard Printing Co., (1926). Reprint. Baltimore: Genealogical Publishing Co., 1987.

Emigration, Immigration, Migration and Naturalization

Eakle, Arlene H., ed. *Kentucky Early Settlers and Stations* Salt Lake City, Utah: Family History World, 1990.

Jillson, Willard Rouse. *Pioneer Kentucky: An Outline of Its Exploration and Settlement, Its Early Cartography and Primitive Geography, Coupled with a Brief Presentation of the Principal Trails, Traces, Forts, Stations, Springs, Licks, Fords and Ferries Used Prior to the Year 1800.* Frankfort, Kentucky: The State Journal Company, 1934.

O'Mallory, Nancy. *Stockading Up: A Study of Pioneer Stations in the Inner Bluegrass Region of Kentucky.* Lexington, Kentucky: Program for Cultural Resources Assessment, Dept. of Anthropology, University of Kentucky, 1987.

Tachau, Mary K. Bonsteel. *Federal Courts in The Early Republic: Kentucky 1789–1816.* Princeton, New Jersey: Princeton University Press, 1978.

United States. District Court (Alabama: Southern District). *Declarations Of Intentions, Naturalizations, and Petitions, 1855–1960.* Microfilm of originals at the National Archives in East Point, Georgia. Salt Lake City: Filmed by the Genealogical Society of Utah, 1987–1989. 9 microfilm.

Land and Property

Brookes-Smith, Joan. *Index for Old Kentucky Surveys and Grants; Index for Tellico Surveys and Grants.* Frankfort: Kentucky Historical Society, 1975.

Cook, Michael L., and Bettie A. Cook. *Kentucky Court of Appeals Deed Books, 1780–1835.* 4 vols. Evansville, Indiana: Cook Publishing, 1985.

Hone, Wade E. *Land and Property Research in the United States.* Salt Lake City: Ancestry Incorporated, 1997.

Jillson, Willard Rouse. *Kentucky Land Grants.* Genealogical Publishing Co., 1972.

Jillson, Willard Rouse. *Old Kentucky Entries and Deeds: A Complete Index to All of the Earliest Land Entries, Military Warrants, Deeds and Wills of the Commonwealth of Kentucky.* 1926. Reprint. Baltimore: Genealogical Publishing Co., 1978.

Jillson, Willard Rouse. *The Kentucky Land Grants: A Systematic Index to All of the Land Grants Recorded in the State Land Office at Frankfort, Kentucky, 1782–1924.* Louisville: Standard Printing Co., 1925.

Jillson, Willard. *Old Kentucky Entries and Deeds.* Filson Club Publication no. 35. Louisville, Kentucky: (1926). Reprint. Baltimore: Genealogical Publishing Co., 1969.

Kentucky. Governor. *County Court Orders, 1836–1955.* Microreproduction of manuscripts, originals in the Kentucky Land Office, Frankfort, Kentucky. Salt Lake City: Filmed by the Genealogical Society of Utah, 1962. 64 microfilm.

Kentucky. Governor. *Grants South of Green River, 1797–1866.* Microreproduction of manuscripts, originals in the Kentucky Land Office, Frankfort, Kentucky. Salt Lake City: Filmed by the Genealogical Society of Utah, 1962. 15 microfilm.

Kentucky. Governor. *Grants West of Tennessee River, 1820–1900.* Microreproduction of manuscript, originals in the Kentucky Land Office, Frankfort, Kentucky. Salt Lake City: Filmed by the Genealogical Society of Utah, 1962. 4 microfilm.

Kentucky. Governor. *Kentucky Land Warrants, 1816–1873; Index, 1812–1836.* Microfilm of original at the state land office in Frankfort, Kentucky. Salt Lake City: Filmed by the Genealogical Society of Utah, 1962. 9 microfilm.

Kentucky. Governor. *Old Kentucky Grants, 1793–1856.* Microreproduction of manuscripts, originals in the Kentucky Land Office, Frankfort, Kentucky. Salt Lake City: Filmed by the Genealogical Society of Utah, 1962. 9 microfilm.

Kentucky. State Land Office. *Tellico Land Grants, 1803–1853, Vol. 1–2.* Microfilm of original at Frankfort, Franklin County, Kentucky. Salt Lake City: Filmed by the Genealogical Society of Utah, 1962. 1 microfilm.

Taylor, Philip Fall and Samuel M. Wilson. *Kentucky Land Warrants, for the French and Indian Revolutionary Wars: A Calendar of Warrants for Land in Kentucky. Granted for Service in the French and Indian Wars; and*

Land Bounty Land Warrants Granted for Military Service in the War for Independence. (1913) Reprint. Greenville, South Carolina: Southern Historical Press, 1917.

Taylor, Philip Fall. *A Calendar of the Warrants for Land In Kentucky. Granted for Service in the French And Indian War.* (1917) Reprint. Baltimore, Maryland: Clearfield Company, 1995.

Virginia. Governor. *Virginia Grants, 1782–1792.* Microreproduction of manuscripts, originals in the Kentucky Land Office, Frankfort, Kentucky. Salt Lake City: Filmed by the Genealogical Society of Utah, 1962. 9 microfilm.

Warrants. The Kentucky Land Grants: A Systematic Index to All of the Land Grants Recorded in the State Land Office at Frankfort, Kentucky, 1782–1924. 1 Vol. In 2. Baltimore: Genealogical Publishing Co., 1971. Originally published as Filson Club Publication no. 33. Louisville: Standard Printing Co., 1925.

Military

Adjutant General State of Kentucky. *Kentucky Soldiers of the War of 1812* (1891) Reprint. Greenville, South Carolina: Southern Historical Press, 1992.

Adjutant General's Office. *Index to Veterans of America Wars from Kentucky.* Frankfort: Kentucky Historical Society, 1966.

Adjutant General's Office. *Kentucky Soldiers of the War of 1812.* Baltimore: Genealogical Publishing Co., 1969.

Clift, G. Glenn. *The Cornstalk Militia of Kentucky, 1792–1811.* (1957) Reprint. Greenville, South Carolina: Southern Historical Press, 1982.

Coleman, J. Winston. *The British Invasion Of Kentucky: with an Account of the Capture of Ruddell's and Martin's Stations, June 1780.* Lexington, Kentucky: Winburn Press, 1951.

Eckenrode, H. J. *List of the Revolutionary Soldiers of Virginia.* n.p., 1912.

Index to Veterans of American Wars from Kentucky. Frankfort, Kentucky: Kentucky Historical Society, 1966.

Kentucky Adjutant General. *Report of the Adjutant General of the State of Kentucky: Mexican War Veterans 1846–1847.* Frankfort, Kentucky: Capital Office, 1889.

Kentucky Adjutant General's Office. *Report of the Adjutant General of Kentucky Soldiers of the War of 1812.* Frankfort, Kentucky: 1891.

Kentucky Adjutant General's Office. *Report of the Adjutant General of the State of Kentucky: Kentucky Volunteers, War with Spain 1898–1899.* Frankfort, Kentucky: Globe Printing, 1908.

Kentucky. Confederate Pension Board. *Civil War Pension Application.* Frankfort: Kentucky Historical Society.

Lafferty, Maude. *The Destruction of Ruddle's and Martin's Forts in the Revolutionary War.* Privately printed, Kentucky Historical Society, Frankfort. 1957.

Lindsay, Kenneth G. *Kentucky's Revolutionary War Pensioners, Under the Acts of 1816, 1832.* Evansville, Maryland: Kenman Publishing Co., 1977.

Quisenberry, Anderson C. *Kentucky in the War of 1812.* (1915), Clearfield Co. Reprint, 1989.

Quisenberry, Anderson C. *Revolutionary Soldiers in Kentucky.* Excerpted from the Year Book, Kentucky Society, Sons of the American Revolution (1896). Baltimore: Genealogical Publishing Co., 1959.

Report of the Adjutant General of the State of Kentucky. *Confederate Kentucky Volunteers, War of 1861–1865.* Frankfort, Kentucky: state printer, 1915.

Simpson, Alicia. *Kentucky Confederate Veteran and Widows Pension Index.* Hartford, Kentucky: Cook and McDowell, 1979.

Speed, Thomas, et al. *The Union Regiments of Kentucky.* 1897. Reprint. Dayton, Ohio: Morningside House, 1984.

United States. Selective Service System. *Kentucky, World War I Selective Service System Draft Registration Cards, 1917–1918. National Archives Microfilm Publications, M1509.* Washington, D.C.: National Archives, 1987–1988.

Volunteer Officers and Soldiers of the Spanish American War, 1898–1899. Frankfort, Kentucky: Kentucky Historical Society, 1966.

Wilder, Minnie S. *Kentucky Soldiers of the War of 1812.* Baltimore: Genealogical Publishing Co., 1969.

Vital and Cemetery Records

Ardery, Julia H. *Kentucky Records: Early Wills and Marriages Copied from Court House Records by Regents, Historians and the State Historian, Old Bible Records and Tombstone Inscriptions, Records from Barren, Bath, Bourbon, Clark, Daviess, Fayette, Harrison, Jessamine, Lincoln, Madison, Mason, Montgomery, Nelson, Nicholas, Ohio, Scott, and Shelby Counties.* 2 vols. Baltimore: Southern Book Co., 1958.

Ardery, Julia H. *Kentucky [Court and Other] Records [Vol. I]. Early Wills and Marriages, Old Bible Records and Tombstone Inscriptions.* (1926) Reprint. Baltimore, Maryland: Genealogical Publishing Co, 1986.

Cemetery Records of Kentucky, 2 vols. Salt Lake City: Genealogical Society, 1962–1968.

Clift, Garrett G. *Kentucky Obituaries, 1787–1854.* Baltimore: Genealogical Publishing Co., 1977.

Daughters of the American Revolution. Fincastle Chapter (Louisville, Kentucky). *Kentucky Wills, Inscriptions, Marriages, and Miscellaneous Records.* Microfilm. Salt Lake City: Genealogical Society of Utah, 1971.

Dodd, Jordan R. *Kentucky Marriages, Early To 1800: A Research Tool.* Bountiful, Utah: Precision Indexing, 1990.

Duff, Jeffrey M. *Inventory of Kentucky Birth, Marriage, and Death Records, 1852–1910.* Rev. ed. Frankfort, Kentucky: Department for Libraries and Archives, 1982.

Green, Karen Mauer, ed. *The Kentucky Gazette. . . Genealogical and Historical Abstracts.* 2 vols. Baltimore: Gateway Press, Inc., 1983–1985.

Guide to Public Vital Statistics Records in Kentucky. Louisville: Historical Records Survey, 1942.

Johnson, Robert Foster. *Wilderness Road Cemeteries in Kentucky, Tennessee and Virginia.* Owensboro, Kentucky: McDowell Publications, 1981.

Kentucky Death Records from 1911 thru 2000. Provo, Utah: MyFamily.com Inc., 1998–2002. online database— http://vitals.rootsweb.com/ky/death/search.cgi

Kentucky Marriage Records from the Register of the Kentucky Historical Society. Baltimore: Genealogical Publishing Co., 1983.

Kentucky Office of Vital Statistics. *Births and Deaths Index, 1911–1954.* Microreproduction of original in Louisville, Kentucky. Salt Lake City: Genealogical Society of Utah, 1960. 92 microfilm.

Kentucky Office of Vital Statistics. *Kentucky Death Index, 1911–1986.* Frankfurt: Kentucky Office of Vital Statistics, 1988. 183 microfiche.

Kentucky. Office of Vital Statistics. *Birth Indexes, 1911–1995.* Frankfort, Kentucky: Kentucky Office of Vital Statistics, 1997. 1038 microfiche.

Kentucky. Office of Vital Statistics. *Divorce Indexes, 1972–1990.* Frankfort, Kentucky: Kentucky Office of Vital Statistics, 1991.

Kentucky. Office of Vital Statistics. *Marriage Indexes, 1973–1995.* Frankfort, Kentucky: Office of Vital Statistics, 1997. 173 microfiche.

County Website	Map Index	Date Created	Parent County or Territory From Which Organized Address/Details
Adair http://columbia-adaircounty.com/	**I8**	**11 Dec 1801**	**Green** Adair County; 424 Public Sq; Columbia, KY 42728-1451; Ph. (270) 384-2801 **Details:** (County Clerk has Marriage, Land, Probate & Military Records from 1802; Clerk Circuit Court has Divorce & Court Records)
Allen www.rootsweb.com/~kyallen/	**J9**	**11 Jan 1815**	**Barren, Warren** Allen County; 201 W Main St.; Scottsville, KY 42164; Ph. (270) 237-3706 **Details:** (County Clerk has Marriage Records from 1815; Clerk of Circuit Court has Divorce Records from 1902 & Probate Records from 1815)
Anderson http://members.aol.com/cbc174/anderson.htm	**H6**	**16 Jan 1827**	**Franklin, Mercer, Washington** Anderson County; 151 S Main St; Lawrenceburg, KY 40342; Ph. (502) 839-3041 **Details:** (County Clerk has Marriage, Probate & Land Records from 1827 & school Records; Clerk Circuit Court has Court Records from 1857)
Ballard www.ballardconet.com/	**Q8**	**15 Feb 1842**	**Hickman, McCracken** Ballard County; 424 Court St; PO Box 145; Wickliffe, KY 42087-0145; Ph. (270) 335-5168 **Details:** (Courthouse burned in 1880) (County Clerk has Marriage & Land Records from 1880; Clerk Circuit Court has Divorce & Probate Records)
Barren www.rootsweb.com/~kybarren/	**J8**	**20 Dec 1798**	**Green, Warren** Barren County; County Courthouse 1st Fl; Glasgow, KY 42141-2812; Ph. (270) 651-3783 **Details:** (County Clerk has Marriage, Land & Probate Records from 1798; Clerk Circuit Court has Divorce & Court Records)

County Website	Map Index	Date Created	Parent County or Territory From Which Organized Address/Details
Bath www.mindspring.com/~kyblue/bath/	E5	15 Jan 1811	**Montgomery** Bath County; PO Box 609; Owingsville, KY 40350; Ph. (606) 674-2613 **Details:** (County Clerk has Marriage, Probate & Land Records from 1811 & Military Discharge Records; Clerk Circuit Court has Divorce & Court Records; County Health Department has Birth & Death Records from 1915)
Bell www.rootsweb.com/~kybell/	E9	28 Feb 1867	**Knox, Harlan** Bell County; Courthouse Sq FL 1; PO Box 156; Pineville, KY 40977; Ph. (606) 337-6143 **Details:** (Formerly Josh Bell; Name changed in 1873) (County Clerk has Marriage & Land Records)
Boone www.boonecountyky.org/	G3	13 Dec 1798	**Campbell** Boone County; 2950 E Washington Sq; Burlington, KY 41005; Ph. (606) 334-2112 **Details:** (County Clerk has Marriage & Probate Records from 1799)
Bourbon www.parisky.com/	F5	17 Oct 1785	**Fayette** Bourbon County; 310 Main St; Paris, KY 40361; Ph. (606) 987-2142 **Details:** (County Clerk has Marriage & Probate Records from 1786; Clerk Circuit Court has Court Records from 1786 & Divorce Records)
Boyd www.rootsweb.com/~kyboyd/	B5	16 Feb 1860	**Carter, Lawrence, Greenup** Boyd County; 2800 Louisa St; Catlettsburg, KY 41129; Ph. (606) 739-5116 **Details:** (County Clerk has Marriage, Land & Military Records from 1860; Clerk Circuit Court has Divorce, Probate & Court Records)
Boyle www.danville-ky.com/	G7	15 Feb 1842	**Mercer, Lincoln** Boyle County; 321 W Main St #123; Danville, KY 40422; Ph. (606) 238-1110 **Details:** (County Clerk has Marriage, Probate, Land & Military Records from 1842; Clerk Circuit Court has Divorce & Court Records)
Bracken www.rootsweb.com/~kybracke/	F4	14 Dec 1796	**Campbell, Mason** Bracken County; 116 W Miami St; PO Box 147; Brooksville, KY 41004; Ph. (606) 735-2952 **Details:** (County Clerk has Marriage, Probate & Land Records from 1797)
Breathitt www.breathittcounty.com/Breathitt1.html	D7	8 Feb 1839	**Clay, Estill, Perry** Breathitt County; 1127 Main St; Jackson, KY 41339-1194; Ph. (606) 666-3810 **Details:** (County Clerk has Marriage, Probate & Land Records from 1875; Clerk Circuit Court has Divorce & Court Records)
Breckinridge www.geocities.com/dabugman.geo/breck.html	K7	9 Dec 1799	**Hardin** Breckinridge County; Courthouse Sq; PO Box 538; Hardinsburg, KY 40143; Ph. (270) 756-2246 **Details:** (County Archives has some Marriage Records from 1800, some Birth Records 1853–1969, some Death Records 1853–1993 & Land Records from 1800; Clerk Circuit Court has Probate & Court Records)

County Website	Map Index	Date Created	Parent County or Territory From Which Organized Address/Details
Bullitt www.ltadd.org/bullitt/	I6	13 Dec 1796	**Jefferson, Nelson** Bullitt County; 149 N Walnut St; Shepherdsville, KY 40165; Ph. (502) 543-2262 **Details:** (County Clerk has Marriage Records from 1795, Land Records from 1796 & Military Discharge Records 1921–1997; Clerk Circuit Court has Divorce & Court Records; Clerk District Court has Probate Records)
Butler www.rootsweb.com/~kybutler/	K7	18 Jan 1810	**Logan, Ohio** Butler County; 110 N Main St; Morgantown, KY 42261-0448; Ph. (270) 526-5676 **Details:** (County Clerk has Marriage & Land Records from 1810; Clerk Circuit Court has Divorce & Court Records)
Caldwell http://home.hiwaay.net/~woliver/caldwell.html	N8	31 Jan 1809	**Livingston** Caldwell County; 100 E Market St Rm 3; Princeton, KY 42445-1675; Ph. (270) 365-6754 **Details:** (County Clerk has Marriage, Land & Probate Records from 1809 & Military Discharge Records; Clerk Circuit Court has Divorce & Court Records)
Calloway http://users.arn.net/~billco/calloway.html	O9	19 Dec 1821	**Hickman** Calloway County; 101 S 5th St; Murray, KY 42071; Ph. (270) 767-0429 **Details:** (County Clerk has Marriage, Probate, Land & Military Discharge Records, minister bonds & election Records; Clerk Circuit Court has Divorce Records)
Campbell www.campbellcountyky.org/	F3	17 Dec 1794	**Harrison, Mason, Scott** Campbell County; 340 York St; Newport, KY 41071; Ph. (606) 292-3850 **Details:** (County Clerk has Marriage, Probate & Land Records from 1785)
Carlisle www.ballardconet.com/GenWeb/carlisle.html	Q9	3 Apr 1886	**Ballard** Carlisle County; W Court St; Bardwell, KY 42023; Ph. (270) 628-3233 **Details:** (County Clerk has Marriage, Probate & Land Records)
Carroll http://gallatinky.tripod.com/Carroll/Carroll.html	H4	9 Feb 1838	**Gallatin** Carroll County; 440 Main St; Carrollton, KY 41008; Ph. (502) 732-7036 **Details:** (County Clerk has Marriage, Probate & Land Records from 1838; Clerk Circuit Court has Divorce & Court Records)
Carter www.rootsweb.com/~kycarter/	C5	9 Feb 1838	**Greenup, Lawrence** Carter County; 300 W Main St; Grayson, KY 41143; Ph. (606) 474-5188 **Details:** (County Clerk has Birth & Death Records 1911–1954 & Marriage Records from 1838; Clerk Circuit Court has Divorce, Probate & Court Records)
Casey www.rootsweb.com/~kycasey/caseypge.htm	G7	14 Nov 1806	**Lincoln** Casey County; PO Box 310; Liberty, KY 42539-0310; Ph. (606) 787-6471 **Details:** (County Health Department has Birth & Death Records; County Clerk has Marriage, Probate & Land Records from 1806; Clerk Circuit Court has Probate Records from 1978, Divorce & Court Records)

County Website	Map Index	Date Created	Parent County or Territory From Which Organized Address/Details
Christian	**N8**	**13 Dec 1796**	**Logan** Christian County; 511 S Main St; Hopkinsville, KY 42240; Ph. (270) 887-4105 mkem@commandnet.net **Details:** (County/Fiscal Court has Land, Marriage, & Estate Records from 1797, County Orders from 1797, Fiscal Court Records from 1908, Military Discharge Records, & County Tax going back 10 years)
Clark www.clarkco.net/	**F6**	**6 Dec 1792**	**Bourbon, Fayette** Clark County; 34 S Main St Rm 103; Winchester, KY 40391-2600; Ph. (606) 745-0282 **Details:** (Clerk Courts has Marriage, Land & Probate Records from 1793; Clerk Circuit Court has Divorce & Court Records)
Clay www.rootsweb.com/~kyclay/clay.html	**E8**	**2 Dec 1806**	**Madison, Floyd, Knox** Clay County; 316 Main St Ste 143; Manchester, KY 40962; Ph. (606) 598-2544 **Details:** (County Clerk has Marriage Records from 1807 & Land Records; Clerk Circuit Court has Divorce Records from 1955 & Probate Records from 1977)
Clinton www.rootsweb.com/~kyclinto/	**H9**	**20 Feb 1836**	**Wayne, Cumberland** Clinton County; 212 Washington; Albany, KY 42602; Ph. (606) 387-5234 **Details:** (County Clerk has Marriage, Land & Probate Records from 1865)
Crittenden http://home.hiwaay.net/~woliver/crittenden.html	**O7**	**26 Jan 1842**	**Livingston** Crittenden County; 107 S Main St; Marion, KY 42064; Ph. (270) 965-3403 **Details:** (County Clerk has Marriage, Probate, Land & Court Records, election returns from 1842; Clerk Circuit Court has Divorce Records)
Cumberland www.geocities.com/Heartland/Trail/1794/	**I9**	**14 Dec 1798**	**Green** Cumberland County; PO Box 275; Burkesville, KY 42717-0275; Ph. (270) 864-3726 **Details:** (County Clerk has some Marriage Records 1882–1923 & from 1927, Probate Records from 1815 & Land Records from 1799; Clerk Circuit Court has Probate Records from 1968, Divorce & Court Records)
Daviess www.geocities.com/gsdownr_2000/daviess1.html	**M6**	**14 Jan 1815**	**Ohio** Daviess County; 212 St Ann St; Owensboro, KY 42303; Ph. (270) 685-8434 **Details:** (County Clerk has Marriage & Land Records from 1815 & Probate Records; Clerk Circuit Court has Divorce & Court Records)
Edmonson http://users.rootsweb.com/~kyedmons/	**K7**	**12 Jan 1825**	**Grayson, Hart, Warren** Edmonson County; Main & Cross St; Brownsville, KY 42210; Ph. (270) 597-2624 **Details:** (County Clerk has Marriage Records from 1840)
Elliott http://home.zoomnet.net/~cbarker/elliott.htm	**C5**	**26 Jan 1869**	**Carter, Lawrence, Morgan** Elliott County; Main St; PO Box 225; Sandy Hook, KY 41171-0225; Ph. (606) 738-4462 **Details:** (County Clerk has Marriage Records from 1934, Probate Records from 1957 & Land Records from 1869; Clerk Circuit Court has Divorce Records from 1957 & Court Records; County Health Department has Birth & Death Records)

County Website	Map Index	Date Created	Parent County or Territory From Which Organized Address/Details
Estill www.estill.net/	F7	27 Jan 1808	**Clark, Madison** Estill County; 130 Main St; Irvine, KY 40336-1098; Ph. (606) 723-5156 **Details:** (County Clerk has Marriage, Burial, Probate & Land Records from 1808; Clerk Circuit Court has Divorce & Court Records)
Fayette www.lfucg.com/	F6	1 May 1780	**Kentucky County., Virginia** Fayette County; 162 E Main St; Lexington, KY 40507-1363; Ph. (859) 253-3344 **Details:** (County Clerk has Marriage Records from 1795, Probate & Land Records from 1794; Clerk Circuit Court has Divorce & Court Records)
Fleming www.flemingcounty.org/	E5	10 Feb 1798	**Mason** Fleming County; Courthouse Sq; Flemingsburg, KY 41041-1399; Ph. (606) 845-8461 **Details:** (County Clerk has Marriage, Probate & Land Records from 1798)
Floyd www.kymtnnet.org/floyd.html	C7	13 Dec 1799	**Fleming, Mason, Montgomery** Floyd County; 3rd Ave; Prestonburg, KY 41653; Ph. (606) 886-3816 **Details:** (County Clerk has Marriage & Land Records from 1800)
Franklin www.rootsweb.com/~kyfrankl/franklin.htm	H5	7 Dec 1794	**Woodford, Mercer, Shelby** Franklin County; PO Box 338; Frankfort, KY 40602-0338; Ph. (502) 875-8702 **Details:** (County Clerk has Marriage, Probate, Land & Court Records from 1795, Confederate Pension Applications; Clerk Circuit Court has Divorce Records)
Fulton www.rootsweb.com/~kyfulton/5642.html	Q10	15 Jan 1845	**Hickman** Fulton County; 201 Moulton St; Hickman, KY 42050; Ph. (270) 236-2061 **Details:** (County Clerk has Marriage, Probate & Land Records from 1845; Clerk Circuit Court has Divorce & Court Records)
Gallatin http://gallatinky.tripod.com/Gallatin.html	H4	14 Dec 1798	**Franklin, Shelby** Gallatin County; 100 Main; PO Box 616; Warsaw, KY 41095-0616; Ph. (859) 567-5411 **Details:** (County Clerk has Marriage, Probate & Land Records from 1799; Clerk Circuit Court has Divorce & Court Records)
Garrard www.angelfire.com/ar2/apeebles/garrard/index.htm	G6	17 Dec 1796	**Madison, Lincoln, Mercer** Garrard County; Public Sq; Lancaster, KY 40444; Ph. (859) 792-3071 **Details:** (County Clerk has Marriage, Probate & Land Records from 1797; Clerk Circuit Court has Court Records from 1813)
Grant http://grantco.org/	G4	12 Feb 1820	**Pendleton** Grant County; Courthouse Basement; PO Box 469; Williamstown, KY 41097-0469; Ph. (859) 824-3321 **Details:** (County Clerk has Marriage, Probate & Land Records from 1820)
Graves	P9	1821	**Hickman** Graves County; 201 E College St; Mayfield, KY 42066; Ph. (270) 247-1733 **Details:** (County Clerk has Marriage, Probate, Court & Land Records from 1888; Clerk Circuit Court has Divorce Records)

County	Map	Date	Parent County or Territory From Which Organized
Website	Index	Created	Address/Details

Grayson   **K7**   **25 Jan 1810**   **Hardin, Ohio**
www.graysoncounty.com/

Grayson County; 10 Public Sq; Leitchfield, KY 42754;
Ph. (270) 259-5295

Details: (County Court House was destroyed by fire in 1896. All records prior to this date were destroyed, A few citizens came forward & refiled records; County Clerk has Election, Land, Plats, Marriage, Military Discharge, Deliquent Propery Tax, Assumed Names, Wills, & Cemetery Records; Circuit Clerk has Divorce & Probate Records; County Historical Society (122 E. Main St.) and County Library (130 Market St.) have other Historical Documents)

Green   **I8**   **20 Dec 1792**   **Lincoln, Nelson**
www.rootsweb.com/~kygreen/

Green County; 203 W Court St; Greensburg, KY 42743-1522;
Ph. (270) 932-5386

Details: (County Clerk has Marriage, Land, Probate & Court Records from 1793; Clerk Circuit Court has Divorce Records; County Health Office has Birth & Death Records)

Greenup   **C4**   **12 Dec 1803**   **Mason**
www.rootsweb.com/~kygreen2/

Greenup County; Main & Harrison; Greenup, KY 41144-1055;
Ph. (606) 473-7394

Details: (County Clerk has Marriage Records from 1803, Probate Records from 1837, Birth & Death Records 1911–1949; Clerk Circuit Court has Divorce & Court Records from 1803)

Hancock   **K6**   **3 Jan 1829**   **Daviess, Ohio, Breckinridge**
www.geocities.com/gsdownr_2000/hancock1.html

Hancock County; 225 Main Cross St; PO Box 146; Hawesville, KY 42348; Ph. (270) 927-6117

Details: (County Clerk has Marriage, Probate & Land Records from 1829; Clerk Circuit Court has Divorce & Court Records)

Hardin   **J6**   **15 Dec 1792**   **Nelson**
www.geocities.com/dabugman.geo/hardin.html

Hardin County; 14 Public Sq; Elizabethtown, KY 42701;
Ph. (270) 765-2171

Details: (County Clerk has Marriage & Land Records)

Harlan   **C9**   **28 Jan 1819**   **Knox, Floyd**
www.rootsweb.com/~kyharlan/

Harlan County; 205 Central St; PO Box 956; Harlan, KY 40831-0956; Ph. (606) 573-3636

Details: (County Clerk has Marriage & Land Records from 1820; Clerk Circuit Court has Divorce & Court Records)

Harrison   **F4**   **21 Dec 1793**   **Bourbon, Scott**
http://home.netcom.com/~jog1/harrison.html

Harrison County; 313 Oddville Ave; Cynthiana, KY 41031;
Ph. (859) 235-0513 harrclrk@setel.com.

Details: (County Clerk has Marriage Records from 1794, Guardianship, Military, Land Records)

Hart   **J8**   **28 Jan 1819**   **Hardin, Barren**
www.hartcounty.com/

Hart County; Main St; Munfordville, KY 42765; Ph. (270) 524-2751

Details: (County Clerk has Birth, Marriage, Death, Land, Probate & Court Records)

County Website	Map Index	Date Created	Parent County or Territory From Which Organized Address/Details
Henderson www.go-henderson.com/	**N6**	**21 Dec 1798**	**Christian** Henderson County; 232 1st St; PO Box 374; Henderson, KY 42420-3146; Ph. (270) 827-5671 **Details:** (County Clerk has Birth & Death Records 1911–1949, Marriage Records from 1806, Land Records from 1797 & Probate Records from 1800; Clerk District Court has Probate Records from 1979; Clerk Circuit Court has Divorce & Court Records)
Henry	**H4**	**14 Dec 1798**	**Shelby** Henry County; 27 S Property Road; PO Box 615; New Castle, KY 40050; Ph. (502) 845-5705 **Details:** (Circuit Clerk has Divorce Records; County Clerk has Land, Marriage, Military Discharge, Tax, & Other Historical Records)
Hickman www.rootsweb.com/~kyhickma/	**Q9**	**19 Dec 1821**	**Caldwell, Livingston** Hickman County; 110 E Clay St; Clinton, KY 42031; Ph. (270) 653-2131 **Details:** (County Clerk has Deed, Mortgage, Marriage, Wills, & Order Records from 1822, Census 1840–1880 & 1910, Birth Records 1852–1909 (incomplete), Death Records 1982–1909(incomplete) Tax Records 1824–1829, Guardianship 1846–1910, 3 Cemetery Books 1984, County Court Orders, Militia Book & Widows Pensions, & Miscellaneous Books; Circuit Clerk has Divorce & Court Records)
Hopkins www.rootsweb.com/~kyhopkin/	**N8**	**9 Dec 1806**	**Henderson** Hopkins County; 10 S Main St; PO Box Drawer 737; Madisonville, KY 42431-2064; Ph. (270) 821-7361 **Details:** (County Clerk has Marriage, Probate, Court & Land Records)
Jackson www.rootsweb.com/~kyjackso/	**E7**	**2 Feb 1858**	**Rockcastle, Owsley, Madison, Clay, Estill, Laurel** Jackson County; Main St; McKee, KY 40447; Ph. (606) 287-7811 **Details:** (County Clerk has Birth, Marriage, Death & Land Records)
Jefferson www.co.jefferson.ky.us/	**I5**	**1 May 1780**	**Kentucky County, Virginia** Jefferson County; 527 W Jefferson St; Louisville, KY 40202-2814; Ph. (502) 574-5700 **Details:** (County Clerk has Marriage & Probate Records from 1781; Clerk Circuit Court has Divorce Records from 1850; Archivist has Court Records from 1780)
Jessamine www.jessaminecounty.org/	**G6**	**19 Dec 1798**	**Fayette** Jessamine County; 400 Park Dr; Nicholasville, KY 40356-0036; Ph. (859) 885-9464 **Details:** (County Clerk has Marriage, Probate & Land Records from 1799; Clerk Circuit Court has Divorce Records)
Johnson www.rootsweb.com/~kyjohnso/johnson.htm	**C6**	**24 Feb 1843**	**Floyd, Morgan, Lawrence** Johnson County; Court St; Paintsville, KY 41240; Ph. (606) 789-2550 **Details:** (County Clerk has Birth, Marriage, Death, Probate & Land Records from 1843; Clerk Circuit Court has Court Records)
Josh Bell		**28 Feb 1867**	**Knox, Harlan** Josh Bell, KY **Details:** Name Changed to Bell County 1873

County Website	Map Index	Date Created	Parent County or Territory From Which Organized Address/Details
Kenton www.kentoncounty.org/	G3	29 Jan 1840	**Campbell** Kenton County; 303 Courthouse; PO Box 1109; Covington, KY 41012; Ph. (859) 491-0702 **Details:** (County Clerk has Marriage, Land & Probate Records from 1860; Clerk Circuit Court has Divorce & Court Records)
Knott www.rootsweb.com/~kyknott/	C7	5 May 1884	**Perry, Breathitt, Floyd, Letcher** Knott County; Main St; Hindman, KY 41822-0446; Ph. (606) 785-5651 **Details:** (County Clerk has Marriage, Court & Land Records from 1886)
Knox www.rootsweb.com/~kyknox/	E9	19 Dec 1799	**Lincoln** Knox County; 401 Court Sq #102; Barbourville, KY 40906-0105; Ph. (606) 546-3568 **Details:** (County Clerk has Marriage & Land Records)
Larue www.rootsweb.com/~kylarue/larue4.htm	I7	4 Mar 1843	**Hardin** Larue County; 209 W High St; Hodgenville, KY 42748; Ph. (270) 358-3544 **Details:** (County Clerk has Marriage & Land Records from 1843 & Probate Records 1843–1979; Clerk Circuit Court has Divorce Records, Probate Records from 1979)
Laurel www.rootsweb.com/~kylaurel/	F8	12 Dec 1825	**Whitley, Clay, Knox, Rockcastle** Laurel County; 101 S Main St; London, KY 40741; Ph. (606) 864-5158 **Details:** (County Clerk has Marriage, Land, Probate & Court Records from 1826)
Lawrence www.rootsweb.com/~kylawren/lawrence.html	C5	14 Dec 1821	**Floyd, Greenup** Lawrence County; 122 S Main Cross St; Louisa, KY 41230; Ph. (606) 638-4102 **Details:** (County Clerk has Marriage & Land Records from 1822 & Probate Records 1822–1977; Clerk Circuit Court has Divorce Records)
Lee www.usgennet.org/usa/ky/county/lee/index.html	E7	29 Jan 1870	**Owsley, Breathitt, Wolfe, Estill** Lee County; Main St Room 11; PO Box 551; Beattyville, KY 41311; Ph. (606) 464-4115 **Details:** (County Clerk has Marriage, Probate & Land Records from 1870; Clerk Circuit Court has Divorce & Court Records)
Leslie www.rootsweb.com/~kyleslie/	D8	29 Mar 1878	**Clay, Harlan, Perry** Leslie County; 22010 Main St; PO Box 916; Hyden, KY 41749; Ph. (606) 672-2193 **Details:** (County Clerk has Marriage, Probate & Land Records; Clerk Circuit Court has Divorce & Court Records)
Letcher www.rootsweb.com/~kyletch/letcher.htm	C8	3 Mar 1842	**Perry, Harlan** Letcher County; 156 Main St Ste 102; Whitesburg, KY 41858; Ph. (606) 633-2432 (County Clerk); (606) 633-7559 (Circuit Clerk); (502) 564-4212 (Frankfort) letcherountyclerk@yahoo.com. **Details:** (County Clerk has Marriage & Land Records from 1845; Circuit Clerk has Divorce Records; State Archives - Frankfort has Birth & Death Records)

County Website	Map Index	Date Created	Parent County or Territory From Which Organized Address/Details
Lewis www.rootsweb.com/~kylewis/	D4	2 Dec 1806	**Mason** Lewis County; 514 Second St; Vanceburg, KY 41179; Ph. (606) 796-3062 **Details:** (County Clerk has Marriage & Land Records from 1807, Probate Records from 1806 & Court Records)
Lincoln www.rootsweb.com/~kylincol/	G7	1 May 1780	**Kentucky County., Virginia** Lincoln County; 102 E Main St; Stanford, KY 40484; Ph. (606) 365-4570 **Details:** (County Clerk has Marriage, Divorce, Probate & Court Records from 1792)
Livingston http://home.hiwaay.net/~woliver/livingston.html	O8	13 Dec 1798	**Christian** Livingston County; 335 Court St; PO Box 400; Smithland, KY 42081-0400; Ph. (270) 928-2162 **Details:** (County Clerk has Marriage Records from 1799, Probate & Land Records from 1800; Clerk Circuit Court has Divorce & Court Records; Records through 1865 have been microfilmed)
Logan www.rootsweb.com/~kylogan/	L9	28 Jun 1792	**Lincoln** Logan County; 229 W 3rd St; Russellville, KY 42276; Ph. (270) 726-6621 **Details:** (County Clerk has Marriage, Probate, Land & Court Records from 1792)
Lyon http://home.hiwaay.net/~woliver/lyon.html	O9	14 Jan 1854	**Caldwell** Lyon County; 200 W Dale Ave; PO Box 698; Eddyville, KY 42038; Ph. (270) 388-2331 **Details:** (County Clerk has Birth Records 1912–1932, Marriage & Land Records from 1854; Clerk Circuit Court has Divorce Records)
Madison www.rootsweb.com/~kymadiso/madison.html	F6	17 Oct 1785	**Lincoln** Madison County; 101 W Main St; Richmond, KY 40475-1415; Ph. (859) 624-4707 **Details:** (County Clerk has Marriage & Land Records from 1787 & Probate Records 1850–1977; Clerk District Court has Probate Records from 1978; Clerk Circuit Court has Divorce & Court Records)
Magoffin www.rootsweb.com/~kymagoff/	D6	22 Feb 1860	**Floyd, Johnson, Morgan** Magoffin County; Court St; Salyersville, KY 41465; Ph. (606) 349-2216 **Details:** (County Clerk has Marriage Records from 1860)
Marion www.rootsweb.com/~kymarion/	H7	25 Jan 1834	**Washington** Marion County; 120 W Main; Lebanon, KY 40033; Ph. (270) 692-2651 **Details:** (County Health Department has Birth & Death Records; County Clerk has Marriage & Land Records from 1863 & Probate Records 1863–1978; Clerk Circuit Court has Probate Records from 1979, Divorce & Court Records)
Marshall http://home.hiwaay.net/~woliver/marshall.html	O9	12 Feb 1842	**Calloway** Marshall County; 1101 Main St; Benton, KY 42025-1498; Ph. (270) 527-4740 **Details:** (County Clerk has Marriage & Land Records from 1848)

County Website	Map Index	Date Created	Parent County or Territory From Which Organized Address/Details
Martin www.kymtnnet.org/martin.html	**B6**	**10 Mar 1870**	**Lawrence, Floyd, Pike, Johnson** Martin County; Main St; Inez, KY 41224; Ph. (606) 298-2810 **Details:** (County Clerk has Birth Records 1903–1949, Marriage Records from 1883 & Death Records 1911–1949; Clerk Circuit Court has Divorce, Probate & Court Records)
Mason www.rootsweb.com/~kymason/mason.htm	**E4**	**5 Nov 1788**	**Bourbon** Mason County; 219 Stanley Reed Court; Maysville, KY 41056-0234; Ph. (606) 564-3341 **Details:** (County Clerk has Marriage, Probate & Land Records from 1789; Clerk Circuit Court has Divorce Records from 1929 & Court Records from 1792)
McCracken www.co.mccracken.ky.us/	**P8**	**1821**	**Hickman** McCracken County; PO Box 609; Paducah, KY 42002; Ph. (270) 444-4700 **Details:** (County Clerk has Marriage & Land Records from 1825; Clerk of Circuit Court has Probate Records from 1826)
McCreary www.pastseeker.com/mccreary/index.html	**G9**	**12 Mar 1912**	**Wayne, Pulaski, Whitley** McCreary County; Main St; PO Box 699; Whitley City, KY 42653; Ph. (606) 376-2411 **Details:** (County Clerk has Marriage Records from 1912, Records 1923–1927 burned & Land Records)
McLean http://lecgbeatlcom.net.home.mindspring.com/	**M7**	**6 Feb 1854**	**Muhlenberg, Daviess, Ohio** McLean County; 210 Main St; Calhoun, KY 42327-0057; Ph. (270) 273-3082 **Details:** (County Clerk has Marriage, Land & Military Records from 1854; Clerk Circuit Court has Probate Records from 1854, Divorce & Court Records)
Meade www.rootsweb.com/~kymeade/	**J6**	**17 Dec 1823**	**Hardin, Breckinridge** Meade County; PO Box 614; Brandenburg, KY 40108-0614; Ph. (270) 422-2152 **Details:** (County Clerk has Marriage Records from 1967, some Marriage, Land & Probate Records from 1824, recent tax Records; Clerk Circuit Court has Divorce & Probate Records)
Menifee (no website)	**E6**	**10 Mar 1869**	**Powell, Wolfe, Bath, Morgan, Montgomery** Menifee County; 12 Main St.; PO Box 123; Frenchburg, KY 40322; Ph. (606) 768-3512 **Details:** (County Clerk has Marriage, Land, & Military Records from 1869; Clerk Circuit Court has Divorce Records from 1869)
Mercer www.rootsweb.com/~kymercer/	**G6**	**17 Oct 1785**	**Lincoln** Mercer County; 235 S Main St; PO Box 426; Harrodsburg, KY 40330-1696; Ph. (606) 734-6310 **Details:** (County Clerk has Marriage, Probate & Land Records from 1786 & Military Discharge Records from 1919; Clerk Circuit Court has Divorce & Court Records)
Metcalfe www.rootsweb.com/~kymetca2/	**I8**	**1 Feb 1860**	**Monroe, Adair, Barren, Cumberland, Green** Metcalfe County; PO Box 850; Edmonton, KY 42129; Ph. (270) 432-4821 **Details:** (County Clerk has Marriage & Land Records)

County Website	Map Index	Date Created	Parent County or Territory From Which Organized Address/Details
Monroe www.geocities.com/Heartland/Plains/4335/ Monroeco/monroe.html	I9	19 Jan 1820	**Barren, Cumberland** Monroe County; PO Box 188; Tompkinsville, KY 42167; Ph. (270) 487-5505 **Details:** (County Clerk has Marriage, Probate & Land Records from 1863; Clerk Circuit Court has Divorce & Court Records)
Montgomery www.rootsweb.com/~kymontgo/montgo.html	E5	14 Dec 1796	**Clark** Montgomery County; 1 Court St; PO Box 414; Mount Sterling, KY 40353; Ph. (859) 498-8700 **Details:** (County Health Department has Birth & Death Records; County Clerk has Marriage Records from 1864, Probate Records from 1797 & Land Records; Clerk Circuit Court has Divorce & Court Records)
Morgan	D6	7 Dec 1822	**Floyd, Bath** Morgan County; 450 Prestonburg St; PO Box 26; West Liberty, KY 41472; Ph. (606) 743-3949 **Details:** (State Records has Birth Records 1852–1910; County Clerk has Divorce, Guardianship, Land, Marriage, Death, Burial, Cemetery, & Probate Records, Military Discharge Records from 1917, Court Records from 1823, Birth Records 1911–1949, Census 1840–1880 & 1900–1920; County Health Department has Birth Records; County Historical Society has Census, Cemetery, & Other Historical Records; City Hall has Business & Commerce Records; Kentucky Vital Statistics has Death Records 1852–1949; Deeds & Wills burned during Civil War, the Clerk had some records at home that were saved.)
Muhlenberg www.geocities.com/Heartland/Park/5159/	M8	14 Dec 1798	**Christian, Logan** Muhlenberg County; 100 S Main St; PO Box 525; Greenville, KY 42345-0525; Ph. (270) 338-1441 **Details:** (County Clerk has Marriage & Land Records; Clerk Circuit Court has Probate & Divorce Records)
Nelson http://bsd.pastracks.com/states/kentucky/nelson/	I6	18 Oct 1784	**Jefferson** Nelson County; 113 E Stephen Foster Ave; Bardstown, KY 40004; Ph. (502) 348-1820 **Details:** (County Clerk has Marriage & Probate Records from 1784)
Nicholas http://brush-arbor.com:8080/jhagee/nichco.html	F5	18 Dec 1799	**Bourbon, Mason** Nicholas County; Main St; Carlisle, KY 40311-0329; Ph. (859) 289-3730 **Details:** (County Clerk has Marriage, Probate & Land Records from 1800; Clerk Circuit Court has Divorce & Court Records)
Ohio www.1bigparty.com/h/myfamily/ohioco.html	L7	17 Dec 1798	**Hardin** Ohio County; Main St; PO Box 85; Hartford, KY 42347-0085; Ph. (270) 298-4422 **Details:** (County Health Department has Death Records from 1911; County Clerk has Marriage & Land Records from 1799, Probate Records from 1801 & Military Discharge Records from 1861; Clerk Circuit Court has Divorce Records, Probate Records from 1978)
Oldham http://oldhamcounty.state.ky.us/	I4	15 Dec 1823	**Henry, Shelby, Jefferson** Oldham County; 100 W Jefferson St; La Grange, KY 40031; Ph. (502) 222-9311 **Details:** (County Clerk has Marriage, Probate & Land Records from 1824; Clerk Circuit Court has Divorce & Court Records)

County	Map	Date	Parent County or Territory From Which Organized
Website	Index	Created	Address/Details

Owen H4 **6 Feb 1819** **Scott, Franklin, Gallatin**
www.rootsweb.com/~kyowen2/owen.html
Owen County; Madison & Seminary St; PO Box 338; Owenton, KY 40359; Ph. (502) 484-2213
Details: (County Clerk has Birth & Death Records 1911–1949, Marriage, Probate & Land Records from 1819; Clerk Circuit Court has Divorce & Court Records at State Archives-Frankfort)

Owsley E7 **23 Jan 1843** **Clay, Estill, Breathitt**
www.rootsweb.com/~kyowsley/owsley.html
Owsley County; 154 Main St; Booneville, KY 41314;
Ph. (606) 593-5735
Details: (County Clerk has Marriage, Probate & Land Records from 1929; Clerk Circuit Court has Divorce & Court Records)

Pendleton F3 **4 Dec 1798** **Bracken, Campbell**
Pendleton County; 233 Main St Room 1; PO Box 112; Falmouth, KY 41040; Ph. (859) 654-3380
Details: (County Clerk has Marriage & Land Records from 1799, Wills from 1800, & Military Records)

Perry D8 **2 Nov 1820** **Clay, Floyd**
www.rootsweb.com/~kyperry/
Perry County; Main St; Hazard, KY 41701; Ph. (606) 436-4614
Details: (County Clerk has Marriage & Land Records from 1821; Clerk Circuit Court has Divorce Records; Clerk District Court has Probate & Court Records)

Pike B7 **19 Dec 1821** **Floyd**
www.rootsweb.com/~kypike/
Pike County; 324 Main St; Pikeville, KY 41501-0631;
Ph. (606) 432-6211
Details: (County Clerk has Birth & Death Records 1911–1949, Marriage & Land Records from 1824, Probate Records from 1822 & school Records 1895–1934)

Powell E6 **7 Jan 1852** **Clark, Estill, Montgomery**
www.usgennet.org/usa/ky/county/powell/
Powell County; 140 Washington St; PO Box 548; Stanton, KY 40380;
Ph. (606) 663-6444
Details: (County Clerk has Marriage, Land & Military Records from 1864; Clerk Circuit Court has Divorce, Probate & Court Records)

Pulaski G8 **10 Dec 1798** **Green, Lincoln**
www.rootsweb.com/~kypulask/
Pulaski County; PO Box 724; Somerset, KY 42501-0724;
Ph. (606) 679-2042
Details: (County Clerk has Marriage, Probate & Land Records from 1799; Clerk Circuit Court has Divorce & Court Records)

Robertson F4 **11 Feb 1867** **Nicholas, Bracken, Mason, Harrison**
http://brush-arbor.com:8080/jhagee/robco.html
Robertson County; PO Box 75; Mount Olivet, KY 41064;
Ph. (606) 724-5212
Details: (County Clerk has Marriage & Land Records from 1867; Clerk Circuit Court has Divorce, Probate & Court Records from 1867)

Rockcastle F7 **8 Jan 1810** **Pulaski, Lincoln, Madison, Knox**
www.rootsweb.com/~kyrockca/rock.htm
Rockcastle County; 205 E Main St; Mount Vernon, KY 40456;
Ph. (606) 256-2831
Details: (County Clerk has Marriage Records from 1852 & Land Records from 1865; Clerk of Circuit Court has Divorce & Court Records from 1873 & Probate Records from 1855)

County Website	Map Index	Date Created	Parent County or Territory From Which Organized Address/Details
Rowan www.rootsweb.com/~kyrowan/	D5	15 Mar 1856	**Fleming, Morgan** Rowan County; 627 E Main St; Morehead, KY 40351; Ph. (606) 784-5212 **Details:** (County Clerk has Marriage, Probate & Land Records from 1890; Clerk Circuit Court has Divorce Records; County Judge has Court Records)
Russell www.rootsweb.com/~kyrussel/russell.html	H8	14 Dec 1825	**Cumberland, Adair, Wayne** Russell County; 101 Monument Sq; PO Box 579; Jamestown, KY 42629-0579; Ph. (270) 343-2125 **Details:** (County Clerk has Marriage, Probate, Court & Land Records from 1826; Clerk Circuit Court has Divorce Records)
Scott http://home.netcom.com/~jog1/ScottCo.html	G5	22 Jun 1792	**Woodford** Scott County; 101 E Main St; Georgetown, KY 40324; Ph. (502) 863-7875 **Details:** (County Clerk has Marriage & Land Records from 1837 & Probate Records from 1796; Clerk Circuit Court has Divorce & Court Records)
Shelby www.shelbycountyclerk.com	H5	23 Jun 1792	**Jefferson** Shelby County; 501 Washington St; Shelbyville, KY 40065; Ph. (502) 663-4410 **Details:** (County Clerk has Records from 1792. County Library has a Kentucky reading room with historical Records. Clerk of Circuit Court has Divorce Records & Other Historical Documents; County Clerk's Office has Death, Guardianship, Land, Marriage, Military, & Probate Records)
Simpson http://simpsonco.bizland.com/index.html	K9	28 Jan 1819	**Allen, Logan, Warren** Simpson County; 103 W Cedar St; Franklin, KY 42134-0268; Ph. (270) 586-8161 **Details:** (County Clerk has Marriage & Land Records from 1882)
Spencer www.rootsweb.com/~kyspence/kyspenc.htm	I5	7 Jan 1824	**Shelby, Bullitt, Nelson** Spencer County; 2 Main St; Taylorsville, KY 40071; Ph. (502) 477-3215 **Details:** (County Clerk has Marriage Records from 1852, Probate & Land Records from 1824; Clerk Circuit Court has Divorce & Court Records)
Taylor www.rootsweb.com/~kytaylor/	I7	13 Jan 1848	**Green** Taylor County; 203 N Court St; Campbellsville, KY 42718; Ph. (270) 465-6677 **Details:** (County Clerk has Marriage, Probate & Land Records from 1848, Birth & Death Records; Clerk Circuit Court has Court Records from 1848)
Todd www.usgennet.org/usa/ky/county/todd/index.htm	M9	30 Dec 1819	**Christian, Logan** Todd County; PO Box 307; Elkton, KY 42220-0157; Ph. (270) 265-2363 **Details:** (County Clerk has Marriage, Divorce, Probate, Court & Land Records)

County Website	Map Index	Date Created	Parent County or Territory From Which Organized Address/Details
Trigg www.kyseeker.com/trigg/index.html	N9	27 Jan 1820	**Christian, Caldwell** Trigg County; 38 Main St; PO Box 1310; Cadiz, KY 42211-0609; Ph. (270) 552-6661 **Details:** (County Health Department has Birth & Death Records; County Clerk has Marriage & Land Records from 1820 & Probate Records 1820–1977; Clerk Circuit Court has Divorce & Court Records)
Trimble www.kyseeker.com/trigg/index.html	I4	9 Feb 1837	**Henry, Oldham, Gallatin** Trimble County; 30 Hwy 42 E; Bedford, KY 40006; Ph. (270) 639-7006 **Details:** (County Clerk has Birth Records 1911–1950, Marriage Records from 1865 & Land Records from 1837)
Union www.ole.net/~maggie/trimble/	O6	15 Jan 1811	**Henderson** Union County; Courthouse; PO Box 119; Morganfield, KY 42437; Ph. (270) 389-1334 **Details:** (County Clerk has Marriage, Probate & Land Records from 1811)
Warren www.rootsweb.com/~kywarren/	K8	14 Dec 1796	**Logan** Warren County; 429 E 10th St; Bowling Green, KY 42101-2250; Ph. (270) 842-9416 **Details:** (County Clerk has Birth, Marriage & Land Records from 1797, Probate Records 1797–1978 & Military Discharge Records from 1917)
Washington http://bsd.pastracks.com/states/kentucky/washington/	H6	22 Jun 1792	**Nelson** Washington County; PO Box 446; Springfield, KY 40069-0446; Ph. (859) 336-5425 **Details:** (County Clerk has Marriage, Probate & Land Records from 1792 & school census 1893–1917; Clerk Circuit Court has Divorce & Court Records from 1792, some Naturalization Records & Military Discharge Records)
Wayne www.rootsweb.com/~kywayne/wayne.html	G9	18 Dec 1800	**Pulaski, Cumberland** Wayne County; 109 N Main St; Monticello, KY 42633; Ph. (606) 348-6661 **Details:** (County Clerk has Marriage & Land Records from 1800 & Probate Records 1800–1978)
Webster www.rootsweb.com/~kywebste/	N7	29 Feb 1860	**Hopkins, Union, Henderson** Webster County; 25 Main St; Dixon, KY 42409-0155; Ph. (270) 639-7006 **Details:** (County Clerk has Marriage & Land Records from 1860 & Probate Records 1860–1977; Clerk Circuit Court has Divorce & Court Records & Probate Records from 1978)
Whitley www.craftheadquartersonline.com/WhitleyCo/Whitley.html	F9	17 Jan 1818	**Knox** Whitley County; Main St; PO Box 8; Williamsburg, KY 40769; Ph. (606) 549-6002 **Details:** (County Clerk has Birth Records 1915–1949, Marriage & Probate Records from 1865 & Land Records from 1818)

County Website	Map Index	Date Created	Parent County or Territory From Which Organized Address/Details
Wolfe http://wolfe.archland.com/	**D6**	**5 Mar 1860**	**Owsley, Breathitt, Powell, Morgan** Wolfe County; PO Box 400; Campton, KY 41301-0400; Ph. (606) 668-3771 **Details:** (County Clerk has Marriage Records from 1913 & Land Records from 1860; Clerk Circuit Court has Divorce, Probate & Court Records)
Woodford http://home.netcom.com/~jog1/woodford.html	**G5**	**12 Nov 1788**	**Fayette** Woodford County; 103 S Main St; Versailles, KY 40383; Ph. (859) 873-3421 **Details:** (County Clerk has Marriage, Probate & Land Records from 1789; Clerk Circuit Court has Divorce & Court Records)

Louisiana

Capital: Baton Rouge

Territory: 1805

State: 1812 (18th)

Union, justice, and confidence

Caddo, Tunica, Choctaw, Chitimacha, and Chawash peoples lived in the region at the time of European contact. Louisiana was discovered early in the 1500s by Spanish explorers Alvar Cabeze de Vaca and Panfile de Narvaez, but the region was claimed by France's Rene Robert de la Salle in 1682. However, it wasn't settled until 1774 when the French settled Natchitoches on the Red River. The first organized migration from France was between 1717 and 1722 under the control of the Compagnie des Indes and a Scottish entrepreneur, John Law. Jean Baptiste Le Moyne, sieur de Bienville, sometimes called the "father of Louisiana," founded New Orleans in 1718, which became the capital in 1722. Other early settlers came from German-speaking areas of Europe, while some were brought from Africa to serve as slaves.

In 1755, the British expelled the French settlers of Acadia, and later, Nova Scotia. As many as 5,000 of these French Acadians, who became known as Cajuns, settled in Louisiana. Descendants of the older French and Spanish settlers became known as Creoles. In 1763, Spain was given all of Louisiana east of the Mississippi, except the area around New Orleans. Taking control of the area in 1769, the Spanish began keeping records in earnest.

During the Revolutionary War, some British sympathizers moved into the area to avoid the conflict. In 1800, Spain ceded Louisiana to the French, although they continued to administer the area until about 1803.

The Louisiana Purchase in 1803 made Louisiana part of the United States. The next year, Louisiana was divided into two sections—the District of Louisiana north of the 33rd parallel, and the Territory of Orleans south of the 33rd parallel. Immediately thereafter, large numbers of Americans from south of the Ohio River moved into the area. In 1805, Louisiana was divided into 12 counties, but smaller civil divisions, called parishes, gradually took over the functions of the counties. By 1807 the Territory of Orleans consisted of 19 parishes, which followed the boundaries of the Old Spanish ecclesiastical parishes. Parishes in Louisiana serve the same function as counties do in other states.

English-speaking settlers occupied Spanish West Florida, between the Mississippi and Pearl rivers, including Baton Rouge, in 1810. When Louisiana was admitted to the Union in 1812, the area was included as part of the state. Baton Rouge became the capital in 1849. Louisiana seceded from the Union in 1861. In May 1862, Union naval forces occupied New Orleans, cutting off nearly all trade. The situation caused severe hardships throughout the state. A military government was established and the courts reorganized. Louisiana furnished more than 77,000 soldiers to the Confederacy and 5,000 to the Union. In 1867, Louisiana became part of the Fifth Military District under General Philip Henry Sheridan. Louisiana was readmitted to the Union in 1868.

Look for vital records in the following locations:

- **Birth and death records:** Vital Records Registry in New Orleans, Louisiana has records of births and deaths since 1914. Delayed registration of births since 1939 are also available.

- **Marriage records:** Colonial marriages were recorded in the judicial records of the French Superior Council and the Spanish Cabildo. Originals are at the Louisiana Historical Center Library and State Museum in New Orleans. They are also kept by royal notaries. Contact the Custodian of Notarial Records in New Orleans. No statewide registration of marriages exists. The parishes keep all marriage records.

- **Court records, wills, deeds and divorce records:** Write to the clerk of each parish.

- **Census records:** Various military and local censuses were taken between 1699 and 1805. A special census of New Orleans was taken in 1805. Most of these census records have been published.

Louisiana

Office of Public Health Vital Records Registry
PO Box 60630
New Orleans, LA 70160
(504) 568-5152 or (800) 454-9570
www.oph.dhh.state.la.us/recordsstatistics/
vitalrecords/

Louisiana State Archives
3851 Essen Lane
Baton Rouge, LA 70809-2137
(225) 922-1000
www.sec.state.la.us/archives/archives/
archivesindex.htm

Notarial Records
Civil District Courts Building
421 Loyola Avenue, Room B-4
New Orleans, LA 70112
(504) 568-8577; Fax (504) 568-8599

Louisiana Historical Center Library and State Museum
400 Esplanade Avenue
New Orleans, Louisiana 70116
Mailing: PO Box 2448
New Orleans, Louisiana 70176-2448
(504) 568-8214

Societies and Repositories

Allen Genealogical & Historical Society; PO Box 789; Kinder, LA 70648-0789.

Amite Genealogy Club; 200 East Mulberry St; Amite, LA 70422-2524.

Ark-La-Tex Genealogical Association; PO Box 4463; Shreveport, LA 71134-0463; aga@softdisk.com; www.rootsweb.com/~laaltgawww.rootsweb.com/~laaltga.

Ascension Heritage Association; PO Box 1085; Donaldsonville, LA 70346-1085.

Attakapas Historical Association; PO Box 43010, USL; Lafayette, LA 70504-3010.

Baton Rouge Genealogical & Historical Society; PO Box 80565 SE Station; Baton Rouge, LA 70898-0565.

Beauregard Historical Society; PO Box 658; De Ridder, LA 70634-0658.

Bienville Historical Society; Rt 1, Box 9; Bienville, LA 71008-9653.

Bossier Restoration Foundation; 231 Mercy Lane; Benton, LA 71006.

Calcasieu Historical Preservation Society; 1635 Hodges St.; Lake Charles, LA 70601-6016.

Central Louisiana Genealogical Society; PO Box 12206; Alexandria, LA 71315-2006; DBrister@aol.com.

Christmas History of Louisiana; 7024 Morgan Rd.; Greenwell Spr., LA 70739.

Claiborne Historical Association; 931 N. Main St.; Homer, LA 71040.

Comité Louisiane-Français; 2717 Massachusetts; Metairie, LA 70003.

Commission des La Avoyelles; PO Box 29; Hamburg, LA 71339-0028.

Czech Heritage Association, Inc.; 14 Locker Rd.; Deville, LA 71329-9318.

Desoto Historical Society, Inc.; PO Box 925; Mansfield, LA 71052-0925; www.rootsweb.com/%7Eladesoto/society.htm.

Diocese of Baton Rouge; Archives Department; PO Box 2028; Baton Rouge, LA 70821.

Division of Historical Preservation; PO Box 44247; Baton Rouge, LA 70804-4247.

East Ascension Genealogical & Historical Society; PO Box 1006; Gonzales, LA 70707-1006.

Edward Livingston Historical Association; PO Box 67; Livingston, LA 70754-0067.

Evangeline Genealogical & Historical Society; PO Box 664; Ville Platte, LA 70586-0664.

Feliciana (West) Historical Society; PO Box 338; St. Francisville, LA 70775.

Foundation for Historical Louisiana, Inc.; 900 North Blvd.; Baton Rouge, LA 70802-5728.

Founders of Natchitoches; PO Box 3; Natchitoches, LA 71457-0003.

Française Comité Louisiana; 2717 Massachusetts; Metairie, LA 70003-5213.

Franklin Parish Genealogical & Historical Society; Rt. 4, Box 150; Winnsboro, LA 71295.

French Settlement Historical Society; General Delivery; French Settlement, LA 70733-9999.

Friends of Genealogy; PO Box 17935; Shreveport, LA 71138-7835.

Friends of the Archives of Louisiana; PO Box 51213; New Orleans, LA 70151-1213.

Genealogical Research Society of New Orleans; PO Box 51791; New Orleans, LA 70151; www.rootsweb.com/%7Elagrsno.

Genealogy West, Inc.; West Bank of the Mississippi River; 5644 Abby Dr.; New Orleans, LA 70131-3808.

General Philemon Thomas Chapter, SAR; 10547 Ridgely; Baton Rouge, LA 70809; (225) 293-2381; ablamm123@aol.com; http://gpt-SAR.freeyellow.com.

German-Acadian Coast Historical & Genealogical Society; PO Box 517; Destrehan, LA 70047-0517; (504) 652-6077; www.rootsweb.com/~lastjohn/geracadn.htm.

Grant Genealogical Society; 300 Main St.; Colfax, LA 71417.

Gretna Historical Society; PO Box 115; 104 Leighton St.; Gretna, LA 70054-0115.

Historical New Orleans Collection; 533 Royal St.; New Orleans, LA 70130-2113.

Historical Preservation of Shreveport; PO Box 857; Shreveport, LA 71162-0857.

Historical Society of North Caddo; PO Box 31; 100 SW Front Street; Vivian, LA 71082; http://pages.prodigy.net/scollier/hsnc.

Iberia Cultural Resources; 924 E. Main St.; New Iberia, LA 70560-3866.

Jackson Assembly of the Felicianas; PO Box 494; Jackson, LA 70748-0494.

Jefferson Genealogical Society, Inc.; PO Box 961; Metairie, LA 70004-0961; jgs@gnofn.org; http://gnofn.org/~jgs.

Jennings Genealogical Society; 136 Greenwood Dr.; Jennings, LA 70546.

Jewish Genealogical Society of New Orleans; PO Box 7811; Metairie, LA 70010; jkarno@karnovsky.com; www.jewishgen.org/jgsno.

Lafayette Historical Society; 324 North Sterling; Lafayette, LA 70501.

Lafourche Heritage Society; PO Box 567; 412 Menard St.; Thibodaux, LA 70392-0567.

Lake Providence Historical Society; 1002 S. Lake St.; Lake Providence, LA 71254-2428.

Le Comité des Archives de la Louisiane; PO Box 44370; Baton Rouge, LA 70804-4370; http://sec.state.la.us/ archives/archives/archives-comite.htm.

LeCircle Historique; 734 West Main St.; New Roads, LA 70760-3522.

Los Isleos de Galvez Heritage& Cultural Society (Canary Island); 7437 Meadowbrook Ave.; Baton Rouge, LA 70810-2014.

Louisiana Division, United Daughters of the Confederacy; LA ; www.rootsweb.com/~laudc/index.htm.

Louisiana Genealogical & Historical Society; PO Box 82060; Baton Rouge, LA 70884-2060; www.rootsweb.com/~la-lghs.

Louisiana Historical Association; PO Box 40931; Lafayette, LA 70504-0831.

Louisiana Historical Society; 5801 St. Charles Ave.; New Orleans, LA 70115-5053; wdr1@home.com; www.acadiacom.net/lahistsoc.

Louisiana State Archives; 3851 Essen Lane; Baton Rouge, LA 70809-2137; (225) 922-1000; archives@sec.state.la.us; www.sec.state.la.us/archives/ archives/archives-index.htm.

Madison Parish Historical Society; 100 South Chestnut St.; Tallulah, LA 71282-4202.

Mt. Lebon Historical Society; General Delivery; Gibsland, LA 71208-9999.

Natchitoches Genealogical & Historical Association; 600 Second Street; PO Box 1349; Natchitoches, LA 71458-1349; (318) 357-2235; ngha@wnonline.net.

North Louisiana Genealogical Society; PO Box 324; Ruston, LA 71273-0324.

North Louisiana Historical Association; PO Box 6701; Shreveport, LA 71106-6701.

Pointe Coupee Historical Society; PO Box 462; New Roads, LA 70760.

Pointe Coupee Parish; Le Circle Historique; 734 Main St.; New Roads, LA 70760.

Pointe de l'Eglise Historical & Genealogical Society; PO Box 160; Church Point, LA 70525-0160.

Red River Heritage; Rt. 4, Box 363; Coushatta, LA 71019-8729.

River Road Historical Society; PO Box 5; Destrehan, LA 70047-0005.

Saint-Domingue Special Interest Group; 1514 Saint Roch Ave.; New Orleans, LA 70117-8347; abe01@www.gnofn.org.

Society of the Sons & Daughters of The Province and Republic of West Florida 1763–1910; 13727 N. Amiss Rd.; Baton Rouge, LA 70810-5042.

Sons of the American Revolution, Louisiana Society; 3059 Belmont Ave.; Baton Rouge, LA 70808.

Southwest Louisiana Genealogical Society, Inc.; PO Box 5652; Lake Charles, LA 70606-5652.

Southwest Louisiana Historical Association; 4201 Alma Lane; Lake Charles, LA 70605.

St. Bernard Genealogical Society, Inc.; PO Box 271; Chalmette, LA 70044; www.rootsweb.com/~lastbern/stbgs.htm.

St. Helena Historical Society; 6370 Hwy 43; Amite, LA 70422.

St. Mary Genealogical & Historical Society; PO Box 662; Morgan City, LA 70381-0662.

St. Tammany Historical Society; 129 Lamarque St.; Mandeville, LA 70448.

State Library of Louisiana; 701 North 4th Street; PO Box 131; Baton Rouge, LA 70802; (225) 342-4923; ladept@pelican.state.lib.la.us; www.state.lib.la.us.

Tangipahoa Parish Historical Society; 77139 North River Rd.; Kentwood, LA 70444.

Terrebonne Genealogical Society; PO Box 295, Station 2; Houma, LA 70360-0295; pchau@cajun.net; www.rootsweb.com/~laterreb/tgs.htm.

Vermillion Genealogical Society; PO Box 117; Abbeville, LA 70511-0117.

Vermillion Historical Society; PO Box 877; Abbeville, LA 70510-0877.

Vernon Historical & Genealogical Society & Library; Hwy. 121, Box 3713; Leesville, LA 71440-0310.

West Bank Genealogy Society; PO Box 872; Harvey, LA 70059-0872; www.rootsweb.com/~lajeffer/wbgs.html.

Louisiana

West Baton Rouge Genealogical Society; PO Box 1126; Port Allen, LA 70767-1126.

West Baton Rouge Historical Society; 845 N. Jefferson Ave.; Port Allen, LA 70767-2417.

Winn Parrish Genealogical & Historical Association; PO Box 652; Winnfield, LA 71483-0652; www.rootsweb.com/~lawpgha.

Bibliography and Record Sources

General

Adams, Donna Burge. *Women in the Florida Parishes.* 5 vols. Baton Rouge, Louisiana: D. B. Adams, 1985–1991.

Arsenault, Bona. *L'Acadie des Ancetres: Avec la Généalogie des Premières Familles Cadiennes.* Québec: Le Conseil de la vie française en Amérique, 1955.

Arthur, Stanley Clisby. *Old Families of Louisiana, 1608–1929, Volume I.* (1931) Reprint. Baltimore: Clearfield Co., 1997.

Arthur, Stanley Clisby. *Index to the Archives of Spanish West Florida, 1782–1810.* New Orleans, Louisiana: Polyanthos, 1975.

Baudier, Roger. *The Catholic Church in Louisiana.* New Orleans: Louisiana Library Association, Public Library Section, 1972.

Beers, H. P. *French and Spanish Records of Louisiana: A Bibliographical Guide to Archive and Manuscript Sources.* Baton Rouge: Louisiana State University Press, 1989.

Biographical and Historical Memoirs of Louisiana: Embracing an Authentic and Comprehensive Account of the Chief Events in the History of the State, a Special Sketch of Every Parish and a Record of the Lives of Many of the Most Worthy and Illustrious Families and Individuals. 2 vols. Chicago: Goodspeed Publishing Co., 1892.

Boling, Yvette G. *A Guide to Printed Sources for Genealogical and Historical Research in the Louisiana Parishes.* Jefferson, Louisiana: the author, 1985.

Bolton, Herbert E. *The Spanish Borderlands: A Chronicle of Old Florida and the Southwest.* (1921) Reprint. Galveston, Texas: Frontier Press.

Brasseaux, Carl A. *Founding of New Acadia: The Beginning of Acadian Life in Louisiana, 1765–1803.* Baton Rouge: Louisiana State University Press, 1987.

Brasseaux, Carl A. *Acadian to Cajun: Transformation of a People, 1803–1877.* Jackson, Mississippi: University Press of Mississippi, 1992.

Brasseaux, Carl A., Keith P. Fontenot, and Claude F. Oubre. *Creoles of Color in the Bayou Country.* Jackson, Mississippi: University Press of Mississippi, 1994.

Conrad. *The Louisiana Purchase Bicentennial Series in Louisiana History, Volume I: The French Experience in Louisiana.* Galveston, Texas: Frontier Press, 1995.

Courts, Kitty. *Down the Old Spanish Trail.* New Iberia, Louisiana: K. Courts, 1999.

Cummins, Light Townsend, and Glen Jeansonne, eds. *A Guide to the History of Louisiana.* Westport, Connecticut: Greenwood Press, 1982.

Davis, Edwin Adams. *Louisiana: A Narrative History.* 2d ed. Baton Rouge: Claitor's Book Store, 1965.

Davis, Ellis Arthur. *The Historical Encyclopedia of Louisiana.* 2 vols. Baton Rogue: Louisiana Historical Bureau.

Deiler, J. Hanno. *A History of the German Churches in Louisiana (1823–1839).* Translated and edited by Marie Stella Condon. (1894, 1983) Reprint. Baltimore: Clearfield, 1995.

DeVille, Winston. *Gulf Coast Colonials. A Compendium of French Families in Early Eighteenth Century Louisiana.* (1968) Reprint. Baltimore: Clearfield Co., 1995.

Dictionary of Louisiana Biography. 2 vols. New Orleans: Louisiana Historical Association, 1988.

Din, Gilbert C. *The Canary Islanders of Louisiana.* Baton Rouge: Louisiana State University Press, 1988.

Eakin, Sue. *Louisiana, the Land and Its People.* 2nd ed. Gretna, Louisiana: Pelican Pub. Co., 1986.

Early Louisiana settlers, 1600s–1800s. S.l.: Brøderbund, 2000. CD-ROM.

Fortier, Alcee. *A History of Louisiana.* 4 vols. New York: Manzi, Joyant, and Co., 1903.

Hall, Gwendolyn Midlo. *Africans in Colonial Louisiana: The Development of Afro-Creole Culture in the Eighteenth Century.* Baton Rouge: Louisiana State University Press, 1992.

Hamer, Collin B. Jr., *Genealogical Materials in the New Orleans Public Library.* New Orleans: Friends of the New Orleans Public Library, 1984.

Hébert, Donald J. *Guide to Church Records in Louisiana.* Eunice, Louisiana, 1976.

Hébert, Donald J. *A Guide to Church Records in Louisiana, 1720–1975.* Eunice, Louisiana: s.n., 1975.

Hébert, Donald J. *South Louisiana Records.* 12 vols. Cecilia, Louisiana: D. J. Hebert, 1978–1985.

Hébert, Donald J. *Southwest Louisiana Records: Church and Civil Records.* 40 vols. Eunice, Louisiana: D. J. Hebert, 1974–1985.

Hébert, Donald J. *Acadian-Cajun Genealogy: Step by Step.* Galveston, Texas: Frontier Press, 1993.

Hirsch, Arnold R., ed. *Creole New Orleans: Race and Americanization.* Baton Rouge: Louisiana State University Press, 1992.

Historical Records Survey (Louisiana*). Inventory of the Church and Synagogue Archives of Louisiana: Jewish Congregations and Organizations.* University, Louisiana: Dept. of Archives, Louisiana State University, 1941.

Inventory of the Louisiana Historical Association Collection on Deposit in the Howard-Tilton Memorial Library, Tulane University. Galveston, Texas: Frontier Press.

Kniffen, Fred B. *Historic Indian Tribes of Louisiana: From 1542 to the Present.* Reprint. Baton Rouge: Louisiana State University Press, 1994.

Labbe, Dolores Egger. *The Louisiana Purchase and Its Aftermath, 1800–1830.* Lafayette, Louisiana: Center for Louisiana Studies, University of Southwestern Louisiana, 1998.

Louisiana Colonials: Soldiers and Vagabonds. (1963), Reprint. Baltimore: Clearfield Co., 1995.

Louisiana History Association. *Louisiana History: The Journal of the Louisiana Historical Association.* Vols. 1-25, 1960–1984. Vols. 26–30, 1985–1989. Galveston, Texas: Frontier Press.

Louisiana Research Outline. Series US States, no. 19, Salt Lake City: Family History Library, 1988.

Louisianans and Their State: A Historical and Biographical Text Book of Louisiana. New Orleans: Louisiana Historical and Biographical Association, 1919.

Malone. *Sweet Chariot: Slave Family and Household Structure in Nineteenth Century Louisiana.* 1992. Galveston, Texas: Frontier Press, 1992.

Martin, François Xavier. *The History of Louisiana, From the Earliest Period.* 2 vols. New Orleans: Lyman and Beardslee, 1827–29.

McAvoy, Thomas Timothy. *Guide to the Microfilm Edition of the Records of the Diocese of Louisiana and the Floridas, 1576–1803.* Notre Dame, Indiana: University of Notre Dame Archives, 1967.

Menn, Joseph Karl. *The Large Slaveholders of the Deep South, 1860.* Ann Arbor, Michigan: UMI Dissertation Services, 1964.

Mills, Gary B. *Forgotten People: Cane River's Creole of Color.* Baton Rouge: Louisiana State University Press, 1977.

Newspaper Files in Louisiana State University Library. Baton Rouge: Louisiana State University, 1961.

Nolan, Charles E. *A Southern Catholic Heritage.* New Orleans: Archdiocese of New Orleans, 1976.

Perkins, A. E. *Who's Who in Colored Louisiana.* Baton Rouge, Louisiana: Douglas Loan Co., 1930.

Perrin, William Henry. *Southwest Louisiana: Biographical and Historical.* Reprint. Baton Rouge: Claitor's Pub. Div., 1971.

Poret, George C. *Vignettes of Louisiana Church History.* Mansura, Louisiana: G. C. Poret, 1985.

Post, Lauren C. *Cajun Sketches from the Prairies of Southwest Louisiana.* Baton Rouge: Louisiana State University Press, 1990.

Resources in Louisiana Libraries: Public, Academic, Special and in Media Centers. Baton Rouge: Louisiana State Library, 1971.

Robichaux, Albert J., Jr. *German Coast Families: European Origins and Settlement in Colonial Louisiana.* Rayne, Louisiana: Hébert Publications, 1997.

Seebold, Herman Boehm de Bachellé. *Old Louisiana Plantation Homes and Family Trees.* 2 vols. New Orleans: Pelican Press, 1941.

Sterkx, H. E. *The Free Negro in Ante-Bellum Louisiana.* Rutherford, New Jersey: Fairleigh Dickinson University Press, 1972.

Tanguay, Cyprien. *Dictionnaire Généalogique des Familles Canadiennes Depuis la Fondation de la Colonie jusqu'a' nos jours.* 7 vols. New York: Ams Press, 1969.

United States. Bureau of Refugees, Freedmen, and Abandoned Lands. *Records of the Assistant Commissioner for the State of Louisiana, Bureau of Refugees, Freedmen, and Abandoned Lands, 1865–1869.* Washington, D.C.: The National Archives, 1976. 36 microfilm.

Usner, Daniel H. *Indians, Settlers & Slaves in a Frontier Exchange Economy: The Lower Mississippi Valley Before 1783.* Galveston, Texas: Frontier Press, 1992.

West, Robert C. *An Atlas of Louisiana Surnames of French and Spanish Origin.* Baton Rouge: Geoscience Pub., Louisiana State University, 1986.

Whittington, Hattie, and Gladys Sandefur. *Louisiana Ahnentafels, Ancestor Charts and Family Group Sheets.* Natchitoches, Louisiana: Natchitoches Genealogical and Historical Association, 1982.

Who's Who in Louisiana and Mississippi: Biographical Sketches of Prominent Men and Women of Louisiana and Mississippi. New Orleans: Times-Picayune, 1918.

Williams, Mary Eleanor. *Black Names in Louisiana.* S.l.: s.n., 1992.

Willie, Leroy Ellis. *German Ancestors and Patriots of Louisiana, 1722–1803.* S.l.: s.n., 1996.

Winzerling, Oscar William. *Acadian Odyssey.* Eunice, Louisiana: Hebert Publications, 1981.

Wood, Gregory. *A Guide to the Acadians in Maryland in the 18th and 19th Centuries.* 1995. Wheaton, Maryland: Maryland Acadian Studies, 1995.

Yoes, Henry E., 3rd, comp. *Biography of Louisiana Materials.* Hohnville, Louisiana, 1973.

Atlases, Maps and Gazetteers

County Parish Boundaries in Louisiana. New Orleans: Historical Records Survey, 1939.

Germann, John J. *Louisiana Post Offices.* Lake Grove, Oregon: The Depot, 1990.

Gibson, Dennis A., ed. *Index to Louisiana Place Names Mentioned in the War of the Rebellion: A Compilation of the Official Records of the Union and Confederate*

Armies. Lafayette: University of Southwestern Louisiana, 1975.

Goins, Charles Robert and John Michael Caldwell. *Historical Atlas of Louisiana.* 1995. Galveston, Texas: Frontier Press, 1995.

Hansen, Harry, ed. *Louisiana: A Guide to the State.* New York: Hastings House, 1971.

Historical Records Survey (Louisiana). *County Parish Boundaries in Louisiana.* New Orleans: Louisiana State University, 1939.

Newton, M. B. *Louisiana, A Geographical Portrait.* Baton Rouge: Geoforensics, 1987.

Spillman, Danell Strickland. *Louisiana Parish Map History.* Baton Rouge, Louisiana: D. Spillman, 1989.

Census Records

Available Census Records and Census Substitutes

Federal Census 1810, 1820, 1830, 1840, 1850, 1860, 1870, 1880, 1900, 1910, 1920, 1930

Federal Mortality Schedules 1850, 1860, 1870, 1880

Union Veterans and Widows 1890

French Colonial Census 1699–1732

State/Territorial Census 1706, 1721, 1726

Confederate Veterans and Widows 1911

Burns, Loretta E., comp. *Louisiana 1911 Census Confederate Veterans* or Widows. The author, 1995.

Dollarhide, William. *The Census Book: A Genealogist's Guide to Federal Census Facts, Schedules and Indexes.* Bountiful, Utah: Heritage Quest, 1999.

Kemp, Thomas Jay. *The American Census Handbook.* Wilmington, Delaware: Scholarly Resources, Inc., 2001.

Lainhart, Ann S. *State Census Records.* Baltimore: Genealogical Publishing Co., Inc., 1992.

Maduell, Charles R., Jr. *The Census Tables for the French Colony of Louisiana from 1699 Through 1732.* (1972) Reprint, Baltimore: Clearfield Co., 1995.

Robichaux, Albert J., Jr. *Louisiana Census and Militia Lists 1770–1789.* 2 vols. Harvey, Louisiana: A. J. Robichaux, 1973 and 1974.

Szucs, Loretto Dennis and Matthew Wright. *Finding Answers in U.S. Census Records.* Ancestry Publishing, 2001.

Thorndale, William, and William Dollarhide. *Map Guide to the U.S. Federal Census, 1790–1920.* Baltimore: Genealogical Publishing Co., 1987.

Court Records, Probate and Wills

Daughters of the American Revolution. Louisiana. *Genealogical Records Committee. Early Court Records and Wills.* Typescript. 1967–1968.

English Language Summaries of the Records of the French Superior Council and the Judicial Records of the Spanish Cabildo, 1714–1800. N.p.: Works Project Administration, n.d.

Gianelloni, Elizabeth Becker. *Calendar of Louisiana Colonial Documents.* 3 vols. S.l.: The Commission, 1961–1967.

Louisiana (Province). Cabildo. *Inventory of the Records of the French Superior Council and Judicial Records of the Spanish Cabildo 1702–1803.* Microfilm of original records in the New Orleans Public Library. Salt Lake City: Filmed by the Genealogical Society of Utah, 1981.

Louisiana (Province). Cabildo. *Judicial Records, 1769–1804.* Microfilm of original records filmed in the Louisiana Historical Center, New Orleans. Salt Lake City: Filmed by the Genealogical Society of Utah, 1979–1980. 239 microfilm.

Louisiana (Province). Conseil Superieur. *Records of the French Superior Court, 1679–1803. Name Card Index to Records of the French Superior Council and Judicial Records of the Spanish Cabildo.* Microfilm of original records in the Louisiana Historical Center, New Orleans. Salt Lake City: Filmed by the Genealogical Society of Utah, 1981. 9 microfilm.

Louisiana. District Court (Fifth District). *Index to Defendant and Plaintiff Dockets, 1846–1880.* Microfilm copy of original records located at the New Orleans Public Library, New Orleans, Louisiana. Salt Lake City: Filmed by the Genealogical Society of Utah, 1985. 4 microfilm.

Louisiana. Judicial District Court (First District). *1st Judicial District Court Records, 1822–1846.* Microfilm copy of original records located at the New Orleans Public Library, New Orleans, Louisiana. Salt Lake City: Filmed by the Genealogical Society of Utah, 1985. 3 microfilm.

National Archives Records Administration. Southwest Region in Fort Worth. *Louisiana, Eastern District, 1806–1982; Western District, 1832–1966; Louisiana, Middle District, 1971–1993; Louisiana, Western District, 1832–1961.* Fort Worth, Texas: National Archives Records Administration. Online database –www.nara.gov/regional/findaids/ftwguid1.html#21

Emigration, Immigration, Migration and Naturalization

Brasseaux, Carl A. *The "Foreign French": Nineteenth-Century French Immigration into Louisiana.* 3 vols. Lafayette: Center for Louisiana Studies, University of Southwestern Louisiana, 1900–1993. Vol. 1, 1820–1839; vol. 2, 1840–1848; vol 3, 1849–1852.

Brasseaux, Carl A. *A Refuge For All Ages, Immigration In Louisiana History.* Lafayette, Louisiana: Center for Louisiana Studies, University of Southwestern Louisiana, 1996.

Conrad, Glen R. *The First Families of Louisiana.* 2 vols. Baton Rouge: Claitor's Pub. Division, 1970.

Early Louisiana settlers, 1600s-1800s. S.l.: Brøderbund, 2000. CD-ROM.

Hébert, Donald J. *Immigration Files Of Southwest Louisiana (1840–1929): Naturalization Records.* Mire, Louisiana: Hebert Pub., 1990.

Passage Index, Louisiana, 1718–1724. Miroreproduction of original published: Center Louisiana State Museum in New Orleans, Louisiana. New Orleans: Center Louisiana State Museum, 1980. 2 microfilm.

Rieder, Milton P., and Norma Gaudet Rieder, eds. *The Acadian Exiles in the American Colonies, 1755–1768.* Metairie, Louisiana: the editors, 1977.

Riviere, Mary Ann. *From Palermo to New Orleans.* New Orleans: M. Riviere, 1987.

Robichaux, Albert J., Jr. *German Coast Families: European Origins And Settlement In Colonial Louisiana.* Rayne, Louisiana: Hébert Publications, 1997.

United States. Circuit Court (Louisiana: Eastern District). *Naturalization Records, 1906–1912.* Microfilm copy of original records located at the district clerks office, New Orleans, Louisiana. Salt Lake City: Filmed by the Genealogical Society of Utah, 1985. 5 microfilm.

United States. District Court (Louisiana: Eastern District). *Naturalization Record, Declaration Of Intent.* Salt Lake City: Filmed by the Genealogical Society of Utah, 1981. 7 microfilm.

United States. District Court (Louisiana: Eastern District). *Naturalization Records, 1906–1932.* Microfilm copy of original records located at the district clerk's office, New Orleans, Louisiana. Salt Lake City: Filmed by the Genealogical Society of Utah, 1985. 30 microfilm.

United States. Immigration and Naturalization Service. *Crew Lists Of Vessels Arriving At New Orleans, Louisiana, 1910–1920.* Washington, D.C.: The National Archives, 1987. 48 microfilm.

United States. Immigration and Naturalization Service. *Passenger Lists of Vessels Arriving At New Orleans, 1820–1921; Index to Passenger Lists of Vessels Arriving in New Orleans, 1853–1952.* (Washington, D.C.: Filmed by the National Archives Record Service, 1947, 1957–1958).

United States. Immigration and Naturalization Service. *Quarterly Abstracts of Passenger Lists of Vessels Arriving At New Orleans, 1820–1875.* (Washington, D.C.: Filmed by the National Archives Record Service, 1959).

Viller`ae, Sidney Louis. *The Canary Islands Migration to Louisiana, 1778–1783: The History and Passenger Lists of the Islenos Volunteer Recruits and Their Families.* Baltimore: Genealogical Publishing Co., 1972.

Land and Property

Deville, Winston. *English Land Grants in West Florida: A Register for the States of Alabama, Mississippi, and Parts of Florida and Louisiana, 1766–1776.* Ville Platte, Louisiana: Winston Deville, 1986.

Exhibit Of Private Land Claims. Microfilm copy of original records located at the Division of State Lands office, Baton Rouge, Louisiana. Salt Lake City: Filmed by the Genealogical Society of Utah, 1983.

First Settlers of the Louisiana Territory: Orleans Territory Grants from American State Papers, Class viii, Public Lands. 2 vols. Nacogdoches, Texas: Ericson Books, and St. Louis: Ingmire Publications, 1983.

Historical Records Survey (Louisiana). *Survey of Federal Archives in Louisiana: From U.S. Land Office Archives.* Baton Rouge, Louisiana: Filmed by Archives and Records Service.

Historical Records Survey, Division of Professional and Service Projects. Works Progress Administration. *Survey of Federal Archives in Louisiana; Land Claims and Other Documents, ca. 1800–1860.* Baton Rouge; Archives and Records Service, n.d.

Hone, Wade E. *Land and Property Research in the United States.* Salt Lake City: Ancestry Incorporated, 1997.

Lowrie, Walter, ed. *Land Claims in the Eastern District of the Orleans Territory. Communicated to the House of Representatives, January 9, 1812.* (1834) reprint Greenville, South Carolina: Southern Historical Press, 1986.

Maudell, Charles R. *Federal Land Grants in the Territory of Orleans: The Delta Parishers.* New Orleans: Polyanthos, 1975.

McMullin, Phillip W., ed. *Grassroots of America: A Computerized Index to the American State Papers: Land Grants and Claims (1789–1837) With Other Aids to Research (Government document serial set numbers 28 through 36).* Greenville, South Carolina: Southern Historical Press, 1994, 1990.

Pintado, Vincente Sebastian. *Pintado Papers, 1795–1842.* Baton Rouge: Archives and Records Service, n.d.

Poret, Ory Gerard. *Louisiana Land Titles: An Inventory of State Land Office Records from the Early Nineteenth Century on File at the State Archives of Louisiana.* Ville Platte, Louisiana: Provincial Press, ©1998.

Tipton, Ennis Mayfield. *Index To U.S. Tract Books, Northwestern Land District, Old Natchitoches District, In The Louisiana State Land Office,* Baton Rouge, Louisiana. Bossier City, Louisiana: Tipton Printing & Pub., 1980.

United States. District Land Office (New Orleans, Louisiana). *Surveys Of Land Claims, 1806–1813 And 1832–1834; Land Records, 1860– 1916 ; Certificates Of Location, 1858–1907.* Microfilm copy of original records located at the Division of State Lands office, Baton Rouge, Louisiana. Salt Lake City: Filmed by the Genealogical Society of Utah, 1983. 3 microfilm.

United States. District Land Office (Opelousas, Louisiana). *Land Records, 1805–1860.* Microfilm copy of original records located at the Division of State Lands office,

Baton Rouge, Louisiana. Salt Lake City: Filmed by the Genealogical Society of Utah, 1983. 6 microfilm.

United States. District Land Office (St. Helena, Louisiana). *Land Records, 1803–1875*. Microfilm copy of original records located at the Division of State Lands office, Baton Rouge, Louisiana. Salt Lake City: Filmed by the Genealogical Society of Utah, 1983. 7 microfilm.

United States. Land Office (Baton Rouge, Louisiana). *Tract Books, 1807–1870*. Salt Lake City: Filmed by the Genealogical Society of Utah, 1983. 24 microfilm.

Military

Adjunct General's Office. *The Compiled Service Records of Louisianans in the War of 1812*. Baton Rouge: Adjunct General's Office, n.d.

Allardice, Bruck. *Other Generals in Gray*. Baton Rouge: Louisiana State University Press, n.d.

Bartlett, Napier. *Military Record of Louisiana: Including Biographical and Historical Papers Relating to the Military Organizations of the State*. 1875. Reprint. Baton Rouge: Louisiana State University Press, 1964.

Bergeron, Arthur W., Jr. *Guide to Louisiana Confederate Military Units, 1861–1865*. Baton Rouge: Louisiana State University Press, 1989.

Booth, Andrew B. *Records of Louisiana Confederate Soldiers and Louisiana Confederate Commands*. (1920, 1984) Reprint. Spartanburg, South Carolina: Reprint Co., 1996.

Casey, Powell A. *Louisiana in the War of 1812*. Baton Rouge: Casey, 1963.

Cunningham, H. H. *Doctors in Gray: The Confederate Medical Service*. Reprint. Baton Rouge: Louisiana State University Press, 1993.

DeVille, Winston. *Louisiana Troops, 1720–1770*. (1965) Reprint. Baltimore: Clearfield Co., 1994.

Enumeration of Ex-Confederate Soldiers and Widows of Deceased Soldiers of Louisiana, Made in 1911. Salt Lake City: Filmed by the Genealogical Society of Utah, 1966.

España. Secretaría de Estado y del Despacho de Guerra. *Hojas de Servicios Militares de América: Floridas Y Luisiana, 1787–1794*. Madrid: Filmado por el Servicio Nacional de Microfilm, 1971.

Gaines, W. Craig. *Confederate Cherokees: John Drew's Regiment of Mounted Rifles*. Baton Rouge: Louisiana State University Press, 1989.

List Of Men Who Died While Serving As Officers In The World War, Louisiana. Salt Lake City: Filmed by the Genealogical Society of Utah, 1990.

Louisiana State Archives. *Confederate Pension Applications Index Database*. Baton Rouge, Louisiana: Louisiana State Archives 2002. Online database— www.sec.state.la.us/archives/gen/cpa-index.htm.

Louisiana. National Guard (New Orleans). *National Guard Records, 1717–1955*. Microreproduction of originals housed at the Louisiana National Guard, New Orleans, Louisiana. Salt Lake City: Filmed by the Genealogical Society of Utah, 1990. 6 microfilm.

Pierson, M. J. B. *Louisiana Soldiers in the War of 1812*. Baton Rouge: Louisiana Genealogical and Historical Society, 1963.

Sifakis, Stewart. *Compendium of the Confederate Armies: Louisiana*. Galveston, Texas: Frontier Press, 1995.

United States Selective Service System, Louisiana. *World War I Selective Service System Draft Registration Cards, 1917–1918. National Archives Microfilm Publications, M1509*. Washington, D.C.: National Archives, 1987–1988.

United States. Adjutant General's Office. *Index to Compiled Service Records of Volunteer Soldiers Who Served During the Florida War in Organizations from the State of Louisiana*. Washington, D.C.: National Archives, 1957.

United States. Adjutant General's Office. *Index to Compiled Service Records of Volunteer Soldiers Who Served During the Mexican War*. Washington, D.C.: The National Archives, 1965.

United States. Adjutant General's Office. *Index to Compiled Service Records of Volunteer Soldiers Who Served During the War of 1812 in Organizations from the State of Louisiana 1812–1815*. Washington, D.C.: The National Archives, 1955.

United States. Adjutant General's Office. *Index to Compiled Service Records of Volunteer Soldiers Who Served During the War with Spain in Organizations from the State of Louisiana*. Washington, D.C.: The National Archives, 1957.

Warner, Ezra J. *Generals in Blue: Lives of the Union Commanders*. Louisiana State University Press, 1964.

Warner, Ezra J. *Generals in Gray: Lives of the Confederate Commanders*. Louisiana State University Press, 1959.

Wiley, Bell Irvin. *Life of Billy Yank: The Common Soldier of the Union*. Reprint. Baton Rouge: Louisiana State University Press, 1971.

Wiley, Bell Irwin. *Life of Johnny Reb: The Common Soldier of the Confederacy*. (1943) Reprint. Baton Rouge: Louisiana State University Press, 1971.

Wright, Nancy Lowrie and Cathy Dantin Shannon. *Louisiana Volunteers in The War Of 1898*. Houma, Louisiana: Wright Shannon Publications, 1989.

Vital and Cemetery Records

Be It Known and Remembered: Bible Records, 4 vols. Baton Rouge: Louisiana Genealogical and Historical Society, 1960.

Bourgard, Shirley Chaisson. *Marriage Dispensations in the Diocese of Louisiana and the Floridas: 1786–1803*. New Orleans; Polyanthos, 1980.

Daughters of the American Revolution. Louisiana (New Orleans). *Louisiana Tombstone Inscriptions*. 22 vols. Salt Lake City: Genealogical Society of Utah, 1970.

DeVille, Winston. *The New Orleans French, 1720–1733, A Collection of Marriage Records Relating to the First Colonists of the Louisiana Province* Baltimore: Genealogical Publishing Co., 1973.

Forsyth, Alice Daly. *Louisiana Marriage Contracts: A Compilation of Abstracts From Records of the Superior Council of Louisiana During the French Regime, 1725–1769.* 2 vols. New Orleans: Polyanthos, 1980.

Frazier, John Purnell. *Tombstone Inscriptions of Northwest Louisiana Cemeteries.* Pittsburg, Texas: John Purnell Fraizer, 1986.

Guide to Public Vital Statistics Records in Louisiana. New Orleans: Historical Records Survey, 1942.

Guide to Vital Statistics Records of Church Archives in Louisiana. New Orleans: Louisiana State Board of Health, 1942.

Hebert, Donald J. *South Louisiana Records.* 12 vols. Cecilia, Louisiana: Donald J. Herbert, 1978.

Louisiana Tombstone Inscriptions. 11 vols. Louisiana Society. Daughters of the American Revolution, 1957.

Marriage Records Index and Contracts (Louisiana), 1718–1900. Microreproduction of original published: Center Louisiana State Museum of New Orleans. New Orleans: Center Louisiana State Museum, 1980.

Mayers, Brenda L., and Gloria L. Kerns. *Death Notices from Louisiana Newspapers, 1811–1919.* vols. 1–6. Baker, Louisiana: Folk Finders, 1984.

Southwest Louisiana Records: Church and Civil Records. 33 vols. Eunice, Louisiana: Donald J. Herbert, 1974–1985.

United States. Bureau of the Census. *Federal Mortality Census Schedules and Related Indexes: Louisiana; 1850; 1860; 1870; 1880.* Washington, D.C.: National Archives and Record Service, 1962. 5 microfilm.

County Website	Map Index	Date Created	Parent County or Territory From Which Organized Address/Details
Acadia County		**10 Apr 1805**	**Original county** Acadia County; LA **Details:** (County Terminated 1845) (Discontinued. Became Ascension & St. James Parishes 31 Mar 1807)
Acadia Parish www.rootsweb.com/~lapehgs/	**K4**	**30 Jun 1886**	**St. Landry** Acadia Parish County; PO Box 922; Crowley, LA 70527-0922; Ph. (337) 788-8881 **Details:** (Parish Clerk has Marriage, Divorce, Probate & Court Records from 1886)
Allen Parish www.rootsweb.com/~laallen/	**I3**	**12 Jun 1912**	**Calcasieu** Allen Parish County; PO Box G; Oberlin, LA 70655-2007; Ph. (337) 639-2803 **Details:** (Parish Clerk has Marriage, Divorce, Probate & Court Records from 1913)
Ascension Parish www.ascensionparish.net/	**K8**	**31 Mar 1807**	**Acadia County** Ascension Parish County; Houmas St; PO Box 192; Donaldsonville, LA 70346; Ph. (225) 773-9866 **Details:** (Parish Clerk has Marriage Records from 1763, Divorce, Probate & Court Records from 1800 & Land Records from 1770)
Assumption Parish www.assumptionclerk.com	**L8**	**31 Mar 1807**	**Lafourche** Assumption Parish County; 4809 Hwy 1; PO Drawer 249; Napoleonville, LA 70390; Ph. (985) 369-6653 dlandry@assumtionclerk.com **Details:** (Parish Clerk has Marriage Records from 1800, Probate Records from 1841, Land Records from 1788, Divorce & Court Records from 1868)

County Website	Map Index	Date Created	Parent County or Territory From Which Organized Address/Details
Attakapas County		**10 Apr 1805**	**Original parish** Attakapas County County; LA **Details:** (County Terminated 1845) (Created as Attakapas Co. Attakapas Parish created 31 Mar 1807. Discontinued & divided into St. Martin & St. Mary 17 Apr 1811, Lafayette 17 Feb 1823 & Vermilion 25 Mar 1844)
Avoyelles Parish H6 www.mindspring.com/~jwbarron/avoyeles.htm		**31 Mar 1807**	**Original Parish** Avoyelles Parish County; 312 N Main St; Marksville, LA 71351; Ph. (318) 253-9208 **Details:** (Parish Clerk has Marriage & Land Records from 1908, Probate Records from 1925, Court Records from 1929, Divorce Records from 1939 & Military Records from 1886)
Baton Rouge Parish		**31 Mar 1807**	**Pointe Coupee** Baton Rouge Parish County; LA **Details:** (see West Baton Rouge) Created as Baton Rouge Parish & became West Baton Rouge 1812)
Beauregard Parish J3 www.rootsweb.com/~labeaure/beaurega.htm		**12 Jun 1919**	**Calcasieu** Beauregard Parish County; 412 Mayeaux Dr; De Ridder, LA 70634-0310; Ph. (337) 463-6146 **Details:** (Parish Clerk has Marriage, Divorce, Probate, Court & Land Records from 1913)
Bienville Parish E3 www.rootsweb.com/~labienvi/		**14 Mar 1848**	**Claiborne** Bienville Parish County; 300 Courthouse Sq; PO Box 746; Arcadia, LA 71001; Ph. (318) 263-2123 **Details:** (Parish Clerk has Marriage, Divorce, Probate & Court Records from 1848)
Bossier Parish D2 www.mybossier.com/index.htm		**24 Feb 1843**	**Claiborne** Bossier Parish County; PO Box 369; Benton, LA 71006; Ph. (318) 965-2336 **Details:** (Parish Clerk has Marriage, Divorce, Probate, Land & Court Records from 1843 & Military Records from 1917)
Caddo Parish E2 www.caddo.org/Parish_Commission/default.htm		**18 Jan 1838**	**Natchitoches** Caddo Parish County; 501 Texas St; Shreveport, LA 71101; Ph. (318) 226-6911 **Details:** (Parish Clerk has Marriage, Divorce, Probate, Court & Land Records from 1835)
Calcasieu Parish K2 www.cppj.net/		**24 Mar 1840**	**St. Landry** Calcasieu Parish County; PO Box 1030; Lake Charles, LA 70602-1030; Ph. (337) 437-3550 **Details:** (Parish Clerk has Marriage, Divorce, Probate, Court & Land Records from 1910)
Caldwell Parish F5 www.rootsweb.com/~lacaldwe/		**6 Mar 1838**	**Catahoula, Ouachita** Caldwell Parish County; 200 Main St; Columbia, LA 71418; Ph. (318) 649-2681 **Details:** (Parish Clerk has Marriage, Divorce, Probate, Land, & Court Records from 1838)

County Website	Map Index	Date Created	Parent County or Territory From Which Organized Address/Details
Cameron Parish www.cameronparish.net/	L3	**15 Mar 1870**	**Calcasieu, Vermilion** Cameron Parish County; 119 Smith Rdg; Cameron, LA 70631-0549; Ph. (337) 775-5316 **Details:** (Parish Clerk has Marriage, Divorce, Probate, Court & Land Records from 1870 & Military Discharge Records from 1918)
Carroll Parish		**14 Mar 1832**	**Concordia, Ouachita** Carroll Parish County; LA **Details:** (see East & West Carroll) Divided into East & West Carroll 28 Mar 1877
Catahoula Parish www.geocities.com/robertce/catahoula/index.html	G6	**23 Mar 1808**	**Rapides** Catahoula Parish County; 301 Bushley St; PO Box 198; Harrisonburg, LA 71340-0198; Ph. (318) 744-5497 **Details:** (Parish Clerk has Marriage Records from 1830, Burial, Probate & Divorce Records from 1800's, Land Records from 1808 & Military Records)
Claiborne Parish www.rootsweb.com/~laclaib2/claibla.htm	D3	**13 Mar 1828**	**Natchitoches** Claiborne Parish County; 512 E Main St; Homer, LA 71040; Ph. (318) 927-9601 **Details:** (Courthouse burned 1849) (Parish Clerk has Marriage, Divorce, Probate, Court & Land Records from 1850)
Concordia County		**10 Apr 1805**	**Original parish** Concordia County, LA **Details:** County Terminated 1845
Concordia Parish www.rootsweb.com/~laconcor/	G6	**1807**	**Original parish** Concordia Parish County; 4001 Carter St, PO Box 790; Vidalia, LA 71373-0790; Ph. (318) 336-4204 **Details:** (Parish Clerk has Marriage Records from 1840, Divorce, Probate, Court & Land Records from 1850)
DeSoto Parish www.rootsweb.com/~ladesoto/index.htm	F2	**1 Apr 1843**	**Natchitoches, Caddo** DeSoto Parish County; Parish Courthouse; Mansfield, LA 71052; Ph. (318) 872-3110 **Details:** (Parish Clerk has Marriage & Land Records from 1843, Divorce, Probate & Court Records)
East Baton Rouge Parish www.ci.baton-rouge.la.us/	J7	**22 Dec 1810**	**Feliciana** East Baton Rouge Parish County; 222 St Louis St; Baton Rouge, LA 70802-5817; Ph. (225) 383-0378 **Details:** (Parish Clerk has Marriage Records from 1840, Divorce, Probate, Court & Land Records from 1782)
East Carroll Parish www.eastcarroll.net/home.htm	D7	**28 Mar 1877**	**Carroll** East Carroll Parish County; 400 1st St; Lake Providence, LA 71254-2616; Ph. (318) 559-2399 **Details:** (Parish Clerk has Marriage, Probate & Land Records)

County Website	Map Index	Date Created	Parent County or Territory From Which Organized Address/Details
East Feliciana Parish www.rootsweb.com/~laeastfe/eastfeliciana.htm	I8	17 Feb 1824	**Feliciana** East Feliciana Parish County; 12305 St Helena St; PO Drawer 599; Clinton, LA 70722; Ph. (225) 683-5145 **Details:** (Parish Clerk has Marriage, Divorce, Probate, Court & Land Records from 1824)
Evangeline Parish www.evangelineparish.com/	J4	15 Jun 1910	**St. Landry** Evangeline Parish County; 200 Court St; Ville Platte, LA 70586; Ph. (337) 363-5671 **Details:** (Parish Clerk has Marriage, Divorce, Probate, Court & Land Records from 1911)
Feliciana County		1810	**Spanish West Florida** Feliciana, LA **Details:** County Terminated 1845
Feliciana Parish		7 Dec 1810	**Spanish West Florida** Feliciana Parish County; LA **Details:** (see East & West Feliciana) Dissolved to form parishes of East & West Feliciana 17 Feb 1824
Franklin Parish www.rootsweb.com/~lafrankl/index.htm	F6	1 Mar 1843	**Catahoula, Ouachita, Madison** Franklin Parish County; 210 Main St; Winnsboro, LA 71295; Ph. (318) 435-9429 **Details:** (Parish Clerk has Marriage, Divorce, Probate, Court & Land Records from 1843)
German Coast County		10 Apr 1805	**Original county** German Coast County; LA **Details:** County Terminated 1845 (Discontinued. Divided to form parishes of St. Charles & St. John the Baptist 31 Mar 1807)
Grant Parish www.rootsweb.com/~lagrant/	G4	4 Mar 1869	**Rapides, Winn** Grant Parish County; Main St; Colfax, LA 71417; Ph. (318) 627-3157 **Details:** (Parish Clerk has Marriage, Divorce, Land, Probate, Military & Court Records from 1878)
Iberia Parish www.intersurf.com/~johnjanr/iberia.htm	M6	30 Oct 1868	**St. Martin, St. Mary** Iberia Parish County; 300 Iberia St Ste 400; New Iberia, LA 70560; Ph. (337) 365-3221 **Details:** (Parish Clerk has Marriage, Divorce, Probate, Court & Land Records from 1868)
Iberville County		1805	**Original parish** Iberville County; LA **Details:** County Terminated 1845
Iberville Parish www.parish.iberville.la.us/	K7	1807	**Original parish** Iberville Parish County; PO Box 423; Plaquemine, LA 70765-0423; Ph. (225) 687-5160 **Details:** (Parish Clerk has Marriage & Land Records from 1770, Divorce, Probate & Court Records from 1807)
Interior Parish		1807	**Original parish** Interior Parish; LA **Details:** Name Changed 1853 to Lafourche Interior

County Website	Map Index	Date Created	Parent County or Territory From Which Organized Address/Details
Jackson Parish E4 www.rootsweb.com/~lajackso/jacksonIndex.htm		**27 Feb 1845**	**Claiborne, Ouachita, Union** Jackson Parish County; 500 E Court St; PO Box 730; Jonesboro, LA 71251; Ph. (318) 259-2424 **Details:** (Parish Clerk has Marriage, Divorce, Land, Probate, Military & Court Records from 1880)
Jefferson Davis Parish K3 www.rootsweb.com/~lajeffda/		**4547**	**Calcasieu** Jefferson Davis Parish County; PO Box 1409; Jennings, LA 70546-1409; Ph. (337) 824-1161 **Details:** (Parish Clerk has Marriage, Divorce, Probate, Court & Land Records from 1913)
Jefferson Parish L9 www.jeffparish.net/		**11 Feb 1825**	**Orleans** Jefferson Parish County; 200 Derbigny St; Gretna, LA 70053; Ph. (504) 364-2800 **Details:** (Parish Clerk has Marriage Records from 1863, Divorce, Probate & Court Records from 1825 & Land Records from 1827)
La Salle Parish G5 www.rootsweb.com/~lalasall/		**3107**	**Catahoula** La Salle Parish County; PO Box 1372; Jena, LA 71342-0057; Ph. (318) 992-2101 **Details:** (Parish Clerk has Marriage, Divorce, Probate, Court & Land Records from 1910)
Lafayette Parish K5 www.lafayettegov.org/index.cfm		**17 Jan 1823**	**St. Martin, Attakapas** Lafayette Parish County; PO Box 4508; Lafayette, LA 70502-4508; Ph. (337) 291-6400 **Details:** (Parish Clerk has Marriage, Divorce, Probate, Court & Land Records from 1823)
Lafourche County		**10 Apr 1805**	**Original parish** Lafourche County; LA **Details:** County Terminated 1845
Lafourche Parish M9 www.lapage.com/parishes/lafou.htm		**10 Apr 1805**	**Original parish** Lafourche Parish County; 309 W 3rd St; Thibodaux, LA 70301-3021; Ph. (985) 447-4841 **Details:** (Formerly Lafourche Interior Parish 1812–1853) (Parish Clerk has Birth, Marriage, Divorce, Probate, Court & Land Records from 1808)
Lafourche Interior Parish		**1807**	**Original parish** Lafourche Interior Parish; LA **Details:** Formerly Interior Parish 1807–1853
Lincoln Parish D4 www.lincolnparish.org/		**27 Feb 1873**	**Bienville, Jackson, Union, Clairborne** Lincoln Parish County; 100 W Texas Ave; Ruston, LA 71270; Ph. (318) 255-3663 **Details:** (Parish Clerk has Marriage, Divorce, Probate & Court Records from 1873)

County Website	Map Index	Date Created	Parent County or Territory From Which Organized Address/Details
Livingston Parish www.lapage.com/parishes/livin.htm	**J8**	**10 Feb 1832**	**St. Helena** Livingston Parish County; 20180 Iowa St; PO Box 427; Livingston, LA 70754; Ph. (225) 686-2266 **Details:** (Parish Clerk has Marriage, Divorce, Probate, Court & Land Records from 1875)
Madison Parish **E7** www.rootsweb.com/~lamadiso/index.htm		**19 Jan 1838**	**Concordia** Madison Parish County; 100 N Cedar St; Tallulah, LA 71282; Ph. (318) 574-0655 **Details:** (Parish Clerk has Marriage Records from 1866, Divorce & Land Records from 1839, Probate Records from 1850 & Court Records from 1882)
Morehouse Parish www.rootsweb.com/~lamoreho/morehouse.htm	**D6**	**25 Mar 1844**	**Ouachita** Morehouse Parish County; 125 E Madison St; Bastrop, LA 71221; Ph. (318) 281-3343 **Details:** (Parish Clerk has Marriage, Divorce, Probate & Court Records from 1870, Land Records from 1844 & Cemetery abstract 1867–1957)
Natchitoches County		**1805**	**Original parish** Natchitoches County; LA **Details:** County Terminated 1845
Natchitoches Parish www.rootsweb.com/~lanatchi/index.htm	**G3**	**10 Apr 1805**	**Original parish** Natchitoches Parish County; PO Box 799; Natchitoches, LA 71458-0799; Ph. (318) 352-2714 **Details:** (Clerk Court has Marriage Records from 1780, Divorce, Probate & Court Records)
Opelousas County		**1805**	**Original county** Opelousas County; LA. **Details:** County Terminated in 1845 (see St. Landry) St. Landry formed from Opelousas Co 31 Mar 1807
Orleans County		**1805**	**Original parish** Orleans County; LA **Details:** County Terminated 1845
Orleans Parish **K10** www.nocitycouncil.com/content/		**1807**	**Original parish** Orleans Parish County; 1300 Perdido St; New Orleans, LA 70112; Ph. (504) 568-5152 **Details:** (Clerk Civic District Court has Divorce, Probate & Court Records from 1805; Register of Conveyances has Land Records from 1832; Public Library has voter registration Records 1895–1941, city directories from 1805 & precinct Books 1895–1952)
Ouachita County		**1805**	**Original parish** Ouachita County; LA **Details:** County Terminated 1845

County Website	Map Index	Date Created	Parent County or Territory From Which Organized Address/Details
Ouachita Parish www.bayou.com/~suelynn/ouachita.html	E5	1807	**Original parish** Ouachita Parish County; 300 St John St; Monroe, LA 71201; Ph. (318) 327-1444 **Details:** (Parish Clerk has Marriage Records from 1800's, Divorce, Court & Probate Records from 1900, Land Records from 1790's & some Military Records)
Plaquemines Parish www.rootsweb.com/~laplaque/laplaque.htm	M11	31 Mar 1807	**Orleans** Plaquemines Parish County; Hwy 39; Pointe a la Hache, LA 70082-9999; Ph. (504) 333-4343 **Details:** (Parish Clerk has Marriage Records from 1809, Divorce, Probate, Court & Land Records from 1800)
Pointe Coupee County		1805	**Original parish** Pointe Coupee County; LA **Details:** County Terminated 1845
Pointe Coupee Parish www.pcpolicejury.org/	J6	1807	**Original parish** Pointe Coupee Parish County; 160 E Main St; New Roads, LA 70760; Ph. (225) 638-9596 **Details:** (Clerk Court has Marriage Records from 1735, Divorce Records from 1800, Probate, Court & Land Records from 1780)
Rapides County		1805	**Original parish** Rapides County; LA **Details:** County Terminated 1845
Rapides Parish www.rapidesclerk.org	H4	1807	**Original parish** Rapides Parish; 701 Murray St; PO Box 952; Alexandria, LA 71301; Ph. (318) 473-8153 **Details:** (District Clerk of Court has Probate, Civil, Criminal, Land, Mortgage, Charter, Plat, Marriage, & Adoption Records)
Red River Parish www.rootsweb.com/~laredriv/index.htm	F2	2 Mar 1871	**Caddo, Bienville, Bossier, DeSoto, Natchitoches** Red River Parish County; 615 E Carroll St; Coushatta, LA 71019; Ph. (318) 932-6741 **Details:** (Clerk Court has Marriage & Probate Records from 1871, Divorce & Court Records from 1904)
Richland Parish www.rootsweb.com/~larichla/home.html	E6	29 Sep 1868	**Ouachita, Carroll, Franklin, Morehouse** Richland Parish County; 108 Courthouse Sq; PO Box 119; Rayville, LA 71269; Ph. (318) 728-4171 **Details:** (Parish Clerk has Marriage, Divorce, Probate, Court & Land Records from 1869)
Sabine Parish www.pastracks.com/states/louisiana/sabine/	G2	7 Mar 1843	**Natchitoches** Sabine Parish County; 400 Court St; PO Box 419; Many, LA 71449-0419; Ph. (318) 256-6223 **Details:** (Parish Clerk has Marriage, Divorce, Land, Probate & Court Records from 1843)

County Website	Map Index	Date Created	Parent County or Territory From Which Organized Address/Details
St. Bernard Parish www.st-bernard.la.us/	L10	31 Mar 1807	**Original parish** St. Bernard Parish County; 8201 W Judge Perez Dr; Chalmette, LA 70043; Ph. (504) 278-1500 **Details:** (Clerk Court has Marriage, Probate, Court & Land Records)
St. Charles Parish www.st-charles.la.us/	L9	31 Mar 1807	**German Coast** St. Charles Parish County; PO Box 302; Hahnville, LA 70057-0302; Ph. (985) 783-6632 **Details:** (Parish Clerk has Marriage, Probate, Land & Court Records)
St. Helena Parish www.rootsweb.com/~lasthele/index.htm	I8	27 Oct 1810	**Spanish West Florida** St. Helena Parish County; Court Sq; Greensburg, LA 70441; Ph. (225) 222-4521 **Details:** (Parish Clerk has Records from 1804)
St. James Parish www.stjamesla.com/	L8	31 Mar 1807	**Original parish** St. James Parish County; River Rd, PO Box 106; Convent, LA 70723; Ph. (225) 562-7497 **Details:** (Parish Clerk has Marriage Records from 1846, Divorce, Probate & Court Records from 1809)
St. John the Baptist Parish www.stjohnclerk.org	K9	31 Mar 1807	**German Coast** St. John the Baptist Parish County; 2393 Hwy 18; P.O. Box 280; Edgard, LA 70049; Ph. (985) 497-3331 eliana@bellsouth.net **Details:** (Parish Clerk has Court Records from 1921, Land Records from 1799, Marriage Records from 1802, Military Records from 1954, Probate Records from 1853, & Tax Rolls from 1850, Divorce, & Guardianship Records)
St. Landry Parish www.slpolicejury.org/	J5	31 Mar 1807	**Opelousas** St. Landry Parish County; Court & Landry St; Opelousas, LA 70570; Ph. (337) 942-5606 **Details:** (Parish Clerk has Marriage Records from 1808, Divorce & Court Records from 1813 & Probate Records from 1809)
St. Martin Parish www.intersurf.com/~johnjanr/stmartin.htm	L7	1807	**Attakapas** St. Martin Parish County; County Courthouse; PO Box 9; Saint Martinville, LA 70582; Ph. (337) 332-4136 **Details:** (Parish Clerk has Marriage, Probate, Court & Land Records)
St. Mary Parish www.parish.st-mary.la.us/	L7	17 Apr 1811	**Attakapas** St. Mary Parish County; 101 Wilson St; Franklin, LA 70538; Ph. (337) 828-4238 **Details:** (Parish Clerk has Marriage, Divorce, Probate, Court & Land Records from 1800)

County Website	Map Index	Date Created	Parent County or Territory From Which Organized Address/Details
St. Tammany Parish www.rootsweb.com/~lasttamm/sttammany.htm	J10	27 Oct 1810	**Spanish West Florida** St. Tammany Parish County; 701 N Columbia St.; PO Box 1090; Covington, LA 70434; Ph. (985) 809-8745 **Details:** (Parish Clerk has Marriage, Divorce, Probate & Court Records from 1812, Land Records from 1810, tax Records from 1880 & Military Discharge Records)
Tangipahoa Parish www.tangicouncil.com/	J9	6 Mar 1869	**Livingston, St. Tammany, St. Helena, Washington** Tangipahoa Parish County; 110 N Bay St; PO Box 667; Amite, LA 70422-0215; Ph. (985) 748-8015 **Details:** (Parish Clerk has Marriage, Divorce, Probate, Court & Land Records from 1869)
Tensas Parish www.rootsweb.com/~latensas/index.html	F7	17 Mar 1843	**Concordia** Tensas Parish County; Courthouse Sq; PO Box 78; Saint Joseph, LA 71366; Ph. (318) 766-3921 **Details:** (Parish Clerk has Marriage, Divorce, Probate & Court Records from 1843)
Terrebonne Parish	M8	22 Mar 1822	**Lafourche** Terrebonne Parish County; PO Box 1569; Houma, LA 70360; Ph. (985) 868-5660 **Details:** (Parish Licensing Department has Marriage & Birth Records; State Vital Records has Death Records; Conveyance Office has Military Records; Civil Department has Divorce & Probate Records; Mortgage Office has Tax Records)
Union Parish www.pastracks.com/states/louisiana/union/	D4	13 Mar 1839	**Ouachita** Union Parish County; Courthouse Bldg; 100 E Bayou St; Farmerville, LA 71241; Ph. (318) 368-3055 **Details:** (Parish Clerk has Marriage, Divorce & Probate Records from 1839 & Court Records)
Vermilion Parish www.vermilion.org/	L5	25 Mar 1844	**Lafayette** Vermilion Parish County; 100 N State St; PO Box 790; Abbeville, LA 70510; Ph. (337) 898-1992 **Details:** (Parish Clerk has Marriage, Divorce, Probate, Court & Land Records from 1885)
Vernon Parish www.rootsweb.com/~lavernon/vernon.htm	H3	30 Mar 1871	**Natchitoches, Rapides, Sabine** Vernon Parish County; 201 S 3rd St; PO Box 40; Leesville, LA 71496-0040; Ph. (337) 238-1384 **Details:** (Parish Clerk has Marriage Records from 1890, Divorce, Probate & Court Records from 1871)
Warren Parish		1811	**Concordia County** Warren Parish; LA **Details:** County Terminated 1814
Washington Parish www.rootsweb.com/~lawashin/	I10	6 Mar 1819	**St. Tammany** Washington Parish County; Courthouse; Franklinton, LA 70438; Ph. (985) 839-4663 **Details:** (Parish Clerk has Marriage, Divorce, Probate, Court & Land Records from 1897)

County Website	Map Index	Date Created	Parent County or Territory From Which Organized Address/Details
Webster Parish www.rootsweb.com/~lawebste/webster.html	D3	27 Feb 1871	**Claiborne, Bienville, Bossier** Webster Parish County; 410 Main St; PO Box 370; Minden, LA 71058-0370; Ph. (318) 371-0366 **Details:** (Parish Clerk has Marriage, Divorce, Probate, Court & Land Records from 1871)
West Baton Rouge Parish www.wbrcouncil.org/	J7	31 Mar 1807	**Pointe Coupee** West Baton Rouge Parish County; PO Box 107; Port Allen, LA 70767-0757; Ph. (225) 383-0378 **Details:** (Formerly Baton Rouge until 1912) (Clerk Court has Birth, Marriage, Probate & Land Records)
West Carrol Parish			**1877 Carroll** West Carroll Parish; LA
West Feliciana Parish www.segenealogy.com/louisiana/la_county/wf.htm	I7	17 Feb 1824	**Feliciana** West Feliciana Parish County; 4789 Prosperity St; PO Box 1845; Saint Francisville, LA 70775; Ph. (225) 635-3794 **Details:** (Parish Clerk has Divorce, Probate, & Court Records from 1900, Marriage Records from 1879, & Land Records from 1811)
Winn Parish www.rootsweb.com/~lawinn/	F4	24 Feb 1852	**Natchitoches, Catahoula, Rapides** Winn Parish County; PO Box 951; Winnfield, LA 71483-0951; Ph. (318) 628-3515 **Details:** (Parish Clerk has Marriage, Divorce, Probate, Court & Land Records from 1886)

Maine

Capital: Augusta
State: 1820 (23rd)

I direct

Vikings and other explorers may have sighted the coast of Maine as early as 1000 AD. The first explorers known to have definitely explored this coast were John and Sebastian Cabot in 1498. When they arrived, the area was populated by Algonquin Indians, including the Abnaki, Penobscot, and Passamaquoddy. Over the next century, English, Portuguese, French, and Spanish expeditions visited the area. Attempts at settlement were made between 1607 and 1625, but all proved unsuccessful. In 1625, the English made the first permanent settlement at Permaquid. Other settlements followed rapidly including York, Saco, Biddeford, Cape Elizabeth, Falmouth (present-day Portland), and Scarboro. Two members of the Plymouth Colony, Sir Ferdinando Gorges and Captain John Mason, were granted the land between the Merrimack and Kennebec rivers in 1622. In 1629, they divided their lands, with Gorges taking the present state of Maine and Mason taking New Hampshire. France likewise claimed the area. Indians sided with the French, which resulted in the French and Indian Wars from about 1632 until 1759.

Massachusetts purchased the province of Maine from Gorges' heirs in 1677 and set up a government in the area. After the death of King Charles in 1685, Massachusetts lost all of its legal standings, forcing landholders to re-secure their land at high fees. These land titles were recorded in Boston; Maine also kept a special land office at York. The area was called the Province of Maine of the Massachusetts Bay Colony until 1779, when it became the District of Maine. Following the Revolution, in which Maine suffered more damage than any other New England area, settlement increased rapidly. The biggest deterrent to settlement was the difficulty of travel in the area, as roads were extremely poor. During the War of 1812, the British captured several Maine cities and the eastern part of Maine came under British control. Desires for separation from Massachusetts intensified, which resulted in statehood as part of the Missouri Compromise of 1820.

The Aroostook War in the 1830's brought approximately 10,000 troops into the area in 1838–1839, but no actual fighting occurred. The War ended in 1842 when a treaty settled the boundary between Maine and New Brunswick. During the Civil War, Maine supplied over 70,000 men to the Union armies. Early settlers were mainly English, Scotch-Irish, and Huguenots. From 1740 to 1800, some German families came to Waldoboro. About 15 percent of the current population descends from two early French groups. The Acadians came from Nova Scotia to the Saint John Valley after 1763 and French Canadians came from Quebec after the Civil War. Artisans from England, Scotland, and Scandinavia came to work in factories and shipyards during the nineteenth century. About 1870, a large number of Swedes settled in the northeast corner of Maine, organizing such cities as New Sweden, Stockholm, Jemtland, and Linneus.

Look for vital records in the following locations:

- **Birth, deaths and marriages:** Very early in their history, Maine towns began keeping records of births, deaths, and marriages. This continued until state registration began in 1892. Selectmen or town clerks kept these records. Many of these records have been printed, while the remainders are available for searching in city offices. State records are kept at the Office of Vital Statistics Department of Human Services, State House in Augusta, Maine.

- **Histories:** Town histories have also been published for the large majority of Maine cities and usually contain genealogical information about early settlers.

- **Adoption records:** Adoption decrees are at the Probate or Superior Court where the adoption was granted. They are sealed after 8 August 1953.

- **Land records:** Land records are in the 16 offices of court clerks. The 16 registrars of probate have settlements of estates.

- **Military records:** War service records, including grave registrations, are at the office of the Adjutant General in

Augusta. Since Maine was part of Massachusetts until 1820, soldiers might be listed with Massachusetts' military records. Lists of many pension and bounty records have also been published.

- **Census records:** In 1827, a state census was taken. Returns exist for only a few areas, including Portland, Bangor, and some unincorporated areas. These returns are available at the Maine State Archives. The returns for Eliot are at the Maine Historical Society, 435 Congress Street, Portland, Maine 04101.

Office of Vital Records Maine
Department of Human Services
221 State Street
#11 State House Station
Augusta, ME 04333-0011
(207) 287-3181
www.maine.gov/portal/facts_history/ vital_records.html

Maine State Archives
84 State House
Augusta, ME 04333-0084
(207) 287-5795
www.state.me.us/sos/arc/

Maine Historical Society
489 Congress Street
Portland, ME 04101
(207) 774-1822

Societies and Repositories

Acton-Shapleigh Historical Society; PO Box 545; Acton, ME 04001-0545; www.actonmaine.com/histscty/histscty.htm.

Albion Historical Society; PO Box 68; Albion, ME 04910; terri@albionmaine.org; www.albionmaine.org.

Allagash Historical Society; Allagash, ME; http://aroostook.me.us/allagash/historical.html.

Androscoggin Historical Society; Court Street Door; County Building; Auburn, ME 04210-5978; www.rootsweb.com/~meandrhs.

Bath Historical Society; Sagadahoc History and Genealogical Rm.; 33 Summer St.; Bath, ME 04530-2687.

Bethel Historical Society; PO Box 12; Bethel, ME 04217; info@bethelhistorical.org; www.bethelhistorical.org.

Boothbay Region Historical Society; 72 Oak Street; PO Box 272; Boothbay Harbor, ME 04538-0272; (207) 633-0820; brhs@gwi.net; www.boothbayhistorical.org/index.htm.

Bridgton Historical Society; PO Box 44; Bridgton, ME 04009; bhs@megalink.net; www.megalink.net/~bhs/index.html.

Camden Historical Society; 80 Mechanic St.; Camden, ME 04843.

Camden-Rockport Historical Society; PO Box 747; Rockport, ME 04856; http://members.mint.net/chmuseum.

Cherryfield-Narraguagus Historical Society; 7 Main St.; PO Box 96; Cherryfield, ME 04622; (207) 546-7979.

Cushing Historical Society, Inc.; PO Box 110; Cushing, ME 04563; www.rootsweb.com/~usgenweb/me/knox/cushing.htm.

Dexter Historical Society; PO Box 481; Dexter, ME 04930; dexhist@ctel.net; www.dextermaine.org/museum/index.html.

Falmouth Historical Society; Falmouth Memorial Library; 5 Lunt Road; Falmouth, ME 04105; www.falmouth.lib.me.us/historical.html.

Finn-Am Society of Mid-Coast Maine; PO Box 488; Warren, ME 04864.

Finnish American Heritage Society of Maine; PO Box 294; West Paris, ME 04289.

Gorham Historical Society; 28 School Street; Gorham, ME 04038; ghs@gorhamcu.com; www.gorhamcu.com/ghs/home.html.

Gray Historical Society; PO Box 544; Gray, ME 04039; cnlknapp@msn.com; www.graymaine.org/history.htm.

Hancock Genealogical Society; PO Box 243; Bass Harbor, ME 04653; http://ellsworthme.org/hcgs.

Hiram Historical Society; 158 Sebago Road; Hiram, ME 04041; (207) 625-4663; hammond@cybertours.com; www.rootsweb.com/~mechiram.

Kennebeck Historical Society; PO Box 5582; Augusta, ME 04332-5582; webmaster@kennebechistorical.org; www.kennebechistorical.org.

Maine Genealogical Society; PO Box 221; Farmington, ME 04938.

Maine Historical Society; 489 Congress St.; Portland, ME 04111; info@mainehistory.org; www.mainehistory.org.

Maine Mayflower Society; PO Box 622; Yarmouth, ME 04096-1164; rthivier@blazenetme.net.

Maine State Archives; 84 State House Station; Augusta, ME 04333-0084; www.state.me.us/sos/arc.

Maine State Library; 64 State House Station; Augusta, ME 04333-0064; (207) 287-5600; msl.webmaster@maine.gov; www.state.me.us/msl.

Milo Historical Society; 12 High Street; Milo, ME 04463; (207) 943-2268; milohist@kynd.com; www.kynd.com/~milohist.

Mount Desert Island Historical Society; PO Box 653; Mount Desert, ME 04660; mdihistory@downeast.net; http://ellsworthme.org/mdihsociety.

Oakland Area Historical Society; Macartney House Museum; Main Street; Oakland, ME ; (207) 465-7549; www.rootsweb.com/~mecoakla.

Old Broad Bay Family History Association; PO Box 1242; Waldoboro, ME 04572; www.rootsweb.com/~meobbfha.

Old York Historical Society; PO Box 312; 207 York Street; York, ME 03909; www.oldyork.org.

Otisfield Historical Society; c/o Ethel Turner; 105 Cape Road; Otisfield, ME 04270; (207) 539-2521; www.rootsweb.com/~mecotisf/otis8.htm.

Pejepscot Chapter Maine Genealogical Society; 35 Grove St; Lisbon Falls, ME 04252-1328.

Pejepscot Historical Society; 159 Park Row; Brunswick, ME 04011; dasmith@gwi.net; www.curtislibrary.com/pejepscot.htm.

Piscataqua Pioneers; 38 Mendum Avenue; Kittery, ME 03904.

Scarborough Historical Society; PO Box 156; Scarborough, ME 04070-0156; www.scarboroughmaine.com/historical.

Sons of the American Revolution, Maine Society; Thing's Corner; PO Box 67; Limerick, ME 04048.

Sullivan & Sorrento Historical Society; PO Box 44; Sullivan, ME 04664; hlm@downeast.net; http://ellsworthme.org/sshs.

The Arnold Expedition Historical Society; RR 4, Box 6895; Gardiner, ME 04345-9112; daniel.h.warren.jr@state.me.us; www.rootsweb.com/~aehs/aehs.htm.

The Kennebunkport Historical Society; PO Box 1173; Kennebunkport, ME 04046; KportHS@gwi.net; www.kporthistory.org.

The Sandy River Valley Chapter of the Maine Genealogical Society; Farmington Public Library; 117 Academy Street; Farmington, ME 04938; www.rootsweb.com/~mesrvmgs.

The Society of Colonial Wars in the State of Maine; ME; egarrett@acadia.net; www.acadia.net/sotcw.

The Thomaston Historical Society; PO Box 384; Thomaston, ME 04861; www.mint.net/thomastonhistoricalsociety.

Union Historical Society; PO Box 154; Union, ME 04862; www.midcoast.com/comespring.

Vinalhaven Historical Society; PO Box 339; Vinalhaven, ME 04863; vhhissoc@midcoast.com; www.midcoast.com/~vhhissoc/home.html.

Washington Co. Genealogical Society; RR 1, Box 28 Shore Rd.; Perry, ME 04667.

Windham, Maine Historical Society; Windham, ME; mainegen@aol.com; www.rootsweb.com/~mewhs.

Woolwich Historical Society; PO Box 98; Woolwich, ME 04579; www.woolwichhistory.org.

Bibliography and Record Sources

General

American Historical Association. *Annual Report of the American Historical Association for the Year 1908.* Washington, D.C.: Government Printing Office, 1909.

Anderson, Joseph C., II. *Maine Families in 1790, Volume 5.* 1996.

Banks, Ronald F. *Maine Becomes A State: The Movement To Separate Maine From Massachusetts, 1785–1820.* Middletown, Connecticut: Published for the Maine Historical Society by Wesleyan University Press, 1970.

Bibliography of the State of Maine. 2 vols. (1896) Reprint. Rockport, Maine: Picton Press, 1985.

Burrage, Henry Sweetser. *Genealogical and Family History of the State of Maine.* 4 vols. New York: Lewis Historical Publishing Company, 1909.

Chase, Henry. *Representative Men of Maine: A Collection of Portraits with Biographical Sketches of Residents of the State, Who Have Achieved Success...to Which Is Added the Portraits and Sketches of All the Governors Since the Formation of the State. . . .* Portland, Maine: Lakeside Press, 1893.

Coe, Harriet B. *Maine Biographies. Excerpted from Maine Resources, Attractions, and Its People: A History.* Baltimore, Maryland: Clearfield Co., Inc., 2002.

Committee for a New England Bibliography. *Maine, A Bibliography of Its History.* Boston: G. K. Hall, 1977.

Crandall, Ralph J., ed. *Genealogical Research in New England.* Baltimore: Genealogical Publishing Co., 1984.

Cutter, William Richard. *New England Families: Genealogical and Memorial.* 4 vols. New York: Lewis Historical Publishing, 1914.

Daughters of the American Revolution (Maine). *Genealogical and Miscellaneous Records Collected 1925–1972.* Microfilm of typescript material at the D.A.R. Library in Washington, D.C. Salt Lake City: Genealogical Society of Utah, 1971–1972. 18 microfilm.

Daughters of the American Revolution. Frances Scott Chapter (District of Columbia). *Maine Records.* Salt Lake City: Genealogical Society of Utah, 1958.

Davis, Walter Goodwin. *Massachusetts and Maine Families.* Baltimore: Genealogical Pub. Co., 1996.

Directory of Maine Pioneer Ancestors. n.p.

Dormer, Mary H. *Directory Of Maine Pioneer Ancestors.* S.l.: s.n., 198–.

Early New England Settlers, 1600s–1800s. S.l.: Brøderbund, 1999. CD-ROM.

English Origins of New England Families: From the New England Historical and Genealogical Register. Second series, 3 vols. Baltimore: Genealogical Publishing, 1985.

Estes, Marie. *Name Index to Maine Local Histories.* Portland: Maine Historical Society, 1985.

French, W. R. *Record of Marriages, 1841–1893, And Funerals, 1840–1893*. Salt Lake City: Filmed by the Genealogical Society of Utah, 1953.

Frost, John Eldridge. *Maine Genealogy: A Bibliographical Guide*. 1985. Rev. ed. Portland, Maine: Maine Historical Society, 1985.

Genealogies of Maine families. 3 vols. Microfilm of original records at the Maine Historical Society in Portland. Salt Lake City: Filmed by the Genealogical Society of Utah, 1956.

Gorn, Michael H., ed. *An Index and Guide to the Microfilm Edition of the Massachusetts and Maine Direct Tax Census of 1798*. Boston: New England Historic Genealogical Society, 1979.

Gray, Philip Howard. *Penobscot Pioneers*. 4 vols. Camden, Maine: Penobscot Press, 1992–1994.

Greenlaw, William Prescott. *The Greenlaw Index of the New England Historic Genealogical Society*. 2 vols. Boston: G. K. Hall, 1979.

Greenleaf, Jonathan. *Sketches of the Ecclesiastical History of the State of Maine from the Earliest Settlement to the Present Time*. Portsmouth N.H.: H. Gray, 1821.

Hall, Lu Verne V. *New England Family Histories: States of Maine and Rhode Island*. Bowie, Maryland: Heritage Books, 2000.

Haskell, John D., Jr., ed. *Maine: A Bibliography of Its History*. Boston: G. K. Hall, 1977.

Hatch, Louis Clinton, ed. *Maine: A History*. 5 vols. New York: American Historical Society, 1919.

Herdon, Richard, et al. *Men of Progress: Biographical Sketches and Portraits of Leaders in Business and Professional Life in and of the State of Maine*. Boston: New England Magazine, 1897.

Historical Records Survey (Maine). *Directory of Churches and Religious Organizations in Maine*. Portland: Maine Historical Records Survey Project, 1940.

Historical Records Survey (Maine). *Town Government in Maine*. Portland, Maine: The Survey, 1940.

Hodgkins, Theodore Roosevelt. *Brief Biographies, Maine: A Biographical Dictionary of Who's Who in Maine, Vol. 1*. Lewiston, Maine: Lewiston Journal, 1926–1927.

Kohl, J. G. *A History of the Discovery of Maine*. Portland, Maine: Maine Historical Society, 1869.

Lawton, R. J. *Franco-Americans of the State of Maine, U.S.A., And Their Achievements: Historical, Descriptive And Biographical*. Lewiston, Maine: H. F. Roy, 1915.

Lindberg, Marcia Wiswall. *Genealogist's Handbook for New England Research*. 3rd ed. Boston, Massachusetts: New England Historic Genealogical Society, 1993.

Little, George Thomas. *Genealogical and Family History of the State of Maine*. 4 vols. New York: Lewis Historical Publishing, 1909.

Maine & New Hampshire Settlers, 1600s–1900s. S.l.: Brøderbund, 2000. CD-ROM.

Maine Families in 1790. 6 vols. Camden, Maine: Picton Press, 1988–1998.

Maine Research Outline. Series US States, no. 20. Salt Lake City: Family History Library, 1988.

Maine State Archives. *Agencies of State Government, 1820–1971, Parts Land II*. Augusta, Maine: Maine State Archives, n.d.

Maine State Archives. *Public Record Repositories in Maine*. Augusta, Maine: Maine State Archives, n.d.

Massachusetts & Maine Genealogies, 1650s–1930s: From The Genealogical Publishing Co., Inc.. S.l.: Brøderbund, 1998. CD-ROM

Moody, Robert Earle. *The Maine Frontier, 1607 to 1763*. Ann Arbor, Michigan.: University Microfilms, 1980.

Moulton, Augustus F. *Maine Historical Sketches*. Lewiston, Maine: Printed for the State, Lewiston Journal Printshop, 1929.

Noyes, Benjamin Lake. *Vital Records Copied From Town, Churches & Cemeteries Records in Various Towns and Counties of Maine Along the Atlantic Seaboard*. 2 vols. Washington, D.C.: D.A.R. Library.

Noyes, Sybil, Charles T. Libby, and Walter G. Davis. *Genealogical Dictionary of Maine and New Hampshire*. (1928-1939) Reprint. Baltimore: Genealogical Publishing, 1996.

Pioneers of Maine. Microfilm of original records (2v) in the Bangor Public Library. Salt Lake City: Genealogical Society of Utah, 1956.

Piscataqua Pioneers. Applications for Membership, 1908–1990. Salt Lake City: Genealogical Society of Utah, 1978, 1980–1990.

Pope, Charles Henry. *The Pioneers of Maine and New Hampshire, 1623–1660*. (1908). Reprint. Baltimore: Clearfield Co., 1997.

Public Record Repositories In Maine. Augusta, Maine: Maine State Archives, 1976.

Ray, Roger B. *The Indians Of Maine And The Atlantic Provinces: A Bibliographical Guide*. Portland, Maine: Maine Historical Society, 1977.

Rider, Fremont, ed. *American Genealogical-Biographical Index. Vols. 1–186+*. Middletown, Connecticut: Godfrey Memorial Library, 1952–.

Ring, Elizabeth. *[Bibliographical] Reference List of Manuscripts Relating to the History of Maine*. (1938). Reprint. Salem, Massachusetts: Higginson Books, 1992.

Savage, James. *A Genealogical Dictionary of the First Settlers of New England Showing Three Generations of Those Who Came Before May 1692, on the Basis of Farmer's Register*. 4 vols. 1860–1862. Reprint. Baltimore: Genealogical Publishing, Co., 1969.

Sawtelle, William Otis. *Historic Trails and Waterways of Maine*. Augusta, Maine: Maine Development Commission, 1932.

Sewall, R. K. *Ancient Dominions of Maine: Embracing The Earliest Facts . . .* Bowie, Maryland: Heritage Books, 1998.

Spencer, Wilbur D. *Pioneers on Maine Rivers. With Lists to 1651.* (1930) Reprint. Baltimore: Clearfield Co., 1995.

Sylvester, Herbert Milton. *Maine Pioneer Settlements.* 5 vols. Boston, Massachusetts: W. B. Clark, 1909.

Taylor, Alan. *Liberty Men and Great Proprietors: The Revolutionary Settlement on the Maine Frontier, 1760–1820.* Galveston, Texas: Frontier Press, 1990.

United States. Commissioner of Internal Revenue. *Internal Revenue Assessment Lists for Maine, 1862– 1866.* Washington, D.C.: National Archives and Records Service, 1970.

Wedda, John. *New England Worships: 100 Drawings of Churches and Temples with Accompanying Text.* New York: Random House, 1965.

Williamson, Joseph. *A Bibliography of the State of Maine from the Earliest Period to 1891.* 2 vols. Portland, Maine: Thurston Print, 1896.

Wright, Norman Edgar. *Genealogy in America.* Salt Lake City: Deseret Book Co., 1968.

Atlases, Maps and Gazetteers

Atlas of Maine, Detailed Back Roads. Galveston, Texas: Frontier Press, n.d.

Attwood, Stanley Bearce. *The Length and Breadth of Maine.* Orono, Maine: University of Maine, 1977.

Carleton, Osgood. *A Map of the District of Maine.* n.p., n.d. Reprint. Originally published 1793.

Chadbourne, Ava Harrie. *Maine Place Names And The Peopling Of Its Towns.* Portland, Maine: Bond Wheelwright Co., 1955.

Denis, Michael J. *Maine Towns And Counties: What Was What, Where And When.* Oakland, Maine: Danbury House Books, 1981.

Dow, Sterling T. *Maine Postal History and Postmarks.* Lawrence, Massachusetts: Quarterman Publications, 1976.

Eckstorm, Fannie Hardy. *Indian Place Names of the Penobscot Valley and the Maine Coast.* Orono, Maine: University of Maine, 1978.

Greenleaf, Moses. *Map Exhibiting the Principal Original Grants and Sales of Lands in the State of Maine.* Ellsworth, Maine: Ellsworth American, 1977.

Historical Records Survey (Maine). *Counties, Cities, Towns, and Plantations of Maine.* Portland, Maine: The Survey, 1940.

Long, John H., ed. *Connecticut, Maine, Massachusetts, and Rhode Island Atlas of Historical County Boundaries.* New York: Simon & Schuster, 1994.

Maine County Subdivisions, Towns, Plantations, Unorganized Territories, and Places. Washington, D.C.: U.S. Government Printing Office, 1977.

Rutherford, Phillip R. *The Dictionary Of Maine Place-Names.* Freeport, Maine: Bond Wheelwright Co., 1970.

United States Office of Geographic Research. *Maine Geographic Names: Alphabetical Finding List.* Reston, Virginia: U.S. Geological Survey, 1985.

Varney, George J. *A Gazetteer of the State of Maine: With Numerous Illustrations.* Bowie, Maryland: Heritage Books, 1991.

Census Records

Available Census Records and Census Substitutes

Federal Census 1790, 1800, 1810, 1820, 1830, 1840, 1850, 1860, 1870, 1880 1900, 1910, 1920, 1930

Federal Mortality Schedules 1850, 1860, 1870, 1880

Union Veterans and Widows 1890

Federal Assessment 1798

Dollarhide, William. *The Census Book: A Genealogist's Guide to Federal Census Facts, Schedules and Indexes.* Bountiful, Utah: Heritage Quest, 1996.

Gorn, Michael H. *An Index and Guide to the Microfilm Edition of the Massachusetts and Maine Direct Tax Census of 1798.* Boston, Massachusetts: New England Historic Genealogical Society, 1979.

Jackson, Ronald Vern. *Maine 1890 Veterans Census Index.* North Salt Lake, Utah: Accelerated Indexing Systems International, 1990.

Kemp, Thomas Jay. *The American Census Handbook.* Wilmington, Deleware: Scholarly Resources, Inc., 2001.

Lainhart, Ann S. *State Census Records.* Baltimore: Genealogical Publishing, 1992.

Maine Census Indexes, 1850–1870. Salt Lake City: Genealogical Society of Utah, 1953.

Maine Genealogical Society. *1790 Census of Maine.* The Society, 1995.

Pruitt, Betty Hobbs, ed. *The Massachusetts Tax Valuation List of 1771.* Boston: G. K. Hall, 1978.

Szucs, Loretto Dennis, and Matthew Wright. *Finding Answers in U.S. Census Records.* Ancestry Publishing, 2001.

Thorndale, William and William Dollarhide. *County Boundary Map Guide to the U.S. Federal Censuses, 1790–1920.* Bountiful, Utah: AGLL, 1987.

United States. Commissioner of Internal Revenue. *Internal Revenue Assessment Lists for Maine, 1862–1866.* Washington, D.C.: National Archives and Records Service, 1970. 15 microfilms.

United States. Secretary of the Treasury. *Massachusetts and Maine Direct Tax Census of 1798.* Cambridge, Massachusetts: New England Historic Genealogical Society, 1978.

Court Records, Probate and Wills

Anderson, Joseph Crook, II. *York County, Maine Wills Abstracts 1801–1858.* Maine Genealogical Society

Special Publication no. 27. 2 vols. Rockport, Maine: Picton Press, 1997.

Frost, John Eldridge. *Maine Probate Abstracts. Vol. 1, 1687–1775; vol. 2, 1775–1800.* Rockport, Maine: Picton Press, 1991.

Libby, Charles T., Robert E. Moody, and Neal W. Allen, eds. *Province and Court Records of Maine.* 6 vols. Portland, Maine: Maine Historical Society, 1928–1975.

Maine Historical Society (Portland, Maine). *Province And Court Records Of Maine.* 6 vols. Portland, Maine: Maine Historical Society, 1928–1975.

Maine State Archives. *Judicial Records.* Augusta, Maine: Maine State Archives, 2002. http://www.state.me.us/sos/arc/archives/judicial/judicial.htm

National Archives Records Administration. Northeast Region (Boston) *U.S. Circuit Court, 1820–1911. (Before 1820, appeals from the district court in Maine were heard in the United States Circuit Court for the District of Massachusetts.* Record Group 21 Records Of The District Courts Of The United States. Waltham, Massachusetts: National Archives Records Administration, Northeast Region (Boston).

National Archives Records Administration. Northeast Region (Boston). Maine, *U.S. District Court, 1789–1973, Including the Northern Division, Bangor, and the Southern Division, Portland.* Record Group 21 Records of the District Courts of the United States. Waltham, Massachusetts: National Archives Records Administration, Northeast Region (Boston).

Sargent, William M. *Maine Wills, 1640–1760.* 1887. Reprint. Baltimore: Clearfield Co., 1996.

Whittier, David Q. *History Of The Court System Of The State Of Maine.* Augusta, Maine: Maine State Archives 198–.

Emigration, Immigration, Migration and Naturalization

Bolton, Ethel Stanwood. *Immigrants to New England, 1700–1775.* Salem, Massachusetts: Essex Institute, 1931.

Coldham, Peter Wilson. *The Complete Book of Emigrants, 1607–1776, and Emigrants in Bondage, 1614–1775.* [Novato, Calif.]: Brøderbund Software, 1996.

Filby, P. William. *Passenger and Immigration Lists Index.* 15 vols. Detroit: Gale research, 1981–.

United States, Bureau of Customs. *A Supplemental Index to Passenger Lists of Vessels Arriving at Atlantic & Gulf Coast Ports (excluding New York) 1820–1874.* Washington, D.C.: National Archives Records Services, 1960.

United States, Bureau of Customs. *Passenger Lists of Vessels Arriving at Boston, 1820–1891: with index 1848–1891.* Washington, D.C.: National Archives Record Service, 1959–1960.

United States, Immigration and Naturalization Service. *Index to Passenger Lists of Vessels Arriving at Boston, Jan. 1, 1902–Dec. 31, 1920; Passenger Lists of Vessels Arriving at Boston, Aug. 1, 1891–1935; Book indexes to Boston Passenger Lists, 1899–1940, National Archives Microfilm Publications.* Washington, D.C.: National Archives and Records Service, 1944–1945, 1956.

United States. Bureau of Customs. *Copies of Lists of Passengers Arriving at Miscellaneous Ports on the Atlantic and Gulf Coasts and at Ports of the Great Lakes, 1820–1873. National Archives Microfilm Publication.* Washington, D.C.: National Archives, 1964.

United States. Immigration and Naturalization Service. *Book Indexes, Portland, Maine Passenger Lists 1907–1930.* Washington, D.C.: National Archives and Record Service, 1944.

United States. Immigration and Naturalization Service. *Index To New England Naturalization Petitions, 1791–1906.* Washington: National Archives. Central Plains Region, 1983. 117 microfilm.

United States. Immigration and Naturalization Service. *Passenger Lists of Vessels Arriving at Portland, Maine, 1893–1943; Index, 1893–1954.* Washington, D.C.: National Archives and Record Service, 1944, 1986.

United States. Immigration and Naturalization Service. *St. Albans District Manifest Records of Aliens Arriving from Foreign Contiguous Territory: Arrivals at Canadian Border Ports from January 1895 to June 30, 1954: Indexes (Soundex), 1895–1924.* Washington, D.C.: National Archives Records Service, 1986.

Land and Property

Annual Report Of The Land Agent Of The State Of Maine, For The Year Ending Nov. 30, 1885. (1886) Reprint. Salem, Massachusetts: Higginson Books, 1994.

Hone, Wade E. *Land and Property Research in the United States.* Salt Lake City: Ancestry Incorporated, 1997.

House, Charles J. *Names of Soldiers of the American Revolution Who Applied for State Bounty, 1893.* Reprint. Baltimore: Genealogical Publishing Co., 1967.

Maine State Archives. *Black House Papers—A Guide to Certain Microfilmed Land Records.* Augusta, Maine: Maine State Archives, n.d.

Maine State Archives. *Counties, Cities, Town and Plantations of Maine.* Augusta, Maine: Maine State Archives, n.d.

Maine. Land Office. *Record of Deeds of the Land Office of Maine, 1824–1861.* Microfilm of original records at Augusta, Maine. Salt Lake City: Filmed by the Genealogical Society of Utah, 1954. 4 microfilm.

Maine. Land Office. *Revolutionary War Veterans Land Records.* Microfilm of original records at the Dept. of Forestry in Augusta, Maine. Microfilm of original records at the Dept. of Forestry in Augusta, Maine. Salt Lake City: Genealogical Society of Utah, 1954. 12 microfilm.

Massachusetts, Land Agent. *Mass. Deeds, 1794–1860.* Microfilm of original records at Augusta, Maine. Salt Lake City: Genealogical Society of Utah, 1954. 5 microfilm.

York Deeds. 18 vols. First Published in Portland, Maine: John T. Hull, 1887. Various Publishers for next 17 vols. 1887–1910. Encompasses the 1642 to 1737 period.

Military

Annual Report of the Adjutant General of the State of Maine Adjutant General, 1861–1866. 5 vols. in 7. Augusta, Maine: Stevens and Sayward, 1862–1867.

Aroostook War: Historical Sketch and Roster of Commissioned Officers and Enlisted Men. . . . Augusta, Maine: Kennebec Journal Print, 1904.

Daughters of the American Revolution. National Society. *Minority Military Service, Maine, 1775–1783.* Washington, D.C.: National Society, Daughters of the American Revolution, 1990.

Fisher, Carleton E. *Soldiers, Sailors, and Patriots of the Revolutionary War, Maine.* Louisville, Kentucky: National Society of the Sons of the American Revolution, 1982.

Flagg, Charles A. *An Alphabetical Index of Revolutionary Pensioners Living in Maine.* Dover, Maine: Reprint. Baltimore: Genealogical Publishing Co., 1967.

Historical Sketch and Roster of Commissioned Officers and Enlisted Men [in the Aroostook War.] (1904) Reprint. Baltimore: Clearfield Co., 1989.

House, Charles L., comp. *Names of Soldiers of the American Revolution Who Applied for State Bounty under the Resolves of March 17, 1835, March 24, 1836, and March 20, 1838, as Appears of Record in Land Office.* Augusta, Maine, 1893. Reprint. Baltimore: Genealogical Publishing Co., 1967.

Johnson, Daniel F. *The American Civil War: the Service Records of Atlantic Canadians with the State of Maine Volunteers.* 2 vols. Saint John, New Brunswick: D. F. Johnson, 1995.

Jordan, William B., comp. *Maine in the Civil War: A Bibliographical Guide.* Portland, Maine: Maine Historical Society, 1976.

Jordan, William B., Jr. *Red Diamond Regiment: The 17th Maine Infantry, 1862–1865.* Galveston, Texas: Frontier Press, 1995.

Maine State Archives. *Dubros Times: Depositions of Revolutionary War Veterans.* Augusta, Maine: Maine State Archives, n.d.

Maine State Archives. *Military Records and Related Sources.* Augusta, Maine: Maine State Archives, 2000. www.state.me.us/sos/arc/archives/military/military.htm

Maine. Adjunct General. *Annual Report.* Augusta, Maine: state printer, 1862–1867.

Maine. Adjutant General. *Report of the Adjutant General of the State of Maine for the Period of the World War, 1917–1919.* Augusta, Maine: Published under the direction of James W. Hanson, the Adjutant General, 1929.

Maine. Adjutant General. *Roster of Maine in the Military Service of the United States and Allies in the World War, 1917–1919.* 2 vols. Augusta, Maine: Published under the direction of James W. Hanson, the Adjutant General, 1929.

Maine. Adjutant General. *Supplement to the Annual Reports of the Adjutant General of the State of Maine for the Years 1861, '62, '63, '64, '65 and 1866.* Augusta, Maine: Stevens & Sayward, 1867.

Society of Colonial Wars. *Register of the Officers and Members of the Society of the Colonial Wars in the State of Maine: also History, Roster and Record of Colonel Jedidiah Preble's Regiment. Campaign of 1758: Together with Capt. Samuel Cobb's Journal.* Portland, Oregon: Marks Printing House, 1905.

United States. Adjutant General's Office. *General Index to Compiled Military Service Records of Revolutionary War Soldiers.* Washington, D.C.: National Archives, 1942.

United States. Adjutant General's Office. *General Index to Compiled Service Records of Volunteer Soldiers Who Served During the War with Spain.* Washington, D.C.: National Archives, 1971.

United States. Adjutant General's Office. *Index to Compiled Service Records of Volunteer Soldiers who Served during the War of 1812.* Washington, D.C.: National Archives, 1965.

United States. Adjutant General's Office. *Index to Compiled Service Records of Volunteer Union Soldiers Who Served in Organizations from the State of Maine.* Washington, D.C.: National Archives, 1964.

United States. Selective Service System. Maine. *World War I Selective Service System Draft Registration Cards, 1917–1918.* Washington, D.C.: National Archives, 1987–1988.

United States. Veterans Administration. *Index to War of 1812 Pension Application Files.* Washington, D.C.: National Archives, 1960.

United States. Veterans Administration. *Registers Of Veterans At The National Home For Disabled Volunteer Soldiers, Eastern Branch In Togus, Maine, 1866–1934.* Microfilm of original records at the National Archives in Washington, D.C. Salt Lake City: Genealogical Society of Utah, 1988. 18 microfilm.

United States. Veterans Administration. *Revolutionary War Pension and Bounty-Land-Warrant Application Files.* Washington, D.C.: National Archives, 1969.

United States. Veterans Administration. *Selected Records from Revolutionary War Pension & Bounty-Land-Warrant Application Files.* Washington, D.C.: National Archives, 1969.

White, Virgil D. *Genealogical Abstracts of the Revolutionary War Pension Files.* 4 vols. Waynesboro, Tennessee: National Historical Publishing, 1990.

White, Virgil D. *Index to Revolutionary War Service Records.* 4 vols. Waynesboro, Tennessee: National Historical Publishing, 1995.

White, Virgil D. *Index to War of 1812 Pension Files.* 2 vols. Waynesboro, Tennessee: National Historical Publishing Co., 1992.

Whitman, William E. S., and Charles H. True. *Maine in the War for the Union.* Lewiston, Maine: Nelson Dingley, Jr., 1865.

Vital and Cemetery Records

Daughters of the American Revolution (Massachusetts). *Grave Locations of Revolutionary Soldiers and Sailors of Maine and Massachusetts.* Salt Lake City: Genealogical Society of Utah, 1991.

Frost, John. *Guide to Maine Vital Records in Transcript.* n.p., 1963.

Maine Division of Vital Statistics. *Index to Vital Records, 1892–1907.* Microfilm of original records in the State Board of Health, Division of Vital Statistics, Augusta, Maine. Salt Lake City: Genealogical Society of Utah, 1954. 184 microfilm.

Maine Old Cemetery Association. *MOCA Revolutionary War Soldiers: Burial Places.* [n.p.], 1987.

Maine Old Cemetery Association. *MOCA Revolutionary War Soldiers.* [n.p.], 1986.

Maine Old Cemetery Association. *MOCA Revolutionary War Soldiers: Birthplaces.* [n.p.], 1987.

Maine State Archives. *Cemetery Index of Veterans.* Photographic Science Corporation. 1975. 11 microfilm.

Maine State Archives. *Maine Town Microfilm List: Town and Vital Records, and Census Reports.* Augusta, Maine: Maine State Archives, n.d.

Maine State Archives. *Delayed Return for Births, Deaths, and Marriages, ca. 1670–1891.* Microfilm of original records in the Maine State Archives. Salt Lake City: Genealogical Society of Utah, 1954. 109 microfilm.

Maine State Archives. *Index to Maine Deaths, 1960–1996.* Augusta, Maine: Maine State Archives, 2002. online database www.state.me.us/sos/arc/geneology/homepage.html

Maine State Archives. *Index to Maine Marriages, 1892–1966, 1976–1996.* Augusta, Maine: Maine State Archive, 2002. online database—www.state.me.us/sos/arc/geneology/homepage.html.

Maine State Archives. *Veterans Cemetery Records.* Microfilm. Photographic Science Corporation, 1975. 15 microfilm.

Maine State Archives. *Vital Records (Births, Marriages, Deaths) before 1892.* Augusta, Maine: Maine State Archives, 2002. Online database—www.state.me.us/sos/arc/geneology/homepage.html.

Maine State Archives. *Vital Records from 1892–1922.* Augusta, Maine: Maine State Archives, 2002. Online database—www.state.me.us/sos/arc/geneology/homepage.html.

Maine State Archives. *Vital Records, 1923– Present.* Augusta, Maine: Maine State Archives, 2002. Online database—www.state.me.us/sos/arc/geneology/homepage.html.

Maine. Division of Vital Statistics. *Deaths of World War II Veterans of Maine.* Microfilm of original records at Augusta, Maine. Salt Lake City: Genealogical Society of Utah, 1954.

Maine. Division of Vital Statistics. *Index to Vital Records Prior to 1892 of. . .Eighty Towns.* Microfilm of original records in the State Board of Health, Division of Vital Statistics, Augusta, Maine. Salt Lake City: Genealogical Society of Utah, 1953. 141 microfilm.

Maine. Division of Vital Statistics. *Index to Vital Records, 1908–1922.* Microfilm of original records in the State Board of Health, Division of Vital Statistics, Augusta, Maine. Salt Lake City: Genealogical Society of Utah, 1954. 148 microfilm.

Maine. Division of Vital Statistics. *Index to Vital Records: Bride Index to Marriages, 1895–1953.* Microfilm of original records in the State Board of Health, Division of Vital Statistics, Augusta, Maine. Salt Lake City: Genealogical Society of Utah, 1954. 111 microfilm.

MOCA Cemetery Inscription Project (MIP): Series One. Bangor, Maine: Northeast Reprographics, 198–

Nathan Hale Cemetery Collection, Surname Index, Series 2. Microfilm of original record in the Maine State Library, Augusta, Maine. Salt Lake City: Filmed by the Genealogical Society of Utah, 1982. Microfilm, 17 rolls.

Nathan Hale Cemetery Collection, Surname Index. Microfilm of original record in the Maine State Library, Augusta, Maine. Salt Lake City: Filmed by the Genealogical Society of Utah, 1982. Microfilm, 210 rolls.

Noyes, Benjamin L. *Vital Records Copied from Town, Church, and Cemetery Records in Various Towns and Counties of Maine Along the Atlantic Coast.* Salt Lake City; Genealogical Society of Utah, 1971. 2 microfilm.

Rohrbach, Lewis Bunker, ed. *Maine Marriages 1892–1966: A Complete List.* Rockport, Maine: Picton Press. 1996. CD-ROM.

The Maine Historical and Genealogical Recorder, 9 vols. Portland, Oregon: S. M. Watson, 1884–1898.

Torrey, Clarence Almon. *New England Marriages Prior to 1700.* Baltimore: Genealogical Publishing Company, ca. 1985.

Townsend, Charles D., ed., *Cemetery Inscriptions and Odd Information of Various Town in the State of Maine: In the Counties of Lincoln, Oxford, Penobscot, Somerset, Waldo.* Sarasota, Florida: Aceto Bookmen, 1995.

Trickey, Katherine W. *Maine Old Cemetery Association Cemetery Inscription Project: Series One, Two and*

Three. Bangor, Maine: Northeast Reprographics, 1982, 1987.

Young, David C., and Elizabeth Keene Young. *Vital Records from Maine Newspapers 1785–1820.* 2 vols. Bowie, Maryland: Heritage Books, 1993.

County Website	Map Index	Date Created	Parent County or Territory From Which Organized / Address/Details
Androscoggin www.rootsweb.com/~meandros/	M4	18 Mar 1854	**Cumberland, Oxford, Kennebec, Lincoln** Androscoggin County; 2 Turner; Auburn, ME 04210; Ph. (207) 784-8390 **Details:** (Clerk Superior Court has Divorce & Court Records from 1854; City Clerk has Birth, Marriage, Death & Burial Records; Register of Probate has Probate Records; Register of Deeds has land Records) Towns Organized Before 1800: Durham 1789, Greene 1788, Lewiston 1795, Lisbon 1799, Livermore 1795, Turner 1786
Aroostook www.aroostook.me.us/	D8	16 Mar 1839	**Washington, Penobscot** Aroostook County; County Courthouse; 144 Swenden St; Caribou, ME 04736; Ph. (207) 493-3318 **Details:** (County Clerk has Divorce & Court Records from 1839; Town Clerks have Birth, Marriage, Death & Burial Records; Probate Court has Probate Records; Register of Deeds has land Records)
Cumberland www.cumberlandcounty.org/	N3	28 May 1760	**York** Cumberland County; 142 Federal St; Portland, ME 04101-4151; Ph. (207) 871-8380 **Details:** (County Clerk has Death, Probate & land Records from 1760; City or Town Clerks have Birth, Marriage, Death & Burial Records) Towns Organized Before 1800: Bridgton 1794, Brunswick 1739, Cape Elizabeth 1765, Falmouth 1718, Freeport 1789, Gorham 1764, Gray 1778, Harpswell 1758, New Gloucester 1774
Devonshire		1673	**Cornwall County NY** Devonshire; ME **Details:** County Terminated 1674 (Unnamed until 1674)
Franklin www.rootsweb.com/~mefrankl/start.htm	J3	20 Mar 1838	**Kennebec, Oxford, Somerset** Franklin County; 140 Main St; Farmington, ME 04938; Ph. (207) 778-6614 **Details:** (Town Clerk has Birth, Marriage, & Death Records; Clerk of District Court has Divorce Records from 1852; Register of Deeds has Land Records from 1838; Probate Court has Probate Records from 1838) Towns Organized Before 1800: Farmington 1794, Jay 1795, New Sharon 1794

County	Map	Date	Parent County or Territory From Which Organized
Website	Index	Created	Address/Details

Hancock   K9   25 Jun 1789   **Lincoln**
www.co.hancock.me.us/

Hancock County; 50 State St; Ellsworth, ME 04605;
Ph. (207) 667-9542
Details: (Town Clerks have Birth, Marriage & Death Records; Clerk Superior Court has Divorce & Court Records; Probate Office has Probate Records; Register of Deeds has land Records; County Clerk has Marriage Records 1789–1891)
    Towns Organized Before 1800: Bar Harbor 1796, Blue Hill 1789, Bucksport 1792, Castine 1796, Deer Isle 1789, Gouldsboro 1789, Mount Desert 1789, Penobscot 1787, Sedjwick 1789, Sullivan 1789, Trenton 1789

Kennebec   M5   20 Feb 1799   **Lincoln, Cumberland**
www.rootsweb.com/~mekenneb/

Kennebec County; 95 State St; Augusta, ME 04330-5611;
Ph. (207) 622-0971
Details: (Register of Deeds has land Records from 1799; Probate Court has Probate Records from 1799; Town Clerks have Birth, Marriage & Death Records)
    Towns Organized Before 1800: Augusta 1797, Belgrade 1796, China 1796, Clinton 1795, Fayette 1795, Hallowell 1771, Litchfield 1795, Monmouth 1792, Mount Vernon 1792, Pittsdan 1779, Readfield 1791, Sidney 1792, Vassalboro 1771, Wayne 1798, Winslow 1771, Winthrop 1771

Knox   M6   9 Mar 1860   **Lincoln, Waldo**
http://members.aol.com/vsena/knox/
KnoxGenWeb.html

Knox County; 62 Union St, PO Box 885; Rockland, ME 04841-0885;
Ph. (207) 594-9379
Details: (Town Clerks have Birth, Marriage & Death Records; Clerk Superior Court has Divorce & Court Records; Probate Court has Probate Records from 1860; Register of Deeds has land Records from 1860)
    Towns Organized Before 1800: Camden 1791, Cushing 1789, Thomaston 1777, Union 1786, Vinalhaven 1789, Warren 1776

Lincoln   N5   28 May 1760   **York**
www.rootsweb.com/~melincol/index.htm

Lincoln County; County Courthouse; High St; PO Box 249; Wiscasset, ME 04578-0000; Ph. (207) 882-6311
Details: (Clerk Courts has Marriage, Probate & land Records from 1860 & Court Records from 1861; Clerk Superior Court has Probate Records from 1760)
    Towns Organized Before 1800: Alno 1794, Boothbay 1764, Bristol 1765, Dresden 1794, Newcastle 1753, Nobleboro 1788, Waldoboro 1773, Wiscasset 1760

Oxford   L2   4 Mar 1805   **York, Cumberland**
www.rootsweb.com/~meoxford/

Oxford County; 26 Western Ave; PO Box 179; South Paris, ME 04281; Ph. (207) 743-6359
Details: (Town Clerks have Birth, Marriage & Death Records; Clerk Courts has Marriage Records 1877–1897, Divorce & Court Records from 1930, Probate & land Records from 1805)
    Towns Organized Before 1800: Bethel 1796, Buckfield 1793, Buxton 1772, Fryeburg 1777, Hartford 1798, Hebron 1792, Norway 1797, Paris 1793, Sumner 1798, Waterford 1797

County Website	Map Index	Date Created	Parent County or Territory From Which Organized Address/Details
Penobscot www.rootsweb.com/~mepenobs/mepenobs.htm	H8	15 Feb 1816	**Hancock** Penobscot County; 97 Hammond St; Bangor, ME 04401; Ph. (207) 942-8535 **Details:** (Clerk Courts has Divorce Records from 1900 & Court Records from 1821; Probate Court has Probate Records; Register of Deeds has land Records) Towns Organized Before 1800: Hampden 1794, Orrington 1788
Piscataquis	F6	23 Mar 1838	**Penobscot, Somerset** Piscataquis County; 159 E. Main St; Dover-Foxcroft, ME 04426; Ph. (207) 564-2431 piscprob@kynd.net **Details:** (Town Clerks have Birth, Marriage & Death Records; Clerk Superior Court has Divorce & Court Records; Probate Court has Probate Records; Register of Deeds has land Records)
Sagadahoc www.rootsweb.com/~mesagada/index.htm	N4	4 Apr 1854	**Lincoln** Sagadahoc County; PO Box 246; Bath, ME 04530-0246; Ph. (207) 443-8200 **Details:** (Town Clerks have Birth, Marriage & Death Records; Clerk District Court has Divorce Records; Clerk Superior Court has Court Records; Register of Probate has Probate Records from 1854; Register of Deeds has land Records from 1854) Towns Organized Before 1800: Bath 1781, Bowdoin 1788, Bowdoinham 1762, Georgetown 1716, Topsham 1764, Woolwich 1759
Somerset www.rootsweb.com/~mesomers/	H4	1 Mar 1809	**Kennebec** Somerset County; Court St; Skowhegan, ME 04976; Ph. (207) 474-9861 **Details:** (Clerk Courts has some Marriage Records from 1800's & Probate Records from 1809) Towns Organized Before 1800: Canaan 1788, Cornville 1798, Fairfield 1788, Norridgewock 1788, Starks 1795
Waldo www.rootsweb.com/~mewaldo/index.htm	L7	7 Feb 1827	**Hancock** Waldo County; 73 Church St; Belfast, ME 04915-1705; Ph. (207) 338-3282 **Details:** (County Clerk has Marriage Records 1828–1887, Divorce & Court Records from 1828; City or Town Clerks have Birth, Marriage, Death & Burial Records; Probate Court has Probate Records; Register of Deeds has land Records) Towns Organized Before 1800: Belfast 1773, Frankfort 1789, Northport 1796, Prospect 1794
Washington www.rootsweb.com/~mewashin/	J10	25 Jun 1789	**Lincoln** Washington County; PO Box 297; Machias, ME 04654-0297; Ph. (207) 255-3127 **Details:** (Town Clerks have Birth, Marriage, Death & Burial Records; Clerk Courts has Divorce & Court Records from 1931, Probate Records from 1785, land Records from 1783 & national Records from 1854; Maine State Archives, Augusta, Maine has Divorce & Court Records before 1931) Towns Organized Before 1800: Addison 1797, Columbia 1796

County	Map	Date	**Parent County or Territory From Which Organized**
Website	Index	Created	Address/Details

York(shire)	P2	**20 Nov 1652**	**Original county**

www.raynorshyn.com/megenweb/york/

Original county

York(shire) County; 45 Kennebank Rd; Alfred, ME 04002;
Ph. (207) 324-1571

Details: (Town Clerks have Birth, Marriage, Death & Burial Records; Clerk Courts has Divorce & Court Records; Register of Probate has Death & Probate Records from 1637; Register of Deeds has land Records from 1636)

Towns Organized Before 1800: Berwick 1713, Biddeford 1718, Cornish 1794, Hollis 1798, Kennebunkport 1653, Kittery 165

Maryland

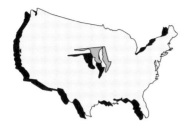

Capital: Annapolis
State: 1788 (7th)

Manly deeds, womanly words

At the time of Giovanni de Verrazano's arrival in 1524, members of the Nanticoke and Piscataway tribes occupied the Maryland woodlands. Verrazano, an Italian navigator who sailed for the French government, became the first European to set foot on Maryland soil. In 1608, Captain John Smith explored the area and made maps of it. The first settlement was on Kent Island, where William Claiborne set up a trading post. Several years later, in 1632, George Calvert and Lord Baltimore secured land from Charles I on both sides of Chesapeake Bay north of Virginia to the 40th parallel. Lord Baltimore, however, died before the charter could be signed. His son, Cecilius Calvert, the second Lord Baltimore, received the grant in his place and began efforts to colonize the area as a haven for persecuted Catholics and those of other religions. The first emigrants left in 1634. There were twenty Catholics and about 200 Protestants. They purchased land from the Indians and settled St. Mary's. The colony experienced great growth, partly due to the passage of the Act Concerning Religion, which outlawed any intolerance of any person professing a belief in Christ. Among the groups attracted by this religious freedom was a large group of Puritans. The Puritans settled Anne Arundel County. Meanwhile, conflicts between Claiborne's group and those controlled by Lord Baltimore led to almost continuous warfare. Not until Claiborne's death in 1677 did hostilities cease.

Settlements during the first century of Maryland's colonization were confined to areas by rivers, streams, and bays. Water provided practically the only efficient means of transportation. Baltimore was founded in 1729. It soon became a major port and commercial center. The Appalachian section of Maryland was not settled until about 1740, when English, Scottish, and Scotch-Irish migrated from St. Mary's, Charles, and Prince George's Counties. Not long afterward, Germans from Pennsylvania also came into the area. The influx of settlers was so great that by 1748 Frederick County was organized in the northwest section of Maryland. Many Acadians driven from Nova Scotia came to Baltimore in 1755. Race riots in Santo Domingo brought about a thousand more French to Baltimore in 1793. Canal diggers from Ireland swelled Baltimore's population between 1817 and 1847. They became farmers and miners in the Appalachians. Baltimore also provided refuge to thousands of Germans who fled their country after the Revolution of 1848.

Maryland adopted a Declaration of Rights in 1776 as well as a state constitution. In 1788, Maryland ratified the Constitution and became the seventh state in the Union. The British ravaged Chesapeake Bay during the War of 1812, but were unable to take Baltimore. Their failed attempt to capture Fort McHenry was the inspiration for Francis Scott Key to write "The Star Spangled Banner." The National Road was completed from Cumberland to Wheeling in 1818. During the Civil War, soldiers from Maryland fought for both sides. More than 46,000 men fought for the Union, while more than 5,000 fought for the Confederacy.

Look for vital records in the following locations:

- **Birth and death records:** Division of Vital Records in Baltimore, Maryland. Civil registration of births and deaths began in 1898, except for Baltimore City, where records began in 1875. Only the individual himself, a parent, or an authorized representative has access to these records if the event occurred within the last 100 years. The Maryland State Archives, Hall of Records in Annapolis, Maryland also has many birth and death records. A few counties have pre-1720 births and deaths in county land records.

- **Marriage records:** The clergy has kept marriage banns and registers since 1640. County clerks have been required to issue marriage licenses since 1777 and to issue ministers' returns since 1865. The circuit court clerk of each county and the State Archives keep these records.

- **Land records:** The earliest land records, 1633–1683, were head rights distributed by the Calvert family. The names of the persons receiving these have been published. Land bounties for military service in the

Revolutionary War and original land records since 1643 are in the Maryland State Archives.

- **Wills:** The county Registrar of Wills kept wills from as early as 1634. They are also available at the State Archives.
- **Census records:** A colonial census was taken in 1776 for most counties. A list of males over 18, who did and did not take oaths of fidelity in 1778, has been published. There are no state census records for Maryland, but there is an 1868 police census for some city wards of Baltimore.

Division of Vital Records

6550 Reisterstown Road
Baltimore, MD 21215
(410) 764-3038
http://mdpublichealth.org.vsa

Maryland State Archives, Hall of Records

350 Rowe Boulevard
Annapolis, MD 21401
(410) 974-3914

Societies and Repositories

Allegany County Historical Society; 219 Washington St.; Cumberland, MD 21502.

American Latvian Association; 400 Hurley Avenue; Rockville, MD 20850-3121; alainfo@alausa.org; www.alausa.org.

Anne Arundel Genealogical Society; PO Box 221; Pasadena, MD 21122.

Baltimore County Genealogical Society, Inc.; PO Box 10085; Towson, MD 21285-0085; www.serve.com/bcgs/bcgs.html.

Baltimore County Historical Society; Agriculture Bldg.; 9811 Van Buren Ln.; Cockeysville, MD 21030.

Calvert County Genealogical Committee Calvert County Historical Society; PO Box 358; Prince Frederick, MD 20678; www.somd.lib.md.us/CALV/cchs.

Calvert County Genealogical Society; PO Box 9; Sunderland, MD 20689.

Captain John Smoot Chapter, SAR; MD ; rjackson@umes-bird.umes.edu; www.intercom.net/user/goldmar/SAR/index.html.

Carroll County Genealogical Society; Box 1752; Westminster, MD 21158; www.carr.lib.md.us/ccgs/ccgs.html.

Catonsville Historical Society, Inc.; PO Box 9311; Catonsville, MD 21228-0311; www.catonsvillehistory.org.

Christian Ardinger, SAR; MD; jrrobinson@aol.com.

Crisfield Heritage Foundation; Somers Cover Marina; Crisfield, MD; www.crisfield.org/Crisfieldheritage.htm.

Dorchester County Historical Society; Meredith House; 902 LaGrange St.; Cambridge, MD 21613; dchs@fastol.com; www.bluecrab.org/dchs/index.html.

Dundalk Patapsco Neck Historical Society; PO Box 9235; Dundalk, MD 21222.

Frederick County Genealogical Society; PO Box 234; Monrovia, MD 21770.

Garrett County Historical Society; PO Box 28; Oakland, MD 21550; www.deepcreektimes.com/gchs.html.

Genealogical Club of the Montgomery County Historical Society; 103W. Montgomery Ave.; Rockville, MD 20850.

Genealogical Society of Allegany County; PO Box 3103; LaVale, MD 21502.

Genealogical Society of Cecil County; Box 11; Charlestown, MD 21914.

Germantown Historical Society; PO Box 475; Germantown, MD 20875; www.clark.net/pub/soderber/ghs.

Governor William Bradford Compact, Descendants of Gov. Wm. Bradford of Plymouth Colony; 5204 Kenwood Ave.; Chevy Chase, MD 20815.

Granite Historical Society; PO Box 43; Granite, MD 21163-0043; granhist@bcpl.net; www.bcpl.net/~granhist.

Harford County Genealogical Society; PO Box 15; Aberdeen, MD 21001; www.rtis.com/reg/md/org/hcgs/default.htm.

Harford County Historical Society; 324 Kenmore Ave.; (The Hayes House); Bel Air, MD 21014; www.rtis.com/reg/md/org/hcgs/default.htm.

Historic Annapolis Foundation; 18 Pinkney Street; Annapolis, MD 21401; alexandb@annapolis.org; www.annapolis.org.

Historical Society of Carroll County, Maryland, Inc.; 210 E. Main St.; Westminster, MD 21157; hscc@carr.org; http://hscc.carr.org.

Historical Society of Cecil County; 135 East Main St.; Elkton, MD 21921; history@cchistory.org; http://cchistory.org.

Historical Society of Frederick County, Inc.; 24 E. Church St.; Frederick, MD 21701; Director@fwp.net; www.fwp.net/hsfc.

Howard County Genealogical Society; Box 274; Columbia, MD 21045-0274; rwbush@att.net; http://users.aol.com/castlewrks/hcgs.

Jewish Genealogical Society of Greater Washington D.C.; PO Box 31122; Bethesda, MD 20824-1122; zakai@aol.com; www.jewishgen.org/jgsgw.

Jewish Historical Society of Maryland; 2707 Moores Valley Dr.; Baltimore, MD 21209; info@jewishmuseummd.org; www.jhsm.org.

Jewish Special Interest Group, Gesher Galicia; 3128 Brooklawn Terrace; Chevy Chase, MD 20815.

Kent County Historical Society; PO Box 665 Church Alley; Chestertown, MD 21620.

Lower Del-Mar, Virginia Genealogical Society; Wicomico County Library; Salisbury, MD 21801.

Maryland Genealogical Society; 201 W Monument St.; Baltimore, MD 21201; president@mdgensoc.org; www.mdgensoc.org.

Maryland Historical Society; 201 W. Monument St.; Baltimore, MD 21201-4674; www.mdhs.org.

Maryland Public Information Network; Sailor Operations Center; 400 Cathedral Street; Baltimore, MD 21201; (410) 396-5551; askus@sailor.lib.md.us; www.sailor.lib.md.us.

Maryland State Archives; 350 Rowe Boulevard; Annapolis, MD 21401; archives@mdarchives.state.md.us; www.mdarchives.state.md.us.

Mid-Atlantic Germanic Society; PO Box 2642; Kensington, MD 20891-2642; www.rootsweb.com/~usmags.

Montgomery County Historical Society; 103 W. Montgomery Ave.; Beall-Dawson House; Rockville, MD 20850; (301) 340-2825; mkharper@montgomeryhistory.org; www.montgomeryhistory.org.

Old Bohemia Historical Society; PO Box 61; Warwick, MD 21912-0061.

Prince George's County Genealogical Society; Box 819; Bowie, MD 20718-0819; http://his.com/~krutar/PGCGS.

Prince George's County, Afro-American Historical and Genealogical Society; PO Box 44722; Ft. Washington, MD 20744-9998.

Prince George's Historical Society; 5626 Bell Station Rd.; Glenn Dale, MD 20769.

Queene Anne's County Historical Society; Wright's Chance; 124 South Commerce St.; Centreville, MD 21617.

Saint Mary's City Historical Society; 11 Courthouse Dr.; PO Box 212; Leonardtown, MD 20650.

Saint Mary's County Genealogical Society, Inc.; PO Box 1109; Leonardtown, MD 20650-1109; julia@olg.com; www.pastracks.com/smcgs.

Silver Spring Historical Society; PO Box 1160; Silver Spring, MD 20910-1160; sshistory@yahoo.com; www.homestead.com/silverspringhistory.

Smithsburg Historical Society; Smithsburg, MD ; http://pilot.wash.lib.md.us/smithsburg/HIST.HTM.

Society for the History of Germans in Maryland; PO Box 22595; Baltimore, MD 21285.

Sons of the American Revolution, Maryland Society; PO Box 92; Woodstock, MD 21163-0082.

The Historical Society of Talbot County; 29 S. Washington St.; Easton, MD 21601; www.hstc.org.

U.S. National Archives & Records Administration (College Park); 8601 Adelphi Road; College Park, MD 20740-6001; www.archives.gov/facilities/md/archives_2.html.

United Methodist Historical Society, Inc.; Lovely Lane United Methodist Church; 2200 St. Paul; Baltimore, MD 21218.

United States Naval Academy Archives; 589 McNair Road; Annapolis, MD 21402-5033; (410) 293-6922; www.archives.gov/facilities/nara_affiliated_archives.html#us_military_academy.

Upper Shore Genealogical Society of Maryland; Box 275; Easton, MD 21601; www.chronography.com/usgs.

Washington County Historical Society; 135 West Washington Street; PO Box 1281; Hagerstown, MD 21741-1281; (301) 797-8782; histsoc@earthlink.net; www.rootsweb.com/~mdwchs.

Washington National Records Center; 4205 Suitland Road; Suitland, MD 20746-8001; (301) 778-1540; center@suitland.nara.gov; www.archives.gov/facilities/md/suitland.htmll.

Bibliography and Record Sources

General

A Guide to Historic Episcopal Churches of Southern Maryland, 1634–1984. Leonardtown, Maryland: Printing Press, 199–.

Andrusko, Samuel M. *Maryland Biographical Sketch Index*. Silver Spring, Maryland: Samuel M. Adrusko, 1983.

Barnes, Robert W., and F. Edward Wright. *Colonial Families of the Eastern Shore of Maryland, Vol. 2*. Westminster, Maryland: Family Line Publications. 1996.

Barnes, Robert. *British Roots of Maryland Families*. Baltimore: Genealogical Publishing Co., 1999.

Barnes, Robert. *British Roots of Maryland Families II*. Baltimore, Maryland: Genealogical Publishing Co., Inc., 2002.

Biographical Cyclopedia of Representative Men of Maryland and District of Columbia. Baltimore: National Biographical Publishing Co., 1879.

Bozeman, John Leeds. *The History of Maryland, from Its First Settlement in 1633 to the Restoration in 1660, Vol. 1*. (1837). Reprint. Baltimore: Heritage Books, Inc., 1990.

Brugger, Robert J. *Maryland: A Middle Temperament, 1634–1980*. (1988). Reprint. Galveston, Texas: Frontier Press. 1990.

Brumbaugh, Gaius Marcus. *Maryland Records: Colonial, Revolutionary, County and Church from Original Sources*. 2 vols. (1915, 1928). Reprint. Baltimore: Genealogical Publishing Co., 1993.

Callcott. *Mistress of Riversdale: the Plantation letters of Rosalie Stier Calvert, 1795–1821*. Galveston, Texas: Frontier Press. 1991.

Carr, Menard, and Walsh. *Robert Cole's World: Agriculture & Society in Early Maryland*. Galveston, Texas: Frontier Press. 1991.

Carr, Morgan, and Russo, eds. *Colonial Chesapeake Society*. Galveston, Texas: Frontier Press. 1988.

Caruthers, Bettie S., comp. *Maryland Oaths of Fidelity*. (1989). Reprint. Westminster, Maryland: Family Line Publications, 1995.

Chapelle, Suzanne Ellery Greene, ed. *Maryland, A History of Its People.* Baltimore: Johns Hopkins University Press, 1986.

Coldham, Peter Wilson. *Settlers of Maryland.* 5 vols. Baltimore: Genealogical Publishing Co., 1995–1996.

Coldham, Peter Wilson. *Settlers of Maryland 1679–1783.* Baltimore, Maryland: Genealogical Publishing Co., 2002.

Cox, Richard J., and Larry E. Sullivan, eds. *Guide to the Research Collections of the Maryland Historical Society.* Baltimore: Maryland Historical Society, 1981.

Dobson, David. *Scots on the Chesapeake, 1607–1830.* Baltimore: Genealogical Publishing Co., 1985.

Ellis, Donna M., and Karen A. Stuart. *The Calvert Papers: Calendar and Guide to the Microfilm Edition.* Baltimore: Maryland Historical Society, 1973.

Forbush, Bliss. *A History of Baltimore Yearly Meeting of Friends: Three Hundred Years of Quakerism in Maryland, Virginia, the District of Colombia, and Central Pennsylvania.* Sandy Spring, Maryland: Baltimore Yearly Meeting of Friends, 1972.

Genealogical Council of Maryland. *Inventory of Maryland Bible Records.* Westminster, Maryland: Family Line Publications, 1989.

Giles, Barbara S. *Selected Maryland Bibliography And Resources.* 2 vols. Seattle: B. S. Giles, ca. 1988–1989.

Green, Karen M. *The Maryland Gazette, 1727–1761: Genealogical and Historical Abstracts.* Galveston, Texas: Frontier Press, 1990.

Hanson, George A. *Old Kent: The Eastern Shore of Maryland.* (1876) Reprint. Baltimore: Clearfield Company, 1996.

Heisey, John W. *Maryland Genealogical Library Guide.* Morgantown, Pennsylvania: Masthof Press, 1998.

Heisey, John W. *Maryland Research Guide.* Indianapolis: Heritage House, 1986.

Henry, J. Maurice. *History Of The Church Of The Brethren In Maryland.* Elgin, Illinois: Brethren Publishing, 1936.

Hofstetter, Eleanor O. *Newspapers In Maryland Libraries: A Union List.* Baltimore: Division of Library Development Services, Maryland State Department of Education, 1977.

Holdcraft, Jacob Mehrling. *Obituaries, Bible Records, Church Records, Family Genealogies, County Records, etc. for Frederick County, Maryland, 1800–1977.* Salt Lake City: Genealogical Society of Utah, 1975, 1977. Microfilm, 59 rolls.

Inventory of Maryland Bible Records. Westminster, Maryland: Family Line Publications, 1989.

Inventory of the Church Archives of Maryland: Protestant Episcopal Diocese of Maryland. Baltimore: Historical Records Survey, 1940.

Jacobsen, Phebe R. *Quaker Records in Maryland.* Annapolis, Maryland: Hall of Records Commission, 1966.

Jordan, Elise Greenup. *Early Families of Southern Maryland.* 5 vols. (1993–1996) Reprint. Westminster, Maryland: Family Line Publications, 1995.

Kanely, Edna A., comp. *Directory of Maryland Church Records.* Westminster, Maryland: Family Line Publications, 1987.

Kanely, Edna Agatha. *Directory of Ministers and the Maryland Churches They Served, 1634–1990,* 2 vols. Westminster, Maryland: Family Line Publications, 1991.

Kulikoff. *Tobacco and Slaves: The Development of Southern Cultures in the Chesapeake, 1680–1800.* Galveston, Texas: Frontier Press, 1986.

Kummer, Frederic Arnold. *The Free State Of Maryland: A History Of The State And Its People, 1634–1941. A Narrative Historical Edition Preserving The Record Of The Growth And Development Of The State, Together With Genealogical And Memorial Records Of Its Prominent Families And Personages.* 4 vols. Ft. Wayne: Allen County Public Library, 198–.

Long, Helen R. *General History Section Index of Scharf's History of Western Maryland.* Manhattan, Kansas: Helen R. Long, 1992.

Maryland Genealogies. (1980) Reprint. Baltimore: Genealogical Publishing Co., Inc., 1997.

Maryland Hall of Records. *Calendar of Maryland State Papers: No. 1—The Black Books.* (1942) Reprint. Baltimore: Clearfield Company, 1995.

Maryland Research Outline. Series U.S.-States, no. 21. Salt Lake City: Family History Library, 1988.

Maryland State Archives. *Archives of Maryland (original Series).* 72 vols. Annapolis, Maryland: Maryland State Archives Publications.

Maryland State Archives. *Archives of Maryland, New Series, Vol. 1.* Annapolis, Maryland: Maryland State Archives Publications, 1990–.

Maryland State Archives. *Church Records at the Maryland State Archives.* Annapolis, Maryland: Maryland State Archives, 2002. Online guide—www.mdarchives .state.md.us/msa/homepage/html/refserv.html

Maryland State Archives. *Guide to State Agency Records— Histories and Series Descriptions.* Annapolis, Maryland: Maryland State Archives Publications, 1994.

Maryland State Archives. *Newspapers at the Maryland State Archives.* Annapolis, Maryland: Maryland State Archives, 2002. Online guide—www.mdarchives.state .md.us/msa/homepage/html/refserv.html

Maryland. State Archives. *A Guide to Government Records at the Maryland State Archives: A Comprehensive List By Agency And Record Series.* Annapolis: Maryland State Archives, 1992.

McCay, Betty L. *Sources for Genealogical Searching in Maryland.* Indianapolis: B. L. McCay, 1972.

Men of Mark in Maryland: Biographies of Leading Men in the State. 4 vols. Washington, D.C.: Johnson-Wynne Co., 1907–1912.

Meyer, Eugene L. *Maryland Lost And Found: People And Places From Chesapeake To Appalachia*. Baltimore: John Hopkins University Press, 1986.

Meyer, Mary Keysor. *Genealogical Research in Maryland: A Guide*. 4th ed. Baltimore: Maryland Historical Society, 1992.

Middleton, Canon Arthur Pierce. *Anglican Maryland, 1692–1792*. Virginia Beach: The Donning Company/Publishers, 1992.

Middleton, Canon Arthur Pierce. *Tobacco Coast: A Maritime History of Chesapeake Bay in the Colonial Era*. Reprint. 1984.

Nead, Daniel Wunderlich. *The Pennsylvania—German in the Settlement of Maryland*. Lancaster, Pennsylvania: 1914. Reprint. Genealogical Publishing Co., 1975.

Newman, Harry Wright. *The Flowering of the Maryland Palatinate*. (1961). Reprint. Baltimore: Clearfield Co., 1985.

Newman, Harry Wright. *To Maryland from Overseas*. Baltimore: Genealogical Publishing Co., (1982). Reprint. 1991.

Papenfuse, Edward C., et al. *A Biographical Dictionary of the Maryland Legislature, 1635–1789*, 2 vols. Baltimore: Johns Hopkins University Press, 1979, 1985.

Papenfuse, Edward C., et al. *A Guide to Government Records at the Maryland State Archives: A Comprehensive List by Agency and Record Series*. Annapolis, Maryland: Maryland State Archives, 1992.

Papenfuse, Edward C., et. al. *A Guide to the Maryland Hall of Records: Local, Judicial and Administrative Records on Microfilm*. Vol. 1. Annapolis, Maryland: Hall of Records Commission, 1978.

Parran, Alice. *Register of Maryland's Heraldic Families 1634–1935*. 2 vols. Baltimore: Parran, 1937.

Passano, Eleanor Phillips. *An Index of the Source Records of Maryland: Genealogical, Biographical, Historical*. (1940). Reprint. Baltimore: Genealogical Publishing Co., 1967.

Peden, Henry C., Jr. *Maryland Deponents, 1634–1799*. Westminster, Maryland: Family Line Publications. 1991.

Peden, Henry C., Jr. *Marylanders to Kentucky, 1775–1825*. Westminster, Maryland: Family Line Publications. 1991.

Peden, Henry C., Jr. *More Maryland Deponents, 1716–1799*. Westminster, Maryland: Family Line Publications. 1992.

Peden, Henry C., Jr. *Quaker Records of Southern Maryland, 1658–1800*. Westminster, Maryland: Family Line Publications. 1992.

Pedley, Avril J. M., comp. *The Manuscript Collections of the Maryland Historical Society*. Baltimore: Maryland Historical Society. 1969.

Portrait and Biographical Record of the Eastern Shore of Maryland: Containing Portraits and Biographies of Many Well Know Citizens of the Past and Present.

Together with Portraits and Biographies of All the Presidents of the United States. New York: Chapman, 1898.

Portrait and Biographical Record of the Sixth Congressional District, Maryland: Containing Portraits and Biographies. . . . New York: Chapman, 1898.

Radoff, Morris Leon. *The Old Line State: A History of Maryland*. Annapolis: Hall of Records Commission, 1971.

Richardson, Hester Dorsey. *Side-lights on Maryland History with Sketches of Early Maryland Families*. 2 vols. (1913). Baltimore: Genealogy Publishing Co. Reprint. 1995.

Rider, Fremont, ed. *American Genealogical—Biographical Index. Vols. 1–186+*. Middletown, Connecticut: Godfrey Memorial Library, 1952–.

Scharf, John T. *History of Western Maryland: Being a History of Frederick, Montgomery, Carroll, Washington, Allegany, and Garrett Counties from the Earliest Period to the Present Day. . . .* 1882. 2 vols. Reprint. Baltimore: Regional Publishing Co., 1968.

Schweitzer, George K. *Maryland Genealogical Research*. Knoxville, Tennessee: George K. Schweitzer, 1991.

Semmes, Raphael T. *Captains and Mariners of Early Maryland*. Baltimore: The John Hopkins Press, 1937.

Sketches of Maryland Eastern Shoremen. (1898). Reprint. Westminster, Maryland: Family Line Publications, 1992.

Skirven, Percy G. *The First Parishes of the Province of Maryland*. (1692, 1923) Reprint. Baltimore: Clearfield Company, 1997.

Skordas, Gust. *The Early Settlers of Maryland*. (1968) Reprint. Baltimore: Genealogical Publishing Co., Inc., 1995.

Smith, Daniel Blake. *Inside the Great House: Planter Family Life in Eighteenth-Century Chesapeake Society*. (1980) Reprint. Galveston, Texas: Frontier Press, 1994.

Southern California Genealogical Society. *Sources of Genealogical Help in Maryland*. Burbank, California: Southern California Genealogical Society.

Spencer, Richard Henry. *Genealogical and Memorial Encyclopedia of the State of Maryland*. (1919). Reprint. Baltimore: Clearfield Company, 1992.

Thomas, James Walter. *Chronicles of Colonial Maryland*. (1900) Reprint. Baltimore: Clearfield Company, 1995.

Torrence, Clayton. *Old Somerset on the Eastern Shore of Maryland*. (1935) Reprint. Baltimore: Clearfield Company, 1996.

Virdin, Donald Odell. *Maryland and Delaware Genealogies and Family Histories: A Bibliography of Books about Maryland and Delaware Families*. Bowie, Maryland: Heritage Books, 1993.

Walsh, Richard, and William Lloyd Fox, eds. *Maryland: A History, 1632–1974*. Reprint, 1974. Baltimore: Maryland Historical Society, 1974.

White, Les. *A Guide to the Microfilm Collection of Newspapers at the Maryland State Archives.* Annapolis: Maryland State Archives, 1990.

Whitman, T. Stephen. *The Price of Freedom: Slavery and Manumission in Baltimore and Early National Maryland.* Lexington, Kentucky.: The University Press of Kentucky, 1997.

Wright, F. Edward. *Quaker Minutes of the Eastern Shore of Maryland 1676–1779.* Lewes, Delaware: Colonial Roots, 2002.

Atlases, Maps and Gazetteers

Brown, Mary R. *An Illustrated Genealogy of the Counties of Maryland and the District of Columbia as a Guide to Locating Records.* Baltimore: French Bray Printing, 1967.

Fisher, Richard Swainson. *Gazetteer of the State of Maryland: Compiled from the Returns of the Seventh Census of the United States and Other Official Documents. To Which is Added, a General Account of the District of Columbia.* New York: J. H. Colton, 1852.

Gannett, Henry. *A Gazetteer of Maryland and Delaware.* (1904) Reprint. Baltimore: Clearfield, Co., 1994.

Kaminkow, Marion J. *Maryland A to Z: A Topographical Dictionary.* Baltimore: Magna Carta Book Co., 1985.

Keatley, J. Kenneth. *Place Names of the Eastern Shore of Maryland.* Queenstown, Maryland: Queen Anne Press, 1987.

Kenny, Hamill. *The Place Names of Maryland: Their Origin and Meaning.* Baltimore: Maryland Historical Society.

Long, John H., ed. *Historical Atlas and Chronology of County Boundaries, 1788–1980. Scale: 1:633,600. Vol. 1–5.* Boston, Massachusetts: G. K. Hall, 1984.

Maryland State Planning Department. *The Counties of Maryland and Baltimore City: Their Origin, Growth, and Development, 1634–1967.* Publication no. 146. Baltimore: Staff Planning commission, 1968.

Maryland/Delaware. Illus. Paper. 80 p. Athens, Georgia: Iberian Publishing Co.

Maryland-Delaware Atlas & Gazetteer. Freeport, Maryland: DeLorme Mapping, 1993.

Papenfuse, Edward C., and Joseph M. Coale. *The Hammond-Harwood House Atlas of Historical Maps of Maryland, 1608–1908.* Baltimore: Johns Hopkins University Press, 1982.

Smith, Chester M. *The Postal History of Maryland, the Delmarva Peninsula and the District of Columbia: The Post Offices and First Postmasters from 1775 to 1984.* Burtonsville, Maryland: The Depot, 1984.

Thompson, Derek, ed. *Atlas of Maryland.* College Park: University of Maryland, 1977.

United States Geological Survey. *Topographic Maps of the United States.* Suitland, Maryland: National Archives and Records Service, 1976.

Census Records

Available Census Records and Census Substitutes

Federal Census 1790, 1800, 1810, 1820, 1830 (except Montgomery, Prince George's, St. Mary's, Queen Annes and Somerset Counties), 1840, 1850, 1860, 1870, 1880, 1900, 1910, 1920, 1930

Federal Mortality Schedules 1850, 1860, 1870, 1880

Union Veterans and Widows 1890

Carothers, Bettie S., comp. *1776 Census of Maryland.* Rev. ed. Westminster, Maryland: Family Line Publications, 1989.

Carothers, Bettie Stirling. *1778 Census of Maryland.* Chesterfield, Missouri: B. S. Carothers, 1975.

Dollahide, William. *The Census Book: A Genealogist's Guide to Federal Census Facts, Schedules and Indexes.* Bountiful, Utah: Heritage Quest, 1999.

Kemp, Thomas Jay. *The American Census Handbook.* Wilmington, Delaware: Scholarly Resources, Inc., 2001.

Lainhart, Ann S. *State Census Records.* Baltimore: Genealogical Publishing Co., Inc., 1992.

Szucs, Loretto Dennis, and Matthew Wright. *Finding Answers in U.S. Census Records.* Ancestry Publishing, 2001.

Thorndale, William and William Dollarhide. *Map Guide to the U.S. Federal Census, 1790–1920.* Baltimore: Genealogical Publishing Co., 1987.

Court Records, Probate and Wills

Cotton, Jane Baldwin. *Index to Wills of the Colonial Period, Books 1–41, 1634–1777.* Annapolis: Hall of Records Commission, 1947.

Cotton, Jane Baldwin. *Maryland Probate Records.* S.l.: Brøderbund, 1998. CD-ROM.

Cotton, Jane Baldwin. *The Maryland Calendar of Wills.* 16 vols. (1904–1928). Reprint. Baltimore: Family Line Publications, 1988.

Cregar, William F. *Index to Chancery Notes, Chancery Dispositions and Testamentary Proceedings.* Microfilm copy of typescript at Maryland Historical Society, Baltimore. Salt Lake City: Filmed by the Genealogical Society of Utah, 1949.

First Laws of the State of Maryland. (1787) Reprint. Washington, D.C.: Scholarly Resources, 1981.

Hooper, Debbie. *Abstracts of Chancery Court Records of Maryland, 1669–1782.* Westminster, Maryland: Family Line Publication, 1996.

Index to Inventories of Estates, 1718–1777. Annapolis, Maryland: Hall of Records Commission, 1947.

Jones, Caleb, comp. *Orderly Book of the "Maryland Loyalists Regiment," June 18, 1778 to October 12, 1778.* (1891) Reprint. Baltimore, Maryland: Clearfield Company, 1996.

Magruder, James M., Jr. *Index of Maryland Colonial Wills, 1634–1777*. 1933. Reprint. Baltimore: Genealogical Publishing Co., 1967.

Magruder, James Mosby. *Magruder's Maryland Colonial Abstracts, Wills, Accounts and Inventories, 1772–1777*. 1934–1939. Reprint. 5 vols. in 1. Baltimore: Genealogical Publishing Co., 1968.

Maryland. Court of Appeals. *Judgements and Decrees*. Annapolis: Hall of Records Commission, 1947.

Maryland. General Court. *Judgements*. Annapolis: Hall of Records Commission, 1947.

Maryland. Provincial Court. *Judicial and Testamentary Business of the Provincial Court: 1637–1683*. Archives of Maryland. Court Series, vols. 1–4, 8, 10–15. Baltimore: Maryland Historical Society, 1887–1964.

Maryland. Provincial Court. *Provincial Court Judgements*. Annapolis: Hall of Records Commission, 1947.

Owen, David R., and Michael C. Tolley. *Courts of Admiralty in Colonial America: The Maryland Experience, 1634–1776*. Baltimore: Maryland Historical Society.

Papenfuse, Edward C. *A Guide to the Maryland Hall of Records: Local, Judicial and Administrative Records on Microform*. Annapolis: Archives Division, Hall of Records Commission, 1978.

Radoff, Morris Leon, et al. *The County Courthouses and Records of Maryland, Part Two: The Records*. Annapolis, Maryland: Hall of Records Commission, 1963.

Skinner, Vernon L. *Abstracts of the Inventories and Accounts of the Prerogative Court* of Maryland. Westminster, Maryland: Family Line Publications, 1988–1991.

United States. Circuit Court (Maryland). *Minutes, 1790–1911*. Washington, D.C.: National Archives, 1973.

Wright, F. Edward. *Maryland Calendar of Wills, Vol. 10: 1748–1753*. Westminster, Maryland: Family Line Publications, 1988.

Wright, F. Edward. *Maryland Calendar of Wills, Vol. 11: 1753–1760*. Westminster, Maryland: Family Line Publications, 1988.

Wright, F. Edward. *Maryland Calendar of Wills, Vol. 9: 1744–1749*. Westminster, Maryland: Family Line Publications, 1988.

Wright, F. Edward. *Maryland Calendar of Wills: From 1744–1779*. 8 vols. Westminster, Maryland: Family Line Publications, 1988.

Emigration, Immigration, Migration and Naturalization

Campbell, Penelope. *Maryland in Africa: The Maryland State Colonization Society, 1831–1857*. Urbana: University of Illinois Press, 1971.

Coldham, Peter Wilson. *The King's Passengers to Maryland and Virginia*. Westminster, Maryland: Family Line, 1997.

Hargreaves-Mawdsley, R. *Bristol and America, a Record of the First Settlers in the Colonies of North America, 1654–1685: Including the Names with Places of Origin of More Than 10,000 Servants to Foreign Plantations Who Sailed from the Port Bristol to Virginia, Maryland, and Other Parts of the Atlantic Coast, and Also to the West Indies from 1654 to 1685*. Reprint. Baltimore: Genealogical Publishing Co., 1978.

Head, Daniel W. *The Pennsylvania-German in the Settlement of Maryland*. Baltimore, Maryland: Clearfield Co., Inc., 2002.

Mortan Allan Directory of European Passenger Steamship Arrivals. 1931. Reprint. Baltimore: Genealogical Publishing Co., 1980.

Oszakiewski, Robert A. *Maryland Naturalization Abstracts, Volume 2*. Westminster, Maryland: Family Line Publications. 1996.

Peden, Henry C., Jr. *Marylanders to Carolina: Migrations of Marylanders to North and South Carolina Prior to 1800*. Westminster, Maryland: Family Line Publications. 1994.

Reamy, Bill and Martha Reamy. *Immigrant Ancestors of Marylanders as Found in Local Histories*. n. p., 1993.

Skordas, Gust. *The Early Settlers of Maryland: An Index to the Names of Immigrants Compiled from Records of Land Patents, 1633–1680, in the Hall of Records, Annapolis, Maryland*. Reprint. Baltimore: Genealogical Publishing Co.,1986.

United States. Bureau of Customs. *Copies of Lists of Passengers Arriving At Miscellaneous Ports on the Atlantic and Gulf Coasts and At Ports on the Great Lakes, 1820–1873*. Washington, D.C.: The National Archives, 1964.

United States. Bureau of Customs. *Index (Soundex) to Passenger Lists of Vessels Arriving At Baltimore, 1897–1952*. Washington, D.C.: National Archives, 1956.

United States. Bureau of Customs. *Passenger Lists of Vessels Arriving At Baltimore, 1820–1921; Quarterly Abstracts of Passenger Lists of Vessels Arriving At Baltimore, 1820–1869*. Washington, D.C.: The National Archives, 1956, 1959, 1969.

United States. Circuit Court (Maryland). Clerk. *Indexes to Naturalization Petitions to the U.S. Circuit and District Courts for Maryland: 1797–1951*. Microfilm of originals at the Federal Archives Records Center, Philadelphia. Washington, D.C.: National Archives. Central Plains Region, 1982. 25 microfilm.

United States. Circuit Court (Maryland). *Naturalization Records, 1906–1911*. Microfilm of records at the National Archives Mid-Atlantic Region, Philadelphia. Salt Lake City: Filmed by the Genealogical Society of Utah, 1991.

United States. District Court (Maryland). *Naturalization Records, 1792–1931*. Microfilms of the originals at the Philadelphia Branch-National Archives. Salt Lake City:

Filmed by the Genealogical Society of Utah, 1990–1991. 67 microfilm.

Wood, Gregory A. *A Guide to the Acadians in Maryland in the 18th and 19th Centuries.* Wheaton, Maryland: Maryland Acadian Studies, 1995.

Wright, F. Edward. *Citizens of the Eastern Shore of Maryland, 1659–1750.* Westminster, Maryland: Family Line Publications, 1986.

Wyand, Jeffrey A., and Florence L. Wyand. *Colonial Maryland Naturalizations.* Reprint. Baltimore: Genealogical Publishing Co., 1986.

Land and Property

Coldham, Peter Wilson. *Settlers of Maryland. [1679–1783].* 5 vols. Baltimore: Genealogical Publishing Company, 1995–1996.

Hartsook, Elisabeth and Gust Skordas. *Land Office and Prerogative Court Records of Colonial Maryland.* (1968) Reprint. Baltimore: Clearfield Company, 1996.

Hone, Wade E. *Land and Property Research in the United States.* Salt Lake City: Ancestry Incorporated, 1997.

Maryland State Archives. *Land Records at the Maryland State Archives.* Annapolis, Maryland: Maryland State Archives, 2002. Online guide—www.mdarchives.state.md.us/msa/homepage/html/refserv.html.

Papers Relating to the Boundary Dispute Between Pennsylvania and Maryland, 1734–1760. Microfilm of original published: Harrisburg, Pennsylvania: C. M. Busch, 1896. Salt Lake City: Filmed by the Genealogical Society of Utah, 1969.

Patents Series: Of the Maryland Land Office. Microfilm copy of original records at Hall of Records, Annapolis, Maryland. Salt Lake City: Filmed by the Genealogical Society of Utah, 1947. 81 microfilm.

Sioussat, Annie Middleton. *Old Manors in the Colony of Maryland.* 2 vols. Ft. Wayne: Allen County Public Library, 198–.

Military

Brumbaugh, Gaius Marcus. *Revolutionary Records of Maryland.* Washington, D.C.: Rufus H. Darby, 1924. Reprint. Baltimore: Clearfield Co., 1996.

Callum, Agnes Kane. *Colored Volunteers of Maryland Civil War, 7th Regiment, United States Colored Troops, 1863–1866.* Baltimore: Mullac Publishers, 1990.

Clark, Murtie June. *Colonial Soldiers of the South, 1732–1774.* Baltimore: Genealogical Publishing Co., 1983.

Clark, Murtie June. *Loyalists in the Southern Campaign of the Revolutionary War.* Baltimore: Genealogical Publishing Company, 1981.

Clements, S. Eugene. *The Maryland Militia in the Revolutionary War.* Westminster, Maryland: Family Line Publications, 1987

Eisenberg, Gerson G. *Marylanders Who Served the Nation: A Biographical Dictionary of Federal Officials From Maryland.* Annapolis, Maryland: Maryland State Archives Publications, 1992.

Goldsborough, William W. *The Maryland Line in the Confederate Army, 1861–1865.* 1900. Reprint, Gaithersburg, Maryland: Olde Soldier Books, 1987.

Hartzler, Daniel D. *Marylanders in the Confederacy.* Silver Spring, Maryland: Family Line Publications, 1986.

Huntsberry, Thomas V., and Joanne M. Huntsberry. *Dartmoor Prison.* Baltimore: J. Mart Publishers, 1984.

Huntsberry, Thomas V., and Joanne M. Huntsberry. *Maryland in the Civil War.* 2 vols. Edgemere, Maryland: J. Mart Publishers, 1985.

Kilbourne, John Dwight. *A Short History of the Maryland Line in the Continental Army.* Baltimore: The Society of the Cincinnati of Maryland, 1992.

Marine, William M. *The British Invasion of Maryland: 1812–1815.* Baltimore, 1913. Reprint. Baltimore: Genealogical Publishing Co., 1977.

Maryland Hall of Records Commission. *Index to the Maryland Line in the Confederate Army, 1867–1865.* Publication no. 3. Annapolis, Maryland.

Maryland Historical Society. *Muster Rolls and Other Records of Service of Maryland Troops in the American Revolution, 1775–1783.* Archives of Maryland, vol. 18. Baltimore. 1900. Reprint. Baltimore: Genealogical Publishing Co., 1972.

Maryland Muster Rolls, Fort Cumberland, 1757–1758. Salt Lake City: Filmed by the Genealogical Society of Utah, 1949.

Maryland War Records Commission. *Maryland in the World War I, 1917–1919. Military and Naval Service Records.* 2 vols. Baltimore: Maryland War Records Commission, 1933.

Maryland. Treasurer's Office. *A List of Invalid Pensioners.* Annapolis, Maryland: J. Hughes, Printer, 1822.

McGhee, Lucy K. *Maryland Revolutionary War Pensions, Revolutionary, 1812, and Indian Wars.* Washington, D.C.: Library of Congress Photoduplication Service, 1987.

Meyer, Mary K. *Westward of Fort Cumberland Military Lots Set Off for Maryland's Revolutionary Soldiers: With an Appended List of Revolutionary Soldiers Granted Pensions by the State of Maryland.* Finksburg, Maryland: Pipe Creek Publication, Inc., 1993.

Muster Rolls and Other Records of Service of Maryland Troops in the American Revolution: 1775–1783. Archives of Maryland. Vol. 18. Baltimore: Maryland Historical Society, 1900.

Newman, Harry Wright. *Maryland Revolutionary Records: Data Obtained From 3,050 Pension Claims and Bounty Land Applications, Including 1,000 Marriages of Maryland Soldiers and a List Of 1,200 Proved Services of Soldiers and Patriots of Other States.* Reprint. Baltimore: Genealogy Publishing Co., 1993.

Register of the Commissioned and Warrant Officers of the Navy of the Confederate States to January 1, 1863. S.l.: s.n., 1863.

Retzer, Henry J. *German Regiment of Maryland and Pennsylvania.* Westminster, Maryland: Family Line Publications. 1991. Rev. ed. 1996.

Roster of the Soldiers and Sailors Who Served in Organizations from Maryland during the Spanish-American War. Reprint. Westminster, Maryland: Family Line Publications, 1990.

Sifakis, Stewart. *Compendium of the Confederate Armies: Kentucky, Maryland, Missouri, the Confederate Units and the Indian Units.* 10 vols. New York: Facts on File, ca. 1992–1995.

United States. Adjutant General's Office. *Index to Compiled Service Records of Volunteer Union Soldiers Who Served in Organizations from the State of Maryland.* Washington, D.C.: The National Archives, 1962.

United States. Record and Pension Office. *Compiled Service Records of Confederate Soldiers Who Served in Organizations from the State of Maryland.* Washington, D.C.: The National Archives, 1960. Microfilm, 22 rolls.

United States. Record and Pension Office. *Compiled Service Records of Volunteer Union Soldiers Who Served in Organizations from the State of Maryland.* Washington, D.C.: The National Archives, 1962. Microfilm, 238 rolls.

United States. Selective Service System. *Maryland, World War I Selective Service System Draft Registration Cards, 1917–1918.* Washington, D.C.: National Archives, 1987–1988.

United States. Veterans Administration. *Pension Index File, Alphabetical; of the Veterans Administrative Contact and Administrative Services, Administrative Operations Services, 1861–1934.* Washington, D.C.: Veterans Administration, Publications Service, 1953.

Wells, Charles J. *Maryland and District of Columbia Volunteers in the Mexican War.* Westminster, Maryland: Family Line Publications, 1991.

Wilmer, L. Allison. *History and Roster of Maryland Volunteers, War of 1861–1865.* Reprint. Silver Spring, Maryland: Family Line Publications, 1987.

Wright, F. Edward. *Maryland Militia, War of 1812.* 8 vols. Silver Spring, Maryland: Family Line Publications. 1979–1992.

Vital and Cemetery Records

Barnes, Robert W. *Maryland Marriages, 1634–1777.* 1978. Reprint. Baltimore: Genealogical Publishing Co., 1975

Barnes, Robert W. *Maryland Marriages, 1778–1800.* 1978. Reprint. Baltimore: Genealogical Publishing Co., 1975.

Barnes, Robert W. *Maryland Marriages, 1801–1820.* 1978. Reprint. Baltimore: Genealogical Pub. Co., 1978.

Barnes, Robert W. *Marriages and Deaths from the Maryland Gazette, 1727–1839.* Baltimore: Genealogical Publishing Co., 1973.

Bell, Annie W. B. *Maryland Marriage Records.* 23 vols. Annapolis, Maryland: Annie W. B. Bell, 1938–1939.

Bell, Annie W. B. *Maryland Records of Deaths, 1718–1777.* Annapolis, Maryland: Annie W. B. Bell, 1936. Indexed.

Brown, Mary Ross. *An Illustrated Genealogy of the Counties of Maryland and the District of Columbia as a Guide to Locating Records. . . .* Baltimore: French-Bray Printing Co., 1967.

Brumbaugh, Gaius Marcus. *Maryland Records: Colonial, Revolutionary, County and Church from Original Sources.* 2 vols. Baltimore: Genealogical Publishing Co., 1967.

Chance, Hilda. *Western Maryland Pioneers: Alphabetical Lists of Marriages, Births, and Deaths of 8,000 Early settlers.* 2 vols. Microreproduction of original published: Liberty, Pennsylvania.: H. Chance, 196–. 2 vols. Salt Lake City: Genealogical Society of Utah, 1968.

Directory of Maryland Burial Grounds. Westminister, Maryland: Family Line Publications, 1996.

Directory of Maryland Cemeteries. Baltimore: Genealogical Council of Maryland, irregular.

Holdcraft, Jacob Mehrling. *Names in Stone: 75,000 Cemetery Inscriptions from Frederick County, Maryland.* 2 vols. Reprint. Baltimore: Genealogical Publishing Co., 1985.

Loudon Park Cemetery (Baltimore, Maryland). *Cemetery Records, 1853–1986.* Salt Lake City: Genealogical Society of Utah, 1986. Microfilm, 66 rolls.

Maryland Genealogies And Marriages, 1634–1820. S.l.: Brøderbund, 1998. CD-ROM.

Maryland State Archives. *Vital and Probate Records at the Maryland State Archives.* Annapolis, Maryland: Maryland State Archives, 2002. Online guide— www.mdarchives.state.md.us/msa/ homepage/html/refserv.html

Meyer, Mary K. *Divorces And Names Changed In Maryland: By Act Of The Legislature, 1634–1867.* Mt. Airy, Maryland: Pipe Creek Pub. 1991.

Ridgely, Helen West, ed. *Historic Graves of Maryland and the District of Columbia: With the Inscriptions Appearing on the Tombstones in Most of the Counties of the State and in Washington and Georgetown.* Baltimore: Genealogical Publishing Co., 1967.

Wright, F. Edward. *Maryland Eastern Shore Vital Records: 1648–1825.* 5 vols. Silver Spring, Maryland: Family Line Publications, 1986.

County Website	Map Index	Date Created	Parent County or Territory From Which Organized Address/Details
Allegany www.allconet.org/	O3	25 Dec 1789	**Washington** Allegany County; 3 Pershing St; Cumberland, MD 21502-3043; Ph. (301) 777-5911 **Details:** (Clerk Circuit Court has Marriage, Divorce, Court & Land Records from 1791 & Naturalization Records 1821–1973; Register of Wills has Probate Records)
Anne Arundel www.co.anne-arundel.md.us/	G5	9 Apr 1650	**St. Mary's** Anne Arundel County; 7 Church Circle; Annapolis, MD 21401; Ph. (410) 222-1397 **Details:** (Clerk Circuit Court has Marriage Records from 1905, Divorce & Court Records from 1870 & Land Records from 1851; Register of Wills has Probate Records; Hall of Records has Marriage Records 1770–1904 & earlier Court & Land Records)
Baltimore www.co.ba.md.us/	G3	30 Jun 1659	**Anne Arundel** Baltimore County; 401 Bosley Ave; Towson, MD 21204-4606; Ph. (410) 887-2601 **Details:** (Clerk Circuit Court has Marriage, Divorce, Court & Land Records from 1851; Register of Wills has Probate Records)
Baltimore City www.rootsweb.com/~mdcbalti/	G4	4 Jul 1851	**Baltimore** Baltimore City County; 6550 Reisterstown Plaza; Baltimore, MD 21202; Ph. (410) 763-3038 **Details:** (City Health Department has Birth, Death & Burial Records; Common Pleas Court has Marriage Records; Clerk Circuit Court has Divorce Records, trust estates, adoptions & name changes from 1853; Register of Wills has Probate Records)
Calvert www.co.cal.md.us/	G7	3 Jul 1654	**St. Mary's** Calvert County; 175 Main St; Prince Frederick, MD 20678; Ph. (410) 535-1600 **Details:** (Name changed to Patuxent 31 Oct 1654. Name changed back to Calvert 31 Dec 1658. Courthouse burned 1882; most Records destroyed) (Clerk Circuit Court has Marriage, Divorce, Court & Land Records from 1882; Register of Wills has Probate Records from 1882; earlier Records available at State Hall of Records)
Caroline www.caroline.md.org	D7	5 Dec 1773	**Dorchester, Queen Anne's** Caroline County; PO Box 458; Denton, MD 21629; Ph. (410) 479-1811 **Details:** (State Archives has Birth & Death Records 1865–1884, 1898–1972, Court Records 1775–1947, Divorce Records 1969–1984, Marriage Records 1774–1972, & Probate Records 1685–1981; Department of Health and Mental Hygiene has Birth Records 1973–1978, Death Records 1972–1987, & Marriage Records 1973–1987)
Carroll http://ccgov.carr.org/	I3	19 Jan 1837	**Baltimore, Frederick** Carroll County; 225 N Center St; Westminster, MD 21157; Ph. (410) 876-2085 **Details:** (Clerk Circuit Court has Marriage Records 1837–1900 not indexed & from 1900 indexed, Divorce, Court & Land Records from 1837)

County Website	Map Index	Date Created	Parent County or Territory From Which Organized Address/Details
Cecil www.registers.state.md.us	D3	31 Dec 1674	**Kent** Cecil County; Suite 101 County Courthouse; PO Box 468; Elkton, MD 21921; Ph. (410) 996-5330 **Details:** (Clerk Circuit Court has Marriage Records from 1777, Divorce, Court & Land Records from 1674; Register of Wills has General Will Index 1675–1953, General Index 1675–1997, Wills Index 1953–1997, From 1997 to Present available on computer at office, & Estate File from 1851)
Charles www.govt.co.charles.md.us/	I8	10 Jul 1658	**Original county** Charles County; PO Box B; La Plata, MD 20646-0167; Ph. (301) 645-0550 **Details:** (Clerk Circuit Court has Marriage Records from 1865, Divorce & Court Records from 1796; Register of Wills has Probate Records; State Hall of Records, Annapolis, MD has Land Records from 1658)
Dorchester www.commissioners.net/	E8	16 Feb 1669	**Original county** Dorchester County; 206 High St; PO Box 26; Cambridge, MD 21613-0026; Ph. (410) 228-0480 **Details:** (Clerk Circuit Court has Marriage Records from 1780, Divorce Records from 1821, Court Records from 1860, Land Records from 1669, plat Records from 1912, equity docket Records from 1821 & corporation Records from 1858)
Durham		1669	**Somerset, Unorganized Territory** Durham County; MD **Details:** County Terminated 1672
Frederick www.fredco-md.net/main/	J3	10 Jun 1748	**Prince George's** Frederick County; 100 W Patrick St; Frederick, MD 21701; Ph. (301) 694-1960 **Details:** (Clerk Circuit Court has Marriage Records from 1778, Probate Records from 1744 & Land Records from 1748)
Garrett www.co.garrett.md.us/	Q3	1 Apr 1872	**Allegany** Garrett County; 203 S 4th St Rm 109; Oakland, MD 21550-1535; Ph. (301) 334-8970 **Details:** (Clerk Circuit Court has Marriage, Divorce, Land & Court Records from 1872, Military Records from 1942 & Naturalization Records 1908–1929; Register of Wills has Probate Records)
Harford www.co.ha.md.us/	F3	2 Mar 1774	**Baltimore** Harford County; 20 W Courtland St; Bel Air, MD 21014-3833; Ph. (410) 838-6000 **Details:** (County Health Department has Birth & Death Records; Clerk Court has Marriage & Land Records from 1779, Divorce & Court Records from 1803)
Howard http://co.ho.md.us/	H4	4 Jul 1851	**Anne Arundel** Howard County; 3430 Courthouse Dr; Ellicott City, MD 21043-4300; Ph. (410) 992-2025 **Details:** (Clerk Circuit Court has Marriage, Divorce, Court & Land Records; Register of Wills has Probate Records)

County Website	Map Index	Date Created	Parent County or Territory From Which Organized Address/Details
Kent www.kentcounty.com/	E4	**2 Aug 1642**	**St. Mary's** Kent County; 103 N Cross St; Chestertown, MD 21620; Ph. (410) 778-7460 **Details:** (Clerk Circuit Court has Marriage Records from 1796, Divorce Records from 1867, Land Records from 1656 & Court Records from early 1800's)
Montgomery www.co.mo.md.us/	J5	**6 Sep 1776**	**Frederick** Montgomery County; 101 Monroe St; Rockville, MD 20850-0000; Ph. (240) 777-9466 **Details:** (Clerk Circuit Court has Marriage Records from 1799, Divorce, Court & Land Records from 1776) (1830 Census missing)
Patuxent		**3 Jul 1654**	**St. Mary's** Patuxent County; MD **Details:** (see Calvert) Formerly Calvert County. Name changed to Patuxent 31 Oct 1654. Name changed back to Calvert 31 Dec 1658
Potomac		**1654**	**St. Mary's** Potomac County; MD **Details:** County Terminated 1658; Formerly St. Mary's
Prince George's www.goprincegeorgescounty.com/index.html	H7	**20 May 1695**	**Charles** Prince George's County; 14735 Main St; Landover, MD 20772; Ph. (301) 350-9700 **Details:** (Clerk Circuit Court has Land & Court Records; Register of Wills has Probate Records) (1830 Census missing)
Providence		**1654**	Providence; MD **Details:** Temporary Name for Anne Arundel 1654–1656
Queen Anne's www.qac.org/	E6	**18 Apr 1706**	**Kent** Queen Anne's County; 107 N Liberty; Centreville, MD 21617; Ph. (410) 758-1773 **Details:** (Clerk Courts has Marriage, Divorce, Court & Land Records; Orphan's Court has Probate Records) (1830 census missing)
Somerset http://skipjack.net/le_shore/visitsomerset/	C9	**22 Aug 1666**	**Kent** Somerset County; 30512 Prince William St; Princess Anne, MD 21853; Ph. (410) 651-1555 **Details:** (State Archive has Birth Records 1649–1720, 1865–1870, 1894, 1898–1972, Death Records 1649–1720, 1898–1972, Divorce Records 1816–1983, Marriage Records 1649–1720, 1796–1972, Military Discharge Records 1956–1973, & Probate Records 1664–1977; Department of Health & Mental Hygiene has Birth Records 1973–1978, Death Records 1972–1987, & Marriage Records 1973–1987; Clerk of Circuit Court has Marriage Records from 1987; State Archives has Land Records from 1665)
St. Mary's www.win.net/~ehayden/states/maryland/stmary/	G9	**9 Feb 1637**	**Original county** St. Mary's County; 23150 Leonard Hall Dr; Leonardtown, MD 20650; Ph. (301) 475-4567 **Details:** (Named Potomac 1654–1658) (Clerk Circuit Court has Marriage & Land Records; Register of Wills has Probate Records) (1830 census missing)

County Website	Map Index	Date Created	Parent County or Territory From Which Organized Address/Details
Talbot www.talbgov.org/	E6	**18 Feb 1662**	**Kent** Talbot County; 11 N Washington St; Easton, MD 21601; Ph. (410) 770-8010 **Details:** (Clerk of Circuit Court has Marriage Records from 1794, Divorce Records from 1908, Court Records from 1818, & Land Records from 1662, Register of Wills has Probate Records)
Washington http://pilot.wash.lib.md.us/washco/	L3	**6 Sep 1776**	**Frederick** Washington County; Summit Ave; Hagerstown, MD 21740; Ph. (301) 790-7991 **Details:** (Clerk Circuit Court has Marriage Records from 1799, Divorce & Land Records from 1776, Court Records from 1797 & Military Discharge Records; other Records may be found at Washington County Free Library, Hagerstown, MD)
Wicomico www.co.wicomico.md.us/	C9	**17 Aug 1867**	**Somerset, Worcester** Wicomico County; PO Box 198; Salisbury, MD 21803; Ph. (410) 548-4801 **Details:** (Clerk Circuit Court has Marriage, Divorce, Land, Military & Court Records from 1867)
Worcester www.worc.lib.md.us/	B10	**29 Oct 1742**	**Somerset** Worcester County; 1 W Market St; Snow Hill, MD 21863; Ph. (401) 632-1194 **Details:** (Clerk Circuit Court has Marriage Records from 1866, Divorce Records from 1900 & Court Records from 1916; Register of Wills has Probate Records)

Notes

Massachusetts

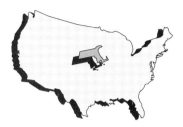

Capital: Boston
State: 1788 (6th)

By the sword we seek peace,
but peace only under liberty

Among the earliest inhabitants of Massachusetts were the Algonquin, Nauset, Wampanoag, Nipmuc, and Pocumtuc peoples. The first English settler, Bartholomew Gosnold, arrived in 1602 and the first permanent settlement was established by the Pilgrims in 1620 at Plymouth.

The Puritans followed within a decade, establishing Salem in 1628 under John Endecott and Boston in 1630 under John Winthrop. The Massachusetts Bay Colony, founded in 1630, provided for a large amount of self-government. Within the next decade, more than 20,000 immigrants, almost entirely British, came to Massachusetts. Religious intolerance in Massachusetts led many to settle elsewhere, such as Rhode Island, Connecticut, New Hampshire, and Maine. In 1691, Plymouth Colony was joined to the Massachusetts Bay Colony, along with parts of Maine and Nova Scotia.

Massachusetts played a prominent role in the Revolutionary War from the Boston Tea Party to Lexington and Concord and the Battle of Bunker Hill. A state constitution was adopted in 1780 and Massachusetts became the sixth state to ratify the United States Constitution, with the proviso that the Bill of Rights be added.

In 1786, the Ohio Land Company was formed, which led many Massachusetts residents to migrate to Ohio. New immigrants, primarily from England, continued to come to Massachusetts for at least two centuries. Maine was separated from Massachusetts in 1819 and became a state in 1820. In the 1830's, factory development began and the demand for workers stimulated renewed immigration. Around mid-century, emigrants from Ireland, Germany and France came to escape disasters and political turmoil in their countries. A few years later, Italians, Russians, Poles, and Portuguese came to work in the factories, mills, and fisheries. During the Civil War, Massachusetts furnished 146,000 men to the Union forces.

Look for vital records in the following locations:

- **Birth, marriage and death records:** Statistics have been kept throughout Massachusetts since the earliest days. To assist researchers, each town has published these records. Statewide registration began in 1841. Early records are available at the Massachusetts State Archives in Boston. A search of town records can yield additional information. Vital records after 1890 are available from the Registrar of Vital Statistics in Boston. You will be asked to state your relationship to the person for whom you seek records and the reason for wanting the records.

- **Divorce records:** Divorce records from 1738 to 1888 are filed in the county court, the governor's council records, the superior court, or the supreme judicial court. After 1888, divorce proceedings were usually filed at the county probate court and superior court.

- **Wills, deeds and land transaction records:** Inquire at county offices. City or county assessors have kept tax records; some are published.

- **Military records:** All war service records following the Revolutionary War are at the office of the Adjutant General in Boston.

- **Naturalization records:** Filed in the various county and district courts. These were copied and indexed in the 1930's for the years 1791 to 1906. The copies and indexes are at the National Archives, Boston Branch, in Waltham, Massachusetts. For records after 1906, contact the National Archives, Boston Branch, or Immigration and Naturalization Service in Boston.

- **Census records:** State censuses were taken in 1855 and 1865. The originals are at the Massachusetts State Archives.

Massachusetts

Registrar of Vital Records and Statistics
150 Mount Vernon Street
1st Floor
Dorchester, MA 02125-3105
(617) 740-2600
www.mass.gov/dph/bhsre/rvr/vrcopies.htm

Massachusetts State Archives
Columbia Point
220 Morrissey Boulevard
Boston, MA 02125
(617) 727-2816
www.state.ma.us/sec/arc/arcidx.htm

Naturalization Service, U.S. Department of Justice
JFK Federal Building, Government Center
Boston, Massachusetts 02203

Societies and Repositories

American-Portuguese Genealogical and Historical Society, Inc.; PO Box 644; Taunton, MA 02780-0644; (508) 822-5664; nestcard@tmlp.com.

Andover Historical Society; 97 Main Street; Andover, MA 01810; andhists@ma.ultranet.com; www.ultranet.com/~andhists.

Berkshire County Historical Society; 780 Holmes Road; Pittsfield, MA 01201; info@berkshirehistory.org; www.berkshirehistory.org.

Beverly Historical Society; 117 Cabot Street; Beverly, MA 01915; proberts@beverlyhistory.org; www.beverlyhistory.org.

Boston Chapter, MASSAR; MA; JManning@masSAR.org; www.massar.org/boston.htm.

Braintree Historical Society; 31 Tenney Road; Braintree, MA 02184; genthayer@aol.com; www.braintreehistoricalsoc.org.

Brockton Historical Society; 216 No. Pearl Street; Brockton, MA 02301; gerryb@brocktonma.com; www.brocktonma.com/bhs/bhs_mus.html.

Canton Historical Society; 1400 Washington Street; Canton, MA 02021; www.canton.org.

Cape Cod Genealogical Society; PO Box 1394; E. Harwich, MA 02645-6394.

Congregational Christian Historical Society; 14 Beacon St.; Boston, MA 02108.

Danvers Historical Society; PO Box 381; Danvers, MA 01923.

Dedham Historical Society; PO Box 215; Dedham, MA 02027; society@DedhamHistorical.org; www.dedhamhistorical.org/index.shtml.

Eastham Historical Society, Inc.; PO Box 8; Eastham, MA 02642.

Easton Historical Society; PO Box 3; North Easton, MA 02356; www.historiceaston.org.

Essex Institute; 132 Essex St.; Salem, MA 01970.

Essex Society of Genealogists, Inc; PO Box 313; Lynnfield, MA 01940-0313.

Falmouth Genealogical Society; PO Box 2107; Teaticket, MA 02536-2107.

Finlandia Foundation, Boston Chapter; 266 Sudbury Street; Marlboro, MA 01752.

Finnish American Society of Cape Cod; PO Box 220; West Barnstable, MA 02668.

Forest Park Station; Springfield, MA 01108-0206; www.rootsweb.com/~mawmgs.

Framingham Historical Society; PO Box 2032; Framingham, MA 01703-2032; (508) 872-3780; www.framingham.com/history/hstsoc_1.htm.

General Society of Mayflower Descendants; Box 3297; Plymouth, MA 02361-3297; www.mayflower.org.

Greater Lowell Genealogy Club; 325 Mammoth Road #2; Lowell, MA 01854; rleachr@aol.com.

Irish Ancestral Research Association (TIARA); PO Box 619; Sudbury, MA 01776.

Italian Genealogical Society of America; PO Box 3572; Peabody, MA 01961-3572.

Jewish Genealogical Society of Greater Boston; PO Box 610366; Newton, MA 02461-0366; info@jgsgb.org; www.jgsgb.org.

Knights and Ladies of Kaleva; PO Box 620; Maynard, MA 01752.

Martha's Vineyard Historical Society; Island of Martha's Vinyard; 59 School St.; PO Box 1310; Edgartown, MA 02539; (508) 627-4441; islebyte@shell.gis.net; www.marthasvineyardhistory.org.

Massachusetts Archives; 220 Morrissey Blvd.; Boston, MA 02125; (617) 727-2816; archives@sec.state.ma.us; www.state.ma.us/sec/arc.

Massachusetts Board of Library Commissioners; 648 Beacon Street; Boston, MA 02215; (617) 267-9400; info@mlin.lib.ma.us; www.mlin.lib.ma.us.

Massachusetts Genealogical Council; PO Box 5393; Cochituate, MA 01778-5393.

Massachusetts Historical Society; 1154 Boylston St.; Boston, MA 02215.

Massachusetts Society of Genealogists, Inc.; PO Box 215; Ashland, MA 01721-0215; harold.odiorne@the-spa.com; www.rootsweb.com/~masgi/msog.

Medford Historical Society; 10 Governors Ave.; Medford, MA 02155.

Middleborough Historical Association, Inc.; PO Box 304; Jackson St.; Middleboro, MA 02346.

NARA, Northeast Region (Boston); 380 Trapelo Road; Waltham, MA 02452-6399; (781) 663-0127; joan.gearin@nara.gov; www.archives.gov/facilities/ma/boston.html.

NARA, Northeast Region (Pittsfield); 10 Conte Drive; Pittsfield, MA 01201-8230; (413) 236-3604; jean.nudd@nara.gov; www.archives.gov/facilities/ma/pittsfield.html.

Needham Historical Society; 53 Glendoon Road; Needham, MA 02192; www.needhamonline.com/HistoricalSociety/home.html.

Old Colony Historical Society; 66 Church Green; Taunton, MA 02780; (508) 822-1622; OldColony@oldcolonyhistoricalsociety.org; www.oldcolonyhistoricalsociety.org.

Peabody Historical Society; 35 Washington St.; Peabody, MA 01960.

Plympton Historical Society; 189 Main Street; Plympton, MA 02367; www.geocities.com/PicketFence/Garden/2578.

Quincy Historical Society; 8 Adams Street; Quincy, MA 02169; qhist@ci.quincy.ma.us; www.key-biz.com/ssn/Quincy/hist_soc.html.

ROOTS Users Group of Cape Cod; PO Box 906; Brewster, MA 02631; mejpa@aol.com.

Sheffield Historical Society; Mark Dewey Research Center; Box 747; Sheffield, MA 01257-0747.

Shirley Historical Society; 182 Center Road; PO Box 217; Shirley, MA 01464-0217.

Sons of the American Revolution, Massachusetts Society; 101 Tremont St.; Suite 608; Boston, MA 02108.

South Shore Genealogical Society; PO Box 396; Norwell, MA 02061-0396.

Southborough Historical Society; PO Box 364; Southborough, MA 01772; www.ultranet.com/~sobohist/index.html.

Supreme Lodge Knights of Pythias; 59 Coddington Street, Suite 202; Quincy, MA 02169-4150; www.pythias.org.

Swedish Ancestry Research Society (SARA); PO Box 70603; Worcester, MA 01607-0603; SARAMembership@Netscape.net; www.members.tripod.com/~SARAssociation/SARa/SARA_Home_Page.htm.

The Association for Gravestone Studies; 278 Main Street, Suite 207; Greenfield, MA 01301; www.gravestonestudies.org.

The Genealogical Roundtable; PO Box 654; Concord, MA 01742-0654; tgo-wmnk@ma.ultranet.com.

The Jamaica Plain Historical Society; PO Box 2924; Jamaica Plain, MA 02130-0024; crosenbe@emerald.tufts.edu; www.geocities.com/jphistoricalsociety.

The Natick Historical Society; 58 Eliot Street; South Natick, MA 01760; elliot@ma.ultranet.com; www.ultranet.com/~elliot.

The Saugus Historical Society; PO Box 1209; Saugus, MA 01906-1209; darren@gbamed.com.; www.saugus.net/HistoricalSociety.

The Society of the War of 1812 in the Commonwealth of Massachusetts; MA; JManning@ma1812society.org; www.ma1812society.org.

Walpole Historical Society; Deacon Willard Lewis House; 33 West St.; Walpole, MA 02081; guyc@post.harvard.edu; www.walpole.ma.us/hhistoric.htm.

Western Massachusetts Genealogical Society; PO Box 206; Springfield, MA 01108-0206.

Winchester Historical Society; PO Box 127; Winchester, MA 01890-0127; president@winchesterhistoricalsociety.org; www.winchesterhistoricalsociety.org.

Bibliography and Record Sources

General

American Historical Society. *Encyclopedia of Massachusetts, Biographical-Genealogical*. 13 vols. New York: The American Historical Society, ca. 1916.

Bacon, Edwin Monroe. *Men Of Progress: One Thousand Biographical Sketches And Portraits Of Leaders In Business And Professional Life In The Commonwealth Of Massachusetts*. Boston: New England Magazine, 1894.

Banks, Charles Edward. *The English Ancestry and Homes of the Pilgrim Fathers Who Came to Plymouth on the 'Mayflower' in 1620, the 'Fortune' in 1621, and the 'Anne' and the 'Little James' in 1623*. (1929). Reprint. Baltimore: Genealogical Publishing Co., 1989.

Banks, Charles Edward. *The Planters of the Commonwealth in Massachusetts, 1620–1640*. (1930) Reprint. Baltimore: Genealogical Publishing, 1996.

Barber, John W. *Historical Collections . . . Relating to the History and Antiquities of Every Town in Massachusetts. With Geographical Descriptions Illustrated by 200 Engravings*. (1839, 1844) Reprint. Baltimore: Clearfield Co., 1995.

Bowman, George Ernest. *The Mayflower Reader. A Selection of Articles from 'The Mayflower Descendant.' (1899–1905)*. Reprint. Baltimore: Clearfield Co., 1996.

Bowman, George Ernest. *Massachusetts Society of Mayflower Descendants: The Bowman Files*. Boston: Massachusetts Society of Mayflower Descendants, 1983.

Brush, John Woolman. *Baptists in Massachusetts*. Valley Forge, Pennsylvania: Judson Press, 1970.

Bushman. *King and People in Provincial Massachusetts*. Galveston, Texas: Frontier Press, 1992.

Catalog of Manuscripts of the Massachusetts Historical Society. 7 vols. Boston: G. K. Hall and Co., 1969.

Central Massachusetts Genealogical Society (Westminster, Massachusetts). *A Guide To Genealogical And Historical Holdings Of Massachusetts Libraries*. Rev.

ed. Westminster, Massachusetts: Central Massachusetts Genealogical Society, 1997.

Colburn, Jeremiah. *Bibliography of the Local History of Massachusetts*. Ann Arbor, Michigan: University Microfilms, 1989.

Colonial Society of Massachusetts. *Medicine in Colonial Massachusetts, 1620–1820*. Galveston, Texas: Frontier Press, 1980.

Colonial Society of Massachusetts. *Seafaring in Colonial Massachusetts*. Galveston, Texas: Frontier Press, 1980.

Corbin, Walter E. *Corbin Manuscript Collection in New England Historic Genealogical Society*. S.l.: s.n., 1982.

Crandall, Ralph J., ed. *Genealogical Research in New England*. Baltimore: Genealogical Publishing, 1984.

Cutter, William Richard. *Genealogical and Personal Memoirs Relating to the Families of the State of Massachusetts*. 4 vols. New York: Lewis Historical Publishing, 1910.

Duffy, Mark J., ed. *The Episcopal Diocese of Massachusetts 1784–1984*. Boston: Episcopal Diocese of Massachusetts, 1984.

Eliot, Samuel Atkins. *Biographical History of Massachusetts*. 10 vols. Boston: Massachusetts Biographical Society, 1911–18.

Flagg, Charles Allcott. *A Guide to Massachusetts Local History: Being a Bibliographic Index to the Literature of the Towns, Cities and Counties of the State, Including Books, Pamphlets, Articles in Periodicals and Collected Works, Books in Preparation, Historical Manuscripts, Newspaper Clippings, Etc.* Salem, Massachusetts: The Salem Press Company, 1907.

Forbes, Abner. *The Rich Men of Massachusetts: Containing a Statement of the Reputed Wealth of About Fifteen Hundred Persons, With Brief Sketches of More Than One Thousand Characters*. Boston: Fetridge and Company, 1851.

Genealogies of Mayflower Families: From the New England Historical and Genealogical Register. 3 vols. Baltimore: Genealogical Publishing, 1985.

Goodwin, John A. *The Pilgrim Republic: An Historical Review of the Colony of New Plymouth, with Sketches of Other New England Settlements, the History of Congregationalism, and the Creeds of the Period*. Boston: Tickner, 1888.

Green, Samuel Abbott. *Centennial Bibliography*. Ann Arbor, Michigan: University Microfilms, 1989.

Greenlaw, William Prescott. *The Greenlaw Index of the New England Historic Genealogical Society*. 2 vols. Boston: G. K. Hall, 1979.

Hallowell, Richard P. *The Quaker Invasion of Massachusetts*. Boston: Houghton Mifflin, 1883.

Hart, Albert Bushnell, ed. *Commonwealth History of Massachusetts: Colony, Province, and State*. 5 vols. New York: The States History, 1927–1930.

Haskell, John D., Jr., ed. *Massachusetts: A Bibliography of Its History*. Hanover, New Hampshire: University Press of New England, 1983.

Historical Records Survey. *Preliminary Edition of Guide to Depositories of Manuscript Collections in Massachusetts*. Boston: Historical Records Survey, 1939.

Jacobson, Judith. *Massachusetts Bay Connections*. (1992). Reprint. Baltimore: Clearfield Co., 1994.

Kaufman, Martin, John W. Ifkovic, and Joseph Carvalho. *A Guide to the History of Massachusetts*. New York: Greenwood Press, 1988.

Lewis, Ella May Swint. *Bible Records for Massachusetts Families*. Springfield, Massachusetts: Lewis, 1960.

Lindberg, Marcia Wiswall, ed. *Genealogist's Handbook for New England Research*. 3rd ed. Boston: New England Historic Genealogical Society, 1993.

Longver, Phyllis O., and Pauline J. Oesterlin. *Surname Guide to Massachusetts Town Histories*. Bowie, Maryland: Heritage Books, 1993.

Massachusetts and Maine Families in the Ancestry of Walter Goodwin Davis. 3 vols. (1916–1963). Reprint. Baltimore: Genealogical Publishing Co., 1996.

Massachusetts Biographical Dictionary: People of All Times and All Places Who Have Been Important to the History and Life of the State. Wilmington, Delaware: American Historical Publications, 1988.

Massachusetts Research Outline. Series U.S.-States, no. 22. Salt Lake City: Family History Library, 1988.

Massachusetts, 1620–1930. S.l.: Brøderbund, 1998. CD-ROM.

Massachusetts. State Archives. *Card Index to the Massachusetts Archives*. Salt Lake City: Filmed by the Genealogical Society of Utah, 1972–1973. Microfilm, 57 rolls.

New England Genealogical Society (Boston, Massachusetts). *Genealogical Card Catalog, A–Z*. Microreproduction of manuscript and typescript at the New England Historic Genealogical Society. Salt Lake City: Genealogical Society of Utah, 1970. 19 microfilm.

New England Historic Genealogical Society. *English Origins of New England Families: from the New England Historical and Genealogical Register*. First Series, 3 vols. 1984. Second Series, 3 vols., 1985. Baltimore: Genealogical Publishing.

Northend, William Dummer. *The Bay Colony: A Civil, Religious and Social History of the Massachusetts Colony and Its Settlements from the Landing at Cape Ann in 1624 to the Death of Governor Winthrop in 1650*. Boston: Estes and Lauriat, 1896.

Pilgrim Genealogies and Histories. S.l.: Brøderbund, 1999. CD-ROM

Pope, Charles Henry. *The Pioneers of Massachusetts 1620–1650*. (1900). Reprint. Baltimore: Genealogical Publishing Co., 1990.

Pope, Charles Henry. *The Plymouth Scrap Book: The Oldest Original Documents Extant in Plymouth Archives Printed Verbatim.* Boston: C. E. Goodspeed, 1918.

Publications of the Colonial Society of Massachusetts, vol. 4, *Collections.* Boston: the society, 1910.

Rider, Fremont, ed. *American Genealogical-Biographical Index. Vols. 1–186+.* Middletown, Connecticut: Godfrey Memorial Library, 1952–.

Savage, James. *A Genealogical Dictionary of the First Settlers of New England Showing Three Generations of Those Who Came Before May 1692, on the Basis of Farmer's Register.* 4 vols. (1860–1862.) Reprint. Baltimore: Genealogical Publishing Company, 1965.

Schweitzer, George K. *Massachusetts Genealogical Research.* Knoxville: George K. Schweitzer, 1990.

Shaw, H. K., comp. *Families of the Pilgrims.* (1956). Reprint. Salem, Massachusetts: Higginson Books, 1994.

Shurtleff, Nathaniel B., and David Pulsifer, eds. *Records of the Colony of New Plymouth in New England.* 12 vols. Boston: William White, 1855–1861.

Southern California Genealogical Society. *Sources of Genealogical Help in Massachusetts.* Burbank, California: The Society, n.d.

Stratton, Eugene Aubrey. *Plymouth Colony: Its History and People, 1620–1691.* Salt Lake City, Utah: Ancestry, 1986.

True, Charles K. *John Winthrop and the Great Colony, or, Sketches of the Settlement of Boston, and of the More Prominent Persons Connected with the Massachusetts Colony.* New York: Nelson & Phillips, 1877.

Tyng, Dudley. *Massachusetts Episcopalians, 1607–1957.* Boston: Episcopal Diocese of Massachusetts, 1960.

Wells, Charles Chauncey and Suzanne Austin Wells. *Preachers, Patriots & Plain Folks: Boston's Guide to King's Chapel, Granary, and Central Cemeteries,* 2004. Oak Park, Illinois: Chauncey Park Press.

Wright, Carroll D. *Report on the Custody and Condition of the Public Records of Parishes, Towns, and Counties.* Boston: Wright and Potter, 1889.

Wright, Norman E. *Genealogy in America. Vol. 1, Massachusetts, Connecticut, and Maine.* Salt Lake City: Deseret Book, 1968.

Young, Alexander. *Chronicles of the First Planters of the Colony of Massachusetts Bay, from 1623 to 1636.* (1846) Reprint. Baltimore: Clearfield Co., 1996.

Young, Alexander. *Chronicles of the Pilgrim Fathers of the Colony of Plymouth from 1602 to 1625.* (1844) Reprint. Baltimore: Clearfield Co., 1995.

Atlases, Maps and Gazetteers

Davis, Charlotte P. *Directory of Massachusetts Place Names, Current and Obsolete.* Lexington, Massachusetts: Bay State News, 1987.

Federal Writer's Program. *The Origin of Massachusetts Place Names of the State, Cities, and Towns.* New York: Harian Publications, 1941.

Gannett, Henry. *A Geographic Dictionary of Massachusetts.* Baltimore, Maryland: Genealogical Publishing Company, 1978.

Guzzi, Paul. *Historical Data Relating to Counties, Cities, and Towns in Massachusetts.* Boston: Secretary of the Commonwealth, 1975.

Hayward, John. *A Gazetteer of Massachusetts: Containing Descriptions of All the Counties, Towns and Districts in the Commonwealth; Also, of Its Principal Mountains, Rivers, Capes, Bays, Harbors, Islands, and Fashionable Resorts. . . .* Washington, D.C.: Library of Congress Photoduplication Service, 1989.

Lindberg, Marcia W. *Genealogist's Handbook for New England Research.* 3rd ed. Boston: New England Historic Genealogical Society, 1993.

Long, John H. *Connecticut, Maine, Massachusetts, and Rhode Island Atlas of Historical County Boundaries.* New York: Simon & Schuster, 1994.

Massachusetts, Harbor and Land Commission. *Massachusetts Town Boundary Atlases, 1898–1916.* Salt Lake City: Genealogical Society of Utah, 1974.

Massachusetts, Secretary of the Commonwealth. *Historical Data Relating to Counties, Cities, and Towns in Massachusetts.* Boston: The Commonwealth, 1975.

Nason, Elias. *Gazetteer of the State of Massachusetts.* Boston: B. B. Russell, 1874.

Spear, Burton W. *Search For the Passengers of the Mary & John, 1630.* 27+ vols. Toledo, Ohio: B.W. Spear, 1985–.

Spofford, Jeremiah. *A Historical and Statistical Gazetteer of Massachusetts: With Sketches of the Principal Events from Its Settlement; a Catalogue of Prominent Characters, and Historical and Statistical Notices of the Several Cities and Towns, Alphabetically Arranged. With a New Map of the State.* 2nd ed., rev. Haverhill, Massachusetts: E. G. Frothingham, 1860.

United States, Geographical Survey. *Topographic Maps of Massachusetts, Rhode Island and Connecticut.* Washington, D.C.: United States Geological Survey, 1950, 1964–1965.

Wilkie, Richard W., and Jack Tager, eds. *Historical Atlas of Massachusetts.* Amherst: University of Massachusetts Press, 1991.

Census Records

Available Census Records and Census Substitutes

Federal Census 1790, 1800, 1810, 1820, 1830, 1840, 1850, 1860, 1870, 1880, 1900, 1910, 1920, 1930

Federal Mortality Schedules 1850, 1860, 1870, 1880

Union Veterans and Widows 1890

Freemen 1630–1691

State/Territorial Census 1779, 1855, 1865

U.S. Direct Tax List 1798

Tax Lists 1760–1771, 1780–1792, 1810–1811

Dollarhide, William. *The Census Book: A Genealogist's Guide to Federal Census Facts, Schedules and Indexes.* Bountiful, Utah: Heritage Quest, 1999.

Kemp, Thomas J. *The American Census Handbook.* Wilmington, Delaware: Scholarly Resources, Inc., 2001.

Lainhart, Ann S. *State Census Records.* Baltimore: Genealogical Publishing Co., Inc., 1992.

List Of Freemen Of Massachusetts, 1630–1691. Baltimore: Genealogical Pub. Co, 1978.

Marnier, Mary Lou and Patricia Rougham Bellows. *A Research Aid for the Massachusetts 1910 Federal Census.* Sudbury, Massachusetts: Computerized Assistance, 1988.

Pruitt, Bettye Hobbs, ed. *The Massachusetts Tax Valuation List of 1771.* Boston: G. K. Hall, 1978.

Szucs, Loretto Dennis and Matthew Wright. *Finding Answers in U.S. Census Records.* Ancestry Publishing, 2001.

Thorndale, William and William Dollarhide. *Map Guides to the U.S. Federal Censuses, 1790–1920: Connecticut, Massachusetts, Rhode Island, 1790–1920.* Baltimore: Genealogical Publishing Co., 1987.

United States, Secretary of the Treasury. *Massachusetts and Maine Direct Tax Census of 1798.* Cambridge, Massachusetts: New England Historic Genealogical Society, 1978.

Court Records, Probate and Wills

Barnes, Thomas G., ed. *The Book of the General Laws and Liberties Concerning the Inhabitants of Massachusetts.* (Reproduction) Galveston, Texas: Frontier Press, n.d.

Busiel, Alice. *Miscellaneous Index and Records (1659–1692) Prior to the Appointment of a Judge of Probate in 1692.* Microfilm of manuscript filmed in Middlesex County, Massachusetts. Salt Lake City: Filmed by the Genealogical Society of Utah, 1964.

Court and probate records for Massachusetts from the Seventeenth through the Twentieth Centuries can be found at the Massachusetts State Archives. For descriptions of collections search online at— www.state.ma.us/sec/arc/arcgen/genidx.htm#military.

Essex County, Massachusetts, Probate Index, 1638–1840. Transcribed by Melinde Lutz Sanborn from the original by W. P. Upham. 2 vols. Boston: Sanborn, 1987.

Konig, David Thomas, ed. *Plymouth Court Records 1686–1859: The Court of Common Pleas and General Sessions of the Peace.* 16 vols. Wilmington, Delaware: Michael Glazier, Inc., 1978–1981.

Law in Colonial Massachusetts, 1630–1800. Boston: Colonial Society of Massachusetts, 1984.

Massachusetts Secretary of the Commonwealth, comp. *List of Persons Whose Names Have Been Changed in Massachusetts, 1780–1892.* (1893) Reprint. Salem, Massachusetts: Higginson Book, Co., 1993.

Massachusetts, Probate Court (Middlesex County). *Index to the Probate Records of the County of Middlesex, Massachusetts: First Series, from 1648 to 1871.* Cambridge, Massachusetts: s.n., 1914.

Massachusetts, Probate Court (Middlesex County). *Index to the Probate Records of the County of Middlesex, Massachusetts: Second Series.* 8 vols. Cambridge, Massachusetts: 1912–1953.

Massachusetts. County Court (Suffolk County). *County Court Files, 1629–1797.* Microfilm of original court files, Boston, Massachusetts. Salt Lake City: Genealogical Society of Utah. Microfilm, 1,639 rolls.

Mayflower Source Records: Primary Data Concerning Southeastern Massachusetts, Cape Cod, and the Islands of Nantucket and Martha's Vineyards. Baltimore: Genealogical Publishing Co., 1986.

McGhan, Judith. *Suffolk County Wills: Abstracts of the Earliest Wills Upon Record in the County of Suffolk, Massachusetts.* Baltimore: Genealogical Publishing Co., 1984.

Paige, L. *List Of Freemen Of Massachusetts, 1630–1691.* Reprint. Baltimore: Genealogical Pub. Co, 1978.

Probate Records of Essex County, Massachusetts. 1635–1681. 3 vols. Salem, Massachusetts: Essex Institute, 1916–20. Reprint, Newburyport, Massachusetts: Parker River Researchers, and Decorah, Iowa: Anundsen Pub, 1988.

Pulsifer, David. *Deeds, Wills, Inventories, etc. 1647–1714: Records of the County of Norfolk, in the Colony of Massachusetts.* Salem, Massachusetts, n.d.

Roser, Susan E. *Mayflower Deeds and Probates: From the Files of George Ernest Bowman at the Massachusetts Society of Mayflower Descendants.* Baltimore: Genealogical Publishing Co., 1994.

Rounds, H. L. Peter. *Abstracts of Bristol County, Massachusetts, Probate Records.* [1687–1762]. 2 vols. Baltimore: Genealogical Publishing Co., 1988.

Shaw, Hubert Kinney. *Plymouth Colony Wills And Inventories: Taken From The Mayflower Descendant.* 3 vols. [n.p. n. p.] Typescripts.

Sherman, Ruth Wilder and Robert S. Wakefield. *Plymouth Colony Probate Guide: Where to Find Wills and Related Data for 800 People of Plymouth Colony, 1620–1691.* Warwick, Rhode Island: Plymouth Colony Research Group, 1983.

Simmons, C. H., Jr. *Plymouth Colony Wills and Inventories,* 2 vols. *1633–1669.* Rockport, Maine: Picton Press, 1996.

Wood, Ralph V., Jr. *Plymouth County Massachusetts, Probate Index 1686–1881.* Camden, Maine: Picton Press, 1988.

Emigration, Immigration, Migration and Naturalization

Note: Emigration and Naturalization records for Massachusetts from the Seventeenth through the Twentieth Centuries can be found at the Massachusetts State Archives. For descriptions of collections search online at www.state.ma.us/sec/arc/arcgen/genidx.htm#military.

Anderson, Robert C., George F. Sanborn Jr., and Melinde Lutz Sanborn. *The Great Migration Begins: Immigrants to New England, 1620–1633*. Boston, Massachusetts: New England Historic Genealogical Society, 1999. See also the online database at www.newenglandancestors.org/research/database/great_migration/.

Banks, Charles Edward. *The Planters of the Commonwealth: A Study of the Emigrants and Emigration in Colonial Times: To Which are Added Lists of Passengers to Boston and to the Bay Colony; the Ships Which Brought Them; Their English Homes, and the Places of Their Settlement in Massachusetts*. (1930). Reprint. Baltimore: Genealogical Publishing Co., 1991.

Banks, Charles Edward. *The Winthrop Fleet of 1630: An Account of the Vessels, the Voyage, the Passengers. . .* (1930). Reprint. Baltimore: Genealogical Publishing Co., 1994.

Bolton, Ethel Stanwood. *Immigrants to New England, 1700–1775*. Salem, Massachusetts: Essex Institute, 1931.

Coldham, Peter Wilson. *The Complete Book of Emigrants, 1607–1776, and Emigrants in Bondage, 1614–1775*. Novato, California: Brøderbund Software, 1996.

Coldham, Peter Wilson. *The Complete Book of Emigrants, 1661–1669*. Baltimore: Genealogical Publishing Co., 1990.

Coldham, Peter Wilson. *The Complete Book of Emigrants, 1700–1750*. Baltimore: Genealogical Publishing Co., 1992.

Colket, Meridith B. *Founders of Early American Families: Emigrants from Europe 1607–1657*. Cleveland, Ohio: General Court of the Order of Founders and Patriots of America, 1985.

Filby, P. William. *Passenger and Immigration Lists Index*. 11 vols. Detroit: Gale Research, 1981–.

Harris, Ruth-Ann and Donald M. Jacobs, eds. *The Search for Missing Friends: Irish Immigrant Advertisements Placed in the Boston Pilot*. Boston. 5 vols. New England Historic Genealogical Society, 1989, 1991, 1993, 1995, 1996.

Massachusetts. Secretary of the Commonwealth. *Indexes to Returns of Naturalization, 1920–1923, 1924–1925*. Microreproduction of card index at Massachusetts State Archives, Boston, Massachusetts. Salt Lake City: Genealogical Society of Utah, 1994. 7 microfilm.

Massachusetts. Secretary of the Commonwealth. *Returns of Naturalization before Various Massachusetts Courts, 1885–1931*. Microreproduction of documents at Massachusetts State Archives, Boston, Massachusetts. Salt Lake City: Genealogical Society of Utah, 1993. 9 microfilm.

Munroe, J. B. *A List of Alien Passengers, Bonded from January 1, 1847 to January 1, 1851, for the Use of the Overseers of the Poor in the Commonwealth of Massachusetts*. (1851) Reprint. Baltimore: Genealogical Publishing Co., 1991.

Thayer, Mrs. Nathaniel. *"The Immigrants (1830–1929)" Commonwealth History of Massachusetts*, vol. 4. New York: The States History Company, 1930.

United States, Bureau of Customs. *A Supplemental Index to Passenger Lists of Vessels Arriving at Atlantic & Gulf Coast Ports (excluding New York) 1820–1874*. Washington, D.C.: National Archives Records Services, 1960.

United States, Bureau of Customs. *Passenger Lists of Vessels Arriving at Boston, 1820–1891: with index 1848–1891*. Washington, D.C.: National Archives Record Service, 1959–1960.

United States, District Court (Massachusetts). *Naturalization Index Cards, 1790–1926*. Microfilm of original records in the offices of the U.S. District Court, Boston, Massachusetts. Salt Lake City: Genealogical Society of Utah, 1985. 17 microfilm.

United States, Immigration and Naturalization Services. *St. Albans District Manifest Records of Aliens Arriving from Foreign Contiguous Territory*. Washington, D.C.: National Archives Records Service, 1986.

United States. District Court (Massachusetts). *Naturalization Records, 1906–1917*. Washington, D.C.: National Archives, 1988.

United States. Immigration and Naturalization Service. *Index To New England Naturalization Petitions, 1791–1906*. Washington, D.C.: National Archives. Central Plains Region, 1983. 117 microfilm.

United States. Immigration and Naturalization Service. *Index to Passenger Lists of Vessels Arriving At Boston, Jan. 1, 1902 to Dec.31, 1920; Passenger Lists of Vessels Arriving At Boston, Aug. 1, 1891–1935; Book Indexes to Boston Passenger Lists, 1899–1940*. Washington, D.C.: National Archives and Records Service, 1944–1945, 1956.

Whitmore, William H. *Port Arrivals and Immigrants to the City of Boston 1715–1716*. (1900) Reprint. Baltimore: Genealogical Publishing, 1989.

Land and Property

Church of Jesus Christ of Latter-day Saints, The. Genealogical Society. Cataloging Section. *Registry of Deeds, Etc. from the Various Counties of Massachusetts, a Register of Contents*. Salt Lake City: Filmed by the Genealogical Society of Utah, 1969.

Hone, Wade E. *Land and Property Research in the United States.* Salt Lake City: Ancestry Incorporated, 1997.

Judd, Sylvester, comp. *Judd Manuscripts (Connecticut).* Microfilm of manuscript at Forbes Public Library, Northampton, Hampshire County, Massachusetts. Salt Lake City: Filmed by the Genealogical Society of Utah, 1960. 5 microfilm.

Massachusetts Archives. Land Court registration decreases. Boston: Massachusetts Archives, 2002. online at— www.state.ma.us/sec/arc/arcgen/genidx.htm

Roser, Susan E. *Mayflower Deeds & Probates: From the Files of George Ernest Bowman at the Massachusetts Society of Mayflower Descendants.* Baltimore, Maryland: Genealogical Publishing co., 1994.

Shaw, Hubert Kinney. *Plymouth Colony Wills and Inventories: Taken from the Mayflower Descendant.* Typescripts. n. p.

Shurtleff, N. B., and David Pulsifer, eds. *Records of the Colony of New Plymouth in New England.* 12 vols. Boston: William White, 1855–61.

Shurtleff, Nathaniel B. *Records of the Governor and Company of the Massachusetts Bay in New England.* 5 vols. Boston: W. White, 1853–54.

Military

Note: Military records for Massachusetts from the Seventeenth through the Twentieth Centuries can be found at the Massachusetts State Archives. For descriptions of collections search online at— www.state.ma.us/sec/arc/arcgen/genidx.htm#military.

Adjutant General of Massachusetts. *Massachusetts Soldiers, Sailors, and Marines of the Civil War.* 9 vols. Norwood, Massachusetts: Norwood Press, 1931–1935.

Adjutant General of Massachusetts. *Records of the Massachusetts Volunteer Militia.* Boston: Gardner W. Pearson, 1913. Boston: Wright and Potter Printing, 1913.

Allen, Gardner, Weld. *Massachusetts Privateers of the Revolution.* Boston: Massachusetts Historical Society, 1927.

Broadfoot Publishing Company. *Papers of the Military Historical Society of Massachusetts.* 15 vols. Wilmington, North Carolina: Broadfoot Pub., n.d.

Budge, George Madison. *Soldiers in King Phillip's War. Official Lists of the Soldiers of Massachusetts Colony Serving in Philip's War, and Sketches of the Principal Officers, Copies of Ancient Documents and Records Relating to the War.* (1906) Reprint. Baltimore: Clearfield Co., 1995.

Doeskin, Carole. *Massachusetts Officers and Soldiers of the Seventeenth Century Conflicts.* Boston: Society of Colonial Wars, 1982.

Donahue, Mary E. *Massachusetts Officers and Soldiers 1702–1722: Queen Anne's War to Dimmer's War.* Boston: Society of Colonial Wars, 1980.

Higginson, Thomas W. *Massachusetts in the Army and Navy during the War of 1861–1865.* 2 vols. Boston: Wright and Potter, 1895–1896.

Jones, Alfred E. *The Loyalists of Massachusetts: Their Memorials, Petitions and Claims.* (1930) Reprint. Baltimore: Clearfield Co., 1995.

MacLean, John P. *Historical Account of the Settlements of Scotch Highlanders in America Prior to the Peace of 1783.* Baltimore: Genealogical Publishing Co., 1968

Massachusetts Adjunct General's Office. R*ecord of Massachusetts Volunteers, 1861–1865.* 2 vols. Boston, Massachusetts: Adjutant General's Office, 1868–1870.

Massachusetts Colonial Wars Database. Boston: Society of Colonial Wars in the Commonwealth of Massachusetts, 2002. Online database—www.newenglandancestors .org/research/database/.

Massachusetts, Adjunct General. *Massachusetts Soldiers, Sailors and Marines in the Civil War.* Brookline, Massachusetts: Adjutant General's Office, 1931–1935.

Massachusetts, Department of the State Secretary. *Massachusetts Soldiers and Sailors of the Revolutionary War.* Boston: Wright & Potter, 1896–1908.

McKay, Robert E. *Massachusetts Soldiers in the French and Indian Wars, 1744–1755.* Boston: Society of Colonial Wars, 1978.

Pearson, Gardner W. *Records of the Massachusetts Volunteer Militia Called Out by the Governor of Massachusetts to Suppress a Threatened Invasion during the War of 1812–1814.* (1913) Reprint. Baltimore: Clearfield Co., 1993.

Pierce, Ebenezer Weaver. *Pierce's Colonial Lists, Civil, Military and Professional Lists of Plymouth and Rhode Island Colonies . . . 1621–1700.* (1881) Reprint. Baltimore: Clearfield Co., 1995.

Stachiw, Myron O. *Massachusetts Officers and Soldiers, 1723–1743: Dummer's War to the War of Jenkin's Ear.* Boston: Society of Colonial Wars in the Commonwealth of Massachusetts and The New England Historic Genealogical Society, 1979.

Stark, J. H. *The Loyalists of Massachusetts, and the Other Side of the American Revolution.* (1910) Reprint. Salem, Massachusetts: Higginson Books, 1990.

United States Veterans Administration. *Index to War of 1812 Pension Application Files.* Washington, D.C.: National Archives, 1960.

United States. Adjutant General's Office. *General Index to Compiled Military Service Records of Revolutionary Ward Soldiers.* Washington, D.C.: National Archives, 1942.

United States. Army. Massachusetts Infantry. "Casualties from Massachusetts in World War I, 1918," *Enlistments, Enrollments, Medical Examinations, Detachments, Oaths, Rosters, Election Returns, Discharges, Desertions, Resignations, Etc.* Microfilm of originals in the National Guard Supply Depot in Natick,

Massachusetts. Salt Lake City: Filmed by the Genealogical Society of Utah, 1988–1991. 120 microfilm.

United States. Selective Service System. *Massachusetts, World War I Selective Service System Draft Registration Cards, 1917–1918.* Washington, D.C.: National Archives, 1987–1988.

United States. Veterans Administration. *Revolutionary War Pension and Bounty-Land-Warrant Application Files.* Washington, D.C.: National Archives, 1969.

United States. Veterans Administration. *Selected Records from Revolutionary War Pension & Bounty-Land-Warrant Application Files.* Washington, D.C.: National Archives, 1969.

Voye, Nancy S., ed. *Massachusetts Officers in the French and Indian Wars 1748–1763. Boston Society of Colonial Wars 1748–1763.* Boston Society of Colonial Wars, 1975.

White, Virgil D. *Genealogical Abstracts of the Revolutionary War Pension Files.* 4 vols. Waynesboro, Tennessee: National Historical Publishing, 1990.

White, Virgil D. *Index to Revolutionary War Service Records.* 4 vols. Waynesboro, Tennessee: National Historical Publishing, 1995.

White, Virgil D., trans. *Index to War of 1812 Pension Files.* Waynesboro, Tennessee: National Historical Publishing Co., 1992.

Vital and Cemetery Records

American Antiquarian Society. *Index of Marriages in Massachusetts Centinel and Columbian Centinel, 1784 to 1840.* Boston: G. K. Hall and Co., 1961.

Bailey, Frederick W. *Early Massachusetts Marriages Prior to 1800: With the Addition of Plymouth Colony Marriages, 1692–1746.* 3 vols in 1. Baltimore: Genealogical Publishing Co., 1968.

Boston Athenaeum. *Index of Obituaries in Boston Newspapers, 1704–1800.* Boston: G. K. Hall and Co., 1968.

Daughters of the American Revolution. *Grave Locations of Revolutionary Soldiers and Sailors of Maine and Massachusetts.* Microfilm of original card index (396 cm., ca., 2500 cards.). Salt Lake City: Genealogical Society of Utah, 1991. 2 microfilm.

Holbrook, Jay Mack. *Bibliography of Massachusetts Vital Records 1620–1905.* Microfiche. Oxford, Massachusetts: Archive Publishing/Microform Books, 1996.

Holbrook, Jay Mack. *Massachusetts Birth, Marriage, & Death Indexes, 1841–1895.* Microfiche. Archive Publishing/Microform Books, 1989.

Holbrook, Jay Mack. *Massachusetts Cemetery Records: Quabbin Park 1741–1984.* Microfiche. Archive Publishing/Microform Books, 1985.

Landis, John T. *Mayflower Descendants and Their Marriage for Two Generations After the Landing.* (1922). Reprint. Baltimore: Clearfield Co., 1990.

Ledogar, Edwin Richard. *Vital Statistics of Eastern Connecticut, Western Rhode Island, South Central Massachusetts.* 2 vols. 1995. Reprint on microfiche. Arvada, Colorado: Ancestor Publishers, 1995.

Massachusetts, Secretary of the Commonwealth. *Births, Marriages (1841–1895), And Deaths (1841–1899); Indexes To Births And Marriages (1841–1905), Deaths (1841–1971).* Microfilm of original records in the Division of Vital Statistics, State House, Boston, Massachusetts. Salt Lake City: Filmed by the Genealogical Society of Utah, 1974, 1985. 398 microfilm.

Massachusetts, Secretary of the Commonwealth. *Divorce Index, 1952–1970.* Microreproduction of original records at the State House in Boston, Massachusetts. Salt Lake City: Genealogical Society of Utah, 1974. 2 microfilm.

Mayflower Source Records: Primary Data Concerning Southeastern Massachusetts, Cape Cod, and the Islands of Nantucket and Martha's Vineyard. Baltimore: Genealogical Publishing Co., 1986.

Stevens, C. J. *The Massachusetts Magazine: Marriage and Death Notices, 1789–1796.* Lambertville, New Jersey: Hunterdon House, 1978.

Torrey, Clarence Almon. *New England Marriages Prior to 1700.* Andover, Massachusetts: Genealogical Publishing Co., 1985.

Vital Records of [town], Massachusetts, to the Year 1850. Boston: New England Historic Genealogical Society, 1902 to ca. 1920. (Series of records for approximately 200 towns.)

County	Map	Date	Parent County or Territory From Which Organized
Website	Index	Created	Address/Details

Barnstable   C8   **2 Jun 1685**

www.barnstablecounty.org/

New Plymouth Colony

Barnstable County; 3195 Main St; Barnstable, MA 2630;
Ph. (508) 362-2511

Details: (Clerk Circuit Court has Divorce & Court Records from 1828; Register of Deeds has Land Records; Probate Judge has Probate Records)

    Towns Organized Before 1800: Barnstable 1638, Chatham 1712, Dennis 1793, Eastham 1646, Falmouth 1694, Harwich 1694, Mashpee 1763, Orleans 1797, Provincetown 1727, Truro 1709, Wellfleet 1763, Yarmouth 1639

Berkshire   Q5   **1761**

www.rootsweb.com/~maberksh/

Hampshire

Berkshire County; 76 East St; Pittsfield, MA 1201;
Ph. (413) 448-8424

Details: (Clerk Courts has Divorce Records 1761–1922 & Court Records from 1761; Probate Judge has Divorce Records from 1922 & Probate Records from 1761; Register of Deeds has Land Records)

    Towns Organized Before 1800: Adams 1778, Alford 1773, Becket 1765, Cheshire 1793, Clarksburg 1798, Dalton 1784, Egremont 1760, Great Barington 1761, Hancock 1776, Lanesborough 1765, Lee 1777, Lenox 1767, Mount Washington 1779, New Ashford 1781, New Marlborough 1759, Otis 1773, Peru 1771, Pittsfield 1761, Richmond 1765, Savoy 1797, Sheffield 1733, Standisfield 1762, Stockbridge 1739, Tyringham 1762, Washington 1777, West Stockbridge 1774, Williamstown 1765

Bristol   G7   **2 Jun 1685**

www.bristol-county.org/bristol_home.htm

New Plymouth Colony

Bristol County; 9 Court St; Taunton, MA 02780-3223;
Ph. (508) 824-9681

Details: (Clerk Courts has Court Records from 1796 & Naturalization Records; Town Clerks have Birth, Marriage & Death Records; Probate Court has Divorce Records from 1921 & Probate Records)

    Towns Organized Before 1800: Attleboro 1694, Berkley 1735, Dartmouth 1652, Dighton 1712, Easton 1725, Freetown 1683, Mansfield 1770, New Bedford 1787, Norton 1710, Raynham 1731, Rehoboth 1645, Sandwich 1638, Somerset 1790, Swansea 1667, Taunton 1639, Westport 1787

Dukes   E10   **22 Jun 1695**

www.vineyard.net/vineyard/history/dukes/

(Martha's Vineyard)

Dukes County; PO Box 190; Edgartown, MA 2539;
Ph. (508) 627-5535

Details: (Clerk Courts has Divorce & Court Records from 1859; Probate Court has Probate Records; Town Clerks have Birth, Marriage, Death & Burial Records)

    Towns Organized Before 1800: Chilmark 1694, Edgartown 1671, Tisbury 1671

Essex   F3   **10 May 1643**

www.essexcountyma.org/

Original county

Essex County; 36 Federal St; Salem, MA 1970; Ph. (978) 741-0200

Details: (Probate Court has Probate Records; Register of Deeds has Land Records from 1640; County Clerk has Birth, Marriage & Death Records)

    Towns Organized Before 1800: Amesbury 1668, Andover 1646, Beverly 1668, Boxford 1694, Danvers 1752, Hamilton 1793, Haverhill 1641, Ipswich 1634, Lynn 1635, Lynnfield 178

County Website	Map Index	Date Created	Parent County or Territory From Which Organized Address/Details
Franklin www.rootsweb.com/~mafrankl/	N3	**24 Jun 1811**	**Hampshire** Franklin County; 425 Main St; Greenfield, MA 01301-3313; Ph. (413) 774-7011 **Details:** (Clerk Courts has Divorce & Court Records from 1811; Register of Probate has Probate Records; Register of Deeds has Land Records) Towns Organized Before 1800: Ashfield 1765, Bernardston 1762, Buckland 1779, Charlemont 1765, Colrain 1761, Conway 1767, Deerfield 1677, Gil 1793, Greenfield 1753, Hawley 1792, Heath 1785, Leverett 1774, Leyden 1784, Montague 1754, New Salem 1753, Northfield 1714, Orange 1783, Rowe 1785, Shelburne 1768, Shuetesbury 1761, Sunderland 1714, Warwick 1763, Wendell 1781, Whately 1771, Williamsburg 1771
Hampden www.rootsweb.com/~mafrankl/	N6	**25 Feb 1812**	**Hampshire** Hampden County; 50 State St; Springfield, MA 1103; Ph. (413) 748-7759 **Details:** (Clerk Courts has Divorce Records 1812–1932 & Court Records; Probate Judge has Probate Records; Register of Deeds has Land Records) Towns Organized Before 1800: Blandford 1741, Brimfield 1714, Chester 1765, Granville 1754, Holland 1783, Longmeadow 1783, Monson 1760, Montgomery 1780, Palmer 1752, Southwick 1770, Springfield 1641, Wales 1762, West Springfield 1774, Westfield 1669, Wilbraham 1763
Hampshire www.rootsweb.com/~mahampsh/	N4	**7 May 1662**	**Middlesex** Hampshire County; 33 King St; Northampton, MA 1060; Ph. (413) 586-8500 **Details:** (City Clerks have Birth, Marriage & Death Records; Probate Court has Probate & Divorce Records; District Court has Court Records; Register of Deeds has Land Records from 1600's) Towns Organized Before 1800: Amherst 1759, Belchertown 1761, Chesterfield 1762, Cummington 1779, Easthampton 1785, Goshen 1781, Granby 1768, Hadley 1661, Middlefield 1783, Northampton 1656, Pelham 1743, Plainfield 1785, Russell 1792, South Hadley 1753, Southapmton 1753, Ware 1761, Westhampton 1778, Worhtington 1768

County Website	Map Index	Date Created	Parent County or Territory From Which Organized Address/Details
Middlesex www.rootsweb.com/~mamiddle/	**H4**	**10 May 1643**	**Original county** Middlesex County; 208 Cambridge St; East Cambridge, MA 2141; Ph. (617) 494-4533 **Details:** (Clerk Courts has Birth Records 1632–1745, Marriage Records 1651–1793, Death Records 1651–1689, Divorce Records from 1888 & Court Records from 1648; Recorder Deeds, P.O. Box 68, E. Cambridge, MA 02141 has Land Records 1632–1855 & for southern district from 1855; Register of Deeds, 360 Gorham St., Lowell, MA 01852 has land records for northern district from 1855) Towns Organized Before 1800; Acton 1735, Ashby 1767, Bedford, 1729, Billerica 1655, Boxborough 1783, Burlington 1799, Cambridge 1631, Carlisle 1780, Chelmsford 1655, Concord 1635, Dracut 1702, Dunstable 1673, Framingham 1675, Groton 1655, Holliston 1724, Hopkinton 715, Lexington 1713, Lincoln 1754, Litleton 715, Malden 1649, Marlborough 1660, Medford 1630, Natick 1650, Newton 1691, Pepperell 1753, Reading 1644, Sherborn 1674, Shirley 1753, Stoneham 1725, Stow 1683, Sudbury 1639, Tewksbury 1734, Townsend 1732, Tyngsboro 1789, Waltham 1738, Watertown 1630, Wayland 1780, Westford 1729, Weston 1713, Wilmington 730, Woburn 1642
Nantucket www.rootsweb.com/~manantuc/nantuckt.htm	**B10**	**22 Jun 1695**	**Original county** Nantucket County; Town and County Bldg, Broad St; Nantucket, MA 2554; Ph. (508) 228-7229 **Details:** (Town Clerks have Birth, Marriage, Death & Burial Records from 1600's; Probate Court has Probate & Divorce Records; Register of Deeds has Land Records; District Court has Court Records) Towns Organized Before 1800: Nantucket 1687
Norfolk www.rootsweb.com/~manorfol/manorfol.htm	**G6**	**26 Mar 1793**	**Suffolk** Norfolk County; 650 High St; Dedham, MA 02026-1855; Ph. (781) 461-6105 **Details:** (Probate Judge has Divorce & Probate Records; Clerk Courts has Court Records from 1928; Register of Deeds has Land Records) (Originally part of the northeastern section of Massachusetts & some towns now part of New Hampshire; The old Records are now at Salem in Essex County which originally included most of Norfolk County)
Plymouth www.plymouth-1620.com/	**E7**	**2 Jun 1685**	**New Plymouth Colony** Plymouth County; County Courthouse; 11 S Russell St; Plymouth, MA 2360; Ph. (781) 830-9100 **Details:** (Town Clerks have Birth, Marriage, Death & Burial Records; Probate Court has Probate & Divorce Records; County Commissioners have Land, Probate & Court Records 1620–1692; Register of Deeds has Land Records) Towns Organized Before 1800: Abinton 1712, Bridgewater 1656, Carver 1790, Duxbury 1637, Halifax 1734, Hanover 1727, Hingham 1635, Hull 1644, Kingston 1726, Marshlfield 1640, Middleborough 1669, Pembroke 1712, Plymouth 1620, Plympton 1707, Rochester 1686, Scituate 1633, Wareham 1739

County Website	Map Index	Date Created	Parent County or Territory From Which Organized Address/Details
Suffolk www.geocities.com/masuffolk/	F5	**10 May 1643**	**Original county** Suffolk County; 1 City Hall Sq; Boston, MA 2201; Ph. (617) 725-8000 **Details:** (Town & City Clerks have Birth, Marriage & Death Records; Clerk Courts has Divorce Records; Register of Probate has Probate & Court Records; Register of Deeds has Land Records; part of 1800 Census missing) Towns Organized Before 1800: Boston 1630, Chelsea 1739, Dorchester 1630, Roxbury 1630
Worcester www.rootsweb.com/~maworces/	K5	**5 Apr 1731**	**Suffolk, Middlesex** Worcester County; 2 Main St; Worcester, MA 01608-1116; Ph. (508) 770-0825 **Details:** (Register of Deeds has Land Records; Probate Court has Probate Records from 1731; Town Clerks have Birth, Marriage & Death Records) Towns Organized Before 1800: Ashburnham 1765, Athol 1762, Auburn 1778, Barre 1753, Berlin 1784, Bolton 1738, Boylston 1786, Brookfield 1673, Charlton 1754, Douglas 1746, Fitchburg 1764, Gardner 1785, Grafton 1735, Greenwich 1754, Hardwick 1739, Harvard 1732, Hubbardston 1767, Lancaster 1653, Leicester 1714, Leominister 1740, Lunenburg 1728, Mendon 1667, Milford 1780, New Braintree 1751, Northborough 1766, Northbridge 1772, Oakham 1762, Oxford 1693, Paxton 1765, Petersham 1754, Phillipston 1786, Princeton 1759, Royalston 1765, Rutland 1714, Shrewsbury 1720, Southborough 1727, Spencer 1753, Sterling 1781, Sutton 1714, Templeton 1762, Upton 1735, Uxbridge 1742, Warren 1742, Westborough 1717, Westminister 1759, Winchendon 1762, Worcester 1684.

Notes

Michigan

Capital: Lansing

Territory: 1805

State: 1837 (26th)

If you seek a pleasant peninsula, look about you

Chippewa, Menominee, Ojibwa, and Miami Indians were Michigan's inhabitants when French explorers arrived about 1610 in search of furs and the fabled Northwest Passage. Jacques Marquette at Sault Ste. Marie organized the first permanent settlement in 1668. In 1701, Antoine de la Mother Cadillac established Fort Pontchartrain, later named Detroit. The French used the area only for fur trading, so when the British gained control in 1763 there were still only a few settlers in the area. The Indians, led by Pontiac, rebelled against the British and laid siege to Detroit for five months. They were ultimately defeated.

In 1774, Michigan became part of the Quebec Territory. The area was used by the British in the Revolutionary War as the base of operations for their attacks on Kentucky. Michigan became part of the United States by the Treaty of Paris in 1783, but the British retained control of the forts at Detroit and Michilimackinac. Michigan became part of the Northwest Territory in 1787. General Anthony Wayne occupied Fort Detroit in 1796 and Jay's Treaty was signed, giving the United States control of all of Michigan.

In 1800, Michigan became part of the Indiana Territory and then became a territory itself in 1805. During the War of 1812, General Hull, who commanded the U.S. forces in Michigan, attempted to invade Canada, failed, and ultimately surrendered Detroit to the British. Only after Admiral Perry's victory in 1813 were the Americans able to take Detroit again. The first public land sales took place in 1818. Work on the Erie Canal started the same year. Steamship travel was soon established between Buffalo and Detroit, which this greatly increased settlement of the area.

Treaties with the Indians in 1819 and 1821 further opened up the area to settlement. Transportation was facilitated by the opening of the Erie Canal in 1825, construction of a road through the Kalamazoo Valley in 1829, and the completion of the Chicago Road in 1835.

In 1835, Michigan lost land along its southern border to Ohio and gained the upper peninsula. Two years later Michigan became the twenty-sixth state.

By 1840, nearly half of the land in the southern peninsula was cultivated by settlers from New York, New England, and Germany. The next 50 years saw tens of thousands of immigrants arrive to work in the lumber and mining camps. They came from Canada, Ireland, Finland, Norway, Sweden, Wales, Poland, Italy, and England, especially the Cornwall area. Religious refugees from Holland also made their way to Michigan, settling around Grand Rapids and the western coast. During the Civil War, more than 87,000 men from Michigan served in the Union forces.

Look for vital records in the following locations:

- **Birth and death records:** County registration of births and deaths began in 1867. General compliance came by 1915. These are available from county clerks, along with delayed registration of birth for many counties. The state also has copies available from the Office of the State Registrar, Michigan Department of Health in Lansing, Michigan. The Clerk of the Circuit Court handled vital records prior to 1867.

- **Marriage and divorce records:** Most counties kept marriage records from the time they were created. Starting in 1805, marriages were required to be registered with the clerk of the local district court. Divorces were first recorded in the Supreme Court, then later by the clerk of the circuit, chancery, or county court. The records are available from county courts.

- **Probate records:** Wayne County began keeping probate records in 1797, while other counties began in about 1817. The clerks of the probate courts keep these records.

- **Naturalizations:** The circuit and district courts handled naturalizations, but the county clerks hold the records.

- **Land records:** The first land office opened in Detroit in 1818. The Registrar of Deeds handles all land matters for each county. The earliest land records are private land claims granted by France and England. These records are at the National Archives, Chicago Branch in Chicago, Illinois. Claims for 1790 to 1837 have been transcribed, indexed, and published. The Michigan State Archives, Department of State in Lansing also has many land and tax records.

- **Census records:** More than 20 early territorial censuses were taken in various areas of Michigan from 1810 to 1830 and are available in published form. Other territorial and state enumerations were made between 1827 and 1904.

Vital Records Request
PO Box 30721
Lansing, Michigan 48909
(517) 373-3740
www.michigan.gov/

Michigan State Archives
3405 North Logan Street
Lansing, Michigan 48906
www.michigan.gov/hal/0,1607,7-160-17445_19273_19313---,00.html

Societies and Repositories

Albion Historical Society; Gardner House Museum; 509 S. Superior St.; Albion, MI 49224.

Auburn Hills Genealogical and Historical Society; MI; www.auburn-hills.org/gen.htm.

Bay County Genealogical Society; PO Box 1366; Bay City, MI 48706-0366; theakergen@home.com; http://community.mlive.com/cc/baygenealogy.

Berrien County Genealogical Society; PO Box 8808; Benton Harbor, MI 49023-8808; coopbecgar@qtm.net; http://w3.qtm.net/bcgensoc.

Branch County Genealogical Society; PO Box 443; Coldwater, MI 49036; www.geocities.com/TheTropics/1050/Gensociety.html.

Cadillac Area Genealogical Society; 411 S. Lake Street; Cadillac, MI 49601; president@cadillac-cags.20m.com; www.cadillac-cags.20m.com.

Calhoun County Genealogical Society; PO Box 879; Marshall, MI 49068; www.rootsweb.com/~micalhou/ccgs.htm.

Cass River Genealogy Society; 359 S. Franklin; Frankenmuth, MI 48734; www.frankenmuthcity.com/library/genealogy.htm.

Cedar Springs Historical Society; 60 Cedar St.; PO Box 296; Cedar Springs, MI 49319; csmuseum@wingsisp.com.

Charlevoix County Genealogical Society; Boyne District Library; 201 E Main St; Boyne City, MI 49712; www.rootsweb.com/~micharle/cx-03.htm.

Cheboygan County Genealogical Society; PO Box 51; Cheboygan, MI 49721; www.rootsweb.com/~miccgs/CCGSmainx.html.

Chippewa County Genealogical Society; PO Box 1686; Sault Ste. Marie, MI 49783-1686; www.rootsweb.com/~michcgs/index.html.

Chippewa County Historical Society; PO Box 342; Sault Ste. Marie, MI 49783; cchs@sault.com.

Dearborn Genealogical Society; PO Box 1112; Dearborn, MI 48121-1112; www.rootsweb.com/~midgs/index.htm.

Delta County Genealogical Society; Box 442; Escanaba, MI 49829-0442; http://grandmastree.com/society.

Dickinson County Genealogical Society; c/o Dickinson County Library; 401 Iron Mountain Str; Iron Mountain, MI 48901-3435.

Downriver Genealogical Society; 1335 Southfield; PO Box 476; Lincoln Park, MI 48146; (313) 381-0507; sherry@plugnplay.com; www.rootsweb.com/~midrgs/drgs.htm.

Eaton County Genealogical Society; PO Box 337; Charlotte, MI 48813-0337; polhamus@pilot.msu.edu; http://userdata.acd.net/mmgs/ecgs.html.

Farmington Genealogical Society; Farmington Community Library; 23500 Liberty Street; Farmington, MI 48335-3570; www.metronet.lib.mi.us/FCL/genealsoc.html.

Finnish American Historical Society of Michigan; 19995 Melrose; Southfield, MI 49075.

Flat River Historical Society; PO Box 188; Greenville, MI 49838.

Flint Genealogical Society; PO Box 1217; Flint, MI 48501-1217; www.rootsweb.com/~mifgs.

Flint Michigan Chapter, AHSGR; 4167 W Four Lakes Dr.; Linden, MI 48451; (810) 629-8710.

Ford Genealogy Club; PO Box 1652; Dearborn, MI 48121-1652; www.wwnet.com/~krugman1/fgc.

Four Flags Area Genealogical Society; PO Box 414; Niles, MI 49120-0414.

Fred Hart Williams Genealogical Society—Detroit Burton Historical Collection; Detroit Public Library; 5201 Woodward Ave.; Detroit, MI 49202.

French Canadian Heritage Society of Michigan; c/o Gail F. Moreau; 9513 Whipple Shores Drive; Clarkston, MI 48348; http://habitant.org/fchsm.

French-Canadian Heritage Society of Michigan, Frenchtown Chapter; c/o Burton Historical Collection; Detroit Public Library; Detroit, MI 48202; annlee@provide.net; www.members.tripod.com/FCHS_FC/index.htm.

Gaylord Fact Finders Genealogical Society; PO Box 1524; Gaylord, MI 49734-5524.

Genealogical Society of Flemish Americans; 18740 Thirteen Mile Rd.; Roseville, MI 48066; www.rootsweb.com/~gsfa.

Genealogical Society of Isabella County; 523 N. Fancher; Mount Pleasant, MI 48858.

Genealogical Society of Monroe County, Michigan; PO Box 1428; Monroe, MI 48161-1428;

jankeeler@ameritech.net;
www.tdi.net/havekost/gsmc.htm.

Genealogical Society of Washtenaw County, Michigan,
Inc.; PO Box 7155; Ann Arbor, MI 48107-7155;
www.hvcn.org/info/gswc.

Genealogists of the Clinton County Historical Society;
PO Box 23; St. Johns, MI 48879-2312;
www.sojourn.com/~mmgs/gofcchs.html.

Grand Haven Genealogical Society; c/o Loutit Library;
407 Columbus Street; Grand Haven, MI 49417.

Grand Traverse Area Genealogical Society; PO Box 2015;
Traverse City, MI 49685-2015; RchrdHayes@aol.com;
www.rootsweb.com/~migtags/gtag.htm.

Gratiot County Historical and Genealogical Society;
PO Box 73; Ithaca, MI 48847-0073;
www.rootsweb.com/~migratio/gchgs/index.html.

Harrison Area Genealogy Society; PO Box 796; Harrison,
MI 48625; www.rootsweb.com/~miclare/harrison.htm.

Hillsdale County Genealogical Society; 22 N. Manning
Street; Hillsdale, MI 49242.

Holland Genealogical Society; c/o Herrick Public Library;
300 River Avenue; Holland, MI 49423.

Huron County Genealogical Society; c/o Marilyn Hebner;
2843 Electric Avenue; Port Huron, MI 48060.

Huron Shores Genealogical Society; c/o Robert J. Parks
Public Library; 6010 N. Skeel Ave. Oscoda, MI 48750-
1577.

Huron Valley Genealogical Society; 1100 Atlantic Street;
Milford, MI 48381; (248) 684-5622;
http://milford.lib.mi.us/MCIN/groups/hvgs.htm.

Ingham County Genealogical Society; PO Box 85; Mason,
MI 48854; icgs@yahoo.com;
http://userdata.acd.net/mmgs/icgs.html.

Ionia County Genealogical Society; 13051 Ainsworth
Road, Rt. 3; Lake Odessa, MI 48849;
pkswiler@juno.com;
www.rootsweb.com/~miionia/icgshome.htm.

Irish Genealogical Society of Michigan; c/o Gaelic League
/Irish-American Club; 2068 Michigan; Detroit, MI
48216; irisha20@aol.com;
www.rootsweb.com/~miigsm.

Isabella County Genealogical Society; 523 N. Faucher St.;
Mt. Pleasant, MI 48858.

Jackson County Genealogical Society; c/o Jackson District
Library; 244 W. Michigan Avenue; Jackson, MI 49201;
www.rootsweb.com/~mijackso/jcgs.htm.

Jewish Genealogical Society of Michigan; 8050 Lincoln
Dr.; Huntington Woods, MI 48070.

Jewish Genealogical Society of Michigan; PO Box 251693;
West Bloomfield, MI 48325-1693; jgsmi@usa.net;
www.jgsmi.org.

Kalamazoo Valley Genealogical Society; PO Box 405;
Comstock, MI 49041; www.rootsweb.com/~mikvgs.

Kalkaska Genealogical Society; PO Box 353; Kalkaska, MI
49646-0353; triplett@gtii.com; http://hometown.aol
.com/fiddlerben/kasgensoc.html.

Kinseekers; 5697 Old Maple Trail; Grawn, MI 49637.

Lapeer County Genealogical Society; c/o City Branch
Library; 921 W. Nepressing St.; Lapeer, MI 48446.

Lenawee County Family Researchers; c/o Corresponding
Secretary; 519 Company Street; Adrian, MI 49221;
lashbrok@aix.cc; http://people.mw.mediaone.net/
coslund/lcfr/index.html.

Lenawee County Genealogical Society; PO Box 511;
Adrain, MI 49221.

Livingston County Genealogical Society; PO Box 1073;
Howell, MI 48844-1073;
www.livgenmi.com/lcgslogo.htm.

Log Cabin Genealogical Society; 103 North Third Street;
Manistique, MI 49854-1018.

Luce-Mackinac Genealogical Society; PO Box 113;
Engadine, MI 49927-0113.

Lyon Township Genealogical Society; c/o Lyon Township
Public Library; 27025 Milford Rd.; New Hudson, MI
48165.

Macomb County Genealogical Group; c/o Mt. Clemens
Public Library; 150 Cass Avenue; Mt. Clemens, MI
48043; www.libcoop.net/mountclemens.

Marquette County Genealogical Society; 217 N. Front
Street; Marquette, MI 49855-3710; MQTCGS@aol.com;
http://members.aol.com/MQTCGS/MCGS/mcgs.html.

Mason County Genealogical Society; PO Box 549;
Ludington, MI 49431.

Mason County Historical Society; Rose Hawley Museum,
115W Loomis St.; Ludington, MI 49431.

Mecosta County Genealogical Society; PO Box 1068; Big
Rapids, MI 49307.

Michigan Genealogical Council; PO Box 80953; Lansing,
MI 48908-0593.

Michigan Historical Commission; 505 State Office Bldg.;
Lansing, MI 48913.

Michigan Society, Order of Founders & Patriots of
America; 2961Woodcreek Way; Bloomfield Hills, MI
48304-1974.

Midland County Historical Society; c/o Midland Center for
the Arts; 1901 W. St. Andrew; Midland, MI 48640.

Midland Genealogical Society; c/o Grace A. Dow Library;
1710 W. St. Andrews Dr.; Midland, MI 48640;
http://users.tm.net/brauschj/mgs.

Mid-Michigan Genealogical Society; PO Box 16033;
Lansing, MI 48901-6033;
http://userdata.acd.net/mmgs/mmgssoc.html.

Monroe County, Genealogical Society of Michigan;
PO Box 1429; Monroe, MI 48161.

Muskegon County Genealogical Society; c/o Hackley
Public Library; 316 W. Webster Avenue; Muskegon, MI

49440-1209; (231) 722-7276; MCGS1972@msn.com; www.rootsweb.com/~mimcgs.

Newaygo County Society of History and Genealogy; PO Box 68; White Cloud, MI 49349-0068; www.rootsweb.com/~minewayg/society.html.

North Oakland Genealogical Society; c/o Orion Township Library; 825 Joslyn Road; Lake Orion, MI 48362; www.pontiac.lib.mi.us/genealog.htm.

Northeast Michigan Genealogical Society; c/o Jesse Besser Museum; 491 Johnson Street; Alpena, MI 49707; http://members.aol.com/alpenaco/migenweb/genealog. htm#Northeast%20Michigan%20Genealogical%20Society.

Northville Genealogical Society; PO Box 932; Northville, MI 48167-0932; www.rootsweb.com/~mings.

Northwest Oakland County Historical Society; 306 South Saginaw St.; Holly, MI 48442; www.pontiac.lib.mi.us/genealog.htm.

Northwestern Michigan College; Mark Osterlin library, 1704 E. Front St.; Traverse City, MI 49684.

Oakland County Genealogical Society; PO Box 1094; Birmingham, MI 48012-1094; www.metronet.lib.mi.us/ROCH/OCGS.

Oceana County Genealogical Chapter; 114 Dryden St.; Hart, MI 49420.

Osceola County Genealogical Society; PO Box 27; Reed City, MI 49677-0027.

Palatines to America, Michigan Chapter; 968 Beechwood St. N.E.; Grand Rapids, MI 49505-3783.

Polish Genealogical Society of Mich.; c/o Burton Historical Collection; 5201 Woodward Ave; Detroit, MI 48202.

Pontiac Area Historical and Genealogical Society; PO Box 901; Pontiac, MI 48056.

Presque Isle County Genealogical Society; c/o Onaway Library; PO Box 742; Onaway, MI 49765-0742.

Redford Township History and Genealogical Society; PO Box 401175; Redford, MI 48240-9175.

Reed City Area Genealogical Society (Osceola County); 4918 Park St.; PO Box 27; Reed City, MI 49677.

Rockwood Area Historical Society; PO Box 68; Rockwood, MI 48171.

Rose City Area Historical Society, Inc.; c/o Ogemaw District Library 107 W. Main, Box 427; Rose City, MI 48654.

Roseville Historical and Genealogical Society; c/o Roseville Public Library; 29777 Gratiot Avenue; Roseville, MI 48066-4196.

Saginaw Genealogical Society; c/o Saginaw Public Library; 505 Janes Avenue; Saginaw, MI 48607.

Saginaw Valley Chapter, AHSGR; 6910 Trowbridge Circle; Saginaw, MI 48603; (517) 799-4266; clniederusa@netscape.net; www.ahsgr.org/saginaw.html.

Shiawassee County Genealogical Society; PO Box 841; Owosso, MI 49967; www.shianet.org/community/orgs/scgs/index.html.

Southwest Michigan Chapter, AHSGR; 3819 E. Bundy Road; Coloma, MI 49038; lhas76@aol.com.

St. Clair County Family History Group; PO Box 611483; Port Huron, MI 48061-1483.

St. Joseph Genealogical Society; PO Box 486; White Pigeon, MI 49099; http://members.tripod.com/ ~tfred/sjgc.html.

State Archives of Michigan; Michigan Historical Center; 702 W. Kalamazoo Stree; Lansing, MI 48909; (517) 373-1414; archives@michigan.gov; www.michigan.gov/hal/0,1607,7-160-17445_19273_19313-51308--,00.html.

Sterling Heights Genealogical and Historical Society; PO Box 1154; Sterling Heights, MI 48311-1154; shghs_mi@yahoo.com; www.rootsweb.com/~mishghs.

The Detroit Society for Genealogical Research, Inc.; Detroit Public Library; 5201 Woodward Ave.; Detroit, MI 48202; cpsrch@aol.com; www.dsgr.org.

The Luce-Mackinac County Genealogical Society; PO Box 113; Engadine, MI 49827-0113; www.rootsweb.com/~miluce/luce-mac.htm.

Then & Now Historical & Genealogical Society of E. Allegan County; 532 N. Main; Wayland, MI 49348-1043.

Three Rivers Genealogical Society; 13724 Spence Road; Three Rivers, MI 49093.

Tri-State Genealogical Society; c/o Sturgis Public Library; 255 North Street; Sturgis, MI 49091; www.rootsweb.com/~intsgs.

Union City Genealogical Society; 680 M-60; Union City, MI 49094.

Van Buren Regional Genealogical Society; PO Box 143; Decatur, MI 49045; (269) 423-8045; tbenson@monroe.lib.mi.us; www.woodlands.lib.mi.us/van/vbrgs.htm.

Vicksburg Historical Society; 7683 East YZ Ave.; Vicksburg, MI 49097.

Western Michigan Genealogical Society; c/o Grand Rapids Public Library; 111 Library Street; Grand Rapids, MI 49503-3268; wmgs@wmgs.org; www.wmgs.org.

Western Wayne County Genealogical Society; PO Box 63; Livonia, MI 49152.

Ypsilanti Historical Society Museum; 220 North Huron St.; Ypsilanti, MI 48197.

Bibliography and Record Sources

General

American Biographical History of Eminent and Self-Made Men: Michigan Volume. Cincinnati, Ohio: Western Biographical Pub. Co., 1878.

Anderson, Alloa Caviness. *Genealogy in Michigan: What, When, Where,* 2nd ed. Ann Arbor, Michigan: A. Anderson, P. Bender, 1978.

Callard, Carole, ed. *Sourcebook of Michigan Census, County Histories, and Vital Records.* Lansing, Michigan: Library of Michigan, 1986.

Centennial Family Certificate Application Files: A Project of the Michigan Genealogical Council. Salt Lake City: Genealogical Society of Utah, 1983. Microfilm, 81 rolls.

Church Record Index. 2 vols. Grand Rapids: The Society, 1993.

DeZeeuw, Donald J., ed. *The Michigan Surname Index.* Lansing, Michigan: Michigan Genealogical Council, 1984.

Fuller, George Newman, *Michigan, a Centennial History of the State and Its People.* 5 vols.: Lewis Publishing Co., 1939.

Genealogist's Guide to Southwestern Michigan. Grawn, Michigan: Kinseeker Publications, 1987.

Genealogist's Guide to the Middle of Michigan. Grawn, Michigan: Kinseeker Publications, 1987.

Genealogist's Guide to the Thumb Area of Michigan. Grawn, Michigan: Kinseeker Publications, 1987.

Genealogist's Guide to Northeastern Michigan. Grawn, Michigan: Kinseeker Publications, 1987.

Genealogist's Guide to Upper Peninsula Michigan. Grawn, Michigan: Kinseeker Publications, 1987.

Hinz, Nelda M. *Genealogical Materials in the Eddy Historical Collection of the Public Libraries of Saginaw.* Saginaw, Michigan: Public Libraries, 1975.

Historical Records Survey (Michigan). *Inventory of the Church Archives of Michigan, The Roman Catholic Church, Archdiocese of Detroit.* Detroit: Michigan Historical Records Survey, 1941.

Kellogg, Lucy Mary. *A Guide to Ancestral Trails in Michigan.* 4th ed. Detroit, Michigan: Detroit Society for Genealogical Research, 1975.

Lanman, Charles. *The Red Book of Michigan: A Civil, Military, and Biographical History.* Detroit: E. B. Smith, 1871.

Library of Michigan (Lansing, Michigan). *Michigan Biographies.* Lansing, Michigan: Microform Systems, Inc., 198–. 24 microfiche.

Library of Michigan (Lansing, Michigan). *Michigan Centennial File Index.* Lansing, Michigan: Microform System, Inc., 198–. 19 microfiches.

Library of Michigan (Lansing, Michigan). *Michigan Surname Index.* Lansing, Michigan: Microform System, Inc., 198–. 136 microfiches.

Loomis, Frances. *Michigan Biography Index.* Detroit Public Library, 1946. Microfilm, 4 rolls.

McGinnis, Carol. *Michigan Genealogy Sources and Resources.* Baltimore: Genealogical Publishing Co., 1987.

Men of Progress: Embracing Biographical Sketches of Representative Michigan Men, With an Outline History of the State: Detroit: Evening New Assoc., 1900.

Michigan Biographies, Including Members of Congress, Elective State Officers, Justices of the Supreme Court, Members of the Michigan Legislature, Board of Regents of the University of Michigan, State Board of Agriculture and State Board of Education. (1924). Reprint. Baltimore: Clearfield Co., 1999.

Michigan Biographies. Lansing, Michigan: Microform Systems, Inc., 198–.

Michigan Bureau of Library Services. *Michigan County Histories: A Bibliography.* Lansing: Michigan Department of Education, Bureau of Library Services, 1978.

Michigan Centennial File Index. Lansing, Michigan: Microform System, Inc., 198–.

Michigan Genealogical Council (Lansing, Michigan). *Guide to the Michigan Genealogical and Historical Collections at the Library of Michigan and the State Archives of Michigan.* Lansing, Michigan: Michigan Genealogical Council, 1996.

Michigan Pioneer Records, 1800–1900. Salt Lake City: Genealogical Society of Utah, 1973, 1974, 1976.

Michigan Research Outline. Series U.S.-States, no. 23. Salt Lake City: Family History Library, 1988.

Michigan Sesquicentennial Pioneer Files and Indexes, ca. 1986–1988. Salt Lake City: Genealogical Society of Utah, 1994.

Michigan State Historical Society. *Michigan Historical Collections.* 40 vols. Lansing, Michigan: W. S. George & Co., 1877–1929.

Michigan. State Library (Lansing, Michigan). *Card File Index to Manuscripts in the Vault, Michigan State Library.* Salt Lake City: Filmed by the Genealogical Society of Utah, 1976. 2 microfilm.

Michigan. State Library (Lansing, Michigan). *Index to Manuscript Materials in the Michigan State Library.* Salt Lake City: Filmed by the Genealogical Society of Utah, 1974. 2 microfilm.

Michigan. State Library (Lansing, Michigan). *Manuscript Index in the Library of Michigan.* Lansing, Michigan: Microform Systems, Inc., 198–. 9 microfiche.

Michigan. State Library. *Link Collection.* Lansing, Michigan: State Library, 1973.

Michigan. State Library. *Pioneer Family Collection.* Salt Lake City: Genealogical Society of Utah, 1973.

Midwest Pioneers, 1600s–1800s. S.l.: Brøderbund, 1999. CD-ROM.

Moore, Charles. *History of Michigan.* 4 vols. Lewis Pub. Co., 1915.

Pilcher, Rev. E. H. *Protestantism in Michigan. Being a Special History of the Methodist Episcopal Church.* Detroit, Michigan. (1878) Reprint. 1st Methodist Church, 1984.

Portrait and Biographical Record of Northern Michigan: Containing Portraits and Biographical Sketches of Prominent and Representative Citizens, Together with

Biographies and Portraits of All the Presidents of the United States: Chicago: Record Pub., 1895.

Powers, Perry F. *A History of Northern Michigan and Its People*. 3 vols. Chicago: Lewis Pub. Co, 1912.

Quigley, Maud. *Index to Family Names in Genealogical Periodicals*. Grand Rapids: Western Michigan Genealogical Society, 1981.

Quigley, Maud. *Index to Michigan Research Found in Genealogical Periodicals*. Grand Rapids: Western Michigan Genealogical Society, 1979.

Sawyer, Alvah Littlefield. *A History of the Northern Peninsula of Michigan and Its People, Its Mining, Lumber and Agricultural Industries*. 3 vols. Chicago: Lewis Publishing Co., 1911.

Sourcebook of Michigan Census, County Histories, and Vital Records. Lansing, Michigan: Library of Michigan, 1986.

Sprenger, Bernice Cox. *Guide to the Manuscripts in the Burton Historical Collection*. Detroit: Detroit Public Library, 1985.

Stevens, Wystan. *Directory of Historical Collections and Societies in Michigan*. Ann Arbor: Historical Society of Michigan, 1973.

Tolzman, Don Heinrich. *Michigan's German Heritage, John Russell's History of the German Influence in the Making of Michigan*. Bowie, Maryland: Heritage Books, 1994.

Tuttle, Charles Richard. *General History of the State of Michigan: With Biographical Sketches, Portrait Engravings and Numerous Illustrations; A Complete History of the Peninsular State from Its Earliest Settlement to the Present Time*. Detroit: R. D. S. Tyler, 1873.

United States. Works Progress Administration (Michigan). *Historical Records Survey. Survey of Records*. Bowling Green, Ohio: Bowling Green University, 1989. 51 microfilm.

Vander Hill, C. Warren. *Settling the Great Lakes Frontier: Immigration to Michigan, 1837–1924*. Lansing: Michigan Historical Commission, 1970.

Warner, Robert M. *Guide to Manuscripts in the Michigan Historical Collections of the University of Michigan*. Ann Arbor: s.n., 1963.

Welch, Richard Warren. *County Evolution in Michigan, 1790–1897*. Lansing: Department of Education, 1972.

Western Michigan Genealogical Society (Grand Rapids, Michigan). *Surname Index, 1600s–1900s*. Salt Lake City: Genealogical Society of Utah, 1976.

Wilson, Victoria. *Genealogist's Guide to the Capitol Region of Michigan*. Grawn, Michigan: Kinseeker Publications, 1987.

Atlases, Maps and Gazetteers

Blois, John T. *Gazetteer of the State of Michigan*. Detroit: S. L. Rood, 1939.

Bowen, B. F. *Bowen's Michigan State Atlas: Containing a Separate Map of Each County, Showing Section, Township and Range Lines, Railroad and Interurban Lines . . .* Indianapolis: B. F. Bowen, 1916.

Ellis, David M. *Michigan Postal History: The Post Offices, 1805–1986*. Lake Grove, Oregon: The Depot, 1993.

Long, John H., ed. *Historical Atlas and Chronology of County Boundaries, 1788–1980. Scale: 1:633,600. Vol. 1–5*. Boston, Massachusetts: G. K. Hall, 1984.

Meints, Graydon M. *Along the Tracks: A Directory of Named Places on Michigan Railroads*. Mount Pleasant, Michigan: Central Michigan University, Clarke Historical Library, 1987.

Michigan Gazetteer. Wilmington, Delaware: American Historical Publications, 1991.

Miles, William. *Michigan Atlases and Plat Books: A Checklist, 1872–1973*. Lansing: State Library Service, 1975.

Puetz, C. J. *Michigan County Map Guide*. Lyndon Station, Wisconsin: Thomas Publications, 199–.

Romig, Walter. *Michigan Place Names: The History of the Founding and the Naming of More Than Five Thousand Past and Present Michigan Communities*. Grosse Pointe, Michigan: Romig, 197–.

Sinko, Peggy Tuck. *Michigan; Atlas of Historical County Boundaries*. New York: Charles Scribner's Sons, 1997.

Taylor, William J. *Upper Michigan Postal History and Postmarks*. Lake Grove, Oregon: The Depot, 1988.

Vogel, Virgil J. *Indian Names in Michigan*. Ann Arbor: The University of Michigan Press, 1986.

Walling, H. F., comp. *Atlas of Michigan . . . Gazetteer of Places, Railroad Stations, Post Offices, Landings, Lakes, Rivers, Islands, Cities, Towns, Villages, Individual Map and Every County. . . .* Detroit: R. M. & S. T. Tackabury, 1873. Reprinted as the *1873 Atlas of Michigan. . . .* Knightstown, Indiana: Bookmark, 1977.

Welch, Richard W. *County Evolution in Michigan, 1790–1897*. Occasional Paper no. 2 Lansing, Michigan: State Library Services, 1972.

Census Records

Available Census Records and Census Substitutes

Federal Census 1820, 1830, 1840, 1850, 1860, 1870, 1880, 1900, 1910, 1920

Federal Mortality Schedules 1850, 1860, 1870, 1880

Union Veterans and Widows 1890

State/Territorial Census 1884, 1894, 1904

Dollarhide, William. *The Census Book: A Genealogist's Guide to Federal Census Facts, Schedules and Indexes*. Bountiful, Utah: Heritage Quest, 1999.

Kemp, Thomas Jay. *The American Census Handbook*. Wilmington, Delaware: Scholarly Resources, 2001.

Lainhart, Ann S. *State Census Records*. Baltimore: Genealogical Publishing Co., Inc., 1992.

McGlynn, Estelle A., ed. *Index to 1840 Federal Population Census of Michigan.* Detroit: Detroit Society for Genealogical Research, 1977.

Michigan Veterans Serving with Allied Forces, 1917–1919: Census of World War I Veterans. Microfilm of original records at the Michigan State Archives in Lansing. Salt Lake City: Filmed by the Genealogical Society of Utah, 1996. 5 microfilm.

Russell, Donna Valley. *Michigan Censuses 1710–1830 Under the French, British, and Americans.* Detroit: Detroit Society for Genealogical Research, 1982.

Szucs, Loretto Dennis and Matthew Wright. *Finding Answers in U.S. Census Records.* Ancestry Publishing, 2001.

Thorndale, William and William Dollarhide. *Map Guide to the U.S.. Federal Census, 1790–1920.* Baltimore: Genealogical Publishing Co., 1987.

United States. Bureau of Internal Revenue. *Internal Revenue Assessment Lists of Michigan, 1862–1866.* Washington, D.C.: The National Archives, 1973. 15 microfilm.

Court, Probate and Wills

Note: Individual county clerks keep court records. See each county listing for further information. Federal district court records are located in the Great Lakes Branch of the National Archives. Their holdings include: Michigan, Eastern District, Bay City, 1894–1973: Michigan, Eastern District, Detroit, 1837–1998; Michigan, Eastern District, Flint, 1895–1975; Michigan, Western District, Grand Rapids, 1863–1978; Michigan, Western District, Kalamazoo, 1967–69; Michigan, Western District, Marquette, 1878–1969; Michigan, Territorial Court, 1815–1837. For additional information online at—www.nara.gov/regional/findaids/chiguid1.html#21.

Michigan. Supreme Court. *Court Records, 1819–1857: Index to Cases, 1805–1857.* Microfilm of original records in the Bentley Library, University of Michigan. Salt Lake City: Genealogical Society of Utah, 1974.

Reed, George Irving. *Bench and Bar of Michigan: A Volume of History and Biography.* Century Pub. and Engraving, ca. 1897.

United States. Territorial Court (Michigan). *Records of the Territorial Court, Michigan, 1816–1836. M1111.* Washington, D.C.: National Archives, 1988.

Emigration, Immigration, Migration and Naturalization

Florer, Warren Washburn. *Early Michigan Settlements.* 3 vols. Ann Arbor: W. W. Florer, ca. 1941–1953.

United States. District Court. (Michigan: Eastern District). *Declarations of Intentions, 1911–1930.* Microfilm of original records housed in the Chicago Branch of the National Archives, Chicago, Illinois. Salt Lake City: Genealogical Society of Utah, 1986. Microfilm, 54 rolls.

United States. District Court. (Michigan: Eastern District). *Naturalization Records, 1913–1928.* Microfilm of original records housed in the Chicago Branch of the National Archives, Chicago, Illinois. Salt Lake City: Genealogical Society of Utah, 1986. 129 microfilm.

United States. District Court. (Michigan: Western District: Northern Division). *Naturalization Records, 1887–1915.* Microfilm of original records housed in the Chicago Branch of the National Archives, Chicago, Illinois. (Salt Lake City: Genealogical Society of Utah, 1986).

United States. District Court. (Michigan: Western District: Southern Division). *Naturalization Records, 1907–1930.* Microfilm of original records housed in the Chicago Branch of the National Archives, Chicago, Illinois. Salt Lake City: Genealogical Society of Utah, 1986. 4 microfilm.

Indexes to Naturalization Records in the State Archives of Michigan. Lansing, Michigan: State Archives of Michigan, 2002. Online database at—www.sos.state.mi.us/history/archive/naturalization/index.html.

United States Immigration and Naturalization Services. *Detroit District Manifest Records of Aliens Arriving from Foreign Contiguous Territory: Arrivals at Detroit, Michigan, 1906–1954.* Washington, D.C.: Immigration and Naturalization Services, 195–. Microfilm, 117 rolls.

Land and Property

Ainsworth, Fern. *Private Land Claims, Illinois, Indiana, Michigan and Wisconsin.* Natchitoches, Louisiana: Fern, Ainsworth, 1985.

Land Records: Alabama, Arkansas, Florida, Louisiana, Michigan, Minnesota, Ohio, Wisconsin. S.l.: Brøderbund, 1996. CD-ROM.

McMullin, Phillip W. *Grassroots of America.* Salt Lake City: Gendex Corp., 1972.

United States. Bureau of Land Management. *Card Files.* Washington, D.C.: Bureau of Land Management, 19–. 160 microfilm.

United States. Congress. *American State Papers.* Salt Lake City; La Crosse, Wisconsin: Genealogical Society of Utah: Brookhaven Press, 1959, 1975, 1977.

United States. Department of State. *Territorial Papers of the United States.* 26 vols. Washington, D.C.: Government Printing Office, 1934–1962.

United States. Department of the Interior. Bureau of Land Management. *Michigan Cash and Homestead Entries, Cadastral Survey Plats.* Version 7.3. Springfield, Virginia: BLM Eastern States, 1994.

Military

Alphabetical General Index to Public Library Sets of 85,271 Names of Michigan Soldiers and Sailors Individual Records. Lansing, Michigan: Michigan Secretary of State, 1915.

Grand Army of the Republic. Department of Michigan. *Records of Posts and Index, 1876–1945.* Microfilm of original records at State Archives of Michigan, Lansing, Michigan. Salt Lake City: Genealogical Society of Utah, 1973, 1991. 90 microfilm.

Landrum, Charles H. *Michigan in the World War: Military and Naval Honors of Michigan Men and Women.* S.l.: Michigan Historical Commission, 1924.

Michigan Adjutant General. *Record of Service of Michigan Volunteers in the Civil War. Indexed in Alphabetical General Index to Public Library Sets of 85,271 Names in the Civil War.* Lansing: Michigan Secretary of State, 1915.

Michigan Adjutant General's Office. *Annual Report of the Adjutant General 1865–1866.* 3 vols. Lansing, Michigan: John A. Kerr & Co., 1866.

Michigan County War Records, 1917–1919: Census of Men Serving in U.S. Forces. Microfilm of original records at the Michigan State Archives in Lansing. Salt Lake City: Filmed by the Genealogical Society of Utah, 1996. 266 microfilm.

Michigan. Adjutant General's Office. *Michigan Volunteers Descriptive Roll, First Regiment, 1847–1848.* Microfilm of originals at the State Archives in Lansing, Michigan. Salt Lake City: Genealogical Society of Utah, 1972.

Michigan. Adjutant General's Office. *Michigan Volunteers Descriptive Rolls, 1861–1866; Index to Michigan Volunteers, 1861–1865.* Microfilm of manuscript (handwritten) at the State Archives, Lansing, Michigan. Salt Lake City: Genealogical Society of Utah, 1972. 5 microfilm.

Michigan. Adjutant General's Office. *Michigan Volunteers, Spanish American War, 1898–1899.* Microfilm of manuscript (handwritten) at the State Archives, Lansing, Michigan. Salt Lake City: Genealogical Society of Utah, 1973. 5 microfilm.

Michigan. Adjutant General's Office. *Records of Michigan Volunteers Mustered into the Service of the United States, 1861–1866.* Microfilm of manuscript (handwritten) at the State Archives, Lansing, Michigan. Salt Lake City: Genealogical Society of Utah, 1973. 7 microfilm.

Michigan. National Guard. *Descriptive Rolls, 1838–1901.* Microfilm of original records at the State Archives, Lansing, Michigan. Salt Lake City: Filmed by the Genealogical Society of Utah, 1972. 4 microfilm.

Michigan. State Archives (Lansing, Michigan). *Deserters From Draft Index, 1917–1918.* Microfilm of original records at the State Archives of Michigan, Lansing, Michigan. Salt Lake City: Filmed by the Genealogical Society of Utah, 1991. 4 microfilm.

Michigan. State Archives (Lansing, Michigan). *Mexican Border Veterans Index, ca.1916–1917.* Microfilm of original records at the State Archives of Michigan, Lansing, Michigan. Salt Lake City: Filmed by the Genealogical Society of Utah, 1991. 2 microfilm.

Michigan. State Archives (Lansing, Michigan). *United Spanish War Veterans Master Index, ca. 1890–1984.* Salt Lake City: Filmed by the Genealogical Society of Utah, 1991. 3 microfilm.

Miller, Alice Turner. *Soldiers of the War of 1812, Who Died in Michigan.* Ithaca, Michigan: Alice Turner Miller, 1962.

Record of Service of Michigan Volunteers in the Civil War, 1861–1865. 46 vols. Kalamazoo, Michigan: Ihling Bros. & Everard, 1905.

Robertson, John. *Michigan in the War,* Revised. Lansing, Michigan: W.S. George, 1882.

Selective Service System. "Registration Card" for men born between April 28, 1877, and February 16, 1897 ("Fourth Registration"), for Illinois, Indiana, Michigan, Ohio, and Wisconsin. *Record Group 147. Chicago: National Archives Records Administration, Great Lakes Region, 1940–.*

Silliman, Sue. *Michigan Military Records.* Baltimore, Maryland: Genealogical Publishing Co., 1969.

Soldiers' Home (Grand Rapids, Michigan). *Historical Register of Inhabitants, 1885–1927.* Microreproduction of original typescript and manuscript at the State Archives, Lansing Michigan. Salt Lake City: Filmed by the Genealogical Society of Utah, 1972. 10 microfilm.

United States Civil War Soldiers Living in Michigan in 1894. St. Johns, Michigan: Genealogists of Clinton County Historical Society, 1988.

United States. Adjutant General's Office. *Index to Compiled Service Records of Volunteer Soldiers Who Served from the State of Michigan for the Patriot War, 1838–1839.* Washington, D.C.: The National Archives, 1965.

United States. Selective Service System. *Michigan, World War I Selective Service System Draft Registration Cards, 1917–1918, M1509.* Washington, D.C.: National Archives, 1987–1988.

United States. War Department. Bureau of Public Relations. *World War II Honor List of Dead and Missing, State of Michigan.* District of Columbia: War Dept. Bureau of Public Relations, 1946.

Welch, Richard Warren. *Michigan in the Mexican War.* S.l.: s.n., 1967.

World War I Card Index for *Michigan.* Microfilm of original records at State Library and Archives of Lansing, Michigan. Salt Lake City: Genealogical Society of Utah, 1976. 37 microfilm.

Vital and Cemetery Records

Burton, Ann and Conrad Burton. *Michigan Quakers, Abstracts of Fifteen Meetings of the Society of Friends 1831–1860.* Glyndwr Resources, 1989.

Grand Army of the Republic (Michigan). *Cemetery Index, 1800s–1900s.* Microfilm of typescripts housed in Grand

Rapids, Michigan. Salt Lake City: Genealogical Society of Utah, 1976. 3 microfilm.

Grand Rapids (Michigan). Public Library. *Cemetery Records of Michigan Soldiers, 1770–1930.* Microfilm of typescript in Grand Rapids, Michigan. Salt Lake City: Genealogical Society of Utah, 1976. 3 microfilm.

Har-Al, Inc. *Michigan Cemetery Compendium.* Spring Arbor, Michigan: Har-Al, 1979.

Historical Records Survey (Michigan). *Vital Statistics Holdings by Government Agencies in Michigan; Birth Records.* Detroit, Michigan: The Project, 1941.

Historical Records Survey (Michigan). *Vital Statistics Holdings by Government Agencies in Michigan; Death Records.* Detroit, Michigan: The Project, 1942.

Historical Records Survey (Michigan). *Vital Statistics Holdings by Government Agencies in Michigan; Marriage Records.* Detroit, Michigan: The Project, 1941.

Library of Michigan (Lansing, Michigan). *Michigan Cemetery Source Book: Companion Volume to the Michigan Cemetery Atlas.* Lansing, Michigan: Library of Michigan, 1994.

Link, Muriel. *Obituaries Index, 1933–1948.* Salt Lake City: Genealogical Society of Utah, 1976.

Michigan. Civil War Centennial Observance Commission. Committee on Civil War Grave Registration. *Civil War Graves Registration Index Cards, ca. 1861–1930.* Microfilm of original records at state archives of Michigan, Lansing, Michigan. Salt Lake City: Genealogical Society of Utah, 1994. 22 microfilm.

Michigan. Department of Community Health. *Michigan Death Index, 1867–1874.* 3 vols. Lansing, Michigan: Michigan Dept. of Community Health, 1997.

Mohnecke, Edward H. *Cemetery Inscriptions. Michigan.* 3 vols. Grand Rapids, Michigan: Edward H. Mohnecke, 1939–1944.

State Library of Michigan. *Michigan Cemetery Source Book.* Lansing: State Library of Michigan, 1994.

The Historical Records Survey (Michigan). *Vital Records from the Detroit Free Press 1831–1868.* Microfilm of typescript at the State Library in Lansing, Michigan. Salt Lake City: Genealogical Society of Utah, 1973. 3 microfilm.

County Website	Map Index	Date Created	Parent County or Territory From Which Organized Address/Details
Aishcum		1 Apr 1840	**Mackinac** Aishcum County; MI **Details:** (see Lake) Name changed to Lake 8 Mar 1843; County Terminated 1843
Alcona www.rootsweb.com/~mialcona/index.htm	E6	1 Apr 1840	**Mackinac, Unorg. Terr.** Alcona County; 106 5th St; Harrisville, MI 48740; Ph. (517) 724-5374 **Details:** (Formerly Negwegon County. Name changed to Alcona 8 Mar 1843. Attached to Mackinac, Cheboygan, Iosco & Alpena Counties prior to organization 12 Mar 1869) (County Clerk has Birth, Marriage, Death, Divorce, Court & Naturalization Records from 1869 & Military Records from 1900; Probate Court has Probate Records; Register of Deeds has Land
Alger www.markovich.info/michigan/algercounty/	K3	17 Mar 1885	**Schoolcraft** Alger County; 101 Court St; Munising, MI 49862; Ph. (906) 387-2076 **Details:** (County Clerk has Birth, Death & Land Records from 1884, Marriage Records from 1887, Divorce & Court Records from 1885; Probate Court has Probate Records)
Allegan www.allegancounty.org/	I11	2 Mar 1831	**Barry** Allegan County; 113 Chestnut St; Allegan, MI 49010-1362; Ph. (616) 673-0450 **Details:** (Organized 7 Sep 1835) (County Clerk has Birth & Death Records from 1867, Marriage Records from 1835, Divorce, Court & Land Records from 1836 & Military Discharge Records; Probate Court has Probate Records from 1836)
Alpena www.alpenacounty.org/alpcnty/index.htm	E6	1 Apr 1840	**Mackinac, Unorg. Terr.** Alpena County; 720 W Chisholm St; Alpena, MI 49707; Ph. (517) 356-0115 **Details:** (Formerly Anamickee County. Name changed to Alpena 8 Mar 1843. Attached to Mackinac & Cheboygan Counties prior to organization 7 Feb 1857) (County Clerk has Birth Records from 1869, Marriage, Death, Divorce & Court Records from 1871; Probate Judge has Probate Records; Register of Deeds has Land Records)
Anamickee		1 Apr 1840	**Mackinac, Unorg. Terr.** Anamickee County; MI **Details:** (see Alpena) Name changed to Alpena 8 Mar 1843
Antrim www.antrimcounty.org/	H5	1 Apr 1840	**Mackinac** Antrim County; 208 E Cayugoa St; PO Box 520; Bellaire, MI 49615-0520; Ph. (616) 533-8607 **Details:** (Formerly Meegisee County. Name changed to Antrim 8 Mar 1843. Attached to Mackinac & Grand Traverse Counties prior to organization 11 Mar 1863) (County Clerk has Birth, Marriage, Death, Divorce & Court Records from 1867 & Military Discharge Records; Probate Judge has Probate Records from 1863; Register of Deeds has Land Records)
Arenac www.rootsweb.com/~miarenac/index.htm	F8	21 Apr 1883	**Bay** Arenac County; 120 N Grove St; PO Box 747; Standish, MI 48658; Ph. (989) 846-4626 **Details:** (County Clerk has Birth, Marriage, Death, Divorce & Court Records from 1883 & Burial Records from 1952)

County Website	Map Index	Date Created	Parent County or Territory From Which Organized Address/Details
Arenac, old		**2 Mar 1831**	**Unorg. Terr.** Arenac, old County; MI **Details:** (Attached to Saginaw. Absorbed by Bay County 20 Apr 1857. Recreated 21 Apr 1883)
Baraga www.rootsweb.com/~mibaraga/	N2	**19 Feb 1875**	**Houghton** Baraga County; 16 N 3rd St; L'Anse, MI 49946; Ph. (906) 524-6183 **Details:** (County Clerk has Birth, Marriage, Death, Divorce, Court & Land Records from 1875 & Burial Records from 1950)
Barry www.barrycounty.org/	H11	**29 Oct 1829**	**Unorg. Terr.** Barry County; 220 W State St; Hastings, MI 49058; Ph. (269) 945-1285, jholtman@barrycounty.org. **Details:** (Attached to St. Joseph & Kalamazoo Counties prior to organization 15 Mar 1839) (County Clerk has Birth & Death Records from 1867, Court Records from 1850, Marriage & Divorce Records from 1839, Military Records from 1950, Burial, Cemetery, Census, & Newspapers)
Bay www.rootsweb.com/~mibay/	F8	**20 Apr 1857**	**Saginaw, Midland, Arenac** Bay County; 515 Center Ave; Bay City, MI 48708-5941; Ph. (517) 892-3528 **Details:** (County Clerk has Birth Records from 1868, Marriage Records from 1857, Death Records from 1867, Divorce Records from 1883 & Court Records from 1965; Probate Court has Probate Records; Register of Deeds has Land Records)
Benzie http://grandtraverseregion.com/benzie/	I6	**27 Feb 1863**	**Leelanau** Benzie County; 448 Court Pl; PO Box 377; Beulah, MI 49617; Ph. (616) 882-9671 **Details:** (Attached to Grand Traverse County prior to organization 30 Mar 1869) (County Clerk has Birth & Death Records from 1868, Marriage & Court Records from 1869, Divorce & Probate Records from 1870, Naturalization Records from 1871 & Burial Records from 1934)
Berrien www.berriencounty.org/	J12	**29 Oct 1829**	**Unorg. Terr.** Berrien County; 701 Main St; St. Joseph, MI 49085-1114; Ph. (616) 983-7111 **Details:** (Attached to Cass County prior to organization 1 Sep 1831) (County Clerk has Birth & Death Records from 1867, Marriage Records from 1831, Naturalization Records 1835–1985 & Military Records from 1918; Probate Court has Probate Records from 1832; Register of Deeds has Land Records from 1831; Clerk Circuit Court has Divorce & Court Records from 1835)
Bleeker		**15 Mar 1861**	**Unorg. Terr.** Bleeker County; MI **Details:** (see Menominee) Name changed to Menominee 19 Mar 1863
Branch http://co.branch.mi.us/	H12	**29 Oct 1829**	**Lenawee, Unorg. Terr.** Branch County; 31 Division St; Coldwater, MI 49036; Ph. (517) 279-4306 **Details:** (Attached to St. Joseph County prior to organization 1 Mar 1833) (County Clerk has Birth & Death Records from 1867, Marriage Records from 1833, Divorce Records, Court Records from 1848 & Naturalization Records from 1847; Probate Court has Probate Records; Register of Deeds has Land Records; City & Town Clerks have Burial Records)

County Website	Map Index	Date Created	Parent County or Territory From Which Organized Address/Details
Calhoun www.calhoun-mi.com/home.htm	**H11**	**29 Oct 1829**	**Unorg. Terr.** Calhoun County; 315 W Green St; Marshall, MI 49068-1585; Ph. (616) 781-0730 **Details:** (Attached to St. Joseph & Kalamazoo Counties prior to organization 1 Apr 1833) (County Clerk has Birth, Marriage, Death, Divorce & Court Records from 1867, Burial Records from 1952, Naturalization Records from 1918, Military Discharge Records from 1919 & election Records from 1972; Probate Court has Probate Records)
Cass http://casscountymi.org/	**I12**	**29 Oct 1829**	**Unorg. Terr.** Cass County; 120 N Broadway; PO Box 355; Cassopolis, MI 49031; Ph. (616) 445-8621 **Details:** (County Clerk/Register has Birth & Death Records from 1867, Marriage Records from 1837, Divorce & Court Records from 1831, Land Records from 1832 & Naturalization Records 1924–1941; Probate Court has Probate Records from 1829)
Charlevoix www.multimag.com/county/mi/charlevoix/	**G5**	**2 Apr 1869**	**Emmet, Antrim, Otsego** Charlevoix County; 203 W Antrim St; Charlevoix, MI 49720; Ph. (616) 547-7200 **Details:** (County Clerk has Birth Records from 1867, Marriage & Death Records from 1868, Divorce, Court & Land Records from 1869 & Probate Records from 1881)
Charlevoix, old		**1843**	**Mackinac** Charlevoix, old County; MI **Details:** (Formerly Keskkauko County. Name changed to Charlevoix 8 Mar 1843. Attached to Mackinac. Eliminated 29 Jan 1853. Recreated 2 Apr 1869)
Cheboygan www.rootsweb.com/~micheboy/micheboy.htm	**G4**	**1 Apr 1840**	**Mackinac** Cheboygan County; 870 S Main St; PO Box 70; Cheboygan, MI 49721; Ph. (616) 627-8808 **Details:** (Attached to Mackinac County prior to organization 29 Jan 1853) (County Clerk has Birth, Marriage & Death Records from 1867, Divorce & Court Records from 1884; Register of Probate has Probate Records from 1854; Register of Deeds has Land Records from 1854)
Cheonoquet Future website at www.rootsweb.com/~migenweb/county_list.htm		**1 Apr 1840**	**Mackinac** Cheonoquet County; MI **Details:** (see Montmorency) Name changed to Montmorency 8 Mar 1843
Chippewa www.sault.com/~chippewa/	**G3**	**1 Feb 1827**	**Mackinac** Chippewa County; 319 Court St; Sault Sainte Marie, MI 49783-2183; Ph. (906) 635-6300 **Details:** (County Clerk has Birth Records from 1869, Marriage Records from 1868, Death Records from 1870, Divorce Records from 1891 & Court Records; Probate Court has Probate Records; Register of Deeds has Land Records)
Clare www.rootsweb.com/~miclare/index.htm	**G8**	**1 Apr 1840**	**Mackinac** Clare County; 225 W Main St; PO Box 438; Harrison, MI 48625-0438; Ph. (517) 539-7131 **Details:** (Formerly Kaykakee County. Name changed to Clare 8 Mar 1843. Attached to Saginaw, Midland, Isabelle & Mecosta Counties prior to organization 13 Mar 1871) (County Clerk has Birth, Marriage, Death, Burial, Divorce, Court & Land Records)

County Website	Map Index	Date Created	Parent County or Territory From Which Organized Address/Details
Clinton www.clinton-county.org/		**2 Mar 1831**	**Unorg. Terr.** Clinton County; 100 E State St; PO Box 69; St. Johns, MI 48879-1571; Ph. (517) 224-5140 **Details:** (Attached to Kent & Shiawassee Counties prior to organization 12 Mar 1839) (County Clerk has Birth & Death Records from 1867, Marriage Records from 1839, Divorce Records from early 1800's & Court Records)
Crawford www.crawfordco.org	**G6**	**1 Apr 1840**	**Mackinac** Crawford County; 200 W Michigan Ave; Grayling, MI 49738-1745; Ph. (989) 348-3200 **Details:** (Formerly Shawano County. Name changed to Crawford 8 Mar 1843. Attached to Mackinac, Cheboygan, Iosco, Antrim & Kalkaska Counties prior to organization 22 Mar 1879) (All Records are from 1876 to Present: County Clerk has Birth, Probate, Marriage, Death, Divorce, Court, & Land Records)
Delta http://grandmastree.com/migenweb/	**K3**	**9 Mar 1843**	**Mackinac, Unorg Terr.** Delta County; 310 Ludington St; Escanaba, MI 49829-4057; Ph. (906) 789-5105 **Details:** (Attached to Mackinac County prior to organization 12 Mar 1861) (County Clerk has Birth, Marriage, Death, Divorce, Court, Probate & Land Records from 1867)
Des Moines		**1 Oct 1834**	**Unorg. Terr.** Des Moines County; MI **Details:** (Disorganized 3 Jul 1836 to Wisconsin Terr.)
Dickinson www.geocities.com/dickinsonco/	**M3**	**21 May 1891**	**Marquette, Menominee, Iron** Dickinson County; 705 S Stephenson Ave; PO Box 609; Iron Mountain, MI 49801-0609; Ph. (906) 774-0988 **Details:** (County Clerk has Birth, Marriage, Death, Divorce, Court & Naturalization Records from 1891; Probate Court has Probate Records; Register of Deeds has Land Records)
Eaton www.co.eaton.mi.us/	**G10**	**29 Oct 1829**	**Unorg. Terr.** Eaton County; 1045 Independence Blvd; Charlotte, MI 48813; Ph. (517) 543-7500 **Details:** (Attached to St. Joseph & Kalamazoo Counties prior to organization 29 Dec 1837) (County Clerk has Birth & Death Records from 1867, Marriage Records from 1838, Divorce & Court Records from 1847 & some Naturalization Records; Probate Court has Probate Records; Register of Deeds has Land Records)
Emmet http://members.tripod.com/~deemamafred/miemmet.html	**G4**	**1 Apr 1840**	**Mackinac** Emmet County; 200 Division St; Petoskey, MI 49770; Ph. (616) 348-1744 **Details:** (Formerly Tonedagana County. Name changed to Emmet 8 Mar 1843. Attached to Mackinac prior to organization 29 Jan 1853) (County Clerk has Birth, Marriage & Death Records from 1867, Divorce Records from 1875, Court & Naturalization Records from 1800's & some Military Records)

County Website	Map Index	Date Created	Parent County or Territory From Which Organized Address/Details
Genesee http://co.genesee.mi.us/	E9	28 Mar 1835	**Lapeer, Saginaw, Shiawassee** Genesee County; 900 S Saginaw St; Flint, MI 48502; Ph. (810) 257-3225 **Details:** (County Clerk has Birth & Death Records from 1867, Marriage & Court Records from 1835 & Divorce Records from 1890; Probate Judge has Probate Records; Cemetery custodians have Burial Records)
Gladwin www.rootsweb.com/~migladwi/	G8	2 Mar 1831	**Unorg. Terr.** Gladwin County; 401 W Cedar Ave; Gladwin, MI 48624-2023; Ph. (517) 426-7351 **Details:** (Attached to Saginaw & Midland Counties prior to organization 18 Apr 1875) (County Clerk has Birth, Marriage, Death, Divorce & Court Records from 1875 & Military Records from 1917; Probate Court has Probate Records from 1875; Register of Deeds has Land Records; County Library has obituary file)
Gogebic www.rootsweb.com/~migogebi/gogebic.com	P3	7 Feb 1887	**Ontonagon** Gogebic County; 200 N Moore St; Bessemer, MI 49911; Ph. (906) 663-4518, gpelissero@gogebic.org **Details:** (County Clerk has Birth, Court, Death, Divorce, Marriage, & Military Records from 1887; Probate Court has Guardianship & Probate Records; Register of Deeds has Land Records from 1887; County Treasurer has Tax Records)
Grand Traverse www.grandtraverse.org/	I6	7 Apr 1851	**Omeena** Grand Traverse County; 400 Boardman Ave; Traverse City, MI 49684; Ph. (231) 922-4760 **Details:** (County Clerk has Birth & Death Records from 1867, Marriage Records from 1853, Divorce & Court Records from 1882; Townships have Burial Records; Register of Deeds has Land Records)
Gratiot www.gratiot.com/	G9	2 Mar 1831	**Unorg. Terr.** Gratiot County; 214 E Center St; Ithaca, MI 48847; Ph. (517) 875-5215 **Details:** (Attached to Saginaw & Clinton Counties prior to organization 3 Feb 1855) (County Clerk has Birth, Death, Divorce & Court Records from 1867 & Marriage Records from 1855; Probate Court has Probate Records; Register of Deeds has Land Records)
Hillsdale www.co.hillsdale.mi.us/	G12	29 Oct 1829	**Unorg. Terr.** Hillsdale County; County Courthouse; 29 N Howell St; Hillsdale, MI 49242-1865; Ph. (517) 437-3391 **Details:** (Attached to Lenawee County prior to organization 11 Feb 1835) (County Clerk has Birth & Death Records from 1867, Marriage Records from 1835, Divorce & Court Records from 1845; Probate Court has Probate Records; Register of Deeds has Land Records)
Houghton Future website at www.rootsweb.com/~migenweb/county_list.htm	N2	19 Mar 1845	**Marquette, Ontonagon** Houghton County; 401 E Houghton Ave; Houghton, MI 49931-2016; Ph. (906) 482-1150 **Details:** (Attached to Chippewa County prior to organization 18 May 1846) (County Clerk has Birth & Death Records from 1867, Marriage Records from 1855, Divorce & Court Records from 1853, Land Records from 1847, Naturalization Records from 1848 & Military Records; Probate Judge has Probate Records)

County Website	Map Index	Date Created	Parent County or Territory From Which Organized Address/Details
Huron www.rootsweb.com/~mihuron/	**D8**	**1 Apr 1840**	**Sanilac** Huron County; 250 E Huron Ave; Bad Axe, MI 48413-1317; Ph. (517) 269-9942 **Details:** (Attached to Saginaw, St. Clair & Sanilac Counties prior to organization 25 Jan 1859) (County Clerk has Birth, Marriage, Death, Divorce & Court Records from 1867; Probate Judge has Probate Records; Register of Deeds has Land Records)
Ingham www.ingham.org/	**G11**	**29 Oct 1829**	**Washtenaw, Shiawassee, Unorg. Terr.** Ingham County; 315 S Jefferson St; Mason, MI 48854; Ph. (517) 676-7201 **Details:** (Attached to Washtenaw County prior to organization 4 June 1838) (County Clerk has Birth & Death Records from 1867, Marriage Records from 1838, Divorce & Court Records from 1839; Probate Court has Probate Records; Town & City Clerks have Burial Records)
Ionia www.ioniacounty.org/	**H10**	**2 Mar 1831**	**Mackinac** Ionia County; 100 E Main St; Ionia, MI 48846; Ph. (616) 527-5322 **Details:** (Attached to Kent County prior to organization 3 Apr 1837) (County Clerk has Birth & Death Records from 1867, Marriage Records from 1837, Divorce & Court Records from 1890)
Iosco www.oscoda.net/ioscocounty/	**E7**	**1 Apr 1840**	**Unorg. Terr.** Iosco County; 422 W Lake St; PO Box 838; Tawas City, MI 48763; Ph. (517) 362-3497 **Details:** (Formerly Kanotin County. Name changed to Iosco 8 Mar 1843. Attached to Mackinac, Saginaw & Cheboygan Counties prior to organization 16 Feb 1857) (County Clerk has Birth Records from 1867, Marriage Records from 1862, Death Records from 1868, Burial Records 1961–1978, Divorce & Court Records from 1859 & Naturalization Records 1859–1906)
Iron www.iron.org/	**N3**	**3 Apr 1885**	**Marquette, Menominee** Iron County; 2 S. 6th St; Crystal Falls, MI 49920-1413; Ph. (906) 875-3221 **Details:** (County Clerk has Birth, Marriage, Death, Divorce & Court Records from 1895; Probate Court has Probate Records; Register of Deeds has Land Records; Towns & Cities have Burial Records)
Isabella www.rootsweb.com/~miisabel/isabella.html	**G8**	**2 Mar 1831**	**Mackinac, Unorg. Terr.** Isabella County; 200 N Main St; Mount Pleasant, MI 48858-2321; Ph. (517) 772-0911 **Details:** (Attached to Saginaw, Ionia & Midland Counties prior to organization 11 Feb 1859) (County Clerk has Birth, Marriage, Death, Divorce & Court Records from 1880)
Isle Royal		**4 Mar 1875**	**Keweenaw** Isle Royal County; MI **Details:** (Attached to Houghton 13 Mar 1885. Absorbed by Keweenaw 9 Apr 1897)
Jackson www.co.jackson.mi.us/	**G11**	**29 Oct 1829**	**Washtenaw, Unorg. Terr.** Jackson County; 312 S Jackson St; Jackson, MI 49201; Ph. (517) 788-4265 **Details:** (Attached to Washtenaw County prior to organization 1 Aug 1832) (County Clerk has Birth & Death Records from 1867, Marriage Records from 1830's, Divorce Records from 1800's & Naturalization Records; Probate Court has Probate Records; Register of Deeds has Land Records; Clerk District Court has Court Records)

County Website	Map Index	Date Created	Parent County or Territory From Which Organized Address/Details
Kalamazoo www.kalcounty.com/	H11	29 Oct 1829	**Unorg. Terr.** Kalamazoo County; 201 W Kalamazoo Ave; Kalamazoo, MI 49007; Ph. (616) 383-8840 **Details:** (Attached to St. Joseph County prior to organization 1 Oct 1830) (County Clerk has Birth & Death Records from 1867, Marriage Records from 1831, Divorce & Court Records from 1800's; Probate Judge has Probate Records; Register of Deeds has Land Records)
Kalkaska http://members.aol.com/fiddlerben/kalkaska.html	H6	1 Apr 1840	**Mackinac** Kalkaska County; 605 N Birch St; Kalkaska, MI 49646; Ph. (616) 258-3300 **Details:** (Formerly Wabassee County. Name changed to Kalkaska 8 Mar 1843. Attached to Mackinac, Grand Traverse & Antrim Counties prior to organization 27 Jan 1871) (County Clerk has Birth, Marriage, Death, Divorce & Court Records from 1871 & Burial Records; Probate Judge has Probate Records; Register of Deeds has Land Records)
Kanotin		1 Apr 1840	**Unorg. Terr.** Kanotin County; MI **Details:** (see Iosco) Name changed to Iosco 8 Mar 1843
Kautawaubet		1 Apr 1840	**Mackinac** Kautawaubet County; MI **Details:** (see Wexford) Name changed to Wexford 8 Mar 1843
Kaykakee		1 Apr 1840	**Mackinac** Kaykakee County; MI **Details:** (see Clare) Name changed to Clare 8 Mar 1843
Kent www.co.kent.mi.us/	H10	2 Mar 1831	**Mackinac, Unorg. Terr.** Kent County; 300 Monroe Ave NW; Grand Rapids, MI 49503; Ph. (616) 336-3550 **Details:** (Organized 4 Apr 1836) (County Clerk has Birth & Death Records from 1867, Marriage Records from 1845 & Burial Records from 1959; Clerk Circuit Court has Divorce & Court Records from 1867; Probate Court has Probate Records; Register of Deeds has Land Records)
Keskkauko		1 Apr 1840	**Mackinac** Keskkauko County; MI **Details:** (see Charlevoix, old) Name changed to Charlevoix 8 Mar 1843
Keweenaw Future website at www.rootsweb.com/ ~migenweb/county_list.htm	M1	11 Mar 1861	**Houghton** Keweenaw County; County Courthouse; 4th St; Eagle River, MI 49924; Ph. (906) 337-2229 **Details:** (County Clerk has Birth, Marriage & Death Records from 1867, Land Records from 1848, Divorce & Court Records; Probate Court has Probate Records)
Lake www.rootsweb.com/~milake/	I8	1 Apr 1840	**Mackinac** Lake County; 800 Tenth St; PO Box B; Baldwin, MI 49304; Ph. (616) 745-4641 **Details:** (Formerly Aishcum County. Name changed to Lake 8 Mar 1843. Attached to Ottawa, Mason & Newaygo Counties prior to organization 1 May 1871) (County Clerk has Birth & Death Records from 1870, Marriage from 1872 & Military Discharge Records; Trial Court has Divorce & Court Records from 1874 & Probate Records; Register of Deeds has land records from 1880)

County Website	Map Index	Date Created	Parent County or Territory From Which Organized Address/Details
Lapeer www.lapeer.lib.mi.us/gov/county/	D10	10 Sep 1822	**Oakland, St. Clair, Unorg. Terr.** Lapeer County; 255 Clay St; Lapeer, MI 48446; Ph. (810) 667-0356 **Details:** (Attached to Oakland County prior to organization 2 Feb 1835) (County Clerk has Birth & Death Records from 1867, Marriage, Divorce & Court Records from 1835)
Leelanau www.leelanaucounty.com/	I6	1 Apr 1840	**Mackinac** Leelanau County; 301 E Cedar St; PO Box 467; Leland, MI 49654; Ph. 231.256.9824 **Details:** (Attached to Mackinac & Grand Traverse Counties prior to organization 27 Feb 1863) (County Clerk has Birth, Marriage & Death Records from 1867, Divorce Records from 1870 & Court Records; Probate Judge has Probate Records)
Lenawee http://dianesgenealogy.com/lenaweemi/index.html	F12	10 Sep 1822	**Monroe** Lenawee County; 425 N Main St; Adrian, MI 49221; Ph. (517) 264-4606 **Details:** (Attached to Monroe County prior to organization 31 Dec 1826; Courthouse burned 1852) (County Clerk has Birth, Marriage & Death Records from 1867, Divorce & Court Records from 1870)
Livingston www.co.livingston.mi.us/	F11	21 Mar 1833	**Shiawassee, Washtenaw** Livingston County; 200 E Grand River Ave; PO Box 377; Howell, MI 48843; Ph. (517) 546-0500 **Details:** (Attached to Shiawassee & Washtenaw Counties prior to organization 4 Apr 1836) (County Clerk has Birth, Court, & Death Records from 1867, Marriage Records from 1836; Register of Deeds has Land Records)
Luce www.rootsweb.com/~miluce/	I3	1 Mar 1887	**Chippewa, Mackinac** Luce County; 407 W Harrie St; Newberry, MI 49868; Ph. (906) 293-5521 **Details:** (County Clerk has Birth, Marriage, Death, Divorce, Court & Land Records from 1887; Probate Judge has Probate Records)
Mackinac www.rootsweb.com/~mimackin/	H3	26 Oct 1818	**Wayne** Mackinac County; 100 S Marley St; St. Ignace, MI 49781; Ph. (906) 643-7300 **Details:** (Formerly Michilimackinac County. Name changed to Mackinac 26 Jan 1837) (County Clerk has Birth & Death Records from 1873, Marriage Records from 1867, Divorce & Court Records from 1808)
Macomb www.macomb.lib.mi.us/macomb/	D11	15 Jan 1818	**Wayne** Macomb County; 40 N Main; Mount Clemens, MI 48043; Ph. (810) 469-5120 **Details:** (County Clerk has Birth & Death Records from 1867, Marriage Records from 1819, Divorce Records from 1847 & Military Records; Probate Court has Probate Records; Register of Deeds has Land Records)
Manistee www.manistee.com/~edo/	J7	1 Apr 1840	**Mackinac** Manistee County; 415 3rd St; Manistee, MI 49660-1606; Ph. (231) 723-3331 **Details:** (Attached to Mackinac, Ottawa & Grand Traverse Counties prior to organization 13 Feb 1855) (County Clerk has Birth & Death Records from 1867, Marriage & Divorce Records from 1856 & Court Records from 1855; Probate Court has Probate Records; Register of Deeds has Land Records)

County Website	Map Index	Date Created	Parent County or Territory From Which Organized Address/Details
Manitou		12 Feb 1855	**Emmet, Leelanau** Manitou County; MI **Details:** (Attached to Mackinac & Leelanau Counties. Disorganized 16 Mar 1861. Eliminated 4 Apr 1895 & absorbed by Charlevoix & Leelanau Counties)
Marquette www.co.marquette.mi.us/	L3	9 Mar 1843	**Chippewa, Mackinac** Marquette County; 234 W Baraga Ave; Marquette, MI 49855; Ph. (906) 225-8330 **Details:** (Attached to Chippewa & Houghton Counties prior to organization 1 Dec 1851) (County Clerk has Birth & Death Records from 1867, Marriage Records from 1851, Divorce & Court Records from 1852)
Mason www.rootsweb.com/~mimason/county.html	J8	1 Apr 1840	**Mackinac** Mason County; 304 E Ludington Ave; Ludington, MI 49431; Ph. (231) 843-8202 **Details:** (Formerly Notipekago County. Name changed to Mason 8 Mar 1843. Attached to Ottawa County prior to organization 13 Feb 1855) (County Clerk has Birth, Marriage, Death, Divorce & Court Records from 1867; City Clerks have burial Records; Probate Court has Probate Records; Register of Deeds has Land Records)
Mecosta www.rootsweb.com/~mimecost/index.html	H8	1 Apr 1840	**Mackinac, Oceana** Mecosta County; 400 Elm St; Big Rapids, MI 49307-1849; Ph. (616) 592-0783 **Details:** (Attached to Newaygo & Kent Counties prior to organization 11 Feb 1858) (County Clerk has Birth & Death Records from 1867, Marriage, Divorce & Court Records from 1859; Probate Court has Probate Records from 1864; Register of Deeds has Land Records from 1859)
Meegisee		1 Apr 1840	**Mackinac** Meegisee County; MI **Details:** (see Antrim) Name changed to Antrim 8 Mar 1843
Menominee www.menomineecounty.com/	L4	15 Mar 1861	**Unorganized Territory** Menominee County; 839 10th Ave; Menominee, MI 49858; Ph. (906) 863-9968 **Details:** (Formerly Bleeker County. Name changed to Menominee 19 Mar 1863) (County Clerk has Birth, Marriage, Death, Divorce & Court Records from 1861; Probate Judge has Probate Records; Register of Deeds has Land Records)
Michilimackinac		26 Oct 1818	**Wayne** Michilimackinac County; MI **Details:** (see Mackinac) Name changed to Mackinac 26 Jan 1837
Midland www.co.midland.mi.us/	F8	2 Mar 1831	**Saginaw, Unorg. Terr.** Midland County; 220 W Ellsworth St; Midland, MI 48640-5180; Ph. (517) 832-6739 **Details:** (Attached to Saginaw County prior to organization 31 Dec 1850) (County Clerk has Birth, Marriage & Death Records from 1867, Burial Records from mid-1800's, Military Discharge Records from 1918 & Naturalization Records 1853–1948; Clerk Circuit Court has Divorce & Court Records from 1800's; Probate Court has Probate Records; Register of Deeds has Land Records from 1855)

County Website	Map Index	Date Created	Parent County or Territory From Which Organized Address/Details
Mikenauk		**1 Apr 1840**	**Mackinac** Mikenauk County; MI **Details:** (see Roscommon) Name changed to Roscommon 8 Mar 1843
Missaukee www.missaukee.org	**H7**	**1 Apr 1840**	**Mackinac** Missaukee County; 111 S Canal St; PO Box 800; Lake City, MI 49651; Ph. (231) 839-4967, clerk@missaukee.org **Details:** (Attached to Mackinac, Grand Traverse, Manistee & Wexford Counties prior to organization 11 Mar 1871) (County Clerk has Birth Records from 1869, Burial Records, Guardianship, Court, & Probate Records from 1873, Death & Divorce Records from 1870, Land & Military Records from 1872, Marriage Records from 1871, & Naturalization Records)
Monroe www.co.monroe.mi.us/	**E12**	**14 Jul 1817**	**Wayne** Monroe County; 106 E 1st St; Monroe, MI 48161-2143; Ph. (734) 240-7020 **Details:** (County Clerk has Birth Records from 1874, Marriage Records from 1818, Death Records from 1867, Divorce & Court Records to 1945; Probate Court has Probate Records; Register of Deeds has Land Records)
Montcalm www.montcalm.org	**H9**	**2 Mar 1831**	**Mackinac** Montcalm County; 211 W Main St; PO Box 368; Stanton, MI 48888; Ph. (989) 831-7339 **Details:** (Attached to Ionia County prior to organization 20 Mar 1850) (County Clerk has Birth & Death Records from 1867, Marriage Records from 1858, Divorce & Court Records from 1865; Probate Court has Probate Records; Register of Deeds has Land Records)
Montmorency www.rootsweb.com/~mimontmo/	**F5**	**1 Apr 1840**	**Mackinac** Montmorency County; County Courthouse; 12265 M-32; PO 789; Atlanta, MI 49709; Ph. (989) 785-8022 **Details:** (Formerly Cheonoquet County. Name changed to Montmorency 8 Mar 1843. Attached to Mackinac, Cheboygan & Alpena Counties prior to organization 21 May 1881. Most Records lost in fire, 1942) (County Clerk has Birth, Marriage & Death Records from 1881, Divorce & Court Records from 1940 & Military Records from 1920)
Muskegon http://co.muskegon.mi.us/	**J9**	**4 Feb 1859**	**Ottawa** Muskegon County; 990 Terrace St; Muskegon, MI 49442; Ph. (616) 724-6221 **Details:** (County Clerk has Birth, Marriage, Death, Divorce & Court Records from 1859; Probate Court has Probate Records; Register of Deeds has Land Records)
Negwegon		**1 Apr 1840**	**Mackinac, Unorg. Terr.** Neewago County; MI **Details:** (see Alcona) Name changed to Alcona 8 Mar 1843

County Website	Map Index	Date Created	Parent County or Territory From Which Organized Address/Details
Newaygo www.countyofnewaygo.com	I8	1 Apr 1840	**Mackinac, Oceana** Newaygo County; 1087 Newell St; White Cloud, MI 49349-0293; Ph. (616) 689-7235 **Details:** (Attached to Kent & Ottawa Counties prior to organization 27 Jan 1851) (County Clerk has Birth & Death Records from 1867, Marriage Records from 1851 & Military Records; Clerk Circuit Court has Divorce, & Court Records; Probate Court has Probate Records; Register of Deeds has Land Records; Naturalization Records were removed to State of Michigan, State Archives)
Notipekago		1 Apr 1840	**Mackinac** Notipekago County; MI **Details:** (see Mason) Name changed to Mason 8 Mar 1843
Oakland www.co.oakland.mi.us/	E10	1820	**Macomb** Oakland County; 1200 N Telegraph Rd; Pontiac, MI 48341; Ph. (248) 858-0572 **Details:** (Attached to Macomb County prior to organization 28 Mar 1820) (County Clerk has Birth & Death Records from 1867, Marriage & Naturalization Records from 1827)
Oceana www.oceana.net/	J8	2 Mar 1831	**Mackinac** Oceana County; 100 Store St; Hart, MI 49420; Ph. (231) 873-4328 **Details:** (Attached to Kent & Ottawa Counties prior to organization 7 Apr 1851) (County Clerk has Birth & Marriage Records from 1867 & Death Records from 1868; Clerk Circuit Court has Divorce & Court Records; Probate Court has Probate Records; Register of Deeds has Land Records)
Ogemaw www.rootsweb.com/~miogemaw/index.htm	F7	1 Apr 1840	**Unorg. Terr.** Ogemaw County; 806 W Houghton Ave; West Branch, MI 48661; Ph. (517) 345-0215 **Details:** (Attached to Mackinac, Cheboygan & Iosco Counties prior to organization. Eliminated 7 Mar 1867 to Iosco. Recreated 28 Mar 1873 from Iosco & organized 27 Apr 1875) (County Clerk has Birth Records from 1879, Marriage Records from 1887, Death Records from 1876, Divorce & Court Records from 1902, Naturalization Records from 1876 & Military Records from 1919; Probate Court has Probate Records from 1873; Register of deeds has Land Records from 1860)
Okkuddo		1 Apr 1840	**Mackinac** Okkuddo County; MI **Details:** (see Otsego) Name changed to Otsego 8 Mar 1843
Omeena		1 Apr 1840	**Mackinac** Omeena County; MI **Details:** County Terminated 1843 (see Grand Traverse) Absorbed by Grand Traverse County 3 Feb 1853
Ontonagon w3.up.net/~edc/	O2	9 Mar 1843	**Chippewa, Mackinac** Ontonagon County; 725 Greenland Rd; Ontonagon, MI 49953; Ph. (906) 884-4255 **Details:** (Attached to Chippewa & Houghton Counties prior to organization 1 Jan 1853) (County Clerk has Birth & Death Records from 1868, Marriage Records from 1861, Divorce & Court Records from 1854 & Land Records from 1850; Probate Court has Probate Records; Cemetery associations have Burial Records)

County Website	Map Index	Date Created	Parent County or Territory From Which Organized Address/Details
Osceola www.rootsweb.com/~miosceol/	H8	1 Apr 1840	**Mackinac** Osceola County; 301 W Upton Ave; PO Box 208; Reed City, MI 49677-1149; Ph. (231) 832-6104 **Details:** (Formerly Unwattin County. Name changed to Osceola 8 Mar 1843. Attached to Ottawa, Mason, Newaygo & Mecosta Counties prior to organization 17 Mar 1869) (County Clerk has Birth & Marriage Records from 1869, Death & Divorce Records from 1870, Court Records from 1963 & Burial Records; Probate Judge has Probate Records; County Treasurer has Land Records)
Oscoda www.rootsweb.com/~mioscoda/	F6	1 Apr 1840	**Mackinac** Oscoda County; 311 Morenci; PO Box 399; Mio, MI 48647; Ph. (989) 826-1110 **Details:** (Attached to Cheboygan, Alpena, Alcona, Iosco & Mackinac Counties prior to organization 10 Mar 1881) (County Clerk has Birth, Circuit Court, Death, Divorce, Marriage, Military Discharge, & Naturalization Records from 1881; Register of Deeds has Land Records from 1850; Probate Court has Guardianship & Probate Records; Township Clerk has Burial Records; Treasurer has Tax Records)
Otsego www.rootsweb.com/~miotsego/index.html	G6	1 Apr 1840	**Mackinac** Otsego County; 225 W Main St; Gaylord, MI 49735-1348; Ph. (517) 732-6484 **Details:** (Formerly Okkuddo County. Name changed to Otsego 8 Mar 1843. Attached to Alpena, Mackinac, Cheboygan, Alpena & Antrim Counties prior to organization 12 Mar 1875) (County Clerk has Birth, Marriage, Death, Divorce & Court Records from 1875; County Treasurer has Land Records)
Ottawa www.co.ottawa.mi.us/	I10	2 Mar 1831	**Mackinac, Unorg. Terr.** Ottawa County; 414 Washington Ave; Grand Haven, MI 49417-1473; Ph. (616) 846-8310 **Details:** (Attached to Kent County prior to organization 29 Dec 1837) (County Clerk has Birth & Death Records from 1867, Marriage & Court Records from 1847 & Divorce Records from 1863)
Presque Isle http://members.aol.com/alpenaco/presque/index.htm	F5	1 Apr 1840	**Mackinac** Presque Isle County; 151 E Huron Ave; PO Box 110; Rogers City, MI 49779-1316; Ph. (517) 734-3288 **Details:** (Attached to Cheboygan & Alpena Counties prior to organization 31 Mar 1871) (County Clerk has Birth & Death Records from 1871, Marriage Records from 1842 & Divorce Records from 1900)
Roscommon www.rootsweb.com/~miroscom/	G7	1 Apr 1840	**Mackinac** Roscommon County; 500 Lake St; Roscommon, MI 48653; Ph. (517) 275-5923 **Details:** (Formerly Mikenauk County. Name changed to Roscommon 8 Mar 1843. Attached to Mackinac, Cheboygan & Midland Counties prior to organization 20 Mar 1875) (County Clerk has Birth & Death Records from 1874, Marriage, Divorce, Probate, Court & Land Records from 1875)

County Website	Map Index	Date Created	Parent County or Territory From Which Organized Address/Details
Saginaw www.saginawcounty.com/	F9	10 Sep 1822	**St. Clair, Unorg. Terr.** Saginaw County; 111 S Michigan Ave; Saginaw, MI 48602; Ph. (517) 790-5251 **Details:** (Attached to Oakland County prior to organization 9 Feb 1835) (County Clerk has Birth & Marriage Records from 1867, Death Records from 1868, Divorce Records from 1886 & Court Records from 1843; Probate Court has Probate Records; Equalization Department has Land Records)
Sanilac www.rootsweb.com/~misanila/	D9	10 Sep 1822	**St. Clair, Unorg. Terr.** Sanilac County; 60 W Sanilac Rd., Rm 203; Sandusky, MI 48471; Ph. (810) 648-3212 **Details:** (Attached to Oakland, St. Clair & Lapeer Counties prior to organization 31 Dec 1849) (County Clerk has Birth Records from 1860, Death Records from 1867, Marriage Records from 1849, Divorce & Court Records from 1854; Probate Court has Probate Records; Register of Deeds has Land Records)
Schoolcraft www.rootsweb.com/~mischool/	J3	9 Mar 1843	**Chippewa, Mackinac** Schoolcraft County; 300 Walnut St #164; Manistique, MI 49854-1491; Ph. (906) 341-3618 **Details:** (Attached to Chippewa, Houghton & Marquette Counties prior to organization 23 Mar 1871) (County Clerk has Birth, Marriage, Death, Divorce, Court & Land Records from 1870; Probate Court has Probate Records from 1870)
Shawano		1818	**Mackinac** Shawano County; MI **Details:** (see Crawford) Name changed to Crawford 8 Mar 1843
Shiawassee www.rootsweb.com/~mishiawa/mishiawa.html	F10	10 Sep 1822	**Oakland, St. Clair, Unorg. Terr.** Shiawassee County; 208 N Shiawasee St; Corunna, MI 48817; Ph. (517) 743-2242 **Details:** (Atttached to Genesee & Oakland Counties prior to organization 18 Mar 1837) (County Clerk has Birth, Marriage & Death Records from 1867, Divorce & Court Records from 1848; Probate Judge has Probate Records; Register of Deeds has Land Records)
St. Clair www.rootsweb.com/~mistclai/index.html	D10	28 Mar 1820	**Macomb** St. Clair County; 201 McMorran Blvd; Port Huron, MI 48060-4006; Ph. (810) 985-2200 **Details:** (Attached to Macomb County prior to organization 8 May 1821) (County Clerk has Birth Records from 1867, Marriage Records from 1834, Death Records from 1868, Divorce & Court Records from 1849)
St. Joseph http://members.tripod.com/~tfred/mistjo.html	I12	29 Oct 1829	**Unorg. Terr.** St. Joseph County; 125 W Main St; Centreville, MI 49032-0189; Ph. (616) 467-5602 **Details:** (County Clerk has Birth & Death Records from 1867, Marriage Records from 1832, Divorce & Court Records from 1900 & Naturalization Records; Probate Court has Probate Records; Register of Deeds has Land Records)
Tonedagana		1 Apr 1840	**Mackinac** Tonedagana County; MI **Details:** (see Emmet) Name changed to Emmet 8 Mar 1843

County	Map	Date	Parent County or Territory From Which Organized
Website	Index	Created	Address/Details

Tuscola E9 **1 Apr 1840** **Sanilac**
www.tuscolacounty.org/

Tuscola County; 440 N State St Suite 1592; Caro, MI 48723;
Ph. (989) 672-3780, white-cormier@tuscolacounty.org
Details: (Attached to Saginaw County prior to organization 2 Mar 1850) (County Clerk has Birth, Court, Death, Divorce, Marriage, & Military Records)

Unwattin **1 Apr 1840** **Mackinac**

Unwattin County; MI
Details: (see Osceola) Name changed to Osceola 8 Mar 1843

Van Buren I11 **29 Oct 1829** **Unorg. Terr.**
www.rootsweb.com/~mivanbur/Mivanbur.html

Van Buren County; 212 E Paw Paw St; Paw Paw, MI 49079-1492;
Ph. (616) 657-8218
Details: (Attached to Cass & Lenawee Counties prior to organization 3 Apr 1837) (County Clerk has Birth & Death Records from 1867, Marriage Records from 1836, Divorce & Court Records from 1837; Probate Court has Probate Records; Register of Deeds has Land Records)

Wabassee **1 Apr 1840** **Mackinac**

Wabassee County; MI
Details: (see Kalkaska) Name changed to Kalkaska 8 Mar 1843

Washtenaw F11 **10 Sep 1822** **Wayne, Oakland**
http://ewashtenaw.org/government/
clerk_register/index_html

Washtenaw County; 200 N Main St, Suite 120; PO Box 8645; Ann Arbor, MI 48107-8645; Ph. (734) 222-6730
Details: (Attached to Wayne County prior to organization 31 Dec 1826) (Vital Records has Birth & Death Records from 1867 & Marriages from 1833; Deeds has Land & Mortgage Records from 1824; Election & Supervisors Records from 1826; Courthouse has Court Records from 1826)

Wayne E11 **21 Nov 1815** **Original county**
www.waynecounty.com/

Wayne County; 201 City Court Bldg; MI 48226; Ph. (313) 224-6262
Details: (County Clerk has Birth, Marriage & Death Records; Probate Court has Probate Records; Register of Deeds has Land Records)

Wexford I7 **1 Apr 1840** **Mackinac**
http://users.netonecom.net/~mgreen/

Wexford County; 437 E Division St; Cadillac, MI 49601;
Ph. (231) 779-9450
Details: (Formerly Kautawaubet County. Name changed to Wexford 8 Mar 1843. Attached to Mackinac, Manistee & Grand Traverse Counties prior to organization 30 Mar 1869) (County Clerk has Birth Records from 1868, Marriage, Death, Divorce & Court Records from 1869)

Wyandot **1840** **Mackinac**

Wyandot; LA
Details: County Terminated 1853

Notes

Minnesota

Capital: St. Paul

Territory: 1849

State: 1858 (23rd)

The star of the North

Ojibwa, Ottawa, Huron, and Dakota Indian tribes were among Minnesota's earliest inhabitants and French fur traders and missionaries preceded settlers. Among the early explorers were Daniel Greysolon and Sieur Du Lhut (Duluth), who built a fort on the shores of Lake Superior and claimed the region for France. Father Louis Hennepin explored the upper Mississippi River in 1680 and discovered the Falls of St. Anthony, where Minneapolis is today. Eastern Minnesota was given to the British in 1763 and fur trading was taken over by the Northwest Company. At the Revolutionary War's end in 1783, this area became part of the United States, and then, part of the Northwest Territory in 1787. The land west of the Mississippi River became part of the United States with the Louisiana Purchase in 1803. Zebulon Pike was sent to explore the area and set up Fort Anthony, later called Fort Snelling, at the junction of the Minnesota and Mississippi rivers. Fort Snelling became the first large settlement, located near present-day St. Paul. By 1823, steamboats were coming up the Mississippi to the fort. The American Fur Company took over the fur trading industry in 1815, ending British control of the area.

In 1836, Minnesota was part of the Wisconsin Territory. The next year, the Sioux and Chippewa Indians sold their claim to the St. Croix Valley, opening the area to lumbering. Real settlement began in earnest with settlers from the eastern United States coming to the eastern part of the state. In 1849, Minnesota became a territory. Further treaties with the Indians between 1851 and 1855 opened up western Minnesota to settlement. Immigration increased with completion of the railroad to the Mississippi River. A 1862 Sioux rebellion that killed more than 500 settlers resulted in the Indians relinquishing the last of their claims.

During the Civil War, Minnesota furnished about 24,000 men to the Union. After the war the state boomed due to its timber, mines, mills, and agriculture. Homesteaders moved into the western and southwestern sections primarily from Germany, Sweden, and Norway. Poland, Lithuania, and the Balkan States furnished much of the labor for the packing plants around the Twin Cities at the turn of the century. Other ethnic groups who came to the state included Danes, Canadians, English, Finns, and Russians.

Look for vital records in the following locations:

- **Birth and death records:** State registration of births began in 1900. Registration of deaths began in 1908. These records are available from the Minnesota Department of Health, Section of Vital Statistics in Minneapolis, Minnesota. Records prior to 1900 are in the offices of the District Court clerks.

- **Marriage and divorce records:** Registration began within a decade of each county's formation. District court administration offices have marriage and divorce records, except for Hennepin County. Hennepin Count records are at the State Department of Health.

- **Probate records:** Probate records are at the Probate Court clerk's office.

- **Land records:** The first general land office was established in Wisconsin in 1848, but was transferred to Stillwater, Minnesota in 1849. These early books and township plats are at the Land Bureau in St. Paul, Minnesota. The National Archives, Chicago Branch in Chicago, Illinois has land entry case files. The registrar of deeds in each county keeps mortgages and deeds.

- **Census records:** Minnesota was included in the Wisconsin and Iowa Territorial censuses in 1836 and 1840. Minnesota Territorial censuses exist for 1849, 1850, 1855, and 1857. State censuses were taken in 1865, 1875, 1885, and 1905.

Minnesota Department of Health, Attention: Office of the State Registrar
PO Box 9441
Minneapolis, Minnesota 55440-9441
(612) 676-5120; Fax (612) 331-5776
www.health.state.mn.us/divs/chs/osr/death.html

Minnesota Historical Society
345 W. Kellogg Blvd.
St. Paul, Minnesota 55102-1906
(651) 296-6126
www.mnhs.org/

Land Bureau
658 Cedar Street
St. Paul, Minnesota 55101

Societies and Repositories

Aitkin County Historical Society; PO Box 215; Aitkin, MN 56431; achs@mlecmn.net; www.aitkin.com/achs.

American Swedish Institute; 2600 Park Ave.; Minneapolis, MN 55407; information@americanswedishinst.org; www.americanswedishinst.org.

Anoka County Genealogical Society; PO Box 48126; Coon Rapids, MN 55448-0126; acgsmn@yahoo.com; http://freepages.genealogy.rootsweb.com/ ~relativememory.

Anoka County Historical Society; 2135 - 3rd Ave., No.; Anoka, MN 55303-2421; www.rootsweb.com/~mnachs.

Becker County Historical Society and Museum; 714 Summit; PO Box 622; Detroit Lakes, MN 56502; bolerud@tekstar.com; www.angelfire.com/mn/bchs39/index.html.

Blue Earth County Historical Society; 415 E. Cherry St.; Mankato, MN 56001; www.bushelboy.com/reg9/bechs.

Brown County Historical Society; 2 North Broadway; New Ulm, MN 56073; bchs@newulmtel.net; http://browncountyhistorymnusa.org.

Carver County Historical Society; 555 West First Street; Waconia, MN; historical@co.carver.mn.us; www.co.carver.mn.us/HistoricalSociety/HistSoc.htm.

Chippewa County Genealogical or Historical Society; 151 Pioneer Dr.; PO Box 303; Montevideo, MN 56265; (320) 269-7636; cchs.june@juno.com; www.montechamber.com/cchs/cchshp.htm.

Clearwater County Historical Society; PO Box 241; Bagley, MN 56621; www.rrv.net/bagleymn/histSoc.htm.

Crow River Genealogical Society; 380 School Road North; Hutchinson, MN 55350.

Crow Wing County Historical Society; PO Box 722; Brainerd, MN 56401; www.mjpdan.com/genweb/ crowwing/general.htm.

Crow Wing County Minnesota Genealogical Society; 2103 Graydon Ave.; Brainerd, MN 56401; www.mjpdan.com/genweb/crowwing/general.htm.

Cuyuna Country Heritage Preservation Society; PO Box 68; Ironton, MN 56455; cchps@emily.net; www.cuyunaheritage.org.

Czechoslovak Genealogical Society International; PO Box 16225; St. Paul, MN 55116-0225; cgsi@aol.com; www.cgsi.org.

Dakota County Genealogical Society; 130 Third Avenue N.; South St. Paul, MN 55075; rthill@isd.net; www.geocities.com/Heartland/Flats/9284.

Danish American Fellowship; 4200 Cedar Ave. S.; Minneapolis, MN 55407; www.daf-mn.org.

Danish American Genealogy Group Minnesota Genealogical Society; 5768 Olson Memorial Hwy.; GoldenValley, MN 55422; wcholm@aol.com; www.mtn.org/mgs/branches/danish.html.

Dodge County Genealogical Society; Box 683; Dodge Center, MN 55927-0683; www.rootsweb.com/~mndodge/resources.htm.

Dodge County Historical Society; PO Box 433; Mantorville, MN 55955; www.rootsweb.com/~mndodge/resources.htm.

Douglas County Genealogical Society; PO Box 197; Henning, MN 56551-0197; www.mtn.org/mgs/branches/douglas.html.

Douglas County Historical Society; 1219 Nokomis Street; Alexandria, MN 56308; bardo@rea-alp.com; www.rea-alp.com/~historic/index.html.

Fillmore County Historical Center; 202 County Road 8; Fountain, MN 55935.

Freeborn County Genealogical Society; 1033 Bridge Ave.; Albert Lee, MN 56007-2205.

German-Bohemian Heritage Society; 311 Linden Street; New Ulm, MN 56073-1519; www.rootsweb.com/~gbhs.

Germanic Genealogy Society; PO Box 16312; Saint Paul, MN 55116-0312; www.mtn.org/mgs/german.

Goodhue County Family Tree Club; c/o Goodhue County Historical Society; 1166 Oak St.; Red Wing, MN 55066.

Great Northern Railway Historical Society; ja.larson@worldnet.att.net; www.gnrhs.org.

Heart-O-Lakes Genealogical Society; PO Box 622; Detroit Lakes, MN 56502-0622; www.angelfire.com/mn/HOLGS/index.html.

Heritage Searchers of Kandiyohi County; PO Box 175; Willmar, MN 56201.

Hubbard County Genealogical Society; 301 Court St. Park Rapids; PO Box 361; Park Rapids, MN 56470; dhensel@eot.com; www.rootsweb.com/~mnhgs.

Icelandic Genealogy Group, Minnesota Genealogical Society; 5769 Olson Memorial Hwy.; Golden Valley, MN 55422.

Irish Genealogical Society, Int'l; PO Box 16585; St. Paul, MN 55116-0585; www.rootsweb.com/~irish.

Iron Range Historical Society; PO Box 786; Gilbert, MN 55741-0786; www.homestead.com/gilbertmn/files/ IronRangeHistoricalSociety.html.

Itasca Genealogical Club; PO Box 261; Bovey, MN 55709-0261.

Jewish Historical Society of the Upper Midwest; 4330 S. Cedar Lake RD; Minneapolis, MN 55416-3700; (952) 381-3360; history@jhsum.org; www.tc.umn.edu/~schlo006.

Kanabec County Historical Society & History Center; PO Box 113, West Forest Ave.; Mora, MN 55051.

Kandiyohi County Historical Society; 617 NE Hwy 71; Willmar, MN 56201; kandhist@wecnet.com; http://freepages.genealogy.rootsweb.com/~kchs123/index.html.

Le Sueur County Historical Society; PO Box 240; Elysian, MN 56028; www.lchs.mus.mn.us.

Maplewood Area Historical Society; 2516 E. Idaho St.; Maplewood, MN 55109; happypebbl@hotmail.com; www.geocities.com/CapeCanaveral/Hall/3649/mahs.html.

Martin County Genealogical Society; 222 E. Blue Earth Ave.; Fairmont, MN 56031-2847; www.geocities.com/Heartland/Hills/4091.

Martin County Historical Society; 304 East Blue Earth Avenue; Fairmont, MN 56031; (507) 235-5178; mchs@bevcomm.net; www.co.martin.mn.us/mchs.

Military Historical Society of Minnesota; 15000 Highway 115; Little Falls, MN 56345-4173; mnmuseum@brainerd.net; www.dma.state.mn.us/cpripley/SpecFeatures/muse1.htm.

Minnesota Genealogical Society; 5768 Olson Memorial Hwy.; Golden Valley, MN 55422; mgsdec@mtm.org.

Minnesota Historical Society; 345 Kellogg Blvd. West; St. Paul, MN 55102-1906; (651) 296-2143; reference@mnhs.org; www.mnhs.org/library.

Minnesota Library Resources; www.state.mn.us/libraries.

Minnesota State Archives; 345 W. Kellogg Blvd.; St. Paul, MN 55102-1906; (651) 297-4502; archives@mnhs.org; www.mnhs.org/preserve/records/index.html.

Minnetonka Historical Society; 13209 E. McGinty Road; Minnetonka, MN 55305; mhs@ci.minnetonka.mn.usg; www.minnetonka-history.org.

MinnKota Genealogical Society; PO Box 126; East Grand Forks, MN 56721; www.rootsweb.com/~minnkota.

Morrison County Historical Society; PO Box 239; 2151 South Lindberg Drive; Little Falls, MN 56345; www.upstel.net/~johns/History/MorrisonCo.html.

Mower County Genealogical Society; PO Box 145; Austin, MN 55912.

Mower County Historical Society; PO Box 804; Austin, MN 55912; www2.smig.net/mchistory.

Nobles County Genealogical Society; Suite 2, 407 12th St.; Worthington, MN 56187-2411.

Nobles County Historical Society; 219 11th Ave.; Worthington, MN 56187.

Norman County Genealogical Society; 100 1st St. E. Apt. 202; Ada, MN 56510; www.rootsweb.com/~mnnorman/NCGenSoc.html.

North Star of Minnesota Chapter, AHSGR; 2479 Churchill St.; Roseville, MN 55113; (612) 787-0408; dochaas@isd.net; www.ahsgr.org/mnnostar.html.

Northwest Territory Canadian and French Heritage Center; PO Box 29397; Brooklyn Center, MN 55429-0397.

Norwegian-American Genealogical Association; c/o Minn. Genealogical Society; 5768 Olson Memorial; Golden Valley, MN 55422; mgsdec@mtn.org.

Norwegian-American Historical Association; 1510 St. Olaf Avenue; Northfield, MN 55057-1097; naha@stolaf.edu; www.naha.stolaf.edu.

Olmsted County Genealogical Society; PO Box 6411; Rochester, MN 55903; www.olmstedhistory.com/ocgs.htm.

Ostfriesen Genealogical Society of Minnesota; PO Box 474; Wyoming, MN 55092; (651) 464-7880; www.rootsweb.com/~mnogsm.

Otter Tail County Historical Society; 1110 Lincoln Avenue West; Fergus Falls, MN 56537; otchs@prtel.com; www.otchs.org.

Pennington County Historical Society; PO Box 127; Thief River Falls, MN 56701.

Pipestone County Genealogical Society; 113 South Hiawatha; Pipestone, MN 56164.

Polish Genealogical Society of Minnesota; 3487 Darrow Ave. SE; Buffalo, MN 55313-5217; www.rootsweb.com/~mnpolgs/pgs-mn.html.

Prairieland Genealogical Society Historical Center; Room 141-Social Science Building; Southwest State U; Marshall, MN 56258; http://freepages.genealogy.rootsweb.com/~cmolitor.

Ramsey County Historical Society; 323 Landmark Center; 75 West Fifth Street; Saint Paul, MN 55102; info@rchs.com; www.rchs.com.

Range Genealogical Society; 801 SW Highway 169 Ste 1; Chisholm, MN 55719-1846.

Redwood County Genealogical Society; 217 West Flynn Street; Redwood Falls, MN 56283; http://freepages.genealogy.rootsweb.com/~corder/RCGS.

Renville County Genealogical Society; 221 North Main Street; PO Box 331; Renville, MN 56284; http://ci.renville.mn.us/rcgs.

Renville County Historical Society and Museum; 411 North Park Drive; PO Box 266; Morton, MN 56270; www.rootsweb.com/~mnrenvil/mus-rchs.htm.

Rice County Genealogical Society; 408 Division St.; Northfield, MN 55057.

Rice County Historical Museum and Genealogical Research Center; 1814 Second Ave.; Faribault, MN 55021.

Roseau County Historical Society; 110 2nd Ave NE; Roseau, MN 56751; roseau@wiktel.com; www.angelfire.com/mn/rchistsocmuseum.

Sherburne County Historical Society; 13122 First St.; Becker, MN 55308; schs@sherbtel.net; www.rootsweb.com/~mnschs/home.htm.

Sibley County Historical Society; PO Box 407; Henderson, MN 56044; http://history.sibley.mn.us/index.htm.

Sons of Norway; 1455 W. Lake St.; Minneapolis, MN 55408.

Sons of the American Revolution, Minnesota Society; 2546 Cedar Ave.; Minneapolis, MN 55404.

St. Cloud Area Genealogists, Inc.; PO Box 213; St. Cloud, MN 56302-0213; www.rootsweb.com/~mnscag/SCAG/Activities.htm.

Stearns County Historical Society (Scandinavian Resources); PO Box 702; 235 S. 33rd Ave.; St. Cloud, MN 56302-0702.

Swedish Genealogical Society of Minnesota; 5768 Olson Memorial Highway; Golden Valley, MN 55422; www.mtn.org/mgs/sweden.

Swift County Historical Society; Box 39; Benson, MN 56215.

Twin Ports Genealogical Society; PO Box 16895; Duluth, MN 55816-0895.

Upsala Area Historical Society; Box 35; Upsala, MN 56384; www.upstel.net/~johns/History.

Verndale Historical Society; PO Box 5; Verndale, MN 56481.

Waseca Area Genealogical Society, Inc.; PO Box 314; Waseca, MN 56093.

Waseca County Historical Society; PO Box 314; Waseca, MN 56093; director@historical.waseca.mn.us; www.historical.waseca.mn.us.

Washington County Historical Society; 602 North Main Street; PO Box 167; Stillwater, MN 55082-0167; (651) 439-5956; BrentWwchsmn.org; http://wchsmn.org.

Watertown Area Historical Society; 309 Lewis Avenue South, PO Box 836; Watertown, MN 55388-0836; http://home.earthlink.net/~lahtinen/wahs.htm.

White Bear Lake Area Historical Society; PO Box 10543; White Bear Lake, MN 55110; (651) 407-5327; wblahistsoc@GoldenGate.net; www.wblareahistoricalsociety.org/index.htm.

Winona County Genealogical Roundtable; PO Box 363; Winona, MN 55987.

Winona County Historical Society; 160 Johnson Street; Winona, MN 55987; wchs@luminet.net; www.winona.msus.edu/historicalsociety.

Yankee Genealogical Society of Minnesota; 5768 Olson Memorial Highway; Golden Valley, MN 55422; www.mtn.org/mgs/branches/yankee.html.

Bibliography and Record Sources

General

Bakeman, Mary Hawker. *Early Presbyterian Church Records from Minnesota 1835–1871 (Including the Church at Fort Snelling).* Roseville, Minnesota: Park Genealogical Books, 1992.

Barnquist, Joseph Alfred Arner. *Minnesota and Its People.* 4 vols. Chicago: S. J. Clarke, 1924.

Bible, Genealogical, Vital Records and Pioneer Stories of Minnesota. Duluth: s.l., s.n., 1946–1947.

Bjørnson, Val. *The History of Minnesota.* 4 vols. West Palm Beach, Florida: Lewis Historical Pub., Co., 1969.

Blatti, Jo. *Women's History in Minnesota: A Survey of Published Sources and Dissertations.* St. Paul: Minnesota Historical Society Press, 1993.

Blegen, Theodore C. *Minnesota: A History of the State.* 2nd ed. Minneapolis: University of Minnesota Press, 1975.

Brook, Michael. *Reference Guide to Minnesota History.* St. Paul: Minnesota Historical Society, 1974.

Castle, Henry Anson. *Minnesota: Its Story and Biography.* 3 vols. Chicago: Lewis Publishing Co., 1915.

Clark, Clifford Edward. *Minnesota in a Century of Change: The State and Its People Since 1900.* St. Paul: Minnesota Historical Society Press, 1989.

Commemorative Biographical Record of the Upper Lake Region: Containing Biographical Sketches of Prominent and Representative Citizens and Many of the Early Settled Families. Chicago: J. H. Beers, 1905.

Compendium of History and Biography of Central and Northern Minnesota, Containing a History of the State of Minnesota . . . and a Compendium of Biography. (1904) Reprint. Salem, Massachusetts: Higginson Books, 1995.

Compendium of History and Biography of Northern Minnesota. Containing a History of the State of Minnesota. (1902) Reprint. Salem, Massachusetts: Higginson Books, 1994.

Daughters of the American Revolution (Minnesota). *Genealogical Collection.* Microfilm. Salt Lake City: Genealogical Society of Utah, 1971.

Directory of Churches and Religious Organizations in Minnesota. Madison, Wisconsin: Historical Records Survey, 1941.

Easton, Augustus B., et al., eds. *History of the St. Croix Valley.* 2 vols. (1909) Reprint. Salem, Massachusetts: Higginson Books, 1996.

Edwards, Rev. Maurice Dwight. *History of the Synod of Minnesota—Presbyterian Church USA.* Introduction by Rev. Robt. Jeambey. (1927) Reprint. Roseville, Minnesota: Park Genealogical Books, 1993.

Folsom, W. H. C. *Fifty Years in the Northwest. With an Introduction and Appendix Containing Reminiscences, Incidents and Notes.* (1888) Reprint. Salem, Massachusetts: Higginson Books, 1994.

Gaynon, D. *A Bibliography of Books and Pamphlets Held in the Northeast Minnesota Historical Center.* Duluth, Minnesota: St. Louis County Historical Society, 1981.

Genealogical Resources of the Minnesota Historical Society, A Guide. Minnesota Historical Society Press, 1989.

Great Northern Railway Company. Personnel Department. *Index to Personnel Files.* Microreproduction of original records at the Minnesota Historical Society in St. Paul, Minnesota. St. Paul: Minnesota Historical Society, 1980. 4 microfilm.

Hage, Anne A. *Church Records in Minnesota: A Guide to Parish Records of Congregational, Evangelical, Reformed, and United Church of Christ Churches, 1851–1981.* Minneapolis: Minnesota Conference, United Church of Christ, 1983.

Hage, George Sigrud. *Newspapers on the Minnesota Frontier, 1849–1860.* Minnesota Historical Society, 1967.

Hamer, Maryanna. *History of the Church of the Brethren on the Northern Plains.* S.1.: s.n., 1977.

Historical Records Survey (Minnesota). *Guide to Depositories of Manuscript Collections in the United States: Minnesota.* St. Paul, Minnesota: Historical Records Survey, 1941.

Historical Records Survey (Minnesota). *Guide to Public Vital Statistics Records in Minnesota.* St. Paul: The Survey, 1941.

Hobart, Chauncey. *History of Methodism in Minnesota.* Introduction by Thelma Boeder. (1887) Reprint. Roseville, Minnesota: Park Genealogical Books, 1992.

Holmquist, June Drenning. *They Chose Minnesota: A Survey of the State's Ethnic Groups.* St. Paul: Minnesota Historical Society, 1981.

Hubbard, Lucius Frederick. *Minnesota in Three Centuries, 1655–1908.* 4 vols. New York: Pub. Society of Minnesota, 1908.

Hyde, C. W. G. *History of the Great Northwest and Its Men of Progress: A Select List of Biographical Sketches and Portraits of the Leaders in Business, Professional and Official Life.* Minneapolis: Minneapolis Journal, 1901.

Illustrated Album of Biography of the Famous Valley of the Red River of the North and the Park Regions . . . Containing the Biographical Sketches of Hundreds of Prominent Old Settlers and Representative Citizens . . . (1889) Reprint. Salem, Massachusetts: Higginson Books, 1996.

Illustrated Historical Atlas of the State of Minnesota. Chicago: A. T. Andreas, 1874.

Jerabek, Esther. *A Bibliography of Minnesota Territorial Documents.* St. Paul, Minnesota: Minnesota Historical Society, 1936.

Jerabek, Esther. *Check list of Minnesota State Documents, 1858–1923.* St. Paul: Minnesota Historical Society, 1972.

Kane, Lucille M. *Guide to the Public Affairs Collection of the Minnesota Historical Society.* St. Paul: Minnesota Historical Society, 1968.

Kirkeby, Lucille L. *Holdings of Genealogical Value in Minnesota's County Museums.* Brainerd, Minnesota: L. Kirkeby, 1986.

Lareau, Paul J., and Elmer Courteau. *French-Canadian Families of the North Central States: A Genealogical Dictionary, 8 vols.* St. Paul, Minnesota: Northwest Territory French and Canadian Heritage Institute, 1980.

Lass, William E. *Minnesota: A Bicentennial History.* New York: W.W. Norton & Co., 1977.

Lind, Marilyn. *Continuing Your Genealogical Research in Minnesota.* Cloquet, Minnesota: The Linden Tree, 1986.

Marquis, Albert Nelson. *The Book of Minnesotans: A Biographical Dictionary of Leading Living Men of the State of Minnesota.* Chicago: A. N. Marquis, 1907.

Memorial Record of Southwestern Minnesota. (1897), Reprint. Salem, Massachusetts: Higginson Books, 1994.

Minnesota Historical Society (St. Paul, Minnesota). *Chippewa and Dakota Indians: A Subject Catalog of Books, Pamphlets, Periodical Articles, and Manuscripts in the Minnesota Historical Society.* St. Paul: Minnesota Historical Society, 1969.

Minnesota Historical Society (St. Paul, Minnesota). *Genealogical Resources of the Minnesota Historical Society: A Guide.* 2nd ed. St. Paul: Minnesota Historical Society Press, 1989, 1993.

Minnesota Historical Society (St. Paul, Minnesota). *Historic Resources in Minnesota: A Report on Their Extent, Location, and Need for Preservation.* St. Paul: The Society, 1979.

Minnesota Historical Society (St. Paul, Minnesota). *Minnesota Historic Resources Survey: Manuscripts: Collection Information Forms, 1973–1979.* Microreproduction of original records at the Division of Archives and Manuscripts, Minnesota Historical Society in St. Paul, Minnesota. St. Paul: Minnesota Historical Society, 1980. 7 microfilm.

Minnesota Historical Society (St. Paul, Minnesota). *Minnesota Historical Society Holdings of Newspapers on Master Negative Microfilm.* St. Paul: Minnesota Historical Society, 1987.

Minnesota Historical Society (St. Paul, Minnesota). *The Oral History Collections of the Minnesota Historical Society.* St. Paul: Minnesota Historical Society Press, 1984.

Minnesota Historical Society. Division of Archives and Manuscripts. *Minnesota State Archives Preliminary Checklist.* Minnesota Historical Society, Division of Archives and Manuscripts, 1979.

Minnesota Research Outline. Series U.S.-States, no. 24. Salt Lake City. Family History Library, 1988.

Moody, Suzanna. *Guide to the Minnesota Finnish American Family History Collection.*

Neill, Rev. Edward D. *History of the Upper Mississippi Valley, Including Explorers and Pioneers of Minnesota, Outlines of the History of Minnesota, Exploration and*

Development Above the Falls of St. Anthony. (1881) Reprint. Salem, Massachusetts: Higginson Books, 1994.

Neill, Rev. Edward D., and Charles S. Bryant. *History of the Minnesota Valley, including the Explorers and Pioneers of Minnesota and History of the Sioux Massacre.* (1882) Reprint. Salem, Massachusetts: Higginson Books, 1994.

Northern Pacific Railway Company. Personnel Department. *Index to Personnel Files.* Microreproduction of original records at the Minnesota Historical Society in St. Paul, Minnesota. St. Paul: Minnesota Historical Society, 1980. 3 microfilm.

Northwest Minnesota Historical Center (Moorhead, Minnesota). *Guide to the Northwest Minnesota Historical Center Collections.* Moorhead, Minnesota: Livingston Lord Library, Moorhead State University, 1988.

Offermann, Glenn W. *Missouri in Minnesota: Centennial History of the Minnesota South District, The Lutheran Church Missouri Synod, 1882–1982.* The Minnesota South District, the Lutheran Church—Missouri Synod, 1982.

Peterson, Ann H. *Every Name Index to Pioneer Chronicles, Stories of Minnesota Territorial Pioneers.* St. Paul: Warren Research & Marketing, 1990.

Pope, Wiley R. *Minnesota Genealogical Index.* St. Paul: Minnesota Family Trees, 1984.

Pope, Wiley R., and Aliss L. Wiener. *Tracing Your Ancestors in Minnesota, A Guide to Sources.* St. Paul, Minnesota: Minnesota Family Trees, 1984.

Porter, Robert B. Porter. *How to Trace Your Minnesota Ancestors.* Center City, Minnesota: Porter Publishing Co., 1985.

Richardson, Antona Hawkins, ed. *Directory of Churches and Religious Organizations in Minnesota. Minnesota Historical Records Survey—Works Progress Administration, 1942.* St. Paul, Minnesota: Paduan Press, 1977.

Shutter, Marion Daniel. *Progressive Men of Minnesota: Biographical Sketches and Portraits of the Leaders in Business, Politics and the Professions; Together with an Historical and Descriptive Sketch of the State.* Minneapolis: The Minneapolis Journal, 1897.

Strand, A. E. *History of the Swedish-Americans of Minnesota.* 3 vols. (1910) Reprint. Salem, Massachusetts: Higginson Books, 1994.

Stuhler, Barbara. *Women of Minnesota: Selected Biographical Essays.* St. Paul: Minnesota Historical Society Press, ca. 1977, corr. reprint 1979.

Taylor, David Vassar. *Blacks in Minnesota: A Preliminary Guide to Historical Sources.* St. Paul: Minnesota Historical Society, 1976.

The United States Biographical Dictionary and Portrait Gallery of Eminent and Self-Made Men: Minnesota Volume. New York: American Biographical Pub. Co., 1879.

Upham, Warren, comp. *Minnesota Biographies, 1655–1912.* Collections of the Minnesota Historical Society, vol. 14. St. Paul: Minnesota Historical Society, 1912.

Warren, Paula Stewart. *An Introduction to Minnesota Research Sources.* Minnesota Genealogical Society, 1988.

Warren, Paula Stewart. *Minnesota Genealogical Reference Guide.* St. Paul, Minnesota: Warren Research & Publishing, 1994.

Warren, Paula Stewart. *Research in Minnesota.* Arlington, Virginia: National Genealogical Society, 1992.

Wasastjerna, Hans R. *History of the Finns in Minnesota.* Duluth, Minnesota: Minnesota Finnish-American Historical Society, 1957.

Atlases, Maps and Gazetteers

Andreas, Alfred T. *Illustrated Historical Atlas of the State of Minnesota.* 1874. Reprint. Evansville, Indiana: Unigraphic, 1976.

Atlas of the State of Minnesota: Containing a Map of Each County, Minnesota and the U.S. . . . . Fergus Falls, Minnesota: Thomas O. Nelson Co., 1982.

Bakeman, Mary Hawker. *Comprehensive Index to AT Andreas' Illustrated Historical Atlas of Minnesota— 1874.* Roseville, Minnesota: Park Genealogical Books, 1992.

Finnell, Arthur Louis. *Minnesota Genealogical Periodical Index.* Marshall, Minnesota: Finnell Richter and Assoc., 1980.

Hage, George Sigrud. *Newspapers on the Minnesota Frontier, 1849–1860.* St. Paul: Minnesota Historical Society, 1967.

Lass, William E. *Minnesota's Boundary with Canada: Its Evolution since 1783.* St. Paul: Minnesota Historical Society Press, 1980.

Leighton, Hudson. *Gazetteer of Minnesota Railroad Towns, 1861–1997.* Roseville, Minnesota: Park Genealogical Books, 1992.

Lewis, Mary Ellen. "The Establishment of County Boundaries in Minnesota." Master's Thesis, University of Minnesota, 1946.

Minnesota Atlas and Gazetteer. 2nd ed. Freeport, Maine: DeLorme Mapping Co., 1995.

Ostendorf, Paul J. *Every Person's Name Index to an Illustrated Atlas of the State of Minnesota.* Winona, Minnesota: St. Mary's College, 1979.

Patera, Alan H., and John S. Gallagher. *The Post Offices of Minnesota.* Burtonville, Maryland: The Depot, 1978.

Rippley, LaVern J. *German Place Names in Minnesota— Deutsche Ortsnamen in Minnesota.* Northfield, Minnesota: St. Olaf College, 1989.

Treude, Mai. *Windows to the Past: A Bibliography of Minnesota County Atlases.* Minneapolis: Center for Urban and Regional Affairs, University of Minnesota, 1980.

Upham, Warren. *Minnesota Geographic Names: Their Origin and Historic Significance.* Minnesota Historical Society 17 (1920). Reprint. St. Paul: Minnesota Historical Society, 1969.

Censuses

Available Census Records and Census Substitutes

Federal Census 1850, 1860, 1870, 1880, 1900, 1910, 1920, 1930

Federal Mortality Schedules 1850, 1860, 1870, 1880, 1900

Union Veterans and Widows 1890

State/Territorial Census 1836, 1849, 1857, 1865, 1875, 1885, 1895, 1905

Bakeman, Mary Hawker. *Guide to the Minnesota State Census Microfilm.* Roseville, Minnesota: Park Genealogical Books, 1992.

Dollarhide, William. *The Census Book: A Genealogist's Guide to Federal Census Facts, Schedules and Indexes.* Bountiful, Utah: Heritage Quest, 1999.

Kemp, Thomas Jay. *The American Census Handbook.* Wilmington, Delaware: Scholarly Resources, Inc., 2001.

Lainhart, Ann S. *State Census Records.* Baltimore: Genealogical Publishing Co., 1992.

Szucs, Loretto Dennis and Matthew Wright. *Finding Answers in U.S. Census Records.* Ancestry Publishing, 2001.

Thorndale, William, and William Dollarhide. *Map Guide to the U.S. Federal Census, 1790–1920.* Baltimore: Genealogical Publishing Co., 1987.

Court Records, Probate and Wills

Note: Probate records are found in individual county court records. Other court records may be found in the Minnesota State Historical Society collections. District court records are found at the National Archives Great Lakes Region Branch, in Chicago.

Green, Stina B. *Adoptions & Name Changes: Minnesota Territory & State, 1851–1881.* Roseville, Minnesota: Park Genealogical Books, 1994.

National Archives Record Administration. Great Lakes Region (Chicago). *Records of the District Courts of the United States, Record Group 21:* Minnesota, Third Division, St. Paul, 1861–1979; Minnesota, Fourth Division, Minneapolis, 1966–69; Minnesota, Fifth Division, Duluth, 1890–1981; Minnesota, Sixth Division, Fergus Falls, 1890–1978. Chicago: National Archives Record Administration. Great Lakes Region (Chicago). www.nara.gov/regional/findaids/chiguid1.html#21.

Emigration, Immigration, Migration and Naturalization

Erickson, James E. *Declarations of Intention (1847–1852) of 262 Minnesota Pioneers.* Roseville, Minnesota: Park Genealogical Books, 1997.

Holmquist, June D., ed., *They Chose Minnesota: A Survey of the State's Ethnic Groups.* St. Paul: Minnesota Historical Society, 1981.

Ljungmark, Lars. *For sale—Minnesota: Organized Promotion of Scandinavian Immigration, 1866–1873.* Chicago: Swedish Pioneer Historical Society, 1971.

United States. Circuit Court (Minnesota: First Division). *Naturalizations, 1897–1899; Declarations of Intentions, 1910.* Microfilm of originals in the National Archives Branch in Kansas City, Missouri. Salt Lake City: Filmed by the Genealogical Society of Utah, 1991. 2 microfilm.

United States. Circuit Court (Minnesota: Fourth Division). *Naturalizations, 1890–1911; Declarations of Intention, 1890–1911.* Microfilm of originals in the National Archives Branch in Kansas City, Missouri. Salt Lake City: Filmed by the Genealogical Society of Utah, 1991. 6 microfilm.

United States. Circuit Court (Minnesota: Second Division). *Naturalizations, 1897–1911; Declarations of Intention, 1900–1911.* Microfilm of originals in the National Archives Branch in Kansas City, Missouri. Salt Lake City: Filmed by the Genealogical Society of Utah, 1991. 2 microfilm.

United States. Circuit Court (Minnesota: Sixth Division). *Naturalizations, 1897–1911.* Microfilm of originals in the National Archives Branch in Kansas City, Missouri. Salt Lake City: Filmed by the Genealogical Society of Utah, 1991.

United States. Circuit Court (Minnesota: Third Division). *Naturalizations, 1875–1911; Declarations of Intention, 1875–1911.* Microfilm of originals in the National Archives Branch in Kansas City, Missouri. Salt Lake City: Filmed by the Genealogical Society of Utah, 1991.

United States. District Court (Minnesota: First Division). *Naturalizations, 1896–1924.* Microfilm of originals in the National Archives Branch in Kansas City, Missouri. Salt Lake City: Filmed by the Genealogical Society of Utah, 1990.

United States. District Court (Minnesota: Fourth Division: Minneapolis). *Naturalizations, 1897–1936.* Microfilm of originals in the National Archives Branch in Kansas City, Missouri. Salt Lake City: Filmed by the Genealogical Society of Utah, 1990–1991. 25 microfilm.

United States. District Court (Minnesota: Second Division). *Declarations of Intention, 1906–1940; Naturalizations, 1897–1944.* Microfilm of originals in the National Archives Branch in Kansas City, Missouri. Salt Lake City: Filmed by the Genealogical Society of Utah, 1990. 4 microfilm.

United States. District Court (Minnesota: Sixth Division). *Naturalizations, 1896–1936; Declarations of Intention, 1896–1936*. Microfilm of originals in the National Archives Branch in Kansas City, Missouri. Salt Lake City: Filmed by the Genealogical Society of Utah, 1991. 3 microfilm.

United States. District Court (Minnesota: Third Division). *Declarations of Intention, 1872–1955; Naturalizations, 1859–1954*. Microfilm of originals in the National Archives Branch in Kansas City, Missouri. Salt Lake City: Filmed by the Genealogical Society of Utah, 1990. 32 microfilm.

Land and Property

Bakeman, Mary Hawker. *Minnesota Land Owner Maps and Directories*. Roseville, Minnesota: Park Genealogical Books, 1994.

Hone, Wade E. *Land and Property Research in the United States*. Salt Lake City: Ancestry Incorporated, 1997.

Iowa. Surveyor General. *Iowa and Minnesota Boundary Records, 1852*. Microfilm made from the originals in the Office of Secretary of State, Des Moines, Iowa. Salt Lake City: Filmed by the Genealogical Society of Utah, 1977. 2 microfilm.

Kinney, Gregory. *A Guide to the Records of Minnesota's Public Lands*. St. Paul: Minnesota Historical Society, 1985.

Land Records: Alabama, Arkansas, Florida, Louisiana, Michigan, Minnesota, Ohio, Wisconsin. S.1.: Brøderbund, 1996. CD-ROM.

National Archives Record Administration. Great Lakes Region (Chicago). *The General Land Office Records, Minnesota, 1855–1882*. Chicago: National Archives Record Administration. Great Lakes Region (Chicago). www.nara.gov/regional/findaids/chiguid1.html

Orfield, Matthias N. *Federal Land Grants to the States with Special Reference to Minnesota*. University of Minnesota Studies in the Social Sciences. Minneapolis: the author, 1915.

United States. Bureau of Land Management. *Card Files*. Microfilm of original card files located at the Bureau of Land Management's Eastern States Office in Alexandria, Virginia. Washington, D.C.: Bureau of Land Management. 160 microfilm.

United States. Department of the Interior. Bureau of Land Management. *Minnesota, 1820–1908: Cash and Homestead Entries*. Springfield, Virginia: BLM Eastern States, 1995. CD-ROM.

Military

Brown, Alonzo L. *History of the Fourth Regiment of Minnesota Infantry Volunteers During the Great Rebellion*. (1892) Reprint. Salem, Massachusetts: Higginson Books, 1995.

Finnell, Arthur Louis. *Known War of 1812 Veterans Buried in Minnesota*: Bloomington, Minnesota: A. L. Finnell, 1996.

Holbrook, Franklin F. *Minnesota in the Spanish-American War and the Philippine Insurrection*. St. Paul: Minnesota War Records Commission, 1923.

Minnesota in the Civil and Indian Wars, 1861–1865. St. Paul: Pioneer Press, 1890–1893.

Minnesota State Historical Society. *Civil and Dakota Wars Collection*. St. Paul, Minnesota: Minnesota State Historical Society, 2000. Online database— www.mnhs.org/library/collections/manuscripts/wars.html.

Minnesota's World War II Army Dead. Roseville, Minnesota: Park Genealogical Books, 1994.

Minnesota's World War II Navy Casualties. Roseville, Minnesota: Park Genealogical Books, 1996.

Pensioners on the Rolls as of 1 January 1883 (Living in Minnesota) with Every Name Index. (1883) Reprint. Roseville, Minnesota: Park Genealogical Books, 1994.

Richardson, Antona Hawkins. *Minnesotans in the Spanish-American War and the Philippine Insurrection, April 21, 1898 to July 4, 1902*. St. Paul, Minnesota: Paduan Press, 1998.

United States. Navy. *Minnesota's W. W. II Combat Connected Naval Casualties (Navy, Marine Corps, Coast Guard)*. Roseville, Minnesota: Park Genealogical Books, 1996.

United States. Selective Service System. *Minnesota, World War I Selective Service System Draft Registration Cards, 1917–1918. National Archives Microfilm Publications, M1509*. Washington, D.C.: National Archives, 1987–1988.

Vital and Cemetery Records

Guide to Church Vital Statistics Records in Minnesota: Baptisms, Marriages, Funerals. St. Paul: Historical Records Survey, 1942.

Guide to Public Vital Statistics Records in Minnesota. St. Paul: Historical Records Survey, 1941.

Hage, Anne A. *Church Records in Minnesota: Guide to Parish Records of Congregational, Evangelical, Reformed & United Church of Christ Churches 1851–1891*. Roseville, Minnesota: Park Genealogical Books, 1983.

Pond Brothers. *Early Presbyterian Church Records from Minnesota 1825–1871*. Transcribed by Mary Hawker Bakeman. Roseville, Minnesota: Park Genealogical Books, 1992.

Pope, Wiley R. *Minnesota Cemeteries in Print: A Bibliography of Minnesota Published Cemetery Inscriptions, and Burials, Etc*. 1st ed. St. Paul: Minnesota Family Trees, 1986.

County Website	Map Index	Date Created	Parent County or Territory From Which Organized Address/Details
Aitkin www.co.aitkin.mn.us/	I6	23 May 1857	**Pine, Ramsey** Aitkin County; 209 2nd St NW; Aitkin, MN 56431-1297; Ph. (218) 927-7336 **Details:** Name spelled Aiken 1857–1862 (Attached to Crow Wing & Morrison Counties prior to organization 6 Feb 1885) (Clerk District Court has Birth Records from 1883, Marriage Records from 1885, Death Records from 1887, Divorce Records from 1886, Probate, Court & Naturalization Records from 1885; County Recorder has Land Records)
Andy Johnson		18 Mar 1858	**Pembina** Andy Johnson County; MN **Details:** (see Wilkin) Formerly Toombs County. Name changed to Andy Johnson 8 Mar 1862. Name changed to Wilkin 6 Mar 1868
Anoka www.co.anoka.mn.us/	I9	23 May 1857	**Ramsey** Anoka County; 325 E Main St; Anoka, MN 55303-2479; Ph. (763) 422-7399 **Details:** (Clerk District Court has Birth & Death Records from 1870, Marriage Records from 1865, Divorce, Court & Land Records from 1866; Probate Judge has Probate Records)
Becker www.co.becker.mn.us/	M5	18 Mar 1858	**Cass, Pembina** Becker County; 913 Lake Ave; PO Box 702; Detroit Lakes, MN 56501-0787; Ph. (218) 846-7304 **Details:** (Attached to Stearns, Crow Wing & Douglas Counties prior to organization 1 Mar 1871) (County Recorder has Birth, Marriage & Death Records from 1871, Divorce, Probate & Court Records from 1940)
Beltrami www.co.beltrami.mn.us	L3	28 Feb 1866	**Unorg. Terr., Itasca, Pembina, Polk** Beltrami County; 701 Minnesota Ave NW, Ste 100; Bemidji, MN 56601-3177; Ph. (218) 333-4148, becky.murphy@co.beltrami.mn.us **Details:** (Attached to Becker County prior to organization 6 Apr 1897) (License Center has Birth, Marriage, & Death Records from 1896; Clerk Courts has Divorce Records from 1951, Probate & Court Records; Recorder Office has Military Records; Historical Society has Land Records prior to 1969)
Benton www.rootsweb.com/~mnbenton/	K8	27 Oct 1849	**St. Croix** Benton County; 531 Dewey St; PO Box 129; Foley, MN 56329; Ph. (320) 968-5037 **Details:** (County Recorder has Birth Records from 1870, Marriage Records from 1887, Death Records from 1871 & Land Records from 1850; Court Administrator has Divorce & Court Records from 1900 & Probate Records from 1850)
Big Sioux		23 May 1857	**Brown** Big Sioux County; MN **Details:** (see South Dakota) Attached to Pipestone County. Eliminated 11 May 1858 when Minn. state was created) County Terminated 1868
Big Stone www.rootsweb.com/~mnbigsto/index.html	O8	20 Feb 1862	**Pierce** Big Stone County; 20 SE 2nd St; Ortonville, MN 56278-1544; Ph. (320) 839-2308 **Details:** (Attached to Renville & Stevens Counties prior to organization 8 Feb 1881) (County Recorder has Birth, Marriage, Death & Land Records from 1881, Divorce & Court Records from 1885; Court Judge has Probate Records)

County Website	Map Index	Date Created	Parent County or Territory From Which Organized Address/Details
Blue Earth www.co.blue-earth.mn.us/	J11	5 Mar 1853	**Unorg. Terr., Dakota** Blue Earth County; 204 S 5th St; PO Box 3524; Mankato, MN 56001-4585; Ph. (507) 389-8343 **Details:** (Clerk District Court has Birth & Death Records from 1870, Marriage Records from 1865, Divorce & Court Records from 1854 & Probate Records from 1858; Register of Deeds has Land Records)
Breckenridge		18 Mar 1858	**Pembina** Breckenridge County; MN **Details:** (see Clay) Name changed to Clay 6 Mar 1862
Brown http://willow.internet-connections.net/web2/brown/	L11	20 Feb 1855	**Blue Earth** Brown County; Center & State Sts; PO Box 248; New Ulm, MN 56073; Ph. (507) 233-6657 **Details:** (Organized 11 Feb 1856) (County Recorder has Birth & Death Records from 1870, Marriage Records from 1857 & Land Records; Clerk District Court has Divorce & Probate Records from 1856 & Court Records from 1885; MN Historical Society has Naturalization Records)
Buchanan		23 May 1857	**Pine** Buchanan County; MN **Details:** County Terminated 1861(see Pine) Attached to Chisago & St. Louis Counties. Eliminated & absorbed by Pine County 8 Oct 1861
Carlton www.mjpdan.com/genweb/carlton/carlton.htm	H6	23 May 1857	**Pine, St. Louis** Carlton County; 301 Walnut Ave; Carlton, MN 55718; Ph. (218) 384-9195 **Details:** (Organized 18 Feb 1870) (Clerk District Court has Birth, Marriage, Death, Burial, Divorce, Probate, Court, Land & Naturalization Records from 1872)
Carver www.rootsweb.com/~mncarver/	J9	20 Feb 1855	**Hennepin, Sibley** Carver County; 600 E 4th St; Chaska, MN 55318; Ph. (612) 361-1930 **Details:** (Court Administrator has Divorce, Probate & Court Records from 1856; County Recorder has Birth, Marriage, Death & Land Records from 1870)
Cass www.mncounties.org/cass/	K6	31 Mar 1851	**Dakota, Pembina, Mahkato, Wahrahta** Cass County; 300 Minnesota Ave; PO Box 3000; Walker, MN 56484; Ph. (218) 547-7247 **Details:** (Attached to Benton, Stearns, Crow Wing & Morrison Counties prior to organization 4 May 1872) (County Treasury has Birth & Death Records from 1896 & Marriage Records from 1897; Clerk District Court has Divorce Records from 1899, Court Records from 1898, Probate & Naturalization Records; City or Town Clerks have Burial Records)
Chippewa www.frontiernet.net/~kmenning/	M9	20 Feb 1862	**Pierce, Davis** Chippewa County; 629 N 11th St; Montevideo, MN 56265; Ph. (320) 269-9431 **Details:** (Attached to Renville County prior to organization 9 Jan 1869) (Clerk District Court has Birth, Marriage, Death, Divorce, Probate & Court Records from 1870; County Recorder has Land Records from 1870; City Clerks have Burial Records)

County Website	Map Index	Date Created	Parent County or Territory From Which Organized Address/Details
Chisago www.co.chisago.mn.us/	**I8**	**31 Mar 1851**	**Washington, Ramsey** Chisago County; 313 N Main St; Center City, MN 55012; Ph. (612) 213-0438 **Details:** (Organized 1 Jan 1852) (Clerk District Court has Birth & Death Records from 1870, Marriage Records from 1852, Court Records from 1880 & Divorce Records; Probate Judge has Probate Records; Register of Deeds has Land Records)
Clay www.rootsweb.com/~mnclay/	**O6**	**18 Mar 1858**	**Pembina** Clay County; 807 11th St; Moorhead, MN 56561; Ph. (218) 299-5031 **Details:** (Formerly Breckenridge County. Name changed to Clay 6 Mar 1862. Attached to Stearns, Crow Wing, Douglas & Becker Counties prior to organization 27 Feb 1872) (County Recorder has Birth, Marriage, Death & Land Records from 1872 & Military Records from 1917; Court Administrator has Divorce & Court Records from 1931 & Probate Records
Clearwater www.co.clearwater.mn.us/	**L4**	**20 Dec 1902**	**Beltrami** Clearwater County; 213 Main Ave N; Bagley, MN 56621; Ph. (218) 694-6129 **Details:** (County Recorder has Birth, Marriage, Death, Land & Military Records from 1903; Court Administrator has Divorce, Probate, Court & Naturalization Records)
Cook www.co.cook.mn.us/	**D4**	**3 Nov 1874**	**Lake** Cook County; PO Box 1150; Grand Marais, MN 55604; Ph. (218) 387-3000 **Details:** (Attached to Lake & St. Louis Counties prior to organization 6 Apr 1897) (County Recorder has Birth & Death Records from 1900, Marriage Records from 1901, Land Records from 1886 & Military Records from 1919; Court Administrator has Divorce, Court & Probate Records)
Cottonwood www.rrcnet.org/~cotton/index.html	**M11**	**23 May 1857**	**Brown** Cottonwood County; 900 3rd Ave; Windom, MN 56101; Ph. (507) 831-1458 **Details:** (Attached to Brown, Redwood & Watonwan Counties prior to organization 4 Jul 1873) (Clerk District Court has Birth, Marriage, Death, Divorce & Court Records from 1871)
Crow Wing www.co.crow-wing.mn.us/	**K6**	**23 May 1857**	**Ramsey** Crow Wing County; 326 Laurel St; Brainerd, MN 56401; Ph. (218) 824-1300 **Details:** (County Treasury has Birth Records from 1873, Marriage Records from 1871 & Death Records from 1874; Court Administrator has Divorce, Probate & Court Records; County Recorder has Land Records from 1867 & Military Discharge Records from 1919)
Dakota www.co.dakota.mn.us/	**H10**	**27 Oct 1849**	**Unorg. Terr.** Dakota County; 1560 Hwy 55 W; Hastings, MN 55033; Ph. (612) 438-4313 **Details:** (Attached to Ramsey County prior to organization 5 Mar 1853) (Clerk District Court has Birth & Death Records from 1870, Marriage Records from 1857, Divorce & Court Records from 1853)
Davis		**20 Feb 1855**	**Cass, Nicollet, Pierce, Sibley** Davis County; MN **Details:** County Terminated 1862 (Attached to Stearns County. Eliminated 20 Feb 1862. Lost to Chippewa & Lac Qui Parle Counties)

County Website	Map Index	Date Created	Parent County or Territory From Which Organized Address/Details
Dodge www.co.dodge.mn.us	I11	**20 Feb 1855**	**Rice, Unorg. Terr.** Dodge County; 22 E 6th St, Dept 101; Mantorville, MN 55955; Ph. (507) 635-6250, sue.alberts@co.dodge.mn.us **Details:** (Recorder's Office has Birth and Death Records from 1870; Marriage Records from 1865)
Doty		**20 Feb 1855**	**Itasca** Doty County; MN **Details:** (see St. Louis) Name changed to Newton 3 Mar 1855. Eliminated to St. Louis County 1 Mar 1856
Douglas www.co.douglas.mn.us/	M7	**8 Mar 1858**	**Cass, Pembina** Douglas County; 305 8th Ave W; Alexandria, MN 56308; Ph. (320) 762-3877 **Details:** (County Recorder has Birth, Marriage & Death Records from 1890, Land Records from late 1800's & Military Records; Clerk of Courts has Divorce, Probate & Court Records)
Faribault www.co.faribault.mn.us/index.cfm	J12	**20 Feb 1855**	**Blue Earth** Faribault County; 415 N Main St; PO Box 130; Blue Earth, MN 56013; Ph. (507) 526-6252 **Details:** (Attached to Blue Earth County prior to organization 1 May 1857) (Court Administrator has Birth, marriage, Death, Divorce, & Probate Records from 1870, Court Records from 1950, & Naturalization Records; Register of Deeds has Land Records)
Fillmore www.co.fillmore.mn.us/	G12	**5 Mar 1853**	**Wabasha** Fillmore County; 101 Fillmore St; Preston, MN 55965; Ph. (507) 765-4701 **Details:** (Court Administrator has Birth & Death Records from 1870, Marriage Records from 1865, Divorce & Court Records from 1885 & Probate Records from 1858; County Recorder has Land Records)
Freeborn www.albertlea.org/	J12	**20 Feb 1855**	**Blue Earth, Rice** Freeborn County; 411 S Broadway Ave; Albert Lea, MN 56007; Ph. (507) 377-5153 **Details:** (Organized 6 Mar 1857) (Clerk District Court has Birth & Death Records from 1870, Marriage & Court Records from 1857; County Recorder has Land Records from 1854; Probate Office has Probate Records from 1866)
Goodhue www.co.goodhue.mn.us/	H10	**5 Mar 1853**	**Wabasha, Dakota** Goodhue County; 509 5th St W; Red Wing, MN 55066; Ph. (651) 385-3148 **Details:** (Attached to Wabasha County prior to organization 15 Jun 1854) (Court Administrator has Birth & Death Records from 1870, Marriage & Probate Records from 1854, Divorce & Court Records from 1951; Minnesota Historical Society has Divorce & Court Records 1854-1950)
Grant www.rootsweb.com/~mngrant/	N7	**6 Mar 1868**	**Stevens, Wilkin, Traverse** Grant County; County Courthouse; Elbow Lake, MN 56531; Ph. (218) 685-4520 **Details:** (Attached to Douglas County prior to organization 1 Mar 1883) (Clerk District Court has Birth & Death Records from 1877, Marriage Records from 1869, Divorce & Court Records from 1883; Probate Judge has Probate Records; Register of Deeds has Land Records)

County Website	Map Index	Date Created	Parent County or Territory From Which Organized Address/Details
Hennepin www.co.hennepin.mn.us/welcome.html	**J9**	**6 Mar 1852**	**Dakota** Hennepin County; 300 S 6th St; Minneapolis, MN 55487-0001; Ph. (612) 348-8241 **Details:** (Clerk District Court has Birth & Death Records from 1870, Marriage, Divorce & Court Records from 1853)
Houston www.geocities.com/houstoncountymn/HC.html	**F12**	**4 Apr 1854**	**Fillmore** Houston County; 304 S Marshall St; Caledonia, MN 55921; Ph. (507) 724-5813 **Details:** (Clerk District Court has Birth & Death Records from 1870, Marriage Records from 1854, Court Records from 1856 & Divorce Records; Probate Judge has Probate Records; Register of Deeds has Land Records)
Hubbard www.co.hubbard.mn.us/	**L5**	**26 Feb 1883**	**Cass** Hubbard County; 301 Court St; Park Rapids, MN 56470; Ph. (218) 732-3552 **Details:** (Attached to Wadena County prior to organization 3 Mar 1887) (County Recorder has Birth, Death & Land Records; License Center has Marriage Records; Clerk District Court has Divorce, Probate & Court Records)
Isanti www.rootsweb.com/~mnisanti/Isanti/	**I8**	**13 Feb 1857**	**Ramsey** Isanti County; 555 18th Ave SW; Cambridge, MN 55008; Ph. (763) 689-1191 **Details:** (Clerk District Court has Birth Records from 1869, Marriage Records from 1871, Death Records from 1873, Burial Records 1900–1908 & 1941–1979, Divorce & Court Records from 1872 & Probate Records from 1892; County Recorder has Land Records)
Itasca www.co.itasca.mn.us/	**J4**	**27 Oct 1849**	**Unorg. Terr.** Itasca County; 123 4th St NE; Grand Rapids, MN 55744; Ph. (218) 327-2856 **Details:** (Attached to Washington, Benton & Chisago Counties prior to organization 6 Mar 1857) (County Recorder-Registrar has Birth & Marriage Records from 1891, Death Records from 1894, Burial Records from 1900, Land Records from 1883 & Military Records from 1919; Court Administrator has Probate Records from 1896, Divorce & Court Records from 1950; MN
Jackson www.rootsweb.com/~mnjackso/	**M12**	**23 May 1857**	**Brown** Jackson County; 405 4th St; PO Box 209; Jackson, MN 56143; Ph. (507) 847-2580 **Details:** (Court Administrator has Birth, Death, Divorce, Probate & Court Records from 1870 & Marriage Records from 1868; County Recorder has Land Records from 1870)
Kanabec www.rootsweb.com/~mnkanabe/	**I8**	**12 Oct 1858**	**Pine** Kanabec County; 18 Vine St N; Mora, MN 55051; Ph. (320) 679-6466 **Details:** (Attached to Pine County prior to organization 4 Nov 1881) (Clerk District Court has Birth & Death Records from 1883, Marriage, Divorce & Court Records from 1882 & Probate Records from 1891; County Recorder has Land Records; Mora City Hall has Burial Records)

County Website	Map Index	Date Created	Parent County or Territory From Which Organized Address/Details
Kandiyohi www.co.kandiyohi.mn.us/	L9	20 Mar 1858	**Meeker, Renville, Pierce, Davis, Stearns** Kandiyohi County; 400 Benson Ave SW; Willmar, MN 56201-3281; Ph. (320) 231-6532 **Details:** (Clerk District Court has Birth, Marriage, Death, Divorce & Court Records from 1870)
Kittson www.rootsweb.com/~mnkittso/	O2	27 Oct 1849	**Unorg. Terr.** Kittson County; 410 S 5th St; PO Box 39; Hallock, MN 56728; Ph. (218) 843-3632 **Details:** (Formerly Pembina County. Name changed to Kittson 9 Mar 1878. Attached to Benton prior to organization 4 Mar 1852. Disorganized 5 Mar 1853. Recreated 24 Apr 1862 from Benton. Attached to Benton, Morrison, Crow Wing, Douglas, Becker, Clay & Polk Counties prior to organization 6 APR 1897) (Clk Dis Ct has b, m, d, div, pro & ct rec from 1880s; Co Rcdr has land rec; MN Hist Soc has nat rec)
Koochiching www.rootsweb.com/~mnkoochi/	J3	19 Dec 1906	**Itasca** Koochiching County; 715 4th St; International Falls, MN 56649; Ph. (218) 283-6260 **Details:** (Clerk District Court has Birth, Marriage, Death, Divorce, Court & Probate Records from 1907)
Lac Qui Parle www.rootsweb.com/~mnlacqui/index.htm	N9	7 Nov 1871	**Redwood** Lac Qui Parle County; 600 6th St; Madison, MN 56256; Ph. (320) 598-3724 **Details:** (Attached to Redwood County prior to organization 7 Jan 1873) (County Recorder has Birth, Marriage, Death & Military Records; Court Administrator has Divorce, Probate & Court Records; County Assesor has Land Records)
Lac Qui Parle, old		20 Feb 1862	**Davis, Pierce** Lac Qui Parle, old County; MN **Details:** (Attached to Renville County. Eliminated 3 Nov 1868 & absorbed by Chippewa County)
Lake www.lakecnty.com/	F4	20 Feb 1855	**Itasca** Lake County; 601 3rd Ave; Two Harbors, MN 55616; Ph. (218) 834-8347 **Details:** (Formerly Superior County. Name changed to St. Louis, old 3 Mar 1855. Name changed to Lake 1 Mar 1856. Attached to Benton & St. Louis Counties prior to organization 27 Feb 1891) (County Registrar has Birth Records from 1898, Marriage & Death Records from 1891, Divorce & Court Records from 1892; Probate Judge has Probate Records; city clerk has Burial Records)
Lake of the Woods www.rootsweb.com/~mnlakeof/	K2	28 Nov 1922	**Beltrami** Lake of the Woods County; 206 SE 8th Ave; PO Box 808; Baudette, MN 56623; Ph. (218) 634-1902 **Details:** (Court Administrator has Birth, Marriage, Death, Divorce, Probate & Court Records from 1923)

County Website	Map Index	Date Created	Parent County or Territory From Which Organized Address/Details
Le Sueur www.co.le-sueur.mn.us/	**J10**	**5 Mar 1853**	**Dakota** Le Sueur County; 88 S Park Ave; Le Center, MN 56057; Ph. (507) 357-2251 **Details:** (Clerk District Court has Birth & Death Records from 1870, Marriage Records from 1854, Divorce & Court Records from 1880 & some school Records 1920–1945; Probate Judge has Probate Records from 1855; Register of Deeds has Land Records from 1850)
Lincoln www.rootsweb.com/~mnlincol/	**O10**	**4 Nov 1873**	**Lyon** Lincoln County; 319 N Rebecca; Ivanhoe, MN 56142; Ph. (507) 694-1360 **Details:** (Attached to Lyon & Redwood Counties prior to organization 9 Feb 1881) (Clerk District Court has Birth & Marriage Records from 1879, Death & Court Records from 1880 & Divorce Records from 1891; Probate Judge has Probate Records from 1877; Register of Deeds has Land Records from 1873)
Lincoln, old		**8 Oct 1861**	**Renville** Lincoln, old County; MN **Details:** (Attached to McLeod County. Eliminated 3 Nov 1868 to Renville County)
Lyon www.lyonco.org/	**N10**	**2 Nov 1869**	**Redwood** Lyon County; 607 W Main; Marshall, MN 56258-3021; Ph. (507) 537-6722 **Details:** (Organized 12 Apr 1870) (Clerk District Court has Birth & Death Records from 1874, Marriage Records from 1872, Divorce, Probate & Court Records from 1880; County Recorder has Land Records)
Mahnomen www.rootsweb.com/~mnmahnom/	**M5**	**27 Dec 1906**	**Norman** Mahnomen County; PO Box 379; Mahnomen, MN 56557; Ph. (218) 935-2251 **Details:** (Clerk District Court has Birth, Marriage, Death, Divorce & Court Records from 1908)
Mankahto		**27 Oct 1849**	**Unorg. Terr.** Mankahto County; MN **Details:** County Terminated 1851 (Attached to Ramsey. Eliminated 1 Sep 1851. Lost to Cass & Pembina Counties)
Manomin		**23 May 1857**	**Ramsey** Manomin County; MN **Details:** County Terminated 1869 (Eliminated 2 Nov 1869 to Anoka County)
Marshall www.rootsweb.com/~mnmarsha/	**N3**	**25 Feb 1879**	**Kittson** Marshall County; 208 E Colvin Ave; Warren, MN 56762; Ph. (218) 745-4816 **Details:** (Attached to Polk County prior to organization 11 Mar 1881) (Court Administrator has Birth, Marriage & Death Records from 1882, Divorce & Probate Records from 1891 & Court Records; County Recorder has Land Records from 1883 & Military Records from 1919)

County Website	Map Index	Date Created	Parent County or Territory From Which Organized Address/Details
Martin www.co.martin.mn.us/	L12	23 May 1857	**Faribault, Brown** Martin County; 201 Lake Ave; Fairmont, MN 56031-1845; Ph. (507) 238-3213 **Details:** (County Recorder has Birth Records from 1874, Marriage Records from 1864, Death Records from 1879 & Land Records; Court Administrator has Divorce, Probate & Court Records)
McLeod www.co.mcleod.mn.us/	K9	1 Mar 1856	**Carver, Sibley** McLeod County; 2389 Hennepin Ave N; Glencoe, MN 55336; Ph. (320) 864-1216 **Details:** (County Recorder has Birth & Death Records from 1870, Marriage Records from 1865, School Census & Land Records; County Administrator has Divorce & Court Records; Veterans Office has Military Records; Probate Office has Probate Records; County Treasurer has Tax Records)
Meeker www.co.meeker.mn.us/	K9	23 Feb 1856	**Davis** Meeker County; 325 Sibley Ave N; Litchfield, MN 55355; Ph. (320) 693-5345, sharon.euerle@co.meeker.mn.us **Details:** (County Treasurer has Birth, Marriage, & Death Records; Clerk of District Court has Divorce & Court Records from 1870, Probate Records from 1858, School Records 1923–1970; Naturalization Index only; County Recorder has Land Records)
Mille Lacs www.co.mille-lacs.mn.us/	J7	23 May 1857	**Ramsey** Mille Lacs County; 635 2nd St SE; Milaca, MN 56353; Ph. (320) 983-8308 **Details:** (Attached to Morrison County prior to organization 30 Apr 1860) (County Recorder has Birth, Marriage, Death & Land Records; Court Administrator has Divorce, Probate & Court Records)
Monongalia		8 Mar 1861	**Davis, Pierce** Monongalia County; MN **Details:** County Terminated 1870 (Discontinued 8 Nov 1870 & became part of Kandyohi County)
Morrison www.co.morrison.mn.us.org	K7	25 Feb 1856	**Benton** Morrison County; 213 SE 1st Ave; Little Falls, MN 56345; Ph. (320) 632-1046, eileen@co.morrison.mn.us **Details:** (County Recorder has Birth, Burial, Cemetery, Census, Court, Death, Divorce, Guardianship, Land, Marriage, & Military Records)
Mower www.rootsweb.com/~mnmower/	H12	20 Feb 1855	**Rice** Mower County; 201 1st St NE; Austin, MN 55912; Ph. (507) 437-9456 **Details:** (Organized 1 Mar 1856) (Clerk District Court has Birth & Death Records from 1870, Marriage Records from 1865, Divorce & Court Records from 1900 & Probate Records from 1856; County Recorder has Land Records)
Murray	N11	23 May 1857	**Brown** Murray County; 2500 28th St; Slayton, MN 56172; Ph. (507) 836-6148 **Details:** (Attached to Brown, Redwood, Watonwan & Cottonwood Counties prior to organization 5 Mar 1879) (Clerk District Court has Divorce, Probate & Court Records; County Recorder has Land Records; County Vital Records has Birth, Death, & Marriage Records from mid-1800s)

County Website	Map Index	Date Created	Parent County or Territory From Which Organized Address/Details
Newton		**20 Feb 1855**	**Itasca** Newton County; MN **Details:** County Terminated 1856 (Formerly Doty County. Name changed to Newton 3 Mar 1855. Eliminated to St. Louis County 1 Mar 1856)
Nicollet www.co.nicollet.mn.us/	I10	**5 Mar 1853**	**Dakota** Nicollet County; 501 S Minnesota Ave; St. Peter, MN 56082; Ph. (507) 934-0325 **Details:** (County Recorder has Birth, Death, & Land Records; Birth Records 1870–1934 in Books, 1935–Current on Statewide Computer; Deaths 1870–1996 in Books, 1997–Current on Statewide Computer; Land Records from 1853 some in Books—Most on County Computer)
Nobles www.co.nobles.mn.us/	N12	**23 May 1857**	**Brown** Nobles County; 315 10th St; Worthington, MN 56187; Ph. (507) 372-8263 **Details:** (Attached to Brown & Martin Counties prior to organization 19 Oct 1870) (County Recorder has Birth, Marriage & Death Records from 1872 & Land Records; Court Administrator has Divorce Records from 1882, Court Records from 1874 & Probate Records)
Norman www.rootsweb.com/~mnnorman/	O5	**8 Nov 1881**	**Polk** Norman County; 16 E 3rd Ave; Ada, MN 56510; Ph. (218) 784-7131 **Details:** (Clerk District Court has Birth & Death Records from 1881, Marriage Records from 1882, some Divorce & Court Records; Probate Judge has Probate Records)
Olmsted www.olmstedcounty.com/	H11	**20 Feb 1855**	**Fillmore, Wabasha, Rice** Olmsted County; 151 SE 4th St; Rochester, MN 55904; Ph. (507) 287-1444 **Details:** (Clerk District Court has incomplete Birth & Death Records from 1871, Marriage Records from 1855, Divorce Records from 1860 & Court Records from 1858; County Court has Probate Records; Coroner & Department of Health have Burial Records)
Otter Tail www.co.otter-tail.mn.us/mainmenu.asp	M6	**18 Mar 1858**	**Pembina, Cass** Otter Tail County; 121 W Junis Ave; Fergus Falls, MN 56537; Ph. (218) 739-2271 **Details:** (Attached to Stearns, Crow Wing & Douglas Counties prior to organization 28 Feb 1870) (Clerk District Court has Birth & Death Records from 1870, Marriage Records from 1869, Divorce Records from 1897, Probate & Court Records from 1872)
Pembina		**27 Oct 1849**	**Unorg. Terr.** Pembina County; MN **Details:** County Terminated 1876 (see Kittson) Name changed to Kittson 9 Mar 1878
Pennington www.rootsweb.com/~mnpennin/mnpennin.htm	N3	**23 Nov 1910**	**Red Lake** Pennington County; 101 Main Ave; PO Box 616; Thief River Falls, MN 56701; Ph. (218) 681-2522 **Details:** (County Recorder has Birth, Marriage, Death, Burial, Land & Military Records from 1910; Court Administrator has Divorce, Probate & Court Records)

County Website	Map Index	Date Created	Parent County or Territory From Which Organized Address/Details
Pierce		5 Mar 1853	**Dakota** Pierce County; MN **Details:** County Terminated 1862 (Eliminated 20 Feb 1862 to Big Stone, Chippewa, Lac Qui Parle, Pope, Stevens & Traverse Counties)
Pine www.pinecounty.com/	H7	1 Mar 1856	**Chisago, Ramsey** Pine County; 315 6th St; Pine City, MN 55063; Ph. (320) 629-5662 **Details:** (Organized 1 Apr 1857) (Clerk District Court has Birth Records from 1874, Death Records from 1879, Marriage, Divorce & Court Records from 1871; Probate Judge has Probate Records; Register of Deeds has Land Records)
Pipestone www.mncounties.org/pipestone/	N11	23 May 1857	**Brown** Pipestone County; 416 S Hiawatha; Pipestone, MN 56164-1562; Ph. (507) 825-6755 **Details:** (Attached to Big Sioux, Brown, Redwood, Watonwan, Rock & Cottonwood Counties prior to organization 27 Jan 1879) (Clerk District Court has Birth, Marriage, Death, Divorce, Probate & Court Records from 1877; County Recorder has Land Records)
Polk www.rootsweb.com/~mnpolk/	O4	20 Jul 1858	**Pembina** Polk County; 612 N Broadway; Crookston, MN 56716; Ph. (218) 281-3464 **Details:** (Attached to Crow Wing, Douglas, Becker & Clay Counties prior to organization 27 Feb 1879) (Court Administrator has Birth, Marriage, Death, Probate & Court Records from 1875; County Recorder has Land Records)
Pope www.mncounties.org/pope/	M8	20 Feb 1862	**Pierce, Cass, Unorg. Terr.** Pope County; 130 Minnesota Ave E; Glenwood, MN 56334; Ph. (320) 634-5723 **Details:** (Organized 28 Feb 1866) (Clerk District Court has Birth, Marriage & Death Records from 1870, Divorce & Court Records from 1880 & Probate Records from 1867)
Ramsey www.co.ramsey.mn.us/	I9	27 Oct 1849	**St. Croix** Ramsey County; 15 Kellogg Blvd W; St. Paul, MN 55102; Ph. (651) 266-4444 **Details:** (Clerk District Court has Birth & Death Records from 1870, Marriage Records from 1850, Divorce & Court Records from 1900 & Probate Records from 1849; Historical Society has Court Records 1858–1899 & Land Records)
Red Lake www.rootsweb.com/~mnredlak/mnredlak.htm	N3	24 Dec 1896	**Polk** Red Lake County; 124 Langevin Ave; PO Box 3; Red Lake Falls, MN 56750; Ph. (218) 253-2997 **Details:** (Organized 6 Apr 1897) (Court Administrator has Birth, Marriage, Death, Divorce, Probate & Court Records from 1897 & school Records 1900–1955; County Recorder has Land Records)
Redwood www.rrcnet.org/~redwood/index.html	M10	4 Nov 1862	**Brown** Redwood County; PO Box 130; Redwood Falls, MN 56283; Ph. (507) 637-4032 **Details:** (Attached to Brown County prior to organization 23 Feb 1865) (Court Administrator has Birth, Marriage & Death Records from 1865, Divorce Records from 1871, Probate Records from 1877 & Court Records from 1867; County Recorder has Land Records)

County Website	Map Index	Date Created	Parent County or Territory From Which Organized Address/Details
Renville www.co.renville.mn.us/	**L10**	**20 Feb 1855**	**Nicollet, Pierce, Sibley** Renville County; 500 DePue Ave E; Olivia, MN 56277; Ph. (320) 523-3669 **Details:** (Attached to Nicollet County prior to organization 31 Jul 1866) (Clerk District Court has Birth, Marriage & Death Records from 1870, Divorce, Probate & Court Records; County Recorder has Land Records)
Rice www.co.rice.mn.us/	**I10**	**5 Mar 1853**	**Dakota, Wabasha** Rice County; 320 NW 3rd St; Faribault, MN 55021-5146; Ph. (507) 332-6114 **Details:** (Attached to Dakota County prior to organization 9 Oct 1855) (Clerk District Court has Birth, Death, Divorce, Probate & Court Records from 1870, Marriage Records from 1856 & Burial Records; County Recorder has Land Records)
Rock www.co.rock.mn.us/	**N12**	**23 May 1857**	**Brown** Rock County; 204 E Brown; PO Box 509; Luverne, MN 56156-0509; Ph. (507) 283-5060 **Details:** (Attached to Brown, Martin & Nobles Counties prior to organization 7 Feb 1874) (County Auditor/Treasury has Birth, Marriage & Death Records from 1875; Clerk District Court has Divorce & Court Records from 1872)
Roseau www.rootsweb.com/~mnroseau/	**M2**	**28 Feb 1894**	**Kittson, Beltrami** Roseau County; 606 5th Ave SW Rm 20; Roseau, MN 56751; Ph. (218) 463-2541 **Details:** (Organized 6 Apr 1896) (Clerk District Court has Birth, Marriage, Death, Divorce, Court & Probate Records from 1895; Register Deeds has Land Records)
Scott www.co.scott.mn.us/xpedio/groups/public/ documents/web_files/scottcountywebframe.hcsp	**J10**	**5 Mar 1853**	**Dakota** Scott County; 428 S Holmes St; Shakopee, MN 55379; Ph. (952) 496-8150 **Details:** (County Recorder has Birth & Death Records from 1871, Marriage Records from 1856, Land Records from 1850's & Military Discharge Records from 1950; Clerk Courts has Divorce & Probate Records from 1850's & Court Records from 1880)
Sherburne www.co.sherburne.mn.us/	**J8**	**25 Feb 1856**	**Benton** Sherburne County; 13880 Hwy 10; Elk River, MN 55330-4601; Ph. (763) 241-2915 **Details:** (Attached to Benton County prior to organization 6 Mar 1862) (Court Administrator has Birth & Death Records from 1870, Marriage Records from 1858, Divorce Records from 1884, Probate Records from 1893 & Court Records from 1877; County Recorder has Land Records)
Sibley www.co.sibley.mn.us/	**K10**	**5 Mar 1853**	**Dakota** Sibley County; 400 Court St; PO Box 44; Gaylord, MN 55334; Ph. (507) 237-4080 **Details:** (Attached to Hennepin County prior to organization 10 Oct 1854) (Court Administrator has Birth, Death & Divorce Records from 1860, Marriage Records from 1856, Probate & Court Records from 1870; County Recorder has Land Records from 1855)

County Website	Map Index	Date Created	Parent County or Territory From Which Organized Address/Details
St. Croix		3 Aug 1840	**Wisconsin Terr.** St. Croix County; MN **Details:** (Eliminated to Benton, Ramsey & Washington Counties 27 Oct 1849)
St. Louis www.co.st-louis.mn.us/	H4	1 Mar 1856	**Itasca, Newton** St. Louis County; 100 N 5th Ave W; Duluth, MN 55802-1202; Ph. (218) 726-2559 **Details:** (Attached to Benton County prior to organization 23 May 1857) (Clerk District Court has Birth, Death & Marriage Records from 1870, Burial permits from 1938, Divorce, Court & Land Records from 1859; County Court has Probate Records)
St. Louis, old		20 Feb 1855	**Itasca** St. Louis, old County; MN **Details:** (Formerly Superior County. Name changed to St. Louis, old 3 Mar 1855. Abolished 1 Mar 1856 & became part of Lake County)
Stearns www.co.stearns.mn.us/	K8	20 Feb 1855	**Cass, Nicollet, Pierce, Sibley** Stearns County; 705 Courthouse Sq; St. Cloud, MN 56303; Ph. (320) 656-3855 **Details:** (Court Administrator has Divorce, Probate & Court Records; County Recorder has Land Records; License Center has Birth, Marriage & Death Records)
Steele www.co.steele.mn.us/	I11	20 Feb 1855	**Rice, Blue Earth, LeSueur** Steele County; 111 E Main St; Owatonna, MN 55060; Ph. (507) 444-7450 **Details:** (Organized 29 Feb 1856) (Clerk District Court has Birth & Death Records from 1870, Marriage Records from 1855, Divorce, Probate & Court Records from 1858; County Recorder has Land Records from 1858)
Stevens www.co.stevens.mn.us/	N8	20 Feb 1862	**Pierce, Unorg. Terr.** Stevens County; 400 Colorado Ave; PO Box 530; Morris, MN 56267; Ph. (320) 589-7414 **Details:** (Attached to Stearns, Douglas & Pope Counties prior to organization 31 Dec 1871) (Clerk District Court has Birth & Death Records from 1872, Marriage Records from 1869, Divorce & Court Records from 1873 & Probate Records from 1901; County Recorder has Land Records from 1871)
Superior www.co.todd.mn.us/		20 Feb 1855	**Itasca** Superior County; MN **Details:** (see Lake) Name changed to Saint Louis, old 3 Mar 1855. Name changed to Lake 1 Mar 1856
Swift www.rootsweb.com/~mnswift/	M9	8 Nov 1870	**Chippewa** Swift County; 301 14th St N; PO Box 50; Benson, MN 56215; Ph. (320) 843-3377 **Details:** (Attached to Pope & Chippewa Counties prior to organization 6 Apr 1897) (County Treasury has Birth Records from 1870, Marriage Records from 1871 & Death Records from 1872; Clerk Courts has Divorce, Court & Probate Records; County Recorder has Land Records)

County Website	Map Index	Date Created	Parent County or Territory From Which Organized Address/Details
Todd www.co.todd.mn.us/	L7	20 Feb 1855	**Cass** Todd County; 221 1st Ave Suite 300; Long Prairie, MN 56347; Ph. (320) 732-4428 **Details:** (Attached to Stearns & Morrison Counties prior to organization 21 Feb 1873) (Clerk District Court has Divorce Records from 1880, Court Records from 1874 & Probate Records; County Recorder has Birth & Death Records from 1870, Marriage Records from 1867, Land Records, school Census from 1914)
Toombs		18 Mar 1858	**Pembina** Toombs County; MN **Details:** (see Wilkin) Name changed to Andy Johnson 8 Mar 1862. Name changed to Wilkin 6 Mar 1868
Traverse www.rootsweb.com/~mntraver/index.html	N8	20 Feb 1862	**Pierce, Unorg. Terr.** Traverse County; 702 2nd Ave N; PO Box 487; Wheaton, MN 56296; Ph. (320) 563-4266 **Details:** (Attached to Stearns, Douglas, Pope & Stevens Counties prior to organization 14 Feb 1881) (Clerk District Court has Birth, Marriage, Death, Divorce, Probate, Court & Land Records from 1881)
Wabasha www.co.wabasha.mn.us/	G11	27 Oct 1849	**Unorg. Terr.** Wabasha County; 625 Jefferson Ave; Wabasha, MN 55981; Ph. (651) 565-3018 **Details:** (Attached to Washington County prior to organization 5 Mar 1853) (County Recorder has Birth & Death Records from 1870, Marriage Records from 1865 & Land Records from 1855; Court Administrator has Divorce, Probate & Court Records from 1858; Veterans Service Office has Military Records)
Wadena www.co.wadena.mn.us/	L6	11 Jun 1858	**Cass, Todd** Wadena County; 415 S Jefferson; PO Box 415; Wadena, MN 56482; Ph. (218) 631-7622 **Details:** (Attached to Crow Wing & Morrison Counties prior to organization 17 Feb 1881) (Clerk District Court has Birth, Marriage & Death Records from 1873, Divorce & Court Records from 1881)
Wahnata		27 Oct 1849	**Unorg. Terr.** Wahnata County; MN **Details:** County Terminated 1851 (Eliminated 1 Sep 1851 to Cass, Dakota & Pembina Counties)
Waseca www.rootsweb.com/~mnwaseca/	J11	27 Feb 1857	**Steele** Waseca County; 307 N State St; Waseca, MN 56093; Ph. (507) 835-0670 **Details:** (Clerk District Court has Birth, Death, Probate & Court Records from 1870, Marriage & Divorce Records from 1858)
Washington www.co.washington.mn.us/	H9	27 Oct 1849	**St. Croix** Washington County; 14949-62nd St N; Stillwater, MN 55082; Ph. (651) 430-6755 **Details:** (Clerk District Court has Birth & Death Records from 1870, Marriage Records from 1845, Divorce & Court Records from 1847 & Probate Records from 1850)

County Website	Map Index	Date Created	Parent County or Territory From Which Organized Address/Details
Watonwan www3.extension.umn.edu/county /main/master.asp?county_id=85	**L11**	**6 Nov 1860**	**Brown** Watonwan County; 710 2nd Ave S; PO Box 518; St. James, MN 56081-0518; Ph. (507) 375-1216 **Details:** (Attached to Brown & Blue Earth Counties prior to organization 15 Jun 1871) (Clerk District Court has Birth, Marriage & Death Records from 1863, Divorce & Court Records from 1865; Probate Judge has Probate Records; Register of Deeds has Land Records)
Wilkin www.co.wilkin.mn.us/	**O6**	**18 Mar 1858**	**Cass, Pembina** Wilkin County; 300 S 5th St; Breckenridge, MN 56520; Ph. (218) 643-5112 **Details:** (Formerly Toombs & Andy Johnson Counties. Name changed to Andy Johnson 8 Mar 1862. Name changed to Wilkin 6 Mar 1868. Attached to Stearns, Crow Wing, Douglas & Otter Tail Counties prior to organization 4 Mar 1872) (Clerk District Court has Birth Records from 1874, Marriage & Divorce Records from 1890, Death Records from 1875 & Court Records from 1858; Probate Judge has Probate Records)
Winona www.rootsweb.com/~mnwinona/	**G11**	**4 Apr 1854**	**Fillmore, Wabasha** Winona County; 171 W 3rd St; Winona, MN 55987; Ph. (507) 457-6340 **Details:** (Clerk District Court has Birth & Death Records from 1870, Marriage, Divorce & Court Records from 1854, Probate Records from 1871 & school Records 1909–1939)
Wright www.co.wright.mn.us/	**J9**	**20 Feb 1855**	**Cass, Sibley** Wright County; 10 2nd St NW; Buffalo, MN 55313-1165; Ph. (763) 682-7357 **Details:** (License Burial has Birth & Death Records from 1871 & Marriage Records from 1866; Court Administrator has Divorce & Court Records from 1870 & Probate Records; Register of Deeds has Land Records)
Yellow Medicine www.rootsweb.com/~mnyellow/	**N10**	**7 Nov 1871**	**Redwood** Yellow Medicine County; 415 9th Ave; Granite Falls, MN 56241-1367; Ph. (320) 564-2529 **Details:** (Organized 25 Feb 1874) (Clerk District Court has Birth, Marriage & Naturalization Records from 1872, Death, Divorce, Probate & Court Records; County Recorder has Land Records)

Mississippi

Capital: Jackson
Territory: 1798
State: 1817 (20th)

By virtue and arms

Chickasaw, Natachez, and Choctaw Indians lived in Mississippi when the first white explorers—the Spaniards, led by Hernando de Soto—arrived between 1539 and 1542. French explorers, led by Marquette and Joliet, toured the area in 1673. They claimed the Mississippi Valley for France in 1682. They established a settlement at Biloxi in 1699 and at Fort Rosalie (now Natchez) in 1716. The British gained control of Mississippi in 1763. Grants of land near Natchez, given to retired English military officers, resulted in migration of Protestants to the formerly Catholic region. During the Revolutionary War, the Natchez District remained loyal to England. Many Tories from the colonies moved into the area at this time. Between 1779 and 1781, Spain took control of the Natchez District. In 1783, Spain gained western Florida, which included part of Mississippi.

The Georgia legislature authorized the Yazoo land sales between 1789 and 1794, bringing hundreds of settlers into the area. Mississippi was made a territory in 1798, with Natchez as the capital. Georgia abandoned claims to the northern portion in 1802 and Spain relinquished the Gulf Coast region during the War of 1812. Thousands of settlers soon entered the area from the eastern and northern states. In 1817, the eastern part of the territory was severed and became the Alabama Territory. Later the same year, Mississippi became the 20th state. Another land boom occurred in 1837 when the last of the Indian lands were opened up to settlement.

By 1860, slaves outnumbered their white owners and Mississippi topped all states in the Union in the production of cotton. In 1861, Mississippi became the second state to secede from the Union and was a leading member of the Confederacy in the Civil War. Approximately 112,000 men served in the Confederate forces, while just more than 500 fought for the Union. Mississippi was readmitted to the Union in 1870.

Look for vital records in the following locations:

- **Birth and death records:** A few counties kept birth and death records from as early as 1879. State registration of births and deaths began in November 1912. General compliance was reached in 1921. Records are available from Vital Records, State Department of Health, in Jackson, Mississippi.
- **Miscellaneous records:** The Mississippi Department of Archives and History in Jackson has early census records and tax rolls, newspaper files, microfilms of the Federal Censuses, records of Mississippi's Confederate soldiers, and some birth and death records.
- **Wills, deeds and probate records:** Wills, deeds, and probate files are held by the chancery clerks or probate courts in each county.
- **Land records:** Some early land records have been published. Federal land case files are at the National Archives, Atlanta Branch in East Point, Georgia.
- **Census records:** Territorial and state censuses were frequently taken between 1792 and 1866 for various counties. Published indexes are available for many of them.

Vital Records Public Health Statistics
PO Box 1700
Jackson, Mississippi 39215-1700
(601) 576-7981
www.health.ms.gov/msdhsite/_static/31,0,109.html

Mississippi Department of Archives and History
200 North Street
PO Box 571
Jackson, Mississippi 39205-0571
(601) 576-6876
www.mdah.state.ms.us/

Mississippi

Societies and Repositories

Aberdeen Genealogical Society; General Delivery; Aberdeen, MS 39730.

Alcorn County Genealogical Society; PO Box 1808; Corinth, MS 38835-1808; www.rootsweb.com/~msacgs/ index.html.

Attala Historical Society; Mary Ricks Thornton Cultural Center; PO Box 127; Kosciusko, MS 39090; www.rootsweb.com/~msahs.

Bolivar County Historical Society; 1615 Terrace Road; Cleveland, MS 38732.

Chickasaw County Historical and Genealogical Society; PO Box 42; Houston, MS 38851; www.rootsweb.com/ ~mschchgs.

Claiborne-Jefferson Genealogical Society; PO Box 1017; Port Gibson, MS 39150.

Family Research Association of Mississippi; PO Box 13334; Jackson, MS 39236-3334; (601) 372-2959; GeoPatWks@aol.com.

Genealogical Society of Desoto County; PO Box 607; Hernando, MS 38632-0632; GSDCMS@hotmail.com; www.rootsweb.com/~msdesoto/gsdcm.htm.

Hancock County Historical Society; 113 Citizen Street; PO Box 1340; Bay Saint Louis, MS 39520.

Hattiesburg Area Historical Society; 127 W Front St.; Hattiesburg, MS 39401-3461.

Historical and Genealogical Society of Panola County; 105 Church St.; Batesville, MS 38606.

Itawamba County Historical Society; PO Box 7G; Mantachie, MS 38855; www.rootsweb.com/~msichs.

Jackson County Genealogical Society; PO Box 994; Pascagoula, MS 39567.

Jones County Genealogical and Historical Organization; PO Box 2644; Laurel, MS 39442-2644.

Marshall County Historical Society; 220 East College Avenue; PO Box 806; Holly Springs, MS 38635.

Mississippi Coast Genealogical and Historical Society; PO Box 513; Biloxi, MS 39530.

Mississippi Department Archives and History; Capers Building; 100 South State Street; PO Box 57; Jackson, MS 39205-0571; (601) 359-6850; pubinfo@mdah.state.ms.us; www.mdah.state.ms.us.

Mississippi Genealogical Society; PO Box 5301; Jackson, MS 39216.

Mississippi Historical Society; PO Box 571; Jackson, MS 39205-0571; mhs@mdah.state.ms.us; www.mdah.state.ms.us/admin/mhistsoc.html.

Mississippi Library Commission; 1221 Ellis Avenue; Jackson, MS 39209-7328; (601) 961-4111; mslib@mlc.lib.ms.us; www.mlc.lib.ms.us.

Mississippi Society of the Sons of the American Revolution; 12 Avery Circle; Jackson, MS 39211.

Natchez Historical Society; 307 South Wall Street; PO Box 49; Natchez, MS 39120.

Northeast Mississippi Historical and Genealogical Society; PO Box 434; Tupelo, MS 38802-0434.

Ocean Springs Genealogical Society; PO Box 1765; Ocean Springs, MS 39566-1765; www.rootsweb.com/~msosgs.

Prentiss County Historical & Genealogical Society; PO Box 491; Booneville, MS 38829; www.rootsweb.com/~mspcgs/Index.html.

Rankin County Historical Society; PO Box 841; Brandon, MS 39042.

Scott County Genealogical Society; PO Box 737; Forest, MS 39074-0737; (601) 469-4799; scottcogensoc@yahoo.com; www.geocities.com/scottcogensoc.

Skipwith Historical and Genealogical Society, Inc.; PO Box 1392; Oxford, MS 38655.

South Mississippi Genealogical Society; PO Box 15271; Hattiesburg, MS 39404-5271; clarise@prodigy.net; www.smsgs.org.

Sunflower County Historical Society; Sunflower County Library; 201 Cypress Drive; Indianola, MS 38751.

Tate County Mississippi Genealogical and Historical Society; PO Box 974; Senatobia, MS 38668.

Tippah County Historical and Genealogical Society; Ripley Public Library; 308 North Commerce Street; Ripley, MS 38663.

Tishomingo County Historical & Genealogical Society; 203 East Quitman Street; PO Box 273; Iuka, MS 38852-2311; (662) 423-3500; tcarchives@nadata.net; www.rootsweb.com/~mstchgs/index.htm.

Vicksburg Genealogical Society, Inc.; PO Box 1161; Vicksburg, MS 39181-1161; www.rootsweb.com/~msvgs/index.htm.

Wayne County Genealogical Organization, Inc.; 712 Wayne St.; Waynesboro, MS 39367.

Webster County Historical Society; Rt. 3, Box 14; Elepora, MS 39744.

West Chickasaw County Genealogical and Historical Society; PO Box 42; Houston, MS 38851.

Winston County Historical and Genealogical Society; PO Box 428; Louisville, MS 39339.

Woodville Civic Club; Friends of the Museum; PO Box 914; Woodville, MS 39669.

Yalobusha County Historical Society; PO Box 258; Coffeeville, MS 38922.

Yazoo Historical Society; 332 North Main Street; PO Box 575; Yazoo City, MS 39194.

Bibliography and Record Sources

General

Adams, Donna Burge. *Women In The Florida Parishes.* 5 vols. Baton Rouge, Louisiana: D. B. Adams, 1985–1991.

Anderson, Hugh George. *Lutheranism in the Southeastern States, 1860–1886: A Social History.* The Hague: Mouton, 1969.

Biographical and Historical Memoirs of Mississippi: Embracing an Authentic and Comprehensive Account of the Chief Events in the History of the State, and a Record of the Lives Of Many of the Most Worthy and Illustrious Families and Individuals. 2 vols. in 4. Chicago: Goodspeed Publishing Co., 1891.

Cain, Cyril Edward. *Four Centuries on the Pascagoula,* 2 vols. State College, Mississippi: C. E. Cain, 1953–1962.

Church of Jesus Christ of Latter-day Saints. Mississippi District. *Annual Genealogical Report, Form E, 1907–1951; Record Of Members, 1874–1943.* Microfilm of original records in the LDS Church Archives, Salt Lake City. Salt Lake City: Filmed by the Genealogical Society of Utah, 1953–1954. 3 microfilm.

Claiborne, J. F. H. *Mississippi as a Province, Territory, and State, with Biographical Notices of Eminent Citizens.* (1880) Reprint. Spartanburg, South Carolina: Reprint Company, 1996.

DeRosier, Arthur H. *The Removal of the Choctaw Indians.* Knoxville: University of Tennessee Press, 1989.

Episcopal Diocese of Mississippi (Jackson, Mississippi). *The Episcopal Church in Mississippi.* Jackson, Mississippi: The Diocese, 1992.

First Settlers of the Mississippi Territory. Nacogdoches, Texas: Ericson Books, n.d.

Gillis, Norman E. *Genealogical Abstract of Biographical Section, Alphabetical Arrangement, A Through Z: Biographical and Historical Memoirs Of Mississippi.* S.1.: Irene S. and Norman E. Gillis, 1962.

Goodspeed Publishing Company. *Biographical and Historical Memoirs of Mississippi, Embracing an Authentic and Comprehensive Account of the Chief Events in the History of the State and a Record of the Lives of Many of the Most Worthy and Illustrious Families and Individuals.* Vols. I and II. (1891) Reprint. Spartanburg, South Carolina: Reprint Company, 1996.

Greenwell, Dale. *Twelve Flags—Triumphs and Tragedies.* 3 vols. Ocean Springs, Mississippi: D. Greenwell, 1968.

Griffin, Benjamin. *History of the Primitive Baptists of Mississippi.* 1853. Reprint. Jonesboro, Arkansas: Sammons Printing, 1958.

Henderson, Thomas W., and Ronald E. Tomlin, comps. *Guide to Official Records in the Mississippi Department of Archives and History.* Jackson, Mississippi: Mississippi Department of Archives and History, 1975.

Jackson, Mississippi: Department of Archives and History, 1969.

Jenkins, William L. *Mississippi, United Methodist Churches: Two Hundred Years of Heritage and Hope.* Franklin, Tennessee: Providence House Pub., 1998.

Johnson, Charles Owen, ed. *The Order of the First Families of Mississippi 1699–1817: 1981 Register.* Ann Arbor, Michigan: Edwards Brothers, Inc., 1981.

Kelly, Thomas E. *Who's Who in Mississippi.,* Mississippi: Tucker Printing House, 1914.

Kidwell, Clara Sue. *Choctaws and Missionaries in Mississippi, 1818–1918.* Norman, Oklahoma: University of Oklahoma Press, 1995.

Lackey, Richard Stephen. *"Mississippi," Genealogical Research: Methods and Sources, vol. 2: 188–218.* Washington, D.C.: American Society of Genealogists, 1980.

Lindsey, J. Allen. *Methodism in the Mississippi Conference.* Jackson, Mississippi: Hawkins Foundation, Mississippi Conference Historical Society, 1964.

Lipscomb, Anne S., and Kathleen S. Hutchison. *Tracing Your Mississippi Ancestors.* Jackson: University Press of Mississippi, 1994.

Lowry, Robert and William H. McCardle. *History of Mississippi from the Discovery of the Great River by Hernando Desoto, Including the Earliest Settlement Made by the French, Under Iberville, to the Death of Jefferson Davis.* (1891) Reprint. Spartanburg, South Carolina: Reprint Company, 1978.

Menn, Joseph Karl. *The Large Slaveholders of the Deep South, 1860.* Thesis (Ph.D).—University of Texas, 1964.

Mississippi Newspapers, 1805–1940: A Preliminary Union List. Jackson, Mississippi: Mississippi Historical Records Survey, 1942.

Mississippi Research Outline. Series U.S.-States, no. 25. Salt Lake City: Family History Library, 1988.

Mississippi. Department of Archives and History. *Mississippi Provincial Archives Spanish Dominion.* Jackson, Mississippi: Photoduplication Div., 1969. 9 microfilm.

Mississippi. Department of Archives and History. *Research in the Mississippi Department of Archives and History.* Salt Lake City: Filmed by the Genealogical Society of Utah, 1972.

Nolan, Charles E. *A Southern Catholic Heritage.* New Orleans: Archdiocese of New Orleans, 1976.

Oakley, Bruce C. *A Postal History Of Mississippi, Stampless Period, 1799–1860.* Baldwyn, Mississippi: Magnolia Pub., 1969.

Owens, Harry P. *Steamboats and the Cotton Economy: River Trade in the Yazoo—Mississippi Delta.* Jackson: University Press of Mississippi, 1990.

Reorganized Church of Jesus Christ of Latter Day Saints. Mobile District (Alabama & Mississippi). *Church Records, 1868–1911.* Microreproduction of originals housed in the RLDS Library Archives, Independence, Missouri. Salt Lake City: Filmed by the Genealogical Society of Utah, 1994.

Rowland, Dunbar, and A. G. Sanders, ed. *Mississippi Provincial Archives, 1612–1763, French Dominion.*

Jackson, Mississippi: Department of Archives and History, 1968.

Rowland, Dunbar. *History of Mississippi, the Heart of the South.* 2 vols. (1925) Reprint. Salem, Massachusetts: Higginson Books, n.d.

Rowland, Dunbar. *Mississippi: Comprising Sketches of Counties, Towns, Events, Institutions, and Persons, Arranged in Cyclopedic Form.* 4 vols. (1907) Reprint. Spartanburg, South Carolina: Reprint Company, 1976.

Rowland, Dunbar. *Mississippi Provincial Archives, 1763–1783; English Dominion: Transcripts of Archives in the Public Record Office, London, England.*

Rowland, Dunbar. *Mississippi.* 4 vols. (1907) Reprint. Spartanburg, South Carolina: The Reprint Co., 1976.

Schilling, T. C. *Abstract History of the Mississippi Baptist Association, 1806–1906.* New Orleans: N.p., 1908.

Strickland, Jean. *Mississippi Biographical Abstracts.* Moss Point, Mississippi: J. Strickland, 1990.

Strickland, Jean. *Residents of the Southeastern Mississippi Territory.* 5 vols. Moss Point, Mississippi: J. Strickland, 1996.

United States. Office of Indian Affairs. *Superintendent of Indian Trade. Records of the Choctaw Trading House, 1803–1824.* Washington D. C.: National Archives. Central Plains Region, 1960. 6 microfilm.

Wallace, Jesse Thomas. *A History of the Negroes of Mississippi From 1865 To 1890.* Clinton, Mississippi: , 1927.

Webster, Anne L. *African Americans: A Mississippi Source Book.* Carrollton, Mississippi: Pioneer Publishing Co., 2002.

Willis, John C. *Forgotten Time: The Yazoo—Mississippi Delta After the Civil War.* Charlottesville, Virginia.: University Press of Virginia, 2000.

Young, Mary Elizabeth. *Redskins, Ruffleshirts and Rednecks: Indian Allotments in Alabama and Mississippi, 1830–1860.* Norman: University of Oklahoma Press, 1961.

Atlases, Maps and Gazetteers

Brieger, James. *Hometown, Mississippi.* 2nd ed. Jackson, Mississippi: Town Square Books, 1997.

Gallagher, John S. *Mississippi Post Offices.* Lake Grove, Oregon: Depot, 1996.

Long, John H., and Peggy Tuck Sinko, comps. *Mississippi Atlas of Historical County Boundaries.* New York: Simon & Schuster, 1993.

Mississippi Maps, 1816–1873. Jackson, Mississippi: Mississippi Department of Archives and History, 1970.

Oakley, Bruce C. *A Postal History of Mississippi— Stampless Period, 1799–1860.* Baldwyn, Mississippi: Magnolia Publishers, 1969.

Rowland, Dunbar. *Mississippi: comprising Sketches of Counties, Towns, Events, Institutions, and Persons,*

Arranged in Cyclopedic Form. 4 vols. Atlanta: Southern Historical Publishing Association, 1907. Reprint. Spartanburg, South Carolina: Reprint Co., 1976.

United States. Office of Geographic Research. Branch of Geographic Names. *Mississippi Geographic Names: Alphabetical Listing.*

Censuses

Available Census Records and Census Substitutes

Federal Census 1820, 1830 (except Pike County), 1840, 1850, 1860 (except Hancock, Washington and Tallahatchie Counties), 1870, 1880, 1900, 1910, 1920, 1930

Federal Mortality Schedules 1850, 1860, 1870, 1880

Union Veterans and Widows 1890

State/Territorial Census 1810, 1816, 1822–1825, 1837, 1841, 1845, 1853, 1866

Dollarhide, William. *The Census Book: A Genealogist's Guide to Federal Census Facts, Schedules and Indexes.* Bountiful, Utah: Heritage Quest, 1999.

Feldman, Lawrence H. *Anglo-Americans in Spanish Archives: Lists of Anglo-American Settlers in the Spanish Colonies of America; a Finding Aid.* Baltimore: Genealogical Publishing Co., 1991.

Kemp, Thomas Jay. *The American Census Handbook.* Wilmington, Delaware: Scholarly Resources, Inc., 2001.

Lainhart, Anne S. *State Census Records.* Baltimore: Genealogical Publishing Co., Inc., 1992.

Szucs, Loretto Dennis and Matthew Wright. *Finding Answers in U.S. Census Records.* Ancestry Publishing, 2001.

Thorndale, William and William Dollarhide. *Map Guide to the U.S. Federal Census, 1790–1920.* Baltimore: Genealogical Publishing Co., 1987.

United States. Bureau of Indian Affairs. *Indian Census Rolls, Choctaw, 1926–1939.* Washington, D.C.: The National Archives, 1965. 2 microfilm.

United States. Bureau of Internal Revenue. *Internal Revenue Lists For Mississippi, 1865–1866.* Washington, D.C.: The National Archives, 1988. 3 microfilm.

Court Records, Probate and Wills

Hendrix, Mary L. *Mississippi Court Records: From the Files of the High Court of Errors and Appeals, 1799–1859.* Jackson, Mississippi: n.d.

King, J. Estelle. *Mississippi Court Records 1799–1835.* (1936) Reprint. Baltimore: Genealogical Publishing Co., 1969.

McBee, May Wilson. *Mississippi County Court Records.* (1858) Reprint. Baltimore: Clearfield Co., 1994.

McBee, May Wilson. *The Natchez Court Records, 1767–1805.* (1953) Reprint. Baltimore: Clearfield Co., 1994.

Mississippi. State Archives. *Mississippi Territorial Land and Court Records, 1798–1817.* Microfilm of original records at the Mississippi State Archives, Jackson, Mississippi. Salt Lake City: Filmed by the Genealogical Society of Utah, 1972. 5 microfilm.

Survey of Records in Mississippi Court Houses. Jackson, Mississippi: Mississippi Genealogical Society, 1957.

Wiltshire, Betty Couch, comp. *Mississippi Index of Wills, 1800–1900.* Bowie, Maryland: Heritage Books, 1989.

Emigration, Immigration, Migration and Naturalization

Index to Naturalization Records, Mississippi Courts, 1798–1906. Jacksonville, Mississippi: Old Law Naturalization Records Project, 1942.

Old Law Naturalization Records Project, Division of Community Service Programs, Work Project Administration. *Index to Naturalization Records Mississippi Courts, 1798–1906.* Washington D.C.: Library of Congress Photoduplication Service, 1989.

Land and Property

Ainsworth, Fern. *Private Land Claims of Mississippi and Missouri.* Natchitoches, Louisiana: Fern Ainsworth, n.d.

DeVille, Winston. *English Land Grants in West Florida: A Register for the States of Alabama, Mississippi, and Parts of Florida and Louisiana, 1766–1776.* Ville Platte, Louisiana: Winston DeVille, 1986.

Guide to Archival Holdings at NARA's Southeast Region (Atlanta). East Point, Georgia: National Archives Records Administration Southeast Region (Atlanta), 2001. Online at—www.nara.gov/regional/atlanta.html

Hone, Wade E. *Land and Property Research in the United States.* Salt Lake City: Ancestry Incorporated, 1997.

Lowrie, Walter. *Early Settlers of Mississippi as Taken from Land Claims in the Mississippi Territory.* (1834) Reprint. Southern Historical Press, 1986.

McMullin, Phillip, ed. *Grassroots of America A Computerized Index to the American State Papers: Land Grants and Claims 1789–1837 with Other Aids to Research (Government Document Serial Set Numbers 28 Through 36).* Salt Lake City: Gendex Corp., 1972.

Mississippi. State Archives. *Mississippi Territorial Land and Court Records, 1798–1817.* Microfilm of original records at the Mississippi State Archives, Jackson, Mississippi. Salt Lake City: Filmed by the Genealogical Society of Utah, 1972. 5 microfilm.

Smith, Clifford Neal. *Spanish And British Land Grants In Mississippi Territory, 1750–1784.* 3 vols. in 1. McNeal, Arizona: Westland, 1996.

United States. Department of the Interior. Bureau of Land Management. *Mississippi Pre 1908 Patents, Cash, Homestead, Chickasaw Indian Treaty and Choctaw Indian Scrip.* Springfield, Virginia: BLM Eastern States, 1997.

Military

Department of Archives and History. *Roster of Mississippi Men Who Served in the War of 1812 and Mexican War.* Jackson, Mississippi: Department of Archives and History, n.d.

Master Alphabetical Index, World War Veterans, Army, 1917–1918. Salt Lake City: Filmed by the Genealogical Society of Utah, 1972.

Mississippi. State Archives. *Master Alphabetical Index, World War Veterans, Army, 1917–1918.* Microreproduction of typescript at the State Archives in Jackson, Mississippi. Salt Lake City: Filmed by the Genealogical Society of Utah, 1972. 2 microfilm.

Rietti, John C. *Military Annals of Mississippi: Military Organizations Which Entered the Service of the Confederate States of America from the State of Mississippi.* (1976) Reprint. Spartanburg, South Carolina: Reprint Co., 1976.

Rowland, Dunbar. *Military History of Mississippi, 1803–1898.* (1908) Reprint. Spartanburg, South Carolina: Reprint Co., 1996.

Rowland, Dunbar. *Official & Statistical Register of the State of Mississippi, Military History Only.* (1908) Reprint. Salem, Massachusetts: Higginson Co., 1995.

Rowland, Eron Opha. *Mississippi Territory in the War of 1812.* (1921) Reprint. Baltimore: Clearfield Co., 1996.

Strickland, Jean and Patricia N. Edwards. *Residents of the Mississippi Territory.* 3 vols. Moss Point, Mississippi: Ben Strickland, n.d.

United States. Adjutant General's Office. *Compiled Service Records of Volunteer Soldiers Who Served During the Mexican War in Organizations from the State of Mississippi.* Washington, D.C.: The National Archives, 1971.

United States. Adjutant General's Office. *Compiled Service Records of Volunteer Soldiers Who Served During the War of 1812 in Organizations from the Territory of Mississippi.* Washington, D.C.: The National Archives, 1967.

United States. Record and Pension Office. *Compiled Service Records of Volunteer Union Soldiers Who Served in Organizations from the State of Mississippi.* Washington, D.C.: The National Archives, 1962.

United States. Selective Service System. *Mississippi, World War I Selective Service System Draft Registration Cards, 1917–1918. National Archives Microfilm Publications, M1509.* Washington, D.C.: National Archives, 1987–1988.

Wiltshire, Betty Crouch. *Mississippi Confederate Grave Registrations.* 2 vols. Bowie, Maryland: Heritage Books, 1991.

Wiltshire, Betty Crouch. *Mississippi Confederate Pension Applications.* 3 vols. Carrollton, Mississippi: Pioneer Publishing Co., 1994.

Vital and Cemetery Records

Birth and death records were not kept until 1912 on the state level. It was not until 1921 that the records were kept on a regular basis. Refer to the county section to locate information for individual counties.

Cemetery Index. Jackson: Mississippi Department of Archives & History, 2002. Online database— www.mdah.state.ms.us/arlib/contents/findaids.html

Dodd, Jordan R. *Mississippi Marriages, Early to 1825: A Research Tool Compiled, Extracted & Transcribed by Liahona Research, Inc.* : Precision Indexing Publishers, ca.1990.

Guide to Vital Statistics in Mississippi: Volume 1, Public Archives. Jackson: Historical Records Survey, 1942.

Ivison, Hazel R. Collins. *These Sacred Places.* S.l.: s.n., 1965.

Marriage Records. Orem, Utah: Automated Archives, 1994. CD-ROM.

Mississippi & Florida, 1800–1900. S.l.: Brøderbund, 1998. CD-ROM.

Mississippi Cemetery and Bible Records. 3 vols. Jackson: Mississippi Genealogical Society, 1954.

Mississippi. State Board of Health. Division of Vital Statistics (Jackson, Mississippi). *Birth Records, 1913–1935; Death Records, 1912–1935.* Microfilm of originals at the Kemper Regional Library, DeKalb, Mississippi. Salt Lake City: Filmed by Genealogical Society of Utah, 2000.

United States. Census Office. *Mississippi Mortality Schedule For 1850, 1860, 1870, And 1880.* Washington, D.C.: The National Archives, 198–. 3 microfilm.

Wiltshire, Betty Couch. *Early Mississippi Records CD-ROM.* Bowie, Maryland: Heritage Books, 1996.

County / Website	Map Index	Date Created	Parent County or Territory From Which Organized / Address/Details
Adams www.rootsweb.com/~msadams/	M2	2 Apr 1799	**Natchez District** Adams County; 115 S Wall St; PO Box 1008; Natchez, MS 39120; Ph. (601) 446-6684 **Details:** (Clerk Chancery Court has Court, Land & Probate Records; Clerk Circuit Court has Marriage & Death Records)
Alcorn www.freedom2000net.com/userpages/ genealogy/alcorn/index.html	B10	15 Apr 1870	**Tippah, Tishomingo** Alcorn County; PO Box 112; Corinth, MS 38834-0112; Ph. (601) 286-7702 **Details:** (Clerk Chancery Court has Divorce Records from 1913; Clerk Circuit Court has Court Records from 1860)
Amite www.rootsweb.com/~msamite/	O4	24 Feb 1809	**Wilkinson** Amite County; 243 W Main St; Liberty, MS 39645-0000; Ph. (601) 657-8022 **Details:** (Clerk Chancery Court has Court, Land & Probate Records from 1809; Clerk Circuit Court has Marriage Records)
Attala www.rootsweb.com/~msattala/	H7	23 Dec 1833	**Choctaw Cession** Attala County; 230 W Washington St; Kosciusko, MS 39090-0000; Ph. (662) 289-2921 **Details:** (Clerk Circuit Court has Marriage Records; Clerk Chancery Court has Divorce, Probate & Land Records & old newspapers)
Bainbridge		17 Jan 1823	**Lawrence, Wayne** Bainbridge County; MS **Details:** County Terminated 1824 (Discontinued 21 Jan 1824 & became Covington County)
Benton www.rootsweb.com/~msbenton/	B8	21 Jul 1870	**Marshall, Tippah** Benton County; Main St; PO Box 218; Ashland, MS 38603-0000; Ph. (662) 224-6300 **Details:** (Clerk Chancery Court has Divorce, Probate & Land Records from 1871)

County Website	Map Index	Date Created	Parent County or Territory From Which Organized Address/Details
Bolivar www.usgw.org/ms/bolivar/	E4	**9 Feb 1836**	**Choctaw Cession** Bolivar County; 401 S Court St; Cleveland, MS 38732-2696; Ph. (662) 843-2071 **Details:** (Clerk Circuit Court, Cleveland, Mississippi has Marriage & Court Records; Clerk Chancery Court has Divorce, Probate & Land Records) (Clerk Circuit Court, Rosedale, Mississippi has Marriage Records from 1866 & Court Records from 1870; Clerk Chancery Court has Divorce, Probate & Land Records) (Chancery & Circuit Clerks Office in both Courthouses. Rosedale Records go back about 20 years earlier than Cleveland)
Calhoun www.rootsweb.com/~mscalhou/	E8	**8 Mar 1852**	**Lafayette, Yalobusha** Calhoun County; PO Box 8; Pittsboro, MS 38951; Ph. (662) 412-3117 **Details:** (Courthouse burned in 1922) (Clerk Chancery Court has Marriage, Divorce, Probate, Court & Land Records from 1922 & Land abstracts from 1852)
Carroll www.rootsweb.com/~mscarrol/	G6	**23 Dec 1833**	**Choctaw Cession** Carroll County; Lexington St; Carrollton, MS 38917; Ph. (662) 237-9274 **Details:** (County Clerk has Marriage, Divorce, Probate, Court & Land Records from 1870)
Chickasaw www.rootsweb.com/~mschicka/	E9	**9 Feb 1836**	**Choctaw Cession, 1832** Chickasaw County; 101 N Jefferson; Houston, MS 38851-0000; Ph. (662) 456-2531 **Details:** (Clerk Circuit Court, Houston has Marriage, Divorce, Probate & Court Records & all Land Records for County) (Clerk Circuit Court, Okolona has Marriage Records from 1877 & Court Records; Clerk Chancery Court has Divorce & Probate Records from 1886)
Choctaw www.rootsweb.com/~mschocta/	G8	**23 Dec 1833**	**Chickasaw Cession, 1832** Choctaw County; 112 Quinn St; PO Box 736; Ackerman, MS 39735-0000; Ph. (662) 285-6329 **Details:** (Clerk Circuit Court has Marriage, Divorce, Probate, Court & Land Records from 1881)
Claiborne www.rootsweb.com/~msclaib2/	L3	**27 Jan 1802**	**Jefferson** Claiborne County; PO Box 449; Port Gibson, MS 39150; Ph. (601) 437-4992 **Details:** (Clerk Chancery Court has Marriage Records from 1816, Divorce Records from 1856, Probate & Court Records from 1802)
Clarke	L9	**1833**	Clarke County; PO Box 689; Quitman, MS 39355; Ph. (662) 776-2126 **Details:** (Clerk Chancery Court has Divorce & Probate Records from 1875)
Clarke (old)		**10 Dec 1812**	**Washington** Clarke County; MS **Details:** County Terminated 1817 into Alabama
Clay www.rootsweb.com/~msclay/	F9	**12 May 1871**	**Chickasaw, Lowndes, Monroe, Oktibbeha** Clay County; PO Box 815; West Point, MS 39773; Ph. (662) 494-3124 **Details:** (Formerly Colfax County. Name changed to Clay 10 Apr 1876) (Clerk Circuit Court has Marriage & Court Records; Clerk Chancery Court has Divorce, Probate & Land Records from 1872)

County Website	Map Index	Date Created	Parent County or Territory From Which Organized Address/Details
Coahoma www.clarksdale.com/county/	**D4**	**9 Feb 1836**	**Chickasaw Cession, 1836** Coahoma County; 115 1st St; PO Box 98; Clarksdale, MS 38614; Ph. (662) 624-3000 **Details:** (Clerk Circuit Court has Marriage & Court Records from 1848 & voter Records from 1949; Clerk Chancery Court has Divorce, Probate & Land Records)
Colfax		**12 May 1871**	**Chickasaw, Lowndes, Monroe, Oktibbeha** Colfax County; MS **Details:** (see Clay) Name changed to Clay 10 Apr 1876
Copiah www.rootsweb.com/~mscopiah/	**L4**	**21 Jan 1823**	**Hinds** Copiah County; PO Box 507; Hazlehurst, MS 39083; Ph. (601) 894-3021 **Details:** (Clerk Chancery Court has Divorce Records from 1840, Probate & Land Records from 1825 & confederate veterans Records; Clerk Circuit Court has Marriage Records from 1825 & Court Records)
Covington www.rootsweb.com/~mscoving/	**M7**	**5 Feb 1819**	**Lawrence, Wayne** Covington County; PO Box 1679; Collins, MS 39428; Ph. (601) 765-6132 **Details:** (Clerk Chancery Court has Marriage, Divorce & Probate Records from 1900, Court & Land Records from 1860)
Davis		**1865**	Davis County; MS **Details:** Name Changed to Jones County
De Soto www.desotonet.com/	**B6**	**9 Feb 1836**	**Indian Lands** De Soto County; 2535 Hwy 51 S; Courthouse Sq; Hernando, MS 38632; Ph. (662) 429-1317 **Details:** (Clerk Chancery Court has Divorce, Probate & Land Records)
Forrest www.co.forrest.ms.us/	**N8**	**19 Apr 1906**	**Perry** Forrest County; 641 Main St; PO Box 951; Hattiesburg, MS 39401; Ph. (601) 545-6014 **Details:** (Clerk Circuit Court has Marriage Records from 1893 & Court Records from 1906; Clerk Chancery Court has Divorce, Land, Probate & Military Records)
Franklin www.rootsweb.com/~msfrankl/	**N3**	**21 Dec 1809**	**Adams** Franklin County; PO Box 297; Meadville, MS 39653; Ph. (601) 384-2330 **Details:** (Clerk Chancery Court has Court, Land & Probate Records; Clerk Circuit Court has Marriage Records)
George www.rootsweb.com/~msgeorge/	**O10**	**16 Mar 1910**	**Greene, Jackson** George County; 355 Cox St; Lucedale, MS 39452-0000; Ph. (601) 947-4801 **Details:** (Clerk Circuit Court has Marriage & Court Records from 1911; Clerk Chancery Court has Divorce, Probate & Land Records from 1911)
Greene www.rootsweb.com/~msgreene/	**N10**	**9 Dec 1811**	**Amite, Franklin, Wayne** Greene County; PO Box 610; Leakesville, MS 39451; Ph. (601) 394-2377 **Details:** (Clerk Chancery Court has Court, Land & Probate Records; Clerk Circuit Court has Marriage Records)

County Website	Map Index	Date Created	Parent County or Territory From Which Organized Address/Details
Grenada www.rootsweb.com/~msgrenad/	F7	9 May 1870	**Carroll, Yalobusha, Choctaw, Talahatchie** Grenada County; PO Box 1208; Grenada, MS 38902; Ph. (662) 226-1821 **Details:** (Clerk Circuit Court has Marriage, Divorce & Probate Records from 1870 & Land Records from 1835)
Hancock www.rootsweb.com/~mshancoc/	Q7	18 Dec 1812	**Mobile District** Hancock County; 150 Main St; Bay St. Louis, MS 39520; Ph. (228) 467-5404 **Details:** (Clerk Circuit Court has Marriage & Court Records; Clerk Chancery Court has Divorce, Probate & Land Records)
Harrison http://co.harrison.ms.us/	Q8	5 Feb 1841	**Hancock, Jackson** Harrison County; 1801 23rd Ave; PO Box Drawer CC; Gulfport, MS 39502; Ph. (228) 865-4118 **Details:** (Clerk Circuit Court has Marriage Records from 1841 & Court Records; Clerk Chancery Court has Divorce, Probate & Land Records)
Hinds www.co.hinds.ms.us/pgs/index.asp	K5	12 Feb 1821	**Choctaw Cession, 1820** Hinds County; PO Box 686; Jackson, MS 39205; Ph. (601) 968-6237 **Details:** (Clerk Circuit Court has Marriage Records from 1823 & Court Records from 1930; Clerk Chancery Court has Divorce, Probate & Land Records)
Holmes www.rootsweb.com/~msholmes/	H6	19 Feb 1833	**Yazoo** Holmes County; PO Box 239; Lexington, MS 39095; Ph. (662) 834-2281 **Details:** (Clerk Chancery Court has Divorce Records from 1894, Probate & Land Records from 1833 & Burial Records; Clerk Circuit Court has Marriage & Court Records)
Humphreys www.rootsweb.com/~mshumphr/	H4	28 Mar 1918	**Holmes, Washington, Yazoo, Sunflower** Humphreys County; PO Box 547; Belzoni, MS 39038; Ph. (662) 247-1740 **Details:** (Clerk Circuit Court has Birth & Marriage Records; Clerk Chancery Court has Divorce, Probate & Land Records from 1918)
Issaquena www.rootsweb.com/~msissaqu/	I4	23 Jan 1844	**Washington** Issaquena County; PO Box 27; Mayersville, MS 39113; Ph. (662) 873-2761 **Details:** (Clerk Chancery Court has Marriage Records from 1866, Divorce, Probate, Court & Land Records from 1850)
Itawamba www.rootsweb.com/~msitawam/	D10	9 Feb 1836	**Chickasaw Cession, 1832** Itawamba County; 201 W Main St; PO Box 776; Fulton, MS 38843; Ph. (662) 862-3421 **Details:** (Clerk Chancery Court has Marriage, Divorce, Probate, Court & Land Records)
Jackson www.co.jackson.ms.us/	Q10	18 Dec 1812	**Mobile District** Jackson County; 3109 Canty St; PO Box 998; Pascaqoula, MS 39567; Ph. (228) 769-3091 **Details:** (Clerk Chancery Court has Divorce & Probate Records, justice of the peace dockets from 1875; Clerk Circuit Court has Marriage Records from 1875)

County Website	Map Index	Date Created	Parent County or Territory From Which Organized Address/Details
Jasper www.rootsweb.com/~msjasper/	**K8**	23 Dec 1833	**Choctaw Cession, 1832** Jasper County; Court St; PO Box 1047; Bay Springs, MS 39422-0000; Ph. (601) 764-3368 **Details:** (County Clerk has Divorce, Probate & Court Records from 1906; Clerk Circuit Court has Marriage Records)
Jefferson www.rootsweb.com/~msjeffer/	**L3**	2 Apr 1799	**Natchez District** Jefferson County; 307 Main St; PO Box 145; Fayette, MS 39069-0000; Ph. (601) 786-3021 **Details:** (Formerly Pickering County. Name changed to Jefferson 11 Jan 1802) (Clerk Chancery Court has Marriage Records from 1798, Divorce Records from 1860, Probate & Land Records from 1798)
Jefferson Davis www.rootsweb.com/~msjdavis/	**M6**	31 Mar 1906	**Covington, Lawrence** Jefferson Davis County; 1025 3rd St; PO Box 1137; Prentiss, MS 39474; Ph. (601) 792-4204 **Details:** (Clerk Chancery Court has Court & Land Records; Clerk Circuit Court has Marriage & Probate Records)
Jones www.edajones.com/	**M8**	24 Jan 1826	**Covington, Wayne** Jones County; PO Box 1468; Laurel, MS 39441; Ph. (601) 428-0527 **Details:** Temporarily name Davis County 1865–1869 (Clerk Circuit Court has Marriage Records from 1882 & Court Records from 1907; Clerk Chancery Court at Laurel & Ellisville, Mississippi has Divorce & Land Records)
Kemper www.rootsweb.com/~mskemper/	**I10**	23 Dec 1833	**Choctaw Cession, 1832** Kemper County; Bell St; PO Box 188; De Kalb, MS 39328; Ph. (601) 743-2560 **Details:** (Clerk Circuit Court has Marriage Records from 1912; Clerk Chancery Court has Divorce, Probate, Court & Land Records from 1912)
Lafayette www.rootsweb.com/~mslafaye/	**D7**	9 Feb 1836	**Chickasaw Cession** Lafayette County; Town Sq; PO Box 1240; Oxford, MS 38655; Ph. (662) 234-2131 **Details:** (Clerk Chancery Court has Marriage, Divorce, Probate & Court Records)
Lamar www.lamarcounty.com/	**N7**	19 Feb 1904	**Marion, Pearl River** Lamar County; 203 Main St; Purvis, MS 39475; Ph. (601) 544-4410 **Details:** (Clerk Circuit Court has Marriage Records; Clerk Chancery Court has Divorce, Probate & Land Records from 1900's; Justice of the Peace has Court Records)
Lauderdale www.lauderdalecounty.org/index.htm	**J9**	23 Dec 1833	**Choctaw Cession** Lauderdale County; 410 Constitution Ave; PO Box 1587; Meridian, MS 39302; Ph. (601) 482-9704 **Details:** (Clerk Chancery Court has Divorce, Probate & Land Records; Clerk Circuit Court has Marriage & Court Records; County Health Department has Birth & Death Records)
Lawrence www.rootsweb.com/~mslawren/	**M6**	22 Dec 1814	**Marion** Lawrence County; PO Box 40; Monticello, MS 39654; Ph. (601) 587-7162 **Details:** (Clerk Circuit Court has Marriage & Court Records; Clerk Chancery Court has Divorce, Probate & Land Records from 1815)

County Website	Map Index	Date Created	Parent County or Territory From Which Organized Address/Details
Leake www.rootsweb.com/~msleake/	I7	23 Dec 1833	**Choctaw Cession** Leake County; Court Sq; PO Box 72; Carthage, MS 39051; Ph. (601) 267-7371 **Details:** (Clerk Chancery Court has Marriage Records, Divorce Records from 1871, Court Records, Land Records from 1833, Probate Records from 1840 & Military Discharge Records from 1918)
Lee www.rootsweb.com/~mslee/	D10	26 Oct 1866	**Itawamba, Pontotoc** Lee County; 200 W Jefferson St; PO Box 7127; Tupelo, MS 38802; Ph. (662) 841-9100 **Details:** (Clerk Chancery Court has Divorce, Probate & Land Records; Clerk Circuit Court has Marriage Records; Justice Court has Court Records)
Leflore www.rootsweb.com/~msleflor/	F5	15 Mar 1871	**Carroll, Sunflower, Tallahatchie** Leflore County; 317 W Market St; PO Box 250; Greenwood, MS 38935; Ph. (662) 453-6203 **Details:** (Clerk Circuit Court has Marriage & Court Records; Clerk Chancery Court has Divorce & Probate Records from 1871 & Land Records from 1834)
Lincoln www.rootsweb.com/~mslincol/	M5	7 Apr 1870	**Franklin, Lawrence, Copiah, Pike, Amite** Lincoln County; 300 S 2nd St; PO Box 555; Brookhaven, MS 39601-3321; Ph. (601) 835-3479 **Details:** (Clerk Chancery Court has Divorce, Probate & Court Records from 1893; Clerk District Court has Marriage Records from 1893)
Lowndes www.rootsweb.com/~mslownde/	G10	30 Jan 1830	**Monroe** Lowndes County; PO Box 684; Columbus, MS 39703; Ph. (662) 329-5805 **Details:** (Department of Archives & History has Marriage, Divorce, Probate, Court & Land Records 1830–1900 & Bible Records)
Madison www.rootsweb.com/~msmadiso/	I6	29 Jan 1828	**Yazoo** Madison County; PO Box 404; Canton, MS 39046; Ph. (601) 859-1177 **Details:** (Clerk Chancery Court has Marriage, Divorce, Probate, Court & Land Records from 1828)
Marion www.rootsweb.com/~msmarion/	N6	9 Dec 1811	**Amite, Wayne, Franklin** Marion County; 250 Broad St Ste 2; Columbia, MS 39429; Ph. (601) 736-2691 **Details:** (Clerk Chancery Court has Marriage, Divorce, Probate, Court & Land Records)
Marshall www.rootsweb.com/~msmarsha/	B7	9 Feb 1836	**Chickasaw Cession, 1832** Marshall County; PO Box 219; Holly Springs, MS 38635; Ph. (662) 252-4431 **Details:** (Clerk Chancery Court has Divorce, Probate & Land Records from 1836)
Monroe www.rootsweb.com/~msmonroe/index.htm	E10	9 Feb 1821	**Chickasaw Cession, 1821** Monroe County; PO Box 578; Aberdeen, MS 39730; Ph. (662) 369-8143 **Details:** (Clerk Circuit Court has Marriage & Court Records; Clerk Chancery Court has Divorce Records, Probate & Land Records from 1821)

County Website	Map Index	Date Created	Parent County or Territory From Which Organized Address/Details
Montgomery www.rootsweb.com/~msmontgo/	G7	13 May 1871	**Carroll, Choctaw** Montgomery County; PO Box 71; Winona, MS 38967; Ph. (662) 283-2333 **Details:** (Clerk Chancery Court has Divorce, Probate, Court & Land Records from 1871; Clerk Circuit Court has Marriage Records)
Neshoba www.neshoba.org/	I8	23 Dec 1833	**Chocktaw Cession, 1830** Neshoba County; 401 E Beacon St Ste 107; Philadelphia, MS 39350; Ph. (601) 656-3581 **Details:** (Clerk Chancery Court has Divorce & Probate Records from 1890; Clerk Circuit Court has Marriage Records from 1912)
Newton www.rootsweb.com/~msnewton/	J8	25 Feb 1836	**Neshoba** Newton County; PO Box 68; Decatur, MS 39327; Ph. (601) 635-2367 **Details:** (Clerk Chancery Court has Divorce, Probate, Court & Land Records from 1876; Clerk Circuit Court has Marriage Records)
Noxubee www.rootsweb.com/~msnoxube/	H10	23 Dec 1833	**Choctaw Cession, 1830** Noxubee County; PO Box 147; Macon, MS 39341; Ph. (662) 726-4243 **Details:** (Clerk Circuit Court has Marriage & Court Records from 1834; Clerk Chancery Court has Divorce, Probate & Land Records from 1834)
Oktibbeha www.eda.co.oktibbeha.ms.us/	G9	23 Dec 1833	**Choctaw Cession, 1830** Oktibbeha County; 101 E Main St; Starkville, MS 39759; Ph. (662) 323-5834 **Details:** (Clerk Chancery Court has Divorce, Probate & Court Records from 1880 & Land Records from 1834; Clerk Circuit Court has Marriage Records)
Panola www.geocities.com/Heartland/Plains/4399/msgenweb/panola.html	D6	9 Feb 1836	**Chickasaw Cession, 1832** Panola County; 151 Public Sq; Batesville, MS 38606-2220; Ph. (601) 563-6205 **Details:** (Clerk Chancery Court has Divorce & Probate Records from 1836; Clerk Circuit Court has Marriage Records from 1885 & Court Records from 1836)
Pearl		1872	**Hancock** Pearl County; MS **Details:** County Terminated 1878
Pearl River www.rootsweb.com/~mspearlr/	P7	22 Feb 1890	**Hancock, Marion** Pearl River County; PO Box 431; Poplarville, MS 39470; Ph. (601) 795-2237 **Details:** (Clerk Chancery Court has Divorce, Probate & Court Records from 1890; Clerk Circuit Court has Marriage Records)
Perry www.usgw.org/ms/perry/	N9	3 Feb 1820	**Greene** Perry County; PO Box 198; New Augusta, MS 39462; Ph. (601) 964-8398 **Details:** (Clerk Chancery Court has Divorce, Probate, Court & Land Records from 1878; Clerk Circuit Court has Marriage Records from 1877)
Pickering		2 Apr 1799	**Natchez District** Pickering County; MS **Details:** (see Jefferson) Name changed to Jefferson 11 Jan 1802

County Website	Map Index	Date Created	Parent County or Territory From Which Organized Address/Details
Pike www.pikeinfo.com/	O5	**9 Dec 1815**	**Marion** Pike County; PO Box 309; Magnolia, MS 39652; Ph. (601) 783-3362 **Details:** (Clerk Chancery Court has Divorce, Probate, Court & Land Records from 1882; Clerk Circuit Court has Marriage Records)
Pontotoc www.geocities.com/dc031888/msgenweb/ pontotoc/pontotoc.htm	D8	**9 Feb 1836**	**Chickasaw Cession, 1832** Pontotoc County; PO Box 209; Pontotoc, MS 38863-0209; Ph. (662) 489-3900 **Details:** (Clerk Circuit Court has Marriage Records; Clerk Chancery Court has Probate, Court & Divorce Records & Land Records from 1836)
Prentiss www.rootsweb.com/~msprenti/	C10	**15 Apr 1870**	**Tishomingo** Prentiss County; PO Box 477; Booneville, MS 38829-0477; Ph. (662) 728-8151 **Details:** (Clerk Chancery Court has Divorce, Probate & Court Records from 1870 & Land Records from 1836; Clerk Circuit Court has Marriage Records)
Quitman www.geocities.com/Heartland/Plains/ 4399/msgenweb/quitman.html	D5	**1 Feb 1877**	**Panola, Coahoma, Tunica, Tallahatchie** Quitman County; 230 Chestnut St; PO Box 100; Marks, MS 38646; Ph. (662) 326-2661 **Details:** (Clerk Chancery Court has Divorce & Probate Records from 1877; Clerk Circuit Court has Marriage & Court Records)
Rankin www.rootsweb.com/~msrankin/	K6	**4 Feb 1828**	**Hinds** Rankin County; 211 E Government St; Brandon, MS 39042; Ph. (601) 825-1469 **Details:** (Clerk Chancery Court has Divorce, Probate & Land Records from 1829)
Scott www.rootsweb.com/~msscott/	J7	**23 Dec 1833**	**Choctaw Cession, 1832** Scott County; PO Box 630; Forest, MS 39074; Ph. (601) 469-1922 **Details:** (Clerk Chancery Court has Divorce & Court Records from 1900, Probate & Land Records from 1835, old church & cemetery Records; Clerk Circuit Court has Marriage Records)
Sharkey www.rootsweb.com/~mssharke/	H4	**29 Mar 1876**	**Warren, Washington, Issaquena** Sharkey County; County Courthouse; PO Box 218; Rolling Fork, MS 39159-0000; Ph. (662) 873-2755 **Details:** (Clerk Chancery Court has Court, Probate & Land Records from 1876; Clerk Circuit Court has Marriage Records from 1876)
Simpson www.rootsweb.com/~mssimpso/	L6	**23 Jan 1824**	**Choctaw Cession, 1820** Simpson County; 109 W Pine Ave; PO Box 367; Mendenhall, MS 39114; Ph. (601) 847-2626 **Details:** (Clerk Circuit Court has Marriage & Court Records; Clerk Chancery Court has Divorce Records from 1880, some Probate & Land Records)
Smith www.rootsweb.com/~mssmith/	L7	**23 Dec 1833**	**Choctaw Cession, 1820** Smith County; Main St; PO Box 39; Raleigh, MS 39153; Ph. (601) 782-9811 **Details:** (Clerk Circuit Court has Marriage Records from 1912 & Court Records; Clerk Chancery Court has Divorce, Probate, Land & Military Records from 1892)

County Website	Map Index	Date Created	Parent County or Territory From Which Organized Address/Details
Stone www.stonecounty.com/	P8	3 Apr 1916	**Harrison** Stone County; PO Box 7; Wiggins, MS 39577; Ph. (601) 928-5266 **Details:** (Clerk Chancery Court has Divorce, Probate, Land & Military Discharge Records from 1916; Clerk Circuit Court has Marriage & Court Records)
Sumner		6 Apr 1874	**Montgomery, Chickasaw, Choctaw, Okitbbeha** Sumner County; MS **Details:** (see Webster) Name changed to Webster 30 Jan 1882
Sunflower www.rootsweb.com/~mssunflo/	F4	15 Feb 1844	**Bolivar, Washington** Sunflower County; 200 Main St; PO Box 988; Indianola, MS 38751-0000; Ph. (662) 887-4703 **Details:** (Clerk Chancery Court has Marriage, Divorce, Probate, Court & Land Records from 1871)
Tallahatchie www.rootsweb.com/~mstallah/	E5	23 Dec 1833	**Choctaw Cession, 1820** Tallahatchie County; PO Box Drawer 350; Charleston, MS 38921; Ph. (662) 647-5551 **Details:** (Clerk Circuit Court has Marriage Records from 1909; Clerk Chancery Court has Divorce & Probate Records from 1909 & Land Records from 1858)
Tate www.rootsweb.com/~mstate/	B6	15 Apr 1873	**Marshall, Tunica, DeSoto** Tate County; 201 Ward St; Senatobia, MS 38668; Ph. (662) 562-5661 **Details:** (Clerk Circuit Court has Marriage Records from 1873; Clerk Chancery Court has Divorce, Probate, Court & Land Records from 1873)
Tippah www.rootsweb.com/~mstippah/	B9	9 Feb 1836	**Chickasaw Cession, 1832** Tippah County; PO Box 99; Ripley, MS 38663; Ph. (662) 837-7374 **Details:** (Clerk Chancery Court or Clerk Circuit Court has Marriage, Divorce, Probate & Court Records from 1856)
Tishomingo www.freedom2000net.com/userpages/ genealogy/Tishom/	B11	9 Feb 1836	**Chickasaw Cession, 1832** Tishomingo County; 1008 Battleground Dr; Iuka, MS 38852-1020; Ph. (662) 423-7010 **Details:** (Clerk Chancery Court has Divorce, Probate, Court & Land Records; Clerk Circuit Court has Marriage Records)
Tunica www.rootsweb.com/~mstunica/	C5	9 Feb 1836	**Chickasaw Cession, 1832** Tunica County; PO Box 217; Tunica, MS 38676; Ph. (662) 363-2451 **Details:** (Clerk Chancery Court has Divorce, Probate, Court & Land Records; Clerk Circuit Court has Marriage Records)
Union www.rootsweb.com/~msunion/	C9	7 Jul 1870	**Pontotoc, Tippah** Union County; 109 Main St E; PO Box 847; New Albany, MS 38652-0000; Ph. (662) 534-1900 **Details:** (Clerk Chancery Court has Divorce, Probate & Court Records; Clerk Circuit Court has Marriage Records)
Walthall www.iocc.com/~swright/walthall/waltmain.html	O6	1912	**Marion, Pike** Walthall County; PO Box 351; Tylertown, MS 39667; Ph. (601) 876-3553 **Details:** (Clerk Circuit Court has Marriage Records from 1914; Clerk Chancery Court has Divorce, Probate, Court & Land Records from 1914)

County Website	Map Index	Date Created	Parent County or Territory From Which Organized Address/Details
Warren www.rootsweb.com/~mswarren/	J4	22 Dec 1809	**Natchez District** Warren County; PO Box 351; Vicksburg, MS 39181-0351; Ph. (601) 636-4415 **Details:** (Clerk Chancery Court has Divorce, Probate, Court & Land Records; Clerk Circuit Court has Marriage Records)
Washington www.usgw.org/ms/washington/	G3	29 Jan 1827	**Warren, Yazoo** Washington County; PO Box 309; Greenville, MS 38701; Ph. (662) 332-1595 **Details:** (Clerk Circuit Court has Marriage Records from 1858 & Court Records from 1890; Clerk Chancery Court has Divorce Records from 1856, Probate & Land Records from 1831)
Washington, old		4 Jun 1800	**Unorg. Terr.** Washington, old County; MS **Details:** (now in Alabama)
Wayne www.wayneco.com/	M9	21 Dec 1809	**Washington, old** Wayne County; 609 Azalea Dr; Waynesboro, MS 39367-0000; Ph. (601) 735-2873 **Details:** (Clerk Chancery Court has Marriage, Burial, Divorce, Probate, Court & Land Records)
Webster www.rootsweb.com/~mswebst2/	F8	6 Apr 1874	**Montgomery, Chickasaw, Choctaw, Oktibbeha** Webster County; Hwy 9 N; PO Box 398; Walthall, MS 39771; Ph. (662) 258-4131 **Details:** (Formerly Sumner County. Name changed to Webster 30 Jan 1882) (Clerk Circuit Court has Marriage & Court Records; Clerk Chancery Court has Divorce, Probate & Land Records from 1800's)
Wilkinson www.rootsweb.com/~mswilkin/	O2	30 Jan 1802	**Adams** Wilkinson County; PO Box 516; Woodville, MS 39669-0516; Ph. (601) 888-4381 **Details:** (Clerk Chancery Court has Marriage, Divorce, Probate, Court & Land Records)
Winston www.rootsweb.com/~mswinsto/	H8	23 Dec 1833	**Choctaw Cession, 1830** Winston County; County Courthouse; PO Box Drawer 69; Louisville, MS 39339; Ph. (662) 773-3631 **Details:** (Clerk Chancery Court has Court, Probate & Land Records from 1834; Clerk Circuit Court has Marriage Records)
Yalobusha www.rootsweb.com/~msyalobu/	E7	23 Dec 1833	**Choctaw Cession, 1830** Yalobusha County; PO Box 664; Water Valley, MS 38965-0664; Ph. (662) 473-2091 **Details:** (Clerk Chancery Court, Water Valley, Mississippi has Divorce, Probate, Court & Land Records; Clerk Circuit Court, Coffeyville, Mississippi has Marriage Records; Clerk Chancery Court has Divorce, Probate, Court & Land Records)
Yazoo http://genealogyamerica.com/msyazoo/	I5	21 Jan 1823	**Hinds** Yazoo County; PO Box 68; Yazoo City, MS 39194; Ph. (601) 746-2213 **Details:** (Clerk Chancery Court has Marriage Records from 1845, Divorce, Probate, Court & Land Records from 1823 & newspapers)

Notes

Missouri

Capital: Jefferson City

Territory: 1812

State: 1821 (24th)

*The welfare of the people
shall be the supreme law*

Missouri's earliest inhabitants, tribes of Sauk, Fox, Algonquin, Osage, and Kansa Indians, were established long before Spanish explorers with Hernando de Soto arrived in 1541. It would be another century-plus before Frenchmen Father Jacques Marquette and Louis Joliet followed and discovered the Missouri River in 1673. Robert Cavelier, Sieur de la Salle, claimed the entire Mississippi River Valley for France in 1682. In 1700, the French made the first settlement near the Des Peres River, south of St. Louis. That settlement lasted for only a short time. The first permanent settlement was Ste. Genevieve, which French lead miners established in 1735. France ceded the area to Spain in 1763. Unaware of the cession, French settlers founded St. Louis the following year.

The first American settlement was in 1787 in Ste. Genevieve County. After 1795, Americans—mainly from Kentucky, Tennessee, Virginia, and the Carolinas—came for the free land Spain was offering. In 1800 Spain returned the region to France. Four years later, the majority of the 10,000 residents were American. The Louisiana Purchase in 1803 made Missouri part of the United States. Two years later Missouri became part of the Territory of Louisiana. Missouri became a territory in 1812. Indian raids continued until about 1815, when treaties were signed and settlement increased. When Missouri became a state in 1821, there were about 57,000 settlers.

Missouri's geographic location made it the gateway to the West, as thousands of settlers departed from Independence (nicknamed the "Queen City of the Trails") en route to New Mexico, Oregon, and California. European immigrants came into the state from Ireland, England, Poland, Switzerland, Bohemia, and Italy to mix with the Americans and descendants of the early French settlers. Members of the Church of Jesus Christ of Latter-day Saints, settled in western Missouri in 1831, but were expelled in 1839. The Platte Purchase of 1837 added six northwestern counties to the state. Missouri was the start of many migrations to the West as both the Santa Fe and Oregon Trails began at

Independence. Even with these migrations, Missouri was the fifth most populous state at the end of the Civil War.

In 1861, the legislature considered secession but voted against it. After the start of the Civil War, the governor repudiated Lincoln's call for troops and called up the state militia to fight for the Confederacy. Federal troops defeated the militia, forcing the governor and legislature to flee to the south. A provisional government was installed until the state government was reorganized in 1864. An estimated 40,000 men fought for the Confederacy, while about 109,000 fought for the Union. Numerous battles were fought in the state, which became one of the important battlegrounds of the war.

Look for vital records in the following locations:

- **Birth and death records:** County clerks were required to register births and deaths from 1883 to 1893. Records still extant can be obtained from the county clerk or the Missouri State Archives in Jefferson City. State registration of births and deaths began in 1863, but did not reach full compliance until 1911. The records after 1910 can be obtained from the Bureau of Vital Records.

- **Marriage and divorce records:** Some marriages from 1825 to the present may be obtained at the office of the Recorder of Deeds in each county. Some of the earliest land claims and grants have been published. Divorce proceedings were filed with a court of common pleas, a circuit court, or the state legislature. Most can be obtained from the circuit court clerk. Unfortunately, many of the county courthouses in Missouri, along with their records, have been burned. The State Historical Society of Missouri, in Columbia, has other records that might be of help to researchers.

- **Land records:** Records of the local land offices are in the Missouri State Archives. Tract book, plat maps, and land patents are at the BLM Eastern States Office in Alexandria, Virginia.

- **Census records:** A few Spanish censuses were taken as early as 1772. Portions of Missouri were included in the 1810 census of Louisiana Territory. Missouri Territory took censuses in 1814, 1817, 1819, and 1820, but the latter was destroyed. Incomplete census records exist for 1821, at four-year intervals from 1825 to 1863, and in 1876. Copies are at the State Historical Society of Missouri and the Missouri State Archives, as well as some county offices.

Missouri Dept of Health and Senior Services
Bureau of Vital Records
PO Box 570
Jefferson City, MO 65102
(573) 751-6387
www.dhss.state.mo.us/BirthAndDeathRecords/
BirthAndDeathRecords.html

Missouri State Archives
Missouri State Archives
600 W. Main
PO Box 1747
Jefferson City, MO 65102
(573) 751-3280
www.sos.mo.gov/archives/Default.asp

State Historical Society of Missouri
1020 Lowry Street
Columbia, MO 65201-7298
(573) 882-7083; fax (573) 884-4950
www.umsystem.edu/shs/

Societies and Repositories

Adair County Historical Society; 211 S. Elson St.; Kirksville, MO 63501-3466; (660) 665-6502; peeve@cableone.net; www.kirksvillecity.com/museums.html.

Alexander Majors Chapter, Sons of the American Revolution; RICHO300@aol.com; www.geocities.com/SARy2k/HomePgOne.html.

American Family Records Association; PO Box 15505; Kansas City, MO 64106.

Andrew County Historical Society; Box 12; Savannah, MO 64485.

Audrain County Area Genealogical Society; c/o Mexico-Audrain County Public Library; 305 West; Mexico, MO 65265.

Audrain County Historical Society; PO Box 3; Mexico, MO 65265.

Baptist Historical Society, Missouri; William Jewell College Library; Liberty, MO 64068.

Barry County Missouri Genealogical & Historical Society; PO Box 291; Cassville, MO 65625; www.rootsweb.com/ ~mobarry/society.html.

Boone County Historical Society; 3801 Ponderosa Street; Columbia, MO 65201; bchs@socket.net; http://members.socket.com/~bchs/index.htm.

Cape Girardeau County Archive Center; 112 East Washington; Jackson, MO 63755; Archive@showme .net; www.showme.net/CapeCounty/archive/index.htm.

Cape Girardeau County, Missouri Genealogical Society; PO Box 389; Jackson, MO 63755; eddleman@clas.net; www.rootsweb.com/~mocgcgs/index.htm.

Carroll County Genealogical Association; PO Box 354; Carrollton, MO 64633-0354; ccga@carolnet.com; www.carolnet.com/ccga.

Carthage, Missouri Genealogical Society; Rt. 3; Carthage, MO 64836.

Cass County Historical Society; 400 East Mechanic; Harrisonville, MO 64701.

Chariton County Historical Society; 115 E. Second St.; PO Box 114; Salisbury, MO 65281; museum@cvalley.net.

Commerce Historical Society; PO Box 93; Commerce, MO 63742; commercemo@clas.net.

Concordia Historical Institute; 301 DeMun Ave.; St. Louis, MO 63105.

Cooper County Historical Society; 5236 Hwy A; Bunceton, MO 65237; www.mo-river.net/Community/ social-services/cooper/historical-society.htm.

Dade County Genealogical Society; PO Box 155; Greenfield, MO 65661-0155.

Dallas County Historical Society; PO Box 594; Buffalo, MO 65622.

Daughters of Union Veterans of the Civil War, 1861–1965, Missouri Dept.; 2615 Porter Ave.; Brentwood, MO 63144.

DeKalb County Historical Society; PO Box 477; Maysville, MO 64469.

Dunklin County, Missouri Genealogical Society; 1101 N. Ricky Rd.; Kennett, MO 63857.

Edson Genealogical Association; 724 S. Whitmer Street; Richmond, MO 64085-2154.

Family Tree Climbers; Box 422; Lawson, MO 64062.

Four Rivers Genealogical Society; 314 W. Main St.; PO Box 146; Washington, MO 63090.

Genealogical Society of Butler County, Missouri, Inc.; PO Box 426; Poplar Bluff, MO 63901; www.rootsweb.com/~mobcgs.

Genealogical Society of Central Missouri; PO Box 26; Columbia, MO 65205-0026; lcrane@coin.org; www.gscm.gen.mo.us/GSCM.HTM.

Genealogical Society of Pulaski County, Missouri; PO Box 226; Crocker, MO 65452.

Genealogical Study Group of the Newton County Historical Society; PO Box 675; Neosho, MO 64950.

Genealogy Friends of the Library; PO Box 314; Neosho, MO 64850.

Graham Historical Society; 417 S. Walnut; Marysville, MO 64468.

Grundy County Genealogical Society; PO Box 223; Trenton, MO 64683; www.rootsweb.com/~mogrundy/gcgen.html.

Grundy County Library; 1331 Main Street; Trenton, MO 64683; (660) 359-3577.

Harrison County Genealogical Society; 2243 Central St.; Bethany, MO 64424-1335.

Heart of America Genealogical Society; c/o Public Library; 311 E. 12th St.; Kansas City, MO 64106.

Historical Society of Maries County, Missouri; PO Box 289; Vienna, MO 65592.

Howard County Genealogical Society; 201 S. Main; Fayette, MO 65248.

Hubbell Family Historical Society; 2051 E. McDaniel St.; PO Box 3813 GS; Springfield, MO 65808-3813.

Iron County Genealogy Society; PO Box 343; Arcadia, MO 63621; jmcclur@mail.tigernet.gen.mo.us; www.angelfire.com/mo3/iron_co_gen/genealogy_society.html.

Jackson County Genealogical Society; Box 2145; Independence, MO 64055.

Jackson County Historical Society; 129 W. Lexington; Independence, MO 64050; info@jchs.org; www.jchs.org/.

Jefferson County Historical Society; c/o De Soto Public Library; 712 So. Main; De Soto, MO 63020-2401; www.rootsweb.com/~mojeffer/jchs.

Jefferson County Missouri Genealogical Society; PO Box 1342; High Ridge, MO 63049; bdiehl@BSDA-transit.org; www.rootsweb.com/~mojcgs/index.html.

Jewish Genealogical Society of St. Louis; United Hebrew Congregation; 13788 Conway Rd; St. Louis, MO 63141; jerfransl@cs.com; www.jewishgen.org/jgs-StLouis.

Kimmswick Historical Society; PO Box 41; Kimmswick, MO 63053.

Laclede County Genealogical Society; PO 350; Lebanon, MO 65536.

Landon Cheek, Afro-American Historical and Genealogical Society; PO Box 23804-0804; St. Louis, MO 63121.

Lawrence County Historical Society; PO Box 406; Mt. Vernon, MO 65712.

Lewis County Historical Society, Inc.; 614 Clark St.; Canton, MO 63435.

Lincoln County, Missouri Genealogical Society; PO Box 192; Hawk Point, MO 63349.

Linn County Genealogical Researchers; 708 McGowan; Brookfield, MO 64628.

Livingston County Genealogical Society; 450 Locust St.; Chillicothe, MO 64601.

Magic Afro-American Historical & Genealogical Society; 3700 Blue Pkwy.; Kansas City, MO 64130.

Mid-Missouri Genealogical Society, Inc.; PO Box 715; Jefferson, MO 65102.

Mine Au Breton Historical Society; Rt. 1, Box 3154; Potosi, MO 63664; www.rootsweb.com/~mowashin/mabhs.html.

Mississippi County Genealogical Society; PO Box 5; Charleston, MO 63834.

Missouri Historical Society Library; 225 S. Skinker; PO Box 11940; St. Louis, MO 63112-0040; (314) 746-4500; library@mohistory.org.

Missouri State Archives; 600 West Main Street; PO Box 1747; Jefferson City, MO 65102; (753) 751-3280; archref@sosmail.state.mo.us; www.sos.mo.gov/archives/Default.asp.

Missouri State Genealogical Association; PO Box 833; Columbia, MO 65205-0833; P.Shackelford@worldnet.att.net; www.mosga.org.

Missouri State Library; 600 W. Main St.; PO Box 38; Jefferson City, MO 65101; (573) 751-3615; libref@sosmail.state.mo.us; www.sos.mo.gov/library.

Missouri Territorial Pioneers; 3929 Milton Dr.; Independence, MO 64055.

Moniteau County, Missouri Historical Society; 201 N. High California, MO 65018.

Montgomery County Genealogical Society; 112 West Second Street; Montgomery City, MO 63361; beverly@ktis.net; www.ktis.net/~nllee/mcgs/index.html.

Morgan County, Missouri Historical Society; PO Box 177; Versailles, MO 65084.

NARA, Central Plains Region (Kansas City); 2312 East Bannister Road; Kansas City, MO 64131-3011; (816) 823-5029; kansascity.reference@nara.gov; www.archives.gov/facilities/mo/kansas_city.html.

NARA, Central Plains Region (Lee's Summit); 200 Space Center Drive; Lee's Summit, MO 64064-1182; (816) 823-5224; kansascitycave.reference@nara.gov; www.archives.gov/facilities/mo/lees_summit.html.

NARA, National Personnel Records Center (Civilian); 9700 Page Avenue; St. Louis, MO 63132-5100; (314) 801-9250; cpr.center@nara.gov; www.archives.gov/facilities/mo/st_louis/civilian_personnel_records.html.

NARA, National Personnel Records Center (Military); Military Personnel Records; 9700 Page Avenue; St. Louis, MO 63132-5100; MPR.center@nara.gov; www.archives.gov/facilities/mo/st_louis/military_personnel_records.html.

Nodaway County Genealogical Society; PO Box 214; Maryville, MO 64468.

Northeast Missouri Genealogical Society; 614 Clark St.; Canton, MO 63435.

Northland Genealogical Society; PO Box 14121; Parkville, MO 64152; jfk@compuserve.com; http://homepages.rootsweb.com/~kcngs.

Northwest Missouri Genealogical Society; PO Box 382; St. Joseph, MO 64502; haskins@ccp.com; www.rootsweb.com/~monwmgs/index.htm.

Old Mines Area Historical Society; Rt. 1, Box 300Z, Cadet; Old Mines, MO 63630.

Oregon County Genealogical Society; Courthouse; Alton, MO 65606.

Osage County, Missouri Historical Society; 402 E. Main St.; PO Box 402; Linn, MO 65051.

Ozark County Genealogical and Historical Society; HCR 2 Box 88; Gainesville, MO 65655.

Ozark Mountain Chapter, Sons of the American Revolution; 1910 N. Lone Pine Ave.; Springfield, MO 65803-5117; (417) 883-2498; William_Bishop@msn.com; www.rootsweb.com/~moomcsam.

Ozarks Genealogical Society; PO Box 3945; Springfield, MO 65808-3945; Ogsoc@dellepro.com; www.rootsweb.com/~ozarksgs.

Perry County Historical Society; PO Box 97; Perryville, MO 63775.

Phelps County Genealogical Society; Box 571; Rolla, MO 65402-0571; pcgs@rollanet.org; www.rollanet.org/~pcgs.

Phelps County Historical Society; PO Box 1535; Rolla, MO 65402-1535; www.umr.edu/~whmcinfo/pchs.

Pike County Genealogical Society; PO Box 313; Bowling Green, MO 63334.

Platte County, Missouri Historical and Genealogical Society, Inc.; 220 Ferrel St.; PO Box 103; Platte City, MO 64079-0103; (816) 431-5121; www.rootsweb.com/~mopchgs.

Polk County Genealogical Society; PO Box 632; Bolivar, MO 65613-0632; www.rootsweb.com/~mopolkgs.

Randolph County Historical Society; Box 116; Moberly, MO 65270.

Ray County Genealogical Association; 901 W. Royle St.; Richmond, MO 64085-1545; kproffitt@raycounty.net; www.rootsweb.org/~morcga.

Ray County Historical Society; Box 2; Richmond, MO 64085.

Reynolds County, Missouri Genealogical and Historical Society; PO Box 281; Ellington, MO 63638.

Ripley County Historical and Genealogical Society; 101 Washington St.; Doniphan, MO 63935.

Scotland County Historical Society; c/o Downing House & Boyer House Museums; 311 S. Main; Memphis, MO 63555.

Scott County Historical & Genealogy Society; PO Box 151; Benton, MO 63736; mcharmon@clas.net; www.scottcountygenealogy.org.

South Vernon Genealogical Society; R-2, Box 280; Sheldon, MO 64784.

South-Central Missouri Genealogical Society; 1043 W. 5th St.; West Plains, MO 65775-2147.

St. Charles County Genealogical Society; 1022 First Capitol Drive; PO Box 715; St. Charles, MO 63302-0715; (636) 724-6668; mroellig@mail.win.org; www.rootsweb.com/~mosccgs.

St. Louis Genealogical Society; PO Box 43010; St. Louis, MO 63143-0010; www.rootsweb.com/~mostlogs/STINDEX.HTM.

State Historical Society of Missouri; 1020 Lowry Street; Columbia, MO 65201-7298; (573) 882-7083; shsofmo@umsystem.edu; www.system.missouri.edu/shs.

Stone County Historical Society; PO Box 63; Galena, MO 65656.

Texas County, Missouri Genealogical & Historical Society; Box 12; Houston, MO 65483.

Tri-County Genealogical Society; PO Box B; Nevada, MO 64772.

Union Cemetery Historical Society; 2727 Main St., Suite 120; Kansas City, MO 64108.

Vernon County Historical Society; 231 N. Main St.; Nevada, MO 64772; info@bushwhacker.org; www.bushwhacker.org.

Warren County Historical Society; PO Box 12; Warrenton, MO 63383.

Webb City Area Genealogical Society; 101 South Liberty St.; Webb City, MO 64870.

West Central Missouri Genealogical Society; 705 Broad St.; Warrensburg, MO 64093.

Westport Historical Society; 4000 Baltimore; Kansas City, MO 64111; www.westporthistorical.org.

White River Valley Historical Society; Box 565; Point Lookout, MO 65726.

Wright County Historical Society; PO Box 66; Hartville, MO 65667.

Bibliography and Record Sources

General

A Guide to County Records on Microfilm. Jefferson City, Missouri: Missouri State Archives, 1990.

A Reminiscent History of the Ozark Region: Comprising a Brief Descriptive History of Each County and Numerous Biographical Sketches of Prominent Citizens of Each County. Easley, South Carolina: Southern Historical Press, 1978.

Bibliography of the Ozarks Books. Salt Lake City: Filmed by the Genealogical Society of Utah, 1977.

Bishop, Beverly D., and Janice L. Fox. *A List of Manuscript Collections in the Archives of the Missouri Historical Society.* St. Louis: Missouri Historical Society, 1982.

Blattner, Teresa. *People of Color: Black Genealogical Records and Abstracts from Missouri Sources.* Bowie, Maryland: Heritage Books, 1998.

Bradley, James LeGrand. *Zion's Camp 1834: Prelude to the Civil War.* Logan, Utah: J. L. Bradley, 1990.

Bryan, William S., and Robert Rose. *A History of the Pioneer Families of Missouri, with Numerous Sketches, Anecdotes, Adventures, Etc. Relating to the Early Days in Missouri. Also the Lives of Daniel Boone and the Celebrated Indian Chief Black Hawk.* (1876, 1935, 1992) Reprint. Baltimore: Clearfield Co., 1996.

Burgess, Roy. *Early Missourians and Kin. A Genealogical Compilation of Inter-related Early Missouri Settlers, Their Ancestors, Descendants, and other Kin.* (1984) Reprint. Bowie, Maryland: Heritage Books, 1992.

Campbell, Robert Allen. *Campbell's Gazetteer of Missouri: from Articles Contributed by Prominent Gentlemen in Each County of The State, and Information Collected and Collated From Official and Other Authentic Sources, by a Corps of Experienced Canvassers, Under the Personal Supervision of the Editor.* Rev. ed. St. Louis: Campbell, 1875.

Catholic Church. Archdiocese of Kansas City and St. Joseph (Missouri). *Parish Register Transcripts, Ca. 1830–1900.* Microreproduction of typescript. Salt Lake City: Filmed by the Genealogical Society of Utah 13 microfilm.

Church of Jesus Christ of Latter-day Saints, The. Historical Department. *Index to Journal History.* Salt Lake City: Filmed by the Historical Dept., 1973. 58 microfilm.

Columbia, Missouri: State Historical Society, 1988.

Conrad, Howard Louis. *Encyclopedia of the History of Missouri, a Compendium of History and Biography for Ready Reference.* New York: Southern History Co., 1901.

Davis, Walter Bickford. *An Illustrated History of Missouri: Comprising Its Early Records, and Civil, Political, and Military History from the First Exploration to the Present Time, Including Biographical Sketches of Prominent Citizens.* St. Louis: A. Hall, 1876.

Directory of Local Historical, Museum and Genealogical Agencies in Missouri. Rev. ed. 1996–1997. Columbia, Missouri: State Historical Society, 1996–1997.

Douglass, Robert Sidney. *Southeast Missouri, a Narrative Account of Its Historical Progress, Its People and Its Principal Interests.* 2 vols. Chicago: Lewis Pub. Co., 1912.

Duncan, R. S. *A History of the Baptists in Missouri, Embracing an Account of the Organization and Growth of Baptist Churches and Associations.* St. Louis: Scammell, 1882.

Dyer, Alvin R. *The Refiner's Fire: The Significance of Events Transpiring in Missouri.* Mormon History. Salt Lake City: Deseret Book, 1968.

Ellsberry, Elizabeth Prather. *Bible Records of Missouri.* 8 vols. in 3. Chillicothe, Missouri: E. P. Ellsberry, 1963–1965.

Gambrill, George. *Genealogical Material and Local Histories in the St. Louis Public Library.* Rev. ed. St. Louis: St. Louis Public Library, 1965.

Gilbert, Joan. *The Trail of Tears Across Missouri.* Columbia, Missouri: University of Missouri Press, 1996.

Goodspeed Publishing Co. *A Reminiscent History of the Ozark Region of Arkansas and Missouri.* (1894) Reprint. Greenville, South Carolina: Southern Historical press, 1988.

Goodspeed Publishing Co. *General History of Missouri from Earliest Times to the Present.* (1888) Reprint. Greenville, South Carolina: Southern Historical Press, 1992.

Goodspeed Publishing Co., *The History of Southeast Missouri, Embracing an Historical Account of the Counties of St. Genevieve, St. Francois, Perry, Cape Giardeau, Bollinger, Madison, New Madrid, Pemiscot, Dunklin, Scott, Mississippi, Stoddard, Butler, Wayne, and Iron.* (1888) Reprint. Greenville, South Carolina: Southern Historical Press, 1990.

Gray, Marcus Lemon. *1806–1906, The Centennial Volume of Missouri Methodism, Methodist Episcopal Church.* South City, Missouri: Press of Burd & Fletcher, ca.1907.

Haley, T. P. *Historical and Biographical Sketches of the Early Churches and Pioneer Preachers of the Christian Church in Missouri.* Kansas City: J. H. Smart, 1888.

Havig, Alan R. *A Centennial History of the State Historical Society of Missouri, 1898–1998.* Columbia, Missouri: University of Missouri Press, 1998.

Hehir, Donald. *Missouri Family Histories and Genealogies, A Bibliography.* Bowie, Maryland: Heritage Books, 1996.

Historical Records Survey (Missouri). *Guide to Public Vital Statistics Records in Missouri.* St. Louis: Historical Records Survey, 1941.

Historical Records Survey (Missouri). *The Organization of Missouri Counties.* St. Louis: Historical Records Survey, 1941.

History of Franklin, Jefferson, Washington, Crawford & Gasconade Counties, Missouri: from the Earliest Time to the Present, Together with Sundry Personal Business and Professional Sketches and Numerous Family Records, Besides a Valuable Fund of [I.E. Fund of] Notes, Original Observations, Etc., Etc. Giradeau, Missouri: Ramfre, 1958.

History of Southeast Missouri: Embracing an Historical Account of the Counties of Ste. Genevieve, St. Francois, Perry, Cape Girardeau, Bollinger, Madison, New Madrid, Pemiscot, Dunklin, Scott, Mississippi, Stoddard,

Butler, Wayne and Iron, Including a Department Devoted to the Preservation of Personal, Professional and Private Records. Chicago: Goodspeed Pub., 1888.

Hodges, Nadine and Audrey L. Woodruff. *Missouri Pioneers: County and Genealogical Records*. 30 vols. Independence: Woodruff, 1967–1976.

Houck, Louis. *A History of Missouri from the Earliest Explorations and Settlements until the Admission of the State into the Union*. 3 vols. Chicago: R. R. Donnelley, 1908.

Houck, Louis. *The Spanish Regime in Missouri: A Collection of Papers and Documents Relating to Upper Louisiana Principally Within the Present Limits of Missouri During the Dominion of Spain, from the Archives of the Indies at Seville*. . . . 2 vols. Chicago: R. R. Donnelley & Sons, 1909.

Ingmire, Frances T. *Pioneer Kentuckians with Missouri Cousins*. 2 vols. Signal Mountain, Tennessee: Mountain Press, n.d..

Luebbering, Patsy. *Publications Relating to Missouri Counties*. Jefferson City, Missouri: Records Management and Archives Service, 1980.

McReynolds, Edwin C. *Missouri, a History of the Crossroads State*. Norman, Oklahoma: University of Oklahoma Press, 1962.

Midwest Pioneers, 1600s–1800s. S.l.: Brøderbund, 1999. CD-ROM.

Missouri Newspapers on Microfilm at the State Historical Society of Missouri. Columbia, Missouri: State Historical Society, n.d.

Missouri Research Outline. Series U.S.-States, no. 26. Salt Lake City: Family History Library, 1988.

Parkin, Robert E. *Guide to Tracing Your Family Tree in Missouri*. St. Louis: Genealogical Research and Productions, 1979.

Patrick, Michael D. *Orphan Trains to Missouri*. Columbia, Missouri: University of Missouri Press, 1997.

Seaton, Richard A. *History of the United Methodist Churches of Missouri*. Missouri: Missouri Methodist Historical Society, 1984.

Selby, Paul O. *A Bibliography of Missouri County Histories and Atlases*. 2d ed. Kirksville, Missouri: Northeast Missouri State Teachers College, 1966.

Sources of Genealogical Help in Missouri. Burbank, California: Southern California Genealogical Society, n.d.

State Historical Society of Missouri. *Directory of Local Historical, Museum and Genealogical Agencies in Missouri*. Columbia, Missouri: State Historical Society, 1994.

State Historical Society of Missouri. *Historic Missouri: A Pictorial Narrative*.

State Historical Society of Missouri. *Missouri Newspapers on Microfilm at the State Historical Society*. Columbia, Missouri: State Historical Society, 1993.

Steele, Edward E. *A Guide to Genealogical Research in St. Louis*. St. Louis: St. Louis Genealogical Society, 1992.

Stevens, Walter Barlow. *Missouri, The Center State, 1821–1915*. 2 vols. Chicago: S. J. Clarke, 1915.

The United States Biographical Dictionary and Portrait Gallery of Eminent and Self-Made Men: Missouri Volume. New York: United States Biographical Pub. Co,, 1878.

Tucker, Frank C. *The Methodist Church in Missouri: 1798–1939, A Brief History*. S.l.: F. C. Tucker, 1966.

United States. Bureau of Marine Inspection and Navigation (Missouri). *Officers License and Related Records, 1905–1942*. Microfilm of originals in the National Archives Branch in Kansas City, Missouri. Salt Lake City: Filmed by the Genealogical Society of Utah, 1991. 25 microfilm.

Van Nada, M. L. *The Book of Missourians: The Achievements and Personnel of Notable Living Men and Women of Missouri in the Opening Decade of the Twentieth Century*. Chicago: T. J. Steele, 1906.

Who's What and Why in Missouri: Library of American Lives; A Reference Edition Recording the Biographies of Contemporary Leaders in Missouri with Special Emphasis on their Achievements in Making the "Show Me" State One of America's Greatest. Hopkinsville, Kentucky: Historical Record Association, 1959.

Wilcox, Pearl. *Saints of the Reorganization in Missouri*. S.l.: s.n., 1974.

Williams, Walter and Floyd Calvin Shoemaker. *Missouri, Mother of the West*. 5 vols. Chicago: American Historical Society, 1930.

Woodruff, Mrs. Howard W. *Missouri Miscellany: Statewide Missouri Genealogical Records*. 16 vols. Independence: Woodruff, 1976–1984.

Atlases, Maps and Gazetteers

Beck, Lewis Caleb. *Gazetteer of the States of Illinois and Missouri*. 1823. Reprint. New York: Arno Press, 1975.

Campbell, Robert Allen. *Gazetteer of Missouri: From Articles Contributed by Prominent Gentlemen in Each County of the State, and Information Collected and Collated from Official and Other Authentic Sources, by a Corps of Experienced Canvassers, Under the Personal Supervision of the Editor*. Rev. ed. St. Louis: Campbell, 1875.

Campbell, Robert Allen. *Campbell's New Atlas of Missouri*. St. Louis: n.p., n.d..

Cohen, Gerald Leonard. *Interesting Missouri Place Names*. Rolla, Missouri: G. Cohen, 1982.

Missouri Atlas [And] Gazetteer. Yarmouth, Massachusetts: DeLorme Mapping Co., 1998.

Ohman, Marian M. "Missouri County Organization 1812–1876." *Missouri Historical Review* 76 (April 1981): 253–281.

Rafferty, Milton D. *Historical Atlas of Missouri*. Norman, Oklahoma: University of Oklahoma Press, 1982.

Ramsay, Robert Lee. *Our Storehouse of Missouri Place Names*. Columbia: University of Missouri, 1952.

Selby, P. O. *A Bibliography of Missouri County Histories and Atlases*. 2nd ed. Kirksville, Missouri: Northeast Missouri State Teachers College, 1966.

Selby, Paul D. *Bibliography of Missouri County Histories and Atlases*. 2d ed. Kirksville, Missouri: Northeast Missouri State Teachers College, 1966.

Wetmore, Alphonso. *Gazetteer of the State of Missouri: with a Map of the State. . . . to Which is Added an Appendix, Containing Frontier Sketches, and Illustrations of Indian Character*. Reprint. New York: Arno Press, 1975.

Censuses

Available Census Records and Census Substitutes

Federal Census 1830, 1840, 1850, 1860, 1870, 1880, 1900, 1910, 1920, 1930

Federal Mortality Schedules 1850, 1860, 1870, 1880

Union Veterans and Widows 1890

State/Territorial Census 1876

Dollarhide, William. *The Census Book: A Genealogist's Guide to Federal Census Facts, Schedules and Indexes*. Bountiful, Utah: Heritage Quest, 1999.

Eddlemon, Sherida. *Ten Thousand Missouri Taxpayers*. Bowie, Maryland: Heritage Books, 1996.

Feldman, Lawrence H. *Anglo-Americans in Spanish Archives: Lists of Anglo-American Settlers in the Spanish Colonies of America; a Finding Aid*. Baltimore: Genealogical Publishing Co., 1991.

Kemp, Thomas Jay. *The American Census Handbook*. Wilmington, Delaware: Scholarly Resources, 2001.

Lainhart, Ann S. *State Census Records*. Baltimore: Genealogical Publishing Co., Inc., 1992.

Stanley, Lois. *Missouri Taxpayers, 1819–1826*. Greenville, South Carolina: Southern Historical Press, 1990.

Szucs, Loretto Dennis and Matthew Wright. *Finding Answers in U.S. Census Records*. Ancestry Publishing, 2001

Thorndale, William and William Dollarhide. *Map Guide to the U.S. Federal Census, 1790–1920*. Baltimore: Genealogical Publishing Co., 1987.

United States. Bureau of Internal Revenue. *Internal Revenue Assessment Lists for the State of Missouri, 1862–1866*. Washington, D.C.: National Archives and Records Services, 1984. 22 microfilm.

Court Records, Probate and Wills

Casselberry, Evans. *A Digest of All the Decisions of the Supreme Court of the State of Missouri, Contained in the First Fifteen Volumes of the Missouri Reports*. Saint Louis: Fisher & Bennett, 1853.

Northwest Missouri Genealogical Society. *Gentry County, Missouri Probate Index, 1885–1902*. St. Joseph, Missouri: the Society, n.d.

St. Louis (Missouri). Archival Library. *French and Spanish Archives, 1766–1816*. St. Louis, Missouri: City of St. Louis, 1962. 5 microfilm.

White, William D. *Preliminary Inventory of the Records of the United States Courts for the Western District of Missouri*. Kansas City, Missouri: Federal Records Center, 1969.

Emigration, Immigration, Migration and Naturalization

Brooks, Linda Barber. *Pioneer Kentuckians with Missouri Cousins*. 2 vols. St. Louis: Ingmire Publications, 1985.

Burnett, Robyn. *German Settlement in Missouri: New Land, Old Ways*. Columbia, Missouri: University of Missouri Press, 1996.

Coppage, A. Maxim and Dorothy Ford Wulfeck. *Virginia Settlers In Missouri*. Owensboro, Kentucky: Cook & McDowell Pub., 1979.

Gerlach, Russel L. *Settlement Patterns in Missouri, a Study of Population Origins, with a Wall Map*. Columbia, Missouri: University of Missouri Press, 1986.

Gerlach, Russel L. *Immigrants in the Ozarks: A Study in Ethnic Geography*. Columbia, Missouri: University of Missouri Press, 1976.

Kamphoefner, Walter D. *The Westfalians: From Germany to Missouri*. Princeton: Princeton University Press, 1987.

United States. Circuit Court (Missouri: Eastern Judicial District: Eastern Division: St. Louis). *Declarations of Intention, 1849–1911*. Salt Lake City: Filmed by the Genealogical Society of Utah, 1991. 5 microfilm.

United States. Circuit Court (Missouri: Western District: Western Division: Kansas City). *Declarations of Intention, 1906–1909*. Microfilm of originals in the National Archives Branch in Kansas City, Missouri. Salt Lake City: Filmed by the Genealogical Society of Utah, 1991.

United States. Circuit Court (Missouri: Western District: Western Division: Kansas City). *Declarations of Intention, 1910–1911*. Microfilm of originals in the National Archives Branch in Kansas City, Missouri. Salt Lake City: Filmed by the Genealogical Society of Utah, 1991.

United States. District Court (Missouri: Central Division). *Index to Naturalization Records, 1876–1906*. Microfilm of originals in the National Archives Branch in Kansas City, Missouri. Salt Lake City: Filmed by the Genealogical Society of Utah, 1991.

United States. District Court (Missouri: Eastern District: Eastern Division: St. Louis). *Naturalization Petitions, Depositions, and Miscellaneous Papers, 1912–1942; Naturalization Certificate Stubs, 1907–1926*. Microfilm of originals in the National Archives Branch in Kansas City, Missouri. Salt Lake City: Filmed by the Genealogical Society of Utah, 1991. 19 microfilm.

United States. District Court (Missouri: Northern Division). *Declarations of Intention, 1909–1929*. Microfilm of originals in the National Archives Branch in Kansas City, Missouri. Salt Lake City: Filmed by the Genealogical Society of Utah, 1991. 5 microfilm.

United States. District Court (Missouri: Northern Division). *Naturalization Petitions, 1907–1929; Naturalization Certificate Stubs, 1907–1929*. Microfilm of originals in the National Archives Branch in Kansas City, Missouri. Salt Lake City: Filmed by the Genealogical Society of Utah, 1991. 6 microfilm.

United States. District Court (Missouri: Southern Division). *Naturalization Petitions and Record, 1911–1937; Citizenship Petitions, 1930–1936; Naturalization Certificate Stubs, 1916–1927*. Microfilm of originals in the National Archives Branch in Kansas City, Missouri. Salt Lake City: Filmed by the Genealogical Society of Utah, 1991. 2 microfilm

United States. District Court (Missouri: Southern Division*). Declaration of Intention, 1895–1985*. Microfilm of originals in the National Archives Branch in Kansas City, Missouri. Salt Lake City: Filmed by the Genealogical Society of Utah, 1991.

United States. District Court (Missouri: Western District: Western Division: Kansas City). *Declarations of Intention, 1892–1936*. Microfilm of originals in the National Archives Branch in Kansas City, Missouri. Salt Lake City: Filmed by the Genealogical Society of Utah, 1991. 6 microfilm.

United States. District Court (Missouri: Western District: Western Division: Kansas City). *Naturalization Petitions, 1909–1929*. Microfilm of originals in the National Archives Branch in Kansas City, Missouri. Salt Lake City: Filmed by the Genealogical Society of Utah, 1991. 11 microfilm.

United States. District Court (Missouri: Western District: Western Division: Kansas City). *Naturalization Petitions and Records, 1920–1926*. Microfilm of originals in the National Archives Branch in Kansas City, Missouri. Salt Lake City: Filmed by the Genealogical Society of Utah, 1991. 8 microfilm.

United States. District Court (Missouri: Western District: Western Division: Kansas City). *Naturalization Petitions, 1929–1935*. Microfilm of originals in the National Archives Branch in Kansas City, Missouri. Salt Lake City: Filmed by the Genealogical Society of Utah, 1994. 4 microfilm.

Land and Property

Beahan, Gary W. *Missouri's Public Domain: United States Land Sales, 1818–1922*. Jefferson City, Missouri: Records Management and Archives Services, 1980.

Boekman, Laurel and Pat B. Weiner, comps. *Missouri Plat Books in the State Historical Society of Missouri*. Columbia, Missouri: State Historical Soc., 1992.

Dunaway, Maxine, comp. *Missouri Military Land Warrants, War of 1812*. Springfield, Missouri: Maxine Dunaway, 1985.

Ericson, Carolyn and Frances Ingmire. *First Settlers of the Missouri Territory*. 2 vols. Nacogdoches, Texas: Ericson Books, ca. 1983.

First Settlers of the Missouri Territory. 2 vols. Nacogdoches, Texas: Ericson Books, 1983.

Hone, Wade E. *Land and Property Research in the United States*. Salt Lake City: Ancestry Incorporated, 1997.

Ingmire, Frances Terry. *Citizens of Missouri*. 3 vols. St. Louis: Frances Ingmire, 1984.

Ingmire, Frances Terry. *Containing Grants in Present States of Missouri, Arkansas and Oklahoma*. St. Louis: the author, 1984.

Louisiana (Territory). Recorder of Land Titles. *Record Books, 1795–1808; Index to French and Spanish Land Grants, 1795– 1812*. Jefferson City, Missouri: State of Missouri, 1970.

Lowrie, Walter, ed. *Early Settlers of Missouri as Taken from Land Claims in the Missouri Territory*. Reprint. Easley, South Carolina: Southern Historical Press, 1986.

Lowrie, Walter, ed. *Land Claims in the Missouri Territory*. (1834) Reprint. Greenville, South Carolina: Southern Historical Press, 1986.

McMullin, Phillip, ed. *Grassroots of America*. Salt Lake City: Gendex Co., 1972.

Missouri Land Claims. 1835. Reprint. New Orleans: Polyanthos, 1976.

Missouri Plat Books in the State Historical Society of Missouri. Columbia, Missouri: State Historical Society, n.d.

Missouri. Governor. *Land Patents, 1800s to Early 1900s*. Jefferson City, Missouri: State of Missouri, 1971.

Missouri. Register of Lands. *Tax Deeds, 1847–1878*. Jefferson City, Missouri: State of Missouri, 1970. 7 microfilm.

Missouri. State Archives. *Miscellaneous Records Relating to Missouri Lands, 1700s, 1800s, 1900s*. Jefferson City, Missouri: State of Missouri, 1969–1972.

Stanley, Lois, George Wilson, and Maryhelen Wilson. *Missouri Taxpayers, 1819–1826*. Greenville, South Carolina: Southern Historical Press.

United States. Bureau of Land Management. *Card Files*. Washington, D.C.: Bureau of Land Management, 160 microfilm.

United States. District Court (Missouri). *Land Proceedings, 1824–1884*. Microfilm of originals in the National Archives Branch in Kansas City, Missouri. Salt Lake City: Filmed by the Genealogical Society of Utah, 1991. 2 microfilm.

United States. General Land Office. *Missouri Land Plats, 1800s*. Jefferson City, Missouri: State of Missouri, 1969.

United States. General Land Office. *Records Of Missouri Swamp Lands: Original Selections, New Selections, and Sales, 1800's*. Jefferson City, Missouri: State of Missouri, 1969. 9 microfilm.

United States. General Land Office. *Records of Missouri Swamp Lands: Original Selections, New Selections, and Sales, 1800's*. Jefferson City, Missouri: State of Missouri, 1969.

United States. General Land Office. *United States Land Sales in Missouri, 1827–1903; Index to Land Sales, 1818–1893*. Jefferson City, Missouri: State of Missouri, 1969.

United States. Veterans Administration. *War of 1812, Military Bounty Land Warrants, 1815–1858*. Washington, D.C.: The National Archives, 1971.

Military

Bartels, Carolyn M. *The Forgotten Men: Missouri State Guards*. Shawnee Mission, Kansas: Two Trails Pub., 1995.

Buss, Karen, comp. *An Every-Name Index to Revolutionary Soldiers and Their Descendants: Missouri Edition*. 1988. Burbank, California: Southern California Genealogical Society, 1988.

Concannon, Marie and Josiah Parkinson. *Grand Army of the Republic—Missouri Division—Index to Death Rolls, 1882–1940*. Columbia, Missouri: State Historical Society, 1995.

Houp, J. Randall. *The 24th Missouri Volunteer Infantry "Lyon Legion."* Alma, Arkansas: J. R. Houp, 1997.

Houts, Alice Kinyoun. *Revolutionary Soldiers Buried in Missouri*. Kansas City, Missouri: Houts, 1966.

Langley, Elizabeth B. *Taney County, Missouri Soldiers Who Fought in the Civil War Including Soldiers of Southwest Missouri and Northwest Arkansas: Also the Cherokees Under Stand Watie*. Billings, Missouri: Elizabeth B. Langley, 1963.

Military Records, 1812–1904. Microfilm of original records at the Missouri Department of Records and Archives, Jefferson City, Missouri. Salt Lake City: Filmed by the Genealogical Society of Utah, 1977–1978. 214 microfilm.

Missouri Confederate Pensions and Confederate Home Applications Index. Hillsboro, Texas: Confederate Research Center, 1996.

Missouri State Archives. *Guide to Military Records*. Jefferson City, Missouri: Missouri State Archives, 2002. Online guide—http://mosl.sos.state.mo.us/rec-man/archives/resources/resources.html.

Missouri. Adjutant General's Office. *Confederate Pension Applications and Soldiers' Home Admission Applications*. Microfilm of original records at the Missouri Department of Records and Archives, Jefferson

City, Missouri. Salt Lake City: Filmed by the Genealogical Society of Utah, 1977. 27 microfilm.

Missouri. Adjutant General's Office. *Military Records, 1812–1904*. Microfilm of original records at the Missouri Department of Records and Archives, Jefferson City, Mo. Salt Lake City: Filmed by the Genealogical Society of Utah, 1977–1978. 214 microfilm.

Missouri. Adjutant General's Office. *Military Records, 1861–1866*. Microfilm of original records at the Missouri Department of Records and Archives, Jefferson City, Mo. Salt Lake City: Filmed by the Genealogical Society of Utah, 1977. 19 microfilm.

Missouri. Adjutant General's Office. *Military Records, Spanish-American War, 1897–1898*. Microfilm of original records at the Missouri Department of Records and Archives, Jefferson City, Mo. Salt Lake City: Filmed by the Genealogical Society of Utah, 1977. 2 microfilm.

Sifakis, Stewart. *Compendium of the Confederate Armies: Kentucky, Maryland, Missouri, the Confederate Units and the Indian Units*. Galveston, Texas: Frontier press, 1995.

State Historical Society of Missouri (Columbia, Missouri). *Index of Residents State Federal Soldiers' Home of Missouri, St. James, Missouri, 1899–1946*. Columbia, Missouri: State Historical Society of Missouri, 1998.

United States. Adjutant General's Office. *Index to Compiled Service Records of Volunteer Union Soldiers Who Served in Organizations from the State of Missouri*. Washington, D.C.: The National Archives, 1962.

United States. Selective Service System. *Missouri, World War I Selective Service System Draft Registration Cards, 1917–1918. National Archives Microfilm Publications, M1509*. Washington, D.C.: National Archives, 1987–1988.

Weant, Kenneth. *The Mexican War, Index to Missouri Militia Volunteers 1*. Kenneth Weant. 2005.

Vital and Cemetery Records

Blattner, Teresa. *Divorces, Separations and Annulments in Missouri 1769 To 1850*. Bowie, Maryland: Heritage Books, 1993.

Brooks, Linda B. *Missouri Marriages to 1850*. 3 vols. St. Louis: Distributed by Ingmire Publishing, 1983.

Campbell, Kathryn H.. *Early Bible and Graveyard Records*. 2 vols. Dallas, Texas: the author, 1972–1974.

Carter, Mrs. J. R. *Early Missouri Marriages to 1840*. 3 vols. Sedalia: Mrs. J. R. Carter, n.d.

Cemetery Records of Missouri. 15 vols. Salt Lake City: Genealogical Society of Utah, 1973.

East Central Missouri Cemetery and Bible Records. 3 vols. Afton, Missouri: John Sappington Chapter, Daughters of the American Revolution, 1974.

Eddlemon, Sherida. *Missouri Birth and Death Records*, 3 vols. Bowie, Maryland: Heritage Books, 2001.

Ellsberry, Elizabeth P. *Bible Records of Missouri*. 8 vols. in 3. Chillicothe, Missouri: Elizabeth P. Ellsberry, 1963.

Ellsberry, Elizabeth P. *Cemetery Records of Missouri*. 3 vols. Chillicothe, Missouri: Elizabeth P. Ellsberry, 1965.

Guide to Public Vital Statistics Records in Missouri. St. Louis: Historical Records Survey, 1941.

Hodges, Nadine, Mrs. John Vineyard, and Mrs. Howard W. Woodruff. *Missouri Pioneers, County and Genealogical Records*. 30 vols. Independence, Missouri: the authors, 1967–.

Kot and Thompson. *Missouri Cemetery Inscription Sources: Print & Microform*. Galveston, Texas: Frontier Press, 1995.

Langley, Elizabeth B. *Bible Records of Missouri*. 3 vols. Billings, Missouri: Elizabeth B. Langley, 1968.

Liahona Research. *Missouri Marriages, Early [ca. 1754] to 1825: A Research Tool*. Bountiful, Utah: Precision Indexing, 1990.

Liahona Research. *Missouri Marriages, 1826 to 1850*. Salt Lake City: AGLL, 1993.

Missouri Cemetery Records. Vol. 1. Kansas City, Missouri: Heart of America Genealogical Society & Library, 1981.

Missouri Mortality Schedules, 1850–1880. Columbia, Missouri: State Historical Society of Missouri. 8 microfilm.

Missouri State Archives. *Guide to Birth and Death Records*. Jefferson City, Missouri: Missouri State Archives, 2002. Online guide—http://mosl.sos.state .mo.us/rec-man/archives/resources/resources.html

Missouri, 1851–1900. S.l.: Brøderbund, 1998. CD-ROM.

Ormesher, Susan. *Missouri Marriages Before 1840*. Baltimore: Genealogical Publishing Co., 1982.

Parker, Ed., comp. *Union Burials—Missouri Units*. 3 vols. Columbia, Missouri: State Historical Society, 1988, 1989, 1993.

Pompey, Sherman L. *List of Missouri Civil War Veteran Burials*. Microfilm. Salt Lake City: Genealogical Society of Utah, 1967.

Stanley, Lois, George F. Wilson, and Maryhelen Wilson. *More Death Records from Missouri Newspapers, 1810–1857*. (1985) Reprint. Greenville, South Carolina, Southern Historical Press, 1990.

Stanley, Lois, George F. Wilson, and Maryhelen Wilson. *1300 "Missing" Missouri Marriage Records from Newspapers, 1812–1853*. (1979) Reprint. Greenville, South Carolina: Southern Historical Press, 1990.

Stanley, Lois, George F. Wilson, and Maryhelen Wilson. *Death Records from the Missouri Newspapers: The Civil War Years, Jan. 1861 to Dec. 1865*. (1983) Reprint, Greenville, South Carolina: Southern Historical Press.

Stanley, Lois, George F. Wilson, and Maryhelen Wilson. *Death Records from Missouri Newspapers, Jan. 1866 to Dec. 1870*. (1984) Reprint. Greenville, South Carolina: Southern Historical Press, 1990.

Stanley, Lois, George F. Wilson, and Maryhelen Wilson. *Death Records of Missouri Men, 1808–1854*. (1981) Reprint. Greenville, South Carolina: Southern Historical Press, 1990.

Stanley, Lois, George F. Wilson, and Maryhelen Wilson. *Death Records of Pioneer Missouri Women, 1808–1853*. (1984) Reprint. Greenville, South Carolina: Southern Historical Press, 1990.

Stanley, Lois, George F. Wilson, and Maryhelen Wilson. *Divorces and Separations in Missouri, 1808–1853*. Greenville, South Carolina: Southern Historical Press, 1990.

Stanley, Lois, George F. Wilson, and Maryhelen Wilson. *Early Missouri Ancestors, Vol. I: From Newspapers, 1808–1822*. (1985) Reprint. Greenville, South Carolina: Southern Historical Press, 1990.

Stanley, Lois, George F. Wilson, and Maryhelen Wilson. *Early Missouri Ancestors, Vol. II: From Newspapers, 1823–1832*. (1987) Reprint. Greenville, South Carolina: Southern Historical Press, 1990.

Stanley, Lois, George F. Wilson, and Maryhelen Wilson. *Early Missouri Marriages in the News, 1820–1853*. (1985) Reprint. Greenville, South Carolina: Southern Historical Press, 1990.

Stanley, Lois, George F. Wilson, and Maryhelen Wilson. *Missouri Marriages in the News, 1851–1865*. (1983) Reprint. Greenville, South Carolina: Southern Historical Press, 1990.

Stanley, Lois, George F. Wilson, and Maryhelen Wilson. *Missouri Marriages in the News, Vol. II, 1866–1870*. (1984) Reprint. Greenville, South Carolina: Southern Historical Press, 1990.

Stanley, Lois, George F. Wilson, and Maryhelen Wilson. *Missouri Taxpayers, 1819–1826*. (1979) Reprint. Greenville, South Carolina: Southern Historical Press, 1990.

Stanley, Lois., George F. Wilson, and Maryhelen Wilson. *Death Records from Missouri Newspapers, January 1854 to December 1860*. (1982) Reprint. Greenville, South Carolina: Southern Historical Press, 1990.

County Website	Map Index	Date Created	Parent County or Territory From Which Organized Address/Details
Adair www.rootsweb.com/~moadair/	I2	29 Jan 1841	**Macon** Adair County; 106 W Washington St; Kirksville, MO 63501; Ph. (660) 665-3350 **Details:** (County Recorder has Marriage & Land Records from 1840; Clerk Circuit Court has Divorce & Court Records; Probate Clerk has Probate Records; County Clerk has school enumeration Records)
Allen		23 Feb 1843	**Holt** Allen County; MO **Details:** (see Atchison) Name changed to Atchison 14 Feb 1845
Andrew www.rootsweb.com/~moandrew/index.html	N2	29 Jan 1841	**Platte Purchase** Andrew County; 411 Court St; Savannah, MO 64485-0206; Ph. (816) 324-3624 **Details:** (County Clerk has Birth & Death Records 1883–1893; Clerk Circuit Court has Marriage, Divorce & Court Records from 1841, Land & Military Records; Probate Judge has Probate Records from 1841)
Arkansas		1813	**New Madrid** Arkansas County; MO **Details:** (abolished 1819 when Territory of Arkansas was formed)
Ashley		17 Feb 1843	**Shannon, Wright** Ashley County; MO **Details:** (see Texas) Name changed to Texas 14 Feb 1845
Atchison www.rootsweb.com/~moatchis/atchison.html	O2	23 Feb 1843	**Holt** Atchison County; 400 S Washington St; Rock Port, MO 64482; Ph. (660) 744-6214 **Details:** (Formerly Allen County. Name changed to Atchison 14 Feb 1845; part of Platte Purchase; attached to Holt County until 1854; lost 10-mile strip to Iowa in 1848) (County Recorder has Marriage & Land Records; Clerk Circuit Court has Death, Divorce & Court Records; County Clerk has Birth Records 1883–1893; Probate Judge has Probate Records)
Audrain www.audrain-county.org/	H4	12 Jan 1831	**Ralls** Audrain County; 101 N Jefferson; Mexico, MO 65265; Ph. (573) 473-5820 **Details:** (Created in 1831, but remained attached to Callaway, Monroe & Ralls Counties until 1836. In 1842 gained an additional 31 sq. miles from Monroe County) (County Clerk has Birth Records 1883–1886; Recorder Deeds has Marriage & Land Records; Clerk Circuit Court has Divorce & Court Records; Probate Judge has Probate Records)
Barry www.rootsweb.com/~mobarry/barry.htm	L11	5 Jan 1835	**Greene** Barry County; 700 Main St; Cassville, MO 65625; Ph. (417) 847-2561 **Details:** (Fire in 1872 destroyed many Records in Circuit Clerks office) (Recorder Deeds has Marriage & Land Records; Clerk Circuit Court has Divorce & Court Records; Probate Judge has Probate Records)
Barton www.rootsweb.com/~mobarton/	M9	12 Dec 1855	**Jasper** Barton County; 1004 Gulf St; Lamar, MO 64759; Ph. (417) 682-3529 **Details:** (Courthouse burned in 1860) (County Clerk has Birth Records 1883–1897 & Death Records 1883–1899; Recorder Deeds has Divorce & Land Records; Probate Court has Probate Records; Magistrate Court, division 2, has Court Records)

County Website	Map Index	Date Created	Parent County or Territory From Which Organized Address/Details
Bates www.rootsweb.com/~mobates/index.htm	M7	29 Jan 1841	**Cass, Van Buren, Jackson** Bates County; 1 N Delaware St; Butler, MO 64730; Ph. (660) 679-3371 **Details:** (22 Feb 1855 the three southern tiers of townships in Cass County were added to Bates; Courthouse burned in 1861) (County Clerk has Birth & Death Records 1883–1887; County Recorder has Marriage Records from 1860 & Land Records from 1840; Clerk Circuit Court has Divorce Records from 1860; Probate Judge has Probate Records)
Benton http://members.aol.com/hrftx/index.htm	K7	3 Jan 1835	**Pettis, St. Clair** Benton County; PO Box 1238; Warsaw, MO 65355-1238; Ph. (660) 438-7326 **Details:** (Benton remained unorganized until Jan 1837; in 1845, 24 sq. miles of northwest part of Benton became part of Pettis County & Hickory County was created, reducing Benton to its present size) (County Clerk has Birth & Death Records from 1883 & Marriage Records from 1839; Clerk Circuit Court has Divorce & Court Records; Probate Court has Probate Records; Recorder Deeds has Land Records)
Bollinger www.rootsweb.com/~mobollin/	D9	1 Mar 1851	**Cape Girardeau, Stoddard, Wayne** Bollinger County; 204 High St; Marble Hill, MO 63764-0046; Ph. (573) 238-2126 **Details:** (Courthouse burned in 1866; Courthouse burned in 1884 while occupied only by the County Clerks office) (County Clerk has Birth & Death Records 1882–1892; Clerk Circuit Court & Recorder has Marriage, Divorce & Land Records; Circuit Judge has Probate Records)
Boone www.showmeboone.com/	I5	16 Nov 1820	**Howard** Boone County; 600 E Broadway; Columbia, MO 65201; Ph. (573) 874-7345 **Details:** (County Clerk has Marriage, Divorce, Probate, Court & Land Records from 1821)
Buchanan www.co.buchanan.mo.us/	N3	31 Dec 1838	**Platte Purchase** Buchanan County; 5th & Jules; St. Joseph, MO 64501; Ph. (816) 271-1412 **Details:** (Recorder Deeds has Marriage Records; Clerk Circuit Court has Divorce Records; Probate Judge has Probate Records; Magistrate Court has Court Records; County Assessor has Land Records)
Butler www.rootsweb.com/~mobutle2/index.html	E11	27 Feb 1849	**Wayne** Butler County; 100 N Main St; Poplar Bluff, MO 63901; Ph. (573) 686-8050 **Details:** (Recorder Deeds has Marriage & Land Records from 1849; Probate Court has Probate Records from 1849; County Clerk has Birth & Death Records 1883–1893)
Caldwell http://members.aol.com/TerR001/Caldwell/caldwell.htm	L3	29 Dec 1836	**Ray** Caldwell County; 49 E Main St; PO Box 67; Kingston, MO 64650-0067; Ph. (816) 586-2571 **Details:** (19 April 1860 courthouse destroyed by fire; all Records destroyed except those of the Probate Court; 28 Nov 1896 courthouse destroyed by fire) (Recorder Office has Marriage & Land Records; Clerk Circuit Court has Divorce Records; Circuit Court, division 2, has Probate Records; Circuit Court, division 1, has Court Records)

County Website	Map Index	Date Created	Parent County or Territory From Which Organized Address/Details
Callaway www.rootsweb.com/~missour/	**H6**	**25 Nov 1820**	**Montgomery** Callaway County; 10 E 5th St; Fulton, MO 65251-1700; Ph. (573) 642-0730 **Details:** (County Clerk has Birth & Death Records 1883–1888; County Recorder has Marriage & Land Records; Clerk Circuit Court has Divorce Records; Probate Judge has Probate Records)
Camden www.rootsweb.com/~mocamden/page1.htm	**J7**	**29 Jan 1841**	**Benton, Pulaski** Camden County; 1 Court Circuit; Camdenton, MO 65020; Ph. (573) 346-4440 **Details:** (Formerly Kinderhook County. Name changed to Camden 23 Feb 1843; line between Camden & Miller changed 1845; Courthouse burned 1902) (County Recorder has Marriage & Divorce Records from 1902; Probate Judge has Probate Records from 1902; Clerk Circuit Court has Court Records from 1902; Tompkins Abstract Office has Land Records)
Cape Girardeau C9 www.showme.net/CapeCounty/		**1804**	**Original District** Cape Girardeau County Archive Center; 112 E Washington; Jackson, MO 63755; Ph. (573) 243-3547 **Details:** (Present size of county since 5 Mar 1849; Courthouse burned in 1870) (County Archive Center has all Government Records from 1797–2000; County Clerk has Birth & Death Records 1883–1893, School, Military, Naturalization, Maps, Marriage, Territorial, & Tax Records; Records has Deed Records)
Carroll http://us-gen.com/mo/carroll/	**K4**	**2 Jan 1833**	**Ray** Carroll County; County Courthouse; Carrollton, MO 64633; Ph. (816) 542-0615 **Details:** (County Clerk has Birth Records 1883–1895 & Death Records 1883–1890; Clerk Circuit Court has Divorce & Court Records from 1833 & Naturalization Records 1843–1919; Recorder Deeds has Marriage Records, Land Records from 1833; Probate Office has Probate Records)
Carter www.rootsweb.com/~mocarter/	**F10**	**10 Mar 1859**	**Ripley, Shannon** Carter County; 105 Main St; Van Buren, MO 63965-0517; Ph. (573) 323-4527 **Details:** (Recorder of Deeds has Marriage & Land Records; Probate Court has Probate Records from 1859)
Cass www.casscounty.com/	**M6**	**3 Mar 1835**	**Jackson** Cass County; 102 E Wall St; Harrisonville, MO 64701; Ph. (816) 380-8102 **Details:** (Formerly Van Buren County. Name changed to Cass 19 Feb 1849; three southern tiers of townships relinquished to Bates 22 Feb 1855) (County Clerk has Birth Records 1861–1896 & Court Records from 1843; Recorder Deeds has Marriage, Divorce & Land Records; Associate Division has Probate Records)
Cedar www.rootsweb.com/~mocedar/index.htm	**L8**	**14 Feb 1845**	**Dade, St Clair** Cedar County; 113 South St; PO Box 158; Stockton, MO 65785-0126; Ph. (417) 276-3514 **Details:** (County Clerk has Marriage, Divorce & Land Records from 1845, Probate & Court Records)

County Website	Map Index	Date Created	Parent County or Territory From Which Organized Address/Details
Chariton	J4	16 Nov 1820	**Howard** Chariton County; 306 S Cherry; Keytesville, MO 65261; Ph. (660) 288-3273 **Details:** (Courthouse burned 20 Sept 1864; only a few Records lost) (County Clerk has Birth & Death Records 1883–1887; Circuit Court Clerk-Recorder has Marriage Records from 1821, Divorce & Court Records from 1872, Land Records from 1827, Naturalization Records from 1877 & Military Discharge Records from 1918; Circuit Court-Probate Division has Probate Records from 1860)
Christian www.rootsweb.com/~mochrist/	K10	8 Mar 1859	**Greene, Taney, Webster** Christian County; 100 W Church; PO Box 278; Ozark, MO 65721; Ph. (417) 581-6372 **Details:** (Courthouse burned 1865) (County Clerk has Birth Records 1840–1904 & Death Records 1883–1884; Circuit Court Clek has Marriage Records from 1866, Land Records from 1861, Probate Records from 1864, Court Records from 1865, & Divorce Records)
Clark www.rootsweb.com/~moclark/clark.htm	H2	16 Dec 1836	**Lewis** Clark County; 111 E Court St; Kahoka, MO 63445-1268; Ph. (660) 727-3283 **Details:** (County Clerk has Marriage, Divorce, Probate, Court & Land Records from 1836)
Clark (old)		1818	**Arkansas** Clark (old) County; MO; **Details:** (never organized; abolished in 1819 when Territory of Arkansas was created)
Clay www.claycogov.com/	M4	2 Jan 1822	**Ray** Clay County; 1 Courthouse Sq; Liberty, MO 64086; Ph. (816) 792-7637 **Details:** (Recorder Deeds has Marriage & Land Records; Clerk Circuit Court has Divorce & Court Records from 1822; Probate Court has Probate Records)
Clinton www.rootsweb.com/~moclinto/	M3	2 Jan 1833	**Clay** Clinton County; 211 N Main St; PO Box 245; Plattsburg, MO 64477-0245; Ph. (816) 539-3719 **Details:** (County Clerk has Marriage, Divorce, Court & Land Records from 1833 & Military Records from 1919; Probate Judge has Probate Records)
Cole www.rootsweb.com/~mocole/cole.html	I6	16 Nov 1820	**Cooper** Cole County; 301 E High St; Jefferson City, MO 65101; Ph. (573) 634-9100 **Details:** (Clerk Circuit Court has Divorce & Court Records from 1821; Probate Judge has Probate Records from 1821; Recorder Deeds has Marriage & Land Records from 1821)
Cooper www.rootsweb.com/~mocooper/index.html	J5	17 Dec 1818	**Howard** Cooper County; 200 Main St; PO Box 123; Boonville, MO 65233-0123; Ph. (660) 882-2626 **Details:** (County Clerk has Birth & Death Records 1883–1893 & Burial Records; Circuit Clerk & Recorder has Marriage, Divorce, Court & Naturalization Records from 1819 & Land Records from 1812; Associate Circuit Court has Probate Records from 1828)

County Website	Map Index	Date Created	Parent County or Territory From Which Organized Address/Details
Crawford www.rootsweb.com/~mocrawfo/index.html	G7	23 Jan 1829	**Gasconade** Crawford County; 302 W Main St; Steelville, MO 65565; Ph. (573) 775-2376 **Details:** (1829–1835 County Court Records lost; Courthouse burned 15 Feb 1873; Courthouse burned 5 Jan 1884) (County Clerk has Marriage, Divorce, Court & Land Records from 1832; Probate Judge has Probate Records from 1889)
Dade www.rootsweb.com/~modade/modade.htm	L9	29 Jan 1841	**Greene** Dade County; Main St; Greenfield, MO 65661; Ph. (417) 637-2724 **Details:** (lost 10-mile strip on northern boundary to Cedar County & 9-mile strip on southern boundary to Lawrence, reducing it to its present size 28 Mar 1845; Courthouse burned in 1863, but no Records lost) (County Recorder has Marriage Records from 1867 & Land Records; Clerk Circuit Court has Divorce Records from 1867; Probate Judge has Probate & Court Records)
Dallas www.rootsweb.com/~modallas/	J8	29 Jan 1841	**Polk** Dallas County; 107 Maple St; PO Box 436; Buffalo, MO 65622-0436; Ph. (417) 345-2632 **Details:** (Formerly Niangua County. Name changed to Dallas 16 Dec 1844; Courthouse burned 18 Oct 1863; second courthouse burned 30 Jul 1864 & Records destroyed; the replaced Records were burned 3 Sep 1867) (County Recorder has Birth, Marriage, Death, Burial, Divorce, Probate, Court & Land Records)
Daviess www.rootsweb.com/~modavies/daviess.htm	L3	29 Dec 1836	**Ray** Daviess County; 102 N Main St; Gallatin, MO 64640; Ph. (660) 663-2641 **Details:** (County Library has Birth & Death Records on microfilm 1883–1893 & local census 1876; Recorder of Deeds has Land Records; Probate Court has Probate Records)
De Kalb www.rootsweb.com/~modekalb/index.html	M3	1843	**Clinton** De Kalb County; 109 W Main St; PO Box 248; Maysville, MO 64469-0248; Ph. (816) 449-5402 **Details:** (Courthouse burned in 1878, many Records lost, but Records of Circuit Clerks Office were preserved along with a few Records from other offices) (County Recorder has Marriage & Divorce Records; County Clerk has Birth Records 1880–1902; Probate Judge has Probate Records)
Decatur		1843	**Ozark** Decatur; MO **Details:** Decatur was a temporary name for Ozark County 1843–1845
Dent www.rootsweb.com/~modent/index.html	G8	10 Feb 1851	**Crawford, Shannon** Dent County; 400 N Main St; Salem, MO 6556; Ph. (573) 729-4144 **Details:** (Courthouse burned in 1864 destroying some Records) (Clerk Circuit Court has Marriage, Divorce & Court Records; Clerk Magistrate Court has Probate Records; County Recorder has Land Records)

County Website	Map Index	Date Created	Parent County or Territory From Which Organized Address/Details
Dodge		1853	**Putnam** Dodge County; MO **Details:** (Discontinued in 1853; had lost Territory when Iowa boundary was established 13 Feb 1849, bringing its area below the constitutional limit of 400 sq miles; its Territory was added to Putnam County 16 Mar 1853)
Douglas www.rootsweb.com/~modougla/doug.htm	I10	29 Oct 1857	**Ozark, Taney** Douglas County; 203 SE 2nd Ave; PO Box 398; Ava, MO 65608; Ph. (417) 683-4714 **Details:** (Territory. increased in 1864 by addition of portions of Taney & Webster Counties) (Clerk Circuit Court & Recorder has Marriage, Divorce & Court Records; Probate & Magistrate Judge has Probate Records)
Dunklin www.rootsweb.com/~modunkl2/dcgenweb.htm	D12	14 Feb 1845	**Stoddard** Dunklin County; PO Box 188; Kennett, MO 63857-0188; Ph. (573) 888-2796 **Details:** (In 1853 a strip one mile wide was taken from Stoddard & added to northern boundary of Dunklin County; Courthouse burned in 1872; all Records lost) (Recorder Deeds has Marriage & Land Records; Clerk Circuit Court has Divorce & Court Records; Probate Judge has Probate Records)
Franklin	F6	11 Dec 1818	**St. Louis** Franklin County; 300 E Main St., Rm 301; Union, MO 63084-0311; Ph. (636) 583-6303 **Details:** (Boundaries not accurately defined until 1845) (County Health Department has Birth & Death Records; County Clerk has Divorce Records; Recorder of Deeds has Land Records; Marriage Licensing Department has Marriage Records; Probate Office has Probate Records; County Assesssor has Tax Records)
Gasconade www.rootsweb.com/~mogascon/index.html	G6	25 Nov 1820	**Franklin** Gasconade County; 119 E 1st St #2; PO Box 295; Hermann, MO 65041; Ph. (573) 486-5427, gchsarc@ktis.net; Gasconade County Historical Society; 315 Schiller St; PO Box 131; Hermann, MO 65041; Ph. (573) 486-4028 **Details:** (In 1869 relinquished 36 sq. miles to Crawford County) (County Historical Society Archives & Records Center has All Historical Records)
Gentry www.rootsweb.com/~mogentry/index.html	M2	12 Feb 1841	**Clinton** Gentry County; 200 Clay St; Albany, MO 64402-1499; Ph. (660) 726-3525 **Details:** (Organization completed 1843; courthouse burned 1885) (County Clerk has Birth & Death Records 1883–1893 & Marriage Records from 1885; Clerk Circuit Court has Divorce, Court & Land Records from 1885; Circuit Court, division 2, has Probate Records from 1885)
Greene www.greenecountymo.org/	K9	2 Jan 1833	**Crawford** Greene County; 940 Boonville Ave; Springfield, MO 65802; Ph. (417) 868-4068 **Details:** (Courthouse burned 1861; few Records lost) (County Archives & Records Center has Probate, Court, tax & Land Records from 1833, Military Discharge Records, Divorce Records 1837–1950, Birth & Death Records 1883–1890 & 1876 local Census Records)

County Website	Map Index	Date Created	Parent County or Territory From Which Organized Address/Details
Grundy	K2	29 Jan 1841	**Livingston** Grundy County; 700 Main St; Trenton, MO 64683; Ph. (660) 359-6305 countyclerk@grundycountymo.com **Details:** (County Clerk has Birth & Death Records 1883–1893, then from 1910, Burial Records, & Tax Records from 1900; Circuit Clerk has Court & Divorce Records from 1841, Immigration & Naturalization Records; County Recorder has Land & Marriage Records from 1841; Probate Clerk has Probate Records from 1864; Jewett Norris Library has Newspapers & Census)
Harrison www.rootsweb.com/~moharris/index.html	L1	14 Feb 1845	**Daviess** Harrison County; 1500 Central St; Bethany, MO 64424; Ph. (660) 425-6424 **Details:** (Courthouse burned Jan 1874, most Records saved; tax Records destroyed) (County Clerk has some Birth Records 1883–1893; Clerk Circuit Court has Marriage & Divorce Records from 1858 & Court Records from 1845; Probate Judge has Probate Records from 1853)
Hempstead		1819	**Arkansas** Hempstead County; MO **Details:** (abolished 1819 when Territory of Arkansas was created)
Henry www.rootsweb.com/~mohenry/henryco.html	L6	13 Dec 1834	**Lafayette** Henry County; Main & Franklin Sts; 100 W Franklin; Clinton, MO 64735-2199; Ph. (660) 885-6963 **Details:** (Formerly Rives County. Name changed to Henry 15 Feb 1841) (County Recorder has Marriage & Land Records from 1830 & Military Discharge Records; County Clerk has Divorce & Court Records; Associate Circuit Court has Probate Records; County Museum has Birth & Burial Records)
Hickory www.rootsweb.com/~mohickor/index.html	K7	14 Feb 1845	**Benton, Polk** Hickory County; PO Box 3; Hermitage, MO 65668; Ph. (417) 745-6450 **Details:** (Courthouse burned 1852 & 1881; many Records lost) (County Clerk has Birth Records 1883–1898; Clerk Circuit Court has Marriage Records from 1872, Divorce & Court Records from 1858; Probate Judge has Probate Records from 1845)
Highland		1843	Highalnd; MO **Details:** Name changed 1845 to Sullivan County
Holt www.geocities.com/Heartland/Plains/4280/HOLTCTY.html	O2	29 Jan 1841	**Platte Purchase** Holt County; 100 W Nodaway St; Oregon, MO 64473; Ph. (660) 446-3303 **Details:** (Formerly Nodaway County. Name changed to Holt 15 Feb 1841. Courthouse burned 30 Jan 1965; most Records undamaged) (County Clerk has incomplete Birth & Death Records 1883–1893, Marriage, Divorce & Land Records from 1841; Clerk Circuit Court has Court Records from 1841; Probate Judge has Probate Records from 1849)

County Website	Map Index	Date Created	Parent County or Territory From Which Organized Address/Details
Howard www.rootsweb.com/~mohoward/	I5	13 Jan 1816	**St. Charles, St. Louis** Howard County; #1 Courthouse Sq; Fayette, MO 65248; Ph. (660) 248-2194 **Details:** (Courthouse burned 1887; few Records lost) (Circuit Clerk & Recorder have Cemetery Books, Military Discharge Records, Marriage & Land Records from 1816, & Circuit Court Records; Probate Clerk has Probate Records from 1835; County Health Nurse has Birth & Death Records)
Howell www.rootsweb.com/~mohowell/intro.htm	H10	2 Mar 1857	**Oregon, Ozark** Howell County; County Courthouse Sq; West Plains, MO 65775; Ph. (417) 256-2591 **Details:** (Courthouse destroyed during Civil War) (County Clerk has Birth Records 1883–1895 & Death Records 1883–1893; Circuit Clerk & Recorder Deeds has Marriage, Divorce, Court & Land Records; Associate Circuit Court has Probate Records)
Iron www.rootsweb.com/~moiron2/index.htm	F8	17 Feb 1857	**Dent, Madison, Reynolds, St. Francis, Washington, Wayne** Iron County; 250 S Main St; PO Box 42; Ironton, MO 63650; Ph. (573) 546-2912 **Details:** (County Clerk has Birth Records 1883–1885, Marriage, Divorce, Probate & Land Records)
Jackson www.co.jackson.mo.us/	M5	15 Dec 1826	**Lafayette** Jackson County; 415 E 12th St; Kansas City, MO 64106-2706; Ph. (816) 881-3333 **Details:** (Nearly all its Territory was acquired from Osage & Kansas Indians 2 Jun 1825) (Department of Records has Marriage & Land Records; Court Administration has Divorce & Court Records; Probate Judge has Probate Records)
Jasper www.rootsweb.com/~mojasper/jcpage.htm	M9	29 Jan 1841	**Newton** Jasper County; 302 S Main St; Carthage, MO 64836-1696; Ph. (417) 358-0441 **Details:** (Courthouse destroyed in 1863; Records had been removed & were returned in 1865; Couthouse burned in 1883; no mention of fate of Records) (County Clerk has Birth Records 1883–1900 & Death Records 1883–1891; Recorder Deeds has Marriage & Land Records; Probate Judge has Probate & Court Records)
Jefferson www.jeffcomo.org/	E6	8 Dec 1818	**Ste. Genevieve, St. Louis** Jefferson County; 300 2nd St; PO Box 100; Hillsboro, MO 63050-0100; Ph. (636) 797-5478 **Details:** (Recorder Deeds has Marriage & Land Records; Probate Court has Probate Records; Clerk Circuit Court has Court Records)
Johnson www.rootsweb.com/~mojohnso/	L6	13 Dec 1834	**Lafayette** Johnson County; 300 N Holden St; Warrensburg, MO 64093; Ph. (660) 747-6161 **Details:** (County Clerk has Birth & Death Records 1883–1893; Recorder of Deeds has Marriage & Land Records from 1835; Clerk Circuit Court has Divorce & Court Records from late 1860's; Probate Judge has Probate Records from mid-1800's)
Kinderhook		29 Jan 1841	**Benton, Pulaski** Kinderhook County; MO **Details:** (see Camden) Name changed to Camden 23 Feb 1843

County	Map	Date	Parent County or Territory From Which Organized
Website	Index	Created	Address/Details

Knox   H2   **14 Feb 1845**   **Scotland**
www.rootsweb.com/~moknox/index.htm
Knox County; 107 N 4th St; Edina, MO 63537; Ph. (660) 397-2184
Details: (County Recorder has Marriage, Divorce & Land Records; Associate Circuit Judge has Probate & Court Records; Historical Society in Courthouse has Birth & Death Records 1883–1890)

Laclede   I8   **24 Feb 1849**   **Camden, Pulaski, Wright**
http://laclede.county.missouri.org/
Laclede County; 200 N Adams Ave; Lebanon, MO 65536; Ph. (417) 532-5471
Details: (County Recorder has Marriage Records; Clerk Circuit Court has Divorce & Court Records; Probate Judge has Probate Records; County Assessor has Land Records)

Lafayette   L5   **16 Nov 1820**   **Cooper**
http://members.aol.com/TerR001/Lafayette/lafayette.htm
Lafayette County; 1001 Main St; PO Box 357; Lexington, MO 64067; Ph. (660) 259-4315
Details: (Formerly Lillard County. Name changed to Lafayette 16 Feb 1825) (County Recorder has Marriage, Divorce, Probate, Court & Land Records from 1821)

Lawrence   L9   **14 Feb 1845**   **Barry, Dade**
www.rootsweb.com/~molawre2/
Lawrence County; PO Box 309; Mount Vernon, MO 65712; Ph. (417) 466-2638
Details: (Recorder Deeds has Marriage & Land Records from 1846; Clerk Circuit Court has Divorce & Court Records from 1846; Probate Judge has Probate Records from 1846)

Lawrence (old)   **1 Mar 1815**   **New Madrid**
Lawrence, old County; MO
Details: (lost Territory to Wayne 1 Feb 1819. Abolished 16 Feb 1825)

Lewis   G2   **2 Jan 1833**   **Marion**
www.rootsweb.com/~molewis/
Lewis County; 100 E Lafayette St; Monticello, MO 63457; Ph. (573) 767-5205
Details: (Clerk Circuit Court has Marriage, Divorce & Land Records; Probate Judge has Probate & Court Records)

Lillard   **16 Nov 1820**   **Cooper**
Lillard County; MO
Details: (see Lafayette) Name changed to Lafayette 16 Feb 1825

Lincoln   F5   **14 Dec 1818**   **St. Charles**
www.rootsweb.com/~molincol/molincoln.htm
Lincoln County; 201 Main St; Troy, MO 63379; Ph. (636) 528-4415
Details: (County Recorder has Marriage Records from 1825, Land, Death & Burial Records; Probate Judge has Probate Records from 1823; Clerk Circuit Court has Divorce Records)

Linn   J3   **6 Jan 1837**   **Chariton**
www.rootsweb.com/~molinn/linn.html
Linn County; 108 N High; Linneus, MO 64653; Ph. (660) 895-5417
Details: (County Clerk has incomplete Birth & Death Records 1883–1888; County Recorder has Marriage & Land Records from 1842; Clerk Circuit Court has Divorce Records from 1837; Probate Office has Probate Records from 1840)

Livingston   K3   **6 Jan 1837**   **Carroll**
www.greenhills.net/~fwoods/
Livingston County; 700 Webster St; Chillicothe, MO 64601; Ph. (660) 646-2293
Details: (County Clerk has Birth & Death Records; Recorder Deeds has Marriage & Land Records; Probate Court has Probate Records; Clerk Circuit Court has Court Records)

County Website	Map Index	Date Created	Parent County or Territory From Which Organized Address/Details
Macon www.rootsweb.com/~momacon/	I3	**6 Jan 1837**	**Randolph** Macon County; 101 E Washington St; Macon, MO 63552-0096; Ph. (660) 385-2913 **Details:** (County Clerk has Birth & Death Records 1883–1893; County Recorder has Marriage & Land Records; Clerk Circuit Court has Divorce Records; Circuit Court, division 2, has Probate Records)
Madison www.pastracks.com/states/missouri/madison/	E9	**14 Dec 1818**	**Cape Girardeau, Ste. Genevieve** Madison County; 1 Courthouse Sq; Fredericktown, MO 63645; Ph. (573) 783-2176 **Details:** (County Clerk has Birth & Death Records 1883–1900 & local Census 1876; Clerk Circuit Court has Marriage, Divorce & Court Records from 1821 & Military Discharge Records from 1943; County Magistrate has Probate Records from 1820; County Assessor has Land Records from 1821)
Maries www.rootsweb.com/~momaries/maries.htm	H7	**2 Mar 1855**	**Osage, Pulaski** Maries County; PO Box 205; Vienna, MO 65582; Ph. (573) 422-3388 **Details:** (In 1859 and 1868 small tracts of Land were exchanged with Phelps County; Courthouse burned 6 Nov 1868, nearly all Records destroyed) (Clerk Circuit Court has Marriage Records from 1873, Divorce & Court Records from 1866, Land Records from 1855 & school Records from 1911; Probate Division has Probate Records from 1880)
Marion www.rootsweb.com/~momarion/index.htm	G3	**14 Dec 1822**	**Ralls** Marion County; 100 S Main St; Palmyra, MO 63461; Ph. (573) 769-2549 **Details:** (Clerk Circuit Court has Marriage, Divorce, Court & Land Records from 1827 & Military Discharge Records; Probate Court has Probate Records)
McDonald www.rootsweb.com/~momcdona/momcdon.htm	M11	**3 Mar 1849**	**Newton** McDonald County; Hwy W; Pineville, MO 64856-0665; Ph. (417) 223-4717 **Details:** (In 1876 an error in survey was corrected, establishing a new eastern line which annexed a 2 1/2 mile strip previously included in Barry County; Courthouse & Records burned in 1863) (Recorder Deeds has Marriage Records; Clerk Circuit Court has Divorce, Court & Land Records; Probate Judge has Probate Records)
Mercer www.rootsweb.com/~momercer/index.html	K1	**14 Feb 1845**	**Grundy** Mercer County; 802 E Main St; Princeton, MO 64673; Ph. (660) 748-3425 **Details:** (Courthouse burned 24 Mar 1898 & nearly all Records of the Circuit Clerk & Recorder, Treasurer & Sheriff were destroyed or badly damaged; Records in office of Probate Judge & County Clerk were saved but many were badly damaged) (County Clerk has Birth Records 1883–1894 & Death Records 1883–1891; Clerk Circuit Court has Marriage, Divorce, Court & Land Records, Curcuit Court, division 2, has Probate Records)

County Website	Map Index	Date Created	Parent County or Territory From Which Organized Address/Details
Miller	**I7**	**6 Feb 1837**	**Cole**

Miller County; PO Box 12; Tuscumbia, MO 65082; Ph. (573) 369-1910

Details: (line between Camden & Miller changed 1845; Territory from Morgan County annexed 1860; minor changes in 1868) (State of Missouri has Birth Records; County Clerk has Burial & Cemetery Records; Circuit Clerk has Court, Divorce, Guardianship, Marriage, & Probate Records; County Assessor has Land & Tax Records)

Mississippi	**B10**	**14 Feb 1845**	**Scott**

www.mississippicountymo-online.com/

Mississippi County; PO Box 304; Charleston, MO 63834-0304; Ph. (573) 683-2146

Details: (Clerk Circuit Court has Marriage, Divorce & Court Records; Probate Judge has Probate Records; County Recorder has Land Records)

Moniteau	**J6**	**14 Feb 1845**	**Cole, Morgan**

www.rootsweb.com/~momonite/moniteauhomepage.htm`

Moniteau County; 200 E Main St; California, MO 65018; Ph. (573) 796-4661

Details: (Recorder Deeds has Marriage & Land Records from 1845; Probate Court has Probate Records from 1845)

Monroe	**H4**	**6 Jan 1831**	**Ralls**

www.pastracks.com/states/missouri/monroe/

Monroe County; 300 N Main St; Paris, MO 65275-1399; Ph. (660) 327-1019

Details: (Clerk Circuit Court has Marriage, Divorce & Court Records; Probate Judge has Probate Records; County Assessor has Land Records)

Montgomery	**G5**	**14 Dec 1818**	**St. Charles**

www.rootsweb.com/~momontgo/index.htm

Montgomery County; 211 E 3rd St; Montgomery City, MO 63361-1956; Ph. (573) 564-3357

Details: (County Records burned 1864) (Clerk Circuit Court has Marriage Records from 1864, Divorce & Court Records from 1886; Probate Judge has Probate Records from 1890)

Morgan	**J6**	**5 Jan 1833**	**Cooper**

www.rootsweb.com/~momorgan/index.htm

Morgan County; 100 E Newton St; Versailles, MO 65084-1298; Ph. (573) 378-5436

Details: (Courthouse burned 1887; no Records lost) (Recorder Deeds has Marriage & Land Records; Probate Court has Probate Records from 1834; Clerk Circuit Court has Court Records; County Clerk has Birth & Death Records)

New Madrid	**D11**	**1804**	**Original district**

www.rootsweb.com/~monewmad/nmgenweb.htm

New Madrid County; PO Box 68; New Madrid, MO 63869; Ph. (573) 748-2524

Details: (Recorder Deeds has Marriage & Land Records; Clerk Circuit Court has Divorce & Court Records; Probate Court has Probate Records)

Newton	**M10**	**30 Dec 1838**	**Barry**

www.rootsweb.com/~monewton/newton.html

Newton County; 101 S Wood St; Neosho, MO 64850; Ph. (417) 451-8220

Details: (In 1846 a strip two miles wide was detached from Newton & attached to Jasper; Courthouse burned 1862, no mention of fate of Records) (County Clerk has Marriage, Divorce, Probate, Court & Land Records)

County Website	Map Index	Date Created	Parent County or Territory From Which Organized Address/Details
Niangua		29 Jan 1841	**Polk** Niangua County; MO **Details:** (see Dallas) Boundaries slightly changed & name changed to Dallas 16 Dec 1844
Nodaway www.rootsweb.com/~monodawa/nodaway.html	N1	2 Jan 1843	**Unorg. Territory.** Nodaway County; 305 N Main St; Maryville, MO 64468-0218; Ph. (660) 582-2251 **Details:** (Attached to Andrew County until organization 14 Feb 1845) (Clerk Circuit Court has Marriage & Divorce Records from 1845; Probate Court has Probate Records)
Oregon www.rootsweb.com/~mooregon/	G10	14 Feb 1845	**Ripley** Oregon County; PO Box 324; Alton, MO 65606; Ph. (417) 778-7475 **Details:** (Courthouse burned during Civil War; Records were removed & most of them saved) (Clerk Circuit Court has Marriage, Divorce & Court Records; Probate Judge has Probate Records; Recorder Deeds has Land Records)
Osage www.osagecountymo.com/	H7	29 Jan 1841	**Gasconade** Osage County; 106 E Main St; Linn, MO 65051; Ph. (573) 897-2139 **Details:** (1 Mar 1855 boundaries between Osage & Pulaski defined; Courthouse burned 15 Nov 1880, Records saved) (Recorder Deeds has Marriage & Land Records from 1841; Probate Court has Probate Records from 1841; County Clerk has Birth & Death Records)
Ozark www.rootsweb.com/~moozark/oz.htm	I11	29 Jan 1841	**Taney** Ozark County; PO Box 416; Gainesville, MO 65655-0416; Ph. (417) 679-3516 **Details:** (Name changed to Decatur 22 Feb 1843; Name changed back to Ozark 24 Mar 1845) (Clerk Circuit Court has Marriage, Divorce & Court Records; County Clerk has County Community minutes; Probate Court has Probate Records; Recorder Deeds has Land Records)
Pemiscot www.rootsweb.com/~mopemis2/pemiscot.htm	D11	19 Feb 1851	**New Madrid** Pemiscot County; 610 Ward Ave; Caruthersville, MO 63830; Ph. (573) 333-4203 **Details:** (Courthouse & Records burned 1883) (Recorder Deeds has Marriage & Land Records from 1883; Clerk Circuit Court has Divorce & Court Records from 1890; Probate Judge has Probate Records)
Perry www.perrycountymo.com/	D8	16 Nov 1820	**Ste. Genevieve** Perry County; 321 N Main St; Perryville, MO 63775; Ph. (573) 547-4242 **Details:** (Clerk Circuit Court has Divorce, Land, Probate & Court Records; County Recorder has Marriage & Military Records; County Clerk has Birth & Death Records 1883–1893 & Naturalization Records from 1821)
Pettis www.rootsweb.com/~mopettis/pettis.htm	K5	26 Jan 1833	**Cooper, Saline** Pettis County; 415 S Ohio Ave; Sedalia, MO 65301; Ph. (660) 826-5395 **Details:** (Recorder Deeds has Marriage & Land Records from 1833; Probate Court has Probate Records from 1833; Clerk Circuit Court has Court Records)

County Website	Map Index	Date Created	Parent County or Territory From Which Organized Address/Details
Phelps www.rollanet.org/~phelps/	H8	13 Nov 1857	**Crawford, Pulaski, Maries** Phelps County; 200 N Main St FL 1; Rolla, MO 65401; Ph. (573) 364-1891 **Details:** (County Clerk has Marriage, Divorce, Court & Land Records from 1857 & Probate Records)
Pike www.pastracks.com/states/missouri/pike/	F4	14 Dec 1818	**St. Charles** Pike County; 115 W Main St; Bowling Green, MO 63334; Ph. (573) 324-2412 **Details:** (Courthouse burned 1864; no mention of fate of Records) (Recorder Deeds has Land Records from 1819 & Marriage Records from 1825; Probate Court has Probate Records from 1825; Clerk Circuit Court has Court Records)
Platte http://co.platte.mo.us/	N4	31 Dec 1838	**Platte Purchase** Platte County; 415 3rd St, Ste 30; Platte City, MO 64079; Ph. (816) 858-2232 **Details:** (Attached to Clay County for civil & Military purposes from Dec 1836 to 31 Dec 1838) (County Clerk has Birth Records 1883–1887 & Death Records 1883–1888; Recorder Deeds has Marriage & Land Records; Clerk Circuit Court has Divorce Records; Probate Judge has Probate & Court Records)
Polk www.rootsweb.com/~mopolk/	K9	5 Jan 1835	**Greene** Polk County; 102 E Broadway St; Bolivar, MO 65613; Ph. (417) 326-4031 **Details:** (County Recorder has Marriage Records from 1835 & Land Records from 1836; Clerk Circuit Court has Divorce & Court Records from 1857; Probate Judge has Probate Records from 1947)
Pulaski www.rootsweb.com/~mopulask/index.htm	I8	19 Jan 1833	**Crawford** Pulaski County; 301 Historic 66 E; Waynesville, MO 65583; Ph. (573) 774-4701 **Details:** (County Clerk has Marriage, Divorce, Probate & Court Records from 1903)
Pulaski (old)		1818	**Franklin** Pulaski, old County; MO **Details:** (organization not perfected & much of its Territory became Gasconade in 1820; abolished 1819 when Territory of Arkansas was created)
Putnam www.rootsweb.com/~moputnam/	J1	22 Feb 1843	**Linn** Putnam County; Main St #204; Unionville, MO 63565; Ph. (660) 947-2674 **Details:** (When the Iowa boundary was established, the areas of both Putnam & Dodge Counties were below the constitutional limit; Dodge disorganized in 1853 & its Territory was regained by Putnam) (Clerk Circuit Court has Birth Records 1878–1903, Marriage Records from 1854, Divorce & Court Records from 1855 & Land Records from 1848; Probate Judge has Probate Records from 1848)

County Website	Map Index	Date Created	Parent County or Territory From Which Organized Address/Details
Ralls www.pastracks.com/states/missouri/ralls/	**G4**	**16 Nov 1820**	**Pike** Ralls County; 311 S Main St; New London, MO 63459; Ph. (573) 985-7111 **Details:** (Bureau of Vital Records has Birth & Death Records from 1910; Clerk Circuit Court & Recorder Deeds has Marriage, Divorce, Court & Land Records from 1821; Probate Judge has Probate Records)
Randolph www.rootsweb.com/~morandol/	**I4**	**22 Jan 1829**	**Chariton** Randolph County; 110 S Main St; Huntsville, MO 65259; Ph. (660) 277-4717 **Details:** (Courthouse burned 1880; a few Records lost) (County Recorder has Marriage & Land Records; Clerk Circuit Court has Divorce Records; Probate Court has Probate Records)
Ray www.rootsweb.com/~moray/index.htm	**L4**	**16 Nov 1820**	**Howard** Ray County; 100 W Main St; PO Box 536; Richmond, MO 64085-0536; Ph. (816) 776-4502 **Details:** (County Clerk has Birth & Death Records 1883–1884; Recorder Deeds has Marriage & Land Records; Clerk Circuit Court has Divorce & Court Records; Probate Judge has Probate Records) (Records of interest to genealogists obtainable from Ray County Historical Society, Richmond, MO 64085)
Reynolds www.rootsweb.com/~moreynol/	**F9**	**25 Feb 1845**	**Shannon** Reynolds County; Courthouse Sq; Centerville, MO 63633; Ph. (573) 648-2494 **Details:** (Courthouse burned 1872; all Records lost) (County Clerk has Birth Records from 1883, Marriage, Divorce, Probate & Court Records from 1872)
Ripley www.rootsweb.com/~moripley/	**F11**	**5 Jan 1833**	**Wayne** Ripley County; County Courthouse; Doniphan, MO 63935; Ph. (573) 996-3215 **Details:** (Recorder Deeds has Marriage & Land Records from 1833; Probate Court has Probate Records)
Rives		**13 Dec 1834**	**Lafayette** Rives County; MO **Details:** (see Henry) Name changed to Henry 15 Feb 1841
Saline www.rootsweb.com/~mosaline/index.html	**K5**	**25 Nov 1820**	**Cooper, Howard** Saline County; 101 E Arrow St; Marshall, MO 65340; Ph. (660) 886-3331 **Details:** (Courthouse burned 1864, but Records were saved) (County Clerk has Birth & Death Records 1883–1885; Marshall Public Library has Cemetary & genealogy Records)
Schuyler www.rootsweb.com/~moschuy2/index.html	**I1**	**14 Feb 1845**	**Adair** Schuyler County; Hwy 136; Lancaster, MO 63548-0187; Ph. (660) 457-3842 **Details:** (County Clerk has Birth & Death Records 1883–1893; Clerk Circuit Court has Marriage & Divorce Records; Probate Judge & Magistrate Courts have Probate & Court Records)

County	Map	Date	Parent County or Territory From Which Organized
Website	Index	Created	Address/Details

Scotland H1 **29 Jan 1841** **Lewis**
www.rootsweb.com/~moscotla/index.htm
Scotland County; 117 S Market St; Memphis, MO 63555;
Ph. (660) 465-7027
Details: (County Clerk has Birth & Death Records 1883–1889; Clerk Circuit Court has Marriage, Divorce, Court & Land Records from 1841; Probate Judge has Probate Records from 1841)

Scott C10 **28 Dec 1821** **New Madrid**
www.rootsweb.com/~moscott/moscott.htm
Scott County; PO Box 188; Benton, MO 63736-0188;
Ph. (573) 545-3549
Details: (Recorder Deeds has Marriage & Land Records; Clerk Circuit Court has Divorce & Court Records; Probate Judge has Probate Records)

Shannon G9 **29 Jan 1841** **Ripley, Washington**
www.rootsweb.com/~moshanno/
Shannon County; PO Box 187; Eminence, MO 65466;
Ph. (573) 226-3414
Details: (Courthouse destroyed during Civil War; Courthouse burned 1863, 1871 & 1938; Recorder Office burned 1893, some Land Records in Ironton, MO prior to 1872) (County Clerk has Marriage Records from 1881, Divorce, Probate, Court & Land Records from 1872)

Shelby H3 **2 Jan 1835** **Marion**
www.rootsweb.com/~moshelby/index.htm
Shelby County; 100 E Main; PO Box 176; Shelbyville, MO 63469;
Ph. (573) 633-2151
Details: (Clerk of Circuit Court has Marriage Records from 1835; Recorders Office has Land Transfers from 1835; County Health Office has Birth Records from 1920; Probate Court has Death & Probate Records from 1850; State Archives has other Records)

St. Charles E6 **1804** **Original district**
www.win.org/county/sccg.htm
St. Charles County; 201 N 2nd St; St. Charles, MO 63301;
Ph. (636) 949-7550
Details: (Recorder Deeds has Marriage & Land Records; Probate Court has Probate Records; Clerk Circuit Court has Court Records)

St. Clair L7 **16 Jan 1833** **Lafayette**
www.rootsweb.com/~mostclai/intro.htm
St. Clair County; PO Box 525; Osceola, MO 64776-0405;
Ph. (417) 646-2315
Details: (Lost Land to Pettis 26 Jan 1833 and attached to Rives until formally organized from Rives County 29 Jan 1841) (County Clerk has Birth & Death Records 1883–1887; Recorders Office has Marriage Records from 1855 & Land Records from 1867; Clerk Circuit Court has Divorce & Probate Records)

St. Francois E8 **19 Dec 1821** **Jefferson, Ste. Genevieve, Washington**
www.pastracks.com/states/missouri/stfrancois/
St. Francois County; County Courthouse Sq; Farmington, MO 63640;
Ph. (573) 756-5411
Details: (County Recorder has Marriage & Land Records; Clerk Circuit Court has Divorce Records; Associate Circuit Court has Probate Records)

St. Louis E6 **1804** **Original district**
www.co.st-louis.mo.us/
St. Louis County; 41 S Central Ave; Clayton, MO 63105;
Ph. (314) 889-2041
Details: (County Clerk has Birth Records 1877–1910; Recorder Deeds has Marriage & Land Records; Clerk Circuit Court has Divorce & Court Records)

County Website	Map Index	Date Created	Parent County or Territory From Which Organized Address/Details
St. Louis City http//stlouis.missouri.org/	E6	5 Mar 1877	**St. Louis** St. Louis City County; 1200 Market St; St. Louis, MO 63103; Ph. (314) 622-4000 or (314) 622-4405 **Details:** (City Recorder has Marriage Records from 1806 & Land Records from 1804; Assessor has tax Records; Probate Judge has Probate Records)
Ste. Genevieve www.geocities.com/Heartland/Estates/4882/ stegmain.html	E8	1804	**Original District** Ste. Genevieve County; 55 S 3rd St; Ste. Genevieve, MO 63670-1601; Ph. (573) 883-5589 **Details:** (County Clerk has Birth & Death Records 1883–1892; Circuit Clerk-Recorder has Marriage, Divorce, Court & Land Records; Circuit Court Judge has Probate Records)
Stoddard www.rootsweb.com/~mostodd2/index.html	D10	2 Jan 1835	**Cape Girardeau** Stoddard County; PO Box 110; Bloomfield, MO 63825; Ph. (573) 568-3339 **Details:** (Courthouse burned 1864 but Records had been removed to safety) (County Clerk has Birth Records 1883–1886 & Military Records; Recorder Deeds has Marriage & Land Records; Clerk Circuit Court has Divorce Records; Probate Judge has Probate Records; Clerk Magistrate Court has Court Records)
Stone www.rootsweb.com/~mostone/stone.htm	K11	10 Feb 1851	**Taney** Stone County; PO Box 45; Galena, MO 65656; Ph. (417) 357-6127 **Details:** (County Clerk has Marriage & Land Records from 1851, Probate & Court Records from 1800's & Military Discharge Records from 1918)
Sullivan www.rootsweb.com/~mosulliv/index.html	J2	17 Feb 1843	**Linn** Sullivan County; 109 N Main St; Milan, MO 63556; Ph. (660) 265-3786 **Details:** (Formerly Highland County 1843–1845) (Recorder Deeds has incomplete Birth Records 1867–1895, Marriage & Land Records from 1845, Death Records 1883–1896; Clerk Circuit Court has Divorce & Court Records from 1845; Probate Judge has Probate Records from 1845)
Taney www.rootsweb.com/~motaney/taney.htm	J11	6 Jan 1837	**Greene** Taney County; 132 David St; Forsyth, MO 65653-0156; Ph. (417) 546-7200 **Details:** (Courthouse burned 1885) (Clerk Circuit Court has Marriage, Divorce, Court & Land Records; Probate Judge has Probate Records; County Clerk has voter registration Records from 1961)
Texas www.rootsweb.com/~motexas/	H9	17 Feb 1843	**Shannon, Wright** Texas County; 210 N Grand Ave; Houston, MO 65483-1226; Ph. (417) 967-2112 **Details:** (Formerly Ashley County. Name changed to Texas 14 Feb 1845) (Recorder Deeds has Marriage Records from 1855 & Land Records from 1845; Clerk Circuit Court has Divorce & Court Records from 1855; Associate Circuit Court has Probate Records from 1850)
Van Buren		3 Mar 1835	**Jackson** Van Buren County; MO **Details:** (see Cass) Name changed to Cass 19 Feb 1849

County	Map	Date	Parent County or Territory From Which Organized
Website	Index	Created	Address/Details

Vernon   M8   17 Feb 1851   **Bates**
www.rootsweb.com/~movernon/
Vernon County; 100 W Cherry St; Nevada, MO 64772;
Ph. (417) 448-2500
Details: (Vernon created 17 Feb 1851, but act was declared unconstitutional since its territory was exactly that of Bates County; legally created 27 Feb 1855; reorganized 17 Oct 1865 after total suspension of civil order during Civil War; Courthouse destroyed during that period, but clerk had taken the records with him when he joined the army and all records were later recovered, except the deed book) (County Clerk has birth & death records 1883–1904; Recorder Deeds has marriage & land records; Clerk Circuit Court has divorce & court records; Probate Court has probate records; County Historical Society has burial records)

Warren   F6   5 Jan 1833   **Montgomery**
www.rootsweb.com/~mowarren/index.html
Warren County; 104 W Market; Warrenton, MO 63383-1903;
Ph. (636) 456-3331
Details: (Recorder Deeds has Marriage & Land Records from 1833; Probate Court has Probate Records from 1833; Clerk Circuit Court has Court Records)

Washington   F7   21 Aug 1813   **Ste. Genevieve**
www.rootsweb.com/~mowashin/index.html
Washington County; 102 N Missouri St; Potosi, MO 63664;
Ph. (573) 438-4901
Details: (County Clerk has Birth Records 1883–1891 & Death Records 1883–1886; Clerk Circuit Court has Marriage, Divorce, Court & Land Records from 1825; Probate Office has Probate Records from 1814)

Wayne   E9   11 Dec 1818   **Cape Girardeau**
www.rootsweb.com/~mowayne/
Wayne County; County Courthouse; PO Box 48; Greenville, MO 63944; Ph. (573) 224-3011
Details: (Courthouse & all Records burned 1854 & again in 1892) (County Clerk has Birth & Death Records 1914–1940; Clerk Circuit Court & Recorder has Marriage, Divorce & Land Records; Associate Circuit Court has Probate Records)

Webster   J9   3 Mar 1855   **Greene, Wright**
www.rootsweb.com/~mowebste/webster.htm
Webster County; 100 Crittenden St; Marshfield, MO 65706;
Ph. (417) 468-2223
Details: (Courthouse burned 1863, but Records were saved, except tax rolls & election returns) (County Clerk has Birth Records 1883–1893 & Death Records 1883–1887; County Recorder has Marriage & Land Records; Clerk Circuit Court has Divorce & Court Records; Probate Judge has Probate Records)

Worth   M1   8 Feb 1861   **Gentry**
www.rootsweb.com/~moworth/worth.html
Worth County; 4th & Front St; Grant City, MO 64456;
Ph. (660) 564-2210
Details: (County Clerk has Birth & Death Records 1883–1893, Marriage, Divorce, Probate, Court & Land Records from 1861)

Wright   I9   29 Jan 1841   **Pulaski**
www.rootsweb.com/~mowright/wright.htm
Wright County; Courthouse Sq; Hartville, MO 65667-0098;
Ph. (417) 741-6661
Details: (Courthouse burned in 1864, destroying many Records; Courthouse & Records destroyed in 1897) (Clerk Circuit Court has Marriage, Divorce & Court Records; Probate Judge has Probate Records; County Recorder has Land Records)

Notes

Montana

Gold and silver

Capital: Helena
Territory: 1864
State: 1889 (41st)

At least sixteen tribes of Indians roamed over the Montana region when the first explorers arrived in the area. Fur traders were in the area before 1800. Obtaining the region in the Louisiana Purchase, President Thomas Jefferson sent Lewis and Clark to explore the new territory. They reached Montana in 1805. Trading posts remained the only settlements until the establishment of Fort Benton, which became the first permanent settlement in 1846. Steamboats first reached Fort Benton in 1859, but the first real influx of people came in 1862 when gold was discovered southeast of Butte. Copper, silver, and other minerals were discovered about 20 years later, which opened up mines and brought Irish, German, Austrian, Polish, and Czech workers to the area.

The western part of Montana became part of the United States in 1846 through the Oregon Treaty. In 1860, this area was made into Missoula County, Washington Territory. By 1864, all of Montana was included in the Idaho Territory. In 1864, Montana became an organized territory, and the 41st state in 1889.

Over the years, cattle and sheep farming prospered. Homestead laws brought families by the droves, but wheat farmers faced a major setback when a drought sent the economy into a depression even before the onslaught of the Great Depression.

Look for vital records in the following locations:

- **Birth and death records:** Some counties began recording births and deaths as early as 1864. Statewide registration began in 1907, reaching general compliance by 1920. These records are available from Montana Vital Records in Helena.
- **Marriage and divorce records:** Kept by individual counties.
- **Probate records:** Kept by counties 1864 to 1889, since then by the district courts.
- **Naturalization records:** Located in county and district courts.

- **Land records:** The earliest land records are at the National Archives, Denver Branch, in Denver, Colorado. Records of patents on homesteads are at county offices. The Bureau of Land Management in Billings, Montana has tract books, township plats, and pre-1908 patent records.
- **Census records:** In 1860, western Montana was part of Washington Territory, and eastern Montana was part of the unorganized area of Nebraska Territory. Federal censuses for Montana Territory are available for 1870 and 1880. Indexes have been published for all of these. Mortality schedules for the 1870 and 1880 censuses are at the Montana Historical Society in Helena.

Office of Vital Statistics Department of Public Health and Human Services
111 N. Sanders Rm 209
PO Box 4210
Billings, MT 59604
(406) 444-2685; Fax (406) 444-1803
http://vhsp.dphhs.mt.gov/dph_12.htm

Montana Historical Society
PO Box 201201
225 North Roberts Street
Helena, MT 59620-1201
(406) 444-2694
www.his.state.mt.us/

Bureau of Land Management
222 North 32nd Street; Box 30157
Helena, MT 59604

Societies and Repositories

Beaver Head-Hunters; 15 S. Montana; Dillon, MT 59725; beaverhh@bmt.net; www.3rivers.net/~abcs/BHH.

Big Horn County Genealogical Society; Box 51; Hardin, MT 59034; mminear11@mcn.net; www.rootsweb.com/~mtmsgs/soc_bhcgs.htm.

Bitterroot Genealogical Society; 702 S. Fifth Street; Hamilton, MT 59840; (406) 961-3159; mahlgren@bitterroot.net; www.rootsweb.com/~mtbgs.

Broken Mountains Genealogical Society; Box 261; Chester, MT 59522; cadyfam@ttc-cmc.net; www.rootsweb.com/~mtmsgs/soc_bmgs.htm.

Carbon County Historical Society; Box 476; Red Lodge, MT 59068.

Fort Assiniboine Genealogical Society; c/o Havre Hill County Library; 402 3 St.; Havre, MT 59501-3644; www.rootsweb.com/~mtmsgs/soc_fags.htm.

Gallatin Genealogical Society; PO Box 1783; Bozeman, MT 59771-1783; www.rootsweb.com/~mtmsgs/soc_ggs.htm.

Great Falls Genealogical Society; High Plains Heritage Center; 422 Second Street South; Great Falls, MT 59405; gfgs@mt.net; www.mt.net/~gfgs.

Lewis and Clark County Genealogical Society; PO Box 5313; Helena, MT 59604; www.mth.mtlib.org/Local%20Information/L&C%20genealogy.htm.

Lewistown Genealogical Society, Inc.; 701 West Main; Lewistown, MT 59457; www.lewistownlibrary.org.

Miles City Genealogical Society; c/o Miles City Public Library; PO Box 711; Miles City, MT 59301; milescity@geocities.com; www.geocities.com/Heartland/Fields/6175.

Milk River Genealogical Society; Box 1000; Chinook, MT 59523; www.rootsweb.com/~mtmsgs/soc_mrgs.htm.

Mineral County Historical Society; Box 533; Superior, MT 59872.

Montana Historical Society Library and Archives; 225 N. Roberts St.; PO Box 201201; Helena, MT 59620-1201; (406) 444-2681; archives@state.mt.us; www.his.state.mt.us/departments/Library-Archives/index.html.

Montana State Genealogical Society; PO Box 555; Chester, MT 59522; bubbles@ttc-cmc.net; www.rootsweb.com/~mtmsgs.

Montana State Library; 1515 East 6th Avenue; PO Box 201800; Helena, MT 59620-1800; (406) 444-3115; http://msl.state.mt.us.

Northwest Montana Historical Society; PO Box 2293; Kalispell, MT 59903; nwmhs@digisys.net; www.digisys.net/museum.

Phillips County Genealogical Society; c/o Delores Messerly; PO Box 334; Malta, MT 59538; www.rootsweb.com/~mtmsgs/soc_phcgs.htm.

Powell County Genealogical Society; 912 Missouri Ave.; Deer Lodge, MT 59722; www.rootsweb.com/~mtmsgs/soc_pcgs.htm.

Root Diggers Genealogical Society; PO Box 249; Glasgow, MT 59230.

Sheridan Daybreakers Genealogical Society; c/o Pamla C. Hendrickson; 318 N Adams St.; Plentywood, MT 59254; daybreakers@petersnn.org; www.petersnn.org/daybreakers/scdgsindex.htm.

Sons of the American Revolution, Montana Society; 408 S. Black; Bozeman, MT 59715.

Tangled Roots Genealogical Society; PO Box 1992; Cut Bank, MT 59427; roncamp@cut-bank.mt.us; www.rootsweb.com/~mtmsgs/soc_trgs.htm.

The Tree Branches, Dawson County, Montana; PO Box 1275; Glendive, MT 59330-1275; www.cheyenneancestors.com/dawson/dwsgens.html.

Western Montana Genealogical Society; PO Box 2714; Missoula, MT 59806-2714; jalf@marsweb.com; www.rootsweb.com/~mtwmgs.

Yellowstone Genealogical Forum; c/o Parmly Billings Library; 510 N. Broadway; Billings, MT 59101; searchandresearch@attbi.com; www.rootsweb.com/~mtygf.

Yellowstone Valley Chapter, AHSGR; 715 W 5th Street; Laurel, MT 59044; (406) 628-6795.

Bibliography and Record Sources

General

A Directory of Churches and Religious Organizations in Montana. Bozeman: Historical Records Survey, 1941.

Borneman, Patricia. *Speaking of Montana: A Guide to the Oral History Collection at the Montana Historical Society, through 1996.* Helena, Montana: Montana Historical Society Press, 1997.

Burlingame, Merrill G., and K. Ross Toole, eds. *A History of Montana, 3 vols.* New York: Lewis Historical Publishing Co., 1957.

Cheney, Roberta Charkeek. *Names on The Face of Montana: The Story of Montana's Place Names.* Missoula, Montana: Mountain Press Pub. Co., 1992, 1983.

Coleman, Julie L. *Golden Opportunities, A Biographical History of Montana's Jewish Communities.*

Edwards, George. *The Pioneer Work of the Presbyterian Church in Montana.* Philadelphia: Microfilmed by the Presbyterian Historical Society, 1992.

Flaherty, Cornelia M. *Go With Haste into the Mountains; A History of the Diocese of Helena.* Helena, Montana: The Diocese, ca.1984.

Historical Records Survey. *A Directory of Churches and Religious Organizations in Montana, 1941.* Bozeman, Montana: s.n., 1941.

Historical Sketch of South-Central Montana. S.l: s.n.

Hyde, C. W. G. *History of the Great Northwest and Its Men of Progress: A Select List of Biographical Sketches and Portraits of the Leaders in Business, Professional and Official Life.* Minneapolis: Minneapolis Journal, 1901.

Johnson, Coburn. *Bibliography of Montana Local Histories.* Montana: Montana Library Association, 1977.

Johnson, Dorothy M. *The Bloody Bozeman: The Perilous Trail to Montana's Gold.* Missoula, Montana: Mountain Press Pub. Co., 1998, 1983.

Lowe, James A. *The Bridger Trail: A Viable Alternative Route to the Gold Fields of Montana Territory in 1864; With Excerpts from Emigrant Diaries, Letters, and Comparative Material from Oregon and Bozeman Trail Diaries.* Spokane: Arthur H. Clark Co., 1999.

Mills, Edward Laird. *Plains, Peaks and Pioneers: Eighty Years of Methodism in Montana.* Portland, Oregon: Binfords & Mort, 1947.

Montana Historical Society, comp. *"List of Early Settlers: A List of All Persons (Except Indians) Who Were in What Is Now Montana During the Winter of 1862–1863," Contributions to the Historical Society of Montana.* 2nd ed. Helena: Rocky Mountain Publishing Co., 1902.

Montana Research Outline. Series U.S.-States, no. 27, Salt Lake City: Family History Library, 1988.

Montana: Inventory of the County Archives: Flathead, Lake, Lincoln, Mineral, Ravalli, Sanders. S.l.: s.n., 1940.

Nicklas, Laurie. *The Montana Locator, A Directory of Public Records for Locating People Dead or Alive.* Modesto, California: the author, 1999.

Palladino, Lawrence Benedict. *Indian and White in the Northwest; or, A History of Catholicity in Montana.* Baltimore: John Murphy & Co., 1894.

Parpart, Paulette K., and Donald E. Spritzer, comps. *Montana Data Index: A Reference Guide to Historical and Genealogical Resources.* Missoula, Montana: Montana Library Association, 1992.

Parpart, Paulette K., and Donald E. Spritzer, comps. *The Montana Historical and Genealogical Data Index.* Missoula, Montana: Montana Library Association Indexing Special Interest Group, 1987.

Progressive Men of the State of Montana. Chicago: A. W. Bowen and Co., 1901.

Richards, Dennis Lee. *Montana's Genealogical and Local History Records: A Selected List of Books, Manuscripts, and Periodicals.* Detroit: Gale Research Co., 1981.

Richards, Dennis. *Montana's Genealogical and Local History Records.* Gale Genealogy.

Sanders, Helen Fitzgerald. *A History of Montana.* 3 vols. Chicago: Lewis Pub. Co., 1913.

Sanders, James U. *Society of Montana Pioneers: Constitution, Members and Officers.*

Schoenberg, Wilfred P. *A History of the Catholic Church in the Pacific Northwest, 1743–1983.* Washington, D.C.: Pastoral Press, 1987.

Schoenberg, Wilfred P. *Jesuits in Montana, 1840–1960.* Portland, Oregon: Oregon-Jesuit, 1960.

Shirley, Gayle Corbett. *More than Petticoats: Remarkable Montana Women.* Helena, Montana: Falcon, 1995.

Southern California Genealogical Society. *Sources of Genealogical Help in Montana.* Burbank, California: SCGS, n.d.

Stoner, Al. *First Families of Montana and Early Settlers.* Lewistown, Montana: Montana State Genealogical Society, 2000.

Stout, Tom. *Montana, Its Story and Biography: A History of Aboriginal and Territorial Montana and Three Decades of Statehood.* 3 vols. Chicago: American Historical Society, 1921.

Toole, K. Ross. *Twentieth Century Montana: A State of Extremes.* Norman Oklahoma: University of Oklahoma Press, 1972.

United States. Department of State. *Territorial Papers of Montana, 1864–1872.* Washington, D.C.: The National Archives, 1963. 2 microfilm.

United States. Work Projects Administration (Montana). *Inventory of the County Archives of Montana: no. 5 Carbon, no. 16 Gallatin, no. 34 Park, no. 48 Stillwater, no. 49 Sweet Grass.* Bozeman, Montana: The Survey, 1942.

VanDersal and Conner's Stockgrowers Directory of Marks and Brands for the State of Montana, 1872–1900: Comprising an Alphabetical List of Names of All Livestock Companies and. . .Sheep and Wool Growers. Glendive, Montana: Review Printing Co., 1974.

Waldron, Ellis. *Montana Legislators, 1864–1979: Profiles and Biographical Directory.* Missoula, Montana: University of Montana, Bureau of Government Research, 1980.

Weisel, George F. *Men and Trade on the Northwest Frontier as Shown by the Fort Owen Ledger.* Missoula, Montana: Montana State University, 1955

Whithorn, Doris. *Bicentennial Tapestry of the Yellowstone Conference. [United Methodist Church from 1784–1984.]* United States: s.n., 1984 (Livingston, Montana: The Livingston Enterprise.) *with Portraits and Maps, vol. 1.* Akron, Ohio: Society of Montana Pioneers, 1899.

Atlases, Maps and Gazetteers

Cheney, Roberta Charkeek. *Names on the Face of Montana: The Story of Montana's Place Names.* Missoula. Montana: Mountain Press Pub. Co., 1992.

Highsmith, Richard M. *Atlas of the Pacific Northwest: Resources and Development.* 4th ed. Corvallis, Oregon: Oregon State University Press, 1968.

Koury, Michael J. *The Military Posts of Montana.* Bellev, Nebraska: Old Army Press, 1970.

Lutz, Dennis and Meryl Lutz. "Montana Post Offices: 1864–1974." *Montana Postal Cache: Research Journal of the Montana Postal History Society* part 1, A–C, 1 (February 1975) M1–M24; part, D-1, 1(May 1975): M25–M49, part 3, J–P, 1 (August 1975): M50–M74; part 4, Q–Z, 1 (November 1975): M75–M103.

Montana Atlas and Gazetteer. Freeport, Maine: DeLorme Mapping Co., 1995.

Montana Historical Society (Helena, Montana). *Catalog of the Map Collection.* Helena, Montana: The Society, 1983. 8 microfiche.

Northwestern Gazetteer, Minnesota, North and South Dakota and Montana Gazetteer and Business Directory. St. Paul: R. L. Polk & Company, 1914.

Censuses

Available Census Records and Census Substitutes

Federal Census 1860 (eastern part with Nebraska, western part with Washington), 1870, 1880, 1900, 1910, 1920, 1930

Federal Mortality Schedules 1870, 1880

Union Veterans and Widows 1890

Dollarhide, William. *The Census Book: A Genealogist's Guide to Federal Census Facts, Schedules and Indexes.* Bountiful, Utah: Heritage Quest, 1999.

Kemp, Thomas J. *The American Census Handbook.* Wilmington, Delaware: Scholarly Resources, Inc., 2001.

Lainhart, Ann S. *State Census Records.* Baltimore: Genealogical Publishing Co., Inc, 1992.

Szucs, Loretto Dennis and Matthew Wright. *Finding Answers in U.S. Census Records.* Ancestry Publishing, 2001.

Thorndale, William and William Dollarhide. *Map Guide to the U.S. Federal Census, 1790–1920.* Baltimore: Genealogical Publishing Co., 1987.

Court Records, Probate and Wills

Note: From 1864 through 1889, probate courts existed in each county. The probate records as well as other court records, are filed in county courthouses. Look for other court records at the National Archives Regional Internet Sites at www.nara.gov.

Emigration, Immigration, Migration and Naturalization

Fuhrman, Diane. *Swedish Immigrants Living in Montana, 1900.* Bozeman, Montana: the author, 1989.

United States. District Court (Montana: Southern District). *Declaration of Intent, 1891–1929; Petition for Naturalization, 1891– 1929; Citizenship Records, 1894–1906; Certificates, 1907–1927.* Microfilm of originals in the Federal Archives, Seattle Branch, Seattle, Washington. Salt Lake City: Filmed by the Genealogical Society of Utah, 1988. 3 microfilm.

United States. Immigration and Naturalization Service. *Indexes to Naturalization Records of the Montana Territorial and Federal Courts, 1868–1929.* Washington, D.C.: National Archives, 1987.

Land and Property

Note: For land entries, including deeds and land patents, contact individual county clerks. Also contact the Montana Office of The Bureau of Land Management at (405) 896-5004. Additional records for land-entry papers prior to 1908 can be found at the National Archives Records Administration, Pacific Alaska Region Branch in Seattle or online at www.nara.gov/regional/seattle.html.

Hone, Wade E. *Land and Property Research in the United States.* Salt Lake City: Ancestry Incorporated, 1997.

MacDonald, Marie Peterson. *After Barbed Wire: A Pictorial History of the Homestead Rush into the Northern Great Plains, 1900–1919.* Glendive, Montana: Frontier Gateway Museum, 1963.

United States. Bureau of Land Management. *Tract Books.* Washington, D.C.: Records Improvement, Bureau of Land Management.

Wollaston, Percy. *Homesteading; A Montana Family Album.* New York: Lyons Press, 1997.

Military

Carroll, John M., and Byron Price. *Roll Call on the Little Big Horn, 28 June 1876.* Fort Collins, Colorado: The Old Army Press, 1974.

Hammer, Kenneth. *Men with Custer: Biographies of the 7th Cavalry, 25 June, 1876.* Fort Collins, Colorado: The Old Army Press, 1972.

Nagles, James C. *U.S. Military Records: A Guide to Federal & State Sources, Colonial America to the Present.* Ancestry Incorporated, 1994.

National Archives Trust Fund Board. *Military Service Records: A Select Catalog of National Archives Microfilm Publications.* Washington, D.C.: National Archives Trust Fund Board, 1985.

United States. Selective Service System. *Montana. World War I Selective Service System Draft Registration Cards, 1917–1918. National Archives Microfilm Publications, M1509.* Washington, D.C.: National Archives, 1987–1988.

Vital and Cemetery Records

Note: Vital records are available at the Montana Department of Public Health and Human Services Vital Statistics Bureau, PO Box 4210, Helena, MT 59604. For current information on holdings and cost visit the website at www.allvitalrecords.com/index.asp?state=MT&tag=genealogy.

Cemetery Records of Montana. 3 vols. Typescript. Salt Lake City: Genealogical Society of Utah, 1947–1961.

Historical Records Survey Project, Division of Professional and Service Projects, Work Projects Administration. *Guide to the Public Vital Statistics in Montana.* Bozeman: Historical Records Survey, 1941.

Inventory of the Vital Statistics Records of Church and Religious Organizations in Montana. Bozeman, Montana: Historical Records Survey, 1942.

Jackson, Ronald Vern. *Montana 1870 Mortality Schedule.* Bountiful, Utah: Accelerated Indexing Systems, ca. 1981.

Lewistown Genealogy Society, prep. *Montana Cemetery Records.* Microfilm of original transcript in possession of the Lewistown Genealogy Society, Lewistown, Montana. Salt Lake City: Filmed by the Genealogical Society of Utah, 1982.

Moog, Una. *Cemetery Inscriptions and Church Records from Hingham, Rudyard, Inverness, Whitlash, Lothair, Joplin and Chester, Montana.* Chester, Montana: Broken Mountains Genealogical Society, 1986.

County / Website	Map Index	Date Created	Parent County or Territory From Which Organized / Address/Details
Beaverhead www.beaverhead.com/	**N9**	**2 Feb 1865**	**Original county** Beaverhead County; 2 S Pacific Cluster 3; Dillon, MT 59725; Ph. (406) 683-2642 **Details:** (County Clerk has Birth Records from 1902, Death Records from 1901 & Land Records from 1864; Clerk District Court has Divorce, Probate & Court Records)
Big Horn www.geocities.com/Heartland/Acres/7759/	**F8**	**13 Jan 1913**	**Rosebud, Yellowstone** Big Horn County; 121 3rd St W; Hardin, MT 59034; Ph. (406) 665-1506 **Details:** (County Clerk has Birth, Death, Naturalization & Land Records from 1913; Clerk District Court has Marriage, Divorce, Probate & Court Records)
Big Horn (old)		**1861**	Big Horn County, MT **Details:** Name Changed 1877 to Custer County
Blaine www.rootsweb.com/~mtblaine/	**H4**	**29 Feb 1912**	**Chouteau** Blaine County; PO Box 908; Chinook, MT 59523; Ph. (406) 357-3240 **Details:** (County Clerk has Deeds from 1912; Clerk of District Court has Marriage, Probate, & Court Records from 1912)
Broadwater www.mtrdp.org/broadwater/	**L7**	**9 Feb 1897**	**Jefferson, Meagher** Broadwater County; 515 Broadway; Townsend, MT 59644; Ph. (406) 266-3443 **Details:** (County Clerk-Recorder has Birth & Death Records from 1900, Land & Military Records; Clerk Court has Marriage, Divorce, Probate, Court & Naturalization Records)
Carbon www.rootsweb.com/~mtcarbon/_crb.html	**H9**	**4 Mar 1895**	**Park, Yellowstone, Custer** Carbon County; PO Box 948; Red Lodge, MT 59068; Ph. (406) 446-1225 **Details:** (County Clerk has Birth Records from 1878, Death Records from 1903, Marriage, Divorce, Probate, Court & Land Records from 1895)
Carter www.rootsweb.com/~mtcarter/index.html	**B8**	**22 Feb 1917**	**Custer** Carter County; 214 Park St; Ekalaka, MT 59324; Ph. (406) 775-8749 **Details:** (County Clerk has Birth, Death & Land Records from 1917; Clerk Courts has Marriage, Divorce, Probate & Court Records)

County Website	Map Index	Date Created	Parent County or Territory From Which Organized Address/Details
Cascade www.rootsweb.com/~mtcascad/	K5	12 Sep 1887	**Chouteau, Meagher, Lewis & Clark** Cascade County; 425 2nd Ave N; Great Falls, MT 59401; Ph. (406) 454-6800 **Details:** (County Clerk & Recorder has Birth, Death & Land Records from 1897 & Military Records from 1918; Clerk Courts has Marriage, Divorce, Probate & Court Records)
Chouteau http://users.eznet.net/~lynch/chouteau/chouteau.html	J4	2 Feb 1865	**Original county** Chouteau County; 1308 Franklin St; Fort Benton, MT 594420000; Ph. (406) 622-5151 **Details:** (County Clerk has Birth & Death Records from 1895, Burial Records & Land Records from 1878; Clerk Courts has Marriage Records from 1888, Divorce & Court Records from 1879 & Probate Records from 1892)
Custer www.rootsweb.com/~mtcuster/	C7	2 Feb 1865	**Original county** Custer County; 1010 Main St; Miles City, MT 593013419; Ph. (406) 232-7800 **Details:** (Formerly Big Horn County (old). Name changed to Custer 16 Feb 1877) (County Clerk has Birth & Death Records from 1907 & Land Records from 1909; Clerk District Court has Marriage, Divorce & Probate Records; Probate Judge has Court Records)
Daniels www.petersnn.org/nemontana/nemont/index.htm	C3	30 Aug 1920	**Valley, Sheridan** Daniels County; 213 Main St; PO Box 247; Scobey, MT 59263; Ph. (406) 487-5561 **Details:** (County Clerk-Recorder has Birth & Death Records from 1920 & Land Records; Clerk Court has Marriage, Divorce & Probate Records from 1920; Clerk District Court has Court Records)
Dawson www.dawsoncountymontana.org	B5	15 Jan 1869	**Original county** Dawson County; 207 W Bell St; Glendive, MT 59330; Ph. (406) 377-3028, commish@midrivers.com **Details:** (County Clerk has Birth & Death Records from 1895 & Land Records from 1882; Clerk Courts has Marriage, Divorce & Court Records from 1882 & Probate Records from 1889; Census Records online; Local Newspaper Office has Newspapers from 1882)
Deer Lodge www.mtech.edu/silverbow/deerlodge.htm	N7	2 Feb 1865	**Original county** Deer Lodge County; 800 S Main St; Anaconda, MT 597112999; Ph. (406) 563-4061 **Details:** (County Clerk has Birth, Death & Land Records; Clerk Courts has Marriage, Divorce, Court & Probate Records)
Edgerton		2 Feb 1865	**Original county** Edgerton County; MT **Details:** (see Lewis & Clark) Name changed to Lewis & Clark 20 Dec 1867
Fallon www.rootsweb.com/~mtfallon/_fll.html	B7	9 Dec 1913	**Custer** Fallon County; 10 W Fallon Ave; Baker, MT 59313; Ph. (406) 778-7106 **Details:** (County Clerk-Recorder has Birth Records from 1884, Death Records from 1919, Land & Military Discharge Records; Clerk Courts has Marriage Records from 1913, Divorce, Probate & Court Records)

County Website	Map Index	Date Created	Parent County or Territory From Which Organized Address/Details
Fergus www.rootsweb.com/~mtfergus/	H5	**12 Mar 1885**	**Meagher, Chouteau** Fergus County; 712 W Main St; Lewistown, MT 594572562; Ph. (406) 538-5119 **Details:** (County Clerk has Birth & Death Records; Clerk Courts has Marriage, Divorce, Probate & Court Records; County Assessor has Land Records)
Flathead www.co.flathead.mt.us/	P4	**6 Feb 1893**	**Missoula** Flathead County; 800 S Main St; Kalispell, MT 59901; Ph. (406) 758-5526 **Details:** (County Clerk & Recorder has Birth & Death Records from 1882, Land Records from 1884 & Burial Records from 1893; Clerk District Court has Marriage, Divorce, Probate & Court Records from 1893)
Gallatin www.rootsweb.com/~mtgallat/Gallatin.htm	K8	**2 Feb 1865**	**Original county** Gallatin County; 311 W Main St; Bozeman, MT 597154576; Ph. (406) 582-3050 **Details:** (County Clerk-Recorder has Birth & Death Records from 1890, Land Records from 1865 & Military Discharge Records from 1900; Clerk District Court has Marriage, Divorce, Probate & Court Records from 1865)
Garfield www.rootsweb.com/~mtgarfie/	E5	**7 Feb 1919**	**Dawson** Garfield County; Hwy 200; PO Box 7; Jordan, MT 593370007; Ph. (406) 557-2760 **Details:** (County Clerk has Birth Records from 1919, Death & Land Records; Clerk Courts has Marriage, Divorce, Probate & Court Records)
Glacier www.rootsweb.com/~mtglacie/	N3	**17 Feb 1919**	**Teton** Glacier County; 512 E Main St; Cut Bank, MT 59427; Ph. (406) 873-5063 **Details:** (County Clerk has Birth, Death & Land Records from 1919; Clerk Courts has Marriage, Divorce, Probate & Court Records)
Golden Valley www.rootsweb.com/~mtgolden/	H7	**4 Oct 1920**	**Musselshell, Sweet Grass** Golden Valley County; PO Box 10; Ryegate, MT 590740010; Ph. (406) 568-2231 **Details:** (County Clerk-Recorder has Birth, Marriage, Death, Divorce, Land, Probate, Military, Court & Naturalization Records from 1920)
Granite www.rootsweb.com/~mtgranit/	O7	**2 Mar 1893**	**Deer Lodge** Granite County; PO Box 925; Philipsburg, MT 59858; Ph. (406) 859-3771 **Details:** (County Recorder has Birth & Death Records from 1895 & Deeds from 1866; Clerk of Courts has Marriage, Probate, & Court Records from 1893)
Hill http://co.hill.mt.us/	J3	**28 Feb 1912**	**Chouteau** Hill County; County Courthouse; 315 4th St; Havre, MT 595013999; Ph. (406) 265-5481 **Details:** (County Clerk & Recorder has Birth & Death Records from 1907 & Land Records from 1865; Clerk Courts has Marriage, Divorce, Probate & Court Records)

Montana

County	Map	Date	Parent County or Territory From Which Organized
Website	Index	Created	Address/Details

Jefferson M7 **2 Feb 1865** **Original county**
www.rootsweb.com/~mtjeffer/index.html
Jefferson County; 201 Centennial; PO Box H; Boulder, MT 59632;
Ph. (406) 225-4020
Details: (County Clerk has Birth & Death Records from 1907 & Land Records from 1865; Clerk District Court has Marriage, Divorce, Probate & Court Records)

Judith Basin J6 **10 Dec 1920** **Fergus, Cascade**
www.rootsweb.com/~mtjudith/
Judith Basin County; 31 1st Ave; PO Box 427; Stanford, MT 59479;
Ph. (406) 553-2301
Details: (County Clerk & Recorder has Birth, Death & Land Records from 1920; Clerk Courts has Marriage, Divorce, Probate & Court Records)

Lake O5 **11 May 1923** **Flathead, Missoula**
www.rootsweb.com/~mtlake/mtlake.html
Lake County; 106 4th Ave E; Polson, MT 598602125;
Ph. (406) 883-6211
Details: (County Clerk-Recorder has Birth, Death & Land Records from 1923; Clerk Courts has Marriage, Divorce, Probate & Court Records from 1923 & Naturalization Records 1923–1953)

Lewis & Clark M5 **2 Feb 1865** **Original county**
www.co.lewis-clark.mt.us/
Lewis & Clark County; 316 N Park Ave; Helena, MT 59624;
Ph. (406) 447-8335
Details: (Formerly Edgerton County. Name changed to Lewis & Clark 20 Dec 1867) (County Clerk has Birth Records from 1907, Death Records from 1895 & Land Records from 1865; Clerk District Court has Marriage, Divorce, Probate & Court Records)

Liberty K3 **11 Feb 1920** **Chouteau, Hill**
www.rootsweb.com/~mtlibert/
Liberty County; 111 1st St E; Chester, MT 59522; Ph. (406) 759-5365
Details: (County Clerk has Birth, Death & Land Records from 1920; Clerk District Court has Marriage Records from 1920, Divorce, Probate & Court Records)

Lincoln Q3 **9 Mar 1909** **Flathead**
www.libby.org/
Lincoln County; 512 California Ave; Libby, MT 59923;
Ph. (406) 293-7781
Details: (County Clerk has Birth, Death & Land Records from 1909; Clerk District Court has Marriage, Divorce, Probate & Court Records; County Clerk also has some transcribed Birth & Death Records prior to 1909)

Madison L9 **2 Feb 1865** **Original county**
www.rootsweb.com/~mtmadiso/madison.html
Madison County; 110 W Wallace St; Virginia City, MT 59755;
Ph. (406) 843-4270
Details: (County Clerk & Recorder has Birth & Death Records from 1909 & Land Records from 1864; Clerk Courts has Marriage Records from 1887, Divorce, Probate & Court Records from 1865)

McCone C5 **20 Feb 1919** **Dawson, Richland**
www.rootsweb.com/~mtmccone/
McCone County; 1004 Ave C; PO Box 199; Circle, MT 59215;
Ph. (406) 485-3505
Details: (County Clerk & Recorder has Birth, Death, Burial & Land Records from 1919; Clerk Courts has Marriage, Divorce, Probate & Court Records)

County Website	Map Index	Date Created	Parent County or Territory From Which Organized Address/Details
Meagher www.rootsweb.com/~mtmeaghe/	K6	16 Nov 1867	**Original county** Meagher County; 15 W Main St; PO Box 309; White Sulphur Springs, MT 59645; Ph. (406) 547-3612 **Details:** (County Clerk & Recorder has Birth & Death Records from 1896, Burial Records from 1884 & Land Records from 1866; Clerk Courts has Marriage & Probate Records from 1866, Divorce, Court & Naturalization Records from 1867)
Mineral www.rootsweb.com/~mtminera/mineral.htm	Q5	7 Aug 1914	**Missoula** Mineral County; 300 River St; PO Box 550; Superior, MT 59872; Ph. (406) 822-4541 **Details:** (County Clerk & Recorder has Birth, Death, Burial & Land Records from 1914; Clerk District Court has Marriage, Divorce, Probate & Court Records from 1914)
Missoula www.co.missoula.mt.us/	O6	2 Feb 1865	**Original county** Missoula County; 200 W Broadway St; Missoula, MT 598024292; Ph. (406) 523-4752 **Details:** (County Clerk has Birth & Death Records from 1895 & Land Records; Clerk Courts has Marriage, Divorce, Probate & Court Records)
Musselshell www.rootsweb.com/~mtmussel/	G6	11 Feb 1911	**Fergus, Yellowstone** Musselshell County; 506 Main St; Roundup, MT 590722498; Ph. (406) 323-1104 **Details:** (County Clerk-Recorder has Birth, Death & Land Records from 1911; Clerk of Courts has Marriage, Divorce, Probate, Military & Court Records from 1911)
Park www.parkcounty.org/	K8	23 Feb 1887	**Gallatin** Park County; 414 E Callender St; Livingston, MT 590472799; Ph. (406) 222-4110 **Details:** (County Clerk has Birth, Death & Land Records from 1907; Clerk District Court has Marriage, Divorce, Probate & Court Records)
Petroleum www.rootsweb.com/~mtpetrol/	G5	24 Nov 1924	**Fergus, Garfield** Petroleum County; 201 E Main; PO Box 226; Winnett, MT 59087; Ph. (406) 429-5311 **Details:** (Director of Records has Birth, Marriage, Death, Burial, Divorce, Probate, Court & Land Records from 1925)
Phillips www.rootsweb.com/~mtphilli/	G4	5 Feb 1915	**Valley** Phillips County; 314 S 2nd Ave W; Malta, MT 59538; Ph. (406) 654-2423 **Details:** (County Clerk has Birth, Death & Land Records; Clerk Courts has Marriage, Divorce, Probate & Court Records)
Pondera www.rootsweb.com/~mtponder/	M4	17 Feb 1919	**Chouteau, Teton** Pondera County; 20 4th Ave SW; Conrad, MT 594252340; Ph. (406) 278-4000 **Details:** (County Clerk has Birth, Death & Land Records from 1919; Clerk Courts has Marriage, Divorce, Probate & Court Records)
Powder River www.rangeweb.net/~emmov/prc.html/	C8	7 Mar 1919	**Custer** Powder River County; PO Box 270; Broadus, MT 59317; Ph. (406) 436-2361 **Details:** (County Clerk has Birth, Death & Election Records from 1919 & Land Records from 1890's; Clerk District Court has Marriage & Divorce Records from 1919, Probate & Court Records)

County	Map	Date	Parent County or Territory From Which Organized
Website	Index	Created	Address/Details

Powell   **N6**   **31 Jan 1901**
www.mtech.edu/silverbow/powell.htm

Missoula, Deer Lodge
Powell County; 409 Missouri Ave; Deer Lodge, MT 597221084;
Ph. (406) 846-3680
Details: (County Clerk has Birth, Death & Land Records from 1907; Clerk Courts has Marriage, Divorce, Probate & Court Records from 1901)

Prairie   **C6**   **5 Feb 1915**
www.rangeweb.net/~emmov/prairie/index2.html

Custer
Prairie County; 217 W Park St; Terry, MT 59349; Ph. (406) 635-5575
Details: (County Clerk has Birth, Death & Land Records from 1915; Clerk Courts has Marriage, Divorce, Probate & Court Records from 1915)

Ravalli   **P7**   **16 Feb 1893**
www.rootsweb.com/~mtravall/

Missoula
Ravalli County; 205 Bedford St; Hamilton, MT 59840;
Ph. (406) 375-6213
Details: (Clerk of Courts has Marriage, Probate, & Court Records from 1893; County Clerk has Deeds from 1866)

Richland   **B4**   **27 May 1914**
www.midrivers.com/~wyldrose/index.html

Dawson
Richland County; 201 W Main St; Sidney, MT 59270;
Ph. (406) 482-1708
Details: (County Clerk has Birth Records from 1910, Death & Land Records from 1914; Clerk District Court has Marriage, Divorce, Probate & Court Records)

Roosevelt   **C3**   **18 Feb 1919**
www.petersnn.org/nemontana/nemont/index.htm

Valley, Richland, Sheridan
Roosevelt County; 400 2nd Ave S; Wolf Point, MT 59201;
Ph. (406) 653-6250
Details: (County Clerk & Recorder has Birth, Death & Land Records from 1919; Clerk District Court has Marriage, Divorce, Probate & Court Records from 1919)

Rosebud   **E7**   **11 Feb 1901**
www.rosebudcounty.homestead.com/

Custer
Rosebud County; 1200 Main St; Forsyth, MT 593270047;
Ph. (406) 356-7318
Details: (County Clerk has Birth & Death Records from 1900 & Land Records; Clerk District Court has Marriage, Divorce, Probate & Court Records)

Sanders   **Q5**   **7 Feb 1905**
www.rootsweb.com/~mtsander/_snd.html

Missoula
Sanders County; PO Box 519; Thompson Falls, MT 59873;
Ph. (406) 827-4392
Details: (County Recorder has Deeds from 1885, Marriage, Probate, & Court Records from 1906)

Sheridan   **B3**   **24 Mar 1913**
www.co.sheridan.mt.us/

Valley
Sheridan County; 100 W Laurel Ave; Plentywood, MT 59254;
Ph. (406) 765-2310
Details: (County Clerk has Birth, Death, Burial & Land Records from 1913; Clerk Courts has Marriage, Divorce, Probate & Court Records from 1913)

County Website	Map Index	Date Created	Parent County or Territory From Which Organized Address/Details
Silver Bow www.co.silverbow.mt.us	M8	**16 Feb 1881**	**Deer Lodge** Silver Bow County; 155 W Granite St; Butte, MT 59701; Ph. (406) 497-6200, clerkrec@co.silverbow.mt.us **Details:** (2 May 1977 the city of Butte & County of Silver Bow were unified to form the Butte-Silver Bow government.) (Clerk & Recorders Office has Birth & Death Records from 1890, Land Records from 1875, & Military Discharge Records from 1918; Clerk of District Court has Court Records from 1871, Marriage & Divorce Records from 1913, Guardianship, & Probate Records; County Archives has Census Records 1900–1970, Immigration, Naturalization & Coroner Registers Records from 1894, Burial Records 1880–1980, Newspapers from 1891, & Other Historical Records)
Stillwater www.rootsweb.com/~mtstillw/	I8	**24 Mar 1913**	**Sweet Grass, Yellowstone, Carbon** Stillwater County; PO Box 149; Columbus, MT 590190149; Ph. (406) 322-8000 **Details:** (County Clerk-Recorder has Birth & Death Records from late 1800's, Land & Military Records; Clerk Courts has Marriage Records from late 1800's, Divorce, Probate, Court & Naturalization Records)
Sweet Grass www.rootsweb.com/~mtsweetg/	I8	**5 Mar 1895**	**Meagher, Park, Yellowstone** Sweet Grass County; 200 W 1st Ave; Big Timber, MT 590110460; Ph. (406) 932-5152 **Details:** (County Clerk & Recorder has Birth Records from 1907, Death & Burial Records from 1900 & Land Records from 1895; Clerk District Court has Marriage, Divorce, Probate & Court Records from 1895)
Teton www.rootsweb.com/~mtteton/index.htm/	M4	**7 Feb 1893**	**Chouteau** Teton County; 915 4th St NW; PO Box 610; Choteau, MT 59422; Ph. (406) 466-2693 **Details:** (County Clerk has Birth, Death & Burial Records from 1899 & Land Records; Clerk District Court has Marriage, Divorce, Probate & Court Records)
Toole www.rootsweb.com/~mttoole/	L3	**7 May 1914**	**Teton, Hill** Toole County; 226 1st St S; Shelby, MT 594741920; Ph. (406) 434-2232 **Details:** (County Clerk & Recorder has Birth, Death & Burial Records from 1914 & Land Records from 1890; Clerk Courts has Marriage Records from 1914, Divorce, Probate & Court Records)
Treasure www.rootsweb.com/~mttreasu/	F7	**7 Feb 1919**	**Rosebud** Treasure County; PO Box 392; Hysham, MT 590380392; Ph. (406) 342-5547 **Details:** (County Clerk & Recorder has Birth, Death & Land Records from 1919; Clerk District Court has Marriage, Divorce, Probate & Court Records)
Valley www.petersnn.org/nemontana/nemont/index.htm	E3	**6 Feb 1893**	**Dawson** Valley County; 501 Court Sq Box 1; Glasgow, MT 592030311; Ph. (406) 228-8221 **Details:** (County Clerk & Recorder has Birth, Death & Land Records from early 1900's; Clerk Courts has Marriage, Divorce, Probate & Court Records)

The Handybook for Genealogists

County Website	Map Index	Date Created	Parent County or Territory From Which Organized Address/Details
Wheatland www.rootsweb.com/~mtwheatl/	I7	**22 Feb 1917**	**Meagher, Sweet Grass** Wheatland County; 201A Ave NW; PO Box 1903; Harlowton, MT 59036; Ph. (406) 632-4891 **Details:** (County Clerk & Recorder has Birth Records from 1917, Death, Burial & Land Records; Clerk Courts has Marriage, Divorce, Probate & Court Records)
Wibaux www.rootsweb.com/~mtwibaux/	A6	**17 Aug 1914**	**Dawson** Wibaux County; 200 S Wilbaux St; Wibaux, MT 59353; Ph. (406) 796-2481 **Details:** (County Clerk-Recorder has Birth & Death Records from 1914, Burial & Land Records from mid-1800's & Military Records from 1917; Clerk District Court has Marriage, Divorce, Probate, Court & Naturalization Records from 1914)
Yellowstone www.co.yellowstone.mt.us/javadefault.asp	G7	**26 Feb 1883**	**Gallatin, Meagher, Custer, Carbon** Yellowstone County; 217 N 27th St; PO Box 35001; Billings, MT 591075001; Ph. (406) 256-2785 **Details:** (County Clerk-Recorder has Birth, Death, Land & Military Records from 1883; Clerk District Court has Marriage, Divorce, Probate & Court Records)

Nebraska

Capital: Lincoln
Territory: 1854
State: 1867 (37th)

Equality before the law

Etienne Veniard de Bourgmond is believed to have been the first European to enter the Nebraska area in 1714 as a French adventurer. His report about the area used the term "Nebraskier," an Indian term meaning "flat water" for the first time. Six years later a Spanish soldier, Pedro de Villasur, led an expedition into Nebraska that was massacred by Pawnee Indians. Only fur traders braved the area until after the Louisiana Purchase in 1803. At that time, a number of expeditions explored the area, some of which reported Nebraska to be a vast wasteland. The first permanent settlement was Bellevue, established in 1823. Other forts and trading posts followed, especially along the Oregon and Mormon trails.

In 1834, Nebraska was placed under the supervision of Arkansas, Michigan, and Missouri. It was termed Indian country from which all others were excluded. Later, Nebraska was made part of the territories of Indiana, Louisiana, and Missouri. Most of the Indian tribes had ceded their land to the United States by 1854 when Nebraska became a territory. It included all territory between 40 and 49 degrees north latitude and between the Missouri River and the crest of the Rocky Mountains. Parts of Colorado, Montana, North Dakota, South Dakota, and Wyoming were then part of Nebraska. In 1861, the Colorado and Dakota Territories were created. In 1863, the formation of the Idaho Territory reduced Nebraska to near its present size.

Many early settlers were stragglers from the California Gold Rush and the Oregon migration. Some of the thousands who traveled the Oregon, California, and Mormon Trails either stopped their migration in Nebraska or returned to Nebraska upon seeing the Rocky Mountains. During the 1850's, many Germans settled in Nebraska. Two decades later, a large group of Germans from Russia settled Lancaster and nearby counties. After the passage of the Homestead Act, many Scandinavians came to the area. Today many Nebraskans are of German, Czech, Swedish, or Russian descent.

During the Civil War, Nebraska sided with the Union and supplied more than 3,000 men to its forces. The first railroad to the Pacific Coast began at Omaha in 1865. It was completed four years later. Nebraska was admitted to the Union in 1867 as the 37th state. Many Civil War veterans came to Nebraska to secure cheap land, which brought about the state's largest population growth.

Look for vital records in the following locations:

- **Birth and death records:** Bureau of Vital Statistics, State Department of Health in Lincoln, Nebraska. Statewide registration of births and deaths began in 1905 and was generally complied with by 1920. Relationship to the individual and the reason for the request must accompany all applications, along with written permission from the individual if the birth occurred within the last 50 years.

- **Marriage records:** Counties kept marriage records. Relationship to the individual and the reason for the request must accompany all applications, along with written permission from the individual if the marriage occurred within the last 50 years.

- **Probate records:** County judges usually keep probate records.

- **Census records:** Territorial and state census records exist for parts of Nebraska for 1854, 1855, 1856, 1860, 1865, and 1869. A detailed census of German immigrants from Russia living in Lincoln was taken from 1913 to 1914. Some of these census records have been transcribed, indexed, and published. Contact the Nebraska State Historical Society, Department of Reference Services.

Vital Records
PO Box 95065
Lincoln, NE 68509
(402) 471-2871
www.hhs.state.ne.us/ced/nevrinfo.htm

Nebraska State Historical Society Department of Reference Services
1500 "R" Street; PO Box 82554
Lincoln, NE 68501-2554
www.nebraskahistory.org/

Societies and Repositories

Adams County Genealogical Society; PO Box 424; Hastings, NE 68902-0424; acgs@inebraska.com; http://incolor.inetnebr.com/achs/acgs.html.

Adams County Historical Society; PO Box 102; Hastings, NE 68902; achs@inebraska.com; http://incolor.inetnebr.com/achs.

American Historical Society of Germans from Russia; 631 D St.; Lincoln, NE 68502-1199; (402) 474-3363; ahsgr@ahsgr.org; www.ahsgr.org.

Boone-Nance County Genealogical Society; PO Box 231; Belgrade, NE 68623; www.rootsweb.com/~nenance/bngensoc.html.

Buffalo County Historical Society; PO Box 523; Kearney, NE 68848-0523; bchs@kearney.net; http://bchs.kearney.net/index.html.

Butler County Historical Society; 3861 MN RD; David City, NE 68632.

Cairo Roots; Rt. 1, Box 42; Cairo, NE 68824.

Chase County Genealogical Society; PO Box 303; Imperial, NE 69033.

Chase County Historical Society; 73989 320th Avenue; Imperial, NE 69033-8616; http://freepages.genealogy.rootsweb.com/~chasecountyne.

Cherry County Genealogical Society; Box 380; Valentine, NE 69201.

Cheyenne County Genealogical Society; Box 802; Sidney, NE 69162.

Cozad Genealogical Club; c/o Cozad Public Library; 910 Meridian Ave.; Cozad, NE 69130.

Cuming County Historical Society; 130 N. River; West Point, NE 68788.

Custer County Historical Society, Inc.; PO Box 334; 445 S. 9th Ave.; Broken Bow, NE 68822-0334; custer.county.history@navix.net; www.rootsweb.com/~necuster/index.htm.

Dakota County Genealogical Society; PO Box 189; Dakota City, NE 68850.

Dawson County Historical Society; PO Box 369; Lexington, NE 68850.

Denton Community Historical Society; PO Box 405; Denton, NE 68339.

Dixon County Historical Society; Box 95; Allen, NE 68710.

Eastern Nebraska Genealogical Society; PO Box 541; Fremont, NE 68025; www.connectfremont.org/CLUB/ENGS.HTM.

Elkhorn Valley Genealogical Society; J.A. Stahl Library; 300 North Colfax; PO Box 258; West Point, NE 68788; (402) 372-3831; wplibrary@cableone.net.

Fillmore Heritage Genealogical Society; Rt. 2, Box 28; Exeter, NE 68351.

Fort Kearney Genealogical Society; PO Box 22; Kearney, NE 68848-0022; garrisonl@charter.net; www.rootsweb.com/~nebuffal/fkgs.htm.

Furnas County Genealogical Society; PO Box 391; Beaver City, NE 68926; www.rootsweb.com/~nefurnas/GenSocResources.html.

Gage County Historical Society; Box 793; Beatrice, NE 68310.

Genealogical Seekers; 462 East 13th St.; Wahoo, NE 68066-1415.

Genealogical Society of Wayne, NE; c/o Steve Gross; 1028 Emerald Drive; Wayne, NE 68787-1000.

Greater Omaha Genealogical Society; PO Box 4011; Omaha, NE 68104-0011; GrOmahaGenSoc@aol.com; http://members.aol.com/_ht_a/gromahagensoc/myhomepage.

Greater York Area Genealogical Society; c/o Kilgore Memorial Library; 6th and Nebraska; York, NE 68467.

Holdrege Area Genealogical Club; PO Box 164; Holdrege, NE 68949.

Holt County Historical Society; 401 E Douglas; O'Neill, NE 68763; www.rootsweb.com/~neholths.

Hooker County Genealogical Society; Box 280; Mullen, NE 69152.

Howard County Historical Society; Howard County Community Hospital; PO Box 406; St. Paul, NE 68873-0406.

Howard County Kinquesters; c/o Mrs. Emma Osterman; 317 7th Street; St. Paul, NE 68873.

Jefferson County Genealogical Society; PO Box 163; Fairbury, NE 68352-0163; JCGS@alltel.net; www.rootsweb.com/~nejeffgs.

Johnson County Historical Society & Museum; 231 Lincoln Street; Tecumseh, NE 68450; JC10928@alltel.net; www.rootsweb.com/~nejohnso/jchstsoc.htm.

Leila Stahl Buffett Genealogy Center; J.A. Stahl Library, 330 N. Colfax; PO Box 258; West Point, NE 68788; (402) 372-3831; wplibrary@cableone.net; www.wplibrary.com.

Lexington Genealogical Society; Box 778; Lexington, NE 68850; eb83217@alltel.net; www.rootsweb.com/~nedawson/lexsoc.html.

Lincoln Nebraska Chapter, AHSGR; 3300 Serenity Circle #10; Lincoln, NE 68506; www.ahsgr.org/nelincol.html.

Lincoln-Lancaster County Genealogical Society; PO Box 30055; Lincoln, NE 68503-0055.

Madison County Genealogical Society; PO Box 1031; Norfolk, NE 68702-1031; madisoncgs@cableone.net.

Midlands Chapter, AHSGR; 9373 Maplewood Blvd.; Omaha, NE 68134-4663; (402) 572-8871.

Naponee Historical Society; PO Box 128; Naponee, NE 68960; http://home.4w.com/pages/psimpson/naponeehist.html.

Nebraska Library Commission; The Atrium; 1200 N Street, Suite 120; Lincoln, NE 68508-2023; (402) 471-2045; webspinner@nlc.state.ne.us; www.nlc.state.ne.us.

Nebraska Panhandle Chapter, AHSGR; 2430 Ave. C; Scottbluff, NE 69361; (308) 632-2459; email: sflack@actcom.com.

Nebraska State Genealogical Society; PO Box 5608; Lincoln, NE 68505; www.rootsweb.com/~nesgs.

Nebraska State Historical Society Library/Archives; 1500 R Street; PO Box 82554; Lincoln, NE 68501; (402) 471-4747; lanshs@nebraskahistory.org; www.nebraskahistory.org.

Nebraskans of Irish and Scotch-Irish Ancestry; Box 5049; Lincoln, NE 68505-5049.

Nemaha Valley Genealogical Society; PO Box 25; Auburn, NE 68305.

North Platte Genealogical Society; PO Box 1452; North Platte, NE 69101.

Northeast Nebraska Chapter, AHSGR; 314 S. 13th Place; Norfolk, NE 68701-1214; ruthelaine@uswest.net; www.ahsgr.org/nenorthe.html.

Northeastern Nebraska Genealogical Society (NENGS); PO Box 249; Lyons, NE 68038.

Northern Antelope County Genealogical Society; Box 267; Orchard, NE 68764.

Northern Nebraska Genealogical Society; 401 E. Douglas; O'Neill, NE 68763.

Nuckolls County Genealogical Society; PO Box 441; Superior, NE 68978-0441.

Omaha Family History Center; 11027 Martha St.; Omaha, NE 68144.

Pawnee Genealogy Scouters; PO Box 231; Belgrade, NE 68623-0231.

Perkins County Genealogical Society; Box 418; Grant, NE 69140.

Plains Genealogical Society; c/o Kimball Public Library; 208 S. Walnut St.; Kimball, NE 69145.

Platte Valley Kin Seekers; PO Box 153; Columbus, NE 60602-0513; pvks@megavision.com; www.megavision.net/pvks.

Prairie Pioneer Genealogical Society; Box 1122; Grand Island, NE 68802.

Ravenna Genealogical Society; 105 Alba St.; Ravenna, NE 68869; johnsten@micrord.com; www.rootsweb.com/~nebuffal/ravenna.htm.

Rebecca Winter's Genealogical Society; PO Box 323; Scottsbluff, NE 69363-0323.

Saline County Genealogical Society; PO Box 24; Crete, NE 68333; th85029@alltel.net.

Sarpy County Genealogical Society; 2402 Sac Place; Bellevue, NE 68005-3932.

Saunders County Genealogy Seekers; c/o G. Cajka; 462 E. 13; Wahoo, NE 68066.

Saunders County Historical Society & Museum; 240 N. Walnut; Wahoo, NE 68066-1858; (402) 443-3090; www.visitsaunderscounty.org.

Schuyler Historical Society and Museum; 1005 B Street; Schuyler, NE 68661.

Seward County Genealogical Society; PO Box 72; Seward, NE 68434.

Sons of the American Revolution, Nebraska Society; 6731 Sumner St.; Lincoln, NE 68506.

South Central Genealogical Society; c/o Jensen Memorial Library; 443 N. Kearney; Minden, NE 68959.

Southeast Nebraska Genealogical Society; PO Box 562; Beatrice, NE 68301.

Southwest Nebraska Genealogical Society; PO Box 156; McCook, NE 69001-0156; rray@swnebr.net; www.rootsweb.com/~neswngs.

Thayer County Genealogical Society; Box 398; Belvidere, NE 68315.

Thomas County Genealogical Society; Box 136; Thedford, NE 69166.

Tri-State Comers Genealogical Society; c/o Lydia BruunWoods Memorial Library; 120 E. 18th; Falls City, NE 68355.

Valley County Genealogical Society; 619 S. 10th; Ord, NE 68862.

Wahoo Genealogical Seekers; 871 West 6th; Wahoo, NE 68066.

Washington County Genealogical Society; c/o Blair Public Library; 210 South 17th Street; Blair, NE 68008.

Washington County Historical Association; PO Box 25; Fort Calhoun, NE 68023; info@newashcohist.org; www.newashcohist.org.

Bibliography and Record Sources

General

A Research Guide to Genealogical Data in Nebraska. Alliance, Nebraska: Nebraska State Genealogical Society, 1980–.

Andreas, A. T. *History of the State of Nebraska.* 2 vols. Chicago: The Western Historical Company, 1882.

Baldwin, Sara Mullin and Robert Morton Mullin. *Nebraskana: Biographical Sketches of Nebraska Men and Women of Achievement.* Hebron, Nebraska: Baldwin Co., 1932.

Bullen, Galen, ed. et. al. *Broken Hoops and Plains People: A Catalogue of Ethnic Resources in the Humanities: Nebraska and Surrounding Area.* Lincoln, Nebraska: Nebraska Curriculum Development Center, 1976.

Casper, Henry Weber. *History of the Catholic Church in Nebraska,* 3 vols. Milwaukee: Catholic Life Pub., 1960–1966.

Compendium of History, Reminiscence and Biography of Nebraska. Chicago: Alden Publishing Co., 1912.

Daniels, Sherrill. *An Index to and Bibliography of Reminiscences in the Nebraska State Historical Society Library.* Lincoln, Nebraska: University of Nebraska Dissertation, 1986.

Diffendal, Anne P. *A Guide to the Newspaper Collection of the State Archives, Nebraska State Historical Society.* Lincoln: Nebraska State Historical Society, 1977.

Early Pioneers of Nebraska, With Allied Lines, Vol. 1. Lincoln: Nebraska State Genealogical Society, 1981.

Historical Records Survey (Nebraska). *Preliminary Edition of Guide to Depositories of Manuscript Collections in the United States—Nebraska.* Lincoln, Nebraska: The Survey, 1940.

Index for Biographical and Genealogical History of Southwestern Nebraska 1904. Lincoln: Lincoln-Lancaster County Genealogical Society.

Morton, Julius Sterling et al. *Illustrated History of Nebraska.* 3 vols. Lincoln: Jacob North and Co., 1905–1913.

Nebraska Newspaper Abstracts: A Computer Index to Names and Events Abstracted from Selected Nebraska Newspapers. Alliance, Nebraska: Nebraska State Genealogical Society, 1983–.

Nebraska Research Outline, Series U.S.-States, No. 28. Salt Lake City: Family History Library, 1988.

Nebraska State Genealogical Society (Lincoln, Nebraska). *Nebraska Newspaper Abstracts, 1930s.* 6 vols. in 1. Lincoln, Nebraska: Nebraska State Genealogical Society, 2000.

Nebraska State Genealogical Society (Lincoln, Nebraska). *Nebraska Newspaper Abstracts, 1940s.* 6 vols. in 1. Lincoln, Nebraska: Nebraska State Genealogical Society, 1999.

Nebraska State Historical Society (Lincoln, Nebraska). *A Guide to the Newspaper Collection of the State Archives, Nebraska State Historical Society.* Lincoln, Nebraska: Nebraska State Historical Soc., 1977.

Nebraska State Historical Society (Lincoln, Nebraska). *Historical Resources for Genealogists in the Nebraska State Historical Society.* Lincoln, Nebraska: Nebraska State Historical Society, 1986.

Nebraska State Historical Society State Archives. *A Guide to the Manuscript Division of the State Archives, Nebraska State Historical Society.* Lincoln: Nebraska State Historical Society, 1974

Nebraska, a Guide to Genealogical Research. Lincoln: Nebraska State Genealogical Society, 1984.

Nimmo, Sylvia, and Mary Cutler. *Nebraska Local History and Genealogical Reference Guide.* Papillion, Nebraska: S. Nimmo.

Nimmo, Sylvia *Nebraska Local History and Genealogy Reference Guide: A Bibliography of County Research Materials in Selected Repositories.* Papillion, Nebraska: the author, 1987.

Olson, James C. *History of Nebraska,* 2nd ed. Lincoln: University of Nebraska Press, 1966.

Perkey, Elton A. *Perkey's Nebraska Place Names.* Lincoln: Nebraska State Genealogical Society, 1982.

Rife, Janet Warkentin. *Germans and German-Russians in Nebraska: A Research Guide to Nebraska Ethnic Studies.* Lincoln: Center for Great Plains Studies, 1980.

Rosicky, Rose. *A History of Czechs (Bohemians) in Nebraska.* Omaha: Czech Historical Society of Nebraska, 1929.

Sandahl, Charles F. *The Nebraska Conference of the Augustana Synod.* n.p.: Nebraska Conference, 1931.

Sheldon, Addison Erwin. *Nebraska: The Land and the People.* 3 vols. Chicago: Lewis Publishing Co., 1931.

Sittler, Melvin. *Sittler Index of Surnames from the Nebraska State Journal.* 5 vols. 1983–1985. Lincoln: Lincoln-Lancaster County Genealogical Society.

Sobotka, Margie. *Nebraska, Kansas Czech Settlers, 1891–1895.* Omaha: the author, 1980.

Source of Genealogical Help in Nebraska. Burbank, California: Southern California Genealogical Society.

Atlases, Maps and Gazetteers

Fitzpatrick, Lillian Linder. *Nebraska Place Names. . . .* New ed. Lincoln: University of Nebraska Press, 1960.

Nebraska Atlas and Gazetteer. Freeport, Maine: DeLorme Mapping Co., 1997.

Nimmo, Sylvia. *Maps Showing Boundaries, Nebraska, 1854–1925.* Papillion, Nebraska: Sylvia Nimmo, 1978.

Perkey, Elton A. *Perkey's Nebraska Place Names.* Lincoln: Nebraska State Historical Society, 1982.

Rapp, William F. *The Post Offices of Nebraska.* Vol. 1. *Territorial Post Offices.* Crete, Nebraska: J-B Publishing Co., 1971.

Searcy, N. D., and A. R. Longwell. *Nebraska Atlas.* Kearney, Nebraska: Nebraska Atlas Publishing Co., 1964.

The Official State Atlas of Nebraska. 1885. Reprint. Evansville, Indiana: Unigraphic, 1976.

Census Records

Available Census Records and Census Substitutes

Federal Census 1860, 1870, 1880, 1900, 1910, 1920, 1930

Federal Mortality Schedules 1860, 1870, 1880

Union Veterans and Widows 1890

State/Territorial Census 1854, 1855, 1856, 1865–1884, 1885

Cox, Eunice Evelyn. *1854, 1855, 1856 Nebraska Territory Censuses.* Ellensburg, Washington: Cox, 1977.

Dollarhide, William. *The Census Book: A Genealogist's Guide to Federal Census Facts, Schedules and Indexes.* Bountiful, Utah: Heritage Quest, 1999.

Kemp, Thomas Jay. *The American Census Handbook.* Wilmington, Delaware: Scholarly Resources, Inc., 2001.

Lainhart, Ann S. *State Census Records.* Baltimore: Genealogical Publishing Co., Inc., 1992.

Szucs, Loretto Dennis and Matthew Wright. *Finding Answers in U.S. Census Records.* Ancestry Publishing, 2001

Thorndale, William and William Dollarhide. *County Boundary Map Guides to the U.S. Federal Censuses, 1790–1920:* Baltimore: Genealogical Publishing Co, 1987.

Court Records, Probate and Wills

Hons, Fred W., and Delbert A. Bishop. *Preliminary Inventory Records of the United States District Court for the District of Nebraska.* Kansas City: Federal Records Center, 1967.

Emigration, Immigration, Migration and Naturalization

Knight, Hal. *111 days to Zion.* Salt Lake City: Deseret News, 1978.

Sobotka, Margie. *Czech Immigrant Passenger List (for Nebraska) 1879.* Omaha, Nebraska: Eastern Nebraska Genealogical Society, 1982.

Land and Property

Homestead Guide of Kansas and Nebraska. Waterville, Kansas: F. G. Adams, 1873.

Hone, Wade E. *Land and Property Research in the United States.* Salt Lake City: Ancestry Incorporated, 1997.

Sheldon, Addison E. *Land Systems and Land Policies in Nebraska: A History of Nebraska Land, Public Domain and Private Property.* Lincoln: Nebraska State Historical Society, 1936.

Military

Dudley, Edgar S. *Roster of Nebraska Volunteers from 1861 to 1869.* Hasting, Nebraska: Wigton & Evans, 1888.

Grand Army of the Republic. Department of Nebraska. *Roster and Indexes of Soldiers, 1911.* Lincoln, Nebraska: Nebraska State Historical Society, 1974. 2 microfilm.

Hartman, Douglas R. *Nebraska's Militia: The History of the Army and Air National Guard, 1854–1991.* Virginia Beach, Virginia: Donning, 1994.

Nebraska Adjutant General. *Roster of Nebraska Volunteers 1861 to 1869.* Hastings, Nebraska: Wigton & Evans, 1888.

Nebraska Secretary of State. *Roster of Soldiers, Sailors, and Marines of the War of 1812, The Mexican War, and*

The War of the Rebellion Residing in Nebraska, Jun 1, 1891. Lincoln: State Journal Co., 1892

Nebraska. Secretary of State. *Roster of Soldiers-Sailors and Marines Who Served in the War of the Rebellion, Spanish-American War and World War.* Omaha: Waters-Barnhart Printing Co., 1925.

Nebraska. Secretary of State. *Roster of Veterans of the Mexican, Civil, and Spanish-American Wars Residing in Nebraska, 1915.* Lincoln: Secretary of State, 1915.

Roster of Nebraska Soldiers. Omaha: Klopp, Bartlett, & Co., 1888.

Sherard, Gerald E. *A Nebraska Civil War Ancestor.* Lakewood, Colorado: G. M. E. Sherard, 1994.

Sherard, Gerald E. *Nebraska Born Veterans Buried in Colorado, 1862–1949.* [Lakewood, Colorado: G. E. Sherard, 1997].

United States. Selective Service System. *Nebraska World War I Selective Service System Draft Registration Cards, 1917–1918.* National Archives Microfilm Publications, M1509. Washington, D.C.: National Archives, 1987–1988.

Vital and Cemetery Records

Daughters of the American Revolution (Nebraska). *Miscellaneous Records: 1856–1972.* Microfilm copy of typescript (301 leaves) made in 1972 in possession of DAR Library, Washington, D.C. Salt Lake City: Filmed by the Genealogical Society of Utah, 1972.

Jackson, Ronald Vern. *Nebraska 1860 Mortality Scheldule.* Bountiful, Utah: Accelerated Indexing Systems, 1980.

Jackson, Ronald Vern. *Nebraska 1870 Mortality* Schedule. Bountiful, Utah: Accelerated Indexing Systems, 1980.

Jackson, Ronald Vern. Nebraska *1880 Mortality Schedule.* Bountiful, Utah: Accelerated Indexing Systems, 1981.

Nebraska Cemeteries and Burial Sites. 2 parts. Lincoln: Nebraska State Genealogical Society, 1984.

Nebraska Cemeteries and Known Burial Sites. Lincoln: Nebraska State Genealogical Society, 1996.

Sherard, Gerald E. *Nebraska Cemetery Index.* Lakewood, Colorado: G. E. Sherard, 199–.

Sones, Georgene Morris. *Nebraska Cemeteries and Burial Sites: In Two Parts.* Lincoln, Nebraska: Nebraska State Genealogy Society, 1996.

The Guide to Public Vital Statistics Records in Nebraska. Lincoln: Historical Records Survey, 1941.

United States. Bureau of Indian Affairs. Winnebago Agency. *Vital Statistics: Births, Marriages and Deaths, 1863–1947.* Kansas City, Missouri: Federal Archives and Records Center, 1977.

County Website	Map Index	Date Created	Parent County or Territory From Which Organized Address/Details
Adams www.rootsweb.com/~neadams/	**G8**	**16 Feb 1867**	**Unorg. Terr.** Adams County; 500 W 5th; Hastings, NE 68901; Ph. (402) 461-7107 **Details:** (County Judge has Marriage & Probate Records; Clerk District Court has Divorce & Land Records)
Antelope www.co.antelope.ne.us	**F5**	**1 Mar 1871**	**L'Eau Qui Court, Unorg. Terr.** Antelope County; 501 Main St; Neligh, NE 68756; Ph. (402) 887-4410, soscou26@nol.org **Details:** (County Clerk has Marriage & Land Records; Judge has Probate & Court Records; Clerk of District Court has Divorce Records; All Birth & Death Records at Bureau of Vital Records)
Arthur www.rootsweb.com/~nearthur/	**M6**	**31 Mar 1887**	**Unorg. Terr.** Arthur County; Main St; Arthur, NE 69121; Ph. (308) 764-2203 **Details:** (Arthur County was formed in 1887, but did not become a county until 1913. Before 1913, Records were kept at McPherson County) (County Clerk has Land Records from 1913; County Court has Marriage, Probate & Court Records from 1913; Clerk District Court has Divorce Records from 1913; County Cemetery Sexton has Burial Records; County Superintendant of schools has School Census from 1913)
Banner www.rootsweb.com/~nebanner/	**R6**	**6 Nov 1888**	**Cheyenne** Banner County; State St; PO Box 67; Harrisburg, NE 69345; Ph. (308) 436-5265 **Details:** (County Clerk has Birth Records from 1920 & Land Records from 1890; County Court has Marriage, Probate & Court Records from 1890; Department of Health has Burial & Divorce Records)
Blackbird		**7 Mar 1855**	**Burt** Blackbird County; NE **Details:** (see Thurston) Name changed to Thurston 28 Mar 1889
Blaine www.rootsweb.com/~neblaine/	**J5**	**5 Mar 1885**	**Custer** Blaine County; PO Box 136; Brewster, NE 68821; Ph. (308) 547-2222 **Details:** (County Judge has Probate & Court Records; County Clerk has Divorce & Land Records from 1887)
Boone www.rootsweb.com/~neboone/	**F6**	**1 Mar 1871**	**Unorg. Terr.** Boone County; 222 S 4th St; Albion, NE 68620; Ph. (402) 395-2055 **Details:** (County Clerk has Marriage Records from 1932, Divorce, Probate & Court Records; Recorder Deeds has Land Records; State Archives, 1500 "R" St., Lincoln, NE 68508 has Marriage Records to 1932)
Box Butte www.rootsweb.com/~neboxbut/	**P5**	**23 Mar 1887**	**Dawes** Box Butte County; 515 Box Butte Ave #203; Alliance, NE 69301; Ph. (308) 762-6565 **Details:** (County Clerk has Marriage & Land Records; County Judge has Probate & Court Records; Clerk District Court has Divorce Records)
Boyd www.rootsweb.com/~neboyd/	**H3**	**20 Mar 1891**	**Holt** Boyd County; 401 Thayer St; Butte, NE 68722; Ph. (402) 775-2391 **Details:** (County Clerk has Marriage, Divorce, Land, Military & Naturalization Records; Clerk District Court has Court Records; Clerk County Court has Probate Records)

County Website	Map Index	Date Created	Parent County or Territory From Which Organized Address/Details
Brown www.co.brown.ne.us/	**J4**	**19 Feb 1883**	**Unorg. Terr.** Brown County; 148 W 4th St; Ainsworth, NE 69210; Ph. (402) 387-2705 **Details:** (Attached to Holt County prior to 1883) (County Clerk has Marriage & Land Records from 1883, Naturalization Records 1884–1922 & Military Discharge Records from 1919; County Judge has Probate Records; Clerk District Court has Divorce & Court Records; County Superintendant of Schools has school Census Records from 1883)
Buffalo www.co.buffalo.ne.us/	**H8**	**14 Mar 1855**	**Original county** Buffalo County; 15th & Central Ave; PO Box 1270; Kearney, NE 68848; Ph. (308) 236-1226 **Details:** (County Clerk has Marriage Records from 1872; County Judge has Probate & Court Records from 1872; Clerk District Court has Divorce Records; Registrar of Deeds has Land Records)
Burt www.rootsweb.com/~neburt/	**C6**	**23 Nov 1854**	**Original county** Burt County; 111 N 13th St; Tekamah, NE 68061; Ph. (402) 374-2955 **Details:** (County Clerk has Marriage & Land Records; County Judge has Probate & Court Records; Clerk District Court has Divorce Records)
Butler www.nol.org/butler	**D7**	**26 Jan 1856**	**Greene** Butler County; 451 5th St; PO Box 289; David City, NE 68632; Ph. (402) 367-7430 **Details:** (County Clerk has Land Records from 1869; County Court has Marriage & Probate Records; Clerk District Court has Divorce & Court Records; Birth & Death Records have been moved to the State Archives)
Calhoun		**26 Jan 1856**	**Lancaster, Douglas** Calhoun County; NE **Details:** (see Saunders) Name changed to Saunders 8 Jan 1862
Cass www.cassne.org	**B8**	**23 Nov 1854**	**Original county** Cass County; 346 Main St #202; Plattsmouth, NE 68048; Ph. (402) 296-9300, barbw@cassne.org **Details:** (County Clerk has Marriage Records from 1855; County Court has Probate & Court Records from 1854; Cemetery Board has Burial Records; Clerk District Court has Divorce Records from 1855; Registrar of Deeds has Land Records)
Cedar www.rootsweb.com/~necedar/	**E4**	**12 Feb 1857**	**Dixon, Pierce** Cedar County; 101 S Broadway Ave; PO Box 47; Hartington, NE 68739; Ph. (402) 254-7411 **Details:** (County Clerk has Marriage & Land Records; County Judge has Probate & Court Records; Clerk District Court has Divorce Records)
Chase www.chasecounty.com/	**M9**	**27 Feb 1873**	**Unorg. Terr.** Chase County; 921 Broadway; Imperial, NE 69033; Ph. (308) 882-5266 **Details:** (County Judge has Marriage, Probate & Court Records from 1886; Clerk District Court has Divorce Records from 1886; County Clerk has Land Records from 1886)

County Website	Map Index	Date Created	Parent County or Territory From Which Organized Address/Details
Cherry www.rootsweb.com/~necherry/	L4	**23 Feb 1883**	**Unorg. Terr.** Cherry County; 365 N Main St; PO Box 120; Valentine, NE 69201; Ph. (402) 376-2771 **Details:** (County Clerk has Marriage & Land Records; County Court has Probate & Court Records; Clerk District Court has Divorce Records)
Cheyenne www.co.cheyenne.ne.us/	P7	**22 Jun 1867**	**Unorg. Terr.** Cheyenne County; 1000 10th Ave; PO Box 217; Sidney, NE 69162; Ph. (308) 254-2141 **Details:** (County Clerk has Marriage & Land Records; County Court has Probate Records; Clerk District Court has Divorce Records)
Clay www.rootsweb.com/~neclay/	F9	**16 Feb 1867**	**Unorg. Terr.** Clay County; 111 W Fairfield St; Clay Center, NE 68933; Ph. (402) 762-3463 **Details:** (County Clerk has Birth & Death Records 1917–1918, Marriage & Land Records from 1871 & Military Records from 1921; Clerk District Court has Divorce, Court & Naturalization Records; County Court has Probate Records)
Clay, old		**7 Mar 1855**	**Original county** Clay, old County; NE **Details:** (absorbed by Gage County in 1864)
Colfax www.colfaxcounty.ne.gob	D6	**15 Feb 1869**	**Platte** Colfax County; 411 E 11th St; Schuyler, NE 68661; Ph. (402) 352-8504, soscou43@nol.org **Details:** (Vital Statistics has Birth & Death Recordsfrom 1904; Historical Society has Burial, Cemetery, & Naturalization Records; Clerk of Courts has Court & Guardianship Records; County Clerk has Land & marriage Records from 1869, & Military Records from 1921; City Library has Newspapers; County Treasury has Tax Records)
Cuming www.co.cuming.ne.us	D5	**16 Mar 1855**	**Burt** Cuming County; 200 S Lincoln St; West Point, NE 68788; Ph. (402) 372-6002 soscou24@nol.org **Details:** (County Clerk has Land & Marriage Records from 1860, & School Census Records; County Court has Probate & Court Records; Clerk of District Court has Immigration & Court Records; Nebraska Department of Vital Statistics has Birth & Death Records)
Custer www.rootsweb.com/~necuste2/	I7	**17 Feb 1877**	**Unorg. Terr.** Custer County; 431 S 10th Ave; Broken Bow, NE 68822; Ph. (308) 872-5701 **Details:** (County Clerk has Birth Records from 1910, Death Records from 1915, obituaries from 1877 & pioneer biographical data; County Historical Society has many other Records; County Judge has Marriage Records from 1878, Probate & Court Records from 1887; Clerk District Court has Divorce Records from 1881; Registrar of Deeds has Land Records from 1880)
Dakota www.sscdc.net/	C4	**7 Mar 1855**	**Burt** Dakota County; 1601 Broadway St; Dakota City, NE 68731; Ph. (402) 987-2126 **Details:** (County Clerk has Marriage Records from 1856 & Military Records from 1921; County Court has Probate Records from 1858; Registrar of Deeds has Land Records from 1856; Clerk District Court has Divorce & Court Records from 1862 & Naturalization Records)

County Website	Map Index	Date Created	Parent County or Territory From Which Organized Address/Details
Dawes www.homestead.com/DawesCountyNE/Home.html	P4	**19 Feb 1885**	**Sioux** Dawes County; 451 Main St; Chadron, NE 69337-2649; Ph. (308) 432-0100 **Details:** (County Clerk has Land Records from 1880; County Judge has Marriage & Probate Records; Clerk District Court has Divorce Records)
Dawson www.rootsweb.com/~nedawson/	J8	**11 Jan 1860**	**Unorg. Terr.** Dawson County; PO Box 370; Lexington, NE 68850; Ph. (308) 324-2127 **Details:** (County Clerk has Marriage Records from 1873; County Court has Probate & Court Records; Clerk District Court has Divorce & Naturalization Records; Registrar of Deeds has Land Records; Veterans Service Office has Military Records)
Deuel www.rootsweb.com/~nedeuel/	O7	**6 Nov 1888**	**Cheyenne** Deuel County; 3rd & Vincent; Chappell, NE 69129; Ph. (308) 874-3308 **Details:** (County Judge has Marriage & Probate Records; County Clerk has Burial, Divorce & Land Records, Court Records from 1890)
Dixon www.co.dixon.ne.us	D4	**26 Jan 1856**	**Blackbird, Izard, Unorg. Terr.** Dixon County; 302 3rd St; PO Box 546; Ponca, NE 68770; Ph. (402) 755-2208, soscou35@nol.org **Details:** (County Clerk has Marriage from 1872, Land Records from 1859; Clerk of District Court has Civic, Divorce, & Naturalization Records from 1862; County Judge has Probate Records from 1872.
Dodge www.rootsweb.com/~nedodge/	C6	**23 Nov 1854**	**Original county** Dodge County; 435 N Park Ave; Fremont, NE 68025; Ph. (402) 727-2767 **Details:** (County Clerk has Marriage Records; County Judge has Probate Records; Clerk District Court has Divorce Records; Registrar of Deeds has Land Records)
Douglas www.co.douglas.ne.us/explorer.shtml	C7	**23 Nov 1854**	**Original county** Douglas County; 1819 Farman St; Omaha, NE 68102; Ph. (402) 444-7143 **Details:** (County Judge has Marriage & Probate Records; Clerk District Court has Divorce Records; County Clerk has Military Discharge Records)
Dundy www.rootsweb.com/~nedundy/	M10	**27 Feb 1873**	**Unorg. Terr.** Dundy County; PO Box 506; Benkelman, NE 69021; Ph. (308) 423-2058 **Details:** (County Clerk has Birth Records from 1907, Death Records from 1904, Burial, Divorce & Court Records; County Judge has Probate Records)
Emmet		**10 Feb 1857**	**Pierce, Unorg. Terr.** Emmet County; NE **Details:** (see Knox) Formerly L'Eau Qui Court County. Name changed to Emmet 18 Feb 1867. Name changed to Knox 21 Feb 1873

County Website	Map Index	Date Created	Parent County or Territory From Which Organized Address/Details
Fillmore www.fillmorecounty.org	E9	26 Jan 1856	**Unorg. Terr.** Fillmore County; 900 G St; PO Box 307; Geneva, NE 68361; Ph. (402) 759-4931, anelson@fillmorecounty.org **Details:** (County Clerk has Marriage & Land Records from 1872, Census & delayed Birth Records; County Court has Probate & Court Records; Clerk District Court has Divorce & Naturalization Records; County Superintendent of Schools has School Census)
Forney		23 Nov 1854	**Original county** Forney County; NE **Details:** (see Nemaha) Name changed to Nemaha 7 Mar 1855
Franklin www.rootsweb.com/~nefrankl/	H10	16 Feb 1867	**Kearney** Franklin County; 405 15th Ave; PO Box 146; Franklin, NE 68939; Ph. (308) 425-6202 **Details:** (County Clerk has Marriage Records from 1872, Divorce & Land Records)
Frontier www.rootsweb.com/~nefronti/	K9	17 Jan 1872	**Unorg. Terr.** Frontier County; 1 Wellington St; PO Box 40; Stockville, NE 69042-0040; Ph. (308) 367-8641 **Details:** (County Clerk has Marriage & Military Records; County Judge has Divorce, Probate, Court & Naturalization Records; Registrar of Deeds has Land Records; Clerk & Treasury have Cemetery Records; Supt Schools has school Census)
Furnas www.rootsweb.com/~nefurnas/	J10	27 Feb 1873	**Unorg. Terr.** Furnas County; 912 R St; PO Box 387; Beaver City, NE 68926-0387; Ph. (308) 268-4145 **Details:** (County Judge has Marriage, Probate & Court Records; Clerk District Court has Divorce Records; County Clerk has Land Records from 1873)
Gage www.usgennet.Organized/usa/ne/county/ gage/index.html	D9	16 Mar 1855	**Original county** Gage County; 612 Grant St; PO Box 429; Beatrice, NE 68310-0429; Ph. (402) 223-1300 **Details:** (County Judge has Marriage & Probate Records from 1860; Clerk District Court has Divorce Records)
Garden www.rootsweb.com/~negarden/	O6	2 Nov 1909	**Deuel** Garden County; 611 Main St; PO Box 486; Oshkosh, NE 69154; Ph. (308) 772-3924 **Details:** (County Clerk has Marriage & Land Records; County Judge has Probate & Court Records; Clerk District Court has Divorce Records)
Garfield www.rootsweb.com/~negarfie/	H5	8 Nov 1884	**Wheeler** Garfield County; 250 S 8th St; PO Box 218; Burwell, NE 68823-0218; Ph. (308) 346-4161 **Details:** (County Clerk has District Court, Divorce, Land Marriage, Military Discharge, & Naturalization Records; County Magistrate has Probate, Register of Wills, & County Court Records; County Treaurer has Tax Records; County Assessors has Land Records; County Library has Newspapers; Historical Society has Burial, Cemetery, Military, Family, & Other Historical Records)

County Website	Map Index	Date Created	Parent County or Territory From Which Organized Address/Details
Gosper www.rootsweb.com/~negosper/	**J9**	**26 Nov 1873**	**Unorg. Terr., Kearney** Gosper County; 507 Smith Ave; PO Box 136; Elwood, NE 68937-0136; Ph. (308) 785-2611 **Details:** (County Judge has Marriage & Probate Records from 1891 & Court Records from 1920; County Clerk has Divorce Records from 1880 & Land Records)
Grant www.rootsweb.com/~negrant/	**N6**	**31 Mar 1887**	**Unorg. Terr.** Grant County; PO Box 139; Hyannis, NE 69350-0139; Ph. (308) 458-2488 **Details:** (County Clerk has Marriage & Land Records from 1888, Court Records from 1897, Naturalization Records 1891–1912, Divorce Records from 1890 & Military Records from 1921; County Judge has Probate Records)
Greeley www.rootsweb.com/~negreele/	**G6**	**1 Mar 1871**	**Unorg. Terr.** Greeley County; PO Box 287; Greeley, NE 68842; Ph. (308) 428-3625 **Details:** (County Clerk has Marriage, Land, Military & Naturalization Records; County Court has Probate Records; Clerk District Court has Divorce & Court Records)
Greene		**6 Mar 1855**	**Cass, Pierce, old** Greene County; NE **Details:** (see Seward) Name changed to Seward 3 Jan 1862
Hall www.rootsweb.com/~nehall/	**G8**	**4 Nov 1858**	**Original county** Hall County; 121 S Pine St; Grand Island, NE 68801; Ph. (308) 385-5080 **Details:** (County Clerk has Marriage Records from 1869; County Judge has Probate Records; Clerk District Court has Divorce & Court Records; Registrar of Deeds has Land Records)
Hamilton www.co.hamilton.ne.us/	**F8**	**16 Feb 1867**	**Unorg. Terr.** Hamilton County; 1111 13th St Ste 1; Aurora, NE 68818; Ph. (402) 694-3443 **Details:** (County Clerk has Marriage & Land Records from 1870; County Judge has Probate & Court Records; Clerk District Court has Divorce Records)
Harlan www.rootsweb.com/~neharlan/	**I10**	**3 Jun 1871**	**Kearney** Harlan County; 706 W 2nd St; Alma, NE 68920; Ph. (308) 928-2173 **Details:** (County Clerk has Marriage & Land Records; County Judge has Probate & Court Records; Clerk District Court has Divorce Records; Registrar of Deeds has Land Records)
Hayes www.rootsweb.com/~nehayes/	**L9**	**19 Feb 1877**	**Unorg. Terr.** Hayes County; Troth St; PO Box 370; Hayes Center, NE 69032; Ph. (308) 286-3413 **Details:** (County Clerk has Death, Burial & Land Records)
Hitchcock www.co.hitchcock.ne.us/	**L10**	**27 Feb 1873**	**Unorg. Terr.** Hitchcock County; 229 E Death St; PO Box 248; Trenton, NE 69044; Ph. (308) 334-5646 **Details:** (County Clerk has Marriage, Land, Divorce & Court Records; County Judge has Probate Records)

Nebraska

County Website	Map Index	Date Created	Parent County or Territory From Which Organized Address/Details
Holt www.rootsweb.com/~neholt/	H4	13 Jan 1860	**Unorg. Terr.** Holt County; 204 N 4th St; PO Box 329; O'Neill, NE 68763; Ph. (402) 336-1762 **Details:** (Formerly West County. Name changed to Holt 9 Jan 1862) (County Clerk has Marriage Records from 1878; County Judge has Probate & Court Records from 1882; Registrar of Deeds has Land Records from 1879; Clerk District Court has Divorce Records from 1879)
Hooker www.rootsweb.com/~nehooker/	L6	29 Mar 1889	**Unorg. Terr.** Hooker County; 303 NE 1st St; PO Box 184; Mullen, NE 69152-0184; Ph. (308) 546-2244 **Details:** (County Clerk has Birth & Death Records from 1919 & Land Records from 1889; County Judge has Marriage & Probate Records)
Howard www.rootsweb.com/~nehoward/	G7	1 Mar 1871	**Hall** Howard County; 612 Indian S; PO Box 25; St. Paul, NE 68873; Ph. (308) 754-4343 **Details:** (County Judge has Marriage, Probate, Court, Land & Naturalization Records from 1872 & Divorce Records from 1873)
Izard		6 Mar 1855	**Unorg. Terr.** Izard County; NE **Details:** (see Stanton) Name changed to Stanton 10 Jan 1862
Jackson		1855	**Unorg. Terr.** Jackson County; NE **Details:** (see Fillmore) Never organized. Changed to Fillmore 26 Jan 1856
Jefferson www.co.jefferson.ne.us	E9	26 Jan 1856	**Unorg. Terr.** Jefferson County; 411 4th St; Fairbury, NE 68352; Ph. (402) 729-2323 soscou33@nol.org **Details:** (Formerly Jones County. Name changed to Jefferson 1864. Boundaries redefined 1867 & 1871) (State Archives has Birth & Death Records; County Clerk has Marriage Records from 1869 & Burial Records, Clerk of District Court has Divorce, Immigraion, & Naturalization Records; County Court has Court, Guardianship, & Probate Records; Register of Deeds has Land Records from 1864; Veterans Service Office has Military Records; Fairbury Journal News has Newspapers; County Treasurer has Tax Records)
Johnson		1857	**Nemaha** Johnson County; 4th & Broadway; PO Box 416; Tecumseh, NE 68450-0416; Ph. (402) 335-3246 **Details:** (New Location) (County Clerk has Marriage & Land Records from 1858; County Judge has Probate & Court Records; Clerk District Court has Divorce Records from 1858)
Johnson, old		2 Mar 1855	**Unorg. Terr.** Johnson County; NE **Details:** County Terminated in 1856
Jones		26 Jan 1856	**Unorg. Terr.** Jones County; NE **Details:** (see Jefferson) Absorbed by Jefferson, 1867

County	Map	Date	Parent County or Territory From Which Organized
Website	Index	Created	Address/Details

Kearney H9 **10 Jan 1860** **Unorg. Terr.**
www.rootsweb.com/~nekearne/
Kearney County; County Courthouse; Minden, NE 68959;
Ph. (308) 832-2723
Details: (County Clerk has Marriage Records from 1872 & Land Records; County Judge has Probate & Court Records; Clerk District Court has Divorce Records)

Keith M7 **27 Feb 1873** **Unorg. Terr.**
www.rootsweb.com/~nekeith/
Keith County; 511 N Spruce St; PO Box 149; Ogallala, NE 69153-0149; Ph. (308) 284-4726
Details: (Vital Records has Birth & Death Records; County Clerk has Land & Marriage Records, Clerk of District Court has Divorce & Court Records)

Keya Paha J3 **4 Nov 1884** **Brown**
www.rootsweb.com/~nekeyapa/
Keya Paha County; PO Box 349; Springview, NE 68778-0349;
Ph. (402) 497-3791
Details: (County Clerk has Marriage, Divorce, Probate, Court & Land Records from 1886 & school Census)

Kimball Q7 **6 Nov 1888** **Cheyenne**
www.rootsweb.com/~nekimbal/
Kimball County; 114 E 3rd St; Kimball, NE 69145;
Ph. (308) 235-2241
Details: (County Clerk has Divorce & Probate Records; County Judge has Marriage & Court Records)

Knox F4 **10 Feb 1857** **Pierce, Unorg. Terr.**
www.rootsweb.com/~neknox/
Knox County; 206 Main St.; PO Box 166; Center, NE 68724;
Ph. (402) 288-5604, joscoula@nol.org
Details: (Formerly L'Eau Qui Court & Emmet Counties. Created as L'Eau Qui Court County. Name changed to Emmet 18 Feb 1867. Name changed to Knox 21 Feb 1873) (County Clerk has Marriage Records from Sept 1, 1865, & Land Records from 1858; County Court has Probate, Guardianship, Conservatorship, Criminal, & Civil Records; District Court has Naturalization Records, Felony Cases, Civil Cases including Domestic Relations from 1872; State Archives has Birth & Death Records)

Lancaster C8 **6 Mar 1855** **Cass, Pierce, old**
http://freepages.genealogy.rootsweb.com/~irishrose/lancindex.html
Lancaster County; 555 S 10th St; Lincoln, NE 68508;
Ph. (402) 441-7484
Details: (County Judge has Marriage & Probate Records; County Clerk has Land Records)

L'Eau Qui Court **10 Feb 1857** **Pierce, Unorg. Terr.**
L'Eau Qui Court County; NE
Details: (see Knox) Name changed to Emmet 18 Feb 1867. Name changed to Knox 21 Feb 1873

Lincoln L8 **7 Jan 1860** **Unorg. Terr.**
www.wathenadesigns.com/Lincoln/index_4.html
Lincoln County; 301 N Jeffers; North Platte, NE 69101;
Ph. (308) 532-4051
Details: (Formerly Shorter County. Name changed to Lincoln 11 Dec 1861) (County Clerk has Marriage Records; Clerk District Court has Divorce Records; County Court has Probate & Court Records; Registrar of Deeds has Land Records)

County Website	Map Index	Date Created	Parent County or Territory From Which Organized Address/Details
Logan www.rootsweb.com/~nelogan/	K6	**24 Feb 1885**	**Unorg. Terr.** Logan County; 317 Main St; PO Box 8; Stapleton, NE 69163-0008; Ph. (308) 636-2311 **Details:** (County Judge has Marriage, Divorce, Probate & Court Records from 1885 & partial Burial Records; County Clerk has Land Records)
Loup www.rootsweb.com/~neloup/	I6	**23 Feb 1883**	**Unorg. Terr.** Loup County; 4th St; PO Box 187; Taylor, NE 68879; Ph. (308) 942-3135 **Details:** (County Judge has Marriage & Probate Records; County Clerk has Divorce, Court & Land Records from 1887)
Loup (old)		**6 Mar 1855**	**Burt** Loup, old County; NE **Details:** (Disorganized in 1856 & became part of Izard, Madison, Monroe & Platte Counties)
Lyon			Lyon County; NE **Details:** (Never Organized. County in southwest corner of state. With Lincoln in 1870 Census)
Madison		**26 Jan 1856**	**McNeale, Loup, old** Madison County; 1313 N Main St; PO Box 290; Madison, NE 68748-0290; Ph. (402) 454-3311 **Details:** (County Clerk has Marriage Records from 1868; Register of Deeds has Land Records from 1868; Clerk Court has Probate Records from 1868; Clerk of District Court has Divorce Records from 1868)
McNeale		**1855**	**Burt** McNeale County; NE **Details:** (Absorbed by Madison & Izard (now Stanton) in 1856)
McPherson www.rootsweb.com/~nemcpher/	L6	**31 Mar 1887**	**Lincoln, Keith, Logan** McPherson County; 5th & Anderson; PO Box 122; Tryon, NE 69167-0122; Ph. (308) 587-2363 **Details:** (County Clerk has Marriage, Divorce & Land Records; County Judge has Probate & Court Records)
Merrick www.rootsweb.com/~nemerric/	F7	**4 Nov 1858**	**Unorg. Terr.** Merrick County; 1510 18th St; PO Box 27; Central City, NE 68826-0027; Ph. (308) 946-2881 **Details:** (County Clerk has Birth & Death Records; County Judge has Marriage, Divorce, Probate & Court Records; Registrar of Deeds has Land Records from 1873)
Monroe		**1856**	**Loup, old** Monroe County; NE **Details:** (Absorbed by Platte County in 1860)
Morrill www.rootsweb.com/~nemorril/index.html	P6	**12 Nov 1908**	**Cheyenne** Morrill County; PO Box 610; Bridgeport, NE 69336-0610; Ph. (308) 262-0860 **Details:** (County Clerk has Birth, Death & Burial Records from 1917 & Land Records from 1909; County Judge has Marriage & Probate Records)

County Website	Map Index	Date Created	Parent County or Territory From Which Organized Address/Details
Nance www.rootsweb.com/~nenance/	F7	13 Feb 1879	**Pawnee Indian Reservation** Nance County; 209 Esther St; Fullerton, NE 68638; Ph. (308) 536-2331 **Details:** (County Clerk has Marriage Records from 1890 & Land Records from 1879; County Judge has Probate Records; Clerk District Court has Divorce & Court Records from 1882)
Nemaha www.rootsweb.com/~nenemaha/	B9	23 Nov 1854	**Original county** Nemaha County; 1824 N St; Auburn, NE 68305; Ph. (402) 274-4213 **Details:** (Formerly Forney County. Name changed to Nemaha 7 Mar 1855) (County Clerk has Marriage Records from 1856, Land & Military Records; County Judge has Probate & Court Records; Clerk District Court has Divorce Records)
Nuckolls www.nuckollscounty.ne.gov	F9	13 Jan 1860	**Unorg. Terr.** Nuckolls County; 150 S Main St; PO Box 366; Nelson, NE 68961; Ph. (402) 225-4361, soscou42@nol.org **Details:** (County Clerk has Census from 1896, Land Records from 1865, Military Discharge Records, Marriage Records from 1872; Clerk of District Court has Immigration & Naturalization Records from 1881, Divorce & Court Records; Clerk Magistration has Guardianship & Probate Records; County Treasury has Tax Records from 1982)
Otoe www.co.otoe.ne.us/	B8	23 Nov 1854	**Cass, Pierce, old** Otoe County; 1021 Central Ave; PO Box 249; Nebraska City, NE 68410; Ph. (402) 873-9505, soscoull@nol.org **Details:** (Formerly Pierce, old. Name changed to Otoe) (County Clerk has Marriage Records from 1855, War Discharge from 1921, School Records 1894–2000; Register of Deeds has Land & Mortgage Records from 1856; Clerk of District Court has Divorce, Civil, & Criminal Court Records from 1857; Clerk of County Court has Probate & Guardianship Records from 1854; All Birth & Death Records are held at the Bureau of Vital Statistics; State Archives has Naturalization & Other Records)
Pawnee www.rootsweb.com/~nepawnee/	C10	6 Mar 1855	**Richardson** Pawnee County; 625 6th St; PO Box 431; Pawnee City, NE 68420; Ph. (402) 852-2962 **Details:** (County Clerk has Marriage Records from 1858, Land, Divorce & Court Records; County Judge has Probate Records)
Perkins www.rootsweb.com/~neperkin/	M8	8 Nov 1887	**Keith** Perkins County; 200 Lincoln Ave; PO Box 156; Grant, NE 69140-0156; Ph. (308) 352-4643 **Details:** (County Clerk has Marriage, Divorce, Court & Land Records; County Judge has Probate Records)
Phelps www.rootsweb.com/~nephelps/	I9	11 Feb 1873	**Kearney** Phelps County; PO Box 404; Holdrege, NE 68949; Ph. (308) 995-4469 **Details:** (County Clerk has Marriage & Land Records; County Judge has Probate Records; Clerk District Court has Divorce Records)

County Website	Map Index	Date Created	Parent County or Territory From Which Organized Address/Details
Pierce www.co.pierce.ne.us/	E5	26 Jan 1856	**Izard, Unorg. Terr.** Pierce County; 111 W Court St Rm 1; Pierce, NE 68767; Ph. (402) 329-4225 **Details:** (Formerly Otoe County) (County Clerk has Marriage, Land & Military Records; Clerk District Court has Divorce & Naturalization Records; County Court has Probate Records; School Superintendant has school attendance Records)
Pierce (old)		1854	**Original county** Pierce, old County; NE **Details:** (see Otoe) Became part of Otoe County 1855
Platte www.rootsweb.com/~neplatte/	E6	26 Jan 1856	**Loup, old** Platte County; 2610 14th St; Columbus, NE 68601; Ph. (402) 563-4904 **Details:** (County Judge has Marriage & Probate Records; Clerk District Court has Divorce & Court Records; County Assessor has Land Records)
Polk www.polkcounty.ne.gov	E7	26 Jan 1856	**York, Unorg. Terr.** Polk County; 400 Hawkeye St; PO Box 276; Osceola, NE 68651; Ph. (402) 747-5431 **Details:** (Previously Part of Butler County, Separated in 1870) (Courthouse Burned in 1881 Few Records Lost) (County Clerk has Book with Burial & Cemetery Records to 1975, Land, Marriage, School Census Records 1886 to 1993; District Court has Court, Divorce, & Naturalization Records; County Court has Probate Records; All Birth & Death Records are with Vital Statistics in Lincoln; Newspapers available at Public Libraries)
Red Willow www.rootsweb.com/~neredwil/	K10	27 Feb 1873	**Unorg. Terr.** Red Willow County; 502 Norris Ave; McCook, NE 69001-2006; Ph. (308) 345-1552 **Details:** (County Clerk has Marriage Records from 1874 & Land Records from 1888; County Court has Probate Records; Clerk District Court has Divorce & Court Records; Veteran Service Office has Military Records; School Superintendant has school Census)
Richardson www.rootsweb.com/~nerichar/	B10	23 Nov 1854	**Original county** Richardson County; 1700 Stone St; Falls City, NE 68355; Ph. (402) 245-2911 **Details:** (County Clerk has Birth & Death Records from 1918; County Judge has Marriage Records from 1800's, Probate & Court Records; Registrar of Deeds has Land Records; Clerk District Court has Divorce Records)
Rock www.co.rock.ne.us/	I5	1889	**Brown** Rock County; 400 State St; PO Box 367; Bassett, NE 68714; Ph. (402) 684-3933 **Details:** (County Judge has Marriage Records; County Clerk has Divorce, Probate, Court & Land Records from 1889)
Saline www.rootsweb.com/~nesaline/	D9	6 Mar 1855	**Original county** Saline County; 215 S Court St; PO Box 865; Wilber, NE 68465; Ph. (402) 821-2374 **Details:** (County Clerk has Birth & Death Records from 1976 & Land Records from 1886; County Court has Marriage Records from 1886 & Probate Records from 1870; Clerk District Court has Divorce & Court Records from 1886)

County Website	Map Index	Date Created	Parent County or Territory From Which Organized Address/Details
Sarpy www.sarpy.com/	**B7**	**7 Feb 1857**	**Douglas** Sarpy County; 1210 Golden Gate Dr; Papillion, NE 68046; Ph. (402) 593-2100 **Details:** (County Judge has Marriage & Probate Records; County Clerk has Land Records)
Saunders www.co.saunders.ne.us/	**D7**	**26 Jan 1856**	**Lancaster, Douglas** Saunders County; PO Box 61; Wahoo, NE 68066; Ph. (402) 443-8101 **Details:** (Formerly Calhoun County. Name changed to Saunders 8 Jan 1862) (County Clerk has Marriage, Burial, Divorce, Probate, Court & Land Records)
Scotts Bluff www.scottsbluffcounty.Organized/	**R6**	**6 Nov 1888**	**Cheyenne** Scotts Bluff County; 1825 10th St; Gering, NE 69341; Ph. (308) 436-6600 **Details:** (County Clerk has Marriage Records; County Judge has Divorce, Probate & Court Records)
Seward http://connectseward.Organized/www/docs/cgov/	**D8**	**6 Mar 1855**	**Cass, Pierce, old** Seward County; 529 Seward St; PO Box 190; Seward, NE 68434; Ph. (402) 643-2883 **Details:** (Formerly Greene County. Name changed to Seward 3 Jan 1862) (County Clerk has Marriage & Land Records from 1866; County Court has Probate Records from 1869; Clerk District Court has Divorce Records from 1868 & Court Records from 1869)
Sheridan www.rootsweb.com/~nesherid/	**O4**	**25 Feb 1885**	**Sioux** Sheridan County; 301 E 2nd St; PO Box 39; Rushville, NE 69360; Ph. (308) 327-2633 **Details:** (County Judge has Marriage, Probate & Court Records; Clerk District Court has Divorce Records)
Sherman www.rootsweb.com/~nesherma/	**H7**	**1 Mar 1871**	**Buffalo, Unorg. Terr.** Sherman County; 630 O Street; PO Box 456; Loup City, NE 68853; Ph. (308) 745-1513 **Details:** (County Clerk has Marriage Records from 1883, Divorce & Court Records from 1882, Land Records from 1873 & Naturalization Records 1882–1920; County Clerk Magistrate has Probate Records; Birth & Death Records moved to State Archives)
Shorter		**7 Jan 1860**	**Unorg. Terr.** Shorter County; NE **Details:** (see Lincoln) Name changed to Lincoln 11 Dec 1861
Sioux www.rootsweb.com/~nesioux/	**Q4**	**19 Feb 1877**	**Unorg. Terr.** Sioux County; 325 Main St; PO Box 158; Harrison, NE 69346; Ph. (308) 668-2443 **Details:** (County Clerk has Land Records; County Judge has Marriage, Probate & Court Records; Clerk District Court has Divorce Records)
Stanton www.stanton.net/county.html	**E6**	**6 Mar 1855**	**Unorg. Terr.** Stanton County; 804 Ivy St; PO Box 347; Stanton, NE 68779; Ph. (402) 439-2222 **Details:** (Formerly Izard County. Name changed to Stanton 20 Jan 1862) (County Clerk has Marriage Records from 1869, Land Records from 1868, Naturalization & Military Records; County Court has Probate Records; Clerk District Court has Divorce & Court Records from 1875)

County Website	Map Index	Date Created	Parent County or Territory From Which Organized Address/Details
Thayer www.rootsweb.com/~nethayer/	E9	26 Jan 1871	**Jefferson** Thayer County; 225 N 4th St; PO Box 208; Hebron, NE 68370-1549; Ph. (402) 768-6126 **Details:** (County Judge has Marriage, Probate & Court Records; Clerk District Court has Divorce Records; County Clerk has Land Records)
Thomas www.rootsweb.com/~nethomas/	K6	31 Mar 1887	**Unorg. Terr.** Thomas County; 503 Main St; Thedford, NE 69166; Ph. (308) 645-2261 **Details:** (County Clerk has Marriage Records from 1887 & Land Records; Clerk District Court has Divorce & Court Records; County Judge has Probate Records)
Thurston www.rootsweb.com/~nethurst/	C5	28 Mar 1889	**Burt** Thurston County; 106 S 5th St; PO Box G; Pender, NE 68047; Ph. (402) 385-2343 **Details:** (Thurston County was originally an Indian reservation & prior to Organized was called Blackbird County, created 7 Mar 1855. From 1884–1889 it was administered by Dakota County. Name changed to Thurston 28 Mar 1889) (County Judge has Marriage & Probate Records from 1889; Clerk District Court has Divorce & Court Records from 1889, County Clerk has Land Records from 1885)
Valley www.rootsweb.com/~nevalley/	H6	1 Mar 1871	**Unorg. Terr.** Valley County; 125 S 15th St; Ord, NE 68862; Ph. (308) 728-3700 **Details:** (County Clerk has Marriage & Land Records from 1883; County Judge has Probate Records; Clerk District Court has Divorce & Court Records)
Washington www.washcone.com/	C6	23 Nov 1854	**Original county** Washington County; 1555 Colfax St; Blair, NE 68008; Ph. (402) 426-6822 **Details:** (County Clerk has Birth, Death, Burial & Land Records; County Judge has Marriage, Probate & Court Records; Clerk District Court has Divorce Records)
Wayne www.rootsweb.com/~newayne/	D5	4 Mar 1871	**Unorg. Terr.** Wayne County; 510 N Pearl St; PO Box 248; Wayne, NE 68787-1939; Ph. (402) 375-2288 **Details:** (County Judge has Marriage, Probate & Court Records from 1871; Clerk District Court has Divorce Records; County Clerk has Land Records from 1870)
Webster www.rootsweb.com/~newebste/	G9	16 Feb 1867	**Unorg. Terr.** Webster County; 621 N Cedar St; Red Cloud, NE 68970; Ph. (402) 746-2716 **Details:** (County Clerk has Marriage, Land, Divorce, Probate & Court Records from 1871 & Naturalization Records from 1874)
West		13 Jan 1860	**Unorg. Terr.** West County; NE **Details:** (see Holt) Name changed to Holt 9 Jan 1862
Wheeler www.rootsweb.com/~newheele/	G6	17 Feb 1877	**Unorg. Terr.** Wheeler County; Main St; PO Box 127; Bartlett, NE 68622; Ph. (308) 654-3235 **Details:** (County Clerk has Court & Land Records)

County Website	Map Index	Date Created	Parent County or Territory From Which Organized Address/Details
York www.rootsweb.com/~neyork/	**E8**	**13 Mar 1855**	**Cass, Pierce, old** York County; 510 Lincoln Ave; York, NE 68467; Ph. (402) 362-7759 **Details:** (County Clerk has Marriage Records; County Court has Probate Records; Registrar of Deeds has Land Records; Clerk District Court has Divorce Records; Veteran Service Office has Military Records)

Notes

Nevada

Capital: Carson City

Territory: 1861

State: 1864 (36th)

All for our country

Explorers began to satisfy their curiosities about the Nevada area in the 1820's. Among those to first visit were Jedediah Smith, Peter Ogden, Kit Carson, and later John C. Fremont. In 1821, Mexico gained its independence from Spain and claimed Nevada as part of its territory. Around 1829, a scout searching for water found an oasis near the current city of Las Vegas. The oasis was an important find because it became possible for travelers to trek across the desert instead of making a detour around the inhospitable land. During the 1840's, numerous wagon trains crossed Nevada on their way to California. In 1848, Nevada, along with other western states, became part of the United States.

The first non-Indian settlement, made at Mormon Station, along with Eagle Ranch and Carson City, met the needs of travelers as more were willing to face the hazards of the trip. Originally part of Mexico, Nevada became part of the Utah Territory in 1850. In 1853 and 1856, residents of the Carson River Valley petitioned to become part of California Territory, claiming that Utah was not protecting them.

Discovery of gold in 1859 at the Comstock Lode brought thousands to Nevada. People from England, Italy, Scandinavia, Germany, France, and Mexico came to join the migrating Americans in the search for gold and silver. Nevada became a territory in 1861 and achieved statehood just two years later.

During the Civil War, more than 1,000 Nevada men served in the Union forces. After the Civil War, Nevada's borders were enlarged slightly, taking away from both Utah and Arizona. The Comstock Lode declined and with it the population of the state during the 1880s. Discoveries of silver at Tonopah, gold at Goldfield and copper at Ely led to new booms that lasted until World War I. Gambling was legalized in 1931, which brought an additional new boom to Nevada.

Look for vital records in the following locations:

- **Birth and death records:** Birth and death records from 1867 to 30 June, 1911 are located in each county recorder's office. Birth and death files from 1 July, 1911 are at the Nevada State Department of Health, Division of Vital Statistics in Carson City, Nevada.

- **Marriage records:** Available at each county recorder's office. Record keeping began there in 1864.

- **Land records:** Deeds and other land records available at each county recorder's office. Record keeping began there in 1864.

- **Court records:** Probate actions were recorded in the Utah Territorial Courts beginning in 1861. These records are now at the Nevada State Library and Archives, Division of Archives and Records in Carson City. Probate records after 1864 are in the district courts.

- **Census records:** Federal census records for 1850 and 1860 are with the Utah Territorial Census. Copies of an 1862 territorial census are at the Nevada State Library and Archives.

Nevada State Department of Health Division of Vital Statistics
505 East King Street, Room 102
Carson City, NV 89710
(775) 684-4242; Fax (775) 684-4156
http:// health2k.state.nv.us/forms/formindex.htm

Nevada State Library and Archives
100 N. Stewart St.
Carson City, NV 89701-4285
(775) 684-3360
http://dmla.clan.lib.nv.us/docs/nsla/

Nevada Historical Society
1650 N. Virginia St.
Reno, NV 89503
(775) 688-1190

Societies and Repositories

Carson Valley Historical Society; 1477 U.S. Highway 395 North; Gardnerville, NV 89410; www.carsonvalleymuseums.com/Pages/staff.html.

Churchill County Historical and Genealogical Society; c/o Churchill County Museum; 1050 S. Main St.; Fallon, NV 89406.

Clark County Heritage Center; 1830 S Boulder Hway; Henderson, NV 89015-8502.

Clark County, Nevada Genealogical Society; PO Box 1929; Las Vegas, NV 89125-1929; CCNGS@Juno.com; www.rootsweb.com/~nvccngs.

Elko Genealogical Society; PO box 5035; Elko, NV 89802.

Eureka Historical Society; PO Box 82; Eureka, NV 89316.

Goldfield Historical Society; PO Box 178; Goldfield, NV 89013.

Humboldt County Genealogical Society; c/o Humboldt County Library; 85 E. 5th St.; Winnemucca, NV 89445.

Jewish Genealogical Society of Las Vegas, Nevada; PO Box 29342; Las Vegas, NV 89126.

Lincoln County Historical Society; PO Box 515; Pioche, NV 89043.

Nevada Historical Society; 1650 North Virginia Street; Reno, NV 89503; plbandur@clan.lib.nv.us; http://dmla.clan.lib.nv.us/docs/museums/reno/his-soc.htm.

Nevada State Genealogical Society; PO Box 20666; Reno, NV 89515; janellemartin@charter.net; www.rootsweb.com/~nvsgs.

Nevada State Library and Archives; 100 North Stewart Street; Carson City, NV 89701-4285; (775) 684-3313; djrallo@clan.lib.nv.us; http://dmla.clan.lib.nv.us/docs/nsla.

Nevada State Museum & Historical Society; 700 Twin Lakes Drive; Las Vegas, NV 89107; http://dmla.clan.lib.nv.us/docs/museums/lv/vegas.htm.

Northeastern Nevada Genealogical Society; 1515 Idaho St.; Elko, NV 89801; www.rootsweb.com/~nvnengs/index.html.

Pahrump, Nevada Genealogical Society; PO Box 66; Pahrump, NV 89048.

Sparks Heritage Society; 814 Victorian Ave.; Sparks, NV 89431.

Town of Round Mountain, Nevada Genealogical Group; PO Box 330; Round Mountain, NV 89045.

Valley of Fire Chapter, DAR; Las Vegas, NV; roseogrady1@lvcm.com; www.rootsweb.com/~nvvfcdar/Index.html.

Wellington Historical Society; PO Box 36; Wellington, NV 89444.

White Pine Historical and Archaeological Society; PO Box 151725; Ely, NV 89315; www.webpanda.com/white_pine_county/historical_society/index.html.

Bibliography and Record Sources

General

Angel, Myron. *History of Nevada: With Illustrations and Biographical Sketches of Its Prominent Men and Pioneers.* Oakland, California: Thompson & West, 1881.

Bancroft, Hubert Howe. *History of Nevada, Colorado and Wyoming, 1540–1888.* San Francisco: History Co., 1890.

Dangberg, Grace. *Carson Valley: Historical Sketches of Nevada's First Settlement.* Reno, Nevada: Carson Valley Historical Society, 1979.

Durham, Michael S. *Desert Between the Mountains: Mormons, Miners, Padres, Mountain Men, and the Opening of the Great Basin, 1772–1869.* New York: Henry Holt, 1997.

Edwards, Elbert B. *200 Years in Nevada: A Story of People Who Opened, Explored and Developed the Land; A Bicentennial History.* Salt Lake City: Publishers Press, 1978.

Elliott, Russell R. *History of Nevada, 1973.* Reprint. Lincoln, Nebraska: University of Nebraska Press, 1984.

Ellison, Marion. *An Inventory and Index to the Records of Carson County, Utah and Nevada Territories, 1855–1861.* Reno: The Grace Dangberg Foundation, 1984.

Ellison, Robert W. *Territorial Lawmen of Nevada: Volume One, the Utah Territorial Period, 1851–1861.* Minden, Nevada: Hot Springs Mountain Press, 1999.

Family History Library. *Family History Centers: Nevada and Utah.* Salt Lake City: Family History Library, n.d..

Greene, Diane E. *Nevada Guide to Genealogical Records.* Baltimore: Clearfield Co., 2000.

History of Nevada, With Illustrations & Biographical Sketches of its Prominent Men & Pioneers. (1881). Reprint. Salem, Massachusetts: Higginson Books, 1992.

Holmes, Kenneth L. *Covered Wagon Women: Diaries & Letters From the Western Trails, 1840–1890.* 11 vols. Glendale, California: Arthur H. Clark Co., ca. 1983–1991.

Inventory of the Church Archives of Nevada: Protestant Episcopal Church. Reno: Historical Records Survey, 1941.

Inventory of the Church Archives of Nevada: Roman Catholic Church. Reno: Historical Records Survey, 1939.

Johnson, David Alan. *Founding the Far West; California, Oregon, and Nevada, 1840–1890.* Berkeley, California: University of California Press, 1992.

Kelly, J. Wells. *First Directory of Nevada Territory: Containing the Names of Residents in the Principal Towns, a Historical Sketch.* Los Gatos, California: The Talisman Press 1962.

Koenig, George. *Beyond This Place There Be Dragons: The Routes of the Tragic Trek of the Death Valley 1849ers Through Nevada, Death Valley, and on to*

Southern California. Glendale, California: Arthur Clark, 1984.

Lee, Joyce C. *Genealogical Prospecting in Nevada: A Guide to Nevada Directories*. Carson City, Nevada: Nevada State Library, 1984.

Lingenfelter, Richard E., and Karen Rix Gash. *The Newspapers of Nevada: A History and Bibliography, 1854–1979*. Reno: University of Nevada Press, 1984.

Loofbourow, Leon L. *Steeples Among the Sage: A Centennial Story of Nevada's Churches*. Oakland: Lake Park Press, 1964.

Mack, Effie Mona. *Nevada: A History of the State from the Earliest Times Through the Civil War*. Glendale, California: Arthur H. Clark Co., 1936.

Nevada Research Outline, Series U.S.-States, no. 29. Salt Lake City: Family History Library, 1988.

Nevada, a Guide to the Silver State. Portland, Oregon: Binfords & Nort, 1940.

Paher, Stanley W. *Nevada: An Annotated Bibliography: Books and Pamphlets Relating to the History and Development of the Silver State*. Las Vegas: Nevada Publications, 1980.

Parker, J. Carlyle and Janet G. Parker. *Nevada Biographical and Genealogical Sketch Index*. 1986.

Parkin, Nona. *Brief Historical Sketches of Nevada Residents, Early 1900's*. Microfilm of typescript (2 v.) in the Nona Parkin collection: Nevada Historical Research, at Reno, Nevada Stake Family History Center, Reno, Nevada. Salt Lake City: Filmed by the Genealogical Society of Utah, 1997.

Patterson, Edna B., Louise A. Ulph, and Victor Goodwin. *Nevada's Northeast Frontier*. S.l.: Western Printing & Pub. Co., 1969.

Robinson, Doreen. *Nevada State Children's Home, Admission Records, 1870–1920*. Pawtucket, Rhode Island: Quintin Publications, 2000.

Scrugham, James G. *Nevada: A Narrative of the Conquest of a Frontier Land*. 3 vols. Chicago: The American Historical Society, 1935.

Shinn, Charles Howard. *The Story of the Mine: As Illustrated by the Great Comstock Lode of Nevada*. New York: D. Appleton, 1897.

Sketches of the Intermountain States: Together with Biographies of Many Prominent and Progressive Citizens Who Have Helped in the Development and History-Making of this Marvelous Region, 1847, 1909, Utah, Idaho, Nevada. Salt Lake City: Salt Lake Tribune, 1909.

Spiros, Joyce V. Hawley. *Genealogical Guide to Arizona and Nevada*. Gallup, New Mexico: Verlene Publishing, 1983.

Thompson, Thomas Hinckley. *Reproduction of Thompson and West's "History of Nevada, 1881" with Illustrations and Biographical Sketches of Its Prominent Men and Pioneers*. Berkeley, California: Howell-North, 1958.

Who's Who in Nevada: Brief Sketches of Men Who are Making History in the Sagebrush State: Los Angeles: Home Printing Co., 1907.

Wiggins, Marvin E. *Mormons and Their Neighbors: An Index of over 75,000 Biographical Sketches from 1820 to the Present*. 2 vols. Provo, Utah: Harold B. Lee Library, Brigham Young University, 1984.

Atlases, Maps and Gazetteers

Averett, Walter R. *Directory of Southern Nevada Place Names*. Rev. ed. S.l.: W. R. Averett, 1962.

Carlson, Helen S. *Nevada Place Names: A Geographical Dictionary*. Reno: University of Nevada Press, 1974.

Gamett, James. *Nevada Post Offices: An Illustrated History*. Las Vegas, Nevada: Nevada Publications, 1983.

Harris, Robert P. *Nevada Postal History, 1861 to 1972*. Santa Cruz, California: Bonanza Press, 1973.

Land Ownership Maps: Nevada. Washington, D.C: Library of Congress, 1967.

Leigh, Rufus Wood. *Nevada Place Names: Their Origin and Significance*. Salt Lake City: Deseret News Press, 1964.

Nevada Atlas and Gazetteer. Freeport, Maine: DeLorme Mapping Co., 1996.

Nevada Maps, Cities and Towns, 1885–1943. New York: Sambo Perris Map Co., 1886. Reprint. Microfilm. Washington, D.C.: Library of Congress, 1980.

Paher, Stanley W. *Nevada Ghost Towns and Mining Camps*. Las Vegas, Nevada: Nevada Publications, 1970.

Census Records

Available Census Records and Census Substitutes

Federal Census 1860 (with Utah), 1870, 1880, 1900, 1910, 1920, 1930

Federal Mortality Schedules 1860, 1870, 1880

Union Veterans and Widows 1890

State/Territorial Census 1862

Inhabitants 1875

Bryan Lee. *1910 Nevada Census Index: Head of Households and Other Surnames in Households*. Bountiful, Utah: AGLL, 1993.

Dollarhide, William. *The Census Book: A Genealogist's Guide to Federal Census Facts, Schedules and Indexes*. Bountiful, Utah: Heritage Quest, 1999.

Kemp, Thomas Jay. *The American Census Handbook*. Wilmington, Delaware: Scholarly Resources, Inc., 2001.

Lainhart, Ann S. *State Census Records*. Baltimore: Genealogical Publishing Co., Inc., 1992.

Scott, Patricia A., comp. *Nevada Tax List, Beginning 1863*. *[ongoing database]*, 2001. www.rootsweb.com/~nvgenweb/nvtax.txt

Szucs, Loretto Dennis and Matthew Wright. *Finding Answers in U.S. Census Records*. Ancestry Publishing, 2001.

Thorndale, William and William Dollarhide. *Map Guide to the U.S. Federal Census, 1790–1920*. Baltimore: Genealogical Publishing Co., 1987.

United States. Census Office. *11th census, 1890. Schedules Enumerating Union Veterans and Widows of Union Veterans of the Civil War*. Washington, D.C.: The National Archives, 1948.

Court Records, Probate and Wills

Note: Probate records are located in the individual counties.

Ellison, Marion. *An Inventory & Index to the Records of Carson County, Utah & Nevada Territories, 1855–1861*. Reno, Nevada: Grace Dangberg Foundation, 1984.

NARA's Pacific Region (San Francisco). *Records of the District Courts of the United States, Record Group 21: Nevada*. San Bruno, California: National Archives Records Administration Pacific Branch. Online at— www.nara.gov/regional/findaids/sanguid1.html#21.

Nevada State Archives and Records Management Archives and Records Management. *The Nevada Supreme Court from the Political History of Nevada*. Carson City, Nevada: Nevada State Archives and Records Management Archives and Records Management, 2001. Online at—http://dmla.clan.lib.nv.us/docs/nsla/archives/archival/exec/scourt.htm.

Nevada Supreme Court Cases at the Nevada State Library and Archives, 1865–1997. Carson City, Nevada: Nevada State Archives and Records Management Archives and Records Management. Online at—http://dmla.clan.lib.nv.us/docs/nsla/archives/court/supcourt.htm.

Emigration, Immigration, Migration and Naturalization

Arrington, Leonard J. *The Mormons in Nevada*. Las Vegas: Las Vegas Sun, 1979.

McCullough, Flavina Maria. *The Basques in the Northwest: A Dissertation, 1945*. Reprint. San Francisco: R and E Research Associates, 1974.

Land and Property

Ellison, Marion. *An Inventory and Index to the Records of Carson County, Utah and Nevada Territories, 1855–1861*. Reno, Nevada: Grace Dangberg Foundation, 1984 (mainly land records).

Hone, Wade E. *Land and Property Research in the United States*. Salt Lake City: Ancestry Incorporated, 1997.

Military

Nevada. Adjutant General. *Annual Reports, 1865–1930*. Microfilm of original: Carson City, Nevada: Nevada State Library and Archives, 1991. S.l.: Filmed by Nevada Printing and Micrographics Division, 1991.

Nevada's Golden Stars. Reno: Nevada Adjutant General's Office 1924.

Pettengill, Cal C., comp. *Nevada Casualties of World War II*. USGenWeb Project Archives, 2000. Online at— ftp://ftp.rootsweb.com/pub/usgenweb/nv/state/WWII.txt.

Revised and Complete Roster of Nevada Veterans, Civil War, Spanish American War, Nevada National Guards to 1914, State Militia, Home Guards. Microfilm of typescript at Reno Family History Center, Reno, Nevada. Original records at Nevada State Library & Archives, Carson City, Nevada. Salt Lake City: Filmed by the Genealogical Society of Utah, 1994.

Sullivan, Maurice J. *Nevada's Golden Stars: A Memorial Volume Designed as a Gift from the State of Nevada to the Relatives of Those Nevada Heroes Who Died in the World War*. Reno, Nevada: A. Carlisle, 1924.

Thompson, J. S. *Records of Early Nevada Military Units and Personnel*. Salt Lake City: Filmed by the Genealogical Society of Utah, 1995.

United States. Adjutant General's Office. *Index to Compiled Service Records of Volunteer Union Soldiers Who Served in Organizations from the State of Nevada*. Washington, D.C.: The National Archives, 1964.

United States. Selective Service System. *Nevada, World War I Selective Service System Draft Registration Cards, 1917–1918*. National Archives Microfilm Publications, M1509. Washington, D.C.: National Archives, 1987–1988.

Vital and Cemetery Records

Arizona, California, Idaho, Nevada, 1850–1951. S.l.: Brøderbund, 1996. CD-ROM.

Family History Center (Reno, Nevada). *Card Index of Persons Buried in Nevada Cemeteries*. Microfilm of cards written and alphabetized by Nevada Family History Center. Salt Lake City: Filmed by the Genealogical Society of Utah, 1990.

Ferrel, Jean, and Roger Ferrel. *Nevada State Cemeteries*. S.l.: s.n., 1997.

Historical Records Survey (Nevada). *Guide to Public Vital Statistics Records in Nevada*. Reno, Nevada: University of Nevada, Las Vegas, 1941.

Ostrander, Edna E. *Index to Marriage Licenses and Marriage Notices in Miscellaneous Nevada Newspapers, 1906–1968*. Microfilm of records at the Office of Vital Statistics, Carson City, Nevada. Salt Lake City: Genealogical Society of Utah, 1968. 293 microfiches.

Paterson, Velma S. *Nevada Cemeteries: Tombstone Inscriptions of Nevada Cemeteries Collected by Local DAR Chapters Throughout Nevada*. Salt Lake City: Genealogical Society of Utah, 1995.

Taylor, Richard B. *The Nevada Tombstone Record Book*. Las Vegas: Nevada Families Project, 1986.

County Website	Map Index	Date Created	Parent County or Territory From Which Organized Address/Details
Carson		17 Jan 1854	**Original county** Carson County; NV **Details:** (Organized as a County in Utah Territory. Discontinued 2 Mar 1861 when Nevada Territory was created. Became part of Douglas, Lyon, Ormsby, Storey, Churchill, Pershing, Humboldt & Washoe Counties)
Carson City www.carson-city.nv.us/ccgov.htm	H1	25 Nov 1861	**Original county** Carson City County; 885 E Musser St; Carson City, NV 89701; Ph. (775) 887-2260 **Details:** (Organized as Ormsby County. Consolidated into Carson City 1969 & Ormsby County discontinued) (County Clerk has Divorce, Probate, Court & Naturalization Records from 1864; County Recorder has Land Records from 1862, Military Records from 1919 & Marriage Records)
Churchill www.governet.net/NV/CO/CHU/home.cfm	G4	25 Nov 1861	**Original county** Churchill County; 155 N Taylor St 110; Fallon, NV 89406; Ph. (775) 423-6028 **Details:** (County Clerk has Marriage, Divorce, Probate & Court Records from 1905)
Clark www.co.clark.nv.us/	N10	5 Feb 1909	**Lincoln** Clark County; 200 S 3rd St; Las Vegas, NV 89155-1601; Ph. (702) 455-3156 **Details:** (County Clerk has Probate, Divorce & Court Records; County Recorder has Marriage & Land Records; County Health Department has Birth & Death Records)
Douglas www.co.douglas.nv.us/	H2	25 Nov 1861	**Original county** Douglas County; 1594 Esmeralda Ave Rm 105; Minden, NV 89423-0218; Ph. (775) 782-9014 **Details:** (County Clerk has Marriage, Divorce, Probate & Court Records)
Elko www.elkocountynv.net	C10	5 Mar 1869	**Eureka** Elko County; 571 Idaho St; Elko, NV 89801-3700; Ph. (775) 753-4600, wsmith@elkocountynv.net **Details:** (County Clerk has Marriage, Divorce, Probate & Court Records from 1876; County Recorder has Birth, Death, Burial & Land Records, & Naturalization Records 1800–1960)
Esmeralda www.accessesmeralda.com	K5	25 Nov 1861	**Original county** Esmeralda County; 233 Crook St.; PO Box 547; Goldfield, NV 89013; Ph. (775) 485-6367 **Details:** (County Clerk & Treasury Office has Marriage Records from 1898, Divorce & Probate Records from 1908, Court Records from 1907 & Naturalization Records from 1904) *(Under Records holdings wrote District Court, but gave no specifics)*
Eureka www.governet.net/NV/CO/EUR/home.cfm	F8	1 Mar 1873	**Lander** Eureka County; 701 S Main St; PO Box 677; Eureka, NV 89316-0677; Ph. (775) 237-5262 **Details:** (County Recorder has Birth, Marriage, Death, Burial & Land Records; County Clerk has Divorce, Probate & Court Records from 1874)

County	Map	Date	Parent County or Territory From Which Organized
Website	Index	Created	Address/Details

Humboldt   C4   **25 Nov 1861**
www.governet.net/NV/CO/HUM/home.cfm

Original county
Humboldt County; 50 W 5th St; Winnemucca, NV 89445;
Ph. (775) 623-6343
Details: (County Clerk has Marriage Records from 1881, Divorce & Court Records from 1863, Probate Records from 1900 & Naturalization Records from 1864; County Recorder has Land Records; see 1860 Utah Census)

Lake   **1861**

Carson
Lake County; NV
Details: Name changed 1862 to Roop County

Lander   F7   **19 Dec 1862**
www.governet.net/NV/CO/LAN/home.cfm

Original county
Lander County; 315 S Humboldt St; Battle Mountain, NV 89820;
Ph. (775) 635-5761
Details: (County Clerk has Marriage Records from 1867, Divorce Records, Probate & Court Records from 1865; County Auditor has some Birth Records)

Lincoln   L10   **26 Feb 1866**
www.governet.net/NV/CO/LIN/home.cfm

Nye
Lincoln County; 1 Main St; Pioche, NV 89043-0000;
Ph. (775) 962-5390
Details: (County Clerk has Marriage, Divorce, Probate, Court & Land Records from 1873)

Lyon   I2   **25 Nov 1861**
www.governet.net/NV/CO/LYO/home.cfm

Original county
Lyon County; 27 S Main St; PO Box 816; Yerington, NV 89447;
Ph. (775) 577-5043
Details: (County Recorder has Marriage & Land Records from 1862; County Clerk has Divorce, Probate & Court Records from 1890)

Mineral   J4   **10 Feb 1911**
www.governet.net/NV/CO/MIN/home.cfm

Esmeralda
Mineral County; PO Box 1450; Hawthorne, NV 89415-1450;
Ph. (775) 945-2446
Details: (County Clerk has Divorce, Probate & Court Records from 1911 with some earlier, Naturalization Records 1911–1956 & Burial Records; County Recorder has Marriage license applications & Military Discharge Records from 1911; County Treasury has Land Records from 1911)

Nye   J7   **16 Feb 1864**
www.governet.net/NV/CO/NYE/home.cfm

Esmeralda
Nye County; 101 Radar Rd; PO Box 1031; Tonopah, NV 89049-1031;
Ph. (775) 482-8127
Details: (County Clerk has Marriage, Divorce, Probate & Court Records from 1860; County Recorder has Land Records)

Ormsby   H1   **25 Nov 1861**

Original county
Ormsby County; NV
Details: (see Carson City) Consolidated with Carson City 1969 & discontinued

Pahute   **1865**

Pahute County; NV
Details: (Terminated 1866)

County Website	Map Index	Date Created	Parent County or Territory From Which Organized Address/Details
Pershing www.pershingcounty.net	E4	18 Mar 1919	**Humboldt** Pershing County;Courthouse: 400 Main St Drawer E; Lovelock, NV 89419; Ph. (775) 273-2208; Administration Building: 398 Main St.; PO Box 820; Lovelock, NV 89419 **Details:** (State Vital Statistics has Birth, Death, Census, & Naturalization Records; Cemetery Office has Burial Records; County Courthouse has Court Records; Clerk of District Court has Divorce, Guardianship, & Probate Records; County Recorder (Administration Building) has Land Records; County Clerk has marriage records; County Recorder has Newspapers; Treasurer (Administration Building) has Tax Records; All records are from March 1919 to Present)
Roop		1860	Roop County; NV **Details:** (see Washoe) Discontinued after a boundary dispute with California Territory. Absorbed by Plumas County, California & Washoe County.
St. Mary's		1856	**Original county** St. Mary's County; NV **Details:** (Organized as a County in Utah Territory. Discontinued 2 Mar 1861 when Nevada Territory was created)
Storey www.governet.net/NV/CO/STO/home.cfm	G2	25 Nov 1861	**Original county** Storey County; PO Box Death; Virginia City, NV 89440-0139; Ph. (755) 847-0969 **Details:** (County Recorder has Birth, Marriage & Death Records from 1875 & Land Records; County Clerk has Divorce & Court Records from 1861 & Probate Records from 1875)
Washoe www.co.washoe.nv.us/	E1	25 Nov 1861	**Original county** Washoe County; 75 Court St; PO Box 11130; Reno, NV 89520; Ph. (775) 328-3260 **Details:** (County Health Department has Birth, Death & Burial Records from 1900; County Clerk has Divorce, Probate, Court & Naturalization Records from 1862; County Recorder has Land Records from 1862 & Marriage Records from 1871)
White Pine www.governet.net/NV/CO/WHP/home.cfm	G10	2 Mar 1869	**Millard, Utah Territory** White Pine County; 953 Campton St; PO Box 659; Ely, NV 89301-1002; Ph. (775) 289-2341 **Details:** (County Clerk has Marriage Records from 1885, Divorce, Probate & Court Records from 1907 & Naturalization Records; County Recorder has Land Records from 1885)

Notes

New Hampshire

Capital: Concord

State: 1788 (9th)

Live free or die

The first Europeans to see New Hampshire were Martin Pring in 1603, Samuel de Champlain in 1605, and Captain John Smith in 1614. In 1622, the King of England granted all of the land between the Merrimac and Kennebec Rivers to Ferdinando Gorges and John Mason. The first settlement occurred three years later at Little Harbor (present-day Rye). Dover was settled about the same time and Strawberry Bank (later Portsmouth), Exeter, and Hampton were all settled by 1638. In 1629, New Hampshire was separated from Maine, and in 1641 was made part of the Massachusetts Colony. It remained so until 1679, when it became a Royal British Province. Seven years later it became part of the Dominion of New England, which lasted three years. Three years of independence followed until a royal government was established in 1692. From 1699 to 1741, the royal governor of Massachusetts governed New Hampshire. Victories over the Indians in 1759 opened New Hampshire to increased settlement. As the population grew, boundary disagreements and land disputes grew more heated. Finally in 1764, the Connecticut River was declared the western boundary.

New Hampshire supported the Revolution, especially following the punitive measures imposed on New England by England. In 1788, New Hampshire was the ninth state to ratify the Constitution. Many settlers heading west from Massachusetts and Connecticut stopped for a time in New Hampshire and Vermont. During the first 200 years of its history, most settlers were English. The next 75 years saw tens of thousands come from Scandinavia, Greece, Italy, and France.

In 1819 the Toleration Act was passed prohibiting taxation to support any church. In 1842, the boundary between New Hampshire and Quebec was settled. During the Civil War, just less than 34,000 men from New Hampshire served in the Union Army. Following the war, industry, transportation, and communications expanded. The textile, leather, and shoe industries brought renewed immigration from French Canadians and others.

Shipping has always played a role in New Hampshire's history. Ships were supplied from Portsmouth during wartime, and the need for military clothing brought renewed immigration and improved the economy.

Look for vital records in the following locations:

- **Birth and death records:** Check the Bureau of Vital Records, Concord, New Hampshire for records after 1901. Towns kept vital statistics from the time they were organized, but they are not complete. Until 1883, less than half of the vital records were recorded with little information. The records are more complete and informative after 1901. Be sure to state your relationship and reason for requesting records when contacting the bureau.

- **Wills, tax records and probate records:** A provincial Registry of Probate kept probate records until 1771 when probate courts were created. Clerks of probate courts in each county are in charge of wills. Tax records are generally found in the town clerk's office and some might be found in the New Hampshire Division of Records Management and Archives in Concord. Almost all towns have published town histories that contain much genealogical information about early settlers.

- **Census records:** The state office in Concord has charge of the census records.

Bureau of Vital Records Registration/Certification
6 Hazen Drive
Concord, New Hampshire 03301
(603) 271-4651 or (800) 852-3345 ext 4651;
Fax (603) 271-3447
http://vitalrec.com/nh.html

Division of Archives and Records Management
71 South Fruit Street
Concord, New Hampshire 03301
(603) 271-2236; Fax (603) 271-2272

Societies and Repositories

American-Canadian Genealogical Society; PO Box 6478; Manchester, NH 03108-6478; cdonais@usa.net; www.acgs.org.

Berlin & Coos County Historical Society; PO Box 52; Berlin, NH 03570.

Conway Historical Society; PO Box 1949; Conway, NH 03818; info@conwayhistory.org; www.conwayhistory .org/index.html.

Dublin Historical Society; 8 Church Street; PO Box 415; Dublin, NH 03444; (603) 563-8545; dublinhistory@monad.net.

Hancock Historical Society; PO Box 138; 7 Main Street; Hancock, NH 03449; hancockhistsoc@mcttelecom.com; www.mv.com/ipusers/hancocknh/hhs/hhs_home.htm.

Historical Society of Cheshire County, New Hampshire; 246 Main St.; PO Box 803; Keene, NH 03431.

Hollis Historical Society; PO Box 138; Hollis, NH 03049.

Merrimack Historical Society; 520 Boston Post Road; Merrimack, NH 03054; http://members.aol.com/merrimackhistory/merhis.html.

Merrimack Society of Genealogists; PO Box 1035; Concord, NH 03302.

N.H. Founders & Patriots; 44 Durham Point Road; Durham, NH 03824-3126.

N.H. Society of Colonial Wars; 19 Pearl Street; Concord, NH 03301-4402.

New Hampshire Division of Records Management and Archives; 71 South Fruit Street; Concord, NH 03301; (603) 271-2236; www.state.nh.us/state.

New Hampshire Historical Society; 30 Park St.; Concord, NH 03301.

New Hampshire Society of Genealogists, (NESOG); RFD 2, Box 668, Wingate Road; Center Barnstead, NH 03225-9103; asnack@worldpath.net; http://nhsog .org/index.htm.

New Hampshire State Library; 20 Park Street; Concord, NH 03301; (603) 271-2144; www.state.nh.us/nhsl.

North Country Genealogical Society; PO Box 618; Littleton, NH 03561.

Northwood Historical Society; PO Box 114; Northwood, NH 03261; www.rootsweb.com/~nhnhs.

Rockingham Society of Genealogists; PO Box 81; 28 Prentiss Way; Exeter, NH 03833-0081.

Strafford County Society Of Genealogists; PO Box 322; Dover, NH 03821-0322.

Bibliography and Record Sources

General

American Baptist Historical Society. *The Records of American Baptists in New Hampshire and Related Organizations.* Rochester, New York: American Baptist Historical Society, 1981.

Belknap, Jeremy. *The History of New Hampshire.* (1831). Reprint. Bowie, Maryland: Heritage Books, 1992.

Bent, Allen H. *Bent's Bibliography of the White Mountains.* (1911) Reprint. Rockport, Maine: Picton Press, 1971.

Biographical Sketches Of Representative Citizens Of The State Of New Hampshire. Boston, Massachusetts: New England Historical Publishing Company, 1902.

Carpenter, Randall C. *Descriptive Inventory of the New Hampshire Collection.* Salt Lake City, Utah: University of Utah Press, 1983.

Carter, Nathan F. *Native Ministry of New Hampshire.* Concord, New Hampshire: Rumford Printing Co., 1906.

Chase, Francis. *Gathered Sketches from the Early History of New Hampshire and Vermont: Containing Vivid and Interesting Accounts of a Great Variety of the Adventures of Our Forefathers, and of Other Incidents of Olden Time, Original and Selected.* Clarmont, New Hampshire: Tracy, Kenney & Co., 1856.

Church of Jesus Christ of Latter-day Saints. Vermont District. *Transcript Of Record/Record Of Members, Early To 1948.* Microfilm of original records in the LDS Church Archives, Salt Lake City. Salt Lake City: Filmed by the Genealogical Society of Utah, 1953–1954. 2 microfilm.

Committee for a New England Bibliography. *New Hampshire, a Bibliography of Its History.* Boston: G. K. Hall, 1979.

Copeley, William N. *Manuscript Church Records At The New Hampshire Historical Society, August 1981.* Salt Lake City: Genealogical Society of Utah, 1985. 1 microfiche.

Copeley, William. *New Hampshire Family Records Vol. I and II.* Bowie, Maryland: Heritage Books, 1994.

Copeley, William. *Index to Genealogies in New Hampshire Town Histories.* Concord, New Hampshire: New Hampshire Historical Society, 1988.

Crandall, Ralph J., ed. *Genealogical Research in New England.* Baltimore: Genealogical Publishing Co., 1984.

Crawford, L. *History of the White Mountains.* (1883) Reprint. Salem, Massachusetts: Higginson Books, 1991.

Daughters of the American Revolution (New Hampshire). *Genealogical Collection.* Microfilm of original records in the D.A.R. Library in Washington, D.C. Salt Lake City: Genealogical Society of Utah, 1971. 15 microfilm.

Drake, Samuel Adams. *The Heart of the White Mountains: Their Legend and Scenery.* (1881) Reprint. Salem, Massachusetts: Higginson Books, 1995.

Early New England Settlers, 1600s–1800s. S.l.: Brøderbund, 1999. CD-ROM.

Fogg, Alonzo J. *The Statistics and Gazetteer of New Hampshire: Containing Descriptions of All the Counties, Towns and Villages, Also, Boundaries and Area of the State, and Its Natural Resources.* Tucson, Arizona: W. C. Cox & Co., 1972.

Green, Scott E. *Directory of Repositories of Family History in New Hampshire*. Baltimore, Maryland: Clearfield Co., 1993.

Hammond, Otis G. *Hammond's Check List of New Hampshire History*. 1971. Reprint. Somersworth, New Hampshire: New Hampshire Publishing Co., 1971.

Haskell, John D., Jr. and T. D. Seymour Bassett, eds. *New Hampshire: A Bibliography of Its History*. Boston: G. K. Hall, 1979.

Hazen, Henry Allen. *The Pastors of New Hampshire, Congregational and Presbyterian: A Chronological Table of the Beginning and Ending of Their Pastorates*. Bristol, New Hampshire: R.W. Musgrove, 1878.

Historical Records Survey (New Hampshire) *Inventory of the Roman Catholic Church Records in New Hampshire*. Manchester, New Hampshire: Diocese of Manchester, 1938.

Historical Records Survey (New Hampshire*). Guide to Church Vital Statistics Records in New Hampshire*. Manchester, New Hampshire: the Survey, 1942.

Historical Records Survey (New Hampshire*). Guide to Depositories of Manuscript Collections in the United States, New Hampshire*. Manchester, New Hampshire: The Survey, 1940.

Historical Records Survey (New Hampshire). *Inventory of the Church Archives of New Hampshire, Protestant Episcopal Diocese of New Hampshire*. Manchester, New Hampshire: the Survey, 1942.

Hurlin, William, et al. *The Baptists of New Hampshire*. Manchester, New Hampshire: New Hampshire Baptist Convention, 1902.

Kern, Charles W. *God, Grace, and Granite: The History of Methodism in New Hampshire, 1768–1988*. Canaan, New Hampshire: Published for the New Hampshire United Methodist Conference by Phoenix Publishing, 1988.

Lawrence, Robert F. *The New Hampshire Churches: Comprising Histories of the Congregational and Presbyterian Churches in the State, with Notices of Other Denominations; Also Containing Many Interesting Incidents Connected with the First Settlement Of Towns*. N.p.: S. L. Claremont Manufacturing Co., 1856.

Maine & New Hampshire Settlers, 1600s–1900s. S.l.: Brøderbund, 2000. CD-ROM.

Metcalf, Henry Harrison. *New Hampshire Women: A Collection of Portraits and Biographical Sketches of Daughters and Residents of the Granite State, Who Are Worthy Representatives of Their Sex in The Various Walks and Conditions of Life*. Concord, New Hampshire: The New Hampshire Publishing Co., 1895.

Moses, George H. *New Hampshire Men: A Collection of Biographical Sketches, with Portraits, of Sons and Residents of the State Who Have Become Known in Commercial, Professional and Political Life*. Concord, New Hampshire: New Hampshire Publishing, 1893.

New Hampshire Historical Society. *Card Index to Genealogies, Published and Manuscript*. Concord, New Hampshire: New Hampshire Historical Society, 1975.

New Hampshire Historical Society. *New Hampshire Notables Card File, 1600 to the Present*. Microfilm of card file in the New Hampshire Historical Society, Concord, New Hampshire. Salt Lake City: Filmed by Genealogical Society of Utah, 1988. 8 microfilm.

New Hampshire. *Research Outline*. Series U.S.-States, no. 30. Salt Lake City: Family History Library, 1988.

New Hampshire. Department of State. Division of Records Management and Archives. *Guide to Early Documents (ca. 1680 to ca. 1900) at tthe New Hampshire Records Management and Archives Center*. Concord, New Hampshire: Division of Records Management and Archives, 1981.

Noyes, Sybil, Charles Thornton Libby, and Walter Goodwin Davis. *Genealogical Dictionary of Maine and New Hampshire. 1928–1939*. Reprint. Baltimore: Genealogical Publishing Co., 1983.

Pettengill, Samuel B. *The Yankee Pioneers: A Saga Of Courage*. Rutland, Vermont: Charles E. Tuttle, 1971.

Pope, Charles H. *Pioneers of Maine and New Hampshire, 1623 to 1660. 1908.* Reprint. Baltimore: Genealogical Publishing Co., 1965.

Roberts, Richard P. *New Hampshire Name Changes 1768–1923*. Bowie, Maryland: Heritage Books, 1993.

Rollock, Rich. *New Hampshire Family Histories*. 3rd ed. Laconia, New Hampshire: Family Histories Directory, 1993.

Sanborn, Edwin D. *History of New Hampshire, from Its First Discovery to the Year 1830: With Dissertations Upon the Rise of Opinions and Institutions, the Growth of Agriculture and Manufactures, and the Influence of Leading Families and Distinguished Men, to the Year 1874*. Manchester, New Hampshire: John B. Clarke, 1875.

Stackpole, Everett S. *History of New Hampshire*. 4 vols. New York: American Historical Society, 1916.

Stearn, Ezra S. *Genealogical and Family History of the State of New Hampshire*. 4 vols. New York: Lewis Publishing Co., 1908.

Tardiff, Olive. *They Paved the Way: A History of New Hampshire Women*. Exeter, New Hampshire: Women for Women Weekly Publishing, 1980.

The First Laws of the State of New Hampshire. (1780) Reprint. Wilmington, Delaware: Scholarly Resources, 1981.

Towle, Glenn C. *New Hampshire Genealogical Digest, 1623–1900*. Vol. 1. Bowie, Maryland: Heritage Books, 1986.

Towle, Laird C. *New Hampshire Genealogical Research Guide*. Bowie, Maryland: Heritage Books, 1983.

Towle, Laird C., and Ann N. Brown. *New Hampshire Genealogical Research Guide.* 2nd ed. Bowie, Maryland: Heritage Books, 1983.

Whiton, John M. *Sketches of the History of New Hampshire, from Its Settlement in 1623 to 1833: Comprising Notices of the Memorable Events and Interesting Incidents of a Period of Two Hundred and Ten Years.* Concord, New Hampshire: Marsh, Capen and Lyon, 1824.

Willey, George F. *State Builders: An Illustrated Historical and Biographical Record of the State of New Hampshire at the Beginning of the Twentieth Century.* Manchester, New Hampshire: New Hampshire Pub. Corp., 1903.

Wilson, Emily S. *Inhabitants of New Hampshire 1776.* (1983) Reprint. Baltimore: Genealogical Publishing Co., 1993.

Atlases, Maps and Gazetteers

Atlas of New Hampshire. Galveston, Texas: Frontier Press, n.d.

Charlton, Edwin A. *New Hampshire as It Is, in Three Parts.* Claremont, New Hampshire: Tracy and Sanford, 1855.

Cobb, David A. *New Hampshire Maps to 1900: An Annotated Checklist.* Hanover, New Hampshire: New Hampshire Historical Society. Distributed by University Press of New England, 1981.

Communities, Settlements and Neighborhood Centers in the State of New Hampshire. Concord: New Hampshire State Planning and Development Commission, 1937. Reprint. 1954.

Farmer, John and Jacob B. Moore. *A Gazetteer of the State of New Hampshire.* Concord, New Hampshire: Jacob B. Moore, 1823.

Fogg, Alonzo J. *The Statistics and Gazetteer of New Hampshire: Containing Descriptions of All the Counties, Towns and Villages, Also, Boundaries and Area of the State, and Its Natural Resources.* Tucson, Arizona: W. C. Cox & Co., 1972.

General Highway Maps: County Series. S.l.: New Hampshire Department of Public Works and Highways, n.d.

Hayward, John. *A Gazetteer of New Hampshire: Containing Descriptions of All the Counties, Towns, and Districts in the State; Also of Its Principal Mountains, Rivers, Waterfalls, Harbors, Islands, and Fashionable Resorts, to Which Are Added Statistical Accounts of Its Agriculture, Commerce and Manufactures.* (1849) Reprint. Bowie, Maryland: Heritage Books, 1993.

Hixon, Robert. *The Place Names of the White Mountains: History and Origins.* Camden, Maine: Down East Books, 1980.

Hunt, Elmer Munson. *New Hampshire Town Names: And Whence They Came.* Peterborough, New Hampshire: Noone House, 1970.

Long, John H., ed. and Gordon DenBoer, comp. *Atlas of Historical County Boundaries: New Hampshire and Vermont.* New York: Simon & Schuster, 1993.

Merrill, Eliphalet. *Gazetteer of the State of New Hampshire.* Bowie, Maryland: Heritage Books, 1987.

New Hampshire Atlas and Gazetteer. 10th ed. Freeport, Maine: DeLorme Mapping Co., 1996.

Simonds, L. W. *New Hampshire Post Offices, 1775–1978.* New London, New Hampshire: Simonds, 1978.

Smith, Chester M. *The Postal History of New Hampshire: The Post Offices and First Postmasters from 1775 to 1985.* Lake Grove, Oregon: The Depot, 1986.

Town and City Atlas of the State of New Hampshire. Boston: D. H. Hurd, Co., 1892.

Census Records

Available Census Records and Census Substitutes

Federal Census 1790, 1800 (except parts of Rockingham and Strafford Counties), 1810, 1820, 1830, 1840, 1850, 1860, 1870, 1880, 1900, 1910, 1920, 1930

Federal Mortality Schedules 1850, 1860, 1870, 1880

Union Veterans and Widows 1890

Residents 1732, 1776

Census of New Hampshire, for the Years 1767 and 1775. Microfilm of original records in the Records & Archives Center, Concord, New Hampshire. Salt Lake City: Filmed by the Genealogical Society of Utah, 1975. 1 microfilm.

Dollarhide, William. *The Census Book: A Genealogist's Guide to Federal Census Facts, Schedules and Indexes.* Bountiful, Utah: Heritage Quest, 1999.

Holbrook, Jay Mack. *New Hampshire 1732 Census.* Oxford, Massachusetts: Holbrook Research Institute, 1981.

Holbrook, Jay Mack. *New Hampshire Residents 1633–1699.* Oxford, Massachusetts: Holbrook Research Institute, 1979.

Kemp, Thomas Jay. *The American Census Handbook.* Wilmington, Delaware: Scholarly Resources, Inc., 2001.

Lainhart, Ann S. *State Census Records.* Baltimore: Genealogical Publishing Co., Inc., 1992.

Szucs, Loretto Dennis and Matthew Wright. *Finding Answers in U.S. Census Records.* Ancestry Publishing, 2001

Thorndale, William and William Dollarhide. *Map Guide to the U.S. Federal Census, 1790–1920.* Baltimore: Genealogical Publishing Co., 1987.

Court Records, Probate and Wills

Batchellor, Albert Stillman. *Probate Records of the Province of New Hampshire.* 9 vols. in 12. Bowie, Maryland: Heritage Books, 1989–1990.

Bell, Charles H. *The Bench and Bar of New Hampshire: Including Biographical Notices of Deceased Judges of the Highest Court, and Lawyers of the Province and*

State and a List of Names of Those Now Living. Boston: Houghton, Mifflin and Co., 1894.

New Hampshire (Colony). *Province Deeds and Probate Records—From 1623–1772.* Microfilm of original records at the Historical Society in Concord, New Hampshire. Salt Lake City: Filmed by the Genealogical Society of Utah, 1975. 118 microfilm.

New Hampshire Provincial and State Papers. 40 vols. Concord, New Hampshire: George E. Jenks, 1867–1943.

New Hampshire. Courts. *Colonial Court Records, 1638–1772 Approx.* Microfilm of original records in Concord, New Hampshire. Salt Lake City: Filmed by the Genealogical Society of Utah, 1975. 207 microfilm.

Probate Records of the Province of New Hampshire, vols. 31–39 of *New Hampshire Provincial and State Papers.* 9 vols. Reprint. Bowie, Maryland: Heritage Books, 1989–1990.

State of New Hampshire. Division of Records Management and Archives. *General Court Records (1680–current).* Concord, New Hampshire: State of New Hampshire. Division of Records Management and Archives, 2002. Online guide—www.state.nh.us/state/archival.html.

State of New Hampshire. Division of Records Management and Archives. *Provincial Probate Records.* Concord, New Hampshire: State of New Hampshire. Division of Records Management and Archives, 2002. Online guide—www.state.nh.us/state/archival.html.

Emigration, Immigration, Migration and Naturalization

Bolton, Ethel Stanwood. *Immigrants to New England, 1700–1775.* Baltimore: Genealogical Publishing, 1966.

Early New England Settlers, 1600s–1800s. S.l.: Brøderbund, 1999. CD-ROM.

National Archives Records Administration: Northeastern Region (Boston). *Records of the Immigration and Naturalization Service, RG 85.* Boston, Massachusetts: National Archives Records Administration: Northeastern Region (Boston). Online guide—www.nara.gov/regional/findaids/bosalrgs.html.

United States. *Immigration and Naturalization Service. Index to New England Naturalization Petitions, 1791–1906.* Washington: National Archives. Central Plains Region, 1983. 117 microfilm.

Land and Property

Hone, Wade E. *Land and Property Research in the United States.* Salt Lake City: Ancestry Incorporated, 1997.

New Hampshire (Colony). *Province Deeds and Probate Records from 1623–1772.* Microfilm of original records at the Historical Society in Concord, New Hampshire. Salt Lake City: Filmed by the Genealogical Society of Utah, 1975. 118 microfilm.

New Hampshire. Proprietors. *Proprietors' Records, 1748–1846.* Microfilm of originals in Concord, New

Hampshire. Salt Lake City: Filmed by the Genealogical Society of Utah, 1975.

State of New Hampshire. Division of Records Management and Archives. *Land Surveyors' Records.* Concord, New Hampshire: State of New Hampshire. Division of Records Management and Archives, 2002. Online guide—www.state.nh.us/state/archival.html.

State of New Hampshire. Division of Records Management and Archives. *Provincial Land Records.* Concord, New Hampshire: State of New Hampshire. Division of Records Management and Archives, 2002. Online guide—www.state.nh.us/state/archival.html.

Military

Draper, Mrs. Amos G. *New Hampshire Pension Records, 1776–1850.* Microfilm of originals at the D.A.R. Library in Washington, D. C. Salt Lake City: Filmed by the Genealogical Society of Utah, 1971. 25 microfilm.

Hammond, Isaac W., ed. *Rolls of the Soldiers in the Revolutionary War.* Provincial and State Papers of New Hampshire, vols. 14–17. Concord and Manchester, New Hampshire, 1885–1889. Reprint. New York: AMS Press, 1973.

New Hampshire. Adjutant General. *Revised Register of New Hampshire Soldiers and Sailors in the War of the Rebellion.* Concord, New Hampshire: adjutant general, 1895.

New Hampshire. *Indian and French Wars and Revolutionary Papers: Collection Of 1880.* Microfilm of originals in Concord, New Hampshire. Salt Lake City: Filmed by the Genealogical Society of Utah, 1975. 2 microfilm.

New Hampshire's Role in the American Revolution, 1763–1789: A Bibliography. Concord, New Hampshire: New Hampshire American Revolution Bicentennial Commission, 1974.

Potter, Chandler E. *The Military History of the State of New Hampshire from its Settlement, in 1623, to the Rebellion in 1861.* 2 vols. New Hampshire Adjutant General's Report. Concord, New Hampshire, 1866–1868. Reprint. Baltimore: Genealogical Publishing Co., 1972.

Revised Register of the Soldiers and Sailors of New Hampshire in the War of the Rebellion. Concord, New Hampshire: Ira C. Evans, 1895.

Rolls and Documents Relating to Soldiers in the Revolutionary War. New Hampshire Provincial and State papers, vols. 14–17. Concord and Manchester, New Hampshire, 1885–1889.

State of New Hampshire. Division of Records Management and Archives. *Military Records.* Concord, New Hampshire: State of New Hampshire. Division of Records Management and Archives, 2002. Online guide—www.state.nh.us/state/archival.html.

United States. Selective Service System. *New Hampshire, World War I Selective Service System Draft Registration*

Cards, 1917–1918. National Archives Microfilm Publications, M1509. Washington, D.C.: National Archives, 1987–1988.

Waite, Otis F. R. *New Hampshire in the Great Rebellion: Containing Histories of the Several New Hampshire Regiments.* Claremont, New Hampshire: Tracy, Chase, & Co., 1870.

Vital and Cemetery Records

Dodge, Nancy L., comp. *Northern New Hampshire Graveyards & Cemeteries.* Salem, Massachusetts: Higginson Books, 1985.

Goss, Winifred L. *Colonial Gravestone Inscriptions in the State of New Hampshire.* Reprint. Baltimore: Clearfield Co., 1997.

Guide to Church Vital Statistics Records in New Hampshire. Manchester, New Hampshire: Historical Records Survey, 1942.

New Hampshire Historical Society. *Card Index to Bible Records.* Microfilm of original records at the New Hampshire Historical Society in Concord, New Hampshire. Salt Lake City: Genealogical Society of Utah, 1975. 1 microfilm.

New Hampshire Historical Society. *Card File Index to Births, Deaths, and Marriages Found in Published Vital Records of Massachusetts to 1850.* Microfilm of original records in the New Hampshire Historical Society, Concord, New Hampshire. Salt Lake City: Filmed by the Genealogical Society of Utah, 1975. 7 microfilm.

New Hampshire Historical Society. *Card File Index to Publishments of Marriage Intention Prior to 1900.* Microfilm of originals at the New Hampshire Historical Society in Concord, New Hampshire. Salt Lake City: Filmed by the Genealogical Society of Utah, 1975.

New Hampshire Registrar of Vital Statistics. *Index of Marriages, Early to 1900.* Salt Lake City: Genealogical Society of Utah, 1975–1976. 102 microfilm.

New Hampshire. Division of Vital Statistics. *Bride's Index, 1640–1900.* Microfilm of original records in the New Hampshire State Department of Health. Salt Lake City: Genealogical Society of Utah, 1975–1976. 17 microfilm.

New Hampshire. Registrar of Vital Statistics. *Index of Births, Early to 1900.* Microfilm of original records in Concord, New Hampshire. Salt Lake City: Genealogical Society of Utah, 1974. 98 microfilm.

New Hampshire. Registrar of Vital Statistics. *Index to Deaths, Early to 1900.* Microfilm of original records in Concord, New Hampshire. Salt Lake City: Genealogical Society of Utah, 1974. 60 microfilm.

New Hampshire. Registrar of Vital Statistics. *Index to Divorces and Annulments Prior to 1938.* Microfilm of original records at Concord, New Hampshire. Salt Lake City: Genealogical Society of Utah, 1975. 8 microfilm.

New Hampshire. Secretary of State. *Index to Early Town Records, New Hampshire, Early to 1850.* Microfilm of original records in the Office of Secretary of State, Concord, New Hampshire. Salt Lake City: Filmed by the Genealogical Society of Utah, 1950. 111 microfilm.

Oesterlin, Pauline Johnson. *New Hampshire Marriage Licenses and Intentions 1709–1961.* Bowie, Maryland: Heritage Books, 1991.

Walterworth, Mrs. E. J. *Location of New Hampshire Revolutionary Soldiers.* n.p., n.d. Copied from the records of the Harold B. Twombly Graves Registration Office by the New Hampshire American Legion.

County Website	Map Index	Date Created	Parent County or Territory From Which Organized Address/Details
Belknap www.belknapcounty.org/	**L7**	**22 Dec 1840**	**Strafford, Merrimac** Belknap County; 64 Court St; Laconia, NH 03246-3679; Ph. (603) 524-3570 **Details:** (Town or City Clerks have Birth, Marriage & Death Records; Clerk Superior Court has Divorce & Court Records; Probate Judge has Probate Records from 1841; Registrar of Deeds has land Records from 1841) Towns Organized Before 1800: Alton 1796, Barnstead 1727, Centre Harbor 1797, Gilmanton 1727, Meredith 1768, New Hampton 1777, Sanbornton 1770
Carroll www.rootsweb.com/~nhcarrol/	**J9**	**22 Dec 1840**	**Strafford** Carroll County; Rt 171; Ossipee, NH 3864; Ph. (603) 539-7751 **Details:** (Clerk Court has Divorce & Court Records from 1859; Town Clerks have Birth, Marriage, Death & Burial Records; Probate Judge has Probate Records; Registrar of Deeds has land Records) Towns Organized Before 1800: Albany 1766, Brookfield 1794, Chatham 1767, Conway 1765, Eaton 1766, Effingham 1788, Moulton-borough 1777
Cheshire www.co.cheshire.nh.us/	**P4**	**29 Apr 1769**	**Original county** Cheshire County; 33 W St; Keene, NH 03431-3355; Ph. (603) 352-6902 **Details:** (Town or City Clerks have Birth, Marriage, Death & Burial Records; County Clerk has Divorce & Court Records; Registrar of Probate has Probate Records; Registrar of Deeds has land Records) Towns Organized Before 1800: Alstead 1763, Chesterfield 1752, Dublin 1771, Fitzwilliam 1773, Gilsum 1763, Hinsdale 1753, Jaffrey 1773, Keene 1753, Marlborough 1776, Marlow 1761, Nelson 1774, Richmond 1752, Rindge 1768, Stoddard 1774, Sullivan 1787, Surry 1769, Swanzey 1753, Walpole 1752, Winchester 1753
Coos http://freepages.genealogy.rootsweb.com/~dickmarston/Coos.html	**E8**	**24 Dec 1803**	**Grafton** Coos County; PO Box 309; Lancaster, NH 03584-0309; Ph. (603) 788-4900 **Details:** (Town or City Clerks have Birth, Marriage, Death & Burial Records; Clerk Superior Court has Divorce & Court Records from 1887; Registrar of Probate has Probate Records; Registrar of Deeds has land Records) Towns Organized Before 1800: Bartlett 1790, Cambridge 1773, Colebrook 1790, Columbia 1797, Dalton 1784, Dummer 1773, Jefferson 1796, Kilkenny 1774, Lancaster 1763, Millsfield 1774, Northumberland 1779, Stratford 1773, Stewartstown 1799, Success 1773, Whitefield 1774

County	Map	Date	Parent County or Territory From Which Organized
Website	Index	Created	Address/Details

Grafton   I6   **29 Apr 1769**   **Original county**

www.geocities.com/Yosemite/2821/grafton.htm

Grafton County; North Haverhill; RR 1 Box 67; North Haverhill, NH 3774; Ph. (603) 787-6941

Details: (Clerk Court has Divorce & Court Records; Probate Judge has Probate Records; Registrar of Deeds has land Records; Town Clerks have Birth, Marriage & Death Records; 1820 census missing)

Towns Organized Before 1800: Alexandria 1782, Bath 1761, Benton 1764, Bethlehem 1799, Bridgewater 1788, Campton 1761, Canaan 1761, Danbury 1795, Dorchester 1761, Enfield 1761, Franconia 1764, Grafton 1778, Groton 1796, Hanover 1761, Haverhill 1763, Hebron 1792, Hill 1778, Holderness 1761, Landaff 1764, Lebanon 1761, Lisbon 1768, Lincoln 1764, Littleton 1784, Lyman 1761, Lyme 1761, Orange 1780, Orford 1761, Plymouth 1763, Rumney 1761, Thornton 1781, Warren 1763, Wentworth 1766, Woodstock 1786

Hillsborough   P6   **29 Apr 1769**   **Original county**

www.hillsboroughcountynh.org/

Hillsborough County; 19 Temple St; Nashua, NH 03060-3472; Ph. (603) 882-9471

Details: (County Clerk has Divorce & Probate Records from 1771; Town Clerks have Birth, Marriage & Death Records; Registrar of Deeds has land Records)

Towns Organized Before 1800: Amherst 1760, Antrim 1777, Bedford 1780, Brookline 1769, Deering 1774, Francestown 1772, Goffstown 1761, Greenfield 1791, Hancock 1779, Hillsborough 1772, Hollis 1746, Hudson 1746, Litchfield 1749, Lyndeborough 1764, Manchester 1751, Mason 1768, Merrimac 1745, Miford 1794, Nashua 1746, New Ipswich 1762, New Boston 1763, Pelham 1746, Peterborough 1760, Sharon 1791, Temple 1769, Weare 1764, Wilton 1762, Windsor 1798

Merrimack   N6   **1 Jul 1823**   **Rockingham, Hillsboro**

www.ci.concord.nh.us/

Merrimack County; 163 N Main St; Concord, NH 3301; Ph. (603) 225-5501

Details: (County Clerk has Divorce Records from 1840 & Court Records from 1823; Town or City Clerks have Birth, Marriage, Death & Burial Records; Probate Judge has Probate Records from 1823; Registrar of Deeds has land Records from 1823)

Towns Organized Before 1800: Andover 1779, Bradford 1787, Bow 1727, Boscawen 1760, Canterbury 1727, Chichester 1727, Concord 1765, Dunbarton 1765, Epsom 1727, Henniker 1768, Hopkinton 1765, Loudon 1773, Newbury 1778, New London 1779, Northfield 1780, Pembroke 1759, Pittsfield 1782, Salisbury 1768, Sutton 1784, Warner 1774

County Website	Map Index	Date Created	Parent County or Territory From Which Organized Address/Details

Rockingham   P9   29 Apr 1769   **Original county**

www.co.rockingham.nh.us/

Rockingham County; 99-119 North Rd; Brentwood, NH 3833; Ph. (603) 679-2256

Details: (Clerk Courts has Divorce & Court Records from 1769; Town or City Clerks have Birth, Marriage, Death & Burial Records; Registrar of Probate has Probate Records from 1770; Registrar of Deeds has land Records from 1643)

Towns Organized Before 1800: Atkinson 1767, Brentwood 1742, Candia 1763, Chester 1722, Danville 1760, Deerfield 1766, East Kingston 1738, Epping 1741, Exeter 1638, Gosport 1715, Greenland 1704, Hampstead 1749, Hampton 1638, Hampton Falls 1712, Kensington 1737, Kingston 1694, Londonderry 1722, New Castle 1692, Newington 1764, New Market 1727, Newtown 1749, North Hampton 1742, Northwood 1773, Nottingham 1722, Plaistow 1749, Poplin 1764, Portsmouth 1653, Raymond 1765, Rye 1726, Salem 1750, Sandown 1756, Seabrook 1763, South Hampton 1742, Stratham 1716, Windham 1742

Strafford   N10   29 Apr 1769   **Original county**

www.usgennet.org/usa/nh/county/strafford/

Strafford County; County Farm Rd; PO Box 799; Dover, NH 3820; Ph. (603) 742-3065

Details: (Town or City Clerk has Birth, Marriage, Death & Burial Records; Clerk Superior Court has Divorce & Court Records; Registrar of Probate has Probate Records; Registrar of Deeds has land Records from 1773)

Towns Organized Before 1800: Barrington 1722, Dover 1623, Durham 1732, Farmington 1798, Lee 1766, Madbury 1755, Middleton 1778, New Durham 1762, Rochester 1722, Somersworth 1754

Sullivan   M4   5 Jul 1827   **Cheshire**

www.usgennet.org/usa/nh/county/sullivan/

Sullivan County; 22 Main St; PO Box 45; Newport, NH 03773-0045; Ph. (603) 863-3450

Details: (Town or City Clerks have Birth, Marriage, Death & Burial Records; Clerk Superior Court has Divorce & Court Records from 1827; Registrar of Probate has Probate Records; Registrar of Deeds has land Records; Richards Library, Newport, New Hampshire has other Records of genealogical interest)

Towns Organized Before 1800: Acworth 1766, Charlestown 1753, Claremont 1764, Cornish 1763, Croydon 1763, Goshen 1791, Grantham 1761, Langdon 1787, Lempster 1761, Newport 1761, Plainfield 1761, Springfield 1794, Unity 1764, Washington 1776, Wendell 1731

Notes

New Jersey

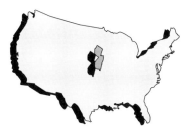

Capital: Trenton
State: 1787 (3rd)

Liberty and prosperity

In 1524, Verrazano became the first European to stand on New Jersey soil. Henry Hudson laid claim in 1609 to the area for the Dutch, who then set up trading posts at present-day Jersey City and Camden in the 1620's. When the first Europeans arrived in New Jersey, they encountered Indians known as the Leni-Lenape, or "original people." The Swedes tried to settle the area as well, but were dominated by the Dutch in 1655. Less than a decade later, in 1664, the British captured the entire area. That same year Lord John Berkeley and Sir George Carteret were granted the land between the Delaware and Hudson rivers. They opened the land to settlers, who came in large numbers. Among those early settlers were British emigrants; Puritans from Connecticut, who established Newark; Scotch-Irish Presbyterians, who settled the eastern counties; and Quakers, who settled in the Delaware River Valley.

The new settlers were diverse in religion but united in opposition to the tax and monetary policies of the proprietors. In 1682, Carteret's heirs sold east Jersey to William Penn. In 1702, New Jersey was put under a royal governor, which it shared with New York until 1738. In 1738, New Jersey had a governor and a legislature of its own. Many important battles of the Revolutionary War took place in New Jersey. Residents supported both sides in the war. New Jersey was the third state to ratify the Constitution and was one of the major forces behind gaining the rights of small states and equal representation in the Senate. The 1790 Census showed New Jersey with a population of 184,139, most of whom were English, Dutch, or Swedish.

Look for vital records in the following locations:

- **Birth and death records:** The New Jersey State Archives holds birth records/registrations/certificates from 1848–1923 and state registered deaths 1848–1940 for in-person research. Mail requests to the Archives are fulfilled for only the years 1848–1878. The New Jersey Department of Vital Statistics holds the records and handles the requests for the subsequent years. The official title of the New Jersey State Archives is "New Jersey State Archives, Division of Archives & Records Management."

- **Marriage and divorce records:** Colonial marriage bonds exist for the years 1711–1795. Marriages were recorded at the county level starting in 1795. The New Jersey State Archives holds state registered marriages from 1848–1940 as well as microfilm of the county recorded marriages for in-person research. Mail requests to the Archives are fulfilled for only the years 1848–1878.

- **Naturalizations:** The New Jersey State Archives has microfilm of pre-1906 county filed records as well as originals of post-1906 records for selected counties.

- **Land records:** The New Jersey State Archives has microfilm of deeds 1795 to about 1900 for almost all counties. Also, the New Jersey State Archives has microfilm of provincial land records for the West Jersey Proprietors as well as the East Jersey Board of Proprietors.

- **Wills and probate records:** The New Jersey State Archives holds the original wills and probate records through 1951. Also, the County Surrogate's Office holds the probate records from 1804 to present. The abstracts of wills and administrations cover the years 1682–1817.

- **Census records:** State censuses exist for 1855–1915. A 1793 militia enrollment census has been published and helps to make up for the destroyed 1790 Census. Also, Tax Lists for 1772–1822 are used to supplement the destroyed/lost censuses of 1790–1820.

New Jersey Vital Statistics Customer Service Unit
PO Box 370
Trenton, New Jersey 08625-0370
(609) 292-4087 ext 582
www.state.nj.us/health/vital/vital.shtml

State Archives
225 West State Street
Trenton, New Jersey 08625-0307
(609) 292-6260; (609) 292-9105 fax
www.njarchives.org

Bureau of Records Management
2300 Stuyvesant Avenue
P.O. Box 307
Trenton, New Jersey 08625-0307
(609) 530-3200; Fax (609) 530-6121

Societies and Repositories

Afro-American Historical and Genealogical Society, New Jersey; 758 Stirling Dr., East; South Orange, NJ 07079-2425.

Association of Jewish Genealogical Societies; 155 N. Washington Ave.; Bergenfield, NJ 07621.

Atlantic County Historical Society; PO Box 301; Somers Point, NJ 08244.

Atlantic Highlands Historical Society; PO Box 108; Atlantic Highlands, NJ 07716; (732) 291-0074; http://community.nj.com/cc/historicalsociety.

Bergen County Historical Society; PO Box 55; River Edge, NJ 07661; http://apollo.carroll.com/bchs/index.html.

Burlington County Historical Society; Delia Biddle Pug Library; 457 High St.; Burlington, NJ 08016.

Camden County Historical Society; PO Box 378; Collingswood, NJ 08108-0378; johnreidseitter@aol.com; www.cchsnj.com.

Cape May Historical Society; Courthouse; Cape May, NJ 08204.

Central Jersey Genealogy Club; PO Box 9903; Hamilton, NJ 08650-1903; CShea70655@aol.com; www.rootsweb.com/~njcjgc.

Cranford Historical Society; The Hanson House; 38 Springfield Avenue; Cranford, NJ 07016; www.bobdevlin.com/crhissoc.html.

Cumberland County Historical Society; PO Box 16; Greenwich, NJ 08323; lummislib@jnlk.com; www.rootsweb.com/~njcumber/webdoc14.html.

Delaware Valley Finnish Americans; 1752 Dixie Line Road; Newark, NJ 19702.

Denville, NJ Genealogy Club; Denville, NJ; huzzah@bigfoot.com; http://members.aol.com/DGenealogy.

Descendants of Founders of New Jersey; 950-A Thornhill Court; Lakewood, NJ 08701.

Estonian American National Council; 21 Shady Lane Drive; Lakewood, NJ 08701; www.estosite.org/eng/eng_home.htm.

Genealogical Club of Metuchen / Edison Regional Historical Society; PO Box 61; Metuchen, NJ 08840.

Genealogical Society of Bergen County, New Jersey; PO Box 432; Midland Park, NJ 07432; ArnieLang@att.net; www.rootsweb.com/~njgsbc.

Genealogical Society of New Jersey; PO Box 1291; New Brunswick, NJ 08903; www.rootsweb.com/~njgsnj/main.htm.

Genealogical Society of Salem County, NJ, Inc.; PO Box 231; Woodstown, NJ 08098; (856) 769-0969; barnaclebill1@comcast.net; www.rootsweb.com/~njsalem/gsscnj.html.

Genealogical Society of the West Fields; c/o Westfield Memorial Library; 550 East Broad St.; Westfield, NJ 07090-2116; www.westfieldnj.com/gswf/index.htm.

Genealogical Society of Westfield; c/o Westfield Memorial Library; 425 East Broad St.; Westfield, NJ 07090.

Gloucester County Historical Society; 17 Hunter St.; Woodbury, NJ 08096-4605; (856) 845-4771; gchs@net-gate.com; www.rootsweb.com/~njglouce/gchs.

Highland Park Historical Society; PO BOX 4255; Highland Park, NJ 08904-4255; www.monmouth.com/~ricekolva.

Historical Society of Boonton Township; RD 2, Box 152; Boonton, NJ 07005.

Historical Society of Moorestown; 12 High Street; PO Box 477; Moorestown, NJ 08057; historical@moorestown.com.

Hunterdon County Historical Society; Hiram E. Deats Memorial Library; 114 Main St.; Flemington, NJ 08822; http://members.aol.com/njysprez/hchs.htm.

Jewish Genealogical Society of North Jersey; 1 Bedford Rd.; Pompton Lakes, NJ 07442.

Jewish Genealogical Society of Greater Philadelphia (JGSGP); 109 Society Hill; Cherry Hill, NJ 08003; jlspector@aol.com; www.jewishgen.org/jgsp.

Jewish Historical Society of Central Jersey; 228 Livingston Ave.; New Brunswick, NJ 08901; jhscj@cs.com; www.jewishgen.org/jhscj.

Jewish Historical Society of MetroWest; 901 Route 10 East; Whippany, NJ 07981-1156; jsettanni@ujfmetrowest.org.

Monmouth County Genealogical Club; PO Box 5; Lincroft, NJ 07738-0005; http://home.infi.net/~kjshelly/mcgs.html.

Monmouth County Historical Association; 70 Court Street; Freehold, NJ 07728; www.monmouth.com/~mcha/index.html.

Morris Area Genealogical Society; PO Box 105; Convent Station, NJ 07961.

Navy Lakehurst Historical Society; PO Box 328; Lakehurst, NJ 08733; (732) 244-8861; info@nlhs.com; www.nlhs.com.

Neptune Township Historical Society; 25 Neptune Blvd.; Neptune, NJ 07753.

New Jersey Historical Society; 52 Park Place; Newark, NJ 07102.

New Jersey State Archives; Department of State Building; 225 West State Str; Trenton, NJ 08625-0307; (609) 292-6260; archives.reference@sos.state.nj.us; www.state.nj.us/state/darm.

New Jersey State Library; PO Box 520; Trenton, NJ 08625-0520; www.njstatelib.org.

Ocean County Genealogical Society; 135 Nautilus Dr.; Manahawkin, NJ 08058-2452.

Ocean County Historical Society; 26 Hadley Ave.; Toms River, NJ 08754-2191.

Ontario & Western Railway Historical Society, Inc.; 1 Rich Ct; Ho-Ho-Kus, NJ 07423; DaveAck1@aol.com; www.nyow.org/main.html.

Passaic County Historical Society Genealogy Club; Lambert Castle Museum; Valley Rd.; Paterson, NJ 07503; mimzil@aol.com; www.rootsweb.com/~njpchsgc.

Phillipsburg Area Historical Society; 675 Corliss Avenue; Phillipsburg, NJ 08865; (908) 454-0816; sherrer@looksmart.com; http://community.nj.com/cc/pburghistsoc.

Plainsboro Historical Society, Inc.; 641 Plainsboro Rd.; Plainsboro, NJ 08536; www.plainsboro.com/historical.

Salem County New Jersey Historical Society; 79-83 Market St.; Salem, NJ 08079; www.salemcounty.com/schs.

Scandinavian American Heritage Society; 32 Hemlock Terrace; Wayne, NJ 07470-4342.

The Howell Historical Society; 427 Lakewood-Farmingdale Rd.; Howell, NJ 07731-8723; howellhist@aol.com; www.howellnj.com/historic.

The Metuchen-Edison Historical Society; PO Box 61; Metuchen, NJ 08840-0061; www.jhalpin.com/metuchen/met-ed.htm.

The Old Mill Hill Society; PO Box 1263; Trenton, NJ 08607-1263; info@oldmillhillsociety.org; www.oldmillhillsociety.org.

Vineland Historical and Antiquarian Society; PO Box 35; Vineland, NJ 08360; sospringrd@aol.com; www.vineland.org/history/society.

Westfield Historical Society Museum and Archives; Box 613; Westfield, NJ 07091-0613; history@westfieldnj.com; www.westfieldnj.com/history/contents.htm.

Bibliography and Record Sources

General

Armstrong, William C. *Pioneer Families of Northwestern New Jersey.* 1979. Reprint. Baltimore: Clearfield Company, 1996.

Bailey, Rosalie Fellows. *Dutch Systems in Family Naming, New York-New Jersey.* Washington, D.C.: National Genealogical Society Bookstore, 1965.

Barber, John W., and Henry Howe. *Historical Collections of New Jersey: Past and Present, Containing a General Collection of the Most Interesting Facts, Traditions, Biographical Sketches, Anecdotes, Etc.* Rev. ed. 1868. Reprint. Baltimore: Clearfield, Co., 1995.

Barker, Bette Marie, Daniel P. Jones, and Karl J. Niederer. *Guide to Family History Sources in the New Jersey State Archives.* 2nd ed. Trenton, New Jersey: Division of Archives and Records Management, 1990.

Burr, Nelson Rollin. *A Narrative and Descriptive Bibliography of New Jersey.* New Jersey Historical Series, vol. 21. Princeton, New Jersey: Van Nostrand, 1964.

Chambers, T. F. *Early Germans of New Jersey, Their History, Churches, and Genealogy.* 1895. Reprint. Baltimore: Genealogical Publishing Co., 1969.

Clark, Patricia L., and Dorothy Huntsman, eds. *American Genealogical Biographical Key Title Index.* Salt Lake City: Genealogical Society of Utah, 1990.

Cohen, David Steven. *New Jersey Ethnic History: A Bibliography.* Trenton: New Jersey Historical Commission, 1986.

Collins, Martha Knowles. *New Jersey Bible Records, 1700's to 1800's, vols. 3–5, 13.* Salt Lake City: Genealogical Society of Utah, 1971.

Cooley, Eli F., and William S. Cooley. *Genealogy of Early Settlers in Trenton and Ewing.* 1883, reprint ed., Baltimore: Genealogical Publishing, 1977.

Cope, Gilbert. *Collection of Family Data.* Salt Lake City: Genealogical Society of Utah, 1966. Microfilm, 75 rolls.

Cyclopedia of New Jersey Biography: Memorial and Biographical. 5 vols. New York: American Historical Society, 1921–23.

Documents Relating to the Colonial History of the State of New Jersey. [Archives of the State of New Jersey, First Series, Second Series]. 42 vols. Newark, New Jersey: Daily Journal Establishment, 1880–1949.

Dornan, John Pickens. *Collection, Family File.* Salt Lake City: Filmed by the Genealogical Society of Utah, 1971.

Flynn, Joseph Michael. *The Catholic Church in New Jersey.* Morristown, New Jersey: N. D., 1904.

Gardiner, Charles C. *Collection of New Jersey Families, 1600–1900: Family Records Taken from Civil, Court, Land and Probate Records, Etc.* New Brunswick, New Jersey: Rutgers University Library, 1970.

Gasero, Russell L., ed. *Guide to Local Church Records in the Archives of the Reformed Church in America and to Genealogical Resources in the Gardner Sage Library, New Brunswick Theological Seminary.* New Brunswick, New Jersey: Historical Society of the Reformed Church in America, 1979.

Genealogical Society of New Jersey. *Genealogical Collection.* Salt Lake City: Genealogical Society of Utah, 1971.

Genealogies of New Jersey Families: From the Genealogical Magazine of New Jersey. 2 vols. Baltimore: Genealogical. Publishing Co., 1996.

Gloucester County Historical Society (Woodury, New Jersey). *Historical and Genealogical Files, 1600's to 1900's*. Salt Lake City: Filmed by the Genealogical Society of Utah, 1976. Microfilm, 33 rolls.

Heston, Alfred M. *South Jersey, a History, 1664–1924*. 5 vols. New York: Lewis Historical, 1924.

Historical Records Survey (New Jersey). *Guide to Depositories of Manuscript Collections in the United States: New Jersey (preliminary volume)*. Newark, New Jersey: Historical Records Survey, 1941.

Historical Records Survey (New Jersey). *Guide to Vital Statistics Records in New Jersey. New Jersey. Bureau of Archives and History*. Trenton: Genealogical Society of New Jersey, 1971.

Historical Records Survey. *Directory of Churches in New Jersey*. 21 vols. Newark, New Jersey: Historical Records Survey, 1940–1941.

Hoelle, Edith. *Genealogical Resources In Southern New Jersey*. Woodbury, New Jersey: Gloucester County Historical Society, 1993.

Honeyman, A. Van Doren, ed. *Northwestern New Jersey, a History of Somerset, Morris, Hunterdon, Warren, and Sussex Counties*. 5 vols. New York: Lewis Historical Publishing, 1927.

Indenture Collection containing Deeds, Bonds, Commissions, etc. of New Jersey Individuals: and other States, 1600–1900. Salt Lake City: Genealogical Society of Utah, 1970.

Index of Names to Various Records in Various New Jersey Counties, 1600–1800s. Salt Lake City: Genealogical Society of Utah, 1972.

Irwin, Barbara S., and Elizabeth B. Turner. *Guide to the Genealogy Chart Collection in the New Jersey Historical Society*.1983, revised ed., Newark, New Jersey: New Jersey Historical Society, 1985.

Jackson, Ronald Vern. *New Jersey Tax Lists, 1772–1822*. 4 vols. Bountiful, Utah: Accelerated Indexing Systems, 1981.

Knapp, Fred D. *The Complete Public Records Guide: Central and Northern New Jersey Region*. New Rochelle, New York: REyn, 1993.

Koehler, Albert F. *The Huguenots or Early French in New Jersey*. 1955. Reprint. Baltimore: Clearfield Co., 1996.

Kull, Irving S. *New Jersey a History*. 5 vols. New York City: The American Historical Society, Inc. 1930–1932.

Lee, Francis Bazley. *Genealogical and Memorial History of the State of New Jersey*. 4 vols. New York: Lewis Historical Publishing, 1910.

Littell, John. *Family Records, or Genealogies of the First Settlers of Passaic Valley*. 1852. Reprint. Baltimore: Clearfield Co. 1981.

McCormick. *New Jersey from Colony to State, 1609–1789*. Galveston, Texas: Frontier Press, 1981.

Mellick, Andrew D., Jr. *The Story of an Old Farm, or, Life in New Jersey in the 18th Century*. 1889. Reprint. Salem, Massachusetts: Higginson Book Co., 1992.

Monnette, Orra Eugene. *First Settlers of Ye Plantations of Piscataway and Woodbridge Olde East New Jersey, 1664–1714*. 7 vols. Los Angeles: Leroy Carman Press, 1930–1935.

Murrin, Mary R., comp. *New Jersey Historical Manuscripts: A Guide to Collections in the State*. Trenton, New Jersey: New Jersey Historical Commission, 1987.

Myers, William Starr. *The Story of New Jersey*. 5 vols. New York: Lewis Historical Pub. Co., 1945.

Nelson, William. *"Church Records in New Jersey," Journal of the Presbyterian Historical Society 2:4 (March 1904): 173–188 and 251–266*. Salt Lake City: Genealogical Society of Utah, 1985.

Nelson, William. *Nelson's Biographical Cyclopedia*. 2 vols. New York: Eastern Historical Publishing Society, 1913.

Nelson, William. *New Jersey Biographical and Genealogical Notes*. 1916. Reprint. Baltimore: Clearfield Co., 1997

New Jersey Research Outline. Series U.S.-States, No. 31. Salt Lake City: Family History Library, 1991.

New Jersey State Archives. *Guide to Family History Sources in the New Jersey State Archives*. Trenton, New Jersey: New Jersey State Archives.

New Jersey State Archives. *Laws of the Royal Colony of New Jersey 1703–1775, vols. II–V*. Trenton, New Jersey: New Jersey State Archives.

Nicholson, Anna Lea. *Nicholson Collection: Ca. 1690–1900*. Salt Lake City: Filmed by the Genealogical Society of Utah, 1987. Microfilm, 22 rolls.

Ogden, Mary Depue. *Memorial Cyclopedia of New Jersey*. 4 vols. Newark, New Jersey: Memorial History, 1915–1921.

Parker, J. Carlyle. *Pennsylvania and Middle Atlantic States Genealogical Manuscripts: A User's Guide to the Manuscript Collections of the Genealogical Society of Pennsylvania as Indexed in Its Manuscript Materials Index*. Turlock, California: Marietta Publishing Co.

Quigley, Mary Alice, Judith A. Fullerton, and Diane E. Kauffman, comps. *Historical Organizations in New Jersey: A Directory*. Rev. ed. Trenton, New Jersey: New Jersey Historical Commission, 1983.

Register of New Jersey County Tax Ratables, Abstracts and Exempt Lists, 1773 to about 1889. Salt Lake City: The Genealogical Society of Utah.

Ricord, Frederick W. *General Index to the Documents Relating to the Colonial History of the State of New Jersey*. Newark, New Jersey: Daily Journal Establishment, 1880.

Rider, Fremont, ed. *American Genealogical Biographical Index.* Vols. 1–186+. Middletown, Connecticut: Godfrey Memorial Library, 1952–.

Rutgers University Library. *A Guide to the Manuscript Collection of the Rutgers University Library.* New Brunswick, New Jersey: Rutgers University Library, 1964.

Shourds, Thomas. *History and Genealogy of Fenwick's Colony.* 1876. Reprint. Baltimore: Clearfield Company, 1991.

Sinclair, Donald A. *A New Jersey Biographical Index Covering Some 100,000 Biographies and Associated Portraits in 237 New Jersey Cyclopedias, Histories, Yearbooks, Periodicals, and Other Collective Biographical Sources Published to about 1980.* Baltimore: Genealogical Publishing, 1993.

Skemer, Don C., and Robert C. Morris. *Guide to the Manuscript Collections of the New Jersey Historical Society.* Newark, New Jersey: New Jersey Historical Society, 1979.

Southern California Genealogical Society. *Sources of Genealogical Help in New Jersey.* Burbank, California: Southern California Genealogical Society.

Stillwell, John E., M.D. *Historical and Genealogical Miscellany: Data Relating to the Settlement & Settlers of New Jersey, vols. I–V.* 1903–1932. Reprint. Baltimore: Genealogical Publishing Co, 1993.

Stockton, Elias Boudinot. *Stockton Collection.* Salt Lake City: Genealogical Society of Utah, 1973. Microfilm, 44 rolls.

Stryker-Rodda, Kenn. *Given Name Index to the Genealogical Magazine of New Jersey, vol. IV.* Hunterdon House.

Stryker-Rodda, Kenn. *New Jersey: Digging for Ancestors in the Garden State.* Detroit: Detroit Society for Genealogical Research, 1970.

The Biographical Encyclopedia of New Jersey of the Nineteenth Century. Philadelphia, Pennsylvania: Galaxy Publishing, 1877.

The First Laws of the State of New Jersey. 1783. Reprint. Wilmington, Delaware: Michael Glazier, 1981.

Trinity Church (Newark, New Jersey: Episcopal). *New Jersey Biographical Card Index, 1790–1900.* Microreproduction of documents at New Jersey Historical Society, Newark, New Jersey. Salt Lake City: Filmed by the Genealogical Society of Utah, 2000. 25 microfilm.

United States. Bureau of Internal Revenue. *Assessment Lists of the Federal Bureau of Internal Revenue, 1862–1866.* Washington, D.C.: National Archives, 1965.

Whitehead, John. *The Judicial and Civil History of New Jersey.* Boston: Boston History Co., 1897.

Wilson, Thomas B. *Notices from New Jersey Newspapers, 1781–1790.* Lambertville, New Jersey: Hunterdon House, 1988.

Works Projects Administration. *The WPA Guide to 1930's New Jersey.* 1939. Reprint. Galveston, Texas: Frontier Press, 1995.

Wright, William C., and Paul A. Stellhorn, eds. *Directory of New Jersey Newspapers, 1765–1970.* Trenton, New Jersey: New Jersey Historical Commission, 1977.

Year Book of The Holland Society of New York, 1912. New York: The Society, 1912.

Atlases, Maps and Gazetteers

An Alphabetical Listing of Local Places and Incorporated Municipalities in the State of New Jersey. New Jersey Dept. of Transportation, 1967.

Gannett, Henry. *Geographic Dictionary of New Jersey.* 1894. Reprint. Baltimore: Genealogical Publishing Co., 1978.

Gordon, Thomas F. *A Gazetteer of the State of New Jersey.* (1834), reprint 2004. Clearfield Company.

Kay, John L., and Chaester M. Smith, Jr. *New Jersey Postal History: The Post Offices and First Postmasters, 1776–1976.* Lawrence, Massachusetts: Quarterman Publications, 1977.

Long, John H., comp. *Historical Atlas and Chronology of County Boundaries, 1788–1980.* Vol. 1, Delaware, Maryland, New Jersey, Pennsylvania. Boston, Massachusetts: G. K. Hall, 1984.

National Gazetteer of the United States of America—New Jersey 1983. Washington, D.C.: Government Printing Office, 1983.

New Jersey Local Names, Municipalities and Counties. Trenton, New Jersey: State Department of Transportation, 1982.

Origin of New Jersey Place Names. Trenton, New Jersey: Public Library Commission, 1945.

Skemer, Don C., comp. *New Jersey Historic Map Portfolio.* Florham Park, New Jersey: Afton Publishing, 1983.

Snyder, John P. *The Story of New Jersey's Civil Boundaries, 1606–1968.* Trenton, New Jersey: Bureau of Geology and Topography, 1969.

Szucs, Loretto Dennis and Matthew Wright. *Finding Answers in U.S. Census Records.* Ancestry Publishing, 2001.

Census Records

Available Census Records and Census Substitutes

Federal Census 1830, 1840, 1850, 1860, 1870, 1880, 1900, 1910, 1920, 1930

Federal Mortality Schedules 1850, 1860, 1870, 1880 Union Veterans and Widows 1890 Militia Census 1793 State/Territorial Census 1885, 1895, 1905, 1915

Craig, Peter Stebbins. *The 1693 Census of the Swedes on the Delaware: Family Histories of the Swedish Lutheran Church Members Residing in Pennsylvania, Delaware, West New Jersey, and Cecil County, Maryland,*

1638–1693. Studies in Swedish American Genealogy 3. Winter Park, Florida: SAG Publications, 1993.

Dollarhide, William. *The Census Book: A Genealogist's Guide to Federal Census Facts, Schedules and Indexes.* Bountiful, Utah: Heritage Quest, 1999.

George, Shirley J., and Sandra E. Glenn. *New Jersey 1850 Mortality Schedule Index.* Columbus, New Jersey: G. & G. Genealogical Book, 1982.

Jackson, Ronald Vern. *New Jersey 1890.* Salt Lake City: Accelerated Indexing Systems, 1990.

Kemp, Thomas Jay. *The American Census Handbook.* Wilmington, Delaware: Scholarly Resources, Inc., 2001.

Lainhart, Ann S. *State Census Records.* Baltimore: Genealogical Publishing Co., Inc., 1992.

New Jersey State Archives. *New Jersey State Census, 1855–1915.* Trenton, New Jersey: New Jersey State Archives.

Stryker-Rodda, Kenn. *Revolutionary Census of New Jersey: An Index Based on Ratables, of the Inhabitants of New Jersey During the Period of the American Revolution.* Rev. ed. Lambertville, New Jersey: Hunterdon House, 1986.

Thorndale, William and William Dollarhide. *Map Guides to the U.S. Federal Censuses, 1790–1920.* Baltimore: Genealogical Publishing Co., 1987.

United States. Census Office. *Census of New Jersey, 1850–1880; Third Series (of Persons Who Died During the Years Ending 30 June 1850, 1 June 1860; 1 June 1870; 31 May 1880.* Trenton, New Jersey: State Library of Archives and History, Department of Education, 1996.

Court Records, Probate and Wills

Index to Wills, Inventories, Etc. in the Office of the Secretary of State Prior to 1901. 3 vols. 1912. Reprinted as *New Jersey Index to Wills.* Baltimore: Genealogical Publishing Co., 1969.

Index to Wills, Office of Secretary of State, State of New Jersey, 1804 to 1830. Trenton, New Jersey: John L. Murphy Publishing Co., 1901.

Jamison, Wallace N. *Religion in New Jersey: A Brief History.* Princeton, New Jersey: D. Van Nostrand, 1964.

Keasbey, Edward Quinton. *The Courts and Lawyers of New Jersey, 1661–1912.* 3 vols. New York: Lewis Historical Publishing Co., 1912.

Miller, George Julius. *The Courts of Chancery in New Jersey, 1684–1696.* Washington, D.C.: Library of Congress Photoduplication Service, 1990.

Nelson, William. *New Jersey Calendar of Wills, 1670–1780.* 1901. Reprint. Arvada, Colorado: Ancestor Publishers.

Nelson, William. *The Law and the Practice of New Jersey from the Earliest Times: Concerning the Probate of Wills, the Administration of Estates, the Protection of Orphans and Minors, and the Control of their Estates; The Prerogative Court, the Ordinary, and the*

Surrogates. Paterson, New Jersey: Paterson History Club, 1909.

New Jersey, Chancery Court. *Chancery Court Cases, 1743–1845.* Salt Lake City: Genealogical Society of Utah, 1978. Microfilm, 86 rolls.

New Jersey, Chancery Court. *Enrolled Decrees, 1825–1850; Index to Enrolled Decrees, 1825–1854.* Salt Lake City: Genealogical Society of Utah, 1979. Microfilm, 298 rolls.

New Jersey, Supreme Court (Burlington County). *Early Index to Supreme Court Minutes, 1681–1842.* n.p. Bibliofilm, 1938.

New Jersey, Supreme Court. *Index to Supreme Court Cases Before and After the Revolution, 1709 to 1842.* Salt Lake City: Genealogical Society of Utah, 1978.

New Jersey. Bureau of Archives and History. *Genealogical Research: A Guide to Source Materials in the Archives and History Bureau of the New Jersey State Library.* Trenton: Genealogical Society of New Jersey, 1971.

New Jersey. Court of Chancery. *Chancery Docket Books, 1824–1900; Index to Chancery Records, 1824–1904.* Microfilm of original records at the Mercer County courthouse. Salt Lake City: Filmed by the Genealogical Society of Utah, 1978. 22 microfilm.

New Jersey. Court of Chancery. *Chancery Register, 1781–1894.* Salt Lake City: Genealogical Society of Utah, 1977.

New Jersey. Court of Chancery. *Court Tickler, 1858–1896.* Microfilms of original records in the New Jersey State Library Trenton. Salt Lake City: Filmed by the Genealogical Society of Utah, 1977. 3 microfilm.

New Jersey. Court of Chancery. *Parchment Rolls, 1755–1806.* Microfilm made from original records in the New Jersey State Library, Trenton. Salt Lake City: Filmed by the Genealogical Society of Utah, 1977. 19 microfilm.

Smeal, Lee and Ronald Vern Jackson. *Index to New Jersey Wills, 1689–1890, The Testators.* Salt Lake City: Accelerated Indexing Systems, 1979.

Stryker-Rodda, Kenn. *New Jersey Index of Wills, Inventories, Etc.* 3 vols. 1912–13. Reprint. Baltimore: Clearfield Company, 1994.

United States. District Court (New Jersey). *Records of the U. S. District Court of New Jersey and Predecessor Courts: 1789–1950.* Washington, D.C.: National Archives.

Emigration, Immigration, Migration and Naturalization

Boyer, Carl, 3rd. *Ship Passenger Lists: New York and New Jersey (1600–1825).* Newhall, California: C. Boyer, ca. 1978.

Chambers, Theodore Frelinghuysen. *The Early Germans of New Jersey: Their History, Churches, and Genealogies. . . 1895, reprint ed.* Baltimore: Genealogical Publishing, 1982.

Coldham, Peter Wilson. *The Complete Book of Emigrants, 1607–1776 and Emigrants in Bondage, 1614–1775.* Novato, California: Brøderbund Software, 1996.

Guide to Naturalization Records in New Jersey. Newark, New Jersey: Historical Records Program, 1941.

Howe, Paul Sturtevant. *Mayflower Pilgrim Descendants in Cape May County, New Jersey—1620–1920.* 1921, reprint ed. Baltimore: Genealogical Publishing, 1977.

Jones, Henry Z., Jr. *More Palatine Families: Some Immigrants to the Middle Colonies 1717–1776 and their European Origins.* Universal City, California: H. Z. Jones, Jr., 1991.

Jones, Henry Z., Jr. *The Palatine Families of New York: A Study of the German Immigrants who arrived in Colonial New York in 1710.* Universal City, California: H. Z. Jones, Jr., 1985.

New Jersey. Bureau of Archives and History. *Index to Naturalization Records, 1703–1862.* Microreproduction of typed index cards at the New Jersey Bureau of Archives and History. Salt Lake City: Genealogical Society of Utah, 1972.

New Jersey. Bureau of Archives and History. *Index to Powers of Attorney, Surveyors Reports, Commissions, etc., Referring to Deeds, ca. 1703–1856.* Microreproduction of manuscript and typescript at the New Jersey Bureau of Archives and History. Salt Lake City: Genealogical Society of Utah, 1969. 2 microfilm.

New Jersey. Supreme Court. *Naturalization Records, 1749–1873; Card Index, 1761–1860.* Salt Lake City: Filmed by the Genealogical Society of Utah, 1978.

Stevenson, John R. *Persons Naturalized in New Jersey Between 1702 and 1776, The New York Genealogical and Biographical Society Record,* vol. 28; April 1897: 86–89.

Winkel, Peter A. *"Naturalizations, Province of New Jersey, 1747–1775," The Genealogical Magazine of New Jersey* 65 (1990): 1–8, 59–66.

Land and Property

Hone, Wade E. *Land and Property Research in the United States.* Salt Lake City: Ancestry Incorporated, 1997.

Index to Powers of Attorney, Surveyor's Reports, Commissions, etc., Referring to Deeds. Salt Lake City: Genealogical Society of Utah, 1972.

Nelson, William. *Patents and Deeds and Other Early Records of New Jersey, 1664–1703.* Baltimore: Genealogical Publishing Co., 1976.

New Jersey State Library (Trenton). *East Jersey Deeds, 1667–1783.* Salt Lake City: Filmed by the Genealogical Society of Utah, 1967.

New Jersey State Library (Trenton). *Index to Deeds, Grantee and Grantor.* Salt Lake City: Filmed by the Genealogical Society of Utah, 1967–1968. 7 microfilm.

New Jersey, Surveyor General. *Perth Amboy Surveys, 1678–1814.* Salt Lake City: Genealogical Society of Utah, 1973.

New Jersey. Supreme Court. *Estates and Partitions, 1712–1866.* Microfilm of originals at the State Archives, Trenton. Salt Lake City: Filmed by the Genealogical Society of Utah, 1993. 2 microfilm.

Stephenson, Richard W. *Land Ownership Maps: A Checklist of Nineteenth Century United States County Maps in the Library of Congress.* Washington, D.C: Library of Congress, 1967.

The Minutes of the Board of Proprietors of the Eastern Division of New Jersey from 1685–1794. 3 vols. Perth Amboy, New Jersey: General Board of Proprietors of the Eastern Division of New Jersey, 1949–1960.

Military

Alphabetical Roll of New Jersey Volunteers in the Civil War. Salt Lake City: Filmed by the Genealogical Society of Utah, 1969.

Bill. *New Jersey and the Revolutionary War.* 1964. Reprint. Galveston, Texas: Frontier Press, 1992.

Campbell, James W. S., comp. *Official Register of the Officers and Men of New Jersey in the Revolutionary War.* 1872. Revised 1911. Reprint. Baltimore: Genealogical Publishing, 1967.

Civil War Pension Claims, New Jersey Soldiers Alphabetical. Salt Lake City: Filmed by the Genealogical Society of Utah, 1969.

General Society of Colonial Wars (Providence, Rhode Island). *Lineage Records, No. 1–14199, 1607–1967; Supplemental Records, 1–13850, 1607–1967; Register of Members.* Salt Lake City: Filmed by the Genealogical Society of Utah, 1967.

Jackson, Ronald V. *Index to Military Men of New Jersey, 1775–1815.* Bountiful, Utah: Accelerated Indexing Systems, 1977.

Jones, Edward Alfred. *The Loyalists of New Jersey: Their Memorials, Petitions, Claims, etc. from English Records.* 1927. Reprint. Lambertville, New Jersey: Hunterdon House, 1988.

McNally, Bernard, comp. *Soldiers and Sailors of New Jersey in the Spanish-American War, Embracing a Chronological Account of the Army and Navy.* Newark, New Jersey: Bernard McNally, 1898.

New Jersey Adjutant General. *Register of the Commissioned Officers and Privates of the New Jersey Volunteers in Service of the United States.* 3 vols. Jersey City, New Jersey: John H. Lyon, 1863–1865.

New Jersey Civil War Records, Books 1–829. Trenton, New Jersey: State Library of Archives & History, 1969.

New Jersey Historical Records Survey. *Index to Stryker's Register of New Jersey in the Revolution.* 1941. Reprint. Baltimore: Clearfield Co., 1995.

New Jersey State Archives. *Index to Revolutionary War Manuscripts*. Trenton, New Jersey: New Jersey State Archives.

New Jersey State Library (Trenton). *Index to Records of Spanish American War, Books 1–122*. Salt Lake City: Genealogical Society of Utah, 1969. 2 microfilm.

New Jersey State Library (Trenton). *Military Officers Recorded in the Office of the Secretary of State, Trenton, New Jersey; Colonial Wars, 1668–1774*. Salt Lake City: Genealogical Society of Utah, 1969.

New Jersey State Library (Trenton). *New Jersey in the War of 1812; Books 1–52*. Microreproduction of original at the State Library of Archives and History. Salt Lake City: Genealogical Society of Utah, 1969. 16 microfilm.

New Jersey State Library (Trenton). *New Jersey Records; French and Indian War, 1757–1764*. Salt Lake City: Genealogical Society of Utah, 1969.

New Jersey, Adjutant General. *Official Register of the Officers and Men of New Jersey in the Revolutionary War*. Trenton, New Jersey: W. T. Nicholson, 1872.

New Jersey, Adjutant General. *Records of Officers and Men of New Jersey in the Civil War, 1861–1865*. Trenton, New Jersey: J. L. Murphy, 1876–1878.

New Jersey, Adjutant General. *Records of Officers and Men of New Jersey in Wars, 1791–1815*. 1909. Reprint. Baltimore: Genealogical Publishing Co., 1970.

Norton, James S. *New Jersey in 1793: An Abstract and Index to the 1793 Militia Census of the State of New Jersey*. Salt Lake City: J. S. Norton, 1973.

Records of Officers and Men of New Jersey in Wars, 1791–1815. 1909. Reprint. Baltimore: Genealogical Publishing, 1970.

Revolutionary War Index: A Compilation of Revolutionary War Slips and Documented Materials from Other Sources. Salt Lake City: Filmed by the Genealogical Society of Utah, 1968.

Revolutionary War Records of New Jersey. Salt Lake City: Genealogical Society of Utah, 1969.

Revolutionary War Slips, Single Citations of the New Jersey Department of Defense Materials. Salt Lake City: Filmed by the Genealogical Society of Utah, 1968.

Second Annual Report of the State Historian of the State of New York. Albany, New York: Wynkoop, Hallenbeck, Crawford, 1897.

Sinclair, Donald A. *A Bibliography, the Civil War and New Jersey*. New Brunswick, New Jersey: Friends of the Rutgers University Library, 1968.

Stratford, Dorothy A., and Thomas B. Wilson. *Certificates and Receipts of Revolutionary New Jersey*. Lambertville, New Jersey: Hunterdon House, 1996.

Stryker, William S. *The New Jersey Volunteers (Loyalists) in the Revolutionary War*. Trenton, New Jersey: Narr, Day & Narr, 1887.

Stryker, William S., comp. *Record of Officers and Men of New Jersey in the Civil War, 1861–1865*. 2 vols. Trenton, New Jersey: John L. Murphy, 1876.

United States. Selective Service System. *New Jersey, World War I Selective Service System Draft Registration Cards, 1917–1918*. Washington, D.C.: National Archives, 1987–1988.

Waldenmaier, Inez. *Revolutionary War Pensioners Living in New Jersey before 1834*. Tulsa, Oklahoma: Inez Waldenmaier, 1983.

White, Virgil D. *Genealogical Abstracts of the Revolutionary War Pension Files*. 4 vols. Waynesboro, Tennessee: National Historical Publishing, 1990.

White, Virgil D. *Index to Revolutionary War Service Records*. 4 vols. Waynesboro, Tennessee: National Historical Publishing, 1995.

Vital and Cemetery Records

An Historical Records Survey of a Miscellany of New Jersey Vital Statistics Records, 1753–1870. Microreproduction of manuscript and typescript records at New Jersey Historical Society, Newark, New Jersey. Salt Lake City: Filmed by the Genealogical Society of Utah, 2000. 2 microfilm.

Card Index to Civil War Soldiers' Graves, 1862. Microreproduction of records at New Jersey Historical Society, Newark, New Jersey. Salt Lake City: Filmed by Genealogical Society of Utah, 2000. 2 microfilm.

County File of Miscellaneous New Jersey Information. Salt Lake City: Genealogical Society of Utah, 1971.

Dirnberger, Janet Drumm. *New Jersey Catholic Baptismal Records from 1759–1781*. Seabrook, Texas: Brambles, 1981.

Guide to Vital Statistics Records in New Jersey. 2 vols. Newark, New Jersey: New Jersey Historical Records Survey, 1941.

Index to Inquisitions on the Dead, 1700s–1800s. Salt Lake City: Genealogical Society of Utah, 1972.

Nelson, William, ed. *Documents Relating to the Colonial History of the State of New Jersey. Marriage Records, 1665–1800*. [Archives of the State of New Jersey, First Series, vol. 22] 1900, reprinted as *New Jersey Marriage Records*. Baltimore: Genealogical Publishing, 1967.

Nelson, William. *New Jersey Marriage Records, 1665–1800*. Baltimore: Genealogical Publishing Co., 1967.

New Jersey Cemetery Inscriptions. Microreproduction of records at the New Jersey Historical Society, Newark, New Jersey. Salt Lake City: Genealogical Society of Utah, 1976. 3 microfilm.

New Jersey Marriage Bonds, W. P. A. Marriage Records, 1670–1800. Salt Lake City: Filmed by the Genealogical Society of Utah, 1969.

New Jersey State Archives. *Colonial Marriage Bonds, 1711–1797*. Trenton, New Jersey: New Jersey State Archives. Microfilm, 8 rolls.

New Jersey Tombstone Inscriptions. Salt Lake City: Genealogical Society of Utah, 1969. Microfilm, 7 rolls.

New Jersey W.P.A. Birth and Death Records, Early to 1900. Salt Lake City: Filmed by the Genealogical Society of Utah, 1969.

New Jersey, 1680–1900. S.l.: Brøderbund, ca. 1998. CD-ROM.

New Jersey. Bureau of Archives and History. *Vital Statistics Index from Trenton Newspapers, 1800–1900.* Salt Lake City: Genealogical Society of Utah, 1969.

New Jersey. Department of Education. Division of State Library Archives and History. *New Jersey Marriages, 1711–1878 (Approx.).* Trenton, New Jersey: Filmed by Microfilm & Record Unit, 1966. 10 microfilm.

New Jersey. Secretary of State. *Marriage Records, 1727–1878.* Trenton, New Jersey: State Library of Archives and History, 1966. 8 microfilm.

Records of Births, Marriages, and Deaths of New Jersey, 1848–1900. Microreproduction of original records at the New Jersey State Library, Trenton. Salt Lake City: Filmed by the Genealogical Society of Utah, 1969. 290 microfilm.

Source Index of New Jersey Families. Salt Lake City: Genealogical Society of Utah, 1971.

Swapin. *Old Burial Grounds of New Jersey: A Guide.* Galveston, Texas: Frontier Press, 1994.

County Website	Map Index	Date Created	Parent County or Territory From Which Organized Address/Details
Atlantic www.aclink.org/	N6	7 Feb 1837	**Gloucester** Atlantic County; 5901 Main St; Mays Landing, NJ 08330-1800; Ph. (609) 625-4011 **Details:** (County Clerk has Divorce Records from 1949, Court, Land & Cemetery Records from 1837; County Surrogate has Probate Records)
Bergen www.co.bergen.nj.us/	D10	1 Mar 1683	**Prov. East Jersey** Bergen County; 1 Bergen County Plaza; Hackensack, NJ 7601; Ph. (201) 336-7000 **Details:** (County Clerk has Divorce Records from 1955, Court & Land Records; County Surrogate has Probate Records)
Burlington http://co.burlington.nj.us/	L7	1681	**Original county** Burlington County; 49 Rancocas Rd; PO Box 6000; Mount Holly, NJ 8060; Ph. (609) 265-5122 **Details:** (County Clerk has Land & Military Records; County Surrogate has Probate Records; County Library has Naturalization Records)
Camden www.co.camden.nj.us/	L5	13 Mar 1844	**Gloucester** Camden County; 520 Market St; Camden, NJ 8102; Ph. (856) 225-5300 **Details:** (County Clerk has Court & Land Records; County Surrogate has Probate Records)
Cape May www.co.cape-may.nj.us/	P6	1685	**West Jersey** Cape May County; 4 Moore Rd; Cape May Court House, NJ 8210; Ph. (609) 465-1010 **Details:** (County Clerk has Marriage Records 1795–1878, Land Records from 1692, Court Records 1793–1948, Military Records from 1919 & Naturalization Records 1900–1960; County Surrogate has Probate Records from 1783)
Cumberland www.co.cumberland.nj.us/	O4	19 Jan 1748	**Salem** Cumberland County; 60 W Broad St; Bridgeton, NJ 8302; Ph. (856) 451-8000 **Details:** (County Clerk has Land Records from 1800's & immigration Records 1840–1989; County Surrogate has Probate Records; Dissolution Office has Divorce Records)

County Website	Map Index	Date Created	Parent County or Territory From Which Organized
			Address/Details
Essex www.co.essex.nj.us/	E9	1 Mar 1683	**Prov. East Jersey** Essex County; 465 Martin Luther King Jr Blvd; Newark, NJ 7102; Ph. (973) 621-4920 **Details:** (County Clerk has Marriage Records 1795–1879, Divorce & Court Records from 1948 & Naturalization Records 1779–1929; City Clerks have Birth & Death Records; County Surrogate has Probate Records; Registrar of Deeds has Land Records)
Gloucester www.co.gloucester.nj.us/	L4	28 May 1686	**Original county** Gloucester County; 1 N Broad St; Woodbury, NJ 08096-4611; Ph. (856) 853-3237 **Details:** (Courthouse burned 1786) (County Clerk has Court & Land Records from 1787; Surrogate Court has Probate Records; Clerk Superior Court has Divorce Records; early Records preserved at Surveyor General's Office, Burlington & Secretary of State Office, Trenton)
Hudson www.hudsoncountynj.org/	E10	22 Feb 1840	**Bergen** Hudson County; 583 Newark Ave; Jersey City, NJ 7306; Ph. (201) 795-6112 **Details:** (Registrar of Deeds has Land Records; Clerk Surrogate Court has Probate Records)
Hunterdon www.co.hunterdon.nj.us/	F5	13 Mar 1714	**Burlington** Hunterdon County; 71 Main St; PO Box 2900; Flemington, NJ 08822-2900; Ph. (908) 788-1221 **Details:** (County Clerk has Marriage Records 1795–1875, Court Records from 1714 & Land Records from 1716; Clerk Surrogate Court has Probate Records; Clerk Superior Court has Divorce Records)
Mercer www.mercercounty.org/	I7	22 Feb 1838	**Somerset, Middlesex, Hunterdon, Burlington** Mercer County; PO Box 8068; Trenton, NJ 08650-0068; Ph. (609) 989-6517 **Details:** (County Surrogate has Probate Records; County Clerk has Court & Land Records from 1838, judgments, tax maps & corporation Records)
Middlesex http://co.middlesex.nj.us/index.asp	H8	1 Mar 1683	**Prov. East Jersey** Middlesex County; PO Box 1110; 235 Ticetown Rd; New Brunswick, NJ 08901; Ph. (732) 745-3005 **Details:** (County Clerk has Marriage, Divorce, Court & Land Records; County Surrogate has Probate Records)
Monmouth http://shore.co.monmouth.nj.us/	I9	1 Mar 1683	**Prov. East Jersey** Monmouth County; Main St Hall of Records; PO Box 1251; Freehold, NJ 7728; Ph. (732) 431-7324 **Details:** (County Clerk has Marriage Records 1795–1892 & Land Records from 1667; County Surrogate has Probate Records)
Morris www.co.morris.nj.us/	E7	15 Mar 1739	**Hunterdon** Morris County; Hall of Records Admin Bldg; Court St; PO Box 315; Morristown, NJ 7963; Ph. (973) 285-6120 **Details:** (County Clerk has Marriage Records 1795–1881, Court Records 1739–1978, Land Records from 1785, slave Records 1804–1820, Naturalization Records from 1816 & Military Discharge Records from 1945; County Surrogate has Probate Records; Clerk Superior Court has Divorce Records)

County Website	Map Index	Date Created	Parent County or Territory From Which Organized Address/Details
Ocean www.oceancountygov.com/	**K9**	**15 Feb 1850**	**Monmouth** Ocean County; 118 Washington St; PO Box 2191; Toms River, NJ 8754; Ph. (732) 929-2018 **Details:** (County Clerk has Probate & Court Records from 1850)
Passaic www.passaiccountynj.org/	**C8**	**7 Feb 1837**	**Bergen, Essex** Passaic County; 401 Grand St #130; Paterson, NJ 7505; Ph. (973) 225-3632 **Details:** (County Clerk has Divorce Records from 1947, Court Records from 1900 & Land Records; County Surrogate has Probate Records)
Salem 	**M3**	**1681**	**Original county** Salem County; 92 Market St; Salem, NJ 08079-1913; Ph. (856) 935-7510 **Details:** (County Clerk has Marriage Records 1675–1912, Court Records from 1707, Land Records from 1695, Naturalization Records 1808–1958, Military Records from 1715 & newspapers from 1819; County Surrogate has Probate Records from 1804; City Clerks have Birth & Death Records)
Somerset www.co.somerset.nj.us/	**F7**	**May 1688**	**Middlesex** Somerset County; 20 Grove St; PO Box 3000; Somerville, NJ 8876; Ph. (908) 231-7006 **Details:** (County Clerk has Court Records from 1777 & Land Records from 1785; County Surrogate has Probate Records)
Sussex www.sussexcountyclerk.com	**B7**	**16 May 1753**	**Morris** Sussex County;83 Spring St; Newton, NJ 07860; Ph. (973) 579-0900, sclerk@nac.net **Details:** (County Clerk has Deeds & Mortgages from 1785, Birth & Manumissions of Slaves, Divisions, Court Records from 1760, Officers Oaths from 1753, Various Maps, Freeholders Minutes from 1753, Road Returns from 1764, Naturalizations Starting 1808 through 1987, Marriages from 1795 through 1850, & Corporations from 1822; State Vital Statistics has Birth, Marriage, Divorce, Land, Estate, Military, Court, & County Records)
Union www.unioncountynj.org/	**F9**	**19 Mar 1857**	**Essex** Union County; 2 Broad St; Elizabeth, NJ 07207-2204; Ph. (908) 527-4966 **Details:** (County Clerk has Land Records from 1857 & Military Discharge Records from 1941; Clerk Superior Court has Divorce Records from 1848 & Court Records; County Surrogate has Probate Records from 1857; Town Clerks have Birth & Death Records)
Warren www.warrennet.org/warrencounty/	**D5**	**20 Nov 1824**	**Sussex** Warren County; 165 County Rd; 519 S; Belvidere, NJ 7823; Ph. (908) 475-6211 **Details:** (Municipal Clerks have Birth & Death Records; County Clerk has Marriage & Land Records from 1825, Divorce & Court Records; County Surrogate has Probate Records)

Notes

New Mexico

Capital: Santa Fe

Territory: 1850

State: 1912 (47th)

It grows as it goes

Although Native Americans had made their home in what we know as New Mexico, Alva Nunez Cabeza de Vaca and his three companions first explored the area in 1536. They had been shipwrecked off the coast of Texas in 1528, and wandered through the Southwest for eight years. During this time, they heard tales of the Seven Cities of Cibola with the gold-studded houses. On returning to Mexico they related these tales and inspired others to explore the area. Among those who followed was Francisco Coronado in 1540. He found only Indian villages, and treated the Indians with hostility.

In 1598, San Juan was founded as the first permanent Spanish settlement in New Mexico. Santa Fe was founded about 1610 and became the capital. Hostilities with the Indians continued for centuries, but became especially fierce around 1680. Pueblo Indians captured Santa Fe and forced the Spaniards to El Paso. The Spanish regained control in 1692–1693, but suffered continued raids. In 1706, Albuquerque was founded.

Mexico gained its independence from Spain in 1821 and claimed New Mexico as one of its provinces. The same year, the Santa Fe Trail was opened and trade commenced between the United States and Mexico. During the Mexican War, General Stephen Kearny occupied New Mexico and declared it part of the United States. New Mexico officially became part of the United States in 1848. Two years later, the New Mexico Territory was formed. It was comprised of the present state of Arizona and part of Colorado, in addition to New Mexico. The Colorado portion was taken away in 1861, and the Arizona section was made into its own territory in 1863. The Gadsden Purchase in 1854 added the Gila Valley in Catron and Grant Counties.

During the Civil War, Confederate forces invaded New Mexico. They were defeated by Union forces in 1862 and forced to withdraw. New Mexico furnished about 6,000 men to the Union forces. The coming of the railroad stimulated settlement in eastern and southern New Mexico along with economic development. In June 1906, Congress passed a bill providing for the admission of Arizona and New Mexico as one state on the condition that the majority of voters in each state approved it. A majority of New Mexican voters approved statehood, but the Arizona voters did not, so both remained as territories. New Mexico finally became a state in 1912.

Look for vital records in the following locations:

- **Birth and death records:** New Mexico Vital Records and Health Statistics, Santa Fe, New Mexico, has birth and death records from 1880 and delayed birth certificates from 1867. Registration was required after 1920. Copies are available only to the registrant, family members, or by court order.

- **Marriage records, wills, property deeds and administrations:** Check with county clerks.

- **Land records:** County clerks also recorded private land grants. The first land grants were given by Spain and Mexico. These records, along with records of public land distributed while New Mexico was a territory, are located at the BLM, New Mexico State office in Santa Fe. Many of these records are available on microfilm.

- **Census records:** Spanish and Mexican colonial censuses exist for 1750–1830, 1823, and 1845, although they are not complete. They are available at the New Mexico Records Center and Archives, University of New Mexico Library in Albuquerque, New Mexico. These have been transcribed, indexed, and published.

New Mexico Vital Records and Health Statistics
PO Box 26110
Santa Fe, New Mexico 87502
(505) 827-2316
http://dohewbs2.health.state.nm.us/VitalRec/
Death%20Certificates.htm

New Mexico State Records Center & Archives
State Archives and Records Management
1205 Camino Carlos Rey
Santa Fe, New Mexico 87505
Archives and Historical Services
(505) 476-7908; Fax (505) 476-7909
www.nmcpr.state.nm.us/

BLM, New Mexico State office
Federal Building
Box 1449
Santa Fe, New Mexico 87501

Societies and Repositories

Artesia Genealogical Society; PO Box 803; Artesia, NM 88210.

Genealogical Club of the Albuquerque Public Library; 423 Central Ave. NE; Albuquerque, NM 87102.

Los Alamos Family History Society; PO Box 900; Los Alamos, NM 87544.

New Mexico Genealogical Society; PO Box 8283; Albuquerque, NM 87123-8283; www.nmgs.org.

New Mexico State Library; 1209 Camino Carlos Rey; Santa Fe, NM 87507; (505) 476-9700; refer@stlib.state.nm.us; www.stlib.state.nm.us.

New Mexico State Records Center and Archives; State Records Center and Archives; 1205 Camino Car; Santa Fe, NM 87507; (505) 476-7900; wdelao@rain.state.nm.us; www.nmcpr.state.nm.us.

Roswell Genealogical Society; 807 North Missouri; Roswell, NM 88201.

Socorro County Genealogical or Historical Society, Inc.; PO Box 923; Socorro, NM 87801-0923; www.rootsweb.com/~nmschs.

Sons of the American Revolution, New Mexico Society; 12429 Chelwood Court N.W.; Albuquerque, NM 87112.

Southeastern New Mexico Genealogical Society; PO Box 5725; Hobbs, NM 88240.

Southern New Mexico Genealogical Society; PO Box 2563; Las Cruces, NM 88004.

The Genealogy Club of Angle Fire; PO Box 503; Angel Fire, NM 87710.

Totah Tracers Genealogical Society; PO Box 1363; Flora Vista, NM 87415.

Bibliography and Record Sources

General

An Illustrated History of New Mexico and Biographical Mention of Many of its Pioneers and Prominent Citizens of Today. . . . Chicago: The Lewis Publishing Co., 1895.

An Illustrated History of New Mexico: Containing a History of this Important Section of the Great Southwest, from the Earliest Period of Its Discovery to the Present Time. . .Portraits of Some of Its Eminent Men, and Biographical Mention of Many of Its Pioneers and Prominent Citizens of Today. Chicago: Lewis Pub. Co., 1895.

Athearn, Frederic J. *A Forgotten Kingdom: The Spanish Frontier in Colorado and New Mexico 1540–1821.* Denver: Bureau of Land Management, Colorado State Office, 1989.

Bahti, Tom. *Southwestern Indian Tribes.* Las Vegas, Nevada: KC Publications, 1968.

Beers, Henry P. *Spanish and Mexican Records of the American Southwest: A Bibliographic Guide to Archive and Manuscript Sources.* Tucson, Arizona: University of Arizona Press, 1979.

Bohme, Frederick G. *A History of the Italians in New Mexico.* New York: Arno Press, 1975.

Bolton, Herbert E. *The Spanish Borderlands: A Chronicle of Old Florida and the Southwest.* Reprint. Galveston, Texas: Frontier Press, 1996.

Brugge, David M. *Navajos in the Catholic Church Records of New Mexico, 1694–1875.* Window Rock, Arizona: Parks and Recreation Dept., 1968.

Chávez, Angélico. *Archives of the Archdiocese of Santa Fe, 1678–1900.* Washington, D.C.: Academy of American Franciscan History, 1957.

Chavez, Fray Angelico. *Origins of New Mexico Families in the Spanish Colonial Period in Two Parts: The Seventeenth (1598–1693) and the Eighteenth (1693–1821) Centuries.* Reprint. Albuquerque: The University of Albuquerque, 1973.

Coan, Charles F. *A History of New Mexico. . .Historical and Biographical.* 3 vols. Chicago: The American Historical Society, 1925.

Coles, Robert. *The Old Ones of New Mexico.* Rev. ed. Albuquerque, New Mexico: University of New Mexico Press, 1973.

Delaney, Robert W. *The Ute Mountain Utes.* Albuquerque, New Mexico: University of New Mexico Press, 1989.

Dominquez, Francisco A. *The Missions of New Mexico, 1776.* Albuquerque: University of New Mexico Press, 1956.

Esterly, Robert E. *Genealogical Resources in New Mexico.* Albuquerque, New Mexico: New Mexico Genealogical Society, 1997.

Foote, Cheryl J. *Women of the New Mexico Frontier, 1846–1912.* Niwot, Colorado: University Press of Colorado, 1990.

Foster, H. Mannie. *History of Mormon Settlements in Mexico and New Mexico.* Logan, Utah: Utah State Agricultural College, 1955.

Grant, Blanche Chloe. *The Taos Indians.* Glorieta, New Mexico: Rio Grande Press, 1976.

Griego, Alfonso. *Voices of the Territory of New Mexico: An Oral History of People of Spanish Descent and Early*

Settlers Born During The Territorial Days. S.l.: Griego, 1985.

Grove, Pearce S. *New Mexico Newspapers: A Comprehensive Guide to Bibliographical Entries and Locations.* Albuquerque: University of New Mexico Press, 1975.

Historical Records Survey (New Mexico). *Directory of Churches and Religious Organizations in New Mexico, 1940.* Albuquerque, New Mexico: New Mexico Historical Records Survey, 1940.

Historical Records Survey (New Mexico). *Inventory of Federal Archives in the States, Series 03, Department of the Treasury, No. 30, New Mexico.* Albuquerque, New Mexico: The Survey, 1941.

History of New Mexico: Its Resources and People. 2 vols. Los Angeles: Pacific States Publishing Co., 1907.

Jefferson, James. *The Southern Utes: A Tribal History.* Ignacio, Colorado: Southern Ute Tribe, ca. 1972.

New Mexico Research Outline, Series U.S.-States, No. 32. Salt Lake City: Family History Library, 1988.

New Mexico State Records Center and Archives (Santa Fe, New Mexico). *Guide to the Microfilm of the Spanish Archives of New Mexico, 1697–1821.* Santa Fe, New Mexico: New Mexico State Records Center and Archives, 1967. 4 microfilm.

Porter, Lyle K. *A History of the Church of Jesus Christ of Latter-day Saints in New Mexico, 1876–1989.* Albuquerque, New Mexico: L. K. and W. H. Porter, 2001.

Prince, Le Baron Bradford. *Spanish Mission Churches of New Mexico.* Glorieta, New Mexico: Rio Grande Press, 1977.

Quintana, Frances Leon. *Pobladores: Hispanic Americans of the Ute Frontier.* Notre Dame, Indiana: University of Notre Dame Press, 1991.

Read, Benjamin M. *Illustrated History of New Mexico:* Santa Fe, New Mexico: New Mexico Print. Co., 1912.

Reorganized Church of Jesus Christ of Latter-day Saints. Eastern Colorado District (Colorado). *Church Records, 1876–1959.* Microreproduction of originals housed in the RLDS Library Archives, Independence, Missouri. Salt Lake City: Filmed by the Genealogical Society of Utah, 1994.

Salpointe, Jean Baptiste. *Soldiers of the Cross: Notes on the Ecclesiastical History of New Mexico, Arizona and Colorado.* Banning, California: St. Boniface's Industrial School, 1898.

Simons, Marc. *Coronado's Land: Daily Life in Colonial New Mexico.* Galveston, Texas: Frontier Press, 1996.

Sources of Genealogical Help in New Mexico. Burbank, California: Southern California Genealogical Society.

Spiros, Joyce V. Hawley. *Handy Genealogical Guide to New Mexico.* Gallup, New Mexico: Verlene Publishing, 1981.

Stratton, Porter A. *The Territorial Press of New Mexico, 1834–1912.* Albuquerque: University of New Mexico Press, 1969.

Svenningsen, Robert. *Preliminary Inventory of the Pueblo Records Created By Field Offices of the Bureau of Indian Affairs.* Washington, D.C.: National Archives and Records Service, 1980.

Swadesh, Frances Leon. *20,000 Years of History: A New Mexico Bibliography.* Santa Fe: Sunstone Press, 1973.

Swadesh, Frances Leon. *Los Primeros Pobladores: Antecesores De Los Chicanos En Nuevo México.* México: Fondo de Cultura Económica, 1977.

Terrell, John Upton. *The Navajos: The Past and Present of A Great People.* New York: Weybright and Talley, 1970.

The Historical Encyclopedia of New Mexico. 2 vols. Albuquerque, New Mexico: New Mexico Historical Association, 1945.

Thomas, Alfred Barnaby. *The Plains Indians and New Mexico, 1751–1778: A Collection of Documents Illustrative of the History of the Eastern Frontier of New Mexico.* Ann Arbor, Michigan: University Microfilms International, 1978.

Thrapp, Dan L. *Victorio and the Mimbres Apaches.* Norman, Oklahoma: University of Oklahoma Press, 1974.

Treib, Marc. *Sanctuaries of Spanish New Mexico.* Berkeley, California: University of California Press, 1993.

Twitchell, Ralph Emerson. *Leading Facts of New Mexican History.* 2 vols. Reprint. Salem, Massachusetts: Higginson Book Co., 1994.

Twitchell, Ralph Emerson. *The Spanish Archives of New Mexico: Compiled and Chronologically Arranged with Historical, Genealogical, Geographical, and Other Annotations, By Authority of the State of New Mexico.* Cedar Rapids, Iowa: Torch Press, 1914.

Tyler, Daniel. *Sources For New Mexican History, 1821–1848.* Santa Fe, New Mexico: Museum of New Mexico Press, 1984.

United States. National Historical Publications and Records Commission. *Spanish Archives of New Mexico, 1621–1821: A Microfilm Project Sponsored by the National Historical Publications Commission.* Microfilm of original manuscript at New Mexico Records Center, Santa Fe, New Mexico. Santa Fe, New Mexico: State of New Mexico Records Center, 1967. 18 microfilm.

Walker, Randi Jones. *Protestantism in the Sangre De Cristos, 1850–1920.* Albuquerque, New Mexico: University of New Mexico Press, 1991.

Weber, David J. *Foreigners in Their Native Land: Historical Roots of the Mexican Americans.* Albuquerque, New Mexico: University of New Mexico Press, 1972.

Wiggins, Marvin E. *Mormons and Their Neighbors: An Index to Over 75,000 Biographical Sketches from 1820 to the Present.* 2 vols. Provo, Utah: Harold B. Lee Library, Brigham Young University, 1984.

Atlases, Maps and Gazetteers

Beck, Warren A., and Ynez D. Haase. *Historical Atlas of New Mexico.* Norman, Oklahoma: University of Oklahoma Press, 1969.

Coan, Charles F. " The County Boundaries of New Mexico." *Southwestern Political Science Quarterly 3* (December 1922): 252–286. Reprint. Santa Fe, New Mexico: Legislative Council Service, 1965.

Dike, Sheldon H. "The Territorial Post Offices of New Mexico." *New Mexico Historical Review 33* (October 1958) 322–327; 34 (January–October 1959): 55–69; 145–152, 203–226, 308–309.

Helbock, Richard W. *Post offices of New Mexico.* Las Cruces, New Mexico: R.W. Helbock, 1981.

Julyan, Robert Hixson. *The Place Names of New Mexico.* Rev., 2nd ed. Albuquerque, New Mexico: University of New Mexico Press, 1998.

New Mexico in Maps. Albuquerque: University of New Mexico Press, 1986.

Pearce, T. M. *New Mexico Place Names: A Geographical Dictionary.* Albuquerque: University of New Mexico Press, 1985.

Census Records

Available Census Records and Census Substitutes

Federal Census 1850, 1860, 1870, 1880, 1900, 1910, 1920, 1930

Union Veterans and Widows 1890

Spanish/Mexican Census 1790, 1823, 1845

State/Territorial Census 1885

Dollarhide, William. *The Census Book: A Genealogist's Guide to Federal Census Facts, Schedules and Indexes.* Bountiful, Utah: Heritage Quest, 1999.

Kemp, Thomas Jay. *The American Census Handbook.* Wilmington, Delaware: Scholarly Resources, Inc., 2001.

Lainhart, Ann S. *State Census Records.* Baltimore: Genealogical Publishing Co., Inc., 1992.

Olmsted, Virginia L. *Spanish and Mexican Colonial Censuses of New Mexico: 1790, 1823, 1845.* Albuquerque: New Mexico Genealogical Society, 1975.

Olmsted, Virginia L. *Spanish and Mexican Censuses of New Mexico: 1750–1830.* Albuquerque: New Mexico Genealogical Society, 1981.

Platt, Lyman D. *Latin American Census Records.* 2nd. ed. Salt Lake City: Instituto Genealógico e Histórico Latinoamericano, 1992.

Szucs, Loretto Dennis and Matthew Wright. *Finding Answers in U.S. Census Records.* Ancestry Publishing, 2001.

Thorndale, William and William Dollarhide. *Map Guide to the U.S. Federal Census, 1790–1920.* Baltimore: Genealogical Publishing Co., 1987.

United States. Bureau of Internal Revenue. *Internal Revenue Assessment Lists For The Territory of New Mexico, 1862–1874.* Washington, D.C.: The National Archives, 1988.

Court Records, Probate and Wills

Historical Records Survey (New Mexico). *Inventory of Federal Archives in the States, Series 02, Federal Courts, No. 30, New Mexico.* Albuquerque, New Mexico: The Survey, 1941.

Howard, E. Stuart. *Preliminary Inventory: Records of the United States District Court for the District of New Mexico.* Record group 21. Denver: Federal Archives and Records Center, 1980.

New Mexico Commission of Public Records. State Records Center and Archives. *List of New Mexico County Courthouses.* Santa Fe, New Mexico: State Records Center and Archives, 002. Online guide— www.nmcpr.state.nm.us/ archives/courthouses.htm.

Emigration, Immigration, Migration and Naturalization

Colligan, John B. *The Juan Páez Hurtado Expedition of 1865: Fraud in Recruiting Colonists for New Mexico.* Albuquerque, New Mexico: University of New Mexico Press, 1995.

Cruz, Gilberto Rafael. *Let There Be Towns: Spanish Municipal Origins in the American Southwest, 1610–1810.* College Station, Texas: Texas A & M University Press, 1988.

Gamio, Manuel. *Mexican Immigration to the United States: A Study of Human Migration and Adjustment.* New York: Arno Press and the New York Times, 1969.

Gamio, Manuel. *The Mexican Immigrant: His Life-Story.* New York: Arno Press and the New York Times, 1969.

Over 1400 Naturalization Records for Various Courts of New Mexico: 1882–1917, Denver Federal Archives. Lakewood, Colorado: Foothills Genealogical Society of Colorado, 1998.

Land and Property

Diaz, Albert James. *A Guide to the Microfilm of Papers Relating to New Mexico Land Grants.* Albuquerque, New Mexico: University of New Mexico Press, 1960.

Hone, Wade E. *Land and Property Research in the United States.* Salt Lake City: Ancestry Incorporated, 1997.

Miscellaneous Archives Relating to New Mexico Land Grants, 1695–1842. Albuquerque: University of New Mexico Library, 1955–1957.

New Mexico (Territory). Secretary's office. *Records of Land Titles, 1847–1852.* Albuquerque: University of New Mexico Library, 1955–1957.

New Mexico (Territory). Surveyor-General's office. *Press Copies of Grant Papers.* Santa Fe: University of New Mexico Library, 1955–57.

New Mexico (Territory). Surveyor-General's office. *Record of Private Land Claims Adjudicated By the U.S.*

Surveyor General, 1855–1890. Albuquerque: University of New Mexico Library, 1955–1957.

New Mexico (Territory). Surveyor-General's office. *Record of Private Land Claims Adjudicated By the U.S. Surveyor General, 1855–1890.* Microfilm of original records in the U.S. Bureau of Land Management, Santa Fe, New Mexico. Albuquerque, New Mexico: University of New Mexico Library, 1955–1957. 25 microfilm.

New Mexico Commission of Public Records. State Records Center and Archives. *Researching New Mexico Land Grants.* Santa Fe, New Mexico: State Records Center and Archives, 002. Online guide— www.nmcpr.state.nm.us/ archives/courthouses.htm.

Salazar, J. Richard. *Calendar to the Microfilm Edition of the Land Records of New Mexico: Spanish Archives of New Mexico, Series 1, Surveyor General Records, and, The Records of the Court of Private Land Claims.* Santa Fe, New Mexico: National Historical Publications and Records Commission, 1987.

Twitchell, Ralph Emerson. *The Twitchell Archives, 1685–1898.* Albuquerque: Filmed by the University of New Mexico Library, 1955–1957.

United States. Court of Private Land Claims. *Private Land Claims Adjudicated By the U.S. Court of Private Land Claims, 1891–1903.*

United States. Surveyor General (New Mexico). *Letters Received, 1854–1892, from the New Mexico Territory.* Albuquerque: University of New Mexico Library, 1955–1957.

United States. Surveyor General (New Mexico). *Pueblo Grants, 1523–1903.* Microfilm of original at the U.S. Bureau of Land Management, Santa Fe, New Mexico. Albuquerque, New Mexico: Filmed by the University of New Mexico Library, 1955–1957.

Van Ness, John R., and Christine M. Van Ness, eds. *Spanish & Mexican Land Grants in New Mexico and Colorado.* S.l.: s.n., ca. 1980. Manhattan, Kansas: AG Press.

Vigil, Donaciano. *Vigil's Index, 1681–1846.* Albuquerque, New Mexico: University of New Mexico Library, 1955–1957.

Westphall, Victor. *The Public Domain in New Mexico, 1854–1891.* Albuquerque: University of New Mexico, 1965.

Military

Billington, Monroe Lee. *New Mexico's Buffalo Soldiers, 1866–1900.* Niwot, Colorado: University Press of Colorado, 1991.

Haulsee, W. M., F. C. Howe, and A. C. Doyle. *Soldiers of the Great War,* 3 vols. Washington, D.C.: Soldiers Record Publishing Association, 1920.

Historical Records Survey (New Mexico). *Inventory of Federal Archives in the States, Series 07, Department of the Navy, No. 30, New Mexico.* Albuquerque, New Mexico: The Survey, 1940.

Historical Records Survey (New Mexico). *Inventory of Federal Archives in the States, Series 04, Department of War, No. 30, New Mexico.* Albuquerque, New Mexico: The Survey, 1940.

Historical Records Survey (New Mexico). *Inventory of Federal Archives in the States, Series 12, Veterans' Administration, No. 30, New Mexico.* Albuquerque, New Mexico: The Survey, 1940.

Matson, Eva Jane. *It Tolled for New Mexico: New Mexicans Captured By the Japanese, 1941–1945.* Las Cruces, New Mexico: Yucca Tree Press, 1994, 1992.

Miller, Darlis A. *Soldiers and Settlers: Military Supply in the Southwest, 1861–1885.* Albuquerque, New Mexico: University of New Mexico Press, 1989.

Twitchell, Ralph E. *The History of the Military Occupation of the Territory of New Mexico From 1846 to 1851 By the Government of the United States: Together With Biographical Sketches of Men Prominent in the Conduct of the Government During That Period.* Tucson, Arizona: W. C. Cox, 1974.

United States. Selective Service System. *New Mexico, World War I Selective Service System Draft Registration Cards, 1917–1918.* National Archives Microfilm Publications, M1509. Washington, D.C.: National Archives, 1987–1988.

Vital and Cemetery Records

Chavez, Angelico. *New Mexico Roots LTD: A Demographic Perspective from Genealogical, Historical, and Geographical Data Found in the Diligencias Matrimoniales or Pre-nuptial Investigations (1678–1869) of the archives of the Archdiocese of Santa Fe.* N.p.: Angelico Chavez, 1982.

Church of Jesus Christ of Latter-day Saints, The. Spanish-American Mission. *Family Group Records: Collected and Compiled By the Former Spanish-American Mission.* 11 vols. Original sheets are now interfiled in the "Patron" section of the Family Group Records Archives in the Family History Library, Salt Lake City. Salt Lake City: Filmed by the Genealogical Society of Utah, 1973, 1980. 8 microfilm.

Guide to Public Vital Statistics Records in New Mexico. Albuquerque: Historical Records Survey, 1942.

Myers, Lee. *Cemetery Records from Southern New Mexico.* The author, 1982.

New Mexico. Department of Health. *Certificate and Record of Death, 1889–1942.* Microfilm of records at Bureau of Vital Records & Health, Department of Health, Santa Fe, New Mexico. Salt Lake City: Filmed by the Genealogical Society of Utah, 1996. 29 microfilm.

New Mexico. Department of Health. *Delayed Certificates of Birth.* Microfilm of records at New Mexico Department of Public Health, Santa Fe, New Mexico. Salt Lake City: Filmed by the Genealogical Society of Utah, 1995. 5 microfilm.

New Mexico. Department of Health. *New Mexico Death Certificates, 1927–1945.* Microfilm of records at New Mexico Dept. of Health, Vital Records & Health Statistics, Santa Fe, New Mexico. Santa Fe, New Mexico: s.n., 1978. 46 microfilm.

Some Marriages of the State of New Mexico, ca. 1880–1920. 2 vols. New Mexico Chapter, Daughters of the American Revolution, 1971–1973.

County Website	Map Index	Date Created	Parent County or Territory From Which Organized Address/Details
Bernalillo www.bernco.gov/	G5	1850	**Original county** Bernalillo County; 1 Civic Plaza NW; Albuquerque, NM 87102; Ph. (505) 768-4090 **Details:** (County Clerk has Marriage Records from 1885, Probate Records from 1895 & Land Records from 1888; Clerk District Court has Divorce & Court Records)
Catron www.mylocalgov.com/CatronCountyNM/	J2	25 Feb 1921	**Socorro** Catron County; 100 Main St; PO Box 197; Reserve, NM 87830; Ph. (505) 533-6400, cclerk@gilanet.com **Details:** (County Clerk has Marriage, Land, & Probate Records from 1921; Clerk of District Court has Divorce & Court Records)
Chaves www.rootsweb.com/~nmchaves/index.html	K10	25 Feb 1889	**Lincoln** Chaves County; 401 N Main St; Roswell, NM 88201-4726; Ph. (505) 624-6614 **Details:** (County Clerk has Marriage, Land & Military Records from 1900; Clerk District Court has Probate Records from 1900, Divorce & Court Records)
Cibola http://bombaci.rootsweb.com/Cibola/	H3	1981	**Valencia** Cibola County; 515 W High Ave; Grants, NM 87020-2526; Ph. (505) 287-8107 **Details:** (County Clerk has Records from 1981)
Colfax http://nenewmexico.com/counties/colfax/index.html	D9	25 Jan 1869	**Mora** Colfax County; 230 N 3rd St; PO Box 1498; Raton, NM 87740-1498; Ph. (505) 445-5551 **Details:** (County Clerk has Marriage Records from 1890, Probate Records from 1903 & Land Records from 1864; Clerk District Court has Divorce & Court Records)
Curry www.currycounty.org/	H11	25 Feb 1909	**Quay, Roosevelt** Curry County; 700 N Main St Ste 7; PO Box 1168; Clovis, NM 88101; Ph. (505) 763-5591 **Details:** (County Clerk has Marriage Records from 1905, Land Records from 1903, Probate Records from 1909 & Military Discharge Records from 1919; Clerk District Court has Divorce, Naturalization & Court Records)
De Baca www.rootsweb.com/~nmdebaca/index.htm	I9	28 Feb 1917	**Chaves, Guadalupe, Roosevelt** De Baca County; 514 Ave C; PO Box 347; Fort Sumner, NM 88119-0347; Ph. (505) 355-2601 **Details:** (County Clerk has Marriage, Probate & Land Records from 1917; Clerk District Court has Divorce Records; Magistrate Judge has Court Records)

County Website	Map Index	Date Created	Parent County or Territory From Which Organized Address/Details
Dona Ana www.co.dona-ana.nm.us/	M5	**9 Jan 1852**	**Original county** Dona Ana County; 180 West Amador; Las Cruces, NM 88001; Ph. (505) 647-7285 **Details:** (County Clerk has Marriage & Probate Records from 1870 & Land Records from 1801; Clerk District Court has Divorce & Court Records)
Eddy www.caverns.net/ecourt/	M10	**25 Feb 1889**	**Lincoln** Eddy County; 101 West Greene; Carlsbad, NM 88220; Ph. (505) 885-3383 **Details:** (County Clerk has Marriage, Probate & Land Records & newspapers from 1891; Clerk District Court has Divorce & Court Records)
Grant www.rootsweb.com/~nmgrant/index.htm	L2	**30 Jan 1868**	**Dona Ana** Grant County; 201 N Cooper St; PO Box 898; Silver City, NM 88062; Ph. (505) 538-2979 **Details:** (County Clerk has Marriage Records from 1872, Probate Records from 1884, Land Records from 1871 & newspapers from 1900; Clerk District Court has Divorce Records; Municipal Court has Court Records)
Guadalupe www.rootsweb.com/~nmguadal/index.htm	H9	**1850**	**Lincoln, San Miguel** Guadalupe County; 420 Parker Ave; Santa Rosa, NM 88435; Ph. (505) 472-3791 **Details:** (Temporarily named Leonard Wood County 1903–1905) (County Clerk has Marriage Records from 1895, Probate Records from 1894 & Land Records from 1893)
Harding http://nenewmexico.com/counties/harding/index.html	E10	**4 Mar 1921**	**Mora, Union** Harding County; 3rd & Pine; PO Box 1002; Mosquero, NM 87733-1002; Ph. (505) 673-2301 **Details:** (County Clerk has Marriage, Divorce, Probate, Court & Land Records from 1921)
Hidalgo www.rootsweb.com/~nmhidalg/	O2	**25 Feb 1919**	**Grant** Hidalgo County; 300 S Shakespeare St; Lordsburg, NM 88045-1939; Ph. (505) 542-9213 **Details:** (County Clerk has Marriage, Probate & Land Records from 1920; Clerk District Court has Divorce & Court Records)
Lea www.leacounty-nm.org/	L11	**7 Mar 1917**	**Chaves, Eddy** Lea County; 100 N Main Ave; PO Box 4C; Lovington, NM 88260; Ph. (505) 396-8532 **Details:** (County Clerk has Marriage & Probate Records from 1917 & Land Records)
Leonard Wood		**17 Mar 1905**	**Guadalupe** Leonard Wood County; NM **Details:** Temporary name for Guadalupe County 1903–1905

County Website	Map Index	Date Created	Parent County or Territory From Which Organized Address/Details
Lincoln www.usgennet.org/usa/nm/county/lincoln/	J8	16 Jan 1869	**Socorro, Dona Ana** Lincoln County; 300 Central Ave; Carrizozo, NM 88301; Ph. (505) 648-2331 **Details:** (County Clerk has Marriage Records from 1882, Probate Records from 1880 & newspapers from 1890)
Los Alamos www.lac.losalamos.nm.us/	E6	16 Mar 1949	**Sandoval, Santa Fe** Los Alamos County; PO Box 30 2300 Trinity Dr; Los Alamos, NM 87544-3051; Ph. (505) 662-8010 **Details:** (County Clerk has Marriage Records from 1940, Land Records from 1949, Probate Records from 1953 & Burial Records from 1961; Clerk District Court has Divorce & Court Records)
Luna www.rootsweb.com/~nmluna/	N4	16 Mar 1901	**Dona Ana, Grant** Luna County; PO Box 1838; Deming, NM 88031-1838; Ph. (505) 546-0491 **Details:** (County Clerk has Marriage, Death, Land, Probate & Military Records from 1901, Deming newspapers from 1901)
McKinley http://bombaci.rootsweb.com/McKinley/	F3	23 Feb 1899	**Bernalillo, Valencia, San Juan, Rio Arriba** McKinley County; 200 W Hill Ave; Gallup, NM 87301-6309; Ph. (505) 863-6866 **Details:** (County Clerk has Birth Records 1907–1958, Marriage, Probate & Land Records from 1901 & voter Registration; Clerk District Court has Divorce Records)
Mora http://nenewmexico.com/counties/mora/ index.html	E8	1 Feb 1860	**Taos** Mora County; PO Box 360; Mora, NM 87732; Ph. (505) 387-2448 **Details:** (County Clerk has Marriage & Probate Records from 1891 & Land Records from 1825; Clerk District Court has Divorce & Court Records)
Otero http://co.otero.nm.us/	L7	30 Jan 1899	**Dona Ana, Lincoln, Socorro** Otero County; 1000 New York Ave #108; Alamogordo, NM 88310; Ph. (505) 437-4942 **Details:** (County Clerk has Land, Marriage, Military Discharge, Probate, & Mining Claims Records)
Quay http://nenewmexico.com/counties/quay/ index.html	H11	28 Feb 1903	**Guadalupe, Union** Quay County; 300 S 3rd St; PO Box 1225; Tucumcari, NM 88401; Ph. (505) 461-0510 **Details:** (County Clerk has Marriage & Land Records from 1893, Probate Records, Military Records from 1945; Clerk District Court has Divorce & Court Records)
Rio Arriba www.usroots.org/~rioarrnm/	D5	1850	**Original county** Rio Arriba County; PO Box 158; Tierra Amarilla, NM 87575; Ph. (505) 588-7254 **Details:** (County Clerk has Marriage & Probate Records from 1852)
Roosevelt www.rootsweb.com/~nmroosev/index.html	J11	28 Feb 1903	**Chaves, Guadalupe** Roosevelt County; 101 W 1st St; Portales, NM 88130; Ph. (505) 356-8562 **Details:** (County Clerk has Marriage, Probate & Land Records from 1903, Military Discharge Records from 1919 & newspapers; Clerk District Court has Divorce & Court Records)

County Website	Map Index	Date Created	Parent County or Territory From Which Organized Address/Details
San Juan http://bombaci.rootsweb.com/SanJuan/	D2	24 Feb 1887	**Rio Arriba** San Juan County; 100 S Oliver Dr; Aztec, NM 87410; Ph. (505) 334-9471 **Details:** (County Clerk has Marriage & Land Records from 1887 & Probate Records from 1899; Clerk District Court has Divorce & Court Records)
San Juan (old)		1861	**Taos** San Juan (old); NM **Details:** County Terminated 1862
San Miguel www.smcounty.net/	G8	9 Jan 1852	**Original county** San Miguel County; 500 W National St; Las Vegas, NM 87701; Ph. (505) 425-9331 **Details:** (Formerly San Miguel del Bado 1850–1852) (County Clerk has Marriage Records from 1880, Probate Records from 1939 & Land Records from 1800's; Clerk District Court has Divorce & Court Records from 1882)
San Miguel del Bado		1850	San Miguel del Bado; NM **Details:** Name changed in 1852 to San Miguel
Sandoval www.rootsweb.com/~nmsandov/	F5	10 Mar 1903	**Bernalillo** Sandoval County; 711 Camino Del Pueblo; PO Box 40; Bernalillo, NM 87004; Ph. (505) 867-2209 **Details:** (County Clerk has Marriage, Probate & Land Records)
Santa Ana		1876	**Original county** Santa Ana County; NM **Details:** (Became part of Bernalillo County, 1876)
Santa Fe www.co.santa-fe.nm.us/	G7	1850	**Original county** Santa Fe County; 102 Grant Ave; Santa Fe, NM 87505; Ph. (505) 986-6280 **Details:** (County Clerk has Marriage Records from 1900, Probate Records from 1894 & Land Records from 1848)
Sierra http://village.globaldrum.com/sierra_newmexico/county.htm	L5	3 Apr 1884	**Socorro, Grant, Dona Ana** Sierra County; 311 N Date St; Truth or Consequences, NM 87901-2362; Ph. (505) 894-2840 **Details:** (County Clerk has Marriage & Land Records from 1884, Probate Records, Military Discharge Records from 1945; Clerk District Court has Divorce & Court Records)
Socorro www.rootsweb.com/~nmsocorr/index.htm	I4	9 Jan 1852	**Original county** Socorro County; 200 Church St; PO Box 1; Socorro, NM 87801; Ph. (505) 835-0589 **Details:** (County Clerk has Marriage Records from 1885, Probate Records from 1912, Land Records from 1859, Birth & Death Records 1907–1941)

County Website	Map Index	Date Created	Parent County or Territory From Which Organized Address/Details
Taos www.rootsweb.com/~nmtaos/index.htm	D7	1850	**Original county** Taos County; 105 Albright St #D, Taos, NM 87571-0676; Ph. (505) 751-8654 **Details:** (County Clerk has Birth, Marriage, Death, Burial & Probate Records from 1846)
Torrance www.rootsweb.com/~nmtaos/index.htm	H7	16 Mar 1903	**Lincoln, San Miguel, Socorro, Santa Fe, Valencia, Bernalillo** Torrance County; 9th & Allen; Estancia, NM 87016; Ph. (505) 384-2221 **Details:** (Courthouse burned in 1910) (County Clerk has Marriage, informal Probate Records & Land Records from 1911; Clerk District Court has Divorce & Court Records)
Union http://nenewmexico.com/counties/union/index.html	D11	23 Feb 1893	**Colfax, Mora, San Miguel** Union County; 200 Court St; PO Box 430; Clayton, NM 88415; Ph. (505) 374-9491 **Details:** (County Clerk has Marriage Records from 1894, Probate, Court & Land Records; Clerk District Court has Divorce Records)
Valencia www.co.valencia.nm.us/	H5	1850	**Original county** Valencia County; 444 Luna Ave; PO Box 1119; Los Lunas, NM 87031-1119; Ph. (505) 866-2073 **Details:** (County Clerk has Marriage Records from 1865 & Probate Records from 1900; Clerk District Court has Divorce & Court Records)

New York

Ever upward

Capital: Albany
State: 1788 (11th)

Giovanni da Verrazano is credited with discovering New York, as he entered New York Harbor in 1524. The next explorers to arrive were Samuel de Champlain, 1603, and Henry Hudson, 1609. Hudson, employed by the Dutch, returned favorable reports about the area, resulting in the formation of the Dutch West Indies Company in 1621. Although its main goal was trade, the company also established settlements at Fort Orange (Albany) in 1624, and New Amsterdam the next year on Manhattan Island.

The Dutch induced settlers from Scandinavia, Great Britain, and Germany to immigrate to the area. Some Puritans migrated from Massachusetts and Connecticut in about 1640. The English also established settlements in the area, notably on Long Island and northeast of New Amsterdam.

In 1664, Charles II granted all the land from the Connecticut River to Delaware Bay, including all of New Netherland, to his brother James. Colonel Richard Nicolls was appointed governor and was ordered to take control of the area from the Dutch. He did so in 1664, when the settlers refused to fight. New York grew slowly due to the hostility of the French, who came from Canada, and the Iroquois. In about 1740, many people from Connecticut settled in Long Island, Dutchess, Westchester, and Orange counties. The end of the French and Indian War—and a treaty with the Indians ceding all their lands east of Rome—opened up Central New York to settlement.

Prior to the Revolutionary War, settlers lived on Long Island, on the banks of the Hudson River, along the Mohawk River (mainly Palatine Germans), and in the extreme southeastern part of the state. Nearly one-third of the battles in the Revolutionary War were fought in New York, including Ethan Allen's victory at Fort Ticonderoga and the victory at Saratoga.

New York became the eleventh state to ratify the Constitution. The state grew rapidly and by 1820 New York City had become the nation's largest city. During the Civil War, New York supplied 448,000 troops to the Union cause.

Growth during the next half century came from the Irish, who settled New York City and the area along the Erie Canal; Germans, who settled upstate in Rochester and Buffalo; and eastern, southern, and central Europeans, who came to work in the factories in Buffalo, Rochester, Schenectady, and New York City. Predominating nationalities include Italian, Russian, German, Polish, Irish, Austrian, English, Hungarian, Swedish, Norwegian, Czech, Greek, French, Finnish, and Danish.

Look for vital records in the following locations:

- **Birth and death records:** Vital Records Section, State Department of Health from 1880 except for the five boroughs of New York City. The Municipal Archives, Archives Division of the Department of Records and Information Center has birth and death records to 1898 for all five boroughs. Individual county offices also have birth and death records for the boroughs. Birth and death records for Albany, Buffalo and Yonkers from 1914 are with the registrars of each city. Other cities and towns generally have birth and death records from 1880. The New York State Archives, Cultural Education Center has vital records mostly from before 1880 scattered among local government records. An inventory of these records is available upon request from the Archives. New York law forbids issuance of any birth record for genealogical research unless it has been on file for at least 75 years. Death records are issued after 50 years.

- **Marriage records:** Vital Records Section, State Department of Health, 1847 to 1865. Marriage records issued only after on file for 50 years. The Municipal Archives, Archives Division of the Department of Records and Information Center has marriage records to 1898 for all five boroughs. Marriage records for Albany, Buffalo and Yonkers from 1914 are with the registrars of each city. Other cities and towns generally have marriage records from 1880 as well. Some old church, cemetery, and marriage records are in the New

York State Library, Department of Education, Manuscripts and History Section. The library also has some published genealogies, and local histories. Marriage bonds, 1753–1783, were extensively damaged in a 1911 fire but have been largely restored. Some of these can be seen at the New York State Archives, Cultural Education Center.

- **Census records:** These censuses show the names and ages of each member of every household and sometimes the county of birth. Most county offices have copies of the returns for their county. The New York State Archives also has the statewide census returns for 1915 and 1925 along with all the earlier state censuses for Albany County.
- **Military records:** Military service, pensions, and land grant records for soldiers who served in the Revolution and the War of 1812 are available through the New York State Archives.

New York State Department of Health Vital Records Section Certification Unit

Certification Unit
800 North Pearl Street, Second floor
Menands, New York 12204
(518) 474-3077
www.health.state.ny.us/vital_records/

New York State Archives New York State Education Department

Cultural Education Center
Albany, New York 12230
(518) 474-6926
www.archives.nysed.gov/aindex.shtml

Municipal Archives, Archives Division of the Department of Records and Information Center

Empire State Plaza
New York, New York 10007
(212) 619-4530

Societies and Repositories

Adirondack Genealogical & Historical Society; 100 Main St.; Saranac Lake, NY 12983; (518) 891-4256; peighta13@adelphia.net; http://freepages.genealogy.rootsweb.com/~adkghs.

Allegany Area Historical Association; PO Box 162; Allegany, NY 14706; oparker2@juno.com; http://bfn.org/~aaha.

Almond Historical Society; PO Box 187; Almond, NY 14804; bakerdk@infoblvd.net; www.rootsweb.com/~nyahs/AlmondHS.html.

American-Scandinavian Foundation; 58 Park Ave.; New York, NY 10016; info@amscan.org; www.amscan.org.

Archivists Round Table of Metropolitian New York; c/o American Express Company; 200 Vesey Street Worl; New York,, NY 10285; Ira.Galtman@AEXP.com; www.nycarchivists.org.

BIGS (Buffalo Irish Genealogical Society); Buffalo Irish Center; 245 Abbott Rd.; Buffalo, NY 14220; Uabriain@aol.com; www.buffalonet.org/army/bigs.htm.

Bridge Line Historical Society; PO Box 13324; Albany, NY 12212; (518) 884-9076; ch952@FreeNet.Buffalo.EDU; www.bridge-line.org.

Brooklyn Genealogical Workshop; c/o The Brooklyn Record; 125 Montague St.; Brooklyn, NY 11201.

Brooklyn Historical Society; 128 Pierrepont St.; Brooklyn, NY 11201; gshaffer@brooklynhistory.org; www.brooklynhistory.org.

Capital District Genealogical Society; PO Box 2175; Empire State Plaza Station; Albany, NY 12220.

Cayuga County Historian; Historic Old Post Office; 157 Genesee St.; Auburn, NY 13021-3423.

Cayuga-Owasco Lakes Historical Society; Box 247; Moravia, NY 13118; www.rootsweb.com/~nycayuga/colhs.htm.

Central New York Genealogical Society; Box 104, Colvin Station; Syracuse, NY 13205; www.rootsweb.com/~nycnygs.

Chautauqua County, New York Genealogical Society; PO Box 404; Fredonia, NY 14063.

Cheektowaga Historical Association; 3329 Broadway; Cheektowaga, NY 14227.

Chemung County Historical Society; 415 E. Water St.; Elmira, NY 14901.

Colonial Dames of America; 421 E. 61st St.; New York, NY 10021.

Columbia County Historical Society; 5 Albany Ave.; PO Box 311; Kinderhook, NY 12106.

Cortland Historical Society; 25 Homer Ave.; Cortland, NY 13045.

Delaware County Historical Association; dcha@catskill.net; www.rootsweb.com/~nydelaha.

Dutchess County Genealogical Society; PO Box 708; Poughkeepsie, NY 12602; www.dcgs-gen.org.

Dutchess County Historical Society; 549 Main Street; PO Box 88; Poughkeepsie, NY 12601; (845) 471-1630; DCHS@earthlink.net.

East Hampton Historical Society; 101 Main Street; East Hampton, NY 11937; www.hamptonsweb.com/ehhs/houstour.htm.

Eastchester Historical Society; Town Hall; 40 Mill Rd., Box 37; Eastchester, NY 10709.

Enchanted Mountains Genealogy Society; enchant@enchantedmountains.com; www.enchantedmountains.com.

Essex County Historical Society; 7590 Court St.; PO Box 428; Elizabethtown, NY 12932; (518) 873-6466; echs@northnet.org; www.adkhistorycenter.org.

Finlandia Foundation, New York Metro Chapter; PO Box 2590; Grand Central Station; New York, NY 10163.

Genealogical Society of Rockland County; PO Box 444; New City, NY 10956; grfee@aol.com; www.rootsweb.com/~nyrockla/GSRC.

General Society of Colonial Wars; 122 E. 58th St.; New York, NY 10022.

Genesee Area Genealogy Society; 25 N. Spruce St.; Batavia, NY 14020; www.rootsweb.com/~nygags.

Geneva Historical Society; 543 South Main Street; Geneva, NY 14456; (315) 789-5151; info@genevahistoricalsociety.com; www.genevahistoricalsociety.com.

German Genealogical Group; PO Box 1004; Kings Park, NY 11754; hans521@optonline.net; http://geocities.com/athens/forum/2833.

Goshen Library and Historical Society; 203 Main St.; Goshen, NY 10924.

Greater New York, Afro-American Historical and Genealogical Society- JSS; PO Box 022340; Brooklyn, NY 11202.

Greater Ridgewood Historical Society; 1820 Flushing Ave.; Ridgewood, NY 11385; http://members.aol.com/ondrdnkhse/grhs.htm.

Heritage Hunters; PO Box 1389; Saratoga Springs, NY 12866-0884.

Herkimer County Historical Society; 400 North Main Street; Herkimer, NY 13350-1955; (315) 866-6413; herkimerhistory@yahoo.com; www.rootsweb.com/~nyhchs.

Historical Society of Middletown and Walkill Precinct, Inc.; 25 East Ave.; Middletown, NY 10940.

Holland Society; 122 E. 58th St.; New York, NY 10022.

Huguenot Historical Society; 18 Broadhead Avenue; New Paltz, NY 12561-0339; hhsoffice@hhs-newpaltz.org; www.hhs-newpaltz.org.

Huntington Historical Society; 209 Main St.; Huntington, NY 11743; www.huntingtonli.org/hunthistorical/about.html.

Irish Family History Forum; PO Box 67; Plainview, NY 11803-0067; President@ifhf.org; www.ifhf.org.

Italian Genealogical Group of New York; 7 Grayon Dr.; Dix Hills, NY 11746.

Jefferson County Genealogical Society; PO Box 6453; Watertown, NY 13601-6453; www.rootsweb.com/~nyjeffer/jeffsoc.htm.

Jefferson County Historical Society; 228 Washington St.; Watertown, NY 13601.

Jewish Genealogical Society of Capital District; 420 Whitehall Rd.; Albany, NY 12208.

Jewish Genealogical Society of Greater Buffalo; 174 Peppertree Dr. #7; Amherst, NY 14228.

Jewish Genealogical Society of Long Island; 37 Westcliff Dr.; Dix Hills, NY 11746; nberman@worldnet.att.net; www.jewishgen.org/jgsli.

Jewish Genealogical Society of Rochester; 265 Viennawood Dr.; Rochester, NY 14618; BKahn@ServTech.com; www.rit.edu/~bekpph/jgsr.

Jewish Genealogical Society, Inc.; PO Box 6398; New York, NY 10128; jgsny@aol.com; www.jgsny.org.

Kodak Genealogical Club; c/o Kodak Park Activities Assoc.; Eastman Kodak Cou; Rochester, NY 14650.

Lancaster New York Historical Society; 40 Clark Street; Lancaster, NY 14086; http://intotem.buffnet.net/lancasterpast/society.

Livingston County Historical Society; 30 Center Street; Geneseo, NY 14454; www.rootsweb.com/~nylchs.

Livingston-Steuben County Genealogical Society; 5 Elizabeth St.; Dansville, NY 14437-1719; www.rootsweb.com/~nyliving/lscgs.htm.

Long Beach Historical Society; PO Box 286; Long Beach, NY 11561-0286; www.longislandnet.com/longbeachhistory.

Longwood Genealogy Group; Longwood Public Library; 800 Middle Country Road; Middle Island, NY; akakarin@aol.com; www.rootsweb.com/~nygglshp/index.html.

Lynbrook Historical & Preservation Society; 28 Hart Street; Lynbrook, NY 11563-1711; lynhistory@aol.com; http://hometown.aol.com/lynhistory/lhps/lynindex.htm.

Madison County Historical Society; 435 Main St., PO Box 415; Cottage Lawn Historic H; Oneida, NY 13421.

Manlius Historical Society; 109 Pleasant Street; Manlius, NY 13104; Manliushistory@aol.com; http://hometown.aol.com/manliushistory/myhomepage/business.html.

Minisink Valley Historical Society; 125-133 West Main St.; PO Box 659; Port Jervis, NY 12771; (845) 856-2375; info@minisink.org; www.minisink.org.

Nanticoke Valley Historical Society; PO Box 75; Maine, NY 13802; (607) 862-4527; mainehistory@tier.net; www.tier.net/mainehistory.

NARA, Northeast Region (New York City); 201 Varick Street; New York, NY 10014-4811; (212) 401-1620; newyork.archives@nara.gov; www.archives.gov/facilities/ny/new_york_city.html.

National Society of Colonial Dames of America in the State of New York; Library; 215 E. 71st St.; New York, NY 10021.

New Castle Historical Society; 100 King Street; Chappaqua, NY 10514; www.newcastle-ny.org/nchs.html.

New York Genealogical and Biographical Society; 122 E. 58th St.; New York, NY 10022-1939; www.nygbs.org.

New York Historical Association; 170 Central Park, West; New York, NY 10024.

New York State Archives and Records Administration; Cultural Education Center Room 3043; Albany, NY 12230; (518) 474-8955; archref@mail.nysed.gov; www.archives.nysed.gov/aindex.shtml.

New York State Council of Genealogical Organizations; PO Box 2593; Syracuse, NY 13220-2593.

New York State Historical Association; PO Box 800; Cooperstown, NY 13326; www.nysha.org.

New York State Library; Cultural Education Center; Empire State Plaza; Albany, NY 12230; (518) 474-5355; www.nysl.nysed.gov.

Newark Valley Historical Society; www.tier.net/nvhistory.

Niagara County Genealogical Society; 215 Niagara Street; Lockport, NY 14094; genealogy@niagaracounty.org.

Northern New York American-Canadian Genealogical Society; PO Box 1256; Plattsburgh, NY 12901; bobino1@Northnet.org; www.rootsweb.com/~nnyacgs.

Oneida County Historical Society; 1608 Genesee Street; Utica, NY 13502-5425; ochs@borg.com; www.midyork.org/ochs.

Onondaga Historical Association; 311 Montgomery St.; Syracuse, NY 13202.

Ontario County Genealogical Society; 55 North Main St; Canandaigua, NY 14424; www.ochs.org/Genealogy/Ocgs/index.html.

Orange County Genealogical Society; 101 Main St.; Goshen, NY 10924; www.rootsweb.com/~nozell/ocgs.

Orleans County Genealogical Society; NY; HollisCan@aol.com; http://members.tripod.com/~ocgs/home.html.

Oswego County Genealogical Society; PO Box 3025; Oswego, NY 13126-0725.

Oyster Bay Historical Society; PO Box 297; Oyster Bay, NY 11771-0297; OBHistory@aol.com; http://members.aol.com/OBHistory.

Palatines to America, New York Chapter; 18 Droms Rd.; Scotia, NY 13202-5304.

Polish Genealogical Society of New York State; 12645 Rt 78; East Aurora, NY 14052; president@pgsnys.org; www.pgsnys.org.

Queens Genealogical Workshop; 1820 Flushing Ave.; Ridgewood, NY 11385; http://home.att.net/~CGohari/index.html.

Queens Historical Society/Kingsland Homestead; Weeping Beech Park; 143-35 37th Avenue; Flushing, NY 11354; (718) 939-0647; info@queenshistoricalsociety.org; www.queenshistoricalsociety.org.

Rensselaer County Historical Society; 57 Second Street; Troy, NY; dhassler@rchsonline.org; www.rchsonline.org.

Rochester Genealogical Society; PO Box 10501; Rochester, NY 14610; (585) 234-2584; www.rootsweb.com/~nyrgs.

Saint Lawrence County Historical Association; PO Box 8; Canton, NY 13617-0008; http://slcha.org.

Saint Lawrence Valley Genealogical Society; PO Box 341; Colton, NY 13625-0341.

Scarsdale Historical Society; PO Box 431; Scarsdale, NY 10583-0431; www.scarsdalenet.com/historicalsociety.

Schenectady County Historical Society; 32 Washington Avenue; Schenectady, NY 12305; www.schist.org.

Schuyler County Historical Society and Library; 108 N. Catherine St., Rt. 14; Montour Falls, NY 14865.

Shaker Heritage Society; 875 Watervliet Shaker Rd. Suite 2; Albany, NY 12211; shakerwv@crisny.org.

Slovak Heritage and Folklore Society International; 151 Colebrook Drive; Rochester, NY 14617; helenezx@aol.com; www.iarelative.com/shfsinfo.htm.

Sons of the American Revolution, Empire State Society; 13 Garden Ave.; Massapequa, NY 11758.

Southold Historical Society; 54325 Main Road; PO Box 1; Southold, NY 11971-0001; sohissoc@optonline.net; www.southoldhistoricalsociety.org.

St. George's Society Of New York; 175 Ninth Avenue; New York, NY 10011-4977; william_r.miller@bms.com; www.stgeorgessociety.org.

Staten Island Historical Society; 441 Clarke Ave.; Staten Island, NY 10306.

Statue of Liberty-Ellis Island Foundation, Inc., The; Attention: History Center; 292 Madison Ave; New York, NY 10017-7769; (212) 561-4588; historycenter@ellisisland.org; www.ellisisland.org.

Steuben County Historical Society; PO Box 349; Bath, NY 14810.

Suffolk County Historical Society; 300 W. Main St.; Riverhead; Long Island, NY 11901.

Sullivan County Historical Society; PO Box 247W; Hurleyville, NY 12747; jmasten@pioneeris.net; www.sullivancountyhistory.org.

The African-Atlantic Genealogical Society; PO Box 7385; Freeport, NY 11520; www.africantic.com.

The American Irish Historical Society; 991 Fifth Ave; New York, NY 10028; www.aihs.org.

The Bronx County Historical Society; 3309 Bainbridge Avenue; Bronx, NY 10467; www.go-newyorkcity.com/0022index.html.

The Buffalo and Erie County Historical Society; 25 Nottingham Court; Buffalo, NY 14216; http://intotem.buffnet.net/bechs.

The Chenango County Historical Society; 45 Rexford Street; Norwich, NY 13815; www.chenangocounty.org/chencohistso.

The Cow Neck Peninsula Historical Society; 336 Port Washington Blvd.; Port Washington, NY 11050-4530; Curator@CowNeck.org; www.cowneck.org.

The Hispanic Genealogical Society of New York; Murray Hill Station - PO Box 818; New York, NY 10156-0602;

president@hispanicgenealogy.com;
www.hispanicgenealogy.com.

The Italian Historical Society of America; 111 Columbia
Heights; Brooklyn, NY 11201;
mail@italianhistorical.org; www.italianhistorical.org.

The Malverne Historical & Preservation Society;
PO Box 393; Malverne, NY 11565; eab371@aol.com;
http://members.aol.com/lynhistory/malverne/
malindex.htm.

The Puerto Rican/Hispanic Genealogical Society Inc.;
PO Box 260118; Bellerose, NY 11426-0118;
miguel_j_hernandez@csi.com;
www.rootsweb.com/~prhgs.

The Southern Tier Genealogical Club of Broome County;
PO Box 690; Vestal, NY 13851-0680;
www.rootsweb.com/~nybroome/stgs/stgs.htm.

Three Village Historical Society, The; PO Box 76; E.
Setauket, NY 11733; TVHistSoc@aol.com;
http://members.aol.com/TVHS1/index.html.

Tioga County Historical Society; 110-112 Front St.;
Owego, NY 13827.

Town of Dayton Historical Society; PO Box 15; Dayton,
NY 14041.

Town of Moriah Historical Society; Port Henry, NY;
iron@porthenry.com;
www.porthenry.com/phframes/MHS.htm.

Town of Watertown NY Historical Society; 22867 County
Route 67; Watertown, NY 13601; TWHS@imcnet.net;
www.usgennet.org/usa/ny/town/watertown/
twhsmain.html.

Twin Tiers Genealogical Society; PO Box 763; Elmira, NY
14902.

Ulster County Genealogical Society; PO Box 536; Hurley,
NY 12443; (845) 331-7453; jderaplie@aol.com;
http://hurley.lib.ny.us/uc_geneological_society.html.

United States Military Academy Archives; Pershing Center,
Bldg. #2107; United States Milita; West Point, NY
10996-2099; (914) 938-7052;
www.archives.gov/facilities/nara_affiliated_archiv.

Wayne County Historical Society; 21 Butternut Street;
Lyons, NY 14489; WCHS4943@aol.com;
www.cgazette.com/common/standing/
WC-historical_society/waynecountyhistorical.htm.

Westchester County Genealogical Society; PO Box 518;
White Plains, NY 10603; KVliddle@aol.com;
www.rootsweb.com/~nywcgs.

Westchester County Historical Society; 2199 Saw Mill
River Road; Elmsford, NY 10523;
www.westchesterhistory.com.

Western New York Genealogical Society; PO Box 338;
Hamburg, NY 14075; (716) 839-1842;
i.m.rupp@worldnet.att.net;
www.pce.net/outram/wny.htm.

Yates County Genealogical and Historical Society;
200 Main St.; Penn Yan, NY 14527; ycghs@linkny.com;
www.yatespast.com.

Yorktown Historical Society; PO Box 355; Yorktown
Heights, NY 10598; www.yorktownhistory.org.

Bibliography and Record Sources

General

Bailey, Rosalie Fellows. *Guide to Genealogical and
Biographical Sources for New York City, Manhattan,
1783–1898.* New York: Bailey, 1954.

Bevier, Louis. *Genealogy of the First Settlers of New Paltz.*
1909. Reprint. Baltimore: Genealogical Publishing Co.,
1965.

Brodhead, John Romeyn. *Documents Relative to the
Colonial History of the State of New York: Procured in
Holland, England, and France.* 15 vols. Albany: Weed,
Parsons & Co., printers, 1853–1887.

Burke, Kate. *Searching in New York: A Reference Guide to
Public and Private Records.* Costa Mesa, California:
ISC Publications, 1987.

Clint, Florence. *New York Area Key: A Guide to the
Genealogical Records of the State of New York.*
Elizabeth, Colorado: Keyline Publishers, 1979.

Cutter, William Richard. *Families of Western New York:
Excerpted from Genealogical and Family History of
Western New York: A Record of the Achievements of her
People in the Making of A Commonwealth and the
Building of a Nation.* 1912. Reprint. Baltimore,
Maryland: Clearfield Co., 1996.

Cutter, William Richard. *Genealogical and Family History
of Central New York. A Record of the Achievements of
Her People in the Making of a Commonwealth and the
Building of a Nation.* 3 vols. 1912. Reprint. Baltimore,
Maryland: Clearfield Co, 1994.

Documentary History of the State of New York. 4 vols. in 8
parts. Albany: Weed, Parsons and Co., 1849–1851.

Epperson, Gwenn F. *New Netherland Roots.* Baltimore:
Genealogical Publishing Co., 1994.

Faibisoff, Sylvia G. *A Bibliography of Newspapers in
Fourteen New York State Counties.* S.l.: s.n., 197–.

Falk, Byron A. *Personal Name Index to the New York
Times Index, 1851–1993: [with additional supplements
to 1996].* Succasunna, New Jersey; Sparks, Nevada:
Roxbury Data Interface, 1976–.

Fitch, Charles Elliot. *Encyclopedia of Biography of New
York: A Life Record of Men and Women of the Past
Whose Sterling Character and Energy and Industry
Have Made Them Preeminent in Their Own and Many
Other States.* 4 vols. New York: American Historical
Society, 1916.

Gehring, Charles T. *New York Historical Manuscripts:
Dutch Land Papers, Volumes GG, HH, II.* Baltimore:
Genealogical Publishing Co., 1980.

Greene, Nelson, ed. *The History of the Mohawk Valley,* 4 vols. Chicago: S. J. Clarke Publishing Co., 1925.

Greene, Nelson. *History of the Valley of the Hudson: River of Destiny, 1609–1930, Covering the Sixteen New York State Hudson River Counties of New York, Bronx, Westchester, Rockland, Orange, Putnam, Dutchess, Ulster, Greene, Columbia, Albany, Rensselaer, Saratoga, Washington, Warren, Essex.* 5 vols. Chicago: S. J. Clarke Pub. Co., 1931.

Guide to Archival Repositories. Buffalo, New York: Western New York Documentary Heritage Program, 1997.

Guzik, Estelle M., ed. *Genealogical Resources in the New York Metropolitan Area.* New York: Jewish Genealogical Society, 1989.

Hamm, Margherita Arlina. *Famous Families of New York: Historical and Biographical Sketches of Families, which in Successive Generations have been Identified with the Development of the Nation.* New York: Putnam, 1902.

Hoff, Henry Bainbridge. *Genealogies of Long Island Families: From the New York Genealogical and Biographical Record.* 2 vols. Baltimore: Genealogical Publishing Co., Inc., 1987.

Ireland, Norma Olin. *Cutter Index: A Consolidated Index of Cutter's 9 Genealogy Series.* Fallbrook, California: Ireland Indexing Service, 197–.

Kronman, Barbara. *The Guide to New York City Public Records.* New York: Public Interest Clearinghouse, 1992.

MacWethy, Lou D. *The Book of Names, Especially Relating to the Early Palatines and the First Settlers of the Mohawk Valley.* 1933. Reprint. Baltimore: Genealogical Publishing Co., 1985.

Nestler, Harold. *A Bibliography of New York State Communities, Counties, Town, and Villages.* 3rd ed. Bowie, Maryland: Heritage Books, 1990.

New York Research Outline. Series U.S.-States, No. 33. Salt Lake City: Family History Library, 1988.

New York State Library Surname Index. Albany: State Library of New York, 1979. 33 Microfiche.

New York Times (New York City). *Obituary Index.* Westport, Connecticut: Meckler, 1989.

New York, Commissioners of Indian Affairs. *Proceedings of the Commissioners of Indian Affairs Appointed by Law for the Extinguishment of Indian Titles in the State of New York.* Albany, New York: J. Munsell, 1861.

New York, Secretary of State. *The Balloting Book and Other Documents Relating to Military Bounty Lands, in the State of New York.* Albany, New York: 1825.

New York, State Historian. *Third Annual Report of the State of New York, 1897; Transmitted to the Legislature, March 14, 1898.* New York City and Albany, New York: Wynkoop, Hahlenbeck and Crawford Co., 1898.

Noyes, J. O. and Morrison's Reprint. *Genesee Valley of Western New York.* Reprint. W.E. Morrison & Co., 1972.

O'Callaghan, Edmund B. *Lists of Inhabitants of Colonial New York (1849–1851).* Reprint. Baltimore, Maryland: Genealogical Publishing Co., 1989.

O'Callaghan, Edmund B. *The Register of New Netherland, 1626–1674.* 1865. Reprint. Baltimore, Maryland: Clearfield Co., 1996.

O'Callaghan, Edmund B. *Calendar of Dutch (and English) Historical Manuscripts in the Office of Secretary of State, Albany, New York.* 2 vols. 1968–1866. Reprint. Ridgewood, New Jersey: The Gregg Press, 1968.

Pearson, Jonathan. *Contributions for the Genealogies of the Descendants of the First Settlers of the Patent and City of Schenectady, from 1662 to 1800.* Baltimore: Reprinted for Clearfield Company Inc. by Genealogical Publishing Co., 1998.

Reynolds, Cuyler. *Genealogical and Family History of Southern New York and the Hudson River Valley.* 1914. Reprint. Baltimore, Maryland: Clearfield Co., 1997.

Reynolds, Helen Wilkinson. *Dutch Houses in the Hudson Valley before 1776.* New York: Payson and Clarke, 1929.

Schwietzer, George K. *New York Genealogical Research.* Knoxville: George K. Schweitzer, 1988.

Scott, Kenneth. *Genealogical Data from Colonial New York Newspapers: A Consolidation of Articles from the New York Genealogical and Biographical Record.* Baltimore: Genealogical Pub. Co., 1977.

Scott, Kenneth. *Genealogical Data From New York Administration Bonds 1753–1799.* New York, New York: New York Genealogical and Biographical Society, 1969.

Scott, Kenneth. *Genealogical Data from the New York Post Boy, 1743–1773.* Arlington, Virginia: National Genealogical Society.

Seversmith, Herbert Furman. *Colonial Families of Long Island, New York and Connecticut: Being the Ancestry & Kindred of Herbert Furman Seversmith.* 5 vols. in 7. Washington: H. F. Seversmith, 1939–1958.

Seversmith, Herbert Furman. *Long Island Genealogical Source Material: A Bibliography.* Washington: National Genealogical Society Bookstore, 1962.

Talcott, Sebastian V. *Genealogical Notes of New York and New England Families.* 1883. Reprint. Baltimore, Maryland: by Clearfield Co., 1994.

Wilson, Thomas B. *Inhabitants of New York, 1774–1776.* Genealogical Publishing Co., 1993.

Worden, Mrs. Jean D., comp. *The New York Genealogical and Biographical Record: 113 Years Master Index, 1870–1892.* Franklin, Ohio: Jean D. Worden, 1983.

Atlases, Maps and Gazetteers

Catalogue of Maps and Surveys in the Offices of the Secretary of State, State Engineer and Surveyor and Comptroller and the New York State Library. Albany, New York: Charles Van Benthuysen, 1859.

French, John Homer. *Gazetteer of the State of New York. (1860) Reprinted with an Index of Names.* (1860, 1983) Reprint. Baltimore, Maryland: Genealogical Publishing Co., 1995.

Gordon, T. F. *Gazetteer of the State of New York, Comprehending Its Colonial History, General Geography, Geology, Internal Improvements; Its Political State; Minute Description of Its Several Counties, Towns, and Villages; Statistical Tables.* (1836) Reprint. Salem, Massachusetts: Higginson Book Co., 1990.

Hough, Franklin B. *Gazetteer of the State of New York, Embracing a Comprehensive Account of the History and Statistics of the State, with Geographical and Topographical Descriptions of Each County, City, Town & Village.* (1872) Reprint. Salem, Massachusetts: Higginson Book Co., 1993.

Long, John H., ed. *New York Atlas of Historical County Boundaries.* Compiled by Kathryn Ford Thorne. New York, New York: Simon & Schuster, 1993.

New York State County Atlases—Post Civil War—Reprint. 46 vols. Ovid, New York: W. E. Morrison & Co.

Wright, Albert H. A. *A Checklist of New York State County Maps Published 1779–1945.* Ithaca, New York: Cornell University, 1965.

Census

Available Census Records and Census Substitutes

Federal Census 1790, 1800, 1810, 1820, 1830, 1840, 1850, 1860, 1870, 1880, 1900, 1910, 1920, 1930

Federal Mortality Schedules 1850, 1860, 1870, 1880

Union Veterans and Widows 1890

State/Territorial Census 1663–1772, 1814, 1835, 1845, 1855, 1865, 1875, 1892, 1905, 1915, 1925

Loyalists 1782

Dollarhide, William. *The Census Book: A Genealogist's Guide to Federal Census Facts, Schedules and Indexes.* Bountiful, Utah: Heritage Quest, 1999.

Inskeep, Carolee. *The Children's Aid Society of New York: An Index to the Federal, State, and Local Census Records of Its Lodging Houses (1855–1925).* Baltimore: Genealogical Publishing Co., Inc., (1996), repr. 2005.

Kemp, Thomas Jay. *The American Census Handbook.* Wilmington, Delaware: Scholarly Resources, Inc., 2001.

Kirkham, E. Kay. *A Handy Guide to Record-Searching in the Larger Cities of the United States: Including a Guide to their Vital Records and Some Maps with Street Indexes with Other Information of Genealogical Value.* Logan, Utah: Everton, 1974.

Lainhart, Ann S. *State Census Records.* Baltimore: Genealogical Publishing Co., Inc., 1992.

Meyers, Carol M. *Early New York State Census Records, 1663–1772.* Gardena, California: RAM Publishers, 1965.

Szucs, Loretto Dennis and Matthew Wright. *Finding Answers in U.S. Census Records.* Ancestry Publishing, 2001.

Thorndale, William and William Dollarhide. *Map Guides to the U.S. Federal Censuses, 1790–1920: New York, 1790-1920.* Genealogical Publishing Co., 1987.

Court, Probate and Wills

Barber, Audrey Gertrude. *Index to Letters of Administration of New York County from 1743–1875.* 6 vols. New York: Audrey Gertrude Barber, 1950–1951.

Christoph, Peter R. *New York Historical Manuscripts, English.* Baltimore: Genealogical Publishing Company, 1980–.

Christoph, Peter R. *New York Historical Manuscripts, English. Records of the Court of Assizes for the Colony of New York, 1665–1682.* Baltimore: Genealogical Publishing Company, 1983.

Cook, William Burt. *Abstracts of Albany County, New York. Probate and Family Records.* Washington, D.C.: Library of the National Society of the Daughters of the American Revolution, 1930.

Fernow, Berthold, comp. *Calendar of Wills on File and Recorded in the Offices of the Clerk of Appeals, of the County Clerk at Albany and the Secretary of State 1626–1836.* New York: Colonial Dames of the State of New York, 1896. Reprint. Baltimore: Genealogical Publishing Co., 1967.

Fernow, Berthold, ed. *The Records of New Amsterdam from 1653 to 1674 Anon Dominic.* 7 vols. New York: Knickerbockers Press, 1897.

New York State Archives. *List of Pre-1847 Court Records in the State Archives.* Albany, New York: Office of Cultural Education, 1984.

Plateau, William Smith, ed. *Abstracts of Wills on File in the Surrogate's Office, City of New York 1665–1801.* New York: New York Historical Society, 1892–1909.

Sawyer, Ray C., comp. and ed. *Index of Wills for New York County 1662–1875.* 6 vols. New York: Ray C. Sawyer, 1930–51.

Scott, Kenneth and Rosanna Conway. *New York Alien Residents 1825–1848.* Baltimore: Genealogical Publishing Co., 1978.

Scott, Kenneth and James A. Owre, eds. *Genealogical Data from Further New York Administration Bonds 1791–1798.* vol. 11. New York: New York Genealogical and Biographical Society, 1971.

Scott, Kenneth and James A. Owre, eds. *Genealogical Data from Inventories of New York Estates, 1666–1825.* New York: New York Genealogical and Biographical Society. 1970.

Scott, Kenneth. *Genealogical Data from New York Administration Bonds, 1753–1799 and Hitherto Unpublished Letters of Administration.* New York: New York Genealogical and Biographical Society, 1969.

Van Lear, Arnold J. F. *Register of the Provincial Secretary; Council Minutes.* 4 vols. Baltimore: Genealogical Publishing, 1974.

Immigration

Bingham, Robert Warwick, ed. *Reports of Joseph Ellicott as Chief of Survey (1797–1800); And As Agent (1800–1821) of the Holland Company's Purchasers in Western New York.* Buffalo, New York: Buffalo Historical Society, 1937–1941.

Bowman, Fred Q. *Landholders of Northeastern New York, 1739–1802.* Reprint. Baltimore: Genealogical Publishing Co., 1987.

Boyer, Carl. *Ship Passenger Lists, New York and New Jersey (1600–1825).* 3rd ed. Newhall, California; Carl Boyer, 1987.

Brownell, Elijah Ellsworth. *Lists of Patents of Lands, Etc. to be Sold in January 1822 for Arrears of Quit Rent.* Philadelphia: s.n., 1937.

Burleigh, H. C. *New York State—Confiscations of Loyalists.* Toronto, Ontario: United Empire Loyalists Association of Canada, 1970.

Calendar of N.Y. Colonial Manuscripts, Indorsed [sic] Land Papers in the Office of the Secretary of State of New York, 1643–1803. Albany, New York: Weed, Parsons and Co. 1864.

Cayman, Eugene W. *Uprooted from Prussia—Transplanted in America.* Buffalo, New York: Aircraft Printing. 1991.

Dixon, Nancy Waggoner. *Palatine Roots: The 1710 German Settlement in NY as Experienced by Johan Peter Wagner.* Rockport, Maine: Piston Press, 1994.

Gehring, Charles T. *New York Historical Manuscripts: Dutch Land Papers, Volumes GG, HH, II.* Baltimore: Genealogical Publishing Co., 1980.

Hewitt, Allen E., and Joyce S. Hewitt. *Naturalization Records, Canadian Extracts.* Hamburg, New York: A.E. Jewitt, Sr.

Jones, Henry Z. *The Palatine Families of New York: A Study of the German Immigrants Who Arrived in Colonial New York in 1710.* 2 vols. Universal City, California: Henry Z. Jones, 1985.

Kim, Sun Bok. *Landlord and Tenant in Colonial New York: Manorial Society 1664–1775.* Chapel Hill: University of North Carolina Press, 1978.

Land

Livsey, Karen E. *Western New York Land Transactions, 1804–1824: Extracted from the Archives of the Holland Land Company.* 2 vols. Baltimore: Genealogical Publishing Co., 1996.

New York, Secretary of State. *The Balloting Book and Other Documents Relating to Military Bounty Lands, in the State of New York.* Albany, New York, 1825.

New York. Secretary of State. *Patents of the State of New York, 1649–1912.* Microfilm of original records at Office of General Services, B.S.R.P., Albany, New York. Salt Lake City: Filmed by the Genealogical Society of Utah, 1973. Microfilm, 60 rolls.

O'Callaghan, E. B. *Calendar of New York Colonial Manuscripts 1643–1803.* 1864, Reprint. Rockport, Maine: Picton Press, 1987.

Pieterse, Wilhelmina C. *Inventory of the Archives of the Holland Land Company: Including the Related Amsterdam Companies and Negotiations Dealing with the Purchase of Land and State Funds in the United States of America 1789–1869.* Amsterdam: Municipal Print Office, 1976.

Scott, Kenneth and Rosanne Conway. *New York Alien Residents 1825–1848.* Baltimore: Genealogical Publishing Co., 1978

Scott, Kenneth and Kenn Stryker-Rodda. *Denizations, Naturalizations, and Oaths of Allegiance in Colonial New York.* Baltimore: Genealogical Publishing Co., 1975.

Scott, Kenneth. *Early New York Naturalizations: Abstracts of Naturalization Records from Federal, State, and Local Courts, 1792–1840.* Baltimore: Genealogical Publishing Company, 1981.

Singleton, Esther. *Dutch New York.* 1909, Reprint. Salem, Massachusetts: Higginson Books, 1994.

Thorne, Kathryn Ford. *New York Atlas of Historical County Boundaries.* New York: Simon & Schuster, 1993.

Yoshpe, Harry B. *The Disposition of Loyalist Estates in the Southern District of the State of New York.* New York: Columbia University Press, 1939.

Military

Adjunct General's Office. *Index of Awards on Claims of the Soldiers of the War of 1812.* Baltimore: Genealogical Publishing Co., 1963.

Bielinski, Stefan. *A Guide to the Revolutionary War Manuscripts in the New York State Library.* Albany: New York State American Revolution Bicentennial Commission, 1976.

Cosgrove, Charles H. *A History of the 134th New York Volunteer Infantry Regiment in the American Civil War, 1862–1865, Long Night's Journey into Day.* Lewiston, New York: Mellen, 1997.

Fernow, Bethold, ed., and New York State Archives. *New York in the Revolution. Documents Relating to the Colonial History of the State of New York, vol. 15.* Albany, New York 1887. Reprint. Baltimore, Maryland: Clearfield Co., 2000.

Hastings, Hugh. State Historian. *Military Minutes of the Council of Appointments of the State of New York.* Albany, New York: State Printer, 1901.

Klein, Milton M. *New York in the American Revolution: A Bibliography.* Albany: New York State American Revolution Bicentennial Commission, 1974.

New York Adjunct General. *Registers in the War of the Rebellion.* Albany, New York: J. B. Lyon, 1894–1906.

New York Adjunct General's Office. *A Record of Commissioned Officers, Non-commissioned Officers and Privates.* Albany, New York: Comstock & Cassidy, 1864–1868.

New York Historical Society. *Muster Rolls of New York Provincial Troops 1755–1764.* New York: The Society, 1892.

New York, Comptroller's Office. *New York in the Revolution as a Colony and State.* 2 vols. Albany, New York: J. B. Lyon and Co., 1904.

New York, Secretary of State. *The Balloting Book and Other Documents Relating to Military Bounty Lands, in the State of New York.* Provo, Utah: Brigham Young University, 1970.

Roberts, James A., and Frederick G. Mather. *New York in the Revolution as Colony and State [Together With Supplement].* 2 vols. in 1. (1898, 1901), Reprint. Baltimore, Maryland: Genealogical Publishing Co., 1996.

Saldana, Richard H., ed. *Index to the New York Spanish-American War Veterans.* 2 vols. Albany, New York: James B. Lyon, 1900.

Sons of the American Revolution. Empire State Society. *Register of the Empire State of the Sons of the American Revolution.* New York: The Society, 1899.

United States. Selective Service System. *New York, World War I Selective Service System Draft Registration Cards, 1917–1918.* Washington, D.C.: National Archives, 1987–1988.

Wilson, Thomas B. *Inhabitants of New York, 1774–1776.* Baltimore: Genealogical Publishing, 1993.

Vital and Cemetery

Bowman, Fred Q. *10,000 Vital Records of Eastern New York, 1777–1834.* Baltimore: Genealogical Publishing Co., 1987.

Bowman, Fred Q. *10,000 Vital Records of New York, 1813–1850.* Baltimore: Genealogical Publishing Co., 1986.

Bowman, Fred Q. *10,000 Vital Records of Western New York, 1809–1850.* Baltimore: Genealogical Publishing Co., 1985.

Bowman, Fred Q. *7,000 Hudson-Mohawk Valley (NY) Vital Records, 1808–1850.* Baltimore, Maryland: Genealogical Publishing Co., 1997.

Bowman, Fred Q. *8000 More Vital Records of Eastern New York State, 1804–1850.* Rhinebeck, New York: Kinship, 1991.

Bowman, Fred Q., and Thomas J. Lynch. *Directory to Collections of New York Vital Records, 1726–1989, with Rare Gazetteer.* Bowie, Maryland: Heritage Books, 1995.

Bowman, Fred. Q. *8,000 More Vital Records of Eastern New York State, 1804–1850.* Rhinebeck, New York: Kinship, 1991.

Cormack, Marie Noll. *New York State Cemetery Inscriptions: Albany County; Herkimer County; Montgomery County; Saratoga County; Schenectady County.* Federal Writers Project of Works Progress Administration of State of New York. Microfilm. Salt Lake City: Genealogical Society of Utah, 1967.

Dilts, Brian Lee, comp. *1890 New York Veterans Census Index.* 2nd ed. Salt Lake City: Index Publishing, 1984.

Historical Records Survey (New York City). *Guide to Vital Statistics in the City of New York, Borough of Manhattan Churches.* New York: Historical Records Survey, 1942.

Historical Records Survey (New York). *Guide to Vital Statistics Records of Churches in New York State, Exclusive of New York City.* 2 vols. Albany: The Survey, 1942.

New York State Cemeteries. 23 vols. Salt Lake City: Genealogical Society of Utah, 1940–69.

New York State Library. *Vital Records Card File.* Microfiche. Albany, New York: New York State Library, Photoduplication Department, 1979.

New York, Secretary of State. *Names of Persons for Whom Marriage Licenses Were Issued By the Secretary of the Province of New York, Prior to 1784.* Albany, New York: Weed, Parsons, and Co., 1860

Robison, Jeannie F. J., and Henrietta C. Bartlett, eds. *Genealogical Records: Manuscript Entries of Births, Deaths and marriages, Taken from Family Bibles, 1581–1917.* (1917) Reprint. Baltimore, Maryland: Clearfield Co., 1995

Scott, Kenneth. *Marriages and Deaths from the New Yorker (Double Quarto Edition) 1836–1841.* Washington, D.C.: National Genealogical Society Bookstore, 1980.

County Website	Map Index	Date Created	Parent County or Territory From Which Organized Address/Details
Albany www.albanycounty.com/	F7	**1 Nov 1683**	**Original county** Albany County; 250 S Pearl St; Albany, NY 12202; Ph. (518) 447-4500 **Details:** (Hall of Records has Land Records from 1630, tax rolls from 1850, Naturalization Records 1827–1991, Albany city directories from 1830 & Marriage Records 1870–1946; Surrogate Court has Probate Records; County Clerk has Divorce & Court Records)
Allegany www.co.allegany.ny.us/	N8	**7 Apr 1806**	**Genesee** Allegany County; 7 Court St; Belmont, NY 14813; Ph. (716) 268-9222 **Details:** (County Clerk has Marriage Records 1908–1935, Divorce & Court Records, Land Records from 1807; Clerk Surrogate Court has Probate Records)
Bronx www.rootsweb.com/~nybronx/	E11	**19 Apr 1912**	**New York** Bronx County; 1780 Grand Concourse; Bronx, NY 10451-2937; Ph. (718) 590-3644 **Details:** (County Clerk has Marriage, Divorce & Court Records from 1914)
Broome www.gobroomecounty.com/index2.php	J8	**28 Mar 1806**	**Tioga** Broome County; 65 Hawley St; Binghamton, NY 13901-3722; Ph. (607) 778-2448 **Details:** (County Clerk has Marriage Records 1908–1935, Military rolls from 1808, Naturalization Records from 1860, Divorce, Court & Land Records & state Census; Surrogate Court has Probate Records from 1806; Town & City Clerks have Birth, Marriage, Death & Burial Records from 1880)
Cattaraugus www.co.cattaraugus.ny.us/	P8	**11 Mar 1808**	**Genesee** Cattaraugus County; 303 Court St; Little Valley, NY 14755; Ph. (716) 938-9111 **Details:** (County Clerk has Divorce & Land Records from 1808, Court Records from 1850 & Naturalization Records; Surrogate Court has Probate Records; Town & City Clerks have Birth, Marriage & Death Records)
Cayuga www.co.cayuga.ny.us/	K6	**8 Mar 1799**	**Onondaga** Cayuga County; 160 Genesee St; Auburn, NY 13021; Ph. (315) 253-1271 **Details:** (County Clerk has Probate & Court Records from 1799, Land Records from 1794 & DAR County Cemetery Records 1790–1960; Town & City Clerks have Birth, Marriage & Death Records)
Charlotte www.rootsweb.com/~nycharlo/charlotte.htm		**12 Mar 1772**	**Albany** Charlotte County; NY **Details:** (see Washington) Name changed to Washington 2 Apr 1784
Chautauqua www.co.chautauqua.ny.us	Q8	**11 Mar 1808**	**Genesee** Chautauqua County; 1 N Erie St; PO Box 170; Mayville, NY 14757; Ph. (716) 753-4857, HenryM@co.chautauqua.ny.us **Details:** (County Clerk has Marriage Records from 1908-1935, Divorce, Court & Land Records from 1811; Surrogate Court has Probate Records; Town or City Clerks have Birth, Marriage, Death & Burial Records)

County Website	Map Index	Date Created	Parent County or Territory From Which Organized Address/Details
Chemung www.chemungcounty.com/	K8	29 Mar 1836	**Tioga** Chemung County; 210 Lake St; PO Box 588; Elmira, NY 14901; Ph. (607) 737-2920 **Details:** (County Clerk has Marriage Records 1908-1936, Divorce, Court & Land Records; Surrogate Court has Probate Records; Town Clerks have Birth, Marriage, & Death Records)
Chenango www.chenango.com/	I7	15 Mar 1798	**Herkimer, Tioga** Chenango County; 5 Court St; Norwich, NY 13815; Ph. (607) 337-4575 **Details:** (County Clerk has Marriage, Divorce, Court & Land Records; Surrogate Court has Probate Records; Town Clerks have Birth, Marriage & Death Records)
Clinton www.co.clinton.ny.us/	E1	7 Mar 1788	**Washington** Clinton County; 137 Margaret St; Plattsburgh, NY 12901; Ph. (518) 565-4700 **Details:** (County Clerk has Divorce Records from 1869, Land Records from 1778 & state Census; Surrogate Court has Probate Records; Town & City Clerks have Birth, Marriage & Death Records)
Columbia www.rootsweb.com/~nycolumb/	E8	4 Apr 1786	**Albany** Columbia County; 560 Warren St.; Hudson, NY 12534; Ph. (518) 828-3339, htanner@govt.co.columbia.ny.us **Details:** (County Clerk has Marriage Records 1908–1934, Court Records from 1825, & Land Records from 1790; Town Clerk has Birth Marriage, & Death Records)
Cortland www2.cortland-co.org/	J7	8 Apr 1808	**Onondaga** Cortland County; 46 Greenbush St; PO Box 5590; Cortland, NY 13045; Ph. (607) 753-5021 **Details:** (County Clerk has Marriage Records 1910–1935, Divorce Records, Court & Land Records from 1808, Naturalization Records 1831–1848 & 1871–1929; Surrogate Court has Probate Records; Town & City Clerks have Birth, Marriage & Death Records)
Delaware www.delawarecounty.net/	H8	10 Mar 1797	**Ulster, Otsego** Delaware County; Courthouse Sq; Delhi, NY 13753-1081; Ph. (607) 746-2123 **Details:** (County Clerk has Marriage Records 1908–1931, Divorce, Court & Land Records from 1797, Naturalization Records from 1810 & state Census; Surrogate Court has Probate Records; Town Clerks have Birth, Marriage, Death & Burial Records)
Dutchess www.dutchessny.gov/	E9	1 Nov 1683	**Original county** Dutchess County; 22 Market St; Poughkeepsie, NY 12601-3233; Ph. (914) 486-2120 **Details:** (County Clerk has Marriage Records 1908–1935, Divorce & Court Records from 1847, Land Records from 1718 & state Census; Surrogate Court has Probate Records; Town & City Clerks have Birth, Marriage & Death Records; County Archives has tax rolls 1854–1954 & colonial Court Records 1730–1799)
Erie www.erie.gov/	P7	2 Apr 1821	**Niagara** Erie County; 25 Delaware Ave; Buffalo, NY 14202-3968; Ph. (716) 858-8785 **Details:** (County Clerk has Marriage Records, Divorce & Court Records from 1809 & Land Records from 1810; Surrogate Court has Probate Records)

County Website	Map Index	Date Created	Parent County or Territory From Which Organized Address/Details
Essex www.rootsweb.com/~nyessex/	**E3**	**1 Mar 1799**	**Clinton** Essex County; 100 Court St; Elizabethtown, NY 12932; Ph. (518) 873-3600 **Details:** (County Clerk has Marriage Records 1908–1936, Divorce Records from 1936, Probate, Court & Land Records from 1799 & state Census; Town & City Clerks have Birth, Marriage, Death & Burial Records)
Franklin www.adirondacklakes.com/	**F2**	**11 Mar 1808**	**Clinton** Franklin County; PO Box 70; Malone, NY 12953; Ph. (518) 481-1671 **Details:** (County Clerk has Marriage Records 1908–1935, some Divorce Records from 1808 & Court Records from 1808; Surrogate Court has Probate Records; Town Clerks have Birth, Marriage & Death Records) *(wrote:There are far too many to detail each & every series. We have all the typical records that most counties have. Our suggestion is to just have researchers give us a call and we can direct their requests as needed. Call about specifics)*
Fulton www.fulton.ny.us/	**F6**	**18 Apr 1838**	**Montgomery** Fulton County; 223 W Main St; Johnstown, NY 12095; Ph. (518) 736-5555 **Details:** (County Clerk has Marriage Records 1900–1926, Land & Court Records; Surrogate Court has Probate Records)
Genesee www.co.genesee.ny.us/	**O6**	**30 Mar 1802**	**Ontario** Genesee County; 15 Main St; Batavia, NY 14020; Ph. (585) 344-2550 ext. 2242 **Details:** (Town/City Clerk has Birth, Death, & Marriage Records from 1880; County Clerk's Office has Land, Civil, & Criminal Records from 1802, Guardianship Records, Census, & Military Records; Surrogate's Court has Probate Records; Real Property Office has Land & Property Records; Chamber of Commerce has Business Records; County Historian has Naturalization & Citizenship Records)
Greene www.greene-ny.com/	**F8**	**25 Mar 1800**	**Ulster, Albany** Greene County; 320 Main St; Catskill, NY 12414-1396; Ph. (518) 943-2050 **Details:** (County Clerk has Marriage Records 1900–1935, Divorce, Court & Land Records from 1800; Surrogate Court has Probate Records; Town Clerks have Birth, Marriage & Death Records)
Hamilton www.hamiltoncounty.com/	**G4**	**12 Apr 1816**	**Montgomery** Hamilton County; RR 8 Box 204; Lake Pleasant, NY 12108; Ph. (518) 548-7111 **Details:** (County Clerk has Divorce, Court & Land Records; Surrogate Court has Probate Records; Town & City Clerks have Birth, Marriage, Death & Burial Records)
Herkimer www.rootsweb.com/~nyherkim/	**H5**	**16 Feb 1791**	**Montgomery** Herkimer County; 109 Mary St; Herkimer, NY 13350; Ph. (315) 867-1002 **Details:** (County Clerk has Marriage Records 1908–1934, Divorce, Court & Land Records; Surrogate Court has Probate Records)

County	Map	Date	Parent County or Territory From Which Organized
Website	Index	Created	Address/Details

Jefferson   J3   **28 Mar 1805**   **Oneida**
www.sunyjefferson.edu/JC/

Jefferson County; 175 Arsenal St; Watertown, NY 13601-2522;
Ph. (315) 785-3081
Details: (County Clerk has Marriage Records 1908–1935, Land & Court Records from 1805, Naturalization Records from early 1800s–1970, Military Discharge Records from 1861 & state Census; Surr Court has Probate Records from early 1800's)

Kings   E12   **1 Nov 1683**   **Original county**
http://community-2.webtv.net/shamrockroots/
kingsny/

Kings County; 360 Adams St; Brooklyn, NY 11201-3712;
Ph. (718) 643-5897
Details: (Department of Health, Brooklyn Borough Office, 295 Flatbush Ave. Extension, Brooklyn, NY 11201 has Birth, Death & Burial Records; City Clerk, Mun. Bldg, Brooklyn, NY 11201 has Marriage Records; County Clerk, Superior Court Bldg, 360 Adams St., Brooklyn, NY 11201 has Divorce Records; Surrogate Court, Superior Court Bldg, 360 Adams St., Brooklyn, NY 11201 has probate records; Clerk Civil Court, 120 Schermerhorn St., Brooklyn NY 11201 has Court Records; County Register, Municipal Building, Joralemon & Court Streets, Brooklyn, NY 11201 has land records)

Lewis   I4   **28 Mar 1805**   **Oneida**
www.adirondacks.org/lewiscounty/

Lewis County; 7660 N State St; Box 232; Lowville, NY 13367-1328;
Ph. (315) 376-5333
Details: (County Clerk has incomplete Birth & Death Records 1847–1852, Divorce & Court Records from 1907, Land Records from 1805, Naturalization Records 1808–1906, Military rolls 1862–1866 & state Census 1825–1925; Surrogate Court has Probate Records)

Livingston   N6   **23 Feb 1821**   **Genesee, Ontario**
www.co.livingston.state.ny.us/

Livingston County; 6 Court St, #201; Genesee, NY 14454;
Ph. (716) 243-7030
Details: (County Clerk has Divorce, Court & Land Records from 1821; Surrogate Court has Probate Records)

Madison   I6   **21 Mar 1806**   **Chenango**
www.madisoncounty.org/

Madison County; N Court St; Wampsville, NY 13163;
Ph. (315) 366-2261
Details: (County Clerk has Marriage Records 1905–1934, Divorce Records from 1900, Court Records from 1889 & Land Records from 1806; Surrogate Court has Probate Records; Town Clerks have Birth, Marriage, Death & Burial Records)

Monroe   N5   **23 Feb 1821**   **Genesee, Ontario**
www.co.monroe.ny.us/

Monroe County; 39 Main St W; Rochester, NY 14614-1408;
Ph. (716) 428-5151
Details: (County Clerk has Marriage Records 1908–1935, Divorce & Court Records from 1860, Land Records from 1821 & Naturalization Records from 1822; Surrogate Court has Probate Records; Town Clerks have Marriage & Burial Records; County Health Department, 111 Westfall Rd., Rochester, NY 14620 has Birth & Death Records; County Historian, 39 Main St. W., Rochester, NY has state census)

County Website	Map Index	Date Created	Parent County or Territory From Which Organized Address/Details
Montgomery www.co.montgomer.ny.us	F6	**12 Mar 1772**	**Albany** Montgomery County; PO Box 1500; Fonda, NY 12068; Ph. (518) 853-4304 **Details:** (Formerly Tryon County. Name changed to Montgomery 2 Apr 1784) (County Clerk has Marriage Records 1908–1935, Assumed business Names & Corporation Papers from 1882, Divorce & Civil Court Records from 1795, Land Records from 1772, State Census, Naturalization Records from 1850, Surveys/Maps; Surrogate Court has Probate & Guardianship Records; History & Archives has Burial/Cemetery Records, State/Federal Census, Court Records from 1772, Military Records, Newspapers, Other Historical & Genealogical Records; Town & City Clerks have Birth, Death, & Marriage Records from 1880)
Nassau www.co.nassau.ny.us/	E12	**27 Apr 1898**	**Queens** Nassau County; 240 Old Country Rd; Mineola, NY 11501; Ph. (516) 571-2663 **Details:** (County Clerk has Marriage Records 1907–1935, Divorce, Court & Land Records from 1899; Surrogate Court has Probate Records; Town Clerks have Birth, Marriage & Death Records)
New York http://home.nyc.gov/portal/ index.jsp?pageID=nyc_home	F12	**1 Nov 1683**	**Original county** New York County; 60 Centre St; New York, NY 10007-1402; Ph. (212) 374-8361 **Details:** (County Clerk has Divorce Records from 1754, Naturalization Records 1794–1924 & state Census; Surrogate Court has Probate Records)
Niagara www.niagaracounty.com/Insight/customindex /NCHome.cfm?SID=2	P6	**11 Mar 1808**	**Genesee** Niagara County; 175 Hawley St; Lockport, NY 14094; Ph. (716) 439-7022 **Details:** (County Clerk has Marriage Records 1908–1935, Divorce Records from 1850, Court & Land Records; Surrogate Court has Probate Records; Town & City Clerks have Birth, Marriage, Death & Burial Records)
Oneida www.oneidacounty.org/	I5	**15 Mar 1798**	**Herkimer** Oneida County; 800 Park Ave; Utica, NY 13501; Ph. (315) 798-5775 **Details:** (County Clerk has Divorce & Court Records, Land Records from 1791; Surr Court has Probate Records; Town Clerks have Birth, Marriage, Death & Burial Records)
Onondaga www.co.onondaga.ny.us/	J6	**5 Mar 1794**	**Herkimer** Onondaga County; 200 Courthouse; Syracuse, NY 13202-2984; Ph. (315) 435-2226 **Details:** (County Clerk has Land, Divorce & Court Records from 1795, Naturalization Records from 1808, state Census 1850–1925 & Military Records from 1917; Surrogate Court has Probate Records; Bureau of Vital Statistics has Birth, Death & Burial Records from 1865; Town & City Clerks have Marriage Records)

County	Map	Date	Parent County or Territory From Which Organized
Website	Index	Created	Address/Details

Ontario M6 **27 Jan 1789** **Montgomery**
www.co.ontario.ny.us/
Ontario County; 20 Ontario St; Canandaigua, NY 14424;
Ph. (716) 396-4200
Details: (Records Management Officer has Marriage Records 1908–1933, Divorce Records from 1887, Probate, Court & Land Records from 1789, Revolutionary War service Records 1820–1832, Military rosters 1862–1920, state Census, County maps from 1798 & Naturalization Records 1803–1954; Town & City Clerks have Birth & Death Records)

Orange F10 **1 Nov 1683** **Original county**
www.co.orange.ny.us/
Orange County; 255-275 Main St; Goshen, NY 10924;
Ph. (845) 291-3000; Orange County Genealogical Society: 101 Main St.; Goshen, NY 10924
Details: (County Clerk has Marriage Records 1908–1933, Divorce & Court Records from 1852, Land Records from 1703 & Census Records; Surrogate Court has Probate Records)

Orleans O5 **12 Nov 1824** **Genesee**
www.orleansny.com/
Orleans County; Courthouse Sq; Albion, NY 14411;
Ph. (716) 589-5334
Details: (County Clerk has Divorce & Court Records from 1880, Land Records from 1826 & state Census; Surrogate Court has Probate Records; Town & City Clerks have Birth, Marriage & Death Records)

Oswego J5 **1 Mar 1816** **Oneida, Onondaga**
www.co.oswego.ny.us/
Oswego County; 46 E Bridge St; Oswego, NY 13126;
Ph. (315) 349-8385
Details: (County Clerk has Marriage Records 1907–1934, some Divorce Records, Court Records, Land Records from 1791 & Military Discharge Records; Records Center has state Census 1850–1925, Naturalization Records 1830's–1950's & some Burial Records; Surrogate Court has Probate Records; City & Town Clerks have Birth & Death Records)

Otsego H7 **16 Feb 1791** **Montgomery**
http://www.otsegocounty.com/
Otsego County; 197 Main St; Cooperstown, NY 13326;
Ph. (607) 547-4276
Details: (County Clerk has Marriage Records 1908–1936, Divorce Records from 1900, Court Records from 1891 & Land Records from 1791; Surrogate Court has Probate Records; Town & City Clerks have Birth, Marriage & Death Records)

Putnam E10 **12 Jun 1812** **Dutchess**
http://putnamcounty@bestweb.net/
Putnam County; 40 Gleneida Ave; Carmel, NY 10512;
Ph. (845) 225-3641
Details: (County Clerk has Divorce Records from 1880, Probate Records, Court Records from 1820 & Land Records from 1814; Town Clerks have Birth, Marriage, Death & Burial Records)

Queens E12 **1 Nov 1683** **Original county**
www.rootsweb.com/~nyqueens/
Queens County; 88-11 Sutphin Blvd; Jamaica, NY 11435-3716;
Ph. (718) 520-3700
Details: (County Clerk has state Census, Divorce Records, Naturalization Records 1794–1941; Surrogate Court has Probate Records; New York City Municipal Archives has Birth, Marriage & Death Records; City Register has Land Records; City of New York has Court Records)

County Website	Map Index	Date Created	Parent County or Territory From Which Organized Address/Details
Rensselaer www.rensco.com/	D7	**7 Feb 1791**	**Albany** Rensselaer County; Courthouse; Troy, NY 12180; Ph. (518) 270-4080 **Details:** (County Clerk has Marriage Records 1908–1930's, Divorce, Court & Land Records from 1791, Naturalization Records from 1830 & maps; Surrogate Court has Probate Records)
Richmond www.rootsweb.com/~nyrichmo/	F12	**1 Nov 1683**	**Original county** Richmond County; 18 Richmond Terr; Staten Island, NY 10301-1935; Ph. (718) 390-5386 **Details:** (Surrogate Court has Probate Records; County Clerk has Land Records; County Health Department has Marriage & Death Records)
Rockland www.co.rockland.ny.us/	F11	**23 Feb 1798**	**Orange** Rockland County; 27 New Hempstead Rd; New City, NY 10956-3636; Ph. (845) 638-5070 **Details:** (County Clerk has Marriage Records 1908–1935, Divorce, Court & Land Records; Surrogate Court has Probate Records)
Saratoga www.co.saratoga.ny.us/	E6	**7 Feb 1791**	**Albany** Saratoga County; 40 McMasters St; Ballston Spa, NY 12020-1999; Ph. (518) 885-2213 **Details:** (County Clerk has Marriage Records 1908–1935, Divorce, Court & Land Records from 1791; Surrogate Court has Probate Records)
Schenectady http://govt.co.schenectady.ny.us/	F6	**7 Mar 1809**	**Albany** Schenectady County; 620 State St; Schenectady, NY 12305-2113; Ph. (518) 388-4220 **Details:** (County Clerk has Marriage Records 1908–1930, Divorce & Court Records from 1858, Land Records & maps from 1630, city directories; Surrogate Court has Probate Records)
Schoharie www.schopeg.org/schcnet/govt/cntygovm.html	F7	**6 Apr 1795**	**Albany, Otsego** Schoharie County; 300 Main St; PO Box 549; Schoharie, NY 12157-0549; Ph. (518) 295-8316 **Details:** (County Clerk has Divorce, Court & Land Records; Surrogate Court has Probate Records; Town Clerks have Birth, Marriage & Death Records)
Schuyler www.lightlink.com/schco/	L8	**17 Apr 1854**	**Tompkins, Steuben, Chemung** Schuyler County; 105 9th St; Watkins Glen, NY 14891; Ph. (607) 535-8133 **Details:** (County Clerk has Divorce, Court & Land Records from 1854 & state Census; Surrogate Court has Probate Records; Town Clerks have Birth, Marriage, Death & Burial Records)
Seneca www.co.seneca.ny.us/	L6	**24 Mar 1804**	**Cayuga** Seneca County; 1 DiPronio Dr; Waterloo, NY 13165; Ph. (315) 539-1770 **Details:** (County Seat is Waterloo; Court is held at Waterloo & Ovid; no Records kept at Ovid; County Clerk has Divorce & Court Records from 1900 & Land Records from 1804; Surrogate Court has Probate Records; Town & City Clerks have Birth, Marriage, Death & Burial Records)

County Website	Map Index	Date Created	Parent County or Territory From Which Organized Address/Details
St. Lawrence www.st-lawrence.ny.us/	H2	3 Mar 1802	**Clinton, Herkimer, Montgomery** St. Lawrence County; 48 Court St; Canton, NY 13617; Ph. (315) 379-2237 **Details:** (County Clerk has Divorce, Court & Land Records from 1802; Surrogate Court has Probate Records; Town Clerks have Birth, Marriage & Death Records)
Steuben www.steubencony.org/	M8	18 Mar 1796	**Ontario** Steuben County; 3 Pulteney Sq; Bath, NY 14810; Ph. (607) 776-9631 **Details:** (County Clerk has Marriage Records 1908–1936, Divorce & Court Records from 1840, Land Records from 1796 & state Census; Surrogate Court has Probate Records; Town & City Clerks have Birth, Marriage & Death Records)
Suffolk www.co.suffolk.ny.us/	D12	1 Nov 1683	**Original county** Suffolk County; 310 Center Dr; Riverhead, NY 11901; Ph. (631) 852-2001 **Details:** (County Clerk has incomplete Birth & Death Records 1847–1849, Marriage Records 1847–1849 & 1908–1935, Court Records from 1725, Land Records from 1666, session Court minutes 1669–1687 & jury lists 1820–1872; Surrogate Court has Probate Records; Town & City Clerks have Birth, Marriage, Death & Burial Records)
Sullivan www.co.sullivan.ny.us/index.asp	G9	27 Mar 1809	**Ulster** Sullivan County; 100 North St; Monticello, NY 12701-1160; Ph. (845) 794-3000 **Details:** (County Clerk has Marriage Records 1908–1933, Divorce Records from 1885 & Land Records from 1809; Surrogate Court has Probate & Court Records; Town Clerks have Birth, Marriage & Death Records)
Tioga www.rootsweb.com/~nytioga/	K8	16 Feb 1791	**Montgomery** Tioga County; 16 Court St; Owego, NY 13827-1515; Ph. (607) 687-8660 **Details:** (County Clerk has Marriage Records 1902–1926, Divorce, Court & Land Records from 1791; Surrogate Court has Probate Records; Town Clerks have Birth, Marriage & Death Records)
Tompkins www.co.tompkins.ny.us/	K7	7 Apr 1817	**Cayuga, Seneca** Tompkins County; 320 N Tioga St; Ithaca, NY 14850; Ph. (607) 274-5431 **Details:** (County Clerk has Marriage Records 1908–1934, Divorce, Court & Land Records from 1817; Surrogate Court has Probate Records from 1817; County Health Department has Birth & Death Records)
Tryon www.rootsweb.com/~nytryon/		12 Mar 1772	**Albany** Tryon County; NY; **Details:** (see Montgomery) Name changed to Montgomery 2 Apr 1784
Ulster www.ulster.ny.us	F9	1 Nov 1683	**Original county** Ulster County; 240 Fair St; PO Box 1800; Kingston, NY 12402; Ph. (845) 340-3288; Ulster County Archives; 300 Foxhall Ave; Kingston, NY 12401 **Details:** (County Clerk has Federal & State Census 1850–1925, Court Records from 1661, Death Records, Divorce Records, Deeds from 1685, Maps from 1746, Naturalization Records 1800–1992; County Treasurer has Tax Records from 1849; Town Clerks have Birth, Death, & Marriage Records; Surrogate Court has Probate Records)

County Website	Map Index	Date Created	Parent County or Territory From Which Organized Address/Details
Warren www.rootsweb.com/~nywarren/	E5	**12 Mar 1813**	**Washington** Warren County; Municipal Center; Lake George, NY 12845; Ph. (518) 761-6429 **Details:** (County Clerk has Divorce Records from 1918, Court & Land Records from 1813, Military Records from 1862, Naturalization Records from 1856 & state Census; Surrogate Court has Probate Records; Town & City Clerks have Birth, Marriage & Death Records)
Washington www.washingtoncounty.org/	D5	**12 Mar 1772**	**Albany** Washington County; Upper Broadway; Fort Edward, NY 12828; Ph. (518) 747-3374 **Details:** (Formerly Charlotte County. Name changed to Washington 2 Apr 1784) (County Clerk-Archives has Birth & Death Records 1847–1849, Marriage Records 1908–1935, state Census 1825–1925, Probate Records 1786–1955, Military pensions 1820–1831, Court Records from 1773 & Naturalization Records 1794–1952; County Clerk has Land Records from 1762 & divorce records from 1918; Town Clerks have birth, marriage & death records from 1881; History Office has burial records to 1995 & military records)
Wayne www.co.wayne.ny.us	L6	**11 Apr 1823**	**Ontario, Seneca** Wayne County; 26 Church St.; Lyons, NY 14489; Ph. (315) 946-5400 **Details:** (Town Clerk has Birth, Death, & Marriage records from 1870, and Burial Records; County Clerk has census records of 1892, 1905, 1915, & 1925; County Historian has other Census Records; County Clerk also has Civil, Criminal, Divorce, & Guardianship Records, Land Records from 1794, Military Discharge Records from 1918, Naturalization Records from 1836–1927, & Marriage Records from 1907–1934)
Westchester www.co.westchester.ny.us/	E10	**1 Nov 1683**	**Original county** Westchester County; 110 Dr Martin Luther King Jr Blvd; White Plains, NY 10601-2504; Ph. (914) 285-3080 **Details:** (County Clerk has Probate Records from 1896, Divorce & Court Records; County Archives has Probate Records to 1895, Land Records, Naturalization Records from 1808, Military Discharge Records & maps from 1776; Town Clerks have Birth, Marriage & Death Records)
Wyoming www.wyomingco.com/	7	**19 May 1841**	**Genesee** Wyoming County; 143 N Main St; Warsaw, NY 14569-1123; Ph. (716) 786-8810 **Details:** (County Clerk has Divorce, Court & Land Records from 1841 & state Census; Surrogate Court has Probate Records; Town Clerks have Birth, Marriage & Death Records)
Yates www.yatesny.com/	L7	**5 Feb 1823**	**Ontario** Yates County; 417 Liberty St Ste 1107; Penn Yan, NY 14527; Ph. (315) 536-5120 **Details:** (Town Clerk has Birth Records from 1908; Surrogate Court has Probate Court Records from 1823; County Clerk has Land, Court, & Naturalization Records from 1823)

North Carolina

Capital: Raleigh

State: 1789 (12th)

To be rather than to seem

Sir Walter Raleigh received a grant from Queen Elizabeth in 1584, which he used to colonize North Carolina. Raleigh's first expedition in 1584 produced glowing reports of Roanoke Island. These reports led to attempts to establish a permanent colony in 1585. Internal and external problems led the settlers to return to England the following year with Sir Francis Drake. In 1587, another group was sent, headed by John White. He returned to England later in the year in desperate need of supplies. It took him three years to return, at which time the settlement had vanished, with only carvings on trees as evidence of inhabitance.

The first permanent settlement was started in 1653, when groups from Virginia occupied the section north of the Albemarle Sound. North Carolina was first differentiated from South Carolina in 1691, but was ruled by governors from South Carolina until 1711. From 1706 to 1725, French Huguenot, German, and Swiss settlers founded towns near the coast. Between 1730 and 1770, with the heaviest influx around 1746, Scottish Highlanders came to North Carolina. Large groups of Scotch-Irish left Pennsylvania via the Shenandoah Valley to settle in Virginia. Many continued on to North Carolina. They settled mostly in the western section of the state around present-day Iredell County and numbered 20,000 in just a few years. By 1760, Germans in Forsyth and Guilford counties numbered 15,000. A colony of English speaking Quakers from Virginia, Pennsylvania, and Nantucket settled in Rockingham, Guilford, and Chatham Counties.

North Carolina was active in the Revolutionary War. But when the convention met on July 21, 1788, to consider a newly drafted Constitution, the document found little favor and was not ratified. As the new United States government was formed, North Carolina was left out as an independent nation. The situation was apparently not acceptable to residents and the Constitution was ratified the following year, making North Carolina the 12th state.

On achieving statehood, North Carolina ceded Tennessee to the United States. By 1850, a quarter of native North Carolinians had left to live in other states or territories. North Carolina seceded from the Union in 1861. It provided the most troops of any state to the Confederacy, an estimated 125,000. North Carolina also had the most casualties, as more than 40,000 were killed. Union forces received more than 3,000 soldiers from North Carolina. North Carolina was readmitted to the Union in 1868. Between 1862 and 1907, 24 counties in southern and western North Carolina lost many records to fire or war.

Look for vital records in the following locations:

Note: Most genealogical county records up to about 1910 can be located in the North Carolina State Archives, Raleigh, North Carolina.

- **Birth and death records:** Counties where births and deaths occurred kept duplicate copies of information sent to the state. None of the parish registers containing records of births or deaths prior to 1820 have survived. North Carolina Vital Records in Raleigh has birth records from October 1913, and death records from 1 January 1930. Death records from 1913 through 1929 are available from the Archives and Records Section, State Records Center in Raleigh.

- **Marriage records:** After 1741, prior to marriage, one had the choice of publishing banns or buying a license, which required posting of a bond. Surviving marriage bonds, except for Granville and Davie counties, are in the North Carolina State Archives. They contain the names of the groom, the bride, the other bondsman, and the witness. None of the marriage records from before 1820 have survived. North Carolina Vital Records in Raleigh has marriage records from January 1962.

- **Land and census records:** Although many early land grants have been lost, there are still many at the Land Office in Raleigh, North Carolina. They are also on microfilm at the State Archives. Many of these records have been transcribed and indexed by the Alvaretta Kenan Register in the book ®*State Censuses of North Carolina, 1784–1787*, published by

Genealogical Publishing Company, 1973. In 1784, the U.S. Continental Congress demanded a list of inhabitants. The surviving lists have been indexed and published.

North Carolina Vital Records
1903 Mail Service Center
Raleigh, North Carolina 27699-1903
(919) 733-3526
http://vitalrecords.dhhs.state.nc.us/vr/index.html

Office of Archives and History
109 E. Jones St.
Raleigh, North Carolina 27601
Mail to: 4610 Mail Service Center
Raleigh, North Carolina 27699-4610
(919) 807-7280; Fax: (919) 733-8807
www.ah.dcr.state.nc.us/

Land Office, Secretary of State
Administration Building
Raleigh, North Carolina 27603

Societies and Repositories

Alamance Battleground Chapter; 804 West Davis Street; Burlington, NC 27215; (336) 228-0766.

Alamance County, North Carolina Genealogical Society; PO Box 3052; Burlington, NC 27215-3052.

Alexander County Ancestry Association; PO Box 241; Hiddenite, NC 28636-0241; www.Alexnews.com.

Alexander County Genealogical Society, Inc; PO Box 545; Hiddenite, NC 28636.

Alleghany Historical-Genealogical Society; Box 817; Sparta, NC 28675.

Anson County Genealogical Society; 108 Sunset Drive 300 Moores Lake Road; Wadesboro, NC 28170; scbailey55@hotmail.com.

Ashe County Historical Society; 148 Library Dr.; West Jefferson, NC 28694; (336) 246-2041; caromwil@skybest.com.

Beaufort County Genealogical Society; PO Box 1089; Washington, NC 27889-1089.

Bethabara Chapter; PO Box 5442; Winston-Salem, NC 27104; (336) 472-2757; foot@netunlimited.net.

Bladen County Historical Society; PO Box 849; Elizabethtown, NC 28337.

Blue Ridge Chapter, Sons of the American Revolution; 337 Vanderbilt Road; Asheville, NC 28803; (828) 274-3169.

Broad River Genealogical Society; PO Box 2261; Shelby, NC 28151-2261.

Burke County Genealogical Society; PO Box 661; Morganton, NC 28655; www.rootsweb.com/~ncburke.

Cabarrus Genealogical Society; PO Box 2981; Concord, NC 28025-2981; cabgensoc@webkorner.com; www.rootsweb.com/~nccgs/index.htm.

Caldwell County Genealogical Society; Box 2476; Lenior, NC 28645-2476.

Carolinas Genealogical Society; PO Box 397; Monroe, NC 28111-0397.

Carteret County Historical Society/The History Place; Jack Spencer Goodwin Library; 1008 Arendell Street; Morehead City, NC 28557; (252) 247-7533; historyplace@starfishnet.com; www.thehistoryplace.org.

Caswell County Historical Association; PO Box 278; Yanceyville, NC 27379.

Catawba County Genealogical Society; PO Box 2406; Hickory, NC 28603; www.co.catawba.nc.us/otheragency/ccgs/ccgsmain.htm.

Catawba Valley Chapter, Sons of the American Revolution; 165 Lakeshore Lane; Taylorsville, NC 28681; (704) 495-4402.

Chatham County Historical Association; PO Box 913; Pittsboro, NC 27312-0913.

Cumberland County Genealogical Society; PO Box 53299; Fayetteville, NC 28305-3299.

Davie County Historical & Genealogical Society; 371 N. Main St.; Mocksville, NC 27038.

Descendants of The Knights of The Bath, North Carolina Society; 1404 Shadyside Dr.; Raleigh, NC 27612.

Duplin County Historical Society; PO Box 220; Rose Hill, NC 28458-0220; www.duplinnet.com/historicalsociety/index.htm.

Durham-Orange Genealogical Society; PO Box 4703; Chapel Hill, NC 27515-4703; ncdogs-admin@rootsweb.com; www.rootsweb.com/~ncdogs.

Eastern North Carolina Genealogical Society; PO Box 395; New Bern, NC 28560.

Edgecombe County Genealogical Society; 909 Main St.; Tarboro, NC 27886.

Family Research Society of Northeastern North Carolina; 106 S. McMorrine St., Suite 6; Elizabeth City, NC 27909-4449; www.geocities.com/heartland/farm/7890.

Federation of North Carolina Historical Societies; 4610 Mail Service Center; Raleigh, NC 27699-4610; (919) 733-7305; tracy.brown@ncmail.net; www.ah.dcr.state.nc.us/affiliates/fnchs/fnchs.htm.

Forsyth County Genealogical Society; Box 5715; Winston-Salem, NC 27113-5715; ccasey@netunlimited.net; www.usgennet.org/alhnncus/ahncfors.

Gaston/Lincoln Genealogical Society; PO Box 584; Mount Holly, NC 28120.

Gates County Historical Society; PO Box 98; Gates, NC 27937.

Genealogical Society of Davidson County; PO Box 1665; Lexington, NC 27292-1665.

Genealogical Society of Iredell County; PO Box 946; Statesville, NC 28677.

Genealogical Society of Rowan County; PO Box 4305; Salisbury, NC 28145-4305.

Genealogical Society of Watauga County; PO Box 126; Boone, NC 28607.

General Francis Nash Chapter, Sons of the American Revolution; 13 Clearwater Drive; Durham, NC 27707; (919) 403-1998; RStevens@stevensmarketing.com.

Granville County Genealogical Society, Inc.; PO Box 1746; Oxford, NC 27565-1746; currin5@gte.net.

Guilford County Genealogical Society; PO Box 9693; Greensboro, NC 27429-0693; w1hlp@aol.com; www.greensboro.com/gcgs.

Halifax County Genealogical Society; PO Box 447; Halifax, NC 27839.

Harnett County Genealogical Society; PO Box 219; Buies Creek, NC 27506-0219.

Haywood County Genealogical Society, Inc.; PO Box 1331; Waynesville, NC 28786-1331; hcgs_nc@yahoo.com; www.rootsweb.com/~nchcgs.

Henderson County Genealogical & Historical Society; 400 North Main Street; Hendersonville, NC 28739; (828) 693-1531; hcgenhis@brinet.com; www.brinet.com/~hcgenhis.

Historic Foundation of the Presbyterian and Reformed Churches; Montreat, NC 28757.

Hyde County Historical & Genealogical Society; 7820 Piney Woods Rd; Fairfield, NC 27826; www.rootsweb.com/~nchyde/HCHGS.HTM.

Independent Order of Odd Fellows, Sovereign Grand Lodge; I.O.O.F.; 422 North Trade St.; Winston-Salem, NC 27101-2830.

Jackson County Genealogical Society; PO Box 2108; Cullowee, NC 28723; www.main.nc.us/jcgs.

Jewish Genealogical Society of Raleigh; 8701 Sleepy Creek Dr.; Raleigh, NC 27612.

Johnston County Genealogical Society; PO Box 2373; Smithfield, NC 27577-2373.

Kinfolk Trackers Genealogical Society; PO Box 1344; New Bern, NC 28563-1344.

Kinfolk Trackers; 8375 HWY 306 South; Arapahoe, NC 28510; cn1197@coastalnet.com; www2.always-online.com/kintracker.

Lee County Genealogical Society; PO Box 3216; Sanford, NC 27331-3216; alvis@clegg.com.

Lower Cape Fear Chapter, Sons of the American Revolution; 900 Seven Oaks Drive; Wilmington, NC 28405; (910) 686-9914; mog@qson.net.

Lt. Col. Felix Walker Chapter, Sons of the American Revolution; 25 Monte Vista Circle; Candler, NC 28715; (828) 665-1887; RWalker96@aol.com.

Lt. Col. John Phifer Chapter, Sons of the American Revolution; 692 Williamsburg Court; Concord, NC 28025-2538; (704) 788-2697; docrandy@prodigy.net.

Marquis de Lafayette Chapter, Sons of the American Revolution; 5360 Amberhill Court; Fayetteville, NC 28311; (910) 482-3991; Joe.Harris@mciworldcom.ne.

Mecklenburg Chapter, Sons of the American Revolution; 9125 B-1 Fishers Pond Drive; Charlotte, NC 28277; (704) 541-0881.

Mecklenburg, North Carolina Genealogical Society; PO Box 32453; Charlotte, NC 28232; omgs002@ibm.net; www.rootsweb.com/~ncomgs/.

Moore County Genealogical Society; PO Box 1183; Pinehurst, NC 28370-1183.

Nathanael Greene Chapter, Sons of the American Revolution; 1106 Gretchen Lane; Greensboro, NC 27410; (336) 292-4690; rebadj@aol.com.

New Bern Chapter, Sons of the American Revolution; 812 Plantation Drive; New Bern, NC 28562; (252) 633-3450; hgnewbern@coastalnet.com.

North Carolina Genealogical Society of Rockingham and Stokes Counties; PO Box 152; Mayodan, NC 27027-0152; DiginRoots@aol.com; http://ns.netmcr.com/~lonabec/gsrsinfo.html.

North Carolina Genealogical Society; PO Box 1492; Raleigh, NC 27602; www.rootsweb.com/~ncgs.

North Carolina Office of Archives and History; 4610 Mail Service Center; Raleigh, NC 27699-4610; (919) 733-7305; ahweb@ncmail.net; www.ah.dcr.state.nc.us.

North Carolina Society of County and Local Historians; 1209 Hill St.; Greensboro, NC 27408.

Old Buncombe County Genealogical Society; PO Box 2122; 85 Tunnel Rd.; Asheville, NC 28802-2122; (828) 253-1894; obcgs@buncombe.main.nc.us; www.obcgs.com.

Old Dobbs County Genealogical Society; PO Box 617; Goldsboro, NC 27530.

Old New Hanover County Genealogical Society; PO Box 2536; Wilmington, NC 28402-2536; cweiss4042@aol.co; www.co.new-hanover.nc.us/lib/oldnew.htm.

Old Tryon County Genealogical Society; Box 938; Forest City, NC 28043.

Olde Mecklenburg Genealogical Society; PO Box 32453; Charlotte, NC 28232-2453; omgs002@ibm.net; www.rootsweb.com/~ncomgs.

Onslow County Genealogical Society; PO Box 1421; Swansboro, NC 28584-1421.

PAF-Finders Club; 8501 Southampton Dr.; Raleigh, NC 27615.

Pitt County Family Researchers; PO Box 20339; Greenville, NC 27858-0339; wbk99@earthlink.net; www.rootsweb.com/~ncpcfr.

Raleigh Chapter, Sons of the American Revolution; 2108 Weybridge Dr.; Raleigh, NC 27615; (919) 954-9956; Hector26@aol.com.

Randolph County Genealogical Society; PO Box 4394; Asheboro, NC 27204; www.rootsweb.com/~ncrcgs.

Rockingham County Historical Society; PO Box 84; Wentworth, NC 27375.

Salisbury Chapter, Sons of the American Revolution; 114 Ridge Creek Road; Salisbury, NC 28147; (704) 639-9845; fgradyhall@msn.com.

Scotland County Genealogical Society, Inc.; PO Box 496; Laurel Hill, NC 28351-0496; www.txdirect.net/~hpeele/society/scgs.htm.

Society of Richmond County Descendants; PO Box 848, Desk 120; Rockingham, NC 28379.

Sons of the American Revolution, North Carolina Society; 2221 Oleander Dr.; Wilmington, NC 28403.

Southeastern North Carolina Genealogical Society; PO Box 468; Chadbourn, NC 28431-0468; tclaw@mailcity.com; www.spiritdesign.net/columbus/sencgs.htm.

Southport Historical Society; 501 N. Atlantic Ave.; Southport, NC 28461.

Stanley County Genealogical Society; Box 31; Albemarle, NC 28001.

State Library of North Carolina; 109 E. Jones Street; 4640 Mail Service Center; Raleigh, NC 27699-4640; (919) 733-2570; statelibrary.dcr.state.nc.us.

Surry County Genealogical Society; Box 997; Dobson, NC 27017-0997.

Swain County, North Carolina Genealogical and Historical Society; PO Box 267; Bryson City, NC 28713.

Tar River Connections Genealogical Society; PO Box 8764; Rocky Mount, NC 27803-8764; turn1104@aol.com; http://necn.ncwc.edu/TRCGS/TRCHP.HTML

Toe Valley Genealogical Society; 491 Beaver Creek Road; Spruce Pine, NC 28777.

Wake County Genealogical Society; PO Box 17713; Raleigh, NC 27619-7713; wcgs@pobox.com; www.rootsweb.com/~ncwcgs.

Wayne County Historical Association; PO Box 665; Goldsboro, NC 27530.

Wilkes Genealogical Society, Inc.; PO Box 1629; North Wilkesboro, NC 28659; http://users.erols.com/fmoran/wilkgen/wilkgen.html.

Wilson County Genealogical Society; PO Box 802; Wilson, NC 27894-0802; ancestor@coastalnet.com; www.wcgs.org.

Yadkin County Historical Society; PO Box 1250; Yadkinville, NC 27055.

Bibliography and Record Sources

General

Anscombe, Francis Charles. *I Called You Friends: The Story of Quakerism in North Carolina.* Boston: Christopher Pub. House, 1959.

Ashe, Samuel A'Court. *Biographical History of North Carolina from Colonial Times to the Present.* 9 vols. Greensboro, North Carolina: C. L. Van Noppen, 1905–1917.

Ball, Bonnie S. *The Melungeons: Their Origin and Kin.* 6th ed. Berryville, Virginia: Virginia Book Co., 1977, 1969.

Bassett, John Spencer. *Slavery in the State of North Carolina.* New York: AMS Press, 1972.

Bernheim, Gotthardt D. *History of the German Settlements and of the Lutheran Church in North and South Carolina.* (1872) Reprint. Baltimore: Clearfield Co., 1996.

Bible, Jean P. *Melungeons—Yesterday and Today.* Signal Mountain, Tennessee: Mountain Press, 1975.

Biographical History of North Carolina from Colonial Times to the Present. vols. 1–8, 10. Greensboro, North Carolina: Charles L. Van Noppen, 1905–1917.

Blosser, Susan Sokol. *The Southern Historical Collection: A Guide to Manuscripts.* Chapel Hill, North Carolina: University of North Carolina Library, 1970.

Broadfoot Publishing. *The Colonial and State Records of North Carolina.* 30 vols. Wilmington, North Carolina: Broadfoot Publishing, 1996.

Bumgarner, George W. *Methodist Episcopal Church in North Carolina, 1865–1939.* Winston-Salem, North Carolina: Hunter Publishing, 1990.

Butler and Watson, eds. *The North Carolina Experience: An Interpretive and Documentary History.* Galveston, Texas: Frontier Press, 1984.

Cain, Barbara T. *Guide to Private Manuscript Collections in the North Carolina State Archives.* 3rd rev. ed. Raleigh: North Carolina Department of Cultural Resources, Division of Archives and History, 1981.

Cain, Barbara T., with Ellen Z. McGrew and Charles E. Morris. *Guide to Private Manuscript Collections in the North Carolina State Archives.* Raleigh, North Carolina: North Carolina Division of Archives and History, 1993.

Cain, Robert J., ed. *Colonial Records of North Carolina [Second Series], Volume IX: Records of the Executive Council, 1755–1775.* Raleigh, North Carolina: North Carolina Division of Archives and History, 1994.

Cain, Robert J., ed. *Colonial Records of North Carolina [Second Series], Volume VI: North Carolina Higher-Court Minutes, 1724–1730.* Raleigh, North Carolina: North Carolina Division of Archives and History, 1981.

Cain, Robert J., ed. *Colonial Records of North Carolina [Second Series], Volume VII: Records of the Executive Council, 1664–1734.* Raleigh, North Carolina: North Carolina Division of Archives and History, 1984.

Cain, Robert J., ed. *Colonial Records of North Carolina [Second Series], Volume VIII: Records of the Executive Council, 1735–1754.* Raleigh, North Carolina. North Carolina Division of Archives and History, 1988.

Chreitzberg, A. M. *Early Methodism in the Carolinas.* Spartanburg, South Carolina: The Reprint Company, 1972.

Colonial Records of North Carolina [Second Series], Volume II: North Carolina Higher-Court Records, 1670–1696. Raleigh, North Carolina: North Carolina Division of Archives and History. Microfilm.

Corbitt, David Leroy. *The Formation of the North Carolina Counties, 1663–1943.* Raleigh, North Carolina: North Carolina Division of Archives and History, 1996.

Crittenden, Charles Christopher. *The Historical Records of North Carolina.* 3 vols. Raleigh, North Carolina: North Carolina Historical Commission, 1938–1939.

Crow, Jeffery J., Paul D. Escott, and Flora J. Hatley. *A History of African Americans in North Carolina.* Raleigh, North Carolina: North Carolina Division of Archives and History, 1994.

DeMond, Robert O. *The Loyalists in North Carolina.* Baltimore, Maryland: Clearfield Co., Inc., 2002.

Dobson, David. *Directory of Scots in the Carolinas, 1680–1830.* (1986) Reprint. Baltimore: Genealogical Publishing Co., 1994.

Draper, L. C. *King's Mountain and Its Heroes: History of the Battle of King's Mountain, October 7th, 1780.* (1881) Reprint. Baltimore: Genealogical Publishing Co., 1993.

Draughon, Wallace R. *North Carolina Genealogical Reference: A Research Guide for All Genealogists, Both Amateur and Professional.* 2nd ed. Durham, North Carolina: Smith Publishing, 1966.

Early North Carolina settlers, 1700s–1900s. S.l.: Brøderbund, 2000. CD-ROM.

Elliott, Wendy L. *Guide to Genealogical Research in North Carolina.* S.l.: W. L. Elliott, 1988.

Emory, Frank. *Paths Toward Freedom: A Biographical History of Blacks and Indians in North Carolina.* Raleigh, North Carolina: Center for Urban Affairs, North Carolina State University, 1976.

Family History Library. *Research Outline; North Carolina.* Salt Lake City: Family History Library.

Fisher, P. W. *One Dozen Pre-Revolutionary Families of Eastern North Carolina and Some of Their Descendants.* (1958) Reprint. Salem, Massachusetts: Higginson Book Co., 1995.

Foote, William Henry. *Sketches of North Carolina, Historical and Biographical, Illustrative of the Principles of a Portion of Her Early Settlers.* New York: Robert Carter, 1846.

Guide to Research Materials in the North Carolina State Archives: State Agency Records. Raleigh, North Carolina: North Carolina Division of Archives and History, 1995.

Hamrick, David O. *Index to the North Carolina Historical and Genealogical Register (Hathaway's Register),* 3 vols. Athens, Georgia: Iberian Publishing Co., 1983.

Hathaway, James Robert Bent. *The North Carolina Historical and Genealogical Register.* Baltimore, Maryland: Clearfield Co., Inc., 2002.

Hehir, Donald M. *Carolina Families: A Bibliography of Books About North and South Carolina Families.* Bowie, Maryland: Heritage Books, 1994.

Henry, Linda Simmons. *The Heritage of Blacks in North Carolina.* Charlotte, North Carolina: North Carolina African-American Heritage Foundation, 1990.

Hickey, Damon D. *Sojourners No More: The Quakers in the New South, 1865–1920.* Greensboro, North Carolina: North Carolina Friends Historical Society: North Carolina Yearly Meeting of Friends, 1997.

Hinshaw, Seth B. *Quaker Women of Carolina: Freedom—Achievement.* North Carolina: United Society of Friends Women, 1994.

Hinshaw, William Wade. *Index to Encyclopedia of American Quaker Genealogy by William Wade Hinshaw.* S.l.: Genealogical Pub. Co., 1999.

Historical Records Survey (North Carolina). *Guide to the Manuscripts in the Archives of the Moravian Church in America, Southern Province.* Raleigh, North Carolina: Historical Records Survey, 1942.

Historical Records Survey (North Carolina). *Guide to the Manuscripts in the Southern Historical Collection of the University of North Carolina.* Chapel Hill: University of North Carolina Press, 1941.

Hofmann, Margaret M. *An Intermediate Short, Short Course in the Use of Some North Carolina Records in Genealogical Research.* The author, 1992.

Hunter, C. L. *Sketches of Western North Carolina.* (1877) Reprint. Baltimore: Genealogical Publishing, 1992.

Inventory of the State Archives of North Carolina. 4 vols. Raleigh, North Carolina: North Carolina Historical Records Survey Project, 1939–1941.

Jones, H. G., and Julius H. Avant. *Union List of North Carolina Newspapers, 1751–1900.* Raleigh: State Department of Archives and History, 1963.

Jones, Roger C., comp., *Guide to North Carolina Newspapers on Microfilm: Titles Available from the Division of Archives and History.* 6th ed. rev. Raleigh: Division of Archives and History, 1984.

Kent, Scotti. *More Than Petticoats: Remarkable North Carolina Women.* Helena, Montana: Falcon, 2000.

Lawson, John. *Lawson's History of North Carolina: Containing the Exact Description and Natural History of that Country, Together with the Present State Thereof and a Journal of a Thousand Miles Traveled through Several Nations of Indians, Giving a Particular Account of their Customs, Manners, Etc., Etc.* Richmond: Garrett and Massie, 1937.

Lawson. *A New Voyage to Carolina.* (1709) Reprint. Galveston, Texas: Frontier Press, 1967.

Leary, Helen F. M., ed. *North Carolina Research.* 2nd ed. Raleigh, North Carolina: North Carolina Genealogical Society, 1996.

Leffer, Hugh Talmage. *History of North Carolina.* 4 vols., New York: Lewis Historical Pub. Co., [1956].

London, Lawrence Foushee. *The Episcopal Church In North Carolina, 1701–1959.* Raleigh, North Carolina: Episcopal Diocese of North Carolina, 1987.

McCubbins, Mamie. *McCubbins Collection.* Microfilm of original and typescript in the Rowan County Public Library at Salisbury, North Carolina. Salt Lake City: Filmed by the Genealogical Society of Utah, 1956. 76 microfilm.

Mooney, Thomas G. *Exploring Your Cherokee Ancestry: A Basic Genealogical Research Guide.* Tahlequah, Oklahoma: Cherokee National Historical Society, Inc., 1990.

Moore, M. H. *Sketches of the Pioneers of Methodism in North Carolina and Virginia.* Nashville, Tennessee: Southern Methodist Publishing House, 1884.

North Carolina Freedmen's Records. North Carolina Genealogical Society.

North Carolina Office of Archives and History. *Guide to Newspapers on Microfilm in the North Carolina State Archives.* Raleigh, North Carolina: North Carolina Office of Archives and History, 2002. Online guide: http://statelibrary.dcr.state.nc.us/ncnp/intro.htm.

North Carolina, Division of Archives and History. *Guide to Research Materials in the North Carolina State Archives. Section B: County Records.* 10th rev. ed. Raleigh: Department of Cultural Resources, Division of Archives and History, 1988.

North Carolina. Division of Archives and History. Archives and Records Section. *Guide to Research Materials in the North Carolina State Archives: State Agency Records.* Raleigh, North Carolina: North Carolina Division of Archives and History, 1995.

North Carolina. Division of Archives and History. Department of Cultural Resources. *Guide to North Carolina Newspapers on Microfilm: Titles Available from the Division of Archives and History.* Raleigh, North Carolina: Division of Archives and History, 1984.

Ormond, Jesse Marvin. *The Country Church in North Carolina: A Study of the Country Churches of North Carolina in Relation to the Material Progress of the State.* Durham, North Carolina: Duke University Press, 1931.

Paschal, George Washington. *History of the North Carolina Baptists.* 2 vols. Gallatin, Tennessee: Church History Research & Archives, 1990.

Powell, William S. *Dictionary of North Carolina Biography.* 6 vols. Chapel Hill, North Carolina: University of North Carolina Press, 1979–.

Powell, William S. *North Carolina through Four Centuries.* Galveston, Texas: Frontier Press, 1989.

Powell, William Stevens. *Dictionary of North Carolina Biography.* 6 vols. Chapel Hill, North Carolina: University of North Carolina Press, 1996.

Powell, William Stevens. *North Carolina Lives: The Tar Heel Who's Who: A Reference Edition Recording the Biographies of Contemporary Leaders in North Carolina with Special Emphasis on their Achievements in Making It One of America's Greatest States.* Hopkinsville, Kentucky: Historical Record Association, 1962.

Protestant Episcopal Church (North Carolina). *History of the Protestant Episcopal Church in North Carolina. Microfilm of Original and Typescript at the State Archives in Raleigh, North Carolina.* Raleigh: North Carolina Department of Archives and History, 1961.

Ramsey. *Carolina Cradle: Settlement of the Northwest Carolina Frontier, 1747–1762.* Galveston, Texas: Frontier Press, 1987.

Ray, Worth S. *Index and Digest to Hathaway's North Carolina Historical and Genealogical Register.* Baltimore, Maryland: Clearfield Co., Inc., 2002.

Ray, Worth S. *Lost Tribes of North Carolina, Part I: Index and Digest to Hathaway's North Carolina Historical and Genealogical Register.* (1945) Reprint. Baltimore: Clearfield Co., 1997.

Ray, Worth S. *Lost Tribes of North Carolina, Part II: Colonial Granville County [North Carolina] and Its People.* (1945) Reprint. Baltimore: Clearfield Co., 1996.

Ray, Worth S. *Lost Tribes of North Carolina, Part III: The Mecklenburg Signers and Their Neighbors.* (1946) Reprint. Baltimore: Clearfield Co., 1995.

Ray, Worth S. *Lost Tribes of North Carolina. Part IV: Old Albemarle and Its Absentee Landlords.* (1947) Reprint. Baltimore: Clearfield Co., 1994.

Read, Motte Alston. *Colonial Families of Virginia and North Carolina.* Microfilm of original manuscript at the South Carolina Historical Society, Charleston, South Carolina. Salt Lake City: Filmed by the Genealogical Society of Utah, 1952.

Rights, Douglas le Tell. *The American Indian in North Carolina.* Durham, North Carolina: Duke University Press, 1947.

Roanoke Island Prisoners—February 1862. Signal Mountain, Tennessee: Mountain Press.

Russell, Anne. *North Carolina Portraits of Faith: A Pictorial History of Religions.* Norfolk, Virginia: Donning Co., 1986.

Saunders, William L., ed. *The Colonial Records of North Carolina: Published Under the Supervision of the Trustees of the Public Libraries, by Order of the General Assembly.* 11 vols. Wilmington, North Carolina: Broadfoot Pub., 1993.

Schweitzer, George K. *North Carolina Genealogical Research*. Knoxville, Tennessee: The author, 1996.

Smallwood, Marilu Burch. *Some Colonial and Revolutionary Families of North Carolina*. 3 vols. Washington, North Carolina: M. B. Smallwood, 1964.

Society of North Carolina Archivists. *Archival and Manuscript Repositories in North Carolina: A Directory*. Galveston, Texas: Frontier Press, 1993.

Spence, Wilma C. *North Carolina Bible Records*. Logan, Utah: Unique Printing Services, 1973.

Spindel, Donna. *Introductory Guide to Indian-Related Records (To 1876) in the North Carolina State Archives*. Raleigh, North Carolina: Division of Archives and History, North Carolina Department of Cultural Resources, 1977.

Starr, Emmet McDonald. *Old Cherokee Families: Old Families and their Genealogy. Reprinted from History of the Cherokee Indians and their Legends and Folklore. with a Comprehensive Index*. Oklahoma City, Oklahoma: The Warden, 1921, 1922.

Stevenson, George. *North Carolina Local History: A Select Bibliography*. Raleigh, North Carolina: State Department of Cultural Resources, 1975.

The Historical Records of North Carolina. 3 vols. Raleigh: North Carolina Historical Commission, 1938–1939.

Thompson, Catherine E. *Selective Guide to Women Related Records in the North Carolina State Archives*. Raleigh, North Carolina: North Carolina Department of Archives and History, 1977.

Thornton, Mary Lindsay. *A Bibliography of North Carolina, 1589–1956*. Westport, Connecticut: Greenwood Press, 1973.

Ware, Charles Crossfield. *North Carolina Disciples of Christ: A History of Their Rise and Progress, and of Their Contribution to Their General Brotherhood*. St. Louis: Christian Board of Publication, 1927.

Watson, Alan D., comp. & ed. *An Index to North Carolina Newspapers, 1784–1789*. Raleigh, North Carolina: North Carolina Department of Archives and History, 1992.

Weeks, Stephen Beauregard. *Index to the Colonial and State Records of North Carolina*. 2 vols. Charlotte, North Carolina: Observer Print. House, 1886.

Weeks, Stephen Beauregard. *The Religious Development in the Province of North Carolina*. New York: Johnson Reprint Corp., 1973.

Wheeler, John Hill. *Historical Sketches of North Carolina from 1584 to 1851*. 2 vols in 1. (1851) Reprint. Baltimore: Clearfield Co., 1993.

Wheeler, John Hill. *Reminiscences and Memoirs of North Carolina and Eminent North Carolinians*. (1884) Reprint. Baltimore: Clearfield Co., 1993.

Woodmason. *The Carolina Backcountry on the Eve of the Revolution*. Galveston, Texas: Frontier Press, 1954.

Atlases, Maps and Gazetteers

Clark, David S. *Index to Maps of North Carolina in Books and Periodicals Illustrating the History of the State from the Voyage of Verrazzano in 1524 to 1975*. Fayetteville, North Carolina: David S. Clark, 1976.

Clay, James W. *North Carolina Atlas*. Chapel Hill, North Carolina: University of North Carolina Press, 1975.

Corbitt, David Leroy. *The Formation of the North Carolina Counties, 1663–1943*. Raleigh, North Carolina: State Department of Archives and History, 1969.

Cumming, William P. *North Carolina in Maps*. Raleigh, North Carolina: North Carolina Division of Archives and History, 1994.

DeLorme Mapping Company. *North Carolina Atlas and Gazetteer: Topographic Maps of the Entire State, Back Roads and Recreational Places*. Freeport, Maine: DeLorme Mapping, 1993.

DePriest, Virginia Greene. *The National Post Road*. Shelby, North Carolina: V. G. DePriest, 1990.

Edwards, Richard, ed. *Statistical Gazetteer of the States of Virginia and North Carolina*. Richmond, Virginia: published by the proprietor, 1856.

Gioe, Joan Colbert. *North Carolina: Her Counties, Her Townships and Her Towns*. Indianapolis: The Researchers, 1981.

Powell. *The North Carolina Gazetteer: A Dictionary of Tar Heel Places*. Galveston, Texas: Frontier Press, 1968.

Puetz, C. J., comp. *North Carolina County Maps*. Lyndon Station, Wisconsin: Thomas Publishing Co., 1991.

Stout, Garland P. *North Carolina Counties*. 5 vols. Greensboro, North Carolina: G. P. Stout, 1973.

Censuses

Available Census Records and Census Substitutes

Federal Census 1790 (supplemented by tax lists for Caswell, Granville and Orange Counties), 1800, 1810 (except Craven, Greene, New Hanover, and Wake Counties), 1820 (except Currituck, Franklin, Martin, Montgomery, Randolph, and Wake Counties), 1830, 1840, 1850, 1860, 1870, 1880, 1900, 1910, 1920, 1930

Federal Mortality Schedules 1850, 1860, 1870, 1880

Union Veterans and Widows 1890

State/Territorial Census 1784–1787

Dollarhide, William. *The Census Book: A Genealogist's Guide to Federal Census Facts, Schedules and Indexes*. Bountiful, Utah: Heritage Quest, 1999.

Kemp, Thomas Jay. *The American Census Handbook*. Wilmington, Delaware: Scholarly Resources, Inc., 2001.

Lainhart, Ann S. *State Census Records*. Baltimore: Genealogical Publishing Co., Inc., 1992.

Ratcliff, Clarence, E. *North Carolina Taxpayers, 1679–1790*. (1987) Reprint. Baltimore: Genealogical Publishing, 1996.

Siler, David W. *Eastern Cherokees: A Census of the Cherokee Nation in North Carolina, Tennessee, Alabama, and Georgia in 1851.* Cottonport, Louisiana: Polyanthos, 1972.

Szucs, Loretto Dennis and Matthew Wright. *Finding Answers in U.S. Census Records.* Ancestry Publishing, 2001.

Thorndale, William and William Dollarhide. *Map Guide to the U.S. Federal Census, 1790–1920.* Baltimore: Genealogical Publishing Co., 1987.

United States. Bureau of Internal Revenue. *Internal Revenue Assessment List for North Carolina, 1864–1866.* Microfilm of originals in the National Archives in Washington, D.C. Salt Lake City: Filmed by the Genealogical Society of Utah, 1988. 2 microfilm.

Wynne, Frances Holloway. *North Carolina Extant Voter Registrations of 1867.* Bowie, Maryland: Heritage Books, 1992.

Court Records, Probate and Wills

Bennett, William Doub. *Catalogue, North Carolina Federal Court Records [at the] National Archives, Atlanta Branch.* Raleigh: W. D. Bennett, 1987.

Clark, Walter. *The State Records of North Carolina.* Goldsboro, North Carolina: Nash Brothers, 1902.

Grimes, J. Bryan. *Abstract of North Carolina Wills [1663-1760].* (1910) Reprint. Baltimore: Clearfield Co., Inc., 1997.

Grimes, J. Bryan. *Abstract of North Carolina Wills: Compiled from Original and Recorded Wills in the Office of the Secretary of State.* (1910) Reprint. Greenville, South Carolina: Southern Historical Press, 1985.

Grimes, J. Bryan. *North Carolina Wills and Inventories.* (1912) Reprint. Baltimore; Clearfield Co., 1994.

McCain, Paul M. *The County Court in North Carolina Before 1750.* New York: AMS Press, 1970.

Mitchell, Thornton W. *North Carolina Wills: A Testator Index, 1665–1900.* (1993) Reprint. Baltimore: Genealogical Publishing, 1996.

North Carolina Higher-Court Records. 5 vols. Raleigh, North Carolina: State Department of Archives and History, 1968–1981.

North Carolina Wills and Court Records, 1679–1775. Microfilm of originals at the Secretary of State's Office in Raleigh, North Carolina. Salt Lake City: Filmed by the Genealogical Society of Utah, 1941. 5 microfilm.

North Carolina. Division of Archives and History (Raleigh, North Carolina). *Colonial Estate Papers, 1669–1759.* Microfilm of original in the North Carolina State Archives in Raleigh, North Carolina. Salt Lake City: Filmed by the Genealogical Society of Utah, 1996. 4 microfilm.

Olds, Fred A. *An Abstract of North Carolina Wills from About 1760 to About 1800 Supplementing Grimes'*

Abstract of North Carolina Wills 1663 to 1760. (1925) Reprint. Baltimore: Clearfield Co., 1996.

The First Laws of the State of North Carolina. 2 vols. (1791) Reprint. Wilmington, Delaware: Scholarly Resources, 1984.

Emigration, Immigration, Migration and Naturalization

Briceland, Alan Vance. *Westward from Virginia: The Exploration of the Virginia-Carolina Frontier, 1650–1710.* Charlottesville, Virginia: University Press of Virginia, 1987.

Camin, Betty J. *North Carolina Naturalization Index, 1792–1862.* Mt. Airy, North Carolina: B. J. Camin, 1989.

Daughters of the American Revolution, North Carolina. *Roster of Soldiers from North Carolina in the American Revolution: With an Appendix Containing a Collection of Miscellaneous Papers.* (1932) Reprint. Baltimore: Genealogical Publishing Co., 1972.

DeMond, Robert O. *The Loyalists in North Carolina During the Revolution.* (1940) Reprint. Baltimore: Clearfield Co., 1994.

Hakluyt, Richard. *Explorations, Descriptions, and Attempted Settlements of Carolina, 1584–1590.* Raleigh: State Department of Archives and History, 1953.

Meyer, Duane. *Highland Scots of North Carolina, 1732–1776.* Chapel Hill, North Carolina: University of North Carolina Press, 1966.

Newsome, A. R., ed. *Record of Emigrants from England and Scotland to North America, 1774–1775.* Raleigh, North Carolina: North Carolina Division of Archives and History, 1989.

Peden, Henry C. *Marylanders to Carolina: Migrations of Marylanders to North and South Carolina Prior to 1800.* Westminster, Maryland: Family Line Publications, 1994.

Reichel, Rev. Levin T. *The Moravians in North Carolina.* (1857) Reprint. Baltimore: Clearfield Co., 1995.

United States. District Court (Alabama: Southern District). *Declarations of Intentions, Naturalizations, and Petitions, 1855–1960.* Microfilm of originals at the National Archives in East Point, Georgia. Salt Lake City: Filmed by the Genealogical Society of Utah, 1987–1989. 9 microfilm.

Land and Property

Burgner, Goldene Fillers. *North Carolina Land Grants in Tennessee, 1778–1791.* Greenville, South Carolina: Southern Historical Press, 1981.

Cartwright, Betty G., and Lillian J. Gardiner. *North Carolina Land Grants in Tennessee, 1778–1791.* Memphis, Tennessee: Division of Archives, 1958.

Church of Jesus Christ of Latter-day Saints, The. Genealogical Department. *North Carolina Land and Property Records: A Register of the Several Counties,*

Alphabetically Arranged, Being a Listing of Deed Records, Mortgages, Trusts, Etc. Salt Lake City: Filmed by the Genealogical Society of Utah, 1969.

Hofmann, Margaret M. *Colony of North Carolina, 1735–1764, 1765–1775; Abstracts of Land Patents,* 2 vols. Weldon, North Carolina: Roanoke New Co., 1982, 1984.

Hofmann, Margaret M. *Province of North Carolina, 1663–1729: Abstracts of Land Patents.* Weldon, North Carolina: Roanoke News Co., 1979.

Hofmann, Margaret M. *The Granville District of North Carolina, 1749–1763: Abstracts of Miscellaneous Land Office Records, Volume 4.* Galveston, Texas: Frontier Press.

Hofmann, Margaret M. *The Granville District of North Carolina, 1748–1763: Abstracts of Land Grants.* 5 vols. Weldon, North Carolina: Roanoke News Co., 1995.

Hone, Wade E. *Land and Property Research in the United States.* Salt Lake City: Ancestry Incorporated, 1997.

North Carolina. Secretary of State. Land Grant Office. *Land Records, 1600 Thru 1957; Land Grant Index, 1693–1959.* Microfilm of originals in the North Carolina State Archives in Raleigh, North Carolina. Raleigh, North Carolina: North Carolina State Archives, 1980. 552 microfilm.

North Carolina. Secretary of State. *Land Grants, Land Entries and Warrants and List of Grants for Various Counties of North Carolina, 1764–1853.* Microfilm of originals at the North Carolina Historical Commission in Raleigh, North Carolina. Salt Lake City: Filmed by the Genealogical Society of Utah, 1941. 3 microfilm.

Powell, William Stevens. *The Proprietors of Carolina.* Raleigh: State Department of Archives and History, 1968.

Pruitt, Albert Bruce. *Colonial Land Entries in North Carolina.* 4 vols. Whitakers, North Carolina: A. B. Pruitt, c1994, 1995.

Smathers, George Henry. *The History of Land Titles in Western North Carolina: A History of the Cherokee Land Laws Affecting the Title to Land Lying West of the Meigs and Freeman Line, and Laws Affecting the Title of Land Lying East of the Meigs and Freeman Line Back to the Top of the Blue Ridge.* Asheville: Miller Printing Co., 1938.

Military

Bradley, Stephen E., Jr., ed. *North Carolina Confederate Militia Officers Roster, as Contained in the Adjunct-General's Officers Roster.* Wilmington, North Carolina: Broadfoot Publishing, 1996.

Burns, Annie W. *Abstracts of Pension Papers of North Carolina Soldiers of the Revolution, 1812, and Indian Wars.* 15 vols. Washington, D.C.: 1960–1966.

Carter, Mary. *North Carolina Revolutionary Soldiers, Sailors, Patriots and Descendants.* 2 vols. Albany, Georgia: Pioneer Publications, 1978.

Clark, Walter, ed. *Histories of the Several Regiments and Battalions from North Carolina in the Great War 1861–1865.* 5 vols. Wilmington, North Carolina: Broadfoot Publishing.

Crow, Jeffery J. *The Black Experience in Revolutionary North Carolina.* Raleigh, North Carolina: North Carolina Division of Archives and History, 1996.

Jordan, Weymouth T., Jr., ed. *North Carolina Troops, 1861–1865: A Roster.* 14 vols. Raleigh, North Carolina: State Department of Archives and History, 1966–.

Kearney, Timothy. *Abstracts of Letters of Resignation of Militia Officers in North Carolina 1779–1840.* Raleigh, North Carolina: North Carolina Genealogical Society, 1992.

Lemmon, Sarah McCulloh. *North Carolina's Role in the First World War.* Raleigh: North Carolina Department of Cultural Resources, Div. of Arch. and Hist., 1975.

North Carolina Adjunct General's Office. *Muster Rolls of the Soldiers of the War of 1812 Detached from the Militia of North Carolina in 1812 and 1814.* Winston-Salem, North Carolina: Barber Publishing Co., 1969.

North Carolina Adjunct General's Office. *Roster of the North Carolina Volunteers in the Spanish-American War, 1898–1899.* Raleigh, North Carolina: Edwards and Broughton, 1900.

North Carolina Office of Archives and History. *Military Records.* Raleigh, North Carolina: North Carolina Office of Archives and History, 2002. Online guide: www.ah.dcr.state.nc.us/sections/archives/arch/military.htm

Pancake. *This Destructive War: The British Campaign in the Carolinas, 1780–1782.* Galveston, Texas: Frontier Press, 1985.

Roster of Soldiers from North Carolina in the American Revolution. (1932) Reprint. Baltimore: Genealogical Publishing Co., 1977.

Roster of the North Carolina Volunteers in the Spanish-American War, 1898–1899. Raleigh, North Carolina: Edwards & Broughton, 1900.

Sifakis, Stewart. *Compendium of the Confederate Armies: North Carolina.* Galveston, Texas: Frontier Press, 1992.

Steelman, Joseph F. *North Carolina's Role in the Spanish-American War.* Raleigh, North Carolina: Department of Cultural Resources, Division of Archives and History, 1975.

Toler, Maurice S. *Muster Rolls of the Soldiers of the War of 1812 Detached from the Militia of North Carolina in 1812 and 1814.* (1851, 1976) Reprint. Baltimore: Clearfield Co., 1996.

United States. Selective Service System. *North Carolina, World War I Selective Service System Draft Registration Cards, 1917–1918. National Archives Microfilm Publications, M1509.* Washington, D.C.: National Archives, 1987–1988.

Volunteer Soldiers in the Cherokee War—1836–1839. Signal Mountain, Tennessee: Mountain Press.

White, Katherine Keogh. *The King's Mountain Men. The Story of Battle, with Sketches of the American Soldiers Who Took Part*. (1924) Reprint. Baltimore: Clearfield Co., 1996.

Yearns and Barrett, eds. *North Carolina Civil War Documentary*. Galveston, Texas: Frontier Press, 1980.

Vital and Cemetery Records

Broughton, Carrie L. *Marriage and Death Notices from Raleigh Register and North Carolina State Gazette, 1799–1825*. (1942–1944) Reprint. Baltimore: Clearfield Co., 1995.

Broughton, Carrie L. *Marriage and Death Notices in Raleigh Register and North Carolina State Gazette, 1826–1845*. (1947) Reprint. Baltimore: Clearfield Co., 1992.

Broughton, Carrie L. *Marriage and Death Notices in Raleigh Register and North Carolina State Gazette, 1846–1867*. 2 vols in one. (1949–1950) Reprint. Baltimore: Clearfield Co., 1992.

Cemetery Records of North Carolina. 8 vols. Salt Lake City: Genealogical Society of Utah, 1947–1961.

Clemens, William Montgomery. *North and South Carolina Marriage Records, from the Earliest Colonial Days to the Civil War*. (1927) Reprint. Baltimore: Genealogical Publishing Co., 1995.

Dodd, Jordan R. *North Carolina Marriages, 1801 to 1825*. Bountiful, Utah: Precision Indexing, 1993.

Dodd, Jordan R. *North Carolina Marriages, Early to 1800*. Bountiful, Utah: Precision Indexing, 1990.

Historical Records Survey (North Carolina). *Guide To Vital Statistics Records In North Carolina*. Raleigh, North Carolina: The Survey, 1942.

Historical Records Survey (North Carolina). *Post-1914 Cemetery Inscription Card Index* Microfilm of originals in the North Carolina Department of Archives and History in Raleigh, North Carolina. Raleigh, North Carolina: North Carolina Department of Archives and History, 1972. 5 microfilm.

Historical Records Survey (North Carolina). *Pre-1914 Cemetery Inscription Card Index*. Microfilm of originals in the North Carolina Department of Archives and History in Raleigh, North Carolina. Raleigh, North Carolina: North Carolina Department of Archives and History, 1972. 23 microfilm.

King, Henry. *Tar Heel Tombstones and the Tales They Tell*. Asheboro, North Carolina: Down Home Press, 1990.

Lucas, Silas Emmett, Jr., and Brent Holcomb. *Marriage and Death Notices from Raleigh, North Carolina Newspapers: 1796–1826*. (1977) Reprint. Greenville, South Carolina: Southern Historical Press, 1984.

McEachern, Leora H. *North Carolina Gravestone Records*. 10 vols. Wilmington, North Carolina: The author, 1971–1981.

Neal, Lois Smathers. *Abstracts of Vital Records from Raleigh, North Carolina, Newspapers, 1799–1829*. 2 vols. Spartanburg, South Carolina: Reprint Company, 1979–.

North Carolina Division of Archives and History. *An Index to Marriage Bonds Filed in the North Carolina State Archives*. Raleigh, North Carolina: North Carolina Department of Cultural Resources, 1977. 88 Microfiche.

North Carolina. Department of Public Health. Vital Records Section. *Death Certificates, 1906–1994; Still Births, 1914–1953; Fetal Deaths, 1960–1974; Index, 1906–1967*. Microfilm of originals in the North Carolina Department of Archives and History in Raleigh, North Carolina. Salt Lake City: Filmed by the Genealogical Society of Utah, 1993–1995. 1022 microfilm.

North Carolina. Department of Public Health. Vital Records Section. *Index To Death Certificates, 1968–1994*. Microfilm of originals at the North Carolina Department of Public Health, Vital Records section in Raleigh, North Carolina. Salt Lake City: Filmed by the Genealogical Society of Utah, 1996. 56 microfiche.

North Carolina. Division of Archives and History (Raleigh, North Carolina). *Birth Certificates, 1913–1918*. Microfilm of originals in the North Carolina State Archives in Raleigh, North Carolina. Salt Lake City: Filmed by the Genealogical Society of Utah, 1998–1999, 2000. 305 microfilm.

Tennessee Valley Authority (Tennessee). *Master File Relocation Card Index For Grave And Cemetery Removal And Relocation, 1934–1954*. Microreproduction of originals housed in the National Archives Record Office, East Point, Georgia. Salt Lake City: Filmed by the Genealogical Society of Utah, 1996.

Wellborn, Mrs. John Scott. *North Carolina Tombstone Records*. Microfilm. 3 vols in 2 reels. Salt Lake City: Genealogical Society of Utah, 1941.

White, Barnetta McGhee. *Somebody Knows My Name: Marriages of Freed People in North Carolina, County by County*. 3 vols. Athens, Georgia: Iberian Publishing Co., 1995.

Works Progress Administration, Historical Records Survey Services Division. *Pre-1914 Cemetery Inscription Card Index*. 26 vols. Raleigh: North Carolina Department of Archives and History, 1972.

County Website	Map Index	Date Created	Parent County or Territory From Which Organized Address/Details
Alamance www.alamance-nc.com/	H5	29 Jan 1849	**Orange** Alamance County; 124 W Elm St; Graham, NC 27253-2802; Ph. (336) 570-6565 **Details:** (Clerk Superior Court has Divorce, Probate & Court Records from 1849; Registrar of Deeds has Birth, Marriage, Death & Land Records)
Albemarle www.usgennet.org/usa/nc/county/albemarle/		1664	**Original county** Albemarle County; NC **Details:** (1 of 3 original counties discontinued in 1739)
Alexander www.co.alexander.nc.us/	L5	15 Jan 1847	**Iredell, Caldwell & Wilkes** Alexander County; 201 1st St SW Ste 1; Taylorsville, NC 28681-2592; Ph. (828) 632-3152 **Details:** (Registrar of Deeds has Birth, Marriage, Death, Burial & Land Records; Clerk Superior Court has Divorce, Probate & Court Records from 1865)
Alleghany www.sparta-nc.com/	L4	1859	**Ashe** Alleghany County; Main St; PO Box 186; Sparta, NC 28675; Ph. (336) 372-4342 **Details:** (Clerk Superior Court has Birth & Death Records from 1914, Marriage Records from 1868, Divorce Records, Probate Records from 1883, Court Records from 1869 & Land Records from 1860)
Anson www.co.anson.nc.us/	J7	1750	**Bladen** Anson County; N Green St; PO Box 352; Wadesboro, NC 28170; Ph. (704) 694-3212 **Details:** (Courthouse burned 1868) (Registrar of Deeds has Birth Records from 1913, Marriage Records from 1869, Death & Land Records; Clerk Superior Court has Divorce Records from 1868, Probate Records from 1750 & Court Records from 1770)
Archdale		1712	**Bath** Archdale County; NC **Details:** (see Craven) Name changed to Craven, 1712
Ashe www.ashecountygov.com	M4	18 Nov 1799	**Wilkes** Ashe County; 150 Government Cir. Ste 2300; Jefferson, NC 28640; Ph. (336) 219-2540 **Details:** (State Archives has Court Records 1849–1920, Divorce Records 1889–1917, Land Records 1793–1905, Probate Records 1856–1949, & Wills 1832–1900; Registrar of Deeds has Land Records from 1905, Birth & Death Records from 1913, & Marriage Records from 1849; Clerk of Superior Court has Divorce Records from 1917, Probate Records from 1949, & Court Records from 1920)
Avery www.banner-elk.com/countown.html	N5	23 Feb 1911	**Caldwell, Mitchell, Watauga** Avery County; Main St; Newland, NC 28657; Ph. (828) 733-8262 **Details:** (Clerk Superior Court has Divorce, Probate, Court & Land Records from 1911)
Bath www.usgennet.org/usa/nc/county/bath/		1705	**Original county** Bath County; NC **Details:** (Divided into Archdale, Pamtecough & Wickham Precincts 3 Dec 1705; County discontinued in 1739)

County Website	Map Index	Date Created	Parent County or Territory From Which Organized Address/Details
Beaufort www.beaufort-county.com/	**D6**	**3 Dec 1705**	**Bath** Beaufort County; 112 W 2nd St; Washington, NC 27889; Ph. (252) 946-2323 **Details:** (Registrar of Deeds has Marriage & Land Records; Clerk Superior Court has Probate & Court Records)
Berkeley		**1671**	**Precinct in Albemarle** Berkeley County; NC **Details:** (see Perquimans) Perquimans County known as Berkeley Precinct from 1671 to 1681
Bertie www.co.bertie.nc.us/	**D5**	**2 Aug 1722**	**Chowan** Bertie County; PO Box 340; Windsor, NC 27983; Ph. (252) 794-5309 **Details:** (State Archives has Court Records 1724–1915, Land Records 1723–1820, Marriage Records 1762–1868, 1870–1903, Probate Records 1728–1920, & Wills 1749–1897; Register of Deeds has Marriage Records from 1902 & Birth & Death Records from 1913; Clerk of Superior Court has Divorce Records)
Bladen www.rootsweb.com/~ncbladen/bladen.htm	**G8**	**1734**	**New Hanover** Bladen County; Courthouse Dr; PO Box 247; Elizabethtown, NC 28337; Ph. (919) 862-6710 **Details:** (Courthouse burned 1800 & 1893) (Registrar of Deeds has Birth & Death Records from 1914, Marriage Records from 1893 & Land Records from 1734; Clerk Superior Court has Divorce & Court Records from 1893 & Probate Records from 1734)
Brunswick www.brunswick.org/	**G9**	**30 Jan 1764**	**New Hanover, Bladen** Brunswick County; PO Box 87; Bolivia, NC 28422-0249; Ph. (910) 253-2690 **Details:** (Registrar of Deeds has Birth, Marriage, Death, Burial & Land Records; Clerk Superior Court has Divorce Records from 1900, Probate Records from 1858 & Court Records from 1882)
Buncombe www.buncombecounty.org/	**O6**	**5 Dec 1791**	**Burke, Rutherford** Buncombe County; 60 Court Plaza Rm 110; Asheville, NC 28801-3519; Ph. (828) 250-4300 **Details:** (Courthouse burned 1830–1835) (Registrar of Deeds has Birth, Marriage, Death, Burial & Land Records; Clerk Superior Court has Divorce & Probate Records from 1832 & Court Records)
Burke www.co.burke.nc.us/	**M5**	**8 Apr 1777**	**Rowan** Burke County; 201 S Green St; PO Box 219; Morganton, NC 28680; Ph. (828) 438-5450 **Details:** (Registrar of Deeds has Birth & Death Records from 1913, Marriage, Land & Military Discharge Records from 1865; Clerk Superior Court has Divorce, Probate & Court Records from 1865)
Bute www.blueridge.net/lds/nc/bute.html		**1779**	**Granville, Northampton** Bute County; NC **Details:** (Discontinued in 1779)
Cabarrus www.co.cabarrus.nc.us/	**K6**	**15 Nov 1792**	**Mecklenburg** Cabarrus County; 65 Church St SE; Concord, NC 28025; Ph. (704) 920-2112 **Details:** (Courthouse burned 1874) (Registrar of Deeds has Birth & Death Records from 1913, Marriage & Land Records from 1792 & Military Discharge Records from 1919; Clerk Superior Court has Divorce, Probate & Court Records)

County Website	Map Index	Date Created	Parent County or Territory From Which Organized Address/Details
Caldwell www.co.caldwell.nc.us/	M5	11 Jan 1841	**Burke, Wilkes** Caldwell County; 905 West Ave NW; Lenoir, NC 28645; Ph. (828) 757-1310 **Details:** (Registrar of Deeds has Birth, Marriage, Death & Land Records; Clerk Superior Court has Divorce, Court & Probate Records from 1841)
Camden www.rootsweb.com/~nccamden/camden.htm	B4	8 Apr 1777	**Pasquotank** Camden County; Hwy 343; PO Box 190; Camden, NC 27921; Ph. (919) 335-4077 **Details:** (Clerk Superior Court has Divorce & Court Records from 1896 & Probate Records from 1912)
Carteret www.mindspring.com/~jsruss/genweb/ NC/carteret.htm	C8	1722	**Craven** Carteret County; Courthouse Sq; Beaufort, NC 28516; Ph. (252) 728-8474 **Details:** (Registrar of Deeds has Birth, Marriage, Death & Land Records; Clerk Superior Court has Divorce, Probate & Court Records)
Caswell www.caswellnc.com/home.htm	H4	8 Apr 1777	**Orange** Caswell County; 139 E Church St; Yanceyville, NC 27379; Ph. (336) 694-4197 **Details:** (Clerk Superior Court has Divorce, Probate & Court Records; Registrar of Deeds has Land Records)
Catawba www.catawbacountync.gov	L6	12 Dec 1842	**Lincoln** Catawba County; 100A Southwest Blvd; PO Box 389; Newton, NC 28658-0389; Ph. (828) 465-1573 **Details:** (Clerk Superior Court has Divorce, Probate & Court Records from 1843; Registrar of Deeds has Marriage & Land Records)
Chatham www.rootsweb.com/~ncchatha/chatham.htm	H6	5 Dec 1770	**Orange** Chatham County; 12 East Rd; Pittsboro, NC 27312; Ph. (919) 542-3240 **Details:** (Registrar of Deeds has Birth & Death Records from 1913, Marriage & Land Records from 1771; Clerk Superior Court has Divorce Records from 1913, Probate Records from 1771 & Court Records from 1869)
Cherokee www.main.nc.us/cherokee/index.html	R7	4 Jan 1839	**Macon** Cherokee County; 53 Peachtree; Murphy, NC 28906; Ph. (282) 837-2613 **Details:** (Clerk Superior Court has Divorce, Probate & Court Records; Registrar of Deeds has Land Records)
Chowan www.co.chowan.nc.us/	C5	1670	**Albemarle** Chowan County; 101 S Broad St; Edenton, NC 27932; Ph. (252) 482-3062 **Details:** (Formerly Shaftesbury 1671–1684) (Registrar of Deeds has Marriage & Land Records; Clerk Superior Court has Probate & Court Records)
Clarendon		1664	**Original County** Clarendon County; NC **Details:** County Terminated 1667
Clay www.rootsweb.com/~ncclay/	Q7	20 Feb 1861	**Cherokee** Clay County; Town Sq; Hayesville, NC 28904-0118; Ph. (828) 389-6301 **Details:** (Registrar of Deeds has Birth, Death & Military Records from 1913, Marriage Records from 1879 & Land Records from 1870)

County	Map	Date	Parent County or Territory From Which Organized
Website	Index	Created	Address/Details

Cleveland M7 **11 Jan 1841** **Rutherford, Lincoln**
www.clevelandcounty.com/nav/index.htm

Cleveland County; 311 E Marion St; PO Box 1210; Shelby, NC 28150; Ph. (704) 484-4834

Details: (Registrar of Deeds has Birth & Death Records from 1914, Marriage Records from 1851 & Land Records from 1841; Clerk Superior Court has Divorce Records from 1921, Probate Records from 1843 & Court Records from 1914)

Columbus G9 **15 Dec 1808** **Bladen, Brunswick**
www.columbus.nc.us/

Columbus County; 612 N Madison St; Whiteville, NC 28472; Ph. (910) 640-6625

Details: (Registrar of Deeds has Birth & Death Records from 1913, Marriage Records from 1867 & Land Records; Clerk Superior Court has Divorce & Court Records from 1868 & Probate Records from 1817)

Craven D7 **3 Dec 1705** **Archdale Precinct of Bath County**
www.cravencounty.com/

Craven County; 406 Craven St; New Bern, NC 28560; Ph. (252) 636-6617

Details: (Formerly Archdale County. Name changed to Craven, 1712) (1810 Census missing) (Registrar of Deeds has Birth & Death Records from 1914, Marriage & Land Records from 1700's & Military Discharge Records; Clerk Superior Court has Divorce Records from 1915; City Clerk has Burial Records)

Cumberland G7 **19 Feb 1754** **Bladen**
www.co.cumberland.nc.us/

Cumberland County; 117 Dick St Rm 114; Fayetteville, NC 28301-5725; Ph. (910) 678-7775

Details: (Registrar of Deeds has Birth, Marriage, Death, Burial & Land Records; Clerk Superior Court has Divorce Records from 1930, Probate Records from 1850 & Court Records from 1900)

Currituck B4 **1684** **Albemarle**
www.co.currituck.nc.us/

Currituck County; PO Box 71; Currituck, NC 27929; Ph. (252) 232-3297

Details: (1820 Census missing; Courthouse burned 1842) (Registrar of Deeds has Birth, Marriage, Death & Land Records; Clerk Superior Court has Divorce, Probate & Court Records)

Dare B5 **3 Feb 1870** **Currituck, Tyrell, Hyde**
www.co.dare.nc.us/

Dare County; 400 Budleigh St; PO Box 70; Manteo, NC 27954; Ph. (252) 473-3438

Details: (Registrar of Deeds has Birth & Death Records from 1913, Marriage Records from 1870 & Land Records; Clerk Superior Court has Divorce, Probate & Court Records from 1870)

Davidson J5 **9 Dec 1822** **Rowan**
www.co.davidson.nc.us/

Davidson County; PO Box 464; Lexington, NC 27293; Ph. (336) 242-2150

Details: (Registrar of Deeds has Birth, Marriage, Death, Burial & Land Records from 1823; Clerk Superior Court has Divorce, Probate & Court Records from 1823)

Davie K5 **20 Dec 1836** **Rowan**
www.co.davie.nc.us/

Davie County; 123 S Main St; Mocksville, NC 27028; Ph. (336) 751-2513

Details: (Registrar of Deeds has Birth, Marriage, Death, Burial & Land Records; Clerk Superior Court has Divorce & Court Records from 1834 & Probate Records from 1837)

County Website	Map Index	Date Created	Parent County or Territory From Which Organized Address/Details
Dobbs www.rootsweb.com/~ncdobbs/dobbs.htm		1791	**Johnston** Dobbs County; NC **Details:** (Discontinued & became part of Wayne County 18 Oct 1779 & Glasgow & Lenoir Counties 5 Dec 1791)
Duplin www.duplincounty.org/	F7	1750	**New Hanover** Duplin County; 118 Duplin St; Kenansville, NC 28349; Ph. (910) 296-2108 **Details:** (Registrar of Deeds has Birth & Death Records from 1913, Marriage Records from 1749, maps & Land Records from 1749 & business Records from 1899; Clerk Superior Court has Probate & Court Records)
Durham www.co.durham.nc.us/	H5	28 Feb 1881	**Orange, Wake** Durham County; 200 E Main St; Durham, NC 27707; Ph. (919) 560-0480 **Details:** (County Health Department has Birth, Death & Burial Records; Registrar of Deeds has Marriage & Land Records; Clerk Superior Court has Divorce, Probate & Court Records from 1881)
Edgecombe www.geocities.com/ncedgecombe/	E5	4 Apr 1741	**Bertie** Edgecombe County; 301 Saint Andrews St; PO Box 386; Tarboro, NC 27886; Ph. (252) 641-7924 **Details:** (Registrar of Deeds has Birth, Marriage & Land Records; Clerk Superior Court has Probate & Court Records)
Forsyth www.co.forsyth.nc.us/	J4	16 Jan 1849	**Stokes** Forsyth County; 102 W 3rd St; PO Box 20639; Winston-Salem, NC 27101; Ph. (336) 727-2903 **Details:** (Registrar of Deeds has Birth, Marriage, Death & Land Records; Clerk Superior Court has Divorce, Probate & Court Records from 1849)
Franklin www.co.franklin.nc.us	F5	1779	**Bute** Franklin County; 113 S Main St; PO Box 545; Louisburg, NC 27549; Ph. (919) 496-3500 **Details:** (Register of Deeds has Birth & Death Records from 1913, Land Records from 1776, & Marriage Records from 1869)
Gaston www.co.gaston.nc.us/	L7	21 Dec 1846	**Lincoln** Gaston County; 325 N Marietta St; PO Box 1578; Gastonia, NC 28053; Ph. (704) 868-7684 **Details:** (Registrar of Deeds has Birth, Marriage & Death Records from 1913 & Land Records from 1847; Clerk Superior Court has Divorce & Court Records)
Gates http://albemarle-nc.com/gates/	C4	1779	**Chowan, Hertford, Perquimans** Gates County; PO Box 345; Gatesville, NC 27938; Ph. (252) 357-0850 **Details:** (Registrar of Deeds has Birth, Marriage, Death, Burial & Land Records; Clerk Superior Court has Divorce, Probate & Court Records from 1780)
Glasgow www.rootsweb.com/~ncglasgo/glasgow.htm		1799	**Dobbs** Glasgow County; NC **Details:** (Discontinued & became part of Greene County 18 Nov 1799)

County Website	Map Index	Date Created	Parent County or Territory From Which Organized Address/Details
Graham www.main.nc.us/graham/index.html	Q6	**30 Jan 1872**	**Cherokee** Graham County; Main St; PO Box 406; Robbinsville, NC 28771-0575; Ph. (828) 479-7971 **Details:** (Registrar of Deeds has Birth & Death Records from 1913, Marriage & Land Records from 1873; Clerk Superior Court has Divorce, Court & Probate Records from 1872)
Granville www.granvillecounty.org/	G4	**28 Jun 1746**	**Edgecombe** Granville County; 101 Main St; Oxford, NC 27565-3318; Ph. (919) 693-6314 **Details:** (Clerk Superior Court has Divorce, Probate & Land Records)
Greene www.co.greene.nc.us/	E6	**18 Nov 1799**	**Glasgow** Greene County; PO Box 86; Snow Hill, NC 28580; Ph. (252) 747-3620 **Details:** (Courthouse burned in 1876) (State Archives has Court Records 1868–1959, Divorce Records 1875–1959, Probate Records 1809–1962, and Wills 1846–1944; Register of Deeds has Birth & Death Records from 1913, & Land & Marriage Records from 1875)
Guilford www.co.guilford.nc.us/	I5	**5 Dec 1770**	**Rowan, Orange** Guilford County; 201 S Eugene St; PO Box 3427; Greensboro, NC 27402; Ph. (336) 641-7556 **Details:** (Courthouse burned 1872; many older Records still available) (Registrar of Deeds has Birth & Death Records from 1913, Marriage Records from 1865, Land Records from 1771 & Military Records; Clerk Courts has Divorce, Probate & Court Records)
Halifax www.halifaxnc.com/	E4	**1759**	**Edgecombe** Halifax County; King St; PO Box 67; Halifax, NC 27839; Ph. (252) 583-2101 **Details:** (Registrar of Deeds has Birth & Death Records from 1913, Marriage Records from 1867, Divorce & Probate Records from 1868, Court Records from 1893, Land Records from 1729 & Military Discharge Records from 1918)
Harnett www.harnett.org/	H6	**7 Feb 1855**	**Cumberland** Harnett County; 729 S Main St; PO Box 279; Lillington, NC 27546; Ph. (910) 893-7540 **Details:** (Registrar of Deeds has Birth, Marriage, Death & Land Records; Clerk Superior Court has Divorce, Probate & Court Records from 1920; Records from 1855 to 1920 were destroyed in a fire)
Haywood http://haywoodnc.org/government/ haywoodcountygovt.html	P6	**15 Dec 1808**	**Buncombe** Haywood County; 215 N Main St; Waynesville, NC 28786; Ph. (828) 452-6635 **Details:** (Registrar of Deeds has Marriage & Land Records; Clerk Superior Court has Probate & Court Records)
Henderson http://mail.henderson.lib.nc.us/county/	O7	**15 Dec 1838**	**Buncombe** Henderson County; 200 N Grove St Ste 129; Hendersonville, NC 28792-5053; Ph. (828) 697-4901 **Details:** (Registrar of Deeds has Birth & Death Records from 1914, Marriage Records from 1800 & Land Records from 1837; Clerk Superior Court has Divorce, Probate & Court Records from 1841)

County Website	Map Index	Date Created	Parent County or Territory From Which Organized Address/Details
Hertford www.rootsweb.com/~nchertfo/	**D4**	**1759**	**Bertie, Chowan, Northampton** Hertford County; King St; PO Box 36; Winton, NC 27986; Ph. (252) 358-7850 **Details:** (Courthouse burned 1832 & 1862) (Registrar of Deeds has Birth, Death & Burial Records from 1913, Marriage Records from 1884 & Land Records from 1866; Clerk Superior Court has Divorce & Court Records from 1883 & Probate Records from 1869)
Hoke www.ncse.org/hoke.html	**H7**	**17 Feb 1911**	**Cumberland, Robeson** Hoke County; 304 N Main St; Raeford, NC 28376; Ph. (919) 875-2035 **Details:** (Registrar of Deeds has Birth, Marriage, Death & Land Records from 1911; Clerk Superior Court has Divorce, Probate & Court Records from 1911)
Hyde http://albemarle-nc.com/hyde/	**B6**	**3 Dec 1705**	**Wickham Precinct of Bath County** Hyde County; 264 Business Hwy; PO Box 297; Swan Quarter, NC 27885; Ph. (252) 926-3011 **Details:** (Formerly Wickham County. Name changed to Hyde, 1712) (Registrar of Deeds has Birth, Death & Burial Records from 1913, Marriage Records from 1850, Land Records from 1736, marriage bonds 1735–1867 & delayed Birth Records from late 1800's; Clerk Superior Court has Divorce & Court Records from 1868 & Probate Records from 1774)
Iredell www.co.iredell.nc.us/	**L6**	**3 Nov 1788**	**Rowan** Iredell County; 201 E Water St; PO Box 904; Statesville, NC 28687; Ph. (704) 872-7468 **Details:** (Courthouse burned in 1854) (Register of Deeds has Birth & Death Records from 1915, Marriage Records from 1893, Burial & Land Records from 1800; Clerk of Superior Court has Divorce Records from 1820, Probate & Court Records from 1788)
Jackson http://main.nc.us/jackson/	**P7**	**29 Jan 1851**	**Haywood, Macon** Jackson County; 401 Grind Stass Rd Rm 103; Sylva, NC 28779; Ph. (828) 586-7532 **Details:** (Registrar of Deeds has Birth, Marriage, Death, Burial & Land Records; Clerk Superior Court has Divorce, Probate & Court Records from 1851)
Johnston www.co.johnston.nc.us/	**F6**	**28 Jun 1746**	**Craven** Johnston County; 207 E Johnston St; PO Box 118; Smithfield, NC 27577-4515; Ph. (919) 989-5160 **Details:** (Registrar of Deeds has Marriage & Land Records; Clerk Superior Court has Probate & Court Records)
Jones www.co.jones.nc.us/	**E7**	**1779**	**Craven** Jones County; PO Box 189; Trenton, NC 28585; Ph. (252) 448-2551 **Details:** (Courthouse burned in 1862) (Registrar of Deeds has Birth & Death Records from 1913, Marriage Records from 1850, Land Records from 1779 & Military Discharge Records; Clerk Courts has Probate Records from 1779, Court & Divorce Records)
Lee www.leencrod.org	**H6**	**6 Mar 1907**	**Chatham, Moore** Lee County; 1408 S Horner Blvd; PO Box 2040; Sanford, NC 27331; Ph. (919) 718-4585 **Details:** (Registrar of Deeds has Birth, Death & Land Records; Clerk Superior Court has Marriage, Divorce, Probate & Court Records from 1907)

County Website	Map Index	Date Created	Parent County or Territory From Which Organized Address/Details
Lenoir www.co.lenoir.nc.us/	E6	5 Dec 1791	**Dobbs** Lenoir County; PO Box 3289; Kinston, NC 28502; Ph. (252) 523-2390 **Details:** (Courthouse burned 1878) (Clerk Superior Court has Divorce, Probate & Court Records from 1880; Registrar of Deeds has Marriage & Land Records)
Lincoln www.lincolncounty.org/	L6	1779	**Tryon** Lincoln County; 115 W Main St; PO Box 218; Lincolnton, NC 28093; Ph. (704) 736-8534 **Details:** (Registrar of Deeds has Birth, Marriage, Death, Burial & Land Records; Clerk Superior Court has Divorce & Court Records from 1920 & Probate Records from 1869)
Macon www.main.nc.us/macon/index.html	Q7	1828	**Haywood** Macon County; Courthouse; Franklin, NC 28734-3005; Ph. (828) 349-2095 **Details:** (Registrar of Deeds has Marriage & Land Records; Clerk Superior Court has Probate & Court Records)
Madison www.madisonrod.com	O5	27 Jan 1851	**Buncombe, Yancey** Madison County;5707 US Hwy 25/70; PO Box 66; Marshall, NC 28753; Ph. (828) 649-3131, susanrector@madisoncountync.org **Details:** (Register of Deeds has Birth & Death Records from 1913, Land, Burial, Cemetery, Marriage, & Military Records from 1851)
Martin http://albemarle-nc.com/martin/	D5	2 Mar 1774	**Halifax, Tyrell** Martin County; 305 E Main St; Williamston, NC 27892-0668; Ph. (252) 792-1683 **Details:** (Courthouse burned in 1884; 1820 Census missing) (Registrar of Deeds has Birth, Marriage, Death & Land Records; Clerk Superior Court has Divorce & Court Records from 1800s & Probate Records from 1700s)
McDowell www.main.nc.us/mcdowell/index.html	N6	19 Dec 1842	**Burke, Rutherford** McDowell County; Courthouse Main St; Marion, NC 28752-4041; Ph. (828) 652-4727 **Details:** (Registrar of Deeds has Birth, Marriage, Death & Land Records; Clerk Superior Court has Divorce, Probate & Court Records from 1842)
Mecklenburg www.charmeck.nc.us/	K7	3 Nov 1762	**Anson** Mecklenburg County; 720 E 4th St; Charlotte, NC 28202-2835; Ph. (704) 336-2443 **Details:** (Registrar of Deeds has Birth & Death Records from 1913, Marriage Records from 1850 & Land Records from 1763; Clerk Superior Court has Divorce, Probate & Court Records from 1930)
Mitchell www.main.nc.us/mitchell/	N5	16 Feb 1861	**Burke, Caldwell, McDowell, Watauga, Yancey** Mitchell County; 26 Crimson Laurel Circle Ste #4; Bakersville, NC 28705; Ph. (828) 688-2139 **Details:** (State Archives has Court Records 1861–1910, Divorce Records 1867–1915, Land Records 1846–1951, Probate Records 1826–1946, and Wills 1823–1927; Register of Deeds has Birth & Death Records from 1913 & Marriage Records from 1861)

County Website	Map Index	Date Created	Parent County or Territory From Which Organized Address/Details
Montgomery www.montgomeryrod.com	I7	1779	**Anson** Montgomery County; 102 E Spring St; PO Box 695; Troy, NC 27371; Ph. (910) 576-4271, montrod@earthlink.net **Details:** (Courthouse burned 1835; 1820 census missing) (Register of Deeds has Birth, Death, Land, Marriage, & Military Records)
Moore www.co.moore.nc.us/	H7	18 Apr 1784	**Cumberland** Moore County; 100 Downstreet; PO Box 936; Carthage, NC 28327-0936; Ph. (910) 947-6370 **Details:** (Courthouse burned in 1889) (Registrar of Deeds has Birth & Death Records from 1913, Marriage & Land Records from 1889 & Land grants from 1784; Clerk Superior Court has Divorce, Probate & Court Records)
Nash www.co.nash.nc.us/	F5	15 Nov 1777	**Edgecombe** Nash County; County Courthouse Rm 104; PO Box 974; Nashville, NC 27856; Ph. (252) 459-9836 **Details:** (Registrar of Deeds has Birth & Death Records from 1913 & Marriage Records from 1872; Clerk Superior Court has Divorce & Court Records from 1876, Probate & Land Records from 1869; oldest wills in Department of Archives, Raleigh, NC)
New Hanover www.co.new-hanover.nc.us/	F9	27 Nov 1729	**Craven** New Hanover County; 3rd & Princess St Rm 103; Wilmington, NC 28401-4090; Ph. (910) 341-7125 **Details:** (Courthouse burned 1798, 1819 & 1840; 1810 Census missing) (Registrar of Deeds has Birth, Marriage, Death & Land Records; Clerk Superior Court has Divorce, Probate & Court Records)
Northampton www.northamptonnc.com/	E4	1741	**Bertie** Northampton County; Jefferson St; PO Box 120; Jackson, NC 27845; Ph. (252) 534-2511 **Details:** (Registrar of Deeds has Birth, Marriage, Death & Land Records; Clerk Superior Court has Divorce Records from 1800, Probate & Court Records from 1761)
Onslow http://co.onslow.nc.us/	E8	1734	**New Hanover** Onslow County; 109 Old Bridge St Rm 107; Jacksonville, NC 28540; Ph. (910) 347-3451 **Details:** (Registrar of Deeds has Birth & Death Records from 1914, Marriage Records from 1893 & Land Records from 1734; Clerk Superior Court has Divorce, Probate & Court Records from 1915, earlier Records at Department of Archives, Raleigh NC 27602)
Orange www.co.orange.nc.us/	H5	31 Mar 1752	**Bladen, Granville, Johnston** Orange County; 200 S Cameron St; Hillsborough, NC 27278; Ph. (919) 245-2675 **Details:** (Courthouse burned 1789) (Registrar of Deeds has Birth & Death Records from 1913, Marriage & Land Records from 1754, Divorce Records from 1869, Probate Records from 1756 & Court Records Records from 1865)
Pamlico www.pamlico.com/	D7	8 Feb 1872	**Beaufort, Craven** Pamlico County; 202 Main St; PO Box 423; Bayboro, NC 28515; Ph. (252) 745-4421 **Details:** (Registrar of Deeds has Birth Records from 1913, Marriage, Death & Land Records from 1872; Clerk Superior Court has Divorce, Probate & Court Records from 1872)

County Website	Map Index	Date Created	Parent County or Territory From Which Organized Address/Details
Pamptecough		1712	**Bath** Pamptecough County; NC **Details:** (see Beaufort) Name changed to Beaufort, 1712
Pasquotank www.co.pasquotank.nc.us/	B4	1684	**Precinct in Albemarle** Pasquotank County; 206 E Main; PO Box 154; Elizabeth City, NC 27907-0039; Ph. (252) 335-4367 **Details:** (Courthouse burned 1862) (Clerk Superior Court has Divorce, Probate & Court Records; Registrar of Deeds has Birth & Death Records from 1913, Marriage Records from 1867 & Land Records from 1700's)
Pender www.pender-county.com/	F9	16 Feb 1875	**New Hanover** Pender County; 300 E Freemont St; PO Box 43; Burgaw, NC 28425; Ph. (910) 259-1225 **Details:** (Registrar of Deeds has Birth, Marriage, Death & Land Records; Clerk Superior Court has Divorce, Probate & Court Records)
Perquimans http://albemarle-nc.com/hertford/	C4	1670	**Precinct in Albemarle** Perquimans County; PO Box 74; Hertford, NC 27944; Ph. (252) 426-5660 **Details:** (Perquimans County was known as Berkeley Precinct from 1671 to 1681) (Registrar of Deeds has Marriage & Land Records; Clerk Superior Court has Probate & Court Records)
Person www2.person.net/person/home.htm	H4	5 Dec 1791	**Caswell** Person County; County Courthouse; Roxboro, NC 27573; Ph. (252) 597-1733 **Details:** (Registrar of Deeds has Birth, Marriage, Death & Land Records; Clerk Superior Court has Divorce, Probate & Court Records from 1791)
Pitt www.co.pitt.nc.us/index.asp	E6	24 Apr 1760	**Beaufort** Pitt County; W 3rd St; PO Box 35; Greenville, NC 27835; Ph. (252) 830-4128 **Details:** (Courthouse burned 1857) (Registrar of Deeds has Birth & Death Records from 1913, Marriage Records from 1866 & Land Records from 1762; Clerk Superior Court has Divorce, Probate & Court Records from 1885)
Polk www.polkcounty.org/	N7	1855	**Henderson, Rutherford** Polk County; PO Box 308; Columbus, NC 28722; Ph. (828) 894-8450 **Details:** (Clerk Superior Court has Divorce Records from 1932, Probate & Court Records from 1872; Registrar of Deeds has Marriage & Land Records)
Randolph www.co.randolph.nc.us/	I6	1779	**Guilford** Randolph County; Shaw Bldg; 158 Worth St; Asheboro, NC 27203; Ph. (336) 318-6960 **Details:** (1820 Census missing) (Registrar of Deeds has Birth & Death Records from 1913, Marriage Records from 1800 & Land Records; Clerk Superior Court has Divorce & Court Records, Probate Records from 1786)

County Website	Map Index	Date Created	Parent County or Territory From Which Organized Address/Details
Richmond www.co.richmond.nc.us/	I7	1779	**Anson** Richmond County; 114 E Franklin St #101; Rockingham, NC 28379; Ph. (910) 997-8250 **Details:** (Registrar of Deeds has Birth & Death Records from 1913, Marriage Records from 1870 & Land Records from 1784; Clerk Superior Court has Divorce Records from 1913 & Probate Records from 1782)
Robeson www.geocities.com/ncrobeson/	H8	1787	**Bladen** Robeson County; 500 N Elm St; PO Box 22; Lumberton, NC 28358; Ph. (919) 671-3044 **Details:** (Registrar of Deeds has Birth Records from 1913, Marriage Records from 1787, Death Records from 1915 & Land Records from 1799; Clerk Superior Court has Divorce & Court Records from 1920 & Probate Records from 1868)
Rockingham www.co.rockingham.nc.us/	I4	19 Nov 1785	**Guilford** Rockingham County; 371 NC 65 #212; PO Box 56; Wentworth, NC 27375; Ph. (336) 342-8820 **Details:** (Courthouse burned 1906) (Registrar of Deeds has Marriage Records from 1868, Birth & Death Records from 1913 & Land Records from 1787; Clerk Superior Court has Probate Records from 1804; North Carolina Historical Commissioner has Marriage Records 1741–1868)
Rowan www.co.rowan.nc.us/	K6	27 Mar 1753	**Anson** Rowan County; 202 N Main St; PO Box 2568; Salisbury, NC 28144-4346; Ph. (704) 636-3102 **Details:** (Registrar of Deeds has Birth, Marriage, Death & Land Records; Clerk Superior Court has Divorce Records from 1881, Probate & Court Records)
Rutherford www.rutherfordgov.org/	N6	14 Apr 1779	**Tryon** Rutherford County; 229 N Main St; PO Box 551; Rutherfordton, NC 28139-0630; Ph. (828) 287-6155 **Details:** (Courthouse burned in 1857) (Clerk Superior Court has Birth Records from 1917, Death Records from 1913, Marriage, Divorce, Probate, Court & Land Records from 1779, tax lists & voter registration)
Sampson www.rootsweb.com/~ncsampso/index.htm	G8	18 Apr 1784	**Duplin** Sampson County; 435 Rowan Rd; PO Box 256; Clinton, NC 28328-4700; Ph. (919) 529-8026 **Details:** (Courthouse burned 1921) (Registrar of Deeds has Marriage & Land Records; Clerk Superior Court has Probate Records)
Scotland www.rootsweb.com/~ncscotla/	I8	20 Feb 1899	**Richmond** Scotland County; 212 Biggs St; Laurinburg, NC 28352; Ph. (910) 277-2577 **Details:** (Registrar of Deeds has Birth Records from 1913, Marriage, Death & Burial Records from 1899 & Land Records; Clerk Superior Court has Divorce, Probate & Court Records from 1899)
Shaftesbury		1671	**Precinct in Albemarle** Shaftesbury; NC **Details:** Name changed in 1684 to Chowan

County Website	Map Index	Date Created	Parent County or Territory From Which Organized Address/Details
Stanly www.co.stanly.nc.us/	J6	11 Jan 1841	**Montgomery** Stanly County; 201 S 2nd St; Albemarle, NC 28001; Ph. (704) 983-3640 **Details:** (Registrar of Deeds has Marriage & Land Records; Clerk Superior Court has Probate Records)
Stokes www.co.stokes.nc.us/	J4	2 Nov 1789	**Surry** Stokes County; PO Box 67; Danbury, NC 27016; Ph. (336) 593-2811 **Details:** (Register of Deeds has Birth & Death Records from 1913, Land Records from 1787, Marriages from 1851, Marriage Bonds Index begins in late 1700's, Military Records from World War I)
Surry www.geocities.com/~surryco/	K4	5 Dec 1770	**Rowan** Surry County; 114 W Atkins St; Dobson, NC 27017-0345; Ph. (336) 401-8150 **Details:** (Registrar of Deeds has Birth, Marriage, Death, Burial & Land Records; Clerk Superior Court has Divorce, Court & Probate Records from 1771)
Swain www.rootsweb.com/~ncswain/	Q6	24 Feb 1871	**Jackson, Macon** Swain County; 1 Mitchell St; PO Box 417; Bryson, NC 28713; Ph. (828) 488-9273 **Details:** (Registrar of Deeds has Birth & Death Records from 1913, Marriage Records from 1907 & Land Records; Clerk Superior Court has Divorce & Court Records from 1900 & Probate Records)
Transylvania www.rootsweb.com/~nctransy/	O7	15 Feb 1861	**Henderson, Jackson** Transylvania County; 12 E Main St; PO Box 417; Brevard, NC 28712; Ph. (828) 884-3162 **Details:** (Registrar of Deeds has Birth & Death Records from 1913, Marriage & Land Records from 1861 & Military Discharge Records; Clerk Superior Court has Divorce, Probate & Court Records)
Tryon www.blueridge.net/lds/nc/tryon.html		1779	**Mecklenburg** Tryon County; NC **Details:** (see Lincoln) Discontinued 1779. Absorbed by Lincoln & Rutherford Counties
Tyrrell http://albemarle-nc.com/columbia/	B5	27 Nov 1729	**Chowan, Currituck, Pasquotank** Tyrrell County; 403 Main St; PO Box 449; Columbia, NC 27925; Ph. (252) 796-2901 **Details:** (Registrar of Deeds has Birth & Death Records from 1913, Marriage Records from 1862 & Land Records; Clerk Superior Court has Divorce Records, Probate Records from 1730 & Court Records from 1900)
Union www.co.union.nc.us/	K7	19 Dec 1842	**Anson, Mecklenburg** Union County; PO Box 248; Monroe, NC 28111; Ph. (704) 283-3727 **Details:** (Registrar of Deeds has Birth, Marriage, Death & Burial Records; Clerk Courts has Divorce, Probate, Military, Court & Naturalization Records; County Assessor has Land Records)
Vance www.vancecounty.org/	G4	5 Mar 1881	**Franklin, Granville, Warren** Vance County; 122 Young St Ste F; Henderson, NC 27536; Ph. (252) 438-4155 **Details:** (Clerk Superior Court has Divorce, Probate & Court Records; Registrar of Deeds has Marriage & Land Records)

County Website	Map Index	Date Created	Parent County or Territory From Which Organized Address/Details
Wake www.co.wake.nc.us/	G5	**5 Dec 1770**	**Cumberland, Johnston, Orange** Wake County; St Garland James Bldg; 300 S Salisbury; PO Box 1897; Raleigh, NC 27602; Ph. (919) 856-5460 **Details:** (1810 & 1820 Census missing) (Registrar of Deeds has Marriage & Land Records; Clerk Superior Court has Probate Records)
Warren www.rootsweb.com/~ncwarren/	F4	**14 Apr 1779**	**Bute** Warren County; PO Box 506; Warrenton, NC 27589-0709; Ph. (252) 257-3265 **Details:** (Registrar of Deeds has Birth & Death Records from 1913, Marriage & Land Records from 1764; Clerk Superior Court has Divorce & Probate Records from 1764 & Court Records from 1968)
Washington www.washingtoncountygov.com/	C5	**15 Nov 1799**	**Tyrell** Washington County; 120 Adams St; Plymouth, NC 27962; Ph. (252) 793-2325 **Details:** (Courthouse burned 1862, 1869 & 1873) (Registrar of Deeds has Birth & Death Records from 1913, Marriage Records from 1851 & Land Records from 1799; Clerk Superior Court has Divorce Records from 1871, Probate & Court Records from 1873)
Watauga www.wataugacounty.org/	M4	**27 Jan 1849**	**Ashe, Caldwell, Wilkes, Yancey** Watauga County; 842 W King St; Boone, NC 28607-3531; Ph. (828) 265-8052 **Details:** (Registrar of Deeds has Birth & Death Records from 1914, Marriage Records from 1872 & Land Records; Clerk Superior Court has Divorce, Probate & Court Records from 1872)
Wayne www.esn.net/waynecounty/	F6	**18 Oct 1779**	**Dobbs** Wayne County; 215 S William St; PO Box 267; Goldsboro, NC 27530-4824; Ph. (919) 731-1449 **Details:** (Registrar of Deeds has Birth, Marriage, Death, Burial & Land Records; Clerk Superior Court has Divorce, Probate & Court Records)
Wickham		**3 Dec 1705**	**Precinct of Bath** Wickham County; NC **Details:** (see Hyde) Name changed to Hyde, 1712
Wilkes www.wilkesnc.org/government/county.htm	L5	**15 Nov 1777**	**Surry, District of Washington** Wilkes County; 110 North St; Wilkesboro, NC 28697; Ph. (336) 651-7351 **Details:** (Registrar of Deeds has Birth & Death Records from 1913, Marriage & Land Records from 1778; Clerk Superior Court has Divorce, Probate & Court Records)
Wilson www.wilson-co.com/	F6	**13 Feb 1855**	**Edgecombe, Johnston, Nash, Wayne** Wilson County; 101 N Goldsboro St; Wilson, NC 27893; Ph. (252) 399-2935 **Details:** (Registrar of Deeds has Birth, Marriage, Death & Land Records; Clerk Superior Court has Divorce & Court Records from 1868 & Probate Records from 1855)
Yadkin www.yadkincounty.gov/	K4	**28 Dec 1850**	**Surry** Yadkin County; 101 State St; Yadkinville, NC 27055; Ph. (336) 679-4225 **Details:** (Registrar of Deeds has Birth & Death Records from 1913, Marriage & Land Records from 1850; Clerk Superior Court has Divorce & Court Records, Probate Records from 1850)

County	Map	Date
Website	Index	Created
Yancey	N6	1833
www.main.nc.us/yancey/index.html		

Parent County or Territory From Which Organized

Address/Details

Buncombe, Burke

Yancey County; County Courthouse; Burnsville, NC 28714;
Ph. (828) 682-2174

Details: (Registrar of Deeds has Birth, Marriage, Death & Burial Records; Clerk Superior Court has Divorce Records from 1875, Probate, Court & Land Records from 1870; Department of Archives & Historical in Raleigh, North Carolina has older Records)

North Dakota

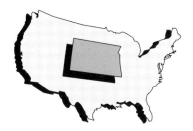

Capital: Bismarck

Territory: 1861

State: 1889 (39th)

Liberty and union, now and forever, one and inseparable

Pierre Gaultier de Varennes was the first French explorer in the area. He reached Indian villages on the Missouri River in 1738. The French laid claim to the area in 1682, but permitted British fur trading. The Louisiana Purchase in 1803 gave the southwestern half of North Dakota to the United States. Lewis and Clark explored the area the following year. The first permanent settlement—besides those of the Native Americans—was made by Scottish pioneers from Canada in 1812 at Pembina.

As Indians were driven westward, settlers came into the eastern regions of the state to farm. The Dakota Territory was organized in 1861 and included the two Dakotas, Montana, and Wyoming. The first Homestead Act offered free land to settlers, but the Civil War and Indian wars delayed settlement. During the Civil War, about 200 men fought for the Union forces. In 1864, the Montana Territory was created, taking the Wyoming and Montana areas from the Dakota Territory.

The possibility of becoming a territory had encouraged more settlers, and there were several well-established communities by the time the first legislature of the newly formed Dakota Territory met in 1862. Over the following years, ongoing battles erupted with the Indians, ending around 1890 with the surrender of Sitting Bull. Farmers had limited success because of scant rainfall and faced the difficulty of getting crops to market. The railroad became a source of ongoing turmoil as some wanted to regulate prices charged for transportation.

As railroads reached completion, settlement in North Dakota began in earnest. In 1871, railroads reached the Red River from St. Paul and Duluth. Dreams of acres of fertile land drew thousands of northern and middle Europeans to North Dakota. Norwegians led the immigration, but large numbers of Swedes, Danes, Icelanders, Czechs, Poles, and Dutch also came. French-Canadians came from Canada. Germans settled around Bismarck and the south central counties, which is evident from the names of the cities in the area, such as Leipzig, Strassburg and Danzig.

The Dakota Territory was divided into North and South Dakota in about 1873. In 1889, North Dakota became the thirty-ninth state in the Union.

Look for vital records in the following locations:

- **Birth and death records:** Registration of births and deaths was required from 1893 to 1895 and after 1899. General compliance with the law was not reached until about 1923. Copies of these records are available from the Division of Vital Records in Bismarck, North Dakota.

- **Marriage, divorce and probate records:** Marriage certificates and licenses are filed in the office of each county judge. Since 1 July 1925, copies of licenses and marriage certificates have been forwarded to the State Registrar, who can issue certified copies. District Court Clerks have charge of civil court, divorce, and probate records.

- **Census records:** North Dakota was included in the 1836 Wisconsin, 1840 Iowa, 1850 Minnesota, and 1860–1880 Dakota Territorial censuses.

- **Land records:** Original patents and copies of township plats are available from the Bureau of Land Management in Billings, Montana. Records of the local land offices are at the State Historical Society of North Dakota in Bismarck, North Dakota. The county registrars of deeds have deeds and land titles dating from the time land became available for private purchase.

Division of Vital Records
600 East Boulevard Avenue, Dept 301
Bismarck, ND 58505-0200
(701) 328-2360; Fax (701) 328-1850
www.vitalnd.com/

State Historical Society of North Dakota State Archives and Library
612 East Boulevard Avenue
Bismarck, ND 58505-0830
(701) 328-2091; Fax (701) 328-2650
www.state.nd.us/hist/sal.htm

North Dakota

Societies and Repositories

Bismarck-Mandan Historical and Genealogical Society; Box 485; Bismarck, ND 58502-0485; dearlsmith2019@msn.com; www.rootsweb.com/~ndbmhgs.

Bottineau County Genealogical Society; 614 W. Pine Circle; Bottineau, ND 58318.

Bowman County Genealogical Society; PO Box 1044; Bowman, ND 58623.

Central North Dakota Genealogical Society; Harvey Public Library; 119 East 10th; Harvey, ND 58341.

Genealogical Guild of Wilkin County, Minnesota and Richland County, North Dakota; c/o Leach Public Library; Wahpeton, ND 58075.

Griggs County Genealogical Society; Box 237, Griggs County Court House; Cooperstown, ND 58425.

James River Genealogical Club; 651 4th St. N.; Carrington, ND 58421; cpaulson@daktel.com; www.rootsweb.com/ ~ndjrjc/index.htm.

McLean County Genealogical Society; PO Box 51; Garrison, ND 58540.

Medora Centennial Commission; Box 212; Medora, ND 58645.

Mouse River Loop Genealogical Society; Box 1391; Minot, ND 58702-1391.

North Dakota Bismarck-Mandan Genealogical Society; PO Box 485; Bismarck, ND 58501.

North Dakota State Archives and Historical Research Library; North Dakota Heritage Center; 612 East Boulevard A; Bismarck, ND 58505-0830; (701) 328-2666; archives@state.nd.us.; www.state.nd.us/ hist/index.html.

North Dakota State Genealogical Society; PO Box 485; Bismarck, ND 58502.

North Dakota State Library; 604 E Blvd Ave - Dept 250; Bismark, ND 58505-0800; (701) 328-2492; tbodvig@state.nd.us; http://ndsl.lib.state.nd.us.

Red River Valley Genealogy Society; PO Box 9284; Fargo, ND 58106-9284; rrvgs@fargocity.com; http://fargocity.com/~rrvgs.

Southwestern North Dakota Genealogical Society; HCR 01, Box 32A; Regent, ND 58650; (701) 563-4672; patrice@pop.ctctel.com.

State Historical Society of North Dakota; Liberty Memorial Bldg.; 612 East Blvd. Ave., Bismarck, ND 58501; histsoc@state.nd.us; www.state.nd.us/hist.

Williams County Genealogical Society; 703W 7th St.; Williston, ND 58801-4908.

Bibliography and Record Sources

General

Aberle, George P. *Pioneers and Their Sons: One Hundred Sixty-Five Family Histories*. Bismarck, North Dakota: Tumbleweed Press, 1980.

Albers, Everett C. *Germans from Russia Settlers*. Fessenden, North Dakota: The Grass Roots Press, 1999.

Compendium of History and Biography of North Dakota Containing a History of North Dakota: Embracing an Account of Early Explorations, Early Settlement, Indian Occupancy . . . and a Concise History of Growth and Development of the State also a Compendium of Biography of North Dakota. (1900) Reprint. Salem, Massachusetts: Higginson Books, 1994.

County Histories for Biographical Information. *Representative Biographical Encyclopedias are: Compendium of History and Biography of North Dakota Containing a History of North Dakota*. Chicago: Geo. A. Ogle & Co., 1900.

Crawford, Lewis Ferandus. *History of North Dakota and North Dakota Biography*. 3 vols. Chicago: American Historical Soc., 1931.

Davenport, John B., and Colleen A. Oihus. *Guide to the Orin G. Libby Manuscript Collection and Related Research Collections*. 2 vols. Grand Forks, North Dakota: Chester Fritz Library, University of North Dakota, 1975, 1983.

History of the Red River Valley, Past and Present. 2 vols. (1909) Reprint. Salem, Maryland: Higginson Books, 1994.

Lareau, Paul J., and Elmer Courteau. *French-Canadian Families of the North Central States: A Genealogical Dictionary*. 8 vols. St. Paul, Minnesota: Northwest Territory French and Canadian Heritage Institute, 1980.

Lounsberry, Clement A. *Early History of North Dakota*. Washington, D.C.: Liberty Press, 1919.

Lounsberry, Clement Augustus. *North Dakota History and People, Outlines of American History*. 3 vols. Chicago: S. J. Clarke, 1916.

North Dakota Research Outline. Series U.S.-States, no. 35. Salt Lake City: Family History Library. 1988.

Rath, George *The Black Sea Germans in the Dakotas*. Freeman, South Dakota: Pine Hill Press, 1977.

Robinson, Elwyn B. *History of North Dakota*. Lincoln: University of Nebraska Press, 1966.

Rylance, Daniel, and J. F. S. Smeall. *Reference Guide to North Dakota History and North Dakota Literature*. Grand Forks: Chester Fritz Library of the University of North Dakota, 1979.

State Historical Society of North Dakota (Bismarck, North Dakota). *Historical Data Project; Pioneer Biography Files*. Bismarck, North Dakota: State Historical Society of North Dakota, 1988–1989. Microfilm, 34 rolls.

Stupnik, Cynthia Ann. *Steppes to New Odessa: Germans from Russia Who Settled in Odessa Township, Dakota Territory*. Bowie, Maryland: Heritage Books, 1996.

The Collections of the State Historical Society of North Dakota. 7 vols. Bismarck, North Dakota: Tribune State Printers, 1906–.

Thorson, Playford V. *Plains Folk: North Dakota's Ethnic History.* Fargo, North Dakota: In cooperation with the North Dakota Humanities Council and the University of North Dakota, 1988.

Vexler, Robert I. *Chronology and Documentary Handbook of the State of North Dakota.* Dobbs Ferry, New York: Oceana Publications, 1978.

Atlases, Maps and Gazetteers

Goodman, Lowell R., and R. J. Eidem. *The Atlas of North Dakota.* Fargo: North Dakota Studies, 1976.

North Dakota County Atlas. Bismark: North Dakota State Highway Dept., Planning Division, 1985.

Patera, Alan H. *North Dakota Post Offices 1850–1982.* Burtonsville, Maryland: The Depot, 1982.

Phillips, George H. *Postoffices and Postmarks of Dakota Territory.* Crete, Nebraska: J-B Publishing Co., 1973.

Wick, Douglas A. *North Dakota Place Names.* Bismark, North Dakota: Hedemarken Collectibles, 1988.

Williams, Mary Ann Barnes. *Origins of North Dakota Place Names.* Washburn, North Dakota: Mary Ann Barnes Williams, 1966.

Census Records

Available Census Records and Census Substitutes

Federal Census 1860, 1870, 1880, 1900, 1910, 1920

Federal Mortality Schedules 1870, 1880

Union Veterans and Widows 1890

State/Territorial 1836, 1885, 1915, 1925

Dollarhide, William. *The Census Book: A Genealogist's Guide to Federal Census Facts, Schedules and Indexes.* Bountiful, Utah: Heritage Quest, 1999.

Kemp, Thomas Jay. *The American Census Handbook.* Wilmington, Delaware: Scholarly Resources, Inc., 2001.

Lainhart, Ann S. *State Census Records.* Baltimore: Genealogical Publishing Co., Inc., 1992.

Szucs, Loretto Dennis and Matthew Wright. *Finding Answers in U.S. Census Records.* Ancestry Publishing, 2001.

Thorndale, William and William Dollarhide. *Map Guides to the U.S. Federal Censuses, 1790–1920: Arkansas, 1810–1920.* Bountiful, Utah, American Genealogical Lending Library, 1987.

Court, Probate and Wills

United States. Bureau of Indian Affairs. *Standing Rock Agency. Heirship Records, Early 1900's.* Kansas City, Missouri: Federal Archives and Records Center, 1977. Microfilm, 3 rolls.

Immigration

Gilman, Rhonda R. *The Red River Trails: Oxcart Routes between St. Paul and the Selkirk Settlement 1820–1870.* St. Paul: Minnesota Historical Society, 1979.

Michels, John M. *North Dakota Pioneers from the Banat.* Bismarck, North Dakota: University of Mary Press, 1992.

Sherman, William C. *Prairie Mosaic: An Ethnic Atlas of Rural North Dakota.* Fargo, North Dakota: North Dakota Institute for Regional Studies, 1983.

United States. Circuit Court (North Dakota: Southeastern Division). *Declarations of Intention, 1890–1924.* Microfilm of original records of Circuit Court held at Fargo. Salt Lake City: Filmed by the Genealogical Society of Utah, 1991.

United States. District Court (North Dakota: Southeastern District). *Naturalization Records, 1906–1924.* Microfilm of original records of the District Court held at Fargo. Salt Lake City: Filmed by the Genealogical Society of Utah, 1991.

Writers' Program (North Dakota). *Ethnic Group Files, ca. 1935–1942.* Bismarck, North Dakota: State Historical Society of North Dakota, 1989.

Land

Brown, Ruth. *Sioux Personal Property Claims from the Original Ledger.* Medford, Oregon: Rogue Genealogical Society, 1987.

Lindgren, H. Elaine. *Land in Her Own Name: Women as Homesteaders in North Dakota.* Fargo, North Dakota: North Dakota Institute for Regional Studies, 1991.

United States. Bureau of Indian Affairs. Standing Rock Agency. *Land Records, 1906–1921.* Kansas City, Missouri: Federal Archives and Records Center, 1977.

Military

Fraser, G. Angus. *Roster of the Men and Women Who Served in the Army or Naval Service (including the Marine Corps) of the United States or its Allies from the State of North Dakota in the World War, 1917–1918,* 4 vols. Bismarck: Bismarck Tribune Co., 1931.

Lounsberry, Clement A. *Early History of North Dakota.* Washington, D.C.: Liberty Press, 1919.

Pensioners on the Roll as of January 1, 1883 (Living in Dakota Territory). Park Genealogical Books, 1996.

United States. Adjutant General's Office. *Index to Compiled Service Records of Volunteer Union Soldiers Who Served in Organizations from the Territory of Dakota.* Washington, D.C.: The National Archives, 1964.

United States. Selective Service System. North Dakota, *World War I Selective Service System Draft Registration Cards, 1917–1918.* National Archives Microfilm Publications, M1509. Washington, D.C.: National Archives, 1987–1988.

United States. Veterans Administration. *Pension Index File, Alphabetical; of the Veterans, 1861–1934.* Washington, D.C.: Veterans Administration, Publications Service, 1953.

Vital and Cemetery Records

Fargo Genealogical Society. *North Dakota Cemeteries,* 16 vols. Fargo, North Dakota. Fargo Genealogical Society, 1972–1977.

Historical Records Survey (North Dakota) *Guide to Public Vital Statistics Records in North Dakota.* Bismarck, North Dakota: The Survey, 1941.

United States. Bureau of Indian Affairs. Standing Rock Agency. *Births, Marriages and Deaths, 1880–1942.* Kansas City, Missouri: Federal Archives and Records Center, 1977.

County Website	Map Index	Date Created	Parent County or Territory From Which Organized Address/Details
Adams www.rootsweb.com/~ndadams/	N9	17 Apr 1907	**Hettinger** Adams County; 602 Adams Ave; Hettinger, ND 58639; Ph. (701) 567-2460 **Details:** (Clerk District Court has Marriage, Divorce, Probate, Court & Land Records from 1907)
Allred		9 Mar 1883	**Howard** Allred County; ND **Details:** (see McKenzie) Eliminated 16 Mar 1905 & absorbed by McKenzie
Barnes www.rootsweb.com/~ndbarnes/	D8	4 Jan 1873	**Pembina** Barnes County; 230 4th S NE; Valley City, ND 58072; Ph. (701) 845-8512 **Details:** (Formerly Burbank County. Name changed to Barnes 14 Jan 1875. Organized 5 Aug 1878) (Clerk District Court has Birth, Death, Burial & Court Records; County Judge has Marriage & Probate Records)
Benson www.state.nd.us	H5	9 Mar 1883	**DeSmet, Ramsey** Benson County; PO Box 206; 311 B Ave S; Minnewaukan, ND 58351; Ph. (701) 473-5340, bserickson@state.nd.us **Details:** (Clerk of District Court has Court, Death, Divorce, Guardianship, Marriage, & Probate Records; Recorder has Land Records; Auditor has Newspapers & Other Historical Records; Treasurer has Tax Records; State Health Department has Birth Records)
Billings www.geocities.com/Athens/Forum/2079/ BILLINGS.HTM	Q8	10 Feb 1879	**Unorg. Terr., Howard** Billings County; 495 4th St; PO Box 138; Medora, ND 58645-0138; Ph. (701) 623-4492 **Details:** (Organized 30 Apr 1886) (Clerk District Court has Marriage Records from 1893, Burial Records from 1922, Divorce Records, Probate Records from 1895, Court Records from 1890 & Land Records from 1886)
Bottineau www.geocities.com/Athens/Forum/2079/ bottine.html	J3	4 Jan 1873	**Buffalo** Bottineau County; 314 W 5th St; Bottineau, ND 58318; Ph. (701) 228-3983 **Details:** (Organized 22 Jul 1884) (Clerk District Court has Birth, Death & Burial Records from 1943, Marriage Records from 1887, Divorce, Probate & Court Records from 1889 & Naturalization Records from 1884; Registrar of Deeds has Land Records)

County	Map	Date	Parent County or Territory From Which Organized
Website	Index	Created	Address/Details

Bowman   **Q10**   **8 Mar 1883**   **Billings**
www.rootsweb.com/~ndbowman/

Bowman County; 104 1st St NW; Bowman, ND 58623; Ph. (701) 523-3450

Details: (Eliminated 30 Nov 1896. Recreated 24 May 1901. Attached to Stark County prior to organization 17 Apr 1907) (Clerk District Court has Marriage Records from 1907, Divorce Records, Probate & Court Records from 1908, Land Records from 1896 & Burial Records)

Buffalo   **6 Jan 1864**   **Brugier, Charles Mix & Unorg. Terr., South Dakota**

Buffalo County; ND

Details: Now in South Dakota (see Burleigh, Kidder, Logan, McHenry, Rolette & Sheridan)

Buford   **9 Mar 1883**   **Wallette**

Buford County; ND

Details: (see Williams) Eliminated 30 Nov 1892 & added to Williams

Burbank   **4 Jan 1873**   **Pembina**

Burbank County; ND

Details: (see Barnes) Name changed to Barnes 14 Jan 1875. Lost to Trail County 12 Jan 1875 & Griggs County 18 Feb 1881 & Discontinued

Burke   **N3**   **8 Feb 1910**   **Ward**
www.rootsweb.com/~ndburke/burke2.htm

Burke County; 103 Main St SW; PO Box 219; Bowbells, ND 58721-0219; Ph. (701) 377-2718

Details: (Clerk District Court has Birth Records from 1905, Marriage, Death, Burial, Divorce, Probate & Court Records from 1910, Land Records from 1900 & homestead patents from 1903)

Burleigh   **J8**   **4 Jan 1873**   **Buffalo**
www.rootsweb.com/~ndburlei/index.htm

Burleigh County; 514 E Thayer Ave; PO Box 5518; Bismarck, ND 58501-4413; Ph. (701) 222-6690

Details: (Clerk District Court has Marriage & Probate Records from 1898, Court Records from 1876 & Burial Records from 1950's)

Cass   **C8**   **4 Jan 1873**   **Pembina**
www.co.cass.nd.us/

Cass County; 211 9th St S; PO Box 2806; Fargo, ND 58103-1833; Ph. (701) 241-5646

Details: (Clerk District Court has Divorce & Court Records from 1885)

Cavalier   **F3**   **4 Jan 1873**   **Pembina**
www.ccjda.org/

Cavalier County; 901 3rd St; Langdon, ND 58249-2457; Ph. (701) 256-2124

Details: (Organized 8 Jul 1884) (Clerk District Court has Marriage, Probate & Court Records Records from 1881 & Divorce Records from 1888; Registrar of Deeds has Land Records)

Chippewa   **24 Apr 1862**   **Unorg. Terr.**

Chippewa County; ND

Details: (Eliminated 17 Dec 1863 to Unorg. Terr.)

County Website	Map Index	Date Created	Parent County or Territory From Which Organized Address/Details
Church		11 Mar 1887	**McHenry, Sheridan, old** Church County; ND **Details:** (see Sheridan) Attached to McHenry. Lost to McHenry, McLean & Pierce Counties. Eliminated 30 Nov 1892 to Sheridan
De Smet		4 Jan 1873	**Buffalo** De Smet County; ND **Details:** (see Pierce) Formerly French County. Name changed to DeSmet 14 Jan 1875. Eliminated 11 Mar 1887 to Pierce
Dickey www.rootsweb.com/~nddickey/dickey.htm	F10	5 Mar 1881	**La Moure, Ransom, Unorg. Terr.** Dickey County; 309 N 2nd St; PO Box 215; Ellendale, ND 58436; Ph. (701) 349-3560 **Details:** (Organized 31 Aug 1882) (Clerk District Court has Marriage, Burial, Divorce, Probate, Military & Court Records; Registrar of Deeds has Land Records; State Historical Society has Naturalization Records)
Divide www.rootsweb.com/~nddivide/divide97.htm	Q3	8 Nov 1910	**Williams** Divide County; 300 N Main St; PO Box 68; Crosby, ND 58730-0068; Ph. (701) 965-6831 **Details:** (Clerk District Court has Birth, Marriage, Death, Burial, Divorce, Probate, Court & Military Records from 1910; Registrar of Deeds has Land Records from 1910; State Historical Society has Naturalization Records)
Dunn www.dunnjda.com/	O7	24 May 1901	**Stark** Dunn County; 205 Owens St; PO Box 136; Manning, ND 58642; Ph. (701) 573-4447 **Details:** (Organized 17 Jan 1908) (Clerk District Court has Marriage, Probate, Divorce & Court Records from 1908 & Military District Records from 1919; Registrar of Deeds has Land Records from 1900; State Historical Society has Naturalization Records)
Dunn, old www.rootsweb.com/~nddunn/		9 Mar 1883	**Howard** Dunn, old County; ND **Details:** (Discontinued & annexed to Stark 30 Nov 1896)
Eddy www.rootsweb.com/~ndeddy/	G6	31 Mar 1885	**Foster** Eddy County; 524 Central Ave; New Rockford, ND 58356; Ph. (701) 947-2813 **Details:** (Clerk District Court has Marriage, Probate & Court Records; Registrar of Deeds has Land Records)
Emmons www.rootsweb.com/~ndemmons/index.htm	I10	10 Feb 1879	**Unorg. Terr., Burleigh, Campbell County, South Dakota** Emmons County; 100 4th St NW; Linton, ND 58552; Ph. (701) 254-4812 **Details:** (Organized 9 Nov 1883) (Clerk District Court has Birth Records from 1889, Marriage Records from 1888, Death, Burial, Divorce & Court Records from 1890, Probate Records from 1884 & Naturalization Records from 1886; Registrar of Deeds has Land Records)
Flanery		9 Mar 1883	**Wallette** Flanery County; ND **Details:** (see Williams) Eliminated 30 Nov 1892 & added to Williams

County Website	Map Index	Date Created	Parent County or Territory From Which Organized Address/Details
Foster www.rootsweb.com/~ndfoster/	F6	4 Jan 1873	**Pembina** Foster County; 1000 5th St N; PO Box 257; Carrington, ND 58421; Ph. (701) 652-1001 **Details:** (Organized 11 Oct 1883) (Clerk District Court has Birth & Death Records from 1900, Marriage, Divorce, Probate & Court Records from 1884, Military & Naturalization Records from 1900 & Burial Records from 1950's; Registrar of Deeds has Land Records)
French		4 Jan 1873	**Buffalo** French County; ND **Details:** (see Pierce) Name changed to De Smet 14 Jan 1875. Eliminated 11 Mar 1887 to Pierce
Garfield		13 Mar 1885	**Mountrail, Stevens** Garfield County; ND **Details:** (Eliminated 30 Nov 1892 to McLean & Ward)
Gingras		4 Jan 1873	**Buffalo** Gingras County; ND **Details:** (see Wells) Name changed to Wells 26 Feb 1881
Golden Valley www.rootsweb.com/~ndgolden/	R8	19 Nov 1912	**Billings** Golden Valley County; 150 1st Ave SE; PO Box 9; Beach, ND 58621-0009; Ph. (701) 872-4352 **Details:** (Clerk District Court has Birth, Marriage, Death, Burial, Divorce, Probate & Court Records from 1912; Registrar of Deeds has Land Records from 1912)
Grand Forks www.grandforkscountygov.com/homepage.htm	C5	4 Jan 1873	**Pembina** Grand Forks County; 151 S 4th St; PO Box 1477; Grand Forks, ND 58201; Ph. (701) 780-8238 **Details:** (Organized 12 Jan 1875) (Clerk District Court has Birth Records from 1903, Death Records from 1908, Divorce Records from 1878, Burial & Court Records, adoption Records & change of name; County Judge has Marriage Records from 1887 & Probate Records from 1880; Registrar of Deeds has Land Records)
Grant www.rootsweb.com/~ndgrant/	L10	7 Nov 1916	**Morton** Grant County; 106 2nd Ave NE; Carson, ND 58529; Ph. (701) 622-3615 **Details:** (Clerk District Court has Birth Records from 1945, Marriage, Death, Burial, Divorce, Probate & Court Records from 1916; Registrar of Deeds has Land Records)
Griggs www.cooperstownnd.com/	E6	18 Feb 1881	**Foster, Burbank, Traill** Griggs County; 808 Rollin Ave SW; Cooperstown, ND 58425; Ph. (701) 797-2772 **Details:** (Organized 16 Jun 1882) (Clerk District Court has Birth Records from 1901, Marriage & Probate Records from 1883, Death Records from 1901, Divorce & Court Records from 1887; Registrar of Deeds has Land Records from 1880)
Hettinger www.hettcnty.com/	N9	24 May 1901	**Stark** Hettinger County; 336 Pacific Ave; Mott, ND 58646; Ph. (701) 824-2645 **Details:** (Attached to Stark County prior to organization 17 Apr 1907) (Clerk District Court has Birth, Death & Burial Records from 1943, Marriage, Divorce, Probate & Court Records from 1907; Registrar of Deeds has Land Records)

County Website	Map Index	Date Created	Parent County or Territory From Which Organized Address/Details
Hettinger, old		9 Mar 1883	**Stark** Hettinger, old County; ND **Details:** (Eliminated 30 Nov 1896 to Stark)
Howard		8 Jan 1873	**Unorg. Terr.** Howard County; ND **Details:** (Eliminated 9 Mar 1883 to Allred, Dunn, McKenzie, old & Wallace)
Kidder www.rootsweb.com/~ndkidder/	H7	4 Jan 1873	**Buffalo** Kidder County; 120 E Broadway; PO Box 66; Steele, ND 58482; Ph. (701) 475-2651 **Details:** (Organized 22 Mar 1881) (Clerk District Court has Birth, Death & Burial Records from 1943, Divorce & Court Records from 1885; County Judge has Marriage Records from 1887 & Probate Records from 1883; Registrar of Deeds has Land Records from 1881)
Kittson		24 Apr 1862	**Unorg. Terr.** Kittson County; ND **Details:** (Organized 1 Jun 1862. Eliminated 17 Dec 1863 to Unorg. Terr.)
La Moure www.rootsweb.com/~ndlamour/	F9	4 Jan 1873	**Pembina** La Moure County; 202 4th Ave NE; PO Box 128; La Moure, ND 58458; Ph. (701) 883-5301 **Details:** (Organized 27 Oct 1881) (Clerk District Court has Birth, Marriage, Death, Burial, Divorce, Probate & Court Records from 1881; Registrar of Deeds has Land Records)
Logan www.rootsweb.com/~ndlogan/	H9	4 Jan 1873	**Buffalo** Logan County; 301 Broadway; Napoleon, ND 58561; Ph. (701) 754-2751 **Details:** (Organized 1 Sep 1884) (Clerk District Court has incomplete Birth & Death Records from 1893, Marriage, Divorce & Court Records from 1890, Probate Records from 1898, Burial Records from 1926 & Military Records from 1920; Registrar of Deeds has Land Records from 1884)
McHenry www.rootsweb.com/~ndmchenr/	J4	4 Jan 1873	**Buffalo** McHenry County; 407 Main St; Towner, ND 58788; Ph. (701) 537-5729 **Details:** (Organized 14 May 1885) (Clerk District Court has Marriage Records from 1903, Divorce, Probate & Court Records from 1900; Registrar of Deeds has Land Records)
McIntosh www.rootsweb.com/~ndmcinto/	H10	9 Mar 1883	**Logan, Unorg. Terr., McPherson County, SD** McIntosh County; 112 NE 1st St; Ashley, ND 58413; Ph. (701) 288-3450 **Details:** (Organized 4 Oct 1884) (Clerk District Court has Birth & Death Records from 1899, Marriage Records from 1885, Probate Records from 1889, Court & Divorce Records from 1937 & Military District Records from 1943; Registrar of Deeds has Land Records; State Historical Society has Naturalization Records)

County Website	Map Index	Date Created	Parent County or Territory From Which Organized Address/Details
McKenzie www.4eyes.net/	Q6	**24 May 1901**	**Billings** McKenzie County; 201 5th St NW; PO Box 523; Watford, ND 58854; Ph. (701) 444-3452 **Details:** (Attached to Stark County prior to organization 16 Mar 1905) (Clerk District Court has Birth & Death Records from 1943, Marriage, Divorce, Probate & Court Records from 1905 & Burial Records; Registrar of Deeds has Land Records)
McKenzie (old)		**9 Mar 1883**	**Howard** McKenzie, old County; ND **Details:** (Annexed to Billings 30 Nov 1896)
McLean www.visitmcleancounty.com/	L6	**8 Mar 1883**	**Stevens, Burleigh, Sheridan, old** McLean County; 712 5th Ave; Washburn, ND 58577; Ph. (701) 462-8541 **Details:** (Clerk District Court has Marriage Records from 1887, Burial Records from 1920, Divorce & Court Records from 1891 & Probate Records from 1900; Registrar of Deeds has Land Records)
Mercer www.rootsweb.com/~ndmercer/	M7	**14 Jan 1875**	**Unorg. Terr.** Mercer County; 1021 Arthur St; Stanton, ND 58571; Ph. (701) 745-3262 **Details:** (Organized 22 Aug 1884) (Clerk District Court has Birth, Death & Burial Records from 1942, Marriage Records from 1894, Divorce & Court Records from 1906 & Probate Records from 1898; Registrar of Deeds has Land Records; State Archives has Naturalization Records)
Morton www.rootsweb.com/%7endmorton/	L8	**8 Jan 1873**	**Unorg. Terr.** Morton County; 210 2nd Ave NW; Mandan, ND 58554; Ph. (701) 667-3355 **Details:** (Organized 28 Feb 1881) (Clerk District Court has Birth Records from 1883, Marriage Records from 1888, Death Records from 1873, Burial Records from 1943, Divorce & Probate Records from 1900's & Court Records from late 1800's; Registrar of Deeds has Land Records from late 1800's)
Mountrail www.rootsweb.com/~ndmountr/mountrail.htm	N5	**4 Jan 1873**	**Buffalo** Mountrail County; PO Box 69; Stanley, ND 58784-0069; Ph. (701) 628-2915 **Details:** (Annexed to Ward in 1891 & eliminated 30 Nov 1892. Recreated 29 Jan 1909 from Ward) (Clerk District Court has Birth, Marriage, Death, Divorce, Probate, Court & Naturalization Records from 1909, Military District Records from 1919 & incomplete Burial Records; Registrar of Deeds has Land Records)
Nelson www.rootsweb.com/~ndnelson/	E5	**2 Mar 1883**	**Foster, Grand Forks, Ramsey, Unorg. Terr.** Nelson County; 210 W B Ave; PO Box 565; Lakota, ND 58344; Ph. (701) 247-2462 **Details:** (Clerk District Court has Birth & Death Records from 1903, Marriage, Probate & Land Records from 1880, Divorce, Court & Burial Records)

County	Map	Date	Parent County or Territory From Which Organized
Website	Index	Created	Address/Details

Oliver   L7   **14 Apr 1885**   **Mercer**
www.rootsweb.com/~ndoliver/
Oliver County; 315 W Main; Center, ND 58530; Ph. (701) 794-8777
Details: (Clerk District Court has Marriage Records from 1915 & Death Records; County Judge has Probate & Court Records; Registrar of Deeds has Land Records)

Pembina   D3   **9 Jan 1867**   **Unorg. Terr.**
www.rootsweb.com/~ndpembin/pembina.htm
Pembina County; 301 Dakota St W #6; Cavalier, ND 58220;
Ph. (701) 265-4275
Details: (Clerk District Court has Birth & Death Records from 1893, Marriage Records from 1882, Divorce, Court & Probate Records from 1883, Military Records from 1945 & Burial Records from 1943; Registrar of Deeds has Land Records)

Pierce   I3   **11 Mar 1887**   **De Smet, Bottineau, McHenry, Rolette**
www.rootsweb.com/~ndpierce/
Pierce County; 240 2nd St; Rugby, ND 58368; Ph. (701) 776-6161
Details: (Organized 11 Apr 1889) (Clerk District Court has Birth, Death & Burial Records from 1943, Marriage Records from 1888, Divorce & Court Records from 1900 & Probate Records from 1898; Registrar of Deeds has Land Records)

Ramsey   F4   **4 Jan 1873**   **Pembina**
www.rootsweb.com/~ndramsey/ramsey.htm
Ramsey County; 524 4th Ave #4; Devils Lake, ND 58301;
Ph. (701) 662-7066
Details: (Organized 25 Jan 1885) (Clerk District Court has Birth, Death & Burial Records from 1890, Divorce & Court Records; County Judge has Marriage & Probate Records; Registrar of Deeds has Land Records)

Ransom   D9   **4 Jan 1873**   **Pembina**
www.rootsweb.com/~ndransom/
Ransom County; 204 5th Ave W; Lisbon, ND 58054;
Ph. (701) 683-5823
Details: (Organized 4 Apr 1881) (Clerk District Court has Birth & Death Records from 1943, Marriage Records from 1882, Divorce, Probate & Court Records; Registrar of Deeds has Land Records)

Renville   M3   **3 Jun 1910**   **Ward**
www.upstel.net/~johns/Renville/renv.html
Renville County; 205 Main St E; PO Box 68; Mohall, ND 58761;
Ph. (701) 756-6398
Details: (Clerk District Court has incomplete Birth & Death Records from 1910, Marriage, Divorce, Probate, Military & Court Records from 1910; Registrar of Deeds has Land Records from 1910)

Renville, old   **4 Jan 1873**   **Buffalo**
www.renvillecounty.org/
Renville, old County; ND
Details: (Part taken to form Ward County 14 Apr 1885. Attached to Ward. Eliminated 30 Nov 1892 to Bottineau & Ward. Recreated 3 Jun 1910)

Richland   B10   **4 Jan 1873**   **Pembina**
www.richlandcounty.org/
RichLand County; 418 2nd Ave N; PO Box 966; Wahpeton, ND 58075; Ph. (701) 642-7818
Details: (Organized 25 Nov 1875) (Clerk District Court has Birth & Death Records from 1900, Divorce & Court Records from 1883 & some Burial Records; County Judge has Marriage Records from 1890 & Probate Records from 1876; Registrar of Deeds has Land Records)

County Website	Map Index	Date Created	Parent County or Territory From Which Organized Address/Details
Rolette www.rootsweb.com/~ndrolett/	**I3**	**4 Jan 1873**	**Buffalo** Rolette County; 102 2nd St NE; Rolla, ND 58367-0460; Ph. (701) 477-3816 **Details:** (Organized 14 Oct 1884) (Clerk District Court has Birth, Death & Burial Records from 1943, Marriage, Divorce & Court Records from 1887 & Probate Records from 1896; Registrar of Deeds has Land Records)
Sargent www.rootsweb.com/~ndsargen/index.htm	**D10**	**9 Apr 1883**	**Ransom** Sargent County; 355 Main St; PO Box 176; Forman, ND 58032; Ph. (701) 724-6241 **Details:** (Clerk District Court has Birth & Death Records from 1943, Marriage Records from 1886, Burial Records from 1948, Probate Records from 1883, Divorce & Court Records; Registrar of Deeds has Land Records)
Sheridan www.rootsweb.com/~ndsherid/	**J6**	**24 Dec 1908**	**McLean** Sheridan County; 215 E 2nd St; PO Box 668; McClusky, ND 58463; Ph. (701) 363-2207 **Details:** (Clerk District Court has Birth Records from 1943, Marriage, Death, Divorce, Probate & Court Records from 1909, Burial Records from 1910 & Military Records from 1918; Registrar of Deeds has Land Records from 1909)
Sheridan, old		**4 Jan 1873**	**Buffalo** Sheridan, old County; ND **Details:** (Part taken to form part of Church 11 Mar 1887. Eliminated 30 Nov 1892 to McLean)
Sheyenne		**24 Apr 1862**	**Unorg. Terr.** Sheyenne County; ND **Details:** (Eliminated 17 Dec 1863 to Unorg. Terr.)
Sioux www.rootsweb.com/~ndsioux/	**K10**	**3 Sep 1914**	**Standing Rock Reservation** Sioux County; 300 2nd Ave; Fort Yates, ND 58538; Ph. (701) 854-3853 **Details:** (Clerk District Court has Marriage Records from 1916, Burial, Divorce, Probate, Court & Land Records)
Slope www.rootsweb.com/~ndslope/	**Q9**	**3 Nov 1914**	**Billings** Slope County; 206 S Main; Amidon, ND 58620-0449; Ph. (701) 879-6260 **Details:** (Organized 14 Jan 1915) (Clerk District Court has Marriage, Death, Burial, Divorce, Probate & Court Records from 1915 & Land Records)
Stark www.rootsweb.com/~ndstark/	**O8**	**10 Feb 1879**	**Unorg. Terr., Howard, Williams (old)** Stark County; 51 3rd St E; PO Box 130; Dickinson, ND 58602-0130; Ph. (701) 264-7639 **Details:** (Organized 30 May 1883) (Clerk District Court has Birth & Death Records from 1898, Burial Records, Divorce & Court Records from 1887 & Naturalization Records 1887–1963; Registrar of Deeds has Land Records)

County Website	Map Index	Date Created	Parent County or Territory From Which Organized Address/Details
Steele	D7	2 Jun 1883	**Griggs, Traill** Steele County; 201 Washington Ave W; PO Box 296; Finley, ND 58230; Ph. (701) 524-2152 **Details:** (Clerk of District Court has Birth & Death Records 1894–1896 & 1900–1901, Court, Probate, & Divorce Records from 1886, & Marriage Records from 1883; Register of Deeds has Land Records)
Stevens		4 Jan 1873	**Buffalo** Stevens County; ND **Details:** (Eliminated 30 Nov 1892 to McLean & Ward)
Stevens, old		24 Apr 1862	**Unorg. Terr.** Stevens, old County; ND **Details:** (Eliminated 17 Dec 1863 to Unorg. Terr.)
Stutsman www.rootsweb.com/~ndstutsm/	G8	4 Jan 1873	**Pembina, Buffalo** Stutsman County; 511 2nd Ave SE; Jamestown, ND 58401; Ph. (701) 252-9042 **Details:** (Clerk District Court has Birth, Death, Burial, Divorce & Court Records; Registrar of Deeds has Land Records; County Judge has Marriage & Probate Records)
Towner www.rootsweb.com/~ndtowner/	G3	8 Mar 1883	**Rolette, Cavalier** Towner County; 315 2nd St; PO Box 517; Cando, ND 58324-0517; Ph. (701) 968-4345 **Details:** (Organized 24 Jan 1884) (Clerk District Court has Marriage Records from 1888, Divorce Records from 1890, Probate Records from 1886, Court Records from 1889, Land Records from 1884 & Burial Records)
Traill www.rootsweb.com/~ndtraill/	B6	12 Jan 1875	**Grand Forks, Burbank, Cass** Traill County; 13 1st St. NW; Hillsboro, ND 58045; Ph. (701) 636-4454 **Details:** (Recorders Office has Land Records from mid-1800's; Clerk of District Court has Marriage Records from 1872, Divorce Records from 1890, & Probate Records from 1882)
Villard		8 Mar 1883	**Billings** Villard County; ND **Details:** (Eliminated 10 Mar 1887 to Billings & Stark)
Wallace		9 Mar 1883	**Howard** Wallace County; ND **Details:** (see McKenzie) Eliminated 30 Nov 1896 to Billings & Stark. Recreated 24 May 1901 from Billings & Stark & attached to Stark County. Eliminated 16 Mar 1905 to McKenzie
Wallette		4 Jan 1873	**Buffalo** Wallette County; ND **Details:** (Eliminated 9 Mar 1883 to Buford & Flannery)
Walsh www.rootsweb.com/~ndwalsh/walsh.htm	D4	20 May 1881	**Grand Forks, Pembina** Walsh County; 600 Cooper Ave; Grafton, ND 58237-1542; Ph. (701) 352-0350 **Details:** (Clerk District Court has Marriage Records from 1884, Divorce, Probate & Court Records from 1881; Registrar of Deeds has Land Records)

County	Map	Date	Parent County or Territory From Which Organized
Website	Index	Created	Address/Details

Ward   L4   **14 Apr 1885**   **Stevens, Wynn, Renville, old**
www.co.ward.nd.us

Ward County; 315 3rd St SE; PO Box 5005; Minot, ND 58701; Ph. (701) 857-6410, sdalen@state.nd.us

Details: (Vital Records has Birth & Death Records; County Records has Burial, Land, Marriage, & Military Records; District Court has Court, Guardianship, & Probate Records; Minot Daily has Newspapers; Auditor's Office has Tax Records)

Wells   H6   **4 Jan 1873**   **Buffalo**
www.rootsweb.com/~ndwells/

Wells County; 700 Railway St N; PO Box 596; Fessenden, ND 58438; Ph. (701) 547-3122

Details: (Formerly Gingras County. Name changed to Wells 26 Feb 1881. Organized 24 Aug 1884) (Clerk District Court has Birth, Marriage, Death, Burial, Divorce, Probate & Court Records; Registrar of Deeds has Land Records)

Williams   P4   **30 Nov 1892**   **Buford, Flannery**
www.rootsweb.com/~ndwillia/

Williams County; Box 2047; Williston, ND 58802; Ph. (701) 572-1729

Details: (Organized 10 Mar 1903) (Clerk District Court has Birth, Marriage, Death, Burial, Probate, Court & Naturalization Records; County Treasury-Recorder has Land Records; Veterans Service Office has Military Records)

Williams, old   **8 Jan 1873**   **Unorg. Terr.**

Williams, old County; ND

Details: (Eliminated 30 Nov 1892 to Mercer)

Wynn   **9 Mar 1883**   **Bottineau, Renville, old**

Wynn County; ND

Details: (Eliminated 11 Mar 1887 to Bottineau, McHenry, Renville, old & Ward)

Notes

Ohio

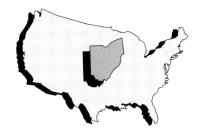

Capital: Columbus
Territory: 1799
State: 1803 (17th)

With God, all things are possible

French traders settled in the western part of Ohio and the English settled in the eastern part in the early 1700's. English expansion toward the West brought the two into conflict by the 1740's. The French and Indian War finally resolved this and the English won control of the area. However, settlement of the region was discouraged, due in part to the hostile Indians in the area. Americans, in their search for space and fertile, inexpensive land, came to the area despite British desires to the contrary. Conflicts between the Indians, who sided with the British, and the Americans were the result. The treaty ending the Revolutionary War ceded the area to the United States.

Following acquisition of the new territory, the eastern seaboard states simply extended their borders to include the new area. The establishment of the Northwest Territory in 1787 put an end to this practice. The following year, the Ohio Company of New England made the first permanent settlement at Marietta. The company, formed by Puritans from Massachusetts and Connecticut, purchased about a million acres of land in southeast Ohio.

In about 1800, the Virginia Bounty—consisting of more than 4 million acres between the Scioto and Little Miami rivers—was set aside for settlers from Virginia and Kentucky. The Chillicothe section in Ross County attracted many settlers from Kentucky and Tennessee. Mid-state, on the eastern border, Germans, Scotch-Irish, and Quakers crossed the Ohio River from Pennsylvania to settle. Another group of settlers from New Jersey traveled down the Ohio River and settled the area between the Little and Big Miami rivers. Here, along with Scotch-Irish and Dutch settlers, they cultivated some 300,000 acres in the southwestern corner of Ohio and established Cincinnati.

Trouble with the Indians continued until 1794, when General Anthony Wayne drove them from the state. The Western Reserve in the northeast corner along Lake Erie was opened to settlers. It included 4 million acres. Connecticut emigrants were the main settlers in this area. In future Erie and Huron counties to the west, Connecticut

refugees who had been burned out by the British during the Revolutionary War began to settle. The area became known as the "Fire Lands" for this reason. A "Refugee Tract" (comprising approximately Franklin, Licking, and Perry counties) was set aside east of the Scioto River for Canadians who had aided the Americans in the Revolutionary War and lost their lands in Canada as a punishment.

Ohio became a territory in 1799. The next year the Indiana Territory was formed, which reduced Ohio to its present size. Ohio was granted statehood in 1803. Steamboat travel brought many settlers up the Ohio River and down Lake Erie. The completion of canals, roads, and railroads opened up the northeastern part of the state after 1815, while the opening of the Erie Canal in 1825 increased settlement from the Northeast. During the Civil War, Ohio had some 313,000 men serving in the Union forces.

Look for vital records in the following locations:

- **Birth and death records:** A few counties have birth and death records from as early as 1840. Individual counties were required to keep these records in 1867. After 1908, birth and death records are at the State Vital Statistics Unit, Ohio Department of Health in Columbus.

- **Marriage and divorce records:** Probate courts have marriage records. A statewide index to marriages since 1949 is at the Division of Vital Statistics. Divorce records were kept by the state Supreme Court until 1852, and then by the Court of Common Pleas in each county.

- **Land records:** The county recorder has land records for each county. Early records of land grants, bounty land, and land purchases are at the Ohio Land Office, Auditor of State in Columbus. Most records of the Western Reserve are at the Connecticut Secretary of State's office. Virginia bounty land warrants are at the Virginia State Library in Richmond, Virginia.

- **Census records:** Town or county censuses were taken between 1798 and 1911 in some counties.

Ohio State Vital Records Office
Revenue Rook
246 North High Street
PO Box 15098
Columbus, Ohio 43216
(614) 466-2531
www.vitalrec.com/oh.html

Ohio Historical Society
State Archives
1982 Velma Avenue, Columbus, Ohio 43211
(614) 297-2300
www.ohiohistory.org/resource/statearc/

Ohio Land Office Auditor of State
88 East Broad Street
Columbus, Ohio 43215

Societies and Repositories

Adams County Genealogical Society; PO Box 231; West Union, OH 45693.

African American Genealogy Group of the Miami Valley; PO Box 485; Yellow Springs, OH 45387; (937) 767-1949; harris175@earthlink.net.

African-American Genealogical Society of Cleveland, Ohio; PO Box 201476; Cleveland, OH 44120-8107.

Ashtabula County Genealogical Society, Inc.; Geneva Public Library; 860 Sherman Street; Geneva, OH 44041-9101; acgs@ashtabulagen.org; www.ashtabulagen.org.

Athens County Chapter, OGS; Athens County Historical Society & Museum; 65 N. C; Athens, OH 45701-2506; (740) 698-3551; achsm@frognet.net; www.frognet.net/~achsm.

Auglaize Co. Genealogical Society; PO Box 2021; Wapakoneta, OH 45895-0521; acgsogs@rootsweb.com; www.rootsweb.com/~ohaugogs/index.html.

Belmont County Chapter, OGS; PO Box 285; Barnesville, OH 43713; (740) 695-3660; bccogs@hotmail.com; www.rootsweb.com/~ohbelogs.

Brookville Historical Society, Inc.; PO Box 82; Brookville, OH 45309-0082.

Brown County Chapter, OGS; PO Box 83; Georgetown, OH 45121-0083.

Butler County Chapter, PGS; PO Box 2011; Middletown, OH 45042-2011; (513) 523-3580; maxiney1106@aol.com; http://da120757.tripod.com/bcogs.

Carroll County Genealogical Society; 24 Second St. N.E.; PO Box 36; Carrollton, OH 44615-1205; carollco@yahoo.com; www.rootsweb.com/~ohcarcgs.

Champaign County Genealogical Society; PO Box 682; Urbana, OH 43078-0680; nleasure@foryou.net; www.rootsweb.com/~ohchampa/society.htm.

Clermont County Genealogical Society; PO Box 394; Batavia, OH 45103-0394; (513) 522-8458; Vgeesner@aol.com; www.rootsweb.com/~ohclecgs.

Clinton County, Ohio Genealogical Society; PO Box 529; Wilmington, OH 45177-0529; (937) 382-5209.

Columbiana Co. Chapter O.G.S.; PO Box 861 Dept I; Salem, OH 44460-0861; (330) 223-1447; frantta@valunet.com; www.rootsweb.com/~ohcolumb.

Columbiana County Historical Society; PO Box 221; Lisbon, OH 44432.

Columbus Jewish Historical Society; 1175 College Avenue; Columbus, OH 43209-2890; cjhs@beol.net; www.gcis.net/cjhs.

Coshocton County Chapter OGS; PO Box 128; Coshocton, OH 43812-0128.

Crawford County Genealogical Society; PO Box 92; Galion, OH 44833-0092.

Cumberland Trail Genealogical Society; PO Box 576; St. Clairesville, OH 43905; (740) 676-4132; CTGS@aol.com.

Cuyahoga Valley Chapter/OGS; PO Box 41414; Brecksville, OH 44141-0414.

Cuyahoga West Chapter, OGS; PO Box 26196; Fairview Park, OH 44126.

Defiance County Chapter, OGS; PO Box 7006; Defiance, OH; ccbrowngenealogy@yahoo.com.

Delaware County Genealogical Society; PO Box 317; 157 East William Street; Delaware, OH 43015-0317; dchsdcgs@midohio.net; www.midohio.net/dchsdcgs.

East Cuyahoga County Genealogical Society; PO Box 24182; Lyndhurst, OH 44124-0182; MorgaBD@msn.com.

East Liverpool Historical Society; 305 Walnut Street; East Liverpool, OH 43920.

East Palestine Historical Society; 555 Bacon Avenue; East Palestine, OH 44413.

Ebenezer Zane Chapter, OHSSAR; 2101 County Road 1; Rayland, OH 43943-7866; grussell@ist.net.

Erie County Chapter, OGS; PO Box 1301; Sandusky, OH 44871-1301.

Ethan Allen Chapter, OHSSAR; 1379 Bradford Street; Warren, OH 44485-1963; (330)395-0310; blackhorse66@hotmail.com.

Ewings Chapter, OHSSAR; 18660 State Route 550; Amesville, OH 45711; (740) 448-7269; www.frognet.net/~asSAR.

Fairfield County Chapter, OGS; PO Box 2268; Lancaster, OH 43130-5268; ksmith@greenapple.com; www.fairfieldgenealogy.org.

Fayette County Chapter, OGS; PO Box 342; Washington CH, OH 43130-0570.

Firelands Bicentennial Chapter, OHSSAR; (440) 323-7156; wmking@ohio.net; www.centurytel.net/lorgen/ovi/SAR.htm.

Franklin County Genealogical & Historical Society;
570 West Broad St.; PO Box 44309; Columbus, OH
43204-0309; (614) 469-1300; FCGHS@yahoo.com;
www.rootsweb.com~ohfcghs.

Friends of the Library, Genealogy Research Group;
1268 Kenwood Avenue; Springfield, OH 45505.

Fulton County Chapter of OGS; PO Box 337; Swanton, OH
43558-0337; (419) 335-0898; kinfolks@bnnorth.net;
www.rootsweb.com/~ohfulton.

Gallia County Historical/Genealogical Society; 410-412
Second Avenue; Gallipolis, OH 45631;
histsoc@zoomnet.net; www.zoomnet.net/~histsoc.

George Rogers Clark Chapter, OHSSAR; Springfield, OH;
PaulS72511@aol.com;
http://grccSAR.homestead.com/grccSAR.html.

Greene County Chapter, Ohio Genealogical Society;
PO Box 706; Xenia, OH 45385; kcline64@woh.rr.com;
www.rootsweb.com/~ohgccogs/main.htm.

Guernsey County Chapter, OGS; PO Box 661; 8583
Georgetown Rd.; Cambridge, OH 43725-0661;
gccogs@earthlink.net; www.usgenet.ogr/usa/oh/county/
guernsey/gcgspub.html.

Hancock County Chapter, OGS; PO Box 672; Findlay, OH
45839-0672; hancock_ogs@hotmail.com;
www.rootsweb.com/~ohhccogs.

Hanover Township Historical Society; PO Box 381;
Hanoverton, OH 44423.

Hardin County Ohio Genealogy Society; Box 520; Kenton,
OH 43326-0520; (419) 675-6230;
www.kenton.com/users/chuck/soc.htm.

Harrison County Genealogical Society; 45507 Unionvale
Road; Cadiz, OH 43907-9723; bjackson@1st.net;
www.rootsweb.com/~ohharris.

Historical Society of Columbiana and Fairfield Townships;
Dept. I, 10 Park Ave.; Columbiana, OH 44408.

Hocking County Chapter, OGS; PO Box 115; Rockbridge,
OH 43149-0115.

Holmes County Chapter, OGS; PO Box 136; Millersburg,
OH 44654-0136; hcgen@valkrie.net.

Hudson Genealogical Study Group; Hudson Library
Archives; 96 Library St.; Hudson, OH 44236-2947;
hgsg1@juno.com;
www.rootsweb.com/~ohhudogs/hudson.htm.

Huron County Chapter, OGS; PO Box 923; Norwalk, OH
44857-0923; www.rootsweb.com/~ohhuron.

Indiana African Historical and Genealogical Society; 11899
Belgreen Ln; Cincinnati, OH 45240-1401.

Jackson County Chapter, OGS; PO Box 807; Jackson, OH
45640-0807; daviska@oplin.lib.oh.us;
http://scioto.org/OGS/Jackson.

Jefferson County Chapter, OGS; PO Box 4712;
Steubenville, OH 43952-8712;
www.rootsweb.com/~ohjefogs.

John Stark Chapter, OHSSAR; 5220 Woodlynn Drive; East
Canton, OH 44730-1756; (330) 488-2227;
jmr@raex.com.

Knox County Chapter, OGS; PO Box 1098; Mt. Vernon,
OH 43050-1098.

LaFayette Chapter, OHSSAR; 899 Hancock Ave.; Akron,
OH 44314-1044; (330) 745-1532; kenlodagoh@att.net;
www.thepchelpers.com.

Lake County Genealogical Society; 184 Phelps Street;
Painesville, OH 44077;
http://131.187.173.99/genealogy_lcgs.htm.

Lawrence County Chapter, OGS; PO Box 945; Ironton, OH
45638-0955; dclark4700@aol.com.

Licking County Genealogical Society; 101 W. Main St.;
Newark, OH 43055-5054; (740) 349-5510;
lcgs@npls.org; www.npls.org/lcgs/index.html.

Lisbon Historical Society; 113 E. Washington St.;
PO Box 221; Lisbon, OH 44432;
lisbonhs@valunet.com; http://countypage.com/lhs.

Logan County Chapter, OGS; PO Box 36; Bellefontaine,
OH 43311-0036; logangs@loganrec.com.

Lorain County Chapter, OGS; PO Box 865; Elyria, OH
44036-0865; www.centuryinter.net/lorgen.

Lucas County Chapter, OGS; c/o Toledo-Lucas Co. Public
Library; Local History; Toledo, OH 43624-1614;
www.utoledo.edu/~gried/lcgs.htm.

Lucasville Historical Society; PO Box 761; Lucasville, OH
45648-0761.

Madison County Genealogy Society; PO Box 102; London,
OH 43140-0102.

Mahoning County Chapter, OGS; PO Box 9333;
Boardman, OH 44513-0333.

Marion Area Genealogical Society; PO Box 844; Marion,
OH 43301-0844; www.genealogy.org/~smoore/marion.

Medina County Chapter, OGS; PO Box 804; Medina, OH
44258-0804.

Meigs County Chapter, OGS; PO Box 346; Pomeroy, OH
45769-0345.

Mercer County Chapter, OGS; PO Box 437; Celina, OH
45822-0437;
www.calweb.com/~wally/mercer/society.htm.

Miami County Historical & Genealogical Society;
PO Box 305; Troy, OH 45373-0305;
www.TDS-NET.com/mchgs.

Miamisburg Historical Society; PO Box 774; Miamisburg,
OH 45343-0774.

Monroe County Genealogical Society; PO Box 641;
Woodsfield, OH 43793-0641; (740) 483-1481;
kromick@1st.net; www.rootsweb.com/~ohmccogs.

Montgomery County Chapter, OGS; 48 Huffman Avenue;
Dayton, OH 45403; (937) 253-2503;
vickers@erinet.com.

Morgan County Chapter, OGS; PO Box 418; McConnelsville, OH 43756-0418.

Morrow County, Ohio Genealogical Society; PO Box 401; Mt. Gilead, OH 43338; b.j.gameier@juno.com; www.rootsweb.com/~ohmorrow.

Muskingum County Chapter, OGS; PO Box 2427; Zanesville, OH 43702-2427; BETW@prodigy.net; www.rootsweb.com/~ohmuskin/mccogs.

NARA, Great Lakes Region (Dayton); 3150 Springboro Road; Dayton, OH 45439-1883; (937) 425-0609; dayton.reference@nara.gov; www.archives.gov/facilities/oh/dayton.html.

Nathan Hale Chapter, OHSSAR; 30 Babic Street; Struthers, OH 44471-3108; (330) 755-8590; PBundy2001@aol.com.

Noble County Chapter, OGS; PO Box 174; Caldwell, OH 43724-0174.

Northeastern Chapter #12, Sons of the American Revolution; 1659 Chapel Road; Jefferson, OH 44047-8716; jtpa@interlacted.net.

Northeastern Ohio Chapter #12, OHSSAR; dickmack@alltel.net; http://acoc.ashtabula.net/srevolution/index.html.

Ohio Historical Society Archives/Library; 1982 Velma Avenue; Columbus, OH 43211; (614) 297-2510; www.ohiohistory.org/resource/statearc.

Old Northwest Historical Society; PO Box 62635; Cincinnati, OH 45262; rrowan@fuse.net; http://home.fuse.net/rrowan.

Palatines to America; 611 E. Weber Rd.; Columbus, OH 43211; pal-am@juno.com; http://palam.org/.

Paulding County Chapter, OGS; 205 E. Main St.; Paulding, OH 45879-1492.

Perry County Chapter, OGS; PO Box 275; Junction City, OH 43748-0275; www.perrygenealogy.net/perryogs.htm.

Pickaway County Historical & Genealogical Society; PO Box 85; Circleville, OH 43113; pkwyhist@bright.net; www.rootsweb.com/~ohpickaw/gen.html.

Pike County Genealogy Society; PO Box 224; Waverly, OH 45690-0224; cmontrose@beol.net; www.rootsweb.com/~ohpcgs/pike.htm.

Polish Genealogical Society of Greater Cleveland, Ohio; PGSGC; 105 Pleasant View Drive; Seville, OH 44273; pulaskipro@aol.com.

Portage County Chapter, OGS; PO Box 821; Ravenna, OH 44266.

Preble County Genealogical Society; Library Administration Center; 450 S. Barron Street; Eaton, OH 45320; (937) 456-4970; pcroom@infinet.com; www.pcdl.lib.oh.us.

Preble County Historical Society; 7693 Swartsel Road; Eaton, OH 45320; prcohs@infinet.com.

Putnam County Chapter, OGS; PO Box 403; Ottawa, OH 45875-0403.

Randolph Township Historical Society, Inc.; PO Box 355; Clayton, OH 45315; Reptar5@aol.com.

Richland County Genealogical Society; PO Box 3823; Mansfield, OH 44907-3823; www.rootsweb.com/~ohrichgs.

Ross County Chapter, OGS; PO Box 6352; Chillicothe, OH 45601-6352; (740) 775-0420; rcgs@bright.net; www.bright.net/~rcgs.

Salem Historical Society; 208 South Broadway Avenue; Salem, OH 44460.

Samuel Huntington Chapter, OHSSAR; 6366 Indian Point Rd.; Painesville, OH 44077-8844; parvlinc@ncweb.com; www.SAR.org/ohsSAR/samuel_huntington_chapter.htm.

Sandusky County Kin Hunters; Spiegle Grove; Fremont, OH 43420-2796.

Scioto County Chapter, OGS; PO Box 812; Portsmouth, OH 45662-0812; gladren@zoomnet.net.

Seneca County Genealogical Society; PO Box 157; Tiffin, OH 44883-0157; seneca09@senecasearchers.org; www.senecasearchers.org/index.html.

Shelby Genealogical Society; PO Box 766; Shelby, OH 44875-0766; www.rootsweb.com/~ohscogs.

Southern Ohio Chapter, OGS; PO Box 414; Hillsboro, OH 45133.

SouthWest Cuyahoga Chapter, OGS; 13305 Pearl Road; Strongsville, OH 44136-3403; gmtjaden@aol.com; http://members.aol.com/gmtjaden.

Stark County, Ohio Chapter, OGS; 1950 Market Avenue North, Apt. B2; Canton, OH 44714-2242; LKLandis@aol.com; www.rootsweb.com/~ohstark/starkogs.htm.

State Library of Ohio; 274 East First Avenue; Columbus, OH 43201; (614) 644-7061; genhelp@sloma.state.oh.us; http://winslo.state.oh.us.

Summit County Chapter, OGS; 239 N. Highland Avenue; Akron, OH 44303; (330) 836-6518; chuckgrnt@aol.com; http://spot.acorn.net/gen.

The Clark County Genealogical Society; PO Box 2524; Springfield, OH 45501-2524; (937) 323-4728; Fhulsizer@aol.com; www.rootsweb.com/~ohcccogs.

The Darke County Genealogical Society; PO Box 908; Greenville, OH 45331-0908.

The Greater Cleveland Genealogical Socitey; PO Box 40234; Cleveland, OH 44140-0254; www.rootsweb.com/~ohgcgg.

The Hamilton County Chapter, OGS; PO Box 15865; Cincinnati, OH 45215-0865; mohrmarg@juno.com; http://members.aol.com/ogshc.

The Henry County Genealogical Society; PO Box 231; Deshler, OH 43516.

The Ottawa County Genealogical Society; PO Box 193;
Port Clinton, OH 43452; (419) 734-3895;
ocgs@altavista.net; www.rootsweb.com/~ohoccgs.

The Wayne County Genealogical Society; PO Box 856;
Wooster, OH 44691;
www.rootsweb.com/~ohwayne/wcgs.htm.

The Wood County Chapter of the Ohio Genealogical
Society; PO Box 722; Bowling Green, OH 43402-0722;
www.rootsweb.com/~ohwood/searchwd.htm#Wood.

Toledo Area Genealogical Society; PO Box 352258;
Toledo, OH 43635-2258.

Trumbull County Chapter, OGS; PO Box 309; Warren, OH
44482-0309.

Tuscarawas County Genealogical Society; PO Box 141;
New Philadelphia, OH 44663-0141; TCGS@aol.com;
http://web1.tusco.net/tuscgen/society.htm.

Union County Genealogical Society; PO Box 438;
Marysville, OH 43040-0438.

Van Wert County Chapter, OGS; PO Box 485; Van Wert,
OH 45891-0485;
www.rootsweb.com/~ohvanwer/vwc_ogs.htm.

Vinton County Historical and Genealogical Society;
PO Box 306; Hamden, OH 45634-0306;
www.rootsweb.com/~ohvinton/ogschapt.htm.

Warren County Genealogical Society; 406 Justice Drive;
Lebanon, OH 45036; (513) 695-1144; wcgs@co
.warren.oh.us; www.co.warren.oh.us/genealogy.

Washington County Chapter, OGS; PO Box 2174; Marietta,
OH 45750-2174.

Wellsville Historical Society; 1003 Riverside Avenue;
PO Box 13; Wellsville, OH 43968.

Williams County Genealogical Society; PO Box 293;
Bryan, OH 43506-0293; www.geocities.com/wmscogen.

Wyandot Tracers OGS; PO Box 414; Upper Sandusky, OH
43351-0414; www.udata.com/users/hsbaker/tracers.htm.

Bibliography and Record Sources

General

Baldwin, Henry R. *The Henry R. Baldwin Genealogy
Records*. 67 vols. Fort Wayne, Indiana: Allen County
Public Library, 1983. (Eastern Ohio and Pennsylvania)

Bell, Carol Willsey. *Ohio Genealogical Guide*. 6th ed.
Youngstown, Ohio: Bell Books, 1995.

Bell, Carol Willsey. *Ohio Guide to Genealogical Sources*.
Reprint. Baltimore: Genealogical Publishing Co., 1993.

Biographical Encyclopedia of Ohio of the 19th Century.
(1876) Reprint. Salem, Massachusetts: Higginson Book
Co., 1995.

Bowers, Ruth and Anita Short. *Gateway to the West*, 2 vols.
(1967–1978) Reprint. Baltimore, Maryland:
Genealogical Publishing Co., 1989.

Buley, R. Carlyle. *The Old Northwest: Pioneer Period,
1815–1840*. 2 vols. Bloomington: Indiana University
Press in association with the Indiana Historical Society,
1983, 1978.

Cayton. *The Frontier Republic: Ideology and Politics in the
Ohio Country, 1780–1825*. Galveston, Texas: Frontier
Press, 1986.

Church of Jesus Christ of Latter-day Saints, The. Historical
Department. *Journal History*. Salt Lake City: Filmed by
the Historical Dept., 1968, 1973. 248 microfilm.

Comley, W. J. *Ohio; The Future Great State: Her
Manufacturers and a History of Her Commercial Cities,
Cincinnati and Cleveland with Portraits and
Biographies of Some of the Old Settlers, and Many of
the Most Prominent Business Men*. Cincinnati, Ohio:
Comley Brothers Manufacturing and Pub. Co., 1875.

Eltscher, Susan M., comp. *The Records of American
Baptists in Ohio, and Related Organizations*. Rochester,
New York: American Baptist Historical Society, 1981.

Family History Library. *Research Outline: Ohio*. Salt Lake
City, Utah: Family History Library.

Finley, James Bradley. *Sketches of Western Methodism:
Biographical, Historical & Miscellaneous, Illustrative
of Pioneer Life*. Cincinnati: Methodist Book Concern,
1856.

Fuller, Sara S. *A Guide to Manuscripts at the Ohio
Historical Society*. Columbus, Ohio: The Society, 1972.

Galbreath, Charles Burleigh. *History of Ohio*. 5 vols.
Chicago: American Historical Society, 1925.

Gerber, David Allison. *Black Ohio and the Color Line,
1860–1915*. Urbana, Illinois: University of Illinois
Press, 1976.

Gilkey, Elliot Howard. *The Ohio Hundred Year Book: A
Handbook of the Public Men and Public Institutions of
Ohio from the Formation of the Northwest Territory
(1787) To July 1, 1901*. Columbus, Ohio: F. J. Heer,
1901.

Gill, Charles Otis and Gifford Pinchot. *Six Thousand
Country Churches*. New York: Macmillan, 1919.

Green, Karen Mauer. *Pioneer Ohio Newspapers,
1793–1810 and 1802–1818: Genealogical and
Historical Abstracts*. 2 vols. Galveston, Texas: Frontier
Press, 1988.

Hall. *The Shane Manuscript Collection: A Genealogical
Guide to the Kentucky and Ohio Papers*. Galveston,
Texas: Frontier Press, 1990.

Harfst, Linda L. *Local History and Genealogy Resources
Guide to Southeastern Ohio*. Wellston, Ohio: Ohio
Valley Area Libraries, 1984.

Harter, Frances D. *Guide to the Manuscript Collection of
Early Ohio Methodism: United Methodist Church of
Ohio*. Delaware, Ohio: United Methodist Archives
Center, 1980.

Harter, Stuart. *Ohio Genealogy and Local History Sources
Index*. Fort Wayne, Indiana: CompuGen Systems, 1986.

Hatcher. *The Western Reserve: The Story of New Connecticut in Ohio.* Galveston, Texas: Frontier Press, 1991.

Hayden, A. S. *The Disciples Early History in Western Reserve 1875.* (1875) Reprint. Knightstown, Indiana: The Bookmark, 1979.

Hehir, Donald M. *Ohio Families: A Bibliography of Books About Ohio Families.* Bowie, Maryland: Heritage Books, 1993.

Heisey, John W. *Ohio Genealogical Research Guide.* Indianapolis, Indiana: Heritage House, 1987.

Hildreth, S. P. *Memoirs of the Early Pioneer Settlers of Ohio, with Narratives of Incidents and Occurrences in 1775.* (1854). Reprint. Baltimore, Maryland: Clearfield Company, 1995.

Historical Records Survey (Ohio). *Inventory of the Church Archives of Ohio Presbyterian Churches.* Microreproduction of Xerox copies of the original papers in the Ohio Historical Society. Salt Lake City: Filmed by the Genealogical Society of Utah, 1972.

Historical Records Survey (Ohio). *Inventory of the State Archives of Ohio.* Columbus, Ohio: Ohio Historical Records Survey Project, 1940.

Hover, John Calvin. *Memoirs of the Miami Valley.* 3 vols. Chicago: R. O. Law Co., 1919.

Howe, Henry. *Historical Collections of Ohio.* 2 vols. Rev. ed. (1888–1908) Reprint. Salem, Massachusetts: Higginson Book Co., 1994.

Hulbert, Archer Butler. *The Ohio River: A Course of Empire.* (1906) Reprint. Salem, Massachusetts: Higginson Book Co., 1996.

Hutslar. *Log Construction in the Ohio Country, 1750–1850.* Galveston, Texas: Frontier Press, 1992.

Kern, Richard. *A History of the Ohio Conference of the Churches of God, General Conference, 1836–1986.* Findlay, Ohio: Richard Kern, 1986.

Larson, David R., ed. *Guide to Manuscript Collections and Institutional Records in Ohio.* N.p.: Society of Ohio Archivists, 1974.

Lentz, Andrea D., ed. *A Guide to Manuscripts at the Ohio Historical Society.* Columbus: The Ohio Historical Society, 1972.

Memoirs of the Lower Ohio Valley: Personal and Genealogical with Portraits. 2 vols. Madison, Wisconsin: Federal Publishing, 1905.

Ohio Genealogical Society. *First Families of Ohio, Official Roster, Vol. 2.* Mansfield, Ohio: Ohio Genealogical Society, 1988.

Ohio Genealogical Society. *Ohio Source Records from the Ohio Genealogical Quarterly.* (1937–1944, 1986) Reprint. Baltimore, Maryland: Genealogical Publishing Co., 1993.

Ohio Historical Society (Columbus, Ohio). *Newspapers: Microfilm Available from the Ohio Historical Society.* Columbus, Ohio: The Society, 1987.

Ohio Historical Society. Archives—Libraries Division. *Ohio County Records Manual.* Rev. ed. Columbus, Ohio: Archives-Library Division, Ohio Historical Society, 1983.

Ohio Historical Society. *Ohio Newspaper Index.* Columbus, Ohio: Ohio Historical Society, 1996–2001. Online guide—www.ohiohistory.org/dindex/.

Ohio Research Outline. Series U.S.-States, no. 36. Salt Lake City: Family History Library, 1988.

Ohio, 1780–1970. S.l.: Brøderbund, 1998. CD-ROM.

Ohio's Progressive Sons, a History of the State: Sketches of Those Who Have Helped to Build Up the Commonwealth. Cincinnati: Queen City Publishing, 1905.

Pike, Kermit J. *A Guide to Shaker Manuscripts in the Library of the Western Reserve Historical Society, With an Inventory of its Shaker Photographs.* Cleveland: Western Reserve Historical Society, 1974.

Pike, Kermit J. *A Guide to the Manuscripts and Archives of the Western Reserve Historical Society.* Cleveland: Western Reserve Historical Society, 1972.

Powell, Esther Weygandt. *Early Ohio Tax Records.* 2 vols. in 1. Reprint. Baltimore, Maryland: Genealogical Publishing Co., 1993.

Progressive Men of Northern Ohio. Cleveland: Plain Dealer Pub. Co., 1906.

Reed, George Irving. *Bench and Bar of Ohio: A Compendium of History and Biography.* 2 vols. Chicago: Century Pub. and Engraving Co., 1897.

Rerick, Rowland H. *State Centennial History of Ohio, Covering the Periods of Indian, French and British Dominion, the Territory Northwest, and the Hundred Years of Statehood.* (1902) Reprint. Salem, Massachusetts: Higginson Book Co., 1995.

Robson, Charles. *The Biographical Encyclopedia of Ohio of the Nineteenth Century.* Cincinnati: Galaxy Pub. Co., 1876.

Rust, Orton G. *History of West Central Ohio.* 3 vols. Indianapolis, Indiana: Historical Pub. Co., 1934.

Sargent, M. P. *Pioneer Sketches: Scenes and Incidents of Former Days.* (1891) Reprint. Salem, Massachusetts: Higginson Book Co., 1993.

Schweitzer, George K. *Ohio Genealogical Research.* Knoxville, Tennessee: George K. Schweitzer, 1995.

Shane, John Dabney. *Shane Manuscript Collection.* Microfilm of the original records in the Presbyterian Historical Society in Philadelphia, Pennsylvania. Salt Lake City: Filmed by the Genealogical Society of Utah, 1966–1967. 36 microfilm.

Short, Mrs. Don R., and Mrs. Denver Eller. *Ohio Bible Records.* 2 vols. 1971. Reprint. Fort Wayne, Indiana: Allen County Public Library, 1983.

Smythe, George Franklin. *A History of the Diocese of Ohio Until the Year 1918.*

Southern Ohio and Its Builders: A Biographical Record of Those Personalities, Who By Reason of Their Achievements Have Merited a Permanent Place in the Story of Twentieth Century Southern Ohio. S.l.: Southern Ohio Biographical Association, 1927.

Sperry, Kip. *Genealogical Research in Ohio.* Baltimore: Genealogical Publishing Co., 1997.

The Encyclopedia of Quaker Genealogy, 1750–1930. S.l.: Brøderbund, 1998. CD-ROM.

Thomson, Peter G. *Bibliography of the State of Ohio, Being a Catalog of the Books and Pamphlets Relating to the History of the State, the West and Northwest.* (1880) Reprint. Salem, Massachusetts: Higginson Book Co., 1993.

Tolzman, Don Heinrich. *Ohio Valley German Biographical Index.* Bowie, Maryland: Heritage Books, 1992.

United Methodist Archives (Ohio). *Methodist Ministers Card Index: All Ohio Conferences, 1797–1981.* Columbus, Ohio: Ohio Historical Society, 1982.

Upton, Harriet T. *History of the Western Reserve.* 3 vols. Reprint. Salem, Massachusetts: Higginson Book Co., 1995.

Western Reserve Historical Society. History Library. *Card Catalog to the Manuscripts Collection in the Library of the Western Reserve Historical Society.* Microfilm of the original records from the Western Reserve Historical Society. Salt Lake City: Filmed by the Genealogical Society of Utah, 1974. 6 microfilm.

Wittke, Carl F., ed. *The History of the State of Ohio.* 6 vols. Columbus, Ohio: The Society, 1941–1944.

Women's Department, Cleveland Centennial Commission, comp. *Genealogical Data Relating to Women in the Western Reserve Before 1840* (1850). Columbus, Ohio: Ohio Historical Society, 1973.

Yon, Paul D. *Guide to Ohio County and Municipal Records for Urban Research.* Columbus: Ohio Historical Society, 1973.

Atlases, Maps and Gazetteers

Atlas of Ohio. Madison, Wisconsin: American Publishing Co., 1975.

Brown, Lloyd Arnold. *Early Maps of the Ohio Valley.* Pittsburgh: University of Pittsburgh Press, 1959.

Burk, Thomas A. *Ohio Lands: A Short History.* 3rd ed. Columbus, Ohio: Auditor of the State, 1991.

Gallagher, John S. *The Post Offices of Ohio.* Burtonsville, Maryland: The Depot, 1979.

Jenkins, Warren. *The Ohio Gazetteer and Traveler's Guide: Containing a Description of the Several Towns, Townships and Counties, with Their Water Courses, Roads, Improvements, Mineral Productions.* Columbus, Ohio: Isaac N. Whiting, 1837.

Kilbourne, John. *1833 Ohio Gazetteer.* (1833) Reprint. Knightstown, Indiana: The Bookmark, 1981.

Long, John H., ed. *Historical Atlas and Chronology of County Boundaries, 1788–1980, Illinois, Indiana, Ohio.* Boston, Massachusetts: G. K. Hall, 1984.

Marzulli, Lawrence J. *The Development of Ohio's Counties and Their Historic Courthouses.* Columbus, Ohio: County Commissioners Assn. of Ohio, 1980?.

Miller, Larry L. *Ohio Place Names.* Bloomington, Indiana: Indiana University Press, 1996.

Ohio Atlas and Gazetteer. 4th ed. Freeport, Maine: DeLorme Mapping Co., 1996.

Overman, William D. *Ohio Town Names.* Akron, Ohio: Atlantic Press, 1958.

Phillips, W. Louis. *Jurisdictional Histories for Ohio's Eighty-Eight Counties, 1788–1985.* Bowie, Maryland: Heritage Books, 1986.

Puerta, C. J., comp. *Ohio County Maps.* Lyndon Station, Wisconsin: Thomas Publishing Co., 1992.

W. L. Howison & Associates. *Maps of Ohio Showing the Development of its Counties.* Columbus, Ohio: W. L. Howison & Assoc., 198–.

Walling, H. F. *1868 Ohio Atlas.* (1868) Reprint. Knightstown, Indiana: The Bookmark, 1995.

Census Records

Available Census Records and Census Substitutes

Federal Census 1820, 1830, 1840, 1850, 1860, 1870, 1880, 1900, 1910, 1920

Federal Mortality Schedules 1850, 1860, 1870

Union Veterans and Widows 1890

Dollarhide, William. *The Census Book: A Genealogist's Guide to Federal Census Facts, Schedules and Indexes.* Bountiful, Utah: Heritage Quest, 1999.

Kemp, Thomas Jay. *The American Census Handbook.* Wilmington, Delaware: Scholarly Resources, Inc., 2001.

Lainhart, Ann S. *State Census Records.* Baltimore: Genealogical Publishing Co., Inc., 1992.

Szucs, Loretto Dennis and Matthew Wright. *Finding Answers in U.S. Census Records.* Ancestry Publishing, 2001.

Thorndale, William and William Dollarhide. *Map Guide to the U.S. Federal Census, 1790–1920.* Baltimore: Genealogical Publishing Co., 1987.

United States. National Archives and Records Administration. *Federal Non-Population Census Schedules, Ohio, 1850–1880, in the Custody of the State Library of Ohio: Products of Agriculture, and Products of Industry.* Washington, D.C.: National Archives & Records Admin., 1988. 104 microfilm.

Court Records, Probate and Wills

Bell, Carol Willsey. *Ohio Wills and Estates to 1850: An Index.* Youngstown, Ohio: Bell Books, 1981.

Bowman, Mary L. *Abstracts and Extracts of the Legislative Acts and Resolutions of the State of Ohio: 1803–1821.* Mansfield, Ohio: Ohio Genealogical Society, 1994.

Daughters of the American Revolution. Independence Pioneers Chapter (Missouri). *Wills, 1655–1871, 1917.* Independence, Missouri: The D.A.R. chapter, 1970–1971.

Historical Records Survey (Ohio). *Inventory of the State Archives of Ohio.* Columbus, Ohio: Ohio Historical Records Survey Project, 1940.

Marshall, Carrington Tanner, ed. *A History of the Courts and Lawyers of Ohio.* 4 vols. New York: American Historical Society, 1934.

Nathan, Jean. *Ohio Marriages Recorded in County Courts Through 1820: An Index.* Mansfield, Ohio: The Society, 1996.

National Archives Records Administration. Great Lakes Region (Dayton). *Ohio Circuit Court Records.* Dayton, Ohio: National Archives Records Administration. Online guide—www.nara.gov/regional/dayton.html.

Ohio Federal Court Orders, 1803–1807. Miami Beach, Florida: TLC Genealogy, 1998.

Ohio Historical Society (Columbus, Ohio). *Ohio County Government Microfilm: Microfilm Available from the Ohio Historical Society.* Columbus, Ohio: Ohio Historical Society, 1987.

Ohio Historical Society. Local Government Records Program. *Guide to Local Government Records at the Ohio University Library.* Athens, Ohio: Ohio University Library, 1986.

Emigration, Immigration, Migration and Naturalization

Aughenbaugh, Gloria L. *Gone to Ohio: Ashland, Brown, Columbiana, Harrison, Jefferson, Richland, Champaign, Crawford, Wood, Logan, Mahoning, Stark and Trumbull Counties, from the Pennsylvania Counties: Adams, Cumberland, Dauphin, Franklin, Lancaster, and York.* 3 vols. York, Pennsylvania: South Central Pennsylvania Genealogical Society, 1990–1996.

Feather, Carl E. *Mountain People in a Flat Land: A Popular History of Appalachian Migration to Northeast Ohio, 1940–1965.* Athens, Ohio: Ohio University Press, 1998.

Ohio Historical Society. *County Naturalizations Held by the Ohio Historical Society.* Columbus, Ohio: Ohio Historical Society, 1996–2001. Online guide— www.ohiohistory.org/resource/archlib/natural.html.

Ohio, Trailways to Highways 1776–1976. Salt Lake City, Utah: Genealogical Society of Utah, 1977.

United States. District Court (Ohio: Southern District). *Naturalization Index, 1852–1991.* Microfilm of original records located at U.S. District Court, Southern District of Ohio, Cincinnati. Salt Lake City: Filmed by the Genealogical Society of Utah, 1992. 16 microfilm.

Wilhelm, Hubert G. H. *The Origin and Distribution of Settlement Groups.* Athens, Ohio: Ohio University, 1982.

Winkle, Kenneth J. *The Politics of Community: Migration and Politics in Antebellum Ohio.* New York: Press Syndicate of the University of Cambridge, 1988.

Land and Property

Berry, Ellen Thomas. *Early Ohio Settlers: Purchasers of Land in Southeastern Ohio, 1800–1840.* Baltimore: Genealogical Publishing Co., 1985.

Berry, Ellen and David Berry. *Early Ohio Settlers Purchasers of Land in East and East Central Ohio, 1800–1840.* Baltimore, Maryland: Genealogical Publishing Co., 1989.

Berry, Ellen and David Berry. *Early Ohio Settlers Purchasers of Land in Southwestern Ohio, 1800–1840.* (1986). Reprint. Baltimore, Maryland: Genealogical Publishing, 1993.

Clark, Marie Taylor. *Ohio Lands South of the Indian Boundary Line.* Chillicothe, Ohio: Marie Taylor Clark, 1984.

Clark, Marie Taylor. *Ohio Lands-Chillicothe Land Office: Entries Encompassing the Lands of Congress Lands, Refuge Tract, United States Military District, and French Grants; Contains Maps and Histories of Land Areas, 1800–1829.* S.l.: Clark, 1984.

Dyer, Albion Morris. *First Ownership of Ohio Lands.* Baltimore: Genealogical Publishing Co., 1982.

Ferguson, Thomas E. *Ohio Lands: A Short History,* 6th ed. Columbus, Ohio: Auditor's Office, State of Ohio, 1995.

Hone, Wade E. *Land and Property Research in the United States.* Salt Lake City: Ancestry Incorporated, 1997.

Hutchinson, William Thomas. *The Bounty Lands of the American Revolution in Ohio.* New York: Arno Press, 1979.

Ohio, 1787–1840. S.l.: Brøderbund, 1999. CD-ROM.

Ohio. Auditor of State. *Canal Lands.* Microfilm of records at the Ohio Historical Society in Columbus. Salt Lake City, Utah: Genealogical Society of Utah, 1959. Microfilm, 50 rolls.

Ohio. Auditor of State. *Governor's Deeds Card Index, 1833–1994.* Microfilm of original records at the Ohio Historical Society, Columbus, Ohio. Salt Lake City: Filmed by the Genealogical Society of Utah, 1995. 4 microfilm.

Ohio. Auditor of State. *Miscellaneous Lands.* Columbus, Ohio: Columbus Microfilm, Inc., 1954–1958, 1995. 23 microfilm.

Ohio. Auditor of State. *Virginia Military District Lands of Ohio; Indexes.* Microfilm of index and original records at the State Auditor's Office in Columbus, Ohio. Salt Lake City: Filmed by the Genealogical Society of Utah, 1995, 1958. 33 microfilm.

Peters, William Edwards. *Ohio Lands and Their History.* Athens, Ohio: W. E. Peters, 1930.

Peters, William Edwards. *Ohio Lands and Their Subdivision.* 2nd ed. Athens, Ohio: William Edwards Peters, 1918.

Petro, Jim. *Ohio Lands: A Short History.* Ohio: The Ohio Auditor of State, 1994.

Powell, Esther Weygandt. *Early Ohio Tax Records.* Reprinted with *The Index to Early Ohio Tax Records.* 2 vols. in 1. (1971, 1973), repr. 2005. Clearfield Company.

Riegel, Mayburt Stephenson. *Early Ohioans' Residences from the Land Grant Records.* Mansfield, Ohio: Ohio Genealogical Society, 1976.

Sherman, C. E. *Original Ohio Land Subdivision Being Volume III: Final Report Ohio Cooperative Topographic Survey.* Columbus: State Reformatory Press, 1925.

United States. Bureau of Land Management. *Card Files.* Microfilm of original card files located at the Bureau of Land Management's Eastern States Office in Alexandria, Virginia. Washington, D.C.: Bureau of Land Management. 160 microfilm.

United States. General Land Office. *U.S. Revolutionary War Bounty Land Warrants Used in the U.S. Military District of Ohio and Related Papers, Acts of 1788, 1803, 1806.* Washington, D.C.: National Archives, 1971.

Military

Broglin, Jana Sloan. *Index to the Official Roster of Ohio Soldiers in the War with Spain.* Mansfield, Ohio: Ohio Genealogical Society, 1990.

Broglin, Jana Sloan. *Roster of the Soldiers of Ohio in the War with Mexico.* (1897) Reprint. Mansfield, Ohio: Ohio Genealogical Society, 1991.

Canfield, Capt. S. S. *History of the 21st Regiment, Ohio Volunteer Infantry, in the War of the Rebellion.* (1893) Reprint. Salem, Massachusetts: Higginson Book Co., 1995.

Dailey, Mrs. Orville D. *The Official Roster of the Soldiers of the American Revolution Who Lived in the State of Ohio: Vol. 2, A–Z.* Columbus, Ohio: State Society DAR, State of Ohio, 1938.

Garner, Grace. *Index to Roster of Ohio Soldiers, War of 1812.* Spokane, Washington: Eastern Washington Genealogical Society, 1974.

Hardesty's Historical and Geographical Encyclopedia, Illustrated . . . Containing . . . Maps of Each State and Territory of the United States, and the Provinces of Canada . . . History of the United States, History of Each State and Territory of the United States . . . Special Military History of Ohio . . . Ohio's Rank and File in the War of the Rebellion. New York: s.n., 1885.

Maxwell, Fay. *Ohio Indian, Revolutionary War, and War of 1812 Trails.* St. Peter, Minnesota: Ohio Genealogy Center, 1974.

Maxwell, Fay. *Ohio Revolutionary War Soldiers 1840 Census and Grave Locations.* St. Peter, Minnesota: Ohio Genealogy Center, 1985.

Maxwell, Fay. *Ohio's Virginia Military Tract Settlers, Also 1801 Tax List.* St. Peter, Minnesota: Ohio Genealogy Center, 1991.

Middle Western Section Records. Colonial and Genealogical Records Committee, Daughters of the American Revolution, Ohio. Fort Wayne, Indiana: Allen County Public Library, 1983.

Ohio Adjutant General's Department. *Roster of Ohio Soldiers in the War of 1812.* (1968) Reprint. Baltimore, Maryland: Clearfield Company, 1989.

Ohio Adjutant General's Office. *The Official Roster of Ohio Soldiers in the War with Spain 1898–1899.* Columbus, Ohio: Edward T. Miller Co., 1916.

Ohio Historical Society. *Civil War Documents.* Columbus, Ohio: Ohio Historical Society, 1996–2001. Online guide—www.ohiohistory.org/dindex/.

Ohio Historical Society. *War of 1812, Roster of Ohio Soldiers.* Columbus, Ohio: Ohio Historical Society, 1996–2001. Online database—www.ohiohistory.org/dindex/.

Ohio Roster Commission. *Official Roster of the Soldiers of the State of Ohio in the War of the Rebellion, 1861–1866.* Akron, Ohio: Werner Co., 1886–1895.

Ohio, Adjutant General's Office. *The Official Roster of the Soldiers of the American Revolution Buried in the State of Ohio.* Columbus, Ohio: F. J. Heer Printing Co., 1929–1959.

Ohio. Adjutant General's Office. *The Official Roster of Ohio Soldiers, Sailors, and Marines in the World War, 1917–1918.* Microfilm of original published: Columbus, Ohio: F. J. Heer Printing Co., 1926–1929. 22 volumes. Salt Lake City: Filmed by the Genealogical Society of Utah, 1959. 23 microfilm.

Phillips, William Louis. *Annotated Bibliography of Ohio Patriots: Revolutionary War & War of 1812.* Bowie, Maryland: Heritage Books, 1985.

Two Hundred Years the Military History of Ohio: Its Border Annals, Its Part in the Indian Wars, in the War of 1812, in the Mexican War, and in the War of the Rebellion, with a Prefix, Giving a Compendium of the History of the United States, History of the Declaration of Independence, Sketches of Its Signers, and of the Presidents, with Portraits and Autographs. New York: H. H. Hardesty, 1886.

United States, Selective Service System. *Ohio, World War I Selective Service System Draft Registration Cards, 1917–1918.* Washington, D.C.: National Archives, 1987–1988.

United States. Navy Department. *State Summary of War Casualties (Ohio), U.S. Navy, 1946: (Includes Navy, Marine, and Coast Guard).* Salt Lake City: Filmed by the Genealogical Society of Utah, 1960.

United States. Veterans Administration. *Revolutionary War Pension and Bounty-Land—Warrant Application Files.* Washington, D.C.: National Archives, 1969.

United States. War Department. *World War II Honor List of Dead and Missing—State of Ohio, June 1946.* Salt Lake City: Filmed by the Genealogical Society of Utah, 1960.

White, Virgil D. *Genealogical Abstracts of the Revolutionary War Pension Files.* 4 vols. Waynesboro, Tennessee: National Historical Publishing, 1990.

Young American Patriots: The Youth of Ohio in World War II. Richmond, Virginia: National Publishing Co., 1947.

Vital and Cemetery Records

Bell, Carol Willsey. *Ohio Divorces: The Early Years.* Boardman, Ohio: Bell Books, 1994.

Caccamo, James F. *Marriage Notices from the Ohio Observer* Series. Apollo, Pennsylvania: Closson Press, 1994.

Daughters of the American Revolution (Ohio). *Early Vital Records of Ohio, 1750–1970.* Microfilm of manuscripts from the DAR Library, Washington, D.C. Salt Lake City: Genealogical Society of Utah, 1972.

Diefenbach, Mrs. H. B., and Mrs. C. O. Ross. *Index to the Grave Records of Soldiers in the War of 1812 Buried in Ohio.* S.l.: s.n., 1945.

Herbert, Jeffrey G. *Index of Death and Other Notices Appearing in the Cincinnati Free Press 1874–1920.* Bowie, Maryland: Heritage Books, 1993.

Index to Grave Records of Servicemen in the War of 1812. State of Ohio. Lancaster, Ohio: Society of the United States Daughters of 1812, 1969.

Marriage Records. Orem, Utah: Automated Archives, 1994. CD-ROM.

Official Roster of the Soldiers of the American Revolution Buried in the State of Ohio. 3 vols. Columbus, Ohio: F. J. Heer Printing, 1929–1959.

Ohio Cemetery Records. Salt Lake City: Filmed by the Genealogical Society of Utah, 1972. 2 microfilm.

Ohio Cemetery Records: Extracted from the "Old Northwest" Genealogical Quarterly. Reprint. Baltimore, Maryland: Genealogical Publishing Co., 1989.

Ohio Historical Society. *Death Certificate Index, 1913–1937.* Columbus, Ohio: Ohio Historical Society, 1992. Online database—www.ohiohistory.org/dindex/.

Ohio. Department of Health. *Certificates of Death, 1908–1944; Index, 1908–1911.* Microfilm of original records at Ohio Historical Society, Columbus, Ohio. Columbus, Ohio: Ohio Historical Society, 1983, 1994–1995. 962 microfilm.

Ohio. Department of Health. *Veteran's Records, 1941–1964.* Microfilm of original records located in the Licking County Courthouse in Newark, Ohio. Salt Lake City: Filmed by the Genealogical Society of Utah, 1974. 7 microfilm.

Smith, Marjorie, ed. *Ohio Marriages: Extracted from the Old Northwest Genealogical Quarterly.* Baltimore: Genealogical Publishing Co., 1980.

Smith, Maxine Hartmann, ed. *Ohio Cemeteries.* Mansfield: Ohio Genealogical Society, 1978. (Addendum, 1990).

State Library of Ohio. *Ohio Birth and Death Records by County.* Columbus, Ohio: State Library of Ohio, 2001. Online guide—http://winslo.state.oh.us/services/genealogy/slogenebir.html.

County Website	Map Index	Date Created	Parent County or Territory From Which Organized Address/Details
Adams www.rootsweb.com/~ohadams/	N4	**10 Jul 1797**	**Hamilton** Adams County; 110 W Main St; West Union, OH 45693-1347; Ph. (937) 544-5547 **Details:** (Courthouse burned in 1910, some Records saved, some as early as 1796; Records of several adjacent Counties prior to their formation included) (Probate Court has Birth & Death Records 1888–1893, Marriage Records 1803–1853 & from 1910, Probate Records 1849–1860 & from 1910; Board of Health has Birth & Death Records from 1908; Clerk Court has Divorce and Court Records from 1910; Court Recorder has Land Records from 1797)
Allen www.co.allen.oh.us/	H3	**12 Feb 1820**	**Shelby** Allen County; 301 N Main St; Lima, OH 45801-4456; Ph. (419) 223-8513 **Details:** (Probate Court has Birth & Death Records from 1867, Marriage Records from 1831 & Probate Records; Clerk Courts has Divorce & Court Records from 1831; County Museum has Naturalization Records 1851–1929)

County Website	Map Index	Date Created	Parent County or Territory From Which Organized Address/Details
Ashland www.ashlandcounty.org/	**H8**	**24 Feb 1846**	**Wayne, Richland, Huron, Lorain** Ashland County; 110 W 2nd St; Ashland, OH 44805; Ph. (419) 289-0000 **Details:** (Clerk Courts has Divorce & Court Records; Probate Court has Marriage & Probate Records; County Recorder has land Records)
Ashtabula www.co.ashtabula.oh.us/	**E12**	**1808**	**Trumbull, Geauga** Ashtabula County; 25 W Jefferson St; Jefferson, OH 44047; Ph. (440) 576-3637 **Details:** (Probate Court has Birth & Death Records 1867–1908, Marriage Records from 1811 & Probate Records from 1800's; County Health Department has Birth & Death Records from 1909; Clerk Courts has Divorce Records from 1811 & Court Records from 1800's; County Recorder has land Records from 1800)
Athens www.seorf.ohiou.edu/athens_county.html	**L8**	**20 Feb 1805**	**Washington** Athens County; Court & Washington Sts; PO Box 290; Athens, OH 45701-0000; Ph. (740) 592-3242 **Details:** (Probate Judge has Birth, Marriage & Probate Records; Clerk Courts has Divorce & Court Records from 1800; County Recorder has land Records)
Auglaize www.genweb.brightusa.net/index.html	**I3**	**14 Feb 1848**	**Allen, Mercer, Darke, Hardin, Logan, Shelby, Van Wert** Auglaize County; 214 S Wagner St; Wapakoneta, OH 45895; Ph. (419) 738-3410 **Details:** (Probate Judge has Birth, Marriage, Death & Probate Records; Clerk Courts has Divorce & Court Records from 1848; County Recorder has land Records)
Belmont www.belmontcountyohio.org/	**K11**	**7 Sep 1801**	**Jefferson, Washington** Belmont County; 100 W Main St; St. Clairsville, OH 43950-1225; Ph. (740) 699-2139 **Details:** (Clerk Courts has Divorce & Court Records from 1820; Probate Court has Birth, Marriage, Death & Probate Records; County Health Department has Burial Records)
Brown www.rootsweb.com/~ohbrown/index.htm	**N3**	**1818**	**Adams, Clermont** Brown County; 101 S Main St; Georgetown, OH 45121-0000; Ph. (937) 378-3100 **Details:** (Probate Judge has Birth, Marriage & Probate Records from 1800's; County Health Department has Death Records from 1800's; Clerk Courts has Divorce & Court Records from 1800's; County Recorder has land Records)
Butler www.butlercountyohio.org/	**L2**	**24 Mar 1803**	**Hamilton** Butler County; 315 High St; Hamilton, OH 45011-2756; Ph. (513) 887-3278 **Details:** (County Health Department has Birth & Death Records; Probate Judge has Marriage & Probate Records; Clerk Courts has Divorce & Court Records; County Auditor has land Records)
Carroll http://pages.eohio.net/carrcomm/	**I11**	**1833**	**Columbiana, Stark, Harrison, Jefferson, Tuscarawas** Carroll County; 119 Public Sq; Carrollton, OH 44615-1448; Ph. (330) 627-4886 **Details:** (Clerk Courts has Divorce & Court Records from 1833; Probate Court has Birth & Death Records 1867–1909, Marriage & Probate Records from 1833; County Recorder has land Records from 1833; Board of Health has Birth & Death Records from 1909)

County Website	Map Index	Date Created	Parent County or Territory From Which Organized Address/Details
Champaign	J3	20 Feb 1805	**Greene, Franklin** Champaign County; 200 N Main St; Urbana, OH 43078; Ph. (937) 484-1028 **Details:** (Probate Court has Birth & Death Records 1867–1909, Guardianship Records from 1867, Marriage Records from 1805, & Probate Records)
Clark www.rootsweb.com/~ohclark/	K3	1818	**Champaign, Madison, Greene** Clark County; Ab Graham Building; Springfield, OH 45502; Ph. (937) 328-2458 **Details:** (Clark County Historical Society, Memorial Hall, Springfield, OH 45502 may assist you in your work, also Warder Public Library, Springfield) (Probate Judge has Birth, Marriage, Death, Probate & Naturalization Records; Clerk Courts has Divorce & Court Records; County Recorder has land Records)
Clermont www.co.clermont.oh.us/	N2	6 Dec 1800	**Hamilton** Clermont County; 212 E Main St; Batavia, OH 45103; Ph. (513) 732-7308 **Details:** (Probate Court has Birth & Death Records 1867–1950, Marriage & Probate Records from 1800 & Naturalization Records from 1860's; Clerk Courts has Divorce Records from 1861 & Court Records from 1803)
Clinton www.rootsweb.com/~ohclinto/	L4	19 Feb 1810	**Highland, Warren** Clinton County; 46 S South St; Wilmington, OH 45177-2214; Ph. (937) 382-2103 **Details:** (Probate Judge has Birth & Death Records 1867–1908, Marriage & Probate Records from 1810; County Health Office has Birth & Death Records from 1908; County Recorder has land Records from 1810; Clerk Courts has Divorce & Court Records from 1810)
Columbiana www.rootsweb.com/~ohcolumb/index.htm	H11	25 Mar 1803	**Jefferson, Washington** Columbiana County; 105 S Market St; Lisbon, OH 44432; Ph. Probate Court (330) 424-9516; County Clerk (330) 424-7777; County Recorder (330) 424-9517; County Auditor (330) 424-9515 **Details:** (County Probate Court has Marriage & Guardianship Records from 1803, Birth & Death Records 1867–1908, & Name Change Records from 1803; County Clerk has Divorce, Court, & Naturalization Records; County Recorder has Land & Military Discharge Records; County Auditor has Tax Records)
Coshocton www.co.coshocton.oh.us/	I8	31 Jan 1810	**Tuscarawas, Muskingum** Coshocton County; 318 Main St Courthouse Square; Coshocton, OH 43812; Ph. (740) 622-1456 **Details:** (Clerk of Courts has Civil/Criminal Cases from 1811 & Naturalization Records from 1811)
Crawford www.rootsweb.com/~ohcrawfo/index.htm	H6	12 Feb 1820	**Delaware** Crawford County; 112 E Mansfield St; Bucyrus, OH 44820; Ph. (419) 562-2766 **Details:** (City & County Health Departments have Birth & Death Records from 1908; Probate Judge has Birth & Death Records 1867–1908, Marriage & Probate Records from 1831; County Recorder has land Records; Clerk Courts has Divorce & Court Records from 1834)

County Website	Map Index	Date Created	Parent County or Territory From Which Organized Address/Details
Cuyahoga www.cuyahoga.oh.us/home/default.asp	F9	10 Feb 1808	**Geauga** Cuyahoga County; 1200 Ontario St; Cleveland, OH 44113; Ph. (216) 443-7950 **Details:** (Probate Court has Birth Records 1859–1901 & Death Records 1868–1908; Western Reserve Historical Society has Marriage Records 1810–1941 & tax Records 1819–1869; Marriage License Bureau has Marriage Records from 1810; County Courthouse has Naturalization Records 1818–1906 & Probate Records from 1810; Clerk Courts has Divorce Records 1837–1925; County Administration Building has Land Records from 1810)
Darke www.calweb.com/~wally/ohdarke/index.htm	J1	3 Jan 1809	**Miami** Darke County; 504 S Broadway St; Greenville, OH 45331-0000; Ph. (937) 547-7335 **Details:** (Probate Judge has Birth & Death Records 1867–1908, Marriage Records from 1817 & Probate Records; Clerk Courts has Divorce & Court Records from 1820; County Recorder has land Records from 1816 & Burial Records (veterans graves) from 1832)
Defiance www.defiance-county.com	F2	4 Mar 1845	**Williams, Henry, Paulding** Defiance County; 510 Court St; Defiance, OH 43512; Ph. (419) 782-4761, recordcenter@defiance-county.com **Details:** (County Records Center has Birth & Death Records 1867–1908, Marriage & Will Records 1845–2003, Naturalization Records 1845–1929, & Military Discharge Records 1865–1974)
Delaware www.co.delaware.oh.us/	J6	10 Feb 1808	**Franklin** Delaware County; 91 N Sandusky St; Delaware, OH 43015; Ph. (740) 369-8761 **Details:** (Clerk Chancery Court has Divorce & Court Records from 1825; Probate Court has Birth, Marriage, Death & Probate Records; County Recorder has land Records)
Erie www.erie-county-ohio.net/	F7	15 Mar 1838	**Huron, Sandusky** Erie County; 323 Columbus Ave; Sandusky, OH 44870; Ph. (419) 627-7705 **Details:** (County Health Department has Birth Records from 1908, Death & Burial Records; Probate Judge has Marriage & Probate Records; Clerk Courts has Divorce & Court Records from 1870; County Recorder has land Records)
Fairfield www.co.fairfield.oh.us/	K7	9 Dec 1800	**Ross, Washington** Fairfield County; 224 E Main St; PO Box 370; Lancaster, OH 43130-3842; Ph. (740) 687-7030 **Details:** (Probate Judge has Birth Records 1867–1907, Marriage, Death & Probate Records; Clerk Courts has Divorce Records from 1860 & Court Records from 1800; County Recorder has land Records from 1803)
Fayette www.fayette-co-oh.com/	L4	19 Feb 1810	**Ross, Highland** Fayette County; 110 E Court St; Washington Court House, OH 43160-1355; Ph. (614) 335-5910 **Details:** (Clerk Courts has Divorce Records from 1853 & Court Records from 1828; Probate Judge has Probate Records; County Recorder has land Records)

County Website	Map Index	Date Created	Parent County or Territory From Which Organized Address/Details
Franklin www.franklincountyclerk.com	**K6**	**30 Mar 1803**	**Ross** Franklin County; 375 S High Street, 23rd FL; Columbus, OH 43215; Ph. (614) 462-3600, franklincountyclerk@co.franklin.oh.us **Details:** (Clerk of Courts has Civil Records from 1803, Criminal Records from 1866, Domestic Relations Records from 1929, and Appeals Records from 1913; Ohio Historical Society has Other Historical Records)
Fulton www.fultoncountyoh.com/	**E3**	**28 Feb 1850**	**Lucas, Henry, Williams** Fulton County; 210 S Fulton St; Wauseon, OH 43567-1355; Ph. (419) 337-9230 **Details:** (Probate Court has Birth & Death Records 1867–1908, Marriage, Probate & Naturalization Records; Clerk Courts has Divorce & Court Records; County Recorder has Military & Burial Records; County Auditor has land Records)
Gallia www.rootsweb.com/~ohgallia/gallia.htm	**N7**	**25 Mar 1803**	**Washington, Adams** Gallia County; 18 Locust St; Gallipolis, OH 45631-1251; Ph. (740) 446-4374 **Details:** (Probate Judge has Birth, Marriage, Death & Probate Records; County Health Department has Burial Records; Clerk Courts has Divorce & Court Records from 1850; County Recorder has land Records)
Geauga www.co.geauga.oh.us/	**F10**	**1806**	**Trumbull** Geauga County; 231 Main St; Chardon, OH 44024-1243; Ph. (216) 285-2222 **Details:** (Probate Judge has Birth, Marriage, Death & Probate Records; County Health Department has Burial Records; Clerk Courts has Divorce & Court Records from 1806; County Recorder has land Records)
Greene www.co.greene.oh.us/	**L3**	**24 Mar 1803**	**Hamilton, Ross** Greene County; 45 N Detroit St; Xenia, OH 45385; Ph. (937) 376-5290 **Details:** (Probate Judge has Birth Records 1869–1908, Marriage & Probate Records from 1803; Clerk Courts has Divorce & Court Records from 1802; County Recorder has land Records from 1803; County Auditor has tax Records from 1803; County Health Department has Birth Records from 1908)
Guernsey www.usgennet.org/usa/oh/county/guernsey/	**K10**	**31 Jan 1810**	**Belmont, Muskingum** Guernsey County; 801 Wheeling Ave; Cambridge, OH 43725-2335; Ph. (740) 432-9230 **Details:** (Clerk Courts has Divorce Records from 1850 & Court Records from 1810; Probate Judge has Birth, Marriage & Probate Records; County Recorder has land Records; City-County Health Department has Death Records)
Hamilton www.hamilton-co.org/	**M1**	**2 Jan 1790**	**Original county** Hamilton County; 1000 Main St; Cincinnati, OH 45202; Ph. (513) 632-5656 **Details:** (Probate Judge has Marriage, Burial & Probate Records; County Health Department has Death Records; Clerk Courts has Divorce & Court Records from 1900; County Recorder has land Records)

County Website	Map Index	Date Created	Parent County or Territory From Which Organized Address/Details
Hancock www.co.hancock.oh.us/	G4	12 Feb 1820	**Logan** Hancock County; 300 S Main St; Findlay, OH 45840-3345; Ph. (419) 424-3911 **Details:** (County Recorder has land Records; Probate Judge has Birth, Marriage, Death & Probate Records)
Hardin www.kenton.com/users/chuck/index.htm	I4	12 Feb 1820	**Logan** Hardin County; Public Sq; Kenton, OH 43326; Ph. (419) 673-6283 **Details:** (Clerk Courts has Divorce & Court Records from 1864; County Health Department has Birth & Death Records; Probate Court has Marriage, Death & Probate Records; County Recorder has land Records)
Harrison Future website at http://scioto.org/OHGenWeb/ohiomap.html	J11	2 Jan 1813	**Jefferson, Tuscarawas** Harrison County; 100 W Market St; Cadiz, OH 43907-1132; Ph. (740) 942-4623 **Details:** (Clerk Courts has Divorce & Court Records from 1813; Probate Judge has Birth Records to 1917, Marriage & Probate Records; County Health Office has Birth Records from 1917, Death & Burial Records; County Recorder has land Records)
Henry www.rootsweb.com/~ohhenry/	F3	12 Feb 1820	**Shelby** Henry County; 660 N Perry St; Napoleon, OH 43545-0546; Ph. (419) 592-4876 **Details:** (Probate Judge has Birth & Death Records 1867–1908, Marriage & Probate Records from 1847; Clerk Courts has Divorce & Court Records from 1880; County Recorder has land Records from 1835)
Highland www.usgennet.org/usa/oh/county/highland/	M4	18 Feb 1805	**Ross, Adams, Clermont** Highland County; 114 Governor Foraker Pl; Hillsboro, OH 45133; Ph. (937) 393-1981 **Details:** (Probate Court has Marriage & Death Records 1867–1909, Birth Records to 1905 & Probate Records; County Health Department has Birth, Marriage & Death Records from 1909; Clerk Courts has Divorce & Court Records from 1832, some Naturalization & adoption Records; County Recorder has land Records)
Hocking www.co.hocking.oh.us/	L7	3 Jan 1818	**Athens, Ross, Fairfield** Hocking County; 1 E Main St; Logan, OH 43138-1207; Ph. (740) 385-3022 **Details:** (Probate Judge has Birth, Marriage & Probate Records; County Health Department has Death Records; Clerk Courts has Divorce & Court Records from 1873; County Recorder has land Records)
Holmes www.holmescounty.com/gov/	I8	20 Jan 1824	**Coshocton, Wayne, Tuscarawas** Holmes County; 1 E Jackson St Suite 203; Millersburg, OH 44654; Ph. (330) 674-5881 **Details:** (Probate Court has Birth and Death Records 1867–1908; Birth Records after 1908 are at the Health Department; Probate Court also has Marriage & Probate Records from 1825)

County Website	Map Index	Date Created	Parent County or Territory From Which Organized Address/Details
Huron www.hccommissioners.com/homepage.htm	G7	7 Feb 1809	**Portage, Cuyahoga** Huron County; 2 E Main St; Norwalk, OH 44857; Ph. (419) 668-5113 **Details:** (Probate Judge has Birth & Death Records 1867–1908, Marriage & Probate Records from 1815 & Naturalization Records from 1859; City & County Health Department have Birth & Death Records from 1908; County Clerk has Court Records from 1815, Divorce & Naturalization Records to 1859; County Recorder has land Records from 1808, Connecticut Fire Sufferers Records 1792–1808 & Military Discharge Records from 1865; County Auditor has Tax Records from 1820; County History Library has Infirmary Records 1848–1900, Tax Records 1815–1825, County Commissioner Journals from 1815, Land Partition Records 1815–1920, County Militia Lists 1864–1865 and Indigent Soldier Burial Records 1880–1920)
Jackson www.rootsweb.com/~ohjackso/jackson.htm	N7	12 Jan 1816	**Scioto, Gallia, Athens, Ross** Jackson County; 226 E Main St; Jackson, OH 45640-0000; Ph. (740) 286-2006 **Details:** (Probate Judge has Birth, Marriage & Probate Records; County Health Department has Death & Burial Records; Clerk Courts has Divorce & Court Records; County Recorder has land Records)
Jefferson www.rootsweb.com/~ohjeffer/	I12	27 Jul 1797	**Washington** Jefferson County; 301 Market St; Steubenville, OH 43952; Ph. (740) 283-8583 **Details:** (Probate Judge has Marriage, Probate & Naturalization Records; Clerk Courts has Divorce & Court Records from 1797; County Recorder has land Records from 1797; Board of Health has Birth & Death Records)
Knox www.knoxcountyohio.org/	I7	30 Jan 1808	**Fairfield** Knox County; 111 E High St; Mount Vernon, OH 43050-3453; Ph. (740) 393-6788 **Details:** (County Health Department has Birth Records from 1908, Death & Burial Records; Probate Judge has Marriage Records from 1803 & Probate Records; Clerk Courts has Divorce & Court Records from 1810; County Recorder has land Records)
Lake www.rootsweb.com/~ohlake/	E10	6 Mar 1840	**Geauga, Cuyahoga** Lake County; 47 N Park Pl; Painesville, OH 44077-3414; Ph. (440) 350-2657 **Details:** (Clerk Courts has Court Records from 1840; Probate Judge has Marriage & Probate Records; County Recorder has land Records)
Lawrence www.db.k12.oh.us/community/lcc_1.htm	O7	21 Dec 1815	**Gallia, Scioto** Lawrence County; 111 N 4th St; Ironton, OH 45638; Ph. (740) 533-4300 **Details:** (Probate Court has Birth Records 1864–1908, Marriage Records from 1900, Death Records 1868–1933 & Probate Records from 1817; County Health Department has Birth & Death Records from 1908; Clerk Courts has Court Records from 1817 & Divorce Records from 1819; County Recorder has land Records from 1817)
Licking www.lcounty.com/	J7	30 Jan 1808	**Fairfield** Licking County; 20 S 2nd St; Newark, OH 43058; Ph. (740) 349-6062 **Details:** (Probate Judge has Birth, Marriage & Probate Records; County Health Department has Death Records; Clerk Courts has Divorce Records from 1876 & Court Records from 1872; County Recorder has land Records)

County Website	Map Index	Date Created	Parent County or Territory From Which Organized Address/Details
Logan www.co.logan.oh.us/	I4	1818	**Champaign** Logan County; 101 S Main St Courthouse; Bellefontaine, OH 43311; Ph. (937) 599-7275 **Details:** (Probate Court has Birth & Death Records 1867–1909, Marriage Records from 1818 & Probate Records from 1820; County Recorder has land, Military & Burial Records; Common Pleas Court has Divorce & Court Records)
Lorain www.centurytel.net/lorgen/	F8	26 Dec 1822	**Huron, Cuyahoga, Medina** Lorain County; 226 Middle Ave; Elyria, OH 44035; Ph. (440) 329-5428 **Details:** (Probate Judge has Birth, Marriage & Probate Records; Clerk Courts has Divorce Records from 1850 & Court Records from 1824; County Recorder has land Records; Elyria Public Library & Lorain County Historical Society have books of genealogical interest)
Lucas http://co.lucas.oh.us/	E4	20 Jun 1835	**Wood, Sandusky, Henry** Lucas County; 700 Adams St; Toledo, OH 43624; Ph. (419) 245-4000 **Details:** (Clerk Courts has Divorce & Court Records from 1850; Probate Judge has Birth Records 1865–1908, Death Records from 1935, Marriage & Probate Records; County Recorder has land Records)
Madison www.co.madison.oh.us/	K5	16 Feb 1810	**Franklin** Madison County; 1 N Main St; London, OH 43140; Ph. (740) 852-9776 **Details:** (Probate Court has Birth & Death Records 1867–1908, Marriage & Probate Records from 1810 & Naturalization Records; County Health Department has Birth Records from 1908; County Recorder has land & Military Discharge Records; Clerk Courts has Divorce & Court Records)
Mahoning http://mahoningcountygov.com/	G11	16 Feb 1846	**Columbiana, Trumbull** Mahoning County; 120 Market St; Youngstown, OH 44503; Ph. (330) 740-2104 **Details:** (County Health Department has Birth & Death Records; Probate Judge has Marriage & Probate Records; Clerk Courts has Divorce & Court Records; County Auditor has land Records)
Marion www.mariononline.com/county/	I5	12 Feb 1820	**Delaware** Marion County; 100 N Main St; Marion, OH 43302; Ph. (740) 387-8128 **Details:** (Probate Court has Marriage & Probate Records; City Health Department has Birth & Death Records from 1908; Public Library has Birth & Death Records 1867–1908; Clerk Courts has Divorce & Court Records; County Recorder has land Records)
Medina www.co.medina.oh.us/	G8	18 Feb 1812	**Portage** Medina County; 93 Public Sq; Medina, OH 44256; Ph. (330) 723-3641 **Details:** (Probate Court has Birth & Death Records to 1909, Marriage & Probate Records; County Health Department has Birth & Death Records from 1909; Clerk Courts has Divorce & Court Records from 1818; County Recorder has land Records)
Meigs http://genealogy.rootsweb.com/~baf/meigs.html	M8	21 Jan 1819	**Gallia, Athens** Meigs County; 100 E 2nd St; Pomeroy, OH 45769-0000; Ph. (740) 992-5290 **Details:** (Probate Judge has Birth, Marriage, Death & Probate Records; Clerk Courts has Divorce & Court Records from 1819; County Recorder has land Records)

County Website	Map Index	Date Created	Parent County or Territory From Which Organized Address/Details
Mercer www.mercercountyohio.org/	I1	12 Feb 1820	**Darke** Mercer County; 101 N Main St; PO Box 28; Celina, OH 45822; Ph. (419) 586-6461 **Details:** (Probate Judge has Birth & Death Records 1867–1908, Marriage Records from 1830 & Probate Records from 1829; Clerk Courts has Divorce & Court Records from 1824; County Recorder has land Records)
Miami www.co.miami.oh.us/	J2	16 Jan 1807	**Montgomery** Miami County; 201 W Main St; Troy, OH 45373-3263; Ph. (937) 332-6855 **Details:** (Clerk Courts has Divorce & Court Records from 1807; Probate Judge has Marriage, Death & Probate Records; County Health Department has Birth Records; County Recorder has land Records)
Monroe www.rootsweb.com/~ohmonroe/	K11	29 Jan 1813	**Belmont, Washington, Guernsey** Monroe County; 101 N Main St; Woodsfield, OH 43793; Ph. (740) 472-0761 **Details:** (Clerk Courts has Divorce & Court Records from early 1800's; Probate Judge has Marriage & Probate Records; County Recorder has land Records)
Montgomery www.co.montgomery.oh.us/	K2	24 Mar 1803	**Hamilton, Wayne, old** Montgomery County; 41 N Perry; Dayton, OH 45422-0002; Ph. (937) 225-6118 **Details:** (Clerk Courts has Divorce & Court Records; Probate Judge has Birth, Marriage, Death & Probate Records; County Recorder has land Records)
Morgan www.rootsweb.com/~ohmorgan/index.htm	L9	29 Dec 1817	**Washington, Guernsey, Muskingum** Morgan County; 19 E Main St; McConnelsville, OH 43756-1198; Ph. (740) 962-4752 **Details:** (County Recorder has land Records; Probate Judge has Birth, Marriage, Death, Probate & Naturalization Records)
Morrow www.rootsweb.com/~ohmorrow/	I6	24 Feb 1848	**Knox, Marion, Delaware, Richland** Morrow County; 48 E High St; Mount Gilead, OH 43338; Ph. (419) 947-2085 **Details:** (Probate Court has Birth & Death Records 1856–1857 & 1867–1908, Marriage & Probate Records from 1848 & Naturalization Records 1848–1894; County Health Department has Birth & Death Records from 1908; County Recorder has land Records from 1848 & Military Records; Common Pleas Court has Divorce & Court Records)
Muskingum www.rootsweb.com/~ohmuskin/	K8	7 Jan 1804	**Washington, Fairfield** Muskingum County; 401 Main St; Zanesville, OH 43701; Ph. (740) 455-7104 **Details:** (Probate Court has Birth & Death Records 1867–1908, Marriage & Probate Records from 1804 & Naturalization Records; County Recorder has land Records from 1803 & Military Records from 1865; Clerk Courts has Divorce & Court Records from 1804)
Noble www.rootsweb.com/~ohnoble/index.htm	K10	11 Mar 1851	**Monroe, Washington, Morgan, Guernsey** Noble County; County Courthouse; Caldwell, OH 43724-0000; Ph. (740) 732-4408 **Details:** (Clerk Courts has Divorce & Court Records from 1851; Probate Judge has Marriage & Probate Records; County Recorder has land Records)

County Website	Map Index	Date Created	Parent County or Territory From Which Organized Address/Details
Ottawa www.co.ottawa.oh.us/OCHome/OCFrameset.htm	E5	**6 Mar 1840**	**Erie, Sandusky, Lucas** Ottawa County; 315 Madison St Rm 103; Port Clinton, OH 43452-1936; Ph. (419) 734-6752 **Details:** (County Health Department has Birth, Death & Burial Records; Probate Judge has Marriage & Probate Records; Clerk Courts has Divorce & Court Records from 1840 & Naturalization Records 1905–1929; County Recorder has land Records)
Paulding Future website at http://scioto.org/OHGenWeb/ohiomap.html	G1	**12 Feb 1820**	**Darke** Paulding County; Perry & N Williams; Paulding, OH 45879-0000; Ph. (419) 399-8210 **Details:** (County Health Department has Birth & Death Records; Probate Judge has Marriage & Probate Records; Clerk Courts has Divorce Records; County Judge has Court Records; County Recorder has land Records)
Perry www.perrygenealogy.net/	K8	**1818**	**Washington, Fairfield, Muskingum** Perry County; 105 N Main St; New Lexington, OH 43764-1241; Ph. (740) 342-1022 **Details:** (Probate Court has Birth & Death Records from 1867, Marriage Records from 1818 & Probate Records; County Recorder has land Records)
Pickaway www.rootsweb.com/~ohpickaw/index.html	L5	**12 Jan 1810**	**Ross, Fairfield, Franklin** Pickaway County; 207 S Court St; Circleville, OH 43113; Ph. (740) 474-5231 **Details:** (County Recorder has land Records from 1810; Probate Court has Birth, Marriage, Death & Probate Records)
Pike www.scioto.org/Pike/	N5	**4 Jan 1815**	**Ross, Scioto, Adams** Pike County; 100 E 2nd St; Waverly, OH 45690; Ph. (740) 947-2715 **Details:** (Probate Judge has Birth, Marriage & Probate Records; Clerk Courts has Divorce & Court Records from 1815; County Recorder has land Records)
Portage www.portageworkforce.org/portagecountydirectory/	G10	**1808**	**Trumbull** Portage County; 449 S Meridian St; PO Box 1035; Ravenna, OH 44266; Ph. (330) 297-3450 **Details:** (Mayor's Office has Birth, Death & Burial Records; Probate Judge has Marriage & Probate Records; Clerk Courts has Divorce & Court Records from 1820; County Treasury has land Records)
Preble www.calweb.com/~wally/preble/index.htm	K1	**15 Feb 1808**	**Montgomery, Butler** Preble County; 100 Main St; Eaton, OH 45320-0000; Ph. (937) 456-8160 **Details:** (Probate Judge has Birth & Death Records from 1867, Probate Records from 1800 & Marriage Records from 1808; Clerk Courts has Divorce & Court Records from 1850; County Recorder has land Records from 1804)
Putnam www.rootsweb.com/~ohputnam/	G3	**12 Feb 1820**	**Shelby** Putnam County; 245 E Main St; Ottawa, OH 45875-1968; Ph. (419) 523-3110 **Details:** (Clerk Courts has Divorce & Court Records from 1834; Probate Judge has Marriage & Probate Records; County Recorder has land Records)

County Website	Map Index	Date Created	Parent County or Territory From Which Organized Address/Details
Richland www.rootsweb.com/~ohrichla/	H7	30 Jan 1808	**Fairfield** Richland County; 50 Park Ave E; Mansfield, OH 44902; Ph. (419) 884-0278 **Details:** (Clerk Courts has Divorce & Court Records from 1815; Probate Judge has Marriage & Probate Records; County Recorder has land Records)
Ross www.co.ross.oh.us/	M5	20 Aug 1798	**Adams, Washington** Ross County; 2 N Paint St; Chillicothe, OH 45601-0000; Ph. (740) 702-3085 **Details:** (Probate Judge has Birth, Marriage, Death & Probate Records; Clerk Courts has Divorce Records from late 1800's & Court Records; County Recorder has land Records)
Sandusky www.sandusky-county.org/	F5	12 Feb 1820	**Huron** Sandusky County; 100 N Park Ave; Fremont, OH 43420-2473; Ph. (419) 334-6100 **Details:** (County Health Department has Birth, Death & Burial Records; Probate Judge has Marriage & Probate Records; Clerk Courts has Divorce Records from 1820 & Court Records; County Recorder has land Records from 1822)
Scioto www.sciotocountyohio.com/	N5	24 Mar 1803	**Adams** Scioto County; 602 7th St; Portsmouth, OH 45662-3948; Ph. (740) 355-8313 **Details:** (Clerk Courts has Divorce & Court Records from 1817; Probate Judge has Marriage & Probate Records; County Recorder has land Records)
Seneca www.rootsweb.com/~ohseneca/seneca.html	G5	12 Feb 1820	**Huron** Seneca County; 103 S Washington St; Tiffin, OH 44883-2354; Ph. (419) 447-0671 **Details:** (Probate Judge has Birth, Marriage & Probate Records; County Health Department has Death Records; Clerk Courts has Divorce & Court Records from 1826; County Recorder has land Records)
Shelby www.co.shelby.oh.us/	J2	7 Jan 1819	**Miami** Shelby County; 129 E Court St; PO Box 809; Sidney, OH 45365; Ph. (937) 498-7221 **Details:** (Clerk Courts has Court Records from 1819; Probate Judge has Birth, Marriage, Death & Probate Records from 1825; County Recorder has land Records from 1819)
Stark www.co.stark.oh.us/	H10	13 Feb 1808	**Columbiana** Stark County; 110 Central Plaza S; Canton, OH 44702-2219; Ph. (330) 438-0796 **Details:** (County Health Department has Birth Records; Probate Court has Marriage & Probate Records; Clerk Courts has Court Records; Family Court has Divorce Records; County Recorder has land Records)
Summit www.co.summit.oh.us/	G10	3 Mar 1840	**Portage, Medina, Stark** Summit County; 53 University Ave; Akron, OH 44301; Ph. (330) 643-2900 **Details:** (County Recorder has land Records from 1840; Probate Court has Birth, Marriage, Death & Probate Records)

County	Map	Date	Parent County or Territory From Which Organized
Website	Index	Created	Address/Details

Trumbull F12   10 Jul 1800   **Jefferson, Wayne, old**
www.co.trumbull.oh.us/
Trumbull County; 160 High St NW; Warren, OH 44481;
Ph. (330) 675-2557
Details: (Clerk Courts has Divorce, Court & Naturalization Records from 1800; Probate Judge has Marriage & Probate Records; County Recorder has land Records)

Tuscarawas I10   13 Feb 1808   **Muskingum**
http://web1.tusco.net/tuscgen/
Tuscarawas County; Public Sq; New Philadelphia, OH 44663;
Ph. (330) 365-3243
Details: (Probate Judge has Birth, Marriage, Death & Probate Records; Clerk Courts has Divorce & Court Records from 1808 & Naturalization Records from 1907; County Recorder has land Records)

Union I5   10 Jan 1820   **Franklin, Madison, Logan, Delaware**
www.co.union.oh.us/
Union County; 215 W 5th St; Marysville, OH 43040-0000;
Ph. (937) 645-3006
Details: (County Recorder has land Records from 1819; Probate Court has Birth, Marriage, Death & Probate Records)

Van Wert H1   12 Feb 1820   **Darke**
www.rootsweb.com/~ohvanwer/
Van Wert County; 121 E Main St 2nd Fl; Van Wert, OH 45891;
Ph. (419) 238-1022
Details: (Clerk Courts has Divorce & Court Records; Probate Judge has Birth & Death Records 1867–1908, Marriage Records from 1840 & Probate Records from 1837; Board of Health has Birth & Death Records from 1908; County Recorder has land Records from 1823)

Vinton M7   23 Mar 1850   **Gallia, Athens, Ross, Jackson, Hocking**
www.rootsweb.com/~ohvinton/vinton.htm
Vinton County; County Courthouse; McArthur, OH 45651-1296;
Ph. (740) 596-4571
Details: (Probate Judge has Birth & Death Records 1867–1950, Marriage Records from 1850 & Probate Records from 1867; County Health Department has Birth Records from 1950; Clerk Courts has Divorce, Court & land Records from 1850)

Warren M3   24 Mar 1803   **Hamilton**
www.co.warren.oh.us/geninfo/index.htm
Warren County; 500 Justice Dr; PO Box 238; Lebanon, OH 45036;
Ph. (513) 695-1120
Details: (Probate Judge has Birth & Death Records from 1867, Marriage & Probate Records from 1803; Clerk Courts has Divorce & Court Records; County Recorder has land Records)

Washington L10   27 Jul 1788   **Original county**
www.washingtongov.org/
Washington County; 205 Putnam St; Marietta, OH 45740;
Ph. (740) 373-6623
Details: (Probate Judge has Birth & Death Records from 1867, Marriage & Probate Records from 1789; Clerk Courts has Divorce & Court Records from 1795; County Recorder has land Records)

Wayne H8   13 Feb 1808   **Columbiana**
www.wooster-wayne.com/county/
Wayne County; 107 W Liberty St; PO Box 507; Wooster, OH 44691;
Ph. (330) 287-5590
Details: (County Clerk has Court & Divorce Records from 1817, & Civil Records)

County Website	Map Index	Date Created	Parent County or Territory From Which Organized Address/Details
Wayne, old		1796	**Original county** Wayne, old County; OH **Details:** (This county disappeared from Ohio in 1803 when Ohio became a state. It ultimately became Wayne County, Michigan)
Williams www.co.williams.oh.us/	E1	12 Feb 1820	**Darke** Williams County; 107 W Butler St; Bryan, OH 43506; Ph. (419) 636-8253 **Details:** (County Records Center has Birth & Death Records 1867–1908, Marriage & Probate Records 1824–1984, Divorce & Court Records 1824–1977 & Naturalization Records 1860–1926; County Health Department has Birth & Death Records from 1909)
Wood www.wcnet.org/wcgovt/	F4	12 Feb 1820	**Logan** Wood County; 1 Courthouse Sq; Bowling Green, OH 43402-2473; Ph. (419) 354-9230 **Details:** (Clerk Courts has Divorce Records from 1851 & Court Records; Probate Judge has Birth Records to 1908, Marriage, Death & Probate Records; County Health Department has Birth Records from 1908; County Recorder has land Records)
Wyandot www.co.wyandot.oh.us/	H5	3 Feb 1845	**Marion, Crawford, Hardin, Hancock** Wyandot County; County Courthouse; Upper Sandusky, OH 43351-0000; Ph. (419) 294-1432 **Details:** (County Health Department has Birth Records 1845–1908; Probate Judge has Marriage & Probate Records from 1845, Death & Burial Records 1845–1908; Clerk Courts has Divorce & Court Records from 1845; County Recorder has land Records from 1845)

Oklahoma

Capital: Oklahoma City

Territory: 1890

State: 1907 (46th)

Work conquers all

In 1541, Coronado became the first non-Native American explorer to enter Oklahoma. French traders passed through the area in the 16th and 17th centuries, but no settlements were established. The United States acquired the area in the Louisiana Purchase in 1803. Oklahoma then became part of the Indiana Territory, except for the Panhandle, which remained under Spanish control. Oklahoma became part of the Missouri Territory in 1812. In 1817, the federal government began sending Indians to the area from Alabama, Georgia, Florida, and Mississippi. The state was divided among five Indian nations: Creek, Cherokee, Chickasaw, Choctaw, and Seminole. Most of Oklahoma became part of the Arkansas Territory in 1819. The Panhandle became part of Mexico following its independence from Spain in 1821.

The western part of the Louisiana Purchase, including the Arkansas Territory, was designated as Indian Territory in 1830. When the United States annexed the Republic of Texas, the Panhandle of Oklahoma (which became "No Man's Land") was included because it was unattached to any territory. During the Civil War, the five Indian nations sided with the Confederacy. About 3,500 Indians helped the Confederates, mostly through the Confederate Indian Brigade and the Indian Home Guard. The Indians suffered horribly during the war as both life and property were wantonly destroyed. The peace treaties forced them to surrender land in western Oklahoma and grant rights-of-way to the railroads. The central part of the state was designated as "Unassigned Lands." By 1872, railroads crossed the area and hordes of settlers arrived. Soldiers drove them away, but these settlers, along with the railroad companies, petitioned Congress to open up these areas. As a result, the government purchased the "Unassigned Lands" and "No Man's Land" from the Indians in 1889.

Oklahoma was unique in its use of land runs. During a land run, an entire district would be opened to settlement on a given day on a first-come basis. The first run in 1889 attracted about 50,000 people. Farmers from Illinois, Iowa, and Kansas chose the western and northwestern sections of

the state, while those from Arkansas, Missouri, and Texas chose the southern and eastern parts of the state. The territorial government was established in 1890, with Guthrie as its capital. Absorption of reservations opened more territory for settlement in the years that followed. The 1893 land run in the northwest section of the state attracted nearly 100,000 new settlers. The first oil boom occurred in 1897 at Bartlesville, bringing thousands more new settlers. More absorption of reservations occurred until only the eastern part of the state remained as Indian Territory. In 1906, the Oklahoma and Indian territories were combined, allowing Oklahoma to be admitted to the Union the following year. The capital was moved to Oklahoma City in 1910.

In the 1920s, deposits of oil and gas helped the economy but the upswing was offset by the onset of the Great Depression of the 1930s. From the early 1900s, wheat and other row crops along with cattle farms became the livelihood of most of the new residents. The fine soil of the region had been held in place by the natural grasses that grew there. In the 1930s, Oklahoma and neighboring states became known as the Dust Bowl as droughts set in and the land—left exposed from the intrusive farming methods—began to erode. The effects would be felt for decades despite efforts to rehabilitate the land.

Look for vital records in the following locations:

- **Birth and death records:** Some early birth and death records from 1891 are scattered among county clerk records. Statewide registration began in 1908, with general compliance by 1930. These records are available from the Registrar of Vital Statistics, State Department of Health in Oklahoma City, Oklahoma.

- **Marriage, court and land records:** County clerks have all marriage, court, and land records. Local land office records are at the Oklahoma Department of Libraries, State Archives Division in Oklahoma City, Oklahoma. The National Archives, Kansas City Branch, in Kansas, and Fort Worth Branch in Texas, have the land entry case files, the original tract books and the township plats of the general land office. The patents and copies of the tract books and township plats are at the Bureau of Land Management, New Mexico State Office in Santa Fe, New Mexico.

Vital Records Service Oklahoma State Department of Health

1000 Northeast 10th
Oklahoma City, Oklahoma 73117
(405) 271-4040
www.health.state.ok.us/program/vital/brec.html

Oklahoma Department of Libraries State Archives Division

200 N.E. 18th Street
Oklahoma City, Oklahoma 73105
www.odl.state.ok.us/oar/index.htm

Societies and Repositories

American Indian Institute; The University of Oklahoma; 555 East Constitution; Norman, OK 73072-7920.

Arbuckle Historical Society; 201 S. 4th; Davis, OK 73030.

Bartlesville Genealogical Society; c/o Bartlesville Public Library; 600 S. Johnstone A; Bartlesville, OK 74003.

Beaver River Genealogical and Historical Society; Rt. 1, Box 79; Hooker, OK 73945.

Broken Arrow Genealogical Society; PO Box 1244; Broken Arrow, OK 74013-1244.

Bryan County Heritage Society; PO Box 153; Calera, OK 74730.

Canadian County Genealogical Society; PO Box 866; El Reno, OK 73036-0866; cancogen@aol.com.

Carter County Genealogical Society; PO Box 1014; Ardmore, OK 73402.

Central Oklahoma Chapter, AHSGR; 1106 W Brooks St.; Norman, OK 73069-4539; (405) 321-7835; lilarwig@swbell.net; www.ahsgr.org/okcentra.html.

Choctaw County Genealogical Society; PO Box 1056; Hugo, OK 74743.

Cleveland County Genealogical Society; PO Box 6176; Norman, OK 73070-6176; ccgs@telepath.com.

Coal County Historical and Genealogical Society; PO Box 436; Coalgate, OK 74538.

Craig County Oklahoma Genealogical Society; PO Box 484; Vinita, OK 74301.

Cushing Genealogical Society; c/o Cushing Public Library; PO Box 551; Cushing, OK 74023; anich@galstar.com.

Delaware County Genealogical Society; c/o Grove Public Library; 1140 Neo Loop; Grove, OK 74344-6046; dcgsinc@hotmail.com.

Delaware County Oklahoma Historical Society; PO Box 855; Jay, OK 74346.

Edmond Genealogical Society; PO Box 1984; Edmond, OK 73093; Gb4886@aol.com; www.rootsweb.com/~okegs.

Garfield County Genealogists, Inc.; PO Box 1106; Enid, OK 73702-1106.

Golden Spread Chapter, AHSGR; RR 2 Box 88; Shattuck, OK 73858.

Greer County Genealogical & Historical Society; 201 W. Lincoln; Mangum, OK 73554; gcghs@hotmail.com.

Haskell County Genealogical Society; 408 N.E. 6th St.; Stigler, OK 74462.

Kiowa County Genealogical Society; Hobart Public Library; PO Box 191; Hobart, OK 73651-0191; kcgenealogy@itlnet.net.

Logan County Genealogical Society; PO Box 1419; Guthrie, OK 73044.

Love County Historical Society; PO Box 134; Marietta, OK 73448.

Major County Genealogical Society; PO Box 74; Fairview, OK 73737.

Mayes County Genealogical Society; PO Box 924; Chouteau, OK 74337.

McClain County Oklahoma Historical and Genealogical Society; 203 Washington St.; Purcell, OK 73090.

McCurtian County Genealogical Society; PO Box 1832; Idabel, OK 74745.

Muskogee County Genealogical Society; 801 W. Okmulgee; Muskogee, OK 74401.

Noble County Genealogical Society; PO Box 785; Perry, OK 73077.

Northwest Oklahoma Genealogical Society; PO Box 834; Woodward, OK 73901.

Oklahoma Department of Libraries; 200 NE 18th St.; Oklahoma City, OK 73105-3298; (405) 521-2502; www.odl.state.ok.us/oklibs.htm.

Oklahoma Genealogical Society; PO Box 12986; Oklahoma City, OK 73157.

Oklahoma Historical Society; Wiley Post Historical Building; 2100 N Lincoln Blv; Oklahoma City, OK 73105-4997; (405) 522-5206; www.ok-history.mus.ok.us.

Oklahoma State Archives and Records Management; 200 NE 18th St.; Oklahoma City, OK 73105; (405) 522-3579; tfugate@oltn.odl.state.ok.us; www.odl.state.ok.us/oar.

Okmulgee County Genealogical Society; PO Box 805; Okmulgee, OK 74447.

Ottawa County Genealogical Society; PO Box 1383; Miami, OK 74355-1383.

Payne County Genealogical Society; PO Box 2708; Stillwater, OK 74076.

Pioneer Genealogical Society; PO Box 1965; Ponca City, OK 74602.

Pioneer Sons and Daughters of the Cherokee Strip; PO Box 465; Enid, OK 73702.

Pittsburg County Genealogical and Historical Society, Inc.; 113 E. Carl Albert Pkwy.; McAlester, OK 74501.

Pocahontas Trails Genealogical Society (Oklahoma-Texas Regional Chapter); Rt. 2, Box 40; Mangum, OK 73554.

Pontotoc County Historical and Genealogical Society; 221 W. 16th St.; Ada, OK 74920.

Poteau Valley Genealogical Society; PO Box 1031; Poteau, OK 74953.

Pushmataha County Historical Society; PO Box 285; Antler, OK 74523.

Roger Mills County Genealogical Society; PO Box 205; Cheyenne, OK 73629.

Rogers County Genealogical Society; PO Box 2493; Claremore, OK 74018.

Southwest Oklahoma Genealogical Society; PO Box 148; Lawton, OK 73502-0148; www.sirinet.net/~lgarris/swogs.

Stephens County Oklahoma Genealogical Society; 301 N. 8th St.; Duncan, OK 73534.

Swink Historical Preservation Association; PO Box 165; Swink, OK 74761; swink1@oio.net.

Three Forks Genealogical Society; 201 South State St.; Wagoner, OK 74467.

Tulsa Genealogical Society; PO Box 585; Tulsa, OK 74101-0585; www.tulsagenealogy.org.

Western Plains Weatherford Genealogical Society; PO Box 1672; Weatherford, OK 73096.

Western Trails Genealogical Society; PO Box 70; Altus, OK 73521.

Bibliography and Record Sources

General

Ashton, Sharron Standifer. *Guide to Cherokee Indian Records Microfilm Collection: Archives and Manuscripts Division, Oklahoma Historical Society.* Norman, Oklahoma: Ashton Books, 1996.

Babcock, Sidney H., and John Y. Bryce. *History of Methodism in Oklahoma: Story of the Indian Mission Annual Conference of the Methodist Episcopal Church, South.* N.p.: 1935.

Baird, W. David. *The Story of Oklahoma.* Norman, Oklahoma: University of Oklahoma Press, 1994.

Bell, George. *Genealogy of Old and New Cherokee Indian Families.* Bartlesville, Oklahoma: George Bell, 1972.

Bernard, Richard M. *The Poles in Oklahoma.* Norman: University of Oklahoma Press, 1980.

Bicha, Karel D. *The Czechs in Oklahoma.* Norman, Oklahoma: University of Oklahoma Press, 1980.

Bingham, Lynetta K. *A History of the Church of Jesus Christ of Latter-day Saints in Eastern Oklahoma: From Oklahoma and Indian Territories to 1980: A History Prepared for the Sesquicentennial of the Organization of the Church.* Tulsa: Tulsa Oklahoma Stake, 1980.

Bivins, Willie Reeves Hardin, et al. *Southwest Oklahoma Keys.* Oklahoma City: Southwest Oklahoma Genealogical Society, 1982.

Blessing, Patrick J. *Oklahoma: Records and Archives.* Tulsa, Oklahoma: University of Tulsa Publications, 1978.

Brown, Jean C. *Oklahoma Research: The Twin Territories.* Sapulpa, Oklahoma: J. C. Brown, 1975.

Brown, Thomas E. *Bible Belt Catholicism: A History of the Roman Catholic Church in Oklahoma, 1905–1945.* New York: United States Catholic Historical Society, 1977.

Burke, Bob. *Like a Prairie Fire: A History of the Assemblies of God in Oklahoma.* Oklahoma City: Oklahoma District Council of the Assemblies of God, 1994.

Carselowey, James Manford. *Cherokee Notes.* Tulsa, Oklahoma: Yesterdays Publications, 1980.

Carselowey, James Manford. *Cherokee Pioneers.* Adair, Oklahoma: J. M. Carselowey, 1961.

Cook, Mrs. John P. *Collection of Oklahoma Bible and Family Records.* N.p., 1954.

Corwin, Hugh D. *The Kiowa Indians: Their History & Life Stories.* Lawton, Oklahoma: H. D. Corwin, 1958.

Dewitt, Donald L. *American Indian Resource Materials in the Western History Collections, University of Oklahoma.* Norman, Oklahoma: University of Oklahoma Press, 1990.

Dewitt, Donald L. *Guide to Manuscript Collections Western History Collections University of Oklahoma.* Bowie, Maryland: Heritage Books, 1994.

England, Stephen J. *Oklahoma Christians: A History of Christian Churches and of the Start of the Christian Church (Disciples Of Christ) in Oklahoma.* S.l.: s.n., 1975 S.l.: Bethany Press.

Federation of Oklahoma Genealogical Societies (Oklahoma City, Oklahoma). *Directory of Oklahoma Sources.* Oklahoma City: Federation of Oklahoma Genealogical Societies, 1993.

Ferguson, Mrs. Tom B. *They Carried the Torch: The Story of Oklahoma's Pioneer Newspapers.* Norman, Oklahoma: Levite of Apache, 1989.

First Families of the Twin Territories: Our Ancestors in Oklahoma before Statehood. Oklahoma Genealogical Society, Special Publication, no. 13. Oklahoma City, Oklahoma: The Society, 1997.

Franklin, Jimmie L. *Journey Toward Hope: A History of Blacks in Oklahoma.* Norman, Oklahoma: University of Oklahoma Press, 1982.

Gard, Wayne. *The Chisholm Trail.* Norman, Oklahoma: University of Oklahoma Press, 1976.

Garrett, Sandi. *Where Are My Cherokees.* Spavinaw, Oklahoma: Cherokee Woman Pub., 1997.

Gaskin, J. M. *Baptist Milestones in Oklahoma.* S.l.: s.n., 1966.

Gibson, Arrell M. *Oklahoma: A Student's Guide to Localized History.* New York: Columbia University, 1965.

Gibson, Arrell Morgan. *A Guide to Regional Manuscript Collections in the Division of Manuscripts, University of Oklahoma Library.* Norman, Oklahoma: University of Oklahoma Press, 1960.

Gray, Robert N. *The Cherokee Strip Of Oklahoma: A Hundred Yesteryears.* Enid, Oklahoma: Sons and Daughters of the Cherokee Strip Pioneers Museum, 1992.

Hale, Duane Kendall. *Tracing Indian Family Histories.* Norman, Oklahoma: OCCE Copy Service, University of Oklahoma, 1983.

Hill, Edward E., comp. *Guide to Records in the National Archives Relating to American Indians.* Washington, D.C.: National Archives, 1981.

Hill, Luther B. *A History of the State of Oklahoma.* 2 vols. Chicago: Lewis Publishing Co., 1908.

Historical Records Survey (Oklahoma). *A List of the Records of the State of Oklahoma.* Oklahoma City: Historical Records Survey, 1938.

Huffman, Mary. *Family History: A Bibliography of the Collection in the Oklahoma Historical Society.* Oklahoma City: The Society, 1992.

Huffman, Mary. *The Five Civilized Tribes: A Bibliography.* Oklahoma City: Oklahoma Historical Society, Library Resources Division, 1991.

Jordan, H. Glenn. *Indian Leaders: Oklahoma's First Statesmen.* Oklahoma City: Oklahoma Historical Society, 1979.

Koplowitz, Bradford. *Guide to the Historical Records of Oklahoma.* Bowie, Maryland: Heritage Books, 1997.

Lemons, Nova A. *Pioneers of Chickasaw Nation, Indian Territory.* 2 vols. Miami, Oklahoma: Timbercreek Ltd., 1997.

Littlefield, Daniel F. *The Chickasaw Freedmen: A People Without A Country.* Westport, Connecticut: Greenwood Press, 1980.

Litton, Gaston. *History of Oklahoma.* 4 vols. New York: Lewis Historical Publishing Co., 1957.

Martin, Laura. *Oklahoma Marriages: A Bibliography.* Oklahoma City, Oklahoma: Library Resources Division, 1996.

McKee, Wilma. *Growing Faith: General Conference Mennonites in Oklahoma.* Newton, Kansas: Faith and Life Press, 1988.

Mooney, Thomas G. *Exploring Your Cherokee Ancestry: A Basic Genealogical Research Guide.* Tahlequah, Oklahoma: Cherokee National Historical Society, 1990.

O'Beirne, Harry F., and Edward S. O'Beirne *The Indian Territory: Its Chiefs, Legislators and Leading Men.* St. Louis: C. B. Woodward Co., 1892.

O'Beirne, Harry F. *Leaders and Leading Men of the Indian Territory with Interesting Biographical Sketches: Choctaws and Chickasaws.* Chicago: American Publishers Association, 1891.

O'Brien, Mary Metzger. *Oklahoma Genealogical Research.* Sand Springs, Oklahoma: M. O'Brien Bookshop, 1986.

Oklahoma Historical Society. *Index to Oklahoma Newspapers.* Oklahoma City, Oklahoma: Oklahoma Historical Society, 2002. Online guide—www.ok-history.mus.ok.us/news/newsindex.htm.

Oklahoma Historical Society. Indian Archives Division. *Catalog of Microfilm Holdings in the Archives & Manuscripts Division Oklahoma Historical Society 1976–1989:* Native American tribal records and special collections. Oklahoma City: The Society, 1976–1989.

Oklahoma Historical Society. Indian Archives Division. *Establishing of Churches in the Cherokee Nation, 1866–1908.* Oklahoma City: The Society, 1976–.

Oklahoma Historical Society. *Oklahoma State, County and Town Records.* Oklahoma City, Oklahoma: Oklahoma Historical Society, 2002. Online guide—www.ok-history.mus.ok.us/lib/staterec.htm.

Oklahoma Research Outline. Series U.S.-States, no 37. Salt Lake City: Family History Library, 1988.

Parker, James W. *All Along the Chisholm Trail.* 2 vols. Yukon, Oklahoma: J. W. Parker, 1988.

Portrait and Biographical Record of Oklahoma: Commemorating the Achievements of Citizens Who Have Contributed to the Progress of Oklahoma and the Development of Its Resources. Chicago: Chapman Publishing Co., 1901.

Preliminary List of Churches and Religious Organizations in Oklahoma. Oklahoma City, Oklahoma: Historical Records Survey, 1942.

Reese, Linda Williams. *Women of Oklahoma, 1890–1920.* Norman, Oklahoma: University of Oklahoma, 1997.

Routh, E. C. *The Story of Oklahoma Baptists.* Oklahoma City: Baptist General Convention, 1932.

Smith's First Directory of Oklahoma Territory, for the Year Commencing August 1, 1890. Oklahoma City, Oklahoma: Oklahoma Historical Society, Research Library, 1986.

Stewart, John and Kenny A. Franks. *State Records, Manuscripts, and Newspapers at the Oklahoma State Archives and Oklahoma Historical Society.* Oklahoma City, Oklahoma: State Department of Libraries and Oklahoma Historical Society, 1975.

Sturtevant, William C. *A Seminole Sourcebook.* New York: Garland Pub., 1987.

Thoburn, Joseph Bradfield. *A Standard History of Oklahoma: An Authentic Narrative of Its Development from the Date of the First European Exploration Down to the Present Time, Including Accounts of the Indian Tribes, Both Civilized and Wild, of the Cattle Range, of the Land Openings and the Achievements of the Most Recent Period.* 5 vols. Chicago: American Historical Society, 1916.

Thoburn, Joseph Bradfield. *Oklahoma, a History of the State and Its People.* 4 vols. New York: Lewis Historical Pub. Co., 1929.

Tobias, Henry J. *The Jews in Oklahoma.* Norman, Oklahoma: University of Oklahoma Press, 1980.

United States. Commission to the Five Civilized Tribes. *Applications for Enrollment of the Commission to the Five Civilized Tribes, 1898–1914.* Washington, D.C.: National Archives and Records Service, 1983.

Walton-Raji, Angela Y. *Black Indian Genealogy Research: African-American Ancestors among the Five Civilized Tribes.* Bowie, Maryland: Heritage Books, 1993.

Welch, W. E. *The Oklahoma Spirit of '17: Biographical Volume.* Oklahoma City, Oklahoma: Historical Pub., 1920.

Welsh, Carol. *An Annotated Guide to the Chronicles of Oklahoma, 1921–1994.* Oklahoma City: Oklahoma Historical Society, 1996.

West, C. W. *Missions and Missionaries of Indian Territory.* Muskogee, Oklahoma: Muscogee Pub., 1990.

Western Oklahoma Historical Society. *Prairie Fire: A Pioneer History of Western Oklahoma.* S.l.: The Society, 1978.

White, James D. *The Souls of the Just: A Necrology of the Catholic Church In Oklahoma.* Tulsa, Oklahoma: Sarto Press, 1983.

Wright, Muriel Hazel. *A Guide to the Indian Tribes of Oklahoma.* Norman, Oklahoma: University of Oklahoma Press, 1951. Reprint. 1986.

Atlases, Maps and Gazetteers

Gannett, Henry A. *A Gazetteer of Indian Territory.* Washington, D.C.: U.S. Government Printing Office, 1905. Reprint. Tulsa, Oklahoma: Oklahoma Yesterday Pub., 1980.

Morris, John W. *Boundaries of Oklahoma.* Oklahoma City: Oklahoma Historical Society, 1980.

Morris, John W. *Ghost Towns of Oklahoma.* Norman, Oklahoma: University of Oklahoma Press, 1977.

Morris, John Wesley and Edwin C. McReynolds. *Historical Atlas of Oklahoma.* Rev. ed. Norman, Oklahoma: University of Oklahoma Press, 1976.

Oklahoma Historical Society (Oklahoma City, Oklahoma). *Boundaries Of Oklahoma.* Oklahoma City: Oklahoma Historical Society, 1980.

Oklahoma. Department of Transportation. *Town and Place Locations.* Oklahoma City: Oklahoma Department of Transportation, 1991.

Shirk, George H. *Oklahoma Place Names.* 2nd ed. Norman, Oklahoma: University of Oklahoma Press, 1974.

Census Records

Available Census Records and Census Substitutes

Federal Census 1860 (with Arkansas), 1900, 1910, 1920

Union Veterans and Widows 1890

Dollarhide, William. *The Census Book: A Genealogist's Guide to Federal Census Facts, Schedules and Indexes.* Bountiful, Utah: Heritage Quest, 1999.

Kemp, Thomas Jay. *The American Census Handbook.* Wilmington, Delaware: Scholarly Resources, Inc., 2001.

Lainhart, Ann S. *State Census Records.* Baltimore: Genealogical Publishing Co., Inc., 1992.

Oklahoma Territory. *First Territorial Census of Oklahoma, 1890.* Oklahoma City: Oklahoma Historical Society, 1961.

Szucs, Loretto Dennis and Matthew Wright. *Finding Answers in U.S. Census Records.* Ancestry Publishing, 2001.

Thorndale, William and William Dollarhide. *Map Guide to the U.S. Federal Census, 1790–1920.* Baltimore: Genealogical Publishing Co., 1987.

United States. Census Office. 11th census, 1890. *Schedules Enumerating Union Veterans and Widows of Union Veterans of the Civil War.* Washington, D.C.: The National Archives, 1948.

Court Records, Probate and Wills

Cook, Mrs. John P. *Collection of Old Wills Assembled by D.A.R. Chapters of Oklahoma.* Salt Lake City: Filmed by the Genealogical Society of Utah, 1970.

Daughters of the American Revolution. Black Beaver Chapter (Norman, Oklahoma). *Abstracts of Wills from Oklahoma Chapters N.S.D.A.R.* Microfilm of original records in the D.A.R. Library in Washington, D.C. Salt Lake City: Filmed by the Genealogical Society of Utah, 1970.

Daughters of the American Revolution. Enid Chapter (Enid, Oklahoma). *Abstracts of Wills of Our Forefathers.* Salt Lake City: Filmed by the Genealogical Society of Utah, 1972.

Louisiana (Territory). Probate Court. *Probate Records, 1808–1812.* Salt Lake City: Filmed by the Genealogical Society of Utah, 1975.

Wever, Orpha Jewell. *Probate Records, 1892–1908. Northern District Cherokee Nation.* 3 vols. Vinita, Oklahoma: Northeast Oklahoma Genealogical Society, 1982–1983.

Emigration, Immigration, Migration and Naturalization

American Historical Society of Germans from Russia. Oklahoma Harvester Chapter (Oklahoma). *German-Russian Heritage, Steppes to America.* Oklahoma: AHSGR, 1991.

Olsen, Monty. *Choctaw Emigration Records.* 2 vols. Calera, Oklahoma: Bryan County Heritage Association, 1990.

Oklahoma

Land and Property

Hinton, Julie Peterson and Louise F. Wilcox. *El Reno District 1901 Land Lottery: Index to Names of Homesteaders Filings.* El Reno, Oklahoma: J. P. Hinton, 1985.

Hoig, Stan. *The Oklahoma Land Rush of 1889.* Oklahoma City: Oklahoma Historical Society, 1984.

Hone, Wade E. *Land and Property Research in the United States.* Salt Lake City: Ancestry Incorporated, 1997.

Ingmire, Frances Terry. *Containing Grants in Present States of Missouri, Arkansas and Oklahoma.* St. Louis: the author, 1984.

Morris, John W. ed. *Boundaries of Oklahoma.* Oklahoma City: Oklahoma Historical Society, 1980.

Oklahoma Historical Society. *Oklahoma Land Records.* Oklahoma City, Oklahoma: Oklahoma Historical Society, 2002. Online guide—www.okhistory.mus.ok.us/lib/landrecords.htm.

Sober, Nancy Hope. *The Intruders: The Illegal Residents of the Cherokee Nation, 1866–1907.* Ponca City, Oklahoma: Cherokee Books, 1991.

Military

A History of the Second World War: A Remembrance, an Appreciation, a Memorial. Oklahoma City: Victory Publishing Co., 1946.

Burton, Arthur T. *Black, Buckskin and Blue: African American Scouts and Soldiers on the Western Frontier.* Austin, Texas: Eaton Press, 1999.

Faulk, Odie B., Kenny A. Franks, and Paul F. Lambert, eds. *Early Military Forts and Posts in Oklahoma.* Oklahoma City: Oklahoma Historical Society, 1978.

Haulsee, W. M., et al, *Soldiers of the Great War.* 3 vols. Washington, D.C.: Soldiers Record Publishing Association, 1920.

Hoffmann, Roy. *Oklahoma Honor Roll, World War I, 1917–1918.* Oklahoma: R. Hoffman.

Index to Applications for Pensions From the State of Oklahoma Submitted by Confederate Soldiers, Sailors and their Widows. Oklahoma City: Oklahoma Genealogical Society, 1969.

Military Information. n.p.: USGenWeb Project, Oklahoma Archives, 2002. Online database—www.rootsweb.com/~usgenweb/ok/military/military.html.

Newman, Stanley. *Oklahoma Air National Guard Pilots in the Korean War.* Oklahoma City: 45th Infantry Division Museum, 1990.

Oklahoma Historical Society. *Oklahoma Military Records.* Oklahoma City, Oklahoma: Oklahoma Historical Society, 2002. Online guide—www.okhistory.mus.ok.us/lib/military.htm.

Pompey, Sherman Lee. *Master Lists of the Cherokee Confederate Indians.* Independence, California: Historical and Genealogical Publishing Co., 1965.

Pompey, Sherman Lee. *Muster Lists of the Creek and Other Confederate Indians.* Independence, California: Historical and Genealogical Publishing Co., 1966.

United States. Adjutant General's Office. *Confederate States Army Casualties: Lists and Narrative Reports.* Washington, D.C.: The National Archives, 1970.

United States. Selective Service System. *Oklahoma, World War I Selective Service System Draft Registration Cards, 1917–1918. National Archives Microfilm Publications, M1509.* Washington, D.C.: National Archives, 1987–1988.

Vital and Cemetery Records

Bode, Frances M. *Oklahoma Territory Weddings.* Geary, Oklahoma: Pioneer Book Committee, 1983.

Bogle, Dixie. *Cherokee Nation Births and Deaths, 1884–1901.* Utica, Kentucky: Cook and McDowell Publishers, 1980.

Bogle, Dixie. *Cherokee Nation Marriages, 1884–1901.* Utica, Kentucky: Cook and McDowell Publishers, 1980.

Cemetery Records of Oklahoma. 9 vols. Typescript. Salt Lake City: Genealogical Society of Utah, 1959–1962.

Guide to Public Vital Statistics Records in Oklahoma. Oklahoma City: Historical Records Survey, 1941.

Index to the Oklahoma County Vital Records Offices. N.p: USGenWeb Project, Oklahoma Archives, 2002. Online Guide—www.vitalrec.com/ok.html.

Mills, Madeline S. and Helen R. Mullenax. *Relocated Cemeteries in Oklahoma and Parts of Arkansas, Kansas, Texas.* Tulsa: Mills and Mullenax, 1974.

Pierce, Barbara and Brian Basore. *Oklahoma Cemeteries: A Bibliography of the Collections in the Oklahoma Historical Society.* Oklahoma City, Oklahoma: Library Resources Division, The Society, 1993.

Talkington, N. Dale. *Birth and Death Notices In Oklahoma And Indian Territories From 1871.* Houston, Texas: N. D. Talkington, 1999.

Tiffee, Ellen and Gloryann Hankins Young. *Oklahoma Marriage Records, Choctaw Nation, Indian Territory.* 10 vols. Norman, Oklahoma: University of Oklahoma, 1969–1978.

Tyner, James W., and Alice Tyner Timmons. *Our People and Where They Rest.* 12 vols. Norman, Oklahoma: University of Oklahoma, 1969–1978.

Union List of Oklahoma Cemeteries. Oklahoma City, Oklahoma: Oklahoma Genealogical Society, 1969.

County Website	Map Index	Date Created	Parent County or Territory From Which Organized Address/Details
A		1891	**Iowa-Sac-Fox & Pottawatomie-Shawnee Lands** A County; OK **Details:** (see Lincoln) Name changed to Lincoln
Adair	**B5**	**16 Jul 1907**	**Cherokee Lands** Adair County; 2nd & Division Sts; PO Box 169; Stilwell, OK 74960-0169; Ph. (918) 696-7198 **Details:** (Clerk Courts has Marriage, Divorce, Probate & Court Records from 1907; County Assessor has Land Records)
www.rootsweb.com/~okadair/adaircty.htm			
Alfalfa	**I3**	**16 Jul 1907**	**Woods** Alfalfa County; County Courthouse; 300 S Grand St; Cherokee, OK 73728-8000; Ph. (580) 596-3158 **Details:** (Clerk of Courts has Marriage, Divorce, Probate, & Court Records; County Clerk has Land Records)
www.rootsweb.com/~okalfalf/main-alfalfa.htm			
Atoka	**D9**	**16 Jul 1907**	**Choctaw Lands** Atoka County; 200 E Court St; Atoka, OK 74525; Ph. (580) 889-5157 **Details:** (Clerk Courts has Marriage Records from 1897, Divorce, Probate & Court Records from 1913; County Clerk has Land Records)
www.rootsweb.com/~okatoka/atoka.htm			
B		1891	**Original county (Pottawatomie-Shawnee Lands)** B County; OK. **Details:** (see Pottawatomie) Name changed to Pottawatomie
Beaver	**M3**	1890	**Original county (Public Lands)** Beaver County; 111 W 2nd St; Beaver, OK 73932-0000; Ph. (580) 625-3418 **Details:** (Clerk Courts has Marriage, Divorce & Court Records from 1890 & Probate Records from 1891)
www.rootsweb.com/~okbeaver/beav.htm			
Beckham	**K7**	**16 Jul 1907**	**Roger Mills, Greer Terr.** Beckham County; 302 E Main St;PO Box 67; Sayre, OK 73662; Ph. (580) 928-3383 **Details:** (County Clerk's Office has Land & Military Records; County Assessor & County Treasurer have Tax Records; County Clerk has Probate, Civil & Criminal Cases)
www.rootsweb.com/~okbeckha/			
Blaine	**I5**	1892	**Original county** Blaine County; 212 N Weigle Ave; PO Box 138; Watonga, OK 73772; Ph. (580) 623-8438, blainecountyclerk@watonga.com **Details:** (Formerly C County. Name changed to Blaine) (Clerk has Court, Divorce, Land, Marriage, Military, Naturalization, Probate, & Other Historical Records; Treasurer has Tax Records)
Bryan	**E9**	**16 Jul 1907**	**Choctaw Lands** Bryan County; 402 W Evergreen St; PO Box 1789; Durant, OK 74701-4703; Ph. (580) 924-1446 **Details:** (County Clerk has Marriage, Divorce & Land Records from 1907, Probate & Court Records)
www.rootsweb.com/~okbryan/			
C		1892	**Original county** C County; OK **Details:** (see Blaine) Name changed to Blaine

County Website	Map Index	Date Created	Parent County or Territory From Which Organized Address/Details
Caddo www.rootsweb.com/~okcaddo/ccpage.htm	I7	1901	**Original Lands** Caddo County; SW 2nd St & Oklahoma Ave; Anadarko, OK 73005-1427; Ph. (405) 247-6609 **Details:** (Formerly I County. Name changed to Caddo 8 Nov 1902) (Clerk Courts has Marriage, Divorce, Probate & Court Records from 1902)
Canadian www.canadiancounty.org/	H6	1890	**Original county** Canadian County; 201 N Choctaw Ave; PO Box 458; El Reno, OK 73036; Ph. (405) 262-1070 **Details:** (Clerk Court has Land, Marriage, Divorce, Probate & Court Records)
Carter www.brightok.net/chickasaw/ardmore/county/	G9	16 Jul 1907	**Chickasaw Lands** Carter County; 1st & B St SW; PO Box 1236; Ardmore, OK 73401-0000; Ph. (580) 223-8162 **Details:** (Clerk Courts has Probate, Court & Land Records; County Clerk has Marriage Records)
Cherokee www.rootsweb.com/~okchero2/	B5	16 Jul 1907	**Cherokee Lands** Cherokee County; 213 W Delaware St; Tahlequah, OK 74464; Ph. (918) 456-3171 **Details:** (Clerk Court has Marriage, Divorce, Probate & Court Records from 1907; County Clerk has Land Records from 1907 & Military Discharge Records from 1917)
Choctaw www.rootsweb.com/~okchocta/	C10	16 Jul 1907	**Choctaw Lands** Choctaw County; 300 E Duke St; Hugo, OK 74743-0000; Ph. (580) 326-3778 **Details:** (Clerk Court has Marriage, Divorce, Probate & Court Records from 1907; County Clerk has Land Records)
Cimarron www.rootsweb.com/~okcimarr/cimarron.htm	Q3	16 Jul 1907	**Beaver** Cimarron County; PO Box 145; Boise City, OK 73933-0145; Ph. (580) 544-2251 **Details:** (Clerk Court has Marriage, Probate & Court Records; County Clerk has Land & Military Records)
Cleveland www.telepath.com/dataman/okcleveland.html	G7	1890	**Unassigned Lands** Cleveland County; 201 S Jones Ave; Norman, OK 73069-6046; Ph. (405) 366-0240 **Details:** (County Clerk has Land & Military Discharge Records from 1889; Clerk Court has Marriage, Divorce, Probate & Court Records)
Coal www.rootsweb.com/~okcoal/	E8	16 Jul 1907	**Cherokee Lands** Coal County; 4 N Main St; Coalgate, OK 74538; Ph. (580) 927-2103 **Details:** (Clerk Court has Marriage, Divorce, Probate & Court Records from 1907; County Clerk has Land Records from 1907 & Military Records from 1917)
Comanche www.comancheco.gen.ok.us/	I8	1901	**Kiowa-Comanche-Apache & Wichita-Caddo Lands** Comanche County; 305 SW 5th St; Lawton, OK 73501-0000; Ph. (580) 355-5214 **Details:** (Clerk Court has Marriage, Divorce, Probate, Court & Land Records from 1901)

County Website	Map Index	Date Created	Parent County or Territory From Which Organized Address/Details
Cotton www.rootsweb.com/~okcotton/	I9	27 Aug 1912	**Comanche** Cotton County; 301 N Broadway St; Walters, OK 73572-1271; Ph. (580) 875-3026 **Details:** (County Clerk has Birth Records 1912–1945, Death & Land Records, surveys & school Census Records; Clerk Court has Marriage, Divorce, Probate & Court Records)
Craig www.rootsweb.com/~okcraig/index.htm	B3	16 Jul 1907	**Cherokee Lands** Craig County; 301 W Canadian Ave; Vinita, OK 74301-3640; Ph. (918) 256-2507 **Details:** (Clerk Court has Marriage Records from 1902, Divorce, Probate & Court Records from 1907; County Clerk has Land Records)
Creek www.rootsweb.com/~okcreek/	E5	16 Jul 1907	**Creek Lands** Creek County; 317 E Lee Ave; Sapulpa, OK 74066; Ph. (918) 227-2525 **Details:** (Clerk Court has Marriage Records from 1907, Divorce, Probate & Court Records; County Clerk has Land Records from 1907; District Court in Bristow has their Marriage & Divorce Records; County Court Clerk in Drumright has their Marriage & Divorce Records)
Custer www.rootsweb.com/~okcuster/custer.htm	J6	1892	**Cheyenne-Arapaho Lands** Custer County; Broadway Ave & B St; Arapaho, OK 73620-0000; Ph. (580) 323-1221 **Details:** (Formerly G County. Name changed to Custer 8 Nov 1892) (County Clerk has Marriage, Divorce & Probate Records from 1899, Court Records from 1894, Land Records, Military Records from 1892, school Census Records from 1913 & County Registrar of electors from 1916; Cemetery Association has Burial Records for each city)
D		1892	**Original county (Cheyenne-Arapaho Lands)** D County; OK **Details:** (see Dewey) Name changed to Dewey 8 Nov 1898
Day http://freepages.genealogy.rootsweb.com/~swokla/day/daycounty.html		1892	**Cheyenne-Arapaho Lands** Day County; OK ; Ph. **Details:** (Formerly E County. Name changed to Day. Discontinued 16 Nov 1907 & became part of Ellis & Roger Mills Counties)
Delaware www.rootsweb.com/~okdelawa/del.htm	B4	16 Jul 1907	**Cherokee Lands** Delaware County; 327 N 5th St; Jay, OK 74346-0000; Ph. (918) 253-4420 **Details:** (Clerk Courts has Probate Records; County Clerk has Marriage & Land Records)
Dewey www.rootsweb.com/~okdewey/okdewey.htm	J5	1892	**Original county (Cheyenne-Arapaho Lands)** Dewey County; Broadway & Ruble St; PO Box 368; Taloga, OK 73667-0368; Ph. (580) 328-5361 **Details:** (Formerly D County. Name changed to Dewey 8 Nov 1898) (Clerk Court has Marriage, Probate & Court Records from 1893 & Divorce Records from 1894; County Clerk has Land Records from 1892)
E		1892	**Cheyenne-Arapaho Lands** E County; OK **Details:** (see Day) Name changed to Day

County Website	Map Index	Date Created	Parent County or Territory From Which Organized Address/Details
Ellis www.rootsweb.com/~okellis/ellis.htm	**L4**	**16 Jul 1907**	**Day, Woodward** Ellis County; Courthouse Sq; 100 S Washington; Arnett, OK 73832-0000; Ph. (580) 885-7301 **Details:** (Clerk Court has Marriage Records from 1892, Divorce Records from 1893, Probate Records from 1908 & Court Records from 1896; County Clerk has Land Records from 1898)
F		**1892**	**Cheyenne-Arapaho Lands** F County; OK **Details:** (see Roger Mills) Name changed to Roger Mills 8 Nov 1892
G		**1892**	**Cheyenne-Arapaho Lands** G County; OK **Details:** (see Custer) Name changed to Custer 8 Nov 1892
Garfield www.rootsweb.com/~okgarfie/gar.htm	**H4**	**1893**	**Original county (Cherokee Outlet)** Garfield County; County Courthouse; Enid, OK 73701; Ph. (580) 237-0225 **Details:** (Originally O County. Name changed to Garfield 6 Nov 1894) (Clerk District Court has Marriage, Divorce, Probate & Court Records from 1893; Registrar of Deeds has Land Records from 1893)
Garvin www.rootsweb.com/~okgarvin/garvin.htm	**G8**	**16 Jul 1907**	**Chickasaw Lands** Garvin County; 201 W Grant Ave; Pauls Valley, OK 73075; Ph. (405) 238-2772 **Details:** (Clerk Court has Marriage, Divorce, Probate & Court Records from 1908; County Clerk has Land Records)
Grady www.telepath.com/dataman/okgrady.html	**H7**	**16 Jul 1907**	**Chickasaw Lands** Grady County; 326 W Choctaw St; PO Box 1009; Chickasha, OK 73023; Ph. (405) 224-7388 **Details:** (County Clerk has Burial & Military Records from 1907; Clerk Court has Marriage, Divorce, Land, Probate & Court Records from 1907)
Grant www.rootsweb.com/~okgrant/okgrant.htm	**H3**	**1893**	**Original county (Cherokee Outlet)** Grant County; 112 Guthrie Rm 104; PO Box 167; Medford, OK 73759; Ph. (580) 395-2274 **Details:** (Formerly L County. Name changed to Grant 6 Nov 1894) (County Clerk has Land & Military Records; Clerk Court has Marriage, Divorce, Probate & Court Records from 1893)
Greer www.rootsweb.com/~okgreer/	**K8**	**1886**	**Org. by Texas, transferred to Okla. by court decision** Greer County; PO Box 207; Mangum, OK 73554; Ph. (580) 782-3664 **Details:** (Organized as Greer County, TX in 1886; an act of Congress on 4 May 1896 declared it Greer County, Okla; A fire in 1901 destroyed the County Records) (Clerk Court has Marriage, Divorce, Probate & Court Records from 1901; County Clerk has Land Records)
H		**1892**	**Cheyenne-Arapaho Lands** H County; OK **Details:** (see Washita) Name changed to Washita 8 Nov 1892
Harmon www.rootsweb.com/~okharmon/harmon.htm	**L8**	**2 Jun 1909**	**Greer** Harmon County; County Courthouse; 114 W Hollis; Hollis, OK 73550-0000; Ph. (580) 688-3658 **Details:** (Clerk Court has Marriage, Divorce, Probate & Court Records)

County Website	Map Index	Date Created	Parent County or Territory From Which Organized Address/Details
Harper www.rootsweb.com/~okharper/index.html	L3	16 Jul 1907	**Woodward** Harper County; 311 SE 1st St; PO Box 369; Buffalo, OK 73834-0000; Ph. (580) 735-2012 **Details:** (Clerk Court has Marriage, Divorce, Probate & Court Records; County Clerk has Land Records from 1895 & school Records 1912–1958)
Haskell www.rootsweb.com/~okhaskel/index.htm	C7	16 Jul 1907	**Choctaw Lands** Haskell County; 202 E Main St; Stigler, OK 74462-2439; Ph. (918) 967-2884 **Details:** (Clerk Court has Marriage, Divorce, Probate & Court Records from 1907; County Clerk has Land Records)
Hughes www.rootsweb.com/~okhughes/hughes.htm	E7	16 Jul 1907	**Creek Lands (Creek & Choctaw Lands)** Hughes County; 200 N Broadway St; Holdenville, OK 74848; Ph. (405) 379-5487 **Details:** (Clerk Court has Marriage, Divorce, Probate & Court Records from 1907; County Clerk has Land Records from 1907)
I		1901	**Original Lands** I County; OK **Details:** (see Caddo) Name changed to Caddo 8 Nov 1902
Jackson www.rootsweb.com/~okjackso/jackson.htm	K8	16 Jul 1907	**Greer** Jackson County; 101 N Main St; Altus, OK 73521; Ph. (580) 482-4070 **Details:** (Clerk Court has Marriage, Divorce, Probate & Court Records from 1907; County Clerk has Land Records)
Jefferson www.rootsweb.com/~okjeffer/	H9	16 Jul 1907	**Comanche (Chickasaw Lands)** Jefferson County; 220 N Main St Rm 103; Waurika, OK 73573; Ph. (580) 228-2029 **Details:** (Clerk Court has Marriage, Divorce, Probate & Court Records from 1908; County Clerk has Land Records)
Johnston www.rootsweb.com/~okjohnst/index.htm	F9	16 Jul 1907	**Chickasaw Lands** Johnston County; 403 W Main; Tishomingo, OK 73460; Ph. (580) 371-3184 **Details:** (Clerk Court has Marriage, Divorce, Probate & Court Records; County Clerk has Land & Military Records)
K		1893	**Original county** K County; OK **Details:** (see Kay) Name changed to Kay
Kay www.courthouse.kay.ok.us/home.html	F3	1893	**Original county (Cherokee Outlet)** Kay County; 201 S Main; PO Box 450; Newkirk, OK 74647-0450; Ph. (580) 362-2537 **Details:** (Formerly K County. Name changed to Kay) (Clerk Court has Marriage, Divorce, Probate & Court Records from 1893; County Clerk has Land Records from 1893)
Kingfisher www.pldi.net/~kgfcounty/	H5	1890	**Original county** Kingfisher County; 101 S Main St; Kingfisher, OK 73750; Ph. (405) 375-3887 **Details:** (County Clerk has Marriage Records from 1900, Divorce, Probate & Court Records from 1896 & Land Records from 1898)

County Website	Map Index	Date Created	Parent County or Territory From Which Organized Address/Details
Kiowa http://rebelcherokee.tripod.com/okkiowa.html	J7	1901	**Kiowa-Comanche-Apache & Caddo-Wichita Lands** Kiowa County; 316 S Main; PO Box 73; Hobart, OK 73651; Ph. (580) 726-5286 **Details:** (Clerk Court has Marriage, Divorce, Probate & Court Records from 1905; County Clerk has Burial, Land & Military Records from 1905)
L		1893	**Chickasaw Lands** L County; OK **Details:** (see Grant) Name changed to Grant 6 Nov 1894
Latimer www.rootsweb.com/~oklatime/	C8	1907	**Choctaw Lands** Latimer County; 109 N Central St; Wilburton, OK 74578; Ph. (918) 465-3543 **Details:** (Clerk Court has Marriage Records from 1906, Divorce, Probate & Court Records)
Le Flore www.rootsweb.com/~okleflor/	B8	16 Jul 1907	**Choctaw Lands** Le Flore County; 100 S Broadway St; Poteau, OK 74953-0607; Ph. (918) 647-5738 **Details:** (Clerk Court has Marriage Records from 1898, Divorce, Probate & Court Records from 1907; County Clerk has Land Records)
Lincoln www.rootsweb.com/~oklincol/	F6	1891	**Iowa-Sac-Fox & Pottawatomie-Shawnee Lands** Lincoln County; 800 Manvel Ave; Chandler, OK 74834-0126; Ph. (405) 258-1264 **Details:** (Formerly A County. Name changed to Lincoln) (Clerk District Court has Marriage, Divorce, Probate & Court Records from 1900; County Clerk has Land Records)
Logan www.rootsweb.com/~oklogan/oklogan.htm	G5	1890	**Original county** Logan County; 301 E Harrison Ave Suite 102; Guthrie, OK 73044; Ph. (405) 282-0266 **Details:** (Clerk Court has Marriage Records from 1889, Divorce, Probate & Court Records; County Clerk has Land Records from 1889; Land Records from 1889)
Love www.rootsweb.com/~oklove/love.htm	G10	16 Jul 1907	**Chickasaw Lands** Love County; 405 W Main St; Marietta, OK 73448; Ph. (580) 276-3059 **Details:** (County Clerk has Birth & Death Records from 1958 & Land Records from 1904; Clerk Court has Marriage, Divorce, Probate & Court Records)
M		1893	**Cherokee Outlet** Marriage County; OK **Details:** (see Woods) Name changed to Woods 6 Nov 1894
Major www.rootsweb.com/~okmajor/major.htm	I4	16 Jul 1907	**Woods** Major County; 500 E Broadway St; Fairview, OK 73737; Ph. (580) 227-4712 **Details:** (Clerk Court has Marriage Records from late 1800s, Divorce, Probate & Court Records from 1908; County Clerk has Land Records)
Marshall www.rootsweb.com/~okmarsha/index.html	F9	16 Jul 1907	**Chickasaw Lands** Marshall County; 1 Courthouse Sq; Madill, OK 73446; Ph. (580) 795-3220 **Details:** (Clerk Court has Marriage, Divorce, Probate & Court Records from 1907; County Clerk has Land Records from 1907 & Military Discharge Records; County Superintendent has school records)

County Website	Map Index	Date Created	Parent County or Territory From Which Organized Address/Details
Mayes www.rootsweb.com/~okmayes/	C4	16 Jul 1907	**Cherokee Lands** Mayes County; NE 1st Adair; Pryor, OK 74361; Ph. (918) 825-2426 **Details:** (Clerk Court has Marriage, Divorce, Probate & Court Records from 1907; County Clerk has Land Records from 1907; County Treasury has tax Records)
McClain www.rootsweb.com/~okmcclai/okmcclain.html	G7	16 Jul 1907	**Chickasaw Lands** McClain County; PO Box 629; Purcell, OK 73080; Ph. (405) 527-3360 **Details:** (County Clerk has Land Records, Military Records from 1918 & school Records 1912–1968)
McCurtain www.rootsweb.com/~okmccurt/mccurt.htm	B9	16 Jul 1907	**Choctaw Lands** McCurtain County; 108 N Central Ave; Idabel, OK 74745; Ph. (580) 286-2370 **Details:** (Clerk Court has Marriage, Divorce, Probate & Court Records from 1907)
McIntosh www.rootsweb.com/~okmccurt/mccurt.htm	D6	16 Jul 1907	**Creek Lands** McIntosh County; 110 N 1st St; Eufaula, OK 74432; Ph. (918) 689-2741 **Details:** (County Clerk has Birth & Death Records 1911–1918 & Land Records; Clerk Court has Marriage, Divorce, Probate & Court Records from 1907)
Murray www.rootsweb.com/~okmurray/	F9	16 Jul 1907	**Chickasaw Lands** Murray County; 10th St & Wyandotte St; Sulphur, OK 73086; Ph. (580) 622-3920 **Details:** (County Clerk has Land Records; Clerk Court has Marriage, Divorce, Probate & Court Records)
Muskogee www.rootsweb.com/~okmuskog/index.htm	C6	1907	**Creek Lands** Muskogee County; 400 W Broadway St; Muskogee, OK 74401; Ph. (918) 682-7781 **Details:** (Clerk Court has Marriage Records from 1890, Divorce, Probate & Court Records from 1907; County Clerk has Land Records)
N		1893	**Cherkoee Outlet** N County; OK **Details:** (see Woodward) Name changed to Woodward 6 Nov 1894
Noble www.rootsweb.com/~oknoble/	G4	1893	**Cherokee Outlet** Noble County; 300 Courthouse Dr; Perry, OK 73077; Ph. (580) 336-2141 **Details:** (Formerly P County. Name changed to Noble 6 Nov 1894) (Clerk Court has Marriage, Divorce, Probate & Court Records from 1893; County Clerk has Land Records from 1893)
Nowata www.rootsweb.com/~oknowata/	D3	16 Jul 1907	**Cherokee Lands** Nowata County; 229 N Maple St; Nowata, OK 74048; Ph. (918) 273-2480, nwcctj@cableone.net **Details:** (Clerk of District Court has Court, Divorce, & Guardianship Records from 1911; County Clerk has Land, Marriage, Military, & Probate Records from 1911; Treasurer has Tax Records from 1911)
O		1893	**Cherokee Outlet** O County; OK **Details:** (see Garfield) Name changed to Garfield 6 Nov 1894

County Website	Map Index	Date Created	Parent County or Territory From Which Organized Address/Details
Okfuskee www.rootsweb.com/~okokfusk/	E6	16 Jul 1907	**Creek Lands** Okfuskee County; 3rd & Atlanta Sts; Okemah, OK 74859-0026; Ph. (918) 623-1724 **Details:** (Clerk Court has Marriage, Divorce, Probate & Court Records; County Clerk has Land Records)
Oklahoma www.oklahomacounty.org/	G6	1890	**Original county** Oklahoma County; 320 Robert S Kerr Ave; Office 409; Oklahoma City, OK 73102; Ph. (405) 713-1721 **Details:** (County Clerk has Marriage, Divorce, Probate & Court Records from 1890)
Okmulgee www.rootsweb.com/~okokmulg/index.html	D5	16 Jul 1907	**Creek Lands** Okmulgee County; 314 W 7th St; Okmulgee, OK 74447-5028; Ph. (918) 756-0788 **Details:** (Clerk Court has Marriage, Divorce, Probate & Court Records; County Clerk has Land & Military Records)
Osage www.rootsweb.com/~okosage2/osage.htm	E4	16 Jul 1907	**Osage Indian Lands** Osage County; 600 Grandview Ave; Pawhuska, OK 74056; Ph. (918) 287-3136 **Details:** (County Clerk has Land Records from 1907; Clerk Court has Marriage, Divorce, Probate & Court Records)
Ottawa www.rootsweb.com/~okottawa/	B3	16 Jul 1907	**Indian Terr.** Ottawa County; 102 E Central; Miami, OK 74354-0000; Ph. (918) 542-3332 **Details:** (Clerk Court has Marriage, Divorce, Probate & Court Records; County Clerk has Land Records from 1890)
P		1893	**Cherokee Outlet** P County; OK **Details:** (see Noble) Name changed to Noble 6 Nov 1894
Pawnee www.rootsweb.com/~okpawnee/pawnee.htm	F4	1895	**Pawnee Lands** Pawnee County; 500 Harrison St Rm 202; Pawnee, OK 74058; Ph. (918) 762-2732 **Details:** (Formerly Q County. Name changed to Pawnee) (County Clerk has Land & Military Records; Clerk Court has Marriage, Divorce, Probate & Court Records)
Payne www.paynecounty.org/	F5	1890	**Original county** Payne County; 606 S Husband St; Stillwater, OK 74074; Ph. (405) 747-8310 **Details:** (Clerk Court has Marriage, Divorce, Probate & Court Records from 1894; County Clerk has Land Records)
Pittsburgh www.rootsweb.com/~okpitts2/	D7	16 Jul 1907	**Choctaw Lands** Pittsburgh County; 115 E Carl Albert Pkwy; McAlester, OK 74501; Ph. (918) 423-6865 **Details:** (County Health Department has Birth, Death & Burial Records; Clerk Court has Marriage, Divorce, Probate & Court Records from 1890; County Clerk has Land Records from 1890)
Pontotoc www.rootsweb.com/~itponca/	F8	16 Jul 1907	**Chickasaw Lands** Pontotoc County; 100 W 13th St; PO Box 1425; Ada, OK 74820; Ph. (580) 332-1425 **Details:** (Clerk Court has Marriage, Divorce, Probate & Court Records from 1907)

County Website	Map Index	Date Created	Parent County or Territory From Which Organized Address/Details
Pottawatomie www.rootsweb.com/~okpottaw/pottawatomie.html	F7	1891	**Original county (Pottawatomie-Shawnee Lands)** Pottawatomie County; 325 N Broadway St; Shawnee, OK 74801; Ph. (405) 273-8222 **Details:** (Formerly B County. Name changed to Pottawatomie) (Clerk Court has Marriage, Divorce, Probate & Court Records; County Clerk has Land Records from 1892)
Pushmataha www.rootsweb.com/~okpushma/	C8	16 Jul 1907	**Choctaw Lands** Pushmataha County; 203 SW 3rd; Antlers, OK 74523-3899; Ph. (580) 298-3626 **Details:** (Clerk Court has Marriage & Probate Records; County Clerk has Land Records)
Q		1893	**Pawnee Lands** Q County; OK **Details:** (see Pawnee) Name changed to Pawnee
Roger Mills www.rootsweb.com/~okrogerm/	L6	1892	**Cheyenne-Arapaho Lands** Roger Mills County; 506 E Broadway; Cheyenne, OK 73628-0000; Ph. (580) 497-3395 **Details:** (Formerly F County. Name changed to Roger Mills 8 Nov 1892) (Clerk Court has Marriage, Probate & Court Records from 1800's & Divorce Records from 1900; County Clerk has Land Records from 1800s)
Rogers http://users.rootsweb.com/~okrogers/	D4	16 Jul 1907	**Cherokee Nation** Rogers County; 219 S Missouri Ave; Claremore, OK 74017; Ph. (918) 341-2518 **Details:** (Clerk Court has Marriage, Divorce, Probate & Court Records from 1907)
Seminole www.rootsweb.com/~oksemino/index.htm	E6	16 Jul 1907	**Seminole Indian Lands** Seminole County; 110 N Wewoka Ave; Wewoka, OK 74884; Ph. (405) 257-2501 **Details:** (Clerk Court has Marriage, Divorce, Probate & Court Records from 1907)
Sequoyah www.rootsweb.com/~oksequo2/	B6	16 Jul 1907	**Cherokee Indian Lands** Sequoyah County; 120 E Chickasaw Ave Box 8; Sallisaw, OK 74955; Ph. (918) 775-4517 **Details:** (Clerk Court has Marriage, Divorce, Probate & Court Records from 1907)
Stephens www.rootsweb.com/~okstephe/stephens.htm	H8	16 Jul 1907	**Comanche, Chickasaw Lands** Stephens County; 101 S 11th St #203; Duncan, OK 73533-0000; Ph. (580) 255-0977 **Details:** (Clerk Court has Marriage & Probate Records; County Clerk has Land Records)
Texas www.texascounty.org/	O3	16 Jul 1907	**Beaver** Texas County; PO Box 197; Guymon, OK 73942; Ph. (580) 335-3141 **Details:** (Clerk Court has Marriage, Divorce, Probate & Court Records from 1907 & Naturalization Records 1864–1929; County Clerk has Cemetery Records, Land Records from 1889 & Military Records from 1917)

County Website	Map Index	Date Created	Parent County or Territory From Which Organized Address/Details
Tillman www.rootsweb.com/~oktillma/	**J9**	**16 Jul 1907**	**Comanche, Kiowa** Tillman County; 201 N 10th St; Frederick, OK 73542; Ph. (580) 335-3421 **Details:** (Clerk Court has Marriage, Divorce, Probate & Court Records from 1907; County Clerk has Land Records from 1907)
Tulsa www.tulsacounty.org/	**D5**	**1907**	**Creek Lands, Cherokee Lands** Tulsa County; 500 S Denver Ave; Tulsa, OK 74103-3835; Ph. (918) 596-5000 **Details:** (Clerk Court has Marriage, Divorce, Probate & Court Records from 1907)
Wagoner www.rootsweb.com/~okwagone/	**C5**	**16 Jul 1907**	**Cherokee Lands** Wagoner County; 307 E Cherokee St; Wagoner, OK 74467-0000; Ph. (918) 485-2216 **Details:** (Clerk Court has Marriage, Divorce, Probate & Court Records from 1908)
Washington www.co.washington.ok.us/	**D3**	**1907**	**Cherokee Lands** Washington County; 420 S Johnstone Ave; Bartlesville, OK 74003-6602; Ph. (918) 337-2840 **Details:** (Clerk Court has Marriage, Divorce, Probate & Court Records from 1907)
Washita www.rootsweb.com/~okwashit/	**J7**	**1900**	**Cheyenne-Arapaho Lands** Washita County; PO Box 380; Cordell, OK 73632-0380; Ph. (580) 832-3548 **Details:** (Formerly H County. Name changed to Washita) (Clerk Court has Marriage, Divorce, Probate & Court Records from 1900)
Woods www.rootsweb.com/~okwoods/main-woods.html	**J3**	**1893**	**Cherokee Outlet** Woods County; 407 Government St; Alva, OK 73717-0000; Ph. (580) 327-0942 **Details:** (Formerly Marriage County. Name changed to Woods 6 Nov 1894) (County Clerk has Marriage Records from 1894, Divorce, Court & Land Records from 1893, Probate Records from 1901 & school Records)
Woodward www.rootsweb.com/~okwoodwa/woodward.htm	**K4**	**1893**	**Cherokee Outlet** Woodward County; 1600 Main St; Woodward, OK 73801; Ph. (580) 256-8097 **Details:** (Formerly N County. Name changed to Woodward 6 Nov 1894) (Clerk Court has Marriage & Probate Records; County Clerk has Land Records)

Oregon

Capital: Salem

Territory: 1848

State: 1859 (33rd)

She flies with her own wings

In 1543, Spanish explorers sighted the Oregon coast; Captain James Cook sighted the shoreline in 1778. But it was Americans—under Captain Robert Gray—who sailed up the Columbia River in 1792 and made the first landing. A few days later, the British sailed further inland and claimed the Columbia and its drainage basin for the British, thereby establishing a rivalry for control of Oregon that lasted until 1846.

Sea otter trade was the basic impetus for settlement in the early years. John Astor's American Fur Company established Fort Astoria on the coast, but due to the War of 1812 sold out to the Northwest Company in 1813. Hudson's Bay Company absorbed the Northwest Company in 1821 and dominated the fur trade for the next two decades. The early fur traders were mainly Canadian, British, and American, and they often married Indian women.

Missionaries entered the area in the 1830's, leading to the first substantial migration along the Oregon Trail in 1842. By 1843, Willamette Valley settlers had set up their own government and were demanding that the British leave the area. Most of these early settlers were from Missouri, Ohio, Illinois, Tennessee, Kentucky, and New England.

President James K. Polk campaigned on the slogan "fifty-four forty, or fight," indicating a desire to have Britain relinquish its claim to Oregon or face a war. In 1846, the British signed the Treaty of Washington, which established the 49th parallel as the international boundary between Canada and the United States.

The Oregon Territory was organized in 1848, comprising present-day Oregon, Washington, Idaho, western Montana, and a corner of Wyoming. Two years later, the Territorial Legislature passed the Donation Land Act of 1850. This act gave 320 acres to every male American over age 18 already in Oregon. If he were to marry by 1 December 1851, his wife would receive an equal amount of land. Men settling in the area by the end of 1853 were granted 160 acres of land and, if married, an equal amount was allotted to their wives. The act encouraged migration to Oregon. Over the next decade, the population quadrupled

due to settlers from the United States, Germany, Sweden, England, Norway, Russia, Finland, Italy, Denmark, Ireland, Austria, Greece, and Czechoslovakia. Statehood was granted in 1859. During the Civil War, the Union received nearly 2,000 soldiers from Oregon. After the war, Indian uprisings resulted in many battles and eventual relegation of the Indians to reservations. The Union Pacific Railroad was completed in 1869, beginning a 30-year expansion in population, which quadrupled Oregon's population.

Look for vital records in the following locations:

- **Birth and death records:** Available from 1903 at the Oregon State Health Division, Center of Health Statistics in Portland. State relationship and reason for the request when writing. Only immediate family members can obtain copies of records. An index to births and deaths from 1903 to 1984 is available from the Oregon State Archives in Salem.

- **Marriage and divorce records:** County clerks have marriage records from the date of organization. Records after 1906 can be obtained from the county or the state. Divorces were granted by the territorial legislature prior to 1853. These records are available at the Oregon State Archives. After 1853, they were recorded in the circuit court of each county. Since 1925, divorces are also stored at the Oregon State Health Division.

- **Probate records:** A probate court handled probate matters in the territorial era. A few early records are at the Oregon State Archives. Since 1859, the probate judge in each county has had jurisdiction over wills. Some records are in the circuit court but county court clerks keep most records.

- **Census records:** The 1850 census for the Oregon Territory indexed and available. Territorial and state censuses also exist for a few counties for many years between 1842 and 1905.

Oregon

Oregon Vital Records
PO Box 14050
Portland, Oregon 97293-0050
(503) 234-8417
http://oregon.gov/DHS/ph/chs/order/index.shtml

Oregon State Archives
800 Summer St. NE
Salem, Oregon 97310
(503) 373-0701; Fax (503) 373-0953
http://arcweb.sos.state.or.us/

Societies and Repositories

ALSI Historical and Genealogical Society, Inc.;
PO Box 922; Waldport, OR 97394.

Baker County Genealogical Group; c/o Baker County
Public Library; 2400 Resort St.; Baker City, OR 97814.

Bend Genealogical Society; PO Box 8254; Bend, OR
97708-8254; www.rootsweb.com/~ordeschu/BGS/
bgsindex.htm.

Benton County Genealogical Society; PO Box 1646;
Philomath, OR 97370-1646; (541) 752-6425.

Blue Mountain Genealogical Society; PO Box 1801;
Pendleton, OR 97801.

Clackamas County Family History Society; PO Box 995;
211 Tumwater Dr.; Oregon City, OR 97045;
www.rootsweb.com/~genepool/ccfhs.htm.

Clatsop County Genealogical Society; c/o Astoria Public
Library; 450 10th St.; Astoria, OR 97103.

Clatsop County Historical Society; 1618 Exchange St.;
Astoria, OR 97103.

Columbia Gorge Genealogical Society; c/o The Dallas
Public Library; 722 Court St.; The Dallas, OR 97058.

Cottage Grove Genealogical Society; PO Box 388; Cottage
Grove, OR 97424;
www.rootsweb.com/~orlane/links/cggs.htm.

Crook County Genealogical Society; 246 North Main
Street; Prineville, OR 97754-1852; (541) 447-3715;
bowlib@crestviewcable.com.

Curry County Historical Society; PO Box 1598; Gold
Beach, OR 97444.

Grant County Genealogical Society; PO Box 418; Canyon
City, OR 97820.

Harney County Genealogical Society; c/o 426 E. Jefferson;
Burns, OR 97720.

Jewish Genealogical Society of Oregon; c/o Mittleman
Jewish Community Center; 6651 SW Capi; Portland,
OR 97219; rondoctor@uswest.net;
www.rootsweb.com/~orjgs.

Juniper Branch of the Family Finders; PO Box 652;
Madras, OR 97741.

Klamath Basin Genealogical Society; 126 S. 3rd St.;
Klamath Falls, OR 97601.

Lake County Historical Society; PO Box 48; Lakeview, OR
97630-0002.

LaPine Genealogical Society; PO Box 1081; LaPine, OR
97739.

Lebanon Genealogical Society; c/o Lebanon Public
Library; 626 2nd St.; Lebanon, OR 97355.

Linn Genealogical Society; PO Box 1222; Albany, OR
97321; www.rootsweb.com/~orlinngs.

Mennonite Historical and Genealogical Society of Oregon;
675 Elma Ave. SE; Salem, OR 97301.

Milton-Freewater Genealogical Club; 127S.E. 6th St.;
Milton-Freewater, OR 97962.

Oregon Chapter, AHSGR; 8618 S.E. 36th Ave.; Portland,
OR 97222-5522; (503) 659-8248; rahaas@uswest.net;
www.ahsgr.org/orportla.html.

Oregon Genealogical Society, Inc.; PO Box 10306; Eugene,
OR 97449-2306;
www.rootsweb.com/~orlncogs/ogsinfo.htm.

Oregon State Archives; 800 Summer St. NE; Salem, OR
97310; (503) 373-0701; reference.archives@state.or.us;
http://arcweb.sos.state.or.us.

Oregon State Library; 250 Winter St. NE; Salem, OR
97301-3950; (503) 378-4243; www.osl.state.or.us/home.

Polk County Genealogical Society; PO Box 320; Dallas,
OR 97338-0220.

Port Orford Genealogical Society; c/o Port Orford Public
Library; 555 W. 20th St.; Port Orford, OR 97465.

Scandinavian Genealogical Society; 9143 Olney St. S.E.;
Salem, OR 97301.

Sherman County Historical Society; PO Box 173; Moro,
OR 97039.

Siuslaw Genealogical Society; c/o Siuslaw Public Library;
PO Box 1540; Florence, OR 97439.

Sons of the American Revolution, Oregon Society;
5190 S.W. Chestnut Ave.; Beaverton, OR 97005.

Sweet Home Oregon Genealogical Society; c/o Sweet
Home Library; PO Box 279; Sweet Home, OR 97386;
(541) 367-5034.

Tillamook County Historical Society Genealogical Study
Group; PO Box 123; Tillamook, OR 97141.

Umatilla County Historical Society; Box 253; Pendleton,
OR 97801.

Willamette Valley Genealogical Society; PO Box 2093;
Salem, OR 97308.

Yamhill County Genealogical Society; PO Box 569;
McMinnville, OR 97128.

Yaquina Chapter, NSDAR; OR; beverlyp@harborside.com;
www.rootsweb.com/~oryaqdar/Yaquina.htm.

Yaquina Genealogical Society; c/o Toledo Public Library;
173 NW Seventh St.; Toledo, OR 97391;
www.rootsweb.com/~orygs.

Bibliography and Record Sources

General

Armstrong, A. N. *Oregon: Comprising a Brief History and Full Description of the Territories of Oregon and Washington. . . Together with Remarks upon the Social Position, Productions, Resources And Prospects of the Country, a Dissertation upon the Climate, and a Full Description of the Indian Tribes of the Pacific Slope. . . Interspersed with Incidents of Travel and Adventure.* Washington, D.C.: Library of Congress, 1989.

Bancroft, Hubert Howe. *History of Oregon.* 2 vols. San Francisco: The History Co., 1886–1888.

Beebe, Ralph K. *A Garden of the Lord: A History of Oregon Yearly Meeting of Friends Church.* S.l.: s.n., 1968.

Book, Betty. *Indians Of Oregon Bibliography, 1966–1983.* Portland, Oregon: Genealogical Council of Oregon, 1991.

Brandt, Patricia and Nancy Guilford, eds. *Oregon Biography Index. Oregon State University Bibliographic Series, no. 11.* Corvallis, Oregon: Oregon State University, 1976.

Capitol's Who's Who for Oregon, 1936–1944. 2 vols. Portland, Oregon: Capitol Pub. Co., 1936–1942.

Carey, Charles Henry. *History of Oregon.* 3 vols. Chicago: Pioneer History Publishing Co., 1922.

Clark, Keith. *Terrible Trail: The Meek Cutoff, 1845.* Caldwell, Idaho: Caxton Printers, 1966.

Cogswell, Philip. *Capitol Names: Individuals Woven Into Oregon's History.* Portland, Oregon: Oregon Historical Society, 1977.

Directory of Churches and Religious Organizations, State of Oregon. Portland: Historical Records Survey, 1940.

Dryden, Cecil Pearl. *Give All to Oregon: Missionary Pioneers of the Far West.* New York: Hastings House, 1968.

Evans, Elwood. *History of the Pacific Northwest: Oregon and Washington; Embracing an Account of the Original Discoveries on the Pacific Coast of North America, and a Description of the Conquest, Settlement and Subjugation of the. . . Original Territory of Oregon; Also Interesting Biographies of the Earliest Settlers.* 2 vols. Portland, Oregon: North Pacific History Co., 1889.

Gaston, Joseph. *The Centennial History of Oregon, 1811–1912,* 4 vols. Chicago: S. J. Clarke Publishing Co., 1912.

Gregg, Jacob Ray. *A History of the Oregon Trail, Santa Fe Trail, and Other Trails.* Portland, Oregon: Binfords & Mort, 1955.

Guide to Depositories of Manuscript Collections in the United States: Oregon-Washington. Portland: Oregon Historical Records Survey, 1940.

Guide to the Manuscript Collections of the Oregon Historical Society. Portland, Oregon: Historical Records Survey, 1940.

Hawthorne, Julian. *The Story of Oregon: A History with Portraits and Biographies.* 2 vols. New York: American Historical Pub. Co., 1892.

Herzberg, Alice Stansfield. *Index to Oregon Newspaper Clippings, 1895–1952.* Medford, Oregon: Rogue Valley Genealogical Society, 1995.

Hines, Harvey K. *An Illustrated History of the State of Oregon: Containing a History of Oregon from the Earliest Period of Its Discovery to the Present Time, Together with Glimpses of Its Auspicious Future; Illustrations and Full-Page Portraits of Some of Its Eminent Men and Biographical Mention of Many of Its Pioneers and Prominent Citizens of Today.* Chicago: Lewis Pub. Co., 1893.

Holmes, Kenneth L. *Covered Wagon Women: Diaries & Letters from the Western Trails, 1840–1890.* 11 vols. Glendale, California: Arthur H. Clark Co., 1983–1991.

Horner, John B. *Oregon History and Early Literature: A Pictorial Narrative of the Pacific Northwest.* Portland, Oregon: The J. K. Gill Company, 1931.

Inventory of Church Archives of Oregon Presbyterian Churches: Microreproductions of original records at the Presbyterian Historical Society, in Philadelphia, Pennsylvania. Salt Lake City: Filmed by the Genealogical Society of Utah, 1967.

Kullberg, Lois G. Gassaway. *Saints to the Columbia: A History of the Church of Jesus Christ of Latter-day Saints In Oregon And Southwestern Washington, 1850–1990.* Vancouver, Washington: L-K Publications, 1991.

Lenzen, Connie Miller. *Research in Oregon.* Arlington, Virginia: National Genealogical Society, 1992.

Lenzen, Connie. *Guide to Genealogical Sources.* Rev. ed. Portland: Genealogical Forum of Oregon, 1994.

Lind, Hope Kauffman. *Apart and Together, Mennonites in Oregon and Neighboring States, 1876–1976.* Scottdale, Pennsylvania: Herald Press, 1990.

Lockley, Fred. *History of the Columbia River Valley from the Dalles to the Sea.* 3 vols. Chicago: S. J. Clarke Publishing Co., 1928.

Lyman, Horace Sumner. *History of Oregon: The Growth of an American State.* New York: North Pacific Pub. Society, 1903.

Mattoon, Charles Hiram. *Baptist Annals of Oregon, 1844–1900.* 2 vols. McMinnville, Oregon: Telephone Register Pub. Co., 1913.

McChesney, Charles E. *Rolls of Certain Indian Tribes in Oregon and Washington.* Fairfield, Washington: Ye Galleon Press, 1969.

Mitchelmore, Lawrence H. *Presbyterianism in Southern Oregon: A History of the Presbytery of Southwest Oregon and Its Forebears 1851–1949.* North Bend, Oregon: L. H. Mitchelmore, 1949.

Munnick, Harriet Duncan. *Catholic Church Records of the Pacific Northwest: Missions of St. Ann and St. Rose of the Cayuse, 1847–1888; Walla Walla and Frenchtown, 1858–1872; Frenchtown, 1872–1888.* Portland, Oregon: Binford & Mort, 1989.

Munnick, Harriet Duncan. *Catholic Church Records of the Pacific Northwest: Grand Ronde Register I (1860–1885), Grand Ronde Register II (1886–1898): St. Michael the Archangel Parish, Grand Ronde Indian Reservation, Grand Ronder, Oregon; St. Patrick's Parish, Muddy Valley, Oregon.* Portland, Oregon: Binford & Mort, 1987.

Nichols, M. Leona. *Mantle of Elias, the Story of Fathers Blanchet and Demers in Early Oregon.* Portland: Binfords and Mort, 1941.

Oregon Genealogical Society (Eugene, Oregon). *Oregon Pioneers.* Eugene, Oregon: The Society, ca. 198–.

Oregon Research Outline. Series U.S.-States, no. 38. Salt Lake City: Family History Library, 1988.

Portrait and Biographical Record of the Willamette Valley, Oregon. Chicago: Chapman Publishing Co., 1903.

Portrait and Biographical Record of Western Oregon: Containing Original Sketches of Many Well Known Citizens of the Past and Present. Chicago: Chapman Publishing Co., 1904.

Rushford, Jerry. *Christians on the Oregon Trail: Churches of Christ and Christian Churches in Early Oregon, 1842–1882.* Joplin, Missouri: College Press Pub. Co., 1997.

Schoenberg, Wilfred P. *Paths to the Northwest: A Jesuit History of the Oregon Province.* Chicago: Loyola University Press, 1982.

Schoenberg, Wilfred P. *These Valiant Women: History of the Sisters of St. Mary of Oregon, 1886–1986.* Beaverton, Oregon: Sisters of St. Mary of Oregon, 1986.

Shacer, F. A. Shaver, Arthur P. Rose, R. F. Steele, and A. E. Adams, comps. *An Illustrated History of Central Oregon: Embracing Wasco, Sherman, Gilliam, Wheeler, Crook, Lake, and Klamath Counties.* Spokane, Washington: Western Historical Pub. Co., 1905.

Southern Oregon Library Federation. *A Guide to the State of Jefferson: A Union List of Historical Materials Relating To Northern California and Southern Oregon.* Portland, Oregon: Filmed by the Oregon Historical Society, 197–.

Steber, Rick. *Oregon Trail: Last of the Pioneers.* Prineville, Oregon: Bonanza Publishing, 1993.

The Oregonian's Handbook of the Pacific Northwest. Portland: Oregonian, 1894.

United States. Bureau of Indian Affairs. Klamath Agency. *Family History and Medical Data, 1904–1937.* Microfilm of originals at the Federal Record Center, Seattle, Washington. Salt Lake City: Filmed by the Genealogical Society of Utah, 1978. 2 microfilm.

United States. Bureau of Indian Affairs. Portland Area Office. *Family Index Cards, 1938–1950.* Microfilm of originals at the Federal Record Center, Seattle, Washington. Salt Lake City: Filmed by the Genealogical Society of Utah, 1978. 2 microfilm.

Vaughn, Thomas. *A Bibliography of Pacific Northwest History.* Oregon Historical Society, n.d.

Who's Who for Idaho, Combined with Who's Who for Oregon and Who's Who for the Western States. Portland, Oregon: Capitol Publishing Co., 1970.

Yarnes, Thomas D. *A History of Oregon Methodism.* Portland: Oregon Methodist Conference Historical Society, 1957.

Atlases, Maps and Gazetteers

Brown, Erma Skyles. *Oregon County Boundary Change Maps, 1843–1916.* Lebanon, Oregon: End of Trail Researchers, 1970.

Loy, William G. *A Preliminary Atlas of Oregon.* Eugene: Geography Department, University of Oregon, 1972.

McArthur, Lewis A. *Oregon Geographic Names.* 6th ed. Portland: Oregon Historical Society, 1992.

Middleton, Lynn. *Places Names of the Pacific Northwest Coast: Origins, Histories and Anecdotes in Bibliographic Form about the Coast of British Columbia, Washington and Oregon.* Seattle, Washington: Superior Pub. Co, 1969.

Oregon Atlas and Gazetteer. 2nd ed. Freeport, Maine: DeLorme Mapping Co., 1995.

Payne, Edwin R. *Oregon Post Offices.* 2nd ed. Rev. to January 1955. Salem, Oregon, 1955.

Preston, Ralph N. *Historical Maps of Oregon: Overland Stage Routes, Old Military Roads, Indian Battle Grounds, Old Forts, and Old Gold Mines.* Corvallis, Oregon: Western Guide Publishers, 1972.

R. L. Polk & Co. Oregon and Washington Gazetteer and Business Directory, 1909–1910. Seattle: R. L. Polk, 1909.

Census Records

Available Census Records and Census Substitutes

Federal Census 1850, 1860, 1870, 1880, 1900, 1910, 1920

Federal Mortality Schedules 1850, 1860, 1870, 1880

Union Veterans and Widows 1890

State/Territorial Census 1845–1857

Dollarhide, William. *The Census Book: A Genealogist's Guide to Federal Census Facts, Schedules and Indexes.* Bountiful, Utah: Heritage Quest, 1999.

Kemp, Thomas Jay. *The American Census Handbook.* Wilmington, Delaware: Scholarly Resources, Inc., 2001.

Lainhart, Ann S. *State Census Records.* Baltimore: Genealogical Publishing Co., Inc., 1992.

Oregon Memorial of Citizens of The U.S. and Miscellaneous Information: Census Records for 1843, Tax Rolls, Newspaper Clippings of Oregon Pioneers,

Government Document on the Boundary Line between the British and United States Territories in Northwestern America. Salt Lake City: Filmed by the Genealogical Society of Utah, 1966.

Szucs, Loretto Dennis and Matthew Wright. *Finding Answers in U.S. Census Records.* Ancestry Publishing, 2001.

Thorndale, William and William Dollarhide. *Map Guide to the U.S. Federal Census, 1790–1920.* Baltimore: Genealogical Publishing Co., 1987.

United States. Bureau of Internal Revenue. *Oregon Internal Revenue Assessment Lists, 1867–1873.* Microfilm of originals in the National Archives Branch in Seattle, Washington. Salt Lake City: Filmed by the Genealogical Society of Utah, 1989. 2 microfilm.

Court Records, Probate and Wills

Note: Court, probate and will records are held in individual courthouses. Additional court records can be found at the Oregon State Archives. For a preview of the collections see their online database at—
http://arcweb.sos.state.or.us/

Reiner, Mary Hedges. *Early Oregon Wills, Multnomah County, 1884–1887.* vol. 3. N.p., 1953.

Reiner, Mary Hedges. *Probated Intestate Estates: Early Oregon, Multnomah County, 1884–1887, with a Few as Early as 1852.* N.p., 1953.

Emigration, Immigration, Migration and Naturalization

Bowen, William Adrian. *The Willamette Valley: Migration and Settlement on the Oregon Frontier.* Seattle: University of Washington Press, 1978.

Lenzen, Connie. *How to Find Oregon Naturalization Records.* S.l.: C. Lenzen, 1991.

Oregon Pioneer Association (Salem, Oregon). *Pioneer Registers, 1818–1859.* Microfilm of originals at the Oregon Historical Society in Portland, Oregon. Salt Lake City: Filmed by the Genealogical Society of Utah, 1999.

Oregon Trail Links. Oregon GenWeb Project, 2002. Online database—www.rootsweb.com/~orgenweb/otlinks.html.

Oregon-California Trails Association Online Database. Independence, Missouri: Oregon-California Trails Association, 2001. Online database—www.octatrails.org/.

Samuelsen, W. David. *Oregon Naturalization Records Index: Declaration of Intention.* 2 vols. Salt Lake City: Sampubco, 1995.

United States. Circuit Court (Oregon). *Indexes to Naturalization Records in the U. S. Circuit and District Courts.* Washington, D.C.: National Archives, 198–. 3 microfilm.

United States. District Court (Oregon). *Declaration of Intentions, 1859–1941; Petitions for Naturalization, 1906–1941; Indexes, 1863–1956; Military Petitions for Naturalization, 1917–1918.* Microfilm of originals at the

National Archives, Seattle Branch, Seattle, Washington. Salt Lake City: Filmed by the Genealogical Society of Utah, 1988. 60 microfilm.

United States. Immigration and Naturalization Service. *Chinese and Japanese Emigrants into Portland, Oregon.* Microfilm of originals in the National Archives Branch in Seattle, Washington. Salt Lake City: Filmed by the Genealogical Society of Utah, 1990. 15 microfilm.

White, Kris. *Overland Passages: A Guide to Overland Documents in the Oregon Historical Society.* Portland, Oregon: Oregon Historical Society Press, 1993.

Land and Property

Genealogical Material in Oregon Donation Land Claims, 5 vols. Portland: Genealogical Forum of Portland, 1957–1975.

Gibson, James R. *Farming the Frontier: The Agricultural Opening of the Oregon Country, 1786–1846.* Vancouver: University of British Columbia Press, 1985.

Hone, Wade E. *Land and Property Research in the United States.* Salt Lake City: Ancestry Incorporated, 1997.

National Archives Records Administration. Pacific Alaska Region. *Records of the District Land Offices For Oregon.* Seattle: National Archives Records Administration. Pacific Alaska Region, 2001. Online database—www.nara.gov/regional/seattle.html.

National Archives Records Administration. Pacific Alaska Region. *Records of Land Offices in Roseburg and Oregon City, Oregon.* Seattle: National Archives Records Administration. Pacific Alaska Region, 2001. Online database—www.nara.gov/regional/seattle.html.

Oregon State Archives, comp. *Index of Oregon Donation Land Claims.* 2nd ed. Portland: Genealogical Forum of Portland, 1987.

United States. General Land Office (Oregon). *Abstracts of Oregon Donation Land Claims, 1852–1903.* Microfilm of original records at the National Archives. Salt Lake City: Filmed by the Genealogical Society of Utah, 1949. 7 microfilm.

United States. General Land Office. *Oregon and Washington Donation Land Files, 1851–1903.* Washington, D.C.: The National Archives, 1970.

Yoshpe, Harry P. and Philip P. Brower, comps. *Preliminary Inventory of the Land-Entry Papers of the General Land Office.* Seattle: National Archives Pacific Alaska Region, 1949.

Military

Drew, Charles S. *An Account of the Origin and Early Prosecution of the Indian War in Oregon.* Fairfield, Washington: Ye Galleon Press, 1972.

Gantenbein, C. U. *The Official Records of the Oregon Volunteers in the Spanish War and Philippine Insurrection.* 2nd ed. Salem, Oregon: J. R. Whitney, 1903.

Indian War Pensions [Index, Oregon]. S.l.: s.n., 1998.

Leonard, Spencer. *A Partial List of Military Casualties and MIA's from the State of Oregon During World War II.* Portland, Oregon: Genealogical Forum of Oregon, Inc., 1993.

Myers, Jane. *Honor Roll of Oregon Grand Army of the Republic, 1881–1935.* Cottage Grove, Oregon: Cottage Grove Genealogical Society, 1980.

Oregon Military Department. Oregon Soldiers Home Applications, 1894–1933. Microfilm of original records at the Oregon State Archives in Salem, Oregon. Salt Lake City: Filmed by the Genealogical Society of Utah, 2000. 16 microfilm.

Oregon State Defense Council. Oregon War Records— Personal Military Service, 1919–1920. Salt Lake City: Filmed by the Genealogical Society of Utah, 2000. 17 microfilm.

Oregon. Division of State Archives. *Oregon Combined Military Alphabetical Index, 1837–1933.* Microfilm of original index at the Oregon State Archives in Salem, Oregon. Salt Lake City: Filmed by the Genealogical Society of Utah, 2000. 37 microfilm.

Oregon. Division of State Archives. *Oregon Combined Military Service Records Index, 1852–1954.* Microfilm of original records at the Oregon State Archives in Salem, Oregon. Salt Lake City: Filmed by the Genealogical Society of Utah, 2000. 44 microfilm.

Pekar, M. A. *Soldiers Who Served in the Oregon Volunteers: Civil War Period, Infantry and Cavalry.* Portland, Oregon: Genealogical Forum of Portland, 1961.

United States. Department of the Interior. *Bureau of Pensions. Indian War Pension Papers, 1897–1902.* Microfilm of original records at the Oregon Historical Society in Portland, Oregon. Salt Lake City: Filmed by the Genealogical Society of Utah, 1998–1999. 14 microfilm.

United States. Selective Service System. *Oregon, World War I Selective Service System Draft Registration Cards, 1917–1918.* National Archives Microfilm Publications, M1509. Washington, D.C.: National Archives, 1987–1988.

Vital and Cemetery Records

Eakley, Barbara Brown. *Episcopal Marriages of the Southern Oregon Coast, 1884–1940.* Coos Bay, Oregon: Bayview Publishers, 1997.

Guide to Public Vital Statistics Records in Oregon. Portland, Oregon: Historical Records Survey, 1942.

Oregon Cemetery Directory. Salem, Oregon: Oregon Heritage Council, 1976.

Oregon Cemetery Records. 2 vols. Salt Lake City: Genealogical Society of Utah, 1956–1961.

Oregon Death Records Index, 1903–1970. Salem, Oregon: Filmed by the Oregon State Archives and Records Center, 197–. 12 microfilm.

Oregon State Archives. Genealogical Information Locator. Salem, Oregon: Oregon State Archives, 2002. Online database—http://159.121.172.88/genealogy/search.lasso.

Oregon. Board of Health. Division of Vital Statistics. *Oregon Statewide Delayed Filings Of Births, 1842–1893.* Microfilm of original records at the Oregon State Archives in Salem, Oregon. Salt Lake City: Filmed by the Genealogical Society of Utah, 2001. 64 microfilm.

Osborn-Ryan, Sharon E. *Cumulative Baptism Index to the Catholic Church Records of the Pacific Northwest.* S.l.: Oregon Heritage Press, 1999.

Osborn-Ryan, Sharon E. *Cumulative Death Index to the Catholic Church Records of the Pacific Northwest.* Portland, Oregon: S. Osborn-Ryan, 1998.

Osborn-Ryan, Sharon E. *Cumulative Marriage Index to the Catholic Church Records of the Pacific Northwest.* S.l.: Oregon Heritage Press, 1998.

County Website	Map Index	Date Created	Parent County or Territory From Which Organized Address/Details
Baker www.bakercounty.org/index.html	**D5**	**22 Sep 1862**	**Wasco** Baker County; 1995 3rd St; Baker, OR 97814; Ph. (541) 523-8207 **Details:** (County Clerk has Marriage, Divorce, Probate & Court Records from 1862)
Benton www.co.benton.or.us/	**P5**	**23 Dec 1847**	**Polk** Benton County; 180 NW 5th St; Corvallis, OR 97330-4777; Ph. (541) 757-6800 **Details:** (County Clerk has Birth & Death Records from 1907, Marriage, Divorce, Probate, Court & Land Records from 1850 & Military Discharge Records from 1919)
Champoeg		**5 Jul 1843**	**Original county** Champoeg County; OR **Details:** (see Marion) Name changed to Marion 3 Sep 1849
Clackamas www.co.clackamas.or.us/	**M4**	**5 Jul 1843**	**Original county** Clackamas County; 104 Eleventh St.; Oregon City, OR 97045; Ph. (503) 722-2745 **Details:** (County Clerk has Birth & Death Records 1902–1920, Land Records 1906–1972, Marriage Records 1853–1966, & Naturalization Records 1890–1905; Oregon State Archives has Birth & Death Records 1915–1945, Circuit Court Records 1846–1986, Divorce Records 1850–1949, Marriage Records 1848–1948, and Naturalization Records 1887–1926; County Clerk has Military Discharge, Land, & Probate Records)
Clark		**27 Jun 1844**	**Original county** Clark County; OR **Details:** (Now part of state of Washington)
Clatsop www.co.clatsop.or.us/	**P2**	**22 Jun 1844**	**Twality** Clatsop County; 749 Commercial St; PO Box 178; Astoria, OR 97103; Ph. (503) 325-8605 **Details:** (County Clerk has Marriage & Land Records from 1860, Divorce & Court Records from 1875 & Probate Records from 1880)
Columbia www.co.columbia.or.us/	**O2**	**16 Jan 1854**	**Washington** Columbia County; 230 Strand St; St. Helens, OR 97051; Ph. (503) 397-3796 **Details:** (County Clerk has Marriage Records from 1890 & Land Records; State Court has Divorce & Court Records from 1854)
Coos www.co.coos.or.us/	**Q8**	**22 Dec 1853**	**Umpqua, Jackson** Coos County; 250 N Baxter St; Coquille, OR 97423; Ph. (541) 396-3121 **Details:** (County Clerk has Birth & Death Records 1906–1929, Marriage Records from 1857, Land Records from 1854, Widows' Military pensions 1929–1950 & some school Records; State Courts have Divorce & Probate Records)
Crook www.rootsweb.com/~orcrook/	**I6**	**24 Oct 1882**	**Wasco** Crook County; 300 E 3rd St; Prineville, OR 97754; Ph. (541) 447-6555 **Details:** (County Clerk has Birth Records 1907–1941, Death Records 1907–1939, Marriage, Divorce & Probate Records from 1883, Land & Court Records from 1882)

County	Map	Date	Parent County or Territory From Which Organized
Website	Index	Created	Address/Details

Curry   **Q10**   **18 Dec 1855**   **Coos**
www.co.curry.or.us/

Curry County; 94235 Moore St; PO Box 746; Gold Beach, OR 97444; Ph. (541) 247-7011

Details: (County Clerk has Marriage & Land Records from 1859; State Court Clerk has Probate & Court Records)

Deschutes   **K7**   **13 Dec 1916**   **Crook**
www.deschutes.org/

Deschutes County; 1300 NW Wall St Ste 200; Bend, OR 97701; Ph. (541) 388-6549, recording@deschutes.org

Details: (County Clerk has Court & Death Records, Land Records from 1871, Marriage Records from 1916, & Military Records from 1845)

Douglas   **O8**   **7 Jan 1852**   **Umpqua 1852 & 1862**
www.co.douglas.or.us/

Douglas County; 1036 SE Douglas St Rm 221; Roseburg, OR 97470; Ph. (541) 440-4324

Details: (Absorbed Umpqua County 1863) (County Clerk has Marriage, Burial, Divorce, Land, Probate, Military Discharge & Court Records from 1853 & Naturalization Records from 1850)

Gilliam   **I3**   **25 Feb 1885**   **Wasco, Morrow**
www.rootsweb.com/~orgillia/gilliam.html

Gilliam County; 221 S Oregon St; Condon, OR 97823-0000; Ph. (541) 384-2311

Details: (County Clerk has Marriage, Divorce, Probate, Court & Land Records from 1885)

Grant   **F5**   **14 Oct 1864**   **Wasco, Umatilla**
www.grantcounty.cc/

Grant County; 200 S Humbolt St; Canyon City, OR 97820; Ph. (541) 575-1675

Details: (County Clerk has Birth & Death Records 1915–1929, Marriage, Land & Probate Records from 1864, Military Records from 1872 & Naturalization Records 1907–1913; Clerk Circuit Court has Divorce & Court Records)

Harney   **G9**   **25 Feb 1889**   **Grant**
www.harneycounty.com/

Harney County; 450 N Buena Vista Ave; Burns, OR 97720; Ph. (541) 573-6641

Details: (County Clerk has Marriage Records from 1911, Land & Probate Records from 1889, Military Records from 1943 & Naturalization Records; Clerk Circuit Court has Divorce & Court Records)

Hood River   **L3**   **23 Jun 1908**   **Wasco**
www.hoodriver.org/

Hood River County; 601 State St; Hood River, OR 97031; Ph. (541) 386-1442

Details: (Vital Records have Birth & Death Records; County Court has Court, Divorce, Guardianship, & Probate Records; Assessment has Land Records; County Clerk has Marriage Records; Assessment has Property Tax Records)

Jackson   **N10**   **12 Jan 1852**   **Umpqua**
www.co.jackson.or.us/

Jackson County; 10 S Oakdale Ave; Medford, OR 97501; Ph. (541) 776-6147

Details: (County Clerk has Marriage Records from 1863, Probate & Land Records from 1853 & voter registration from 1952)

County Website	Map Index	Date Created	Parent County or Territory From Which Organized Address/Details
Jefferson www.rootsweb.com/~orjeffer/	**K5**	**12 Dec 1914**	**Crook** Jefferson County; 75 SE C St; Madras, OR 97741-1709; Ph. (541) 475-4451 **Details:** (County Clerk has Marriage, Divorce, Probate, Court & Land Records from 1914)
Josephine www.co.josephine.or.us/	**P11**	**22 Jan 1856**	**Jackson** Josephine County; 500 NW 6th St; Grants Pass, OR 97526; Ph. (541) 474-5243 **Details:** (County Clerk has Marriage & Land Records from 1857; Clerk Circuit Court has Divorce, Probate & Court Records)
Klamath www.co.klamath.or.us/	**L10**	**17 Oct 1882**	**West part of Lake County.** Klamath County; 305 Main St; Klamath Falls, OR 97601-6385; Ph. (541) 883-5134 **Details:** (County Clerk has Marriage & Land Records from 1882 & Military Records from 1919; Clerk Circuit Court has Divorce, Probate & Court Records)
Lake www.lakecountyinfo.com/	**J9**	**24 Oct 1874**	**Jackson, Wasco** Lake County; 513 Center St; Lakeview, OR 97630; Ph. (541) 947-6006 **Details:** (County Clerk has Marriage & Land Records; Clerk Circuit Court has Divorce, Probate & Court Records)
Lane www.co.lane.or.us/	**N7**	**28 Jan 1851**	**Benton, Linn** Lane County; 125 E 8th; Eugene, OR 97401; Ph. (541) 682-4234 **Details:** (Deeds & Records Archives has Marriage, Land, Military & Naturalization Records from 1855; Court Archives has Probate & Divorce Records; Clerk Circuit Court has Court Records)
Lewis		**21 Dec 1845**	**Original county** Lewis County; OR **Details:** (Now part of state of Washington)
Lincoln www.co.lincoln.or.us/	**Q5**	**20 Feb 1893**	**Benton, Polk** Lincoln County; 225 W Olive St; Newport, OR 97365; Ph. (541) 265-4131 **Details:** (County Clerk has Birth & Death Records 1907–1916, Marriage Records from 1905, Land Records from 1893, Military Discharge Records from 1945 & Voter Registration from 1920; District Court has Divorce, Probate & Court Records)
Linn www.co.linn.or.us/	**M5**	**28 Dec 1847**	**Original county** Linn County; 300 4th Ave SW; PO Box 100; Albany, OR 97321; Ph. (541) 967-3831 **Details:** (County Clerk has Marriage Records from 1850, Divorce, Probate & Court Records from 1854 & Military enumeration from 1905)
Malheur www.malheurco.org/	**D8**	**17 Feb 1887**	**Baker** Malheur County; 251 B St W; Vale, OR 97918; Ph. (541) 473-5151 **Details:** (County Clerk has Marriage, Probate & Land Records from 1887)

County Website	Map Index	Date Created	Parent County or Territory From Which Organized Address/Details
Marion www.open.org/~marion/	N4	5 Jul 1843	**Original county** Marion County; Courthouse Square; 555 Court St NE; Salem, OR 97309; Ph. (503) 588-5225 **Details:** (Formerly Champoeg County. Name changed to Marion 3 Sep 1849) (County Clerk has Marriage Records from 1849 & Land Records from 1850; District Court has Divorce, Probate & Court Records; State Archives has wills 1853–1951, Naturalization Records 1849–1975 & assessment rolls 1857–1925)
Morrow www.rootsweb.com/~ormorrow/	H3	16 Feb 1885	**Umatilla** Morrow County; 100 N Court St; Heppner, OR 97836; Ph. (541) 676-5603 **Details:** (County Clerk has Marriage, Probate, Divorce & Court Records from 1885)
Multnomah www.co.multnomah.or.us/	M3	22 Dec 1854	**Washington, Clackamas** Multnomah County; 1021 SW 4th Ave; Portland, OR 97204-1123; Ph. (503) 248-3511 **Details:** (County Clerk has Divorce, Court & Land Records from 1854)
Polk www.co.polk.or.us/	O4	22 Dec 1845	**Yamhill** Polk County; 850 Main St Rm 201; Dallas, OR 97338; Ph. (503) 623-9217 **Details:** (County Clerk has Marriage, Probate & Land Records)
Sherman www.rootsweb.com/~orsherma/	J3	25 Feb 1889	**Wasco** Sherman County; 500 Court St; Moro, OR 97039; Ph. (541) 565-3606 **Details:** (County Clerk has Marriage & Probate Records from 1889, Birth Records 1904–1939, Death Records 1905–1952 & Court Records from 1894)
Tillamook http://arcweb.sos.state.or.us/county/cptillamookdescrip.html	P3	15 Dec 1853	**Clatsop, Polk, Yamhill** Tillamook County; 201 Laurel Ave; Tillamook, OR 97141; Ph. (503) 842-3402
Tuality		5 Jul 1843	**Original county** Twality County; OR **Details:** (see Washington) Name changed to Washington 3 Sep 1849
Umatilla www.co.umatilla.or.us/	F3	27 Sep 1862	**Wasco** Umatilla County; 216 SE 4th St; Pendleton, OR 97801-2590; Ph. (541) 276-7111 **Details:** (County Clerk has Marriage, Divorce, Probate, Court & Land Records from 1862)
Umpqua		1851	**Benton, Linn** Umpqua County; OR **Details:** (absorbed by Douglas County 1863)
Union www.usgennet.org/usa/or/county/union1/union.htm	E3	14 Oct 1864	**Baker** Union County; 1106 K Ave; LaGrande, OR 97850; Ph. (541) 963-1006 **Details:** (County Clerk has Marriage & Land Records from 1875 & Naturalization Records 1900–1975; Clerk Circuit Court has Divorce, Probate & Court Records from 1854)

County Website	Map Index	Date Created	Parent County or Territory From Which Organized Address/Details
Wallowa www.co.wallowa.or.us/	**C3**	**11 Feb 1887**	**Union** Wallowa County; 101 S River St; Enterprise, OR 97828-1300; Ph. (541) 426-4543 **Details:** (County Clerk has Birth Records 1907–1943, Marriage, Land & Military Records from 1897, Divorce, Probate & Court Records from 1897–1970 & Naturalization Records 1897–1920; Circuit Court has Divorce, Probate & Court Records from 1971)
Wasco www.historysavers.com/orwasco/	**K4**	**11 Jan 1854**	**Clackamas, Marion, Linn** Wasco County; 511 Washington St; The Dalles, OR 97058; Ph. (541) 504-2530 **Details:** (All Records from 1854: State Vital Statistics has Birth & Death Records; Circuit Court has Court, Divorce, Guardianship, & Probate Records; County Clerk has Land & Military Discharge Records; County Assessor has Land & Tax Records)
Washington www.co.washington.or.us/cgi/home/washco.pl	**O3**	**5 July 1843**	**Original county** Washington County; 155 N 1st Ave Ste 130; Hillsboro, OR 97124-3072; Ph. (503) 864-8741 **Details:** (Formerly Twality [or Falatine County]. Name changed to Washington 3 Sep 1849) (Records Section, Assessment & Taxation has Marriage, Land & Military Records from 1850; Clerk Circuit Court has Divorce & Court Records from 1896, Probate Records from 1871 & Naturalization Records from 1906)
Wheeler Future website at www.rootsweb.com/ ~orgenweb/counties.html	**I5**	**17 Feb 1899**	**Crook, Gilliam, Grant** Wheeler County; 701 Adams St; PO Box 327; Fossil, OR 97830; Ph. (541) 763-2400 **Details:** (County Clerk has Probate Records from 1899 & Land Records; Clerk Circuit Court has Divorce & Court Records)
Yamhill www.co.yamhill.or.us/	**O3**	**5 Jul 1843**	**Original county** Yamhill County; 535 NE 5th St; McMinnville, OR 97128; Ph. (503) 434-7518 **Details:** (County Clerk has Marriage Records from 1881 & Land Records from 1853)

The Handybook for Genealogists

Notes

Pennsylvania

Capital: Harrisburg
State: 1787 (2nd)

*Virtue, liberty, and
independence*

The Swedes made the first permanent settlement in Pennsylvania in 1643 and built the first log cabins in America. These settlers became the nucleus for William Penn's colony, despite being conquered by the Dutch and the English. In 1681, King Charles II granted William Penn a charter, which made Penn proprietor and governor of Pennsylvania. He first visited the colony in 1682 and set up a General Assembly at Chester. Penn named his capital Philadelphia, and before allowing settlers into any area, bought the land from the Indians. On Penn's second visit (1699–1701), he granted the Charter of Privileges, which made the legislature independent and virtually in control of the colony.

Penn established the colony as a refuge for those who were persecuted for their religious beliefs. The persecuted from throughout Europe came, including Quakers from England, Scotland, Ireland, and Wales; Palatines from the Rhine Valley; Anabaptists (Mennonites) from Germany and Switzerland; Dunkards (members of the Church of the Brethren) from Germany in 1721; Roman Catholics from England in 1732; Moravians via Georgia in 1740; Welsh, Swiss, and Scotch-Irish between 1700 and 1728; and the Pennsylvania Dutch (who were Germans) around 1740. Indian relations remained peaceable until the French arrived in 1753. Their arrival lead to the French and Indian War and Pontiac's War.

Philadelphia played an important role during the Revolution and in the drafting of the Constitution. Pennsylvania was among the greatest contributors of men, money, and supplies to the Revolutionary War and was the site of many important battles, such as Washington's crossing of the Delaware, the battles of Brandywine and Germantown, and the winter camp at Valley Forge. In 1787, Pennsylvania was the second state to ratify the Constitution. Philadelphia served as the capital of the United States from 1790 to 1800.

Boundary disputes were nearly constant until 1800. The boundary with Maryland was settled by the Mason and Dixon survey, 1763–1767. The Pennamite War between 1769 and 1775 was fought between settlers from Connecti-

cut and Pennsylvania over the Wyoming Valley. This was finally settled in 1782 by the Decree of Trenton, which gave the land to Pennsylvania. Connecticut finally yielded in 1784. Southwestern Pennsylvania was also claimed by Virginia, but this dispute was settled in 1785. In 1792, Pennsylvania bought the Erie triangle to gain a port on Lake Erie.

Tens of thousands of settlers came in the early 1800's to work in mines and industry. These came from Italy, Poland, Russia, Austria, Germany, Czechoslovakia, England, Ireland, Hungary, Sweden, Greece, France, Norway, Denmark, and Finland. By 1811, steamboats began traveling from Pittsburgh to New Orleans. The railroad canal line extended from Philadelphia to Pittsburgh by 1834. With these improvements came more immigrants, so that by 1840 there was no longer a frontier in Pennsylvania. Pennsylvania had the first anti-slavery society in 1775. It is no wonder that the state was so pro-Union. Nearly 400,000 men served for the Union, and the battle of Gettysburg was fought on Pennsylvania soil.

Look for vital records in the following locations:

- **Birth and death records:** Statewide registration of births and deaths began in January 1906. Copies are available from the Division of Vital Statistics, State Department of Health in Newcastle, Pennsylvania. Records prior to 1906 were kept (by the registrar of wills) in individual counties or cities, some as early as 1852.

- **Marriage records:** Individual counties or cities also kept marriage records, some from the early 1800's, through most of 1885.

- **Naturalizations:** Original Oaths of Allegiance, 1727 to 1794, are at the Bureau of Archives and History, Harrisburg, Pennsylvania. Most later immigrants filed for naturalization in a county court.

- **Land records:** The state land office, established in 1682, is now the Bureau of Land Records. The Bureau of Archives and History in Harrisburg, Pennsylvania sells warrantee township maps which show the original land grants within present township boundaries, as well as names and other information for the original warrantee and patentee. Records about the Wyoming Valley prior to 1782 are kept in Hartford, Connecticut.

Division of Vital Statistics State Department of Health
101 South Mercer Street, Room 401
PO Box 1528
New Castle, Pennsylvania 16101
(724) 656-3100
www.dsf.health.state.pa.us

Bureau of Archives and History
PO Box 1026
Harrisburg, Pennsylvania 17108
www.phmc.state.pa.us/bah/DAM/overview.htm

Pennsylvania Historical & Museum Commission
Pennsylvania State Archives
350 North Street
Harrisburg, Pennsylvania 17120-0090
(717) 783-3281
www.phmc.state.pa.us/overview.asp

Societies and Repositories

Adams County Pennsylvania Historical Society; PO Box 4325; Gettysburg, PA 17325.

African-American Historical & Genealogical Society, Western Pennsylvania; 1307 Pointview St.; Pittsburgh, PA 15206.

Allegheny Foothills Historical Society; Boyce Park Adm. Bldg.; 675 Old Franklin Rd.; Pittsburgh, PA 15239.

American Canal Society, The; c/o Charles W. Derr; 117 Main Street; Freemansburg, PA 18017; www.americancanals.org.

American Swedish Historical Foundation; 1900 Pattison Ave.; Philadelphia, PA 19145; ashm@libertynet.org; www.americanswedish.org.

Ancient Order of Hiberians; McKeesport Heritage Center; 190 W. Schwab Ave.; Munhall, PA 15120.

Armstrong County Genealogical Society; 300 North McKean Street; PO Box 735; Kittanning, PA 16201-1345; www.angelfire.com/pa2/acgs.

Beaver County Genealogical Society; 3225 Dutch Ridge Road; Beaver, PA 15009; www.rootsweb.com/~pabecgs.

Bedford County, Pioneer Historical Society, Inc.; 242 E. John St.; Bedford, PA 15522.

Berks County Genealogical Society; 3618 Kutztown Road; Laureldale, PA 19605; kermgoda@epix.net; www.berksgenes.org.

Berwick Historical Society; 102 Fast Second St.; Berwick, PA 18603-4827; www.berwickhistoricalsociety.org.

Blair County Genealogical Society; 431 Scotch Valley Rd.; Hollidaysburg, PA 16648; www.rootsweb.com/~pabcgs.

Blair County Historical Society; PO Box 1083; Altoona, PA 16603.

Bradford Landmark Society; 45 E. Corydon; Bradford, PA 16701.

Brownsville Historical Society; Box 24; Brownsville, PA 15417.

Bucks County Genealogical Society; PO Box 1092; Doylestown, PA 18901; bucksgen@juno.com.

Bucks County Historical Society; 94 S. Pine St.; Doylestown, PA 18901.

Cambria County Historical Society; Box 274 West High St.; Ebensburg, PA 15931.

Cameron County Historical Society; 139 E. Fourth St.; Emporium, PA 15834.

Capital Area Genealogical Society; PO Box 4502; Harrisburg, PA 17111-0502; www.maley.net/cags.

Central Pennsylvania Genealogical Pioneers; 1150 N. Front St.; Sunbury, PA 17801.

Centre County Genealogical Society; PO Box 1135; State College, PA 16804-1135; BakerGen@aol.com; www.rootsweb.com/~paccgs.

Centre County Historical Society; 1001 E. College Ave.; State College, PA 16801.

Chester County Historical Society; 225 N. High St.; West Chester, PA 19380.

Clarion County Historical and Genealogical Society; Courthouse Square; 186 Grant St.; Clarion, PA 16214.

Clearfield County Historical Society; 104 E. Pine St.; Clearfield, PA 16830.

Clinton County Genealogical Society; PO Box 193; Castanea, PA 17726.

Clinton County Historical Society; 362 E. Water St.; Lock Haven, PA 17740.

Cocalico Valley Historical Society; 249 W. Main St.; Ephrata, PA 17522.

Columbia County Historical and Genealogical Society; 225 Market Street; PO Box 360; Bloomsburg, PA 17815-0360; (570) 784-1600; research @colcohist-gensoc.org; www.colcohist-gensoc.org.

Connellsville Area Historical Society; 410 E. Cedar Ave.; Connellsville, PA 15425.

Cornerstone Genealogical Society; PO Box 547; Waynesburg, PA 15370; www.vicoa.com/cornerstone.

Crawford County Genealogical Society; 848 N. Main St.; Meadville, PA 16335.

Cumberland County Historical Society; PO Box 626; Carlisle, PA 17013.

Delaware County Historical Society; 991 Palmers Mill Rd.; Media, PA 19063-1049.

Elizabeth Township Historical Society; 5811 Smithfield St.; Boston, PA 15135.

Elk County Historical Society; 109 Center St.; County Courthouse; Ridgway, PA 15853.

Erie County Historical Society; 417 State St.; Erie, PA 16501.

Erie Society for Genealogical Research; PO Box 1403; Erie, PA 16512.

Evangelical and Reformed Historical Society; 555 W. James St.; Lancaster, PA 17603.

Fayette County Genealogical Society; 24 Jefferson Street; Uniontown, PA 15401; www.fforward.com/gene/fcgene.htm.

Forest County Historical Society; c/o Courthouse; Tionesta, PA 16353.

Frackville Area Historical Society; 104 Broad Mountain Avenue; Frackville, PA 17931; www.geocities.com/Heartland/Acres/5200.

Friends Historical Association; Haverford College; Haverford, PA 19041.

Fulton County Historical Society; Box 115; McConnellsburg, PA 17233.

Genealogical Research Society of Northeastern Pennsylvania; PO Box 1; Olyphant, PA 18447-0001; genealogy@usnetway.com; www.cfrobbins.com/grsnp.

Genealogical Society of Pennsylvania; 215 S. Broad St., 7th Floor; Philadelphia, PA 19107-5325; gsppa@aol.com; www.libertynet.org/gspa.

Genealogical Society of Southwestern Pennsylvania; PO Box 894; Washington, PA 15301-0894.

Greene County Historical Society; Rd #2; Waynesburg, PA 15370.

Heritage Society of Pennsylvania; PO Box 146; Laugblintown, PA 15655.

Historic Schaefferstown, Inc.; Box 1776; Schaefferstown, PA 17088.

Historical & Genealogical Society of Indiana County, Pennsylvania; 200 S. Sixth Street; Indiana, PA 15701; (724) 463-9600; ichs@ptd.net; www.rootsweb.com/~paicgs.

Historical and Genealogical Society of Jefferson County; Box 51; Brookville, PA 15825.

Historical Society of Berks County; 940 Centre Ave.; Reading, PA 19601; (610) 375-4375; society.library @verizon.net; www.berksweb.com/histsoc.

Historical Society of Dauphin County; 219 S. Front St.; Harrisburg, PA 17104.

Historical Society of Green Tree; 10 W. Manilla Ave.; Pittsburgh, PA 15220.

Historical Society of Pennsylvania; Thirteen Hundred Locust St.; Philadelphia, PA 19107.

Historical Society of Perry County, Headquarters and Museum; 129 N. Second St.; Newport, PA 17074.

Historical Society of Westmoreland; 151 Old Salem Rd.; Greensburg, PA 15601.

Homestead Historical Society; 1110 Silvan Ave.; Homestead, PA 15120.

Huntingdon County Historical Society; PO Box 305; Huntingdon, PA 16652.

Indiana County Historical & Genealogical Society; So. 6th & Wayne Ave.; Indiana, PA 15701.

Jewish Genealogical Society of Philadelphia; 332 Harrison Ave.; Elkins Park, PA 19117-2662.

Jewish Genealogical Society of Pittsburgh; 2131 Fifth Ave.; Pittsburgh, PA 15219; (412) 471-0772; julfalk@aol.com; www.jewishgen.org/jgs-pittsburgh.

Juniata County Historical Society; 498 Jefferson St., Suite B; Mifflintown, PA 17059-1424.

Kittochtinny Historical Society, Inc.; 175 E. King St.; Chambersburg, PA 17201.

Lackawanna County Historical Society; 232 Monroe Ave.; Scranton, PA 18510.

Lancaster County Historical Society; 230 N. President Ave.; Lancaster, PA 17603.

Lancaster Mennonite Historical Society; 2215 Millstream Road; Lancaster, PA 17602-1499.

Lawrence County Historical Society; 2nd Floor, Box 1745; Public Library; 408 N. Jefferson St.; New Castle, PA 16103.

Lebanon County Historical Society; 924 Cumberland St.; Lebanon, PA 17042.

Lehigh County Historical Society; PO Box 1548; Allentown, PA 18105.

Ligonier Valley Historical Society; Star Route East; Ligonier, PA 15658.

Lycoming County Genealogical Society; PO Box 3625; Williamsport, PA 17701; LCGSgen@aol.com; http://members.aol.com/LCGSgen/lcgs.htm.

Lycoming County Historical Society and Museum; 958 W. 4th St.; Williamsport, PA 17701.

Mahanoy and Mahantongo Historical & Preservation Society; PO Box 143; Dalmatia, PA 17017; www.mahantongo.org.

Masontown Historical Society; Box 769; Masontown, PA 15461.

McKean County Genealogical Society; PO Box 207A; Derrick City, PA 16727.

McKean County Historical Society; Courthouse; Smethport, PA 16749.

Mennonite Historical Society; 2215 Millstream Road; Lancaster, PA 17602.

Mercer County Genealogical Society; Box 812; Sharon, PA 16146.

Mercer County Historical Society; 119 S. Pitt St.; Mercer, PA 16137.

Mifflin County Historical Society; 1 W. Market St., Ste. 1; Lewistown, PA 17044-2128.

Montgomery County Historical Society; 1654 Dekalb St.; Norristown, PA 19401.

Montour County Historical Society; PO Box 8, 1 Bloom St.; Danville, PA 17821.

Muncy Historical Society and Museum of History; 40 N. Main St.; Muncy, PA 17756; muncyhistorical@aol.com.

NARA, Mid Atlantic Region (Center City Philadelphia); 900 Market Street; Philadelphia, PA 19107-4292; (215) 606-0100; philadelphia.archives@nara.gov; www.archives.gov/midatlantic/public_services/public_services.html.

NARA, Mid Atlantic Region (Northeast Philadelphia); 14700 Townsend Road; Philadelphia, PA 19154-1096; (215) 305-2000; www.archives.gov/midatlantic/fed_agency_services/fed_agency_services.html.

Northampton County Historical and Genealogical Society; 101 So. 4th St.; Easton, PA 18042.

Northeastern Pennsylvania Genealogical Society; PO Box 1776; Shavertown, PA 18708-0776; www.rootsweb.com/~panepgs.

Northeastern Pennsylvania, Genealogical Research Society, Inc.; 210 Grant St.; Olyphant, PA 18447.

Northumberland County Historical Society; 1150 N. Front St.; Sunbury, PA 17801.

Old York Road Genealogical Society; 1030 Old York Road; Abington, PA 19001.

Palatines to America, Pennsylvania Chapter; PO Box 280; Strasburg, PA 17579-0280.

Palmyra Area Genealogical Society; PO Box 544; Palmyra, PA 17078.

Pennsylvania State Archives; 350 North Street; Harrisburg, PA 17120-0090; (717) 783-3281; www.phmc.state.pa.us/bah/dam/overview.htm.

Perry Historian Genealogical Society; PO Box 73; Newport, PA 17074.

Pike County Historical Society; 608 Broad St.; Milford, PA 18337.

Pinegrove Historical Society; PO Box 65; Pine Grove, PA 17963; www.rootsweb.com/~papghs/index.htm.

Pioneer Historical Society of Bedford County; Box 421; Bedford, PA 15522.

Pittsburgh, North Hills Genealogists; c/o Northland Public Library; 300 Cumberland Rd.; Pittsburgh, PA 15237-5455.

Potter County Historical Society; 308 N. Main St.; Coudersport, PA 16915.

Presbyterian Historical Society; 425 Lombard St.; Philadelphia, PA 19147.

Punxsutawney Area Historical and Genealogical Society; 401 W. Mahoning Street; Punxsutawney, PA 15767; punxsyhistory@usachoice.net; http://users.penn.com/~mweimer/historcl.html.

Scottish Historic and Research Society of the Delaware Valley, Inc.; 102 St. Paul's Rd.; Ardmore, PA 19003.

Sewickley Valley Historical Society; 200 Broad; Sewickley, PA 15143.

Snyder County Historical Society; 30 E. Market St.; PO Box 276; Middleburg, PA 17842.

Sons of the American Revolution, Pennsylvania Society; 510 Vine St.; Perkasie, PA 18944.

Sons of Union Veterans of the Civil War; PO Box 1865; Harrisburg, PA 17105; CinCSUVCW@aol.com; http://suvcw.org.

South Central Pennsylvania Genealogical Society, Inc.; PO Box 1824; York, PA 17405; www.innernet.net/hively/SouthCentralPAGenealogicalSociety.htm.

St. Marys and Benzinger Township Historical Society, Genealogical Dept.; 319 Eric Ave.; St. Marys, PA 15857.

State Library of Pennsylvania; Office of Commonwealth Libraries; Bureau of State; Harrisburg, PA 17126-1745; (717) 787-4440; ra-reference@state.pa.us; www.statelibrary.state.pa.us/libraries/site/default.asp.

Sullivan County Historical Society; Courthouse Square; Meylert St., Box 252; LaPorte, PA 18626.

Susquehanna County Historical Society; 2 Monument Square; Montrose, PA 18801.

Susquehanna Depot Historical Society, Inc.; PO Box 161; Susquehanna, PA 18847.

Tarentum Genealogical Society; PO Box 66; Tarentum, PA 15084; www.targensoc.homestead.com/home.html.

The Genealogical Society of Southwestern Pennsylvania; PO Box 0894; Washington, PA 15301-0894.

The Historical Society of Schuylkill County; 14 N. 3rd St.; Pottsville, PA 17901.

The Pennsylvania German Society; PO Box 244; Kutztown, PA 19530-0244; pgs@fast.net; www.pgs.org.

Tioga County Historical Society; 120 Main St., Box 724; Wellsboro, PA 16901.

Tri-County Heritage Society; PO Box 352; Morgantown, PA 19543; tchslibrary@juno.com.

Tulpehocken Settlement Historical Society; 116 N. Front St.; PO Box 53; Womelsdorf, PA 19567.

Tuscarora Township Historical Society, Bradford County; R.D. #2, Box 105-C; Laceyville, PA 18623.

Union County Historical Society; South Second and St. Louis Streets; Lewisburg, PA 17837; (570) 524-8666; hstoricl@ptd.net; www.rootsweb.com/~paunion/society.html.

Venango County Genealogy Club; 2 Central Ave.; Oil City, PA 16301.

Venango County Historical Society; PO Box 101; 301 S. Park St.; Franklin, PA 16323.

Warren County Genealogical Society; 6 Main St.; Warren, PA 16365.

Warren County Historical Society; Box 427; Warren, PA 16365.

Washington County Historical Society and Library; LeMoyne House, 49 E. Maiden St.; Washington, PA 15301.

Wattsburg Area Historical Society; PO Box 240; Wattsburg, PA 16442-0240.

Wayne County Historical Society; PO Box 446; Honesdale, PA 18431; (570) 253-3420; wchspa@ptd.net.

Western Pennsylvania Afro-American Historical & Genealogical Society; 1307 Point View St.; Pittsburgh, PA 15206.

Western Pennsylvania Genealogical Society; c/o Carnegie Library; 4400 Forbes Ave.; Pittsburgh, PA 15213-4080.

Windber-Johnstown Area Genealogical Society; PO Box 5048; Johnstown, PA 15904-5048; www.ccacc.cc.pa.us/library/genealogy.htm.

Wyoming County Historical Society; PO Box 309; Tunkhannock, PA 18657-9998; http://wyshs.org.

York County Historical Society; 250 E. Market St.; York, PA 17403.

Bibliography and Record Sources

General

Baumann, Roland M. *Guide to the Microfilm of the Records of Pennsylvania's Revolutionary Governments, 1775–1790: (record group 27) in the Pennsylvania State Archives.* Harrisburg: Pennsylvania Historical and Museum Commission, 1978, 1979.

Bining, Arthur C., et al. *Writing on Pennsylvania History: A Bibliography.* Harrisburg, Pennsylvania: Pennsylvania Historical and Museum Commission, 1946.

Blockson, Charles L. *African Americans in Pennsylvania: A History and Guide.* Baltimore, Maryland: A DuForcelf book published by Black Classic Press, 1994.

Brecht, Samuel Kriebel. *The Genealogical Record of the Schwenkfelder Families: Seekers of Religious Liberty Who Fled from Silesia to Saxony and Thence to Pennsylvania in the Years 1731 to 1737.* New York: Rand McNally, printed for the Board of Publication of the Schwenkfelder Church, Pennsburg, Pennsylvania, 1923.

Bricker, Florence M., comp. and ed. *Church and Pastoral Records in the Archives of the United Church of Christ and the Evangelical and Reformed Historical Society, Lancaster, Pennsylvania.* Lancaster, Pennsylvania: The Society, 1982.

Browing, Charles Henry. *Welsh Settlement of Pennsylvania.* Philadelphia, Pennsylvania: William J. Campbell, 1912.

Card Index to Pennsylvania Germans in the Magazines: Proceedings and Addresses (Pennsylvania German Society); Pennsylvania Dutchman; PGFS or Pennsylvania German Folklore Society; Penn-Germania; the Pennsylvania-German; Historical Review of Berks County. Salt Lake City: Genealogical Society of Utah, 1978. Microfilm, 38 rolls.

Chester County Historical Society (West Chester, Pennsylvania). *Genealogical Clippings File, up to 1968.* Microfilm, 151 rolls.

Chester County Historical Society (West Chester, Pennsylvania). *Genealogical Manuscripts Up to 1968.* Salt Lake City: Filmed by the Genealogical Society of Utah, 1968. Microfilm, 104 rolls.

Clint, Florence. *Pennsylvania Area Key: A Guide to the Genealogical Records of the State of Pennsylvania; Including Maps, Histories, Charts and Other Helpful Materials.* 2nd ed. Denver: Area Keys, 1976.

Colonial Society of Pennsylvania (Philadelphia, Pennsylvania). *Applications for Membership in Alphabetical Order by Member With a Complete Genealogy Back to Original Ancestor.* Salt Lake City: Genealogical Society of Utah, 1968

Crist, Robert Grant. *Penn's Example to the Nations: 300 Years of the Holy Experiment.* Harrisburg, Pennsylvania: Pennsylvania Council of Churches, Inc. for the Pennsylvania Religious Tercentenary Committee, 1987.

Cutler, Jean H. *Directory of Museums and Historical Organizations in Pennsylvania.* Harrisburg, Pennsylvania: The Federation, 1991.

Donehoo, George P. *Pennsylvania; A History.* 9 vols. New York: Lewis Historical Pub. Co., 1926–1931.

Downey, Dennis B., and Francis J. Bremer. *A Guide to the History of Pennsylvania.* Westport, Connecticut: Greenwood Press, 1993.

Dunaway, Wayland Fuller. *The Scotch-Irish of Colonial Pennsylvania.* Chapel Hill, North Carolina: The University of North Carolina Press, 1944.

Egle, William Henry, ed. *Notes and Queries: Historical, Biographical, and Genealogical, Relating Chiefly to Interior Pennsylvania. 1894–1904.* Reprint. Baltimore: Genealogical Publishing, 1971.

Egle, William Henry. *An Illustrated History of the Commonwealth of Pennsylvania: Civil, Political, and Military from its Earliest Settlement to the Present Time, Including Historical Descriptions of Each County in the State, Their Towns, and Industrial Resources.* Philadelphia: E. M. Gardner, 1880.

Egle, William Henry. *Pennsylvania Genealogies, Chiefly Scotch-Irish and German.* Reprint. Baltimore: Genealogical Publishing, 1969.

Elliot, Margaret Sherburne. *Guide to Depositories of Manuscript Collections in Pennsylvania.* Harrisburg, Pennsylvania: Pennsylvania Historical Commission, 1939.

Ely, Warren S. *Warren S. Ely Collection, Genealogical Data, Letters.* Salt Lake City: Filmed by the Genealogical Society of Utah, 1967. Microfilm, 46 rolls.

Eshleman, Frank. *Historic Background and Annals of the Swiss and German Pioneer Settlers of Southeastern Pennsylvania and of their Remote Ancestors from the Middle of the Dark Ages, Down to the Time of the Revolutionary War . . . With Particular Reference to the German-Swiss Mennonites or Anabaptists, the Amish and Other Non-resistant Sects.* 1917. Reprint. Baltimore: Genealogical Publishing Co., 1969.

Evans, Frank B., and Martha L. Simonetti, eds. *Summary Guide to the Pennsylvania State Archives.* Harrisburg, Pennsylvania: Pennsylvania Historical and Museum Commission, 1970.

Genealogical and Biographical Records File, Up to 1968. Salt Lake City: Filmed by the Genealogical Society of Utah, 1968. Microfilm, 41 rolls.

Genealogies of Pennsylvania Families: From the Pennsylvania Genealogical Magazine. 3 vols. Baltimore, Maryland: Genealogical Publishing, 1982.

Genealogies of Pennsylvania Families: From the Pennsylvania Magazine of History and Biography. Baltimore: Genealogical Publishing, 1981.

Gerberich, Albert Henry. *Pennsylvania German Families.* Salt Lake City: Filmed by the Genealogical Society of Utah, 1967. Microfilm, 16 rolls.

Gibson, Gail M. *Pennsylvania Directory of Historical Organizations, 1970.* Harrisburg, Pennsylvania: Pennsylvania Historical and Museum Commission, 1970.

Glenn, Thomas Allen. *Merion in the Welsh Tract: With Sketches of the Townships of Haverford and Radnor, Historical and Genealogical Collections Concerning the Welsh Barony in the Province of Pennsylvania, Settled by the Cymric Quaker in 1682.* Norristown, Pennsylvania: Herald Press, 1896.

Glenn, Thomas Allen. *Welsh Founders of Pennsylvania.* 2 vols. Oxford: Fox, Jones and Co., 1911–1913.

Godcharles, Frederic Antes. *Index to the Encyclopedia of Pennsylvania Biography.* Philadelphia: W. D. Stock, 1996. Baltimore, Maryland: Printed for Clearfield Co. by Genealogical Pub. Co.

Grand Army of the Republic, Department of Pennsylvania. *Record of Eligibility of Ladies of the Grand Army of the Republic, Department of Pennsylvania 1883–1992.* Salt Lake City: Genealogical Society of Utah, 1993.

Heisey, John W. *Handbook for Genealogical Research in Pennsylvania.* Indianapolis: Heritage House, 1985.

Hinshaw, William Wade. *The William Wade Hinshaw Index to Quaker Meeting Records in the Friends Library in Swarthmore College, Pennsylvania.* Salt Lake City: Filmed by the Genealogical Society of Utah, 1957. Microfilm, 73 rolls.

Historical Records Survey (Pennsylvania). *Inventory of Church Archives in Pennsylvania.* Microfilm of original records in the State Archives in Harrisburg. Salt Lake City: Filmed by the Genealogical Society of Utah, 1977. 72 microfilm.

Historical Records Survey (Pennsylvania). *Inventory of Church Archives, Society of Friends in Pennsylvania.* Philadelphia: Friends' Historical Association, 1941.

Historical Records Survey (Pennsylvania). *Inventory of the Church Archives of Pennsylvania Presbyterian Churches.*

Microreproductions of original records at the Presbyterian Historical Society, in Philadelphia, Pennsylvania. Salt Lake City: Filmed by the Genealogical Society of Utah, 1967, 1972. 24 microfilm.

Historical Records Survey (Pennsylvania). *Inventory of the County Archives of Pennsylvania: Records of the Works Project Administration, Pennsylvania Historical Writer's Project.* Microfilms of original records in the Pennsylvania State Archives. Salt Lake City: Filmed by the Genealogical Society of Utah, 1977. 5 microfilm.

Historical Society of Pennsylvania. *Guide to the Manuscript Collections of the Historical Society of Pennsylvania.* Philadelphia: The Society, 1991.

Hocker, Edward W. *Genealogical Data Relating to the German Settlers of Pennsylvania. 1743–1800.* 1935.

Hoenstine, Floyd G. *Guide to Genealogical and Historical Research in Pennsylvania.* Hollidaysburg, Pennsylvania: the author, 1978. Supplements 1985, 1990.

Huguenot Society of Pennsylvania. *Application Papers; Ancestor Index.* Salt Lake City: Filmed by the Genealogical Society of Utah, 1967. Microfilm, 12 rolls.

Iscrupe, William L., and Shirley G. M. Iscrupe, comps. *Pennsylvania Line: A Research Guide to Pennsylvania Genealogy and Local History.* 4th ed. Laughlintown, Pennsylvania: Southwest Pennsylvania Genealogical Services, 1990.

Jordan, John W. *Genealogical and Personal History of the Allegheny Valley, Pennsylvania.* 3 vols. New York: Lewis Historical Publishing, 1913.

Jordan, John W., ed. *Genealogical and Personal History of Northern Pennsylvania.* 3 vols. New York: Lewis Historical Publishing, 1913.

Jordan, John W., et al. *Encyclopedia of Pennsylvania Biography.* 32 vols. New York: Lewis Historical Publishing Co, 1914–1967.

Jordan, John W., et. al. *Colonial and Revolutionary Families of Pennsylvania.* 11 vols. New York: Lewis Publishing, 1911–1965.

Manning, Barbara. *Genealogical Abstracts from Newspapers of the German Reformed Church, 1830–1839.* Bowie, Maryland: Heritage Books, 1992.

Manning, Barbara. *Genealogical Abstracts from Newspapers of the German Reformed Church 1840–1843.* Bowie, Maryland: Heritage Books, Inc., 1995.

Manuscript Card Catalog of the Genealogical Society of Pennsylvania. Salt Lake City: Genealogical Society of Utah, 1964.

McConnell, Michael N. *A Country Between: The Upper Ohio Valley and Its Peoples, 1724–1774.* Lincoln, Nebraska: University of Nebraska Press, 1992.

Meyen, Emil. *Bibliography on the Colonial Germans of North America: Especially the Pennsylvania Germans and their Descendants.* Reprint. Baltimore, Maryland: Genealogical Publishing, 1982.

Parker, J. Carlyle. *Pennsylvania and Middle Atlantic States Genealogical Manuscripts: A User's Guide to the Manuscript Collections of the Genealogical Society of Pennsylvania.* Turlock, California: Marietta Publishing, 1986.

Parsons, William T. *The Pennsylvania Dutch: A Persistent Minority.* Boston: Twayne Publishers, 1976.

Pennsylvania Archives. Philadelphia: J. Severns, 1852–1856, 1874–1935.

Pennsylvania Biographical Dictionary: People of All Times and Places Who Have Been Important to the History and Life of the State. Wilmington, Delaware: American Historical Publications, 1989.

Pennsylvania Historical Society. *Genealogical Collections; Families of Pennsylvania, New Jersey, Etc., 1700–1950.* Salt Lake City: Genealogical Society of Utah, 1966.

Pennsylvania Historical Survey, Division of Community Service Programs, Work Projects Administration. *A Checklist of Pennsylvania Newspapers, Philadelphia County.* Harrisburg, Pennsylvania: Pennsylvania Historical Commission, 1944.

Pennsylvania Historical Survey. *County Government and Archives in Pennsylvania.* Harrisburg, Pennsylvania: Pennsylvania Historical and Museum Commission, 1947.

Presbyterian Historical Society (Philadelphia, Pennsylvania). *Miscellaneous Biographical Collection.* Salt Lake City: Filmed by the Genealogical Society of Utah, 1967.

Rauco, Louis F. *Pennsylvania Newspapers and Selected Out-of-State Newspapers.* S. l.: s. n., 1984.

Richman, Irwin. *Historical Manuscript Depositories in Pennsylvania.* Harrisburg: The Pennsylvania Historical and Museum Commission, 1965.

Rider, Fremont, ed. *American Genealogical-Biographical Index.* Vols. 1–186+. Middletown, Connecticut: Godfrey Memorial Library, 1952–.

Robson, Charles, ed. *The Biographical Encyclopedia of Pennsylvania of the Nineteenth Century.* Philadelphia, Pennsylvania: Galaxy, 1874.

Rosenberger, Homer Tope. *The Pennsylvania Germans, 1891–1965 Frequently known as the "Pennsylvania Dutch".* S.l.: H. T. Rosenberger, 1966, Lancaster, Pennsylvania: Printed for the Pennsylvania German Society.

Salisbury, Ruth, ed. *Pennsylvania Newspapers, a Bibliography and Union List.* Pittsburgh: Pennsylvania Library Association, 1969

Schory, Eva Draegert. *Every Name Index to Egle's Notes and Queries.* 2 vols. Decatur, Illinois: Decatur Genealogical Society, 1982–1986.

Schweitzer, George K. *Pennsylvania Genealogical Research.* Knoxville, Tennessee: G. Schweitzer, 1986.

Stapleton, Ammon. *Memorials of the Huguenots in America, With Special Reference to Their Emigration [sic] to Pennsylvania.* 1901. Reprint: Baltimore: Genealogical Publishing, 1969.

State Library of Pennsylvania (Harrisburg). *Genealogical Surname Card Index.* Microfilm of records in the Pennsylvania State Library. Salt Lake City: Filmed by the Genealogical Society of Utah, 1977. Microfilm, 42 rolls.

State Library of Pennsylvania (Harrisburg, Pennsylvania). *County Records Card File, 1651–1977.* Microfilm of original records in the Pennsylvania State Library. Salt Lake City: Filmed by the Genealogical Society of Utah, 1977.

Stevens, Sylvester Kirby and Donald H. Kent, ed. *Bibliography of Pennsylvania History.* 2nd ed. Harrisburg, Pennsylvania: Pennsylvania Historical and Museum Commission, 1957.

Stevens, Sylvester Kirby. *Pennsylvania: The Heritage of a Commonwealth.* 4 vol. West Palm Beach, Florida: The American Historical Company, 1968.

Suran, Frank M. *Guide to the Record Groups in the Pennsylvania State Archives.* Harrisburg, Pennsylvania: Pennsylvania Historical and Museum Commission, 1980.

Trussell, John B. B., Jr. *Pennsylvania Historical Bibliography.* Vols. 1–6. Harrisburg, Pennsylvania: Pennsylvania Historical and Museum Commission, 1979–1989.

Turner, Edward Raymond. *The Negro in Pennsylvania: Slavery-Servitude-Freedom, 1639–1861.* New York: Negro Universities Press, 1969.

United States. Commissioner of Internal Revenue. *Internal Revenue Assessment Lists for Pennsylvania, 1862–1865.* Washington, D.C.: National Archives and Record Service, 1975. Microfilm, 106 rolls.

United States. Secretary of the Treasury. *United States Direct Tax of 1798: Tax Lists for the State of Pennsylvania.* Salt Lake City: Genealogical Society of Utah, 1962. Microfilm, 23 rolls.

Virdin, Donald Odell. *Pennsylvania Family Histories and Genealogies.* Bowie, Maryland: Heritage Books, 1992.

Wall, Carol, ed. *Bibliography of Pennsylvania History: A Supplement.* Harrisburg, Pennsylvania: Pennsylvania Historical and Museum Commission, 1976.

Whipkey, Harry E. *Guide to the Manuscript Groups in the Pennsylvania State Archives.* Harrisburg, Pennsylvania: Pennsylvania Historical and Museum Commission, 1976.

Wilkinson, Norman B. *Bibliography of Pennsylvania History.* 2nd ed. Harrisburg, Pennsylvania: Pennsylvania Historical and Museum Commission, 1957.

Woodroofe, Helen Hutchison, comp. *A Genealogist's Guide to Pennsylvania Records.* Reprinted from the Pennsylvania Genealogical Magazine. Philadelphia: Genealogical Society of Pennsylvania, 1995.

Works Progress Administration. *Inventory of the Church Archives of Pennsylvania Presbyterian Churches.* Salt

Lake City: Filmed by the Genealogical Society of Utah, 1967, 1972.

Atlases, Maps and Gazetteers

Atlas of Pennsylvania. Philadelphia: Temple University, 1989.

Bien, Joseph R. *Atlas of the State of Pennsylvania: From Original Surveys and Various Local Surveys Revised and Corrected.* New York: Julius Bein & Co., 1900.

County Historical Maps. Harrisburg, Pennsylvania: Archives Publishing of Pennsylvania.

Espenschade, Abraham H. *Pennsylvania Place Names.* 1925. Reprint. Baltimore, Maryland: Genealogical Publishing, 1970.

Gordon, Thomas F. *A Gazetteer of the State of Pennsylvania.* Philadelphia: T. Belknap, 1832.

Historical Collections of the State of Pennsylvania: Containing a Copious Selection of the Most Interesting Facts, Traditions, Biographical Sketches, Anecdotes, etc., Relating to its History and Antiquities, Both General and Local, with Topographical Descriptions of Every County and all the Larger Towns in the State. Philadelphia: G. W. Gorton, 1843. (New Haven, Connecticut: Durrie and Peck 1843).

Kay, John L., and Chester M. Smith, Jr. *Pennsylvania Postal History.* Lawrence, Massachusetts: Quarterman Publications, 1976.

Long, John H., ed. *Historical Atlas and Chronology of County Boundaries, 1788–1980.* Vol. 1, Delaware, Maryland, New Jersey, Pennsylvania. Boston: G. K. Hall, 1984.

Long, John H., ed. *Pennsylvania: Atlas of Historical County Boundaries.* New York: Charles Scribner's Sons, Simon and Schuster Macmillan, 1996.

Pennsylvania Gazetteer. Wilmington, Delaware: American Historical Publications, 1989.

Russ, William A., Jr. *How Pennsylvania County Maps.* Lyndon Station, University Park: Pennsylvania Historical Association, 1966.

Scott, Joseph. *A Geographical Description of Pennsylvania: Also of the Counties Respectively, in the Order in Which They Were Established by the Legislature: With an Alphabetical List of the Townships in Each County; and Their Population in 1800.* Philadelphia: Robert Cochran, 1806. Reprint, Microfiche, Early American Imprints, Second Series, no. 11331.

Simonetti, Martha L. comp., Donald H. Kent, and Harry E. Whipkey, eds., *Descriptive List of the Map Collection in the Pennsylvania State Archives.* Harrisburg, Pennsylvania; Pennsylvania Historical and Museum Commission, 1976.

United States, Geological Survey, *Pennsylvania: Index to Topographic and Other Map Coverage.* Reston, Virginia: The Survey, 1983.

Walling, H. F., and O. W. Gray. *Historical Topographical Atlas of the State of Pennsylvania.* 1872; Reprint. Knightstown, Indiana: Bookmark, 1977.

Census Records

Available Census Records and Census Substitutes

Federal Census 1790, 1800, 1810, 1820, 1830, 1840, 1850, 1860, 1870, 1880, 1900, 1910, 1920, 1930

Federal Mortality Schedules 1850, 1860, 1870, 1880

Union Veterans and Widows 1890

U.S. Direct Tax 1798

Dollarhide, William. *The Census Book: A Genealogist's Guide to Federal Census Facts, Schedules and Indexes.* Bountiful, Utah: Heritage Quest, 1999.

Kemp, Thomas Jay. *The American Census Handbook.* Wilmington, Delaware: Scholarly Resources, Inc., 2001.

Szucs, Loretto Dennis and Matthew Wright. *Finding Answers in U.S. Census Records.* Ancestry Publishing, 2001

Thorndale, William and William Dollarhide. *Map Guide to the U.S. Federal Census, 1790–1920.* Baltimore: Genealogical Publishing Co., 1987.

United States, Census Office. *Non-population Census Schedules for Pennsylvania; Agricultural Schedules, 1850–1880.* Washington, D. C.: National Archives, 1970. Microfilm, 61 rolls.

United States, Census Office. *Non-population Census Schedules for Pennsylvania; Manufacturers Schedules 1850–1880.* Washington, D. C.: National Archives, 1971; Wooster, Ohio: Microfilmed by Micro Photo Division of Bell & Howell. Microfilm, 21 rolls.

Court Records, Probate and Wills

Armstrong, Edward, ed. *Record of Upland Court from the 14th of November, 1676, to the 14th of June, 1681.* Salt Lake City: Filmed by the Genealogical Society of Utah, 1969.

Beers, Donna. *Pennsylvania in the 1700s: An Index to Who Was There and Where.* Warrensburg, Missouri: D. Beers, 1998.

Brodhead, John Romeyn, agent; and E. B. O'Callaghan, ed. *Documents Relative to the Colonial History of the State of New York: Procured in Holland, England, and France.* Albany, New York: Weed, Parsons & Co., Print, 1853–1887.

Catanese, Lynn Ann. *Guide to Records of the Court of Common Pleas, Chester County, Pennsylvania, 1681–1900: Records of the Prothonotary, Civil Records of the Sheriff, Select Civil Records of the Circuit Court of Chester County and the Supreme Court of Pennsylvania.* West Chester, Pennsylvania: Chester County Historical Society, 1987.

Catanese, Lynn Ann. *Guide to Records of the Court of Quarter Sessions, Chester County, Pennsylvania, 1681–1969: Records of the Clerk of Courts, Records of* the Court of Oyer and Terminer and General Jail Delivery, Criminal Records of the Sheriff. West Chester, Pennsylvania: Chester County Historical Society, 1988.

Pennsylvania. Court of Quarter Sessions (Philadelphia County). *Court Docket, 1753–1879*. Salt Lake City: Filmed by the Genealogical Society of Utah, 1974.

Pennsylvania. Orphans' Court (Philadelphia County). *Orphans' Court Records, 1719–1880: Orphans' Court Index, 1719–1938*. Salt Lake City: Genealogical Society of Utah, 1947, 1980–1981. Microfilm, 417 rolls.

Philadelphia County (Pennsylvania). *Register of Wills. Wills, 1682–1916; Indexes to Wills, 1682–1924*. Salt Lake City: Genealogical Society of Utah, 1947, 1981–1982. Microfilm, 327 rolls.

Registrar's Book of Governor Keith's Court of Chancery of the Province of Pennsylvania, 1720–1735. Reprint. Harrisburg, Pennsylvania: Pennsylvania Bar Association, 1941.

United States. District Court (Pennsylvania: Eastern District). *Law Records, 1789–1844*. Washington, D.C.: National Archives. Central Plains Region, 1977. 32 microfilm.

Emigration, Immigration, Migration and Naturalization

Adams, Raymond D. *An Alphabetical Index to Ulster Emigrants to Philadelphia 1803–1850*. 1992, Reprinted 2004. Clearfield Company.

Bentley, Elizabeth P., and Michael H. Tepper. *Passenger Arrivals at the Port of Philadelphia, 1800–1819*. Baltimore, Maryland: Genealogical Publishing, 1986.

Boyer, Carl. *Ship Passenger Lists, Pennsylvania and Delaware, 1641–1825*. Newhall, California: C. Boyer, 1980.

Egle, William Henry. *Names of Foreigners Who Took the Oath of Allegiance to the Province and State of Pennsylvania, 1727–1775, with Foreign Arrivals, 1786–1808*. Reprint. Baltimore: Genealogical Publishing Co., 1967.

Emigrants to Pennsylvania, 1641–1819: A Consolidation of Ship Passenger Lists from the Pennsylvania Magazine of History and Biography. Baltimore, Maryland: Genealogical Publishing, 1975.

Filby, P. William and Mary K. Meyer. *Philadelphia Naturalization Records, an Index to Records of Aliens' Declarations of Intentions and/or Oaths of Allegiance, 1789–1880*. Detroit, Michigan: Gale Research, 1982.

Filby, P. William. *Passenger and Immigration Lists Index*. 15 vols. Detroit: Gale Research, 1981–.

Giuseppi, M. S., ed. *Naturalizations of Foreign Protestants in the American And West Indian Colonies (Pursuant to Statute 13 George II, c. 7)*. (Originally published as Publications of the Huguenot Society of London, volume XXIV, London, 1921). Reprint, Baltimore: Genealogical Pub. Co., 1969.

Hull, William I. *William Penn and the Dutch Quaker Migration to Pennsylvania*. Baltimore, Maryland: Clearfield Co., Inc., 2002.

Immigrants to Pennsylvania, 1600s–1800s. S.l.: Brøderbund, 1999. CD-ROM.

Koger, M. V. *Index to the Names of 30,000 Immigrants—German, Swiss, Dutch and French—into Pennsylvania, 1727–1776*. Salt Lake City: Filmed by Genealogical Society of Utah, 1972.

Kuhns, Oscar. *The German and Swiss Settlements of Colonial Pennsylvania. A Study of the So-Called Pennsylvania Dutch*. 1900, repr. 2004. Clearfield Company.

Myers, Albert C., comp. *Notes on Immigrants to Pennsylvania, 1681–1737*. Microfilm of manuscripts (54 vols.) at the Chester County Historical Society, West Chester, Pennsylvania. Salt Lake City: Filmed by the Genealogical Society of Utah, 1968. Microfilm, 14 rolls.

Pennsylvania. Court of Common Pleas (Philadelphia County). *Declarations of Intention, 1821–1911*. Microfilm of original records at the Philadelphia City Archives. Salt Lake City: Genealogical Society of Utah, 1974. Microfilm, 38 rolls.

Pennsylvania. Court of Common Pleas (Philadelphia County). *Petitions for Naturalization 1793–1906; Indexes 1793–1930*. Microfilm of original records at the Philadelphia City Archives. Salt Lake City: Genealogical Society of Utah, 1974. Microfilm, 176 rolls.

Pennsylvania. Court of Quarter Sessions (Philadelphia County). *Declarations of Intentions, 1810–1932; Index, 1810–1887*. Microfilm of original records at the Philadelphia City Archives. Salt Lake City: Genealogical Society of Utah, 1974, 1991. Microfilm, 48 rolls.

Pennsylvania. Court of Quarter Sessions (Philadelphia County). *Petitions for Naturalization 1800–1929; Indexes 1802–1930*. Microfilm of original records at the Philadelphia City Archives. Salt Lake City: Genealogical Society of Utah, 1974. Microfilm, 185 rolls.

Pennsylvania. Supreme Executive Council. *Application for Passes, 1775–1790*. Harrisburg, Pennsylvania: Pennsylvania Historical & Museum Commission, 1978.

Reaman, George Elmore. *The Trail of the Black Walnut*. Reprint. Baltimore, Maryland: Genealogical Pub. Co., Inc., 1993.

Sheppard, Walter Lee, Jr. *Passengers and Ships Prior to 1684, Penn's Colony: Volume I*. 1992 facsimile reprint. Willow Bend Books.

Strassburger, Ralph Beaver and William John Hinke. *Pennsylvania German Pioneers: A Publication of the Original Lists of Arrivals in the Port of Philadelphia from 1727 to 1808*. Norristown, Pennsylvania: Pennsylvania German Society, 1934.

United States. Circuit Court (Pennsylvania: Eastern District). *Naturalization Petitions and Records, 1795–1911*. Microfilm of original records at the

National Archives, Philadelphia Branch, Philadelphia, Pennsylvania. Salt Lake City: Genealogical Society of Utah, 1987, 1990–1991. Microfilm, 53 rolls.

Westcott, Thompson. *Names of Persons Who Took the Oath of Allegiance to the State of Pennsylvania Between the Years 1777 and 1789: With a History of the "Test Laws" of Pennsylvania.* 1865. Reprint, Baltimore: Genealogical Pub. Co., 1965.

Land and Property

Boyd, Julian P., and Robert J. Taylor. *Susquehanna Company Papers.* 11 vols. Ithaca, New York: Cornell University Press, 1962–1971.

Egle, William Henry, ed. *Early Pennsylvania Land Records: Minutes of The Board of Property.* Baltimore: Genealogical Publishing, 1976.

Egle, William Henry. *Warrantees of Land in the Several Counties of the State of Pennsylvania, 1730–1898.* 3 vols. Harrisburg, Pennsylvania: W. S. Ray, State Printer, 1897.

Hone, Wade E. *Land and Property Research in the United States.* Salt Lake City: Ancestry Incorporated, 1997.

Munger, Donna Bingham. *Pennsylvania Land Records: A History and Guide for Research.* Wilmington, Delaware: Scholarly Resources, 1991.

Pennsylvania, Bureau of Land Records. *Patent Books, 1676–1960.* Harrisburg, Pennsylvania: Bureau of Land Records, 1957–1972.

Pennsylvania, Bureau of Land Records. *Warrant Register, 1682–1950.* Microfilm of original records found in the Bureau of Land Records in Harrisburg, Pennsylvania. Salt Lake City: Genealogical Society of Utah, 1976. 6 microfilm.

Pennsylvania, Land Office. *Caveats. 1699–1890.* Salt Lake City: Genealogical Society of Utah, 1976. Microfilm, 19 rolls.

Pennsylvania, Land Office. *Depositions, 1683–1881.* Microfilm of original records in the Pennsylvania Bureau of Land Records, Harrisburg, Pennsylvania. Salt Lake City: Genealogical Society of Utah, 1976.

Pennsylvania, Land Office. *Original Warrants of Depreciation Lands, 1780–1800.* Microfilm of original records in the Pennsylvania Bureau of Land Records, Harrisburg, Pennsylvania. Salt Lake City: Genealogical Society of Utah, 1976.

Pennsylvania, Land Office. *Proof of Settlement Records, 1797–1869.* Salt Lake City: Genealogical Society of Utah, 1976. Microfilm, 15 rolls.

Pennsylvania, Surveyor General. *Original Surveys, 1682–1920.* Microfilm of original records in the Bureau of Land Records in Harrisburg, Pennsylvania. Salt Lake City: Genealogical Society of Utah, 1976. Microfilm, 499 rolls.

Pennsylvania, Surveyor General's Office. *Donation Lands Records, 1780–1800.* Microfilm of original records in the Pennsylvania Bureau of Land Records, Harrisburg,

Pennsylvania. Salt Lake City: Genealogical Society of Utah, 1976.

Pennsylvania. Board of Property. *Board of Property Papers, 1682–1850.* Microfilm of original records in the Pennsylvania Bureau of Land Records, Harrisburg, Pennsylvania. Salt Lake City: Genealogical Society of Utah, 1976. Microfilm, 19 rolls.

Pennsylvania. Secretary of the Land Office. *Rent Rolls, 1703–1744.* Microfilm of original records in the State Archives in Harrisburg. Salt Lake City: Genealogical Society of Utah, 1979.

Pennsylvania. Supreme Court. *Sheriff's Deed Book for the Eastern District, 1796–1876.* Microfilms of original records in the Pennsylvania State Archives. Salt Lake City: Filmed by the Genealogical Society of Utah, 1977. 4 microfilm.

Weinberg, Allen and Thomas E. Slatterly. *Warrants and Surveys of the Province of Pennsylvania Including the Three Lower Counties, 1759.* Philadelphia: City of Philadelphia, Department of Records, 1965.

Military

Bates, Samuel P. *History of Pennsylvania Volunteers.* Harrisburg, Pennsylvania: state printer, 1869–1871.

Cope, Harry E. *Soldiers and Widows of Soldiers of the Revolutionary War Granted Pensions by the Commonwealth of Pennsylvania.*

Hackenburg, Randy W. *Pennsylvania in the War with Mexico.* Shippensburg, Pennsylvania: White Mane Pub. Co., 1992.

Historical Society of Pennsylvania. *Index to Pennsylvania in the War of the Revolution: Battalions and Line, 1775–1783; Associated Battalions and Militia, 1775–1783.* Microfilm of the original records at the Historical Society of Pennsylvania in Philadelphia, Pennsylvania. Salt Lake City: Genealogical Society of Utah, 1966. 10 microfilm.

Linn, John Blair. *Pennsylvania in the War of the Revolution, Battalions and Line 1775–1783.* Harrisburg, Pennsylvania: state printer, 1880.

Military Abstract Card File for the Revolutionary War, 1775–1783. Salt Lake City: Filmed by the Genealogical Society of Utah, 1978. Microfilm, 48 rolls.

Muster Rolls of the Pennsylvania Volunteers in the War of 1812–1814, 1895. Reprint. Baltimore: Genealogical Publishing, 1967.

Myers, Harold L. *Pennsylvania and the War of 1812.* Harrisburg, Pennsylvania: Pennsylvania Historical and Museum Commission, 1964.

Nettling, Dan A. *Pennsylvania Military History: A Bibliography. Part II, The Civil War.* Carlisle Barracks, Pennsylvania: U. S. Army Military History Institute, 1992.

Nolan, James B. *Officers and Soldiers in the Service of the Province of Pennsylvania, 1744–1764.* Philadelphia: University of Pennsylvania, 1936.

Pennsylvania, Auditor General. Board of Military Claims. *Military Claims Settled, 1862–1905*. Microfilm of original records in the Pennsylvania State Archives. Salt Lake City: Genealogical Society of Utah, 1977. Microfilm, 63 rolls.

Pennsylvania, Auditor General. *Revolutionary War Pension File, 1809–1893*. Microfilm of original records in Pennsylvania State Archives. Salt Lake City: Genealogical Society of Utah, 1966. 4 microfilm.

Pennsylvania, Comptroller General. *Revolutionary War Pension Accounts, 1785–1809, 1834–1838*. Microfilm of original records in the Pennsylvania State Archives. Salt Lake City: Genealogical Society of Utah, 1978.

Pennsylvania, State of. *Pennsylvania Archives*. 138 vols. Harrisburg, Pennsylvania: Pennsylvania Historical and Museum Commission, 1857–1914.

Pennsylvania, Supreme Executive Council. *Forfeited Estates File, 1777–1790*. Harrisburg, Pennsylvania: Pennsylvania Historical and Museum Commission, 1978

Pennsylvania. Adjutant General. *Mexican Service Index, 1846–1848*. Microfilm of original records in the Pennsylvania Bureau of Archives and History. Salt Lake City: Genealogical Society of Utah, 1979.

Pennsylvania. Adjutant General. *United States Volunteers of the Spanish American War, 1893–1901*. Microfilm of original records in the Bureau of Archives & History in Harrisburg. Salt Lake City: Genealogical Society of Utah, 1979.

Pennsylvania. Auditor General. *War of 1812 Pension Records, 1866–1896*. Microfilm of original records in the Pennsylvania State Archives. Salt Lake City: Genealogical Society of Utah, 1977. Microfilm, 26 rolls.

Pennsylvania. Auditor General. *War of 1812, List of Soldiers*. Microfilm of original records in the Pennsylvania State Archives. Salt Lake City: Genealogical Society of Utah, 1978. 2 microfilm

Pennsylvania. Auditor General's Office. *Military Claims Not Settled, 1862–1905*. Microfilm of original records in the Pennsylvania State Archives. Salt Lake City: Filmed by the Genealogical Society of Utah, 1977, 1978. 5 microfilm.

Pennsylvania. Bureau of Audits. *Mexican War Military Accounts, 1846–1880*. Microfilm of original records in the Pennsylvania State Archives. Salt Lake City: Genealogical Society of Utah, 1978. 5 microfilm.

Pennsylvania. Bureau of Audits. *War of 1812 Militia Accounts, 1812–1827*. Microfilm of original records in the Pennsylvania State Archives. Salt Lake City: Genealogical Society of Utah, 1978. 8 microfilm

Pennsylvania. Comptroller General. *Military Accounts, Line, 1775–1809*. Microfilm of original records in the State Archives in Harrisburg. Salt Lake City: Filmed by the Genealogical Society of Utah, 1978. 9 microfilm.

Pennsylvania. Comptroller General. *Militia Military Accounts, 1777–1794*. Microfilm of original records in the Pennsylvania State Archives in Harrisburg. Salt Lake City: Filmed by the Genealogical Society of Utah. 38 microfilm 1978.

Pennsylvania. Department of Military Affairs State Veteran's Compensation Division. *Spanish American War Veteran's Compensation File*. Microfilm of original records in the Bureau of Archives and History in Harrisburg. Salt Lake City: Genealogical Society of Utah, 1979. Microfilm, 46 rolls.

Provincial Council. *Colonial Records*. 16 vols. Philadelphia: the state, 1853.

Stevens, S. K., Marvin W. Schlegel, and Joseph T. Kingston. *Pennsylvania's Second Year at War; December 7, 1942 to December 7, 1943*. Harrisburg, Pennsylvania: Pennsylvania Historical and Museum Commission, 1945.

Stewart, Thomas J. *Record of Pennsylvania Volunteers in the Spanish-American War, 1898*, 2nd ed. Harrisburg, Pennsylvania: Wm. Stanley Ray, 1901.

Trussell, John B. B., Jr. *The Pennsylvania Line, Regimental Organization and Operations, 1776–1783*. Harrisburg, Pennsylvania: Pennsylvania Historical and Museum Commission, 1977.

United States, Adjutant General's Office. *Index to Compiled Service Records of Volunteer Union Soldiers Who Served in Organizations from the State of Pennsylvania*. Washington, D.C.: National Archives, 1964. Microfilm, 135 rolls.

United States, Adjutant General's Office. *General Index to Compiled Military Service Records of Revolutionary War Soldiers*. Washington, D.C.: National Archives, 1942.

United States, Selective Service System. *Pennsylvania, World War I Selective Service System Draft Registration Cards, 1917–1918*. Washington, D.C.: National Archives, 1987–1988.

United States, War Department. *Revolutionary War Rolls 1775–1783, Pennsylvania Jackets 1–93*. Washington, D.C.: The National Archives, 1957.

United States. Adjutant General's Office. *World War II Honor List of Dead and Missing: State of Pennsylvania*. Washington, D.C.: Government Printing Office, 1946.

United States. Record and Pension Office. *Compiled Service Records of Volunteer Soldiers Who Served During the Mexican War in Organizations from the State of Pennsylvania*. Washington, D.C.: National Archives and Records Service, 1976.

White, Virgil D. *Genealogical War Abstracts of the Revolutionary Pension Files*. 4 vols. Waynesboro, Tennessee: National Historical Publishing, 1990.

White, Virgil D. *Index to Revolutionary War Service Records*. 4 vols. Waynesboro, Tennessee: National Historical Publishing, 1995.

Pennsylvania

Vital and Cemetery Records

Bucks County (Pennsylvania). Coroner. *Coroner's Views and Inquisitions, 1710–1906; Index, 1722–1946.* Salt Lake City: Genealogical Society of Utah, 1973.

Cemetery Records of Pennsylvania, 9 vols. Salt Lake City: Genealogical Society, 1946–1968.

Fisher. Charles Adam. *Early Pennsylvania Births, 1675–1875.* Reprint of 1947 edition; Baltimore: Genealogical Publishing Co., 1979.

Inventory of Vital Statistics within Each County. Harrisburg, Pennsylvania: Historical Records Survey, N.d.

Ledoux, Albert H. *Catholic Vital Records of Central Pennsylvania,* 4 vols. Altoona, Pennsylvania: A. H. Ledoux, 1993–1996.

Marriage Register of Pennsylvania, 1684 to 1689. Salt Lake City: Genealogical Society of Utah, 1948. Microfilm of original records in the Department of Records in Philadelphia. Salt Lake City: Genealogical Society of Utah, 1962. Microfilm, 56 rolls.

Pennsylvania Historical Survey. Work Projects Administration. *Index to Registration of Deaths, City of Philadelphia, 1803–1860.* Philadelphia: Department of Records, 1962.

Pennsylvania Marriages Prior to 1790. 1968. Reprint, Baltimore, Pennsylvania: Genealogical Publishing, 1968.

Pennsylvania Vital Records From the Pennsylvania Genealogical Magazine and The Pennsylvania Magazine of History and Biography. Volumes I, II, and III. Pub. 1983, Reprinted 2004. Clearfield Company.

Pennsylvania, Secretary of the Commonwealth. *Births, Marriages, and Deaths on File at the State Archives, 1852–1854.* Salt Lake City: Genealogical Society of Utah, 1977.

Pennsylvania. Bureau of Vital Statistics. *Marriage Records, 1885–1889.* Microfilm of the original records at the State Archives in Harrisburg. Salt Lake City: Genealogical Society of Utah, 1978.

Pennsylvania. Bureau of Vital Statistics. *Registration of Births, 1852–1908; Delayed Record of Birth, Filed 1941– 1965.* Salt Lake City: Filmed by the Genealogical Society of Utah, 1968. 6 microfilm.

Pennsylvania. Governor. *Death Warrants, 1794–1873.* Microfilm of the original records at the State Archives in Harrisburg. Salt Lake City: Genealogical Society of Utah, 1977.

Pennsylvania. Supreme Executive Council. *Marriage Bonds, 1784–1786.* Harrisburg, Pennsylvania: Pennsylvania Historical & Museum Commission, 1978.

Philadelphia (Pennsylvania) Department of Public Health. *Birth Correction Cards 1872–1915, 1967–1981.* Microfilm of original records in the City Hall, Philadelphia, Pennsylvania. Salt Lake City: Filmed by the Genealogical Society of Utah, 1982. 26 microfilm.

Philadelphia (Pennsylvania) Department of Public Health. *Death Records, 1832–1860.* Microreproduction of original at the Historical Society of Pennsylvania. Salt Lake City: Genealogical Society of Utah, 1964. 7 microfilm.

Philadelphia (Pennsylvania). Board of Health. *Birth Registers, 1860–1903, For the City of Philadelphia.*

Philadelphia (Pennsylvania). Board of Health. *Birth Returns, 1904–1915, Filed by Physician, Midwife, or Hospital.* Microfilm of original records at the Philadelphia City Archives. Salt Lake City: Genealogical Society of Utah, 1954–1962, 1983, 1985–1986. Microfilm, 197 rolls.

Philadelphia (Pennsylvania). Board of Health. *Death Registers, 1860–1903.* Microfilm of original records in the Philadelphia Department of Records. Philadelphia: Microfilmed by Department of Records, 1962. Microfilm, 54 rolls.

Philadelphia (Pennsylvania). *Board of Health. Registration of Deaths, 1803–1903; Arranged by Year and Cemetery.* Microfilm of original records in the City Archives, Philadelphia. Salt Lake City: Filmed by the Genealogical Society of Utah, 1991–1997. 1029 microfilm.

Philadelphia (Pennsylvania). Bureau of Health. *Birth Index Cards, 1904–1915, for Philadelphia.* Microfilm of original records at the Philadelphia City Archives. Salt Lake City: Genealogical Society of Utah, 1983. Microfilm, 174 rolls.

Philadelphia (Pennsylvania). Bureau of Health. *Death Certificates, 1904–1915: Death Indexes, 1904–1915.* Philadelphia, Pennsylvania: Microfilmed by Department of Records, 1962–1963. Microfilm, 781 rolls.

Philadelphia (Pennsylvania). Department of Public Health. *Burial Records, 1807–1840.* Microreproduction of original at the Historical Society of Pennsylvania. Salt Lake City: Genealogical Society of Utah, 1964. 10 microfilm.

Record of Pennsylvania Marriages, Prior to 1810. 2 vols. 1880. Reprint. Baltimore: Genealogical Pub. Co., 1968.

Scott, Kenneth. *Abstracts (Mainly Deaths) From the Pennsylvania Gazette, 1775–1783.* Baltimore: Genealogical Publishing Co., 1976.

County Website	Map Index	Date Created	Parent County or Territory From Which Organized Address/Details
Adams www.rootsweb.com/~paadams/adams.htm	**H10**	**22 Jan 1800**	**York** Adams County; 111 Baltimore St; Gettysburg, PA 17325-2312; Ph. (717) 334-6781 **Details:** (Clerk Court has Birth & Death Records 1852–1855 & 1893–1905, Marriage Records 1852–1855 & from 1856; Prothonotary Office has Divorce & Court Records from 1800; County Divorce has Probate & Land Records from 1800)
Allegheny www.county.allegheny.pa.us/	**Q8**	**24 Sep 1788**	**Westmoreland, Washington** Allegheny County; 436 Grant St; Pittsburgh, PA 15219-2403; Ph. (412) 355-5322 **Details:** (Registrar of Wills has Marriage Records; Prothonotary Office, 1st Floor, City County Building has Divorce Records; Clerk Court has Probate & Court Records; Divorce Deeds has Land Records)
Armstrong www.armstrongcounty.com/	**O6**	**12 Mar 1800**	**Allegheny, Lycoming, Westmoreland** Armstrong County; 450 Market St; Kittanning, PA 16201; Ph. (724) 548-3256 **Details:** (County Registrar & Divorce has Birth, Death & Burial Records 1893–1905, Marriage Records from 1895, Probate & Land Records from 1805)
Beaver www.co.beaver.pa.us/	**R7**	**12 Mar 1800**	**Allegheny, Washington** Beaver County; 810 3rd St; Beaver, PA 15009-2187; Ph. (724) 728-3934 **Details:** (Registrar of Wills has Birth Records 1893–1906, Death Records 1852–1854 & 1893–1906, Marriage Records 1852–1854 & from 1886 & Probate Records from 1800; Divorce Deeds has Land Records from 1800; Prothonotary has Divorce, Court & Naturalization Records; Veterans Office has Military Records)
Bedford www.rootsweb.com/~pabedfor/bedford.html	**L9**	**9 Mar 1771**	**Cumberland** Bedford County; 230 S Juliana St; Bedford, PA 15522; Ph. (814) 623-4833 **Details:** (Prothonotary has Birth & Death Records 1852–1854 & 1893–1906, Marriage Records 1852–1854 & from 1885, Divorce Records from 1804, Probate & Court Records from 1771)
Berks www.co.berks.pa.us	**D8**	**1752**	**Lancaster, Philadelphia, Chester** Berks County; 633 Court St; Reading, PA 19601; Ph. (610) 478-6600 **Details:** (County Clerk has Birth & Death Records 1894–1905, Marriage Records from 1885 & Probate Records from 1752; Prothonotary Office has Divorce & Court Records; Divorce Deeds has Land Records)
Blair www.rootsweb.com/~pablair/	**K8**	**26 Feb 1846**	**Huntingdon, Bedford** Blair County; 423 Allegheny St; Hollidaysburg, PA 16648-2022; Ph. (814) 693-3000 **Details:** (Prothonotary Office has Divorce, Probate & Court Records from 1846, Naturalization Records from 1848, Marriage Records from 1885 & Birth & Death Records 1893–1905)

County Website	Map Index	Date Created	Parent County or Territory From Which Organized Address/Details
Bradford www.rootsweb.com/~pabradfo/bradweb.htm	F3	21 Feb 1810	**Luzerne, Lycoming** Bradford County; 301 Main St; Towanda, PA 18848-1884; Ph. (570) 265-1727 **Details:** (Formerly Ontario County. Name changed to Bradford 24 Mar 1812) (Prothonotary & Clerk Courts has Divorce Records from 1878, Court Records from 1813 & Naturalization Records 1832–1960; Registrar & Divorce Office has Birth & Death Records 1895–1905, Marriage Records from 1885, Probate & Land Records from 1812 & Military Records from 1940)
Bucks www.buckscounty.org/	B8	10 Mar 1682	**Original county** Bucks County; 55 E Court St; Doylestown, PA 18901; Ph. (215) 348-6265 **Details:** (Common Wealth of Pennsylvania has Birth & Death Records from 1910; Prothonotory Office has Court & Divorce Records; Register of Wills has Guardianship, Marriage, & Probate Records; Recorder of Deeds has Land Records)
Butler www.co.butler.pa.us/	P6	12 Mar 1800	**Allegheny** Butler County; 124 W Diamond St; PO Box 1208; Butler, PA 16001; Ph. (724) 284-5348 **Details:** (County Clerk has Birth & Death Records 1893–1906, Marriage Records from 1885, Divorce Records from 1805 & Naturalization Records from 1804; Orphans Court has Probate Records from 1804; Prothonotary Office has Court & Land Records from 1804)
Cambria www.co.cambria.pa.us/	M8	26 Mar 1804	**Somerset, Bedford, Huntingdon** Cambria County; 200 S Center St; Edensburg, PA 15931-1936; Ph. (814) 472-5440 **Details:** (County Clerk has Birth & Death Records 1893–1906, Marriage Records from 1885, Divorce Records from 1866, Probate Records from 1819, Court Records from 1849 & Land Records from 1846)
Cameron www.rootsweb.com/~pacamero/	K4	29 Mar 1860	**Clinton, Elk, McKean, Potter** Cameron County; 20 E 5th St; Emporium, PA 15834; Ph. (814) 486-2315 **Details:** (County Clerk has Birth & Death Records 1860–1905, Marriage, Divorce, Probate, Court & Land Records from 1860)
Carbon www.rootsweb.com/~pacarbon/	D6	13 Mar 1843	**Northampton, Monroe** Carbon County; 44 Susquehanna St.; PO Box 129; Jim Thorpe, PA 18229; Ph. (570) 325-5713 **Details:** (Register of Wills has Index to Wills & Administration from 1834, Birth & Death Records 1894–1905, Marriage Records from 1885; Prothonotary has Fictitious Names Records 1921–1979, & Naturalization Records 1843–1958; Clerk of Courts has Indexes to the Court of Quarter Sessions from 1843; Department of Health has Birth & Death Records from 1906)

County Website	Map Index	Date Created	Parent County or Territory From Which Organized Address/Details
Centre http://county.centreconnect.org/index.htm	**J6**	**13 Feb 1800**	**Lycoming, Mifflin, Northumberland** Centre County; Willowbank County Bldg; 414 Holmes Ave.; Bellefonte, PA 16823; Ph. (814) 355-6724 **Details:** (County Clerk has Birth & Death Records 1893–1905 & Marriage Records from 1885; Prothonotary Office has Divorce Records from 1890, Court & Naturalization Records from 1800; Registrar of Wills has Probate Records from 1800; Divorce Deeds has Land Records from 1801) *(Mailed a letter telling of their change of address, but did not return our requested information. Did give new address & phone number, inserted above)*
Chester www.chesco.org/	**D9**	**10 Mar 1682**	**Original county** Chester County; 601 W Town Rd; PO Box 2747; West Chester, PA 19380; Ph. (610) 344-6760 **Details:** (County Archives has Birth & Death Records 1852–1855 & 1893–1906, Marriage Records 1852–1855 & 1885–1930, Divorce Records 1804–1828, Probate Records 1714–1923, Court Records 1681–1900, Land Records 1716–1905, tax Records 1715–1939 & poorhouse Records 1798–1937)
Clarion www.co.clarion.pa.us/	**O5**	**11 Mar 1839**	**Venango, Armstrong** Clarion County; 421 Main St; Clarion, PA 16214-1028; Ph. (814) 226-4000 **Details:** (Registrar and Divorce has Birth & Death Records 1893–1906, Marriage Records from 1885, Probate & Land Records from 1840; Prothonotary Clerk has Divorce Records from 1880 & Court Records from 1874)
Clearfield www.landex.com	**L5**	**26 Mar 1804**	**Huntingdon, Lycoming** Clearfield County; 1 N Second St. Suite #103; PO Box 361; Clearfield, PA 16830; Ph. (814) 765-2641 Ext. 1850 **Details:** (County Registrar & Divorce has Birth & Death Records 1893–1905 & Marriage Records from 1885; Prothonotary Office has Divorce & Court Records from 1828; County Divorce has Probate Records from 1875; County Commissioner has Land Records)
Clinton www.clintoncountypa.com/	**J5**	**21 Jun 1839**	**Lycoming, Centre** Clinton County; County Courthouse; Lock Haven, PA 17745; Ph. (717) 893-4000 **Details:** (County Clerk has Birth, Marriage, Death, Divorce, Probate, Court & Land Records)
Columbia www.columbiapa.org/	**F5**	**22 Mar 1813**	**Northumberland** Columbia County; PO Box 380; Bloomsburg, PA 17815; Ph. (570) 389-5632 **Details:** (County Clerk has Birth & Death Records 1893–1905, Marriage Records from 1888, Court Records from 1814 & Divorce Records)
Crawford www.co.crawford.pa.us/	**Q3**	**12 Mar 1800**	**Allegheny** Crawford County; 903 Diamond Park; Meadville, PA 16335; Ph. (814) 336-1151 **Details:** (County Clerk has Birth, Death & Burial Records 1893–1905, Marriage Records from 1885, Divorce Records, Probate, Court & Land Records from 1800)

County Website	Map Index	Date Created	Parent County or Territory From Which Organized Address/Details
Cumberland www.co.cumberland.pa.us/	H9	**27 Jan 1750**	**Lancaster** Cumberland County; 1 Courthouse Sq; Carlisle, PA 17013; Ph. (717) 240-6370 **Details:** (Registrar of Wills has Birth & Death Records 1894–1905, Marriage Records from 1885 & Probate Records from 1750; Prothonotary Office has Divorce & Court Records from 1751; Divorce Deeds has Land Records from 1751)
Dauphin www.dauphinc.org/	G8	**4 Mar 1785**	**Lancaster** Dauphin County; Front & Market Sts; Harrisburg, PA 17101-2012; Ph. (717) 255-2692 **Details:** (County Clerk has Birth & Death Records 1893–1906, Marriage Records from 1885 & Probate Records from 1795; Prothonotary Office has Divorce & Court Records; Divorce Deeds has Land Records)
Delaware www.co.delaware.pa.us/	C10	**26 Sep 1789**	**Chester** Delaware County; 201 W Front St; Media, PA 19063; Ph. (610) 891-4260 **Details:** (County Clerk has Birth & Death Records 1893–1906, Marriage Records from 1885, Divorce Records from 1927, Probate Records from 1790, Court Records from 1897, Land Records from 1789, orphans Court Records from 1865 & delayed Birth Records 1875–1900)
Elk www.co.elk.pa.us/	M4	**18 Apr 1843**	**Jefferson, McKean, Clearfield** Elk County; Main St; Ridgway, PA 15853; Ph. (814) 776-1161 **Details:** (Registrar & Divorce has Birth & Death Records 1893–1906, Marriage Records from 1895, Probate Records from 1847 & Land Records from 1861; Prothonotary Office has Divorce & Court Records from 1843)
Erie www.eriecountygov.org/	Q2	**12 Mar 1800**	**Allegheny** Erie County; 140 W 6th St; Erie, PA 16501; Ph. (814) 451-6080 **Details:** (Courthouse burned 1824; all Records destroyed) (County Clerk has Birth & Death Records 1893–1905 & Marriage Records from 1885; Prothonotary Office has Divorce & Court Records from 1823; Registrar of Wills has Probate Records from 1823; Recorder of Deeds Land Records from 1823)
Fayette www.fforward.com/	P10	**26 Sep 1783**	**Westmoreland** Fayette County; 61 E Main St; Uniontown, PA 15401-3514; Ph. (724) 430-1206 **Details:** (Clerk Orphans Court has Birth & Death Records 1893–1905, Marriage Records from 1885 & Probate Records from 1784; Prothonotary Office has Divorce Records & Court Records from 1784; Divorce Deeds has Land Records from 1784)
Forest http://forestcounty.com/	N4	**11 Apr 1848**	**Jefferson** Forest County; 526 Elm St; PO Box 423; Tionesta, PA 16353; Ph. (814) 755-3526 **Details:** (County Registrar & Divorce has Birth Records 1893–1906, Marriage, Divorce & Land Records)

County Website	Map Index	Date Created	Parent County or Territory From Which Organized Address/Details
Franklin www.franklinco.pa.net/	**J9**	**9 Sep 1784**	**Cumberland** Franklin County; 157 Lincoln Way E; Chambersburg, PA 17201-2211; Ph. (717) 261-3805 **Details:** (County Clerk has Birth & Death Records 1894–1906, Marriage Records from 1885, Divorce Records from 1884, Probate & Land Records from 1785)
Fulton www.rootsweb.com/~pafulton/index.htm	**K9**	**19 Apr 1850**	**Bedford** Fulton County; 201 N 2nd St; McConnellsburg, PA 17233; Ph. (717) 485-4212 **Details:** (Clerk Orphans Court has Birth & Death Records 1895–1905, Marriage Records from 1885 & orphans Court Records from 1850; Prothonotary Office has Divorce & Court Records from 1850; Registrar of Wills has Probate Records from 1850; Divorce Deeds has Land Records from 1850)
Greene http://county.greenepa.net/	**R10**	**9 Feb 1796**	**Washington** Greene County; 93 E High St; County Office Bldg; Waynesburg, PA 15370; Ph. (724) 852-5281 **Details:** (County Clerk has Birth & Death Records 1893–1915 & Marriage Records from 1885; Prothonotary Office has Divorce Records from 1816 & Court Records from 1797; County Registrar has Probate Records from 1796; Divorce Deeds has Land Records from 1796)
Huntingdon www.huntingdoncounty.net/	**K8**	**20 Sep 1787**	**Bedford** Huntingdon County; 223 Penn St; PO Box 39; Huntingdon, PA 16652; Ph. (814) 543-1610 (Clerk of Court) ((814) 643-2740) **Details:** (Prothonotary/Clerk of Court has Court, Divorce, Naturalization & Citizenship Records from 1788; County Clerk has Birth Records 1894–1906, Death Records 1894–1905, Marriage Records from 1885, Divorce, & Probate Records)
Indiana www.rootsweb.com/~paindian/	**N7**	**30 Mar 1803**	**Westmoreland, Lycoming** Indiana County; 825 Philadelphia St; Indiana, PA 15701-3934; Ph. (724) 465-3860 **Details:** (Prothonotary & Clerk Courts has Divorce, Land & Court Records from 1807 & Naturalization Records 1806–1958; Registrar of Wills has Probate Records)
Jefferson	**N5**	**26 Mar 1804**	**Lycoming** Jefferson County; 200 Main St; Brookville, PA 15825; Ph. (814) 849-1610 **Details:** (Recorder of Deeds has Property Deeds, Maps, & Military Records from 1828; Register of Wills has Probate Records from early 1800's; Clerk of the Orphans' Court has Birth & Death Records 1893–1906, Marriage Records from 1885)
Juniata www.co.juniata.pa.us/	**I8**	**2 Mar 1831**	**Mifflin** Juniata County; Bridge St; PO Box 68; Mifflintown, PA 17059-0068; Ph. (717) 436-8991 **Details:** (County Clerk has Birth & Death Records 1893–1907, Marriage Records from 1885, Divorce Records from 1900, Probate, Court & Land Records from 1831 & Naturalization Records from early 1800's to 1930)

County Website	Map Index	Date Created	Parent County or Territory From Which Organized Address/Details
Lackawanna www.rootsweb.com/~palackaw/	**D4**	**21 Aug 1878**	**Luzerne** Lackawanna County; 200 Adams Ave; Scranton, PA 18503; Ph. (570) 963-6723 **Details:** (County Commisioner Office has Marriage, Divorce, Probate & Court Records from 1878)
Lancaster www.co.lancaster.pa.us/lanco/site/default.asp	**E9**	**1729**	**Chester** Lancaster County; 50 N Duke St; PO Box 3480; Lancaster, PA 17602-2805; Ph. (717) 299-8319 **Details:** (Registrar of Wills has Birth Records 1893–1905, Marriage Records from 1885, Probate & Court Records from 1729; Prothonotary Court has Records of Common Pleas Court & Divorce Records; Clerk Orphans Court has orphans Court Records; Divorce Deeds has Land Records from 1729; Court Common Pleas has Death Records 1894–1927)
Lawrence www.lawrencecounty.com/	**R6**	**20 Mar 1849**	**Beaver, Mercer** Lawrence County; 433 Court St; New Castle, PA 16101-3599; Ph. (724) 656-2127 **Details:** (County Clerk has Birth, Death & Burial Records 1893–1905, Marriage Records from 1893, Divorce & Court Records from 1855; Registrar & Divorce has Probate & Land Records)
Lebanon http://dfs.pacounties.org/lebanon/site/default.asp	**F8**	**16 Feb 1813**	**Dauphin, Lancaster** Lebanon County; 400 S 8th St; Lebanon, PA 17042-6794; Ph. (717) 274-2801, clerkofcourts102@lebcnty.org (Clerk of Court) **Details:** (Board of Assessment has Property & Tax Records; Clerk of Courts has Juvenile & Criminal Records; Register of Wills has Marriage, Probate, Adoption, & Guardianship Records)
Lehigh www.lehighcounty.org/	**C7**	**6 Mar 1812**	**Northampton** Lehigh County; 455 W Hamilton St; Allentown, PA 18105; Ph. (610) 782-3148 **Details:** (Clerk Orphans Court has Birth Records 1895–1905, Death Records 1893–1904 & Marriage Records from 1885; Prothonotary Court has Divorce & Court Records from 1812; Registrar of Wills has Probate Records from 1812; Divorce Deeds has Land Records from 1812)
Luzerne www.rootsweb.com/~paluzern/	**E5**	**25 Sep 1786**	**Northumberland** Luzerne County; 200 N River St; Wilkes-Barre, PA 18711; Ph. (570) 825-1585 **Details:** (Registrar of Wills has Birth, Death & Burial Records 1893–1906, Marriage Records from 1885 & Probate Records from 1786; Prothonotary Office has Divorce & Court Records; Divorce Deeds has Land Records)
Lycoming www.lyco.org/	**H4**	**13 Apr 1795**	**Northumberland** Lycoming County; 48 W 3rd St; Williamsport, PA 17701; Ph. (570) 327-2263 **Details:** (County Clerk has Birth Records 1893–1905, Death Records 1893–1898, Marriage Records from 1885, Probate Records from 1850 & Land Records from 1795; Prothonotary Court has Divorce & Court Records from 1795; The James V. Brown Library, 19 E. Fourth St., Williamsport, PA is the major source of Lycoming County genealogical info)

County Website	Map Index	Date Created	Parent County or Territory From Which Organized Address/Details
McKean www.rootsweb.com/~pamckean/	L3	26 Mar 1804	**Lycoming** McKean County; 500 W Main St; PO Box 202; Smethport, PA 16749; Ph. (814) 887-3260 **Details:** (Clerk of Orphans' Court has Marriage Records from 1885; Register of Wills has Wills from 1827; Birth & Death Records 1892 to 1905)
Mercer www.mcc.co.mercer.pa.us/	R5	12 Mar 1800	**Allegheny** Mercer County; 138 S Diamond St; Mercer, PA 16137; Ph. (724) 662-3800 **Details:** (County Clerk has Birth & Death Records 1893–1905, Marriage Records from 1885 & Probate Records from 1800; Prothonotary Office has Divorce & Court Records; Divorce Deeds has Land Records)
Mifflin http://mifflincounty.lcworkshop.com/	J7	19 Sep 1789	**Cumberland, Northumberland** Mifflin County; 20 N Wayne St; Lewistown, PA 17044; Ph. (717) 248-6733 **Details:** (County Clerk has Birth Records 1893–1905, Marriage Records from 1885, Probate & Land Records from 1789; Prothonotary Office has Divorce & Court Records)
Monroe www.co.monroe.pa.us/	C6	1 Apr 1836	**Pike, Northampton** Monroe County; 7 Monroe St; Stroudsburg, PA 18360; Ph. (570) 420-3710 **Details:** (County Clerk has Birth Records 1892–1905, Marriage Records from 1885, Court Records from 1845 & Divorce Records from 1900; Registrar of Wills has Probate Records; Divorce Deeds has Land Records)
Montgomery www.montcopa.org/	C8	10 Sep 1784	**Philadelphia** Montgomery County; Airy & Swede St; Norristown, PA 19404; Ph. (610) 278-3020 **Details:** (Clerk Orphans Court has Birth & Death Records 1893–1913 & Marriage Records from 1885; Registrar of Wills has Probate Records from 1784; Divorce Deeds has Land Records from 1784; Prothonotary Office has Divorce & Court Records from 1784)
Montour www.montourco.org/	G6	3 May 1850	**Columbia** Montour County; 29 Mill St; Danville, PA 17821-1945; Ph. (570) 271-3012 **Details:** (Prothonotary & Clerk Courts has Birth & Death Records 1893–1905, Marriage Records from 1885, Divorce & Court Records from 1850; Registrar of Wills has Probate Records; Divorce Deeds has Land Records)
Northampton www.northamptoncounty.org/	C7	1752	**Bucks** Northampton County; 7th & Washington St; Easton, PA 18042-7411; Ph. (610) 559-3000 **Details:** (Clerk Orphan Court has Birth Records 1893–1936 & Marriage Records from 1885; Prothonotary Office has Divorce & Court Records; Registrar of Wills has Probate Records; Divorce Deeds has Land Records)

Pennsylvania

County Website	Map Index	Date Created	Parent County or Territory From Which Organized Address/Details
Northumberland F6 www.northumberlandco.org/		21 Mar 1772	**Lancaster, Berks, Cumberland, Bedford, Northampton** Northumberland County; 2nd & Market St; Sunbury, PA 17801; Ph. (570) 988-4100 **Details:** (Registrar and Divorce has Birth & Death Records 1893–1905, Marriage Records from 1885, Probate & Land Records from 1772; Prothonotary Office has Divorce & Court Records)
Ontario		21 Feb 1810	**Luzerne, Lycoming** Ontario County; PA **Details:** (see Bradford) Name changed to Bradford 24 Mar 1812
Perry H8 www.perryco.org/		22 Mar 1820	**Cumberland** Perry County; PO Box 37; New Bloomfield, PA 17068; Ph. (717) 582-2131 **Details:** (County Clerk has Birth Records 1893–1918, Marriage Records from 1870 & Land Records from 1820; Registrar of Wills has Probate Records)
Philadelphia B9 www.phila.gov/		10 Mar 1682	**Original county** Philadelphia County; Broad & Market St; Philadelphia, PA 19107; Ph. (215) 686-1776 **Details:** (Clerk Orphans Court has Marriage Records; Prothonotary Office has Divorce & Court Records from 1874; Registrar of Wills has Probate Records; Department Records has Land Records)
Pike B5 www.pa-roots.com/~pike/		26 Mar 1814	**Wayne** Pike County; 506 Broad St; Milford, PA 18337-1511; Ph. (570) 296-7231 **Details:** (Clerk Commissioner has Birth & Death Records 1893–1905, Marriage Records from 1885, Divorce, Probate, Court & Land Records from 1814)
Potter J3 www.pottercountypa.net/		26 Mar 1804	**Lycoming** Potter County; 1 E 2nd St; Coudersport, PA 16915; Ph. (814) 274-8290 **Details:** (Prothonotary has Birth, Death & Burial Records 1893–1905, Marriage & Divorce Records from 1885; Registrar of Wills has Probate Records; Divorce Deeds has Land Records)
Schuylkill E7 www.co.schuylkill.pa.us/		1 Mar 1811	**Berks, Northampton** Schuylkill County; N 2nd St & Laurel Blvd; Pottsville, PA 17901; Ph. (570) 622-5570 **Details:** (Clerk Commissioner has Birth & Death Records 1893–1905, Marriage Records from 1885, Divorce Records from 1878, Probate, Court & Land Records from 1811)
Snyder H7 www.rootsweb.com/~pasnyder/		2 Mar 1855	**Union** Snyder County; 11 W Market St; Middleburg, PA 17842; Ph. (570) 837-4207 **Details:** (Clerk Courts has Birth, Death & Burial Records 1893–1905, Marriage Records from 1885, Divorce & Court Records from 1855; County Registrar & Divorce has Probate & Land Records; Susquehanna University Library in Selinsgrove has local Census Records)

County Website	Map Index	Date Created	Parent County or Territory From Which Organized Address/Details
Somerset www.rootsweb.com/~pasomers/	N9	**17 Apr 1795**	**Bedford** Somerset County; 111 E Union St; Somerset, PA 15501; Ph. (814) 445-5154 **Details:** (Registrar of Wills has Birth & Death Records 1893–1906, Marriage Records from 1885 & Probate Records from 1795; Divorce Deeds has Land Records from 1795 & Military Discharge Records from 1865; Prothonotary Office has Divorce & Court Records from 1795 & Naturalization Records 1795–1955)
Sullivan www.sullivancountypa.org/	F4	**15 Mar 1847**	**Lycoming** Sullivan County; Main & Muncy; Laporte, PA 18626; Ph. (570) 946-5201 **Details:** (Clerk Orphans Court has Birth & Death Records 1893–1905 & Marriage Records from 1885; Prothonotary Office has Divorce & Court Records from 1847; Registrar of Wills has Probate Records from 1847; Divorce Deeds has Land Records)
Susquehanna www.susquehanna.pa.us/	D3	**21 Feb 1810**	**Luzerne** Susquehanna County; County Courthouse; Montrose, PA 18801; Ph. (570) 278-4600 **Details:** (Registrar & Divorce has Birth & Death Records 1893–1906, Marriage Records from 1885, Probate Records from 1810 & Military Records from 1918; Prothonotary & Clerk Courts has Divorce Records from 1877, Court Records from 1812 & Naturalization Records 1844–1956)
Tioga www.rootsweb.com/~patioga/tiogaweb.htm	H3	**26 Mar 1804**	**Lycoming** Tioga County; 116 Main St; Wellsboro, PA 16901; Ph. (717) 724-1906 **Details:** (Registrar & Divorce has Birth & Death Records 1893–1905, Marriage Records from 1885, Probate Records from 1806, Land Records from 1807 & Military Records from 1868; Prothonotary & Clerk Courts has Divorce & Court Records from 1813 & Naturalization Records from 1818)
Union www.unionco.org/	H6	**22 Mar 1813**	**Northumberland** Union County; 103 S 2nd St; Lewisburg, PA 17837; Ph. (570) 524-8751 **Details:** (Prothonotary Office has Orphans Court Records from 1813, Marriage Records from 1885, Divorce Records, Death Records from 1852–1885 and 1893–1905, Birth Records from 1893–1905, Naturalization Records from 1813–1950, Census, Registrar has Wills & Letters of Administration from 1813, Deed Books, from 1813; Historical Society has Census, Tax Assessments, Agricultural Census, Manufacturers Reports, Mortality Reports, Social Security Records, Newspaper, Other Miscellaneous Records)
Venango www.co.venango.pa.us	P4	**12 Mar 1800**	**Allegheny, Lycoming** Venango County; 1168 Liberty St; Franklin, PA 16323; Ph. (814) 432-9534, sbuchan@co.venango.pa.us **Details:** (Clerk Courts & Divorce Deeds has Birth & Death Records 1893–1905, Marriage Records from 1885, Probate & Land Records from 1806, Divorce & Court Records)
Warren www.warren-county.net/	N3	**12 Mar 1800**	**Allegheny, Lycoming** Warren County; 204 4th Ave; Warren, PA 16365-2399; Ph. (814) 723-7550 **Details:** (Registrar and Divorce has Birth & Death Records 1893–1906, Marriage Records from 1885, Probate & Land Records from 1819; Prothonotary Office has Divorce & Court Records)

County Website	Map Index	Date Created	Parent County or Territory From Which Organized Address/Details
Washington www.co.washington.pa.us/	R9	28 Mar 1781	**Westmoreland** Washington County; 100 W Beau St; Washington, PA 15301; Ph. (724) 228-6723 **Details:** (Registrar of Wills has Birth & Death Records 1893–1906, Marriage Records from 1885 & Probate Records from 1781; Divorce Deeds has Land & Military Records from 1781; Prothonotary & Clerk Courts has Divorce & Court Records from 1781 & Naturalization Records 1802–1964)
Wayne www.co.wayne.pa.us	C4	21 Mar 1798	**Northampton** Wayne County; 925 Court St; Honesdale, PA 18431; Ph. (570) 253-5970 ext 212 **Details:** (Prothonotary Office has Birth & Death Records 1893–1906, Marriage Records from 1885, Divorce Records from 1900 & Court Records from 1798; Recorder of Deeds has Land Records from 1798; Register of Wills has Estate & Probate Records from 1798)
Westmoreland www.co.westmoreland.pa.us/index.shtml	O8	26 Feb 1773	**Bedford** Westmoreland County; 2 N Main St; Greensburg, PA 15601-2405; Ph. (724) 830-3000 **Details:** (County Clerk has Birth Records 1893–1905, Marriage Records from 1893 & Probate Records from 1800; Prothonotary Office has Divorce Records; Clerk Courts has Court Records; Registrar of Deeds has Land Records)
Wyoming www.wycopa.com/	E4	4 Apr 1842	**Luzerne** Wyoming County; 1 Courthouse Sq; Tunkhannock, PA 18657; Ph. (570) 836-3200 **Details:** (Clerk Courts has Birth & Death Records 1893–1905, Marriage Records from 1885, Divorce, Probate, Court & Land Records from 1842)
York www.york-county.org/	G10	1749	**Lancaster** York County; 28 E Market St; York, PA 17401; Ph. (717) 771-9675 **Details:** (County Clerk has Birth & Death Records 1893–1907, Marriage Records from 1885, Divorce, Court & Land Records from 1749; Registrar of Wills has Probate Records)

Rhode Island

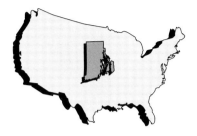

Hope

Capital: Providence
State: 1790 (13th)

Giovanni da Verrazano was the first proven explorer to visit Rhode Island, arriving at Block Island in 1524. The first non-Native American settler was the Reverend William Blackstone. He came from Boston to Cumberland in 1634. Two years later, Roger Williams established the first permanent settlement at Providence and bought land from the Indians to settle. Banned from the Massachusetts Bay Colony because of his religious and political views, Williams helped other refugees from the colony to settle in Rhode Island. Among these were Anne Hutchinson, John Clarke, and William Coddington. With Williams' help, Coddington bought the island of Aquidneck and founded Portsmouth. The next year, internal dissension led to the founding of Newport at the other end of the island. In 1642, Samuel Gorton settled Warwick. These four settlements united and sent Roger Williams to England to obtain a charter. The grant he obtained from Parliament in 1644 permitted them to choose their own form of government. In 1647, the four settlements created a government under the name of Providence Plantations. In 1663, King Charles II granted "Rhode Island and Providence Plantations" a new charter, which guaranteed religious freedom and democratic government.

Early settlers included Quakers and refugees from Massachusetts. The towns of Bristol, Little Compton, Tiverton, and Warren, all from Massachusetts, became part of Rhode Island in 1747. Newport became a shipping center due to the triangular trade between the West Indies and Africa. Rum was taken to Africa in exchange for slaves. These slaves were taken to the West Indies in exchange for molasses, which was taken to Newport to be made into rum.

Border disputes arose between Rhode Island, Massachusetts, and Connecticut. Rhode Island was the first colony to declare independence from England, in May 1776. The British occupied Newport for nearly three years during the Revolutionary War. Rhode Island was the last to accept the Constitution, fearful of a strong central government and high taxes.

Slavery was gradually abolished, starting in 1784. The decline in trade, agriculture (due to more fertile lands opening in the west), and whaling led to the growth of factories in the state. Thousands of foreign laborers entered the state to fill the new jobs. They were of all nationalities, but especially Italian, English, Irish, Polish, Russian, Swedish, German, and Austrian.

In 1843, the Freeman's Constitution was adopted, which entitled anyone born in the United States, instead of just landowners, to vote. During the Civil War, about 23,000 men served in the Union armed forces. In 1862, Rhode Island gained the town of East Providence and part of the town of Pawtucket from Massachusetts and gave Fall River to Massachusetts.

Look for vital records in the following locations:

- **Birth, death and marriage records:** Contact Rhode Island Department of Health, Division of Vital Statistics in Providence, Rhode Island. Town clerks have kept records of births, marriages, and deaths since the 1630's. The records are more complete after 1700. Statewide registration began in January 1853 with general compliance by 1915.

- **Divorce records:** The Supreme Court kept early divorce records. Those made before 1962 are at the Providence Archives, Phillips Memorial Library in Providence.

- **Census records:** Colonial censuses and lists exist for 1747 to 1754, 1774, and 1782. State censuses were taken at 10-year intervals from 1865 to 1935, but the 1895 census is missing. Originals are at the Rhode Island State Archives, State House in Providence. The Rhode Island Historical Society Library in Providence has one of the largest collections of early records in New England.

**Office of Vital Records Rhode Island
Department of Health**
3 Capitol Hill, Room 101
Providence, Rhode Island 02908-5097
(401) 222-2811
www.health.ri.gov/chic/vital/index.php

Rhode Island State Archives
337 Westminster Street
Providence, Rhode Island 02903
(401) 222-2353
www.sec.state.ri.us/Archives/

Providence Archives Phillips Memorial Library
River Avenue and Eaton Street
Providence, Rhode Island 02918

Rhode Island Historical Society Library
121 Hope Street
Providence, Rhode Island 02903

Societies and Repositories

American-French Genealogical Society; PO Box 830;
Woonsocket, RI 02895-0870; rogerafgs@home.com;
www.afgs.org.

Mayflower Descendants of Rhode Island; 128 Massasoit;
Warwick, RI 02903.

Newport Historical Society; 82 Touro St.; Newport, RI
2840.

Rhode Island Genealogical Society; PO Box 433;
Greenville, RI 2828; RIGenSociety@myfamily.com;
http://users.ids.net/~ricon/rigs.html.

Rhode Island Jewish Historical Association; 130 Sessions
St.; Providence, RI 2906; www.dowtech.com/rijha.

Rhode Island Office of Libraries and Information Services;
Ground Floor; One Capitol Hill; Providence, RI 02908;
(401) 222-5768; www.olis.state.ri.us.

Rhode Island State Archives and Public Records
Administration; 337 Westminster St.; Providence, RI
02903; (401) 222-2353; reference@archives.state.ri.us;
www.state.ri.us/archives.

Rhode Island State Historical Society; 52 Power St.;
Providence, RI 2906; www.rihs.org.

Sons of the American Revolution, Rhode Island Society;
PO Box 137; East Greenwich, RI 2818.

State Archives and Public Records Administration;
337 Westminster St.; Providence, RI 2903;
reference@archives.state.ri.us; www.state.ri.us/archives.

Bibliography and Record Sources

General

A Guide to Newspaper Indexes in New England. Holden,
Massachusetts: New England Library Association, 1978.

American Baptist Historical Society. *The Records of
American Baptists in Rhode Island and Related
Organizations.* Rochester, New York: American Baptist
Historical Society, 1981.

Arnold, Samuel Greene. *History of the State of Rhode
Island and Providence Plantations: 1636–1790.* 2 vols.
Spartanburg, South Carolina: The Reprint Co., 1970.

Austin, John Osborne. *The Genealogical Dictionary of
Rhode Island: Comprising Three Generations of Settlers
Who Came Before 1690 (with Many Families Carried to
the Fourth Generation).* Reprint with additions and
corrections. Baltimore: Genealogical Publishing Co.,
1978.

Bartlett, John Russell. *Bibliography of Rhode Island:
A Catalogue of Books and Other Publications Relating
to the State of Rhode Island, With Notes, Historical,
Biographical and Critical.* Ann Arbor, Michigan:
University Microfilms Inc., 1987. 3 microfiche.

Bates, Louise Prosser. *Bates Collection of Genealogical
Data of Rhode Island Families: with General Index to
Surnames, A–Z.* Salt Lake City: Filmed by the
Genealogical Society of Utah, 1950. Microfilm, 23 rolls.

Benns, Martha A. (Martha Adela Halton). *Rhode Island
Family Records: Vol. 1–3.* Salt Lake City: Filmed by the
Genealogical Society of Utah, 1950.

Bicknell, Thomas Williams. *The History of the State of
Rhode Island and Providence Plantations.* Tucson,
Arizona: Filmed by W. C. Cox, 1974.

*Biographical Cyclopedia of Representative Men of Rhode
Island.* 2 vols. Providence: National Biographical
Publishing Co., 1881.

Briggs, Anthony Tarbox. *Briggs Collection of Cemetery
Records, Wills, Record Books of Genealogy and
Scrapbooks of Vital Records and Historical Events: With
General Index to Surnames, A–Z.* Salt Lake City: Filmed
by the Genealogical Society of Utah, 1950. Microfilm,
24 rolls.

Brigham, Clarence Saunders. *Bibliography of Rhode Island
History.* Ann Arbor, Michigan: University Microfilms
Inc., 1987.

Brigham, Clarence Saunders. *Report on the Archives of
Rhode Island.* Ann Arbor, Michigan: University
Microfilms Inc., 1989.

Calef, Frank T. *Genealogical Index Rhode Island Records.*
Salt Lake City: Filmed by the Genealogical Society of
Utah, 1950. Microfilm, 41 rolls.

Chapin, Howard Millar. *Documentary History of Rhode
Island.* 2 vols. Providence: Preston and Rounds, 1916,
1919.

Conley, Patrick T. *An album of Rhode Island History, 1636–1986*. Norfolk, Virginia: Donning, 1986.

Cox, Lynn T. *Rhode Island Register*. S.l.: s.n., 19–.

Cullen, Thomas F. *The Catholic Church in Rhode Island*. North Providence, Rhode Island: Franciscan Missionaries of Mary, 1936.

Cutter, William Richard. *New England Families: Genealogical and Memorial*. 4 vols. 1913. Reprint. New York: Lewis Historical Publishing Co., 1914.

Farnham, Charles W. *Rhode Island Colonial Records*. Salt Lake City: Genealogical Society, 1969.

Field, Edward, ed. *State of Rhode Island and Providence Plantations at the End of the Century*, 3 vols. Boston: Mason Publishing Co, 1902.

Genealogies of Rhode Island Families: From Rhode Island Periodicals. 2 vols. Baltimore: Genealogical Publishing Co., 1983.

Greenlaw, William Prescott. *The Greenlaw Index of the New England Historic Genealogical Society*. 2 vols. Boston: G. K. Hall, 1979.

Hall, Lu Verne V. *New England Family Histories: States of Maine and Rhode Island*. Bowie, Maryland: Heritage Books, 2000.

Herndon, Richard. *Men of Progress: Biographical Sketches and Portraits of Leaders in Business and Professional Life in the State of Rhode Island and Providence Plantations*. Boston: New England Magazine, 1896.

Historical Records Survey (Rhode Island). *Inventory of the Church Archives of Rhode Island; Society of Friends*. Providence: The Survey, 1939.

Kirkham, E. Kay. *An Index to Some of the Bibles and Family Records of the United States*, vol. 2. Logan, Utah: Everton Publishers, 1984.

Munro, Wilfred H. *Memorial Encyclopedia of the State of Rhode Island*. Boston: American Historical Society, 1916.

New England Historic Genealogical Society. *English Origins of New England Families: From the New England Historical and Genealogical Register*. First Series, 3 vols., 1984. Second Series, 3 vols., 1985. Baltimore: Genealogical Publishing Co.

Parker, J. Carlyle. *Rhode Island Biographical and Genealogical Sketch Index*. Turlock, California: Marietta Pub. Co., 1991.

Parks, Roger, ed. *Rhode Island: A Bibliography of Its History*. Hanover, New Hampshire: University Press of New England, 1983.

Pierce, Ebenezer Weaver. *Civil, Military and Professional Lists of Plymouth and Rhode Island Colonies: Comprising Colonial, County, and Town Officers, Clergymen, Physicians and Lawyers . . .1881*. Reprint. Baltimore: Genealogical Publishing Co., 1968.

Representative Men and Old Families of Rhode Island: Genealogical and Historical Sketches of Prominent and Representative Citizens of Many of the Old Families, 3 vols. Chicago: J. H. Beers & Co., 1908.

Rhode Island Baptist State Convention. *Inventory of the Church Archives of Rhode Island (Baptist)*. Providence: The Survey, 1941.

Rhode Island Conference of Business Associations. *The Book of Rhode Island: An Illustrated Description of the Advantages and Opportunities of the State of Rhode Island and the Progress That Has Been Achieved, with Historical Sketches of Many Leading Industries and a Biographical Record of Citizens Who Have Helped to Produce the Superb Structure—Historical, Commercial, Industrial, Agricultural and Recreational—Which Comprises the Strength of this Charming State*. Providence: Rhode Island Conference of Business Associations, 1930.

Rhode Island Genealogies. S.l.: Brøderbund, 1996. CD-ROM.

Rhode Island Research Outline. Series U.S.-States, no. 40. Salt Lake City: Family History Library, 1988.

Rhode Island Society of Colonial Dames. *Genealogical Chart about Many Rhode Island families. Microfilm of Manuscripts in the Rhode Island Historical Society*. Salt Lake City: Filmed by the Genealogical Society of Utah, 1950. 3 microfilm.

Rhode Island State Archives, coll. *Certificates for Deputies and Freemen of Rhode Island Towns, 1663–1778*.

Rider, Fremont, ed. *American Genealogical-Biographical Index*. Vols. 1–186+. Middletown, Connecticut: Godfrey Memorial Library, 1952–. Salt Lake City: Filmed by the Genealogical Society of Utah, 1974.

Savage, James. *A Genealogical Dictionary of the First Settlers of New England*. 4 vols. 1860–1862. Reprint. Baltimore: Genealogical Publishing Co., 1965.

Short, Josephine Keefer and Mrs. Bentley W. Morse. *Rhode Island Bible Records*. Salt Lake City: Filmed by the Genealogical Society of Utah, 1950.

Sperry, Kip. *Rhode Island Sources for Family Historians and Genealogists*. Logan, Utah: Everton Publishers, 1986.

The Early Records of the Town of Providence, 21 vols. Providence: Snow and Farnham, City Printers, 1892–1915.

Works Projects Administration. *Inventory of Church Archives in Rhode Island: Baptist Bodies*. Providence: Historical Records Survey, 1939.

Atlases, Maps and Gazetteers

Cady, John H. *Rhode Island Boundaries, 1636–1936*. Providence: State of Rhode Island and Providence Plantations, 1936.

Gallagher, John S. *The Post Offices of Rhode Island*. Burtonsville, Maryland: The Depot, 1977.

Gannett, Henry. *A Geographic Dictionary of Connecticut and Rhode Island*. 1894. Reprint. Baltimore: Genealogical Publishing Co., 1978.

Long, John H. *Connecticut, Maine, Massachusetts, Rhode Island, Atlas of Historical County Boundaries.* New York: Simon & Schuster, 1994.

Merolla, Lawrence M., Arthur B. Jackson, and Frank M. Crowther. *Rhode Island Postal History: The Post Offices.* Providence: Rhode Island Postal History Society, 1977.

Pease, John Chauncey and John M. Niles. *A Gazetteer of the State of Connecticut and Rhode Island.* Hartford, Connecticut: Heritage Books, 1991.

Rhode Island—A Guide to the Smallest State. Boston: Houghton Mifflin Co., 1937.

Wright, Marion I., and Robert J. Sullivan. *Rhode Island Atlas.* Providence: Rhode Island Publications Society, 1982.

Census Records

Available Census Records and Census Substitutes

Federal Census, 1790, 1800, 1810, 1820, 1830, 1840, 1850, 1860, 1870, 1880, 1900, 1910, 1920, 1930

Union Veteran and Widows 1890

State/Territorial Census 1747, 1770, 1774, 1777, 1779, 1782, 1865, 1875, 1885, 1905, 1915, 1925, 1935

Bartlett, John R., comp. *Census of the Inhabitants of the Colony of Rhode Island and Providence Plantations, 1774.* Baltimore: Genealogical Publishing Co., 1969.

Beers, Daniel G. *Atlas of the State of Rhode and Providence Plantations.* Philadelphia: Pomeroy & Beers, 1870.

Chamberlain, Mildred M. *The Rhode Island 1777 Military Census.* Baltimore: Genealogical Publishing Co., 1985.

Dollarhide, William. *The Census Book: A Genealogist's Guide to Federal Census Facts, Schedules and Indexes.* Bountiful, Utah: Heritage Quest, 1999.

Kemp, Thomas Jay. *The American Census Handbook.* Wilmington, Delaware: Scholarly Resources, Inc., 2001.

Lainhart, Ann S. *State Census Records.* Baltimore: Genealogical Publishing Co., Inc., 1992.

Szucs, Loretto Dennis and Matthew Wright. *Finding Answers in U.S. Census Records.* Ancestry Publishing, 2001.

Thorndale, William and William Dollarhide. *Map Guide to the U.S. Federal Census, 1790–1920.* Baltimore: Genealogical Publishing Co., 1987.

United States. Census Office. *Rhode Island, 1790 thru 1840 Federal Census: Population Schedules.* Washington, D.C.: The National Archives, 1938, 1949, 1950, 1958–1961, 1969. 12 microfilm.

Court Records, Probate and Wills

Bartlett, John R. *Records of the Colony of Rhode Island and Providence Plantations in New England.* 10 vols. Providence: A. C. Green, 1856–1865.

Beaman, Nellie M. C. *Index of Wills, 1636–1850.* Vol. 16 in *Rhode Island Genealogical Register.* New Series. Princeton, Massachusetts: Rhode Island Families Association, 1992.

Calef, Frank T. *The Providence Probate Records to 1775 with Index.* Salt Lake City: Filmed by the Genealogical Society of Utah, 1950.

Field, Edward, ed. *Index to the Probate Records of the Municipal Court of the City of Providence, Rhode Island: From 1646 to and including the Year 1899.* Providence, Rhode Island: Providence Press, 1902.

Records of the Vice-Admiralty Court of Rhode Island: 1716–1752. Millwood, New York: Kraus Reprint, 1975.

Rhode Island Court Records: Records of the Court of Trials of the Colony of Providence Plantations, 1647–1670. 2 vols. Providence: Rhode Island Historical Society, 1920–1922.

Rhode Island General Court of Trials, 1671–1704. Boxford, Massachusetts: J. F. Fiske, 1998, 1998.

Rhode Island. General Council. *General Council Meeting Minutes and Documents.* Salt Lake City: Filmed by the Genealogical Society of Utah, 1974.

Rhode Island. Supreme Court. *Court Records, 1671–1879.* Microfilm of records in Newport, Rhode Island. Salt Lake City: Filmed by the Genealogical Society of Utah, 1973. 9 microfilm.

Wakefield, Robert S. *Index to Wills in Rhode Island Genealogical Register, vol. 1–4.* Warwick, Rhode Island: Plymouth Colony Research Group, 1982.

Emigration, Immigration, Migration and Naturalization

Bolton, Ethel Stanwood. *Immigrants to New England, 1700–1775.* Salem, Massachusetts: The Essex Institute, 1931.

Deputies & Freemen Index, 1664–1778 [i.e. 1806]. Microfilm of typed index cards at the Rhode Island State Archives in Providence at the statehouse. Salt Lake City: Filmed by the Genealogical Society of Utah, 1974. 3 microfilm.

Filby, P. William. *Passenger and Immigration Lists Index.* 15 vols. Detroit: Gale Research, 1981–.

List of American Seamen of Providence District Pursuant to the Act for the Relief and Protection of American Seamen: Found At U.S. Customs House, Providence, Rhode Island. Salt Lake City: Filmed by the Genealogical Society of Utah, 1950.

Taylor, Maureen. *Rhode Island Passenger Lists: Port of Providence 1798–1808: 1820–1872 and Port of Bristol and Warren 1820–1871.* Baltimore: Genealogical Publishing Co., 1993.

United States. Bureau of Customs. *Copies of Lists of Passengers Arriving at Miscellaneous Ports on the Atlantic and Gulf Coasts and at Ports on the Great*

Lakes, 1820–1873. Washington, D.C.: The National Archives, 1964.

United States. Bureau of Customs. *Passenger Lists of Vessels Arriving At Boston, 1820–1891: with Index 1848–1891.* Washington, D.C.: National Archives Record Service, 1959–1960.

United States. Immigration and Naturalization Service. *Passenger Lists, Providence, Rhode Island, 1911–1916; Book Indexes, 1911–1934; Card Indexes, 1911–1954.* Washington, D.C.: National Archives and Records Service, 1944–1945.

United States. Immigration and Naturalization Service. *Index to New England Naturalization Petitions, 1791–1906.* Washington, D.C.: National Archives. Central Plains Region, 1983. 117 microfilm.

United States. Immigration and Naturalization Service. *St. Albans District Manifest Records of Aliens Arriving from Foreign Contiguous Territory: Arrivals at Canadian Border Ports from January 1895 to June 30, 1954: Indexes (Soundex), 1895–1924.* Washington, D.C.: National Archives Records Service, 1986. Microfilm, 400 rolls.

Land and Property

Arnold, James N. *The Records of the Proprietors of the Narragansett, Otherwise Called the Fones Record.* Providence, Rhode Island: Narragansett Historical Publishing, 1894.

Dougine, Genevieve N. *Index to Rhode Island Land Evidences, 1648–1696: Also Record of Marriages, 1800.* Microfilm of manuscripts at the New York Genealogical and Biographical Society in New York. Salt Lake City: Filmed by the Genealogical Society of Utah, 1941.

Field, Edward. *Revolutionary Defenses in Rhode Island: An Historical Account of the Fortifications and Deacons Erected during the American Revolution, with Muster Rolls of the Companies Stationed along the Shores of Narragansett Bay: Preston and Rounds, 1896.* Salt Lake City: Filmed by the Genealogical Society of Utah, 1992.

Hone, Wade E. *Land and Property Research in the United States.* Salt Lake City: Ancestry Incorporated, 1997.

Land and Public Notary Records of Rhode Island, 1648–1795. Microfilm of manuscripts from the Rhode Island State Archives, Providence, Rhode Island. Salt Lake City: Filmed by the Genealogical Society of Utah, 1973. 4 microfilm.

Records of Rhode Island, 1638–1644. Microfilm of manuscripts in the Rhode Island State Archives in Providence, Rhode Island. Salt Lake City: Filmed by the Genealogical Society of Utah, 1974.

Rhode Island Miscellaneous Records, ca. 1600–1900. Salt Lake City: Filmed by the Genealogical Society of Utah, 1992.

Rhode Island. General Assembly. *Proceedings of the General Assembly: 1646–1851.* Microfilm of manuscripts in the Rhode Island State Archives in Providence. Salt Lake City: Filmed by the Genealogical Society of Utah, 1974. 18 microfilm.

Rhode Island. State Archives. *Rhode Island Militia and National Guard Enlistment Papers, 1890–1919.* Microreproduction of documents in State Archives, Providence, Rhode Island. Salt Lake City: Filmed by the Genealogical Society of Utah, 1993. 41 microfilm.

Worthington, Dorothy, comp. *Rhode Island Land Evidences, Vol. 1, 1648–1696.* Providence, Rhode Island: Rhode Island Historical Society, 1921. Reprinted with a preface by Albert T. Klyberg. Baltimore: Genealogical Publishing Co., 1970.

Military

Chapin, Howard Miller. *Rhode Island in the Colonial Wars: A List of Rhode Island Soldiers and Sailors in King George's War, 1740–1748.* Providence, Rhode Island: Rhode Island Historical Society, 1920.

Chapin, Howard Miller. *Rhode Island in the Colonial Wars: A List of Rhode Island Soldiers and Sailors in the Old French and Indian Wars, 1755–1762.* Providence, Rhode Island: Rhode Island Historical Society, 1918.

Cowell, Benjamin. *Spirit of '76 in Rhode Island.* Boston: A. J. Wright, 1850.

Index to Register of Seamen's Protection, 1796–1868. Microfilm of manuscripts at the Rhode Island Historical Society in Providence. Salt Lake City: Filmed by the Genealogical Society of Utah, 1974. 3 microfilm.

Military papers—War of 1812: 1792–1794, 1812–1815. Microfilm of manuscripts filmed at the Rhode Island State Archives in Providence. Salt Lake City: Filmed by the Genealogical Society of Utah, 1974. 2 microfilm.

Rhode Island. Adjutant General's Office. *Military Records, 1847–1900.* Microreproduction of documents at Rhode Island State Archives, Providence, Rhode Island. Salt Lake City: Filmed by the Genealogical Society of Utah, 1994. 7 microfilm.

Rhode Island. State Archives. *Card Index to Military and Naval Records, 1774–1805.* Microfilm of original records in the State Archives, Providence, Rhode Island. Salt Lake City: Filmed by the Genealogical Society of Utah, 1974, 1980. 19 microfilm.

Smith, Joseph J. *Civil and Military List of Rhode Island, 1647–1800.* 3 vols. Providence, Rhode Island: Preston and Rounds, 1901.

United States. Selective Service System. *Rhode Island, World War I Selective Service System Draft Registration Cards, 1917–1918.* National Archives Microfilm Publications, M1509. Washington, D.C.: National Archives, 1987–1988.

Walker, Anthony. *So Few the Brave: Rhode Island Continentals, 1775–1783.* Newport, Rhode Island: Seafield, 1981.

Vital and Cemetery Records

_____. *Index to Arnold's Rhode Island Vital Records: Rhode Island Cemetery Records.* Salt Lake City: Genealogical Society of Utah, 1950. Microfilm, 11 rolls.

Arnold, James N. *Coventry Rhode Island Headstone Inscriptions.* Salt Lake City: Filmed by the Genealogical Society of Utah, 1950.

Arnold, James N. *Vital Records of Rhode Island, 1636–1850: A Family Register for the People.* 20 vols. Providence, Rhode Island: Narragansett Historical Publishing Co., 1891–1912.

Beaman, Alden G. *Vital Records of Rhode Island, New Series.* 13 vols. Princeton, Massachusetts: the compiler, 1975–1987.

Benns, Charles P., and Martha A. Benns. *Rhode Island Cemetery Records, 1931–1941.* 6 vols. N.p., n.d. Salt Lake City: Genealogical Society of Utah, 1950. Microfilm.

Briggs, Anthony T. *Briggs Collection of Cemetery Records, Wills, Record Books of Genealogy and Scrapbooks of Vital Records and Historical Events.* Salt Lake City: Genealogical Society of Utah, 1950. Microfilm.

Brown, Clarence I. *Rhode Island Cemetery and Genealogical Records.* Salt Lake City: Genealogical Society of Utah, 1950. Microfilm.

Calef, Frank T. *Genealogical Index Rhode Island Records.* Salt Lake City: Filmed by the Genealogical Society of Utah, 1950. 42 microfilm.

Calef, Frank T. *Rehoboth Cemetery Records.* Salt Lake City: Filmed by the Genealogical Society of Utah, 1950.

Guide to the Public Vital Statistics Records: Births, Marriages, Deaths, in the State of Rhode Island and Providence Plantations. Providence: Historical Records Survey, 1941.

Miscellaneous Vital Records, 1700–1850. Microfilm of records in James Arnold's family notes—town notes collection at the Knight Memorial Library, Providence, Rhode Island. Salt Lake City: Filmed by the Genealogical Society of Utah, 1992.

Potter, Nellie Brownell. *Rhode Island Burial Grounds.* Salt Lake City: Filmed by the Genealogical Society of Utah, 1950.

Rhode Island Returns of Birth (1893–1898), Certificates of Death (1946–1948), Out of State Deaths (1946–1947), and out of State Death Index (1900–1948). Microreproduction of records at Rhode Island State Archives, Providence. Salt Lake City: The Genealogical Society of Utah, 1999. 24 microfilm.

Rhode Island. Department of State. Record Commissioner. *Guide to the Public Vital Statistics Records (Births, Marriages, Deaths) in the State of Rhode Island and Providence Plantations: Containing Chronologies of the Legislation Relating to or Affecting the Records Together with an Outline of the Civic Division of the State.* Providence: The Survey, 1941.

Rhode Island. Division of Vital Records. *Vital records & Indexes for Births, Deaths, and Marriages: 1853 Through 1900.* Microreproduction of computer printout at the Rhode Island Department of Health, Division of Vital Records, Providence. Salt Lake City: Filmed by the Genealogical Society of Utah, 1991. 72 microfilm.

Rhode Island. State Archives. *Deaths (1901–1943) and Index of Deaths (1901–1920).* Microreproduction of documents at Rhode Island State Archives, Providence, Rhode Island. Salt Lake City: Filmed by the Genealogical Society of Utah, 1993–1994. 158 microfilm.

Rhode Island. State Archives. *Delayed Births, 1846–1892, 1896–1898; Index 1846–1898.* Microreproduction of documents at Rhode Island State Archives, Providence, Rhode Island. Salt Lake City: Filmed by the Genealogical Society of Utah, 1994. 5 microfilm.

Snow, Edwin M., Charles V. Chapin, Dennett L. Richardson, and Michael J. Nestor. *Alphabetical Index of the Births, Marriages and Deaths Recorded in Providence.* 32 vols. Providence, Rhode Island, 1879–1946.

Torrey, Clarence Almon. *New England Marriages Prior to 1700.* Baltimore: Genealogical Publishing Co., 1985.

Turner, H. E. *Cemetery Records of Rhode Island.* Salt Lake City: Filmed by the Genealogical Society of Utah, 1950.

County Website	Map Index	Date Created	Parent County or Territory From Which Organized Address/Details
Bristol www.rootsweb.com/~ribristo/	I10	17 Feb 1747	**Newport** Bristol County; 1 Dorrance Plaza; Warren, RI 02885-4369; Ph. (508) 823-588 **Details:** (There is no County Clerk in Bristol County; Town & City Clerks have Birth, Marriage, Death, Burial & Probate Records; Clerk District Court has Court Records) (Four Towns in Bristol County) Towns Organized Before 1800: Barrington 1717, Bristol 1681, Warren 1746–1747
Kent www.rootsweb.com/~rikent/kent.html	I5	11 Jun 1750	**Providence** Kent County; 222 Quaker Ln; West Warwick, RI 2893; Ph. (401) 841-835 **Details:** (Town & City Clerks have Birth, Marriage, Death, Burial, Probate & land Records) (Five Towns in Kent County) Towns Organized Before 1800: Coventry 1741, East Greenwich 1677, Warwick 1642–1643, West Greenwich 1741
King's		3 Jun 1729	**Newport** King's County; RI **Details:** (see Washington) Name changed to Washington 29 Oct 1781
Newport www.rootsweb.com/~rinewpor/	K10	22 Jun 1703	**Original county** Newport County; 8 Washington Sq; Newport, RI 02840-7199; Ph. (401) 841-835 **Details:** (Formerly Rhode Island County. Name changed to Newport 16 Jun 1729. 1746–1747 eastern boundary adjusted under decree of the King of England) (City & Town Clerks have Birth, Marriage, Death & Burial Records; Family & Superior Courts have Divorce Records; Probate Court has Probate Records from 1784, District Court has Court Records; Recorder Deeds has land records from 1780; Newport Historical Society, 82 Truro St., Newport, RI has early church, land, & probate records) (Five towns & one city in Newport County) Towns Organized Before 1800: Jamestown 1678, Little Compton 1746–1747, Middletown 1743, New Shoreham 1672, Portsmouth 1638, Tiverton 1746–1747
Providence www.rootsweb.com/~riprovid/	E5	22 Jun 1703	**Original county** Providence County; 250 Benefit St; Providence, RI 2903; Ph. (401) 277-671 **Details:** (Formerly Providence Plantations. Name changed to Providence County 16 Jun 1729) (Probate Judge has Probate Records; Family Court has Divorce Records; Municipal Court has Court Records; Recorder Deeds has land Records; Town & City Clerks have Birth, Marriage & Death Records) (22 Towns in Providence County) Towns Organized Before 1800: Cranston 1754, Cumberland 1746–1747, Foster 1781, Glouchester 1730–1731, Johnston 1759, North Providence 1765, Providence 1636, Scituate 1730–1731, Smithfield 1730–1731,
Providence Plantations		22 Jun 1703	**Original county** Providence Plantations County; RI **Details:** (see Providence) Name changed to Providence County 16 Jun 1729
Rhode Island		22 Jun 1703	**Original county** Rhode Island County; RI **Details:** (see Newport) Name changed to Newport 16 Jun 1729

County Website	Map Index	Date Created	Parent County or Territory From Which Organized Address/Details
Washington www.rootsweb.com/~riwashin/riwash.html	L5	**3 Jun 1729**	

Newport
Washington County; 4800 Tower Hill Rd; Wakefield, RI 02879-2239; Ph. (401) 841-835

Details: (Formerly King's County. Name changed to Washington 29 Oct 1781) (Town & City Clerks have Birth, Marriage, Death, Probate & land Records) (Twenty Towns in Washington County)

Towns Organized Before 1800: Charlestown 1738, Exeter 1742–1743, Hopkinton 1757, North Kingstown 1641, Richmond 1747

South Carolina

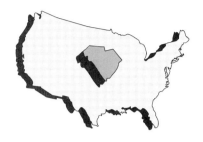

Capital: Columbia
State: 1788 (8th)

While I breathe, I hope
(Prepared in mind and resources)

The Spanish and French attempted to settle South Carolina, from its discovery in 1521 until 1663, but they failed. In 1663, King Charles II granted the territory between the 31st and 36th parallels, from ocean to ocean, to eight noblemen. The first permanent settlement, called Charles Town, was situated on the Ashley River. It was settled by a group from England and Barbados. A group of Dutch settlers came from New York after a few months, and were later joined by others from Holland. Ten years later, the town was moved to the present site of Charleston.

Other early settlers include Quakers in 1675, Huguenots in 1680, dissenters from the Episcopal Church in Somerset in 1683, Irish in 1675, and Scotch Presbyterians in 1684 who settled at Port Royal. In 1729, Carolina was divided into North and South Carolina. In 1732, part of South Carolina became Georgia. In 1730, the colonial government provided incentives for landowners in new townships, so settlers gathered along the banks of the Santee and Edisto Rivers. From 1732 to 1763, a number of families came from England, Scotland, Ireland, Wales, Switzerland and Germany into the central section of South Carolina. The "Up Country," or western half of the state, was first settled between 1745 and 1760 by immigrants from the Rhine area of Germany, the Northern American colonies, and the Ulster section of Ireland.

Battles with Spanish, French, Indians, and pirates occupied the settlers prior to the Revolutionary War. A treaty in 1760 ended the Cherokee War and opened up more land for settlement. With the offer of tax-free land for a decade, Scotch-Irish immigrants and settlers from other colonies swelled the western lands. South Carolina entered the Union in 1788 as the eighth state. Overseas immigration dwindled about 1815 and virtually ceased between 1830 and 1840. Political refugees from Germany immigrated to South Carolina in 1848.

South Carolina was the first state to secede from the Union in 1860. The first shots of the Civil War were fired by South Carolina troops on Fort Sumter on 12 April 1861. The state was devastated by General William Tecumseh Sherman during the war. An estimated 63,000 men served in the Confederate forces from South Carolina. Readmission to the Union came in 1868. After the Civil War, agriculture declined and employment shifted to the textile industry.

In 1769, nine judicial districts were established—Charleston, Georgetown, Beaufort, Orangeburg, Ninety-Six, Camden, and Cheraws. Records were kept at Charleston until 1780. In 1790, the capital was moved from Charleston to Columbia, although some functions remained at Charleston until after the Civil War. In 1795, Pinckney and Washington districts were created. Three years later the nine districts were divided into several more including the following:

- **Ninety-Sixth District:** Abbeville, Edgefield, Newberry, Laurens, and Spartanburg (all formed in 1795)
- **Washington District:** Pendleton and Greenville
- **Pinckney District:** Union and York
- **Camden District:** Chester, Lancaster, Fairfield, Kershaw, and Sumter
- **Cheraws District:** Chesterfield, Darlington, and Marlborough
- **Georgetown District:** Georgetown and Marion
- **Charleston District:** Charleston and Colleton
- **Orangeburg District:** Orangeburg and Barnwell

Districts were changed to counties in 1868.

Look for vital records in the following locations:

- **Birth and death records:** Contact the Office of Vital Records in Columbia, South Carolina and with individual county clerks for birth and death records from 1915 to present. City of Charleston birth records, beginning in 1877, are at the City Health Department. Death records for the city are also available from 1821.
- **Marriage and divorce records:** Contact the Office of Vital Records in Columbia for marriage records beginning with 1 July 1850. Marriage records from about July 1910, plus some in the early 1800's, are at the offices of Probate Judges in each county. Before

statewide registration, the ordinary of the province could issue a marriage license or banns could be published in a church. Some marriage settlements from the 1760's to the 1800's are at the South Carolina Department of Archives and History in Capitol Station, Columbia, South Carolina. Divorce was illegal in South Carolina until 1949. Proceedings are kept by the county court, but there are restrictions on availability.

- **Probate and court records**: Before 1732, the secretary of the province kept probate records. After that, they were kept by the clerks of ordinary and probate courts in each county.

- **Census records**: No colonial censuses remain. State censuses exist for 1829 (Fairfield and Laurens districts) and 1839 (Kershaw District) along with the 1869 population returns and 1875 agricultural and population returns. These are all kept at the South Carolina Department of Archives and History.

South Carolina DHEC Office of Vital Records

2600 Bull Street, Columbia
South Carolina 29201
(803) 896-6104
www.scdhec.net/vr/death.htm

South Carolina Archives and History Center

8301 Parklane Road
Columbia, SC 29223
(803) 896-6100; Fax (803) 896-6198
www.state.sc.us/scdah/

Societies and Repositories

Aiken-Barnwell Genealogical Society; PO Box 415; Aiken, SC 29802; lhutto@home.ifx.net; www.ifx.net/~lhutto/page2.html.

Allendale County Historical Society; PO Box 523; Allendale, SC 29810.

Anderson County Chapter, South Carolina Genealogical Society; PO Box 74; Anderson, SC 29622-0074; www.rootsweb.com/~scanders/andgensoc.html.

Beaufort Chapter, South Carolina Genealogical Society; PO Box 1070; St. Helena Island, SC 29920.

Bluffton Historical Preservation Society, Inc.; PO Box 742; Bluffton, SC 29910; www.heywardhouse.org.

Catawba Wateree Genealogical Society Chapter, South Carolina Genealogical Society; Camden Archives and Museum; 1314 Broad Street; Camden, SC 29020; CatawbaWatereeGS@aol.com; http://hometown.aol.com/catawbawatereegs/index.html.

Charleston Chapter, South Carolina Genealogical Society; PO Box 20266; Charleston, SC 29413-0266; sassy2sid@aol.com; www.scgen.org/charlestonmain.htm.

Chester County Genealogical Society; PO Box 336; Richburg, SC 29729.

Chesterfield District Chapter, South Carolina Genealogical Society; PO Box 167; Chesterfield, SC 29709-0167; (843) 623-2244; www.chesterfielddistrictchapter.org/chesterfieldsc.

Clarendon County Archives and History Center; 211 North Brooks Street; Manning, SC 29102; http://home.sc.rr.com/clarendonarchive.

Columbia Chapter, South Carolina Genealogical Society; PO Box 11353; Columbia, SC 29211-1353; ozzie_29223@yahoo.com; www.rootsweb.com/~scccscgs.

Darlington County Historical Commission; 204 Hewitt St.; Darlington, SC 29532; (843) 398-4710.

Dutch Fork Chapter, South Carolina Genealogical Society; PO Box 481; Chapin, SC 29036-0481.

Fairfield Chapter, South Carolina Genealogical Society; PO Box 93; Winnsboro, SC 29180; (803) 781-2679; JHollis@Conterra.com; www.rootsweb.com/~scfairfi/gensoc.html.

Greenville Chapter, South Carolina Genealogical Society; PO Box 16236; Greenville, SC 29606; www.greenvillegenealogy.org.

Greenville County Historical Society; PO Box 10472; Greenville, SC 29603-0472; www.greenvillehistory.org.

Hilton Head Island Genealogical Society Chapter, South Carolina Genealogical Society; 32 Office Park Rd Ste 300; Hilton Head Island, SC 29928-4640; (843) 785-6834; hhigs@heritagelib.org; http://ourtown.islandpacket.com/32.

Horry County Historical Society; 606 Main Street; Conway, SC 29526-4340; www.hchsonline.org.

Huguenot Society of South Carolina; 138 Logan St.; Charleston, SC 29401; huguenot@cchat.com; www.huguenotsociety.org.

Jasper County Historical Society; PO Box 2111; Ridgeland, SC 29936.

Kershaw County Historical Society; 811 Fair Street; PO Box 501; Camden, SC 29020; kchistory@mindspring.com; www.mindspring.com/%7ekchistory.

Laurens District Chapter, South Carolina Genealogical Society; PO Box 1217; Laurens, SC 29360-1217.

Lexington County, South Carolina Genealogical Association; PO Box 1442; Lexington, SC 29072.

Maj. General William Moultrie Chapter, Sons of the American Revolution; Charleston, SC; rmikell@aol.com.

Matthew Singleton Chapter, Sons of the American Revolution; Sumter, SC; flimfly@earthlink.net.

Old 96 Chapter, South Carolina Genealogical Society; 203 McElhaney Road; Travelers Rest, SC 29690; http://scgen.org/oldninetysix.htm.

Old Darlington District Chapter, South Carolina Genealogical Society; PO Box 175; Hartsville, SC 29551-0175; JAndr45985@aol.com; www.geocities.com/Heartland/Estates/7212.

Old Edgefield District Chapter, South Carolina Genealogical Society; PO Box 546; Edgefield, SC 29824-0546; www.rootsweb.com/~scedgefi/oedgs.html.

Old Newberry District Chapter, South Carolina Genealogical Society; PO Box 154; Newberry, SC 29108-0154; www.rootsweb.com/~scondc.

Old Pendleton District Chapter, South Carolina Genealogical Society; 228 Ivydale Drive; Greenville, SC 29609; http://oldpendleton.homestead.com.

Old St. Bartholomew Chapter, South Carolina Genealogical Society; 104 Wade Hampton Avenue; Walterboro, SC 29488; (843) 549-5757; osbcscgc@yahoo.com; www.rootsweb.com/~scosbc.

Orangeburg German-Swiss Genealogical Society; PO Box 974; Orangeburg, SC 29116-0974; www.rootsweb.com/~scogsgs.

Parris Island Historical and Museum Society; PO Box 5202; Parris Island, SC 29905-5202; www.parrisisland.com/historic.htm.

Pee Dee Chapter, South Carolina Genealogical Society; PO Box 1428; Marion, SC 29571-1428; http://scgen.org/peedee.htm.

Piedmont Historical Society; PO Box 8096; Spartanburg, SC 29305; fbjrgphs@spartanburg.net; www.angelfire.com/sc/piedmonths/info.html.

Pinckney District Chapter, South Carolina Genealogical Society; PO Box 5281; Spartanburg, SC 29304; www.scgen.org/pinckneymain.htm.

Saluda County Historical Society; PO Box 22; Saluda, SC 29138; www.saludaschistorical.org.

Sons of the American Revolution, South Carolina Society; 2805 Hwy. 414; Taylors, SC 29687.

South Carolina Department of Archives and History; Archives & History Center; 8301 Parklane Road; Columbia, SC 29223; (803) 896-6104; www.state.sc.us/scdah/homepage.htm.

South Carolina Division Sons of Confederate Veterans; 1309 Fairlawn Drive; Sumter, SC 29154; (803) 481-3223; scscvcommander@aol.com; www.scscv.org.

South Carolina Genealogical Society; PO Box 492; Columbia, SC 29202; scgen@peoplepc.com; www.scgen.org.

South Carolina Historical Society; 100 Meeting St.; Charleston, SC 29401; (843) 723-3225; info@schistory.org; www.schistory.org.

South Carolina State Library; PO Box 11469; Columbia, SC 29211; (803) 734-8666; www.state.sc.us/scsl.

Spartanburg County Historical Association; PO Box 887; Spartanburg, SC 29304; scha@mindspring.com; www.spartanarts.org/history.

Sumter County Genealogical Society Chapter, South Carolina Genealogical Society; 219 West Liberty Street; PO Box 2543; Sumter, SC 29151-2543; (803) 773-9144; SumterGenSoc@aol.com; www.rootsweb.com/~scscgs.

Three Rivers Historical Society; 414 N. Main St.; Hemingway, SC 29554; johnmgregg@threerivershistsoc.org; www.threerivershistsoc.org/index.htm.

Bibliography and Record Sources

General

Andrea, Leonardo. *Genealogical Correspondence: Collection of the Late Leonardo Andrea.* Microfilm of ms. and typescript collection in possession of Connie Andrea, Columbia, South Carolina. Salt Lake City: Filmed by the Genealogical Society of Utah, 1974. 21 microfilm.

Andrea, Leonardo. *Genealogical Folders in the Leonardo Andrea Collection: Collection of the Late Leonardo Andrea.* Microfilm of manuscript, typescript, and printed materials collection in possession of Connie Andrea, Columbia, South Carolina. Salt Lake City: Filmed by the Genealogical Society of Utah, 1974. 51 microfilm.

Austin, Jeannette H. *North Carolina—South Carolina Bible Records.* Riverdale, Georgia: J. H. Austin, 1987.

Bodie, Idella. *South Carolina Women.* 2nd ed. Orangeburg, South Carolina: Sandlapper Pub., 1991.

Carson, Helen C. *Records in the British Public Records Office Relating to South Carolina, 1663–1782.* Columbia, South Carolina: South Carolina Department of Archives and History, 1973.

Chandler, Marion C. *The South Carolina Archives: A Temporary Summary Guide.* 2nd ed. Columbia: South Carolina Department of Archives and History, 1976.

Cote, Richard N. *Local and Family History in South Carolina: A Bibliography.* Easley, South Carolina: Southern Historical Press, 1981.

Cote, Richard N. and Patricia H. Williams. *Dictionary of South Carolina Biography, vol. 1.* Easley, South Carolina: Southern Historical Press, 1985.

Cyclopedia of Eminent and Representative Men of the Carolinas of the Nineteenth Century. Madison, Wisconsin: Brant & Fuller, 1892.

Easterby, James H. *Guide to the Study and Reading of South Carolina History.* 2 vols. Columbia, South Carolina: Historical Commission of South Carolina, 1949–1950.

Hehir, Donald M. *Carolina Families: A Bibliography of Books about North and South Carolina Families.* Bowie, Maryland: Heritage Books, 1994.

Hemphill, James C. *Men of Mark in South Carolina . . . A Collection of Biographies of Leading Men of the State.* 4 vols. Washington, D.C.: Men of Mark Publishing Co., 1907–1909.

Hendrix, Ge Lee Corley. *Research in South Carolina.* Arlington, Virginia: National Genealogical Society, 1992.

Hicks, Theresa. *South Carolina: A Guide for Genealogists.* Rev. ed. Columbia, South Carolina: Columbian Chapter, South Carolina Genealogical Society, 1996.

Holcomb, Brent Howard. *A Guide to South Carolina Genealogical Research and Records.* Rev. ed. Columbia, South Carolina: Brent Howard Holcomb, 1991.

Jones, Lewis P. *Books and Articles on South Carolina History.* 2nd ed. Columbia, South Carolina: University of South Carolina Press, 1991.

Journal of the Commons House of Assembly, 1736–1754. Columbia: Historical Commission of South Carolina, 1951–.

Kirkham, E. Kay. *An Index to Some of the Family Records of the Southern States.* Logan, Utah: Everton Publishers, 1979.

Lester, Memory Aldridge. *Bible Records from the Southern States*, 7 vols. in 6. Chapel Hill, North Carolina: Memory Aldridge Lester, 1956–1962.

Lineage Charts South Carolina Genealogical Society Chapters. 4 vols. Greenville, South Carolina: Greenville Chapter, The South Carolina Genealogical Society, 1976–1987.

Mizell, M. Hayes. *A Checklist of South Carolina State Publications.* 3 vol. in 1. Columbia, South Carolina: Archives Department of South Carolina, 1962.

Moore, John Hammond. *Research Materials in South Carolina: A Guide Compiled and Edited for the South Carolina State Library Board with the Cooperation of the South Carolina Library Association.* Columbia, South Carolina: University of South Carolina Press, 1967.

Moore, John Hammond. *South Carolina Newspapers.* Columbia, South Carolina: University of South Carolina Press, 1988.

Neuffer, Claude. *Correct Mispronunciations of Some South Carolina Names.* Columbia, South Carolina: University of South Carolina Press, 1983.

Petty, Julian J. *The Growth and Distribution of Population in South Carolina.* Spartanburg, South Carolina: The Reprint Co., 1975.

Read, Motte Alston, comp. *Colonial Families of South Carolina.* Salt Lake City: Filmed by the Genealogical Society of Utah, 1952.

Rivers, William James. *A Sketch of the History of South Carolina to the Close of the Proprietary Government by the Revolution of 1719: With an Appendix Containing Many Valuable Records Hitherto Unpublished.* Charleston, South Carolina: McCarter & Co., 1856.

Sass, Herbert Ravenel. *The Story of the South Carolina Lowcountry.* 3 vols. West Columbia, South Carolina: J. F. Hyer Pub., 1956.

Schweitzer, George K. *South Carolina Genealogical Research.* Knoxville: the author, 1985.

Snowden, Yates and Harry G. Cutler. *History of South Carolina.* 5 vols. Chicago: Lewis Publishing Co., 1920.

South Carolina Genealogies: Articles from the South Carolina Historical and Genealogical Magazine. 5 vols. Spartanburg, South Carolina: The Reprint Co., 1983.

South Carolina Research Outline. Series U.S.-States, no. 41. Salt Lake City: Family History Library, 1988.

South Carolina. Department of Archives and History. *A Guide to Local Government Records in the South Carolina Archives.* South Carolina: University of South Carolina Press, 1988.

South Carolina. Department of Archives and History. *Combined Alphabetical Index, 1695–1925: Consolidated Index & Spandex.* Microreproduction of original manuscript at the South Carolina Department of Archives and History, Columbia, South Carolina. ca. 1992. S.l.: s.n., 199–. 19 microfilm.

Stampp, Kenneth M. *Records of Ante-Bellum Southern Plantations from the Revolution through the Civil War: Series A, Selections from the South Caroliniana Library, University of South Carolina.* Microfilm of original records in the South Caroliniana Library, University of South Carolina, Columbia, South Carolina. Frederick, Maryland: University Publications of America, 1985. 41 microfilm.

Stampp, Kenneth M. *Records of Ante-Bellum Southern Plantations from the Revolution through the Civil War: Series B, Selections from the South Carolina Historical Society.* Microfilm of original records in the South Carolina Historical Society. Frederick, Maryland: University Publications of America, 1985. 10 microfilm.

Stokes, Allen H. *A Guide to the Manuscript Collection of the South Caroliniana Library.* Columbia, South Carolina: The Library, 1982.

The Huguenots of South Carolina and their Descendants. Microfilm of originals in Charleston, South Carolina. Salt Lake City: Filmed by the Genealogical Society of Utah, 1952.

Wallace, David Duncan. *South Carolina: A Short History 1520–1948.* Columbia, South Carolina: University of South Carolina Press, 1951.

Weston, Plowden Charles Jennett. *Documents Connected with the History of South Carolina.* Woodbridge, Connecticut: Research Publications, 197–.

Wooley, James E., ed. *A Collection of Upper South Carolina Genealogical and Family Records.* 3 vols. Easley, South Carolina: Southern Historical Press, 1979–1982.

Atlases, Maps and Gazetteers

Black, James. "The Counties and Districts of South Carolina," in *Genealogical Journal, vol. 5, no. 3, pp. 100–113.* Salt Lake City: Utah Genealogical Association, 1976.

Cropper, Mariam D. *South Carolina Waterways as They Appear in Mill's Atlas.* Salt Lake City: Accelerated Indexing Systems, 1977.

Mills, Robert. *Atlas of the State of South Carolina.* Reprinted as *Atlas of the States of South Carolina, 1825.* Easley, South Carolina: Southern Historical Press, 1980.

Names in South Carolina, 1954–. Columbia: University of South Carolina, 1954–1983.

Neuffer, Claude H., ed. *Names of South Carolina.* Vols. 1–12, 1954–1965. Columbia: Department of English, University of South Carolina, 1967. Reprint. Spartanburg, South Carolina: Reprint Co., 1976.

Puetz, C. J., comp. *South Carolina County Maps.* Lyndon Station, Wisconsin: Thomas Publishing Co., 1989.

Salley, Olin J. *Post Offices of Yesteryear, Interesting Old Lists Reveals Many Unusual Place Names and Changes Wrought by a Century of Progress.* Salt Lake City: Filmed by the Genealogical Society of Utah, 1974.

Sheriff, G. Anne Campbell. *Pickens and Oconee Counties Post Offices, 1797–1971: Including South Carolina Post Offices, 1793–1832.* S.l.: Oconee County Historical Society, 1995.

Work Projects Administration. *Palmetto Place Names.* 1941. Reprint. Spartanburg, South Carolina: The Reprint Co., 1975.

Census Records

Available Census Records and Census Substitutes

Federal Census 1790, 1800, 1810, 1830, 1840, 1850, 1860, 1870, 1880, 1900, 1910, 1920

Federal Mortality Schedules 1850, 1860, 1870, 1880

Union Veterans and Widows 1890

Dollarhide, William. *The Census Book: A Genealogist's Guide to Federal Census Facts, Schedules and Indexes.* Bountiful, Utah: Heritage Quest, 1999.

Kemp, Thomas Jay. *The American Census Handbook.* Wilmington, Delaware: Scholarly Resources, Inc., 2001.

Lainhart, Ann S. *State Census Records.* Baltimore: Genealogical Publishing Co., Inc., 1992.

Szucs, Loretto Dennis and Matthew Wright. *Finding Answers in U.S. Census Records.* Ancestry Publishing, 2001

Thorndale, William and William Dollarhide. *Map Guide to the U.S. Federal Census, 1790–1920.* Baltimore: Genealogical Publishing Co., 1987.

United States. Bureau of Internal Revenue. *Internal Revenue Assessment Lists for South Carolina, 1864–1866.* Washington, D.C.: The National Archives, 1972.

Court Records, Probate and Wills

Esker, Katie-Prince Ward. *South Carolina Wills and Other Court Records.* Salt Lake City: Filmed by the Genealogical Society of Utah, 1998.

Gregorie, Anne King. *Records of the Court of Chancery of South Carolina, 1671–1779.* Washington, D.C.: American Historical Association, 1950.

Holcomb, Brent H. *Probate Records of South Carolina.* 3 vols. Easley, South Carolina: Southern Historical Press, 1977.

Houston, Martha Lou, comp. *Indexes to the County Wills of South Carolina.* 1939. Reprint. Baltimore: Genealogical Publishing Co., 1964.

Lesser, Charles H. *South Carolina Begins: The Records of a Proprietary Colony, 1663–1721.* Columbia, South Carolina: South Carolina Department of Archives and History, 1995.

Moore, Carolina T., and Agatha Aimar Simmons. *Abstracts of the Wills of the State of South Carolina.* 3 vols. Columbia, South Carolina: the compilers, 1960–1969.

Moore, Caroline T. *Records of the Secretary of the Province of South Carolina, 1692–1721.* Columbia, South Carolina: R. L. Bryan Co, 1978.

South Carolina Will Transcripts, 1782–1868. Columbia, South Carolina: South Carolina Department of Archives and History, 1978. 31 microfilm.

South Carolina. Court of Vice-Admiralty. *Pre-federal Admiralty Court Records, Province and State of South Carolina, 1716–1789.* Washington, D.C.: The National Archives, 1981. 3 microfilm.

Warren, Mary B. *South Carolina Jury Lists, 1718 Through 1783.* Danielsville, Georgia: Heritage Papers, 1977.

Warren, Mary B. *South Carolina Wills, 1670–1853, or Later: Compiled from C.W.A., W.P.A. Microfilms, and Original Volumes.* Danielsville, Georgia: Heritage Papers, 1981.

Young, Willie Pauline. *A Genealogical Collection of South Carolina Wills and Records.* 2 vols. 1955. Reprint, Easley, South Carolina: Southern Historical Press, 1981.

Emigration, Immigration, Migration and Naturalization

Baldwin, Agnes Lelans. *First Settlers of South Carolina 1670–1700.* Easley, South Carolina: Southern Historical Press, 1985.

Filby, P. William. *Passenger and Immigration Lists Index.* Detroit: Gale Research Co., 1981, 1985, 1986.

Holcomb, Brent H. *South Carolina Naturalizations, 1783–1850.* Baltimore: Genealogical Publishing Co., 1985.

Jones, Jack Moreland and Mary Bondurant Warren. *South Carolina Immigrants, 1760 to 1770.* Danielsville, Georgia: Heritage Papers, 1988.

Revill, Janie. *A Compilation of the Original Lists of Protestant Immigrants to South Carolina, 1763–1773.* 1939. Reprint. Baltimore: Genealogical Publishing Co., 1968.

Stephenson, Jean. *Scotch-Irish Migration to South Carolina, 1772.* Strasburg, Virginia: Shenandoah Publishing House, 1971.

United States. District Court (Alabama: Southern District). *Declarations of Intentions, Naturalizations, and Petitions, 1855–1960.* Microfilm of originals at the National Archives in East Point, Georgia. Salt Lake City: Filmed by the Genealogical Society of Utah, 1987–1989. 9 microfilm.

United States. District Court (South Carolina). *Record of Admissions to Citizenship, District of South Carolina, 1790–1906.* Microfilm of original records in the Federal Archives and Records Center, Atlanta, Georgia. Washington, D.C.: National Archives and Records Service, 1981.

United States. District Court. *Naturalization Records, South Carolina, 1790–1906.* Microfilm of originals at the National Archives in East Point, Georgia. Salt Lake City: Filmed by the Genealogical Society of Utah, 1987–1989.

United States. Immigration and Naturalization Service. *Index to Passenger Lists of Vessels Arriving at Miscellaneous Ports in Alabama, Florida, Georgia, and South Carolina, 1890–1924.* Microreproduction of original records at the National Archives. Washington, D.C.: Microphotographed by Immigration and Naturalization Service, 1957. 26 microfilm.

Warren, Mary Bondurant. *Citizens and Immigrants— South Carolina, 1768.* Danielsville, Georgia: Heritage Papers, ca. 1980.

Land and Property

Bleser, Carol K. Rothrock. *The Promised Land: The History of the South Carolina Land Commission 1869–1890.* Columbia, South Carolina: University of South Carolina Press, 1969.

Bratcher, R. Wayne. *Index to Commissioner of Locations, Plat Books A and B, 1784–1788: In Addition to Families Naming Swamps, Branches, Creeks, Ponds, Rivers, Roads, and Counties of the Lower Ninety-Six District from the Coast of South Carolina as Far Inland as There Were Settlements.* Greenville, South Carolina: A Press, 1986.

Charleston County (South Carolina), Register of Mesne Conveyance. *An Index to Deeds of the Province State of South Carolina, 1719–1785, and Charlestown District, 1785–1800.* Easley, South Carolina: Southern Historical Press, 1977.

Early South Carolina Settlers, 1600s–1800s. S.l.: Brøderbund, 2000. CD-ROM.

Esker, Katie-Prince Ward. *South Carolina Memorials, 1731–1776: Abstracts of Selected Land Records from a Collection in the Department of Archives and History.* 2 vols. New Orleans: Polyanthos, 1973–1977.

Holcomb, Brent H. *North Carolina Land Grants in South Carolina,* 2 vols. Clinton, South Carolina: the author, 1975, 1976.

Holcomb, Brent H. *Petitions for Land from the South Carolina Council Journals.* Columbia, South Carolina: SCMAR, 1996–1999.

Holcomb, Brent H. *South Carolina Deed Abstracts.* 3 vols. Columbia, South Carolina: SCMAR, 1996.

Hone, Wade E. *Land and Property Research in the United States.* Salt Lake City: Ancestry Incorporated, 1997.

Jackson, Ronald Vern. *Index to South Carolina Land Grants, 1784–1800.* Bountiful, Utah: Accelerated Indexing Systems, 1977.

Langley, Clara A. *South Carolina Deed Abstracts, 1719–1772.* 4 vols. Easley, South Carolina: Southern Historical Press, 1983–1984.

Lucas, Silas Emmett, Jr. *An Index to Deeds of the Province and State of South Carolina 1719–1785 and Charleston District 1785–1800.* Easley, South Carolina: Southern Historical Press, 1977.

Motes, Jesse Hogan. *South Carolina Memorials, Abstracts of Land Titles.* Greenville, South Carolina: Southern Historical Press, 1996.

Salley, A. S., Jr., and R. N. Olsberg, eds. *Warrants for Land in South Carolina 1672–1711.* Rev. ed. Columbia, South Carolina: University of South Carolina Press, 1973.

Salley, Alexander S. *Records of the Secretary of the Province and the Register of the Province of South Carolina, 1671–1675.* Columbia, South Carolina: Historical Commission of South Carolina, 1944.

Smith, William Roy. *South Carolina as a Royal Province, 1719–1776.* New York: Macmillan, 1903.

South Carolina Memorials; Registration of Land Grants, 1704–1776 and Index. Salt Lake City: Genealogical Society of Utah, 1950. 9 microfilm.

South Carolina. Secretary of State. *Miscellaneous Records, 1771–1868.* Microfilm of original records filmed at the Historical Commission of South Carolina located in Columbia, South Carolina. Salt Lake City: Filmed by the Genealogical Society of Utah, 1950–1951. 56 microfilm.

South Carolina. Secretary of State. *Mortgage Records, 1734–1860; Index, 1709–1840.* Microfilm of original records filmed at the Historical Commission in Columbia, South Carolina. Salt Lake City: Filmed by the Genealogical Society of Utah, 1951. 27 microfilm.

South Carolina. Secretary of State. *Royal Land Grants, 1731–1775; Index, 1695–1775.* Microfilm of original records filmed at the Secretary of State's Office in Columbia, South Carolina. Salt Lake City: Filmed by the Genealogical Society of Utah, 1951. 17 microfilm.

South Carolina. Surveyor General. *Land Grants, 1784–1882.* Microfilm of original records filmed in the Secretary of State's Office at Columbia, South Carolina. Salt Lake City: Filmed by the Genealogical Society of Utah, 1950–1951. 50 microfilm.

South Carolina. Surveyor General. *South Carolina Land Plats, 1731–1861; Indexes, 1688–1872.* Microfilm of original records filmed at the Secretary of State's Office in Columbia, South Carolina. Salt Lake City: Filmed by the Genealogical Society of Utah, 1950. 28 microfilm.

Military

Andrea, Leonardo. *South Carolina Colonial Soldiers and Patriots.* Columbia, South Carolina: N.p., 1952.

Clark, Murtie June, comp. *Colonial Soldiers of the South, 1732–1774.* Baltimore: Genealogical Publishing Co., 1983.

Ervin, Sara A., ed. *South Carolinians in the Revolution, with Service Records and Miscellaneous Data . . . 1775–1855.* Ypsilanti, Michigan. 1959. Reprint. Baltimore: Genealogical Publishing Co., 1971.

Ervin, Sara Sullivan. *South Carolinians in the Revolution.* 1949. Reprint. Baltimore: Genealogical Publishing Co., 1965.

Flynn, Jean Martin. *The Militia in Antebellum South Carolina Society.* Spartanburg, South Carolina: The Reprint Co., ca. 1991.

Haulsee, W. M., F. C. Howe, and Alfred C. Doyle. *Soldiers of the Great War*, 3 vols. Washington, D.C.: Soldiers Record Publishing Association, 1920.

Meyer, Jack Allen. *South Carolina in the Mexican War: A Regiment of Volunteers, 1846–1917.* Columbia, South Carolina: South Carolina Department of Archives and History, 1996.

Moss, Bobby Gilmer. *Roster of South Carolina Patriots in the American Revolution.* Baltimore: Genealogical Publishing Co., 1983.

Pierce, Alycon Trubey. *South Carolina Revolutionary Records, Selected Final Pension Payment Vouchers, 1818–1864*: South Carolina: Charleston. Athens, Georgia: Iberian Pub. Co., 1996.

Pruitt, Janye C. G. *Revolutionary War Pension Applicants Who Served from South Carolina.* N.p.: 1946.

Revill, Janie. *Copy of the Original Index Book Showing the Revolutionary Claims Filed in South Carolina between August 20, 1783 and August 31, 1786, 1941.* Reprint. Baltimore: Genealogical Publishing Co., 1969.

Salley, A. S., Jr. *South Carolina Troops in Confederate Service.* Columbia, South Carolina: R. L. Bryan, 1913–1930.

Salley, Alexander S., comp. *Records of the Regiments of the South Carolina Line in the Revolutionary War.* Clearfield Company, 2005.

South Carolina, Department of Archives and History. *Stub Entries to Indents Issues in Payment of Claims Against South Carolina Growing Out of the Revolution.* 12 vols. Columbia, South Carolina, 1919–1957.

United Daughters of the Confederacy. *South Carolina Division. Recollections and Reminiscences, 1861–1865 through World War.* S.l.: The Society, ca. 1990–.

United States. Adjutant General's Office. *Index to Compiled Service Records of Confederate Soldiers Who Served in Organizations from the State of South Carolina.* Washington, D.C.: The National Archives, 1962. 35 microfilm.

United States. Adjutant General's Office. *Index to Compiled Service Records of Volunteer Soldiers Who Served During the War of 1812 in Organizations from the State of South Carolina.* Washington, D.C.: The National Archives, 1966. 7 microfilm.

United States. Selective Service System. *South Carolina, World War I Selective Service System Draft Registration Cards, 1917–1918.* National Archives Microfilm Publications, M1509. Washington, D.C.: National Archives, 1987–1988.

Vital and Cemetery Records

Cemetery Records of Confederate Soldiers Buried in South Carolina. Typescript. Salt Lake City: Genealogical Society of Utah, 1947.

Clemens, William M. *North and South Carolina Marriage Records: From the Earliest Colonial Days to the Civil War.* Baltimore, Maryland: Genealogical Publishing Company, 1981.

Holcomb, Brent H. *South Carolina Marriages: 1688–1799.* 3 vols. Baltimore: Genealogical Publishing Co., 1980–1981, 1984.

Holcomb, Brent H. *Supplement to South Carolina Marriages, 1688–1820.* Baltimore: Genealogical Publishing Co., 1984.

Huey, Olga Crosland. *South Carolina Cemetery Epitaphs.* Microfilm. Salt Lake City: Genealogical Society of Utah, 1974.

King, Susan L. *Charleston, South Carolina, Marriages 1877–1895.*

South Carolina Cemetery Records, 3 vols. Salt Lake City: Genealogical Society, 1941–1954.

South Carolina Marriage Settlements, 1785–1889. Microfilm of originals in Columbia, South Carolina. Salt Lake City: Filmed by the Genealogical Society of Utah, 1950. 9 microfilm.

South Carolina. State Board of Health. *Death Certificate Indexes, 1915–1944.* Columbia, South Carolina. Columbia, South Carolina: State Records Center. 53 microfiche.

South Carolina. State Board of Health. *South Carolina Death Certificates, 1915–1944.* Columbia, South Carolina. Columbia, South Carolina: State Records Center. 418 microfilm.

Works Progress Administration, South Carolina Historical Records Survey. *Index to Tombstone Inscriptions, 1930s.* Spartanburg, North Carolina: Historical Records Survey, n.d.

County Website	Map Index	Date Created	Parent County or Territory From Which Organized Address/Details
Abbeville www.sccounties.org/counties/abbeville.htm	**O4**	**12 Mar 1785**	**District 96** Abbeville County; 102 Court Sq; PO Box 99; Abbeville, SC 29620-0099; Ph. (864) 459-5074 **Details:** (Clerk Court has Land Records from 1873, Divorce & Court Records; Probate Judge has Marriage & Probate Records)
Aiken www.aikencounty.net/	**M7**	**10 Mar 1871**	**Edgefield, Orangeburg, Barnwell, Lexington** Aiken County; 828 Richland Ave W; Aiken, SC 29801-3834; Ph. (803) 642-1715 **Details:** (County Health Department has Birth & Death Records; Probate Judge has Marriage Records from 1911 & Probate Records from 1875; Clerk Court has Divorce, Court & Land Records)
Allendale www.allendalecounty.com/	**L9**	**6 Feb 1919**	**Barnwell, Hampton** Allendale County; 526 Memorial Ave; PO Box 126; Allendale, SC 29810-0126; Ph. (803) 584-2737 **Details:** (Probate Judge has Marriage & Probate Records; Clerk Courts has Court & Land Records)
Anderson www.andersoncountysc.org/	**P3**	**20 Dec 1826**	**Pendleton District** Anderson County; 100 S Main St; PO Box 8002; Anderson, SC 29624; Ph. (864) 260-4053 **Details:** (County Health Department has Birth, Death & Burial Records; Probate Judge has Marriage & Probate Records; Clerk Court has Divorce Records from 1949, Land Records from 1788 & Court Records)
Bamberg www.sccounties.org/counties/Bamberg.htm	**K8**	**25 Feb 1897**	**Barnwell** Bamberg County; 110 N Main St; PO Box 150; Bamberg, SC 29003-0150; Ph. (803) 245-3025 **Details:** (Clerk Court has Divorce, Court & Land Records; Probate Judge has Marriage & Probate Records; County Health Department has Birth & Death Records)
Barnwell www.sccounties.org/counties/Barnwell.htm	**L8**	**1798**	**Orangeburg District** Barnwell County; Main St; PO Box 723; Barnwell, SC 29812-0723; Ph. (803) 541-1020 **Details:** (County Clerk has Court & Land Records from mid-1700's & Divorce Records; Probate Judge has Marriage & Probate Records)
Beaufort www.co.beaufort.sc.us/	**J12**	**1769**	**Granville** Beaufort County; 100 Ribaut Rd; Beaufort, SC 29902; Ph. (843) 470-5227 **Details:** (Created 1769 from Granville County as an original judicial district) (County Clerk has Birth & Death Records from 1915; Probate Judge has Marriage & Probate Records; Records prior to 1785 are filed in Charleston)
Berkeley www.berkeley.Library.sc.us/gov.html	**G8**	**31 Jan 1882**	**Charleston** Berkeley County; 223 N Live Oak Dr; Moncks Corner, SC 29461-3707; Ph. (843) 761-6900 **Details:** (Clerk Court has Divorce, Court & Land Records; Probate Judge has Marriage & Probate Records; County Health Department has Birth, Death & Burial Records)
Berkeley, old		**1683**	**Original county (not present Berkeley County.)** Berkeley, old County; SC **Details:** (One of 4 original counties. Discontinued, 1769)

County Website	Map Index	Date Created	Parent County or Territory From Which Organized Address/Details
Calhoun www.sccounties.org/counties/calhoun.htm	J6	14 Feb 1908	**Lexington, Orangeburg** Calhoun County; 302 S Huff Dr.; St. Matthews, SC 29135; Ph. (803) 874-3524 **Details:** (Probate Judge has Marriage Records 1911–1956 & Probate Records 1908–1950; Department of Health has Birth & Death Records from 1915; Clerk of Courts has Court Records from 1908 & Divorce Records from 1949; Historical Commission has Land, Bible, & Cemetery Records from 1735)
Camden District		1769	**Craven, Berkeley, old** Camden District County; SC **Details:** (Created from portions of Berkeley, old & Craven Counties as one of 7 original judicial districts. Discontinued in 1798 to form Chester, Lancaster, Fairfield, Kershaw & Sumter Counties)
Carteret District		1685	**Unorganized Territory** Carteret District County; SC **Details:** (Name changed to Granville 1700)
Charleston www.charlestoncounty.org/	H10	1769	**Colleton, Berkeley, old** Charleston County; 2144 Melbourne Ave; Charleston, SC 29405; Ph. (843) 740-5700 **Details:** (Created in 1769 from portions of Colleton & Berkeley, old, as one of 7 original judicial districts; Split in 1798 to form Charleston & Colleton Counties) (County Health Department has Birth & Death Records; Probate Judge has Marriage, Probate & Court Records; Clerk Court has Divorce Records; County Registrar has Land Records)
Cheraws District			**1769 Craven** Cheraws District County; SC **Details:** County Terminated 1800 (Created in 1769 from Craven County as one of 7 original judicial districts. Discontinued in 1798 to form Chesterfield, Darlington & Marlboro Counties)
Cherokee www.sccounties.org/counties/Cherokee.htm	L1	25 Feb 1897	**Union, York, Spartanburg** Cherokee County; 125 E Floyd Baker Blvd; PO Box Drawer 2289; Gaffney, SC 29340; Ph. (864) 487-2574 **Details:** (County Health Department has Birth & Death Records; Probate Judge has Marriage & Probate Records; Clerk Court has Divorce, Court & Land Records)
Chester www.sccounties.org/counties/Chester.htm	K3	1785	**Camden District** Chester County; 140 Main St; PO Box Drawer 580; Chester, SC 29706; Ph. (803) 385-2605 **Details:** (Probate Judge has Probate Records from 1789 & Marriage Records from 1911; Clerk Court has Land Records from 1785, Divorce & Court Records)
Chesterfield www.sccounties.org/counties/Chesterfield.htm	H3	1785	**Cheraws District** Chesterfield County; 200 W Main St; PO Box 529; Chesterfield, SC 29709; Ph. (843) 623-2574, clerkofcourt4@yahoo.com **Details:** (Health Department has Birth & Death Records; Clerk has Military, Land, & Divorce Records; Probate's Office has Marriage Records; Library has other Historical Records)
Claremont		1785	Claremont County; SC **Details:** (see Sumter) County Terminated 1800

County Website	Map Index	Date Created	Parent County or Territory From Which Organized Address/Details
Clarendon www.clarendoncounty.com/	**H6**	1855	**Sumter District** Clarendon County; W Boyce St; PO Box E; Manning, SC 29102-0136; Ph. (803) 435-4443 **Details:** (Census schedules missing for 1820, 1830, 1840 & 1850) (County Health Department has Birth, Death & Burial Records from 1915; Probate Judge has Marriage Records from 1911 & Probate Records from 1856; Clerk Court has Divorce Records from 1947, Court & Land Records from 1856)
Colleton www.sccounties.org/counties/Colleton.htm	**I9**	1798	**Charleston District** Colleton County; PO Box 620; Walterboro, SC 29488; Ph. (843) 549-5791 **Details:** (Probate Court has Marriage Records from 1911 & Probate Records from 1865; County Health Department has Birth & Death Records from 1915; Clerk Court has Divorce Records from 1949, Land & Court Records from 1865; Veterans Affairs Office has Military Records from 1865; County Library has Cemetery & other genealogical Records; Records prior to 1785 are filed)
Colleton (old)		1682	**Original county** Colleton, old County; SC **Details:** (One of 4 original counties. Discontinued, 1769)
Craven (old)		1682	**Original county** Craven, old County; SC **Details:** (One of 4 original counties. Terminated 1800)
Darlington www.sccounties.org/counties/Darlington.htm	**G4**	1785	**Cheraws District** Darlington County; 1 Public Sq; Darlington, SC 29532; Ph. (843) 398-4330 **Details:** (County Clerk has Marriage Records from 1912, Divorce Records from 1950, Land Records from 1806 & Court Records; Probate Judge has Marriage & Probate Records)
Dillon www.sccounties.org/counties/Dillon.htm	**E4**	5 Feb 1910	**Marion** Dillon County; PO Drawer 1220; Dillon, SC 29536-0449; Ph. (843) 774-1425 **Details:** (Clerk Courts has Court & Land Records from 1910; Probate Judge has Marriage & Probate Records)
Dorchester www.sccounties.org/counties/Dorchester.htm	**I8**	25 Feb 1897	**Berkeley, Colleton** Dorchester County; PO Box 158; St. George, SC 29477; Ph. (843) 563-0120 **Details:** (County Clerk has Birth Records from 1915; Probate Judge has Marriage & Probate Records)
Edgefield www.edgefieldcounty.org/	**N6**	1785	**District 96** Edgefield County; 129 Courthouse Sq; Edgefield, SC 29824-0663; Ph. (803) 637-4080 **Details:** (small portion of Aiken County added to Edgefield in 1966) (County Health Department has Birth, Death & Burial Records; Probate Judge has Marriage & Probate Records; County Clerk has Land, Divorce & Court Records)

County Website	Map Index	Date Created	Parent County or Territory From Which Organized Address/Details
Fairfield www.sccounties.org/counties/Fairfield.htm	K3	1785	**Camden District** Fairfield County; PO Drawer 299; Winnsboro, SC 29180; Ph. (803) 712-6526 **Details:** (Clerk Court has Divorce, Land & Court Records; County Health Department has Birth & Death Records; Probate Judge has Marriage & Probate Records)
Florence www.florenceco.org/index.html	E5	22 Dec 1888	**Marion, Darlington, Clarendon, Williamsburg** Florence County; 180 N Irby St; Florence, SC 29501-3456; Ph. (843) 665-3031 **Details:** (County Health Department has Birth & Death Records; Probate Judge has Marriage & Probate Records; Clerk Court has Divorce, Court & Land Records)
Georgetown www.co.georgetown.sc.us/	E7	1769	**Craven** Georgetown County; 715 Prince St; Georgetown, SC 29440-3631; Ph. (843) 546-5011 **Details:** (Created in 1769 from Craven County as one of 7 original judicial districts; Split in 1798 to form Georgetown & Marion Counties) (County Health Department has Birth & Death Records; Probate Judge has Marriage Records from 1911 & Probate Records; Clerk Court has Divorce Records from 1949, Land Records from 1866 & Court Records; Records prior to 1785 are filed in Charleston)
Granville www.co.greenville.sc.us/		1683	**Original county** Granville County; SC **Details:** (One of 4 original counties. Discontinued, 1769; Formerly Carteret County 1685–1708)
Greenville www.co.greenville.sc.us/	O2	1786	**Washington District** Greenville County; 301 University Ridge Ste 100; Greenville, SC 29601-3665; Ph. (864) 467-8551 **Details:** (Clerk Court has Birth & Death Records from 1915, Marriage Records from 1911, Divorce & Probate Records)
Greenwood www.co.greenwood.sc.us/	N5	2 Mar 1897	**Abbeville, Edgefield** Greenwood County; 528 Monument St; Greenwood, SC 29646; Ph. (864) 942-8546 **Details:** (County Health Department has Birth & Death Records; Probate Judge has Marriage & Probate Records; Clerk Court has Divorce Records from 1937, Court & Land Records from 1897)
Hampton www.sccounties.org/counties/Hampton.htm	K10	18 Feb 1878	**Beaufort** Hampton County; 1 Elm St; PO Box 7; Hampton, SC 29924-0007; Ph. (803) 943-7510 **Details:** (County Health Department has Birth & Death Records; Clerk Court has Court & Land Records; Probate Judge has Marriage & Probate Records)
Hilton		1785	Hilton County; SC **Details:** County Terminated 1800
Horry www.horrycounty.org/	D5	19 Dec 1801	**Georgetown District** Horry County; 1201 3rd Ave; Conway, SC 29526; Ph. (803) 248-1885 **Details:** (County Health Department has Birth, Death & Burial Records; Clerk Court has Divorce Records from 1947, Court & Land Records; Probate Judge has Marriage & Probate Records)

County	Map	Date	Parent County or Territory From Which Organized
Website	Index	Created	Address/Details

Jasper   K11   30 Jan 1912   **Beaufort, Hampton**
www.sccounties.org/counties/Jasper.htm

Jasper County; 305 Russell St; PO Box 248; Ridgeland, SC 29936-0248; Ph. (843) 726-7781
Details: (County Health Department has Birth & Death Records; Probate Judge has Marriage & Probate Records; Clerk Court has Divorce, Court & Land Records)

Kershaw   I3   1791   **Camden District**
www.camden-sc.org/

Kershaw County; 1121 Broad St; Camden, SC 29020-3638;
Ph. (803) 425-1527
Details: (Clerk Court has Divorce Records from 1949, Court & Land Records from 1791; Probate Judge has Marriage & Probate Records)

Lancaster   I3   1785   **Camden District**
www.sccounties.org/counties/Lancaster.htm

Lancaster County; PO Box 1809; Lancaster, SC 29720-1585;
Ph. (803) 285-1585
Details: (County Health Department has Birth & Death Records; Probate Judge has Marriage & Probate Records; Clerk Court has Divorce Records from 1958, Court Records from 1800 & Land Records from 1762)

Laurens   N3   1785   **District 96**
www.geocities.com/BourbonStreet/4492/

Laurens County; PO Box 445; Laurens, SC 29360-0445;
Ph. (864) 984-3538
Details: (County Health Department has Birth & Death Records; Probate Judge has Marriage & Probate Records; Clerk Court has Divorce Records, Court Records from 1900 & Land Records from 1790)

Lee   G4   25 Feb 1902   **Darlington, Sumter, Kershaw**
www.rootsweb.com/~sclee/index.html

Lee County; 11 Courthouse Sq; PO Box 281; Bishopville, SC 29010;
Ph. (803) 484-5341
Details: (County Health Department has Birth Records from 1915, Death Records from 1902, Divorce & Burial Records; Probate Judge has Marriage & Probate Records from 1902; Clerk Court has Court & Land Records from 1902)

Lexington   K5   1785   **Orangeburg District**
www.lex-co.com/my_lex.html

Lexington County; 139 E Main St; Lexington, SC 29072;
Ph. (803) 359-8235
Details: (County Health Department has Birth & Death Records; Probate Judge has Marriage & Probate Records; Clerk Court has Divorce Records from 1949, Land Records from 1839 & Court Records)

Liberty   1785

Liberty County; SC
Details: (see Marion) (used briefly as a subdivision of Marion County) County Terminated 1800

Marion   D5   1785   **Georgetown District**
www.geocities.com/BourbonStreet/1786/marion.html

Marion County; PO Box 295; Marion, SC 29571-0183;
Ph. (843) 423-8240
Details: (County Health Department has Birth, Death & Burial Records; Probate Judge has Marriage & Probate Records; Clerk Court has Divorce Records from 1948, Court & Land Records from 1800)

County Website	Map Index	Date Created	Parent County or Territory From Which Organized Address/Details
Marlboro www.rootsweb.com/~scmarlbo/	F3	1785	**Cheraws District** Marlboro County; 205 Usher St; Bennettsville, SC 29512-0996; Ph. (843) 479-5613 **Details:** (County Clerk has Birth, Death, Burial, Divorce & Court Records; Probate Judge has Marriage & Probate Records)
McCormick www.geocities.com/BourbonStreet/6420/	O5	19 Feb 1916	**Greenwood, Abbeville** McCormick County; 133 S Mine St; McCormick, SC 29835; Ph. (864) 465-2195 **Details:** (Clerk Court has Divorce, Land & Court Records from 1916; Probate Judge has Marriage & Probate Records from 1916; County Health Department has Birth & Death Records from 1916)
Newberry www.rootsweb.com/~scnewbe2/	M4	1785	**District 96** Newberry County; 1226 College St; PO Box 278; Newberry, SC 29108-0278; Ph. (803) 321-2110 **Details:** (Clerk Court has Birth & Death Records from 1915, Marriage Records from 1911, Divorce Records from 1949, Probate, Court & Land Records from 1776)
Ninety-Six Dist		1769	**Granville, Colleton, old** Ninety-Six Dist County; SC **Details:** (Created in 1769 from Colleton, old & Granville as one of 7 original judicial districts. Discontinued in 1798 to form Abbeville, Edgefield, Newberry, Laurens & Spartanburg Counties)
Oconee www.rootsweb.com/~scoconee/oconee.html	Q2	29 Jan 1868	**Pickens** Oconee County; W Main St; PO Box 678; Walhalla, SC 29691; Ph. (864) 638-4280 **Details:** (County Health Department has Birth & Death Records from 1915; Probate Judge has Marriage Records from 1911 & Probate Records from 1868; Clerk Court has Divorce Records from 1949, Court & Land Records from 1868)
Orange		1785	**Orangeburg District** Orange County; SC **Details:** (Former county in Orangeburg District about 1800, mostly in present-day Orangeburg County, with parts in present-day counties of Bamberg, Calhoun & Lexington)
Orangeburg www.orangeburgsc.net/	I7	1769	**Colleton, old, Berkeley, old** Orangeburg County; 190 Gibson St; Orangeburg, SC 29115-5463; Ph. (803) 533-6260 **Details:** (Created in 1769 from Colleton, old & Berkeley, old as one of 7 original judicial districts; Split in 1798 to form Orangeburg & Barnwell Counties) (Clerk Court has Divorce Records from 1949, Court & Land Records from 1865; County Health Department has Birth, Death & Burial Records; Probate Judge has Marriage & Probate Records)
Pendleton		1786	**Washington District** Pendleton County; SC **Details:** County Terminated 1800 (see Pickens & Anderson) (Discontinued in 1826 to form Pickens & Anderson Counties)

County Website	Map Index	Date Created	Parent County or Territory From Which Organized Address/Details
Pickens www.rootsweb.com/~scpicke2/	P2	20 Dec 1826	**Pendleton District** Pickens County; 214 E Main St; Pickens, SC 29671-0215; Ph. (864) 898-5862 **Details:** (Clerk Court has Birth & Death Records from 1915, Divorce Records from 1949, Court Records from 1868 & Land Records; Probate Judge has Marriage & Probate Records)
Pickney District		1791	**Original District** Pickney District County; SC **Details:** County Terminated 1800 (Discontinued in 1798 to form Union & York Counties)
Richland www.geocities.com/frankoclark/richland/	J5	1785	**Kershaw District** Richland County; 1701 Main St #205; Columbia, SC 29202; Ph. (803) 748-4684 **Details:** (1800 Census schedules missing) (Probate Judge has Marriage, Probate & Court Records; County Auditor has Land Records)
Salem		1792	**Sumter District** Salem County; SC **Details:** County Terminated 1800 (see Sumter) (Former county in Sumter District about 1800; part of Sumter County about 1810. Parts lay in the present-day counties of Lee, Sumter, Clarendon & Florence)
Saluda www.rootsweb.com/~scsaluda/index.htm	M5	25 Feb 1896	**Edgefield** Saluda County; 100 E Church St; Saluda, SC 29138; Ph. (864) 445-3303 **Details:** (Clerk Court has Divorce, Court & Land Records; Probate Judge has Marriage & Probate Records)
Spartanburg www.rootsweb.com/~scsparta/	N2	1785	**District 96** Spartanburg County; 180 Magnolia St; Spartanburg, SC 29306; Ph. (864) 596-2591 **Details:** (County Health Department has Birth & Death Records; Probate Judge has Marriage Records from 1911 & Probate Records from 1700; Clerk Court has Divorce Records & Court Records from 1785; RMC Office has Land Records)
Sumter www.rootsweb.com/~scsumter/index.html	I5	1798	**Camden District** Sumter County; 141 N Main St; Sumter, SC 29150-4965; Ph. (803) 773-1581 **Details:** (County Health Department has Birth & Death Records; Probate Judge has Marriage Records from 1910 & Probate Records from 1900; Clerk Court has Divorce, Court & Land Records)
Union www.rootsweb.com/~scunion/union.html	M3	1785	**Pinckney District** Union County; 210 W Main St; PO Box 200; Union, SC 29379-0200; Ph. (864) 429-1630 **Details:** (Clerk Court has Court Records from 1785, Divorce & Land Records; Probate Judge has Marriage & Probate Records)
Washington		1785	**Original District** Washington County; SC **Details:** County Terminated 1800 (Discontinued in 1798 to form Pendleton & Greenville Counties)

County Website	Map Index	Date Created	Parent County or Territory From Which Organized Address/Details
Williamsburg www.rootsweb.com/~scwillia/html.htm	F6	1802	**Georgetown District** Williamsburg County; 125 W Main St; Kingstree, SC 29556-3347; Ph. (843) 354-9321 **Details:** (Clerk Court has Divorce Records from 1948, Court & Land Records from 1806; Probate Judge has Marriage Records from 1911 & Probate Records)
Winyaw		1785	Winyaw County; SC **Details:** County Terminated 1800 (Formerly a county in Georgetown District, later became Georgetown County)
York www.rootsweb.com/~scyork/	K1	1785	**Pickney District** York County; S Congress; PO Box 649; York, SC 29745; Ph. (803) 684-8505 **Details:** (County Health Department has Birth Records from 1915, Death & Burial Records; Probate Judge has Marriage & Probate Records; Clerk Court has Divorce Records from 1942, Court & Land Records from 1786)

Notes

South Dakota

Capital: Pierre
Territory: 1861
State: 1889 (40th)

Under God, the people rule

French explorers entered South Dakota in 1742, but French interest waned after the French and Indian War. The United States gained the region with the Louisiana Purchase in 1803. Lewis and Clark made their exploration of the area between 1804 and 1806. Only hardy fur traders ventured into the area before 1858. In that year, the Yankton Sioux Indians ceded their claim to southeastern Dakota to the United States. Settlements sprang up at Yankton, Vermillion, and other sites between the Big Sioux and Missouri rivers. In 1861, the Dakotas were made into one territory, after years in the Missouri, Minnesota, Iowa, Wisconsin, Michigan and Nebraska territories. The Dakota Territory covered all of North and South Dakota, Montana, and northern Wyoming. Montana was taken away in 1864, Wyoming in 1868, and the territory divided into North and South Dakota in 1867.

About 200 men from the Dakota Territory served with the Union during the Civil War. Discovery of gold in the Black Hills in 1875 led to an upswing in settlement. Railroads came into the area between 1878 and 1888 and stimulated the Dakota land boom. South Dakota entered the Union in 1889 and all but three of its 68 counties were formed. Railroads reached the western part of the state during the first decade of the 20th century, bringing thousands of homesteaders to the area. The predominating nationalities in South Dakota are Norwegian, German, Russian, Swedish, Danish, Czech, English, Austrian, Irish, Finnish, Polish, Greek, and Italian.

Look for vital records in the following locations:

- **Birth and death records:** Contact Registrar of Deeds for some records created before 1905. Records of births, marriages, divorces, and deaths from 1905 on file with the State Department of Health, Vital Records in Pierre, South Dakota.
- **Wills and probate matters:** Kept by district court clerks. Probate records prior to statehood were kept by the Territorial Probate Court and are available from the Archives Division of the South Dakota State Historical Society in Pierre.
- **Census records:** South Dakota was included in the 1836 Wisconsin, 1840 Iowa, 1850 Minnesota (Pembina District), and 1860 to 1880 Dakota territorial censuses. Indexes have been published for some of these censuses. State and territorial censuses for 1885, 1895, 1905, 1915, 1925, 1935, and 1945 are available at the State Historical Society.

South Dakota Department of Health Vital Records
600 East Capitol
Pierre, South Dakota 57501-2536
(605) 773-4961
www.state.sd.us/doh/vitalrec/vital.htm

South Dakota State Historical Society State Archives
900 Governors Drive
Pierre, South Dakota 57501-2217
(605) 773-3804, Fax: (605) 773-6041
www.sdhistory.org/arc/archives.htm

South Dakota

Societies and Repositories

Aberdeen Area Genealogical Society; Box 493; Aberdeen, SD 57402-0493.

Brookings Area Genealogical Society; 524 Fourth St.; Brookings, SD 57006.

Center of the Nation, AHSGR; 7 Swan Lane; Spearfish, SD 57783; (605) 642-1149; jhi@rushmore.com.

East River Genealogical Forum; 554 Montana Ave SW; Huron, SD 57350-2326.

Family Tree Genealogical Society; Box 202; Winner, SD 57580-0202.

Heritage Club - Platte; Rt. 2, Box 128; Platte, SD 57369-0128.

Homestead Chapter, AHSGR; PO Box 98; Freeman, SD 57029-0098; (605) 925-7834.

Hyde County Historical & Genealogical Society; PO Box 392; Highmore, SD 57345-0392.

Kingsbury Genealogical Society; PO Box 330; DeSmet, SD 57231-0330.

Lake County Genealogical Society; c/o Karl Mundt Library; Dakota State College; Madison, SD 57042.

Lyman-Brule Genealogical Society; 110 E. Lawler; Chamdberlain, SD 57325; lymanbrule2@yahoo.com; www.rootsweb.com/~sdlbgs.

Mitchell Area Genealogical Society; 620 N. Edmunds; Mitchell, SD 57301.

Moody County Genealogical Society; 501 W. First Ave.; Flandreau, SD 57028-1003; (605) 997-2786; duncana@iw.net.

Pierre-Ft. Pierre Genealogical Society; PO Box 925; Pierre, SD 57501-0925.

Platte Heritage Club; Rt. 2, Box 128; Platte, SD 57369.

Rapid City Society for Genealogical Research; PO Box 1495; Rapid City, SD 57709-1495.

Sioux Valley Genealogical Society; 200 W. 6th St.; Sioux Falls, SD 57104-6001.

South Dakota Genealogical Society; PO Box 1101; Pierre, SD 57501-1101; www.rootsweb.com/~sdgenweb/gensoc/sdgensoc.html.

South Dakota State Historical Society and Archives; 900 Governors Drive; Pierre, SD 57501-2217; (605) 773-3458; www.sdhistory.org/Default.asp.

South Dakota State Library; 800 Governors Drive; Pierre, SD 57501-2294; (605) 773-3131; library@state.sd.us; www.sdstatelibrary.com/askfor.htm.

Tri-State Genealogical Society; c/o Public Library; 905 5th St.; Belle Fourche, SD 57717-1705; http://scream.iw.net/~shepherd.

Union County Historical Society; PO Box 552; Elk Point, SD 57025.

Watertown Genealogical Society; 611 N.E. B Ave.; Watertown, SD 57201.

Yankton Genealogical Society; PO Box 71; Missions Hills, SD 57406.

Bibliography and Record Sources

General

Alexander, Ruth A., et al., comps. *South Dakota: Changing, Changeless, 1889–1989 [sic].* South Dakota Library Association, 1985.

Fox's Who's Who Among South Dakotans: A Biographical Directory of Citizens Who Are Prominent in Professional, Political, Business and Civic Affairs of the State. 2 vols. Pierre, South Dakota: Fox Kindley, 1929.

Holley, Frances Chamberlain. *Once Their Home: Or Our Legacy from the Dahkotahs.* Chicago: Donohue & Henneberry, 1892.

Kingsbury, George Washington. *History of Dakota Territory and South Dakota: Its History and Its People By George Martin Smith.* 5 vols. Chicago: S. J. Clarke Co., 1915.

Memorial and Biographical Record and Illustrated Compendium of Biography [Central South Dakota]: Containing a Compendium of Local Biography . . . of Central South Dakota . . . Also a Compendium of the National Biography, Containing Biographical Sketches of Hundreds of the Greatest Men and Celebrities America has Produced. Chicago: George A. Ogle, 1899. Salt Lake City: Genealogical Society of Utah, 1963. Microfilm.

Memorial and Biographical Record, the Black Hills Region: An Illustrated Compendium of Biography Containing a Compendium of Local Biography, including Biographical Sketches of Prominent Old Settlers and Representative Citizens of the Black Hills Region . . . Also a Compendium of National Biography. Chicago: Geo. A. Ogle & Co., 1898. Salt Lake City: Genealogical Society of Utah, 1976. Microfilm.

Memorial and Biographical Record: An Illustrated Compendium of Biography Containing a Compendium of Local Biography. Chicago: George A. Ogle Co., 1897. Tucson, Arizona: W. C. Cox Co., 1974. Microfilm.

Prairie Progress in West Central South Dakota. Sioux Falls, South Dakota: Historical Society of Old Stanley County, South Dakota, 1968.

Schell, Herbert S. *History of South Dakota.* 2nd ed. Lincoln, Nebraska: University of Nebraska Press, 1968.

Sioux Valley Genealogical Society. *Pioneer Certificates.* Salt Lake City: Filmed by the Genealogical Society of Utah, 1990. 20 Microfilm.

South Dakota Research Outline. Series U.S.-States, no. 41. Salt Lake City: Family History Library, 1988.

State Historical Society of North Dakota. *Historical Data Project; Pioneer Biography Files.* Bismarck, North Dakota: State Historical Society of North Dakota, 1988–1989. 34 Microfilm.

Wagner, Sally Roesch. *Daughters of Dakota*. 6 vols. Yankton, South Dakota: Daughters of Dakota, ca. 1989.

Atlases, Maps and Gazetteers

Federal Writer's Project. *South Dakota Place Names*. Vermillion: University of South Dakota, 1940.

Phillips, George H. *Postoffices and Postmarks of Dakota Territory*. Crete, Nebraska: J-B Publishing, 1973.

Phillips, George H. *The Postoffices of South Dakota, 1861–1930*. Crete, Nebraska: J-B Publishing, 1975.

R. L. Polk & Company. *Northwestern Gazetteer: Minnesota, North and South Dakota and Montana Gazetteer and Business Directory*. St. Paul, Minnesota: R. L. Polk & Company, 1914.

Sneve, Virginia D. H. *South Dakota Geographic Names*. Vermillion: University of South Dakota, 1941. Reprint. Sioux Falls, South Dakota: Brevet Press, 1973.

Census Records

Available Census Records and Census Substitutes

Federal Census 1860, 1870, 1880, 1900, 1910, 1920, 1930

Federal Mortality Schedules 1860, 1870, 1880

Union Veterans and Widows 1890

State/Territorial Census 1836, 1885, 1895, 1905, 1915, 1925, 1935, 1945

Dollarhide, William. *The Census Book: A Genealogist's Guide to Federal Census Facts, Schedules and Indexes*. Bountiful, Utah: Heritage Quest, 1999.

Kemp, Thomas Jay. *The American Census Handbook*. Wilmington, Delaware: Scholarly Resources, Inc., 2001.

Lainhart, Ann S. *State Census Records*. Baltimore: Genealogical Publishing Co., Inc., 1992.

Szucs, Loretto Dennis and Matthew Wright. *Finding Answers in U.S. Census Records*. Ancestry Publishing, 2001.

Thorndale, William and William Dollarhide. *Map Guide to the U.S. Federal Census, 1790–1920*. Baltimore: Genealogical Publishing Co., 1987.

Court Records, Probate and Wills

Note: For these records search the individual counties.

Emigration, Immigration, Migration and Naturalization

Lareau, Paul J., and Elmer Courteau. *French-Canadian Families of the North Central States: A Genealogical Dictionary*. 8 vols. St. Paul, Minnesota: Northwest Territory French and Canadian Heritage Institute, 1980.

University of Minnes. *The Immigration History Research Center: a guide to collections*. New York: Greenwood Press, 1991.

Land and Property

Bureau of Land Management. *South Dakota BLM Database*. South Dakota: SDGENWEB, 2002. Online database—www.rootsweb.com/~usgenweb/sd/land/sdland.htm

Gates, Paul Wallace. *Fifty Million Acres: Conflicts over Kansas Land Policy, 1854–1890*. Norman, Oklahoma: University of Oklahoma Press, 1997.

Green, Charles L. *The Administration of the Public Domain in South Dakota*. Pierre, South Dakota: Hipple Printing, 1939.

Hibbard, Benjamin Horace. *A History of the Public Land Policies*. Madison: University of Wisconsin Press, 1965.

Hone, Wade E. *Land and Property Research in the United States*. Salt Lake City: Ancestry Incorporated, 1997.

Skogen, Larry C. *Indian Depredation Claims, 1796–1920*. Norman: University of Oklahoma Press, ca. 1996.

Military

Haulsee, W. M., F. G. Howe, A. C. Doyle. *Soldiers of the Great War*. 3 vols. Washington, D.C.: Soldiers Record Publishing Association, 1920.

United States Selective Service System. *South Dakota, World War I Selective Service System Draft Registration Cards, 1917–1918. National Archives Microfilm Publications, M1509*. Washington, D.C.: National Archives, 1987–1988.

United States. Adjutant General's Office. *Index to Compiled Service Records of Volunteer Union Soldiers Who Served in Organizations from the Territory of Dakota*. Washington, D.C.: The National Archives, 1964.

United States. Army. *Registers of Enlistments in the United States Army, 1798–1914*. Washington, D.C.: National Archives, 1956.

United States. Veterans Administration. *Pension Index File, Alphabetical; of the Veterans Administrative Contact and Administrative Services, Administrative Operations Services, 1861–1934*. Washington, D.C.: Veterans Administration, Publications Service, 1953.

United States. Veterans Administration. *Pension Index Files, Indian Wars, 1892–1926*. Washington, D.C.: Veterans Administration, 1959.

Vital and Cemetery

Krueger, Maurice and Florence Krueger. *South Dakota Cemeteries, 1990*. Mina, South Dakota: the authors, 1990.

Rapid City Society for Genealogical Research. *Some Black Hills Area Cemeteries, South Dakota*. 6 vols. Rapid City, South Dakota: Rapid City Society for Genealogical Research, 1993.

United States. Bureau of Indian Affairs. Cheyenne River Agency. *Agency records, 1869–1951*. Kansas City,

Missouri: Filmed by the National Archives, 1978. 14 Microfilm.

United States. Bureau of Indian Affairs. Crow Creek Agency. *Birth and Death Records, 1919–1939*. Kansas City, Missouri: Federal Archives and Records Center, 1976. Microfilm.

United States. Bureau of Indian Affairs. Pine Ridge Agency. *Birth and Death Records, 1895–1950*. Kansas City, Missouri: Federal Archives and Records Center, 1976. 2 Microfilm.

United States. Bureau of Indian Affairs. Rosebud Agency. *Birth and Death Records, 1900–1946*. Salt Lake City: Filmed by the Genealogical Society of Utah, 1976. 2 Microfilm.

United States. Bureau of Indian Affairs. Sisseton Agency. *Birth and Death Records, 1928–1945*. Kansas City,

Missouri: Federal Archives and Records Center, 1977. Microfilm.

United States. Bureau of Indian Affairs. Standing Rock Agency. *Births, Marriages and Deaths, 1880–1942*. Kansas City, Missouri: Federal Archives and Records Center, 1977. 2 Microfilm.

United States. Work Projects Administration (South Dakota). *South Dakota Grave Registration Project; Cemetery Information*. Salt Lake City: Genealogical Society of Utah. 1980. 17 Microfilm.

United States. Work Projects Administration (South Dakota). *South Dakota Graves Registration Service; Field Data—Veterans*. Salt Lake City: Genealogical Society of Utah, 1980. 12 Microfilm.

County Website	Map Index	Date Created	Parent County or Territory From Which Organized Address/Details
Armstrong		8 Mar 1883	**Cheyenne, Rusk, Stanley** Armstrong County; SD **Details:** (see Dewey) Formerly Pyatt County. Name changed to Armstrong 6 Jan 1895. Eliminated 4 Nov 1952 to Dewey
Armstrong (old)		8 Jan 1873	**Charles Mix, Hutchinson** Armstrong, old County; SD **Details:** (see Hutchinson) Eliminated 1 Oct 1879 to Hutchinson
Ashmore		8 Jan 1873	**Buffalo** Ashmore County; SD **Details:** (see Potter) Name changed to Potter 14 Jan 1875
Aurora www.rootsweb.com/~sdaurora/	F8	1 Oct 1879	**Cragin, Wetmore** Aurora County; 401 S Main St; PO Box 366; Plankinton, SD 57368; Ph. (605) 942-7165 **Details:** (Organized 29 Aug 1881) (Clerk Court has Divorce, Probate & Court Records from 1879; Registrar of Deeds has Birth, Marriage, Death & Burial Records; County Assessor has Land Records)
Beadle www.rootsweb.com/~sdbeadle/	E6	1 Oct 1879	**Spink, Clark, Burchard, Kingsbury** Beadle County; 450 3rd St SW; Huron, SD 57350; Ph. (605) 353-7165 **Details:** (Organized 9 Jul 1880) (Clerk Courts has Divorce Records from 1884, Probate & Court Records from 1893 & Land Records; Registrar of Deeds has Birth, Marriage, Death & Burial Records)
Beadle, old		8 Jan 1873	**Hanson** Beadle, old County; SD **Details:** (see Brown) Eliminated 1 Oct 1879 to Brown & Unorganized Territory
Bennett www.rootsweb.com/~sdbennet/	M10	3 Jun 1909	**Lugenbeel, Shannon, Washington, Washabaugh** Bennett County; 202 Main St; Martin, SD 57551; Ph. (605) 685-6969 **Details:** (Attached to Fall River County prior to organization 27 Apr 1912) (Registrar of Deeds has Land Records from 1907, Marriage Records from 1912, Birth & Death Records from 1913 & Burial Records from 1943; Clerk Courts has Divorce, Probate & Court Records)

County Website	Map Index	Date Created	Parent County or Territory From Which Organized Address/Details
Big Sioux		**23 May 1857**	**Brown County, Minnesota** Big Sioux County; SD **Details:** (Attached to Pipestone County, Minnesota. Eliminated 11 May 1858 when Minnesota state was created)
Bon Homme www.rootsweb.com/~sdbonhom/	D10	**5 Apr 1862**	**Unorg. Terr.** Bon Homme County; PO Box 6; Tyndall, SD 57066; Ph. (605) 589-4215 **Details:** (Clerk Court has Probate Records from 1900, Court Records from 1878 & Divorce Records; Registrar of Deeds has Birth, Marriage, Death & Military Records)
Boreman		**8 Jan 1873**	**Unorg. Terr.** Boreman County; SD **Details:** (see Corson) Attached to Campbell County. Eliminated 2 Mar 1909 to Corson
Bramble		**8 Jan 1873**	**Hanson** Bramble County; SD **Details:** (Eliminated 1 Oct 1879 to Miner)
Brookings www.rootsweb.com/~sdbrooki/	B7	**5 Apr 1862**	**Unorg. Terr.** Brookings County; 314 6th Ave; Brookings, SD 57006; Ph. (605) 692-6284 **Details:** (Organized 13 Jan 1871) (Clerk Court has Divorce, Probate & Court Records; Registrar of Deeds has Birth, Marriage & Death Records from 1905, Burial Records from 1940, Land & Military Records)
Brown www.brown.sd.us/	E3	**1 Oct 1879**	**Mills, Stone, Beadle, old** Brown County; 101 1st Ave SE; Aberdeen, SD 57401-4203; Ph. (605) 622-2266 **Details:** (Organized 14 Sep 1880) (Clerk Courts has Birth, Marriage, Death, Burial, Divorce, Probate & Court Records; Registrar of Deeds has Land Records)
Bruguier		**8 May 1862**	**Unorg. Terr.** Bruguier County; SD **Details:** (Attached to Charles Mix. Eliminated 6 Jan 1864 to Buffalo & Charles Mix)
Brule www.rootsweb.com/~sdbrule/	G8	**14 Jan 1875**	**Charles Mix** Brule County; 300 S Courtland St; Chamberlain, SD 57325; Ph. (605) 734-5443 **Details:** (Registrar of Deeds has Birth & Death Records from 1905, Burial Records from 1941 & Land Records from 1880; County Treasury has Marriage Records from 1882; County Clerk has Divorce Records from 1885, Probate & Naturalization Records from 1880 & Court Records from 1882)
Buffalo www.geocities.com/lynettet.geo/buffalo/ buffalo.html	G7	**6 Jan 1864**	**Brugier, Charles Mix, Unorg. Terr.** Buffalo County; PO Box 148; Gann Valley, SD 57341-0148; Ph. (605) 293-3234 **Details:** (Attached to Bon Homme County prior to organization 13 Jan 1871) (Registrar of Deeds has Birth & Death Records from 1905, Burial Records from 1941 & Land Records; County Treasury has Marriage Records from 1887; County Clerk has Divorce Records from 1915, Probate & Court Records from 1885)

County Website	Map Index	Date Created	Parent County or Territory From Which Organized Address/Details
Burchard		8 Jan 1873	**Hanson** Burchard County; SD **Details:** (Eliminated 1 Oct 1879 to Beadle & Hand)
Burdick		8 Mar 1883	**Harding** Burdick County; SD **Details:** (Eliminated 28 Feb 1889 to Harding)
Butte	P5	6 May 1883	**Lawrence, Mandan** Butte County; 839 5th Ave; Belle Fourche, SD 57717; Ph. (605) 892-2912, paula_rod@rushmore.com **Details:** (Register of Deeds has Birth Records from 1905; Burial & Cememtery Records from 1930, Death Records from 1905, Land Records from 1883, Marrige Records from 1890, & Military Records)
Campbell www.ehrman.net/campbell/index.html	I3	8 Jan 1873	**Buffalo** Campbell County; PO Box 146; Mound City, SD 57646; Ph. (605) 955-3536 **Details:** (Organized 17 Apr 1884) (Registrar of Deeds has Birth, Marriage & Cemetery Records from late 1800's, Death Records from 1905, Land Records from 1884 & Military Discharge Records from 1921; Clerk Court has Divorce & Court Records from 1890, Probate Records from 1891 & Naturalization Records from 1884; County Auditor has School Census Records from early 1900's)
Charles Mix www.rootsweb.com/~sdcharle/	E10	8 May 1862	**Unorg. Terr.** Charles Mix County; 400 Main St E; PO Box 490; Lake Andes, SD 57356; Ph. (605) 487-7511 **Details:** (Clerk Courts has Birth, Marriage & Death Records from 1905, Burial Records, Divorce, Probate & Court Records from 1890)
Cheyenne		11 Jan 1875	**Pratt, Rusk, Stanley, Unorg. Terr.** Cheyenne County; SD **Details:** (Eliminated 8 Mar 1883 to Jackson, Nowlin, Pyatt & Sterling)
Choteau		9 Mar 1883	**Martin** Choteau County; SD **Details:** (Attached to Lawrence & Butte Counties. Eliminated 8 Nov 1898 to Butte & Meade)
Clark www.rootsweb.com/~sdclark/index.htm	D6	8 Jan 1873	**Hanson** Clark County; PO Box 294; Clark, SD 57225; Ph. (605) 532-5363 **Details:** (Organized 23 May 1881) (Registrar of Deeds has Marriage Records from 1884, Birth & Death Records from 1905, Burial Records from 1941, Military Discharge Records from 1919 & Land Records; Clerk Courts has Divorce, Probate & Court Records)
Clay www.rootsweb.com/~sdclay/	B10	10 Apr 1862	**Unorg. Terr.** Clay County; 211 W Main St; PO Box 403; Vermillion, SD 57069; Ph. (605) 677-2871 **Details:** (Registrar of Deeds has Birth & Death Records from 1905, Marriage Records from 1880, Land Records from 1863 & Burial Records from 1962; Clerk Court has Probate Records from 1875, Court Records from 1866 & Divorce Records from 1889)

County Website	Map Index	Date Created	Parent County or Territory From Which Organized Address/Details
Codington www.rootsweb.com/~sdcoding/	**C5**	**15 Feb 1877**	**Clark, Grant, Hamlin, Unorg. Terr.** Codington County; 14 1st Ave SW; Watertown, SD 57201; Ph. (605) 882-4850 **Details:** (Organized 7 Aug 1878) (Clerk Courts has Birth, Death, Burial & Divorce Records from 1905, Marriage Records from 1900, Probate Records from 1893 & Court Records from 1883)
Cole		**10 Apr 1862**	**Unorg. Terr.** Cole County; SD **Details:** (see Union) Name changed to Union 7 Jan 1864
Corson www.rootsweb.com/~sdcorson/	**L3**	**2 Mar 1909**	**Boreman, Dewey, Schnasse** Corson County; 200 1st St E; McIntosh, SD 57641; Ph. (605) 273-4201 **Details:** (Registrar of Deeds has Birth, Death & Land Records from 1909; County Treasury has Marriage Records; Clerk Court has Divorce, Probate & Court Records)
Cragin		**8 Jan 1873**	**Hanson** Cragin County; SD **Details:** (Eliminated 1 Oct 1879 to Aurora & Unorg. Terr.)
Custer www.rapidnet.com/~saj/custer/	**P8**	**11 Jan 1875**	**Unorg. Terr.** Custer County; 420 Mt Rushmore Rd; Custer, SD 57730; Ph. (605) 673-4816 **Details:** (Organized 26 Apr 1877) (Clerk Courts has Birth & Death Records from 1905, Marriage Records from 1887, Divorce, Probate & Court Records from 1890)
Davison www.davisoncounty.org/	**E9**	**8 Jan 1873**	**Hanson** Davison County; 200 E 4th Ave; Mitchell, SD 57301; Ph. (605) 995-8616 **Details:** (Organized 31 Jul 1874) (Registrar of Deeds has Birth & Death Records from 1905, Marriage, Burial & Land Records; Clerk Court has Divorce, Probate & Court Records from 1880)
Day http://curie.bcc.louisville.edu/~cps/dayco/	**D4**	**1 Oct 1879**	**Greeley, Stone** Day County; 710 W 1st St; Webster, SD 57274-1391; Ph. (605) 345-3771 **Details:** (Organized 2 Jan 1882) (Registrar of Deeds has Birth & Death Records from 1905, Land Records from 1879 & Burial Records from 1930; County Treasury has Marriage Records from 1880; Clerk Court has Divorce & Court Records from 1885 & Probate Records from 1898)
Delano		**11 Jan 1875**	**Unorg. Terr.** Delano County; SD **Details:** (Attached to Lawrence & Butte Counties. Eliminated 8 Nov 1898 to Meade)
Deuel www.rootsweb.com/~sddeuel/index.html	**A6**	**5 Apr 1862**	**Unorg. Terr.** Deuel County; PO Box 307; Clear Lake, SD 57226; Ph. (605) 874-2268 **Details:** (Organized 20 May 1878) (Clerk of Courts has Divorce Records from 1879, Probate & Court Records from 1878; Register of Deeds has Burial Records from 1941, Marriage Records from 1879, Land Records from 1885, Birth & Death Records from 1905)

County Website	Map Index	Date Created	Parent County or Territory From Which Organized
			Address/Details

Dewey K5 — 8 Jan 1873 — **Unorg. Terr.**
Dewey County; 710 C St; PO Box 117; Timber Lake, SD 57656;
Ph. (605) 865-3661
Details: (Formerly Rusk County. Name changed to Dewey 9 Mar 1883. Attached to Walworth County prior to organization 3 Dec 1910) (Registrar of Deeds has Birth, Marriage & Land Records from 1910, Death Records from 1911, Cemetery Records from 1941 & Military Records from 1919; Clerk Court has Divorce & Probate Records from 1911 & Court Records from 1910, County Auditor has School Census Records 1911–1972)
www.rootsweb.com/~sddewey/

Douglas E9 — 10 Jan 1873 — **Charles Mix**
Douglas County; 706 Braddock St; Armour, SD 57313;
Ph. (605) 724-2585
Details: (Organized 7 Jun 1882) (Registrar of Deeds has Birth & Death Records from 1905 & Land Records; County Treasury has Marriage Records from 1884; Clerk Courts has Court Records from 1884, Divorce & Probate Records from 1887)
www.rootsweb.com/~sddougla/

Edmunds G4 — 8 Jan 1873 — **Buffalo**
Edmunds County; 2nd St; Ipswich, SD 57451; Ph. (605) 426-6671
Details: (Organized 27 Jul 1883) (Registrar of Deeds has Birth Records from 1905, Death Records from 1887, Land Records from 1883, Burial Records from 1941 & Marriage Records from 1887; Clerk Court has Divorce Records from 1887, Court & Probate Records from 1884)
www.rootsweb.com/~sdedmund/

Ewing — 8 Mar 1883 — **Harding**
Ewing County; SD
Details: County Terminated 1884 (Attached to Butte County. Eliminated 6 Nov 1894 to Harding)

Fall River Q10 — 3 Apr 1883 — **Custer**
Fall River County; 906 N River St; Hot Springs, SD 57747-1387;
Ph. (605) 745-5132
Details: (Registrar of Deeds has Land Records from 1883, Birth & Death Records from 1905 & Marriage Records; Clerk Courts has Divorce, Probate & Court Records from 1890)
www.rootsweb.com/~sdfallsr/

Faulk G5 — 8 Jan 1873 — **Buffalo**
Faulk County; PO Box 309; Faulkton, SD 57438-0309;
Ph. (605) 598-6223
Details: (Organized 5 Nov 1883) (Registrar of Deeds has Birth, Marriage, Death, Burial & Land Records from 1888 & Military Records; Clerk Court has Divorce & Court Records from 1900 & Probate Records from 1888)
www.rootsweb.com/~sdfaulk/findex.htm

Forsythe — 11 Jan 1875 — **Unorg. Terr.**
Forsythe County; SD
Details: (Eliminated 19 Feb 1881 to Custer)

Grant B5 — 8 Jan 1873 — **Deuel, Hanson**
Grant County; 210 E 5th Ave; PO Box 509; Milbank, SD 57252-2433; Ph. (605) 432-5482
Details: (Organized 17 Jun 1878) (Clerk Courts has Birth & Death Records from 1905, Marriage Records from 1890, Divorce, Probate & Court Records from 1897 & newspapers from 1880; Registrar of Deeds has Land Records)
www.rootsweb.com/~sdgrant/

County Website	Map Index	Date Created	Parent County or Territory From Which Organized Address/Details
Greeley		8 Jan 1873	**Hanson** Greely County; SD **Details:** (Eliminated 1 Oct 1879 to Day)
Gregory www.rootsweb.com/~sdgregor/Gregory_websit/ Page_1x.html	G10	8 May 1862	**Unorg. Terr.** Gregory County; PO Box 413; Burke, SD 57523; Ph. (605) 775-2664 **Details:** (Attached to Todd & Charles Mix Counties prior to organization 5 Sep 1898) (Registrar of Deeds has Marriage Records from 1898, Birth, Death, Land & Military Discharge Records from 1905 & Burial Records from 1941; Clerk Court has Divorce, Probate & Court Records from 1899)
Haakon www.rootsweb.com/~sdhaakon/	L7	3 Nov 1914	**Stanley** Haakon County; 140 S Howard; Philip, SD 57567; Ph. (605) 859-2627 **Details:** (Organized 8 Feb 1915) (Clerk Courts has Birth, Marriage, Death, Burial, Divorce, Probate, Court & adoption Records from 1915)
Hamlin www.rootsweb.com/~sdhamlin/	C6	8 Jan 1873	**Deuel, Hanson** Hamlin County; PO Box 237; Hayti, SD 57241; Ph. (605) 783-3201 **Details:** (Organized 10 Sep 1878) (Registrar of Deeds has Birth, Death & Burial Records from 1905, Land Records, Marriage Records from 1879; Clerk Court has Divorce & Court Records from 1885, Probate Records from 1890, Naturalization Records from 1880, School Census Records from 1903 & School Records from 1890)
Hand www.geocities.com/lynettet.geo/hand/hand.html	G6	8 Jan 1873	**Buffalo** Hand County; 415 W 1st Ave; Miller, SD 57362-1346; Ph. (605) 853-3512 **Details:** (Organized 1 Sep 1882) (Registrar of Deeds has Birth & Death Records from 1905, Burial & Land Records; County Treasury has Marriage Records from 1883; Clerk Court has Divorce Records from late 1800's, Probate Records from 1880's & Court Records from 1889)
Hanson www.rootsweb.com/~sdhanson/index.html	D8	13 Jan 1871	**Buffalo, Deuel, Brookings, Charles Mix, Hutchinson, Jayne, Minnehaha** Hanson County; 720 5th St; Alexandria, SD 57311; Ph. (605) 239-4446 **Details:** (Organized 16 Aug 1873) (Clerk Courts has Birth, Marriage, Death, Burial, Divorce, Probate & Court Records from 1905)
Harding		1908	**Butte, Unorg. Terr.** Harding County; 901 Ramsland St; Buffalo, SD 57720; Ph. (605) 375-3351 **Details:** (Attached to Butte County. Eliminated 8 Nov 1898 to Butte. Recreated 3 Nov 1908 from Butte. Organized 30 Jan 1911) (Registrar of Deeds has Birth, Death, Burial & Land Records from 1909; County Treasury has Marriage Records from 1909; Clerk Court has Divorce, Probate, Court & School Census Records from 1909)
Harding (old)		5 Mar 1881	**Unorg. Terr.** Harding County; SD **Details:** County Terminated 1898

County Website	Map Index	Date Created	Parent County or Territory From Which Organized Address/Details
Hughes www.rootsweb.com/~sdhughes/	I7	8 Jan 1873	**Buffalo** Hughes County; 104 E Capitol Ave; Pierre, SD 57501-2563; Ph. (605) 773-3713 **Details:** (Organized 26 Nov 1880) (Clerk Courts has Divorce & Court Records from 1880 & Probate Records from 1890; Registrar of Deeds has Birth, Marriage, Death, Burial & Land Records)
Hutchinson www.rootsweb.com/~sdhutchi/	D9	8 May 1862	**Unorg. Terr.** Hutchinson County; 140 Euclid St; Olivet, SD 57052; Ph. (605) 387-2838 **Details:** (Organized 13 Jan 1871) (Registrar of Deeds has Land Records from 1876, Marriage Records from 1887, Birth & Death Records from 1905 & Burial Records from 1914; Clerk Courts has Divorce & Court Records from 1883 & Probate Records from 1899; County Auditor has School Records from 1924)
Hyde www.rootsweb.com/~sdhyde/	H6	8 Jan 1873	**Buffalo** Hyde County; PO Box 306; Highmore, SD 57345-0306; Ph. (605) 852-2512 **Details:** (Organized 1 Oct 1883) (Clerk Court has Birth & Death Records from 1905, Marriage Records from 1887, Burial Records from 1936, Divorce & Court Records from 1884 & Probate Records from 1892; Registrar of Deeds has Land Records from 1880's)
Jackson www.rootsweb.com/~sdjackso/	M9	1914	**Cheyenne, Lugenbeel, White River** Jackson County; 1 S Main St; Kadoka, SD 57543; Ph. (605) 837-2420 **Details:** (Attached to Stanley & Pennington Counties. Eliminated 3 Jun 1909 to Mellette & Washabaugh. Recreated 3 Nov 1914 from Stanley. Organized 9 Feb 1915) (Registrar of Deeds has Birth, Marriage, Death, Burial, Divorce, Probate, Court & Land Records)
Jackson (old)	M9	8 Mar 1883	**Cheyenne, Lugenbeel, White River** Jackson County (old); SD **Details:** County Terminated 1909
Jayne		8 May 1862	**Unorg. Terr.** Jayne County; SD **Details:** (Attached to Yankton County. Eliminated 13 Jan 1871 to Hanson, Hutchinson & Turner Counties)
Jerauld	F8	17 Apr 1883	**Aurora, Buffalo** Jerauld County; 205 S Wallace Ave S.; PO Box 452; Wessington Springs, SD 57382; Ph. (605) 539-1712 **Details:** (Register of Deeds has Birth, Cemetery, Death, Marriage, & Military Records; Area Development has Business & Commerce Records; County Auditor has Census Records; Clerk of Courts has Court, Divorce, Guardianship, Immigration, Naturalization, & Probate Records; Director of Equilization has Land Records; Local Newspapers have Old Newspapers; Treasurer has Tax Records; Library has other historical documents, contact them at (605) 539-1803)
Jones www.rootsweb.com/~sdjones/	K7	1916	**Lyman** Jones County; 310 Main; Murdo, SD 57559; Ph. (605) 669-2361 **Details:** (Registrar of Deeds has Birth, Marriage, Death & Land Records; Clerk Court has Divorce, Probate & Court Records from 1917)

County Website	Map Index	Date Created	Parent County or Territory From Which Organized Address/Details
Kingsbury www.rootsweb.com/~sdkingsb/	C7	8 Jan 1873	**Hanson** Kingsbury County; 102 2nd St SE; De Smet, SD 57231; Ph. (605) 854-3832 **Details:** (Organized 18 Feb 1880) (Register of Deeds has Birth, Death & Burial Records from 1905, & Marriage Records from 1890, Clerk of Courts has Divorce & Court Records from 1920, & Probate Records)
Lake www.rootsweb.com/~sdlake/	B8	8 Jan 1873	**Brookings, Hanson, Minnehaha** Lake County; County Courthouse; 200 E Center; Madison, SD 57042; Ph. (605) 256-4876 **Details:** (Clerk Courts has Birth & Death Records from 1905, Marriage Records from 1874, Burial Records from 1941, Divorce & Court Records from 1881 & Probate Records from 1884)
Lawrence www.lawrence.sd.us/	R7	11 Jan 1875	**Unorg. Terr.** Lawrence County; 644 Main St; Deadwood, SD 57732; Ph. (605) 578-2040 **Details:** (Organized 5 Mar 1877) (Registrar of Deeds has Birth Records from 1905 & Death Records from 1906; County Treasury has Marriage Records from 1887; Clerk Court has Divorce, Probate, Court & Land Records from 1895; City Auditor has Burial Records)
Lincoln www.rootsweb.com/~sdlincol/	B10	5 Apr 1862	**Unorg. Terr.** Lincoln County; 100 E 5th St; Carton, SD 57013-1732; Ph. (605) 987-5661 **Details:** (Organized 30 Dec 1867) (Registrar of Deeds has Birth & Death Records from 1905, Land & Burial Records; County Treasury has Marriage Records from 1890; Clerk Court has Probate Records from 1890, Court & Divorce Records from 1872)
Lugenbeel		11 Jan 1875	**Meyer, Pratt** Lugenbeel County; SD **Details:** (see Washabaugh) Attached to Fall River. Eliminated 3 Jun 1909 to Bennett & Todd
Lyman www.rootsweb.com/~sdlyman/	I8	8 Jan 1873	**Gregory, Unorg. Terr.** Lyman County; PO Box 235; Kennebec, SD 57544; Ph. (605) 869-2277 **Details:** (Attached to Brule County prior to organization 21 May 1893) (Registrar of Deeds has Birth Records from 1905, Death Records from 1920, Burial & Land Records; County Treasury has Marriage Records from 1905; Clerk Court has Divorce, Probate & Court Records from 1880)
Mandan		11 Jan 1875	**Unorg. Terr.** Mandan County; SD **Details:** (Eliminated 10 Mar 1887 to Lawrence)
Marshall www.rootsweb.com/~sdmarsha/mindex.htm	D3	2 May 1885	**Day** Marshall County; County Courthouse; Britton, SD 57430; Ph. (605) 448-5213 **Details:** (Registrar of Deeds has Birth & Death Records from 1905, Marriage Records from 1887, Burial & Land Records; Clerk Court has Divorce Records from 1888, Probate Records from 1889 & Court Records)

County Website	Map Index	Date Created	Parent County or Territory From Which Organized Address/Details
Martin		5 Mar 1881	**Unorg. Terr.** Martin County; SD **Details:** (Attached to Butte County. Eliminated 8 Nov 1898 to Butte)
McCook www.rootsweb.com/~sdmccook/index.htm	C8	8 Jan 1873	**Hanson** McCook County; 130 W Essex Ave; Salem, SD 57058; Ph. (605) 425-2781 **Details:** (Organized 15 Jun 1878) (Registrar of Deeds has Marriage Records from 1882, Burial Records from 1895, Birth & Death Records from 1905 & Land Records; Clerk Courts has Court & Naturalization Records from 1880, Probate Records from 1881 & some School Census Records from 1900)
McPherson www.rootsweb.com/~sdmcpher/	G3	8 Jan 1873	**Buffalo** McPherson County; County Courthouse; PO Box L; Leola, SD 57456; Ph. (605) 439-3351 **Details:** (Organized 6 Mar 1884) (Clerk Court has Probate Records from 1893, Court Records from 1889, Naturalization Records from 1884 & Divorce Records; Registrar of Deeds has Birth & Death Records from 1905, Burial Records from 1941, Marriage & Land Records)
Meade www.rootsweb.com/~sdmeade/Meade%20Co/	O6	7 Feb 1889	**Lawrence** Meade County; 1425 Sherman St; PO Box 939; Sturgis, SD 57785; Ph. (605) 347-2356 **Details:** (Registrar of Deeds has Marriage & Land Records; Clerk Courts has Probate & Court Records)
Mellette www.rootsweb.com/~sdmellet/	K9	3 Jun 1909	**Jackson, Meyer, Pratt, Washabaugh, Unorg. Terr.** Mellette County; S 1st St; PO Box C; White River, SD 57579; Ph. (605) 259-3230 **Details:** (Organized 31 May 1911) (Registrar of Deeds has Birth & Death Records from 1912, Burial Records from 1913 & Land Records; County Treasury has Marriage Records from 1912; Clerk Court has Divorce, Probate & Court Records from 1911)
Meyer		8 Jan 1873	**Unorg. Terr.** Meyer County; SD **Details:** (Attached to Lyman. Eliminated 3 Jun 1909 to Mellette & Todd)
Midway		23 May 1857	**Brown County, Minnesota** Midway County; SD **Details:** (Eliminated 11 May 1858 when Minnesota became a state)
Mills		8 Jan 1873	**Hanson** Mills County; SD **Details:** (Eliminated 1 Oct 1879 to Brown & Unorg. Terr.)
Miner www.geocities.com/lynettet.geo/miner/miner.html	D8	8 Jan 1873	**Hanson** Miner County; 401 N Main St; PO Box 265; Howard, SD 57349; Ph. (605) 772-4612 **Details:** (Organized 2 Dec 1880) (Registrar of Deeds has Birth & Death Records from 1905, Marriage Records from 1886, Burial & Land Records; Clerk Court has Probate & Court Records from 1886 & Divorce Records)

County Website	Map Index	Date Created	Parent County or Territory From Which Organized Address/Details
Minnehaha www.minnehahacounty.org/	**B8**	**5 Apr 1862**	**Unorg. Terr.** Minnehaha County; 415 N Dakota Ave; Sioux Falls, SD 57102; Ph. (605) 367-4223 **Details:** (Attached to Union County prior to organization 4 Jan 1868) (Clerk Courts has Divorce, Probate & Court Records from 1876; Registrar of Deeds has Marriage Records from 1876, Birth & Death Records from 1905 & Land Records)
Moody www.rootsweb.com/~sdmoody/	**B7**	**8 Jan 1873**	**Brookings, Minnehaha** Moody County; 101 E Pipestone Ave; PO Box 152; Flandreau, SD 57028; Ph. (605) 997-3181 **Details:** (Registrar of Deeds has Birth & Death Records from 1905, Burial & Land Records; County Treasury has Marriage Records from 1873; Clerk Court has Probate Records from 1890, Court Records from 1905, Divorce Records, newspapers from 1880's)
Nowlin		**8 Mar 1883**	**Cheyenne, White River** Nowlin County; SD **Details:** (Attached to Pennington, Hughes, Meade & Stanley Counties. Eliminated 8 Nov 1898 to Lyman & Stanley)
Pennington www.co.pennington.sd.us/	**P8**	**11 Jan 1875**	**Unorg. Terr.** Pennington County; 315 St Joseph St; Rapid City, SD 57709-0230; Ph. (605) 394-2575 **Details:** (Organized 19 Apr 1877) (Registrar of Deeds has Birth & Death Records from 1905 & Land Records; County Treasury has Marriage Records from 1887; Clerk Court has Divorce & Court Records from 1877 & Probate Records from 1884)
Perkins www.rootsweb.com/~sdperkin/	**N4**	**3 Nov 1908**	**Butte** Perkins County; PO Box 27; Bison, SD 57620; Ph. (605) 244-5626 **Details:** (Organized 9 Feb 1909) (Registrar of Deeds has Birth, Death & Burial Records from 1909 & Land Records; County Treasury has Marriage Records from 1909; Clerk Court has Probate, Court, Divorce & Naturalization Records from 1909)
Potter www.rootsweb.com/~sdpotter/potterindex.htm	**I5**	**8 Jan 1873**	**Buffalo** Potter County; 201 S Exene St; Gettysburg, SD 57442; Ph. (605) 765-9472 **Details:** (Formerly Ashmore County. Name changed to Potter 14 Jan 1875. Organized 27 Dec 1883) (Clerk Courts has Birth & Death from 1885, Court Records from 1884 & adoption Records from 1941; Registrar of Deeds has Land Records)
Pratt		**8 Jan 1873**	**Unorg. Terr.** Pratt County; SD **Details:** (Attached to Brule & Lyman Counties. Eliminated 3 Jun 1909 to Mellette)
Presho		**8 Jan 1873**	**Unorg. Terr.** Presho County; SD. **Details:** (Attached to Brule & Lyman Counties. Eliminated 6 June 1907 to Tripp)
Pyatt		**8 Mar 1883**	**Cheyenne, Rusk, Stanley** Pyatt County; SD **Details:** (see Dewey) Name changed to Armstrong 6 Jan 1895. Armstrong eliminated 4 Nov 1952 to Dewey

County Website	Map Index	Date Created	Parent County or Territory From Which Organized Address/Details
Rinehart		**9 Mar 1883**	**Martin** Rinehart County; SD **Details:** (Attached to Lawrence & Butte Counties. Eliminated 8 Nov 1898 to Butte & Meade)
Roberts www.rootsweb.com/~sdrobert/	**B3**	**8 Mar 1883**	**Grant, Sisseton/Wahpeton Indian Reserve** Roberts County; 411 2nd Ave E; Sisseton, SD 57262; Ph. (605) 698-7152 **Details:** (Clerk Courts has Birth, Death & Burial Records from 1905, Marriage & Divorce Records from 1890, Probate & Court Records from 1889; Registrar of Deeds has Land Records)
Rusk		**8 Jan 1873**	**Unorg. Terr.** Rusk County; SD **Details:** (see Dewey) Name changed to Dewey 9 Mar 1883
Sanborn www.rootsweb.com/~sdsanbor/	**E7**	**1 May 1883**	**Miner** Sanborn County; 604 W 6th St; PO Box 7; Woonsocket, SD 57385; Ph. (605) 796-4515 **Details:** (Clerk Courts has Divorce, Probate & Court Records from 1905; Registrar of Deeds has Birth, Marriage, Death, Burial & Land Records)
Schnasse		**9 Mar 1883**	**Boreman, Unorg. Terr.** Schnasse County; SD **Details:** (Attached to Walworth County. Eliminated 1 Feb 1911 to Ziebach)
Scobey		**8 Mar 1883**	**Delano** Scobey County; SD **Details:** (Attached to Lawrence & Meade Counties. Eliminated 8 Nov 1898 to Meade)
Shannon www.rootsweb.com/~sdshanno/index.htm	**N9**	**11 Jan 1875**	**Unorg. Terr.** Shannon County; 906 N River St; Hot Springs, SD 57747-1387; Ph. (605) 745-5131 **Details:** (Attached to Fall River County) (Registrar of Deeds has Marriage & Land Records; Clerk Courts has Probate & Court Records)
Spink www.rootsweb.com/~sdspink/sindex.htm	**E5**	**8 Jan 1873**	**Hanson** Spink County; 210 E 7th Ave; Redfield, SD 57469; Ph. (605) 472-1825 **Details:** (Organized 1 Aug 1879) (Clerk Courts has Birth & Death Records from 1905, Marriage Records from 1887, Burial Records from 1941, Divorce & Court Records from 1882 & Probate Records from 1880; Registrar of Deeds has Land Records)
Stanley www.rootsweb.com/~sdstanle/	**K7**	**8 Jan 1873**	**Unorg. Terr.** Stanley County; 40 E 2nd Ave; Fort Pierre, SD 57532; Ph. (605) 223-2673 **Details:** (Attached to Hughes County prior to organization 23 Apr 1890) (Registrar of Deeds has Marriage Records from 1890, Burial Records from 1892, Birth & Death Records from 1905 & Land Records; Clerk Courts has Divorce, Probate & Court Records from 1890)
Sterling		**8 Mar 1883**	**Cheyenne** Sterling County; SD **Details:** (Attached to Lawrence, Hughes, Meade & Stanley Counties. Eliminated 1 Feb 1911 to Ziebach)

County Website	Map Index	Date Created	Parent County or Territory From Which Organized Address/Details
Stone		**8 Jan 1873**	**Hanson** Stone County; SD **Details:** (Eliminated 1 Oct 1879 to Brown, Day & Unorg. Terr.)
Sully www.sdcounties.org/sully/	I6	**8 Jan 1873**	**Buffalo** Sully County; 700 Ash Ave; Onida, SD 57564; Ph. (605) 258-2535 **Details:** (Organized 19 Apr 1883) (Registrar of Deeds has Birth, Marriage, Death, Burial & Land Records; Clerk Courts has Probate & Court Records)
Thompson		**8 Jan 1873**	**Hanson** Thompson County; SD **Details:** (Eliminated 1 Oct 1879 to Spink & Unorg. Terr.)
Todd www.rootsweb.com/~sdtodd/	K10	**9 Mar 1909**	**Lugenbeel, Meyer, Washabaugh, Unorg. Terr.** Todd County; 200 E 3rd St; Winner, SD 57580; Ph. (605) 842-2266 **Details:** (Though created by legislative act 9 Mar 1909, Todd has never been fully organized. Part of the Unorg. County of Bennett, comprising part of Rosebud Indian Reservation, annexed in 1911; within the limits of Rosebud Indian Reservation. Attached to Lyman & Trip Counties) (Register of Deeds has Marriage and Land Records; Clerk of Courts has Probate and Court Records)
Todd (old)		**8 May 1862**	**Unorg. Terr.** Todd, old County; SD **Details:** (Disorganized 7 Mar 1890 & attached to Charles Mix County. Eliminated 3 Jun 1897 to Gregory)
Tripp www.rootsweb.com/~sdtripp/	I9	**8 Jan 1873**	**Unorg. Terr., Gregory, Todd, old** Tripp County; 200 E 3rd St; Winner, SD 57580; Ph. (605) 842-2266 **Details:** (Organized 15 Jun 1909) (Registrar of Deeds has Birth Records from 1909, Burial Records from 1941 & Land Records; County Treasury has Marriage Records from 1909; Clerk Court has Divorce, Probate & Court Records from 1912)
Turner www.rootsweb.com/~sdturner/	C9	**13 Jan 1871**	**Lincoln, Jayne** Turner County; 400 S Main St; Parker, SD 57053-0446; Ph. (605) 297-3115 **Details:** (Clerk Courts has Birth & Death Records from 1905, Marriage Records from 1872, Divorce Records from 1907, Probate Records from 1886 & Court Records from 1900; Registrar of Deeds has Land Records)
Union www.rootsweb.com/~sdunion/	A10	**10 Apr 1862**	**Unorg. Terr.** Union County; PO Box 757; Elk Point, SD 57025-0757; Ph. (605) 356-2132 **Details:** (Formerly Cole County. Name changed to Union 7 Jan 1864) (Registrar of Deeds has Birth Records from 1866, Marriage Records from 1886, Death Records from 1905, Burial Records from 1961, Land Records from 1863 & Military Discharge Records from 1919; Clerk Court has Probate Records from 1875, Court Records from 1890 & Divorce Records)
Wagner		**9 Mar 1883**	**Martin** Wagner County; SD **Details:** (Attached to Lawrence & Butte Counties. Eliminated 8 Nov 1898 to Butte)

South Dakota

County	Map	Date	Parent County or Territory From Which Organized
Website	Index	Created	Address/Details

Walworth I4 **8 Jan 1873** **Buffalo**
www.rootsweb.com/~sdwalwor/
Walworth County; PO Box 199; Selby, SD 57472-0199;
Ph. (605) 649-7878
Details: (Organized 28 Mar 1883) (Registrar of Deeds has Birth, Death & Burial Records from 1905 & Land Records; County Treasury has Marriage Records from 1889; Clerk Court has Divorce Records from 1889, Probate & Court Records from 1892)

Washabaugh **9 Mar 1883** **Lugenbeel, Shannon**
Washabaugh County; SD
Details: County Terminated 1979 (Unorganized; Attached to Custer County; within limits of Pine Ridge Indian Reservation; part taken to form parts of Bennet, Mellette & Todd 3 Jun 1909 & part comprising part of Rosebud Indian Reservation; annexed to Mellette in 2 Mar 1911. Attached to Jackson 3 Jun 1915)

Washington **9 Mar 1883** **Shannon, Lugenbeel**
Washington County; SD
Details: (Unorganized; Attached to Custer & Pennington Counties; within limits of Pine Ridge Indian Reservation; part taken to form part of Bennet 3 Jun 1909; Eliminated 2 Nov 1943 to Shannon)

Wetmore **8 Jan 1873** **Hanson**
Wetmore County; SD
Details: (Eliminated 1 Oct 1879 to Aurora & Miner)

White River **11 Jan 1875** **Pratt, Unorg. Terr.**
White River County; SD
Details: (Eliminated 8 Mar 1883 to Jackson & Nowlin)

Wood **8 Jan 1883** **Hanson**
Wood County; SD
Details: (Eliminated 1 Oct 1879 to Kingsbury)

Yankton C10 **10 Apr 1862** **Unorg. Terr.**
Yankton County; 410 Walnut St; PO Box 155; Yankton, SD 57078;
Ph. (605) 668-3080
Details: (All Records from 1900 to Present: Clerk of Courts has Court, Divorce, Guardianship, & Probate Records)

Ziebach L5 **1 Feb 1911** **Schnasse, Sterling, Armstrong, Unorg. Terr.**
www.rootsweb.com/~sdziebac/index.html
Ziebach County; PO Box 68; Dupree, SD 57623; Ph. (605) 365-5159
Details: (within limits of Cheyenne River Indian Reservation) (Registrar of Deeds has Birth, Marriage, Death, Burial & Land Records from 1911; Clerk Courts has Divorce, Probate & Court Records from 1911)

Ziebach, old **10 Feb 1877** **Pennington**
Ziebach, old County; SD
Details: (Attached to Pennington County. Eliminated 8 Nov 1898 to Pennington)

Tennessee

Capital: Nashville
State: 1796 (16th)

Agriculture and commerce

The Spanish first visited Tennessee in the mid-1500s, but they made no attempt to colonize the area. King Charles II included Tennessee in his grant of the Carolinas in 1663. The first English visited the area a decade later. That same year, Marquette and Joliet landed at the site of the future city of Memphis. In 1682, La Salle built a fort at the mouth of the Hatchie River in west Tennessee. Rivalry between the French and the English continued until the end of the French and Indian War in 1763. After explorations of the area by the likes of Daniel Boone, the first settlers entered the area in 1769 from North Carolina and Virginia. They settled in the Watauga Valley and banded together as the Watauga Association in 1771. By 1772, there were four areas of settlement: north of the Holstein River, near Bristol; along the Watauga River, near Elizabethton; west of the Holstein River, near Rogersville, and along the Nolichucky River, near Erwin. North Carolina formally annexed Tennessee in 1776 as Washington County.

During the Revolutionary War, there were a number of volunteers from the state and some notable battles, including the Battle of Kings Mountain in 1780, which was the turning point of the war in the South. In 1784, North Carolina ceded Tennessee to the United States in order to secure federal protection for the area. When the federal government refused to acknowledge the cession, the people in Tennessee organized the State of Franklin. This lasted only four years, as North Carolina regained control of the area in 1789. North Carolina again ceded the area to the United States in 1789, which formed the Southwest Territory in 1790.

Settlement of middle Tennessee began with the founding of Nashville in 1779. The west Tennessee area was the last to be settled. In 1796, Tennessee became a state. Twenty years later, the first steamboat reached Nashville. Early white settlers of Tennessee were predominantly English, but there were many Scotch-Irish, Germans, and Irish, as well as some French and Dutch. Most of the Americans came from South Carolina, Virginia, and North Carolina. Many of the Scotch-Irish came through the Shenandoah Valley, while the Germans settled in several of the counties west of Chattanooga.

In 1861, Tennessee seceded from the Union. The Confederacy received about 110,000 soldiers from Tennessee and the Union about 31,000, mostly from east Tennessee. Tennessee was readmitted to the Union in 1866.

Look for vital records in the following locations:

- **Birth and death records:** Contact the Division of Vital Records in Nashville, Tennessee. Official registration of births and deaths began in 1914. Birth records from 1908 and death records since 1936 are available. State relationship to the individual for whom you are seeking records and the reason for the request. Certified copies of records of births and deaths in Nashville, Knoxville, and Chattanooga between 1881 and 1914 are also available at the Division of Vital Records. Certified copies of births and deaths in Memphis are available from the Shelby County Health Department in Memphis. Certified copies of the records of the District School Enumeration Census for 1908–1912 are available from the Division of Vital Records.

- **Marriage and divorce records:** Certificates of marriage prior to 1 July 1945 are available from county court clerks. Marriage records after 1945 are available from the Division of Vital Records. Some marriage records have been published. Divorce records are usually kept by the circuit court of each county.

- **Wills, deeds, taxpayer lists, guardianships and court records:** Maintained by individual counties. Some of these records have been transcribed and are in the Tennessee State Library and Archives in Nashville.

- **Census records:** No state or territorial censuses were taken by Tennessee; however, there was an 1897 census for Memphis.

Tennessee Vital Records
Central Services Building
First Floor, 421 Fifth Avenue North
Nashville, Tennessee 37247

(615) 741-1763; Fax: (615) 741-9860
www2.state.tn.us/health/vr/index.htm

Tennessee State Library and Archives
403 Seventh Avenue North
Nashville, Tennessee 37243
(615) 741-2764; Fax: (615) 532-2472
www.tennessee.gov/tsla/

Societies and Repositories

Bedford County Historical Society; 624 S. Brittain St.; Shelbyville, TN 37160.

Blount County Genealogical and Historical Society; PO Box 4986; Maryville, TN 37902-4986.

Bradley County Genealogical Society; PO Box 1384; Cleveland, TN 37364-1384.

Campbell County Historical Society; 101 Sixth St.; LaFollette, TN 37766.

Civil War Plymouth Pilgrims Descendants Society; c/o Scott Holmes, Treasurer; 1037 Whitehall Drive; Franklin, TN 37064; edboots@worldnet.att.net; http://home.att.net/~cwppds/homepage.htm.

Claiborne County Historical Society; PO Box 32; Tazewell, TN 37879.

Coffee County Historical Society; Box 524; Manchester, TN 37355.

East Tennessee Historical Society; 500 W. Church Ave.; Knoxville, TN 37902-2505.

Fentress County Genealogical Society; PO Box 178; Jamestown, TN 38556.

Franklin County Historical Society; PO Box 130; Winchester, TN 37398.

Genealogy Friends; PO Box 863; Hendersonville, TN 37077.

Giles County Historical Society; PO Box 693; Pulaski, TN 38478.

Hamblen County Genealogical Society; PO Box 1213; Morristown, TN 37816-1213.

Hancock County Historical & Genealogical Society; PO Box 307; Sneedville, TN 37869; www.korrnet.org/overhome/page3.html.

Hawkins County Genealogical and Historical Society; PO Box 429; Rogersville, TN 37857-3424.

Henry County Genealogical Society of Tennessee; PO Box 1411; Paris, TN 38242.

Isaac Shelby Chapter, Sons of the American Revolution; 48 Redthorn Cove; Cordova, TN 38018-7244; ttb2@bellsouth.net; http://members.aol.com/memphisar/htmls/memsarww.htm.

Jefferson County Genealogical Society; PO Box 267; Jefferson City, TN 37760.

John Sevier Chapter, Sons of the American Revolution; 7825 Hixson Pike; Hixson, TN 37343; (423) 842-1810; hixsoncl@cdc.net; www.SAR.org/tnsSAR/js-tn.htm.

Jonesborough Genealogical Society; c/o Washington County-Jonesborough Library; 200 Sab; Jonesborough, TN 37659.

Kings Mountain Chapter, Sons of the American Revolution; 1314 Woodland Dr.; Johnson City, TN 37601; (423) 928-1341; wpb1314@worldnet.att.net; www.SAR.org/tnsSAR/km-tn.htm.

Lawrence County Genealogical Society; 218 N. Military Ave., Suite B-1; Lawrenceburg, TN 38464.

Lincoln County Genealogical Society; 1508 West Washington St.; Fayetteville, TN 37334.

Macon County Historical Society; 4233 Green Grove Rd.; Hartsville, TN 37074.

Marion County Genealogical Group; 6611 Old Dunlap Rd.; Whitwell, TN 37397.

Maury County, Tennessee Historical Society; PO Box 147; Columbia, TN 38401.

Mid-West Tennessee Genealogical Society; PO Box 3343; Jackson, TN 38301.

Obion County Genealogical Society; PO Box 241; Union City, TN 38261.

Old James County Historical Society; PO Box 203; Ooltewah, TN 37363.

Pellissippi Genealogical and Historical Society; c/o Clinton Public Library; Anderson County; 118 South Hicks St.; Clinton, TN 37716.

Polk County Historical and Genealogical Society; PO Box 636; Benton, TN 37307-0636.

Sons of the American Revolution, Society of Tennessee; 1712 Natchez Trace; Nashville, TN 37212.

Signal Mountain Genealogical Society, Inc.; 103 Florida Ave.; Signal Mountain, TN 37377.

Stephen Holston Chapter, Sons of the American Revolution; 102 Case Ln.; Oak Ridge, TN 37830; (865) 483-3337; bobkemper@worldnet.att.net; www.sar.org/tnssar/sh-tn.htm.

Stones River Chapter, Sons of the American Revolution; 2808 Clearview Ct.; Murfreesboro, TN 37129; NCarr36550@aol.com; www.SAR.org/tnsSAR/sr-tn.htm.

Tennessee Genealogical Society; PO Box 247; Brunswick, TN 38014-0247; tngensociety@yahoo.com.

Tennessee State Library and Archives; 403 Seventh Avenue North; Nashville, TN 37243-0312; (615) 741-2764; www.state.tn.us/sos/statelib/tslahome.htm.

The Andrew Jackson Chapter, Sons of the American Revolution; 1605 Craggie Hope Rd.; Kingston Springs, TN 37082; (615) 952-9552; Roy_Miles @email.msn.com; www.sar.org/tnssar/aj-tn.htm.

The Central of Georgia Railway Historical Society; 4403 Sunnybrook Dr.; Nashville, TN 37205; allen@cofg.org; www.cofg.org.

Tombigbee Chapter, Sons of the American Revolution; 117 Seventh Avenue; Columbia, TN 38401; (931) 381-5150; www.SAR.org/tnsSAR/t-tn.htm.

Trousdale County Historical Society; 4233 Green Grove Rd.; Hartsville, TN 37074.

Union County Historical Society, Inc.; PO Box 95; Maynardville, TN 37807.

Upper Cumberland Genealogical Association; Putnam Library; 48 E. Broad St.; Cookeville, TN 38501.

Upper Cumberland Genealogical Support Group; Art Circle Public Library; 306 E. First St.; Crossville, TN 38555.

Valentine Sevier Chapter, Sons of the American Revolution; 331 Grassland Dr.; Clarksville, TN 37043; (931) 647-0954; James.Thweatt@mcmail.vanderbilt.edu; www.SAR.org/tnsSAR/vs-tn.htm.

Van Buren County Historical Society; PO Box 126; Spencer, TN 38585.

Vardy Community Historical Society; PO Box 554; Sneedville, TN 37869; http://hometown.aol.com/vardyvalley/index.html.

Watauga Association of Genealogists, Upper East Tennessee; PO Box 117; Johnson City, TN 37605-0117.

White County Genealogical-Historical Society; PO Box 721; Sparta, TN 38583-0721.

Bibliography and Record Sources

General

Allison, John Roy V. *Notable Men of Tennessee: Personal and Genealogical With Portraits.* 2 vols. Atlanta: Southern Historical Association, 1905.

Bamman, Gale Williams. *Research in Tennessee.* Arlington, Virginia: National Genealogical Society, 1993.

Bible Records of Families in East Tennessee and Their Connections in Other Areas. 3 vols. Genealogical Record Committee, Daughters of the American Revolution, 1959–1960.

Carr, John. *Early Times in Middle Tennessee.* Nashville, Tennessee: R. H. Horsley and Associates, 1958.

Crutchfield, James A. *Timeless Tennesseans.* Huntsville, Alabama: Strode Publishers, 1984.

Folmsbee, Stanley John. *History of Tennessee.* 4 vols. New York: Lewis Historical Publishing Co., 1960.

Fulcher, Richard Carlton. *Guide to County Records and Genealogical Resources in Tennessee.* Baltimore: Genealogical Publishing Co, 1987.

Guide to Microfilmed Manuscript Holdings of the Tennessee State Library and Archives. 3rd ed. Nashville: Tennessee State Library and Archives, 1983.

Hale, William T., and Dixon L. Merritt. *A History of Tennessee and Tennesseans.* 8 vols. Chicago: Lewis Publishing Co., 1913.

Hathaway, Beverly W. *Genealogy Research Sources in Tennessee.* West Jordan, Utah: Allstates Research Co., 1972.

Historical Records Survey (Tennessee). *Check List of Tennessee Imprints, 1841–1850.* Nashville, Tennessee: Tennessee Historical Records Survey, 1941.

Historical Records Survey (Tennessee). *List of Tennessee Imprints, 1793–1840, in Tennessee Libraries.* Nashville, Tennessee: Tennessee Historical Records Survey, 1941.

Inventory of the Church Archives of Tennessee: Nashville Baptist Association. Nashville: Historical Records Survey, WPA, 1939.

Inventory of the Church Archives of Tennessee: Tennessee Baptist Convention, Ocoee Baptist Association. Nashville: Historical Records Survey, WPA, 1942.

Moore, John Trotwood and Austin P. Foster. *Tennessee, the Volunteer State, 1760–1923.* 4 vols. Chicago: S. J. Clark Publishing Co., 1923.

Ray, Worth Stickley. *Tennessee Cousins: A History of Tennessee People.* 1950. Reprint. Baltimore: Genealogical Publishing Co., 1968.

Schweitzer, George K. *Tennessee Genealogical Research.* Knoxville: George K. Schweitzer, 1986.

Sistler, Byron and Barbara Sistler. *Vital Statistics from Nineteenth Century Tennessee Church Records.* Nashville: B. Sistler and Assoc., 1979.

Smith, Sam B., and Luke H. Banker, ed. and comp. *Tennessee History: A Bibliography.* Knoxville: University of Tennessee Press, 1974.

Sneed, Adele Weiss. *Bible Records of Families of East Tennessee and Their Connections From Other Areas.* 3 vols. N.p., Knoxville Chapter of the Daughters of the American Colonists and James White Chapter of the Daughters of the American Revolution, 1959–1960.

Speer, Ed. *The Tennessee Handbook.* Jefferson, North Carolina: McFarland & Co., Inc., Publishers, 2002.

Speer, William S. *Sketches of Prominent Tennesseans.* Nashville: A. B. Tavel, 1888.

Stanley J. Folmsbee, et al. *History of Tennessee.* 4 vols. New York: Lewis Historical Publishing Co., 1960.

Tennessee County Records Manual. Nashville: Tennessee State Library and Archives, 1968.

Tennessee Newspapers: A Cumulative List of Microfilmed Tennessee Newspapers in the Tennessee State Library. Nashville: Tennessee State Library and Archives, 1978.

Tennessee Research Outline. Series U.S.-States, no. 42. Salt Lake City: Family History Library. 1988.

United States. Court of Claims. *Eastern Cherokee Applications, August 29, 1906 to May 26, 1909.* Washington, D.C.: National Archives, 1981.

Whitley, Edythe. *Tennessee Genealogical Records: Records of Early Settlers from State and County Archives.* Baltimore: Genealogical Publishing Co., 1981.

Atlases, Maps and Gazetteers

Foster, Austin P. *Counties of Tennessee.* Nashville: Department of Education, Division of history, State of Tennessee, 1923.

Fullerton, Ralph O. *Place Names of Tennessee.* Nashville: Tennessee Department of Conservation, Division of Geology, 1974.

McBride, Robert M., and Owen Meredith, ed. *Eastin Morris' Tennessee Gazetteer 1834 and Matthew Rhea's Map of the State of Tennessee, 1832.* Nashville: The Gazetteer Press, 1971.

Puetz, C. J., comp. *Tennessee County Maps.* Lyndon Station, Wisconsin: Thomas Publishing Co., 1992.

Tennessee Atlas and Gazetteer. 3rd ed. Freeport, Maine: DeLorme Mapping Co., 1995.

Census Records

Available Census Records and Census Substitutes

Federal Census 1810 (Rutherford and Grainger Counties only), 1820, 1830, 1840, 1850, 1860, 1870, 1880, 1900, 1910, 1920

Federal Mortality Schedules 1850, 1860, 1880

Union Veterans and Widows 1890

Allen, Maud Bliss. *Census Records and Cherokee Muster Rolls.* Washington: N.p., 1935.

Dollarhide, William. *The Census Book: A Genealogist's Guide to Federal Census Facts, Schedules and Indexes.* Bountiful, Utah: Heritage Quest, 1999.

Early Tennessee Tax Lists. Evanston, Illinois: Byron Sistler and Assoc., 1977.

East Tennessee Tax Lists. Fort Worth, Texas: Arrow Printing Co., 1964.

Kemp, Thomas Jay. *The American Census Handbook.* Wilmington, Delaware: Scholarly Resources, Inc., 2001.

Lainhart, Ann S. *State Census Records.* Baltimore: Genealogical Publishing Co., Inc., 1992.

McGhee, Lucy Kate. *Partial Census of 1787 to 1791 of Tennessee as taken from the North Carolina Land Grants.* Salt Lake City: Filmed by the Genealogical Society of Utah, 1990. Microfilm, 2 rolls.

Siler, David W. *Eastern Cherokees: A Census of the Cherokee Nation, 1851.* Cottonport, Louisiana: Polyanthos, 1972.

Thorndale, William and William Dollarhide. *Map Guide to the U.S. Federal Census, 1790–1920.* Baltimore: Genealogical Publishing Co., 1987.

Court, Probate and Wills

Fischer, Marjorie Hood and Ruth Blake Burns. *Tennessee Tidbits, 1778–1914.* Vol. 2. Vista, California: Ram Press, 1988.

Fischer, Marjorie Hood. *Tennessee Tidbits, 1778–1914.* Vol. 1. Easley, South Carolina: Southern Historical Press, 1986.

Fischer, Marjorie Hood. *Tennessee Tidbits, 1778–1914.* Vol. 3. Vista, California: RAM Press, 1989.

Historical Records Survey (Tennessee). *Survey to Tennessee County Court Records, Prior to 1860, in the Second, Third and Fourth Districts.* Microfilm of typescript in Nashville, Tennessee. Salt Lake City: Filmed by the Genealogical Society of Utah, 1943. Microfilm.

Sistler, Byron and Barbara Sistler. *Index to Tennessee Wills and Administrations, 1779–1861.* Nashville, Tennessee: Byron Sistler & Associates, 1990.

Survey to Tennessee County Court Records, Prior to 1860, in the Second, Third and Fourth Districts. Nashville: Historical Records Survey, 1943.

Emigration, Immigration, Migration and Naturalization

Naturalization Index Cards for Chattanooga, Tennessee. Microfilm of originals in the National Archives Branch in East Point, Georgia. Salt Lake City: Filmed by the Genealogical Society of Utah, 1989. Microfilm.

United States. District Court (Alabama: Southern District*).* *Declarations of Intentions, Naturalizations, and Petitions, 1855–1960.* Microfilm of originals at the National Archives in East Point, Georgia. Salt Lake City: Filmed by the Genealogical Society of Utah, 1987–1989. Microfilm, 9 rolls.

Land

Goldene F. Burgner, *North Carolina Land Grants in Tennessee, 1778–1791.* N.p.: Southern Historical Press, 1981.

Griffey, Irene M. *Earliest Tennessee Land Records & Earliest Tennessee Land History.* Baltimore: Clearfield Co., 2000.

Land Grants, 1775–1905, 1911. Nashville, Tennessee: Tennessee State Library and Archives, 1976. Microfilm, multiple rolls.

McNamara, Billie R. *Tennessee Land: Its Early History and Laws.* Knoxville, Tennessee: B. R. McNamara, 1997.

North Carolina. Secretary of State. Land Grant Office. *Land Records, 1600 thru 1957; Land Grant Index, 1693–1959.* Raleigh, North Carolina: North Carolina State Archives, 1980. Microfilm, 552 rolls.

Pruitt, Albert Bruce. *Tennessee Land Entries Military Bounty Land (1783–1841).* 7 vols. Whitakers, North Carolina: Pruitt, A. Bruce, 1997.

Pruitt, Albert Bruce. *Tennessee Land Entries: John Armstrong's Office.* 2 vols. S.l.: A. B. Pruitt, 1995.

Pruitt, Albert Bruce. *Tennessee Land Warrants.* Whitakers, North Carolina: A. B. Pruitt, 1999.

Rice, Shirley Hollis. *The Hidden Revolutionary War Land Grants in the Tennessee Military Reservation.* Lawrenceburg, Tennessee: Family Tree Press, 1992.

Sistler, Byron. *Tennessee Land Grants, Surnames.* 17 vols. Nashville, Tennessee: Byron Sistler, 1997.

Tennessee Valley Authority (Tennessee). *Tennessee Population Relocation Files, 1934–1954.* Microreproduction of originals housed in the National Archives Record Office, East Point, Georgia. Salt Lake City: Filmed by the Genealogical Society of Utah, 1996. Microfilm, 41 rolls.

United States. District Court (Tennessee). *Final Record Books, 1803–1850; Land Claim Records, 1807–1820.* Washington, D.C.: National Archives. Central Plains Region, 1982.

Military

Allen, Penelope J. *Tennessee Soldiers in the Revolution.* Baltimore: Genealogical Publishing Co., 1975.

Armstrong, Zella, comp. *Some Tennessee Heroes of the Revolution Compiled from Pension of the Republic of Texas. Muster Rolls of the Texas Revolution.* Austin, Texas: Daughters of the Republic of Texas, 1986.

Armstrong, Zella, comp. *Twenty-four Hundred Tennessee Pensioners of the Revolution, War of 1812.* Chattanooga, Tennessee: Lookout Publishing Co., 1937.

Barron, John C., et al. *Republic of Texas Pension Application Abstracts.* Austin, Texas: Austin Genealogical Society, 1987.

Barton, Henry W. *Texas Volunteers in the Mexican War.* Wichita Falls, Texas: Texan Press, 1970.

Bates, Lucy W. *Roster of Soldiers and Patriots of the American Revolution Buried in Tennessee.* 1974. Chattanooga, Tennessee: Lookout Publishing Co., 1933. Reprint. Baltimore: Genealogical Publishing Co., 1975.

Brock, Reid. *Volunteers: Tennesseans in the War with Mexico.* 2 vols. Salt Lake City: Kitchen Table Press, 1986.

Confederate Patriot Index (1894–1978) 2 vols., S.p.: Tennessee Division, United Daughters of the Confederacy, 1976, 1978.

Dyer, Gustavus. *The Tennessee Civil War Veterans Questionnaires.* 5 vols. Easley, South Carolina: Southern Historical Press, 1985.

Haywood, John. "List of North Carolina Revolutionary Soldiers Given Land in Tennessee, by the Act of 1782–1783." In *The History of Tennessee.* Reprint. New York: Arno Press, 1971.

McCown, M. H., and I. E. Burns. *Soldiers of the War of 1812 Buried in Tennessee.* Johnson City, Tennessee: Society of U.S. Daughters of 1812, 1959.

Moore, Mrs. J. T. *Record of Commissions of Officers in the 1796–1815 Tennessee Militia.* Baltimore: Genealogical Publishing Co., 1977.

Rosenthal, Phil and Bill Groneman. *Roll Call at the Alamo.* Fort Collins, Colorado: Old Army Press, 1985.

Sistler, Samuel. *Index to Tennessee Confederate Pension Applications.* Nashville: Byron Sistler, 1995.

Spurlin, Charles D. *Texas Veterans in the Mexican War.* St. Louis: Ingmire Pub., 1984.

Tennesseeans in the Civil War. Nashville: Civil War Commission, 1965.

United States Selective Service System. *Tennessee World War I Selective Service System Draft Registration Cards, 1917–1918.* National Archives Microfilm Publications, M1509. Washington, D.C.: National Archives, 1987–1988.

United States. Adjutant General's Office. *Compiled Service Records of Volunteer Soldiers Who Served During the Mexican War in Organizations from the State of Tennessee.* Washington, D.C.: The National Archives, 1965. Microfilm, multiple rolls.

Wiefering, Edna. *Tennessee Confederate Widows and Their Families: Abstracts of 11,190 Confederate Widows' Applications.* Cleveland, Tennessee: Cleveland Public Library, 1992.

Vital and Cemetery

Acklen, Jeannette T. *Tennessee Records: Bible Records and Marriages Bonds.* Reprint. Baltimore, Maryland: Clearfield Co., 1997.

Acklen, Jeannette T. *Tennessee Records: Tombstone Inscriptions and Manuscripts, Historical and Biographical.* Nashville, Tennessee: Cullom and Ghertner, 1976.

Acklen, Jeannette Tillotson. *Tennessee Records: Bible Records and Marriage Bonds.* Baltimore: Genealogical Publishing Co., 1967.

Baker, Russell Pierce. *Obituaries and Marriage Notices From the Tennessee Baptist: 1844–1862.* Easley, South Carolina: Southern Historical Press, 1979.

Cemetery Records of Tennessee. 2 vols. Salt Lake City: Genealogical Society, 1951–1962.

Gale W. Bamman. *Tennessee Divorces, 1797–1858.* Nashville: G. Bamman, 1985.

Garrett, Jill L. *Obituaries from Tennessee Newspapers.* Easley, South Carolina: Southern Historical Press, 1980.

Guide to Church Vital Statistics in Tennessee. Nashville: War Services Section, WPA, 1942.

Historical Records Project and Historical Records Survey. *Church, Cemetery, Bible, and Family Records from Tennessee.* Salt Lake City: Filmed by the Genealogical Society of Utah, 1943.

Lucas, Silas E., and Ella L. Sheffield, *35,000 Tennessee Marriage Records and Bonds, 1783–1870.* 3 vols. Easley, South Carolina: Southern Historical Press, 1981.

Lucas, Silas Emmett. *Marriages from Early Tennessee Newspapers, 1794–1851.* Easley, South Carolina: Southern Historical Press, 1978.

Meier, Oveda. *Tennessee Ancestors: The Brave and the Dead, Probate and Death Records of Early Middle Tennessee, 1780–1805.* Salt Lake City: O. Meier, 1990.

Sistler, Byron and Barbara Sistler. *Early East Tennessee Marriages.* 2 vols. Nashville: Byron Sistler & Assoc., 1987.

Sistler, Byron and Barbara Sistler. *Early Middle Tennessee Marriages.* 2 vols. Nashville: Byron Sistler and Assoc., 1988.

Sistler, Byron and Barbara Sistler. *Early West Tennessee Marriages.* 2 vols. Nashville: B. Sistler & Assoc. 1989.

Tennessee. Division of Vital Records. *Births (Enumerator Record Series), 1908–1912.* Nashville, Tennessee: Tennessee State Library and Archives, 1980. Microfilm, 85 rolls.

Tennessee. State Library and Archives *Marriages, 1919–1974; Marriage Indexes for Several Counties, 1837–1987, 1837–1987.* Nashville, Tennessee: Tennessee State Library and Archives, 1988. Microfilm, 262 rolls.

Tennessee. State Library and Archives. *Births & Deaths, 1925–1940; Wills, 1889 to Sept. 1958.* Nashville, Tennessee: Tennessee State Library and Archives, 1988.

Tennessee. State Library and Archives. *Record of Deaths, 1920–1939.* Tennessee. Nashville, Tennessee: Tennessee State Library and Archives, 1988. Microfilm, 277 rolls.

County Website	Map Index	Date Created	Parent County or Territory From Which Organized / Address/Details
Anderson www.korrnet.org/anderson/	F5	**6 Nov 1801**	**Knox, Grainger** Anderson County; 100 N Main St; Clinton, TN 37716-3615; Ph. (865) 457-6232 **Details:** (County Clerk has Marriage & Probate Records)
Bedford www.tngenweb.org/bedford/	K7	**3 Dec 1807**	**Rutherford** Bedford County; 100 N Side Sq; Shelbyville, TN 37160; Ph. (931) 684-1921 **Details:** (Courthouse destroyed by fire & by a tornado in the past) (County Clerk has Marriage Records from 1863 & Probate Records; Clerk Circuit Court has Divorce Records)
Benton www.rootsweb.com/~tnbenton/index.htm	N5	**19 Dec 1835**	**Henry, Humphreys** Benton County; Court Sq; Camden, TN 38320; Ph. (901) 584-6053 **Details:** (County Clerk has Marriage Records from 1836 & Probate Records from 1840; Clerk Circuit Court has Divorce & Court Records; Registrar of Deeds has Land Records)
Bledsoe www.tngenweb.org/bledsoe/	H6	**30 Nov 1807**	**Roane** Bledsoe County; Main St; PO Box 149; Pikeville, TN 37367-0212; Ph. (423) 447-2137 **Details:** (Courthouse burned in 1908) (County Clerk has Marriage & Probate Records from 1908; Registrar of Deeds has Land Records)
Blount www.korrnet.org/blountco/	F6	**11 Jul 1795**	**Knox** Blount County; 345 Court St; Maryville, TN 37804; Ph. (865) 273-5800 **Details:** (County Clerk has Marriage & Probate Records from 1795; Clerk Circuit Court has Divorce Records; Registrar of Deeds has Land Records)

County Website	Map Index	Date Created	Parent County or Territory From Which Organized Address/Details
Bradley www.bradleyco.net/	H7	10 Feb 1836	**Cherokee Indian Lands** Bradley County; PO Box 46; Cleveland, TN 37364-0046; Ph. (423) 476-0520 **Details:** (Courthouse Records destroyed by fire in Nov 1864) (County Clerk has Marriage Records from 1864; Clerk & Master has Probate Records from 1864; Registrar of Deeds has Land & Military Discharge Records from 1864; Circuit & Session Court has Divorce & Court Records from 1864; Cleveland Public Library has early Court Records, Census, Probate, Marriage & Death Records)
Campbell www.rootsweb.com/~tncampbe/	F5	11 Sep 1806	**Anderson, Claiborne** Campbell County; Main St; Jacksboro, TN 37757; Ph. (423) 562-3496 **Details:** (County Clerk has Marriage Records from 1838; Registrar of Deeds has Land Records)
Cannon www.cafes.net/jlewis/cannon.htm	J6	31 Jan 1836	**Coffee, Warren, Wilson, Rutherford** Cannon County; County Courthouse; Woodbury, TN 37190; Ph. (615) 563-5936 **Details:** (County Clerk has Marriage Records from 1838; Registrar of Deeds has Land Records)
Carroll www.rootsweb.com/~tncarrol/	O5	7 Nov 1821	**Chickasaw Indian Lands** Carroll County; 625 High St; PO Box 110; Huntingdon, TN 38344; Ph. (731) 986-1960 **Details:** (County Clerk has Marriage Records from 1838; Registrar of Deeds has Land Records)
Carter www.tngenweb.org/carter/	B5	9 Apr 1796	**Washington** Carter County; 801 E Elk Ave; Elizabethton, TN 37643; Ph. (423) 542-1814 **Details:** (County Clerk has Probate Records from 1800; Chancery & Circuit Court has Divorce & Court Records; Registrar of Deeds has Land Records)
Cheatham www.cheathamcounty.net/	L5	28 Feb 1856	**Davidson, Dickson, Montgomery, Robertson** Cheatham County; 100 Public Sq; Ashland City, TN 37015; Ph. (615) 792-5179 **Details:** (County Clerk has Marriage & Probate Records from 1865; Clerk Circuit Court has Divorce & Court Records; Registrar of Deeds has Land Records)
Chester www.rootsweb.com/~tncheste/chester.htm	O7	1879	**Hardeman, Madison, Henderson, McNairy** Chester County; 126 Crook Ave; Henderson, TN 38340; Ph. (731) 989-7171 **Details:** (County Clerk has Marriage & Probate Records from 1890; Clerk Circuit Court has Divorce & Court Records; Registrar of Deeds has Land Records)

County Website	Map Index	Date Created	Parent County or Territory From Which Organized
			Address/Details

Claiborne   E4   29 Oct 1801
www.tngenweb.org/claiborne/

Grainger, Hawkins
Claiborne County; PO Box 173; Tazewell, TN 37879;
Ph. (423) 626-3283 (County Clerk); (423) 626-3334 (Circuit Court Clerk); (423) 626-3284 (Clerk & Master); (423) 626-3325 (Register of Deeds); (423) 626-3276 (Property Assessor)
Details: (County Clerk has Marriage Records from 1838, Wills from from 1837–Aug 1982 (probate); County Magistrates & Justice of Peace Court Records from 1801; Circuit Court Clerk has Civil, Circuit, Criminal Court, & Divorce Records; Clerk & Master has Chancery & Probate Court Records; Register of Deeds has Land Records; Assessor of Property has Land Maps/Assessment of Property Records: Some Records were destroyed by fire in 1932)

Clay   I4   24 Jun 1870
www.tngenweb.org/clay/

Jackson, Overton
Clay County; 100 Courthouse Sq; Celina, TN 38551;
Ph. (931) 243-3145
Details: (County Clerk has Marriage Records from 1870; Clerk & Master has Probate Records from 1870; County Assessor has Land Records; Clerk Circuit Court has Divorce & Court Records from 1870)

Cocke   D6   9 Oct 1797
www.rootsweb.com/~tncocke/Index.html

Jefferson
Cocke County; 111 Court Ave; Newport, TN 37821;
Ph. (423) 623-6176
Details: (County Clerk has Birth & Death Records 1909–1911 & 1928–1930 & Marriage Records; Clerk & Master has Divorce & Probate Records from 1877; Clerk Circuit Court has Court Records; Registrar of Deeds has Land Records; Stokely Memorial Library has a genealogical section)

Coffee   J6   8 Jan 1836
www.cafes.net/jlewis/

Franklin, Warren, Bedford
Coffee County; 300 Hillsboro Blvd; Box 8; Manchester, TN 37355;
Ph. (931) 723-5106
Details: (County Clerk has Marriage Records from 1854 & Probate Records from 1836; Clerk Circuit Court has Divorce & Court Records; Registrar of Deeds has Land Records)

Crockett   P6   20 Dec 1845
www.rootsweb.com/~tncrocke/

Dyer, Madison, Gibson, Haywood
Crockett County; 1 S Bells St, Ste 1; Alamo, TN 38001;
Ph. (731) 696-5452
Details: (County Terminated in 1846 and Restored in 1872) (Clerk of Court has Marriage Records from 1872, Birth & Death Records from 1925, & Probate Records up to 1980; Clerk of Circuit Court as Divorce Records; Chancery Court has Divorce Records from 1872 & Probate Records from 1980; Register of Deeds has Boundry Line Dispute from 1872; County Health Department has Death Records; Library has Birth Records 1940–1960)

Cumberland   H6   16 Nov 1855
www.upper-cumberland.net/users/mboniol/

Bledsoe, Morgan, Roane, White, Rhea, Van Buren, Putnam
Cumberland County; 2 N Main St; #206; Crossville, TN 38555;
Ph. (931) 484-6442
Details: (County Clerk has Marriage & Probate Records from 1905; Clerk & Master & Clerk Circuit Court have Divorce Records; Registrar of Deeds has Land Records)

County Website	Map Index	Date Created	Parent County or Territory From Which Organized Address/Details

Davidson   K5   18 Apr 1783
www.rootsweb.com/~tndavids/nashgene.htm

Washington

Davidson County; 700 2nd Ave S; Nashville, TN 37210;
Ph. (615) 862-5710

Details: (County Clerk has Marriage Records from 1789 & Probate Records from 1783; Clerk Circuit Court has Divorce & Court Records; Registrar of Deeds has Land Records)

De Kalb   I5   11 Dec 1837
www.tngenweb.org/dekalb/

Cannon, Warren, White, Wilson, Jackson

De Kalb County; County Courthouse; Rm 205; Smithville, TN 37166;
Ph. (615) 597-5159

Details: (County Clerk has Marriage Records from 1848 & Probate Records from 1854; Clerk Chancery Court has Divorce Records; Registrar of Deeds has Land Records)

Decatur   N7   Nov 1845
www.netease.net/decatur/

Perry

Decatur County; PO Box 488; Decaturville, TN 38329-0488;
Ph. (731) 852-3417

Details: (County Clerk has Marriage Records from 1869; Registrar of Deeds has Land Records)

Dickson   M5   25 Oct 1803
www.rootsweb.com/~tndickso/

Montgomery, Robertson

Dickson County; 4 Court Sq; Charlotte, TN 37036; Ph. (615) 789-4171

Details: (Courthouse was destoryed by tornado about 1835; many Records were destroyed) (County Clerk has Birth & Death Records 1908–1912 & 1925–1939, Marriage Records from 1817 & Probate Records from 1977; Registrar Office has Land Records from 1804 & Military Discharge Records from 1946)

Dyer   Q5   16 Oct 1823
www.rootsweb.com/~tndyer/

Chickasaw Indian Lands

Dyer County; PO Box 1360; Dyersburg, TN 38025-1360;
Ph. (731) 286-7814

Details: (County Clerk has Marriage & Probate Records from 1850, Divorce & Court Records from 1927 & funeral Records 1914–1956; Registrar of Deeds has Land Records)

Fayette   Q7   29 Sep 1824
www.wdbj.net/~wdbj/fayette/index.html

Shelby, Hardeman

Fayette County; 1 Court Sq; County Courthouse; Somerville, TN 38068; Ph. (901) 465-2871

Details: (County Clerk has Birth & Death Records 1925–1929, Marriage Records from 1838 except Marriage Records 1918–1925 lost in fire; Clerk & Master has Probate Records; Registrar of Deeds has Land Records)

Fentress   H5   28 Nov 1823
www.rootsweb.com/~tnfentre/fent.htm

Morgan, Overton

Fentress County; 101 S Main St; Jamestown, TN 38556;
Ph. (931) 879-8615

Details: (County Clerk has Marriage Records from 1905; Registrar of Deeds has Land Records)

Franklin   J8   3 Dec 1807
www.tngenweb.org/franklin/

Bedford, Warren

Franklin County; 1 So Jefferson St; Winchester, TN 37398;
Ph. (931) 967-2541

Details: (County Clerk has Marriage Records from 1838 & Probate Records from 1808; Registrar of Deeds has Land Records)

County Website	Map Index	Date Created	Parent County or Territory From Which Organized Address/Details
Gibson www.rootsweb.com/~tngibson/	P5	21 Oct 1823	**Chickasaw Indian Lands** Gibson County; County Courthouse; PO Box 228; Trenton, TN 38382; Ph. (731) 855-7639 **Details:** (County Clerk has Marriage Records from 1824 & Probate Records 1824–1981; Registrar of Deeds has Land Records)
Giles	L7	14 Nov 1809	**Maury** Giles County; PO Box 678; Pulaski, TN 38478-0678; Ph. (931) 363-8434 **Details:** (Old Records Dept has all County Records 1810–1900; Chancery Clerk, County Clerk, Circuit Clerk hold records from 1900; Register of Deeds has Land Records from 1900; Trustee has Tax Records from 1900; Destroyed Records include: Marriages 1810–1865, Wills & Settlement 1810–1865, & Tax Books 1910–1878)
Grainger www.rootsweb.com/~tngraing/	E5	22 Apr 1796	**Hawkins, Knox** Grainger County; County Courthouse; PO Box 116; Rutledge, TN 37861; Ph. (865) 828-3511 **Details:** (County Clerk has Marriage Records from 1796; Registrar of Deeds has Land Records)
Greene www.rootsweb.com/~tngreene/	D5	18 Apr 1783	**Washington** Greene County; 101 S Main St; Greenville, TN 37743; Ph. (423) 798-1708 **Details:** (County Clerk has Marriage & Probate Records; Registrar of Deeds has Land Records)
Grundy www.tngenweb.org/grundy/	I7	29 Jan 1844	**Coffee, Warren** Grundy County; Hwy 56 & 108; Altamont, TN 37301; Ph. (931) 692-3455 **Details:** (County Clerk has Marriage & Probate Records from 1850; Registrar of Deeds has Land Records)
Hamblen www.tngenweb.org/hamblen/	D5	8 Jun 1870	**Grainger, Hawkins, Jefferson** Hamblen County; 511 W 2nd N St; Morristown, TN 37814; Ph. (423) 586-9112 **Details:** (County Clerk has Marriage & Probate Records from 1870; Clerk & Master has Divorce Records; Clerk Circuit Court has Court Records; Registrar of Deeds has Land Records)
Hamilton www.hamiltontn.gov/	H7	25 Oct 1819	**Cherokee Indian Lands** Hamilton County; County Courthouse; Rm 201; Chattanooga, TN 37402; Ph. (423) 209-6500 **Details:** (County Clerk has Marriage Records from 1857; County Health Department has Birth Records from 1949 & Death Records from 1972; Circuit Court & Clerk & Masters has Divorce Records; Clerk & Masters has Probate Records from 1865; Clerk & Masters & Registrar of Deeds has Land Records; Registrar of Deeds has Military Discharge Records; Clerk Circuit Court has Court Records)
Hancock www.rootsweb.com/~tnhancoc/	D4	7 Jan 1844	**Claiborne, Hawkins** Hancock County; PO Box 347; Sneedville, TN 37869; Ph. (423) 733-4341 **Details:** (County Clerk has Marriage, Divorce, Probate & Court Records from 1930, Land Records from 1875 & Military Records from 1917)

County Website	Map Index	Date Created	Parent County or Territory From Which Organized Address/Details
Hardeman www.tngenweb.org/hardeman/	P7	16 Oct 1823	**Chickasaw Indian Lands** Hardeman County; 100 N Main St; Bolivar, TN 38008-2322; Ph. (901) 658-3541 **Details:** (County Clerk has Marriage & Probate Records from 1823; Registrar of Deeds has Land Records)
Hardin www.hardinhistory.com/history/genealog.htm	N7	13 Nov 1819	**Chickasaw Indian Lands** Hardin County; 601 Main St; Savannah, TN 38372; Ph. (901) 925-8166 **Details:** (County Clerk has Marriage Records from 1864, Divorce, Land, Probate & Court Records)
Hawkins www.rootsweb.com/~tnhawkin/index.html	D5	18 Nov 1787	**Sullivan** Hawkins County; 100 E Main St; Rogersville, TN 37857-3390; Ph. (423) 272-8150 **Details:** (County Clerk has Marriage Records from 1789 & Probate Records; Clerk Circuit Court has Divorce & Court Records; Registrar of Deeds has Land Records)
Haywood www.rootsweb.com/~tnhaywoo/	P6	3 Nov 1823	**Chickasaw Indian Lands** Haywood County; 1 N Washington St; Brownsville, TN 38012; Ph. (731) 772-2362 **Details:** (County Clerk has Marriage Records from 1859, Divorce Records 1941–1965 & Probate Records from 1826; Registrar of Deeds has Land Records)
Henderson www.tngenweb.org/henderson/	O6	7 Nov 1821	**Chickasaw Indian Lands** Henderson County; 17 Monroe St; Lexington, TN 38351; Ph. (731) 968-2801 **Details:** (Courthouse burned 1863 & 1895; some Records saved) (Clerk Chancery Court has Birth Records; County Clerk has Marriage Records from 1893; Clerk Circuit Court has Divorce & Court Records; Registrar of Deeds has Land Records)
Henry www.rootsweb.com/~tnhenry/	N5	7 Nov 1821	**Chickasaw Indian Lands** Henry County; 100 W Washington St; Paris, TN 38242-0024; Ph. (731) 642-2412 **Details:** (Registrar of Deeds has Land Records; County Clerk has Birth, Marriage, Death & Probate Records; Clerk Circuit Court has Court Records)
Hickman www.rootsweb.com/~tnhickma/	M6	3 Dec 1807	**Dickson** Hickman County; Public Square; Centerville, TN 37033; Ph. (931) 729-2621 **Details:** (Courthouse burned 1865; all Records lost) (County Clerk has Marriage & Probate Records from 1867; Clerk Circuit Court has Divorce & Court Records; Registrar of Deeds has Land Records from 1807)
Houston www.rootsweb.com/~tnhousto/	M5	23 Jan 1871	**Dickson, Stewart, Humphreys** Houston County; PO Box 388; Erin, TN 37061-0388; Ph. (931) 289-3870 **Details:** (County Clerk has Marriage Records; Clerk Circuit Court has Divorce & Court Records; County Court has Probate Records; Registrar of Deeds has Land Records)

County Website	Map Index	Date Created	Parent County or Territory From Which Organized Address/Details
Humphreys www.tngenweb.org/humphreys/	M5	19 Oct 1809	**Stewart** Humphreys County; 102 Thompson St; Waverly, TN 37185; Ph. (931) 296-7671 **Details:** (Courthouse burned in 1876 & 1898; many Records lost; only Land Records are complete) (County Clerk has Land Records from 1809, Marriage Records from 1861 & Probate Records from 1838)
Jackson www.tngenweb.org/jackson/	I5	6 Nov 1801	**Smith** Jackson County; 101 E Hill Rd; PO Box 346; Gainesboro, TN 38562-0346; Ph. (931) 268-9516 **Details:** (County Clerk has Marriage & Probate Records from 1870; Registrar of Deeds has Land Records)
James		1870	**Hamilton, Bradley** James County; TN **Details:** County Terminated 1920
Jefferson www.tngenweb.org/jefferson/	E5	11 Jun 1792	**Green, Hawkins** Jefferson County; 214 W Main St; Dandridge, TN 37725-0710; Ph. (865) 397-2935 **Details:** (County Clerk has Marriage & Probate Records from 1792; Clerk & Master has Divorce Records; Clerk Circuit Court has Court Records; Registrar of Deeds has Land Records)
Johnson www.jacksonco.com/	B4	2 Jan 1836	**Carter** Johnson County; 210 College St; Mountain City, TN 37683; Ph. (423) 727-7853 **Details:** (County Clerk has Marriage & Probate Records from 1836; Clerk Chancery Court has Divorce & Court Records; Registrar of Deeds has Land Records)
Knox www.korrnet.org/knox/	F5	11 Jun 1792	**Greene, Hawkins** Knox County; Old Knox County Courthouse; Knoxville, TN 37902-1805; Ph. (865) 215-2390 **Details:** (County Archives has Probate Records from 1789, Marriage, Divorce & Court Records from 1792 & tax Records from 1806; Registrar of Deeds has Land Records)
Lake www.ecsis.net/lakecounty/history/	Q5	24 Jun 1870	**Obion** Lake County; 229 Church St; Tiptonville, TN 38079-1162; Ph. (731) 253-8926 **Details:** (County Clerk has Probate Records from 1870 & Marriage Records from 1883; Clerk Chancery & Circuit Court have Divorce Records; Registrar & Tax Assessor have Land Records)
Lauderdale www.rootsweb.com/~tnlauder/	Q6	24 Nov 1835	**Dyer, Tipton, Haywood** Lauderdale County; County Courthouse; Ripley, TN 38063; Ph. (731) 635-2561 **Details:** (County Clerk has Marriage Records from 1838 & Probate Records; Clerk Chancery Court has Divorce Records; General Sessions Court has Court Records; Registrar of Deeds has Land Records)
Lawrence www.tngenweb.org/lawrence/	M7	21 Oct 1817	**Hickman, Maury** Lawrence County; 240 W Gaines St; Lawrenceburg, TN 38464; Ph. (931) 762-7700 **Details:** (County Health Department has Birth Records; County Clerk has Marriage Records from 1818 & Probate Records from 1829; Clerk Circuit Court has Divorce Records; Registrar of Deeds has Land Records)

County Website	Map Index	Date Created	Parent County or Territory From Which Organized Address/Details
Lewis www.tngenweb.org/lewis/	M6	21 Dec 1843	**Hickman, Maury, Wayne, Lawrence** Lewis County; 110 N Park St; Hohenwald, TN 38462; Ph. (931) 796-3734 **Details:** (County completely abolished in 1866 following the Civil War; for that year Records will be found in Maury, Lawrence, Hickman & Wayne Counties; County was Restored in 1867) (County Clerk has Marriage Records from 1881, Probate & Court Records; Clerk Circuit Court has Divorce Records; Registrar of Deeds has Land Records)
Lincoln www.rootsweb.com/~tnlincol/	K7	14 Nov 1809	**Bedford** Lincoln County; 112 Main Ave S; PO Box 577; Fayetteville, TN 37334-0577; Ph. (931) 433-2454 **Details:** (County Clerk has Marriage & Probate Records; Clerk Circuit Court has Divorce Records; Clerk & Master has Court Records; Registrar of Deeds has Land Records)
Loudon www.rootsweb.com/~tnloudon/	F6	2 Jun 1870	**Blount, Monroe, Roane** Loudon County; 601 Grove St; Loudon, TN 37774; Ph. (423) 458-2630 **Details:** (County Clerk has Marriage Records from 1870; Clerk Circuit Court has Divorce & Court Records from 1870; Registrar of Deeds has Land Records from 1870)
Macon http://maconcountytennessee.com/	J4	18 Jan 1842	**Smith, Sumner** Macon County; 106 County Courthouse; Lafayette, TN 37083; Ph. (615) 666-2000 **Details:** (County Clerk has Birth Records 1908–1912, Marriage Records from 1901 & Probate Records from 1900; Clerk Circuit Court has Divorce & Court Records; Registrar of Deeds has Land Records)
Madison www.co.madison.tn.us/	O6	7 Nov 1821	**Chickasaw Indian Lands** Madison County; 100 E Main St; Rm 105; Jackson, TN 38301; Ph. (731) 423-6022 **Details:** (County Clerk has Marriage Records from 1823 [except 1833–1845]; Probate Office has Probate Records from 1825; Registrar of Deeds has Land Records)
Marion www.rootsweb.com/~tnmarion/	I7	20 Nov 1817	**Cherokee Indian Lands** Marion County; 24 County Courthouse Sq; Jasper, TN 37347; Ph. (423) 942-2515 **Details:** (Courthouse burned 1822; Marriage Records destroyed) (County Clerk has Marriage Records from 1919 & Probate Records from 1874; Registrar of Deeds has Land Records)
Marshall www.tngenweb.org/marshall/	K7	20 Feb 1836	**Bedford, Lincoln, Maury** Marshall County;1107 Courthouse Annex; Lewisburg, TN 37091; Ph. (931) 359-1072, daphne.fagan@state.tn.us **Details:** (County Clerk has Marriage & Probate Records from 1836; Marriage & County Commission Minutes from 1950; Clerk and Master has Probate Records and Earlier Minute Books; Registrar of Deeds has Land Records)
Maury www.tngenweb.org/maury/	L6	16 Nov 1807	**Williamson** Maury County; Courthouse; Columbia, TN 38401; Ph. (931) 381-3690 **Details:** (County Clerk has Marriage Records; Clerk & Master has Divorce, Probate & Court Records; Registrar of Deeds has Land Records)

County Website	Map Index	Date Created	Parent County or Territory From Which Organized Address/Details
McMinn www.mcminnco.org/	G7	13 Nov 1819	**Cherokee Indian Lands** McMinn County; 6 E Madison Ave; Athens, TN 37303; Ph. (423) 745-1281 **Details:** (County Clerk has Marriage, Probate & Court Records from 1820; Registrar of Deeds has Land Records)
McNairy www.rootsweb.com/~tnmcnair/	O7	8 Oct 1823	**Hardin** McNairy County; County Courthouse; Selmer, TN 38375; Ph. (731) 645-3511 **Details:** (County Clerk has Marriage Records from 1861, some Birth, Death & Cemetery Records; Clerk Circuit Court has Divorce Records; Registrar of Deeds has Land Records)
Meigs www.tngenweb.org/meigs/	H7	20 Jan 1836	**Cherokee Indian Lands** Meigs County; Main St; PO Box 218; Decatur, TN 37322; Ph. (423) 334-5747 **Details:** (County Clerk has Marriage & Probate Records from 1836; Clerk Circuit Court has Divorce & Court Records; Registrar of Deeds has Land Records)
Monroe www.monroegovernment.org/	F7	13 Nov 1819	**Cherokee Indian Lands** Monroe County; 105 College St; Madisonville, TN 37354; Ph. (423) 442-5940 **Details:** (County Clerk has Marriage Records from 1838, Probate Records from 1833 & Court Records from 1868; Registrar of Deeds has Land Records)
Montgomery www.tngenweb.org/montgomery/	M4	9 Apr 1796	**Tennessee** Montgomery County; 350 Pagent Ln; Clarksville, TN 37040; Ph. (931) 648-5711 **Details:** (County Archives has Marriage Records from 1838, Probate Records from 1797 & Court Records; Clerk Circuit Court has Divorce Records from 1930; Registrar of Deeds has Land Records)
Moore www.knology.net/~jparkes/genealogy/ mooretn/moore.htm	J7	14 Dec 1871	**Bedford, Franklin, Lincoln, Coffee** Moore County; Public Sq; Lynchburg, TN 37352; Ph. (931) 759-7028 **Details:** (Registrar of Deeds has Land Records; County Clerk has Birth, Marriage, Death & Probate Records; Clerk Circuit Court has Court Records)
Morgan www.tngenweb.org/morgan/	G5	15 Oct 1817	**Roane** Morgan County; Main St; Wartburg, TN 37887; Ph. (423) 346-3480 **Details:** (County Clerk has Birth Records 1908–1912, Marriage Records from 1862, Divorce & Probate Records, Land Records from 1818)
Obion www.rootsweb.com/~tnobion/	P5	24 Oct 1823	**Chickasaw Indian Lands** Obion County; 6 Bill Burnett Circle; Union City, TN 38261; Ph. (731) 885-2562 **Details:** (County Clerk has Marriage Records from 1824 & Probate Records from 1833; Circuit & Chancery Court has Divorce Records; Circuit & General Sessions Court has Court Records; Registrar of Deeds has Land Records)

County Website	Map Index	Date Created	Parent County or Territory From Which Organized Address/Details
Overton www.rootsweb.com/~tnoverto/overton.htm	**H5**	**11 Sep 1806**	**Jackson** Overton County; 100 E Court St; Livingston, TN 38570; Ph. (931) 823-2536 **Details:** (County Clerk has Marriage & Probate Records from 1867; Clerk Circuit Court has Divorce & Court Records; Registrar of Deeds has Land Records)
Perry www.netease.net/perry/	**N6**	**14 Nov 1818**	**Hickman** Perry County; Main St; PO Box 16; Linden, TN 37096-0016; Ph. (931) 589-2219 **Details:** (County Clerk has Birth Records 1908–1912 & 1925–1939 & Marriage Records from 1899; Registrar of Deeds has Land Records)
Pickett www.rootsweb.com/~tnpicket/pick.htm	**H4**	**27 Feb 1879**	**Fentress, Overton** Pickett County; 1 Courthouse Sq; Byrdstown, TN 38549; Ph. (931) 864-3359 **Details:** (County Health Department has Birth Records; County Clerk has Marriage & Probate Records from 1935; Clerk & Master & Clerk Circuit Court has Divorce Records; Clerk Circuit Court has Court Records; Registrar of Deeds has Land Records)
Polk www.tngenweb.org/polk/	**G8**	**28 Nov 1839**	**Bradley, McMinn** Polk County; Hwy 411; Benton, TN 37307; Ph. (423) 338-4526 **Details:** (Registrar of Deeds has Land Records; County Clerk has Marriage & Probate Records)
Putnam www.tngenweb.org/putnam/	**I5**	**2 Feb 1842**	**White, Jackson, Overton, DeKalb, Smith** Putnam County; 421 E Spring St; Cookeville, TN 38501; Ph. (931) 526-6321 **Details:** (County Abandoned in 1844, Restored in 1854) (Courthouse burned in 1899) (County Clerk has Birth & Death Records 1925–1940, incomplete Birth & Death Records 1908–1912, Marriage Records from 1879 & Probate Records from 1876; Clerk Chancery Court has Divorce & Court Records from 1900; Registrar of Deeds has Land Records from 1854; Clerk Circuit Court has Circuit Court Records from 1900; County Historian; Route 2, Box 408; Cookeville, TN 38501, has miscellaneous County Records)
Rhea www.tngenweb.org/rhea/	**H6**	**30 Nov 1807**	**Roane** Rhea County; 1475 Market St; Dayton, TN 37321; Ph. (423) 775-7808 **Details:** (County Clerk has Marriage Records from 1808; Registrar of Deeds has Land Records)
Roane www.tngenweb.org/roane/	**G6**	**6 Nov 1801**	**Knox** Roane County; 200 E Race St; Kingston, TN 37763; Ph. (423) 376-5556 **Details:** (County Clerk has Marriage & Probate Records from 1801; Registrar of Deeds has Land Records)
Robertson http://members.aol.com/tngenweb/robtco.htm	**L4**	**9 Apr 1796**	**Tennessee** Robertson County; 509 S Brown St; Springfield, TN 37172; Ph. (615) 384-5895 **Details:** (State Library in Nashville has Birth & Death Records from 1925, Marriage Records from 1839, Probate Records from 1796, Court Records from 1832 & Divorce Records from 1844; Registrar of Deeds has Land Records from 1796)

County Website	Map Index	Date Created	Parent County or Territory From Which Organized Address/Details
Rutherford www.rutherfordcounty.org/	K6	25 Oct 1803	**Davidson** Rutherford County; 319 N Maple St; Murfreesboro, TN 37130; Ph. (615) 898-7799 **Details:** (County Clerk has Marriage & Probate Records from 1804; Registrar of Deeds has Land Records)
Scott www.scottcounty.com/	G5	17 Dec 1849	**Fentress, Morgan, Anderson, Campbell** Scott County; 283 Court St; Huntsville, TN 37756-0087; Ph. (423) 663-2627 **Details:** (Registrar of Deeds has Land Records; County Clerk has Marriage & Probate Records)
Sequatchie www.tngenweb.org/sequatchie/	I7	9 Dec 1857	**Hamilton** Sequatchie County; 308 Cherry St; Dunlap, TN 37327; Ph. (423) 949-2522 **Details:** (County Clerk has Birth, Marriage, Death & Probate Records from 1858; Clerk Circuit Court has Divorce & Court Records; Registrar of Deeds has Land Records)
Sevier www.tngenweb.org/sevier/	E6	28 Sep 1794	**Jefferson** Sevier County; 125 Court Ave; Sevierville, TN 37862; Ph. (423) 453-5502 **Details:** (County Clerk has Marriage Records from 1856 & Probate Records from 1850; Registrar of Deeds has Land Records)
Shelby www.co.shelby.tn.us/index.htm	Q7	24 Nov 1819	**Hardin** Shelby County; 150 Washington St; Memphis, TN 38103; Ph. (901) 545-4244 **Details:** (County Health Department has Birth, Death & Burial Records; County Clerk has Marriage Records from 1820; Clerk Cir- cuit Court has Divorce Records; Probate Judge has Probate Records; General Sessions Court has Court Records; Registrar of Deeds has Land Records)
Smith www.rootsweb.com/~tnsmith/	J5	26 Oct 1799	**Sumner** Smith County; 211 Main St; Carthage, TN 37030; Ph. (615) 735-2092 **Details:** (State Library & Archives have microfilm Records; Regis- trar of Deeds has Land Records; County Clerk has Birth, Marriage, Death & Probate Records)
Stewart www.rootsweb.com/~tnstewar/index.htm	N4	1 Nov 1803	**Montgomery** Stewart County; Main St; PO Box 67; Dover, TN 37058; Ph. (931) 232-7616 **Details:** (Courthouse burned during Civil War) (County Clerk has Marriage & Probate Records from 1898; Registrar of Deeds has Land Records from 1803)
Sullivan www.sullivancounty.org/	B4	18 Oct 1779	**Washington** Sullivan County; 3411 Hwy 126; PO Box 530; Blountville, TN 37617; Ph. (423) 323-6428 **Details:** (County Clerk has Marriage Records from 1863, Birth Records 1908–1912 & Death Records 1925–1938; Clerk & Master has Probate Records; Registrar of Deeds has Land Records)

County Website	Map Index	Date Created	Parent County or Territory From Which Organized Address/Details
Sumner www.sumnertn.org	**K4**	**18 Nov 1786**	**Davidson** Sumner County; 355 N. Belvedere Dr; Gallatin, TN 37066; Ph. (615) 452-4282 **Details:** (County Archives has original Marriage Records from 1786–1969, Probate Records/Wills prior to 1985, Chancery Court Records prior to 1989, Circuit Court Records prior to 1983, County Court Records prior to 1985, Microfilm documents include Marriage Records prior to 2004, Probate Records/Wills prior to 2003, Chancery Court Records prior to 2004, Circuit Court Records prior to 2004 and Deeds prior to 1965; Register of Deeds has original Deed Books, Death Records from 1908-1925, & Birth Records from 1908–1912)
Tennessee		**1796**	Tennessee County; TN **Details:** (County surrendered name when state became Tennessee, 1796)
Tipton www.tiptonco.com	**Q7**	**29 Oct 1823**	**Chickasaw Indian Lands** Tipton County; 220 Hwy 51 N; PO Box 528; Covington, TN 38019; Ph. (901) 476-0207 pdeen@tiptonco.com **Details:** (County Clerk has Marriage Records from 1840; General Sessions Court has Divorce Records from 1823 & Court Records; Clerk Chancery Court has Probate Records 1823–1982; Registrar of Deeds has Land Records)
Trousdale www.rootsweb.org/~tntrousd/	**J5**	**21 Jun 1870**	**Macon, Smith, Wilson, Sumner** Trousdale County; Main St & Court Sq; Hartsville, TN 37074; Ph. (615) 374-2906 **Details:** (County Clerk has Marriage & Probate Records from 1906; Clerk Circuit Court has Divorce & Court Records; Registrar of Deeds has Land Records)
Unicoi www.rootsweb.com/~tnunicoi/	**C5**	**23 Mar 1875**	**Carter, Washington** Unicoi County; 100 N Main Ave; PO Box 340; Erwin, TN 37650-0340; Ph. (423) 743-9541 **Details:** (County Clerk has Marriage & Probate Records from 1875; Clerk Circuit Court & Chancery Court has Divorce & Court Records; Registrar of Deeds has Land Records from 1875)
Union www.unioncountytn.org/	**F5**	**3 Jan 1850**	**Anderson, Campbell, Claiborne, Grainger, Knox** Union County; 901 Main St; PO Box 395; Maynardville, TN 37807; Ph. (423) 992-8043 **Details:** (County Clerk has Birth Records from 1863, Marriage & Probate Records; County Assessor has Land Records)
Van Buren www.rootsweb.com/~tnvanbur/	**I6**	**3 Jan 1840**	**Bledsoe, Warren, White** Van Buren County; Courthouse Sq; PO Box 126; Spencer, TN 38585; Ph. (931) 946-2121 **Details:** (County Clerk has Birth Records 1925–1938, Death Records 1926–1938, Marriage & Probate Records from 1840; Clerk & Master has Divorce Records from 1840; General Sessions Court has Court Records from 1840; Registrar of Deeds has Land Records from 1840)

County Website	Map Index	Date Created	Parent County or Territory From Which Organized Address/Details
Warren www.tngenweb.org/warren/	**I6**	**26 Nov 1807**	**White** Warren County; 111 S Court Sq; McMinnville, TN 37110; Ph. (931) 473-2623 **Details:** (County Clerk has Marriage Records from 1852, Death Records from 1925 & Probate Records from 1827; Clerk Circuit Court has Divorce & Court Records; Registrar of Deeds has Land Records)
Washington www.rootsweb.com/~tnwashin/	**C5**	**15 Nov 1777**	**Washington District** Washington County; PO Box 219; Jonesborough, TN 37659; Ph. (423) 753-1621 **Details:** (Covered present state. Many counties formed from it. This County also embraced parts of present North Carolina Counties) (County Clerk has Birth Records 1908–1912 & 1925–1938, Marriage Records from 1787 & Probate Records from 1779; Registrar of Deeds has Land Records)
Wayne www.tngenweb.org/union/		**1785**	**State of Franklin** Wayne County; 100 Court Circle; PO Box 206; Waynesboro, TN 38485-0206; Ph. (931) 722-5517 **Details:** (Abolished 1 Jun 1796) (This Wayne County created under the state of Franklin. Included present Carter County & part of Johnson County)
Wayne www.netease.net/wayne/	**M7**	**24 Nov 1817**	**Hickman, Humphreys** Wayne County; 100 Court Circuit; PO Box 206; Waynesboro, TN 38485-0206; Ph. (931) 722-5517 **Details:** (County Clerk has Marriage Records from 1857 & Probate Records from 1848; Registrar of Deeds has Land Records)
Weakley www.rootsweb.com/~tnweakle/	**O5**	**21 Oct 1823**	**Chickasaw Indian Lands** Weakley County; 1 Courthouse Sq #107; PO Box 587; Dresden, TN 38225; Ph. (731) 364-2285 **Details:** (County Clerk has Marriage Records from 1840 & Probate Records from 1828; Clerk Circuit Court has Divorce Records; Registrar of Deeds has Land Records)
White web.blomand.net/~wcolley/WCGHS.html	**I6**	**11 Sep 1806**	**Smith** White County; County Courthouse; Sparta, TN 38583; Ph. (931) 836-3203; County Archives: Rm 304 Courthouse; Ph. (931) 837-4066; wcarchives@blomand.net; Historical Society: PO Box 721; Ph. (931) 837-4066 **Details:** (County Archives has Marriage Records 1838–1933, Probate Records 1833–1885; Historical Society has other Miscellaneous Records)
Williamson www.williamsoncounty-tn.gov/live/default.asp	**L6**	**26 Oct 1799**	**Davidson** Williamson County; 510 Columbia Ave; PO Box 1006; Franklin, TN 37065; Ph. (615) 790-5462, louisel@williamson-tn.org **Details:** (Williamson County Archives has Military Records; Deeds from 1800–1972; Tax Books 1800–1963; Chancery Court Records 1825–1998; Circuit Court Records 1810–1999; County Court Records 1816–1966; Guardian Bonds 1856–1897; Wills from 1800–1999; Probate Court Records from 1973–1999; Marriage Records 1800–1987; Death Records 1914–1954; Newspapers; and Miscellaneous bound books)

County	Map	Date	Parent County or Territory From Which Organized
Website	Index	Created	Address/Details
Wilson	**J5**	**26 Oct 1799**	**Sumner**
www.wilsoncountytn.com/			Wilson County; 228 E Main St; Lebanon, TN 37087; Ph. (615) 444-2835

Details: (County Clerk has Marriage Records from 1802 & Probate Records from 1800; Clerk & Master & Clerk Circuit Court has Divorce Records; Registrar of Deeds has Land Records)

Notes

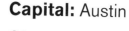

Texas

Capital: Austin
State: 1845 (28th)

Friendship

Following a shipwreck in 1528, Alvar Nunez Cabeza de Vaca and others wandered across Texas and the Southwest for eight years. On returning to Mexico, the tales they told of the Seven Cities of Cibola inspired other explorers to search for the golden cities. In so doing, they crossed many parts of the state but had no interest in settling the area. The French also came to the area around 1685, but their attempt at settlement failed. Seeing a threat from the French, the Spanish sent missionaries into Texas to establish missions. Their goal was to convert the Indians and to civilize the frontier. The first permanent settlement began in 1682 near El Paso. By 1820, there were still only a few thousand non-native settlers in all of Texas.

Texas became part of Mexico in 1821, when Mexico achieved independence from Spain. Stephen Austin reached an agreement with Mexico that same year to bring American settlers into the area. The first colony was started in 1821 on the lower Brazos. Former residents of Alabama, Louisiana, Mississippi, and Tennessee came to the area, and that by 1832 there were more than 20,000 Americans in Texas. In 1835, the Battle of Gonzales began the revolution against Mexico. The Texans quickly took San Antonio, but Santa Anna recaptured it and destroyed the small force at the Alamo. Sam Houston led the Texas army to victory over the Mexicans in 1836.

The Republic of Texas lasted from 1836 to 1845. The United States annexed Texas in 1845, making Texas the 28th state. The following year, Mexico declared war on the United States in an effort to reclaim Texas and other territory. More than 6,000 Texans fought against Mexico during the war. Mexico was defeated and gave up its claim to Texas. In 1850, Texas gave up its claims to Colorado, Wyoming, Kansas, and Oklahoma. In 1861, Texas seceded from the Union. During the Civil War, some 60,000 Texans fought for the Confederacy and only about 1,200 for the Union. Texas was readmitted to the Union in 1870. During the 1870's, most Indians moved to the Indian Territory in Oklahoma.

Establishment of railroads provided a boost to the economy. Cotton plantations and cattle became more prevalent as the railroad provided easier access to markets. The Great Depression witnessed continuing conflicts, including the deportation of many immigrants.

Look for vital records in the following locations:

- **Birth and death records:** Bureau of Vital Statistics, Texas Department of Health in Austin, Texas. Statewide registration of births and deaths began in 1903. Cities also have had requirements to register births and deaths at various times, which have been forwarded to the state and county clerks.

- **Marriage and divorce records:** Marriage records have been forwarded to the Bureau of Vital Statistics only since 1966. Records prior to that time are available from the county clerk. Prior to 1836, only Catholic Churches could perform marriages, so some Protestant marriages will be found in Catholic records. Reports of divorce or annulment began to be filed with the Bureau of Vital Statistics in 1968. Prior to then, the district clerk of each county kept these records. Probate clerks have kept probate records in each county.

- **Naturalization records:** Naturalization records were filed with the district court clerk. The National Archives, Fort Worth Branch in Texas has naturalization records.

- **Census records:** Several censuses were taken in Texas prior to statehood, including municipality censuses and some mission and military district censuses between 1792 and 1836. Many are published. Available mission censuses have been translated and are available on microfilm at the University of Texas, Institute of Texas in San Antonio. School censuses were taken in 1854 and 1855 by some counties and are available at the Texas State Archives in Austin.

Vital Statistics Unit
Department of State Health Services
PO Box 12040
Austin, Texas 78711-2040
(888) 963-7111; Fax (512) 458-7711
www.tdh.state.tx.us/bvs/registra/certcop.htm

Texas State Library and Archives
PO Box 12927
Austin, Texas 78711
www.tsl.state.tx.us/

National Archives Fort Worth Branch
501 Felix Street, PO Box 6216
Fort Worth, Texas 76115

Societies and Repositories

Alexander Hodge #49, TXSSAR; PO Box 485; Missouri City, TX 77459-0485; alexanderhodge@hotmail.com.

Amarillo Genealogical Society; 413 E. 4th St.; Amarillo, TX 79189.

Angelina County Genealogical Society; PO Box 150631; Lufkin, TX 75915-0631; rudel@lcc.net.

Archer County Historical Commission; Rt. 1; Windthorst, TX 76389.

Arkansas Division United Daughters of the Confederacy; 6 Trammells Trace; Texarkana, TX 75503; http://hometown.aol.com/retteacher/AR_UDC.html.

Arlington Genealogical Society; 4319 Waycross Dr.; Arlington, TX 76016-3007; (817) 451-5764; www.rootsweb.com/~txags/ags.htm.

Atascosa County Genealogical Society Library; Aigner-Mumme Memorial Building; 4th and H Avenue P.; Poteet, TX 78065; acgsl@aol.com, poteetlib@aol.com; http://members.aol.com/poteetlib/gen/index.html.

Athens Genealogical Organization; c/o Henderson Public Library; 121 Prairieville St.; Athens, TX 75751.

Austin County Historical Commission; 206 S. Masonic St; Bellville, TX 77418.

Austin Genealogical Society; PO Box 1507; Austin, TX 78767-1507; (512) 378-4735; marilyn@ahenley.com; www.austintxgensoc.org.

Bay Area Genealogical Society; PO Box 891447; Houston, TX 77289-1447; (281) 486-0406; CRHellen@worldnet.att.net; www.rootsweb.com/~txbags/baygen.html.

Bay Area Heritage Society; Library & Museum; 220 W. Defee Ave.; Baytown, TX 77520-4010.

Baytown Genealogical Society; PO Box 2486; Baytown, TX 77522-2486; (281) 424-8388; librarian@BaytownGenealogyResearchLibrary.org; www.baytowngenealogyresearchlibrary.org.

Bear Creek Genealogical Society; 8922 Rockhurst Dr.; Houston, TX 77080-3018.

Beaumont Heritage Society; 2985 French Rd.; Beaumont, TX 77706.

Bellville Historical Society Resource Center; 15 North Masonic; Bellville, TX 77418; bellhist@industryinet.com.

Bellville Historical Society; PO Box 67; Bellville, TX 77418.

Boerne Area Historical Society; Box 178; Boerne, TX 78006.

Borden County Historical Commission; Box 23; Gail, TX 79738.

Bosque County Historical Commission; PO Box 534; Meridian, TX 76665.

Brazos Genealogical Association; PO Box 5493; Bryan, TX 77805-5493; http://user.txcyber.com/~bga.

Brazosport Genealogical Society; PO Box 813; Lake Jackson, TX 77566.

Brooks County Historical Commission; 604 W. Blucher; Falfurrias, TX 78355.

Brown County Historical Society; PO Box 146; Brownwood, TX 76801.

Burkburnett Genealogical Society; c/o Burkburnett Library; 215 East 4th St.; Burkburnett, TX 76354.

Burnet County Genealogical Society; c/o Herman Brown Free Library; 100 Washington Stree; Burnet, TX 78611; rgsmith@moment.net; www.rootsweb.com/~txburnet/index.htm.

Caldwell County Genealogical and Historical Society; 215 South Pecan Avenue; Luling, TX 78648; www.rootsweb.com/~txcaldwe/socpage.htm.

Camp County Genealogical Society; PO Box 1083; Pittsburg, TX 75686-3083; www.rootsweb.com/~txccgs/members.htm.

Cass County Genealogical Society; PO Box 880 Dept. CCW; Atlanta, TX 75551-0880; (903) 796-2107; fourpines@juno.com; http://homepages.rootsweb.com/~danasite/CCGS.

Central Texas Genealogical Society; Waco-McLennan County Library System; 1717 Austin Ave; Waco, TX 76701; www.rootsweb.com/~txmclenn.

Chaparral Genealogical Society; PO Box 606; Tomball, TX 77377-0606; www.rootsweb.com/~txwaller/chap.htm.

Cherokee County Genealogical Society; PO Box 1332; Jacksonville, TX 75766-1332; (903) 586-0135; ccgs@tyler.net; www.tyler.net/ccgs/default.html.

Childress Genealogical Society; 117 Ave. B., N.E.; Childress, TX 79201.

Clayton Library Friends; PO Box 271078; Houston, TX 77277-1078; www.hpl.lib.tx.us/clayton/clf.html.

Cleveland Area Gen. Enterprises (CAGE); c/o Mrs. Barbara Smith; Austin Memorial Library 220 S. Bonham; Cleveland, TX 77327.

Collin County Genealogical Society; PO Box 865052; Plano, TX 75086-5052.

Cooke County Heritage Society; PO Box 150; Gainesville, TX 76240.

Corral County Genealogy; PO Box 310160; New Braunfels, TX 78131-0160.

Coryell County Genealogical Society; c/o Gatesville Public Library; 811 Main St.; Gatesville, TX 76528.

Cottle County Genealogical Society; Box 1005; Paducah, TX 79248.

Crockett County Historical Society; PO Drawer B; Ozona, TX 76943.

Cross Timbers Genealogical Society, Inc.; PO Box 197; Gainsville, TX 76241.

Cypress Basin Genealogical and Historical Society; PO Box 403; Mt. Pleasant, TX 75455.

Czech Heritage Society of Texas; 7411 Kite Hill; Houston, TX 77041.

Dallas County East Genealogical Society; 7637 Mary Dan Dr.; Dallas, TX 75217-4603.

Dallas Genealogical Society; PO Box 12648; Dallas, TX 75225-0446; info@dallasgenealogy.org; www.dallasgenealogy.org.

Dallas Jewish Historical Society; 7900 Northaven Rd.; Dallas, TX 75230; www.dvjc.org/history/genealogy.shtml.

Deaf Smith County Genealogical Society; 211 E. 4th St.; Hereford, TX 79045.

Denton County Genealogical Society; PO Box 424707; Denton, TX 76204-4707; www.iglobal.net/pub/dcgs.

Descendants of Mexican War Veterans; PO Box 830482; Richardson, TX 75083-0482; www.dmwv.org/dmwv/home.htm.

Duncanville Texas Genealogical Society; 622 W. Camp Wisdom Rd.; Duncanville, TX 75116.

East Bell County Genealogical Society; 3219 Meadow Oaks Dr.; Temple, TX 76502-1752.

East End Historical Association; PO Box 2424; Galveston, TX 77550.

East Texas Genealogical Society; PO Box 6967; Tyler, TX 75711-6967; scottfitzgerald@tyler.net; www.rootsweb.com/~txetgs.

El Paso Genealogical Society; c/o El Paso Main Public Library; 501 N. Oregon St.; El Paso, TX 79901.

Ellis County Genealogical Society; Box 385; Waxahachie, TX 75165.

Fort Brown Genealogical Society; 608 E. Adams; Brownsville, TX 78520.

Fort Clark Historical Society; PO Box 1061; Brackettville, TX 78832.

Fort Worth Genealogical Society; PO Box 9767; Fort Worth, TX 76147-2767.

Fredricksburg Genealogical Society; PO Box 164; 108 N. Edison St.; Fredricksburg, TX 78624; fbggenealogy@fbg.net.

Freestone County Genealogical Society; PO Box 14; Fairfield, TX 75840.

Galveston County Genealogical Society; PO Box 1141; Galveston, TX 77553-1141.

Genealogical Society of Aransas County; PO Box 1642; Fulton, TX 78358.

Genealogical Society of Big Springs; c/o Howard County Library; Big Spring, TX 79720.

Genealogical Society of Kendall County; PO Box 623; Boerne, TX 78006-0623.

Genealogical Society of Kerrville; 505 Water St.; Kerrville, TX 78028.

German-Texan Heritage Society; 507 E. 10th St.; PO Box 684171; Austin, TX 78768-4171.

Gillespie County Historical Society; 312 West San Antonio; Fredricksburg, TX 78624.

Golden Spread Chapter, AHSGR; PO Box 207; Darrouzett, TX 79024; (806) 624-2217.

Grand Prairie Genealogical Society; PO Box 532026; Grand Prairie, TX 75053.

Grayson County Texas Genealogical Society; 421 N. Travis; Sherman, TX 75090.

Gregg County Historical & Genealogical Society; PO Box 2985; Longview, TX 75606-2985.

Grimes County Heritage Association; 1215 E. Washington Ave.; Navasota, TX 77868.

Guadalupe County Genealogical Society; 707 East College St.; Sequin, TX 78155.

Guadalupe Victoria Chapter, DAR; 607 Ave. D.; Victoria, TX 77901.

Harris County Genealogical Society; PO Box 391; Pasadena, TX 77501.

Harrison County Historical Society; Old Courthouse Museum; Peter Whetstone Square; Marshall, TX 75670.

Heart of Texas Genealogical Society; PO Box 133; Rochelle, TX 76872.

Hemphill County Historical & Genealogical Society; Rt. 2; Canadian, TX 79014.

Henderson County Historical Society; PO Box 943; Athens, TX 75751.

Heritage Association of San Marcos; PO Box 1806; San Marcos, TX 78666.

Heritage Society of Washington County; PO Box 1123; Brenham, TX 77833.

Hi Plains Genealogical Society; c/o Unger Memorial Library; 825 Austin; Plainview, TX 79072.

High Plains Genealogical Society; 1807 Ennis St.; Plainview, TX 79072.

Hill College Harold B. Simpson Center / Confederate Research Center; 112 Lamar Drive; PO Box 619;

Hillsboro, TX 76645; (254) 582-2555;
patterson@hill-college.cc.tx.us;
www.hill-college.cc.tx.us/ museum/crc.html.

Hill County Genealogical Society; PO Box 636; Hillsboro, TX 76645-0636.

Hillsboro Heritage League; PO Box 2; Hillsboro, TX 76645.

Hispanic Genealogical Society; 2932 Barksdale; Houston, TX 77093.

Hood County Genealogical Society; PO Box 1623; Granbury, TX 76048.

Hopkins County Genealogical Society; PO Box 624; Sulphur Springs, TX 75483-0624.

Houston Afro-American Historical & Genealogical Society; 302 Harbor Dr.; Houston, TX 77062.

Houston Area Genealogical Association; 2507 Tannehill; Houston, TX 77008-3052.

Houston Genealogical Forum; PO Box 271466; Houston, TX 77277-1466.

Houston Polish Genealogical Society; c/o 3606 Maroneal; Houston, TX 77025.

Houston Public Library; Clayton Library Center for Genealogical Research; 5300 Caroline; Houston, TX 77004-6896; (832) 393-2600.

Humble Area Genealogical Society; PO Box 2723; Humble, TX 77347.

Hunt County Genealogical Society; PO Box 398; Greenville, TX 75401.

Hutchinson County Genealogical Society; Hutchinson County Library; 625 Weatherly St.; Borger, TX 79007.

Iowa Park Genealogical and Historical Society; 400 West Alameda; Iowa Park, TX 76367.

Jewish Genealogical Society of Houston; 11727 Riverview Dr.; Houston, TX 77077.

Johnson County Genealogical Society; PO Box 1256; Cleburne, TX 76033.

Karnes County Historical Society; Box 162; Karnes City, TX 78118.

Kaufman County Genealogical Society; Box 337; Terrell, TX 75160.

Kent County Genealogical and Historical Society; Box 414; Jayton, TX 79528.

Kingsland Genealogical Society; PO Box 952; Kingsland, TX 78639.

Lake Jackson Historical Association; PO Box 242; Lake Jackson, TX 77566.

Lamar County Genealogical Society Library; 1125 Bonham St; Paris, TX 75460; (903) 784-5020; http://gen.1starnet.com.

Lamesa Area Genealogical Society; Box 1264; Lamesa, TX 79331.

Leon County Genealogical Society; PO Box 400; Centerville, TX 75833-0400.

Liberty County Historical Commission; PO Box 23; Liberty, TX 77575.

Los Bexarenos Genealogical Society; PO Box 1935; San Antonio, TX 78297.

Lubbock Heritage Society; PO Box 5443; Lubbock, TX 79417.

Lufkin Genealogical & Historical Society; PO Box 150631; Lufkin, TX 75915-0631.

Madison County Genealogical Society; Box 26; Madisonville, TX 77864.

Marion County Genealogical Society; Box 224; Jefferson, TX 75657.

Matagorda County African-American Historical Society; PO Box 1386; Bay City, TX 77404-1386; tdsmith@wcnet.net.

Matagorda County Genealogical Society; PO Box 264; Bay City, TX 77404-0264; mcgs264@yahoo.com; www.rootsweb.com/~txmatago/gensoc.htm.

McAllen Genealogical Society; c/o McAllen Memorial Library; 601 N. Main St.; McAllen, TX 78501.

Menard Genealogical Society; PO Box 94; Menard, TX 76859-0094.

Mesquite Historical and Genealogical Society; c/o PO Box 850165; Mesquite, TX 75185-0165.

Methodist Historical Society; Fondren Library; Southern Methodist University; Dallas, TX 75275.

Mid-Cities Genealogical Society; PO Box 407; Bedford, TX 76095-0407.

Midland Genealogical Society; 301 W. Missouri; Midland, TX 79701-5108; aauburg@apex2000.net.

Milam County Genealogical Society; c/o Lucy Patterson Memorial Library; 201 Ackerman; Rockdale, TX 76567.

Montgomery County Genealogical & Historical Society, Inc.; PO Box 867; Conroe, TX 77305-0867.

Motley County Genealogical and Historical Society; 1105 Main; PO Box 557; Matador, TX 79244.

Nacogdoches Genealogical Society; PO Box 4634; Nacogdoches, TX 75962; jhancock@lcc.net; www.rootsweb.com/~txngs.

NARA, Southwest Region (Fort Worth); 501 West Felix Street, Building 1; PO 6216; Fort Worth, TX 76115-0216; (817) 334-5525; ftworth.reference@nara.gov; www.archives.gov/facilities/tx/fort_worth.html.

Navarro County Genealogical Society; PO Box 2278; Corsicana, TX 75151.

New Boston Genealogical Society; c/o New Boston Public Library; 127 North Ellis; New Boston, TX 75570-2905.

Newton County Historical Commission; Box 56; Burkeville, TX 75932.

North Texas Genealogical and Historical Association; Box 4602; Wichita Falls, TX 76308.

Orange County Historical Society; PO Box 1345; Orange, TX 77630.

Palo Pinto County Historical Association; PO Box 105; Palo Pinto, TX 76484-0105.

Parker County Genealogical Society; 1214 Charles St.; Weatherford, TX 76086.

Pecan Valley Genealogical Society; 1707 3rd; Brownwood, TX 76801.

Permian Basin Genealogical Society; 321 W. 5th St.; Odessa, TX 79761.

Plano Heritage Association; 1900 West 15th St.; Plano, TX 75075.

Polish Genealogical Society of Texas; 218 Beaver Bend; Houston, TX 77037.

Polish Genealogical Society of Texas; Rt. 1, Box 475-S; Navasota, TX 77868.

Randolph Area Genealogical Society; PO Box 2134; Universal City, TX 78148-1134.

Red River County Texas Genealogical Society; PO Drawer D; Clarksville, TX 75426.

Refugio County Historical Society; Refugio County Museum; 102 West St.; Refugio, TX 78377.

Roberts County Historical Commission; Roberts County Museum; Box 306; Miami, TX 79059.

Root Seekers Genealogical Society; Tri-County Library; PO Box 1770; Mabank, TX 75147-1770.

Rusk County Historical Commission; PO Box 1773; Henderson, TX 75652.

Salado Historical Society; PO Box 251; Salado, TX 76571.

San Angelo Genealogical and Historical Society, Inc.; PO Box 3453; San Angelo, TX 76901.

San Antonio Genealogical and Historical Society; PO Box 790087; San Antonio, TX 78279-0087.

San Jacinto County Heritage Society; PO Box 505; Coldspring, TX 77331.

San Marcos/Hays County Genealogical Society; PO Box 503; San Marcos, TX 78666.

Sons of the American Revolution, Texas Society; 3342 Dartmoor Dr.; Dallas, TX 75229.

Schleicher County Historical Society; Box 473; Eldorado, TX 76936.

Scurry County Genealogical Society; PO Box 195; Snyder, TX 79550.

Smith County Historical Society; 125 S. College; Tyler, TX 75702.

Somervell County Genealogical and Heritage Society; PO Box 1097; Glen Rose, TX 76043.

South Plains Genealogical Society; PO Box 6607; Lubbock, TX 79493.

South Texas Genealogical Society; PO Box 754; Beeville, TX 78104.

Southeast Texas Genealogical & Historical Society; c/o Tyrrell Historical Library; PO Box 3827; Beaumont, TX 77704.

Southwest Texas Genealogical Society; PO Box 295; Uvalde, TX 78802.

Stephens County Genealogical Society; PO Box 350; Breckenridge, TX 76024.

Stephens County Historical Association; 201 N. Harding; Breckenridge, TX 76024.

Taylor Heritage Society; PO Box 385; Taylor, TX 76574.

Terrell County Historical Commission; PO Box 7; Sanderson, TX 79848.

Texarkana USA Genealogical Society; PO Box 5825; Texarkana, TX 75505-5825.

Texas City Ancestry Searchers; PO Box 3301; Texas City, TX 77592.

Texas Czech Heritage and Cultural Center, Inc.; PO Box 6; La Grange, TX 78945; czech@cvtv.net; www.genealogy.org/~czech/tchcc.html.

Texas State Genealogical Society; 3219 Meadow Oaks Dr.; Temple, TX 76502-1752; www.rootsweb.com/~txsgs.

Texas State Library and Archives Commission; 1201 Brazos; PO Box 12927; Austin, TX 78711-2927; (512) 463-5463; geninfo@tsl.state.tx.us; www.tsl.state.tx.us.

Texas Wendish Heritage Society; PO Box 311; Giddings, TX 78942.

Tex-Ok Panhandle Genealogical Society; 1010 S. Harvard St.; Perryton, TX 79070.

The Erath County Genealogical Society; PO Box 1587; Stephenville, TX 76401; www.rootsweb.com/~txerath/gene_soc_temp.htm.

The Society of Descendants of Goliad; PO Box 1208; San Antonio, TX 78294.

The Texas State Historical Association; 2/306 Sid Richardson Hall; University of Texas; Austin, TX 78712; www.tsha.utexas.edu.

Timpson Area Genealogical and Heritage Society; PO Box 726; Timpson, TX 75975.

Tip O'Texas Genealogical Society; Harlingen Public Library; 410 76 Drive; Harlingen, TX 78550.

Tom Green County Historical Preservation League; PO Box 1625; San Angelo, TX 76902.

Tri-County Genealogical Society; Leonard Library; PO Box 107; Leonard, TX 75452.

Troup Genealogical/ Historical Society; PO Box 173; Troup, TX 75789.

Val Verde County Genealogical Society; PO Box 442052; DelRio, TX 78842.

Van Alstyne Genealogical Society; 3212 Knob Hill Rd.; Van Alstyne, TX 75495-5112.

Van Zandt County Genealogical Society; PO Box 716; Canton, TX 75103-0716.

Victoria County Genealogical Society; 302 N. Main St.; Victoria, TX 77901.

Walker County, Texas, Genealogical Society; Huntsville
Public Library; 1216 14th St.; PO Box 1295; Huntsville,
TX 77342-1295; (936) 291-5472; info@wcgen.com;
www.wcgen.com.

Wallisville Heritage; PO Box 16; Wallisville, TX 77597.

Ward County Genealogical Society; 400 E. Fourth St.;
Monahans, TX 79756.

Webb County Heritage Foundation; PO Drawer 29; Laredo,
TX 78042.

West Bell Genealogical Society; PO Box 851; Killeen, TX
76540.

West Texas Genealogical Society; PO Box 2307; Abilene,
TX 79604.

Wharton County Chapter Texas German Society;
PO Box 1236; El Campo, TX 77437.

Wharton County Czech Society; 1601 Michael St.;
El Campo, TX 77437.

Williamson County Genealogical Society; PO Box 585;
Round Rock, TX 78680.

Wise County Genealogical Society; PO Box 126; Rhome,
TX 76078.

Wise County Historical Society; Box 427; Decatur, TX
76234; DecaturGenealogicalSociety@msn.com;
www.rootsweb.com/~ildecgs.

Wood County Genealogical Society; PO Box 832;
Quitman, TX 75783.

Yorktown Historical Society; Yorktown Historical
Museum; PO Box 884; Yorktown, TX 78164.

Zapata County Historical Commission; Box 6305; Zapata,
TX 78076.

Bibliography and Record Sources

General

Bailey, Emory E., et al. *Who's Who in Texas.* Dallas: Who's
Who Publishing, 1931.

Bailey, Ernest Emory. *Texas Historical and Biographical
Record with a Genealogical Study of Historical Family
Records.* Austin: Texas historical and Biographical
Record, n.d.

Beers, Henry P. *Spanish and Mexican Records of the
American Southwest: A Bibliographic Guide to Archive
and Manuscript Sources.* Tucson: University of Arizona
Press, 1979.

*Biographical Gazetteer of Texas: Publication of the
Biographical Sketch File of the Texas Collection At
Baylor University, an Ongoing Project.* 6 vols. Austin,
Texas: Morrison Books, 1985–.

Biographical Souvenir of the State of Texas. 1889. Reprint.
Easley, South Carolina: Southern Historical Press, 1978.

Bockstruck, Lloyd DeWitt. *Research in Texas.* Arlington,
Virginia: National Genealogical Society, 1992.

Brown, John Henry. *Indian Wars and Pioneers of Texas.*
1880. Reprint. Easley, South Carolina: Southern
Historical Press, 1978.

Carroll, James M. *A History of Texas Baptists.* Dallas:
Baptist Standard Publishing Co., 1923.

Chamblin, Thomas S., ed. *The Historical Encyclopedia of
Texas.* 2 vols. Dallas: Texas Historical Institute, 1982.

Connor, Seymour V. *Who's Who in Texas Today: A New
Biographical Survey of Texas.* Austin, Texas: Pemberton
Press, 1968.

Corbin, John. *Catalog of Genealogical Materials in Texas
Libraries.* Austin, Texas: Texas State Library and
Historical Commission, 1965.

Daughters of the Republic of Texas. *A Guide to the Texana
Holdings of the Texas History Library of the Daughters
of the Republic of Texas.* 2 vol. San Antonio, Texas: s.n.,
1978.

Davis, Ellis Arthur and Edwin H. Grobe. *Encyclopedia of
Texas.* Dallas: Texas Development Bureau, 190–.

Ericson, Carolyn Reeves, and Joe E. Ericson. *A Guide to
Texas Research.* Nacogdoches, Texas: Ericson Books,
1993.

Fey, Everett Anthony. *New Braunfels: The First Founders.*
2 vols. N.p., 1995.

Fitzmorris, Mary Angela. *Four Decades of Catholicism in
Texas 1820–1860.* Washington, D.C.: Catholic
University of America, 1926.

*Founders and Patriots of the Republic of Texas: Lineages
of the Members of the Daughters of the Republic of
Texas.* 3 vols. Austin, Texas: Daughters of the Republic
of Texas, 1963–1985.

Hanna, Archibald. *Bibliography of Texas, 1795–1845.* 2nd
ed., rev. Woodbridge, Connecticut: Research Pub., 1983.

Holley, Edward G. *Resources of Texas Libraries.* Austin,
Texas: Texas State Library, 1968.

Jenkins, John Holmes. *Cracker Barrel Chronicles:
A Bibliography of Texas Town and County Histories.*
Austin, Texas: Pemberton Press, 1965.

Johnson, Frank W. *History of Texas and Texans.* 5 vols.
Chicago: American Historical Society, 1914.

Kennedy, Imogene K., and J. Leon Kennedy. *Genealogical
Records in Texas.* Reprint. Baltimore: Genealogical
Publishing Co., 1992.

McQueen, Clyde. *Black Churches in Texas: A Guide to
Historic Congregations.* College Station, Texas: Texas
A & M University, 2000.

Morris, Mrs. Harry Joseph. *Citizens of the Republic of
Texas.* Dallas: Texas State Genealogical Society, 1977.

Munnerlyn, Tom. *Texas Local History: A Source Book for
Available Town and County Histories, Local Memoirs
and Genealogical Records.* Austin, Texas: Eakin Press,
1983.

Phelan, Macum. *History of Early Methodism in Texas, 1817–1866.* Nashville: Cokesbury Press, 1924.

Pylant, James. *Genealogies of Texas Families: Biographical Notes of Pioneer Settlers.* Stephenville, Texas: Datatrace Systems, 1989.

Residents of Texas, 1782–1836. 3 vols. San Antonio, Texas: The University of Texas, Institute of Texan Cultures, 1984.

Reynolds. Bess. *Records of Southern Families: From Bibles, Tombstones, Sketches, Newspapers, 1740–1957.* Dallas, Texas: Microfilm Sales & Service, 1961. Microfilm.

Texas Family Land Heritage Registry. 8 vols. Austin, Texas: Texas Department of Agriculture, 1974–.

Texas Newspapers, 1813–1939: A Union List of Newspaper Files Available in Offices of Publishers, Libraries, and a Number of Private Collections. Houston, Texas: San Jacinto Museum of History Association, 1941.

Texas Research Outline. Series U.S.-States, no. 43. Salt Lake City: Family History Library, 1988.

Webb, Walter Prescott, ed. *The Handbook of Texas.* 3 vols. Austin: Texas State Historical Association, 1952–1976.

Atlases, Maps and Gazetteers

Bartholomew, Ed. *800 Texas Ghost Towns.* Fort Davis, Texas: Frontier Book, 1971.

Day, James M. *Maps of Texas, 1527–1900: The Map Collection of the Texas State Archives.* Austin, Texas: Pemberton Press, 1964.

Day, James M., comp. *Maps of Texas 1527–1900: The Map Collection of the Texas State Archives.* Austin, Texas: Pemberton Press, 1974.

Gannett, Henry. *A Gazetteer of Texas.* 2nd ed. Washington, D.C.: Government Printing Office, 1904.

Madison, Virginia and Hallie Stillwell. *How Come It's Called That?: Place Names in the Big Bend Country.* Albuquerque: University of New Mexico Press, 1958.

Martin, James C., and Robert S. Martin. *Maps of Texas and the Southwest, 1513–1900.* Albuquerque: University of New Mexico Press, 1984.

Massengill, Fred I. *Texas Towns: Origin of Names and Location of Each of the 2,148 Post Offices in Texas.* Terrell, Texas: 1936.

Ming, Virginia H., and William L. Ming. *Biographical Gazetteer of Texas.* 6 vols. Austin, Texas: W. M. Morrison Books, 1985–1987.

Pool, William C. *A Historical Atlas of Texas.* Austin, Texas: Encino Press, 1975.

Tarpley, Fred. *1,001 Texas Place Names.* Austin: University of Texas Press, 1980.

Texas Atlas and Gazetteer. Freeport, Maine: DeLorme Mapping, 1995.

United States. Geological Survey. *Texas Index to Topographic and Other Map Coverage.* Reston, Virginia: Geological Survey, 1972.

Williams, J. W. *Old Texas Trails.* Burnet, Texas: Eakin Press, 1979.

Census Records

Available Census Records and Census Substitutes

Federal Census 1850, 1860, 1870, 1880, 1900, 1910, 1920

Federal Mortality Schedules 1850, 1860, 1870, 1880

Union Veterans and Widows 1890

State/Territorial Census 1829–1836

School Census 1854–1855

Dollarhide, William. *The Census Book: A Genealogist's Guide to Federal Census Facts, Schedules and Indexes.* Bountiful, Utah: Heritage Quest, 1999.

Jackson, Ronald Vern, et al. *Texas, 1840–1849.* North Salt Lake, Utah: Accelerated Indexing Systems International, 1981.

Jackson, Ronald Vern. *Texas, 1830–1839, Census Index.* North Salt Lake, Utah: Accelerated Indexing Systems International, 1981.

Kemp, Thomas Jay. *The American Census Handbook.* Wilmington, Delaware: Scholarly Resources, Inc., 2001.

Lainhart, Ann S. *State Census Records.* Baltimore: Genealogical Publishing Co., Inc., 1992.

Mullins, Marion D. *The First Census of Texas, 1829–1836: To Which are Added Texas Citizenship Lists, 1821–1845, and Other Early Records of the Republic of Texas.* Washington, D.C.: National Genealogical Society, 1962.

Thorndale, William and William Dollarhide. *Map Guide to the U.S. Federal Census, 1790–1920.* Baltimore: Genealogical Publishing Co., 1987.

White, Gifford E. *1830 Citizens of Texas.* Austin, Texas: Eakin Press, 1983.

Court Records, Probate and Wills

Daughters of the American Revolution. *Texas Records from Bibles, Probate Records, Wills, Cemeteries, 1639–1954.* Dallas, Texas: Filmed by Microfilm Sales & Service, 1961. Microfilm.

Index to Probate Cases of Texas. 1940. Reprint. San Antonio: Bureau of Research in the Social Sciences, University of Texas, 1980. Compiled by the Work Projects Administration for 31 counties.

Emigration, Immigration, Migration and Naturalization

Blaha, Albert J. *Passenger Lists for Galveston, 1850–1855.* Houston, Texas: A. J. Blaha, 1985.

Geue, Chester W., and Ethel H. Geue. *A New Land Beckoned: German Immigration to Texas, 1844–1847.* Enlarged ed. Waco: Texian Press, 1972.

Geue, Ethel H. *New Homes in a New Land German Immigration to Texas 1847–1861*. Baltimore, Maryland: Clearfield Co., Inc., 2002.

Hejl, Edmond H. *Czech Footprints Across the Bluebonnet Fields of Texas: Villages of Origin*. N.p., 1983.

Marsh, Helen and Timothy Marsh. *Tennesseans in Texas*. Easley, South Carolina: Southern Historical Press, 1986.

McManus, J. *Comal County, Texas, and New Braunfels, Texas, German Immigrant Ships, 1845–1846*. St. Louis, Missouri: F. T. Ingmire, 1985.

Ships Passenger Lists, Port of Galveston, Texas, 1846–1871. Easley, South Carolina: Southern Historical Press, 1984.

Williams, Villamae, ed. *Stephen F. Austin's Register of Families*. Baltimore: Genealogical Publishing Co., 1989.

Land and Property

Abstract of Land Claims, Compiled From the Records of the General Land Office. Galveston: Civilian Book Office, 1852.

Abstract of Land Titles of Texas Comprising the Titled, Patented, and Located Lands in the State. Galveston: Shaw and Blaylock, 1878.

An Abstract of the Original Titles of Records in the General Land Office. 1838. Reprint. Austin, Texas: Pemberton Press, 1964.

Bowden, J. J. *Spanish and Mexican Land Grants in the Chihuahuan Acquisition*. El Paso, Texas: Texas Western Press, 1971.

Early Texas Settlers, 1700s–1800s. S.l.: Brøderbund, 2000. CD-ROM.

Ericson, Carolyn Reeves. *First Settlers of the Republic of Texas: Headright Land Grants which were Reported as Genuine and Legal by the Traveling Commissioners, January 1840*. 2 vols. Reprint. Nacogdoches, Texas: Carolyn Reeves Ericson, 1982.

First Settlers of the Republic of Texas: Headright Land Grants, 1840. 2 vols., 1841, Reprint. Nacogdoches, Texas: Carolyn R. Ericson, 1982–.

Geue, Chester W., and Ethel H. Geue. *A New Land Beckoned. German Immigration to Texas, 1844–1847*. Baltimore, Maryland: Clearfield Co., Inc., 2002.

Gould, Florence C. *Claiming Their Land: Women Homesteaders in Texas*. El Paso, Texas: Texas Western Press, 1991.

Mauro, Garry. *The Land Commissioners of Texas: 150 Years of the General Land Office*. Austin: Texas General Land Office, 1986.

Miller, Thomas Lloyd. *Bounty and Donation Land Grants of Texas 1835–1888*. Austin: University of Texas Press, 1967.

Miller, Thomas Lloyd. *Texas Confederate Scrip Grantees*. N.p., 1985.

Miller, Thomas Lloyd. *The Public Lands of Texas 1519–1970*. Norman, Oklahoma: University of Oklahoma Press, 1972.

Miller, Thomas Lloyd. *The Public Lands of Texas, 1519–1970*. Norman: University of Oklahoma Press, 1971.

Taylor, Virginia H. *Index to Spanish and Mexican Land Grants in Texas*. Austin, Texas: Lone Star Press, 1974.

University of Texas (San Antonio). Institute of Texan Cultures. *Residents of Texas, 1782–1836*. 3 vol. San Antonio, Texas: The Institute, 1984.

White, Gifford. *Character Certificates in the General Land Office of Texas*. Austin: G. White, 1985.

Military

Barron, John C., et al. *Republic of Texas Pension Application Abstracts*. Austin, Texas: Austin Genealogical Society, 1987.

Barton, Henry W. *Texas Volunteers in the Mexican War*. Wichita Falls, Texas: Texican Press, 1970.

Dixon, Sam Houston and Louis Wiltz Kemp. *The Heroes of San Jacinto*. Houston: The Anson Jones Press, 1932.

Fay, Mary Smith. *War of 1812 Veterans in Texas*. New Orleans: Polyanthos, 1979.

Ingmire, Frances Terry. *Texas Frontiersmen, 1839–1860: Minute Men, Militia, Home Guard, Indian Fighters*. St. Louis: F. T. Ingmire, 1982.

Ingmire, Frances Terry. *Texas Rangers: Frontier Battalion, Minute Men, Commanding Officers, 1847–1900*. 6 vols. St. Louis: Ingmire Publications, 1982.

Kinney, John M. *Index to Applications for Texas Confederate Pensions*. Austin, Texas: Archives Division, Texas State Library, 1977.

Muster Rolls of the Texas Revolution. Austin, Texas: Daughters of the Republic of Texas, Inc., 1986.

Pompey, Sherman L. *Muster Lists of the Texas Confederate Troops*. Independence, California: Historical and Genealogical Publishing Co., 1966.

Roll Call at the Alamo. Ft. Collins, Colorado: The Old Army Press, 1985.

Sibley, Marilyn McAdams. *Lone Stars and State Gazettes: Texas Newspapers Before the Civil War*. College Station, Texas: Texas A & M University Press, 1983.

Stephens, Robert W. *Texas Ranger Indian War Pensions*. Quanah, Texas: Nortex Press, 1975.

Texas Confederate Index: Confederate Soldiers of the State of Texas. Dallas, Texas: Presidial Press, 1978. Microfiche.

Texas Newspapers, 1813–1939: A Union List. Houston: N.p.: San Jacinto Museum of History Association, 1951.

United States. Record and Pension Office. *Compiled Service Records of Volunteer Soldiers Who Served During the Mexican War in Organizations from the State of Texas*. Washington, D.C.: The National Archives, 1959. Microfilm, multiple rolls.

United States. Selective Service System. *Texas, World War I Selective Service System Draft Registration Cards, 1917–1918*. National Archives Microfilm Publications, M1509. Washington, D.C.: National Archives, 1987–1988.

White, Virgil D. *Index to Texas CSA Pension Files*. Waynesboro, Tennessee: National Historical Publishing Co., 1989.

Vital and Cemetery

An Index to Texas Probate Birth Records, ca. 1900–1945, ca. 1900–1945. Austin: Texas State Library, 1988. Microfilm, 11 rolls.

Biggerstaff, Mrs. Malcolm B. *4000 Tombstone Inscriptions from Texas. 1745–1870: Along the Old San Antonio Road and the Trail of Austin's Colonists*. Oklahoma City, Oklahoma: Oklahoma Historical Society, 1952.

Cemetery Records of Texas. 6 vols. Typescript. Salt Lake City: Genealogical Society of Utah, 1956–1963.

Crofford-Gould, Sharry. *Texas Cemetery Inscriptions: A Source Index*. San Antonio: Limited Editions, 1977.

Daughters of the American Revolution. Alamo Chapter (San Antonio, Texas). *Texas Cemetery Records,*

Miscellaneous Bible Records, 1782–1955. San Antonio, Texas: Microfilm Center, 1973.

Dodd, Jordan R. *Texas Marriages, Early to 1850: A Research Tool*. Bountiful, Utah: Precision Indexing, 1990.

Frazier, John P. *Northeast Texas Cemeteries*. Shreveport, California: S. and W. Enterprises, 1984.

Gracy, Alice D., Emma G. S. Gentry, and Jane Sumner. *Early Texas Birth Records, 1838–1878*. 2 vols. Austin, Texas: the authors, 1969, 1971.

Grammer, Norma R. *Marriage Records of Early Texas, 1826–1846*. Fort Worth, Texas: Fort Worth Genealogical Society, 1971.

Guide to Public Vital Statistics Records in Texas. N.p.: Historical Records Survey, 1941.

Inscriptions from Texas, 1745–1870: Along the Old San Antonio Road and the Trail of Austin's Colonists. Oklahoma City: Oklahoma Historical Society, 1952.

Parsons, Kim. *A Reference to Texas Cemetery Records*. Humble, Texas: the author, 1988.

Swenson, Helen S. *8,800 Texas Marriages, 1824–1850*. 2 vols. Round Rock, Texas: Helen S. Swanson, 1981.

County Website	Map Index	Date Created	Parent County or Territory From Which Organized Address/Details
Anderson www.wwits.net/counties/anderson.phtml	**F10**	**24 Mar 1846**	**Houston** Anderson County; 500 N Church St; Palestine, TX 75801-3024; Ph. (903) 723-7432 **Details:** (District Clerk has Divorce Records; County Clerk has Birth & Death Records from 1903, Marriage, Probate & Land Records from 1846 & Court Records; cities have Birth & Death Records from 1953)
Andrews www.rootsweb.com/~txandrew/	**F4**	**21 Aug 1876**	**Bexar Land District** Andrews County; 215 NW 1st St; Andrews, TX 79714; Ph. (915) 524-1426 **Details:** (County Clerk has Birth, Marriage & Court Records from 1910, Probate Records from 1911 & Land Records from 1884; District Clerk has Divorce Records)
Angelina www.rootsweb.com/~txangeli/	**G11**	**22 Apr 1846**	**Nacogdoches** Angelina County; PO Box 908; Lufkin, TX 75902-0908; Ph. (936) 634-8339 **Details:** (County Clerk has some Birth Records from 1875, Death Records from 1903, Marriage, Probate & Land Records from 1846; District Clerk has Divorce Records; County Clerk & District Court have Court Records from 1920)

County Website	Map Index	Date Created	Parent County or Territory From Which Organized Address/Details
Aransas www.rootsweb.com/~txaransa/	K9	18 Sep 1871	**Refugio** Aransas County; 301 N Liveoak St; Rockport, TX 78382-2744; Ph. (361) 790-0122 **Details:** (County Clerk has Birth & Death Records from 1901, Marriage, Probate, Court & Land Records from 1871)
Archer www.rootsweb.com/~txarcher/archer.htm	D8	22 Jan 1858	**Fannin Land District** Archer County; 112 E Walnut; PO Box 458; Archer City, TX 76351; Ph. (940) 574-4615 **Details:** (County Clerk has Birth Records from 1880, Marriage, Death, Burial, Divorce, Probate, Court & Land Records)
Armstrong www.rootsweb.com/~txarmstr/	C5	21 Aug 1876	**Bexar Land District** Armstrong County; PO Box 309; ClAuditore, TX 79019; Ph. (806) 226-2081 **Details:** (County Clerk has Birth & Death Records from 1903, Marriage & Probate Records from 1890, Court Records from 1898 & Land Records from 1883; Clerk Circuit Court has Divorce Records)
Atascosa www.pastracks.com/states/texas/atascosa	J8	25 Jan 1856	**Bexar Land District** Atascosa County; Circle Dr Room 6-1; Jourdanton, TX 78026; Ph. (830) 767-2511 **Details:** (District Clerk has Court Records 1857–1910 & Naturalization Records 1888–1903; County Clerk has Land Records 1856–1907, Marriage Records 1856–1911, Probate Records 1873–1910, Birth Records from 1856, Death Records from 1903, & Divorce Records from 1857)
Austin www.austincounty.com/	H10	17 Mar 1836	**Old Mexican Municipality** Austin County; 1 E Main St; Bellville, TX 77418; Ph. (979) 865-5911, cbilski@austincounty.com **Details:** (County Clerk has Birth & Death Records from 1903, Marriage, Land & Probate Records from early 1800's, Cemetery, Court, Military Discharge & Naturalization Records; District Court has Divorce Records)
Bailey www.rootsweb.com/~txbailey/index.htm	D4	21 Aug 1876	**Bexar Land District** Bailey County; 300 S 1st St; Muleshoe, TX 79347-3621; Ph. (806) 272-3044 **Details:** (County Clerk has Birth, Marriage, Probate & Court Records from 1918 & Land Records from 1882; District Clerk has Divorce Records)
Bandera www.rootsweb.com/~txbander/	I7	26 Jan 1856	**Bexar Land District** Bandera County; County Courthouse; Bandera, TX 78003; Ph. (830) 796-3332 **Details:** (County/District Clerk has Birth & Death Records from 1904, Marriage, Divorce, Land, Probate, Court & Naturalization Records from 1856 & Military Discharge Records from 1900)
Bastrop www.rootsweb.com/~txbastro/bastrop.htm	H9	17 Mar 1836	**Old Mexican Municipality** Bastrop County; 804 Pecan St; PO Box 577; Bastrop, TX 78602; Ph. (512) 332-7234 **Details:** (Formerly Mina County 1834–1837) (County Clerk has Birth & Death Records from 1903, Marriage Records from 1860, Probate Records from 1850, Court Records from 1890, Land Records from 1837, Military Discharge Records from 1919 & Naturalization Records from 1855; District Clerk has Divorce Records)

County Website	Map Index	Date Created	Parent County or Territory From Which Organized Address/Details
Baylor www.rootsweb.com/~txbaylor/baylor.htm	**D7**	**1 Feb 1858**	**Fannin Land District** Baylor County; 101 S Washington; PO Box 689; Seymour, TX 76380-0689; Ph. (940) 888-3322 **Details:** (County Clerk has Birth & Death Records from 1903, Marriage Records from 1879, Divorce Records from 1881, Probate & Court Records from 1880)
Bee http://bsd.pastracks.com/states/texas/bee/	**J8**	**8 Dec 1857**	**Goliad, Refugio, Live Oak, San Patricio, Karnes** Bee County; 105 W Corpus Christi St; Beeville, TX 78102-5684; Ph. (361) 362-3245 **Details:** (County Clerk has Birth & Death Records from 1903, Marriage, Probate & Land Records from 1858 & Court Records from 1876; District Clerk has Divorce Records)
Bell www.bellcountytx.com/	**G9**	**22 Jan 1850**	**Milam** Bell County; 550 E 2nd St; PO Box 480; Belton, TX 76513; Ph. (254) 933-5174 **Details:** (County Clerk has Birth & Death Records from 1903, Marriage, Probate & Land Records from 1850, Military Records & school Census; Clerk District Court has Divorce Records from 1850, Court & Naturalization Records)
Bevil		**1834**	**Old Mexican Municipality** Bevil County; TX **Details:** County Name changed in 1835 to Jasper
Bexar www.co.bexar.tx.us/	**I8**	**1836**	**Old Mexican Municipality (established 1731)** Bexar County; 100 Dolorosa St Ste 108; San Antonio, TX 78205-3083; Ph. (210) 335-2585 **Details:** (County Clerk has Birth Records from 1838, Marriage Records from 1837, Death Records from 1903, Probate Records from 1843, Land Records from 1700's, Spanish church Records 1737–1859 & Spanish City Council minutes 1815–1820)
Blanco www.moment.net/~blancoco/	**H8**	**12 Feb 1858**	**Gillespie, Comal, Burnet, Hays** Blanco County; PO Box 65; Johnson City, TX 78636-0117; Ph. (830) 868-7357 **Details:** (County Clerk has Birth & Death Records from 1903, Marriage, Divorce, Probate, Court & Land Records from 1876)
Borden www.pastracks.com/states/texas/borden/	**E5**	**21 Aug 1876**	**Bexar Land District** Borden County; 117 E Wasson; PO Box 124; Gail, TX 79738; Ph. (806) 756-4312 **Details:** (Clerks Office has Land, Birth, Death, Marriage, Probate, Military Discharge Records. As Combination Clerk we have both County & District Court Records)
Bosque 	**F9**	**4 Feb 1854**	**McLennan, Milam** Bosque County; 104 W Morgan St.; PO Box 617; Meridian, TX 76665; Ph. (254) 435-2201, room106@htcomp.net **Details:** (County Clerk has Birth & Death Records from 1903, Marriage Records from 1860, Probate & Deed Records from 1854; District Clerk has Divorce Records)

County Website	Map Index	Date Created	Parent County or Territory From Which Organized Address/Details
Bowie www.usroots.com/~jmautrey/	E12	17 Dec 1840	**Red River** Bowie County; PO Box 248; New Boston, TX 75570; Ph. (903) 628-2571 **Details:** (County Clerk has Birth, Marriage, Death, Probate, Land & Military Records, school Census; Clerk District Court has Divorce & Court Records)
Brazoria www.brazoria.tx.us.landata.com	I10	17 Mar 1836	**Old Mexican Municipality** Brazoria County; 111 E Locust St Ste 200; Angleton, TX 77515; Ph. (979) 864-1355 **Details:** (County Clerk has Birth Records from 1901, Court Records from 1896, Death Records from 1903, Land Records from 1826, Marriage Records from 1829, Military Records from 1919, Probate records from 1837, Statewide Birth Records from 1930, Delayed Birth Records from the 1800's)
Brazos	H10	30 Jan 1841	**Washington, Robertson** Brazos County; 300 E 26th St, Ste 120; PO Box 111; Bryan, TX 77803; Ph. (979) 361-4528 **Details:** (Formerly Navasota County. Name changed to Brazos 28 Jan 1842) (County Clerk has Birth, Death, Land, Marriage, Military, & Probate Records from 1890, Business Records from 1940, Court Records from 1950; City has Cemetery Records; Library has Census; District Clerk has Divorce & Naturalization Records; Tax Assessor has Tax Records)
Brewster www.rootsweb.com/~txbrewst/	I3	2 Feb 1887	**Presidio** Brewster County; 201 W Ave E; Alpine, TX 79830; Ph. ((915) 837-3366 **Details:** (County Clerk has Birth, Probate, Military & Court Records from 1900, Marriage Records from 1887, Death Records from 1903 & Land Records from 1800; District Court has Divorce Records)
Briscoe www.rootsweb.com/~txbrisco/	C5	21 Aug 1876	**Bexar Land District** Briscoe County; 415 Main; PO Box 375; Silverton, TX 79257; Ph. (806) 823-2134 **Details:** (County Clerk has Birth & Land Records from 1887, Marriage, Death, Probate & Military Records from 1900 & Court Records from 1945; District Court has Divorce Records)
Brooks http://bsd.pastracks.com/states/texas/brooks/	L8	11-Mar-11	**Starr, Zapata, Hidalgo** Brooks County; PO Box 427; Falfurrias, TX 78355; Ph. (361) 325-3053 **Details:** (County Clerk has Birth, Marriage, Death, Probate & Court Records from 1911)
Brown www.rootsweb.com/~txbrown/	F7	27 Aug 1856	**Travis, Comanche** Brown County; 200 S Broadway St; Brownwood, TX 76801; Ph. (915) 643-2594 **Details:** (County Clerk has Birth Records from 1900, Death Records from 1903, Marriage, Land, Probate, Court & Military Records from 1880; District Court has Divorce Records from 1880)
Buchanan		22 Jan 1858	**Bosque** Buchanan County; TX **Details:** (see Stephens) Name changed to Stephens 17 Dec 1861

County Website	Map Index	Date Created	Parent County or Territory From Which Organized Address/Details
Burleson www.rootsweb.com/~txburles/burles.htm	H9	15 Jan 1846	**Milam, Washington** Burleson County; PO Box 57; Caldwell, TX 77836; Ph. (409) 567-2329 **Details:** (County Clerk has Birth & Death Records from 1903, Marriage, Probate, Court & Land Records from 1845; District Clerk has Divorce Records from 1845)
Burnet www.rootsweb.com/~txburnet/	G8	5 Feb 1852	**Travis, Bell, Williamson** Burnet County; 220 S Pierce St; Burnet, TX 78611-3136; Ph. (512) 756-5420 **Details:** (County Clerk has Birth & Death Records from 1903, Marriage, Burial, Probate & Land Records from 1852 & Court Records from 1876; District Clerk has Divorce Records)
Caldwell www.rootsweb.com/~txcaldwe/index.htm	I9	6 Mar 1848	**Gonzales, Bastrop** Caldwell County; 110 S Main St; Lockhart, TX 78644; Ph. (512) 398-1804 **Details:** (County Clerk has Birth & Death Records from 1903, Marriage & Land Records from 1848 & Court Records; District Clerk has Divorce Records)
Calhoun www.tisd.net/~calhoun/	J10	4 Apr 1846	**Victoria, Matagorda, Jackson** Calhoun County; 211 S Ann St; Port Lavaca, TX 77979-4249; Ph. (361) 553-4411 **Details:** (County Clerk has Birth & Death Records from 1903, probated Birth Records from 1863, Marriage & Land Records from 1846, Probate Records from 1849, Court Records from 1850 & Military Discharge Records from 1919)
Callahan www.rootsweb.com/~txcallah/	F7	1 Feb 1858	**Bexar, Travis, Bosque** Callahan County; 400 Market St; Baird, TX 79504-5305; Ph. (915) 854-1217 **Details:** (County Clerk has Birth & Death Records from 1903, Marriage, Probate & Land Records from 1877; District Clerk has Divorce & Court Records)
Cameron www.CameronCountyClerk.org	M9	12 Feb 1848	**Nueces** Cameron County;964 E. Harrison; PO Box 2178; Brownsville, TX 78520; Ph. (956) 544-0815, lgperez@co.cameron.tx.us **Details:** (County Clerk has Birth, Death & Military Records from 1848, Marriage Records from 1900, Land Records from 1845, Probate Records from 1850 & Court Records from 1964)
Camp www.rootsweb.com/~txcamp/	E11	6 Apr 1874	**Upshur** Camp County; 126 Church St; Pittsburg, TX 75686; Ph. (903) 856-2731 **Details:** (County Clerk has Birth & Death Records from 1903, Marriage, Probate & Court Records from 1874 & Land Records from 1854)
Carson www.rootsweb.com/~txcarson/	B5	21 Aug 1876	**Bexar Land District** Carson County; PO Box 487; Panhandle, TX 79068; Ph. (806) 537-3873 **Details:** (County Clerk has Birth & Death Records from 1903, Marriage Records from 1888, Divorce Records from 1902, Probate Records from 1907 & Land Records from 1883)

County Website	Map Index	Date Created	Parent County or Territory From Which Organized Address/Details
Cass www.rootsweb.com/~txcass/	E12	25 Apr 1846	**Bowie** Cass County; PO Box 468; Linden, TX 75563; Ph. (903) 756-5071 **Details:** (Name changed to Davis 17 Dec 1861; Name changed back to Cass 16 May 1871) (County Clerk has some delayed Birth Records from 1873, Death Records 1903–1933, Marriage, Probate & Land Records from 1846, school Census 1932–1971 & Military Discharge Records from 1917; District Court has Divorce & Court Records)
Castro www.rootsweb.com/~txcastro/castro/index.htm	C4	21 Aug 1876	**Bexar Land District** Castro County; 100 E Bedford St; Dimmitt, TX 79027-2643; Ph. (806) 647-3338 **Details:** (County Clerk has Birth & Death Records from 1903, Marriage, Divorce & Court Records from 1892, Land Records from 1911, Probate Records from 1948 & Military Records from 1917)
Chambers http://co.chambers.tx.us/	I11	12 Feb 1858	**Jefferson, Libraryerty** Chambers County; 404 Washington; Anahuac, TX 77514; Ph. (409) 267-8309 **Details:** (County Clerk has Birth Records from 1903, Death Records from 1908, Marriage, Probate, Court & Land Records from 1875 & Divorce Records from 1910)
Cherokee www.tyler.net/ccgs/default.html	F11	11 Apr 1846	**Nacogdoches** Cherokee County; 520 N Main St; PO Drawer 420; Rusk, TX 75785; Ph. (903) 683-2350 **Details:** (County Clerk has Birth & Death Records from 1903, Marriage, Probate & Land Records from 1846, Court & Divorce Records)
Childress www.rootsweb.com/~txchildr/	C6	21 Aug 1876	**Bexar Land District** Childress County; Courthouse Box 4; Childress, TX 79201-3755; Ph. (940) 937-6143 **Details:** (County Clerk has Birth & Death Records from 1903, Marriage Records from 1893, Divorce & Court Records from 1900, Probate Records from 1894 & Land Records from 1895)
Cibilo		1869	**Wilson** Cibilo County; TX **Details:** Temporary Name given to Wilson County 1869–1874
Clay www.co.clay.tx.us/	D8	24 Dec 1857	**Cooke** Clay County; 100 N Bridge St; PO Box 548; Henrietta, TX 76365-2858; Ph. (940) 538-4631 **Details:** (County Clerk has Birth & Death Records from 1903, Marriage Records from 1874, Probate & Land Records from 1873 & Court Records from 1876)
Cochran	D4	21 Aug 1876	**Bexar Land District** Cochran County; 100 N Main, Rm 102; Morton, TX 79346; Ph. (806) 266-5450 **Details:** (County Clerk has Birth, Death, Divorce, Probate & Court Records from 1926, Marriage Records from 1924 & Land Records from 1884)

County Website	Map Index	Date Created	Parent County or Territory From Which Organized Address/Details
Coke www.cvcog.org/coke/coke.htm	**F6**	**13 Mar 1889**	**Tom Green** Coke County; PO Box 150; Robert Lee, TX 76945; Ph. (915) 453-2631 **Details:** (County Clerk has Birth & Death Records from 1903, Marriage, Divorce, Probate & Court Records from 1891 & Land Records from 1875)
Coleman www.rootsweb.com/~txcolema/	**F7**	**1 Feb 1858**	**Travis, Brown** Coleman County; PO Box 591; Coleman, TX 76834-0591; Ph. (915) 625-2889 **Details:** (County Clerk has Birth & Death Records from 1900, Marriage Records from 1878, Land Records from 1849, Probate Records from 1876, Military Records from 1918 & Court Records from 1977; District Court has Divorce Records)
Collin www.collincountytexas.gov	**E9**	**3 Apr 1846**	**Fannin** Collin County; 200 S McDonald St Ste 120; McKinney, TX 75069-5655; Ph. (972) 548-4185 **Details:** (County Clerk has Birth, Burial, Cemetery, Business, Court, Death, Land, Marriage, Military, Probate, & Other Historical Records)
Collingsworth www.rootsweb.com/~txcollin/	**C6**	**21 Aug 1876**	**Bexar Land District** Collingsworth County; County Courthouse Rm 3; Wellington, TX 79095; Ph. (806) 447-2408 **Details:** (County Clerk has Birth Records from 1891, Marriage Records from 1890, Death Records from 1892, Divorce & Court Records from 1903 & Land Records)
Colorado www.rtis.com/reg/colorado-cty/gov.htm	**I10**	**1835**	**Old Mexican Municipality** Colorado County; PO Box 68; Columbus, TX 78934; Ph. (979) 732-2155 **Details:** (County Clerk has Birth & Death Records from 1903, Marriage & Probate Records from 1837 & Land Records; District Clerk has Divorce & Court Records)
Comal www.co.comal.tx.us/	**I8**	**24 Mar 1846**	**Bexar, Gonzales, Travis** Comal County; 150 N Seguin Ste 101; New Braunfels, TX 78130; Ph. (830) 620-5513 **Details:** (County Clerk has Birth Records 1903–1910 & 1930–1950, Marriage Records from 1846, Death Records from 1903, Probate, Land, Naturalization & Court Records from 1846 & Military Discharge Records from 1919)
Comanche www.rootsweb.com/~txcomanc/comanche.htm	**F8**	**25 Jan 1856**	**Bosque, Coryell** Comanche County; County Courthouse; Comanche, TX 76442; Ph. (915) 356-2655 **Details:** (County Clerk has Birth, Death & Burial Records from 1903, Marriage Records from 1856, Probate Records from 1897, Court Records from 1934 & Land Records from 1859)
Concho www.rootsweb.com/~txconcho/	**G7**	**1 Feb 1858**	**Bexar** Concho County; 152 N. Roberts; PO Box 98; Paint Rock, TX 76866 **Details:** (County Clerk has Birth, Death, Marriage, Land, & Court Records from July 1, 1879)

County Website	Map Index	Date Created	Parent County or Territory From Which Organized Address/Details
Cooke www.rootsweb.com/~txcooke/index.html	**D9**	**20 Mar 1848**	**Fannin** Cooke County; 100 Dixon St; Gainesville, TX 76240; Ph. (940) 668-5420 **Details:** (County Clerk has Birth & Death Records from 1903, Marriage, Probate, Court & Land Records from 1850; District Clerk has Divorce Records)
Coryell www.rootsweb.com/~txcoryel/	**G8**	**4 Feb 1854**	**Bell, McLennan** Coryell County; PO Box 237; Gatesville, TX 76528; Ph. (254) 865-5016 **Details:** (County Clerk has Birth & Death Records from 1903, Marriage, Probate, Court & Land Records from 1854)
Cottle www.rootsweb.com/~txcottle/	**D6**	**21 Aug 1876**	**Fannin Land District** Cottle County; PO Box 717; Paducah, TX 78248; Ph. (806) 492-3823 **Details:** (County Clerk has Birth, Marriage, Death, Burial, Divorce, Probate, Court & Land Records from 1892)
Crane www.rootsweb.com/~txcrane/	**G4**	**26 Feb 1887**	**Tom Green** Crane County; PO Box 578; Crane, TX 79731; Ph. (432) 558-3581 **Details:** (County Clerk has Birth Records from 1928, Marriage, Death, Divorce, Probate, Court & Land Records from 1927 & Burial Records from 1953)
Crockett www.rootsweb.com/~txcrocke/	**H5**	**22 Jan 1875**	**Bexar Land District** Crockett County; PO Drawer C; Ozona, TX 76943; Ph. (915) 392-2022 **Details:** (County Clerk has Birth & Death Records from 1903, Divorce, Probate & Court Records from 1892 & Burial Records after 1980)
Crosby www.rootsweb.com/~txcrosby/	**G5**	**21 Aug 1876**	**Bexar Land District** Crosby County; PO Box 218; Crosbyton, TX 79322; Ph. (806) 675-2334 **Details:** (County Clerk has Birth & Death Records from 1903, Marriage, Probate & Court Records from 1887 & Land Records from 1886; District Clerk has Divorce Records)
Culberson www.rootsweb.com/~txculber/	**G2**	**10 Mar 1911**	**El Paso** Culberson County; PO Box 158; Van Horn, TX 79855-0158; Ph. (915) 283-2058 **Details:** (County Clerk has Birth, Marriage, Death, Burial, Divorce, Land, Probate, Military & Court Records from 1911)
Dallam www.dallam.org/county/	**A4**	**21 Aug 1876**	**Bexar Land District** Dallam County; PO Box 1352; Dalhart, TX 79022; Ph. (806) 249-4751 **Details:** (County Clerk has Birth & Death Records from 1903, Marriage & Court Records from 1891, Divorce Records from 1892, Probate Records from 1900 & Land Records from 1876)
Dallas www.dallascounty.org/	**E9**	**30 Mar 1846**	**Nacogdoches, Robertson** Dallas County; 500 Main St; Dallas, TX 75202; Ph. (214) 653-7131 **Details:** (County Clerk has Birth & Death Records from 1903, Marriage Records from 1846, Probate, Court & Land Records; District Court has Divorce Records)

County Website	Map Index	Date Created	Parent County or Territory From Which Organized Address/Details
Davis		25 Apr 1846	**Bowie** Davis County; TX **Details:** (Formerly Cass County. Name changed to Davis 17 Dec 1861. Name changed back to Cass 16 May 1871)
Dawson		1 Feb 1858	**Bexar Land District** Dawson County; TX **Details:** County Terminated in 1866
De Witt www.rootsweb.com/~txdewitt/	I9	24 Mar 1846	**Goliad, Gonzales, Victoria** De Witt County; 307 N Gonzales St; Cuero, TX 77954-2870; Ph. (512) 275-3724 **Details:** (County Clerk has Birth & Death Records from 1903, Marriage, Probate, Court & Land Records from 1846; Civil War muster rolls from 1861)
Deaf Smith www.rootsweb.com/~txdeafsm/	C4	21 Aug 1876	**Bexar Land District** Deaf Smith County; 235 E 3rd Rm 203; Hereford, TX 79045; Ph. (806) 364-1746 **Details:** (County Clerk has Birth & Death Records from 1903, Marriage, Probate & Court Records from 1891, Land Records from 1882 & Military Discharge Records from 1919; District Clerk has Divorce Records & doctor Records from 1903)
Delta http://gen.1starnet.com/delta/	E10	29 Jul 1870	**Hopkins, Lamar** Delta County; 200 W Dallas Ave; Cooper, TX 75432; Ph. (903) 395-4110 **Details:** (County Clerk has Birth, Probate & Court Records from 1903, Marriage Records from 1870, Death Records from 1916 & Land Records)
Denton http://dentoncounty.com/default1001.htm	E9	11 Apr 1846	**Fannin** Denton County; PO Box 2187; Denton, TX 76202; Ph. (940) 349-2021 **Details:** (Courthouse burned 1875; a few Records saved) (County Clerk has Birth, Death & Burial Records from 1903, Marriage, Probate, Court & Land Records from 1876; District Clerk has Divorce Records from 1876)
Dickens www.rootsweb.com/~txdicken/	D6	21 Aug 1876	**Bexar Land District** Dickens County; PO Box 179; Dickens, TX 79229; Ph. (806) 623-5531 **Details:** (County Clerk has Birth, Marriage, Death, Burial, Divorce, Probate, Court & Land Records from 1891)
Dimmit www.Historicaloricdistrict.com/Genealogy/dimmit/dimmit.htm	J7	1 Feb 1858	**Uvalde, Bexar, Maverick, Webb** Dimmit County; 103 N 5th St; Carrizo Springs, TX 78834; Ph. (830) 876-3569 **Details:** (County Clerk has Birth & Death Records from 1903, Marriage & Court Records from 1881, Probate Records from 1882 & Land Records; District Clerk has Divorce Records)
Donley www.rootsweb.com/~txdonley/	C6	21 Aug 1876	**Bexar Land District** Donley County; 300 S Sally; Clarendon, TX 79226; Ph. (806) 874-3436 **Details:** (County Clerk has Birth Records from 1877, Marriage & Land Records from 1882, Death Records from 1903, Probate Records from 1923 & Military Discharge Records from 1919)

County Website	Map Index	Date Created	Parent County or Territory From Which Organized Address/Details
Duval www.vsta.com/~rlblack/duvalpage.html	**K8**	**1 Feb 1858**	**Live Oak, Starr, Neuces** Duval County; PO Box 248; San Diego, TX 78384-1816; Ph. (512) 279-3322 **Details:** (County Clerk has Birth & Death Records from 1903, Marriage, Probate & Land Records from 1877 & Court Records)
Eastland www.rootsweb.com/~txeastla/	**F8**	**1 Feb 1858**	**Bosque, Coryell, Travis** Eastland County; PO Box 110; Eastland, TX 76448; Ph. (254) 629-1583 **Details:** (County Clerk has Birth & Death Records 1903–1930 & 1940–1950, Marriage Records from 1874, Land Records from 1870, Probate Records from 1882 & Military Discharge Records from 1919; District Court has Divorce Records from 1903)
Ector www.rootsweb.com/~txector/index.htm	**F4**	**26 Feb 1887**	**Tom Green** Ector County; 300 N Grant Ave; Odessa, TX 79761; Ph. (915) 335-3030 **Details:** (County Clerk has Birth, Marriage, Death, Burial, Probate, Court & Land Records from 1896; District Clerk has Divorce Records)
Edwards www.rootsweb.com/~txedward/	**I6**	**1 Feb 1858**	**Bexar Land District** Edwards County; PO Box 184; Rocksprings, TX 78880-0184; Ph. (830) 683-2235 **Details:** (County Clerk has Birth & Death Records from 1903, Marriage, Divorce, Probate, Court & Land Records from 1884)
El Paso www.co.el-paso.tx.us/	**I1**	**3 Jan 1850**	**Bexar Land District** El Paso County; 500 E San Antonio St; El Paso, TX 79901-2421; Ph. (915) 546-2071 **Details:** (County Clerk has Birth, Death & Burial Records from 1903, Marriage Records from 1880, Military Discharge Records from 1919, Probate, Court & Land Records)
Ellis www.rootsweb.com/~txellis/	**F9**	**20 Dec 1849**	**Navarro** Ellis County; 115 W Franklin; Waxahachie, TX 75165; Ph. (972) 923-5070 **Details:** (County Clerk has Birth, Marriage, Death, Land, Probate, Military & Court Records)
Encinal		**1 Feb 1858**	**Webb** Encinal County; TX **Details:** (see Webb) Never organized. Discontinued 12 Mar 1899 & returned to Webb County
Erath www.rootsweb.com/~txerath/erath.htm	**F8**	**25 Jan 1856**	**Bosque, Coryell** Erath County; 100 W Washington St; Stephenville, TX 76401; Ph. (254) 965-1482 **Details:** (County Clerk has Birth & Death Records from 1903, Marriage Records from 1869, Probate Records from 1876 & Land Records from 1867)
Falls	**G9**	**28 Jan 1850**	**Limestone, Milam** Falls County; 125 Bridge St; PO Box 458; Marlin, TX 76661; Ph. (254) 883-1408 **Details:** (County Clerk has Birth & Death Records from 1903, Land Records from 1835, Marriage Records from 1854, Military Discharges from 1917, & Probate Records from 1880)

County Website	Map Index	Date Created	Parent County or Territory From Which Organized Address/Details
Fannin www.rootsweb.com/~txfannin/	D10	14 Dec 1837	**Red River** Fannin County; 101 Sam Rayburn Dr; Bonham, TX 75418; Ph. (903) 583-7486 **Details:** (County Clerk has Birth Records from 1903 with a few 1874–1876, Death Records from 1903, Marriage Records from 1852, Probate, Land & Court Records from 1838)
Fayette www.co.fayette.tx.us/	I9	14 Dec 1837	**Bastrop, Colorado** Fayette County; 246 W Colorado; PO Box 59; La Grange, TX 78945; Ph. (979) 968-3251 **Details:** (County Court has Birth & Death Rrecords from 1903, Court, Guardianship, Land, Marriage, & Probate Records from 1838; District Clerks Office has Indexes for Naturalization & Citizenship)
Fisher www.rootsweb.com/~txfisher/	E6	21 Aug 1876	**Bexar Land District** Fisher County; PO Box 368; Roby, TX 79543; Ph. (915) 776-2401 **Details:** (County Clerk has Birth, Death & Marriage Records from 1903, Land Records from 1886, Probate & Court Records from 1920)
Floyd www.rootsweb.com/~txfloyd/	D5	21 Aug 1876	**Bexar Land District** Floyd County; 100 S Main St; PO Box 476; Floydada, TX 79235; Ph. (806) 983-4900 **Details:** (County Clerk has Birth, Marriage, Death, Probate & Court Records from 1903 & Land Records from 1876; District Clerk has Divorce Records)
Foard www.foardcounty.org/	D7	3 Mar 1891	**Hardeman, Knox, King, Cottle** Foard County; PO Box 539; Crowell, TX 79227; Ph. (940) 684-1365 **Details:** (County Clerk has Birth & Death Records from 1903, Marriage, Divorce, Probate, Court & Land Records from 1891)
Fort Bend www.co.fort-bend.tx.us/	I10	29 Dec 1837	**Austin** Fort Bend County; 301 Jackson St; PO Box 520; Richmond, TX 77469; Ph. (281) 341-8685 **Details:** (County Clerk has Birth & Death Records from 1903, Marriage & Land Records from 1838, Probate Records from 1836 & Court Records from 1876)
Franklin www.mt-vernon.com/~skelly/	E11	6 Mar 1875	**Titus** Franklin County; 200 N Kaufman St; Mount Vernon, TX 75457; Ph. (903) 537-4252 Ext. 6, fcclerk@mt-vernon.com **Details:** (County Clerk has Divorce Records from 1884, Birth & Death Records from 1903, Marriage & Probate Records from 1875 & Land Records from 1843)
Freestone www.rootsweb.com/~txfreest/	G10	6 Sep 1850	**Limestone** Freestone County; PO Box 307; Fairfield, TX 75840; Ph. (903) 389-2635 **Details:** (County Clerk has Birth & Death Records from 1903, Marriage Records from 1853, Land, Probate, Military Discharge & Court Records from 1851)
Frio www.rootsweb.com/~txfrio/	J7	1 Feb 1858	**Atascosa, Bexar, Uvalde** Frio County; PO Box 847; Pearsall, TX 79360; Ph. (830) 334-2214 **Details:** (County Clerk has Birth & Death Records from 1903, Marriage Records from 1876, Probate Records from 1874, Court Records from 1907 & Land Records from 1871)

County Website	Map Index	Date Created	Parent County or Territory From Which Organized Address/Details
Gaines www.gainescounty.org/	E4	21 Aug 1876	**Bexar Land District** Gaines County; 101 S Main St; PO Box 847; Seminole, TX 79360-4342; Ph. (432) 758-4003 **Details:** (County Clerk has Birth, Marriage, Death, Burial, Probate, & Court Records from 1905 & Land Records)
Galveston www.co.galveston.tx.us/	I11	15 May 1838	**Brazoria, Libraryerty** Galveston County; 722 Moody; Galveston, TX 77550; Ph. (409) 766-2210 **Details:** (County Clerk has Birth & Death Records 1903–1910 & 1941–1951, Marriage, Probate & Land Records from 1838 & Court Records from 1875)
Garza www.angelfire.com/tx/gcounty/index.html	E5	21 Aug 1876	**Bexar Land District** Garza County; 300 W Main St; Post, TX 79356; Ph. (806) 495-4430 **Details:** (County Clerk has Birth, Marriage, Death, Divorce, Probate & Court Records from 1907 & Land Records)
Gillespie www.rootsweb.com/~txgilles/	H7	23 Feb 1848	**Bexar, Travis** Gillespie County; 101 W Main St; PO Box 551; Fredericksburg, TX 78624; Ph. (830) 997-6515 **Details:** (County Clerk has Birth, Marriage & Probate Records from 1850, Death Records from 1902, Land Records from 1848 & Court Records from 1954; District Clerk has Divorce Records)
Glasscock www.rootsweb.com/~txglassc/	F5	4 Apr 1887	**Tom Green** Glasscock County; PO Box 190; Garden City, TX 79739-0190; Ph. (915) 354-2371 **Details:** (County Clerk has Birth & Death Records from 1903, Marriage & Court Records from 1893, Probate Records from 1895 & Land Records from 1883; District Clerk has Divorce Records; County Judge has recent Burial Records)
Goliad www.goliad.org/goliad.html	J9	17 Mar 1836	**Old Mexican Municipality** Goliad County; 127 S Courthouse Square; PO Box 5; Goliad, TX 77963-0005; Ph. (361) 645-3294 **Details:** (County Clerk has Birth & Death Records from 1903, Marriage, Probate, Court & Land Records from 1870 & Divorce Records)
Gonzales www.rootsweb.com/~txgonzal/	I9	17 Mar 1836	**Old Mexican Municipality** Gonzales County; 1709 Dewitt Dr; PO Box 77; Gonzales, TX 78629-0077; Ph. (830) 672-2801 **Details:** (County Clerk has Birth & Death Records from 1903, Marriage, Probate & Land Records from 1829; District Clerk has Divorce Records; Archives & Records Censuster has all older Records from County & District Clerks, Cemetery Records & School Census)
Gray www.rootsweb.com/~txgray/	B6	21 Aug 1876	**Bexar Land District** Gray County; 200 N Russell St; PO Box 1902; Pampa, TX 79066; Ph. (806) 669-8004 **Details:** (County Clerk has Birth Records from 1903, Marriage, Death, Probate & Court Records from 1902, Burial Records from 1930, Land Records from 1887 & Military Discharge Records from 1919; District Clerk has Divorce Records)

The Handybook for Genealogists

County Website	Map Index	Date Created	Parent County or Territory From Which Organized Address/Details
Grayson www.co.grayson.tx.us/	D9	17 Mar 1846	**Fannin Land District** Grayson County; 100 W Houston St; Sherman, TX 75090; Ph. (903) 813-4243 **Details:** (County Clerk has Birth & Death Records from 1900, Marriage, Probate, Court & Land Records from 1846; District Clerk has Divorce Records)
Gregg www.co.gregg.tx.us/	F11	12 Apr 1873	**Rusk, Upshur** Gregg County; 101 E Methvin St; PO Box 3049; Longview, TX 75606-3049; Ph. (903) 236-8430 **Details:** (County Clerk has Birth, Marriage, Court & Land Records from 1873, Death Records from 1900 & Probate Records)
Grimes www.rootsweb.com/~txgrimes/	H10	6 Apr 1846	**Montgomery** Grimes County; PO Box 209; Anderson, TX 77830; Ph. (409) 873-2111 **Details:** (County Clerk has Birth, Death & Court Records from 1903, Marriage & Probate Records from 1848 & Land Records from 1843)
Guadalupe www.co.guadalupe.tx.us/	I8	30 Mar 1846	**Bexar, Gonzales** Guadalupe County; 101 E Court St; PO Box 990; Seguin, TX 78156-0990; Ph. (830) 303-4188 ext. 239 **Details:** (County Court has Marriage, Probate, Cattle Brand from 1846, & Deed Records from 1853; County Clerk has Birth & Death Records from 1903, Business Records from 1995, Guardianship Records from 1846, Land Records from 1853, Marriage Records from 1846, Military Records 1919, & Probate Records from 1846)
Hale www.texasonline.net/halecounty/	D5	21 Aug 1876	**Bexar Land District** Hale County; 500 Broadway; Plainview, TX 79072-8050; Ph. (806) 291-5261 **Details:** (County Clerk has Marriage & Land Records from 1888 & Probate Records from 1889; District Clerk has Divorce & Court Records)
Hall www.rootsweb.com/~txhall/	C6	21 Aug 1876	**Bexar Land District** Hall County; County Courthouse Box 8; Memphis, TX 79245; Ph. (806) 259-2627 **Details:** (County Clerk has Birth, Marriage, Death, Divorce, Probate, Court & Land Records from 1890)
Hamilton www.rootsweb.com/~txhamilt/main.htm	G8	22 Jun 1858	**Bosque, Comanche, Lampasas, Coryell** Hamilton County; County Courthouse; Hamilton, TX 76531-1859; Ph. (254) 386-3518 **Details:** (Created 2 Feb 1842, but not organized until 1858) (County Clerk has incomplete Birth & Death Records from 1903, Marriage Records from 1885, Divorce Records from 1875, Probate Records from 1870 & Land Records)
Hansford www.rootsweb.com/~txhansfo/	A5	21 Aug 1876	**Bexar Land District** Hansford County; PO Box 397; Spearman, TX 79081-3499; Ph. (806) 659-4110 **Details:** (County Clerk has Land Records from 1875, Birth, Marriage, Death, Divorce, Probate & Court Records from 1900)

County Website	Map Index	Date Created	Parent County or Territory From Which Organized Address/Details
Hardeman www.rootsweb.com/~txhardem/	D7	1 Feb 1858	**Fannin Land District** Hardeman County; PO Box 30; Quanah, TX 79252-0030; Ph. (940) 663-2901 **Details:** (County Clerk has Birth & Death Records from 1903, Marriage Records from 1885, Probate & Court Records from 1886 & Land Records from 1871; District Clerk has Divorce Records)
Hardin www.rootsweb.com/~txhardin/index.htm	H11	22 Jan 1858	**Jefferson, Libraryerty** Hardin County; PO Box 38; Kountze, TX 77625; Ph. (409) 246-5185 **Details:** (County Clerk has Birth Records from 1892, Marriage, Death & Land Records from 1859 & Probate Records from 1888; District Clerk has Divorce Records)
Harris www.co.harris.tx.us/	I10	17 Mar 1836	**Old Mexican Municipality** Harris County; 1001 Preston 4th Floor; Houston, TX 77251-1525; Ph. (713) 755-6405 **Details:** (Formerly Harrisburg County. Name changed to Harris 28 Dec 1839) (County Clerk has Birth & Death Records from 1903, Marriage & Land Records from 1836, Probate Records from late 1800's, Court Records from 1920's & immigration Records 1880–1890; District Clerk has Divorce Records)
Harrisburg		17 Mar 1836	**Old Mexican Municipality** Harrisburg County; TX **Details:** (see Harris) Name changed to Harris 28 Dec 1839
Harrison www.rootsweb.com/~txharris/	F12	28 Jan 1839	**Shelby** Harrison County; PO Box 1365; Marshall, TX 75671; Ph. (903) 935-4858 **Details:** (County Clerk has Birth & Death Records from 1903, Marriage, Land & Probate Records from 1800)
Hartley www.rootsweb.com/~txhartle/	B4	21 Aug 1876	**Bexar Land District** Hartley County; PO Box Q; Channing, TX 79018; Ph. (806) 235-3582 **Details:** (County Clerk has Birth Records from 1898, Marriage & Probate Records from 1891, Death Records from 1903, Land Records from 1888 & Military Discharge Records from 1919; District Court has Divorce Records from 1891 & Court Records from 1892)
Haskell www.rootsweb.com/~txhaskel/haskell.htm	E7	1 Feb 1858	**Fannin, Milam** Haskell County; PO Box 725; Haskell, TX 79521-0905; Ph. (940) 864-2451 **Details:** (County Clerk has Birth Records from late 1800's, Marriage & Probate Records from 1885, Death Records from 1903, Military Records from 1917, Land & Court Records; District Court has Divorce Records)
Hays www.co.hays.tx.us/	H8	1 Mar 1848	**Travis** Hays County; 137 N Guadalupe St; San Marcos, TX 78666; Ph. (512) 393-7330 **Details:** (County Clerk has Probate Records from 1839, Birth Records from 1865, Marriage, Court & Land Records from 1848 & Military Records from 1919; District Clerk has Divorce Records from 1897)

County Website	Map Index	Date Created	Parent County or Territory From Which Organized Address/Details
Hemphill www.rootsweb.com/~txhemphi/	**B6**	**21 Aug 1876**	**Bexar Land District** Hemphill County; PO Box 867; Canadian, TX 79014-0867; Ph. (806) 323-6212 **Details:** (County Clerk has Birth Records from 1876, Death Records from 1910, Marriage, Divorce, Probate, Court & Land Records from 1887)
Henderson www.hendersoncotx.com/	**F10**	**27 Apr 1846**	**Houston, Nacogdoches** Henderson County; 100 E Tyler St Ste 107; Athens, TX 75751; Ph. (903) 675-6140 **Details:** (County Clerk has Birth & Death Records from 1903, Marriage Records from 1880, Probate Records from 1860, Court Records from 1910 & Land Records from 1846)
Hidalgo www.co.hidalgo.tx.us/	**M8**	**24 Jan 1852**	**Cameron, Starr** Hidalgo County; PO Box 58; Edinburg, TX 78540; Ph. (956) 318-2100 **Details:** (County Clerk has Birth, Marriage, Death, Probate, Court & Land Records; District Clerk has Divorce Records)
Hill www.rootsweb.com/~txhill/index.html	**F9**	**7 Feb 1853**	**Navarro** Hill County; PO Box 398; Hillsboro, TX 76645-0398; Ph. (254) 582-4030 **Details:** (Courthouse burned between 1874 & 1878) (County Clerk has Birth & Marriage Records from 1876, Probate Records from 1879 & Land Records from 1853; District Clerk has Divorce Records)
Hockley www.rootsweb.com/~txhockle/index.htm	**D4**	**21 Aug 1876**	**Bexar Land District** Hockley County; County Courthouse Box 1; Levelland, TX 79336; Ph. (806) 894-3185 **Details:** (attached to Lubbock County from 1891 to 1921) (County Clerk has Birth, Marriage, Death, Probate, Court & Land Records from 1921)
Hood www.granburydepot.org/	**F8**	**3 Nov 1865**	**Johnson** Hood County; 100 E Pearl St; PO Box 339; Granbury, TX 76048-0339; Ph. (817) 579-3222 **Details:** (County Clerk has Birth & Death Records from 1903, Marriage, Divorce, Probate, Court & Land Records from 1875; Hood Public Library in Granbury has many Records of the late Judge Henry Davis)
Hopkins www.hopkinscountytx.org	**E10**	**25 Mar 1846**	**Lamar, Nacogdoches** Hopkins County; 411 College St.; PO Box 288; Sulphur Springs, TX; Ph. (903) 438-4074, hopcoclk@yahoo.com75482 **Details:** (County Clerk has Probate, Guardianship, Land, & Marriage Records from 1846, Birth & Death Records from 1903, Military Discharge & County Court Records; District Clerk has Divorce Records starting from 1800 & District Court Records; County Genealogical Society has Burial, Cemetery, Census, Newspapers, & Other Historical Records)

County Website	Map Index	Date Created	Parent County or Territory From Which Organized Address/Details
Houston www.io.com/~dwhite/more.html	**G10**	**12 Jun 1837**	**Nacogdoches** Houston County; PO Box 370; Crockett, TX 75835; Ph. (936) 544-3255 **Details:** (County Clerk has Birth, Marriage & Death Records from 1903, Probate, Court & Land Records from 1882; District Clerk has Divorce Records from 1920; County Historical Commission has Burial Records, family & local Histories)
Howard	**F5**	**21 Aug 1876**	**Bexar Land District** Howard County; 300 Main St; PO Box 1468; Big Spring, TX 79720; Ph. (915) 264-2213, dwright@howard-county.org **Details:** (County Clerk has Birth, Court, Death, Guardianship, Land, Marriage, Military, & Probate Records from 1896)
Hudspeth www.rootsweb.com/~txhudspe/	**I2**	**16 Feb 1917**	**El Paso** Hudspeth County; PO Drawer A; Sierra Blanca, TX 79851; Ph. (915) 369-2301 **Details:** (County Clerk has Birth, Marriage, Death, Divorce, Probate & Court Records from 1917 & Land Records from 1836)
Hunt www.rootsweb.com/~txhunt/	**E10**	**11 Apr 1846**	**Fannin, Nacogdoches** Hunt County; PO Box 1316; Greenville, TX 75401; Ph. (903) 408-4130 **Details:** (County Clerk has Birth, Death & Burial Records from 1903, Marriage & Land Records from 1846, Probate Records from 1800's, Military Records from early 1900's & Court Records from 1967; District Clerk has Divorce Records)
Hutchinson www.usroots.org/~hutchitx/	**B5**	**21 Aug 1876**	**Bexar Land District** Hutchinson County; PO Box 1186; Stinnett, TX 79083-0580; Ph. (806) 878-4002 **Details:** (County Clerk has Marriage, Probate, Court & Land Records from 1901, Birth Records from 1876 & Death Records; District Clerk has Divorce Records)
Irion www.rootsweb.com/~txirion/	**G6**	**7 Mar 1889**	**Tom Green** Irion County; PO Box 736; Mertzon, TX 76941-0736; Ph. (915) 835-2421 **Details:** (County Clerk has Birth, Marriage, Death, Divorce, Land, Probate, Military & Court Records from 1889; Tax Assessor has poll tax Records)
Jack www.rootsweb.com/~txjack/	**E8**	**27 Aug 1856**	**Cooke** Jack County; 100 Main St, Ste. 208; Jacksboro, TX 76458; Ph. (940) 567-2111 **Details:** (County Clerk has Birth & Death Records from 1903, Probate Records from 1857, Land Records from 1860, Marriage & Court Records; District Clerk has Divorce Records)
Jackson www.rootsweb.com/~txjackso/index.htm	**J10**	**17 Mar 1836**	**Old Mexican Municipality** Jackson County; 115 W Main St; Edna, TX 77957-2733; Ph. (361) 782-3563 **Details:** (County Clerk has Birth & Death Records from 1903, Marriage, Probate & Land Records from 1836 & Court Records from 1910; District Clerk has Divorce Records)

County Website	Map Index	Date Created	Parent County or Territory From Which Organized Address/Details
Jasper www.rootsweb.com/~txjasper/index.htm	**H12**	**17 Mar 1836**	**Old Mexican Municipality** Jasper County; PO Box 2070; Jasper, TX 75951; Ph. (409) 384-2632 **Details:** (Formerly Bevil County 1834–1836) (County Clerk has Marriage, Probate & Land Records from 1849, Birth Records from 1874, Death Records from 1903, Court Records from 1911 & Cemetery Records; District Clerk has Divorce Records)
Jeff Davis www.rootsweb.com/~txjeffda/	**G3**	**15 Mar 1887**	**Presidio** Jeff Davis County; PO Box 398; Fort Davis, TX 79734-0398; Ph. (915) 426-3251 **Details:** (County Clerk has Death Records from 1904, Birth Records from 1883, Divorce Records from 1946, Marriage, Probate, Court & Land Records from 1887)
Jefferson www.co.jefferson.tx.us/	**I12**	**17 Mar 1836**	**Old Mexican Municipality** Jefferson County; PO Box 1151; Beaumont, TX 77704; Ph. (409) 835-8475 **Details:** (County Clerk has Birth & Death Records 1903–1966, Marriage, Land, Probate, Court & Military Discharge Records from 1836; District Clerk has Divorce Records)
Jim Hogg	**L8**	**31 Mar 1913**	**Brooks, Duval** Jim Hogg County; 102 E. Tilley; PO Box 878; Hebbronville, TX 78361; Ph. (361) 527-4031 **Details:** (County Clerk has Birth, Court, Death, Divorce, Guardianship, Land, Marriage, Military, & Probate Records from 1913)
Jim Wells http://bsd.pastracks.com/states/texas/jimwells/	**K8**	**25 Mar 1911**	**Nueces** Jim Wells County; 200 N Almond St; Alice, TX 78332; Ph. (361) 668-5702 **Details:** (County Clerk has Birth, Death, Marriage, Probate & Court Records from 1911 & Land Records from 1848; District Clerk has Divorce Records)
Johnson www.htcomp.net/jcgs/	**F9**	**13 Feb 1854**	**Ellis, Hill, Navarro, McLennan** Johnson County; PO Box 662; Cleburne, TX 76031; Ph. (817) 556-6311 **Details:** (County Clerk has Marriage, Land & Probate Records from 1854, Birth & Death Records from 1903; District Clerk has Divorce Records)
Jones www.rootsweb.com/~txjones/	**E7**	**1 Feb 1858**	**Bexar Land District, Bosque** Jones County; PO Box 552; Anson, TX 79501; Ph. (915) 823-3762 **Details:** (County Clerk has Birth & Death Records from 1903, Marriage & Land Records from 1881 & Probate Records from 1882; District Clerk has Divorce & Court Records)
Karnes www.rootsweb.com/~txkarnes/	**J8**	**4 Feb 1854**	**Bexar, DeWitt, Goliad, San Patricio** Karnes County; 101 N Panna Maria St; Karnes City, TX 78118; Ph. (830) 780-3938 (County Clerk); (830) 780-2562 (District Clerk) **Details:** (County Clerk has Birth, Death & Court Records from 1900, Marriage Records from 1875, Probate Records from 1870 & Land Records from 1854; District Clerk has Divorce Records from 1858)

County Website	Map Index	Date Created	Parent County or Territory From Which Organized Address/Details
Kaufman www.kaufmancounty.net/	F10	**26 Feb 1848**	**Henderson** Kaufman County; County Courthouse; Kaufman, TX 75142; Ph. (972) 932-4331 **Details:** (County Clerk has Birth & Death Records from 1903, Court, Land, Maps, Marriage, Probate, & Other Historical Records from 1850; District Clerk has Court & Divorce Records; County Judge has Census Records)
Kendall www.rootsweb.com/~txkendal/index.htm	I8	**10 Jan 1862**	**Kerr, Blanco** Kendall County; 204 E San Antonio St; Boerne, TX 78006; Ph. (830) 249-9343 **Details:** (County Clerk has Marriage, Probate & Land Records)
Kenedy http://bsd.pastracks.com/states/texas/kenedy/	L9	**2 Apr 1921**	**Willacy, Hidalgo, Cameron** Kenedy County; PO Box 37; Sarita, TX 78385; Ph. (361) 294-5220 **Details:** (County Clerk has Birth Records from 1926, Marriage Records from 1923, Death Records from 1929, Divorce & Court Records from 1914, Probate & Land Records)
Kent www.rootsweb.com/~txkent/	E6	**21 Aug 1876**	**Bexar Land District** Kent County; PO Box 9; Jayton, TX 79528; Ph. (806) 237-3881 **Details:** (County Clerk has Birth, Marriage, Death, Divorce, Land, Probate, Military & Court Records from 1876)
Kerr www.ktc.net/kgs/	H7	**26 Jan 1856**	**Bexar** Kerr County; 700 Main St; Kerrville, TX 78028-5323; Ph. (830) 792-2255 **Details:** (County Clerk has Birth & Death Records from 1903, Marriage, Probate, Land & Court Records from 1856; District Clerk has Divorce Records)
Kimble www.rootsweb.com/~txkimble/	H7	**22 Jan 1858**	**Bexar Land District** Kimble County; 501 Main St Courthouse; Junction, TX 76849-4763; Ph. (915) 446-3353 **Details:** (County Clerk has Birth & Death Records from 1900, Marriage, Divorce, Land & Court Records from 1884, Probate Records from early 1900's & Military Records from 1915)
King www.rootsweb.com/~txking/	D6	**21 Aug 1876**	**Bexar Land District** King County; PO Box 135; Guthrie, TX 79236; Ph. (806) 596-4412 **Details:** (County Clerk has Birth, Divorce & Court Records from 1914, Marriage Records from 1891, Death Records from 1925, Probate Records from 1915 & Land Records from 1878)
Kinney www.rootsweb.com/~txkinney/	I6	**28 Jan 1850**	**Bexar Land District** Kinney County; PO Drawer 9; Brackettville, TX 78832; Ph. (830) 563-2521 **Details:** (County Clerk has Birth & Death Records from 1903, Marriage Records from 1872, Divorce, Probate, Court & Land Records from 1873; St. Mary's Catholic Church, Brackettville, TX has Burial Records)
Kleberg http://bsd.pastracks.com/states/texas/kleberg/	K9	**27 Feb 1913**	**Nueces** Kleberg County; PO Box 1327; Kingsville, TX 78364-1327; Ph. (361) 595-8548 **Details:** (County Clerk has Birth, Marriage, Death, Probate, Court & Land Records from 1913; District Clerk has Divorce Records)

County	Map	Date	Parent County or Territory From Which Organized
Website	Index	Created	Address/Details

Knox   **D7**   **1 Feb 1858**   **Fannin Land District**
www.knoxcountytexas.com/

Knox County; PO Box 196; Benjamin, TX 79505;
Ph. (940) 454-2441

Details: (County Clerk has Birth Records from 1905, Marriage Records from 1886, Death Records from 1917, Divorce Records from 1900's, Probate, Court & Land Records from 1887)

Lamar   **D11**   **17 Dec 1840**   **Red River**
http://gen.1starnet.com/

Lamar County; 119 N Main St; Paris, TX 75460-4265;
Ph. (903) 737-2420

Details: (County Clerk has Birth & Death Records from 1903, Marriage, Probate, Court & Land Records from 1843; District Clerk has Divorce Records)

Lamb   **D4**   **21 Aug 1876**   **Bexar Land District**
www.rootsweb.com/~txlamb/index.htm

Lamb County; 100 6th St; Littlefield, TX 79339-3366;
Ph. (806) 385-5173

Details: (County Clerk has Birth, Marriage, Death & Probate Records from 1920, Land Records from 1915 & Court Records)

Lampasas   **G8**   **1 Feb 1856**   **Bell, Travis**
www.rootsweb.com/~txlampas/lampasas.html

Lampasas County; PO Box 231; Lampasas, TX 76550-0231;
Ph. (512) 556-8271

Details: (County Clerk has Birth Records from 1895, Death Records from 1910, Marriage Records from 1879, Probate Records from 1876, Court Records from 1899 & Land Records from 1872)

LaSalle   **J7**   **1 Feb 1858**   **Bexar, Webb**
www.Historicaloricdistrict.com/Genealogy/
lasalle/lasalle.htm

LaSalle County; PO Box 340; Cotulla, TX 78014-0340;
Ph. (210) 879-2117

Details: (County & District Clerk has Marriage, Death, Divorce, Land, Probate, Military & Court Records from 1881)

Lavaca   **I9**   **6 Apr 1846**   **Colorado, Victoria, Jackson, Gonzales, Fayette**
www.rootsweb.com/~txlavaca/index.htm

Lavaca County; PO Box 326; Hallettsville, TX 77964;
Ph. (361) 798-3612

Details: (County Clerk has Birth & Death Records from 1903, Marriage & Probate Records from 1847, Land Records from 1846, Military Records from 1918, Court & Naturalization Records)

Lee   **H9**   **14 Apr 1874**   **Bastrop, Burleson, Washington, Fayette**
www.jamesdavidwalker.com/lee/

Lee County; PO Box 419; Giddings, TX 78942; Ph. (409) 542-3684

Details: (County Clerk has Birth & Death Records from 1903, Marriage, Probate, Court & Land Records from 1874; District Clerk has Divorce Records)

Leon   **G10**   **17 Mar 1846**   **Robertson**
www.rootsweb.com/~txleon/

Leon County; PO Box 98; Censusterville, TX 75833-0098;
Ph. (903) 536-2352

Details: (County Clerk has Birth & Death Records from 1903, Marriage Records from 1885, Probate Records from 1846, Court & Land Records)

County Website	Map Index	Date Created	Parent County or Territory From Which Organized Address/Details
Liberty www.rootsweb.com/~txLibraryert/	H11	17 Mar 1836	**Old Mexican Municipality** Liberty County; 1923 Sam Houston St; Libraryerty, TX 77575; Ph. (409) 336-4670 **Details:** (Courthouse burned 11 Dec 1874; Records destroyed) (County Clerk has Birth & Death Records from 1903, Marriage Records from 1875, Probate, Court & Land Records from 1874; District Clerk has Divorce Records)
Limestone www.rootsweb.com/~txlimest/index.html	G9	11 Apr 1846	**Robertson** Limestone County; 200 W State St; PO Box 350; Groesbeck, TX 76642; Ph. (254) 729-5504 **Details:** (County Clerk has Birth & Death Records from 1903, Marriage Records from 1873, Probate Records from 1880's, Land Records from late 1800's, Court Records from 1900's & Military Records from 1920's; District Clerk has Divorce Records)
Lipscomb www.rootsweb.com/~txlipsco/	A6	21 Aug 1876	**Bexar Land District** Lipscomb County; PO Box 70; Lipscomb, TX 79056; Ph. (806) 862-3091 **Details:** (County Clerk has Birth, Marriage, Death, Divorce, Probate, Court & Land Records from 1887, Military Discharge Records from 1919 & Naturalization Records 1926–1927)
Live Oak www.rootsweb.com/~txliveoa/	J8	2 Feb 1856	**Nueces, San Patricio** Live Oak County; PO Box 280; George West, TX 78022; Ph. (512) 449-2733 **Details:** (County Clerk has Birth & Death Records from 1903, Marriage & Land Records from 1856, Probate Records from 1857 & Court Records; District Clerk has Divorce Records)
Llano www.rootsweb.com/~txllano/	H8	1 Feb 1856	**Bexar, Gillespie** Llano County; 801 Ford; Llano, TX 78643; Ph. (915) 247-4455 **Details:** (County Clerk has Birth & Death Records from 1903, Marriage, Land, Probate & Court Records from 1880 & Military Records from 1919; District Clerk has Divorce & Naturalization Records)
Loving www.rootsweb.com/~txloving/	F3	26 Feb 1887	**Tom Green** Loving County; PO Box 194; Mentone, TX 79754-9999; Ph. (915) 377-2441 **Details:** (Attached to Reeves County. Reorganized 1931) (County Clerk has Birth, Marriage, Death, Divorce, Probate & Court Records from 1931 & Land Records from 1920)
Lubbock www.co.lubbock.tx.us/	D5	21 Aug 1876	**Bexar Land District** Lubbock County; PO Box 10536; Lubbock, TX 79408; Ph. (806) 775-1054 **Details:** (Attached to Crosby County at one time) (County Clerk has Birth & Death Records from 1903, Marriage Records from 1891, Probate & Court Records from 1904 & Land Records)
Lynn www.rootsweb.com/~txlynn/index.htm	E5	21 Aug 1876	**Bexar Land District** Lynn County; PO Box 1256; Tahoka, TX 79373; Ph. (806) 998-4750 **Details:** (County Clerk has Birth, Marriage & Death Records from 1910, Land, Probate, Military & Court Records; District Clerk has Divorce Records)

County Website	Map Index	Date Created	Parent County or Territory From Which Organized Address/Details
Madison www.rootsweb.com/~txmadiso/	G10	27 Jan 1853	**Leon, Grimes, Walker** Madison County; 101 W Main St; Madisonville, TX 77864; Ph. (936) 348-2638 **Details:** (County Clerk has Birth & Death Records from 1903, Marriage, Probate, Land, Military & Court Records from 1873)
Marion www.rootsweb.com/~txmarion/	E12	8 Feb 1860	**Cass, Harrison** Marion County; 102 W Austin St Rm 206; PO Box F; Jefferson, TX 75657-0420; Ph. (903) 665-3971 **Details:** (County Clerk has Birth & Death Records from 1903, Marriage, Probate & Land Records from 1860)
Martin www.rootsweb.com/~txmartin/	F5	21 Aug 1876	**Bexar Land District** Martin County; PO Box 906; Stanton, TX 79782; Ph. (915) 756-3412 **Details:** (County Clerk has Birth & Death Records from 1910, Marriage, Court, Divorce & Probate Records from 1885 & Land Records)
Mason www.rootsweb.com/~txmason/	H7	22 Jan 1858	**Gillespie, Bexar Land District** Mason County; 201 Ft. McKavitt St; PO Box 702; Mason, TX 76856; Ph. (325) 347-5253 **Details:** (County Clerk has Birth, Death & Burial Records from 1903, Marriage, Divorce, Probate & Court Records from 1877 & Land Records from 1858; All Records are in the same office in the Mason County Courthouse)
Matagorda www.rootsweb.com/~txmatago/	J10	17 Mar 1836	**Old Mexican Municipality** Matagorda County; 1700 7th St; Bay City, TX 77414; Ph. (979) 244-7680 **Details:** (County Clerk has Birth Records from 1903, Marriage Records from 1838, Death Records from 1917, Land Records from 1827, Probate Records from late 1800's, Military Records from 1919 & Court Records from 1981)
Maverick www.geocities.com/maverickcotx/	J6	2 Feb 1856	**Kinney** Maverick County; 500 Quarry St; PO Box 4050; Eagle Pass, TX 78853; Ph. (830) 773-2829 **Details:** (County Clerk has Birth & Death Records from 1903, Marriage Records from 1871, Probate, Court & Land Records)
McCulloch www.rootsweb.com/~txmccull/	G7	27 Aug 1856	**Bexar** McCulloch County; County Courthouse; Brady, TX 76825; Ph. (915) 597-0733 **Details:** (County Clerk has Birth & Death Records from 1903, Marriage Records from 1878, Land Records from 1860, Court Records from 1876 & Military Records from 1918)
McLennan www.co.mclennan.tx.us/	G9	22 Jan 1850	**Milam, Limestone, Navarro** McLennan County; PO Box 1727; Waco, TX 76703; Ph. (254) 757-5078 **Details:** (County Clerk has Birth & Death Records from 1929, Marriage, Probate, Court & Land Records from 1850; District Clerk has Divorce Records)
McMullen www.rootsweb.com/~txmcmull/	J8	1 Feb 1858	**Bexar, Live Oak, Atascosa** McMullen County; PO Box 235; Tilden, TX 78072; Ph. (512) 274-3215 **Details:** (County Clerk has Birth & Death Records from 1903, Marriage, Probate, Court & Land Records from 1850)

County Website	Map Index	Date Created	Parent County or Territory From Which Organized Address/Details
Medina www.summitsoftware.com/medina/	**I7**	**12 Feb 1848**	**Bexar Land District** Medina County; County Courthouse; 2516 McHaughten; Hondo, TX 78861; Ph. (830) 741-6041 **Details:** (County Clerk has Birth & Death Records from 1903, Marriage, Probate & Land Records from 1848 & Court Records from 1876)
Menard www.menardtexas.com/	**G7**	**22 Jan 1858**	**Bexar Land District** Menard County; PO Box 1028; Menard, TX 76859; Ph. (915) 396-4682 **Details:** (County Clerk has Birth & Court Records from 1900, Marriage Records from 1878, Death Records from 1917, Divorce Records from 1889, Probate & Land Records from 1880)
Midland www.co.midland.tx.us/	**F5**	**4 Mar 1885**	**Tom Green** Midland County; PO Box 211; Midland, TX 79702; Ph. (915) 688-1059 **Details:** (County Clerk has Birth & Death Records from 1917, Marriage & Land Records from 1885 & Probate Records from 1911; District Clerk has Divorce & Court Records)
Milam www.milamcounty.org/	**G9**	**17 Mar 1836**	**Old Mexican Municipality** Milam County; 107 W Main St.; Cameron, TX 76520; Ph. (254) 697-7049 **Details:** (Formerly Viesca County 1834–1836) (County Clerk has Birth & Death Records from 1903, Land, Marriage & Probate Records from 1874, Court Records from 1872, & School Census 1909–1970)
Mills www.rootsweb.com/~txmills/mills.html	**G8**	**15 Mar 1887**	**Comanche, Brown, Hamilton, Lampasas** Mills County; PO Box 646; Goldthwaite, TX 76844-0646; Ph. (915) 648-2711 **Details:** (County Clerk has Birth & Death Records from 1903, Marriage, Divorce, Probate, Court & Land Records from 1887)
Mitchell www.rootsweb.com/~txmitche/	**F6**	**21 Aug 1876**	**Bexar Land District** Mitchell County; 349 Oak St., Rm 103; Colorado City, TX 79512; Ph. (915) 728-3481 **Details:** (County Clerk has Birth & Death Records from 1903, Marriage, Probate, Court, & Land Records from 1881)
Montague www.co.montague.tx.us	**D9**	**24 Dec 1857**	**Cooke** Montague County; PO Box 77; 100 Rush; Montague, TX 76251; Ph. (940) 894-2461 **Details:** (County Clerk has Birth & Death Records from 1903, Marriage, Probate & Court Records from 1873 & Land Records)
Montgomery www.co.montgomery.tx.us/	**H10**	**14 Dec 1837**	**Washington** Montgomery County; 301 N Main; PO Box 959; Conroe, TX 77305-0959; Ph. (936) 539-7885 **Details:** (County Clerk has Birth, Death & Burial Records from 1903, Marriage, Probate & Land Records from 1838 & Court Records from 1929; District Clerk has Divorce Records from 1914)
Moore www.rootsweb.com/~txmoore/moore.htm	**B5**	**21 Aug 1876**	**Bexar Land District** Moore County; 715 Dumas Ave; Dumas, TX 79029-0396; Ph. (806) 935-6164 **Details:** (County Clerk has Birth, Death, Burial, Probate & Court Records from 1901, Marriage Records from 1894 & Land Records from 1877; District Clerk has Divorce Records)

County	Map	Date	Parent County or Territory From Which Organized
Website	Index	Created	Address/Details

Morris   E11   **6 Mar 1875**   **Titus**
www.rootsweb.com/~txmorris/morris.htm

Morris County; 500 Broadnax St; Daingerfield, TX 75638-1315;
Ph. (903) 645-3911
Details: (County Clerk has Birth & Death Records from 1903, Marriage & Probate Records from 1875, Land Records from 1849 & some delayed Birth Records; District Clerk has Divorce & Court Records)

Motley   D6   **21 Aug 1876**   **Bexar Land District**
www.rootsweb.com/~txmotley/

Motley County; PO Box 66; Matador, TX 79244; Ph. (806) 347-2621
Details: (County Clerk has Birth & Death Records from 1903, Marriage, Divorce, Probate & Court Records from 1891 & Land Records from 1891 with some earlier)

Nacogdoches   G11   **17 Mar 1836**   **Old Mexican Municipality**
www.rootsweb.com/~txnacogd/

Nacogdoches County; 101 W Main St; Nacogdoches, TX
75961-5119; Ph. (936) 560-7733
Details: (County Clerk has Birth & Death Records from 1903, Marriage Records from 1793, Land Records from 1833, Probate Records from 1837, Court Records from late 1800's & Military Records from 1918; District Clerk has Divorce Records)

Navarro   F10   **25 Apr 1846**   **Robertson**
www.navarrocounty.org

Navarro County; 300 W 3rd Ave; Corsicana, TX 75110;
Ph. (903) 654-3035
Details: (County Clerk has Birth, Burial, Cemetery, Death, Guardianship, Land, Marriage, Military & Probate Records; Tax Office has Tax Records; District Clerk has Divorce Records)

Navasota   **30 Jan 1841**   **Washington, Robertson**

Navasota County; TX
Details: (see Brazos) Name changed to Brazos in 28 Jan 1842

Newton   G12   **22 Apr 1846**   **Jasper**
www.jas.net/~newton/

Newton County; PO Box 484; Newton, TX 75966;
Ph. (409) 379-5341
Details: (County Clerk has Birth & Death Records from 1903, Marriage Records from 1846, Probate Records from 1870, Court & Land Records)

Nolan   F6   **21 Aug 1876**   **Bexar Land District**
www.rootsweb.com/~txnolan/

Nolan County; 100 E 3rd St; PO Box 98; Sweetwater, TX
79556-4511; Ph. (915) 235-2462
Details: (County Clerk has Birth, Death & Court Records from 1900, Marriage Records from 1881, Probate Records from 1884 & Land Records from 1889; District Clerk has Divorce Records; County Justice of the Peace has Burial Records)

Nueces   K9   **18 Apr 1846**   **San Patricio**
www.County.nueces.tx.us/

Nueces County; 901 Leopard St; Corpus Christi, TX 78401;
Ph. (361) 888-0580
Details: (County Clerk has Marriage, Probate, Court & Land Records)

County Website	Map Index	Date Created	Parent County or Territory From Which Organized Address/Details
Ochiltree www.rootsweb.com/~txochilt/	A6	21 Aug 1876	**Bexar Land District** Ochiltree County; 511 S Main St; Perryton, TX 79070-3154; Ph. (806) 435-8039 **Details:** (County Clerk has Birth Records from 1903, Death & Burial Records from 1904, Marriage Records from 1889, Probate Records from 1906, Land Records from 1890, Court Records from 1909 & Military Records from 1918; District Clerk has Divorce Records from 1891)
Oldham www.rootsweb.com/~txoldham/	B4	21 Aug 1876	**Bexar Land District** Oldham County; PO Box 469; Vega, TX 79092-0469; Ph. (806) 267-2667 **Details:** (County Clerk has Birth Records from 1917, Death Records from 1918, Marriage & Divorce Records from 1881, Burial & Probate Records from 1887, Court Records from 1911 & Land Records from 1878)
Orange www.County.orange.tx.us/	H12	5 Feb 1852	**Jefferson** Orange County; 801 W Division St; PO Box 1536; Orange, TX 77631; Ph. (409) 882-7055 **Details:** (County Clerk has Birth Records from 1878, Death Records from 1903, Marriage, Land & Probate Records from 1852, Military Records from 1898 & Court Records from 1896; District Clerk has Divorce Records)
Palo Pinto www.rootsweb.com/~txpalopi/	E8	27 Aug 1856	**Navarro, Bosque** Palo Pinto County; 520 Oak St.; PO Box 219; Palo Pinto, TX 76484; Ph. (940) 659-1277 **Details:** (County Clerk has Birth & Death Records from 1903, Court, Land, Marriage, Probate & Guardianship Records from 1857; District Clerk has Divorce Records from 1900)
Panola www.carthagetexas.com/county.htm	F12	30 Mar 1846	**Harrison, Shelby** Panola County; 110 S Sycamore St; Carthage, TX 75633; Ph. (903) 693-0302 **Details:** (County Clerk has Birth & Death Records from 1903, Marriage Records from 1846, Probate, Court & Land Records)
Parker www.rootsweb.com/~txparker/	E9	12 Dec 1855	**Bosque, Navarro** Parker County; 1112 Santa Fe; PO Box 819; Weatherford, TX 76086-0819; Ph. (817) 594-7461 **Details:** (County Clerk has Birth, Marriage & Death Records from 1903, Land Records from 1874, Probate, Military & Court Records; District Clerk has Divorce Records)
Parmer www.rootsweb.com/~txparmer/	C4	21 Aug 1876	**Bexar Land District** Parmer County; 401 3rd St; PO Box 356; Farwell, TX 79325; Ph. (806) 481-3691 **Details:** (County Clerk has Birth, Marriage, Death, Probate, Court & Land Records from 1908; District Clerk has Divorce Records from 1908)
Pecos www.co.pecos.tx.us/	H4	3 May 1871	**Presidio** Pecos County; 103 W Callaghan St; Fort Stockton, TX 79735-7101; Ph. (915) 336-7555 **Details:** (County Clerk has Birth, Marriage, Death, Probate & Land Records)

County Website	Map Index	Date Created	Parent County or Territory From Which Organized Address/Details
Polk www.co.polkcountyclerk.com	**H11**	**30 Mar 1846**	**Liberty** Polk County; 101 Church Ste 100; PO Drawer 2119; Livingston, TX 77351; Ph. (936) 327-6804 or (936) 327-6805 **Details:** (County Clerk has Birth, Burial, Cemetery, Death, Guardianship, Probate, Land, Marriage, & Military Discharge Records, State & Federal Tax Liens, Lispendens, Assumed Name Certificates, Commissioner Court Minutes, & Cattle Brands; Any Records that have been removed are stored at the Texas State Library & Archives Commission, PO Box 310, Liberty, TX 77575-0310, Ph. (936) 336-8821)
Potter www.co.potter.tx.us/countyclerk	**B5**	**21 Aug 1876**	**Bexar Land District** Potter County; 500 S Fillmore, Room 205; PO Box 9638; Amarillo, TX 79105; Ph. (806) 379-2275 **Details:** (County Clerk has Marriage Reccords from 1959, Military Records from 1949, Birth & Death Records from 1941 to May 1951, Delayed Birth Records for Potter County, Land Records from 1890, Probate Records from 1885)
Presidio www.rootsweb.com/~txpresid/	**I3**	**3 Jan 1850**	**Bexar Land District** Presidio County; PO Box 789; Marfa, TX 79843; Ph. (915) 729-4812 **Details:** (County & District Clerk has Birth & Death Records from 1903, Marriage & Land Records from 1875, Divorce & Court Records from 1886, Probate Records from 1884 & Military Records from 1944)
Rains www.rootsweb.com/~txrains/rains.htm	**E10**	**9 Jun 1870**	**Hopkins, Hunt, Wood** Rains County; PO Box 187; Emory, TX 75440-0187; Ph. (903) 473-2461 **Details:** (County Clerk has Birth Records from 1902, Death Records from 1903, Marriage, Divorce & Land Records from 1880 & Probate Records from 1894)
Randall www.randallcounty.org/	**C5**	**21 Aug 1876**	**Bexar Land District** Randall County; PO Box 660; Canyon, TX 79015-0660; Ph. (806) 468-5505 **Details:** (County Clerk has Marriage, Probate, Court & Land Records; District Clerk has Divorce Records)
Reagan www.cvcog.org/reagan/reagan.htm	**G5**	**7 Mar 1903**	**Tom Green** Reagan County; PO Box 100; Big Lake, TX 76932-0100; Ph. (915) 884-2442 **Details:** (County Clerk has Birth, Marriage, Death, Divorce, Probate, Court & Land Records from 1903, some Records from 1883 transferred from Tom Green County)
Real www.rootsweb.com/~txreal/	**I7**	**3 Apr 1913**	**Bandera, Kerr, Edwards** Real County; PO Box 656; Leakey, TX 78873-0656; Ph. (830) 232-6888 **Details:** (County Clerk has Birth, Marriage, Death, Divorce, Probate, Court & Land Records from 1913)
Red River www.rootsweb.com/~txredriv/	**D11**	**7 Mar 1836**	**Old Mexican Municipality** Red River County; 200 N Walnut St; Clarksville, TX 75426; Ph. (903) 427-2401 **Details:** (County Clerk has Birth & Death Records from 1903, Marriage Records from 1845, Probate & Land Records from 1835; District Clerk has Divorce & Court Records)

County Website	Map Index	Date Created	Parent County or Territory From Which Organized Address/Details
Reeves www.rootsweb.com/~txreeves/	**G3**	**14 Apr 1883**	**Pecos** Reeves County; PO Box 867; Pecos, TX 79772-0867; Ph. (915) 445-5467 **Details:** (County Clerk has Birth & Death Records from 1903, Marriage, Probate, Court & Land Records from 1885 & some deferred Birth Records from the 1800's)
Refugio http://bsd.pastracks.com/states/texas/refugio/	**J9**	**17 Mar 1836**	**Old Mexican Municipality** Refugio County; 808 Commerce St; Refugio, TX 78377-0704; Ph. (361) 526-2727 **Details:** (County Clerk has Birth & Death Records from 1903, Marriage Records from 1851, Probate Records from 1840, Court Records from 1881 & Land Records from 1835)
Roberts www.rootsweb.com/~txrobert/	**B6**	**21 Aug 1876**	**Bexar Land District** Roberts County; PO Box 477; Miami, TX 79059; Ph. (806) 868-2341 **Details:** (County Clerk has Birth & Death Records from 1903, Marriage, Divorce, Probate, Court & Land Records from 1889 & Burial Records from 1900)
Robertson www.rootsweb.com/~txrober2/	**G10**	**14 Dec 1837**	**Milam** Robertson County; PO Box 1029; Franklin, TX 77856; Ph. (979) 828-4130 **Details:** (County Clerk has Birth & Death Records from 1903, Marriage & Probate Records from 1837 & Land Records; District Clerk has Divorce & Court Records)
Rockwall www.rockwall.net/	**E10**	**1 Mar 1873**	**Kaufman** Rockwall County; 1101 Ridge Rd Ste 101; Rockwall, TX 75087; Ph. (972) 882-0240 **Details:** (County Clerk has Birth, Marriage & Death Records from 1875, Land from 1890, Probate Records from 1877 & Court Records)
Runnels www.rootsweb.com/~txrunnel/	**F7**	**1 Feb 1858**	**Bexar Land District, Travis** Runnels County; PO Box 189; Ballinger, TX 76821; Ph. (915) 365-2720 **Details:** (County Clerk has Birth, Death & Court Records from 1903, Marriage, Probate & Land Records from 1880, Military Discharge Records from 1918 & school Census Records 1925–1970; District Clerk has Divorce Records)
Rusk www.rootsweb.com/~txrusk/index.htm	**F11**	**16 Jan 1843**	**Nacogdoches** Rusk County; PO Box 758; Henderson, TX 75653; Ph. (903) 657-0330 **Details:** (Courthouse fire in 1878 destroyed some Records) (County Clerk has Birth & Death Records from 1903, Marriage, Land & Probate Records from 1843, Court Records from 1844 & Military Discharge Records from 1917; District Court has Divorce Records from 1844)
Sabine www.rootsweb.com/~txsabine/index.htm	**G12**	**17 Mar 1836**	**Old Mexican Municipality** Sabine County; PO Drawer 580; Hemphill, TX 75948; Ph. (409) 787-3786 **Details:** (County Clerk has Birth & Death Records from 1903, Marriage Records from 1880, Land Records from 1875 & Probate Records; District Clerk has Divorce & Court Records)

County Website	Map Index	Date Created	Parent County or Territory From Which Organized Address/Details
San Augustine www.rootsweb.com/~txsanaug/index_1.htm	G12	17 Mar 1836	**Old Mexican Municipality** San Augustine County; 106 Courthouse; San Augustine, TX 75972; Ph. (936) 275-2452 **Details:** (County Clerk has Birth Records from 1905, Death Records from 1903, Marriage Records from 1837, Probate Records from 1828 & Land Records from 1833; District Clerk has Divorce & Court Records from 1837)
San Jacinto www.County.san-jacinto.tx.us/	H11	13 Aug 1870	**Libraryerty, Polk, Montgomery, Walker** San Jacinto County; PO Box 669; Cold Spring, TX 77331; Ph. (936) 653-2324 **Details:** (County Clerk has Birth, Marriage & Death Records from 1888, Land & Probate Records from 1800's, Military Discharge Records from 1919 & Court Records from 1907; District Clerk has Divorce Records)
San Patricio http://bsd.pastracks.com/states/texas/sanpatricio/	K9	17 Mar 1836	**Old Mexican Municipality** San Patricio County; 400 W Sinton Rm 105; Sinton, TX 78387-0578; Ph. (361) 364-6290 **Details:** (County Clerk has Birth Records from 1893, Death Records from 1903, Marriage Records from 1858, Probate Records from 1847, Court Records from 1876 & Land Records from 1848)
San Saba www.rootsweb.com/~txssaba/	G8	1 Feb 1856	**Bexar Land District** San Saba County; County Courthouse; San Saba, TX 76877; Ph. (915) 372-3301 **Details:** (County Clerk has Birth & Death Records from 1903, Marriage, Divorce, Court & Land Records from 1856 & Probate Records from 1890)
Schleicher www.cvcog.org/schlcher/eldorado.htm	G6	1 Apr 1887	**Crockett** Schleicher County; PO Drawer 580; Eldorado, TX 76936; Ph. (915) 853-2833 **Details:** (County Clerk has Birth & Death Records from 1903, Marriage, Divorce, Probate & Court Records from 1901 & Land Records from 1889)
Scurry www.rootsweb.com/~txscurry/	E6	21 Aug 1876	**Bexar Land District** Scurry County; 1806 25th St Ste 300; Snyder, TX 79549; Ph. (915) 573-5332 **Details:** (County Clerk has Birth & Death Records from 1903, Marriage, Land & Probate Records from 1884, Court Records from 1909 & Military Records from 1918; District Clerk has Divorce Records)
Shackelford www.albanytexas.com/	E7	1 Feb 1858	**Bosque** Shackelford County; PO Box 247; Albany, TX 76430-0247; Ph. (915) 762-2232 **Details:** (County Clerk has Birth Records from 1903, Marriage & Land Records from 1874, Death & Probate Records from 1875, Court Records from 1899 & Divorce Records)
Shelby www.rootsweb.com/~txshelby/	F12	17 Mar 1836	**Old Mexican Municipality** Shelby County; 200 San Augustine St; PO Box 1987; Censuster, TX 75935-3945; Ph. (936) 598-6361 **Details:** (County Clerk has Birth, Marriage, Probate, Court & Land Records from 1882, Death & Burial Records from 1903; District Clerk has Divorce Records)

County Website	Map Index	Date Created	Parent County or Territory From Which Organized Address/Details
Sherman www.rootsweb.com/~txshelby/	A5	21 Aug 1876	**Bexar Land District** Sherman County; 701 N 3rd; PO Box 270; Stratford, TX 79084; Ph. (806) 396-2371 **Details:** (County Clerk has Birth, Death, Probate & Court Records from 1903, Marriage & Land Records from 1901, Burial Records from 1895, Divorce Records from 1914 & commission Court minutes from 1889)
Smith www.smith-county.com/	F11	11 Apr 1846	**Nacogdoches** Smith County; 100 N Broadway Ave; Tyler, TX 75702-1018; Ph. (903) 535-0630 **Details:** (County Clerk has Birth & Death Records from 1903, Marriage Records from 1848, Probate Records from 1847, Court & Land Records from 1846)
Somervell http://vip.hpnc.com/~clerk/	F8	13 Mar 1875	**Hood, Johnson** Somervell County; PO Box 1098; Glen Rose, TX 76043-1098; Ph. (254) 897-4427 **Details:** (County Clerk has Birth & Death Records from 1903, Marriage Records from 1885, Divorce & Court Records from 1889, Probate & Land Records from 1875)
Starr www.rootsweb.com/~txstarr/	M8	10 Feb 1848	**Nueces** Starr County; County Courthouse Rm 201; Rio Grande City, TX 78582; Ph. (956) 487-2101 **Details:** (County Clerk has Birth Records from 1880, Death Records from 1903, Marriage Records from 1858, Probate Records from 1853, Land Records from 1848, Court Records from 1932, Naturalization Records 1883–1898 & Military Discharge Records from 1919)
Stephens www.rootsweb.com/~txstephe/	E8	22 Jan 1858	**Bosque** Stephens County; County Courthouse; 200 W Walker; Breckenridge, TX 76424; Ph. (254) 559-3700 **Details:** (Formerly Buchanan County. Name changed to Stephens 17 Dec 1861) (County Clerk has Birth & Death Records from 1903, Marriage Records from 1876, Probate Records from 1886 & Land Records from 1858; District Clerk has Divorce & Court Records)
Sterling www.rootsweb.com/~txsterli/	F6	4 Mar 1891	**Tom Green** Sterling County; 615 4th; PO Box 55; Sterling City, TX 76951-0055; Ph. (915) 378-5191 **Details:** (County Clerk has Birth & Death Records from 1903, Marriage Records from 1913, Divorce, Probate, Court & Land Records from 1891)
Stonewall www.rootsweb.com/~txstonew/	E6	21 Aug 1876	**Bexar Land District** Stonewall County; PO Drawer P; Aspermont, TX 79502-0914; Ph. (940) 989-2272 **Details:** (County Clerk has Birth, Marriage, Death, Divorce, Probate, Court & Land Records from 1900's)
Sutton www.rootsweb.com/~txsutton/	H6	1 Apr 1887	**Crockett** Sutton County; 300 E Oak St Ste 3; Sonora, TX 76950; Ph. (915) 387-3815 **Details:** (County Clerk has Birth & Death Records from 1903, Marriage, Divorce, Probate, Court & Land Records from 1891)

County Website	Map Index	Date Created	Parent County or Territory From Which Organized Address/Details
Swisher www.rootsweb.com/~txswishe/Swisher.html	**C5**	**21 Aug 1876**	**Bexar Land District** Swisher County; County Courthouse; Tulia, TX 79088; Ph. (806) 995-3294 **Details:** (County Clerk has Birth Records from 1904, Marriage, Death & Burial Records from 1900, Divorce Records from 1905, Probate & Court Records from 1890 & Land Records from 1888)
Tarrant www.County.tarrant.tx.us/tarrantco/site/default.asp	**E9**	**20 Dec 1849**	**Navarro** Tarrant County; 100 W Weatherford Rm 130; Fort Worth, TX 76196; Ph. (817) 884-1195 **Details:** (County Clerk has Birth, Marriage, Land & Probate Records from 1876 & Death Records from 1903; District Clerk has Divorce & Court Records; 1860 Census missing)
Taylor www.rootsweb.com/~txtaylor/	**F7**	**1 Feb 1858**	**Bexar, Travis** Taylor County; 300 Oak St; Abilene, TX 79602; Ph. (915) 674-1202 **Details:** (County Clerk has Marriage, Probate & Land Records)
Terrell www.rootsweb.com/~txterrel/	**H5**	**8 Apr 1905**	**Pecos** Terrell County; PO Drawer 410; Sanderson, TX 79848-0410; Ph. (915) 345-2391 **Details:** (County Clerk has Marriage, Probate & Land Records)
Terry www.rootsweb.com/~txterry/index.htm	**E4**	**21 Aug 1876**	**Bexar Land District** Terry County; 500 W Main Rm 105; Brownfield, TX 79316; Ph. (806) 637-8551 **Details:** (attached to Martin County from 1889 to 1904) (County Clerk has Birth, Marriage, Death, Land, Probate, Military & Court Records from 1904)
Throckmorton www.rootsweb.com/~txthrock/throck.htm	**E7**	**13 Jan 1858**	**Fannin Land District, Bosque** Throckmorton County; PO Box 309; Throckmorton, TX 76483-0309; Ph. (940) 849-2501 **Details:** (County Clerk has Birth Records from 1903, Marriage, Death, Divorce & Probate Records from 1879, Court & Land Records; 1870 Census missing)
Titus www.rootsweb.com/~txtitus/	**E11**	**11 May 1846**	**Red River, Bowie** Titus County; 100 W 1st St Ste 204; Mt. Pleasant, TX 75455; Ph. (903) 577-6796 **Details:** (County Clerk has Birth, Marriage, Death, Land, Probate, Court & Military Records from 1895; District Clerk has Divorce Records from 1895)
Tom Green www.County.tom-green.tx.us/	**G6**	**13 Mar 1874**	**Bexar Land District** Tom Green County; 124 W Beauregard Ave; San Angelo, TX 76903-5850; Ph. (915) 659-6553 **Details:** (County Clerk has Birth & Death Records from 1903, Marriage, Probate & Court Records from 1875 & Land Records from 1860)
Travis www.County.travis.tx.us/	**H8**	**25 Jan 1840**	**Bastrop** Travis County; 100 Guadalupe St #222; PO Box 1748; Austin, TX 78767; Ph. (512) 473-9188 **Details:** (County Clerk has Birth & Death Records from 1903, Marriage, Probate, Court & Land Records from 1840)

County Website	Map Index	Date Created	Parent County or Territory From Which Organized Address/Details
Trinity http://people.txucom.net/dford/tcp.html	G11	11 Feb 1850	**Houston** Trinity County; PO Box 456; Groveton, TX 75845; Ph. (936) 642-1208 **Details:** (Courthouse burned 1876; some deeds refiled) (County Clerk has Birth Records from 1911, Death Records from 1919, Marriage & Land Records from 1876, Divorce Records from 1920, Probate & Court Records; County Judge has school Records)
Tyler www.rootsweb.com/~txtyler/index_1.htm	H12	3 Apr 1846	**Libraryerty** Tyler County; 100 W Bluff St; Woodville, TX 75979; Ph. (409) 283-2281 **Details:** (County Clerk has Birth Records from 1838, Marriage Records from 1849, Death & Burial Records from 1903, Probate Records from 1845 & Land Records from 1846; District Clerk has Divorce & Court Records)
Upshur www.upshurcounty.com/	E11	27 Apr 1846	**Harrison, Nacogdoches** Upshur County; 100 W Tyler St; PO Box 730; Gilmer, TX 75644-2198; Ph. (903) 843-4015 **Details:** (County Clerk has Birth & Death Records from 1903, Marriage Records from 1873, Land Records from 1845, Probate Records from 1853 & Military Records from 1919; District Clerk has Divorce Records)
Upton www.rootsweb.com/~txupton/	G5	26 Feb 1887	**Tom Green** Upton County; 205 E 10; PO Box 465; Rankin, TX 79778-0465; Ph. (915) 693-2861 **Details:** (County Clerk has Birth, Marriage, Divorce, Land, Probate & Military Records from 1910; District Clerk has Court Records)
Uvalde www.uvaldecounty.com/	I7	8 Feb 1850	**Bexar** Uvalde County; PO Box 284; Uvalde, TX 78802; Ph. (830) 278-6614 **Details:** (County Clerk has Birth, Marriage, Death, Probate, Court & Land Records from 1856; District Clerk has Divorce Records)
Val Verde www.rootsweb.com/~txvalver/	I5	20 Feb 1885	**Crockett, Kinney, Pecos** Val Verde County; PO Box 1267; Del Rio, TX 78841-1267; Ph. (830) 774-7564 **Details:** (County Clerk has Marriage, Land, Probate, Military & Court Records from 1885; District Clerk has Divorce Records)
Van Zandt www.rootsweb.com/~txvanzan/vzcpage.htm	F10	20 Mar 1848	**Henderson** Van Zandt County; 121 E Dallas St Rm 202; Canton, TX 75103; Ph. (903) 567-6503 **Details:** (County Clerk has Birth & Death Records from 1903, Marriage, Land, Probate & Court Records from 1848 & Military Discharge Records from 1918; District Clerk has Divorce Records from 1848)
Victoria www.viptx.net/vcgs/	K9	17 Mar 1836	**Old Mexican Municipality** Victoria County; 115 N Bridge; Victoria, TX 77901; Ph. (361) 575-1478 **Details:** (County Clerk has Birth & Death Records from 1903, Marriage, Probate & Land Records from 1838 & Court Records from 1867; District Clerk has Divorce Records)

County Website	Map Index	Date Created	Parent County or Territory From Which Organized Address/Details
Walker www.walker.tx.us.org	H11	**6 Apr 1846**	**Montgomery** Walker County; 1100 University Ave; PO Box 210; Huntsville, TX 77342-0210; Ph. (936) 436-4922 **Details:** (County Clerk has Birth & Death Records from 1903, Business Records from 1920; Court, Guardianship, Land, Marriage, & Probate Records from 1846; Immigration, Tax, & Naturalization Records from 1880)
Waller www.rootsweb.com/~txwaller/	H10	**28 Apr 1873**	**Austin, Grimes** Waller County; 836 Austin St #217; Hempstead, TX 77445-4667; Ph. (979) 826-7711 **Details:** (County Clerk has Birth & Death Records from 1903, Marriage, Probate, Court & Land Records from 1873)
Ward www.rootsweb.com/~txward/	G4	**26 Feb 1887**	**Tom Green** Ward County; 400 S Allen St; Monahans, TX 79756; Ph. (915) 943-3294 **Details:** (County Clerk has Birth, Marriage, Death, Probate, Court & Land Records from 1892 & Military Records; District Clerk has Divorce Records)
Washington www.startel.net/users/awhart/wgenweb/ washiton.htm	H10	**17 Mar 1836**	**Texas Municipality** Washington County; 100 E Main St; Brenham, TX 77834; Ph. (409) 277-6200 **Details:** (County Clerk has Birth & Death Records from 1903, Marriage Records from 1837, Probate & Land Records; District Clerk has Divorce Records)
Webb http://webbcounty.com/	K7	**28 Jan 1848**	**Bexar, Nueces** Webb County; 1110 Victoria St; PO Box 29; Laredo, TX 78042; Ph. (956) 721-2645 **Details:** (County Clerk has Birth & Death Records from 1856, Marriage Records from 1850, Probate Records from 1870 & Land Records)
Wharton www.rootsweb.com/~txwharto/	I10	**3 Apr 1846**	**Matagorda, Jackson, Colorado,** Wharton County; 100 E Milam St; PO Box 69; Wharton, TX 77488; Ph. (979) 532-2381 **Details:** (County Clerk has Birth & Death Records from 1903, Marriage Records from 1857, Land Records from 1846, Probate Records from 1849, Court Records from 1909 & Military Records from 1919)
Wheeler www.rootsweb.com/~txwheele/	B6	**21 Aug 1876**	**Bexar Land District** Wheeler County; PO Box 465; Wheeler, TX 79096-0465; Ph. (806) 826-5544 **Details:** (County Clerk has Birth & Death Records from 1906, Marriage, Probate, Court & Land Records from 1879; District Clerk has Divorce Records)
Wichita www.rootsweb.com/~txwichit/	D8	**1 Feb 1858**	**Fannin Land District** Wichita County; 900 7th St; PO Box 1679; Wichita Falls, TX 76307-1679; Ph. (940) 766-8144 **Details:** (County Clerk has incomplete Birth Records from 1890, incomplete Death Records from 1900, Marriage, Probate & Land Records from 1882; District Clerk has Divorce & Court Records)

County Website	Map Index	Date Created	Parent County or Territory From Which Organized Address/Details
Wilbarger www.County.wilbarger.tx.us/	**D7**	**1 Feb 1858**	**Bexar Land District** Wilbarger County; 1700 Wilbarger St; Vernon, TX 76384-4742; Ph. (940) 552-5486 **Details:** (County Clerk has Birth, Marriage, Death, Probate, Court & Land Records from 1900; District Clerk has Divorce Records; City Secretary has Burial Records)
Willacy www.pastracks.com/states/texas/willacy/	**L9**	**11 Mar 1911**	**Hidalgo, Cameron** Willacy County; Courthouse Annex Bldg; 190 N 3rd St; Raymondville, TX 78580; Ph. (956) 689-2710 **Details:** (County Clerk had Birth, Marriage, Death, Probate & Court Records from 1921 & Land Records from 1891)
Williamson www.wilco.org/	**H9**	**13 Mar 1848**	**Milam** Williamson County; PO Box 18; Georgetown, TX 78627; Ph. (512) 943-1515 **Details:** (County Clerk has Birth & Death Records from 1903, Marriage, Land, Probate & Court Records from 1848 & Military Discharge Records from 1917; District Clerk has Divorce Records)
Wilson	**I8**	**13 Feb 1860**	**Bexar, Karnes** Wilson County; 1420 3rd St, Rm 105; PO Box 27; Floresville, TX 78114; Ph. (830) 393-7308 **Details:** (Name changed in 1869 to Cibilo. Wilson name Restored in 1874) (County Clerk has Birth, Burial, Cemetery, Court, Death, Guardianship, Land, Marriage, Military Discharge, & Probate Records; City Clerk has Business & Commerce Records; County Library has Census Records; District Clerk has Divorce Records; County Assessor has Tax Records)
Winkler www.rootsweb.com/~txwinkle/	**F4**	**26 Feb 1887**	**Tom Green** Winkler County; PO Box 1007; Kermit, TX 79745-4236; Ph. (915) 586-3401 **Details:** (County Clerk has Birth Records from 1919, Death & Probate Records from 1912, Marriage & Court Records from 1911 & Land Records from 1887; District Clerk has Divorce Records)
Wise www.co.wise.tx.us	**E9**	**23 Jan 1856**	**Cooke** Wise County; 200 N Trinity St; PO Box 359; Decatur, TX 76234; Ph. (940) 627-3351, sherry.parker-lemon@co.wise.tx.us **Details:** (County Clerk has Birth & Death Records from 1903, Marriage Records from 1881, Probate Records from 1882, Land Records from 1852 & Court Records)
Wood www.rootsweb.com/~txwood/index.htm	**E11**	**5 Feb 1850**	**Van Zandt** Wood County; 1 Main St.; PO Box 1796; Quitman, TX 75783; Ph. (903) 763-2711 **Details:** (County Clerk has Birth Records 1903–1995, Death Records 1903–1999, Land Records 1878–1909, Marriage Records 1879–2002, Military Discharge Records 1918–1949, & Probate Records 1878–1932; District Clerk has Court Records 1860–1936 & Divorce Records 1897–1935; County Courthouse & all Records burned in 1878)

County Website	Map Index	Date Created	Parent County or Territory From Which Organized Address/Details
Yoakum www.pastracks.com/states/texas/yoakum/	E4	**21 Aug 1876**	**Bexar Land District** Yoakum County; PO Box 309; Plains, TX 79355; Ph. (806) 456-2721 **Details:** (Attached to Martin County from 1904 to 1907) (County Clerk has Birth Records from 1878, Marriage & Death Records from 1908, Probate Records from 1907, Court Records from 1930 & Land Records from 1898; District Clerk has Divorce Records)
Young www.rootsweb.com/~txyoung/young.htm	E8	**2 Feb 1856**	**Bosque, Fannin** Young County; 516 4th St Rm 104; Graham, TX 76450; Ph. (940) 549-8432 **Details:** (County Clerk has Birth & Death Records from 1903, Marriage, Probate, Court & Land Records from 1856; District Clerk has Divorce Records)
Zapata www.vsta.com/~rlblack/zapata.html	L7	**22 Jan 1858**	**Starr, Webb** Zapata County; PO Box 789; Zapata, TX 78076; Ph. (956) 765-9915 **Details:** (County Clerk has Birth Records 1870's-1930's, Marriage & Land Records from 1800's, Probate & Court Records from 1900's; District Clerk has Divorce Records; Justice of the Peace Office has Birth Records from 1930's & Death Records)
Zavala www.Historicaloricdistrict.com/Genealogy/zavala/zavala.htm	J7	**1 Feb 1858**	**Uvalde, Maverick** Zavala County; County Courthouse; Crystal City, TX 78839; Ph. (830) 374-2331 **Details:** (County Clerk has Birth, Marriage, Death, Probate & Court Records from 1884, Land & Military Records; District Clerk has Divorce Records)

Notes

Utah

Capital: Salt Lake City
Territory: 1850
State: 1896 (45th)

Industry

Early Utah was home to two distinct cultures—the Freemonts and the Anasazi, also known as the Basket Weavers or Pueblos. These two cultures died out around 1300, but left behind evidence of their lifestyles, including rock art, buildings, and artifacts. The first documented explorers in Utah were Father Silvestre Escalante and Father Francisco Dominguez in 1776. Between 1811 and 1840, fur trappers entered Utah and prepared the way for future settlers. The first permanent settlers were members of the Church of Jesus Christ of Latter-day Saints, also known as Mormons. They entered the Salt Lake Valley on 24 July 1847, led by their church president Brigham Young. They had been forced out of their homes in Nauvoo, Illinois and crossed the plains to the desert. New groups arrived several times each month, so that by 1850, there were 11,380 residents. Most of the early settlers came from New England, Ohio, Illinois, Missouri, and Canada. Most of the Europeans were English, Germans, Danes, Swedes, Norwegians, Swiss, Hollanders, Welsh, and Scottish. Despite warnings from Jim Bridger that corn could never grow in Utah, the Mormons were able to irrigate the land and develop a healthy agriculture.

With the end of the Mexican War, Utah became a part of the United States. The Mormons created the State of Deseret in 1849 and petitioned Congress for admission to the Union. Deseret included parts of present-day California, Oregon, Idaho, Wyoming, Nevada, Arizona, New Mexico, and Utah. Congress denied the petition, but did create the Territory of Utah in 1850, which included parts of Nevada, Wyoming, Colorado, and Utah. With the creation of the territories of Nevada and Colorado in 1861, and Wyoming in 1868, Utah reached it present size.

In the decade following their arrival in Utah, the Mormon settlers founded some 100 towns in Utah, Nevada, Idaho, California, and Wyoming. Between 1856 and 1860, another 8,000 immigrants came to Utah in handcart companies. The Utah War of 1857–1858, which occurred when United States troops were sent to suppress a rebellion that never existed, was peaceably settled. Federal troops, however, remained in Utah after the war until 1861. Another wave of Mormon settlement occurred between 1858 and 1868, which established communities in southern Utah, southern Idaho, southeastern Nevada and northern Arizona. The first transcontinental railroad was completed at Promontory Point in Utah in 1869.

A series of acts passed by Congress were aimed at the Mormons and their practice of polygamy. Additionally, these acts abolished women's suffrage and certain civil rights so that prosecution of polygamists would be easier. As a result of these laws, many Mormons fled the area to Sonora and Chihuahua, Mexico and to Alberta, Canada. Mormon Church President Wilford Woodruff made a proclamation known as the Manifesto in 1890, which discontinued the practice of polygamy. With this roadblock to statehood removed, Utah became a state in 1896.

Look for vital records in the following locations:

- **Birth and death records:** Bureau of Vital Records, Utah State Department of Health. Registration began in 1905. Most counties began keeping ledger entries of births and deaths in 1898. Salt Lake City, Ogden, and Logan also have some birth and death records.
- **Marriage records:** Most marriage records since 1887 are at the county clerk's office or the Utah State Archives.
- **Census records:** An 1856 territorial census is at the Historical Department of the LDS Church. The Family History Library of The Church of Jesus Christ of Latter-day Saints has one of the largest collections of genealogical resources, records, books, microfilm, and microfiche in the world. These resources are also available through Family History Centers (branches) located throughout the world.

Office of Vital Records and Statistics
288 North 1460 West
PO Box 141012

Salt Lake City, Utah 84114-1012
(801) 538-6105
http://health.utah.gov/vitalrecords/silver/deathinfo.htm

Utah State Archives and Records Service

346 S Rio Grande
Salt Lake City, UT 84101-1106
(801) 531-3848; Fax (801) 531-3854
http://archives.utah.gov/

Utah State Historical Society (Division of State History)

300 South Rio Grande St.
Salt Lake City, UT 84101-1182
(801) 533-3500; Fax (801) 533-3504
http://history.utah.gov

Family History Library of The Church of Jesus Christ of Latter-day Saints

35 North West Temple
Salt Lake City, Utah 84150-3400
(801) 240-2584 or (800) 346-6044; Fax (801) 240-3718
www.FamilySearch.org

LDS Church Historical Department

50 East North Temple
Salt Lake City, Utah 84150
Archives Search Room (801) 240-2272
Library: (801) 240-2745
www.lds.org/churchhistory/archives
www.lds.org/churchhistory/library

Societies and Repositories

Bridgerland Chapter, Utah Genealogical Association; (208) 847-0519; bridgerland@infouga.org.

Cuban Genealogical Society; PO Box 2650; Salt Lake City, UT 84110-2650; Mayra@Utah-Inter.Net; www.rootsweb.com/~utcubangs.

Daughters of the American Revolution, Utah Society; 6855 So. Willow Way; Salt Lake City, UT 84121.

Genealogical Society of Utah; 35 North West Temple; Salt Lake City, UT 84150.

German Chapter, UGA; PO Box 1144; Salt Lake City, UT 84110; (801) 963-8401; info@infouga.org; www.infouga.org/german.html.

Icelandic Association of Utah; 84 N. 1120 E.; Spanish Fork, UT 84660.

Institute of Genealogy and History for Latin America; 2191 S. 2200 E.; Mt. Springs, UT 84757; lplatt@infowest.com; www.genealogy.com/00000140.html?Welcome=1010690722.

International Society Daughters of Utah Pioneers; 300 N. Main St.; Salt Lake City, UT 84103; (801) 538-1050; info@dupinternational.org; www.dupinternational.org.

Jewish Genealogical Society of Salt Lake City; 3510 Fleetwood Dr.; Salt Lake City, UT 94109.

Ogden Region Chapter, UGA; 5584 S. 4225 W.; Roy, UT 84067; (801) 985-9237; ugaogdenchapter@yahoo.com; www.infouga.org/ogden.html.

Salt Lake Chapter, UGA; PO Box 1144; Salt Lake City, UT 84110; (801) 359-2499; dcyphergen@aol.com; www.infouga.org/saltlake.html.

Snake River Chapter, UGA; PO Box 1144; Salt Lake City, UT 84110; info@infouga.org; www.rootsweb.com/~idsrfhc.

South Salt Lake Valley Chapter, UGA; PO Box 1144; Salt Lake City, UT 84110; southslchapter@infouga.org.

Tooele/Magna Chapter, UGA; PO Box 1144; Salt Lake City, UT 84110; info@infouga.org; www.infouga.org/tooelemagna.html.

Utah Chapter, AHSGR; 259 E. 500 North; Lehi, UT 84043-1638; (801) 731-3054.

Utah Genealogical Association; PO Box 1144; Salt Lake City, UT 84110; president@infouga.org; www.infouga.org.

Utah State Archives and Records Service; State Capitol, Archives Building; PO Box 141021; Salt Lake City, UT 84114-1021; (801) 538-3012; archivesresearch@utah.gov; www.archives.state.ut.us.

Utah State Historical Society; 300 South Rio Grande; Salt Lake City, UT 84101-1143; ushs@history.state.ut.us; www.dced.state.ut.us/history.

Utah State Library; 250 N. 1950 W., Suite A; Salt Lake City, UT 84116-7901; (801) 715-6777; http://library.utah.gov.

Utah Valley Chapter, UGA; PO Box 1144; Salt Lake City, UT 84110; (801) 225-3266; utahvalley@infouga.org; www.infouga.org/utahvalley.html.

Bibliography and Record Sources

General

A Guide to the Oral History Collection, Utah State Historical Society. Salt Lake City: Utah State Historical Society Library, 1980.

Allen, James B., and Glen M. Leonard. *The Story of the Latter-day Saints*. Salt Lake City: Deseret Book Co., 1976.

Alter, J. Cecil. *Early Utah Journalism*. Salt Lake City: Utah State Historical Society, 1938.

Alter, J. Cecil. *Utah, The Storied Domain, A Documentary History of Utah's Eventful Career.* 3 vol. Chicago & New York: American Historical Society, Inc, 1932.

Bennett, Archibald F. Bennett, comp. *Family Genealogical Records Alphabetically Arranged. Research Notes by Benjamin F. Cummings Jr. on the Ancestry of Some*

Early Utah Families: Abt. 1898–1900. Salt Lake City: Filmed by the Genealogical Society of Utah, 1954. Microfilm, multiple rolls.

Bitton, Davis. *Guide to Mormon Diaries and Autobiographies.* Provo, Utah: Brigham Young University Press, 1977.

Carter, Kate B., comp. *Daughters of the Utah Pioneer Lessons.* 31 vols. Salt Lake City: Daughters of the Utah Pioneers, 1937–1968.

Carter, Kate B., comp. *Heart Throbs of the West.* 12 vols. Salt Lake City: Daughters of the Utah Pioneers, 1939–.

Carter, Kate B., comp. *Our Pioneer Heritage.* 20 vols. Salt Lake City: Daughters of the Utah Pioneers, 1958–1977.

Carter, Kate B., comp. *Treasures of Pioneer History.* 6 vols. Salt Lake City: Daughters of the Utah Pioneers, 1952–1957.

Church Almanac. Salt Lake City: Deseret News, 1974–. Annual 1974–1987, biannual 1989–.

Directory of Special Information Resources in Utah, 1982. Rev. Salt Lake City: Utah Library Association, 1987.

Episcopal Church. Diocese of Utah. *Episcopal Register of the Bishop of Utah (Bishop's Personal Register) 1899–1946, 1951–1967.* Salt Lake City: Filmed by the Genealogical Society of Utah, 1975. Microfilm, multiple rolls.

Esshom, Frank. *Pioneers and Prominent Men of Utah.* 1913. Reprint. Salt Lake City: Western Epics Inc, 1966.

Genealogical Society of Utah. *Genealogical Surveys of LDS Members: Autobiographies and Ancestors.* Salt Lake City: The Society, 1924–1929. Microfilm, multiple rolls.

Historical Records Survey (Utah). *Inventory of the Church Archives of Utah.* 3 vols. Salt Lake City: Utah Historical Records Survey, 1940.

Holley, Robert P., ed. *Utah's Newspapers—Traces of Her Past.* Salt Lake City: University of Utah, 1984.

Jaussi, Laureen and Gloria Chaston. *Genealogical Records of Utah.* Salt Lake City: Deseret Book Co., 1974.

Jenson, Andrew. *Encyclopedic History of the Church.* Salt Lake City: Deseret News Publishing Company, 1941.

Jenson, Andrew. *Latter-day Saint Biographical Encyclopedia.* Salt Lake City: A. Jenson History Co., 1901–1936.

May, Dean L. *Utah: A People's History.* Salt Lake City: University of Utah Press, 1987.

Mooney, Bernice. *Salt of the Earth.* Salt Lake City: Catholic Diocese of Salt Lake City, 1987.

Name Index to the Library of Congress Collection of Mormon Diaries. Logan, Utah: Utah State University, 1971.

Portrait, Genealogical and Biographical Record of the State of Utah. Chicago: National Historical Board, 1902.

Reorganized Church of Jesus Christ of Latter Day Saints. Utah District. *Church Records, 1868–1940.* Salt Lake City: Filmed by the Genealogical Society of Utah, 1994. Microfilm, 2 rolls.

Smith, Joseph. *History of the Church of Jesus Christ of Latter-day Saints.* 7 vols. 1902. Reprint. Salt Lake City: Deseret Book Co., 1970.

Sutton, Wain, ed. *Utah: A Centennial History.* 3 vols. New York: Lewis Historical Publishing Co., 1949.

Thatcher, Linda. *Guide to Newspapers Located in the Utah State Historical Society Library.* Salt Lake City: Utah State Historical Society, 1985.

Utah Pioneer Biographies. 44 vols. N.p., 1935–1964.

Utah State Historical Society. *Guide to Archives and Manuscript Collections in Selected Utah Repositories.* Salt Lake City: Utah State Historical Society, 1990. CD-ROM.

Utah State Historical Society. *A Guide to Unpublished Materials at the Utah State Historical Society.* Salt Lake City: Utah State Historical Society Library, 1989;

Utah State Archives and Record Services. *Guide to Official Records of Genealogical Value in the State of Utah.* Salt Lake City: Utah State Archives and Record Services, 1980.

Utah State Archives and Record Services. *Municipal Records Manual, 1983.* Utah State Archives and Record Services, 1983.

Utah Research Outline. Series U.S.-States, no. 44. Salt Lake City: Family History Library, 1988.

Wasatch Presbyterian Church (Salt Lake City, Utah). *Wasatch Presbyterian Church Records, 1885–1955.* Salt Lake City: Filmed by the Genealogical Society of Utah, 2000. Microfilm.

Wiggins, Marvin E. *Mormons and Their Neighbors: An Index of Over 75,000 Biographical Sketches from 1820 to the Present.* 2 vols. Provo, Utah: Brigham Young University, 1984.

Atlases, Maps and Gazetteers

Gallagher, John S. *The Post Offices of Utah.* Burtonsville, Maryland: The Depot, 1977.

Gannett, Henry A. *A Gazetteer of Utah.* Washington, D.C.: U.S. Government Printing Office, 1900.

Greer, Deon C., et al. *Atlas of Utah.* Ogden, Utah Weber State College, 1981.

Gruber, Ted. *Postal History of Utah, 1849–1976.* Crete, New Brunswick: J-B Publishing Co., 1978.

Leigh, Rufus Wood. *Five Hundred Utah Place Names.* Salt Lake City: Deseret News Press, 1961.

Miller, David E. *Utah History Atlas.* 2nd ed. n.p.: Miller, 1968.

Moffat, Riley Moore. *Printed Maps of Utah to 1900: An Annotated Cartobibliography.* Western Association of Map Librarians, 1981.

Sloan, Robert W. *Utah Gazetteer and Directory of Logan, Ogden, Provo and Salt Lake City for 1884.* Salt Lake City: Herald Printing and Publishing Co., 1884.

Utah: A Guide to the State. New York: Hastings House, 1941.

Utah Writer's Project. *Origins of Utah Place Names*. Salt Lake City: State Department of Instruction, 1940.

VanCott, John E., comp. *Utah Place Names: A Comprehensive Guide to the Origins of Geographic Names*. Salt Lake City: University of Utah Press, 1990.

Ward, Jill Anderson. *LDS Place Names Gazetteer*. Salt Lake City: Family History Library, 1986.

Censuses

Available Census Records and Census Substitutes

History Library of the Church of Jesus Christ of Latter-day Saints, 35 North West Temple, Salt Lake City, Utah 84150,

Federal Census 1850, 1860, 1870, 1880, 1900, 1910, 1920, 1930

Federal Mortality Schedules 1870

Union Veterans and Widows 1890

State/Territorial Census 1851, 1856

Church of Jesus Christ of Latter-day Saints, The. *Church Census Records, 1914–1960*. Salt Lake City: Filmed by the Genealogical Society of Utah, 1962. Microfilm, multiple rolls.

Dollarhide, William. *The Census Book: A Genealogist's Guide to Federal Census Facts, Schedules and Indexes*. Bountiful, Utah: Heritage Quest, 1999.

Lainhart, Ann S. *State Census Records*. Baltimore: Genealogical Publishing Co., Inc., 1992.

Kemp, Thomas Jay. *The American Census Handbook*. Wilmington, Delaware: Scholarly Resources, Inc., 2001.

Szucs, Loretto Dennis and Matthew Wright. *Finding Answers in U.S. Census Records*. Ancestry Publishing, 2001.

Thorndale, William and William Dollarhide. *Map Guide to the U.S. Federal Census, 1790–1920*. Baltimore: Genealogical Publishing Co., 1987.

United States. Bureau of Indian Affairs. *Indian Census Rolls, Fort Hall, 1885–1939*. Washington, D.C.: The National Archives, 1965.

Court Records, Probate and Wills

District Court (Utah County). *Appearance Docket Records 1859–1872*. Salt Lake City: Filmed by the Genealogical Society of Utah, 1959.

Interior Department Territorial Papers, Utah, 1850–1902. Washington, D.C.: National Archives. Central Plains Region, 1963. Microfilm, 6 rolls.

Utah. District Court (Salt Lake County). *Probate Records; Estates and Guardianship, 1852–1910, and Index to Books A–F*. Salt Lake City: Filmed by the Genealogical Society of Utah, 1966. Microfilm, multiple rolls.

United States. Supreme Court. *A Record of the Decisions of the United States Supreme Court for the Territory of*

Utah: Book A, 1861–1893. Salt Lake City: Utah State Records and Archives Service, 1975.

Immigration

Bashore, Melvin Lee. *Mormon Pioneer Companies Crossing the Plains (1847–1868) Narratives: Guide to Sources in Utah Libraries and Archives*. 3rd rev. ed. Salt Lake City: The Church of Jesus Christ of Latter-day Saints. Historical Dept., 1990.

Bashore, Melvin L., and Linda L. Haslam. *Mormons on the High Seas: Ocean Voyage Narratives to America (1840–1890)*. Salt Lake City: Historical Department of The Church of Jesus Christ of Latter-day Saints, 1990.

Emigration Records, Scandinavian Mission (Denmark, Norway, Sweden) 1852– 1920. Salt Lake City: Filmed by the Genealogical Society of Utah, 1951–1953. Microfilm, multiple rolls.

European Emigration Card Index, 1849–1925. Salt Lake City: Filmed by the Genealogical Society of Utah, 1951. Microfilm, multiple rolls.

Hafen, LeRoy R., and Ann W. Hafen. *Handcarts to Zion: The Story of a Unique Western Migration, 1856–1860, with Contemporary Journals, Accounts, Reports, and Rosters of Members of the Ten Handcart Companies*. Glendale, California: Arthur H. Clark, 1960.

Naturalization Records, 1853–1936. Salt Lake City: Utah State Archives and Records Service, 1980–1981, 1989– 1990. Microfilm, multiple copies.

Naturalization Index, ca 1860–1989. Utah District Court (Utah County). Salt Lake City: Genealogical Society of Utah. 1989. Microfilm, multiple copies.

Perpetual Emigrating Fund Company. *Names of Persons and Sureties Indebted to the Perpetual Emigrating Fund Company from 1850 to 1877 Inclusive*. Salt Lake City: Filmed by the Genealogical Society of Utah, 1950. Microfilm.

Sonne, Conway B. *Saints on the Seas: A Maritime History of Mormon Migration, 1830–1890*. Salt Lake City: University of Utah Press, 1983.

Sonne, Conway B. *Ships, Saints, and Mariners: A Maritime Encyclopedia of Mormon Migration, 1830–1890*. Salt Lake City: University of Utah Press, 1987.

Taylor, Margery. *Worldwide LDS Ship Register 1840–1913*. Salt Lake City: Family History Library, 1991.

United States. Supreme Court (Utah Territory). *Declarations of Intentions to Become Citizens, vol. B–C, 1872–1893*. Salt Lake City: Utah State Archives and Records Service, 1982.

Utah Immigration Card Index, 1847–1868. Salt Lake City: Filmed by the Genealogical Society of Utah, 1963. Microfilm, multiple rolls.

Land

Barker, Joel. *Preliminary Inventory of Land Management—Utah.* Denver: Denver Archives and Records Center, 1979.

Fox, Feramorz Young. *The Mormon Land System, A Study of the Settlement and Utilization of Land Under the Direction of the Mormon Church.* Logan: Utah State Agricultural College, 1955.

Linford, Lawrence L. "Establishing and Maintaining Land Ownership in Utah Prior to 1869." Salt Lake City: *Utah Historical Society Quarterly,* vol. 42 (1974): 126–143.

Nelson, Lowry. *The Mormon Village: A Pattern and Technique of Land Settlement.* Salt Lake City: University of Utah Press, 1952.

Military

Correspondence Records Concerning Indian War Pensions, 1914–1928.

Fisher, Margaret May Merrill. *Utah and the Civil War.* Salt Lake City: Deseret Book Co., 1929.

Hance, Watson and Irene Warr. *Johnston, Connor and the Mormons: An Outline of Military History in Northern Utah.* Salt Lake City: n.p., 1962.

Larson, Carl V. *A Database of the Mormon Battalion.* Providence, Utah: K. W. Watkins, 1987.

Mabey, Charles R. *The Utah Batteries: A History. [Spanish American War 1898].* Salt Lake City: n.p., 1900.

Mexican Border Service, Muster Rolls, 1916–1917. Salt Lake City: Genealogical Society of Utah, 1966. Microfilm.

Prentiss, A., ed. *The History of the Utah Volunteers in the Spanish-American War and in the Philippine Islands.* Salt Lake City: W. F. Ford, 1900.

United States. Bureau of Pensions. *Selected Pension Application Files for Members of the Mormon [sic] Battalion, Mexican War, 1846–1848.* Washington, D.C.: National Archives and Records Service, 1934.

United States. Record and Pension Office. *Compiled Service Records of Volunteer Soldiers Who Served During the Mexican War in Mormon Organizations.* Washington, D.C.: National Archives, 1961.

United States. Selective Service System. *Utah World War I Selective Service System Draft Registration Cards, 1917–1918.* Washington, D.C.: National Archives, 1987–1988.

Utah State Archives. *Card Index to Military Records of the Indian Wars, 1866–1867; A–Z.* Salt Lake City: Filmed by the Genealogical Society of Utah, 1966. Microfilm, multiple rolls.

Utah State Archives. *Spanish-American War; Index to Utah Units.* Salt Lake City: Filmed by the Genealogical Society of Utah, 1966. Microfilm.

Utah. Board of Commissioners of Indian War Records. *Service Records of Indian Wars in Utah, 1853–1868.*

Salt Lake City: Filmed by the Genealogical Society of Utah, 1966. Microfilm, multiple rolls.

Utah. Secretary of State. *Applications for Indian War Medals, 1905–1912.* Salt Lake City: Filmed by the Utah State Archives, 1980. Microfilm, multiple rolls.

Warrum, Noble. *Utah in the World War.* Salt Lake City: Utah State Council of Defense, 1924.

Vital and Cemetery

Cemetery Listing (Utah). Salt Lake City: Utah State Archives and Records Service, 1986.

Cemetery Records of Utah. 13 vols. Salt Lake City: Genealogical Society of Utah, 1953.

Church of Jesus Christ of Latter-day Saints, The. Church Historian's Office. *Obituary Index File to the Salt Lake Tribune and Deseret News as of 31 December 1970.* Salt Lake City: Church Historian's Office, 1971. Microfilm, 64 rolls.

Ellison, Marion. *An Inventory and Index to the Records of Carson County, Utah and Nevada Territories, 1855–1861.* Reno, Nevada: Grace Dangberg Foundation, 1984.

Guide to Public Vital Statistics of Utah. Salt Lake City: Utah Historical Records Survey, 1941.

Hansen, Judith Woolstenhulme. *Marriages in Utah Territory, 1850–1884: From the Deseret News, 1850–1872, and the Elias Smith Journals, 1850–1884.* Salt Lake City: Utah Genealogical Association, 1998.

Historical Records Survey (Utah). *Guide to Public Vital Statistics of Utah.* Salt Lake City: Historical Records Survey, 1941.

McClay, Irvin C. *Cemeteries in Utah.* Salt Lake City: Utah State Archives and Records Service, 1980

Miscellaneous Marriage Records Index: Compiled From Civil Records. Microfilm. 19 reels. Salt Lake City: Genealogical Society of Utah, 1972.

Salt Lake City (Utah). Office of Vital Statistics. *Birth Records, 1890–1950, 1953.* Salt Lake City: Filmed by the Genealogical Society of Utah, 1950. Microfilm, multiple rolls.

Salt Lake City (Utah). Office of Vital Statistics. *Death Records of Salt Lake City, Utah, 1848 to Sept. 1950.* Salt Lake City: Filmed by the Genealogical Society of Utah, 1950. Microfilm, multiple rolls.

Salt Lake County (Utah). County Clerk. *Alphabetic Marriage Listing, 1887–1987.* Salt Lake City: Management Information Systems, 1987. Microfilm, multiple rolls.

Territorial Vital Records: Births, Divorces, Guardianship, Marriages, Naturalization, Wills; 1800s thru 1906 Utah Territory, Arizona, Colorado, Idaho, Nevada, Wyoming, Indian Terr.; LDS Branches, Wards; Deseret News Vital Recs.; J.P. Marriages; Meth. Marriages. St. George, Utah Genealogical CD Publishing, 1994. CD-ROM.

Utah

United States. Bureau of Indian Affairs. Uintah and Ouray Agency. *Vital Records of the Ute Indians to 1946.* Salt Lake City: Filmed by the Genealogical Society of Utah, 1953. Microfilm.

Utah Death Index: 1891–1905 (Excluding Salt Lake County). Edited by Judith W. Hansen. Monograph Series, no. 2. Salt Lake City: Professional Chapter, Utah Genealogical Association, 1995.

Utah State Historical Society. *Burials Database.* Salt Lake City: Utah State Historical Society, 2001. online database—www.dced.state.ut.us/history/Services/lcburials.html

Utah. Department of Health. Bureau of Vital Records. *Utah Death Certificates, 1904–1943.* Salt Lake City: Filmed by the Genealogical Society of Utah, 2001. Microfilm, 127 rolls.

County Website	Map Index	Date Created	Parent County or Territory From Which Organized Address/Details
Beaver www.lofthouse.com/USA/Utah/beaver/index.html	M2	1856	**Iron, Millard** Beaver County; 105 E Center; PO Box 392; Beaver, UT 84713-0392; Ph. (435) 438-6463 **Details:** (County Clerk has Birth Records 1897–1905, Marriage Records from 1887, Death Records 1900–1905, Divorce Records from 1871, Probate Records from 1872 & Court Records from 1856; Beaver City Office has Burial Records)
Box Elder www.lofthouse.com/boxelder/	C2	5 Jan 1856	**Unorg. Terr., Weber, Green River** Box Elder County; 1 S Main St; Brigham City, UT 84302; Ph. (435) 734-3388 **Details:** (County Clerk has Birth & Death Records 1898–1905, Marriage Records from 1887, Divorce, Probate, Court & Land Records from 1856)
Cache www.cachecounty.org	C6	5 Jan 1856	**Unorg. Terr., Green River** Cache County; 179 N Main St; Logan, UT 84321; Ph. (435) 716-7150 **Details:** (County Clerk has Marriage Records from 1888; Clerk District Court has Divorce, Probate & Court Records; County Recorder has Land Records; Bear River Health Department has Birth & Death Records)
Carbon www.co.carbon.ut.us/	I9	8 Mar 1894	**Emery** Carbon County; 120 E Main St; Price, UT 84501-3057; Ph. (435) 636-3224 **Details:** (County Clerk has Marriage Records; Clerk District Court has Divorce, Probate & Court Records; County Recorder has Land Records)
Carson		17 Jan 1854	**Tooele, Juab, Millard, Iron** Carson County; UT **Details:** (Transferred to Nevada Terr., 1861)
Cedar		1856	**Utah County** Cedar County; UT **Details:** (Absorbed by Utah County, 1862)
Daggett www.rootsweb.com/~utdagget/index.html	F11	4 Mar 1917	**Uintah** Daggett County; 95 N 1st St W; PO Box 219; Manila, UT 84046-0218; Ph. (435) 784-3154 **Details:** (County Clerk has Marriage, Burial, Divorce, Probate, Court & Land Records from 1918)

County Website	Map Index	Date Created	Parent County or Territory From Which Organized Address/Details
Davis www.co.davis.ut.us/	E5	1850	**Original county** Davis County; PO Box 618; Farmington, UT 84025-0618; Ph. (801) 451-3420 **Details:** (County Clerk has Marriage Records; Clerk District Court has Divorce, Probate & Court Records)
Desert		1852	**Unorg. Terr.** Desert County; UT **Details:** (Absorbed by Tooele County, 1862)
Duchesne www.duchesnegov.net/	G9	7 Mar 1913	**Uintah** Duchesne County; PO Box 910; Duchesne, UT 84021-0910; Ph. (435) 738-1100 **Details:** (County Clerk has Marriage Records from 1915; County Recorder has Land Records from 1915; Clerk at 8th District Court has Divorce, Probate, & Court Records from 1915)
Emery www.co.emery.ut.us/	K8	12 Feb 1880	**Sanpete, Sevier** Emery County; 95 E Main St; Castle Dale, UT 84513; Ph. (435) 381-5106 **Details:** (County Clerk has Marriage Records from 1888; State Court has Divorce, Probate & Court Records; County Recorder has Land Records)
Garfield www.rootsweb.com/~utgarfie/ Garfield_index.html	N7	1 Mar 1882	**Iron, Kane, Washington** Garfield County; 55 S Main St; PO Box 77; Panguitch, UT 84759-0077; Ph. (435) 676-8826 **Details:** (Created in 1864 but not organized until 9 Mar 1882) (County Clerk has Marriage Records from 1890, Divorce, Probate & Court Records from 1896; County Recorder has Land Records from 1882 & Death Records 1896–1905)
Grand www.lofthouse.com/USA/Utah/grand/index.html	J11	13 Mar 1890	**Emery, Uintah** Grand County; 125 E Center St; Moab, UT 84532-2449; Ph. (435) 259-1321 **Details:** (County Clerk has Marriage & Probate Records from 1890, Divorce & Court Records from 1896 & Land Records)
Greasewood		1856	**Box Elder** Greasewood County; UT **Details:** (Absorbed by Box Elder County, 1862)
Great Salt Lake		3 Mar 1852	**Original county** Great Salt Lake County; UT **Details:** (see Salt Lake) Name changed to Salt Lake 29 Jan 1868
Green River		1852	**Original county** Green River County; UT **Details:** (Transferred to Wyoming Terr., 1868)
Humboldt		1856	Humboldt County; UT **Details:** (Transferred to Nevada Terr., 1861)

County Website	Map Index	Date Created	Parent County or Territory From Which Organized Address/Details
Iron www.co.iron.ut.us/	N2	31 Jan 1850	**Original county** Iron County; 68 S 100 E; PO Box 429; Parowan, UT 84761; Ph. (435) 477-8341 **Details:** (Formerly Little Salt Lake County. Name changed to Iron 3 Dec 1850) (County Clerk has Marriage Records from 1887; County Recorder has Land Records from 1852; Clerk District Court has Divorce, Probate & Court Records)
Juab www.co.juab.ut.us/	I4	3 Mar 1852	**Original county** Juab County; 160 N Main St; Nephi, UT 84648-1412; Ph. (435) 623-3410 **Details:** (County Clerk has Birth, Marriage, Death, Divorce, Probate, Court & Land Records from 1898)
Kane www.kaneutah.com/	P6	16 Jan 1864	**Washington** Kane County; 76 N Main St; Kanab, UT 84741; Ph. (435) 644-2458 **Details:** (County Clerk has Marriage, Divorce, Probate & Court Records; County Recorder has Land Records)
Little Salt Lake		31 Jan 1850	**Original county** Little Salt Lake County; UT **Details:** (see Iron) Name changed to Iron 3 Dec 1850
Malad		1856	Malad County; UT **Details:** (Absorbed by Box Elder County, 1862)
Millard www.millardcounty.com/	K3	4 Oct 1851	**Iron** Millard County; 765 S Hwy 99; Fillmore, UT 84631; Ph. (435) 743-6223 **Details:** (County Clerk has Marriage Records from 1887, Divorce, Probate & Court Records from 1852; County Recorder has Land & Military Records)
Morgan www.rootsweb.com/~utmorgan/	E6	17 Jan 1862	**Summit, Weber, Cache** Morgan County; 48 W Young St; Morgan, UT 84050; Ph. (801) 845-4011 **Details:** (County Clerk has Marriage Records from 1888, Divorce & Court Records from 1896 & Probate Records from 1869; County Recorder has Land Records)
Piute www.piute-county.org/	M5	16 Jan 1865	**Beaver** Piute County; 550 N Main St; PO Box 99; Junction, UT 84740; Ph. (435) 577-2840 **Details:** (County Clerk has Birth & Death Records from 1898, Marriage Records from 1887, Divorce, Probate & Court Records from 1872)
Rich http://richcountyut.homestead.com/genweb.html	C7	16 Jan 1864	**Original county** Rich County; 20 N Main St; PO Box 218; Randolph, UT 84064-0218; Ph. (435) 793-2415 **Details:** (Formerly Richland County. Name changed to Rich 29 Jan 1868) (County Clerk has Marriage Records from 1888, Divorce, Probate & Court Records from 1872; County Recorder has Land Records)
Richland		16 Jan 1864	**Original county** Richland County; UT **Details:** (see Rich) Name changed to Rich 29 Jan 1868

County Website	Map Index	Date Created	Parent County or Territory From Which Organized Address/Details
Rio Virgin		1869	**Washington** Rio Virgin County; UT **Details:** (Absorbed by Washington County, 1872)
Salt Lake www.co.slc.ut.us/	F6	1849	**Original county** Salt Lake County; 2001 State St Rm S2200; Salt Lake City, UT 84190; Ph. (801) 468-3519 **Details:** (Formerly Great Salt Lake County. Name changed to Salt Lake 29 Jan 1868) (County Clerk has Marriage Records from 1887, Divorce & Court Records from 1896 & Probate Records from 1852; County Recorder has Land Records)
San Juan http://utahreach.usu.edu/sanjuan/index.htm	N11	17 Feb 1880	**Kane, Iron, Piute** San Juan County; 117 S Main St; PO Box 338; Monticello, UT 84535; Ph. (435) 587-3223 **Details:** (County Clerk has Marriage & Probate Records from 1888, Divorce & Court Records from 1891)
Sanpete http://utahreach.usu.edu/sanpete/index.htm	J6	3 Mar 1852	**Original county** Sanpete County; 160 N Main St; Manti, UT 84642; Ph. (435) 835-2131 **Details:** (County Clerk has Birth Records 1897–1905, Death Records 1898–1905, Marriage Records from 1888, Divorce, Probate & Court Records from 1878 & Land Records from 1870)
Sevier http://utahreach.usu.edu/sevier/index.htm	L6	16 Jan 1865	**Sanpete** Sevier County; 250 N Main; PO Box 517; Richfield, UT 84701; Ph. (435) 893-0401 **Details:** (County Clerk has Birth & Death Records 1898–1905, Marriage Records, Naturalization Records 1850–1898; State Court has Divorce, Probate & Court Records; County Recorder has Land Records, Military Discharge Records from 1942)
Shambip		1857	**Tooele, Juab** Shambip County; UT **Details:** (Absorbed by Tooele County, 1862)
St. Marys		1856	St. Marys County; UT **Details:** (Transferred to Nevada Terr., 1866)
Summit www.co.summit.ut.us/	F8	13 Jan 1854	**Salt Lake, Green River** Summit County; PO Box 128; Coalville, UT 84017; Ph. (435) 336-3203 **Details:** (County Clerk has Birth Records 1898–1905, Death Records 1898–1901, Marriage Records from 1888, Divorce, Probate & Court Records from 1896; County Recorder has Land Records)
Tooele www.co.tooele.ut.us/	F3	1849	**Original county** Tooele County; 47 S Main St; Tooele, UT 84074; Ph. (435) 843-3140 **Details:** (County Clerk has Birth & Death Records 1897–1905 & Marriage Records from 1887; Clerk District Court has Divorce, Probate & Court Records; County Recorder has Land Records)
Uintah http://utahreach.usu.edu/uintah/index.htm	H11	18 Feb 1880	**Wasatch** Uintah County; 147 E Main St; Vernal, UT 84078; Ph. (435) 781-5360 **Details:** (County Clerk has Marriage, Divorce, Probate & Court Records; County Recorder has Land Records)

County Website	Map Index	Date Created	Parent County or Territory From Which Organized Address/Details
Utah www.co.utah.ut.us/	H6	1849	**Original county** Utah County; 100 E Center Rm 3600; Provo, UT 84606; Ph. (801) 851-8109 **Details:** (4th District Court has Divorce, Probate, & Court Records; Clerk/Auditor's Office has Marriage Records from 1888)
Wasatch www.co.wasatch.ut.us/	G7	17 Jan 1862	**Davis, Green River** Wasatch County; 25 N Main St; Heber City, UT 84032; Ph. (435) 654-3211 **Details:** (County Clerk has Birth & Death Records 1898–1905, Marriage Records from 1879, Divorce & Court Records from 1898, Probate Records from 1897 & Land Records from 1862)
Washington www.washco.state.ut.us/	P2	3 Mar 1852	**Unorg. Terr.** Washington County; 197 E Tabernacle St; St. George, UT 84770; Ph. (435) 634-5712 **Details:** (County Clerk has Marriage Records from 1887, Divorce Records from 1878, Probate & Court Records from 1874; County Recorder has Land Records)
Wayne www.rootsweb.com/~utwayne/ Wayne_index.html	M8	10 Mar 1892	**Piute** Wayne County; 18 S Main; PO Box 189; Loa, UT 84747; Ph. (435) 836-2731 **Details:** (County Clerk has some Birth & Death Records 1898–1927 & Marriage, Divorce, Court & Probate Records from 1898; County Recorder has Land Records from 1898)
Weber www.co.weber.ut.us/	D6	1849	**Original county** Weber County; 2380 Washington Blvd #320; Ogden, UT 84401; Ph. (801) 399-8400 **Details:** (County Clerk has Marriage Records from 1887; Clerk District Court has Divorce, Probate & Court Records; County Recorder has Land Records)

Vermont

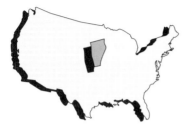

Capital: Montpelier
State: 1791 (14th)

Freedom and unity

Before the first Europeans settled in Vermont, the Iroquois Confederacy and the Algonquian-speaking tribes battled for control of Vermont. By the 1600s, the Iroquois had pushed several groups out of the area, but the struggle continued. The first French explorer, Samuel de Champlain, arrived in 1609 and sided with the Algonquian tribes, returning them to power. As Europeans began to explore the area and establish forts, the struggle shifted and countries vied for control of the land. Over the next century, French, Dutch and British posts were established though there were few permanent settlers. The quarrel between the French and British eventually included Indian tribes that sided with each country and culminated in the French and Indian War. In 1763, the French lost a key battle and the British took control of the region.

With the defeat of the French, settlement began in earnest. New Hampshire granted land for 129 towns in Vermont between 1749 and 1764. New York's claim to the area was validated by King George III, resulting in a nullification of all grants made by New Hampshire. Although some grantees obtained new grants from New York, the others banded together under Ethan Allen to form the Green Mountain Boys. They resisted New York's efforts to evict those who did not receive New York grants. The Revolutionary War prevented major conflicts between the Green Mountain Boys and New York. However, Ethan Allen and his men did fight for the colonies, capturing forts Ticonderoga and Crown Point from the British.

In 1776, Vermont held a convention and declared its independence from New York. The next year a constitution was approved making Vermont an independent republic. Vermont remained a republic until statehood was granted in 1791. The settlers in Vermont carried on substantial trade with Canada, most of it avoiding British revenue officers. The War of 1812 severely restricted this smuggling, so Vermont was very antiwar. When the war ended, many Vermonters left the state to farm better lands in Ohio and a few New Englanders came to replace them.

The Champlain Canal opened in 1823, connecting Vermont with New York City. In 1825, the Erie Canal opened, carrying Vermont settlers to Ohio and other western areas. Irish laborers came to work on Vermont railroads, the first of which opened in 1848. During the Civil War, Vermont supplied more than 34,000 men to the Union armies.

Most of the early settlers came from the New England colonies. Other large groups of immigrants came from Ireland in the mid-1800s and French Canada later in the century. Farmers from Finland came into the Markham Mountain region in southwestern Windsor County and the Equinox Mountain section of northern Bennington County. Welsh came to the midwest section of Rutland County to work in the slate quarries. Scottish and Italian stonecutters came to the quarries southeast of Montpelier. Russians, Poles, Czechs, Austrians, and Swedes came to the granite quarries of Rutland County. About half of the foreign-born population in Vermont came from Canada.

- **Birth, death, marriage and divorce records:** Town clerks have kept these records since 1760. Many of these records have been indexed for the entire state. The Vital Records Section, Department of Health will search these indexes for a fee. This office also has divorce records from 1861 to 1968. For birth, marriage, and death records since 1955 and divorce records since 1968, contact the Division of Vital Statistics.
- **Census records:** The Vermont Historical Society Library has the largest genealogical collection in the state. Portions of some colonial censuses are available and have been published.
- **Land records:** Many colonial land records are at the Vermont State Archives, Division of State Papers. Later land transactions are kept by the town clerks.
- **Naturalization records:** Filed primarily in county and district courts.

Vermont Department of Health Vital Records Section
PO Box 70
108 Cherry Street
Burlington, VT 05402-0070
(802) 863-7200 or (800) 464-4343; Fax (802) 865-7754
www.healthyvermonters.info/hs/vital/vitalhome.shtml

Vermont State Archives
Office of Secretary of State
109 State Street
Montpelier, Vermont 05602
(802) 828-2308
http://vermont-archives.org/

Public Records General Services Department
(802) 828-3288
www.state.vt.us/gsd/pubrec.htm

Vermont Historical Society
Vermont History Center
60 Washington Street
Barre, Vermont 05641-4209
(802) 479-8500; Fax (802) 479-8510
www.vermonthistory.org/

Societies and Repositories

Addison Town Historical Society; 288 Cedar Drive; Addison, VT 05491-8732.

Alburgh Historical Society, Inc.; PO Box 453; Alburg, VT 05440; tepper@together.net.

Barnet Historical Society; RR 1, Box 241; Barnet, VT 05821.

Bennington Historical Society; 7 Main Street; Bennington, VT 05201; bennmuse@sover.net; www.benningtonmuseum.com/BHS.html.

Berlin Historical Society Inc.; 1921 Scott Hill Road; Berlin, VT 05602.

Bethel Historical Society; 223 N. Main St.; Bethel, VT 05032.

Bradford Historical Society; PO Box 301; Bradford, VT 05033; L_C_Coffin@kingcon.com.

Braintree Historical Society; RFD 1, Thayer Brook Road; Randolph, VT 05060; www.braintreehistoricalsoc.org.

Brattleboro Historical Society, Inc.; 23 West Street; Brattleboro, VT 05301; histsoc@together.net.

Bridport Historical Society; c/o Marjorie Huestis; 2947 Basin Harbor Road; Bridport, VT 05734.

Bristol Historical Society Museum; Howden Hall Community Center; 19 W. Street; Bristol, VT 05443.

Cabot Historical Society; PO Box 63; Marshfield, VT 05658.

Canaan Historical Society; PO Box 371; Canaan, VT 05903.

Cavendish Historical Society; PO Box 110; Cavendish, VT 05142.

Charlotte Historical Society; 613 Hill's Point Road; Charlotte, VT 05445.

Chelsea Historical Society; PO Box 206; Chelsea, VT 05038.

Chester Historical Society; Main Street; Chester, VT 05143.

Concord Historical Society; PO Box 195; Concord, VT 05824-0195.

Crystal Lake Falls Historical Association; PO Box 253; Barton, VT 05822.

Derby Historical Society; PO Box 357; Derby, VT 05829; gardyne@together.net.

Dorset Historical Society; PO Box 52; Dorset, VT 05251; jhardman@dorsethistory.com; www.dorsethistory.org.

Dover Historical Society; PO Box 53; East Dover, VT 05341-7705.

Elmore Historical Society; PO Box 53; Lake Elmore, VT 05657.

Enosburg Historical Society; PO Box 98; Enosburg Falls, VT 05450.

Fairfax Historical Society; PO Box 145; Fairfax, VT 05454; (802) 849-6638; mcain@together.net; www.geocities.com/Heartland/Farm/9445/index.html.

Fairfield Historical Society; 1345 Northrup Road; Enosburg Falls, VT 05450.

Fairlee Historical Society; PO Box 95; Fairlee, VT 05045.

Franklin Historical Society; 1787 Riley Road; Franklin, VT 05457.

Genealogical Society of Vermont; PO Box 1553; St. Albans, VT 05478-1006; jtyler@bennington.edu; www.rootsweb.com/~vtgsv.

Georgia Historical Society Museum; PO Box 2072; Georgia, VT 05468.

Glover Historical Society; Municipal Building; PO Box 208; Glover, VT 05839; (802) 525-8855.

Grafton Historical Society; PO Box 202; Grafton, VT 05146.

Greensboro Historical Society; Highland Lodge; PO Box 151; Greensboro, VT 05841.

Groton Historical Society; PO Box 89; Groton, VT 05046; (802) 584-3417.

Guilford Historical Society; 236 School Road; Guilford, VT 05301.

Halifax Historical Society; RR 4, Box 531; Brattleboro, VT 05301.

Hartford Historical Society; PO Box 547; Hartford, VT 05047.

Historical Society of Peru; PO Box 153; Peru, VT 05152.

Historical Society of Windham County; PO Box 246; Newfane, VT 05345.

Holland Historical Society; RD 1, Box 37, Derby Line; Holland, VT 05830.

Huntington Historical Society; PO Box 147; Huntington, VT 05462.

Hyde Park Historical Society; 97 Eden Street; Hyde Park, VT 05655.

Island Pond Historical Society; PO Box 408; Island Pond, VT 05846.

Isle La Motte Historical Society; Isle La Motte, VT 05463.

Jamaica Historical Foundation; PO Box 287; Jamaica, VT 05343; jdickson@sover.net.

Jericho Historical Society; PO Box 35; Jericho, VT 05465; info@snowflakebentley.com; http://snowflakebentley.com/jhs.htm.

Lincoln Historical Society; c/o Town Clerk; Lincoln, VT 05443.

Londonderry Historical Society; PO Box 114; So. Londonderry, VT 05155.

Lowell Historical Society; 636 Irish Hill Road; Lowell, VT 05847.

Lunenburg Historical Society; PO Box 5; Lunenburg, VT 05906; lunenburgvt@yahoo.com.

Lyndon Historical Society; PO Box 85; Lyndon Center, VT 05850; (802) 626-8746; www.sover.net/~boerad/historic.htm.

Manchester Historical Society; PO Box 363; Manchester, VT 05254.

Marlboro Historical Society; PO Box 131; Marlboro, VT 05344.

Memphremagog Historical Society; Goodrich Memorial Library; 70 Main Street; Newport, VT 05855; smckenny@sunet.net.

Middlesex Historical Society; 84 McCullough Hill Road; Middlesex, VT 05602.

Milton Historical Society; PO Box 2; Milton, VT 05468.

Missisquoi Valley Historical Society; PO Box 237; East Main Street; North Troy, VT 05859.

Montgomery Historical Society; PO Box 47; Montgomery, VT 05470.

Moretown Historical Society; Moretown, VT 05660; (802) 496-2090; www.moretownvt.com/history3.html.

New Haven Historical Society; 70 East Street; New Haven, VT 05472.

Northfield Historical Society; PO Box 88; Northfield, VT 05663.

Norwich Historical Society; PO Box 1680; Norwich, VT 05055.

Orleans County Historical Society; Old Stone House Museum; 28 Old Stone House Road; Brownington, VT 05860; (802) 754-2022; osh@together.net; www.oldstonehousemuseum.org.

Peacham Historical Association; 104 Thaddeus Stevens Road; Peacham, VT 05862; www.peacham.net/historical.

Pittsford Historical Society; PO Box 423; Pittsford, VT 05763; www.pittsford-historical.org.

Poultney Historical Society; 2625 Vermont Route 140; Poultney, VT 05764-9281.

Pownal Historical Society, Inc.; PO Box 313; Pownal, VT 05261; www.pownal.org.

Randolph Historical Society; PO Box 15; Randolph Center, VT 05061; lwleonardsthall@aol.com.

Reading Historical Society; PO Box 252; Reading, VT 05062.

Readsboro Historical Society; PO Box 158; Readsboro, VT 05350.

Richford Historical Society; 186 So. Main St.; Richford, VT 05476.

Rochester Historical Society; PO Box 7; Rochester, VT 05767; edavis@sover.net.

Royalton Historical Society; 4184 Route 14; Royalton, VT 05068; jdumville@dca.state.vt.us.

Rupert Historical Society; Box 2, Lewis Rd.; Rupert, VT 05768; R.K.Kittay@sover.net.

Rutland Historical Society; 96 Center Street; Rutland, VT 05701.

Salisbury Historical Society; 7 Forbes Circle; Middlebury, VT 05753.

Saxtons River Historical Society; PO Box 18; Saxtons River, VT 05154; luring@sover.net.

Shaftsbury Historical Society; PO Box 401; Shaftsbury, VT 05262.

Shoreham Historical Society; Route 22-A; Shoreham, VT 05770; vtbasket@shoreham.net; http://steveworld.ksci.com/ShorehamHS/SHShome.htm.

Shrewsbury Historical Society; 996 Lincoln Hill Road; Cuttingsville, VT 05738.

Springfield Art & Historical Society; PO Box 313; Springfield, VT 05156.

St. Albans Historical Society; PO Box 722; St. Albans, VT 05478.

St. Johnsbury Historical Society; c/o Fairbanks Museum, 1302 Main St.; St. Johnsbury, VT 05819.

Stannard Historical Society; 9 Willey Road; Greensboro Bend, VT 05842.

Swanton Historical Society; 11 Lake St.; Swanton, VT 05488; rkilburn@together.net.

Thetford Historical Society; PO Box 33; Thetford, VT 05074.

Tinmouth Historical & Genealogical Society; 43 Chipmunk Crossing Dr.; Tinmouth, VT 05773-1179.

Townshend Historical Society; PO Box 202; Townshend, VT 05353; ths@dugrenier.com; www.townshendvt.com.

Tunbridge Historical Society; 24 The Crossroad; Tunbridge, VT 05077.

Vermont French-Canadian Genealogical Society; PO Box 65128; Burlington, VT 05406-5128; http://members.aol.com/vtfcgs/genealogy.

Vermont Historical Society; Pavilion Office Bldg.; 109 State St.; Montpelier, VT 05609-0901; vhs@vhs.state.vt.us; www.state.vt.us/vhs.

Vermont State Archives; Redstone Building; 26 Terrace Street, Drawer 09; Montpelier, VT 05609-1101; (802) 828-2363; gsanford@sec.state.vt.us; http://vermont-archives.org.

Vernon Historians; PO Box 282; Vernon, VT 05354.

Waitsfield Historical Society; PO Box 816; Waitsfield, VT 05673.

Wallingford Historical Society; PO Box 327; Wallingford, VT 05773.

Waterbury Historical Society; 28 North Main Street; Waterbury, VT 05676.

Weathersfield Historical Society; PO Box 126; Weathersfield, VT 05151.

Wells Historical Society; 8 Capron Lane; Wells, VT 05774.

Welsh-American Genealogical Society; 60 Norton Ave.; Poultney, VT 05764-1011; wagsjan@sover.net; www.rootsweb.com/~vtwags.

West Haven Historical Society, Inc.; 834 Main St; West Haven, VT 05743; kellis@rrmc.org.

West Windsor Historical Society; PO Box 12; Brownsville, VT 05037; (802) 484-7249.

Westford Historical Society; PO Box 21; Westford, VT 05494; www.geocities.com/westford_05494.

Westminster Historical Society, Inc.; PO Box 2; Westminster, VT 05158-0002; www.microserve.net/~rduffalo/wrhistsoc.html.

Whitingham Historical Society; PO Box 125; Jacksonville, VT 05342.

Williamstown Historical Society; PO Box 338; Williamstown, VT 05679-0338.

Williston Historical Society; PO Box 995; Williston, VT 05495.

Winooski Historical Society; 21 Park Street; Winooski, VT 05404; (802) 655-3561.

Woodstock Historical Society; 26 Elm Street; Woodstock, VT 05091; whs@sover.net; www.uvm.edu/~histpres/ vtiana/woodstockhs.html.

Bibliography and Record Sources

General

A Guide to Newspaper Indexes in New England. Holden, Massachusetts: New England Library Association, 1978.

A Guide to Vermont's Repositories. Montpelier, Vermont: Vermont State Archives, 1986.

Basic Sources for Vermont Historical Research. Montpelier, Vermont: Office of the Secretary of State, 1981.

Bassett, T. D. Seymour, ed. *Vermont: A Bibliography of Its History.* Boston: G. K. Hall & Co.; 1981.

Brigham, Loriman S. *A Calendar of Manuscripts in Certain Boxes at the Vermont Historical Society.* Montpelier, Vermont: S.n., 1970.

Brigham, Loriman S. *Guide to the "Miscellaneous File" of Uncatalogued Material in the Vermont Historical Society . . .* Montpelier, Vermont: S.n., 1969.

Carleton, Hiram. *Genealogical and Family History of the State of Vermont.* 2 vols. New York: Lewis Publishing Co., 1903.

Comstock, John Moore. *The Congregational Churches of Vermont and Their Ministry.* St. Johnsbury, Vermont: Caledonian Co., 1915.

Crandall, Ralph J., ed. *Genealogical Research in New England.* Baltimore: Genealogical Publishing Co., 1984.

Crocker, Henry. *History of the Baptists in Vermont.* Bellows Falls, Vermont: P. H. Gobie Press, 1913.

Cutter, William Richard. *New England Families, Genealogical and Memorial.* 4 vols. 1913. Reprinted and enlarged. New York: Lewis Historical Publishing Co., 1914.

Directory of Churches and Religious Organizations in the State of Vermont. Montpelier, Vermont: Historical Records Survey, 1939.

Dodge, Prentiss Cutler. *Encyclopedia, Vermont Biography.* Burlington, Vermont: Ullery Publishing Co., 1912.

Eichholz, Alice. *Collecting Vermont Ancestors.* Montpelier, Vermont: New Trails, 1986.

Final Report and Inventory of the Vermont Historical Records Survey, W.P.A. Rutland, Vermont: Works Progress Administration, 1942.

Genealogist's Handbook for New England Research. 3rd. ed. Boston: New England Historic Genealogical Society, 1993.

Greenlaw, William Prescott. *The Greenlaw Index of the New England Historic Genealogical Society.* 2 vols. Boston: G. K. Hall, 1979.

Hall, Hiland. *The History of Vermont, from its Discovery to its Administration into the Union in 1791.* Albany, New York: J. Munsell, 1868.

Hall, Lu Verne V. *New England Family Histories and Genealogies: States of New Hampshire and Vermont.* Bowie, Maryland: Heritage Books, 2000.

Hemenway, Abby Maria, ed. *Vermont Historical Gazetteer: A Magazine Embracing a History of Each Town, Civil, Ecclesiastical, Biographical and Military.* 6 vols. Burlington, Vermont: A. M. Hemenway, 1868–1891.

Historical Records Survey (Vermont). *A Directory of Churches and Religious Organizations in the State of Vermont.* Montpelier, Vermont: The Survey, 1939.

Historical Records Survey (Vermont). *Inventory of the Church Archives of Vermont, no. 1, Diocese of Vermont, Protestant Episcopal.* Montpelier, Vermont: The Survey, 1940.

Holbrook, Jay Mack. *Vermont's First Settlers*. Oxford, Massachusetts: Holbrook Research Institute, 1976. Alphabetically arranged land grants in Vermont, 1763 to 1803

Index to the Burlington Free Press. 6 vols. Montpelier, Vermont: Historical Records Survey, 1941.

Ireland, Norma Olin and Winifred Irving. *Cutter Index: A Consolidated Index of Cutter's Nine Genealogy Series*. Fallbrook, California: Ireland Indexing Service, 197–.

Kent, Dorman B. E. *Vermonters*. Montpelier, Vermont: Vermont Historical Society, 1937.

New England Historic Genealogical Society. *English Origins of New England Families: From the New England Historical and Genealogical Register*. First Series, 3 vols. Boston, Massachusetts: The Society, 1984.

Rider, Fremont, ed. *American Genealogical-Biographical Index*. Vols. 1–186. Middletown, Connecticut: The Godfrey Memorial Library, 1952–.

Rising, Marsh Hoffman. *Vermont Newspaper Abstract: Vermont Gazette, The Vermont Gazette: Epitome of the World, The World, The Green-Mountain Farmer*. Boston: The New England Historic Genealogical Society, 2001.

Savage, James. *A Genealogical Dictionary of the First Settlers of New England: Showing Three Generations of Those Who Came Before May 1692*. 4 vols. 1860–1862. Reprint. Baltimore: Genealogical Publishing Company, 1981.

The American Genealogical Index. Middletown, Connecticut: Published by a committee representing the cooperating subscribing libraries [at] Wesleyan University Station, 1942–1951.

Thompson, Zadock. *History of Vermont*. Burlington, Vermont: Thompson, 1853.

Ullery, Jacob G. *Men of Vermont:* Brattleboro, Vermont: Transcript Publishing Co., 1894.

Vermont Research Outline. Series U.S.-States, no. 45. Salt Lake City: Family History Library, 1988.

Atlases, Maps and Gazetteers

Graffagnino, J. Kevin. *The Shaping of Vermont: 1749–1877*. Rutland, Vermont: Vermont Heritage Press, 1983.

Hancock, William. *The Vermont Atlas and Gazetteer*. Yarmouth, Maine: D. Delorme, 1978.

Hayward, John. *A Gazetteer of Vermont: Containing Descriptions of All the Counties, Towns, and Districts in the State, and of Its Principal Mountains, Rivers, Waterfalls, Harbors, Islands, and Curious Places*. Bowie, Maryland: Heritage Books, 1990.

Long, John H., ed. *Atlas of Historical County Boundaries: New Hampshire and Vermont*. New York: Simon & Schuster, 1993.

Slawson, George C., Arthur W. Bingham, and Sprague W. Drenan. *The Postal History of Vermont*. Collectors Club Handbook, no. 21. New York: Collectors Club, 1969.

Swift, Ester Munroe. *Vermont Place-Names: Footprints of History*. Brattleboro, Vermont: Stephen Greene Press, 1977.

Vermont Atlas and Gazetteer. 9th ed. Freeport, Maine: DeLorme Mapping Co., 1996.

Censuses

Available Census Records and Census Substitutes

Federal Census 1790, 1800, 1810, 1820, 1830, 1840, 1850, 1860, 1870, 1880, 1900, 1910, 1920, 1930

Federal Mortality Schedules 1880

Union Veterans and Widows 1890

Dollarhide, William. *The Census Book: A Genealogist's Guide to Federal Census Facts, Schedules and Indexes*. Bountiful, Utah: Heritage Quest, 1999.

Holbrook, Jay Mack. *Vermont 1771 Census*. Oxford, Massachusetts: Holbrook Research Institute, 1982.

Kemp, Thomas Jay. *The American Census Handbook*. Wilmington, Delaware: Scholarly Resources, Inc., 2001.

Lainhart, Ann S. *State Census Records*. Baltimore: Genealogical Publishing Co., Inc., 1992.

Szucs, Loretto Dennis and Matthew Wright. *Finding Answers in U.S. Census Records*. Ancestry Publishing, 2001.

Thorndale, William and William Dollarhide. *Map Guide to the U.S. Federal Census, 1790–1920*. Baltimore: Genealogical Publishing Co., 1987.

Court Records, Probate and Wills

Note: Each county has one county court and one supreme court. Probate records are filed in a probate district. The probate district does not necessarily adhere to the county boundaries. Most records have not been microfilmed and each county must be contacted to search the court and probate records.

Vermont. Secretary of State. *State Papers of Vermont*. Montpelier, Vermont: Published by authority of Secretary of State, 1939–.

Immigration

Filby, P. William. *Passenger and Immigration Lists Index*. 15 vols. Detroit: Gale Research, 1981–.

Stilwell, Lewis D. *Migration from Vermont*. Montpelier, Vermont: Vermont Historical Society, 1948.

United States. Bureau of Customs. *A Supplemental Index to Passenger Lists of Vessels Arriving At Atlantic & Gulf Coast Ports (Excluding New York) 1820–1874*. Washington, D.C.: Filmed by the National Archives Record Services, 1960. National Archives Microfilm, M 334.

United States. Immigration and Naturalization Service. *Index to New England Naturalization Petitions, 1791–1906*. Washington, D.C.: National Archives, 1983. Microfilm.

United States. Immigration and Naturalization Service. *St. Albans District Manifest Records of Aliens Arriving from Foreign Contiguous Territory: Arrivals At Canadian Border Ports from January 1895 to June 30, 1954: Indexes (Soundex), 1895–1924*. Washington, D.C.: National Archives Records Service, 1986.

Land

Bogart, Walter Thompson. *The Vermont Lease Lands*. Montpelier: Vermont Historical Society, 1950.

Charters Granted by the State of Vermont, 1779–1846. 2 vols. Vermont Public Records Division, 1974.

Denio, Herbert Williams. *Massachusetts Land Grants in Vermont*. Cambridge, Massachusetts: John Wilson and Son, University Press, 1920. Reprinted from *Publications of the Colonial Society of Massachusetts* 24 (March 1920): 35–99.

Holbrook, Jay Mack. *Vermont's First Settlers*. Oxford, Massachusetts: Holbrook Research Institute, 1976.

Index to the Papers of the Surveyors-General. 2nd ed. Reprint. Montpelier, Vermont: Secretary of State, 1918. S.l.: s.n., 1973.

State Papers of Vermont. 17 vols. Montpelier: Secretary of State 1918–69. Volumes have separate subjects. Vol. 5 is entitled *Petitions for Land Grants, 1778–1881*. Vol. 7 covers *New York Land Patents, 1668–1768, Covering Land and Included in the State of Vermont*.

Vermont. Secretary of State. *State Papers of Vermont*. Montpelier, Vermont: Published by authority of Secretary of State, 1939–.

Military

Clark, Byron N. *A List of Pensioners of the War of 1812. Vermont Claimants*. Baltimore: Genealogical Publishing Co., 1969.

Crockett, Walter Hill. *Revolutionary Soldiers Buried in Vermont*. 1903–1907. Reprint. Baltimore: Genealogical Publishing Co., 1959.

Daughters of the American Revolution (Vermont). *Genealogical Collection*. Microfilm. Washington, D.C.: Reproduction Systems for the Genealogical Society of Utah, 1971.

Fisher, Carleton E. *Soldiers, Sailors, and Patriots of the Revolutionary War, Vermont*. Camden, Maine: Picton Press, 1992

Goodrich, John E., comp. and ed. *Rolls of Soldiers in the Revolutionary War, 1775–1783*. Rutland, Vermont: Tuttle Co., 1904.

Johnson. Herbert T. *Vermont in the Spanish-American War*. Montpelier, Vermont: Adjutant General. 1929.

Peck, Theodore S. *Revised Roster of Vermont Volunteers: and Lists of Vermonters Who Served in the Army and Navy of the United States During the War of the Rebellion, 1861–1866*. Montpelier, Vermont: Watchman Publishing Co., 1892.

United States. Selective Service System. *Vermont, World War I Selective Service System Draft Registration Cards, 1917–1918*. National Archives Microfilm Publications, M1509. Washington, D.C.: National Archives, 1987–1988.

Vermont Adjutant General's Office. *Roster of Soldiers in the War of 1812–1814*. Montpelier, Vermont: Herbert T. Johnson, Adjutant General, 1933.

Vermont. Adjutant General. *Revised Roster of Vermont Volunteers and Lists of Vermonters Who Served in the Army and Navy of the United States during the War of the Rebellion, 1861–1866*. Montpelier, Vermont: Watchman, 1892.

Vital and Cemetery

Arnold, James N. *Index to James N. Arnold Tombstone Records' Collection*. [Knight Memorial Library] Providence, Rhode Island. Salt Lake City: Filmed by the Genealogical Society of Utah, 1992. Microfilm.

Hyde, Arthur L. *Burial Grounds of Vermont*. Townshend, Vermont: Vermont Old Cemetery Association, 1991.

Jones, Gertrude H. *Cemetery Records, Eastern States Mission*. 11 vols. Typescript. n.p.: n.p.

Nichols, Joann H. *Index to Known Cemetery Listings in Vermont*. Brattleboro, Vermont: the author, 1976.

Proceedings of the Vermont Historical Society.— 1860–1929; New Ser., vol. 1, No. 1 (Jan. 1930); vol. 11, No. 3–4 (Sept. 1943). Brattleboro, Vermont: The Society, 1860–1943.

Rollins, Alden M. *Vermont Warnings Out*. 2 vols. Camden, Maine: Picton Press, 1995–1997.

Vermont, Secretary of State. *General Index to Vital Records of Vermont, 1871–1908*. Salt Lake City: Genealogical Society of Utah, 1967. Microfilm, 120 rolls.

Vermont, Secretary of State. *General Index to Vital Records of Vermont, to 1870*. Salt Lake City: Genealogical Society of Utah, 1951. Microfilm, 287 rolls.

Vermont. Secretary of State. *State Records of Births, Marriages, and Deaths, 1909–1942*. Salt Lake City: Filmed by the Genealogical Society of Utah, 1994–1997. Microfilm, 278 rolls.

Vermont. Secretary of State. *State Records of Births, Marriages, and Deaths, 1942–1954*. Salt Lake City: Filmed by the Genealogical Society of Utah, 1994–1996. Microfilm, 133 rolls.

County Website	Map Index	Date Created	Parent County or Territory From Which Organized Address/Details

Addison   **I3**   **18 Oct 1785**

http://home.att.net/~swaitela/Default.htm

Rutland

Addison County; 5 Court St; Middlebury, VT 05753-1405;
Ph. (802) 388-4237

Details: (Town Clerks have Birth, Marriage, Death & Burial Records; County Clerk has Divorce & Court Records from 1797; Probate Judge has Probate Records)

   Towns Organized Before 1800: Addison 1761, Bridport 1761, Cornwall 1761, Ferrisburgh 1762, Leicester 1761, Lincoln 1780, Middlebury 1761, Monkton 1762, New Haven 1761, Orwell 1763, Panton 1761, Ripton 1781, Salisbury 1761, Shoreham 1761, Starksboro 1780, Vergennes 1788, Waltham 1796, Weybridge 1761, Whiting 1763

Bennington   **O3**   **11 Feb 1779**

www.rootsweb.com/~vtbennin/index.html

Original county

Bennington County; 207 South St; Bennington, VT 5201;
Ph. (802) 447-2700

Details: (Town Clerks have Birth, Marriage, Death & Burial Records; County Clerk has Divorce Records from 1899 & Court Records from 1861; Probate Judge has Probate Records)

   Towns Organized Before 1800: Arlington 1761, Bennington 1749, Dorset 1761, Glastenbury 1761, Landgrove 1780, Manchester 1761, Peru 1761, Pownal 1760, Rupert 1761, Sandgate 1761, Shaftsbury 1761, Sunderland 1761, Winhall 1761

Caledonia   **F9**   **5 Nov 1792**

http://home.att.net/~local_history/
Caledonia-Co-VT.htm

Orange

Caledonia County; 27 Main St; St. Johnsbury, VT 5819;
Ph. (802) 748-3813

Details: (Town Clerks have Birth, Marriage, Death, Burial & Land Records; County Clerk has Divorce & Court Records from 1797; Probate Judge has Probate Records)

   Towns Organized Before 1800: Barnet 1763, Burke 1782, Cabot 1780, Danville 1786, Groton 1789, Hardwick 1781, Lyndon 1780, Peacham 1763, Ryegate 1763, Sheffield 1793, St. Johnsbury 1785, Sutton 1782, Walden 1780, Waterford 1781, Wheelock 1785

Chittenden   **F3**   **22 Oct 1787**

http://home.att.net/~local_history/
Chittenden-Co-VT.htm

Addison

Chittenden County; 175 Main St; Burlington, VT 05401-8310;
Ph. (802) 863-7481

Details: (Town Clerks have Birth, Marriage, Death, Burial, Probate & Land Records; County Clerk has Divorce Records from 1829 & Court Records from 1798)

   Towns Organized Before 1800: Bolton 1763, Burlington 1763, Charlotte 1762, Colchester 1763, Essex 1763, Hinesburg, 1762, Huntington 1763, Jericho 1763, Milton 1763, Richmond 1794, Shelburne 1763, St. George 1763, Underhill 1763, Williston 1763

Cumberland   **1779**

Cumberland County; VT
Details: County Terminated 1781

Essex   **D11**   **5 Nov 1792**

www.rootsweb.com/~vtessex/index.htm

Orange

Essex County; PO Box 75; Guildhall, VT 5905; Ph. (802) 676-3910
Details: (County Clerk has Birth & Death Records from 1884, Marriage & Burial Records, a few Divorce Records, Court Records from 1800 & Land Records from 1762; Probate Judge has Probate Records from 1800)

   Towns Organized Before 1800: Bloomfield 1762, Brunswick 1761, Canaan 1782, Concord 1780, Guildhall 1761, Lunenburg 1763

County	Map	Date	Parent County or Territory From Which Organized
Website	Index	Created	Address/Details

Franklin   **C5**   **5 Nov 1792**
www.rootsweb.com/~vtfrankl/Franklin.html

Chittenden
Franklin County; PO Box 808; St. Albans, VT 5478;
Ph. (802) 524-3863
Details: (County Clerk has Divorce & Court Records from 1900;
Town Clerks have Birth, Marriage, Death, Burial & Land Records;
Probate Judge has Probate Records)
   Towns Organized Before 1800: Bakersfield 1791, Berkshire 1781,
Enosburg 1780, Fairfax 1763, Fairfield 1763, Fletcher 1781, Franklin
1789, Georgia 1763, Highgate 1763, Montgomery 1789, Richford
1780, Sheldon 1763, Swanton 1763, St. Albans 1763

Grand Isle   **C2**   **9 Nov 1802**
http://Death_larose.tripod.com/GrandIsleVT/

Franklin, Chittenden
Grand Isle County; Rt 2; PO Box 7; North Hero, VT 5474;
Ph. (802) 372-8350
Details: (Probate Judge has Probate Records; Town Clerks have
Birth, Marriage, Death & Land Records)
   Towns Organized Before 1800: Alburg 1781, Grand Isle 1779, Isles
La Motte 1779, North Hero 1779, South Hero 1779

Jefferson   **1 Nov 1810**

Addison, Orange, Caledonia, Orleans
Jefferson County; VT
Details: (see Washington) Name changed to Washington 8 Nov
1814

Lamoille   **E6**   **26 Oct 1835**
www.usgennet.org/usa/vt/county/lamoille1/
index.htm

Chittenden, Orleans, Franklin, Washington
Lamoille County; PO Box 303; Hyde Park, VT 05655-0303;
Ph. (802) 888-2207
Details: (County Clerk has Divorce & Court Records from 1837;
Town Clerks have Birth, Marriage, Death, Burial & Land Records;
Probate Judge has Probate Records)
   Towns Organized Before 1800: Cambridge 1781, Elmore 1781,
Hyde Park 1781, Johnson 1792, Morristown 1763, Stowe 1763, Wol-
cott 1781

Orange   **I7**   **22 Feb 1781**
www.usgennet.org/usa/vt/county/orange/

Original county
Orange County; PO Box 95; Chelsea, VT 5038; Ph. (802) 685-4610
Details: (Town Clerks have Birth, Marriage, Death, Burial & Land
Records; County Clerk has Divorce & Court Records from 1781 &
Land Records from 1771; Probate Judge has Probate Records from
1771)
   Towns Organized Before 1800: Bradford 1770, Braintree 1781,
Brookfield 1781, Chelsea 1781, Corinth 1764, Fairlee 1761, Newbury
1763, Orange 1781, Randolph 1781, Stratford 1761, Thetford 1761,
Topsham 1763, Turnbridge 1761, Vershire 1781, Washington 1781,
West Fairlee 1779, Williamstown 1781

Orleans   **D8**   **5 Nov 1792**
http://users.rootsweb.com/~vtorlean/
VTGenWeb.SM.htm

Chittenden
Orleans County; PO Box 787; Newport, VT 05855-0787;
Ph. (802) 334-2711
Details: (Town & City Clerks have Birth, Marriage, Death & Land
Records; District Probate Court has Probate Records; County Clerk
has Divorce & Court Records from 1800)
   Towns Organized Before 1800: Barton 1789, Craftsbury 1781,
Derby 1779, Glover 1783, Greensboro 1781, Holland 1779, Jay 1792,
Westfield 1780

County	Map	Date	Parent County or Territory From Which Organized
Website	Index	Created	Address/Details

Rutland   K3   **22 Feb 1781**
www.rootsweb.com/~vtrutlan/index.html

Bennington

Rutland County; 83 Center St; Rutland, VT 5701; Ph. (802) 775-4394

Details: (Secretary of State Office, Montpelier has Birth, Marriage & Death Records 1760–1955 & Divorce Records 1760–1968; Town Clerks have Land Records from 1826; County Clerk has Land Records 1779–1826 & Court Records; Probate Court has Probate Records)

Towns Organized Before 1800: Benson 1780, Brandon 1761, Castleton 1761, Chittenden 1780, Clarendon 1761, Danby 1761, Fair Haven 1779, Hubbardton 1764, Ira 1781, Mendon 1781, Middletown Springs 1784, Mt. Holly 1792, Mt. Tabor 1761, Pawlet 1761, Pittsford 1761, Poultney 1761, Rutland 1761, Sherburn 1761, Shrewsbury 1761, Sudbury 1763, Wallingford 1761, Wells 1761 West Haven 1792

Washington   G6   **1 Nov 1810**
www.rootsweb.com/~vtwashin/index.htm

Addison, Orange, Caledonia, Orleans

Washington County; PO Box 426; Montpelier, VT 05602-0426; Ph. (802) 223-2091

Details: (Formerly Jefferson County. Name changed to Washington 8 Nov 1814) (Secretary of State, Montpelier has Birth, Marriage & Death Records; County Clerk has Divorce & Court Records; Probate Court has Probate Records; Town & City Clerks have Land Records)

Towns Organized Before 1800: Barre 1781, Berlin 1763, Calais 1781, Duxbury 1763, Marshfield 1782, Middlesex 1763, Montpelier 1781, Moretown 1763, Northfield 1781, Plainfield 1797, Roxbury 1781, Waitsfield 1782, Warren 1780, Waterbury 1763, Worcester 1763

Windham   P5   **22 Feb 1781**
www.rootsweb.com/~vtwashin/index.htm

Original county

Windham County; PO Box 207; Newfane, VT 05345-0207; Ph. (802) 365-7979

Details: (Town Clerks have Birth, Marriage, Death, Burial & Land Records; County Clerk has Divorce & Court Records from 1825; Probate Judge has Probate Records)

Towns Organized Before 1800: Athens 1780, Brattleboro 1753, Brookline 1794, Grafton 1754, Guilford 1754, Halifax 1750, Jamaica 1780, Londonderry 1780, Marlboro 1751, Newfane 1753, Putney 1753, Rockingham 1752, Townshend 1753, Woodbury 1781, Westminster 1752, Whitingham 1770, Wilmington 1751, Windham 1795

Windsor   K6   **22 Feb 1781**
www.usgennet.org/usa/vt/county/windsor/

Original county

Windsor County; 12 The Green; Woodstock, VT 05091-1212; Ph. (802) 457-2121

Details: (County Clerk has Divorce & Court Records from 1782; Town Clerks have Birth, Marriage, Death, Burial & Land Records; Probate Judge has Probate Records)

Towns Organized Before 1800: Andover 1761, Baltimore 1793, Barnard 1761, Bethel 1779, Bridgewater 1761, Cavendish 1761, Chester 1754, Hartford 1761, Hartland 1761, Ludlow 1761, Norwich 1761, Plymouth 1761, Pomfret 1761, Reading 1761, Royalton 1769, Sharon 1761, Springfield 1761, Stockbridge 1761, Weathersfield 1761, Weston 1799, Windsor 1761, Woodstock 1761

Notes

Virginia

Capital: Richmond

State: 1788 (10th)

Thus always to tyrants

James I granted a charter to the Virginia Company in 1606 to colonize Virginia. The first ships left in 1607 and formed the first permanent English settlement in the New World at Jamestown. Captain John Smith provided the strong leadership needed by the fledgling settlement. Through several harsh winters, the colony struggled to stay alive. New supplies and immigrants came each year, with the most crucial being in 1610, when the 65 surviving settlers were about to give up and return to England. In 1612, John Rolfe cultured the first commercial tobacco and later married Pocahontas. In 1618, the Virginia Company granted land to all free settlers and allowed a general assembly to be held. An Indian massacre in 1622 and internal disputes in the colony led James I to revoke the Virginia Company's charter and to make Virginia a royal colony in 1624.

Immigrants arrived nearly every month. By 1700, Virginia had 80,000 residents in the Tidewater area. Settlers began scattering over the coastal plain and the Piedmont Plateau before 1700. During the 1700's, the tobacco industry flourished, due to the fertile soil and the use of slave labor. As the soil was exhausted by the tobacco crops, westward expansion began with the search for farmable land past the Blue Ridge Mountains. Between 1710 and 1740, passes were discovered across the Blue Ridge Mountains into the Shenandoah Valley. Emigrants from Pennsylvania and New Jersey began to enter the valley. In about 1730, there was a heavy immigration of Scotch-Irish, Germans, and Welsh from Pennsylvania into Virginia, most of whom settled in the upper valleys. They brought with them their religions– Presbyterian, Baptist, and Quaker. Methodist churches were established around 1800. By the mid-18th century, Virginia's population had grown to more than 280,000 people.

Between 1750 and 1784, land grants made to the Ohio Company encouraged exploration beyond the Alleghenies. Virginia organized the new area southeast of the Ohio River in 1775 and called it the District of West Augusta. Much of this area was ceded to Pennsylvania in 1779. In the 1770's the Wilderness Road across the Cumberland Gap opened up Kentucky. Kentucky County, which later became the state

of Kentucky, was organized in 1776. Virginia was prominent in the Revolutionary War due to its great leaders like Thomas Jefferson, George Washington, Patrick Henry, George Mason, and Richard Henry Lee. Little fighting occurred on Virginian soil until the final years of the war and the final surrender at Yorktown.

In 1784, Virginia ceded its claims north of the Ohio River to the United States. Virginia entered the Union in 1788. Virginia seceded from the Union in 1861. Robert E. Lee was placed in command of the Confederate troops for Virginia, with Richmond as the capital of the Confederacy. The northwestern counties of the state refused to join in the secession and were admitted to the Union in 1863 as the state of West Virginia. Virginia was the central battlefield for the Civil War, with the first major battle at Bull Run (Manassas) and the final surrender at Appomattox. An estimated 155,000 men from Virginia fought for the Confederacy. Virginia was readmitted to the Union in 1870. The majority of foreign-born immigrants include Russians, English, Germans, Italians, Greeks, Polish, Czechs, Irish, Austrians, and Hungarians.

Look for vital records in the following locations:

Note: In Virginia, all cities are politically independent of a county, though a city and county can share physical facilities.

- **Birth and death records:** Few such records survive before 1854 for the two major Virginia denominations, Anglican/Episcopal and Presbyterian, who kept them. Until 1786, the Anglican Church was the state church of Virginia. In accordance with English law, the church kept parish registers of vital statistics. Unfortunately, most of these are no longer in existence. A fire in 1844 at a Presbyterian Church headquarters in Philadelphia destroyed many of their records. Extant registers are generally available on microfilm at the state library or appropriate church archive, and also at the LDS Family History Library. Civil registrations begin in 1854 but were voluntary, thus incomplete, and officially ceased in 1896. Indices are available for births only. Registration resumed in 1912, with a 50 year restriction on access for deaths and 100 year restriction on births. Microfilm of actual certificates and indices to records in the public domain available at the state and some local libraries. Requests by mail/phone for certificates or search of index must be directed to the Division of Vital Statistics. Expect a minimum of 90 days for reply.

- **Marriages:** Prior to 1854, most marriages were recorded either in church registers or in civil bonds, with few surviving prior to 1782. Many extant bonds have been published, but on a county by county basis. Starting in 1854, marriages were recorded by license at the Division of Vital Statistics with registers of the same available at the county where the license was issued. For the period 1854 to 1935, check the state library. State library also has a statewide index to grooms and brides, generally by decade, but will *not* fill phone/mail requests for copies.

- **Land records:** Colonial and state grants, and indexes to the same, are available at the state library on microfilm. Deeds are recorded at the county/city level, with microfilm copies of same at the state library, and grantor/grantee indices available at both locations. Years covered vary by locale. Virginia law has always required the wife of a grantor to give formal consent, but said consent was not always recorded with or at the same time as the deed.

- **Probate records:** Wills and other probate records are recorded at the local level, except for the period in the 1800's when multi-jurisdiction District courts existed. Microfilm copies of originals are available, along with testator indices (years covered vary by jurisdiction; some jurisdictions also have legatee indices).

- **Tax records:** Land and personal property taxes are extant for all localities from 1783 or year of formation of locality, whichever is earlier. Some lists called "tithables" survive prior to 1783, as does a 1704 quit rent roll which excludes the "Northern Neck" counties of Lancaster, Northumberland, Richmond, Stafford and Westmoreland. Originals not retired to the state archives will typically be in the custody of the Commissioner of Revenue. Microfilm is available to about 1880 for all localities at state library.

Virginia Department of Health,
Office of Vital Records and Health Statistics
PO Box 1000
Richmond, Virginia 23218-1000
(804) 662-6200
www.vdh.state.va.us/vitalrec/index.asp

The Library of Virginia
800 East Broad Street
Richmond, Virginia
(804) 692-3888
www.lva.lib.va.us/

BLM Eastern States Office
7450 Boston Blvd, Springfield VA 22153
(703) 440-1600

Societies and Repositories

Albemarle County Historical Society; 220 Court Square; Charlottesville, VA 22901.

Alleghany Highlands Genealogical Society; 1011 N. Rockbridge St.; Covington, VA 24426.

Augusta County Genealogical Society; 2002 Lyndhurst Rd.; Waynesboro, VA 22980-5226.

Augusta County, Virginia Historical Society; PO Box 686; Staunton, VA 24401.

Bath County Historical Society, Inc.; PO Box 212; Warm Springs, VA 24484.

Bedford Historical Society, Inc.; PO Box 602; Bedford, VA 24523.

Caroline County Genealogical Society; PO Box 9; Bowling Green, VA 22427.

Carroll County Genealogical Club; PO Box 395; Hillsville, VA 24343.

Carroll County Historical Society; PO Box 937; Hillsville, VA 24343.

Central Virginia Genealogical Association; PO Box 5583; Charlottesville, VA 22905-5583.

Chesterfield Historical Society of Virginia; PO Box 40; Chesterfield, VA 23832.

Clan MacLaren Society of North America, Ltd.; 7810 Kincardine Ct.; Alexandria, VA 22315-4025; (703) 971-6924; genealogy@ClanMacLarenNA.org.

Clark County Historical Association; PO Box 306; Berryville, VA 22611.

Clinch Mountain Militia Chapter, Sons of the American Revolution; 5 Windswept; Tazewell, VA 24651; (540) 979-8251; bluridge@netscope.net.

Col. Fielding Lewis Chapter, Sons of the American Revolution; 1314 Sophia Street; Fredericksburg, VA 22401-3742; (540) 371-2370; wjscmsmas@aol.com; http://members.home.net/sarfielding.

Colonel George Waller Chapter, Sons of the American Revolution; 1100 Mulberry Road; Martinsville, VA 24112-5220; (540) 673-6057; mark@markcrabtree.org; www.sar.org/vassar/waller.htm.

Culpeper Historical Society, Inc.; PO Box 785; Culpeper, VA 22701.

Culpeper Minute Men Chapter, Sons of the American Revolution; 11201 Springfield; Fredericksburg, VA 22408; (540) 710-6764; mmelyman@earthlink.net; www.home.earthlink.net/~mmelyman.

Cumberland County Historical Society; Box 88; Cumberland, VA 23040.

Dan River Chapter, Sons of the American Revolution; 4618 Black Stump Road; Weems, VA 22576-2003; (804) 435-7088; laprade@rivnet.net.

Fairfax Genealogical Society; PO Box 2290; Merrifield, VA 22116-2290.

Fairfax Historical Society; PO Box 415; Fairfax, VA 22030.

Fincastle Resolutions Chapter, Sons of the American Revolution; 3161 Stoneridge Rd., SW; Roanoke, VA 24014-4217; (540) 345-8521; Hokie69@aol.com.

Fort Harrison Chapter, Sons of the American Revolution; 879 Airport Road; Bridgewater, VA 22812-3500; (540) 828-4669; cnsheap@prodigy.net.

Franklin County Genealogical Society; PO Box 316; Ferrum, VA 24088.

Fredericksburg Regional Genealogical Society; PO Box 42013; Fredericksburg, VA 22404.

Ft. Eustis Historical and Archaeological Association; PO Box 4408; Ft. Eustis, VA 23604.

Gen. William Campbell Chapter, Sons of the American Revolution; 19770 McCray Drive; Abingdon, VA 24211; (540) 623-2442.

Genealogical Research Institute of Virginia; PO Box 29178; Richmond, VA 23242-0178.

Genealogical Society of Page County, Virginia; Page Public Library; 100 Zerkel St.; Luray, VA 22835.

George Mason Chapter, Sons of the American Revolution; 1740 Key West Lane; Vienna, VA 22182-2318; (703) 281-5915; albeatty@erols.com.

George Washington Chapter, Sons of the American Revolution; 2202 Guildmore Road; Reston, VA 20191-4902; (703) 620-9879; guildmore@aol.com.

Goochland County Historical Society; PO Box 602; Goochland, VA 23063.

Grayson County Historical Society, Inc.; PO Box 529; Independence, VA 24348-0529.

Greene County Historical Society; PO Box 185; Stanardsville, VA 22973.

Historical Society of Washington County, Virginia; Box 484; Abingdon, VA 24210.

Holston Territory Genealogical Society; PO Box 433; Bristol, VA 24203-0433.

Isle of Wight County Historical Society; PO Box 121; Smithfield, VA 23431.

Jewish Genealogical Society of Tidewater; Jewish Community Center; 7300 Newport Ave.; Norfolk, VA 23505.

King and Queen Historical Society; PO Box 129, King and Queen C. H., VA 23085.

King George County Historical Society; PO Box 424; King George, VA 22485.

Lee County Historical and Genealogical Society; PO Box 231; Jonesville, VA 24263.

Lt. David Cox Chapter, Sons of the American Revolution; 1939 Englewood Road; Galax, VA 24333; (540) 236-4682; cdphilen@ls.net.

Martinsville Henry County Historical Society; PO Drawer 432; Martinsville, VA 24114.

Mathews County Historical Society; PO Box 885; Mathews, VA 23109.

Mount Vernon Genealogical Society; 1500 Shenandoah Rd.; Alexandria, VA 22308.

New River Historical Society; PO Box 373; Newbern, VA 24126.

New River Valley Chapter, Sons of the American Revolution; PO Box 638; Pembroke, VA 24136; (540) 626-7193; clybne@gva.net.

Norfolk Chapter, Sons of the American Revolution; 637 E. Lynn Shores Circle; Virginia Beach, VA 23452; (757) 340-2536.

Norfolk County Historical Society; Chesapeake Public Library; 298 Cedar Rd.; Chesapeake, VA 23320-5512.

Northern Neck Historical Society; Westmoreland County; PO Box 716; Montross, VA 22520.

Orange County Historical Society; 130 Caroline St.; Orange, VA 22960.

Palatines to America, Virginia Chapter; 3249 Cambridge Court; Fairfax, VA 22032-1942.

Patrick County Genealogical Society; PO Drawer 1016; Stuart, VA 24171.

Patrick Henry Chapter, Sons of the American Revolution; 158 Rosecliff Farms; Amherst, VA 24521; (804) 946-2050; gfgould@hotmail.com.

Pittsylvania Historical Society; PO Box 846; Chatham, VA 24531.

Prince William County Genealogical Society; PO Box 2019; Manassas, VA 20108-0812.

Richmond Chapter, Sons of the American Revolution; 5815 West Club Lane; Richmond, VA 23226; (804) 288-2135.

Roanoke Valley Historical Society; PO Box 1904; Roanoke, VA 24008.

Rockbridge Volunteers Chapter, Sons of the American Revolution; Route 724, Box 76; Brownsburg, VA 24415; (540) 348-5698.

Rockingham County Historical Society; 301 S. Main St.; Dayton, VA 22812.

Sergeant-Major John Champe Chapter, Sons of the American Revolution; 19433 Loudoun Orchard Road; Leesburg, VA 20175; lmoison137@aol.com.

Society of the Old Creek Cross; 9501 4th Place; Lorton, VA 22079.

Southwest Virginia Historical Society; PO Box 3877; Wise, VA 24293.

Southwestern Virginia Genealogical Society; PO Box 12485; Roanoke, VA 24026.

Stewart Bell Jr. Archives/Handley Regional Library; 100 W. Piccadilly St.; PO Box 58; Winchester, VA 22604; archives@hrl.lib.state.va.us; www.hrl.lib.state.va.us.

Surry County Historical Society and Museum; PO Box 262; Surry, VA 23883.

The Library of Virginia; 800 East Broad Street; Richmond, VA 23219-8000; (804) 692-3500; www.lva.lib.va.us.

Thomas Jefferson Chapter, Sons of the American Revolution; 3115 Dundee Road; Earlysville, VA 22936-9623; (804) 975-0569; nm2n@virginia.edu; http://monticello.avenue.org/tjcsar.

Thomas Nelson, Jr. Chapter, Sons of the American Revolution; 821 Sharpley Avenue; Hampton, VA 23666-2818; (757) 826-8644; RebMixon@juno.com.

Tidewater Genealogical Society; PO Box 7650; Hampton, VA 23666.

Tidewater, Afro-American Historical and Genealogical Society; 2200 Crossroad Trail; Virginia Beach, VA 23456.

United Daughters of the Confederacy; UDC General Headquarters; 328 North Boulevard; Richmond, VA 23220-4057; hqudc@rcn.com; www.hqudc.org.

Virginia Beach Genealogical Society; PO Box 62901; Virginia Beach, VA 23466-2901.

Virginia Division, United Daughters of the Confederacy; VA; jslougheed@erols.com.

Virginia Genealogical Society; 5001 W. Broad St. # 115; Richmond, VA 23230-3023; mail@vgs.org; www.vgs.org.

Virginia Historical Society; 428 North Boulevard; Richmond, VA 23220; www.vahistorical.org/index.htm.

Virginia-North Carolina, Piedmont Genealogical Society; PO Box 2272; Danville, VA 24541-2272; vancsoc@juno.com.

Williamsburg Chapter, Sons of the American Revolution; 47 Whittaker's Mills Road; Williamsburg, VA 23185-5534; (757) 229-0496; thomascamsr@aol.com.

Bibliography and Record Sources

General

A Key to Survey Reports and Microfilm of the Virginia Colonial Records Project. Richmond: Virginia State Library and Archives, 1990.

Axelson, Edith F. *A Guide to Episcopal Church Records in Virginia.* Athens, Georgia: Iberian Publishing, 1988.

Bible Records From Virginia. Salt Lake City: Genealogical Society of Utah, 1947. Microfilm, 4 rolls.

Brigham, Clarence Saunders. *History and Bibliography of American Newspapers, 1690–1820.* 2 vols. Worcester, Massachusetts: American Antiquarian Society, 1947, 1975.

Brock, Robert Alonza. *Virginia and Virginians.* 2 vols. Richmond, Virginia and Toledo, Ohio: H. H. Hardesty, 1888.

Brown, Stuart E., Jr. *Virginia Genealogies: A Trial List of Printed Books and Pamphlets.* 2 vols. Berryville, Virginia: Virginia Book, 1967, 1980.

Cappon, Lester J. *Virginia Newspapers 1821–1935: A Bibliography with Historical Introduction and Notes.* New York: D. Appleton Century, 1936.

Cerny, Johni and Gary J. Zimmerman. *Before Germanna: The Origins and Ancestry of Those Affiliated with the Second Germanna Colony of Virginia.* Monograph series, 1–12. Bountiful, Utah: American Genealogical Lending Library, 1990.

Clark, Jewell T., and Elizabeth Terry Long. *A Guide to Church Records in the Archives Branch, Virginia State Library.* Richmond: Virginia State Library, Archives and Records Division, 1981.

Clay, Robert Young. *Virginia Genealogical Resources.* Detroit: Detroit Society of Genealogical Research, 1980.

Dabney Virginius. *Virginia: The New Dominion.* Charlottesville: University Press of Virginia, 1971.

Daughters of the American Revolution. Virginia. Genealogical Records Committee. *Miscellaneous Bible, Tombstone and Court Records Submitted by Various Virginia Chapters of the Daughters of the American Revolution.* Salt Lake City: Genealogical Society of Utah, 1970. Microfilm.

Des Cognet, Louis, Jr., comp. *English Duplicates of Lost Virginia Records.* Baltimore: Genealogical Publishing Co., 1981.

Executive Journals of the Council of Colonial Virginia. 6 vols. Richmond: Virginia State Library, 1966–1978.

Finkelman, Paul. *State Slavery Statutes: Guide to the Microfiche Collection.* Frederick, Maryland: University Publications of America, 1989

Fleet, Beverley. *Virginia Colonial Abstracts.* 34 vols. 1937–1949. Reprint. Baltimore: Genealogical Publishing, 1988.

Foley, Louise Pledge Heath. *Early Virginia Families along the James River.* 2 vols. 1978. Reprint. Baltimore: Genealogical Publishing Co., 1990.

Foote, William Henry. *Sketches of Virginia: Historical and Biographical.* 2 vols. Philadelphia: William S. Marten, 1850–1856.

French, S. Bassett. *Biographical Sketches [of Virginia].* Richmond, Virginia: Virginia State Library, 1949.

Genealogies of Virginia Families: From the William and Mary College Quarterly. 5 vols. Baltimore: Genealogical Publishing, 1982.

Genealogies of Virginia Families: From Tyler's Quarterly. 4 vols. Baltimore: Genealogical Publishing, 1981.

Goodwin, Edward L. *The Colonial Church in Virginia.* Milwaukee: Morehouse Pub., 1927.

Gray, Gertrude E. *Virginia Northern Neck Land Grants.* 4 vols. Baltimore, Maryland: Genealogical Pub. Co., 1993.

Grundset, Eric. *Research in Virginia.* Arlington, Virginia: National Genealogical Society, 1998.

Hart, Lyndon H. *A Preliminary Guide to Pre-1904 Municipal Records in the Archives Branch, Virginia State Library and Archives.* Richmond, Virginia: Library and Archives, 1988.

Hart, Lyndon H., III. *Guide to Bible Records in the Archives Branch, Virginia State Library.* Richmond: Virginia State Library and Archives. 1985.

Hart, Lyndon H., III, comp. *A Guide to Genealogical Notes and Charts in the Archives Branch, Virginia State Library.* Richmond: Virginia State Library, 1983.

History of Virginia. 6 vols. Chicago: American Historical Society, 1924.

Howard, H. E. *The Virginia Battles and Leaders Series.* Lynchburg, Virginia: H. E. Howard, 1984.

Jester, Annie Lash and Martha Woodruff Hiden. *Adventurers of Purse and Person, Virginia, 1607–1624/5.* 3rd ed. 1956. Reprint, n.l.: Order of the First Families of Virginia, 1987.

Kercheval, Samuel. *A History of the Valley of Virginia.* Baltimore, Maryland: Clearfield Co., Inc., 2002.

Journals of the Council of the State of Virginia. 5 vols. Richmond: Virginia State Library, 1931–1982.

McGinnis, Carol. *Virginia Genealogy: Sources and Resources.* Baltimore: Genealogical Publishing Co., 1993.

Meade, William. *Old Churches, Ministers and Families of Virginia,* 1857. Reprint. Baltimore: Genealogical Publishing, 1966.

Men of Mark in Virginia. 5 vols. Washington, D.C.: Men of Mark Publishing Co., 1906–1909.

Neville, John D. *Bacon's Rebellion.* Jamestown Foundation, n.d.

Oliver, Harold, comp. and ed. *Virginia in the 1600s: An Index to Who Was There! — and Where!* Riverside, California: D&H Publishing Co., 1992.

Palmer, William P., ed. *Calendar of Virginia State Papers and Other Manuscripts. Preserved in the Capitol.* 3 vols. Richmond, Virginia: 1875–1883.

Pecquet du Bellet, Louise. *Some Prominent Virginia Families.* 4 vols. 1907. Reprint. Baltimore: Genealogical Publishing, 1976.

Ray, Suzanne Smith. *A Preliminary Guide to Pre-1904 County Records in the Archives Branch, Virginia State Library and Archives.* Richmond, Virginia: Library and Archives, 1988.

Records of the Assistant Commissioner for the State of Virginia, Bureau of Refugees. *Freedmen, and Abandoned Lands, 1865–1869.* Washington, D.C.: National Archives, 1988.

Records of the Superintendent of Education for the State of Virginia, Bureau of Refugees. *Freedmen, and Abandoned Lords, 1865–1870.* Washington, D.C.: National Archives, 1977.

Registers of Signatures of Depositors in Branches of the Freedman's Savings and Trust Company, 1865–1874. Washington, D.C.: National Archives, 1969.

Salmon, Emily J., and Edward D. C. Campbell. *The Hornbook of Virginia History: A Ready Reference Guide to the Old Dominion's People, Places, and Past.* 4th ed. Richmond, Virginia: The Library of Virginia, 1994.

Salmon, John. S., comp. *A Guide to State Records in the Archives Branch.* Richmond: Virginia State Library, 1985.

Schweitzer, George K. *Virginia Genealogical Research.* Knoxville: George K. Schweitzer, 1982.

Stewart, Robert Armistead. *Index to Printed Virginia Genealogies.* 1930. Reprint. Baltimore: Genealogical Publishing Co, 1970.

Summers, Lewis Preston. *Annals of Southwest Virginia, 1769–1800.* 1929. Reprint. 1 vol. In two parts. Baltimore: Genealogical Publishing Co., 1996.

Swem, Earl Gregg. *Virginia Historical Index.* 2 vols. in 4. 1934–1936. Reprint. Gloucester, Massachusetts: Peter Smith, 1965.

Taylor, Philip F. *A Calendar of the Warrants for Land in Kentucky, Granted for Service in the French and Indian War, Excerpted from the Year Book of the Society of Colonial Wars of Kentucky.* 1917. Reprint. Baltimore: Genealogical Publishing Co. 1967.

True, Ransom B. *Biographical Dictionary of Early Virginia, 1607–1660.* Jamestown: Association for the Preservation of Virginia Antiquities, 1982. 19 microfiche.

Tyler, Lyon Gardiner. *Encyclopedia of Virginia Biography.* 5 vols. New York: Lewis Historical Pub., 1915.

Virginia Genealogy, A Guide to Resources in the University of Virginia Library. Charlottesville, Virginia: The University Press of Virginia, 1983.

Virginia Historical Society. *Index of Bible Records on File in the Virginia Historical Society.* Salt Lake City: Genealogical Society of Utah, 1987.

Virginia Local History: A Bibliography. Richmond: Virginia State Library, 1971. Supplement, 1976.

Virginia Research Outline. Series U.S.-States, no. 46. Salt Lake City: Family History Library, 1988.

Wardell, Patrick G. *Timesaving Aid to Virginia—West Virginia Ancestors.* 4 vols. Athens, Georgia: Iberian Publishing Co., 1985–1990.

Wardell, Patrick G. *Virginians and West Virginians, 1607–1870.* 3 vols. Bowie, Maryland: Heritage Books, 1986–1992.

Weisiger, Benjamin B., III. *Burned County Data 1809–1848: As Found in the Virginia Contested Elected Files.* Richmond, Virginia: Benjamin B. Weisiger, 1986.

Atlases, Maps and Gazetteers

Axelson, Edith F. *Virginia Postmasters and Post Offices, 1789–1832.* Athens, Georgia: Iberian Pub. Co., 1991.

Doran, Michael F. *Atlas of County Boundary Changes in Virginia, 1634–1895.* Athens, Georgia: Iberian Publishing, 1987.

Gannett, Henry. *A Gazetteer of Virginia*. Washington: Government Printing Office, 1904. Reprint as *A Gazetteer of Virginia and West Virginia*. Baltimore: Genealogical Publishing Co., 1975.

Hale, John S. *A Historical Atlas of Colonial Virginia*. Staunton, Virginia: Old Dominion Publications, 1978.

Hanson, Raus McDill. *Virginia Place Names*. Verona, Virginia: McClure Press, 1969.

Hiden, Martha W. *How Justice Grew: Virginia Counties, an Abstract of Their Formation*. Charlottesville: University Press of Virginia, 1957. Reprint. Baltimore: Clearfield Co., 1992.

Martin, Joseph. *A New and Comprehensive Gazetteer of Virginia, and the District of Columbia*. Charlottesville: J. Martin, 1835.

Sames, James W., III. *Index of Kentucky and Virginia Maps, 1562 to 1900*. Frankfurt, Kentucky: Kentucky Historical Society, 1976.

Stephenson, Richard W. *The Cartography of Northern Virginia: Facsimile Reproductions of Maps Dating From 1608 to 1915*. Fairfax, Virginia: Fairfax County, Virginia, 1981.

Topping, Mary, et al. *Approved Place Names in Virginia*. Charlottesville, Virginia: University Press of Virginia, 1971.

Virginia Atlas and Gazetteer. 3rd ed. Freeport, Maine: Delorme Mapping Co., 1995.

Censuses

Available Census Records and Census Substitutes

Federal Census 1810 (except Grayson, Greenbrier, Halifax, Hardy, Henry, James City, King William, Louisa, Mecklenburg, Nansemond, Northampton, Orange, Patrick, Pittsylvania, Russell, and Tazewell Counties), 1820, 1830, 1840, 1850, 1860, 1870, 1880, 1900, 1910, 1920, 1930

Federal Mortality Schedules 1850, 1860, 1870, 1880

Union Veterans and Widows 1890

Dollarhide, William. *The Census Book: A Genealogist's Guide to Federal Census Facts, Schedules and Indexes*. Bountiful, Utah: Heritage Quest, 1999.

Finkelman, Paul. *State Slavery Statutes: Guide to the Microfiche Collection*. Frederick, Maryland: University Publications of America, 1989.

Fothergill, Augusta B. *Virginia Taxpayers, 1782–1787*. 1940. Reprint. Baltimore: Genealogical Publishing, 1974.

Kemp, Thomas Jay. *The American Census Handbook*. Wilmington, Delaware: Scholarly Resources, Inc., 2001.

Lainhart, Ann S. *State Census Records*. Baltimore: Genealogical Publishing Co., Inc., 1992.

Schreiner-Yantis, Netti and Florence Speakman Love, comps. *The 1787 Census of Virginia: An Accounting of the Names of Every White Male Tithable Over 21 Years, the Number of White Males Between 16 & 21 Years, the Number of Slaves Over 16 & Those Under 16 Years*. 3 vols. Springfield, Virginia: Genealogical Books in Print, 1987.

Schreiner-Yantis, Netti. *A Supplement to the 1810 Census of Virginia: Tax Lists of the Counties for Which the Census is Missing*. Springfield, Virginia: Genealogical Books in Print, 1971.

Smith, Annie Laurie Wright. *The Quit Rents of Virginia*: Richmond: Expert Letter Writing, 1957.

Szucs, Loretto Dennis and Matthew Wright. *Finding Answers in U.S. Census Records*. Ancestry Publishing, 2001.

Thorndale, William and William Dollarhide. *Map Guide to the U.S. Federal Census, 1790–1920*. Baltimore: Genealogical Publishing Co., 1987.

Virginia in 1740: A Reconstructed Census. Miami Beach, Florida: T. L. C. Genealogy, 1992.

Virginia Tax Records: From the Virginia Magazine of History and Biography, The William and Mary College Quarterly, and Tyler's Quarterly. Baltimore: Genealogical Publishing Company, 1983.

Woodson, Robert F., and Isobel B. Virginia. *Tithables from Burned Record Counties*. Richmond, Virginia: Isobel B. Woodson, 1970.

Court Records, Probate and Wills

Chalkley, Lyman. *Chronicles of the Scotch-Irish Settlement in Virginia: Extracted from the Original Court Records of Augusta County, 1754–1800*. 3 vols. 1912. Reprint. Baltimore: Genealogical Publishing, 1980.

Clemens, William Montgomery, comp. *Virginia Wills Before 1799: A Complete Abstract Register of All Names Mentioned in Over Six Hundred Recorded Wills*. Pompton Lakes, New Jersey: Biblio Co., 1924.

Cocke, William Ronald. *Hanover County Chancery Wills and Notes: A Compendium of Genealogical, Biographical and Historical Material as Contained in Cases of the Chancery Suits of Hanover county, Virginia*. 1940. Reprint. Baltimore: Genealogical Publishing Co., 1978.

Currier-Briggs, Noel. *Virginia Settlers and English Adventurers: Abstracts of Wills, 1484–1798, and Legal Proceedings, 1560–1700, Relating to Early Virginia Families*. 3 vols. Baltimore: Genealogical Publishing Co., 1970.

Hopkins, William Lindsay. *Some Wills from Burned Counties of Virginia and Other Wills Not Listed in the Virginia Wills and Administrations, 1632–1800*. Richmond, Virginia: W. L. Hopkins, 1987.

McGhan, Judith. *Virginia Will Records*. Baltimore: Genealogical Publishing, 1982.

McIlwaine, H. R. *Minutes of the Council and General Court of Colonial Virginia*. 2nd ed. Richmond, Virginia State Library, 1979.

Nugent, Nell Marion. *Caveat Proceedings*. n.p., 1970.

Sparacio, Ruth and Sam Sparacio. *Surname Index of Antient Press Publications.* 11 vols. McLean, Virginia: R. & S. Sparacio, 1993–1997.

Torrence, Clayton, comp. *Virginia Wills and Administrations 1632–1800: An Index of Wills Recorded in Local Courts of Virginia, 1632–1800, and of Administrations on Estates Shown by Inventories of the Estates of Intestates Recorded in Will (and Other) Books of Local Courts, 1632–1800.* 1931. Reprint. Baltimore: Genealogical Publishing Co., 1985.

Vogt, John and T. William Kethley, Jr. *Will and Estate Records in the Virginia State Library: A Researcher's Guide.* Athens, Georgia: Iberian Publishing Co., 1987.

Emigration, Immigration, Migration and Naturalization

Brock, Robert A. *Documents, Chiefly Unpublished, Relating to the Huguenot Emigration to Virginia and to the Settlement at Manakintown.* 1886. Reprint. Baltimore: Genealogical Publishing Co., 1979.

Coldham, Peter Wilson. *The Complete Book of Emigrants, 1607–1776, and Emigrants in Bondage, 1614–1775.* Novato, California: Brøderbund Software, 1996.

Greer, George C. *Early Virginia Immigrants, 1623–1666.* 1912. Reprint. Baltimore: Genealogical Publishing Co., 1982.

Hume, Robert. *Early Child Immigrants to Virginia, 1618–1642.* Baltimore: Magna Carta Book Co., 1986.

Stanard, William Glover. *Some Emigrants to Virginia: Memoranda in Regard to Several Hundred Emigrants to Virginia During the Colonial Period Whose Parentage is Shown or Former Residence Indicated by Authentic Records.* 1911. Reprint. Baltimore: Genealogical Publishing Co., 1979.

Withington, Lathrop. *Virginia Gleanings in England: Abstracts of 17th- and 18th-Century English Wills and Administrations Relating to Virginia and Virginians.* Baltimore: Genealogical Publishing, 1980.

Land and Property

Auditor's Office. *Pay Rolls of Militia Entitled to Land Bounty Under Act of Congress of 1850.* Richmond, Virginia: Auditor's Office, 1851.

Brookes-Smith, Joan E. *Master Index Virginia Surveys and Grants 1774–1791.* Frankfort: Kentucky Historical Society, 1976.

Burgess, Louis A., comp. and ed. *Virginia Soldiers of 1776, Compiled from Documents on File in the Virginia Land Office; Together with Material Found in the Archives Department of the Virginia State Library and Other Reliable Sources.* 3 vols. Reprint. Spartanburg, South Carolina: Reprint Co., 1973.

Cabell, Priscilla Harriss. *Turff and Twigg: The French Lands.* Richmond, Virginia: Priscilla Harriss Cabell, 1988.

Egle, William Henry. *Old Rights, Property Rights, Virginia Entries and Soldiers Entitled to Donation Lands.* Harrisburg, Virginia: C. M. Busch, State Printer, 1896.

Hone, Wade E. *Land and Property Research in the United States.* Salt Lake City: Ancestry Incorporated, 1997.

Hopkins, William Lindsay. "*Virginia Land Patent Books.*" *Magazine of Virginia Genealogy.* Richmond: Virginia Genealogical Society, 1984–.

Hopkins, William Lindsay. *Virginia Revolutionary War Land Grant Claims 1783–1850 (Rejected).* Richmond: Gen-N-Dex, 1988.

Hudgins, Dennis, ed. *Cavaliers and Pioneers: Abstracts of Virginia Land Patents and Grants, 1732–1741.* Vol. 4 of 5. Richmond: Virginia Genealogical Society, 1994.

Hudgins, Dennis, ed. *Cavaliers and Pioneers: Abstracts of Virginia Land Patents and Grants, 1741–1749.* Vol. 5 of 5. Richmond: Virginia Genealogical Society, 1994.

Kaylor, Peter Cline. *Abstract of Land Grant Surveys, 1761–1791.* 1938. Baltimore: Clearfield Co., 1991.

Nugent, Nell Marion. *Cavaliers and Pioneers: Abstracts of Virginia Land Patents and Grants.* 5 vols. Richmond: Dietz Print: Virginia State Library: Virginia Genealogical Society, 1934, 1963, 1977–1979, 1994.

Parks, Gary. *Virginia Land Records: From the Virginia Magazine of History and Biography, the William and Mary College Quarterly, and Tyler's Quarterly.* Baltimore: Genealogical Publishing Co., 1982.

Robinson, W. Stitt. *Mother Earth—Land Grants in Virginia, 1607–1699.* Williamsburg: 350th Anniversary Celebration Corp., 1957.

Schreiner-Yantis, Netti. *Montgomery County, Virginia—Circa 1790: A Comprehensive Study, including the 1789 Tax Lists, Abstracts of Over 800 Land Surveys and Data Concerning Migration.* Springfield, Virginia, 1972.

Smith, Annie Laurie Wright, comp. *The Quit Rents of Virginia, 1704.* Baltimore: Genealogical Publishing Co., 1980.

Wardell, Patrick G. *War of 1812 Virginia Bounty Land and Pension Applicants.* Bowie, Maryland: Heritage Books, 1987.

Military

Abercrombie, Janice L. *Virginia Publick Claims.* 3 vols. Athens, Georgia: Iberian Publishing Co., 1992.

Auditor's Office. *Muster Rolls of the Virginia Militia in the War of 1812.* Richmond, Virginia: Auditor's Office, 1852.

Bockstruck, Lloyd DeWitt. *Virginia's Colonial Soldiers.* Baltimore: Genealogical Publishing Co., 1988.

Brumbaugh, Gaius M. *Revolutionary War Records: Virginia Army and Navy Forces with Bounty Land Warrants for Virginia Military District of Ohio and Virginia Scrip, From Federal and State Archives.* 1936. Reprint. Baltimore: Genealogical Publishing Co., 1967.

Butler, Stuart Lee. *Guide to Virginia Militia Units in the War of 1812*. Athens, Georgia: Iberian Publishing Co; 1988.

Butler, Stuart Lee. *Virginia Soldiers in the United States Army, 1800–1815*. Atlanta: Iberian Publishing Co., 1986.

Confederate Pension Applications, Virginia, Acts of 1888, 1900, 1902; Index, 1888–1934. Microreproduction of original records at the Virginia State Library and Archives in Richmond, Virginia. Salt Lake City: Filmed by the Genealogical Society of Utah, 1988.

Crozier, William Armstrong. *Virginia Colonial Militia, 1651–1776*. 1905. Reprint. Baltimore: Genealogical Publishing Co., 1982.

Dorman, John Frederick, comp. *Virginia 1958–1995 Revolutionary Pension Applications*. 51 vols. Washington, D.C.: n.p., 1958–1995.

Eckenrode, H. J. *List of the Colonial Soldiers of Virginia*. 1905. Reprint. Baltimore: Genealogical Publishing Co., 1974.

Eckenrode, H. J. *List of the Revolutionary Soldiers of Virginia*. Richmond: D. Bottom, 1912.

Egle, William Henry. *Old Rights, Property Rights, Virginia Entries and Soldiers Entitled to Donation Lands*. Harrisburg, Virginia: C. M. Busch, State Printer, 1896.

Gwathmey, John H. *Historical Register of Virginians in the Revolution: Soldiers, Sailors, Marines: 1775–1783*. Richmond, Virginia: Deitz Press, 1938. Reprint. Baltimore: Genealogical Publishing Co., 1973.

Haulsee, W. M., F. G. Howe, and A. C. Dayle, comps. *Soldiers of the Great War*. 3 vols. Washington, D.C.: Soldiers Record Publishing Association, 1920.

Hemphill, W. Edwin, ed. *Gold Star Honor Roll of Virginians in the Second World War*. Charlottesville, Virginia: Virginia World War II History Commission, 1947.

Howard, H. E. *Virginia Regimental History Series*. Lynchburg, Virginia: H. E. Howard, 1982–.

Lewis, Virgil A. *Soldiery of West Virginia in the French and Indian War: Lord Dunmore's War: The Revolution: The Later Indian Wars: The Whiskey Insurrection: The Second War with England: The War with Mexico, and Addenda Relating to West Virginians in the Civil War*. Baltimore: Genealogical Publishing Co., 1967.

McCallister, Joseph T. *Index to Saffell's List of Virginia Soldiers in the Revolution*. Hot Springs, Virginia: McAllister Publishing Co., 1913.

Muster Rolls, Payrolls, and Index of the Virginia Militia in the War of 1812. Salt Lake City: Genealogical Society of Utah, 1955.

Taylor, Philip F. *A Calendar of the Warrants for Land in Kentucky, Granted for Service in the French and Indian War*. 1917. Reprint. Baltimore: Genealogical Publishing Company, 1967.

United States. Selective Service System. *Virginia, World War I Selective Service System Draft Registration Cards, 1917–1918*. Washington, D.C.: National Archives, 1987–1988.

Virginia Military Organizations in the World War: with Supplement of Distinguished Service. Richmond: n.p., 1927.

Virginia Military Records: From the Virginia Magazine of History and Biography, the William and Mary College Quarterly, and Tyler's Quarterly. Baltimore: Genealogical Publishing, 1983.

Virginia Regimental Histories Series. Lynchburg, Virginia: H. E. Howard, 1982–.

Virginia Revolutionary War State Pensions 1980; Reprint. Easley, South Carolina: Southern Historical Press, 1982.

Virginia. Office of the Secretary of Virginia Military Records. *Index to Confederate Service Records of Virginia; Confederate Service Records of Virginia, 1861–1865*. Microfilm of original at the State Library in Richmond, Virginia. Salt Lake City: Filmed by the Genealogical Society of Utah, 1954.

Wallace, Lee A. *A Guide to Virginia Military Organizations, 1861–1865*. Lynchburg, Virginia: H. E. Howard, 1986.

Wardell, Patrick G. *War of 1812: Virginia Bounty Land and Pension Applications*. Bowie, Maryland: Heritage Books, 1987.

Wilson, Samuel M. *Catalogue of Revolutionary Soldiers and Sailors of the Commonwealth of Virginia to Whom Land Bounty Warrants Were Granted*. Baltimore, Maryland: Clearfield Co., Inc., 2002.

Vital and Cemetery Records

Borden, Duane L. *Tombstone Inscriptions (Virginia)*. 9 vols. Ozark, Missouri: Yates Pub. Co., 1986.

Crozier, William A. *Early Virginia Marriages*. Baltimore: Genealogical Publishing Co., 1982.

Hall, Virginius Cornick. *Abstracts of Marriage and Obituary Notices in Virginia Newspapers Before 1820*. Salt Lake City: Genealogical Society of Utah, 1987.

Hogg, Anne M., and Dennis A. Tosh. *Virginia Cemeteries: A Guide to Resources*. Charlottesville: University of Virginia, 1986.

McDonald, Cecil D. *Some Virginia Marriages, 1800–1825*. 12 vols. in 1. Seattle: Cecil D. McDonald, 1973.

McDonald, Cecil D. *Some Virginia Marriages, 1700–1799*. 25 vols. in 2. Seattle: Cecil D. McDonald, 1972.

McIlwaine, H. R. *Index to Obituary Notices in the Richmond Enquirer from May 9, 1804 through 1828, and the Richmond Whig from January 1824 to 1838*. 1921. Reprint. Baltimore: Genealogical Publishing, 1974.

Some Marriages in the Burned Record Counties of Virginia. Richmond: Virginia Genealogical Society, 1979.

True, Ransom B. *Some Virginia Marriages, 1826–1850.* 2 vols. in 1. Seattle: Cecil D. McDonald, 1975.

Virginia Marriage Records: From the Virginia Magazine of History and Biography, the William and Mary's College Quarterly, and the Tyler's Quarterly. Baltimore: Genealogical Publishing Co., 1982.

Virginia Vital Records: From the Virginia Magazine of History and Biography, the William and Mary's College Quarterly, and the Tyler's Quarterly. Baltimore: Genealogical Publishing Co., 1982.

Virginia. Bureau of Vital Statistics. *Birth records, 1853–1941; indexes, 1853–1950.* Microfilm of the original records at the Virginia State Library in Richmond, Virginia. Salt Lake City: Filmed by the Genealogical Society of Utah, 1996. Microfilm, 99 rolls.

Vogt, John and T. William Kethley. *Marriage Records in the Virginia State Library: A Researcher's Guide.* Athens, Georgia: Iberian Press, 1984.

Wulfeck, Dorothy F. *Marriages of Some Virginia Residents, 1607–1800.* 2 vols. Baltimore: Genealogical Publishing Co., 1986.

County / Website	Map Index	Date Created	Parent County or Territory From Which Organized / Address/Details
Accawmack www.rootsweb.com/~vanortha/		1634	**Original Shire** Accawmack County; VA **Details:** (see Northampton) Name changed to Northampton, 1643
Accomack www.esva.net/~accomack/	A7	1661	**Northampton** Accomack County; PO Box 288; 23296 Courthouse Ave; 2nd Floor, Suite 203; Accomack, VA 23301; Ph. (757) 787-5776, accomac@esva.net **Details:** (Clerk Circuit Court has Marriage Records from 1784, Divorce Records from 1850, Probate, Court & Land Records from 1663)
Albemarle	H6	6 May 1744	**Goochland, Louisa** Albemarle County; 401 McIntire Rd; Charlottesville, VA 22902; Ph. (434) 296-5841, smarshal@albemarle.org **Details:** (Clerk Circuit Court has Marriage Records from 1870, Land Records from 1748, Divorce, Probate & Court Records)
Alexandria (Ind. City) www.ci.alexandria.va.us		13 Mar 1847	**Fairfax** Alexandria (Ind. City) County; PO Box 178; 301 King St; Alexandria, VA 22314; Ph. (703) 838-4000 **Details:** (County name changed to Arlington 16 Mar 1920; Part of District of Columbia 1791–1846; see District of Columbia for Census Records 1800–1840) (Alexandria Health Center has Birth, Death & Burial Records; Clerk Circuit Court has Marriage & Divorce Records from 1870, Probate, Court & Land Records from 1783)
Alleghany www.co.alleghany.va.us	K7	5 Jan 1822	**Bath, Botetourt, Monroe** Alleghany County; 9212 Winterberry Ave, Ste C; Covington, VA 24426; Ph. (540) 863-6600, alegclk@intelos.net **Details:** (Clerk Circuit Court has Marriage Records from 1845, Divorce, Probate, Court & Land Records from 1822)
Amelia www.rootsweb.com/~vaamelia/	F8	1 Feb 1734	**Brunswick, Prince George** Amelia County; 1630 Dunn Street, Ste 101; PO Box A; Amelia, VA 23002; Ph. (804) 561-3039 **Details:** (Clerk Circuit Court has Marriage, Divorce, Land, Probate, Military & Court Records from 1734)

Virginia

County Website	Map Index	Date Created	Parent County or Territory From Which Organized Address/Details
Amherst www.countyofamherst.com	I7	1761	**Albemarle** Amherst County; PO Box 462; 113 Taylor St.; Amherst, VA 24521; Ph. (434) 946-9321 **Details:** (Clerk of Circuit Court has Divorce, Land, Probate, & Court Records from 1761, & Marriage Records from 1763; Library of Virginia has Birth & Death Records from 1912)
Appomattox www.appomattox.com/	H8	8 Feb 1845	**Buckingham, Campbell, Charlotte, Prince Edward** Appomattox County; PO Box 863; Moton Lane; Appomattox, VA 24522; Ph. (434) 352-2637 **Details:** (Clerk Circuit Court has Marriage, Divorce & Probate Records from 1892, Court & Land Records)
Arlington www.co.arlington.va.us	D4	13 Mar 1847	**Fairfax** Arlington County; 2100 Clarendon Blvd; Arlington, VA 22201; Ph. (703) 228-3000 **Details:** (Formerly Alexandria County. Name changed to Arlington 16 Mar 1920) (Clerk Circuit Court has Birth, Marriage, Death, Probate, Land & Court Records)
Augusta www.co.augusta.va.us/	I5	1 Aug 1738	**Orange** Augusta County; PO Box 590; 18 Government Center; Verona, VA 24482; Ph. (540) 245-5610 **Details:** (Clerk Circuit Court has Birth & Death Records 1853–1896, Marriage Records from 1785, Probate & Land Records from 1745, property tax Records 1800–1851, Land tax Records from 1786 & Court claims 1782–1785)
Barbour www.rootsweb.com/~wvgenweb/			Barbour County; VA **Details:** (See West Virginia)
Bath www.bathcountyva.org/	J6	14 Dec 1790	**Augusta, Botetourt, Greenbrier** Bath County; PO Box 309; Route 619, Courthouse; Hot Springs, VA 24484; Ph. (540) 839-7221, bathcc@tds.net **Details:** (Clerk Circuit Court has Birth Records 1854–1880, Death Records 1854–1870, Divorce, Probate, Land & Court Records from 1791)
Bedford www.co.bedford.va.us/	I7	27 Feb 1752	**Albemarle, Lunenburg** Bedford County; 122 E Main St; Bedford, VA 24523; Ph. (540) 586-7601 **Details:** (Clerk Circuit Court has Birth Records 1853–1897 & 1912–1918, Death Records 1853–1918, Marriage, Divorce, Probate, Court & Land Records from 1754)
Bedford (Ind. City) www.bedfordva.gov		1890	**Bedford** Bedford (Ind. City) County; PO Box 807; 215 E Main St; Bedford, VA 24523; Ph. (540) 587-6001 **Details:** (County seat of Bedford County) (Clerk Circuit Court has Marriage, Probate & Land Records)
Berkeley www.rootsweb.com/~wvgenweb/		1772	**Frederick** Berkeley County; VA **Details:** (See West Virginia) County lost to West Virginia 1863
Bermuda		1617	**Original County** Bermuda County; VA **Details:** County Terminated 1634

County Website	Map Index	Date Created	Parent County or Territory From Which Organized Address/Details
Bland www.bland.org	M8	30 Mar 1861	**Giles, Tazewell, Wythe** Bland County; PO Box 510; 654 Main St; Bland, VA 24315; Ph. (276) 688-4622 **Details:** (Clerk Circuit Court has Marriage, Probate & Land Records from 1861 & Divorce Records from 1900)
Boone www.rootsweb.com/~wvgenweb/		1847	**Kanawah, Cabell, Logan** Boone County; VA **Details:** (See West Virginia) County lost to West Virgina 1863
Botetourt www.co.botetourt.va.us	J7	7 Nov 1769	**Augusta** Botetourt County; 1 W Main St., #1 Intersection of Main & Roanoke Streets; Fincastle, VA 24090; Ph. (540) 473-8233 **Details:** (Clerk Circuit Court has Birth & Death Records 1853–1870, Marriage, Divorce, Probate, Land, Court & Cemetery Records from 1770)
Braxton www.rootsweb.com/~wvgenweb/		1836	**Kanawah, Lewis, Nichols** Braxton County; VA **Details:** (See West Virginia) County lost to West Virgina 1863
Bristol (Ind. City) www.bristolva.org/		12 Feb 1890	**Washington** Bristol (Ind. City) County; 300 Lee St; Bristol, VA 24201; Ph. (276) 645-7300 **Details:** (Clerk Circuit Court has Marriage, Divorce, Land, Probate, Military & Court Records from 1890)
Brooke www.rootsweb.com/~wvgenweb/			Brooke County; VA **Details:** (See West Virginia)
Brunswick	F9	2 Nov 1720	**Prince George, Isle of Wight, Surry** Brunswick County; PO Box 399; 102 Tobacco St.; Lawrence, VA 23868; Ph. (434) 848-3107 **Details:** (Clerk Circuit Court has Marriage, Divorce & Probate Records from 1732 & Land Records from 1900)
Buchanan	O8	13 Feb 1858	**Russell, Tazewell** Buchanan County;PO Box 950; Main Street, 4th Floor; Grundy, VA 24614; Ph. (276) 935-6500 **Details:** (Courthouse burned 1885) (Clerk Circuit Court has Mar- riage, Divorce, Probate, Court & Land Records from 1885)
Buckingham	H7	1761	**Albemarle** Buckingham County; PO Box 252; Highway 60; Administration Building; Buckingham, VA 23921; Ph. (434) 969-4242 **Details:** (Clerk Circuit Court has Birth & Death Records from 1896, Marriage, Divorce & Probate Records from 1869)
Buena Vista (Ind. City) www.buenavistavirginia.org		1892	**Rockbridge** Buena Vista (Ind. City) County; 2039 Sycamore Ave; Buena Vista, VA 24416; Ph. (540) 261-8600 **Details:** (Clerk Circuit Court has Marriage, Divorce, Probate, Court, Land & Military Discharge Records from 1892)
Cabell www.rootsweb.com/~wvgenweb/		1809	**Kanawah** Cabell County; VA **Details:** (See West Virginia) County lost to West Virginia 1863

County Website	Map Index	Date Created	Parent County or Territory From Which Organized Address/Details
Calhoun www.rootsweb.com/~wvgenweb/		1856	**Gilmer** Calhoun County; VA **Details:** (See West Virginia) County lost to West Virginia 1863
Campbell www.co.campbell.va.us	I8	5 Nov 1781	**Bedford** Campbell County; PO Box 100; 47 Courthouse Land; Rustburg, VA 24588; Ph. (434) 332-9525 **Details:** (Clerk Circuit Court has Birth & Death Records 1912–1918, Marriage, Divorce, Probate, Court & Land Records from 1782)
Caroline www.co.caroline.va.us/	E6	1 Feb 1727	**Essex, King and Queen, King William** Caroline County; PO Box 309; Bowling Green, VA 22427; Ph. (804) 633-5800 **Details:** (Clerk Circuit Court has Marriage Records 1787–1853, Land Records from 1836, Divorce, Probate & Court Records)
Carroll www.co.carroll.va.us/	L9	17 Jan 1842	**Grayson, Patrick** Carroll County; 605 Pine St.; PO Box 218; Hillsville, VA 24343-0515; Ph. (276) 730-3070 **Details:** (Clerk Circuit Court has Birth Records 1842–1896, Marriage, Divorce, Probate & Land Records from 1842)
Charles River www.rootsweb.com/~vayork/		1634	**Original Shire** Charles River County; VA **Details:** (see York) Name changed to York, 1643
Charles City 	D8	1634	**Original Shire** Charles City County; PO Box 128; 10900 Courthouse Road; Charles City, VA 23030; Ph. (804) 829-9201 **Details:** (Clerk Circuit Court has Birth, Marriage, Death, Probate & Land Records)
Charlotte www.co.charlotte.va.us/	H8	26 May 1764	**Lunenburg** Charlotte County; PO Box 608; 250 LeGrande Ave., Ste A; Charlotte Court House, VA 23923; Ph. (434) 542-5117 **Details:** (County Clerk has Birth & Death Records 1853–1870, Marriage, Probate, Court & Land Records from 1765 & Divorce Records)
Charlottesville (Ind. City) www.charlottesville.org		1762	**Albemarle** Charlottesville (Ind. City) County; PO Box 911; 605 E Main St; Charlottesville, VA 22902; Ph. (434) 970-3113 **Details:** (County seat of Albemarle County) (Clerk Circuit Court has Marriage, Probate & Land Records)
Chesapeake (Ind. City) www.cityofchesapeake.net	C9	1 Jan 1963	**Norfolk** Chesapeake (Ind. City) County; PO Box 15225; 306 Cedar Rd; Chesapeake, VA 23328; Ph. (757) 382-6166 **Details:** (Formerly Norfolk County. Changed to Chesapeake City 1 Jan 1963) (Clerk Circuit Court, PO Box 15205, has Birth & Death Records 1853–1870, Marriage Records from 1706, Divorce Records from 1800, Probate & Land Records from 1637)
Chesterfield www.co.chesterfield.va.us/	F7	1 May 1749	**Henrico** Chesterfield County; PO Box 40; 9901 Lori Road; Chesterfield, VA 23832; Ph. (804) 748-1000 **Details:** (Clerk Circuit Court has Marriage Records from 1771, Land Records from 1749, Divorce, Probate & Court Records)

County Website	Map Index	Date Created	Parent County or Territory From Which Organized Address/Details
Clarke www.co.clarke.va.us/	F3	8 Mar 1836	**Frederick** Clarke County; 102 N Church St, 2nd Floor; Berryville, VA 22611; Ph. (540) 955-5100 **Details:** (Clerk Circuit Court has Marriage, Divorce, Probate, Court & Land Records from 1836)
Clay www.rootsweb.com/~wvgenweb/		1858	**Braxton, Nicholas** Clay County; VA **Details:** (See West Virginia) County lost to West Virginia 1863
Clifton Forge (Ind. City)			**1906 Alleghany** Clifton Forge (Ind. City) County; PO Box 631; Clifton Forge, VA 24422-0631; Ph. (540) 863-5091 **Details:** (City Clerk has Marriage, Divorce & Land Records from 1906 & Probate Records)
Colonial Heights (Ind. City) www.colonial-heights.com			**1948 Chesterfield** Colonial Heights (Ind. City) County; PO Box 3401; 201 James Ave; Colonial Heights, VA 23834; Ph. (804) 520-9265 **Details:** (Clerk Circuit Court has Marriage, Divorce, Probate, Court & Land Records from 1961; Clerk Circuit Court, Chesterfield County, has Divorce, Probate Court & Land Records to 1961)
Covington (Ind. City) www.covington.va.us		1952	**Alleghany** Covington (Ind. City) County; 333 W Locust St; Covington, VA 24426; Ph. (540) 965-6300 **Details:** (County seat of Alleghany County) (Clerk Circuit Court has Marriage, Probate & Land Records)
Craig www.co.craig.va.us/	K7	21 Mar 1851	**Botetourt, Giles, Roanoke, Monroe** Craig County; PO Box 308; Corner of Court & Main St., 2nd Floor; New Castle, VA 24127; Ph. (540) 864-5010 **Details:** (Clerk Circuit Court has Birth Records 1864–1896, Marriage, Divorce, Probate, Court & Land Records from 1851)
Culpeper www.co.culpeper.va.us	F5	23 Mar 1748	**Orange** Culpeper County; 302 N Main St.; Culpeper, VA 22701; Ph. (540) 727-3427 **Details:** (Clerk Circuit Court has Birth Records 1864–1896 & 1912–1917, Death Records 1864–1896, Marriage Records from 1781, Land & Probate Records from 1749 & Court Records from 1831; Town Clerks have Burial Records)
Cumberland www.rootsweb.com/~vacumber/	G7	1749	**Goochland** Cumberland County; County Courthouse; 1 Courthouse Circle; PO Box 8; Cumberland, VA 23040; Ph. (804) 492-4442 **Details:** (Clerk Circuit Court has Marriage, Divorce, Probate & Court Records from 1749, Birth & Death Records 1853–1870)
Danville (Ind. City) www.ci.danville-va.gov		1890	**Pittsylvania** Danville (Ind. City) County; PO Box 3300; 427 Patton St; Danville, VA 24541; Ph. (434) 799-5100 **Details:** (Clerk Circuit Court has Marriage, Divorce, Land & Court Records from 1841, Probate Records from 1857 & Military Records from 1942)

County Website	Map Index	Date Created	Parent County or Territory From Which Organized Address/Details
Dickenson www.dickensonctyva.com	P8	3 Mar 1880	**Buchanan, Russell, Wise** Dickenson County; PO Box 1098; Main Street Courthouse; Clintwood, VA 24228; Ph. (276) 926-1676 **Details:** (County Health Department has Birth, Death & Burial Records; Clerk Circuit Court has Marriage, Divorce, Court & Land Records from 1880, Probate & Military Discharge Records)
Dinwiddie	F8	27 Feb 1752	**Prince George** Dinwiddie County; PO Box 70; 14016 Boydton Plank Road; Pamplin Administration Building; Dinwiddie, VA 23841; Ph. (804) 469-4500 **Details:** (Clerk Circuit Court has Birth & Death Records 1865–1896, Marriage, Probate, Court & Land Records from 1833 & Divorce Records from 1870)
Doddridge www.rootsweb.com/~wvgenweb/		1845	**Harrison, Ritchie, Tyler, Lewis** Doddridge County; VA **Details:** (See West Virginia) County lost to West Virginia 1863
Dunmore www.rootsweb.com/~vashenan/vashenan.html		24 Mar 1772	**Frederick** Dunmore County; VA **Details:** (see Shenandoah) Name changed to Shenandoah 1 Feb 1778
Elizabeth City www.rootsweb.com/~vaelizab/		1634	**Original Shire** Elizabeth City County; VA **Details:** (see Hampton) Absorbed by Hampton Jul 1952
Emporia (Ind. City) www.ci.emporia.va.us	D6	16 Apr 1692	**Rappahannock, old** Emporia (Ind. City); PO Box 511; 201 S Main St; Emporia VA 23847; Ph. (434) 634-3332, jprince.cor@ci.emporia.va.us
Essex www.essex-virginia.org/	D6	16 Apr 1692	**Rappahannock, old** Essex County; PO Box 1079; 205 Cross St.; Tappanhannock, VA 22560; Ph. (804) 443-4331 **Details:** (Clerk Circuit Court has Marriage Records from 1814, Divorce & Land Records from 1865, Probate Records from 1656 & Court Records from 1692)
Fairfax www.fairfaxcounty.gov/court/circuit/archives.htm	E4	6 May 1742	**Prince William** Fairfax County; 4110 Chain Bridge Rd; Fairfax, VA 22030; Ph. (703) 246-4168, arch@fairfaxcounty.gov **Details:** (Circuit Court Clerk has Birth & Death Records 1912–1917, Court Records from 1749, Divorce & Tax Records from 1850, Guardianship, Land, & Probate Records from 1742, Marriage Records from 1853, Military Records from 1861, & Minute Books/Court Orders from 1749)
Fairfax (Ind. City) www.fairfaxva.gov		1961	**Fairfax** Fairfax (Ind. City) County; 10455 Armstrong St; Fairfax, VA 22030-3630; Ph. (703) 385-7855 **Details:** (County seat of Fairfax County) (See Fairfax County)
Falls Church (Ind. City) www.ci.falls-church.va.us		1948	**Fairfax** Falls Church (Ind. City) County; 300 Park Ave; Falls Church, VA 22046; Ph. (703) 248-5001 **Details:** (Fairfax County Clerk Circuit Court has Birth, Marriage, Divorce, Probate, Court & Land Records)

County Website	Map Index	Date Created	Parent County or Territory From Which Organized Address/Details
Fauquier www.fauquiercounty.gov	**F4**	**14 Sep 1758**	**Prince William** Fauquier County; 40 Culpeper St, 4th Floor; Warrenton, VA 20186; Ph. (540) 347-8680 **Details:** (Clerk Circuit Court has Birth Records 1853–1896, Death Records 1853–1896 & 1912–1917, Marriage, Land & Probate Records from 1759, Divorce Records from 1831, Court Records from 1975 & Military Discharge Records from 1944)
Fayette www.rootsweb.com/~vagenweb/kentucky.htm www.rootsweb.com/~wvgenweb		**1831**	**Kanawah, Greenbrier, Logan** Fayette County; VA **Details:** (See West Virginia) (2 Counties, Fayette 1, split to Kentucky, & Fayette 2, split to West Virginia) Lost to West Virginia 1863
Fincastle		**1772**	**Botetourt** Fincastle County; VA **Details:** (see Montgomery) Discontinued 1776 (Divided into Kentucky, Montgomery, and Washington County)
Floyd www.fin.org/	**K8**	**15 Jan 1831**	**Montgomery, Franklin** Floyd County; PO Box 218; 120 W Oxford St.; Floyd, VA 24091; Ph. (540) 745-9300 **Details:** (Clerk Circuit Court has Birth & Death Records 1852–1872, Marriage, Divorce, Probate, Court & Land Records from 1831)
Fluvanna www.co.fluvanna.va.us/	**G6**	**5 May 1777**	**Albemarle** Fluvanna County; PO Box 540; 132 Main St; Palmyra, VA 22963; Ph. (434) 591-1910 **Details:** (Clerk Circuit Court has Birth & Death Records 1853–1896, Marriage, Divorce, Probate, Court & Land Records from 1777 & some Burial Records)
Franklin www.franklincountyva.org/	**J8**	**17 Oct 1785**	**Bedford, Henry** Franklin County; 40 E Court St.; Rocky Mount, VA 24151; Ph. (540) 483-3030 **Details:** (Clerk Circuit Court has Birth, Marriage, Death, Probate, Land & Court Records)
Franklin (Ind. City) www.franklinva.com		**1788**	**Southampton** Franklin (Ind. City) County; PO Box 179; 207 W Second Ave.; Franklin, VA 23851; Ph. (757) 562-8503 **Details:** (Southampton County Clerk Circuit Court has Divorce, Probate, Court & Land Records)
Frederick www.co.frederick.va.us/	**G3**	**1 Aug 1738**	**Orange** Frederick County; 107 N Kent St; County Administration Building; Ph. (540) 665-5600 **Details:** (Nine square miles of Frederick County annexed to city of Winchester) (Clerk Circuit Court has Birth Records 1853–1912, Marriage Records from 1782, Death Records 1853–1896, Divorce Records from 1870, Probate & Land Records from 1743)
Fredericksburg (Ind. City) www.efredericksburg.net		**1879**	**Spotsylvania** Fredericksburg (Ind. City) County; PO Box 7447; 715 Princess Anne St; Fredericksburg, VA 22404; Ph. (540) 372-1010 **Details:** (Clerk Circuit Court has Birth, Marriage, Death, Probate, Court & Land Records)

County Website	Map Index	Date Created	Parent County or Territory From Which Organized Address/Details
Galax (Ind. City) www.ingalax.net		1954	**Carroll, Grayson** Galax (Ind. City) County; 111 E Grayson St.; Fries, VA 24333; Ph. (276) 236-5773 **Details:** (Galax, Virginia 24333 is on the line between Grayson & Carroll Counties, contact both counties for their Records of Galax)
Giles www.gilescounty.org/	L8	16 Jan 1806	**Montgomery, Monroe, Tazewell, Wythe** Giles County; 315 N Main St; Pearisburg, VA 24134; Ph. (540) 921-2525 **Details:** (Clerk Circuit Court has Marriage Records from 1806, Birth & Death Records 1858–1896, Divorce, Probate, Court & Land Records)
Gilmer www.rootsweb.com/~wvgenweb/		1845	**Kanawah, Lewis** Gilmer County; VA **Details:** (See West Virginia) County lost to West Virginia 1863
Gloucester www.gloucesterva.info	C7	1651	**York** Gloucester County; PO Box 329; 6467 Main St; Gloucester, VA 23061; Ph. (804) 693-4042 **Details:** (Clerk Circuit Court has Birth Records 1863–1890 & 1912–1916, Death Records 1865–1890, Marriage Records from 1853, Divorce, Probate, Court & Land Records from 1865)
Goochland www.co.goochland.va.us/	F7	1 Feb 1727	**Henrico** Goochland County; PO Box 10; 2983 River Road West; Goochland, VA 23063; Ph. (804) 556-5300 **Details:** (Clerk Circuit Court has Marriage & Probate Records from 1730, Divorce & Court Records from 1800 & Land Records from 1862)
Grayson www.graysoncounty.va.com	M9	7 Nov 1792	**Wythe, Patrick** Grayson County; PO Box 217; 129 Davis St; Independence, VA 24348; Ph. (540) 773-2471 **Details:** (Clerk Circuit Court has Marriage, Divorce, Probate, Court & Land Records from 1793)
Greenbrier www.rootsweb.com/~wvgenweb/			Greenbrier County; VA **Details:** (See West Virginia)
Greene	G5	24 Jan 1838	**Orange** Greene County; PO Box 358; 40 Celt Road; Stanardsville, VA 22973; Ph. (434) 985-5201 **Details:** (Clerk Circuit Court has Birth Records 1853–1896 & 1912–1919, Death Records 1838–1860, Marriage, Divorce, Probate, Court & Land Records from 1838)
Greensville www.greensvillecountyva.gov/	E9	16 Oct 1780	**Brunswick, Sussex** Greensville County; 1750 E Atlantic St; Emporia, VA 23847; Ph. (434) 348-4205 **Details:** (Clerk Circuit Court has Marriage, Land & Probate Records from 1781, Divorce & Court Records from 1900)
Halifax www.oldhalifax.com/county	H9	27 Feb 1752	**Lunenburg** Halifax County; PO Box 699; 134 S Main St; Halifax, VA 24558; Ph. (434) 476-3305 **Details:** (Clerk Circuit Court has Marriage Records from 1753, Divorce & Court Records from 1752, Probate Records from 1762 & Land Records from 1761)

County Website	Map Index	Date Created	Parent County or Territory From Which Organized Address/Details
Hampshire www.rootsweb.com/~wvgenweb/		1753	**Frederick** Hampshire County; VA **Details:** (See West Virginia) County lost to West Virginia 1863
Hampton **(Ind. City)**	C8	1908	**Elizabeth City** Hampton (Ind. City) County; 22 Lincoln St; Hampton, VA 23669; Ph. (757) 727-6392 **Details:** (Formerly Elizabeth City. Absorbed by Hampton Jul 1952) (Clerk Circuit Court has Marriage, Probate, Land & Court Records)
Hancock www.rootsweb.com/~wvgenweb/		1848	**Brooke** Hancock County; VA **Details:** (See West Virginia) County lost to West Virginia 1863
Hanover www.co.hanover.va.us/	E6	2 Nov 1720	**New Kent** Hanover County; PO Box 470; 7516 County Complex; Hanover, VA 23069; Ph. (804) 365-6000 **Details:** (Clerk Circuit Court has Marriage, Divorce, Probate, Land & Court Records from 1865)
Hardy www.rootsweb.com/~wvgenweb/		1785	**Hampshire** Hardy County; VA **Details:** (See West Virginia) County lost to West Virgina 1863
Harrison www.rootsweb.com/~wvgenweb/		1784	**Monongalia** Harrison County; VA **Details:** (See West Virginia) County lost to West Virginia 1863
Harrisonburg (Ind. City) www.ci.harisonburg.va.us		1916	**Rockingham** Harrisonburg (Ind. City) County; 345 S Main St; Harrisonburg, VA 22801; Ph. (540) 432-7701 **Details:** (County seat of Rockingham County) (City Clerk has Birth & Death Records 1862–1894, Marriage, Court & Land Records from 1778 & Probate Records from 1803)
Henrico www.co.henrico.va.us/	E7	1617	**Original Shire** Henrico County; PO Box 27032; 4301 E Parham Road; Glenside, VA 23273; Ph. (804) 501-4206 **Details:** (Clerk Circuit Court has Marriage, Probate & Land Records from 1781, Divorce & Court Records)
Henry www.henrycounty.neocom.net	J9	7 Oct 1776	**Pittsylvania** Henry County; PO Box 7; 3300 King's Mountain Road; Martinsville, VA 24112; Ph. (276) 634-4601 **Details:** (Clerk Circuit Court has Marriage & Land Records from 1777, Divorce Records from 1909 & Probate Records)
Highland www.highlandcova.org	J5	19 Mar 1847	**Bath, Pendleton** Highland County; PO Office 130; Main & Spruce St, 1st Floor, Courthouse; Monterey, VA 24465; Ph. (540) 468-2347 **Details:** (Clerk Circuit Court has Birth Records 1850–1898, Marriage, Divorce & Land Records from 1850, Probate Records from 1860 & Court Records from 1937)
Hopewell (Ind. City) www.ci.hopewell.va.us		1911	**Prince George** Hopewell (Ind. City) County; 300 N Main St; Hopewell, VA 23860; Ph. (804) 541-2270 **Details:** (Clerk Circuit Court has Marriage, Divorce, Probate & Land Records; Clerk District Court has Court Records)

County Website	Map Index	Date Created	Parent County or Territory From Which Organized Address/Details
Illinois www.rootsweb.com/~vagenweb/illinois.htm		1778	**Augusta** Illinois County; VA **Details:** (Discontinued 1784 and became Northwest Terr.)
Isle of Wight www.co.isle-of-wight.va.us/	D9	1634	**Original Shire** Isle of Wight County; County Courthouse; Hwy 258; PO Box 110; Isle of Wight, VA 23397; Ph. (757) 365-6233 **Details:** (Formerly Warrosquyoacke. Name changed to Isle of Wight 1637) (Clerk Circuit Court has Birth Records 1853–1876, Death Records 1853–1874, Marriage Records from 1772, Divorce Records from 1853, Probate Records from 1647, Court Records from 1746 & Land Records)
Jackson www.rootsweb.com/~wvgenweb/		1831	**Kanawah, Mason, Wood** Jackson County; VA **Details:** (See West Virginia) County lost to West Virginai 1863
James City www.james-city.va.us/	D8	1617	**Original Shire** James City County; 5201 Monticello Ave., Ste 6; Williamsburg, VA 23188; Ph. (757) 564-2242 **Details:** (Clerk of Circuit Court has Marriage, Divorce, Probate, & Court Records from 1865, & Land Records from 1854)
Jefferson www.rootsweb.com/~wvgenweb/		1801	**Berkeley** Jefferson County; VA **Details:** (See West Virginia) County lost to West Virginia 1863
Kanawah www.rootsweb.com/~wvgenweb/		1788	**Greenbrier, Montgomery** Kanawah County; VA **Details:** (See West Virginia) County lost to West Virginia 1863
Kentucky www.rootsweb.com/~vagenweb/kentucky.htm		1776	**Fincastle** Kentucky County; VA **Details:** (Discontinued 1780 and became Fayette, Jefferson & Lincoln Counties, Kentucky)
King & Queen www.iocc.com/~swright/kqmain.html	D6	16 Apr 1691	**New Kent** King & Queen County; PO Box 67; King & Queen Courthouse, VA 23085; Ph. (804) 785-5984 **Details:** (Clerk of Circuit Cour has Marriage Records from 1867, Divorce & Court Records from 1831, Land Records from 1719, Probate Records from 1864, Birth & Death Records from 1865)
King George www.king-george.va.us	E5	2 Nov 1720	**Richmond, Westmoreland** King George County; 9483 Kings Hwy, #3; King George, VA 22485; Ph. (540) 775-3322 **Details:** (Clerk of Circuit Court has Birth Records 1871–1917, Military Records 1824–1860, Marriage Records from 1786, Divorce Records from 1811, Land, Probate, & Court Records from 1721)
King William www.co.king-william.us	D7	5 Dec 1700	**King and Queen** King William County; PO Box 215; 180 Horse Landing Road; King William, VA 23086; Ph. (804) 769-4927 **Details:** (Fire in 1855 burned most Records; some Records to 1702 have been photocopied) (Clerk Circuit Court has Marriage, Divorce, Probate & Court Records from 1885 & Land Records)

County Website	Map Index	Date Created	Parent County or Territory From Which Organized Address/Details
Lancaster www.lancova.com/	C7	1652	**Northumberland, York** Lancaster County; 8311 Mary Ball Road; Lancaster, VA 22503; Ph. (804) 462-5129 **Details:** (County Health Department has Birth Records; Clerk Circuit Court has Marriage Records from 1715, Death, Probate & Land Records from 1652, Divorce Records from 1800 & Court Records from 1910)
Lee	Q9	25 Oct 1792	**Russell** Lee County; PO Box 367; Corner of Church & Main Sts, Rm 111; Jonesville, VA 24263; Ph. (276) 346-7714 **Details:** (Clerk Circuit Court has Birth & Death Records 1853–1877, Marriage Records from 1830, Divorce Records from 1832, Probate Records from 1800, Court & Land Records from 1793)
Lewis www.rootsweb.com/~wvgenweb/		1816	**Harrison** Lewis County; VA **Details:** (See West Virginia) County lost to West Virginia 1863
Lexington (Ind. City) www.ci.lexington.va.us		1778	**Rockbridge** Lexington (Ind. City) County; PO Box 922; 300 E Washington; Lexington, VA 24450; Ph. (540) 462-3700 **Details:** (County seat ot Rockbridge County) (Clerk Circuit Court has Marriage, Probate & Land Records)
Lincoln www.rootsweb.com/~vagenweb/kentucky.htm		1780	**Kentucky County** Lincoln County; VA **Details:** (See West Virginia)
Logan www.rootsweb.com/~wvgenweb/		1824	**Cabell, Giles, Kanawah** Logan County; VA **Details:** (See West Virginia) County lost to West Virginia 1863
Loudoun www.loudoun.gov	F3	25 Mar 1757	**Fairfax** Loudoun County; PO Box 7000; 1 Harrison St., South; Leesburg, VA 20177; Ph. (703) 777-0100 **Details:** (Clerk Circuit Court has Birth Records 1853–1859, 1864–1866 & 1869–1879, Death Records 1853–1866, Marriage Records from 1793, Divorce, Probate & Land Records from 1757, Court Records from 1858 & tithables 1758–1786)
Louisa www.louisacounty.com/	F6	6 May 1742	**Hanover** Louisa County; PO Box 160; 1 Woolfolk Ave; Louisa, VA 23093; Ph. (540) 967-0401 **Details:** (Clerk Circuit Court has Birth Records 1867–1896, Marriage, Divorce & Probate Records from 1742 & Land Records)
Lower Norfolk		1637	**New Norfolk** Lower Norfolk County; VA **Details:** (See Princess Anne and Norfolk) Abolished 1691 & divided between Princess Anne & Norfolk Counties
Lunenburg	G8	6 May 1745	**Brunswick** Lunenburg County; 11409 Courthouse Road; Lunenburg, VA 23952; Ph. (804) 696-2230 **Details:** (Clerk Circuit Court has Marriage, Divorce, Probate, Court & Land Records from 1746)

County Website	Map Index	Date Created	Parent County or Territory From Which Organized Address/Details
Lynchburg (Ind. City) www.lynchburgva.gov		1852	**Campbell** Lynchburg (Ind. City) County; PO Box 60; 900 Church St, 3rd; Lynchburg, VA 24505; Ph. (434) 455-3990 **Details:** (Clerk Circuit Court has Birth & Death Records 1853–1868, Marriage, Divorce, Probate, Court & Land Records from 1805, Military Discharge Records from 1919, Military Records from Civil War & slave register)
Madison	G5	4 Dec 1792	**Culpeper** Madison County; 1 Main St; PO Box 220; Madison, VA 22727-0220; Ph. (540) 948-6888 **Details:** (Clerk Circuit Court has Marriage, Divorce, Probate, Court & Land Records from 1793)
Manassas (Ind. City) www.ci.manassescity.org		1975	**Prince William** Manassas (Ind. City) County; Po Box 560; 9027 Center St; Manassas, VA 20110; Ph. (703) 257-8200
Manassas Park (Ind. City) www.ci.manasses-park.va.us		1975	**Prince William** Manassas Park (Ind. City) County; 1 Park Center Court; Manassas, VA 22111; Ph. (703) 335-8800 **Details:** (County seat of Prince William County) (Clerk Circuit Court has Marriage, Probate & Land Records)
Marion www.rootsweb.com/~wvgenweb/		1842	**Harrison, Monogalia** Marion County; VA **Details:** (See West Virginia) County lost to West Virginia 1863
Marshall www.rootsweb.com/~wvgenweb/		1835	**Ohio** Marshall County; VA **Details:** (See West Virginia) County lost to West Virginia 1863
Martinsville (Ind. City) www.ci.martinsville.va.us		1928	**Henry** Martinsville (Ind. City) County; PO Box 1112; 55 W Church St.; Martinsville, VA 24114; Ph. (276) 656-5000 **Details:** (County seat of Henry County) (Clerk Circuit Court has Marriage, Divorce, Probate, Court & Land Records from 1942)
Mason www.rootsweb.com/~wvgenweb/		1804	**Kanawah** Mason County; VA **Details:** (See West Virginia) County lost to West Virginia 1863
Mathews www.co.mathews.va.us/	C7	16 Dec 1790	**Gloucester** Mathews County; PO Box 839; Route 1001; Cobbs Creek, VA 23109; Ph. (804) 725-7172 **Details:** (Clerk Circuit Court has Marriage, Divorce, Probate, Court & Land Records from 1865)
McDowell www.rootsweb.com/~wvgenweb/		1858	**Kanawah** McDowell County; VA **Details:** (See West Virginia) County lost to West Virginia 1863
Mecklenburg www.mecklenburgva.com	G9	26 May 1764	**Lunenburg** Mecklenburg County; PO Box 307; 350 Washington St; Boydton, VA 23917; Ph. (434) 738-6191 **Details:** (Clerk Circuit Court has Marriage, Probate, Land & Court Records)

County	Map	Date	Parent County or Territory From Which Organized
Website	Index	Created	Address/Details

Mercer
www.rootsweb.com/~vagenweb/kentucky.htm

Mercer County; VA
Details: (See West Virginia)

Middlesex   C7   1669
www.co.middlesex.va.us/

Lancaster
Middlesex County; PO Box 428; 877 General Puller Highway; Saluda, VA 23149; Ph. (804) 758-4330
Details: (Clerk Circuit Court has Birth & Marriage Records from 1840, Probate, Court & Land Records from 1673)

Monongalia   1776
www.rootsweb.com/~wvgenweb/

Augusta
Monongalia County; VA
Details: (See West Virginia) County lost to West Virginia 1863

Monroe   1799
www.rootsweb.com/~wvgenweb/

Greenbrier
Monroe County; VA
Details: (See West Virginia) County lost to West Virginia 1863

Montgomery   K8   7 Oct 1776
www.montva.com/

Fincastle, Botetourt
Montgomery County; 755 Roanoke Street, Ste 2E; Christiansburg, VA 24073; Ph. (540) 382-6954
Details: (Clerk Circuit Court has Birth & Death Records 1853–1871, Marriage, Divorce, Probate, Court & Land Records from 1773)

Morgan   1820
www.rootsweb.com/~wvgenweb/

Berkeley, Hampshire
Morgan County; VA
Details: (See West Virginia) County lost to West Virginia 1863

Nansemond   1637
www.rootsweb.com/~vanansem/

Upper Norfolk
Nansemond County; VA
Details: (see Suffolk City) Became an independent city, 1972. Nansemond County and Suffolk City merged 1 Jan 1974

Nelson   H6   25 Dec 1807
www.nelsoncounty.com/

Amherst
Nelson County; 84 Courthouse Sq; PO Box 336; Lovingston, VA 22949; Ph. (434) 263-7000
Details: (Clerk Circuit Court has Marriage, Divorce, Probate, Court & Land Records from 1808)

New Kent   D7   20 Nov 1654
www.co.newkent.state.va.

York, James City
New Kent County; PO Box 50; 12007 Courthouse Cir, Ste 201; New Kent, VA 23124; Ph. (804) 966-9863
Details: (Clerk Circuit Court has Birth & Death Records 1865–1888, Marriage, Divorce, Probate, Court & Land Records from 1865)

New Norfolk   1636

Elizabeth City
New Norfolk County; VA
Details: Abolished 1637. Divided to Upper Norfolk (now Suffolk) & Lower Norfolk (now Chesapeake)

Newport News (Ind. City)   C8   1896
www.nngov.com

Warwick
Newport News (Ind. City) County; 2400 Washington Ave; Newport News, VA 23607; Ph. (757) 926-8411
Details: (Incorporated with Warwick 1 Jul 1958) (Clerk Circuit Court has Marriage, Probate & Land Records)

County Website	Map Index	Date Created	Parent County or Territory From Which Organized Address/Details
Nicholas www.rootsweb.com/~wvgenweb/		1818	**Greenbrier, Kanawah** Nicholas County; VA **Details:** (See West Virginia) County lost to West Virginia 1863
Norfolk (Ind. City) www.norfolk.gov	C9	1691	**Lower Norfolk** Norfolk County; PO Box 1531; 810 Union St; Norfolk, VA 23510; Ph. (757) 664-4000 **Details:** (changed to Chesapeake City 1 Jan 1963) (Clerk Circuit Court has Marriage, Probate, Land & Court Records)
Northampton www.co.northampton.va.us	B7	1634	**Original Shire** Northampton County; 16404 Courthouse Rd; PO Box 66; Eastville, VA 23347; Ph. (757) 678-0440 **Details:** (Formerly Accawmack County. Name changed to Northampton, 1643) (Clerk Circuit Court has Marriage Records from 1706, Probate, Court & Land Records from 1632 & Divorce Records from 1904)
Northumberland C6 www.co.northumberland.va.co		1645	**Indian Dist. of Chickacoan** Northumberland County; PO Box 217; Heathsville, VA 22473-0217; Ph. (804) 580-3777 **Details:** (Clerk Circuit Court has Marriage, Divorce, Probate, Court & Land Records)
Norton (Ind. City) www.nortonva.org		1954	**Wise** Norton (Ind. City) County; PO Box 618; 618 Virginia Ave, NW; Norton, VA 24273; Ph. (276) 679-1160 **Details:** (all Records with Wise County)
Nottoway www.nottoway.org	F8	22 Dec 1788	**Amelia** Nottoway County; PO Box 92; 344 W Court House Road; Nottoway, VA 23955; Ph. (434) 645-8696 **Details:** (Some Records were destroyed during the Civil War. Clerk Circuit Court has Marriage, Divorce & Court Records from 1865, Land, Probate & Military Records from 1789)
Ohio www.rootsweb.com/~wvgenweb/		1776	**Augusta** Ohio County; VA **Details:** (See West Virginia) County lost to West Virginia 1863
Orange www.orangecova.com	F5	1 Feb 1734	**Spotsylvania** Orange County; PO Box 111; 112 W Main St; Orang, VA 22960; Ph. (540) 672-3313 **Details:** (Clerk Circuit Court has Birth Records 1860–1895, Marriage Records from 1757, Probate, Court & Land Records from 1734)
Page www.co.page.va.us/	G4	30 Mar 1831	**Rockingham, Shenandoah** Page County; 117 S Court St; Shenandoah, VA 22835; Ph. (540) 743-4142 **Details:** (Clerk Circuit Court has Marriage, Divorce, Land, Probate & Court Records from 1831)
Patrick www.co.patrick.va.us/	K9	26 Nov 1790	**Henry** Patrick County; 106 Rucker St; PO Box 466; Stuart, VA 24171; Ph. (276) 694-6094 **Details:** (Clerk Circuit Court has Birth & Death Records 1853–1896, Marriage, Divorce, Probate, Court & Land Records from 1791)

County Website	Map Index	Date Created	Parent County or Territory From Which Organized Address/Details
Pendleton www.rootsweb.com/~wvgenweb/		1787	**Augusta, Hardy** Pendleton County; VA **Details:** (See West Virginia) County lost to West Virginia 1863
Petersburg (Ind. City) www.petersburg-va.org		16 Mar 1850	**Dinwiddie, Prince George, Chesterfield** Petersburg (Ind. City) County; 135 N Union St, Rm 202; Petersburg, VA 23803; Ph. (804) 733-2301 **Details:** (City Clerk has Birth Records 1853–1896, Death Records from 1853, Marriage, Divorce, Probate & Land Records from 1784)
Pittsylvania www.pitgov.org	I9	6 Nov 1766	**Halifax** Pittsylvania County; PO Box 426; 21 N Main St; Chatham, VA 24531; Ph. (434) 432-7710 **Details:** (Clerk Circuit Court has Marriage, Divorce, Probate, Court & Land Records from 1767)
Pleasants www.rootsweb.com/~wvgenweb/		1851	**Ritchie, Tyler, Wood** Pleasants County; VA **Details:** (See West Virginia) County lost to West Virginia 1863
Pocahontas www.rootsweb.com/~wvgenweb/		1821	**Pendleton** Pocahontas County; VA **Details:** (See West Virginia) County lost to West Virginia 1863
Poquoson (Ind. City) www.ci.poquoson.va.us		1952	**York** Poquoson (Ind. City) County;500 City hall Ave; Poquoson, VA 23662; Ph. (757) 868-3000 **Details:** (Clerk Circuit Court has Marriage, Probate & Land Records)
Portsmouth (Ind. City) www.portsmouthva.gov		1858	**Norfolk** Portsmouth (Ind. City) County; PO Box 820; 801 Crawford St, 6th; Portsmouth, VA 23704; Ph. (757) 393-8641 **Details:** (Territory taken from Norfolk County & annexed to Portsmouth in 1848, 1960 & 1968) (Clerk Circuit Court has Birth & Death Records 1858–1896, Marriage, Divorce, Probate, Court & Land Records from 1848; Portsmouth Public Health Department, PO Box 250, Portsmouth, VA 23705 has Birth, Death & Burial Records)
Powhatan www.powhatanva.com	F7	5 May 1777	**Chesterfield, Cumberland** Powhatan County; 3834 Old Buckingham Road, Ste A; Powhatan, VA 23139; Ph. (804) 598-5611 **Details:** (Clerk Circuit Court has Marriage, Divorce, Probate, Court & Land Records from 1777)
Preston www.rootsweb.com/~wvgenweb/		1818	**Monongallia** Preston County; VA **Details:** (See West Virginia) County lost to West Virginia 1863
Prince Edward www.co.prince-edward.va.us/	G8	27 Feb 1752	**Amelia** Prince Edward County; PO Box 382; 111 S Street; Farmville, VA 23901; Ph. (434) 392-8837 **Details:** (Clerk Circuit Court has Birth Records 1853–1896, Death Records 1853–1869, Marriage, Divorce, Probate, Court & Land Records from 1754)

Virginia

County Website	Map Index	Date Created	Parent County or Territory From Which Organized Address/Details
Prince George www.princegeorgeva.org	E8	1702	**Charles City** Prince George County; 6400 Courthouse Rd; PO Box 68; Prince George, VA 23875; Ph. (804) 733-2600 **Details:** (Clerk Circuit Court has incomplete Birth Records 1865–1896, Marriage, Divorce & Probate Records from 1865, Court Records from 1945 & Land Records)
Prince William www.pwcgov.org/	E4	1730	**King George, Stafford** Prince William County; 1 County Complex Court; Dumfries, VA 22192; Ph. (703) 792-6600 **Details:** (Clerk Circuit Court has Marriage Records from 1856, Divorce & Court Records from 1823, Probate Records from 1734 & Land Records from 1731)
Princess Anne www.rootsweb.com/~vaprinc2/pa.htm		1691	**Lower Norfolk** Princess Anne County; VA **Details:** (see Virginia Beach) Annexed to Norfolk County, 1950. Now part of Ind. City of Virginia Beach; consolidated, 1963
Pulaski www.pulaskicounty.org/	L8	30 Mar 1839	**Montgomery, Wythe** Pulaski County; 45 3rd St NW Suite 101; Pulaski, VA 24301; wlooka Ph. (540) 980-7825, bill@pulaskicounty.org **Details:** (Clerk Circuit Court has Marriage Records from 1882, Divorce, Probate, Court & Land Records from 1839)
Putnam www.rootsweb.com/~wvgenweb/		1848	**Kanawah, Mason, Cabell** Putnam County; VA **Details:** (See West Virginia) County lost to West Virginia 1863
Radford (Ind. City) www.radford.va.us		1887	**Pulaski** Radford (Ind. City) County; 619 2nd St; Radford, VA 24141; Ph. (540) 731-3603 **Details:** (Clerk Circuit Court has Marriage, Divorce, Probate, Court & Land Records from 1892)
Raleigh www.rootsweb.com/~wvgenweb/		1850	**Fayette** Raleigh County; VA **Details:** (See West Virginia) County lost to West Virginia 1863
Randolph www.rootsweb.com/~wvgenweb/		1786	**Harrison** Randolph County; VA **Details:** (See West Virginia) County lost to West Virginia 1863
Rappahannock 	G4	8 Feb 1833	**Culpeper** Rappahannock County; PO Box 519; 290 Gay St; Washington, VA 22747; Ph. (540) 675-5330 **Details:** (Clerk Circuit Court has Marriage, Divorce, Probate & Court Records from 1833, Land Records from 1838 & some personal property Records from 1834)
Rappahannock (old)		1656	**Lancaster** Rappahannock, old County; VA **Details:** (see Essex) Abolished 1692
Richmond www.co.richmond.va.us	D6	16 Apr 1692	**Rappahannock, old** Richmond County; 101 Court Cir; PO Box 1000; Warsaw, VA 22572; Ph. (804) 333-3415 **Details:** (Clerk Circuit Court has Birth & Death Records 1853–1895, Marriage Records from 1853, Divorce, Probate & Land Records from 1693)

County Website	Map Index	Date Created	Parent County or Territory From Which Organized Address/Details
Richmond (Ind. City) www.richmondgov.com		1782	**Henrico** Richmond (Ind. City) County; 900 E Broad St; City Hall; Richmond, VA 23219; Ph. (804) 646-7970 **Details:** (County seat of Henrico County) (Department of Health, Bureau of Vital Records, Madison Bldg., Richmond, VA 23219, has Divorce Records 1870–1954; Clerk Chancery Court, City Hall, Richmond, VA 23219 has Probate & Land Records; Clerk Civil Court has Court Records)
Ritchie www.rootsweb.com/~wvgenweb/		1843	**Harrison, Lewis, Wood** Ritchie County; VA **Details:** (See West Virginia) County lost to West Virginia 1863
Roane www.rootsweb.com/~wvgenweb/		1856	**Kanawah, Jackson, Gilmer, Witt** Roane County; VA **Details:** (See West Virginia) County lost to West Virginia 1863
Roanoke www.co.roanoke.va.us/	K8	30 Mar 1838	**Botetourt, Montgomery** Roanoke County; 5204 Bernard Dr, SW; PO Box 29800; Roanoke, VA 24018; Ph. (540) 772-2006 **Details:** (Clerk Circuit Court has Marriage, Divorce, Probate, Court & Land Records from 1838)
Roanoke (Ind. City) www.roanokegov.com		1884	**Roanoke** Roanoke (Ind. City) County; 215 Church Ave; Roanoke, VA 24011; Ph. (540) 853-2333 **Details:** (Clerk of Courts has Birth Records 1884–1896, Marriage, Divorce, Probate, Court & Land Records from 1884)
Rockbridge www.co.rockbridge.va.us	I6	20 Oct 1777	**Augusta, Botetourt** Rockbridge County; 150 S Main St, 2nd Floor; Lexington, VA 24450; Ph. (540) 463-4361 **Details:** (Clerk Circuit Court has Birth Records 1853–1896, Death Records 1853–1870, Marriage, Divorce, Probate, Court & Land Records from 1778)
Rockingham www.co.rockingham.va.us/	H4	20 Oct 1777	**Augusta** Rockingham County; PO Box 1252; 20 E Gay Street; Harrisonburg, VA 22803; Ph. (540) 564-3111 **Details:** (Clerk Circuit Court has Birth Records 1862–1894, Death Records 1890–1894, Marriage, Probate, Court & Land Records from 1778 & Divorce Records from 1833. Some Records burned in 1864)
Russell 	O8	17 Oct 1785	**Washington** Russell County; PO Box 1208; 121 E Main St.; Lebanon, VA 24266; Ph. (276) 889-8000 **Details:** (Clerk Circuit Court has Marriage Records from 1853, Divorce & Court Records from 1786, Probate Records from 1803 & Land Records from 1787)
Salem (Ind. City) www.ci.salem.va.us		1802	**Roanoke** Salem (Ind. City) County; PO Box 869; 114 N Broad St; Salem, VA 24153; Ph. (540) 375-3000 **Details:** (County seat of Roanoke County) (Clerk Circuit Court has Marriage, Probate, Land & Court Records)

County Website	Map Index	Date Created	Parent County or Territory From Which Organized Address/Details
Scott www.scottcountyva.com/	P9	24 Nov 1814	**Lee, Russell, Washington** Scott County; 112 Water Street, Ste 1; Gate City, VA 24251; Ph. (276) 286-6521 **Details:** (Clerk Circuit Court has Birth Records 1853–1895, Death Records 1853–1892, Marriage, Divorce, Probate, Court & Land Records from 1815)
Shenandoah	H4	24 Mar 1772	**Frederick** Shenandoah County; 600 N Main St, Ste 102; Woodstock, VA 22664; Ph. (540) 459-6165, www.shenco@co.shenandoah.va.us **Details:** (Formerly Dunmore County. Name changed to Shenandoah 1 Feb 1778) (Clerk Circuit Court has Marriage, Divorce, Probate, Court & Land Records from 1772)
Smyth www.smythcounty.com	N8	23 Feb 1832	**Washington, Wythe** Smyth County; 121 Bagley Cir, Ste 100; Marion, VA 24354; Ph. (276) 783-3298 **Details:** (Clerk Circuit Court has Marriage, Divorce, Probate, Court & Land Records from 1832)
Southampton	E9	30 Apr 1749	**Isle of Wight, Nansemond** Southampton County; PO Box 400; 26022 Administration Center Dr.; Courtland, VA 23837; Ph. (757) 653-3015 **Details:** (Clerk Circuit Court has Marriage, Court, Land & Probate Records)
Spotsylvania www.spotsylvania.va.us/	F5	2 Nov 1720	**Essex, King and Queen, King William** Spotsylvania County; PO Box 99; 9105 Courthouse Road; Spotslyvania, VA 22553; Ph. (540) 582-7010 **Details:** (Clerk Circuit Court has Marriage & Probate Records from 1722, Birth Records 1864–1895 & 1911–1915, Death Records 1911–1915, Court Records from 1724, Land Records from 1856, Military pension Records 1898–1926 & coroners inquests 1879–1912)
Stafford www.co.stafford.va.us/	E5	1664	**Westmoreland** Stafford County; PO Box 339; 1300 Courthouse Road; Stafford, VA 22555; Ph. (540) 658-8600 **Details:** (Clerk Circuit Court has Marriage Records from 1854, Divorce & Court Records from 1664, Probate & Land Records from 1699)
Staunton (Ind. City)		16 Jan 08	**Augusta** Staunton (Ind. City) County; PO Box 58; 116 W Beverley St; Staunton, VA 24402; Ph. (540) 332-3800 **Details:** (Clerk Circuit Court has Birth Records 1853–1896, Death Records 1853–1892, Marriage, Divorce, Probate, Court & Land Records from 1802)
Suffolk (Ind. City)	D9	1910	**Nansemond** Suffolk (Ind. City) County; PO Box 1858; 441 Market St; Suffolk, VA 23439; Ph. (757) 923-2085 **Details:** (Nansemond County & Suffolk City merged 1 Jan 1974) (Clerk City Court has Marriage, Divorce, Probate & Land Records from 1866)

County Website	Map Index	Date Created	Parent County or Territory From Which Organized Address/Details
Surry www.co.surry.state.va.us	**D8**	1652	**James City** Surry County; PO Box 65; 45 School St; Surry, VA 23883; Ph. (757) 294-5271 **Details:** (Clerk Circuit Court has Birth & Death Records 1853–1896, Marriage Records from 1768, Probate & Land Records from 1652, Court Records from 1671 & Divorce Records)
Sussex	**E9**	27 Feb 1752	**Surry** Sussex County; PO Box 1337; 15088 Courthouse Rd. Rt. 735; Sussex, VA 23884; Ph. (434) 246-5511 **Details:** (Clerk of Circuit Court has Birth & Death Records 1853–1869, Marriage, Land, Probate, & Court Records from 1754)
Taylor www.rootsweb.com/~wvgenweb/		1844	**Barbour, Harrison, Marion, Preston** Taylor County; VA **Details:** (See West Virginia) County lost to West Virginia 1863
Tazewell www.tazewellcounty.org/	**N8**	17 Dec 1799	**Russell, Wythe** Tazewell County; 106 E Main St; Tazewell, VA 24651; Ph. (276) 988-1200 **Details:** (Clerk Circuit Court has Birth & Death Records 1853–1870, Marriage, Probate & Land Records from 1800 & Court Records from 1832)
Tucker www.rootsweb.com/~wvgenweb/		1856	**Randolph** Tucker County; VA **Details:** (See West Virginia) County lost to West Virginia 1863
Tyler www.rootsweb.com/~wvgenweb/		1814	**Ohio** Tyler County; VA **Details:** (See West Virginia) County lost to West Virginia 1863
Upper Norfolk		1637	**New Norfolk** Upper Norfolk County; VA **Details:** (see Nansemond) Name changed to Nansemond 1645
Upshur www.rootsweb.com/~wvgenweb/		1851	**Barbour, Lewis** Upshur County; VA **Details:** (See West Virginia) County lost to West Virginia 1863
Virginia Beach (Ind. City) www.vbgov.com	**B9**	1 Jan 1963	**Princess Anne** Virginia Beach (Ind. City) County; Municipal Ctr Bldg #1; Virginia Beach, VA 23456; Ph. (757) 427-4242 **Details:** (Clerk Circuit Court has Birth & Death Records 1864–1894, Marriage Records from 1749 except Marriage Records 1822–1852 which were destroyed in fire, Divorce Records from 1814, Probate, Court & Land Records from 1691)
Warren www.warrencountyva.net	**G4**	9 Mar 1836	**Frederick, Shenandoah** Warren County; 220 N Commerce, Ste 100; Front Royal, VA 22630; Ph. (540) 636-4600 **Details:** (Clerk Circuit Court has Marriage, Divorce, Probate, Court & Land Records from 1836)
Warrosquoyacke www.rootsweb.com/~vaisleof/		1634	**Original Shire** Warrosquoyacke County; VA **Details:** (see Isle of Wight) Name changed to Isle of Wight 1637

County Website	Map Index	Date Created	Parent County or Territory From Which Organized Address/Details
Warwick www.rootsweb.com/~vawarwic/warwick.htm		1634	**Original Shire** Warwick County; VA **Details:** (see Newport News, Ind. City) Formerly Warwick River. Name changed to Warwick 1642. Incorporated as an independent city 1952. Merged with city of Newport News 1 Jul 1958
Warwick River www.rootsweb.com/~vawarwic/warwick.htm		1634	**Original Shire** Warwick River County; VA **Details:** (Name changed to Warwick 1642; merged with city of Newport News 1 Jul 1958)
Washington www.washcova.com	O9	7 Oct 1776	**Fincastle** Washington County; 205 Academy Dr; Abingdon, VA 24210; Ph. (276) 676-6202 **Details:** (In 1974 nine square miles of Washington County were annexed to the city of Bristol, which is an independent city with its own Clerks office & Records) (Clerk Circuit Court has Marriage, Divorce, Probate, Court & Land Records from 1777)
Wayne www.rootsweb.com/~wvgenweb/		1842	**Cabell** Wayne County; VA **Details:** (See West Virginia) County lost to West Virginia
Waynesboro (Ind. City) www.waynesboro.va.us		Feb 1948	**Augusta** Waynesboro (Ind. City) County; PO Box 1028; 503 W Main St; Waynesboro, VA 22980; Ph. (540) 942-6600 **Details:** (Clerk Circuit Court has Marriage, Divorce, Probate, Court & Land Records from 1948)
Webster www.rootsweb.com/~wvgenweb/		1860	**Braxton, Nicholas, Randolph** Webster County; VA **Details:** (See West Virginia) County lost to West Virginia
Westmoreland www.westmoreland-county.org	D6	5 Jul 1653	**Northumberland** Westmoreland County; PO Box 1000; 111 Polk St; Montross, VA 22520; Ph. (804) 493-0130 **Details:** (Clerk Circuit Court has Birth & Death Records 1855–1895, Marriage Records from 1786, Divorce Records from 1850, Probate, Court & Land Records from 1653)
Wetzel www.rootsweb.com/~wvgenweb/		1846	**Tyler** Wetzel County; VA **Details:** (See West Virginia) County lost to West Virginia 1863
Williamsburg (Ind. City) www.ci.williamsburg.va.us		1884	**James City** Williamsburg (Ind. City) County; 401 Lafayette St; Williamsburg, VA 23185; Ph. (757) 220-6100 **Details:** (Clerk Circuit Court has Marriage, Divorce, Probate & Land Records from 1865 & Court Records from 1953)
Winchester (Ind. City) www.ci.winchester.va.us		1874	**Frederick** Winchester (Ind. City) County; 5 N Caomeron St; Winchester, VA 22601; Ph. (540) 667-1815 **Details:** (City Clerk has Marriage, Probate & Land Records)°
Wirt www.rootsweb.com/~wvgenweb/		1848	**Wood, Jackson** Wirt County; VA **Details:** (See West Virginia) County lost to West Virginia 1863

County	Map	Date	Parent County or Territory From Which Organized
Website	Index	Created	Address/Details

Wise   P8   **16 Feb 1856**

www.wisecounty.org/

Lee, Russell, Scott
Wise County; 206 E Main St; PO Box 570; Wise, VA 24293;
Ph. (276) 328-2321
Details: (Clerk Circuit Court has Marriage & Divorce Records from 1856, Probate & Land Records)

Wood   **1798**

www.rootsweb.com/~wvgenweb/

Harrison
Wood County; VA
Details: (See West Virginia) County lost to West Virginia 1863

Wyoming   **1850**

www.rootsweb.com/~wvgenweb/

Logan
Wyoming County; VA
Details: (See West Virginia) County lost to West Virginia 1863

Wythe   M9   **1 Dec 1789**

www.wytheco.org/

Montgomery
Wythe County; 345 S Fourth St, Ste A; Wytheville, VA 24382;
Ph. (276) 223-6020
Details: (Clerk Circuit Court has Marriage, Divorce, Probate, Court & Land Records from 1790)

Yohogania   **1776**

www.rootsweb.com/~vayohoga/

Augusta District
Yohogania County; VA
Details: (Discontinued & ceded to Pennsylvania 1786)

York   C8   **1634**

www.yorkcounty.gov

Original Shire
York County; PO box 532; 224 Ballard St; Yorktown, VA 23690-0532; Ph. (757) 890-3320
Details: (Formerly Charles River County Name changed to York 1642)
(Clerk Circuit Court has Marriage, Probate, Land & Court Records)

Notes

Washington

Capital: Olympia

Territory: 1853

State: 1889 (42nd)

By and by

In 1775 Spaniards became the first non-natives to touch Washington soil. American fur traders came between 1789 and 1792, claiming much of the Northwest for America. The British explored Puget Sound in 1792, claiming the whole area for England. The first settlement of the area was at Astoria, a trading post established by John Jacob Astor. The British, however, controlled the area for the most part until the 1840's. Spain withdrew its claim in 1819. In 1836, Marcus Whitman established the second settlement near Walla Walla. Once Whitman and other missionaries had come, other settlers soon followed, with the Willamette Valley and Columbia Valley the main points of settlement. In 1846, the present boundary was established between the United States and Canada as Britain withdrew its claim to the area.

The Oregon Territory was created in 1848, including the present states of Oregon, Washington, Idaho, and parts of Montana and Wyoming. Settlers went farther north in 1849 to obtain food and lumber for the California gold fields. The Oregon Donation Act of 1850 guaranteed from 160 to 640 acres of land to those who settled and cultivated land before 1855. Some 30,000 settlers came as a result of this act, which prompted Congress to organize the Washington Territory in 1853. During the Civil War, Washington supplied nearly 1,000 men to the Union forces. Prospectors entered the area in 1860, when gold was discovered near Walla Walla. The Idaho Territory was created in 1863 from parts of eastern Washington Territory. In 1888, the transcontinental railroads reached Washington, bringing with them a new influx of settlers. Washington became the forty-second state in 1889. Seattle was its largest city and the chief supply point for the Alaskan gold rush.

During its peak growth years, settlers from Wisconsin, Minnesota, and other western states came by the thousands. Canadian farmers came to obtain good land at a low price. Most of the newcomers were Canadian, Swedish, Norwegian, English, German, Finnish, Italian, Russian, Danish, and Scottish.

Look for vital records in the following locations:

- **Birth and death records:** State Department of Health, Center for Health Statistics since 1907. Records prior to that are in the offices of county auditors, and usually go back to 1891. City health departments in Seattle, Spokane, Bellingham, and Tacoma also have birth and death records.

- **Marriage and land records:** County Auditors have marriage and land records. County clerks have wills and probate records.

- **Census records:** Territorial and state censuses exist for a few counties for various years prior to 1892. These partial censuses are available at the Washington State Library in Olympia.

Department of Health Center for Health Statistics
PO Box 9709
Olympia, Washington 98507-9709
(360) 236-4300
www.doh.wa.gov/ehsphl/chs/cert.htm

Washington State Archives
1129 Washington Street SE
Olympia, Washington 98504
Mail to: PO Box 40238
Olympia, Washington 98507-9709
(360) 586-1492
www.secstate.wa.gov/archives/

Washington State Library
Point Plaza East
6880 Capitol Blvd Tumwater
Mail: PO Box 42460
Olympia, Washington 98504-2460
(360) 704-5200
www.secstate.wa.gov/library/

National Archives Seattle Branch
6125 Sand Point Way NE
Seattle, Washington 98115-7999

Societies and Repositories

Alexander Hamilton Chapter, WASAR; Bremerton, WA; (360) 692-8478; hbhouston@telebyte.com.

Big Bend Chapter, AHSGR; 202 W 2nd; Ritzville, WA 99169-1704; (509) 659-1537; tjspreng@ritzcom.net.

Big Bend Chapter, Germans from Russia; 202 West 2nd; Ritzville, WA 99169.

Blue Mountain Chapter, AHSGR; 2111 Gemstone; Walla Walla, WA 99362; (509) 529-2253; lfrank@bmi.net.

Blue Mountain Chapter, Germans from Russia; 240 Bald Rd.; Touchet, WA 99360.

Central Washington Chapter, AHSGR; 306 N. Alder; Toppenish, WA 98948; (509) 865-2059; huscoord@wolfenet.com; www.ahsgr.org/wacentra.html.

Chehalis Valley Historical Society; 268-11 Oak Meadows Rd.; Oakville, WA 98568.

Chelan Valley Genealogical Society; PO Box "Y"; Chelan, WA 98816.

Clallam County Genealogical Society; c/o Genealogical Library, Clallam County Museum; Port Angeles, WA 98362.

Clark County Genealogical Society; PO Box 5249; Vancouver, WA 98668-5249.

Columbia Basin Chapter, AHSGR; 1820 West Part St.; Pasco, WA 99301; (509) 545-9423.

Columbia Basin Chapter, Germans from Russia; 1820 W. Park; Pasco, WA 99301.

Douglas County Genealogical Society; PO Box 63; Waterville, WA 98858.

Eastern Washington Genealogical Society; PO Box 1826; Spokane, WA 99210-1826; http://onlinepub.net/ewgs.

Eastside Genealogical Society; PO Box 374; Bellevue, WA 98009.

Ellensburg, Washington Genealogical Group; 507 E. Tacoma St.; Ellensburg, WA 98926.

Genealogical Society of Pierce County; PO Box 189; Dupont, WA 98327-0189.

Grant County Genealogical Society; c/o Ephrata Public Library; 45 Alder St. N.W.; Ephrata, WA 98823.

Grays Harbor Genealogical Society; PO Box 867; Cosmopolis, WA 98537-0867.

Greater Seattle Chapter, AHSGR; 7010 17th Avenue NE; Seattle, WA 98115; (206) 523-4136; www.ahsgr.org/waseattl.html.

Greater Seattle Chapter, Germans from Russia; 7010 17th Ave., NE; Seattle, WA 98115.

Italian Interest Group of the Eastside Genealogical Society; PO Box 374; Bellevue, WA 98009-0374.

Jewish Genealogical Society of Washington; 14222 NE 1st Lane; Bellevue, WA 98007.

Kittitas County Genealogical Society; PO Box 1342; Ellensburg, WA 98926.

Lewis County Genealogical Society; PO Box 782; Chelalis, WA 98532.

Lower Columbia Genealogical Society; PO Box 472; Longview, WA 98632.

Maple Valley Historical Society; PO Box 123; Maple Valley, WA 98038.

Mason County Genealogical Society; PO Box 333; Hoodspont, WA 98548.

NARA's Pacific Alaska Region (Seattle); 6125 Sand Point Way NE; Seattle, WA 98115-7999; (907) 526-6501; seattle.reference@nara.gov; www.archives.gov/facilities/wa/seattle.html.

Northeast Washington Genealogical Society; c/o Colville Public Library; 195 S. Oak; Colville, WA 99114.

Okanogan County Genealogical Society; 263 Old Riverside Hwy.; Omak, WA 98841.

Olympia Genealogical Society; c/o Olympia Public Library; 8th and Franklin; Olympia, WA 98501.

Olympic Peninsula Chapter, AHSGR; 30 Raccoon Rd.; Sequim, WA 98382; (360) 683-1765; marva @olypen.com; www.ahsgr.org/waolypen.html.

Olympic Peninsula Chapter, Germans from Russia; 2551 Fir Ave.; Bremerton, WA 98310.

Pacific County Genealogical Society; 1312 265th PL; Ocean Park, WA 98640-4230.

Rainier Chapter, AHSGR; 1007 No. Meridian; Puyallup, WA 98371; (253) 845-0136; www.ahsgr.org/warainer.html.

Rainier Chapter, Germans from Russia; 1007 N. Meridian; Puyallup, WA 98371-4408.

Redmond Historical Society; The Old Redmond Schoolhouse; 16600 NE 80 St., Rm. 1; Redmond, WA 98052.

Seattle Chapter, Sons of the American Revolution; Seattle, WA; (206) 242-6323; emanders@uswest.net.

Seattle Genealogical Society; 8511 15 Ave. NE; Seattle, WA 98115.

Skagit Valley Genealogical Society; PO Box 715; Conway, WA 98238.

Sno-Isle Genealogical Society; PO Box 63; Edmonds, WA 98020.

Sons of the American Revolution, Washington Society; 12233 9th Ave., NW.; Seattle, WA 98177.

South King County Genealogical Society; PO Box 3174; Kent, WA 98032.

South Pierce County Historical Society; PO Box 1966; Eatonville, WA 98328.

Spokane Chapter #1, Sons of the American Revolution; Millwood, WA; (509) 924-9990; Wmpeachee@aol.com.

State Capitol Historical Association; 211 W. 21st Ave.; Olympia, WA 98501.

Stillaguamish Valley Genealogical Society of North Snohomish County; PO Box 34; Arlington, WA 98223.

Tacoma-Pierce County Genealogical Society; PO Box 1952; Tacoma, WA 98401.

Tri-City Genealogical Society; PO Box 1410; Richland, WA 99352-1410.

Walla Walla Valley Genealogical Society; PO Box 115; Walla Walla, WA 99362-0115.

Washington State Archives; PO BOX 40238; Olympia, WA 98504-0238; (360) 586-1492; archives@secstate.wa.gov; www.secstate.wa.gov/archives.

Washington State Genealogical Society; Box 1422; Olympia, WA 98507-1422; www.rootsweb.com/~wasgs.

Washington State Historical Society Library; State Historical Bldg.; 315 N. Stadium Way; Tacoma, WA 98403; www.wshs.org.

Washington State Historical Society; 1911 Pacific Avenue; Tacoma, WA 98402; www.wshs.org.

Washington State Library; PO Box 42460; Olympia, WA 98504-2460; (360) 704-5200; askalibrarian@secstate.wa.gov; www.statelib.wa.gov.

Wenatchee Area Genealogical Society; 133 S. Mission St.; PO Box 5280; Wenatchee, WA 98807-5280.

Whatcom Genealogical Society; PO Box 1493; Bellingham, WA 98227-1493.

Whitman County Genealogical Society; PO Box 393; Pullman, WA 99163; bluejean@wsu.edu; www.completebbs.com/simonsen/wcgsindex.html.

Willapa Harbor Genealogical Society; c/o Raymond Public Library; 507 Duryea St.; Raymond, WA 98577.

Yakima Valley Genealogical Society; PO Box 445; Yakima, WA 98907.

Bibliography and Record Sources

General

Abbott, Newton Carl. *The Evolution of Washington Counties.* S.l.: Yakima Valley Genealogical Society & Klickitat County Historical Society, 1978.

Avery, Mary Williamson. *Washington: A History of the Evergreen State.* Seattle: University of Washington Press, 1967.

Boyd, Robert. *History of the Synod of Washington of the Presbyterian Church in the United States of America 1835–1909.* Seattle: The Synod, 1910.

Brulotte, Frieda Eichler. *Germans from Russia in the Yakima Valley, Prior to 1940.* Yakima, Washington: The Society, 1990.

Clubb, Mrs. Robert Earl. *Family Records of Washington Pioneers Prior to 1891.* Daughters of the American Revolution of the State of Washington. Salt Lake City: Genealogical Society of Utah, 1960. Microfilm.

Dahlie, Jorgen. *A Social History of Scandinavian Immigration, Washington State, 1895–1910.* New York: Arno Press, 1980.

Evans, Elwood. *History of the Pacific Northwest: Oregon and Washington; Embracing an Account of the Original Discoveries on the Pacific Coast of North America, and a Description of the Conquest, Settlement and Subjugation of the Original Territory of Oregon; also Interesting Biographies of the Earliest Settlers.* 2 vols. Portland, Oregon: North Pacific History Co., 1889.

Genealogical Resources in Washington State: A Guide to Genealogical Records Held at Repositories, Government Agencies and Archives. Olympia, Washington: Secretary of State, Division of Archives and Records Management, 1983.

Hines, Harvey K. *An Illustrated History of the State of Washington: Containing . . . Biographical Mention of . . . its Pioneers and Prominent Citizens.* Chicago: Lewis Pub. Co., 1893.

Hunt, Herbert. *Washington West of the Cascades: Historical and Descriptive, the Explorers, the Indians, the Modern.* Tucson, Arizona: W. C. Cox, 1974.

Missionary History of the Pacific Northwest: Containing the Wonderful Story of Jason Lee, with Sketches of Many of his Co-Laborers all Illustrating Life on the Plains and in the Mountains in Pioneer Days. Washington, D.C.: Library of Congress, 1990.

Historical Records of Washington State: Records and Papers Held at Repositories. Olympia, Washington: Washington State Historical Records Advisory Board, 1981.

Howell, Erle. *Methodisim in the Northwest.* Nashville, Tennessee: Pacific Northwest Conference Historical Society, 1966.

Kirkham, E. Kay. *An Index to Some of the Bibles and Family Records of the United States.* vol. 2. Logan, Utah: Everton Publishers, 1984.

Miller, Frances Caldwell. *Celebrating the History of the Pioneer Families of Washington, 1853–1889.* Wenatchee, Washington: Native Daughters of Washington Territorial Pioneers, 1989.

Newton Carl Abbott and Fred E. Carver. *The Evolution of Washington Counties.* n.p.: Yakima Valley Genealogical Society & Klickitat County Historical Society, 1978.

Osborn-Ryan, Sharon E. *Cumulative Baptism Index to the Catholic Church Records of the Pacific Northwest.* S.l.: Oregon Heritage Press, 1999.

Pollard, Lancaster. *A History of Washington.* 4 vols. New York: American Historical Society, 1937.

Preston, Ralph N. *Early Washington: Overland Stage Routes, Old Military Roads, Indian Battle Grounds, Old Forts, Old Gold Mines.* Corvallis, Oregon: Western Guide Publishers, 1974.

Prosch, Charles. *Reminiscences of Washington Territory.* Fairfield, Washington: Ye Galleon Press, 1969.

Priestley, Marilyn. *Comprehensive Guide to the Manuscripts Collection and to the Personal Papers in the University Archives.* Seattle, Washington: The Library, 1980.

Schoenberg, Wilfred P. *A History of the Catholic Church in the Pacific Northwest, 1743–1983.* Washington, D.C.: Pastoral Press, 1987.

Sketches of Washingtonians. Seattle: W. C. Wolfe & Co., 1906.

Swart, Shirley, comp. *Index to Washington State Daughters of the American Revolution.* Yakima, Washington: Yakima Valley Genealogical Society, 1983.

Tacoma-Pierce County Genealogical Society. *Bibliography of Washington State Historical Society Library.* 3 vols. Tacoma, Washington: The Society, 1986.

The Dictionary Catalog of the Pacific Northwest Collection of the University of Washington. 6 vols. Boston: G. K. Hall and Co., 1972.

Washington Research Outline. Series U.S.-States, no. 47. Salt Lake City: Family History Library, 1988.

Washington State Historical Records and Archives Projects. *Historical Records of Washington State: Records and Papers held at Repositories.* Olympia, Washington: Washington State Historical Records Advisory Board, 1981.

Washington State Union List of Newspapers: On Microfilm. Olympia, Washington: Washington State Library, 1991. 11 microfiche.

Washington West of the Cascades. 3 vols. Chicago: S. J. Clarke, 1917.

Who's Who in Washington State: A Compilation of Biographical Sketches of Men and Women Prominent in the Affairs of Washington State. Seattle: H. Allen Pub., 1927.

Atlases, Maps and Gazetteers

Abbott, Newton Carl, Fred E. Carver, and J. W. Helm, comp. *The Evolution of Washington Counties.* Yakima, Washington: Yakima Valley Genealogical Society and Klickitat County Historical Society, 1978.

Landes, Henry. *A Geographic Dictionary of Washington.* Washington Geological Survey. Bulletin no. 17. Olympic, Washington: F. M. Lamborn, 1917.

Meany, Edmond S. *Origin of Washington Geographic Names.* 1923. Reprint. Detroit: Gale Research Co., 1968.

Phillips, James W. *Washington State Place Names.* Seattle: University of Washington Press, 1971.

Preston, Ralph N. *Early Washington: Overland Stage Routes, Old Military Roads, Indian Battle Grounds, Old Forts, Old Gold Miners.* Corvallis, Oregon: Western Guide Publishers, 1974. Reprinted as *Early Washington Atlas.* 2nd ed. Binford & Mort Publishers, 1974.

R. L. Polk & Co. Oregon & Washington Gazetteer and Business Directory, 1909–1910. Seattle: R. L. Polk, 1909.

Scott, James R. *Washington: A Centennial Atlas.* Bellingham: Western Washington University, 1989.

Scott, James R. and Roland L. DeLorme. *Historical Atlas of Washington.* Norman: University of Oklahoma Press, 1988.

Washington Atlas and Gazetteer. 3rd ed. Freeport, Maine: DeLorme Mapping Co., 1996.

Censuses

Available Census Records and Census Substitutes

Federal Census 1860, 1870, 1880, 1900, 1910, 1920, 1930

Federal Mortality Schedules 1850, 1860, 1870, 1880

Union Veterans and Widows 1890

State/Territorial Census 1857–1892, 1872–1888

Dollarhide, William. *The Census Book: A Genealogist's Guide to Federal Census Facts, Schedules and Indexes.* Bountiful, Utah: Heritage Quest, 1999.

Lainhart, Ann S. *State Census Records.* Baltimore: Genealogical Publishing Co., Inc., 1992.

Kemp, Thomas Jay. *The American Census Handbook.* Wilmington, Delaware: Scholarly Resources, Inc., 2001

Szucs, Loretto Dennis and Matthew Wright. *Finding Answers in U.S. Census Records.* Ancestry Publishing, 2001.

Thorndale, William and William Dollarhide. *Map Guide to the U.S. Federal Census, 1790–1920.* Baltimore: Genealogical Publishing Co., 1987.

United States. Bureau of Indian Affairs. Portland Area Office. *Tribal Census Information, 1877–1952.* Microfilm of originals at the Federal Record Center, Seattle, Washington. Salt Lake City: Filmed by the Genealogical Society of Utah, 1978. 2 microfilm.

Washington. Secretary of State. *Washington Territorial Census Rolls, 1857–1892.* Olympia, Washington: Washington State Archives, 1987. Microfilm, 20 rolls.

Court Records, Probate and Wills

Frontier Justice Records Project (Washington state). *Frontier Justice: Guide to the Court Records of Washington Territory, 1853–1889.* 2 vols. Olympia, Washington: National Historical Publications and Records Commission, 1987.

Hopkins, Pat. *A Guide to the Records of Washington Territorial Supreme Court, 1853–1889.* Olympia, Washington: Washington State Archives, 1983.

United States. Bureau of Indian Affairs. Portland Area Office. *Heirship and Probate Information, 1887–1952.* Microfilm of originals at the Federal Record Center, Seattle, Washington. Salt Lake City: Filmed by the Genealogical Society of Utah, 1978. Microfilm, 10 rolls.

Immigration

United States. District Court (Washington: Eastern District). *Declaration of Intention, 1890–1972; Petition for Naturalization, 1907–1 950; Repatriations, 1940–1942; Application for Citizenship, 1879–1906; Indexes, 1890–1947.* Microfilm of originals in the National Archives, Seattle Branch in Seattle, Washington. Salt Lake City: Filmed by the Genealogical Society of Utah, 1988. Microfilm, 26 rolls.

United States. District Court (Washington: Western District: Southern Division). *Naturalization Indexes, 1896–1953.* Microfilm of originals at the Archives Branch of the Federal Archives and Records Center at Seattle, Washington. Salt Lake City: Filmed by the Genealogical Society of Utah, 1984. Microfilm, 2 rolls.

United States. Immigration and Naturalization Service. *Passenger and Crew Lists of Vessels Arriving At Seattle, Washington, 1890– 1921.* Washington, D.C.: National Archives Records Service, 1957. Microfilm, multiple rolls.

United States. Immigration and Naturalization Service. *Crew Lists of Vessels Arriving at Seattle, Washington, 1903–1917.* Washington, D.C.: The National Archives, 1988. Microfilm, 15 rolls.

Land

United States. Bureau of Indian Affairs. Tulalip Agency. *Allotment and Land Records, 1883–1932.* Microfilm of original records in the Federal Record Center, Seattle, Washington. Salt Lake City: Filmed by the Genealogical Society of Utah, 1978. 4 microfilm.

United States. General Land Office. *Abstracts of Washington Donation Land Claims, 1855–1902.* Washington, D.C.: The National Archives, 1951. Microfilm, multiple rolls.

United States. General Land Office. *Oregon and Washington Donation Land Files, 1851–1903.* Washington, D.C.: The National Archives, 1970. Microfilm, 108 rolls.

United States. Land Office. *Donation Land Claims by Orphans in Oregon and Washington, 1867–1873.* Microfilm of originals in the National Archives Branch in Seattle, Washington. Salt Lake City: Filmed by the Genealogical Society of Utah, 1989.

United States. Land Office (Washington). *Land records.* Microfilm of Originals in the National Archives Pacific Northwest Region Office in Seattle, Washington. Salt Lake City: Filmed by the Genealogical Society of Utah, 1989. Microfilm 72 rolls.

Washington Territory Donation Land Claims: An Abstract of Information in the Land Claim Papers of Persons Who Settled in Washington Territory Before 1856. Seattle: Seattle Genealogical Society, 1980

Waugh, Kathleen. *Index to Mining Surveys, 1883–1964.* Olympia, Washington: K. Waugh, 1985.

Military

Field, Virgil F. *Washington National Guard Pamphlet: The Official History of the Washington National Guard.* 7 vols. in 3. Tacoma: Office of the Adjutant General, 1961.

Pompey, Sherman Lee. *Burial List of the Members of the 1st Washington Territory Infantry.* Kingsburg, California: Pacific Specialties, 1972.

Pompey, Sherman Lee. *Civil War Veteran Burials from the Arizona Territory, Nebraska, Nevada, New Mexico, Oregon, Utah and the Washington Territory.* Salt Lake City: Filmed by the Genealogical Society of Utah, 1975. Microfilm.

Taylor, John. *Indian War Muster Rolls, 1855–1856.* Microfilm of originals in the Washington State Archives in Olympia, Washington. Salt Lake City: Filmed by the Genealogical Society of Utah, 1991. Microfilm.

United States. Adjutant General's Office. *Index to Compiled Service Records of Volunteer Union Soldiers Who Served in Organizations from the Territory of Washington.* Washington, D.C.: The National Archives, 1964. Microfilm.

United States. Army. *Registers of Enlistments in the United States Army, 1798–1914.* Washington, D.C.: National Archives, 1956. Microfilm, Multiple rolls.

United States. Selective Service System. *Washington World War I Selective Service System Draft Registration Cards, 1917–1918.* National Archives Microfilm Publications, M1509. Washington, D.C.: National Archives, 1987–1988.

United States. Veterans Administration. *Pension Index Files, Indian Wars, 1892–1926.* Washington: Veterans' Administration, 1959. Microfilm, multiple rolls.

Vital and Cemetery

A Directory of Cemeteries and Funeral Homes in Washington State. Washington Interment Association and the Washington State Funeral Directors Association. Orting, Washington: Heritage Quest, 1990.

Carter, John D., ed. *Washington's First Marriages of the Thirty-Nine Counties.* Spokane: Eastern Washington Genealogical Society, 1986

Cemetery Records of Washington. 6 vols. Salt Lake City: Genealogical Society of Utah. 1957–1960.

Guide to Public Vital Statistics Records in Washington. Seattle, Washington: Washington Historical Records Survey, 1941.

United States. Bureau of Indian Affairs. Northern Idaho Agency. *Agency Records, 1887–1947.* Salt Lake City: Filmed by the Genealogical Society of Utah, 1979. 7 microfilm rolls.

Washington Bureau of Vital Statistics. *Index to Birth Certificates, 1907–1959.* Olympia, Washington: Bureau of Vital Statistics, 1960.

Washington Bureau of Vital Statistics. *Index to Death Certificates, 1907–1959, 1960–1979*. Olympia, Washington: Bureau of Vital Statistics, 1954–1960.

Washington. Department of Health. Bureau of Vital Statistics. *Index to Delayed Birth Records, 1900–1980*. Olympia, Washington: Bureau of Vital Statistics, 1996. 12 microfiche.

County Website	Map Index	Date Created	Parent County or Territory From Which Organized Address/Details
Adams www.co.adams.wa.us/	**D7**	**28 Nov 1883**	**Whitman** Adams County; 210 W Broadway Ave; Ritzville, WA 99169-1860; Ph. (509) 659-325 **Details:** (County Auditor has Birth & Death Records to 1907 & Marriage Records; County Clerk has Divorce & Probate Records; County Assessor has Land Records)
Asotin www.palouse.org/asotin.htm	**A9**	**27 Oct 1883**	**Garfield** Asotin County; PO Box 159; Asotin, WA 99402-0159; Ph. (509) 243-418 **Details:** (County Auditor has Birth & Marriage Records from 1891 & Death Records 1891–1907; County Clerk has Divorce & Probate Records; County Assessor has Land Records from 1891)
Benton www.co.benton.wa.us/	**G9**	**8 Mar 1905**	**Yakima, Klickitat** Benton County; 600 Market St; Prosser, WA 99350-0190; Ph. (509) 786-562 **Details:** (County Auditor has Birth Records 1905–1907 & Marriage Records from 1905; County Clerk has Divorce, Probate & Court Records; County Assessor has Land Records)
Chehalis		**14 Apr 1854**	**Thurston** Chehalis County; WA **Details:** (see Grays Harbor) Name changed to Grays Harbor 15 Mar 1915
Chelan www.co.chelan.wa.us/	**I5**	**13 Mar 1899**	**Kittitas, Okanogan** Chelan County; 350 Douglas St; Wenatchee, WA 98801; Ph. (509) 667-638 **Details:** (County Auditor has Birth & Death Records 1900–1907 & Marriage Records from 1900; City Clerk has Burial Records; County Clerk has Divorce, Probate & Court Records)
Clallam www.clallam.net/	**Q4**	**26 Apr 1854**	**Jefferson** Clallam County; 223 E 4th St; PO Box 863; Port Angeles, WA 98362-3025; Ph. (360) 417-250 **Details:** (County Auditor has Marriage & Land Records; County Clerk has Probate Records)
Clark www.co.clark.wa.us/	**M11**	**27 Jun 1844**	**Original county** Clark County; 1200 Franklin St; Vancouver, WA 98660; Ph. (360) 397-229 **Details:** (Formerly Vancouver County. Name changed to Clark 3 Sep 1849) (County Auditor has Birth & Death Records 1890–1906, Marriage Records from 1890 & Land Records from 1850; County Clerk has Divorce, Probate & Court Records from 1890)

County Website	Map Index	Date Created	Parent County or Territory From Which Organized Address/Details
Columbia www.columbiaco.com/	C9	11 Nov 1875	**Walla Walla** Columbia County; 341 E Main St; Dayton, WA 99328-1361; Ph. (509) 382-432 **Details:** (County Clerk has Probate, Divorce & Court Records from 1891; County Auditor has Birth & Death Records 1891–1906, Marriage Records from 1876, Land Records from 1864 & Military Discharge Records)
Cowlitz www.co.cowlitz.wa.us/	N10	21 Apr 1854	**Lewis** Cowlitz County; 207 4th Ave N; Kelso, WA 98626-1798; Ph. (360) 577-301 **Details:** (County Auditor has Marriage Records from 1867, Death Records 1891–1907 & Land Records; County Clerk has Divorce, Probate & Court Records from 1874, Naturalization & adoption Records from 1869)
Douglas www.douglascountywa.net/	G5	28 Nov 1883	**Lincoln** Douglas County; 213 S Rainier; Waterville, WA 98858; Ph. (509) 745-852 **Details:** (County Auditor has Birth Records to 1907, Burial Records to 1909, Land Records to 1925, Marriage, Death, Divorce, Probate & Court Records)
Ferry www.wa.gov/ferry/	E3	18 Feb 1899	**Stevens** Ferry County; 350 E Delaware; PO Box 302; Republic, WA 99166; Ph. (509) 775-523 **Details:** (County Clerk has Divorce, Probate & Court Records from 1899)
Franklin www.co.franklin.wa.us/	E9	28 Nov 1883	**Whitman** Franklin County; 1016 N 4th Ave; Pasco, WA 99301; Ph. (509) 545-352 **Details:** (County Auditor has Birth, Death & Burial Records 1891–1910, Marriage Records from 1891 & Land Records; County Clerk has Divorce, Probate & Court Records from 1891)
Garfield www.palouse.org/garfield.htm	B9	29 Nov 1881	**Columbia** Garfield County; PO Box 915; Pomeroy, WA 99347-0915; Ph. (509) 843-373 **Details:** (County Auditor has Birth & Death Records 1891–1907, Marriage & Land Records from 1891 & Burial Records 1891–1918; County Clerk has Divorce, Probate & Court Records from 1882)
Grant www.grantcounty-wa.com/	F7	24 Feb 1909	**Douglas** Grant County; 35 C St NW; PO Box 37; Ephrata, WA 98823-0037; Ph. (509) 754-201 **Details:** (County Auditor has Marriage & Land Records from 1909; County Clerk has Divorce, Probate & Court Records)
Grays Harbor www.co.grays-harbor.wa.us/	P7	14 Apr 1854	**Thurston** Grays Harbor County; 102 W Broadway Rm 203; Montesano, WA 98563; Ph. (360) 249-384 **Details:** (Formerly Chehalis County. Name changed to Grays Harbor 15 Mar 1915) (County Clerk has Probate, Divorce & Court Records from 1860; County Auditor has Marriage Records from 1891; County Assessor has Land Records from 1855; County Health Department has Birth & Death Records)

Washington

County Website	Map Index	Date Created	Parent County or Territory From Which Organized Address/Details
Island www.islandcounty.net/	M4	6 Jan 1853	**Thurston** Island County; NE 6th & Main St; PO Box 5000; Coupeville, WA 98239-5000; Ph. (360) 679-735 **Details:** (County Auditor has Birth & Death Records 1870–1907, Marriage Records from 1855 & Land Records from 1853; County Clerk has Divorce, Probate & Court Records)
Jefferson www.co.jefferson.wa.us/	P6	22 Dec 1852	**Thurston, Lewis** Jefferson County; 1820 Jefferson St; PO Box 1220; Port Townsend, WA 98368-0920; Ph. (360) 385-912 **Details:** (County Clerk has Divorce Records from 1886, Probate Records from 1891 & Court Records from 1890; County Auditor has Birth & Death Records 1891–1907 & Marriage Records from 1853)
King www.metrokc.gov/	L6	22 Dec 1852	**Thurston** King County; 516 3rd Ave; Seattle, WA 98104; Ph. (206) 296-102 **Details:** (Records & Elections Divorce, Records Secretary has Birth, Marriage, Death & Land Records from 1853; Clerk Superior Court has Divorce, Probate & Court Records)
Kitsap www.kitsapgov.com/	N6	16 Jan 1857	**King, Jefferson** Kitsap County; 614 Division St; Port Orchard, WA 98366; Ph. (360) 337-716 **Details:** (Formerly Slaughter County. Name changed to Kitsap 13 Jul 1857) (County Auditor has Birth Records 1891–1907, Death Records 1892–1907 & Marriage Records from 1892; County Clerk has Divorce & Court Records from 1888, Probate & adoption Records from 1861 & Land Records from 1857)
Kittitas www.co.kittitas.wa.us/	I7	24 Nov 1883	**Yakima** Kittitas County; 205 W 5th Ave; Ellensburg, WA 98926; Ph. (509) 962-762 **Details:** (County Auditor has Birth & Death Records 1891–1907, Marriage Records from 1884 & Land Records from 1882; County Clerk has Divorce, Probate & Court Records from 1890's)
Klickitat http://klickitatcounty.org/	J11	20 Dec 1859	**Skamania** Klickitat County; 205 S Columbus Ave Rm 204; Goldendale, WA 98620; Ph. (509) 773-455 **Details:** (County Clerk has Divorce, Probate & Court Records; County Auditor has Marriage Records)
Lewis www.co.lewis.wa.us/	M9	21 Dec 1845	**Original county** Lewis County; 351 NW North St; Chehalis, WA 98532; Ph. (360) 740-270 **Details:** (County Auditor has Birth & Death Records 1891–1907 & Marriage Records from 1850; County Clerk has Divorce, Probate & Court Records from 1870's)
Lincoln www.rootsweb.com/~walincol/lincoln.htm	E6	24 Nov 1883	**Spokane** Lincoln County; 450 Logan St; PO Box 68; Davenport, WA 99122; Ph. (509) 725-140 **Details:** (County Auditor has Birth & Death Records 1891–1907, Marriage Records from 1884, & Land Records from 1883; County Clerk has Naturalization Records 1886–1924, Divorce, Probate, & Court Records from 1907)

County Website	Map Index	Date Created	Parent County or Territory From Which Organized Address/Details
Mason www.co.mason.wa.us/	O7	**13 Mar 1854**	**Thurston** Mason County; 411 N 5th; PO Box 340; Shelton, WA 98584; Ph. (360) 427-967 **Details:** (Formerly Sawamish County. Name changed to Mason 8 Jan 1864) (County Auditor has Marriage Records from 1892, Death Records 1891–1906 & Land Records from 1850's; County Clerk has Divorce, Probate & Court Records)
Okanogan www.okanogancounty.org/	H3	**2 Feb 1888**	**Stevens** Okanogan County; 149 3rd N; PO Box 72; Okanogan, WA 98840; Ph. (509) 422-727 **Details:** (County Auditor has Birth & Death Records 1891–1908, Marriage & Land Records from 1891 & patents from 1892; County Clerk has Divorce, Probate & Court Records from 1896)
Pacific www.co.pacific.wa.us/	P9	**4 Feb 1851**	**Lewis** Pacific County; 300 Memorial Ave; PO Box 67; South Bend, WA 98586-0067; Ph. (360) 875-932 **Details:** (County Auditor has Birth & Death Records 1891–1905 & Marriage Records from 1868; County Clerk has Divorce, Probate & Court Records; County Assessor has Land Records)
Pend Oreille www.usgennet.org/usa/wa/county/pendoreille/	B3	**1 Mar 1911**	**Stevens** Pend Oreille County; 625 W 4th; PO Box 5020; Newport, WA 99156-5000; Ph. (509) 447-243 **Details:** (County Auditor has Birth, Marriage & Land Records from 1911; County Clerk has Divorce, Probate & Court Records from 1911)
Pierce www.co.pierce.wa.us/PC/	L8	**22 Dec 1852**	**Thurston** Pierce County; 930 Tacoma Ave S; Tacoma, WA 98402; Ph. (253) 798-745 **Details:** (County Auditor has Marriage & Land Records; County Clerk has Divorce, Probate & Court Records from 1890 & adoptions)
San Juan www.co.san-juan.wa.us/	O4	**31 Oct 1873**	**Whatcom** San Juan County; 350 Court St #7; Friday Harbor, WA 98250-1249; Ph. (360) 378-216 **Details:** (County Clerk has Divorce, Probate & Court Records; County Auditor has Birth Records 1892–1907, Death Records 1890–1907 & Marriage Records from 1878)
Sawamish		**13 Mar 1854**	**Thurston** Sawamish County; WA **Details:** (see Mason) Name changed to Mason 8 Jan 1864
Shoshone		**1858**	**Walla Walla** Shoshone County; WA **Details:** Name changed in 1860 to Spokane County (old)
Skagit www.skagitcounty.net/index.htm	K4	**28 Nov 1883**	**Whatcom** Skagit County; 700 S 2nd St; PO Box 837; Mount Vernon, WA 98273; Ph. (360) 336-944 **Details:** (County Auditor has Birth & Death Records 1891–1907, Marriage Records from 1884 & Land Records from 1872; County Clerk has Divorce, Probate & Court Records from 1870)

County Website	Map Index	Date Created	Parent County or Territory From Which Organized Address/Details
Skamania Future website at http://usgenweb.com/	L10	9 Mar 1854	**Clark** Skamania County; 240 Vancouver Ave; Stevenson, WA 98648-0790; Ph. (509) 427-943 **Details:** (County Auditor has Land Records; County Clerk has Marriage, Divorce, Probate & Court Records from 1856)
Slaughter		16 Jan 1857	**King, Jefferson** Slaughter County; WA **Details:** (see Kitsap) Name changed to Kitsap 13 Jul 1857
Snohomish www.County.snohomish.wa.us/	L5	14 Jan 1861	**Island** Snohomish County; 3000 Rockefeller Ave MS 605; Everett, WA 98201-4046; Ph. (425) 388-358 **Details:** (County Auditor has Birth & Death Records 1891–1907 & Marriage Records from 1891; County Clerk has Divorce, Probate & Court Records)
Spokane www.spokanecounty.org/	B6	29 Jan 1858	**Walla Walla** Spokane County; W 1116 Broadway; Spokane, WA 99260; Ph. (509) 477-224 **Details:** (Spokane County was organized in 1858 from Walla Walla, then disorganized & reorganized in 1879 from Stevens County) (County Auditor has Birth & Death Records 1890–1907, Marriage Records from 1890 & Land Records; County Clerk has Divorce, Probate & Court Records)
Spokane (old)		1860	**Walla Walla** Spokane County (old); WA **Details:** County Terminated in 1864
Stevens www.co.stevens.wa.us/	C4	20 Jan 1863	**Walla Walla** Stevens County; 215 S Oak St Rm 206; Colville, WA 99114; Ph. (509) 684-757 **Details:** (County Auditor has Birth & Death Records 1891–1907, Marriage Records from 1861 & Land Records from 1883; County Clerk has Probate, Divorce & Court Records from 1889)
Thurston www.co.thurston.wa.us/	N8	12 Jan 1852	**Lewis** Thurston County; 2000 Lakeridge Dr SW; Olympia, WA 98502; Ph. (360) 786-543 **Details:** (County Auditor has Birth & Death Records 1891–1907 & Marriage Records from 1891; County Clerk has Divorce, Probate & Court Records)
Vancouver		27 Jun 1844	**Original county** Vancouver County; WA **Details:** (see Clark) Name changed to Clark 3 Sep 1849
Wahkiakum www.cwcog.org/	O10	24 Apr 1854	**Pacific** Wahkiakum County; 64 Main St; PO Box 116; Cathlamet, WA 98612; Ph. (360) 795-355 **Details:** (County Auditor has Birth Records 1891–1907 & Marriage Records from 1891; County Clerk has Burial, Divorce, Probate, Court & Land Records from 1868)

County	Map	Date	Parent County or Territory From Which Organized
Website	Index	Created	Address/Details

Walla Walla E9

www.co.walla-walla.wa.us/

25 Apr 1854

Clark

Walla Walla County; 315 West Main St; PO Box 836; Walla Walla, WA 99362-0259; Ph. (509)   527-322

Details: (County Clerk has Divorce, Probate & Court Records from 1860)

Whatcom L3

www.co.whatcom.wa.us/

9 Mar 1854

Island

Whatcom County; 311 Grand Ave; PO Box 1144; Bellingham, WA 98227; Ph. (360)   676-677

Details: (County Auditor has Birth & Death Records 1891–1907, Marriage Records from 1869 & Land Records; County Clerk has Divorce, Probate & Court Records)

Whitman B8

www.palouse.org/whitman.htm

29 Nov 1871

Stevens

Whitman County; N 404 Main St; Box 390; Colfax, WA 99111-2031; Ph. (509)   397-624

Details: (County Clerk has Marriage Records 1872–1891, Probate Records from 1870, Divorce & Court Records from 1864 & Naturalization Records 1862–1942; County Auditor has Birth & Death Records 1891–1907 & Land Records)

Yakima J9

http://co.yakima.wa.us/

21 Jan 1865

Walla Walla

Yakima County; 128 N 2nd St; Yakima, WA 98901; Ph. (509)   574-143

Details: (County Auditor had Birth & Death Records 1891–1907, Marriage Records from 1880 & Land Records; County Clerk has Probate, Divorce & Court Records from 1882)

Notes

West Virginia

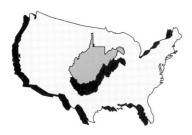

Capital: Charleston

State: 1863 (35th)

Mountaineers are always free

Fur traders entered western Virginia by the mid-1600's, with the first expedition across the Blue Ridge and Allegheny mountains occurring in 1671. In 1712, Baron de Graffenreid visited the eastern Panhandle to find land for Swiss families. In 1730, Virginia began to grant land to settlers. Many of these were immigrants who were promised religious freedom. Welsh, German, and Scotch-Irish settlers from Pennsylvania built the first settlements by 1734. Other early settlers came from Maryland to create Berkeley and Jefferson counties.

During the French and Indian War, attacks on settlers were so common that many fled back to the more populated areas of Virginia. A series of forts were built, but the attacks continued until about 1758. Over the next decades, battles with the Native Tribes of the region continued to be a problem for settlers, but the population and prosperity of the region continued to grow.

In 1775, the West Augusta District was established by Virginia, which included all of present West Virginia and part of western Pennsylvania. Most of the northern part of the county was ceded to Pennsylvania in 1779 in exchange for Pennsylvania relinquishing its claims to the rest of the county.

When Virginia seceded from the Union in 1861, western counties objected. Fifty western counties united to form "The Restored Government of Virginia" and petitioned Congress for re-admittance to the Union. The state of West Virginia was admitted to the Union in 1863, after several Union victories in the area. During the Civil War, West Virginia had about 32,000 soldiers in the Union army and 9,000 in the Confederate army. In the 1870's industrial expansion in West Virginia attracted immigrants from the southern states and European immigrants, especially Italians, Poles, Hungarians, Austrians, English, Germans, Greeks, Russians, and Czechs.

Look for vital records in the following locations:

- **Birth and death records:** Contact the Division of Vital Statistics of the State Department of Health in Charleston, West Virginia. Statewide registration of births and deaths began in 1917.
- **Marriage and divorce records:** Although most state records were destroyed in a 1921 fire, most counties have records from 1853. Some counties also have marriage records from 1870. County clerks of individual circuit courts keep divorce records.
- **Probate records:** Contact individual county court administrations. These records are found in deed books and court order books.
- **Naturalization records:** Naturalization proceedings were recorded in the minutes and dockets of the courts until 1906. After 1929, only federal courts handled naturalizations.
- **Census records**: State censuses were taken in some counties between 1782 and 1785, and have been published along with tax records.

Vital Registration Office
Room 165
350 Capitol Street
Charleston, WV 25301-3701
(304) 558-2931; Fax: (304) 558-8001
www.wvdhhr.org/bph/oehp/hsc/vr/birtcert.htm

Archives and History Library
The Cultural Center
1900 Kanawha Boulevard, E.
Charleston, WV 25305-0300
www.wvculture.org/history/index.html

Societies and Repositories

Allegheny Regional Family History Society; PO Box 1804; Elkins, WV 26241; www.swcp.com/~dhickman.

Berkelely County Genealogical-Historical Society; PO Box 1624; Martinsburg, WV 25401.

Boone County, West Virginia Genealogical Society; PO Box 295; Madison, WV 25130.

Brooke County Genealogical Society, Inc.; PO Box 144; Beech Bottom, WV 26030.

Doddridge County Historical Society; Box 23; West Union, WV 26456.

Genealogical Society of Fayette and Raleigh Counties, Inc.; PO Box 68; Oak Hill, WV 25901-0068.

Gilmer County Historical Society; 706 Mineral Rd.; Glenville, WV 26351.

Hacker's Creek Pioneer Desc.; 23 Abbotts Run Rd.; Horner, WV 26372; hcpd@access.mountain.net.

Hardy County Genealogical-Historical Society; Moorefield, WV 26836.

Jackson County Historical Society; PO Box 22; Ripley, WV 25271.

Kanawha Valley Genealogical Society; PO Box 8555; South Charleston, WV 25303.

KYOWVA Genealogical Society; PO Box 1254; Huntington, WV 25715.

Lincoln County Genealogical Society; 7999 Lynn Ave.; Hamlin, WV 25523.

Logan County Genealogical Society; PO Box 1959; Logan, WV 25601.

Marion County Genealogical Club, Inc.; Marion County Library, 321 Monroe St.; Fairmont, WV 26554.

Mercer County Historical Society; Box 5012; Princeton, WV 24740.

Mineral County Historical Landmark Commission; Rt. One, Box 94; Burlington, WV 26710.

Mingo County Genealogical Society; Box 2581; Williamson, WV 25661.

Monroe County Historical Society; PO Box 465; Union, WV 24983.

Morgan County Historical and Genealogical Society; Box 52; Berkeley Springs, WV 25411.

Palatines to America, West Virginia Chapter; 572 Plymouth Ave.; Morgantown, WV 26505-2142.

Pendleton County Historical Society; PO Box 549; Franklin, WV 26807.

Ritchie County Historical Society; Rt. 1 Box 53; Harrisville, WV 26362.

Roane County Historical Society; PO Box 161; Spencer, WV 25276.

Sons of the American Revolution, West Virginia Society; 132 N Court St.; Lewisburg, WV 24901.

Taylor County Historical and Genealogical Society, Inc.; PO Box 522; Grafton, WV 26354.

Tri-State Genealogical and Historical Society; PO Box 454; Newell, WV 26050-0454; www.rootsweb.com/~wvtsghs/indext.htm.

Tyler County Historical Society; Box 317; Middleboume, WV 26149.

Upshur County, West Virginia Historical Society; PO Box 2082; Buckhannon, WV 26201.

West Augusta Historical & Genealogical Society; 251510th Ave.; Parkersburg, WV 26101.

West Virginia Historical Society; Cultural Center, Capitol Complex; Charleston, WV 25305.

West Virginia Library Commission; 1900 Kanawha Blvd. E.; Charleston, WV 25305; (304) 558-2041; web_one@wvlc .lib.wv.us; http://librarycommission.lib.wv.us.

West Virginia State Archives; The Cultural Center; 1900 Kanawha Boulevard, East; Charleston, WV 25305-0300; (304) 558-0230; www.wvculture.org/history/wvsamenu.html.

Wetzel County Genealogical Society; PO Box 464; New Martinsville, WV 26155-0464.

Wheeling Area Genealogical Society; 2237 Marshall Ave.; Wheeling, WV 26003-7444; LEWELLENNJ@aol.com; www.rootsweb.com/~wvwags/index.htm.

Wyoming County Genealogical Society; PO Box 1456; Pineville, WV 24874.

Bibliography and Record Sources

General

Atkinson, George Wesley. *Prominent Men of West Virginia*. Wheeling, West Virginia: W. L. Callin, 1890.

Brown, Stuart E., Jr. *Virginia Genealogies, a Trial List of Printed Books and Pamphlets*. 3 vols. Berryville, Virginia: Virginia Book Co., 1967–1989.

Butcher, Bernard Lee. *Genealogical and Personal History of the Upper Monongahela Valley, West Virginia*. 3 vols. New York: Lewis Historical Publishing Co., 1912.

Callaham, James Morton. *History of West Virginia, Old and New*. 3 vols. Chicago: American Historical Society, 1923.

Clark, Newell T., and Elizabeth Terry Long. *A Guide to Church Records in the Archives Branch of the Virginia State Library*. Richmond: Virginia State Library, 1981.

Comstock, Jim, comp. and ed. *The West Virginia Heritage Encyclopedia*. Richwood, West Virginia: Comstock, 1976. Microfiche.

Daughters of the American Revolution (West Virginia). *Genealogical Collection*. Microfilm. Salt Lake City: Genealogical Society of Utah, 1970.

Davis, Innis C. *A Bibliography of West Virginia*. Parts 1, 2, Charleston: West Virginia Department of Archives and History, 1939.

Ebert, Rebecca A. *Finding Your People in the Shenandoah Valley of Virginia and West Virginia*. Winchester, Virginia: The Rebecca Co., 1984.

Forbes, Harold M. *West Virginia History: A Guide to Research.* Morgantown: West Virginia University Press, 1981.

Genealogies of West Virginia Families. *West Virginia Historical Magazine Quarterly.* Reprint. Clearfield Co, 1992.

Ham, F. Gerald. *Guide to Manuscripts and Archives in the West Virginia Collection, Number II, 1958–1962.* Morgantown, West Virginia: West Virginia University Library, 1965.

Hess, James W. *Guide to Manuscripts and Archives in the West Virginia Collection.* Morgantown, West Virginia: West Virginia University Library, 1974.

Historical Records Survey (West Virginia). *Church Records Survey, West Virginia, Episcopal.* Salt Lake City: Filmed by the Genealogical Society of Utah, 1961.

Historical Records Survey (West Virginia). *An Inventory of the Records of the West Virginia Counties Which have been Deposited in the West Virginia University Library: Archives Section, at Morgantown, West Virginia.* S.l.: s.n., 198–.

Historical Records Survey (West Virginia). *Church Records Survey, West Virginia, Methodist.* (Protestant). Salt Lake City: Filmed by the Genealogical Society of Utah, 1961. 9 microfilm.

Historical Records Survey (West Virginia). *Inventory of the Church Archives of West Virginia: the Protestant Episcopal Church.* Wheeling, West Virginia: Diocese of West Virginia, 1939.

Historical Records Survey (West Virginia). *Survey of Baptist Churches, West Virginia.* Salt Lake City: Filmed by the Genealogical Society of Utah, 1961.

Historical Records Survey (West Virginia). *Survey of Church Records, West Virginia, Presbyterian.* Salt Lake City: Filmed by the Genealogical Society of Utah, 1961. 7 microfilm.

History of the Great Kanawha Valley: With Family History and Biographical Sketches. 2 vols. Madison, Wisconsin: Brant, Fuller & Co., 1891.

Lang, Theodore F. *Loyal West Virginia from 1861 to 1865.* Baltimore: Deutsch, 1895.

McGinnis, Carol. *West Virginia Genealogy: Sources and Resources.* Baltimore: Genealogical Publishing Co., 1988

Men of West Virginia. 2 vols. Chicago: Biographical Publishing Co., 1903.

Miller, Thomas Condit and Hu Maxwell. *West Virginia and Its People.* 3 vols. New York: Lewis Historical Publishing Co., 1913.

Peterkin, George W. *A History and Record of the Protestant Episcopal Church in the Diocese of West Virginia.* Charleston, West Virginia: Tribune Co., 1902

Rice, Otis K. *West Virginia: A History.* Lexington, Kentucky: University Press of Kentucky, 1985.

Shetler, Charles. *Guide to the Study of West Virginia History.* Morgantown: West Virginia University Library, 1960.

Stewart, Robert Armistead. *Index to Printed Virginia Genealogies.* 1930. Reprint. Baltimore: Genealogical Publishing Co, 1970.

Stinson, Helen S. *A Handbook for Genealogical Research in West Virginia.* Rev. and exp. South Charleston, West Virginia: Kanawha Valley Genealogical Society, 1991.

Tetrick, W. Guy, comp. *Obituaries from Newspapers; Clarksburg Exponent, Clarksburg Telegram and Other Papers of Northern West Virginia.* Salt Lake City: Genealogical Society of Utah, 1958. Microfilm, multiple rolls.

Tetrick, W. Guy. *Obituaries from Newspapers of Northern West Virginia.* 2 vols. Clarksburg, West Virginia: W. G. Tetrick, 1933.

The West Virginia Heritage Encyclopedia. Richwood, West Virginia: Comstock, 1976. Microfiche.

Wardell, P. G. *Timesaving Aid to Virginia-West Virginia Ancestors: A Genealogical Index of Surnames from Published Sources.* 4 vols. Athens, Georgia: Iberian Publishing Co., 1990.

Wardell, Patrick G. *Virginians & West Virginians, 1607–1870.* Bowie, Maryland: Heritage Books, 1986–1992.

West Virginia Research Outline. Series U.S.-States, no. 48. Salt Lake City: Family History Library, 1988.

Atlases, Maps and Gazetteers

Gannett, Henry. *Gazetteer of West Virginia.* Washington, D.C: U.S. Government Printing Office, 1904. Reprinted as *A Gazetteer of Virginia and West Virginia.* Baltimore: Genealogical Publishing Co., 1975.

Kenny, Hamill. *West Virginia Place Names, Their Origin and Meaning, Including the Nomenclature of the Streams and Mountains.* Piedmont, West Virginia: Place Name Press, 1945.

New Descriptive Atlas of West Virginia. Clarksburg, West Virginia: Clarksburg Publishing Co., 1933.

Puetz, C. J., comp. *West Virginia County Maps.* Lyndon Station, Wisconsin: Thomas Publishing Co., 1990.

Sims, Edgar B. *Making a State: Formation of West Virginia.* Charleston, West Virginia: Edgar B. Sims, 1956.

West Virginia Historical Records Survey. *West Virginia County Formations and Boundary Changes.* Charleston, West Virginia: Historical Survey. 1938.

Census Records

Available Census Records and Census Substitutes
Federal Census 1870, 1880, 1900, 1910, 1920

Federal Mortality Schedules 1850, 1860, 1870, 1880

Union Veterans and Widows 1890

Bridges, Steven A. *Virginians in 1800: Counties of West Virginia.* Trumbull, Connecticut: Steven A. Bridges, 1987.

Dollarhide, William. *The Census Book: A Genealogist's Guide to Federal Census Facts, Schedules and Indexes.* Bountiful, Utah: Heritage Quest, 1999.

Fothergill, Augusta B., and John Mark Naugle. *Virginia Tax Payers, 1782–87, Other than Those Published by the United States Census Bureau.* 1940. Reprint. Baltimore: Genealogical Publishing Co., 1966.

Heads of Families . . . Records of the State Enumerations: 1782 to 1785, Virginia. 1908. Reprint. Baltimore: Southern Book Co., 1952.

Kemp, Thomas Jay. *The American Census Handbook.* Wilmington, Delaware: Scholarly Resources, Inc., 2001.

Schreiner-Yantis, Netti and Florence Speakman Love, comps. *The 1787 Census of Virginia: An Accounting of the Names of Every White Male Tithable Over 21 Years.* 3 vols. Springfield, Virginia: Genealogical Books in Print, 1987.

Schreiner-Yantis, Netti. *A Supplement to the 1810 Census of Virginia: Tax Lists of the Counties for Which the Census is Missing.* Springfield, Virginia: Genealogical Books in Print, 1971.

Thorndale, William and William Dollarhide. *Map Guide to the U.S. Federal Census, 1790–1920.* Baltimore: Genealogical Publishing Co., 1987.

Court Records, Probate and Wills

Chalkley, Lyman. *Chronicles of the Scots-Irish Settlement in Virginia: Extracted from the Original Court Records of Augusta County, 1754–1800.* 3 vols., 1912, Reprint. Baltimore: Genealogical Publishing Co., 1980.

Johnston, Ross B. *West Virginia Estate Settlements, 1753–1850: An Index to Wills, Inventories, Appraisements, Land Grants and Surveys to 1850.* Excerpted from West Virginia History, vols. 17–24. 1955–1963. Reprint. Baltimore: Genealogical Publishing Co., 1977.

McFarland, K. T. H. *Early West Virginia Wills.* Apollo, Pennsylvania: Closson Press, 1993.

Torrence, Clayton. *Virginia Wills and Administrations, 1632–1800.* 1930. Reprint. Baltimore: Genealogical Publishing Co., 1965.

United States. District Court (West Virginia: Northern District). *Accounts: 1865–1880.* Microfilm of originals at the West Virginia University Library, Morgantown. Salt Lake City: Filmed by the Genealogical Society of Utah, 1958. Microfilm.

Emigration, Immigration, Migration and Naturalization

Chalkley, Lyman. *Chronicles of the Scotch-Irish Settlement in Virginia: Extracted from the Original Court Records of Augusta County, 1754–1800.* Salt Lake City: Genealogical Society, 1958.

Filby, P. William, *Passenger and Immigration Lists Index.* 15 vols. Detroit: Gale Research, 1981–.

United States. District Court (West Virginia). *Naturalization Records, 1943–1954.* Northern District Microfilm of originals at the federal building, Elkins. Salt Lake City: Filmed by the Genealogical Society of Utah, 1987. 2 microfilm.

United States. District Court (West Virginia: Northern District). *Declarations of Intention, 1908–1938.* Microfilm copy of originals at federal building, Elkins. Salt Lake City: Filmed by the Genealogical Society of Utah, 1987. 3 microfilm.

United States. District Court (West Virginia: Northern District). *Naturalization Records, 1844–1875.* Copies of original materials at the National Archives Record Center, Philadelphia. Salt Lake City: Filmed by the Genealogical Society of Utah, 1990. 2 microfilm.

United States. District Court (West Virginia: Northern District). *Petitions Granted: 1929–1957.* Microfilm copy of originals at federal building, Elkins. Salt Lake City: Filmed by the Genealogical Society of Utah, 1987.

Land

Dyer, M. H. *Dyer's Index to Land Grants in West Virginia.* Salem, Massachusetts: Higginson Book Company, 1996.

Northern Neck Surveys, 1721–1779. Richmond: Virginia State Library, 1995. 36 microfilm.

Sims, Edgar B. *Sims Index to Land Grants in West Virginia.* Charleston: Auditor's Office, 1952. Supplement, 1963.

Sims, Edgar Barr. *Making a State: Formation of West Virginia.* Charleston: E. B. Sims, 1956.

Sims, Edgar Barr. *Sims Index to Land Grants in West Virginia.* Charleston: E. B. Sims, 1952.

West Virginia. State Auditor. *Land Grants, 1748–1912.* Salt Lake City: Filmed by the Genealogical Society of Utah, 1967. Microfilm, multiple rolls.

West Virginia. State Auditor. *Land Sales, 1860–1875.* Salt Lake City: Filmed by the Genealogical Society of Utah, 1860–1875. Microfilm, multiple rolls.

West Virginia. State Auditor. *Plats and Surveys, 1863–1889.* Salt Lake City: Filmed by the Genealogical Society of Utah, 1967. Microfilm.

Military

Dawson, Francis Warrington. *Reminiscences of Confederate Service, 1861–1865.* Bethesda, Maryland: University Publications of America, 1990.

Hansrote, Hazel Groves. *Military Records of Maryland, Pennsylvania, Virginia and West Virginia, 1775–1920.* Salt Lake City: Filmed by the Genealogical Society of Utah, 1975.

Johnston, Ross B. *West Virginians in the American Revolution.* Baltimore, Maryland: Clearfield Co., Inc., 2002.

Lewis, Virgil A. "The Soldiery of West Virginia in the French and Indian War, Lord Dunmore's War, The Revolution . . . the War with Mexico." In *Third Biennial*

Report of the State Department of Archives and History, pp. 39–118. Charleston, West Virginia: News-Mail Co., 1910. Reprint. Baltimore: Genealogical Publishing Co., n.d.

Reddy, Anne Waller. *West Virginia Revolutionary Ancestors Whose Services were Non-military. 1930.* Reprint. Baltimore: Genealogical Publishing Co., 1963.

Stutler, Boyd B. *West Virginia in the Civil War.* Charleston, West Virginia: Educational Foundation, 1963.

United States. Record and Pension Office. *Compiled Service Records of Volunteer Union Soldiers Who Served in Organizations from the State of West Virginia.* Washington, D.C.: The National Archives, 1963. Microfilm, multiple copies.

United States. Selective Service System. *West Virginia, World War I Selective Service System Draft Registration Cards, 1917–1918.* National Archives Microfilm Publications, M1509. Washington, D.C.: National Archives, 1987–1988.

Virginia. Governor. *Militia Commission Papers, Governor's Office, 1784–1856.* Microfilm of the original records at the Virginia State Library in Richmond, Virginia. Richmond: Virginia State Library, 1996. 121 microfilm.

Virginia/West Virginia Genealogical Data from Revolutionary War Pension and Bounty Land Warrant Records. Bowie, Maryland: Heritage Books, 1988–.

Wardell, Patrick G. *War of 1812: Virginia Bounty Land & Pension Applicants: A Quick Reference Guide to Ancestors Having War of 1812 Service Who Served, Lived, Died, or Married in Virginia or West Virginia.* Bowie, Maryland: Heritage Books, 1987.

Watkins, Raymond W. *Confederate Burials in West Virginia Cemeteries.* Typescript. Salt Lake City: Genealogical Society of Utah, 1978.

Vital and Cemetery

Historical Records Survey (West Virginia*). Inventory of Public Vital Statistics Records in West Virginia.* 2 vols. Charleston, West Virginia: West Virginia Historical Records Survey, 1941–1942.

Pegram, G. A. *Cemeteries in Various Counties in West Virginia.* Microfilm of material at the West Virginia University Library, Morgantown, prepared by the Historical Records Survey. Salt Lake City: Filmed by the Genealogical Society of Utah, 1961. Microfilm.

Tetrick, W. Guy. *Obituaries from Newspapers of Northern West Virginia: Principally from the Counties of Barbour, Braxton, Calhoun, Doddridge, Gilmer, Harrison, Lewis, Nicholas, Pocahontas, Preston, Randolph, Ritchie, Taylor, Tucker, Tyler, Upshur, Webster and Parts of Marion, Wetzel and Wirt.* 2 vols. Clarksburg, West Virginia: W. G. Tetrick, 1933.

United Daughters of the Confederacy. Georgia Division. *Roster of Confederate Graves.* 7 vols. Atlanta: United Daughters of the Confederacy, Georgia Division, 1995.

Vital Statistics, 1853–1860 of West Virginia. Microreproduction of original manuscript at the Virginia State Library, Richmond, Virginia. Salt Lake City: Filmed by the Genealogical Society of Utah, 1954. 10 microfilm.

West Virginia, 1863–1900 [Marriages]. S.l.: Brøderbund, 1999. CD-ROM.

West Virginia. Division of Vital Statistics. *Birth Certificates and Delayed Birth Certificates, 1852–1930.* Microfilm of the original records at Vital Registration Office, Division of Health, Charleston, West Virginia. Salt Lake City: Filmed by the Genealogical Society of Utah, 1994–1995. 315 microfilm.

West Virginia. Division of Vital Statistics. *Certificates of Deaths, 1917–1973.* Microfilm of original records at the West Virginia State Archives and the Vital Registration Office, West Virginia Division of Health, in Charleston, West Virginia. Salt Lake City: Filmed by the Genealogical Society of Utah, 1994–1995, 1998. 361 microfilm.

West Virginia. Division of Vital Statistics. *Disinterment and Reburials, 1980–1991.* Microfilm of the original records at state registrar's office in Charleston, West Virginia. Salt Lake City: Filmed by the Genealogical Society of Utah, 1994. 10 microfilm.

County Website	Map Index	Date Created	Parent County or Territory From Which Organized Address/Details
Barbour www.rootsweb.com/~wvbarbou/	I6	3 Mar 1843	**Harrison, Lewis, Randolph** Barbour County; 8 N Main St; Philippi, WV 26416; Ph. (304) 457-2232 **Details:** (County Clerk has Birth, Marriage, Death & Probate Records from 1843 & Land Records from 1845; Clerk Circuit Court has Divorce & Court Records)
Berkeley www.berkeleycountycomm.org/	C5	10 Feb 1772	**Frederick, VA** Berkeley County; 400 W Stephen St, Ste 201; Martinsburg, WV 25401; Ph. (304) 264-1923 **Details:** (County Clerk has Birth & Death Records from 1865, Marriage Records from 1781, Probate Records from 1772 & Land Records from 1880; Clerk Circuit Court has Divorce Records)
Boone www.rootsweb.com/~wvboone/	M10	11 Mar 1847	**Kanawha, Cabell, Logan** Boone County; 200 State St; Madison, WV 25130-1152; Ph. (304) 369-7331 **Details:** (County Clerk has Birth, Marriage, Death, Probate & Land Records from 1865; Clerk Circuit Court has Divorce & Court Records)
Braxton www.braxtonwv.org/CourtHouse.htm	K7	15 Jan 1836	**Kanawha, Lewis, Nicholas** Braxton County; 300 Main St; PO Box 486; Sutton, WV 26601; Ph. (304) 765-2833 **Details:** (County Clerk has Birth, Marriage & Death indexes 1853–1886, Probate & Land Records; Clerk Circuit Court has Divorce & Court Records)
Brooke www.rootsweb.com/~wvbrooke/brooke.htm	J2	30 Nov 1796	Brooke County; 632 Main St; Wellsburg, WV 26070; Ph. (304) 737-3661 **Details:** (County Clerk has Birth & Death Records from 1853, Marriage, Probate & Land Records from 1797 & Military Records from 1917; Clerk Circuit Court has Divorce & Court Records)
Cabell www.rootsweb.com/~wvcabell/cabell.html	O8	2 Jan 1809	**Kanawha** Cabell County; 8th St & 4th Ave; Huntington, WV 25701; Ph. (304) 526-8625 **Details:** (County Clerk has Birth & Death Records from 1853, Marriage Records from 1809, Land Records from 1808 & Probate Records; Clerk Circuit Court has Divorce & Court Records from 1809)
Calhoun www.rootsweb.com/~wvcalhou/index2.htm	L7	5 Mar 1856	**Gilmer** Calhoun County; Main St; PO Box 230; Grantsville, WV 26147; Ph. (304) 354-6725 **Details:** (County Clerk has Birth, Marriage, Death, Probate & Land Records from 1856)
Clay www.rootsweb.com/~wvclay/index.htm	K8	29 Mar 1858	**Nicholas** Clay County; 207 Main St; Clay, WV 25043; Ph. (304) 587-4283 **Details:** (County Clerk has Birth, Marriage, Death & Probate Records from 1858 & Land Records)

County Website	Map Index	Date Created	Parent County or Territory From Which Organized Address/Details
Doddridge www.rootsweb.com/~wvdoddri/	**J5**	**4 Feb 1845**	**Harrison, Tyler, Ritchie, Lewis** Doddridge County; 118 E Court St; West Union, WV 26456; Ph. (304) 873-2631 **Details:** (County Clerk has Birth & Death Records from 1853, Marriage, Probate & Land Records from 1845; Clerk Circuit Court has Court Records)
Fayette www.fayettecounty.com/	**K10**	**28 Feb 1831**	**Kanawha, Greenbrier, Logan, Nicholas** Fayette County; 100 Church St; Fayetteville, WV 25840; Ph. (304) 574-1200 **Details:** (County Clerk has Birth & Death Records from 1866, Marriage, Probate & Land Records from 1831; Clerk Circuit Court has Divorce & Court Records)
Gilmer www.rootsweb.com/~wvgilmer/	**K6**	**3 Feb 1845**	**Lewis, Kanawha** Gilmer County; 10 Howard St; Glenville, WV 26351; Ph. (304) 462-7641 **Details:** (County Clerk has Birth, Death & Court Records from 1853, Marriage, Probate & Land Records from 1845)
Grant www.rootsweb.com/~wvgrant/grant.htm	**F6**	**14 Feb 1866**	Grant County; 5 Highland Ave; Petersburg, WV 26847-1705; Ph. (304) 257-4550 **Details:** (County Clerk has Birth, Marriage, Death, Divorce, Probate, Court & Land Records from 1866)
Greenbrier www.rootsweb.com/~wvgreenb/	**J10**	**20 Oct 1777**	**Montgomery & Botetourt, VA** Greenbrier County; 200 N Court St; PO Box 506; Lewisburg, WV 24901-0506; Ph. (304) 647-6602 **Details:** (County Clerk has Birth & Death Records from 1853, Marriage Records from 1781, Probate & Land Records from 1780 & Court Records)
Hampshire www.rootsweb.com/~wvhampsh/	**D5**	**27 Feb 1752**	**Frederick & Augusta, VA** Hampshire County; Main St; Romney, WV 26757-1696; Ph. (304) 822-5112 **Details:** (County Clerk has Birth, Marriage & Death Records from 1865, Probate Records from 1780, Court Records from 1831 & Land Records)
Hancock www.rootsweb.com/~wvhancoc/index.htm	**J1**	**15 Jan 1848**	**Brooke** Hancock County; PO Box 367; New Cumberland, WV 26047; Ph. (304) 564-3311 **Details:** (County Clerk has Birth, Marriage, Death, Probate & Land Records from 1848; Clerk Circuit Court has Divorce Records)
Hardy www.rootsweb.com/~wvhardy/	**E6**	**17 Oct 1785**	**Hampshire** Hardy County; 204 Washington St; Moorefield, WV 26836; Ph. (304) 538-2929 **Details:** (County Clerk has Birth, Marriage, Death & Burial Records from 1853, Probate & Land Records from 1786, Court Records from 1960 & Divorce Records)

County Website	Map Index	Date Created	Parent County or Territory From Which Organized Address/Details
Harrison www.rootsweb.com/~wvharris/	J5	3 May 1784	**Monongalia** Harrison County; 301 W Main St; Clarksburg, WV 26301-2909; Ph. (304) 624-8611 **Details:** (County Clerk has Birth & Death Records from 1853, Marriage Records from 1784, Probate Records from 1788 & Land Records from 1786)
Jackson www.rootsweb.com/~wvjackso/JACK.HTM	M7	1 Mar 1831	**Kanawha, Mason, Wood** Jackson County; PO Box 800; Ripley, WV 25271; Ph. (304) 372-2011 **Details:** (County Clerk has Birth & Death Records from 1853, Marriage Records from 1831, Land Records from early 1800's, Probate Records from 1861 & Military Records from 1918; Clerk Circuit Court has Divorce & Court Records from 1831)
Jefferson jeffersoncountyclerk.net	B5	8 Jan 1801	**Berkeley** Jefferson County; PO Box 208; Charles Town, WV 25414; Ph. (304) 728-3215, clerkjeff@yahoo.com **Details:** (County Clerk has Birth & Death Records from 1853 (except Civil War Years), Marriage, Land, & Probate Records from 1801)
Kanawha www.kancocomm.com/	L8	14 Nov 1788	**Greenbrier, Montgomery, VA** Kanawha County; 409 Virginia St E; Charleston, WV 25301; Ph. (304) 357-0130 **Details:** (County Clerk has Birth & Death Records from 1853, Marriage Records from 1824, Probate Records from 1831 & Land Records from 1790)
Lewis www.rootsweb.com/~wvlewis/	J6	18 Dec 1816	Lewis County; 110 Center Ave; Weston, WV 26452; Ph. (304) 269-8215 **Details:** (County Clerk has Birth & Death Records from 1853, Marriage, Probate & Land Records from 1816; Clerk Circuit Court has Divorce Records)
Lincoln www.rootsweb.com/~wvlincol/	N9	23 Feb 1867	**Cabell, Kanawha, Putnam** Lincoln County; 8000 Court Ave; Hamlin, WV 25523; Ph. (304) 824-3336 **Details:** (County Clerk has Birth, Marriage, Death, Probate & Land Records from 1909)
Logan www.rootsweb.com/~wvlogan/logan.htm	N10	12 Jan 1824	**Kanawha & Cabell, WV; Giles & Tazewell, VA** Logan County; County Courthouse Rm 101; Logan, WV 25601; Ph. (304) 792-8600 **Details:** (County Clerk has Birth, Marriage & Death Records from 1872, Burial, Probate, Land & Military Records; Clerk Circuit Court has Divorce, Court & Naturalization Records)
Marion www.rootsweb.com/~wvmarion/marion.html	I4	14 Jan 1842	**Harrison, Monongalia** Marion County; 217 Adams St; PO Box 1267; Fairmont, WV 26554-1267; Ph. (304) 367-5440 **Details:** (County Clerk has Birth, Death, Marriage, Probate, Deeds, & Military Records from 1842)

County Website	Map Index	Date Created	Parent County or Territory From Which Organized Address/Details
Marshall www.rootsweb.com/~wvmarsha/marsh.htm	**J3**	**12 Mar 1835**	Marshall County; 7th St; PO Box 459; Moundsville, WV 26041; Ph. (304) 845-1220 **Details:** (County Clerk has Birth & Death Records from 1853, Marriage & Land Records from 1835 & Probate Records from 1850; Clerk Circuit Court has Divorce & Court Records)
Mason www.rootsweb.com/~wvmason/mason.htm	**N7**	**2 Jan 1804**	**Kanawha** Mason County; 200 6th St; Point Pleasant, WV 25550; Ph. (304) 675-1997 **Details:** (County Clerk has Birth & Death Records from 1853, Marriage, Probate & Land Records from 1804 & Military Records from 1918; Clerk Circuit Court has Divorce & Court Records)
McDowell www.geocities.com/mcdowellcounty/	**M12**	**20 Feb 1858**	**Tazewell, VA** McDowell County; 90 Wyoming St #109; Welch, WV 24801; Ph. (304) 436-8344 **Details:** (County seat was first Perryville; changed to Welch in 1892) (County Clerk has Birth Records from 1872, Marriage Records from 1861, Death Records from 1894, Probate Records from 1897 & Land Records; Clerk Circuit Court has Divorce Records)
Mercer www.rootsweb.com/~wvmercer/mercer.htm	**K12**	**17 Mar 1837**	**Tazewell, VA** Mercer County; PO Box 1716; Princeton, WV 24740; Ph. (304) 487-8311 **Details:** (County Clerk has Birth, Marriage & Death Records from 1853, Probate & Land Records from 1837; Clerk Circuit Court has Divorce & Court Records from 1837)
Mineral www.mineralcountywv.com/	**E5**	**1 Feb 1866**	**Hampshire** Mineral County; 150 Armstrong St; Keyser, WV 26726-3505; Ph. (304) 788-3924 **Details:** (County Clerk has Birth, Marriage, Death, Probate & Land Records from 1866)
Mingo www.rootsweb.com/~wvmingo/mingo.htm	**O10**	**30 Jan 1895**	**Logan** Mingo County; PO Box 1197; WIlliamson, WV 25661-1197; Ph. (304) 235-0330 **Details:** (County Clerk has Birth, Marriage, Death & Land Records from 1895 & Burial Records from 1959; Clerk Circuit Court has Divorce, Probate & Court Records)
Monongalia www.co.monongalia.wv.us/	**I4**	**7 Oct 1776**	**W. Augusta** Monongalia County; 243 High St #123; Morgantown, WV 26505; Ph. (304) 291-7230 **Details:** (County Clerk has Birth & Death Records from 1853, Marriage Records from 1796, Probate Records from early 1800's & Land Records from 1843; Clerk Circuit Court has Divorce & Court Records from 1845 & Naturalization Records 1906–1953)
Monroe www.rootsweb.com/~wvmonroe/	**J11**	**14 Jan 1799**	**Greenbrier** Monroe County; Main St; Union, WV 24983; Ph. (304) 772-3096 **Details:** (County Clerk has Birth & Death Records from 1853, Marriage & Land Records from 1799 & Probate Records)

County Website	Map Index	Date Created	Parent County or Territory From Which Organized Address/Details
Morgan www.rootsweb.com/~wvmonroe/	C4	**9 Feb 1820**	**Berkeley, Hampshire** Morgan County; 202 Fairfax St Ste 100; Berkeley Springs, WV 25411; Ph. (304) 258-8547 **Details:** (County Clerk has Birth, Marriage, Death & Probate Records from 1865, Land & some Marriage & Probate Records from 1820; Clerk Circuit Court has Divorce & Court Records)
Nicholas www.rootsweb.com/~wvnichol/index.html	K8	**30 Jan 1818**	**Greenbrier, Kanawha, Randolph** Nicholas County; 700 Main St; Summersville, WV 26651; Ph. (304) 872-7820 **Details:** (County Clerk has Birth Records from 1855, Marriage & Land Records from 1812, Death Records from 1890 & Probate Records from 1880; Clerk Circuit Court has Divorce & Court Records)
Ohio www.hostville.com/wvoh/	J2	**7 Oct 1776**	**Dist. of W. Augusta** Ohio County; 1500 Chapline St; Wheeling, WV 26003; Ph. (304) 234-3729 **Details:** (County Clerk has Birth & Death Records from 1853, Marriage Records from 1793, Probate Records from 1777 & Land Records from 1778; Clerk Circuit Court has Divorce & Court Records from 1884)
Pendleton http://franklinwv.com/	F7	**4 Dec 1787**	**Augusta, Hardy & Rockingham, VA** Pendleton County; Main St; Franklin, WV 26807; Ph. (304) 358-2505 **Details:** (County Clerk has Birth & Death Records from 1853, Marriage Records from 1800, Probate & Land Records from 1789)
Pleasants www.geocities.com/CapitolHill/Lobby/3918/	L5	**29 Mar 1851**	**Tyler, Wood** Pleasants County; 301 Court Ln #101; St. Marys, WV 26170; Ph. (304) 684-3542 **Details:** (County Clerk has Birth, Marriage, Death & Probate Records from 1853 & Land Records from 1851; Clerk Circuit Court has Divorce & Court Records)
Pocahontas www.neumedia.net./~pocahontascc/	H8	**21 Dec 1821**	**Pendleton & Randolph, WV & Bath, VA** Pocahontas County; 900 10th Ave; Marlinton, WV 24954; Ph. (304) 799-4549 **Details:** (County Clerk has Birth Records from 1853, Death Records from 1854, Marriage, Probate & Land Records from 1822; Clerk Circuit Court has Divorce & Court Records)
Preston www.rootsweb.com/~wvpresto/	H5	**19 Jan 1818**	**Monongalia** Preston County; 101 W Main St #201; Kingwood, WV 26537; Ph. (304) 329-0070 **Details:** (County Clerk has Birth, Marriage, Death, Probate & Land Records from 1869; Clerk Circuit Court has Divorce & Court Records)
Putnam www.putnamcounty.org/commission/	N8	**11 Mar 1848**	**Kanawha, Mason, Cabell** Putnam County; 3389 Winfield Rd; Winfield, WV 25213; Ph. (304) 586-0202 **Details:** (County Clerk has Birth Records from 1848, Death Records from 1853, Marriage & Probate Records from 1849 & Land Records from 1841; Clerk Circuit Court has Divorce & Court Records)

County Website	Map Index	Date Created	Parent County or Territory From Which Organized Address/Details
Raleigh www.rootsweb.com/~wvraleig/	**L10**	**23 Jan 1850**	**Fayette** Raleigh County; County Courthouse; 215 Main St; Beckley, WV 25801; Ph. (304) 255-9123 **Details:** (County Clerk has Birth, Marriage, Death, Probate & Land Records from 1850; Clerk Circuit Court has Divorce & Court Records)
Randolph www.randolphcountywv.com/core.htm	**H7**	**16 Oct 1786**	**Harrison** Randolph County; 2 Randolph Ave; Elkins, WV 26241; Ph. (304) 636-0543 **Details:** (County Clerk has Birth Records from 1856, Marriage & Probate Records from 1787, Death Records from 1853 & Land Records)
Ritchie www.rootsweb.com/~wvritchi/indexr.htm	**K6**	**18 Feb 1843**	**Harrison, Lewis, Wood** Ritchie County; 115 E Main St Rm 201; Harrisville, WV 26362; Ph. (304) 643-2164 **Details:** (County Clerk has Birth, Marriage, Death, Probate, Land & Military Records from 1853; Clerk Circuit Court has Divorce Records; Magistrate Court has Court Records)
Roane www.pa-roots.com/~roane/	**L7**	**11 Mar 1856**	**Kanawha, Jackson, Gilmer** Roane County; 200 Main St; Spencer, WV 25276-1497; Ph. (304) 927-2860 **Details:** (County Clerk has Birth, Marriage, Death, Probate & Land Records from 1856)
Summers www.rootsweb.com/~wvsummer/summers.htm	**K11**	**27 Feb 1871**	**Greenbrier, Monroe, Mercer, Fayette** Summers County; PO Box 97; Hinton, WV 25951; Ph. (304) 466-7104 **Details:** (County Clerk has Birth, Marriage, Death, Probate & Land Records from 1871; Clerk Circuit Court has Divorce & Court Records)
Taylor www.rootsweb.com/~wvtaylor/	**I5**	**19 Jan 1844**	**Barbour, Harrison, Marion** Taylor County; 214 W Main St; Grafton, WV 26354-1387; Ph. (304) 265-1401 **Details:** (County Clerk has Birth, Marriage, Death, Probate & Land Records from 1853; Clerk Circuit Court has Divorce & Court Records)
Tucker www.tuckercounty.com/	**G6**	**7 Mar 1856**	**Randolph** Tucker County; 215 1st St; Parsons, WV 26287; Ph. (304) 478-2414 **Details:** (County Clerk has Birth, Marriage, Death, Probate & Land Records from 1856; Clerk Circuit Court has Divorce, Court & Naturalization Records)
Tyler www.tylercounty.net/Default.htm	**K5**	**6 Dec 1814**	**Ohio** Tyler County; Main St; PO Box 66; Middlebourne, WV 26149-0066; Ph. (304) 758-2102 **Details:** (County Clerk has Birth, Marriage & Death Records from 1853 with incomplete Marriage Records from 1815, Probate & Land Records from 1815; Clerk Circuit Court has Divorce & Court Records)

County Website	Map Index	Date Created	Parent County or Territory From Which Organized Address/Details
Upshur www.rootsweb.com/~wvupshur/	I7	**26 Mar 1851**	**Randolph, Barbour, Lewis** Upshur County; 40 W Main St #101; Buckhannon, WV 26201; Ph. (304) 472-1068 **Details:** (County Clerk has Birth, Marriage, Death & Land Records from 1853; Clerk Circuit Court has Divorce, Probate & Court Records)
Wayne www.rootsweb.com/~wvwayne/wayne.htm	O9	**18 Jan 1842**	**Cabell** Wayne County; 700 Hendricks St; Wayne, WV 25570; Ph. (304) 272-6371 **Details:** (County Clerk has Birth & Death Records from 1853, Marriage Records from 1854, Probate & Land Records)
Webster www.websterwv.com/index1.html	J8	**10 Jan 1860**	**Braxton, Nicholas, Randolph** Webster County; 2 Court Sq #G1; Webster Springs, WV 26288; Ph. (304) 847-2508 **Details:** (County Clerk has Birth, Marriage, Death, Burial, Probate & Land Records from 1887)
Wetzel	J4	**10 Jan 1846**	**Tyler** Wetzel County; 200 Main St.; PO Box 156; New Martinsville, WV 26155; Ph. (304) 455-8224 **Details:** (County Clerk has Birth, Burial, Death, Land, Marriage, Military, & Probate Records; Clerk of Circuit Court has Court, Divorce, & Guardianship Records; County Treasurer has Tax Records; Genealogical Society has Census & Other Historical Records)
Wirt www.rootsweb.com/~wvwirt/index.htm	L6	**19 Jan 1848**	**Wood, Jackson** Wirt County; Washington St; PO Box 53; Elizabeth, WV 26143-0053; Ph. (304) 275-4271 **Details:** (County Clerk has Birth & Death Records from 1870, Marriage Records from 1854, Probate & Land Records from 1848; Clerk Circuit Court has Divorce Records)
Wood www.rootsweb.com/~wvwood/index.htm	L6	**21 Dec 1798**	Wood County; 1 Court Sq; Parkersburg, WV 26101; Ph. (304) 424-1844 **Details:** (County Clerk has Birth, Marriage & Death Records from 1850, Probate Records, Military Records from 1900; County Assessor has Land Records from 1798; Clerk Circuit Court has Divorce & Court Records)
Wyoming www.rootsweb.com/~wvwyomin/	M11	**26 Jan 1850**	**Logan** Wyoming County; Bank St; Pineville, WV 24874; Ph. (304) 732-8000 **Details:** (County Clerk has Birth, Marriage, Death, Probate & Land Records, bond Books & County Court order Books from 1850; Clerk Circuit Court has Divorce & Court Records)

Wisconsin

Capital: Madison

Territory: 1836

State: 1848 (30th)

Forward

Jean Nicolet, a French explorer, first toured Wisconsin in 1634. Many other Frenchmen explored the area over the next few decades, leading to the first trading post at La Baye in 1648.

A conflict between the French and the Fox tribes over a strategic trade route led to a series of battles during the first half of the 1700s, eventually culminating in the French and Indian War. The Fox tribe was seriously depleted during the battles but the French also faced heavy casualties and the French were further weakened by the ongoing conflicts with the English. At the end of the French and Indian War, in 1763, France ceded its holdings—including Wisconsin—to Great Britain. Great Britain then signed the land to America at the end of the American Revolution. Wisconsin was included in the Northwest Territory, established in 1787, but the government exercised no official control over the land or the settlers and the British continued to monopolize trade from the area.

During the War of 1812, many natives of the area sided with the British against America. After the war ended, American settlement of the region finally began, though the fur trade continued to dominate the economy. Following inclusion in the Indiana Territory in 1800 and the Illinois Territory in 1809, Wisconsin became part of the Michigan Territory in 1818.

The first large-scale immigration took place in the 1820's, due to a lead-mining boom in the mines of southern Wisconsin. Following several Indian wars that eliminated Indian threats, settlers flocked to the southeastern areas of the state along Lake Michigan. The cities of Milwaukee, Racine, and Kenosha were settled during the 1830's. In 1836, Congress created the Wisconsin Territory, which included land from west of the Mississippi River to the Missouri River. The creation of the Iowa Territory in 1838 took away much of the western portion.

In the 1840's many families arrived from Germany and New York. The biggest influx of people came around 1848 when the last Indian lands were relinquished and Wisconsin became a state. They came from the northern European countries, doubling the population between 1850 and 1860. In the Civil War, Wisconsin provided about 90,000 men to the Union. The leading nationalities in Wisconsin are German (by nearly three to one), Polish, Norwegian, Russian, Austrian, Swedish, Czech, Italian, Danish, Hungarian, English, Finnish, Greek, Irish, and French.

Look for vital records in the following locations:

- **Birth and death records:** Contact the State Historical Society of Wisconsin in Madison. Statewide registration began in 1907. A few counties began keeping birth and death records in the 1850's. Both pre- and post-1907 records are at the State Historical Society. To obtain copies write to Vital Records at the address below. Be sure to state the reason for your request.
- **Wills, deeds, land grants, and taxpayer lists:** Available at most county courthouses.
- **Military records:** Contact the Office of the Adjutant General in Madison.
- **Census records:** Residents of Wisconsin were included in the territorial censuses of Indiana in 1820, Michigan in 1830, and Wisconsin in 1849. Special censuses were taken by the territory or state in 1836, 1838, 1840, 1842, 1846, 1847, 1855, 1865, 1875, 1885, 1895, and 1905.

Wisconsin Vital Records Office
PO Box 309
Madison, Wisconsin 53701-0309
(608) 266-1371
www.dhfs.state.wi.us/vitalrecords/index.htm

Wisconsin Historical Society
816 State Street
Madison, Wisconsin 53706
Archives: (608) 264-6460
Library: (608)264-6535

Office of the Adjutant General
Madison, Wisconsin 53702

Societies and Repositories

Afro-American Genealogical Society of Milwaukee; 2620 W. Center St.; Milwaukee, WI 53206.

Ancestors of Richland County Hills; 23783 Covered Bridge Dr.; Richland Center, WI 53581.

Barron County Genealogical Society; 1122 Knapp St.; Chetek, WI 54728.

Bay Area Genealogical Society; PO Box 283; Green Bay, WI 54305-0283.

Chippewa County Genealogical Society; 123 Allen St.; Chippewa Falls, WI 54729-2898; www.chippewacounty.com/home/history.html.

Dodge and Jefferson Counties Genealogical Society; PO Box 91; Watertown, WI 53094-0091.

Dunn County Genealogical Society; PO Box 633; Menomonie, WI 54751.

Eagle River Historical Society; PO Box 2011; Eagle River, WI 54521.

Fond du Lac County Genealogical Society; PO Box 1284; Fond du Lac, WI 54936-1284; www.rootsweb.com/~wifonddu/resources/organizations/fdlgensoc.htm.

Fond du Lac County Historical Society; PO Box 1294; Fond du Lac, WI 54935.

Fox Valley Genealogical Society; PO Box 1592; Appleton, WI 54913-1592.

Fox Valley of Wisconsin Chapter, AHSGR; 945 Anchorage Court; Oshkosh, WI 54901; (920) 235-7231.

French-Canadian/Acadian Genealogists of Wisconsin; PO Box 414; Hales Corners, WI 53130-0414.

Genealogical Research Society of Eau Claire; c/o Chippewa Valley Museum; PO Box 1204; Eau Claire, WI 54702-1204; www.rootsweb.com/~wigrsec.

German Interest Group-Wisconsin; 3730 Kennedy Road; GIG-WI, PO Box 2185; Janesville, WI 53547-2185; www.rootsweb.com/~wigig/index.html.

Grant County, Wisconsin Genealogical Society; Box 281; Dickeyville, WI 53808-0281; reese@mwci.net; www.rootsweb.com/~wigrant/gcgensoc.htm.

Hartford History Room; Hartford Public Library; 115 North Main Street; Hartford, WI 53027; (262) 673-8240; hpl@hnet.net; www.hnet.net/~hpl.

Heart O'Wisconsin Genealogical Society; PO Box 516; Wisconsin Rapids, WI 54494-0516; www.rootsweb.com/~wiwood/HeartOWi/h-master.htm.

Huguenot Society of Wisconsin; 8920 North Lake Drive; Bayside, WI 53217-1940; (414) 351-0644; CChew@execpc.com; www.execpc.com/~drg/wihs.html.

Iowa County Wisconsin Genealogical Society; PO Box 321; Dodgeville, WI 53533-0321; www.friendsnfamily.net/wiiowagensoc/index.html.

Irish Genealogical Society of Wisconsin, (I.G.S.W.); PO Box 13766; Wauwatosa, WI 53213-0766.

Jackson County Historical Society; 13 South 1st St.; Black River Falls, WI 54615.

Jackson County Wisconsin Footprints; W11770 Cty. Rd. P; Black River Falls, WI 54615-5926.

Jewish Genealogical Society, Wisconsin; 9280 N. Fairway Dr.; Milwaukee, WI 53217.

Kenosha County Genealogical Society; 4902 52nd St.; Kenosha, WI 53142.

Kewaunee County Historical Society; PO Box 232; Courthouse Square; Kewaunee, WI 54216.

La Crosse Area Genealogical Society; PO Box 1782; La Crosse, WI 54602-1782; ajlquist@acegroup.cc; www.rootsweb.com/~wilacgs.

Lafayette County Genealogical Society; PO Box 443; Shullsburg, WI 53586; janiceronnerud@hotmail.com; www.rootsweb.com/~wilafcgs.

Langlade County Genealogical Society; PO Box 307; Antigo, WI 54409; www.rootsweb.com/~wilcgs/index.html.

Lower Wisconsin River Genealogical & Historical Research Center; PO Box 202; Wauzeka, WI 53826; www.mwt.net/~bcobe/genealogy.html.

Manitowoc County Genealogical Society; PO Box 1745; Manitowoc, WI 54221-1745.

Marathon County Genealogical Society; PO Box 1512; Wausau, WI 54402-1512; prmorse@dwave.net; www.geocities.com/mcgsociety.

Marshfield Area Genealogical Group; PO Box 337; Marshfield, WI 54449.

Menomonee Falls Historical Society; Box 91; Menomonee Falls, WI 53051.

Milwaukee County Genealogical Society; PO Box 27326; Milwaukee, WI 53227.

Milwaukee County Historical Society; 910 N. 3rd St.; Milwaukee, WI 53203.

Northwoods Genealogical Society; PO Box 1132; Rhinelander, WI 54501.

Oconomowoc Genealogical Club of Waukesha County; 733 E. Sherman Ave.; Oconomowoc, WI 53066.

Polish Genealogical Society of Wisconsin; 3731 Turnwood Dr.; Richfield, WI 53076.

Pornmerscher Verein Freistadt Rundschreiben (Pomeranian Society of Freistadt); PO Box 204; Germantown, WI 53022.

Rock County Genealogical Society; Library at 440 N. Jackson St.; PO Box 711; Janesville, WI 53547-0711; www.rootsweb.com/~wircgs/index.html.

Sons of the American Revolution, Wisconsin Society; 5677 N. Consaul Place; Milwaukee, WI 53217.

Sauk County Historical Society; PO Box 651; Baraboo, WI 53913; schist@shopstop.net; www.saukcounty.com/schs.

Seventh Day Baptist Historical Society; PO Box 1678; Janesville, WI 53547.

Sheboygan County Historical Research Center; 518 Water St. #3; Sheboygan Falls, WI 53085-1455.

South Central Chapter of WSGS; PO Box 5652; Madison, WI 53705-0652; a.r.mclaughlin@worldnet.att.net; www.rootsweb.com/~wisccwsgs.

Southeastern Wisconsin Chapter, AHSGR; 3121 Pioneer Rd.; Mequon, WI 53097-1620; lustyal@aol.com; www.ahsgr.org/wisouthe.html.

St. Croix Valley Genealogical Society; PO Box 396; River Falls, WI 54022; www.pressenter.com/~scvgs.

State Historical Society of Wisconsin; Univ. of Wisconsin; 816 State St.; Madison, WI 53706; (608) 264-6400; www.wisconsinhistory.org.

Stevens Point Area Genealogical Society; c/o Portage County Library; 1001 Main St.; Stevens Point, WI 54481-2860.

Taylor County Genealogical Society; 224 S. Second Street; Medford, WI 54451-1899; tcgs16@hotmail.com; www.rootsweb.com/~witcgs.

Walworth County Genealogical Society; PO Box 159; Delavan, WI 53115-0159; (608) 752-8816; pgleich@ticon.net; www.rootsweb.com/~wiwalwor/wcgs.html.

Washington County Historical Society Museum, Inc.; 340 S. 5th Ave.; West Bend, WI 53095.

Waukesha County Genealogical Society; PO Box 1541; Waukesha, WI 53187-1541.

Waupaca Area Genealogical Society (WAGS); PO Box 42; King, WI 54946-0042; freistedt@gglbbs.com.

White Pine Genealogical Society; PO Box 512; Marienette, WI 54143.

Winnebagoland Genealogical Society; c/o Oshkosh Public Library; 106 Washington Ave.; Oshkosh, WI 54901-4985.

Wisconsin Division for Libraries; WI; www.dpi.state.wi.us/dpi/dltcl/pld/wis_lib.html.

Wisconsin Genealogical Council, Inc.; N9307 Abitz Ln.; Luxemburg, WI 54217-9628.

Wisconsin State Genealogical Society, Inc.; 2109 20th Ave.; Monroe, WI 53566; www.wsgs.org.

Wisconsin State Old Cemetery Society; 6100 West Mequon Rd.; Mequon, WI 53092.

Bibliography and Record Sources

General

Aikens, Andrew J. *Men of Progress, Wisconsin: A Selected List of Biographical Sketches and Portraits of the Leaders in Business, Professional and Official Life,* *Together with Short Notes on the History and Character of Wisconsin*. Milwaukee: Evening Wisconsin Co., 1897.

Alderson, Jo Bartels. *Wisconsin's Early French*. Bowie, Maryland: Heritage Books, 1998.

Bennett, Pansy S. *History of Methodism in Wisconsin*. Cincinnati: Cranston & Stowe, 1890.

Blake, William. *Cross and Flame in Wisconsin: The Story of United Methodism in the Badger State*. Sun Prairie, Wisconsin: United Methodist Church, Wisconsin Conference, 1973.

Cooper, Zachary. *Black Settlers in Rural Wisconsin*. Madison, Wisconsin: State Historical Society of Wisconsin, 1997.

Danky, James P. *Genealogical Research: An Introduction to the Resources of the State Historical Society of Wisconsin*. Rev. ed. Madison: State Historical Society of Wisconsin, 1986.

Danky, James P. *Newspapers in the State Historical Society of Wisconsin: A Bibliography with Holdings*. 2 vols. New York: Norman Ross, 1994.

Dexter, Frank N. *A Hundred Years of Congregational History in Wisconsin*. S.l.: Wisconsin Congregation Conference, 1933 (K & K Print Shop.)

Dictionary of Wisconsin Biography. Madison: State Historical Society, 1960.

Draper, Lyman Copeland. *Collections of the State Historical Society of Wisconsin*. 24 vols. Madison, Wisconsin: State Historical Society of Wisconsin, 1855–.

Draper, Lyman Copeland. *Draper Manuscript Collection*. Chicago: Filmed by the University of Chicago Library, 197–. 147 microfilm.

Gleason, Margaret. *Printed Resources for Genealogical Searching in Wisconsin: A Selective Bibliography*. Detroit: Detroit Society for Genealogical Research, 1964.

Heckman, John. *Brethren in Northern Illinois and Wisconsin*. Elgin, Illinois: Brethren Publishing House, 1941.

Heming, Harry H. *The Catholic Church in Wisconsin: A History of the Catholic Church in Wisconsin from the Earliest Tie to the Present Day Including an Account of the First Churches, Organization of Parishes, Dioceses and Archdiocese, Statement of Present Condition of the Church; Illustrated by Portraits of Archbishop, Bishops, Priests, Prominent Laymen an Pictures of Churches, Educational and Other Religious Institutions*. Milwaukee, Wisconsin: Catholic Historical Publishing Co., 1895–1898.

Herrick, Linda M. *Wisconsin Genealogical Research*. Janesville, Wisconsin: Origins, 1996.

Historical Records Survey (Wisconsin). *Directory of Churches and Religious Organizations in Wisconsin*. Madison, Wisconsin: The Wisconsin Historical Records Survey, 1941.

Historical Records Survey (Wisconsin). *Guide to Church Vital Statistics Records in Wisconsin*. Madison, Wisconsin: Wisconsin Historical Records Survey, 1942.

History of Northern Wisconsin: Containing an Account of its Settlement, Growth, Development Resources; an Extensive Sketch of its Counties, Cities, Towns and Villages, Their Improvement, Industries, Manufactories; Biographical Sketches, Portraits of Prominent Men and Early Settlers; Views of County Seats, etc. Chicago, Illinois: Western Historical, 1881.

History of Wisconsin. Vols. 1–3, 5–6. Madison: State Historical Society, 1973–1988.

Lareau, Paul J., and Elmer Courteau. *French-Canadian Families of the North Central States: A Genealogical Dictionary*. 8 vols. St. Paul, Minnesota: Northwest Territory French and Canadian Heritage Institute, 1980.

Lurie, Nancy Oestreich. *Wisconsin Indians*. Madison, Wisconsin: State Historical Society of Wisconsin, 1980.

Mason, Carol I. *Introduction to Wisconsin Indians: Prehistory to Statehood*. Salem, Wisconsin: Sheffield Publishing, 1988.

Nelke, David I. *Columbian Biographical Dictionary and Portrait Gallery*. Chicago: Lewis Publishing Co., 1895.

Nennett, Pansey S. F. *History of Methodism in Wisconsin*. Cincinnati: Cranston & Stowe, 1980.

Noonan, Barry Christopher. *Index to Green Bay Newspapers, 1833–1840*. Madison, Wisconsin: Wisconsin State Historical Society, 1987.

Notable Men of Wisconsin. Tucson, Arizona: W. C. Cox Co., 1974.

Oehlerts, Donald E. *Guide to Wisconsin Newspapers, 1833–1957*. Madison: State Historical Society of Wisconsin, 1958.

Patterson, Betty. *Some Pioneer Families of Wisconsin: An Index*. Madison: State Genealogical Society, 1977.

Paul, Barbara Dotts. *Wisconsin History: An Annotated Bibliography*. Westport, Connecticut: Greenwood Press, 1999.

Peet, Stephen. *History of the Presbyterian and Congregational Churches and Ministers in Wisconsin*. Milwaukee: S. Chapman, 1851.

Quaife, Milo Milton. *Wisconsin: Its History and Its People, 1634–1924*. 4 vols. Chicago: S. J. Clarke Publishing Co., 1924.

Reed, Parker McCobb. *The Bench and Bar of Wisconsin: History and Biography*. Milwaukee: P. M. Reed, 1882.

Rentmeester, Les. *The Wisconsin Fur-Trade People*. Melbourne, Florida: L & J Rentmeester, 1991.

Rummel, Leo. *History of the Catholic Church in Wisconsin*. Madison, Wisconsin: Wisconsin State Council, Knights of Columbus, 1976.

Ryan, Carol Ward. *Searching for Your Wisconsin Ancestors in the Wisconsin Libraries*. 2nd ed. Green Bay, Wisconsin: Carol Ward Ryan, 1988

Schlinkert, Leroy. *Subject Bibliography of Wisconsin History*. Madison: State Historical Society of Wisconsin, 1947.

Smith, Alice E., ed. *Guide to the Manuscripts of the Wisconsin Historical Society*. Madison, Wisconsin: State Historical Society of Wisconsin, 1944, 1957.

Soldiers' and Citizens' Album of Biographical Record (of Wisconsin): Containing Personal Sketches of Army Men and Citizens Prominent in Loyalty of the Union: Also a Chronological and Statistical History of the Civil War and a History of the Grand Army of the Republic: With Portraits of Soldiers and Prominent Citizens. 2 vols. Bethesda, Maryland: University Publications of America, 1993. 19 microfiches.

Some Pioneer Families of Wisconsin: An Index, Volume 2. Madison: State Genealogical Society, 1987.

Stark, William F. *Ghost Towns of Wisconsin*. Sheboygan, Wisconsin: Zimmermann Press, 1977.

State Historical Society of Wisconsin. *Annotated Catalogue of Newspaper Files of the Library of the State Historical Society of Wisconsin*. Madison: Wisconsin State Historical Society, 1911.

Territorial Papers of the United States: the Territory of Wisconsin, 1836–1848: A Microfilm Supplement. Washington, D.C.: National Archives, 1959.

Tuttle, Charles Richard. *An Illustrated History of the State of Wisconsin: Being a Complete Civil, Political, and Military History of the State, from its First Exploration Down to 1875*. Boston: B. B. Russell, 1875.

United States Biographical Dictionary and Portrait: Gallery of Eminent and Self-made Men: Wisconsin Volume. Chicago: American Biographical Pub., 1877.

University of Wisconsin-Green Bay. *Guide to Archives and Manuscripts in the University of Wisconsin-Green Bay Area Research Center*. Rev. ed. Green Bay, Wisconsin: University of Wisconsin-Green Bay Area Research Center, 1992.

Usher, Ellis B. *Wisconsin: Its Story and Biography, 1848–1913*. 8 vols. Chicago: Lewis Publishing Co., 1914.

Waterstreet, Darlene E. *Biography Index to the Wisconsin Blue Books*. Milwaukee, Wisconsin: Badger Infosearch, 1974.

Wilcox, Pearl. *Regathering of the Scattered Saints in Wisconsin and Illinois*. Independence, Missouri: P. Wilcox, 1984.

Wisconsin Domesday Book: Town Studies. Publications of the State Historical Society of Wisconsin. Minasha, Wisconsin: George Santa Publishing Co., 1924.

Wisconsin Research Outline. Series U.S.-States, no. 49. Salt Lake City: Family History Library, 1988.

Wisconsin. State Historical Society. *Guide to Archives and Manuscripts in the University of Wisconsin-Platteville Area Research Center*. Madison, Wisconsin: State Historical Society of Wisconsin, 1990.

Yearbook of the Wisconsin Evangelical Lutheran Synod. Milwaukee: Northwestern Publishing House, 1989–.

Atlases, Maps and Gazetteers

DeLorme Mapping Company. *Wisconsin Atlas & Gazetteer*. Freeport, Maine: DeLorme Mapping Co., 1988.

DenBoer, Gordon. *Wisconsin, Atlas of Historical County Boundaries*. New York: Charles Scribner's Sons, 1997.

Fox, Michael J., comp. *Maps and Atlases Showing Land Ownership in Wisconsin*. Madison: State historical Society of Wisconsin, 1978.

Gard, Robert E., and L. G. Sorden. *The Romance of Wisconsin Place Names*. New York: October House, 1968. Reprint. Minocqua, Wisconsin: Heartland Press, 1988.

Hale, James B., comp. *Wisconsin Post Office Handbook, 1921–1971*. Wisconsin Postal History Society. Bulletin no. 10. Madison: Wisconsin Postal History Society, 1971.

Hunt, John W. *Wisconsin Gazetteer*. Madison, Wisconsin: P. Brown, 1853. Reprint. Microfiche. Louisville, Kentucky: Lost Cause Press, 1974. Ann Arbor, Michigan: University Microfilm.

Long, John H., ed. Historical *Atlas and Chronology of County Boundaries, 1788–1980*. Vols. 1–5. Boston, Massachusetts: G. K. Hall, 1984.

Peck, George W., ed. *Wisconsin: Comprising Sketches of Counties, Towns, Events, Institutions and persons Arranged in Cyclopedic Form*. Madison, Wisconsin: Western Historical Association, 1906.

Puetz, C. J., comp. *Wisconsin County Maps*. Lyndon Station, Wisconsin: Thomas Publishing Co., 1992.

Robinson, Arthur and Jerry B. Culver. *Atlas of Wisconsin: General Maps and Gazetteers*. Madison: University of Wisconsin Press, 1974.

Snyder, Van Vechten & Co. *Historical Atlas of Wisconsin*. Janesville, Wisconsin: Origins, 1995.

Walling, H. F. *Atlas of the State of Wisconsin*. Detroit: Walling, Tackabury and Co., 1876.

Census Records

Available Census Records and Census Substitutes

Federal Census 1820 (with Michigan), 1830 (with Michigan), 1840, 1850, 1860, 1870, 1880, 1900, 1910, 1920, 1930

Federal Mortality Schedules 1850, 1880

Union Veterans and Widows 1890

State/Territorial Census 1836, 1838, 1842, 1846, 1847, 1855, 1875, 1885 1895, 1905

Dollarhide, William. *The Census Book: A Genealogist's Guide to Federal Census Facts, Schedules and Indexes*. Bountiful, Utah: Heritage Quest, 1999.

Kemp, Thomas Jay. *The American Census Handbook*. Wilmington, Delaware: Scholarly Resources, Inc., 2001.

Lainhart, Ann S. *State Census Records*. Baltimore: Genealogical Publishing Co., Inc., 1992.

Thorndale, William and William Dollarhide. *Map Guide to the U.S. Federal Census, 1790–1920*. Baltimore: Genealogical Publishing Co., 1987.

Court Records, Probate and Wills

Note: Many court records are housed at the Wisconsin State Archives. Court records including probate, wills, inventories, guardianship and administrations are found in the individual county court records.

Delgado, David J. *Guide to the Wisconsin State Archives*. Madison, Wisconsin: State Historical Society of Wisconsin, 1966.

Emigration, Immigration, Migration and Naturalization

Current, Richard Nelson. *"A German State?" in Wisconsin: A Bicentennial History*. New York: W. W. Norton & Co., 1977.

Sachtjen, Maude. *Immigration to Wisconsin: A Thesis*. Madison: University of Wisconsin, 1928.

State Historical Society of Wisconsin (Madison, Wisconsin). *Index to Citizenship*. Microfilm of Original card index at the Wisconsin State Historical Society, Madison. Salt Lake City: Filmed by the Genealogical Society of Utah, 1989.

United States. District Court. (Illinois: Northern District). *Soundex Index to Naturalization Petitions for U.S. District & Circuit Courts, Northern District of Illinois and Immigration and Naturalization Service District 9, 1840–1950*. Salt Lake City: Filmed by the Genealogical Society of Utah, 1988. 183 microfilm.

Wisconsin. Circuit Court (Dane County). *Admission to Citizenship Records, 1855–1906*. Salt Lake City: Filmed by the Genealogical Society of Utah, 1980. Microfilm.

Wisconsin. Circuit Court (Dane County). *Declarations of Intention, 1848–1906*. Salt Lake City: Filmed by the Genealogical Society of Utah, 1980. Microfilm.

Wisconsin. Circuit Court (Dane County). *Petitions and Oaths, 1841–1905*. Salt Lake City: Filmed by the Genealogical Society of Utah, 1980. Microfilm.

Wisconsin. Municipal Court (Madison). *Declarations of Intent, 1861–1906*. Salt Lake City: Filmed by the Genealogical Society of Utah, 1980.

Wisconsin. Municipal Court (Madison). *Declarations of Intent, 1875–1906; Applications for Admission, 1906*. Salt Lake City: Filmed by the Genealogical Society of Utah, 1980. Microfilm.

Wisconsin. Supreme Court. *Naturalization Records, 1840–1900*. Salt Lake City: Filmed by the Genealogical Society of Utah, 1979, 1984. 7 microfilm.

Wisconsin

Land and Property

Bureau of Land Management. *Wisconsin, 1820–1908 Cash and Homestead Entries, Cadastral Survey Plats.* Springfield, Virginia: BLM Eastern States, 1994.

English, William Hayden. *Conquest of the Country Northwest of the River Ohio, 1778–1783, and Life of General George Rogers Clark: With Numerous Sketches of Men Who Served under Clark and Full List of Those Allotted Lands in Clark's Grant for Service in the Campaigns against the British Posts, Showing Exact Land Allotted Each.* 2 vols. Indiana: Bowen–Merrill, 1896.

Land Records: Alabama, Arkansas, Florida, Louisiana, Michigan, Minnesota, Ohio, Wisconsin. S.l.: Brøderbund, 1996. CD-ROM.

Military

Grand Army of the Republic. *Soldiers' and Citizens' Album.* 2 vols. Chicago, Illinois: Grand Army Publishing Co., 1888, 1890.

Miljat, Leslie Elizabeth. *Admission Applications, 1867–1872, National Home for Disabled Volunteer Soldiers, Northwestern Branch. Milwaukee, Wisconsin.* Wauwatosa, Wisconsin: L. E. Miljat, 1991.

Moore, Dennis R. *Researching Your Civil War Ancestors in Wisconsin.* Manitowoc, Wisconsin: Bivouac Publications, 1994.

Revolutionary War Veterans, 1775–1784, Buried in Wisconsin. Salt Lake City: Filmed by the Genealogical Society of Utah, 1975.

Soldiers' and Citizens' Album of Biographical Record, 2 vols. Chicago: Grand Army Pub., 1888, 1890;

United States Veterans Administration. *Pension Index File, Alphabetical; of the Veterans Administration.* Washington, D.C.: Veterans Administration, Publications Service, 1953.

United States. Adjutant General's Office. *Index to Compiled Service Records of Volunteer Union Soldiers Who Served in Organizations from the State of Wisconsin.* Washington, D.C.: The National Archives, 1964. Microfilm.

United States. Selective Service System. *Wisconsin, World War I Selective Service System Draft Registration Cards, 1917–1918.* Washington, D.C.: National Archives, 1987–1988.

Wisconsin Adjutant General's Office. *Annual Report of the Adjutant General, 1865.* Madison, Wisconsin: Democrat Printing. 1912.

Wisconsin. Adjutant General. *Roster of Wisconsin Volunteers, War of the Rebellion 1861–1865.* Madison: Democrat Print Co., 1886.

Wisconsin. Adjutant General's Office. *Military Records, 1861–1865.* Salt Lake City: Filmed by the Genealogical Society of Utah, 1981. Microfilm.

Wisconsin's Gold Star List: Soldiers, Sailors, Marines and Nurses from the Badger State. Madison: State Historical Society of Wisconsin, 1925.

Vital and Cemetery Records

Bookstaff, Manning M. *Index to Deaths Reported in "The Wisconsin Jewish Chronicle," 1921–1961.* Milwaukee: M. M. Bookstaff, 1994.

Daughters of the American Revolution. Wisconsin. *Bible and Cemetery Inscriptions from Wisconsin.* Salt Lake City: Genealogical Society of Utah, 1970. Microfilm.

Daughters of the American Revolution. Wisconsin. *Bible and Cemetery Records, 1700–1940.* Microfilm. Salt Lake City: Genealogical Society of Utah, 1970.

Daughters of the American Revolution. Wisconsin. *Bible and Cemetery Records, 1800–1940.* Microfilm. Salt Lake City: Genealogical Society of Utah, 1970.

Herrick, Linda M., and Wendy K. Uncapher. *Cemetery Locations in Wisconsin.* Origins. Janesville, Wisconsin, 1998.

Wisconsin, Bureau of Health Statistics. *Index to Registration of Births, 1852–1907.* 41 microfiche. Madison: Wisconsin State Historical Society, 1979.

Wisconsin, Bureau of Health Statistics. *Index to Registration of Marriages, 1852–1907.* 77 microfiche. Madison: Wisconsin State Historical Society, 1980.

Wisconsin, Bureau of Health Statistics. *Pre-1907 Death Index By Name.* Madison: Wisconsin State Historical Society, 1981. Microfiche.

Wisconsin, Bureau of Health Statistics. *Unedited Index to Registration of Births, 1852–1907.* 38 microfiche. Madison: Wisconsin State Historical Society, 1979.

Wisconsin. Bureau of Vital Statistics. *Delayed Births, Ca. 1937–1941; Affidavit Delayed Births, Ca. 1940–1942.* Salt Lake City: Filmed by the Genealogical Society of Utah, 1981. Microfilm.

Wisconsin. Bureau of Vital Statistics. *Registration of Deaths, ca. 1862–1907.* Microfilm of original records of the Bureau of Health Statistics in Madison, Wisconsin. Salt Lake City: Filmed by the Genealogical Society of Utah, 1981. 68 microfilm.

Wisconsin. Center for Health Statistics. *Death Records Index, 1959–1984.* Madison, Wisconsin: Wisconsin Center for Health Statistics, 198–. Microfilm.

County Website	Map Index	Date Created	Parent County or Territory From Which Organized Address/Details

Adams   J7   **11 Mar 1848**   **Portage**
www.adamscountywi.com/
Adams County; 400 N Main St; Friendship, WI 53934-0278;
Ph. (608) 339-4200
Details: (Registrar of Deeds has Birth Records from 1860, Marriage Records from 1859, Death Records from 1873 & Land Records from 1853; Clerk Court has Divorce & Court Records; Registrar in Probate has Probate Records)

Ashland   E5   **27 Mar 1860**   **LaPointe**
http://travelbayfieldcounty.com/
Ashland County; 201 Main St W; Ashland, WI 54806-1652;
Ph. (715) 682-7000
Details: (Registrar of Deeds has Birth Records from 1863, Marriage Records from 1879, Death Records from 1877 & Land Records from 1860; Clerk Circuit Court has Divorce & Court Records from 1873; Registrar in Probate has Probate Records from 1890)

Bad Axe   **1 Mar 1851**   **Crawford**
Bad Axe County; WI
Details: (see Vernon) Name changed to Vernon 22 Mar 1862

Barron   G3   **19 Mar 1859**   **Polk**
www.co.barron.wi.us/
Barron County; 330 E La Salle Ave; Barron, WI 54812-1591;
Ph. (715) 537-6200
Details: (Formerly Dallas County. Name changed to Barron 4 Mar 1869) (Registrar of Deeds has Birth, Marriage, Death & Land Records; Registrar in Probate has Probate Records; Clerk Courts has Court Records)

Bayfield   D4   **19 Feb 1845**   **St. Croix**
http://travelbayfieldcounty.com/
Bayfield County; 117 E 5th St; Washburn, WI 54891-9464;
Ph. (715) 373-6100
Details: (Formerly La Pointe County. Name changed to Bayfield 12 Apr 1866) (Registrar of Deeds has Birth, Marriage & Death Records, Land Records from 1850; Clerk Circuit Court has Divorce Records from 1889, Probate Records from 1870 & Court Records from 1888)

Brown   I10   **26 Oct 1818**   **Michigan Terr.**
www.co.brown.wi.us/
Brown County; 305 E Walnut St; PO Box 23600; Green Bay, WI 54305-3600; Ph. (920) 448-4016
Details: (Registrar of Deeds has Birth Records from 1846, Marriage Records from 1821, Death Records from 1834 & Land Records; Clerk Court has Divorce & Court Records from 1832; Registrar in Probate has Probate Records from 1828; see Michigan for 1820–1830 Census)

Buffalo   I3   **6 Jul 1853**   **Jackson**
www.buffalocounty.com/
Buffalo County; 407 S 2nd St; Alma, WI 54610; Ph. (608) 685-6206
Details: (Registrar of Deeds has Birth, Marriage, Death, Burial & Land Records; Clerk Circuit Court has Divorce & Court Records; Registrar in Probate has Probate Records)

Burnett   F2   **31 Mar 1856**   **Polk, Douglas**
www.mwd.com/burnett/
Burnett County; 7410 County Rd K; Siren, WI 54872;
Ph. (715) 349-2173
Details: (Registrar of Deeds has Birth, Marriage & Death Records from 1861, Burial Records, Land Records from 1856 & Military Discharge Records from 1919; Clerk Court has Divorce, Court & Naturalization Records from 1856; Registrar in Probate has Probate Records from 1856)

County Website	Map Index	Date Created	Parent County or Territory From Which Organized Address/Details
Calumet www.co.calumet.wi.us/	J10	7 Dec 1836	**Brown** Calumet County; 206 Court St; Chilton, WI 53014-1198; Ph. (920) 849-1458 **Details:** (Registrar of Deeds has Birth Records from 1851, Marriage Records from 1846, Death Records from 1866 & Land Records from 1840; Clerk Circuit Court has Divorce Records from 1880 & Court Records from 1877; Registrar in Probate has Probate Records from 1868)
Chippewa www.co.chippewa.wi.us/	G4	3 Feb 1845	**Crawford** Chippewa County; 711 N Bridge St; Chippewa Falls, WI 54729-1876; Ph. (715) 726-7980 **Details:** (Registrar of Deeds has Birth Records from 1858, Marriage Records from 1860, Death Records from 1870, Land Records from 1856, Naturalization Records 1895–1955 & 1905 state Census; Registrar in Probate has Probate Records)
Clark www.clark-cty-wi.org/	H5	6 Jul 1853	**Jackson** Clark County; 517 Court St; Neillsville, WI 54456-1992; Ph. (715) 743-5148 **Details:** (County Clerk has Birth & Death Records, Marriage Records from 1866, Land Records from 1855 & Naturalization Records 1857–1954; Registrar in Probate has Probate Records from 1854)
Columbia www.co.columbia.wi.us/defaultt.asp	K8	3 Feb 1846	**Portage** Columbia County; PO Box 177; Portage, WI 53901-0177; Ph. (608) 742-9654 **Details:** (Registrar of Deeds has Land, Birth, Marriage, Death & Burial Records; Clerk Circuit Court has Divorce & Court Records; Registrar in Probate has Probate Records)
Crawford www.rootsweb.com/~wicrawfo/	L4	26 Oct 1818	**Michigan Terr.** Crawford County; 220 N Beaumont Rd; Prairie du Chien, WI 53821-1405; Ph. (608) 326-0200 **Details:** (County Clerk has Birth Records from 1866, Marriage Records from 1820, Death & Burial Records from 1880, Divorce & Court Records from 1848 & Probate Records from 1819; see Michigan for 1820–1830 Census)
Dallas		19 Mar 1859	**Polk** Dallas County; WI **Details:** (see Barron) Name changed to Barron 4 Mar 1869
Dane www.co.dane.wi.us/	L7	7 Dec 1836	**Crawford, Iowa, Milwaukee** Dane County; 210 Martin Luther King Blvd; Madison, WI 53709; Ph. (608) 266-4121 **Details:** (Registrar of Deeds has Birth, Marriage, Death, Land & Military Records; Clerk Court has Divorce, Probate & Court Records)
Dodge www.co.dodge.wi.us/	K9	7 Dec 1836	**Brown, Milwaukee** Dodge County; 127 E Oak St; Juneau, WI 53039; Ph. (920) 386-3600 **Details:** (Registrar of Deeds has Birth, Marriage, Death & Land Records from 1877; Clerk Court has Divorce & Court Records; Registrar in Probate has Probate Records from 1854)

County Website	Map Index	Date Created	Parent County or Territory From Which Organized Address/Details
Door www.co.door.wi.us/	H12	**11 Feb 1851**	**Brown** Door County; 421 Nebraska St; Sturgeon Bay, WI 54235-2204; Ph. (920) 746-2200 **Details:** (Registrar of Deeds has Birth, Marriage, Death & Land Records from 1850; Clerk Court has Divorce Records from 1900 & Court Records from 1860; Registrar in Probate has Probate Records from 1863)
Douglas www.douglascountywi.org/	D3	**9 Feb 1854**	**LaPointe** Douglas County; 1313 Belknap St; Superior, WI 54880-2769; Ph. (715) 395-1341 **Details:** (Registrar of Deeds has Birth, Marriage & Death Records from 1878 & Land Records; Clerk Court has Divorce, Probate & Court Records from 1878)
Dunn www.rootsweb.com/~widunn/	H3	**3 Feb 1854**	**Chippewa** Dunn County; 800 Wilson Ave; Menomonie, WI 54751-2785; Ph. (715) 232-1677 **Details:** (Registrar of Deeds has Birth, Marriage & Death Records from 1860 & Land Records)
Eau Claire www.co.eau-claire.wi.us/	H4	**6 Oct 1856**	**Chippewa** Eau Claire County; 721 Oxford Ave; Eau Claire, WI 54703-5481; Ph. (715) 839-4803 **Details:** (Registrar of Deeds has Birth, Marriage, Death & Land Records from 1856; Clerk Court has Divorce Records from 1856 & Court Records from 1929)
Florence www.florencewisconsin.com/	E9	**18 Mar 1882**	**Marinette, Oconto** Florence County; 501 Lake Ave; Florence, WI 54121-0410; Ph. (715) 528-3201 **Details:** (Registrar of Deeds has Birth, Marriage, Death & Land Records; Clerk Circuit Court has Divorce, Probate & Court Records)
Fond du Lac www.rootsweb.com/~wifonddu/index.htm	K9	**7 Dec 1836**	**Brown** Fond du Lac County; 160 S Macy St; Fond du Lac, WI 54935-4241; Ph. (920) 929-3000 **Details:** (Registrar of Deeds has Birth Records from 1847, Marriage Records from 1844, Death Records from 1868 & Land Records; Clerk Courts has Divorce & Court Records; Probate Office has Probate Records; Veterans Office has Military Records)
Forest www.co.forest.wi.gov	F9	**11 Apr 1885**	**Langlade** Forest County; 200 E Madison St; Crandon, WI 54520; Ph. (715) 478-2422 **Details:** (Register of Deeds has Birth, Death, Marriage & Military Records; Clerk of Courts has Court Records; Clerk of Circuit Court has Divorce Records; County Treasurer has Land & Tax Records; County Clerk has Marriage Records; State Historical Society has Naturalization Records; Probate Court has Probate Records)
Gates		**15 May 1901**	**Chippewa** Gates County; WI **Details:** (see Rusk) Name changed to Rusk 19 Jun 1905

County	Map	Date	Parent County or Territory From Which Organized
Website	Index	Created	Address/Details

Grant M5 **8 Dec 1836** **Iowa**
http://grantcounty.org/

Grant County; 111 S Jefferson; Lancaster, WI 53813;
Ph. (608) 723-2675
Details: (Registrar of Deeds has Birth & Death Records from 1876, Marriage Records from 1840 & Land Records from 1837; Registrar in Probate has Probate Records from 1840; Clerk Court has Divorce & Court Records; Veterans Service Officer has Military Records)

Green M7 **8 Dec 1836** **Iowa**
www.greencounty.org/

Green County; 1016 16th Ave; Monroe, WI 53566-2098;
Ph. (608) 328-9430
Details: (Registrar of Deeds has Birth Records from 1907, Marriage Records from 1846, Death Records from 1878 & Land Records; Clerk Circuit Court has Divorce & Court Records; County Judge has Probate Records)

Green Lake K8 **5 Mar 1858** **Marquette**
www.co.green-lake.wi.us/

Green Lake County; PO Box 3188; Green Lake, WI 54941;
Ph. (920) 294-4005
Details: (Registrar of Deeds has Birth & Death Records from 1876, Marriage & Land Records from 1852 & Military Discharge Records from 1945; Clerk Courts has Divorce & Court Records; Registrar in Probate has Probate Records)

Iowa L6 **9 Oct 1829** **Crawford**
www.iowacounty.org/

Iowa County; 222 N Iowa St; Dodgeville, WI 53533;
Ph. (608) 935-3024
Details: (Registrar of Deeds has Birth & Death Records from 1866, Marriage Records from 1852 & Land Records from 1835; Clerk Circuit Court has Divorce Records from 1860 & Court Records; Registrar in Probate has Probate Records from 1890; see Michigan for 1830 Census)

Iron E6 **1 Mar 1893** **Ashland**
http://ironcountywi.com/

Iron County; 300 Taconite St; Hurley, WI 54534-1546;
Ph. (715) 561-3375
Details: (Registrar of Deeds has Birth, Marriage, Death & Land Records from 1893; Clerk Courts has Divorce & Court Records; Registrar in Probate has Probate Records)

Jackson I5 **11 Feb 1853** **LaCrosse**
www.co.jackson.wi.us/

Jackson County; 307 Main St; Black River Falls, WI 54615;
Ph. (715) 284-0201
Details: (Registrar of Deeds has Birth, Marriage, Death, Burial & Land Records; Clerk Court has Divorce & Court Records; Registrar in Probate has Probate Records)

Jefferson L8 **7 Dec 1836** **Milwaukee**
www.co.jefferson.wi.us/

Jefferson County; 320 S Main St; Jefferson, WI 53549-1718;
Ph. (920) 674-7140
Details: (Registrar of Deeds has Birth & Marriage Records from 1850, Death Records from 1840 & Land Records from 1838; Clerk Circuit Court has Divorce Records from 1851 & Court Records from 1843; Registrar in Probate has Probate Records from 1840)

County Website	Map Index	Date Created	Parent County or Territory From Which Organized Address/Details
Juneau www.juneaucounty.com/	**J6**	**13 Oct 1856**	**Adams** Juneau County; 220 E State St; Mauston, WI 53948; Ph. (608) 847-9300 **Details:** (Registrar of Deeds has Birth, Marriage & Death Records from 1880 & Land Records from 1854; Clerk Court has Divorce & Court Records; Registrar in Probate has Probate Records)
Kenosha www.co.kenosha.wi.us/	**N10**	**30 Jan 1850**	**Racine** Kenosha County; 1010 56th St; Kenosha, WI 53140; Ph. (262) 653-2552 **Details:** (County Clerk has Marriage Records from 1900; Registrar of Deeds has Land Records; Registrar in Probate has Probate Records)
Kewaunee www.gokewaunee.net/	**I11**	**16 Apr 1852**	**Door** Kewaunee County; 613 Dodge St; Kewaunee, WI 54216; Ph. (920) 388-7133 **Details:** (Registrar of Deeds has Birth & Land Records from 1873, Marriage & Death Records from 1874; Registrar in Probate has Probate Records from 1867)
La Crosse www.co.la-crosse.wi.us	**K4**	**1 Mar 1851**	**Crawford** La Crosse County; 400 4th St; La Crosse, WI 54601; Ph. (608) 785-9644, flock.deb@co.la-crosse.wi.us **Details:** (Registrar of Deeds has Birth Records from 1877, Death Records from 1876, Marriage & Land Records from 1851, & Military Records from 1899)
La Pointe http://wicip.uwplatt.edu/lafayette/index.html		**19 Feb 1845**	**St. Croix** La Pointe County; WI **Details:** (see Bayfield) Name changed to Bayfield 12 Apr 1866
Lafayette http://wicip.uwplatt.edu/lafayette/index.html	**M6**	**31 Jan 1846**	**Iowa** Lafayette County; 626 Main St; Darlington, WI 53530; Ph. (608) 776-4850 **Details:** (Registrar of Deeds has Birth Records from 1860, Marriage Records from 1847, Death Records from 1877 & Land Records from 1840; Clerk Court has Divorce & Court Records; Registrar in Probate has Probate Records)
Langlade www.rootsweb.com/~wilangl2/	**G8**	**27 Feb 1879**	**Oconto** Langlade County; 800 Clermont St; Antigo, WI 54409-1985; Ph. (715) 627-6200 **Details:** (Formerly New County. Name changed to Langlade 19 Feb 1880) (Registrar of Deeds has Birth & Death Records; County Clerk has Marriage Records from 1918; Clerk Circuit Court has Divorce & Court Records; Registrar in Probate has Probate Records; County Assessor has Land Records)
Lincoln www.co.lincoln.wi.us/	**G7**	**4 Mar 1874**	**Marathon** Lincoln County; 1110 E Main St; Merrill, WI 54452-2554; Ph. (715) 536-0312 **Details:** (Registrar of Deeds has Marriage & Land Records; Registrar in Probate has Probate Records; Clerk Courts has Court Records)

County Website	Map Index	Date Created	Parent County or Territory From Which Organized Address/Details
Manitowoc www.manitowoc-county.com/	J11	7 Dec 1836	**Brown** Manitowoc County; 1010 S 8th St, Ste 115; Manitowoc, WI 54220; Ph. (920) 683-4004, charpeterson@co.manitowoc.wi.us **Details:** (Register of Deeds has Birth, Death, & Marriage Records from 1850; Clerk of Circuit Court has Divorce & Other Court Records; Register of Probate has Guardianship & Probate Records)
Marathon www.co.marathon.wi.us/	H7	9 Feb 1850	**Portage** Marathon County; 500 Forest St; Wausau, WI 54403; Ph. (715) 261-1500 **Details:** (Registrar of Deeds has Birth, Marriage & Death Records from 1900 & Land Records from 1850; Clerk Circuit Court has Divorce & Court Records from 1900; County Court has Probate Records from 1900)
Marinette www.rootsweb.com/~wimarine/	G10	27 Feb 1879	**Oconto** Marinette County; 1926 Hall Ave; Marinette, WI 54143; Ph. (715) 732-7532 **Details:** (Registrar of Deeds has Birth, Marriage, Death & Land Records from 1879; Clerk Circuit Court has Divorce & Court Records from 1879; Registrar in Probate has Probate Records from 1879)
Marquette http://co.marquette.wi.us/	J7	7 Dec 1836	**Brown** Marquette County; 77 W Park St; Montello, WI 53949; Ph. (608) 297-9136 **Details:** (Registrar of Deeds has Birth Records from 1876, Marriage & Death Records from 1869 & Land Records; Clerk Circuit Court has Divorce & Court Records from 1878 & Naturalization Records 1868–1936; Registrar in Probate has Probate Records from 1890)
Menominee www.rootsweb.com/~wimenomi/	H9	1 May 1961	**Oconto, Shawano** Menominee County; PO Box 279; Keshena, WI 54135; Ph. (715) 799-3311 **Details:** (County Clerk has Birth, Marriage, Death & Land Records; Registrar in Probate has Probate Records)
Milwaukee http://204.194.250.11/	M11	6 Sep 1834	**Brown, Iowa** Milwaukee County; 901 N 9th St; Milwaukee, WI 53233; Ph. (414) 278-4987 **Details:** (Registrar of Deeds has Birth, Marriage & Death Records, Land Records from 1835; Registrar in Probate has Probate Records from 1838)
Monroe www.co.monroe.wi.us/	J5	21 Mar 1854	**La Crosse** Monroe County; 202 S K St; Sparta, WI 54656; Ph. (608) 269-8705 **Details:** (Registrar of Deeds has Birth, Marriage, Death & Land Records; Clerk Court has Divorce, Probate, Court & Naturalization Records; Veterans Service Office has Military Records)
New		27 Feb 1879	**Oconto** New County; WI **Details:** (see Langlade) Name changed to Langlade 19 Feb 1880

County Website	Map Index	Date Created	Parent County or Territory From Which Organized Address/Details

Oconto   H10   6 Feb 1851
www.co.oconto.wi.us/

Brown
Oconto County; 301 Washington St; Oconto, WI 54153-1621;
Ph. (920) 834-6800
Details: (Registrar of Deeds has Birth, Marriage, Death, Burial & Land Records; Clerk Courts has Divorce & Court Records; Registrar in Probate has Probate Records; Oconto Historical Society has Historical Records)

Oneida   F8   1887
www.rootsweb.com/~wigenweb/oneida/

Lincoln
Oneida County; 1 Courthouse Sq; Rhinelander, WI 54501;
Ph. (715) 369-6144
Details: (Registrar of Deeds has Birth, Marriage, Death & Land Records; Clerk Circuit Court has Divorce & Court Records; Registrar in Probate has Probate Records)

Outagamie   I10   17 Feb 1851
www.co.outagamie.wi.us/

Brown, Winnebago
Outagamie County; 410 S Walnut St; Appleton, WI 54911;
Ph. (920) 832-5095
Details: (Register of Deeds has Birth, Death, Marriage, & Land Records & Plot Maps; School Records moved to Green Bay Area Research Center)

Ozaukee   L11   7 Mar 1853
www.co.ozaukee.wi.us/

Washington
Ozaukee County; 121 W Main St; PO Box 994; Port Washington, WI 53074; Ph. (262) 284-8100
Details: (Registrar of Deeds has Birth, Marriage, Death & Land Records from 1853; Clerk Circuit Court has Divorce, Probate & Court Records; County Treasury has tax rolls from 1851)

Pepin   H3   25 Feb 1858
www.co.pepin.wi.us/

Dunn
Pepin County; 740 7th Ave W; Durand, WI 54736-1628;
Ph. (715) 672-8857
Details: (Registrar of Deeds has Birth, Marriage, Death & Land Records; Clerk Circuit Court has Divorce & Court Records; Registrar in Probate has Probate Records)

Pierce   H2   1853
www.co.pierce.wi.us/

Saint Croix
Pierce County; 414 W Main; PO Box 119; Ellsworth, WI 54011;
Ph. (715) 273-3531
Details: (County Clerk has Birth & Death Records from 1876, Marriage Records from 1855, Divorce Records from 1875, Probate Records from 1878 & Court Records from 1869)

Polk   F1   14 Mar 1853
www.co.polk.wi.us/

Saint Croix
Polk County; 100 Polk County Plaza; Balsam Lake, WI 54810;
Ph. (715) 485-9226
Details: (Registrar of Deeds has Birth Records from 1858, Marriage Records from 1861, Death Records from 1866 & Land Records; Clerk Court has Divorce & Court Records; Registrar in Probate has Probate Records)

Portage   I7   7 Dec 1836
www.co.portage.wi.us/

Brown, Crawford, Iowa, Milwaukee
Portage County; 1516 Church St; Stevens Point, WI 54481;
Ph. (715) 346-1351
Details: (Registrar of Deeds has Birth Records from 1863, Marriage Records from 1860, Death Records from 1856 & Land Records; Clerk Circuit Court has Divorce & Court Records from 1844; County Judge has Probate Records from 1890)

County Website	Map Index	Date Created	Parent County or Territory From Which Organized Address/Details
Price www.pricecounty.org/	F6	**26 Feb 1879**	**Chippewa, Lincoln** Price County; 126 Cherry St; Phillips, WI 54555; Ph. (715) 339-3325 **Details:** (Registrar of Deeds has Birth & Marriage Records from 1880, Death Records from 1884 & Land Records from 1867; Clerk Circuit Court has Divorce & Court Records from 1882; Registrar in Probate has Probate Records from 1879; County Clerk has Marriage applications)
Racine www.racineco.com/	M10	**7 Dec 1836**	**Milwaukee** Racine County; 730 Wisconsin Ave; Racine, WI 53403; Ph. (262) 636-3121 **Details:** (Registrar of Deeds has Birth Records from 1876, Marriage & Land Records from 1837, Death Records from 1853 & veterans Records from 1918; Family Court has Divorce Records from 1940; Probate Court has Probate Records from 1846; Clerk Courts has Court Records from 1970)
Richland www.richlandcounty.com/	L5	**18 Feb 1842**	**Crawford, Sauk** Richland County; 181 W Seminary St; Richland Center, WI 53581; Ph. (608) 647-2197 **Details:** (Registrar of Deeds has Birth & Death Records from 1870, Marriage & Land Records from 1850; Clerk Court has Divorce & Court Records from 1860; Registrar in Probate has Probate Records from 1851; City Clerks have Burial Records)
Rock www.co.rock.wi.us/	M8	**7 Dec 1836**	**Milwaukee** Rock County; 51 S Main St; Janesville, WI 53545-3978; Ph. (608) 757-5660 **Details:** (Registrar of Deeds has Birth, Marriage & Death Records from 1849 & Land Records from 1839; Registrar in Probate has Probate Records)
Rusk www.ruskcounty.org/	F4	**15 May 1901**	**Chippewa** Rusk County; 311 Miner Ave E; Ladysmith, WI 54848-1862; Ph. (715) 532-2100 **Details:** (Formerly Gates County. Name changed to Rusk 19 Jun 1905) (Registrar of Deeds has Birth, Marriage, Death & Land Records from 1872; County Court has Divorce, Probate & Court Records)
Sauk www.co.sauk.wi.us/	L6	**11 Jan 1840**	**Crawford, Dane, Portage** Sauk County; 515 Oak St; Baraboo, WI 53913; Ph. (608) 355-3286 **Details:** (Registrar of Deeds has Birth Records from 1860, Marriage Records from 1850, Death Records from 1870 & Land Records; Clerk Circuit Court has Divorce & Court Records; Registrar in Probate has Probate Records)
Sawyer www.sawyercountygov.org/	F4	**10 Mar 1883**	**Ashland, Chippewa** Sawyer County; 10610 Main; PO Box 273; Hayward, WI 54843; Ph. (715) 634-4866 **Details:** (Registrar of Deeds has Birth, Marriage, Death, Burial, Divorce, Probate, Court & Land Records)
Shawano www.co.shawano.wi.us/	H8	**16 Feb 1853**	**Oconto, Waupaca, Winnebago** Shawano County; 311 N Main St; Shawano, WI 54166; Ph. (715) 526-9150 **Details:** (Registrar of Deeds has Birth, Marriage, Death & Land Records; Registrar in Probate has Probate Records)

County Website	Map Index	Date Created	Parent County or Territory From Which Organized Address/Details
Sheboygan www.rootsweb.com/~wisheboy/	K10	7 Dec 1836	**Brown** Sheboygan County; 615 N 6th St; Sheboygan, WI 53081; Ph. (920) 459-3003 **Details:** (Registrar of Deeds has Birth, Marriage, Death & Land Records from 1872; County Court has Divorce, Court & Naturalization Records from 1850; Registrar in Probate has Probate Records from 1850)
St. Croix www.co.saint-croix.wi.us/	H2	9 Jan 1840	**Crawford** St. Croix County; 1101 Carmichael Rd; Hudson, WI 54016; Ph. (715) 386-4609 **Details:** (Registrar of Deeds has Birth, Marriage, Death & Land Records; Clerk Circuit Court has Divorce & Court Records; Registrar in Probate has Probate Records)
Taylor www.taylor-county.com	G5	4 Mar 1875	**Clark, Lincoln, Marathon, Chippewa** Taylor County; 224 S 2nd St; Medford, WI 54451; Ph. (715) 748-1483 **Details:** (Registrar of Deeds has Birth, Marriage, & Death Records from 1875, School Census Records & Platbooks; Clerk Court has Divorce & Court Records; Cicuit Court has Probate Records; Frances L. Simek Memorial Library has Cemetery Indexes, & Microfilms of Census, Naturalization Records, & Newspapers)
Trempealeau www.tremplocounty.com/	I4	27 Jan 1854	**LaCrosse, Jackson, Buffalo, Chippewa** Trempealeau County; PO Box 67; Whitehall, WI 54773-0067; Ph. (715) 538-2311 **Details:** (Registrar of Deeds has Birth, Marriage, Death, Burial & Land Records; Clerk Circuit Court has Divorce & Court Records; Registrar in Probate has Probate Records)
Vernon www.rootsweb.com/~wivernon/	K4	1 Mar 1851	**Crawford** Vernon County; 400 Courthouse Sq St; Viroqua, WI 54665; Ph. (608) 637-5380 **Details:** (Formerly Bad Axe County. Name changed to Vernon 22 Mar 1862) (Registrar of Deeds has Birth, Marriage, Death & Land Records; Clerk Circuit Court has Divorce & Court Records; Registrar in Probate has Probate Records)
Vilas http://co.vilas.wi.us/	E7	12 Apr 1893	**Oneida** Vilas County; 330 Court St; Eagle River, WI 54521; Ph. (715) 479-3600 **Details:** (Registrar of Deeds has Birth, Marriage, Death & Land Records; Registrar in Probate has Probate Records)
Walworth www.walworthcounty.org/	M9	7 Dec 1836	**Milwaukee** Walworth County; 100 W Walworth; PO Box 1001; Elkhorn, WI 53121; Ph. (262) 741-4241 **Details:** (Registrar of Deeds has Birth Records from 1845, Marriage & Land Records from 1839, Death Records from 1872, Burial Records from 1969, Divorce & Court Records from 1850 & Probate Records from 1800's)
Washburn www.rootsweb.com/~wiwashbu/	F3	27 Mar 1883	**Burnett** Washburn County; 10 W 4th Ave; Shell Lake, WI 54871; Ph. (715) 468-4600 **Details:** (Registrar of Deeds has Birth, Marriage, Death & Land Records from 1883; Clerk Courts has Divorce, Probate & Court Records from 1883)

County Website	Map Index	Date Created	Parent County or Territory From Which Organized Address/Details
Washington www.co.washington.wi.us/	L10	7 Dec 1836	**Brown, Milwaukee** Washington County; 432 E Washington St; West Bend, WI 53095; Ph. (262) 335-4301 **Details:** (County Clerk has Birth, Marriage & Death Records from 1850, Divorce & Court Records from 1849; Registrar in Probate has Probate Records from 1851)
Waukesha www.waukeshacounty.gov/	L10	31 Jan 1846	**Milwaukee** Waukesha County; 1320 Pewaukee Rd; Waukesha, WI 53188; Ph. (262) 548-7010 **Details:** (Registrar of Deeds has Birth Records from 1860, Marriage Records from 1846, Death Records from 1879 & Land Records; Clerk Courts has Divorce Records from 1847 & Court Records from 1962; Registrar in Probate has Probate Records from 1846; County Clerk has Marriage applications from 1899)
Waupaca www.rootsweb.com/~wiwaupac/index.htm	I9	17 Feb 1851	**Brown, Winnebago** Waupaca County; 811 Harding St; Waupaca, WI 54981; Ph. (715) 258-6200 **Details:** (Registrar of Deeds has Birth, Marriage, Death & Land Records from 1852; Clerk Court has Divorce Records from 1907 & Court Records from 1880; Clerk Circuit Court has Probate Records from 1857)
Waushara www.1waushara.com/	J8	15 Feb 1851	**Marquette** Waushara County; 209 S Saint Marie St; PO Box 488; Wautoma, WI 54982; Ph. (920) 787-0442 **Details:** (Registrar of Deeds has Birth & Death Records from 1876, Marriage & Land Records from 1852; Clerk Court has Divorce & Court Records; Registrar in Probate has Probate Records)
Winnebago www.co.winnebago.wi.us/	J9	6 Jan 1840	**Brown, Calumet, Fond du Lac, Marquette** Winnebago County; 415 Jackson St; Oshkosh, WI 54901; Ph. (920) 236-4888 **Details:** (Attached to Brown & Fond du Lac Cos prior to organization 1 Jan 1848) (Registrar of Deeds has Birth & Land Records from 1861, Marriage Records from 1870 & Death Records; Registrar in Probate has Probate Records)
Wood www.co.wood.wi.us/	I6	29 Mar 1856	**Portage** Wood County; 400 Market St; Wisconsin Rapids, WI 54494; Ph. (715) 421-8460 **Details:** (Registrar of Deeds has Birth, Marriage & Death Records from 1875 & Land Records; Clerk Courts has Divorce & Court Records from 1875; Registrar in Probate has Probate Records from 1875)
http://co.la-crosse.wi.us			**LaCrosse** LaCrosse County; 400 N. 4th St. LaCrosse, WI, 54601; Ph. (608) 785-9644 **Details:** (Register of Deeds has Birth 1877, Death 1876, Marriage 1851, Military (confidential) 1899, Land Records 1851)

Wyoming

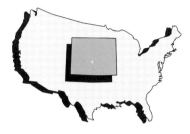

Capital: Cheyenne

Territory: 1868

State: 1890 (44th)

Equal rights

Before 1800, only a few fur traders and explorers entered the Wyoming region. After the Louisiana Purchase, Lewis and Clark and others explored the area. The American and Rocky Mountain Fur Companies explored the area extensively over the next three decades and opened the Overland Trail. In 1834, Fort Laramie became the first permanent settlement in Wyoming. In 1849, it became a supply depot on the Oregon Trail, with up to 50,000 individuals going through the fort in 1850 alone. The second settlement in the state was at Fort Bridger, in 1842.

When the Dakota Territory was established in 1861, Wyoming was included. Laramie County was organized in 1867 and included all of the present state of Wyoming. Between 1867 and 1869, the transcontinental Union Pacific Railway was built through southern Wyoming, bringing the towns of Laramie, Cheyenne, Rawlins, Rock Springs, Green River, and Evanston into existence. Wyoming Territory was created in 1868 with 6,000 to 7,000 inhabitants. Yellowstone Park was established in 1872. Arapaho and Cheyenne Indians moved to reservations. The Sioux Indians were defeated in 1877, after which northern Wyoming was opened to cattle grazing. A cattle boom followed, which reached its peak in the 1880's.

In 1890, Wyoming became a state. The Carey Act of 1894 provided for the reclamation and homesteading of desert land, which stimulated new settlements in northern Wyoming. Mormons established towns in the Big Horn Basin. By 1940, Wyoming's foreign-born residents came from England, Germany, Sweden, Russia, Italy, Austria, Greece, Denmark, Norway, Ireland, Poland, Finland, Czechoslovakia, France, and Hungary.

Look for vital records in the following locations:

- **Birth, death and marriage records:** Contact Vital Records Services, Cheyenne, Wyoming. Birth and death records are available beginning in 1909. Marriage records start on 1 May 1941. Earlier records are filed with the county courts.
- **Probate, land and naturalization records:** Prior to statehood, probate records were kept by the territorial probate court. After statehood, they were kept by the district court in each county, as were naturalization and land records.
- **Census records:** A state census exists for 1905, and is available at the Wyoming State Archives, Museums and Historical Department in Cheyenne.

Vital Records Services
Room 172
Hathaway Building
Cheyenne, Wyoming 82002
(307) 777-7591; Fax: (307) 635-4103
http://wdh.state.wy.us/vital_records/certificate.asp

Wyoming State Archives
2301 Central Avenue
Cheyenne, WY 82002
(307) 777-7826; Fax: (307) 777-7044
http://wyoarchives.state.wy.us/

Societies and Repositories

Cheyenne Genealogical Society; Laramie County Library; Central Ave.; Cheyenne, WY 82001.

Fremont County Genealogical Society; c/o Riverton Branch Library; 1330 W. Park Ave.; Riverton, WY 82501.

Lander Valley (Fremont County) Genealogical Society; 1015 Black Blvd.; Lander, WY 82520; www.fortunecity.com/millenium/bluepeter/119.

Laramie County Library System—Genealogy Department; 2800 Central Avenue; Cheyenne, WY 82001-2799; (307) 634-3561; sseniawski@larm.lib.wy.us; www.lclsonline.org.

Laramie Peekers Genealogical Society of Platte County; 1108 21st St.; Wheatland, WY 82201.

Natrona County Genealogical Society; PO Box 50665; Casper, WY 82605.

Park County Genealogical Society; PO Box 3056; Cody, WY 82414.

Powell Valley Genealogical Club; PO Box 184; Powell, WY 82435.

Sons of the American Revolution, Wyoming Society; 1040 S. Thurmond; Sheridan, WY 82801.

Sheridan Genealogical Society, Inc.; Wyoming Rm., Sheridan County Library; 335 W. Alger; Sheridan, WY 82801.

Southeastern Wyoming Chapter, AHSGR; 2415 Van Lennen; Cheyenne, WY 82001; (307) 634-0309; dennisguil@aol.com.

Sublette County Genealogical Society; PO Box 1186; Pindale, WY 82941.

Weston County Genealogical Society; 23 W. Main; Newcastle, WY 82701.

Wyoming State Archives; Barrett Building; 2301 Central Avenue; Cheyenne, WY 82002; (307) 777-7826; wyarchive@state.wy.us; http://wyoarchives.state.wy.us.

Wyoming State Historical Society; PMB #184; 1740H Dell Range Blvd.; Cheyenne, WY 82009-4946; executive@wyshs.org; http://wyshs.org.

Wyoming State Library; 2301 Capitol Avenue; Cheyenne, WY 82002-0060; (307) 777-6333; refdesk@state.wy.us; www-wsl.state.wy.us.

Yellowstone National Park Archives; PO Box 168; Yellowstone Nat'l Pa, WY 82190; (307) 344-2261; www.nps.gov/yell/technical/museum/index.htm.

Bibliography and Record Sources

General

A Directory of Church and Religious Organizations in the State of Wyoming. Cheyenne: Historical Records Survey, 1939.

Bartlett, Ichabod S. *History of Wyoming.* 3 vols. Chicago: S. J. Clarke Publishing Co., 1918.

Beach, Cora May Brown. *Women of Wyoming: Including a Short History of Some of the Early Activities of Women of Our State, Together with Biographies of those Women Who Were Our Early Pioneers as well as of Women Who Have Been Prominent in Public Affairs and in Civil Organizations and Service Work.* 2 vols. Casper, Wyoming: S. E. Boyer, 1927.

Beard, Frances B. *Wyoming from Territorial Days to the Present.* 3 vols. Chicago: American Historical Society, 1933.

Bird, Twila. *A Century of Saints: A Front Range History of the Church of Jesus Christ of Latter-day Saints.* Aurora, Colorado: Front Range Centennial Committee, 1997.

Chaffin, Lorah. *Sons of the West: Biographical Account of Early-Day Wyoming.* Caldwell, Idaho: Caxton Printers, 1941.

Chamblin, Thomas S. *The Historical Encyclopedia of Wyoming.* 2 vols. Cheyenne, Wyoming: Published by Wyoming Historical Institute, 1970.

Donahue, Jim, ed. *Guide to the County Archives of Wyoming.* Cheyenne, Wyoming: Wyoming State Archives, 1991.

Donahue, Jim, ed. *Guide to the State Government and Municipal Archives of Wyoming.* Cheyenne, Wyoming: Wyoming State Archives, 1991.

Engebretson, Doug. *Empty Saddles, Forgotten Names: Outlaws of the Black Hills and Wyoming.* Aberdeen, South Dakota: North Plains Press, 1982.

Federal Postal Employees and Contractors in Wyoming, 1869–1911. Cheyenne, Wyoming: Medicine Bow Publications, 1985.

Gorzalka, Ann. *Wyoming's Territorial Sheriffs.* Glendo, Wyoming: High Plains Press, 1998.

Guide to Vital Statistics Records in Wyoming: Church Archives. Cheyenne: Historical Records Survey, 1942.

"Guide to Wyoming Frontier Newspapers," *Annals of Wyoming,* vols. 33–35 (1961–1963). Cheyenne: Wyoming State Archives, 1923–.

Hendrickson, Gordon Olaf. *Peopling the High Plains: Wyoming's European Heritage.* Cheyenne, Wyoming: Wyoming State Archives and Historical Department, 1977.

Historical Records Survey (Wyoming). *Inventory of the Church Archives of Wyoming Presbyterian Churches.* Salt Lake City: Filmed by the Genealogical Society of Utah, 1967.

Homsher, Lola. *Guide to Wyoming Newspapers, 1867–1967.* Cheyenne: Wyoming State Library, 1971.

Hoy, Billie. *A History of the Covenant Church in the Midwest and Southwest Conferences.* Salina, Kansas: Arrow Printing Co., 1961.

Inventory of the Church Archives of Wyoming Presbyterian Churches. N.p.: Historical Records Survey, N.d.

Lester, Margaret Moore. *From Rags to Riches: A History of Hilliard and Bear River, 1890–1990.* Evanston, Wyoming: 1st Impressions, 1992.

Peterson, C. S. *Men of Wyoming, The National Newspaper Reference Book of Wyoming: Containing Photographs and Biographies of over Three Hundred Men Residents.* Denver, Colorado: s.n., 1915.

Progressive Men of the State of Wyoming. Chicago: A. W. Bowen, 1903.

Sandahl, Charles Frederick. *The Nebraska Conference of the Augustana Synod: Survey of its Work with Sketches of its Congregations, Institutions, Organizations and Pioneers.* S.l.: Nebraska Conference, 1931.

Spiros, Joyce V. H. G*enealogical Guide to Wyoming.* Gallup, New Mexico: Verlene Publisher, 1982.

Taft, Alfred Larson. *History of Wyoming.* Lincoln: University of Nebraska Press, 1965.

Trenholm, Virginia Cole, ed. *Wyoming Blue Book.* 5 vol. in 6. Cheyenne, Wyoming: Wyoming State Archives and Historical Department, 1991.

United States. Work Projects Administration. *Guide to Public Vital Statistics Records in Wyoming.* Cheyenne, Wyoming: s.n., 1941.

Welch, Charles Arthur. *History of the Big Horn Basin: With Stories of Early Days, Sketches of Pioneers and Writings of the Author.* Salt Lake City: Deseret News Press, 1940.

Wheeler, Denice. *The Feminine Frontier: Wyoming Women, 1850–1900.* S.l.: s.n., 1987.

Wiggins, Marvin E. *Mormons and Their Neighbors: An Index to Over 75,000 Biographical Sketches from 1820 to the Present.* 2 vols. Provo, Utah: Harold B. Lee Library, Brigham Young University, 1984.

Woods, Lawrence M. *Wyoming Biographies.* Worland, Wyoming: High Plains Pub. Co., 1991.

Wyoming Research Outline. Series U.S.-States, no. 50. Salt Lake City: Family History Library, 1988.

Atlases, Maps and Gazetteers

Bishop, Loren C. *Maps of Wyoming Trails, Roads, Migration Routes and Forts.* Cheyenne, Wyoming: Wyoming State Archives & Historical Dept., 1963.

Gallagher, John S. *Wyoming Post Offices, 1850–1980.* Burtonsville, Maryland: The Depot, 1980.

Urbanek, Mae B. *Wyoming Place Names.* Reprint. Missoula, Montana: Mountain Press Publishing Co., 1988.

Wyoming Atlas and Gazetteer. Freeport, Maine: DeLorme Mapping Co., 1993.

Census Records

Dollarhide, William. *The Census Book: A Genealogist's Guide to Federal Census Facts, Schedules and Indexes.* Bountiful, Utah: Heritage Quest, 1999.

Kemp, Thomas Jay. *The American Census Handbook.* Wilmington, Delaware: Scholarly Resources, Inc., 2001.

Lainhart, Ann S. *State Census Records.* Baltimore: Genealogical Publishing Co., Inc., 1992.

Thorndale, William and William Dollarhide. *Map Guide to the U.S. Federal Census, 1790–1920.* Baltimore: Genealogical Publishing Co., 1987.

Court Records, Probate and Wills

Note: Court, probate and will records are kept at the county level. See county pages for individual references.

Emigration, Immigration, Migration and Naturalization

Cornwall, Rebecca. *Rescue of the 1856 Handcart Companies.* Provo, Utah: Brigham Young University Press, 1981.

Knight, Hal. *111 Days to Zion.* Salt Lake City: Deseret News, 1978.

Land and Property

Bolger, Eile. *Preliminary Inventory of the Records of the Bureau of Land Management, Wyoming: Record Group 49.* Denver: Federal Archives and Records Center, 1983.

Stockmen's Gazateer [sic] of Wyoming, 1909. Cheyenne, Wyoming: State of Wyoming Microfilm Dept., 1959.

Military

Johnson, Dorothy M. *The Bloody Bozeman: The Perilous Trail to Montana's Gold.* Missoula, Montana: Mountain Press Pub. Co., 1998.

Murray, Robert A. *Military Posts of Wyoming.* Fort Collins, Colorado: The Old Army Press, 1974.

Sanchez, Leo R. *Reflections of World War II, 115th U.S. Cavalry Wyoming National Guard.* Casper, Wyoming: The School, 1994.

United States. Adjutant General's Office. *Index to Compiled Service Records of Volunteer Union Soldiers Who Served in Organizations From the Territory of Nebraska.* Washington, D.C.: The National Archives, 1964. 2 microfilm.

United States. Selective Service System. *Wyoming, World War I Selective Service System Draft Registration Cards, 1917–1918.* Washington, D.C.: The National Archives, 1987–1988. 14 microfilm.

Vital and Cemetery

Lovell, Evelyn and Marlys Albert Bias. *Davis Funeral Homes Records for 1918–1951, Riverton, Wyoming: Master Index.* Riverton, Wyoming: Fremont County Genealogical Society, 1987.

Martin, Phyllis J. *Uinta County, Wyoming Cemetery Records.* Evanston, Wyoming: the author, 1982.

Territorial Vital Records: Births, Divorces, Guardianship, Marriages, Naturalization, Wills; 1800's thru 1906 Utah

Territory, Arizona, Colorado, Idaho, Nevada, Wyoming, Indian Terr.; LDS Branches, Wards; Deseret News Vital Recs.; J.P. Marriages; Meth. Marriages. St. George, Utah: Genealogical CD Publishing, ca. 1994. CD-ROM.

United States. Work Projects Administration. *Guide to Public Vital Statistics Records in Wyoming.* Cheyenne, Wyoming: s.n., 1941.

Whittlesey, Lee H. *Death in Yellowstone: Accidents and Foolhardiness in the First National Park.* Boulder, Colorado: Roberts Rinehart Pub., 1995.

Wyoming. State Hospital. *Burial Records.* Salt Lake City: Genealogical Society of Utah, 1969.

County Website	Map Index	Date Created	Parent County or Territory From Which Organized Address/Details
Albany www.rootsweb.com/~wyalbany/	**E10**	**16 Dec 1868**	**Original county** Albany County; County Courthouse Rm 202; Laramie, WY 82070; Ph. (307) 721-2541 **Details:** (County Clerk has Marriage Records from 1869, Burial Records from 1885, Land Records from 1868 & Military Records from 1919; Clerk District Court has Divorce, Probate, Court & Naturalization Records)
Big Horn www.rootsweb.com/~wybighor/	**K2**	**12 Mar 1890**	**Fremont, Johnson, Sheridan** Big Horn County; 420 W C St; Basin, WY 82410; Ph. (307) 568-2357 **Details:** (County Clerk has Marriage & Land Records from 1896; Clerk District Court has Divorce, Probate & Court Records from 1896)
Campbell http://ccg.co.campbell.wy.us/	**E3**	**13 Feb 1911**	**Crook, Weston** Campbell County; 500 S Gillette Ave Ste 220; Gillette, WY 82716; Ph. (307) 682-7285 **Details:** (County Clerk has Marriage & Land Records from 1912 & election Records; Clerk Court has Divorce, Probate & Court Records)
Carbon www.rootsweb.com/~wycarbon/	**H10**	**16 Dec 1868**	**Original county** Carbon County; PO Box 6; Rawlins, WY 82301; Ph. (307) 328-2668 **Details:** (County Clerk has Marriage Records from 1876 & Land Records from 1880; Clerk District Court has Divorce, Probate & Court Records; see Nebraska for 1860 Census)
Carter		**27 Dec 1867**	**Original county** Carter County; WY **Details:** (see Sweetwater) Name changed to Sweetwater 13 Dec 1869
Converse www.rootsweb.com/~wyconver/	**E6**	**9 Mar 1888**	**Laramie, Albany** Converse County; 107 N 5th St; PO Box 990; Douglas, WY 82633; Ph. (307) 358-2244 **Details:** (County Clerk has Marriage, Land, Military Discharge & tax Records from 1888 & poll Records from 1930; Clerk Court has Divorce, Probate & Court Records from 1888)
Crook www.rootsweb.com/~wycrook/	**C3**	**8 Dec 1875**	**Laramie, Albany** Crook County; 309 Cleveland St; PO Box 37; Sundance, WY 82729-0037; Ph. (307) 283-1323 **Details:** (County Clerk has Marriage & Land Records from 1855; Clerk Court has Divorce, Probate & Court Records)

County Website	Map Index	Date Created	Parent County or Territory From Which Organized Address/Details
Fremont www.fremontcounty.org	**K7**	**5 Mar 1884**	**Sweetwater** Fremont County; 450 N 2nd St, Rm 220; Lander, WY 82520; Ph. (307) 332-1127; fcclerkfreese@yahoo.com **Details:** (County Clerk has Cemetery, Land, Marriage, & Military Records from 1884; Clerk of District Court has Court, Divorce, & Estate Records)
Goshen www.prairieweb.com/goshen_cty_wy/ gc_home.htm	**B9**	**9 Feb 1911**	**Laramie** Goshen County; 2125 E A St; PO Box 160; Torrington, WY 82240; Ph. (307) 532-4051 **Details:** (County Clerk has Marriage & Land Records; Clerk District Court has Divorce, Probate & Court Records)
Hot Springs www.rootsweb.com/~wyhotspr/	**L5**	**9 Feb 1911**	**Park, Big Horn** Hot Springs County; 415 Arapahoe St; Thermopolis, WY 82443; Ph. (307) 864-3515 **Details:** (County Clerk has Marriage Records from 1913 & Land Records; Clerk District Court has Divorce, Probate & Court Records; Land Records transcribed from Fremont County)
Johnson www.johnsoncountywyoming.org/	**G4**	**8 Dec 1875**	**Carbon** Johnson County; 76 N Main St; Buffalo, WY 82834; Ph. (307) 684-7272 **Details:** (Formerly Pease County. Name changed to Johnson 13 Dec 1879) (County Clerk has Marriage & Land Records; Clerk District Court has Divorce, Probate & Court Records)
Laramie http://webgate.co.laramie.wy.us/	**C11**	**9 Jan 1867**	**Original county** Laramie County; 309 W 20th St; Cheyenne, WY 82001; Ph. (307) 633-4268 **Details:** (County Clerk has Marriage Records from 1868 & Land Records; Clerk District Court has Divorce, Probate & Court Records; see Nebraska for 1860 Census)
Lincoln www.co.lincoln.wy.us/	**P9**	**1911**	**Uinta** Lincoln County; PO Box 670; Kemmerer, WY 83101; Ph. (307) 877-9056 **Details:** (County Clerk has Marriage Records from 1913 & Land Records; Clerk District Court has Divorce & Probate Records from 1913 & Court Records)
Natrona www.rootsweb.com/~wynatron/	**G6**	**9 Mar 1888**	**Carbon** Natrona County; 200 N Center St Rm 157; Casper, WY 82601; Ph. (307) 235-9200 **Details:** (County Clerk has Marriage & Land Records from 1888, Military Discharge Records, power of attorney, notary & commissions tax license-state & federal; Clerk District Court has Divorce, Probate & Court Records)
Niobrara www.rootsweb.com/~wyniobra/	**C6**	**14 Feb 1911**	**Converse** Niobrara County; 424 S Elm; PO Box 420; Lusk, WY 82225; Ph. (307) 334-2211 **Details:** (County Clerk has Marriage & Land Records from 1888; Clerk District Court has Divorce, Probate & Court Records)

County Website	Map Index	Date Created	Parent County or Territory From Which Organized Address/Details
Park www.rootsweb.com/~wypark/	N3	15 Feb 1909	**Big Horn** Park County; 1002 Sheridan Ave; PO Box 160; Cody, WY 82414; Ph. (307) 587-5548 **Details:** (County Clerk has Marriage & Land Records from 1911; Clerk Court has Divorce, Probate & Court Records)
Pease		8 Dec 1875	**Carbon** Pease County; WY **Details:** (see Johnson) Name changed to Johnson 13 Dec 1879
Platte www.rootsweb.com/~wyplatte/	D9	9 Feb 1911	**Laramie** Platte County; 800 9th St; PO Box 728; Wheatland, WY 82201; Ph. (307) 322-2315 **Details:** (Vital Statistics has Birth, Death, & Marriage Records; City Clerk has Burial Records; Clerk of Courts has Court Records; Clerk of District Court has Divorce, Guardianship, & Probate Records; County Clerk has Land & Military Discharge Records; County Library has Newspapers; Federal Level has Natuarlization & Census Records; County Treasurer has Tax Records)
Sheridan www.sheridancounty.com/	G2	9 Mar 1888	**Johnson** Sheridan County; 224 S Main St Ste B2; Sheridan, WY 82801; Ph. (307) 674-2500 **Details:** (County Clerk has Marriage & Land Records from 1888; Clerk District Court has Divorce, Probate & Court Records)
Sublette www.sublette.com	N8	15 Feb 1921	**Fremont, Lincoln** Sublette County; PO Box 250; Pinedale, WY 82941; Ph. (307) 367-4372 **Details:** (State Archives has Land Records 1922–1967, & Marriage Records 1923–1967; Clerk of District Court has Divore, Probate, & Court Records from 1923)
Sweetwater www.co.sweet.wy.us/	L9	27 Dec 1867	Sweetwater County; 80 W Flaming Gorge Way; PO Box 730; Green River, WY 82935; Ph. (307) 872-6400 **Details:** (Formerly Carter County. Name changed to Sweetwater 13 Dec 1869) (County Clerk has Marriage Records from 1864 & Land Records from 1876; Clerk District Court has Divorce, Probate & Court Records; see Nebraska for 1860 Census)
Teton www.rootsweb.com/~wyteton/	P4	15 Feb 1921	**Lincoln** Teton County; 200 S Willow; PO Box 1727; Jackson, WY 83001; Ph. (307) 733-4430 **Details:** (County Clerk has Marriage, Divorce, Probate, Land & Court Records)
Uinta www.uintacounty.com/	P11	1 Dec 1869	**Original county** Uinta County; 225 9th St; PO Box 810; Evanston, WY 82931; Ph. (307) 783-0306 **Details:** (County Clerk has Marriage Records from 1872, Land Records from 1870 & Military Discharge Records from 1902; Clerk District Court has Divorce & Probate Records; see Nebraska for 1860 Census)

County Website	Map Index	Date Created	Parent County or Territory From Which Organized Address/Details
Washakie www.rootsweb.com/~wywashak/	**J4**	**9 Feb 1911**	**Big Horn** Washakie County; 10th St & Big Horn Ave; Worland, WY 82401; Ph. (307) 347-6491 **Details:** (County Clerk has Marriage & Land Records; Clerk District Court has Divorce, Probate & Court Records)
Weston www.rootsweb.com/~wyweston/	**C5**	**12 Mar 1890**	**Crook** Weston County; 1 W Main St; Newcastle, WY 82701; Ph. (307) 746-4744 **Details:** (County Clerk has Marriage Records from 1890 & Land Records from 1886; Clerk District Court has Divorce, Probate & Court Records from 1890)

County Index

A, Oklahoma, 611
Abbeville, South Carolina, 670
Acadia County, Louisiana, 315
Acadia Parish, Louisiana, 315
Accawmack, Virginia, 785
Accomack, Virginia, 785
Ada, Idaho, 186
Adair, Iowa, 244
Adair, Kentucky, 292
Adair, Missouri, 437
Adair, Oklahoma, 611
Adams, Colorado, 87
Adams, Idaho, 186
Adams, Illinois, 200
Adams, Indiana, 223
Adams, Iowa, 244
Adams, Mississippi, 416
Adams, Nebraska, 472
Adams, North Dakota, 572
Adams, Ohio, 592
Adams, Pennsylvania, 645
Adams, Washington, 812
Adams, Wisconsin, 837
Addison, Vermont, 773
Aiken, South Carolina, 670
Aishcum, Michigan, 374
Aitkin, Minnesota, 397
Alachua, Florida, 132
Alamance, North Carolina, 555
Alameda, California, 75
Alamosa, Colorado, 87
Albany, New York, 536
Albany, Wyoming, 850
Albemarle, North Carolina, 555
Albemarle, Virginia, 785
Alcona, Michigan, 374
Alcorn, Mississippi, 416
Aleutians East Borough, Alaska, 40
Aleutians West Census Area, Alaska, 40
Alexander, Illinois, 200
Alexander, North Carolina, 555
Alexandria (Ind. City), Virginia, 785
Alfalfa, Oklahoma, 611
Alger, Michigan, 374
Allamakee, Iowa, 244
Allegan, Michigan, 374
Allegany, Maryland, 346
Allegany, New York, 536
Alleghany, North Carolina, 555
Alleghany, Virginia, 785
Allegheny, Pennsylvania, 645
Allen, Indiana, 223
Allen, Kansas, 267
Allen, Kentucky, 292
Allen, Missouri, 437
Allen, Ohio, 592
Allen Parish, Louisiana, 315
Allendale, South Carolina, 670
Allred, North Dakota, 572
Alpena, Michigan, 374
Alpine, California, 75
Alturas, Idaho, 186
Amador, California, 75
Amelia, Virginia, 785
Amherst, Virginia, 786
Amite, Mississippi, 416
Anamickee, Michigan, 374
Anchorage Borough, Alaska, 40
Anderson, Kansas, 267
Anderson, Kentucky, 292
Anderson, South Carolina, 670
Anderson, Tennessee, 700
Anderson, Texas, 723
Andrew, Missouri, 437
Andrews, Texas, 723
Androscoggin, Maine, 333
Andy Johnson, Minnesota, 397
Angelina, Texas, 723
Anne Arundel, Maryland, 346
Anoka, Minnesota, 397
Anson, North Carolina, 555
Antelope, Nebraska, 472
Antrim, Michigan, 374
Apache, Arizona, 47
Appanoose, Iowa, 244
Appling, Georgia, 153
Appomattox, Virginia, 786
Aransas, Texas, 724
Arapahoe, Colorado, 87
Arapahoe, Kansas, 267
Archdale, North Carolina, 555

Archer, Texas, 724
Archuleta, Colorado, 88
Arenac, Michigan, 374
Arenac, old, Michigan, 375
Arkansas, Arkansas, 54
Arkansas, Missouri, 437
Arlington, Virginia, 786
Armstrong, Pennsylvania, 645
Armstrong, South Dakota, 682
Armstrong, Texas, 724
Armstrong, old, South Dakota, 682
Aroostook, Maine, 333
Arthur, Nebraska, 472
Ascension Parish, Louisiana, 315
Ashe, North Carolina, 555
Ashland, Ohio, 593
Ashland, Wisconsin, 837
Ashley, Arkansas, 54
Ashley, Missouri, 437
Ashmore, South Dakota, 682
Ashtabula, Ohio, 593
Asotin, Washington, 812
Assumption Parish, Louisiana, 315
Atascosa, Texas, 724
Atchison, Kansas, 267
Atchison, Missouri, 437
Athens, Ohio, 593
Atkinson, Georgia, 153
Atlantic, New Jersey, 513
Atoka, Oklahoma, 611
Attakapas County, Louisiana, 316
Attala, Mississippi, 416
Audrain, Missouri, 437
Audubon, Iowa, 244
Auglaize, Ohio, 593
Augusta, Virginia, 786
Aurora, South Dakota, 682
Austin, Texas, 724
Autauga, Alabama, 28
Avery, North Carolina, 555
Avoyelles Parish, Louisiana, 316

B, Oklahoma, 611
Baca, Colorado, 88
Bacon, Georgia, 153
Bad Ax, Wisconsin, 837
Bailey, Texas, 724
Bainbridge, Mississippi, 416
Baine, Alabama, 28
Baker, Alabama, 28
Baker, Florida, 132
Baker, Georgia, 153
Baker, Oregon, 627
Baldwin, Alabama, 28
Baldwin, Georgia, 153
Ballard, Kentucky, 292
Baltimore, Maryland, 346
Baltimore City, Maryland, 346
Bamberg, South Carolina, 670
Bancroft, Iowa, 245
Bandera, Texas, 724
Banks, Georgia, 153
Banner, Nebraska, 472
Bannock, Idaho, 186
Baraga, Michigan, 375
Barber, Kansas, 267
Barbour, Alabama, 28
Barbour, Virginia, 786
Barbour, West Virginia, 824
Barnes, North Dakota, 572
Barnstable, Massachusetts, 360
Barnwell, South Carolina, 670
Barren, Kentucky, 292
Barron, Wisconsin, 837
Barrow, Georgia, 153
Barry, Michigan, 375
Barry, Missouri, 437
Bartholomew, Indiana, 223
Barton, Kansas, 267
Barton, Missouri, 437
Bartow, Georgia, 153
Bastrop, Texas, 724
Bates, Missouri, 438
Bath, Kentucky, 293
Bath, North Carolina, 555
Bath, Virginia, 786
Baton Rouge Parish, Louisiana, 316
Baxter, Arkansas, 55
Bay, Florida, 132
Bay, Michigan, 375
Bayfield, Wisconsin, 837

Baylor, Texas, 725
Beadle, South Dakota, 682
Beadle, old, South Dakota, 682
Bear Lake, Idaho, 186
Beaufort, North Carolina, 556
Beaufort, South Carolina, 670
Beauregard Parish, Louisiana, 316
Beaver, Oklahoma, 611
Beaver, Pennsylvania, 645
Beaver, Utah, 762
Beaverhead, Montana, 459
Becker, Minnesota, 397
Beckham, Oklahoma, 611
Bedford, Pennsylvania, 645
Bedford, Tennessee, 700
Bedford, Virginia, 786
Bedford (Ind. City), Virginia, 786
Bee, Texas, 725
Belknap, New Hampshire, 501
Bell, Kentucky, 293
Bell, Texas, 725
Belmont, Ohio, 593
Beltrami, Minnesota, 397
Benewah, Idaho, 186
Ben Hill, Georgia, 154
Bennett, South Dakota, 682
Bennington, Vermont, 773
Benson, North Dakota, 572
Bent, Colorado, 88
Benton, Alabama, 28
Benton, Arkansas, 55
Benton, Florida, 132
Benton, Indiana, 223
Benton, Iowa, 245
Benton, Minnesota, 397
Benton, Mississippi, 416
Benton, Missouri, 438
Benton, Oregon, 627
Benton, Tennessee, 700
Benton, Washington, 812
Benzie, Michigan, 375
Bergen, New Jersey, 513
Berkeley, North Carolina, 556
Berkeley, South Carolina, 670
Berkeley, Virginia, 786
Berkeley, West Virginia, 824
Berkeley, old, South Carolina, 670
Berks, Pennsylvania, 645
Berkshire, Massachusetts, 360
Bermuda, Virginia, 786
Bernalillo, New Mexico, 522
Berrien, Georgia, 154
Berrien, Michigan, 375
Bertie, North Carolina, 556
Bethel Census Area, Alaska, 40
Bevil, Texas, 725
Bexar, Texas, 725
Bibb, Alabama, 28
Bibb, Georgia, 154
Bienville Parish, Louisiana, 316
Big Horn, Montana, 459
Big Horn, Wyoming, 850
Big Horn, old, Montana, 459
Big Sioux, Minnesota, 397
Big Sioux, South Dakota, 683
Big Stone, Minnesota, 397
Billings, Kansas, 267
Billings, North Dakota, 572
Bingham, Idaho, 186
Black Hawk, Iowa, 245
Blackbird, Nebraska, 472
Blackford, Indiana, 223
Bladen, North Carolina, 556
Blaine, Idaho, 186
Blaine, Montana, 459
Blaine, Nebraska, 472
Blaine, Oklahoma, 611
Blair, Pennsylvania, 645
Blanco, Texas, 725
Bland, Virginia, 787
Bleckley, Georgia, 154
Bledsoe, Tennessee, 700
Bleeker, Michigan, 375
Blount, Alabama, 28
Blount, Tennessee, 700
Blue Earth, Minnesota, 398
Boise, Idaho, 186
Bolivar, Mississippi, 417
Bollinger, Missouri, 438
Bon Homme, South Dakota, 683
Bond, Illinois, 200

Bonner, Idaho, 187
Bonneville, Idaho, 187
Boone, Arkansas, 55
Boone, Illinois, 201
Boone, Indiana, 224
Boone, Iowa, 245
Boone, Kentucky, 293
Boone, Missouri, 438
Boone, Nebraska, 472
Boone, Virginia, 787
Boone, West Virginia, 824
Borden, Texas, 725
Boreman, South Dakota, 683
Bosque, Texas, 725
Bossier Parish, Louisiana, 316
Botetourt, Virginia, 787
Bottineau, North Dakota, 572
Boulder, Colorado, 88
Boundary, Idaho, 187
Bourbon, Kansas, 267
Bourbon, Kentucky, 293
Bowie, Texas, 726
Bowman, North Dakota, 573
Box Butte, Nebraska, 472
Box Elder, Utah, 762
Boyd, Kentucky, 293
Boyd, Nebraska, 472
Boyle, Kentucky, 293
Bracken, Kentucky, 293
Bradford, Florida, 132
Bradford, Pennsylvania, 646
Bradley, Arkansas, 55
Bradley, Tennessee, 701
Bramble, South Dakota, 683
Branch, Michigan, 375
Branciforte, California, 75
Brantley, Georgia, 154
Braxton, Virginia, 787
Braxton, West Virginia, 824
Brazoria, Texas, 726
Brazos, Texas, 726
Breathitt, Kentucky, 293
Breckenridge, Kansas, 267
Breckenridge, Minnesota, 398
Breckinridge, Kentucky, 293
Bremer, Iowa, 245
Brevard, Florida, 132
Brewster, Texas, 726
Briscoe, Texas, 726
Bristol, Massachusetts, 360
Bristol, Rhode Island, 661
Bristol (Ind. City), Virginia, 787
Bristol Bay Borough, Alaska, 40
Broadwater, Montana, 459
Bronx, New York, 536
Brooke, Virginia, 787
Brooke, West Virginia, 824
Brookings, South Dakota, 683
Brooks, Georgia, 154
Brooks, Texas, 726
Broome, New York, 536
Broomfield, Colorado, 88
Broward, Florida, 132
Brown, Illinois, 201
Brown, Indiana, 224
Brown, Kansas, 268
Brown, Minnesota, 398
Brown, Nebraska, 473
Brown, Ohio, 593
Brown, South Dakota, 683
Brown, Texas, 726
Brown, Wisconsin, 837
Bruguier, South Dakota, 683
Brule, South Dakota, 683
Brunswick, North Carolina, 556
Brunswick, Virginia, 787
Bryan, Georgia, 154
Bryan, Oklahoma, 611
Buchanan, Iowa, 245
Buchanan, Minnesota, 398
Buchanan, Missouri, 438
Buchanan, Texas, 726
Buchanan, Virginia, 787
Buckingham, Virginia, 787
Bucks, Pennsylvania, 646
Buena Vista, Iowa, 245
Buena Vista (Ind. City), Virginia, 787
Buffalo, Kansas, 268
Buffalo, Nebraska, 473
Buffalo, North Dakota, 573
Buffalo, South Dakota, 683

Geauga, Ohio, 596
Gem, Idaho, 188
Genesee, Michigan, 378
Genesee, New York, 538
Geneva, Alabama, 32
Gentry, Missouri, 442
George, Mississippi, 418
Georgetown, South Carolina, 673
German Coast County, Louisiana, 318
Gibson, Indiana, 226
Gibson, Tennessee, 704
Gila, Arizona, 47
Gilchrist, Florida, 134
Giles, Tennessee, 704
Giles, Virginia, 792
Gillespie, Texas, 734
Gilliam, Oregon, 628
Gilmer, Georgia, 160
Gilmer, Virginia, 792
Gilmer, West Virginia, 825
Gilpin, Colorado, 90
Gingras, North Dakota, 575
Glacier, Montana, 461
Glades, Florida, 134
Gladwin, Michigan, 378
Glascock, Georgia, 160
Glasgow, North Carolina, 559
Glasscock, Texas, 734
Glenn, California, 76
Gloucester, New Jersey, 514
Gloucester, Virginia, 792
Glynn, Georgia, 160
Godfrey, Kansas, 271
Gogebic, Michigan, 378
Golden Valley, Montana, 461
Golden Valley, North Dakota, 575
Goliad, Texas, 734
Gonzales, Texas, 734
Goochland, Virginia, 792
Goodhue, Minnesota, 400
Gooding, Idaho, 188
Gordon, Georgia, 160
Goshen, Wyoming, 851
Gosper, Nebraska, 477
Gove, Kansas, 271
Grady, Georgia, 160
Grady, Oklahoma, 614
Grafton, New Hampshire, 502
Graham, Arizona, 47
Graham, Kansas, 272
Graham, North Carolina, 560
Grainger, Tennessee, 704
Grand, Colorado, 90
Grand, Utah, 763
Grand Forks, North Dakota, 575
Grand Isle, Vermont, 774
Grand Traverse, Michigan, 378
Granite, Montana, 461
Grant, Arkansas, 57
Grant, Indiana, 226
Grant, Kansas, 272
Grant, Kentucky, 296
Grant, Minnesota, 400
Grant, Nebraska, 477
Grant, New Mexico, 523
Grant, North Dakota, 575
Grant, Oklahoma, 614
Grant, Oregon, 628
Grant, South Dakota, 686
Grant, Washington, 813
Grant, Wisconsin, 840
Grant, West Virginia, 825
Grant Parish, Louisiana, 318
Granville, North Carolina, 560
Granville, South Carolina, 673
Gratiot, Michigan, 378
Graves, Kentucky, 296
Gray, Kansas, 272
Gray, Texas, 734
Gray, old, Kansas, 272
Grays Harbor, Washington, 813
Grayson, Kentucky, 297
Grayson, Texas, 735
Grayson, Virginia, 792
Greasewood, Utah, 763
Great Salt Lake, Utah, 763
Greeley, Kansas, 272
Greeley, Nebraska, 477
Greeley, South Dakota, 687
Green, Kentucky, 297
Green, Wisconsin, 840
Green Lake, Wisconsin, 840
Green River, Utah, 763
Greenbrier, Virginia, 792
Greenbrier, West Virginia, 825
Greene, Alabama, 32
Greene, Arkansas, 57
Greene, Georgia, 161
Greene, Illinois, 204
Greene, Indiana, 226
Greene, Iowa, 250
Greene, Mississippi, 418
Greene, Missouri, 442

Greene, North Carolina, 560
Greene, Nebraska, 477
Greene, New York, 538
Greene, Ohio, 596
Greene, Pennsylvania, 649
Greene, Tennessee, 704
Greene, Virginia, 792
Greenlee, Arizona, 47
Greensville, Virginia, 792
Greenville, South Carolina, 673
Greenwood, Colorado, 90
Greenwood, Kansas, 272
Greenwood, South Carolina, 673
Greer, Oklahoma, 614
Gregg, Texas, 735
Gregory, South Dakota, 687
Grenada, Mississippi, 419
Griggs, North Dakota, 575
Grimes, Texas, 735
Grundy, Illinois, 204
Grundy, Iowa, 250
Grundy, Missouri, 443
Grundy, Tennessee, 704
Guadalupe, Colorado, 91
Guadalupe, New Mexico, 523
Guadalupe, Texas, 735
Guernsey, Ohio, 596
Guilford, North Carolina, 560
Gulf, Florida, 134
Gunnison, Colorado, 91
Guthrie, Iowa, 250
Gwinnett, Georgia, 161

H, Oklahoma, 614
Haakon, South Dakota, 687
Habersham, Georgia, 161
Haines Borough, Alaska, 40
Hale, Alabama, 32
Hale, Texas, 735
Halifax, North Carolina, 560
Halifax, Virginia, 792
Hall, Georgia, 161
Hall, Nebraska, 477
Hall, Texas, 735
Hamblen, Tennessee, 704
Hamilton, Florida, 134
Hamilton, Illinois, 204
Hamilton, Indiana, 227
Hamilton, Iowa, 250
Hamilton, Kansas, 272
Hamilton, Nebraska, 477
Hamilton, New York, 538
Hamilton, Ohio, 596
Hamilton, Tennessee, 704
Hamilton, Texas, 735
Hamlin, South Dakota, 687
Hampden, Massachusetts, 361
Hampshire, Massachusetts, 361
Hampshire, Virginia, 793
Hampshire, West Virginia, 825
Hampton, South Carolina, 673
Hampton (Ind. City), Virginia, 793
Hancock, Alabama, 32
Hancock, Georgia, 161
Hancock, Illinois, 204
Hancock, Indiana, 227
Hancock, Iowa, 250
Hancock, Kentucky, 297
Hancock, Maine, 334
Hancock, Mississippi, 419
Hancock, Ohio, 597
Hancock, Tennessee, 704
Hancock, Virginia, 793
Hancock, West Virginia, 825
Hand, South Dakota, 687
Hanover, Virginia, 793
Hansford, Texas, 735
Hanson, South Dakota, 687
Haralson, Georgia, 161
Hardee, Florida, 135
Hardeman, Tennessee, 705
Hardeman, Texas, 736
Hardin, Illinois, 205
Hardin, Iowa, 250
Hardin, Kentucky, 297
Hardin, Ohio, 597
Hardin, Tennessee, 705
Hardin, Texas, 736
Harding, New Mexico, 523
Harding, South Dakota, 687
Harding, old, South Dakota, 687
Hardy, Virginia, 793
Hardy, West Virginia, 825
Harford, Maryland, 347
Harlan, Kentucky, 297
Harlan, Nebraska, 477
Harmon, Oklahoma, 614
Harnett, North Carolina, 560
Harney, Oregon, 628
Harper, Kansas, 273
Harper, Oklahoma, 615
Harris, Georgia, 161

Harris, Texas, 736
Harrisburg, Texas, 736
Harrison, Indiana, 227
Harrison, Iowa, 250
Harrison, Kentucky, 297
Harrison, Mississippi, 443
Harrison, Mississippi, 419
Harrison, Ohio, 597
Harrison, Texas, 736
Harrison, Virginia, 793
Harrison, West Virginia, 825
Harrisonburg (Ind. City), Virginia, 793
Hart, Georgia, 162
Hart, Kentucky, 297
Hartford, Connecticut, 106
Hartley, Texas, 736
Harvey, Kansas, 273
Haskell, Kansas, 273
Haskell, Oklahoma, 615
Haskell, Texas, 736
Hawaii, Hawaii, 179
Hawkins, Tennessee, 705
Hayes, Nebraska, 477
Hays, Texas, 736
Haywood, North Carolina, 560
Haywood, Tennessee, 705
Heard, Georgia, 162
Hemphill, Texas, 737
Hempstead, Arkansas, 58
Hempstead, Missouri, 443
Henderson, Illinois, 205
Henderson, Kentucky, 298
Henderson, North Carolina, 560
Henderson, Tennessee, 705
Henderson, Texas, 737
Hendricks, Indiana, 227
Hendry, Florida, 135
Hennepin, Minnesota, 401
Henrico, Virginia, 793
Henry, Alabama, 32
Henry, Georgia, 162
Henry, Illinois, 205
Henry, Indiana, 227
Henry, Iowa, 251
Henry, Kentucky, 298
Henry, Missouri, 443
Henry, Ohio, 597
Henry, Tennessee, 705
Henry, Virginia, 793
Herkimer, New York, 538
Hernando, Florida, 135
Hertford, North Carolina, 561
Hettinger, North Dakota, 575
Hettinger, old, North Dakota, 576
Hickman, Kentucky, 298
Hickman, Tennessee, 705
Hickory, Missouri, 443
Hidalgo, New Mexico, 523
Hidalgo, Texas, 737
Highland, Missouri, 443
Highland, Ohio, 597
Highland, Virginia, 793
Highlands, Florida, 135
Hill, Montana, 461
Hill, Texas, 737
Hillsborough, Florida, 135
Hillsborough, New Hampshire, 502
Hillsdale, Michigan, 378
Hilton, South Carolina, 673
Hinds, Mississippi, 419
Hinsdale, Colorado, 91
Hitchcock, Nebraska, 477
Hoarekill, Delaware, 115
Hocking, Ohio, 597
Hockley, Texas, 737
Hodgeman, Kansas, 273
Hoke, North Carolina, 561
Holmes, Florida, 135
Holmes, Mississippi, 419
Holmes, Ohio, 597
Holt, Missouri, 443
Holt, Nebraska, 478
Honolulu, Hawaii, 179
Hood, Texas, 737
Hood River, Oregon, 628
Hooker, Nebraska, 478
Hopewell (Ind. City), Virginia, 793
Hopkins, Kentucky, 298
Hopkins, Texas, 737
Horry, South Carolina, 673
Hot Spring, Arkansas, 58
Hot Springs, Wyoming, 851
Houghton, Michigan, 378
Houston, Alabama, 32
Houston, Georgia, 162
Houston, Minnesota, 401
Houston, Tennessee, 705
Houston, Texas, 738
Howard, Arkansas, 58
Howard, Indiana, 227
Howard, Iowa, 251
Howard, Kansas, 273
Howard, Maryland, 347

Howard, Missouri, 444
Howard, Nebraska, 478
Howard, North Dakota, 576
Howard, Texas, 738
Howell, Missouri, 444
Hubbard, Minnesota, 401
Hudson, New Jersey, 514
Hudspeth, Texas, 738
Huerfano, Colorado, 91
Hughes, Oklahoma, 615
Hughes, South Dakota, 688
Humboldt, California, 76
Humboldt, Iowa, 251
Humboldt, Nevada, 492
Humboldt, Utah, 763
Humboldt, old, Iowa, 251
Humphreys, Mississippi, 419
Humphreys, Tennessee, 706
Hunt, Texas, 738
Hunter, Kansas, 273
Hunterdon, New Jersey, 514
Huntingdon, Pennsylvania, 649
Huntington, Indiana, 227
Huron, Michigan, 379
Huron, Ohio, 598
Hutchinson, South Dakota, 688
Hutchinson, Texas, 738
Hyde, North Carolina, 561
Hyde, South Dakota, 688

I, Oklahoma, 615
Iberia Parish, Louisiana, 318
Iberville County, Louisiana, 318
Iberville Parish, Louisiana, 318
Ida, Iowa, 251
Idaho, Idaho, 188
Illinois, Virginia, 794
Imperial, California, 76
Independence, Arkansas, 58
Indian River, Florida, 135
Indiana, Pennsylvania, 649
Ingham, Michigan, 379
Interior Parish, Louisiana, 318
Inyo, California, 76
Ionia, Michigan, 379
Iosco, Michigan, 379
Iowa, Iowa, 251
Iowa, Wisconsin, 840
Iredell, North Carolina, 561
Irion, Texas, 738
Iron, Michigan, 379
Iron, Missouri, 444
Iron, Utah, 764
Iron, Wisconsin, 840
Iroquois, Illinois, 205
Irving, Kansas, 273
Irwin, Georgia, 162
Isabella, Michigan, 379
Isanti, Minnesota, 401
Island, Washington, 814
Isle of Wight, Virginia, 794
Isle Royal, Michigan, 379
Issaquena, Mississippi, 419
Itasca, Minnesota, 401
Itawamba, Mississippi, 419
Izard, Arkansas, 58
Izard, Nebraska, 478

Jack, Texas, 738
Jackson, Alabama, 32
Jackson, Arkansas, 58
Jackson, Colorado, 91
Jackson, Florida, 135
Jackson, Georgia, 162
Jackson, Illinois, 205
Jackson, Indiana, 227
Jackson, Iowa, 251
Jackson, Kansas, 273
Jackson, Kentucky, 298
Jackson, Michigan, 379
Jackson, Minnesota, 401
Jackson, Mississippi, 419
Jackson, Missouri, 444
Jackson, Nebraska, 478
Jackson, North Carolina, 561
Jackson, Ohio, 598
Jackson, Oklahoma, 615
Jackson, Oregon, 628
Jackson, South Dakota, 688
Jackson, Tennessee, 706
Jackson, Texas, 738
Jackson, Virginia, 794
Jackson, West Virginia, 825
Jackson, Wisconsin, 840
Jackson Parish, Louisiana, 319
Jackson, old, South Dakota, 688
James, Tennessee, 706
James City, Virginia, 794
Jasper, Georgia, 162
Jasper, Illinois, 205
Jasper, Indiana, 228
Jasper, Iowa, 252
Jasper, Mississippi, 420

The Handybook for Genealogists

Madison, Illinois, 207
Madison, Iowa, 253
Madison, Indiana, 229
Madison, Kansas, 275
Madison, Kentucky, 300
Madison, Mississippi, 421
Madison, Missouri, 446
Madison, Montana, 462
Madison, Nebraska, 480
Madison, New York, 539
Madison, North Carolina, 562
Madison, Ohio, 599
Madison, Tennessee, 707
Madison, Texas, 743
Madison, Virginia, 796
Madison Parish, Louisiana, 320
Magoffin, Kentucky, 300
Mahaska, Iowa, 253
Mahnomen, Minnesota, 403
Mahoning, Ohio, 599
Major, Oklahoma, 616
Malad, Utah, 764
Malheur, Oregon, 629
Manassas Park (Ind. City), Virginia, 796
Manatee, Florida, 136
Mandan, South Dakota, 689
Manistee, Michigan, 381
Manitou, Michigan, 382
Manitowoc, Wisconsin, 842
Mankahto, Minnesota, 403
Manomin, Minnesota, 403
Marathon, Wisconsin, 842
Marengo, Alabama, 34
Maricopa, Arizona, 47
Maries, Missouri, 446
Marin, California, 77
Marinette, Wisconsin, 842
Marion, Alabama, 34
Marion, Arkansas, 60
Marion, Florida, 137
Marion, Georgia, 164
Marion, Illinois, 207
Marion, Indiana, 229
Marion, Iowa, 254
Marion, Kansas, 275
Marion, Kentucky, 300
Marion, Mississippi, 421
Marion, Missouri, 446
Marion, Ohio, 599
Marion, Oregon, 630
Marion, South Carolina, 674
Marion, Tennessee, 707
Marion, Texas, 743
Marion, Virginia, 796
Marion, West Virginia, 825
Mariposa, California, 77
Marlboro, South Carolina, 675
Marquette, Michigan, 382
Marquette, Wisconsin, 842
Marshall, Alabama, 34
Marshall, Illinois, 208
Marshall, Indiana, 229
Marshall, Iowa, 254
Marshall, Kansas, 275
Marshall, Kentucky, 300
Marshall, Minnesota, 403
Marshall, Mississippi, 421
Marshall, Oklahoma, 616
Marshall, South Dakota, 689
Marshall, Tennessee, 707
Marshall, Virginia, 796
Marshall, West Virginia, 827
Martin, Florida, 137
Martin, Indiana, 229
Martin, Kentucky, 301
Martin, Minnesota, 404
Martin, North Carolina, 562
Martin, South Dakota, 690
Martin, Texas, 743
Martinsville (Ind. City), Virginia, 796
Mason, Illinois, 208
Mason, Kentucky, 301
Mason, Michigan, 382
Mason, Texas, 743
Mason, Virginia, 796
Mason, Washington, 815
Mason, West Virginia, 827
Massac, Illinois, 208
Matagorda, Texas, 743
Matanuska-Susitna Borough, Alaska, 41
Mathews, Virginia, 796
Maui, Hawaii, 179
Maury, Tennessee, 707
Maverick, Texas, 743
Mayes, Oklahoma, 617
McClain, Oklahoma, 617
McCone, Montana, 462
McCook, South Dakota, 690
McCormick, South Carolina, 675
McCracken, Kentucky, 301
McCreary, Kentucky, 301
McCulloch, Texas, 743
McCurtain, Oklahoma, 617

McDonald, Missouri, 446
McDonough, Illinois, 208
McDowell, North Carolina, 562
McDowell, Virginia, 796
McDowell, West Virginia, 827
McDuffie, Georgia, 165
McGee, Kansas, 275
McHenry, Illinois, 208
McHenry, North Dakota, 576
McIntosh, Georgia, 165
McIntosh, North Dakota, 576
McIntosh, Oklahoma, 617
McKean, Pennsylvania, 651
McKenzie, North Dakota, 577
McKenzie, old, North Dakota, 577
McKinley, New Mexico, 524
McLean, Illinois, 208
McLean, Kentucky, 301
McLean, North Dakota, 577
McLennan, Texas, 743
McLeod, Minnesota, 404
McMinn, Tennessee, 708
McMullen, Texas, 743
McNairy, Tennessee, 708
McNeale, Nebraska, 480
McPherson, Kansas, 275
McPherson, Nebraska, 480
McPherson, South Dakota, 690
Meade, Kansas, 275
Meade, Kentucky, 301
Meade, South Dakota, 690
Meagher, Montana, 463
Mecklenburg, North Carolina, 562
Mecklenburg, Virginia, 796
Mecosta, Michigan, 382
Medina, Ohio, 599
Medina, Texas, 744
Meegisee, Michigan, 382
Meeker, Minnesota, 404
Meigs, Ohio, 599
Meigs, Tennessee, 708
Mellette, South Dakota, 690
Menard, Illinois, 208
Menard, Texas, 744
Mendocino, California, 78
Menifee, Kentucky, 301
Menominee, Michigan, 382
Menominee, Wisconsin, 842
Merced, California, 78
Mercer, Illinois, 209
Mercer, Kentucky, 301
Mercer, Missouri, 446
Mercer, New Jersey, 514
Mercer, North Dakota, 577
Mercer, Ohio, 600
Mercer, Pennsylvania, 651
Mercer, Virginia, 797
Mercer, West Virginia, 827
Meriwether, Georgia, 165
Merrick, Nebraska, 480
Merrimack, New Hampshire, 502
Mesa, Colorado, 92
Mesilla, Arizona, 48
Metcalfe, Kentucky, 301
Meyer, South Dakota, 690
Miami, Indiana, 229
Miami, Kansas, 275
Miami, Ohio, 600
Miami-Dade, Florida, 137
Michilimackinac, Michigan, 382
Middlesex, Connecticut, 106
Middlesex, Massachusetts, 362
Middlesex, New Jersey, 514
Middlesex, Virginia, 797
Midland, Michigan, 382
Midland, Texas, 744
Midway, South Dakota, 690
Mifflin, Pennsylvania, 651
Mikenauk, Michigan, 383
Milam, Texas, 744
Millard, Utah, 764
Mille Lacs, Minnesota, 404
Miller, Arkansas, 60
Miller, Georgia, 165
Miller, Missouri, 447
Miller, old, Arkansas, 60
Mills, Iowa, 254
Mills, South Dakota, 690
Mills, Texas, 744
Milton, Georgia, 165
Milwaukee, Wisconsin, 842
Miner, South Dakota, 690
Mineral, Colorado, 92
Mineral, Montana, 463
Mineral, Nevada, 492
Mineral, West Virginia, 827
Mingo, West Virginia, 827
Minidoka, Idaho, 189
Minnehaha, South Dakota, 691
Missaukee, Michigan, 383
Mississippi, Arkansas, 60
Mississippi, Missouri, 447
Missoula, Montana, 463

Mitchell, Georgia, 165
Mitchell, Iowa, 254
Mitchell, Kansas, 275
Mitchell, North Carolina, 562
Mitchell, Texas, 744
Mobile, Alabama, 34
Modoc, California, 78
Moffat, Colorado, 92
Mohave, Arizona, 48
Moniteau, Missouri, 447
Monmouth, New Jersey, 514
Mono, California, 78
Monona, Iowa, 254
Monongalia, Minnesota, 404
Monongalia, Virginia, 797
Monongalia, West Virginia, 827
Monroe, Alabama, 34
Monroe, Arkansas, 60
Monroe, Florida, 137
Monroe, Georgia, 165
Monroe, Illinois, 209
Monroe, Indiana, 230
Monroe, Iowa, 254
Monroe, Kentucky, 302
Monroe, Michigan, 383
Monroe, Mississippi, 421
Monroe, Missouri, 447
Monroe, Nebraska, 480
Monroe, New York, 539
Monroe, Ohio, 600
Monroe, Pennsylvania, 651
Monroe, Tennessee, 708
Monroe, Virginia, 797
Monroe, West Virginia, 827
Monroe, Wisconsin, 742
Montague, Texas, 744
Montcalm, Michigan, 383
Monterey, California, 78
Montezuma, Colorado, 93
Montgomery, Alabama, 34
Montgomery, Arkansas, 60
Montgomery, Georgia, 165
Montgomery, Illinois, 209
Montgomery, Indiana, 230
Montgomery, Iowa, 254
Montgomery, Kansas, 275
Montgomery, Kentucky, 302
Montgomery, Maryland, 348
Montgomery, Mississippi, 422
Montgomery, Missouri, 447
Montgomery, New York, 540
Montgomery, North Carolina, 563
Montgomery, Ohio, 600
Montgomery, Pennsylvania, 651
Montgomery, Tennessee, 708
Montgomery, Texas, 744
Montgomery, Virginia, 797
Montmorency, Michigan, 383
Montour, Pennsylvania, 651
Montrose, Colorado, 93
Moody, South Dakota, 391
Moore, North Carolina, 563
Moore, Tennessee, 708
Moore, Texas, 744
Mora, New Mexico, 524
Morehouse Parish, Louisiana, 320
Morgan, Alabama, 34
Morgan, Colorado, 93
Morgan, Georgia, 166
Morgan, Illinois, 209
Morgan, Indiana, 230
Morgan, Kentucky, 302
Morgan, Missouri, 447
Morgan, Ohio, 600
Morgan, Tennessee, 708
Morgan, Utah, 764
Morgan, Virginia, 797
Morgan, West Virginia, 828
Morrill, Nebraska, 480
Morris, Kansas, 277
Morris, New Jersey, 514
Morris, Texas, 745
Morrison, Minnesota, 404
Morrow, Ohio, 600
Morrow, Oregon, 630
Morton, Kansas, 277
Morton, North Dakota, 577
Mosquito, Florida, 137
Motley, Texas, 745
Moultrie, Illinois, 209
Mountrail, North Dakota, 577
Mower, Minnesota, 404
Muhlenberg, Kentucky, 302
Multnomah, Oregon, 630
Murray, Georgia, 166
Murray, Minnesota, 404
Murray, Oklahoma, 617
Muscatine, Iowa, 255
Muscogee, Georgia, 166
Muskegon, Michigan, 383
Muskingum, Ohio, 600
Muskogee, Oklahoma, 617
Musselshell, Montana, 463

N, Oklahoma, 617
Nacogdoches, Texas, 745
Nance, Nebraska, 481
Nansemond, Virginia, 797
Nantucket, Massachusetts, 362
Napa, California, 78
Nash, North Carolina, 563
Nassau, Florida, 137
Nassau, New York, 540
Natchitoches County, Louisiana, 320
Natchitoches Parish, Louisiana, 320
Natrona, Wyoming, 851
Navajo, Arizona, 48
Navarro, Texas, 745
Navasota, Texas, 745
Newegon, Michigan, 383
Nelson, Kentucky, 302
Nelson, North Dakota, 577
Nelson, Virginia, 797
Nemaha, Kansas, 277
Nemaha, Nebraska, 481
Neosho, Kansas, 277
Neshoba, Mississippi, 422
Ness, Kansas, 277
Nevada, Arkansas, 60
Nevada, California, 78
New, Wisconsin, 842
New Amstel, Delaware, 115
New Castle, Delaware, 115
New Hanover, North Carolina, 563
New Haven, Connecticut, 106
New Kent, Virginia, 797
New London, Connecticut, 107
New Madrid, Missouri, 447
New Norfolk, Virginia, 797
New River, Florida, 137
New York, New York, 540
Newaygo, Michigan, 384
Newberry, South Carolina, 675
Newport, Rhode Island, 661
Newport News (Ind. City), Virginia, 797
Newton, Arkansas, 60
Newton, Georgia, 166
Newton, Indiana, 230
Newton, Minnesota, 405
Newton, Mississippi, 422
Newton, Missouri, 447
Newton, Texas, 745
Nez Perce, Idaho, 189
Niagara, New York, 540
Niangua, Missouri, 448
Nicholas, Kentucky, 302
Nicholas, Virginia, 798
Nicholas, West Virginia, 828
Nicollet, Minnesota, 405
Ninety-Six Dist, South Carolina, 675
Niobrara, Wyoming, 851
Noble, Indiana, 230
Noble, Ohio, 600
Noble, Oklahoma, 617
Nobles, Minnesota, 405
Nodaway, Missouri, 448
Nolan, Texas, 745
Nome Census Area, Alaska, 41
Norfolk, Massachusetts, 362
Norfolk, Virginia, 798
Norman, Minnesota, 405
North Slope Borough, Alaska, 41
Northampton, North Carolina, 563
Northampton, Pennsylvania, 651
Northampton, Virginia, 798
Northumberland, Pennsylvania, 652
Northumberland, Virginia, 798
Northwest Arctic Borough, Alaska, 41
Norton, Kansas, 277
Norton (Ind. City), Virginia, 798
Notipekago, Michigan, 384
Nottoway, Virginia, 798
Nowata, Oklahoma, 617
Nowlin, South Dakota, 691
Noxubee, Mississippi, 422
Nuckolls, Nebraska, 481
Nueces, Texas, 745
Nye, Nevada, 492

O, Oklahoma, 617
Oahu, Hawaii, 179
Oakland, Michigan, 384
Obion, Tennessee, 708
O'Brien, Iowa, 255
Ocean, New Jersey, 515
Oceana, Michigan, 384
Ochiltree, Texas, 746
Oconee, Georgia, 166
Oconee, South Carolina, 675
Oconto, Wisconsin, 843
Ogemaw, Michigan, 384
Ogle, Illinois, 209
Oglethorpe, Georgia, 166
Ohio, Indiana, 230
Ohio, Kentucky, 302
Ohio, Virginia, 798
Ohio, West Virginia, 828

Rusk, Wisconsin, 844
Russell, Alabama, 35
Russell, Kansas, 279
Russell, Kentucky, 304
Russell, Virginia, 801
Rutherford, North Carolina, 565
Rutherford, Tennessee, 710
Rutland, Vermont, 775

Sabine, Texas, 748
Sabine Parish, Louisiana, 321
Sac, Iowa, 256
Sacramento, California, 79
Sagadahoc, Maine, 335
Saginaw, Michigan, 386
Saguache, Colorado, 94
Salem, New Jersey, 515
Salem, South Carolina, 676
Salem (Ind. City), Virginia, 801
Saline, Arkansas, 62
Saline, Illinois, 211
Saline, Kansas, 279
Saline, Missouri, 450
Saline, Nebraska, 482
Salt Lake, Utah, 765
Saluda, South Carolina, 676
Sampson, North Carolina, 565
San Augustine, Texas, 749
San Benito, California, 79
San Bernardino, California, 79
San Diego, California, 79
San Francisco, California, 79
San Jacinto, Texas, 749
San Joaquin, California, 79
San Juan, Colorado, 94
San Juan, New Mexico, 525
San Juan, Utah, 765
San Juan, old, New Mexico, 525
San Juan, Washington, 815
San Luis Obispo, California, 80
San Mateo, California, 80
San Miguel, Colorado, 94
San Miguel, New Mexico, 525
San Miguel del Bado, New Mexico, 525
San Patricio, Texas, 749
San Saba, Texas, 749
Sanborn, South Dakota, 692
Sanders, Montana, 464
Sandoval, New Mexico, 525
Sandusky, Ohio, 602
Sanford, Alabama, 35
Sangamon, Illinois, 211
Sanilac, Michigan, 386
Sanpete, Utah, 765
Santa Ana, New Mexico, 525
Santa Barbara, California, 80
Santa Clara, California, 80
Santa Cruz, Arizona, 48
Santa Cruz, California, 80
Santa Fe, New Mexico, 525
Santa Rosa, Florida, 138
Sarasota, Florida, 138
Saratoga, New York, 542
Sarber, Arkansas, 62
Sargent, North Dakota, 579
Sarpy, Nebraska, 483
Sauk, Wisconsin, 844
Saunders, Nebraska, 483
Sawamish, Washington, 815
Sawyer, Wisconsin, 844
Schenectady, New York, 542
Schleicher, Texas, 749
Schley, Georgia, 168
Schnasse, South Dakota, 692
Schoharie, New York, 542
Schoolcraft, Michigan, 386
Schuyler, Illinois, 211
Schuyler, Missouri, 450
Schuyler, New York, 542
Schuylkill, Pennsylvania, 652
Scioto, Ohio, 602
Scobey, South Dakota, 692
Scotland, Missouri, 451
Scotland, North Carolina, 565
Scott, Arkansas, 62
Scott, Illinois, 211
Scott, Indiana, 232
Scott, Iowa, 256
Scott, Kansas, 279
Scott, Kentucky, 304
Scott, Minnesota, 407
Scott, Mississippi, 423
Scott, Missouri, 451
Scott, Tennessee, 710
Scott, Virginia, 802
Scotts Bluff, Nebraska, 483
Screven, Georgia, 168
Scurry, Texas, 749
Searcy, Arkansas, 62
Sebastian, Arkansas, 62
Sedgwick, Colorado, 95
Sedgwick, Kansas, 279
Seminole, Florida, 139

Seminole, Georgia, 168
Seminole, Oklahoma, 619
Seneca, New York, 542
Seneca, Ohio, 602
Sequatchie, Tennessee, 710
Sequoyah, Kansas, 279
Sequoyah, Oklahoma, 619
Sevier, Arkansas, 62
Sevier, Tennessee, 710
Sevier, Utah, 765
Seward, Kansas, 279
Seward, Nebraska, 483
Seward, old, Kansas, 279
Shackelford, Texas, 749
Shaftesbury, North Carolina, 565
Shambip, Utah, 765
Shannon, Missouri, 451
Shannon, South Dakota, 692
Sharkey, Mississippi, 423
Sharp, Arkansas, 62
Shasta, California, 80
Shawano, Michigan, 386
Shawano, Wisconsin, 844
Shawnee, Kansas, 279
Sheboygan, Wisconsin, 845
Shelby, Alabama, 35
Shelby, Illinois, 211
Shelby, Indiana, 232
Shelby, Iowa, 257
Shelby, Kentucky, 304
Shelby, Missouri, 451
Shelby, Ohio, 602
Shelby, Tennessee, 710
Shelby, Texas, 749
Shenandoah, Virginia, 802
Sherburne, Minnesota, 407
Sheridan, Kansas, 279
Sheridan, Montana, 464
Sheridan, North Dakota, 579
Sheridan, Nebraska, 483
Sheridan, Wyoming, 852
Sheridan, old, North Dakota, 579
Sherman, Kansas, 281
Sherman, Nebraska, 483
Sherman, Oregon, 630
Sherman, Texas, 750
Sheyenne, North Dakota, 579
Shiawassee, Michigan, 386
Shirley, Kansas, 281
Shorter, Nebraska, 483
Shoshone, Idaho, 190
Shoshone, Washington, 815
Sibley, Minnesota, 407
Sierra, New Mexico, 525
Sierra, California, 80
Silver Bow, Montana, 465
Simpson, Kentucky, 304
Simpson, Mississippi, 423
Sioux, Iowa, 257
Sioux, North Dakota, 579
Sioux, Nebraska, 483
Siskiyou, California, 81
Sitka Borough, Alaska, 41
Skagit, Washington, 815
Skagway-Hoonah-Angoon Census Area,
    Alaska, 41
Skamania, Washington, 816
Slaughter, Iowa, 257
Slaughter, Washington, 816
Slope, North Dakota, 579
Smith, Kansas, 281
Smith, Mississippi, 423
Smith, Tennessee, 710
Smith, Texas, 750
Smyth, Virginia, 802
Snohomish, Washington, 816
Snyder, Pennsylvania, 652
Socorro, New Mexico, 525
Solano, California, 81
Somerset, Maryland, 348
Somerset, Maine, 335
Somerset, New Jersey, 515
Somerset, Pennsylvania, 653
Somervell, Texas, 750
Sonoma, California, 81
South Arapahoe, California, 95
Southampton, Virginia, 802
Southeast Fairbanks Census Area, Alaska, 42
Spalding, Georgia, 168
Spartanburg, South Carolina, 676
Spencer, Indiana, 232
Spencer, Kentucky, 304
Spink, South Dakota, 692
Spokane, Washington, 816
Spotsylvania, Virginia, 802
St. Andrew, Georgia, 168
St. Bernard Parish, Louisiana, 322
St. Charles, Missouri, 451
St. Charles Parish, Louisiana, 322
St. Clair, Alabama, 35
St. Clair, Illinois, 211
St. Clair, Michigan, 386
St. Croix, Minnesota, 408

St. Clair, Missouri, 451
St. Croix, Wisconsin, 845
St. David, Georgia, 168
St. Francis, Arkansas, 62
St. Francois, Missouri, 451
St. George, Georgia, 168
St. Helena Parish, Louisiana, 322
St. James, Georgia, 168
St. James Parish, Louisiana, 322
St. John, Georgia, 169
St. John, Kansas, 281
St. John the Baptist Parish, Louisiana, 322
St. Johns, Florida, 139
St. Jones, Delaware, 115
St. Joseph, Indiana, 233
St. Joseph, Michigan, 386
St. Landry Parish, Louisiana, 322
St. Lawrence, New York, 543
St. Louis, Minnesota, 408
St. Louis, Missouri, 451
St. Louis, old, Minnesota, 408
St. Louis City, Missouri, 452
St. Lucie, Florida, 139
St. Martin Parish, Louisiana, 322
St. Mary, Georgia, 169
St. Mary Parish, Louisiana, 322
St. Mary's, Maryland, 348
St. Mary's, Nevada, 493
St. Marys, Utah, 65
St. Matthew, Georgia, 169
St. Patrick, Georgia, 169
St. Paul, Georgia, 169
St. Philip, Georgia, 169
St. Tammany Parish, Louisiana, 323
St. Thomas, Georgia, 169
Stafford, Kansas, 281
Stafford, Virginia, 802
Stanislaus, California, 81
Stanley, South Dakota, 692
Stanly, North Carolina, 566
Stanton, Kansas, 281
Stanton, Nebraska, 483
Stark, Illinois, 211
Stark, North Dakota, 579
Stark, Ohio, 602
Starke, Indiana, 233
Starr, Texas, 750
Staunton (Ind. City), Virginia, 802
Ste. Genevieve, Missouri, 452
Stearns, Minnesota, 408
Steele, Minnesota, 408
Steele, North Dakota, 580
Stephens, Georgia, 169
Stephens, Oklahoma, 619
Stephens, Texas, 750
Stephenson, Illinois, 212
Sterling, South Dakota, 692
Sterling, Texas, 750
Steuben, Indiana, 233
Steuben, New York, 543
Stevens, Kansas, 281
Stevens, Minnesota, 408
Stevens, North Dakota, 580
Stevens, Washington, 816
Stevens, old, North Dakota, 580
Stewart, Georgia, 169
Stewart, Tennessee, 710
Stillwater, Montana, 465
Stoddard, Missouri, 452
Stokes, North Carolina, 566
Stone, Arkansas, 62
Stone, Mississippi, 424
Stone, Missouri, 452
Stone, South Dakota, 693
Stonewall, Texas, 750
Storey, Nevada, 493
Story, Iowa, 257
Strafford, New Hampshire, 503
Stutsman, North Dakota, 580
Sublette, Wyoming, 852
Suffolk, Massachusetts, 362
Suffolk, New York, 543
Suffolk (Ind. City), Virginia, 802
Sullivan, Indiana, 233
Sullivan, Missouri, 452
Sullivan, New Hampshire, 503
Sullivan, New York, 543
Sullivan, Pennsylvania, 653
Sullivan, Tennessee, 710
Sully, South Dakota, 693
Summers, West Virginia, 829
Summit, Colorado, 95
Summit, Ohio, 602
Summit, Utah, 765
Sumner, Kansas, 281
Sumner, Mississippi, 424
Sumner, Tennessee, 711
Sumter, Alabama, 35
Sumter, Florida, 139
Sumter, Georgia, 169
Sumter, South Carolina, 676
Sunflower, Mississippi, 424
Superior, Minnesota, 408

Surry, North Carolina, 566
Surry, Virginia, 803
Susquehanna, Pennsylvania, 653
Sussex, Delaware, 115
Sussex, New Jersey, 515
Sussex, Virginia, 803
Sutter, California, 81
Sutton, Texas, 750
Suwannee, Florida, 139
Swain, North Carolina, 566
Sweet Grass, Montana, 465
Sweetwater, Wyoming, 852
Swift, Minnesota, 408
Swisher, Texas, 751
Switzerland, Indiana, 233

Talbot, Georgia, 170
Talbot, Maryland, 349
Taliaferro, Georgia, 170
Talladega, Alabama, 36
Tallahatchie, Mississippi, 424
Tallapoosa, Alabama, 36
Tama, Iowa, 257
Taney, Missouri, 452
Tangipahoa Parish, Louisiana, 323
Taos, New Mexico, 526
Tarrant, Texas, 751
Tate, Mississippi, 424
Tattnall, Georgia, 170
Taylor, Florida, 139
Taylor, Georgia, 170
Taylor, Iowa, 257
Taylor, Kentucky, 304
Taylor, Texas, 751
Taylor, Virginia, 803
Taylor, West Virginia, 829
Taylor, Wisconsin, 845
Tazewell, Illinois, 212
Tazewell, Virginia, 803
Tehama, California, 81
Telfair, Georgia, 170
Teller, Colorado, 95
Tennessee, Tennessee, 711
Tensas Parish, Louisiana, 323
Terrebonne Parish, Louisiana, 323
Terrell, Georgia, 170
Terrell, Texas, 751
Terry, Texas, 751
Teton, Idaho, 190
Teton, Montana, 465
Teton, Wyoming, 852
Texas, Missouri, 452
Texas, Oklahoma, 619
Thayer, Nebraska, 484
Thomas, Georgia, 170
Thomas, Kansas, 282
Thomas, Nebraska, 484
Thompson, South Dakota, 693
Throckmorton, Texas, 751
Thurston, Nebraska, 484
Thurston, Washington, 816
Tift, Georgia, 170
Tillamook, Oregon, 630
Tillman, Oklahoma, 620
Tioga, New York, 543
Tioga, Pennsylvania, 653
Tippah, Mississippi, 424
Tippecanoe, Indiana, 233
Tipton, Indiana, 233
Tipton, Tennessee, 711
Tishomingo, Mississippi, 424
Titus, Texas, 751
Todd, Kentucky, 304
Todd, Minnesota, 409
Todd, South Dakota, 693
Todd, old, South Dakota, 693
Tolland, Connecticut, 107
Tom Green, Texas, 751
Tompkins, New York, 543
Tonedagana, Michigan, 386
Tooele, Utah, 765
Toole, Montana, 465
Toombs, Georgia, 171
Toombs, Minnesota, 409
Torrance, New Mexico, 526
Towner, North Dakota, 580
Towns, Georgia, 171
Traill, North Dakota, 580
Transylvania, North Carolina, 566
Traverse, Minnesota, 409
Travis, Texas, 751
Treasure, Montana, 465
Trego, Kansas, 282
Trempealeau, Wisconsin, 845
Treutlen, Georgia, 171
Trigg, Kentucky, 305
Trimble, Kentucky, 305
Trinity, California, 81
Trinity, Texas, 752
Tripp, South Dakota, 693
Troup, Georgia, 171
Trousdale, Tennessee, 711
Trumbull, Ohio, 603

Full-color Maps

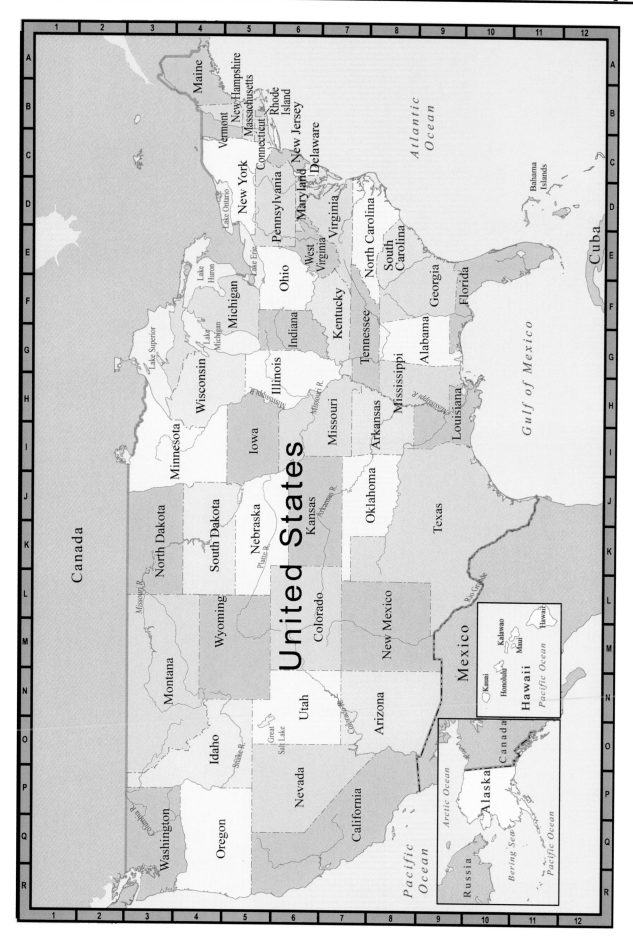

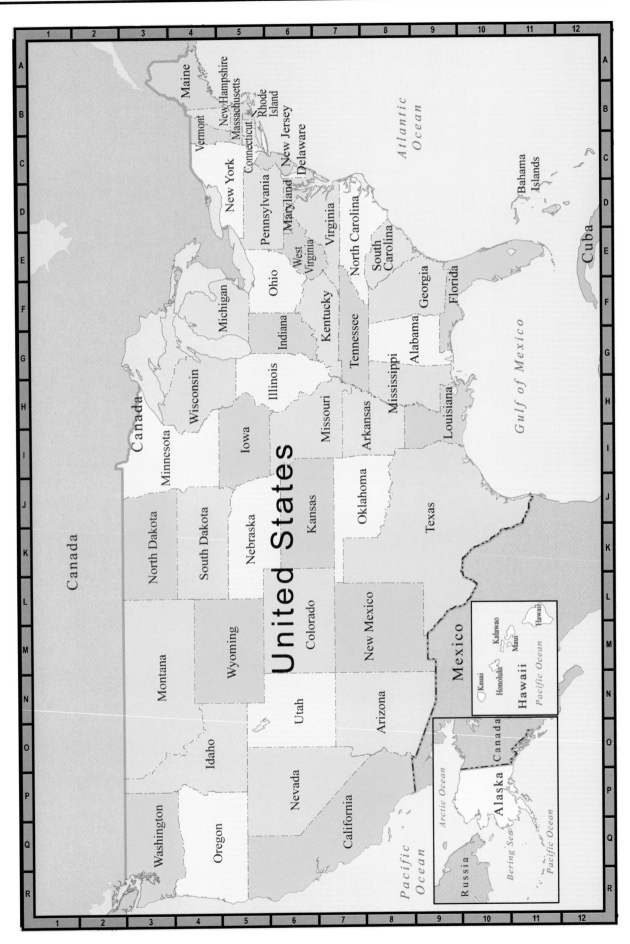

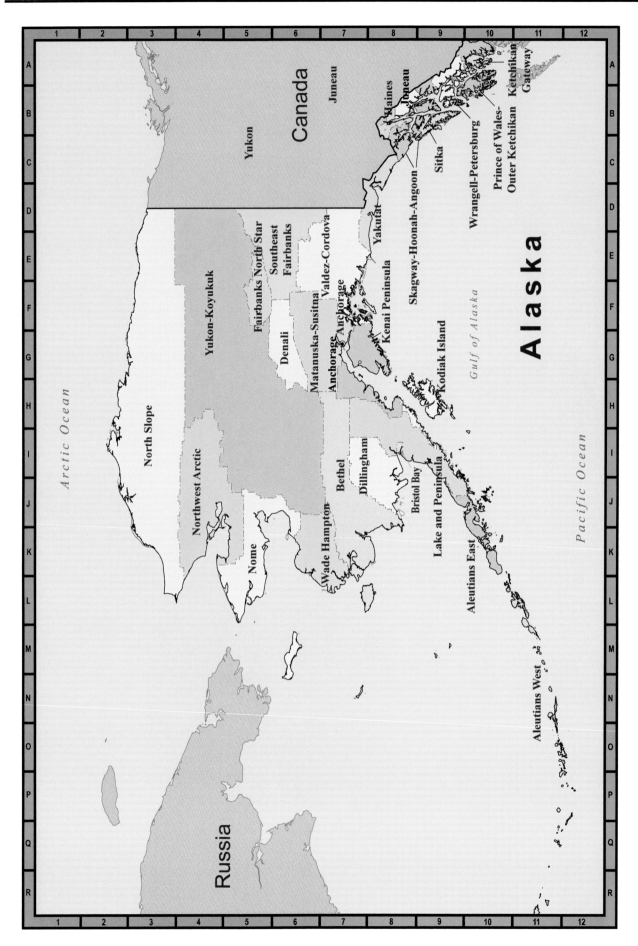

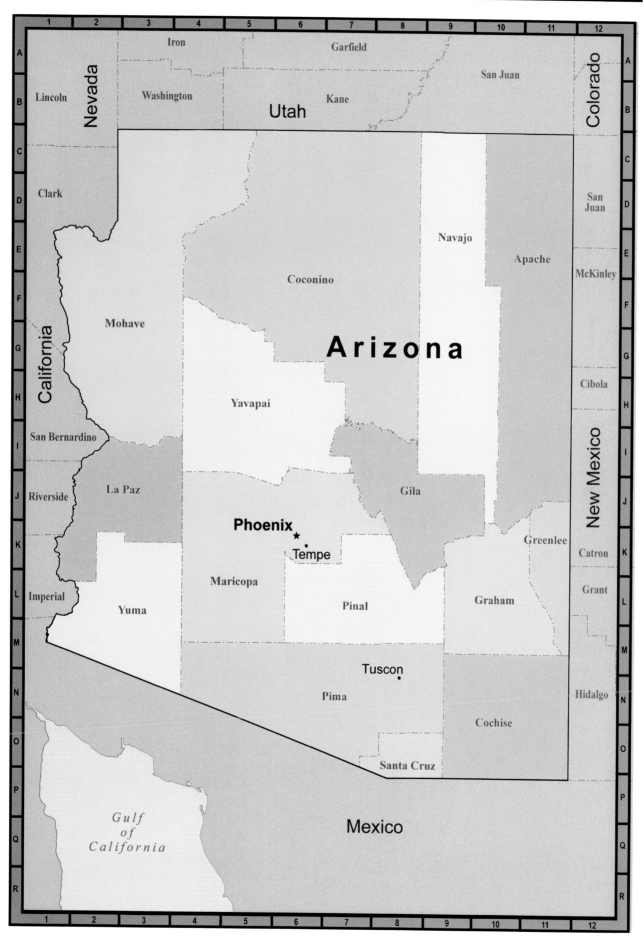

California

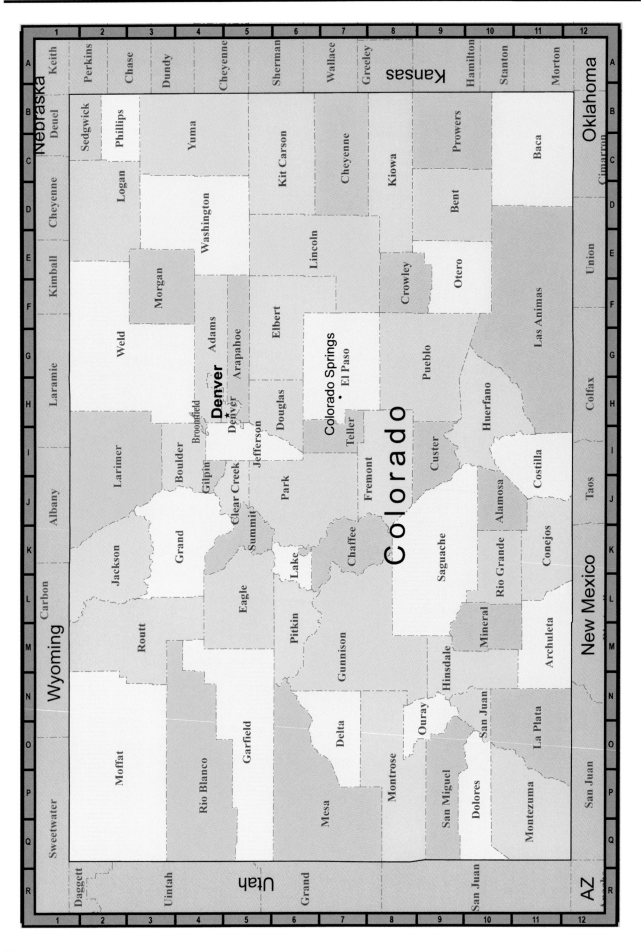

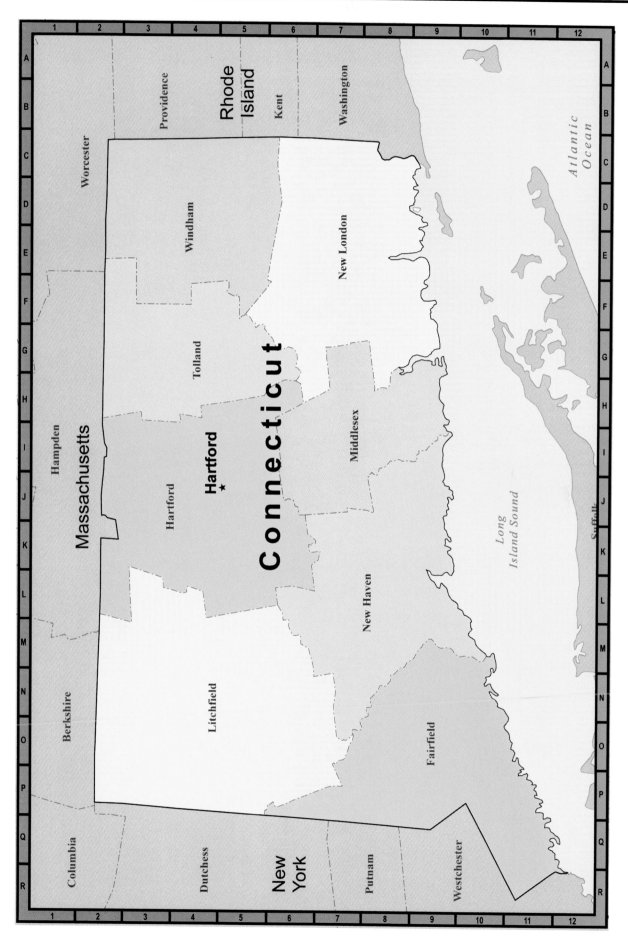

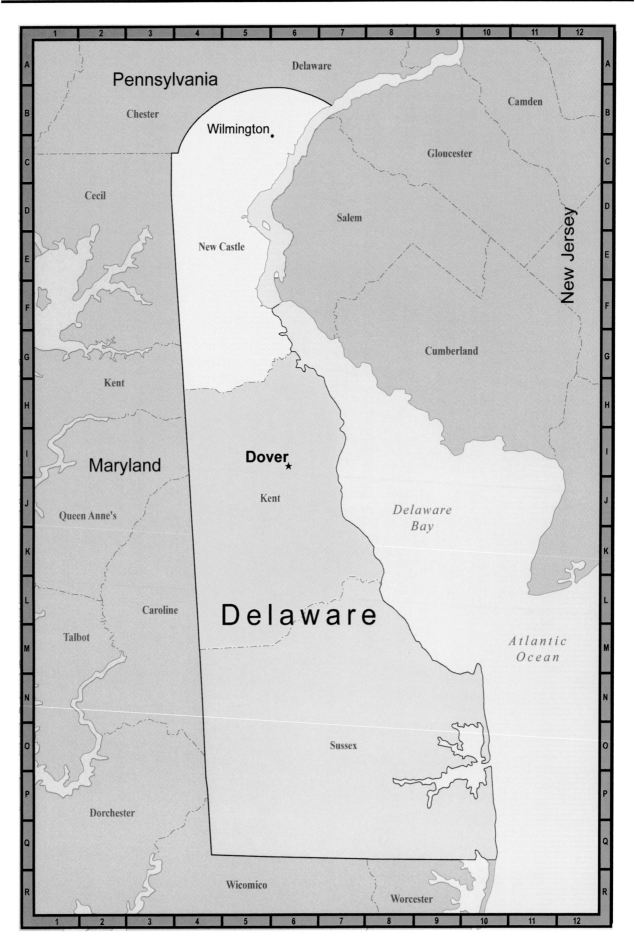

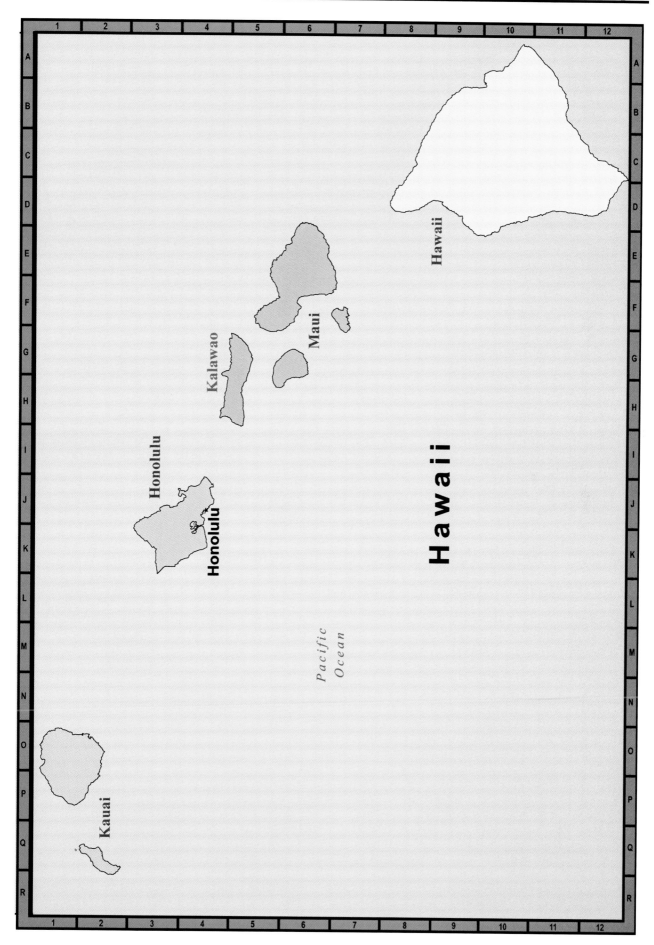

Hawaii

Kalawao

Maui

Honolulu

Honolulu

Hawaii

Pacific Ocean

Kauai

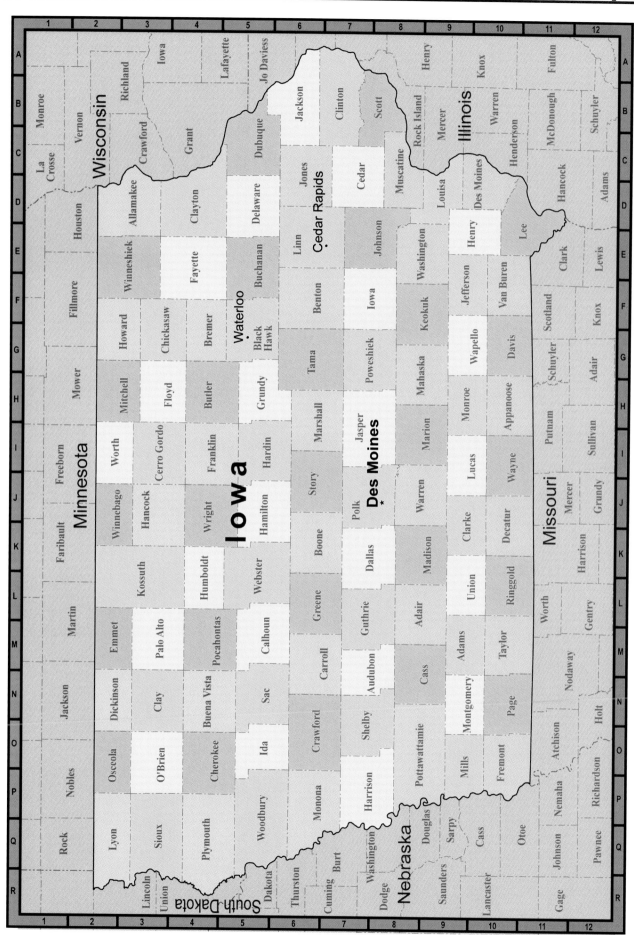

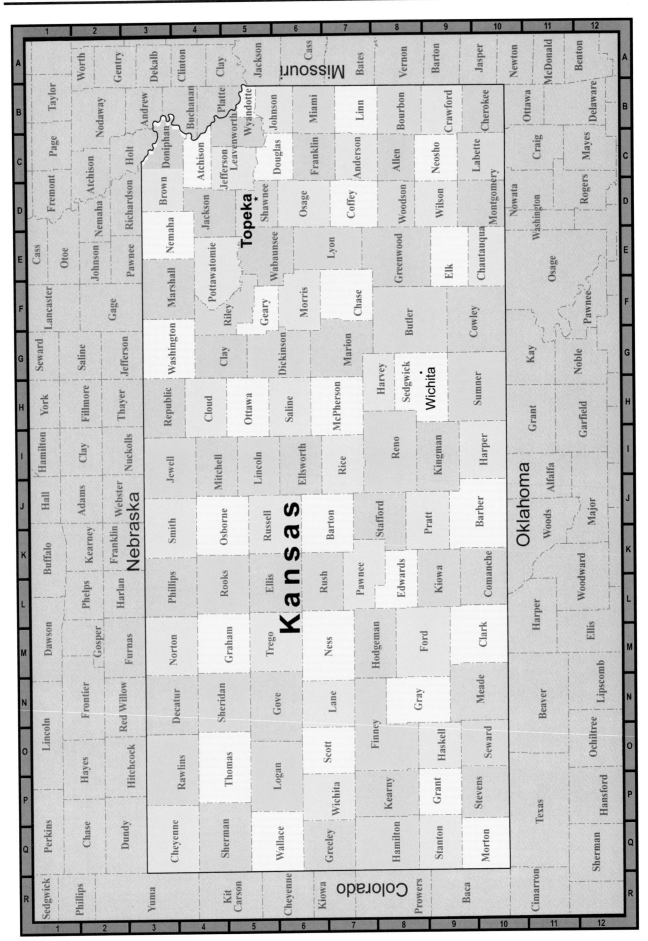

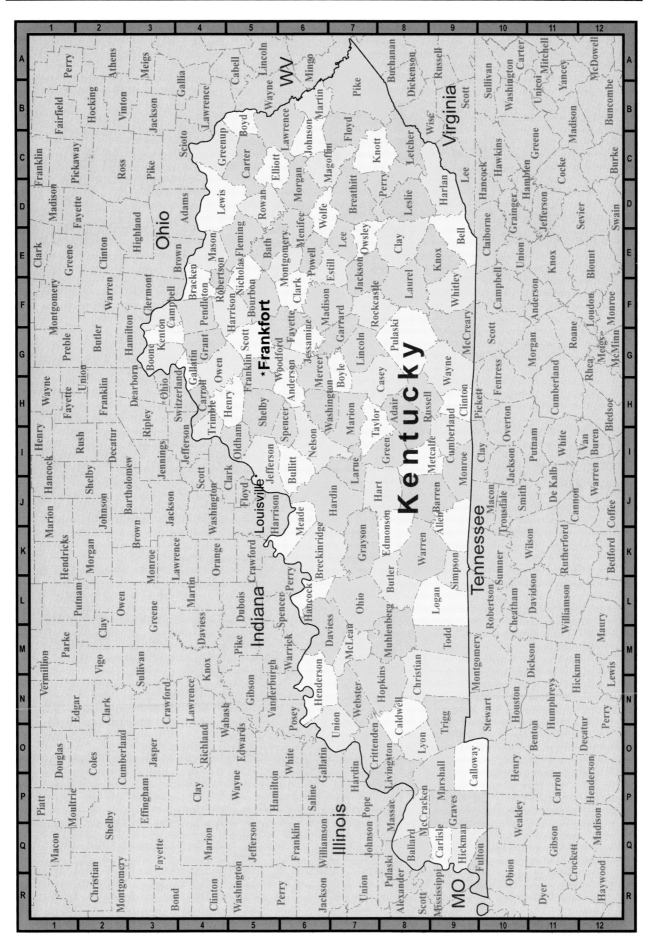

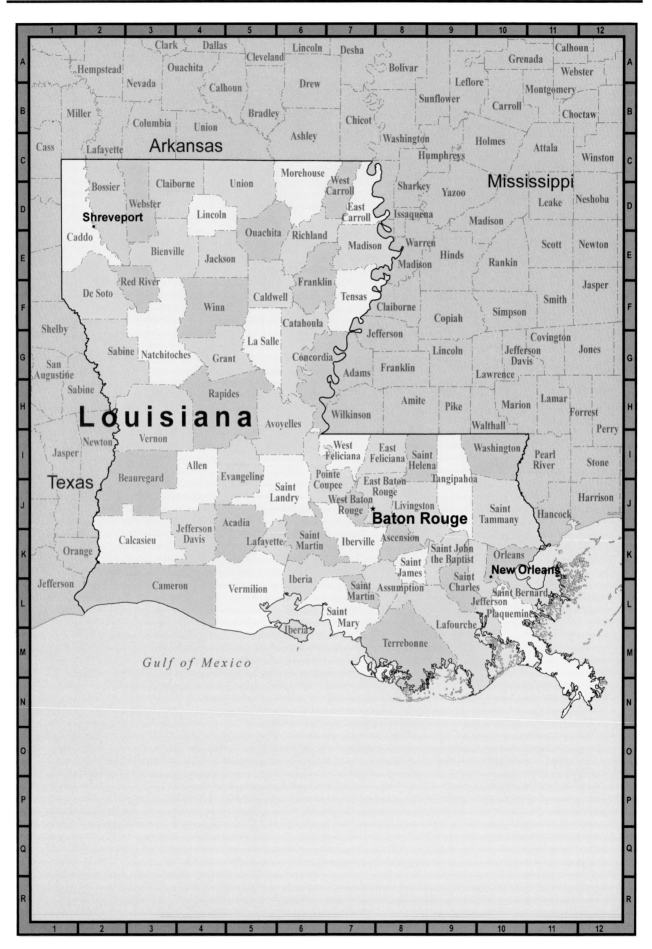

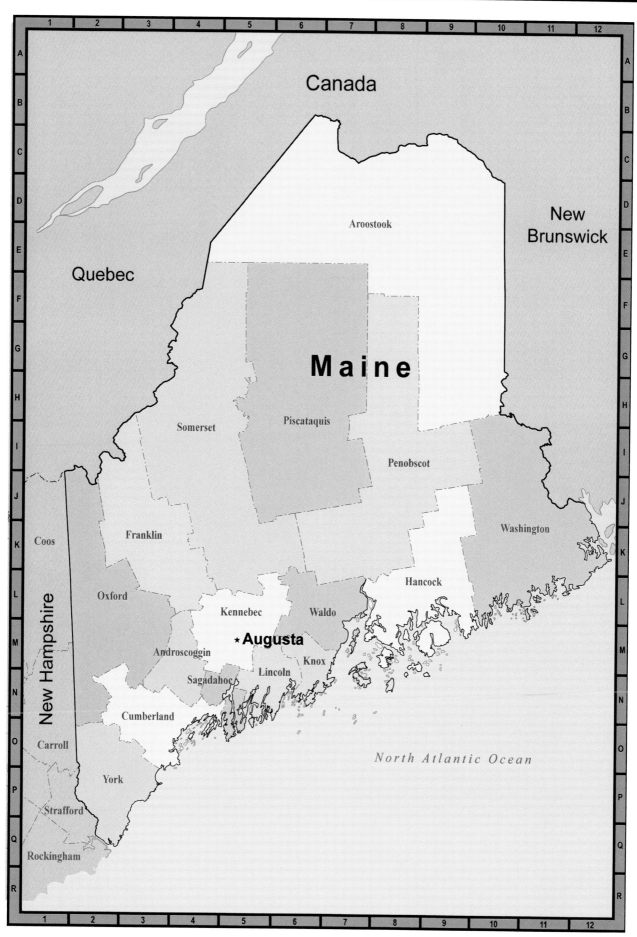

Canada

Quebec

New Brunswick

Aroostook

Maine

Somerset

Piscataquis

Penobscot

Washington

Franklin

Hancock

Coos

Oxford

Kennebec

Waldo

New Hampshire

★ Augusta

Androscoggin

Knox

Lincoln

Sagadahoc

Carroll

Cumberland

North Atlantic Ocean

York

Strafford

Rockingham

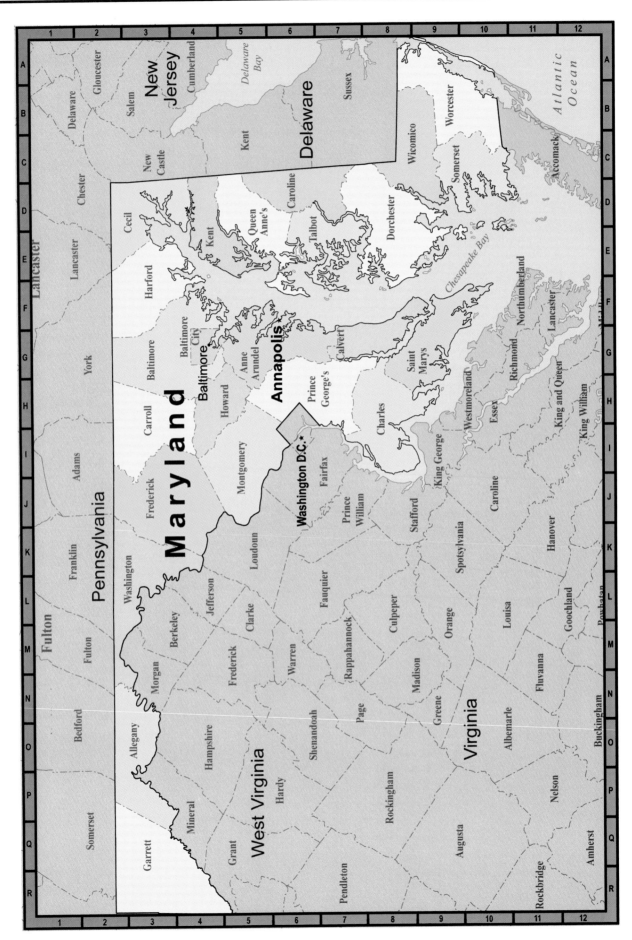

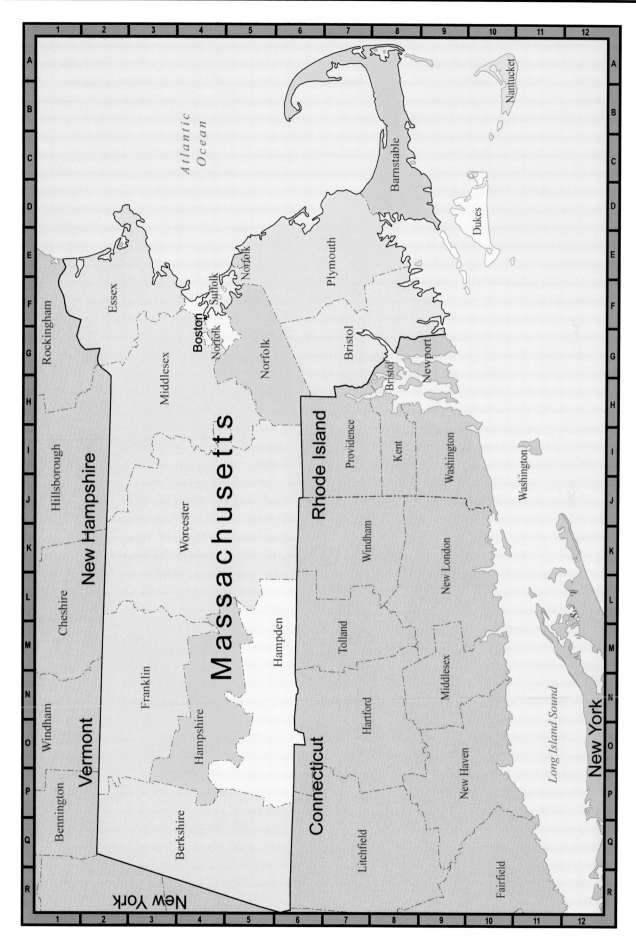

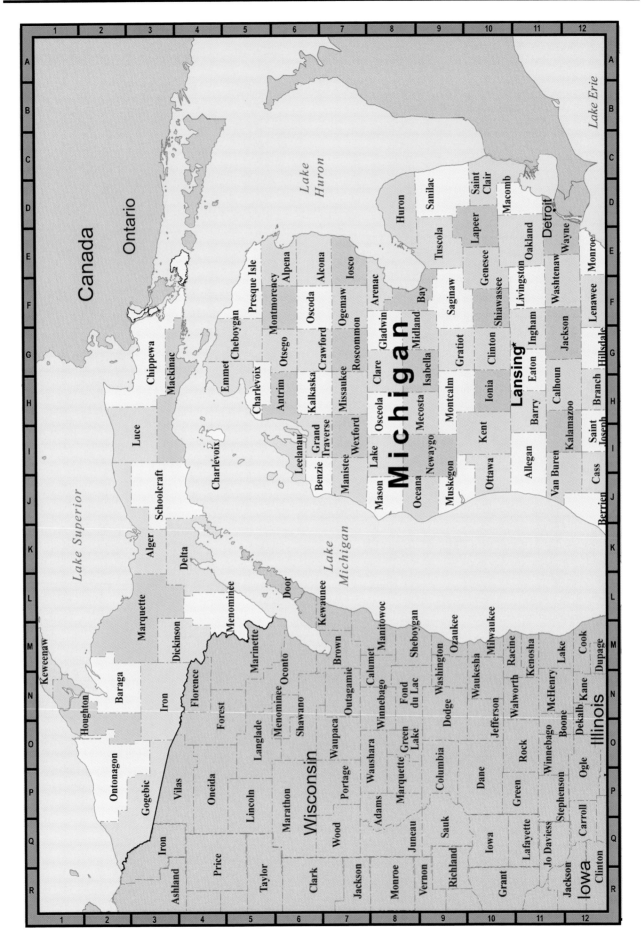

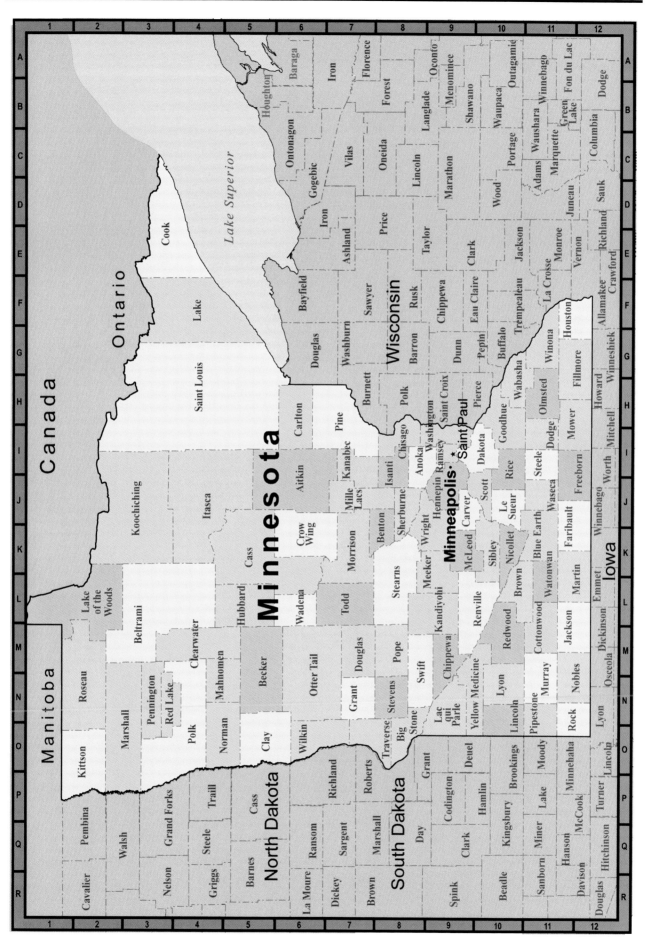

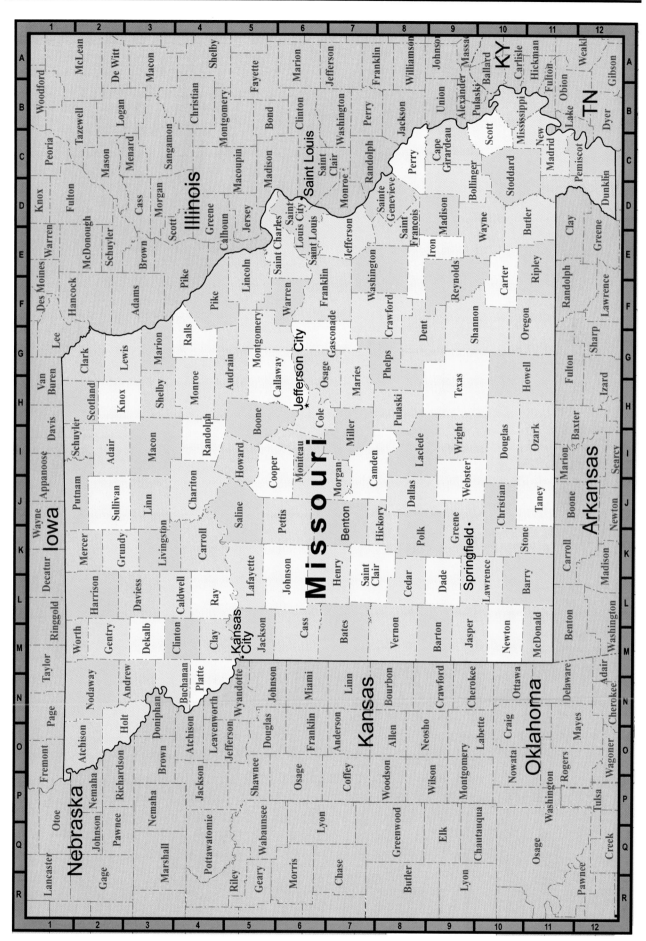

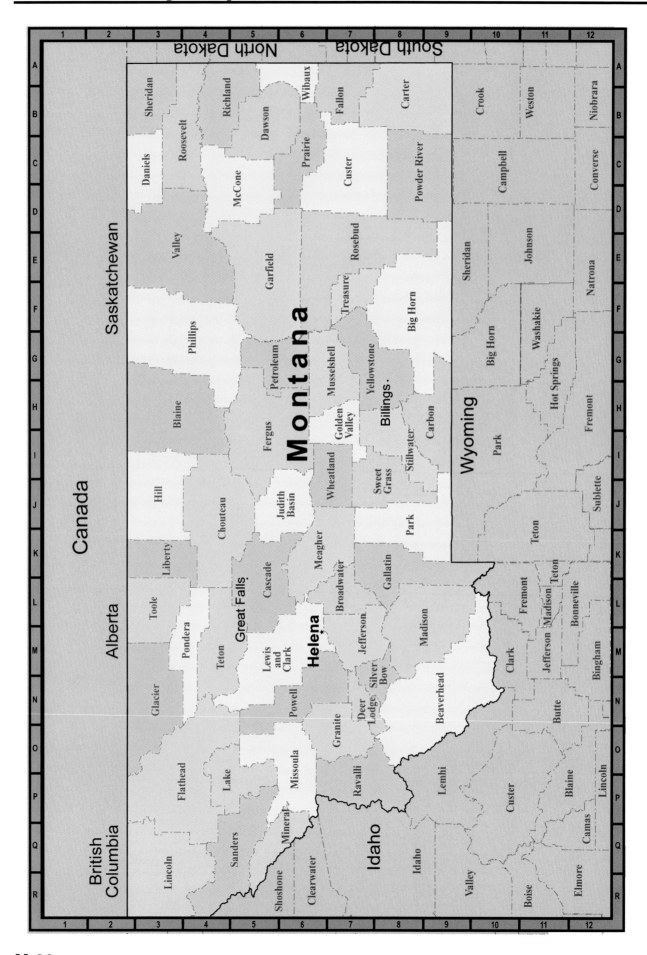

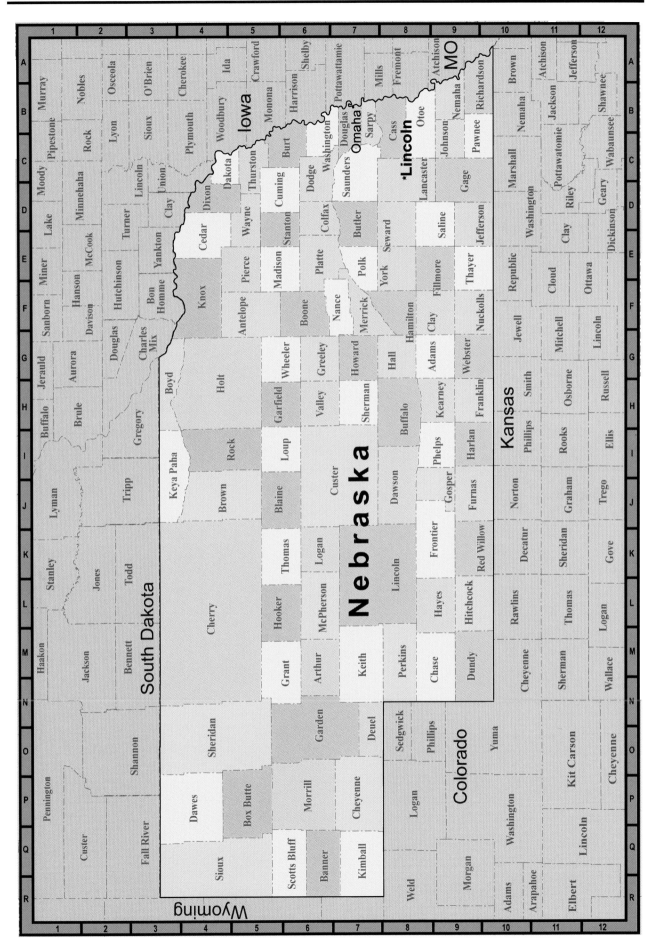

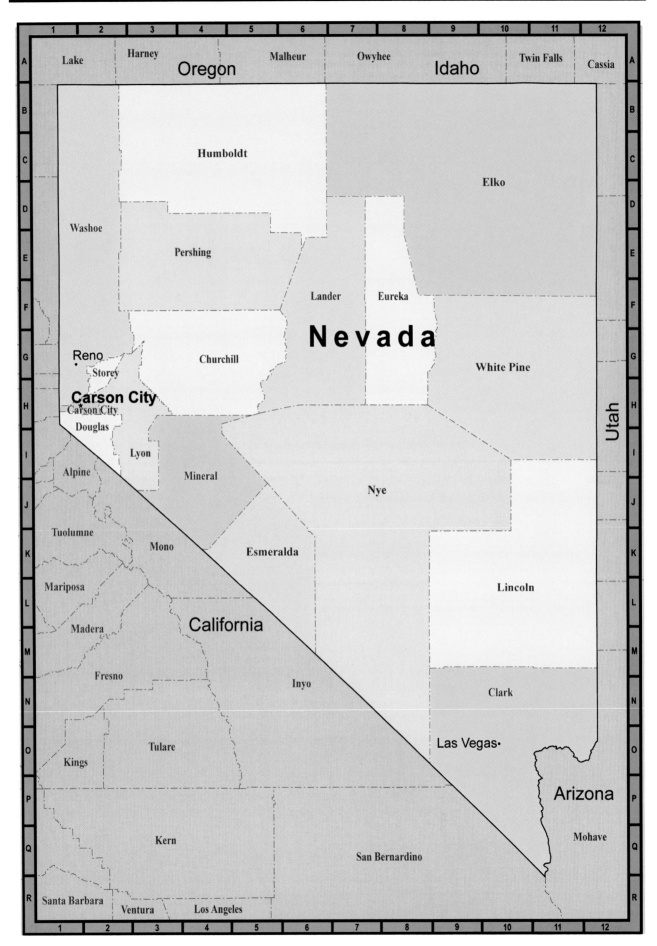

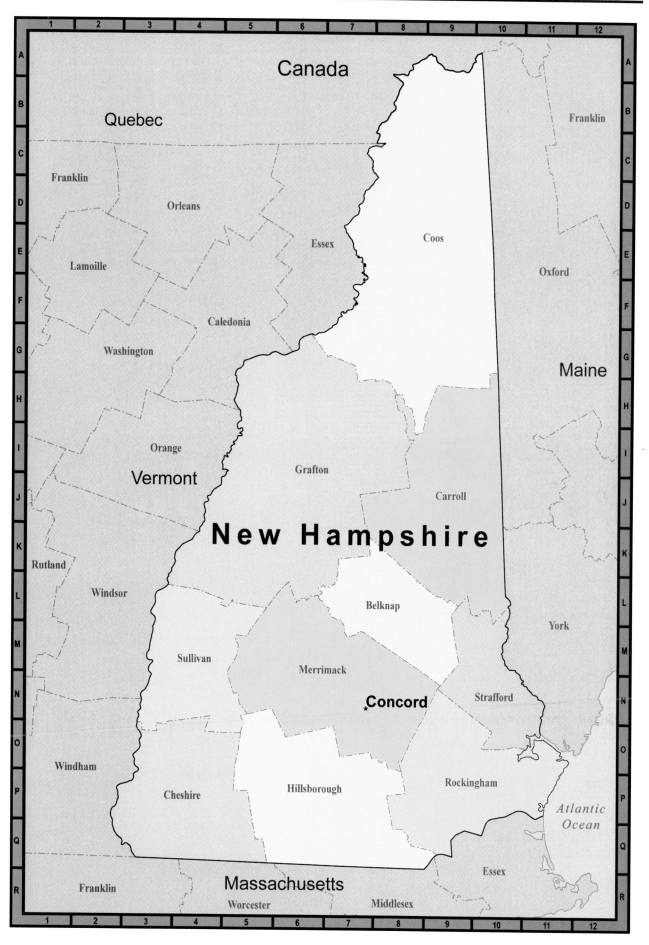

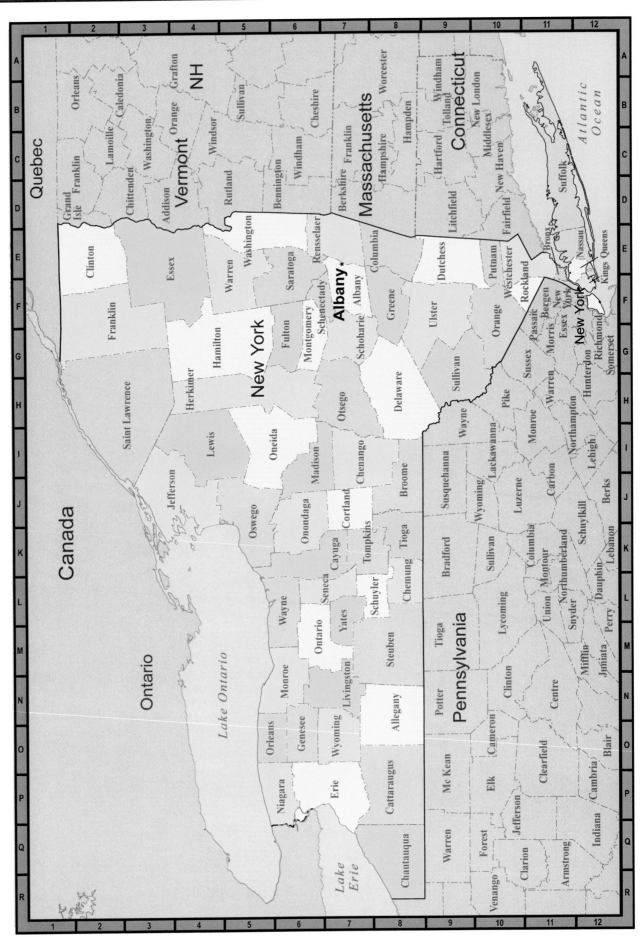

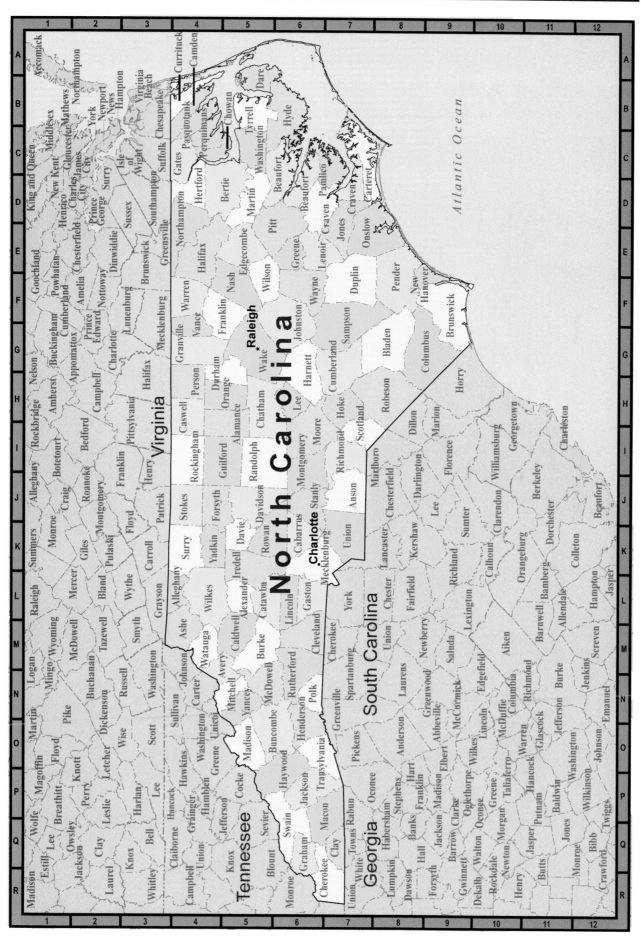

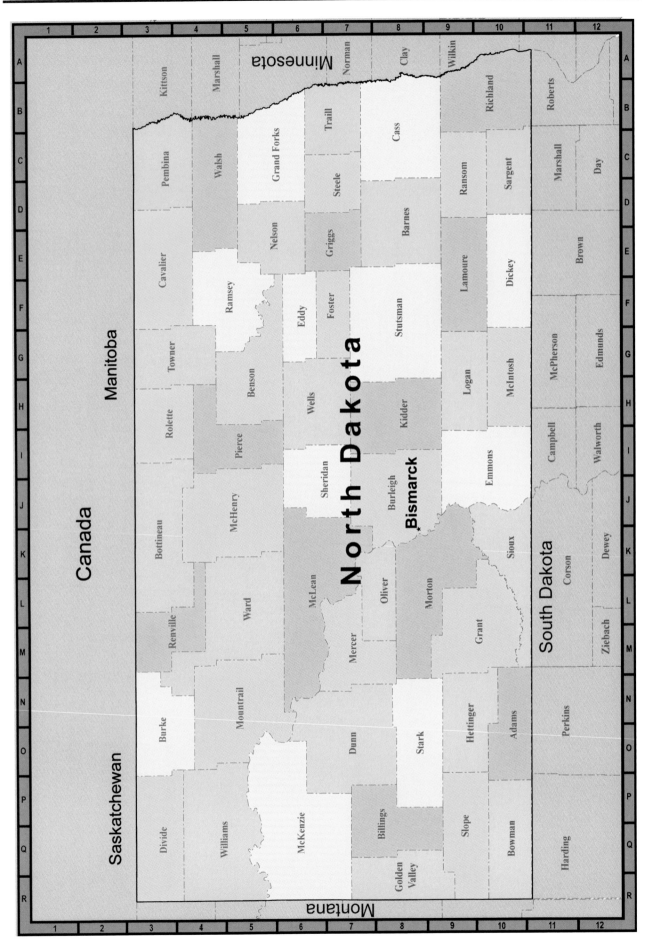

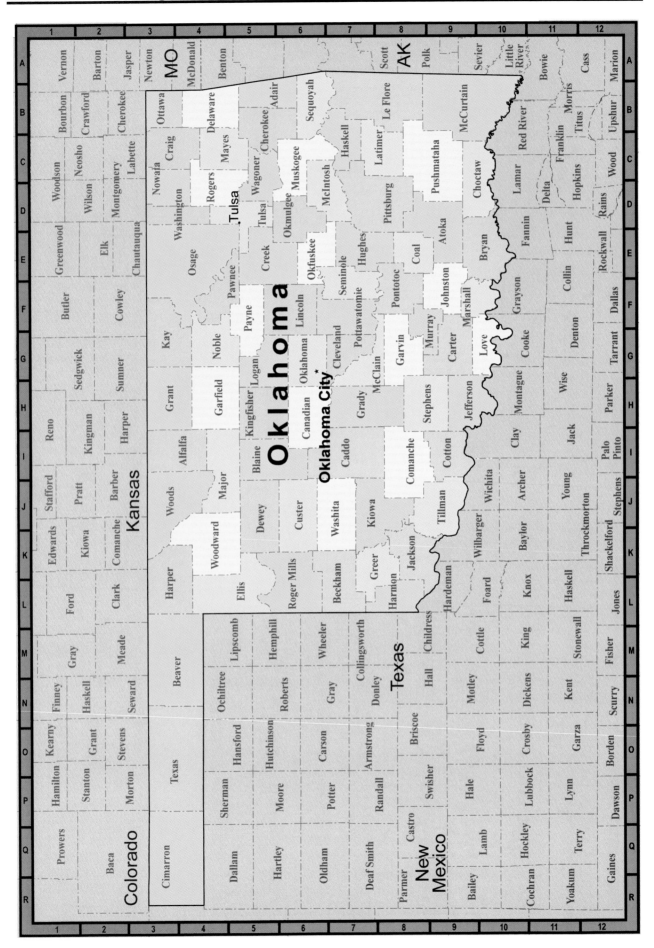

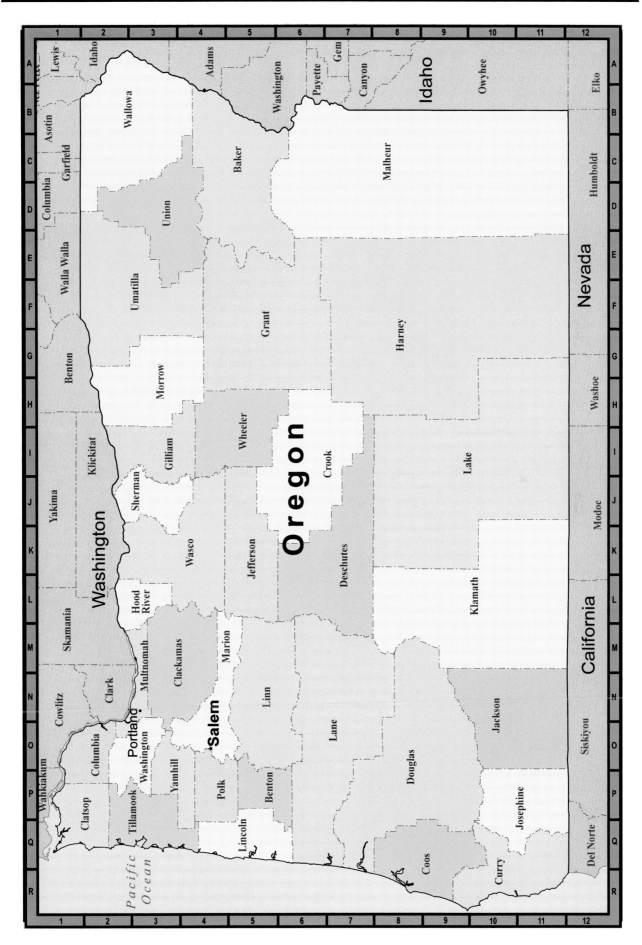

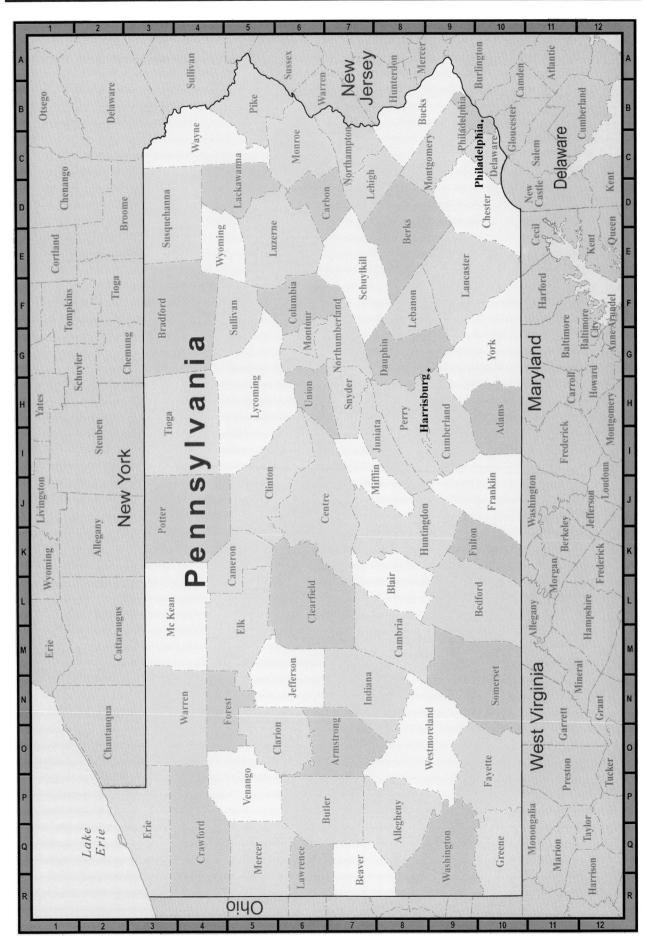

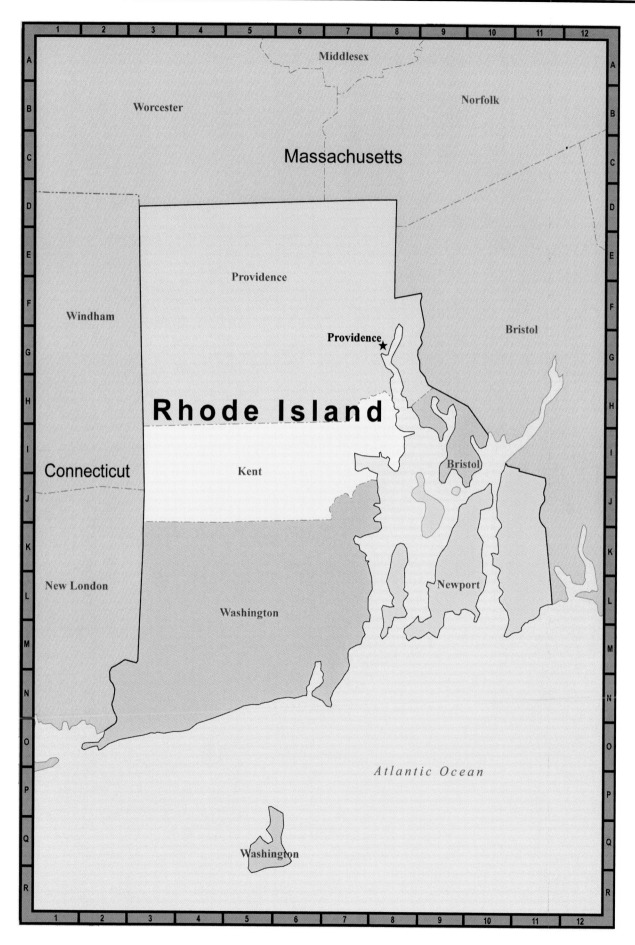

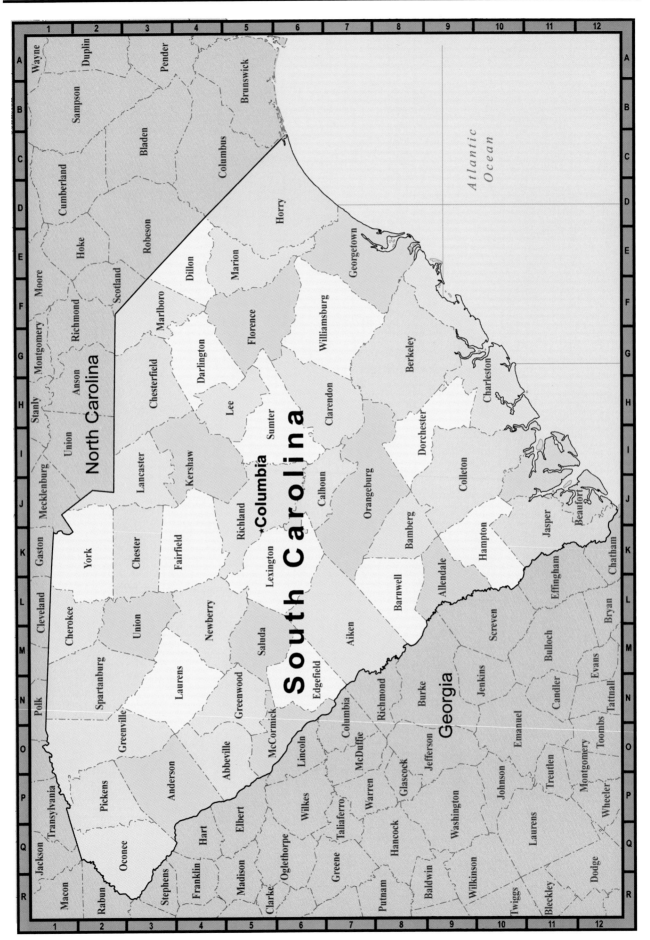

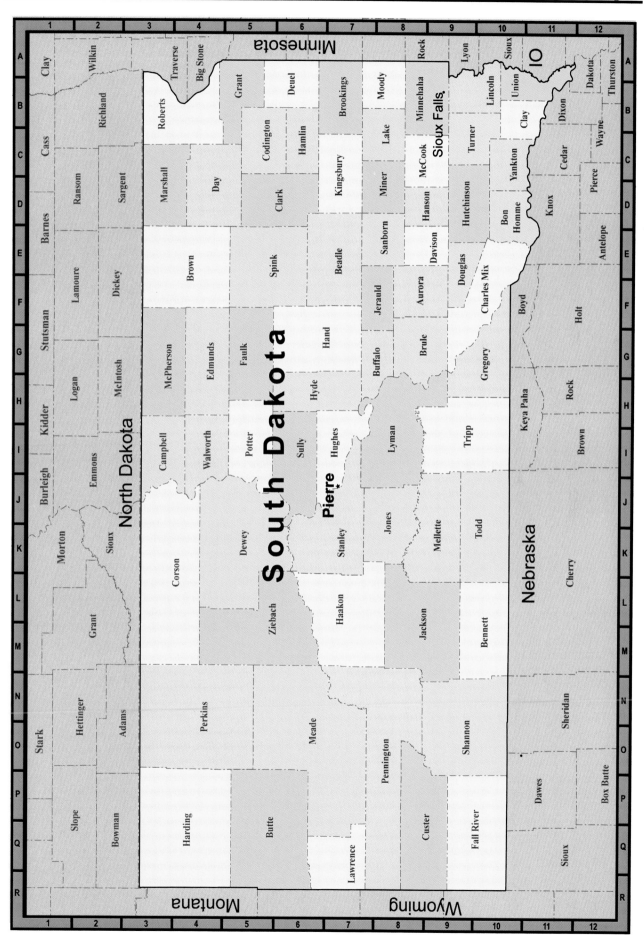

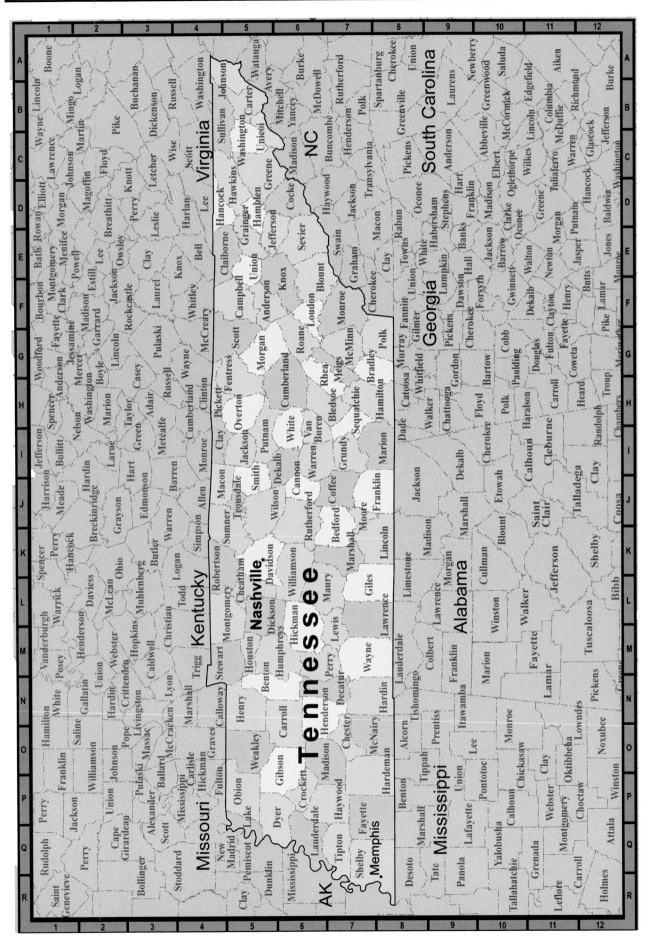

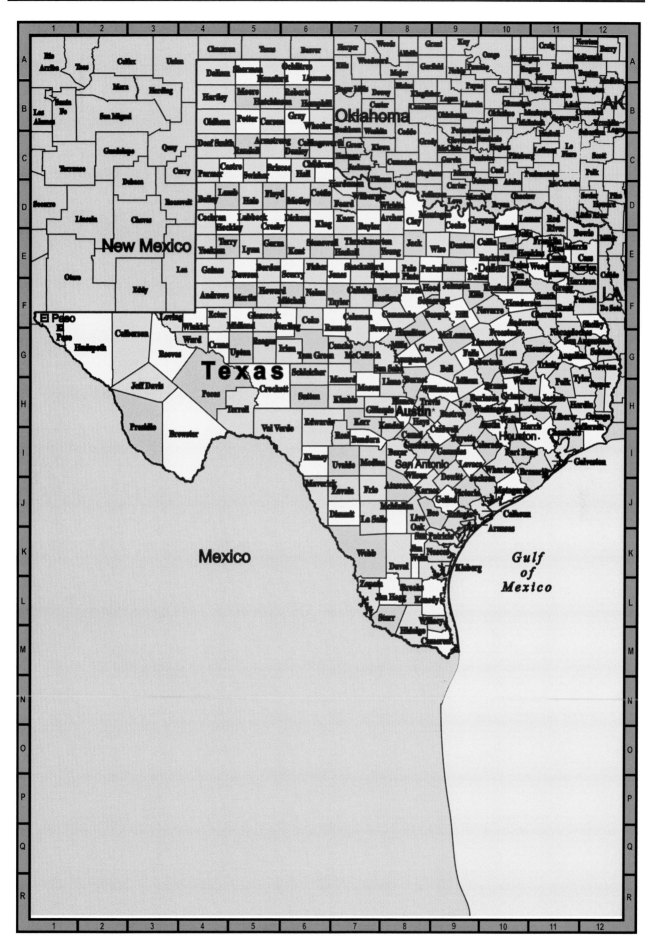

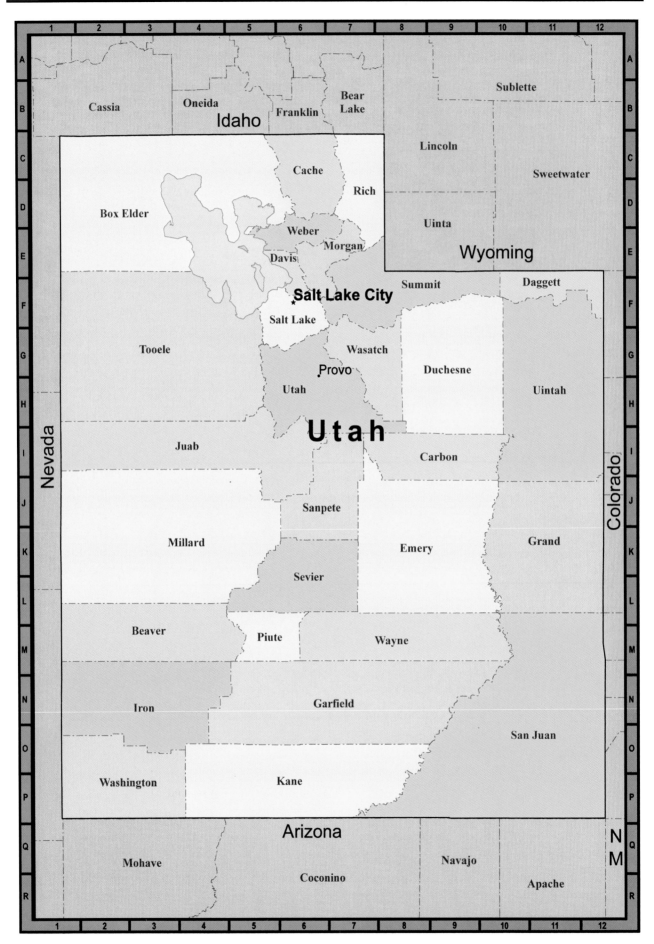

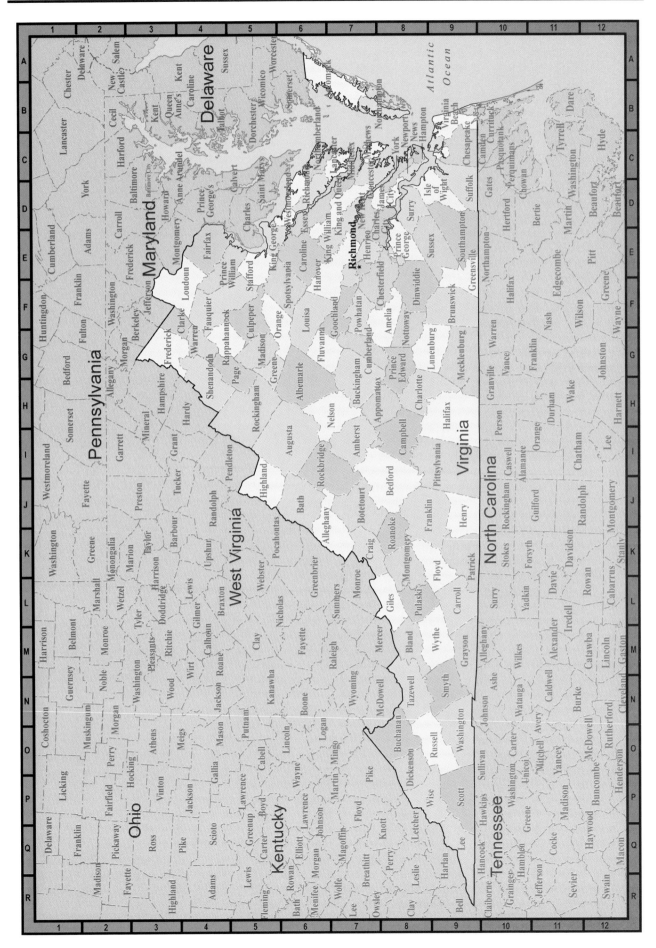

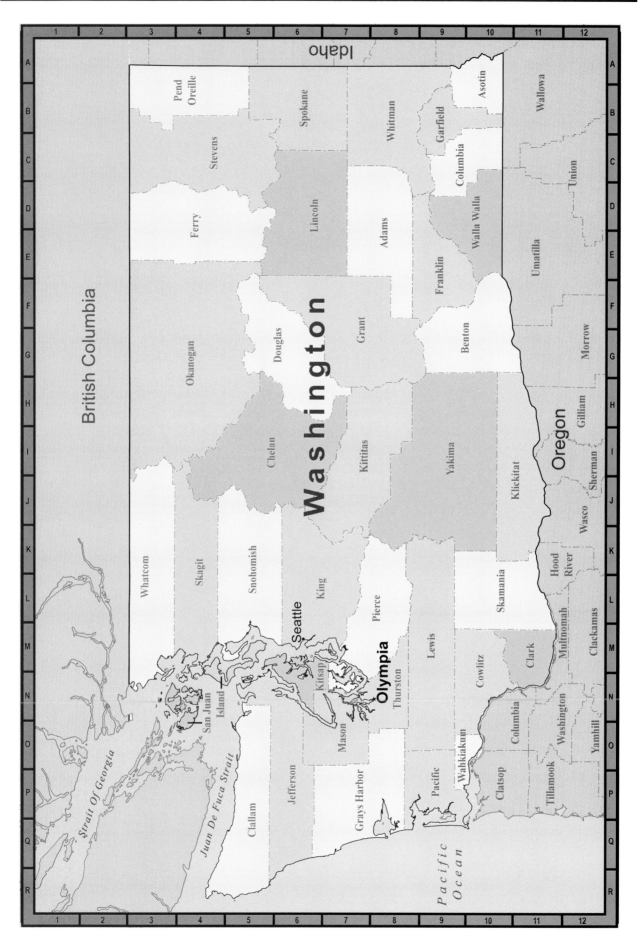

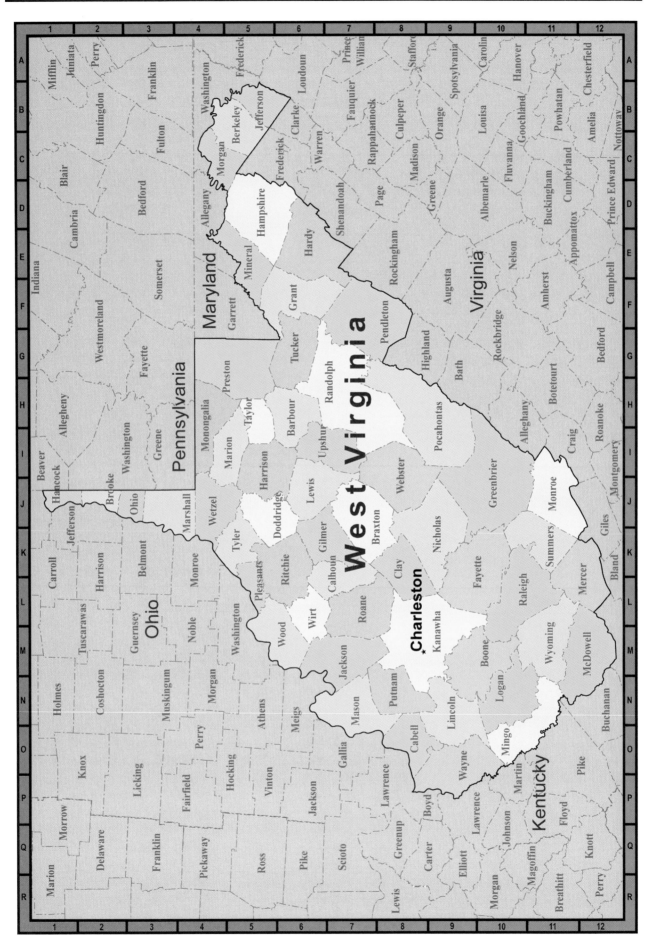

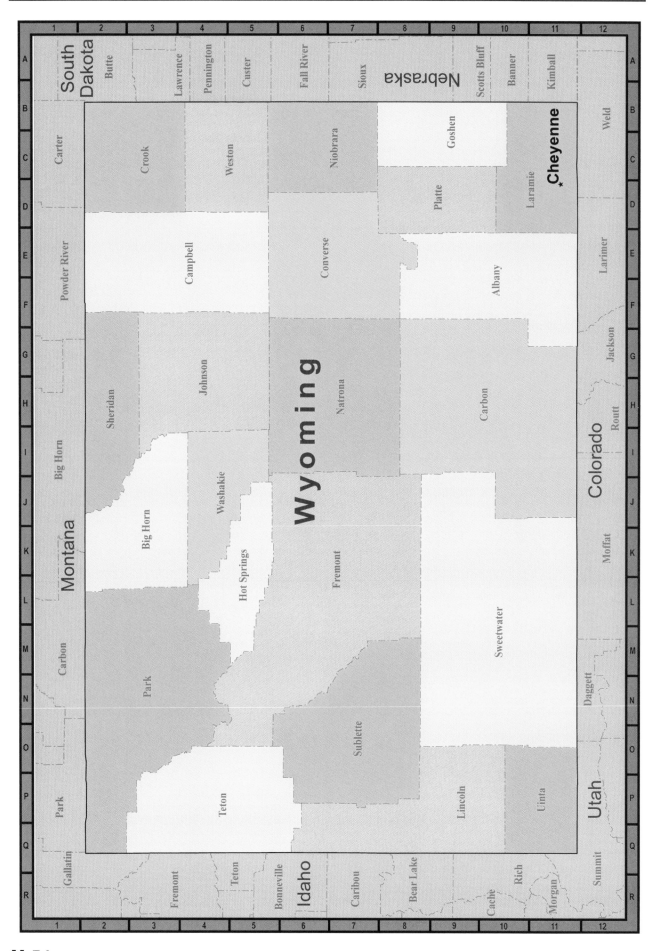

ALABAMA-CHICKASAW TRAIL: From Montgomery, Alabama in a northwest direction to the Tombigbee River in Mississippi. Approximately 170 miles. **Map page M-68.**

Alabama: Montgomery, Autauga, Chilton, Bibb, Tuscaloosa, Fayette, Lamar

Mississippi: Monroe

ALABAMA, CHOCTAW and NATCHEZ TRAIL: From Montgomery, Alabama west through Jackson, Mississippi to Vicksburg, Mississippi. Approximately 290 miles. **Map page M-68.**

Alabama: Montgomery, Lowndes, Dallas, Marengo, Choctaw

Mississippi: Lauderdale, Newton, Scott, Rankin, Hinds, Warren

ALABAMA and MOBILE TRAIL: From Montgomery, Alabama southwest to Mobile, Alabama. Approximately 150 miles. **Map page M-68.**

Alabama: Montgomery, Lowndes, Butler, Monroe, Clark, Baldwin

ALACHUA-TAMPA BAY TRAIL: From Alachua, Florida trailhead south to Tampa Bay, Florida. Approximately 140 miles. **Map page M-68.**

Florida: Alachua, Marion, Sumter, Hernando, Pasco, Hillsborough, Pinellas

AUGUSTA and CHEROKEE TRAIL: Northwest on the west side of the Savannah River from Augusta, Georgia to where it intersects with the Lower Cherokee Traders Path, continues until it joins the trailhead at Tallulah Falls, Georgia with Coosa-Tugaloo Indian Path and Unicoi Turnpike. Approximately 100 miles. **Map page M-67.**

Georgia: Richmond, Columbia, Lincoln, Wilkes, Elbert, Hart, Franklin, Stephens, Habersham

AUGUSTA-SAVANNAH TRAIL: South by southeast from Augusta, Georgia along the Savannah River on the Georgia side to Savannah, Georgia. Approximately 125 miles. **Map page M-65.**

Georgia: Richmond, Burke, Screven, Effingham, Chatham

AUGUSTA-ST. AUGUSTINE TRAIL: From Augusta, Georgia south to join the Old Trading Path through several counties, then southeast to St. Augustine, Florida. Approximately 290 miles. **Map page M-68.**

Georgia: Richmond, Burke, Jenkins, Candler, Evans, Taftnall, Appling, Bacon, Ware, Clinch, Echols

Florida: Hamilton, Columbia, Union, Bradford, Clay, St. Johns

BAY ROAD: From Boston to Taunton and New Bedford, Massachusetts traveling in a south direction. Approximately 60 miles. **Map page M-64.**

Massachusetts: Suffolk, Norfolk, Bristol

BLACK FOX TRAIL: Northeast form the Hiwassee River in North Carolina to the Stone River in Tennessee, where it junctions with the Cisca and St. Augustine Trail. Approximately 140 miles. **Map page M-67.**

North Carolina: Cherokee

Tennessee: Polk, Bradley, Hamilton, Bledsoe, Van Buren, Warren, Cannon, Rutherford

BOSTON POST ROAD: From Boston, Massachusetts to New York City. There are at least two different routes. One follows the Old Connecticut Path to Hartford, Connecticut continuing south to New Haven, then west by southwest through Bridgeport and Stamford, Connecticut to New York City. The other follows the Old Roebuck Road to Providence, Rhode Island, then continuing south by southwest, then following the coastal line across Connecticut to New Haven, west by southwest through Bridgeport and Stamford to New York City. Approximately 275 miles. **Map page M-64.**

Route 1

Massachusetts: Suffolk, Middlesex, Worchester, Hampden

Connecticut: Hartford, Middlesex, New Haven, Fairfield

New York: Westchester, Bronx, New York, Kings, Queens

Route 2

Massachusetts: Suffolk, Norfolk, Bristol

Rhode Island: Providence, Kent, Washington

Connecticut: New London, Middlesex, New Haven, Fairfield

New York: Westchester, Bronx, New York, Kings, Queens

BOLIVAR and MEMPHIS TRAIL: West from Bolivar, Tennessee to Memphis and the Mississippi River. Approximately 60 miles. **Map page M-67.**

Tennessee: Hardeman, Fayette, Shelby

BRADDOCKS ROAD: West by northwest from Cumberland, Maryland along part of the Gist's Trace and on to Ft. Duquesne at Pittsburgh, Pennsylvania. Approximately 100 miles. **Map page M-65.**

Maryland: Allegany, Garrett

Pennsylvania: Somerset, Fayette, Allegheny

BUFFALO TRACE: From Louisville, Kentucky west by northwest across southern Indiana to Vincennes, through Centralia, Illinois, then west by southwest to Kaskaskia, Illinois on the Missouri River. Approximately 320 Miles. **Map page M-66.**

Kentucky: Jefferson

Indiana: Floyd, Harrison, Washington, Orange, Martin, Daviess, Knox

Illinois: Lawrence, Richland, Clay, Marion, Jefferson, Washington, Perry, Randolph

BURD'S ROAD: Northwest From Gist's Plantation to Ft. Burd and Brownsville on the Monongahela River, Pennsylvania. It became a link in the National Road. Approximately 35 miles. **Map page M-63.**

Pennsylvania: Fayette

CAMDEN-CHARLESTON PATH: Southeast direction from Camden, to Charleston, South Carolina. Approximately 150 miles. **Map page M-65.**

South Carolina: Kershaw, Sumter, Calhoun, Orangeburg, Dorchester, Charleston

CATAWBA and NORTHERN TRAIL: Starting in York County, South Carolina at the point where it intersects the lower Cherokee Traders Path running north along the

Catawba River, then cross country to the Yadkin River in North Carolina to join the New River and Southern Trail. Approximately 100 miles. **Map page M-65.**

South Carolina: York

North Carolina: Gaston, Lincoln, Catawba, Alexander, Wilkes

CATAWBA TRAIL: A continuation of the Old South Carolina State Road in a northwest direction across the small part of North Carolina, through the Great Smoky Mountains into the Great Valley of Tennessee, crossing the Great Indian Warpath and the Holston River at the western tip of Virginia, then to the Cumberland Gap, where it joins the Warrior's Path of Kentucky. Approximately 120 Miles. **Map page M-67.**

North Carolina: Polk, Henderson, Buncombe, Madison

Tennessee: Cocke, Greene, Hamblen, Grainger, Claiborne, Hancock

Virginia: Lee

CATSKILL ROAD: West from Springfield, Massachusetts to Hudson River, then to Wattle's Ferry on the Susquehanna River. Approximately 90 miles. **Map page M-64.**

Massachusetts: Hampden, Berkshire

New York: Columbia, Greene

CHARLESTON-FT. CHARLOTTE TRAIL: West by northwest from Charleston, South Carolina across southeast South Carolina to the Savannah River, where it joins the Ft. Charlotte and Cherokee Old Path. Approximately 105 miles. **Map page M-63.**

South Carolina: Charleston, Dorchester, Orangeburg, Aiken, Edgefiele, McCormick

CHARLESTON-SAVANNAH TRAIL: Southwest along the cost from Charleston, South Carolina to Savannah, Georgia. Approximately 120 miles. **Map page M-65.**

South Carolina: Charleston, Collection, Beaufort, Jasper

Georgia: Chatham

CHATTANOOGA-WILLSTOWN ROAD: North by northeast from the junction with the Tallapoosa Trail to Chattanooga, Tennessee. Approximately 70 miles. **Map page M-68.**

Alabama: Etowah, DeKalb

Tennessee: Hamilton

CHICAGO-DUBUQUE HIGHWAY: West by northwest from Chicago, Illinois to the Mississippi River at Dubuque, Iowa. Approximately 170 miles. **Map page M-66.**

Illinois: Cook, DuPage, Kane, McHenry, Boon, Winnebago, Stephenson, Jo Daviess

Iowa: Dubuque

CHICAGO-KASKASKIA ROAD: A road from Lake Michigan, south by southwest, through Peoria and Springfield, Illinois east of St. Louis to Kaskaskia on the Missouri River. Approximately 350 miles. **Map page M-66.**

Illinois: Cook, Will, Grundy, Marshall, Woodford, Tazewell. Logan, Sangamon, Montgomery, Bond, Madison, St. Clair, Randolph

CHOCTAW-BAY ST. LOUIS TRAIL: From Meridian, Mississippi south by southwest to Bay St. Louis, Mississippi. Approximately 155 miles. **Map page M-68.**

Mississippi: Lauderdale, Clarke, Jasper, Jones, Forest, Lamar, Pearl River, Hancock

CISCO and MIDDLE TENNESSEE TRAIL: A continuation of West Tennessee Chickasaw Trail, northeast from Bolivar, Tennessee to the Tennessee River in Benton County Tennessee. Approximately 65 miles. **Map page M-67.**

Tennessee: Hardeman, Chester, Henderson, Carroll, Benton

CISCA and ST.AUGUSTINE TRAIL or NICKAJACK TRAIL: Northwest from Augusta, Georgia through Athens, Georgia and through Chattanooga to Nashville, Tennessee. Approximately 240 miles. **Map page M-63.**

Georgia: Richmond, Columbia, McDuffie, Warren, Taliaferro, Greene, Morgan, Walton, Barrow, Hall, Forsyth, Cherokee, Bartow, Gordon, Whitfield, Catoosa

Tennessee: Hamilton, Marion, Franklin, Coffee, Bedford, Rutherford, Davidson

COASTAL PATH: Coastal road from Boston to Plymouth, Massachusetts, Traveling in a south by southeast direction. Approximately 35 miles. **Map page M-64.**

Massachusetts: Suffolk, Norfolk, Plymouth

COOSA-TUGALOO INDIAN WARPATH: Northeast from Birmingham, Alabama through eastern Alabama then northern Georgia to the Tugaloo River between Georgia and South Carolina. Approximately 200 miles. **Map page M-67.**

Alabama: Jefferson, St. Clair, Etowah, Cherokee

Georgia: Floyd, Bartow, Cherokee, Dawson, Hall, Banks, Stephens

CUMBERLAND and GREAT LAKES TRAIL: North by northwest from Nashville, Tennessee to near Lexington, Kentucky where it joins the Tennessee, Ohio, and Great Lakes Trail. Approximately 214 miles. **Map page M-67.**

Tennessee: Davidson, Sumner, Macon

Kentucky: Monroe, Cumberland, Adair, Casey, Boyle, Mercer

CUMBERLAND and OHIO FALLS TRAIL: North by northwest from Nashville, Tennessee to Louisville, Kentucky on the Ohio River. Approximately 175 miles. **Map page M-67.**

Tennessee: Davidson, Robertson

Kentucky: Logan, Warren, Edmonson, Hart, Hardin, Bullitt, Jefferson

CUMBERLAND ROAD: West from Brownsville, Pennsylvania to Ft. Henry at Wheeling, West Virginia. Approximately 50 miles. **Map page M-67.**

Pennsylvania: Fayette, Washington

West Virginia: Ohio

CUMBERLAND TRACE: West from Knoxville to Nashville, Tennessee. Approximately 180 miles. **Map page M-67.**

Tennessee: Knox, Loudon, Roane, Cumberland, White, Putnam, Smith, Trousdale, Wilson, Davidson

DETROIT-CHICAGO ROAD: From Detroit, Michigan in a west by southwest direction to Chicago, Illinois. Approximately 275 miles. **Map page M-66.**

Michigan: Wayne, Monroe, Lenawee, Hillsdale, Branch, St. Joseph, Cass, Berrien

Indiana: LaPorte, Porter, Luke

Illinois: Cook

FALL LINE or SOUTHERN ROAD: South by southwest form Philadelphia, Pennsylvania through Baltimore, Maryland, Richmond, Virginia, Raleigh and Fayetteville, North Carolina: Cheraw, Camden, and Columbia, South Carolina, and west Augusta, Georgia, passing through Macon and Columbus, Georgia to Montgomery, Alabama. Approximately 1,200 miles. **Map page M-63.**
Pennsylvania: Delaware, Philadelphia
Delaware: New Castle
Maryland: Cecil, Harford, Baltimore, Anne Arundel, Howard, Prince George's
Virginia: Arlington, Fairfax, Prince William, Stafford, Spotsylvania, Caroline, Hanover, Richmond, Henrico, Chesterfield, Dinwiddie, Brunswick
North Carolina: Warren, Franklin, Wake, Johnson, Harnett, Cumberland, Hoke, Scotland
South Carolina: Marlboro, Chesterfield, Kershaw, Richland, Lexington, Aiken
Georgia: Richmond, McDuffie, Warren, Hancock, Baldwin, Jones, Bibb, Crawford, Taylor, Talbot, Muscogee
Alabama: Russell, Lee, Macon, Montgomery

FAYETEVILLE, ELIZABETHTOWN, and WILMINGTON TRAIL of NORTH CAROLINA: Southeast direction from Fayetteville through Elizabethville to Wilmington, North Carolina. Approximately 95 miles. **Map page M-65.**
North Carolina: Cumberland, Bladen, Columbus, Brunswick

FORBIDEN PATH or CATSKILL TURNPIKE: West from Albany, New York across the state to Lake Erie, New York. Approximately 220 miles. **Map page M-64.**
New York: Albany, Schoharie, Otsego, Chenango, Cortland, Tompkins, Schuyler, Steuben, Allegany, Cattaraugus, Erie

FT. CHARLOTTE and CHEROKEE OLD PATH: Northwest from Ft. Charlotte, South Carolina along the east side of the Savannah River where it intersects with the Lower Cherokee Traders Path, continuing on to the trailhead where Coosa-Tugaloo Path and Old Cherokee Path come together. Approximately 70 miles. **Map page M-67.**
South Carolina: McCormick, Abbeville, Anderson, Oconee

FT. MOORE-CHARLESTON TRAIL: West by northwest from Charleston, South Carolina to Augusta, Georgia, where it joins a trailhead junction. Approximately 150 miles. **Map page M-65.**
South Carolina: Charleston, Dorchester, Colleton, Bamberg, Barnwell, Aiken

GAINE'S TRACE: From the Tombigbee River in Monroe County, Mississippi northeast to the Tennessee River near Decatur, Alabama. Approximately 120 miles. **Map page M-67.**
Mississippi: Monroe
Alabama: Lamar, Marion, Winston, Lawrence, Morgan

GIST'S TRACE or NEMACOLINIS PATH: West by northwest from Cumberland, Maryland to Christopher Gist's plantation between the Youghiogheny and Mononga-

hela Rivers in Pennsylvania. Portions would become part of the Braddock's Road and the National Road. Approximately 60 miles. **Map page M-65.**
Maryland: Allegany, Garrett
Pennsylvania: Somerset, Fayette

GREAT GENESEE ROAD: West from Utica, New York to the Genesee River and on to Fort Niagara, New York. Approximately 195 miles. **Map page M-64.**
New York: Oneida, Madison, Onondaga, Cayuga, Wayne, Monroe, Genesee, Niagara

GREAT INDIAN WARPATH: Southwest direction from Philadelphia, through Lancaster, Pennsylvania; Hagerstown, Maryland; Martinsburg, West Virginia, Harrisonburg and Roanoke, Virginia, to Chattanooga, Tennessee. This great trunk trail has had many names for various sections and branches. Approximately 550 miles. **Map page M-63.**
Pennsylvania: Philadelphia, Delaware, Chester, Lancaster, York, Adams
Maryland: Washington
West Virginia: Berkeley
Virginia: Frederick, Shenandoah, Rockingham, Augusta, Rockbridge, Botetourt, Roanoke, Montgomery, Pulaski, Wythe, Smyth, Washington
Tennessee: Sullivan, Washington, Greene, Cocke, Sevier, Blount, Monroe, McMinn, Bradley

GREAT SHAMOKIN PATH: Northwest from New York City through New Jersey to Susquehannah County, Pennsylvania, then west to Lake Erie. Approximately 440 miles. **Map page M-64.**
New York: Kings, Queens, New York
New Jersey: Essex, Morris, Sussex
Pennsylvania: Pike, Wayne, Susquehanna, Bradford, Tioga, Potter, McKean, Warren, Erie

GREAT SOUTH TRAIL: From Nashville, Tennessee south through Huntsville and Birmingham, Alabama to Mobile, Alabama. Approximately 435 miles. **Map page M-63.**
Tennessee: Davidson, Rutherford, Bedford, Lincoln
Alabama: Madison, Morgan, Cullman, Blount, Jefferson, Bibb, Perry, Marengo, Clarke, Washington, Mobile

GREAT TRADING PATH: Southwest direction from Roanoke, Virginia into northeast Tennessee (part of the Great Indian Warpath). The section from Roanoke to the Cumberland Gap was later part of the Wilderness Road. Approximately 190 miles. **Map page M-65.**
Virginia: Roanoke, Montgomery, Pulaski, Wythe, Smyth, Washington
Tennessee: Sullivan, Hawkins, Hancock, Clairborne

GREAT TRAIL or GREAT PATH: From Pittsburgh, Pennsylvania in west by northwest direction to Detroit, Michigan. Approximately 270 miles. **Map page M-66.**
Pennsylvania: Allegheny, Beaver, Lawrence
Ohio: Mahoning, Stark, Wayne, Ashland, Huron, Seneca, Sandusky, Ottawa, Lucas
Michigan: Monroe, Wayne

GREAT VALLEY ROAD or GREAT WAGON ROAD: Southwest direction from Hagerstown, Maryland though the Shenandoah Valley to Roanoke, Virginia (part of the Great Indian Warpath) Approximately 150 miles. **Map page M-65.**

Maryland: Washington

West Virginia: Berkley

Virginia: Frederick, Shenandoah, Rockingham, Augusta, Rockbridge, Botetourt, Roanoke

GREENWOOD ROAD: Hartford, Connecticut to Albany, New York traveling in a northwest direction. Approximately 70 miles. **Map page M-64.**

Connecticut: Hartford, Litchfield

Massachusetts: Berkshire

New York: Columbia, Rensselaer, Albany

JACKSON'S MILITARY ROAD: From Nashville, Tennessee south by southwest through Florence, Alabama to Columbus, Mississippi, joining the Lake Ponchartrain Trail and ending at Lake Ponchartrain, Louisiana. Approximately 445 miles. **Map page M-63.**

Tennessee: Davidson, Williamson, Maury, Giles, Lawrence

Alabama: Lauderdale, Colbert, Franklin, Marion

Mississippi: Monroe, Lowndes, Noxubee, Winston, Neshoba, Jasper, Smith, Covington, Jefferson, Davis, Marion, Walthall

Louisiana: Washington, St. Tammany

JACKSONVILLE-APALACHEE BAY TRAIL: From Jacksonville, Florida west across Florida to meet the Tugaloo-Apalachee Bay Trail, then south to Apalachee Bay. Approximately 170 miles. **Map page M-68.**

Florida: Duval, Baker, Hamilton, Madison, Jefferson, Wakulla

JACKSONVILLE-ST. AUGUSTINE TRAIL: From Jacksonville, Florida south along the coastline to St. Augustine. Approximately 40 miles. **Map page M-68.**

Florida: Duval, St. Johns

JONESBORO ROAD: Staring on the coast at the New Bern, North Carolina running in a northwest direction above Raleigh through Greensboro and Salem to the Catawba River, there joining Rutherford's War Trace to Asheville, then along the Broad River into Tennessee on the Catawba Trail to Knoxville, Tennessee. Approximately 345 miles. **Map page M-65.**

North Carolina: Craven, Lenoir, Greene, Wilson, Nash, Durham, Orange, Allamance, Guilford, Forsyth, Davie, Iredell, Alexander, Catawba, Burke, McDowell, Buncombe, Madison

Tennessee: Cocke, Jefferson, Knox

KANAWHA BRANCH of the GREAT INDIAN WARPATH: Starting at Chillicothe, Ohio in a southeast direction crossing the Ohio River at Gallipolis, Ohio and following the Kanawha River past Charlestown, West Virginia, then following the New River of the Chiswets, and joining the main path. Approximately 205 miles. **Map page M-65.**

Ohio: Ross, Jackson, Gallia

West Virginia: Mason, Putnam, Kanawha, Fayette, Raleigh, Summers, Mercer

Virginia: Giles, Pulaski

KELLOG TRAIL: A continuation of the Pecatonica Trail in a southeast direction from the Illinois River in Putnam County, Illinois to Terre Haute, Indiana. Approximately 160 miles. **Map page M-66.**

Illinois: Putnam, Marshall, LaSalle, Livingston, Ford, Iroquois, Vermillion

Indiana: Parke, Vigo

KENNEBUNK ROAD: Coastal road from Boston, Massachusetts through Kennebunk and Portland to Augusta, Maine traveling in a north by northeast direction. Approximately 180 miles. **Map page M-64.**

Massachusetts: Suffolk, Middlesex, Essex

New Hampshire: Rockingham

Maine: York, Cumberland, Sagadahoc, Kennebec

KITTANNING PATH: West by northwest form the Tuscarora Path through Altoona and Kittanning, to the Allegheny River, all in Pennsylvania. Approximately 115 miles. **Map page M-64.**

Pennsylvania: Mifflin, Huntingdon, Blair, Cambria, Indiana, Armstrong

LAFAYETTE ROAD: South by southeast from Lafayette, Indiana to the Ohio River on Crawford County, Indiana. Approximately 170 miles. **Map page M-66.**

Indiana: Tippecanoe, Montgomery, Putnam, Owen, Monroe, Lawrence, Orange, Crawford

LAKE CHAMPLAIN TRAIL: A continuation of the Hudson River Path from Albany, New York to the St. Lawrence River in Canada. Approximately 200 miles. **Map page M-64.**

New York: Albany, Saratoga, Warren, Essex, Clinton

Canada: Quebec

LAKE PONCHARTRAIN TRAIL: Southeast from Wilkinson, Mississippi to Lake Pontchartrain, then northeast until the trail joins Jackson's Military Road. Approximately 80 miles. **Map page M-68.**

Mississippi: Wilkinson

Louisiana: East Feliciana, St. Helena, Livingston, Tangipahoa, St. Tammany, Washington

LAKE TRAIL or LAKE SHORE PATH: West by southwest from Buffalo, New York along the shore of Lake Erie to Cleveland, Ohio, continuing west to Sandusky Country, Ohio, where it joins and becomes part of the Great Trail or Great Path. Approximately 260 miles. **Map page M-66.**

New York: Erie, Chautauqua

Pennsylvania: Erie

Ohio: Ashtabula, Lake, Cuyahoga, Lorain, Erie, Sandusky

LEHIGH and LACKAWANNA PATHS: South from the Forbidden Path or Catskill Turnpike in Otsego County, New York, through Scranton, Pennsylvania to Northampton County, where it joins the Minsi Path. Approximately 90 miles. **Map page M-64.**

New York: Otsego, Delaware

Pennsylvania: Wayne, Susquehanna, Lackawanna, Monroe, Northampton

LOWER CHEROKEE TRADER'S PATH: West by southwest from Charlotte, North Carolina across the northern section of South Carolina to the Tugaloo River, where it joins the Tugaloo-Apalachee Bay Trail. Approximately 215 miles. **Map page M-67.**

South Carolina: York, Cherokee, Spartanburg, Greenville, Anderson, Oconee

North Carolina: Mecklenburg, Gaston

LOWER CREEK TRADING POST: West by southwest from Augusta, Georgia to Macon, Georgia, then west to Birmingham, Alabama; then west by northwest to the Tombigbee River in eastern Mississippi, continuing west by northwest to Oxford, Mississippi. Then west by southwest through Clarksdale to the Mississippi River. Approximately 540 miles. **Map page M-63.**

Georgia: Richmond, McDuffie, Warren, Hancock, Baldwin, Jones, Bibb, Monroe, Upson, Meriwether, Troup

Alabama: Randolph, Clay, Talladega, Shelby, Jefferson, Walker, Fayette, Lamar

Mississippi: Monroe, Lee, Pontotoc, Lafayette, Panola, Quitman, Coahoma

LOWER WARPATH or WEST TENNESSEE TRAIL: West from Nashville, Tennessee to the Tennessee River. As the trail continues beyond the Tennessee River, it becomes the Mississippi and Tennessee River Trail. Approximately 60 miles. **Map page M-67.**

Tennessee: Davidson, Cheatham, Dickson, Humphreys

MACON and MONTGOMERY TRAIL: From Montgomery, Alabama east through Columbus then east by northeast to Macon, Georgia. Approximately 120 miles. **Map page M-68.**

Alabama: Montgomery, Macon, Russell, Lee

Georgia: Muskogee, Talbot, Taylor, Crawford, Bibb

MARYLAND ROAD: West from Baltimore, to Cumberland, Maryland. This was the first section of the National Road. Approximately 110 miles. **Map page M-65.**

Maryland: Baltimore, Carroll, Fredrick, Washington, Allegany

MAYSVILLE TURNPIKE: A continuation of Zane's Trace form Maysville, Kentucky southwest to Elizabethtown, Kentucky. Approximately 165 miles. **Map page M-66.**

Kentucky: Mason, Robertson, Nicholas, Bourbon, Fayette, Woodford, Anderson, Washington, Nelson, Hardin.

MEMPHIS, PONTOTOC and MOBILE TRAIL: From Memphis, Tennessee south by southeast through Pontotoc, Mississippi, then southwest to Grenada, then south by southeast to Mobile, Alabama. Approximately 360 miles. **Map page M-63.**

Tennessee: Shelby

Mississippi: DeSoto, Marshall, Union, Pontotoc, Calhoun, Grenada, Montgomery, Attala, Leake, Neshoba, Newton, Jasper, Clarke, Wayne, Greene

Alabama: Washington, Mobile

MIAMI PATH: North form Cincinnati, Ohio through western Ohio to Defiance, Ohio, where the trail joins the Vincennes and Indianapolis Road. Approximately 180 miles. **Map page M-66.**

Ohio: Hamilton, Butler, Preble, Drake, Mercer, Van Wert, Paulding, Defiance

MICHIGAN ROAD: Straight south from South Bend, Indiana to Indianapolis, Indiana. Approximately 140 miles. **Map page M-66.**

Indiana: St. Joseph, Marshall, Fulton, Miami, Howard, Tipton, Hamilton, Marion

MIDDLE CREEK TRADING PATH: West by southwest from McCormack, South Carolina across Georgia to eastern Alabama. Approximately 230 miles. **Map page M-63.**

South Carolina: McCormack

Georgia: Lincoln, Wilkes, Taliaferro, Greene, Morgan, Jasper, Buffs, Spalding, Pike, Meriwether, Troup

Alabama: Chambers

MIHOAUKEE TRAIL: North from Chicago, Illinois along the shore of Lake Michigan to Milwaukee, Wisconsin, then continuing north by northwest to Fond du Lac, Wisconsin. Approximately 110 miles. **Map page M-66.**

Illinois: Cook. Lake

Wisconsin: Kenosha, Racine, Milwaukee, Washington, Fond du Lac

MINSI PATH: South by southwest from Kingston, New York to Port Jervis, then on the west side of the Delaware River to Philadelphia, Pennsylvania. Approximately 110 miles. **Map page M-64.**

New York: Ulster, Sullivan, Orange

Pennsylvania: Pike, Monroe, Northampton, Bucks, Montgomery, Philadelphia

MISSISSIPPI and TENNESSEE RIVER TRAIL: West from the Tennessee River to the Mississippi River. Approximately 90 miles. **Map page M-67.**

Tennessee: Benton, Carroll, Gibson, Dyer

MOBILE and NATCHEZ TRAIL: From Mobile, Alabama across lower Mississippi in a west by northwest direction to Natchez, Mississippi. Approximately 220 miles. **Map page M-68.**

Alabama: Mobile

Mississippi: George, Perry, Forest, Lamar, Marion, Walthall, Pike, Amite, Franklin, Adams

MOHAWK or IROQUOIS TRAIL: West by northwest from Albany, New York along the Mohawk River Utica and Rome, diverging with a branch to Fort Oswego on Lake Ontario. Approximately 190 miles. **Map page M-64.**

New York: Albany, Schenectady, Herkimer, Oneida, Oswego

NASHVILLE ROAD: West by northwest from Knoxville, Tennessee to near Monterey, where it joins the Cumberland Trace. Approximately 86 miles. **Map page M-67.**

Tennessee: Knox, Anderson, Morgan, Fentress, Overton, Putnam

NASHVILLE-SALINE RIVER TRAIL: Northwest from Nashville, Tennessee through the small part of Kentucky, crossing the Ohio river near Paducah into Illinois, then to Kaskaskia on the Mississippi River. Approximately 200 miles. **Map page M-67.**

Tennessee: Davidson, Cheatham, Montgomery

Kentucky: Christian, Trigg, Lyon, Marshall, McCracken

Illinois: Massac, Johnson, Union, Jackson, Randolph

NATCHEZ-LOWER CREEKS TRAIL: From Natchez east across lower Mississippi and lower Alabama to Montgomery, Alabama. Approximately 310 miles. **Map page M-68.**

Mississippi: Adams, Franklin, Lincoln, Lawrence, Jefferson, Davis, Covington, Jones, Wayne

Alabama: Washington, Clark, Monroe

NATCHEZ TRACE or CHICKASAW TRAIL: From Natchez, Mississippi north by northeast to Nashville, Tennessee. Approximately 380 miles. **Map page M-68.**

Mississippi: Adams, Jefferson, Claiborne, Hinds, Madison, Leake, Winston, Oktibbeha, Clay, Monroe

Tennessee: Lawrence, Giles, Maury, Williamson, Davidson

NATCHEZ-NEW ORLEANS TRAIL: From Natchez, Mississippi south along the Mississippi River, then east to New Orleans, Louisiana. Approximately 125 miles. **Map page M-68.**

Mississippi: Adams, Wilkinson

Louisiana: West Feliciana, East Feliciana, East Baton Rouge, Ascension, St. James, St. John the Baptist, St. Charles, Jefferson, Orleans

NEW RIVER and SOUTHERN TRAIL: Starting at the Yadkin River, it is a continuation of the Catawba and Northern Trail. North across the small part of Virginia into West Virginia, where it connects with the Kanooba Branch of the Great Indian Warpath in Mercer County. Approximately 165 miles. **Map page M-65.**

North Carolina: Wilkes, Alleghany

Virginia: Grayson, Carroll, Wythe, Pulaski, Giles

West Virginia: Mercer

OCCANEECHI PATH: Southwest direction from the Bermuda Hundred on the James River near Richmond, Virginia through Salisbury, North Carolina; Camden, South Carolina; to Augusta, Georgia. Approximately 500 miles. **Map page M-63.**

Virginia: Prince George, Dinwiddie, Brunswick, Lundenburg, Mecklenburg

North Carolina: Granville, Durham, Orange, Alamance, Guilford, Randolph, Davidson, Rowan, Cabarrus, Mecklenburg

South Carolina: York, Chester, Lancaster, Kershaw, Fairfield, Richland, Lexington, Aiken

Georgia: Columbia, Richmond

OKFUSKEE TRAIL: North to south trail along the Tallapoosa River in eastern Alabama. Approximately 70 miles. **Map page M-68.**

Alabama: Randolph, Cleburne, Cherokee

OLD CHEROKEE PATH: From Seneca, South Carolina runs north by northeast across North Carolina to the Great Indian Warpath in Virginia. Approximately 150 miles. **Map page M-65.**

South Carolina: Oconee, Pickens, Greenville

North Carolina: Polk, Rutherford, McDowell, Burke, Caldwell, Watauga

Tennessee: Johnson

Virginia: Washington

OLD CHICAGO ROAD: South by southeast from Chicago, Illinois to Indianapolis, Indiana. Approximately 165 miles. **Map page M-66.**

Illinois: Cook

Indiana: Lake, Newton, Benton, Tippecanoe, Clinton, Boone, Marion

OLD CONNECTICUT PATH: From Boston traveling in a west by southwest direction to Springfield, where it splits. One branch goes straight south to Hartford, Connecticut. The other goes to Albany, New York traveling in a west by northwest direction. Approximately 290 miles. **Map page M-64.**

Massachusetts: Suffolk, Middlesex, Worcester, Hampden, Hampshire, Berkshire

Connecticut: Hartford

New York: Columbia, Rensselaer, Albany

OLD NORTHWESTERN TURNPIKE: From Alexandria (Washington D.C. area) west in the upper countries of Virginia, into two counties in West Virginia, then across Garrett Country, Maryland, back into West Virginia to Parkersburg on the Ohio River. Approximately 180 miles. **Map page M-65.**

Virginia: Fairfax, Arlington, Loudoun, Clarke, Frederick

West Virginia: Hampshire, Mineral

Maryland: Garrett

West Virginia: Preston, Taylor, Harrison, Doddridge, Ritchie, Wood

OLD ROEBUCK ROAD: from Boston, Massachusetts to Providence, Rhode Island traveling in a south by southwest direction. Approximately 60 miles. **Map page M-64.**

Massachusetts: Suffolk, Norfolk, Bristol

Rhode Island: Providence

OLD SOUTH CAROLINA STATE ROAD: Northwest from Charleston, South Carolina through Columbia and Greenville to the North Carolina border where it joins the Catawba Trail. Approximately 180 miles. **Map page M-63.**

South Carolina: Charleston, Dorchester, Orangeburg, Calhoun, Lexington, Newberry, Laurens, Spartanburg, Greenville

OLD TRADING PATH: From the Savannah River southwest across Georgia to the Apalachicola River in Florida, then west through the Florida panhandle to Pensacola Bay, Florida. Approximately 335 miles. **Map page M-68.**

Georgia: Effingham, Bullock, Evans, Taftnall, Appling, Bacon, Coffee, Atkinson, Berrien, Cook, Colquitt, Grady, Decatur

Florida: Jackson, Washington, Holmes, Walton, Okaloosa, Santa Rosa

PAMUNKEY-NEW RIVER TRAIL: West from the Pamunkey River north of Richmond, Virginia through Charlottesville and Staunton, Virginia into West Virginia to the New River in Fayette County where in connects with the Kanawha Branch of the Great Indian Warpath. Approximately 135 miles. **Map page M-65.**

Virginia: Hanover, Louisa, Albemarle, Augusta, Bath

West Virginia: Greenbriar, Fayette

PECATONICA TRAIL: From Lake Michigan at Green Bay south by southwest to Madison, Wisconsin, then south to Illinois, then southeast to the Illinois River in

Bureau County, Illinois. Approximately 290 miles. **Map page M-66.**

Wisconsin: Brown, Calumet, Fond du Lac, Dodge, Columbia, Dane, Rock

Illinois: Winnebago, Stephenson, Ogle, lee, Bureau

PHILIDELPHIA WAGON ROAD: West by southwest from Philadelphia through Lancaster, Pennsylvania to Hagerstown Maryland (part of the Great Indian Warpath into the Shenandoah Valley) Approximately 140 Miles. **Map page M-65.**

Pennsylvania: Philadelphia, Delaware, Chester, Lancaster, York, Adams

Maryland: Washington

West Virginia: Berkley

Virginia: Frederick, Shenandoah

RAYSTOWN PATH or FORBE'S ROAD or OLD TRADING PATH: West from Philadelphia, through Harrisburg and Bedford to Pittsburgh, Pennsylvania. Approximately 210 miles. **Map page M-64.**

Pennsylvania: Philadelphia, Chester, Delaware, Lancaster, Lebanon, Dauphin, Cumberland, Franklin, Fulton, Bedford, Somerset, Westmoreland, Allegheny

RICHMOND ROAD or CHESAPEAKE BRANCH of the GREAT INDIAN WARPATH: Beginning at Richmond, Virginia running in a west by southwest direction through Lynchburg and Roanoke, becoming the Great Indian Warpath at Ft. Chissel on the New River. Approximately 135 miles. **Map page M-65.**

Virginia: Henrico, Powhatan, Cumberland, Buckingham, Appomattox, Amherst, Bedford, Roanoke, Montgomery.

RICHMOND-WILLIAMSBURG ROAD: East by southeast from Richmond, Virginia along the James River to Williamsburg, Virginia. Approximately 45 miles. **Map page M-65.**

Virginia: Henrico, Charles City, James City

RUSSELLVILLE-SHAWNEETOWN TRAIL: Northwest from Russellville, Kentucky to Shawneetown, Illinois on the Ohio River. Approximately 110 miles. **Map page M-67.**

Kentucky: Logan, Todd, Muhlenberg, Hopkins, Webster, Union

Illinois: Gallatin

RUTHERFORD'S WAR TRACE: A continuation of the Jonesboro Road from the Catawba River north of Salisbury, North Carolina in a southwest direction through Asheville to the Little Tennessee River near Franklin, where it joins the Black Fox Trail. Approximately 180 miles. **Map page M-65.**

North Carolina: Davie, Rowan, Iredell, Catawba, Burke, McDowell, Buncombe, Haywood, Jackson, Macon, Cherokee

SAURA-SAPONI TRAIL: South by Southwest direction from Charlottesville, Virginia to the area of Greensboro, North Carolina. Approximately 120 miles. **Map page M-65.**

Virginia: Albemarle, Nelson, Amherst, Campbell, Pittsylvania

SAVANNAH-JACKSONVILLE TRAIL: South from Savannah, Georgia along the Atlantic Coast to Jacksonville, Florida. Approximately 135 miles. **Map page M-68.**

Georgia: Chatham, Bryan, Liberty, McIntosh, Glynn, Camden

Florida: Nassau, Duval

SCIOTO TRAIL: Straight south from Sandusky Bay, on Lake Erie along the Scioto River to Portsmouth on the Ohio River, being the northernmost extension of the Warriors Path. Approximately 220 miles. **Map page M-66.**

Ohio: Sandusky, Seneca, Crawford, Marion, Delaware, Franklin, Pickaway, Ross, Pike, Scioto

SECONDARY COAST ROAD: South by southwest direction form Peterburg, Virginia along the coast to Charleston, South Carolina, Approximately 475 miles. **Map page M-63.**

Virginia: Prince George's Sussex, Southampton, Isle of Wight, Suffolk

North Carolina: Gates, Hertford, Bertie, Martin, Beaufort, Craven, Jones, Onslow, Pender, New Hanover, Brunswick

South Carolina: Horry, Georgetown, Charleston

ST. AUGUSTINE-APALACHEE TRAIL: West from St. Augustine, Florida to Alachua, then west by northwest to Tallahassee, Florida. Approximately 205 miles. **Map page M-68.**

Florida: St. Johns, Clay, Alachua, Gilchrist, Lafayette, Taylor, Jefferson, Leon

ST. AUGUSTINE-FLINT RIVER TRAIL: From St. Augustine, Florida west to a junction with the Jacksonville Apalachee Bay Trail, past Tallahassee to the Chattahoochee on the Apalachicola River. Approximately 170 miles. **Map page M-68.**

Florida: St. Johns, Clay, Bradford, Union, Columbia, Hamilton, Madison, Jefferson, Leon, Gadsden, Jackson

TALLAPOOSA TRAIL: From Montgomery, Alabama north through Birmingham, then in a north by northeast direction to join the Chattanooga-Willstown Road. Approximately 190 miles. **Map page M-68.**

Alabama: Montgomery, Elmore, Autauga, Chilton, Shelby, Jefferson, St. Clair, Etowah

TENNESSEE, OHIO AND GREAT LAKES TRAIL: North from Chattanooga, Tennessee to Detroit, Michigan, Approximately 480 miles. **Map page M-63.**

Tennessee: Hamilton, Rhea, Roane, Morgan, Fentress, Pickett

Kentucky: Wayne, Russell, Adair, Casey, Boyle, Mercer, Jessamine, Fayette, Bourbon, Nicholas, Robertson, Mason

Ohio: Brown, Highland, Clinton, Green, Clark, Champaign, Logan, Hardin, Hancock, Wood, Lucas

Michigan: Monroe, Wayne

THE NATIONAL ROAD: West from Baltimore, Maryland to St. Lois, Missouri, linking the Maryland Road, Gist's Trace, Braddock's Road, Burd's Road, and the Cumberland Road to Wheeling, West Virginia; then continuing through Columbus, Ohio; Indianapolis and Terre

Haute, Indiana; Vandalia, Illinois to St. Louis, Missouri. Approximately 755 miles. **Map page M-63.**

Maryland: Baltimore, Carroll, Frederick, Washington, Allegany, Garrett

Pennsylvania: Somerset, Fayette, Washington

West Virginia: Ohio

Ohio: Belmont, Guernsey, Muskingum. Licking, Franklin, Madison, Clark, Montgomery, Preble

Indiana: Wayne, Henry, Hancock, Marion, Hendricks, Morgan, Putnam, Clay, Vigo

Illinois: Clark, Cumberland, Jasper, Effingham, Fayette, Bond, Madison

Missouri: St. Louis

TOMBIGBEE and ARKANSAS RIVER TRAIL: West from the Tombigbee River in Monroe County, Mississippi across the state to the mouth of the Arkansas River. Approximately 180 miles. **Map page M-68.**

Mississippi: Monroe, Chickasaw, Calhoun, Yalobusha, Tallahatchie, Sunflower, Bolivar

TUGALOO-APALACHEE BAY TRAIL: South by southwest from the Tugaloo River in Georgia across the Florida panhandle to the Gulf of Mexico. Approximately 310 miles. **Map page M-63.**

Georgia: Stephens, Franklin, Madison, Jackson, Clarke, Oconee, Walton, Newton, Buffs, Lamar, Upson, Taylor, Schley, Sumter, Lee, Dougherty, Baker, Mitchell, Grady

Florida: Leon, Wakulla

TUSCARORA PATH: Southwest from Scranton, Pennsylvania to Bedford, Pennsylvania. Approximately 215 miles. **Map page M-64.**

Pennsylvania: Lackawanna, Luzerne, Columbia, Northumberland, Snyder, Mifflin, Huntingdon, Bedford

TUSCARORA PATH: Southwest from Scranton, Pennsylvania to Bedford, Pennsylvania. Approximately 106 miles. **Map page M-64.**

New York: Kings, Queens, New York

New Jersey: Hudson, Union, Middlesex, Mercer, Burlington

Pennsylvania: Philadelphia

UNICOI TURNPIKE: Northwest from the trailhead at Tallulah Falls, to the trailhead in North Carolina, intersects with Black Fox Trail and Rutherford War Trace on the Hiwassee River. Approximately 60 miles. **Map page M-67.**

Georgia: Rabun, Towns

North Carolina: Clay, Cherokee

UPPER CREEKS-PENSCOLA TRAIL: From Montgomery, Alabama in a southwesterly direction around the boundary of the panhandle of Florida, then turning southeast to Pensacola Bay, Florida. Approximately 235 miles. **Map page M-68.**

Alabama: Montgomery, Lowndes, Butler, Conecuh, Escambia, Baldwin

Florida: Escambia

VENANGO PATH: North from Kittanning, to the Great Shamokin Path, Joining together near Corry, Pennsylvania, then turning west to Erie, Pennsylvania. Approximately 110 miles. **Map page M-66.**

Pennsylvania: Butler, Venango, Forest, Warren, Erie.

VINCENNES AND INDIANAPOLIS ROAD: South by southwest from Detroit, Michigan through Defiance, Ohio, Ft. Wayne and Indianapolis to Vincennes, Indiana. Approximately 360 miles. **Map page M-66.**

Michigan: Wayne, Monroe

Ohio: Lucas, Wood, Henry, Defiance, Paulding

Indiana: Allen, Wells, Huntington, Grant, Madison, Hamilton, Marion, Morgan, Monroe, Greene, Knox

WARRIORS PATH of KENTUCKY: A Continuation of the Scioto Trail in a southern direction from the Ohio River at Portsmouth, Ohio, to the Cumberland Gap, Kentucky. Approximately 190 miles. **Map page M-67.**

Kentucky: Greenup, Carter, Rowan, Bath, Montgomery, Powell, Estell, Jackson, Laurel, Knox, Bell

WEST TENNESSEE CHICKASAW TRAIL: South from Bolivar, Tennessee to the junction point with Natchez Trace Trail in Mississippi. Approximately 160 miles. **Map page M-67.**

Tennessee: Hardeman

Mississippi: Tippah, Union, Pontotoc

WILDERNESS ROAD: Cleared by Daniel Boone and 30 ax-men, followed the Great Indian Warpath on the North Fork of the Holston River on the Virginia-Tennessee border, west to the Cumberland Gap, then taking the Warriors Path into Kentucky. From there continuing northwest through Harrodsburg, on to Louisville, Kentucky. Approximately 180 miles. **Map page M-67.**

Tennessee: Sullivan, Hawkins, Hancock, Clairborne

Kentucky: Bell, Knox, Laurel, Rockcastle, Lincoln, Boyle, Mercer, Washington, Spencer, Jefferson

WIMINGTON, HIGHPOINT and NORTHERN TRAIL: Starting at Wilmington, North Carolina running in a northwest direction to the Greensboro aea, then north into Virginia where it joins the Great Indian Warpath near Roanoke, Virginia. Approximately 255 miles. **Map page M-65.**

North Carolina: Brunswick, Columbus, Robeson, Scotland, Richmond, Moore, Randolph, Guilford, Rockingham

Virginia: Henry, Franklin, Roanoke

ZANE'S TRACE: In general southwest direction from Wheeling, West Virginia through Chillicothe, Ohio to Maysville, Kentucky. Approximately 255 miles. **Map page M-66.**

West Virginia: Ohio

Ohio: Belmont, Guernsey, Muskingum, Perry, Fairfield, Hocking, Ross, Pike, Adams, Brown

Kentucky: Maso

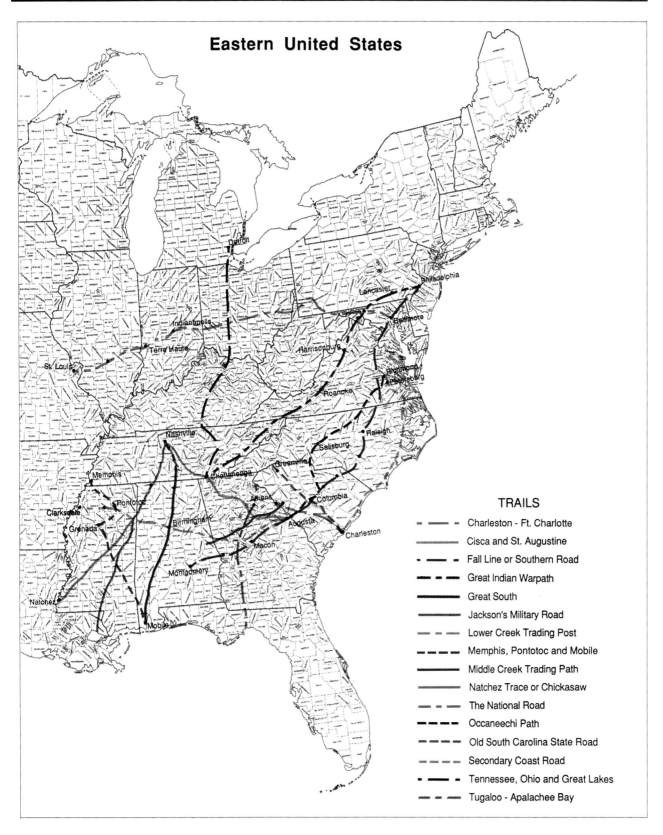

Eastern United States

TRAILS

- – · – · Charleston - Ft. Charlotte
- ———— Cisca and St. Augustine
- · —— · —— Fall Line or Southern Road
- ▬ ▬ ▬ Great Indian Warpath
- ▬▬▬▬ Great South
- ———— Jackson's Military Road
- – – – Lower Creek Trading Post
- ▬ ▬ ▬ ▬ Memphis, Pontotoc and Mobile
- ———— Middle Creek Trading Path
- ———— Natchez Trace or Chickasaw
- – · — · — The National Road
- ▬ ▬ ▬ ▬ Occaneechi Path
- ▬ ▬ ▬ Old South Carolina State Road
- – – – Secondary Coast Road
- · ▬ · ▬ · Tennessee, Ohio and Great Lakes
- – – – Tugaloo - Apalachee Bay

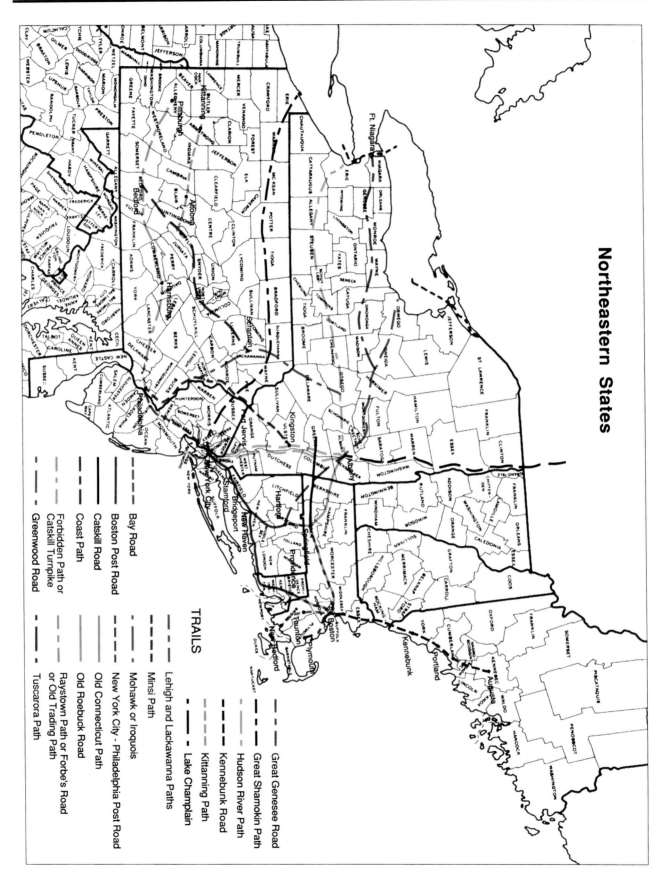

Northeastern States

TRAILS

- Bay Road
- Boston Post Road
- Catskill Road
- Coast Path
- Forbidden Path or Catskill Turnpike
- Greenwood Road
- Lehigh and Lackawanna Paths
- Minsi Path
- Mohawk or Iroquois
- New York City - Philadelphia Post Road
- Old Connecticut Path
- Old Roebuck Road
- Raystown Path or Forbe's Road or Old Trading Path
- Tuscarora Path
- Great Genesee Road
- Great Shamokin Path
- Hudson River Path
- Kennebunk Road
- Kittanning Path
- Lake Champlain

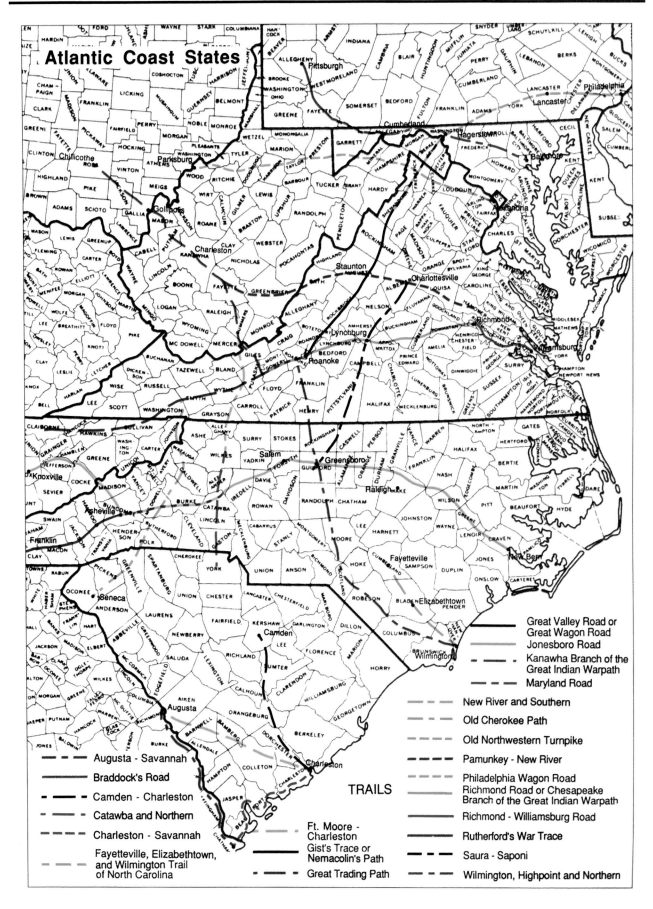

Atlantic Coast States

TRAILS

Great Valley Road or Great Wagon Road
Jonesboro Road
Kanawha Branch of the Great Indian Warpath
Maryland Road

New River and Southern
Old Cherokee Path
Old Northwestern Turnpike
Pamunkey - New River
Philadelphia Wagon Road
Richmond Road or Chesapeake Branch of the Great Indian Warpath
Richmond - Williamsburg Road
Rutherford's War Trace
Saura - Saponi
Wilmington, Highpoint and Northern

Augusta - Savannah
Braddock's Road
Camden - Charleston
Catawba and Northern
Charleston - Savannah
Fayetteville, Elizabethtown, and Wilmington Trail of North Carolina

Ft. Moore - Charleston
Gist's Trace or Nemacolin's Path
Great Trading Path

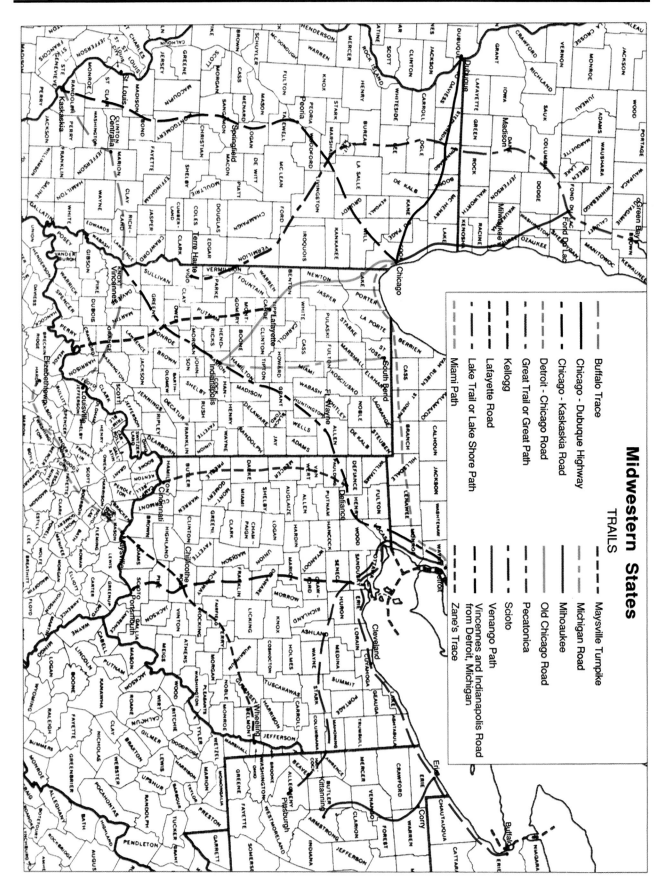

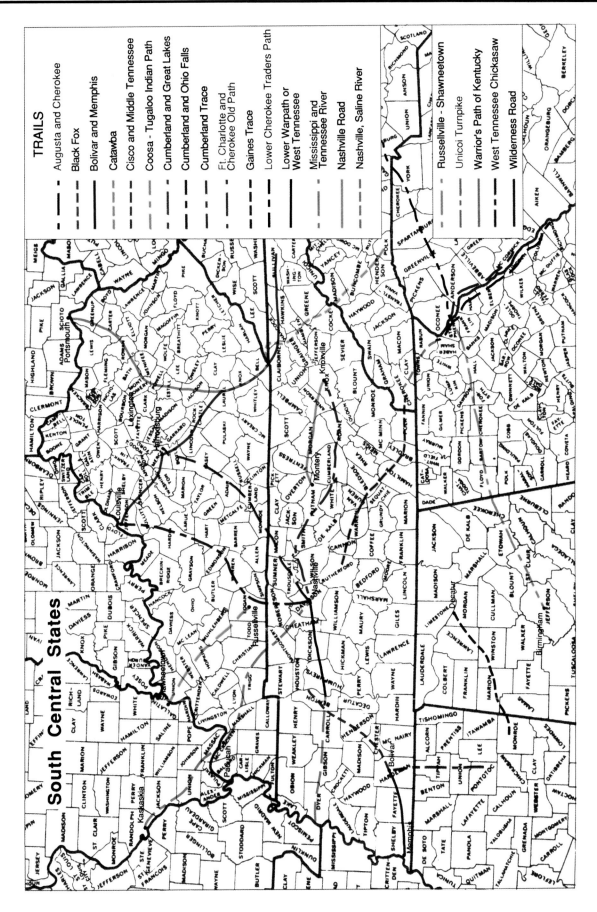

TRAILS

- Augusta and Cherokee
- Black Fox
- Bolivar and Memphis
- Catawba
- Cisco and Middle Tennessee
- Coosa - Tugaloo Indian Path
- Cumberland and Great Lakes
- Cumberland and Ohio Falls
- Cumberland Trace
- Ft. Charlotte and Cherokee Old Path
- Gaines Trace
- Lower Cherokee Traders Path
- Lower Warpath or West Tennessee
- Mississippi and Tennessee River
- Nashville Road
- Nashville, Saline River
- Russellville - Shawneetown
- Unicoi Turnpike
- Warrior's Path of Kentucky
- West Tennessee Chickasaw
- Wilderness Road

South Central States

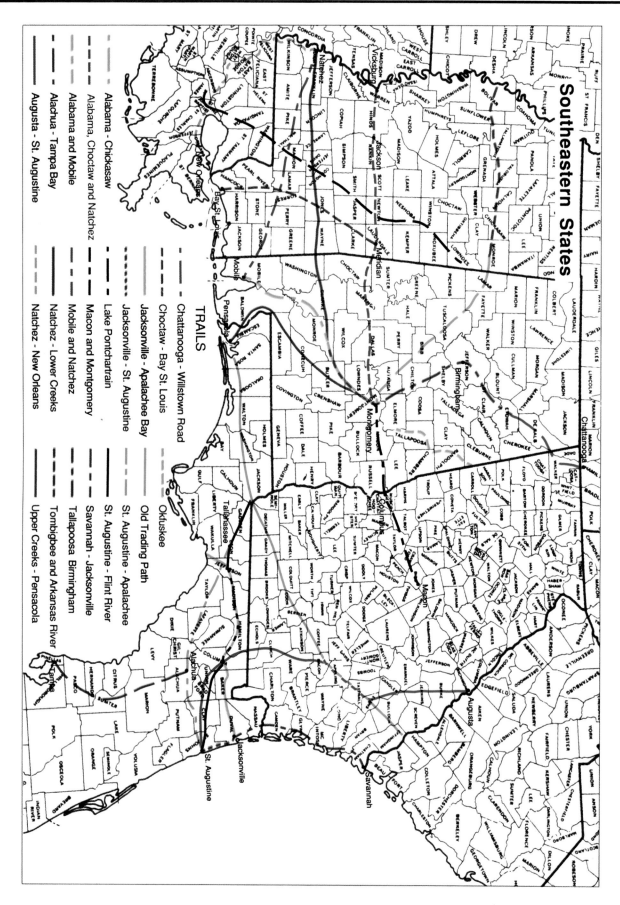

TRAILS

— — — — Alabama - Chickasaw
— · — · — Alabama, Choctaw and Natchez
————— Alabama and Mobile
— · · — · · Alachua - Tampa Bay
————— Augusta - St. Augustine

— — — — Chattanooga - Willstown Road
— · — · — Choctaw - Bay St. Louis
————— Jacksonville - Apalachee Bay
— · · — · · Jacksonville - St. Augustine
————— Lake Pontchartrain

— — — — Macon and Montgomery
— · — · — Mobile and Natchez
————— Natchez - Lower Creeks
— · · — · · Natchez - New Orleans
————— Old Trading Path

— — — — St. Augustine - Apalachee
— · — · — St. Augustine - Flint River
————— Savannah - Jacksonville
— · · — · · Tallapoosa Birmingham
————— Tombigbee and Arkansas River
————— Upper Creeks - Pensacola

Southeastern States

CANALS AND THE CUMBERLAND ROAD, 1785 - 1850

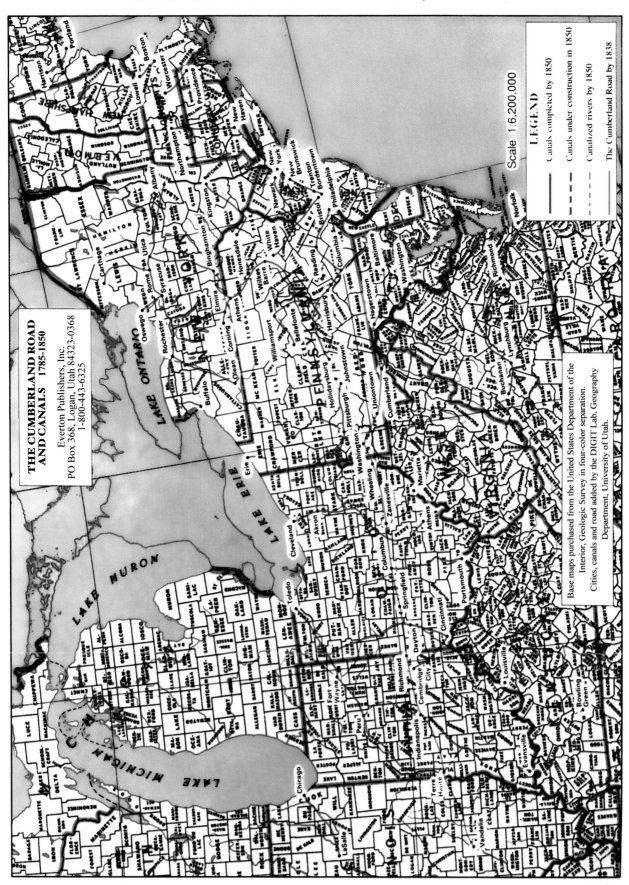

RAILROADS BY 1860

RAILROADS BY 1860

Everton Publishers, Inc.
PO Box 368, Logan, Utah 84323-0368
1-800-443-6325

Scale 1:9,170,000

Base map purchased from the United State Department of the Interior, Geologic Survey in four-color separation. Cities adn railroads added by the DIGIT Lab, Geography Department, University of Utah.

TERRITORIAL GROWTH 1775 – 1820

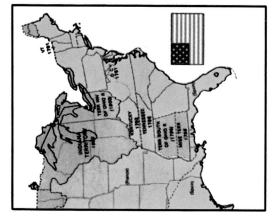

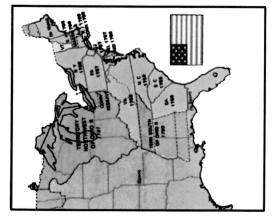

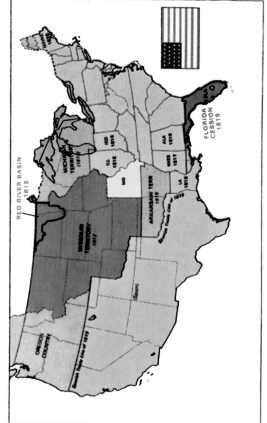

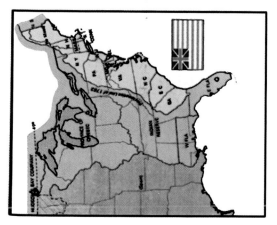

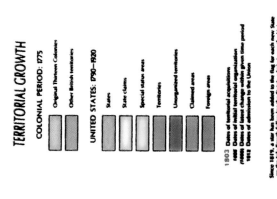

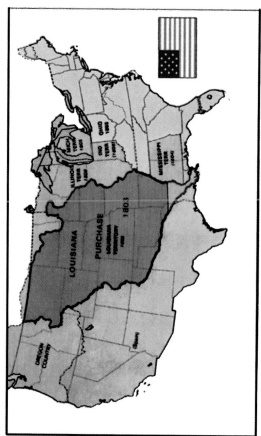

TERRITORIAL GROWTH, 1830 - 1860

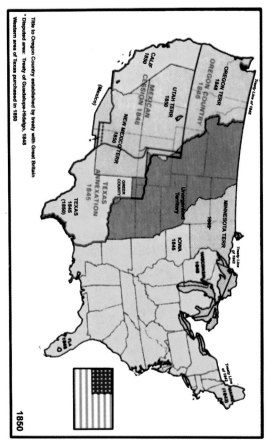

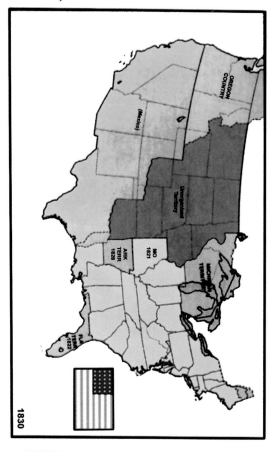

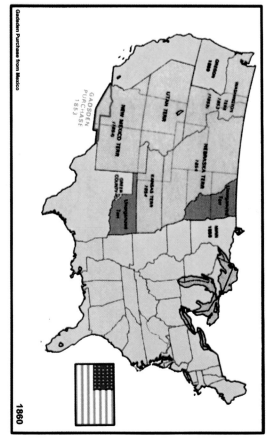

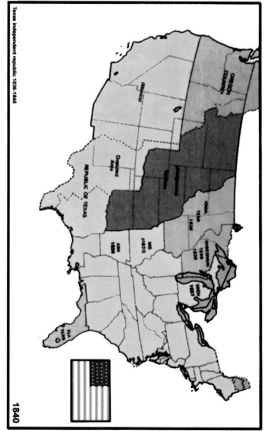